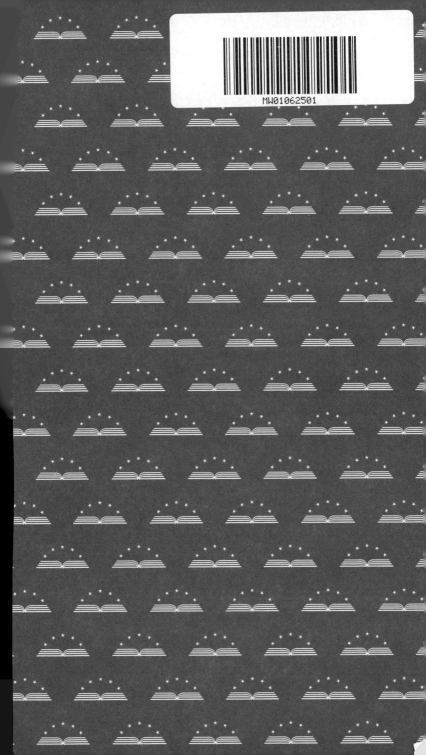

Library of America, a nonprofit organization,
champions our nation's cultural heritage
by publishing America's greatest writing in
authoritative new editions and providing resources
for readers to explore this rich, living legacy.

WILLIAM TECUMSEH SHERMAN

WILLIAM TECUMSEH SHERMAN

Memoirs of General W. T. Sherman

Charles Royster, *editor*

THE LIBRARY OF AMERICA

Published in the United States by Library of America.
Visit our website at www.loa.org.

This paper exceeds the requirements of
ANSI/NISO z39.48–1992 (Permanence of Paper).

Distributed to the trade in the United States
by Penguin Random House Inc.
and in Canada by Penguin Random House Canada, Ltd.

Library of Congress Catalog Card Number: 90–60012
For cataloging information, see end of Notes.
ISBN 978-0-940450-65-3
ISBN 0-940450-65-8

———

Twelfth Printing
The Library of America—51

Manufactured in the United States of America

Contents

MEMOIRS

OF

GENERAL WILLIAM T. SHERMAN.

IN TWO VOLUMES.

VOL. I.

GENERAL W. T. SHERMAN

TO

HIS COMRADES IN ARMS,

VOLUNTEERS AND REGULARS.

NEARLY TEN YEARS have passed since the close of the civil war in America, and yet no satisfactory history thereof is accessible to the public; nor should any be attempted until the Government has published, and placed within the reach of students, the abundant materials that are buried in the War Department at Washington. These are in process of compilation; but, at the rate of progress for the past ten years, it is probable that a new century will come before they are published and circulated, with full indexes to enable the historian to make a judicious selection of materials.

What is now offered is not designed as a history of the war, or even as a complete account of all the incidents in which the writer bore a part, but merely his recollection of events, corrected by a reference to his own memoranda, which may assist the future historian when he comes to describe the whole, and account for the motives and reasons which influenced some of the actors in the grand drama of war.

I trust a perusal of these pages will prove interesting to the survivors, who have manifested so often their intense love of the "cause" which moved a nation to vindicate its own authority; and, equally so, to the rising generation, who therefrom may learn that a country and government such as ours are worth fighting for, and dying for, if need be.

If successful in this, I shall feel amply repaid for departing from the usage of military men, who seldom attempt to publish their own deeds, but rest content with simply contributing by their acts to the honor and glory of their country.

WILLIAM T. SHERMAN,
General.

ST. LOUIS, MISSOURI, *January* 21, 1875.

Preface to the Second Edition.

ANOTHER TEN YEARS have passed since I ventured to publish my Memoirs, and, being once more at leisure, I have revised them in the light of the many criticisms public and private.

My habit has been to note in pencil the suggestions of critics, and to examine the substance of their differences; for critics must differ from the author, to manifest their superiority.

Where I have found material error I have corrected; and I have added two chapters, one at the beginning, another at the end, both of the most general character, and an appendix.

I wish my friends and enemies to understand that I disclaim the character of historian, but assume to be a witness on the stand before the great tribunal of history, to assist some future Napier, Alison, or Hume to comprehend the feelings and thoughts of the actors in the grand conflicts of the recent past, and thereby to lessen his labors in the compilation necessary for the future benefit of mankind.

In this free country every man is at perfect liberty to publish his own thoughts and impressions, and any witness who may differ from me should publish his own version of facts in the truthful narration of which he is interested. I am publishing my own memoirs, not *theirs*, and we all know that no three honest witnesses of a simple brawl can agree on all the details. How much more likely will be the difference in a great battle covering a vast space of broken ground, when each division, brigade, regiment, and even company, naturally and honestly believes that it was the focus of the whole affair! Each of them won the battle. None ever lost. That was the fate of the old man who unhappily commanded.

In this edition I give the best maps which I believe have ever been prepared, compiled by General O. M. Poe, from personal knowledge and official surveys, and what I chiefly aim to establish is the true *cause* of the *results* which are already known to the whole world; and it may be a relief to many to know that I shall publish no other, but, like the player at cards, will "stand;" not that I have accomplished perfection, but because I can do no better with the cards in hand. Of omissions there are plenty, but of wilful perversion of facts, none.

In the preface to the first edition, in 1875, I used these words: "Nearly ten years have passed since the close of the civil war in America, and yet no satisfactory history thereof is accessible to the public; nor should any be attempted until the Government has published, and placed within the reach of students, the abundant materials that are buried in the War Department at Washington. These are in process of compilation; but, at the rate of progress for the past ten years, it is probable that a new century will come before they are published and circulated, with full indexes to enable the historian to make a judicious selection of materials."

Another decade is past, and I am in possession of all these publications, my last being Volume XI, Part 3, Series 1, the last date in which is August 30, 1862. I am afraid that if I assume again the character of prophet, I must extend the time deep into the next century, and pray meanwhile that the official records of the war, "Union and Confederate," may approach completion before the "next war," or rather that we, as a people, may be spared another war until the last one is officially recorded. Meantime the rising generation must be content with memoirs and histories compiled from the best sources available.

In this sense I offer mine as to the events of which I was an eye-witness and participant, or for which I was responsible.

W. T. SHERMAN,
General (retired).

St. Louis, Missouri, *March 30, 1885.*

Contents.

VOLUME I.

Chapter I.

ACCORDING TO Cothren, in his "History of Ancient Wood-bury, Connecticut," the Sherman family came from Dedham, Essex County, England. The first recorded name is of Edmond Sherman, with his three sons, Edmond, Samuel, and John, who were at Boston before 1636; and further it is distinctly recorded that Hon. Samuel Sherman, *Rev. John*, his brother, and Captain John, his first cousin, arrived from Dedham, Essex County, England, in 1634. Samuel afterward married Sarah Mitchell, who had come (in the same ship) from England, and finally settled at Stratford, Connecticut. The other two (Johns) located at Watertown, Massachusetts.

From Captain John Sherman are descended Roger Sherman, the signer of the Declaration of Independence, Hon. William M. Evarts, the Messrs. Hoar, of Massachusetts, and many others of national fame. Our own family are descended from the Hon. Samuel Sherman and his son, the Rev. John, who was born in 1650–'51; then another John, born in 1687; then Judge Daniel, born in 1721; then Taylor Sherman, our grandfather, who was born in 1758. Taylor Sherman was a lawyer and judge in Norwalk, Connecticut, where he resided until his death, May 4, 1815; leaving a widow, Betsey Stoddard Sherman, and three children, Charles R. (our father), Daniel, and Betsey.

When the State of Connecticut, in 1786, ceded to the United States her claim to the western part of her public domain, as defined by her Royal Charter, she reserved a large district in what is now northern Ohio, a portion of which (five hundred thousand acres) composed the "Fire-Land District," which was set apart to indemnify the parties who had lost property in Connecticut by the raids of Generals Arnold, Tryon, and others during the latter part of the Revolutionary War.

Our grandfather, Judge Taylor Sherman, was one of the commissioners appointed by the State of Connecticut to quiet the Indian title, and to survey and subdivide this Fire-Land District, which includes the present counties of Huron and Erie. In his capacity as commissioner he made several trips to Ohio in the early part of this century, and it is supposed that he then contracted the disease which proved fatal. For his labor and losses he received a title to two sections of land, which fact was probably the prime cause of the migration of our family to the West. My father received a good education, and was admitted to the bar at Norwalk, Connecticut, where, in 1810, he, at twenty years of age, married Mary Hoyt, also of Norwalk, and at once migrated to Ohio, leaving his wife (my mother) for a time. His first purpose was to settle at Zanesville, Ohio, but he finally chose Lancaster, Fairfield County, where he at once engaged in the practice of his profession. In 1811 he returned to Norwalk, where, meantime, was born Charles Taylor Sherman, the eldest of the family, who with his mother was carried to Ohio on horseback.

Judge Taylor Sherman's family remained in Norwalk till 1815, when his death led to the emigration of the remainder of the family, viz., of Uncle Daniel Sherman, who settled at Monroeville, Ohio, as a farmer, where he lived and died quite recently, leaving children and grandchildren; and an aunt, Betsey, who married Judge Parker, of Mansfield, and died in 1851, leaving children and grandchildren; also Grandmother Elizabeth Stoddard Sherman, who resided with her daughter, Mrs. Betsey Parker, in Mansfield until her death, August 1, 1848.

Thus my father, Charles R. Sherman, became finally established at Lancaster, Ohio, as a lawyer, with his own family in the year 1811, and continued there till the time of his death, in 1829. I have no doubt that he was in the first instance attracted to Lancaster by the natural beauty of its scenery, and the charms of its already established society. He continued in the practice of his profession, which in those days was no sinecure, for the ordinary circuit was made on horseback, and embraced Marietta, Cincinnati, and Detroit. Hardly was the family established there when the War of 1812 caused great alarm and distress in all Ohio. The English captured Detroit and the shores of Lake Erie down to the Maumee River; while the Indians still occupied the greater part of the State.

Nearly every man had to be somewhat of a soldier, but I think my father was only a commissary; still, he seems to have caught a fancy for the great chief of the Shawnees, "Tecumseh."

Perry's victory on Lake Erie was the turning-point of the Western campaign, and General Harrison's victory over the British and Indians at the river Thames in Canada ended the war in the West, and restored peace and tranquillity to the exposed settlers of Ohio. My father at once resumed his practice at the bar, and was soon recognized as an able and successful lawyer. When, in 1816, my brother James was born, he insisted on engrafting the Indian name "Tecumseh" on the usual family list. My mother had already named her first son after her own brother *Charles*; and insisted on the second son taking the name of her other brother James, and when I came along, on the 8th of February, 1820, mother having no more brothers, my father succeeded in his original purpose, and named me William *Tecumseh*.

The family rapidly increased till it embraced six boys and five girls, all of whom attained maturity and married; of these six are still living.

In the year 1821 a vacancy occurred in the Supreme Court of Ohio, and I find this petition:

SOMERSET, OHIO, *July* 6, 1821.
May it please your Excellency:

We ask leave to recommend to your Excellency's favorable notice Charles R. Sherman, Esq., of Lancaster, as a man possessing in an eminent degree those qualifications so much to be desired in a Judge of the Supreme Court.

From a long acquaintance with Mr. Sherman, we are happy to be able to state to your Excellency that our minds are led to the conclusion that that gentleman possesses a disposition noble and generous, a mind discriminating, comprehensive, and combining a heart pure, benevolent and humane. Manners dignified, mild, and complaisant, and a firmness not to be shaken and of unquestioned integrity.

But Mr. Sherman's character cannot be unknown to your Excellency, and on that acquaintance without further comment we might safely rest his pretensions.

We think we hazard little in assuring your Excellency that his appointment would give almost universal satisfaction to the citizens of Perry County.

With great consideration, we have the honor to be
  Your Excellency's most obedient humble servants,

       CHARLES A. HOOD,
       GEORGE TREAT,
       PETER DITTOE,
       P. ODLIN,
       J. B. ORTEN,
       T. BECKWITH,
       WILLIAM P. DORST,
       JOHN MURRAY,
       JACOB MOINS,
       B. EATON,
       DANIEL GRIGGS,
       HENRY DITTOE,
       NICHOLAS McCARTY.

His Excellency ETHAN A. BROWN,
 Governor of Ohio, Columbus.

He was soon after appointed a Judge of the Supreme Court, and served in that capacity to the day of his death.

My memory extends back to about 1827, and I recall him, returning home on horseback, when all the boys used to run and contend for the privilege of riding his horse from the front door back to the stable. On one occasion, I was the first, and being mounted rode to the stable; but "Old Dick" was impatient because the stable-door was not opened promptly, so he started for the barn of our neighbor Mr. King; there, also, no one was in waiting to open the gate, and, after a reasonable time, "Dick" started back for home somewhat in a hurry, and threw me among a pile of stones, in front of preacher Wright's house, where I was picked up apparently a dead boy; but my time was not yet, and I recovered, though the scars remain to this day.

The year 1829 was a sad one to our family. We were then ten children, my eldest brother Charles absent at the State University, Athens, Ohio; my next brother, James, in a store at Cincinnati; and the rest were at home, at school. Father was away on the circuit. One day Jane Sturgeon came to the school, called us out, and when we reached home all was lamentation: news had come that father was ill unto death, at Lebanon, a hundred miles away. Mother started at once, by coach, but met the news of his death about Washington, and returned home. He had ridden on horseback from Cincinnati to Lebanon to hold court, during a hot day in June. On the next day he took his seat on the bench, opened court in the forenoon, but in the afternoon, after recess, was seized with a severe chill and had to adjourn the court. The best medical aid was called in, and for three days with apparent success, but the fever then assumed a more dangerous type, and he gradually yielded to it, dying on the sixth day, viz., June 24, 1829.

My brother James had been summoned from Cincinnati, and was present at his bedside, as was also Henry Stoddard, Esq., of Dayton, Ohio, our cousin. Mr. Stoddard once told me that the cause of my father's death was cholera; but at that time, 1829, there was no Asiatic cholera in the United States, and the family attributed his death to exposure to the hot sun of June, and a consequent fever, "typhoid."

From the resolutions of the bench, bar, and public generally, now in my possession, his death was universally deplored; more especially by his neighbors in Lancaster, and by the Society of Freemasons, of which he was the High-Priest of Arch Chapter No. 11.

His death left the family very poor, but friends rose up with proffers of generous care and assistance; for all the neighbors knew that mother could not maintain so large a family without help. My eldest brother, Charles, had nearly completed his education at the university at Athens, and concluded to go to his uncle, Judge Parker, at Mansfield, Ohio, to study law. My eldest sister, Elizabeth, soon after married William J. Reese, Esq.; James was already in a store at Cincinnati; and, with the exception of the three youngest children, the rest of us were scattered. I fell to the charge of the Hon. Thomas Ewing, who took me to his family, and ever after treated me as his own son.

I continued at the Academy in Lancaster, which was the

best in the place; indeed, as good a school as any in Ohio. We studied all the common branches of knowledge, including Latin, Greek, and French. At first the school was kept by Mr. Parsons; he was succeeded by Mr. Brown, and he by two brothers, Samuel and Mark How. These were all excellent teachers, and we made good progress, first at the old academy and afterward at a new school-house, built by Samuel How, in the orchard of Hugh Boyle, Esq.

Time passed with us as with boys generally. Mr. Ewing was in the United States Senate, and I was notified to prepare for West Point, of which institution we had little knowledge, except that it was very strict, and that the army was its natural consequence. In 1834 I was large for my age, and the construction of canals was the rage in Ohio. A canal was projected to connect with the great Ohio Canal at Carroll (eight miles above Lancaster), down the valley of the Hock Hocking to Athens (forty-four miles), and thence to the Ohio River by slack water.

Preacher Carpenter, of Lancaster, was appointed to make the preliminary surveys, and selected the necessary working party out of the boys of the town. From our school were chosen —— Wilson, Emanuel Geisy, William King, and myself. Geisy and I were the rod-men. We worked during that fall and next spring, marking two experimental lines, and for our work we each received a silver half-dollar for each day's actual work, the first money any of us had ever earned.

In June, 1835, one of our school-fellows, William Irvin, was appointed a cadet to West Point, and, as it required sixteen years of age for admission, I had to wait another year. During the autumn of 1835 and spring of 1836 I devoted myself chiefly to mathematics and French, which were known to be the chief requisites for admission to West Point.

Some time in the spring of 1836 I received through Mr. Ewing, then at Washington, from the Secretary of War, Mr. Poinsett, the letter of appointment as a cadet, with a list of the articles of clothing necessary to be taken along, all of which were liberally provided by Mrs. Ewing; and with orders to report to Mr. Ewing, at Washington, by a certain date, I left Lancaster about the 20th of May in the stage-coach for Zanesville. There we transferred to the coaches of the Great

National Road, the highway of travel from the West to the East. The stages generally travelled in gangs of from one to six coaches, each drawn by four good horses, carrying nine passengers inside and three or four outside.

In about three days, travelling day and night, we reached Frederick, Maryland. There we were told that we could take rail-cars to Baltimore, and thence to Washington; but there was also a two-horse hack ready to start for Washington direct. Not having full faith in the novel and dangerous railroad, I stuck to the coach, and in the night reached Gadsby's Hotel in Washington City.

The next morning I hunted up Mr. Ewing, and found him boarding with a mess of Senators at Mrs. Hill's, corner of Third and C Streets, and transferred my trunk to the same place. I spent a week in Washington, and think I saw more of the place in that time than I ever have since in the many years of residence there. General Jackson was President, and was at the zenith of his fame. I recall looking at him a full hour, one morning, through the wood railing on Pennsylvania Avenue, as he paced up and down the gravel walk on the north front of the White House. He wore a cap and an overcoat so full that his form seemed smaller than I had expected. I also recall the appearance of Postmaster-General Amos Kendall, of Vice-President Van Buren, Messrs. Calhoun, Webster, Clay, Cass, Silas Wright, etc.

In due time I took my departure for West Point with Cadets Belt and Bronaugh. These were appointed cadets as from Ohio, although neither had ever seen that State. But in those days there were fewer applicants from Ohio than now, and near the close of the term the vacancies unasked for were usually filled from applicants on the spot. Neither of these parties, however, graduated, so the State of Ohio lost nothing. We went to Baltimore by rail, there took a boat up to Havre de Grace, then the rail to Wilmington, Delaware, and up the Delaware in a boat to Philadelphia. I staid over in Philadelphia one day at the old Mansion House, to visit the family of my brother-in-law, Mr. Reese. I found his father a fine sample of the old merchant gentleman, in a good house in Arch Street, with his accomplished daughters, who had been to Ohio, and whom I had seen there. From Philadelphia we took boat to Bordentown, rail to Amboy, and boat again to New York City, stopping at the American Hotel. I staid a week in New York City, visiting my uncle, Charles Hoyt, at his beautiful place on Brooklyn Heights, and my uncle James, then living in White Street. My friend William Scott was there, the young husband of my cousin, Louise Hoyt; a neatly-dressed young fellow, who looked on me as an un-tamed animal just caught in the far West—"fit food for gun-powder," and good for nothing else.

About June 12th I embarked in the steamer Cornelius Vanderbilt for West Point; registered in the office of Lieuten-ant C. F. Smith, Adjutant of the Military Academy, as a new cadet of the class of 1836, and at once became installed as the "plebe" of my fellow-townsman, William Irvin, then entering his Third Class.

Colonel R. E. De Russy was Superintendent; Major John Fowle, Sixth United States Infantry, Commandant. The prin-cipal Professors were: Mahan, Engineering; Bartlett, Natural Philosophy; Bailey, Chemistry; Church, Mathematics; Weir, Drawing; and Berard, French.

The routine of military training and of instruction was then fully established, and has remained almost the same ever since. To give a mere outline would swell this to an inconve-nient size, and I therefore merely state that I went through the regular course of four years, graduating in June, 1840, number six in a class of forty-three. These forty-three were all that remained of more than one hundred which originally constituted the class. At the Academy I was not considered a good soldier, for at no time was I selected for any office, but remained a private throughout the whole four years. Then, as now, neatness in dress and form, with a strict conformity to the rules, were the qualifications required for office, and I suppose I was found not to excel in any of these. In studies I always held a respectable reputation with the professors, and generally ranked among the best, especially in drawing, chem-istry, mathematics, and natural philosophy. My average de-merits, per annum, were about one hundred and fifty, which reduced my final class standing from number four to six.

In June, 1840, after the final examination, the class gradu-ated and we received our diplomas. Meantime, Major Delafield, United States Engineers, had become Superintendent; Major C. F. Smith, Commandant of Cadets; but the corps of professors and assistants remained almost unchanged during our whole term. We were all granted the usual furlough of three months, and parted for our homes, there to await assignment to our respective corps and regiments. In due season I was appointed and commissioned second-lieutenant, Third Artillery, and ordered to report at Governor's Island, New York Harbor, at the end of September. I spent my furlough mostly at Lancaster and Mansfield, Ohio; toward the close of September returned to New York, reported to Major Justin Dimock, commanding the recruiting rendezvous at Governor's Island, and was assigned to command a company of recruits preparing for service in Florida. Early in October this company was detailed, as one of four, to embark in a sailing-vessel for Savannah, Georgia, under command of Captain and Brevet Major Penrose. We embarked and sailed, reaching Savannah about the middle of October, where we transferred to a small steamer and proceeded by the inland route to St. Augustine, Florida. We reached St. Augustine at the same time with the Eighth Infantry, commanded by Colonel and Brevet Brigadier-General William J. Worth. At that time General Zachary Taylor was in chief command in Florida, and had his headquarters at Tampa Bay. My regiment, the Third Artillery, occupied the posts along the Atlantic coast of Florida, from St. Augustine south to Key Biscayne, and my own company, A, was at Fort Pierce, Indian River. At St. Augustine I was detached from the company of recruits, which was designed for the Second Infantry, and was ordered to join my proper company at Fort Pierce. Colonel William Gates commanded the regiment, with Lieutenant William Austine Brown as adjutant of the regiment. Lieutenant Bragg commanded the post of St. Augustine with his own company, E, and G (Garner's), then commanded by Lieutenant Judd. In a few days I embarked in the little steamer William Gaston down the coast, stopping one day at New Smyrna, held by John R. Vinton's company (B), with which was serving Lieutenant William H. Shover.

In due season we arrived off the bar of Indian River and anchored. A whale-boat came off with a crew of four men, steered by a character of some note, known as the Pilot Ashlock. I transferred self and baggage to this boat, and, with the mails, was carried through the surf over the bar, into the mouth of Indian River Inlet. It was then dark; we transferred to a smaller boat, and the same crew pulled us up through a channel in the middle of Mangrove Islands, the roosting-place of thousands of pelicans and birds that rose in clouds and circled above our heads. The water below was alive with fish, whose course through it could be seen by the phosphoric wake; and Ashlock told me many a tale of the Indian war then in progress, and of his adventures in hunting and fishing, which he described as the best in the world. About two miles from the bar, we emerged into the lagoon, a broad expanse of shallow water that lies parallel with the coast, separated from it by a narrow strip of sand, backed by a continuous series of islands and promontories, covered with a dense growth of mangrove and saw-palmetto. Pulling across this lagoon, in about three more miles we approached the lights of Fort Pierce. Reaching a small wharf, we landed, and were met by the officers of the post, Lieutenants George Taylor and Edward J. Steptoe, and Assistant-Surgeon James Simons. Taking the mail-bag, we walked up a steep sand-bluff on which the fort was situated, and across the parade-ground to the officers' quarters. These were six or seven log-houses, thatched with palmetto-leaves, built on high posts, with a porch in front, facing the water. The men's quarters were also of logs forming the two sides of a rectangle, open toward the water; the intervals and flanks were closed with log stockades. I was assigned to one of these rooms, and at once began service with my company, A, then commanded by Lieutenant Taylor.

The season was hardly yet come for active operations against the Indians, so that the officers were naturally attracted to Ashlock, who was the best fisherman I ever saw. He soon initiated us into the mysteries of shark-spearing, trolling for red-fish, and taking the sheep's-head and mullet. These abounded so that we could at any time catch an unlimited quantity at pleasure. The companies also owned nets for catching green turtles. These nets had meshes about a foot square, were set across channels in the lagoon, the ends secured to stakes driven into the mud, the lower line sunk with lead or stone weights and the upper line floated with cork. We usually visited these nets twice a day, and found from one to six green turtles entangled in the meshes. Disengaging them, they were carried to pens, made with stakes stuck in the mud, where they were fed with mangrove-leaves, and our cooks had at all times an ample supply of the best of green turtles. They were so cheap and common that the soldiers regarded it as an imposition when compelled to eat green turtle steaks, instead of poor Florida beef, or the usual barrelled mess-pork. I do not recall in my whole experience a spot on earth where fish, oysters, and green turtles so abound as at Fort Pierce, Florida.

In November, Major Childs arrived with Lieutenant Van Vliet and a detachment of recruits to fill our two companies, and preparations were at once begun for active operations in the field. At that time the Indians in the Peninsula of Florida were scattered, and the war consisted in hunting up and se-curing the small fragments, to be sent to join the others of their tribe of Seminoles already established in the Indian Ter-ritory west of Arkansas. Our expeditions were mostly made in boats in the lagoons extending from the "Haul-over," near two hundred miles above the fort, down to Jupiter Inlet, about fifty miles below, and in the many streams which emp-tied therein. Many such expeditions were made during that winter, with more or less success, in which we succeeded in picking up small parties of men, women, and children. On one occasion, near the "Haul-over," when I was not present, the expedition was more successful. It struck a party of nearly fifty Indians, killed several warriors, and captured others. In this expedition my classmate, Lieutenant Van Vliet, who was an excellent shot, killed a warrior who was running at full speed among trees, and one of the sergeants of our company (Broderick) was said to have dispatched three warriors, and it was reported that he took the scalp of one and brought it in to the fort as a trophy. Broderick was so elated that, on reach-ing the post, he had to celebrate his victory by a big drunk.

There was at the time a poor, weakly soldier of our com-pany whose wife cooked for our mess. She was somewhat of a flirt, and rather fond of admiration. Sergeant Broderick was attracted to her, and hung around the mess-house more than the husband fancied; so he reported the matter to Lieutenant Taylor, who reproved Broderick for his behavior. A few days afterward the husband again appealed to his commanding officer (Taylor), who exclaimed: "Haven't you got a musket? Can't you defend your own family?" Very soon after a shot was heard down by the mess-house, and it transpired that the husband had actually shot Broderick, inflicting a wound which proved mortal. The law and army regulations required that the man should be sent to the nearest civil court, which was at St. Augustine; accordingly, the prisoner and necessary witnesses were sent up by the next monthly steamer. Among the latter were Lieutenant Taylor and the pilot Ashlock.

After they had been gone about a month, the sentinel on the roof-top of our quarters reported the smoke of a steamer approaching the bar, and, as I was acting quartermaster, I took a boat and pulled down to get the mail. I reached the log-hut in which the pilots lived, and saw them start with their boat across the bar, board the steamer, and then return. Ashlock was at his old post at the steering-oar, with two ladies, who soon came to the landing, having passed through a very heavy surf, and I was presented to one as *Mrs. Ashlock*, and the other as her sister, a very pretty little Minorcan girl of about fourteen years of age. Mrs. Ashlock herself was probably eighteen or twenty years old, and a very handsome woman. I was hurriedly informed that the murder trial was in progress at St. Augustine; that Ashlock had given his testimony, and had availed himself of the chance to take a wife to share with him the solitude of his desolate hut on the beach at Indian River. He had brought ashore his wife, her sister, and their chests, with the mail, and had orders to return immediately to the steamer (Gaston or Harney) to bring ashore some soldiers belonging to another company, E (Braggs), which had been ordered from St. Augustine to Fort Pierce. Ashlock left his wife and her sister standing on the beach near the pilot-hut, and started back with his whale-boat across the bar. I also took the mail and started up to the fort, and had hardly reached the wharf when I observed another boat following me. As soon as this reached the wharf the men reported that Ashlock and all his crew, with the exception of one man, had been drowned a few minutes after I had left the beach. They said his surf-boat had reached the steamer, had taken on board a load of soldiers, some eight or ten, and had started back through the surf, when on the bar a heavy breaker upset the boat, and all were lost except the boy who pulled the bow-oar, who clung to the rope or painter, hauled himself to the upset boat, held on, drifted with it outside the breakers, and was finally beached near a mile down the coast. They reported also that the steamer had got up anchor, run in as close to the bar as she could, paused awhile, and then had started down the coast.

I instantly took a fresh crew of soldiers and returned to the bar; there sat poor Mrs. Ashlock on her chest of clothes, a weeping widow, who had seen her husband perish amid sharks and waves; she clung to the hope that the steamer had picked him up, but, strange to say, he could not swim, although he had been employed on the water all his life.

Her sister was more demonstrative, and wailed as one lost to all hope and life. She appealed to us all to do miracles to save the struggling men in the waves, though two hours had already passed, and to have gone out then among those heavy breakers, with an inexperienced crew, would have been worse than suicide. All I could do was to reorganize the guard at the beach, take the two desolate females up to the fort, and give them the use of my own quarters. Very soon their anguish was quieted, and they began to look for the return of their steamer with Ashlock and his rescued crew. The next day I went again to the beach with Lieutenant Ord, and we found that one or two bodies had been washed ashore, torn all to pieces by the sharks, which literally swarmed the inlet at every new tide. In a few days the weather moderated, and the steamer returned from the south, but the surf was so high that she anchored a mile off. I went out myself, in the whale or surf boat, over that terrible bar with a crew of soldiers, boarded the steamer, and learned that none other of Ashlock's crew except the one before mentioned had been saved; but, on the contrary, the captain of the steamer had sent one of his own boats to their rescue, which was likewise upset in the surf, and, out of the three men in her, one had drifted back outside the breakers, clinging to the upturned boat, and was picked up. This sad and fatal catastrophe made us all *afraid* of that bar, and in returning to the shore I adopted the more prudent course of beaching the boat below the inlet, which insured us a good ducking, but was attended with less risk to life.

I had to return to the fort and bear to Mrs. Ashlock the absolute truth, that her husband was lost forever.

Meantime her sister had entirely recovered her equilibrium, and being the guest of the officers, who were extremely courteous to her, she did not lament so loudly the calamity that saved them a long life of banishment on the beach of Indian River. By the first opportunity they were sent back to St. Augustine, the possessors of all of Ashlock's worldly goods and effects, consisting of a good rifle, several cast-nets, hand-lines, etc., etc., besides some three hundred dollars in money, which was due him by the quartermaster for his services as pilot. I afterward saw these ladies at St. Augustine, and years afterward the younger one came to Charleston, South Carolina, the wife of the somewhat famous Captain Thistle, agent for the United States for live-oak in Florida, who was noted as the first of the troublesome class of inventors of modern artillery. He was the inventor of a gun that "did not recoil at all," or "if anything it recoiled a little forward."

One day, in the summer of 1841, the sentinel on the house-top at Fort Pierce called out, "Indians! Indians!" Everybody sprang to his gun, the companies formed promptly on the parade-ground, and soon were reported as approaching the post, from the pine-woods in rear, four Indians on horseback. They rode straight up to the gateway, dismounted, and came in. They were conducted by the officer of the day to the commanding officer, Major Childs, who sat on the porch in front of his own room. After the usual pause, one of them, a black man named Joe, who spoke English, said they had been sent in by Coacoochee (Wild Cat), one of the most noted of the Seminole chiefs, to see the big chief of the post. He gradually unwrapped a piece of paper, which was passed over to Major Childs, who read it, and it was in the nature of a "Safe Guard" for "Wild Cat" to come into Fort Pierce to receive provisions and assistance while collecting his tribe, with the purpose of emigrating to their reservation west of Arkansas. The paper was signed by General Worth, who had succeeded

General Taylor, at Tampa Bay, in command of all the troops in Florida. Major Childs inquired, "Where is Coacoochee?" and was answered, "Close by," when Joe explained that he had been sent in by his chief to see if the paper was all right. Major Childs said it was "all right," and that Coacoochee ought to come in himself. Joe offered to go out and bring him in, when Major Childs ordered me to take eight or ten mounted men and go out to escort him in. Detailing ten men to saddle up, and taking Joe and one Indian boy along on their own ponies, I started out under their guidance.

We continued to ride five or six miles, when I began to suspect treachery, of which I had heard so much in former years, and had been specially cautioned against by the older officers; but Joe always answered, "Only a little way." At last we approached one of those close hammocks, so well known in Florida, standing like an island in the interminable pine-forest, with a pond of water near it. On its edge I noticed a few Indians loitering, which Joe pointed out as *the place*. Apprehensive of treachery, I halted the guard, gave orders to the sergeant to watch me closely, and rode forward alone with the two Indian guides. As we neared the hammock, about a dozen Indian warriors rose up and waited for us. When in their midst I inquired for the chief, Coacoochee. He approached my horse and, slapping his breast, said, "Me Coacoochee." He was a very handsome young Indian warrior, not more than twenty-five years old, but in his then dress could hardly be distinguished from the rest. I then explained to him, through Joe, that I had been sent by my "chief" to escort him into the fort. He wanted me to get down and "talk." I told him that I had no "talk" in me, but that, on his reaching the post, he could talk as much as he pleased with the "big chief," Major Childs. They all seemed to be indifferent, and in no hurry; and I noticed that all their guns were leaning against a tree. I beckoned to the sergeant, who advanced rapidly with his escort, and told him to secure the rifles, which he proceeded to do. Coacoochee pretended to be very angry, but I explained to him that his warriors were tired and mine were not, and that the soldiers would carry the guns on their horses. I told him I would provide him a horse to ride, and the sooner he was ready the better for all. He then stripped, washed himself in the pond, and began to dress in all his Indian finery, which consisted of buckskin leggins, moccasins, and several shirts. He then began to put on vests, one after another, and one of them had the marks of a bullet, just above the pocket, with the stain of blood. In the pocket was a one-dollar Tallahassee Bank note, and the rascal had the impudence to ask me to give him silver coin for that dollar. He had evidently killed the wearer, and was disappointed because the pocket contained a paper dollar instead of one in silver. In due time he was dressed with turban and ostrich-feathers, and mounted the horse reserved for him, and thus we rode back together to Fort Pierce. Major Childs and all the officers received him on the porch, and there we had a regular "talk." Coacoochee "was tired of the war." "His people were scattered and it would take a 'moon' to collect them for emigration," and he "wanted rations for that time," etc., etc.

All this was agreed to, and a month was allowed for him to get ready with his whole band (numbering some one hundred and fifty or one hundred and sixty) to migrate. The "talk" then ceased, and Coacoochee and his envoys proceeded to get regularly drunk, which was easily done by the agency of commissary whiskey. They staid at Fort Pierce during the night, and the next day departed. Several times during the month there came into the post two or more of these same Indians, always to beg for something to eat or drink, and after a full month Coacoochee and about twenty of his warriors came in with several ponies, but with none of their women or children. Major Childs had not from the beginning the least faith in his sincerity; had made up his mind to seize the whole party and compel them to emigrate. He arranged for the usual council, and instructed Lieutenant Taylor to invite Coacoochee and his uncle (who was held to be a principal chief) to his room to take some good brandy, instead of the common commissary whiskey. At a signal agreed on I was to go to the quarters of Company A, to dispatch the first-sergeant and another man to Lieutenant Taylor's room, there to seize the two chiefs and secure them; and with the company I was to enter Major Childs's room and secure the remainder of the party. Meantime Lieutenant Van Vliet was ordered to go to the quarters of his company, F, and at the same signal to march rapidly to the rear of the officers' quarters, so as to catch any who might attempt to escape by the open windows to the rear.

All resulted exactly as prearranged, and in a few minutes the whole party was in irons. At first they claimed that we had acted treacherously, but very soon they admitted that for a month Coacoochee had been quietly removing his women and children toward Lake Okeechobee and the Everglades; and that this visit to our post was to have been their last. It so happened that almost at the instant of our seizing these Indians a vessel arrived off the bar with reënforcements from St. Augustine. These were brought up to Fort Pierce, and we marched that night and next day rapidly, some fifty miles, to Lake Okeechobee, in hopes to capture the balance of the tribe, especially the families, but they had taken the alarm and escaped. Coacoochee and his warriors were sent by Major Childs in a schooner to New Orleans *en route* to their reservation, but General Worth recalled them to Tampa Bay, and by sending out Coacoochee himself the women and children came in voluntarily, and then all were shipped to their destination. This was a heavy loss to the Seminoles, but there still remained in the Peninsula a few hundred warriors with their families scattered into very small parcels, who were concealed in the most inaccessible hammocks and swamps. These had no difficulty in finding plenty of food anywhere and everywhere. Deer and wild turkey were abundant, and as for fish there was no end to them. Indeed, Florida was the Indian's paradise, was of little value to us, and it was a great pity to remove the Seminoles at all, for we could have collected there all the Choctaws, Creeks, Cherokees, and Chickasaws, in addition to the Seminoles. They would have thrived in the Peninsula, whereas they now occupy lands that are very valuable, which are coveted by their white neighbors on all sides, while the Peninsula of Florida still remains with a population less than should make a good State.

During that and preceding years General W. S. Harney had penetrated and crossed through the Everglades, capturing and hanging Chekika and his band, and had brought in many prisoners, who were also shipped West. We at Fort Pierce made several other excursions to Jupiter, Lake Worth, Lauderdale, and into the Everglades, picking up here and there a family, so that it was absurd any longer to call it a "war." These excursions, however, possessed to us a peculiar charm, for the fragrance of the air, the abundance of game and fish, and just enough of adventure, gave to life a relish. I had just returned to Lauderdale from one of these scouts with Lieutenants Rankin, Ord, George H. Thomas, Field, Van Vliet, and others, when I received notice of my promotion to be first-lieutenant of Company G, which occurred November 30, 1841, and I was ordered to return to Fort Pierce, turn over the public property for which I was accountable to Lieutenant H. S. Burton, and then to join my new company at St. Augustine.

I reached St. Augustine before Christmas, and was assigned to command a detachment of twenty men stationed at Picolata, on the St. John's River, eighteen miles distant. At St. Augustine were still the headquarters of the regiment, Colonel William Gates, with Company E, Lieutenant Bragg, and Company G, Lieutenant H. B. Judd. The only buildings at Picolata were the one occupied by my detachment, which had been built for a hospital, and the dwelling of a family named Williams, with whom I boarded. On the other hand, St. Augustine had many pleasant families, among whom was prominent that of United States Judge Bronson. I was half my time in St. Augustine or on the road, and remember the old place with pleasure. In February we received orders transferring the whole regiment to the Gulf posts, and our company, G, was ordered to escort Colonel Gates and his family across to the Suwanee River *en route* for Pensacola. The company, with the colonel and his family, reached Picolata (where my detachment joined), and we embarked in a steamboat for Pilatka. Here Lieutenant Judd discovered that he had forgotten something and had to return to St. Augustine, so that I commanded the company on the march, having with me Second-Lieutenant George B. Ayres. Our first march was to Fort Russell, then Micanopy, Wacahoota, and Wacasassee, all which posts were garrisoned by the Second or Seventh Infantry. At Wacasassee we met General Worth and his staff, *en route* for Pilatka. Lieutenant Judd overtook us about the Suwanee, where we embarked on a small boat for Cedar Keys, and there took a larger one for Pensacola, where the colonel and his family landed, and our company proceeded on in the same vessel to our post—Fort Morgan, Mobile Point.

This fort had not been occupied by troops for many years, was very dirty, and we found little or no stores there. Major Ogden, of the engineers, occupied a house outside the fort. I was quartermaster and commissary, and, taking advantage of one of the engineer schooners engaged in bringing materials for the fort, I went up to Mobile city, and, through the agency of Messrs. Deshon, Taylor, and Myers, merchants, procured all essentials for the troops, and returned to the post. In the course of a week or ten days arrived another company, H, commanded by Lieutenant James Ketchum, with Lieutenants Rankin and Sewall L. Fish, and an assistant surgeon (Wells). Ketchum became the commanding officer, and Lieutenant Rankin quartermaster. We proceeded to put the post in as good order as possible; had regular guard-mounting and parades, but little drill. We found magnificent fishing with the seine on the outer beach, and sometimes in a single haul we would take ten or fifteen barrels of the best kind of fish, embracing pompinos, red-fish, snappers, etc.

We remained there till June, when the regiment was ordered to exchange from the Gulf posts to those on the Atlantic, extending from Savannah to North Carolina. The brig Wetumpka was chartered, and our company (G) embarked and sailed to Pensacola, where we took on board another company (D) (Burke's), commanded by Lieutenant H. S. Burton, with Colonel Gates, the regimental headquarters, and some families. From Pensacola we sailed for Charleston, South Carolina. The weather was hot, the winds light, and we made a long passage; but at last reached Charleston Harbor, disembarked, and took post in Fort Moultrie.

Soon after two other companies arrived, Bragg's (B) and Keyes's (K). The two former companies were already quartered inside of Fort Moultrie, and these latter were placed in gun-sheds, outside, which were altered into barracks. We remained at Fort Moultrie nearly five years, until the Mexican War scattered us forever. Our life there was of strict garrison duty, with plenty of leisure for hunting and social entertainments. We soon formed many and most pleasant acquaintances in the city of Charleston; and it so happened that many of the families resided at Sullivan's Island in the summer season, where we could reciprocate the hospitalities extended to us in the winter.

During the summer of 1843, having been continuously on duty for three years, I applied for and received a leave of absence for three months, which I spent mostly in Ohio. In November I started to return to my post at Charleston by way of New Orleans; took the stage to Chillicothe, Ohio, November 16th, having Henry Stanberry, Esq., and wife, as travelling companions. We continued by stage next day to Portsmouth, Ohio.

At Portsmouth Mr. Stanberry took a boat up the river, and I one down to Cincinnati. There I found my brothers Lampson and Hoyt employed in the "Gazette" printing-office, and spent much time with them and Charles Anderson, Esq., visiting his brother Larz, Mr. Longworth, some of his artist friends, and especially Miss Sallie Carneal, then quite a belle, and noted for her fine voice.

On the 20th I took passage on the steamboat Manhattan for St. Louis; reached Louisville, where Dr. Conrad, of the army, joined me, and in the Manhattan we continued on to St. Louis, with a mixed crowd. We reached the Mississippi at Cairo the 23d, and St. Louis, Friday, November 24, 1843. At St. Louis we called on Colonel S. W. Kearney and Major Cooper, his adjutant-general, and found my classmate, Lieutenant McNutt, of the ordnance, stationed at the arsenal; also Mr. Deas, an artist, and Pacificus Ord, who was studying law. I spent a week at St. Louis, visiting the arsenal, Jefferson Barracks, and most places of interest, and then became impressed with its great future. It then contained about forty thousand people, and my notes describe thirty-six good steamboats receiving and discharging cargo at the levee.

I took passage December 4th in the steamer John Aull for New Orleans. As we passed Cairo the snow was falling, and the country was wintery and devoid of verdure. Gradually, however, as we proceeded south, the green color came; grass and trees showed the change of latitude, and when in the course of a week we had reached New Orleans, the roses were in full bloom, the sugar-cane just ripe, and a tropical air prevalent. We reached New Orleans December 11, 1843, where I spent about a week visiting the barracks, then occupied by the Seventh Infantry; the theatres, hotels, and all the usual places of interest of that day.

On the 16th of December I continued on to Mobile in the steamer Fashion by way of Lake Pontchartrain; saw there most of my personal friends, Mr. and Mrs. Bull, Judge Bragg and his brother Dunbar, Deshon, Taylor, and Myers, etc., and on the 19th of December took passage in the steamboat Bourbon for Montgomery, Alabama, by way of the Alabama River. We reached Montgomery at noon, December 23d, and took cars at 1 P.M. for Franklin, forty miles, which we reached at 7 P.M., thence stages for Griffin, Georgia, *via* La Grange and Greenville. This took the whole night of the 23d and the day of the 24th. At Griffin we took cars for Macon, and thence to Savannah, which we reached Christmas-night, finding Lieutenants Ridgley and Ketchum at tea, where we were soon joined by Rankin and Beckwith.

On the 26th I took the boat for Charleston, reaching my post, and reported for duty Wednesday morning, December 27, 1843.

I had hardly got back to my post when, on the 21st of January, 1844, I received from Lieutenant R. P. Hammond, at Marietta, Georgia, an intimation that Colonel Churchill, Inspector-General of the Army, had applied for me to assist him in taking depositions in upper Georgia and Alabama concerning certain losses by volunteers in Florida of horses and equipments by reason of the failure of the United States to provide sufficient forage, and for which Congress had made an appropriation. On the 4th of February the order came from the Adjutant-General in Washington for me to proceed to Marietta, Georgia, and report to Inspector-General Churchill. I was delayed till the 14th of February by reason of being on a court-martial, when I was duly relieved and started by rail to Augusta, Georgia, and as far as Madison, where I took the mail-coach, reaching Marietta on the 17th. There I reported for duty to Colonel Churchill, who was already engaged on his work, assisted by Lieutenant R. P. Hammond, Third Artillery, and a citizen named Stockton. The colonel had his family with him, consisting of Mrs. Churchill, Mary, now Mrs. Professor Baird, and Charles Churchill, then a boy of about fifteen years of age.

We all lived in a tavern, and had an office convenient. The duty consisted in taking individual depositions of the officers and men who had composed two regiments and a battalion of mounted volunteers that had served in Florida. An oath was administered to each man by Colonel Churchill, who then turned the claimant over to one of us to take down and record his deposition according to certain forms, which enabled them to be consolidated and tabulated. We remained in Marietta about six weeks, during which time I repeatedly rode to *Kenesaw Mountain*, and over the very ground where afterward, in 1864, we had some hard battles.

After closing our business at Marietta the colonel ordered us to transfer our operations to Bellefonte, Alabama. As he proposed to take his family and party by the stage, Hammond lent me his riding-horse, which I rode to Allatoona and the Etowah River. Hearing of certain large Indian mounds near the way, I turned to one side to visit them, stopping a couple of days with Colonel Lewis Tumlin, on whose plantation these mounds were. We struck up such an acquaintance that we corresponded for some years, and as I passed his plantation during the war, in 1864, I inquired for him, but he was not at home. From Tumlin's I rode to Rome, and by way of Wills Valley over Sand Mountain and the Raccoon Range to the Tennessee River at Bellefonte, Alabama. We all assembled there in March, and continued our work for nearly two months, when, having completed the business, Colonel Churchill, with his family, went North by way of Nashville; Hammond, Stockton, and I returning South on horseback, by Rome, Allatoona, Marietta, Atlanta, and Madison, Georgia. Stockton stopped at Marietta, where he resided. Hammond took the cars at Madison, and I rode alone to Augusta, Georgia, where I left the horse and returned to Charleston and Fort Moultrie by rail.

Thus by a mere accident I was enabled to traverse on horseback the very ground where in after-years I had to conduct vast armies and fight great battles. That the knowledge thus acquired was of infinite use to me, and consequently to the Government, I have always felt and stated.

During the autumn of 1844, a difficulty arose among the officers of Company B, Third Artillery (John R. Vinton's), garrisoning Augusta Arsenal, and I was sent up from Fort Moultrie as a sort of peace-maker. After staying there some months, certain transfers of officers were made, which reconciled the difficulty, and I returned to my post, Fort Moultrie. During that winter, 1844–'45, I was visiting at the plantation of Mr. Poyas, on the east branch of the Cooper, about fifty miles from Fort Moultrie, hunting deer with his son James, and Lieutenant John F. Reynolds, Third Artillery. We had taken our stands, and a deer came out of the swamp near that of Mr. James Poyas, who fired, broke the leg of the deer, which turned back into the swamp and came out again above mine. I could follow his course by the cry of the hounds, which were in close pursuit. Hastily mounting my horse, I struck across the pine-woods to head the deer off, and when at full career my horse leaped a fallen log and his fore-foot caught one of those hard, unyielding pine-knots that brought him with violence to the ground. I got up as quick as possible, and found my right arm out of place at the shoulder, caused by the weight of the double-barrelled gun. Seeing Reynolds at some distance, I called out lustily and brought him to me. He soon mended the bridle and saddle, which had been broken by the fall, helped me on my horse, and we followed the course of the hounds. At first my arm did not pain me much, but it soon began to ache so that it was almost unendurable. In about three miles we came to a negro hut, where I got off and rested till Reynolds could overtake Poyas and bring him back. They came at last, but by that time the arm was so swollen and painful that I could not ride. They rigged up an old gig belonging to the negro, in which I was carried six miles to the plantation of Mr. Poyas, Sr. A neighboring physician was sent for, who tried the usual methods of setting the arm, but without success; each time making the operation more painful. At last he sent off, got a set of double pulleys and cords, with which he succeeded in extending the muscles and in getting the bone into place. I then returned to Fort Moultrie, but being disabled, applied for a short leave and went North.

I started January 25, 1845; went to Washington, Baltimore,

and Lancaster, Ohio, whence I went to Mansfield, and thence back by Newark to Wheeling, Cumberland, Baltimore, Philadelphia, and New York, whence I sailed back for Charleston on the ship Sullivan, reaching Fort Moultrie March 9, 1845.

About that time (March 1, 1845) Congress had, by a joint resolution, provided for the annexation of Texas, then an independent Republic, subject to certain conditions requiring the acceptance of the Republic of Texas to be final and conclusive. We all expected war as a matter of course. At that time General Zachary Taylor had assembled a couple of regiments of infantry and one of dragoons at Fort Jessup, Louisiana, and had orders to extend military protection to Texas against the Indians, or a "foreign enemy," the moment the terms of annexation were accepted. He received notice of such acceptance July 7th, and forthwith proceeded to remove his troops to Corpus Christi, Texas, where, during the summer and fall of 1845, was assembled that force with which, in the spring of 1846, was begun the Mexican War.

Some time during that summer came to Fort Moultrie orders for sending Company E, Third Artillery, Lieutenant Bragg, to New Orleans, there to receive a battery of field-guns, and thence to the camp of General Taylor at Corpus Christi. This was the first company of our regiment sent to the seat of war, and it embarked on the brig Hayne. This was the only company that left Fort Moultrie till after I was detached for recruiting service on the 1st of May, 1846.

Inasmuch as Charleston afterward became famous, as the spot where began our civil war, a general description of it, as it was in 1846, will not be out of place.

The city lies on a long peninsula between the Ashley and Cooper Rivers—a low, level peninsula of sand. Meeting Street is its Broadway, with King Street, next west and parallel, the street of shops and small stores. These streets are crossed at right angles by many others, of which Broad Street was the principal; and the intersection of Meeting and Broad was the heart of the city, marked by the Guard-House and St. Michael's Episcopal Church. The Custom-House, Post-Office, etc., were at the foot of Broad Street, near the wharves of the Cooper River front. At the extremity of the peninsula was a drive, open to the bay, and faced by some of the handsomest houses of the city, called the "Battery." Looking down the bay on the right, was James Island, an irregular triangle of about seven miles, the whole island in cultivation with sea-island cotton. At the lower end was Fort Johnson, then simply the station of Captain Bowman, United States Engineers, engaged in building Fort Sumter. This fort (Sumter) was erected on an artificial island nearly in mid-channel, made by dumping rocks, mostly brought as ballast in cotton-ships from the North. As the rock reached the surface it was levelled, and made the foundation of Fort Sumter. In 1846 this fort was barely above the water. Still farther out beyond James Island, and separated from it by a wide space of salt marsh with crooked channels, was Morris Island, composed of the sand-dunes thrown up by the wind and the sea, backed with the salt marsh. On this was the lighthouse, but no people.

On the left, looking down the bay from the Battery of Charleston, was, first, Castle Pinckney, a round brick fort, of two tiers of guns, one in embrasure, the other in barbette, built on a marsh island, which was not garrisoned. Farther down the bay a point of the mainland reached the bay, where there was a group of houses, called Mount Pleasant; and at the extremity of the bay, distant six miles, was Sullivan's Island, presenting a smooth sand-beach to the sea, with the line of sand-hills or dunes thrown up by the waves and winds, and the usual backing of marsh and crooked salt-water channels.

At the shoulder of this island was Fort Moultrie, an irregular fort, without ditch or counterscarp, with a brick scarp wall about twelve feet high, which could be scaled anywhere, and this was surmounted by an earth parapet capable of mounting about forty twenty-four and thirty-two pounder smooth-bore iron guns. Inside the fort were three two-story brick barracks, sufficient to quarter the officers and men of two companies of artillery.

At sea was the usual "bar," changing slightly from year to year, but generally the main ship-channel came from the south, parallel to Morris Island, till it was well up to Fort Moultrie, where it curved, passing close to Fort Sumter and up to the wharves of the city, which were built mostly along the Cooper River front.

Charleston was then a proud, aristocratic city, and assumed

a leadership in the public opinion of the South far out of proportion to her population, wealth, or commerce. On more than one occasion previously, the inhabitants had almost inaugurated civil war, by their assertion and professed belief that each State had, in the original compact of government, reserved to itself the right to withdraw from the Union at its own option, whenever the people supposed they had sufficient cause. We used to discuss these things at our own mess-tables, vehemently and sometimes quite angrily; but I am sure that I never feared it would go further than it had already gone in the winter of 1832–'33, when the attempt at "nullification" was promptly suppressed by President Jackson's famous declaration, "The Union must and shall be preserved!" and by the judicious management of General Scott.

Still, civil war was to be; and, now that it has come and gone, we can rest secure in the knowledge that as the chief cause, slavery, has been eradicated forever, it is not likely to come again.

Chapter II.

EARLY RECOLLECTIONS OF CALIFORNIA.

1846–1848.

IN THE SPRING of 1846 I was a first-lieutenant of Company G, Third Artillery, stationed at Fort Moultrie, South Carolina. The company was commanded by Captain Robert Anderson; Henry B. Judd was the senior first-lieutenant, and I was the junior first-lieutenant, and George B. Ayres the second-lieutenant. Colonel William Gates commanded the post and regiment, with First-Lieutenant William Austine as his adjutant. Two other companies were at the post, viz., Martin Burke's and E. D. Keyes's, and among the officers were T. W. Sherman, Morris Miller, H. B. Field, William Churchill, Joseph Stewart, and Surgeon McLaren.

The country now known as Texas had been recently acquired, and war with Mexico was threatening. One of our companies (Bragg's), with George H. Thomas, John F. Reynolds, and Frank Thomas, had gone the year previous and was at that time with General Taylor's army at Corpus Christi, Texas.

In that year (1846) I received the regular detail for recruiting service, with orders to report to the general superintendent at Governor's Island, New York; and accordingly left Fort Moultrie in the latter part of April, and reported to the superintendent, Colonel R. B. Mason, First Dragoons, at New York, on the 1st day of May. I was assigned to the Pittsburg rendezvous, whither I proceeded and relieved Lieutenant Scott. Early in May I took up my quarters at the St. Charles Hotel, and entered upon the discharge of my duties. There was a regular recruiting-station already established, with a sergeant, corporal, and two or three men, with a citizen physician, Dr. McDowell, to examine the recruits. The threatening war with Mexico made a demand for recruits, and I received authority to open another sub-rendezvous at Zanesville, Ohio, whither I took the sergeant and established him. This was very handy to me, as my home was at

Lancaster, Ohio, only thirty-six miles off, so that I was thus enabled to visit my friends there quite often.

In the latter part of May, when at Wheeling, Virginia, on my way back from Zanesville to Pittsburg, I heard the first news of the battle of Palo Alto and Resaca de la Palma, which occurred on the 8th and 9th of May, and, in common with everybody else, felt intensely excited. That I should be on recruiting service, when my comrades were actually fighting, was intolerable, and I hurried on to my post, Pittsburg. At that time the railroad did not extend west of the Alleghanies, and all journeys were made by stage-coaches. In this instance I traveled from Zanesville to Wheeling, thence to Washington (Pennsylvania), and thence to Pittsburg by stage-coach. On reaching Pittsburg I found many private letters; one from Ord, then a first-lieutenant in Company F, Third Artillery, at Fort McHenry, Baltimore, saying that his company had just received orders for California, and asking me to apply for it. Without committing myself to that project, I wrote to the Adjutant-General, R. Jones, at Washington, D. C., asking him to consider me as an applicant for any active service, and saying that I would willingly forego the recruiting detail, which I well knew plenty of others would jump at. Impatient to approach the scene of active operations, without authority (and I suppose wrongfully), I left my corporal in charge of the rendezvous, and took all the recruits I had made, about twenty-five, in a steamboat to Cincinnati, and turned them over to Major N. C. McCrea, commanding at Newport Barracks. I then reported in Cincinnati, to the superintendent of the Western recruiting service, Colonel Fanning, an old officer with one arm, who inquired by what authority I had come away from my post. I argued that I took it for granted he wanted all the recruits he could get to forward to the army at Brownsville, Texas; and did not know but that he might want me to go along. Instead of appreciating my volunteer zeal, he cursed and swore at me for leaving my post without orders, and told me to go back to Pittsburg. I then asked for an order that would entitle me to transportation back, which at first he emphatically refused, but at last he gave the order, and I returned to Pittsburg, all the way by stage, stopping again at Lancaster, where I attended the wedding of my school-mate

Mike Effinger, and also visited my sub-rendezvous at Zanesville. R. S. Ewell, of my class, arrived to open a cavalry
rendezvous, but, finding my depot there, he went on to
Columbus, Ohio. Tom Jordan afterward was ordered to Zanesville, to take charge of that rendezvous, under the general War
Department orders increasing the number of recruiting-
stations. I reached Pittsburg late in June, and found the order
relieving me from recruiting service, and detailing my class-
mate H. B. Field to my place. I was assigned to Company F,
then under orders for California. By private letters from Lieutenant Ord, I heard that the company had already started
from Fort McHenry for Governor's Island, New York Harbor, to take passage for California in a naval transport. I
worked all that night, made up my accounts current, and
turned over the balance of cash to the citizen physician, Dr.
McDowell; and also closed my clothing and property returns,
leaving blank receipts with the same gentleman for Field's
signature, when he should get there, to be forwarded to the
Department at Washington, and the duplicates to me. These I
did not receive for more than a year. I remember that I got
my orders about 8 P.M. one night, and took passage in the
boat for Brownsville, the next morning traveled by stage from
Brownsville to Cumberland, Maryland, and thence by cars to
Baltimore, Philadelphia, and New York, in a great hurry lest
the ship might sail without me. I found Company F at
Governor's Island, Captain C. Q. Tompkins in command,
Lieutenant E. O. C. Ord senior first-lieutenant, myself junior
first-lieutenant, Lucien Loeser and Charles Minor the second-
lieutenants.

The company had been filled up to one hundred privates,
twelve non-commissioned officers, and one ordnance sergeant
(Layton), making one hundred and thirteen enlisted men and
five officers. Dr. James L. Ord had been employed as acting
assistant surgeon to accompany the expedition, and Lieutenant H. W. Halleck, of the engineers, was also to go along.
The United States store-ship Lexington was then preparing at
the Navy-Yard, Brooklyn, to carry us around Cape Horn to
California. She was receiving on board the necessary stores
for the long voyage, and for service after our arrival there.
Lieutenant-Commander Theodorus Bailey was in command

of the vessel, Lieutenant William H. Macomb executive officer, and Passed-Midshipmen Muse, Spotts, and J. W. A. Nicholson, were the watch-officers; Wilson purser, and Abernethy surgeon. The latter was caterer of the mess, and we all made an advance of cash for him to lay in the necessary mess-stores. To enable us to prepare for so long a voyage and for an indefinite sojourn in that far-off country, the War Department had authorized us to draw six months' pay in advance, which sum of money we invested in surplus clothing and such other things as seemed to us necessary. At last the ship was ready, and was towed down abreast of Fort Columbus, where we were conveyed on board, and on the 14th of July, 1846, we were towed to sea by a steam-tug, and cast off. Colonel R. B. Mason, still superintendent of the general recruiting service, accompanied us down the bay and out to sea, returning with the tug. A few other friends were of the party, but at last they left us, and we were alone upon the sea, and the sailors were busy with the sails and ropes. The Lexington was an old ship, changed from a sloop-of-war to a store-ship, with an after-cabin, a "ward-room," and "between-decks." In the cabin were Captains Bailey and Tompkins, with whom messed the purser, Wilson. In the ward-room were all the other officers, two in each state-room; and Minor, being an extra lieutenant, had to sleep in a hammock slung in the ward-room. Ord and I roomed together; Halleck and Loeser and the others were scattered about. The men were arranged in bunks "between-decks," one set along the sides of the ship, and another, double tier, amidships. The crew were slung in hammocks well forward. Of these there were about fifty. We at once subdivided the company into four squads, under the four lieutenants of the company, and arranged with the naval officers that our men should serve on deck by squads, after the manner of their watches; that the sailors should do all the work aloft, and the soldiers on deck.

On fair days we drilled our men at the manual, and generally kept them employed as much as possible, giving great attention to the police and cleanliness of their dress and bunks; and so successful were we in this, that, though the voyage lasted nearly two hundred days, every man was able to leave the ship and march up the hill to the fort at Monterey, California, carrying his own knapsack and equipments.

The voyage from New York to Rio Janeiro was without accident or any thing to vary the usual monotony. We soon settled down to the humdrum of a long voyage, reading some, not much; playing games, but never gambling; and chiefly engaged in eating our meals regularly. In crossing the equator we had the usual visit of Neptune and his wife, who, with a large razor and a bucket of soapsuds, came over the sides and shaved some of the greenhorns; but naval etiquette exempted the officers, and Neptune was not permitted to come aft of the mizzen-mast. At last, after sixty days of absolute monotony, the island of Raza, off Rio Janeiro, was descried, and we slowly entered the harbor, passing a fort on our right hand, from which came a hail, in the Portuguese language, from a huge speaking-trumpet, and our officer of the deck answered back in gibberish, according to a well-understood custom of the place. Sugar-loaf Mountain, on the south of the entrance, is very remarkable and well named; is almost conical, with a slight lean. The man-of-war anchorage is about five miles inside the heads, directly in front of the city of Rio Janeiro. Words will not describe the beauty of this perfect harbor, nor the delightful feeling after a long voyage of its fragrant airs, and the entire contrast between all things there and what we had left in New York.

We found the United States frigate Columbia anchored there, and after the Lexington was properly moored, nearly all the officers went on shore for sight-seeing and enjoyment. We landed at a wharf opposite which was a famous French restaurant, Faroux, and after ordering supper we all proceeded to the Rua da Ouvador, where most of the shops were, especially those for making feather flowers, as much to see the pretty girls as the flowers which they so skillfully made; thence we went to the theatre, where, besides some opera, we witnessed the audience and saw the Emperor Dom Pedro, and his Empress, the daughter of the King of Sicily. After the theatre we went back to the restaurant, where we had an excellent supper, with fruits of every variety and excellence, such as we had never seen before, or even knew the names of.

Supper being over, we called for the bill, and it was rendered in French, with Brazilian currency. It footed up some twenty-six thousand reis. The figures alarmed us, so we all put on the waiters' plate various coins in gold, which he took to the counter and returned the change, making the total about sixteen dollars. The millreis is about a dollar, but being a paper-money was at a discount, so as only to be worth about fifty-six cents in coin.

The Lexington remained in Rio about a week, during which we visited the Palace, a few miles in the country, also the Botanic Gardens, a place of infinite interest, with its specimens of tropical fruits, spices, etc., etc., and indeed every place of note. The thing I best recall is a visit Halleck and I made to the *Corcovado*, a high mountain whence the water is conveyed for the supply of the city. We started to take a walk, and passed along the aqueduct, which approaches the city by a series of arches; thence up the point of the hill to a place known as the *Madre*, or fountain, to which all the water that drips from the leaves is conducted by tile gutters, and is carried to the city by an open stone aqueduct.

Here we found Mr. Henry A. Wise, of Virginia, the United States minister to Brazil, and a Dr. Garnett, United States Navy, his intended son-in-law. We had a very interesting conversation, in which Mr. Wise enlarged on the fact that Rio was supplied from the "dews of heaven," for in the dry season the water comes from the mists and fogs which hang around the *Corcovado*, drips from the leaves of the trees, and is conducted to the *Madre* fountain by miles of tile gutters. Halleck and I continued our ascent of the mountain, catching from points of the way magnificent views of the scenery round about Rio Janeiro. We reached near the summit what was called the emperor's coffee-plantation, where we saw coffee-berries in their various stages, and the scaffolds on which the berries were dried before being cleaned. The coffee-tree reminded me of the red haw-tree of Ohio, and the berries were somewhat like those of the same tree, two grains of coffee being inclosed in one berry. These were dried and cleaned of the husk by hand or by machinery. A short, steep ascent from this place carried us to the summit, from which is beheld one of the most picturesque views on earth. The Organ

Mountains to the west and north, the ocean to the east, the city of Rio with its red-tiled houses at our feet, and the entire harbor like a map spread out, with innumerable bright valleys, make up a landscape that cannot be described by mere words. This spot is universally visited by strangers, and has often been described. After enjoying it immeasurably, we returned to the city by another route, tired but amply repaid by our long walk.

In due time all had been done that was requisite, and the Lexington put to sea and resumed her voyage. In October we approached Cape Horn, the first land descried was Staten Island, white with snow, and the ship seemed to be aiming for the channel to its west, straits of Le Maire, but her course was changed and we passed around to the east. In time we saw Cape Horn; an island rounded like an oven, after which it takes its name (*Ornos*) oven. Here we experienced very rough weather, buffeting about under storm stay-sails, and spending nearly a month before the wind favored our passage and enabled the course of the ship to be changed for Valparaiso. One day we sailed parallel with a French sloop-of-war, and it was sublime to watch the two ships rising and falling in those long deep swells of the ocean. All the time we were followed by the usual large flocks of Cape-pigeons and albatrosses of every color. The former resembled the common barn-pigeon exactly, but are in fact gulls of beautiful and varied colors, mostly dove-color. We caught many with fishing-lines baited with pork. We also took in the same way many albatrosses. The white ones are very large, and their down is equal to that of the swan. At last Cape Horn and its swelling seas were left behind, and we reached Valparaiso in about sixty days from Rio. We anchored in the open roadstead, and spent there about ten days, visiting all the usual places of interest, its foretop, main-top, mizzen-top, etc. Halleck and Ord went up to Santiago, the capital of Chili, some sixty miles inland, but I did not go. Valparaiso did not impress me favorably at all. Seen from the sea, it looked like a long string of houses along the narrow beach, surmounted with red banks of earth, with little verdure, and no trees at all. Northward the space widened out somewhat, and gave room for a plaza, but the mass of houses in that quarter were poor. We were there in

November, corresponding to our early spring, and we enjoyed the large strawberries which abounded. The Independence frigate, Commodore Shubrick, came in while we were there, having overtaken us, bound also for California. We met there also the sloop-of-war Levant, from California, and from the officers heard of many of the events that had transpired about the time the navy, under Commodore Sloat, had taken possession of the country.

All the necessary supplies being renewed in Valparaiso, the voyage was resumed. For nearly forty days we had uninterrupted favorable winds, being in the "trades," and, having settled down to sailor habits, time passed without notice. We had brought with us all the books we could find in New York about California, and had read them over and over again: Wilkes's "Exploring Expedition;" Dana's "Two Years before the Mast;" and Forbes's "Account of the Missions." It was generally understood we were bound for Monterey, then the capital of Upper California. We knew, of course, that General Kearney was *en route* for the same country overland; that Fremont was there with his exploring party; that the navy had already taken possession, and that a regiment of volunteers, Stevenson's, was to follow us from New York; but nevertheless we were impatient to reach our destination. About the middle of January the ship began to approach the California coast, of which the captain was duly cautious, because the English and Spanish charts differed some fifteen miles in the longitude, and on all the charts a current of two miles an hour was indicated northward along the coast. At last land was made one morning, and here occurred one of those accidents so provoking after a long and tedious voyage. Macomb, the master and regular navigator, had made the correct observations, but Nicholson during the night, by an observation on the north star, put the ship some twenty miles farther south than was the case by the regular reckoning, so that Captain Bailey gave directions to alter the course of the ship more to the north, and to follow the coast up, and to keep a good lookout for Point Pinos that marks the location of Monterey Bay. The usual north wind slackened, so that when noon allowed Macomb to get a good observation, it was found that we were north of Año Nuevo, the northern headland of

Monterey Bay. The ship was put about, but little by little arose one of those southeast storms so common on the coast in winter, and we buffeted about for several days, cursing that unfortunate observation on the north star, for, on first sighting the coast, had we turned for Monterey, instead of away to the north, we would have been snugly anchored before the storm. But the southeaster abated, and the usual northwest wind came out again, and we sailed steadily down into the roadstead of Monterey Bay. This is shaped somewhat like a fish-hook, the barb being the harbor, the point being Point Pinos, the southern headland. Slowly the land came out of the water, the high mountains about Santa Cruz, the low beach of the Salinas, and the strongly-marked ridge terminating in the sea in a point of dark pine-trees. Then the line of whitewashed houses of adobe, backed by the groves of dark oaks, resembling old apple-trees; and then we saw two vessels anchored close to the town. One was a small merchant-brig and another a large ship apparently dismasted. At last we saw a boat coming out to meet us, and when it came alongside, we were surprised to find Lieutenant Henry Wise, master of the Independence frigate, that we had left at Valparaiso. Wise had come off to pilot us to our anchorage. While giving orders to the man at the wheel, he, in his peculiar fluent style, told to us, gathered about him, that the Independence had sailed from Valparaiso a week after us and had been in Monterey a week; that the Californians had broken out into an insurrection; that the naval fleet under Commodore Stockton was all down the coast about San Diego; that General Kearney had reached the country, but had had a severe battle at San Pascual, and had been worsted, losing several officers and men, himself and others wounded; that war was then going on at Los Angeles; that the whole country was full of guerrillas, and that recently at Yerba Buena the alcalde, Lieutenant Bartlett, United States Navy, while out after cattle, had been lassoed, etc., etc. Indeed, in the short space of time that Wise was piloting our ship in, he told us more news than we could have learned on shore in a week, and, being unfamiliar with the great distances, we imagined that we should have to debark and begin fighting at once. Swords were brought out, guns oiled and made ready, and every thing was in a bustle when the old Lexington dropped her anchor on January 26, 1847, in Monterey Bay, after a voyage of one hundred and ninety-eight days from New York. Every thing on shore looked bright and beautiful, the hills covered with grass and flowers, the live-oaks so serene and homelike, and the low adobe houses, with red-tiled roofs and whitened walls, contrasted well with the dark pine-trees behind, making a decidedly good impression upon us who had come so far to spy out the land. Nothing could be more peaceful in its looks than Monterey in January, 1847. We had already made the acquaintance of Commodore Shubrick and the officers of the Independence in Valparaiso, so that we again met as old friends. Immediate preparations were made for landing, and, as I was quartermaster and commissary, I had plenty to do. There was a small wharf and an adobe custom-house in possession of the navy; also a barrack of two stories, occupied by some marines, commanded by Lieutenant Maddox; and on a hill to the west of the town had been built a two-story block-house of hewed logs occupied by a guard of sailors under command of Lieutenant Baldwin, United States Navy. Not a single modern wagon or cart was to be had in Monterey, nothing but the old Mexican cart with wooden wheels, drawn by two or three pairs of oxen, yoked by the horns. A man named Tom Cole had two or more of these, and he came into immediate requisition. The United States consul, and most prominent man there at the time, was Thomas O. Larkin, who had a store and a pretty good two-story house occupied by his family. It was soon determined that our company was to land and encamp on the hill at the block-house, and we were also to have possession of the warehouse, or custom-house, for storage. The company was landed on the wharf, and we all marched in full dress with knapsacks and arms, to the hill and relieved the guard under Lieutenant Baldwin. Tents and camp-equipage were hauled up, and soon the camp was established. I remained in a room at the custom-house, where I could superintend the landing of the stores and their proper distribution. I had brought out from New York twenty thousand dollars commissary funds, and eight thousand dollars quartermaster funds, and as the ship contained about six months' supply of provisions, also a saw-mill, grist-mill, and almost every thing needed, we were soon established comfortably. We found the people of Monterey a mixed set of Americans, native Mexicans, and Indians, about one thousand all told. They were kind and pleasant, and seemed to have nothing to do, except such as owned ranches in the country for the rearing of horses and cattle. Horses could be bought at any price from four dollars up to sixteen, but no horse was ever valued above a doubloon or Mexican ounce (sixteen dollars). Cattle cost eight dollars fifty cents for the best, and this made beef net about two cents a pound, but at that time nobody bought beef by the pound, but by the carcass.

Game of all kinds—elk, deer, wild geese, and ducks—was abundant; but coffee, sugar, and small stores, were rare and costly.

There were some half-dozen shops or stores, but their shelves were empty. The people were very fond of riding, dancing, and of shows of any kind. The young fellows took great delight in showing off their horsemanship, and would dash along, picking up a half-dollar from the ground, stop their horses in full career and turn about on the space of a bullock's hide, and their skill with the lasso was certainly wonderful. At full speed they could cast their lasso about the horns of a bull, or so throw it as to catch any particular foot. These fellows would work all day on horseback in driving cattle or catching wild-horses for a mere nothing, but all the money offered would not have hired one of them to walk a mile. The girls were very fond of dancing, and they did dance gracefully and well. Every Sunday, regularly, we had a *baile*, or dance, and sometimes interspersed through the week.

I remember very well, soon after our arrival, that we were all invited to witness a play called "Adam and Eve." Eve was personated by a pretty young girl known as Dolores Gomez, who, however, was dressed very unlike Eve, for she was covered with a petticoat and spangles. Adam was personated by her brother ——, the same who has since become somewhat famous as the person on whom is founded the McGarrahan claim. God Almighty was personated, and heaven's occupants seemed very human. Yet the play was pretty, interesting, and elicited universal applause. All the month of February we were by day preparing for our long stay in the country, and at

night making the most of the balls and parties of the most
primitive kind, picking up a smattering of Spanish, and extending our acquaintance with the people and the *costumbres
del pais*. I can well recall that Ord and I, impatient to look
inland, got permission and started for the Mission of San Juan
Bautista. Mounted on horses, and with our carbines, we took
the road by El Toro, quite a prominent hill, around which
passes the road to the south, following the Salinas or Monterey River. After about twenty miles over a sandy country
covered with oak-bushes and scrub, we entered quite a pretty
valley in which there was a ranch at the foot of the Toro.
Resting there a while and getting some information, we again
started in the direction of a mountain to the north of the
Salinas, called the Gavillano. It was quite dark when we
reached the Salinas River, which we attempted to pass at several points, but found it full of water, and the quicksands
were bad. Hearing the bark of a dog, we changed our course
in that direction, and, on hailing, were answered by voices
which directed us where to cross. Our knowledge of the language was limited, but we managed to understand, and to
flounder through the sand and water, and reached a small
adobe-house on the banks of the Salinas, where we spent the
night. The house was a single room, without floor or glass;
only a rude door, and window with bars. Not a particle of
food but meat, yet the man and woman entertained us with
the language of lords, put themselves, their house, and every
thing, at our "disposition," and made little barefoot children
dance for our entertainment. We made our supper of beef,
and slept on a bullock's hide on the dirt-floor. In the morning
we crossed the Salinas Plain, about fifteen miles of level
ground, taking a shot occasionally at wild-geese, which
abounded there, and entering the well-wooded valley that
comes out from the foot of the Gavillano. We had cruised
about all day, and it was almost dark when we reached the
house of a Señor Gomez, father of those who at Monterey
had performed the parts of Adam and Eve. His house was a
two-story adobe, and had a fence in front. It was situated well
up among the foot-hills of the Gavillano, and could not be
seen until within a few yards. We hitched our horses to the
fence and went in just as Gomez was about to sit down to a

tempting supper of stewed hare and tortillas. We were officers and *caballeros* and could not be ignored. After turning our horses to grass, at his invitation we joined him at supper. The allowance, though ample for one, was rather short for three, and I thought the Spanish grandiloquent politeness of Gomez, who was fat and old, was not over-cordial. However, down we sat, and I was helped to a dish of rabbit, with what I thought to be an abundant sauce of tomato. Taking a good mouthful, I felt as though I had taken liquid fire; the tomato was *chile colorado*, or red pepper, of the purest kind. It nearly killed me, and I saw Gomez's eyes twinkle, for he saw that his share of supper was increased. I contented myself with bits of the meat, and an abundant supply of tortillas. Ord was better case-hardened, and stood it better. We staid at Gomez's that night, sleeping, as all did, on the ground, and the next morning we crossed the hill by the bridle-path to the old Mission of San Juan Bautista. The Mission was in a beautiful valley, very level, and bounded on all sides by hills. The plain was covered with wild-grasses and mustard, and had abundant water. Cattle and horses were seen in all directions, and it was manifest that the priests who first occupied the country were good judges of land. It was Sunday, and all the people, about a hundred, had come to church from the country round about. Ord was somewhat of a Catholic, and entered the church with his clanking spurs and kneeled down, attracting the attention of all, for he had on the uniform of an American officer. As soon as church was out, all rushed to the various sports. I saw the priest, with his gray robes tucked up, playing at billiards, others were cock-fighting, and some at horse-racing. My horse had become lame, and I resolved to buy another. As soon as it was known that I wanted a horse, several came for me, and displayed their horses by dashing past and hauling them up short. There was a fine black stallion that attracted my notice, and, after trying him myself, I concluded a purchase. I left with the seller my own lame horse, which he was to bring to me at Monterey, when I was to pay him ten dollars for the other. The Mission of San Juan bore the marks of high prosperity at a former period, and had a good pear-orchard just under the plateau where stood the church. After spending the day, Ord and I returned to Monterey, about thirty-five miles, by a shorter route. Thus passed the month of February, and, though there were no mails or regular expresses, we heard occasionally from Yerba Buena and Sutter's Fort to the north, and from the army and navy about Los Angeles at the south. We also knew that a quarrel had grown up at Los Angeles, between General Kearney, Colonel Fremont, and Commodore Stockton, as to the right to control affairs in California. Kearney had with him only the fragments of the two companies of dragoons, which had come across from New Mexico with him, and had been handled very roughly by Don Andreas Pico, at San Pascual, in which engagement Captains Moore and Johnson, and Lieutenant Hammond, were killed, and Kearney himself wounded. There remained with him Colonel Swords, quartermaster; Captain H. S. Turner, First Dragoons; Captains Emory and Warner, Topographical Engineers; Assistant Surgeon Griffin, and Lieutenant J. W. Davidson. Fremont had marched down from the north with a battalion of volunteers; Commodore Stockton had marched up from San Diego to Los Angeles, with General Kearney, his dragoons, and a battalion of sailors and marines, and was soon joined there by Fremont, and they jointly received the surrender of the insurgents under Andreas Pico. We also knew that General R. B. Mason had been ordered to California; that Colonel John D. Stevenson was coming out to California with a regiment of New York Volunteers; that Commodore Shubrick had orders also from the Navy Department to control matters afloat; that General Kearney, by virtue of his rank, had the right to control all the land-forces in the service of the United States; and that Fremont claimed the same right by virtue of a letter he had received from Colonel Benton, then a Senator, and a man of great influence with Polk's Administration. So that among the younger officers the query was very natural, "Who the devil is Governor of California?" One day I was on board the Independence frigate, dining with the ward-room officers, when a war-vessel was reported in the offing, which in due time was made out to be the Cyane, Captain DuPont. After dinner, we were all on deck, to watch the new arrival, the ships meanwhile exchanging signals, which were interpreted that General Kearney was on board. As the Cyane approached, a boat was sent to meet her, with Commodore Shubrick's flag-officer, Lieutenant Lewis, to carry the usual messages, and to invite General Kearney to come on board the Independence as the guest of Commodore Shubrick. Quite a number of officers were on deck, among them Lieutenants Wise, Montgomery Lewis, William Chapman, and others, noted wits and wags of the navy. In due time the Cyane anchored close by, and our boat was seen returning with a stranger in the stern-sheets, clothed in army-blue. As the boat came nearer, we saw that it was General Kearney with an old dragoon coat on, and an army-cap, to which the general had added the broad *visor*, cut from a full-dress hat, to shade his face and eyes against the glaring sun of the Gila region. Chapman exclaimed: "Fellows, the problem is solved; there is the grand-vizier (visor) by G—d! *He* is Governor of California."

All hands received the general with great heartiness, and he soon passed out of our sight into the commodore's cabin. Between Commodore Shubrick and General Kearney existed from that time forward the greatest harmony and good feeling, and no further trouble existed as to the controlling power on the Pacific coast. General Kearney had dispatched from San Diego his quartermaster, Colonel Swords, to the Sandwich Islands, to purchase clothing and stores for his men, and had come up to Monterey, bringing with him Turner and Warner, leaving Emory and the company of dragoons below. He was delighted to find a full strong company of artillery, subject to his orders, well supplied with clothing and money in all respects, and, much to the disgust of our Captain Tompkins, he took half of his company clothing and part of the money held by me for the relief of his worn-out and almost naked dragoons left behind at Los Angeles. In a few days he moved on shore, took up his quarters at Larkin's house, and established his headquarters, with Captain Turner as his adjutant-general. One day Turner and Warner were at my tent, and, seeing a store-box full of socks, drawers, and calico shirts, of which I had laid in a three years' supply, and of which they had none, made known to me their wants, and I told them to help themselves, which Turner and Warner did. The latter, however, insisted on paying me the cost, and from that date to this Turner and I have been close friends. Warner, poor fellow, was afterward killed by Indians. Things gradually came into shape, a semi-monthly courier line was established from Yerba Buena to San Diego, and we were thus enabled to keep pace with events throughout the country. In March Stevenson's regiment arrived. Colonel Mason also arrived by sea from Callao in the store-ship Erie, and P. St. George Cooke's battalion of Mormons reached San Luis Rey. A. J. Smith and George Stoneman were with him, and were assigned to the company of dragoons at Los Angeles. All these troops and the navy regarded General Kearney as the rightful commander, though Fremont still remained at Los Angeles, styling himself as Governor, issuing orders and holding his battalion of California Volunteers in apparent defiance of General Kearney. Colonel Mason and Major Turner were sent down by sea with a paymaster, with muster-rolls and orders to muster this battalion into the service of the United States, to pay and then to muster them out; but on their reaching Los Angeles Fremont would not consent to it, and the controversy became so angry that a challenge was believed to have passed between Mason and Fremont, but the duel never came about. Turner rode up by land in four or five days, and Fremont, becoming alarmed, followed him, as we supposed, to overtake him, but he did not succeed. On Fremont's arrival at Monterey, he camped in a tent about a mile out of town and called on General Kearney, and it was reported that the latter threatened him very severely and ordered him back to Los Angeles immediately, to disband his volunteers, and to cease the exercise of authority of any kind in the country. Feeling a natural curiosity to see Fremont, who was then quite famous by reason of his recent explorations and the still more recent conflicts with Kearney and Mason, I rode out to his camp, and found him in a conical tent with one Captain Owens, who was a mountaineer, trapper, etc., but originally from Zanesville, Ohio. I spent an hour or so with Fremont in his tent, took some tea with him, and left, without being much impressed with him. In due time Colonel Swords returned from the Sandwich Islands and relieved me as quartermaster. Captain William G. Marcy, son of the Secretary of War, had also come out in one of Stevenson's ships as an assistant commissary of subsistence, and was stationed at Monterey and relieved me as commissary, so that I reverted to the condition of a company-officer. While acting as a staff officer I had lived at the custom-house in Monterey, but when relieved I took a tent in line with the other company-officers on the hill, where we had a mess.

Stevenson's regiment reached San Francisco Bay early in March, 1847. Three companies were stationed at the Presidio under Major James A. Hardie; one company (Brackett's) at Sonoma; three, under Colonel Stevenson, at Monterey; and three, under Lieutenant-Colonel Burton, at Santa Barbara. One day I was down at the headquarters at Larkin's house, when General Kearney remarked to me that he was going down to Los Angeles in the ship Lexington, and wanted me to go along as his aide. Of course this was most agreeable to me. Two of Stevenson's companies, with the headquarters and the colonel, were to go also. They embarked, and early in May we sailed for San Pedro. Before embarking, the United States line-of-battle-ship Columbus had reached the coast from China with Commodore Biddle, whose rank gave him the supreme command of the navy on the coast. He was busy in calling in—"lassooing"—from the land-service the various naval officers who under Stockton had been doing all sorts of military and civil service on shore. Knowing that I was to go down the coast with General Kearney, he sent for me and handed me two unsealed parcels addressed to Lieutenant Wilson, United States Navy, and Major Gillespie, United States Marines, at Los Angeles. These were written orders pretty much in these words: "On receipt of this order you will repair at once on board the United States ship Lexington at San Pedro, and on reaching Monterey you will report to the undersigned.—JAMES BIDDLE." Of course, I executed my part to the letter, and these officers were duly "lassooed." We sailed down the coast with a fair wind, and anchored inside the kelp, abreast of Johnson's house. Messages were forthwith dispatched up to Los Angeles, twenty miles off, and preparations for horses made for us to ride up. We landed, and, as Kearney held to my arm in ascending the steep path up the bluff, he remarked to himself, rather than to me, that it was strange that Fremont did not want to return north by the

Lexington on account of sea-sickness, but preferred to go by land over five hundred miles. The younger officers had been discussing what the general would do with Fremont, who was supposed to be in a state of mutiny. Some thought he would be tried and shot, some that he would be carried back *in irons*; and all agreed that if any one else than Fremont had put on such airs, and had acted as he had done, Kearney would have shown him no mercy, for he was regarded as the strictest sort of a disciplinarian. We had a pleasant ride across the plain which lies between the seashore and Los Angeles, which we reached in about three hours, the infantry following on foot. We found Colonel P. St. George Cooke living at the house of a Mr. Pryor, and the company of dragoons, with A. J. Smith, Davidson, Stoneman, and Dr. Griffin, quartered in an adobe-house close by. Fremont held his court in the only two-story frame-house in the place. After some time spent at Pryor's house, General Kearney ordered me to call on Fremont to notify him of his arrival, and that he desired to see him. I walked round to the house which had been pointed out to me as his, inquired of a man at the door if the colonel was in, was answered "Yes," and was conducted to a large room on the second floor, where very soon Fremont came in, and I delivered my message. As I was on the point of leaving, he inquired where I was going to, and I answered that I was going back to Pryor's house, where the general was, when he remarked that if I would wait a moment he would go along. Of course I waited, and he soon joined me, dressed much as a Californian, with the peculiar high, broad-brimmed hat, with a fancy cord, and we walked together back to Pryor's, where I left him with General Kearney. We spent several days very pleasantly at Los Angeles, then, as now, the chief *pueblo* of the south, famous for its grapes, fruits, and wines. There was a hill close to the town, from which we had a perfect view of the place. The surrounding country is level, utterly devoid of trees, except the willows and cotton-woods that line the Los Angeles Creek and the *acequias*, or ditches, which lead from it. The space of ground cultivated in vineyards seemed about five miles by one, embracing the town. Every house had its inclosure of vineyard, which resembled a miniature orchard, the vines being very old, ranged in rows, trimmed very close, with irrigating ditches so arranged that a stream of water could be diverted between each row of vines. The Los Angeles and San Gabriel Rivers are fed by melting snows from a range of mountains to the east, and the quantity of cultivated land depends upon the amount of water. This did not seem to be very large; but the San Gabriel River, close by, was represented to contain a larger volume of water, affording the means of greatly enlarging the space for cultivation. The climate was so moderate that oranges, figs, pomegranates, etc., were generally to be found in every yard or inclosure.

At the time of our visit, General Kearney was making his preparations to return overland to the United States, and he arranged to secure a volunteer escort out of the battalion of Mormons that was then stationed at San Luis Rey, under Colonel Cooke and a Major Hunt. This battalion was only enlisted for one year, and the time for their discharge was approaching, and it was generally understood that the majority of the men wanted to be discharged so as to join the Mormons who had halted at Salt Lake, but a lieutenant and about forty men volunteered to return to Missouri as the escort of General Kearney. These were mounted on mules and horses, and I was appointed to conduct them to Monterey by land. Leaving the party at Los Angeles to follow by sea in the Lexington, I started with the Mormon detachment and traveled by land. We averaged about thirty miles a day, stopped one day at Santa Barbara, where I saw Colonel Burton, and so on by the usually traveled road to Monterey, reaching it in about fifteen days, arriving some days in advance of the Lexington. This gave me the best kind of an opportunity for seeing the country, which was very sparsely populated indeed, except by a few families at the various Missions. We had no wheeled vehicles, but packed our food and clothing on mules driven ahead, and we slept on the ground in the open air, the rainy season having passed. Fremont followed me by land in a few days, and, by the end of May, General Kearney was all ready at Monterey to take his departure, leaving to succeed him in command Colonel R. B. Mason, First Dragoons. Our Captain (Tompkins), too, had become discontented at his separation from his family, tendered his resignation to General

Kearney, and availed himself of a sailing-vessel bound for Callao to reach the East. Colonel Mason selected me as his adjutant-general; and on the very last day of May General Kearney, with his Mormon escort, with Colonel Cooke, Colonel Swords (quartermaster), Captain Turner, and a naval officer, Captain Radford, took his departure for the East overland, leaving us in full possession of California and its fate. Fremont also left California with General Kearney, and with him departed all cause of confusion and disorder in the country. From that time forth no one could dispute the authority of Colonel Mason as in command of all the United States forces on shore, while the senior naval officer had a like control afloat. This was Commodore James Biddle, who had reached the station from China in the Columbus, and he in turn was succeeded by Commodore T. Ap Catesby Jones in the line-of-battle-ship Ohio. At that time Monterey was our headquarters, and the naval commander for a time remained there, but subsequently San Francisco Bay became the chief naval rendezvous.

Colonel R. B. Mason, First Dragoons, was an officer of great experience, of stern character, deemed by some harsh and severe, but in all my intercourse with him he was kind and agreeable. He had a large fund of good sense, and, during our long period of service together, I enjoyed his unlimited confidence. He had been in his day a splendid shot and hunter, and often entertained me with characteristic anecdotes of Taylor, Twiggs, Worth, Harney, Martin Scott, etc., etc., who were then in Mexico, gaining a national fame. California had settled down to a condition of absolute repose, and we naturally repined at our fate in being so remote from the war in Mexico, where our comrades were reaping large honors. Mason dwelt in a house not far from the Custom-House, with Captain Lanman, United States Navy; I had a small adobe-house back of Larkin's. Halleck and Dr. Murray had a small log-house not far off. The company of artillery was still on the hill, under the command of Lieutenant Ord, engaged in building a fort whereon to mount the guns we had brought out in the Lexington, and also in constructing quarters out of hewn pine-logs for the men. Lieutenant Minor, a very clever young officer, had taken violently sick and died

about the time I got back from Los Angeles, leaving Lieutenants Ord and Loeser alone with the company, with Assistant-
Surgeon Robert Murray. Captain William G. Marcy was the
quartermaster and commissary. Naglee's company of Stevenson's regiment had been mounted and was sent out against
the Indians in the San Joaquin Valley, and Shannon's company occupied the barracks. Shortly after General Kearney
had gone East, we found an order of his on record, removing
one Mr. Nash, the Alcalde of Sonoma, and appointing to his
place ex-Governor L. W. Boggs. A letter came to Colonel and
Governor Mason from Boggs, whom he had personally
known in Missouri, complaining that, though he had been
appointed alcalde, the then incumbent (Nash) utterly denied
Kearney's right to remove him, because he had been elected
by the people under the proclamation of Commodore Sloat,
and refused to surrender his office or to account for his acts as
alcalde. Such a proclamation had been made by Commodore
Sloat shortly after the first occupation of California, announcing that the people were free and enlightened American citizens, entitled to all the rights and privileges as such, and
among them the right to elect their own officers, etc. The
people of Sonoma town and valley, some forty or fifty immigrants from the United States, and very few native Californians, had elected Mr. Nash, and, as stated, he refused to
recognize the right of a mere military commander to eject him
and to appoint another to his place. Neither General Kearney
nor Mason had much respect for this kind of "buncombe,"
but assumed the true doctrine that California was yet a Mexican province, held by right of conquest, that the military
commander was held responsible to the country, and that the
province should be held *in statu quo* until a treaty of peace.
This letter of Boggs was therefore referred to Captain Brackett, whose company was stationed at Sonoma, with orders to
notify Nash that Boggs was the rightful alcalde; that he must
quietly surrender his office, with the books and records
thereof, and that he must account for any moneys received
from the sale of town-lots, etc., etc.; and in the event of refusal he (Captain Brackett) must compel him by the use of
force. In due time we got Brackett's answer, saying that the
little community of Sonoma was in a dangerous state of effer-

vescence caused by his orders; that Nash was backed by most of the Americans there who had come across from Missouri with American ideas; that as he (Brackett) was a volunteer officer, likely to be soon discharged, and as he designed to settle there, he asked in consequence to be excused from the execution of this (to him) unpleasant duty. Such a request, coming to an old soldier like Colonel Mason, aroused his wrath, and he would have proceeded rough-shod against Brackett, who, by-the-way, was a West Point graduate, and ought to have known better; but I suggested to the colonel that, the case being a test one, he had better send me up to Sonoma, and I would settle it quick enough. He then gave me an order to go to Sonoma to carry out the instructions already given to Brackett.

I took one soldier with me, Private Barnes, with four horses, two of which we rode, and the other two we drove ahead. The first day we reached Gilroy's and camped by a stream near three or four adobe-huts known as Gilroy's ranch. The next day we passed Murphy's, San José, and Santa Clara Mission, camping some four miles beyond, where a kind of hole had been dug in the ground for water. The whole of this distance, now so beautifully improved and settled, was then scarcely occupied, except by poor ranches producing horses and cattle. The *pueblo* of San José was a string of low adobe-houses festooned with red peppers and garlic; and the Mission of Santa Clara was a dilapidated concern, with its church and orchard. The long line of poplar-trees lining the road from San José to Santa Clara bespoke a former period when the priests had ruled the land. Just about dark I was lying on the ground near the well, and my soldier Barnes had watered our horses and picketed them to grass, when we heard a horse crushing his way through the high mustard-bushes which filled the plain, and soon a man came to us to inquire if we had seen a saddle-horse pass up the road. We explained to him what we had heard, and he went off in pursuit of his horse. Before dark he came back unsuccessful, and gave his name as Bidwell, the same gentleman who has since been a member of Congress, who is married to Miss Kennedy, of Washington City, and now lives in princely style at Chico, California.

He explained that he was a surveyor, and had been in the lower country engaged in surveying land; that the horse had escaped him with his saddle-bags containing all his notes and papers, and some six hundred dollars in money, all the money he had earned. He spent the night with us on the ground, and the next morning we left him there to continue the search for his horse, and I afterward heard that he had found his saddle-bags all right, but never recovered the horse. The next day toward night we approached the Mission of San Francisco, and the village of Yerba Buena, tired and weary—the wind as usual blowing a perfect hurricane, and a more desolate region it was impossible to conceive of. Leaving Barnes to work his way into the town as best he could with the tired animals, I took the freshest horse and rode forward. I fell in with Lieutenant Fabius Stanley, United States Navy, and we rode into Yerba Buena together about an hour before sundown, there being nothing but a path from the Mission into the town, deep and heavy with drift-sand. My horse could hardly drag one foot after the other when we reached the old Hudson Bay Company's house, which was then the store of Howard and Mellus. There I learned where Captain Folsom, the quartermaster, was to be found. He was staying with a family of the name of Grimes, who had a small house back of Howard's store, which must have been near where Sacramento Street now crosses Kearney. Folsom was a classmate of mine, had come out with Stevenson's regiment as quartermaster, and was at the time the chief-quartermaster of the department. His office was in the old custom-house standing at the northwest corner of the Plaza. He had hired two warehouses, the only ones there at the time, of one Liedsdorff, the principal man of Yerba Buena, who also owned the only publichouse, or tavern, called the City Hotel, on Kearney Street, at the southeast corner of the Plaza. I stopped with Folsom at Mrs. Grimes's, and he sent my horse, as also the other three when Barnes had got in after dark, to a *corral* where he had a little barley, but no hay. At that time nobody fed a horse, but he was usually turned out to pick such scanty grass as he could find on the side-hills. The few government horses used in town were usually sent out to the Presidio, where the grass was somewhat better. At that time (July, 1847), what is now called San Francisco was called Yerba Buena. A naval officer, Lieutenant Washington A. Bartlett, its first alcalde, had caused it to be surveyed and laid out into blocks and lots, which were being sold at sixteen dollars a lot of fifty *varas* square; the understanding being that no single person could purchase of the alcalde more than one in-lot of fifty varas, and one out-lot of a hundred varas. Folsom, however, had got his clerks, orderlies, etc., to buy lots, and they, for a small consideration, conveyed them to him, so that he was nominally the owner of a good many lots. Lieutenant Halleck had bought one of each kind, and so had Warner. Many naval officers had also invested, and Captain Folsom advised me to buy some, but I felt actually insulted that he should think me such a fool as to pay money for property in such a horrid place as Yerba Buena, especially ridiculing his quarter of the city, then called Happy Valley. At that day Montgomery Street was, as now, the business street, extending from Jackson to Sacramento, the water of the bay leaving barely room for a few houses on its east side, and the public warehouses were on a sandy beach about where the Bank of California now stands, viz., near the intersection of Sansome and California Streets. Along Montgomery Street were the stores of Howard & Mellus, Frank Ward, Sherman & Ruckel, Ross & Co., and it may be one or two others. Around the Plaza were a few houses, among them the City Hotel and the Custom-House, single-story adobes with tiled roofs, and they were by far the most substantial and best houses in the place. The population was estimated at about four hundred, of whom Kanakas (natives of the Sandwich Islands) formed the bulk. At the foot of Clay Street was a small wharf which small boats could reach at high tide; but the principal landing-place was where some stones had fallen into the water, about where Broadway now intersects Battery Street. On the steep bluff above had been excavated, by the navy, during the year before, a bench, wherein were mounted a couple of navy-guns, styled *the battery*, which, I suppose, gave name to the street. I explained to Folsom the object of my visit, and learned from him that he had no boat in which to send me to Sonoma, and that the only chance to get there was to borrow a boat from the navy. The line-of-battle-ship Columbus was then lying at anchor off the town, and he said if I would get up early the next morning I could go off to her in one of the *market*-boats.

Accordingly, I was up bright and early, down at the wharf, found a boat, and went off to the Columbus to see Commodore Biddle. On reaching the ship and stating to the officer of the deck my business, I was shown into the commodore's cabin, and soon made known to him my object. Biddle was a small-sized man, but vivacious in the extreme. He had a perfect contempt for all humbug, and at once entered into the business with extreme alacrity. I was somewhat amused at the importance he attached to the step. He had a chaplain, and a private secretary, in a small room latticed off from his cabin, and he first called on them to go out, and, when we were alone, he enlarged on the folly of Sloat's proclamation, giving the people the right to elect their own officers, and commended Kearney and Mason for nipping that idea in the bud, and keeping the power in their own hands. He then sent for the first lieutenant (Drayton), and inquired if there were among the officers on board any who had ever been in the Upper Bay, and learning that there was a midshipman (Whittaker) he was sent for. It so happened that this midshipman had been on a frolic on shore a few nights before, and was accordingly much frightened when summoned into the commodore's presence, but as soon as he was questioned as to his knowledge of the bay, he was sensibly relieved, and professed to know every thing about it.

Accordingly, the long-boat was ordered with this midshipman and eight sailors, prepared with water and provisions for several days' absence. Biddle then asked me if I knew any of his own officers, and which one of them I would prefer to accompany me. I knew most of them, and we settled down on Louis McLane. He was sent for, and it was settled that McLane and I were to conduct this *important* mission, and the commodore enjoined on us complete secrecy, so as to insure success, and he especially cautioned us against being pumped by his ward-room officers, Chapman, Lewis, Wise, etc., while on board his ship. With this injunction I was dismissed to the ward-room, where I found Chapman, Lewis, and Wise, dreadfully exercised at our profound secrecy. The fact that McLane and I had been closeted with the commo-

dore for an hour, that orders for the boat and stores had been
made, that the chaplain and clerk had been sent out of the
cabin, etc., etc., all excited their curiosity; but McLane and I
kept our secret well. The general impression was, that we had
some knowledge about the fate of Captain Montgomery's
two sons and the crew that had been lost the year before. In
1846 Captain Montgomery commanded at Yerba Buena, on
board the St. Mary sloop-of-war, and he had a detachment of
men stationed up at Sonoma. Occasionally a boat was sent up
with provisions or intelligence to them. Montgomery had
two sons on board his ship, one a midshipman, the other his
secretary. Having occasion to send some money up to
Sonoma, he sent his two sons with a good boat and crew.
The boat started with a strong breeze and a very large sail,
was watched from the deck until she was out of sight, and has
never been heard of since. There was, of course, much speculation as to their fate, some contending that the boat must
have been capsized in San Pablo Bay, and that all were lost;
others contending that the crew had murdered the officers for
the money, and then escaped; but, so far as I know, not a
man of that crew has ever been seen or heard of since. When
at last the boat was ready for us, we started, leaving all hands,
save the commodore, impressed with the belief that we were
going on some errand connected with the loss of the missing
boat and crew of the St. Mary. We sailed directly north, up
the bay and across San Pablo, reached the mouth of Sonoma
Creek about dark, and during the night worked up the creek
some twelve miles by means of the tide, to a landing called
the *Embarcadero*. To maintain the secrecy which the commodore had enjoined on us, McLane and I agreed to keep up the
delusion by pretending to be on a marketing expedition to
pick up chickens, pigs, etc., for the mess of the Columbus,
soon to depart for home.

Leaving the midshipman and four sailors to guard the boat,
we started on foot with the other four for Sonoma Town,
which we soon reached. It was a simple open square, around
which were some adobe-houses, that of General Vallejo occupying one side. On another was an unfinished two-story
adobe building, occupied as a barrack by Brackett's company.
We soon found Captain Brackett, and I told him that I

intended to take Nash a prisoner and convey him back to Monterey to answer for his mutinous behavior. I got an old sergeant of his company, whom I had known in the Third Artillery, quietly to ascertain the whereabouts of Nash, who was a bachelor, stopping with the family of a lawyer named Green. The sergeant soon returned, saying that Nash had gone over to Napa, but would be back that evening; so McLane and I went up to a farm of some pretensions, occupied by one Andreas Hoepner, with a pretty Sitka wife, who lived a couple of miles above Sonoma, and we bought of him some chickens, pigs, etc. We then visited Governor Boggs's family and that of General Vallejo, who was then, as now, one of the most prominent and influential natives of California. About dark I learned that Nash had come back, and then, giving Brackett orders to have a cart ready at the corner of the plaza, McLane and I went to the house of Green. Posting an armed sailor on each side of the house, we knocked at the door and walked in. We found Green, Nash, and two women, at supper. I inquired if Nash were in, and was first answered "No," but one of the women soon pointed to him, and he rose. We were armed with pistols, and the family was evidently alarmed. I walked up to him and took his arm, and told him to come along with me. He asked me, "Where?" and I said, "Monterey." "Why?" I would explain that more at leisure. Green put himself between me and the door, and demanded, in theatrical style, why I dared arrest a peaceable citizen in his house. I simply pointed to my pistol, and told him to get out of the way, which he did. Nash asked to get some clothing, but I told him he should want for nothing. We passed out, Green following us with loud words, which brought the four sailors to the front-door, when I told him to hush up or I would take him prisoner also. About that time one of the sailors, handling his pistol carelessly, discharged it, and Green disappeared very suddenly. We took Nash to the cart, put him in, and proceeded back to our boat. The next morning we were gone.

Nash being out of the way, Boggs entered on his office, and the right to appoint or remove from civil office was never again questioned in California during the military *régime*. Nash was an old man, and was very much alarmed for his personal safety. He had come across the Plains, and had never yet seen the sea. While on our way down the bay, I explained fully to him the state of things in California, and he admitted he had never looked on it in that light before, and professed a willingness to surrender his office; but, having gone so far, I thought it best to take him to Monterey. On our way down the bay the wind was so strong, as we approached the Columbus, that we had to take refuge behind Yerba Buena Island, then called Goat Island, where we landed, and I killed a gray seal. The next morning, the wind being comparatively light, we got out and worked our way up to the Columbus, where I left my prisoner on board, and went on shore to find Commodore Biddle, who had gone to dine with Frank Ward. I found him there, and committed Nash to his charge, with the request that he would send him down to Monterey, which he did in the sloop-of-war Dale, Captain Selfridge commanding. I then returned to Monterey by land, and, when the Dale arrived, Colonel Mason and I went on board, found poor old Mr. Nash half dead with sea-sickness and fear, lest Colonel Mason would treat him with extreme military rigor. But, on the contrary, the colonel spoke to him kindly, released him as a prisoner on his promise to go back to Sonoma, surrender his office to Boggs, and account to him for his acts while in office. He afterward came on shore, was provided with clothing and a horse, returned to Sonoma, and I never have seen him since.

Matters and things settled down in Upper California, and all moved along with peace and harmony. The war still continued in Mexico, and the navy authorities resolved to employ their time with the capture of Mazatlan and Guaymas. Lower California had already been occupied by two companies of Stevenson's regiment, under Lieutenant-Colonel Burton, who had taken post at La Paz, and a small party of sailors was on shore at San Josef, near Cape San Lucas, detached from the Lexington, Lieutenant-Commander Bailey. The orders for this occupation were made by General Kearney before he left, in pursuance of instructions from the War Department, merely to subserve a political end, for there were few or no people in Lower California, which is a miserable, wretched, dried-up peninsula. I remember the proclamation made by

Burton and Captain Bailey, in taking possession, which was in the usual florid style. Bailey signed his name as the senior naval officer at the station, but, as it was necessary to put it into Spanish to reach the inhabitants of the newly-acquired country, it was interpreted, "El mas antiguo de todos los oficiales de la marina," etc., which, literally, is "the most ancient of all the naval officers," etc., a translation at which we made some fun.

The expedition to Mazatlan was, however, for a different purpose, viz., to get possession of the ports of Mazatlan and Guaymas, as a part of the war against Mexico, and not for permanent conquest.

Commodore Shubrick commanded this expedition, and took Halleck along as his engineer-officer. They captured Mazatlan and Guaymas, and then called on Colonel Mason to send soldiers down to hold possession, but he had none to spare, and it was found impossible to raise other volunteers either in California or Oregon, and the navy held these places by detachments of sailors and marines till the end of the war. Burton also called for reënforcements, and Naglee's company was sent to him from Monterey, and these three companies occupied Lower California at the end of the Mexican War. Major Hardie still commanded at San Francisco and above; Company F, Third Artillery, and Shannon's company of volunteers, were at Monterey; Lippett's company at Santa Barbara; Colonel Stevenson, with one company of his regiment, and the company of the First Dragoons, was at Los Angeles; and a company of Mormons, reënlisted out of the Mormon Battalion, garrisoned San Diego—and thus matters went along throughout 1847 into 1848. I had occasion to make several trips to Yerba Buena and back, and in the spring of 1848 Colonel Mason and I went down to Santa Barbara in the sloop-of-war Dale.

I spent much time in hunting deer and bear in the mountains back of the Carmel Mission, and ducks and geese in the plains of the Salinas. As soon as the fall rains set in, the young oats would sprout up, and myriads of ducks, brant, and geese, made their appearance. In a single day, or rather in the evening of one day and the morning of the next, I could load a pack-mule with geese and ducks. They had grown somewhat wild from the increased number of hunters, yet, by marking well the place where a flock lighted, I could, by taking advantage of gullies or the shape of the ground, creep up within range; and, giving one barrel on the ground, and the other as they rose, I have secured as many as nine at one discharge. Colonel Mason on one occasion killed eleven geese by one discharge of small shot. The seasons in California are well marked. About October and November the rains begin, and the whole country, plains and mountains, becomes covered with a bright-green grass, with endless flowers. The intervals between the rains give the finest weather possible. These rains are less frequent in March, and cease altogether in April and May, when gradually the grass dies and the whole aspect of things changes, first to yellow, then to brown, and by midsummer all is burnt up and dry as an ash-heap.

When General Kearney first departed we took his office at Larkin's; but shortly afterward we had a broad stairway constructed to lead from the outside to the upper front porch of the barracks. By cutting a large door through the adobe-wall, we made the upper room in the centre our office; and another side-room, connected with it by a door, was Colonel Mason's private office.

I had a single clerk, a soldier named Baden; and William E. P. Hartnell, citizen, also had a table in the same room. He was the government interpreter, and had charge of the civil archives. After Halleck's return from Mazatlan, he was, by Colonel Mason, made Secretary of State; and he then had charge of the civil archives, including the land-titles, of which Fremont first had possession, but which had reverted to us when he left the country.

I remember one day, in the spring of 1848, that two men, Americans, came into the office and inquired for the Governor. I asked their business, and one answered that they had just come down from Captain Sutter on special business, and they wanted to see Governor Mason *in person*. I took them in to the colonel, and left them together. After some time the colonel came to his door and called to me. I went in, and my attention was directed to a series of papers unfolded on his table, in which lay about half an ounce of *placer*-gold. Mason said to me, "What is that?" I touched it and examined one or two of the larger pieces, and asked, "Is it gold?" Mason asked me if I had ever seen native gold. I answered that, in 1844, I was in Upper Georgia, and there saw some native gold, but it was much finer than this, and that it was in phials, or in transparent quills; but I said that, if this were gold, it could be easily tested, first, by its malleability, and next by acids. I took a piece in my teeth, and the metallic lustre was perfect. I then called to the clerk, Baden, to bring an axe and hatchet from the backyard. When these were brought, I took the largest piece and beat it out flat, and beyond doubt it was metal, and a pure metal. Still, we attached little importance to the fact, for gold was known to exist at San Fernando, at the south, and yet was not considered of much value.

Colonel Mason then handed me a letter from Captain Sutter, addressed to him, stating that he (Sutter) was engaged in erecting a saw-mill at Coloma, about forty miles up the American Fork, above his fort at New Helvetia, for the general benefit of the settlers in that vicinity; that he had incurred considerable expense, and wanted a "preëmption" to the quarter-section of land on which the mill was located, embracing the tail-race in which this particular gold had been found. Mason instructed me to prepare a letter, in answer, for his signature. I wrote off a letter, reciting that California was yet a Mexican province, simply held by us as a conquest; that no laws of the United States yet applied to it, much less the land laws or preëmption laws, which could only apply after a public survey. Therefore it was impossible for the Governor to promise him (Sutter) a title to the land; yet, as there were no settlements within forty miles, he was not likely to be disturbed by trespassers. Colonel Mason signed the letter, handed it to one of the gentlemen who had brought the sample of gold, and they departed.

That gold was the *first* discovered in the Sierra Nevada, which soon revolutionized the whole country, and actually moved the whole civilized world. About this time (May and June, 1848), far more importance was attached to quicksilver. One mine, the New Almaden, twelve miles south of San José, was well known, and was in possession of the agent of a Scotch gentleman named Forbes, who at the time was British consul at Tepic, Mexico. Mr. Forbes came up from San Blas in a small brig, which proved to be a Mexican vessel; the vessel was seized, condemned, and actually sold, but Forbes was wealthy, and bought her in. His title to the quicksilver-mine was, however, never disputed, as he had bought it regularly, before our conquest of the country, from another British subject, also named Forbes, a resident of Santa Clara Mission, who had purchased it of the discoverer, a priest; but the boundaries of the land attached to the mine were even then in dispute. Other men were in search of quicksilver; and the whole range of mountains near the New Almaden mine was stained with the brilliant red of the sulphuret of mercury (cinnabar). A company composed of T. O. Larkin, J. R. Snyder, and others, among them one John Ricord (who was quite a character), also claimed a valuable mine near by. Ricord was a lawyer from about Buffalo, and by some means had got to the Sandwich Islands, where he became a great favorite of the king, Kamehameha; was his attorney-general, and got into a difficulty with the Rev. Mr. Judd, who was a kind of prime-minister to his majesty. One or the other had to go, and Ricord left for San Francisco, where he arrived while Colonel Mason and I were there on some business connected with the customs. Ricord at once made a dead set at Mason with flattery, and all sorts of spurious arguments, to convince him that our military government was too simple in its forms for the new state of facts, and that he was the man to remodel it. I had heard a good deal to his prejudice, and did all I could to prevent Mason taking him into his confidence. We then started back for Monterey. Ricord was along, and night and day he was harping on his scheme; but he disgusted Colonel Mason with his flattery, and, on reaching Monterey, he opened what he called a law-office, but there were neither courts nor clients, so necessity forced him to turn his thoughts to something else, and quicksilver became his hobby. In the spring of 1848 an appeal came to our office from San José, which compelled the Governor to go up in person. Lieutenant Loeser and I, with a couple of soldiers, went along. At San José the Governor held some kind of a court, in which Ricord and the alcalde had a warm dispute about a certain mine which Ricord, as a member of the Larkin Company, had opened within the limits claimed by the

New Almaden Company. On our way up we had visited the ground, and were therefore better prepared to understand the controversy. We had found at New Almaden Mr. Walkinshaw, a fine Scotch gentleman, the resident agent of Mr. Forbes. He had built in the valley, near a small stream, a few board-houses, and some four or five furnaces for the distillation of the mercury. These were very simple in their structure, being composed of whalers' kettles, set in masonry. These kettles were filled with broken ore about the size of McAdam-stone, mingled with lime. Another kettle, reversed, formed the lid, and the seam was luted with clay. On applying heat, the mercury was volatilized and carried into a chimney-stack, where it condensed and flowed back into a reservoir, and then was led in pipes into another kettle outside. After witnessing this process, we visited the mine itself, which outcropped near the apex of the hill, about a thousand feet above the furnaces. We found wagons hauling the mineral down the hill and returning empty, and in the mines quite a number of Sonora miners were blasting and driving for the beautiful ore (cinnabar). It was then, and is now, a most valuable mine. The adit of the mine was at the apex of the hill, which drooped off to the north. We rode along this hill, and saw where many openings had been begun, but these, proving of little or no value, had been abandoned. Three miles beyond, on the west face of the hill, we came to the opening of the "Larkin Company." There was evidence of a good deal of work, but the mine itself was filled up by what seemed a land-slide. The question involved in the lawsuit before the alcalde at San José was, first, whether the mine was or was not on the land belonging to the New Almaden property; and, next, whether the company had complied with all the conditions of the mining laws of Mexico, which were construed to be still in force in California.

These laws required that any one who discovered a valuable mine on private land should first file with the alcalde, or judge of the district, a notice and claim for the benefits of such discovery; then the mine was to be opened and followed for a distance of at least one hundred feet within a specified time, and the claimants must take out samples of the mineral and deposit the same with the alcalde, who was then required to inspect *personally* the mine, to see that it fulfilled all the conditions of the law, before he could give a written title. In this case the alcalde had been to the mine and had possession of samples of the ore; but, as the mouth of the mine was closed up, as alleged, from the act of God, by a land-slide, it was contended by Ricord and his associates that it was competent to prove by good witnesses that the mine had been opened into the hill one hundred feet, and that, by no negligence of theirs, it had caved in. It was generally understood that Robert J. Walker, United States Secretary of the Treasury, was then a partner in this mining company; and a vessel, the bark Gray Eagle, was ready at San Francisco to sail for New York with the title-papers on which to base a joint-stock company for speculative uses. I think the alcalde was satisfied that the law had been complied with, that he had given the necessary papers, and, as at that time there was nothing developed to show fraud, the Governor (Mason) did not interfere. At that date there was no public house or tavern in San José where we could stop, so we started toward Santa Cruz and encamped about ten miles out, to the west of the town, where we fell in with another party of explorers, of whom Ruckel, of San Francisco, was the head; and after supper, as we sat around the camp-fire, the conversation turned on quicksilver in general, and the result of the contest in San José in particular. Mason was relating to Ruckel the points and the arguments of Ricord, that the company should not suffer from an act of God, viz., the caving in of the mouth of the mine, when a man named Cash, a fellow who had once been in the quartermaster's employ as a teamster, spoke up: "Governor Mason, did Judge Ricord say that?" "Yes," said the Governor; and then Cash related how he and another man, whose name he gave, had been employed by Ricord to undermine a heavy rock that rested above the mouth of the mine, so that it tumbled down, carrying with it a large quantity of earth, and completely filled it up, as we had seen; "and," said Cash, "it took us three days of the hardest kind of work." This was the act of God, and on the papers procured from the alcalde at that time, I understand, was built a huge speculation, by which thousands of dollars changed hands in the United States and were lost. This happened long before the celebrated McGarrahan claim, which has produced so much noise, and which still is being prosecuted in the courts and in Congress.

On the next day we crossed over the Santa Cruz Mountains, from which we had sublime views of the scenery, first looking east toward the lower Bay of San Francisco, with the bright plains of Santa Clara and San José, and then to the west upon the ocean, the town of Monterey being visible sixty miles off. If my memory is correct, we beheld from that mountain the firing of a salute from the battery at Monterey, and counted the number of guns from the white puffs of smoke, but could not hear the sound. That night we slept on piles of wheat in a mill at Soquel, near Santa Cruz, and, our supplies being short, I advised that we should make an early start next morning, so as to reach the ranch of Don Juan Antonio Vallejo, a particular friend, who had a large and valuable cattle-ranch on the Pajaro River, about twenty miles on our way to Monterey. Accordingly, we were off by the first light of day, and by nine o'clock we had reached the ranch. It was on a high point of the plateau, overlooking the plain of the Pajaro, on which were grazing numbers of horses and cattle. The house was of adobe, with a long range of adobe-huts occupied by the semi-civilized Indians, who at that time did all the labor of a ranch, the herding and marking of cattle, breaking of horses, and cultivating the little patches of wheat and vegetables which constituted all the farming of that day. Every thing about the house looked deserted, and, seeing a small Indian boy leaning up against a post, I approached him and asked him in Spanish, "Where is the master?" "Gone to the Presidio" (Monterey). "Is anybody in the house?" "No." "Is it locked up?" "Yes." "Is no one about who can get in?" "No." "Have you any meat?" "No." "Any flour or grain?" "No." "Any chickens?" "No." "Any eggs?" "No." "What do you live on?" "*Nada*" (nothing). The utter indifference of this boy, and the tone of his answer "*Nada,*" attracted the attention of Colonel Mason, who had been listening to our conversation, and who knew enough of Spanish to catch the meaning, and he exclaimed with some feeling, "So we get *nada* for our breakfast." I felt mortified, for I had held out the prospect of a splendid breakfast of meat and *tortillas* with rice, chickens, eggs, etc., at the ranch of my friend José Antonio, as a justification for taking the Governor, a man of sixty years of age, more than twenty miles at a full canter for his breakfast. But there was no help for it, and we accordingly went a short distance to a pond, where we unpacked our mules and made a slim breakfast on some scraps of hard bread and a bone of pork that remained in our *alforjas*. This was no uncommon thing in those days, when many a *ranchero* with his eleven leagues of land, his hundreds of horses and thousands of cattle, would receive us with all the grandiloquence of a Spanish lord, and confess that he had nothing in his house to eat except the carcass of a beef hung up, from which the stranger might cut and cook, without money or price, what he needed. That night we slept on Salinas Plain, and the next morning reached Monterey. All the missions and houses at that period were alive with fleas, which the natives looked on as pleasant titillators, but they so tortured me that I always gave them a wide berth, and slept on a saddle-blanket, with the saddle for a pillow and the *serape*, or blanket, for a cover. We never feared rain except in winter. As the spring and summer of 1848 advanced, the reports came faster and faster from the gold-mines at Sutter's saw-mill. Stories reached us of fabulous discoveries, and spread throughout the land. Everybody was talking of "Gold! gold!!" until it assumed the character of a fever. Some of our soldiers began to desert; citizens were fitting out trains of wagons and pack-mules to go to the mines. We heard of men earning fifty, five hundred, and thousands of dollars per day, and for a time it seemed as though somebody would reach solid gold. Some of this gold began to come to Yerba Buena in trade, and to disturb the value of merchandise, particularly of mules, horses, tin pans, and articles used in mining. I of course could not escape the infection, and at last convinced Colonel Mason that it was our duty to go up and see with our own eyes, that we might report the truth to our Government. As yet we had no regular mail to any part of the United States, but mails had come to us at long intervals, around Cape Horn, and one or two overland. I well remember the first overland mail. It was brought by Kit Carson in saddle-bags from Taos in New Mexico. We heard of his arrival at Los Angeles, and waited patiently for his arrival at headquarters. His fame then was at its height, from the publication of Fremont's books, and I was very anxious to see a man who had achieved such feats of daring among the wild animals of the Rocky Mountains, and still wilder Indians of the Plains. At last his arrival was reported at the tavern at Monterey, and I hurried to hunt him up. I cannot express my surprise at beholding a small, stoop-shouldered man, with reddish hair, freckled face, soft blue eyes, and nothing to indicate extraordinary courage or daring. He spoke but little, and answered questions in monosyllables. I asked for his mail, and he picked up his light saddle-bags containing the great overland mail, and we walked together to headquarters, where he delivered his parcel into Colonel Mason's own hands. He spent some days in Monterey, during which time we extracted with difficulty some items of his personal history. He was then by commission a lieutenant in the regiment of Mounted Rifles serving in Mexico under Colonel Sumner, and, as he could not reach his regiment from California, Colonel Mason ordered that for a time he should be assigned to duty with A. J. Smith's company, First Dragoons, at Los Angeles. He remained at Los Angeles some months, and was then sent back to the United States with dispatches, traveling two thousand miles almost alone, in preference to being encumbered by a large party.

Toward the close of June, 1848, the gold-fever being at its height, by Colonel Mason's orders I made preparations for his trip to the newly-discovered gold-mines at Sutter's Fort. I selected four good soldiers, with Aaron, Colonel Mason's black servant, and a good outfit of horses and pack-mules, we started by the usually traveled route for Yerba Buena. There Captain Folsom and two citizens joined our party. The first difficulty was to cross the bay to Saucelito. Folsom, as quartermaster, had a sort of scow with a large sail, with which to discharge the cargoes of ships, that could not come within a mile of the shore. It took nearly the whole day to get the old scow up to the only wharf there, and then the water was so shallow that the scow, with its load of horses, would not float at the first high tide, but by infinite labor on the next tide she was got off and safely crossed over to Saucelito. We followed in a more comfortable schooner. Having safely landed our horses and mules, we packed up and rode to San Rafael

Mission, stopping with Don Timoteo Murphy. The next day's journey took us to Bodega, where lived a man named Stephen Smith, who had the only steam saw-mill in California. He had a Peruvian wife, and employed a number of absolutely naked Indians in making adobes. We spent a day very pleasantly with him, and learned that he had come to California some years before, at the personal advice of Daniel Webster, who had informed him that sooner or later the United States would be in possession of California, and that in consequence it would become a great country. From Bodega we traveled to Sonoma, by way of Petaluma, and spent a day with General Vallejo. I had been there before, as related, in the business of the alcalde Nash. From Sonoma we crossed over by way of Napa, Suisun, and Vaca's ranch, to the Puta. In the rainy season, the plain between the Puta and Sacramento Rivers is impassable, but in July the waters dry up; and we passed without trouble, by the trail for Sutter's *Embarcadero*. We reached the Sacramento River, then full of water, with a deep, clear current. The only means of crossing over was by an Indian dugout canoe. We began by carrying across our packs and saddles, and then our people. When all things were ready, the horses were driven into the water, one being guided ahead by a man in the canoe. Of course, the horses and mules at first refused to take to the water, and it was nearly a day's work to get them across, and even then some of our animals after crossing escaped into the woods and undergrowth that lined the river, but we secured enough of them to reach Sutter's Fort, three miles back from the *embarcadero*, where we encamped at the old slough, or pond, near the fort. On application, Captain Sutter sent some Indians back into the bushes, who recovered and brought in all our animals. At that time there was not the sign of a habitation there or thereabouts, except the fort, and an old adobe-house, east of the fort, known as the hospital. The fort itself was one of adobe-walls, about twenty feet high, rectangular in form, with two-story block-houses at diagonal corners. The entrance was by a large gate, open by day and closed at night, with two iron ship's guns near at hand. Inside there was a large house, with a good shingle-roof, used as a storehouse, and all round the walls were ranged rooms, the fort-wall being the outer wall of the house. The inner wall also was of adobe. These rooms were used by Captain Sutter himself and by his people. He had a blacksmith's shop, carpenter's shop, etc., and other rooms where the women made blankets. Sutter was monarch of all he surveyed, and had authority to inflict punishment even unto death, a power he did not fail to use. He had horses, cattle, and sheep, and of these he gave liberally and without price to all in need. He caused to be driven into our camp a beef and some sheep, which were slaughtered for our use. Already the gold-mines were beginning to be felt. Many people were then encamped, some going and some coming, all full of gold-stories, and each surpassing the other. We found preparations in progress for celebrating the Fourth of July, then close at hand, and we agreed to remain over to assist on the occasion; of course, being the high officials, we were the honored guests. People came from a great distance to attend this celebration of the Fourth of July, and the tables were laid in the large room inside the storehouse of the fort. A man of some note, named Sinclair, presided, and after a substantial meal and a reasonable supply of *aguardiente* we began the toasts. All that I remember is that Folsom and I spoke for our party; others, Captain Sutter included, made speeches, and before the celebration was over Sutter was enthusiastic, and many others showed the effects of the *aguardiente*. The next day (namely, July 5, 1848) we resumed our journey toward the mines, and, in twenty-five miles of as hot and dusty a ride as possible, we reached Mormon Island. I have heretofore stated that the gold was first found in the tail-race of the saw-mill at Coloma, forty miles above Sutter's Fort, or fifteen above Mormon Island, in the bed of the American Fork of the Sacramento River. It seems that Sutter had employed an American named Marshall, a sort of millwright, to do this work for him, but Marshall afterward claimed that in the matter of the saw-mill they were copartners. At all events, Marshall and the family of Mr. Wimmer were living at Coloma, where the pine-trees afforded the best material for lumber. He had under him four white men, Mormons, who had been discharged from Cooke's battalion, and some Indians. These were engaged in hewing logs, building a mill-dam, and putting up a saw-mill. Marshall, as the architect, had made the "tub-wheel," and had set it in

motion, and had also furnished some of the rude parts of machinery necessary for an ordinary up-and-down saw-mill.

Labor was very scarce, expensive, and had to be econo-
mized. The mill was built over a dry channel of the river
which was calculated to be the tail-race. After arranging his
head-race, dam, and *tub-wheel*, he let on the water to test the
goodness of his machinery. It worked very well until it was
found that the tail-race did not carry off the water fast
enough, so he put his men to work in a rude way to clear out
the tail-race. They scratched a kind of ditch down the middle
of the dry channel, throwing the coarser stones to one side;
then, letting on the water again, it would run with velocity
down the channel, washing away the dirt, thus saving labor.
This course of action was repeated several times, acting exactly like the long Tom afterward resorted to by the miners.
As Marshall himself was working in this ditch, he observed
particles of yellow metal which he gathered up in his hand,
when it seemed to have suddenly flashed across his mind that
it was *gold*. After picking up about an ounce, he hurried down
to the fort to report to Captain Sutter his discovery. Captain
Sutter himself related to me Marshall's account, saying that,
as he sat in his room at the fort one day in February or
March, 1848, a knock was heard at his door, and he called out,
"Come in." In walked Marshall, who was a half-crazy man at
best, but then looked strangely wild. "What is the matter,
Marshall?" Marshall inquired if any one was within hearing,
and began to peer about the room, and look under the bed,
when Sutter, fearing that some calamity had befallen the party
up at the saw-mill, and that Marshall was really crazy, began
to make his way to the door, demanding of Marshall to explain what was the matter. At last he revealed his discovery,
and laid before Captain Sutter the pellicles of gold he had
picked up in the ditch. At first, Sutter attached little or no
importance to the discovery, and told Marshall to go back
to the mill, and say nothing of what he had seen to Mr.
Wimmer, or any one else. Yet, as it might add value to the
location, he dispatched to our headquarters at Monterey, as I
have already related, the two men with a written application
for a preëmption to the quarter-section of land at Coloma.
Marshall returned to the mill, but could not keep out of his

wonderful ditch, and by some means the other men employed
there learned his secret. They then wanted to gather the gold,
and Marshall threatened to shoot them if they attempted it;
but these men had sense enough to know that if "placer"-
gold existed at Coloma, it would also be found farther down-
stream, and they gradually "prospected" until they reached
Mormon Island, fifteen miles below, where they discovered
one of the richest placers on earth. These men revealed the
fact to some other Mormons who were employed by Captain
Sutter at a grist-mill he was building still lower down the
American Fork, and six miles above his fort. All of them
struck for higher wages, to which Sutter yielded, until they
asked ten dollars a day, which he refused, and the two mills
on which he had spent so much money were never built, and
fell into decay.

In my opinion, when the Mormons were driven from Nau-
voo, Illinois, in 1844, they cast about for a land where they
would not be disturbed again, and fixed on California. In the
year 1845 a ship, the Brooklyn, sailed from New York for California, with a colony of Mormons, of which Sam Brannan
was the leader, and we found them there on our arrival in
January, 1847. When General Kearney, at Fort Leavenworth,
was collecting volunteers early in 1846, for the Mexican War,
he, through the instrumentality of Captain James Allen,
brother to our quartermaster, General Robert Allen, raised
the battalion of Mormons at Kanesville, Iowa, now Council
Bluffs, on the express understanding that it would facilitate
their migration to California. But when the Mormons
reached Salt Lake, in 1846, they learned that they had been
forestalled by the United States forces in California, and they
then determined to settle down where they were. Therefore,
when this battalion of five companies of Mormons (raised by
Allen, who died on the way, and was succeeded by Cooke)
was discharged at Los Angeles, California, in the early summer of 1847, most of the men went to their people at Salt
Lake, with all the money received, as pay from the United
States, invested in cattle and breeding-horses; one company
reënlisted for another year, and the remainder sought work in
the country. As soon as the fame of the gold discovery spread
through California, the Mormons naturally turned to Mor-

mon Island, so that in July, 1848, we found about three hundred of them there at work. Sam Brannan was on hand as the high-priest, collecting the tithes. Clark, of Clark's Point, an early pioneer, was there also, and nearly all the Mormons who had come out in the Brooklyn, or who had staid in California after the discharge of their battalion, had collected there. I recall the scene as perfectly to-day as though it were yesterday. In the midst of a broken country, all parched and dried by the hot sun of July, sparsely wooded with live-oaks and straggling pines, lay the valley of the American River, with its bold mountain-stream coming out of the Snowy Mountains to the east. In this valley is a flat, or gravel-bed, which in high water is an island, or is overflown, but at the time of our visit was simply a level gravel-bed of the river. On its edges men were digging, and filling buckets with the finer earth and gravel, which was carried to a machine made like a baby's cradle, open at the foot, and at the head a plate of sheet-iron or zinc, punctured full of holes. On this metallic plate was emptied the earth, and water was then poured on it from buckets, while one man shook the cradle with violent rocking by a handle. On the bottom were nailed cleats of wood. With this rude machine four men could earn from forty to one hundred dollars a day, averaging sixteen dollars, or a gold ounce, per man per day. While the sun blazed down on the heads of the miners with tropical heat, the water was bitter cold, and all hands were either standing in the water or had their clothes wet all the time; yet there were no complaints of rheumatism or cold. We made our camp on a small knoll, a little below the island, and from it could overlook the busy scene. A few bush-huts near by served as stores, boarding-houses, and for sleeping; but all hands slept on the ground, with pine-leaves and blankets for bedding. As soon as the news spread that the Governor was there, persons came to see us, and volunteered all kinds of information, illustrating it by samples of the gold, which was of a uniform kind, "scale-gold," bright and beautiful. A large variety, of every conceivable shape and form, was found in the smaller gulches round about, but the gold in the river-bed was uniformly "scale-gold." I remember that Mr. Clark was in camp, talking to Colonel Mason about matters and things generally, when he inquired, "Governor, what business has Sam Brannan to collect the tithes here?" Clark admitted that Brannan was the head of the Mormon church in California, and he was simply questioning as to Brannan's right, as high-priest, to compel the Mormons to pay him the regular tithes. Colonel Mason answered, "Brannan has a perfect right to collect the tax, if you Mormons are fools enough to pay it." "Then," said Clark, "I for one won't pay it any longer." Colonel Mason added: "This is public land, and the gold is the property of the United States; all of you here are trespassers, but, as the Government is benefited by your getting out the gold, I do not intend to interfere." I understood, afterward, that from that time the payment of the tithes ceased, but Brannan had already collected enough money wherewith to hire Sutter's hospital, and to open a store there, in which he made more money than any merchant in California, during that summer and fall. The understanding was, that the money collected by him as tithes was the foundation of his fortune, which is still very large in San Francisco. That evening we all mingled freely with the miners, and witnessed the process of cleaning up and "panning" out, which is the last process for separating the pure gold from the fine dirt and black sand.

The next day we continued our journey up the valley of the American Fork, stopping at various camps, where mining was in progress; and about noon we reached Coloma, the place where gold had been first discovered. The hills were higher, and the timber of better quality. The river was narrower and bolder, and but few miners were at work there, by reason of Marshall's and Sutter's claim to the site. There stood the saw-mill unfinished, the dam and tail-race just as they were left when the Mormons ceased work. Marshall and Wimmer's family of wife and half a dozen children were there, guarding their supposed treasure; living in a house made of clapboards. Here also we were shown many specimens of gold, of a coarser grain than that found at Mormon Island. The next day we crossed the American River to its north side, and visited many small camps of men, in what were called the "dry diggings." Little pools of water stood in the beds of the streams, and these were used to wash the dirt; and there the gold was in every conceivable shape and size, some of the specimens weighing several ounces. Some of these "diggings" were extremely rich, but as a whole they were more precarious in results than at the river. Sometimes a lucky fellow would hit on a "pocket," and collect several thousand dollars in a few days, and then again he would be shifting about from place to place, "prospecting," and spending all he had made. Little stores were being opened at every point, where flour, bacon, etc., were sold; every thing being a dollar a pound, and a meal usually costing three dollars. Nobody paid for a bed, for he slept on the ground, without fear of cold or rain. We spent nearly a week in that region, and were quite bewildered by the fabulous tales of recent discoveries, which at the time were confined to the several forks of the American and Yuba Rivers. All this time our horses had nothing to eat but the sparse grass in that region, and we were forced to work our way down toward the Sacramento Valley, or to see our animals perish. Still we contemplated a visit to the Yuba and Feather Rivers, from which we had heard of more wonderful "diggings;" but met a courier, who announced the arrival of a ship at Monterey, with dispatches of great importance from Mazatlan. We accordingly turned our horses back to Sutter's Fort. Crossing the Sacramento again by swimming our horses, and ferrying their loads in that solitary canoe, we took our back track as far as the Napa, and then turned to Benicia, on Carquinez Straits. We found there a solitary adobe-house, occupied by Mr. Hastings and his family, embracing Dr. Semple, the proprietor of the ferry. This ferry was a ship's-boat, with a latteen-sail, which could carry across at one tide six or eight horses.

It took us several days to cross over, and during that time we got well acquainted with the doctor, who was quite a character. He had come to California from Illinois, and was brother to Senator Semple. He was about seven feet high, and very intelligent. When we first reached Monterey, he had a printing-press, which belonged to the United States, having been captured at the custom-house, and had been used to print custom-house blanks. With this Dr. Semple, as editor, published the *Californian*, a small sheet of news, once a week; and it was a curiosity in its line, using two *v*'s for a *w*, and other combinations of letters, made necessary by want of type. After some time he removed to Yerba Buena with his paper, and it grew up to be the *Alta California* of to-day. Foreseeing, as he thought, the growth of a great city somewhere on the Bay of San Francisco, he selected Carquinez Straits as its location, and obtained from General Vallejo a title to a league of land, on condition of building up a city thereon to bear the name of Vallejo's wife. This was Francisca Benicia; accordingly, the new city was named "Francisca." At this time, the town near the mouth of the bay was known universally as Yerba Buena; but that name was not known abroad, although San Francisco was familiar to the whole civilized world. Now, some of the chief men of Yerba Buena, Folsom, Howard, Leidesdorf, and others, knowing the importance of a *name*, saw their danger, and, by some action of the *ayuntamiento*, or town council, changed the name of Yerba Buena to "San Francisco." Dr. Semple was outraged at their changing the name to one so like his of *Francisca*, and he in turn changed his town to the other name of Mrs. Vallejo, viz., "Benicia;" and Benicia it has remained to this day. I am convinced that this little circumstance was big with consequences. That Benicia has the best natural site for a commercial city, I am satisfied; and had half the money and half the labor since bestowed upon San Francisco been expended at Benicia, we should have at this day a city of palaces on the Carquinez Straits. The name of "San Francisco," however, fixed the city where it now is; for every ship in 1848–'49, which cleared from any part of the world, knew the name of San Francisco, but not Yerba Buena or Benicia; and, accordingly, ships consigned to California came pouring in with their contents, and were anchored in front of Yerba Buena, the first town. Captains and crews deserted for the gold-mines, and now half the city in front of Montgomery Street is built over the hulks thus abandoned. But Dr. Semple, at that time, was all there was of Benicia; he was captain and crew of his ferry-boat, and managed to pass our party to the south side of Carquinez Straits in about two days.

Thence we proceeded up Amador Valley to Alameda Creek, and so on to the old mission of San José; thence to the *pueblo* of San José, where Folsom and those belonging in Yerba Buena went in that direction, and we continued on to Monterey, our party all the way giving official sanction to the news from the gold-mines, and adding new force to the "fever."

On reaching Monterey, we found dispatches from Commodore Shubrick, at Mazatlan, which gave almost positive assurance that the war with Mexico was over; that hostilities had ceased, and commissioners were arranging the terms of peace at Guadalupe Hidalgo. It was well that this news reached California at that critical time; for so contagious had become the "gold-fever" that everybody was bound to go and try his fortune, and the volunteer regiment of Stevenson's would have deserted *en masse*, had the men not been assured that they would very soon be entitled to an honorable discharge.

Many of our regulars did desert, among them the very men who had escorted us faithfully to the mines and back. Our servants also left us, and nothing less than three hundred dollars a month would hire a man in California; Colonel Mason's black boy, Aaron, alone of all our then servants proving faithful. We were forced to resort to all manner of shifts to live. First, we had a mess with a black fellow we called Bustamente as cook; but he got the fever, and had to go. We next took a soldier, but he deserted, and carried off my double-barreled shot-gun, which I prized very highly. To meet this condition of facts, Colonel Mason ordered that liberal furloughs should be given to the soldiers, and promises to all in turn, and he allowed all the officers to draw their rations in kind. As the actual value of the ration was very large, this enabled us to live. Halleck, Murray, Ord, and I, boarded with Doña Augustias, and turned in our rations as pay for our board.

Some time in September, 1848, the official news of the treaty of peace reached us, and the Mexican War *was* over. This treaty was signed in May, and came to us all the way by land by a courier from Lower California, sent from La Paz by Lieutenant-Colonel Burton. On its receipt, orders were at once made for the muster-out of all of Stevenson's regiment, and our military forces were thus reduced to the single company of dragoons at Los Angeles, and the one company of artillery at Monterey. Nearly all business had ceased, except that connected with gold; and, during that fall, Colonel Mason, Captain Warner, and I, made another trip up to Sutter's Fort, going also to the newly-discovered mines on the Stanislaus, called "Sonora," named from the miners of Sonora, Mexico, who had first discovered them. We found there pretty much the same state of facts as before existed at Mormon Island and Coloma, and we daily received intelligence of the opening of still other mines north and south.

But I have passed over a very interesting fact. As soon as we had returned from our first visit to the gold-mines, it became important to send home positive knowledge of this valuable discovery. The means of communication with the United States were very precarious, and I suggested to Colonel Mason that a special courier ought to be sent; that Second-Lieutenant Loeser had been promoted to first-lieutenant, and was entitled to go home. He was accordingly detailed to carry the news. I prepared with great care the letter to the adjutant-general of August 17, 1848, which Colonel Mason modified in a few particulars; and, as it was important to send not only the specimens which had been presented to us along our route of travel, I advised the colonel to allow Captain Folsom to purchase and send to Washington a large sample of the commercial gold in general use, and to pay for the same out of the money in his hands known as the "civil fund," arising from duties collected at the several ports in California. He consented to this, and Captain Folsom bought an oyster-can full at ten dollars the ounce, which was the rate of value at which it was then received at the custom-house. Folsom was instructed further to contract with some vessel to carry the messenger to South America, where he could take the English steamers as far east as Jamaica, with a conditional charter giving increased payment if the vessel could catch the October steamer. Folsom chartered the bark La Lambayecana, owned and navigated by Henry D. Cooke, who has since been the Governor of the District of Columbia. In due time this vessel reached Monterey, and Lieutenant Loeser, with his report and specimens of gold, embarked and sailed. He reached the South American Continent at Payta, Peru, in time, took the English steamer of October to Panama, and thence went on to Kingston, Jamaica, where he found a sailing-vessel bound for New Orleans. On reaching New Orleans, he telegraphed to the War Department his arrival; but so many delays had occurred that he did not reach

Washington in time to have the matter embraced in the President's regular message of 1848, as we had calculated. Still, the President made it the subject of a special message, and thus became "official" what had before only reached the world in a very indefinite shape. Then began that wonderful development, and the great emigration to California, by land and by sea, of 1849 and 1850.

As before narrated, Mason, Warner, and I, made a second visit to the mines in September and October, 1848. As the winter season approached, Colonel Mason returned to Monterey, and I remained for a time at Sutter's Fort. In order to share somewhat in the riches of the land, we formed a partnership in a store at Coloma, in charge of Norman S. Bestor, who had been Warner's clerk. We supplied the necessary money, fifteen hundred dollars (five hundred dollars each), and Bestor carried on the store at Coloma for his share. Out of this investment, each of us realized a profit of about fifteen hundred dollars. Warner also got a regular leave of absence, and contracted with Captain Sutter for surveying and locating the town of Sacramento. He received for this sixteen dollars per day for his services as surveyor; and Sutter paid all the hands engaged in the work. The town was laid off mostly up about the fort, but a few streets were staked off along the river-bank, and one or two leading to it. Captain Sutter always contended, however, that no town could possibly exist on the immediate bank of the river, because the spring freshets rose over the bank, and frequently it was necessary to swim a horse to reach the boat-landing. Nevertheless, from the very beginning the town began to be built on the very river-bank, viz., First, Second, and Third Streets, with J and K Streets leading back. Among the principal merchants and traders of that winter, at Sacramento, were Sam Brannan and Hensley, Reading & Co. For several years the site was annually flooded; but the people have persevered in building the levees, and afterward in raising all the streets, so that Sacramento is now a fine city, the capital of the State, and stands where, in 1848, was nothing but a dense mass of bushes, vines, and submerged land. The old fort has disappeared altogether.

During the fall of 1848, Warner, Ord, and I, camped on the

bank of the American River, abreast of the fort, at what was known as the "Old Tan-Yard." I was cook, Ord cleaned up the dishes, and Warner looked after the horses; but Ord was deposed as scullion because he would only wipe the tin plates with a tuft of grass, according to the custom of the country, whereas Warner insisted on having them washed after each meal with hot water. Warner was in consequence promoted to scullion, and Ord became the hostler. We drew our rations in kind from the commissary at San Francisco, who sent them up to us by a boat; and we were thus enabled to dispense a generous hospitality to many a poor devil who otherwise would have had nothing to eat.

The winter of 1848–'49 was a period of intense activity throughout California. The rainy season was unfavorable to the operations of gold-mining, and was very hard upon the thousands of houseless men and women who dwelt in the mountains, and even in the towns. Most of the natives and old inhabitants had returned to their ranches and houses; yet there were not roofs enough in the country to shelter the thousands who had arrived by sea and by land. The news had gone forth to the whole civilized world that gold in fabulous quantities was to be had for the mere digging, and adventurers came pouring in blindly to seek their fortunes, without a thought of house or food. Yerba Buena had been converted into San Francisco. Sacramento City had been laid out, lots were being rapidly sold, and the town was being built up as an entrepot to the mines. Stockton also had been chosen as a convenient point for trading with the lower or southern mines. Captain Sutter was the sole proprietor of the former, and Captain Charles Weber was the owner of the site of Stockton, which was as yet known as "French Camp."

Chapter III.

EARLY RECOLLECTIONS OF CALIFORNIA— (CONTINUED).

1849 – 1850.

THE DEPARTMENT HEADQUARTERS still remained at Monterey, but, with the few soldiers, we had next to nothing to do. In midwinter we heard of the approach of a battalion of the Second Dragoons, under Major Lawrence Pike Graham, with Captains Rucker, Coutts, Campbell, and others, along. So exhausted were they by their long march from Upper Mexico that we had to send relief to meet them as they approached. When this command reached Los Angeles, it was left there as the garrison, and Captain A. J. Smith's company of the First Dragoons was brought up to San Francisco. We were also advised that the Second Infantry, Colonel B. Riley, would be sent out around Cape Horn in sailing-ships; that the Mounted Rifles, under Lieutenant-Colonel Loring, would march overland to Oregon; and that Brigadier-General Persifer F. Smith would come out in chief command on the Pacific coast. It was also known that a contract had been entered into with parties in New York and New Orleans for a monthly line of steamers from those cities to California, *via* Panama. Lieutenant-Colonel Burton had come up from Lower California, and, as captain of the Third Artillery, he was assigned to command Company F, Third Artillery, at Monterey. Captain Warner remained at Sacramento, surveying; and Halleck, Murray, Ord, and I, boarded with Doña Augustias. The season was unusually rainy and severe, but we passed the time with the usual round of dances and parties. The time fixed for the arrival of the mail-steamer was understood to be about January 1, 1849, but the day came and went without any tidings of her. Orders were given to Captain Burton to announce her arrival by firing a national salute, and each morning we listened for the guns from the fort. The month of January passed, and the greater part of February, too. As was usual, the army officers celebrated the 22d of February with a grand ball, given in the new stone school-house, which Alcalde Walter Colton had built. It was the largest and best hall then in California. The ball was really a handsome affair, and we kept it up nearly all night. The next morning we were at breakfast: present, Doña Augustias, and Manuelita, Halleck, Murray, and myself. We were dull and stupid enough until a gun from the fort aroused us, then another and another. "The steamer!" exclaimed all, and, without waiting for hats or any thing, off we dashed. I reached the wharf hatless, but the doña sent my cap after me by a servant. The white puffs of smoke hung around the fort, mingled with the dense fog, which hid all the water of the bay, and well out to sea could be seen the black spars of some unknown vessel. At the wharf I found a group of soldiers and a small row-boat, which belonged to a brig at anchor in the bay. Hastily ordering a couple of willing soldiers to get in and take the oars, and Mr. Larkin and Mr. Hartnell asking to go along, we jumped in and pushed off. Steering our boat toward the spars, which loomed up above the fog clear and distinct, in about a mile we came to the black hull of the strange monster, the long-expected and most welcome steamer California. Her wheels were barely moving, for her pilot could not see the shore-line distinctly, though the hills and Point of Pines could be clearly made out over the fog, and occasionally a glimpse of some white walls showed where the town lay. A "Jacob's ladder" was lowered for us from the steamer, and in a minute I scrambled up on deck, followed by Larkin and Hartnell, and we found ourselves in the midst of many old friends. There was Canby, the adjutant-general, who was to take my place; Charley Hoyt, my cousin; General Persifer F. Smith and wife; Gibbs, his aide-de-camp; Major Ogden, of the Engineers, and wife; and, indeed, many old Californians, among them Alfred Robinson, and Frank Ward with his pretty bride. By the time the ship was fairly at anchor we had answered a million of questions about gold and the state of the country; and, learning that the ship was out of fuel, had informed the captain (Marshall) that there was abundance of pine-wood, but no willing hands to cut it; that no man could be hired at less than an ounce of gold a day, unless the soldiers would volunteer to do it for some agreed-upon price. As for coal, there was not a pound in Monterey, or anywhere else in California.

Vessels with coal were known to be *en route* around Cape Horn, but none had yet reached California.

The arrival of this steamer was the beginning of a new epoch on the Pacific coast; yet there she lay, helpless, without coal or fuel. The native Californians, who had never seen a steamship, stood for days on the beach looking at her, with the universal exclamation, *"Tan feo!"*—how ugly!—and she was truly ugly when compared with the clean, well-sparred frigates and sloops-of-war that had hitherto been seen on the North Pacific coast. It was first supposed it would take ten days to get wood enough to prosecute her voyage, and therefore all the passengers who could took up their quarters on shore. Major Canby relieved me, and took the place I had held so long as adjutant-general of the Department of California. The time seemed most opportune for me to leave the service, as I had several splendid offers of employment and of partnership, and, accordingly, I made my written resignation; but General Smith put his veto upon it, saying that he was to command the Division of the Pacific, while General Riley was to have the Department of California, and Colonel Loring that of Oregon. He wanted me as his adjutant-general, because of my familiarity with the country, and knowledge of its then condition. At the time, he had on his staff Gibbs as aide-de-camp, and Fitzgerald as quartermaster. He also had along with him quite a retinue of servants, hired with a clear contract to serve him for a whole year after reaching California, every one of whom deserted, except a young black fellow named Isaac. Mrs. Smith, a pleasant but delicate Louisiana lady, had a white maid-servant, in whose fidelity she had unbounded confidence; but this girl was married to a perfect stranger, and off before she had even landed in San Francisco. It was, therefore, finally arranged that, on the California, I was to accompany General Smith to San Francisco as his adjutant-general. I accordingly sold some of my horses, and arranged for others to go up by land; and from that time I became fairly enlisted in the military family of General Persifer F. Smith.

I parted with my old commander, Colonel Mason, with sincere regret. To me he had ever been kind and considerate, and, while stern, honest to a fault, he was the very embodiment of the principle of fidelity to the interests of the General Government. He possessed a native strong intellect, and far more knowledge of the principles of civil government and law than he got credit for. In private and public expenditures he was extremely economical, but not penurious. In cases where the officers had to contribute money for parties and entertainments, he always gave a double share, because of his allowance of double rations. During our frequent journeys, I was always caterer, and paid all the bills. In settling with him he required a written statement of the items of account, but never disputed one of them. During our time, California was, as now, full of a bold, enterprising, and speculative set of men, who were engaged in every sort of game to make money. I know that Colonel Mason was beset by them to use his position to make a fortune for himself and his friends; but he never bought land or town-lots, because, he said, it was his place to hold the public estate for the Government as free and unencumbered by claims as possible; and when I wanted him to stop the public-land sales in San Francisco, San José, etc., he would not; for, although he did not believe the titles given by the alcaldes worth a cent, yet they aided to settle the towns and public lands, and he thought, on the whole, the Government would be benefited thereby. The same thing occurred as to the gold-mines. He never took a title to a town-lot, unless it was one, of no real value, from Alcalde Colton, in Monterey, of which I have never heard since. He did take a share in the store which Warner, Bestor, and I, opened at Coloma, paid his share of the capital, five hundred dollars, and received his share of the profits, fifteen hundred dollars. I think also he took a share in a venture to China with Larkin and others; but, on leaving California, he was glad to sell out without profit or loss. In the stern discharge of his duty he made some bitter enemies, among them Henry M. Naglee, who, in the newspapers of the day, endeavored to damage his fair fame. But, knowing him intimately, I am certain that he is entitled to all praise for having so controlled the affairs of the country that, when his successor arrived, all things were so disposed that a civil form of government was an easy matter of adjustment. Colonel Mason was relieved by General Riley some time in April, and left California in the steamer of the 1st May

for Washington and St. Louis, where he died of cholera in the
summer of 1850, and his body is buried in Bellefontaine Cemetery. His widow afterward married Major (since General)
Don Carlos Buell, and is now living in Kentucky.

In overhauling the hold of the steamer California, as she lay
at anchor in Monterey Bay, a considerable amount of coal
was found under some heavy duplicate machinery. With this,
and such wood as had been gathered, she was able to renew
her voyage. The usual signal was made, and we all went on
board. About the 1st of March we entered the Heads, and
anchored off San Francisco, near the United States line-of-
battle-ship Ohio, Commodore T. Ap Catesby Jones. As was
the universal custom of the day, the crew of the California
deserted her; and she lay for months unable to make a trip
back to Panama, as was expected of her. As soon as we
reached San Francisco, the first thing was to secure an office
and a house to live in. The weather was rainy and stormy, and
snow even lay on the hills back of the Mission. Captain Folsom, the quartermaster, agreed to surrender for our office the
old adobe custom-house, on the upper corner of the plaza, as
soon as he could remove his papers and effects down to one
of his warehouses on the beach; and he also rented for us as
quarters the old Hudson Bay Company house on Montgomery Street, which had been used by Howard & Mellus as a
store, and at that very time they were moving their goods
into a larger brick building just completed for them. As these
changes would take some time, General Smith and Colonel
Ogden, with their wives, accepted the hospitality offered by
Commodore Jones on board the Ohio. I opened the office at
the custom-house, and Gibbs, Fitzgerald, and some others of
us, slept in the loft of the Hudson Bay Company house until
the lower part was cleared of Howard's store, after which
General Smith and the ladies moved in. There we had a general mess, and the efforts at house-keeping were simply ludicrous. One servant after another, whom General Smith had
brought from New Orleans, with a solemn promise to stand
by him for one whole year, deserted without a word of notice
or explanation, and in a few days none remained but little
Isaac. The ladies had no maid or attendants; and the general,
commanding all the mighty forces of the United States on the

Pacific coast, had to scratch to get one good meal a day for his family! He was a gentleman of fine social qualities, genial and gentle, and joked at every thing. Poor Mrs. Smith and Mrs. Ogden did not bear it so philosophically. Gibbs, Fitzgerald, and I, could cruise around and find a meal, which cost three dollars, at some of the many restaurants which had sprung up out of red-wood boards and cotton lining; but the general and ladies could not go out, for ladies were *rara aves* at that day in California. Isaac was cook, chamber-maid, and every thing, thoughtless of himself, and struggling, out of the slimmest means, to compound a breakfast for a large and hungry family. Breakfast would be announced any time between ten and twelve, and dinner according to circumstances. Many a time have I seen General Smith, with a can of preserved meat in his hands, going toward the house, take off his hat on meeting a negro, and, on being asked the reason of his politeness, he would answer that they were the only real gentlemen in California. I confess that the fidelity of Colonel Mason's boy "Aaron," and of General Smith's boy "Isaac," at a time when every white man laughed at promises as something made to be broken, has given me a kindly feeling of respect for the negroes, and makes me hope that they will find an honorable "status" in the jumble of affairs in which we now live. That was a dull, hard winter in San Francisco; the rains were heavy, and the mud fearful. I have seen mules stumble in the street, and drown in the liquid mud! Montgomery Street had been filled up with brush and clay, and I always dreaded to ride on horseback along it, because the mud was so deep that a horse's legs would become entangled in the bushes below, and the rider was likely to be thrown and drowned in the mud. The only sidewalks were made of stepping-stones of empty boxes, and here and there a few planks with barrel-staves nailed on. All the town lay along Montgomery Street, from Sacramento to Jackson, and about the plaza. Gambling was the chief occupation of the people. While they were waiting for the cessation of the rainy season, and for the beginning of spring, all sorts of houses were being put up, but of the most flimsy kind, and all were stores, restaurants, or gambling-saloons. Any room twenty by sixty feet would rent for a thousand dollars a month. I had, as my pay, seventy dollars a month, and no one would even try to hire a servant under three hundred dollars. Had it not been for the fifteen hundred dollars I had made in the store at Coloma, I could not have lived through the winter. About the 1st of April arrived the steamer Oregon; but her captain (Pearson) knew what was the state of affairs on shore, and ran his steamer alongside the line-of-battle-ship Ohio at Saucelito, and obtained the privilege of leaving his crew on board as "prisoners" until he was ready to return to sea. Then, discharging his passengers and getting coal out of some of the ships which had arrived, he retook his crew out of limbo and carried the first regular mail back to Panama early in April. In regular order arrived the third steamer, the Panama; and, as the vessels were arriving with coal, the California was enabled to hire a crew and get off. From that time forward these three ships constituted the regular line of mail-steamers, which has been kept up ever since. By the steamer Oregon arrived out Major R. P. Hammond, J. M. Williams, James Blair, and others; also the gentlemen who, with Major Ogden, were to compose a joint commission to select the sites for the permanent forts and navy-yard of California. This commission was composed of Majors Ogden, Smith, and Leadbetter, of the army, and Captains Goldsborough, Van Brunt, and Blunt, of the navy. These officers, after a most careful study of the whole subject, selected Mare Island for the navy-yard, and "Benicia" for the storehouses and arsenals of the army. The Pacific Mail Steamship Company also selected Benicia as their depot. Thus was again revived the old struggle for supremacy of these two points as the site of the future city of the Pacific. Meantime, however, San Francisco had secured the *name*. About six hundred ships were anchored there without crews, and could not get away; and there the city *was*, and *had* to be.

Nevertheless, General Smith, being disinterested and unprejudiced, decided on Benicia as the point where the city ought to be, and where the army headquarters should be. By the Oregon there arrived at San Francisco a man who deserves mention here—Baron Steinberger. He had been a great cattle-dealer in the United States, and boasted that he had helped to break the United States Bank, by being indebted to it five million dollars! At all events, he was a splendid-looking fellow, and brought with him from Washington a letter to General Smith and another for Commodore Jones, to the effect that he was a man of enlarged experience in beef; that the authorities in Washington knew that there existed in California large herds of cattle, which were only valuable for their hides and tallow; that it was of great importance to the Government that this beef should be cured and salted so as to be of use to the army and navy, obviating the necessity of shipping salt-beef around Cape Horn. I know he had such a letter from the Secretary of War, Marcy, to General Smith, for it passed into my custody, and I happened to be in Commodore Jones's cabin when the baron presented the one for him from the Secretary of the Navy. The baron was anxious to pitch in at once, and said that all he needed to start with were salt and barrels. After some inquiries of his purser, the commodore promised to let him have the barrels with their salt, as fast as they were emptied by the crew. Then the baron explained that he could get a nice lot of cattle from Don Timoteo Murphy, at the Mission of San Rafael, on the north side of the bay, but he could not get a boat and crew to handle them. Under the authority from the Secretary of the Navy, the commodore then promised him the use of a boat and crew, until he (the baron) could find and purchase a suitable one for himself. Then the baron opened the first regular butcher-shop in San Francisco, on the wharf about the foot of Broadway or Pacific Street, where we could buy at twenty-five or fifty cents a pound the best roasts, steaks, and cuts of beef, which had cost him nothing, for he never paid anybody if he could help it, and he soon cleaned poor Don Timoteo out. At first, every boat of his, in coming down from the San Rafael, touched at the Ohio, and left the best beefsteaks and roasts for the commodore, but soon the baron had enough money to dispense with the borrowed boat, and set up for himself, and from this small beginning, step by step, he rose in a few months to be one of the richest and most influential men in San Francisco; but in his wild speculations he was at last caught, and became helplessly bankrupt. He followed General Fremont to St. Louis in 1861, where I saw him, but soon afterward he died a pauper in one of the hospitals. When General Smith had his headquarters in San Francisco, in the spring of 1849, Steinberger gave dinners worthy any baron of old; and when, in after-years, I was a banker there, he used to borrow of me small sums of money in repayment for my share of these feasts; and somewhere among my old packages I hold one of his confidential notes for two hundred dollars, but on the whole I got off easily. I have no doubt that, if this man's history could be written out, it would present phases as wonderful as any of romance; but in my judgment he was a dangerous man, without any true sense of honor or honesty.

Little by little the rains of that season grew less and less, and the hills once more became green and covered with flowers. It became perfectly evident that no family could live in San Francisco on such a salary as Uncle Sam allowed his most favored officials; so General Smith and Major Ogden concluded to send their families back to the United States, and afterward we men-folks could take to camp and live on our rations. The Second Infantry had arrived, and had been distributed, four companies to Monterey, and the rest somewhat as Stevenson's regiment had been. A. J. Smith's company of dragoons was sent up to Sonoma, whither General Smith had resolved to move our headquarters. On the steamer which sailed about May 1st (I think the California), we embarked, the ladies for home and we for Monterey. At Monterey we went on shore, and Colonel Mason, who meantime had been relieved by General Riley, went on board, and the steamer departed for Panama. Of all that party I alone am alive.

General Riley had, with his family, taken the house which Colonel Mason had formerly used, and Major Canby and wife had secured rooms at Alvarado's. Captain Kane was quartermaster, and had his family in the house of a man named Garner, near the redoubt. Burton and Company F were still at the fort; the four companies of the Second Infantry were quartered in the barracks, the same building in which we had had our headquarters; and the company officers were quartered in hired buildings near by. General Smith and his aide, Captain Gibbs, went to Larkin's house, and I was at my old rooms at Doña Augustias. As we intended to go back to San Francisco by land and afterward to travel a good deal, General Smith gave me the necessary authority to fit out the party. There happened to be several trains of horses and mules in town, so I purchased about a dozen horses and mules at two hundred dollars a head, on account of the Quartermaster's Department, and we had them kept under guard in the quartermaster's *corral*.

I remember one night being in the quarters of Lieutenant Alfred Sully, where nearly all the officers of the garrison were assembled, listening to Sully's stories. Lieutenant Derby, "Squibob," was one of the number, as also Fred Steele, "Neighbor" Jones, and others, when, just after "tattoo," the orderly-sergeants came to report the result of "tattoo" roll-call; one reported five men absent, another eight, and so on, until it became certain that twenty-eight men had deserted; and they were so bold and open in their behavior that it amounted to defiance. They had deliberately slung their knapsacks and started for the gold-mines. Dr. Murray and I were the only ones present who were familiar with the country, and I explained how easy they could all be taken by a party going out at once to Salinas Plain, where the country was so open and level that a rabbit could not cross without being seen; that the deserters could not go to the mines without crossing that plain, and could not reach it before daylight. All agreed that the whole regiment would desert if these men were not brought back. Several officers volunteered on the spot to go after them; and, as the soldiers could not be trusted, it was useless to send any but officers in pursuit. Some one went to report the affair to the adjutant-general, Canby, and he to General Riley. I waited some time, and, as the thing grew cold, I thought it was given up, and went to my room and to bed.

About midnight I was called up and informed that there were seven officers willing to go, but the difficulty was to get horses and saddles. I went down to Larkin's house and got General Smith to consent that we might take the horses I had bought for our trip. It was nearly three o'clock A.M. before we were all mounted and ready. I had a musket which I used for hunting. With this I led off at a canter, followed by the others. About six miles out, by the faint moon, I saw ahead of us in the sandy road some blue coats, and, fearing lest they might resist or escape into the dense bushes which lined the road, I halted and found with me Paymaster Hill, Captain

N. H. Davis, and Lieutenant John Hamilton. We waited some time for the others, viz., Canby, Murray, Gibbs, and Sully, to come up, but as they were not in sight we made a dash up the road and captured six of the deserters, who were Germans, with heavy knapsacks on, trudging along the deep, sandy road. They had not expected pursuit, had not heard our horses, and were accordingly easily taken. Finding myself the senior officer present, I ordered Lieutenant Hamilton to search the men and then to march them back to Monterey, suspecting, as was the fact, that the rest of our party had taken a road that branched off a couple of miles back. Daylight broke as we reached the Salinas River, twelve miles out, and there the trail was broad and fresh leading directly out on the Salinas Plain. This plain is about five miles wide, and then the ground becomes somewhat broken. The trail continued very plain, and I rode on at a gallop to where there was an old adobe-ranch on the left of the road, with the head of a lagoon, or pond, close by. I saw one or two of the soldiers getting water at the pond, and others up near the house. I had the best horse and was considerably ahead, but on looking back could see Hill and Davis coming up behind at a gallop. I motioned to them to hurry forward, and turned my horse across the head of the pond, knowing the ground well, as it was a favorite place for shooting geese and ducks. Approaching the house, I ordered the men who were outside to go in. They did not know me personally, and exchanged glances, but I had my musket cocked, and, as the two had seen Davis and Hill coming up pretty fast, they obeyed. Dismounting, I found the house full of deserters, and there was no escape for them. They naturally supposed that I had a strong party with me, and when I ordered them to "fall in" they obeyed from habit. By the time Hill and Davis came up I had them formed in two ranks, the front rank facing about, and I was taking away their bayonets, pistols, etc. We disarmed them, destroying a musket and several pistols, and, on counting them, we found that we three had taken eighteen, which, added to the six first captured, made twenty-four. We made them sling their knapsacks and begin their homeward march. It was near night when we got back, so that these deserters had traveled nearly forty miles since "tattoo" of the night before. The other party had captured three, so that only one man had escaped. I doubt not this prevented the desertion of the bulk of the Second Infantry that spring, for at that time so demoralizing was the effect of the gold-mines that everybody not in the military service justified desertion, because a soldier, if free, could earn more money in a day than he received per month. Not only did soldiers and sailors desert, but captains and masters of ships actually abandoned their vessels and cargoes to try their luck at the mines. Preachers and professors forgot their creeds and took to trade, and even to keeping gambling-houses. I remember that one of our regular soldiers, named Reese, in deserting stole a favorite double-barreled gun of mine, and when the orderly-sergeant of the company, Carson, was going on furlough, I asked him when he came across Reese to try and get my gun back. When he returned he told me that he had found Reese and offered him a hundred dollars for my gun, but Reese sent me word that he liked the gun, and would not take a hundred dollars for it. Soldiers or sailors who could reach the mines were universally shielded by the miners, so that it was next to useless to attempt their recapture. In due season General Persifer Smith, Gibbs, and I, with some hired packers, started back for San Francisco, and soon after we transferred our headquarters to Sonoma. About this time Major Joseph Hooker arrived from the East—the regular adjutant-general of the division—relieved me, and I became thereafter one of General Smith's regular aides-de-camp.

As there was very little to do, General Smith encouraged us to go into any business that would enable us to make money. R. P. Hammond, James Blair, and I, made a contract to survey for Colonel J. D. Stevenson his newly-projected city of "New York of the Pacific," situated at the mouth of the San Joaquin River. The contract embraced, also, the making of soundings and the marking out of a channel through Suisun Bay. We hired, in San Francisco, a small metallic boat, with a sail, laid in some stores, and proceeded to the United States ship Ohio, anchored at Saucelito, where we borrowed a sailor-boy and lead-lines with which to sound the channel. We sailed up to Benicia, and, at General Smith's request, we surveyed and marked the line dividing the city of Benicia from the government reserve. We then sounded the bay back and forth, and staked out the best channel up Suisun Bay, from which Blair made out sailing directions. We then made the preliminary surveys of the city of "New York of the Pacific," all of which were duly plotted; and for this work we each received from Stevenson five hundred dollars and ten or fifteen lots. I sold enough lots to make up another five hundred dollars, and let the balance go; for the city of "New York of the Pacific" never came to any thing. Indeed, cities at the time were being projected by speculators all round the bay and all over the country.

While we were surveying at "New York of the Pacific," occurred one of those little events that showed the force of the gold-fever. We had a sailor-boy with us, about seventeen years old, who cooked our meals and helped work the boat. On shore, we had the sail spread so as to shelter us against the wind and dew. One morning I awoke about daylight, and looked out to see if our sailor-boy was at work getting breakfast; but he was not at the fire at all. Getting up, I discovered that he had converted a *tule-bolsa* into a sail-boat, and was sailing for the gold-mines. He was astride this *bolsa*, with a small parcel of bread and meat done up in a piece of cloth; another piece of cloth, such as we used for making our signal-stations, he had fixed into a sail; and with a paddle he was directing his precarious craft right out into the broad bay, to follow the general direction of the schooners and boats that he knew were ascending the Sacramento River. He was about a hundred yards from the shore. I jerked up my gun, and hailed him to come back. After a moment's hesitation, he let go his sheet and began to paddle back. This *bolsa* was nothing but a bundle of *tule*, or bullrush, bound together with grass-ropes in the shape of a cigar, about ten feet long and about two feet through the butt. With these the California Indians cross streams of considerable size. When he came ashore, I gave him a good overhauling for attempting to desert, and put him to work getting breakfast. In due time we returned him to his ship, the Ohio.

Subsequently, I made a bargain with Mr. Hartnell to survey his ranch at Cosumnes River, Sacramento Valley. Ord and a young citizen, named Seton, were associated with me in this. I bought of Rodman M. Price a surveyor's compass, chain, etc., and, in San Francisco, a small wagon and harness. Availing ourselves of a schooner, chartered to carry Major Miller and two companies of the Second Infantry from San Francisco to Stockton, we got up to our destination at little cost. I recall an occurrence that happened when the schooner was anchored in Carquinez Straits, opposite the soldiers' camp on shore. We were waiting for daylight and a fair wind; the schooner lay anchored at an ebb-tide, and about daylight Ord and I had gone ashore for something. Just as we were pulling off from shore, we heard the loud shouts of the men, and saw them all running down toward the water. Our attention thus drawn, we saw something swimming in the water, and pulled toward it, thinking it a coyote; but we soon recognized a large grizzly bear, swimming directly across the channel. Not having any weapon, we hurriedly pulled for the schooner, calling out, as we neared it, "A bear! a bear!" It so happened that Major Miller was on deck, washing his face and hands. He ran rapidly to the bow of the vessel, took the musket from the hands of the sentinel, and fired at the bear, as he passed but a short distance ahead of the schooner. The bear rose, made a growl or howl, but continued his course. As we scrambled up the port-side to get our guns, the mate, with a crew, happened to have a boat on the starboard-side, and, armed only with a hatchet, they pulled up alongside the bear, and the mate struck him in the head with the hatchet. The bear turned, tried to get into the boat, but the mate struck his claws with repeated blows, and made him let go. After several passes with him, the mate actually killed the bear, got a rope round him, and towed him alongside the schooner, where he was hoisted on deck. The carcass weighed over six hundred pounds. It was found that Major Miller's shot had struck the bear in the lower jaw, and thus disabled him. Had it not been for this, the bear would certainly have upset the boat and drowned all in it. As it was, however, his meat served us a good turn in our trip up to Stockton. At Stockton we disembarked our wagon, provisions, and instruments.

There I bought two fine mules at three hundred dollars each, and we hitched up and started for the Cosumnes River.

About twelve miles off was the Mokelumne, a wide, bold stream, with a canoe as a ferry-boat. We took our wagon to pieces, and ferried it and its contents across, and then drove our mules into the water. In crossing, one mule became entangled in the rope of the other, and for a time we thought he was a gone mule; but at last he revived and we hitched up. The mules were both pack-animals; neither had ever before seen a wagon. Young Seton also was about as green, and had never handled a mule. We put on the harness, and began to hitch them in, when one of the mules turned his head, saw the wagon, and started. We held on tight, but the beast did not stop until he had shivered the tongue-pole into a dozen fragments. The fact was, that Seton had hitched the traces before he had put on the blind-bridle. There was considerable swearing done, but that would not mend the pole. There was no place nearer than Sutter's Fort to repair damages, so we were put to our wits' end. We first sent back a mile or so, and bought a raw-hide. Gathering up the fragments of the pole and cutting the hide into strips, we fished it in the rudest manner. As long as the hide was green, the pole was very shaky; but gradually the sun dried the hide, tightened it, and the pole actually held for about a month. This cost us nearly a day of delay; but, when damages were repaired, we harnessed up again, and reached the crossing of the Cosumnes, where our survey was to begin. The *expediente*, or title-papers, of the ranch described it as containing nine or eleven leagues on the Cosumnes, south side, and between the San Joaquin River and Sierra Nevada Mountains. We began at the place where the road crosses the Cosumnes, and laid down a line four miles south, perpendicular to the general direction of the stream; then, surveying up the stream, we marked each mile so as to admit of a subdivision of one mile by four. The land was dry and very poor, with the exception of here and there some small pieces of bottom-land, the great bulk of the bottom-land occurring on the north side of the stream. We continued the survey up some twenty miles into the hills above the mill of Dailor and Sheldon. It took about a month to make this survey, which, when finished, was duly plotted; and for it we received one-tenth of the land, or two subdivisions. Ord and I took the land, and we paid Seton for his labor in cash. By the sale of my share of the land, subsequently, I realized three thousand dollars. After finishing Hartnell's survey, we crossed over to Dailor's, and did some work for him at five hundred dollars a day for the party. Having finished our work on the Cosumnes, we proceeded to Sacramento, where Captain Sutter employed us to connect the survey of Sacramento City, made by Lieutenant Warner, and that of Sutterville, three miles below, which was then being surveyed by Lieutenant J. W. Davidson, of the First Dragoons. At Sutterville, the plateau of the Sacramento approached quite near the river, and it would have made a better site for a town than the low, submerged land where the city now stands; but it seems to be a law of growth that all natural advantages are disregarded wherever once business chooses a location. Old Sutter's *embarcadero* became Sacramento City, simply because it was the first point used for unloading boats for Sutter's Fort, just as the site for San Francisco was fixed by the use of Yerba Buena as the hide-landing for the Mission of "San Francisco de Asis."

I invested my earnings in this survey in three lots in Sacramento City, on which I made a fair profit by a sale to one McNulty, of Mansfield, Ohio. I only had a two months' leave of absence, during which General Smith, his staff, and a retinue of civil friends, were making a tour of the gold-mines, and hearing that he was *en route* back to his headquarters at Sonoma, I knocked off my work, sold my instruments, and left my wagon and mules with my cousin Charley Hoyt, who had a store in Sacramento, and was on the point of moving up to a ranch, for which he had bargained, on Bear Creek, on which was afterward established Camp "Far West." He afterward sold the mules, wagon, etc., for me, and on the whole I think I cleared, by those two months' work, about six thousand dollars. I then returned to headquarters at Sonoma, in time to attend my fellow aide-de-camp Gibbs through a long and dangerous sickness, during which he was on board a store-ship, guarded by Captain George Johnson, who now resides in San Francisco. General Smith had agreed that on the first good opportunity he would send me to the United States as a bearer of dispatches, but this he could not do until he had made the examination of Oregon, which was also in his command. During the summer of 1849 there continued to pour into California a perfect stream of people. Steamers came, and a line was established from San Francisco to Sacramento, of which the Senator was the pioneer, charging sixteen dollars a passage, and actually coining money. Other boats were built, out of materials which had either come around Cape Horn or were brought from the Sandwich Islands. Wharves were built, houses were springing up as if by magic, and the Bay of San Francisco presented as busy a scene of life as any part of the world. Major Allen, of the Quartermaster's Department, who had come out as chief-quartermaster of the division, was building a large warehouse at Benicia, with a row of quarters, out of lumber at one hundred dollars per thousand feet, and the work was done by men at sixteen dollars a day. I have seen a detailed soldier, who got only his monthly pay of eight dollars a month, and twenty cents a day for extra duty, nailing on weather-boards and shingles, alongside a citizen who was paid sixteen dollars a day. This was a real injustice, made the soldiers discontented, and it was hardly to be wondered at that so many deserted. While the mass of people were busy at gold and in mammoth speculations, a set of busy politicians were at work to secure the prizes of civil government. Gwin and Fremont were there, and T. Butler King, of Georgia, had come out from the East, scheming for office. He staid with us at Sonoma, and was generally regarded as the Government candidate for United States Senator. General Riley as Governor, and Captain Halleck as Secretary of State, had issued a proclamation for the election of a convention to frame a State constitution. In due time the elections were held, and the convention was assembled at Monterey. Dr. Semple was elected president; and Gwin, Sutter, Halleck, Butler King, Sherwood, Gilbert, Shannon, and others, were members. General Smith took no part in this convention, but sent me down to watch the proceedings, and report to him. The only subject of interest was the slavery question. There were no slaves then in California, save a few who had come out as servants, but the Southern people at that time claimed their share of territory, out of that acquired by the common labors of all sections of the Union in the war with Mexico. Still, in California there was little feeling on the subject. I never heard

General Smith, who was a Louisianian, express any opinion about it. Nor did Butler King, of Georgia, ever manifest any particular interest in the matter. A committee was named to draft a constitution, which in due time was reported, with the usual clause, then known as the Wilmot Proviso, excluding slavery; and during the debate which ensued very little opposition was made to this clause, which was finally adopted by a large majority, although the convention was made up in large part of men from our Southern States. This matter of California being a free State, afterward, in the national Congress, gave rise to angry debates, which at one time threatened civil war. The result of the convention was the election of State officers, and of the Legislature which sat in San José in October and November, 1849, and which elected Fremont and Gwin as the first United States Senators in Congress from the Pacific coast.

Shortly after returning from Monterey, I was sent by General Smith up to Sacramento City to instruct Lieutenants Warner and Williamson, of the Engineers, to push their surveys of the Sierra Nevada Mountains, for the purpose of ascertaining the possibility of passing that range by a railroad, a subject that then elicited universal interest. It was generally assumed that such a road could not be made along any of the immigrant roads then in use, and Warner's orders were to look farther north up the Feather River, or some one of its tributaries. Warner was engaged in this survey during the summer and fall of 1849, and had explored, to the very end of Goose Lake, the source of Feather River. Then, leaving Williamson with the baggage and part of the men, he took about ten men and a first-rate guide, crossed the summit to the east, and had turned south, having the range of mountains on his right hand, with the intention of regaining his camp by another pass in the mountain. The party was strung out, single file, with wide spaces between, Warner ahead. He had just crossed a small valley and ascended one of the spurs covered with sage-brush and rocks, when a band of Indians rose up and poured in a shower of arrows. The mule turned and ran back to the valley, where Warner fell off dead, punctured by five arrows. The mule also died. The guide, who was next to Warner, was mortally wounded; and one or two men had arrows in their bodies, but recovered. The party gathered about Warner's body, in sight of the Indians, who whooped and yelled, but did not venture away from their cover of rocks. This party of men remained there all day without bury-ing the bodies, and at night, by a wide circuit, passed the mountain, and reached Williamson's camp. The news of Warner's death cast a gloom over all the old Californians, who knew him well. He was a careful, prudent, and honest officer, well qualified for his business, and extremely accurate in all his work. He and I had been intimately associated dur-ing our four years together in California, and I felt his loss deeply. The season was then too far advanced to attempt to avenge his death, and it was not until the next spring that a party was sent out to gather up and bury his scattered bones.

As winter approached, the immigrants overland came pour-ing into California, dusty and worn with their two thousand miles of weary travel across the plains and mountains. Those who arrived in October and November reported thousands still behind them, with oxen perishing, and short of food. Appeals were made for help, and General Smith resolved to attempt relief. Major Rucker, who had come across with Pike Graham's Battalion of Dragoons, had exchanged with Major Fitzgerald, of the Quartermaster's Department, and was de-tailed to conduct this relief. General Smith ordered him to be supplied with one hundred thousand dollars out of the civil fund, subject to his control, and with this to purchase at Sac-ramento flour, bacon, etc., and to hire men and mules to send out and meet the immigrants. Major Rucker fulfilled this duty perfectly, sending out pack-trains loaded with food by the many routes by which the immigrants were known to be ap-proaching, went out himself with one of these trains, and re-mained in the mountains until the last immigrant had got in. No doubt this expedition saved many a life which has since been most useful to the country. I remained at Sacramento a good part of the fall of 1849, recognizing among the immi-grants many of my old personal friends—John C. Fall, William King, Sam Stambaugh, Hugh Ewing, Hampton Denman, etc. I got Rucker to give these last two employment along with the train for the relief of the immigrants. They had proposed to begin a ranch on my land on the Cosumnes, but afterward changed their minds, and went out with Rucker.

While I was at Sacramento General Smith had gone on his contemplated trip to Oregon, and promised that he would be back in December, when he would send me home with dispatches. Accordingly, as the winter and rainy season was at hand, I went to San Francisco, and spent some time at the Presidio, waiting patiently for General Smith's return. About Christmas a vessel arrived from Oregon with the dispatches, and an order for me to deliver them in person to General Winfield Scott, in New York City. General Smith had sent them down, remaining in Oregon for a time. Of course I was all ready, and others of our set were going home by the same conveyance, viz., Rucker, Ord, A. J. Smith—some under orders, and the others on leave. Wanting to see my old friends in Monterey, I arranged for my passage in the steamer of January 1, 1850, paying six hundred dollars for passage to New York, and went down to Monterey by land, Rucker accompanying me. The weather was unusually rainy, and all the plain about Santa Clara was under water; but we reached Monterey in time. I again was welcomed by my friends, Doña Augustias, Manuelita, and the family, and it was resolved that I should take two of the boys home with me and put them at Georgetown College for education, viz., Antonio and Porfirio, thirteen and eleven years old. The doña gave me a bag of gold-dust to pay for their passage and to deposit at the college. On the 2d day of January punctually appeared the steamer Oregon. We were all soon on board and off for home. At that time the steamers touched at San Diego, Acapulco, and Panama. Our passage down the coast was unusually pleasant. Arrived at Panama, we hired mules and rode across to Gorgona, on the Cruces River, where we hired a boat and paddled down to the mouth of the river, off which lay the steamer Crescent City. It usually took four days to cross the isthmus, every passenger taking care of himself, and it was really funny to watch the efforts of women and men unaccustomed to mules. It was an old song to us, and the trip across was easy and interesting. In due time we were rowed off to the Crescent City, rolling back and forth in the swell, and we scrambled aboard by a "Jacob's ladder" from the stern. Some of the women had to be hoisted aboard by lowering a tub from the end of a boom; fun to us who looked on, but awkward enough to the poor women, especially to a very fat one, who attracted much notice. General Fremont, wife and child (Lillie) were passengers with us down from San Francisco; but Mrs. Fremont not being well, they remained over one trip at Panama.

Senator Gwin was one of our passengers, and went through to New York. We reached New York about the close of January, after a safe and pleasant trip. Our party, composed of Ord, A. J. Smith, and Rucker, with the two boys, Antonio and Porfirio, put up at Delmonico's, on Bowling Green; and, as soon as we had cleaned up somewhat, I took a carriage, went to General Scott's office in Ninth Street, delivered my dispatches, was *ordered* to dine with him next day, and then went forth to hunt up my old friends and relations, the Scotts, Hoyts, etc., etc.

On reaching New York, most of us had rough soldier's clothing, but we soon got a new outfit, and I dined with General Scott's family, Mrs. Scott being present, and also their son-in-law and daughter (Colonel and Mrs. H. L. Scott). The general questioned me pretty closely in regard to things on the Pacific coast, especially the politics, and startled me with the assertion that "our country was on the eve of a terrible civil war." He interested me by anecdotes of my old army comrades in his recent battles around the city of Mexico, and I felt deeply the fact that our country had passed through a foreign war, that my comrades had fought great battles, and yet I had not heard a hostile shot. Of course, I thought it the last and only chance in my day, and that my career as a soldier was at an end. After some four or five days spent in New York, I was, by an order of General Scott, sent to Washington, to lay before the Secretary of War (Crawford, of Georgia) the dispatches which I had brought from California. On reaching Washington, I found that Mr. Ewing was Secretary of the Interior, and I at once became a member of his family. The family occupied the house of Mr. Blair, on Pennsylvania Avenue, directly in front of the War Department. I immediately repaired to the War Department, and placed my dispatches in the hands of Mr. Crawford, who questioned me somewhat about California, but seemed little interested in the subject, except so far as it related to slavery and the routes through Texas. I then went to call on the President at the White House. I found Major Bliss, who had been my teacher in mathematics at West Point, and was then General Taylor's son-in-law and private secretary. He took me into the room, now used by the President's private secretaries, where President Taylor was. I had never seen him before, though I had served under him in Florida in 1840–'41, and was most agreeably surprised at his fine personal appearance, and his pleasant, easy manners. He received me with great kindness, told me that Colonel Mason had mentioned my name with praise, and that he would be pleased to do me any act of favor. We were with him nearly an hour, talking about California generally, and of his personal friends, Persifer Smith, Riley, Canby, and others. Although General Scott was generally regarded by the army as the most accomplished soldier of the Mexican War, yet General Taylor had that blunt, honest, and stern character, that endeared him to the masses of the people, and made him President. Bliss, too, had gained a large fame by his marked skill and intelligence as an adjutant-general and military adviser. His manner was very unmilitary, and in his talk he stammered and hesitated, so as to make an unfavorable impression on a stranger; but he was wonderfully accurate and skillful with his pen, and his orders and letters form a model of military precision and clearness.

Chapter IV.

Missouri, Louisiana, and California.

1850–1855.

Having returned from California in January, 1850, with dispatches for the War Department, and having delivered them in person first to General Scott in New York City, and afterward to the Secretary of War (Crawford) in Washington City, I applied for and received a leave of absence for six months. I first visited my mother, then living at Mansfield, Ohio, and returned to Washington, where, on the 1st day of May, 1850, I was married to Miss Ellen Boyle Ewing, daughter of the Hon. Thomas Ewing, Secretary of the Interior. The marriage ceremony was attended by a large and distinguished company, embracing Daniel Webster, Henry Clay, T. H. Benton, President Taylor, and all his cabinet. This occurred at the house of Mr. Ewing, the same now owned and occupied by Mr. F. P. Blair, senior, on Pennsylvania Avenue, opposite the War Department. We made a wedding-tour to Baltimore, New York, Niagara, and Ohio, and returned to Washington by the 1st of July. General Taylor participated in the celebration of the Fourth of July, a very hot day, by hearing a long speech from the Hon. Henry S. Foote, at the base of the Washington Monument. Returning from the celebration much heated and fatigued, he partook too freely of his favorite iced milk with cherries, and during that night was seized with a severe colic, which by morning had quite prostrated him. It was said that he sent for his son-in-law, Surgeon Wood, United States Army, stationed in Baltimore, and declined medical assistance from anybody else. Mr. Ewing visited him several times, and was manifestly uneasy and anxious, as was also his son-in-law, Major Bliss, then of the army, and his confidential secretary. He rapidly grew worse, and died in about four days.

At that time there was a high state of political feeling pervading the country, on account of the questions growing out of the new Territories just acquired from Mexico by the war. Congress was in session, and General Taylor's sudden death evidently created great alarm. I was present in the Senate-gallery, and saw the oath of office administered to the Vice-President, Mr. Fillmore, a man of splendid physical proportions and commanding appearance; but on the faces of Senators and people could easily be read the feelings of doubt and uncertainty that prevailed. All knew that a change in the cabinet and general policy was likely to result, but at the time it was supposed that Mr. Fillmore, whose home was in Buffalo, would be less liberal than General Taylor to the politicians of the South, who feared, or pretended to fear, a crusade against slavery; or, as was the political cry of the day, that slavery would be prohibited in the Territories and in the places exclusively under the jurisdiction of the United States. Events, however, proved the contrary.

I attended General Taylor's funeral as a sort of aide-de-camp, at the request of the Adjutant-General of the army, Roger Jones, whose brother, a militia-general, commanded the escort, composed of militia and some regulars. Among the regulars I recall the names of Captains John Sedgwick and W. F. Barry.

Hardly was General Taylor decently buried in the Congressional Cemetery when the political struggle recommenced, and it became manifest that Mr. Fillmore favored the general compromise then known as Henry Clay's "Omnibus Bill," and that a general change of cabinet would at once occur. Webster was to succeed Mr. Clayton as Secretary of State, Corwin to succeed Mr. Meredith as Secretary of the Treasury, and A. H. H. Stuart to succeed Mr. Ewing as Secretary of the Interior. Mr. Ewing, however, was immediately appointed by the Governor of the State to succeed Corwin in the Senate. These changes made it necessary for Mr. Ewing to discontinue house-keeping, and Mr. Corwin took his house and furniture off his hands. I escorted the family out to their home in Lancaster, Ohio; but, before this had occurred, some most interesting debates took place in the Senate, which I regularly attended, and heard Clay, Benton, Foote, King of Alabama, Dayton, and the many real orators of that day. Mr. Calhoun was in his seat, but he was evidently approaching his end, for he was pale and feeble in the extreme. I heard Mr. Webster's last speech on the floor of the Senate, under circumstances that warrant a description. It was publicly known that he was to leave the Senate, and enter the new cabinet of Mr. Fillmore, as his Secretary of State, and that prior to leaving he was to make a great speech on the "Omnibus Bill." Resolved to hear it, I went up to the Capitol on the day named, an hour or so earlier than usual. The speech was to be delivered in the old Senate-chamber, now used by the Supreme Court. The galleries were much smaller than at present, and I found them full to overflowing, with a dense crowd about the door, struggling to reach the stairs. I could not get near, and then tried the reporters' gallery, but found it equally crowded; so I feared I should lose the only possible opportunity to hear Mr. Webster.

I had only a limited personal acquaintance with any of the Senators, but had met Mr. Corwin quite often at Mr. Ewing's house, and I also knew that he had been extremely friendly to my father in his lifetime; so I ventured to send in to him my card, "W. T. S., First-Lieutenant, Third Artillery." He came to the door promptly, when I said, "Mr. Corwin, I believe Mr. Webster is to speak to-day." His answer was, "Yes, he has the floor at one o'clock." I then added that I was extremely anxious to hear him. "Well," said he, "why don't you go into the gallery?" I explained that it was full, and I had tried every access, but found all jammed with people. "Well," said he, "what do you want of me?" I explained that I would like him to take me on the floor of the Senate; that I had often seen from the gallery persons on the floor, no better entitled to it than I. He then asked in his quizzical way, "Are you a foreign embassador?" "No." "Are you the Governor of a State?" "No." "Are you a member of the other House?" "Certainly not." "Have you ever had a vote of thanks by name?" "No." "Well, these are the only privileged members." I then told him he knew well enough who I was, and that if he chose he could take me in. He then said, "Have you any impudence?" I told him, "A reasonable amount if occasion called for it." "Do you think you could become so interested in my conversation as not to notice the door-keeper?" (pointing to him). I told him that there was not the least doubt of it, if he would tell me one of his funny stories. He then took my arm, and led me a turn in the vestibule, talking about some indifferent matter, but all the time directing my looks to his left hand, toward which he was gesticulating with his right; and thus we approached the door-keeper, who began asking me, "Foreign embassador? Governor of a State? Member of Congress?" etc.; but I caught Corwin's eye, which said plainly, "Don't mind him, pay attention to me," and in this way we entered the Senate-chamber by a side-door. Once in, Corwin said, "Now you can take care of yourself," and I thanked him cordially. I found a seat close behind Mr. Webster, and near General Scott, and heard the whole of the speech. It was heavy in the extreme, and I confess that I was disappointed and tired long before it was finished. No doubt the speech was full of fact and argument, but it had none of the fire of oratory, or intensity of feeling, that marked all of Mr. Clay's efforts.

Toward the end of July, as before stated, all the family went home to Lancaster. Congress was still in session, and the bill adding four captains to the Commissary Department had not passed, but was reasonably certain to, and I was equally sure of being one of them. At that time my name was on the muster-roll of (Light) Company C, Third Artillery (Bragg's), stationed at Jefferson Barracks, near St. Louis. But, as there was cholera at St. Louis, on application, I was permitted to delay joining my company until September. Early in that month, I proceeded to Cincinnati, and thence by steamboat to St. Louis, and then to Jefferson Barracks, where I reported for duty to Captain and Brevet-Colonel Braxton Bragg, commanding (Light) Company C, Third Artillery. The other officers of the company were First-Lieutenant James A. Hardie, and afterward Hackaliah Brown. New horses had just been purchased for the battery, and we were preparing for work, when the mail brought the orders announcing the passage of the bill increasing the Commissary Department by four captains, to which were promoted Captains Shiras, Blair, Sherman, and Bowen. I was ordered to take post at St. Louis, and to relieve Captain A. J. Smith, First Dragoons, who had been acting in that capacity for some months. My commission bore date September 27, 1850. I proceeded forthwith to the city, relieved Captain Smith, and entered on the discharge of the duties of the office.

Colonel N. S. Clarke, Sixth Infantry, commanded the department; Major D. C. Buell was adjutant-general, and Captain W. S. Hancock was regimental quartermaster; Colonel Thomas Swords was the depot quartermaster, and we had our offices in the same building, on the corner of Washington Avenue and Second. Subsequently Major S. Van Vliet relieved Colonel Swords. I remained at the Planters' House until my family arrived, when we occupied a house on Chouteau Avenue, near Twelfth.

During the spring and summer of 1851, Mr. Ewing and Mr. Henry Stoddard, of Dayton, Ohio, a cousin of my father, were much in St. Louis, on business connected with the estate of Major Amos Stoddard, who was of the old army, as early as the beginning of this century. He was stationed at the village of St. Louis at the time of the Louisiana purchase, and when Lewis and Clarke made their famous expedition across the continent to the Columbia River. Major Stoddard at that early day had purchased a small farm back of the village, of some Spaniard or Frenchman, but, as he was a bachelor, and was killed at Fort Meigs, Ohio, during the War of 1812, the title was for many years lost sight of, and the farm was covered over by other claims and by occupants. As St. Louis began to grow, his brothers and sisters, and their descendants, concluded to look up the property. After much and fruitless litigation, they at last retained Mr. Stoddard, of Dayton, who in turn employed Mr. Ewing, and these, after many years of labor, established the title, and in the summer of 1851 they were put in possession by the United States marshal. The ground was laid off, the city survey extended over it, and the whole was sold in partition. I made some purchases, and acquired an interest, which I have retained more or less ever since.

We continued to reside in St. Louis throughout the year 1851, and in the spring of 1852 I had occasion to visit Fort Leavenworth on duty, partly to inspect a lot of cattle which a Mr. Gordon, of Cass County, had contracted to deliver in New Mexico, to enable Colonel Sumner to attempt his scheme of making the soldiers in New Mexico self-supporting, by raising their own meat, and in a measure their own vegetables. I found Fort Leavenworth then, as now, a most beautiful spot, but in the midst of a wild Indian country.

There were no whites settled in what is now the State of Kansas. Weston, in Missouri, was the *great* town, and speculation in town-lots there and thereabout burnt the fingers of some of the army-officers, who wanted to plant their scanty dollars in a fruitful soil. I rode on horseback over to Gordon's farm, saw the cattle, concluded the bargain, and returned by way of Independence, Missouri. At Independence I found F. X. Aubrey, a noted man of that day, who had just made a celebrated ride of six hundred miles in six days. That spring the United States quartermaster, Major L. C. Easton, at Fort Union, New Mexico, had occasion to send some message east by a certain date, and contracted with Aubrey to carry it to the nearest post-office (then Independence, Missouri), making his compensation conditional on the time consumed. He was supplied with a good horse, and an order on the outgoing trains for an exchange. Though the whole route was infested with hostile Indians, and not a house on it, Aubrey started alone with his rifle. He was fortunate in meeting several outward-bound trains, and thereby made frequent changes of horses, some four or five, and reached Independence in six days, having hardly rested or slept the whole way. Of course, he was extremely fatigued, and said there was an opinion among the wild Indians that if a man "sleeps out his sleep," after such extreme exhaustion, he will never awake; and, accordingly, he instructed his landlord to wake him up after eight hours of sleep. When aroused at last, he saw by the clock that he had been asleep twenty hours, and he was dreadfully angry, threatened to murder his landlord, who protested he had tried in every way to get him up, but found it impossible, and had let him "sleep it out." Aubrey, in describing his sensations to me, said he took it for granted he was a dead man; but in fact he sustained no ill effects, and was off again in a few days. I met him afterward often in California, and always esteemed him one of the best samples of that bold race of men who had grown up on the Plains, along with the Indians, in the service of the fur companies. He was afterward, in 1856, killed by R. C. Weightman, in a bar-room row, at Santa Fé, New Mexico, where he had just arrived from California.

In going from Independence to Fort Leavenworth, I had to

swim Milk Creek, and sleep all night in a Shawnee camp. The next day I crossed the Kaw or Kansas River in a ferry-boat, maintained by the blacksmith of the tribe, and reached the fort in the evening. At that day the whole region was unsettled, where now exist many rich counties, highly cultivated, embracing several cities of from ten to forty thousand inhabitants. From Fort Leavenworth I returned by steamboat to St. Louis.

In the summer of 1852, my family went to Lancaster, Ohio; but I remained at my post. Late in the season, it was rumored that I was to be transferred to New Orleans, and in due time I learned the cause. During a part of the Mexican War, Major Seawell, of the Seventh Infantry, had been acting commissary of subsistence at New Orleans, then the great depot of supplies for the troops in Texas, and of those operating beyond the Rio Grande. Commissaries at that time were allowed to purchase in open market, and were not restricted to advertising and awarding contracts to the lowest bidders. It was reported that Major Seawell had purchased largely of the house of Perry Seawell & Co., Mr. Seawell being a relative of his. When he was relieved in his duties by Major Waggaman, of the regular Commissary Department, the latter found Perry Seawell & Co. so prompt and satisfactory that he continued the patronage; for which there was a good reason, because stores for the use of the troops at remote posts had to be packed in a particular way, to bear transportation in wagons, or even on pack-mules; and this firm had made extraordinary preparations for this exclusive purpose. Some time about 1849, a brother of Major Waggaman, who had been clerk to Captain Casey, commissary of subsistence, at Tampa Bay, Florida, was thrown out of office by the death of the captain, and he naturally applied to his brother in New Orleans for employment; and he, in turn, referred him to his friends, Messrs. Perry Seawell & Co. These first employed him as a clerk, and afterward admitted him as a partner. Thus it resulted, in fact, that Major Waggaman was dealing largely, if not exclusively, with a firm of which his brother was a partner.

One day, as General Twiggs was coming across Lake Pontchartrain, he fell in with one of his old cronies, who was an extensive grocer. This gentleman gradually led the conversation to the downward tendency of the times since he and Twiggs were young, saying that, in former years, all the merchants of New Orleans had a chance at government patronage; but now, in order to sell to the army commissary, one had to take a brother in as a partner. General Twiggs resented this, but the merchant again affirmed it, and gave names. As soon as General Twiggs reached his office, he instructed his adjutant-general, Colonel Bliss—who told me this—to address a categorical note of inquiry to Major Waggaman. The major very frankly stated the facts as they had arisen, and insisted that the firm of Perry Seawell & Co. had enjoyed a large patronage, but deserved it richly by reason of their promptness, fairness, and fidelity. The correspondence was sent to Washington, and the result was, that Major Waggaman was ordered to St. Louis, and I was ordered to New Orleans.

I went down to New Orleans in a steamboat in the month of September, 1852, taking with me a clerk, and, on arrival, assumed the office, in a bank-building facing Lafayette Square, in which were the offices of all the army departments. General D. Twiggs was in command of the department, with Colonel W. W. S. Bliss (son-in-law of General Taylor) as his adjutant-general. Colonel A. C. Myers was quartermaster, Captain John F. Reynolds aide-de-camp, and Colonel A. J. Coffee paymaster. I took rooms at the St. Louis Hotel, kept by a most excellent gentleman, Colonel Mudge.

Mr. Perry Seawell came to me in person, soliciting a continuance of the custom which he had theretofore enjoyed; but I told him frankly that a change was necessary, and I never saw or heard of him afterward. I simply purchased in open market, arranged for the proper packing of the stores, and had not the least difficulty in supplying the troops and satisfying the head of the department in Washington.

About Christmas, I had notice that my family, consisting of Mrs. Sherman, two children, and nurse, with my sister Fanny (now Mrs. Moulton, of Cincinnati, Ohio), were *en route* for New Orleans by steam-packet; so I hired a house on Magazine Street, and furnished it. Almost at the moment of their arrival, also came from St. Louis my personal friend Major Turner, with a parcel of documents, which, on examination, proved to be articles of copartnership for a bank in California under the title of "Lucas, Turner & Co.," in which my name was embraced as a partner. Major Turner was, at the time, actually *en route* for New York, to embark for San Francisco, to inaugurate the bank, in the nature of a branch of the firm already existing at St. Louis under the name of "Lucas & Symonds." We discussed the matter very fully, and he left with me the papers for reflection, and went on to New York and California.

Shortly after arrived James H. Lucas, Esq., the principal of the banking-firm in St. Louis, a most honorable and wealthy gentleman. He further explained the full programme of the branch in California; that my name had been included at the instance of Major Turner, who was a man of family and property in St. Louis, unwilling to remain long in San Francisco, and who wanted me to succeed him there. He offered me a very tempting income, with an interest that would accumulate and grow. He also disclosed to me that, in establishing a branch in California, he was influenced by the apparent prosperity of Page, Bacon & Co., and further that he had received the principal data, on which he had founded the scheme, from B. R. Nisbet, who was then a teller in the firm of Page, Bacon & Co., of San Francisco; that he also was to be taken in as a partner, and was fully competent to manage all the details of the business; but, as Nisbet was comparatively young, Mr. Lucas wanted me to reside in San Francisco permanently, as the head of the firm. All these matters were fully discussed, and I agreed to apply for a six months' leave of absence, go to San Francisco, see for myself, and be governed by appearances there. I accordingly, with General Twiggs's approval, applied to the adjutant-general for a six months' leave, which was granted; and Captain John F. Reynolds was named to perform my duties during my absence.

During the stay of my family in New Orleans, we enjoyed the society of the families of General Twiggs, Colonel Myers, and Colonel Bliss, as also of many citizens, among whom was the wife of Mr. Day, sister to my brother-in-law, Judge Bartley. General Twiggs was then one of the oldest officers of the army. His history extended back to the War of 1812, and he had served in early days with General Jackson in Florida and in the Creek campaigns. He had fine powers of description, and often entertained us, at his office, with accounts of his experiences in the earlier settlements of the Southwest. Colonel Bliss had been General Taylor's adjutant in the Mexican War, and was universally regarded as one of the most finished and accomplished scholars in the army, and his wife was a most agreeable and accomplished lady.

Late in February, I dispatched my family up to Ohio in the steamboat Tecumseh (Captain Pearce); disposed of my house and furniture; turned over to Major Reynolds the funds, property, and records of the office; and took passage in a small steamer for Nicaragua, *en route* for California. We embarked early in March, and in seven days reached Greytown, where we united with the passengers from New York, and proceeded, by the Nicaragua River and Lake, for the Pacific Ocean.

The river was low, and the little steam canal-boats, four in number, grounded often, so that the passengers had to get into the water, to help them over the bars. In all there were about six hundred passengers, of whom about sixty were women and children. In four days we reached Castillo, where there is a decided fall, passed by a short railway, and above this fall we were transferred to a larger boat, which carried us up the rest of the river, and across the beautiful lake Nicaragua, studded with volcanic islands. Landing at Virgin Bay, we rode on mules across to San Juan del Sur, where lay at anchor the propeller S. S. Lewis (Captain Partridge, I think). Passengers were carried through the surf by natives to small boats, and rowed off to the Lewis. The weather was very hot, and quite a scramble followed for state-rooms, especially for those on deck. I succeeded in reaching the purser's office, got my ticket for a berth in one of the best state-rooms on deck, and, just as I was turning from the window, a lady who was a fellow-passenger from New Orleans, a Mrs. D——, called to me to secure her and her lady-friend berths on deck, saying that those below were unendurable. I spoke to the purser, who, at the moment perplexed by the crowd and clamor, answered: "I must put their names down for the other two berths of *your* state-room; but, as soon as the confusion is over, I will make some change whereby you shall not suffer."

As soon as these two women were assigned to a state-room, they took possession, and I was left out. Their names were recorded as "Captain Sherman and ladies." As soon as things were quieted down I remonstrated with the purser, who at last gave me a lower berth in another and larger state-room on deck, with five others, so that my two ladies had the state-room all to themselves. At every meal the steward would come to me and say, "Captain Sherman, will you bring your ladies to the table?" and we had the best seats in the ship. This continued throughout the voyage, and I assert that "my ladies" were of the most modest and best-behaved in the ship; but some time after we had reached San Francisco one of our fellow-passengers came to me and inquired if I personally knew Mrs. D——, with flaxen tresses, who sang so sweetly for us, and who had come out under my especial escort. I replied I did not, more than the chance acquaintance of the voyage, and what she herself had told me, viz., that she expected to meet her husband, who lived about Mokelumne Hill. He then informed me that she was a woman of the town. Society in California was then decidedly mixed.

In due season the steamship Lewis got under weigh. She was a wooden ship, long and narrow, bark-rigged, and a propeller; very slow, moving not over eight miles an hour. We stopped at Acapulco, and, in eighteen days, passed in sight of Point Pinos at Monterey, and at the speed we were traveling expected to reach San Francisco at 4 A.M. the next day. The cabin-passengers, as was usual, bought of the steward some champagne and cigars, and we had a sort of ovation for the captain, purser, and surgeon of the ship, who were all very clever fellows, though they had a slow and poor ship.

Late at night all the passengers went to bed, expecting to enter the port at daylight. I did not undress, as I thought the captain could and would run in at night, and I lay down with my clothes on. About 4 A.M. I was awakened by a bump and sort of grating of the vessel, which I thought was our arrival at the wharf in San Francisco; but instantly the ship struck heavily; the engines stopped, and the running to and fro on deck showed that something was wrong. In a moment I was out of my state-room, at the bulwark, holding fast to a stanchion, and looking over the side at the white and seething water caused by her sudden and violent stoppage. The sea was comparatively smooth, the night pitch-dark, and the fog deep and impenetrable; the ship would rise with the swell, and come down with a bump and quiver that was decidedly unpleasant. Soon the passengers were out of their rooms, undressed, calling for help, and praying as though the ship were going to sink immediately. Of course she could not sink, being already on the bottom, and the only question was as to the strength of hull to stand the bumping and straining. Great confusion for a time prevailed, but soon I realized that the captain had taken all proper precautions to secure his boats, of which there were six at the davits. These are the first things that steerage-passengers make for in case of shipwreck, and right over my head I heard the captain's voice say in a low tone, but quite decided: "Let go that falls, or, damn you, I'll blow your head off!" This seemingly harsh language gave me great comfort at the time, and on saying so to the captain afterward, he explained that it was addressed to a passenger who attempted to lower one of the boats. Guards, composed of the crew, were soon posted to prevent any interference with the boats, and the officers circulated among the passengers the report that there was no immediate danger; that, fortunately, the sea was smooth; that we were simply aground, and must quietly await daylight.

They advised the passengers to keep quiet, and the ladies and children to dress and sit at the doors of their state-rooms, there to await the advice and action of the officers of the ship, who were perfectly cool and self-possessed. Meantime the ship was working over a reef—for a time I feared she would break in two; but, as the water gradually rose inside to a level with the sea outside, the ship swung broadside to the swell, and all her keel seemed to rest on the rock or sand. At no time did the sea break over the deck—but the water below drove all the people up to the main-deck and to the promenade-deck, and thus we remained for about three hours, when daylight came; but there was a fog so thick that nothing but water could be seen. The captain caused a boat to be carefully lowered, put in her a trustworthy officer with a boat-compass, and we saw her depart into the fog. During her absence the ship's bell was kept tolling. Then the fires were all out, the ship full of water, and gradually breaking up, wriggling with every swell like a willow basket—the sea all round us full of the floating fragments of her sheeting, twisted and torn into a spongy condition. In less than an hour the boat returned, saying that the beach was quite near, not more than a mile away, and had a good place for landing. All the boats were then carefully lowered, and manned by crews belonging to the ship; a piece of the gangway, on the leeward side, was cut away, and all the women, and a few of the worst-scared men, were lowered into the boats, which pulled for shore. In a comparatively short time the boats returned, took new loads, and the debarkation was afterward carried on quietly and systematically. No baggage was allowed to go on shore except bags or parcels carried in the hands of passengers. At times the fog lifted so that we could see from the wreck the tops of the hills, and the outline of the shore; and I remember sitting on the upper or hurricane deck with the captain, who had his maps and compass before him, and was trying to make out where the ship was. I thought I recognized the outline of the hills below the mission of Dolores, and so stated to him; but he called my attention to the fact that the general line of hills bore northwest, whereas the coast south of San Francisco bears due north and south. He therefore concluded that the ship had overrun her reckoning, and was then to the north of San Francisco. He also explained that, the passage up being longer than usual, viz., eighteen days, the coal was short; that at the time the firemen were using some cut-up spars along with the slack of coal, and that this fuel had made more than usual steam, so that the ship must have glided along faster than reckoned. This proved to be the actual case, for, in fact, the steamship Lewis was wrecked April 9, 1853, on "Duckworth Reef," Baulinas Bay, about eighteen miles above the entrance to San Francisco.

The captain had sent ashore the purser in the first boat, with orders to work his way to the city as soon as possible, to report the loss of his vessel, and to bring back help. I remained on the wreck till among the last of the passengers, managing to get a can of crackers and some sardines out of the submerged pantry, a thing the rest of the passengers did not have, and then I went quietly ashore in one of the boats.

The passengers were all on the beach, under a steep bluff; had built fires to dry their clothes, but had seen no human being, and had no idea where they were. Taking along with me a fellow-passenger, a young chap about eighteen years old, I scrambled up the bluff, and walked back toward the hills, in hopes to get a good view of some known object. It was then the month of April, and the hills were covered with the beautiful grasses and flowers of that season of the year. We soon found horse paths and tracks, and following them we came upon a drove of horses grazing at large, some of which had saddle-marks. At about two miles from the beach we found a *corral*; and thence, following one of the strongest-marked paths, in about a mile more we descended into a valley, and, on turning a sharp point, reached a board shanty, with a horse picketed near by. Four men were inside eating a meal. I inquired if any of the Lewis's people had been there; they did not seem to understand what I meant, when I explained to them that about three miles from them, and beyond the old *corral*, the steamer Lewis was wrecked, and her passengers were on the beach. I inquired where we were, and they answered, "At Baulinas Creek;" that they were employed at a saw-mill just above, and were engaged in shipping lumber to San Francisco; that a schooner loaded with lumber was then about two miles down the creek, waiting for the tide to get out, and doubtless if we would walk down they would take us on board.

I wrote a few words back to the captain, telling him where he was, and that I would hurry to the city to send him help. My companion and I then went on down the creek, and soon descried the schooner anchored out in the stream. On being hailed, a small boat came in and took us on board. The "captain" willingly agreed for a small sum to carry us down to San Francisco; and, as his whole crew consisted of a small boy about twelve years old, we helped him to get up his anchor and pole the schooner down the creek and out over the bar on a high tide. This must have been about 2 P.M. Once over the bar, the sails were hoisted, and we glided along rapidly with a strong, fair, northwest wind. The fog had lifted, so we could see the shores plainly, and the entrance to the bay. In a couple of hours we were entering the bay, and running "wing-and-wing." Outside the wind was simply the usual strong breeze; but, as it passes through the head of the Golden Gate, it increases, and there, too, we met a strong ebb-tide.

The schooner was loaded with lumber, much of which was on deck, lashed down to ring-bolts with raw-hide thongs. The captain was steering, and I was reclining on the lumber, looking at the familiar shore, as we approached Fort Point, when I heard a sort of cry, and felt the schooner going over. As we got into the throat of the "Heads," the force of the wind, meeting a strong ebb-tide, drove the nose of the schooner under water; she dove like a duck, went over on her side, and began to drift out with the tide. I found myself in the water, mixed up with pieces of plank and ropes; struck out, swam round to the stern, got on the keel, and clambered up on the side. Satisfied that she could not sink, by reason of her cargo, I was not in the least alarmed, but thought two shipwrecks in one day not a good beginning for a new, peaceful career. Nobody was drowned, however; the captain and crew were busy in securing such articles as were liable to float off, and I looked out for some passing boat or vessel to pick us up. We were drifting steadily out to sea, while I was signaling to a boat about three miles off, toward Saucelito, and saw her tack and stand toward us. I was busy watching this sail-boat, when I heard a Yankee's voice, close behind, saying, "This is a nice mess you've got yourselves into," and looking about I saw a man in a small boat, who had seen us upset, and had rowed out to us from a schooner anchored close under the fort. Some explanations were made, and when the sail-boat coming from Saucelito was near enough to be spoken to, and the captain had engaged her to help his schooner, we bade him good-by, and got the man in the small boat to carry us ashore, and land us at the foot of the bluff, just below the fort. Once there, I was at home, and we footed it up to the Presidio. Of the sentinel I inquired who was in command of the post, and was answered, "Major Merchant." He was not then in, but his adjutant, Lieutenant Gardner, was. I sent my card to him; he came out, and was much surprised to find me covered with sand, and dripping with water, a good specimen of a shipwrecked mariner. A few words of explanation sufficed; horses were provided, and we rode hastily into the city, reaching the office of the Nicaragua Steamship Company (C. K. Garrison, agent) about dark, just as the purser had arrived, by a totally different route. It was too late to send relief that night, but by daylight next morning two steamers were *en route* for and reached the place of wreck in time to relieve the passengers and bring them, and most of the baggage. I lost my carpet-bag, but saved my trunk. The Lewis went to pieces the night after we got off, and, had there been an average sea during the night of our shipwreck, none of us probably would have escaped. That evening in San Francisco I hunted up Major Turner, whom I found boarding, in company with General E. A. Hitchcock, at a Mrs. Ross's, on Clay Street, near Powell. I took quarters with them, and began to make my studies, with a view to a decision whether it was best to undertake this new and untried scheme of banking, or to return to New Orleans and hold on to what I then had, a good army commission.

At the time of my arrival, San Francisco was on the top wave of speculation and prosperity. Major Turner had rented at six hundred dollars a month the office formerly used and then owned by Adams & Co., on the east side of Montgomery Street, between Sacramento and California Streets. B. R. Nisbet was the active partner, and James Reilly the teller. Already the bank of Lucas, Turner & Co. was established, and was engaged in selling bills of exchange, receiving deposits, and loaning money at three per cent. a month.

Page, Bacon & Co., and Adams & Co., were in full blast across the street, in Parrott's new granite building, and other bankers were doing seemingly a prosperous business, among them Wells, Fargo & Co.; Drexel, Sather & Church; Burgoyne & Co.; James King of Wm.; Sanders & Brenham; Davidson & Co.; Palmer, Cook & Co., and others. Turner and I had rooms at Mrs. Ross's, and took our meals at restaurants down-town, mostly at a Frenchman's named Martin, on the southwest corner of Montgomery and California Streets. General Hitchcock, of the army, commanding the Department of California, usually messed with us; also a Captain Mason, and Lieutenant Whiting, of the Engineer Corps. We soon secured a small share of business, and became satisfied there was room for profit. Everybody seemed to be making money fast; the city was being rapidly extended and improved; people paid their three per cent. a month interest without fail, and without deeming it excessive. Turner, Nisbet, and I, daily discussed the prospects, and gradually settled down to the conviction that with two hundred thousand dollars capital, and a credit of fifty thousand dollars in New York, we could build up a business that would help the St. Louis house, and at the same time pay expenses in California, with a reasonable profit. Of course, Turner never designed to remain long in California, and I consented to go back to St. Louis, confer with Mr. Lucas and Captain Simonds, agree upon further details, and then return permanently.

I have no memoranda by me now by which to determine the fact, but think I returned to New York in July, 1853, by the Nicaragua route, and thence to St. Louis by way of Lancaster, Ohio, where my family still was. Mr. Lucas promptly agreed to the terms proposed, and further consented, on the expiration of the lease of the Adams & Co. office, to erect a new banking-house in San Francisco, to cost fifty thousand dollars. I then returned to Lancaster, explained to Mr. Ewing and Mrs. Sherman all the details of our agreement, and, meeting their approval, I sent to the Adjutant-General of the army my letter of resignation, to take effect at the end of the six months' leave, and the resignation was accepted, to take effect September 6, 1853. Being then a citizen, I engaged a passage out to California by the Nicaragua route, in the steamer leaving New York September 20th, for myself and family, and accordingly proceeded to New York, where I had a conference with Mr. Meigs, cashier of the American Exchange Bank, and with Messrs. Wadsworth & Sheldon, bankers, who were our New York correspondents; and on the 20th embarked for San Juan del Norte, with the family, composed of Mrs. Sherman, Lizzie, then less than a year old, and her nurse, Mary Lynch. Our passage down was uneventful, and, on the boats up the Nicaragua River, pretty much the same as before. On reaching Virgin Bay, I engaged a native with three mules to carry us across to the Pacific, and as usual the trip partook of the ludicrous—Mrs. Sherman mounted on a donkey about as large as a Newfoundland dog; Mary Lynch on another, trying to carry Lizzie on a pillow before her, but her mule had a fashion of lying down, which scared her, till I exchanged mules, and my California spurs kept that mule on his legs. I carried Lizzie some time till she was fast asleep, when I got our native man to carry her awhile. The child woke up, and, finding herself in the hands of a dark-visaged man, she yelled most lustily till I got her away. At the summit of the pass, there was a clear-running brook, where we rested an hour, and bathed Lizzie in its sweet waters. We then continued to the end of our journey, and, without going to the tavern at San Juan del Sur, we passed directly to the vessel, then at anchor about two miles out. To reach her we engaged a native boat, which had to be kept outside the surf. Mrs. Sherman was first taken in the arms of two stout natives; Mary Lynch, carrying Lizzie, was carried by two others; and I followed, mounted on the back of a strapping fellow, while fifty or a hundred others were running to and fro, cackling like geese.

Mary Lynch got scared at the surf, and began screaming like a fool, when Lizzie became convulsed with fear, and one of the natives rushed to her, caught her out of Mary's arms, and carried her swiftly to Mrs. Sherman, who, by that time, was in the boat, but Lizzie had fainted with fear, and for a long time sobbed as though permanently injured. For years she showed symptoms that made us believe she had never entirely recovered from the effects of the scare. In due time we reached the steamer Sierra Nevada, and got a good stateroom. Our passage up the coast was pleasant enough; we reached San Francisco on the 15th of October, and took quarters at an hotel on Stockton Street, near Broadway.

Major Turner remained till some time in November, when he also departed for the East, leaving me and Nisbet to manage the bank. I endeavored to make myself familiar with the business, but of course Nisbet kept the books, and gave his personal attention to the loans, discounts, and drafts, which yielded the profits. I soon saw, however, that the three per cent. charged as premium on bills of exchange was not all profit, but out of this had to come one and a fourth to one and a half for freight, one and a third for insurance, with some indefinite promise of a return premium; then, the cost of blanks, boxing of the bullion, etc., etc. Indeed, I saw no margin for profit at all. Nisbet, however, who had long been familiar with the business, insisted there was a profit, in the fact that the gold-dust or bullion shipped was more valuable than its cost to us. We, of course, had to remit bullion to meet our bills on New York, and bought crude gold-dust, or bars refined by Kellogg & Humbert or E. Justh & Co., for at that time the United States Mint was not in operation. But, as the reports of our shipments came back from New York, I discovered that I was right, and Nisbet was wrong; and, although we could not help selling our checks on New York and St. Louis at the same price as other bankers, I discovered that, at all events, the exchange business in San Francisco was rather a losing business than profitable. The same as to loans. We could loan, at three per cent. a month, all our own money, say two hundred and fifty thousand dollars, and a part of our deposit account. This latter account in California was decidedly uncertain. The balance due depositors would run down to a mere nominal sum on steamer-days, which were the 1st and 15th of each month, and then would increase till the next steamer-day, so that we could not make use of any reasonable part of this balance for loans beyond the next steamer-day; or, in other words, we had an expensive bank, with expensive clerks, and all the machinery for taking care of other people's money for their benefit, without corresponding profit. I also saw that loans were attended with *risk* commensurate with the rate; nevertheless, I could not attempt to reform the rules and customs established by others before me, and had to drift along with the rest toward that Niagara that none foresaw at the time.

Shortly after arriving out in 1853, we looked around for a site for the new bank, and the only place then available on Montgomery Street, the Wall Street of San Francisco, was a lot at the corner of Jackson Street, facing Montgomery, with an alley on the north, belonging to James Lick. The ground was sixty by sixty-two feet, and I had to pay for it thirty-two thousand dollars. I then made a contract with the builders, Keyser & Brown, to erect a three-story brick building, with finished basement, for about fifty thousand dollars. This made eighty-two thousand instead of fifty thousand dollars, but I thought Mr. Lucas could stand it and would approve, which he did, though it resulted in loss to him. After the civil war, he told me he had sold the building for forty thousand dollars, about half its cost, but luckily gold was then at 250, so that he could use the forty thousand dollars gold as the equivalent of one hundred thousand dollars currency. The building was erected; I gave it my personal supervision, and it was strongly and thoroughly built, for I saw it two years ago, when several earthquakes had made no impression on it; still, the choice of site was unfortunate, for the city drifted in the opposite direction, viz., toward Market Street. I then thought that all the heavy business would remain toward the foot of Broadway and Jackson Street, because there were the deepest water and best wharves, but in this I made a mistake. Nevertheless, in the spring of 1854, the new bank was finished, and we removed to it, paying rents thereafter to our Mr. Lucas instead of to Adams & Co. A man named Wright, during the same season, built a still finer building just across the street from us; Pioche, Bayerque & Co. were already established on another corner of Jackson Street, and the new Metropolitan Theatre was in progress diagonally opposite us. During the whole of 1854 our business steadily grew, our average deposits going up to half a million, and our sales of exchange and consequent shipment of bullion averaging two hundred thousand dollars per steamer. I signed all bills of exchange, and insisted on Nisbet consulting me on loans and discounts. Spite of every caution, however, we lost occasionally by bad loans, and worse by the steady depreciation of real estate. The city of San Francisco was then extending her streets, sewering them, and planking them, with three-inch lumber. In payment for the lumber and the work of contractors, the city authorities paid scrip in even sums of one hundred, five hundred, one thousand, and five thousand dollars. These formed a favorite collateral for loans at from fifty to sixty cents on the dollar, and no one doubted their ultimate value, either by redemption or by being converted into city bonds. The notes also of H. Meiggs, Neeley Thompson & Co., etc., lumber-dealers, were favorite notes, for they paid their interest promptly, and lodged large margins of these street-improvement warrants as collateral. At that time, Meiggs was a prominent man, lived in style in a large house on Broadway, was a member of the City Council, and owned large saw-mills up the coast about Mendocino. In him Nisbet had unbounded faith, but, for some reason, I feared or mistrusted him, and remember that I cautioned Nisbet not to extend his credit, but to gradually contract his loans. On looking over our bills receivable, then about six hundred thousand dollars, I found Meiggs, as principal or indorser, owed us about eighty thousand dollars—all, however, secured by city warrants; still, he kept bank accounts elsewhere, and was generally a borrower. I instructed Nisbet to insist on his reducing his line as the notes matured, and, as he found it indelicate to speak to Meiggs, I instructed him to refer him to me; accordingly, when, on the next steamer-day, Meiggs appeared at the counter for a draft on Philadelphia, of about twenty thousand dollars, for which he offered his note and collateral, he was referred to me, and I explained to him that our draft was the same as money; that he could have it for cash, but that we were already in advance to him some seventy-five or eighty thousand dollars, and that instead of increasing the amount I must insist on its reduction. He inquired if I mistrusted his ability, etc. I explained, certainly not, but that our duty was to assist those who did *all* their business with us, and, as our means were necessarily limited, I must restrict him to some reasonable sum, say, twenty-five thousand dollars. Meiggs invited me to go with him to a rich mercantile house on Clay Street, whose partners belonged in Hamburg, and there, in the presence of the principals of the house, he demonstrated, as clearly as a proposition in mathematics, that his business at Mendocino was based on calculations that could not fail. The bill of exchange which he wanted, he said would make the last payment on a propeller already built in Philadelphia, which would be sent to San Francisco, to tow into and out of port the schooners and brigs that were bringing his lumber down the coast. I admitted all he said, but renewed my determination to limit his credit to twenty-five thousand dollars. The Hamburg firm then agreed to accept for him the payment of all his debt to us, except the twenty-five thousand dollars, payable in equal parts for the next three steamer-days. Accordingly, Meiggs went back with me to our bank, wrote his note for twenty-five thousand dollars, and secured it by mortgage on real estate and city warrants, and substituted the three acceptances of the Hamburg firm for the overplus. I surrendered to him all his former notes, except one for which he was indorser. The three acceptances duly matured and were paid; one morning Meiggs and family were missing, and it was discovered they had embarked in a sailing-vessel for South America. This was the beginning of a series of failures in San Francisco, that extended through the next two years. As soon as it was known that Meiggs had fled, the town was full of rumors, and everybody was running to and fro to secure his money. His debts amounted to nearly a million dollars. The Hamburg house, which had been humbugged, were heavy losers and failed, I think. I took possession of Meiggs's dwelling-house and other property for which I held his mortgage, and in the city warrants thought I had an overplus; but it transpired that Meiggs, being in the City Council, had issued various quantities of street scrip, which was adjudged a forgery, though, beyond doubt, most of it, if not all, was properly signed, but fraudulently issued. On this city scrip our bank must have lost about ten thousand dollars. Meiggs subsequently turned up in Chili, where again he rose to wealth and has paid much of his San Francisco debts, but none to us. He is now in Peru, living like a prince. With Meiggs fell all the lumber-dealers, and many persons dealing in city scrip. Compared with others, our loss was a trifle. In a short time things in San Francisco resumed their wonted course, and we generally laughed at the escapade of Meiggs, and the cursing of his deluded creditors.

Shortly after our arrival in San Francisco, I rented of a Mr. Marryat, son of the English Captain Marryat, the author, a small frame-house on Stockton Street, near Green, buying of him his furniture, and we removed to it about December 1, 1853. Close by, around on Green Street, a man named Dickey was building two small brick-houses, on ground which he had leased of Nicholson. I bought one of these houses, subject to the ground-rent, and moved into it as soon as finished. Lieutenant T. H. Stevens, of the United States Navy, with his family, rented the other; we lived in this house throughout the year 1854, and up to April 17, 1855.

Chapter V.

DURING THE WINTER of 1854—'55, I received frequent intimations in my letters from the St. Louis house, that the bank of Page, Bacon & Co. was in trouble, growing out of their relations to the Ohio & Mississippi Railroad, to the contractors for building which they had made large advances, to secure which they had been compelled to take, as it were, an assignment of the contract itself, and finally to assume all the liabilities of the contractors. Then they had to borrow money in New York, and raise other money from time to time, in the purchase of iron and materials for the road, and to pay the hands. The firm in St. Louis and that in San Francisco were different, having different partners, and the St. Louis house naturally pressed the San Francisco firm to ship largely of "gold-dust," which gave them a great name; also to keep as large a balance as possible in New York to sustain their credit. Mr. Page was a very wealthy man, but his wealth consisted mostly of land and property in St. Louis. He was an old man, and a good one; had been a baker, and knew little of banking as a business. This part of his general business was managed exclusively by his son-in-law, Henry D. Bacon, who was young, handsome, and generally popular. How he was drawn into that affair of the Ohio & Mississippi road I have no means of knowing, except by hearsay. Their business in New York was done through the American Exchange Bank, and through Duncan, Sherman & Co. As we were rival houses, the St. Louis partners removed our account from the American Exchange Bank to the Metropolitan Bank; and, as Wadsworth & Sheldon had failed, I was instructed to deal in time bills, and in European exchange, with Schuchardt & Gebhard, bankers in Nassau Street.

In California the house of Page, Bacon & Co. was composed of the same partners as in St. Louis, with the addition of Henry Haight, Judge Chambers, and young Frank Page. The latter had charge of the "branch" in Sacramento. Haight was the real head-man, but he was too fond of lager-beer to be intrusted with so large a business. Beyond all comparison, Page, Bacon & Co. were the most prominent bankers in California in 1853–'55. Though I had notice of danger in that quarter, from our partners in St. Louis, nobody in California doubted their wealth and stability. They must have had, during that winter, an average deposit account of nearly two million dollars, of which seven hundred thousand dollars was in "certificates of deposit," the most stable of all accounts in a bank. Thousands of miners invested their earnings in such certificates, which they converted into drafts on New York, when they were ready to go home or wanted to send their "pile" to their families. Adams & Co. were next in order, because of their numerous offices scattered throughout the mining country. A gentleman named Haskell had been in charge of Adams & Co. in San Francisco, but in the winter of 1854–'55 some changes were made, and the banking department had been transferred to a magnificent office in Halleck's new Metropolitan Block. James King of Wm. had discontinued business on his own account, and been employed by Adams & Co. as their cashier and banker, and Isaiah C. Wood had succeeded Haskell in chief control of the express department. Wells, Fargo & Co. were also bankers as well as expressmen, and William J. Pardee was the resident partner.

As the mail-steamer came in on February 17, 1855, according to her custom, she ran close to the Long Wharf (Meiggs's) on North Beach, to throw ashore the express-parcels of news for speedy delivery. Some passenger on deck called to a man of his acquaintance standing on the wharf, that Page & Bacon had failed in New York. The news spread like wild-fire, but soon it was met by the newspaper accounts to the effect that some particular acceptances of Page & Bacon, of St. Louis, in the hands of Duncan, Sherman & Co., in New York, had gone to protest. All who had balances at Page, Bacon & Co.'s, or held certificates of deposit, were more or less alarmed, wanted to secure their money, and a general excitement pervaded the whole community. Word was soon passed round that the matter admitted of explanation, viz., that the two houses were distinct and separate concerns, that every draft of the *California* house had been paid in New York, and would continue to be paid. It was expected that this assertion would quiet the fears of the California creditors, but for the next three days there was a steady "run" on that bank. Page, Bacon & Co. stood the first day's run very well, and, as I afterward learned, paid out about six hundred thousand dollars in gold coin. On the 20th of February Henry Haight came to our bank, to see what help we were willing to give him; but I was out, and Nisbet could not answer positively for the firm. Our condition was then very strong. The deposit account was about six hundred thousand dollars, and we had in our vault about five hundred thousand dollars in coin and bullion, besides an equal amount of good bills receivable. Still I did not like to weaken ourselves to help others; but in a most friendly spirit, that night after bank-hours, I went down to Page, Bacon & Co., and entered their office from the rear. I found in the cashier's room Folsom, Parrott, Dewey and Payne, Captain Ritchie, Donohue, and others, citizens and friends of the house, who had been called in for consultation. Passing into the main office, where all the book-keepers, tellers, etc., with gas-lights, were busy writing up the day's work, I found Mr. Page, Henry Haight, and Judge Chambers. I spoke to Haight, saying that I was sorry I had been out when he called at our bank, and had now come to see him in the most friendly spirit. Haight had evidently been drinking, and said abruptly that "all the banks would break," that "no bank could instantly pay all its obligations," etc. I answered he could speak for himself, but not for me; that I had come to offer to buy with cash a fair proportion of his bullion, notes, and bills; but, if they were going to fail, I would not be drawn in. Haight's manner was extremely offensive, but Mr. Page tried to smooth it over, saying they had had a bad day's run, and could not answer for the result till their books were written up.

I passed back again into the room where the before-named gentlemen were discussing some paper which lay before them, and was going to pass out, when Captain Folsom, who was an officer of the army, a class-mate and intimate friend of mine, handed me the paper the contents of which they were discussing. It was very short, and in Henry Haight's handwriting, pretty much in these terms: "We, the undersigned property-holders of San Francisco, having *personally* examined the books, papers, etc., of Page, Bacon & Co., do hereby certify that the house is solvent and able to pay all its debts," etc. Haight had drawn up and asked them to sign this paper, with the intention to publish it in the next morning's papers, for effect. While I was talking with Captain Folsom, Haight came into the room to listen. I admitted that the effect of such a publication would surely be good, and would probably stave off immediate demand till their assets could be in part converted or realized; but I naturally inquired of Folsom, "Have you personally examined the accounts, as herein recited, and the assets, enough to warrant your signature to this paper?" for, "thereby you in effect become indorsers." Folsom said they had not, when Haight turned on me rudely and said, "Do you think the affairs of such a house as Page, Bacon & Co. can be critically examined in an hour?" I answered: "These gentlemen can do what they please, but they have twelve hours before the bank will open on the morrow, and if the ledger is written up" (as I believed it was or could be by midnight), "they can (by counting the coin, bullion on hand, and notes or stocks of immediate realization) approximate near enough for them to indorse for the remainder." But Haight pooh-poohed me, and I left. Folsom followed me out, told me he could not afford to imperil all he had, and asked my advice. I explained to him that my partner Nisbet had been educated and trained in that very house of Page, Bacon & Co.; that we kept our books exactly as they did; that every day the ledger was written up, so that from it one could see exactly how much actual money was due the depositors and certificates; and then by counting the money in the vault, estimating the bullion on hand, which, though not actual money, could easily be converted into coin, and supplementing these amounts by "bills receivable," they ought to arrive at an approximate result. After Folsom had left me, John Parrott also stopped and talked with me to the same effect. Next morning I looked out for the notice, but no such notice appeared in the morning papers, and I afterward learned that, on Parrott and Folsom demanding an actual count of the money in the vault, Haight angrily refused unless they would accept his word for it, when one after the other declined to sign his paper.

The run on Page, Bacon & Co. therefore continued throughout the 21st, and I expected all day to get an invitation to close our bank for the next day, February 22, which we could have made a holiday by concerted action; but each banker waited for Page, Bacon & Co. to ask for it, and, no such circular coming, in the then state of feeling no other banker was willing to take the initiative. On the morning of February 22, 1855, everybody was startled by receiving a small slip of paper, delivered at all the houses, on which was printed a short notice that, for "want of coin," Page, Bacon & Co. found it necessary to close their bank for a short time. Of course, we all knew the consequences, and that every other bank in San Francisco would be tried. During the 22d we all kept open, and watched our depositors closely; but the day was generally observed by the people as a holiday, and the firemen paraded the streets of San Francisco in unusual strength. But, on writing up our books that night, we found that our deposit account had diminished about sixty-five thousand dollars. Still, there was no run on us, or any other of the banks, that day; yet, observing little knots of men on the street, discussing the state of the banks generally, and overhearing Haight's expression quoted, that, in case of the failure of Page, Bacon & Co., "all the other banks would break," I deemed it prudent to make ready. For some days we had refused all loans and renewals, and we tried, without success, some of our call-loans; but, like Hotspur's spirits, they would not come.

Our financial condition on that day (February 22, 1855) was: Due depositors and demand certificates, five hundred and twenty thousand dollars; to meet which, we had in the vault—coin, three hundred and eighty thousand dollars; bullion, seventy-five thousand dollars; and bills receivable, about six hundred thousand dollars. Of these, at least one hundred thousand dollars were on demand, with stock collaterals. Therefore, for the extent of our business, we were stronger than the Bank of England, or any bank in New York City.

Before daylight next morning, our door-bell was rung, and

I was called down-stairs by E. Casserly, Esq. (an eminent lawyer of the day, since United States Senator), who informed me
he had just come up from the office of Adams & Co., to tell
me that their affairs were in such condition that they would
not open that morning at all; and that this, added to the suspension of Page, Bacon & Co., announced the day before,
would surely cause a general run on all the banks. I informed
him that I expected as much, and was prepared for it.

In going down to the bank that morning, I found Montgomery Street full; but, punctually to the minute, the bank
opened, and in rushed the crowd. As usual, the most noisy
and clamorous were men and women who held small certificates; still, others with larger accounts were in the crowd,
pushing forward for their balances. All were promptly met
and paid. Several gentlemen of my personal acquaintance
merely asked my word of honor that their money was safe,
and went away; others, who had large balances, and no immediate use for coin, gladly accepted gold-bars, whereby we
paid out the seventy-five thousand dollars of bullion, relieving
the coin to that amount.

Meantime, rumors from the street came pouring in that
Wright & Co. had failed; then Wells, Fargo & Co.; then
Palmer, Cook & Co., and indeed all, or nearly all, the banks
of the city; and I was told that parties on the street were
betting high, first, that we would close our doors at eleven
o'clock; then twelve, and so on; but we did not, till the usual
hour that night. We had paid every demand, and still had a
respectable amount left.

This run on the bank (the only one I ever experienced)
presented all the features, serious and comical, usual to such
occasions. At our counter happened that identical case, narrated of others, of the Frenchman, who was nearly squeezed
to death in getting to the counter, and, when he received his
money, did not know what to do with it. "If you got the
money, I no want him; but if you no got him, I want it like
the devil!"

Toward the close of the day, some of our customers deposited, rather ostentatiously, small amounts, not aggregating
more than eight or ten thousand dollars. Book-keepers and
tellers were kept at work to write up the books; and these

showed: Due depositors and certificates, about one hundred and twenty thousand dollars, for which remained of coin about fifty thousand dollars. I resolved not to sleep until I had collected from those owing the bank a part of their debts; for I was angry with them that they had stood back and allowed the panic to fall on the banks alone. Among these were Captain Folsom, who owed us twenty-five thousand dollars, secured by a mortgage on the American Theatre and Tehama Hotel; James Smiley, contractor for building the Custom-House, who owed us two notes of twenty thousand and sixteen thousand dollars, for which we held, as collateral, two acceptances of the collector of the port, Major R. P. Hammond, for twenty thousand dollars each; besides other private parties that I need not name. The acceptances given to Smiley were for work done on the Custom-House, but could not be paid until the work was actually laid in the walls, and certified by Major Tower, United States Engineers; but Smiley had an immense amount of granite, brick, iron, etc., on the ground, in advance of construction, and these acceptances were given him expressly that he might raise money thereon for the payment of such materials.

Therefore, as soon as I got my dinner, I took my saddle-horse, and rode to Captain Folsom's house, where I found him in great pain and distress, mental and physical. He was sitting in a chair, and bathing his head with a sponge. I explained to him the object of my visit, and he said he had expected it, and had already sent his agent, Van Winkle, down-town, with instructions to raise what money he could at any cost; but he did not succeed in raising a cent. So great was the shock to public confidence, that men slept on their money, and would not loan it for ten per cent. a week, on any security whatever—even on mint certificates, which were as good as gold, and only required about ten days to be paid in coin by the United States Mint. I then rode up to Hammond's house, on Rincon Hill, and found him there. I explained to him exactly Smiley's affairs, and only asked him to pay one of his acceptances. He inquired, "Why not both?" I answered that was so much the better; it would put me under still greater obligations. He then agreed to meet me at our bank at 10 P.M. I sent word to others that I demanded them to pay what they could on their paper, and then returned to the bank, to meet Hammond. In due time, he came down with Palmer (of Palmer, Cook & Co.), and there he met Smiley, who was, of course, very anxious to retire his notes. We there discussed the matter fully, when Hammond said, "Sherman, give me up my two acceptances, and I will substitute therefor my check of forty thousand dollars," with "the distinct understanding that, if the money is not needed by you, it shall be returned to me, and the transaction then to remain *statu quo*." To this there was a general assent. Nisbet handed him his two acceptances, and he handed me his check, signed as collector of the port, on Major J. R. Snyder, United States Treasurer, for forty thousand dollars. I afterward rode out, that night, to Major Snyder's house on North Beach, saw him, and he agreed to meet me at 8 A.M. next day, at the United States Mint, and to pay the check, so that I could have the money before the bank opened. The next morning, as agreed on, we met, and he paid me the check in two sealed bags of gold-coin, each marked twenty thousand dollars, which I had carried to the bank, but never opened them, or even broke the seals.

That morning our bank opened as usual, but there was no appearance of a continuation of the "run;" on the contrary, money began to come back on deposit, so that by night we had a considerable increase, and this went on from day to day, till nearly the old condition of things returned. After about three days, finding I had no use for the money obtained on Hammond's check, I took the identical two bags back to the cashier of the Custom-House, and recovered the two acceptances which had been surrendered as described; and Smiley's two notes were afterward paid in their due course, out of the cash received on those identical acceptances. But, years afterward, on settling with Hammond for the Custom-House contract when completed, there was a difference, and Smiley sued Lucas, Turner & Co. for money had and received for his benefit, being the identical forty thousand dollars herein explained, but he lost his case. Hammond, too, was afterward removed from office, and indicted in part for this transaction. He was tried before the United States Circuit Court, Judge McAlister presiding, for a violation of the sub-Treasury Act, but was acquitted. Our bank, having thus passed so well through the crisis, took at once a first rank; but these bank failures had caused so many mercantile losses, and had led to such an utter downfall in the value of real estate, that everybody lost more or less money by bad debts, by depreciation of stocks and collaterals, that became unsalable, if not worthless.

About this time (viz., February, 1855) I had exchanged my house on Green Street, with Mr. Sloat, for the half of a fifty-vara lot on Harrison Street, between Fremont and First, on which there was a small cottage, and I had contracted for the building of a new frame-house thereon, at six thousand dollars. This house was finished on the 9th of April, and my family moved into it at once.

For some time Mrs. Sherman had been anxious to go home to Lancaster, Ohio, where we had left our daughter Minnie, with her grandparents, and we arranged that S. M. Bowman, Esq., and wife, should move into our new house and board us, viz., Lizzie, Willie with the nurse Biddy, and myself, for a fair consideration. It so happened that two of my personal friends, Messrs. Winters and Cunningham of Marysville, and a young fellow named Eagan, now a captain in the Commissary Department, were going East in the steamer of the middle of April, and that Mr. William H. Aspinwall, of New York, and Mr. Chauncey, of Philadelphia, were also going back; and they all offered to look to the personal comfort of Mrs. Sherman on the voyage. They took passage in the steamer Golden Age (Commodore Watkins), which sailed on April 17, 1855. Their passage down the coast was very pleasant till within a day's distance of Panama, when one bright moonlit night, April 29th, the ship, running at full speed, between the Islands Quibo and Quicara, struck on a sunken reef, tore out a streak in her bottom, and at once began to fill with water. Fortunately she did not stick fast, but swung off into deep water, and Commodore Watkins happening to be on deck at the moment, walking with Mr. Aspinwall, learning that the water was rushing in with great rapidity, gave orders for a full head of steam, and turned the vessel's bow straight for the Island Quicara. The water rose rapidly in the hold, the passengers were all assembled, fearful of going down, the fires were out, and the last revolution of the wheels made, when her bow touched gently on the beach, and the vessel's stern sank in deep water. Lines were got out, and the ship held in an upright position, so that the passengers were safe, and but little incommoded. I have often heard Mrs. Sherman tell of the boy Eagan, then about fourteen years old, coming to her state-room, and calling to her not to be afraid, as he was a good swimmer; but on coming out into the cabin, partially dressed, she felt more confidence in the cool manner, bearing, and greater strength of Mr. Winters. There must have been nearly a thousand souls on board at the time, few of whom could have been saved had the steamer gone down in mid-channel, which surely would have resulted, had not Commodore Watkins been on deck, or had he been less prompt in his determination to beach his ship. A sail-boat was dispatched toward Panama, which luckily met the steamer John L. Stephens, just coming out of the bay, loaded with about a thousand passengers bound for San Francisco, and she at once proceeded to the relief of the Golden Age. Her passengers were transferred in small boats to the Stephens, which vessel, with her two thousand people crowded together with hardly standing-room, returned to Panama, whence the passengers for the East proceeded to their destination without further delay. Luckily for Mrs. Sherman, Purser Goddard, an old Ohio friend of ours, was on the Stephens, and most kindly gave up his own room to her, and such lady friends as she included in her party. The Golden Age was afterward partially repaired at Quicara, pumped out, and steamed to Panama, when, after further repairs, she resumed her place in the line. I think she is still in existence, but Commodore Watkins afterward lost his life in China, by falling down a hatchway.

Mrs. Sherman returned in the latter part of November of the same year, when Mr. and Mrs. Bowman, who meantime had bought a lot next to us and erected a house thereon, removed to it, and we thus continued close neighbors and friends until we left the country for good in 1857.

During the summer of 1856, in San Francisco, occurred one of those unhappy events, too common to new countries, in which I became involved in spite of myself.

William Neely Johnson was Governor of California, and resided at Sacramento City; General John E. Wool commanded the Department of California, having succeeded General Hitchcock, and had his headquarters at Benicia; and a Mr. Van Ness was mayor of the city. Politics had become a regular and profitable business, and politicians were more than suspected of being corrupt. It was reported and currently believed that the sheriff (Scannell) had been required to pay the Democratic Central Committee a hundred thousand dollars for his nomination, which was equivalent to an election, for an office of the nominal salary of twelve thousand dollars a year for four years. In the election all sorts of dishonesty were charged and believed, especially of "ballot-box stuffing," and too generally the better classes avoided the elections and dodged jury-duty, so that the affairs of the city government necessarily passed into the hands of a low set of professional politicians. Among them was a man named James Casey, who edited a small paper, the printing office of which was in a room on the third floor of our banking-office. I hardly knew him by sight, and rarely if ever saw his paper; but one day Mr. Sather, of the excellent banking firm of Drexel, Sather & Church, came to me, and called my attention to an article in Casey's paper so full of falsehood and malice, that we construed it as an effort to black-mail the banks generally. At that time we were all laboring to restore confidence, which had been so rudely shaken by the panic, and I went up-stairs, found Casey, and pointed out to him the objectionable nature of his article, told him plainly that I could not tolerate his attempt to print and circulate slanders in our building, and, if he repeated it, I would cause him and his press to be thrown out of the windows. He took the hint and moved to more friendly quarters. I mention this fact, to show my estimate of the man, who became a figure in the drama I am about to describe. James King of Wm., as before explained, was in 1853 a banker on his own account, but some time in 1854 he had closed out his business, and engaged with Adams & Co., as cashier. When this firm failed, he, in common with all the employés, was thrown out of employment, and had to look around for something else. He settled down to the publication of an evening paper, called the *Bulletin*, and, being a man of fine manners and address, he at once constituted himself the champion of society against the public and private characters whom he saw fit to arraign.

As might have been expected, this soon brought him into the usual newspaper war with other editors, and especially with Casey, and epithets *à la* "Eatanswill" were soon bandying back and forth between them. One evening of May, 1856, King published, in the *Bulletin*, copies of papers procured from New York, to show that Casey had once been sentenced to the State penitentiary at Sing Sing. Casey took mortal offense, and called at the *Bulletin* office, on the corner of Montgomery and Merchant Streets, where he found King, and violent words passed between them, resulting in Casey giving King notice that he would shoot him on sight. King remained in his office till about 5 or 6 P.M., when he started toward his home on Stockton Street, and, as he neared the corner of Washington, Casey approached him from the opposite direction, called to him, and began firing. King had on a short cloak, and in his breast-pocket a small pistol, which he did not use. One of Casey's shots struck him high up in the breast, from which he reeled, was caught by some passing friend, and carried into the express-office on the corner, where he was laid on the counter, and a surgeon sent for. Casey escaped up Washington Street, went to the City Hall, and delivered himself to the sheriff (Scannell), who conveyed him to jail and locked him in a cell. Meantime, the news spread like wildfire, and all the city was in commotion, for King was very popular. Nisbet, who boarded with us on Harrison Street, had been delayed at the bank later than usual, so that he happened to be near at the time, and, when he came out to dinner, he brought me the news of this affair, and said that there was every appearance of a riot down-town that night. This occurred toward the evening of May 14, 1856.

It so happened that, on the urgent solicitation of Van Winkle and of Governor Johnson, I had only a few days before agreed to accept the commission of major-general of the Second Division of Militia, embracing San Francisco. I had received the commission, but had not as yet formally accepted it, or even put myself in communication with the volunteer companies of the city. Of these, at that moment of time, there was a company of artillery with four guns, commanded by a

Captain Johns, formerly of the army, and two or three uniformed companies of infantry. After dinner I went downtown to see what was going on; found that King had been removed to a room in the Metropolitan Block; that his life was in great peril; that Casey was safe in jail, and the sheriff had called to his assistance a *posse* of the city police, some citizens, and one of the militia companies. The people were gathered in groups on the streets, and the words "Vigilance Committee" were freely spoken, but I saw no signs of immediate violence. The next morning, I again went to the jail, and found all things quiet, but the militia had withdrawn. I then went to the City Hall, saw the mayor, Van Ness, and some of the city officials, agreed to do what I could to maintain order with such militia as were on hand, and then formally accepted the commission, and took the "oath." In 1851 (when I was not in California) there had been a Vigilance Committee, and it was understood that its organization still existed. All the newspapers took ground in favor of the Vigilance Committee, except the *Herald* (John Nugent, editor), and nearly all the best people favored that means of redress. I could see they were organizing, hiring rendezvous, collecting arms, etc., without concealment. It was soon manifest that the companies of volunteers would go with the "committee," and that the public authorities could not rely on them for aid or defense. Still, there were a good many citizens who contended that, if the civil authorities were properly sustained by the people at large, they could and would execute the law. But the papers inflamed the public mind, and the controversy spread to the country. About the third day after the shooting of King, Governor Johnson telegraphed me that he would be down in the evening boat, and asked me to meet him on arrival for consultation. I got C. K. Garrison to go with me, and we met the Governor and his brother on the wharf, and walked up to the International Hotel on Jackson Street, above Montgomery. We discussed the state of affairs fully; and Johnson, on learning that his particular friend, William T. Coleman, was the president of the Vigilance Committee, proposed to go and see him. *En route* we stopped at King's room, ascertained that he was slowly sinking, and could not live long; and then near midnight we walked to the Turnverein Hall, where the committee was known to be sitting in consultation. This hall was on Bush Street, at about the intersection of Stockton. It was all lighted up within, but the door was locked.

The Governor knocked at the door, and on inquiry from inside—"Who's there?"—gave his name. After some delay we were admitted into a sort of vestibule, beyond which was a large hall, and we could hear the suppressed voices of a multitude. We were shown into a bar-room to the right, when the Governor asked to see Coleman. The man left us, went into the main hall, and soon returned with Coleman, who was pale and agitated. After shaking hands all round, the Governor said, "Coleman, what the devil is the matter here?" Coleman said, "Governor, it is time this shooting on our streets should stop." The Governor replied, "I agree with you perfectly, and have come down from Sacramento to assist." Coleman rejoined that "the people were tired of it, and had no faith in the officers of the law." A general conversation then followed, in which it was admitted that King would die, and that Casey *must* be executed; but the manner of execution was the thing to be settled, Coleman contending that the people would do it without trusting the courts or the sheriff. It so happened that at that time Judge Norton was on the bench of the court having jurisdiction, and he was universally recognized as an able and upright man, whom no one could or did mistrust; and it also happened that a grand-jury was then in session. Johnson argued that the time had passed in California for mobs and vigilance committees, and said if Coleman and associates would use their influence to support the law, he (the Governor) would undertake that, as soon as King died, the grand-jury should indict, that Judge Norton would try the murderer, and the whole proceeding should be as speedy as decency would allow. Then Coleman said "the people had no confidence in Scannell, the sheriff," who was, he said, in collusion with the rowdy element of San Francisco. Johnson then offered to be personally responsible that Casey should be safely guarded, and should be forthcoming for trial and execution at the proper time. I remember very well Johnson's assertion that he had no right to make these stipulations, and maybe no power to fulfill them; but he did it to save the city and state from the disgrace of a mob. Coleman disclaimed that the vigilance organization was a "mob," admitted that the proposition of the Governor was fair, and all he or any one should ask; and added, if we would wait awhile, he would submit it to the council, and bring back an answer.

We waited nearly an hour, and could hear the hum of voices in the hall, but no words, when Coleman came back, accompanied by a committee, of which I think the two brothers Arrington, Thomas Smiley the auctioneer, Seymour, Truett, and others, were members. The whole conversation was gone over again, and the Governor's proposition was positively agreed to, with this further condition, that the Vigilance Committee should send into the jail a small force of their own men, to make certain that Casey should not be carried off or allowed to escape.

The Governor, his brother William, Garrison, and I, then went up to the jail, where we found the sheriff and his *posse-comitatus* of police and citizens. These were styled the "Law-and-Order party," and some of them took offense that the Governor should have held communication with the "damned rebels," and several of them left the jail; but the sheriff seemed to agree with the Governor that what he had done was right and best; and, while we were there, some eight or ten armed men arrived from the Vigilance Committee, and were received by the sheriff (Scannell) as a part of his regular *posse*.

The Governor then, near daylight, went to his hotel, and I to my house for a short sleep. Next day I was at the bank, as usual, when about noon the Governor called, and asked me to walk with him down-street. He said he had just received a message from the Vigilance Committee to the effect that they were not bound by Coleman's promise not to do any thing till the regular trial by jury should be had, etc. He was with reason furious, and asked me to go with him to Truett's store, over which the Executive Committee was said to be in session. We were admitted to a front-room up-stairs, and heard voices in the back-room. The Governor inquired for Coleman, but he was not forthcoming. Another of the committee, Seymour, met us, denied *in toto* the promise of the night before, and the Governor openly accused him of treachery and falsehood.

The quarrel became public, and the newspapers took it up, both parties turning on the Governor; one, the Vigilantes, denying the promise made by Coleman, their president; and the other, the "Law-and-Order party," refusing any further assistance, because Johnson had stooped to make terms with rebels. At all events, he was powerless, and had to let matters drift to a conclusion.

King died about Friday, May 20th, and the funeral was appointed for the next Sunday. Early on that day the Governor sent for me at my house. I found him on the roof of the International, from which we looked down on the whole city, and more especially the face of Telegraph Hill, which was already covered with a crowd of people, while others were moving toward the jail on Broadway. Parties of armed men, in good order, were marching by platoons in the same direction, and formed in line along Broadway, facing the jail-door. Soon a small party was seen to advance to this door, and knock; a parley ensued, the doors were opened, and Casey was led out. In a few minutes another prisoner was brought out, who proved to be Cora, a man who had once been tried for killing Richardson, the United States Marshal, when the jury disagreed, and he was awaiting a new trial. These prisoners were placed in carriages, and escorted by the armed force down to the rooms of the Vigilance Committee, through the principal streets of the city. The day was exceedingly beautiful, and the whole proceeding was orderly in the extreme. I was under the impression that Casey and Cora were hanged that same Sunday, but was probably in error; but in a very few days they were hanged by the neck—dead—suspended from beams projecting from the windows of the committee's rooms, without other trial than could be given in secret, and by night.

We all thought the matter had ended there, and accordingly the Governor returned to Sacramento in disgust, and I went about my business. But it soon became manifest that the Vigilance Committee had no intention to surrender the power thus usurped. They took a building on Clay Street, near Front, fortified it, employed guards and armed sentinels, sat in midnight council, issued writs of arrest and banishment, and utterly ignored all authority but their own. A good many men were banished and forced to leave the country, but they were of that class we could well spare. Yankee Sullivan, a prisoner in their custody, committed suicide, and a feeling of general insecurity pervaded the city. Business was deranged; and the *Bulletin*, then under control of Tom King, a brother of James, poured out its abuse on some of our best men, as well as the worst. Governor Johnson, being again appealed to, concluded to go to work regularly, and telegraphed me about the 1st of June to meet him at General Wool's headquarters at Benicia that night. I went up, and we met at the hotel where General Wool was boarding. Johnson had with him his Secretary of State. We discussed the state of the country generally, and I had agreed that if Wool would give us arms and ammunition out of the United States Arsenal at Benicia, and if Commodore Farragut, of the navy, commanding the navy-yard on Mare Island, would give us a ship, I would call out volunteers, and, when a sufficient number had responded, I would have the arms come down from Benicia in the ship, arm my men, take possession of a thirty-two-pound-gun battery at the Marine Hospital on Rincon Point, thence command a dispersion of the unlawfully-armed force of the Vigilance Committee, and arrest some of the leaders.

We played cards that night, carrying on a conversation, in which Wool insisted on a proclamation commanding the Vigilance Committee to disperse, etc., and he told us how he had on some occasion, as far back as 1814, suppressed a mutiny on the Northern frontier. I did not understand him to make any distinct promise of assistance that night, but he invited us to accompany him on an inspection of the arsenal the next day, which we did. On handling some rifled muskets in the arsenal storehouse he asked me how they would answer our purpose. I said they were the very things, and that we did not want cartridge boxes or belts, but that I would have the cartridges carried in the breeches-pockets, and the caps in the vest-pockets. I knew that there were stored in that arsenal four thousand muskets, for I recognized the boxes which we had carried out in the Lexington around Cape Horn in 1846. Afterward we all met at the quarters of Captain D. R. Jones of the army, and I saw the Secretary of State, D. F. Douglass, Esq., walk out with General Wool in earnest conversation, and this Secretary of State afterward asserted that Wool there and then promised us the arms and ammunition, provided the Governor would make his proclamation for the committee to disperse, and that I should afterward call out the militia, etc. On the way back to the hotel at Benicia, General Wool, Captain Callendar of the arsenal, and I, were walking side by side, and I was telling him (General Wool) that I would also need some ammunition for the thirty-two-pound guns then in position at Rincon Point, when Wool turned to Callendar and inquired, "Did I not order those guns to be brought away?" Callendar said: "Yes, general. I made a requisition on the quartermaster for transportation, but his schooner has been so busy that the guns are still there." Then said Wool: "Let them remain; we may have use for them." I therefrom inferred, of course, that it was all agreed to so far as he was concerned.

Soon after we had reached the hotel, we ordered a buggy, and Governor Johnson and I drove to Vallejo, six miles, crossed over to Mare Island, and walked up to the commandant's house, where we found Commodore Farragut and his family. We stated our business fairly, but the commodore answered very frankly that he had no authority, without orders from his department, to take any part in civil broils; he doubted the wisdom of the attempt; said he had no ship available except the John Adams, Captain Boutwell, and that she needed repairs. But he assented at last to the proposition to let the sloop John Adams drop down abreast of the city after certain repairs, to lie off there for *moral effect*, which afterward actually occurred.

We then returned to Benicia, and Wool's first question was, "What luck?" We answered, "Not much," and explained what Commodore Farragut could and would do, and that, instead of having a naval vessel, we would seize and use one of the Pacific Mail Company's steamers, lying at their dock in Benicia, to carry down to San Francisco the arms and munitions when the time came.

As the time was then near at hand for the arrival of the evening boats, we all walked down to the wharf together, where I told Johnson that he could not be too careful; that I had not heard General Wool make a positive promise of assistance. Upon this, Johnson called General Wool to one side, and we three drew together. Johnson said: "General Wool, General Sherman is very particular, and wants to know exactly what you propose to do." Wool answered: "I understand, Governor, that in the first place a writ of *habeas corpus* will be issued commanding the jailers of the Vigilance Committee to produce the body of some one of the prisoners held by them (which, of course, will be refused); that you then issue your proclamation commanding them to disperse, and, failing this, you will call out the militia, and command General Sherman with it to suppress the Vigilance Committee as an unlawful body;" to which the Governor responded, "Yes." "Then," said Wool, "on General Sherman's making his requisition, approved by you, I will order the issue of the necessary arms and ammunition." I remember well that I said, emphatically: "That is all I want.—Now, Governor, you may go ahead." We soon parted; Johnson and Douglas taking the boat to Sacramento, and I to San Francisco.

The Chief-Justice, Terry, came to San Francisco the next day, issued a writ of *habeas corpus* for the body of one Maloney, which writ was resisted, as we expected. The Governor then issued his proclamation, and I published my orders, dated June 4, 1855. The Quartermaster-General of the State, General Kibbe, also came to San Francisco, took an office in the City Hall, engaged several rooms for armories, and soon the men began to enroll into companies. In my general orders calling out the militia, I used the expression, "When a sufficient number of men are enrolled, arms and ammunition will be supplied." Some of the best men of the "Vigilantes" came to me and remonstrated, saying that collision would surely result; that it would be terrible, etc. All I could say in reply was, that it was for them to get out of the way. "Remove your fort; cease your midnight councils; and prevent your armed bodies from patrolling the streets." They inquired where I was to get arms, and I answered that I had them *certain*. But personally I went right along with my business at the bank, conscious that at any moment we might have trouble. Another committee of citizens, a conciliatory body, was formed to prevent collision if possible, and the newspapers boiled over with vehement vituperation. This second committee was composed of such men as Crockett, Ritchie, Thornton, Bailey Peyton, Foote, Donohue, Kelly, and others, a class of the most intelligent and wealthy men of the city, who earnestly and honestly desired to prevent bloodshed. They also came to me, and I told them that our men were enrolling very fast, and that, when I deemed the right moment had come, the Vigilance Committee must disperse, else bloodshed and destruction of property would inevitably follow. They also had discovered that the better men of the Vigilance Committee itself were getting tired of the business, and thought that in the execution of Casey and Cora, and the banishment of a dozen or more rowdies, they had done enough, and were then willing to stop. It was suggested that, if our Law-and-Order party would not arm, by a certain day near at hand the committee would disperse, and some of their leaders would submit to an indictment and trial by a jury of citizens, which they knew would acquit them of crime. One day in the bank a man called me to the counter and said, "If you expect to get arms of General Wool, you will be mistaken, for I was at Benicia yesterday, and heard him say he would not give them." This person was known to me to be a man of truth, and I immediately wrote to General Wool a letter telling him what I had heard, and how any hesitation on his part would compromise me as a man of truth and honor; adding that I did not believe we should ever need the arms, but only the *promise* of them, for "the committee was letting down, and would soon disperse and submit to the law," etc. I further asked him to answer me categorically that very night, by the Stockton boat, which would pass Benicia on its way down about midnight, and I would sit up and wait for his answer. I did wait for his letter, but it did not come, and the next day I got a telegraphic dispatch from Governor Johnson, who, at Sacramento, had also heard of General Wool's "back-down," asking me to meet him again at Benicia that night.

I went up in the evening boat, and found General Wool's aide-de-camp, Captain Arnold, of the army, on the wharf, with a letter in his hand, which he said was for me. I asked for it, but he said he knew its importance, and preferred we should go to General Wool's room together, and the general could hand it to me in person. We did go right up to General

Wool's, who took the sealed parcel and laid it aside, saying that it was literally a copy of one he had sent to Governor Johnson, who would doubtless give me a copy; but I insisted that I had made a written communication, and was entitled to a written answer.

At that moment several gentlemen of the "Conciliation party," who had come up in the same steamer with me, asked for admission and came in. I recall the names of Crockett, Foote, Bailey Peyton, Judge Thornton, Donohue, etc., and the conversation became general, Wool trying to explain away the effect of our misunderstanding, taking good pains not to deny his promise made to me personally *on the wharf.* I renewed my application for the letter addressed to me, then lying on his table. On my statement of the case, Bailey Peyton said, "General Wool, I think General Sherman has a right to a written answer from you, for he is surely compromised." Upon this Wool handed me the letter. I opened and read it, and it denied any promise of arms, but otherwise was extremely evasive and non-committal. I had heard of the arrival at the wharf of the Governor and party, and was expecting them at Wool's room, but, instead of stopping at the hotel where we were, they passed to another hotel on the block above. I went up and found there, in a room on the second floor over the bar-room, Governor Johnson, Chief-Justice Terry, Jones, of Palmer, Cooke & Co., E. D. Baker, Volney E. Howard, and one or two others. All were talking furiously against Wool, denouncing him as a d——d liar, and not sparing the severest terms. I showed the Governor General Wool's letter to me, which he said was in effect the same as the one addressed to and received by him at Sacramento. He was so offended that he would not even call on General Wool, and said he would never again recognize him as an officer or gentleman. We discussed matters generally, and Judge Terry said that the Vigilance Committee were a set of d——d pork-merchants; that they were getting scared, and that General Wool was in collusion with them to bring the State into contempt, etc. I explained that there were no arms in the State except what General Wool had, or what were in the hands of the Vigilance Committee of San Francisco, and that the part of wisdom for us was to be patient and cautious. About that time Crockett and his associates sent up their cards, but Terry and the more violent of the Governor's followers denounced them as no better than "Vigilantes," and wanted the Governor to refuse even to receive them. I explained that they were not "Vigilantes," that Judge Thornton was a "Law-and-Order" man, was one of the first to respond to the call of the sheriff, and that he went actually to the jail with his one arm the night we expected the first attempt at rescue, etc. Johnson then sent word for them to reduce their business to *writing*. They simply sent in a written request for an audience, and they were then promptly admitted. After some general conversation, the Governor said he was prepared to hear them, when Mr. Crockett rose and made a prepared speech embracing a clear and fair statement of the condition of things in San Francisco, concluding with the assertion of the willingness of the committee to disband and submit to trial after a certain date not very remote. All the time Crockett was speaking, Terry sat with his hat on, drawn over his eyes, and with his feet on a table. As soon as Crockett was through, they were dismissed, and Johnson began to prepare a written answer. This was scratched, altered, and amended, to suit the notions of his counselors, and at last was copied and sent. This answer amounted to little or nothing. Seeing that we were powerless for good, and that violent counsels would prevail under the influence of Terry and others, I sat down at the table, and wrote my resignation, which Johnson accepted in a complimentary note on the spot, and at the same time he appointed to my place General Volney E. Howard, then present, a lawyer who had once been a member of Congress from Texas, and who was expected to drive the d——d pork-merchants into the bay at short notice.

I went soon after to General Wool's room, where I found Crockett and the rest of his party; told them that I was out of the fight, having resigned my commission; that I had neglected business that had been intrusted to me by my St. Louis partners; and that I would thenceforward mind my own business, and leave public affairs severely alone. We all returned to San Francisco that night by the Stockton boat, and I never afterward had any thing to do with politics in California, perfectly satisfied with that short experience.

Johnson and Wool fought out their quarrel of veracity in the newspapers and on paper. But, in my opinion, there is not a shadow of doubt that General Wool did deliberately deceive us; that he had authority to issue arms, and that, had he adhered to his promise, we could have checked the committee before it became a fixed institution, and a part of the common law of California. Major-General Volney E. Howard came to San Francisco soon after; continued the organization of militia which I had begun; succeeded in getting a few arms from the country; but one day the Vigilance Committee sallied from their armories, captured the arms of the "Law-and-Order party," put some of their men into prison, while General Howard, with others, escaped to the country; after which the Vigilance Committee had it all their own way. Subsequently, in July, 1856, they arrested Chief-Justice Terry, and tried him for stabbing one of their constables, but he managed to escape at night, and took refuge on the John Adams. In August, they hanged Hetherington and Brace in broad daylight, without any jury-trial; and, soon after, they quietly disbanded. As they controlled the press, they wrote their own history, and the world generally gives them the credit of having purged San Francisco of rowdies and roughs; but their success has given great stimulus to a dangerous principle, that would at any time justify the mob in seizing all the power of government; and who is to say that the Vigilance Committee may not be composed of the worst, instead of the best, elements of a community? Indeed, in San Francisco, as soon as it was demonstrated that the real power had passed from the City Hall to the committee-room, the same set of bailiffs, constables, and rowdies that had infested the City Hall were found in the employment of the "Vigilantes;" and, after three months' experience, the better class of people became tired of the midnight sessions and left the business and power of the committee in the hands of a court, of which a Sydney man was reported to be the head or chief-justice.

During the winter of 1855–'56, and indeed throughout the year 1856, all kinds of business became unsettled in California. The mines continued to yield about fifty millions of gold a year; but little attention was paid to agriculture or to any business other than that of "mining," and, as the placer-gold

was becoming worked out, the miners were restless and uneasy, and were shifting about from place to place, impelled by
rumors put afloat for speculative purposes. A great many extensive enterprises by joint-stock companies had been begun,
in the way of water-ditches, to bring water from the head of
the mountain-streams down to the richer alluvial deposits,
and nearly all of these companies became embarrassed or
bankrupt. Foreign capital, also, which had been attracted to
California by reason of the high rates of interest, was being
withdrawn, or was tied up in property which could not be
sold; and, although our bank's having withstood the panic
gave us great credit, still the community itself was shaken, and
loans of money were risky in the extreme. A great many merchants, of the highest name, availed themselves of the extremely liberal bankrupt law to get discharged of their old
debts, without sacrificing much, if any, of their stocks of
goods on hand, except a lawyer's fee; thus realizing Martin
Burke's saying that "many a clever fellow had been ruined by
paying his debts." The merchants and business-men of San
Francisco did not intend to be ruined by such a course. I
raised the rate of exchange from three to three and a half,
while others kept on at the old rate; and I labored hard to
collect old debts, and strove, in making new loans, to be on
the safe side. The State and city both denied much of their
public debt; in fact, repudiated it; and real estate, which the
year before had been first-class security, became utterly unsalable.

The office labor and confinement, and the anxiety attending
the business, aggravated my asthma to such an extent that at
times it deprived me of sleep, and threatened to become
chronic and serious; and I was also conscious that the first
and original cause which had induced Mr. Lucas to establish
the bank in California had ceased. I so reported to him, and
that I really believed that he could use his money more safely
and to better advantage in St. Louis. This met his prompt
approval, and he instructed me gradually to draw out, preparatory to a removal to New York City. Accordingly, early in
April, 1857, I published an advertisement in the San Francisco
papers, notifying our customers that, on the 1st day of May,
we would discontinue business and remove East, requiring all

to withdraw their accounts, and declaring that, if any remained on the 1st day of May, their balances would be transferred to the banking-house of Parrott & Co. Punctually to the day, this was done, and the business of Lucas, Turner & Co., of San Francisco, was discontinued, except the more difficult and disagreeable part of collecting their own moneys and selling the real estate, to which the firm had succeeded by purchase or foreclosure. One of the partners, B. R. Nisbet, assisted by our attorney, S. M. Bowman, Esq., remained behind to close up the business of the bank.

Chapter VI.

CALIFORNIA, NEW YORK, AND KANSAS.

1857–1859.

HAVING CLOSED the bank at San Francisco on the 1st day of May, 1857, accompanied by my family I embarked in the steamer Sonora for Panama, crossed the isthmus, and sailed to New York, whence we proceeded to Lancaster, Ohio, where Mrs. Sherman and the family stopped, and I went on to St. Louis. I found there that some changes had been made in the parent-house, that Mr. Lucas had bought out his partner, Captain Symonds, and that the firm's name had been changed to that of James H. Lucas & Co.

It had also been arranged that an office or branch was to be established in New York City, of which I was to have charge, on pretty much the same terms and conditions as in the previous San Francisco firm.

Mr. Lucas, Major Turner, and I, agreed to meet in New York, soon after the 4th of July. We met accordingly at the Metropolitan Hotel, selected an office, No. 12 Wall Street, purchased the necessary furniture, and engaged a teller, bookkeeper, and porter. The new firm was to bear the same title of Lucas, Turner & Co., with about the same partners in interest, but the nature of the business was totally different. We opened our office on the 21st of July, 1857, and at once began to receive accounts from the West and from California, but our chief business was as the resident agents of the St. Louis firm of James H. Lucas & Co. Personally I took rooms at No. 100 Prince Street, in which house were also quartered Major J. G. Barnard, and Lieutenant J. B. McPherson, United States Engineers, both of whom afterward attained great fame in the civil war.

My business relations in New York were with the Metropolitan Bank and Bank of America; and with the very wealthy and most respectable firm of Schuchhardt & Gebhard, of Nassau Street. Every thing went along swimmingly till the 21st of August, when all Wall Street was thrown into a spasm by the failure of the Ohio Life and Trust Company, and the panic so resembled that in San Francisco, that, having nothing seemingly at stake, I felt amused. But it soon became a serious matter even to me. Western stocks and securities tumbled to such a figure, that all Western banks that held such securities, and had procured advances thereon, were compelled to pay up or substitute increased collaterals. Our own house was not a borrower in New York at all, but many of our Western correspondents were, and it taxed my time to watch their interests. In September, the panic extended so as to threaten the safety of even some of the New York banks not connected with the West; and the alarm became general, and at last universal.

In the very midst of this panic came the news that the steamer Central America, formerly the George Law, with six hundred passengers and about sixteen hundred thousand dollars of treasure, coming from Aspinwall, had foundered at sea, off the coast of Georgia, and that about sixty of the passengers had been providentially picked up by a Swedish bark, and brought into Savannah. The absolute loss of this treasure went to swell the confusion and panic of the day.

A few days after, I was standing in the vestibule of the Metropolitan Hotel, and heard the captain of the Swedish bark tell his singular story of the rescue of these passengers. He was a short, sailor-like-looking man, with a strong German or Swedish accent. He said that he was sailing from some port in Honduras for Sweden, running down the Gulf Stream off Savannah. The weather had been heavy for some days, and, about nightfall, as he paced his deck, he observed a man-of-war hawk circle about his vessel, gradually lowering, until the bird was as it were aiming at him. He jerked out a belaying-pin, struck at the bird, missed it, when the hawk again rose high in the air, and a second time began to descend, contract his circle, and make at him again. The second time he hit the bird, and struck it to the deck. This strange fact made him uneasy, and he thought it betokened danger; he went to the binnacle, saw the course he was steering, and without any particular reason he ordered the steersman to alter the course one point to the east.

After this it became quite dark, and he continued to promenade the deck, and had settled into a drowsy state, when as in a dream he thought he heard voices all round his ship. Waking up, he ran to the side of the ship, saw something struggling in the water, and heard clearly cries for help. Instantly heaving his ship to, and lowering all his boats, he managed to pick up sixty or more persons who were floating about on skylights, doors, spars, and whatever fragments remained of the Central America. Had he not changed the course of his vessel by reason of the mysterious conduct of that man-of-war hawk, not a soul would probably have survived the night. It was stated by the rescued passengers, among whom was Billy Birch, that the Central America had sailed from Aspinwall with the passengers and freight which left San Francisco on the 1st of September, and encountered the gale in the Gulf Stream somewhere off Savannah, in which she sprung a leak, filled rapidly, and went down. The passengers who were saved had clung to doors, skylights, and such floating objects as they could reach, and were thus rescued; all the rest, some five hundred in number, had gone down with the ship.

The panic grew worse and worse, and about the end of September there was a general suspension of the banks of New York, and a money crisis extended all over the country. In New York, Lucas, Turner & Co. had nothing at risk. We had large cash balances in the Metropolitan Bank and in the Bank of America, all safe, and we held, for the account of the St. Louis house, at least two hundred thousand dollars, of St. Louis city and county bonds, and of acceptances falling due right along, none extending beyond ninety days. I was advised from St. Louis that money matters were extremely tight; but I did not dream of any danger in that quarter. I knew well that Mr. Lucas was worth two or three million dollars in the best real estate, and inferred from the large balances to their credit with me that no mere panic could shake his credit; but, early on the morning of October 7th, my cousin, James M. Hoyt, came to me in bed, and read me a paragraph in the morning paper, to the effect that James H. Lucas & Co., of St. Louis, had suspended. I was, of course, surprised, but not sorry; for I had always contended that a man of so much visible wealth as Mr. Lucas should not be engaged in a business subject to such vicissitudes. I hurried down to the office, where I received the same information officially, by telegraph, with instructions to make proper disposition of the affairs of the bank, and to come out to St. Louis, with such assets as would be available there. I transferred the funds belonging to all our correspondents, with lists of outstanding checks, to one or other of our bankers, and with the cash balance of the St. Louis house and their available assets started for St. Louis. I may say with confidence that no man lost a cent by either of the banking-firms of Lucas, Turner & Co., of San Francisco or New York; but, as usual, those who owed us were not always as just.

I reached St. Louis October 17th, and found the partners engaged in liquidating the balances due depositors as fast as collections could be forced; and, as the panic began to subside, this process became quite rapid, and Mr. Lucas, by making a loan in Philadelphia, was enabled to close out all accounts without having made any serious sacrifices. Of course, no person ever lost a cent by him: he has recently died, leaving an estate of eight million dollars. During his lifetime, I had opportunities to know him well, and take much pleasure in bearing testimony to his great worth and personal kindness. On the failure of his bank, he assumed personally all the liabilities, released his partners of all responsibility, and offered to assist me to engage in business, which he supposed was due to me because I had resigned my army commission.

I remained in St. Louis till the 7th of December, 1857, assisting in collecting for the bank, and in controlling all matters which came from the New York and San Francisco branches. B. R. Nisbet was still in San Francisco, but had married a Miss Thornton, and was coming home. There still remained in California a good deal of real estate, and notes, valued at about two hundred thousand dollars in the aggregate; so that, at Mr. Lucas's request, I agreed to go out again, to bring matters, if possible, nearer a final settlement. I accordingly left St. Louis, reached Lancaster, where my family was, on the 10th, staid there till after Christmas, and then went to New York, where I remained till January 5th, when I embarked on the steamer Moses Taylor (Captain McGowan) for Aspinwall; caught the Golden Gate (Captain Whiting) at

Panama, January 15, 1858; and reached San Francisco on the 28th of January. I found that Nisbet and wife had gone to St. Louis, and that we had passed each other at sea. He had carried the ledger and books to St. Louis, but left a schedule, notes, etc., in the hands of S. M. Bowman, Esq., who passed them over to me.

On the 30th of January I published a notice of the dissolution of the partnership, and called on all who were still indebted to the firm of Lucas, Turner & Co. to pay up, or the notes would be sold at auction. I also advertised that all the real property was for sale.

Business had somewhat changed since 1857. Parrott & Co.; Garrison, Fritz & Ralston; Wells, Fargo & Co.; Drexel, Sather & Church, and Tallant & Wilde, were the principal bankers. Property continued almost unsalable, and prices were less than a half of what they had been in 1853–'54. William Blanding, Esq., had rented my house on Harrison Street; so I occupied a room in the bank, No. 11, and boarded at the Meiggs House, corner of Broadway and Montgomery, which we owned. Having reduced expenses to a minimum, I proceeded, with all possible dispatch, to collect outstanding debts, in some instances making sacrifices and compromises. I made some few sales, and generally aimed to put matters in such a shape that time would bring the best result. Some of our heaviest creditors were John M. Rhodes & Co., of Sacramento and Shasta; Langton & Co., of Downieville; and E. M. Strange, of Murphy's. In trying to put these debts in course of settlement, I made some arrangement in Downieville with the law-firm of Spears & Thornton, to collect, by suit, a certain note of Green & Purdy for twelve thousand dollars. Early in April, I learned that Spears had collected three thousand seven hundred dollars in money, had appropriated it to his own use, and had pledged another good note taken in part payment of three thousand and fifty-three dollars. He pretended to be insane. I had to make two visits to Downieville on this business, and there made the acquaintance of Mr. Stewart, now a Senator from Nevada. He was married to a daughter of Governor Foote; was living in a small frame-house on the bar just below the town; and his little daughter was playing about the door in the sand.

Stewart was then a lawyer in Downieville, in good practice; afterward, by some lucky stroke, became part owner of a valuable silver-mine in Nevada, and is now accounted a millionaire. I managed to save something out of Spears, and more out of his partner Thornton. This affair of Spears ruined him, because his insanity was manifestly feigned.

I remained in San Francisco till July 3d, when, having collected and remitted every cent that I could raise, and got all the property in the best shape possible, hearing from St. Louis that business had revived, and that there was no need of further sacrifice, I put all the papers, with a full letter of instructions, and power of attorney, in the hands of William Blanding, Esq., and took passage on the good steamer Golden Gate, Captain Whiting, for Panama and home. I reached Lancaster on July 28, 1858, and found all the family well. I was then perfectly unhampered, but the serious and greater question remained, what was I to do to support my family, consisting of a wife and four children, all accustomed to more than the average comforts of life?

I remained at Lancaster all of August, 1858, during which time I was discussing with Mr. Ewing and others what to do next. Major Turner and Mr. Lucas, in St. Louis, were willing to do any thing to aid me, but I thought best to keep independent. Mr. Ewing had property at Chauncey, consisting of salt-wells and coal-mines, but for that part of Ohio I had no fancy. Two of his sons, Hugh and T. E., Jr., had established themselves at Leavenworth, Kansas, where they and their father had bought a good deal of land, some near the town, and some back in the country. Mr. Ewing offered to confide to me the general management of his share of interest, and Hugh and T. E., Jr., offered me an equal copartnership in their law-firm. Accordingly, about the 1st of September, I started for Kansas, stopping a couple of weeks in St. Louis, and reached Leavenworth. I found about two miles below the fort, on the river-bank, where in 1851 was a tangled thicket, quite a handsome and thriving city, growing rapidly in rivalry with Kansas City, and St. Joseph, Missouri. After looking about and consulting with friends, among them my classmate Major Stewart Van Vliet, quartermaster at the fort, I concluded to accept the proposition of Mr. Ewing, and accordingly the firm of Sherman & Ewing was duly announced, and our services to the public offered as attorneys-at-law.

We had an office on Main Street, between Shawnee and Delaware, on the second floor, over the office of Hampton Denman, Esq., mayor of the city. This building was a mere shell, and our office was reached by a stairway on the outside. Although in the course of my military reading I had studied a few of the ordinary law-books, such as Blackstone, Kent, Starkie, etc., I did not presume to be a lawyer; but our agreement was that Thomas Ewing, Jr., a good and thorough lawyer, should manage all business in the courts, while I gave attention to collections, agencies for houses and lands, and such business as my experience in banking had qualified me for. Yet, as my name was embraced in a law-firm, it seemed to me proper to take out a license. Accordingly, one day when United States Judge Lecompte was in our office, I mentioned the matter to him; he told me to go down to the clerk of his court, and he would give me the license. I inquired what examination I would have to submit to, and he replied, "None at all;" he would admit me on the ground of general intelligence.

During that summer we got our share of the business of the profession, then represented by several eminent law-firms, embracing names that have since flourished in the Senate, and in the higher courts of the country. But the most lucrative single case was given me by my friend Major Van Vliet, who employed me to go to Fort Riley, one hundred and thirty-six miles west of Fort Leavenworth, to superintend the repairs to the military road. For this purpose he supplied me with a four-mule ambulance and driver. The country was then sparsely settled, and quite as many Indians were along the road as white people; still there were embryo towns all along the route, and a few farms sprinkled over the beautiful prairies. On reaching Indianola, near Topeka, I found everybody down with the chills and fever. My own driver became so shaky that I had to act as driver and cook. But in due season I reconnoitred the road, and made contracts for repairing some bridges, and for cutting such parts of the road as needed it. I then returned to Fort Leavenworth, and reported, receiving a fair compensation. On my way up I met Colonel Sumner's column, returning from their summer scout on the plains, and spent the night with the officers, among whom were Captains Sackett, Sturgis, etc. Also at Fort Riley I was cordially received and entertained by some old army-friends, among them Major Sedgwick, Captains Totten, Eli Long, etc.

Mrs. Sherman and children arrived out in November, and we spent the winter very comfortably in the house of Thomas Ewing, Jr., on the corner of Third and Pottawottamie Streets. On the 1st of January, 1859, Daniel McCook, Esq., was admitted to membership in our firm, which became Sherman, Ewing & McCook. Our business continued to grow, but, as the income hardly sufficed for three such expensive personages, I continued to look about for something more certain and profitable, and during that spring undertook for the Hon. Thomas Ewing, of Ohio, to open a farm on a large tract of land he owned on Indian Creek, forty miles west of Leavenworth, for the benefit of his grand-nephew, Henry Clark, and his grand-niece, Mrs. Walker. These arrived out in the spring, by which time I had caused to be erected a small frame dwelling-house, a barn, and fencing for a hundred acres. This helped to pass away time, but afforded little profit; and on the 11th of June, 1859, I wrote to Major D. C. Buell, assistant adjutant-general, on duty in the War Department with Secretary of War Floyd, inquiring if there was a vacancy among the army paymasters, or any thing in his line that I could obtain. He replied promptly, and sent me the printed programme for a military college about to be organized in Louisiana, and advised me to apply for the superintendent's place, saying that General G. Mason Graham, the half-brother of my old commanding general, R. B. Mason, was very influential in this matter, and would doubtless befriend me on account of the relations that had existed between General Mason and myself in California. Accordingly, I addressed a letter of application to the Hon. R. C. Wickliffe, Baton Rouge, Louisiana, asking the answer to be sent to me at Lancaster, Ohio, where I proposed to leave my family. But, before leaving this branch of the subject, I must explain a little matter of which I have seen an account in print, complimentary or otherwise of the firm of Sherman, Ewing & McCook, more especially of the senior partner.

One day, as I sat in our office, an Irishman came in and said he had a case and wanted a lawyer. I asked him to sit down and give me the points of his case, all the other members of the firm being out. Our client stated that he had rented a lot of an Irish landlord for five dollars a month; that he had erected thereon a small frame shanty, which was occupied by his family; that he had paid his rent regularly up to a recent period, but to his house he had appended a shed which extended over a part of an adjoining vacant lot belonging to the same landlord, for which he was charged two and a half dollars a month, which he refused to pay. The consequence was, that his landlord had for a few months declined even his five dollars monthly rent until the arrears amounted to about seventeen dollars, for which he was sued. I told him we would undertake his case, of which I took notes, and a fee of five dollars in advance, and in due order I placed the notes in the hands of McCook, and thought no more of it.

A month or so after, our client rushed into the office and said his case had been called at Judge Gardner's (I think), and he wanted his lawyer right away. I sent him up to the Circuit Court, Judge Pettit's, for McCook, but he soon returned, saying he could not find McCook, and accordingly I hurried with him up to Judge Gardner's office, intending to ask a continuance, but I found our antagonist there, with his lawyer and witnesses, and Judge Gardner would not grant a continuance, so of necessity I had to act, hoping that at every minute McCook would come. But the trial proceeded regularly to its end; we were beaten, and judgment was entered against our client for the amount claimed, and costs. As soon as the matter was explained to McCook, he said "execution" could not be taken for ten days, and, as our client was poor, and had nothing on which the landlord could levy but his house, McCook advised him to get his neighbors together, to pick up the house, and carry it on to another vacant lot, belonging to a non-resident, so that even the house could not be taken in execution. Thus the grasping landlord, though successful in his judgment, failed in the execution, and our client was abundantly satisfied.

In due time I closed up my business at Leavenworth, and went to Lancaster, Ohio, where, in July, 1859, I received notice from Governor Wickliffe that I had been elected super-intendent of the proposed college, and inviting me to come down to Louisiana as early as possible, because they were anx-ious to put the college into operation by the 1st of January following. For this honorable position I was indebted to Ma-jor D. C. Buell and General G. Mason Graham, to whom I have made full and due acknowledgment. During the civil war, it was reported and charged that I owed my position to the personal friendship of Generals Bragg and Beauregard, and that, in taking up arms against the South, I had been guilty of a breach of hospitality and friendship. I was not in-debted to General Bragg, because he himself told me that he was not even aware that I was an applicant, and had favored the selection of Major Jenkins, another West Point graduate. General Beauregard had nothing whatever to do with the matter.

Chapter VII.

Louisiana.

1859–1861.

IN THE AUTUMN of 1859, having made arrangements for my family to remain in Lancaster, I proceeded, *via* Columbus, Cincinnati, and Louisville, to Baton Rouge, Louisiana, where I reported for duty to Governor Wickliffe, who, by virtue of his office, was the president of the Board of Supervisors of the new institution over which I was called to preside. He explained to me the act of the Legislature under which the institution was founded; told me that the building was situated near Alexandria, in the parish of Rapides, and was substantially finished; that the future management would rest with a Board of Supervisors, mostly citizens of Rapides Parish, where also resided the Governor-elect, T. O. Moore, who would soon succeed him in his office as Governor and president *ex officio*; and advised me to go at once to Alexandria, and put myself in communication with Moore and the supervisors. Accordingly I took a boat at Baton Rouge, for the mouth of Red River. The river being low, and its navigation precarious, I there took the regular mail-coach, as the more certain conveyance, and continued on toward Alexandria. I found, as a fellow-passenger in the coach, Judge Henry Boyce, of the United States District Court, with whom I had made acquaintance years before, at St. Louis, and, as we neared Alexandria, he proposed that we should stop at Governor Moore's and spend the night. Moore's house and plantation were on Bayou Robert, about eight miles from Alexandria. We found him at home, with his wife and a married daughter, and spent the night there. He sent us forward to Alexandria the next morning, in his own carriage. On arriving at Alexandria, I put up at an inn, or boarding-house, and almost immediately thereafter went about ten miles farther up Bayou Rapides, to the plantation and house of General G. Mason Graham, to whom I looked as the principal man with whom I had to deal. He was a high-toned gentleman, and his whole heart was in the enterprise. He at once put me at ease. We acted together most cordially from that time forth, and it was at his house that all the details of the seminary were arranged. We first visited the college-building together. It was located on an old country place of four hundred acres of pineland, with numerous springs, and the building was very large and handsome. A carpenter, named James, resided there, and had the general charge of the property; but, as there was not a table, chair, black-board, or any thing on hand, necessary for a beginning, I concluded to quarter myself in one of the rooms of the seminary, and board with an old black woman who cooked for James, so that I might personally push forward the necessary preparations. There was an old rail-fence about the place, and a large pile of boards in front. I immediately engaged four carpenters, and set them at work to make out of these boards mess-tables, benches, black-boards, etc. I also opened a correspondence with the professors-elect, and with all parties of influence in the State, who were interested in our work. At the meeting of the Board of Supervisors, held at Alexandria, August 2, 1859, five professors had been elected: 1. W. T. Sherman, Superintendent, and Professor of Engineering, etc.; 2. Anthony Vallas, Professor of Mathematics, Philosophy, etc.; 3. Francis W. Smith, Professor of Chemistry, etc.; 4. David F. Boyd, Professor of Languages, English and Ancient; 5. E. Berti St. Ange, Professor of French and Modern Languages.

These constituted the Academic Board, while the general supervision remained in the Board of Supervisors, composed of the Governor of the State, the Superintendent of Public Education, and twelve members, nominated by the Governor, and confirmed by the Senate. The institution was bound to educate sixteen beneficiary students, free of any charge for tuition. These had only to pay for their clothing and books, while all others had to pay their entire expenses, including tuition.

Early in November, Profs. Smith, Vallas, St. Ange, and I, met a committee of the Board of Supervisors, composed of T. C. Manning, G. Mason Graham, and W. W. Whittington, at General Graham's house, and resolved to open the institution to pupils on the 1st day of January, 1860. We adopted a series of by-laws for the government of the institution, which was styled the "Louisiana Seminary of Learning and Military Academy." This title grew out of the original grant, by the Congress of the United States, of a certain township of public land, to be sold by the State, and dedicated to the use of a "seminary of learning." I do not suppose that Congress designed thereby to fix the name or title; but the subject had so long been debated in Louisiana that the name, though awkward, had become familiar. We appended to it "Military Academy," as explanatory of its general design.

On the 17th of November, 1859, the Governor of the State, Wickliffe, issued officially a general circular, prepared by us, giving public notice that the "Seminary of Learning" would open on the 1st day of January, 1860; containing a description of the locality, and the general regulations for the proposed institution; and authorizing parties to apply for further information to the "Superintendent," at Alexandria, Louisiana.

The Legislature had appropriated for the sixteen beneficiaries at the rate of two hundred and eighty-three dollars per annum, to which we added sixty dollars as tuition for pay cadets; and, though the price was low, we undertook to manage for the first year on that basis.

Promptly to the day, we opened, with about sixty cadets present. Major Smith was the commandant of cadets, and I the superintendent. I had been to New Orleans, where I had bought a supply of mattresses, books, and every thing requisite, and we started very much on the basis of West Point and of the Virginia Military Institute, but without uniforms or muskets; yet with roll-calls, sections, and recitations, we kept as near the standard of West Point as possible. I kept all the money accounts, and gave general directions to the steward, professors, and cadets. The other professors had their regular classes and recitations. We all lived in rooms in the college-building, except Vallas, who had a family, and rented a house near by. A creole gentleman, B. Jarreau, Esq., had been elected steward, and he also had his family in a house not far off. The other professors had a mess in a room adjoining the mess-hall. A few more cadets joined in the course of the winter, so that we had in all, during the first term, seventy-three cadets, of whom fifty-nine passed the examination on the 30th

of July, 1860. During our first term many defects in the original act of the Legislature were demonstrated, and, by the advice of the Board of Supervisors, I went down to Baton
Rouge during the session of the Legislature, to advocate and
urge the passage of a new bill, putting the institution on a
better footing. Thomas O. Moore was then Governor, Bragg
was a member of the Board of Public Works, and Richard
Taylor was a Senator. I got well acquainted with all of these,
and with some of the leading men of the State, and was always treated with the greatest courtesy and kindness. In conjunction with the proper committee of the Legislature, we
prepared a new bill, which was passed and approved on the
7th of March, 1860, by which we were to have a beneficiary
cadet for each parish, in all fifty-six, and fifteen thousand dollars annually for their maintenance; also twenty thousand dollars for the general use of the college. During that session we
got an appropriation of fifteen thousand dollars for building
two professors' houses, for the purchase of philosophical and
chemical apparatus, and for the beginning of a college library.
The seminary was made a State Arsenal, under the title of
State Central Arsenal, and I was allowed five hundred dollars
a year as its superintendent. These matters took me several
times to Baton Rouge that winter, and I recall an event of
some interest, which must have happened in February. At
that time my brother, John Sherman, was a candidate, in the
national House of Representatives, for Speaker, against Bo-
cock, of Virginia. In the South he was regarded as an "abolitionist," the most horrible of all monsters; and many people
of Louisiana looked at me with suspicion, as the brother of
the abolitionist, John Sherman, and doubted the propriety of
having me at the head of an important State institution. By
this time I was pretty well acquainted with many of their
prominent men, was generally esteemed by all in authority,
and by the people of Rapides Parish especially, who saw that I
was devoted to my particular business, and that I gave no
heed to the political excitement of the day. But the members
of the State Senate and House did not know me so well, and
it was natural that they should be suspicious of a Northern
man, and the brother of him who was the "abolition" candidate for Speaker of the House.

One evening, at a large dinner-party at Governor Moore's, at which were present several members of the Louisiana Legislature, Taylor, Bragg, and the Attorney-General Hyams, after the ladies had left the table, I noticed at Governor Moore's end quite a lively discussion going on, in which my name was frequently used; at length the Governor called to me, saying: "Colonel Sherman, you can readily understand that, with your brother the abolitionist candidate for Speaker, some of our people wonder that you should be here at the head of an important State institution. Now, you are at my table, and I assure you of my confidence. Won't you speak your mind freely on this question of slavery, that so agitates the land? You are under my roof, and, whatever you say, you have my protection."

I answered: "Governor Moore, you mistake in calling my brother, John Sherman, an abolitionist. We have been separated since childhood—I in the army, and he pursuing his profession of law in Northern Ohio; and it is possible we may differ in general sentiment, but I deny that he is considered at home an abolitionist; and, although he prefers the free institutions under which he lives to those of slavery which prevail here, he would not of himself take from you by law or force any property whatever, even slaves."

Then said Moore: "Give us your own views of slavery as you see it here and throughout the South."

I answered in effect that "the people of Louisiana were hardly responsible for slavery, as they had inherited it; that I found two distinct conditions of slavery, domestic and field hands. The domestic slaves, employed by the families, were probably better treated than any slaves on earth; but the condition of the field-hands was different, depending more on the temper and disposition of their masters and overseers than were those employed about the house;" and I went on to say that, "were I a citizen of Louisiana, and a member of the Legislature, I would deem it wise to bring the legal condition of the slaves more near the status of human beings under all Christian and civilized governments. In the first place, I argued that, in sales of slaves made by the State, I would forbid the separation of families, letting the father, mother, and children, be sold together to one person, instead of each to the highest bidder. And, again, I would advise the repeal of the statute which enacted a severe penalty for even the owner to teach his slave to read and write, because that actually qualified property and took away a part of its value; illustrating the assertion by the case of Henry Sampson, who had been the slave of Colonel Chambers, of Rapides Parish, who had gone to California as the servant of an officer of the army, and who was afterward employed by me in the bank at San Francisco. At first he could not write or read, and I could only afford to pay him one hundred dollars a month; but he was taught to read and write by Reilley, our bank-teller, when his services became worth two hundred and fifty dollars a month, which enabled him to buy his own freedom and that of his brother and his family."

What I said was listened to by all with the most profound attention; and, when I was through, some one (I think it was Mr. Hyams) struck the table with his fist, making the glasses jingle, and said, "By God, he is right!" and at once he took up the debate, which went on, for an hour or more, on both sides with ability and fairness. Of course, I was glad to be thus relieved, because at the time all men in Louisiana were dreadfully excited on questions affecting their slaves, who constituted the bulk of their wealth, and without whom they honestly believed that sugar, cotton, and rice, could not possibly be cultivated.

On the 30th and 31st of July, 1860, we had an examination at the seminary, winding up with a ball, and as much publicity as possible to attract general notice; and immediately thereafter we all scattered—the cadets to their homes, and the professors wherever they pleased—all to meet again on the 1st day of the next November. Major Smith and I agreed to meet in New York on a certain day in August, to purchase books, models, etc. I went directly to my family in Lancaster, and after a few days proceeded to Washington, to endeavor to procure from the General Government the necessary muskets and equipments for our cadets by the beginning of the next term. I was in Washington on the 17th day of August, and hunted up my friend Major Buell, of the Adjutant-General's Department, who was on duty with the Secretary of War, Floyd. I had with me a letter of Governor Moore's, authorizing me to act in his name. Major Buell took me into Floyd's room at the War Department, to whom I explained my business, and I was agreeably surprised to meet with such easy success. Although the State of Louisiana had already drawn her full quota of arms, Floyd promptly promised to order my requisition to be filled, and I procured the necessary blanks at the Ordnance-Office, filled them with two hundred cadet muskets, and all equipments complete, and was assured that all these articles would be shipped to Louisiana in season for our use that fall. These assurances were faithfully carried out.

I then went on to New York, there met Major Smith according to appointment, and together we selected and purchased a good supply of uniforms, clothing, and text-books, as well as a fair number of books of history and fiction, to commence a library.

When this business was completed, I returned to Lancaster, and remained with my family till the time approached for me to return to Louisiana. I again left my family at Lancaster, until assured of the completion of the two buildings designed for the married professors for which I had contracted that spring with Mr. Mills, of Alexandria, and which were well under progress when I left in August. One of these was designed for me and the other for Vallas. Mr. Ewing presented me with a horse, which I took down the river with me, and *en route* I ordered from Grimsley & Co. a full equipment of saddle, bridle, etc., the same that I used in the war, and which I lost with my horse, shot under me at Shiloh.

Reaching Alexandria early in October, I pushed forward the construction of the two buildings, some fences, gates, and all other work, with the object of a more perfect start at the opening of the regular term November 1, 1860.

About this time Dr. Powhatan Clark was elected Assistant Professor of Chemistry, etc., and acted as secretary of the Board of Supervisors, but no other changes were made in our small circle of professors.

November came, and with it nearly if not quite all our first set of cadets, and others, to the number of about one hundred and thirty. We divided them into two companies, issued arms and clothing, and began a regular system of drills and instruction, as well as the regular recitations. I had moved into my new house, but prudently had not sent for my family, nominally on the ground of waiting until the season was further advanced, but really because of the storm that was lowering heavy on the political horizon. The presidential election was to occur in November, and the nominations had already been made in stormy debates by the usual conventions. Lincoln and Hamlin (to the South utterly unknown) were the nominees of the Republican party, and for the first time both these candidates were from Northern States. The Democratic party divided—one set nominating a ticket at Charleston, and the other at Baltimore. Breckenridge and Lane were the nominees of the Southern or Democratic party; and Bell and Everett, a kind of compromise, mostly in favor in Louisiana. Political excitement was at its very height, and it was constantly asserted that Mr. Lincoln's election would imperil the Union. I purposely kept aloof from politics, would take no part, and remember that on the day of the election in November I was notified that it would be advisable for me to vote for Bell and Everett, but I openly said I would not, and I did not. The election of Mr. Lincoln fell upon us all like a clap of thunder. People saw and felt that the South had threatened so long that, if she quietly submitted, the question of slavery in the Territories was at an end forever. I mingled freely with the members of the Board of Supervisors, and with the people of Rapides Parish generally, keeping aloof from all cliques and parties, and I certainly hoped that the threatened storm would blow over, as had so often occurred before, after similar threats. At our seminary the order of exercises went along with the regularity of the seasons. Once a week, I had the older cadets to practise reading, reciting, and elocution, and noticed that their selections were from Calhoun, Yancey, and other Southern speakers, all treating of the defense of their slaves and their home institutions as the very highest duty of the patriot. Among boys this was to be expected; and among the members of our board, though most of them declaimed against politicians generally, and especially abolitionists, as pests, yet there was a growing feeling that danger was in the wind. I recall the visit of a young gentleman who had been sent from Jackson, by the Governor of Mississippi, to confer

with Governor Moore, then on his plantation at Bayou Robert, and who had come over to see our college. He spoke to
me openly of secession as a fixed fact, and that its details were
only left open for discussion. I also recall the visit of some
man who was said to be a high officer in the order of
"Knights of the Golden Circle," of the existence of which order I was even ignorant, until explained to me by Major
Smith and Dr. Clark. But in November, 1860, no man ever
approached me offensively, to ascertain my views, or my proposed course of action in case of secession, and no man in or
out of authority ever tried to induce me to take part in steps
designed to lead toward disunion. I think my general opinions were well known and understood, viz., that "secession
was treason, was *war*;" and that in no event could the North
and West permit the Mississippi River to pass out of their
control. But some men at the South actually supposed at the
time that the Northwestern States, in case of a disruption of
the General Government, would be drawn in self-interest to
an alliance with the South. What I now write I do not offer as
any thing like a history of the important events of that time,
but rather as my memory of them, the effect they had on me
personally, and to what extent they influenced my personal
conduct.

South Carolina seceded December 20, 1860, and Mississippi
soon after. Emissaries came to Louisiana to influence the
Governor, Legislature, and people, and it was the common
assertion that, if all the Cotton States would follow the lead
of South Carolina, it would diminish the chances of civil war,
because a bold and determined front would deter the General
Government from any measures of coercion. About this time
also, viz., early in December, we received Mr. Buchanan's annual message to Congress, in which he publicly announced
that the General Government had no constitutional power to
"coerce a State." I confess this staggered me, and I feared that
the prophecies and assertions of Alison and other European
commentators on our form of government were right, and
that our Constitution was a mere rope of sand, that would
break with the first pressure.

The Legislature of Louisiana met on the 10th of December,
and passed an act calling a convention of delegates from the

people, to meet at Baton Rouge, on the 8th of January, to take into consideration the state of the Union; and, although it was universally admitted that a large majority of the voters of the State were opposed to secession, disunion, and all the steps of the South Carolinians, yet we saw that they were powerless, and that the politicians would sweep them along rapidly to the end, prearranged by their leaders in Washington. Before the ordinance of secession was passed, or the convention had assembled, on the faith of a telegraphic dispatch sent by the two Senators, Benjamin and Slidell, from their seats in the United States Senate at Washington, Governor Moore ordered the seizure of all the United States forts at the mouth of the Mississippi and Lake Pontchartrain, and of the United States arsenal at Baton Rouge. The forts had no garrisons, but the arsenal was held by a small company of artillery, commanded by Major Haskins, a most worthy and excellent officer, who had lost an arm in Mexico. I remember well that I was strongly and bitterly impressed by the seizure of the arsenal, which occurred on January 10, 1861.

When I went first to Baton Rouge, in 1859, *en route* to Alexandria, I found Captain Rickett's company of artillery stationed in the arsenal, but soon after there was somewhat of a clamor on the Texas frontier about Brownsville, which induced the War Department to order Rickett's company to that frontier. I remember that Governor Moore remonstrated with the Secretary of War because so much dangerous property, composed of muskets, powder, etc., had been left by the United States unguarded, in a parish where the slave population was as five or six to one of whites; and it was on his official demand that the United States Government ordered Haskins's company to replace Rickett's. This company did not number forty men. In the night of January 9th, about five hundred New Orleans militia, under command of a Colonel Wheat, went up from New Orleans by boat, landed, surrounded the arsenal, and demanded its surrender. Haskins was of course unprepared for such a step, yet he at first resolved to defend the post as he best could with his small force. But Bragg, who was an old army acquaintance of his, had a parley with him, exhibited to him the vastly superior force of his assailants, embracing two field-batteries, and

offered to procure for him honorable terms, to march out
with drums and colors, and to take unmolested passage in a
boat up to St. Louis; alleging, further, that the old Union was
at an end, and that a just settlement would be made between
the two new fragments for all the property stored in the arsenal. Of course it was Haskins's duty to have defended his post
to the death; but up to that time the national authorities in
Washington had shown such pusillanimity, that the officers of
the army knew not what to do. The result, anyhow, was that
Haskins surrendered his post, and at once embarked for St.
Louis. The arms and munitions stored in the arsenal were
scattered—some to Mississippi, some to New Orleans, some
to Shreveport; and to me, at the Central Arsenal, were consigned two thousand muskets, three hundred Jäger rifles, and
a large amount of cartridges and ammunition. The invoices
were signed by the former ordnance-sergeant, Olodowski, as
a captain of ordnance, and I think he continued such on General Bragg's staff through the whole of the subsequent civil
war. These arms, etc., came up to me at Alexandria, with orders from Governor Moore to receipt for and account for
them. Thus I was made the receiver of stolen goods, and
these goods the property of the United States. This grated
hard on my feelings as an ex-army-officer, and on counting
the arms I noticed that they were packed in the old familiar
boxes, with the "U. S." simply scratched off. General G. Mason Graham had resigned as the chairman of the Executive
Committee, and Dr. S. A. Smith, of Alexandria, then a member of the State Senate, had succeeded him as chairman, and
acted as head of the Board of Supervisors. At the time I was
in most intimate correspondence with all of these parties, and
our letters must have been full of politics, but I have only
retained copies of a few of the letters, which I will embody in
this connection, as they will show, better than by any thing I
can now recall, the feelings of parties at that critical period.
The seizure of the arsenal at Baton Rouge occurred January
10, 1861, and the secession ordinance was not passed until
about the 25th or 26th of the same month. At all events, after
the seizure of the arsenal, and before the passage of the ordinance of secession, viz., on the 18th of January, I wrote as
follows:

LOUISIANA STATE SEMINARY OF LEARNING AND ⎱
MILITARY ACADEMY, *January* 18, 1861. ⎰

Governor THOMAS O. MOORE, *Baton Rouge, Louisiana.*

SIR: As I occupy a *quasi*-military position under the laws of the State, I deem it proper to acquaint you that I accepted such position when Louisiana was a State in the Union, and when the motto of this seminary was inserted in marble over the main door: "By the liberality of the General Government of the United States. The Union—*esto perpetua.*"

Recent events foreshadow a great change, and it becomes all men to choose. If Louisiana withdraw from the Federal Union, I prefer to maintain my allegiance to the Constitution as long as a fragment of it survives, and my longer stay here would be wrong in every sense of the word.

In that event, I beg you will send or appoint some authorized agent to take charge of the arms and munitions of war belonging to the State, or advise me what disposition to make of them.

And furthermore, as president of the Board of Supervisors, I beg you to take immediate steps to relieve me as superintendent, the moment the State determines to secede, for on no earthly account will I do any act or think any thought hostile to or in defiance of the old Government of the United States.

With great respect, your obedient servant,

W. T. SHERMAN, *Superintendent.*

[PRIVATE.]

January 18, 1861.

To Governor MOORE.

MY DEAR SIR: I take it for granted that you have been expecting for some days the accompanying paper from me (the above official letter). I have repeatedly and again made known to General Graham and Dr. Smith that, in the event of a severance of the relations hitherto existing between the Confederate States of this Union, I would be forced to choose the old Union. It is barely possible all the States may secede, South and North, that new combinations may result, but this process will be one of time and uncertainty, and I cannot with my opinions await the subsequent development.

I have never been a politician, and therefore undervalue the excited feelings and opinions of present rulers, but I do think, if this people cannot execute a form of government like the present, that a worse one will result.

I will keep the cadets as quiet as possible. They are nervous, but I think the interest of the State requires them here, guarding this property, and acquiring a knowledge which will be useful to your State in after-times.

When I leave, which I now regard as certain, the present professors can manage well enough, to afford you leisure time to find a suitable successor to me. You might order Major Smith to receipt for the arms, and to exercise military command, while the academic exercises could go on under the board. In time, some gentleman will turn up, better qualified than I am, to carry on the seminary to its ultimate point of success. I entertain the kindest feelings toward all, and would leave the State with much regret; only in great events we must choose, one way or the other.

Truly, your friend,

W. T. SHERMAN.

January 19, 1861 — *Saturday.*

Dr. S. A. SMITH, *President Board of Supervisors, Baton Rouge, Louisiana.*

DEAR SIR: I have just finished my quarterly reports to the parents of all the cadets here, or who have been here. All my books of account are written up to date. All bills for the houses, fences, etc., are settled, and nothing now remains but the daily routine of recitations and drills. I have written officially and unofficially to Governor Moore, that with my opinions of the claimed right of seccession, of the seizure of public forts, arsenals, etc., and the ignominious capture of a United States garrison, stationed in your midst, as a guard to the arsenal and for the protection of your own people, it would be highly improper for me longer to remain. No great inconvenience can result to the seminary. I will be the chief loser. I came down two months before my pay commenced. I made sacrifices in Kansas to enable me thus to obey the call of Governor Wickliffe, and you know that last winter I declined a most advantageous offer of employment abroad; and thus far I have received nothing as superintendent of the arsenal, though I went to Washington and New York (at my own expense) on the faith of the five hundred dollars salary promised.

These are all small matters in comparison with those involved in the present state of the country, which will cause sacrifices by millions, instead of by hundreds. The more I think of it, the more I think I should be away, the sooner the better; and therefore I hope you will join with Governor Moore in authorizing me to turn over to Major Smith the military command here, and to the academic board the control of the daily exercises and recitations.

There will be no necessity of your coming up. You can let Major Smith receive the few hundreds of cash I have on hand, and I can meet you on a day certain in New Orleans, when we can settle the bank account. Before I leave, I can pay the steward Jarreau his account for the month, and there would be no necessity for other payments till about the close of March, by which time the board can meet, and elect a treasurer and superintendent also.

At present I have no class, and there will be none ready till about the month of May, when there will be a class in "surveying." Even if you do not elect a superintendent in the mean time, Major Smith could easily teach this class, as he is very familiar with the subject-matter. Indeed, I think you will do well to leave the subject of a new superintendent until one perfectly satisfactory turns up.

There is only one favor I would ask. The seminary has plenty of money in bank. The Legislature will surely appropriate for my salary as superintendent of this arsenal. Would you not let me make my drafts on the State Treasury, send them to you, let the Treasurer note them for payment when the appropriation is made, and then pay them out of the seminary fund? The drafts will be paid in March, and the seminary will lose nothing. This would be just to me; for I actually spent two hundred dollars and more in going to Washington and New York, thereby securing from the United States, in advance, three thousand dollars' worth of the very best arms; and clothing and books, at a clear profit to the seminary of over eight hundred dollars. I may be some time in finding new employment, and will stand in need of this money (five hundred dollars); otherwise I would abandon it.

I will not ask you to put the Board of Supervisors to the trouble of meeting, unless you can get a quorum at Baton Rouge.

With great respect, your friend,
W. T. SHERMAN.

By course of mail, I received the following answer from Governor Moore, the original of which I still possess. It is all in General Bragg's handwriting, with which I am familiar:

EXECUTIVE OFFICE, }
BATON ROUGE, LOUISIANA, *January* 23, 1861.}

MY DEAR SIR: It is with the deepest regret I acknowledge receipt of your communication of the 18th inst. In the pressure of official business, I can now only request you to transfer to Prof. Smith the arms, munitions, and funds in your hands, whenever you conclude to withdraw from the position you have filled with so much distinction. You cannot regret more than I do the necessity which deprives us of your services, and you will bear with you the respect, confidence, and admiration, of all who have been associated with you. Very truly, your friend,

THOMAS O. MOORE.

Colonel W. T. SHERMAN, Superintendent
Military Academy, Alexandria.

I must have received several letters from Bragg, about this time, which have not been preserved; for I find that, on the 1st of February, 1861, I wrote him thus:

SEMINARY OF LEARNING, ⎫
ALEXANDRIA, LOUISIANA, *February* 1, 1861. ⎭

Colonel BRAXTON BRAGG, Baton Rouge, Louisiana.

DEAR SIR: Yours of January 23d and 27th are received. I thank you most kindly, and Governor Moore through you, for the kind manner in which you have met my wishes.

Now that I cannot be compromised by political events, I will so shape my course as best to serve the institution, which has a strong hold on my affections and respect.

The Board of Supervisors will be called for the 9th instant, and I will coöperate with them in their measures to place matters here on a safe and secure basis. I expect to be here two weeks, and will make you full returns of money and property belonging to the State Central Arsenal. All the arms and ammunition are safely stored here. Then I will write you more at length. With sincere respect, your friend,

W. T. SHERMAN.

Major Smith's receipt to me, for the arms and property belonging both to the seminary and to the arsenal, is dated February 19, 1861. I subjoin also, in this connection, copies of one or two papers that may prove of interest:

BATON ROUGE, *January* 28, 1861.

To Major SHERMAN, Superintendent, Alexandria.

MY DEAR SIR: Your letter was duly received, and would have been answered ere this time could I have arranged sooner the matter of the five hundred dollars. I shall go from here to New Orleans to-day or to-morrow, and will remain there till Saturday after next, perhaps. I shall expect to meet you there, as indicated in your note to me.

I need not tell you that it is with no ordinary regret that I view your determination to leave us, for really I believe that the success of our institution, now almost assured, is jeopardized thereby. I am sure that we will never have a superintendent with whom I shall have more pleasant relations than those which have existed between yourself and me.

I fully appreciate the motives which have induced you to give up a position presenting so many advantages to yourself, and sincerely hope that you may, in any future enterprise, enjoy the success which your character and ability merit and deserve.

Should you come down on the Rapides (steamer), please look after my wife, who will, I hope, accompany you on said boat, or some other good one.

Colonel Bragg informs me that the necessary orders have been given for the transfer and receipt by Major Smith of the public property.

I herewith transmit a request to the secretary to convene the Board of Supervisors, that they may act as seems best to them in the premises.

In the mean time, Major Smith will command by seniority the cadets, and the Academic Board will be able to conduct the scientific exercises of the institution until the Board of Supervisors can have time to act. Hoping to meet you soon at the St. Charles, I am,

Most truly, your friend and servant,

S. A. SMITH.

P. S.—Governor Moore desires me to express his profound regret that the State is about to lose one who we all fondly hoped had cast his destinies for weal or for woe among us; and that he is sensible that we lose thereby an officer whom it will be difficult, if not impossible, to replace.

S. A. S.

BATON ROUGE, *February* 11, 1861.

To Major SHERMAN, *Alexandria.*

DEAR SIR: I have been in New Orleans for ten days, and on returning here find two letters from you, also your prompt answer to the resolution of the House of Representatives, for which I am much obliged.

The resolution passed the last day before adjournment. I was purposing to respond, when your welcome reports came to hand. I have arranged to pay you your five hundred dollars.

I will say nothing of general politics, except to give my opinion that there is not to be any war.

In that event, would it not be possible for you to become a citizen of our State? Every one deplores your determination to leave us. At the same time, your friends feel that you are abandoning a position that might become an object of desire to any one.

I will try to meet you in New Orleans at any time you may indicate; but it would be best for you to stop here, when, if possible, I will accompany you. Should you do so, you will find me just above the State-House, and facing it.

Bring with you a few copies of the "Rules of the Seminary."

Yours truly,
S. A. SMITH.

LOUISIANA STATE SEMINARY OF LEARNING AND }
MILITARY ACADEMY, *February* 14, 1861. }

Colonel W. T. SHERMAN.

SIR: I am instructed by the Board of Supervisors of this institution to present a copy of the resolutions adopted by them at their last meeting:

"*Resolved,* That the thanks of the Board of Supervisors are due, and are hereby tendered, to Colonel William T. Sherman for the able and efficient manner in which he has conducted the affairs of the seminary during the time the institution has been under his control—a period attended with unusual difficulties, requiring on the part of the superintendent to successfully overcome them a high order of administrative talent. And the board further bear willing testimony to the valuable services that Colonel Sherman has rendered them in their efforts to establish an institution of learning in accordance with the beneficent design of the State and Federal Governments; evincing at all times a readiness to adapt himself to the ever-varying requirements of an institution of learning in its infancy, struggling to attain a position of honor and usefulness.

"*Resolved, further,* That, in accepting the resignation of Colonel Sherman as Superintendent of the State Seminary of Learning and Military Academy, we tender to him assurances of our high personal regard, and our sincere regret at the occurrence of causes that render it necessary to part with so esteemed and valued a friend, as well as co-laborer in the cause of education."

POWHATAN CLARKE, *Secretary to the Board.*

A copy of the resolution of the Academic Board, passed at their session of April 1, 1861:

"*Resolved,* That in the resignation of the late superintendent, Colonel W. T. Sherman, the Academic Board deem it not improper to express their deep conviction of the loss the institution has sustained in being thus deprived of an able head. They cannot fail to appreciate the manliness of character which has always marked the actions of Colonel Sherman. While he is personally endeared to many of them as a friend, they consider it their high pleasure to tender to him in this resolution their regret on his separation, and their sincere wish for his future welfare."

I have given the above at some length, because, during the civil war, it was in Southern circles asserted that I was guilty of a breach of hospitality in taking up arms against the South. They were manifestly the aggressors, and we could only defend our own by assailing them. Yet, without any knowledge of what the future had in store for me, I took unusual precautions that the institution should not be damaged by my withdrawal. About the 20th of February, having turned over all property, records, and money, on hand, to Major Smith, and taking with me the necessary documents to make the final settlement with Dr. S. A. Smith, at the bank in New Orleans, where the funds of the institution were deposited to my credit, I took passage from Alexandria for that city, and arrived there, I think, on the 23d. Dr. Smith met me, and we went to the bank, where I turned over to him the balance, got him to audit all my accounts, certify that they were correct and just, and that there remained not one cent of balance in my hands. I charged in my account current for my salary up to the end of February, at the rate of four thousand dollars a year, and for the five hundred dollars due me as superintendent of the Central Arsenal, all of which was due and had been fairly earned, and then I stood free and discharged of any and every obligation, honorary or business, that was due by me to the State of Louisiana, or to any corporation or individual in that State.

This business occupied two or three days, during which I staid at the St. Louis Hotel. I usually sat at table with Colonel and Mrs. Bragg, and an officer who wore the uniform of the State of Louisiana, and was addressed as captain. Bragg wore a colonel's uniform, and explained to me that he was a colonel in the State service, a colonel of artillery, and that some companies of his regiment garrisoned Forts Jackson and St. Philip, and the arsenal at Baton Rouge.

Beauregard at the time had two sons at the Seminary of Learning. I had given them some of my personal care at the father's request, and, wanting to tell him of their condition and progress, I went to his usual office in the Custom-House Building, and found him in the act of starting for Montgomery, Alabama. Bragg said afterward that Beauregard had been sent for by Jefferson Davis, and that it was rumored that he had been made a brigadier-general, of which fact he seemed jealous, because in the old army Bragg was the senior.

Davis and Stephens had been inaugurated President and Vice-President of the Confederate States of America, February 18, 1861, at Montgomery, and those States only embraced the seven cotton States. I recall a conversation at the tea-table, one evening, at the St. Louis Hotel. When Bragg was speaking of Beauregard's promotion, Mrs. Bragg, turning to me, said, "You know that my husband is not a favorite with the new President." My mind was resting on Mr. Lincoln as the *new* President, and I said I did not know that Bragg had ever met Mr. Lincoln, when Mrs. Bragg said, quite pointedly, "I didn't mean *your* President, but *our* President." I knew that Bragg hated Davis bitterly, and that he had resigned from the army in 1855, or 1856, because Davis, as Secretary of War, had ordered him, with his battery, from Jefferson Barracks, Missouri, to Fort Smith or Fort Washita, in the Indian country, as Bragg expressed it, "to chase Indians with six-pounders."

I visited the quartermaster, Colonel A. C. Myers, who had resigned from the army, January 28, 1861, and had accepted service under the new *régime*. His office was in the same old room in the Lafayette Square building, which he had in 1853, when I was there a commissary, with the same pictures on the wall, and the letters "U. S." on every thing, including his desk, papers, etc. I asked him if he did not feel funny. "No, not at all. The thing was inevitable, secession was a complete success; there would be no war, but the two Governments would settle all matters of business in a friendly spirit, and each would go on in its allotted sphere, without further confusion." About this date, February 16th, General Twiggs, Myers's father-in-law, had surrendered his entire command, in the Department of Texas, to some State troops, with all the Government property, thus consummating the first serious step in the drama of the conspiracy, which was to form a confederacy of the cotton States, before working upon the other slave or border States, and before the 4th of March, the day for the inauguration of President Lincoln.

I walked the streets of New Orleans, and found business going along as usual. Ships were strung for miles along the lower levee, and steamboats above, all discharging or receiving cargo. The Pelican flag of Louisiana was flying over the Custom-House, Mint, City Hall, and everywhere. At the levee ships carried every flag on earth except that of the United States, and I was told that during a procession on the 22d of February, celebrating their emancipation from the despotism of the United States Government, only one national flag was shown from a house, and that the house of Cuthbert Bullitt, on Lafayette Square. He was commanded to take it down, but he refused, and defended it with his pistol.

The only officer of the army that I can recall, as being there at the time, who was faithful, was Colonel C. L. Kilburn, of the Commissary Department, and he was preparing to escape North.

Everybody regarded the change of Government as final; that Louisiana, by a mere declaration, was a free and independent State, and could enter into any new alliance or combination she chose.

Men were being enlisted and armed, to defend the State, and there was not the least evidence that the national Administration designed to make any effort, by force, to vindicate the national authority. I therefore bade adieu to all my friends, and about the 25th of February took my departure by railroad, for Lancaster, *via* Cairo and Cincinnati.

Before leaving this subject, I will simply record the fate of some of my associates. The seminary was dispersed by the war, and all the professors and cadets took service in the Confederacy, except Vallas, St. Ange, and Cadet Taliaferro. The latter joined a Union regiment, as a lieutenant, after New Orleans was retaken by the United States fleet, under Farragut. I think that both Vallas and St. Ange have died in poverty since the war. Major Smith joined the rebel army in Virginia, and was killed in April, 1865, as he was withdrawing his garrison, by night, from the batteries at Drury's Bluff, at the time

General Lee began his final retreat from Richmond. Boyd became a captain of engineers on the staff of General Richard Taylor, was captured, and was in jail at Natchez, Mississippi, when I was on my Meridian expedition. He succeeded in getting a letter to me on my arrival at Vicksburg, and, on my way down to New Orleans, I stopped at Natchez, took him along, and enabled him to effect an exchange through General Banks. As soon as the war was over, he returned to Alexandria, and reorganized the old institution, where I visited him in 1867; but, the next winter, the building took fire and burned to the ground. The students, library, apparatus, etc., were transferred to Baton Rouge, where the same institution now is, under the title of the Louisiana University. I have been able to do them many acts of kindness, and am still in correspondence with Colonel Boyd, its president.

General G. Mason Graham is still living on his plantation, on Bayou Rapides, old and much respected.

Dr. S. A. Smith became a surgeon in the rebel army, and at the close of the war was medical director of the trans-Mississippi Department, with General Kirby Smith. I have seen him since the war, at New Orleans, where he died about a year ago.

Dr. Clark was in Washington recently, applying for a place as United States consul abroad. I assisted him, but with no success, and he is now at Baltimore, Maryland.

After the battle of Shiloh, I found among the prisoners Cadet Barrow, fitted him out with some clean clothing, of which he was in need, and from him learned that Cadet Workman was killed in that battle.

Governor Moore's plantation was devastated by General Banks's troops. After the war he appealed to me, and through the Attorney-General, Henry Stanbery, I aided in having his land restored to him, and I think he is now living there.

Bragg, Beauregard, and Taylor, enacted high parts in the succeeding war, and now reside in Louisiana or Texas.

Chapter VIII.

MISSOURI.

April and May, 1861.

URING THE TIME of these events in Louisiana, I was in constant correspondence with my brother, John Sherman, at Washington; Mr. Ewing, at Lancaster, Ohio; and Major H. S. Turner, at St. Louis. I had managed to maintain my family comfortably at Lancaster, but was extremely anxious about the future. It looked like the end of my career, for I did not suppose that "civil war" could give me an employment that would provide for the family. I thought, and may have said, that the national crisis had been brought about by the politicians, and, as it was upon us, they "might fight it out." Therefore, when I turned North from New Orleans, I felt more disposed to look to St. Louis for a home, and to Major Turner to find me employment, than to the public service.

I left New Orleans about the 1st of March, 1861, by rail to Jackson and Clinton, Mississippi, Jackson, Tennessee, and Columbus, Kentucky, where we took a boat to Cairo, and thence, by rail, to Cincinnati and Lancaster. All the way, I heard, in the cars and boats, warm discussions about politics; to the effect that, if Mr. Lincoln should attempt coercion of the seceded States, the other slave or border States would make common cause, when, it was believed, it would be madness to attempt to reduce them to subjection. In the South, the people were earnest, fierce and angry, and were evidently organizing for action; whereas, in Illinois, Indiana, and Ohio, I saw not the least sign of preparation. It certainly looked to me as though the people of the North would tamely submit to a disruption of the Union, and the orators of the South used, openly and constantly, the expressions that there would be no war, and that a lady's thimble would hold all the blood to be shed. On reaching Lancaster, I found letters from my brother John, inviting me to come to Washington, as he wanted to see me; and from Major Turner, at St. Louis, that he was trying to secure for me the office of president of the Fifth Street Railroad, with a salary of twenty-five hundred dollars; that Mr. Lucas and D. A. January held a controlling interest of stock, would vote for me, and the election would occur in March. This suited me exactly, and I answered Turner that I would accept, with thanks. But I also thought it right and proper that I should first go to Washington, to talk with my brother, Senator Sherman.

Mr. Lincoln had just been installed, and the newspapers were filled with rumors of every kind indicative of war; the chief act of interest was that Major Robert Anderson had taken by night into Fort Sumter all the troops garrisoning Charleston Harbor, and that he was determined to defend it against the demands of the State of South Carolina and of the Confederate States. I must have reached Washington about the 10th of March. I found my brother there, just appointed Senator, in place of Mr. Chase, who was in the cabinet, and I have no doubt my opinions, thoughts, and feelings, wrought up by the events in Louisiana, seemed to him gloomy and extravagant. About Washington I saw but few signs of preparation, though the Southern Senators and Representatives were daily sounding their threats on the floors of Congress, and were publicly withdrawing to join the Confederate Congress at Montgomery. Even in the War Department and about the public offices there was open, unconcealed talk, amounting to high-treason.

One day, John Sherman took me with him to see Mr. Lincoln. He walked into the room where the secretary to the President now sits, we found the room full of people, and Mr. Lincoln sat at the end of the table, talking with three or four gentlemen, who soon left. John walked up, shook hands, and took a chair near him, holding in his hand some papers referring to minor appointments in the State of Ohio, which formed the subject of conversation. Mr. Lincoln took the papers, said he would refer them to the proper heads of departments, and would be glad to make the appointments asked for, if not already promised. John then turned to me, and said, "Mr. President, this is my brother, Colonel Sherman, who is just up from Louisiana, he may give you some information you want." "Ah!" said Mr. Lincoln, "how are they getting along down there?" I said, "They think they are getting along swimmingly—they are preparing for war."

"Oh, well!" said he, "I guess we'll manage to keep house." I was silenced, said no more to him, and we soon left. I was sadly disappointed, and remember that I broke out on John, d—ning the politicians generally, saying, "You have got things in a hell of a fix, and you may get them out as you best can," adding that the country was sleeping on a volcano that might burst forth at any minute, but that I was going to St. Louis to take care of my family, and would have no more to do with it. John begged me to be more patient, but I said I would not; that I had no time to wait, that I was off for St. Louis; and off I went. At Lancaster I found letters from Major Turner, inviting me to St. Louis, as the place in the Fifth Street Railroad was a sure thing, and that Mr. Lucas would rent me a good house on Locust Street, suitable for my family, for six hundred dollars a year.

Mrs. Sherman and I gathered our family and effects together, started for St. Louis March 27th, where we rented of Mr. Lucas the house on Locust Street, between Tenth and Eleventh, and occupied it on the 1st of April. Charles Ewing and John Hunter had formed a law-partnership in St. Louis, and agreed to board with us, taking rooms on the third floor. In the latter part of March, I was duly elected president of the Fifth Street Railroad, and entered on the discharge of my duties April 1, 1861. We had a central office on the corner of Fifth and Locust, and also another up at the stables in Bremen. The road was well stocked and in full operation, and all I had to do was to watch the economical administration of existing affairs, which I endeavored to do with fidelity and zeal. But the whole air was full of wars and rumors of wars. The struggle was going on politically for the border States. Even in Missouri, which was a slave State, it was manifest that the Governor of the State, Claiborne Jackson, and all the leading politicians, were for the South in case of a war. The house on the northwest corner of Fifth and Pine was the rebel headquarters, where the rebel flag was hung publicly, and the crowds about the Planters' House were all more or less rebel. There was also a camp in Lindell's Grove, at the end of Olive Street, under command of General D. M. Frost, a Northern man, a graduate of West Point, in open sympathy with the Southern leaders. This camp was nominally a State camp of instruction, but, beyond doubt, was in the interest of the Southern cause, designed to be used against the national authority in the event of the General Government's attempting to coerce the Southern Confederacy. General William S. Harney was in command of the Department of Missouri, and resided in his own house, on Fourth Street, below Market; and there were five or six companies of United States troops in the arsenal, commanded by Captain N. Lyon; throughout the city, there had been organized, almost exclusively out of the German part of the population, four or five regiments of "Home Guards," with which movement Frank Blair, B. Gratz Brown, John M. Schofield, Clinton B. Fisk, and others, were most active on the part of the national authorities. Frank Blair's brother Montgomery was in the cabinet of Mr. Lincoln at Washington, and to him seemed committed the general management of affairs in Missouri.

The newspapers fanned the public excitement to the highest pitch, and threats of attacking the arsenal on the one hand, and the mob of d——d rebels in Camp Jackson on the other, were bandied about. I tried my best to keep out of the current, and only talked freely with a few men; among them Colonel John O'Fallon, a wealthy gentleman who resided above St. Louis. He daily came down to my office in Bremen, and we walked up and down the pavement by the hour, deploring the sad condition of our country, and the seeming drift toward dissolution and anarchy. I used also to go down to the arsenal occasionally to see Lyon, Totten, and other of my army acquaintance, and was glad to see them making preparations to defend their post, if not to assume the offensive.

The bombardment of Fort Sumter, which was announced by telegraph, began April 12th, and ended on the 14th. We then knew that the war was actually begun, and though the South was openly, manifestly the aggressor, yet her friends and apologists insisted that she was simply acting on a justifiable defensive, and that in the forcible seizure of the public forts within her limits the people were acting with reasonable prudence and foresight. Yet neither party seemed willing to invade, or cross the border. Davis, who ordered the bombardment of Sumter, knew the temper of his people well, and foresaw that it would precipitate the action of the border States; for almost immediately Virginia, North Carolina, Arkansas, and Tennessee, followed the lead of the cotton States, and conventions were deliberating in Kentucky and Missouri.

On the night of Saturday, April 6th, I received the following dispatch:

WASHINGTON, *April* 6, 1861.

Major W. T. SHERMAN:

Will you accept the chief clerkship of the War Department? We will make you assistant Secretary of War when Congress meets.

M. Blair, *Postmaster-General.*

To which I replied by telegraph, Monday morning, "I cannot accept;" and by mail as follows:

OFFICE ST. LOUIS RAILROAD COMPANY,
Monday, April 8, 1861.

Hon. M. BLAIR, *Washington, D. C.:*

I received, about nine o'clock Saturday night, your telegraph dispatch, which I have this moment answered, "I cannot accept."

I have quite a large family, and when I resigned my place in Louisiana, on account of secession, I had no time to lose; and, therefore, after my hasty visit to Washington, where I saw no chance of employment, I came to St. Louis, have accepted a place in this company, have rented a house, and incurred other obligations, so that I am not at liberty to change.

I thank you for the compliment contained in your offer, and assure you that I wish the Administration all success in its almost impossible task of governing this distracted and anarchical people.

Yours truly,
W. T. SHERMAN.

I was afterward told that this letter gave offense, and that some of Mr. Lincoln's cabinet concluded that I too would prove false to the country.

Later in that month, after the capture of Fort Sumter by the Confederate authorities, a Dr. Cornyn came to our house on Locust Street, one night after I had gone to bed, and told me he had been sent by Frank Blair, who was not well, and wanted to see me that night at his house. I dressed and walked over to his house on Washington Avenue, near Fourteenth, and found there, in the front-room, several gentlemen, among whom I recall Henry T. Blow. Blair was in the back-room, closeted with some gentleman, who soon left, and I was called in. He there told me that the Government was mistrustful of General Harney, that a change in the command of the department was to be made; that he held it in his power to appoint a brigadier-general, and put him in command of the department, and he offered me the place. I told him I had once offered my services, and they were declined; that I had made business engagements in St. Louis, which I could not throw off at pleasure; that I had long deliberated on my course of action, and must decline his offer, however tempting and complimentary. He reasoned with me, but I persisted. He told me, in that event, he should appoint Lyon, and he did so.

Finding that even my best friends were uneasy as to my political status, on the 8th of May I addressed the following official letter to the Secretary of War:

OFFICE OF ST. LOUIS RAILROAD COMPANY, }
May 8, 1861. }

Hon. S. CAMERON, *Secretary of War, Washington, D. C.*

DEAR SIR: I hold myself now, as always, prepared to serve my country in the capacity for which I was trained. I did not and will not volunteer for *three months*, because I cannot throw my family on the cold charity of the world. But for the *three-years* call, made by the President, an officer can prepare his command and do good service.

I will not volunteer as a soldier, because rightfully or wrongfully I feel unwilling to take a mere private's place, and, having for many years lived in California and Louisiana, the men are not well enough acquainted with me to elect me to my appropriate place.

Should my services be needed, the records of the War Department will enable you to designate the station in which I can render most service.

Yours truly,
W. T. SHERMAN.

To this I do not think I received a direct answer; but, on

the 14th of the same month, I was appointed colonel of the Thirteenth Regular Infantry.

I remember going to the arsenal on the 9th of May, taking my children with me in the street-cars. Within the arsenal wall were drawn up in parallel lines four regiments of the "Home Guards," and I saw men distributing cartridges to the boxes. I also saw General Lyon running about with his hair in the wind, his pockets full of papers, wild and irregular, but I knew him to be a man of vehement purpose and of determined action. I saw of course that it meant business, but whether for defense or offense I did not know. The next morning I went up to the railroad-office in Bremen, as usual, and heard at every corner of the streets that the "Dutch" were moving on Camp Jackson. People were barricading their houses, and men were running in that direction. I hurried through my business as quickly as I could, and got back to my house on Locust Street by twelve o'clock. Charles Ewing and Hunter were there, and insisted on going out to the camp to see "the fun." I tried to dissuade them, saying that in case of conflict the by-standers were more likely to be killed than the men engaged, but they would go. I felt as much interest as anybody else, but staid at home, took my little son Willie, who was about seven years old, and walked up and down the pavement in front of our house, listening for the sound of musketry or cannon in the direction of Camp Jackson. While so engaged Miss Eliza Dean, who lived opposite us, called me across the street, told me that her brother-in-law, Dr. Scott, was a surgeon in Frost's camp, and she was dreadfully afraid he would be killed. I reasoned with her that General Lyon was a regular officer; that if he had gone out, as reported, to Camp Jackson, he would take with him such a force as would make resistance impossible; but she would not be comforted, saying that the camp was made up of the young men from the first and best families of St. Louis, and that they were proud, and would fight. I explained that young men of the best families did not like to be killed better than ordinary people. Edging gradually up the street, I was in Olive Street just about Twelfth, when I saw a man running from the direction of Camp Jackson at full speed, calling, as he went, "They've surrendered, they've surrendered!" So I

turned back and rang the bell at Mrs. Dean's. Eliza came to
the door, and I explained what I had heard; but she angrily
slammed the door in my face! Evidently she was disappointed
to find she was mistaken in her estimate of the rash courage of
the best families.

I again turned in the direction of Camp Jackson, my boy
Willie with me still. At the head of Olive Street, abreast of
Lindell's Grove, I found Frank Blair's regiment in the street,
with ranks opened, and the Camp Jackson prisoners inside. A
crowd of people was gathered around, calling to the prisoners
by name, some hurrahing for Jeff Davis, and others encouraging the troops. Men, women, and children, were in the
crowd. I passed along till I found myself inside the grove,
where I met Charles Ewing and John Hunter, and we stood
looking at the troops on the road, heading toward the city. A
band of music was playing at the head, and the column made
one or two ineffectual starts, but for some reason was halted.
The battalion of regulars was abreast of me, of which Major
Rufus Saxton was in command, and I gave him an evening
paper, which I had bought of the newsboy on my way out.
He was reading from it some piece of news, sitting on his
horse, when the column again began to move forward, and he
resumed his place at the head of his command. At that part of
the road, or street, was an embankment about eight feet high,
and a drunken fellow tried to pass over it to the people opposite. One of the regular sergeant file-closers ordered him back,
but he attempted to pass through the ranks, when the sergeant barred his progress with his musket "a-port." The
drunken man seized his musket, when the sergeant threw him
off with violence, and he rolled over and over down the bank.
By the time this man had picked himself up and got his hat,
which had fallen off, and had again mounted the embankment, the regulars had passed, and the head of Osterhaus's
regiment of Home Guards had come up. The man had in his
hand a small pistol, which he fired off, and I heard that the
ball had struck the leg of one of Osterhaus's staff; the regiment stopped; there was a moment of confusion, when the
soldiers of that regiment began to fire over our heads in the
grove. I heard the balls cutting the leaves above our heads,
and saw several men and women running in all directions,

some of whom were wounded. Of course there was a general stampede. Charles Ewing threw Willie on the ground and covered him with his body. Hunter ran behind the hill, and I also threw myself on the ground. The fire ran back from the head of the regiment toward its rear, and as I saw the men reloading their pieces, I jerked Willie up, ran back with him into a gulley which covered us, lay there until I saw that the fire had ceased, and that the column was again moving on, when I took up Willie and started back for home round by way of Market Street. A woman and child were killed outright; two or three men were also killed, and several others were wounded. The great mass of the people on that occasion were simply curious spectators, though men were sprinkled through the crowd calling out, "Hurrah for Jeff Davis!" and others were particularly abusive of the "damned Dutch." Lyon posted a guard in charge of the vacant camp, and marched his prisoners down to the arsenal; some were paroled, and others held, till afterward they were regularly exchanged.

A very few days after this event, May 14th, I received a dispatch from my brother Charles in Washington, telling me to come on at once; that I had been appointed a colonel of the Thirteenth Regular Infantry, and that I was wanted at Washington immediately.

Of course I could no longer defer action. I saw Mr. Lucas, Major Turner, and other friends and parties connected with the road, who agreed that I should go on. I left my family, because I was under the impression that I would be allowed to enlist my own regiment, which would take some time, and I expected to raise the regiment and organize it at Jefferson Barracks. I repaired to Washington, and there found that the Government was trying to rise to a level with the occasion. Mr. Lincoln had, without the sanction of law, authorized the raising of ten new regiments of regulars, each infantry regiment to be composed of three battalions of eight companies each; and had called for seventy-five thousand State volunteers. Even this call seemed to me utterly inadequate; still it was none of my business. I took the oath of office, and was furnished with a list of officers, appointed to my regiment, which was still incomplete. I reported in person to General

Scott, at his office on Seventeenth Street, opposite the War Department, and applied for authority to return West, and raise my regiment at Jefferson Barracks, but the general said my lieutenant-colonel, Burbank, was fully qualified to super-intend the enlistment, and that he wanted me there; and he at once dictated an order for me to report to him in person for inspection duty.

Satisfied that I would not be permitted to return to St. Louis, I instructed Mrs. Sherman to pack up, return to Lan-caster, and trust to the fate of war.

I also resigned my place as president of the Fifth Street Railroad, to take effect at the end of May, so that in fact I received pay from that road for only two months' service, and then began my new army career.

Chapter IX.

FROM THE BATTLE OF BULL RUN
TO PADUCAH—KENTUCKY AND MISSOURI.

1861–1862.

AND NOW THAT, in these notes, I have fairly reached the period of the civil war, which ravaged our country from 1861 to 1865—an event involving a conflict of passion, of prejudice, and of arms, that has developed results which, for better or worse, have left their mark on the world's history—I feel that I tread on delicate ground.

I have again and again been invited to write a history of the war, or to record for publication my personal recollections of it, with large offers of money therefor; all of which I have heretofore declined, because the truth is not always palatable, and should not always be told. Many of the actors in the grand drama still live, and they and their friends are quick to controversy, which should be avoided. The great end of peace has been attained, with little or no change in our form of government, and the duty of all good men is to allow the passions of that period to subside, that we may direct our physical and mental labor to repair the waste of war, and to engage in the greater task of continuing our hitherto wonderful national development.

What I now propose to do is merely to group some of my personal recollections about the historic persons and events of the day, prepared not with any view to their publication, but rather for preservation till I am gone; and then to be allowed to follow into oblivion the cords of similar papers, or to be used by some historian who may need them by way of illustration.

I have heretofore recorded how I again came into the military service of the United States as a colonel of the Thirteenth Regular Infantry, a regiment that had no existence at the time, and that, instead of being allowed to enlist the men and instruct them, as expected, I was assigned in Washington City, by an order of Lieutenant-General Winfield Scott, to inspection duty near him on the 20th of June, 1861.

At that time Lieutenant-General Scott commanded the army in chief, with Colonel E. D. Townsend as his adjutant-general, Major G. W. Cullum, United States Engineers, and Major Schuyler Hamilton, as aides-de-camp. The general had an office up-stairs on Seventeenth Street, opposite the War Department, and resided in a house close by, on Pennsylvania Avenue. All fears for the immediate safety of the capital had ceased, and quite a large force of regulars and volunteers had been collected in and about Washington. Brigadier-General J. K. Mansfield commanded in the city, and Brigadier-General Irvin McDowell on the other side of the Potomac, with his headquarters at Arlington House. His troops extended in a semicircle from Alexandria to above Georgetown. Several forts and redoubts were either built or in progress, and the people were already clamorous for a general forward movement. Another considerable army had also been collected in Pennsylvania under General Patterson, and, at the time I speak of, had moved forward to Hagerstown and Williamsport, on the Potomac River. My brother, John Sherman, was a volunteer aide-de-camp to General Patterson, and, toward the end of June, I went up to Hagerstown to see him. I found that army in the very act of moving, and we rode down to Williamsport in a buggy, and were present when the leading division crossed the Potomac River by fording it waist-deep. My friend and classmate, George H. Thomas, was there, in command of a brigade in the leading division. I talked with him a good deal, also with General Cadwalader, and with the staff-officers of General Patterson, viz., Fitz-John Porter, Belger, Beckwith, and others, all of whom seemed encouraged to think that the war was to be short and decisive, and that, as soon as it was demonstrated that the General Government meant in earnest to defend its rights and property, some general compromise would result.

Patterson's army crossed the Potomac River on the 1st or 2d of July, and, as John Sherman was to take his seat as a Senator in the called session of Congress, to meet July 4th, he resigned his place as aide-de-camp, presented me his two horses and equipment, and we returned to Washington together.

The Congress assembled punctually on the 4th of July, and the message of Mr. Lincoln was strong and good: it recognized the fact that civil war was upon us, that compromise of any kind was at an end; and he asked for four hundred thousand men, and four hundred million dollars, wherewith to vindicate the national authority, and to regain possession of the captured forts and other property of the United States.

It was also immediately demonstrated that the tone and temper of Congress had changed since the Southern Senators and members had withdrawn, and that we, the military, could now go to work with some definite plans and ideas.

The appearance of the troops about Washington was good, but it was manifest they were far from being soldiers. Their uniforms were as various as the States and cities from which they came; their arms were also of every pattern and calibre; and they were so loaded down with overcoats, haversacks, knapsacks, tents, and baggage, that it took from twenty-five to fifty wagons to move the camp of a regiment from one place to another, and some of the camps had bakeries and cooking establishments that would have done credit to Delmonico.

While I was on duty with General Scott, viz., from June 20th to about June 30th, the general frequently communicated to those about him his opinions and proposed plans. He seemed vexed with the clamors of the press for immediate action, and the continued interference in details by the President, Secretary of War, and Congress. He spoke of organizing a grand army of invasion, of which the regulars were to constitute the "iron column," and seemed to intimate that he himself would take the field in person, though he was at the time very old, very heavy, and very unwieldy. His age must have been about seventy-five years.

At that date, July 4, 1861, the rebels had two armies in front of Washington; the one at Manassas Junction, commanded by General Beauregard, with his advance guard at Fairfax Court-House, and indeed almost in sight of Washington. The other, commanded by General Joe Johnston, was at Winchester, with its advance at Martinsburg and Harper's Ferry; but the advance had fallen back before Patterson, who then occupied Martinsburg and the line of the Baltimore & Ohio Railroad.

The temper of Congress and the people would not permit the slow and methodical preparation desired by General

Scott; and the cry of "On to Richmond!" which was shared by the volunteers, most of whom had only engaged for ninety days, forced General Scott to hasten his preparations, and to order a general advance about the middle of July. McDowell was to move from the defenses of Washington, and Patterson from Martinsburg. In the organization of McDowell's army into divisions and brigades, Colonel David Hunter was assigned to command the Second Division, and I was ordered to take command of his former brigade, which was composed of five regiments in position in and about Fort Corcoran, and on the ground opposite Georgetown. I assumed command on the 30th of June, and proceeded at once to prepare it for the general advance. My command constituted the Third Brigade of the First Division, which division was commanded by Brigadier-General Daniel Tyler, a graduate of West Point, but who had seen little or no actual service. I applied to General McDowell for some staff-officers, and he gave me, as adjutant-general, Lieutenant Piper, of the Third Artillery, and, as aide-de-camp, Lieutenant McQuesten, a fine young cavalry-officer, fresh from West Point.

I selected for the field the Thirteenth New York, Colonel Quinby; the Sixty-ninth New York, Colonel Corcoran; the Seventy-ninth New York, Colonel Cameron; and the Second Wisconsin, Lieutenant-Colonel Peck. These were all good, strong, volunteer regiments, pretty well commanded; and I had reason to believe that I had one of the best brigades in the whole army. Captain Ayres's battery of the Third Regular Artillery was also attached to my brigade. The other regiment, the Twenty-ninth New York, Colonel Bennett, was destined to be left behind in charge of the forts and camps during our absence, which was expected to be short. Soon after I had assumed the command, a difficulty arose in the Sixty-ninth, an Irish regiment. This regiment had volunteered in New York, early in April, for ninety days; but, by reason of the difficulty of passing through Baltimore, they had come *via* Annapolis, had been held for duty on the railroad as a guard for nearly a month before they actually reached Washington, and were then mustered in about a month after enrollment. Some of the men claimed that they were entitled to their discharge in ninety days from the time of enrollment, whereas the muster-roll read ninety days from the date of muster-in. One day, Colonel Corcoran explained this matter to me. I advised him to reduce the facts to writing, and that I would submit it to the War Department for an authoritative decision. He did so, and the War Department decided that the muster-roll was the only contract of service, that it would be construed literally; and that the regiment would be held till the expiration of three months from the date of muster-in, viz., to about August 1, 1861. General Scott at the same time wrote one of his characteristic letters to Corcoran, telling him that we were about to engage in battle, and he knew his Irish friends would not leave him in such a crisis. Corcoran and the officers generally wanted to go to the expected battle, but a good many of the men were not so anxious. In the Second Wisconsin, also, was developed a personal difficulty. The actual colonel was S. P. Coon, a good-hearted gentleman, who knew no more of the military art than a child; whereas his lieutenant-colonel, Peck, had been to West Point, and knew the drill. Preferring that the latter should remain in command of the regiment, I put Colonel Coon on my personal staff, which reconciled the difficulty.

In due season, about July 15th, our division moved forward, leaving our camps standing; Keyes's brigade in the lead, then Schenck's, then mine, and Richardson's last. We marched *via* Vienna, Germantown, and Centreville, where all the army, composed of five divisions, seemed to converge. The march demonstrated little save the general laxity of discipline; for with all my personal efforts I could not prevent the men from straggling for water, blackberries, or any thing on the way they fancied.

At Centreville, on the 18th, Richardson's brigade was sent by General Tyler to reconnoitre Blackburn's Ford across Bull Run, and he found it strongly guarded. From our camp, at Centreville, we heard the cannonading, and then a sharp musketry-fire. I received orders from General Tyler to send forward Ayres's battery, and very soon after another order came for me to advance with my whole brigade. We marched the three miles at the double-quick, arrived in time to relieve Richardson's brigade, which was just drawing back from the ford, worsted, and stood for half an hour or so under a fire of artillery, which killed four or five of my men. General Tyler was there in person, giving directions, and soon after he ordered us all back to our camp in Centreville. This reconnoissance had developed a strong force, and had been made without the orders of General McDowell; however, it satisfied us that the enemy was in force on the other side of Bull Run, and had no intention to leave without a serious battle. We lay in camp at Centreville all of the 19th and 20th, and during that night began the movement which resulted in the battle of Bull Run, on July 21st. Of this so much has been written that more would be superfluous; and the reports of the opposing commanders, McDowell and Johnston, are fair and correct. It is now generally admitted that it was one of the best-planned battles of the war, but one of the worst-fought. Our men had been told so often at home that all they had to do was to make a bold appearance, and the rebels would run; and nearly all of us for the first time then heard the sound of cannon and muskets in anger, and saw the bloody scenes common to all battles, with which we were soon to be familiar. We had good organization, good men, but no cohesion, no real discipline, no respect for authority, no real knowledge of war. Both armies were fairly defeated, and, whichever had stood fast, the other would have run. Though the North was overwhelmed with mortification and shame, the South really had not much to boast of, for in the three or four hours of fighting their organization was so broken up that they did not and could not follow our army, when it was known to be in a state of disgraceful and causeless flight. It is easy to criticise a battle after it is over, but all now admit that none others, equally raw in war, could have done better than we did at Bull Run; and the lesson of that battle should not be lost on a people like ours.

I insert my official report, as a condensed statement of my share in the battle:

HEADQUARTERS THIRD BRIGADE, FIRST DIVISION, }
FORT CORCORAN, *July 25, 1861.* }

To Captain A. BAIRD, *Assistant Adjutant-General, First Division* (*General Tyler's*).

SIR: I have the honor to submit this my report of the operations of my brigade during the action of the 21st instant. The brigade is composed of the Thirteenth New York Volunteers, Colonel Quinby; Sixty-ninth New York, Colonel Corcoran; Seventy-ninth New York, Colonel Cameron; Second Wisconsin, Lieutenant-Colonel Peck; and Company E, Third Artillery, under command of Captain R. B. Ayres, Fifth Artillery. We left our camp near Centreville, pursuant to orders, at half-past 2 A.M., taking place in your column, next to the brigade of General Schenck, and proceeded as far as the halt, before the enemy's position, near the stone bridge across Bull Run. Here the brigade was deployed in line along the skirt of timber to the right of the Warrenton road, and remained quietly in position till after 10 A.M. The enemy remained very quiet, but about that time we saw a rebel regiment leave its cover in our front, and proceed in double-quick time on the road toward Sudley Springs, by which we knew the columns of Colonels Hunter and Heintzelman were approaching. About the same time we observed in motion a large mass of the enemy, below and on the other side of the stone bridge. I directed Captain Ayres to take position with his battery near our right, and to open fire on this mass; but you had previously detached the two rifle-guns belonging to this battery, and, finding that the smooth-bore guns did not reach the enemy's position, we ceased firing, and I sent a request that you would send to me the thirty-pounder rifle-gun attached to Captain Carlisle's battery. At the same time I shifted the New York Sixty-ninth to the extreme right of the brigade. Thus we remained till we heard the musketry-fire across Bull Run, showing that the head of Colonel Hunter's column was engaged. This firing was brisk, and showed that Hunter was driving before him the enemy, till about noon, when it became certain the enemy had come to a stand, and that our forces on the other side of Bull Run were all engaged, artillery and infantry.

Here you sent me the order to cross over with the whole brigade, to the assistance of Colonel Hunter. Early in the day, when reconnoitring the ground, I had seen a horseman descend from a bluff in our front, cross the stream, and show himself in the open field on this side; and, inferring that we could cross over at the same point, I sent forward a company as skirmishers, and followed with the whole brigade, the New York Sixty-ninth leading.

We found no difficulty in crossing over, and met with no opposition in ascending the steep bluff opposite with our infantry, but it was impassable to the artillery, and I sent word back to Captain Ayres to follow if possible, otherwise to use his discretion. Captain Ayres did not cross Bull Run, but remained on that side, with the rest of your division. His report herewith describes his operations during the remainder of the day. Advancing slowly and cautiously with the head of the column, to give time for the regiments in succession to close up their ranks, we first encountered a party of the enemy retreating along a cluster of pines; Lieutenant-Colonel Haggerty, of the Sixty-ninth, without orders, rode out alone, and endeavored to intercept their retreat. One of the enemy, in full view, at short range, shot Haggerty, and he fell dead from his horse. The Sixty-ninth opened fire on this party, which was returned; but, determined to effect our junction with Hunter's division, I ordered this fire to cease, and we proceeded with caution toward the field where we then plainly saw our forces engaged. Displaying our colors conspicuously at the head of our column, we succeeded in attracting the attention of our friends, and soon formed the brigade in rear of Colonel Porter's. Here I learned that Colonel Hunter was disabled by a severe wound, and that General McDowell was on the field. I sought him out, and received his orders to join in pursuit of the enemy, who was falling back to the left of the road by which the army had approached from Sudley Springs. Placing Colonel Quinby's regiment of rifles in front, in column, by division, I directed the other regiments to follow in line of battle, in the order of the Wisconsin Second, New York Seventy-ninth, and New York Sixty-ninth. Quinby's regiment advanced steadily down the hill and up the ridge, from which he opened fire upon the enemy, who had made another stand on ground very favorable to him, and the regiment continued advancing as the enemy gave way, till the head of the column reached the point near which Rickett's battery was so severely cut up. The other regiments descended the hill in line of battle, under a severe cannonade; and, the ground affording comparative shelter from the enemy's artillery, they changed direction, by the right flank, and followed the road before mentioned. At the point where this road crosses the ridge to our left front, the ground was swept by a most severe fire of artillery, rifles, and musketry, and we saw, in succession, several regiments driven from it; among them the Zouaves and battalion of marines. Before reaching the crest of this hill, the roadway was worn deep enough to afford shelter, and I kept the several regiments in it as long as possible; but when the Wisconsin Second was abreast of the enemy, by order of Major Wadsworth, of General McDowell's staff, I ordered it to leave the roadway, by the left flank, and to attack the enemy.

This regiment ascended to the brow of the hill steadily, received the severe fire of the enemy, returned it with spirit, and advanced, delivering its fire. This regiment is uniformed in gray cloth, almost identical with that of the great bulk of the secession army; and, when the regiment fell into confusion and retreated toward the road, there was a universal cry that they were being fired on by our own men. The regiment rallied again, passed the brow of the hill a second time, but was again repulsed in disorder. By this time the New York Seventy-ninth had closed up, and in like manner it was ordered to cross the brow of the hill, and drive the enemy from cover. It was impossible to get a good view of this ground. In it there was one battery of artillery, which poured an incessant fire upon our advancing column, and the ground was very irregular with small clusters of pines, affording shelter, of which the enemy took good advantage. The fire of rifles and musketry was very severe. The Seventy-ninth, headed by its colonel, Cameron, charged across the hill, and for a short time the contest was severe; they rallied several times under fire, but finally broke, and gained the cover of the hill.

This left the field open to the New York Sixty-ninth, Colonel Corcoran, who, in his turn, led his regiment over the crest, and had in full, open view the ground so severely contested; the fire was very severe, and the roar of cannon, musketry, and rifles, incessant; it was manifest the enemy was here in great force, far superior to us at that point. The Sixty-ninth held the ground for some time, but finally fell back in disorder.

All this time Quinby's regiment occupied another ridge, to our left, overlooking the same field of action, and similarly engaged. Here, about half-past 3 P.M., began the scene of confusion and disorder that characterized the remainder of the day. Up to that time, all had kept their places, and seemed perfectly cool, and used to the shell and shot that fell, comparatively harmless, all around us; but the short exposure to an intense fire of small-arms, at close range, had killed many, wounded more, and had produced disorder in all of the battalions that had attempted to encounter it. Men fell away from their ranks, talking, and in great confusion. Colonel Cameron had been mortally wounded, was carried to an ambulance, and reported dying. Many other officers were reported dead or missing, and many of the wounded were making their way, with more or less assistance, to the buildings used as hospitals, on the ridge to the west. We succeeded in partially reforming the regiments, but it was manifest that they would not stand, and I directed Colonel Corcoran to move along the ridge to the rear, near the position where we had first formed the brigade. General McDowell was there in person, and used all possible efforts to reassure the men. By the active exertions of Colonel Corcoran, we formed an irregular square against the cavalry which were then seen to issue from the position from which we had been driven, and we began our retreat toward the same ford of

Bull Run by which we had approached the field of battle. There was
no positive order to retreat, although for an hour it had been going
on by the operation of the men themselves. The ranks were thin and
irregular, and we found a stream of people strung from the hospital
across Bull Run, and far toward Centreville. After putting in motion
the irregular square in person, I pushed forward to find Captain
Ayres's battery at the crossing of Bull Run. I sought it at its last
position, before the brigade had crossed over, but it was not there;
then passing through the woods, where, in the morning, we had first
formed line, we approached the blacksmith's shop, but there found a
detachment of the secession cavalry and thence made a circuit, avoiding Cub Run Bridge, into Centreville, where I found General Mc-
Dowell, and from him understood that it was his purpose to rally
the forces, and make a stand at Centreville.

But, about nine o'clock at night, I received from General Tyler, in
person, the order to continue the retreat to the Potomac. This retreat
was by night, and disorderly in the extreme. The men of different
regiments mingled together, and some reached the river at Arlington, some at Long Bridge, and the greater part returned to their
former camp, at or near Fort Corcoran. I reached this point at noon
the next day, and found a miscellaneous crowd crossing over the
aqueduct and ferries. Conceiving this to be demoralizing, I at once
commanded the guard to be increased, and all persons attempting to
pass over to be stopped. This soon produced its effect; men sought
their proper companies and regiments. Comparative order was restored, and all were posted to the best advantage.

I herewith inclose the official report of Captain Kelly, commanding officer of the New York Sixty-ninth; also, full lists of the killed,
wounded, and missing.

Our loss was heavy, and occurred chiefly at the point near where
Rickett's battery was destroyed. Lieutenant-Colonel Haggerty was

REGIMENTS, Etc.	Killed.	Wounded.	Missing.	Total.
Ayres's Battery	6	3	. . .	9
New York Thirteenth	11	27	20	58
New York Sixty-ninth. . . .	38	59	95	192
New York Seventy-ninth. . .	32	51	115	198
Wisconsin Second	24	65	63	152
	111	205	293	609

killed about noon, before we had effected a junction with Colonel Hunter's division. Colonel Cameron was mortally wounded leading his regiment in the charge, and Colonel Corcoran has been missing since the cavalry-charge near the building used as a hospital.

For names, rank, etc., of the above, I refer to the lists herewith.

Lieutenants Piper and McQuesten, of my personal staff, were under fire all day, and carried orders to and fro with as much coolness as on parade. Lieutenant Bagley, of the New York Sixty-ninth, a volunteer aide, asked leave to serve with his company, during the action, and is among those reported missing. I have intelligence that he is a prisoner, and slightly wounded.

Colonel Coon, of Wisconsin, a volunteer aide, also rendered good service during the day.

W. T. SHERMAN, *Colonel commanding Brigade.*

This report, which I had not read probably since its date till now, recalls to me vividly the whole scene of the affair at Blackburn's Ford, when for the first time in my life I saw cannonballs strike men and crash through the trees and saplings above and around us, and realized the always sickening confusion as one approaches a fight from the rear; then the night-march from Centreville, on the Warrenton road, standing for hours wondering what was meant; the deployment along the edge of the field that sloped down to Bull Run, and waiting for Hunter's approach on the other side from the direction of Sudley Springs, away off to our right; the terrible scare of a poor negro who was caught between our lines; the crossing of Bull Run, and the fear lest we should be fired on by our own men; the killing of Lieutenant-Colonel Haggerty, which occurred in plain sight; and the first scenes of a field strewed with dead men and horses. Yet, at that period of the battle, we were the victors and felt jubilant. At that moment, also, my brigade passed Hunter's division; but Heintzelman's was still ahead of us, and we followed its lead along the road toward Manassas Junction, crossing a small stream and ascending a long hill, at the summit of which the battle was going on. Here my regiments came into action well, but successively, and were driven back, each in its turn. For two hours we continued to dash at the woods on our left front, which were full of rebels; but I was convinced their organization was broken, and that they had simply halted there and taken advantage of these woods as a cover, to reach which we had to pass over the intervening fields about the Henry House, which were clear, open, and gave them a decided advantage. After I had put in each of my regiments, and had them driven back to the cover of the road, I had no idea that we were beaten, but reformed the regiments in line in their proper order, and only wanted a little rest, when I found that my brigade was almost alone, except Syke's regulars, who had formed square against cavalry and were coming back. I then realized that the whole army was "in retreat," and that my own men were individually making back for the stone bridge. Corcoran and I formed the brigade into an irregular square, but it fell to pieces; and, along with a crowd, disorganized but not much scared, the brigade got back to Centreville to our former camps. Corcoran was captured, and held a prisoner for some time; but I got safe to Centreville. I saw General McDowell in Centreville, and understood that several of his divisions had not been engaged at all, that he would reorganize them at Centreville, and there await the enemy. I got my four regiments in parallel lines in a field, the same in which we had camped before the battle, and had lain down to sleep under a tree, when I heard some one asking for me. I called out where I was, when General Tyler in person gave me orders to march back to our camps at Fort Corcoran. I aroused my aides, gave them orders to call up the sleeping men, have each regiment to leave the field by a flank and to take the same road back by which we had come. It was near midnight, and the road was full of troops, wagons, and batteries. We tried to keep our regiments separate, but all became inextricably mixed. Toward morning we reached Vienna, where I slept some hours, and the next day, about noon, we reached Fort Corcoran.

A slow, mizzling rain had set in, and probably a more gloomy day never presented itself. All organization seemed to be at an end; but I and my staff labored hard to collect our men into their proper companies and into their former camps, and, on the 23d of July, I moved the Second Wisconsin and Seventy-ninth New York closer in to Fort Corcoran, and got things in better order than I had expected. Of course, we took it for granted that the rebels would be on our heels, and we accordingly prepared to defend our posts. By the 25th I had collected all the materials, made my report, and had my brigade about as well governed as any in that army; although most of the ninety-day men, especially the Sixty-ninth, had become extremely tired of the war, and wanted to go home. Some of them were so mutinous, at one time, that I had the battery to unlimber, threatening, if they dared to leave camp without orders, I would open fire on them. Drills and the daily exercises were resumed, and I ordered that at the three principal roll-calls the men should form ranks with belts and muskets, and that they should keep their ranks until I in person had received the reports and had dismissed them. The Sixty-ninth still occupied Fort Corcoran, and one morning, after reveille, when I had just received the report, had dismissed the regiment, and was leaving, I found myself in a crowd of men crossing the drawbridge on their way to a barn close by, where they had their sinks; among them was an officer, who said: "Colonel, I am going to New York to-day. What can I do for you?" I answered: "How can you go to New York? I do not remember to have signed a leave for you." He said, "No; he did not want a leave. He had engaged to serve three months, and had already served more than that time. If the Government did not intend to pay him, he could afford to lose the money; that he was a lawyer, and had neglected his business long enough, and was then going home." I noticed that a good many of the soldiers had paused about us to listen, and knew that, if this officer could defy me, they also would. So I turned on him sharp, and said: "Captain, this question of your term of service has been submitted to the rightful authority, and the decision has been published in orders. You are a soldier, and must submit to orders till you are properly discharged. If you attempt to leave without orders, it will be mutiny, and I will shoot you like a dog! Go back into the fort *now*, instantly, and don't dare to leave without my consent." I had on an overcoat, and may have had my hand about the breast, for he looked at me hard, paused a moment, and then turned back into the fort. The men scattered, and I returned to the house where I was quartered, close by.

That same day, which must have been about July 26th, I

was near the river-bank, looking at a block-house which had
been built for the defense of the aqueduct, when I saw a carriage coming by the road that crossed the Potomac River at
Georgetown by a ferry. I thought I recognized in the carriage
the person of President Lincoln. I hurried across a bend, so as
to stand by the road-side as the carriage passed. I was in uniform, with a sword on, and was recognized by Mr. Lincoln
and Mr. Seward, who rode side by side in an open hack. I
inquired if they were going to my camps, and Mr. Lincoln
said: "Yes; we heard that you had got over the big scare, and
we thought we would come over and see the 'boys.'" The
roads had been much changed and were rough. I asked if I
might give directions to his coachman, he promptly invited
me to jump in and to tell the coachman which way to drive.
Intending to begin on the right and follow round to the left, I
turned the driver into a side-road which led up a very steep
hill, and, seeing a soldier, called to him and sent him up hurriedly to announce to the colonel (Bennett, I think) that the
President was coming. As we slowly ascended the hill, I discovered that Mr. Lincoln was full of feeling, and wanted to
encourage our men. I asked if he intended to speak to them,
and he said he would like to. I asked him then to please discourage all cheering, noise, or any sort of confusion; that we
had had enough of it before Bull Run to ruin any set of men,
and that what we needed were cool, thoughtful, hard-fighting
soldiers—no more hurrahing, no more humbug. He took my
remarks in the most perfect good-nature. Before we had
reached the first camp, I heard the drum beating the "assembly," saw the men running for their tents, and in a few
minutes the regiment was in line, arms presented, and then
brought to an order and "parade rest!"

Mr. Lincoln stood up in the carriage, and made one of the
neatest, best, and most feeling addresses I ever listened to,
referring to our late disaster at Bull Run, the high duties that
still devolved on us, and the brighter days yet to come. At one
or two points the soldiers began to cheer, but he promptly
checked them, saying: "Don't cheer, boys. I confess I rather
like it myself, but Colonel Sherman here says it is not
military; and I guess we had better defer to his opinion."
In winding up, he explained that, as President, he was

commander-in-chief; that he was resolved that the soldiers should have every thing that the law allowed; and he called on one and all to appeal to him personally in case they were wronged. The effect of this speech was excellent.

We passed along in the same manner to all the camps of my brigade; and Mr. Lincoln complimented me highly for the order, cleanliness, and discipline, that he observed. Indeed, he and Mr. Seward both assured me that it was the first bright moment they had experienced since the battle.

At last we reached Fort Corcoran. The carriage could not enter, so I ordered the regiment, without arms, to come outside, and gather about Mr. Lincoln, who would speak to them. He made to them the same feeling address, with more personal allusions, because of their special gallantry in the battle under Corcoran, who was still a prisoner in the hands of the enemy; and he concluded with the same general offer of redress in case of grievance. In the crowd I saw the officer with whom I had had the passage at reveille that morning. His face was pale, and lips compressed. I foresaw a scene, but sat on the front seat of the carriage as quiet as a lamb. This officer forced his way through the crowd to the carriage, and said: "Mr. President, I have a cause of grievance. This morning I went to speak to Colonel Sherman, and he threatened to shoot me." Mr. Lincoln, who was still standing, said, "Threatened to shoot you?" "Yes, sir, he threatened to shoot me." Mr. Lincoln looked at him, then at me, and stooping his tall, spare form toward the officer, said to him in a loud stage-whisper, easily heard for some yards around: "Well, if I were you, and he threatened to shoot, I would not trust him, for I believe he would do it." The officer turned about and disappeared, and the men laughed at him. Soon the carriage drove on, and, as we descended the hill, I explained the facts to the President, who answered, "Of course I didn't know any thing about it, but I thought you knew your own business best." I thanked him for his confidence, and assured him that what he had done would go far to enable me to maintain good discipline, and it did.

By this time the day was well spent. I asked to take my leave, and the President and Mr. Seward drove back to Washington. This spirit of mutiny was common to the whole army, and was not subdued till several regiments or parts of regiments had been ordered to Fort Jefferson, Florida, as punishment.

General McDowell had resumed his headquarters at the Arlington House, and was busily engaged in restoring order to his army, sending off the ninety-days men, and replacing them by regiments which had come under the three-years call. We were all trembling lest we should be held personally accountable for the disastrous result of the battle. General McClellan had been summoned from the West to Washington, and changes in the subordinate commands were announced almost daily. I remember, as a group of officers were talking in the large room of the Arlington House, used as the adjutant-general's office, one evening, some young officer came in with a list of the new brigadiers just announced at the War Department, which embraced the names of Heintzelman, Keyes, Franklin, Andrew Porter, W. T. Sherman, and others, who had been colonels in the battle, and all of whom had shared the common stampede. Of course, we discredited the truth of the list; and Heintzelman broke out in his nasal voice, "By —— ——, it's all a lie! Every mother's son of you will be cashiered." We all felt he was right, but, nevertheless, it was true; and we were all announced in general orders as brigadier-generals of volunteers.

General McClellan arrived, and, on assuming command, confirmed McDowell's organization. Instead of coming over the river, as we expected, he took a house in Washington, and only came over from time to time to have a review or inspection. I had received several new regiments, and had begun two new forts on the hill or plateau, above and farther out than Fort Corcoran; and I organized a system of drills, embracing the evolutions of the line, all of which was new to me, and I had to learn the tactics from books; but I was convinced that we had a long, hard war before us, and made up my mind to begin at the very beginning to prepare for it.

August was passing, and troops were pouring in from all quarters; General McClellan told me he intended to organize an army of a hundred thousand men, with one hundred field-batteries, and I still hoped he would come on our side of the Potomac, pitch his tent, and prepare for real hard work, but his headquarters still remained in a house in Washington City. I then thought, and still think, that was a fatal mistake. His choice as general-in-chief at the time was fully justified by his high reputation in the army and country, and, if he then had any political views or ambition, I surely did not suspect it.

About the middle of August I got a note from Brigadier-General Robert Anderson, asking me to come and see him at his room at Willard's Hotel. I rode over and found him in conversation with several gentlemen, and he explained to me that events in Kentucky were approaching a crisis; that the Legislature was in session, and ready, as soon as properly backed by the General Government, to take open sides for the Union cause; that he was offered the command of the Department of the Cumberland, to embrace Kentucky, Tennessee, etc., and that he wanted help, and that the President had offered to allow him to select out of the new brigadiers four of his own choice. I had been a lieutenant in Captain Anderson's company, at Fort Moultrie, from 1843 to 1846, and he explained that he wanted me as his right hand. He also indicated George H. Thomas, D. C. Buell, and Burnside, as the other three. Of course, I always wanted to go West, and was perfectly willing to go with Anderson, especially in a subordinate capacity. We agreed to call on the President on a subsequent day, to talk with him about it, and we did. It hardly seems probable that Mr. Lincoln should have come to Willard's Hotel to meet us, but my impression is that he did, and that General Anderson had some difficulty in prevailing on him to appoint George H. Thomas, a native of Virginia, to be brigadier-general, because so many Southern officers had already played false; but I was still more emphatic in my indorsement of him by reason of my talk with him at the time he crossed the Potomac with Patterson's army, when Mr. Lincoln promised to appoint him and to assign him to duty with General Anderson. In this interview with Mr. Lincoln, I also explained to him my extreme desire to serve in a subordinate capacity, and in no event to be left in a superior command. He promised me this with promptness, making the jocular remark that his chief trouble was to find places for the too many generals who wanted to be at the head of affairs, to command armies, etc.

The official order is dated—

[Special Order No. 114.]

HEADQUARTERS OF THE ARMY, ⎫
WASHINGTON, *August* 24, 1861.⎰

The following assignment is made of the general officers of the volunteer service, whose appointment was announced in General Orders No. 62, from the War Department:

To the Department of the Cumberland, Brigadier-General Robert Anderson commanding:

Brigadier-General W. T. Sherman,
Brigadier-General George H. Thomas.

. . . .

By command of Lieutenant-General Scott:

E. D. TOWNSEND, *Assistant Adjutant-General.*

After some days, I was relieved in command of my brigade and post by Brigadier General Fitz-John Porter, and at once took my departure for Cincinnati, Ohio, *via* Cresson, Pennsylvania, where General Anderson was with his family; and he, Thomas, and I, met by appointment at the house of his brother, Larz Anderson, Esq., in Cincinnati. We were there on the 1st and 2d of September, when several prominent gentlemen of Kentucky met us to discuss the situation, among whom were Jackson, Harlan, Speed, and others. At that time, William Nelson, an officer of the navy, had been commissioned a brigadier-general of volunteers, and had his camp at Dick Robinson, a few miles beyond the Kentucky River, south of Nicholasville; and Brigadier-General L. H. Rousseau had another camp at Jeffersonville, opposite Louisville. The State Legislature was in session at Frankfort, and was ready to take definite action as soon as General Anderson was prepared, for the State was threatened with invasion from Tennessee, by two forces: one from the direction of Nashville, commanded by Generals Albert Sidney Johnston and Buckner; and the other from the direction of Cumberland Gap, commanded by Generals Crittenden and Zollicoffer. General Anderson saw that he had not force enough to resist these two columns, and concluded to send me in person for help to Indianapolis and Springfield, to confer with the Governors of

Indiana, and Illinois, and to General Fremont, who commanded in St. Louis.

McClellan and Fremont were the two men toward whom the country looked as the great Union leaders, and toward them were streaming the newly-raised regiments of infantry and cavalry, and batteries of artillery; nobody seeming to think of the intervening link covered by Kentucky. While I was to make this tour, Generals Anderson and Thomas were to go to Louisville and initiate the department. None of us had a staff, or any of the machinery for organizing an army, and, indeed, we had no army to organize. Anderson was empowered to raise regiments in Kentucky, and to commission a few brigadier-generals.

At Indianapolis I found Governor Morton and all the State officials busy in equipping and providing for the new regiments, and my object was to divert some of them toward Kentucky; but they were called for as fast as they were mustered in, either for the army of McClellan or Fremont. At Springfield also I found the same general activity and zeal, Governor Yates busy in providing for his men; but these men also had been promised to Fremont. I then went on to St. Louis, where all was seeming activity, bustle, and preparation. Meeting R. M. Renick at the Planters' House (where I stopped), I inquired where I could find General Fremont. Renick said, "What do you want with General Fremont?" I said I had come to see him on business; and he added, "You don't suppose that he will see such as you?" and went on to retail all the scandal of the day: that Fremont was a great potentate, surrounded by sentries and guards; that he had a more showy court than any real king; that he kept senators, governors, and the first citizens, dancing attendance for days and weeks before granting an audience, etc.; that if I expected to see him on business, I would have to make my application in writing, and submit to a close scrutiny by his chief of staff and by his civil surroundings. Of course I laughed at all this, and renewed my simple inquiry as to where was his office, and was informed that he resided and had his office at Major Brant's new house on Chouteau Avenue. It was then late in the afternoon, and I concluded to wait till the next morning; but that night I received a dispatch from General Anderson in

Louisville to hurry back, as events were pressing, and he needed me.

Accordingly, I rose early next morning before daybreak, got breakfast with the early railroad-passengers, and about sunrise was at the gate of General Fremont's headquarters. A sentinel with drawn sabre paraded up and down in front of the house. I had on my undress uniform indicating my rank, and inquired of the sentinel, "Is General Fremont up?" He answered, "I don't know." Seeing that he was a soldier by his bearing, I spoke in a sharp, emphatic voice, "Then find out." He called for the corporal of the guard, and soon a fine-looking German sergeant came, to whom I addressed the same inquiry. He in turn did not know, and I bade him find out, as I had immediate and important business with the general. The sergeant entered the house by the front-basement door, and after ten or fifteen minutes the main front-door above was slowly opened from the inside, and who should appear but my old San Francisco acquaintance Isaiah C. Woods, whom I had not seen or heard of since his flight to Australia, at the time of the failure of Adams & Co. in 1855! He ushered me in hastily, closed the door, and conducted me into the office on the right of the hall. We were glad to meet, after so long and eventful an interval, and mutually inquired after our respective families and special acquaintances. I found that he was a commissioned officer, a major on duty with Fremont, and Major Eaton, now of the Paymaster's Department, was in the same office with him. I explained to them that I had come from General Anderson, and wanted to confer with General Fremont in person. Woods left me, but soon returned, said the general would see me in a very few minutes, and within ten minutes I was shown across the hall into the large parlor, where General Fremont received me very politely. We had met before, as early as 1847, in California, and I had also seen him several times when he was senator. I then in a rapid manner ran over all the points of interest in General Anderson's new sphere of action, hoped he would spare us from the new levies what troops he could, and generally act in concert with us. He told me that his first business would be to drive the rebel General Price and his army out of Missouri, when he would turn his attention down the Mississippi. He asked my opinion about the various kinds of field-artillery which manufacturers were thrusting on him, especially the then newly-invented James gun, and afterward our conversation took a wide turn about the character of the principal citizens of St. Louis, with whom I was well acquainted.

Telling General Fremont that I had been summoned to Louisville, and that I should leave in the first train, viz., at 3 P.M., I took my leave of him. Returning to Wood's office, I found there two more Californians, viz., Messrs. Palmer and Haskell, so I felt that, while Fremont might be suspicious of others, he allowed free ingress to his old California acquaintances.

Returning to the Planters' House, I heard of Beard, another Californian, a Mormon, who had the contract for the line of redoubts which Fremont had ordered to be constructed around the city, before he would take his departure for the interior of the State; and while I stood near the office-counter, I saw old Baron Steinberger, a prince among our early California adventurers, come in and look over the register. I avoided him on purpose, but his presence in St. Louis recalled the maxim, "Where the vultures are, there is a carcass close by;" and I suspected that the profitable contracts of the quartermaster, McKinstry, had drawn to St. Louis some of the most enterprising men of California. I suspect they can account for the fact that, in a very short time, Fremont fell from his high estate in Missouri, by reason of frauds, or supposed frauds, in the administration of the affairs of his command.

I left St. Louis that afternoon and reached Louisville the next morning. I found General Anderson quartered at the Louisville Hotel, and he had taken a dwelling house on —— Street as an office. Captain O. D. Greene was his adjutant-general, Lieutenant Throckmorton his aide, and Captain Prime, of the Engineer Corps, was on duty with him. General George H. Thomas had been dispatched to camp Dick Robinson, to relieve Nelson.

The city was full of all sorts of rumors. The Legislature, moved by considerations purely of a political nature, had taken the step, whatever it was, that amounted to an adherence to the Union, instead of joining the already-seceded

States. This was universally known to be the signal for action. For it we were utterly unprepared, whereas the rebels were fully prepared. General Sidney Johnston immediately crossed into Kentucky, and advanced as far as Bowling Green, which he began to fortify, and thence dispatched General Buckner with a division forward toward Louisville; General Zollicoffer, in like manner, entered the State and advanced as far as Somerset. On the day I reached Louisville the excitement ran high. It was known that Columbus, Kentucky, had been occupied, September 7th, by a strong rebel force, under Generals Pillow and Polk, and that General Grant had moved from Cairo and occupied Paducah in force on the 6th. Many of the rebel families expected Buckner to reach Louisville at any moment. That night, General Anderson sent for me, and I found with him Mr. Guthrie, president of the Louisville & Nashville Railroad, who had in his hands a dispatch to the effect that the bridge across the Rolling Fork of Salt Creek, less than thirty miles out, had been burned, and that Buckner's force, *en route* for Louisville, had been detained beyond Green River by a train thrown from the track. We learned afterward that a man named Bird had displaced a rail on purpose to throw the train off the track, and thereby give us time.

Mr. Guthrie explained that in the ravine just beyond Salt Creek were several high and important trestles which, if destroyed, would take months to replace, and General Anderson thought it well worth the effort to save them. Also, on Muldraugh's Hill beyond, was a strong position, which had in former years been used as the site for the State "Camp of Instruction," and we all supposed that General Buckner, who was familiar with the ground, was aiming for a position there, from which to operate on Louisville.

All the troops we had to counteract Buckner were Rousseau's Legion, and a few Home Guards in Louisville. The former were still encamped across the river at Jeffersonville; so General Anderson ordered me to go over, and with them, and such Home Guards as we could collect, make the effort to secure possession of Muldraugh's Hill before Buckner could reach it. I took Captain Prime with me, and crossed over to Rousseau's camp. The long-roll was beaten, and within an hour the men, to the number of about one thousand, were marching for the ferry-boat and for the Nashville depot. Meantime General Anderson had sent to collect some Home Guards, and Mr. Guthrie to get the trains ready. It was after midnight before we began to move. The trains proceeded slowly, and it was daybreak when we reached Lebanon Junction, twenty-six miles out, where we disembarked, and marched to the bridge over Salt River, which we found had been burnt; whether to prevent Buckner coming into Louisville, or us from going out, was not clear. Rousseau's Legion forded the stream and marched up to the State Camp of Instruction, finding the high trestles all secure. The railroad-hands went to work at once to rebuild the bridge. I remained a couple of days at Lebanon Junction, during which General Anderson forwarded two regiments of volunteers that had come to him. Before the bridge was done we advanced the whole camp to the summit of Muldraugh's Hill, just back of Elizabethtown. There I learned definitely that General Buckner had not crossed Green River at all, that General Sidney Johnston was fortifying Bowling Green, and preparing for a systematic advance into Kentucky, of which he was a native, and with whose people and geography he must have been familiar.

As fast as fresh troops reached Louisville, they were sent out to me at Muldraugh's Hill, where I was endeavoring to put them into shape for service, and by the 1st of October I had the equivalent of a division of two brigades preparing to move forward toward Green River. The daily correspondence between General Anderson and myself satisfied me that the worry and harassment at Louisville were exhausting his strength and health, and that he would soon leave. On a telegraphic summons from him, about the 5th of October, I went down to Louisville, when General Anderson said he could not stand the mental torture of his command any longer, and that he must go away, or it would kill him. On the 8th of October he actually published an order relinquishing the command, and, by reason of my seniority, I had no alternative but to assume command, though much against the grain, and in direct violation of Mr. Lincoln's promise to me. I am certain that, in my earliest communication to the War Department, I renewed the expression of my wish to remain in a subordinate position, and that I received the assurance that Brigadier-General Buell would soon arrive from California, and would be sent to relieve me.

By that time I had become pretty familiar with the geography and the general resources of Kentucky. We had parties all over the State raising regiments and companies; but it was manifest that the young men were generally inclined to the cause of the South, while the older men of property wanted to be let alone—i. e., to remain neutral. As to a forward movement that fall, it was simply impracticable; for we were forced to use divergent lines, leading our columns farther and farther apart; and all I could attempt was to go on and collect force and material at the two points already chosen, viz., Dick Robinson and Elizabethtown. General George H. Thomas still continued to command the former, and on the 12th of October I dispatched Brigadier-General A. McD. McCook to command the latter, which had been moved forward to Nolin Creek, fifty-two miles out of Louisville, toward Bowling Green. Staff-officers began to arrive to relieve us of the constant drudgery which, up to that time, had been forced on General Anderson and myself; and these were all good men. Colonel Thomas Swords, quartermaster, arrived on the 13th; Paymaster Larned on the 14th; and Lieutenant Smyzer, Fifth Artillery, acting ordnance-officer, on the 20th; Captain Symonds was already on duty as the commissary of subsistence; Captain O. D. Greene was the adjutant-general, and completed a good working staff.

The everlasting worry of citizens complaining of every petty delinquency of a soldier, and forcing themselves forward to discuss politics, made the position of a commanding general no sinecure. I continued to strengthen the two corps forward and their routes of supply; all the time expecting that Sidney Johnston, who was a real general, and who had as correct information of our situation as I had, would unite his force with Zollicoffer, and fall on Thomas at Dick Robinson, or McCook at Nolin. Had he done so in October, 1861, he could have walked into Louisville, and the vital part of the population would have hailed him as a deliverer. Why he did not, was to me a mystery then and is now; for I know that he saw the move, and had his wagons loaded up at one time for a start toward Frankfort, passing between our two camps. Conscious of our weakness, I was unnecessarily unhappy, and doubtless exhibited it too much to those near me; but it did seem to me that the Government at Washington, intent on the larger preparations of Fremont in Missouri and McClellan in Washington, actually ignored us in Kentucky.

About this time, say the middle of October, I received notice, by telegraph, that the Secretary of War, Mr. Cameron (then in St. Louis), would visit me at Louisville, on his way back to Washington. I was delighted to have an opportunity to properly represent the actual state of affairs, and got Mr. Guthrie to go with me across to Jeffersonville, to meet the Secretary of War and escort him to Louisville. The train was behind time, but Mr. Guthrie and I waited till it actually arrived. Mr. Cameron was attended by Adjutant-General Lorenzo Thomas, and six or seven gentlemen who turned out to be newspaper reporters. Mr. Cameron's first inquiry was, when he could start for Cincinnati, saying that, as he had been detained at St. Louis so long, it was important he should hurry on to Washington. I explained that the regular mail-boat would leave very soon—viz., at 12 M.—but I begged him to come over to Louisville; that I wanted to see him on business as important as any in Washington, and hoped he would come and spend at least a day with us. He asked if every thing was not well with us, and I told him far from it; that things were actually bad, as bad as bad could be. This seemed to surprise him, and Mr. Guthrie added his persuasion to mine; when Mr. Cameron, learning that he could leave Louisville by rail *via* Frankfort next morning early, and make the same connections at Cincinnati, consented to go with us to Louisville, with the distinct understanding that he must leave early the next morning for Washington.

We accordingly all took hacks, crossed the river by the ferry, and drove to the Galt House, where I was then staying. Brigadier-General T. J. Wood had come down from Indianapolis by the same train, and was one of the party. We all proceeded to my room on the first floor of the Galt House, where our excellent landlord, Silas Miller, Esq., sent us a good lunch and something to drink. Mr. Cameron was not well, and lay on my bed, but joined in the general conversation. He and his party seemed to be full of the particulars of the developments in St. Louis of some of Fremont's extravagant contracts and expenses, which were the occasion of Cameron's trip to St. Louis, and which finally resulted in Fremont's being relieved, first by General Hunter, and after by General H. W. Halleck.

After some general conversation, Mr. Cameron called to me, "Now, General Sherman, tell us of your troubles." I said I preferred not to discuss business with so many strangers present. He said, "They are all friends, all members of my family, and you may speak your mind freely and without restraint." I am sure I stepped to the door, locked it to prevent intrusion, and then fully and fairly represented the state of affairs in Kentucky, especially the situation and numbers of my troops. I complained that the new levies of Ohio and Indiana were diverted East and West, and we got scarcely any thing; that our forces at Nolin and Dick Robinson were powerless for invasion, and only tempting to a general such as we believed Sidney Johnston to be; that, if Johnston chose, he could march to Louisville any day. Cameron exclaimed: "You astonish me! Our informants, the Kentucky Senators and members of Congress, claim that they have in Kentucky plenty of men, and all they want are arms and money." I then said it was not true; for the young men were arming and going out openly in broad daylight to the rebel camps, provided with good horses and guns by their fathers, who were at best "neutral;" and as to arms, he had, in Washington, promised General Anderson forty thousand of the best Springfield muskets, instead of which we had received only about twelve thousand Belgian muskets, which the Governor of Pennsylvania had refused, as had also the Governor of Ohio, but which had been adjudged good enough for Kentucky. I asserted that volunteer colonels raising regiments in various parts of the State had come to Louisville for arms, and when they saw what I had to offer had scorned to receive them—to confirm the truth of which I appealed to Mr. Guthrie, who said that every word I had spoken was true, and he repeated what I had often heard him say, that no man who owned a slave or a mule in Kentucky could be trusted.

Mr. Cameron appeared alarmed at what was said, and

turned to Adjutant-General L. Thomas, to inquire if he knew
of any troops available, that had not been already assigned.
He mentioned Negley's Pennsylvania Brigade, at Pittsburg,
and a couple of other regiments that were then *en route* for St.
Louis. Mr. Cameron ordered him to divert these to Louisville, and Thomas made the telegraphic orders on the spot.
He further promised, on reaching Washington, to give us
more of his time and assistance.

In the general conversation which followed, I remember
taking a large map of the United States, and assuming the
people of the whole South to be in rebellion, that our task
was to subdue them, showed that McClellan was on the left,
having a frontage of less than a hundred miles, and Fremont
the right, about the same; whereas I, the centre, had from the
Big Sandy to Paducah, over three hundred miles of frontier;
that McClellan had a hundred thousand men, Fremont sixty
thousand, whereas to me had only been allotted about eighteen thousand. I argued that, for the purpose of defense, we
should have sixty thousand men at once, and for offense,
would need two hundred thousand, before we were done.
Mr. Cameron, who still lay on the bed, threw up his hands
and exclaimed, "Great God! where are they to come from?" I
asserted that there were plenty of men at the North, ready
and willing to come, if he would only accept their services;
for it was notorious that regiments had been formed in all the
Northwestern States, whose services had been refused by the
War Department, on the ground that they would not be
needed. We discussed all these matters fully, in the most
friendly spirit, and I thought I had aroused Mr. Cameron to a
realization of the great war that was before us, and was in fact
upon us. I heard him tell General Thomas to make a note
of our conversation, that he might attend to my requests
on reaching Washington. We all spent the evening together
agreeably in conversation, many Union citizens calling to pay
their respects, and the next morning early we took the train
for Frankfort; Mr. Cameron and party going on to Cincinnati
and Washington, and I to Camp Dick Robinson to see General Thomas and the troops there.

I found General Thomas in a tavern, with most of his regiments camped about him. He had sent a small force some

miles in advance toward Cumberland Gap, under Brigadier-General Schoepf. Remaining there a couple of days, I returned to Louisville; on the 22d of October, General Negley's brigade arrived in boats from Pittsburg, was sent out to Camp Nolin; and the Thirty-seventh Indiana, Colonel Hazzard, and Second Minnesota, Colonel Van Cleve, also reached Louisville by rail, and were posted at Elizabethtown and Lebanon Junction. These were the same troops which had been ordered by Mr. Cameron when at Louisville, and they were all that I received thereafter, prior to my leaving Kentucky. On reaching Washington, Mr. Cameron called on General Thomas, as he himself afterward told me, to submit his memorandum of events during his absence, and in that memorandum was mentioned my *insane* request for two hundred thousand men. By some newspaper man this was seen and published, and, before I had the least conception of it, I was universally published throughout the country as "insane, crazy," etc. Without any knowledge, however, of this fact, I had previously addressed to the Adjutant-General of the army at Washington this letter:

HEADQUARTERS DEPARTMENT OF THE CUMBERLAND, }
LOUISVILLE, KENTUCKY, *October* 22, 1861. }

To General L. THOMAS, *Adjutant-General, Washington, D. C.*

SIR: On my arrival at Camp Dick Robinson, I found General Thomas had stationed a Kentucky regiment at Rock Castle Hill, beyond a river of the same name, and had sent an Ohio and an Indiana regiment forward in support. He was embarrassed for transportation, and I authorized him to hire teams, and to move his whole force nearer to his advance-guard, so as to support it, as he had information of the approach of Zollicoffer toward London. I have just heard from him, that he had sent forward General Schoepf with Colonel Wolford's cavalry, Colonel Steadman's Ohio regiment, and a battery of artillery, followed on a succeeding day by a Tennessee brigade. He had still two Kentucky regiments, the Thirty-eighth Ohio and another battery of artillery, with which he was to follow yesterday. This force, if concentrated, should be strong enough for the purpose; at all events, it is all he had or I could give him.

I explained to you fully, when here, the supposed position of our adversaries, among which was a force in the valley of Big Sandy, supposed to be advancing on Paris, Kentucky. General Nelson at

Maysville was instructed to collect all the men he could, and Colonel Gill's regiment of Ohio Volunteers. Colonel Harris was already in position at Olympian Springs, and a regiment lay at Lexington, which I ordered to his support. This leaves the line of Thomas's operations exposed, but I cannot help it. I explained so fully to yourself and the Secretary of War the condition of things, that I can add nothing new until further developments. You know my views that this great centre of our field is too weak, far too weak, and I have begged and implored till I dare not say more.

Buckner still is beyond Green River. He sent a detachment of his men, variously estimated at from two to four thousand toward Greensburg. General Ward, with about one thousand men, retreated to Campbellsburg, where he called to his assistance some partially-formed regiments to the number of about two thousand. The enemy did not advance, and General Ward was at last dates at Campbellsburg. The officers charged with raising regiments must of necessity be near their homes to collect men, and for this reason are out of position; but at or near Greensburg and Lebanon, I desire to assemble as large a force of the Kentucky Volunteers as possible. This organization is necessarily irregular, but the necessity is so great that I must have them, and therefore have issued to them arms and clothing during the process of formation. This has facilitated their enlistment; inasmuch as the Legislature has provided money for organizing the Kentucky Volunteers, and intrusted its disbursement to a board of loyal gentlemen, I have endeavored to coöperate with them to hasten the formation of these corps.

The great difficulty is, and has been, that as volunteers offer, we have not arms and clothing to give them. The arms sent us are, as you already know, European muskets of uncouth pattern, which the volunteers will not touch.

General McCook has now three brigades—Johnson's, Wood's, and Rousseau's. Negley's brigade arrived to-day, and will be sent out at once. The Minnesota regiment has also arrived, and will be sent forward. Hazzard's regiment of Indiana troops I have ordered to the mouth of Salt Creek, an important point on the turnpike-road leading to Elizabethtown.

I again repeat that our force here is out of all proportion to the importance of the position. Our defeat would be disastrous to the nation; and to expect of new men, who never bore arms, to do miracles, is not right.

I am, with much respect, yours truly,

W. T. SHERMAN, *Brigadier-General commanding.*

About this time my attention was drawn to the publication in all the Eastern papers, which of course was copied at the West, of the report that I was "crazy, insane, and mad," that "I had demanded two hundred thousand men for the defense of Kentucky;" and the authority given for this report was stated to be the Secretary of War himself, Mr. Cameron, who never, to my knowledge, took pains to affirm or deny it. My position was therefore simply unbearable, and it is probable I resented the cruel insult with language of intense feeling. Still I received no orders, no reënforcements, not a word of encouragement or relief. About November 1st, General Mc-Clellan was appointed commander-in-chief of all the armies in the field, and by telegraph called for a report from me. It is herewith given:

HEADQUARTERS DEPARTMENT OF THE CUMBERLAND, }
LOUISVILLE, KENTUCKY, *November* 4, 1861. }

General L. THOMAS, *Adjutant-General, Washington, D. C.*

SIR: In compliance with the telegraphic orders of General McClellan, received late last night, I submit this report of the forces in Kentucky, and of their condition.

The tabular statement shows the position of the several regiments. The camp at Nolin is at the present extremity of the Nashville Railroad. This force was thrown forward to meet the advance of Buckner's army, which then fell back to Green River, twenty-three miles beyond. These regiments were substantially without means of transportation, other than the railroad, which is guarded at all dangerous points, yet is liable to interruption at any moment, by the tearing up of a rail by the disaffected inhabitants or a hired enemy. These regiments are composed of good materials, but devoid of company officers of experience, and have been put under thorough drill since being in camp. They are generally well clad, and provided for. Beyond Green River, the enemy has masked his forces, and it is very difficult to ascertain even the approximate numbers. No pains have been spared to ascertain them, but without success, and it is well known that they far outnumber us. Depending, however, on the railroads to their rear for transportation, they have not thus far advanced this side of Green River, except in marauding parties. This is the proper line of advance, but will require a very large force, certainly fifty thousand men, as their railroad facilities south enable them to concentrate at

Munfordsville the entire strength of the South. General McCook's command is divided into four brigades, under Generals Wood, R. W. Johnson, Rousseau, and Negley.

General Thomas's line of operations is from Lexington, toward Cumberland Gap and Ford, which are occupied by a force of rebel Tennesseeans, under the command of Zollicoffer. Thomas occupies the position at London, in front of two roads which lead to the fertile part of Kentucky, the one by Richmond, and the other by Crab Orchard, with his reserve at Camp Dick Robinson, eight miles south of the Kentucky River. His provisions and stores go by railroad from Cincinnati to Nicholasville, and thence in wagons to his several regiments. He is forced to hire transportation.

Brigadier-General Nelson is operating by the line from Olympian Springs, east of Paris, on the Covington & Lexington Railroad, toward Prestonburg, in the valley of the Big Sandy, where is assembled a force of from twenty-five to thirty-five hundred rebel Kentuckians waiting reënforcements from Virginia. My last report from him was to October 28th, at which time he had Colonel Harris's Ohio Second, nine hundred strong; Colonel Norton's Twenty-first Ohio, one thousand; and Colonel Sill's Thirty-third Ohio, seven hundred and fifty strong; with two irregular Kentucky regiments, Colonels Marshall and Metcalf. These troops were on the road near Hazel Green and West Liberty, advancing toward Prestonburg.

Upon an inspection of the map, you will observe these are all divergent lines, but rendered necessary, from the fact that our enemies choose them as places of refuge from pursuit, where they can receive assistance from neighboring States. Our lines are all too weak, probably with the exception of that to Prestonburg. To strengthen these, I am thrown on the raw levies of Ohio and Indiana, who arrive in detachments, perfectly fresh from the country, and loaded down with baggage, also upon the Kentuckians, who are slowly forming regiments all over the State, at points remote from danger, and whom it will be almost impossible to assemble together. The organization of this latter force is, by the laws of Kentucky, under the control of a military board of citizens, at the capital, Frankfort, and they think they will be enabled to have fifteen regiments toward the middle of this month, but I doubt it, and deem it unsafe to rely on them. There are four regiments forming in the neighborhood of Owensboro', near the mouth of Green River, who are doing good service, also in the neighborhood of Campbellsville, but it is unsafe to rely on troops so suddenly armed and equipped.

They are not yet clothed or uniformed. I know well you will think our force too widely distributed, but we are forced to it by the attitude of our enemies, whose force and numbers the country never has and probably never will comprehend.

I am told that my estimate of troops needed for this line, viz., two hundred thousand, has been construed to my prejudice, and therefore leave it for the future. This is the great centre on which our enemies can concentrate whatever force is not employed elsewhere. Detailed statement of present force inclosed with this.

With great respect, your obedient servant,

W. T. SHERMAN, *Brigadier-General commanding.*

BRIGADIER-GENERAL M^CCOOK'S CAMP, AT NOLIN, FIFTY-TWO
MILES FROM LOUISVILLE, KENTUCKY, NOVEMBER 4, 1861.

First Brigade (General ROUSSEAU).—Third Kentucky, Colonel Bulkley; Fourth Kentucky, Colonel Whittaker; First Cavalry, Colonel Board; Stone's battery; two companies Nineteenth United States Infantry, and two companies Fifteenth United States Infantry, Captain Gilman.

Second Brigade (General T. J. WOOD).—Thirty-eighth Indiana, Colonel Scribner; Thirty-ninth Indiana, Colonel Harrison; Thirtieth Indiana, Colonel Bass; Twenty-ninth Indiana, Colonel Miller.

Third Brigade (General JOHNSON).—Forty-ninth Ohio, Colonel Gibson; Fifteenth Ohio, Colonel Dickey; Thirty-fourth Illinois, Colonel King; Thirty-second Indiana, Colonel Willach.

Fourth Brigade (General NEGLEY).—Seventy-seventh Pennsylvania, Colonel Hambright; Seventy-eighth Pennsylvania, Colonel Sinnell; Seventy-ninth Pennsylvania, Colonel Stambaugh; Battery ——, Captain Mueller.

Camp Dick Robinson (General G. H. THOMAS).— —— Kentucky, Colonel Bramlette; —— Kentucky, Colonel Fry; —— Kentucky Cavalry, Colonel Woolford; Fourteenth Ohio, Colonel Steadman; First Artillery, Colonel Barnett; Third Ohio, Colonel Carter; —— East Tennessee, Colonel Byrd.

Bardstown, Kentucky.—Tenth Indiana, Colonel Manson.

Crab Orchard.—Thirty-third Indiana, Colonel Coburn.

Jeffersonville, Indiana.—Thirty-fourth Indiana, Colonel Steele; Thirty-sixth Indiana, Colonel Grose; First Wisconsin, Colonel Starkweather.

Mouth of Salt River.—Ninth Michigan, Colonel Duffield; Thirty-seventh Indiana, Colonel Hazzard.

Lebanon Junction.—Second Minnesota, Colonel Van Cleve.

Olympian Springs. —Second Ohio, Colonel Harris.
Cynthiana, Kentucky. —Thirty-fifth Ohio, Colonel Vandever.
Nicholasville, Kentucky. —Twenty-first Ohio, Colonel Norton; Thirty-eighth Ohio, Colonel Bradley.
Big Hill. —Seventeenth Ohio, Colonel Connell.
Colesburg. —Twenty-fourth Illinois, Colonel Hecker.
Elizabethtown, Kentucky. —Nineteenth Illinois, Colonel Turchin.
Owensboro' or Henderson. —Thirty-first Indiana, Colonel Cruft; Colonel Edwards, forming Rock Castle; Colonel Boyle, Harrodsburg; Colonel Barney, Irvine; Colonel Hazzard, Burksville; Colonel Haskins, Somerset.

And, in order to conclude this subject, I also add copies of two telegraphic dispatches, sent for General McClellan's use about the same time, which are all the official letters received at his headquarters, as certified by the Adjutant-General, L. Thomas, in a letter of February 1, 1862, in answer to an application of my brother, Senator John Sherman, and on which I was adjudged insane:

LOUISVILLE, *November* 3, 10 P.M.
To General McCLELLAN, *Washington, D. C.:*
Dispatch just received. We are forced to operate on three lines, all dependent on railroads of doubtful safety, requiring strong guards. From Paris to Prestonburg, three Ohio regiments and some militia—enemy variously reported from thirty-five hundred to seven thousand. From Lexington toward Cumberland Gap, Brigadier-General Thomas, one Indiana and five Ohio regiments, two Kentucky and two Tennessee; hired wagons and badly clad. Zollicoffer, at Cumberland Ford, about seven thousand. Lee reported on the way with Virginia reënforcements. In front of Louisville, fifty-two miles, McCook, with four brigades of about thirteen thousand, with four regiments to guard the railroad, at all times in danger. Enemy along the railroad from Green River to Bowling Green, Nashville, and Clarksville. Buckner, Hardee, Sidney Johnston, Polk, and Pillow, the two former in immediate command, the force as large as they want or can subsist, from twenty-five to thirty thousand. Bowling Green strongly fortified. Our forces too small to do good, and too large to sacrifice.

W. T. SHERMAN, *Brigadier-General.*

HEADQUARTERS DEPARTMENT OF THE CUMBERLAND, ⎫
LOUISVILLE, KENTUCKY, *November* 6, 1861. ⎭

General L. THOMAS, *Adjutant-General.*

SIR: General McClellan telegraphs me to report to him daily the situation of affairs here. The country is so large that it is impossible to give clear and definite views. Our enemies have a terrible advantage in the fact that in our midst, in our camps, and along our avenues of travel, they have active partisans, farmers and business-men, who seemingly pursue their usual calling, but are in fact spies. They report all our movements and strength, while we can procure information only by circuitous and unreliable means. I inclose you the copy of an intercepted letter, which is but the type of others. Many men from every part of the State are now enrolled under Buckner— have gone to him—while ours have to be raised in neighborhoods, and cannot be called together except at long notice. These volunteers are being organized under the laws of the State, and the 10th of November is fixed for the time of consolidating them into companies and regiments. Many of them are armed by the United States as home guards, and many by General Anderson and myself, because of the necessity of being armed to guard their camps against internal enemies. Should we be overwhelmed, they would scatter, and their arms and clothing will go to the enemy, furnishing the very material they so much need. We should have here a very large force, sufficient to give confidence to the Union men of the ability to do what should be done—possess ourselves of all the State. But all see and feel we are brought to a stand-still, and this produces doubt and alarm. With our present force it would be simple madness to cross Green River, and yet hesitation may be as fatal. In like manner the other columns are in peril, not so much in front as rear, the railroads over which our stores must pass being much exposed. I have the Nashville Railroad guarded by three regiments, yet it is far from being safe; and, the moment actual hostilities commence, these roads will be interrupted, and we will be in a dilemma. To meet this in part I have put a cargo of provisions at the mouth of Salt River, guarded by two regiments. All these detachments weaken the main force, and endanger the whole. Do not conclude, as before, that I exaggerate the facts. They are as stated, and the future looks as dark as possible. It would be better if some man of sanguine mind were here, for I am forced to order according to my convictions. Yours truly,

W. T. SHERMAN, *Brigadier-General commanding.*

After the war was over, General Thomas J. Wood, then in command of the district of Vicksburg, prepared a statement addressed to the public, describing the interview with the Secretary of War, which he calls a "Council of War." I did not then deem it necessary to renew a matter which had been swept into oblivion by the war itself; but, as it is evidence by an eye-witness, it is worthy of insertion here.

STATEMENT.

On the 11th of October, 1861, the writer, who had been personally on mustering duty in Indiana, was appointed a brigadier-general of volunteers, and ordered to report to General Sherman, then in command of the Department of the Cumberland, with his headquarters at Louisville, having succeeded General Robert Anderson. When the writer was about leaving Indianapolis to proceed to Louisville, Mr. Cameron, returning from his famous visit of inspection to General Fremont's department, at St. Louis, Missouri, arrived at Indianapolis, and announced his intention to visit General Sherman.

The writer was invited to accompany the party to Louisville. Taking the early morning train from Indianapolis to Louisville on the 16th of October, 1861, the party arrived in Jeffersonville shortly after mid-day. General Sherman met the party in Jeffersonville, and accompanied it to the Galt House, in Louisville, the hotel at which he was stopping.

During the afternoon General Sherman informed the writer that a council of war was to be held immediately in his private room in the hotel, and desired him to be present at the council. General Sherman and the writer proceeded directly to the room. The writer entered the room first, and observed in it Mr. Cameron, Adjutant-General L. Thomas, and some other persons, all of whose names he did not know, but whom he recognized as being of Mr. Cameron's party. The name of one of the party the writer had learned, which he remembers as Wilkinson, or Wilkerson, and who he understood was a writer for the *New York Tribune* newspaper. The Hon. James Guthrie was also in the room, having been invited, on account of his eminent position as a citizen of Kentucky, his high civic reputation, and his well-known devotion to the Union, to meet the Secretary of War in the council. When General Sherman entered the room he closed the door, and turned the key in the lock.

Before entering on the business of the meeting, General Sherman remarked substantially: "Mr. Cameron, we have met here to discuss matters and interchange views which should be known only by persons high in the confidence of the Government. There are persons present whom I do not know, and I desire to know, before opening the business of the council, whether they are persons who may be properly allowed to hear the views which I have to submit to you." Mr. Cameron replied, with some little testiness of manner, that the persons referred to belonged to his party, and there was no objection to their knowing whatever might be communicated to him.

Certainly the legitimate and natural conclusion from this remark of Mr. Cameron's was that whatever views might be submitted by General Sherman would be considered under the protection of the seal of secrecy, and would not be divulged to the public till all apprehension of injurious consequences from such disclosure had passed. And it may be remarked, further, that justice to General Sherman required that if, at any future time, his conclusions as to the amount of force necessary to conduct the operations committed to his charge should be made public, the grounds on which his conclusions were based should be made public at the same time.

Mr. Cameron then asked General Sherman what his plans were. To this General Sherman replied that he had no plans; that no sufficient force had been placed at his disposition with which to devise any plan of operations; that, before a commanding general could project a plan of campaign, he must know what amount of force he would have to operate with.

The general added that he had views which he would be happy to submit for the consideration of the Secretary. Mr. Cameron desired to hear General Sherman's views.

General Sherman began by giving his opinion of the people of Kentucky, and the then condition of the State. He remarked that he believed a very large majority of the people of Kentucky were thoroughly devoted to the Union, and loyal to the Government, and that the Unionists embraced almost all the older and more substantial men in the State; but, unfortunately, there was no organization nor arms among the Union men; that the rebel minority, thoroughly vindictive in its sentiments, was organized and armed (this having been done in advance by their leaders), and, beyond the reach of the Federal forces, overawed and prevented the Union men from organizing; that, in his opinion, if Federal protection were extended throughout the State to the Union men, a large force could be raised for the service of the Government.

General Sherman next presented a *résumé* of the information in his possession as to the number of the rebel troops in Kentucky. Commencing with the force at Columbus, Kentucky, the reports varied, giving the strength from ten to twenty thousand. It was commanded by Lieutenant-General Polk. General Sherman fixed it at the lowest estimate; say, ten thousand. The force at Bowling Green, commanded by General A. S. Johnston, supported by Hardee, Buckner, and others, was variously estimated at from eighteen to thirty thousand. General Sherman estimated this force at the lowest figures given to it by his information—eighteen thousand.

He explained that, for purposes of defense, these two forces ought, owing to the facility with which troops might be transported from one to the other, by the net-work of railroads in Middle and West Tennessee, to be considered almost as one. General Sherman remarked, also, on the facility with which reënforcements could be transported by railroad to Bowling Green, from the other rebellious States.

The third organized body of rebel troops was in Eastern Kentucky, under General Zollicoffer, estimated, according to the most reliable information, at six thousand men. This force threatened a descent, if unrestrained, on the blue-grass region of Kentucky, including the cities of Lexington, and Frankfort, the capital of the State; and if successful in its primary movements, as it would gather head as it advanced, might endanger the safety of Cincinnati.

General Sherman said that the information in his possession indicated an intention, on the part of the rebels, of a general and grand advance toward the Ohio River. He further expressed the opinion that, if such advance should be made, and not checked, the rebel force would be swollen by at least twenty thousand recruits from the disloyalists in Kentucky. His low computation of the organized rebel soldiers then in Kentucky fixed the strength at about thirty-five thousand. Add twenty thousand for reënforcements gained in Kentucky, to say nothing of troops drawn from other rebel States, and the effective rebel force in the State, at a low estimate, would be fifty-five thousand men.

General Sherman explained forcibly how largely the difficulties of suppressing the rebellion would be enhanced, if the rebels should be allowed to plant themselves firmly, with strong fortifications, at commanding points on the Ohio River. It would be facile for them to carry the war thence into the loyal States north of the river.

To resist an advance of the rebels, General Sherman stated that he did not have at that time in Kentucky more than some twelve to fourteen thousand effective men. The bulk of this force was posted at camp Nolin, on the Louisville & Nashville Railway, fifty miles south of Louisville. A part of it was in Eastern Kentucky, under General George H. Thomas, and a very small force was in the lower valley of Green River.

This disposition of the force had been made for the double pur-

pose of watching and checking the rebels, and protecting the raising
and organization of troops among the Union men of Kentucky.

Having explained the situation from the defensive point of
view, General Sherman proceeded to consider it from the offensive
stand-point. The Government had undertaken to suppress the rebellion; the *onus faciendi*, therefore, rested on the Government.
The rebellion could never be put down, the authority of the paramount Government asserted, and the union of the States declared
perpetual, by force of arms, by maintaining the defensive; to accomplish these grand desiderata, it was absolutely necessary the Government should adopt, and maintain until the rebellion was crushed, the
offensive.

For the purpose of expelling the rebels from Kentucky, General
Sherman said that at least sixty thousand soldiers were necessary.
Considering that the means of accomplishment must always be pro-
portioned to the end to be achieved, and bearing in mind the array
of rebel force then in Kentucky, every sensible man must admit that
the estimate of the force given by General Sherman, for driving the
rebels out of the State, and reëstablishing and maintaining the authority of the Government, was a very low one. The truth is that,
before the rebels were driven from Kentucky, many more than sixty
thousand soldiers were sent into the State.

Ascending from the consideration of the narrow question of the
political and military situation in Kentucky, and the extent of force
necessary to redeem the State from rebel thraldom, forecasting in his
sagacious intellect the grand and daring operations which, three
years afterward, he realized in a campaign, taken in its entirety, without a parallel in modern times, General Sherman expressed the opinion that, to carry the war to the Gulf of Mexico, and destroy all
armed opposition to the Government, in the entire Mississippi Valley, at least two hundred thousand troops were absolutely requisite.

So soon as General Sherman had concluded the expression of his
views, Mr. Cameron asked, with much warmth and apparent irrita-
tion, "Where do you suppose, General Sherman, all this force is to
come from?" General Sherman replied that he did not know; that it
was not his duty to raise, organize, and put the necessary military
force into the field; that duty pertained to the War Department. His
duty was to organize campaigns and command the troops after they
had been put into the field.

At this point of the proceedings, General Sherman suggested that
it might be agreeable to the Secretary to hear the views of Mr. Guthrie. Thus appealed to, Mr. Guthrie said he did not consider himself,
being a civilian, competent to give an opinion as to the extent of

force necessary to carry the war to the Gulf of Mexico; but, being well informed of the condition of things in Kentucky, he indorsed fully General Sherman's opinion of the force required to drive the rebels out of the State.

The foregoing is a circumstantial account of the deliberations of the council that were of any importance.

A good deal of desultory conversation followed, on immaterial matters; and some orders were issued by telegraph, by the Secretary of War, for some small reënforcements to be sent to Kentucky immediately, from Pennsylvania and Indiana.

A short time after the council was held—the exact time is not now remembered by the writer—an imperfect narrative of it appeared in the *New York Tribune.* This account announced to the public the conclusions uttered by General Sherman in the council, without giving the reasons on which his conclusions were based. The unfairness of this course to General Sherman needs no comment. All military men were shocked by the gross breach of faith which had been committed.

TH. J. WOOD, *Major-General Volunteers.*
VICKSBURG, MISSISSIPPI, *August* 24, 1866.

Brigadier-General Don Carlos Buell arrived at Louisville about the middle of November, with orders to relieve me, and I was transferred for duty to the Department of the Missouri, and ordered to report in person to Major-General H. W. Halleck at St. Louis. I accompanied General Buell to the camp at Nolin, where he reviewed and inspected the camp and troops under the command of General A. McD. McCook, and on our way back General Buell inspected the regiment of Hazzard at Elizabethtown. I then turned over my command to him, and took my departure for St. Louis.

At the time I was so relieved I thought, of course, it was done in fulfillment of Mr. Lincoln's promise to me, and as a necessary result of my repeated demand for the fulfillment of that promise; but I saw and felt, and was of course deeply moved to observe, the manifest belief that there was more or less of truth in the rumor that the cares, perplexities, and anxiety of the situation had unbalanced my judgment and mind. It was, doubtless, an incident common to all civil wars, to which I could only submit with the best grace possible, trusting to the future for an opportunity to redeem my fortune and good name. Of course I could not deny the fact, and had to submit to all its painful consequences for months; and, moreover, I could not hide from myself that many of the officers and soldiers subsequently placed under my command looked at me askance and with suspicion. Indeed, it was not until the following April that the battle of Shiloh gave me personally the chance to redeem my good name.

On reaching St. Louis and reporting to General Halleck, I was received kindly, and was shortly afterward (viz., November 23d) sent up to Sedalia to inspect the camp there, and the troops located along the road back to Jefferson City, and I was ordered to assume command in a certain contingency. I found General Steele at Sedalia with his regiments scattered about loosely; and General Pope at Otterville, twenty miles back, with no concert between them. The rebel general, Sterling Price, had his forces down about Osceola and Warsaw. I advised General Halleck to collect the whole of his men into one camp on the La Mine River, near Georgetown, to put them into brigades and divisions, so as to be ready to be handled, and I gave some preliminary orders looking to that end. But the newspapers kept harping on my insanity and paralyzed my efforts. In spite of myself, they tortured from me some words and acts of imprudence. General Halleck telegraphed me on November 26th: "Unless telegraph-lines are interrupted, make no movement of troops without orders;" and on November 29th: "No forward movement of troops on Osceola will be made; only strong reconnoitring-parties will be sent out in the supposed direction of the enemy; the bulk of the troops being held in position till more reliable information is obtained."

About the same time I received the following dispatch:

HEADQUARTERS, ST. LOUIS, MISSOURI,
November 28, 1861.

Brigadier-General SHERMAN, *Sedalia:*

Mrs. Sherman is here. General Halleck is satisfied, from reports of scouts received here, that no attack on Sedalia is intended. You will therefore return to this city, and report your observations on the condition of the troops you have examined. Please telegraph when you will leave.

SCHUYLER HAMILTON, *Brigadier-General and Aide-de-Camp.*

I accordingly returned to St. Louis, where I found Mrs. Sherman, naturally and properly distressed at the continued and reiterated reports of the newspapers of my insanity, and she had come from Lancaster to see me. This recall from Sedalia simply swelled the cry. It was alleged that I was recalled by reason of something foolish I had done at Sedalia, though in fact I had done absolutely nothing, except to recommend what was done immediately thereafter on the advice of Colonel McPherson, on a subsequent inspection. Seeing and realizing that my efforts were useless, I concluded to ask for a twenty days' leave of absence, to accompany Mrs. Sherman to our home in Lancaster, and to allow the storm to blow over somewhat. It also happened to be mid-winter, when nothing was doing; so Mrs. Sherman and I returned to Lancaster, where I was born, and where I supposed I was better known and appreciated.

The newspapers kept up their game as though instigated by malice, and chief among them was the *Cincinnati Commercial*, whose editor, Halsted, was generally believed to be an honorable man. P. B. Ewing, Esq., being in Cincinnati, saw him and asked him why he, who certainly knew better, would reiterate such a damaging slander. He answered, quite cavalierly, that it was one of the news-items of the day, and he had to keep up with the time; but he would be most happy to publish any correction I might make, as though I could deny such a malicious piece of scandal affecting myself. On the 12th of November I had occasion to write to General Halleck, and I have a copy of his letter in answer:

ST. LOUIS, *December* 18, 1861.
Brigadier-General W. T. SHERMAN, *Lancaster, Ohio.*

MY DEAR GENERAL: Yours of the 12th was received a day or two ago, but was mislaid for the moment among private papers, or I should have answered it sooner. The newspaper attacks are certainly shameless and scandalous, but I cannot agree with you, that they have us in their power "to destroy us as they please." I certainly get my share of abuse, but it will not disturb me.

Your movement of the troops was not countermanded by me because I thought it an unwise one in itself, but because I was not then ready for it. I had better information of Price's movements than you had, and I had no apprehension of an attack. I intended to concentrate the forces on that line, but I wished the movement delayed until I could determine on a better position.

After receiving Lieutenant-Colonel McPherson's report, I made precisely the location you had ordered. I was desirous at the time not to prevent the advance of Price by any movement on our part, hoping that he would move on Lexington; but finding that he had determined to remain at Osceola for some time at least, I made the movement you proposed. As you could not know my plans, you and others may have misconstrued the reason of my countermanding your orders. . . .

I hope to see you well enough for duty soon. Our organization goes on slowly, but we will effect it in time. Yours truly,

H. W. HALLECK.

And subsequently, in a letter to Hon. Thomas Ewing, in answer to some inquiries involving the same general subject, General Halleck wrote as follows:

ST. LOUIS, *February* 15, 1862.

Hon. THOMAS EWING, *Lancaster, Ohio.*

DEAR SIR: Your note of the 13th, and one of this date, from Mr. Sherman, in relation to Brigadier-General Sherman's having being relieved from command in Sedalia, in November last, are just received. General Sherman was not put in command at Sedalia; he was authorized to assume it, and did so for a day or two. He did not know my plans, and his movement of troops did not accord with them. I therefore directed him to leave them as they were, and report here the result of his *inspection*, for which purpose he had been ordered there.

No telegram or dispatch of any kind was sent by me, or by any one with my knowledge or authority, in relation to it. After his return here, I gave him a leave of absence of twenty days, for the benefit of his health. As I was then pressing General McClellan for more officers, I deemed it necessary to explain why I did so. I used these words: "I am satisfied that General Sherman's physical and mental system is so completely broken by labor and care as to render him, for the present, unfit for duty; perhaps a few weeks' rest may restore him." This was the only communication I made on the subject. On no occasion have I ever expressed an opinion that his mind was affected otherwise than by over-exertion; to have said so would have done him the greatest injustice.

After General Sherman returned from his short leave, I found that his health was nearly restored, and I placed him temporarily in command of the camp of instruction, numbering over fifteen thousand men. I then wrote to General McClellan that he would soon be able to again take the field. I gave General Sherman a copy of my letter. This is the total of my correspondence on the subject. As evidence that I have every confidence in General Sherman, I have placed him in command of Western Kentucky—a command only second in importance in this department. As soon as divisions and columns can be organized, I propose to send him into the field where he can render most efficient service. I have seen newspaper squibs charging him with being "crazy," etc. This is the grossest injustice; I do not, however, consider such attacks worthy of notice. The best answer is General Sherman's present position, and the valuable services he is rendering to the country. I have the fullest confidence in him.

Very respectfully, your obedient servant,

H. W. HALLECK, *Major-General.*

On returning to St. Louis, on the expiration of my leave of absence, I found that General Halleck was beginning to move his troops: one part, under General U. S. Grant, up the Tennessee River; and another part, under General S. R. Curtis, in the direction of Springfield, Missouri. General Grant was then at Paducah, and General Curtis was under orders for Rolla. I was ordered to take Curtis's place in command of the camp of instruction, at Benton Barracks, on the ground back of North St. Louis, now used as the Fair Grounds, by the following order:

[Special Order No. 87].

HEADQUARTERS DEPARTMENT OF THE MISSOURI, ⎫
ST. LOUIS, *December* 23, 1861.   ⎬
                                            ⎭

[EXTRACT.]

Brigadier-General W. T. Sherman, United States Volunteers, is hereby assigned to the command of the camp of instruction and post of Benton Barracks. He will have every armed regiment and company in his command ready for service at a moment's warning, and will notify all concerned that, when marching orders are received, it is expected that they will be instantly obeyed; no excuses for delay will be admitted. General Sherman will immediately report to these headquarters what regiments and companies, at Benton Barracks, are ready for the field.

By order of Major-General Halleck,

J. C. KELTEN, *Assistant Adjutant-General.*

I immediately assumed command, and found, in the building constructed for the commanding officer, Brigadier-
General Strong, and the family of a captain of Iowa cavalry,
with whom we boarded. Major Curtis, son of General Curtis,
was the adjutant-general, but was soon relieved by Captain
J. H. Hammond, who was appointed assistant adjutant-
general, and assigned to duty with me.

Brigadier-General Hurlbut was also there, and about a
dozen regiments of infantry and cavalry. I at once gave all
matters pertaining to the post my personal attention, got the
regiments in as good order as possible, kept up communication with General Halleck's headquarters by telegraph, and,
when orders came for the movement of any regiment or detachment, it moved instantly. The winter was very wet, and
the ground badly drained. The quarters had been erected by
General Fremont, under contract; they were mere shells, but
well arranged for a camp, embracing the Fair Grounds, and
some forty acres of flat ground west of it. I instituted drills,
and was specially ordered by General Halleck to watch Generals Hurlbut and Strong, and report as to their fitness for
their commissions as brigadier-generals. I had known Hurlbut as a young lawyer, in Charleston, South Carolina, before
the Mexican War, at which time he took a special interest in
military matters, and I found him far above the average in the
knowledge of regimental and brigade drill, and so reported.
General Strong had been a merchant, and he told me that he
never professed to be a soldier, but had been urged on the
Secretary of War for the commission of a brigadier-general,
with the expectation of becoming quartermaster or commissary-general. He was a good, kind-hearted gentleman, boiling
over with patriotism and zeal. I advised him what to read
and study, was considerably amused at his receiving instruction from a young lieutenant who knew the company and
battalion drill, and could hear him practise in his room
the words of command, and tone of voice, "Break from
the right, to march to the left!" "Battalion, halt!" "Forward
into line!" etc. Of course I made a favorable report in his case.
Among the infantry and cavalry colonels were some who afterward rose to distinction—David Stuart, Gordon Granger,
Bussey, etc., etc.

Though it was mid-winter, General Halleck was pushing his preparations most vigorously, and surely he brought order out of chaos in St. Louis with commendable energy. I remember, one night, sitting in his room, on the second floor of the Planters' House, with him and General Cullum, his chief of staff, talking of things generally, and the subject then was of the much-talked-of "advance," as soon as the season would permit. Most people urged the movement down the Mississippi River; but Generals Polk and Pillow had a large rebel force, with heavy guns in a very strong position, at Columbus, Kentucky, about eighteen miles below Cairo. Commodore Foote had his gunboat fleet at Cairo; and General U. S. Grant, who commanded the district, was collecting a large force at Paducah, Cairo, and Bird's Point. General Halleck had a map on his table, with a large pencil in his hand, and asked, "Where is the rebel line?" Cullum drew the pencil through Bowling Green, Forts Donelson and Henry, and Columbus, Kentucky. "That is their line," said Halleck. "Now, where is the proper place to break it?" And either Cullum or I said, "*Naturally* the centre." Halleck drew a line perpendicular to the other, near its middle, and it coincided nearly with the general course of the Tennessee River; and he said, "That's the true line of operations." This occurred more than a month before General Grant began the movement, and, as he was subject to General Halleck's orders, I have always given Halleck the full credit for that movement, which was skillful, successful, and extremely rich in military results; indeed, it was the first real success on our side in the civil war. The movement up the Tennessee began about the 1st of February, and Fort Henry was captured by the joint action of the navy under Commodore Foote, and the land-forces under General Grant, on the 6th of February, 1862. About the same time, General S. R. Curtis had moved forward from Rolla, and, on the 8th of March, defeated the rebels under McCulloch, Van Dorn, and Price, at Pea Ridge.

As soon as Fort Henry fell, General Grant marched straight across to Fort Donelson, on the Cumberland River, invested the place, and, as soon as the gunboats had come round from the Tennessee, and had bombarded the water-front, he assaulted; whereupon Buckner surrendered the garrison of twelve thousand men; Pillow and ex-Secretary of War General Floyd having personally escaped across the river at night, occasioning a good deal of fun and criticism at their expense.

Before the fall of Donelson, but after that of Henry, I received, at Benton Barracks, the following orders:

HEADQUARTERS DEPARTMENT OF THE MISSOURI,
ST. LOUIS, *February* 13, 1862.

Brigadier-General SHERMAN, *Benton Barracks:*
You will immediately repair to Paducah, Kentucky, and assume command of that post. Brigadier-General Hurlbut will accompany you. The command of Benton Barracks will be turned over to General Strong.

H. W. HALLECK, *Major-General.*

I started for Paducah the same day, and think that General Cullum went with me to Cairo; General Halleck's purpose being to push forward the operations up the Tennessee River with unusual vigor. On reaching Paducah, I found this dispatch:

HEADQUARTERS DEPARTMENT OF THE MISSOURI,
ST. LOUIS, *February* 15, 1862.

Brigadier-General SHERMAN, *Paducah, Kentucky:*
Send General Grant every thing you can spare from Paducah and Smithland; also General Hurlbut.

Bowling Green has been evacuated entirely.

H. W. HALLECK, *Major-General.*

The next day brought us news of the surrender of Buckner, and probably at no time during the war did we all feel so heavy a weight raised from our breasts, or so thankful for a most fruitful series of victories. They at once gave Generals Halleck, Grant, and C. F. Smith, great fame. Of course, the rebels let go their whole line, and fell back on Nashville and Island No. Ten, and to the Memphis & Charleston Railroad. Everybody was anxious to help. Boats passed up and down constantly, and very soon arrived the rebel prisoners from Donelson. I saw General Buckner on the boat, he seemed self-sufficient, and thought their loss was not really so serious to their cause as we did.

About this time another force of twenty or twenty-five

thousand men was collected on the west bank of the Mississippi, above Cairo, under the command of Major-General John Pope, designed to become the "Army of the Mississippi," and to operate, in conjunction with the navy, down the river against the enemy's left flank, which had held the strong post of Columbus, Kentucky, but which, on the fall of Fort Donelson, had fallen back to New Madrid and Island No. 10.

Chapter X.

BY THE END of February, 1862, Major-General Halleck commanded all the armies in the valley of the Mississippi, from his headquarters in St. Louis. These were, the Army of the Ohio, Major-General Buell, in Kentucky; the Army of the Tennessee, Major-General Grant, at Forts Henry and Donelson; the Army of the Mississippi, Major-General Pope; and that of General S. R. Curtis, in Southwest Missouri. He posted his chief of staff, General Cullum, at Cairo, and me at Paducah, chiefly to expedite and facilitate the important operations then in progress up the Tennessee and Cumberland Rivers.

Fort Donelson had surrendered to General Grant on the 16th of February, and there must have been a good deal of confusion resulting from the necessary care of the wounded, and disposition of prisoners, common to all such occasions, and there was a real difficulty in communicating between St. Louis and Fort Donelson.

General Buell had also followed up the rebel army, which had retreated hastily from Bowling Green to and through Nashville, a city of so much importance to the South, that it was at one time proposed as its capital. Both Generals Grant and Buell looked to its capture as an event of great importance. On the 21st General Grant sent General Smith with his division to Clarksville, fifty miles above Donelson, toward Nashville, and on the 27th went himself to Nashville to meet and confer with General Buell, but returned to Donelson the next day.

Meantime, General Halleck at St. Louis must have felt that his armies were getting away from him, and began to send dispatches to me at Paducah, to be forwarded by boat, or by a rickety telegraph-line up to Fort Henry, which lay entirely in a hostile country, and was consequently always out of repair. On the 1st of March I received the following dispatch, and forwarded it to General Grant, both by the telegraph and boat:

ST. LOUIS, *March* 1, 1862.

To General GRANT, *Fort Henry:*

Transports will be sent you as soon as possible, to move your column up the Tennessee River. The main object of this expedition will be to destroy the railroad-bridge over Bear Creek, near Eastport, Mississippi; and also the railroad connections at Corinth, Jackson, and Humboldt. It is thought best that these objects be attempted in the order named. Strong detachments of cavalry and light artillery, supported by infantry, may by rapid movements reach these points from the river, without any serious opposition.

Avoid any general engagements with strong forces. It will be better to retreat than to risk a general battle. This should be strongly impressed on the officers sent with expeditions from the river. General C. F. Smith or some very discreet officer should be selected for such commands. Having accomplished these objects, or such of them as may be practicable, you will return to Danville, and move on Paris.

Perhaps the troops sent to Jackson and Humboldt can reach Paris by land as easily as to return to the transports. This must depend on the character of the roads and the position of the enemy. All telegraphic lines which can be reached must be cut. The gunboats will accompany the transports for their protection. Any loyal Tennesseeans who desire it, may be enlisted and supplied with arms. Competent officers should be left to command Forts Henry and Donelson in your absence. I have indicated in general terms the object of this.

H. W. HALLECK, *Major-General.*

Again on the 2d:

CAIRO, *March* 2, 1862.

To General GRANT:

General Halleck, February 25th, telegraphs me: "General Grant will send no more forces to Clarksville. General Smith's division will come to Fort Henry, or a point higher up on the Tennessee River; transports will also be collected at Paducah. Two gunboats in Tennessee River with Grant. General Grant will immediately have small garrisons detailed for Forts Henry and Donelson, and all other forces made ready for the field."

From your letter of the 28th, I learn you were at Fort Donelson, and General Smith at Nashville, from which I infer you could not

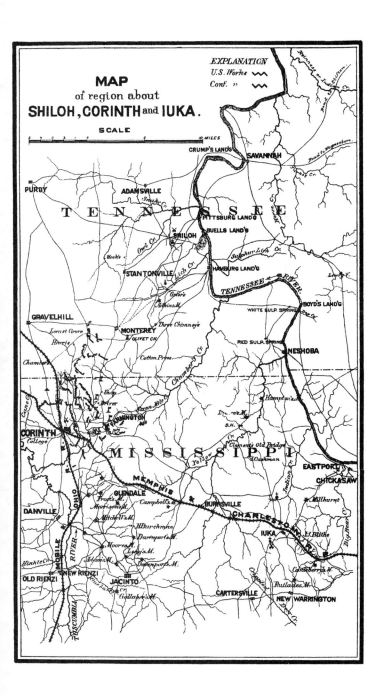

MAP
of region about
SHILOH, CORINTH and IUKA.

SCALE

EXPLANATION
U.S. Works ⌇⌇
Conf. „ ⌇⌇

TENNESSEE

MISSISSIPPI

PURDY
ADAMSVILLE
CRUMP'S LAND'G
SAVANNAH
PITTSBURG LAND'G
SHILOH
BUELLS LAND'S
HAMBURG LAND'G
STANTONVILLE
GRAVELHILL
MONTEREY
OLIVET CH.
BOYD'S LAND'G
WHITE SULP. SPRING
RED SULP. SPRING
NESHOBA
FARMINGTON
CORINTH
EASTPORT
CHICKASAW
GLENDALE
BURNSVILLE
DANVILLE
Millburnt
IUKA
CHARLESTON
OLD RIENZI
NEW RIENZI
JACINTO
CARTERSVILLE
NEW WARRINGTON

TENNESSEE RIVER
MEMPHIS
OHIO
MOBILE
RIVER

have received orders. Halleck's telegram of last night says: "Who sent Smith's division to Nashville? I ordered it across to the Tennessee, where they are wanted immediately. Order them back. Send all spare transports up Tennessee to General Grant." Evidently the general supposes you to be on the Tennessee. I am sending all the transports I can find for you, reporting to General Sherman for orders to go up the Cumberland for you, or, if you march across to Fort Henry, then to send them up the Tennessee.

G. W. CULLUM, *Brigadier-General.*

On the 4th came this dispatch:

ST. LOUIS, *March* 4, 1862.

To Major-General U. S. GRANT:

You will place Major-General C. F. Smith in command of expedition, and remain yourself at Fort Henry. Why do you not obey my orders to report strength and positions of your command?

H. W. HALLECK, *Major-General.*

Halleck was evidently working himself into a passion, but he was too far from the seat of war to make due allowance for the actual state of facts. General Grant had done so much, that General Halleck should have been patient. Meantime, at Paducah, I was busy sending boats in every direction—some under the orders of General Halleck, others of General Cullum; others for General Grant, and still others for General Buell at Nashville; and at the same time I was organizing out of the new troops that were arriving at Paducah a division for myself when allowed to take the field, which I had been promised by General Halleck. His purpose was evidently to operate up the Tennessee River, to break up Bear Creek Bridge and the railroad communications between the Mississippi and Tennessee Rivers, and no doubt he was provoked that Generals Grant and Smith had turned aside to Nashville. In the mean time several of the gunboats, under Captain Phelps, United States Navy, had gone up the Tennessee as far as Florence, and on their return had reported a strong Union feeling among the people along the river. On the 10th of March, having received the necessary orders from General Halleck, I embarked my division at Paducah. It was composed of four brigades. The First, commanded by Colonel S. G. Hicks, was composed of the Fortieth Illinois, Forty-sixth

Ohio, and Morton's Indiana Battery, on the boats Sallie List, Golden Gate, J. B. Adams, and Lancaster.

The Second Brigade, Colonel D. Stuart, was composed of the Fifty-fifth Illinois, Seventy-first Ohio, and Fifty-fourth Ohio; embarked on the Hannibal, Universe, Hazel Dell, Cheeseman, and Prairie Rose.

The Third Brigade, Colonel Hildebrand, was composed of the Seventy-seventh Ohio, Fifty-seventh Ohio, and Fifty-third Ohio; embarked on the Poland, Anglo-Saxon, Ohio No. Three, and Continental.

The Fourth Brigade, Colonel Buckland, was composed of the Seventy-second Ohio, Forty-eighth Ohio, and Seventieth Ohio; embarked on the Empress, Baltic, Shenango, and Marengo.

We steamed up to Fort Henry, the river being high and in splendid order. There I reported in person to General C. F. Smith, and by him was ordered a few miles above, to the remains of the burned railroad bridge, to await the rendezvous of the rest of his army. I had my headquarters on the Continental.

Among my colonels I had a strange character—Thomas Worthington, colonel of the Forty-sixth Ohio. He was a graduate of West Point, of the class of 1827; was, therefore, older than General Halleck, General Grant, or myself, and claimed to know more of war than all of us put together. In ascending the river he did not keep his place in the column, but pushed on and reached Savannah a day before the rest of my division. When I reached that place, I found that Worthington had landed his regiment, and was flying about giving orders, as though he were commander-in-chief. I made him get back to his boat, and gave him to understand that he must thereafter keep his place. General C. F. Smith arrived about the 13th of March, with a large fleet of boats, containing Hurlbut's division, Lew. Wallace's division, and that of himself, then commanded by Brigadier-General W. H. L. Wallace.

General Smith sent for me to meet him on his boat, and ordered me to push on under escort of the two gunboats, Lexington and Tyler, commanded by Captains Gwin and Shirk, United States Navy. I was to land at some point below Eastport, and make a break of the Memphis & Charleston

Railroad, between Tuscumbia and Corinth. General Smith was quite unwell, and was suffering from his leg, which was swollen and very sore, from a mere abrasion in stepping into a small-boat. This actually mortified, and resulted in his death about a month after, viz., April 25, 1862. He was adjutant of the Military Academy during the early part of my career there, and afterward commandant of cadets. He was a very handsome and soldierly man, of great experience, and at Donelson had acted with so much personal bravery that to him many attributed the success of the assault. I immediately steamed up the Tennessee River, following the two gunboats, and, in passing Pittsburg Landing, was told by Captain Gwin that, on his former trip up the river, he had found a rebel regiment of cavalry posted there, and that it was the usual landing-place for the people about Corinth, distant thirty miles. I sent word back to General Smith that, if we were detained up the river, he ought to post some troops at Pittsburg Landing. We went on up the river cautiously, till we saw Eastport and Chickasaw, both of which were occupied by rebel batteries and a small rebel force of infantry.

We then dropped back quietly to the mouth of Yellow River, a few miles below, whence led a road to Burnsville, a place on the Memphis & Charleston road, where were the company's repair-shops. We at once commenced disembarking the command: first the cavalry, which started at once for Burnsville, with orders to tear up the railroad-track, and burn the depots, shops, etc; and I followed with the infantry and artillery as fast as they were disembarked. It was raining very hard at the time. Daylight found us about six miles out, where we met the cavalry returning. They had made numerous attempts to cross the streams, which had become so swollen that mere brooks covered the whole bottom; and my aide-de-camp, Sanger, whom I had dispatched with the cavalry, reported the loss, by drowning, of several of the men. The rain was pouring in torrents, and reports from the rear came that the river was rising very fast, and that, unless we got back to our boats soon, the bottom would be simply impassable. There was no alternative but to regain our boats; and even this was so difficult, that we had to unharness the artillery-horses, and drag the guns under water through the bayous, to

reach the bank of the river. Once more embarked, I concluded to drop down to Pittsburg Landing, and to make the
attempt from there. During the night of the 14th, we dropped
down to Pittsburg Landing, where I found Hurlbut's division in boats. Leaving my command there, I steamed down to
Savannah, and reported to General Smith in person, who saw
in the flooded Tennessee the full truth of my report; and he
then instructed me to disembark my own division, and that of
General Hurlbut, at Pittsburg Landing; to take positions well
back, and to leave room for his whole army; telling me that
he would soon come up in person, and move out in force to
make the lodgment on the railroad, contemplated by General
Halleck's orders.

Lieutenant-Colonel McPherson, of General C. F. Smith's,
or rather General Halleck's, staff, returned with me, and on
the 16th of March we disembarked and marched out about
ten miles toward Corinth, to a place called Monterey or Pea
Ridge, where the rebels had a cavalry regiment, which of
course decamped on our approach, but from the people we
learned that trains were bringing large masses of men from
every direction into Corinth. McPherson and I reconnoitred
the ground well, and then returned to our boats. On the 18th,
Hurlbut disembarked his division and took post about a mile
and a half out, near where the roads branched, one leading to
Corinth and the other toward Hamburg. On the 19th I disembarked my division, and took post about three miles back,
three of the brigades covering the roads to Purdy and
Corinth, and the other brigade (Stuart's) temporarily at a
place on the Hamburg Road, near Lick Creek Ford, where
the Bark Road came into the Hamburg Road. Within a few
days, Prentiss's division arrived and camped on my left, and
afterward McClernand's and W. H. L. Wallace's divisions,
which formed a line to our rear. Lew Wallace's division remained on the north side of Snake Creek, on a road leading
from Savannah or Crump's Landing to Purdy.

General C. F. Smith remained back at Savannah, in chief
command, and I was only responsible for my own division. I
kept pickets well out on the roads, and made myself familiar
with all the ground inside and outside my lines. My personal
staff was composed of Captain J. H. Hammond, assistant

adjutant-general; Surgeons Hartshorn and L'Hommedieu; Lieutenant Colonels Hascall and Sanger, inspector-generals; Lieutenants McCoy and John Taylor, aides-de-camp. We were all conscious that the enemy was collecting at Corinth, but in what force we could not know, nor did we know what was going on behind us. On the 17th of March, General U. S. Grant was restored to the command of all the troops up the Tennessee River, by reason of General Smith's extreme illness, and because he had explained to General Halleck satisfactorily his conduct after Donelson; and he too made his headquarters at Savannah, but frequently visited our camps. I always acted on the supposition that we were an invading army; that our purpose was to move forward in force, make a lodgment on the Memphis & Charleston road, and thus repeat the grand tactics of Fort Donelson, by separating the rebels in the interior from those at Memphis and on the Mississippi River. We did not fortify our camps against an attack, because we had no orders to do so, and because such a course would have made our raw men timid. The position was naturally strong, with Snake Creek on our right, a deep, bold stream, with a confluent (Owl Creek) to our right front; and Lick Creek, with a similar confluent, on our left, thus narrowing the space over which we could be attacked to about a mile and a half or two miles.

At a later period of the war, we could have rendered this position impregnable in one night, but at this time we did not do it, and it may be it is well we did not. From about the 1st of April we were conscious that the rebel cavalry in our front was getting bolder and more saucy; and on Friday, the 4th of April, it dashed down and carried off one of our picket-guards, composed of an officer and seven men, posted a couple of miles out on the Corinth road. Colonel Buckland sent a company to its relief, then followed himself with a regiment, and, fearing lest he might be worsted, I called out his whole brigade and followed some four or five miles, when the cavalry in advance encountered artillery. I then, after dark, drew back to our lines, and reported the fact by letter to General Grant, at Savannah; but thus far we had not positively detected the presence of infantry, for cavalry regiments generally had a couple of guns along, and I supposed the guns that

opened on us on the evening of Friday, April 4th, belonged
to the cavalry that was hovering along our whole front.

Saturday passed in our camps without any unusual event,
the weather being wet and mild, and the roads back to the
steamboat-landing being heavy with mud; but on Sunday
morning, the 6th, early, there was a good deal of picket-firing,
and I got breakfast, rode out along my lines, and, about four
hundred yards to the front of Appler's regiment, received
from some bushes in a ravine to the left front a volley which
killed my orderly, Holliday. About the same time I saw the
rebel lines of battle in front coming down on us as far as the
eye could reach. All my troops were in line of battle, ready,
and the ground was favorable to us. I gave the necessary
orders to the battery (Waterhouse's) attached to Hildebrand's brigade, and cautioned the men to reserve their fire
till the rebels had crossed the ravine of Owl Creek, and
had begun the ascent; also, sent staff-officers to notify Generals McClernand and Prentiss of the coming blow. Indeed,
McClernand had already sent three regiments to the support
of my left flank, and they were in position when the onset
came.

In a few minutes the battle of "Shiloh" began with extreme
fury, and lasted two days. Its history has been well given, and
it has been made the subject of a great deal of controversy.
Hildebrand's brigade was soon knocked to pieces, but Buckland's and McDowell's kept their organization throughout.
Stuart's was driven back to the river, and did not join me in
person till the second day of the battle. I think my several
reports of that battle are condensed and good, made on the
spot, when all the names and facts were fresh in my memory,
and are herewith given entire:

HEADQUARTERS FIRST DIVISION, ⎱
PITTSBURG LANDING, *March* 17, 1862.⎰

Captain Wm. McMICHAEL, *Assistant Adjutant-General to General*
C. F. SMITH, *Savannah, Tennessee.*

SIR: Last night I dispatched a party of cavalry, at 6 P.M., under the
command of Lieutenant-Colonel Heath, Fifth Ohio Cavalry, for a
strong reconnoissance, if possible, to be converted into an attack

upon the Memphis road. The command got off punctually, followed at twelve o'clock at night by the First Brigade of my division, commanded by Colonel McDowell, the other brigades to follow in order.

About one at night the cavalry returned, reporting the road occupied in force by the enemy, with whose advance-guard they skirmished, driving them back about a mile, taking two prisoners, and having their chief guide, Thomas Maxwell, Esq., and three men of the Fourth Illinois wounded.

Inclosed please find the report of Lieutenant-Colonel Heath; also a copy of his instructions, and the order of march. As soon as the cavalry returned, I saw that an attempt on the road was frustrated, and accordingly have placed McDowell's brigade to our right front, guarding the pass of Snake Creek; Stuart's brigade to the left front, to watch the pass of Lick Creek; and I shall this morning move directly out on the Corinth road, about eight miles to or toward Pea Ridge, which is a key-point to the southwest.

General Hurlbut's division will be landed to-day, and the artillery and infantry disposed so as to defend Pittsburg, leaving my division entire for any movement by land or water.

As near as I can learn, there are five regiments of rebel infantry at Purdy; at Corinth, and distributed along the railroad to Iuca, are probably thirty thousand men; but my information from prisoners is very indistinct. Every road and path is occupied by the enemy's cavalry, whose orders seem to be, to fire a volley, retire, again fire and retire. The force on the Purdy road attacked and driven by Major Bowman yesterday, was about sixty strong. That encountered last night on the Corinth road was about five companies of Tennessee cavalry, sent from Purdy about 2 P.M. yesterday.

I hear there is a force of two regiments on Pea Ridge, at the point where the Purdy and Corinth roads come together.

I am satisfied we cannot reach the Memphis & Charleston road without a considerable engagement, which is prohibited by General Halleck's instructions, so that I will be governed by your orders of yesterday, to occupy Pittsburg strongly, extend the pickets so as to include a semi-circle of three miles, and push a strong reconnoissance as far out as Lick Creek and Pea Ridge.

I will send down a good many boats to-day, to be employed as you may direct; and would be obliged if you would send a couple of thousand sacks of corn, as much hay as you can possibly spare, and, if possible, a barge of coal.

I will send a steamboat under care of the gunboat, to collect corn from cribs on the river-bank.

I have the honor to be your obedient servant,

W. T. SHERMAN,
Brigadier-General commanding First Division.

HEADQUARTERS, STEAMBOAT CONTINENTAL, }
PITTSBURG, *March* 18, 1862. }

Captain RAWLINS, *Assistant Adjutant-General to General* GRANT.

SIR: The division surgeon having placed some one hundred or more sick on board the Fanny Bullitt, I have permitted her to take them to Savannah. There is neither house nor building of any kind that can be used for a hospital here.

I hope to receive an order to establish floating hospitals, but in the mean time, by the advice of the surgeon, allow these sick men to leave. Let me hope that it will meet your approbation.

The order for debarkation came while General Sherman was absent with three brigades, and no men are left to move the effects of these brigades.

The landing, too, is small, with scarcely any chance to increase it; therefore there is a great accumulation of boats. Colonel McArthur has arrived, and is now cutting a landing for himself.

General Sherman will return this evening. I am obliged to transgress, and write myself in the mean time,

Respectfully your obedient servant,
J. H. HAMMOND, *Assistant Adjutant-General.*

P. S.—4 P.M.—Just back; have been half-way to Corinth and to Purdy. All right. Have just read this letter, and approve all but floating hospitals; regimental surgeons can take care of all sick, except chronic cases, which can always be sent down to Paducah.

Magnificent plain for camping and drilling, and a military point of great strength. The enemy has felt us twice, at great loss and demoralization; will report at length this evening; am now much worn out.

W. T. SHERMAN, *Brigadier-General.*

HEADQUARTERS FIRST DIVISION, }
PITTSBURG LANDING, *March* 19, 1862. }

Captain RAWLINS, *Assistant Adjutant-General to General* GRANT,
    Savannah, Tennessee.

SIR: I have just returned from an extensive reconnoissance toward Corinth and Purdy, and am strongly impressed with the importance of this position, both for its land advantages and its strategic position. The ground itself admits of easy defense by a small command,

and yet affords admirable camping-ground for a hundred thousand men. I will as soon as possible make or cause to be made a topographical sketch of the position. The only drawback is that, at this stage of water, the space for landing is contracted too much for the immense fleet now here discharging.

I will push the loading and unloading of boats, but suggest that you send at once (Captain Dodd, if possible) the best quartermaster you can, that he may control and organize this whole matter. I have a good commissary, and will keep as few provisions afloat as possible. Yours, etc.,

W. T. SHERMAN, *Brigadier-General commanding.*

HEADQUARTERS SHERMAN'S DIVISION, CAMP SHILOH, }
NEAR PITTSBURG LANDING, TENNESSEE, *April* 2, 1862. }

Captain J. A. RAWLINS, *Assistant Adjutant-General to General*
GRANT.

SIR: In obedience to General Grant's instructions of March 31st, with one section of Captain Muench's Minnesota Battery, two twelve-pound howitzers, a detachment of Fifth Ohio Cavalry of one hundred and fifty men, under Major Ricker, and two battalions of infantry from the Fifty-seventh and Seventy-seventh Ohio, under the command of Colonels Hildebrand and Mungen, I marched to the river, and embarked on the steamers Empress and Tecumseh. The gunboat Cairo did not arrive at Pittsburg, until after midnight, and at 6 A.M. Captain Bryant, commanding the gunboat, notified me that he was ready to proceed up the river. I followed, keeping the transports within about three hundred yards of the gunboat. About 1 P.M., the Cairo commenced shelling the battery above the mouth of Indian Creek, but elicited no reply. She proceeded up the river steadily and cautiously, followed close by the Tyler and Lexington, all throwing shells at the points where, on former visits of the gunboats, enemy's batteries were found. In this order all followed, till it was demonstrated that all the enemy's batteries, including that at Chickasaw, were abandoned.

I ordered the battalion of infantry under Colonel Hildebrand to disembark at Eastport, and with the other battalion proceeded to Chickasaw and landed. The battery at this point had evidently been abandoned some time, and consisted of the remains of an old Indian mound, partly washed away by the river, which had been fashioned into a two-gun battery, with a small magazine. The ground to its rear had evidently been overflowed during the late freshet, and led to the removal of the guns to Eastport, where the batteries were on high, elevated ground, accessible at all seasons from the country to the rear.

Upon personal inspection, I attach little importance to Chickasaw as a military position. The people, who had fled during the approach of the gunboats, returned to the village, and said the place had been occupied by one Tennessee regiment and a battery of artillery from Pensacola. After remaining at Chickasaw some hours, all the boats dropped back to Eastport, not more than a mile below, and landed there. Eastport Landing during the late freshet must have been about twelve feet under water, but at the present stage the landing is the best I have seen on the Tennessee River.

The levee is clear of trees or snags, and a hundred boats could land there without confusion.

The soil is of sand and gravel, and very firm. The road back is hard, and at a distance of about four hundred yards from the water begin the gravel hills of the country. The infantry scouts sent out by Colonel Hildebrand found the enemy's cavalry mounted, and watching the Iuca road, about two miles back of Eastport. The distance to Iuca is only eight miles, and Iuca is the nearest point and has the best road by which the Charleston & Memphis Railroad can be reached. I could obtain no certain information as to the strength of the enemy there, but am satisfied that it would have been folly to have attempted it with my command. Our object being to dislodge the enemy from the batteries recently erected near Eastport, and this being attained, I have returned, and report the river to be clear to and beyond Chickasaw.

I have the honor to be, your obedient servant,

W. T. SHERMAN,
Brigadier-General commanding Division.

HEADQUARTERS FIFTH DIVISION, ⎱
CAMP SHILOH, *April* 5, 1862.⎰

Captain J. A. RAWLINS, *Assistant Adjutant-General, District of Western Tennessee.*

SIR: I have the honor to report that yesterday, about 3 P.M., the lieutenant commanding and seven men of the advance pickets imprudently advanced from their posts and were captured. I ordered Major Ricker, of the Fifth Ohio Cavalry, to proceed rapidly to the picket-station, ascertain the truth, and act according to circumstances. He reached the station, found the pickets had been captured as reported, and that a company of infantry sent by the brigade commander had gone forward in pursuit of some cavalry. He rapidly advanced some two miles, and found them engaged, charged the enemy, and drove them along the Ridge road, till he met and received three discharges of artillery, when he very properly wheeled under cover, and returned till he met me.

As soon as I heard artillery, I advanced with two regiments of infantry, and took position, and remained until the scattered companies of infantry and cavalry had returned. This was after night.

I infer that the enemy is in some considerable force at Pea Ridge, that yesterday morning they crossed a brigade of two regiments of infantry, one regiment of cavalry, and one battery of field-artillery, to the ridge on which the Corinth road lies. They halted the infantry and artillery at a point about five miles in my front, sent a detachment to the lane of General Meaks, on the north of Owl Creek, and the cavalry down toward our camp. This cavalry captured a part of our advance pickets, and afterward engaged the two companies of Colonel Buckland's regiment, as described by him in his report herewith inclosed. Our cavalry drove them back upon their artillery and Infantry, killing many, and bringing off ten prisoners, all of the First Alabama Cavalry, whom I send to you.

We lost of the pickets one first-lieutenant and seven men of the Ohio Seventieth Infantry (list inclosed); one major, one lieutenant, and one private of the Seventy-second Ohio, taken prisoners; eight privates wounded (names in full, embraced in report of Colonel Buckland, inclosed herewith).

We took ten prisoners, and left two rebels wounded and many killed on the field.

I have the honor to be, your obedient servant,

W. T. SHERMAN,
Brigadier-General, commanding Division.

HEADQUARTERS FIFTH DIVISION, ⎫
CAMP SHILOH, *April* 10, 1862.⎰

Captain J. A. RAWLINS, *Assistant Adjutant-General to General*
GRANT.

SIR: I had the honor to report that, on Friday the 4th inst., the enemy's cavalry drove in our pickets, posted about a mile and a half in advance of my centre, on the main Corinth road, capturing one first-lieutenant and seven men; that I caused a pursuit by the cavalry of my division, driving them back about five miles, and killing many. On Saturday the enemy's cavalry was again very bold, coming well down to our front; yet I did not believe they designed any thing but a strong demonstration. On Sunday morning early, the 6th inst., the enemy drove our advance-guard back on the main body, when I ordered under arms all my division, and sent word to General Mc-

Clernand, asking him to support my left; to General Prentiss, giving him notice that the enemy was in our front in force, and to General Hurlbut, asking him to support General Prentiss. At that time— 7 A.M.—my division was arranged as follows:

First Brigade, composed of the Sixth Iowa, Colonel J. A. McDowell; Fortieth Illinois, Colonel Hicks; Forty-sixth Ohio, Colonel Worthington; and the Morton battery, Captain Behr, on the extreme right, guarding the bridge on the Purdy road over Owl Creek.

Second Brigade, composed of the Fifty-fifth Illinois, Colonel D. Stuart; the Fifty-fourth Ohio, Colonel T. Kilby Smith; and the Seventy-first Ohio, Colonel Mason, on the extreme left, guarding the ford over Lick Creek.

Third Brigade, composed of the Seventy-seventh Ohio, Colonel Hildebrand; the Fifty-third Ohio, Colonel Appler; and the Fifty-seventh Ohio, Colonel Mungen, on the left of the Corinth road, its right resting on Shiloh meeting-house.

Fourth Brigade, composed of the Seventy-second Ohio, Colonel Buckland; the Forty-eighth Ohio, Colonel Sullivan; and the Seventieth Ohio, Colonel Cockerill, on the right of the Corinth road, its left resting on Shiloh meeting-house.

Two batteries of artillery—Taylor's and Waterhouse's—were posted, the former at Shiloh, and the latter on a ridge to the left, with a front-fire over open ground between Mungen's and Appler's regiments. The cavalry, eight companies of the Fourth Illinois, under Colonel Dickey, were posted in a large open field to the left and rear of Shiloh meeting-house, which I regarded as the centre of my position.

Shortly after 7 A.M., with my entire staff, I rode along a portion of our front, and when in the open field before Appler's regiment, the enemy's pickets opened a brisk fire upon my party, killing my orderly, Thomas D. Holliday, of Company H, Second Illinois Cavalry. The fire came from the bushes which line a small stream that rises in the field in front of Appler's camp, and flows to the north along my whole front.

This valley afforded the enemy partial cover; but our men were so posted as to have a good fire at them as they crossed the valley and ascended the rising ground on our side.

About 8 A.M. I saw the glistening bayonets of heavy masses of infantry to our left front in the woods beyond the small stream alluded to, and became satisfied for the first time that the enemy designed a determined attack on our whole camp.

All the regiments of my division were then in line of battle at their proper posts. I rode to Colonel Appler, and ordered him to hold his ground at all hazards, as he held the left flank of our first line of battle, and I informed him that he had a good battery on his right, and strong support to his rear. General McClernand had promptly and energetically responded to my request, and had sent me three regiments which were posted to protect Waterhouse's battery and the left flank of my line.

The battle opened by the enemy's battery, in the woods to our front, throwing shells into our camp. Taylor's and Waterhouse's batteries promptly responded, and I then observed heavy battalions of infantry passing obliquely to the left, across the open field in Appler's front; also, other columns advancing directly upon my division. Our infantry and artillery opened along the whole line, and the battle became general. Other heavy masses of the enemy's forces kept passing across the field to our left, and directing their course on General Prentiss. I saw at once that the enemy designed to pass my left flank, and fall upon Generals McClernand and Prentiss, whose line of camps was almost parallel with the Tennessee River, and about two miles back from it. Very soon the sound of artillery and musketry announced that General Prentiss was engaged; and about 9 A.M. I judged that he was falling back. About this time Appler's regiment broke in disorder, followed by Mungen's regiment, and the enemy pressed forward on Waterhouse's battery thereby exposed.

The three Illinois regiments in immediate support of this battery stood for some time; but the enemy's advance was so vigorous, and the fire so severe, that when Colonel Raith, of the Forty-third Illinois, received a severe wound and fell from his horse, his regiment and the others manifested disorder, and the enemy got possession of three guns of this (Waterhouse's) battery. Although our left was thus turned, and the enemy was pressing our whole line, I deemed Shiloh so important, that I remained by it and renewed my orders to Colonels McDowell and Buckland to hold their ground; and we did hold these positions until about 10 A.M., when the enemy had got his artillery to the rear of our left flank and some change became absolutely necessary. Two regiments of Hildebrand's brigade—Appler's and Mungen's—had already disappeared to the rear, and Hildebrand's own regiment was in disorder. I therefore gave orders for Taylor's battery—still at Shiloh—to fall back as far as the Purdy and Hamburg road, and for McDowell and Buckland to adopt that road as their new line. I rode across the angle and met Behr's battery at the cross-roads, and ordered it immediately to come into battery, action right. Captain Behr gave the order, but he was almost immediately shot from his horse, when drivers and gunners fled in disorder, carrying off the caissons, and abandoning five out of six guns, without firing a shot. The enemy pressed on, gaining this battery, and we were again forced to choose a new line of defense. Hildebrand's brigade had substantially disappeared from the field, though he himself bravely remained. McDowell's and Buckland's brigades maintained their organizations, and were conducted by my aides, so as to join on General McClernand's right, thus abandoning my original camps and line. This was about 10½ A.M., at which time the enemy had made a furious attack on General McClernand's whole front. He struggled most determinedly, but, finding him pressed, I moved McDowell's brigade directly against the left flank of the enemy, forced him back some distance, and then directed the men to avail themselves of every cover—trees, fallen timber, and a wooded valley to our right. We held this position for four long hours, sometimes gaining and at others losing ground; General McClernand and myself acting in perfect concert, and struggling to maintain this line. While we were so hard pressed, two Iowa regiments approached from the rear, but could not be brought up to the severe fire that was raging in our front, and General Grant, who visited us on that ground, will remember our situation about 3 P.M.; but about 4 P.M. it was evident that Hurlbut's line had been driven back to the river; and knowing that General Lew Wallace was coming with reënforcements from Crump's Landing, General McClernand and I, on consultation, selected a new line of defense, with its right covering a bridge by which General Wallace had to approach. We fell back as well as we could, gathering in addition to our own such scattered forces as we could find, and formed the new line.

During this change the enemy's cavalry charged us, but were handsomely repulsed by the Twenty-ninth Illinois Regiment. The Fifth Ohio Battery, which had come up, rendered good service in holding the enemy in check for some time, and Major Taylor also came up with another battery and got into position, just in time to get a good flank-fire upon the enemy's column, as he pressed on General McClernand's right, checking his advance; when General McClernand's division made a fine charge on the enemy and drove him back into the ravines to our front and right. I had a clear field, about two hundred yards wide, in my immediate front, and contented myself with keeping the enemy's infantry at that distance during the rest of the day. In this position we rested for the night. My command had become decidedly of a mixed character. Buckland's brigade was the only one that retained its organization. Colonel Hildebrand was personally there, but his brigade was not. Colonel McDowell had been severely injured by a fall off his horse, and had gone to the river, and the three regiments of his brigade were not in line. The Thirteenth Missouri, Colonel Crafts J. Wright, had reported to me on the field, and fought well, retaining its regimental organization; and it formed a part of my line during Sunday night and all Monday. Other fragments of regiments and companies had also fallen into my division, and acted with it during the remainder of the battle. Generals Grant and Buell visited me in our bivouac that evening, and from them I learned the situation of affairs on other parts of the field. General Wallace arrived from Crump's Landing shortly after dark, and formed his line to my right rear. It rained hard during the night, but our men were in good spirits, lay on their arms, being satisfied with such bread and meat as could be gathered at the neighboring camps, and determined to redeem on Monday the losses of Sunday.

At daylight of Monday I received General Grant's orders to advance and recapture our original camps. I dispatched several members of my staff to bring up all the men they could find, especially the brigade of Colonel Stuart, which had been separated from the division all the day before; and at the appointed time the division, or rather what remained of it, with the Thirteenth Missouri and other fragments, moved forward and reoccupied the ground on the extreme right of General McClernand's camp, where we attracted the fire of a battery located near Colonel McDowell's former headquarters. Here I remained, patiently waiting for the sound of General Buell's advance upon the main Corinth road. About 10 A.M. the heavy firing in that direction, and its steady approach, satisfied me; and General Wallace being on our right flank with his well-conducted division, I led the head of my column to General McClernand's right, formed line of battle, facing south, with Buckland's brigade directly across the ridge, and Stuart's brigade on its right in the woods; and thus advanced, steadily and slowly, under a heavy fire of musketry and artillery. Taylor had just got to me from the rear, where he had gone for ammunition, and brought up three guns, which I ordered into position, to advance by hand firing. These guns belonged to Company A, Chicago Light Artillery, commanded by Lieutenant P. P. Wood, and did most excellent service. Under cover of their fire, we advanced till we reached the point where the Corinth road crosses the line of McClernand's camp, and here I saw for the first time the well-ordered and compact columns of General Buell's Kentucky forces, whose soldierly movements at once gave confidence to our newer and less disciplined men. Here I saw Willich's regiment advance upon a point of water-oaks and thicket, behind which I knew the enemy was in great strength, and enter it in beautiful style. Then arose the severest musketry-fire I ever heard, and lasted some twenty minutes, when this splendid regiment had to fall back. This green point of timber is about five hundred yards east of Shiloh meeting-house, and it was evident here was to be the struggle. The enemy could also be seen forming his lines to the south. General McClernand sending to me for artillery, I detached to him the three guns of Wood's battery, with which he speedily drove them back, and, seeing some others to the rear, I sent one of my staff to bring them forward, when, by almost providential decree, they proved to be two twenty-four-pound howitzers belonging to McAlister's battery, and served as well as guns ever could be.

This was about 2 P.M. The enemy had one battery close by Shiloh, and another near the Hamburg road, both pouring grape and canister upon any column of troops that advanced upon the green point of water-oaks. Willich's regiment had been repulsed, but a whole brigade of McCook's division advanced beautifully, deployed, and entered this dreaded wood. I ordered my second brigade (then commanded by Colonel T. Kilby Smith, Colonel Stuart being wounded) to form on its right, and my fourth brigade, Colonel Buckland, on its right; all to advance abreast with this Kentucky brigade before mentioned, which I afterward found to be Rousseau's brigade of McCook's division. I gave personal direction to the twenty-four-pounder guns, whose well-directed fire first silenced the enemy's guns to the left, and afterward at the Shiloh meeting-house.

Rousseau's brigade moved in splendid order steadily to the front, sweeping every thing before it, and at 4 P.M. we stood upon the ground of our original front line; and the enemy was in full retreat. I directed my several brigades to resume at once their original camps.

Several times during the battle, cartridges gave out; but General Grant had thoughtfully kept a supply coming from the rear. When I appealed to regiments to stand fast, although out of cartridges, I did so because, to retire a regiment for any cause, has a bad effect on others. I commend the Fortieth Illinois and Thirteenth Missouri for thus holding their ground under heavy fire, although their cartridge-boxes were empty.

I am ordered by General Grant to give personal credit where I think it is due, and censure where I think it merited. I concede that General McCook's splendid division from Kentucky drove back the enemy along the Corinth road, which was the great centre of this field of battle, where Beauregard commanded in person, supported by Bragg's, Polk's, and Breckenridge's divisions. I think Johnston was killed by exposing himself in front of his troops, at the time of their attack on Buckland's brigade on Sunday morning; although in this I may be mistaken.

My division was made up of regiments perfectly new, nearly all having received their muskets for the first time at Paducah. None of them had ever been under fire or beheld heavy columns of an enemy bearing down on them as they did on last Sunday.

To expect of them the coolness and steadiness of older troops would be wrong. They knew not the value of combination and organization. When individual fears seized them, the first impulse was to get away. My third brigade did break much too soon, and I am not yet advised where they were during Sunday afternoon and Monday morning. Colonel Hildebrand, its commander, was as cool as any man I ever saw, and no one could have made stronger efforts to hold his men to their places than he did. He kept his own regiment with individual exceptions in hand, an hour after Appler's and Mungen's regiments had left their proper field of action. Colonel Buckland managed his brigade well. I commend him to your notice as a cool, intelligent, and judicious gentleman, needing only confidence and experience to make a good commander. His subordinates, Colonels Sullivan and Cockerill, behaved with great gallantry; the former receiving a severe wound on Sunday, and yet commanding and holding his regiment well in hand all day, and on Monday, until his right arm was broken by a shot. Colonel Cockerill held a larger proportion of his men than any colonel in my division, and was with me from first to last.

Colonel J. A. McDowell, commanding the first brigade, held his ground on Sunday, till I ordered him to fall back, which he did in line of battle; and when ordered, he conducted the attack on the enemy's left in good style. In falling back to the next position, he was thrown from his horse and injured, and his brigade was not in position on Monday morning. His subordinates, Colonels Hicks and Worthington, displayed great personal courage. Colonel Hicks led his regiment in the attack on Sunday, and received a wound, which it is feared may prove mortal. He is a brave and gallant gentleman, and deserves well of his country. Lieutenant-Colonel Walcutt, of the Ohio Forty-sixth, was severely wounded on Sunday, and has been disabled ever since. My second brigade, Colonel Stuart, was detached nearly two miles from my headquarters. He had to fight his own battle on Sunday, against superior numbers, as the enemy interposed between him and General Prentiss early in the day. Colonel Stuart was wounded severely, and yet reported for duty on Monday morning, but was compelled to leave during the day, when the command devolved on Colonel T. Kilby Smith, who was always in the thickest of the fight, and led the brigade handsomely.

I have not yet received Colonel Stuart's report of the operations of his brigade during the time he was detached, and must therefore forbear to mention names. Lieutenant-Colonel Kyle, of the Seventy-first, was mortally wounded on Sunday, but the regiment itself I did not see, as only a small fragment of it was with the brigade when it joined the division on Monday morning. Great credit is due the fragments of men of the disordered regiments who kept in the advance. I observed and noticed them, but until the brigadiers and colonels make their reports, I cannot venture to name individuals, but will in due season notice all who kept in our front line, as well as those who preferred to keep back near the steamboat-landing. I will also send a full list of the killed, wounded, and missing, by name, rank, company, and regiment. At present I submit the result in figures:

REGIMENTS, Etc.	KILLED.		WOUNDED.		MISSING.	
	Officers.	Men.	Officers.	Men.	Officers.	Men.
Sixth Iowa	2	49	3	117	. .	39
Fortieth Illinois	1	42	7	148	. .	2
Forty-sixth Ohio	2	32	3	147	. .	52
Fifty-fifth Illinois	1	45	8	183	. .	41
Fifty-fourth Ohio	2	22	5	128	. .	32
Seventy-first Ohio	1	12	. .	52	1	45
Seventy-seventh Ohio . .	1	48	7	107	3	53
Fifty-seventh Ohio . . .	2	7	. .	82	. .	33
Fifty-third Ohio	. .	7	. .	39	. .	5
Seventy-second Ohio . . .	2	13	5	85	. .	49
Forty-eighth Ohio	1	13	3	70	1	45
Seventieth Ohio	. .	9	1	53	1	39
Taylor's battery, no report .	. .	. .	. .	. .	. .	. .
Behr's	1	. .	. .	. .	. .	. .
Barrett's	. .	1	. .	5	. .	. .
Waterhouse's	. .	1	3	14	. .	. .
Orderly Holliday	. .	1	. .	. .	. .	. .
Total.	16	302	45	1,230	6	435

RECAPITULATION.

Officers killed	16
Officers wounded.	45
Officers missing	6
Soldiers killed	302
Soldiers wounded.	1,230
Soldiers missing	435
Aggregate loss in the division	2,034

The enemy captured seven of our guns on Sunday, but on Monday we recovered seven; not the identical guns we had lost, but enough in number to balance the account. At the time of recovering our camps our men were so fatigued that we could not follow the retreating masses of the enemy; but on the following day I followed up with Buckland's and Hildebrand's brigade for six miles, the result of which I have already reported.

Of my personal staff, I can only speak with praise and thanks. I think they smelled as much gunpowder and heard as many cannon-balls and bullets as must satisfy their ambition. Captain Hammond, my chief of staff, though in feeble health, was very active in rallying broken troops, encouraging the steadfast and aiding to form the lines of defense and attack. I recommend him to your notice. Major Sanger's intelligence, quick perception, and rapid execution, were of very great value to me, especially in bringing into line the batteries that coöperated so efficiently in our movements. Captains McCoy and Dayton, aides-de-camp, were with me all the time, carrying orders, and acting with coolness, spirit, and courage. To Surgeon Hartshorne and Dr. L'Hommedieu hundreds of wounded men are indebted for the kind and excellent treatment received on the field of battle and in the various temporary hospitals created along the line of our operations. They worked day and night, and did not rest till all the wounded of our own troops as well as of the enemy were in safe and comfortable shelter. To Major Taylor, chief of artillery, I feel under deep obligations, for his good sense and judgment in managing the batteries, on which so much depended. I inclose his report and indorse his recommendations. The cavalry of my command kept to the rear, and took little part in the action; but it would have been madness to have exposed horses to the musketry-fire under which we were compelled to remain from Sunday at 8 A.M. till Monday at 4 P.M.

Captain Kossack, of the engineers, was with me all the time, and was of great assistance. I inclose his sketch of the battle-field, which is the best I have seen, and which will enable you to see the various positions occupied by my division, as well as of the others that participated in the battle. I will also send in, during the day, the detailed reports of my brigadiers and colonels, and will indorse them with such remarks as I deem proper.

I am, with much respect, your obedient servant,

W. T. SHERMAN,
Brigadier-General commanding Fifth Division.

HEADQUARTERS FIFTH DIVISION,
Tuesday, April 8, 1862.

SIR: With the cavalry placed at my command and two brigades of my fatigued troops, I went this morning out on the Corinth road. One after another of the abandoned camps of the enemy lined the roads, with hospital-flags for their protection; at all we found more or less wounded and dead men. At the forks of the road I found the head of General T. J. Wood's division of Buell's Army. I ordered cavalry to examine both roads leading toward Corinth, and found the enemy on both. Colonel Dickey, of the Fourth Illinois Cavalry, asking for reënforcements, I ordered General Wood to advance the head of his column cautiously on the left-hand road, while I conducted the head of the third brigade of my division up the right-hand road. About half a mile from the forks was a clear field, through which the road passed, and, immediately beyond, a space of some two hundred yards of fallen timber, and beyond that an extensive rebel camp. The enemy's cavalry could be seen in this camp; after reconnoissance, I ordered the two advance companies of the Ohio Seventy-seventh, Colonel Hildebrand, to deploy forward as skirmishers, and the regiment itself forward into line, with an interval of one hundred yards. In this order we advanced cautiously until the skirmishers were engaged. Taking it for granted this disposition would clear the camp, I held Colonel Dickey's Fourth Illinois Cavalry ready for the charge. The enemy's cavalry came down boldly at a charge, led by General Forrest in person, breaking through our line of skirmishers; when the regiment of infantry, without cause, broke, threw away their muskets, and fled. The ground was admirably adapted for a defense of infantry against cavalry, being miry and covered with fallen timber.

As the regiment of infantry broke, Dickey's Cavalry began to discharge their carbines, and fell into disorder. I instantly sent orders to the rear for the brigade to form line of battle, which was promptly executed. The broken infantry and cavalry rallied on this line, and, as the enemy's cavalry came to it, our cavalry in turn charged and drove them from the field. I advanced the entire brigade over the same ground and sent Colonel Dickey's cavalry a mile farther on the road. On examining the ground which had been occupied by the Seventy-seventh Ohio, we found fifteen of our men dead and about twenty-five wounded. I sent for wagons and had all the wounded carried back to camp, and caused the dead to be buried, also the whole rebel camp to be destroyed.

Here we found much ammunition for field-pieces, which was destroyed; also two caissons, and a general hospital, with about two hundred and eighty Confederate wounded, and about fifty of our own wounded men. Not having the means of bringing them off, Colonel Dickey, by my orders, took a surrender, signed by the medical director (Lyle) and by all the attending surgeons, and a pledge to report themselves to you as prisoners of war; also a pledge that our wounded should be carefully attended to, and surrendered to us to-morrow as soon as ambulances could go out. I inclose this written document, and request that you cause wagons or ambulances for our wounded to be sent to-morrow, and that wagons be sent to bring in the many tents belonging to us which are pitched along the road for four miles out. I did not destroy them, because I knew the enemy could not move them. The roads are very bad, and are strewed with abandoned wagons, ambulances, and limber-boxes. The enemy has succeeded in carrying off the guns, but has crippled his batteries by abandoning the hind limber-boxes of at least twenty caissons. I am satisfied the enemy's infantry and artillery passed Lick Creek this morning, traveling all of last night, and that he left to his rear all his cavalry, which has protected his retreat; but signs of confusion and disorder mark the whole road. The check sustained by us at the fallen timber delayed our advance, so that night came upon us before the wounded were provided for and the dead buried, and our troops being fagged out by three days' hard fighting, exposure, and privation, I ordered them back to their camps, where they now are.

I have the honor to be, your obedient servant,

W. T. SHERMAN,
Brigadier-General commanding Division.

General Grant did not make an official report of the battle of Shiloh, but all its incidents and events were covered by the reports of division commanders and subordinates. Probably no single battle of the war gave rise to such wild and damaging reports. It was publicly asserted at the North that our army was taken completely by surprise; that the rebels caught us in our tents; bayoneted the men in their beds; that General Grant was drunk; that Buell's opportune arrival saved the Army of the Tennessee from utter annihilation, etc. These reports were in a measure sustained by the published opinions of Generals Buell, Nelson, and others, who had reached the steamboat-landing from the east, just before nightfall of the 6th, when there was a large crowd of frightened, stampeded men, who clamored and declared that our army was all destroyed and beaten. Personally I saw General Grant, who with his staff visited me about 10 A.M. of the 6th, when we were desperately engaged. But we had checked the headlong assault of our enemy, and then held our ground. This gave him great satisfaction, and he told me that things did not look as well over on the left. He also told me that on his way up from Savannah that morning he had stopped at Crump's Landing, and had ordered Lew Wallace's division to cross over Snake Creek, so as to come up on my right, telling me to look out for him. He came again just before dark, and described the last assault made by the rebels at the ravine, near the steamboat-landing, which he had repelled by a heavy battery collected under Colonel J. D. Webster and other officers, and he was convinced that the battle was over for that day. He ordered me to be ready to assume the offensive in the morning, saying that, as he had observed at Fort Donelson at the crisis of the battle, both sides seemed defeated, and whoever assumed the offensive was sure to win. General Grant also explained to me that General Buell had reached the bank of the Tennessee River opposite Pittsburg Landing, and was in the act of ferrying his troops across at the time he was speaking to me.

About half an hour afterward General Buell himself rode up to where I was, accompanied by Colonels Fry, Michler, and others of his staff. I was dismounted at the time, and General Buell made of me a good many significant inquiries about matters and things generally. By the aid of a manuscript map made by myself, I pointed out to him our positions as they had been in the morning, and our then positions; I also explained that my right then covered the bridge over Snake Creek by which we had all day been expecting Lew Wallace; that McClernand was on my left, Hurlbut on his left, and so on. But Buell said he had come up from the landing, and had not seen our men, of whose existence in fact he seemed to doubt. I insisted that I had five thousand good men still left in line, and thought that McClernand had as many more, and that with what was left of Hurlbut's, W. H. L. Wallace's, and Prentiss's divisions, we ought to have eighteen thousand men fit for battle. I reckoned that ten thousand of our men were dead, wounded, or prisoners, and that the enemy's loss could not be much less. Buell said that Nelson's, McCook's, and

Crittenden's divisions of his army, containing eighteen thousand men, had arrived and could cross over in the night, and be ready for the next day's battle. I argued that with these reënforcements we could sweep the field. Buell seemed to mistrust us, and repeatedly said that he did not like the looks of things, especially about the boat-landing, and I really feared he would not cross over his army that night, lest he should become involved in our general disaster. He did not, of course, understand the shape of the ground, and asked me for the use of my map, which I lent him on the promise that he would return it. He handed it to Major Michler to have it copied, and the original returned to me, which Michler did two or three days after the battle. Buell did cross over that night, and the next day we assumed the offensive and swept the field, thus gaining the battle decisively. Nevertheless, the controversy was started and kept up, mostly to the personal prejudice of General Grant, who as usual maintained an imperturbable silence.

After the battle, a constant stream of civilian surgeons, and sanitary commission agents, men and women, came up the Tennessee to bring relief to the thousands of maimed and wounded soldiers for whom we had imperfect means of shelter and care. These people caught up the camp-stories, which on their return home they retailed through their local papers, usually elevating their own neighbors into heroes, but decrying all others. Among them was Lieutenant-Governor Stanton, of Ohio, who published in Belfontaine, Ohio, a most abusive article about General Grant and his subordinate generals. As General Grant did not and would not take up the cudgels, I did so. My letter in reply to Stanton, dated June 10, 1862, was published in the *Cincinnati Commercial* soon after its date. To this Lieutenant-Governor Stanton replied, and I further rejoined in a letter dated July 12, 1862. These letters are too personal to be revived. By this time the good people of the North had begun to have their eyes opened, and to give us in the field more faith and support. Stanton was never again elected to any public office, and was commonly spoken of as "the late Mr. Stanton." He is now dead, and I doubt not in life he often regretted his mistake in attempting to gain popular fame by abusing the army-leaders, then as now an easy and favorite mode of gaining notoriety, if not popularity. Of course, subsequent events gave General Grant and most of the other actors in that battle their appropriate place in history, but the danger of sudden popular clamors is well illustrated by this case.

The battle of Shiloh, or Pittsburg Landing, was one of the most fiercely contested of the war. On the morning of April 6, 1862, the five divisions of McClernand, Prentiss, Hurlbut, W. H. L. Wallace, and Sherman, aggregated about thirty-two thousand men. We had no intrenchments of any sort, on the theory that as soon as Buell arrived we would march to Corinth to attack the enemy. The rebel army, commanded by General Albert Sidney Johnston, was, according to their own reports and admissions, forty-five thousand strong, had the momentum of attack, and beyond all question fought skillfully from early morning till about 2 P.M., when their commander-in-chief was killed by a Minié-ball in the calf of his leg, which penetrated the boot and severed the main artery. There was then a perceptible lull for a couple of hours, when the attack was renewed, but with much less vehemence, and continued up to dark. Early at night the division of Lew Wallace arrived from the other side of Snake Creek, not having fired a shot. A very small part of General Buell's army was on our side of the Tennessee River that evening, and their loss was trivial.

During that night, the three divisions of McCook, Nelson, and Crittenden, were ferried across the Tennessee, and fought with us the next day (7th). During that night, also, the two wooden gunboats, Tyler, commanded by Lieutenant Gwin, and Lexington, Lieutenant Shirk, both of the regular navy, caused shells to be thrown toward that part of the field of battle known to be occupied by the enemy. Beauregard afterward reported his entire loss as ten thousand six hundred and ninety-nine. Our aggregate loss, made up from official statements, shows seventeen hundred killed, seven thousand four hundred and ninety-five wounded, and three thousand and twenty-two prisoners; aggregate, twelve thousand two hundred and seventeen, of which twenty-one hundred and sixty-seven were in Buell's army, leaving for that of Grant ten thousand and fifty. This result is a fair measure of the amount of fighting done by each army.

Chapter XI.

SHILOH TO MEMPHIS.

April to July, 1862.

WHILE THE "Army of the Tennessee," under Generals Grant and C. F. Smith, was operating up the Tennessee River, another force, styled the "Army of the Mississippi," commanded by Major-General John Pope, was moving directly down the Mississippi River, against that portion of the rebel line which, under Generals Polk and Pillow, had fallen back from Columbus, Kentucky, to Island Number Ten and New Madrid. This army had the full coöperation of the gunboat fleet, commanded by Admiral Foote, and was assisted by the high flood of that season, which enabled General Pope, by great skill and industry, to open a canal from a point above Island Number Ten to New Madrid below, by which he interposed between the rebel army and its available line of supply and retreat. At the very time that we were fighting the bloody battle on the Tennessee River, General Pope and Admiral Foote were bombarding the batteries on Island Number Ten, and the Kentucky shore abreast of it; and General Pope having crossed over by steamers a part of his army to the east bank, captured a large part of this rebel army, at and near Tiptonville.

General Halleck still remained at St. Louis, whence he gave general directions to the armies of General Curtis, Generals Grant, Buell, and Pope; and instead of following up his most important and brilliant successes directly down the Mississippi, he concluded to bring General Pope's army around to the Tennessee, and to come in person to command there. The gunboat fleet pushed on down the Mississippi, but was brought up again all standing by the heavy batteries at Fort Pillow, about fifty miles above Memphis. About this time Admiral Farragut, with another large sea-going fleet, and with the coöperating army of General Butler, was entering the Mississippi River by the Passes, and preparing to reduce Forts Jackson and St. Philip in order to reach New Orleans; so that all minds were turned to the conquest of the Mississippi

River, and surely adequate means were provided for the undertaking.

The battle of Shiloh had been fought, as described, on the 6th and 7th of April; and when the movement of the 8th had revealed that our enemy was gone, in full retreat, leaving killed, wounded, and much property by the way, we all experienced a feeling of relief. The struggle had been so long, so desperate and bloody, that the survivors seemed exhausted and nerveless; we appreciated the value of the victory, but realized also its great cost of life. The close of the battle had left the Army of the Tennessee on the right, and the Army of the Ohio on the left; but I believe neither General Grant nor Buell exercised command, the one over the other; each of them having his hands full in repairing damages. All the division, brigade, and regimental commanders were busy in collecting stragglers, regaining lost property, in burying dead men and horses, and in providing for their wounded. Some few new regiments came forward, and some changes of organization became necessary. Then, or very soon after, I consolidated my four brigades into three, which were commanded: First, Brigadier-General Morgan L. Smith; Second, Colonel John A. McDowell; Third, Brigadier-General J. W. Denver. About the same time I was promoted to major-general of volunteers.

The Seventy-first Ohio was detached to Clarksville, Tennessee, and the Sixth and Eighth Missouri were transferred to my division.

In a few days after the battle, General Halleck arrived by steamboat from St. Louis, pitched his camp near the steamboat-landing, and assumed personal command of all the armies. He was attended by his staff, composed of General G. W. Cullum, U. S. Engineers, as his chief of staff; Colonel George Thom, U. S. Engineers; and Colonels Kelton and Kemper, adjutants-general. It soon became manifest that his mind had been prejudiced by the rumors which had gone forth to the detriment of General Grant; for in a few days he issued an order, reorganizing and rearranging the whole army. General Buell's Army of the Ohio constituted the centre; General Pope's army, then arriving at Hamburg Landing, was the left; the right was made up of mine and Hurlbut's divisions, belonging to the old Army of the Tennessee, and two new ones, made up from the fragments of the divisions of Prentiss and C. F. Smith, and of troops transferred thereto, commanded by Generals T. W. Sherman and Davies. General George H. Thomas was taken from Buell, to command the right. McClernand's and Lew Wallace's divisions were styled the reserve, to be commanded by McClernand. General Grant was substantially left out, and was named "second in command," according to some French notion, with no clear, well-defined command or authority. He still retained his old staff, composed of Rawlins, adjutant-general; Riggin, Lagow, and Hilyer, aides; and he had a small company of the Fourth Illinois Cavalry as an escort. For more than a month he thus remained, without any apparent authority, frequently visiting me and others, and rarely complaining; but I could see that he felt deeply the indignity, if not insult, heaped upon him.

General Thomas at once assumed command of the right wing, and, until we reached Corinth, I served immediately under his command. We were classmates, intimately acquainted, had served together before in the old army, and in Kentucky, and it made to us little difference who commanded the other, provided the good cause prevailed.

Corinth was about thirty miles distant, and we all knew that we should find there the same army with which we had so fiercely grappled at Shiloh, reorganized, reënforced, and commanded in chief by General Beauregard in place of Johnston, who had fallen at Shiloh. But we were also reënforced by Buell's and Pope's armies; so that before the end of April our army extended from Snake Creek on the right to the Tennessee River, at Hamburg, on the left, and must have numbered nearly one hundred thousand men.

Ample supplies of all kinds reached us by the Tennessee River, which had a good stage of water; but our wagon transportation was limited, and much confusion occurred in hauling supplies to the several camps. By the end of April, the several armies seemed to be ready, and the general forward movement on Corinth began. My division was on the extreme right of the right wing, and marched out by the "White House," leaving Monterey or Pea Ridge to the south. Crossing Lick Creek, we came into the main road about a mile south of Monterey, where we turned square to the right, and came into the Purdy road, near "Elams." Thence we followed the Purdy road to Corinth, my skirmishers reaching at all times the Mobile & Ohio Railroad. Of course our marches were governed by the main centre, which followed the direct road from Pittsburg Landing to Corinth; and this movement was provokingly slow. We fortified almost every camp at night, though we had encountered no serious opposition, except from cavalry, which gave ground easily as we advanced. The opposition increased as we neared Corinth, and at a place called Russell's we had a sharp affair of one brigade, under the immediate direction of Brigadier-General Morgan L. Smith, assisted by the brigade of General Denver. This affair occurred on the 19th of May, and our line was then within about two miles of the northern intrenchments of Corinth.

On the 27th I received orders from General Halleck "to send a force the next day to drive the rebels from the house in our front, on the Corinth road, to drive in their pickets as far as possible, and to make a strong demonstration on Corinth itself;" authorizing me to call on any adjacent division for assistance.

I reconnoitred the ground carefully, and found that the main road led forward along the fence of a large cotton-field to our right front, and ascended a wooded hill, occupied in some force by the enemy, on which was the farm-house referred to in General Halleck's orders. At the farther end of the field was a double log-house, whose chinking had been removed; so that it formed a good block-house from which the enemy could fire on any person approaching from our quarter.

General Hurlbut's division was on my immediate left, and General McClernand's reserve on our right rear. I asked of each the assistance of a brigade. The former sent General Veatch's, and the latter General John A. Logan's brigade. I asked the former to support our left flank, and the latter our right flank. The next morning early, Morgan L. Smith's brigade was deployed under cover on the left, and Denver's on the right, ready to move forward rapidly at a signal. I had a battery of four twenty-pound Parrott guns, commanded by Captain Silversparre. Colonel Ezra Taylor, chief of artillery, had two of these guns moved up silently by hand behind a small knoll, from the crest of which the enemy's block-house and position could be distinctly seen; when all were ready, these guns were moved to the crest, and several quick rounds were fired at the house, followed after an interval by a single gun. This was the signal agreed on, and the troops responded beautifully, crossed the field in line of battle, preceded by their skirmishers who carried the position in good style, and pursued the enemy for half a mile beyond.

The main line halted on the crest of the ridge, from which we could look over the parapets of the rebel works at Corinth, and hear their drum and bugle calls. The rebel brigade had evidently been taken by surprise in our attack; it soon rallied and came back on us with the usual yell, driving in our skirmishers, but was quickly checked when it came within range of our guns and line of battle. Generals Grant and Thomas happened to be with me during this affair, and were well pleased at the handsome manner in which the troops behaved. That night we began the usual entrenchments, and the next day brought forward the artillery and the rest of the division, which then extended from the Mobile & Ohio Railroad, at Bowie Hill Cut, to the Corinth & Purdy road, there connecting with Hurlbut's division. That night, viz., May 29th, we heard unusual sounds in Corinth, the constant whistling of locomotives, and soon after daylight occurred a series of explosions followed by a dense smoke rising high over the town. There was a telegraph line connecting my headquarters with those of General Halleck, about four miles off, on the Hamburg road. I inquired if he knew the cause of the explosions and of the smoke, and he answered to "advance with my division and feel the enemy if still in my front." I immediately dispatched two regiments from each of my three brigades to feel the immediate front, and in a very short time advanced with the whole division. Each brigade found the rebel parapets abandoned, and pushed straight for the town, which lies in the northeast angle of intersection of the Mobile & Ohio and Memphis & Charleston Railroads. Many buildings had been burned by the enemy on evacuation, which had begun the night before at 6 P.M., and continued through the night, the rear-guard burning their magazine at the time of withdrawing, about daybreak. Morgan L. Smith's brigade followed the retreating rear-guard some four miles to the Tuscumbia Bridge, which was found burned. I halted the other brigades at the college, about a mile to the southwest of the town, where I was overtaken by General Thomas in person.

The heads of all the columns had entered the rebel lines about the same time, and there was some rather foolish clamor for the first honors, but in fact there was no honor in the event. Beauregard had made a clean retreat to the south, and was only seriously pursued by cavalry from General Pope's flank. But he reached Tupelo, where he halted for reorganization; and there is no doubt that at the moment there was much disorganization in his ranks, for the woods were full of deserters whom we did not even take prisoners, but advised them to make their way home and stay there. We spent the day at and near the college, when General Thomas, who applied for orders at Halleck's headquarters, directed me to conduct my division back to the camp of the night before, where we had left our trains. The advance on Corinth had occupied all of the month of May, the most beautiful and valuable month of the year for campaigning in this latitude. There had been little fighting, save on General Pope's left flank about Farmington; and on our right. I esteemed it a magnificent drill, as it served for the instruction of our men in guard and picket duty, and in habituating them to out-door life; and by the time we had reached Corinth I believe that army was the best then on this continent, and could have gone where it pleased. The four subdivisions were well commanded, as were the divisions and brigades of the whole army. General Halleck was a man of great capacity, of large acquirements, and at the time possessed the confidence of the country, and of most of the army. I held him in high estimation, and gave him credit for the combinations which had resulted in placing this magnificent army of a hundred thousand men, well equipped and provided, with a good base, at Corinth, from which he could move in any direction.

Had he held his force as a unit, he could have gone to Mobile, or Vicksburg, or anywhere in that region, which would by one move have solved the whole Mississippi problem;

and, from what he then told me, I believe he intended such a campaign, but was overruled from Washington. Be that as it may, the army had no sooner settled down at Corinth before it was scattered: General Pope was called to the East, and his army distributed among the others; General Thomas was relieved from the command of the right wing, and reassigned to his division in the Army of the Ohio; and that whole army under General Buell was turned east along the Memphis & Charleston road, to march for Chattanooga. McClernand's "reserve" was turned west to Bolivar and Memphis. General Halleck took post himself at Corinth, assigned Lieutenant-Colonel McPherson to take charge of the railroads, with instructions to repair them as far as Columbus, Kentucky, and to collect cars and locomotives to operate them to Corinth and Grand Junction. I was soon dispatched with my own and Hurlbut's divisions northwest fourteen miles to Chewalla, to save what could be of any value out of six trains of cars belonging to the rebels which had been wrecked and partially burned at the time of the evacuation of Corinth.

A short time before leaving Corinth I rode from my camp to General Halleck's headquarters, then in tents just outside of the town, where we sat and gossiped for some time, when he mentioned to me casually that General Grant was going away the next morning. I inquired the cause, and he said that he did not know, but that Grant had applied for a thirty days' leave, which had been given him. Of course we all knew that he was chafing under the slights of his anomalous position, and I determined to see him on my way back. His camp was a short distance off the Monterey road, in the woods, and consisted of four or five tents, with a sapling railing around the front. As I rode up, Majors Rawlins, Lagow, and Hilyer, were in front of the camp, and piled up near them were the usual office and camp chests, all ready for a start in the morning. I inquired for the general, and was shown to his tent, where I found him seated on a camp-stool, with papers on a rude camp-table; he seemed to be employed in assorting letters, and tying them up with red tape into convenient bundles. After passing the usual compliments, I inquired if it were true that he was going away. He said, "Yes." I then inquired the reason, and he said: "Sherman, you know. You know that I am in the way here. I have stood it as long as I can, and can endure it no longer." I inquired where he was going to, and he said, "St. Louis." I then asked if he had any business there, and he said, "Not a bit." I then begged him to stay, illustrating his case by my own.

Before the battle of Shiloh, I had been cast down by a mere newspaper assertion of "crazy;" but that single battle had given me new life, and now I was in high feather; and I argued with him that, if he went away, events would go right along, and he would be left out; whereas, if he remained, some happy accident might restore him to favor and his true place. He certainly appreciated my friendly advice, and promised to wait awhile; at all events, not to go without seeing me again, or communicating with me. Very soon after this, I was ordered to Chewalla, where, on the 6th of June, I received a note from him, saying that he had reconsidered his intention, and would remain. I cannot find the note, but my answer I have kept.

CHEWALLA, *June* 6, 1862.

Major-General GRANT.

MY DEAR SIR: I have just received your note, and am rejoiced at your conclusion to remain; for you could not be quiet at home for a week when armies were moving, and rest could not relieve your mind of the gnawing sensation that injustice had been done you.

.   .   .   .

My orders at Chewalla were to rescue the wrecked trains there, to reconnoitre westward and estimate the amount of damage to the railroad as far as Grand Junction, about fifty miles. We camped our troops on high, healthy ground to the south of Chewalla, and after I had personally reconnoitred the country, details of men were made and volunteer locomotive-engineers obtained to superintend the repairs. I found six locomotives and about sixty cars, thrown from the track, parts of the machinery detached and hidden in the surrounding swamp, and all damaged as much by fire as possible. It seems that these trains were inside of Corinth during the night of evacuation, loading up with all sorts of commissary stores, etc., and about daylight were started west; but the cavalry-picket stationed at the Tuscumbia bridge had, by mistake or panic, burned the bridge before the trains got to them. The trains, therefore, were caught, and the engineers and guards hastily scattered the stores into the swamp, and disabled the trains as far as they could, before our cavalry had discovered their critical situation. The weather was hot, and the swamp fairly stunk with the putrid flour and fermenting sugar and molasses; I was so much exposed there in the hot sun, pushing forward the work, that I got a touch of malarial fever, which hung on me for a month, and forced me to ride two days in an ambulance, the only time I ever did such a thing during the whole war. By the 7th I reported to General Halleck that the amount of work necessary to reëstablish the railroad between Corinth and Grand Junction was so great, that he concluded not to attempt its repair, but to rely on the road back to Jackson (Tennessee), and forward to Grand Junction; and I was ordered to move to Grand Junction, to take up the repairs from there toward Memphis.

The evacuation of Corinth by Beauregard, and the movements of General McClernand's force toward Memphis, had necessitated the evacuation of Fort Pillow, which occurred about June 1st; soon followed by the further withdrawal of the Confederate army from Memphis, by reason of the destruction of the rebel gunboats in the bold and dashing attack by our gunboats under command of Admiral Davis, who had succeeded Foote. This occurred June 7th. Admiral Farragut had also captured New Orleans after the terrible passage of Forts Jackson and St. Philip on May 24th, and had ascended the river as high as Vicksburg; so that it seemed as though, before the end of June, we should surely have full possession of the whole river. But it is now known that the progress of our Western armies had aroused the rebel government to the exercise of the most stupendous energy. Every man capable of bearing arms at the South was declared to be a soldier, and forced to act as such. All their armies were greatly reënforced, and the most despotic power was granted to enforce discipline and supplies. Beauregard was replaced by Bragg, a man of more ability—of greater powers of organization, of action, and discipline—but naturally exacting and severe, and not possessing the qualities to attract the love of his officers and men. He had a hard task to bring into order and discipline that mass of men to whose command he succeeded at Tupelo, with which he afterward fairly outmanœuvred General Buell, and forced him back from Chattanooga to Louisville. It was a fatal mistake, however, that halted General Halleck at Corinth, and led him to disperse and scatter the best materials for a fighting army that, up to that date, had been assembled in the West.

During the latter part of June and first half of July, I had my own and Hurlbut's divisions about Grand Junction, La-grange, Moscow, and Lafayette, building railroad-trestles and bridges, fighting off cavalry detachments coming from the south, and waging an everlasting quarrel with planters about their negroes and fences—they trying, in the midst of moving armies, to raise a crop of corn. On the 17th of June I sent a detachment of two brigades, under General M. L. Smith, to Holly Springs, in the belief that I could better protect the railroad from some point in front than by scattering our men along it; and, on the 23d, I was at Lafayette Station, when General Grant, with his staff and a very insignificant escort, arrived from Corinth *en route* for Memphis, to take command of that place and of the District of West Tennessee. He came very near falling into the hands of the enemy, who infested the whole country with small but bold detachments of cavalry. Up to that time I had received my orders direct from General Halleck at Corinth, but soon after I fell under the immediate command of General Grant, and so continued to the end of the war; but, on the 29th, General Halleck notified me that "a division of troops under General C. S. Hamilton of 'Rosecrans's army corps,' had passed the Hatchie from Corinth," and was destined for Holly Springs, ordering me to "coöperate as far as advisable," but "not to neglect the protection of the road." I ordered General Hurlbut to leave detachments at Grand Junction and Lagrange, and to march for Holly Springs. I left detachments at Moscow and Lafayette, and, with about four thousand men, marched for the same point. Hurlbut and I met at Hudsonville, and thence marched to the Coldwater, within four miles of Holly Springs. We encountered only small detachments of rebel cavalry under Colonels Jackson and Pierson, and drove them into and through Holly Springs; but they hung about, and I kept an infantry brigade in Holly Springs to keep them out. I heard nothing from General Hamilton till the 5th of July, when I received a letter from him dated Rienzi, saying that he had been within nineteen miles of Holly Springs and had turned back for Corinth; and on the next day, July 6th, I got a tele-graph order from General Halleck, of July 2d, sent me by cou-rier from Moscow, "not to attempt to hold Holly Springs, but to fall back and protect the railroad." We accordingly marched back twenty-five miles—Hurlbut to Lagrange, and I to Moscow. The enemy had no infantry nearer than the Talla-hatchee bridge, but their cavalry was saucy and active, supe-rior to ours, and I despaired of ever protecting a railroad, presenting a broad front of one hundred miles, from their dashes.

About this time, we were taunted by the Confederate sol-diers and citizens with the assertion that Lee had defeated McClellan at Richmond; that he would soon be in Washing-ton; and that our turn would come next. The extreme caution of General Halleck also indicated that something had gone wrong, and, on the 16th of July, at Moscow, I received a dis-patch from him, announcing that he had been summoned to Washington, which he seemed to regret, and which at that moment I most deeply deplored. He announced that his command would devolve on General Grant, who had been summoned around from Memphis to Corinth by way of Columbus, Kentucky, and that I was to go into Memphis to take command of the District of West Tennessee, vacated by General Grant. By this time, also, I was made aware that the great army that had assembled at Corinth at the end of May had been scattered and dissipated, and that terrible disasters had befallen our other armies in Virginia and the East.

I soon received orders to move to Memphis, taking Hurl-but's division along. We reached Memphis on the 21st, and on the 22d I posted my three brigades mostly in and near Fort Pickering, and Hurlbut's division next below on the river-bank by reason of the scarcity of water, except in the Missis-sippi River itself. The weather was intensely hot. The same order that took us to Memphis required me to send the divi-sion of General Lew Wallace (then commanded by Brigadier-General A. P. Hovey) to Helena, Arkansas, to report to

General Curtis, which was easily accomplished by steamboat. I made my own camp in a vacant lot, near Mr. Moon's house, and gave my chief attention to the construction of Fort Pickering, then in charge of Major Prime, United States Engineers; to perfecting the drill and discipline of the two divisions under my command; and to the administration of civil affairs.

At the time when General Halleck was summoned from Corinth to Washington, to succeed McClellan as commander-in-chief, I surely expected of him immediate and important results. The Army of the Ohio was at the time marching toward Chattanooga, and was strung from Eastport by Huntsville to Bridgeport, under the command of General Buell. In like manner, the Army of the Tennessee was strung along the same general line, from Memphis to Tuscumbia, and was commanded by General Grant, with no common commander for both these forces: so that the great army which General Halleck had so well assembled at Corinth, was put on the defensive, with a frontage of three hundred miles. Soon thereafter the rebels displayed peculiar energy and military skill. General Bragg had reorganized the army of Beauregard at Tupelo, carried it rapidly and skillfully toward Chattanooga, whence he boldly assumed the offensive, moving straight for Nashville and Louisville, and compelling General Buell to fall back to the Ohio River at Louisville.

The army of Van Dorn and Price had been brought from the trans-Mississippi Department to the east of the river, and was collected at and about Holly Springs, where, reënforced by Armstrong's and Forrest's cavalry, it amounted to about forty thousand brave and hardy soldiers. These were General Grant's immediate antagonists, and so many and large detachments had been drawn from him, that for a time he was put on the defensive. In person he had his headquarters at Corinth, with the three divisions of Hamilton, Davies, and McKean, under the immediate orders of General Rosecrans. General Ord had succeeded to the division of McClernand (who had also gone to Washington), and held Bolivar and Grand Junction. I had in Memphis my own and Hurlbut's divisions, and other smaller detachments were strung along the Memphis & Charleston road. But the enemy's detachments could strike this road at so many points, that no use could be made of it, and General Grant had to employ the railroads, from Columbus, Kentucky, to Corinth and Grand Junction, by way of Jackson, Tennessee, a point common to both roads, and held in some force.

In the early part of September the enemy in our front manifested great activity, feeling with cavalry at all points, and on the 13th General Van Dorn threatened Corinth, while General Price seized the town of Iuka, which was promptly abandoned by a small garrison under Colonel Murphy. Price's force was about eight thousand men, and the general impression was that he was *en route* for Eastport, with the purpose to cross the Tennessee River in the direction of Nashville, in aid of General Bragg, then in full career for Kentucky. General Grant determined to attack him in force, prepared to regain Corinth before Van Dorn could reach it. He had drawn Ord to Corinth, and moved him, by Burnsville, on Iuka, by the main road, twenty-six miles. General Grant accompanied this column as far as Burnsville. At the same time he had dispatched Rosecrans by roads to the south, *via* Jacinto, with orders to approach Iuka by the two main roads, coming into Iuka from the south, viz., the Jacinto and Fulton roads.

On the 18th General Ord encountered the enemy about four miles out of Iuka. His orders contemplated that he should not make a serious attack, until Rosecrans had gained his position on the south; but, as usual, Rosecrans had encountered difficulties in the confusion of roads, his head of column did not reach the vicinity of Iuka till 4 P.M. of the 19th, and then his troops were long drawn out on the single Jacinto road, leaving the Fulton road clear for Price's use. Price perceived his advantage, and attacked with vehemence the head of Rosecrans's column, Hamilton's division, beating it back, capturing a battery, and killing and disabling seven hundred and thirty-six men, so that when night closed in Rosecrans was driven to the defensive, and Price, perceiving his danger, deliberately withdrew by the Fulton road, and the next morning was gone. Although General Ord must have been within four or six miles of this battle, he did not hear a sound; and he or General Grant did not know of it till advised the next morning by a courier who had made a wide circuit to reach them. General Grant was much offended with General Rosecrans because of this affair, but in my experience these concerted movements generally fail, unless with the very best kind of troops, and then in a country on whose roads some reliance can be placed, which is not the case in Northern Mississippi. If Price was aiming for Tennessee, he failed, and was therefore beaten. He made a wide circuit by the south, and again joined Van Dorn.

On the 6th of September, at Memphis, I received an order from General Grant dated the 2d, to send Hurlbut's division to Brownsville, in the direction of Bolivar, thence to report by letter to him at Jackson. The division started the same day, and, as our men and officers had been together side by side from the first landing at Shiloh, we felt the parting like the breaking up of a family. But General Grant was forced to use every man, for he knew well that Van Dorn could attack him at pleasure, at any point of his long line. To be the better prepared, on the 23d of September he took post himself at Jackson, Tennessee, with a small reserve force, and gave Rosecrans command of Corinth, with his three divisions and some detachments, aggregating about twenty thousand men. He posted General Ord with his own and Hurlbut's divisions at Bolivar, with outposts toward Grand Junction and Lagrange. These amounted to nine or ten thousand men, and I held Memphis with my own division, amounting to about six thousand men. The whole of General Grant's men at that time may have aggregated fifty thousand, but he had to defend a frontage of a hundred and fifty miles, guard some two hundred miles of railway, and as much river. Van Dorn had forty thousand men, united, at perfect liberty to move in any direction, and to choose his own point of attack, under cover of woods, and a superior body of cavalry, familiar with every foot of the ground. Therefore General Grant had good reason for telegraphing to General Halleck, on the 1st of October, that his position was precarious, "but I hope to get out of it all right." In Memphis my business was to hold fast that important flank, and by that date Fort Pickering had been made very strong, and capable of perfect defense by a single brigade. I therefore endeavored by excursions to threaten Van Dorn's detachments to the southeast and east. I repeatedly sent out strong detachments toward Holly Springs, which was his main depot of supply; and General Grierson, with his Sixth Illinois, the only cavalry I had, made some bold and successful dashes at the Coldwater, compelling Van Dorn to cover it by Armstrong's whole division of cavalry. Still, by the 1st of October, General Grant was satisfied that the enemy was meditating an attack in force on Bolivar or Corinth; and on the 2d Van Dorn made his appearance near Corinth, with his entire army. On the 3d he moved down on that place from the north and northwest. General Rosecrans went out some four miles to meet him, but was worsted and compelled to fall back within the line of his forts. These had been begun under General Halleck, but were much strengthened by General Grant, and consisted of several detached redoubts, bearing on each other, and inclosing the town and the depots of stores at the intersection of the two railroads. Van Dorn closed down on the forts by the evening of the 3d, and on the morning of the 4th assaulted with great vehemence. Our men, covered by good parapets, fought gallantly, and defended their posts well, inflicting terrible losses on the enemy, so that by noon the rebels were repulsed at all points, and drew off, leaving their dead and wounded in our hands. Their losses, were variously estimated, but the whole truth will probably never be known, for in that army reports and returns were not the fashion. General Rosecrans admitted his own loss to be three hundred and fifteen killed, eighteen hundred and twelve wounded, and two hundred and thirty-two missing or prisoners, and claimed on the part of the rebels fourteen hundred and twenty-three dead, two thousand and twenty-five prisoners and wounded. Of course, most of the wounded must have gone off or been carried off, so that, beyond doubt, the rebel army lost at Corinth fully six thousand men.

Meantime, General Grant, at Jackson, had dispatched Brigadier-General McPherson, with a brigade, directly for Corinth, which reached General Rosecrans after the battle; and, in anticipation of his victory, had ordered him to pursue instantly, notifying him that he had ordered Ord's and Hurlbut's divisions rapidly across to Pocahontas, so as to strike the rebels in flank. On the morning of the 5th, General Ord reached the Hatchie River, at Davis's bridge, with four thousand men; crossed over and encountered the retreating army, captured a battery and several hundred prisoners, dispersing the rebel advance, and forcing the main column to make a wide circuit by the south in order to cross the Hatchie River. Had General Rosecrans pursued promptly, and been on the heels of this mass of confused and routed men, Van Dorn's army would surely have been utterly ruined; as it was, Van Dorn regained Holly Springs somewhat demoralized.

General Rosecrans did not begin his pursuit till the next morning, the 5th, and it was then too late. General Grant was again displeased with him, and never became fully reconciled. General Rosecrans was soon after relieved, and transferred to the Army of the Cumberland, in Tennessee, of which he afterward obtained the command, in place of General Buell, who was removed.

The effect of the battle of Corinth was very great. It was, indeed, a decisive blow to the Confederate cause in our quarter, and changed the whole aspect of affairs in West Tennessee. From the timid defensive we were at once enabled to assume the bold offensive. In Memphis I could see its effects upon the citizens, and they openly admitted that their cause had sustained a death-blow. But the rebel government was then at its maximum strength; Van Dorn was reënforced, and very soon Lieutenant-General J. C. Pemberton arrived and assumed the command, adopting for his line the Tallahatchie River, with an advance-guard along the Coldwater, and smaller detachments forward at Grand Junction and Hernando. General Grant, in like manner, was reënforced by new regiments.

Out of those which were assigned to Memphis I organized two new brigades, and placed them under officers who had gained skill and experience during the previous campaign.

Chapter XII.

July, 1862, to January, 1863.

WHEN WE FIRST entered Memphis, July 21, 1862, I found the place dead; no business doing, the stores closed, churches, schools, and every thing shut up. The people were all more or less in sympathy with our enemies, and there was a strong prospect that the whole civil population would become a dead weight on our hands. Inasmuch as the Mississippi River was then in our possession northward, and steamboats were freely plying with passengers and freight, I caused all the stores to be opened, churches, schools, theatres, and places of amusement, to be reëstablished, and very soon Memphis resumed its appearance of an active, busy, prosperous place. I also restored the mayor (whose name was Parks) and the city government to the performance of their public functions, and required them to maintain a good civil police.

Up to that date neither Congress nor the President had made any clear, well-defined rules touching the negro slaves, and the different generals had issued orders according to their own political sentiments. Both Generals Halleck and Grant regarded the slave as still a slave, only that the labor of the slave belonged to his owner, if faithful to the Union, or to the United States, if the master had taken up arms against the Government, or adhered to the fortunes of the rebellion. Therefore, in Memphis, we received all fugitives, put them to work on the fortifications, supplied them with food and clothing, and reserved the question of payment of wages for future decision. No force was allowed to be used to restore a fugitive slave to his master in any event; but if the master proved his loyalty, he was usually permitted to see his slave, and, if he could persuade him to return home, it was permitted. Cotton, also, was a fruitful subject of controversy. The Secretary of the Treasury, Mr. Chase, was extremely anxious at that particular time to promote the purchase of cotton, because each bale was worth, in gold, about three hundred dollars, and answered the purpose of coin in our foreign exchanges. He therefore encouraged the trade, so that hundreds of greedy speculators flocked down the Mississippi, and resorted to all sorts of measures to obtain cotton from the interior, often purchasing it from negroes who did not own it, but who knew where it was concealed. This whole business was taken from the jurisdiction of the military, and committed to Treasury agents appointed by Mr. Chase.

Other questions absorbed the attention of military commanders; and by way of illustration I here insert a few letters from my "letter-book," which contains hundreds on similar subjects:

HEADQUARTERS FIFTH DIVISION, }
MEMPHIS, TENNESSEE, *August* 11, 1862.}

Hon. S. P. CHASE, *Secretary of the Treasury.*

SIR: Your letter of August 2d, just received, invites my discussion of the cotton question.

I will write plainly and slowly, because I know you have no time to listen to trifles. This is no trifle; when one nation is at war with another, all the people of the one are enemies of the other: then the rules are plain and easy of understanding. Most unfortunately, the war in which we are now engaged has been complicated with the belief on the one hand that all on the other are *not* enemies. It would have been better if, at the outset, this mistake had not been made, and it is wrong longer to be misled by it. The Government of the United States may now safely proceed on the proper rule that all in the South *are* enemies of all in the North; and not only are they unfriendly, but all who can procure arms now bear them as organized regiments, or as guerrillas. There is not a garrison in Tennessee where a man can go beyond the sight of the flag-staff without being shot or captured. It so happened that these people had cotton, and, whenever they apprehended our large armies would move, they destroyed the cotton in the belief that, of course, we would seize it, and convert it to our use. They did not and could not dream that we would pay money for it. It had been condemned to destruction by their own acknowledged government, and was therefore lost to their people; and could have been, without injustice, taken by us, and sent away, either as absolute prize of war, or for future compensation. But the commercial enterprise of the Jews soon discovered that ten cents would buy a pound of cotton behind our army; that four cents would take it to Boston, where they could receive thirty cents in

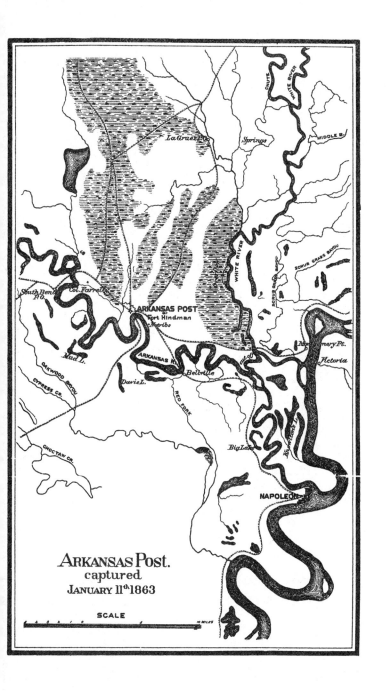

ARKANSAS POST.
captured
JANUARY 11th 1863

SCALE

10 MILES

gold. The bait was too tempting, and it spread like fire, when here they discovered that salt, bacon, powder, fire-arms, percussion-caps, etc., etc., were worth as much as gold; and, strange to say, this traffic was not only permitted, but encouraged. Before we in the interior could know it, hundreds, yea thousands of barrels of salt and millions of dollars had been disbursed; and I have no doubt that Bragg's army at Tupelo, and Van Dorn's at Vicksburg, received enough salt to make bacon, without which they could not have moved their armies in mass; and that from ten to twenty thousand fresh arms, and a due supply of cartridges, have also been got, I am equally satisfied. As soon as I got to Memphis, having seen the effect in the interior, I ordered (only as to my own command) that gold, silver, and Treasury notes, were contraband of war, and should not go into the interior, where all were hostile. It is idle to talk about Union men here: many want peace, and fear war and its results; but all prefer a Southern, independent government, and are fighting or working for it. Every gold dollar that was spent for cotton, was sent to the seaboard, to be exchanged for bank-notes and Confederate scrip, which will buy goods here, and are taken in ordinary transactions. I therefore required cotton to be paid for in such notes, by an obligation to pay at the end of the war, or by a deposit of the price in the hands of a trustee, viz., the United States Quartermaster. Under these rules cotton is being obtained about as fast as by any other process, and yet the enemy receives no "aid or comfort." Under the "gold" rule, the country people who had concealed their cotton from the burners, and who openly scorned our greenbacks, were willing enough to take Tennessee money, which will buy their groceries; but now that the trade is to be encouraged, and gold paid out, I admit that cotton will be sent in by our open enemies, who can make better use of gold than they can of their hidden bales of cotton.

I may not appreciate the foreign aspect of the question, but my views on this may be ventured. If England ever threatens war because we don't furnish her cotton, tell her plainly if she can't employ and feed her own people, to send them here, where they cannot only earn an honest living, but soon secure independence by moderate labor. We are not bound to furnish her cotton. She has more reason to fight the South for burning that cotton, than us for not shipping it. To aid the South on this ground would be hypocrisy which the world would detect at once. Let her make her ultimatum, and there are enough generous minds in Europe that will counteract her in the balance. Of course her motive is to cripple a power that rivals her in commerce and manufactures, that threatenes even to usurp her history. In twenty more years of prosperity, it will require a close calculation to determine whether England, her laws and history, claim for a home the Continent of America or the Isle of Britain. Therefore, finding us in a death-struggle for existence, she seems to seek a quarrel to destroy both parts in detail.

Southern people know this full well, and will only accept the alliance of England in order to get arms and manufactures in exchange for their cotton. The Southern Confederacy will accept no other mediation, because she knows full well that in *Old* England her slaves and slavery will receive no more encouragement than in *New* England.

France certainly does not need our cotton enough to disturb her equilibrium, and her mediation would be entitled to a more respectful consideration than on the part of her present ally. But I feel assured the French will not encourage rebellion and secession anywhere as a political doctrine. Certainly all the German states must be our ardent friends; and, in case of European intervention, they could not be kept down.

With great respect, your obedient servant,

W. T. SHERMAN, *Major-General.*

HEADQUARTERS FIFTH DIVISION, ARMY OF THE TENNESSEE,
MEMPHIS, *July* 23, 1862.

Dr. E. S. PLUMMER *and others, Physicians in Memphis,*
   Signers to a Petition.

GENTLEMEN: I have this moment received your communication, and assure you that it grieves my heart thus to be the instrument of adding to the seeming cruelty and hardship of this unnatural war.

On my arrival here, I found my predecessor (General Hovey) had issued an order permitting the departure south of all persons subject to the conscript law of the Southern Confederacy. Many applications have been made to me to modify this order, but I regarded it as a condition precedent by which I was bound in honor, and therefore I have made no changes or modifications; nor shall I determine what action I shall adopt in relation to persons unfriendly to our cause who remain after the time limited by General Hovey's order has expired. It is now sunset, and all who have not availed themselves of General Hovey's authority, and who remain in Memphis, are supposed to be loyal and true men.

I will only say that I cannot allow the personal convenience of even a large class of ladies to influence me in my determination to make Memphis a safe place of operations for an army, and all people who are unfriendly should forthwith prepare to depart in such direction as I may hereafter indicate.

Surgeons are not liable to be made prisoners of war, but they should not reside within the lines of an army which they regard as hostile. The situation would be too delicate.

I am, with great respect, your obedient servant,

W. T. SHERMAN, *Major-General*.

HEADQUARTERS, MEMPHIS, *July* 24, 1862.

SAMUEL SAWYER, *Esq., Editor Union Appeal, Memphis*.

DEAR SIR: It is well I should come to an understanding at once with the press as well as the people of Memphis, which I am ordered to command; which means, to control for the interest, welfare, and glory of the *whole* Government of the United States.

Personalities in a newspaper are wrong and criminal. Thus, though you meant to be complimentary in your sketch of my career, you make more than a dozen mistakes of fact, which I need not correct, as I don't desire my biography to be written till I am dead. It is enough for the world to know that I live and am a soldier, bound to obey the orders of my superiors, the laws of my country, and to venerate its Constitution; and that, when discretion is given me, I shall exercise it wisely and account to my superiors.

I regard your article headed "City Council—General Sherman and Colonel Slack," as highly indiscreet. Of course, no person who can jeopardize the safety of Memphis can remain here, much less exercise public authority; but I must take time, and be satisfied that injustice be not done.

If the parties named be the men you describe, the fact should not be published, to put them on their guard and thus to encourage their escape. The evidence should be carefully collected, authenticated, and then placed in my hands. But your statement of facts is entirely qualified, in my mind, and loses its force by your negligence of the very simple facts within your reach as to myself: I had been in the army six years in 1846; am not related by blood to any member of Lucas, Turner & Co.; was associated with them in business six years (instead of two); am not colonel of the Fifteenth Infantry, but of the Thirteenth. Your correction, this morning, of the acknowledged error as to General Denver and others, is still erroneous. General Morgan L. Smith did not belong to my command at the battle of Shiloh at all, but he was transferred to my division just before reaching Corinth. I mention these facts in kindness, to show you how wrong it is to speak of persons.

I will attend to the judge, mayor, Boards of Aldermen, and policemen, all in good time.

Use your influence to reëstablish system, order, government. You may rest easy that no military commander is going to neglect internal safety, or to guard against external danger; but to do right requires time, and more patience than I usually possess. If I find the press of Memphis actuated by high principle and a sole devotion to their country, I will be their best friend; but, if I find them personal, abusive, dealing in innuendoes and hints at a blind venture, and looking to their own selfish aggrandizement and fame, then they had better look out; for I regard such persons as greater enemies to their country and to mankind than the men who, from a mistaken sense of State pride, have taken up muskets, and fight us about as hard as we care about. In haste, but in kindness, yours, etc.

W. T. SHERMAN, *Major-General.*

HEADQUARTERS FIFTH DIVISION, }
MEMPHIS, TENNESSEE, *July* 27, 1862.}

JOHN PARK, *Mayor of Memphis, present.*

SIR: Yours of July 24th is before me, and has received, as all similar papers ever will, my careful and most respectful consideration. I have the most unbounded respect for the civil law, courts, and authorities, and shall do all in my power to restore them to their proper use, viz., the protection of life, liberty, and property.

Unfortunately, at this time, civil war prevails in the land, and necessarily the military, for the time being, must be superior to the civil authority, but it does not therefore destroy it. Civil courts and executive officers should still exist and perform duties, without which civil or municipal bodies would soon pass into disrespect—an end to be avoided. I am glad to find in Memphis a mayor and municipal authorities not only in existence, but in the co-exercise of important functions, and I shall endeavor to restore one or more civil tribunals for the arbitration of contracts and punishment of crimes, which the military have neither time nor inclination to interfere with. Among these, first in importance is the maintenance of order, peace, and quiet, within the jurisdiction of Memphis. To insure this, I will keep a strong provost guard in the city, but will limit their duty to guarding public property held or claimed by the United States, and for the arrest and confinement of State prisoners and soldiers who are disorderly or improperly away from their regiments. This guard ought not to arrest citizens for disorder or minor crimes. This should be done by the city police. I understand that the city police is too weak in numbers to accomplish this perfectly, and I therefore recommend that the City Council at once take steps to increase this force to a number which, in their judgment, day and night can enforce your ordinances as to peace, quiet, and order; so that any change in our military dispositions will not have a tendency to leave your people unguarded. I am willing to instruct the provost guard to assist the police force when any combination is made too strong for them to overcome; but the city police should be strong enough for any probable contingency. The cost of maintaining this police force must necessarily fall upon all citizens equitably.

I am not willing, nor do I think it good policy, for the city authorities to collect the taxes belonging to the State and County, as you recommend; for these would have to be refunded. Better meet the expenses at once by a new tax on all interested. Therefore, if you, on consultation with the proper municipal body, will frame a good bill for the increase of your police force, and for raising the necessary means for their support and maintenance, I will approve it and aid you in the collection of the tax. Of course, I cannot suggest how this tax should be laid, but I think that it should be made uniform on all interests, real estate, and personal property, including money and merchandise.

All who are protected should share the expenses in proportion to the interests involved. I am, with respect, your obedient servant,

W. T. SHERMAN, *Major-General commanding*.

HEADQUARTERS FIFTH DIVISION, ⎱
MEMPHIS, *August* 7, 1862. ⎰

Captain FITCH, *Assistant Quartermaster, Memphis, Tennessee.*

SIR: The duties devolving on the quartermaster of this post, in addition to his legitimate functions, are very important and onerous, and I am fully aware that the task is more than should devolve on one man. I will endeavor to get you help in the person of some commissioned officer, and, if possible, one under bond, as he must handle large amounts of money in trust; but, for the present, we must execute the duties falling to our share as well as possible. On the subject of vacant houses, General Grant's orders are: "Take possession of all vacant stores and houses in the city, and have them rented at reasonable rates; rent to be paid monthly in advance. These buildings, with their tenants, can be turned over to proprietors on proof of loyalty; also take charge of such as have been leased out by disloyal owners."

I understand that General Grant takes the rents and profits of this class of real property under the rules and laws of war, and not under the confiscation act of Congress; therefore the question of title is not involved—simply the possession, and the rents and profits of houses belonging to our enemies, which are not vacant, we hold in trust for them or the Government, according to the future decisions of the proper tribunals.

Mr. McDonald, your chief agent in renting and managing this business, called on me last evening and left with me written questions, which it would take a volume to answer and a Webster to elucidate; but as we can only attempt plain, substantial justice, I will answer these questions as well as I can, briefly and to the point:

First. When ground is owned by parties who have gone south, and have leased the ground to parties now in the city who own the improvements on the ground?

Answer. The United States takes the rents due the owner of the land; does not disturb the owner of the improvements.

Second. When parties owning houses have gone south, and the tenant has given his notes for the rent in advance?

Answer. Notes are mere evidence of the debt due landlord. The tenant pays the rent to the quartermaster, who gives a bond of indemnity against the notes representing the debt for the particular rent.

Third. When the tenant has expended several months' rent in repairs on the house?

Answer. Of course, allow all such credits on reasonable proof and showing.

Fourth. When the owner has gone south, and parties here hold liens on the property and are collecting the rents to satisfy their liens?

Answer. The rent of a house can only be mortgaged to a person in possession. If a loyal tenant be in possession and claim the rent from himself as due to himself on some other debt, allow it; but, if not in actual possession of the property, rents are not good liens for a debt, but must be paid to the quartermaster.

Fifth. Of parties claiming foreign protection?

Answer. Many claim foreign protection who are not entitled to it. If they are foreign subjects residing for business in this country, they are entitled to consideration and protection so long as they obey the laws of the country. If they occupy houses belonging to absent rebels, they must pay rent to the quartermaster. If they own property, they must occupy it by themselves, tenants, or servants.

Eighth. When houses are occupied and the owner has gone south, leaving an agent to collect rent for his benefit?

Answer. Rent must be paid to the quartermaster. No agent can collect and remit money south without subjecting himself to arrest and trial for aiding and abetting the public enemy.

Ninth. When houses are owned by loyal citizens, but are un-occupied?

Answer. Such should not be disturbed, but it would be well to advise them to have some servant at the house to occupy it.

Tenth. When parties who occupy the house are creditors of the owner, who has gone south?

Answer. You only look to collection of rents. Any person who transmits money south is liable to arrest and trial for aiding and abetting the enemy; but I do not think it our business to collect debts other than rents.

Eleventh. When the parties who own the property have left the city under General Hovey's Order No. 1, but are in the immediate neighborhood, on their plantations?

Answer. It makes no difference where they are, so they are absent.

Twelfth. When movable property is found in stores that are closed?

Answer. The goods are security for the rent. If the owner of the goods prefers to remove the goods to paying rent, he can do so.

Thirteenth. When the owner lives in town, and refuses to take the oath of allegiance?

Answer. If the house be occupied, it does not fall under the order. If the house be vacant, it does. The owner can recover his property by taking the oath.

All persons in Memphis residing within our military lines are presumed to be loyal, good citizens, and may at any moment be called to serve on juries, *posses comitatus*, or other civil service required by the Constitution and laws of our country. Should they be called upon to do such duty, which would require them to acknowledge their allegiance and subordination to the Constitution of the United States, it would then be too late to refuse. So long as they remain quiet and conform to these laws, they are entitled to protection in their property and lives.

We have nothing to do with confiscation. We only deal with possession, and therefore the necessity of a strict accountability, because the United States assumes the place of trustee, and must account to the rightful owner for his property, rents, and profits. In due season courts will be established to execute the laws, the confiscation act included, when we will be relieved of this duty and trust. Until that time, every opportunity should be given to the wavering and disloyal to return to their allegiance to the Constitution of their birth or adoption. I am, etc.,

W. T. SHERMAN,
Major-General commanding.

HEADQUARTERS FIFTH DIVISION, ⎱
MEMPHIS, TENNESSEE, *August* 26, 1862.⎰

Major-General GRANT, *Corinth, Mississippi.*

SIR: In pursuance of your request that I should keep you advised of matters of interest here, in addition to the purely official matters, I now write.

I dispatched promptly the thirteen companies of cavalry, nine of Fourth Illinois, and four of Eleventh Illinois, to their respective destinations, punctually on the 23d instant, although the order was only received on the 22d. I received at the same time, from Colonel Dickey, the notice that the bridge over Hatchie was burned, and therefore I prescribed their order of march *via* Bolivar. They started at 12 M. of the 23d, and I have no news of them since. None of the cavalry ordered to me is yet heard from.

The guerrillas have destroyed several bridges over Wolf Creek; one at Raleigh, on the road by which I had prescribed trade and travel to and from the city. I have a strong guard at the lower bridge over Wolf River, by which we can reach the country to the north of that stream; but, as the Confederates have burned their own bridges, I will hold them to my order, and allow no trade over any other road than the one prescribed, using the lower or Randolph road for our own convenience. I am still satisfied there is no large force of rebels anywhere in the neighborhood. All the navy gunboats are below except the St. Louis, which lies off the city. When Commodore Davis passes down from Cairo, I will try to see him, and get him to exchange the St. Louis for a fleeter boat not iron-clad; one that can move up and down the river, to break up ferry-boats and canoes, and to prevent all passing across the river. Of course, in spite of all our efforts, smuggling is carried on. We occasionally make hauls of clothing, gold-lace, buttons, etc., but I am satisfied that salt and arms are got to the interior somehow. I have addressed the Board of Trade a letter on this point, which will enable us to control it better.

You may have been troubled at hearing reports of drunkenness here. There was some after pay-day, but generally all is as quiet and orderly as possible. I traverse the city every day and night, and assert that Memphis is and has been as orderly a city as St. Louis, Cincinnati, or New York.

Before the city authorities undertook to license saloons, there was as much whiskey here as now, and it would take all my command as custom-house inspectors, to break open all the parcels and packages containing liquor. I can destroy all groggeries and shops where soldiers get liquor just as we would in St. Louis.

The newspapers are accusing me of cruelty to the sick; as base a charge as was ever made. I would not let the Sanitary Committee carry off a boat-load of sick, because I have no right to. We have good hospitals here, and plenty of them. Our regimental hospitals are in the camps of the men, and the sick do much better there than in the general hospitals; so say my division surgeon and the regimental surgeons. The civilian doctors would, if permitted, take away our entire command. General Curtis sends his sick up here, but usually no nurses; and it is not right that nurses should be taken from my command for his sick. I think that, when we are endeavoring to raise soldiers and to instruct them, it is bad policy to keep them at hospitals as attendants and nurses.

I send you Dr. Derby's acknowledgment that he gave the leave of absence of which he was charged. I have placed him in arrest, in obedience to General Halleck's orders, but he remains in charge of the Overton Hospital, which is not full of patients.

The State Hospital also is not full, and I cannot imagine what Dr. Derby wants with the Female Academy on Vance Street. I will see him again, and now that he is the chief at Overton Hospital, I think he will not want the academy. Still, if he does, under your orders I will cause it to be vacated by the children and Sisters of Mercy. They have just advertised for more scholars, and will be sadly disappointed. If, however, this building or any other be needed for a hospital, it must be taken; but really, in my heart, I do not see what possible chance there is, under present circumstances, of filling with patients the two large hospitals now in use, besides the one asked for. I may, however, be mistaken in the particular building asked for by Dr. Derby, and will go myself to see.

The fort is progressing well, Captain Jenney having arrived. Sixteen heavy guns are received, with a large amount of shot and shell, but the platforms are not yet ready; still, if occasion should arise for dispatch, I can put a larger force to work. Captain Prime, when here, advised that the work should proceed regularly under the proper engineer officers and laborers.

I am, etc.,

W. T. SHERMAN, *Major-General commanding.*

HEADQUARTERS FIFTH DIVISION,
MEMPHIS, TENNESSEE, *September* 4, 1862.

Colonel J. C. KELTON, *Assistant Adjutant-General, Headquarters of the Army, Washington, D. C.*

DEAR COLONEL: Please acknowledge to the major-general commanding the receipt by me of his letter, and convey to him my assurrances that I have promptly modified my first instructions about cotton, so as to conform to his orders. Trade in cotton is now free, but in all else I endeavor so to control it that the enemy shall receive no contraband goods, or any aid or comfort; still I feel sure that the officers of steamboats are sadly tempted by high prices to land salt and other prohibited articles at way-points along the river. This, too, in time will be checked.

All seems well here and hereabout; no large body of the enemy within striking distance. A force of about two thousand cavalry passed through Grand Junction north last Friday, and fell on a detachment of the Bolivar army at Middleburg, the result of which is doubtless reported to you. As soon as I heard of the movement, I dispatched a force to the southeast by way of diversion, and am satisfied that the enemy's infantry and artillery fell back in consequence behind the Tallahatchie.

The weather is very hot, country very dry, and dust as bad as possible. I hold my two divisions ready, with their original complement of transportation, for field service.

Of course all things must now depend on events in front of Washington and in Kentucky.

The gunboat Eastport and four transports loaded with prisoners of war destined for Vicksburg have been lying before Memphis for two days, but are now steaming up to resume their voyage.

Our fort progresses well, but our guns are not yet mounted. The engineers are now shaping the banquette to receive platforms. I expect Captain Prime from Corinth in two or three days.

I am, with great respect, yours,

W. T. SHERMAN, *Major-General commanding*.

HEADQUARTERS FIFTH DIVISION, }
MEMPHIS, TENNESSEE, *September* 21, 1862.}

Editor Bulletin.

SIR: Your comments on the recent orders of Generals Halleck and McClellan afford the occasion appropriate for me to make public the fact that there is a law of Congress, as old as our Government itself, but reënacted on the 10th of April, 1806, and in force ever since. That law reads:

"All officers and soldiers are to behave themselves orderly in quarters and on the march; and whoever shall commit any waste or spoil, either in walks of trees, parks, warrens, fish-ponds, houses and gardens, cornfields, inclosures or meadows, or shall maliciously destroy any property whatever belonging to the inhabitants of the United States, unless by order of the commander-in-chief of the armies of said United States, shall (besides such penalties as they are liable to by law) be punished according to the nature and degree of the offense, by the judgment of a general or regimental court-martial."

Such is the law of Congress; and the orders of the commander-in-chief are, that officers or soldiers convicted of straggling and pillaging shall be punished with death. These orders have not come to me officially, but I have seen them in newspapers, and am satisfied that they express the determination of the commander-in-chief. Straggling and pillaging have ever been great military crimes; and every officer and soldier in my command knows what stress I have laid upon them, and that, so far as in my power lies, I will punish them to the full extent of the law and orders.

The law is one thing, the execution of the law another. God himself has commanded: "Thou shalt not kill," "thou shalt not steal," "thou shalt not covet thy neighbor's goods," etc. Will any one say these things are not done now as well as before these laws were announced at Sinai? I admit the law to be that "no officer or soldier of the United States shall commit waste or destruction of cornfields, orchards, potato-patches, or any kind of pillage on the property of friend or foe near Memphis," and that I stand prepared to execute the law as far as possible.

No officer or soldier should enter the house or premises of any peaceable citizen, no matter what his politics, unless on business; and no such officer or soldier can force an entrance unless he have a written order from a commanding officer or provost-marshal, which written authority must be exhibited if demanded. When property such as forage, building or other materials are needed by the United States, a receipt will be given by the officer taking them, which receipt should be presented to the quartermaster, who will substitute therefor a regular voucher, to be paid according to the circumstances of the case. If the officer refuse to give such receipt, the citizen may fairly infer that the property is wrongfully taken, and he should, for his own protection, ascertain the name, rank, and regiment of the officer, and report him in writing. If any soldier commits waste or destruction, the person whose property is thus wasted must find out the name, company, and regiment of the actual transgressor. In order to punish there must be a trial, and there must be testimony. It is not sufficient that a general accusation be made, that soldiers are doing this or that. I cannot punish my whole command, or a whole battalion, because one or two bad soldiers do wrong. The punishment must reach the perpetrators, and no one can identify them as well as the party who is interested. The State of Tennessee does not hold itself responsible for acts of larceny committed by her citizens, nor does the United States or any other nation. These are individual acts of wrong, and punishment can only be inflicted on the wrong-doer. I know the difficulty of identifying particular soldiers, but difficulties do not alter the importance of principles of justice. They should stimulate the parties to increase their efforts to find out the actual perpetrators of the crime.

Colonels of regiments and commanders of corps are liable to severe punishment for permitting their men to leave their camps to commit waste or destruction; but I know full well that many of the acts attributed to soldiers are committed by citizens and negroes, and are charged to soldiers because of a desire to find fault with them; but this only reacts upon the community and increases the mischief. While every officer would willingly follow up an accusation against any one or more of his men whose names or description were given immediately after the discovery of the act, he would naturally resent any general charge against his *good* men, for the criminal conduct of a few bad ones.

I have examined into many of the cases of complaint made in this general way, and have felt mortified that our soldiers should do acts which are nothing more or less than stealing, but I was powerless without some clew whereby to reach the rightful party. I know that the great mass of our soldiers would scorn to steal or commit crime, and I will not therefore entertain vague and general complaints, but stand prepared always to follow up any reasonable complaint when the charge is definite and the names of witnesses furnished.

I know, moreover, in some instances when our soldiers are complained of, that they have been insulted by sneering remarks about "Yankees," "Northern barbarians," "Lincoln's hirelings," etc. People who use such language must seek redress through some one else, for I will not tolerate insults to our country or cause. When people forget their obligations to a Government that made them respected among the nations of the earth, and speak contemptuously of the flag which is the silent emblem of that country, I will not go out of my way to protect them or their property. I will punish the soldiers for trespass or waste if adjudged by a court-martial, because they disobey orders; but soldiers are men and citizens as well as soldiers, and should promptly resent any insult to their country, come from what quarter it may. I mention this phase because it is too common. Insult to a soldier does not justify pillage, but it takes from the officer the disposition he would otherwise feel to follow up the inquiry and punish the wrong-doers.

Again, armies in motion or stationary must commit some waste. Flankers must let down fences and cross fields; and, when an attack is contemplated or apprehended, a command will naturally clear the ground of houses, fences, and trees. This is waste, but is the natural consequence of war, chargeable on those who caused the war. So in fortifying a place, dwelling-houses must be taken, materials used, even wasted, and great damage done, which in the end may prove useless. This, too, is an expense not chargeable to us, but to those who made the war; and generally war is destruction and nothing else.

We must bear this in mind, that however peaceful things look, we are really *at war*; and much that looks like waste or destruction is only the removal of objects that obstruct our fire, or would afford cover to an enemy.

This class of waste must be distinguished from the wanton waste committed by army-stragglers, which is wrong, and can be punished by the death-penalty if proper testimony can be produced.

Yours, etc.,

W. T. SHERMAN, *Major-General commanding*.

Satisfied that, in the progress of the war, Memphis would become an important depot, I pushed forward the construction of Fort Pickering, kept most of the troops in camps back of the city, and my own headquarters remained in tents on the edge of the city, near Mr. Moon's house, until, on the approach of winter, Mrs. Sherman came down with the children to visit me, when I took a house nearer the fort.

All this time battalion and brigade drills were enforced, so that, when the season approached for active operations farther south, I had my division in the best possible order, and about the 1st of November it was composed as follows:

First Brigade, Brigadier-General M. L. SMITH. — Eighth Missouri, Colonel G. A. Smith; Sixth Missouri, Colonel Peter E. Bland; One Hundred and Thirteenth Illinois, Colonel George B. Hoge; Fifty-fourth Ohio, Colonel T. Kilby Smith; One Hundred and Twentieth Illinois, Colonel G. W. McKeaig.

Second Brigade, Colonel JOHN ADAIR McDOWELL. — Sixth Iowa, Lieutenant-Colonel John M. Corse; Fortieth Illinois, Colonel J. W. Booth; Forty-sixth Ohio, Colonel C. C. Walcutt; Thirteenth United States Infantry, First Battalion, Major D. Chase.

Third Brigade, Brigadier-General J. W. DENVER. — Forty-eighth

Ohio, Colonel P. J. Sullivan; Fifty-third Ohio, Colonel W. S. Jones; Seventieth Ohio, Colonel J. R. Cockerill.

Fourth Brigade, Colonel DAVID STUART. — Fifty-fifth Illinois, Colonel O. Malmburg; Fifty-seventh Ohio, Colonel W. Mungen; Eighty-third Indiana, Colonel B. Spooner; One Hundred and Sixteenth Illinois, Colonel Tupper; One Hundred and Twenty-seventh Illinois, Lieutenant-Colonel Eldridge.

Fifth Brigade, Colonel R. P. BUCKLAND. — Seventy-second Ohio, Lieutenant-Colonel D. W. C. Loudon; Thirty-second Wisconsin, Colonel J. W. Howe; Ninety-third Indiana, Colonel Thomas; Ninety-third Illinois, Major J. M. Fisher.

Subsequently, Brigadier-General J. G. Lauman arrived at Memphis, and I made up a sixth brigade, and organized these six brigades into three divisions, under Brigadier-Generals M. L. Smith, J. W. Denver, and J. G. Lauman.

About the 17th of November I received an order from General Grant, dated —

LAGRANGE, *November* 15, 1862.

Meet me at Columbus, Kentucky, on Thursday next. If you have a good map of the country south of you, take it up with you.

U. S. GRANT, *Major-General.*

I started forthwith by boat, and met General Grant, who had reached Columbus by the railroad from Jackson, Tennessee. He explained to me that he proposed to move against Pemberton, then intrenched on a line behind the Tallahatchie River below Holly Springs; that he would move on Holly Springs and Abberville, from Grand Junction; that McPherson, with the troops at Corinth, would aim to make junction with him at Holly Springs; and that he wanted me to leave in Memphis a proper garrison, and to aim for the Tallahatchie, so as to come up on his right by a certain date. He further said that his ultimate object was to capture Vicksburg, to open the navigation of the Mississippi River, and that General Halleck had authorized him to call on the troops in the Department of Arkansas, then commanded by General S. R. Curtis, for coöperation. I suggested to him that if he would request General Curtis to send an expedition from some point on the Mississippi near Helena, then held in force, toward Grenada, to the rear of Pemberton, it would alarm him for the safety of his communications, and would assist us materially in the proposed attack on his front. He authorized me to send to the commanding officer at Helena a request to that effect, and, as soon as I reached Memphis, I dispatched my aide, Major McCoy, to Helena, who returned, bringing me a letter from General Frederick Steele, who had just reached Helena with Osterhaus's division, and who was temporarily in command, General Curtis having gone to St. Louis. This letter contained the assurance that he "would send from Friar's Point a large force under Brigadier-General A. P. Hovey in the direction of Grenada, aiming to reach the Tallahatchie at Charleston, on the next Monday, Tuesday, or Wednesday (December 1st) at furthest." My command was appointed to start on Wednesday, November 24th, and meantime Major-General S. A. Hurlbut, having reported for duty, was assigned to the command of Memphis, with four regiments of infantry, one battery of artillery, two companies of Thielman's cavalry, and the certain prospect of soon receiving a number of new regiments, known to be *en route*.

I marched out of Memphis punctually with three small divisions, taking different roads till we approached the Tallahatchie, when we converged on Wyatt to cross the river, there a bold, deep stream, with a newly-constructed fort behind. I had Grierson's Sixth Illinois Cavalry with me, and with it opened communication with General Grant when we were abreast of Holly Springs. We reached Wyatt on the 2d day of December without the least opposition, and there learned that Pemberton's whole army had fallen back to the Yalabusha, near Grenada, in a great measure by reason of the exaggerated reports concerning the Helena force, which had reached Charleston; and some of General Hovey's cavalry, under General Washburn, having struck the railroad in the neighborhood of Coffeeville, naturally alarmed General Pemberton for the safety of his communications, and made him let go his Tallahatchie line with all the forts which he had built at great cost in labor. We had to build a bridge at Wyatt, which consumed a couple of days, and on the 5th of December my whole command was at College Hill, ten miles from Oxford, whence I reported to General Grant in Oxford.

On the 8th I received the following letter:

OXFORD, MISSISSIPPI, *December* 8, 1862.—*Morning.*
General SHERMAN, *College Hill.*

DEAR GENERAL: The following is a copy of dispatch just received from Washington:

WASHINGTON, *December* 7, 1862.—12 M.
General GRANT:

The capture of Grenada may change our plans in regard to Vicksburg. You will move your troops as you may deem best to accomplish the great object in view. You will retain, till further orders, all troops of General Curtis now in your department. Telegraph to General Allen in St. Louis for all steamboats you may require. Ask Porter to coöperate. Telegraph what are your present plans.

H. W. HALLECK, *General-in-Chief.*

I wish you would come over this evening and stay to-night, or come in the morning. I would like to talk with you about this matter. My notion is to send two divisions back to Memphis, and fix upon a day when they should effect a landing, and press from here with this command at the proper time to coöperate. If I do not do this I will move our present force to Grenada, including Steele's, repairing road as we proceed, and establish a depot of provisions there. When a good ready is had, to move immediately on Jackson, Mississippi, cutting loose from the road. Of the two plans I look most favorably on the former.

Come over and we will talk this matter over.

Yours truly,

U. S. GRANT, *Major-General.*

I repaired at once to Oxford, and found General Grant in a large house with all his staff, and we discussed every possible chance. He explained to me that large reënforcements had been promised, which would reach Memphis very soon, if not already there; that the entire gunboat fleet, then under the command of Admiral D. D. Porter, would coöperate; that we could count on a full division from the troops at Helena; and he believed that, by a prompt movement, I could make a lodgment up the Yazoo and capture Vicksburg from the rear; that its garrison was small, and he, at Oxford, would so handle his troops as to hold Pemberton away from Vicksburg. I also understood that, if Pemberton should retreat south, he would follow him up, and would expect to find me at the Yazoo River, if not inside of Vicksburg. I confess, at that

moment I did not dream that General McClernand, or anybody else, was scheming for the mere honor of capturing
Vicksburg. We knew at the time that General Butler had been
reënforced by General Banks at New Orleans, and the latter
was supposed to be working his way up-stream from New
Orleans, while we were working down. That day General
Grant dispatched to General Halleck, in Washington, as
follows:

OXFORD, *December* 8, 1862.
Major-General H. W. HALLECK, *Washington, D. C.:*
General Sherman will command the expedition down the Mississippi. He will have a force of about forty thousand men; will land
above Vicksburg (up the Yazoo, if practicable), and cut the Mississippi Central road and the road running east from Vicksburg, where
they cross Black River. I will coöperate from here, my movements
depending on those of the enemy. With the large cavalry force now
at my command, I will be able to have them show themselves at
different points on the Tallahatchie and Yalabusha; and, when an
opportunity occurs, make a real attack. After cutting the two roads,
General Sherman's movements to secure the end desired will necessarily be left to his judgment.
I will occupy this road to Coffeeville.

U. S. GRANT, *Major-General.*

I was shown this dispatch before it was sent, and afterward
the general drew up for me the following letter of instructions
in his own handwriting, which I now possess:

HEADQUARTERS THIRTEENTH ARMY CORPS,
DEPARTMENT OF THE TENNESSEE,
OXFORD, MISSISSIPPI, *December* 8, 1862.

Major-General W. T. SHERMAN, *commanding Right Wing Army in
    the Field, present.*
GENERAL: You will proceed with as little delay as practicable to
Memphis, Tennessee, taking with you one division of your present
command. On your arrival at Memphis you will assume command of
all the troops there, and that portion of General Curtis's forces at
present east of the Mississippi River, and organize them into brigades and divisions in your own way.
As soon as possible move with them down the river to the vicinity
of Vicksburg, and, with the coöperation of the gunboat fleet under
command of Flag-Officer Porter, proceed to the reduction of that

place in such manner as circumstances and your own judgment may dictate.

The amount of rations, forage, land transportation, etc., necessary to take, will be left entirely to yourself.

The quartermaster in St. Louis will be instructed to send you transportation for thirty thousand men. Should you still find yourself deficient, your quartermaster will be authorized to make up the deficiency from such transports as may come into the port of Memphis.

On arriving in Memphis put yourself in communication with Admiral Porter, and arrange with him for his coöperation.

Inform me at the earliest practicable day of the time when you will embark, and such plans as may then be matured. I will hold the forces here in readiness to coöperate with you in such manner as the movements of the enemy may make necessary.

Leave the District of Memphis in the command of an efficient officer and with a garrison of four regiments of infantry, the siege-guns, and whatever cavalry force may be there.

One regiment of infantry and at least a section of artillery will also be left at Friar's Point or Delta, to protect the stores of the cavalry post that will be left there. Yours truly,

U. S. GRANT, *Major-General.*

I also insert here another letter, dated the 14th instant, sent afterward to me at Memphis, which completes all instructions received by me governing the first movement against Vicksburg:

HEADQUARTERS DEPARTMENT OF THE TENNESSEE, ⎱
OXFORD, MISSISSIPPI, *December* 14, 1862. ⎰

Major-General SHERMAN, *commanding, etc., Memphis, Tennessee:*

I have not had one word from Grierson since he left, and am getting uneasy about him. I hope General Gorman will give you no difficulty about retaining the troops on this side the river, and Steele to command them. The twenty-one thousand men you have, with the twelve thousand from Helena, will make a good force. The enemy are as yet on the Yalabusha. I am pushing down on them slowly, but so as to keep up the impression of a continuous move. I feel particularly anxious to have the Helena cavalry on this side of the river; if not now, at least after you start. If Gorman will send them, instruct them where to go and how to communicate with me. My headquarters will probably be in Coffeeville one week hence. In the mean time I will order transportation, etc. . . . It would be well if you could have two or three small boats suitable for navigating the

Yazoo. It may become necessary for me to look to that base for supplies before we get through. . . .

U. S. GRANT, *Major-General.*

When we rode to Oxford from College Hill, there happened a little circumstance which seems worthy of record.
While General Van Dorn had his headquarters in Holly
Springs, viz., in October, 1862, he was very short of the comforts and luxuries of life, and resorted to every possible device
to draw from the abundant supplies in Memphis. He had no
difficulty whatever in getting spies into the town for information, but he had trouble in getting bulky supplies out through
our guards, though sometimes I connived at his supplies of
cigars, liquors, boots, gloves, etc., for his individual use; but
medicines and large supplies of all kinds were confiscated, if
attempted to be passed out. As we rode that morning toward
Oxford, I observed in a farmer's barn-yard a wagon that
looked like a city furniture-wagon with springs. We were always short of wagons, so I called the attention of the quartermaster, Colonel J. Condit Smith, saying, "There is a good
wagon; go for it." He dropped out of the retinue with an
orderly, and after we had ridden a mile or so he overtook us,
and I asked him, "What luck?" He answered, "All right; I
have secured that wagon, and I also got another," and explained that he had gone to the farmer's house to inquire
about the furniture-wagon, when the farmer said it did not
belong to him, but to some party in Memphis, adding that in
his barn was another belonging to the same party. They went
to the barn, and there found a handsome city hearse, with pall
and plumes. The farmer said they had had a big funeral out of
Memphis, but when it reached his house, the coffin was
found to contain a fine assortment of medicines for the use of
Van Dorn's army. Thus under the pretense of a first-class funeral, they had carried through our guards the very things we
had tried to prevent. It was a good trick, but diminished our
respect for such pageants afterward.

As soon as I was in possession of General Grant's instructions of December 8th, with a further request that I should
dispatch Colonel Grierson, with his cavalry, across by land
to Helena, to notify General Steele of the general plan, I

returned to College Hill, selected the division of Brigadier-
General Morgan L. Smith to return with me to Memphis;
started Grierson on his errand to Helena, and ordered Generals Denver and Lauman to report to General Grant for further
orders. We started back by the most direct route, reached
Memphis by noon of December 12th, and began immediately
the preparations for the Vicksburg movement. There I found
two irregular divisions which had arrived at Memphis in my
absence, commanded respectively by Brigadier-General A. J.
Smith and Brigadier-General George W. Morgan. These were
designated the First and Third Divisions, leaving the Second
Division of Morgan L. Smith to retain its original name and
number.

I also sent orders, in the name of General Grant, to
General Gorman, who meantime had replaced General Steele
in command of Helena, in lieu of the troops which had
been east of the Mississippi and had returned, to make up
a strong division to report to me on my way down. This division was accordingly organized, and was commanded by
Brigadier-General Frederick Steele, constituting my Fourth
Division.

Meantime a large fleet of steamboats was assembling from
St. Louis and Cairo, and Admiral Porter dropped down to
Memphis with his whole gunboat fleet, ready to coöperate in
the movement. The preparations were necessarily hasty in the
extreme, but this was the essence of the whole plan, viz., to
reach Vicksburg as it were by surprise, while General Grant
held in check Pemberton's army about Grenada, leaving me to
contend only with the smaller garrison of Vicksburg and its
well-known strong batteries and defenses. On the 19th the
Memphis troops were embarked, and steamed down to Helena, where on the 21st General Steele's division was also embarked; and on the 22d we were all rendezvoused at Friar's
Point, in the following order, viz.:

Steamer Forest Queen, general headquarters, and battalion Thirteenth United States Infantry.
First Division, Brigadier-General A. J. SMITH. — Steamers Des Arc,
division headquarters and escort; Metropolitan, Sixth Indiana; J. H.

Dickey, Twenty-third Wisconsin; J. C. Snow, Sixteenth Indiana; Hiawatha, Ninety-sixth Ohio; J. S. Pringle, Sixty-seventh Indiana; J. W. Cheeseman, Ninth Kentucky; R. Campbell, Ninety-seventh Indiana; Duke of Argyle, Seventy-seventh Illinois; City of Alton, One Hundred and Eighth and Forty-eighth Ohio; City of Louisiana, Mercantile Battery; Ohio Belle, Seventeenth Ohio Battery; Citizen, Eighty-third Ohio; Champion, commissary-boat; General Anderson, Ordnance.

Second Division, Brigadier-General M. L. SMITH. — Steamers Chancellor, headquarters, and Thielman's cavalry; Planet, One Hundred and Sixteenth Illinois; City of Memphis, Batteries A and B (Missouri Artillery), Eighth Missouri, and section of Parrott guns; Omaha, Fifty-seventh Ohio; Sioux City, Eighty-third Indiana; Spread Eagle, One Hundred and Twenty-seventh Illinois; Ed. Walsh, One Hundred and Thirteenth Illinois; Westmoreland, Fifty-fifth Illinois, headquarters Fourth Brigade; Sunny South, Fifty-fourth Ohio; Universe, Sixth Missouri; Robert Allen, commissary-boat.

Third Division, Brigadier-General G. W. MORGAN. — Steamers Empress, division headquarters; Key West, One Hundred and Eighteenth Illinois; Sam Gaty, Sixty-ninth Indiana; Northerner, One Hundred and Twentieth Ohio; Belle Peoria, headquarters Second Brigade, two companies Forty-ninth Ohio, and pontoons; Die Vernon, Third Kentucky; War Eagle, Forty-ninth Indiana (eight companies), and Foster's battery; Henry von Phul, headquarters Third Brigade, and eight companies Sixteenth Ohio; Fanny Bullitt, One Hundred and Fourteenth Ohio, and Lamphere's battery; Crescent City, Twenty-second Kentucky and Fifty-fourth Indiana; Des Moines, Forty-second Ohio; Pembina, Lamphere's and Stone's batteries; Lady Jackson, commissary-boat.

Fourth Division, Brigadier-General FREDERICK STEELE. — Steamers Continental, headquarters, escort and battery; John J. Roe, Fourth and Ninth Iowa; Nebraska, Thirty-first Iowa; Key West, First Iowa Artillery; John Warner, Thirteenth Illinois; Tecumseh, Twenty-sixth Iowa; Decatur, Twenty-eighth Iowa; Quitman, Thirty-fourth Iowa; Kennett, Twenty-ninth Missouri; Gladiator, Thirtieth Missouri; Isabella, Thirty-first Missouri; D. G. Taylor, quartermaster's stores and horses; Sucker State, Thirty-second Missouri; Dakota, Third Missouri; Tutt, Twelfth Missouri; Emma, Seventeenth Missouri; Adriatic, First Missouri; Meteor, Seventy-sixth Ohio; Polar Star, Fifty-eighth Ohio.

At the same time were communicated the following instructions:

HEADQUARTERS RIGHT WING,
THIRTEENTH ARMY CORPS,
FOREST QUEEN, *December* 23, 1862.

To Commanders of Divisions, Generals F. STEELE, GEORGE W.
MORGAN, A. J. SMITH, *and* M. L. SMITH:

With this I hand to each of you a copy of a map, compiled from the best sources, and which in the main is correct. It is the same used by Admiral Porter and myself. Complete military success can only be accomplished by united action on some *general plan*, embracing usually a large district of country. In the present instance, our object is to secure the navigation of the Mississippi River and its main branches, and to hold them as military channels of communication and for commercial purposes. The river, above Vicksburg, has been gained by conquering the country to its rear, rendering its possession by our enemy useless and unsafe to him, and of great value to us. But the enemy still holds the river from Vicksburg to Baton Rouge, navigating it with his boats, and the possession of it enables him to connect his communications and routes of supply, east and west. To deprive him of this will be a severe blow, and, if done effectually, will be of great advantage to us, and probably the most decisive act of the war. To accomplish this important result we are to act our part—an important one of the great *whole*. General Banks, with a large force, has reënforced General Butler in Louisiana, and from that quarter an expedition, by water and land, is coming northward. General Grant, with the Thirteenth Army Corps, of which we compose the right wing, is moving southward. The naval squadron (Admiral Porter) is operating with his gunboat fleet by water, each in perfect harmony with the other.

General Grant's left and centre were at last accounts approaching the Yalabusha, near Grenada, and the railroad to his rear, by which he drew his supplies, was reported to be seriously damaged. This may disconcert him somewhat, but only makes more important our line of operations. At the Yalabusha General Grant may encounter the army of General Pemberton, the same which refused him *battle* on the line of the Tallahatchie, which was strongly fortified; but, as he will not have time to fortify it, he will hardly stand there; and, in that event, General Grant will immediately advance down the high ridge between the Big Black and Yazoo, and will expect to meet us on the Yazoo and receive from us the supplies which he needs, and which he knows we carry along. Parts of this general plan are to coöperate with the naval squadron in the reduction of Vicksburg; to secure possession of the land lying between the Yazoo and Big Black; and to act in concert with General Grant against Pemberton's forces, supposed to have Jackson, Mississippi, as a point of concentration. Vicksburg is doubtless very strongly fortified, both against the river and land approaches. Already the gunboats have secured the Yazoo up for twenty-three miles, to a fort on the Yazoo at Haines's Bluff, giving us a choice for a landing-place at some point up the Yazoo below this fort, or on the island which lies between Vicksburg and the present mouth of the Yazoo. (*See* map [*b, c, d*], Johnson's plantation.)

But, before any actual collision with the enemy, I purpose, after our whole *land-force* is rendezvoused at Gaines's Landing, Arkansas, to proceed in order to Milliken's Bend (*a*), and there dispatch a brigade, without wagons or any incumbrances whatever, to the Vicksburg & Shreveport Railroad (at *h* and *k*), to destroy that effectually, and to cut off that fruitful avenue of supply; then to proceed to the mouth of the Yazoo, and, after possessing ourselves of the latest and most authentic information from naval officers now there, to land our whole force on the Mississippi side, and then to reach the point where the Vicksburg & Jackson Railroad crosses the Big Black (*f*); after which to attack Vicksburg *by land*, while the gunboats assail it by water. It may be necessary (looking to Grant's approach), before attacking Vicksburg, to reduce the battery at *Haines's Bluff* first, so as to enable some of the lighter gunboats and transports to ascend the Yazoo and communicate with General Grant. The detailed manner of accomplishing all these results will be communicated in due season, and these general points are only made known at this time, that commanders may study the maps, and also that in the event of non-receipt of orders all may act in perfect concert by following the general movement, unless specially detached.

You all now have the same map, so that no mistakes or confusion need result from different names of localities. All possible preparations as to wagons, provisions, axes, and intrenching-tools, should be made in advance, so that when we do land there will be no want of them. When we begin to act on shore, we must do the work quickly and effectually. The gunboats under Admiral Porter will do their full share, and I feel every assurance that the army will not fall short in its work.

Division commanders may read this to regimental commanders, and furnish brigade commanders a copy. They should also cause as many copies of the map to be made on the same scale as possible, being very careful in copying the names.

The points marked *e* and *g* (Allan's and Mount Albans) are evidently strategical points that will figure in our future operations, and these positions should be well studied.

I am, with great respect, your obedient servant,

W. T. SHERMAN, *Major-General.*

The Mississippi boats were admirably calculated for handling troops, horses, guns, stores, etc., easy of embarkation and disembarkation, and supplies of all kinds were abundant, except fuel. For this we had to rely on wood, but most of the wood-yards, so common on the river before the war, had been exhausted, so that we had to use fence-rails, old dead timber, the logs of houses, etc. Having abundance of men and plenty of axes, each boat could daily procure a supply.

In proceeding down the river, one or more of Admiral Porter's gunboats took the lead; others were distributed throughout the column, and some brought up the rear. We manœuvred by divisions and brigades when in motion, and it was a magnificent sight as we thus steamed down the river. What few inhabitants remained at the plantations on the river-bank were unfriendly, except the slaves; some few guerrilla-parties infested the banks, but did not dare to molest so strong a force as I then commanded.

We reached Milliken's Bend on Christmas-day, when I detached one brigade (Burbridge's), of A. J. Smith's division, to the southwest, to break up the railroad leading from Vicksburg toward Shreveport, Louisiana. Leaving A. J. Smith's division there to await the return of Burbridge, the remaining three divisions proceeded, on the 26th, to the mouth of the Yazoo, and up that river to Johnson's plantation, thirteen miles, and there disembarked—Steele's division above the mouth of Chickasaw Bayou, Morgan's division near the house of Johnson (which had been burned by the gunboats on a former occasion), and M. L. Smith's just below. A. J. Smith's division arrived the next night, and disembarked below that of M. L. Smith. The place of our disembarkation was in fact an island, separated from the high bluff known as Walnut Hills, on which the town of Vicksburg stands, by a broad and shallow bayou—evidently an old channel of the Yazoo. On our right was another wide bayou, known as Old River; and on the left still another, much narrower, but too deep to be forded, known as Chickasaw Bayou. All the island was densely wooded, except Johnson's plantation, immediately on the bank of the Yazoo, and a series of old cotton-fields along Chickasaw Bayou. There was a road from Johnson's plantation directly to Vicksburg, but it crossed numerous bayous and deep swamps by bridges, which had been destroyed; and this road debouched on level ground at the foot of the Vicksburg bluff, opposite strong forts, well prepared and defended by heavy artillery. On this road I directed General A. J. Smith's division, not so much by way of a direct attack as a diversion and threat.

Morgan was to move to his left, to reach Chickasaw Bayou, and to follow it toward the bluff, about four miles above A. J. Smith. Steele was on Morgan's left, across Chickasaw Bayou, and M. L. Smith on Morgan's right. We met light resistance at all points, but skirmished, on the 27th, up to the main bayou, that separated our position from the bluffs of Vicksburg, which were found to be strong by nature and by art, and seemingly well defended. On reconnoitring the front in person, during the 27th and 28th, I became satisfied that General A. J. Smith could not cross the intervening obstacles under the heavy fire of the forts immediately in his front, and that the main bayou was impassable, except at two points— one near the head of Chickasaw Bayou, in front of Morgan, and the other about a mile lower down, in front of M. L. Smith's division.

During the general reconnoissance of the 28th General Morgan L. Smith received a severe and dangerous wound in his hip, which completely disabled him and compelled him to go to his steamboat, leaving the command of his division to Brigadier-General D. Stuart; but I drew a part of General A. J. Smith's division, and that general himself, to the point selected for passing the bayou, and committed that special task to his management.

General Steele reported that it was physically impossible to reach the bluffs from his position, so I ordered him to leave but a show of force there, and to return to the west side of

Chickasaw Bayou in support of General Morgan's left. He had to countermarch and use the steamboats in the Yazoo to get on the firm ground on our side of the Chickasaw.

On the morning of December 29th all the troops were ready and in position. The first step was to make a lodgment on the foot-hills and bluffs abreast of our position, while diversions were made by the navy toward Haines's Bluff, and by the first division directly toward Vicksburg. I estimated the enemy's forces, then strung from Vicksburg to Haines's Bluff, at fifteen thousand men, commanded by the rebel Generals Martin Luther Smith and Stephen D. Lee. Aiming to reach firm ground beyond this bayou, and to leave as little time for our enemy to reënforce as possible, I determined to make a show of attack along the whole front, but to break across the bayou at the two points named, and gave general orders accordingly. I pointed out to General Morgan the place where he could pass the bayou, and he answered, "General, in ten minutes after you give the signal I'll be on those hills." He was to lead his division in person, and was to be supported by Steele's division. The front was very narrow, and immediately opposite, at the base of the hills about three hundred yards from the bayou, was a rebel battery, supported by an infantry force posted on the spurs of the hill behind. To draw attention from this, the real point of attack, I gave instructions to commence the attack at the flanks.

I went in person about a mile to the right rear of Morgan's position, at a place convenient to receive reports from all other parts of the line; and about noon of December 29th gave the orders and signal for the main attack. A heavy artillery-fire opened along our whole line, and was replied to by the rebel batteries, and soon the infantry-fire opened heavily, especially on A. J. Smith's front, and in front of General George W. Morgan. One brigade (De Courcey's) of Morgan's troops crossed the bayou safely, but took to cover behind the bank, and could not be moved forward. Frank Blair's brigade, of Steele's division, in support, also crossed the bayou, passed over the space of level ground to the foot of the hills; but, being unsupported by Morgan, and meeting a very severe cross-fire of artillery, was staggered and gradually fell back, leaving about five hundred men behind, wounded and prisoners; among them Colonel Thomas Fletcher, afterward Governor of Missouri. Part of Thayer's brigade took a wrong direction, and did not cross the bayou at all; nor did General Morgan cross in person. This attack failed; and I have always felt that it was due to the failure of General G. W. Morgan to obey his orders, or to fulfill his promise made in person. Had he used with skill and boldness one of his brigades, in addition to that of Blair's, he could have made a lodgment on the bluff, which would have opened the door for our whole force to follow. Meantime the Sixth Missouri Infantry, at heavy loss, had also crossed the bayou at the narrow passage lower down, but could not ascend the steep bank; right over their heads was a rebel battery, whose fire was in a measure kept down by our sharpshooters (Thirteenth United States Infantry) posted behind legs, stumps, and trees, on our side of the bayou.

The men of the Sixth Missouri actually scooped out with their hands caves in the bank, which sheltered them against the fire of the enemy, who, right over their heads, held their muskets outside the parapet vertically, and fired down. So critical was the position, that we could not recall the men till after dark, and then one at a time. Our loss had been pretty heavy, and we had accomplished nothing, and had inflicted little loss on our enemy. At first I intended to renew the assault, but soon became satisfied that, the enemy's attention having been drawn to the only two practicable points, it would prove too costly, and accordingly resolved to look elsewhere for a point below Haines's Bluff, or Blake's plantation. That night I conferred with Admiral Porter, who undertook to cover the landing; and the next day (December 30th) the boats were all selected, but so alarmed were the captains and pilots, that we had to place sentinels with loaded muskets to insure their remaining at their posts. Under cover of night, Steele's division, and one brigade of Stuart's, were drawn out of line, and quietly embarked on steamboats in the Yazoo River. The night of December 30th was appointed for this force, under the command of General Fred Steele, to proceed up the Yazoo just below Haines's Bluff, there to disembark about daylight, and make a dash for the hills. Meantime we had strengthened our positions near Chickasaw Bayou, had all our guns in good position with parapets, and had every thing ready to renew our attack as soon as we heard the sound of battle above.

At midnight I left Admiral Porter on his gunboat; he had his fleet ready and the night was propitious. I rode back to camp and gave orders for all to be ready by daybreak; but when daylight came I received a note from General Steele reporting that, before his boats had got up steam, the fog had settled down on the river so thick and impenetrable, that it was simply impossible to move; so the attempt had to be abandoned. The rain, too, began to fall, and the trees bore water-marks ten feet above our heads, so that I became convinced that the part of wisdom was to withdraw. I ordered the stores which had been landed to be reëmbarked on the boats, and preparations made for all the troops to regain their proper boats during the night of the 1st of January, 1863. From our camps at Chickasaw we could hear the whistles of the trains arriving in Vicksburg, could see battalions of men marching up toward Haines's Bluff, and taking post at all points in our front. I was more than convinced that heavy reënforcements were coming to Vicksburg; whether from Pemberton at Grenada, Bragg in Tennessee, or from other sources, I could not tell; but at no point did the enemy assume the offensive; and when we drew off our rear-guard, on the morning of the 2d, they simply followed up the movement, timidly. Up to that moment I had not heard a word from General Grant since leaving Memphis; and most assuredly I had listened for days for the sound of his guns in the direction of Yazoo City. On the morning of January 2d, all my command were again afloat in their proper steamboats, when Admiral Porter told me that General McClernand had arrived at the mouth of the Yazoo in the steamboat Tigress, and that it was rumored he had come down to supersede me. Leaving my whole force where it was, I ran down to the mouth of the Yazoo in a small tug-boat, and there found General McClernand, with orders from the War Department to command the expeditionary force on the Mississippi River. I explained what had been done, and what was the actual state of facts; that the heavy reënforcements pouring into Vicksburg must be Pemberton's army, and that General Grant must be near at hand.

He informed me that General Grant was not coming at all; that his depot at Holly Springs had been captured by Van Dorn, and that he had drawn back from Coffeeville and Oxford to Holly Springs and Lagrange; and, further, that Quinby's division of Grant's army was actually at Memphis for stores when he passed down. This, then, fully explained how Vicksburg was being reënforced. I saw that any attempt on the place from the Yazoo was hopeless; and, with General McClernand's full approval, we all came out of the Yazoo, and on the 3d of January rendezvoused at Milliken's Bend, about ten miles above. On the 4th General McClernand issued his General Order No. 1, assuming command of the Army of the Mississippi, divided into two corps; the first to be commanded by General Morgan, composed of his own and A. J. Smith's divisions; and the second, composed of Steele's and Stuart's divisions, to be commanded by me. Up to that time the army had been styled the right wing of (General Grant's) Thirteenth Army Corps, and numbered about thirty thousand men. The aggregate loss during the time of my command, mostly on the 29th of December, was one hundred and seventy-five killed, nine hundred and thirty wounded, and seven hundred and forty-three prisoners. According to Badeau, the rebels lost sixty-three killed, one hundred and thirty-four wounded, and ten prisoners.

It afterward transpired that Van Dorn had captured Holly Springs on the 20th of December, and that General Grant fell back very soon after. General Pemberton, who had telegraphic and railroad communication with Vicksburg, was therefore at perfect liberty to reënforce the place with a garrison equal, if not superior, to my command. The rebels held high, commanding ground, and could see every movement of our men and boats, so that the only possible hope of success consisted in celerity and surprise, and in General Grant's holding all of Pemberton's army hard pressed meantime. General Grant was perfectly aware of this, and had sent me word of the change, but it did not reach me in time; indeed, I was not aware of it until after my assault of December 29th, and until the news was brought me by General McClernand as related. General McClernand was appointed to this command by President Lincoln in person, who had no knowledge of what was then going on down the river. Still, my relief, on the heels of a failure, raised the usual cry, at the North, of "repulse, failure, and bungling." There was no bungling on my part, for I never worked harder or with more intensity of purpose in my life; and General Grant, long after, in his report of the operations of the siege of Vicksburg, gave us all full credit for the skill of the movement, and described the almost impregnable nature of the ground; and, although in all official reports I assumed the whole responsibility, I have ever felt that had General Morgan promptly and skillfully sustained the lead of Frank Blair's brigade on that day, we should have broken the rebel line, and effected a lodgment on the hills behind Vicksburg. General Frank Blair was outspoken and indignant against Generals Morgan and De Courcey at the time, and always abused me for assuming the whole blame. But, had we succeeded, we might have found ourselves in a worse trap, when General Pemberton was at full liberty to turn his whole force against us.

While I was engaged at Chickasaw Bayou, Admiral Porter was equally busy in the Yazoo River, threatening the enemy's batteries at Haines's and Snyder's Bluffs above. In a sharp engagement he lost one of his best officers, in the person of Captain Gwin, United States Navy, who, though on board an iron-clad, insisted on keeping his post on deck, where he was struck in the breast by a round shot, which carried away the muscle, and contused the lung within, from which he died a few days after. We of the army deplored his loss quite as much as his fellows of the navy, for he had been intimately associated with us in our previous operations on the Tennessee River, at Shiloh and above, and we had come to regard him as one of us.

On the 4th of January, 1863, our fleet of transports was collected at Milliken's Bend, about ten miles above the mouth of the Yazoo, Admiral Porter remaining with his gunboats at the Yazoo. General John A. McClernand was in chief command, General George W. Morgan commanded the First Corps and I the Second Corps of the Army of the Mississippi.

I had learned that a small steamboat, the Blue Wing, with a mail, towing coal-barges and loaded with ammunition, had left Memphis for the Yazoo, about the 20th of December, had been captured by a rebel boat which had come out of the Arkansas River, and had been carried up that river to Fort Hindman. We had reports from this fort, usually called the "Post of Arkansas," about forty miles above the mouth, that it was held by about five thousand rebels, was an inclosed work, commanding the passage of the river, but supposed to be easy of capture from the rear. At that time I don't think General McClernand had any definite views or plans of action. If so, he did not impart them to me. He spoke in general terms of opening the navigation of the Mississippi, "cutting his way to the sea," etc., etc., but the *modus operandi* was not so clear. Knowing full well that we could not carry on operations against Vicksburg as long as the rebels held the Post of Arkansas, whence to attack our boats coming and going without convoy, I visited him on his boat, the Tigress, took with me a boy who had been on the Blue Wing, and had escaped, and asked leave to go up the Arkansas, to clear out the Post. He made various objections, but consented to go with me to see Admiral Porter about it. We got up steam in the Forest Queen, during the night of January 4th, stopped at the Tigress, took General McClernand on board, and proceeded down the river by night to the admiral's boat, the Black Hawk, lying in the mouth of the Yazoo. It must have been near midnight, and Admiral Porter was in *déshabille*. We were seated in his cabin and I explained my views about Arkansas Post, and asked his coöperation. He said that he was short of coal, and could not use wood in his iron-clad boats. Of these I asked for two, to be commanded by Captain Shirk or Phelps, or some officer of my acquaintance. At that moment, poor Gwin lay on his bed, in a state-room close by, dying from the effect of the cannon shot received at Haines's Bluff, as before described. Porter's manner to McClernand was so curt that I invited him out into a forward-cabin where he had his charts, and asked him what he meant by it. He said that "he did not like him;" that in Washington, before coming West, he had been introduced to him by President Lincoln, and he had taken a strong prejudice against him. I begged him, for the sake of harmony, to waive that, which he promised to do. Returning to the cabin, the conversation was resumed, and, on our offering to tow his gunboats up the river to save coal, and on renewing the request for Shirk to command the detachment, Porter said, "Suppose I go along myself?" I answered, if he would do so, it would insure the success of the enterprise. At that time I supposed General McClernand would send me on this business, but he concluded to go himself, and to take his whole force. Orders were at once issued for the troops not to disembark at Milliken's Bend, but to remain as they were on board the transports. My two divisions were commanded—the First, by Brigadier-General Frederick Steele, with three brigades, commanded by Brigadier-Generals F. P. Blair, C. E. Hovey, and J. M. Thayer; the Second, by Brigadier-General D. Stuart, with two brigades, commanded by Colonels G. A. Smith and T. Kilby Smith.

The whole army, embarked on steamboats convoyed by the gunboats, of which three were iron-clads, proceeded up the Mississippi River to the mouth of White River, which we reached January 8th. On the next day we continued up White River to the "Cut-off;" through this to the Arkansas, and up the Arkansas to Notrib's farm, just below Fort Hindman. Early the next morning we disembarked. Stuart's division, moving up the river along the bank, soon encountered a force of the enemy intrenched behind a line of earthworks, extending from the river across to the swamp. I took Steele's division, marching by the flank by a road through the swamp to the firm ground behind, and was moving up to get to the rear of Fort Hindman, when General McClernand overtook me, with the report that the rebels had abandoned their first position, and had fallen back into the fort. By his orders, we countermarched, recrossed the swamp, and hurried forward to overtake Stuart, marching for Fort Hindman. The first line of the rebels was about four miles below Fort Hindman, and the intervening space was densely wooded and obscure, with the exception of some old fields back of and close to the fort. During the night, which was a bright moonlight one, we reconnoitred close up, and found a large number of huts which had been abandoned, and the whole rebel force had fallen back into and about the fort. Personally I crept up to a stump so close that I could hear the enemy hard at work, pulling down houses, cutting with axes, and building intrenchments.

I could almost hear their words, and I was thus listening when, about 4 A.M. the bugler in the rebel camp sounded as pretty a reveille as I ever listened to.

When daylight broke it revealed to us a new line of parapet straight across the peninsula, connecting Fort Hindman, on the Arkansas River bank, with the impassable swamp about a mile to its left or rear. This peninsula was divided into two nearly equal parts by a road. My command had the ground to the right of the road, and Morgan's corps that to the left. McClernand had his quarters still on the Tigress, back at Notrib's farm, but moved forward that morning (January 11th) to a place in the woods to our rear, where he had a man up a tree, to observe and report the movements.

There was a general understanding with Admiral Porter that he was to attack the fort with his three ironclad gunboats directly by its water-front, while we assaulted by land in the rear. About 10 A.M. I got a message from General McClernand, telling me where he could be found, and asking me what we were waiting for. I answered that we were then in close contact with the enemy, viz., about five or six hundred yards off; that the next movement must be a direct assault; that this should be simultaneous along the whole line; and that I was waiting to hear from the gunboats; asking him to notify Admiral Porter that we were all ready. In about half an hour I heard the clear ring of the navy-guns; the fire gradually increasing in rapidity and advancing toward the fort. I had distributed our field-guns, and, when I judged the time had come, I gave the orders to begin. The intervening ground between us and the enemy was a dead level, with the exception of one or two small gullies, and our men had no cover but the few standing trees and some logs on the ground. The troops advanced well under a heavy fire, once or twice falling to the ground for a sort of rest or pause. Every tree had its group of men, and behind each log was a crowd of sharpshooters, who kept up so hot a fire that the rebel troops fired wild. The fire of the fort proper was kept busy by the gunboats and Morgan's corps, so that all my corps had to encounter was the direct fire from the newly-built parapet across the peninsula. This line had three sections of field-guns, that kept things pretty lively, and several round-shot came so near me that I realized that they were aimed at my staff; so I dismounted, and made them scatter.

As the gunboats got closer up I saw their flags actually over the parapet of Fort Hindman, and the rebel gunners scamper out of the embrasures and run down into the ditch behind. About the same time a man jumped up on the rebel parapet just where the road entered, waving a large white flag, and numerous smaller white rags appeared above the parapet along the whole line. I immediately ordered, "Cease firing!" and sent the same word down the line to General Steele, who had made similar progress on the right, following the border of the swamp. I ordered my aide, Colonel Dayton, to jump on his horse and ride straight up to the large white flag, and when his horse was on the parapet I followed with the rest of my staff. All firing had ceased, except an occasional shot away to the right, and one of the captains (Smith) of the Thirteenth Regulars was wounded after the display of the white flag. On entering the line, I saw that our muskets and guns had done good execution; for there was a horse-battery, and every horse lay dead in the traces. The fresh-made parapet had been knocked down in many places, and dead men lay around very thick. I inquired who commanded at that point, and a Colonel Garland stepped up and said that he commanded that brigade. I ordered him to form his brigade, stack arms, hang the belts on the muskets, and stand waiting for orders. Stuart's division had been halted outside the parapet. I then sent Major Hammond down the rebel line to the right, with orders to stop Steele's division outside, and to have the other rebel brigade stack its arms in like manner, and to await further orders. I inquired of Colonel Garland who commanded in chief, and he said that General Churchill did, and that he was inside the fort. I then rode into the fort, which was well built, with good parapets, drawbridge, and ditch, and was an inclosed work of four bastions. I found it full of soldiers and sailors, its parapets toward the river well battered in, and Porter's gunboats in the river, close against the fort, with their bows on shore. I soon found General Churchill, in conversation with Admiral Porter and General A. J. Smith, and about this time my adjutant-general, Major J. H. Hammond, came and reported that General Deshler, who commanded the rebel brigade facing and opposed to Steele, had refused to stack arms and surrender, on the ground that he had received no orders from his commanding general; that nothing separated this brigade from Steele's men except the light parapet, and that there might be trouble there at any moment. I advised General Churchill to send orders at once, because a single shot might bring the whole of Steele's division on Deshler's brigade, and I would not be responsible for the consequences; soon afterward, we both concluded to go in person. General Churchill had the horses of himself and staff in the ditch; they were brought in, and we rode together to where Garland was standing, and Churchill spoke to him in an angry tone, "Why did you display the white flag!" Garland replied, "I received orders to do so from one of your staff." Churchill denied giving such an order, and angry words passed between them. I stopped them, saying that it made little difference then, as they were in our power. We continued to ride down the line to its extreme point, where we found Deshler in person, and his troops were still standing to the parapet with their muskets in hand. Steele's men were on the outside. I asked Deshler: "What does this mean? You are a regular officer, and ought to know better." He answered, snappishly, that "he had received no orders to surrender;" when General Churchill said: "You see, sir, that we are in their power, and you may surrender." Deshler turned to his staff-officers and ordered them to repeat the command to "stack arms," etc., to the colonels of his brigade. I was on my horse, and he was on foot. Wishing to soften the blow of defeat, I spoke to him kindly, saying that I knew a family of Deshlers in Columbus, Ohio, and inquired if they were relations of his. He disclaimed any relation with people living north of the Ohio, in an offensive tone, and I think I gave him a piece of my mind that he did not relish. He was a West Point graduate, small but very handsome, and was afterward killed in battle. I never met him again.

Returning to the position where I had first entered the rebel line, I received orders from General McClernand, by one of his staff, to leave General A. J. Smith in charge of the fort and prisoners, and with my troops to remain outside. The officer explained that the general was then on the Tigress, which had moved up from below, to a point in the river just above the fort; and not understanding his orders, I concluded to go and see him in person. My troops were then in possession of two of the three brigades which composed the army opposed to us; and my troops were also in possession of all the ground of the peninsula outside the "fort proper" (Hindman). I found General McClernand on the Tigress, in high spirits. He said repeatedly: "Glorious! glorious! my star is ever in the ascendant!" He spoke complimentarily of the troops, but was extremely jealous of the navy. He said: "I'll make a splendid report;" "I had a man up a tree;" etc. I was very hungry and tired, and fear I did not appreciate the honors in reserve for us, and asked for something to eat and drink. He very kindly ordered something to be brought, and explained to me that by his "orders" he did not wish to interfere with the actual state of facts; that General A. J. Smith would occupy "Fort Hindman," which his troops had first entered, and I could hold the lines outside, and go on securing the prisoners and stores as I had begun. I returned to the position of Garland's brigade and gave the necessary orders for marching all the prisoners, disarmed, to a pocket formed by the river and two deep gullies just above the fort, by which time it had become quite dark. After dark another rebel regiment arrived from Pine Bluff, marched right in, and was also made prisoners. There seemed to be a good deal of feeling among the rebel officers against Garland, who asked leave to stay with me that night, to which I of course consented. Just outside the rebel parapet was a house which had been used for a hospital. I had a room cleaned out, and occupied it that night. A cavalry-soldier lent me his battered coffee-pot with some coffee and scraps of hard bread out of his nose-bag; Garland and I made some coffee, ate our bread together, and talked politics by the fire till quite late at night, when we lay down on straw that was saturated with the blood of dead or wounded men. The next day the prisoners were all collected on their boats, lists were made out, and orders given for their transportation to St. Louis, in charge of my aide, Major Sanger. We then proceeded to dismantle and level the forts, destroy or remove the stores, and we found in the magazine the very ammunition which had been sent for us in the Blue

Wing, which was secured and afterward used in our twenty-pound Parrott guns.

On the 13th we reëmbarked; the whole expedition returned out of the river by the direct route down the Arkansas during a heavy snow-storm, and rendezvoused in the Mississippi, at Napoleon, at the mouth of the Arkansas. Here General Mc-Clernand told me he had received a letter from General Grant at Memphis, who disapproved of our movement up the Arkansas; but that communication was made before he had learned of our complete success. When informed of this, and of the promptness with which it had been executed, he could not but approve. We were then ordered back to Milliken's Bend, to await General Grant's arrival in person. We reached Milliken's Bend January 21st.

McClernand's report of the capture of Fort Hindman almost ignored the action of Porter's fleet altogether. This was unfair, for I know that the admiral led his fleet in person in the river-attack, and that his guns silenced those of Fort Hindman, and drove the gunners into the ditch.

The aggregate loss in my corps at Arkansas Post was five hundred and nineteen, viz., four officers and seventy-five men killed, thirty-four officers and four hundred and six men wounded. I never knew the losses in the gunboat fleet, or in Morgan's corps; but they must have been less than in mine, which was more exposed. The number of rebel dead must have been nearly one hundred and fifty; of prisoners, by actual count, we secured four thousand seven hundred and ninety-one, and sent them north to St. Louis.

Chapter XIII.

VICKSBURG.

January to July, 1863.

THE CAMPAIGN OF 1863, resulting in the capture of Vicksburg, was so important, that its history has been well studied and well described in all the books treating of the civil war, more especially by Dr. Draper, in his "History of the Civil War in America," and in Badeau's "Military History of General Grant." In the latter it is more fully and accurately given than in any other, and is well illustrated by maps and original documents. I now need only attempt to further illustrate Badeau's account by some additional details. When our expedition came out of the Arkansas River, January 18, 1863, and rendezvoused at the river-bank, in front of the town of Napoleon, Arkansas, we were visited by General Grant in person, who had come down from Memphis in a steamboat. Although at this time Major-General J. A. McClernand was in command of the Army of the Mississippi, by virtue of a confidential order of the War Department, dated October 21, 1862, which order bore the indorsement of President Lincoln, General Grant still exercised a command over him, by reason of his general command of the Department of the Tennessee. By an order (No. 210) of December 18, 1862, from the War Department, received at Arkansas Post, the Western armies had been grouped into five *corps d'armée*, viz.: the Thirteenth, Major-General McClernand; the Fourteenth, Major-General George H. Thomas, in Middle Tennessee; the Fifteenth, Major-General W. T. Sherman; the Sixteenth, Major-General Hurlbut, then at or near Memphis; and the Seventeenth, Major-General McPherson, also at and back of Memphis. General Grant when at Napoleon, on the 18th of January, ordered McClernand with his own and my corps to return to Vicksburg, to disembark on the west bank, and to resume work on a canal across the peninsula, which had been begun by General Thomas Williams the summer before, the object being to turn the Mississippi River at that point, or at least to make a passage for our fleet of gunboats and transports across

326

Expedition
to
STEELE'S BAYOU
DEER CREEK
etc.
in connection with the
Gunboat Fleet
March 1863.

the peninsula, opposite Vicksburg. General Grant then returned to Memphis, ordered to Lake Providence, about sixty miles above us, McPherson's corps, the Seventeenth, and then came down again to give his personal supervision to the whole movement.

The Mississippi River was very high and rising, and we began that system of canals on which we expended so much hard work fruitlessly: first, the canal at Young's plantation, opposite Vicksburg; second, that at Lake Providence; and third, at the Yazoo Pass, leading into the head-waters of the Yazoo River. Early in February the gunboats Indianola and Queen of the West ran the batteries of Vicksburg. The latter was afterward crippled in Red River, and was captured by the rebels; and the Indianola was butted and sunk about forty miles below Vicksburg. We heard the booming of the guns, but did not know of her loss till some days after. During the months of January and February, we were digging the canal and fighting off the water of the Mississippi, which continued to rise and threatened to drown us. We had no sure place of refuge except the narrow levee, and such steamboats as remained abreast of our camps. My two divisions furnished alternately a detail of five hundred men a day, to work on the canal. So high was the water in the beginning of March, that McClernand's corps was moved to higher ground, at Milliken's Bend, but I remained at Young's plantation, laid off a due proportion of the levee for each subdivision of my command, and assigned other parts to such steamboats as lay at the levee. My own headquarters were in Mrs. Grove's house, which had the water all around it, and could only be reached by a plank-walk from the levee, built on posts.

General Frederick Steele commanded the first division, and General D. Stuart the second; this latter division had been reënforced by General Hugh Ewing's brigade, which had arrived from West Virginia.

At the time of its date I received the following note from General Grant:

MILLIKEN'S BEND, *March* 16, 1863

General SHERMAN.

DEAR SIR: I have just returned from a reconnoissance up Steele's Bayou, with the admiral (Porter), and five of his gunboats. With some labor in cutting tree-tops out of the way, it will be navigable for any class of steamers.

I want you to have your pioneer corps, or one regiment of good men for such work, detailed, and at the landing as soon as possible.

The party will want to take with them their rations, arms, and sufficient camp and garrison equipage for a few days. I will have a boat at any place you may designate, as early as the men can be there. The Eighth Missouri (being many of them boatmen) would be excellent men for this purpose.

As soon as you give directions for these men to be in readiness, come up and see me, and I will explain fully. The tug that takes this is instructed to wait for you. A full supply of axes will be required.

Very respectfully,

U. S. GRANT, *Major-General.*

This letter was instantly (8 A.M.) sent to Colonel Giles A. Smith, commanding the Eighth Missouri, with orders to prepare immediately. He returned it at 9.15, with an answer that the regiment was all ready. I went up to Milliken's Bend in the tug, and had a conference with the general, resulting in these orders:

HEADQUARTERS DEPARTMENT OF THE TENNESSEE, ⎫
  BEFORE VICKSBURG, *March* 16, 1863.   ⎬

Major-General W. T. SHERMAN, *commanding Fifteenth Army Corps.*

GENERAL: You will proceed as early as practicable up Steele's Bayou, and through Black Bayou to Deer Creek, and thence with the gunboats now there by any route they may take to get into the Yazoo River, for the purpose of determining the feasibility of getting an army through that route to the east bank of that river, and at a point from which they can act advantageously against Vicksburg.

Make such details from your army corps as may be required to clear out the channel of the various bayous through which transports would have to run, and to hold such points as in your judgment should be occupied.

I place at your disposal to-day the steamers Diligent and Silver Wave, the only two suitable for the present navigation of this route. Others will be supplied you as fast as required, and they can be got.

I have given directions (and you may repeat them) that the party going on board the steamer Diligent push on until they reach Black Bayou, only stopping sufficiently long at any point before reaching there to remove such obstructions as prevent their own progress.

Captain Kossak, of the Engineers, will go with this party. The other boat-load will commence their work in Steele's Bayou, and make the navigation as free as possible all the way through.

There is but little work to be done in Steele's Bayou, except for about five miles about midway of the bayou. In this portion many overhanging trees will have to be removed, and should be dragged out of the channel.

Very respectfully,

U. S. GRANT, *Major-General.*

On returning to my camp at Young's Point, I started these two boats up the Yazoo and Steele's Bayou, with the Eighth Missouri and some pioneers, with axes, saws, and all the tools necessary. I gave orders for a part of Stuart's division to proceed in the large boats up the Mississippi River to a point at Gwin's plantation, where a bend of Steele's Bayou neared the main river; and the next day, with one or two staff-officers and orderlies, got a navy-tug, and hurried up to overtake Admiral Porter. About sixty miles up Steele's Bayou we came to the gunboat Price, Lieutenant Woodworth, United States Navy, commanding, and then turned into Black Bayou, a narrow, crooked channel, obstructed by overhanging oaks, and filled with cypress and cotton-wood trees. The gunboats had forced their way through, pushing aside trees a foot in diameter. In about four miles we overtook the gunboat fleet just as it was emerging into Deer Creek. Along Deer Creek the alluvium was higher, and there was a large cotton-plantation belonging to a Mr. Hill, who was absent, and the negroes were in charge of the place. Here I overtook Admiral Porter, and accompanied him a couple of miles up Deer Creek, which was much wider and more free of trees, with plantations on both sides at intervals. Admiral Porter thought he had passed the worst, and that he would be able to reach the Rolling Fork and Sunflower. He requested me to return and use all possible means to clear out Black Bayou. I returned to Hill's plantation, which was soon reached by Major Coleman, with a part of the Eighth Missouri; the bulk of the regiment and the pioneers had been distributed along the bayous, and set to work under the general supervision of Captain Kossak. The Diligent and Silver Wave then returned to Gwin's plantation and brought up Brigadier-General Giles A. Smith, with the

Sixth Missouri, and part of the One Hundred and Sixteenth Illinois. Admiral Porter was then working up Deer Creek with his iron-clads, but he had left me a tug, which enabled me to reconnoitre the country, which was all under water except the narrow strip along Deer Creek. During the 19th I heard the heavy navy-guns booming more frequently than seemed consistent with mere guerrilla operations; and that night I got a message from Porter, written on tissue-paper, brought me through the swamp by a negro, who had it concealed in a piece of tobacco.

The admiral stated that he had met a force of infantry and artillery which gave him great trouble by killing the men who had to expose themselves outside the iron armor to shove off the bows of the boats, which had so little headway that they would not steer. He begged me to come to his rescue as quickly as possible. Giles A. Smith had only about eight hundred men with him, but I ordered him to start up Deer Creek at once, crossing to the east side by an old bridge at Hill's plantation, which we had repaired for the purpose; to work his way up to the gunboat-fleet, and to report to the admiral that I would come up with every man I could raise as soon as possible. I was almost alone at Hill's, but took a canoe, paddled down Black Bayou to the gunboat Price, and there, luckily, found the Silver Wave with a load of men just arrived from Gwin's plantation. Taking some of the parties who were at work along the bayou into an empty coal-barge, we tugged it up by a navy-tug, followed by the Silver Wave, crashing through the trees, carrying away pilot-house, smoke-stacks, and every thing above-deck; but the captain (McMillan, of Pittsburg) was a brave fellow, and realized the necessity. The night was absolutely black, and we could only make two and a half of the four miles. We then disembarked, and marched through the canebrake, carrying lighted candles in our hands, till we got into the open cotton-fields at Hill's plantation, where we lay down for a few hours' rest. These men were a part of Giles A. Smith's brigade, and part belonged to the brigade of T. Kilby Smith, the senior officer present being Lieutenant-Colonel Rice, Fifty-fourth Ohio, an excellent young officer. We had no horses.

On Sunday morning, March 21st, as soon as daylight appeared, we started, following the same route which Giles A. Smith had taken the day before; the battalion of the Thirteenth United States Regulars, Major Chase, in the lead. We could hear Porter's guns, and knew that moments were precious. Being on foot myself, no man could complain, and we generally went at the double-quick, with occasional rests. The road lay along Deer Creek, passing several plantations; and occasionally, at the bends, it crossed the swamp, where the water came above my hips. The smaller drummer-boys had to carry their drums on their heads, and most of the men slung their cartridge-boxes around their necks. The soldiers generally were glad to have their general and field officers afoot, but we gave them a fair specimen of marching, accomplishing about twenty-one miles by noon. Of course, our speed was accelerated by the sounds of the navy-guns, which became more and more distinct, though we could see nothing. At a plantation near some Indian mounds we met a detachment of the Eighth Missouri, that had been up to the fleet, and had been sent down as a picket to prevent any obstructions below. This picket reported that Admiral Porter had found Deer Creek badly obstructed, had turned back; that there was a rebel force beyond the fleet, with some six-pounders, and nothing between us and the fleet. So I sat down on the door-sill of a cabin to rest, but had not been seated ten minutes when, in the wood just ahead, not three hundred yards off, I heard quick and rapid firing of musketry. Jumping up, I ran up the road, and found Lieutenant-Colonel Rice, who said the head of his column had struck a small force of rebels with a working gang of negroes, provided with axes, who on the first fire had broken and run back into the swamp. I ordered Rice to deploy his brigade, his left on the road, and extending as far into the swamp as the ground would permit, and then to sweep forward until he uncovered the gunboats. The movement was rapid and well executed, and we soon came to some large cotton-fields and could see our gunboats in Deer Creek, occasionally firing a heavy eight-inch gun across the cotton-field into the swamp behind. About that time Major Kirby, of the Eighth Missouri, galloped down the road on a horse he had picked up the night before, and met me. He explained the situation of affairs, and offered me his horse. I got on *bareback*, and rode up the levee, the sailors coming out of their iron-clads and cheering most vociferously as I rode by, and as our men swept forward across the cotton-field in full view. I soon found Admiral Porter, who was on the deck of one of his iron-clads, with a shield made of the section of a smoke-stack, and I doubt if he was ever more glad to meet a friend than he was to see me. He explained that he had almost reached the Rolling Fork, when the woods became full of sharp-shooters, who, taking advantage of trees, stumps, and the levee, would shoot down every man that poked his nose outside the protection of their armor; so that he could not handle his clumsy boats in the narrow channel. The rebels had evidently dispatched a force from Haines's Bluff up the Sun-flower to the Rolling Fork, had anticipated the movement of Admiral Porter's fleet, and had completely obstructed the channel of the upper part of Deer Creek by felling trees into it, so that further progress in that direction was simply impos-sible. It also happened that, at the instant of my arrival, a party of about four hundred rebels, armed and supplied with axes, had passed around the fleet and had got below it, in-tending in like manner to block up the channel by the felling of trees, so as to cut off retreat. This was the force we had struck so opportunely at the time before described. I inquired of Admiral Porter what he proposed to do, and he said he wanted to get out of that scrape as quickly as possible. He was actually working back when I met him, and, as we then had a sufficient force to cover his movement completely, he continued to back down Deer Creek. He informed me at one time things looked so critical that he had made up his mind to blow up the gunboats, and to escape with his men through the swamp to the Mississippi River. There being no longer any sharp-shooters to bother the sailors, they made good progress; still, it took three full days for the fleet to back out of Deer Creek into Black Bayou, at Hill's plantation, whence Admiral Porter proceeded to his post at the mouth of the Yazoo, leaving Captain Owen in command of the fleet. I re-ported the facts to General Grant, who was sadly disap-pointed at the failure of the fleet to get through to the Yazoo above Haines's Bluff, and ordered us all to resume our camps at Young's Point. We accordingly steamed down, and regained our camps on the 27th. As this expedition up Deer Creek was but one of many efforts to secure a footing from which to operate against Vicksburg, I add the report of Brigadier-General Giles A. Smith, who was the first to reach the fleet:

HEADQUARTERS FIRST BRIGADE, SECOND DIVISION,
FIFTEENTH ARMY CORPS, YOUNG'S POINT, LOUISIANA,
March 28, 1863.

Captain L. M. DAYTON, *Assistant Adjutant-General.*

CAPTAIN: I have the honor to report the movements of the First Brigade in the expedition up Steele's Bayou, Black Bayou, and Deer Creek.

The Sixth Missouri and One Hundred and Sixteenth Illinois regiments embarked at the mouth of Muddy Bayou on the evening of Thursday, the 18th of March, and proceeded up Steele's Bayou to the mouth of Black; thence up Black Bayou to Hill's plantation, at its junction with Deer Creek, where we arrived on Friday at four o'clock P.M., and joined the Eighth Missouri, Lieutenant-Colonel Coleman commanding, which had arrived at that point two days before. General Sherman had also established his headquarters there, having preceded the Eighth Missouri in a tug, with no other escort than two or three of his staff, reconnoitring all the different bayous and branches, thereby greatly facilitating the movements of the troops, but at the same time exposing himself beyond precedent in a commanding general. At three o'clock of Saturday morning, the 20th instant, General Sherman having received a communication from Admiral Porter at the mouth of Rolling Fork, asking for a speedy coöperation of the land forces with his fleet, I was ordered by General Sherman to be ready, with all the available force at that point, to accompany him to his relief; but before starting it was arranged that I should proceed with the force at hand (eight hundred men), while he remained, again entirely unprotected, to hurry up the troops expected to arrive that night, consisting of the Thirteenth Infantry and One Hundred and Thirteenth Illinois Volunteers, completing my brigade, and the Second Brigade, Colonel T. Kilby Smith commanding.

This, as the sequel showed, proved a very wise measure, and resulted in the safety of the whole fleet. At daybreak we were in motion, with a regular guide. We had proceeded but about six miles, when we found the enemy had been very busy felling trees to obstruct the creek.

All the negroes along the route had been notified to be ready at nightfall to continue the work. To prevent this as much as possible, I ordered all able-bodied negroes to be taken along, and warned some of the principal inhabitants that they would be held responsible for any more obstructions being placed across the creek. We reached the admiral about four o'clock P.M., with no opposition save my advance-guard (Company A, Sixth Missouri) being fired into from the opposite side of the creek, killing one man, and slightly wounding another; having no way of crossing, we had to content ourselves with driving them beyond musket-range. Proceeding with as little loss of time as possible, I found the fleet obstructed in front by fallen trees, in rear by a sunken coal-barge, and surrounded by a large force of rebels with an abundant supply of artillery, but wisely keeping their main force out of range of the admiral's guns. Every tree and stump covered a sharp-shooter, ready to pick off any luckless marine who showed his head above-decks, and entirely preventing the working-parties from removing obstructions.

In pursuance of orders from General Sherman, I reported to Admiral Porter for orders, who turned over to me all the land-forces in his fleet (about one hundred and fifty men), together with two howitzers, and I was instructed by him to retain a sufficient force to clear out the sharp-shooters, and to distribute the remainder along the creek for six or seven miles below, to prevent any more obstructions being placed in it during the night. This was speedily arranged, our skirmishers capturing three prisoners. Immediate steps were now taken to remove the coal-barge, which was accomplished about daylight on Sunday morning, when the fleet moved back toward Black Bayou. By three o'clock P.M. we had only made about six miles, owing to the large number of trees to be removed; at this point, where our progress was very slow, we discovered a long line of the enemy filing along the edge of the woods, and taking position on the creek below us, and about one mile ahead of our advance. Shortly after, they opened fire on the gunboats from batteries behind the cavalry and infantry. The boats not only replied to the batteries, which they soon silenced, but poured a destructive fire into their lines. Heavy skirmishing was also heard in our front, supposed to be by three companies from the Sixth and Eighth Missouri, whose position, taken the previous night to guard the creek, was beyond the point reached by the enemy, and consequently liable to be cut off or captured. Captain Owen, of the Louisville, the leading boat, made every effort to go through the obstructions and aid in the rescuing of the men. I ordered Major Kirby, with four companies of the Sixth Missouri, forward, with two companies deployed. He soon met General Sherman, with the Thirteenth Infantry and One Hundred and Thirteenth Illinois, driving the enemy before them, and opening communication along the creek with the gunboats. Instead of our three companies referred to as engaging the enemy, General Sherman had arrived at a very opportune moment with the two regiments mentioned above, and the Second Brigade. The enemy, not expecting an attack from that quarter, after some hot skirmishing, retreated. General Sherman immediately ordered the Thirteenth Infantry and One Hundred and Thirteenth Illinois to pursue; but, after following their trace for about two miles, they were recalled.

We continued our march for about two miles, when we bivouacked for the night. Early on Monday morning (March 22d) we continued our march, but owing to the slow progress of the gunboats did not reach Hill's plantation until Tuesday, the 23d instant, where we remained until the 25th; we then reëmbarked, and arrived at Young's Point on Friday, the 27th instant.

Below you will find a list of casualties. Very respectfully,

GILES A. SMITH,
Colonel Eighth Missouri, commanding First Brigade.

P. S.—I forgot to state above that the Thirteenth Infantry and One Hundred and Thirteenth Illinois being under the immediate command of General Sherman, he can mention them as their conduct deserves.

On the 3d of April, a division of troops, commanded by Brigadier-General J. M. Tuttle, was assigned to my corps, and was designated the Third Division; and, on the 4th of April, Brigadier-General D. Stuart was relieved from the command of the Second Division, to which Major-General Frank P. Blair was appointed by an order from General Grant's headquarters. Stuart had been with me from the time we were at Benton Barracks, in command of the Fifty-fifth Illinois, then of a brigade, and finally of a division; but he had failed in securing a confirmation by the Senate to his nomination as brigadier-general, by reason of some old affair at Chicago, and, having resigned his commission as colonel, he was out of service. I esteemed him very highly, and was actually mortified that the service should thus be deprived of so excellent and gallant an officer. He afterward settled in New Orleans as a lawyer, and died about 1867 or 1868.

On the 6th of April, my command, the Fifteenth Corps, was composed of three divisions:

The First Division, commanded by Major-General Fred Steele; and his three brigades by Colonel Manter, Colonel Charles R. Wood, and Brigadier-General John M. Thayer.

The Second Division, commanded by Major-General Frank P. Blair; and his three brigades by Colonel Giles A. Smith, Colonel Thomas Kilby Smith, and Brigadier-General Hugh Ewing.

The Third Division, commanded by Brigadier-General J. M. Tuttle; and his three brigades by Brigadier-General R. P. Buckland, Colonel J. A. Mower, and Brigadier-General John E. Smith.

My own staff then embraced: Dayton, McCoy, and Hill, aides; J. H. Hammond, assistant adjutant-general; Sanger, inspector-General; McFeeley, commissary; J. Condit Smith, quartermaster; Charles McMillan, medical director; Ezra Taylor, chief of artillery; Jno. C. Neely, ordnance-officer; Jenney and Pitzman, engineers.

By this time it had become thoroughly demonstrated that we could not divert the main river Mississippi, or get practicable access to the east bank of the Yazoo, in the rear of Vicksburg, by any of the passes; and we were all in the habit of discussing the various chances of the future. General Grant's headquarters were at Milliken's Bend, in tents, and his army was strung along the river all the way from Young's Point up to Lake Providence, at least sixty miles. I had always contended that the best way to take Vicksburg was to resume the movement which had been so well begun the previous November, viz., for the main army to march by land down the country inland of the Mississippi River; while the gunboat-fleet and a minor land-force should threaten Vicksburg on its river-front.

I reasoned that, with the large force then subject to General Grant's orders—viz., four army corps—he could easily resume the movement from Memphis, by way of Oxford and Grenada, to Jackson, Mississippi, or down the ridge between the Yazoo and Big Black; but General Grant would not, for reasons other than military, take any course which looked like a step backward; and he himself concluded on the river movement below Vicksburg, so as to appear like connecting with

General Banks, who at the same time was besieging Port Hudson from the direction of New Orleans.

Preliminary orders had already been given, looking to the digging of a canal, to connect the river at Duckport with Willow Bayou, back of Milliken's Bend, so as to form a channel for the conveyance of supplies, by way of Richmond, to New Carthage; and several steam dredge-boats had come from the upper rivers to assist in the work. One day early in April, I was up at General Grant's headquarters, and we talked over all these things with absolute freedom. Charles A. Dana, Assistant Secretary of War, was there, and Wilson, Rawlins, Frank Blair, McPherson, etc. We all knew, what was notorious, that General McClernand was still intriguing against General Grant, in hopes to regain the command of the whole expedition, and that others were raising a clamor against General Grant in the newspapers at the North. Even Mr. Lincoln and General Halleck seemed to be shaken; but at no instant of time did we (his personal friends) slacken in our loyalty to him. One night, after such a discussion, and believing that General McClernand had no real plan of action shaped in his mind, I wrote my letter of April 8, 1863, to Colonel Rawlins, which letter is embraced in full at page 616 of Badeau's book, and which I now reproduce here:

HEADQUARTERS FIFTEENTH ARMY CORPS,
CAMP NEAR VICKSBURG, *April* 8, 1863.

Colonel J. A. RAWLINS, *Assistant Adjutant-General to General* GRANT.

SIR: I would most respectfully suggest (for reasons which I will not name) that General Grant call on his corps commanders for their opinions, concise and positive, on the best general plan of a campaign. Unless this be done, there are men who will, in any result falling below the popular standard, claim that *their* advice was unheeded, and that fatal consequence resulted therefrom. My own opinions are—

First. That the Army of the Tennessee is now far in advance of the other grand armies of the United States.

Second. That a corps from Missouri should forthwith be moved from St. Louis to the vicinity of Little Rock, Arkansas; supplies collected there while the river is full, and land communication with

Memphis opened *via* Des Arc on the White, and Madison on the St. Francis River.

Third. That as much of the Yazoo Pass, Coldwater, and Tallahatchie Rivers, as can be gained and fortified, be held, and the main army be transported thither by land and water; that the road back to Memphis be secured and reopened, and, as soon as the waters subside, Grenada be attacked, and the swamp-road across to Helena be patrolled by cavalry.

Fourth. That the line of the Yalabusha be the base from which to operate against the points where the Mississippi Central crosses Big Black, above Canton; and, lastly, where the Vicksburg & Jackson Railroad crosses the same river (Big Black). The capture of Vicksburg would result.

Fifth. That a minor force be left in this vicinity, not to exceed ten thousand men, with only enough steamboats to float and transport them to any desired point; this force to be held always near enough to act with the gunboats when the main army is known to be near Vicksburg—Haines's Bluff or Yazoo City.

Sixth. I do doubt the capacity of Willow Bayou (which I estimate to be fifty miles long and very tortuous) as a military channel, to supply an army large enough to operate against Jackson, Mississippi, or the Black River Bridge; and such a channel will be very vulnerable to a force coming from the west, which we must expect. Yet this canal will be most useful as the way to convey coals and supplies to a fleet that should navigate the lower reach of the Mississippi between Vicksburg and the Red River.

Seventh. The chief reason for operating *solely* by water was the season of the year and high water in the Tallahatchie and Yalabusha Rivers. The spring is now here, and soon these streams will be no serious obstacle, save in the ambuscades of the forest, and whatever works the enemy may have erected at or near Grenada. North Mississippi is too valuable for us to allow the enemy to hold it and make crops this year.

I make these suggestions, with the request that General Grant will read them and give them, as I know he will, a share of his thoughts. I would prefer that he should not answer this letter, but merely give it as much or as little weight as it deserves. Whatever plan of action he may adopt will receive from me the same zealous coöperation and energetic support as though conceived by myself. I do not believe General Banks will make any serious attack on Port Hudson this spring. I am, etc.,

W. T. SHERMAN, *Major-General.*

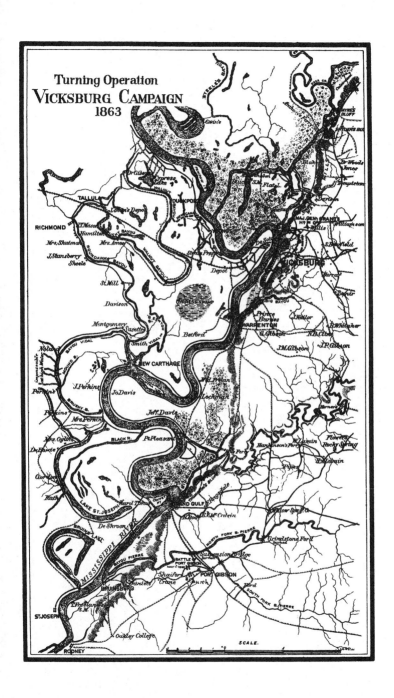

Turning Operation
VICKSBURG CAMPAIGN
1863

This is the letter which some critics have styled a "protest." We never had a council of war at any time during the Vicksburg campaign. We often met casually, regardless of rank or power, and talked and gossiped of things in general, as officers do and should. But my letter speaks for itself. It shows my opinions clearly at that stage of the game, and was meant partially to induce General Grant to call on General McClernand for a similar expression of opinion, but, so far as I know, he did not. He went on quietly to work out his own designs; and he has told me, since the war, that had we possessed in December, 1862, the experience of marching and maintaining armies without a regular base, which we afterward acquired, he would have gone on from Oxford as first contemplated, and would not have turned back because of the destruction of his depot at Holly Springs by Van Dorn. The distance from Oxford to the rear of Vicksburg is little greater than by the circuitous route we afterward followed, from Bruinsburg to Jackson and Vicksburg, during which we had neither depot nor train of supplies. I have never criticised General Grant's strategy on this or any other occasion, but I thought then that he had lost an opportunity, which cost him and us six months' extra-hard work, for we might have captured Vicksburg from the direction of Oxford in January, quite as easily as was afterward done in July, 1863.

General Grant's orders for the general movement past Vicksburg, by Richmond and Carthage, were dated April 20, 1863. McClernand was to lead off with his corps, McPherson next, and my corps (the Fifteenth) to bring up the rear. Preliminary thereto, on the night of April 16th, seven iron-clads led by Admiral Porter in person, in the Benton, with three transports, and ten barges in tow, ran the Vicksburg batteries by night. Anticipating a scene, I had four yawl-boats hauled across the swamp, to the reach of the river below Vicksburg, and manned them with soldiers, ready to pick up any of the disabled wrecks as they floated by. I was out in the stream when the fleet passed Vicksburg, and the scene was truly sublime. As soon as the rebel gunners detected the Benton, which was in the lead, they opened on her, and on the others in succession, with shot and shell; houses on the Vicksburg side and on the opposite shore were set on fire, which lighted up the whole river; and the roar of cannon, the bursting of shells, and finally the burning of the Henry Clay, drifting with the current, made up a picture of the terrible not often seen. Each gunboat returned the fire as she passed the town, while the transports hugged the opposite shore. When the Benton had got abreast of us, I pulled off to her, boarded, had a few words with Admiral Porter, and as she was drifting rapidly toward the lower batteries at Warrenton, I left, and pulled back toward the shore, meeting the gunboat Tuscumbia towing the transport Forest Queen into the bank out of the range of fire. The Forest Queen, Captain Conway, had been my flag-boat up the Arkansas, and for some time after, and I was very friendly with her officers. This was the only transport whose captain would not receive volunteers as a crew, but her own officers and *crew* stuck to their boat, and carried her safely below the Vicksburg batteries, and afterward rendered splendid service in ferrying troops across the river at Grand Gulf and Bruinsburg. In passing Vicksburg, she was damaged in the hull and had a steam-pipe cut away, but this was soon repaired. The Henry Clay was set on fire by bursting shells, and burned up; one of my yawls picked up her pilot floating on a piece of wreck, and the bulk of her crew escaped in their own yawl-boat to the shore above. The Silver Wave, Captain McMillan, the same that was with us up Steele's Bayou, passed safely, and she also rendered good service afterward.

Subsequently, on the night of April 26th, six other transports with numerous barges loaded with hay, corn, freight, and provisions, were drifted past Vicksburg; of these the Tigress was hit, and sunk just as she reached the river-bank below, on our side. I was there with my yawls, and saw Colonel Lagow, of General Grant's staff, who had passed the batteries in the Tigress, and I think he was satisfied never to attempt such a thing again. Thus General Grant's army had below Vicksburg an abundance of stores, and boats with which to cross the river. The road by which the troops marched was very bad, and it was not until the 1st of May that it was clear for my corps. While waiting my turn to march, I received a letter from General Grant, written at Carthage, saying that he proposed to cross over and attack Grand Gulf, about the end of April, and he thought I could put in my time usefully by making a "feint" on Haines's Bluff, but he did not like to order me to do it, because it might be reported at the North that I had again been "repulsed, etc." Thus we had to fight a senseless clamor at the North, as well as a determined foe and the obstacles of Nature. Of course, I answered him that I would make the "feint," regardless of public clamor at a distance, and I did make it most effectually; using all the old boats I could get about Milliken's Bend and the mouth of the Yazoo, but taking only ten small regiments, selected out of Blair's division, to make a show of force. We afterward learned that General Pemberton in Vicksburg had previously dispatched a large force to the assistance of General Bowen, at Grand Gulf and Port Gibson, which force had proceeded as far as Hankinson's Ferry, when he discovered our ostentatious movement up the Yazoo, recalled his men, and sent them up to Haines's Bluff to meet us. This detachment of rebel troops must have marched nearly sixty miles without rest, for afterward, on reaching Vicksburg, I heard that the men were perfectly exhausted, and lay along the road in groups, completely fagged out. This diversion, made with so much pomp and display, therefore completely fulfilled its purpose, by leaving General Grant to contend with a minor force, on landing at Bruinsburg, and afterward at Port Gibson and Grand Gulf.

In May the waters of the Mississippi had so far subsided that all our canals were useless, and the roads had become practicable. After McPherson's corps had passed Richmond, I took up the route of march, with Steele's and Tuttle's divisions. Blair's division remained at Milliken's Bend to protect our depots there, till relieved by troops from Memphis, and then he was ordered to follow us. Our route lay by Richmond and Roundabout Bayou; then, following Bayou Vidal we struck the Mississippi at Perkins's plantation. Thence the route followed Lake St. Joseph to a plantation called Hard Times, about five miles above Grand Gulf. The road was more or less occupied by wagons and detachments belonging to McPherson's corps; still we marched rapidly and reached Hard Times on the 6th of May. Along the Bayou or Lake St. Joseph were many very fine cotton-plantations, and I recall

that of a Mr. Bowie, brother-in-law of the Hon. Reverdy
Johnson, of Baltimore. The house was very handsome, with a
fine, extensive grass-plot in front. We entered the yard, and,
leaving our horses with the headquarters escort, walked to the
house. On the front-porch I found a magnificent grand-piano,
with several satin-covered arm-chairs, in one of which sat a
Union soldier (one of McPherson's men), with his feet on the
keys of the piano, and his musket and knapsack lying on the
porch. I asked him what he was doing there, and he answered
that he was "taking a rest;" this was manifest and I started
him in a hurry to overtake his command. The house was ten-
antless, and had been completely ransacked; articles of dress
and books were strewed about, and a handsome boudoir with
mirror front had been cast down, striking a French bedstead,
shivering the glass. The library was extensive, with a fine collection of books; and hanging on the wall were two full-
length portraits of Reverdy Johnson and his wife, one of the
most beautiful ladies of our country, with whom I had been
acquainted in Washington at the time of General Taylor's administration. Behind the mansion was the usual double row
of cabins called the "quarters." There I found an old negro (a
family servant) with several women, whom I sent to the house
to put things in order; telling the old man that other troops
would follow, and he must stand on the porch to tell any
officers who came along that the property belonged to Mr.
Bowie, who was the brother-in-law of our friend Mr.
Reverdy Johnson, of Baltimore, asking them to see that no
further harm was done. Soon after we left the house I saw
some negroes carrying away furniture which manifestly belonged to the house, and compelled them to carry it back; and
after reaching camp that night, at Hard Times, I sent a wagon
back to Bowie's plantation, to bring up to Dr. Hollings-
worth's house the two portraits for safe keeping; but before
the wagon had reached Bowie's the house was burned,
whether by some of our men or by negroes I have never
learned.

At the river there was a good deal of scrambling to get
across, because the means of ferriage were inadequate; but by
the aid of the Forest Queen and several gunboats I got my
command across during the 7th of May, and marched out to

Hankinson's Ferry (eighteen miles), relieving General Crocker's division of McPherson's corps. McClernand's corps and McPherson's were still ahead, and had fought the battle of Port Gibson, on the 11th. I overtook General Grant in person at Auburn, and he accompanied my corps all the way into Jackson, which we reached May 14th. McClernand's corps had been left in observation toward Edwards's Ferry. McPherson had fought at Raymond, and taken the left-hand road toward Jackson, *via* Clinton, while my troops were ordered by General Grant in person to take the right-hand road leading through Mississippi Springs. We reached Jackson at the same time; McPherson fighting on the Clinton road, and my troops fighting just outside the town, on the Raymond road, where we captured three entire field-batteries, and about two hundred prisoners of war. The rebels, under General Joe Johnston, had retreated through the town northward on the Canton road. Generals Grant, McPherson, and I, met in the large hotel facing the State-House, where the former explained to us that he had intercepted dispatches from Pemberton to Johnston, which made it important for us to work smart to prevent a junction of their respective forces. McPherson was ordered to march back early the next day on the Clinton road to make junction with McClernand, and I was ordered to remain one day to break up railroads, to destroy the arsenal, a foundery, the cotton-factory of the Messrs. Green, etc., etc., and then to follow McPherson.

McPherson left Jackson early on the 15th, and General Grant during the same day. I kept my troops busy in tearing up railroad-tracks, etc., but early on the morning of the 16th received notice from General Grant that a battle was imminent near Edwards's Depot; that he wanted me to dispatch one of my divisions immediately, and to follow with the other as soon as I had completed the work of destruction. Steele's division started immediately, and later in the day I followed with the other division (Tuttle's). Just as I was leaving Jackson, a very fat man came to see me, to inquire if his hotel, a large, frame-building near the depot, were doomed to be burned. I told him we had no intention to burn it, or any other house, except the machine-shops, and such buildings as could easily be converted to hostile uses. He professed to be a law-abiding Union man, and I remember to have said that this fact was manifest from the sign of his hotel, which was the "Confederate Hotel;" the sign "United States" being faintly painted out, and "Confederate" painted over it! I remembered that hotel, as it was the supper-station for the New Orleans trains when I used to travel the road before the war. I had not the least purpose, however, of burning it, but, just as we were leaving the town, it burst out in flames and was burned to the ground. I never found out exactly who set it on fire, but was told that in one of our batteries were some officers and men who had been made prisoners at Shiloh, with Prentiss's division, and had been carried past Jackson in a railroad-train; they had been permitted by the guard to go to this very hotel for supper, and had nothing to pay but greenbacks, which were refused, with insult, by this same law-abiding landlord. These men, it was said, had quietly and stealthily applied the fire underneath the hotel just as we were leaving the town.

About dark we met General Grant's staff-officer near Bolton Station, who turned us to the right, with orders to push on to Vicksburg by what was known as the upper Jackson Road, which crossed the Big Black at Bridgeport. During that day (May 16th) the battle of Champion Hills had been fought and won by McClernand's and McPherson's corps, aided by one division of mine (Blair's), under the immediate command of General Grant; and McPherson was then following the mass of Pemberton's army, disordered and retreating toward Vicksburg by the Edwards's Ferry road. General Blair's division had come up from the rear, was temporarily attached to McClernand's corps, taking part with it in the battle of Champion Hills, but on the 17th it was ordered by General Grant across to Bridgeport, to join me there.

Just beyond Bolton there was a small hewn-log house, standing back in a yard, in which was a well; at this some of our soldiers were drawing water. I rode in to get a drink, and, seeing a book on the ground, asked some soldier to hand it to me. It was a volume of the Constitution of the United States, and on the title-page was written the name of Jefferson Davis. On inquiry of a negro, I learned that the place belonged to the then President of the Southern Confederation. His brother Joe Davis's plantation was not far off; one of my staff-officers went there, with a few soldiers, and took a pair of carriage-horses, without my knowledge at the time. He found Joe Davis at home, an old man, attended by a young and affectionate niece; but they were overwhelmed with grief to see their country overrun and swarming with Federal troops.

We pushed on, and reached the Big Black early, Blair's troops having preceded us by an hour or so. I found General Blair in person, and he reported that there was no bridge across the Big Black; that it was swimming-deep; and that there was a rebel force on the opposite side, intrenched. He had ordered a detachment of the Thirteenth United States Regulars, under Captain Charles Ewing, to strip some artillery-horses, mount the men, and swim the river above the ferry, to attack and drive away the party on the opposite bank. I did not approve of this risky attempt, but crept down close to the brink of the river-bank, behind a corn-crib belonging to a plantation-house near by, and saw the parapet on the opposite bank. Ordering a section of guns to be brought forward by hand behind this corn-crib, a few well-directed shells brought out of their holes the little party that was covering the crossing, viz., a lieutenant and ten men, who came down to the river-bank and surrendered. Blair's pontoon-train was brought up, consisting of India-rubber boats, one of which was inflated, used as a boat, and brought over the prisoners. A pontoon-bridge was at once begun, finished by night, and the troops began the passage. After dark, the whole scene was lit up with fires of pitch-pine. General Grant joined me there, and we sat on a log, looking at the passage of the troops by the light of those fires; the bridge swayed to and fro under the passing feet, and made a fine war-picture. At daybreak we moved on, ascending the ridge, and by 10 A.M. the head of my column, long drawn out, reached the Benton road, and gave us command of the peninsula between the Yazoo and Big Black. I dispatched Colonel Swan, of the Fourth Iowa Cavalry, to Haines's Bluff, to capture that battery from the rear, and he afterward reported that he found it abandoned, its garrison having hastily retreated into Vicksburg, leaving their guns partially disabled, a magazine full of ammunition, and a hospital full of wounded and sick men.

Colonel Swan saw one of our gunboats lying about two miles below in the Yazoo, to which he signaled. She steamed up, and to its commander the cavalry turned over the battery at Haines's Bluff, and rejoined me in front of Vicksburg. Allowing a couple of hours for rest and to close up the column, I resumed the march straight on Vicksburg. About two miles before reaching the forts, the road forked; the left was the main Jackson road, and the right was the "graveyard" road, which entered Vicksburg near a large cemetery. General Grant in person directed me to take the right-hand road, but, as McPherson had not yet got up from the direction of the railroad-bridge at Big Black, I sent the Eighth Missouri on the main Jackson road, to push the rebel skirmishers into town, and to remain until relieved by McPherson's advance, which happened late that evening, May 18th. The battalion of the Thirteenth United States Regulars, commanded by Captain Washington, was at the head of the column on the right-hand road, and pushed the rebels close behind their parapets; one of my staff, Captain Pitzman, receiving a dangerous wound in the hip, which apparently disabled him for life. By night Blair's whole division had closed up against the defenses of Vicksburg, which were found to be strong and well manned; and, on General Steele's head of column arriving, I turned it still more to the right, with orders to work its way down the bluff, so as to make connection with our fleet in the Mississippi River. There was a good deal of desultory fighting that evening, and a man was killed by the side of General Grant and myself, as we sat by the road-side looking at Steele's division passing to the right. General Steele's men reached the road which led from Vicksburg up to Haines's Bluff, which road lay at the foot of the hills, and intercepted some prisoners and wagons which were coming down from Haines's Bluff.

All that night McPherson's troops were arriving by the main Jackson road, and McClernand's by another near the railroad, deploying forward as fast as they struck the rebel works. My corps (the Fifteenth) had the right of the line of investment; McPherson's (the Seventeenth) the centre; and McClernand's (the Thirteenth) the left, reaching from the river above to the railroad below. Our lines connected, and invested about three-quarters of the land-front of the fortifications of Vicksburg. On the supposition that the garrison of Vicksburg was demoralized by the defeats at Champion Hills and at the railroad crossing of the Big Black, General Grant ordered an assault at our respective fronts on the 19th. My troops reached the top of the parapet, but could not cross over. The rebel parapets were strongly manned, and the enemy fought hard and well. My loss was pretty heavy, falling chiefly on the Thirteenth Regulars, whose commanding officer, Captain Washington, was killed, and several other regiments were pretty badly cut up. We, however, held the ground up to the ditch till night, and then drew back only a short distance, and began to counter-trench. On the graveyard road, our parapet was within less than fifty yards of the rebel ditch.

On the 20th of May, General Grant called the three corps commanders together, viz., McClernand, McPherson, and Sherman. We compared notes, and agreed that the assault of the day before had failed, by reason of the natural strength of the position, and because we were forced by the nature of the ground to limit our attacks to the strongest parts of the enemy's line, viz., where the three principal roads entered the city. It was not a council of war, but a mere consultation, resulting in orders from General Grant for us to make all possible preparations for a renewed assault on the 22d, simultaneously, at 10 A.M. I reconnoitred my front thoroughly in person, from right to left, and concluded to make my real attack at the right flank of the bastion, where the graveyard road entered the enemy's intrenchments, and at another point in the curtain about a hundred yards to its right (our left); also to make a strong demonstration by Steele's division, about a mile to our right, toward the river. All our field-batteries were put in position, and were covered by good epaulements; the troops were brought forward, in easy support, concealed by the shape of the ground; and to the minute, viz., 10 A.M. of May 22d, the troops sprang to the assault. A small party, that might be called a forlorn hope, provided with plank to cross the ditch, advanced at a run, up to the very ditch; the lines of infantry sprang from cover, and advanced rapidly in line of battle. I took a position within two hundred yards of the rebel parapet, on the off slope of a spur of ground, where by advancing two or three steps I could see every thing. The rebel line, concealed by the parapet, showed no sign of unusual activity, but as our troops came in fair view, the enemy rose behind their parapet and poured a furious fire upon our lines; and, for about two hours, we had a severe and bloody battle, but at every point we were repulsed. In the very midst of this, when shell and shot fell furious and fast, occurred that little episode which has been celebrated in song and story, of the boy Orion P. Howe, badly wounded, bearing me a message for cartridges, calibre 54, described in my letter to the Hon. E. M. Stanton, Secretary of War. This boy was afterward appointed a cadet to the United States Naval Academy, at Annapolis, but he could not graduate, and I do not now know what has become of him.

After our men had been fairly beaten back from off the parapet, and had got cover behind the spurs of ground close up to the rebel works, General Grant came to where I was, on foot, having left his horse some distance to the rear. I pointed out to him the rebel works, admitted that my assault had failed, and he said the result with McPherson and McClernand was about the same. While he was with me, an orderly or staff-officer came and handed him a piece of paper, which he read and handed to me. I think the writing was in pencil, on a loose piece of paper, and was in General McClernand's handwriting, to the effect that "his troops had captured the rebel parapet in his front," that "the flag of the Union waved over the stronghold of Vicksburg," and asking him (General Grant) to give renewed orders to McPherson and Sherman to press their attacks on their respective fronts, lest the enemy should concentrate on him (McClernand). General Grant said, "I don't believe a word of it;" but I reasoned with him, that this note was official, and must be credited, and I offered to renew the assault at once with new troops. He said he would instantly ride down the line to McClernand's front, and if I did not receive orders to the contrary, by 3 o'clock P.M., I might try it again. Mower's fresh brigade was brought up under cover, and some changes were made in Giles Smith's brigade; and, punctually at 3 P.M., hearing heavy firing down along the line to my left, I ordered the second assault. It was a repetition of the first, equally unsuccessful and bloody. It also transpired that the same thing had occurred with General McPherson, who lost in this second assault some most valuable officers and men, without adequate result; and that General McClernand, instead of having taken any single point of the rebel main parapet, had only taken one or two small outlying lunettes open to the rear, where his men were at the mercy of the rebels behind their main parapet, and most of them were actually thus captured. This affair caused great feeling with us, and severe criticisms on General McClernand, which led finally to his removal from the command of the Thirteenth Corps, to which General Ord succeeded. The immediate cause, however, of General McClernand's removal was the publication of a sort of congratulatory order addressed to his troops, first published in St. Louis, in which he claimed that he had actually succeeded in making a lodgment in Vicksburg, but had lost it, owing to the fact that McPherson and Sherman did not fulfill their parts of the general plan of attack. This was simply untrue. The two several assaults made May 22d, on the lines of Vicksburg, had failed, by reason of the great strength of the position and the determined fighting of its garrison. I have since seen the position at Sevastopol, and without hesitation I declare that at Vicksburg to have been the more difficult of the two.

Thereafter our proceedings were all in the nature of a siege. General Grant drew more troops from Memphis, to prolong our general line to the left, so as completely to invest the place on its land-side, while the navy held the river both above and below. General Mower's brigade of Tuttle's division was also sent across the river to the peninsula, so that by May 31st Vicksburg was completely beleaguered. Good roads were constructed from our camps to the several landing-places on the Yazoo River, to which points our boats brought us ample supplies; so that we were in a splendid condition for a siege, while our enemy was shut up in a close fort, with a large civil population of men, women, and children to feed, in addition to his combatant force. If we could prevent sallies, or relief from the outside, the fate of the garrison of Vicksburg was merely a question of time.

I had my headquarters camp close up to the works, near the centre of my corps, and General Grant had his bivouac behind a ravine to my rear. We estimated Pemberton's whole force in Vicksburg at thirty thousand men, and it was well known that the rebel General Joseph E. Johnston was engaged in collecting another strong force near the Big Black, with the intention to attack our rear, and thus to afford Pemberton an opportunity to escape with his men. Even then the ability of General Johnston was recognized, and General Grant told me that he was about the only general on that side whom he feared. Each corps kept strong pickets well to the rear; but, as the rumors of Johnston's accumulating force reached us, General Grant concluded to take stronger measures. He had received from the North General J. G. Parkes's corps (Ninth), which had been posted at Haines's Bluff; then, detailing one division from each of the three *corps d'armée* investing Vicksburg, he ordered me to go out, take a general command of all, and to counteract any movement on the part of General Johnston to relieve Vicksburg. I reconnoitred the whole country, from Haines's Bluff to the railroad bridge, and posted the troops thus: Parkes's two divisions from Haines's Bluff out to the Benton or ridge road; Tuttle's division, of my corps, joining on and extending to a plantation called Young's, overlooking Bear Creek valley, which empties into the Big Black above Messinger's Ferry; then McArthur's division, of McPherson's corps, took up the line, and reached to Osterhaus's division of McClernand's corps, which held a strong fortified position at the railroad-crossing of the Big Black River. I was of opinion that, if Johnston should cross the Big Black, he could by the favorable nature of the country be held in check till a concentration could be effected by us at the point threatened. From the best information we could gather, General Johnston had about thirty or forty thousand men. I took post near a plantation of one Trible, near Markham's, and frequently reconnoitred the whole line, and could see the enemy engaged in like manner, on the east side of Big Black; but he never attempted actually to cross over, except with some cavalry, just above Bear Creek, which was easily driven back. I was there from June 20th to the 4th of July. In a small log-house near Markham's was the family of Mr. Klein, whose wife was the daughter of Mrs. Day, of New Orleans, who in turn was the sister of Judge T. W. Bartley, my brother-in-law. I used frequently to drop in and take a meal with them, and Mrs. Klein was generally known as the general's cousin, which doubtless saved her and her family from molestation, too common on the part of our men.

One day, as I was riding the line near a farm known as Parson Fox's, I heard that the family of a Mr. Wilkinson, of New Orleans, was "refugeeing" at a house near by. I rode up, inquired, and found two young girls of that name, who said they were the children of General Wilkinson, of Louisiana, and that their brother had been at the Military School at Alexandria. Inquiring for their mother, I was told she was spending the day at Parson Fox's. As this house was on my route, I rode there, went through a large gate into the yard, followed by my staff and escort, and found quite a number of ladies sitting on the porch. I rode up and inquired if that were Parson Fox's. The parson, a fine-looking, venerable old man, rose, and said that he was Parson Fox. I then inquired for Mrs. Wilkinson, when an elderly lady answered that she was the person. I asked her if she were from Plaquemine Parish, Louisiana, and she said she was. I then inquired if she had a son who had been a cadet at Alexandria when General Sherman was superintendent, and she answered yes. I then announced myself, inquired after the boy, and she said he was inside of Vicksburg, an artillery lieutenant. I then asked about her husband, whom I had known, when she burst into tears, and cried out in agony, "You killed him at Bull Run, where he was fighting for his country!" I disclaimed killing anybody at Bull Run; but all the women present (nearly a dozen) burst into loud lamentations, which made it most uncomfortable for me, and I rode away. On the 3d of July, as I sat at my bivouac by the road-side near Trible's, I saw a poor, miserable horse, carrying a lady, and led by a little negro boy, coming across a cotton-field toward me; as they approached I recognized poor Mrs. Wilkinson, and helped her to dismount. I inquired what had brought her to me in that style, and she answered that she *knew* Vicksburg was going to surrender, and she wanted to go right away to see her boy. I had a telegraph-wire to General Grant's headquarters, and had heard that there were symptoms of surrender, but as yet nothing definite. I tried to console and dissuade her, but she was resolved, and I could not help giving her a letter to General Grant, explaining to him who she was, and asking him to give her the earliest opportunity to see her son. The distance was fully twenty miles, but off she started, and I afterward learned that my letter had enabled her to see her son, who had escaped unharmed. Later in the day I got by telegraph General Grant's notice of the negotiations for surrender; and, by his directions, gave general orders to my troops to be ready at a moment's notice to cross the Big Black, and go for Joe Johnston.

The next day (July 4, 1863) Vicksburg surrendered, and orders were given for at once attacking General Johnston. The Thirteenth Corps (General Ord) was ordered to march rapidly, and cross the Big Black at the railroad-bridge; the Fifteenth by Messinger's, and the Ninth (General Parkes) by Birdsong's Ferry—all to converge on Bolton. My corps crossed the Big Black during the 5th and 6th of July, and marched for Bolton, where we came in with General Ord's troops; but the Ninth Corps was delayed in crossing at Birdsong's. Johnston had received timely notice of Pemberton's surrender, and was in full retreat for Jackson. On the 8th all our troops reached the neighborhood of Clinton, the weather fearfully hot, and water scarce. Johnston had marched rapidly, and in retreating had caused cattle, hogs, and sheep, to be driven into the ponds of water, and there shot down; so that we had to haul their dead and stinking carcasses out to use the water. On the 10th of July we had driven the rebel army into Jackson, where it turned at bay behind the intrenchments, which had been enlarged and strengthened since our former visit in May. We closed our lines about Jackson; my corps (Fifteenth) held the centre, extending from the Clinton to the Raymond road; Ord's (Thirteenth) on the right, reaching Pearl River below the town; and Parkes's (Ninth) the left, above the town.

On the 11th we pressed close in, and shelled the town from every direction. One of Ord's brigades (Lauman's) got too close, and was very roughly handled and driven back in disorder. General Ord accused the commander (General Lauman) of having disregarded his orders, and attributed to him personally the disaster and heavy loss of men. He requested his relief, which I granted, and General Lauman went to the rear, and never regained his division. He died after the war, in Iowa, much respected, as before that time he had been universally esteemed a most gallant and excellent officer. The weather was fearfully hot, but we continued to press the siege day and night, using our artillery pretty freely; and on the morning of July 17th the place was found evacuated. General Steele's division was sent in pursuit as far as Brandon (fourteen miles), but General Johnston had carried his army safely off, and pursuit in that hot weather would have been fatal to my command.

Reporting the fact to General Grant, he ordered me to return, to send General Parkes's corps to Haines's Bluff, General Ord's back to Vicksburg, and he consented that I should encamp my whole corps near the Big Black, pretty much on the same ground we had occupied before the movement, and with the prospect of a period of rest for the remainder of the summer. We reached our camps on the 27th of July.

Meantime, a division of troops, commanded by Brigadier-General W. Sooy Smith, had been added to my corps. General Smith applied for and received a sick-leave on the 20th of July; Brigadier-General Hugh Ewing was assigned to its command; and from that time it constituted the Fourth Division of the Fifteenth Army Corps.

Port Hudson had surrendered to General Banks on the 8th of July (a necessary consequence of the fall of Vicksburg), and thus terminated probably the most important enterprise of the civil war—the recovery of the complete control of the Mississippi River, from its source to its mouth—or, in the language of Mr. Lincoln, the Mississippi went "unvexed to the sea."

I put my four divisions into handsome, clean camps, looking to health and comfort alone, and had my headquarters in a beautiful grove near the house of that same Parson Fox where I had found the crowd of weeping rebel women waiting for the fate of their friends in Vicksburg.

The loss sustained by the Fifteenth Corps in the assault of May 19th, at Vicksburg, was mostly confined to the battalion of the Thirteenth Regulars, whose commanding officer, Captain Washington, was mortally wounded, and afterward died in the hands of the enemy, which battalion lost seventy-seven men out of the two hundred and fifty engaged; the Eighty-third Indiana (Colonel Spooner), and the One Hundred and Twenty-seventh Illinois (Lieutenant-Colonel Eldridge), the aggregate being about two hundred.

In the assaults of the 22d, the loss in the Fifteenth Corps was about six hundred.

In the attack on Jackson, Mississippi, during the 11th–16th of July, General Ord reported the loss in the Thirteenth Army Corps seven hundred and sixty-two, of which five hundred and thirty-three were confined to Lauman's division; General Parkes reported, in the Ninth Corps, thirty-seven killed, two hundred and fifty-eight wounded, and thirty-three missing: total, three hundred and twenty-eight. In the Fifteenth Corps the loss was less; so that, in the aggregate, the loss as reported by me at the time was less than a thousand men, while we took that number alone of prisoners.

In General Grant's entire army before Vicksburg, composed of the Ninth, part of the Sixteenth, and the whole of the Thirteenth, Fifteenth, and Seventeenth Corps, the aggregate loss, as stated by Badeau, was—

Killed	1,243
Wounded	7,095
Missing	535
Total	8,873

Whereas the Confederate loss, as stated by the same author, was:

Surrendered at Vicksburg	32,000
Captured at Champion Hills	3,000
Captured at Big Black Bridge	2,000
Captured at Port Gibson	2,000
Captured with Loring	4,000
Killed and wounded	10,000
Stragglers	3,000
Total	56,000

Besides which, "a large amount of public property, consisting of railroads, locomotives, cars, steamers, cotton, guns, muskets, ammunition, etc., etc., was captured in Vicksburg."

The value of the capture of Vicksburg, however, was not measured by the list of prisoners, guns, and small-arms, but by the fact that its possession secured the navigation of the great central river of the continent, bisected fatally the Southern Confederacy, and set the armies which had been used in its conquest free for other purposes; and it so happened that the event coincided as to time with another great victory which crowned our arms far away, at Gettysburg, Pennsylvania. That was a defensive battle, whereas ours was offensive in the highest acceptation of the term, and the two, occurring at the same moment of time, should have ended the war; but the rebel leaders were mad, and seemed determined that their people should drink of the very lowest dregs of the cup of war, which they themselves had prepared.

The campaign of Vicksburg, in its conception and execution, belonged exclusively to General Grant, not only in the great whole, but in the thousands of its details. I still retain many of his letters and notes, all in his own handwriting, prescribing the routes of march for divisions and detachments, specifying even the amount of food and tools to be carried along. Many persons gave his adjutant-general, Rawlins, the credit for these things, but they were in error; for no commanding general of an army ever gave more of his personal attention to details, or wrote so many of his own orders, reports, and letters, as General Grant. His success at Vicksburg justly gave him great fame at home and abroad. The President conferred on him the rank of major-general in the regular army, the highest grade then existing by law; and General McPherson and I shared in his success by receiving similar commissions as brigadier-generals in the regular army.

But our success at Vicksburg produced other results not so favorable to our cause—a general relaxation of effort, and desire to escape the hard drudgery of camp: officers sought leaves of absence to visit their homes, and soldiers obtained furloughs and discharges on the most slender pretexts; even the General Government seemed to relax in its efforts to replenish our ranks with new men, or to enforce the draft, and the politicians were pressing their schemes to reorganize or patch up some form of civil government, as fast as the armies gained partial possession of the States.

In order to illustrate this peculiar phase of our civil war, I give at this place copies of certain letters which have not heretofore been published:

[PRIVATE.]

WASHINGTON, *August* 29, 1863.

Major-General W. T. SHERMAN, *Vicksburg, Mississippi.*

MY DEAR GENERAL: The question of reconstruction in Louisiana, Mississippi, and Arkansas, will soon come up for decision of the Government, and not only the length of the war, but our ultimate and complete success, will depend upon its decision. It is a difficult matter, but I believe it can be successfully solved, if the President will consult opinions of cool and discreet men, who are capable of looking at it in all its bearings and effects. I think he is disposed to receive the advice of our generals who have been in these States, and know much more of their condition than gassy politicians in Congress. General Banks has written pretty fully on the subject. I wrote to General Grant, immediately after the fall of Vicksburg, for his views in regard to Mississippi, but he has not yet answered.

I wish you would consult with Grant, McPherson, and others of cool, good judgment, and write me your views fully, as I may wish to use them with the President. You had better write me unofficially, and then your letter will not be put on file, and cannot hereafter be used against you. You have been in Washington enough to know how every thing a man writes or says is picked up by his enemies and misconstrued. With kind wishes for your further success,

I am yours truly,

H. W. HALLECK.

[PRIVATE AND CONFIDENTIAL.]

HEADQUARTERS, FIFTEENTH ARMY CORPS, CAMP ON BIG BLACK, MISSISSIPPI, *September* 17, 1863.

H. W. HALLECK, *Commander-in-Chief, Washington, D. C.*

DEAR GENERAL: I have received your letter of August 29th, and with pleasure confide to you fully my thoughts on the important matters you suggest, with absolute confidence that you will use what is valuable, and reject the useless or superfluous.

That part of the continent of North America known as Louisiana, Mississippi, and Arkansas, is in my judgment the key to the whole interior. The valley of the Mississippi is America, and, although railroads have changed the economy of intercommunication, yet the water-channels still mark the lines of fertile land, and afford cheap carriage to the heavy products of it.

The inhabitants of the country on the Monongahela, the Illinois, the Minnesota, the Yellowstone, and Osage, are as directly concerned in the security of the Lower Mississippi as are those who dwell on its very banks in Louisiana; and now that the nation has recovered its possession, this generation of men will make a fearful mistake if they again commit its charge to a people liable to misuse their position, and assert, as was recently done, that, because they dwelt on the banks of this mighty stream, they had a right to control its navigation.

I would deem it very unwise at this time, or for years to come, to revive the State governments of Louisiana, etc., or to institute in this quarter any civil government in which the local people have much to say. They had a government so mild and paternal that they gradually forgot they had any at all, save what they themselves controlled; they asserted an absolute right to seize public moneys, forts, arms, and even to shut up the natural avenues of travel and commerce. They chose *war*—they ignored and denied all the obligations of the solemn contract of government and appealed to force.

We accepted the issue, and now they begin to realize that war is a two-edged sword, and it may be that many of the inhabitants cry for *peace*. I know them well, and the very impulses of their nature; and to deal with the inhabitants of that part of the South which borders on the great river, we must recognize the classes into which they have divided themselves:

First. The large planters, owning lands, slaves, and all kinds of personal property. These are, on the whole, the ruling class. They are educated, wealthy, and easily approached. In some districts they are bitter as gall, and have given up slaves, plantations, and all, serving in the armies of the Confederacy; whereas, in others, they are conservative. None dare admit a friendship for us, though they say freely that they were at the outset opposed to war and disunion. I *know* we can manage this class, but only by *action*. Argument is exhausted, and words have lost their usual meaning. Nothing but the logic of events touches their understanding; but, of late, this has worked a wonderful change. If our country were like Europe, crowded with people, I would say it would be easier to replace this class than to reconstruct it, subordinate to the policy of the nation; but, as this is not the case, it is better to allow the planters, with individual exceptions, gradually to recover their plantations, to hire any species of labor, and to adapt themselves to the new order of things. Still, their friendship and assistance to reconstruct order out of the present ruin cannot be depended on. They watch the operations of our armies, and hope still for a Southern Confederacy that will restore to them the slaves and privileges which they feel are otherwise lost forever. In my judgment, we have two more battles to win before we should even bother our minds with the idea of restoring civil order—viz., one near Meridian, in November, and one near Shreveport, in February and March next, when Red River is navigable by our gunboats. When these are done, then, and not until then, will the planters of Louisiana, Arkansas, and Mississippi, submit. Slavery is already gone, and, to cultivate the land, negro or other labor must be hired. This, of itself, is a vast revolution, and time must be afforded to allow men to adjust their minds and habits to this new order of things. A civil government of the representative type would suit this class far less than a pure military rule, readily adapting itself to actual occurrences, and able to enforce its laws and orders promptly and emphatically.

Second. The smaller farmers, mechanics, merchants, and laborers. This class will probably number three-quarters of the whole; have, in fact, no real interest in the establishment of a Southern Confederacy, and have been led or driven into war on the false theory that they were to be benefited somehow—they knew not how. They are essentially tired of the war, and would slink back home if they could. These are the real *tiers état* of the South, and are hardly worthy a thought; for they swerve to and fro according to events which they do not comprehend or attempt to shape. When the time for reconstruction comes, they will want the old political system of caucuses, Legislatures, etc., to amuse them and make them believe they are real sovereigns; but in all things they will follow blindly the lead of the planters. The Southern politicians, who understand this class, use them as the French do their masses—seemingly consult their prejudices, while they make their orders and enforce them. We should do the same.

Third. The Union men of the South. I must confess I have little respect for this class. They allowed a clamorous set of demagogues to muzzle and drive them as a pack of curs. Afraid of shadows, they submit tamely to squads of dragoons, and permit them, without a murmur, to burn their cotton, take their horses, corn, and every thing; and, when we reach them, they are full of complaints if our men take a few fence-rails for fire, or corn to feed our horses. They give us no assistance or information, and are loudest in their complaints at the smallest excesses of our soldiers. Their sons, horses, arms, and every thing useful, are in the army against us, and they stay at home, claiming all the exemptions of peaceful citizens. I account them as nothing in this great game of war.

Fourth. The young bloods of the South: sons of planters, lawyers about towns, good billiard-players and sportsmen, men who never did work and never will. War suits them, and the rascals are brave, fine riders, bold to rashness, and dangerous subjects in every sense. They care not a sou for niggers, land, or any thing. They hate Yankees *per se*, and don't bother their brains about the past, present, or future. As long as they have good horses, plenty of forage, and an open country, they are happy. This is a larger class than most men suppose, and they are the most dangerous set of men that this war has turned loose upon the world. They are splendid riders, first-rate shots, and utterly reckless. Stewart, John Morgan, Forrest, and Jackson, are the types and leaders of this class. These men must all be killed or employed by us before we can hope for peace. They have no property or future, and therefore cannot be influenced by any thing, except personal considerations. I have two brigades of these fellows in my front, commanded by Cosby, of the old army, and Whitfield, of Texas. Stephen D. Lee is in command of the whole. I have frequent interviews with their officers, a good understanding with them, and am inclined to think, when the resources of their country are exhausted, we must employ them. They are the best cavalry in the world, but it will tax Mr. Chase's genius for finance to supply them with horses. At present horses cost them nothing; for they take where they find, and don't bother their brains as to who is to pay for them; the same may be said of the cornfields, which have, as they believe, been cultivated by a good-natured people for their special benefit. We propose to share with them the free use of these cornfields, planted by willing hands, that will never gather the crops.

Now that I have sketched the people who inhabit the district of country under consideration, I will proceed to discuss the future.

A civil government now, for any part of it, would be simply ridiculous. The people would not regard it, and even the military commanders of the antagonistic parties would treat it lightly. Governors would be simply petitioners for military assistance, to protect supposed friendly interests, and military commanders would refuse to disperse and weaken their armies for military reasons. Jealousies would arise between the two conflicting powers, and, instead of contributing to the end of the war, would actually defer it. Therefore, I contend that the interests of the United States, and of the real parties concerned, demand the continuance of the simple military rule, till after *all* the organized armies of the South are dispersed, conquered, and subjugated.

The people of all this region are represented in the Army of

Virginia, at Charleston, Mobile, and Chattanooga. They have sons and relations in each of the rebel armies, and naturally are interested in their fate. Though we hold military possession of the key-points of their country, still they contend, and naturally, that should Lee succeed in Virginia, or Bragg at Chattanooga, a change will occur here also. We cannot for this reason attempt to reconstruct parts of the South as we conquer it, till all idea of the establishment of a Southern Confederacy is abandoned. We should avail ourselves of the present lull to secure the strategical points that will give us an advantage in the future military movements, and we should treat the idea of civil government as one in which we as a nation have a minor or subordinate interest. The opportunity is good to impress on the population the truth that they are more interested in civil government than we are; and that, to enjoy the protection of laws, they must not be passive observers of events, but must aid and sustain the constituted authorities in enforcing the laws; they must not only submit themselves, but should pay their share of taxes, and render personal services when called on.

It seems to me, in contemplating the history of the past two years, that all the people of our country, North, South, East, and West, have been undergoing a salutary political schooling, learning lessons which might have been acquired from the experience of other people; but we had all become so wise in our own conceit that we would only learn by actual experience of our own. The people even of small and unimportant localities, North as well as South, had reasoned themselves into the belief that their opinions were superior to the aggregated interest of the whole nation. Half our territorial nation rebelled, on a doctrine of secession that they themselves now scout; and a real numerical majority actually believed that a little State was endowed with such sovereignty that it could defeat the policy of the great whole. I think the present war has exploded that notion, and were this war to cease now, the experience gained, though dear, would be worth the expense.

Another great and important natural truth is still in contest, and can only be solved by war. Numerical majorities by vote have been our great arbiter. Heretofore all men have cheerfully submitted to it in questions left open, but numerical majorities are not necessarily physical majorities. The South, though numerically inferior, contend they can whip the Northern superiority of numbers, and therefore by natural law they contend that they are not bound to submit. This issue is the only real one, and in my judgment all else should be deferred to it. War alone can decide it, and it is the only question now left for us as a people to decide. Can we whip the South? If we can, our numerical majority has both the natural and constitutional right to govern them. If we cannot whip them, they contend for the natural right to select their own government, and they have the argument. Our armies must prevail over theirs; our officers, marshals, and courts, must penetrate into the innermost recesses of their land, before we have the natural right to demand their submission.

I would banish all minor questions, assert the broad doctrine that as a nation the United States has the right, and also the physical power, to penetrate to every part of our national domain, and that we will do it—that we will do it in our own time and in our own way; that it makes no difference whether it be in one year, or two, or ten, or twenty; that we will remove and destroy every obstacle, if need be, take every life, every acre of land, every particle of property, every thing that to us seems proper; that we will not cease till the end is attained; that all who do not aid us are enemies, and that we will not account to them for our acts. If the people of the South oppose, they do so at their peril; and if they stand by, mere lookers-on in this domestic tragedy, they have no right to immunity, protection, or share in the final results.

I even believe and contend further that, in the North, every member of the nation is bound by both natural and constitutional law to "maintain and defend the Government against all its enemies and opposers whomsoever." If they fail to do it they are derelict, and can be punished, or deprived of all advantages arising from the labors of those who do. If any man, North or South, withholds his share of taxes, or his physical assistance in this, the crisis of our history, he should be deprived of all voice in the future elections of this country, and might be banished, or reduced to the condition of a mere denizen of the land.

War is upon us, none can deny it. It is not the choice of the Government of the United States, but of a faction; the Government was forced to accept the issue, or to submit to a degradation fatal and disgraceful to all the inhabitants. In accepting war, *it* should be "pure and simple" as applied to the belligerents. I would keep it so, till all traces of the war are effaced; till those who appealed to it are sick and tired of it, and come to the emblem of our nation, and sue for peace. I would not coax them, or even meet them half-way, but make them so sick of war that generations would pass away before they would again appeal to it.

I know what I say when I repeat that the insurgents of the South sneer at all overtures looking to their interests. They scorn the alliance with the Copperheads; they tell me to my face that they respect

Grant, McPherson, and our brave associates who fight manfully and well for a principle, but despise the Copperheads and sneaks at the North, who profess friendship for the South and opposition to the war, as mere covers for their knavery and poltroonery.

God knows that I deplore this fratricidal war as much as any man living, but it is upon us, a physical fact; and there is only one honorable issue from it. We must fight it out, army against army, and man against man; and I know, and you know, and civilians begin to realize the fact, that reconciliation and reconstruction will be easier through and by means of strong, well-equipped, and organized armies than through any species of conventions that can be framed. The issues are made, and all discussion is out of place and ridiculous. The section of thirty-pounder Parrott rifles now drilling before my tent is a more convincing argument than the largest Democratic meeting the State of New York can possibly assemble at Albany; and a simple order of the War Department to draft enough men to fill our skeleton regiments would be more convincing as to our national perpetuity than an humble pardon to Jeff. Davis and all his misled host.

The only government needed or deserved by the States of Louisiana, Arkansas, and Mississippi, now exists in Grant's army. This needs, simply, enough privates to fill its ranks; all else will follow in due season. This army has its well-defined code of laws and practice, and can adapt itself to the wants and necessities of a city, the country, the rivers, the sea, indeed to all parts of this land. It better subserves the interest and policy of the General Government, and the people here prefer it to any weak or servile combination that would at once, from force of habit, revive and perpetuate local prejudices and passions. The people of this country have forfeited all right to a voice in the councils of the nation. They know it and feel it, and in after-years they will be the better citizens from the dear-bought experience of the present crisis. Let them learn now, and learn it well, that good citizens must obey as well as command. Obedience to law, absolute—yea, even abject—is the lesson that this war, under Providence, will teach the free and enlightened American citizen. As a nation, we shall be the better for it.

I never have apprehended foreign interference in our family quarrel. Of course, governments founded on a different and it may be an antagonistic principle with ours naturally feel a pleasure at our complications, and, it may be, wish our downfall; but in the end England and France will join with us in jubilation at the triumph of constitutional government over faction. Even now the English manifest this. I do not profess to understand Napoleon's design in

Mexico, and I do not see that his taking military possession of Mexico concerns us. We have as much territory now as we want. The Mexicans have failed in self-government, and it was a question as to what nation she should fall a prey. That is now solved, and I don't see that we are damaged. We have the finest part of the North American Continent, all we can people and can take care of; and, if we can suppress rebellion in our own land, and compose the strife generated by it, we shall have enough people, resources, and wealth, if well combined, to defy interference from any and every quarter.

I therefore hope the Government of the United States will continue, as heretofore, to collect, in well-organized armies, the physical strength of the nation; applying it, as heretofore, in asserting the national authority; and in persevering, without relaxation, to the end. This, whether near or far off, is not for us to say; but, fortunately, we have no choice. We must succeed—no other choice is left us except degradation. The South must be ruled by us, or she will rule us. We must conquer them, or ourselves be conquered. There is no middle course. They ask, and will have, nothing else, and talk of compromise is bosh; for we know they would even scorn the offer.

I wish the war could have been deferred for twenty years, till the superabundant population of the North could flow in and replace the losses sustained by war; but this could not be, and we are forced to take things as they are.

All therefore I can now venture to advise is to raise the draft to its maximum, fill the present regiments to as large a standard as possible, and push the war, pure and simple. Great attention should be paid to the discipline of our armies, for on them may be founded the future stability of the Government.

The cost of the war is, of course, to be considered, but finances will adjust themselves to the actual state of affairs; and, even if we would, we could not change the cost. Indeed, the larger the cost now, the less will it be in the end; for the end must be attained somehow, regardless of loss of life and treasure, and is merely a question of time.

Excuse so long a letter. With great respect, etc.,

W. T. SHERMAN, *Major-General.*

General Halleck, on receipt of this letter, telegraphed me that Mr. Lincoln had read it carefully, and had instructed him to obtain my consent to have it published. At the time, I preferred not to be drawn into any newspaper controversy, and so wrote to General Halleck; and the above letter has never been, to my knowledge, published; though Mr. Lincoln more than once referred to it with marks of approval.

HEADQUARTERS FIFTEENTH ARMY CORPS, ⎱
CAMP ON BIG BLACK, *September* 17, 1863.⎰

Brigadier-General J. A. RAWLINS, *Acting Assistant Adjutant-General, Vicksburg.*

DEAR GENERAL: I inclose for your perusal, and for you to read to General Grant such parts as you deem interesting, letters received by me from Prof. Mahan and General Halleck, with my answers. After you have read my answer to General Halleck, I beg you to inclose it to its address, and return me the others.

I think Prof. Mahan's very marked encomium upon the campaign of Vicksburg is so flattering to General Grant, that you may offer to let him keep the letter, if he values such a testimonial. I have never written a word to General Halleck since my report of last December, after the affair at Chickasaw, except a short letter a few days ago, thanking him for the kind manner of his transmitting to me the appointment of brigadier-general. I know that in Washington I am incomprehensible, because at the outset of the war I would not go it blind and rush headlong into a war unprepared and with an utter ignorance of its extent and purpose. I was then construed *unsound*; and now that I insist on war pure and simple, with no admixture of civil compromises, I am supposed vindictive. You remember what *Polonius* said to his son *Laertes*: "Beware of entrance to a quarrel; but, being in, bear it, that the opposed may beware of thee." What is true of the single man, is equally true of a nation. Our leaders seemed at first to thirst for the quarrel, willing, even anxious, to array against us all possible elements of opposition; and now, being in, they would hasten to quit long before the "opposed" has received that lesson which he needs. I would make this war as severe as possible, and show no symptoms of tiring till the South begs for mercy; indeed, I know, and you know, that the end would be reached quicker by such a course than by any seeming yielding on our part. I don't want our Government to be bothered by patching up local governments, or by trying to reconcile any class of men. The South has done her worst, and now is the time for us to pile on our blows thick and fast.

Instead of postponing the draft till after the elections, we ought now to have our ranks full of drafted men; and, at best, if they come at all, they will reach us when we should be in motion.

I think General Halleck would like to have the honest, candid opinions of all of us, viz., Grant, McPherson, and Sherman. I have given mine, and would prefer, of course, that it should coincide with the others. Still, no matter what my opinion may be, I can easily adapt my conduct to the plans of others, and am only too happy when I find theirs better than mine.

If no trouble, please show Halleck's letter to McPherson, and ask him to write also. I know his regiments are like mine (mere squads), and need filling up. Yours truly,

W. T. SHERMAN, *Major-General*.

Chapter XIV.

CHATTANOOGA AND KNOXVILLE.

July to December, 1863.

AFTER THE FALL of Vicksburg, and its corollary, Port Hudson, the Mississippi River was wholly in the possession of the Union forces, and formed a perfect line of separation in the territories of our opponents. Thenceforth, they could not cross it save by stealth, and the military affairs on its west bank became unimportant. Grant's army had seemingly completed its share of the work of war, and lay, as it were, idle for a time. In person General Grant went to New Orleans to confer with General Banks, and his victorious army was somewhat dispersed. Parke's corps (Ninth) returned to Kentucky, and afterward formed part of the Army of the Ohio, under General Burnside; Ord's corps (Thirteenth) was sent down to Natchez, and gradually drifted to New Orleans and Texas; McPherson's (Seventeenth) remained in and near Vicksburg; Hurlbut's (Sixteenth) was at Memphis; and mine (Fifteenth) was encamped along the Big Black, about twenty miles east of Vicksburg. This corps was composed of four divisions: Steele's (the First) was posted at and near the railroad-bridge; Blair's (the Second), next in order, near Parson Fox's; the Third Division (Tuttle's) was on the ridge about the head of Bear Creek; and the Fourth (Ewing's) was at Messinger's Ford. My own headquarters were in tents in a fine grove of old oaks near Parson Fox's house, and the battalion of the Thirteenth Regulars was the headquarters guard.

All the camps were arranged for health, comfort, rest, and drill. It being midsummer, we did not expect any change till the autumn months, and accordingly made ourselves as comfortable as possible. There was a short railroad in operation from Vicksburg to the bridge across the Big Black, whence supplies in abundance were hauled to our respective camps. With a knowledge of this fact Mrs. Sherman came down from Ohio with Minnie, Lizzie, Willie, and Tom, to pay us a visit in our camp at Parson Fox's. Willie was then nine years old, was well advanced for his years, and took the most intense interest in the affairs of the army. He was a great favorite with the soldiers, and used to ride with me on horseback in the numerous drills and reviews of the time. He then had the promise of as long a life as any of my children, and displayed more interest in the war than any of them. He was called a "sergeant" in the regular battalion, learned the manual of arms, and regularly attended the parade and guard-mounting of the Thirteenth, back of my camp. We made frequent visits to Vicksburg, and always stopped with General McPherson, who had a large house, and boarded with a family (Mrs. Edwards's) in which were several interesting young ladies. General Grant occupied another house (Mrs. Lum's) in Vicksburg during that summer, and also had his family with him. The time passed very agreeably, diversified only by little events of not much significance, among which I will recount only one.

While we occupied the west bank of the Big Black, the east bank was watched by a rebel cavalry-division, commanded by General Armstrong. He had four brigades, commanded by Generals Whitfield, Stark, Cosby, and Wirt Adams. Quite frequently they communicated with us by flags of truce on trivial matters, and we reciprocated, merely to observe them. One day a flag of truce, borne by a Captain B——, of Louisville, Kentucky, escorted by about twenty-five men, was reported at Messinger's Ferry, and I sent orders to let them come right into my tent. This brought them through the camps of the Fourth Division, and part of the Second; and as they drew up in front of my tent, I invited Captain B—— and another officer with him (a major from Mobile) to dismount, to enter my tent, and to make themselves at home. Their escort was sent to join mine, with orders to furnish them forage and every thing they wanted. B—— had brought a sealed letter for General Grant at Vicksburg, which was dispatched to him. In the evening we had a good supper, with wine and cigars, and, as we sat talking, B—— spoke of his father and mother, in Louisville, got leave to write them a long letter without its being read by any one, and then we talked about the war. He said: "What is the use of your persevering? It is simply impossible to subdue eight millions of people;" asserting that "the feeling in the South had become so embittered that a reconciliation was impossible." I answered that, "sitting as we then were, we appeared very comfortable, and surely there was no trouble in our becoming friends." "Yes," said he, "that is very true of us, but we are gentlemen of education, and can easily adapt ourselves to any condition of things; but this would not apply equally well to the common people, or to the common soldiers." I took him out to the camp-fires behind the tent, and there were the men of his escort and mine mingled together, drinking their coffee, and happy as soldiers always seem. I asked B—— what he thought of that, and he admitted that I had the best of the argument. Before I dismissed this flag of truce, his companion consulted me confidentially as to what disposition he ought to make of his family, then in Mobile, and I frankly gave him the best advice I could.

While we were thus lying idle in camp on the Big Black, the Army of the Cumberland, under General Rosecrans, was moving against Bragg at Chattanooga; and the Army of the Ohio, General Burnside, was marching toward East Tennessee. General Rosecrans was so confident of success that he somewhat scattered his command, seemingly to surround and capture Bragg in Chattanooga; but the latter, reënforced from Virginia, drew out of Chattanooga, concentrated his army at Lafayette, and at Chickamauga fell on Rosecrans, defeated him, and drove him into Chattanooga. The whole country seemed paralyzed by this unhappy event; and the authorities in Washington were thoroughly stampeded. From the East the Eleventh Corps (Slocum), and the Twelfth Corps (Howard), were sent by rail to Nashville, and forward under command of General Hooker; orders were also sent to General Grant, by Halleck, to send what reënforcements he could spare immediately toward Chattanooga.

Bragg had completely driven Rosecrans's army into Chattanooga; the latter was in actual danger of starvation, and the railroad to his rear seemed inadequate to his supply. The first intimation which I got of this disaster was on the 22d of September, by an order from General Grant to dispatch one of my divisions immediately into Vicksburg, to go toward Chattanooga, and I designated the First, General Osterhaus— Steele meantime having been appointed to the command of the Department of Arkansas, and had gone to Little Rock. General Osterhaus marched the same day, and on the 23d I was summoned to Vicksburg in person, where General Grant showed me the alarming dispatches from General Halleck, which had been sent from Memphis by General Hurlbut, and said, on further thought, that he would send me and my whole corps. But, inasmuch as one division of McPherson's corps (John E. Smith's) had already started, he instructed me to leave one of my divisions on the Big Black, and to get the other two ready to follow at once. I designated the Second, then commanded by Brigadier-General Giles A. Smith, and the Fourth, commanded by Brigadier-General Corse.

On the 25th I returned to my camp on Big Black, gave all the necessary orders for these divisions to move, and for the Third (Tuttle's) to remain, and went into Vicksburg with my family. The last of my corps designed for this expedition started from camp on the 27th, reached Vicksburg the 28th, and were embarked on boats provided for them. General Halleck's dispatches dwelt upon the fact that General Rosecrans's routes of supply were overtaxed, and that we should move from Memphis eastward, repairing railroads as we progressed, as far as Athens, Alabama, whence I was to report to General Rosecrans, at Chattanooga, by letter.

I took passage for myself and family in the steamer Atlantic, Captain Henry McDougall. When the boat was ready to start, Willie was missing. Mrs. Sherman supposed him to have been with me, whereas I supposed he was with her. An officer of the Thirteenth went up to General McPherson's house for him, and soon returned, with Captain Clift leading him, carrying in his hands a small double-barreled shot-gun; and I joked him about carrying away captured property. In a short time we got off. As we all stood on the guards to look at our old camps at Young's Point, I remarked that Willie was not well, and he admitted that he was sick. His mother put him to bed, and consulted Dr. Roler, of the Fifty-fifth Illinois, who found symptoms of typhoid fever. The river was low; we made slow progress till above Helena; and, as we approached Memphis, Dr. Roler told me that Willie's life was in danger, and he was extremely anxious to reach Memphis for certain medicines and for consultation. We arrived at Memphis on the 2d of October, carried Willie up to the Gayoso Hotel, and got the most experienced physician there, who acted with Dr. Roler, but he sank rapidly, and died the evening of the 3d of October. The blow was a terrible one to us all, so sudden and so unexpected, that I could not help reproaching myself for having consented to his visit in that sickly region in the summer-time. Of all my children, he seemed the most precious. Born in San Francisco, I had watched with intense interest his development, and he seemed more than any of the children to take an interest in my special profession. Mrs. Sherman, Minnie, Lizzie, and Tom, were with him at the time, and we all, helpless and overwhelmed, saw him die. Being in the very midst of an important military enterprise, I had hardly time to pause and think of my personal loss. We procured a metallic casket, and had a military funeral, the battalion of the Thirteenth United States Regulars acting as escort from the Gayoso Hotel to the steamboat Grey Eagle, which conveyed him and my family up to Cairo, whence they proceeded to our home at Lancaster, Ohio, where he was buried. I here give my letter to Captain C. C. Smith, who commanded the battalion at the time, as exhibiting our intense feelings:

GAYOSO HOUSE, MEMPHIS, TENNESSEE, }
October 4, 1863 —*Midnight.* }

Captain C. C. SMITH, *commanding Battalion Thirteenth United States Regulars.*

MY DEAR FRIEND: I cannot sleep to-night till I record an expression of the deep feelings of my heart to you, and to the officers and soldiers of the battalion, for their kind behavior to my poor child. I realize that you all feel for my family the attachment of kindred, and I assure you of full reciprocity.

Consistent with a sense of duty to my profession and office, I could not leave my post, and sent for the family to come to me in that fatal climate, and in that sickly period of the year, and behold the result! The child that bore my name, and in whose future I reposed with more confidence than I did in my own plan of life, now floats a mere corpse, seeking a grave in a distant land, with a weeping mother, brother, and sisters, clustered about him. For myself, I ask no sympathy. On, on I must go, to meet a soldier's fate, or live to see our country rise superior to all factions, till its flag is adored and respected by ourselves and by all the powers of the earth.

But Willie was, or thought he was, a sergeant in the Thirteenth. I have seen his eye brighten, his heart beat, as he beheld the battalion under arms, and asked me if they were not *real* soldiers. Child as he was, he had the enthusiasm, the pure love of truth, honor, and love of country, which should animate all soldiers.

God only knows why he should die thus young. He is dead, but will not be forgotten till those who knew him in life have followed him to that same mysterious end.

Please convey to the battalion my heart-felt thanks, and assure each and all that if in after-years they call on me or mine, and mention that they were of the Thirteenth Regulars when Willie was a sergeant, they will have a key to the affections of my family that will open all it has; that we will share with them our last blanket, our last crust! Your friend,

W. T. SHERMAN, *Major-General.*

Long afterward, in the spring of 1867, we had his body disinterred and brought to St. Louis, where he is now buried in a beautiful spot, in Calvary Cemetery, by the side of another child, "Charles," who was born at Lancaster, in the summer of 1864, died early, and was buried at Notre Dame, Indiana. His body was transferred at the same time to the same spot. Over Willie's grave is erected a beautiful marble monument, designed and executed by the officers and soldiers of that battalion which claimed him as a sergeant and comrade.

During the summer and fall of 1863 Major-General S. A. Hurlbut was in command at Memphis. He supplied me copies of all dispatches from Washington, and all the information he possessed of the events about Chattanooga. Two of these dispatches cover all essential points:

WASHINGTON CITY, *September* 15, 1863 — 5 P.M.
Major-General S. A. HURLBUT, *Memphis:*

All the troops that can possibly be spared in West Tennessee and on the Mississippi River should be sent without delay to assist General Rosecrans on the Tennessee River.

Urge Sherman to act with all possible promptness.

If you have boats, send them down to bring up his troops.

Information just received indicates that a part of Lee's army has been sent to reënforce Bragg.

H. W. HALLECK, *General-in-Chief.*

WASHINGTON, *September* 19, 1863—4 P.M.
Major-General S. A. HURLBUT, *Memphis, Tennessee:*

Give me definite information of the number of troops sent toward Decatur, and where they are. Also, what other troops are to follow, and when.

Has any thing been heard from the troops ordered from Vicksburg?

No efforts must be spared to support Rosecrans's right, and to guard the crossings of the Tennessee River.

H. W. HALLECK, *General-in-Chief.*

My special orders were to repair the Memphis & Charleston Railroad eastward as I progressed, as far as Athens, Alabama, to draw supplies by that route, so that, on reaching Athens, we should not be dependent on the roads back to Nashville, already overtaxed by the demand of Rosecrans's army.

On reaching Memphis, October 2d, I found that Osterhaus's division had already gone by rail as far as Corinth, and that John E. Smith's division was in the act of starting by cars. The Second Division, then commanded by Brigadier-General Giles A. Smith, reached Memphis at the same time with me; and the Fourth Division, commanded by Brigadier-General John M. Corse, arrived a day or two after. The railroad was in fair condition as far as Corinth, ninety-six miles, but the road was badly stocked with locomotives and cars, so that it took until the 9th to get off the Second Division, when I gave orders for the Fourth Division and wagon-trains to march by the common road.

On Sunday morning, October 11th, with a special train loaded with our orderlies and clerks, the horses of our staff, the battalion of the Thirteenth United States Regulars, and a few officers going forward to join their commands, among them Brigadier-General Hugh Ewing, I started for Corinth.

At Germantown, eight miles, we passed Corse's division (Fourth) on the march, and about noon the train ran by the depot at Colliersville, twenty-six miles out. I was in the rear car with my staff, dozing, but observed the train slacking speed and stopping about half a mile beyond the depot. I noticed some soldiers running to and fro, got out at the end of the car, and soon Colonel Anthony (Sixty-sixth Indiana), who commanded the post, rode up and said that his pickets had just been driven in, and there was an appearance of an attack by a large force of cavalry coming from the southeast. I ordered the men to get off the train, to form on the knoll near the railroad-cut, and soon observed a rebel officer riding toward us with a white flag. Colonel Anthony and Colonel Dayton (one of my aides) were sent to meet him, and to keep him in conversation as long as possible. They soon returned, saying it was the adjutant of the rebel general Chalmers, who demanded the surrender of the place. I instructed them to return and give a negative answer, but to delay him as much as possible, so as to give us time for preparation. I saw Anthony, Dayton, and the rebel bearer of the flag, in conversation, and the latter turn his horse to ride back, when I ordered Colonel McCoy to run to the station, and get a message over the wires as quick as possible to Memphis and Germantown, to hurry forward Corse's division. I then ordered the train to back to the depot, and drew back the battalion of regulars to the small earth redoubt near it. The depot-building was of brick, and had been punctured with loop-holes. To its east, about two hundred yards, was a small square earthwork or fort, into which were put a part of the regulars along with the company of the Sixty-sixth Indiana already there. The rest of the men were distributed into the railroad-cut, and in some shallow rifle-trenches near the depot. We had hardly made these preparations when the enemy was seen forming in a long line on the ridge to the south, about four hundred yards off, and soon after two parties of cavalry passed the railroad on both sides of us, cutting the wires and tearing up some rails. Soon they opened on us with artillery (of which we had none), and their men were dismounting and preparing to assault. To the south of us was an extensive cornfield, with the corn still standing, and on the other side was the town of Colliersville. All the houses near, that could give shelter to the enemy, were ordered to be set on fire, and the men were instructed to keep well under cover and to reserve their fire for the assault, which seemed inevitable. A long line of rebel skirmishers came down through the cornfield, and two other parties approached us along the railroad on both sides.

In the fort was a small magazine containing some cartridges. Lieutenant James, a fine, gallant fellow, who was ordnance-officer on my staff, asked leave to arm the orderlies and clerks with some muskets which he had found in the depot, to which I consented; he marched them into the magazine, issued cartridges, and marched back to the depot to assist in its defense. Afterward he came to me, said a party of the enemy had got into the woods near the depot, and was annoying him, and he wanted to charge and drive it away. I advised him to be extremely cautious, as our enemy vastly outnumbered us, and had every advantage in position and artillery; but instructed him, if they got too near, he might make a sally. Soon after, I heard a rapid fire in that quarter, and Lieutenant James was brought in on a stretcher, with a ball through his breast, which I supposed to be fatal.* The enemy closed down on us several times, and got possession of the rear of our train, from which they succeeded in getting five of our horses, among them my favorite mare Dolly; but our men were cool and practised shots (with great experience acquired at Vicksburg), and drove them back. With their artillery they knocked to pieces our locomotive and several of the cars, and set fire to the train; but we managed to get possession again, and extinguished the fire. Colonel Audenreid, aide-de-camp, was provoked to find that his valise of nice shirts had been used to kindle the fire. The fighting continued all round us for three or four hours, when we observed signs of drawing off, which I attributed to the rightful cause, the rapid approach of Corse's division, which arrived about dark, having marched the whole distance from Memphis, twenty-six miles, on the double-quick. The next day we repaired damages to the railroad and locomotive, and went on to Corinth.

At Corinth, on the 16th, I received the following important dispatches:

*After the fight we sent him back to Memphis, where his mother and father came from their home on the North River to nurse him. Young James was recovering from his wound, but was afterward killed by a fall from his horse, near his home, when riding with the daughters of Mr. Hamilton Fish, now Secretary of State.

MEMPHIS, *October* 14, 1863—11 A.M.
Arrived this morning. Will be off in a few hours. My orders are only to go to Cairo, and report from there by telegraph. McPherson will be in Canton to-day. He will remain there until Sunday or Monday next, and reconnoitre as far eastward as possible with cavalry, in the mean time.

U. S. GRANT, *Major-General.*

WASHINGTON, *October* 14, 1863—1 P.M.
Major-General W. T. SHERMAN, *Corinth:*
Yours of the 10th is received. The important matter to be attended to is that of supplies. When Eastport can be reached by boats, the use of the railroad can be dispensed with; but until that time it must be guarded as far as used. The Kentucky Railroad can barely supply General Rosecrans. All these matters must be left to your judgment as circumstances may arise. Should the enemy be so strong as to prevent your going to Athens, or connecting with General Rosecrans, you will nevertheless have assisted him greatly by drawing away a part of the enemy's forces.

H. W. HALLECK, *Major-General.*

On the 18th, with my staff and a small escort, I rode forward to Burnsville, and on the 19th to Iuka, where, on the next day, I was most agreeably surprised to hear of the arrival at Eastport (only ten miles off) of two gunboats, under the command of Captain Phelps, which had been sent up the Tennessee River by Admiral Porter, to help us.

Satisfied that, to reach Athens and to communicate with General Rosecrans, we should have to take the route north of the Tennessee River, on the 24th I ordered the Fourth Division to cross at Eastport with the aid of the gunboats, and to move to Florence. About the same time, I received the general orders assigning General Grant to command the Military Division of the Mississippi, authorizing him, on reaching Chattanooga, to supersede General Rosecrans by General George H. Thomas, with other and complete authority, as set forth in the following letters of General Halleck, which were sent to me by General Grant; and the same orders devolved on me the command of the Department and Army of the Tennessee.

HEADQUARTERS OF THE ARMY, }
WASHINGTON, D. C., *October* 16, 1863.}

Major-General U. S. GRANT, *Louisville*.

GENERAL: You will receive herewith the orders of the President of the United States, placing you in command of the Departments of the Ohio, Cumberland, and Tennessee. The organization of these departments will be changed as you may deem most practicable. You will immediately proceed to Chattanooga, and relieve General Rosecrans. You can communicate with Generals Burnside and Sherman by telegraph. A summary of the orders sent to these officers will be sent to you immediately. It is left optional with you to supersede General Rosecrans by General G. H. Thomas or not. Any other changes will be made on your request by telegram.

One of the first objects requiring your attention is the supply of your armies. Another is the security of the passes in the Georgia mountains, to shut out the enemy from Tennessee and Kentucky. You will consult with General Meigs and Colonel Scott in regard to transportation and supplies.

Should circumstances permit, I will visit you personally in a few days for consultation.

H. W. HALLECK, *General-in-Chief*.

HEADQUARTERS OF THE ARMY, }
WASHINGTON, D. C., *October* 20, 1863.}

Major-General GRANT, *Louisville*.

GENERAL: In compliance with my promise, I now proceed to give you a brief statement of the objects aimed at by General Rosecrans and General Burnside's movement into East Tennessee, and of the measures directed to be taken to attain these objects.

It has been the constant desire of the government, from the beginning of the war, to rescue the loyal inhabitants of East Tennessee from the hands of the rebels, who fully appreciated the importance of continuing their hold upon that country. In addition to the large amount of agricultural products drawn from the upper valley of the Tennessee, they also obtained iron and other materials from the vicinity of Chattanooga. The possession of East Tennessee would cut off one of their most important railroad communications, and threaten their manufactories at Rome, Atlanta, etc.

When General Buell was ordered into East Tennessee in the summer of 1862, Chattanooga was comparatively unprotected; but Bragg reached there before Buell, and, by threatening his communications, forced him to retreat on Nashville and Louisville. Again, after the battle of Perryville, General Buell was urged to pursue Bragg's defeated army, and drive it from East Tennessee. The same was urged upon his successor, but the lateness of the season or other causes prevented further operations after the battle of Stone River.

Last spring, when your movements on the Mississippi River had drawn out of Tennessee a large force of the enemy, I again urged General Rosecrans to take advantage of that opportunity to carry out his projected plan of campaign, General Burnside being ready to coöperate, with a diminished but still efficient force. But he could not be persuaded to act in time, preferring to lie still till your campaign should be terminated. I represented to him, but without avail, that by this delay Johnston might be able to reënforce Bragg with the troops then operating against you.

When General Rosecrans finally determined to advance, he was allowed to select his own lines and plans for carrying out the objects of the expedition. He was directed, however, to report his movements daily, till he crossed the Tennessee, and to connect his left, so far as possible, with General Burnside's right. General Burnside was directed to move simultaneously, connecting his right, as far as possible, with General Rosecrans's left, so that, if the enemy concentrated upon either army, the other could move to its assistance. When General Burnside reached Kingston and Knoxville, and found no considerable number of the enemy in East Tennessee, he was instructed to move down the river and coöperate with General Rosecrans.

These instructions were repeated some fifteen times, but were not carried out, General Burnside alleging as an excuse that he believed that Bragg was in retreat, and that General Rosecrans needed no reënforcements. When the latter had gained possession of Chattanooga he was directed not to move on Rome as he proposed, but simply to hold the mountain-passes, so as to prevent the ingress of the rebels into East Tennessee. That object accomplished, I considered the campaign as ended, at least for the present. Future operations would depend upon the ascertained strength and movements of the enemy. In other words, the main objects of the campaign were the restoration of East Tennessee to the Union, and by holding the two extremities of the valley to secure it from rebel invasion.

The moment I received reliable information of the departure of Longstreet's corps from the Army of the Potomac, I ordered forward to General Rosecrans every available man in the Department of the Ohio, and again urged General Burnside to move to his assistance. I also telegraphed to Generals Hurlbut, Sherman, and yourself, to send forward all available troops in your department. If these forces had been sent to General Rosecrans by Nashville, they could not have been supplied; I therefore directed them to move by Corinth and the Tennessee River. The necessity of this has been proved by the fact that the reënforcements sent to him from the Army of the Potomac have not been able, for the want of railroad transportation, to reach General Rosecrans's army in the field.

In regard to the relative strength of the opposing armies, it is believed that General Rosecrans when he first moved against Bragg had double, if not treble, his force. General Burnside, also, had more than double the force of Buckner; and, even when Bragg and Buckner united, Rosecrans's army was very greatly superior in number. Even the eighteen thousand men sent from Virginia, under Longstreet, would not have given the enemy the superiority. It is now ascertained that the greater part of the prisoners parolled by you at Vicksburg, and General Banks at Port Hudson, were illegally and improperly declared exchanged, and forced into the ranks to swell the rebel numbers at Chickamauga. This outrageous act, in violation of the laws of war, of the cartel entered into by the rebel authorities, and of all sense of honor, gives us a useful lesson in regard to the character of the enemy with whom we are contending. He neither regards the rules of civilized warfare, nor even his most solemn engagements. You may, therefore, expect to meet in arms thousands of unexchanged prisoners released by you and others on parole, not to serve again till duly exchanged.

Although the enemy by this disgraceful means has been able to concentrate in Georgia and Alabama a much larger force than we anticipated, your armies will be abundantly able to defeat him. Your difficulty will not be in the want of men, but in the means of supplying them at this season of the year. A single-track railroad can supply an army of sixty or seventy thousand men, with the usual number of cavalry and artillery; but beyond that number, or with a large mounted force, the difficulty of supply is very great.

I do not know the present condition of the road from Nashville to Decatur, but, if practicable to repair it, the use of that triangle will be of great assistance to you. I hope, also, that the recent rise of water in the Cumberland and Tennessee Rivers will enable you to employ water transportation to Nashville, Eastport, or Florence.

If you reoccupy the passes of Lookout Mountain, which should never have been given up, you will be able to use the railroad and river from Bridgeport to Chattanooga. This seems to me a matter of vital importance, and should receive your early attention.

I submit this summary in the hope that it will assist you in fully understanding the objects of the campaign, and the means of attaining these objects. Probably the Secretary of War, in his interviews with you at Louisville, has gone over the same ground.

Whatever measures you may deem proper to adopt under existing circumstances, you will receive all possible assistance from the authorities at Washington. You have never, heretofore, complained that such assistance has not been afforded you in your operations, and I think you will have no cause of complaint in your present campaign. Very respectfully, your obedient servant,

H. W. HALLECK, *General-in-Chief.*

General Frank P. Blair, who was then ahead with the two divisions of Osterhaus and John E. Smith, was temporarily assigned to the command of the Fifteenth Corps. General Hurlbut remained at Memphis in command of the Sixteenth Corps, and General McPherson at Vicksburg with the Seventeenth. These three corps made up the Army of the Tennessee.

I was still busy in pushing forward the repairs to the railroad-bridge at Bear Creek, and in patching up the many breaks between it and Tuscumbia, when on the 27th of October, as I sat on the porch of a house, I was approached by a dirty, black-haired individual with mixed dress and strange demeanor, who inquired for me, and, on being assured that I was in fact the man, he handed me a letter from General Blair at Tuscumbia, and another short one, which was a telegraph-message from General Grant at Chattanooga, addressed to me through General George Crook, commanding at Huntsville, Alabama, to this effect:

Drop all work on Memphis & Charleston Railroad, cross the Tennessee, and hurry eastward with all possible dispatch toward Bridgeport, till you meet further orders from me.

U. S. GRANT.

The bearer of this message was Corporal Pike, who described to me, in his peculiar way, that General Crook had sent him in a canoe; that he had pulled down the Tennessee River, over Muscle Shoals, was fired at all the way by guerrillas, but on reaching Tuscumbia he had providentially found it in possession of our troops. He had reported to General Blair, who sent him on to me at Iuka. This Pike proved to be a singular character; his manner attracted my notice at once, and I got him a horse, and had him travel with us eastward to about Elkton, whence I sent him back to General Crook at Huntsville; but told him, if I could ever do him a personal service, he might apply to me. The next spring when I was in Chattanooga, preparing for the Atlanta campaign, Corporal Pike made his appearance and asked a fulfillment of my promise. I inquired what he wanted, and he said he wanted to do something *bold*, something that would make him a hero. I explained to him, that we were getting ready to go for Joe Johnston at Dalton, that I expected to be in the neighborhood of Atlanta about the 4th of July, and wanted the bridge across the Savannah River at Augusta, Georgia, to be burnt about that time, to produce alarm and confusion behind the rebel army. I explained to Pike that the chances were three to one that he would be caught and hanged; but the greater the danger the greater seemed to be his desire to attempt it. I told him to select a companion, to disguise himself as an East Tennessee refugee, work his way over the mountains into North Carolina, and at the time appointed to float down the Savannah River and burn that bridge. In a few days he had made his preparations and took his departure. The bridge was not burnt, and I supposed that Pike had been caught and hanged.

When we reached Columbia, South Carolina, in February, 1865, just as we were leaving the town, in passing near the asylum, I heard my name called, and saw a very dirty fellow followed by a file of men running toward me, and as they got near I recognized Pike. He called to me to identify him as one of *my* men; he was then a prisoner under guard, and I instructed the guard to bring him that night to my camp some fifteen miles up the road, which was done. Pike gave me a graphic narrative of his adventures, which would have filled a volume; told me how he had made two attempts to burn the bridge, and failed; and said that at the time of our entering Columbia he was a prisoner in the hands of the rebels, under trial for his life, but in the confusion of their retreat he made his escape and got into our lines, where he was again made a prisoner by our troops because of his looks. Pike got some clothes, cleaned up, and I used him afterward to communicate with Wilmington, North Carolina. Some time after the war, he was appointed a lieutenant of the Regular Cavalry, and was killed in Oregon, by the accidental discharge of a pistol. Just before his death he wrote me, saying that he was tired of the monotony of garrison-life, and wanted to turn Indian, join the Cheyennes on the Plains, who were then giving us great trouble, and, after he had gained their confidence, he would betray them into our hands. Of course I wrote him that he must try and settle down and become a gentleman as well as an officer, apply himself to his duties, and forget the wild desires of his nature, which were well enough in time of war, but not suited to his new condition as an officer; but, poor fellow! he was killed by an accident, which probably saved him from a slower but harder fate.

At Iuka I issued all the orders to McPherson and Hurlbut necessary for the Department of the Tennessee during my absence, and, further, ordered the collection of a force out of the Sixteenth Corps, of about eight thousand men, to be commanded by General G. M. Dodge, with orders to follow as far east as Athens, Tennessee, there to await instructions. We instantly discontinued all attempts to repair the Charleston Railroad; and the remaining three divisions of the Fifteenth Corps marched to Eastport, crossed the Tennessee River by the aid of the gunboats, a ferry-boat, and and a couple of transports which had come up, and hurried eastward.

In person I crossed on the 1st of November, and rode forward to Florence, where I overtook Ewing's division. The other divisions followed rapidly. On the road to Florence I was accompanied by my staff, some clerks, and mounted orderlies. Major Ezra Taylor was chief of artillery, and one of his sons was a clerk at headquarters. The latter seems to have dropped out of the column, and gone to a farm-house near the road. There was no organized force of the rebel army north of the Tennessee River, but the country was full of guerrillas. A party of these pounced down on the farm, caught young Taylor and another of the clerks, and after reaching Florence, Major Taylor heard of the capture of his son, and learned that when last seen he was stripped of his hat and coat, was tied to the tail-board of a wagon, and driven rapidly to the north of the road we had traveled. The major appealed to me to do something for his rescue. I had no cavalry to send in pursuit, but knowing that there was always an understanding between these guerrillas and their friends who staid at home, I sent for three or four of the principal men of Florence (among them a Mr. Foster, who had once been a Senator in Congress), explained to them the capture of young Taylor and his comrade, and demanded their immediate restoration. They, of course, remonstrated, denied all knowledge of the acts of these guerrillas, and claimed to be peaceful citizens of Alabama, residing at home. I insisted that these guerrillas were their own sons and neighbors; that they knew their haunts, and could reach them if they wanted, and they could effect the restoration to us of these men; and I said, moreover, they must do it within twenty-four hours, or I would take them, strip them of their hats and coats, and tie them to the tail-boards of our wagons till they were produced. They sent off messengers at once, and young Taylor and his comrade were brought back the next day.

Resuming our march eastward by the large road, we soon reached Elk River, which was wide and deep, and could only be crossed by a ferry, a process entirely too slow for the occasion; so I changed the route more by the north, to Elkton, Winchester, and Deckerd. At this point we came in communication with the Army of the Cumberland, and by telegraph with General Grant, who was at Chattanooga. He reiterated his orders for me and my command to hurry forward with all possible dispatch, and in person I reached Bridgeport during the night of November 13th, my troops following behind by several roads. At Bridgeport I found a garrison guarding the railroad-bridge and pontoon-bridge there, and staid with the quartermaster, Colonel William G. Le Duc (who was my school-mate at How's School in 1836). There I received a dispatch from General Grant, at Chattanooga, to come up in person, leaving my troops to follow as fast as possible. At that time there were two or three small steamboats on the river, engaged in carrying stores up as far as Kelly's Ferry. In one of these I took passage, and on reaching Kelly's Ferry found orderlies, with one of General Grant's private horses, waiting for me, on which I rode into Chattanooga, November 14th. Of course, I was heartily welcomed by Generals Grant,

Thomas, and all, who realized the extraordinary efforts we had made to come to their relief.

The next morning we walked out to Fort Wood, a prominent salient of the defenses of the place, and from its parapet we had a magnificent view of the panorama. Lookout Mountain, with its rebel flags and batteries, stood out boldly, and an occasional shot fired toward Wauhatchee or Moccasin Point gave life to the scene. These shots could barely reach Chattanooga, and I was told that one or more shot had struck a hospital inside the lines. All along Missionary Ridge were the tents of the rebel beleaguering force; the lines of trench from Lookout up toward the Chickamauga were plainly visible; and rebel sentinels, in a continuous chain, were walking their posts in plain view, not a thousand yards off. "Why," said I, "General Grant, you are besieged;" and he said, "It is too true." Up to that moment I had no idea that things were so bad. The rebel lines actually extended from the river, below the town, to the river above, and the Army of the Cumberland was closely held to the town and its immediate defenses. General Grant pointed out to me a house on Missionary Ridge, where General Bragg's headquarters were known to be. He also explained the situation of affairs generally; that the mules and horses of Thomas's army were so starved that they could not haul his guns; that forage, corn, and provisions, were so scarce that the men in hunger stole the few grains of corn that were given to favorite horses; that the men of Thomas's army had been so demoralized by the battle of Chickamauga that he feared they could not be got out of their trenches to assume the offensive; that Bragg had detached Longstreet with a considerable force up into East Tennessee, to defeat and capture Burnside; that Burnside was in danger, etc.; and that he (Grant) was extremely anxious to attack Bragg in position, to defeat him, or at least to force him to recall Longstreet. The Army of the Cumberland had so long been in the trenches that he wanted my troops to hurry up, to take the offensive *first*; after which, he had no doubt the Cumberland army would fight well. Meantime the Eleventh and Twelfth Corps, under General Hooker, had been advanced from Bridgeport along the railroad to Wauhatchee, but could not as yet pass Lookout Mountain. A pontoon-bridge had been thrown across the Tennessee River at Brown's Ferry, by which supplies were hauled into Chattanooga from Kelly's and Wauhatchee.

Another bridge was in course of construction at Chattanooga, under the immediate direction of Quartermaster-General Meigs, but at the time all wagons, etc., had to be ferried across by a flying-bridge. Men were busy and hard at work everywhere inside our lines, and boats for another pontoon-bridge were being rapidly constructed under Brigadier-General W. F. Smith, familiarly known as "Baldy Smith," and this bridge was destined to be used by my troops, at a point of the river about four miles above Chattanooga, just below the mouth of the Chickamauga River. General Grant explained to me that he had reconnoitred the rebel line from Lookout Mountain up to Chickamauga, and he believed that the northern portion of Missionary Ridge was not fortified at all; and he wanted me, as soon as my troops got up, to lay the new pontoon-bridge by night, cross over, and attack Bragg's right flank on that part of the ridge abutting on Chickamauga Creek, near the tunnel; and he proposed that we should go at once to look at the ground. In company with Generals Thomas, W. F. Smith, Brannan, and others, we crossed by the flying-bridge, rode back of the hills some four miles, left our horses, and got on a hill overlooking the whole ground about the mouth of the Chickamauga River, and across to the Missionary Hills near the tunnel. Smith and I crept down behind a fringe of trees that lined the river-bank, to the very point selected for the new bridge, where we sat for some time, seeing the rebel pickets on the opposite bank, and almost hearing their words.

Having seen enough, we returned to Chattanooga; and in order to hurry up my command, on which so much depended, I started back to Kelly's in hopes to catch the steamboat that same evening; but on my arrival the boat had gone. I applied to the commanding officer, got a rough boat manned by four soldiers, and started down the river by night. I occasionally took a turn at the oars to relieve some tired man, and about midnight we reached Shell Mound, where General Whittaker, of Kentucky, furnished us a new and good crew, with which we reached Bridgeport by daylight. I started Ewing's division in advance, with orders to turn aside toward Trenton, to make the enemy believe we were going to turn Bragg's left by pretty much the same road Rosecrans had followed; but with the other three divisions I followed the main road, *via* the Big Trestle at Whitesides, and reached General Hooker's headquarters, just above Wauhatchee, on the 20th; my troops strung all the way back to Bridgeport. It was on this occasion that the Fifteenth Corps gained its peculiar badge: as the men were trudging along the deeply-cut, muddy road, of a cold, drizzly day, one of our Western soldiers left his ranks and joined a party of the Twelfth Corps at their camp-fire. They got into conversation, the Twelfth-Corps men asking what troops we were, etc., etc. In turn, our fellow (who had never seen a corps-badge, and noticed that every thing was marked with a star) asked if they were all brigadier-generals. Of course they were not, but the star was their corps-badge, and every wagon, tent, hat, etc., had its star. Then the Twelfth-Corps men inquired what corps he belonged to, and he answered, "The Fifteenth Corps." "What is your badge?" "Why," said he (and he was an Irishman), suiting the action to the word, "forty rounds in the cartridge-box, and twenty in the pocket!" At that time Blair commanded the corps; but Logan succeeded soon after, and, hearing the story, adopted the cartridge-box and forty rounds as the corps-badge.

The condition of the roads was such, and the bridge at Brown's so frail, that it was not until the 23d that we got three of my divisions behind the hills near the point indicated above Chattanooga for crossing the river. It was determined to begin the battle with these three divisions, aided by a division of Thomas's army, commanded by General Jeff. C. Davis, that was already near that point. All the details of the battle of Chattanooga, so far as I was a witness, are so fully given in my official report herewith, that I need add nothing to it. It was a magnificent battle in its conception, in its execution, and in its glorious results; hastened somewhat by the supposed danger of Burnside, at Knoxville, yet so completely successful, that nothing is left for cavil or fault-finding. The first day was lowering and overcast, favoring us greatly, because we wanted to be concealed from Bragg, whose position on the mountain-tops completely overlooked us and our movements. The second day was beautifully clear, and many a time, in the midst of its carnage and noise, I could not help stopping to look across that vast field of battle, to admire its sublimity.

The object of General Hooker's and my attacks on the extreme flanks of Bragg's position was, to disturb him to such an extent, that he would naturally detach from his centre as against us, so that Thomas's army could break through his centre. The whole plan succeeded admirably; but it was not until after dark that I learned the complete success at the centre, and received General Grant's orders to pursue on the north side of Chickamauga Creek.

HEADQUARTERS MILITARY DIVISION OF THE MISSISSIPPI, }
CHATTANOOGA, TENNESSEE, *November* 25, 1863. }

Major-General SHERMAN.

GENERAL: No doubt you witnessed the handsome manner in which Thomas's troops carried Missionary Ridge this afternoon, and can feel a just pride, too, in the part taken by the forces under your command in taking first so much of the same range of hills, and then in attracting the attention of so many of the enemy as to make Thomas's part certain of success. The next thing now will be to relieve Burnside. I have heard from him to the evening of the 23d. At that time he had from ten to twelve days' supplies, and spoke hopefully of being able to hold out that length of time.

My plan is to move your forces out gradually until they reach the railroad between Cleveland and Dalton. Granger will move up the south side of the Tennessee with a column of twenty thousand men, taking no wagons, or but few, with him. His men will carry four days' rations, and the steamer Chattanooga, loaded with rations, will accompany the expedition.

I take it for granted that Bragg's entire force has left. If not, of course, the first thing is to dispose of him. If he has gone, the only thing necessary to do to-morrow will be to send out a reconnoissance to ascertain the whereabouts of the enemy. Yours truly,

U. S. GRANT, *Major-General.*

P. S.—On reflection, I think we will push Bragg with all our strength to-morrow, and try if we cannot cut off a good portion of his rear troops and trains. His men have manifested a strong disposition to desert for some time past, and we will now give them a chance. I will instruct Thomas accordingly. Move the advance force early, on the most easterly road taken by the enemy.

U. S. G.

This compelled me to reverse our column, so as to use the bridge across the Chickamauga at its mouth. The next day we struck the rebel rear at Chickamauga Station, and again near Graysville. There we came in contact with Hooker's and Palmer's troops, who had reached Ringgold. There I detached Howard to cross Taylor's Ridge, and strike the railroad which comes from the north by Cleveland to Dalton. Hooker's troops were roughly handled at Ringgold, and the pursuit was checked. Receiving a note from General Hooker, asking help, I rode forward to Ringgold to explain the movement of Howard; where I met General Grant, and learned that the rebels had again retreated toward Dalton. He gave orders to discontinue the pursuit, as he meant to turn his attention to General Burnside, supposed to be in great danger at Knoxville, about one hundred and thirty miles northeast. General Grant returned and spent part of the night with me, at Graysville. We talked over matters generally, and he explained that he had ordered General Gordon Granger, with the Fourth Corps, to move forward rapidly to Burnside's help, and that he must return to Chattanooga to push him. By reason of the scarcity of food, especially of forage, he consented that, instead of going back, I might keep out in the country; for in motion I could pick up some forage and food, especially on the Hiawassee River, whereas none remained in Chattanooga.

Accordingly, on the 29th of November, my several columns marched to Cleveland, and the next day we reached the Hiawassee at Charleston, where the Chattanooga & Knoxville Railroad crosses it. The railroad-bridge was partially damaged by the enemy in retreating, but we found some abandoned stores. There and thereabouts I expected some rest for my weary troops and horses; but, as I rode into town, I met Colonel J. H. Wilson and C. A. Dana (Assistant Secretary of War), who had ridden out from Chattanooga to find me, with the following letter from General Grant, and copies of several dispatches from General Burnside, the last which had been received from him by way of Cumberland Gap:

HEADQUARTERS MILITARY DIVISION OF THE MISSISSIPPI,
CHATTANOOGA, TENNESSEE, *November* 29, 1863.

Major-General W. T. SHERMAN:

News are received from Knoxville to the morning of the 27th. At that time the place was still invested, but the attack on it was not vigorous. Longstreet evidently determined to starve the garrison out. Granger is on the way to Burnside's relief, but I have lost all faith in his energy or capacity to manage an expedition of the importance of this one. I am inclined to think, therefore, I shall have to send you. Push as rapidly as you can to the Hiawassee, and determine for yourself what force to take with you from that point. Granger has his corps with him, from which you will select in conjunction with the force now with you. In plain words, you will assume command of all the forces now moving up the Tennessee, including the garrison at Kingston, and from that force organize what you deem proper to relieve Burnside. The balance send back to Chattanooga. Granger has a boat loaded with provisions, which you can issue, and return the boat. I will have another loaded, to follow you. Use, of course, as sparingly as possible from the rations taken with you, and subsist off the country all you can.

It is expected that Foster is moving, by this time, from Cumberland Gap on Knoxville. I do not know what force he will have with him, but presume it will range from three thousand five hundred to five thousand. I leave this matter to you, knowing that you will do better acting upon your discretion than you could trammeled with instructions. I will only add, that the last advices from Burnside himself indicated his ability to hold out with rations only to about the 3d of December.

Very respectfully,
U. S. GRANT, *Major-General commanding.*

This showed that, on the 27th of November, General Burnside was in Knoxville, closely besieged by the rebel General Longstreet; that his provisions were short, and that, unless relieved by December 3d, he might have to surrender. General Grant further wrote that General Granger, instead of moving with great rapidity as ordered, seemed to move "slowly, and with reluctance;" and, although he (General Grant) hated to call on me and on my tired troops, there was no alternative.

He wanted me to take command of every thing within reach, and to hurry forward to Knoxville.

All the details of our march to Knoxville are also given in my official report. By extraordinary efforts Long's small brigade of cavalry reached Knoxville during the night of the 3d, purposely to let Burnside know that I was rapidly approaching with an adequate force to raise the siege.

With the head of my infantry column I reached Marysville, about fifteen miles short of Knoxville, on the 5th of December, when I received official notice from Burnside that Longstreet had raised the siege, and had started in retreat up the valley toward Virginia. Halting all the army, except Granger's two divisions, on the morning of the 6th, with General Granger and some of my staff I rode into Knoxville. Approaching from the south and west, we crossed the Holston on a pontoon-bridge, and in a large pen on the Knoxville side I saw a fine lot of cattle, which did not look much like starvation. I found General Burnside and staff domiciled in a large, fine mansion, looking very comfortable, and in a few words he described to me the leading events of the previous few days, and said he had already given orders looking to the pursuit of Longstreet. I offered to join in the pursuit, though in fact my men were worn out, and suffering in that cold season and climate. Indeed, on our way up I personally was almost frozen, and had to beg leave to sleep in the house of a family at Athens.

Burnside explained to me that, reënforced by Granger's two divisions of ten thousand men, he would be able to push Longstreet out of East Tennessee, and he hoped to capture much of his artillery and trains. Granger was present at our conversation, and most unreasonably, I thought, remonstrated against being left; complaining bitterly of what he thought was hard treatment to his men and himself. I know that his language and manner at that time produced on my mind a bad impression, and it was one of the causes which led me to relieve him as a corps commander in the campaign of the next spring. I asked General Burnside to reduce his wishes to writing, which he did in the letter of December 7th, embodied in my official report. General Burnside and I then walked along his lines and examined the salient, known as

Fort Sanders, where, some days before, Longstreet had made his assault, and had sustained a bloody repulse.

Returning to Burnside's quarters, we all sat down to a good dinner, embracing roast-turkey. There was a regular dining-table, with clean table-cloth, dishes, knives, forks, spoons, etc., etc. I had seen nothing of this kind in my field experience, and could not help exclaiming that I thought "they were starving," etc.; but Burnside explained that Longstreet had at no time completely invested the place, and that he had kept open communication with the country on the south side of the river Holston, more especially with the French Broad settlements, from whose Union inhabitants he had received a good supply of beef, bacon, and corn-meal. Had I known of this, I should not have hurried my men so fast; but until I reached Knoxville I thought his troops there were actually in danger of starvation. Having supplied General Burnside all the help he wanted, we began our leisurely return to Chattanooga, which we reached on the 16th; when General Grant in person ordered me to restore to General Thomas the divisions of Howard and Davis, which belonged to his army, and to conduct my own corps (the Fifteenth) to North Alabama for winter-quarters.

HEADQUARTERS DEPARTMENT AND ARMY OF THE TENNESSEE, }
BRIDGEPORT, ALABAMA, *December* 19, 1863. }

Brigadier-General JOHN A. RAWLINS, *Chief of Staff to General*
GRANT, *Chattanooga.*

GENERAL: For the first time, I am now at leisure to make an official record of events with which the troops under my command have been connected during the eventful campaign which has just closed.

During the month of September last, the Fifteenth Army Corps, which I had the honor to command, lay in camps along the Big Black, about twenty miles east of Vicksburg, Mississippi. It consisted of four divisions. The First, commanded by Brigadier-General P. J. Osterhaus, was composed of two brigades, led by Brigadier-General C. R. Woods and Colonel J. A. Williamson (of the Fourth Iowa).

The Second, commanded by Brigadier-General Morgan L. Smith, was composed of two brigades, led by Brigadier-Generals Giles A. Smith and J. A. J. Lightburn.

The Third, commanded by Brigadier-General J. M. Tuttle, was composed of three brigades, led by Brigadier-Generals J. A. Mower and R. P. Buckland, and Colonel J. J. Wood (of the Twelfth Iowa).

The Fourth, commanded by Brigadier-General Hugh Ewing, was composed of three brigades, led by Brigadier-General J. M. Corse, Colonel Loomis (Twenty-sixth Illinois), and Colonel J. R. Cockerill (of the Seventieth Ohio).

On the 22d day of September I received a telegraphic dispatch from General Grant, then at Vicksburg, commanding the Department of the Tennessee, requiring me to detach one of my divisions to march to Vicksburg, there to embark for Memphis, where it was to form a part of an army to be sent to Chattanooga, to reënforce General Rosecrans. I designated the First Division, and at 4 P.M. the same day it marched for Vicksburg, and embarked the next day.

On the 23d of September I was summoned to Vicksburg by the general commanding, who showed me several dispatches from the general-in-chief, which led him to suppose he would have to send me and my whole corps to Memphis and eastward, and I was instructed to prepare for such orders. It was explained to me that, in consequence of the low stage of water in the Mississippi, boats had arrived irregularly, and had brought dispatches that seemed to conflict in their meaning, and that General John E. Smith's division (of General McPherson's corps) had been ordered up to Memphis, and that I should take that division and leave one of my own in its stead, to hold the line of the Big Black. I detailed my third division (General Tuttle) to remain and report to Major-General McPherson, commanding the Seventeenth Corps, at Vicksburg; and that of General John E. Smith, already started for Memphis, was styled the Third Division, Fifteenth Corps, though it still belongs to the Seventeenth Army Corps. This division is also composed of three brigades, commanded by General Matthias, Colonel J. B. Raum (of the Fifty-sixth Illinois), and Colonel J. I. Alexander (of the Fifty-ninth Indiana).

The Second and Fourth Divisions were started for Vicksburg the moment I was notified that boats were in readiness, and on the 27th of September I embarked in person in the steamer Atlantic, for Memphis, followed by a fleet of boats conveying these two divisions. Our progress was slow, on account of the unprecedentedly low water in the Mississippi, and the scarcity of coal and wood. We were compelled at places to gather fence-rails, and to land wagons and haul wood from the interior to the boats; but I reached Memphis during the night of the 2d of October, and the other boats came in on the 3d and 4th.

On arrival at Memphis I saw General Hurlbut, and read all the dispatches and letters of instruction of General Halleck, and therein derived my instructions, which I construed to be as follows:

To conduct the Fifteenth Army Corps, and all other troops which could be spared from the line of the Memphis & Charleston Railroad, to Athens, Alabama, and thence report by letter for orders to General Rosecrans, commanding the Army of the Cumberland, at Chattanooga; to follow substantially the railroad eastward, repairing it as I moved; to look to my own line for supplies; and in no event to depend on General Rosecrans for supplies, as the roads to his rear were already overtaxed to supply his present army.

I learned from General Hurlbut that General Osterhaus's division was already out in front of Corinth, and that General John E. Smith was still at Memphis, moving his troops and material by railroad as fast as its limited stock would carry them. General J. D. Webster was superintendent of the railroad, and was enjoined to work night and day, and to expedite the movement as rapidly as possible; but the capacity of the road was so small, that I soon saw that I could move horses, mules, and wagons faster by land, and therefore I dispatched the artillery and wagons by the road under escort, and finally moved the entire Fourth Division by land.

The enemy seems to have had early notice of this movement, and he endeavored to thwart us from the start. A considerable force assembled in a threatening attitude at Salem, south of Salisbury Station; and General Carr, who commanded at Corinth, felt compelled to turn back and use a part of my troops, that had already reached Corinth, to resist the threatened attack.

On Sunday, October 11th, having put in motion my whole force, I started myself for Corinth, in a special train, with the battalion of the Thirteenth United States Regulars as escort. We reached Collierville Station about noon, just in time to take part in the defense made of that station by Colonel D. C. Anthony, of the Sixty-sixth Indiana, against an attack made by General Chalmers with a force of about three thousand cavalry, with eight pieces of artillery. He was beaten off, the damage to the road repaired, and we resumed our journey the next day, reaching Corinth at night.

I immediately ordered General Blair forward to Iuka, with the First Division, and, as fast as I got troops up, pushed them forward of Bear Creek, the bridge of which was completely destroyed, and an engineer regiment, under command of Colonel Flad, was engaged in its repairs.

Quite a considerable force of the enemy was assembled in our front, near Tuscumbia, to resist our advance. It was commanded by General Stephen D. Lee, and composed of Roddy's and Ferguson's brigades, with irregular cavalry, amounting in the aggregate to about five thousand.

In person I moved from Corinth to Burnsville on the 18th, and to Iuka on the 19th of October.

Osterhaus's division was in the advance, constantly skirmishing with the enemy; he was supported by General Morgan L. Smith's, both divisions under the general command of Major-General Blair. General John E. Smith's division covered the working-party engaged in rebuilding the railroad.

Foreseeing difficulty in crossing the Tennessee River, I had written to Admiral Porter, at Cairo, asking him to watch the Tennessee and send up some gunboats the moment the stage of water admitted; and had also requested General Allen, quartermaster at St. Louis, to dispatch to Eastport a steam ferry-boat.

The admiral, ever prompt and ready to assist us, had two fine gunboats at Eastport, under Captain Phelps, the very day after my arrival at Iuka; and Captain Phelps had a coal-barge decked over, with which to cross our horses and wagons before the arrival of the ferry-boat.

Still following literally the instructions of General Halleck, I pushed forward the repairs of the railroad, and ordered General Blair, with the two leading divisions, to drive the enemy beyond Tuscumbia. This he did successfully, after a pretty severe fight at Cane Creek, occupying Tuscumbia on the 27th of October.

In the mean time many important changes in command had occurred, which I must note here, to a proper understanding of the case.

General Grant had been called from Vicksburg, and sent to Chattanooga to command the military division of the Mississippi, composed of the three Departments of the Ohio, Cumberland, and Tennessee; and the Department of the Tennessee had been devolved on me, with instructions, however, to retain command of the army in the field. At Iuka I made what appeared to me the best disposition of matters relating to the department, giving General McPherson full powers in Mississippi and General Hurlbut in West Tennessee, and assigned General Blair to the command of the Fifteenth Army Corps; and summoned General Hurlbut from Memphis, and General Dodge from Corinth, and selected out of the Sixteenth Corps a force of about eight thousand men, which I directed General Dodge to organize with all expedition, and with it to follow me eastward.

On the 27th of October, when General Blair, with two divisions, was at Tuscumbia, I ordered General Ewing, with the Fourth Division, to cross the Tennessee (by means of the gunboats and scow) as rapidly as possible at Eastport, and push forward to Florence, which he did; and the same day a messenger from General Grant floated down the Tennessee over Muscle Shoals, landed at Tuscumbia, and was sent to me at Iuka. He bore a short message from the general to this effect: "Drop all work on the railroad east of Bear Creek; push your command toward Bridgeport till you meet orders;" etc. Instantly the order was executed; the order of march was reversed, and all the columns were directed to Eastport, the only place where we could cross the Tennessee. At first we only had the gunboats and coal-barge; but the ferry-boat and two transports arrived on the 31st of October, and the work of crossing was pushed with all the vigor possible. In person I crossed, and passed to the head of the column at Florence on the 1st of November, leaving the rear divisions to be conducted by General Blair, and marched to Rogersville and Elk River. This was found impassable. To ferry would have consumed too much time, and to build a bridge still more; so there was no alternative but to turn up Elk River by way of Gilbertsboro, Elkton, etc., to the stone bridge at Fayetteville, where we crossed the Elk, and proceeded to Winchester and Deckerd.

At Fayetteville I received orders from General Grant to come to Bridgeport with the Fifteenth Army Corps, and to leave General Dodge's command at Pulaski, and along the railroad from Columbia to Decatur. I instructed General Blair to follow with the Second and First Divisions by way of New Market, Larkinsville, and Bellefonte, while I conducted the other two divisions by way of Deckerd; the Fourth Division crossing the mountain to Stevenson, and the Third by University Place and Swedon's Cove.

In person I proceeded by Swedon's Cove and Battle Creek, reaching Bridgeport on the night of November 13th. I immediately telegraphed to the commanding general my arrival, and the positions of my several divisions, and was summoned to Chattanooga. I took the first steamboat during the night of the 14th for Kelly's Ferry, and rode into Chattanooga on the 15th. I then learned the part assigned me in the coming drama, was supplied with the necessary maps and information, and rode, during the 16th, in company with Generals Grant, Thomas, W. F. Smith, Brannan, and others, to the positions occupied on the west bank of the Tennessee, from which could be seen the camps of the enemy, compassing Chattanooga and the line of Missionary Hills, with its terminus on Chickamauga Creek, the point that I was expected to take, hold, and fortify. Pontoons, with a full supply of balks and chesses, had been prepared for the bridge over the Tennessee, and all things had been prearranged with a foresight that elicited my admiration. From the hills we looked down on the amphitheatre of Chattanooga as on a map, and nothing remained but for me to put my troops in the desired position. The plan contemplated that, in addition to crossing the Tennessee River and making a lodgment on the terminus of Missionary Ridge, I should demonstrate against Lookout Mountain, near Trenton, with a part of my command.

All in Chattanooga were impatient for action, rendered almost acute by the natural apprehensions felt for the safety of General Burnside in East Tennessee.

My command had marched from Memphis, three hundred and thirty miles, and I had pushed them as fast as the roads and distance would admit, but I saw enough of the condition of men and animals in Chattanooga to inspire me with renewed energy. I immediately ordered my leading division (General Ewing's) to march *via* Shellmound to Trenton, demonstrating against Lookout Ridge, but to be prepared to turn quickly and follow me to Chattanooga and in person I returned to Bridgeport, rowing a boat down the Tennessee from Kelly's Ferry, and immediately on arrival put in motion my divisions in the order in which they had arrived. The bridge of boats at Bridgeport was frail, and, though used day and night, our passage was slow; and the road thence to Chattanooga was dreadfully cut up and encumbered with the wagons of the other troops stationed along the road. I reached General Hooker's headquarters during a rain, in the afternoon of the 20th, and met General Grant's orders for the general attack on the next day. It was simply impossible for me to fulfill my part in time; only one division (General John E. Smith's) was in position. General Ewing was still at Trenton, and the other two were toiling along the terrible road from Shellmound to Chattanooga. No troops ever were or could be in better condition than mine, or who labored harder to fulfill their part. On a proper representation, General Grant postponed the attack. On the 21st I got the Second Division over Brown's-Ferry Bridge, and General Ewing got up; but the bridge broke repeatedly, and delays occurred which no human sagacity could prevent. All labored night and day, and General Ewing got over on the 23d; but my rear division was cut off by the broken bridge at Brown's Ferry, and could not join me. I offered to go into action with my three divisions, supported by General Jeff. C. Davis, leaving one of my best divisions (Osterhaus's) to act with General Hooker against Lookout Mountain. That division has not joined me yet, but I know and feel that it has served the country well, and that it has reflected honor on the Fifteenth Army Corps and the Army of the Tennessee. I leave the record of its history to General Hooker, or whomsoever has had its services during the late memorable events, confident that all will do it merited honor.

At last, on the 23d of November, my three divisions lay behind the hills opposite the mouth of the Chickamauga. I dispatched the brigade of the Second Division, commanded by General Giles A. Smith, under cover of the hills, to North Chickamauga Creek, to man the boats designed for the pontoon-bridge, with orders (at midnight) to drop down silently to a point above the mouth of the South Chickamauga, there land two regiments, who were to move along the river-bank quietly, and capture the enemy's river-pickets.

General Giles A. Smith then was to drop rapidly below the mouth of the Chickamauga, disembark the rest of his brigade, and dispatch the boats across for fresh loads. These orders were skillfully executed, and every rebel picket but one was captured. The balance of General Morgan L. Smith's division was then rapidly ferried across; that of General John E. Smith followed, and by daylight of November 24th two divisions of about eight thousand men were on the east bank of the Tennessee, and had thrown up a very respectable rifle-trench as a *tête du pont*. As soon as the day dawned, some of the boats were taken from the use of ferrying, and a pontoon-bridge was begun, under the immediate direction of Captain Dresser, the whole planned and supervised by General William F. Smith in person. A pontoon-bridge was also built at the same time over Chickamauga Creek, near its mouth, giving communication with the two regiments which had been left on the north side, and fulfilling a most important purpose at a later stage of the drama. I will here bear my willing testimony to the completeness of this whole business. All the officers charged with the work were present, and manifested a skill which I cannot praise too highly. I have never beheld any work done so quietly, so well; and I doubt if the history of war can show a bridge of that extent (viz., thirteen hundred and fifty feet) laid so noiselessly and well, in so short a time. I attribute it to the genius and intelligence of General William F. Smith. The steamer Dunbar arrived up in the course of the morning, and relieved Ewing's division of the labor of rowing across; but by noon the pontoon-bridge was done, and my three divisions were across, with men, horses, artillery, and every thing.

General Jeff. C. Davis's division was ready to take the bridge, and I ordered the columns to form in order to carry the Missionary Hills. The movement had been carefully explained to all division commanders, and at 1 P.M. we marched from the river in three columns in echelon: the left, General Morgan L. Smith, the column of direction, following substantially Chickamauga Creek; the centre, General

John E. Smith, in columns, doubled on the centre, at one brigade interval to the right and rear; the right, General Ewing, in column at the same distance to the right rear, prepared to deploy to the right, on the supposition that we would meet an enemy in that direction. Each head of column was covered by a good line of skirmishers, with supports. A light drizzling rain prevailed, and the clouds hung low, cloaking our movement from the enemy's tower of observation on Lookout Mountain. We soon gained the foot-hills; our skirmishers crept up the face of the hills, followed by their supports, and at 3.30 P.M. we had gained, with no loss, the desired point. A brigade of each division was pushed rapidly to the top of the hill, and the enemy for the first time seemed to realize the movement, but too late, for we were in possession. He opened with artillery, but General Ewing soon got some of Captain Richardson's guns up that steep hill and gave back artillery, and the enemy's skirmishers made one or two ineffectual dashes at General Lightburn, who had swept round and got a farther hill, which was the real continuation of the ridge. From studying all the maps, I had inferred that Missionary Ridge was a continuous hill; but we found ourselves on two high points, with a deep depression between us and the one immediately over the tunnel, which was my chief objective point. The ground we had gained, however, was so important, that I could leave nothing to chance, and ordered it to be fortified during the night. One brigade of each division was left on the hill, one of General Morgan L. Smith's closed the gap to Chickamauga Creek, two of General John E. Smith's were drawn back to the base in reserve, and General Ewing's right was extended down into the plain, thus crossing the ridge in a general line, facing southeast.

The enemy felt our left flank about 4 P.M., and a pretty smart engagement with artillery and muskets ensued, when he drew off; but it cost us dear, for General Giles A. Smith was severely wounded, and had to go to the rear; and the command of the brigade devolved on Colonel Tupper (One Hundred and Sixteenth Illinois), who managed it with skill during the rest of the operations. At the moment of my crossing the bridge, General Howard appeared, having come with three regiments from Chattanooga, along the east bank of the Tennessee, connecting my new position with that of the main army in Chattanooga. He left the three regiments attached temporarily to General Ewing's right, and returned to his own corps at Chattanooga. As night closed in, I ordered General Jeff. C. Davis to keep one of his brigades at the bridge, one close up to my position, and one intermediate. Thus we passed the night, heavy details being kept busy at work on the intrenchments on the hill. During the night the sky cleared away bright, a cold frost filled the air, and our camp-fires revealed to the enemy and to our friends in Chattanooga our position on Missionary Ridge. About midnight I received, at the hands of Major Rowley (of General Grant's staff), orders to attack the enemy at "dawn of day," with notice that General Thomas would attack in force *early* in the day. Accordingly, before day I was in the saddle, attended by all my staff; rode to the extreme left of our position near Chickamauga Creek; thence up the hill, held by General Lightburn; and round to the extreme right of General Ewing. Catching as accurate an idea of the ground as possible by the dim light of morning, I saw that our line of attack was in the direction of Missionary Ridge, with wings supporting on either flank. Quite a valley lay between us and the next hill of the series, and this hill presented steep sides, the one to the west partially cleared, but the other covered with the native forest. The crest of the ridge was narrow and wooded. The farther point of this hill was held by the enemy with a breastwork of logs and fresh earth, filled with men and two guns. The enemy was also seen in great force on a still higher hill beyond the tunnel, from which he had a fine plunging fire on the hill in dispute. The gorge between, through which several roads and the railroad-tunnel pass, could not be seen from our position, but formed the natural *place d'armes*, where the enemy covered his masses to resist our contemplated movement of turning his right flank and endangering his communications with his depot at Chickamauga Station.

As soon as possible, the following dispositions were made: The brigades of Colonels Cockrell and Alexander, and General Lightburn, were to hold our hill as the key-point. General Corse, with as much of his brigade as could operate along the narrow ridge, was to attack from our right centre. General Lightburn was to dispatch a good regiment from his position to coöperate with General Corse; and General Morgan L. Smith was to move along the east base of Missionary Ridge, connecting with General Corse; and Colonel Loomis, in like manner, to move along the west base, supported by the two reserve brigades of General John E. Smith.

The sun had hardly risen before General Corse had completed his preparations and his bugle sounded the "forward!" The Fortieth Illinois, supported by the Forty-sixth Ohio, on our right centre, with the Thirtieth Ohio (Colonel Jones), moved down the face of our hill, and up that held by the enemy. The line advanced to within about eighty yards of the intrenched position, where General Corse found a secondary crest, which he gained and held. To this point he called his reserves, and asked for reënforcements, which were sent; but the space was narrow, and it was not well to crowd the men, as the enemy's artillery and musketry fire swept the approach to his position, giving him great advantage. As soon as General Corse had made his preparations, he assaulted, and a close, severe contest ensued, which lasted more than an hour, gaining and losing ground, but never the position first obtained, from which the enemy in vain attempted to drive him. General Morgan L. Smith kept gaining ground on the left spurs of Missionary Ridge, and Colonel Loomis got abreast of the tunnel and railroad embankment on his side, drawing the enemy's fire, and to that extent relieving the assaulting party on the hill-crest. Captain Callender had four of his guns on General Ewing's hill, and Captain Woods his Napoleon battery on General Lightburn's; also, two guns of Dillon's battery were with Colonel Alexander's brigade. All directed their fire as carefully as possible, to clear the hill to our front, without endangering our own men. The fight raged furiously about 10 A.M., when General Corse received a severe wound, was brought off the field, and the command of the brigade and of the assault at that key-point devolved on that fine young, gallant officer, Colonel Walcutt, of the Forty-sixth Ohio, who fulfilled his part manfully. He continued the contest, pressing forward at all points. Colonel Loomis had made good progress to the right, and about 2 P.M. General John E. Smith, judging the battle to be most severe on the hill, and being required to support General Ewing, ordered up Colonel Raum's and General Matthias's brigades across the field to the summit that was being fought for. They moved up under a heavy fire of cannon and musketry, and joined Colonel Walcutt; but the crest was so narrow that they necessarily occupied the west face of the hill. The enemy, at the time being massed in great strength in the tunnel-gorge, moved a large force under cover of the ground and the thick bushes, and suddenly appeared on the right rear of this command. The suddenness of the attack disconcerted the men, exposed as they were in the open field; they fell back in some disorder to the lower edge of the field, and reformed. These two brigades were in the nature of supports, and did not constitute a part of the real attack. The movement, seen from Chattanooga (five miles off) with spy-glasses, gave rise to the report, which even General Meigs has repeated, that we were repulsed on the left. It was *not so*. The real attacking columns of General Corse, Colonel Loomis, and General Smith, were not repulsed. They engaged in a close struggle all day persistently, stubbornly, and well. When the two reserve brigades of General John E. Smith fell back as described, the enemy made a show of pursuit, but were in their turn caught in flank by the well-directed fire of our brigade on the wooded crest, and hastily sought cover behind the hill.

Thus matters stood about 3 P.M. The day was bright and clear, and the amphitheatre of Chattanooga lay in beauty at our feet. I had watched for the attack of General Thomas *"early in the day."*

Column after column of the enemy was streaming toward me; gun after gun poured its concentric shot on us, from every hill and spur that gave a view of any part of the ground held by us. An occasional shot from Fort Wood and Orchard Knob, and some musketry-fire and artillery over about Lookout Mountain, was all that I could detect on our side; but about 3 P.M. I noticed the white line of musketry-fire in front of Orchard Knoll extending farther and farther right and left and on. We could only hear a faint echo of sound, but enough was seen to satisfy me that General Thomas was at last moving on the *centre.* I knew that our attack had drawn vast masses of the enemy to our flank, and felt sure of the result. Some guns which had been firing on us all day were silent, or were turned in a different direction.

The advancing line of musketry-fire from Orchard Knoll disappeared to us behind a spur of the hill, and could no longer be seen; and it was not until night closed in that I knew that the troops in Chattanooga had swept across Missionary Ridge and broken the enemy's centre. Of course, the victory was won, and pursuit was the next step.

I ordered General Morgan L. Smith to feel to the tunnel, and it was found vacant, save by the dead and wounded of our own and the enemy commingled. The reserve of General Jeff. C. Davis was ordered to march at once by the pontoon-bridge across Chickamauga Creek, at its mouth, and push forward for the depot.

General Howard had reported to me in the early part of the day, with the remainder of his army corps (the Eleventh), and had been posted to connect my left with Chickamauga Creek. He was ordered to repair an old broken bridge about two miles up the Chickamauga, and to follow General Davis at 4 A.M., and the Fifteenth Army Corps was ordered to follow at daylight. But General Howard found that to repair the bridge was more of a task than was at first supposed, and we were all compelled to cross the Chickamauga on the new pontoon-bridge at its mouth. By about 11 A.M. General Jeff. C. Davis's division reached the depot, just in time to see it in flames. He found the enemy occupying two hills, partially intrenched, just beyond the depot. These he soon drove away. The depot presented a scene of desolation that war alone exhibits—corn-meal and corn in huge burning piles, broken wagons, abandoned caissons, two thirty-two-pounder rifled-guns with carriages burned, pieces of pontoons, balks and chesses, etc., destined doubtless for the famous invasion of Kentucky, and all manner of things, burning and broken. Still, the enemy kindly left us a good supply of forage for our horses, and meal, beans, etc., for our men.

Pausing but a short while, we passed on, the road filled with broken wagons and abandoned caissons, till night. Just as the head of the column emerged from a dark, miry swamp, we encountered the rear-guard of the retreating enemy. The fight was sharp, but the night closed in so dark that we could not move. General Grant came up to us there. At daylight we resumed the march, and at Graysville, where a good bridge spanned the Chickamauga, we found the corps of General Palmer on the south bank, who informed us that General Hooker was on a road still farther south, and we could hear his guns near Ringgold.

As the roads were filled with all the troops they could possibly accommodate, I turned to the east, to fulfill another part of the general plan, viz., to break up all communication between Bragg and Longstreet.

We had all sorts of rumors as to the latter, but it was manifest that we should interpose a proper force between these two armies. I therefore directed General Howard to move to Parker's Gap, and thence send rapidly a competent force to Red Clay, or the Council-Ground, there to destroy a large section of the railroad which connects Dalton and Cleveland. This work was most successfully and fully accomplished that day. The division of General Jeff. C. Davis was moved close up to Ringgold, to assist General Hooker if needed, and the Fifteenth Corps was held at Graysville, for any thing that might turn up. About noon I had a message from General Hooker, saying he had had a pretty hard fight at the mountain-pass just beyond Ringgold, and he wanted me to come forward to turn the position. He was not aware at the time that Howard, by moving through Parker's Gap toward Red Clay, had already turned it. So I rode forward to Ringgold in person, and found the enemy had already fallen back to Tunnel Hill. He was already out of the valley of the Chickamauga, and on ground whence the waters flow to the Coosa. He was out of Tennessee.

I found General Grant at Ringgold, and, after some explanations as to breaking up the railroad from Ringgold back to the State line, as soon as some cars loaded with wounded men could be pushed back to Chickamauga depot, I was ordered to move slowly and leisurely back to Chattanooga.

On the following day the Fifteenth Corps destroyed absolutely and effectually the railroad from a point half-way between Ringgold and Graysville, back to the State line; and General Grant, coming to Graysville, consented that, instead of returning direct to Chattanooga, I might send back all my artillery-wagons and impediments, and make a circuit by the north as far as the Hiawassee River.

Accordingly, on the morning of November 29th, General Howard moved from Parker's Gap to Cleveland, General Davis by way of McDaniel's Gap, and General Blair with two divisions of the Fifteenth Corps by way of Julien's Gap, all meeting at Cleveland that night. Here another good break was made in the Dalton & Cleveland road. On the 30th the army moved to Charleston, General Howard approaching so rapidly that the enemy evacuated with haste, leaving the bridge but partially damaged, and five car-loads of flour and provisions on the north bank of the Hiawassee.

This was to have been the limit of our operations. Officers and men had brought no baggage or provisions, and the weather was bitter cold. I had already reached the town of Charleston, when General Wilson arrived with a letter from General Grant, at Chattanooga, informing me that the latest authentic accounts from Knoxville were to the 27th, at which time General Burnside was completely invested, and had provisions only to include the 3d of December; that General Granger had left Chattanooga for Knoxville by the river-road, with a steamboat following him in the river; but he feared that General Granger could not reach Knoxville in time, and ordered me to take command of all troops moving for the relief of Knoxville, and hasten to General Burnside. Seven days before, we had left our camps on the other side of the Tennessee with two days' rations, without a change of clothing—stripped for the fight, with but a single blanket or coat per man, from myself to the private included.

Of course, we then had no provisions save what we gathered by the road, and were ill supplied for such a march. But we learned that twelve thousand of our fellow-soldiers were beleaguered in the mountain town of Knoxville, eighty-four miles distant; that they needed relief, and must have it in three days. This was enough—and it had to be done. General Howard that night repaired and planked the railroad-bridge, and at daylight the army passed over the Hiawassee and marched to Athens, fifteen miles. I had supposed rightly that General Granger was about the mouth of the Hiawassee, and had sent him notice of my orders; that General Grant had sent me a copy of his written instructions, which were full and complete, and that he must push for Kingston, near which we would make a junction. But by the time I reached Athens I had better studied the

geography, and sent him orders, which found him at Decatur, that
Kingston was out of our way; that he should send his boat to Kingston, but with his command strike across to Philadelphia, and report
to me there. I had but a small force of cavalry, which was, at the time
of my receipt of General Grant's orders, scouting over about Benton
and Columbus. I left my aide, Major McCoy, at Charleston, to communicate with this cavalry and hurry it forward. It overtook me in
the night at Athens.

On the 2d of December the army moved rapidly north toward
Loudon, twenty-six miles distant. About 11 A.M. the cavalry passed to
the head of the column, was ordered to push to Loudon, and, if
possible, to save a pontoon-bridge across the Tennessee, held by a
brigade of the enemy commanded by General Vaughn. The cavalry
moved with such rapidity as to capture every picket; but the brigade
of Vaughn had artillery in position, covered by earthworks, and displayed a force too respectable to be carried by a cavalry dash, so that
darkness closed in before General Howard's infantry got up. The
enemy abandoned the place in the night, destroying the pontoons,
running three locomotives and forty-eight cars into the Tennessee
River, and abandoned much provision, four guns, and other material, which General Howard took at daylight. But the bridge was
gone, and we were forced to turn east and trust to General Burnside's bridge at Knoxville. It was all-important that General Burnside
should have notice of our coming, and but one day of the time
remained.

Accordingly, at Philadelphia, during the night of the 2d of December, I sent my aide (Major Audenried) forward to Colonel Long,
commanding the brigade of cavalry at Loudon, to explain to him
how all-important it was that notice of our approach should reach
General Burnside within twenty-four hours, ordering him to select
the best materials of his command, to start at once, ford the Little
Tennessee, and push into Knoxville at whatever cost of life and
horse-flesh. Major Audenried was ordered to go along. The distance
to be traveled was about forty miles, and the roads villainous. Before
day they were off, and at daylight the Fifteenth Corps was turned
from Philadelphia for the Little Tennessee at Morgantown, where
my maps represented the river as being very shallow; but it was
found too deep for fording, and the water was freezing cold—width
two hundred and forty yards, depth from two to five feet; horses
could ford, but artillery and men could not. A bridge was indispensable. General Wilson (who accompanied me) undertook to superintend the bridge, and I am under many obligations to him, as I was
without an engineer, having sent Captain Jenny back from Graysville

to survey our field of battle. We had our pioneers, but only such tools as axes, picks, and spades. General Wilson, working partly with cut wood and partly with square trestles (made of the houses of the late town of Morgantown), progressed apace, and by dark of December 4th troops and animals passed over the bridge, and by daybreak of the 5th the Fifteenth Corps (General Blair's) was over, and Generals Granger's and Davis's divisions were ready to pass; but the diagonal bracing was imperfect for want of spikes, and the bridge broke, causing delay. I had ordered General Blair to move out on the Marysville road five miles, there to await notice that General Granger was on a parallel road abreast of him, and in person I was at a house where the roads parted, when a messenger rode up, bringing me a few words from General Burnside, to the effect that Colonel Long had arrived at Knoxville with his cavalry, and that all was well with him there; Longstreet still lay before the place, but there were symptoms of his speedy departure.

I felt that I had accomplished the first great step in the problem for the relief of General Burnside's army, but still urged on the work. As soon as the bridge was mended, all the troops moved forward. General Howard had marched from Loudon, had found a pretty good ford for his horses and wagons at Davis's, seven miles below Morgantown, and had made an ingenious bridge of the wagons left by General Vaughn at Loudon, on which to pass his men. He marched by Unitia and Louisville. On the night of the 5th all the heads of columns communicated at Marysville, where I met Major Van Buren (of General Burnside's staff), who announced that Longstreet had the night before retreated on the Rutledge, Rogersville, and Bristol road, leading to Virginia; that General Burnside's cavalry was on his heels; and that the general desired to see me in person as soon as I could come to Knoxville. I ordered all the troops to halt and rest, except the two divisions of General Granger, which were ordered to move forward to Little River, and General Granger to report in person to General Burnside for orders. His was the force originally designed to reënforce General Burnside, and it was eminently proper that it should join in the stern-chase after Longstreet.

On the morning of December 6th I rode from Marysville into Knoxville, and met General Burnside. General Granger arrived later in the day. We examined his lines of fortifications, which were a wonderful production for the short time allowed in their selection of ground and construction of work. It seemed to me that they were nearly impregnable. We examined the redoubt named "Sanders," where, on the Sunday previous, three brigades of the enemy had assaulted and met a bloody repulse. Now, all was peaceful and quiet; but a few hours before, the deadly bullet sought its victim all round about that hilly barrier.

The general explained to me fully and frankly what he had done, and what he proposed to do. He asked of me nothing but General Granger's command; and suggested, in view of the large force I had brought from Chattanooga, that I should return with due expedition to the line of the Hiawassee, lest Bragg, reënforced, might take advantage of our absence to resume the offensive. I asked him to reduce this to writing, which he did, and I here introduce it as part of my report:

HEADQUARTERS ARMY OF THE OHIO, }
KNOXVILLE, *December* 7, 1863. }

Major-General W. T. SHERMAN, *commanding, etc.*

GENERAL: I desire to express to you and your command my most hearty thanks and gratitude for your promptness in coming to our relief during the siege of Knoxville, and I am satisfied your approach served to raise the siege. The emergency having passed, I do not deem, for the present, any other portion of your command but the corps of General Granger necessary for operations in this section; and, inasmuch as General Grant has weakened the forces immediately with him in order to relieve us (thereby rendering the position of General Thomas less secure), I deem it advisable that all the troops now here, save those commanded by General Granger, should return at once to within supporting distance of the forces in front of Bragg's army. In behalf of my command, I desire again to thank you and your command for the kindness you have done us.

I am, general, very respectfully, your obedient servant,
A. E. BURNSIDE, *Major-General commanding.*

Accordingly, having seen General Burnside's forces move out of Knoxville in pursuit of Longstreet, and General Granger's move in, I put in motion my own command to return. General Howard was ordered to move, *via* Davis's Ford and Sweetwater, to Athens, with a guard forward at Charleston, to hold and repair the bridge which the enemy had retaken after our passage up. General Jeff. C. Davis moved to Columbus, on the Hiawassee, *via* Madisonville, and the two divisions of the Fifteenth Corps moved to Tellico Plains, to cover a movement of cavalry across the mountains into Georgia, to overtake a wagon-train which had dodged us on our way up, and had escaped by way of Murphy. Subsequently, on a report from General Howard that the enemy held Charleston, I diverted General Ewing's division to Athens, and went in person to Tellico with

General Morgan L. Smith's division. By the 9th all our troops were in position, and we held the rich country between the Little Tennessee and the Hiawassee. The cavalry, under Colonel Long, passed the mountain at Tellico, and proceeded about seventeen miles beyond Murphy, when Colonel Long, deeming his farther pursuit of the wagon-train useless, returned on the 12th to Tellico. I then ordered him and the division of General Morgan L. Smith to move to Charleston, to which point I had previously ordered the corps of General Howard.

On the 14th of December all of my command in the field lay along the Hiawassee. Having communicated to General Grant the actual state of affairs, I received orders to leave, on the line of the Hiawassee, all the cavalry, and come to Chattanooga with the rest of my command. I left the brigade of cavalry commanded by Colonel Long, reënforced by the Fifth Ohio Cavalry (Lieutenant-Colonel Heath)—the only cavalry properly belonging to the Fifteenth Army Corps—at Charleston, and with the remainder moved by easy marches, by Cleveland and Tyner's Depot, into Chattanooga, where I received in person from General Grant orders to transfer back to their appropriate commands the corps of General Howard and the division commanded by General Jeff. C. Davis, and to conduct the Fifteenth Army Corps to its new field of operations.

It will thus appear that we have been constantly in motion since our departure from the Big Black, in Mississippi, until the present moment. I have been unable to receive from subordinate commanders the usual full, detailed reports of events, and have therefore been compelled to make up this report from my own personal memory; but, as soon as possible, subordinate reports will be received and duly forwarded.

In reviewing the facts, I must do justice to the men of my command for the patience, cheerfulness, and courage which officers and men have displayed throughout, in battle, on the march, and in camp. For long periods, without regular rations or supplies of any kind, they have marched through mud and over rocks, sometimes barefooted, without a murmur. Without a moment's rest after a march of over four hundred miles, without sleep for three successive nights, we crossed the Tennessee, fought our part of the battle of Chattanooga, pursued the enemy out of Tennessee, and then turned more than a hundred and twenty miles north and compelled Longstreet to raise the siege of Knoxville, which gave so much anxiety to the whole country. It is hard to realize the importance of these events without recalling the memory of the general feeling which pervaded all minds at Chattanooga prior to our arrival. I cannot speak of the Fifteenth Army Corps without a seeming vanity; but as I am no longer its commander, I assert that there is no better body of soldiers in America than it. I wish all to feel a just pride in its real honors.

To General Howard and his command, to General Jeff. C. Davis and his, I am more than usually indebted for the intelligence of commanders and fidelity of commands. The brigade of Colonel Bushbeck, belonging to the Eleventh Corps, which was the first to come out of Chattanooga to my flank, fought at the Tunnel Hill, in connection with General Ewing's division, and displayed a courage almost amounting to rashness. Following the enemy almost to the tunnel-gorge, it lost many valuable lives, prominent among them Lieutenant-Colonel Taft, spoken of as a most gallant soldier.

In General Howard throughout I found a polished and Christian gentleman, exhibiting the highest and most chivalric traits of the soldier. General Davis handled his division with artistic skill, more especially at the moment we encountered the enemy's rear-guard, near Graysville, at nightfall. I must award to this division the credit of the best order during our movement through East Tennessee, when long marches and the necessity of foraging to the right and left gave some reason for disordered ranks.

Inasmuch as exception may be taken to my explanation of the temporary confusion, during the battle of Chattanooga, of the two brigades of General Matthias and Colonel Raum, I will here state that I saw the whole, and attach no blame to any one. Accidents will happen in battle, as elsewhere; and at the point where they so manfully went to relieve the pressure on other parts of our assaulting line, they exposed themselves unconsciously to an enemy vastly superior in force, and favored by the shape of the ground. Had that enemy come out on equal terms, those brigades would have shown their mettle, which has been tried more than once before and *stood* the test of fire. They reformed their ranks, and were ready to support General Ewing's division in a very few minutes; and the circumstance would have hardly called for notice on my part, had not others reported what was seen from Chattanooga, a distance of nearly five miles, from where could only be seen the troops in the open field in which this affair occurred.

I now subjoin the best report of casualties I am able to compile from the records thus far received:

CORPS, DIVISIONS, ETC.	Killed.	Wounded.	Missing.	Total.
FIFTEENTH ARMY CORPS:				
First Division	67	364	66	497
Second Division	No report.	62 (in hosp.)	. . . .	62
Third Division.	89	288	122	499
Fourth Division	72	535	21	628
Total				1,686
ELEVENTH ARMY CORPS:				
Bushbeck's Brigade . . .	37	145	81	263
Aggregate Loss. . . .				1,949

No report from General Davis's division, but loss is small.

Among the killed were some of our most valuable officers: Colonels Putnam, Ninety-third Illinois; O'Meara, Ninetieth Illinois; and Torrence, Thirtieth Iowa; Lieutenant-Colonel Taft, of the Eleventh Corps; and Major Bushnell, Thirteenth Illinois.

Among the wounded are Brigadier-Generals Giles A. Smith, Corse, and Matthias; Colonel Raum; Colonel Waugelin, Twelfth Missouri; Lieutenant-Colonel Partridge, Thirteenth Illinois; Major P. I. Welsh, Fifty-sixth Illinois; and Major Nathan McAlla, Tenth Iowa.

Among the missing is Lieutenant-Colonel Archer, Seventeenth Iowa.

My report is already so long, that I must forbear mentioning acts of individual merit. These will be recorded in the reports of division commanders, which I will cheerfully indorse; but I must say that it is but justice that colonels of regiments, who have so long and so well commanded brigades, as in the following cases, should be commissioned to the grade which they have filled with so much usefulness and credit to the public service, viz.: Colonel J. R. Cockerell, Seventieth Ohio; Colonel J. M. Loomis, Twenty-sixth Illinois; Colonel C. C. Walcutt, Forty-sixth Ohio; Colonel J. A. Williamson, Fourth Iowa; Colonel G. B. Raum, Fifty-sixth Illinois; Colonel J. I. Alexander, Fifty-ninth Indiana.

My personal staff, as usual, have served their country with fidelity, and credit to themselves, throughout these events, and have received my personal thanks.

Inclosed you will please find a map of that part of the battle-field of Chattanooga fought over by the troops under my command, surveyed and drawn by Captain Jenney, engineer on my staff. I have the honor to be, your obedient servant,

W. T. SHERMAN, *Major-General commanding.*

[General Order No. 68.]
WAR DEPARTMENT, ADJUTANT-GENERAL'S OFFICE, ⎫
WASHINGTON, *February* 21, 1864. ⎭

PUBLIC RESOLUTION — No. 12.

Joint resolution tendering the thanks of Congress to Major-General W. T. Sherman and others.

Be it resolved by the Senate and House of Representatives of the United States of America in Congress assembled, That the thanks of Congress and of the people of the United States are due, and that the same are hereby tendered, to Major-General W. T. Sherman, commander of the Department and Army of the Tennessee, and the officers and soldiers who served under him, for their gallant and arduous services in marching to the relief of the Army of the Cumberland, and for their gallantry and heroism in the battle of Chattanooga, which contributed in a great degree to the success of our arms in that glorious victory.

Approved February 19, 1864.

By order of the Secretary of War:

E. D. TOWNSEND, *Assistant Adjutant-General.*

On the 19th of December I was at Bridgeport, and gave all the orders necessary for the distribution of the four divisions of the Fifteenth Corps along the railroad from Stevenson to Decatur, and the part of the Sixteenth Corps, commanded by General Dodge, along the railroad from Decatur to Nashville, to make the needed repairs, and to be in readiness for the campaign of the succeeding year; and on the 21st I went up to Nashville, to confer with General Grant and conclude the arrangements for the winter. At that time General Grant was under the impression that the next campaign would be up the valley of East Tennessee, in the direction of Virginia; and as it was likely to be the last and most important campaign of the war, it became necessary to set free as many of the old troops serving along the Mississippi River as possible. This was the real object and purpose of the Meridian campaign, and of Banks's expedition up Red River to Shreveport during that winter.

Chapter XV.

MERIDIAN CAMPAIGN.

January and February, 1864.

THE WINTER of 1863–'64 opened very cold and severe; and it was manifest after the battle of Chattanooga, November 25, 1863, and the raising of the siege of Knoxville, December 5th, that military operations in that quarter must in a measure cease, or be limited to Burnside's force beyond Knoxville. On the 21st of December General Grant had removed his headquarters to Nashville, Tennessee, leaving General George H. Thomas at Chattanooga, in command of the Department of the Cumberland, and of the army round about that place; and I was at Bridgeport, with orders to distribute my troops along the railroad from Stevenson to Decatur, Alabama, and from Decatur up toward Nashville.

General G. M. Dodge, who was in command of the detachment of the Sixteenth Corps, numbering about eight thousand men, had not participated with us in the battle of Chattanooga, but had remained at and near Pulaski, Tennessee, engaged in repairing that railroad, as auxiliary to the main line which led from Nashville to Stevenson, and Chattanooga. General John A. Logan had succeeded to the command of the Fifteenth Corps, by regular appointment of the President of the United States, and had relieved General Frank P. Blair, who had been temporarily in command of that corps during the Chattanooga and Knoxville movement.

At that time I was in command of the Department of the Tennessee, which embraced substantially the territory on the east bank of the Mississippi River, from Natchez up to the Ohio River, and thence along the Tennessee River as high as Decatur and Bellefonte, Alabama. General McPherson was at Vicksburg and General Hurlbut at Memphis, and from them I had the regular reports of affairs in that quarter of my command. The rebels still maintained a considerable force of infantry and cavalry in the State of Mississippi, threatening the river, whose navigation had become to us so delicate and

MERIDIAN
CAMPAIGN

EXPLANATION

15th Army Corps
16th ,,   ,,
17th ,,   ,,
Cavalry

SCALE

important a matter. Satisfied that I could check this by one or two quick moves inland, and thereby set free a considerable body of men held as local garrisons, I went up to Nashville and represented the case to General Grant, who consented that I might go down the Mississippi River, where the bulk of my command lay, and strike a blow on the east of the river, while General Banks from New Orleans should in like manner strike another to the west; thus preventing any further molestation of the boats navigating the main river, and thereby widening the gap in the Southern Confederacy.

After having given all the necessary orders for the distribution, during the winter months, of that part of my command which was in Southern and Middle Tennessee, I went to Cincinnati and Lancaster, Ohio, to spend Christmas with my family; and on my return I took Minnie with me down to a convent at Reading, near Cincinnati, where I left her, and took the cars for Cairo, Illinois, which I reached January 3d, a very cold and bitter day. The ice was forming fast, and there was great danger that the Mississippi River would become closed to navigation. Admiral Porter, who was at Cairo, gave me a small gunboat (the Juliet), with which I went up to Paducah, to inspect that place, garrisoned by a small force, commanded by Colonel S. G. Hicks, Fortieth Illinois, who had been with me and was severely wounded at Shiloh. Returning to Cairo, we started down the Mississippi River, which was full of floating ice. With the utmost difficulty we made our way through it, for hours floating in the midst of immense cakes, that chafed and ground our boat so that at times we were in danger of sinking. But about the 10th of January we reached Memphis, where I found General Hurlbut, and explained to him my purpose to collect from his garrisons and those of McPherson about twenty thousand men, with which in February to march out from Vicksburg as far as Meridian, break up the Mobile & Ohio Railroad, and also the one leading from Vicksburg to Selma, Alabama. I instructed him to select two good divisions, and to be ready with them to go along. At Memphis I found Brigadier-General W. Sooy Smith, with a force of about twenty-five hundred cavalry, which he had by General Grant's orders brought across from Middle Tennessee, to assist in our general purpose, as well as to punish the rebel General Forrest, who had been most active in harassing our garrisons in West Tennessee and Mississippi.

After staying a couple of days at Memphis, we continued on in the gunboat Silver Cloud to Vicksburg, where I found General McPherson, and, giving him similar orders, instructed him to send out spies to ascertain and bring back timely information of the strength and location of the enemy. The winter continued so severe that the river at Vicksburg was full of floating ice, but in the Silver Cloud we breasted it manfully, and got back to Memphis by the 20th. A chief part of the enterprise was to destroy the rebel cavalry commanded by General Forrest, who were a constant threat to our railway communications in Middle Tennessee, and I committed this task to Brigadier-General W. Sooy Smith. General Hurlbut had in his command about seven thousand five hundred cavalry, scattered from Columbus, Kentucky, to Corinth, Mississippi, and we proposed to make up an aggregate cavalry force of about seven thousand "effective," out of these and the twenty-five hundred which General Smith had brought with him from Middle Tennessee. With this force General Smith was ordered to move from Memphis straight for Meridian, Mississippi, and to start by February 1st. I explained to him personally the nature of Forrest as a man, and of his peculiar force; told him that in his route he was sure to encounter Forrest, who always attacked with a vehemence for which he must be prepared, and that, after he had repelled the first attack, he must in turn assume the most determined offensive, overwhelm him and utterly destroy his whole force. I knew that Forrest could not have more than four thousand cavalry, and my own movement would give employment to every other man of the rebel army not immediately present with him, so that he (General Smith) might safely act on the hypothesis I have stated.

Having completed all these preparations in Memphis, being satisfied that the cavalry force would be ready to start by the 1st of February, and having seen General Hurlbut with his two divisions embark in steamers for Vicksburg, I also reëmbarked for the same destination on the 27th of January.

On the 1st of February we rendezvoused in Vicksburg,

where I found a spy who had been sent out two weeks before, had been to Meridian, and brought back correct information of the state of facts in the interior of Mississippi. Lieutenant-General (Bishop) Polk was in chief command, with head-quarters at Meridian, and had two divisions of infantry, one of which (General Loring's) was posted at Canton, Mississippi, the other (General French's) at Brandon. He had also two divisions of cavalry—Armstrong's, composed of the three brigades of Ross, Stark, and Wirt Adams, which were scattered from the neighborhood of Yazoo City to Jackson and below; and Forrest's, which was united, toward Memphis, with headquarters at Como. General Polk seemed to have no suspicion of our intentions to disturb his serenity.

Accordingly, on the morning of February 3d, we started in two columns, each of two divisions, preceded by a light force of cavalry, commanded by Colonel E. F. Winslow. General McPherson commanded the right column, and General Hurl-but the left. The former crossed the Big Black at the railroad-bridge, and the latter seven miles above, at Messinger's. We were lightly equipped as to wagons, and marched without deployment straight for Meridian, distant one hundred and fifty miles. We struck the rebel cavalry beyond the Big Black, and pushed them pell-mell into and beyond Jackson during the 6th. The next day we reached Brandon, and on the 9th Morton, where we perceived signs of an infantry concentration, but the enemy did not give us battle, and retreated before us. The rebel cavalry were all around us, so we kept our columns compact and offered few or no chances for their dashes. As far as Morton we had occupied two roads, but there we were forced into one. Toward evening of the 12th, Hurlbut's column passed through Decatur, with orders to go into camp four miles beyond at a creek. McPherson's head of column was some four miles behind, and I personally detached one of Hurlbut's regiments to guard the cross-roads at Decatur till the head of McPherson's column should come in sight. Intending to spend the night in Decatur, I went to a double log-house, and arranged with the lady for some supper. We unsaddled our horses, tied them to the fence inside the yard, and, being tired, I lay down on a bed and fell asleep. Presently I heard shouts and hallooing, and then heard pistol-shots close to the house. My aide, Major Audenried, called me and said we were attacked by rebel cavalry, who were all around us. I jumped up and inquired where was the regiment of infantry I had myself posted at the cross-roads. He said a few moments before it had marched past the house, following the road by which General Hurlbut had gone, and I told him to run, overtake it, and bring it back. Meantime, I went out into the back-yard, saw wagons passing at a run down the road, and horsemen dashing about in a cloud of dust, firing their pistols, their shots reaching the house in which we were. Gathering the few orderlies and clerks that were about, I was preparing to get into a corn-crib at the back side of the lot, wherein to defend ourselves, when I saw Audenried coming back with the regiment, on a run, deploying forward as they came. This regiment soon cleared the place and drove the rebel cavalry back toward the south, whence they had come.

It transpired that the colonel of this infantry regiment, whose name I do not recall, had seen some officers of McPherson's staff (among them Inspector-General Strong) coming up the road at a gallop, raising a cloud of dust; supposing them to be the head of McPherson's column, and being anxious to get into camp before dark, he had called in his pickets and started down the road, leaving me perfectly exposed. Some straggling wagons, escorted by a New Jersey regiment, were passing at the time, and composed the rear of Hurlbut's train. The rebel cavalry, seeing the road clear of troops, and these wagons passing, struck them in flank, shot down the mules of three or four wagons, broke the column, and began a general skirmish. The escort defended their wagons as well as they could, and thus diverted their attention; otherwise I would surely have been captured. In a short time the head of McPherson's column came up, went into camp, and we spent the night in Decatur.

The next day we pushed on, and on the 14th entered Meridian, the enemy retreating before us toward Demopolis, Alabama. We at once set to work to destroy an arsenal, immense storehouses, and the railroad in every direction. We staid in Meridian five days, expecting every hour to hear of General Sooy Smith, but could get no tidings of him whatever. A large force of infantry was kept at work all the time in

breaking up the Mobile & Ohio Railroad south and north;
also the Jackson & Selma Railroad, east and west. I was determined to damage these roads so that they could not be used
again for hostile purposes during the rest of the war. I never
had the remotest idea of going to Mobile, but had purposely
given out that idea to the people of the country, so as to
deceive the enemy and to divert their attention. Many persons
still insist that, because we did not go to Mobile on this occasion, I had failed; but in the following letter to General
Banks, of January 31st, written from Vicksburg before starting
for Meridian, it will be seen clearly that I indicated my intention to keep up the delusion of an attack on Mobile by land,
whereas I promised him to be back to Vicksburg by the 1st of
March, so as to coöperate with him in his contemplated attack on Shreveport:

HEADQUARTERS DEPARTMENT OF THE TENNESSEE,
VICKSBURG, *January* 31, 1864.

Major-General N. P. BANKS, *commanding Department of the Gulf,*
New Orleans.

GENERAL: I received yesterday, at the hands of Captain Dunham,
aide-de-camp, your letter of the 25th inst., and hasten to reply. Captain Dunham has gone to the mouth of White River, *en route* for
Little Rock, and the other officers who accompanied him have gone
up to Cairo, as I understand, to charter twenty-five steamboats for
the Red River trip. The Mississippi River, though low for the season, is free of ice and in good boating order; but I understand that
Red River is still low. I had a man in from Alexandria yesterday,
who reported the falls or rapids at that place impassable save by the
smallest boats. My inland expedition is now moving, and I will be
off for Jackson and Meridian to-morrow. The only fear I have is in
the weather. All the other combinations are good. I want to keep up
the delusion of an attack on Mobile and the Alabama River, and
therefore would be obliged if you would keep up an irritating foraging or other expedition in that direction.

My orders from General Grant will not, as yet, justify me in embarking for Red River, though I am very anxious to move in that
direction. The moment I learned that you were preparing for it, I
sent a communication to Admiral Porter, and dispatched to General
Grant at Chattanooga, asking if he wanted me and Steele to coöperate with you against Shreveport; and I will have his answer in time,
for you cannot do any thing till Red River has twelve feet of water

on the rapids at Alexandria. That will be from March to June. I have lived on Red River, and know somewhat of the phases of that stream. The expedition on Shreveport should be made rapidly, with simultaneous movements from Little Rock on Shreveport, from Opelousas on Alexandria, and a combined force of gunboats and transports directly up Red River. Admiral Porter will be able to have a splendid fleet by March 1st. I think Steele could move with ten thousand infantry and five thousand cavalry. I could take about ten thousand, and you could, I suppose, have the same. Your movement from Opelousas, simultaneous with mine up the river, would compel Dick Taylor to leave Fort De Russy (near Marksville), and the whole combined force could appear at Shreveport about a day appointed beforehand.

I doubt if the enemy will risk a siege at Shreveport, although I am informed they are fortifying the place, and placing many heavy guns in position. It would be better for us that they should stand there, as we might make large and important captures. But I do not believe the enemy will fight a force of thirty thousand men, acting in concert with gunboats.

I will be most happy to take part in the proposed expedition, and hope, before you have made your final dispositions, that I will have the necessary permission. Half the Army of the Tennessee is near the Tennessee River, beyond Huntsville, Alabama, awaiting the completion of the railroad, and, by present orders, I will be compelled to hasten there to command it in person, unless meantime General Grant modifies the plan. I have now in this department only the force left to hold the river and the posts, and I am seriously embarrassed by the promises made the veteran volunteers for furlough. I think, by March 1st, I can put afloat for Shreveport ten thousand men, provided I succeed in my present movement in cleaning out the State of Mississippi, and in breaking up the railroads about Meridian.

I am, with great respect, your obedient servant,

W. T. SHERMAN, *Major-General commanding.*

The object of the Meridian expedition was to strike the roads inland, so to paralyze the rebel forces that we could take from the defense of the Mississippi River the equivalent of a corps of twenty thousand men, to be used in the next Georgia campaign; and this was actually done. At the same time, I wanted to destroy General Forrest, who, with an irregular force of cavalry, was constantly threatening Memphis and the river above, as well as our routes of supply in Middle Tennessee. In this we failed utterly, because General W. Sooy Smith did not fulfill his orders, which were clear and specific, as contained in my letter of instructions to him of January 27th, at Memphis, and my personal explanations to him at the same time. Instead of starting at the date ordered, February 1st, he did not leave Memphis till the 11th, waiting for Waring's brigade that was ice-bound near Columbus, Kentucky; and then, when he did start, he allowed General Forrest to head him off and to defeat him with an inferior force, near West Point, below Okalona, on the Mobile & Ohio Railroad.

We waited at Meridian till the 20th to hear from General Smith, but hearing nothing whatever, and having utterly destroyed the railroads in and around that junction, I ordered General McPherson to move back slowly toward Canton. With Winslow's cavalry, and Hurlbut's infantry, I turned north to Marion, and thence to a place called "Union," whence I dispatched the cavalry farther north to Philadelphia and Louisville, to feel as it were for General Smith, and then turned all the infantry columns toward Canton, Mississippi. On the 26th we all reached Canton, but we had not heard a word of General Smith, nor was it until some time after (at Vicksburg) that I learned the whole truth of General Smith's movement and of his failure. Of course I did not and could not approve of his conduct, and I know that he yet chafes under the censure. I had set so much store on his part of the project that I was disappointed, and so reported officially to General Grant. General Smith never regained my confidence as a soldier, though I still regard him as a most accomplished gentleman and a skillful engineer. Since the close of the war he has appealed to me to relieve him of that censure, but I could not do it, because it would falsify history.

Having assembled all my troops in and about Canton, on the 27th of February I left them under the command of the senior major-general, Hurlbut, with orders to remain till about the 3d of March, and then to come into Vicksburg leisurely; and, escorted by Winslow's cavalry, I rode into Vicksburg on the last day of February. There I found letters from General Grant, at Nashville, and General Banks, at New Orleans, concerning his (General Banks's) projected movement up Red River. I was authorized by the former to contribute aid to General Banks for a limited time; but General Grant insisted on my returning in person to my own command about Huntsville, Alabama, as soon as possible, to prepare for the spring campaign.

About this time we were much embarrassed by a general order of the War Department, promising a thirty-days furlough to all soldiers who would "veteranize"—viz., reënlist for the rest of the war. This was a judicious and wise measure, because it doubtless secured the services of a very large portion of the men who had almost completed a three-years enlistment, and were therefore veteran soldiers in feeling and in habit. But to furlough so many of our men at that instant of time was like disbanding an army in the very midst of battle.

In order to come to a perfect understanding with General Banks, I took the steamer Diana and ran down to New Orleans to see him. Among the many letters which I found in Vicksburg on my return from Meridian was one from Captain D. F. Boyd, of Louisiana, written from the jail in Natchez, telling me that he was a prisoner of war in our hands; had been captured in Louisiana by some of our scouts; and he bespoke my friendly assistance. Boyd was Professor of Ancient Languages at the Louisiana Seminary of Learning during my administration in 1859–'60; was an accomplished scholar, of moderate views in politics, but, being a Virginian, was drawn, like all others of his kind, into the vortex of the rebellion by the events of 1861, which broke up colleges and every thing at the South. Natchez, at this time, was in my command, and was held by a strong division, commanded by Brigadier-General J. W. Davidson. In the Diana we stopped at Natchez, and I made a hasty inspection of the place. I sent for Boyd, who was in good health, but quite dirty, and begged me to take him out of prison, and to effect his exchange. I receipted for him; took him along with me to New Orleans; offered him money, which he declined; allowed him to go free in the city; and obtained from General Banks a promise to effect his exchange, which was afterward done. Boyd is now my legitimate successor in Louisiana, viz., President of the Louisiana University, which is the present title of what had been the Seminary of Learning. After the war was over, Boyd went back to Alexandria, reorganized the old institution, which I visited in 1866; but the building was burnt down by an accident or by an incendiary about 1868, and the institution was then removed to Baton Rouge, where it now is, under its new title of the University of Louisiana.

We reached New Orleans on the 2d of March. I found General Banks, with his wife and daughter, living in a good house, and he explained to me fully the position and strength of his troops, and his plans of action for the approaching campaign. I dined with him, and, rough as I was—just out of the woods—attended, that night, a very pleasant party at the house of a lady, whose name I cannot recall, but who is now the wife of Captain Arnold, Fifth United States Artillery. At this party were also Mr. and Mrs. Frank Howe. I found New Orleans much changed since I had been familiar with it in 1853 and in 1860—'61. It was full of officers and soldiers. Among the former were General T. W. Sherman, who had lost a leg at Port Hudson, and General Charles P. Stone, whom I knew so well in California, and who is now in the Egyptian service as chief of staff. The bulk of General Banks's army was about Opelousas, under command of General Franklin, ready to move on Alexandria. General Banks seemed to be all ready, but intended to delay his departure a few days to assist in the inauguration of a civil government for Louisiana, under Governor Hahn. In Lafayette Square I saw the arrangements of scaffolding for the fireworks and benches for the audience. General Banks urged me to remain over the 4th of March, to participate in the ceremonies, which he explained would include the performance of the "Anvil Chorus" by all the bands of his army, and during the performance the church-bells were to be rung, and cannons were to be fired by electricity. I regarded all such ceremonies as out of place at a time when it seemed to me every hour and every minute were due to the war. General Banks's movement, however, contemplated my sending a force of ten thousand men in boats up Red River from Vicksburg, and that a junction should occur at Alexandria by March 17th. I therefore had no time to wait for the grand pageant of the 4th of March, but took my departure from New Orleans in the Diana the evening of March 3d.

On the next day, March 4th, I wrote to General Banks a

letter, which was extremely minute in conveying to him how far I felt authorized to go under my orders from General Grant. At that time General Grant commanded the Military Division of the Mississippi, embracing my own Department of the Tennessee and that of General Steele in Arkansas, but not that of General Banks in Louisiana. General Banks was acting on his own powers, or under the instructions of General Halleck in Washington, and our assistance to him was designed as a loan of ten thousand men for a period of thirty days. The instructions of March 6th to General A. J. Smith, who commanded this detachment, were full and explicit on this point. The Diana reached Vicksburg on the 6th, where I found that the expeditionary army had come in from Canton. One division of five thousand men was made up out of Hurlbut's command, and placed under Brigadier-General T. Kilby Smith; and a similar division was made out of McPherson's and Hurlbut's troops, and placed under Brigadier-General Joseph A. Mower; the whole commanded by Brigadier-General A. J. Smith. General Hurlbut, with the rest of his command, returned to Memphis, and General McPherson remained at Vicksburg. General A. J. Smith's command was in due season embarked, and proceeded to Red River, which it ascended, convoyed by Admiral Porter's fleet. General Mower's division was landed near the outlet of the Atchafalaya, marched up by land and captured the fort below Alexandria known as Fort De Russy, and the whole fleet then proceeded up to Alexandria, reaching it on the day appointed, viz., March 17th, where it waited for the arrival of General Banks, who, however, did not come till some days after. These two divisions participated in the whole of General Banks's unfortunate Red River expedition, and were delayed so long up Red River, and subsequently on the Mississippi, that they did not share with their comrades the successes and glories of the Atlanta campaign, for which I had designed them; and, indeed, they did not join our army till just in time to assist General George H. Thomas to defeat General Hood before Nashville, on the 15th and 16th of December, 1864.

General Grant's letter of instructions, which was brought me by General Butterfield, who had followed me to New Orleans, enjoined on me, after concluding with General

Banks the details for his Red River expedition, to make all necessary arrangements for furloughing the men entitled to that privilege, and to hurry back to the army at Huntsville, Alabama. I accordingly gave the necessary orders to General McPherson, at Vicksburg, and continued up the river toward Memphis. On our way we met Captain Badeau, of General Grant's staff, bearing the following letter, of March 4th, which I answered on the 10th, and sent the answer by General Butterfield, who had accompanied me up from New Orleans. Copies of both were also sent to General McPherson, at Vicksburg.

[PRIVATE.]

NASHVILLE, TENNESSEE, *March* 4, 1864.

DEAR SHERMAN: The bill reviving the grade of lieutenant-general in the army has become a law, and my name has been sent to the Senate for the place.

I now receive orders to report at Washington immediately, *in person*, which indicates either a confirmation or a likelihood of confirmation. I start in the morning to comply with the order, but I shall say very distinctly on my arrival there that I shall accept no appointment which will require me to make that city my headquarters. This, however, is not what I started out to write about.

While I have been eminently successful in this war, in at least gaining the confidence of the public, no one feels more than I how much of this success is due to the energy, skill, and the harmonious putting forth of that energy and skill, of those whom it has been my good fortune to have occupying subordinate positions under me.

There are many officers to whom these remarks are applicable to a greater or less degree, proportionate to their ability as soldiers; but what I want is to express my thanks to you and McPherson, as *the men* to whom, above all others, I feel indebted for whatever I have had of success. How far your advice and suggestions have been of assistance, you know. How far your execution of whatever has been given you to do entitles you to the reward I am receiving, you cannot know as well as I do. I feel all the gratitude this letter would express, giving it the most flattering construction.

The word *you* I use in the plural, intending it for McPherson also. I should write to him, and will some day, but, starting in the morning, I do not know that I will find time just now. Your friend,

U. S. GRANT, *Major-General.*

[PRIVATE AND CONFIDENTIAL.]

NEAR MEMPHIS, *March* 10, 1864.

General GRANT.

DEAR GENERAL: I have your more than kind and characteristic letter of the 4th, and will send a copy of it to General McPherson at once.

You do yourself injustice and us too much honor in assigning to us so large a share of the merits which have led to your high advancement. I know you approve the friendship I have ever professed to you, and will permit me to continue as heretofore to manifest it on all proper occasions.

You are now Washington's legitimate successor, and occupy a position of almost dangerous elevation; but if you can continue as heretofore to be yourself, simple, honest, and unpretending, you will enjoy through life the respect and love of friends, and the homage of millions of human beings who will award to you a large share for securing to them and their descendants a government of law and stability.

I repeat, you do General McPherson and myself too much honor. At Belmont you manifested your traits, neither of us being near; at Donelson also you illustrated your whole character. I was not near, and General McPherson in too subordinate a capacity to influence you.

Until you had won Donelson, I confess I was almost cowed by the terrible array of anarchical elements that presented themselves at every point; but that victory admitted the ray of light which I have followed ever since.

I believe you are as brave, patriotic, and just, as the great prototype Washington; as unselfish, kind-hearted, and honest, as a man should be; but the chief characteristic in your nature is the simple faith in success you have always manifested, which I can liken to nothing else than the faith a Christian has in his Saviour.

This faith gave you victory at Shiloh and Vicksburg. Also, when you have completed your best preparations, you go into battle without hesitation, as at Chattanooga—no doubts, no reserve; and I tell you that it was this that made us act with confidence. I knew wherever I was that you thought of me, and if I got in a tight place you would come—if alive.

My only points of doubt were as to your knowledge of grand strategy, and of books of science and history; but I confess your common-sense seems to have supplied all this.

Now as to the future. Do not stay in Washington. Halleck is better qualified than you are to stand the buffets of intrigue and policy.

Come out West; take to yourself the whole Mississippi Valley; let us make it dead-sure, and I tell you the Atlantic slope and Pacific shores will follow its destiny as sure as the limbs of a tree live or die with the main trunk! We have done much; still much remains to be done. Time and time's influences are all with us; we could almost afford to sit still and let these influences work. Even in the seceded States your word *now* would go further than a President's proclamation, or an act of Congress.

For God's sake and for your country's sake, come out of Washington! I foretold to General Halleck, before he left Corinth, the inevitable result to him, and I now exhort you to come out West. Here lies the seat of the coming empire; and from the West, when our task is done, we will make short work of Charleston and Richmond, and the impoverished coast of the Atlantic. Your sincere friend,

W. T. SHERMAN.

We reached Memphis on the 13th, where I remained some days, but on the 14th of March received from General Grant a dispatch to hurry to Nashville in person by the 17th, if possible. Disposing of all matters then pending, I took a steamboat to Cairo, the cars thence to Louisville and Nashville, reaching that place on the 17th of March, 1864.

I found General Grant there. He had been to Washington and back, and was ordered to return East to command all the armies of the United States, and personally the Army of the Potomac. I was to succeed him in command of the Military Division of the Mississippi, embracing the Departments of the Ohio, Cumberland, Tennessee, and Arkansas. General Grant was of course very busy in winding up all matters of business, in transferring his command to me, and in preparing for what was manifest would be the great and closing campaign of our civil war. Mrs. Grant and some of their children were with him, and occupied a large house in Nashville, which was used as an office, dwelling, and every thing combined.

On the 18th of March I had issued orders assuming command of the Military Division of the Mississippi, and was seated in the office, when the general came in and said they were about to present him a sword, inviting me to come and see the ceremony. I went back into what was the dining-room of the house; on the table lay a rose-wood box, containing a sword, sash, spurs, etc., and round about the table were grouped Mrs. Grant, Nelly, and one or two of the boys. I was introduced to a large, corpulent gentleman, as the mayor, and another citizen, who had come down from Galena to make this presentation of a sword to their fellow-townsman. I think that Rawlins, Bowers, Badeau, and one or more of General Grant's personal staff, were present. The mayor rose and in the most dignified way read a finished speech to General Grant, who stood, as usual, very awkwardly; and the mayor closed his speech by handing him the resolutions of the City Council engrossed on parchment, with a broad ribbon and large seal attached. After the mayor had fulfilled his office so well, General Grant said: "Mr. Mayor, as I knew that this ceremony was to occur, and as I am not used to speaking, I have written something in reply." He then began to fumble in his pockets, first his breast-coat pocket, then his pants, vest, etc., and after considerable delay he pulled out a crumpled piece of common yellow cartridge-paper, which he handed to the mayor. His whole manner was awkward in the extreme, yet perfectly characteristic, and in strong contrast with the elegant parchment and speech of the mayor. When read, however, the substance of his answer was most excellent, short, concise, and, if it had been delivered by word of mouth, would have been all that the occasion required.

I could not help laughing at a scene so characteristic of the man who then stood prominent before the country, and to whom all had turned as the only one qualified to guide the nation in a war that had become painfully critical. With copies of the few letters referred to, and which seem necessary to illustrate the subject-matter, I close this chapter.

> HEADQUARTERS DEPARTMENT OF THE TENNESSEE, }
> STEAMER DIANA (UNDER WEIGH), *March* 4, 1864.}

Major-General N. P. BANKS, *commanding Department of the Gulf,*
   New Orleans.

GENERAL: I had the honor to receive your letter of the 2d instant yesterday at New Orleans, but was unable to answer, except verbally, and I now reduce it to writing.

I will arrive at Vicksburg the 6th instant, and I expect to meet there my command from Canton, out of which I will select two divisions of about ten thousand men, embark them under a good commander, and order him:

1st. To rendezvous at the mouth of Red River, and, in concert with Admiral Porter (if he agree), to strike Harrisonburg a *hard* blow.

2d. To return to Red River and ascend it, aiming to reach Alexandria on the 17th of March, to report to you.

3d. That, as this command is designed to operate by water, it will not be encumbered with much land transportation, say two wagons to a regiment, but with an ample supply of stores, including mortars and heavy rifled guns, to be used against fortified places.

4th. That I have calculated, and so reported to General Grant, that this detachment of his forces in no event is to go beyond Shreveport, and that you will spare them the moment you can, trying to get them back to the Mississippi River in thirty days from the time they actually enter Red River.

The year is wearing away fast, and I would like to carry to General Grant at Huntsville, Alabama, every man of his military division, as early in April as possible, for I am sure we ought to move from the base of the Tennessee River to the south before the season is too far advanced, say as early as April 15th next.

I feel certain of your complete success, provided you make the concentration in time, to assure which I will see in person to the embarkation and dispatch of my quota, and I will write to General Steele, conveying to him my personal and professional opinion that the present opportunity is the most perfect one that will ever offer itself to him to clean out his enemies in Arkansas.

Wishing you all honor and success, I am, with respect, your friend and servant,

W. T. SHERMAN, *Major-General.*

HEADQUARTERS DEPARTMENT OF THE TENNESSEE, ⎫
VICKSBURG, *March* 6, 1864. ⎭

Brigadier-General A. J. SMITH, *commanding Expedition up Red River, Vicksburg, Mississippi.*

GENERAL: By an order this day issued, you are to command a strong, well-appointed detachment of the Army of the Tennessee, sent to reënforce a movement up Red River, but more especially against the fortified position at Shreveport.

You will embark your command as soon as possible, little encumbered with wagons or wheeled vehicles, but well supplied with fuel, provisions, and ammunition. Take with you the twelve mortars, with their ammunition, and all the thirty-pound Parrotts the ordnance-officer will supply. Proceed to the mouth of Red River and confer with Admiral Porter. Consult with him, and in all the expedition rely on him implicitly, as he is the approved friend of the Army of the Tennessee, and has been associated with us from the beginning. I have undertaken with General Banks that you will be at Alexandria, Louisiana, on or before the 17th day of March; and you will, if time allows, coöperate with the navy in destroying Harrisonburg, up Black River; but as I passed Red River yesterday I saw Admiral Porter, and he told me he had already sent an expedition to Harrisonburg, so that I suppose that part of the plan will be accomplished before you reach Red River; but, in any event, be careful to reach Alexandria about the 17th of March.

General Banks will start by land from Franklin, in the Têche country, either the 5th or 7th, and will march *via* Opelousas to Alexandria. You will meet him there, report to him, and act under his orders. My understanding with him is that his forces will move by land, *via* Natchitoches, to Shreveport, while the gunboat-fleet is to ascend the river with your transports in company. Red River is very low for the season, and I doubt if any of the boats can pass the falls or rapids at Alexandria. What General Banks proposes to do in that event I do not know; but my own judgment is that Shreveport ought not to be attacked until the gunboats can reach it. Not that a force marching by land cannot do it alone, but it would be bad economy in war to invest the place with an army so far from heavy guns, mortars, ammunition, and provisions, which can alone reach Shreveport by water. Still, I do not know about General Banks's plans in that event; and whatever they may be, your duty will be to conform, in the most hearty manner.

My understanding with General Banks is that he will not need the coöperation of your force beyond thirty days from the date you reach Red River. As soon as he has taken Shreveport, or as soon as he can spare you, return to Vicksburg with all dispatch, gather up your detachments, wagons, tents, transportation, and all property pertaining to so much of the command as belongs to the Sixteenth Army Corps, and conduct it to Memphis, where orders will await you. My present belief is your division, entire, will be needed with the Army of the Tennessee, about Huntsville or Bridgeport. Still, I will leave orders with General Hurlbut, at Memphis, for you on your return.

I believe if water will enable the gunboats to cross the rapids at Alexandria, you will be able to make a quick, strong, and effective blow at our enemy in the West, thus widening the belt of our territory, and making the breach between the Confederate Government and its outlying trans-Mississippi Department more perfect.

It is understood that General Steele makes a simultaneous move from Little Rock, on Shreveport or Natchitoches, with a force of about ten thousand men. Banks will have seventeen thousand, and you ten thousand. If these can act concentrically and simultaneously, you will make short work of it, and then General Banks will have enough force to hold as much of the Red River country as he deems wise, leaving you to bring to General Grant's main army the seven thousand five hundred men of the Sixteenth Corps now with you. Having faith in your sound judgment and experience, I confide this important and delicate command to you, with certainty that you will harmonize perfectly with Admiral Porter and General Banks, with whom you are to act, and thereby insure success.

I am, with respect, your obedient servant,
W. T. Sherman, *Major-General commanding.*

Headquarters Department of the Tennessee, }
Memphis, *March* 14, 1864. }

Major-General McPherson, *commanding, etc., Vicksburg, Mississippi.*

Dear General: I wrote you at length on the 11th, by a special bearer of dispatches, and now make special orders to cover the movements therein indicated. It was my purpose to await your answer, but I am summoned by General Grant to be in Nashville on the 17th, and it will keep me moving night and day to get there by that date. I must rely on you, for you understand that we *must* reënforce the great army at the centre (Chattanooga) as much as possible, at the same time not risking the safety of any point on the Mississippi which is fortified and armed with heavy guns. I want you to push matters as rapidly as possible, and to do all you can to put two handsome divisions of your own corps at Cairo, ready to embark up the Tennessee River by the 20th or 30th of April at the *very furthest.* I wish it could be done quicker; but the promise of these thirty-days furloughs in the States of enlistment, though politic, is very unmilitary. It deprives us of our ability to calculate as to time; but do the best you can. Hurlbut can do nothing till A. J. Smith returns from Red River. I will then order him to occupy Grenada temporarily, and to try and get those locomotives that we need here. I may also order him with cavalry and infantry to march toward Tuscaloosa, at the same time that we move from the Tennessee River about Chattanooga.

I don't know as yet the grand strategy of the next campaign, but on arrival at Nashville I will soon catch the main points, and will advise you of them.

Steal a furlough and run to Baltimore *incog.*; but get back in time to take part in the next grand move.

Write me fully and frequently of your progress. I have ordered the quartermaster to send down as many boats as he can get, to facilitate your movements. Mules, wagons, etc., can come up afterward by transient boats. I am truly your friend,

W. T. SHERMAN, *Major-General commanding.*

[Special Field Order No. 28.]

HEADQUARTERS DEPARTMENT OF THE TENNESSEE,⎫
MEMPHIS, TENN., *March* 14, 1864.   ⎭

1. Major-General McPherson will organize two good divisions of his corps (Seventeenth) of about five thousand men, each embracing in part the reënlisted veterans of his corps whose furloughs will expire in April, which he will command in person, and will rendezvous at Cairo, Illinois, and report by telegraph and letter to the general commanding at department headquarters, wherever they may be. These divisions will be provided with new arms and accoutrements, and land transportation (wagons and mules) out of the supplies now at Vicksburg, which will be conveyed to Cairo by or before April 15th.

.   .   .   .

4. During the absence of General McPherson from the district of Vicksburg, Major-General Hurlbut will exercise command over all the troops in the Department of the Tennessee from Cairo to Natchez, inclusive, and will receive special instructions from department headquarters.

By order of Major-General W. T. Sherman:

L. M. DAYTON, *Aide-de-Camp.*

Appendix to Volume I.

CHICKASAW BAYOU.

Report of Brigadier-General G. W. Morgan.

HEADQUARTERS THIRD DIVISION, RIGHT WING,
THIRTEENTH ARMY CORPS,
STEAMER EMPRESS, *January 3,* 1863.

Major J. H. HAMMOND, *Chief of Staff.*

SIR: On the 1st instant, while pressed by many arduous duties, I was requested to report to the commanding general the operations of my division during the affair of the 27th, the action of the 28th, and the battle of the 29th ult.

I had not received the report of subordinate commanders, nor had I time to review the report I have the honor to submit.

Herewith I have the honor to forward these reports, connected with which I will submit a few remarks.

Brigadier-General Blair speaks of having discovered, while on his retreat from the enemy's works, a broad and easy road running from the left of my position to the enemy's lines. The road is neither broad nor easy, and was advanced over by De Courcey when leading his brigade to the charge. The road General Blair speaks of is the one running from Lake's Landing and intersecting with the Vicksburg road on the Chickasaw Bluffs. Its existence was known to me on the 28th ult., but it was left open intentionally by the enemy, and was commanded by a direct and cross fire from batteries and rifle-pits. The withdrawal of his brigade from the assault by Colonel De Courcey was justified by the failure of the corps of A. J. Smith, and the command of Colonel Lindsey, to advance simultaneously to the assault. Both had the same difficulties to encounter—impassable bayous. The enemy's line of battle was concave, and De Courcey advanced against his centre—hence he sustained a concentric fire, and the withdrawal of Steele from the front of the enemy's right on the 28th ult. enabled the enemy on the following day to concentrate his right upon his centre.

I regret to find, from the report of Brigadier-General Thayer, some one regiment skulked; this I did not observe, nor is it mentioned by General Blair, though his were the troops which occupied that portion of the field. As far as my observation extended, the troops bore themselves nobly; but the Sixteenth Ohio Infantry was peerless on the field, as it had ever been in camp or on the march. Lieutenant-Colonel Kershner, commanding, was wounded and taken prisoner. He is an officer of rare merit, and deserves to command a brigade. Lieutenant-Colonel Dister, commanding the Fifty-eighth Ohio, was killed within the enemy's works; and Lieutenant-Colonel Monroe, Twenty-second Kentucky, was struck down at the head of his regiment.

I again express my profound acknowledgments to Brigadier-Generals Blair and Thayer, and Colonels De Courcey, Lindsey, and Sheldon, brigade commanders. Also to Major M. C. Garber, assistant quartermaster; Captain S. S. Lyon, acting topographical engineer; Lieutenant Burdick, acting ordnance officer; Lieutenant Hutchins, acting chief of staff; Lieutenants H. G. Fisher and Smith, of Signal Corps; Lieutenant E. D. Saunders, my acting assistant adjutant-general; and Lieutenants English and Montgomery, acting aides-de-camp, for the efficient services rendered me.

Nor can I close this report without speaking in terms of high praise of the meritorious and gallant services of Captains Foster and Lamphier. Their batteries silenced several of the enemy's works, and throughout the operations rendered good service. My sincere acknowledgments are also due to Captain Griffith, commanding First Iowa Battery, and Captain Hoffman, commanding Fourth Ohio Battery.

I am, sir, very respectfully, your obedient servant,
GEORGE W. MORGAN, *Brigadier-General Volunteers.*

CINCINNATI, *February* 3, 1876.
MY DEAR GENERAL: Regarding the attack at Chickasaw Bayou, my record shows the position of Steele on the left; Morgan to his right; Morgan L. Smith to his right, and A. J. Smith on the extreme right; the latter not expected to accomplish much more than a diversion, the result to come from the three other divisions, Morgan having the best opportunity. Saturday night they were in position; you were at Lake's plantation, right and rear of Morgan.

The attack for lodgment on the hills was ordered for Sunday morning, December 28th. I was sent to A. J. Smith before daylight, and returned to you soon after. You were with Morgan. You had fully explained to him the importance of *his* success, and that he should be *present* with the attacking column, which was to be a part of his division, supported by the remainder, and by Blair's brigade of Steele's division coöperating. The attack was to be simultaneous, by the four divisions, on a signal.

Morgan's answer to you was that, when the signal was given, he would *lead* his attack, and with his life he would be on the bluffs in fifteen minutes. He seemed of positive knowledge, and as sure of success. You then retired to a central point, to be in easy communi-

cation with Steele and Morgan L. Smith. The attack was made, and
developed, in the case of Steele, M. L. Smith, and A. J. Smith, that
to cross the bayou was impossible, if opposed by any force, and in
each they were by a strong one. Morgan's attacking force succeeded
in getting across the causeway and marsh, but he did *not* go with it,
nor *support* it with more men, and a large number were captured
from Blair's brigade *after* gaining the enemy's last line of works
covering the bayou. At the time everybody blamed and criticised
Morgan with the failure. You felt from the advance of his attack it
must be successful, and, as it pushed forward, you sent me to urge
on M. L. Smith, as Morgan was over, and he, Smith, must aid by
persistent attack, and give Morgan as good a chance as could be to
make his lodgment. . . .

I am, etc.,   L. M. Dayton,
Late Colonel of the Staff, now of Cincinnati, Ohio.
General W. T. Sherman, *St. Louis, Missouri.*

[Copy.]

". . . . The expedition was wonderfully well provided with provisions, transportation, and munitions, and even axes, picks, and shov-
els, so much in use later in the war, evidenced the forethought that
governed this force. The boats, from their open lower deck construction, proved admirable for transports, but their tinder-box construction made fire-traps of them, requiring unremitting vigilance. These
points were well understood, and the readiness with which the
troops adapted themselves to circumstances was a constant source of
wonder and congratulations.

"The fleet collected at Friar's Point for final orders, and there the
order of sailing was laid down with great minuteness, and private
instructions issued to commanders of divisions, all of whom had
personal interviews with the commanding general, and received
personal explanations on pretty much every point involved. Our
headquarters boat, the Forest Queen, was not very comfortable, nor
well provided, but General Sherman submitted cheerfully, on the
grounds of duty, and thought Conway a fine fellow. I was only able
to concede that he was a good steamboat captain. . . .

"Our camp appointments were Spartan in the extreme, and in
their simplicity would have met the demands of any demagogue in
the land. The nights were cold and damp, and General Sherman
uncomfortably active in his preparations, so that the assistant
adjutant-general had no very luxurious post just then. We were surrounded with sloughs. The ground was wet, and the water, although
in winter, was very unwholesome. Many of our men, to this day,
have reminders of the Yazoo in ague, fevers, and diseases of the

bowels. Cavalry was useless. One battalion of Illinois cavalry was strongly suspected of camping in the timber, until time passed enough to justify the suspicion of having been somewhere. Really the strength of Vicksburg was in being out of reach of attack. . . .

"My orders were to learn and report what was going on on the right, particularly to try and form an idea of the enemy's force in front of M. L. Smith's division, and at the sand-bar. Leaving my horse close in the rear of the Sixth Missouri, when the fire became too heavy for riding, I succeeded, by taking frequent cover, in reaching unhurt the verge of the bayou among the drift-logs. There, by concert of action with Lieutenant-Colonel Blood, of the Sixth Missouri, his regiment, and the Thirteenth Regular Infantry, kept up a heavy fire on everything that showed along the levee and earthworks in front. The enemy were behind the embankment, not over one hundred and fifty yards across the bayou. Several officers, including Colonel Blood, Colonel Kilby Smith, and myself, managed, by getting on the piles of drift, to see over the levee through the cleared fields beyond, even to the foot of the bluff. The chips and twigs flew around lively enough, but we staid up long enough to make sure that the enemy had as many men behind the levee as could get cover. We saw, also, a line of rifle-pits in the rear, commanding the rear of the levee, and still beyond, winding along the foot of the bluff, a road worn by long use deep into the side-hill, and with the side next us strengthened with a good earthwork, affording a covered line of communication in the rear. The fire of our men was so well maintained that we were able to see all these things, say a minute or more. Some of those who ventured were wounded, but those mentioned and myself escaped unhurt. I advised that men enough to hold the position, once across—say three hundred—should make a rush (protected as our lookout had been by a heavy fire) across the sand-bar, and get a footing under the other bank of the bayou, as the nucleus of an attacking force, if General Sherman decided to attack there, or to make a strong diversion if the attack was made at the head of Chickasaw Bayou, in front of Morgan. General A. J. Smith, commanding First and Second Divisions, approved of this. While returning to General Sherman, I passed along the Second and part of the Third Division. On the left of the Second I found a new Illinois regiment, high up in numbers, working its way into position. The colonel, a brave but inexperienced officer, was trying to lead his men according to the popular pictorial idea, viz., riding in advance waving his sword. I was leading my horse, and taking advantage of such cover as I could find on my course, but this man acted so bravely that I tried to save him. He did not accept my expostulations with very good grace, but was not rough about it. While I was begging him to dismount, he waved his sword and advanced. In a second he was shot through the chest, and dropped from his horse, plucky to the last. He died, I was told, within the hour.* Many of the regiments were new and inexperienced, but as a rule behaved well. The fire along the bayou was severe, but not very fatal, on account of the cover. I was constantly asked what news from Grant, for from the moment of our arrival in the Yazoo we were in expectation of either hearing his guns in the rear, or of having communication with him. This encouraged the men greatly, but the long waiting was disappointing, as the enemy was evidently in large force in the plenty of works, and a very strong position. Careful estimates and available information placed their force at fifteen to twenty thousand men. I returned to headquarters about the middle of the afternoon, and made my report to the general. We were busy till after midnight, and again early in the morning of the 29th, in preparing orders for the attack. These were unusually minute in detail. It seemed as though no contingency was left unprovided for. Urgent orders and cautions as to rations and ammunition were given. Drawings of the line of attack, orders for supports, all and everything was foreseen and given in writing, with personal explanations to commanders of divisions, brigades, and even commanders of regiments. Indeed, the commanding general, always careful as to detail, left nothing to chance, and with experienced and ordinate officers we would have succeeded, for the troops were good. The general plan involved a feint on our left toward Haines's Bluff, by the navy, under Admiral Porter, with whom we were in constant communication, while between him and General Sherman perfect harmony existed. On the right a demonstration by A. J. Smith was to be made. The Second Division (Stuart's) was to cross the sand-bar, and the Third (General Morgan's) was to cross on a small bridge over the slough at the head of Chickasaw Bayou, and, supported by Steele, was to push straight for the Bluff at the nearest spur where there was a battery in position, and to effect a lodgment there and in the earthworks. General Sherman gave his orders in person to Morgan and Steele. I understood Morgan to promise that he would lead his division in person, and he seemed to expect an easy victory, and expressed himself freely to that effect. The aides were sent out, until I was left alone with the general and a couple of orderlies. He located himself in a position easy of access, and the most convenient afforded to the point of attack. He directed me to see what I could, and report if I met any-

---

*Colonel Wyman, Thirteenth Illinois Infantry.

thing that he should know. I galloped as fast as possible to the right, and found part of the Sixth Missouri pushing over the sand-bar covered by the Thirteenth Regulars with a heavy fire. We supposed, if once across, they could get up the bank and turn the levee against the enemy, and left with that impression. Being in heavy timber, I was not quite sure of my way back to the general, his location being new, and therefore pushed full gallop for Morgan's front, catching a good many stray shots from the sharp-shooters behind the levee, as I was compelled to keep in sight of the bayou to hold direction. Something over half-way along Morgan's division front, the commander of a Kentucky regiment hailed me and said he must have support, as he was threatened by a masked battery, and the enemy was in force in his front, and might cross any moment. I answered, rather shortly: 'How the devil do you know there is a masked battery? If you can't get over, how can the rebels get at you?' He insisted on the battery, and danger. I finally told him the bayou was utterly impassable there, but, if he insisted the enemy could cross, I would insist on an advance on our side at that point. Hurrying on to make up lost time, I soon reached Morgan. He was making encouraging speeches in a general way, but stopped to ask me questions as to Steele's rank, date of commission, etc. I was very much disturbed at this, fearing want of harmony, and rode on to Steele, whom I found cursing Morgan so fiercely that I could not exactly make out the source of the trouble, or reason why; but saw want of concert clearly enough. I hastened back to General Sherman, and endeavored to impress my ideas on him and my fears; but, while he admitted the facts, he could not be made to believe that any jealousy or personal quarrel could lead to a failure to support each other, and a neglect of duty. The signal for attack had already been given, and the artillery had opened, when I left him again for Morgan's front. I found Morgan where I left him, and the troops advancing. I had understood that he was to lead his division, and asked about it, but, getting no satisfaction, pushed for the front, crossing the slough at the little bridge at the head of the bayou. I found the willows cut off eighteen inches or two feet long, with sharp points above the mud, making it slow and difficult to pass, save at the bridge. I overtook the rear of the advance about two or three hundred feet up the gentle slope, and was astonished to find how small a force was making the attack. I was also surprised to find that they were Steele's men instead of Morgan's. I also saw several regiments across the bayou, but not advancing; they were near the levee. A heavy artillery and infantry fire was going on all this time. While making my way along the column, from which there were very few falling back, a shell burst

near me, and the concussion confused me at the time and left me
with a headache for several months. When I got my wits about me
again I found a good many coming back, but the main part of the
force was compact and keeping up the fight. I did not get closer to
the woods than about five hundred feet, and found that a large number had penetrated into the enemy's works. When our men fell back,
very few ran, but came slowly and sullenly, far more angry than
frightened. I found General Frank Blair on foot, and with him Colonel Sea, of Southwest Missouri, and learned that Colonel Thomas
Fletcher, afterward Governor of Missouri, was captured with many
of his men. They both insisted there on the spot, with those around
us, that if all the men ordered up had gone up, or even all that
crossed the bayou had moved forward, we could have readily established ourselves in the enemy's works. I was firmly of the same opinion at the time on the ground; and, an entrance effected, we could
have brought the whole force on dry ground, and had a base of
operations against Vicksburg—though probably, in view of later
events, we would have had to stand a siege from Pemberton's army.
After explanations with Blair, I rode to where the men were, who
had crossed the bayou, but had not advanced with the others. I
found them to be De Courcey's brigade, of Morgan's division,
which General Sherman supposed to be in advance. In fact, it was
the intended support that made the attack. A correspondence and
controversy followed between General Blair and Colonel De
Courcey, most of which I have, but nothing came of it. On reaching
the bayou, I found that Thayer's brigade, of Steele's division, had in
some way lost its direction and filed off to the right. Remembering
the 'masked battery,' I suspected that had something to do with the
matter, and, on following it up, I learned that the Kentucky colonel
before mentioned had appealed for aid against the masked battery
and invisible force of rebels, and that a regiment had been ordered to
him. This regiment, filing off into the timber, had been followed by
Thayer's brigade, supposing it to be advancing to the front, and thus
left a single brigade to attack a superior force of the enemy in an
intrenched and naturally strong position. By the time the mistake
could be rectified, it was too late. Our loss was from one hundred
and fifty to two hundred killed, and about seven hundred prisoners
and wounded. During the afternoon I went with a flag of truce, with
reference to burying the dead. I saw between eighty and one hundred of our men dead, all *stripped*. There were others closer into the
enemy's works than I was allowed to go. On going later to where
the Sixth Missouri crossed, I found that they were under the bank,
and had dug in with their hands and bayonets, or anything in reach,

to protect themselves from a vertical fire from the enemy overhead, who had a heavy force there. With great difficulty they were withdrawn at night. Next day arrangements were made to attempt a lodgment below Haines's Bluff. This was to be done by Steele's command, while the rest of the force attacked again where we had already tried. During the day locomotives whistled, and a great noise and fuss went on in our front, and we supposed that Grant was driving in Pemberton, and expected firing any moment up the Yazoo or in the rear of Vicksburg. Not hearing this, we concluded that Pemberton was throwing his forces into Vicksburg. A heavy fog prevented Steele from making his movement. Rain began to fall, and our location was not good to be in after a heavy rain, or with the river rising. During the night (I think) of January 1, 1863, our troops were embarked, material and provisions having been loaded during the day. A short time before daylight of the 2d, I went, by order of the general commanding, to our picket lines and carefully examined the enemy's lines, wherever a camp-fire indicated their presence. They were not very vigilant, and I once got close enough to hear them talk, but could understand nothing. Early in the morning I came in with the rear-guard, the enemy advancing his pickets and main guards only, and making no effort at all to press us. Once I couldn't resist the temptation to fire into a squad that came bolder than the rest, and the two shots were good ones. We received a volley in return that did come very close among us, but hurt none of my party. Very soon after our rear-guard was aboard, General Sherman learned from Admiral Porter that McClernand had arrived at the mouth of the Yazoo. He went, taking me and one other staff-officer, to see McClernand, and found that, under an order from the President, he had taken command of the Army of the Mississippi. He and his staff, of whom I only remember two— Colonels Scates and Braham, assistant adjutant-general and aide-de-camp—seemed to think they had a big thing, and, so far as I could judge, they had just that. All hands thought the country expected them to cut their way to the Gulf; and to us, who had just come out of the swamp, the cutting didn't seem such an easy job as to the new-comers. Making due allowance for the elevation they seemed to feel in view of their job, everything passed off pleasantly, and we learned that General Grant's communications had been cut at Holly Springs by the capture of Murphy and his force (at Holly Springs), and that he was either in Memphis by that time or would soon be. So that, everything considered, it was about as well that we did not get our forces on the bluffs of Walnut Hill."

The above statement was sent to General Sherman in a letter dated "Chicago, February 5, 1876," and signed "John H. Hammond." Hammond* was General Sherman's assistant adjutant-general at the Chickasaw Bayou.

J. E. TOURTELOTTE, *Colonel and Aide-de-Camp.*

On 29th December, 1862, at Chickasaw Bayou, I was in command of the Thirty-first Missouri Volunteer Infantry, First Brigade, First Division, Fifteenth Army Corps (Blair's brigade). Colonel Wyman, of the Thirteenth Illinois Volunteer Infantry, having been killed, I was the senior colonel of the brigade. General Blair rode up to where my regiment lay, and said to me: "We are to make a charge here; we will charge in two lines; your regiment will be in the first line, and the Twenty-ninth (Cavender's) will support you. Form here in the timber, and move out across the bayou on a double-quick, and go right on to the top of the heights in your front." He then told me to await a signal. I then attempted to make a reconnaissance of the ground over which we would have to charge, and rode out to the open ground in my front, and saw that there was water and soft mud in the bayou, and was fired upon by the sharp-shooters of the enemy, and turned and went back into the woods where my command lay. Soon after that General Blair came near me, and I told him there was water and mud in the bayou, and I doubted if we could get across. He answered me that General Morgan told him there was no water nor mud to hinder us. I remarked that I had seen it myself, and General Morgan, or any one else, could see it if he would risk being shot at pretty lively. I then told General Blair that it was certain destruction to us if we passed over the abatis upon the open ground where there had once been a corn-field; that we could never reach the base of the hill. He turned to me and said, "Can't you take your regiment up there?" I told him, "Yes, I can take my regiment anywhere, because the men do not know any better than to go," but remarked that old soldiers could not be got to go up there. General Blair then said: "Tom, if we succeed, this will be a grand thing; you will have the glory of leading the assault." He then went on to say that General Morgan's division would support us, and they were heroes of many battles, and pointed to the Fifty-eighth Ohio, then forming in the rear of the Thirteenth Illinois on my right, and said: "See these men? They are a part of Morgan's division, and are heroes of many battles." I laughingly said that they might be heroes, but the regiment did not number as many as one of my companies. He again

---

*Still living.

assured me we would be supported by Morgan's division, and all I had to do was to keep right on and "keep going till you get into Vicksburg." I took my position in advance of my regiment and awaited the signal. When we heard it, we raised a shout, and started at a double-quick, the Thirteenth Illinois on my right. I saw no troops on my left. When we emerged from the woods, the enemy opened upon us; crossing the bayou under fire, and many of the men sinking in the mud and water, our line was very much disordered, but we pretty well restored it before reaching the abatis. Here we were greatly disordered, but somewhat restored the line on reaching the plateau or corn-field. The Twenty-ninth Missouri came on, gallantly supporting us. The Thirteenth Illinois came out upon the corn-field, and the Fifty-eighth Ohio followed close upon it. There was firing to my left, and as I afterward learned was from the Fourth Iowa of Thayer's brigade (and I believe of Steele's division). I was struck and fell, and my regiment went back in great disorder. The fire was terrific. I saw beyond the Thirteenth Illinois, to my right, a disordered line, and learned afterward it was the Sixteenth Ohio. When I was taken from the field by the enemy and taken into Vicksburg, I found among the wounded and prisoners men and officers of the Sixteenth and Fifty-eighth Ohio, and of the Twenty-ninth and Thirty-first Missouri, and Thirteenth Illinois. After I was exchanged and joined my command, General Blair laughingly remarked to me that I had literally obeyed his order and gone "straight on to Vicksburg." He lamented the cutting to pieces of our force on that day. We talked the whole matter over at his headquarters during the siege of Vicksburg. He said that if the charge had been made along our whole line with the same vigor of attack made by his brigade, and if we had been supported as Morgan promised to do, we might have succeeded. I dissented from the opinion that we could even then have succeeded. I asked him what excuse Morgan gave for failing to support us, and he said that Colonel or General De Courcey was in some manner to blame for that, but he said Morgan was mistaken as to the nature of the ground and generally as to the feasibility of the whole thing, and was responsible for the failure to afford us the support he had promised; that he and General Sherman and all of them were misled by the statements and opinions of Morgan as to the situation in our front, and Morgan was, on his part, deceived by the reports of his scouts about other matters as well as the matter of the water in the bayou.

THOMAS C. FLETCHER.

ARKANSAS POST.

Extracts from Admiral Porter's Journal.

SHERMAN and I had made arrangements to capture Arkansas Post.

On the 31st of December, while preparing to go out of the Yazoo, an army officer called to see me, and said that he belonged to General McClernand's staff, and that the general was at the mouth of the Yazoo River, and desired to see me at once. I sent word to the general that if he wished to see me he could have an opportunity by calling on board my flag-ship.

A few moments after I had heard the news of McClernand's arrival, I saw Sherman pulling about in a boat, and hailed him, informing him that McClernand was at the mouth of the Yazoo. Sherman then came on board, and, in consequence of this unexpected news, determined to postpone the movement out of the Yazoo River, and let McClernand take that upon himself.

General McClernand took my hint and came on board the flag-ship, but I soon discovered that any admiral, Grant, Sherman, or all the generals in the army, were nobody in his estimation. Sherman had been at McClernand's headquarters to see him and state the condition of affairs, and *he then suggested to the latter the plan of going to Arkansas Post.*

I had a number of fine maps hanging up in my cabin, and when McClernand came on board he examined them all with the eye of a connoisseur. He then stated to me as a new thing the plan *he proposed* (*!*) of going to Arkansas Post and stirring up our troops, which had been "demoralized by the *late defeat*" (Sherman was present, looking daggers at him). I answered, "Yes, General Sherman and myself have already arranged for going to Arkansas Post." Sherman then made some remark about the disposition of the troops in the coming expedition, when McClernand gave him rather a curt answer. McClernand then remarked, "If you will let me have three gunboats, I will go and take the place." Now General McClernand had about as much idea of what a gunboat was, or could do, as the man in the moon. He did not know the difference between an ironclad and a "tinclad." He had heard that gunboats had taken Fort Henry, and that was all he knew about them. I said to him: "I'll tell you what I will do, General McClernand. If General Sherman goes in command of the troops, I will go myself in command of a proper force, and will insure the capture of the post." McClernand winced under this, and Sherman quietly walked off into the after-cabin. He beckoned me to come there, while McClernand was apparently deeply engaged in studying out a chart, making believe he was interested, in order to conceal his temper. Sherman said to me: "Admiral, how could you make such a remark to McClernand? He hates me already, and you have made him an enemy for life."

"I don't care," said I; "he shall not treat you rudely in my cabin, and I was glad of the opportunity of letting him know my sentiments." By this time, General McClernand having bottled up his wrath, or cooled down, I went in to him and we discussed the matter. He consented that Sherman should go in command of the troops, and the interview ended pleasantly enough.

The above extracts from Admiral Porter's journal were sent by the admiral to General Sherman, inclosed in a letter dated "Washington, May 29, 1875," and signed "David D. Porter."

J. E. TOURTELOTTE.

After leaving the Yazoo, the Army of the Mississippi rendezvous was at Milliken's Bend. During the night of January 4th or 5th, General McClernand came on board the Forest Queen, and with General Sherman went to the Black Hawk flag-boat. There an interview took place, during which the expedition to Arkansas Post took shape. General Sherman having asked leave to take the post, and Admiral Porter having decided to go along, McClernand thought best to go with his entire army, although the enemy were supposed to have only about four or five thousand men, and the fort was little more than a large earthwork commanding the river.

General Sherman's command was then entitled the Second Corps, Army of the Mississippi, and was comprised of the First Division, Blair's, Hovey's, and Thayer's brigades, commanded by Steele; and the Second Division, commanded by David Stuart, with Colonels Giles A. and Kilby Smith commanding brigades.

Our fleet was convoyed by three ironclads and several other gunboats. The weather was bitterly cold for that latitude; we were four days getting into the Arkansas River, which we entered by the White River cut-off; and my recollection is, that our passing the mouth of the main river deceived the enemy as to our destination. The entrance through the cut-off was feasible by reason of high water, and I think made our appearance a surprise to the force at the post. We disembarked on the morning of the 10th of January. Stuart's division first encountered the enemy behind an earthwork about four miles from the fort, running across the solid ground from the river to a swamp. General Sherman in person took Steele's division, and followed a road leading to the rear of the earthwork just mentioned. We had got fairly under way when the rebels fell back to the fort, and McClernand, coming up, ordered us to fall back, and march up the river. It seemed to me then, and afterward, that it would have been better to have marched straight to the rear of the fort, as we started to do. We soon overtook Stuart and closed in, General Sherman on the right, Morgan's force on the left, reaching to the river, where the gunboats were, while Sherman reached from the road which connected the post with the back country, toward where the earthworks reached the river above the fort, and threatened their communications with Little Rock. The night was cold and cloudy, with some snow. There were a good many abandoned huts to our rear, but our forces in position lay on the frozen ground, sheltered as best they could, among the bushes and timber. We were so close that they could have reached us any time during the night with light artillery. The gunboats threw heavy shells into the fort and behind the earthworks all night, keeping the enemy awake and anxious. The heavy boom of the artillery was followed by the squeak, squeak of Admiral Porter's little tug, as he moved around making his arrangements for the morrow. The sounds were ridiculous by comparison. General Sherman and staff lay on the roots of an old oak-tree, that kept them partly clear of mud. The cold was sharp, my right boot being frozen solid in a puddle in the morning. About half-past two or three o'clock, General Sherman, with another and myself, crept in as close as possible and reconnoitred the position. The general managed to creep in much closer than the rest of us—in fact, so close as to cause us anxiety. The enemy worked hard all night on their abatis and intrenchments, and in the morning we found a ditch and parapet running clear across the point on which the post was situated. This point was cut by a road from the back country, across which was a heavy earthwork and a battery. This road was at the extremity of our left. General McClernand kept his headquarters on his boat, the Tigress. He came up in the morning to a place in the woods in our rear. One of his staff, a cavalry-officer, climbed a tree to report movements; but from that point there was very little to be seen. Between ten and eleven o'clock the fire opened from the fleet, and we opened along the whole line from infantry and field-guns. Our men soon worked in close enough to keep down the fire of the enemy to a very marked degree.

. . . .

After reporting to General Sherman, and while explaining the position of the fleet, the smoke-stacks and flags appeared above the fort. What firing was going on in our immediate front ceased. A good many rebels were in plain sight, running away from the fort and scattering. While we were still surprised, the cry was raised that a white flag was hung out. I did not see it, but in a few minutes saw others along the line, and just as the general started for the fort I saw the flag not far from the white house, near the parapet. Orders were given to cease firing. Captain Dayton was sent to the fort where the first flag was raised. Some shots were fired and some men hurt after this. The first rebel officer we encountered was Colonel or General Garland, commanding brigade, who was ordered to put his men in line and stack arms, which was done. I was directed to pass along the line to the right, and cause the prisoners to stack arms and form our men in line, just outside the work. This I did till I reached Deshler's brigade, on our extreme right, or nearly so, and who was opposed to the right of Steele's force. Steele's men had rushed up to the very foot of the parapet, and some were on it, though they did not fire. The commander of the enemy (Deshler) refused to obey my orders to stack arms, and asked a good many questions as to "how it happened;" said he was not whipped, but held us in check, etc. I told him there were eight or nine thousand men right there, that a shot from me, or a call, would bring down on him, and that we had entire possession of the place. After sending two officers from the nearest troops to explain the condition to Steele, and to warn every officer they met to pass the word for everybody to be on the sharp lookout, I arranged with Deshler to keep quiet until I could bring his own commander, or orders from him. Returning to General Sherman, I found a party of young rebel officers, including Robert Johnston's son (rebel Senate) and Captain Wolf, quartermaster, of New Orleans, who declined to surrender except to gentlemen. Some German Missouri soldiers didn't relish the distinction, and were about clubbing them over the head, when I interfered and received their surrender. Hurrying back to the general, I reported the dangerous condition of things. He and General Churchill, commanding officer of the enemy, started for Deshler's brigade; meeting Garland, a quarrel and some recrimination followed between him and Churchill, as to where the fault of the surrender belonged, which was rather promptly silenced by General Sherman, who hurried to the scene of trouble. There, after some ill-natured talk, Deshler ordered his men to lay down their arms. I rode into the fort, and found the parapet badly torn up by the fire from the fleet. On going to the embrasure where I had seen the gun while on the river-bank talking to Captain Shirk, the piece was found split back about eighteen inches, and the lower half of the muzzle dropped out. A battered but unexploded shell lying with the piece explained that it must have struck the gun in the muzzle, almost squarely. On passing along the inside I saw from the torn condition of the earthworks

how tremendous our fire was, and how the fire of the enemy was
kept down. The fire of the navy had partly torn down the side of the
fort next the river. A good many sailors were in the fort. General
A. J. Smith, Admiral Porter, and General Burbridge were there—all
in high spirits, but in some contention as to who got in first. Toward
dark, or nearly so, an Arkansas regiment came in as reënforcements,
but surrendered without any trouble. About the same time General
Sherman received orders to put General A. J. Smith in charge of the
fort, and stay outside with his men. As his troops were nearly all
inside, and had four-fifths of the prisoners in charge, these orders
were not very clear, and the general left for headquarters to find out
what was meant. I went on collecting arms, and as our men were
scattering a good deal and were greatly excited, I took the precaution
to pass along the line and march the prisoners far enough from the
stacked arms to be out of temptation. I was especially urged to
this by hearing several rebel officers speak of their guns being still
loaded. It was dark before all the prisoners were collected and under
guard, including the regiment that arrived after the fight. I am confident that all the prisoners were under guard by General Sherman's
troops.

Everything being secure, the staff-officers, all of whom had been
busily engaged, scattered to compare notes and enjoy the victory. I
found my way on board the Tigress, where every one was greatly
excited, and in high feather regarding our victory, the biggest thing
since Donelson. I also obtained some food and small comforts for a
few rebel officers, including young Johnston, Wolfe, and the Colonel
Deshler already mentioned. Then hunted up General Sherman,
whom I found sitting on a cracker-box in the white house already
mentioned, near where the white flag first appeared. Garland was
with him, and slept with him that night, while the rest of us laid
around wherever we could. It was a gloomy, bloody house, and suggestive of war. Garland was blamed by the other Confederate officers
for the white flag, and remained with us for safety. Next day was
very cold. We worked hard at the lists of prisoners—nearly five
thousand in number—all of whom were sent to St. Louis, in charge
of our inspector-general, Major Sanger. Our loss was less than one
hundred. The enemy, although behind intrenchments, lost more
than double what we did. Their wounded were much worse hurt
than ours, who were mostly hit around the head and arms.

The losses were nearly all in General Sherman's wing of the army.
The loss in the fleet amounted to little, but their service was very
valuable, and deserved great credit, though they received little. There
was a good deal of sympathy between our part of the forces and the

fleet people, and I then thought, and still think, if we had been on the left next the river, that in connection with the tremendous fire from the navy, we could have carried the work in an hour after we opened on it. Their missiles traversed the whole fortification, clear through to the hospitals at the upper end, and I stood five minutes in rifle-range of the fort next the river—not hit, and but seldom shot at, and no one hit near me.

On the 13th we embarked, in a snow-storm; collected at Napoleon, which seemed to be washing away; and then steamed to Milliken's Bend, where we arrived on January 21st, and soon after went to Young's plantation, near Vicksburg.

The above statement from General Hammond was received by General Sherman, inclosed in a letter dated "Chicago, February 5, 1876," and signed "John H. Hammond," who was adjutant-general to General Sherman during the winter of 1862–'63.

J. E. TOURTELOTTE.

CINCINNATI, February 3, 1876.

MY DEAR GENERAL: At Arkansas Post the troops debarked from steamer January 9th, from one o'clock to dark, in the vicinity of Notrib's farm, and on the 10th moved out to get position; Steele to the right, crossing the low ground to the north, to get a higher ground, avoid crowding the moving columns, and gain the left (our right) and rear of the "post," and the river-bank above the post. Stuart took the river-road—the movement commencing at 11 o'clock A.M. After crossing the low ground covered with water, you were called back with Steele, as Stuart had driven out the enemy's rifle-trench pickets, this giving more and feasible room for moving. Stuart was pushed forward, and by dark he and Steele were well up to their expected positions. Before daylight on the 11th you directed me to accompany you for a personal inspection of the ground to your front, which we made on foot, going so far forward that we could easily hear the enemy at work and moving about. Discovering the open fields, you at once directed Steele to move to the right and front, and pushed Stuart out so as to fully command them and the field-work of the enemy extending from the fort, to prevent further strengthening, as it was evident these works were the product of a recent thought. Stuart and Steele were prompt in taking position, but Morgan's command (not under your control) did not seem to work up, or keep in junction with you. At ten o'clock you sent me to McClernand to ascertain why the delay of attack. He attributed it to Admiral Porter, which was really unjust. The attack began at 1 P.M. by Admiral Porter, and the sound of his first gun had not died till your men were engaged—Wood's, Barrett's, and the Parrott batteries and infantry. It was lively for a time, and Stuart pushed clear up to the enemy's rifle-trenches, and forced them to keep sheltered. Hammond was mostly with Steele; Sanger sent to McClernand, and McCoy, myself, and John Taylor were with you and Stuart. At about half-past three I got your permission to go to Giles Smith's skirmish-line, and, thinking I saw evidence of the enemy weakening, I hurried back to you and reported my observations. I was so confident that a demand for it would bring a surrender, that I *asked permission* to make it, and, as you granted me, but refused to let another member of your staff, at his request, go with me, I rode directly down the road with only an orderly. Colonel Garland, commanding a brigade, was the first officer I saw, to whom, for you, I made the demand. All firing ceased at once, or in a few moments. I sent the orderly back to you, and you rode forward. It was then four o'clock.

During the attack, nobody seemed to think McClernand had any clear idea of what or how it was to be done. During the day he gave you no directions, nor came where you were; he was well to the rear, with his "man up a tree," who in the capacity of a lookout gave McClernand information, *from which* he based such instructions as he made to his subordinates. He was free to express himself as being a man of "destiny," and his "star" was in the ascendance. I am, etc.,

L. M. DAYTON, *late Colonel of the Staff,*
now of Cincinnati, Ohio.

General W. T. SHERMAN.

MERIDIAN CAMPAIGN.

[Special Field Orders, No. 11.]

HEADQUARTERS DEPARTMENT OF THE TENNESSEE, ⎱
MEMPHIS, *January* 27, 1864 ⎰

.   .   .   .

V. The expedition is one of celerity, and all things must tend to that. Corps commanders and staff-officers will see that our movements are not encumbered by wheeled vehicles improperly loaded. Not a tent, from the commander-in-chief down, will be carried. The sick will be left behind, and the surgeons can find houses and sheds for all hospital purposes.

VI. All the cavalry in this department is placed under the orders and command of Brigadier-General W. S. Smith, who will receive special instructions.

.   .   .   .

By order of Major-General W. T. Sherman:

L. M. DAYTON, *Aide-de-Camp*.

NOTE.—That same evening I started in a steamboat for Vicksburg.

W. T. S.

ST. LOUIS, 1885.

HEADQUARTERS DEPARTMENT OF THE TENNESSEE, ⎫
MEMPHIS, *January* 27, 1864. ⎰

Brigadier-General W. S. SMITH, *commanding Cavalry, etc., present.*

DEAR GENERAL: By an order issued this day I have placed all the cavalry of this department subject to your command. I estimate you can make a force of full seven thousand men, which I believe to be superior and better in all respects than the combined cavalry which the enemy has in all the State of Mississippi. I will in person start for Vicksburg to-day, and with four divisions of infantry, artillery, and cavalry move out for Jackson, Brandon, and Meridian, aiming to reach the latter place by February 10th. General Banks will feign on Pascagoula and General Logan on Rome. I want you with your cavalry to move from Colliersville on Pontotoc and Okolona; thence sweeping down near the Mobile & Ohio Railroad, disable that road as much as possible, consume or destroy the resources of the enemy along that road, break up the connection with Columbus, Mississippi, and finally reach me at or near Meridian as near the date I have mentioned as possible. This will call for great energy of action on your part, but I believe you are equal to it, and you have the best and most experienced troops in the service, and they will do anything that is possible. General Grierson is with you, and is familiar with the whole country. I will send up from Haines's Bluff an expedition of gunboats and transports combined, to feel up the Yazoo as far as the present water will permit. This will disconcert the enemy. My movement on Jackson will also divide the enemy, so that by no combination can he reach you with but a part of his force. I wish you to attack any force of cavalry you meet and follow them southward, but in no event be drawn into the forks of the streams that make up the Yazoo nor over into Alabama. Do not let the enemy draw you into minor affairs, but look solely to the greater object to destroy his communication from Okolona to Meridian, and thence eastward to Selma. From Okolona south you will find abundance of forage collected along the railroad, and the farmers have corn standing in the fields. Take liberally of all these, as well as horses, mules, cattle, etc. As a rule, respect dwellings and families as something too sacred to be disturbed by soldiers, but mills, barns, sheds, stables, and such like things use for the benefit or convenience of your command. If convenient, send into Columbus, Mississippi, and destroy all machinery there, and the bridge across the Tombigbee, which enables the enemy to draw the resources of the east side of the valley, but this is not of sufficient importance to delay your movement. Try and communicate with me by scouts and spies from the time you reach Pontotoc. Avoid any large force of infantry, leaving them to me. We have talked over this matter so much that the above covers all points not provided for in my published orders of to-day. I am, etc.,

W. T. SHERMAN, *Major-General, commanding.*

MEMPHIS, TENNESSEE, *January* 27, 1864.
Brigadier-General J. P. HATCH, *in charge of Cavalry Bureau,*
   St. Louis, Missouri.

SIR: Your favor of the 21st inst. is just received. Up to the present time eight hundred and eighteen horses have arrived here since Captain Hudson's visit to St. Louis. I wrote you upon his return several days ago that it would not be necessary to divert shipments to this point which could not reach us before February 1st. We shall certainly get off on our contemplated expedition before that time. The number of horses estimated for in this department by its chief quartermaster was two thousand, and this number, including those already sent, will, I think, completely mount all the dismounted cavalry of this department. Recruits for cavalry regiments are arriving freely, and this will swell our requisitions for a couple of months to come. I will as far as possible procure horses from the regions of country traversed by our cavalry.

.   .   .   .

Yours truly,
W. SOOY SMITH, *Brigadier-General,*
Chief of Cavalry, Military Division of the Mississippi.

MEMPHIS, TENNESSEE, *January* 28, 1864.
Brigadier-General GEORGE CROOK, *commanding Second Cavalry*
   Division, Huntsville, Alabama.

I start in about three days with seven thousand men to Meridian *via* Pontotoc. Demonstrate on Decatur, to hold Roddy.

W. SOOY SMITH, *Brigadier-General,*
Chief of Cavalry, Military Division of the Mississippi.

MAYWOOD, ILLINOIS, *July* 9, 1875.
General W. T. SHERMAN, *Commander-in-Chief, United States Army.*

SIR: Your letter of July 7th is just received.

Your entire statement in the "Memoirs" concerning my part in the Meridian campaign is incorrect.

You overstate my strength, placing it at seven thousand effective, when it was but six. The nominal strength of my command was seven thousand.

You understate the strength of my enemy, putting Forrest's force at four thousand. On our return to Nashville, you stated it, in General Grant's presence, to have been but twenty-five hundred. Before and during my movement I positively knew Forrest's strength to be full six thousand, and he has since told me so himself.

Instead of delaying from the 1st to the 11th of February for "some regiment that was ice-bound near Columbus, Kentucky," it was an entire brigade, Colonel Waring's, without which your orders to me were peremptory not to move. I asked you if I should wait its arrival, and you answered: "Certainly; if you go without it, you will be too weak, and I want you strong enough to go where you please."

The time set for our arrival at Meridian, the 10th of February, had arrived before it was possible for me, under your orders, to move from Memphis, and I would have been entirely justifiable if I had not started at all. But I was at that time, and at all times during the war, as earnest and anxious to carry out my orders, and do my full duty, as you or any other officer could be, and I set out to make a march of two hundred and fifty miles into the Confederacy, having to drive back a rebel force equal to my own. After the time had arrived for the full completion of my movement, I drove this force before me, and penetrated one hundred and sixty miles into the Confederacy—did more hard fighting, and killed, wounded, and captured more of the enemy than you did during the campaign—did my work most thoroughly, as far as I could go without encountering the rebel cavalry set loose by your return from Meridian, and brought off my command, with all the captured property and rescued negroes, with very small loss, considering that inflicted on the enemy, and the long-continued and very severe fighting. If I had disobeyed your orders, and started without Waring's brigade, I would have been "too weak," would probably have been defeated, and would have been subjected to just censure. Having awaited its arrival, as I was positively and distinctly ordered to do, it only remained for me to start upon its arrival, and accomplish all that I could of the work allotted to me. To have attempted to penetrate farther into the enemy's country, with the cavalry of Polk's army coming up to reënforce Forrest, would have insured the destruction of my entire command, situated as it was. I cannot now go into all the particulars, though I assure you that they make the proof of the correctness of my conduct as conclusive as I could desire it to be. I was not headed off and defeated by an inferior force near West Point. We had the fighting all our own way near West Point, and at all other points except at Okalona, on our return, when we had the worst of it for a little while, but finally checked the enemy handsomely, and continued our return march, fighting at the rear and on both flanks, repulsing all attacks and moving in perfect order. And so my movement was not a failure, except that I did not reach Meridian as intended, for the reason stated, and for many more which it is not necessary for me to detail here. On the other hand, it was a very decided success, inflicting a terrible destruction of supplies of every kind, and a heavy loss of men upon the enemy. You should have so reported it in the beginning. You should so amend your report and "Memoirs" now. This, and no less than this, is due from one soldier to another. It is due to the exalted position which you occupy, and, above all, it is due to that truthfulness in history which you claim to revere. If you desire it, I will endeavor to visit you, and in a friendly manner "fight our battles o'er again," and endeavor to convince you that you have always been mistaken as to the manner in which my part in the "Meridian campaign" was performed. But I will never rest until the wrong statements regarding it are fully and fairly corrected. Yours truly,

WILLIAM SOOY SMITH.

HEADQUARTERS ARMY OF THE UNITED STATES, ⎱
ST. LOUIS, MISSOURI, *July* 11, 1875. ⎰

General J. D. WEBSTER, *Chicago, Illinois.*

DEAR GENERAL: General W. Sooy Smith feels aggrieved and wronged by my account of his part in the Meridian campaign, in my "Memoirs," page 423, and properly appeals to me for correction. I have offered to modify any words or form of expression that he may point out, but he asks me to completely change the whole that concerns him. This, of course, I will not do, as his part was material to the whole, and cannot be omitted or materially altered without changing the remainder, for his failure to reach Meridian by February 10th was the reason for other movements distant from him. I now offer him, what seems to me fair and liberal, that we submit the points at issue to you as arbitrator. You are familiar with the ground, the coincident history, and most, if not all, the parties.

I propose to supply you with—

1. Copy of my orders placing all the cavalry under General Smith's orders (with returns).

2. My letter of instructions to him of January 27th.

3. My official report of the campaign, dated Vicksburg, March 7, 1864.

4. General W. Sooy Smith's report of his operations, dated Nashville, Tennessee, March 4, 1864.

After reading these, I further propose that you address us questions which we will answer in writing, when you are to make us a concise, written decision, which I will have published in close connection with the subject in controversy. If General Smith will show you my letter to him of this date, and also deliver this with his written assent, I will promptly furnish you the above documents, and also procure from the official files a return of the cavalry force available at and near Memphis on the date of my orders, viz., January 27, 1864.

With great respect, your friend and servant,

W. T. SHERMAN, *General.*

NOTE.—General Smith never submitted his case to the arbitration offered. The whole will be made clear by the publication of the official records, which are already in print, though not yet issued. His orders were in writing, and I have no recollection of the "peremptory" verbal orders to which he refers, and quotes as from me.

ST. LOUIS, MISSOURI, 1885.   W. T. S.

MAYWOOD, ILLINOIS, *July* 14, 1875.
General W. T. SHERMAN, *Commander-in-Chief, etc.*

DEAR GENERAL: Your letter of the 11th of July reaches me just as I am starting to spend the first vacation I have ever allowed myself—in the Territories, with my wife and son.

It indicates a spirit of fairness from which we have better things than an arbitration to hope for. Though, if we should reach such a necessity, there is no one living to whom our differences might more properly be referred than to General Webster. I make no objection to your writing *your* "Memoirs," and, as long as they refer to your own conduct, you are at liberty to write them as you like; but, when they refer to mine, and deal unjustly with my reputation, I, of right, object.

Neither do I wish to write *my* "Memoirs," unless compelled to do so to vindicate my good name. There were certain commands which were to make up mine. These, Waring's brigade included, were spoken of by us in the long conversation to which you refer. This brigade we knew was having a hard time of it in its movement from Columbus to Memphis. I asked you if I should move without it if it did not arrive, and you answered me as stated in my last letter to you. Those who immediately surrounded me during the painful delay that occurred will inform you how sorely I chafed under the restraint of that peremptory order.

In the conversation that occurred between us at Nashville, while all the orders, written and verbal, were still fresh in your memory, you did not censure me for waiting for Waring, but for allowing myself to be encumbered with fugitive negroes to such an extent that my command was measurably unfit for active movement or easy handling, and for turning back from West Point, instead of pressing on toward Meridian. Invitations had been industriously circulated, by printed circulars and otherwise, to the negroes to come into our lines, and to seek our protection wherever they could find it, and I considered ourselves pledged to receive and protect them. Your censure for so doing, and your remarks on that subject to me in Nashville, are still fresh in my memory, and of a character which you would now doubtless gladly disavow.

But we must meet and talk the whole matter over, and I will be at any trouble to see you when I return.

Meantime I will not let go the hope that I will convince you absolutely of your error, for the facts are entirely on my side. Yours truly,

WILLIAM SOOY SMITH.

END OF VOL. I.

MEMOIRS

OF

GENERAL WILLIAM T. SHERMAN.

IN TWO VOLUMES.

VOL. II.

Contents.

VOLUME II.

Chapter XVI.

ATLANTA CAMPAIGN—NASHVILLE AND CHATTANOOGA
TO KENESAW.

March, April, and May, 1864.

O N THE 18th day of March, 1864, at Nashville, Tennessee,
I relieved Lieutenant-General Grant in command of the
Military Division of the Mississippi, embracing the Departments of the Ohio, Cumberland, Tennessee, and Arkansas,
commanded respectively by Major-Generals Schofield, Thomas, McPherson, and Steele. General Grant was in the act of
starting East to assume command of all the armies of the
United States, but more particularly to give direction in person to the Armies of the Potomac and James, operating
against Richmond; and I accompanied him as far as Cincinnati on his way, to avail myself of the opportunity to discuss
privately many little details incident to the contemplated
changes, and of preparation for the great events then impending. Among these was the intended assignment to duty of
many officers of note and influence, who had, by the force of
events, drifted into inactivity and discontent. Among these
stood prominent Generals McClellan, Burnside, and Fremont,
in the East; and Generals Buell, McCook, Negley, and Crittenden, at the West. My understanding was that General
Grant thought it wise and prudent to give all these officers
appropriate commands, that would enable them to regain the
influence they had lost; and, as a general reorganization of all
the armies was then necessary, he directed me to keep in mind
especially the claims of Generals Buell, McCook, and Crittenden, and endeavor to give them commands that would be
as near their rank and dates of commission as possible; but I
was to do nothing until I heard further from him on the subject, as he explained that he would have to consult the Secretary of War before making final orders. General Buell and his
officers had been subjected to a long ordeal by a court of
inquiry, touching their conduct of the campaign in Tennessee
and Kentucky, that resulted in the battle of Perryville, or

Chaplin's Hills, October 8, 1862, and they had been substantially acquitted; and, as it was manifest that we were to have some hard fighting, we were anxious to bring into harmony every man and every officer of skill in the profession of arms. Of these, Generals Buell and McClellan were prominent in rank, and also by reason of their fame acquired in Mexico, as well as in the earlier part of the civil war.

After my return to Nashville I addressed myself to the task of organization and preparation, which involved the general security of the vast region of the South which had been already conquered, more especially the several routes of supply and communication with the active armies at the front, and to organize a large army to move into Georgia, coincident with the advance of the Eastern armies against Richmond. I soon received from Colonel J. B. Fry—now of the Adjutant-General's Department, but then at Washington in charge of the Provost-Marshal-General's office—a letter asking me to do something for General Buell. I answered him frankly, telling him of my understanding with General Grant, and that I was still awaiting the expected order of the War Department, assigning General Buell to my command. Colonel Fry, as General Buell's special friend, replied that he was very anxious that I should make specific application for the services of General Buell by name, and inquired what I proposed to offer him. To this I answered that, after the agreement with General Grant that he would notify me from Washington, I could not with propriety press the matter, but if General Buell should be assigned to me specifically I was prepared to assign him to command all the troops on the Mississippi River from Cairo to Natchez, comprising about three divisions, or the equivalent of a *corps d'armée*. General Grant never afterward communicated to me on the subject at all; and I inferred that Mr. Stanton, who was notoriously vindictive in his prejudices, would not consent to the employment of these high officers. General Buell, toward the close of the war, published a bitter political letter, aimed at General Grant, reflecting on his general management of the war, and stated that both Generals Canby and Sherman had offered him a subordinate command, which he had declined because he had once outranked us. This was not true as to me, or Canby either, I think, for both General Canby and I ranked him at West Point and in the old army, and he (General Buell) was only superior to us in the date of his commission as major-general, for a short period in 1862. This newspaper communication, though aimed at General Grant, reacted on himself, for it closed his military career. General Crittenden afterward obtained authority for service, and I offered him a division, but he declined it for the reason, as I understood it, that he had at one time commanded a corps. He is now in the United States service, commanding the Seventeenth Infantry. General McCook obtained a command under General Canby, in the Department of the Gulf, where he rendered good service, and he is also in the regular service, lieutenant-colonel Tenth Infantry.

I returned to Nashville from Cincinnati about the 25th of March, and started at once, in a special car attached to the regular train, to inspect my command at the front, going to Pulaski, Tennessee, where I found General G. M. Dodge; thence to Huntsville, Alabama, where I had left a part of my personal staff and the records of the department during the time we had been absent at Meridian; and there I found General McPherson, who had arrived from Vicksburg, and had assumed command of the Army of the Tennessee. General McPherson accompanied me, and we proceeded by the cars to Stevenson, Bridgeport, etc., to Chattanooga, where we spent a day or two with General George H. Thomas, and then continued on to Knoxville, where was General Schofield. He returned with us to Chattanooga, stopping by the way a few hours at Loudon, where were the headquarters of the Fourth Corps (Major-General Gordon Granger). General Granger, as usual, was full of complaints at the treatment of his corps since I had left him with General Burnside, at Knoxville, the preceding November; and he stated to me personally that he had a leave of absence in his pocket, of which he intended to take advantage very soon. About the end of March, therefore, the three army commanders and myself were together at Chattanooga. We had nothing like a council of war, but conversed freely and frankly on all matters of interest then in progress or impending. We all knew that, as soon as the spring was fairly open, we should have to move directly against our antagonist, General Jos. E. Johnston, then securely intrenched at Dalton, thirty miles distant; and the purpose of our conference at the time was to ascertain our own resources, and to distribute to each part of the army its appropriate share of work. We discussed every possible contingency likely to arise, and I simply instructed each army commander to make immediate preparations for a hard campaign, regulating the distribution of supplies that were coming up by rail from Nashville as equitably as possible. We also agreed on some subordinate changes in the organization of the three separate armies which were destined to take the field; among which was the consolidation of the Eleventh and Twelfth Corps (Howard and Slocum) into a single corps, to be commanded by General Jos. Hooker. General Howard was to be transferred to the Fourth Corps, *vice* Gordon Granger to avail himself of his leave of absence; and General Slocum was to be ordered down the Mississippi River, to command the District of Vicksburg. These changes required the consent of the President, and were all in due time approved.

The great question of the campaign was one of supplies. Nashville, our chief depot, was itself partially in a hostile country, and even the routes of supply from Louisville to Nashville by rail, and by way of the Cumberland River, had to be guarded. Chattanooga (our starting-point) was one hundred and thirty-six miles in front of Nashville, and every foot of the way, especially the many bridges, trestles, and culverts, had to be strongly guarded against the acts of a local hostile population and of the enemy's cavalry. Then, of course, as we advanced into Georgia, it was manifest that we should have to repair the railroad, use it, and guard it likewise. General Thomas's army was much the largest of the three, was best provided, and contained the best corps of engineers, railroad managers, and repair parties, as well as the best body of spies and provost-marshals. On him we were therefore compelled in a great measure to rely for these most useful branches of service. He had so long exercised absolute command and control over the railroads in his department, that the other armies were jealous, and these thought the Army of the Cumberland got the lion's share of the supplies and other advantages of the railroads. I found a good deal of

feeling in the Army of the Tennessee on this score, and therefore took supreme control of the roads myself, placed all the
army commanders on an equal footing, and gave to each the
same control, so far as orders of transportation for men and
stores were concerned. Thomas's spies brought him frequent
and accurate reports of Jos. E. Johnston's army at Dalton,
giving its strength anywhere between forty and fifty thousand
men, and these were being reënforced by troops from Mississippi, and by the Georgia militia, under General G. W. Smith.
General Johnston seemed to be acting purely on the defensive,
so that we had time and leisure to take all our measures deliberately and fully. I fixed the date of May 1st, when all things
should be in readiness for the grand forward movement, and
then returned to Nashville; General Schofield going back to
Knoxville, and McPherson to Huntsville, Thomas remaining
at Chattanooga.

On the 2d of April, at Nashville, I wrote to General Grant,
then at Washington, reporting to him the results of my visit
to the several armies, and asked his consent to the several
changes proposed, which was promptly given by telegraph. I
then addressed myself specially to the troublesome question
of transportation and supplies. I found the capacity of the
railroads from Nashville forward to Decatur, and to Chattanooga, so small, especially in the number of locomotives and
cars, that it was clear that they were barely able to supply the
daily wants of the armies then dependent on them, with no
power of accumulating a surplus in advance. The cars were
daily loaded down with men returning from furlough, with
cattle, horses, etc.; and, by reason of the previous desolation
of the country between Chattanooga and Knoxville, General
Thomas had authorized the issue of provisions to the suffering inhabitants.

We could not attempt an advance into Georgia without
food, ammunition, etc.; and ordinary prudence dictated that
we should have an accumulation at the front, in case of interruption to the railway by the act of the enemy, or by common
accident. Accordingly, on the 6th of April, I issued a general
order, limiting the use of the railroad-cars to transporting
only the essential articles of food, ammunition, and supplies
for the army proper, forbidding any further issues to citizens,

and cutting off all civil traffic; requiring the commanders of posts within thirty miles of Nashville to haul out their own stores in wagons; requiring all troops destined for the front to march, and all beef-cattle to be driven on their own legs. This was a great help, but of course it naturally raised a howl. Some of the poor Union people of East Tennessee appealed to President Lincoln, whose kind heart responded promptly to their request. He telegraphed me to know if I could not modify or repeal my orders; but I answered him that a great campaign was impending, on which the fate of the nation hung; that our railroads had but a limited capacity, and could not provide for the necessities of the army and of the people too; that one or the other must quit, and we could not until the army of Jos. Johnston was conquered, etc., etc. Mr. Lincoln seemed to acquiesce, and I advised the people to obtain and drive out cattle from Kentucky, and to haul out their supplies by the wagon-road from the same quarter, by way of Cumberland Gap. By these changes we nearly or quite doubled our daily accumulation of stores at the front, and yet even this was not found enough.

I accordingly called together in Nashville the master of transportation, Colonel Anderson, the chief quartermaster, General J. L. Donaldson, and the chief commissary, General Amos Beckwith, for conference. I assumed the strength of the army to move from Chattanooga into Georgia at one hundred thousand men, and the number of animals to be fed, both for cavalry and draught, at thirty-five thousand; then, allowing for occasional wrecks of trains, which were very common, and for the interruption of the road itself by guerrillas and regular raids, we estimated it would require one hundred and thirty cars, of ten tons each, to reach Chattanooga daily, to be reasonably certain of an adequate supply. Even with this calculation, we could not afford to bring forward hay for the horses and mules, nor more than five pounds of oats or corn per day for each animal. I was willing to risk the question of forage in part, because I expected to find wheat and corn fields, and a good deal of grass, as we advanced into Georgia at that season of the year. The problem then was to deliver at Chattanooga and beyond one hundred and thirty car-loads daily, leaving the beef-cattle to be driven on the hoof, and all the troops in excess of the usual train-guards to march by the ordinary roads. Colonel Anderson promptly explained that he did not possess cars or locomotives enough to do this work. I then instructed and authorized him to hold on to all trains that arrived at Nashville from Louisville, and to allow none to go back until he had secured enough to fill the requirements of our problem. At the time he only had about sixty serviceable locomotives, and about six hundred cars of all kinds, and he represented that to provide for all contingencies he must have at least one hundred locomotives and one thousand cars. As soon as Mr. Guthrie, the President of the Louisville & Nashville Railroad, detected that we were holding on to all his locomotives and cars, he wrote me, earnestly remonstrating against it, saying that he would not be able with diminished stock to bring forward the necessary stores from Louisville to Nashville. I wrote to him, frankly telling him exactly how we were placed, appealed to his patriotism to stand by us, and advised him in like manner to hold on to all trains coming into Jeffersonville, Indiana. He and General Robert Allen, then quartermaster-general at Louisville, arranged a ferry-boat so as to transfer the trains over the Ohio River from Jeffersonville, and in a short time we had cars and locomotives from almost every road at the North; months afterward I was amused to see, away down in Georgia, cars marked "Pittsburg & Fort Wayne," "Delaware & Lackawanna," "Baltimore & Ohio," and indeed with the names of almost every railroad north of the Ohio River. How these railroad companies ever recovered their property, or settled their transportation accounts, I have never heard, but to this fact, as much as to any other single fact, I attribute the perfect success which afterward attended our campaigns; and I have always felt grateful to Mr. Guthrie, of Louisville, who had sense enough and patriotism enough to subordinate the interests of his railroad company to the cause of his country.

About this time, viz., the early part of April, I was much disturbed by a bold raid made by the rebel General Forrest up between the Mississippi and Tennessee Rivers. He reached the

Ohio River at Paducah, but was handsomely repulsed by Colonel Hicks. He then swung down toward Memphis, assaulted and carried Fort Pillow, massacring a part of its garrison, composed wholly of negro troops. At first I discredited the story of the massacre, because, in preparing for the Meridian campaign, I had ordered Fort Pillow to be evacuated, but it transpired afterward that General Hurlbut had retained a small garrison at Fort Pillow to encourage the enlistment of the blacks as soldiers, which was a favorite political policy at that day. The massacre at Fort Pillow occurred April 12, 1864, and has been the subject of congressional inquiry. No doubt Forrest's men acted like a set of barbarians, shooting down the helpless negro garrison after the fort was in their possession; but I am told that Forrest personally disclaims any active participation in the assault, and that he stopped the firing as soon as he could. I also take it for granted that Forrest did not lead the assault in person, and consequently that he was to the rear, out of sight if not of hearing at the time, and I was told by hundreds of our men, who were at various times prisoners in Forrest's possession, that he was usually very kind to them. He had a desperate set of fellows under him, and at that very time there is no doubt the feeling of the Southern people was fearfully savage on this very point of our making soldiers out of their late slaves, and Forrest may have shared the feeling.

I also had another serious cause of disturbance about that time. I wanted badly the two divisions of troops which had been loaned to General Banks in the month of March previously, with the express understanding that their absence was to endure only one month, and that during April they were to come out of Red River, and be again within the sphere of my command. I accordingly instructed one of my inspector-generals, John M. Corse, to take a fleet steamboat at Nashville, proceed *via* Cairo, Memphis, and Vicksburg, to General Banks up the Red River, and to deliver the following letter of April 3d, as also others, of like tenor, to Generals A. J. Smith and Fred Steele, who were supposed to be with him:

Major-General N. P. BANKS, *commanding Department of the Gulf,
Red River.*

GENERAL: The thirty days for which I loaned you the command
of General A. J. Smith will expire on the 10th instant. I send with
this Brigadier-General J. M. Corse, to carry orders to General A. J.
Smith, and to give directions for a new movement, which is preliminary to the general campaign. General Corse may see you and explain in full, but, lest he should not find you in person, I will simply
state that Forrest, availing himself of the absence of our furloughed
men and of the detachment with you, has pushed up between the
Mississippi and Tennessee Rivers, even to the Ohio. He attacked
Paducah, but got the worst of it, and he still lingers about the place.
I hope that he will remain thereabouts till General A. J. Smith can
reach his destined point, but this I can hardly expect; yet I want him
to reach by the Yazoo a position near Grenada, thence to operate
against Forrest, after which to march across to Decatur, Alabama.
You will see that he has a big job, and therefore should start at once.
From all that I can learn, my troops reached Alexandria, Louisiana,
at the time agreed on, viz., March 17th, and I hear of them at Natchitoches, but cannot hear of your troops being above Opelousas.

Steele is also moving. I leave Steele's entire force to coöperate with
you and the navy, but, as I before stated, I must have A. J. Smith's
troops now as soon as possible.

I beg you will expedite their return to Vicksburg, if they have not
already started, and I want them if possible to remain in the same
boats they have used up Red River, as it will save the time otherwise
consumed in transfer to other boats.

All is well in this quarter, and I hope by the time you turn against
Mobile our forces will again act toward the same end, though from
distant points. General Grant, now having lawful control, will
doubtless see that all minor objects are disregarded, and that all the
armies act on a common plan.

Hoping, when this reaches you, that you will be in possession of
Shreveport, I am, with great respect, etc.,

W. T. SHERMAN, *Major-General commanding.*

Rumors were reaching us thick and fast of defeat and disaster in that quarter; and I feared then, what afterward actually
happened, that neither General Banks nor Admiral Porter
could or would spare those two divisions. On the 23d of
April, General Corse returned, bringing full answers to my

letters, and I saw that we must go on without them. This was a serious loss to the Army of the Tennessee, which was also short by two other divisions that were on their veteran furlough, and were under orders to rendezvous at Cairo, before embarking for Clifton, on the Tennessee River.

On the 10th of April, 1864, the headquarters of the three Armies of the Cumberland, Tennessee, and Ohio, were at Chattanooga, Huntsville, and Knoxville, and the tables on page 474, *et seq.*, give their exact condition and strength.

The Department of the Arkansas was then subject to my command, but General Fred Steele, its commander, was at Little Rock, remote from me, acting in coöperation with General Banks, and had full employment for every soldier of his command; so that I never depended on him for any men, or for any participation in the Georgia campaign. Soon after, viz., May 8th, that department was transferred to the Military Division of "the Gulf," or "Southwest," Major-General E. R. S. Canby commanding, and General Steele served with him in the subsequent movement against Mobile.

In Generals Thomas, McPherson, and Schofield, I had three generals of education and experience, admirably qualified for the work before us. Each has made a history of his own, and I need not here dwell on their respective merits as men, or as commanders of armies, except that each possessed special qualities of mind and of character which fitted them in the highest degree for the work then in contemplation.

By the returns of April 10, 1864, it will be seen that the Army of the Cumberland had on its muster-rolls—

	Men.
Present and absent	171,450
Present for duty	88,883

The Army of the Tennessee—

	Men.
Present and absent	134,763
Present for duty	64,957

The Army of the Ohio—

	Men.
Present and absent	46,052
Present for duty	26,242

The department and army commanders had to maintain strong garrisons in their respective departments, and also to guard their respective lines of supply. I therefore, in my mind, aimed to prepare out of these three armies, by the 1st of May, 1864, a compact army for active operations in Georgia, of about the following numbers:

	Men.
Army of the Cumberland	50,000
Army of the Tennessee	35,000
Army of the Ohio	15,000
Total.	100,000

and, to make these troops as mobile as possible, I made the strictest possible orders in relation to wagons and all species of incumbrances and impedimenta whatever. Each officer and soldier was required to carry on his horse or person food and clothing enough for five days. To each regiment was allowed but one wagon and one ambulance, and to the officers of each company one pack-horse or mule.

Each division and brigade was provided a fair proportion of wagons for a supply-train, and these were limited in their loads to carry food, ammunition, and clothing. Tents were forbidden to all save the sick and wounded, and one tent only was allowed to each headquarters for use as an office. These orders were not absolutely enforced, though in person I set the example, and did not have a tent, nor did any officer about me have one; but we had wall tent-flies, without poles, and no tent-furniture of any kind. We usually spread our flies over saplings, or on fence-rails or posts improvised on the spot. Most of the general officers, except Thomas, followed my example strictly; but he had a regular headquarters-camp. I frequently called his attention to the orders on this subject, rather jestingly than seriously. He would break out against his officers for having such luxuries, but, needing a tent himself, and being good-natured and slow to act, he never enforced my orders perfectly. In addition to his regular wagon-train, he had a big wagon which could be converted into an office, and this we used to call "Thomas's circus." Several times during the campaign I found quartermasters hid away in some comfortable nook to the rear, with tents and mess-fixtures which

Transcript from the Tri-Monthly Return of the Department of the Cumberland, commanded by Major-General THOMAS, for April 10, 1864.

COMMANDS	Number of Regiments	Number of Companies	For Duty — General Officers	For Duty — General Staff-Officers	For Duty — Field, Staff, and Company Officers	For Duty — Total commissioned	For Duty — Enlisted Men	For Duty — Aggregate	Special, Extra, or Daily Duty — Commissioned Officers	Special, Extra, or Daily Duty — Enlisted Men	Sick — Commissioned Officers	Sick — Enlisted Men	In Arrest or Confinem't — Commissioned Officers	In Arrest or Confinem't — Enlisted Men	Aggregate	On Detached Service — Within the Department — Commissioned Officers	On Detached Service — Within the Department — Enlisted Men	On Detached Service — Without the Department — Commissioned Officers	On Detached Service — Without the Department — Enlisted Men	With Leave — Commissioned Officers	With Leave — Enlisted Men
Department Staff	.	.	8	19	.	22	.	22	.	.	.	.	.	.	22	1	.	1	.	2	.
Fourth Army Corps	75	751	6	17	826	849	15,323	16,172	80	1,505	27	726	5	82	18,597	301	4,484	95	384	782	8,266
Fourteenth Army Corps	60	600	7	13	686	706	18,931	19,637	126	1,866	53	1,210	11	132	23,035	326	4,823	114	457	408	5,724
Eleventh and Twelfth Ar'y Crps*	55	561	9	8	864	919	20,028	20,947	82	1,874	37	1,378	12	161	24,491	207	2,628	120	627	189	2,614
District of Nashville	18	196	5	12	396	409	8,820	9,229	74	2,221	26	907	9	216	12,682	104	1,431	36	175	23	796
Cavalry Command	26	293	1	.	542	555	10,472	11,027	49	1,442	23	404	6	72	13,023	175	2,762	62	847	136	1,899
Reserve Artillery	.	12	.	.	31	31	1,073	1,104	.	17	1	35	.	.	1,162	4	10	13	6	6	159
Tenth Ohio Sharp-shooters	.	14	.	.	30	30	596	626	5	154	5	50	1	18	854	33	57	.	.	2	12
Post of Chattanooga	1	.	1	3	123	127	3,153	3,280	18	296	.	155	.	49	3,803	17	574	17	76	21	342
Engineer Brigade	.	40	.	.	30	30	1,020	1,050	13	345	.	53	.	8	1,469	25	162	10	36	40	520
Unassigned Infantry	4	42	.	.	102	102	2,975	3,077	16	282	.	324	.	24	3,723	.	152	.	11	36	559
" Cavalry	4	33	.	.	79	79	1,388	1,667	3	204	9	168	4	26	2,081	9	184	4	5	4	108
" Artillery	3	9	.	.	20	20	871	891	1	16	2	38	1	4	953	5	4	6	3	4	145
Signal Corps	.	.	.	.	.	24	130	154	.	.	.	1	.	.	155	3	36	.	.	.	4
Grand Total	252	2,626	32	142	3,729	3,903	84,980	88,883	467	10,222	183	5,449	49	797	106,050	1,215	17,307	478	2,627	1,653	21,148

*Consolidated, and named Twentieth Army Corps.

Geo H Thomas

Transcript from the Tri-Monthly Return of the Department of the Cumberland—(Continued.)

COMMANDS	ABSENT — Sick		ABSENT — Without Authority		PRESENT AND ABSENT			Aggregate Last Return	PRESENT FOR DUTY EQUIPPED — Infantry		Cavalry		Artillery		HORSES		GUNS	
	Comm. Officers	Enlisted Men	Comm. Officers	Enlisted Men	Comm. Officers	Enlisted Men	Aggregate		Comm. Officers	Enlisted Men	Comm. Officers	Enlisted Men	Comm. Officers	Enlisted Men	Serviceable	Unserviceable	Number	
Department Staff	1				27		27	27										Brig.-Gen. W. D. Whipple.
Fourth Army Corps	82	5,685	27	408	2,248	36,863	39,111	39,112	785	14,115			12	381	295	25	24	Maj.-Gen. O. O. Howard.
Fourteenth Army Corps	50	4,004	26	369	1,820	37,516	39,336	38,941	686	18,406			23	782	664	52	42	Maj.-Gen. J. M. Palmer.
Eleventh and Twelfth Army Corps	41	3,728	11	371	1,618	33,409	35,027	34,858	838	18,297	1	50	25	988	802	44	52	Maj.-Gen. J. Hooker.
District of Nashville	7	983	5	357	693	15,906	16,599	18,074	362	8,006	2	89	24	739	539	10	65	Maj.-Gen. L. H. Rousseau.
Cavalry Command	44	2,800	17	237	1,067	20,935	22,002	22,002	104	1,376	363	6,786	6	188	9,022	1,969	12	Brig.-Gen. K. Garrard.
Reserve Artillery	1	116	2	49	59	1,470	1,529	3,074					27	940	481	4	38	Brig.-Gen. J. M. Brannan.
Fourth Ohio Sharp-shooters	2	43	2	3	46	933	979	980	30	596								Capt. G. M. Barber.
Post of Chattanooga	3	518	31	35	255	5,198	5,453	3,981	56	1,189			20	1,050			89	Maj.-Gen. J. B. Steedman.
Engineer Brigade	3	270	2	15	115	2,429	2,544	2,572	30	1,020					218	7		Gen. O. M. Poe.
Unassigned Infantry	1	244	1	40	181	4,611	4,792	4,010	96	3,001								Maj.-Gen. Carl Schurz.
" Cavalry		174		70	112	2,527	2,639	2,265			79	1,204			668	545		{ In the field with other divisions of cavalry.
" Artillery		83		8	39	1,172	1,211	775					20	871	54	11	28	Col. J. Barnett, 1st Ohio L.A.
Signal Corps	1			1	28	173	201	192										Capt. P. Babcock, Jr.
Grand Total	236	18,649	124	1,963	8,308	163,142	171,450	170,863	2,987	66,006	445	8,129	161	5,939	12,733	2,667	350	

Official: E. D. TOWNSEND, Adjutant-General.   GEO. H. THOMAS, Major-General commanding.

Transcript from the Tri-Monthly Return of the Department and Army of the Tennessee, commanded by Major-General McPHERSON, for April 10, 1864.

COMMANDS.	Number of Regiments.	Number of Companies.	For Duty — General Officers.	General Staff-Officers.	Field, Staff, and Company Officers.	Total commissioned.	Enlisted Men.	Aggregate.	Special, Extra, or Daily Duty. Commissioned Officers.	Enlisted Men.	Sick. Commissioned Officers.	Enlisted Men.	In Arrest or Confineme't. Commissioned Officers.	Enlisted Men.	PRESENT Aggregate.	On Detached Service. Within the Department. Commissioned Officers.	Enlisted Men.	Without the Department. Commissioned Officers.	Enlisted Men.	With Leave. Commissioned Officers.	Enlisted Men.	Sick. Commissioned Officers.	Enlisted Men.
Department Staff	.	.	1	4	.	5	.	5	.	.	.	.	.	.	5	.	.	.	.	.	.	.	.
Fifteenth Army Corps . .	56	571	9	13	728	750	14,919	15,669	94	1,925	52	1,302	7	152	19,201	215	3,055	102	354	394	5,069	56	3,316
Sixteenth Army Corps . .	71	811	10	33	1,355	1,400	31,345	32,745	169	4,402	81	3,042	23	193	40,655	299	3,191	195	1,560	494	8,208	84	4,058
Seventeenth Army Corps .	58	627	6	30	598	634	15,890	16,524	76	2,134	58	2,348	15	96	21,251	461	7,660	128	534	660	10,148	23	1,585
Signal Detachment	.	.	.	.	1	1	13	14	.	.	.	.	.	.	14	1	7	1	2	1	.	.	.
Total Force — Department and Army of the Tennessee . .	185	2,009	26	82	2,681	2,790	62,167	64,957	339	8,461	191	6,692	45	441	81,126	976	13,913	426	2,450	1,549	23,515	163	8,959

Transcript from the Tri-Monthly Return of the Department and Army of the Tennessee—(Continued.)

COMMANDS.	ABSENT. Without Authority.		PRESENT AND ABSENT.				PRESENT FOR DUTY EQUIPPED.						HORSES.		GUNS.	
	Commissioned Officers.	Enlisted Men.	Commissioned Officers.	Enlisted Men.	Aggregate.	Aggregate Last Return.	Infantry. Commissioned Officers.	Enlisted Men.	Cavalry. Commissioned Officers.	Enlisted Men.	Artillery. Commissioned Officers.	Enlisted Men.	Serviceable.	Unserviceable.	Number.	
Department Staff			5		5	5										Colonel W. T. Clark.
Fifteenth Army Corps . . .	19	262	1,689	30,354	32,043	31,522	689	11,053	27	350	31	1,165	1,086	243	57	Major-General J. A. Logan.
Sixteenth Army Corps . . .	23	966	2,768	57,055	59,823	58,245	554	11,107	152	3,081	80	2,840	5,779	1,064	173	Major-General G. M. Dodge.
Seventeenth Army Corps . .	14	395	2,069	40,790	42,859	42,859	400	8,545	91	2,187	59	2,005	2,911	1,016	58	Major-General Frank P. Blair.
Signal Detachment		7	4	29	33	26							31			Captain O. H. Howard.
Total Force — Department and Army of the Tennessee . .	56	1,630	6,535	128,228	134,763	132,657	1,643	30,705	270	6,168	170	6,010	9,807	2,323	288	

Official: E. D. TOWNSEND, Adjutant-General.   J. B. McPHERSON, Major-General commanding.

Transcript from the Tri-Monthly Return of the Department of the Ohio, commanded by Major-General SCHOFIELD, for April 10, 1864.

COMMANDS.	Number of Regiments.	Number of Companies.	PRESENT. For Duty — General Officers.	For Duty — General Staff-Officers.	For Duty — Field, Staff, and Company Officers.	For Duty — Total commissioned.	For Duty — Enlisted Men.	Aggregate.	Special, Extra, or Daily Duty — Commissioned Officers.	Special, Extra, or Daily Duty — Enlisted Men.	Sick — Commissioned Officers.	Sick — Enlisted Men.	In Arrest or Confinem't — Commissioned Officers.	In Arrest or Confinem't — Enlisted Men.	Aggregate.	ABSENT. On Detached Service Within the Department — Commissioned Officers.	Within the Department — Enlisted Men.	On Detached Service Without the Department — Commissioned Officers.	Without the Department — Enlisted Men.	With Leave — Commissioned Officers.	With Leave — Enlisted Men.	Sick — Commissioned Officers.	Sick — Enlisted Men.
Twenty-third Army Corps	24	326	4	7	675	686	14,733	15,419	88	1,968	50	1,490	8	313	19,336	221	3,365	15	133	36	512	24	2,408
Cavalry Corps	14	167	1	4	209	214	5,419	5,633	42	673	19	557	4	37	6,965	141	1,660	14	35	32	270	29	1,375
District of the Clinch	4	37	1	3	79	83	1,406	1,489	9	118	5	120	2	21	1,764	9	69	1	14	4	3	5	229
Defenses of Knoxville	2	42			123	123	3,507	3,630	19	354	4	552	4	16	4,579	31	314	3	78	7	54	4	441
Newport Barracks					2	2	69	71		5		1		10	87						1		1
Total Force—Department of the Ohio	44	572	6	14	1,088	1,108	25,134	26,242	158	3,118	78	2,720	18	397	32,731	402	5,408	33	260	79	840	62	4,454

Transcript from the Tri-Monthly Return of the Department of the Ohio—(Continued.)

COMMANDS.	ABSENT. Without Authority.		PRESENT AND ABSENT.			Aggregate Last Return.	PRESENT FOR DUTY EQUIPPED.						HORSES.		GUNS.	
	Commissioned Officers.	Enlisted Men.	Commissioned Officers.	Enlisted Men.	Aggregate.		Infantry Commissioned Officers.	Infantry Enlisted Men.	Cavalry Commissioned Officers.	Cavalry Enlisted Men.	Artillery Commissioned Officers.	Artillery Enlisted Men.	Serviceable.	Unserviceable.	Number.	
Twenty-third Army Corps . . .	13	970	1,141	25,892	27,033	26,999	545	11,500	76	1,180	49	1,614	427	67	...	Major-General J. D. Cox.
Cavalry Corps	9	314	504	10,340	10,844	10,844	57	1,184	125	2,917	...	...	1,888	424	...	Major-General G. Stoneman.
District of the Clinch . .	1	373	119	2,353	2,472	2,478	54	897	16	245	9	291	5	...	...	Brig.-General T. T. Garrard.
Defenses of Knoxville . . .	3	99	198	5,415	5,613	5,613	21	455	...	...	57	1,834	12	...	602	Brigadier-General D. Tillson.
Newport Barracks	...	1	2	88	90	224	...	...	...	...	...	...	...	...	...	Colonel J. P. Sanderson.
Total Force— Department of the Ohio	26	1,757	1,964	44,088	46,052	46,158	677	14,036	217	4,342	115	3,739	2,032	491	602	

Official: E. D. TOWNSEND, Adjutant-General.   J. M. SCHOFIELD, Major-General commanding.

were the envy of the passing soldiers; and I frequently broke them up, and distributed the tents to the surgeons of brigades. Yet my orders actually reduced the transportation, so that I doubt if any army ever went forth to battle with fewer impedimenta, and where the regular and necessary supplies of food, ammunition, and clothing, were issued, as called for, so regularly and so well.

My personal staff was then composed of Captain J. C. Mc-Coy, aide-de-camp; Captain L. M. Dayton, aide-de-camp; Captain J. C. Audenried, aide-de-camp; Brigadier-General J. D. Webster, chief of staff; Major R. M. Sawyer, assistant adjutant-general; Captain Montgomery Rochester, assistant adjutant-general. These last three were left at Nashville in charge of the office, and were empowered to give orders in my name, communication being generally kept up by telegraph.

Subsequently were added to my staff, and accompanied me in the field, Brigadier-General W. F. Barry, chief of artillery; Colonel O. M. Poe, chief of engineers; Colonel L. C. Easton, chief quartermaster; Colonel Amos Beckwith, chief commissary; Captain Thos. G. Baylor, chief of ordnance; Surgeon E. D. Kittoe, medical director; Brigadier-General J. M. Corse, inspector-general; Lieutenant-Colonel C. Ewing, inspector-general; and Lieutenant-Colonel Willard Warner, inspector-general.

These officers constituted my staff proper at the beginning of the campaign, which remained substantially the same till the close of the war, with very few exceptions; viz.: Surgeon John Moore, United States Army, relieved Surgeon Kittoe of the volunteers (about Atlanta) as medical director; Major Henry Hitchcock joined as judge-advocate, and Captain G. Ward Nichols reported as an extra aide-de-camp (after the fall of Atlanta) at Gaylesville, just before we started for Savannah.

During the whole month of April the preparations for active war were going on with extreme vigor, and my letter-book shows an active correspondence with Generals Grant, Halleck, Thomas, McPherson, and Schofield on thousands of matters of detail and arrangement, most of which are embraced in my testimony before the Committee on the Conduct of the War, vol. i., Appendix.

When the time for action approached, viz., May 1, 1864, the actual armies prepared to move into Georgia resulted as follows, present for battle:

Army of the Cumberland, Major-General THOMAS.

	Men.
Infantry.	54,568
Artillery	2,377
Cavalry	3,828
Aggregate	60,773

Number of field-guns, 130.

Army of the Tennessee, Major-General McPHERSON.

	Men.
Infantry.	22,437
Artillery	1,404
Cavalry	624
Aggregate	24,465

Guns, 96.

Army of the Ohio, Major-General SCHOFIELD.

	Men.
Infantry.	11,183
Artillery	679
Cavalry	1,697
Aggregate	13,559

Guns, 28.

Grand aggregate, 98,797 men and 254 guns.

These figures do not embrace the cavalry divisions which were still incomplete, viz., of General Stoneman, at Lexington, Kentucky, and of General Garrard, at Columbia, Tennessee, who were then rapidly collecting horses, and joined us in the early stage of the campaign. General Stoneman, having a division of about four thousand men and horses, was attached to Schofield's Army of the Ohio. General Garrard's division, of about four thousand five hundred men and horses, was attached to General Thomas's command; and he had another irregular division of cavalry, commanded by Brigadier-General E. McCook. There was also a small brigade of cavalry,

belonging to the Army of the Cumberland, attached temporarily to the Army of the Tennessee, which was commanded
by Brigadier-General Judson Kilpatrick. These cavalry commands changed constantly in strength and numbers, and were
generally used on the extreme flanks, or for some special detached service, as will be hereinafter related. The Army of the
Tennessee was still short by the two divisions detached with
General Banks, up Red River, and two other divisions on
furlough in Illinois, Indiana, and Ohio, but which were rendezvousing at Cairo, under Generals Leggett and Crocker, to
form a part of the Seventeenth Corps, which corps was to be
commanded by Major-General Frank P. Blair, then a member
of Congress, in Washington. On the 2d of April I notified him
by letter that I wanted him to join and to command these two
divisions, which ought to be ready by the 1st of May. General
Blair, with these two divisions, constituting the Seventeenth
Army Corps, did not actually overtake us until we reached
Acworth and Big Shanty, in Georgia, about the 9th of June,
1864.

In my letter of April 4th to General John A. Rawlins,
chief of staff to General Grant at Washington, I described at
length all the preparations that were in progress for the
active campaign thus contemplated, and therein estimated
Schofield at twelve thousand, Thomas at forty-five thousand,
and McPherson at thirty thousand. At first I intended to open
the campaign about May 1st, by moving Schofield on Dalton
from Cleveland, Thomas on the same objective from Chattanooga, and McPherson on Rome and Kingston from
Gunter's Landing. My intention was merely to threaten
Dalton in front, and to direct McPherson to act vigorously
against the railroad below Resaca, far to the rear of the
enemy. But by reason of his being short of his estimated
strength by the four divisions before referred to, and thus
being reduced to about twenty-four thousand men, I did not
feel justified in placing him so far away from the support of
the main body of the army, and therefore subsequently
changed the plan of campaign, so far as to bring that army up
to Chattanooga, and to direct it thence through Ship's Gap
against the railroad to Johnston's rear, at or near Resaca,
distant from Dalton only eighteen miles, and in full commu-

nication with the other armies by roads behind Rockyface Ridge, of about the same length.

On the 10th of April I received General Grant's letter of April 4th from Washington, which formed the basis of all the campaigns of the year 1864, and subsequently received another of April 19th, written from Culpepper, Virginia, both of which are now in my possession, in his own handwriting, and are here given entire. These letters embrace substantially all the orders he ever made on this particular subject, and these, it will be seen, devolved on me the details both as to the plan and execution of the campaign by the armies under my immediate command. These armies were to be directed against the rebel army commanded by General Joseph E. Johnston, then lying on the defensive, strongly intrenched at Dalton, Georgia; and I was required to follow it up closely and persistently, so that in no event could any part be detached to assist General Lee in Virginia; General Grant undertaking in like manner to keep Lee so busy that he could not respond to any calls of help by Johnston. Neither Atlanta, nor Augusta, nor Savannah, was the objective, but the "army of Jos. Johnston," go where it might.

[Private and Confidential.]

Headquarters Armies of the United States, ⎱
    Washington, D. C., *April* 4, 1864. ⎰

Major-General W. T. Sherman, *commanding Military Division of the Mississippi.*

General: It is my design, if the enemy keep quiet and allow me to take the initiative in the spring campaign, to work all parts of the army together, and somewhat toward a common centre. For your information I now write you my programme, as at present determined upon.

I have sent orders to Banks, by private messenger, to finish up his present expedition against Shreveport with all dispatch; to turn over the defense of Red River to General Steele and the navy, and to return your troops to you, and his own to New Orleans; to abandon all of Texas, except the Rio Grande, and to hold that with not to exceed four thousand men; to reduce the number of troops on the Mississippi to the lowest number necessary to hold it, and to collect from his command not less than twenty-five thousand men. To this I will add five thousand from Missouri. With this force he is to commence operations against Mobile as soon as he can. It will be impossible for him to commence too early.

Gillmore joins Butler with ten thousand men, and the two operate against Richmond from the south side of James River. This will give Butler thirty-three thousand men to operate with, W. F. Smith commanding the right wing of his forces, and Gillmore the left wing. I will stay with the Army of the Potomac, increased by Burnside's corps of not less than twenty-five thousand effective men, and operate directly against Lee's army, wherever it may be found.

Sigel collects all his available force in two columns, one, under Ord and Averill, to start from Beverly, Virginia, and the other, under Crook, to start from Charleston, on the Kanawha, to move against the Virginia & Tennessee Railroad.

Crook will have all cavalry, and will endeavor to get in about Saltville, and move east from there to join Ord. His force will be all cavalry, while Ord will have from ten to twelve thousand men of all arms.

You I propose to move against Johnston's army, to break it up, and to get into the interior of the enemy's country as far as you can, inflicting all the damage you can against their war resources.

I do not propose to lay down for you a plan of campaign, but simply to lay down the work it is desirable to have done, and leave you free to execute it in your own way. Submit to me, however, as early as you can, your plan of operations.

As stated, Banks is ordered to commence operations as soon as he can. Gillmore is ordered to report at Fortress Monroe by the 18th inst., or as soon thereafter as practicable. Sigel is concentrating now. None will move from their places of rendezvous until I direct, except Banks. I want to be ready to move by the 25th inst., if possible; but all I can now direct is that you get ready as soon as possible. I know you will have difficulties to encounter in getting through the mountains to where supplies are abundant, but I believe you will accomplish it.

From the expedition from the Department of West Virginia I do not calculate on very great results; but it is the only way I can take troops from there. With the long line of railroad Sigel has to protect, he can spare no troops, except to move directly to his front. In this way he must get through to inflict great damage on the enemy, or the enemy must detach from one of his armies a large force to prevent it. In other words, if Sigel can't skin himself, he can hold a leg while some one else skins.

I am, general, very respectfully, your obedient servant,

U. S. GRANT, *Lieutenant-General*.

HEADQUARTERS MILITARY DIVISION OF THE MISSISSIPPI, ⎫
NASHVILLE, TENNESSEE, *April* 10, 1864. ⎭
Lieutenant-General U. S. GRANT, *Commander-in-Chief,*
Washington, D. C.

DEAR GENERAL: Your two letters of April 4th are now before me, and afford me infinite satisfaction. That we are now all to act on a common plan, converging on a common centre, looks like enlightened war.

Like yourself, you take the biggest load, and from me you shall have thorough and hearty coöperation. I will not let side issues draw me off from your main plans in which I am to knock Jos. Johnston, and to do as much damage to the resources of the enemy as possible. I have heretofore written to General Rawlins and to Colonel Comstock (of your staff) somewhat of the method in which I propose to act. I have seen all my army, corps, and division commanders, and have signified only to the former, viz., Schofield, Thomas, and McPherson, our general plans, which I inferred from the purport of our conversation here and at Cincinnati.

First, I am pushing stores to the front with all possible dispatch, and am completing the army organization according to the orders from Washington, which are ample and perfectly satisfactory.

It will take us all of April to get in our furloughed veterans, to bring up A. J. Smith's command, and to collect provisions and cattle on the line of the Tennessee. Each of the armies will guard, by detachments of its own, its rear communications.

At the signal to be given by you, Schofield, leaving a select garrison at Knoxville and Loudon, with twelve thousand men will drop down to the Hiawassee, and march against Johnston's right by the old Federal road. Stoneman, now in Kentucky, organizing the cavalry forces of the Army of the Ohio, will operate with Schofield on his left front — it may be, pushing a select body of about two thousand cavalry by Ducktown or Elijah toward Athens, Georgia.

Thomas will aim to have forty-five thousand men of all arms, and move straight against Johnston, wherever he may be, fighting him cautiously, persistently, and to the best advantage. He will have two divisions of cavalry, to take advantage of any offering.

McPherson will have nine divisions of the Army of the Tennessee, if A. J. Smith gets here, in which case he will have full thirty thousand of the best men in America. He will cross the Tennessee at Decatur and Whitesburg, march toward Rome, and feel for Thomas. If Johnston falls behind the Coosa, then McPherson will push for Rome; and if Johnston falls behind the Chattahoochee, as I believe he will, then McPherson will cross over and join Thomas.

McPherson has no cavalry, but I have taken one of Thomas's divisions, viz., Garrard's, six thousand strong, which is now at Columbia, mounting, equipping, and preparing. I design this division to operate on McPherson's right, rear, or front, according as the enemy appears. But the moment I detect Johnston falling behind the Chattahoochee, I propose to cast off the effective part of this cavalry division, after crossing the Coosa, straight for Opelika, West Point, Columbus, or Wetumpka, to break up the road between Montgomery and Georgia. If Garrard can do this work well, he can return to the Union army; but should a superior force interpose, then he will seek safety at Pensacola and join Banks, or, after rest, will act against any force that he can find east of Mobile, till such time as he can reach me.

Should Johnston fall behind the Chattahoochee, I will feign to the right, but pass to the left and act against Atlanta or its eastern communications, according to developed facts.

This is about as far ahead as I feel disposed to look, but I will ever bear in mind that Johnston is at all times to be kept so busy that he cannot in any event send any part of his command against you or Banks.

If Banks can at the same time carry Mobile and open up the Alabama River, he will in a measure solve the most difficult part of my problem, viz., "provisions." But in that I must venture. Georgia has a million of inhabitants. If they can live, we should not starve. If the enemy interrupt our communications, I will be absolved from all obligations to subsist on our own resources, and will feel perfectly justified in taking whatever and wherever we can find.

I will inspire my command, if successful, with the feeling that beef and salt are all that is absolutely necessary to life, and that parched corn once fed General Jackson's army on that very ground.

As ever, your friend and servant,

W. T. SHERMAN, *Major-General.*

HEADQUARTERS ARMIES IN THE FIELD, ⎰
CULPEPPER COURT-HOUSE, VIRGINIA, *April* 19, 1864. ⎱

Major-General W. T. SHERMAN, *commanding Military Division of the Mississippi.*

GENERAL: Since my letter to you of April 4th I have seen no reason to change any portion of the general plan of campaign, if the enemy remain still and allow us to take the initiative. Rain has continued so uninterruptedly until the last day or two that it will be impossible to move, however, before the 27th, even if no more should fall in the mean time. I think Saturday, the 30th, will probably be the day for our general move.

Colonel Comstock, who will take this, can spend a day with you, and fill up many little gaps of information not given in any of my letters.

What I now want more particularly to say is, that if the two main attacks, yours and the one from here, should promise great success, the enemy may, in a fit of desperation, abandon one part of their line of defense, and throw their whole strength upon the other, believing a single defeat without any victory to sustain them better than a defeat all along their line, and hoping too, at the same time, that the army, meeting with no resistance, will rest perfectly satisfied with their laurels, having penetrated to a given point south, thereby enabling them to throw their force first upon one and then on the other.

With the majority of military commanders they might do this.

But you have had too much experience in traveling light, and subsisting upon the country, to be caught by any such *ruse*. I hope my experience has not been thrown away. My directions, then, would be, if the enemy in your front show signs of joining Lee, follow him up to the full extent of your ability. I will prevent the concentration of Lee upon your front, if it is in the power of this army to do it.

The Army of the Potomac looks well, and, so far as I can judge, officers and men feel well. Yours truly,

U. S. GRANT, *Lieutenant-General.*

HEADQUARTERS MILITARY DIVISION OF THE MISSISSIPPI, ⎱
NASHVILLE, TENNESSEE, *April* 24, 1864. ⎰

Lieutenant-General GRANT, *commanding Armies of the United States, Culpepper, Virginia.*

GENERAL: I now have, at the hands of Colonel Comstock, of your staff, the letter of April 19th, and am as far prepared to assume the offensive as possible. I only ask as much time as you think proper, to enable me to get up McPherson's two divisions from Cairo. Their furloughs will expire about this time, and some of them should now be in motion for Clifton, whence they will march to Decatur, to join General Dodge.

McPherson is ordered to assemble the Fifteenth Corps near Larkin's, and to get the Sixteenth and Seventeenth Corps (Dodge and Blair) at Decatur at the earliest possible moment. From these two points he will direct his forces on Lebanon, Summerville, and Lafayette, where he will act against Johnston, if he accept battle at Dalton; or move in the direction of Rome, if the enemy give up Dalton, and fall behind the Oostenaula or Etowah. I see that there is some risk in dividing our forces, but Thomas and Schofield will have strength enough to cover all the valleys as far as Dalton; and, should Johnston turn his whole force against McPherson, the latter will have his bridge at Larkin's, and the route to Chattanooga *via* Wills's Valley and the Chattanooga Creek, open for retreat; and if Johnston attempt to leave Dalton, Thomas will have force enough to push on through Dalton to Kingston, which will checkmate him. My own opinion is that Johnston will be compelled to hang to his railroad, the only possible avenue of supply to his army, estimated at from forty-five to sixty thousand men.

At Lafayette all our armies will be together, and if Johnston stands at Dalton we must attack him in position. Thomas feels certain that he has no material increase of force, and that he has not sent away Hardee, or any part of his army. Supplies are the great question. I have materially increased the number of cars daily. When I got here, the average was from sixty-five to eighty per day. Yesterday the report was one hundred and ninety-three; to-day, one hundred and thirty-four; and my estimate is that one hundred and forty-five cars per day will give us a day's supply and a day's accumulation.

McPherson is ordered to carry in wagons twenty day's rations, and to rely on the depot at Ringgold for the renewal of his bread. Beeves are now being driven on the hoof to the front; and the commissary, Colonel Beckwith, seems fully alive to the importance of the whole matter.

Our weakest point will be from the direction of Decatur, and I will be forced to risk something from that quarter, depending on the fact that the enemy has no force available with which to threaten our communications from that direction.

Colonel Comstock will explain to you personally much that I cannot commit to paper. I am, with great respect,

W. T. SHERMAN, *Major-General.*

On the 28th of April I removed my headquarters to Chattanooga, and prepared for taking the field in person. General Grant had first indicated the 30th of April as the day for the simultaneous advance, but subsequently changed the day to May 5th. McPherson's troops were brought forward rapidly to Chattanooga, partly by rail and partly by marching. Thomas's troops were already in position (his advance being out as far as Ringgold—eighteen miles), and Schofield was marching down by Cleveland to Red Clay and Catoosa Springs. On the 4th of May, Thomas was in person at Ringgold, his left at Catoosa, and his right at Leet's Tan-yard. Schofield was at Red Clay, closing upon Thomas's left; and McPherson was moving rapidly into Chattanooga, and out toward Gordon's Mill.

On the 5th I rode out to Ringgold, and on the very day appointed by General Grant from his headquarters in Virginia the great campaign was begun. To give all the minute details will involve more than is contemplated, and I will endeavor only to trace the principal events, or rather to record such as weighed heaviest on my own mind at the time, and which now remain best fixed in my memory.

My general headquarters and official records remained back at Nashville, and I had near me only my personal staff and inspectors-general, with about half a dozen wagons, and a single company of Ohio sharp-shooters (commanded by Lieutenant McCrory) as headquarters or camp guard. I also had a small company of irregular Alabama cavalry (commanded by Lieutenant Snelling), used mostly as orderlies and couriers. No wall-tents were allowed, only the flies. Our mess establishment was less in bulk than that of any of the brigade commanders; nor was this from an indifference to the ordinary comforts of life, but because I wanted to set the example, and gradually to convert all parts of that army into a mobile machine, willing and able to start at a minute's notice, and to subsist on the scantiest food. To reap absolute success might involve the necessity even of dropping all wagons, and to subsist on the chance food which the country was known to contain. I had obtained not only the United States census-tables of 1860, but a compilation made by the Controller of the State of Georgia for the purpose of taxation, containing in considerable detail the "population and statistics" of every county in Georgia. One of my aides (Captain Dayton) acted as assistant adjutant-general, with an order-book, letter-book, and writing-paper, that filled a small chest not much larger than an ordinary candle-box. The only reports and returns called for were the ordinary tri-monthly returns of "effective strength." As these accumulated they were sent back to Nashville, and afterward were embraced in the archives of the Military Division of the Mississippi, changed in 1865 to the Military Division of the Missouri, and I suppose they were burned in the Chicago fire of 1870. Still, duplicates remain of all essential papers in the archives of the War Department.

The 6th of May was given to Schofield and McPherson to get into position, and on the 7th General Thomas moved in force against Tunnel Hill, driving off a mere picket-guard of the enemy, and I was agreeably surprised to find that no damage had been done to the tunnel or the railroad. From Tunnel Hill I could look into the gorge by which the railroad passed through a straight and well-defined range of mountains, presenting sharp palisade faces, and known as "Rocky Face." The gorge itself was called the "Buzzard Roost." We could plainly see the enemy in this gorge and behind it, and Mill Creek which formed the gorge, flowing toward Dalton, had been dammed up, making a sort of irregular lake, filling the road, thereby obstructing it, and the enemy's batteries crowned the cliffs on either side. The position was very strong, and I knew that such a general as was my antagonist (Jos. Johnston), who had been there six months, had fortified it to the maximum. Therefore I had no intention to attack the position seriously in front, but depended on McPherson to capture and hold the railroad to its rear, which would force Johnston to detach largely against him, or rather, as I expected, to evacuate his position at Dalton altogether. My orders to Generals Thomas and Schofield were merely to press strongly at all points in front, ready to rush in on the first appearance of "let go," and, if possible, to catch our enemy in the confusion of retreat.

All the movements of the 7th and 8th were made exactly as ordered, and the enemy seemed quiescent, acting purely on the defensive.

I had constant communication with all parts of the army, and on the 9th McPherson's head of column entered and passed through Snake Creek, perfectly undefended, and accomplished a complete surprise to the enemy. At its farther *débouché* he met a cavalry brigade, easily driven, which retreated hastily north toward Dalton, and doubtless carried to Johnston the first serious intimation that a heavy force of infantry and artillery was to his rear and within a few miles of his railroad. I got a short note from McPherson that day (written at 2 P.M., when he was within a mile and a half of

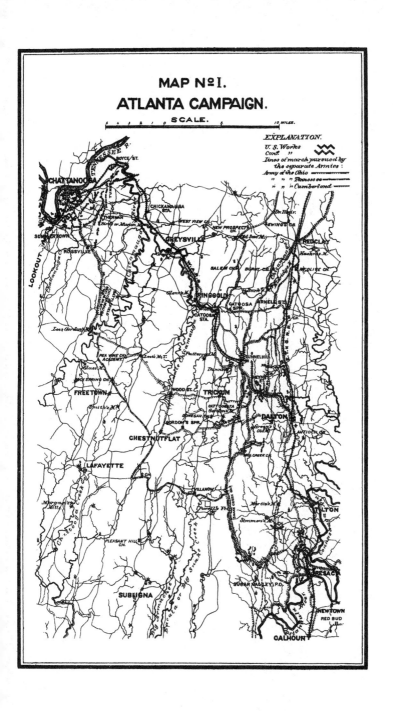

the railroad, above and near Resaca), and we all felt jubilant. I renewed orders to Thomas and Schofield to be ready for the instant pursuit of what I expected to be a broken and disordered army, forced to retreat by roads to the east of Resaca, which were known to be very rough and impracticable.

That night I received further notice from McPherson that he had found Resaca too strong for a surprise; that in consequence he had fallen back three miles to the mouth of Snake-Creek Gap, and was there fortified. I wrote him the next day the following letters, copies of which are in my letter-book; but his to me were mere notes in pencil, not retained:

HEADQUARTERS MILITARY DIVISION OF THE MISSISSIPPI, ⎱
IN THE FIELD, TUNNEL HILL, GEORGIA, *May* 11, 1864—*Morning.*⎰

Major-General McPHERSON, *commanding Army of the Tennessee,*
    Sugar Valley, Georgia.

GENERAL: I received by courier (in the night) yours of 5 and 6:30 P.M. of yesterday.

You now have your twenty-three thousand men, and General Hooker is in close support, so that you can hold all of Jos. Johnston's army in check should he abandon Dalton. He cannot afford to abandon Dalton, for he has fixed it up on purpose to receive us, and he observes that we are close at hand, waiting for him to quit. He cannot afford a detachment strong enough to fight you, as his army will not admit of it.

Strengthen your position; fight any thing that comes; and threaten the safety of the railroad all the time. But, to tell the truth, I would rather the enemy would stay in Dalton two more days, when he may find in his rear a larger party than he expects in an open field. At all events, we can then choose our own ground, and he will be forced to move out of his works. I do not intend to put a column into Buzzard-Roost Gap at present.

See that you are in easy communication with me and with all headquarters. After to-day the supplies will be at Ringgold. Yours,

W. T. SHERMAN, *Major-General commanding.*

HEADQUARTERS MILITARY DIVISION OF THE MISSISSIPPI, ⎱
IN THE FIELD, TUNNEL HILL, GEORGIA, *May* 11, 1864—*Evening.*⎰

General McPHERSON, *Sugar Valley.*

GENERAL: The indications are that Johnston is evacuating Dalton. In that event, Howard's corps and the cavalry will pursue; all the rest will follow your route. I will be down early in the morning.

Try to strike him if possible about the forks of the road.

Hooker must be with you now, and you may send General Garrard by Summerville to threaten Rome and that flank. I will cause all the lines to be felt at once.

W. T. SHERMAN, *Major-General commanding.*

McPherson had startled Johnston in his fancied security, but had not done the full measure of his work. He had in hand twenty-three thousand of the best men of the army, and could have walked into Resaca (then held only by a small brigade), or he could have placed his whole force astride the railroad above Resaca, and there have easily withstood the attack of all of Johnston's army, with the knowledge that Thomas and Schofield were on his heels. Had he done so, I am certain that Johnston would not have ventured to attack him in position, but would have retreated eastward by Spring Place, and we should have captured half his army and all his artillery and wagons at the very beginning of the campaign.

Such an opportunity does not occur twice in a single life, but at the critical moment McPherson seems to have been a little cautious. Still, he was perfectly justified by his orders, and fell back and assumed an unassailable defensive position in Sugar Valley, on the Resaca side of Snake-Creek Gap. As soon as informed of this, I determined to pass the whole army through Snake-Creek Gap, and to move on Resaca with the main army.

But during the 10th, the enemy showed no signs of evacuating Dalton, and I was waiting for the arrival of Garrard's and Stoneman's cavalry, known to be near at hand, so as to secure the full advantages of victory, of which I felt certain. Hooker's Twentieth Corps was at once moved down to within easy supporting distance of McPherson; and on the 11th, perceiving signs of evacuation of Dalton, I gave all the orders for the general movement, leaving the Fourth Corps (Howard) and Stoneman's cavalry in observation in front of Buzzard-Roost Gap, and directing all the rest of the army to march through Snake-Creek Gap, straight on Resaca. The roads were only such as the country afforded, mere rough wagon-ways, and these converged to the single narrow track through Snake-Creek Gap; but during the 12th and 13th the

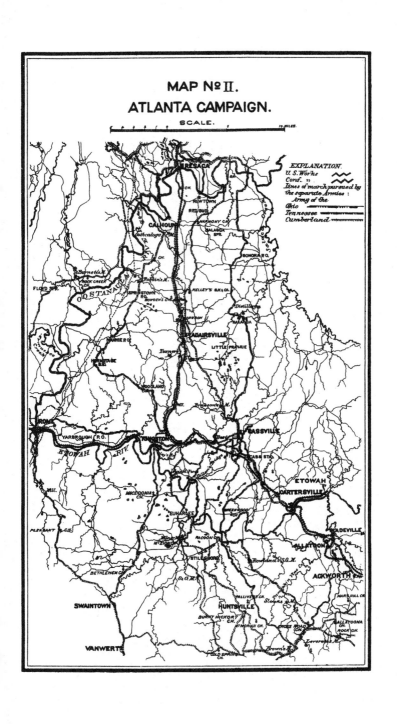

MAP No II.

ATLANTA CAMPAIGN.

SCALE.

EXPLANATION.
U. S. Works
Conf. "
Lines of march pursued by
the separate Armies:
Army of the
Ohio
Tennessee
Cumberland

bulk of Thomas's and Schofield's armies were got through, and deployed against Resaca, McPherson on the right, Thomas in the centre, and Schofield on the left. Johnston, as I anticipated, had abandoned all his well-prepared defenses at Dalton, and was found inside of Resaca with the bulk of his army, holding his divisions well in hand, acting purely on the defensive, and fighting well at all points of conflict. A complete line of intrenchments was found covering the place, and this was strongly manned at all points. On the 14th we closed in, enveloping the town on its north and west, and during the 15th we had a day of continual battle and skirmish. At the same time I caused two pontoon-bridges to be laid across the Oostenaula River at Lay's Ferry, about three miles below the town, by which we could threaten Calhoun, a station on the railroad seven miles below Resaca. At the same time, May 14th, I dispatched General Garrard, with his cavalry division, down the Oostenaula by the Rome road, with orders to cross over, if possible, and to attack or threaten the railroad at any point below Calhoun and above Kingston.

During the 15th, without attempting to assault the fortified works, we pressed at all points, and the sound of cannon and musketry rose all day to the dignity of a battle. Toward evening McPherson moved his whole line of battle forward, till he had gained a ridge overlooking the town, from which his field-artillery could reach the railroad-bridge across the Oostenaula. The enemy made several attempts to drive him away, repeating the sallies several times, and extending them into the night; but in every instance he was repulsed with bloody loss.

Hooker's corps had also some heavy and handsome fighting that afternoon and night on the left, where the Dalton road entered the intrenchments, capturing a four-gun intrenched battery, with its men and guns; and generally all our men showed the finest fighting qualities.

Howard's corps had followed Johnston down from Dalton, and was in line; Stoneman's division of cavalry had also got up, and was on the extreme left, beyond the Oostenaula.

On the night of May 15th Johnston got his army across the bridges, set them on fire, and we entered Resaca at daylight. Our loss up to that time was about six hundred dead and thirty-three hundred and seventy-five wounded—mostly light wounds that did not necessitate sending the men to the rear for treatment. That Johnston had deliberately designed in advance to give up such strong positions as Dalton and Resaca, for the purpose of drawing us farther south, is simply absurd. Had he remained in Dalton another hour, it would have been his total defeat, and he only evacuated Resaca because his safety demanded it. The movement by us through Snake-Creek Gap was a total surprise to him. My army about doubled his in size, but he had all the advantages of natural positions, of artificial forts and roads, and of concentrated action. We were compelled to grope our way through forests, across mountains, with a large army, necessarily more or less dispersed. Of course, I was disappointed not to have crippled his army more at that particular stage of the game; but, as it resulted, these rapid successes gave us the initiative, and the usual impulse of a conquering army.

Johnston having retreated in the night of May 15th, immediate pursuit was begun. A division of infantry (Jeff. C. Davis's) was at once dispatched down the valley toward Rome, to support Garrard's cavalry, and the whole army was ordered to pursue, McPherson by Lay's Ferry, on the right, Thomas directly by the railroad, and Schofield by the left, by the old road that crossed the Oostenaula above Echota or Newtown. We hastily repaired the railroad-bridge at Resaca, which had been partially burned, and built a temporary floating-bridge out of timber and materials found on the spot; so that Thomas got his advance corps over during the 16th, and marched as far as Calhoun, where he came into communication with McPherson's troops, which had crossed the Oostenaula at Lay's Ferry by our pontoon-bridges, previously laid. Inasmuch as the bridge at Resaca was overtaxed, Hooker's Twentieth Corps was also diverted to cross by the fords and ferries above Resaca, in the neighborhood of Echota.

On the 17th, toward evening, the head of Thomas's column, Newton's division, encountered the rear-guard of Johnston's army near Adairsville. I was near the head of column at the time, trying to get a view of the position of the enemy from an elevation in an open field. My party attracted the fire of a battery; a shell passed through the group of staff-officers and burst just beyond, which scattered us promptly. The next morning the enemy had disappeared, and our pursuit was continued to Kingston, which we reached during Sunday forenoon, the 19th.

From Resaca the railroad runs nearly due south, but at Kingston it makes junction with another railroad from Rome, and changes direction due east. At that time McPherson's head of column was about four miles to the west of Kingston, at a country place called "Woodlawn;" Schofield and Hooker were on the direct roads leading from Newtown to Cassville, diagonal to the route followed by Thomas. Thomas's head of column, which had followed the country roads alongside of the railroad, was about four miles east of Kingston, toward Cassville, when about noon I got a message from him that he had found the enemy, drawn up in line of battle, on some extensive, open ground, about half-way between Kingston and Cassville, and that appearances indicated a willingness and preparation for battle.

Hurriedly sending orders to McPherson to resume the march, to hasten forward by roads leading to the south of Kingston, so as to leave for Thomas's troops and trains the use of the main road, and to come up on his right, I rode forward rapidly, over some rough gravel hills, and about six miles from Kingston found General Thomas, with his troops deployed; but he reported that the enemy had fallen back in echelon of divisions, steadily and in superb order, into Cassville. I knew that the roads by which Generals Hooker and Schofield were approaching would lead them to a seminary near Cassville, and that it was all-important to secure the point of junction of these roads with the main road along which we were marching. Therefore I ordered General Thomas to push forward his deployed lines as rapidly as possible; and, as night was approaching, I ordered two field-batteries to close up at a gallop on some woods which lay between us and the town of Cassville. We could not see the town by reason of these woods, but a high range of hills just back of the town was visible over the tree-tops. On these hills could be seen fresh-made parapets, and the movements of men, against whom I directed the artillery to fire at long range. The stout resistance made by the enemy along our whole front of a couple of miles indicated a purpose to fight at Cassville; and, as the night was closing in, General Thomas and I were together, along with our skirmish-lines near the seminary, on the edge of the town, where musket-bullets from the enemy were cutting the leaves of the trees pretty thickly about us. Either Thomas or I remarked that that was not the place for the two senior officers of a great army, and we personally went back to the battery, where we passed the night on the ground. During the night I had reports from McPherson, Hooker, and Schofield. The former was about five miles to my right rear, near the "nitre-caves;" Schofield was about six miles north, and Hooker between us, within two miles. All were ordered to close down on Cassville at daylight, and to attack the enemy wherever found. Skirmishing was kept up all night, but when day broke the next morning, May 20th, the enemy was gone, and our cavalry was sent in pursuit. These reported him beyond the Etowah River. We were then well in advance of our railroad-trains, on which we depended for supplies; so I determined to pause a few days to repair the railroad, which had been damaged but little, except at the bridge at Resaca, and then to go on.

Nearly all the people of the country seemed to have fled with Johnston's army; yet some few families remained, and from one of them I procured the copy of an order which Johnston had made at Adairsville, in which he recited that he had retreated as far as strategy required, and that his army must be prepared for battle at Cassville. The newspapers of the South, many of which we found, were also loud in denunciation of Johnston's falling back before us without a serious battle, simply resisting by his skirmish-lines and by his rear-guard. But his friends proclaimed that it was all *strategic*; that he was deliberately drawing us farther and farther into the meshes, farther and farther away from our base of supplies, and that in due season he would not only halt for battle, but assume the bold offensive. Of course it was to my interest to bring him to battle as soon as possible, when our numerical superiority was at the greatest; for he was picking up his detachments as he fell back, whereas I was compelled to make similar and stronger detachments to repair the railroads as we advanced, and to guard them. I found at Cassville many evidences of preparation for a grand battle, among them a long line of fresh intrenchments on the hill beyond the town, extending nearly three miles to the south, embracing the railroad-crossing. I was also convinced that the whole of Polk's corps had joined Johnston from Mississippi, and that he had in hand three full corps, viz., Hood's, Polk's, and Hardee's, numbering about sixty thousand men, and could not then imagine why he had declined battle, and did not learn the real reason till after the war was over, and then from General Johnston himself.

In the autumn of 1865, when in command of the Military Division of the Missouri, I went from St. Louis to Little Rock, Arkansas, and afterward to Memphis. Taking a steamer for Cairo, I found as fellow-passengers Generals Johnston and Frank Blair. We were, of course, on the most friendly terms, and on our way up we talked over our battles again, played cards, and questioned each other as to particular parts of our mutual conduct in the game of war. I told Johnston that I had seen his order of preparation, in the nature of an address to his army, announcing his purpose to retreat no more, but to accept battle at Cassville. He answered that such was his purpose; that he had left Hardee's corps in the open fields to check Thomas, and gain time for his formation on the ridge, just behind Cassville; and it was this corps which General Thomas had seen deployed, and whose handsome movement in retreat he had reported in such complimentary terms. Johnston described how he had placed Hood's corps on the right, Polk's in the centre, and Hardee's on the left. He said he had ridden over the ground, given to each corps commander his position, and orders to throw up parapets during the night; that he was with Hardee on his extreme left as the night closed in, and as Hardee's troops fell back to the position assigned them for the intended battle of the next day; and that, after giving Hardee some general instructions, he and his staff rode back to Cassville. As he entered the town, or village, he met Generals Hood and Polk. Hood inquired of him if he had had any thing to eat, and he said no, that he was both hungry and tired, when Hood invited him to go and share a supper which had been prepared for him at a house close by. At the supper they discussed the chances of the impending battle, when Hood spoke of the ground assigned him as being enfiladed by our (Union) artillery, which Johnston disputed, when General Polk chimed in with the remark that General Hood was right; that the cannon-shots fired by us at nightfall had enfiladed their general line of battle, and that for this reason he feared they could not hold their men. General Johnston was surprised at this, for he understood General Hood to be one of those who professed to criticise his strategy, contending that, instead of retreating, he should have risked a battle. General Johnston said he was provoked, accused them of having been in conference, with being beaten before battle, and added that he was unwilling to engage in a critical battle with an army so superior to his own in numbers, with two of his three corps commanders dissatisfied with the ground and positions assigned them. He then and there made up his mind to retreat still farther south, to put the Etowah River and the Allatoona range between us; and he at once gave orders to resume the retrograde movement.

This was my recollection of the substance of the conversation, of which I made no note at the time; but, at a meeting of the Society of the Army of the Cumberland some years after, at Cleveland, Ohio, about 1868, in a short after-dinner speech, I related this conversation, and it got into print. Subsequently, in the spring of 1870, when I was at New Orleans, *en route* for Texas, General Hood called to see me at the St. Charles Hotel, explained that he had seen my speech reprinted in the newspapers and gave me his version of the same event, describing the halt at Cassville, the general orders for battle on that ground, and the meeting at supper with Generals Johnston and Polk, when the chances of the battle to be fought the next day were freely and fully discussed; and he stated that he had argued against fighting the battle purely on the defensive, but had asked General Johnston to permit him with his own corps and part of Polk's to quit their lines, and to march rapidly to attack and overwhelm Schofield, who was known to be separated from Thomas by an interval of nearly five miles, claiming that he could have defeated Schofield, and got back to his position in time to meet General Thomas's attack in front. He also stated that he had then contended

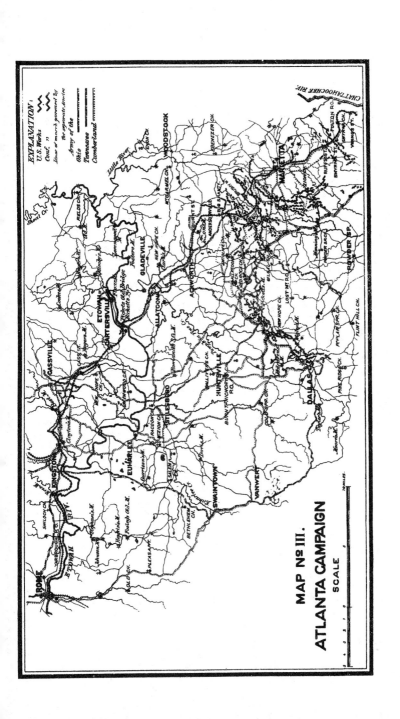

MAP Nº III.
ATLANTA CAMPAIGN
SCALE

with Johnston for the "offensive-defensive" game, instead of the "pure defensive," as proposed by General Johnston; and he said that it was at this time that General Johnston had taken offense, and that it was for this reason he had ordered the retreat that night. As subsequent events estranged these two officers, it is very natural they should now differ on this point; but it was sufficient for us that the rebel army did retreat that night, leaving us masters of all the country above the Etowah River.

For the purposes of rest, to give time for the repair of the railroads, and to replenish supplies, we lay by some few days in that quarter—Schofield with Stoneman's cavalry holding the ground at Cassville Depot, Cartersville, and the Etowah Bridge; Thomas holding his ground near Cassville, and McPherson that near Kingston. The officer intrusted with the repair of the railroads was Colonel W. W. Wright, a railroad-engineer, who, with about two thousand men, was so industrious and skillful that the bridge at Resaca was rebuilt in three days, and cars loaded with stores came forward to Kingston on the 24th. The telegraph also brought us the news of the bloody and desperate battles of the Wilderness, in Virginia, and that General Grant was pushing his operations against Lee with terrific energy. I was therefore resolved to give my enemy no rest.

In early days (1844), when a lieutenant of the Third Artillery, I had been sent from Charleston, South Carolina, to Marietta, Georgia, to assist Inspector-General Churchill to take testimony concerning certain losses of horses and accoutrements by the Georgia Volunteers during the Florida War; and after completing the work at Marietta we transferred our party over to Bellefonte, Alabama. I had ridden the distance on horseback, and had noted well the topography of the country, especially that about Kenesaw, Allatoona, and the Etowah River. On that occasion I had stopped some days with a Colonel Tumlin, to see some remarkable Indian mounds on the Etowah River, usually called the "Hightower." I therefore knew that the Allatoona Pass was very strong, would be hard to force, and resolved not even to attempt it, but to turn the position, by moving from Kingston to Marietta *via* Dallas; accordingly I made orders on the 20th to get ready for the march to begin on the 23d. The Army of the Cumberland was ordered to march for Dallas, by Euharlee and Stilesboro'; Davis's division, then in Rome, by Van Wert; the Army of the Ohio to keep on the left of Thomas, by a place called Burnt Hickory; and the Army of the Tennessee to march for a position a little to the south, so as to be on the right of the general army, when grouped about Dallas.

The movement contemplated leaving our railroad, and to depend for twenty days on the contents of our wagons; and as the country was very obscure, mostly in a state of nature, densely wooded, and with few roads, our movements were necessarily slow. We crossed the Etowah by several bridges and fords, and took as many roads as possible, keeping up communication by cross-roads, or by couriers through the woods. I personally joined General Thomas, who had the centre, and was consequently the main column, or "column of direction." The several columns followed generally the valley of the Euharlee, a tributary coming into the Etowah from the south, and gradually crossed over a ridge of mountains, parts of which had once been worked over for gold, and were consequently full of paths and unused wagon-roads or tracks. A cavalry picket of the enemy at Burnt Hickory was captured, and had on his person an order from General Johnston, dated at Allatoona, which showed that he had detected my purpose of turning his position, and it accordingly became necessary to use great caution, lest some of the minor columns should fall into ambush, but, luckily the enemy was not much more familiar with that part of the country than we were. On the other side of the Allatoona range, the Pumpkin-Vine Creek, also a tributary of the Etowah, flowed north and west; Dallas, the point aimed at, was a small town on the other or east side of this creek, and was the point of concentration of a great many roads that led in every direction. Its possession would be a threat to Marietta and Atlanta, but I could not then venture to attempt either, till I had regained the use of the railroad, at least as far down as its *débouché* from the Allatoona range of mountains. Therefore, the movement was chiefly designed to compel Johnston to give up Allatoona.

On the 25th all the columns were moving steadily on Dallas—McPherson and Davis away off to the right, near Van

Wert; Thomas on the main road in the centre, with Hooker's Twentieth Corps ahead, toward Dallas; and Schofield to the left rear. For the convenience of march, Hooker had his three divisions on separate roads, all leading toward Dallas, when, in the afternoon, as he approached a bridge across Pumpkin-Vine Creek, he found it held by a cavalry force, which was driven off, but the bridge was on fire. This fire was extinguished, and Hooker's leading division (Geary's) followed the retreating cavalry on a road leading due east toward Marietta, instead of Dallas. This leading division, about four miles out from the bridge, struck a heavy infantry force, which was moving down from Allatoona toward Dallas, and a sharp battle ensued. I came up in person soon after, and as my map showed that we were near an important cross-road called "New Hope," from a Methodist meeting-house there of that name, I ordered General Hooker to secure it if possible that night. He asked for a short delay, till he could bring up his other two divisions, viz., of Butterfield and Williams, but before these divisions had got up and were deployed, the enemy had also gained corresponding strength. The woods were so dense, and the resistance so spirited, that Hooker could not carry the position, though the battle was noisy, and prolonged far into the night. This point, "New Hope," was the accidental intersection of the road leading from Allatoona to Dallas with that from Van Wert to Marietta, was four miles northeast of Dallas, and from the bloody fighting there for the next week was called by the soldiers "Hell-Hole."

The night was pitch-dark, it rained hard, and the convergence of our columns toward Dallas produced much confusion. I am sure similar confusion existed in the army opposed to us, for we were all mixed up. I slept on the ground, without cover, alongside of a log, got little sleep, resolved at daylight to renew the battle, and to make a lodgment on the Dallas and Allatoona road if possible, but the morning revealed a strong line of intrenchments facing us, with a heavy force of infantry and guns. The battle was renewed, and without success. McPherson reached Dallas that morning, viz., the 26th, and deployed his troops to the southeast and east of the town, placing Davis's division of the Fourteenth Corps, which had joined him on the road from Rome, on his left;

but this still left a gap of at least three miles between Davis and Hooker. Meantime, also, General Schofield was closing up on Thomas's left.

Satisfied that Johnston in person was at New Hope with all his army, and that it was so much nearer my "objective," the railroad, than Dallas, I concluded to draw McPherson from Dallas to Hooker's right, and gave orders accordingly; but McPherson also was confronted with a heavy force, and, as he began to withdraw according to his orders, on the morning of the 28th he was fiercely assailed on his right; a bloody battle ensued, in which he repulsed the attack, inflicting heavy loss on his assailants, and it was not until the 1st of June that he was enabled to withdraw from Dallas, and to effect a close junction with Hooker in front of New Hope. Meantime Thomas and Schofield were completing their deployments, gradually overlapping Johnston on his right, and thus extending our left nearer and nearer to the railroad, the nearest point of which was Acworth, about eight miles distant. All this time a continual battle was in progress by strong skirmish-lines, taking advantage of every species of cover, and both parties fortifying each night by rifle-trenches, with head-logs, many of which grew to be as formidable as first-class works of defense. Occasionally one party or the other would make a dash in the nature of a sally, but usually it sustained a repulse with great loss of life. I visited personally all parts of our lines nearly every day, was constantly within musket-range, and though the fire of musketry and cannon resounded day and night along the whole line, varying from six to ten miles, I rarely saw a dozen of the enemy at any one time; and these were always skirmishers dodging from tree to tree, or behind logs on the ground, or who occasionally showed their heads above the hastily-constructed but remarkably strong rifle-trenches. On the occasion of my visit to McPherson on the 30th of May, while standing with a group of officers, among whom were Generals McPherson, Logan, Barry, and Colonel Taylor, my former chief of artillery, a Minié-ball passed through Logan's coat-sleeve, scratching the skin, and struck Colonel Taylor square in the breast; luckily he had in his pocket a famous memorandum-book, in which he kept a sort of diary, about which we used to joke him a good deal; its thickness and size saved his life, breaking the force of the ball, so that after traversing the book it only penetrated the breast to the ribs, but it knocked him down and disabled him for the rest of the campaign. He was a most competent and worthy officer, and now lives in poverty in Chicago, sustained in part by his own labor, and in part by a pitiful pension recently granted.

On the 1st of June General McPherson closed in upon the right, and, without attempting further to carry the enemy's strong position at New Hope Church, I held our general right in close contact with it, gradually, carefully, and steadily working by the left, until our strong infantry-lines had reached and secured possession of all the wagon-roads between New Hope, Allatoona, and Acworth, when I dispatched Generals Garrard's and Stoneman's divisions of cavalry into Allatoona, the first around by the west end of the pass, and the latter by the direct road. Both reached their destination without opposition, and orders were at once given to repair the railroad forward from Kingston to Allatoona, embracing the bridge across the Etowah River. Thus the real object of my move on Dallas was accomplished, and on the 4th of June I was preparing to draw off from New Hope Church, and to take position on the railroad in front of Allatoona, when, General Johnston himself having evacuated his position, we effected the change without further battle, and moved to the railroad, occupying it from Allatoona and Acworth forward to Big Shanty, in sight of the famous Kenesaw Mountain.

Thus, substantially in the month of May, we had steadily driven our antagonist from the strong positions of Dalton, Resaca, Cassville, Allatoona, and Dallas; had advanced our lines in strong, compact order from Chattanooga to Big Shanty, nearly a hundred miles of as difficult country as was ever fought over by civilized armies; and thus stood prepared to go on, anxious to fight, and confident of success as soon as the railroad communications were complete to bring forward the necessary supplies. It is now impossible to state accurately our loss of life and men in any one separate battle; for the fighting was continuous, almost daily, among trees and bushes, on ground where one could rarely see a hundred yards ahead.

The aggregate loss in the several corps for the month of May is reported as follows in the usual monthly returns sent to the Adjutant-General's office, which are, therefore, official:

Casualties during the Month of May, 1864 (Major-General SHERMAN commanding).

ARMY OF THE CUMBERLAND (MAJOR-GENERAL THOMAS).

CORPS.	Killed and Missing.	Wounded.	Total.
Fourth (Howard)	576	1,910	2,486
Fourteenth (Palmer).	147	655	802
Twentieth (Hooker)	571	2,997	3,568
Total	1,294	5,562	6,856

ARMY OF THE TENNESSEE (MAJOR-GENERAL M^cPHERSON).

CORPS.	Killed and Missing.	Wounded.	Total.
Fifteenth (Logan)	122	624	746
Sixteenth (Dodge)	94	430	524
Seventeenth (Blair)	(Not yet up.)	1	1
Total	216	1,055	1,271

ARMY OF THE OHIO (MAJOR-GENERAL SCHOFIELD).

CORPS.	Killed and Missing.	Wounded.	Total.
Twenty-third (Schofield)	226	757	983
Cavalry	127	62	189
Total	353	819	1,172
Grand aggregate.	1,863	7,436	9,299

General Joseph E. Johnston, in his "Narrative of his Military Operations," just published (March 27, 1874), gives the

effective strength of his army at and about Dalton on the 1st
of May, 1864 (page 302), as follows:

Infantry	37,652
Artillery	2,812
Cavalry	2,392
Total.	42,856

During May, and prior to reaching Cassville, he was further
reënforced (page 352):

Polk's corps of three divisions. . . .	12,000
Martin's division of cavalry	3,500
Jackson's division of cavalry.	3,900

And at New Hope Church, May 26th:

Brigade of Quarles	2,200
Grand total	64,456

His losses during the month of May are stated by him, as
taken from the report of Surgeon Foard (page 325):

FROM DALTON TO CASSVILLE.

CORPS.	Killed.	Wounded.	Total.
Hardee's	116	850	966
Hood's.	283	1,564	1,847
Polk's.	46	529	575
Total	445	2,943	3,388

AT NEW HOPE CHURCH (PAGE 335.)

CORPS.	Killed.	Wounded.	Total.
Hardee's	156	879	1,035
Hood's	103	756	859
Polk's.	17	94	111
Total	276	1,729	2,005
Total killed and wounded during May . .	721	4,672	5,393

These figures include only the killed and wounded, whereas my statement of losses embraces the "missing," which are usually "prisoners," and of these we captured, during the whole campaign of four and a half months, exactly 12,983, whose names, rank, and regiments, were officially reported to the Commissary-General of Prisoners; and assuming a due proportion for the month of May, viz., one-fourth, makes 3,245 to be added to the killed and wounded given above, making an aggregate loss in Johnston's army, from Dalton to New Hope, inclusive, of 8,638, against ours of 9,299.

Therefore General Johnston is greatly in error, in his estimates on page 357, in stating our loss, as compared with his, at six or ten to one.

I always estimated my force at about double his, and could afford to lose two to one without disturbing our relative proportion; but I also reckoned that, in the natural strength of the country, in the abundance of mountains, streams, and forests, he had a fair offset to our numerical superiority, and therefore endeavored to act with reasonable caution while moving on the vigorous "offensive."

With the drawn battle of New Hope Church, and our occupation of the natural fortress of Allatoona, terminated the month of May, and the first stage of the campaign.

Chapter XVII.

ATLANTA CAMPAIGN — BATTLES ABOUT KENESAW
MOUNTAIN.
June, 1864.

O N THE 1ST of June our three armies were well in hand, in the broken and densely-wooded country fronting the enemy intrenched at New Hope Church, about five miles north of Dallas. General Stoneman's division of cavalry had occupied Allatoona, on the railroad, and General Garrard's division was at the western end of the pass, about Stilesboro'. Colonel W. W. Wright, of the Engineers, was busily employed in repairing the railroad and rebuilding the bridge across the Etowah (or Hightower) River, which had been destroyed by the enemy on his retreat; and the armies were engaged in a general and constant skirmish along a front of about six miles — McPherson the right, Thomas the centre, and Schofield on the left. By gradually covering our front with parapet, and extending to the left, we approached the railroad toward Acworth and overlapped the enemy's right. By the 4th of June we had made such progress that Johnston evacuated his lines in the night, leaving us masters of the situation, when I deliberately shifted McPherson's army to the extreme left, at and in front of Acworth, with Thomas's about two miles on his right, and Schofield's on his right — all facing east. Heavy rains set in about the 1st of June, making the roads infamous; but our marches were short, as we needed time for the repair of the railroad, so as to bring supplies forward to Allatoona Station. On the 6th I rode back to Allatoona, seven miles, found it all that was expected, and gave orders for its fortification and preparation as a "secondary base." General Blair arrived at Acworth on the 8th with his two divisions of the Seventeenth Corps — the same which had been on veteran furlough — had come up from Cairo by way of Clifton, on the Tennessee River, and had followed our general route to Allatoona, where he had left a garrison of about fifteen hundred men. His effective strength, as reported, was nine thousand. These, with new regiments and furloughed

519

men who had joined early in the month of May, equaled our losses from battle, sickness, and by detachments; so that the three armies still aggregated about one hundred thousand effective men.

On the 10th of June the whole combined army moved forward six miles, to "Big Shanty," a station on the railroad, whence we had a good view of the enemy's position, which embraced three prominent hills, known as Kenesaw, Pine Mountain, and Lost Mountain. On each of these hills the enemy had signal-stations and fresh lines of parapets. Heavy masses of infantry could be distinctly seen with the naked eye, and it was manifest that Johnston had chosen his ground well, and with deliberation had prepared for battle; but his line was at least ten miles in extent—too long, in my judgment, to be held successfully by his force, then estimated at sixty thousand. As his position, however, gave him a perfect view over our field, we had to proceed with due caution. McPherson had the left, following the railroad, which curved around the north base of Kenesaw; Thomas the centre, obliqued to the right, deploying below Kenesaw and facing Pine Hill; and Schofield, somewhat refused, was on the general right, looking south, toward Lost Mountain.

On the 11th the Etowah bridge was done; the railroad was repaired up to our very skirmish-line, close to the base of Kenesaw, and a loaded train of cars came to Big Shanty. The locomotive, detached, was run forward to a water-tank within the range of the enemy's guns on Kenesaw, whence the enemy opened fire on the locomotive; but the engineer was not afraid, went on to the tank, got water, and returned safely to his train, answering the guns with the screams of his engine, heightened by the cheers and shouts of our men.

The rains continued to pour, and made our developments slow and dilatory, for there were no roads, and these had to be improvised by each division for its own supply-train from the depot in Big Shanty to the camps. Meantime each army was deploying carefully before the enemy, intrenching every camp, ready as against a sally. The enemy's cavalry was also busy in our rear, compelling us to detach cavalry all the way back as far as Resaca, and to strengthen all the infantry posts as far as Nashville. Besides, there was great danger, always in

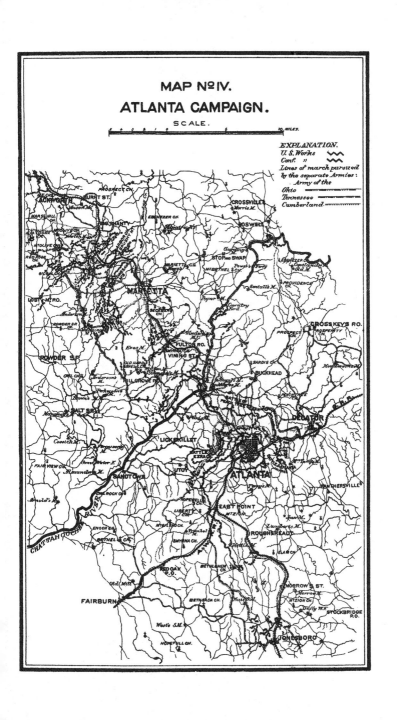

MAP Nº IV.

ATLANTA CAMPAIGN.

SCALE.

EXPLANATION.
U. S. Works
Conf. "
Lines of march pursued
by the separate Armies:
Army of the
Ohio
Tennessee
Cumberland

my mind, that Forrest would collect a heavy cavalry command in Mississippi, cross the Tennessee River, and break up our railroad below Nashville. In anticipation of this very danger, I had sent General Sturgis to Memphis to take command of all the cavalry in that quarter, to go out toward Pontotoc, engage Forrest and defeat him; but on the 14th of June I learned that General Sturgis had himself been defeated on the 10th of June, and had been driven by Forrest back into Memphis in considerable confusion. I expected that this would soon be followed by a general raid on all our roads in Tennessee. General A. J. Smith, with the two divisions of the Sixteenth and Seventeenth Corps which had been with General Banks up Red River, had returned from that ill-fated expedition, and had been ordered to General Canby at New Orleans, who was making a diversion about Mobile; but, on hearing of General Sturgis's defeat, I ordered General Smith to go out from Memphis and renew the offensive, so as to keep Forrest off our roads. This he did finally, defeating Forrest at Tupelo, on the 13th, 14th, and 15th days of July; and he so stirred up matters in North Mississippi that Forrest could not leave for Tennessee. This, for a time, left me only the task of covering the roads against such minor detachments of cavalry as Johnston could spare from his immediate army, and I proposed to keep these too busy in their own defense to spare detachments.

By the 14th the rain slackened, and we occupied a continuous line of ten miles, intrenched, conforming to the irregular position of the enemy, when I reconnoitred, with a view to make a break in their line between Kenesaw and Pine Mountain. When abreast of Pine Mountain I noticed a rebel battery on its crest, with a continuous line of fresh rifle-trench about half-way down the hill. Our skirmishers were at the time engaged in the woods about the base of this hill between the lines, and I estimated the distance to the battery on the crest at about eight hundred yards. Near it, in plain view, stood a group of the enemy, evidently observing us with glasses. General Howard, commanding the Fourth Corps, was near by, and I called his attention to this group, and ordered him to compel it to keep behind its cover. He replied that his orders from General Thomas were to spare artillery-ammunition. This was right, according to the general policy, but I explained to him that we must keep up the *morale* of a bold offensive, that he must use his artillery, force the enemy to remain on the timid defensive, and ordered him to cause a battery close by to fire three volleys. I continued to ride down our line, and soon heard, in quick succession, the three volleys. The next division in order was Geary's, and I gave him similar orders. General Polk, in my opinion, was killed by the second volley fired from the first battery referred to.

In a conversation with General Johnston, after the war, he explained that on that day he had ridden in person from Marietta to Pine Mountain, held by Bates's division, and was accompanied by Generals Hardee and Polk. When on Pine Mountain, reconnoitring, quite a group of soldiers, belonging to the battery close by, clustered about him. He noticed the preparations of our battery to fire, and cautioned these men to scatter. They did so, and he likewise hurried behind the parapet, from which he had an equally good view of our position; but General Polk, who was dignified and corpulent, walked back slowly, not wishing to appear too hurried or cautious in the presence of the men, and was struck across the breast by an unexploded shell, which killed him instantly. This is my memory of the conversation, and it is confirmed by Johnston himself in his "Narrative," page 337, except that he calculated the distance of our battery at six hundred yards, and says that Polk was killed by the third shot; I know that our guns fired by volley, and believe that he was hit by a shot of the second volley. It has been asserted that I fired the gun which killed General Polk, and that I knew it was directed against that general. The fact is, at that distance we could not even tell that the group were officers at all; I was on horseback, a couple of hundred yards off, before my orders to fire were executed, had no idea that our shot had taken effect, and continued my ride down along the line to Schofield's extreme flank, returning late in the evening to my headquarters at Big Shanty, where I occupied an abandoned house. In a cottonfield back of that house was our signal-station, on the roof of an old gin-house. The signal-officer reported that by studying the enemy's signals he had learned the "key," and that he could read their signals. He explained to me that he had translated a signal about noon, from Pine Mountain to

Marietta, "Send an ambulance for General Polk's body;" and later in the day another, "Why don't you send an ambulance for General Polk?" From this we inferred that General Polk had been killed, but how or where we knew not; and this inference was confirmed later in the same day by the report of some prisoners who had been captured.

On the 15th we advanced our general lines, intending to attack at any weak point discovered between Kenesaw and Pine Mountain; but Pine Mountain was found to be abandoned, and Johnston had contracted his front somewhat, on a direct line, connecting Kenesaw with Lost Mountain. Thomas and Schofield thereby gained about two miles of most difficult country, and McPherson's left lapped well around the north end of Kenesaw. We captured a good many prisoners, among them a whole infantry regiment, the Fourteenth Alabama, three hundred and twenty strong.

On the 16th the general movement was continued, when Lost Mountain was abandoned by the enemy. Our right naturally swung round, so as to threaten the railroad below Marietta, but Johnston had still further contracted and strengthened his lines, covering Marietta and all the roads below.

On the 17th and 18th the rain again fell in torrents, making army movements impossible, but we devoted the time to strengthening our positions, more especially the left and centre, with a view gradually to draw from the left to add to the right; and we had to hold our lines on the left extremely strong, to guard against a sally from Kenesaw against our depot at Big Shanty. Garrard's division of cavalry was kept busy on our left, McPherson had gradually extended to his right, enabling Thomas to do the same still farther; but the enemy's position was so very strong, and everywhere it was covered by intrenchments, that we found it as dangerous to assault as a permanent fort. We in like manner covered our lines of battle by similar works, and even our skirmishers learned to cover their bodies by the simplest and best forms of defensive works, such as rails or logs, piled in the form of a simple lunette, covered on the outside with earth thrown up at night.

The enemy and ourselves used the same form of rifle-trench, varied according to the nature of the ground, viz.: the trees and bushes were cut away for a hundred yards or more in front, serving as an abatis or entanglement; the parapets varied from four to six feet high, the dirt taken from a ditch outside and from a covered way inside, and this parapet was surmounted by a "head-log," composed of the trunk of a tree from twelve to twenty inches at the butt, lying along the interior crest of the parapet and resting in notches cut in other trunks which extended back, forming an inclined plane, in case the head-log should be knocked inward by a cannon-shot. The men of both armies became extremely skillful in the construction of these works, because each man realized their value and importance to himself, so that it required no orders for their construction. As soon as a regiment or brigade gained a position within easy distance for a sally, it would set to work with a will, and would construct such a parapet in a single night; but I endeavored to spare the soldiers this hard labor by authorizing each division commander to organize out of the freedmen who escaped to us a pioneer corps of two hundred men, who were fed out of the regular army supplies, and I promised them ten dollars a month, under an existing act of Congress. These pioneer detachments became very useful to us during the rest of the war, for they could work at night while our men slept; they in turn were not expected to fight, and could therefore sleep by day. Our enemies used their slaves for a similar purpose, but usually kept them out of the range of fire by employing them to fortify and strengthen the position to their rear *next* to be occupied in their general retrograde. During this campaign hundreds if not thousands of miles of similar intrenchments were built by both armies, and, as a rule, whichever party attacked got the worst of it.

On the 19th of June the rebel army again fell back on its flanks, to such an extent that for a time I supposed it had retreated to the Chattahoochee River, fifteen miles distant; but as we pressed forward we were soon undeceived, for we found it still more concentrated, covering Marietta and the railroad. These successive contractions of the enemy's line encouraged us and discouraged him, but were doubtless justified by sound reasons. On the 20th Johnston's position was unusually strong. Kenesaw Mountain was his salient; his two flanks were refused and covered by parapets and by Noonday and Nose's Creeks. His left flank was his weak point, so long as he acted on the "defensive," whereas, had he designed to contract the extent of his line for the purpose of getting in reserve a force with which to strike "offensively" from his right, he would have done a wise act, and I was compelled to presume that such was his object. We were also so far from Nashville and Chattanooga that we were naturally sensitive for the safety of our railroad and depots, so that the left (McPherson) was held *very strong*.

About this time came reports that a large cavalry force of the enemy had passed around our left flank, evidently to strike this very railroad somewhere below Chattanooga. I therefore reënforced the cavalry stationed from Resaca to Cassville, and ordered forward from Huntsville, Alabama, the infantry division of General John E. Smith, to hold Kingston securely.

While we were thus engaged about Kenesaw, General Grant had his hands full with Lee, in Virginia. General Halleck was the chief of staff at Washington, and to him I communicated almost daily. I find from my letter-book that on the 21st of June I reported to him tersely and truly the condition of facts on that day: "This is the nineteenth day of rain, and the prospect of fair weather is as far off as ever. The roads are impassable; the fields and woods become quagmires after a few wagons have crossed over. Yet we are at work all the time. The left flank is across Noonday Creek, and the right is across Nose's Creek. The enemy still holds Kenesaw, a conical mountain, with Marietta behind it, and has his flanks retired, to cover that town and the railroad behind. I am all ready to attack the moment the weather and roads will permit troops and artillery to move with any thing like life."

The weather has a wonderful effect on troops: in action and on the march, rain is favorable; but in the woods, where all is blind and uncertain, it seems almost impossible for an army covering ten miles of front to act in concert during wet and stormy weather. Still I pressed operations with the utmost earnestness, aiming always to keep our fortified lines in absolute contact with the enemy, while with the surplus force we felt forward, from one flank or the other, for his line of communication and retreat. On the 22d of June I rode the whole line, and ordered General Thomas in person to advance his extreme right corps (Hooker's); and instructed General Schofield, by letter, to keep his entire army, viz., the Twenty-third Corps, as a strong right flank in close support of Hooker's deployed line. During this day the sun came out, with some promise of clear weather, and I had got back to my bivouac about dark, when a signal-message was received, dated—

KULP HOUSE, 5.30 P.M.

General SHERMAN:

We have repulsed two heavy attacks, and feel confident, our only apprehension being from our extreme right flank. Three entire corps are in front of us.

Major-General HOOKER.

Hooker's corps (the Twentieth) belonged to Thomas's army; Thomas's headquarters were two miles nearer to Hooker than mine; and Hooker, being an old army officer, knew that he should have reported this fact to Thomas and not to me; I was, moreover, specially disturbed by the assertion in his report that he was uneasy about his *right flank*, when Schofield had been specially ordered to protect that. I first inquired of my adjutant, Dayton, if he were certain that General Schofield had received his orders, and he answered that the envelope in which he had sent them was receipted by General Schofield himself. I knew, therefore, that General Schofield must be near by, in close support of Hooker's right flank. General Thomas had before this occasion complained to me of General Hooker's disposition to "switch off," leaving wide gaps in his line, so as to be independent, and to make *glory* on his own account. I therefore resolved not to overlook this breach of discipline and propriety. The rebel army was only composed of three corps; I had that very day ridden six miles of their lines, found them everywhere strongly occupied, and therefore Hooker could not have encountered "three entire corps." Both McPherson and Schofield had also complained to me of this same tendency of Hooker to widen the gap between his own corps and his proper army (Thomas's), so as to come into closer contact with one or other of the wings, asserting that he was the senior by commission to both McPherson and Schofield, and that in the event of battle he should assume command over them, by virtue of his older commission.

They appealed to me to protect them. I had heard during that day some cannonading and heavy firing down toward the "Kulp House," which was about five miles southeast of where I was, but this was nothing unusual, for at the same moment there was firing along our lines full ten miles in extent. Early the next day (23d) I rode down to the "Kulp House," which was on a road leading from Powder Springs to Marietta, about three miles distant from the latter. On the way I passed through General Butterfield's division of Hooker's corps, which I learned had not been engaged at all in the battle of the day before; then I rode along Geary's and Williams's divisions, which occupied the field of battle, and the men were engaged in burying the· dead. I found General Schofield's corps on the Powder Springs road, its head of column abreast of Hooker's right, therefore constituting "a strong right flank," and I met Generals Schofield and Hooker together. As rain was falling at the moment, we passed into a little church standing by the road-side, and I there showed General Schofield Hooker's signal-message of the day before. He was very angry, and pretty sharp words passed between them, Schofield saying that his head of column (Hascall's division) had been, at the time of the battle, actually in advance of Hooker's line; that the attack or sally of the enemy struck his troops before it did Hooker's; that General Hooker knew of it at the time; and he offered to go out and show me that the dead men of his advance division (Hascall's) were lying farther out than any of Hooker's. General Hooker pretended not to have known this fact. I then asked him why he had called on me for help, until he had used all of his own troops; asserting that I had just seen Butterfield's division, and had learned from him that he had not been engaged the day before at all; and I asserted that the enemy's sally must have been made by one corps (Hood's), in place of three, and that it had fallen on Geary's and Williams's divisions, which had repulsed the attack handsomely. As we rode away from that church General Hooker was by my side, and I told him that such a thing must not occur again; in other words, I reproved him more gently than the occasion demanded, and from that time he began to sulk. General Hooker had come from the East with great fame as a "fighter," and at Chattanooga he was glorified by his "battle above the clouds," which I fear turned his head. He seemed jealous of all the army commanders, because in years, former rank, and experience, he thought he was our superior.

On the 23d of June I telegraphed to General Halleck this summary, which I cannot again better state:

We continue to press forward on the principle of an advance against fortified positions. The whole country is one vast fort, and Johnston must have at least fifty miles of connected trenches, with abatis and finished batteries. We gain ground daily, fighting all the time. On the 21st General Stanley gained a position near the south end of Kenesaw, from which the enemy attempted in vain to drive him; and the same day General T. J. Wood's division took a hill, which the enemy assaulted three times at night without success, leaving more than a hundred dead on the ground. Yesterday the extreme right (Hooker and Schofield) advanced on the Powder Springs road to within three miles of Marietta. The enemy made a strong effort to drive them away, but failed signally, leaving more than two hundred dead on the field. Our lines are now in close contact, and the fighting is incessant, with a good deal of artillery-fire. As fast as we gain one position the enemy has another all ready, but I think he will soon have to let go Kenesaw, which is the key to the whole country. The weather is now better, and the roads are drying up fast. Our losses are light, and, notwithstanding the repeated breaks of the road to our rear, supplies are ample.

During the 24th and 25th of June General Schofield extended his right as far as prudent, so as to compel the enemy to thin out his lines correspondingly, with the intention to make two strong assaults at points where success would give us the greatest advantage. I had consulted Generals Thomas, McPherson, and Schofield, and we all agreed that we could not with prudence stretch out any more, and therefore there was no alternative but to attack "fortified lines," a thing carefully avoided up to that time. I reasoned, if we could make a breach anywhere near the rebel centre, and thrust in a strong head of column, that with the one moiety of our army we could hold in check the corresponding wing of the enemy, and with the other sweep in flank and overwhelm the other half. The 27th of June was fixed as the day for the attempt, and in order to oversee the whole, and to be in close communication with all parts of the army, I had a place cleared on the top of a hill to the rear of Thomas's centre, and had the telegraph-wires laid to it. The points of attack were chosen, and the troops were all prepared with as little demonstration as possible. About 9 A.M. of the day appointed, the troops moved to the assault, and all along our lines for ten miles a furious fire of artillery and musketry was kept up. At all points the enemy met us with determined courage and in great force. McPherson's attacking column fought up the face of the lesser Kenesaw, but could not reach the summit. About a mile to the right (just below the Dallas road) Thomas's assaulting column reached the parapet, where Brigadier-General Harker was shot down mortally wounded, and Brigadier-General Daniel McCook (my old law-partner) was desperately wounded, from the effects of which he afterward died. By 11.30 the assault was in fact over, and had failed. We had not broken the rebel line at either point, but our assaulting columns held their ground within a few yards of the rebel trenches, and there covered themselves with parapet. McPherson lost about five hundred men and several valuable officers, and Thomas lost nearly two thousand men. This was the hardest fight of the campaign up to that date, and it is well described by Johnston in his "Narrative" (pages 342, 343), where he admits his loss in killed and wounded as—

	Men.
Hood's corps (not reported)	. . .
Hardee's corps.	286
Loring's (Polk's)	522
Total.	808

This, no doubt, is a true and fair statement; but, as usual, Johnston overestimates our loss, putting it at six thousand, whereas our entire loss was about twenty-five hundred, killed and wounded.

While the battle was in progress at the centre, Schofield crossed Olley's Creek on the right, and gained a position threatening Johnston's line of retreat; and, to increase the

effect, I ordered Stoneman's cavalry to proceed rapidly still farther to the right, to Sweetwater. Satisfied of the bloody cost
of attacking intrenched lines, I at once thought of moving the
whole army to the railroad at a point (Fulton) about ten miles
below Marietta, or to the Chattahoochee River itself, a movement similar to the one afterward so successfully practised at
Atlanta. All the orders were issued to bring forward supplies
enough to fill our wagons, intending to strip the railroad back
to Allatoona, and leave that place as our depot, to be covered
as well as possible by Garrard's cavalry. General Thomas, as
usual, shook his head, deeming it risky to leave the railroad;
but something had to be done, and I had resolved on this move,
as reported in my dispatch to General Halleck on July 1st:

> General Schofield is now south of Olley's Creek, and on the head
> of Nickajack. I have been hurrying down provisions and forage, and
> to-morrow night propose to move McPherson from the left to the
> extreme right, back of General Thomas. This will bring my right within
> three miles of the Chattahoochee River, and about five miles from
> the railroad. By this movement I think I can force Johnston to move
> his whole army down from Kenesaw to defend his railroad and the
> Chattahoochee, when I will (by the left flank) reach the railroad be-
> low Marietta; but in this I must cut loose from the railroad with ten
> days' supplies in wagons. Johnston may come out of his intrench-
> ments to attack Thomas, which is exactly what I want, for General
> Thomas is well intrenched on a line parallel with the enemy south of
> Kenesaw. I think that Allatoona and the line of the Etowah are
> strong enough for me to venture on this move. The movement is
> substantially down the Sandtown road straight for Atlanta.

McPherson drew out of his lines during the night of July
2d, leaving Garrard's cavalry, dismounted, occupying his
trenches, and moved to the rear of the Army of the Cumberland, stretching down the Nickajack; but Johnston detected
the movement, and promptly abandoned Marietta and Kenesaw. I expected as much, for, by the earliest dawn of the 3d of
July, I was up at a large spy-glass mounted on a tripod, which
Colonel Poe, United States Engineers, had at his bivouac close
by our camp. I directed the glass on Kenesaw, and saw some
of our pickets crawling up the hill cautiously; soon they stood
upon the very top, and I could plainly see their movements as
they ran along the crest just abandoned by the enemy. In a

minute I roused my staff, and started them off with orders in every direction for a pursuit by every possible road, hoping to catch Johnston in the confusion of retreat, especially at the crossing of the Chattahoochee River.

I must close this chapter here, so as to give the actual losses during June, which are compiled from the official returns by months. These losses, from June 1st to July 3d, were all substantially sustained about Kenesaw and Marietta, and it was really a continuous battle, lasting from the 10th day of June till the 3d of July, when the rebel army fell back from Marietta toward the Chattahoochee River. Our losses were:

ARMY OF THE CUMBERLAND.

CORPS.	Killed and Missing.	Wounded.	Total.
Fourth (Howard)	602	1,542	2,144
Fourteenth (Palmer).	353	1,466	1,819
Twentieth (Hooker)	322	1,246	1,568
Total, Army of the Cumberland. .	1,277	4,254	5,531

ARMY OF THE TENNESSEE.

CORPS.	Killed and Missing.	Wounded.	Total.
Fifteenth (Logan)	179	687	866
Sixteenth (Dodge)	52	157	209
Seventeenth (Blair)	47	212	259
Total, Army of the Tennessee . . .	278	1,056	1,334

ARMY OF THE OHIO.

CORPS.	Killed and Missing.	Wounded.	Total.
Twenty-third (Schofield)	105	362	467
Cavalry	130	68	198
Total, Army of the Ohio.	235	430	665
Loss in June, aggregate	1,790	5,740	7,530

Johnston makes his statement of losses from the report of his surgeon Foard, for pretty much the same period, viz., from June 4th to July 4th (page 576):

CORPS.	Killed.	Wounded.	Total.
Hardee's	200	1,433	1,633
Hood's	140	1,121	1,261
Polk's	128	926	1,054
Total	468	3,480	3,948

In the tabular statement the "missing" embraces the prisoners; and, giving two thousand as a fair proportion of prisoners captured by us for the month of June (twelve thousand nine hundred and eighty-three in all the campaign), makes an aggregate loss in the rebel army of fifty-nine hundred and forty-eight, to ours of seventy-five hundred and thirty—a less proportion than in the relative strength of our two armies, viz., as six to ten, thus maintaining our relative superiority, which the desperate game of war justified.

Chapter XVIII.

As BEFORE EXPLAINED, on the 3d of July, by moving McPherson's entire army from the extreme left, at the base of Kenesaw to the right, below Olley's Creek, and stretching it down the Nickajack toward Turner's Ferry of the Chattahoochee, we forced Johnston to choose between a direct assault on Thomas's intrenched position, or to permit us to make a lodgment on his railroad below Marietta, or even to cross the Chattahoochee. Of course, he chose to let go Kenesaw and Marietta, and fall back on an intrenched camp prepared by his orders in advance on the north and west bank of the Chattahoochee, covering the railroad-crossing and his several pontoon-bridges. I confess I had not learned beforehand of the existence of this strong place, in the nature of a *tête-du-pont*, and had counted on striking him an effectual blow in the expected confusion of his crossing the Chattahoochee, a broad and deep river then to his rear. Ordering every part of the army to pursue vigorously on the morning of the 3d of July, I rode into Marietta, just quitted by the rebel rear-guard, and was terribly angry at the cautious pursuit by Garrard's cavalry, and even by the head of our infantry columns. But Johnston had in advance cleared and multiplied his roads, whereas ours had to cross at right angles from the direction of Powder Springs toward Marietta, producing delay and confusion. By night Thomas's head of column ran up against a strong rear-guard intrenched at Smyrna camp-ground, six miles below Marietta, and there on the next day we celebrated our Fourth of July, by a noisy but not a desperate battle, designed chiefly to hold the enemy there till Generals McPherson and Schofield could get well into position below him, near the Chattahoochee crossings.

It was here that General Noyes, late Governor of Ohio, lost his leg. I came very near being shot myself while reconnoitring in the second story of a house on our picket-line, which was struck several times by cannon-shot, and perfectly riddled with musket-balls.

During the night Johnston drew back all his army and trains inside the *tête-du-pont* at the Chattahoochee, which proved one of the strongest pieces of field-fortification I ever saw. We closed up against it, and were promptly met by a heavy and severe fire. Thomas was on the main road in immediate pursuit; next on his right was Schofield; and McPherson on the extreme right, reaching the Chattahoochee River below Turner's Ferry. Stoneman's cavalry was still farther to the right, along down the Chattahoochee River as far as opposite Sandtown; and on that day I ordered Garrard's division of cavalry up the river eighteen miles, to secure possession of the factories at Roswell, as well as to hold an important bridge and ford at that place.

About three miles out from the Chattahoochee the main road forked, the right branch following substantially the railroad, and the left one leading straight for Atlanta, *via* Paice's Ferry and Buckhead. We found the latter unoccupied and unguarded, and the Fourth Corps (Howard's) reached the river at Paice's Ferry. The right-hand road was perfectly covered by the *tête-du-pont* before described, where the resistance was very severe, and for some time deceived me, for I was pushing Thomas with orders to fiercely assault his enemy, supposing that he was merely opposing us to gain time to get his trains and troops across the Chattahoochee; but, on personally reconnoitring, I saw the abatis and the strong redoubts, which satisfied me of the preparations that had been made by Johnston in anticipation of this very event. While I was with General Jeff. C. Davis, a poor negro came out of the abatis, blanched with fright, said he had been hidden under a log all day, with a perfect storm of shot, shells, and musket-balls, passing over him, till a short lull had enabled him to creep out and make himself known to our skirmishers, who in turn had sent him back to where we were. This negro explained that he with about a thousand slaves had been at work a month or more on these very lines, which, as he explained, extended from the river about a mile above the railroad-bridge to Turner's Ferry below, being in extent from five to six miles.

Therefore, on the 5th of July we had driven our enemy to

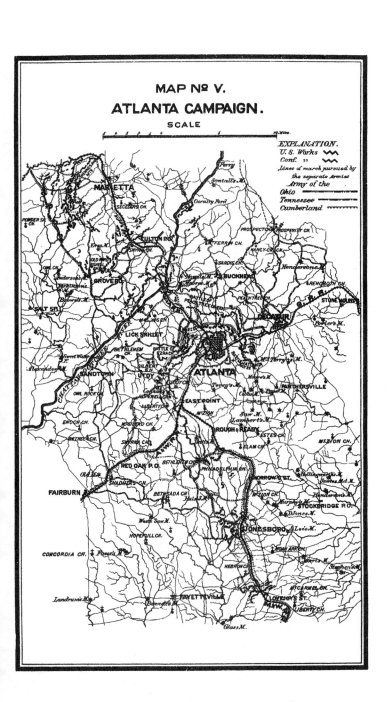

MAP Nº V.
ATLANTA CAMPAIGN.
SCALE

cover in the valley of the Chattahoochee, and we held possession of the river above for eighteen miles, as far as Roswell,
and below ten miles to the mouth of the Sweetwater. Moreover, we held the high ground and could overlook his movements, instead of his looking down on us, as was the case at
Kenesaw.

From a hill just back of Vining's Station I could see the
houses in Atlanta, nine miles distant, and the whole intervening valley of the Chattahoochee; could observe the preparations for our reception on the other side, the camps of men
and large trains of covered wagons; and supposed, as a matter
of course, that Johnston had passed the river with the bulk of
his army, and that he had only left on our side a corps to
cover his bridges; but in fact he had only sent across his
cavalry and trains. Between Howard's corps at Paice's Ferry
and the rest of Thomas's army pressing up against this *tête-
du-pont*, was a space concealed by dense woods, in crossing
which I came near riding into a detachment of the enemy's
cavalry; and later in the same day Colonel Frank Sherman, of
Chicago, then on General Howard's staff, did actually ride
straight into the enemy's camp, supposing that our lines were
continuous. He was carried to Atlanta, and for some time the
enemy supposed they were in possession of the commander-
in-chief of the opposing army.

I knew that Johnston would not remain long on the west
bank of the Chattahoochee, for I could easily practise on that
ground to better advantage our former tactics of intrenching
a moiety in his front, and with the rest of our army cross
the river and threaten either his rear or the city of Atlanta
itself, which city was of vital importance to the existence not
only of his own army, but of the Confederacy itself. In my
dispatch of July 6th to General Halleck, at Washington, I state
that—

Johnston (in his retreat from Kenesaw) has left two breaks in the
railroad—one above Marietta and one near Vining's Station. The
former is already repaired, and Johnston's army has heard the sound
of our locomotives. The telegraph is finished to Vining's Station,
and the field-wire has just reached my bivouac, and will be ready
to convey this message as soon as it is written and translated into
cipher.

I propose to study the crossings of the Chattahoochee, and, when all is ready, to move quickly. As a beginning, I will keep the troops and wagons well back from the river, and only display to the enemy our picket-line, with a few field-batteries along at random. I have already shifted Schofield to a point in our left rear, whence he can in a single move reach the Chattahoochee at a point above the railroad-bridge, where there is a ford. At present the waters are turbid and swollen from recent rains; but if the present hot weather lasts, the water will run down very fast. We have pontoons enough for four bridges, but, as our crossing will be resisted, we must manœuvre some. All the regular crossing-places are covered by forts, apparently of long construction; but we shall cross in due time, and, instead of attacking Atlanta direct, or any of its forts, I propose to make a circuit, destroying all its railroads. This is a delicate movement, and must be done with caution. Our army is in good condition and full of confidence; but the weather is intensely hot, and a good many men have fallen with sunstroke. The country is high and healthy, and the sanitary condition of the army is good.

At this time Stoneman was very active on our extreme right, pretending to be searching the river below Turner's Ferry for a crossing, and was watched closely by the enemy's cavalry on the other side. McPherson, on the right, was equally demonstrative at and near Turner's Ferry. Thomas faced substantially the intrenched *tête-du-pont*, and had his left on the Chattahoochee River, at Paice's Ferry. Garrard's cavalry was up at Roswell, and McCook's small division of cavalry was intermediate, above Soap's Creek. Meantime, also, the railroad-construction party was hard at work, repairing the railroad up to our camp at Vining's Station.

Of course, I expected every possible resistance in crossing the Chattahoochee River, and had made up my mind to feign on the right, but actually to cross over by the left. We had already secured a crossing-place at Roswell, but one nearer was advisable; General Schofield had examined the river well, found a place just below the mouth of Soap's Creek which he deemed advantageous, and was instructed to effect an early crossing there, and to intrench a good position on the other side, viz., the east bank. But, preliminary thereto, I had ordered General Rousseau, at Nashville, to collect, out of the scattered detachments of cavalry in Tennessee, a force of a couple of thousand men, to rendezvous at Decatur, Alabama, thence to make a rapid march for Opelika, to break up the railroad-links between Georgia and Alabama, and then to make junction with me about Atlanta; or, if forced, to go on to Pensacola, or even to swing across to some of our posts in Mississippi. General Rousseau asked leave to command this expedition himself, to which I consented, and on the 6th of July he reported that he was all ready at Decatur, and I gave him orders to start. He moved promptly on the 9th, crossed the Coosa below the "Ten Islands" and the Tallapoosa below "Horseshoe Bend," having passed through Talladega. He struck the railroad west of Opelika, tore it up for twenty miles, then turned north and came to Marietta on the 22d of July, whence he reported to me. This expedition was in the nature of a raid, and must have disturbed the enemy somewhat; but, as usual, the cavalry did not work hard, and their destruction of the railroad was soon repaired. Rousseau, when he reported to me in person before Atlanta, on the 23d of July, stated his entire loss to have been only twelve killed and thirty wounded. He brought in four hundred captured mules and three hundred horses, and also told me a good story. He said he was far down in Alabama, below Talladega, one hot, dusty day, when the blue clothing of his men was gray with dust; he had halted his column along a road, and he in person, with his staff, had gone to the house of a planter, who met him kindly on the front-porch. He asked for water, which was brought, and as the party sat on the porch in conversation he saw, in a stable-yard across the road, quite a number of good mules. He remarked to the planter, "My good sir, I fear I must take some of your mules." The planter remonstrated, saying he had already contributed liberally to the *good cause*; that it was only last week he had given to General Roddy ten mules. Rousseau replied, "Well, in this war you should be at least neutral—that is, you should be as liberal to us as to Roddy" (a rebel cavalry general). "Well, ain't you on our side?" "No," said Rousseau; "I am General Rousseau, and all these men you see are Yanks." "Great God! is it possible? Are these Yanks? Who ever supposed they would come away down here in Alabama?" Of course, Rousseau took his ten mules.

Schofield effected his crossing at Soap's Creek very handsomely on the 9th, capturing the small guard that was watching the crossing. By night he was on the high ground beyond, strongly intrenched, with two good pontoon-bridges finished, and was prepared, if necessary, for an assault by the whole Confederate army. The same day Garrard's cavalry also crossed over at Roswell, drove away the cavalry-pickets, and held its ground till relieved by Newton's division of Howard's corps, which was sent up temporarily, till it in turn was relieved by Dodge's corps (Sixteenth) of the Army of the Tennessee, which was the advance of the whole of that army.

That night Johnston evacuated his trenches, crossed over the Chattahoochee, burned the railroad-bridge and his pontoon and trestle bridges, and left us in full possession of the north or west bank—besides which, we had already secured possession of the two good crossings at Roswell and Soap's Creek. I have always thought Johnston neglected his opportunity there, for he had lain comparatively idle while we got control of both banks of the river above him.

On the 13th I ordered McPherson, with the Fifteenth Corps, to move up to Roswell, to cross over, prepare good bridges, and to make a strong *tête-du-pont* on the farther side. Stoneman had been sent down to Campbellton, with orders to cross over and to threaten the railroad below Atlanta, if he could do so without too much risk; and General Blair, with the Seventeenth Corps, was to remain at Turner's Ferry, demonstrating as much as possible, thus keeping up the feint below while we were actually crossing above. Thomas was also ordered to prepare his bridges at Powers's and Paice's Ferries. By crossing the Chattahoochee above the railroad-bridge, we were better placed to cover our railroad and depots than below, though a movement across the river below the railroad, to the south of Atlanta, might have been more decisive. But we were already so far from home, and would be compelled to accept battle whenever offered, with the Chattahoochee to *our* rear, that it became imperative for me to take all prudential measures the case admitted of, and I therefore determined to pass the river above the railroad-bridge—McPherson on the left, Schofield in the centre, and Thomas on the right.

On the 13th I reported to General Halleck as follows:

All is well. I have now accumulated stores at Allatoona and Marietta, both fortified and garrisoned points. Have also three places at which to cross the Chattahoochee in our possession, and only await General Stoneman's return from a trip down the river, to cross the army in force and move on Atlanta.

Stoneman is now out two days, and had orders to be back on the fourth or fifth day at furthest.

From the 10th to the 15th we were all busy in strengthening the several points for the proposed passage of the Chattahoochee, in increasing the number and capacity of the bridges, rearranging the garrisons to our rear, and in bringing forward supplies. On the 15th General Stoneman got back to Powder Springs, and was ordered to replace General Blair at Turner's Ferry, and Blair, with the Seventeenth Corps, was ordered up to Roswell to join McPherson.

On the 17th we began the general movement against Atlanta, Thomas crossing the Chattahoochee at Powers's and Paice's, by pontoon-bridges; Schofield moving out toward Cross Keys, and McPherson toward Stone Mountain. We encountered but little opposition except by cavalry. On the 18th all the armies moved on a general right wheel, Thomas to Buckhead, forming line of battle facing Peach-Tree Creek; Schofield was on his left, and McPherson well over toward the railroad between Stone Mountain and Decatur, which he reached at 2 P.M. of that day, about four miles from Stone Mountain, and seven miles east of Decatur, and there he turned toward Atlanta, breaking up the railroad as he progressed, his advance-guard reaching Decatur about night, where he came into communication with Schofield's troops, which had also reached Decatur. About 10 A.M. of that day (July 18th), when the armies were all in motion, one of General Thomas's staff-officers brought me a citizen, one of our spies, who had just come out of Atlanta, and had brought a newspaper of the same day, or of the day before, containing Johnston's order relinquishing the command of the Confederate forces in Atlanta, and Hood's order assuming the command. I immediately inquired of General Schofield, who was his classmate at West Point, about Hood, as to his general character, etc., and learned that he was bold even to rashness, and courageous in the extreme; I inferred that the change of commanders meant "fight." Notice of this important change was at once sent to all parts of the army, and every division commander was cautioned to be always prepared for battle in any shape. This was just what we wanted, viz., to fight in open ground, on any thing like equal terms, instead of being forced to run up against prepared intrenchments; but, at the same time, the enemy having Atlanta behind him, could choose the time and place of attack, and could at pleasure mass a superior force on our weakest points. Therefore, we had to be constantly ready for sallies.

On the 19th the three armies were converging toward Atlanta, meeting such feeble resistance that I really thought the enemy intended to evacuate the place. McPherson was moving astride of the railroad, near Decatur; Schofield along a road leading toward Atlanta, by Colonel Howard's house and the distillery; and Thomas was crossing "Peach-Tree" in line of battle, building bridges for nearly every division as deployed. There was quite a gap between Thomas and Schofield, which I endeavored to close by drawing two of Howard's divisions nearer Schofield. On the 20th I was with General Schofield near the centre, and soon after noon heard heavy firing in front of Thomas's right, which lasted an hour or so, and then ceased. I soon learned that the enemy had made a furious sally, the blow falling on Hooker's corps (the Twentieth), and partially on Johnson's division of the Fourteenth, and Newton's of the Fourth. The troops had crossed Peach-Tree Creek, were deployed, but at the time were resting for noon, when, without notice, the enemy came pouring out of their trenches down upon them, they became commingled, and fought in many places hand to hand. General Thomas happened to be near the rear of Newton's division, and got some field-batteries in a good position, on the north side of Peach-Tree Creek, from which he directed a furious fire on a mass of the enemy, which was passing around Newton's left and exposed flank. After a couple of hours of hard and close conflict, the enemy retired slowly within his trenches, leaving his dead and many wounded on the field. Johnson's and Newton's losses were light, for they had partially covered their

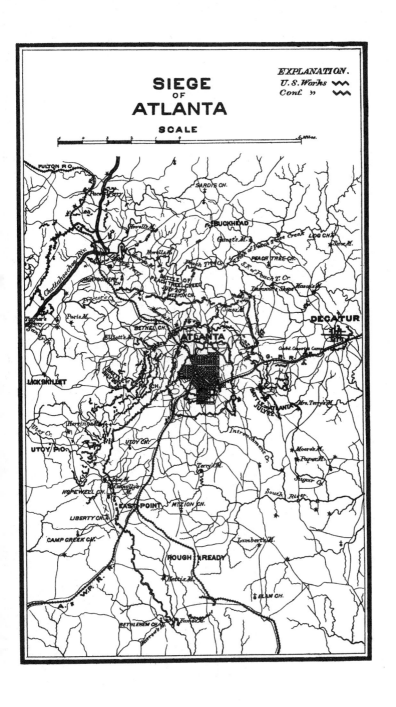

SIEGE
OF
ATLANTA

SCALE

EXPLANATION.
U.S.Works
Conf. "

fronts with light parapet; but Hooker's whole corps fought in open ground, and lost about fifteen hundred men. He reported four hundred rebel dead left on the ground, and that the rebel wounded would number four thousand; but this was conjectural, for most of them got back within their own lines. We had, however, met successfully a bold sally, had repelled it handsomely, and were also put on our guard; and the event illustrated the future tactics of our enemy. This sally came from the Peach-Tree line, which General Johnston had carefully prepared in advance, from which to fight us *outside* of Atlanta. We then advanced our lines in compact order, close up to these finished intrenchments, overlapping them on our left. From various parts of our lines the houses inside of Atlanta were plainly visible, though between us were the strong parapets, with ditch, *fraise, chevaux-de-frise* and abatis, prepared long in advance by Colonel Jeremy F. Gilmer, formerly of the United States Engineers. McPherson had the Fifteenth Corps astride the Augusta Railroad, and the Seventeenth deployed on its left. Schofield was next on his right, then came Howard's, Hooker's, and Palmer's corps, on the extreme right. Each corps was deployed with strong reserves, and their trains were parked to their rear. McPherson's trains were in Decatur, guarded by a brigade commanded by Colonel Sprague of the Sixty-third Ohio. The Sixteenth Corps (Dodge's) was crowded out of position on the right of McPherson's line, by the contraction of the circle of investment; and, during the previous afternoon, the Seventeenth Corps (Blair's) had pushed its operations on the farther side of the Augusta Railroad, so as to secure possession of a hill, known as Leggett's Hill, which Leggett's and Force's divisions had carried by assault. Giles A. Smith's division was on Leggett's left, deployed with a weak left flank "in air," in military phraseology. The evening before General Gresham, a great favorite, was badly wounded; and there also Colonel Tom Reynolds, now of Madison, Wisconsin, was shot through the leg. When the surgeons were debating the propriety of amputating it in his hearing, he begged them to spare the leg, as it was very valuable, being an "imported leg." He was of Irish birth, and this well-timed piece of wit saved his leg, for the surgeons thought, if he could perpetrate a joke at such a time, they would trust to his vitality to save his limb.

During the night, I had full reports from all parts of our line, most of which was partially intrenched as against a sally, and finding that McPherson was stretching out too much on his left flank, I wrote him a note early in the morning not to extend so much by his left; for we had not troops enough to completely invest the place, and I intended to destroy utterly all parts of the Augusta Railroad to the east of Atlanta, then to withdraw from the left flank and add to the right. In that letter I ordered McPherson not to extend any farther to the left, but to employ General Dodge's corps (Sixteenth), then forced out of position, to destroy every rail and tie of the railroad, from Decatur up to his skirmish-line, and I wanted him (McPherson) to be ready, as soon as General Garrard returned from Covington (whither I had sent him), to move to the extreme right of Thomas, so as to reach if possible the railroad below Atlanta, viz., the Macon road. In the morning we found the strong line of parapet, "Peach-Tree line," to the front of Schofield and Thomas, abandoned, and our lines were advanced rapidly close up to Atlanta. For some moments I supposed the enemy intended to evacuate, and in person was on horseback at the head of Schofield's troops, who had advanced in front of the Howard House to some open ground, from which we could plainly see the whole rebel line of parapets, and I saw their men dragging up from the intervening valley, by the distillery, trees and saplings for abatis. Our skirmishers found the enemy down in this valley, and we could see the rebel main line strongly manned, with guns in position at intervals. Schofield was dressing forward his lines, and I could hear Thomas farther to the right engaged, when General McPherson and his staff rode up. We went back to the Howard House, a double frame-building with a porch, and sat on the steps, discussing the chances of battle, and of Hood's general character. McPherson had also been of the same class at West Point with Hood, Schofield, and Sheridan. We agreed that we ought to be unusually cautious and prepared at all times for sallies and for hard fighting, because Hood, though not deemed much of a scholar, or of great mental capacity, was undoubtedly a brave, determined, and rash man; and the change of commanders at that particular crisis argued the displeasure of the Confederate Government with the cautious but prudent conduct of General Jos. Johnston.

McPherson was in excellent spirits, well pleased at the progress of events so far, and had come over purposely to see me about the order I had given him to use Dodge's corps to break up the railroad, saying that the night before he had gained a position on Leggett's Hill from which he could look over the rebel parapet, and see the high smoke-stack of a large foundery in Atlanta; that before receiving my order he had diverted Dodge's two divisions (then in motion) from the main road, along a diagonal one that led to his extreme left flank, then held by Giles A. Smith's division (Seventeenth Corps), for the purpose of strengthening that flank; and that he had sent some intrenching-tools there, to erect some batteries from which he intended to knock down that foundery, and otherwise to damage the buildings inside of Atlanta. He said he could put all his pioneers to work, and do with them in the time indicated all I had proposed to do with General Dodge's two divisions. Of course I assented at once, and we walked down the road a short distance, sat down by the foot of a tree where I had my map, and on it pointed out to him Thomas's position and his own. I then explained minutely that, after we had sufficiently broken up the Augusta road, I wanted to shift his whole army around by the rear to Thomas's extreme right, and hoped thus to reach the other railroad at East Point. While we sat there we could hear lively skirmishing going on near us (down about the distillery), and occasionally round-shot from twelve or twenty-four pound guns came through the trees in reply to those of Schofield, and we could hear similar sounds all along down the lines of Thomas to our right, and his own to the left; but presently the firing appeared a little more brisk (especially over about Giles A. Smith's division), and then we heard an occasional gun back toward Decatur. I asked him what it meant. We took my pocket-compass (which I always carried), and by noting the direction of the sound, we became satisfied that the firing was too far to our left rear to be explained by known facts, and he hastily called for his horse, his staff, and his orderlies.

McPherson was then in his prime (about thirty-four years old), over six feet high, and a very handsome man in every way, was universally liked, and had many noble qualities. He had on his boots outside his pantaloons, gauntlets on his hands, had on his major-general's uniform, and wore a sword-belt, but no sword. He hastily gathered his papers (save one, which I now possess) into a pocket-book, put it in his breast-pocket, and jumped on his horse, saying he would hurry down his line and send me back word what these sounds meant. His adjutant-general, Clark, Inspector-General Strong, and his aides, Captains Steele and Gile, were with him. Although the sound of musketry on our left grew in volume, I was not so much disturbed by it as by the sound of artillery back toward Decatur. I ordered Schofield at once to send a brigade back to Decatur (some five miles) and was walking up and down the porch of the Howard House, listening, when one of McPherson's staff, with his horse covered with sweat, dashed up to the porch, and reported that General McPherson was either "killed or a prisoner." He explained that when they had left me a few minutes before, they had ridden rapidly across to the railroad, the sounds of battle increasing as they neared the position occupied by General Giles A. Smith's division, and that McPherson had sent first one, then another of his staff to bring some of the reserve brigades of the Fifteenth Corps over to the exposed left flank; that he had reached the head of Dodge's corps (marching by the flank on the diagonal road as described), and had ordered it to hurry forward to the same point; that then, almost if not entirely alone, he had followed this road leading across the wooded valley behind the Seventeenth Corps, and had disappeared in these woods, doubtless with a sense of absolute security. The sound of musketry was there heard, and McPherson's horse came back, bleeding, wounded, and riderless. I ordered the staff-officer who brought this message to return at once, to find General Logan (the senior officer present with the Army of the Tennessee), to report the same facts to him, and to instruct him to drive back this supposed small force, which had evidently got around the Seventeenth Corps through the blind woods in rear of our left flank. I soon dispatched one of my own staff (McCoy, I think) to General Logan with similar orders, telling him to refuse his left flank, and to fight the battle (holding fast to Leggett's Hill) with the Army of the Tennessee; that I would personally look to Decatur and to the safety of his rear, and would reënforce him if he needed it. I dispatched orders to General Thomas on our right, telling him of this strong sally, and my inference that the lines in his front had evidently been weakened by reason thereof, and that he ought to take advantage of the opportunity to make a lodgment in Atlanta, if possible.

Meantime the sounds of the battle rose on our extreme left more and more furious, extending to the place where I stood, at the Howard House. Within an hour an ambulance came in (attended by Colonels Clark and Strong, and Captains Steele and Gile), bearing McPherson's body. I had it carried inside of the Howard House, and laid on a door wrenched from its hinges. Dr. Hewitt, of the army, was there, and I asked him to examine the wound. He opened the coat and shirt, saw where the ball had entered and where it came out, or rather lodged under the skin, and he reported that McPherson must have died in a few seconds after being hit; that the ball had ranged upward across his body, and passed near the heart. He was dressed just as he left me, with gauntlets and boots on, but his pocket-book was gone. On further inquiry I learned that his body must have been in possession of the enemy some minutes, during which time it was rifled of the pocket-book, and I was much concerned lest the letter I had written him that morning should have fallen into the hands of some one who could read and understand its meaning. Fortunately the spot in the woods where McPherson was shot was re-gained by our troops in a few minutes, and the pocket-book found in the haversack of a prisoner of war captured at the time, and it and its contents were secured by one of McPherson's staff.

While we were examining the body inside the house, the battle was progressing outside, and many shots struck the building, which I feared would take fire; so I ordered Captains Steele and Gile to carry the body to Marietta. They reached that place the same night, and, on application, I ordered his personal staff to go on and escort the body to his home, in Clyde, Ohio, where it was received with great honor, and it is now buried in a small cemetery, close by his mother's house, which cemetery is composed in part of the family orchard, in which he used to play when a boy. The foundation is ready laid for the equestrian monument now in progress, under the auspices of the Society of the Army of the Tennessee.

The reports that came to me from all parts of the field revealed clearly what was the game of my antagonist, and the ground somewhat favored him. The railroad and wagon-road from Decatur to Atlanta lie along the summit, from which the waters flow, by short, steep valleys, into the "Peach-Tree" and Chattahoochee, to the west, and by other valleys, of gentler declivity, toward the east (Ocmulgee). The ridges and level ground were mostly cleared, and had been cultivated as corn or cotton fields; but where the valleys were broken, they were left in a state of nature—wooded, and full of undergrowth. McPherson's line of battle was across this railroad, along a general ridge, with a gentle but cleared valley to his front, between him and the defenses of Atlanta; and another valley, behind him, was clear of timber in part, but to his left rear the country was heavily wooded. Hood, during the night of July 21st, had withdrawn from his Peach-Tree line, had occupied the fortified line of Atlanta, facing north and east, with Stewart's—formerly Polk's—corps and part of Hardee's, and with G. W. Smith's division of militia. His own corps, and part of Hardee's, had marched out to the road leading from McDonough to Decatur, and had turned so as to strike the left and rear of McPherson's line "in air." At the same time he had sent Wheeler's division of cavalry against the trains parked in Decatur. Unluckily for us, I had sent away the whole of Garrard's division of cavalry during the night of the 20th, with orders to proceed to Covington, thirty miles east, to burn two important bridges across the Ulcofauhatchee and Yellow Rivers, to tear up the railroad, to damage it as much as possible from Stone Mountain eastward, and to be gone four days; so that McPherson had no cavalry in hand to guard that flank.

The enemy was therefore enabled, under cover of the forest, to approach quite near before he was discovered; indeed, his skirmish-line had worked through the timber and got into the field to the rear of Giles A. Smith's division of the Seventeenth Corps unseen, had captured Murray's battery of regular artillery, moving through these woods entirely unguarded, and had got possession of several of the hospital camps. The right of this rebel line struck Dodge's troops in motion; but, fortunately, this corps (Sixteenth) had only to halt, face to the left, and was in line of battle; and this corps not only held in check the enemy, but drove him back through the woods. About the same time this same force had struck General Giles A. Smith's left flank, doubled it back, captured four guns in position and the party engaged in building the very battery which was the special object of McPherson's visit to me, and almost enveloped the entire left flank. The men, however, were skillful and brave, and fought for a time with their backs to Atlanta. They gradually fell back, compressing their own line, and gaining strength by making junction with Leggett's division of the Seventeenth Corps, well and strongly posted on the hill. One or two brigades of the Fifteenth Corps, ordered by McPherson, came rapidly across the open field to the rear, from the direction of the railroad, filled up the gap from Blair's new left to the head of Dodge's column—now facing to the general left—thus forming a strong left flank, at right angles to the original line of battle. The enemy attacked, boldly and repeatedly, the whole of this flank, but met an equally fierce resistance; and on that ground a bloody battle raged from little after noon till into the night. A part of Hood's plan of action was to sally from Atlanta at the same moment; but this sally was not, for some reason, simultaneous, for the first attack on our extreme left flank had been checked and repulsed before the sally came from the direction of Atlanta. Meantime, Colonel Sprague, in Decatur, had got his teams harnessed up, and safely conducted his train to the rear of Schofield's position, holding in check Wheeler's cavalry till he had got off all his trains, with the exception of three or four wagons. I remained near the Howard House, receiving reports and sending orders, urging Generals Thomas and Schofield to take advantage of the absence from their front of so considerable a body as was evidently engaged on our left, and, if possible, to make a lodgment in Atlanta itself; but they reported that the lines to their front, at all accessible points, were strong, by nature and by art, and were fully manned. About 4 P.M. the expected sally came from Atlanta, directed mainly against Leggett's Hill and along the Decatur road. At Leggett's Hill they were met and bloodily repulsed. Along the railroad they were more successful. Sweeping over a small force with two guns, they reached our main line, broke through it, and got possession of De Gress's battery of four twenty-pound Parrotts, killing every horse, and turning the guns against us. General Charles R. Wood's division of the Fifteenth Corps was on the extreme right of the Army of the Tennessee, between the railroad and the Howard House, where he connected with Schofield's troops. He reported to me in person that the line on his left had been swept back, and that his connection with General Logan, on Leggett's Hill, was broken. I ordered him to wheel his brigades to the left, to advance in echelon, and to catch the enemy in flank. General Schofield brought forward all his available batteries, to the number of twenty guns, to a position to the left front of the Howard House, whence we could overlook the field of action, and directed a heavy fire over the heads of General Wood's men against the enemy; and we saw Wood's troops advance and encounter the enemy, who had secured possession of the old line of parapet which had been held by our men. His right crossed this parapet, which he swept back, taking it in flank; and, at the same time, the division which had been driven back along the railroad was rallied by General Logan in person, and fought for their former ground. These combined forces drove the enemy into Atlanta, recovering the twenty-pound Parrott guns—but one of them was found "bursted" while in the possession of the enemy. The two six-pounders farther in advance were, however, lost, and had been hauled back by the enemy into Atlanta. Poor Captain de Gress came to me in tears, lamenting the loss of his favorite guns; when they were regained he had only a few men left, and not a single horse. He asked an order for a reëquipment, but I told him he must beg and borrow of others till he could restore his battery, now reduced to three guns. How he did so I do not know, but in a short time he did get horses, men, and finally another gun, of the same special pattern, and served them with splendid effect till the very close of the war. This battery had also been with me from Shiloh till that time.

The battle of July 22d is usually called the battle of Atlanta. It extended from the Howard House to General Giles A. Smith's position, about a mile beyond the Augusta Railroad, and then back toward Decatur, the whole extent of ground being fully seven miles. In part the ground was clear and in part densely wooded. I rode over the whole of it the next day, and it bore the marks of a bloody conflict. The enemy had retired during the night inside of Atlanta, and we remained masters of the situation outside. I purposely allowed the Army of the Tennessee to fight this battle almost unaided, save by demonstrations on the part of General Schofield and Thomas against the fortified lines to their immediate fronts, and by detaching, as described, one of Schofield's brigades to Decatur, because I knew that the attacking force could only be a part of Hood's army, and that, if any assistance were rendered by either of the other armies, the Army of the Tennessee would be jealous. Nobly did they do their work that day, and terrible was the slaughter done to our enemy, though at sad cost to ourselves, as shown by the following reports:

HEADQUARTERS MILITARY DIVISION OF THE MISSISSIPPI,
IN THE FIELD, NEAR ATLANTA, *July* 23, 1864.

General HALLECK, *Washington, D. C.*

Yesterday morning the enemy fell back to the intrenchments proper of the city of Atlanta, which are in a general circle, with a radius of one and a half miles, and we closed in. While we were forming our lines, and selecting positions for our batteries, the enemy appeared suddenly out of the dense woods in heavy masses on our extreme left, and struck the Seventeenth Corps (General Blair) in flank, and was forcing it back, when the Sixteenth Corps (General Dodge) came up and checked the movement, but the enemy's cavalry got well to our rear, and into Decatur, and for some hours our left flank was completely enveloped. The fight that resulted was continuous until night, with heavy loss on both sides. The enemy took one of our batteries (Murray's, of the Regular Army) that was marching in its place in column in the road, unconscious of danger. About 4 P.M. the enemy sallied against the division of General Morgan L. Smith, of the Fifteenth Corps, which occupied an abandoned line of rifle-trench near the railroad east of the city, and forced it back some four hundred yards, leaving in his hands for the time two batteries, but the ground and batteries were immediately after recovered by the same troops reënforced. I cannot well approximate our loss, which fell heavily on the Fifteenth and Seventeenth Corps, but count it as three thousand; I know that, being on the defensive, we have inflicted equally heavy loss on the enemy.

General McPherson, when arranging his troops about 11 A.M., and passing from one column to another, incautiously rode upon an ambuscade without apprehension, at some distance ahead of his staff and orderlies, and was shot dead.

W. T. SHERMAN, Major-General commanding.

HEADQUARTERS MILITARY DIVISION OF THE MISSISSIPPI, ⎫
IN THE FIELD, NEAR ATLANTA, GEORGIA, *July* 25, 1864 — 8 A.M.⎭

Major-General HALLECK, *Washington, D. C.*

GENERAL: I find it difficult to make prompt report of results, coupled with some data or information, without occasionally making mistakes. McPherson's sudden death, and Logan succeeding to the command as it were in the midst of battle, made some confusion on our extreme left; but it soon recovered and made sad havoc with the enemy, who had practised one of his favorite games of attacking our left when in motion, and before it had time to cover its weak flank. After riding over the ground and hearing the varying statements of the actors, I directed General Logan to make an official report of the actual result, and I herewith inclose it.

Though the number of dead rebels seems excessive, I am disposed to give full credit to the report that our loss, though only thirty-five hundred and twenty-one killed, wounded, and missing, the enemy's dead alone on the field nearly equaled that number, viz., thirty-two hundred and twenty. Happening at that point of the line when a flag of truce was sent in to ask permission for each party to bury its dead, I gave General Logan authority to permit a temporary truce on that flank *alone*, while our labors and fighting proceeded at all others.

I also send you a copy of General Garrard's report of the breaking of the railroad toward Augusta. I am now grouping my command to attack the Macon road, and with that view will intrench a strong line of circumvallation with flanks, so as to have as large an infantry column as possible, with all the cavalry to swing round to the south and east, to strike that road at or below East Point.

I have the honor to be, your obedient servant,

W. T. SHERMAN, *Major-General commanding.*

HEADQUARTERS DEPARTMENT AND ARMY OF THE TENNESSEE,
BEFORE ATLANTA, GEORGIA, *July* 24, 1864.

Major-General W. T. SHERMAN, *commanding Military Division of the Mississippi.*

GENERAL: I have the honor to report the following general summary of the result of the attack of the enemy on this army on the 22d inst.

Total loss, killed, wounded, and missing, thirty-five hundred and twenty-one, and ten pieces of artillery.

We have buried and delivered to the enemy, under a flag of truce sent in by them, in front of the Third Division, Seventeenth Corps, one thousand of their killed.

The number of their dead in front of the Fourth Division of the same corps, including those on the ground not now occupied by our troops, General Blair reports, will swell the number of their dead on his front to two thousand.

The number of their dead buried in front of the Fifteenth Corps, up to this hour, is three hundred and sixty, and the commanding officer reports that at least as many more are yet unburied, burying-parties being still at work.

The number of dead buried in front of the Sixteenth Corps is four hundred and twenty-two. We have over one thousand of their wounded in our hands, the larger number of the wounded being carried off during the night, after the engagement, by them.

We captured eighteen stands of colors, and have them now. We also captured five thousand stands of arms.

The attack was made on our lines seven times, and was seven times repulsed. Hood's and Hardee's corps and Wheeler's cavalry engaged us.

We have sent to the rear one thousand prisoners, including thirty-three commissioned officers of high rank.

We still occupy the field, and the troops are in fine spirits. A detailed and full report will be furnished as soon as completed.

Recapitulation.

Our total loss   3,521
Enemy's dead, thus far reported, buried,
    and delivered to them   3,220
Total prisoners sent North   1,017
Total prisoners, wounded, in our hands . . .   1,000
Estimated loss of the enemy, at least   10,000

Very respectfully, your obedient servant,

                JOHN A. LOGAN, *Major-General.*

On the 22d of July General Rousseau reached Marietta, having returned from his raid on the Alabama road at Opelika, and on the next day General Garrard also returned from Covington, both having been measurably successful. The former was about twenty-five hundred strong, the latter about four thousand, and both reported that their horses were jaded and tired, needing shoes and rest. But, about this time, I was advised by General Grant (then investing Richmond) that the rebel Government had become aroused to the critical condition of things about Atlanta, and that I must look out for Hood being greatly reënforced. I therefore was resolved to push matters, and at once set about the original purpose of transferring the whole of the Army of the Tennessee to our right flank, leaving Schofield to stretch out so as to rest his left on the Augusta road, then torn up for thirty miles eastward; and, as auxiliary thereto, I ordered all the cavalry to be ready to pass around Atlanta on both flanks, to break up the Macon road at some point below, so as to cut off all supplies to the rebel army inside, and thus to force it to evacuate, or come out and fight us on equal terms.

But it first became necessary to settle the important question of who should succeed General McPherson? General Logan had taken command of the Army of the Tennessee by virtue of his seniority, and had done well; but I did not consider him equal to the command of three corps. Between him and General Blair there existed a natural rivalry. Both were men of great courage and talent, but were politicians by nature and experience, and it may be that for this reason they were mistrusted by regular officers like Generals Schofield,

Thomas, and myself. It was all-important that there should exist a perfect understanding among the army commanders, and at a conference with General George H. Thomas at the headquarters of General Thomas J. Woods, commanding a division in the Fourth Corps, he (Thomas) remonstrated warmly against my recommending that General Logan should be regularly assigned to the command of the Army of the Tennessee by reason of his accidental seniority. We discussed fully the merits and qualities of every officer of high rank in the army, and finally settled on Major-General O. O. Howard as the best officer who was present and available for the purpose; on the 24th of July I telegraphed to General Halleck this preference, and it was promptly ratified by the President. General Howard's place in command of the Fourth Corps was filled by General Stanley, one of his division commanders, on the recommendation of General Thomas. All these promotions happened to fall upon West-Pointers, and doubtless Logan and Blair had some reason to believe that we intended to monopolize the higher honors of the war for the regular officers. I remember well my own thoughts and feelings at the time, and feel sure that I was not intentionally partial to any class. I wanted to succeed in taking Atlanta, and needed commanders who were purely and technically soldiers, men who would obey orders and execute them promptly and on time; for I knew that we would have to execute some most delicate manœuvres, requiring the utmost skill, nicety, and precision. I believed that General Howard would do all these faithfully and well, and I think the result has justified my choice. I regarded both Generals Logan and Blair as "volunteers," that looked to personal fame and glory as auxiliary and secondary to their political ambition, and not as professional soldiers.

As soon as it was known that General Howard had been chosen to command the Army of the Tennessee, General Hooker applied to General Thomas to be relieved of the command of the Twentieth Corps, and General Thomas forwarded his application to me approved and *heartily* recommended. I at once telegraphed to General Halleck, recommending General Slocum (then at Vicksburg) to be his successor, because Slocum had been displaced from the command of his corps at the time when the Eleventh and Twelfth were united and made the Twentieth.

General Hooker was offended because he was not chosen to succeed McPherson; but his chances were not even considered; indeed, I had never been satisfied with him since his affair at the Kulp House, and had been more than once disposed to relieve him of his corps, because of his repeated attempts to interfere with Generals McPherson and Schofield. I had known Hooker since 1836, and was intimately associated with him in California, where we served together on the staff of General Persifer F. Smith. He had come to us from the East with a high reputation as a "fighter," which he had fully justified at Chattanooga and Peach-Tree Creek, at which latter battle I complimented him on the field for special gallantry, and afterward in official reports. Still, I did feel a sense of relief when he left us. We were then two hundred and fifty miles in advance of our base, dependent on a single line of railroad for our daily food. We had a bold, determined foe in our immediate front, strongly intrenched, with communication open to his rear for supplies and reënforcements, and every soldier realized that we had plenty of hard fighting ahead, and that all honors had to be fairly earned.

Until General Slocum joined (in the latter part of August), the Twentieth Corps was commanded by General A. S. Williams, the senior division commander present. On the 25th of July the army, therefore, stood thus: the Army of the Tennessee (General O. O. Howard commanding) was on the left, pretty much on the same ground it had occupied during the battle of the 22d, all ready to move rapidly by the rear to the extreme right beyond Proctor's Creek; the Army of the Ohio (General Schofield) was next in order, with its left flank reaching the Augusta Railroad; next in order, conforming closely with the rebel intrenchments of Atlanta, was General Thomas's Army of the Cumberland, in the order of—the Fourth Corps (Stanley's), the Twentieth Corps (Williams's), and the Fourteenth Corps (Palmer's). Palmer's right division (Jefferson C. Davis's) was strongly refused along Proctor's Creek. This line was about five miles long, and was intrenched as against a sally about as strong as was our enemy. The cavalry was assembled in two strong divisions; that of McCook (including the brigade of Harrison which had been brought in from Opelika by General Rousseau) numbered about thirty-five hundred effective cavalry, and was posted to our right rear, at Turner's Ferry, where we had a good pontoon-bridge; and to our left rear, at and about Decatur, were the two cavalry divisions of Stoneman, twenty-five hundred, and Garrard, four thousand, united for the time and occasion under the command of Major-General George Stoneman, a cavalry-officer of high repute. My plan of action was to move the Army of the Tennessee to the right rapidly and boldly against the railroad below Atlanta, and at the same time to send all the cavalry around by the right and left to make a lodgment on the Macon road about Jonesboro'.

All the orders were given, and the morning of the 27th was fixed for commencing the movement. On the 26th I received from General Stoneman a note asking permission (after having accomplished his orders to break up the railroad at Jonesboro') to go on to Macon to rescue our prisoners of war known to be held there, and then to push on to Andersonville, where was the great depot of Union prisoners, in which were penned at one time as many as twenty-three thousand of our men, badly fed and harshly treated. I wrote him an answer consenting substantially to his proposition, only modifying it by requiring him to send back General Garrard's division to its position on our left flank after he had broken up the railroad at Jonesboro'. Promptly, and on time, all got off, and General Dodge's corps (the Sixteenth, of the Army of the Tennessee) reached its position across Proctor's Creek the same evening, and early the next morning (the 28th) Blair's corps (the Seventeenth) deployed on his right, both corps covering their front with the usual parapet; the Fifteenth Corps (General Logan's) came up that morning on the right of Blair, strongly refused, and began to prepare the usual cover. As General Jeff. C. Davis's division was, as it were, left out of line, I ordered it on the evening before to march down toward Turner's Ferry, and then to take a road laid down on our maps which led from there toward East Point, ready to engage any enemy that might attack our general right flank, after the same manner as had been done to the left flank on the 22d.

Personally on the morning of the 28th I followed the movement, and rode to the extreme right, where we could hear some skirmishing and an occasional cannon-shot. As we approached the ground held by the Fifteenth Corps, a cannon-ball passed over my shoulder and killed the horse of an orderly behind; and seeing that this gun enfiladed the road by which we were riding, we turned out of it and rode down into a valley, where we left our horses and walked up to the hill held by Morgan L. Smith's division of the Fifteenth Corps. Near a house I met Generals Howard and Logan, who explained that there was an intrenched battery to their front, with the appearance of a strong infantry support. I then walked up to the ridge, where I found General Morgan L. Smith. His men were deployed and engaged in rolling logs and fence-rails, preparing a hasty cover. From this ridge we could overlook the open fields near a meeting-house known as "Ezra Church," close by the Poor-House. We could see the fresh earth of a parapet covering some guns (that fired an occasional shot), and there was also an appearance of activity beyond. General Smith was in the act of sending forward a regiment from his right flank to feel the position of the enemy, when I explained to him and to Generals Logan and Howard that they must look out for General Jeff. C. Davis's division, which was coming up from the direction of Turner's Ferry.

As the skirmish-fire warmed up along the front of Blair's corps, as well as along the Fifteenth Corps (Logan's), I became convinced that Hood designed to attack this right flank, to prevent, if possible, the extension of our line in that direction. I regained my horse, and rode rapidly back to see that Davis's division had been dispatched as ordered. I found General Davis in person, who was unwell, and had sent his division that morning early, under the command of his senior brigadier, Morgan; but, as I attached great importance to the movement, he mounted his horse, and rode away to overtake and to hurry forward the movement, so as to come up on the left rear of the enemy, during the expected battle.

By this time the sound of cannon and musketry denoted a severe battle as in progress, which began seriously at 11½ A.M., and ended substantially by 4 P.M. It was a fierce attack by the enemy on our extreme right flank, well posted and partially covered. The most authentic account of the battle is given by General Logan, who commanded the Fifteenth Corps, in his official report to the Adjutant-General of the Army of the Tennessee, thus:

HEADQUARTERS FIFTEENTH ARMY CORPS, ⎱
  BEFORE ATLANTA, GEORGIA, *July* 29, 1864.⎰

Lieutenant-Colonel WILLIAM T. CLARK, *Assistant Adjutant-General,*
    Army of the Tennessee, present.

COLONEL: I have the honor to report that, in pursuance of orders, I moved my command into position on the right of the Seventeenth Corps, which was the extreme right of the army in the field, during the night of the 27th and morning of the 28th; and, while advancing in line of battle to a more favorable position, we were met by the rebel infantry of Hardee's and Lee's corps, who made a determined and desperate attack on us at 11½ A.M. of the 28th (yesterday).

My lines were only protected by logs and rails, hastily thrown up in front of them.

The first onset was received and checked, and the battle commenced and lasted until about three o'clock in the evening. During that time six successive charges were made, which were six times gallantly repulsed, each time with fearful loss to the enemy.

Later in the evening my lines were several times assaulted vigorously, but each time with like result.

The worst of the fighting occurred on General Harrow's and Morgan L. Smith's fronts, which formed the centre and right of the corps.

The troops could not have displayed greater courage, nor greater determination not to give ground; had they shown less, they would have been driven from their position.

Brigadier-Generals C. R. Woods, Harrow, and Morgan L. Smith, division commanders, are entitled to equal credit for gallant conduct and skill in repelling the assault.

My thanks are due to Major-Generals Blair and Dodge for sending me reënforcements at a time when they were much needed.

My losses were fifty killed, four hundred and forty-nine wounded, and seventy-three missing: aggregate, five hundred and seventy-two.

The division of General Harrow captured five battle-flags. There were about fifteen hundred or two thousand muskets left on the ground. One hundred and six prisoners were captured, exclusive of seventy-three wounded, who were sent to our hospital, and are being cared for by our surgeons.

Five hundred and sixty-five rebels have up to this time been buried, and about two hundred are supposed to be yet unburied.

A large number of their wounded were undoubtedly carried away in the night, as the enemy did not withdraw till near daylight. The enemy's loss could not have been less than six or seven thousand men.

A more detailed report will hereafter be made.

I am, very respectfully,

Your obedient servant,

JOHN A. LOGAN,

Major-General, commanding Fifteenth Army Corps.

General Howard, in transmitting this report, added:

I wish to express my high gratification with the conduct of the troops engaged. I never saw better conduct in battle. General Logan, though ill and much worn out, was indefatigable, and the success of the day is as much attributable to him as to any one man.

This was, of course, the first fight in which General Howard had commanded the Army of the Tennessee, and he evidently aimed to reconcile General Logan in his disappointment, and to gain the heart of his army, to which he was a stranger. He very properly left General Logan to fight his own corps, but exposed himself freely; and, after the firing had ceased, in the afternoon he walked the lines; the men, as reported to me, gathered about him in the most affectionate way, and he at once gained their respect and confidence. To this fact I at the time attached much importance, for it put me at ease as to the future conduct of that most important army.

At no instant of time did I feel the least uneasiness about the result on the 28th, but wanted to reap fuller results, hoping that Davis's division would come up at the instant of defeat, and catch the enemy in flank; but the woods were dense, the roads obscure, and as usual this division got on the wrong road, and did not come into position until about dark. In like manner, I thought that Hood had greatly weakened his main lines inside of Atlanta, and accordingly sent repeated orders to Schofield and Thomas to make an attempt to break in; but both reported that they found the parapets very strong and full manned.

Our men were unusually encouraged by this day's work, for they realized that we could compel Hood to come out from behind his fortified lines to attack us at a disadvantage. In conversation with me, the soldiers of the Fifteenth Corps, with whom I was on the most familiar terms, spoke of the affair of the 28th as the easiest thing in the world; that, in fact, it was a common slaughter of the enemy; they pointed out where the rebel lines had been, and how they themselves had fired deliberately, had shot down their antagonists, whose bodies still lay unburied, and marked plainly their lines of battle, which must have halted within easy musket-range of our men, who were partially protected by their improvised line of logs and fence-rails. All bore willing testimony to the courage and spirit of the foe, who, though repeatedly repulsed, came back with increased determination some six or more times.

The next morning the Fifteenth Corps wheeled forward to the left over the battle-field of the day before, and Davis's division still farther prolonged the line, which reached nearly to the ever-to-be-remembered "Sandtown road."

Then, by further thinning out Thomas's line, which was well intrenched, I drew another division of Palmer's corps (Baird's) around to the right, to further strengthen that flank. I was impatient to hear from the cavalry raid, then four days out, and was watching for its effect, ready to make a bold push for the possession of East Point. General Garrard's division returned to Decatur on the 31st, and reported that General Stoneman had posted him at Flat Rock, while he (Stoneman) went on. The month of July therefore closed with our infantry line strongly intrenched, but drawn out from the Augusta road on the left to the Sandtown road on the right, a distance of full ten measured miles.

The enemy, though evidently somewhat intimidated by the results of their defeats on the 22d and 28th, still presented a bold front at all points, with fortified lines that defied a direct assault. Our railroad was done to the rear of our camps, Colonel W. W. Wright having reconstructed the bridge across the Chattahoochee in six days; and our garrisons and detachments to the rear had so effectually guarded the railroad that the trains from Nashville arrived daily, and our substantial wants were well supplied.

The month, though hot in the extreme, had been one of constant conflict, without intermission, and on four several occasions—viz., July 4th, 20th, 22d, and 28th—these affairs had amounted to real battles, with casualty lists by the thousands. Assuming the correctness of the rebel surgeon Foard's report, on page 577 of Johnston's "Narrative," commencing with July 4th and terminating with July 31st, we have:

CORPS.	Killed.	Wounded.	Total.
Hardee's	523	2,774	3,297
Lee's	351	2,408	2,759
Stewart's	436	2,141	2,577
Wheeler's Cavalry	29	156	185
Engineers.	2	21	23
Total	1,341	7,500	8,841

To these I add as prisoners, at least   2,000
Aggregate loss of the enemy in July, 1864   10,841

Our losses, as compiled from the official returns for July, 1864, are:

ARMY OF THE CUMBERLAND.

CORPS.	Killed and Missing.	Wounded.	Total.
Fourth	116	432	548
Fourteenth	317	1,084	1,401
Twentieth	541	1,480	2,021
Total, Army of the Cumberland. .	974	2,996	3,970

ARMY OF THE TENNESSEE.

CORPS.	Killed and Missing.	Wounded.	Total.
Fifteenth	590	797	1,387
Sixteenth	289	721	1,010
Seventeenth	1,361	1,203	2,564
Total, Army of the Tennessee . . .	2,240	2,721	4,961

ARMY OF THE OHIO.

CORPS.	Killed and Missing.	Wounded.	Total.
Twenty-third.	95	167	262
Cavalry	495	31	526
Total, Army of the Ohio	590	198	788
Aggregate loss for July	3,804	5,915	9,719

In this table the column of "killed and missing" embraces the prisoners that fell into the hands of the enemy, mostly lost in the Seventeenth Corps, on the 22d of July, and does not embrace the losses in the cavalry divisions of Garrard and McCook, which, however, were small for July. In all other respects the statement is absolutely correct. I am satisfied, however, that Surgeon Foard could not have been in possession of data sufficiently accurate to enable him to report the losses in actual battle of men who never saw the hospital. During the whole campaign I had rendered to me tri-monthly statements of "effective strength," from which I carefully eliminated the figures not essential for my conduct, so that at all times I knew the exact fighting-strength of each corps, division, and brigade, of the whole army, and also endeavored to bear in mind our losses both on the several fields of battle and by sickness, and well remember that I always estimated that during the month of July we had inflicted heavier loss on the enemy than we had sustained ourselves, and the above figures prove it conclusively. Before closing this chapter, I must record one or two minor events that occurred about this time, that may prove of interest.

On the 24th of July I received a dispatch from Inspector-General James A. Hardie, then on duty at the War Department in Washington, to the effect that Generals Osterhaus and Alvan P. Hovey had been appointed major-generals. Both of these had begun the campaign with us in command of divisions, but had gone to the rear—the former by reason of sickness, and the latter dissatisfied with General Schofield and myself about the composition of his division of the Twenty-third Corps. Both were esteemed as first-class officers, who had gained special distinction in the Vicksburg campaign. But up to that time, when the newspapers announced daily promotions elsewhere, no prominent officers serving with me had been advanced a peg, and I felt hurt. I answered Hardie on the 25th, in a dispatch which has been made public, closing with this language: "If the rear be the post of honor, then we had better all change front on Washington." To my amazement, in a few days I received from President Lincoln himself an answer, in which he caught me fairly. I have not preserved a copy of that dispatch, and suppose it was burned up in the Chicago fire; but it was characteristic of Mr. Lincoln, and was dated the 26th or 27th day of July, contained unequivocal expressions of respect for those who were fighting hard and unselfishly, offering us a full share of the honors and rewards of the war, and saying that, in the cases of Hovey and Osterhaus, he was influenced mainly by the recommendations of Generals Grant and Sherman. On the 27th I replied direct, apologizing somewhat for my message to General Hardie, saying that I did not suppose such messages ever reached him personally, explaining that General Grant's and Sherman's recommendations for Hovey and Osterhaus had been made when the events of the Vicksburg campaign were fresh with us, and that my dispatch of the 25th to General Hardie had reflected chiefly the feelings of the officers then present with me before Atlanta. The result of all this, however, was good, for another dispatch from General Hardie, of the 28th, called on me to nominate eight colonels for promotion as brigadier-generals. I at once sent a circular note to the army-commanders to nominate two colonels from the Army of the Ohio and three from each of the others; and the result was, that on the 29th of July I telegraphed the names of—Colonel William Gross, Thirty-sixth Indiana; Colonel Charles C. Walcutt, Forty-sixth Ohio; Colonel James W. Riley, One Hundred and Fourth Ohio; Colonel L. P. Bradley, Fifty-first Illinois; Colonel J. W. Sprague, Sixty-third Ohio; Colonel Joseph A. Cooper, Sixth East Tennessee; Colonel John T. Croxton, Fourth Kentucky; Colonel William W. Belknap, Fifteenth Iowa. These were promptly appointed brigadier-generals, were already in command of brigades or divisions; and I doubt if eight promotions were ever made fairer, or were more honestly earned, during the whole war.

Chapter XIX.

CAPTURE OF ATLANTA.

August and September, 1864.

THE MONTH of August opened hot and sultry, but our position before Atlanta was healthy, with ample supply of wood, water, and provisions. The troops had become habituated to the slow and steady progress of the siege; the skirmish-lines were held close up to the enemy, were covered by rifle-trenches or logs, and kept up a continuous clatter of musketry. The main lines were held farther back, adapted to the shape of the ground, with muskets loaded and stacked for instant use. The field-batteries were in select positions, covered by handsome parapets, and occasional shots from them gave life and animation to the scene. The men loitered about the trenches carelessly, or busied themselves in constructing ingenious huts out of the abundant timber, and seemed as snug, comfortable, and happy, as though they were at home. General Schofield was still on the extreme left, Thomas in the centre, and Howard on the right. Two divisions of the Fourteenth Corps (Baird's and Jeff. C. Davis's) were detached to the right rear, and held in reserve.

I thus awaited the effect of the cavalry movement against the railroad about Jonesboro', and had heard from General Garrard that Stoneman had gone on to Macon; during that day (August 1st) Colonel Brownlow, of a Tennessee cavalry regiment, came in to Marietta from General McCook, and reported that McCook's whole division had been overwhelmed, defeated, and captured at Newnan. Of course, I was disturbed by this wild report, though I discredited it, but made all possible preparations to strengthen our guards along the railroad to the rear, on the theory that the force of cavalry which had defeated McCook would at once be on the railroad about Marietta. At the same time Garrard was ordered to occupy the trenches on our left, while Schofield's whole army moved to the extreme right, and extended the line toward East Point. Thomas was also ordered still further to thin out his lines, so as to set free the other division (Johnson's) of the

Fourteenth Corps (Palmer's), which was moved to the extreme right rear, and held in reserve ready to make a bold push from that flank to secure a footing on the Macon Railroad at or below East Point.

These changes were effected during the 2d and 3d days of August, when General McCook came in and reported the actual results of his cavalry expedition. He had crossed the Chattahoochee River below Campbellton, by his pontoon-bridge; had then marched rapidly across to the Macon Railroad at Lovejoy's Station, where he had reason to expect General Stoneman; but, not hearing of him, he set to work, tore up two miles of track, burned two trains of cars, and cut away five miles of telegraph-wire. He also found the wagon-train belonging to the rebel army in Atlanta, burned five hundred wagons, killed eight hundred mules, and captured seventy-two officers and three hundred and fifty men. Finding his progress eastward, toward McDonough, barred by a superior force, he turned back to Newnan, where he found himself completely surrounded by infantry and cavalry. He had to drop his prisoners and fight his way out, losing about six hundred men in killed and captured, and then returned with the remainder to his position at Turner's Ferry. This was bad enough, but not so bad as had been reported by Colonel Brownlow. Meantime, rumors came that General Stoneman was down about Macon, on the east bank of the Ocmulgee. On the 4th of August Colonel Adams got to Marietta with his small brigade of nine hundred men belonging to Stoneman's cavalry, reporting, as usual, all the rest lost, and this was partially confirmed by a report which came to me all the way round by General Grant's headquarters before Richmond. A few days afterward Colonel Capron also got in, with another small brigade perfectly demoralized, and confirmed the report that General Stoneman had covered the escape of these two small brigades, himself standing with a reserve of seven hundred men, with which he surrendered to a Colonel Iverson. Thus another of my cavalry divisions was badly damaged, and out of the fragments we hastily reorganized three small divisions under Brigadier-Generals Garrard, McCook, and Kilpatrick.

Stoneman had not obeyed his orders to attack the railroad

first before going to Macon and Andersonville, but had crossed the Ocmulgee River high up near Covington, and had gone down that river on the east bank. He reached Clinton, and sent out detachments which struck the railroad leading from Macon to Savannah at Griswold Station, where they found and destroyed seventeen locomotives and over a hundred cars; then went on and burned the bridge across the Oconee, and reunited the division before Macon. Stoneman shelled the town across the river, but could not cross over by the bridge, and returned to Clinton, where he found his retreat obstructed, as he supposed, by a superior force. There he became bewildered, and sacrificed himself for the safety of his command. He occupied the attention of his enemy by a small force of seven hundred men, giving Colonels Adams and Capron leave, with their brigades, to cut their way back to me at Atlanta. The former reached us entire, but the latter was struck and scattered at some place farther north, and came in by detachments. Stoneman surrendered, and remained a prisoner until he was exchanged some time after, late in September, at Rough and Ready.

I now became satisfied that cavalry could not, or would not, make a sufficient lodgment on the railroad below Atlanta, and that nothing would suffice but for us to reach it with the main army. Therefore the most urgent efforts to that end were made, and to Schofield, on the right, was committed the charge of this special object. He had his own corps (the Twenty-third), composed of eleven thousand and seventy-five infantry and eight hundred and eighty-five artillery, with McCook's broken division of cavalry, seventeen hundred and fifty-four men and horses. For this purpose I also placed the Fourteenth Corps (Palmer) under his orders. This corps numbered at the time seventeen thousand two hundred and eighty-eight infantry and eight hundred and twenty-six artillery; but General Palmer claimed to rank General Schofield in the date of his commission as major-general, and denied the latter's right to exercise command over him. General Palmer was a man of ability, but was not enterprising. His three divisions were compact and strong, well commanded, admirable on the defensive, but slow to move or to act on the offensive. His corps (the Fourteenth) had sustained, up to that time, fewer hard knocks than any other corps in the whole army, and I was anxious to give it a chance. I always expected to have a desperate fight to get possession of the Macon road, which was then the vital objective of the campaign. Its possession by us would, in my judgment, result in the capture of Atlanta, and give us the fruits of victory, although the destruction of Hood's army was the real object to be desired. Yet Atlanta was known as the "Gate-City of the South," was full of founderies, arsenals, and machine-shops, and I knew that its capture would be the death-knell of the Southern Confederacy.

On the 4th of August I ordered General Schofield to make a bold attack on the railroad, anywhere about East Point, and ordered General Palmer to report to him for duty. He at once denied General Schofield's right to command him; but, after examining the dates of their respective commissions, and hearing their arguments, I wrote to General Palmer.

August 4th — 10.45 P.M.

From the statements made by yourself and General Schofield to-day, my decision is, that he ranks you as a major-general, being of the same date of present commission, by reason of his previous superior rank as *brigadier-general*. The movements of to-morrow are so important that the orders of the superior on that flank must be regarded as military orders, and not in the nature of coöperation. I did hope that there would be no necessity for my making this decision; but it is better for all parties interested that no question of rank should occur in actual battle. The Sandtown road, and the railroad, if possible, must be gained to-morrow, if it costs half your command. I regard the loss of time this afternoon as equal to the loss of two thousand men.

I also communicated the substance of this to General Thomas, to whose army Palmer's corps belonged, who replied on the 5th:

I regret to hear that Palmer has taken the course he has, and I know that he intends to offer his resignation as soon as he can properly do so. I recommend that his application be granted.

And on the 5th I again wrote to General Palmer, arguing the point with him, advising him, as a friend, not to resign at that crisis lest his motives might be misconstrued, and because it might damage his future career in civil life; but, at the same time, I felt it my duty to say to him that the operations on that flank, during the 4th and 5th, had not been satisfactory—not imputing to him, however, any want of energy or skill, but insisting that "the events did not keep pace with my desires." General Schofield had reported to me that night:

I am compelled to acknowledge that I have totally failed to make any aggressive movement with the Fourteenth Corps. I have ordered General Johnson's division to replace General Hascall's this evening, and I propose to-morrow to take my own troops (Twenty-third Corps) to the right, and try to recover what has been lost by two days' delay. The force may likely be too small.

I sanctioned the movement, and ordered two of Palmer's divisions—Davis's and Baird's—to follow *en échelon* in support of Schofield, and summoned General Palmer to meet me in person. He came on the 6th to my headquarters, and insisted on his resignation being accepted, for which formal act I referred him to General Thomas. He then rode to General Thomas's camp, where he made a written resignation of his office as commander of the Fourteenth Corps, and was granted the usual leave of absence to go to his home in Illinois, there to await further orders. General Thomas recommended that the resignation be accepted; that Johnson, the senior division commander of the corps, should be ordered back to Nashville as chief of cavalry, and that Brigadier-General Jefferson C. Davis, the next in order, should be promoted major-general, and assigned to command the corps. These changes had to be referred to the President, in Washington, and were, in due time, approved and executed; and thenceforward I had no reason to complain of the slowness or inactivity of that splendid corps. It had been originally formed by General George H. Thomas, had been commanded by him in person, and had imbibed somewhat his personal character, viz., steadiness, good order, and deliberation—nothing hasty or rash, but always safe, "slow, and sure."

On August 7th I telegraphed to General Halleck:

Have received to-day the dispatches of the Secretary of War and of General Grant, which are very satisfactory. We keep hammering away all the time, and there is no peace, inside or outside of Atlanta.

To-day General Schofield got round the line which was assaulted yesterday by General Reilly's brigade, turned it and gained the ground where the assault had been made, and got possession of all our dead and wounded. He continued to press on that flank, and brought on a noisy but not a bloody battle. He drove the enemy behind his main breastworks, which cover the railroad from Atlanta to East Point, and captured a good many of the skirmishers, who are of his best troops—for the militia hug the breastworks close. I do not deem it prudent to extend any more to the right, but will push forward daily by parallels, and make the inside of Atlanta too hot to be endured. I have sent back to Chattanooga for two thirty-pound Parrotts, with which we can pick out almost any house in town. I am too impatient for a siege, and don't know but this is as good a place to fight it out on, as farther inland. One thing is certain, whether we get inside of Atlanta or not, it will be a used-up community when we are done with it.

In Schofield's extension on the 5th, General Reilly's brigade had struck an outwork, which he promptly attacked, but, as usual, got entangled in the trees and bushes which had been felled, and lost about five hundred men, in killed and wounded; but, as above reported, this outwork was found abandoned the next day, and we could see from it that the rebels were extending their lines, parallel with the railroad, about as fast as we could add to our line of investment. On the 10th of August the Parrott thirty-pounders were received and placed in position; for a couple of days we kept up a sharp fire from all our batteries converging on Atlanta, and at every available point we advanced our infantry-lines, thereby shortening and strengthening the investment; but I was not willing to order a direct assault, unless some accident or positive neglect on the part of our antagonist should reveal an opening. However, it was manifest that no such opening was intended by Hood, who felt secure behind his strong defenses. He had repelled our cavalry attacks on his railroad, and had damaged us seriously thereby, so I expected that he would attempt the same game against our rear. Therefore I made extraordinary exertions to recompose our cavalry divisions, which were so essential, both for defense and offense. Kilpatrick was given that on our right rear, in support of Schofield's exposed flank; Garrard retained that on our general left; and McCook's division was held somewhat in reserve, about Marietta and the railroad. On the 10th, having occasion to telegraph to General Grant, then in Washington, I used this language:

Since July 28th Hood has not attempted to meet us outside his parapets. In order to possess and destroy effectually his communications, I may have to leave a corps at the railroad-bridge, well intrenched, and cut loose with the balance to make a circle of desolation around Atlanta. I do not propose to assault the works, which are too strong, nor to proceed by regular approaches. I have lost a good many regiments, and will lose more, by the expiration of service; and this is the only reason why I want reënforcements. We have killed, crippled, and captured more of the enemy than we have lost by his acts.

On the 12th of August I heard of the success of Admiral Farragut in entering Mobile Bay, which was regarded as a most valuable auxiliary to our operations at Atlanta; and learned that I had been commissioned a major-general in the regular army, which was unexpected, and not desired until successful in the capture of Atlanta. These did not change the fact that we were held in check by the stubborn defense of the place, and a conviction was forced on my mind that our enemy would hold fast, even though every house in the town should be battered down by our artillery. It was evident that we must decoy him out to fight us on something like equal terms, or else, with the whole army, raise the siege and attack his communications. Accordingly, on the 13th of August, I gave general orders for the Twentieth Corps to draw back to the railroad-bridge at the Chattahoochee, to protect our trains, hospitals, spare artillery, and the railroad-depot, while the rest of the army should move bodily to some point on the Macon Railroad below East Point.

Luckily, I learned just then that the enemy's cavalry, under General Wheeler, had made a wide circuit around our left flank, and had actually reached our railroad at Tilton Station, above Resaca, captured a drove of one thousand of our beef-cattle, and was strong enough to appear before Dalton, and demand of its commander, Colonel Raum, the surrender of the place. General John E. Smith, who was at Kingston, collected together a couple of thousand men, and proceeded in cars to the relief of Dalton, when Wheeler retreated north-

ward toward Cleveland. On the 16th another detachment of
the enemy's cavalry appeared in force about Allatoona and
the Etowah bridge, when I became fully convinced that Hood
had sent *all* of his cavalry to raid upon our railroads. For
some days our communication with Nashville was interrupted
by the destruction of the telegraph-lines, as well as railroad. I
at once ordered strong reconnoissances forward from our
flanks on the left by Garrard, and on the right by Kilpatrick.
The former moved with so much caution that I was displeased; but Kilpatrick, on the contrary, displayed so much
zeal and activity that I was attracted to him at once. He
reached Fairburn Station, on the West Point road, and tore it
up, returning safely to his position on our right flank. I summoned him to me, and was so pleased with his spirit and
confidence, that I concluded to suspend the general movement of the main army, and to send him with his small division of cavalry to break up the Macon road about Jonesboro',
in the hopes that it would force Hood to evacuate Atlanta,
and that I should thereby not only secure possession of the
city itself, but probably could catch Hood in the confusion of
retreat; and, further to increase the chances of success, I ordered General Thomas to detach two brigades of Garrard's
division of cavalry from the left to the right rear, to act as a
reserve in support of General Kilpatrick. Meantime, also, the
utmost activity was ordered along our whole front by the infantry and artillery. Kilpatrick got off during the night of the
18th, and returned to us on the 22d, having made the complete circuit of Atlanta. He reported that he had destroyed
three miles of the railroad about Jonesboro', which he reckoned would take ten days to repair; that he had encountered a
division of infantry and a brigade of cavalry (Ross's); that he
had captured a battery and destroyed three of its guns, bringing one in as a trophy, and he also brought in three battle-
flags and seventy prisoners. On the 23d, however, we saw
trains coming into Atlanta from the south, when I became
more than ever convinced that cavalry could not or would not
work hard enough to disable a railroad properly, and therefore resolved at once to proceed to the execution of my original plan. Meantime, the damage done to our own railroad
and telegraph by Wheeler, about Resaca and Dalton, had

been repaired, and Wheeler himself was too far away to be of any service to his own army, and where he could not do us much harm, viz., up about the Hiawassee. On the 24th I rode down to the Chattahoochee bridge, to see in person that it could be properly defended by the single corps proposed to be left there for that purpose, and found that the rebel works, which had been built by Johnston to resist us, could be easily utilized against themselves; and on returning to my camp, at 7.15 P.M. that same evening, I telegraphed to General Halleck as follows:

Heavy fires in Atlanta all day, caused by our artillery. I will be all ready, and will commence the movement around Atlanta by the south, to-morrow night, and for some time you will hear little of us. I will keep open a courier line back to the Chattahoochee bridge, by way of Sandtown. The Twentieth Corps will hold the railroad-bridge, and I will move with the balance of the army, provisioned for twenty days.

Meantime General Dodge (commanding the Sixteenth Corps) had been wounded in the forehead, had gone to the rear, and his two divisions were distributed to the Fifteenth and Seventeenth Corps. The real movement commenced on the 25th, at night. The Twentieth Corps drew back and took post at the railroad-bridge, and the Fourth Corps (Stanley) moved to his right rear, closing up with the Fourteenth Corps (Jeff. C. Davis) near Utoy Creek; at the same time Garrard's cavalry, leaving their horses out of sight, occupied the vacant trenches, so that the enemy did not detect the change at all. The next night (26th) the Fifteenth and Seventeenth Corps, composing the Army of the Tennessee (Howard), drew out of their trenches, made a wide circuit, and came up on the extreme right of the Fourth and Fourteenth Corps of the Army of the Cumberland (Thomas) along Utoy Creek, facing south. The enemy seemed to suspect something that night, using his artillery pretty freely; but I think he supposed we were going to retreat altogether. An artillery-shot, fired at random, killed one man and wounded another, and the next morning some of his infantry came out of Atlanta and found our camps abandoned. It was afterward related that there was great rejoicing in Atlanta "that the Yankees were gone;" the fact was telegraphed all over the South, and several trains of cars (with ladies) came up from Macon to assist in the celebration of their grand victory.

On the 28th (making a general left-wheel, pivoting on Schofield) both Thomas and Howard reached the West Point Railroad, extending from East Point to Red-Oak Station and Fairburn, where we spent the next day (29th) in breaking it up thoroughly. The track was heaved up in sections the length of a regiment, then separated rail by rail; bonfires were made of the ties and of fence-rails on which the rails were heated, carried to trees or telegraph-poles, wrapped around and left to cool. Such rails could not be used again; and, to be still more certain, we filled up many deep cuts with trees, brush, and earth, and commingled with them loaded shells, so arranged that they would explode on an attempt to haul out the bushes. The explosion of one such shell would have de-moralized a gang of negroes, and thus would have prevented even the attempt to clear the road.

Meantime Schofield, with the Twenty-third Corps, pre-sented a bold front toward East Point, daring and inviting the enemy to sally out to attack him in position. His first move-ment was on the 30th, to Mount Gilead Church, then to Morrow's Mills, facing Rough and Ready. Thomas was on his right, within easy support, moving by cross-roads from Red Oak to the Fayetteville road, extending from Couch's to Renfrew's; and Howard was aiming for Jonesboro'.

I was with General Thomas that day, which was hot but otherwise very pleasant. We stopped for a short noon-rest near a little church (marked on our maps as Shoal-Creek Church), which stood back about a hundred yards from the road, in a grove of native oaks. The infantry column had halted in the road, stacked their arms, and the men were scat-tered about—some lying in the shade of the trees, and others were bringing corn-stalks from a large corn-field across the road to feed our horses, while still others had arms full of the roasting-ears, then in their prime. Hundreds of fires were soon started with the fence-rails, and the men were busy roasting the ears. Thomas and I were walking up and down the road which led to the church, discussing the chances of the movement, which he thought were extra-hazardous, and our path carried us by a fire at which a soldier was roasting his corn. The fire was built artistically; the man was stripping the ears of their husks, standing them in front of his fire, watching them carefully, and turning each ear little by little, so as to roast it nicely. He was down on his knees intent on his business, paying little heed to the stately and serious deliberations of his leaders. Thomas's mind was running on the fact that we had cut loose from our base of supplies, and that seventy thousand men were then dependent for their food on the chance supplies of the country (already impoverished by the requisitions of the enemy), and on the contents of our wagons. Between Thomas and his men there existed a most kindly relation, and he frequently talked with them in the most familiar way. Pausing awhile, and watching the operations of this man roasting his corn, he said, "What are you doing?" The man looked up smilingly: "Why, general, I am laying in a supply of provisions." "That is right, my man, but don't waste your provisions." As we resumed our walk, the man remarked, in a sort of musing way, but loud enough for me to hear: "There he goes, there goes the old man, economizing as usual." "Economizing" with corn, which cost only the labor of gathering and roasting!

As we walked, we could hear General Howard's guns at intervals, away off to our right front, but an ominous silence continued toward our left, where I was expecting at each moment to hear the sound of battle. That night we reached Renfrew's, and had reports from left to right (from General Schofield, about Morrow's Mills, to General Howard, within a couple of miles of Jonesboro'). The next morning (August 31st) all moved straight for the railroad. Schofield reached it near Rough and Ready, and Thomas at two points between there and Jonesboro'. Howard found an intrenched foe (Hardee's corps) covering Jonesboro', and his men began at once to dig their accustomed rifle-pits. Orders were sent to Generals Thomas and Schofield to turn straight for Jonesboro', tearing up the railroad-track as they advanced. About 3 P.M. the enemy sallied from Jonesboro' against the Fifteenth corps, but was easily repulsed, and driven back within his lines. All hands were kept busy tearing up the railroad, and it was not until toward evening of the 1st day of September that the Fourteenth Corps (Davis) closed down on the north front of Jonesboro', connecting on his right with Howard, and his left reaching the railroad, along which General Stanley was moving, followed by Schofield. General Davis formed his divisions in line about 4 P.M., swept forward over some old cotton-fields in full view, and went over the rebel parapet handsomely, capturing the whole of Govan's brigade, with two field-batteries of ten guns. Being on the spot, I checked Davis's movement, and ordered General Howard to send the two divisions of the Seventeenth Corps (Blair) round by his right rear, to get below Jonesboro', and to reach the railroad, so as to cut off retreat in that direction. I also dispatched orders after orders to hurry forward Stanley, so as to lap around Jonesboro' on the east, hoping thus to capture the whole of Hardee's corps. I sent first Captain Audenried (aide-de-camp), then Colonel Poe, of the Engineers, and lastly General Thomas himself (and that is the only time during the campaign I can recall seeing General Thomas urge his horse into a gallop). Night was approaching, and the country on the farther side of the railroad was densely wooded. General Stanley had come up on the left of Davis, and was deploying, though there could not have been on his front more than a skirmish-line. Had he moved straight on by the flank, or by a slight circuit to his left, he would have inclosed the whole ground occupied by Hardee's corps, and that corps could not have escaped us; but night came on, and Hardee did escape.

Meantime General Slocum had reached his corps (the Twentieth), stationed at the Chattahoochee bridge, had relieved General A. S. Williams in command, and orders had been sent back to him to feel forward occasionally toward Atlanta, to observe the effect when we had reached the railroad. That night I was so restless and impatient that I could not sleep, and about midnight there arose toward Atlanta sounds of shells exploding, and other sound like that of musketry. I walked to the house of a farmer close by my bivouac, called him out to listen to the reverberations which came from the direction of Atlanta (twenty miles to the north of us), and inquired of him if he had resided there long. He said he had, and that these sounds were just like those of a battle. An interval of quiet then ensued, when again, about 4 A.M., arose other similar explosions, but I still remained in doubt whether the enemy was engaged in blowing up his own magazines, or whether General Slocum had not felt forward, and become engaged in a real battle.

The next morning General Hardee was gone, and we all pushed forward along the railroad south, in close pursuit, till we ran up against his lines at a point just above Lovejoy's Station. While bringing forward troops and feeling the new position of our adversary, rumors came from the rear that the enemy had evacuated Atlanta, and that General Slocum was in the city. Later in the day I received a note in Slocum's own handwriting, stating that he had heard during the night the very sounds that I have referred to; that he had moved rapidly up from the bridge about daylight, and had entered Atlanta unopposed. His letter was dated inside the city, so there was no doubt of the fact. General Thomas's bivouac was but a short distance from mine, and, before giving notice to the army in general orders, I sent one of my staff-officers to show him the note. In a few minutes the officer returned, soon followed by Thomas himself, who again examined the note, so as to be perfectly certain that it was genuine. The news seemed to him too good to be true. He snapped his fingers, whistled, and almost danced, and, as the news spread to the army, the shouts that arose from our men, the wild hallooing and glorious laughter, were to us a full recompense for the labor and toils and hardships through which we had passed in the previous three months.

A courier-line was at once organized, messages were sent back and forth from our camp at Lovejoy's to Atlanta, and to our telegraph-station at the Chattahoochee bridge. Of course, the glad tidings flew on the wings of electricity to all parts of the North, where the people had patiently awaited news of their husbands, sons, and brothers, away down in "Dixie Land;" and congratulations came pouring back full of goodwill and patriotism. This victory was most opportune; Mr. Lincoln himself told me afterward that even he had previously felt in doubt, for the summer was fast passing away; that General Grant seemed to be checkmated about Richmond and Petersburg, and my army seemed to have run up against an impassable barrier, when, suddenly and unexpectedly, came the news that "Atlanta was ours, and fairly won." On this text many a fine speech was made, but none more eloquent than that by Edward Everett, in Boston. A presidential election then agitated the North. Mr. Lincoln represented the national cause, and General McClellan had accepted the nomination of the Democratic party, whose platform was that the war was a failure, and that it was better to allow the South to go free to establish a separate government, whose cornerstone should be slavery. Success to our arms at that instant was therefore a political necessity; and it was all-important that something startling in our interest should occur before the election in November. The brilliant success at Atlanta filled that requirement, and made the election of Mr. Lincoln certain. Among the many letters of congratulation received, those of Mr. Lincoln and General Grant seem most important:

EXECUTIVE MANSION, ⎫
WASHINGTON, D. C., *September* 3, 1864.⎭
   The national thanks are rendered by the President to Major-General W. T. Sherman and the gallant officers and soldiers of his command before Atlanta, for the distinguished ability and perseverance displayed in the campaign in Georgia, which, under Divine favor, has resulted in the capture of Atlanta. The marches, battles, sieges, and other military operations, that have signalized the campaign, must render it famous in the annals of war, and have entitled those who have participated therein to the applause and thanks of the nation.

ABRAHAM LINCOLN,
President of the United States

CITY POINT, VIRGINIA, *September* 4, 1864—9 P.M.
Major-General SHERMAN:
   I have just received your dispatch announcing the capture of Atlanta. In honor of your great victory, I have ordered a salute to be fired with *shotted* guns from every battery bearing upon the enemy. The salute will be fired within an hour, amid great rejoicing.

U. S. GRANT, *Lieutenant-General.*

   These dispatches were communicated to the army in general orders, and we all felt duly encouraged and elated by the praise of those competent to bestow it.
   The army still remained where the news of success had first

found us, viz., Lovejoy's; but, after due reflection, I resolved not to attempt at that time a further pursuit of Hood's army, but slowly and deliberately to move back, occupy Atlanta, enjoy a short period of rest, and to think well over the next step required in the progress of events. Orders for this movement were made on the 5th September, and three days were given for each army to reach the place assigned it, viz.: the Army of the Cumberland in and about Atlanta; the Army of the Tennessee at East Point; and the Army of the Ohio at Decatur.

Personally I rode back to Jonesboro' on the 6th, and there inspected the rebel hospital, full of wounded officers and men left by Hardee in his retreat. The next night we stopped at Rough and Ready, and on the 8th of September we rode into Atlanta, then occupied by the Twentieth Corps (General Slocum). In the Court-House Square was encamped a brigade, embracing the Massachusetts Second and Thirty-third Regiments, which had two of the finest bands of the army, and their music was to us all a source of infinite pleasure during our sojourn in that city. I took up my headquarters in the house of Judge Lyons, which stood opposite one corner of the Court-House Square, and at once set about a measure already ordered, of which I had thought much and long, viz., to remove the entire civil population, and to deny to all civilians from the rear the expected profits of civil trade. Hundreds of sutlers and traders were waiting at Nashville and Chattanooga, greedy to reach Atlanta with their wares and goods, with which to drive a profitable trade with the inhabitants. I gave positive orders that none of these traders, except three (one for each separate army), should be permitted to come nearer than Chattanooga; and, moreover, I peremptorily required that all the citizens and families resident in Atlanta should go away, giving to each the option to go south or north, as their interests or feelings dictated. I was resolved to make Atlanta a pure military garrison or depot, with no civil population to influence military measures. I had seen Memphis, Vicksburg, Natchez, and New Orleans, all captured from the enemy, and each at once was garrisoned by a full division of troops, if not more; so that success was actually crippling our armies in the field by detachments to guard and protect the interests of a hostile population.

I gave notice of this purpose, as early as the 4th of September, to General Halleck, in a letter concluding with these words:

> If the people raise a howl against my barbarity and cruelty, I will answer that war is war, and not popularity-seeking. If they want peace, they and their relatives must stop the war.

I knew, of course, that such a measure would be strongly criticised, but made up my mind to do it with the absolute certainty of its justness, and that time would sanction its wisdom. I knew that the people of the South would read in this measure two important conclusions: one, that we were in earnest; and the other, if they were sincere in their common and popular clamor "to die in the last ditch," that the opportunity would soon come.

Soon after our reaching Atlanta, General Hood had sent in by a flag of truce a proposition, offering a general exchange of prisoners, saying that he was authorized to make such an exchange by the Richmond authorities, out of the vast number of our men then held captive at Andersonville, the same whom General Stoneman had hoped to rescue at the time of his raid. Some of these prisoners had already escaped and got in, had described the pitiable condition of the remainder, and, although I felt a sympathy for their hardships and sufferings as deeply as any man could, yet as nearly all the prisoners who had been captured by us during the campaign had been sent, as fast as taken, to the usual depots North, they were then beyond my control. There were still about two thousand, mostly captured at Jonesboro', who had been sent back by cars, but had not passed Chattanooga. These I ordered back, and offered General Hood to exchange them for Stoneman, Buell, and such of my own army as would make up the equivalent; but I would not exchange for his prisoners *generally*, because I knew these would have to be sent to their own regiments, away from my army, whereas all we could give him could at once be put to duty in his immediate army. Quite an angry correspondence grew up between us, which was published at the time in the newspapers, but it is not to be found in any book of which I have present knowledge, and therefore is given here, as illustrative of the events referred to, and of the feelings of the actors in the game of war at that particular crisis, together with certain other original letters of Generals Grant and Halleck, never hitherto published.

HEADQUARTERS ARMIES OF THE UNITED STATES, ⎱
CITY POINT, VIRGINIA, *September* 12, 1864.⎰

Major-General W. T. SHERMAN, *commanding Military Division of the Mississippi.*

GENERAL: I send Lieutenant-Colonel Horace Porter, of my staff, with this. Colonel Porter will explain to you the exact condition of affairs here, better than I can do in the limits of a letter. Although I feel myself strong enough now for offensive operations, I am holding on quietly, to get advantage of recruits and convalescents, who are coming forward very rapidly. My lines are necessarily very long, extending from Deep Bottom, north of the James, across the peninsula formed by the Appomattox and the James, and south of the Appomattox to the Weldon road. This line is very strongly fortified, and can be held with comparatively few men; but, from its great length, necessarily takes many in the aggregate. I propose, when I do move, to extend my left so as to control what is known as the Southside, or Lynchburg & Petersburg road; then, if possible, to keep the Danville road cut. At the same time this move is made, I want to send a force of from six to ten thousand men against Wilmington. The way I propose to do this is to land the men north of Fort Fisher, and hold that point. At the same time a large naval fleet will be assembled there, and the iron-clads will run the batteries as they did at Mobile. This will give us the same control of the harbor of Wilmington that we now have of the harbor of Mobile. What you are to do with the forces at your command, I do not exactly see. The difficulties of supplying your army, except when they are constantly moving beyond where you are, I plainly see. If it had not been for Price's movement, Canby could have sent twelve thousand more men to Mobile. From your command on the Mississippi, an equal number could have been taken. With these forces, my idea would have been to divide them, sending one-half to Mobile, and the other half to Savannah. You could then move as proposed in your telegram, so as to threaten Macon and Augusta equally. Whichever one should be abandoned by the enemy, you could take and open up a new base of supplies. My object now in sending a staff-officer to you is not so much to suggest operations for you as to get your views, and to have plans matured by the time every thing can be got ready. It would probably be the 5th of October before any of the plans here indicated will be executed. If you have any promotions to recommend, send the names forward, and I will approve them.

In conclusion, it is hardly necessary for me to say that I feel you have accomplished the most gigantic undertaking given to any general in this war, and with a skill and ability that will be acknowledged in history as unsurpassed, if not unequaled. It gives me as much pleasure to record this in your favor as it would in favor of any living man, myself included.

Truly yours,

U. S. GRANT, *Lieutenant-General.*

HEADQUARTERS MILITARY DIVISION OF THE MISSISSIPPI, ⎫
    IN THE FIELD, ATLANTA, GEORGIA, *September* 20, 1864.⎭

Lieutenant-General U. S. GRANT, *Commander-in-Chief, City Point, Virginia.*

GENERAL: I have the honor to acknowledge, at the hands of Lieutenant-Colonel Porter, of your staff, your letter of September 12th, and accept with thanks the honorable and kindly mention of the services of this army in the great cause in which we are all engaged.

I send by Colonel Porter all official reports which are completed, and will in a few days submit a list of names which are deemed worthy of promotion.

I think we owe it to the President to save him the invidious task of selection among the vast number of worthy applicants, and have ordered my army commanders to prepare their lists with great care, and to express their preferences, based upon claims of actual capacity and services rendered.

These I will consolidate, and submit in such a form that, if mistakes are made, they will at least be sanctioned by the best contemporaneous evidence of merit, for I know that vacancies do not exist equal in number to that of the officers who really deserve promotion.

As to the future, I am pleased to know that your army is being steadily reënforced by a good class of men, and I hope it will go on until you have a force that is numerically double that of your antagonist, so that with one part you can watch him, and with the other push out boldly from your left flank, occupy the Southside Railroad, compel him to attack you in position, or accept battle on your own terms.

We ought to ask our country for the largest possible armies that can be raised, as so important a thing as the self-existence of a great nation should not be left to the fickle chances of war.

Now that Mobile is shut out to the commerce of our enemy, it calls for no further effort on our part, unless the capture of the city can be followed by the occupation of the Alabama River and the railroad to Columbus, Georgia, when that place would be a magnificent auxiliary to my further progress into Georgia; but, until General Canby is much reënforced, and until he can more thoroughly subdue the scattered armies west of the Mississippi, I suppose that much cannot be attempted by him against the Alabama River and Columbus, Georgia.

The utter destruction of Wilmington, North Carolina, is of importance only in connection with the necessity of cutting off all foreign trade to our enemy, and if Admiral Farragut can get across the bar, and move quickly, I suppose he will succeed. From my knowledge of the mouth of Cape Fear River, I anticipate more difficulty in getting the heavy ships across the bar than in reaching the town of Wilmington; but, of course, the soundings of the channel are well known at Washington, as well as the draught of his iron-clads, so that it must be demonstrated to be feasible, or else it would not be attempted. If successful, I suppose that Fort Caswell will be occupied, and the fleet at once sent to the Savannah River. Then the reduction of that city is the next question. It once in our possession, and the river open to us, I would not hesitate to cross the State of Georgia with sixty thousand men, hauling some stores, and depending on the country for the balance. Where a million of people find subsistence, my army won't starve; but, as you know, in a country like Georgia, with few roads and innumerable streams, an inferior force can so delay an army and harass it, that it would not be a formidable object; but if the enemy knew that we had our boats in the Savannah River I could rapidly move to Milledgeville, where there is abundance of corn and meat, and could so threaten Macon and Augusta that the enemy would doubtless give up Macon for Augusta; then I would move so as to interpose between Augusta and Savannah, and force him to give us Augusta, with the only powder-mills and factories remaining in the South, or let us have the use of the Savannah River. Either horn of the dilemma will be worth a battle. I would prefer his holding Augusta (as the probabilities are); for then, with the Savannah River in our possession, the taking of Augusta would be a mere matter of time. This campaign can be made in the winter.

But the more I study the game, the more am I convinced that it would be wrong for us to penetrate farther into Georgia without an objective beyond. It would not be productive of much good. I can start east and make a circuit south and back, doing vast damage to the State, but resulting in no permanent good; and by mere threatening to do so, I hold a rod over the Georgians, who are not over-loyal to the South. I will therefore give it as my opinion that your army and Canby's should be reënforced to the maximum; that, after you get Wilmington, you should strike for Savannah and its river; that General Canby should hold the Mississippi River, and send a force to take Columbus, Georgia, either by way of the Alabama or Appalachicola River; that I should keep Hood employed and put my army in fine order for a march on Augusta, Columbia, and Charleston; and start as soon as Wilmington is sealed to commerce, and the city of Savannah is in our possession.

I think it will be found that the movements of Price and Shelby, west of the Mississippi, are mere diversions. They cannot hope to enter Missouri except as raiders; and the truth is, that General Rosecrans should be ashamed to take my troops for such a purpose. If you will secure Wilmington and the city of Savannah from your centre, and let General Canby have command over the Mississippi River and country west of it, I will send a force to the Alabama and Appalachicola, provided you give me one hundred thousand of the drafted men to fill up my old regiments; and if you will fix a day to be in Savannah, I will insure our possession of Macon and a point on the river below Augusta. The possession of the Savannah River is more than fatal to the possibility of Southern independence. They may stand the fall of Richmond, but not of all Georgia.

I will have a long talk with Colonel Porter, and tell him every thing that may occur to me of interest to you.

In the mean time, know that I admire your dogged perseverance and pluck more than ever. If you can whip Lee and I can march to the Atlantic, I think Uncle Abe will give us a twenty days' leave of absence to see the young folks. Yours as ever,

W. T. SHERMAN, *Major-General.*

HEADQUARTERS OF THE ARMY, ⎫
WASHINGTON, *September* 16, 1864.⎰

General W. T. SHERMAN, *Atlanta, Georgia.*

MY DEAR GENERAL: Your very interesting letter of the 4th is just received. Its perusal has given me the greatest pleasure. I have not written before to congratulate you on the capture of Atlanta, the objective point of your brilliant campaign, for the reason that I have been suffering from my annual attack of "coryza," or hay-cold. It affects my eyes so much that I can scarcely see to write. As you suppose, I have watched your movements most attentively and critically, and I do not hesitate to say that your campaign has been the most brilliant of the war. Its results are less striking and less complete than those of General Grant at Vicksburg, but then you have had greater difficulties to encounter, a longer line of communications to keep up, and a longer and more continuous strain upon yourself and upon your army.

You must have been very considerably annoyed by the State negro recruiting-agents. Your letter was a capital one, and did much good. The law was a ridiculous one; it was opposed by the War Department, but passed through the influence of Eastern manufacturers, who hoped to escape the draft in that way. They were making immense fortunes out of the war, and could well afford to *purchase* negro recruits, and thus save their employés at home.

I fully agree with you in regard to the policy of a stringent draft; but, unfortunately, political influences are against us, and I fear it will not amount to much. Mr. Seward's speech at Auburn, again prophesying, for the twentieth time, that the rebellion would be crushed in a few months, and saying that there would be no draft, as we now had enough soldiers to end the war, etc., has done much harm, in a military point of view. I have seen enough of politics here to last me for life. You are right in avoiding them. McClellan may possibly reach the White House, but he will lose the respect of all honest, high-minded patriots, by his affiliation with such traitors and Copperheads as B——, V——, W——, S——, & Co. He would not stand upon the traitorous Chicago platform, but he had not the manliness to oppose it. A major-general in the United States Army, and yet not one word to utter against rebels or the rebellion! I had much respect for McClellan before he became a politician, but very little after reading his letter accepting the nomination.

Hooker certainly made a mistake in leaving before the capture of Atlanta. I understand that, when here, he said that you would fail; your army was discouraged and dissatisfied, etc., etc. He is most unmeasured in his abuse of me. I inclose you a specimen of what he publishes in Northern papers, wherever he goes. They are dictated by himself and written by W. B. and such worthies. The funny part of the business is, that I had nothing whatever to do with his being relieved on either occasion. Moreover, I have never said any thing to the President or Secretary of War to injure him in the slightest degree, and he knows that perfectly well. His animosity arises from another source. He is aware that I know some things about his character and conduct in California, and, fearing that I may use that information against him, he seeks to ward off its effect by making it appear that I am his personal enemy, am jealous of him, etc. I know of no other reason for his hostility to me. He is welcome to abuse me as much as he pleases; I don't think it will do him much good, or me much harm. I know very little of General Howard, but believe him to be a true, honorable man. Thomas is also a noble old war-horse. It is true, as you say, that he is slow, but he is always sure.

I have not seen General Grant since the fall of Atlanta, and do not know what instructions he has sent you. I fear that Canby has not the means to do much by way of Mobile. The military effects of Banks's disaster are now showing themselves by the threatened operations of Price & Co. toward Missouri, thus keeping in check our armies west of the Mississippi.

With many thanks for your kind letter, and wishes for your future success, yours truly,

H. W. HALLECK.

HEADQUARTERS MILITARY DIVISION OF THE MISSISSIPPI, }
ATLANTA, GEORGIA, *September* 20, 1864. }

Major-General HALLECK, *Chief of Staff, Washington, D. C.*

GENERAL: I have the honor herewith to submit copies of a correspondence between General Hood, of the Confederate Army, the Mayor of Atlanta, and myself, touching the removal of the inhabitants of Atlanta.

In explanation of the tone which marks some of these letters, I will only call your attention to the fact that, after I had announced my determination, General Hood took upon himself to question my motives. I could not tamely submit to such impertinence; and I have also seen that, in violation of all official usage, he has published in the Macon newspapers such parts of the correspondence as suited his purpose. This could have had no other object than to create a feeling on the part of the people; but if he expects to resort to such artifices, I think I can meet him there too.

It is sufficient for my Government to know that the removal of the inhabitants has been made with liberality and fairness, that it has been attended with no force, and that no women or children have suffered, unless for want of provisions by their natural protectors and friends.

My real reasons for this step were:

We want all the houses of Atlanta for military storage and occupation.

We want to contract the lines of defense, so as to diminish the garrison to the limit necessary to defend its narrow and vital parts, instead of embracing, as the lines now do, the vast suburbs. This contraction of the lines, with the necessary citadels and redoubts, will make it necessary to destroy the very houses used by families as residences.

Atlanta is a fortified town, was stubbornly defended, and fairly captured. As captors, we have a right to it.

The residence here of a poor population would compel us, sooner or later, to feed them or to see them starve under our eyes.

The residence here of the families of our enemies would be a temptation and a means to keep up a correspondence dangerous and hurtful to our cause; a civil population calls for provost-guards, and absorbs the attention of officers in listening to everlasting complaints and special grievances that are not military.

These are my reasons; and, if satisfactory to the Government of the United States, it makes no difference whether it pleases General Hood and *his* people or not. I am, with respect, your obedient servant,

W. T. SHERMAN, *Major-General commanding.*

HEADQUARTERS MILITARY DIVISION OF THE MISSISSIPPI, }
IN THE FIELD, ATLANTA, GEORGIA, *September* 7, 1864. }

General HOOD, *commanding Confederate Army.*

GENERAL: I have deemed it to the interest of the United States that the citizens now residing in Atlanta should remove, those who prefer it to go south, and the rest north. For the latter I can provide food and transportation to points of their election in Tennessee, Kentucky, or farther north. For the former I can provide transportation by cars as far as Rough and Ready, and also wagons; but, that their removal may be made with as little discomfort as possible, it will be necessary for you to help the families from Rough and Ready to the cars at Lovejoy's. If you consent, I will undertake to remove all the families in Atlanta who prefer to go south to Rough and Ready, with all their movable effects, viz., clothing, trunks, reasonable furniture, bedding, etc., with their servants, white and black, with the proviso that no force shall be used toward the blacks, one way or the other. If they want to go with their masters or mistresses, they may do so; otherwise they will be sent away, unless they be men, when they may be employed by our quartermaster. Atlanta is no place for families or non-combatants, and I have no desire to send them north if you will assist in conveying them south. If this proposition meets your views, I will consent to a truce in the neighborhood of Rough and Ready, stipulating that any wagons, horses, animals, or persons sent there for the purposes herein stated, shall in no manner be harmed or molested; you in your turn agreeing that any cars, wagons, or carriages, persons or animals sent to the same point, shall not be interfered with. Each of us might send a guard of, say, one hundred men, to maintain order, and limit the truce to, say, two days after a certain time appointed.

I have authorized the mayor to choose two citizens to convey to you this letter, with such documents as the mayor may forward in explanation, and shall await your reply. I have the honor to be your obedient servant.

W. T. SHERMAN, *Major-General commanding.*

HEADQUARTERS ARMY OF TENNESSEE, }
OFFICE CHIEF OF STAFF, *September* 9, 1864.}

Major-General W. T. SHERMAN, *commanding United States Forces in Georgia.*

GENERAL: Your letter of yesterday's date, borne by James M. Ball and James R. Crew, citizens of Atlanta, is received. You say therein, "I deem it to be to the interest of the United States that the citizens now residing in Atlanta should remove," etc. I do not consider that I have any alternative in this matter. I therefore accept your proposition to declare a truce of two days, or such time as may be necessary to accomplish the purpose mentioned, and shall render all assistance in my power to expedite the transportation of citizens in this direction. I suggest that a staff-officer be appointed by you to superintend the removal from the city to Rough and Ready, while I appoint a like officer to control their removal farther south; that a guard of one hundred men be sent by either party as you propose, to maintain order at that place, and that the removal begin on Monday next.

And now, sir, permit me to say that the unprecedented measure you propose transcends, in studied and ingenious cruelty, all acts ever before brought to my attention in the dark history of war.

In the name of God and humanity, I protest, believing that you will find that you are expelling from their homes and firesides the wives and children of a brave people. I am, general, very respectfully, your obedient servant,

J. B. HOOD, *General.*

HEADQUARTERS MILITARY DIVISION OF THE MISSISSIPPI, }
IN THE FIELD, ATLANTA, GEORGIA, *September* 10, 1864.}

General J. B. HOOD, *commanding Army of Tennessee, Confederate Army.*

GENERAL: I have the honor to acknowledge the receipt of your letter of this date, at the hands of Messrs. Ball and Crew, consenting to the arrangements I had proposed to facilitate the removal south of the people of Atlanta, who prefer to go in that direction. I inclose you a copy of my orders, which will, I am satisfied, accomplish my purpose perfectly.

You style the measures proposed "unprecedented," and appeal to the dark history of war for a parallel, as an act of "studied and ingenious cruelty." It is not unprecedented; for General Johnston himself very wisely and properly removed the families all the way from Dalton down, and I see no reason why Atlanta should be excepted. Nor is it necessary to appeal to the dark history of war, when recent and modern examples are so handy. You yourself burned dwelling-houses along your parapet, and I have seen to-day fifty houses that you have rendered uninhabitable because they stood in the way of your forts and men. You defended Atlanta on a line so close to town that every cannon-shot and many musket-shots from our line of investment, that overshot their mark, went into the habitations of women and children. General Hardee did the same at Jonesboro', and General Johnston did the same, last summer, at Jackson, Mississippi. I have not accused you of heartless cruelty, but merely instance these cases of very recent occurrence, and could go on and enumerate hundreds of others, and challenge any fair man to judge which of us has the heart of pity for the families of a "brave people."

I say that it is kindness to these families of Atlanta to remove them now, at once, from scenes that women and children should not be exposed to, and the "brave people" should scorn to commit their wives and children to the rude barbarians who thus, as you say, violate the laws of war, as illustrated in the pages of its dark history.

In the name of common-sense, I ask you not to appeal to a just God in such a sacrilegious manner. You who, in the midst of peace and prosperity, have plunged a nation into war—dark and cruel war—who dared and badgered us to battle, insulted our flag, seized our arsenals and forts that were left in the honorable custody of peaceful ordnance-sergeants, seized and made "prisoners of war" the very garrisons sent to protect your people against negroes and Indians, long before any overt act was committed by the (to you) hated Lincoln Government; tried to force Kentucky and Missouri into rebellion, spite of themselves; falsified the vote of Louisiana; turned loose your privateers to plunder unarmed ships; expelled Union families by the thousands, burned their houses, and declared, by an act of your Congress, the confiscation of all debts due Northern men for goods had and received! Talk thus to the marines, but not to me, who have seen these things, and who will this day make as much sacrifice for the peace and honor of the South as the best-born Southerner among you! If we must be enemies, let us be men, and fight it out as we propose to do, and not deal in such hypocritical appeals to God and humanity. God will judge us in due time, and he will pronounce whether it be more humane to fight with a town full of women and the families of a brave people at our back, or to remove them in time to places of safety among their own friends and people. I am, very respectfully, your obedient servant,

W. T. SHERMAN, *Major-General commanding.*

HEADQUARTERS ARMY OF TENNESSEE, }
September 12, 1864. }

Major-General W. T. SHERMAN, *commanding Military Division of the Mississippi.*

GENERAL: I have the honor to acknowledge the receipt of your letter of the 9th inst., with its inclosure in reference to the women, children, and others, whom you have thought proper to expel from their homes in the city of Atlanta. Had you seen proper to let the matter rest there, I would gladly have allowed your letter to close this correspondence, and, without your expressing it in words, would have been willing to believe that, while "the interests of the United States," in your opinion, compelled you to an act of barbarous cruelty, you regretted the necessity, and we would have dropped the subject; but you have chosen to indulge in statements which I feel compelled to notice, at least so far as to signify my dissent, and not allow silence in regard to them to be construed as acquiescence.

I see nothing in your communication which induces me to modify the language of condemnation with which I characterized your order. It but strengthens me in the opinion that it stands "preëminent in the dark history of war for studied and ingenious cruelty." Your original order was stripped of all pretenses; you announced the edict for the sole reason that it was "to the interest of the United States." This alone you offered to us and the civilized world as an all-sufficient reason for disregarding the laws of God and man. You say that "General Johnston himself very wisely and properly removed the families all the way from Dalton down." It is due to that gallant soldier and gentleman to say that no act of his distinguished career gives the least color to your unfounded aspersions upon his conduct. He depopulated no villages, nor towns, nor cities, either friendly or hostile. He offered and extended friendly aid to his unfortunate fellow-citizens who desired to flee from your fraternal embraces. You are equally unfortunate in your attempt to find a justification for this act of cruelty, either in the defense of Jonesboro', by General

Hardee, or of Atlanta, by myself. General Hardee defended his position in front of Jonesboro' at the expense of injury to the houses; an ordinary, proper, and justifiable act of war. I defended Atlanta at the same risk and cost. If there was any fault in either case, it was your own, in not giving notice, especially in the case of Atlanta, of your purpose to shell the town, which is usual in war among civilized nations. No inhabitant was expelled from his home and fireside by the orders of General Hardee or myself, and therefore your recent order can find no support from the conduct of either of us. I feel no other emotion other than pain in reading that portion of your letter which attempts to justify your shelling Atlanta without notice under pretense that I defended Atlanta upon a line so close to town that every cannon-shot and many musket-balls from your line of investment, that overshot their mark, went into the habitations of women and children. I made no complaint of your firing into Atlanta in any way you thought proper. I make none now, but there are a hundred thousand witnesses that you fired into the habitations of women and children for weeks, firing far above and miles beyond my line of defense. I have too good an opinion, founded both upon observation and experience, of the skill of your artillerists, to credit the insinuation that they for several weeks unintentionally fired too high for my modest field-works, and slaughtered women and children by accident and want of skill.

The residue of your letter is rather discussion. It opens a wide field for the discussion of questions which I do not feel are committed to me. I am only a general of one of the armies of the Confederate States, charged with military operations in the field, under the direction of my superior officers, and I am not called upon to discuss with you the causes of the present war, or the political questions which led to or resulted from it. These grave and important questions have been committed to far abler hands than mine, and I shall only refer to them so far as to repel any unjust conclusion which might be drawn from my silence. You charge my country with "daring and badgering you to battle." The truth is, we sent commissioners to you, respectfully offering a peaceful separation, before the first gun was fired on either side. You say we insulted your flag. The truth is, we fired upon it, and those who fought under it, when you came to our doors upon the mission of subjugation. You say we seized upon your forts and arsenals, and made prisoners of the garrisons sent to protect us against negroes and Indians. The truth is, we, by force of arms, drove out insolent intruders and took possession of our own forts and arsenals, to resist your claims to dominion over masters, slaves, and Indians, all of whom are to this day, with a unanimity unexampled in the history of the world, warring against your attempts to become their masters. You say that we tried to force Missouri and Kentucky into rebellion in spite of themselves. The truth is, my Government, from the beginning of this struggle to this hour, has again and again offered, before the whole world, to leave it to the unbiased will of these States, and all others, to determine for themselves whether they will cast their destiny with your Government or ours; and your Government has resisted this fundamental principle of free institutions with the bayonet, and labors daily, by force and fraud, to fasten its hateful tyranny upon the unfortunate freemen of these States. You say we falsified the vote of Louisiana. The truth is, Louisiana not only separated herself from your Government by nearly a unanimous vote of her people, but has vindicated the act upon every battle-field from Gettysburg to the Sabine, and has exhibited an heroic devotion to her decision which challenges the admiration and respect of every man capable of feeling sympathy for the oppressed or admiration for heroic valor. You say that we turned loose pirates to plunder your unarmed ships. The truth is, when you robbed us of our part of the navy, we built and bought a few vessels, hoisted the flag of our country, and swept the seas, in defiance of your navy, around the whole circumference of the globe. You say we have expelled Union families by thousands. The truth is, not a single family has been expelled from the Confederate States, that I am aware of; but, on the contrary, the moderation of our Government toward traitors has been a fruitful theme of denunciation by its enemies and well-meaning friends of our cause. You say my Government, by acts of Congress, has confiscated "all debts due Northern men for goods sold and delivered." The truth is, our Congress gave due and ample time to your merchants and traders to depart from our shores with their ships, goods, and effects, and only sequestrated the property of our enemies in retaliation for their acts—declaring us traitors, and confiscating our property wherever their power extended, either in their country or our own. Such are your accusations, and such are the facts known of all men to be true.

You order into exile the whole population of a city; drive men, women, and children from their homes at the point of the bayonet, under the plea that it is to the interest of your Government, and on the claim that it is an act of "kindness to these families of Atlanta." Butler only banished from New Orleans the registered enemies of his Government, and acknowledged that he did it as a punishment. You issue a sweeping edict, covering all the inhabitants of a city, and add insult to the injury heaped upon the defenseless by assuming that you have done them a kindness. This you follow by the assertion that you will "make as much sacrifice for the peace and honor of the South as the best-born Southerner." And, because I characterize what you call a kindness as being real cruelty, you presume to sit in judgment between me and my God; and you decide that my earnest prayer to the Almighty Father to save our women and children from what you call kindness, is a "sacrilegious, hypocritical appeal."

You came into our country with your army, avowedly for the purpose of subjugating free white men, women, and children, and not only intend to rule over them, but you make negroes your allies, and desire to place over us an inferior race, which we have raised from barbarism to its present position, which is the highest ever attained by that race, in any country, in all time. I must, therefore, decline to accept your statements in reference to your kindness toward the people of Atlanta, and your willingness to sacrifice every thing for the peace and honor of the South, and refuse to be governed by your decision in regard to matters between myself, my country, and my God.

You say, "Let us fight it out like men." To this my reply is—for myself, and I believe for all the true men, ay, and women and children, in my country—we will fight you to the death! Better die a thousand deaths than submit to live under you or your Government and your negro allies!

Having answered the points forced upon me by your letter of the 9th of September, I close this correspondence with you; and, notwithstanding your comments upon my appeal to God in the cause of humanity, I again humbly and reverently invoke his almighty aid in defense of justice and right. Respectfully, your obedient servant,

J. B. HOOD, *General.*

ATLANTA, GEORGIA, *September* 11, 1864.
Major-General W. T. SHERMAN.

SIR: We the undersigned, Mayor and two of the Council for the city of Atlanta, for the time being the only legal organ of the people of the said city, to express their wants and wishes, ask leave most earnestly but respectfully to petition you to reconsider the order requiring them to leave Atlanta.

At first view, it struck us that the measure would involve extraordinary hardship and loss, but since we have seen the practical execution of it so far as it has progressed, and the individual condition of the people, and heard their statements as to the inconveniences, loss, and suffering attending it, we are satisfied that the amount of it will involve in the aggregate consequences appalling and heart-rending.

Many poor women are in advanced state of pregnancy, others now having young children, and whose husbands for the greater part are either in the army, prisoners, or dead. Some say: "I have such a one sick at my house; who will wait on them when I am gone?" Others say: "What are we to do? We have no house to go to, and no means to buy, build, or rent any; no parents, relatives, or friends, to go to." Another says: "I will try and take this or that article of property, but such and such things I must leave behind, though I need them much." We reply to them: "General Sherman will carry your property to Rough and Ready, and General Hood will take it thence on." And they will reply to that: "But I want to leave the railroad at such a place, and cannot get conveyance from there on."

We only refer to a few facts, to try to illustrate in part how this measure will operate in practice. As you advanced, the people north of this fell back; and before your arrival here, a large portion of the people had retired south, so that the country south of this is already crowded, and without houses enough to accommodate the people, and we are informed that many are now staying in churches and other out-buildings.

This being so, how is it possible for the people still here (mostly women and children) to find any shelter? And how can they live through the winter in the woods—no shelter or subsistence, in the midst of strangers who know them not, and without the power to assist them much, if they were willing to do so?

This is but a feeble picture of the consequences of this measure. You know the woe, the horrors, and the suffering, cannot be described by words; imagination can only conceive of it, and we ask you to take these things into consideration.

We know your mind and time are constantly occupied with the duties of your command, which almost deters us from asking your attention to this matter, but thought it might be that you had not considered this subject in all of its awful consequences, and that on more reflection you, we hope, would not make this people an exception to all mankind, for we know of no such instance ever having occurred—surely never in the United States—and what has this *helpless* people done, that they should be driven from their homes, to wander strangers and outcasts, and exiles, and to subsist on charity?

We do not know as yet the number of people still here; of those who are here, we are satisfied a respectable number, if allowed to remain at home, could subsist for several months without assistance, and a respectable number for a much longer time, and who might not need assistance at any time.

In conclusion, we most earnestly and solemnly petition you to reconsider this order, or modify it, and suffer this unfortunate people to remain at home, and enjoy what little means they have.

Respectfully submitted:

> JAMES M. CALHOUN, *Mayor*.
> E. E. RAWSON, *Councilman*.
> S. C. WELLS, *Councilman*.

HEADQUARTERS MILITARY DIVISION OF THE MISSISSIPPI, }
IN THE FIELD, ATLANTA, GEORGIA, *September* 12, 1864. }

JAMES M. CALHOUN, *Mayor,* E. E. RAWSON *and* S. C. WELLS,
representing City Council of Atlanta.

GENTLEMEN: I have your letter of the 11th, in the nature of a petition to revoke my orders removing all the inhabitants from Atlanta. I have read it carefully, and give full credit to your statements of the distress that will be occasioned, and yet shall not revoke my orders, because they were not designed to meet the humanities of the case, but to prepare for the future struggles in which millions of good people outside of Atlanta have a deep interest. We must have peace, not only at Atlanta, but in all America. To secure this, we must stop the war that now desolates our once happy and favored country. To stop war, we must defeat the rebel armies which are arrayed against the laws and Constitution that all must respect and obey. To defeat those armies, we must prepare the way to reach them in their recesses, provided with the arms and instruments which enable us to accomplish our purpose. Now, I know the vindictive nature of our enemy, that we may have many years of military operations from this quarter; and, therefore, deem it wise and prudent to prepare in time. The use of Atlanta for warlike purposes is inconsistent with its character as a home for families. There will be no manufactures, commerce, or agriculture here, for the maintenance of families, and sooner or later want will compel the inhabitants to go. Why not go now, when all the arrangements are completed for the transfer, instead of waiting till the plunging shot of contending armies will renew the scenes of the past month? Of course, I do not apprehend any such thing at this moment, but you do not suppose this army will be here until the war is over. I cannot discuss this subject with you fairly, because I cannot impart to you what we propose to do, but I assert that our military plans make it necessary for the inhabitants to go away, and I can only renew my offer of services to make their exodus in any direction as easy and comfortable as possible.

You cannot qualify war in harsher terms than I will. War is cruelty, and you cannot refine it; and those who brought war into our country deserve all the curses and maledictions a people can pour out. I know I had no hand in making this war, and I know I will make more sacrifices to-day than any of you to secure peace. But you cannot have peace and a division of our country. If the United States submits to a division now, it will not stop, but will go on until we reap the fate of Mexico, which is eternal war. The United States does and must assert its authority, wherever it once had power; for, if it relaxes one bit to pressure, it is gone, and I believe that such is the national feeling. This feeling assumes various shapes, but always comes back to that of Union. Once admit the Union, once more acknowledge the authority of the national Government, and, instead of devoting your houses and streets and roads to the dread uses of war, I and this army become at once your protectors and supporters, shielding you from danger, let it come from what quarter it may. I know that a few individuals cannot resist a torrent of error and passion, such as swept the South into rebellion, but you can point out, so that we may know those who desire a government, and those who insist on war and its desolation.

You might as well appeal against the thunder-storm as against these terrible hardships of war. They are inevitable, and the only way the people of Atlanta can hope once more to live in peace and quiet at home, is to stop the war, which can only be done by admitting that it began in error and is perpetuated in pride.

We don't want your negroes, or your horses, or your houses, or your lands, or any thing you have, but we do want and will have a just obedience to the laws of the United States. That we will have, and, if it involves the destruction of your improvements, we cannot help it.

You have heretofore read public sentiment in your newspapers, that live by falsehood and excitement; and the quicker you seek for truth in other quarters, the better. I repeat then that, by the original compact of Government, the United States had certain rights in Georgia, which have never been relinquished and never will be; that the South began war by seizing forts, arsenals, mints, custom-houses, etc., etc., long before Mr. Lincoln was installed, and before the South had one jot or tittle of provocation. I myself have seen in Missouri, Kentucky, Tennessee, and Mississippi, hundreds and thousands of women and children fleeing from your armies and desperadoes, hungry and with bleeding feet. In Memphis, Vicksburg, and Mississippi, we fed thousands upon thousands of the families of rebel soldiers left on our hands, and whom we could not see starve.

Now that war comes home to you, you feel very different. You deprecate its horrors, but did not feel them when you sent car-loads of soldiers and ammunition, and moulded shells and shot, to carry war into Kentucky and Tennessee, to desolate the homes of hundreds and thousands of good people who only asked to live in peace at their old homes, and under the Government of their inheritance. But these comparisons are idle. I want peace, and believe it can only be reached through union and war, and I will ever conduct war with a view to perfect and early success.

But, my dear sirs, when peace does come, you may call on me for any thing. Then will I share with you the last cracker, and watch with you to shield your homes and families against danger from every quarter.

Now you must go, and take with you the old and feeble, feed and nurse them, and build for them, in more quiet places, proper habitations to shield them against the weather until the mad passions of men cool down, and allow the Union and peace once more to settle over your old homes at Atlanta. Yours in haste,

W. T. SHERMAN, *Major-General commanding*.

HEADQUARTERS MILITARY DIVISION OF THE MISSISSIPPI, }
IN THE FIELD, ATLANTA, GEORGIA, *September* 14, 1864. }

General J. B. HOOD, *commanding Army of the Tennessee, Confederate Army.*

GENERAL: Yours of September 12th is received, and has been carefully perused. I agree with you that this discussion by two soldiers is out of place, and profitless; but you must admit that you began the controversy by characterizing an official act of mine in unfair and improper terms. I reiterate my former answer, and to the only new matter contained in your rejoinder add: We have no "negro allies" in this army; not a single negro soldier left Chattanooga with this army, or is with it now. There are a few guarding Chattanooga, which General Steedman sent at one time to drive Wheeler out of Dalton.

I was not bound by the laws of war to give notice of the shelling of Atlanta, a "fortified town, with magazines, arsenals, founderies, and public stores;" you were bound to take notice. See the books.

This is the conclusion of our correspondence, which I did not begin, and terminate with satisfaction. I am, with respect, your obedient servant,

W. T. SHERMAN, *Major-General commanding*.

HEADQUARTERS OF THE ARMY, }
WASHINGTON, *September* 28, 1864.}

Major-General SHERMAN, *Atlanta, Georgia.*

GENERAL: Your communications of the 20th in regard to the removal of families from Atlanta, and the exchange of prisoners, and also the official report of your campaign, are just received. I have not had time as yet to examine your report. The course which you have pursued in removing rebel families from Atlanta, and in the exchange of prisoners, is fully approved by the War Department. Not only are you justified by the laws and usages of war in removing these people, but I think it was your duty to your own army to do so. Moreover, I am fully of opinion that the nature of your position, the character of the war, the conduct of the enemy (and especially of non-combatants and women of the territory which we have heretofore conquered and occupied), will justify you in gathering up all the forage and provisions which your army may require, both for a siege of Atlanta and for your supply in your march farther into the enemy's country. Let the disloyal families of the country, thus stripped, go to their husbands, fathers, and natural protectors, in the rebel ranks; we have tried three years of conciliation and kindness without any reciprocation; on the contrary, those thus treated have acted as spies and guerrillas in our rear and within our lines. The safety of our armies, and a proper regard for the lives of our soldiers, require that we apply to our inexorable foes the severe rules of war. We certainly are not required to treat the so-called non-combatant rebels better than they themselves treat each other. Even here in Virginia, within fifty miles of Washington, they strip their own families of provisions, leaving them, as our army advances, to be fed by us, or to starve within our lines. We have fed this class of people long enough. Let them go with their husbands and fathers in the rebel ranks; and if they won't go, we must send them to their friends and natural protectors. I would destroy every mill and factory within reach which I did not want for my own use. This the rebels have done, not only in Maryland and Pennsylvania, but also in Virginia and other rebel States, when compelled to fall back before our armies. In many sections of the country they have not left a mill to grind grain for their own suffering families, lest we might use them to supply our armies. We must do the same.

I have endeavored to impress these views upon our commanders for the last two years. You are almost the only one who has properly applied them. I do not approve of General Hunter's course in burning private houses or uselessly destroying private property. That is barbarous. But I approve of taking or destroying whatever may serve as supplies to us or to the enemy's army.

Very respectfully, your obedient servant,

H. W. HALLECK, *Major-General, Chief of Staff.*

In order to effect the exchange of prisoners, to facilitate the exodus of the people of Atlanta, and to keep open communication with the South, we established a neutral camp, at and about the railroad-station next south of Atlanta, known as "Rough and Ready," to which point I dispatched Lieutenant-Colonel Willard Warner, of my staff, with a guard of one hundred men, and General Hood sent Colonel Clare, of his staff, with a similar guard; these officers and men harmonized perfectly, and parted good friends when their work was done. In the mean time I also had reconnoitred the entire rebel lines about Atlanta, which were well built, but were entirely too extensive to be held by a single corps or division of troops, so I instructed Colonel Poe, United States Engineers, on my staff, to lay off an inner and shorter line, susceptible of defense by a smaller garrison.

By the middle of September all these matters were in progress, the reports of the past campaign were written up and dispatched to Washington, and our thoughts began to turn toward the future. Admiral Farragut had boldly and successfully run the forts at the entrance to Mobile Bay, which resulted in the capture of Fort Morgan, so that General Canby was enabled to begin his regular operations against Mobile City, with a view to open the Alabama River to navigation. My first thoughts were to concert operations with him, either by way of Montgomery, Alabama, or by the Appalachicola; but so long a line, to be used as a base for further operations eastward, was not advisable, and I concluded to await the initiative of the enemy, supposing that he would be forced to resort to some desperate campaign by the clamor raised at the South on account of the great loss to them of the city of Atlanta.

General Thomas occupied a house on Marietta Street, which had a veranda with high pillars. We were sitting there one evening, talking about things generally, when General

Thomas asked leave to send his trains back to Chattanooga, for the convenience and economy of forage. I inquired of him if he supposed we would be allowed much rest at Atlanta, and he said he thought we would, or that at all events it would not be prudent for us to go much farther into Georgia because of our already long line of communication, viz., three hundred miles from Nashville. This was true; but there we were, and we could not afford to remain on the defensive, simply holding Atlanta and fighting for the safety of its railroad. I insisted on his retaining all trains, and on keeping all his divisions ready to move at a moment's warning. All the army, officers and men, seemed to relax more or less, and sink into a condition of idleness. General Schofield was permitted to go to Knoxville, to look after matters in his Department of the Ohio; and Generals Blair and Logan went home to look after politics. Many of the regiments were entitled to, and claimed, their discharge, by reason of the expiration of their term of service; so that with victory and success came also many causes of disintegration.

The rebel General Wheeler was still in Middle Tennessee, threatening our railroads, and rumors came that Forrest was on his way from Mississippi to the same theatre, for the avowed purpose of breaking up our railroads and compelling us to fall back from our conquest. To prepare for this, or any other emergency, I ordered Newton's division of the Fourth Corps back to Chattanooga, and Corse's division of the Seventeenth Corps to Rome, and instructed General Rousseau at Nashville, Granger at Decatur, and Steadman at Chattanooga, to adopt the most active measures to protect and insure the safety of our roads.

Hood still remained about Lovejoy's Station, and, up to the 15th of September, had given no signs of his future plans; so that with this date I close the campaign of Atlanta, with the following review of our relative losses during the months of August and September, with a summary of those for the whole campaign, beginning May 6 and ending September 15, 1864. The losses for August and September are added together, so as to include those about Jonesboro':

ARMY OF THE CUMBERLAND—(MAJOR-GENERAL THOMAS.)

CORPS.	Killed and Missing.	Wounded.	Total.
Fourth (Stanley).	166	416	582
Fourteenth (Davis, Palmer)	444	1,809	2,253
Twentieth (Williams, Slocum)	71	189	260
Total	681	2,414	3,095

ARMY OF THE TENNESSEE—(MAJOR-GENERAL O. O. HOWARD.)

CORPS.	Killed and Missing.	Wounded.	Total.
Fifteenth (Logan)	143	430	573
Sixteenth (Dodge)	40	217	257
Seventeenth (Blair)	102	258	360
Total	285	905	1,190

ARMY OF THE OHIO—(MAJOR-GENERAL SCHOFIELD.)

CORPS.	Killed and Missing.	Wounded.	Total.
Twenty-third (Cox)	146	279	425
Cavalry (Garrard, McCook, Kilpatrick).	296	133	429
Total	442	412	854
Grand Aggregate	1,408	3,731	5,139

Hood's losses, as reported for the same period, page 577, Johnston's "Narrative:"

CORPS.	Killed.	Wounded.	Total.
Hardee's	141	1,018	1,159
Lee's	248	1,631	1,879
Stewart's	93	574	667
Total	482	3,223	3,705

To which should be added:

Prisoners captured by us	3,738
Giving his total loss.	7,443

On recapitulating the entire losses of each army during the entire campaign, from May to September, inclusive, we have, in the Union army, as per table appended:

Killed	4,423
Wounded.	22,822
Missing	4,442
Aggregate loss	31,687

In the Southern army, according to the reports of Surgeon Foard (pp. 576, 577, Johnston's "Narrative"):

Killed (Johnston)	1,221
" (Hood)	1,823
Total killed	3,044
Wounded (Johnston)	8,229
" (Hood)	10,723
Total killed and wounded.	21,996
Add prisoners captured by us, and officially reported at the time (*see* table)	12,983
Aggregate loss to Southern army. .	34,979

The foregoing figures are official, and are very nearly correct. I see no room for error save in the cavalry, which was very much scattered, and whose reports are much less reliable than of the infantry and artillery; but as Surgeon Foard's tables do not embrace Wheeler's, Jackson's, and Martin's divisions of cavalry, I infer that the comparison, as to cavalry losses, is a "stand-off."

I have no doubt that the Southern officers flattered themselves that they had killed and crippled of us two and even six to one, as stated by Johnston; but they were simply mistaken, and I herewith submit official tabular statements made up from the archives of the War Department, in proof thereof:

Statement showing the Losses sustained in Battle by the Army under Command of General W. T. SHERMAN, from May to September, 1864, inclusive.

COMMANDS.	MAY.		JUNE.		JULY.		AUGUST.		SEPTEMBER.		Total Killed or Missing.	Total Wounded.	Aggregate.	REMARKS.
	Killed or Missing	Wounded	Killed or Missing	Wounded	Killed or Missing	Wounded	Killed or Missing	Wounded	Killed or Missing	Wounded				
Fourth Corps	576	1,910	602	1,542	116	432	106	152	60	264	1,460	4,300	5,760	
Fourteenth Corps	147	655	353	1,466	317	1,084	180	801	264	1,008	1,261	5,014	6,275	
Twentieth Corps	571	2,997	322	1,246	541	1,480	70	189	1		1,505	5,912	7,417	
Total—Army of the Cumberland .	1,294	5,562	1,277	4,254	974	2,996	356	1,142	325	1,272	4,226	15,226	19,452	
Fifteenth Corps	122	624	179	687	590	797	108	367	35	63	1,034	2,538	3,572	
Sixteenth Corps	a94	a430	a52	a157	a289	a721	a40	a217			475	1,525	2,000	Left wing broken up September, 1864, and troops transferred to Fifteenth and Seventeenth Corps.
Seventeenth Corps	b40	b209	c20	c102	d26	d146	74	212	28	46	*86	*460	*546	
Total—Army of the Tennessee .	256	1,264	298	1,158	2,266	2,867	222	799	63	109	3,105	6,197	9,302	
Twenty-third Corps	226	757	105	362	95	167	142	270	4	9	572	1,565	2,137	
Cavalry	127	62	130	68	495	31	199	110	97	23	1,048	294	1,342	
Grand Total	1,903	7,645	1,810	5,842	3,830	6,061	919	2,321	489	1,413	*8,951	*23,282	*32,233	

a Left wing in Atlanta campaign. b Right wing on Red River expedition. c Right wing at Lake Chicot, La. d Right wing skirmishes in Mississippi. e Right wing at Tupelo, Miss.

*These figures have been obtained principally from the monthly returns of the several army corps, and are believed to be approximately correct. The killed and missing, being reported in the same column on the returns, cannot be shown separately in this table, but from another source of information (Regimental Rolls and Returns) the aggregate number of missing during the period in question is found to have been 4,442. Deducting this number from the 8,951 of both classes would give 4,508 as the number killed. Then subtracting the casualties (86 killed and 460 wounded) of the right wing, Sixteenth Army Corps, not engaged in the Atlanta campaign, would give the losses of General Sherman's immediate command from Chattanooga to Atlanta as follows: Killed, 4,423; wounded, 22,822; missing, 4,442—total 31,687.

E. D. TOWNSEND, *Adjutant-General.*

*Prisoners and Deserters taken by "Army in the Field," Military Division
of the Mississippi, during May, June, and August,* 1864.

COMMANDS.	PRISONERS.		DESERTERS.		Aggregate.
	Commis-sioned Officers.	Enlisted Men.	Commis-sioned Officers.	Enlisted Men.	
Army of the Cumberland	121	3,838	21	1,543	5,523
Army of the Tennessee	133	2,591	5	576	3,305
Army of the Ohio	16	781	1	292	1,090
Total	270	7,210	27	2,411	9,918

To which add the prisoners and deserters
taken by the Army of the Cumberland,
September 1st to 20th.   3,065
                                                                                        ─────
        Making aggregate.   12,983

Reports from armies of the Tennessee and Ohio include the whole
campaign, to September 15, 1864.

W. T. SHERMAN,
Major-General United States Army commanding.

I have also had a careful tabular statement compiled from
official records in the adjutant-general's office, giving the "effective strength" of the army under my command for each of
the months of May, June, July, August, and September, 1864,
which enumerate every man (infantry, artillery, and cavalry)
for duty. The recapitulation clearly exhibits the actual truth.
We opened the campaign with 98,797 (ninety-eight thousand
seven hundred and ninety-seven) men. Blair's two divisions
joined us early in June, giving 112,819 (one hundred and
twelve thousand eight hundred and nineteen), which number
gradually became reduced to 106,070 (one hundred and six

Statement showing the Effective Strength of the Army under General W. T. SHERMAN, during the Campaign against Atlanta, Georgia, 1864.

COMMANDS	Jun — Inf. Off.	Jun — Inf. Men	Jun — Cav. Off.	Jun — Cav. Men	Jun — Art. Off.	Jun — Art. Men	Jul — Inf. Off.	Jul — Inf. Men	Jul — Cav. Off.	Jul — Cav. Men	Jul — Art. Off.	Jul — Art. Men	Aug — Inf. Off.	Aug — Inf. Men	Aug — Cav. Off.	Aug — Cav. Men	Aug — Art. Off.	Aug — Art. Men	Sep — Inf. Off.	Sep — Inf. Men	Sep — Cav. Off.	Sep — Cav. Men	Sep — Art. Off.	Sep — Art. Men
Fourth Army Corps	999	15,453	.	.	21	754	878	13,338	.	.	16	724	827	11,837	.	.	20	835	736	10,678	.	.	22	682
Fourteenth Army Corps	1,007	21,618	.	.	21	802	906	17,900	.	.	21	780	847	16,441	.	.	19	707	720	13,733	.	.	22	774
Twentieth Army Corps	808	15,071	3	68	25	826	734	13,057	3	68	24	786	645	11,112	3	40	27	751	649	10,955	3	35	31	740
Total—Ar'y of the Cmb'r'l'd	2,814	52,142	3	68	67	2,382	2,518	44,295	3	68	61	2,290	2,319	39,390	3	40	66	2,293	2,105	35,366	3	35	75	2,196
Fifteenth Army Corps	636	11,044	.	.	25	792	612	10,396	.	.	23	757	508	8,033	.	.	14	578	523	7,691	.	.	9	447
Sixteenth A. C. (left wing)	408	9,053	26	322	12	540	441	9,625	4	38	16	620	402	8,111	29	370	11	422	322	7,054	3	27	11	401
Seventeenth Army Corps	387	8,380	4	83	17	904	380	7,812	9	91	23	947	280	5,541	5	29	22	923	225	4,962	4	23	16	705
Total—Army of the Tenn.	1,431	28,477	30	405	54	2,236	1,433	27,833	13	129	62	2,324	1,190	21,685	34	399	47	1,923	1,070	19,707	7	50	36	1,553
Twenty-third Army Corps	406	9,040	.	.	20	505	498	11,509	.	.	24	875	490	10,585	.	.	25	860	407	9,019	.	.	15	540
Garrard's Cavalry	.	.	200	4,822	3	130	.	.	180	4,047	3	122	.	.	179	3,699	3	111	.	.	166	2,911	3	104
Stoneman's Cavalry	.	.	138	2,753	.	.	.	.	128	2,530	.	.	.	.	96	1,803	.	.	.	.	101	1,835	.	.
McCook's Cavalry	.	.	152	2,570	3	79	.	.	161	2,169	3	75	.	.	120	1,634	3	60	.	.	132	1,720	3	73
Kilpatrick's Cavalry	.	.	89	1,678	5	117	.	.	128	2,483	4	102	.	.	144	2,366	4	104	.	.	166	2,268	4	88
Grand Aggregate	4,651	89,659	612	12,296	152	5,449	4,449	83,637	613	11,426	157	5,788	3,999	71,660	676	9,941	148	5,351	3,582	64,092	575	8,819	136	4,354

RECAPITULATION—ATLANTA CAMPAIGN.

ARM.	June 1.	July 1.	August 1.	September 1.
Infantry.	94,310	88,086	75,659	67,674
Cavalry	12,908	12,039	10,517	9,394
Artillery	5,601	5,945	5,499	4,690
Aggregate	112,819	106,070	91,675	81,758

thousand and seventy men), 91,675 (ninety-one thousand six hundred and seventy-five), and 81,758 (eighty-one thousand seven hundred and fifty-eight) at the end of the campaign. This gradual reduction was not altogether owing to death and wounds, but to the expiration of service, or by detachments sent to points at the rear.

Chapter XX.

B Y THE MIDDLE of September, matters and things had settled down in Atlanta, so that we felt perfectly at home.
The telegraph and railroads were repaired, and we had uninterrupted communication to the rear. The trains arrived with
regularity and dispatch, and brought us ample supplies. General Wheeler had been driven out of Middle Tennessee, escaping south across the Tennessee River at Bainbridge; and
things looked as though we were to have a period of repose.

One day, two citizens, Messrs. Hill and Foster, came into
our lines at Decatur, and were sent to my headquarters. They
represented themselves as former members of Congress, and
particular friends of my brother John Sherman; that Mr. Hill
had a son killed in the rebel army as it fell back before us
somewhere near Cassville, and they wanted to obtain the
body, having learned from a comrade where it was buried. I
gave them permission to go by rail to the rear, with a note to
the commanding officer, General John E. Smith, at Cartersville, requiring him to furnish them an escort and an ambulance for the purpose. I invited them to take dinner with our
mess, and we naturally ran into a general conversation about
politics and the devastation and ruin caused by the war. They
had seen a part of the country over which the army had
passed, and could easily apply its measure of desolation to the
remainder of the State, if necessity should compel us to go
ahead.

Mr. Hill resided at Madison, on the main road to Augusta,
and seemed to realize fully the danger; said that further resistance on the part of the South was madness, that he hoped
Governor Brown, of Georgia, would so proclaim it, and withdraw his people from the rebellion, in pursuance of what was
known as the policy of "separate State action." I told him, if
he saw Governor Brown, to describe to him fully what he had
seen, and to say that if he remained inert, I would be compelled to go ahead, devastating the State in its whole length

and breadth; that there was no adequate force to stop us, etc.; but if he would issue his proclamation withdrawing his State troops from the armies of the Confederacy, I would spare the State, and in our passage across it confine the troops to the main roads, and would, moreover, pay for all the corn and food we needed. I also told Mr. Hill that he might, in my name, invite Governor Brown to visit Atlanta; that I would give him a safeguard, and that if he wanted to make a speech, I would guarantee him as full and respectable an audience as any he had ever spoken to. I believe that Mr. Hill, after reaching his home at Madison, went to Milledgeville, the capital of the State, and delivered the message to Governor Brown. I had also sent similar messages by Judge Wright of Rome, Georgia, and by Mr. King, of Marietta. On the 15th of September I telegraphed to General Halleck as follows:

My report is done, and will be forwarded as soon as I get in a few more of the subordinate reports. I am awaiting a courier from General Grant. All well; the troops are in good, healthy camps, and supplies are coming forward finely. Governor Brown has disbanded his militia, to gather the corn and sorghum of the State. I have reason to believe that he and Stephens want to visit me, and have sent them a hearty invitation. I will exchange two thousand prisoners with Hood, but no more.

Governor Brown's action at that time is fully explained by the following letter, since made public, which was then only known to us in part by hearsay:

EXECUTIVE DEPARTMENT, }
MILLEDGEVILLE, GEORGIA, *September* 10, 1864.}

General J. B. HOOD, *commanding Army of Tennessee.*

GENERAL: As the militia of the State were called out for the defense of Atlanta during the campaign against it, which has terminated by the fall of the city into the hands of the enemy, and as many of these left their homes without preparation (expecting to be gone but a few weeks), who have remained in service over three months (most of the time in the trenches), justice requires that they be permitted, while the enemy are preparing for the winter campaign, to return to their homes, and look for a time after important interests, and prepare themselves for such service as may be required when another campaign commences against other important points in the State. I therefore hereby withdraw said organization from your command. . . .

JOSEPH C. BROWN.

This militia had composed a division under command of Major-General Gustavus W. Smith, and were thus dispersed to their homes, to gather the corn and sorghum, then ripe and ready for the harvesters.

On the 17th I received by telegraph from President Lincoln this dispatch:

WASHINGTON, D. C., *September* 17, 1864—10 A.M.
Major-General SHERMAN:
I feel great interest in the subjects of your dispatch, mentioning corn and sorghum, and the contemplated visit to you.

A. LINCOLN, *President of the United States.*

I replied at once:

HEADQUARTERS MILITARY DIVISION OF THE MISSISSIPPI, ⎱
IN THE FIELD, ATLANTA, GEORGIA, *September* 17, 1864. ⎰

President LINCOLN, *Washington, D. C.:*
I will keep the department fully advised of all developments connected with the subject in which you feel interested.

Mr. Wright, former member of Congress from Rome, Georgia, and Mr. King, of Marietta, are now going between Governor Brown and myself. I have said to them that some of the people of Georgia are engaged in rebellion, begun in error and perpetuated in pride, but that Georgia can now save herself from the devastations of war preparing for her, only by withdrawing her quota out of the Confederate Army, and aiding me to expel Hood from the borders of the State; in which event, instead of desolating the land as we progress, I will keep our men to the high-roads and commons, and pay for the corn and meat we need and take.

I am fully conscious of the delicate nature of such assertions, but it would be a magnificent stroke of policy if we could, without surrendering principle or a foot of ground, arouse the latent enmity of Georgia against Davis.

The people do not hesitate to say that Mr. Stephens was and is a Union man at heart; and they say that Davis will not trust him or let him have a share in his Government.

W. T. SHERMAN, *Major-General.*

I have not the least doubt that Governor Brown, at that

time, seriously entertained the proposition; but he hardly felt
ready to act, and simply gave a furlough to the militia, and
called a special session of the Legislature, to meet at Milledgeville, to take into consideration the critical condition of
affairs in the State.

On the 20th of September Colonel Horace Porter arrived
from General Grant, at City Point, bringing me the letter of
September 12th, asking my general views as to what should
next be done. He staid several days at Atlanta, and on his
return carried back to Washington my full reports of the past
campaign, and my letter of September 20th to General Grant
in answer to his of the 12th.

About this time we detected signs of activity on the part of
the enemy. On the 21st Hood shifted his army across from the
Macon road, at Lovejoy's, to the West Point road, at Palmetto
Station, and his cavalry appeared on the west side of the
Chattahoochee, toward Powder Springs; thus, as it were,
stepping aside, and opening wide the door for us to enter
Central Georgia. I inferred, however, that his real purpose
was to assume the offensive against our railroads, and on the
24th a heavy force of cavalry from Mississippi, under General
Forrest, made its appearance at Athens, Alabama, and cap-
tured its garrison.

General Newton's division (of the Fourth Corps), and
Corse's (of the Seventeenth), were sent back by rail, the
former to Chattanooga, and the latter to Rome. On the 25th I
telegraphed to General Halleck:

> Hood seems to be moving, as it were, to the Alabama line, leaving
> open the road to Macon, as also to Augusta; but his cavalry is busy
> on all our roads. A force, number estimated as high as eight thou-
> sand, are reported to have captured Athens, Alabama; and a regi-
> ment of three hundred and fifty men sent to its relief. I have sent
> Newton's division up to Chattanooga in cars, and will send another
> division to Rome. If I were sure that Savannah would soon be in our
> possession, I should be tempted to march for Milledgeville and Au-
> gusta; but I must first secure what I have. Jeff. Davis is at Macon.
>
> W. T. SHERMAN, *Major-General*.

On the next day I telegraphed further that Jeff. Davis was
with Hood at Palmetto Station. One of our spies was there at

the time, who came in the next night, and reported to me the substance of his speech to the soldiers. It was a repetition of those he had made at Columbia, South Carolina, and Macon, Georgia, on his way out, which I had seen in the newspapers. Davis seemed to be perfectly upset by the fall of Atlanta, and to have lost all sense and reason. He denounced General Jos. Johnston and Governor Brown as little better than traitors; attributed to them personally the many misfortunes which had befallen their cause, and informed the soldiers that now the tables were to be turned; that General Forrest was already on our roads in Middle Tennessee; and that Hood's army would soon be there. He asserted that the Yankee army would have to retreat or starve, and that the retreat would prove more disastrous than was that of Napoleon from Moscow. He promised his Tennessee and Kentucky soldiers that their feet should soon tread their "native soil," etc., etc. He made no concealment of these vainglorious boasts, and thus gave us the full key to his future designs. To be forewarned was to be forearmed, and I think we took full advantage of the occasion.

On the 26th I received this dispatch:

CITY POINT, VIRGINIA, *September* 26, 1864—10 A.M.
Major-General SHERMAN, *Atlanta:*

It will be better to drive Forrest out of Middle Tennessee as a first step, and do any thing else you may feel your force sufficient for. When a movement is made on any part of the sea-coast, I will advise you. If Hood goes to the Alabama line, will it not be impossible for him to subsist his army?

U. S. GRANT, *Lieutenant-General.*

Answer:

HEADQUARTERS MILITARY DIVISION OF THE MISSISSIPPI, }
IN THE FIELD, ATLANTA, GEORGIA, *September* 26, 1864.}

GENERAL: I have your dispatch of to-day. I have already sent one division (Newton's) to Chattanooga, and another (Corse's) to Rome.

Our armies are much reduced, and if I send back any more, I will not be able to threaten Georgia much. There are men enough to the rear to whip Forrest, but they are necessarily scattered to defend the roads.

Can you expedite the sending to Nashville of the recruits that are in Indiana and Ohio? They could occupy the forts.

Hood is now on the West Point road, twenty-four miles south of this, and draws his supplies by that road. Jefferson Davis is there to-day, and superhuman efforts will be made to break my road.

Forrest is now lieutenant-general, and commands all the enemy's cavalry.

W. T. SHERMAN, *Major-General.*

General Grant first thought I was in error in supposing that Jeff. Davis was at Macon and Palmetto, but on the 27th I received a printed copy of his speech made at Macon on the 22d, which was so significant that I ordered it to be telegraphed entire as far as Louisville, to be sent thence by mail to Washington, and on the same day received this dispatch:

WASHINGTON, D. C., *September* 27, 1864 — 9 A.M.
Major-General SHERMAN, *Atlanta:*
You say Jeff. Davis is on a visit to General Hood. I judge that Brown and Stephens are the objects of his visit.

A. LINCOLN, *President of the United States.*

To which I replied:

HEADQUARTERS MILITARY DIVISION OF THE MISSISSIPPI, ⎱
IN THE FIELD, ATLANTA, GEORGIA, *September* 28, 1864.⎰

President LINCOLN, *Washington, D. C.:*
I have positive knowledge that Mr. Davis made a speech at Macon, on the 22d, which I mailed to General Halleck yesterday. It was bitter against General Jos. Johnston and Governor Brown. The militia are on furlough. Brown is at Milledgeville, trying to get a Legislature to meet next month, but he is afraid to act unless in concert with other Governors. Judge Wright, of Rome, has been here, and Messrs. Hill and Nelson, former members of Congress, are here now, and will go to meet Wright at Rome, and then go back to Madison and Milledgeville.

Great efforts are being made to reënforce Hood's army, and to break up my railroads, and I should have at once a good reserve force at Nashville. It would have a bad effect, if I were forced to send back any considerable part of my army to guard roads, so as to weaken me to an extent that I could not act offensively if the occasion calls for it.

W. T. SHERMAN, *Major-General.*

All this time Hood and I were carrying on the foregoing correspondence relating to the exchange of prisoners, the removal of the people from Atlanta, and the relief of our prisoners of war at Andersonville. Notwithstanding the severity of their imprisonment, some of these men escaped from Andersonville, and got to me at Atlanta. They described their sad condition: more than twenty-five thousand prisoners confined in a stockade designed for only ten thousand; debarred the privilege of gathering wood out of which to make huts; deprived of sufficient healthy food, and the little stream that ran through their prison-pen poisoned and polluted by the offal from their cooking and butchering houses above. On the 22d of September I wrote to General Hood, describing the condition of our men at Andersonville, purposely refraining from casting odium on him or his associates for the treatment of these men, but asking his consent for me to procure from our generous friends at the North the articles of clothing and comfort which they wanted, viz., under-clothing, soap, combs, scissors, etc.—all needed to keep them in health— and to send these stores with a train, and an officer to issue them. General Hood, on the 24th, promptly consented, and I telegraphed to my friend Mr. James E. Yeatman, Vice-President of the Sanitary Commission at St. Louis, to send us all the under-clothing and soap he could spare, specifying twelve hundred fine-tooth combs, and four hundred pairs of shears to cut hair. These articles indicate the plague that most afflicted our prisoners at Andersonville.

Mr. Yeatman promptly responded to my request, expressed the articles, but they did not reach Andersonville in time, for the prisoners were soon after removed; these supplies did, however, finally overtake them at Jacksonville, Florida, just before the war closed.

On the 28th I received from General Grant two dispatches:

CITY POINT, VIRGINIA, *September* 27, 1864—8.30 A.M.
Major-General SHERMAN:

It is evident, from the tone of the Richmond press and from other sources of information, that the enemy intend making a desperate effort to drive you from where you are. I have directed all new troops from the West, and from the East too, if necessary, in case none are ready in the West, to be sent to you. If General Burbridge is not too far on his way to Abingdon, I think he had better be recalled and his surplus troops sent into Tennessee.

U. S. GRANT, *Lieutenant-General.*

CITY POINT, VIRGINIA, *September* 27, 1864 — 10.30 A.M.
Major-General SHERMAN:

I have directed all recruits and new troops from all the Western States to be sent to Nashville, to receive their further orders from you. I was mistaken about Jeff. Davis being in Richmond on Thursday last. He was then on his way to Macon.

U. S. GRANT, *Lieutenant-General.*

Forrest having already made his appearance in Middle Tennessee, and Hood evidently edging off in that direction, satisfied me that the general movement against our roads had begun. I therefore determined to send General Thomas back to Chattanooga, with another division (Morgan's, of the Fourteenth Corps), to meet the danger in Tennessee. General Thomas went up on the 29th, and Morgan's division followed the same day, also by rail. And I telegraphed to General Halleck:

I take it for granted that Forrest will cut our road, but think we can prevent him from making a serious lodgment. His cavalry will travel a hundred miles where ours will ten. I have sent two divisions up to Chattanooga and one to Rome, and General Thomas started to-day to drive Forrest out of Tennessee. Our roads should be watched from the rear, and I am glad that General Grant has ordered reserves to Nashville. I prefer for the future to make the movement on Milledgeville, Millen, and Savannah. Hood now rests twenty-four miles south, on the Chattahoochee, with his right on the West Point road. He is removing the iron of the Macon road. I can whip his infantry, but his cavalry is to be feared.

There was great difficulty in obtaining correct information about Hood's movements from Palmetto Station. I could not get spies to penetrate his camps, but on the 1st of October I was satisfied that the bulk of his infantry was at and across the Chattahoochee River, near Campbellton, and that his cavalry

was on the west side, at Powder Springs. On that day I telegraphed to General Grant:

Hood is evidently across the Chattahoochee, below Sweetwater. If
he tries to get on our road, this side of the Etowah, I shall attack
him; but if he goes to the Selma & Talladega road, why will it not do
to leave Tennessee to the forces which Thomas has, and the reserves
soon to come to Nashville, and for me to destroy Atlanta and march
across Georgia to Savannah or Charleston, breaking roads and doing
irreparable damage? We cannot remain on the defensive.

The Selma & Talladega road herein referred to was an unfinished railroad from Selma, Alabama, through Talladega, to
Blue Mountain, a terminus sixty-five miles southwest of
Rome and about fifteen miles southeast of Gadsden, where
the rebel army could be supplied from the direction of Montgomery and Mobile, and from which point Hood could easily
threaten Middle Tennessee. My first impression was, that
Hood would make for that point; but by the 3d of October
the indications were that he would strike our railroad nearer
us, viz., about Kingston or Marietta.

Orders were at once made for the Twentieth Corps (Slocum's) to hold Atlanta and the bridges of the Chattahoochee, and the other corps were put in motion for Marietta.

The army had undergone many changes since the capture
of Atlanta. General Schofield had gone to the rear, leaving
General J. D. Cox in command of the Army of the Ohio
(Twenty-third Corps). General Thomas, also, had been dispatched to Chattanooga, with Newton's division of the
Fourth Corps and Morgan's of the Fourteenth Corps, leaving
General D. S. Stanley, the senior major-general of the two
corps of his Army of the Cumberland, remaining and available for this movement, viz., the Fourth and Fourteenth,
commanded by himself and Major-General Jeff. C. Davis; and
after General Dodge was wounded, his corps (the Sixteenth)
had been broken up, and its two divisions were added to the
Fifteenth and Seventeenth Corps, constituting the Army of
the Tennessee, commanded by Major-General O. O. Howard.
Generals Logan and Blair had gone home to assist in the
political canvass, leaving their corps, viz., the Fifteenth and

Seventeenth, under the command of Major-Generals Osterhaus and T. E. G. Ransom.

These five corps were very much reduced in strength, by
detachments and by discharges, so that for the purpose of
fighting Hood I had only about sixty thousand infantry and
artillery, with two small divisions of cavalry (Kilpatrick's and
Garrard's). General Elliott was the chief of cavalry to the
Army of the Cumberland, and was the senior officer of that
arm of service present for duty with me.

We had strong railroad guards at Marietta and Kenesaw,
Allatoona, Etowah Bridge, Kingston, Rome, Resaca, Dalton,
Ringgold, and Chattanooga. All the important bridges were
likewise protected by good block-houses, admirably constructed, and capable of a strong defense against cavalry or
infantry; and at nearly all the regular railroad-stations we had
smaller detachments intrenched. I had little fear of the enemy's cavalry damaging our roads seriously, for they rarely
made a break which could not be repaired in a few days; but
it was absolutely necessary to keep General Hood's infantry
off our main route of communication and supply. Forrest had
with him in Middle Tennessee about eight thousand cavalry,
and Hood's army was estimated at from thirty-five to forty
thousand men, infantry and artillery, including Wheeler's cavalry, then about three thousand strong.

We crossed the Chattahoochee River during the 3d and 4th
of October, rendezvoused at the old battle-field of Smyrna
Camp, and the next day reached Marietta and Kenesaw. The
telegraph-wires had been cut above Marietta, and learning
that heavy masses of infantry, artillery, and cavalry, had been
seen from Kenesaw (marching north), I inferred that Allatoona was their objective point; and on the 4th of October I
signaled from Vining's Station to Kenesaw, and from Kenesaw to Allatoona, over the heads of the enemy, a message for
General Corse, at Rome, to hurry back to the assistance of the
garrison at Allatoona. Allatoona was held by a small brigade,
commanded by Lieutenant-Colonel Tourtellotte, my present
aide-de-camp. He had two small redoubts on either side of
the railroad, overlooking the village of Allatoona, and the
warehouses, in which were stored over a million rations of
bread.

Reaching Kenesaw Mountain about 8 A.M. of October 5th (a beautiful day), I had a superb view of the vast panorama to the north and west. To the southwest, about Dallas, could be seen the smoke of camp-fires, indicating the presence of a large force of the enemy, and the whole line of railroad from Big Shanty up to Allatoona (full fifteen miles) was marked by the fires of the burning railroad. We could plainly see the smoke of battle about Allatoona, and hear the faint reverberation of the cannon.

From Kenesaw I ordered the Twenty-third Corps (General Cox) to march due west on the Burnt Hickory road, and to burn houses or piles of brush as it progressed, to indicate the head of column, hoping to interpose this corps between Hood's main army at Dallas and the detachment then assailing Allatoona. The rest of the army was directed straight for Allatoona, northwest, distant eighteen miles. The signal-officer on Kenesaw reported that since daylight he had failed to obtain any answer to his call for Allatoona; but, while I was with him, he caught a faint glimpse of the tell-tale flag through an embrasure, and after much time he made out these letters—"C.," "R.," "S.," "E.," "H.," "E.," "R.," and translated the message—"Corse is here." It was a source of great relief, for it gave me the first assurance that General Corse had received his orders, and that the place was adequately garrisoned.

I watched with painful suspense the indications of the battle raging there, and was dreadfully impatient at the slow progress of the relieving column, whose advance was marked by the smokes which were made according to orders, but about 2 P.M. I noticed with satisfaction that the smoke of battle about Allatoona grew less and less, and ceased altogether about 4 P.M. For a time I attributed this result to the effect of General Cox's march, but later in the afternoon the signal-flag announced the welcome tidings that the attack had been fairly repulsed, but that General Corse was wounded. The next day my aide, Colonel Dayton, received this characteristic dispatch:

ALLATOONA, GEORGIA, *October* 6, 1864—2 P.M.
Captain L. M. DAYTON, *Aide-de-Camp:*
I am short a cheek-bone and an ear, but am able to whip all h—l

yet! My losses are very heavy. A force moving from Stilesboro' to Kingston gives me some anxiety. Tell me where Sherman is.

JOHN M. CORSE, Brigadier-General.

Inasmuch as the enemy had retreated southwest, and would probably next appear at Rome, I answered General Corse with orders to get back to Rome with his troops as quickly as possible.

General Corse's report of this fight at Allatoona is very full and graphic. It is dated Rome, October 27, 1864; recites the fact that he received his orders by signal to go to the assistance of Allatoona on the 4th, when he telegraphed to Kingston for cars, and a train of thirty empty cars was started for him, but about ten of them got off the track and caused delay. By 7 P.M. he had at Rome a train of twenty cars, which he loaded up with Colonel Rowett's brigade, and part of the Twelfth Illinois Infantry; started at 8 P.M., reached Allatoona (distant thirty-five miles) at 1 A.M. of the 5th, and sent the train back for more men; but the road was in bad order, and no more men came in time. He found Colonel Tourtellotte's garrison composed of eight hundred and ninety men; his reenforcement was one thousand and fifty-four: total for the defense, nineteen hundred and forty-four. The outposts were already engaged, and as soon as daylight came he drew back the men from the village to the ridge on which the redoubts were built.

The enemy was composed of French's division of three brigades, variously reported from four to five thousand strong. This force gradually surrounded the place by 8 A.M., when General French sent in by flag of truce this note:

AROUND ALLATOONA, October 5, 1864.

Commanding Officer, United States Forces, Allatoona:

I have placed the forces under my command in such positions that you are surrounded, and to avoid a needless effusion of blood I call on you to surrender your forces at once, and unconditionally.

Five minutes will be allowed you to decide. Should you accede to this, you will be treated in the most honorable manner as prisoners of war.

I have the honor to be, very respectfully yours,

S. G. FRENCH,
Major-General commanding forces Confederate States.

General Corse answered immediately:

HEADQUARTERS FOURTH DIVISION, FIFTEENTH CORPS,⎱
ALLATOONA, GEORGIA, 8.30 A.M., *October* 5, 1864. ⎰

Major-General S. G. FRENCH, *Confederate States, etc.:*
Your communication demanding surrender of my command I acknowledge receipt of, and respectfully reply that we are prepared for the "needless effusion of blood" whenever it is agreeable to you.
I am, very respectfully, your obedient servant,

JOHN M. CORSE,
Brigadier-General commanding forces United States.

Of course the attack began at once, coming from front, flank, and rear. There were two small redoubts, with slight parapets and ditches, one on each side of the deep railroad-cut. These redoubts had been located by Colonel Poe, United States Engineers, at the time of our advance on Kenesaw, the previous June. Each redoubt overlooked the storehouses close by the railroad, and each could aid the other defensively by catching in flank the attacking force of the other. Our troops at first endeavored to hold some ground outside the redoubts, but were soon driven inside, when the enemy made repeated assaults, but were always driven back. About 11 A.M., Colonel Redfield, of the Thirty-ninth Iowa, was killed, and Colonel Rowett was wounded, but never ceased to fight and encourage his men. Colonel Tourtellotte was shot through the hips, but continued to command. General Corse was, at 1 P.M., shot across the face, the ball cutting his ear, which stunned him, but he continued to encourage his men and to give orders. The enemy (about 1.30 P.M.) made a last and desperate effort to carry one of the redoubts, but was badly cut to pieces by the artillery and infantry fire from the other, when he began to draw off, leaving his dead and wounded on the ground.

Before finally withdrawing, General French converged a heavy fire of his cannon on the block-house at Allatoona Creek, about two miles from the depot, set it on fire, and captured its garrison, consisting of four officers and eighty-five men. By 4 P.M. he was in full retreat south, on the Dallas road, and got by before the head of General Cox's column had reached it; still several ambulances and stragglers were picked up by this command on that road. General Corse reported two hundred and thirty-one rebel dead, four hundred and eleven prisoners, three regimental colors, and eight hundred muskets captured.

Among the prisoners was a Brigadier-General Young, who thought that French's aggregate loss would reach two thousand. Colonel Tourtellotte says that, for days after General Corse had returned to Rome, his men found and buried at least a hundred more dead rebels, who had doubtless been wounded, and died in the woods near Allatoona. I know that when I reached Allatoona, on the 9th, I saw a good many dead men, which had been collected for burial.

Corse's entire loss, officially reported, was:

GARRISON.	Killed.	Wounded.	Missing.	Total.
Officers	6	23	6	35
Men.	136	330	206	672
Total	142	353	212	707

I esteemed this defense of Allatoona so handsome and important, that I made it the subject of a general order, viz., No. 86, of October 7, 1864:

The general commanding avails himself of the opportunity, in the handsome defense made of Allatoona, to illustrate the most important principle in war, that fortified posts should be defended to the last, regardless of the relative numbers of the party attacking and attacked. . . . The thanks of this army are due and are hereby accorded to General Corse, Colonel Tourtellotte, Colonel Rowett, officers, and men, for their determined and gallant defense of Allatoona, and it is made an example to illustrate the importance of preparing in time, and meeting the danger, when present, boldly, manfully, and well.

Commanders and garrisons of the posts along our railroad are hereby instructed that they must hold their posts to the last minute, sure that the time gained is valuable and necessary to their comrades at the front.

By order of Major-General W. T. Sherman,

L. M. DAYTON, *Aide-de-Camp*.

The rebels had struck our railroad a heavy blow, burning every tie, bending the rails for eight miles, from Big Shanty to above Acworth, so that the estimate for repairs called for thirty-five thousand new ties, and six miles of iron. Ten thousand men were distributed along the break to replace the ties, and to prepare the road-bed, while the regular repair-party, under Colonel W. W. Wright, came down from Chattanooga with iron, spikes, etc., and in about seven days the road was all right again. It was by such acts of extraordinary energy that we discouraged our adversaries, for the rebel soldiers felt that it was a waste of labor for them to march hurriedly, on wide circuits, day and night, to burn a bridge and tear up a mile or so of track, when they knew that we could lay it back so quickly. They supposed that we had men and money without limit, and that we always kept on hand, distributed along the road, duplicates of every bridge and culvert of any importance.

A good story is told of one who was on Kenesaw Mountain during our advance in the previous June or July. A group of rebels lay in the shade of a tree, one hot day, overlooking our camps about Big Shanty. One soldier remarked to his fellows:

"Well, the Yanks will have to git up and git now, for I heard General Johnston himself say that General Wheeler had blown up *the tunnel* near Dalton, and that the Yanks would have to retreat, because they could get no more rations."

"Oh, hell!" said a listener, "don't you know that old Sherman carries a *duplicate* tunnel along?"

After the war was over, General Johnston inquired of me who was our chief railroad-engineer. When I told him that it was Colonel W. W. Wright, a civilian, he was much surprised, said that our feats of bridge-building and repairs of roads had excited his admiration; and he instanced the occasion at Kenesaw in June, when an officer from Wheeler's cavalry had reported to him in person that he had come from General Wheeler, who had made a bad break in our road about Tilton Station, which he said would take at least a fortnight to repair; and, while they were talking, a train was seen coming down the road, which had passed that very break, and had reached me at Big Shanty as soon as the fleet horseman had reached him (General Johnston) at Marietta!

I doubt whether the history of war can furnish more examples of skill and bravery than attended the defense of the railroad from Nashville to Atlanta during the year 1864.

In person I reached Allatoona on the 9th of October, still in doubt as to Hood's immediate intentions. Our cavalry could do little against his infantry in the rough and wooded country about Dallas, which masked the enemy's movements; but General Corse, at Rome, with Spencer's First Alabama Cavalry and a mounted regiment of Illinois Infantry, could feel the country south of Rome about Cedartown and Villa Rica; and reported the enemy to be in force at both places. On the 9th I telegraphed to General Thomas, at Nashville, as follows:

I came up here to relieve our road. The Twentieth Corps remains at Atlanta. Hood reached the road and broke it up between Big Shanty and Acworth. He attacked Allatoona, but was repulsed. We have plenty of bread and meat, but forage is scarce. I want to destroy all the road below Chattanooga, including Atlanta, and to make for the sea-coast. We cannot defend this long line of road.

And on the same day I telegraphed to General Grant, at City Point:

It will be a physical impossibility to protect the roads, now that Hood, Forrest, Wheeler, and the whole batch of devils, are turned loose without home or habitation. I think Hood's movements indicate a diversion to the end of the Selma & Talladega road, at Blue Mountain, about sixty miles southwest of Rome, from which he will threaten Kingston, Bridgeport, and Decatur, Alabama. I propose that we break up the railroad from Chattanooga forward, and that we strike out with our wagons for Milledgeville, Millen, and Savannah. Until we can repopulate Georgia, it is useless for us to occupy it; but the utter destruction of its roads, houses, and people, will cripple their military resources. By attempting to hold the roads, we will lose a thousand men each month, and will gain no result. I can make this march, and make Georgia howl! We have on hand over eight thousand head of cattle and three million rations of bread, but no corn. We can find plenty of forage in the interior of the State.

Meantime the rebel General Forrest had made a bold circuit in Middle Tennessee, avoiding all fortified points, and breaking up the railroad at several places; but, as usual, he did his work so hastily and carelessly that our engineers soon repaired the damage—then, retreating before General Rousseau, he left the State of Tennessee, crossing the river near Florence, Alabama, and got off unharmed.

On the 10th of October the enemy appeared south of the Etowah River at Rome, when I ordered all the armies to march to Kingston, rode myself to Cartersville with the Twenty-third Corps (General Cox), and telegraphed from there to General Thomas at Nashville:

> It looks to me as though Hood was bound for Tuscumbia. He is now crossing the Coosa River below Rome, looking west. Let me know if you can hold him with your forces now in Tennessee and the expected reënforcements, as, in that event, you know what I propose to do.
>
> I will be at Kingston to-morrow. I think Rome is strong enough to resist any attack, and the rivers are all high. If he turns up by Summerville, I will get in behind him.

And on the same day to General Grant, at City Point:

> Hood is now crossing the Coosa, twelve miles below Rome, bound west. If he passes over to the Mobile & Ohio Railroad, had I not better execute the plan of my letter sent you by Colonel Porter, and leave General Thomas, with the troops now in Tennessee, to defend the State? He will have an ample force when the reënforcements ordered reach Nashville.

I found General John E. Smith at Cartersville, and on the 11th rode on to Kingston, where I had telegraphic communications in all directions.

From General Corse, at Rome, I learned that Hood's army had disappeared, but in what direction he was still in doubt; and I was so strongly convinced of the wisdom of my proposition to change the whole tactics of the campaign, to leave Hood to General Thomas, and to march across Georgia for Savannah or Charleston, that I again telegraphed to General Grant:

> We cannot now remain on the defensive. With twenty-five thousand infantry and the bold cavalry he has, Hood can constantly break my road. I would infinitely prefer to make a wreck of the road and of

the country from Chattanooga to Atlanta, including the latter city; send back all my wounded and unserviceable men, and with my effective army move through Georgia, smashing things to the sea. Hood may turn into Tennessee and Kentucky, but I believe he will be forced to follow me. Instead of being on the defensive, I will be on the offensive. Instead of my guessing at what he means to do, he will have to guess at my plans. The difference in war would be fully twenty-five per cent. I can make Savannah, Charleston, or the mouth of the Chattahoochee (Appalachicola). Answer quick, as I know we will not have the telegraph long.

I received no answer to this at the time, and the next day went on to Rome, where the news came that Hood had made his appearance at Resaca, and had demanded the surrender of the place, which was commanded by Colonel Weaver, reënforced by Brevet Brigadier-General Raum. General Hood had evidently marched with rapidity up the Chattooga Valley, by Summerville, Lafayette, Ship's Gap, and Snake-Creek Gap, and had with him his whole army, except a small force left behind to watch Rome. I ordered Resaca to be further reënforced by rail from Kingston, and ordered General Cox to make a bold reconnoissance down the Coosa Valley, which captured and brought into Rome some cavalrymen and a couple of field-guns, with their horses and men. At first I thought of interposing my whole army in the Chattooga Valley, so as to prevent Hood's escape south; but I saw at a glance that he did not mean to fight, and in that event, after damaging the road all he could, he would be likely to retreat eastward by Spring Place, which I did not want him to do; and, hearing from General Raum that he still held Resaca safe, and that General Edward McCook had also got there with some cavalry reënforcements, I turned all the heads of columns for Resaca, viz., General Cox's, from Rome; General Stanley's, from McGuire's; and General Howard's, from Kingston. We all reached Resaca during that night, and the next morning (13th) learned that Hood's whole army had passed up the valley toward Dalton, burning the railroad and doing all the damage possible.

On the 12th he had demanded the surrender of Resaca in the following letter:

HEADQUARTERS ARMY OF TENNESSEE, ⎫
IN THE FIELD, *October* 12, 1864.   ⎭

To the Officer commanding the United States Forces at Resaca, Georgia.

SIR: I demand the immediate and unconditional surrender of the post and garrison under your command, and, should this be acceded to, all white officers and soldiers will be parolled in a few days. If the place is carried by assault, no prisoners will be taken. Most respectfully, your obedient servant,

J. B. HOOD, *General.*

To this Colonel Weaver, then in command, replied:

HEADQUARTERS SECOND BRIGADE, THIRD DIVISION, ⎫
FIFTEENTH CORPS, RESACA, GEORGIA, *October* 12, 1864.   ⎭

To General J. B. HOOD:

Your communication of this date just received. In reply, I have to state that I am somewhat surprised at the concluding paragraph, to the effect that, if the place is carried by assault, no prisoners will be taken. In my opinion I can hold this post. If you want it, come and take it.

I am, general, very respectfully, your most obedient servant,
CLARK R. WEAVER, *Commanding Officer.*

This brigade was very small, and as Hood's investment extended only from the Oostenaula, below the town, to the Connesauga above, he left open the approach from the south, which enabled General Raum and the cavalry of Generals McCook and Watkins to reënforce from Kingston. In fact, Hood, admonished by his losses at Allatoona, did not attempt an assault at all, but limited his attack to the above threat, and to some skirmishing, giving his attention chiefly to the destruction of the railroad, which he accomplished all the way up to Tunnel Hill, nearly twenty miles, capturing *en route* the regiment of black troops at Dalton (Johnson's Forty-fourth United States colored). On the 14th, I turned General Howard through Snake-Creek Gap, and sent General Stanley around by Tilton, with orders to cross the mountain to the west, so as to capture, if possible, the force left by the enemy in Snake-Creek Gap. We found this gap very badly obstructed by fallen timber, but got through that night, and the next day the main army was at Villanow. On the morning of the 16th, the leading division of General Howard's column, commanded by General Charles R. Woods, carried Ship's Gap, taking prisoners part of the Twenty-fourth South Carolina Regiment, which had been left there to hold us in check.

The best information there obtained located Hood's army at Lafayette, near which place I hoped to catch him and force him to battle; but, by the time we had got enough troops across the mountain at Ship's Gap, Hood had escaped down the valley of the Chattooga, and all we could do was to follow him as closely as possible. From Ship's Gap I dispatched couriers to Chattanooga, and received word back that General Schofield was there, endeavoring to coöperate with me, but Hood had broken up the telegraph, and thus had prevented quick communication. General Schofield did not reach me till the army had got down to Gaylesville, about the 21st of October.

It was at Ship's Gap that a courier brought me the cipher message from General Halleck which intimated that the authorities in Washington were willing I should undertake the march across Georgia to the sea. The translated dispatch named "Horse-i-bar Sound" as the point where the fleet would await my arrival. After much time I construed it to mean, "Ossabaw Sound," below Savannah, which was correct.

On the 16th I telegraphed to General Thomas, at Nashville:

Send me Morgan's and Newton's old divisions. Reëstablish the road, and I will follow Hood wherever he may go. I think he will move to Blue Mountain. We can maintain our men and animals on the country.

General Thomas's reply was:

NASHVILLE, *October* 17, 1864—10.30 A.M.
Major-General SHERMAN:
Your dispatch from Ship's Gap, 5 P.M. of the 16th, just received. Schofield, whom I placed in command of the two divisions (Wagner's and Morgan's), was to move up Lookout Valley this A.M., to intercept Hood, should he be marching for Bridgeport. I will order him to join you with the two divisions, and will reconstruct the road as soon as possible. Will also reorganize the guards for posts and block-houses. . . . Mower and Wilson have arrived, and are on their

way to join you. I hope you will adopt Grant's idea of turning Wilson loose, rather than undertake the plan of a march with the whole force through Georgia to the sea, inasmuch as General Grant cannot coöperate with you as at first arranged.

GEORGE H. THOMAS, *Major-General.*

So it is clear that at that date neither General Grant nor General Thomas heartily favored my proposed plan of campaign. On the same day, I wrote to General Schofield at Chattanooga:

Hood is not at Dear Head Cove. We occupy Ship's Gap and Lafayette. Hood is moving south *via* Summerville, Alpine, and Gadsden. If he enters Tennessee, it will be to the west of Huntsville, but I think he has given up all such idea. I want the road repaired to Atlanta; the sick and wounded men sent north of the Tennessee; my army recomposed; and I will then make the interior of Georgia feel the weight of war. It is folly for us to be moving our armies on the reports of scouts and citizens. We must maintain the offensive. Your first move on Trenton and Valley Head was right—the move to defend Caperton's Ferry is wrong. Notify General Thomas of these my views. We must follow Hood till he is beyond the reach of mischief, and then resume the offensive.

The correspondence between me and the authorities at Washington, as well as with the several army commanders, given at length in the report of the Committee on the Conduct of the War, is full on all these points.

After striking our road at Dalton, Hood was compelled to go on to Chattanooga and Bridgeport, or to pass around by Decatur and abandon altogether his attempt to make us let go our hold of Atlanta by attacking our communications. It was clear to me that he had no intention to meet us in open battle, and the lightness and celerity of his army convinced me that I could not possibly catch him on a stern-chase. We therefore quietly followed him down the Chattooga Valley to the neighborhood of Gadsden, but halted the main armies near the Coosa River, at the mouth of the Chattooga, drawing our supplies of corn and meat from the farms of that comparatively rich valley and of the neighborhood.

General Slocum, in Atlanta, had likewise sent out, under strong escort, large trains of wagons to the east, and brought back corn, bacon, and all kinds of provisions, so that Hood's efforts to cut off our supplies only reacted on his own people. So long as the railroads were in good order, our supplies came full and regular from the North; but when the enemy broke our railroads we were perfectly justified in stripping the inhabitants of all they had. I remember well the appeal of a very respectable farmer against our men driving away his fine flock of sheep. I explained to him that General Hood had broken our railroad; that we were a strong, hungry crowd, and needed plenty of food; that Uncle Sam was deeply interested in our continued health and would soon repair these roads, but meantime we must eat; we preferred Illinois beef, but mutton would have to answer. Poor fellow! I don't believe he was convinced of the wisdom or wit of my explanation. Very soon after reaching Lafayette we organized a line of supply from Chattanooga to Ringgold by rail, and thence by wagons to our camps about Gaylesville. Meantime, also, Hood had reached the neighborhood of Gadsden, and drew his supplies from the railroad at Blue Mountain.

On the 19th of October I telegraphed to General Halleck, at Washington:

Hood has retreated rapidly by all the roads leading south. Our advance columns are now at Alpine and Melville Post-Office. I shall pursue him as far as Gaylesville. The enemy will not venture toward Tennessee except around by Decatur. I propose to send the Fourth Corps back to General Thomas, and leave him, with that corps, the garrisons, and new troops, to defend the line of the Tennessee River; and with the rest I will push into the heart of Georgia and come out at Savannah, destroying all the railroads of the State. The break in our railroad at Big Shanty is almost repaired, and that about Dalton should be done in ten days. We find abundance of forage in the country.

On the same day I telegraphed to General L. C. Easton, chief-quartermaster, who had been absent on a visit to Missouri, but had got back to Chattanooga:

Go in person to superintend the repairs of the railroad, and make all orders in my name that will expedite its completion. I want it finished, to bring back from Atlanta to Chattanooga the sick and wounded men and surplus stores. On the 1st of November I want nothing in front of Chattanooga except what we can use as food and clothing and haul in our wagons. There is plenty of corn in the country, and we only want forage for the posts. I allow ten days for all this to be done, by which time I expect to be at or near Atlanta.

I telegraphed also to General Amos Beckwith, chief-commissary in Atlanta, who was acting as chief-quartermaster during the absence of General Easton:

Hood will escape me. I want to prepare for my big raid. On the 1st of November I want nothing in Atlanta but what is necessary for war. Send all trash to the rear at once, and have on hand thirty days' food and but little forage. I propose to abandon Atlanta, and the railroad back to Chattanooga, to sally forth to ruin Georgia and bring up on the sea-shore. Make all dispositions accordingly. I will go down the Coosa until I am sure that Hood has gone to Blue Mountain.

On the 21st of October I reached Gaylesville, had my bivouac in an open field back of the village, and remained there till the 28th. During that time General Schofield arrived, with the two divisions of Generals Wagner (formerly Newton's) and Morgan, which were returned to their respective corps (the Fourth and Fourteenth), and General Schofield resumed his own command of the Army of the Ohio, then on the Coosa River, near Cedar Bluff. General Joseph A. Mower also arrived, and was assigned to command a division in the Seventeenth Corps; and General J. H. Wilson came, having been sent from Virginia by General Grant, for the purpose of commanding all my cavalry. I first intended to organize this cavalry into a corps of three small divisions, to be commanded by General Wilson; but the horses were well run down, and, at Wilson's instance, I concluded to retain only one division of four thousand five hundred men, with selected horses, under General Kilpatrick, and to send General Wilson back with all the rest to Nashville, to be reorganized and to act under General Thomas in the defense of Tennessee. Orders to this effect were made on the 24th of October.

General Grant, in designating General Wilson to command my cavalry, predicted that he would, by his personal activity, increase the effect of that arm "fifty per cent.," and he advised that he should be sent south, to accomplish all that I had proposed to do with the main army; but I had not so much faith in cavalry as he had, and preferred to adhere to my original intention of going myself with a competent force.

About this time I learned that General Beauregard had reached Hood's army at Gadsden; that, without assuming direct command of that army, he had authority from the Confederate Government to direct all its movements, and to call to his assistance the whole strength of the South. His orders, on assuming command, were full of alarm and desperation, dated—

HEADQUARTERS MILITARY DIVISION OF THE WEST,
October 17, 1864.

In assuming command, at this critical juncture, of the Military Division of the West, I appeal to my countrymen, of all classes and sections, for their generous support. In assigning me to this responsible position, the President of the Confederate States has extended to me the assurance of his earnest support. The Executives of your States meet me with similar expressions of their devotion to our cause. The noble army in the field, composed of brave men and gallant officers, are strangers to me, but I know they will do all that patriots can achieve. . . .

The army of Sherman still defiantly holds Atlanta. He can and must be driven from it. It is only for the good people of Georgia and surrounding States to speak the word, and the work is done. We have abundant provisions. There are men enough in the country, liable to and able for service, to accomplish the result. . . .

My countrymen, respond to this call as you have done in days that are past, and, with the blessing of a kind and overruling Providence, the enemy shall be driven from your soil. The security of your wives and daughters from the insults and outrages of a brutal foe shall be established soon, and be followed by a permanent and honorable peace. The claims of home and country, wife and children, uniting with the demands of honor and patriotism, summon us to the field. We cannot, dare not, will not fail to respond. Full of hope and confidence, I come to join you in your struggles, sharing your privations, and, with your brave and true men, to strike the blow that shall bring success to our arms, triumph to our cause, and peace to our country!

. . . .

G. T. BEAUREGARD, *General.*

Notwithstanding this somewhat boastful order or appeal, General Beauregard did not actually accompany General

Hood on his disastrous march to Nashville, but took post at Corinth, Mississippi, to control the movement of his supplies and to watch me.

At Gaylesville the pursuit of Hood by the army under my immediate command may be said to have ceased. During this pursuit, the Fifteenth Corps was commanded by its senior major-general present, P. J. Osterhaus, in the absence of General John A. Logan; and the Seventeenth Corps was commanded by Brigadier-General T. E. G. Ransom, the senior officer present, in the absence of General Frank P. Blair.

General Ransom was a young, most gallant, and promising officer, son of the Colonel Ransom who was killed at Chapultepec, in the Mexican War. He had served with the Army of the Tennessee in 1862 and 1863, at Vicksburg, where he was severely wounded. He was not well at the time we started from Atlanta, but he insisted on going along with his command. His symptoms became more aggravated on the march, and when we were encamped near Gaylesville, I visited him in company with Surgeon John Moore, United States Army, who said that the case was one of typhoid fever, which would likely prove fatal. A few days after, viz., the 28th, he was being carried on a litter toward Rome; and as I rode from Gaylesville to Rome, I passed him by the way, stopped, and spoke with him, but did not then suppose he was so near his end. The next day, however, his escort reached Rome, bearing his dead body. The officer in charge reported that, shortly after I had passed, his symptoms became so much worse that they stopped at a farm-house by the road-side, where he died that evening. His body was at once sent to Chicago for burial, and a monument has been ordered by the Society of the Army of the Tennessee to be erected in his memory.

On the 26th of October I learned that Hood's whole army had made its appearance about Decatur, Alabama, and at once caused a strong reconnoissance to be made down the Coosa to near Gadsden, which revealed the truth that the enemy was gone, except a small force of cavalry, commanded by General Wheeler, which had been left to watch us. I then finally resolved on my future course, which was to leave Hood to be encountered by General Thomas, while I should carry into full effect the long-contemplated project of marching for the sea-coast, and thence to operate toward Richmond. But it was all-important to me and to our cause that General Thomas should have an ample force, equal to any and every emergency.

He then had at Nashville about eight or ten thousand new troops, and as many more civil employés of the Quartermaster's Department, which were not suited for the field, but would be most useful in manning the excellent forts that already covered Nashville. At Chattanooga, he had General Steedman's division, about five thousand men, besides garrisons for Chattanooga, Bridgeport, and Stevenson; at Murfreesboro' he also had General Rousseau's division, which was full five thousand strong, independent of the necessary garrisons for the railroad. At Decatur and Huntsville, Alabama, was the infantry division of General R. S. Granger, estimated at four thousand; and near Florence, Alabama, watching the crossings of the Tennessee, were General Edward Hatch's division of cavalry, four thousand; General Croxton's brigade, twenty-five hundred; and Colonel Capron's brigade, twelve hundred; besides which, General J. H. Wilson had collected in Nashville about ten thousand dismounted cavalry, for which he was rapidly collecting the necessary horses for a remount. All these aggregated about forty-five thousand men. General A. J. Smith at that time was in Missouri, with the two divisions of the Sixteenth Corps which had been diverted to that quarter to assist General Rosecrans in driving the rebel General Price out of Missouri. This object had been accomplished, and these troops, numbering from eight to ten thousand, had been ordered to Nashville. To these I proposed at first to add only the Fourth Corps (General Stanley), fifteen thousand; and that corps was ordered from Gaylesville to march to Chattanooga, and thence report for orders to General Thomas; but subsequently, on the 30th of October, at Rome, Georgia, learning from General Thomas that the new troops promised by General Grant were coming forward very slowly, I concluded to further reënforce him by General Schofield's corps (Twenty-third), twelve thousand, which corps accordingly marched for Resaca, and there took the cars for Chattanooga. I then knew that General Thomas would have

an ample force with which to encounter General Hood anywhere in the open field, besides garrisons to secure the railroad to his rear and as far forward as Chattanooga. And,
moreover, I was more than convinced that he would have
ample time for preparation; for, on that very day, General
R. S. Granger had telegraphed me from Decatur, Alabama:

> I omitted to mention another reason why Hood will go to Tus-
> cumbia before crossing the Tennessee River. He was evidently out of
> supplies. His men were all grumbling; the first thing the prisoners
> asked for was something to eat. Hood could not get any thing if he
> should cross this side of Rogersville.

I knew that the country about Decatur and Tuscumbia,
Alabama, was bare of provisions, and inferred that General
Hood would have to draw his supplies, not only of food, but
of stores, clothing, and ammunition, from Mobile, Montgomery, and Selma, Alabama, by the railroad around by
Meridian and Corinth, Mississippi, which we had most effectually disabled the previous winter.

General Hood did not make a serious attack on Decatur,
but hung around it from October 26th to the 30th, when he
drew off and marched for a point on the south side of the
Tennessee River, opposite Florence, where he was compelled
to remain nearly a month, to collect the necessary supplies for
his contemplated invasion of Tennessee and Kentucky.

The Fourth Corps (Stanley) had already reached Chattanooga, and had been transported by rail to Pulaski, Tennessee; and General Thomas ordered General Schofield, with the
Twenty-third Corps, to Columbia, Tennessee, a place intermediate between Hood (then on the Tennessee River, opposite Florence) and Forrest, opposite Johnsonville.

On the 31st of October General Croxton, of the cavalry,
reported that the enemy had crossed the Tennessee River four
miles above Florence, and that he had endeavored to stop
him, but without success. Still, I was convinced that Hood's
army was in no condition to march for Nashville, and that a
good deal of further delay might reasonably be counted on. I
also rested with much confidence on the fact that the Tennessee River below Muscle Shoals was strongly patrolled by gunboats, and that the reach of the river above Muscle Shoals,

from Decatur as high up as our railroad at Bridgeport, was also guarded by gunboats, so that Hood, to cross over, would be compelled to select a point inaccessible to these gunboats. He actually did choose such a place, at the old railroad-piers, four miles above Florence, Alabama, which is below Muscle Shoals and above Colbert Shoals.

On the 31st of October Forrest made his appearance on the Tennessee River opposite Johnsonville (whence a new railroad led to Nashville), and with his cavalry and field-pieces actually crippled and captured two gunboats with five of our transports, a feat of arms which, I confess, excited my admiration.

There is no doubt that the month of October closed to us looking decidedly squally; but, somehow, I was sustained in the belief that in a very few days the tide would turn.

On the 1st of November I telegraphed very fully to General Grant, at City Point, who must have been disturbed by the wild rumors that filled the country, and on the 2d of November received (at Rome) this dispatch:

CITY POINT, *November* 1, 1864—6 P.M.
Major-General SHERMAN:
Do you not think it advisable, now that Hood has gone so far north, to entirely ruin him before starting on your proposed campaign? With Hood's army destroyed, you can go where you please with impunity. I believed and still believe, if you had started south while Hood was in the neighborhood of you, he would have been forced to go after you. Now that he is far away he might look upon the chase as useless, and he will go in one direction while you are pushing in the other. If you can see a chance of destroying Hood's army, attend to that first, and make your other move secondary.
U. S. GRANT, *Lieutenant-General*.

My answer is dated—

ROME, GEORGIA, *November* 2, 1864.
Lieutenant-General U. S. GRANT, *City Point, Virginia:*
Your dispatch is received. If I could hope to overhaul Hood, I would turn against him with my whole force; then he would retreat to the southwest, drawing me as a decoy away from Georgia, which is his chief object. If he ventures north of the Tennessee River, I may turn in that direction, and endeavor to get below him on his line of retreat; but thus far he has not gone above the Tennessee River. General Thomas will have a force strong enough to prevent his

reaching any country in which we have an interest; and he has orders, if Hood turns to follow me, to push for Selma, Alabama. No single army can catch Hood, and I am convinced the best results will follow from our defeating Jeff. Davis's cherished plan of making me leave Georgia by manœuvring. Thus far I have confined my efforts to thwart this plan, and have reduced baggage so that I can pick up and start in any direction; but I regard the pursuit of Hood as useless. Still, if he attempts to invade Middle Tennessee, I will hold Decatur, and be prepared to move in that direction; but, unless I let go of Atlanta, my force will not be equal to his.

W. T. SHERMAN, *Major-General.*

By this date, under the intelligent and energetic action of Colonel W. W. Wright, and with the labor of fifteen hundred men, the railroad break of fifteen miles about Dalton was repaired so far as to admit of the passage of cars, and I transferred my headquarters to Kingston as more central; and from that place, on the same day (November 2d), again telegraphed to General Grant.

KINGSTON, GEORGIA, *November* 2, 1864.
Lieutenant-General U. S. GRANT, *City Point, Virginia:*
If I turn back, the whole effect of my campaign will be lost. By my movements I have thrown Beauregard (Hood) well to the west, and Thomas will have ample time and sufficient troops to hold him until the reënforcements from Missouri reach him. We have now ample supplies at Chattannooga and Atlanta, and can stand a month's interruption to our communications. I do not believe the Confederate army can reach our railroad-lines except by cavalry-raids, and Wilson will have cavalry enough to checkmate them. I am clearly of opinion that the best results will follow my contemplated movement through Georgia.

W. T. SHERMAN, *Major-General.*

That same day I received, in answer to the Rome dispatch, the following:

CITY POINT, VIRGINIA, *November* 2, 1864—11:30 A.M.
Major-General SHERMAN:
Your dispatch of 9 A.M. yesterday is just received. I dispatched you the same date, advising that Hood's army, now that it had worked so far north, ought to be looked upon now as the "object." With the

force, however, that you have left with General Thomas, he must be able to take care of Hood and destroy him.

I do not see that you can withdraw from where you are to follow Hood, without giving up all we have gained in territory. I say, then, go on as you propose.

U. S. GRANT, *Lieutenant-General.*

This was the first time that General Grant ordered the "march to the sea," and, although many of his warm friends and admirers insist that he was the author and projector of that march, and that I simply executed his plans, General Grant has never, in my opinion, thought so or said so. The truth is fully given in an original letter of President Lincoln, which I received at Savannah, Georgia, and have at this instant before me, every word of which is in his own familiar handwriting. It is dated—

WASHINGTON, *December* 26, 1864.

.   .   .   .

When you were about leaving Atlanta for the Atlantic coast, I was anxious, if not fearful; but, feeling that you were the better judge, and remembering "nothing risked, nothing gained," I did not interfere. Now, the undertaking being a success, the honor is all yours; for I believe none of us went further than to acquiesce; and, taking the work of General Thomas into account, as it should be taken, it is indeed a great success. Not only does it afford the obvious and immediate military advantages, but, in showing to the world that your army could be divided, putting the stronger part to an important new service, and yet leaving enough to vanquish the old opposing force of the whole, Hood's army, it brings those who sat in darkness to see a great light. But what next? I suppose it will be safer if I leave General Grant and yourself to decide.

A. LINCOLN.

Of course, this judgment, made after the event, was extremely flattering and was all I ever expected, a recognition of the truth and of its importance. I have often been asked, by well-meaning friends, when the thought of that march first entered my mind. I knew that an army which had penetrated Georgia as far as Atlanta could not turn back. It must go ahead, but when, how, and where, depended on many considerations. As soon as Hood had shifted across from Lovejoy's to Palmetto, I saw the move in my "mind's eye;" and, after Jeff. Davis's speech at Palmetto, of September 26th, I was more positive in my conviction, but was in doubt as to the time and manner. When General Hood first struck our railroad above Marietta, we were not ready, and I was forced to watch his movements further, till he had "carromed" off to the west of Decatur. Then I was perfectly convinced, and had no longer a shadow of doubt. The only possible question was as to Thomas's strength and ability to meet Hood in the open field. I did not suppose that General Hood, though rash, would venture to attack fortified places like Allatoona, Resaca, Decatur, and Nashville; but he did so, and in so doing he played into our hands perfectly.

On the 2d of November I was at Kingston, Georgia, and my four corps—the Fifteenth, Seventeenth, Fourteenth, and Twentieth—with one division of cavalry, were strung from Rome to Atlanta. Our railroads and telegraph had been repaired, and I deliberately prepared for the march to Savannah, distant three hundred miles from Atlanta. All the sick and wounded men had been sent back by rail to Chattanooga; all our wagon-trains had been carefully overhauled and loaded, so as to be ready to start on an hour's notice, and there was no serious enemy in our front.

General Hood remained still at Florence, Alabama, occupying both banks of the Tennessee River, busy in collecting shoes and clothing for his men, and the necessary ammunition and stores with which to invade Tennessee, most of which had to come from Mobile, Selma, and Montgomery, Alabama, over railroads that were still broken. Beauregard was at Corinth, hastening forward these necessary preparations.

General Thomas was at Nashville, with Wilson's dismounted cavalry and a mass of new troops and quartermaster's employés amply sufficient to defend the place. The Fourth and Twenty-third Corps, under Generals Stanley and Schofield, were posted at Pulaski, Tennessee, and the cavalry of Hatch, Croxton, and Capron, were about Florence, watching Hood. Smith's (A. J.) two divisions of the Sixteenth Corps were still in Missouri, but were reported as ready to embark at Lexington for the Cumberland River and Nashville. Of course, General Thomas saw that on him would likely fall the real blow, and was naturally anxious. He still kept Granger's division at Decatur, Rousseau's at Murfrees-boro', and Steedman's at Chattanooga, with strong railroad guards at all the essential points intermediate, confident that by means of this very railroad he could make his concentration sooner than Hood could possibly march up from Florence.

Meantime, General F. P. Blair had rejoined his corps (Seventeenth), and we were receiving at Kingston recruits and returned furlough-men, distributing them to their proper companies. Paymasters had come down to pay off our men before their departure to a new sphere of action, and commissioners were also on hand from the several States to take the vote of our men in the presidential election then agitating the country.

On the 6th of November, at Kingston, I wrote and telegraphed to General Grant, reviewing the whole situation, gave him my full plan of action, stated that I was ready to march as soon as the election was over, and appointed November 10th as the day for starting. On the 8th I received this dispatch.

CITY POINT, VIRGINIA, *November 7*, 1864—10.30 P.M.
Major-General SHERMAN:

Your dispatch of this evening received. I see no present reason for changing your plan. Should any arise, you will see it, or if I do I will inform you. I think every thing here is favorable now. Great good fortune attend you! I believe you will be eminently successful, and, at worst, can only make a march less fruitful of results than hoped for.

U. S. GRANT, *Lieutenant-General.*

Meantime trains of cars were whirling by, carrying to the rear an immense amount of stores which had accumulated at Atlanta, and at the other stations along the railroad; and General Steedman had come down to Kingston, to take charge of the final evacuation and withdrawal of the several garrisons below Chattanooga.

On the 10th of November the movement may be said to have fairly begun. All the troops designed for the campaign were ordered to march for Atlanta, and General Corse, before evacuating his post at Rome, was ordered to burn all the mills, factories, etc., etc., that could be useful to the enemy, should he undertake to pursue us, or resume military possession of the country. This was done on the night of the 10th, and next day Corse reached Kingston. On the 11th General Thomas and I interchanged full dispatches. He had heard of the arrival of General A. J. Smith's two divisions at Paducah, which would surely reach Nashville much sooner than General Hood could possibly do from Florence, so that he was perfectly satisfied with his share of the army.

On the 12th, with a full staff, I started from Kingston for Atlanta; and about noon of that day we reached Cartersville, and sat on the edge of a porch to rest, when the telegraph operator, Mr. Van Valkenburg, or Eddy, got the wire down from the poles to his lap, in which he held a small pocket instrument. Calling "Chattanooga," he received this message from General Thomas, dated—

NASHVILLE, *November* 12, 1864—8.30. A.M.

Major-General SHERMAN:

Your dispatch of twelve o'clock last night is received. I have no fears that Beauregard can do us any harm now, and, if he attempts to follow you, I will follow him as far as possible. If he does not follow you, I will then thoroughly organize my troops, and believe I shall have men enough to ruin him unless he gets out of the way very rapidly.

The country of Middle Alabama, I learn, is teeming with supplies this year, which will be greatly to our advantage. I have no additional news to report from the direction of Florence.

I am now convinced that the greater part of Beauregard's army is near Florence and Tuscumbia, and that you will have at least a clear road before you for several days, and that your success will fully equal your expectations.

GEORGE H. THOMAS, *Major-General.*

I answered simply: "Dispatch received—all right." About that instant of time, some of our men burnt a bridge, which severed the telegraph-wire, and all communication with the rear ceased thenceforth.

As we rode on toward Atlanta that night, I remember the railroad-trains going to the rear with a furious speed; the engineers and the few men about the trains waving us an affectionate adieu. It surely was a strange event—two hostile armies marching in opposite directions, each in the full belief that it was achieving a final and conclusive result in a great war; and I was strongly inspired with the feeling that the movement on our part was a direct attack upon the rebel army and the rebel capital at Richmond, though a full thousand miles of hostile country intervened, and that, for better or worse, it would end the war.

Chapter XXI.

THE MARCH TO THE SEA—FROM ATLANTA TO SAVANNAH.

November and December, 1864.

O N THE 12th of November the railroad and telegraph communications with the rear were broken, and the army stood detached from all friends, dependent on its own resources and supplies. No time was to be lost; all the detachments were ordered to march rapidly for Atlanta, breaking up the railroad *en route*, and generally to so damage the country as to make it untenable to the enemy. By the 14th all the troops had arrived at or near Atlanta, and were, according to orders, grouped into two wings, the right and left, commanded respectively by Major-Generals O. O. Howard and H. W. Slocum, both comparatively young men, but educated and experienced officers, fully competent to their command.

The right wing was composed of the Fifteenth Corps, Major-General P. J. Osterhaus commanding, and the Seventeenth Corps, Major-General Frank P. Blair commanding.

The left wing was composed of the Fourteenth Corps, Major-General Jefferson C. Davis commanding, and the Twentieth Corps, Brigadier-General A. S. Williams commanding.

The Fifteenth Corps had four divisions, commanded by Brigadier-Generals Charles R. Woods, W. B. Hazen, John E. Smith, and John M. Corse.

The Seventeenth Corps had three divisions, commanded by Major-General J. A. Mower, and Brigadier-Generals M. D. Leggett and Giles A. Smith.

The Fourteenth Corps had three divisions, commanded by Brigadier-Generals W. P. Carlin, James D. Morgan, and A. Baird.

The Twentieth Corps had also three divisions, commanded by Brigadier-Generals N. J. Jackson, John W. Geary, and W. T. Ward.

The cavalry division was held separate, subject to my own orders. It was commanded by Brigadier-General Judson

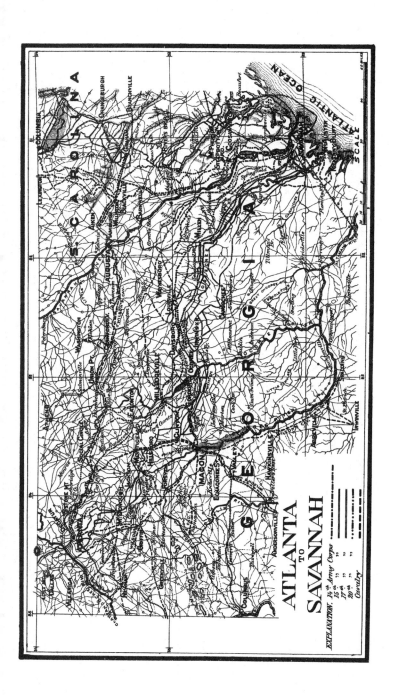

ATLANTA
TO
SAVANAH

EXPLANATION. 14th Army Corps
15th " "
17th " "
20th " "
Cavalry

Kilpatrick, and was composed of two brigades, commanded by Colonels Eli H. Murray, of Kentucky, and Smith D. Atkins, of Illinois.

The strength of the army, as officially reported, is given in the following tables, and shows an aggregate of fifty-five thousand three hundred and twenty-nine infantry, five thousand and sixty-three cavalry, and eighteen hundred and twelve artillery—in all, sixty-two thousand two hundred and four officers and men. (*See* table for December 1st.)

RECAPITULATION—ATLANTA TO SAVANNAH.

ARM.	November 10.	December 1.	December 20.
Infantry.	52,796	55,329	54,255
Cavalry	4,961	5,063	4,584
Artillery	1,788	1,812	1,759
Aggregate	59,545	62,204	60,598

The most extraordinary efforts had been made to purge this army of non-combatants and of sick men, for we knew well that there was to be no place of safety save with the army itself; our wagons were loaded with ammunition, provisions, and forage, and we could ill afford to haul even sick men in the ambulances, so that all on this exhibit may be assumed to have been able-bodied, experienced soldiers, well armed, well equipped and provided, as far as human foresight could, with all the essentials of life, strength, and vigorous action.

The two general orders made for this march appear to me, even at this late day, so clear, emphatic, and well-digested, that no account of that historic event is perfect without them, and I give them entire, even at the seeming appearance of repetition; and, though they called for great sacrifice and labor on the part of the officers and men, I insist that these orders were obeyed as well as any similar orders ever were, by an army operating wholly in an enemy's country, and dispersed, as we necessarily were, during the subsequent period of nearly six months.

Effective Strength of the Army commanded by General W. T. SHERMAN, during the March from Atlanta to Savannah, Georgia, 1864.

COMMANDS.	NOVEMBER 10.						DECEMBER 1.						DECEMBER 20.					
	Infantry.		Cavalry.		Artillery.		Infantry.		Cavalry.		Artillery.		Infantry.		Cavalry.		Artillery.	
	Commissioned Officers.	Enlisted Men.	Commissioned Officers.	Enlisted Men.	Commissioned Officers.	Enlisted Men.	Commissioned Officers.	Enlisted Men.	Commissioned Officers.	Enlisted Men.	Commissioned Officers.	Enlisted Men.	Commissioned Officers.	Enlisted Men.	Commissioned Officers.	Enlisted Men.	Commissioned Officers.	Enlisted Men.
Fifteenth Army Corps . .	724	14,568	..	..	11	376	750	15,144	..	..	17	362	753	14,441	..	..	12	367
Seventeenth Army Corps .	420	10,667	2	43	5	266	418	11,314	2	30	10	318	436	11,293	2	30	7	278
Total—Right Wing. .	1,144	25,235	2	43	16	642	1,168	26,458	2	30	27	680	1,189	25,734	2	30	19	645
Fourteenth Army Corps .	566	12,397	..	..	11	388	623	13,339	..	..	11	443	621	13,170	..	..	11	434
Twentieth Army Corps .	602	12,862	..	..	25	607	638	13,103	..	..	22	529	631	12,910	..	..	24	526
Total—Left Wing . .	1,158	25,259	..	..	36	995	1,261	26,442	..	..	33	972	1,252	26,080	..	..	35	960
Kilpatrick's Cavalry . . .	..	..	244	4,672	4	95	..	..	251	4,780	4	96	..	..	201	4,351	4	96
Grand Aggregate . . .	2,302	50,494	246	4,715	56	1,732	2,429	52,900	253	4,810	64	1,748	2,441	51,814	203	4,381	58	1,701

[Special Field Orders, No. 119.]
HEADQUARTERS MILITARY DIVISION OF THE MISSISSIPPI, ⎰
IN THE FIELD, KINGSTON, GEORGIA, *November* 8, 1864.⎱

The general commanding deems it proper at this time to inform the officers and men of the Fourteenth, Fifteenth, Seventeenth, and Twentieth Corps, that he has organized them into an army for a special purpose, well known to the War Department and to General Grant. It is sufficient for you to know that it involves a departure from our present base, and a long and difficult march to a new one. All the chances of war have been considered and provided for, as far as human sagacity can. All he asks of you is to maintain that discipline, patience, and courage, which have characterized you in the past; and he hopes, through you, to strike a blow at our enemy that will have a material effect in producing what we all so much desire, his complete overthrow. Of all things, the most important is, that the men, during marches and in camp, keep their places and do not scatter about as stragglers or foragers, to be picked up by a hostile people in detail. It is also of the utmost importance that our wagons should not be loaded with any thing but provisions and ammunition. All surplus servants, non-combatants, and refugees, should now go to the rear, and none should be encouraged to encumber us on the march. At some future time we will be able to provide for the poor whites and blacks who seek to escape the bondage under which they are now suffering. With these few simple cautions, he hopes to lead you to achievements equal in importance to those of the past.

By order of Major-General W. T. Sherman,

L. M. DAYTON, *Aide-de-Camp.*

[Special Field Orders, No. 120.]
HEADQUARTERS MILITARY DIVISION OF THE MISSISSIPPI, ⎰
IN THE FIELD, KINGSTON, GEORGIA, *November* 9, 1864.⎱

1. For the purpose of military operations, this army is divided into two wings viz.:

The right wing, Major-General O. O. Howard commanding, composed of the Fifteenth and Seventeenth Corps; the left wing, Major-General H. W. Slocum commanding, composed of the Fourteenth and Twentieth Corps.

2. The habitual order of march will be, wherever practicable, by four roads, as nearly parallel as possible, and converging at points hereafter to be indicated in orders. The cavalry, Brigadier-General Kilpatrick commanding, will receive special orders from the commander-in-chief.

3. There will be no general train of supplies, but each corps will

have its ammunition-train and provision-train, distributed habitually as follows: Behind each regiment should follow one wagon and one ambulance; behind each brigade should follow a due proportion of ammunition-wagons, provision-wagons, and ambulances. In case of danger, each corps commander should change this order of march, by having his advance and rear brigades unencumbered by wheels. The separate columns will start habitually at 7 A.M., and make about fifteen miles per day, unless otherwise fixed in orders.

4. The army will forage liberally on the country during the march. To this end, each brigade commander will organize a good and sufficient foraging party, under the command of one or more discreet officers, who will gather, near the route traveled, corn or forage of any kind, meat of any kind, vegetables, corn-meal, or whatever is needed by the command, aiming at all times to keep in the wagons at least ten days' provisions for his command, and three days' forage. Soldiers must not enter the dwellings of the inhabitants, or commit any trespass; but, during a halt or camp, they may be permitted to gather turnips, potatoes, and other vegetables, and to drive in stock in sight of their camp. To regular foraging-parties must be intrusted the gathering of provisions and forage, at any distance from the road traveled.

5. To corps commanders alone is intrusted the power to destroy mills, houses, cotton-gins, etc.; and for them this general principle is laid down: In districts and neighborhoods where the army is unmolested, no destruction of such property should be permitted; but should guerrillas or bushwhackers molest our march, or should the inhabitants burn bridges, obstruct roads, or otherwise manifest local hostility, then army commanders should order and enforce a devastation more or less relentless, according to the measure of such hostility.

6. As for horses, mules, wagons, etc., belonging to the inhabitants, the cavalry and artillery may appropriate freely and without limit; discriminating, however, between the rich, who are usually hostile, and the poor and industrious, usually neutral or friendly. Foraging-parties may also take mules or horses, to replace the jaded animals of their trains, or to serve as pack-mules for the regiments or brigades. In all foraging, of whatever kind, the parties engaged will refrain from abusive or threatening language, and may, where the officer in command thinks proper, give written certificates of the facts, but no receipts; and they will endeavor to leave with each family a reasonable portion for their maintenance,

7. Negroes who are able-bodied and can be of service to the several columns may be taken along; but each army commander will

bear in mind that the question of supplies is a very important one, and that his first duty is to see to those who bear arms.

8. The organization, at once, of a good pioneer battalion for each army corps, composed if possible of negroes, should be attended to. This battalion should follow the advance-guard, repair roads and double them if possible, so that the columns will not be delayed after reaching bad places. Also, army commanders should practise the habit of giving the artillery and wagons the road, marching their troops on one side, and instruct their troops to assist wagons at steep hills or bad crossings of streams.

9. Captain O. M. Poe, chief-engineer, will assign to each wing of the army a pontoon-train, fully equipped and organized; and the commanders thereof will see to their being properly protected at all times.

By order of Major-General W. T. Sherman,

L. M. DAYTON, *Aide-de-Camp.*

The greatest possible attention had been given to the artillery and wagon trains. The number of guns had been reduced to sixty-five, or about one gun to each thousand men, and these were generally in batteries of four guns each.

Each gun, caisson, and forge, was drawn by four teams of horses. We had in all about twenty-five hundred wagons, with teams of six mules to each, and six hundred ambulances, with two horses to each. The loads were made comparatively light, about twenty-five hundred pounds net; each wagon carrying in addition the forage needed by its own team. Each soldier carried on his person forty rounds of ammunition, and in the wagons were enough cartridges to make up about two hundred rounds per man, and in like manner two hundred rounds of assorted ammunition were carried for each gun.

The wagon-trains were divided equally between the four corps, so that each had about eight hundred wagons, and these usually on the march occupied five miles or more of road. Each corps commander managed his own train; and habitually the artillery and wagons had the road, while the men, with the exception of the advance and rear guards, pursued paths improvised by the side of the wagons, unless they were forced to use a bridge or causeway in common.

I reached Atlanta during the afternoon of the 14th, and found that all preparations had been made—Colonel Beckwith, chief commissary, reporting one million two hundred thousand rations in possession of the troops, which was about twenty days' supply, and he had on hand a good supply of beef-cattle to be driven along on the hoof. Of forage, the supply was limited, being of oats and corn enough for five days, but I knew that within that time we would reach a country well stocked with corn, which had been gathered and stored in cribs, seemingly for our use, by Governor Brown's militia.

Colonel Poe, United States Engineers, of my staff, had been busy in his special task of destruction. He had a large force at work, had leveled the great depot, round-house, and the machine-shops of the Georgia Railroad, and had applied fire to the wreck. One of these machine-shops had been used by the rebels as an arsenal, and in it were stored piles of shot and shell, some of which proved to be loaded, and that night was made hideous by the bursting of shells, whose fragments came uncomfortably near Judge Lyon's house, in which I was quartered. The fire also reached the block of stores near the depot, and the heart of the city was in flames all night, but the fire did not reach the parts of Atlanta where the court-house was, or the great mass of dwelling-houses.

The march from Atlanta began on the morning of November 15th, the right wing and cavalry following the railroad southeast toward Jonesboro', and General Slocum with the Twentieth Corps leading off to the east by Decatur and Stone Mountain, toward Madison. These were divergent lines, designed to threaten both Macon and Augusta at the same time, so as to prevent a concentration at our intended destination, or "objective," Milledgeville, the capital of Georgia, distant southeast about one hundred miles. The time allowed each column for reaching Milledgeville was seven days. I remained in Atlanta during the 15th with the Fourteenth Corps, and the rear-guard of the right wing, to complete the loading of the trains, and the destruction of the buildings of Atlanta which could be converted to hostile uses, and on the morning of the 16th started with my personal staff, a company of Alabama cavalry, commanded by Lieutenant Snelling, and an infantry company, commanded by Lieutenant McCrory, which guarded our small train of wagons.

My staff was then composed of Major L. M. Dayton, aide-de-camp and acting adjutant-general, Major J. C. McCoy, and Major J. C. Audenried, aides. Major Ward Nichols had joined some weeks before at Gaylesville, Alabama, and was attached as an acting aide-de-camp. Also Major Henry Hitchcock had joined at the same time as judge-advocate. Colonel Charles Ewing was inspector-general, and Surgeon John Moore medical director. These constituted our mess. We had no tents, only the flies, with which we nightly made bivouacs with the assistance of the abundant pine-boughs, which made excellent shelter, as well as beds.

Colonel L. C. Easton was chief-quartermaster; Colonel Amos Beckwith, chief-commissary; Colonel O. M. Poe, chief-engineer; and Colonel T. G. Baylor, chief of ordnance. These invariably rode with us during the day, but they had a separate camp and mess at night.

General William F. Barry had been chief of artillery in the previous campaign, but at Kingston his face was so swollen with erysipelas that he was reluctantly compelled to leave us for the rear, and he could not, on recovering, rejoin us till we had reached Savannah.

About 7 A.M. of November 16th we rode out of Atlanta by the Decatur road, filled by the marching troops and wagons of the Fourteenth Corps; and reaching the hill, just outside of the old rebel works, we naturally paused to look back upon the scenes of our past battles. We stood upon the very ground whereon was fought the bloody battle of July 22d, and could see the copse of wood where McPherson fell. Behind us lay Atlanta, smouldering and in ruins, the black smoke rising high in air, and hanging like a pall over the ruined city. Away off in the distance, on the McDonough road, was the rear of Howard's column, the gun-barrels glistening in the sun, the white-topped wagons stretching away to the south; and right before us the Fourteenth Corps, marching steadily and rapidly, with a cheery look and swinging pace, that made light of the thousand miles that lay between us and Richmond. Some band, by accident, struck up the anthem of "John Brown's soul goes marching on;" the men caught up the strain, and never before or since have I heard the chorus of "Glory, glory, hallelujah!" done with more spirit, or in better harmony of time and place.

Then we turned our horses' heads to the east; Atlanta was soon lost behind the screen of trees, and became a thing of the past. Around it clings many a thought of desperate battle, of hope and fear, that now seem like the memory of a dream; and I have never seen the place since. The day was extremely beautiful, clear sunlight, with bracing air, and an unusual feeling of exhilaration seemed to pervade all minds—a feeling of something to come, vague and undefined, still full of venture and intense interest. Even the common soldiers caught the inspiration, and many a group called out to me as I worked my way past them, "Uncle Billy, I guess Grant is waiting for us at Richmond!" Indeed, the general sentiment was that we were marching for Richmond, and that there we should end the war, but how and when they seemed to care not; nor did they measure the distance, or count the cost in life, or bother their brains about the great rivers to be crossed, and the food required for man and beast, that had to be gathered by the way. There was a "devil-may-care" feeling pervading officers and men, that made me feel the full load of responsibility, for success would be accepted as a matter of course, whereas, should we fail, this "march" would be adjudged the wild adventure of a crazy fool. I had no purpose to march direct for Richmond by way of Augusta and Charlotte, but always designed to reach the sea-coast first at Savannah or Port Royal, South Carolina, and even kept in mind the alternative of Pensacola.

The first night out we camped by the road-side near Lithonia. Stone Mountain, a mass of granite, was in plain view, cut out in clear outline against the blue sky; the whole horizon was lurid with the bonfires of rail-ties, and groups of men all night were carrying the heated rails to the nearest trees, and bending them around the trunks. Colonel Poe had provided tools for ripping up the rails and twisting them when hot; but the best and easiest way is the one I have described, of heating the middle of the iron-rails on bonfires made of the cross-ties, and then winding them around a telegraph-pole or the trunk of some convenient sapling. I attached much importance to this destruction of the railroad, gave it my own personal attention, and made reiterated orders to others on the subject.

The next day we passed through the handsome town of Covington, the soldiers closing up their ranks, the color-bearers unfurling their flags, and the bands striking up patriotic airs. The white people came out of their houses to behold the sight, spite of their deep hatred of the invaders, and the negroes were simply frantic with joy. Whenever they heard my name, they clustered about my horse, shouted and prayed in their peculiar style, which had a natural eloquence that would have moved a stone. I have witnessed hundreds, if not thousands, of such scenes; and can now see a poor girl, in the very ecstasy of the Methodist "shout," hugging the banner of one of the regiments, and jumping up to the "feet of Jesus."

I remember, when riding around by a by-street in Covington, to avoid the crowd that followed the marching column, that some one brought me an invitation to dine with a sister of Sam. Anderson, who was a cadet at West Point with me; but the messenger reached me after we had passed the main part of the town. I asked to be excused, and rode on to a place designated for camp, at the crossing of the Ulcofauhachee River, about four miles to the east of the town. Here we made our bivouac, and I walked up to a plantation-house close by, where were assembled many negroes, among them an old, gray-haired man, of as fine a head as I ever saw. I asked him if he understood about the war and its progress. He said he did; that he had been looking for the "angel of the Lord" ever since he was knee-high, and, though we professed to be fighting for the Union, he supposed that slavery was the cause, and that our success was to be his freedom. I asked him if all the negro slaves comprehended this fact, and he said they surely did. I then explained to him that we wanted the slaves to remain where they were, and not to load us down with useless mouths, which would eat up the food needed for our fighting-men; that our success was their assured freedom; that we could receive a few of their young, hearty men as pioneers; but that, if they followed us in swarms of old and young, feeble and helpless, it would simply load us down and cripple us in our great task. I think Major Henry Hitchcock was with me on that occasion, and made a note of the conversation, and I believe that old man spread this message to the slaves, which was carried from mouth to mouth, to the very end of our journey, and that it in part saved us from the great danger we incurred of swelling our numbers so that famine would have attended our progress. It was at this very plantation that a soldier passed me with a ham on his musket, a jug of sorghum-molasses under his arm, and a big piece of honey in his hand, from which he was eating, and, catching my eye, he remarked *sotto voce* and carelessly to a comrade, "Forage liberally on the country," quoting from my general orders. On this occasion, as on many others that fell under my personal observation, I reproved the man, explained that foraging must be limited to the regular parties properly detailed, and that all provisions thus obtained must be delivered to the regular commissaries, to be fairly distributed to the men who kept their ranks.

From Covington the Fourteenth Corps (Davis's), with which I was traveling, turned to the right for Milledgeville, *via* Shady Dale. General Slocum was ahead at Madison, with the Twentieth Corps, having torn up the railroad as far as that place, and thence had sent Geary's division on to the Oconee, to burn the bridges across that stream, when this corps turned south by Eatonton, for Milledgeville, the common "objective" for the first stage of the "march." We found abundance of corn, molasses, meal, bacon, and sweet-potatoes. We also took a good many cows and oxen, and a large number of mules. In all these the country was quite rich, never before having been visited by a hostile army; the recent crop had been excellent, had been just gathered and laid by for the winter. As a rule, we destroyed none, but kept our wagons full, and fed our teams bountifully.

The skill and success of the men in collecting forage was one of the features of this march. Each brigade commander had authority to detail a company of foragers, usually about fifty men, with one or two commissioned officers selected for their boldness and enterprise. This party would be dispatched before daylight with a knowledge of the intended day's march and camp; would proceed on foot five or six miles from the route traveled by their brigade, and then visit every plantation and farm within range. They would usually procure a wagon or family carriage, load it with bacon, corn-meal, turkeys, chickens, ducks, and every thing that could be used as food or forage, and would then regain the main road, usually in advance of their train. When this came up, they would deliver to the brigade commissary the supplies thus gathered by the way. Often would I pass these foraging-parties at the roadside, waiting for their wagons to come up, and was amused at their strange collections—mules, horses, even cattle, packed with old saddles and loaded with hams, bacon, bags of corn-meal, and poultry of every character and description. Although this foraging was attended with great danger and hard work, there seemed to be a charm about it that attracted the soldiers, and it was a privilege to be detailed on such a party. Daily they returned mounted on all sorts of beasts, which were at once taken from them and appropriated to the general use; but the next day they would start out again on foot, only to repeat the experience of the day before. No doubt, many acts of pillage, robbery, and violence, were committed by these parties of foragers, usually called "bummers;" for I have since heard of jewelry taken from women, and the plunder of articles that never reached the commissary; but these acts were exceptional and incidental. I never heard of any cases of murder or rape; and no army could have carried along sufficient food and forage for a march of three hundred miles; so that foraging in some shape was necessary. The country was sparsely settled, with no magistrates or civil authorities who could respond to requisitions, as is done in all the wars of Europe; so that this system of foraging was simply indispensable to our success. By it our men were well supplied with all the essentials of life and health, while the wagons retained enough in case of unexpected delay, and our animals were well fed. Indeed, when we reached Savannah, the trains were pronounced by experts to be the finest in flesh and appearance ever seen with any army.

Habitually each corps followed some main road, and the foragers, being kept out on the exposed flank, served all the military uses of flankers. The main columns gathered, by the roads traveled, much forage and food, chiefly meat, corn, and sweet-potatoes, and it was the duty of each division and brigade quartermaster to fill his wagons as fast as the contents were issued to the troops. The wagon-trains had the right to the road *always*, but each wagon was required to keep closed up, so as to leave no gaps in the column. If for any purpose any wagon or group of wagons dropped out of place, they had to wait for the rear. And this was always dreaded, for each brigade commander wanted his train up at camp as soon after reaching it with his men as possible.

I have seen much skill and industry displayed by these quartermasters on the march, in trying to load their wagons with corn and fodder by the way without losing their place in column. They would, while marching, shift the loads of wagons, so as to have six or ten of them empty. Then, riding well ahead, they would secure possession of certain stacks of fodder near the road, or cribs of corn, leave some men in charge, then open fences and a road back for a couple of miles, return to their trains, divert the empty wagons out of column, and conduct them rapidly to their forage, load up and regain their place in column without losing distance. On one occasion I remember to have seen ten or a dozen wagons thus loaded with corn from two or three full cribs, almost without halting. These cribs were built of logs, and roofed. The train-guard, by a lever, had raised the whole side of the crib a foot or two; the wagons drove close alongside, and the men in the cribs, lying on their backs, kicked out a wagon-load of corn in the time I have taken to describe it.

In a well-ordered and well-disciplined army, these things might be deemed irregular, but I am convinced that the ingenuity of these younger officers accomplished many things far better than I could have ordered, and the marches were thus made, and the distances were accomplished, in the most admirable way. Habitually we started from camp at the earliest break of dawn, and usually reached camp soon after noon. The marches varied from ten to fifteen miles a day, though sometimes on extreme flanks it was necessary to make as much as twenty, but the rate of travel was regulated by the wagons; and, considering the nature of the roads, fifteen miles per day was deemed the limit.

The pontoon-trains were in like manner distributed in about equal proportions to the four corps, giving each a section of about nine hundred feet. The pontoons were of the skeleton pattern, with cotton-canvas covers, each boat, with its proportion of balks and chesses, constituting a load for one wagon. By uniting two such sections together, we could make a bridge of eighteen hundred feet, enough for any river we had to traverse; but habitually the leading brigade would, out of the abundant timber, improvise a bridge before the pontoon-train could come up, unless in the cases of rivers of considerable magnitude, such as the Ocmulgee, Oconee, Ogeechee, Savannah, etc.

On the 20th of November I was still with the Fourteenth Corps, near Eatonton Factory, waiting to hear of the Twentieth Corps; and on the 21st we camped near the house of a man named Vann; the next day, about 4 P.M., General Davis had halted his head of column on a wooded ridge, overlooking an extensive slope of cultivated country, about ten miles short of Milledgeville, and was deploying his troops for camp when I got up. There was a high, raw wind blowing, and I asked him why he had chosen so cold and bleak a position. He explained that he had accomplished his full distance for the day, and had there an abundance of wood and water. He explained further that his advance-guard was a mile or so ahead; so I rode on, asking him to let his rear division, as it came up, move some distance ahead into the depression or valley beyond. Riding on some distance to the border of a plantation, I turned out of the main road into a cluster of wild-plum bushes, that broke the force of the cold November wind, dismounted, and instructed the staff to pick out the place for our camp.

The afternoon was unusually raw and cold. My orderly was at hand with his invariable saddle-bags, which contained a change of under-clothing, my maps, a flask of whiskey, and bunch of cigars. Taking a drink and lighting a cigar, I walked to a row of negro-huts close by, entered one and found a soldier or two warming themselves by a wood-fire. I took their place by the fire, intending to wait there till our wagons had got up, and a camp made for the night. I was talking to the old negro woman, when some one came and explained to me that, if I would come farther down the road, I could find a better place. So I started on foot, and found on the main road a good double-hewed-log house, in one room of which

Colonel Poe, Dr. Moore, and others, had started a fire. I sent back orders to the "plum-bushes" to bring our horses and saddles up to this house, and an orderly to conduct our head-quarter wagons to the same place. In looking around the room, I saw a small box, like a candle-box, marked "Howell Cobb," and, on inquiring of a negro, found that we were at the plantation of General Howell Cobb, of Georgia, one of the leading rebels of the South, then a general in the South-ern army, and who had been Secretary of the United States Treasury in Mr. Buchanan's time. Of course, we confiscated his property, and found it rich in corn, beans, pea-nuts, and sorghum-molasses. Extensive fields were all round the house; I sent word back to General Davis to explain whose planta-tion it was, and instructed him to spare nothing. That night huge bonfires consumed the fence-rails, kept our soldiers warm, and the teamsters and men, as well as the slaves, car-ried off an immense quantity of corn and provisions of all sorts.

In due season the headquarter wagons came up, and we got supper. After supper I sat on a chair astride, with my back to a good fire, musing, and became conscious that an old negro, with a tallow-candle in his hand, was scanning my face closely. I inquired, "What do you want, old man?" He an-swered, "Dey say you is Massa Sherman." I answered that such was the case, and inquired what he wanted. He only wanted to look at me, and kept muttering, "Dis nigger can't sleep dis night." I asked him why he trembled so, and he said that he wanted to be sure that we were in fact "Yankees," for on a former occasion some rebel cavalry had put on light-blue overcoats, personating Yankee troops, and many of the ne-groes were deceived thereby, himself among the number— had shown them sympathy, and had in consequence been unmercifully beaten therefor. This time he wanted to be cer-tain before committing himself; so I told him to go out on the porch, from which he could see the whole horizon lit up with camp-fires, and he could then judge whether he had ever seen any thing like it before. The old man became convinced that the "Yankees" had come at last, about whom he had been dreaming all his life; and some of the staff-officers gave him a strong drink of whiskey, which set his tongue going. Lieu-tenant Snelling, who commanded my escort, was a Georgian, and recognized in this old negro a favorite slave of his uncle, who resided about six miles off; but the old slave did not at first recognize his young master in our uniform. One of my staff-officers asked him what had become of his young master, George. He did not know, only that he had gone off to the war, and he supposed him killed, as a matter of course. His attention was then drawn to Snelling's face, when he fell on his knees and thanked God that he had found his young master alive and along with the Yankees. Snelling inquired all about his uncle and the family, asked my permission to go and pay his uncle a visit, which I granted, of course, and the next morning he described to me his visit. The uncle was not cordial, by any means, to find his nephew in the ranks of the host that was desolating the land, and Snelling came back, having exchanged his tired horse for a fresher one out of his uncle's stables, explaining that surely some of the "bummers" would have got the horse had he not.

The next morning, November 23d, we rode into Milledgeville, the capital of the State, whither the Twentieth Corps had preceded us; and during that day the left wing was all united, in and around Milledgeville. From the inhabitants we learned that some of Kilpatrick's cavalry had preceded us by a couple of days, and that all of the right wing was at and near Gordon, twelve miles off, viz., the place where the branch railroad came to Milledgeville from the Macon & Savannah road. The first stage of the journey was, therefore, complete, and absolutely successful.

General Howard soon reported by letter the operations of his right wing, which, on leaving Atlanta, had substantially followed the two roads toward Macon, by Jonesboro' and McDonough, and reached the Ocmulgee at Planters' Factory, which they crossed, by the aid of the pontoon-train, during the 18th and 19th of November. Thence, with the Seventeenth Corps (General Blair's) he (General Howard) had marched *via* Monticello toward Gordon, having dispatched Kilpatrick's cavalry, supported by the Fifteenth Corps (Osterhaus's), to feign on Macon. Kilpatrick met the enemy's cavalry about four miles out of Macon, and drove them rapidly back into the bridge-defenses held by infantry. Kilpatrick charged these, got inside the parapet, but could not hold it, and retired to his infantry supports, near Griswold Station. The Fifteenth Corps tore up the railroad-track eastward from Griswold, leaving Charles R. Wood's division behind as a rear-guard—one brigade of which was intrenched across the road, with some of Kilpatrick's cavalry on the flanks. On the 22d of November General G. W. Smith, with a division of troops, came out of Macon, attacked this brigade (Walcutt's) in position, and was handsomely repulsed and driven back into Macon. This brigade was in part armed with Spencer repeating-rifles, and its fire was so rapid that General Smith insists to this day that he encountered a whole division; but he is mistaken; he was beaten by one brigade (Walcutt's), and made no further effort to molest our operations from that direction. General Walcutt was wounded in the leg, and had to ride the rest of the distance to Savannah in a carriage.

Therefore, by the 23d, I was in Milledgeville with the left wing, and was in full communication with the right wing at Gordon. The people of Milledgeville remained at home, except the Governor (Brown), the State officers, and Legislature, who had ignominiously fled, in the utmost disorder and confusion; standing not on the order of their going, but going at once—some by rail, some by carriages, and many on foot. Some of the citizens who remained behind described this flight of the "brave and patriotic" Governor Brown. He had occupied a public building known as the "Governor's Mansion," and had hastily stripped it of carpets, curtains, and furniture of all sorts, which were removed to a train of freight-cars, which carried away these things—even the cabbages and vegetables from his kitchen and cellar—leaving behind muskets, ammunition, and the public archives. On arrival at Milledgeville I occupied the same public mansion, and was soon overwhelmed with appeals for protection. General Slocum had previously arrived with the Twentieth Corps, had taken up his quarters at the Milledgeville Hotel, established a good provost-guard, and excellent order was maintained. The most frantic appeals had been made by the Governor and Legislature for help from every quarter, and the people of the State had been called out *en masse* to resist and destroy the invaders of their homes and firesides. Even the prisoners and convicts of the penitentiary were released on condition of serving as soldiers, and the cadets were taken from their military college for the same purpose. These constituted a small battalion, under General Harry Wayne, a former officer of the United States Army, and son of the then Justice Wayne of the Supreme Court. But these hastily retreated east across the Oconee River, leaving us a good bridge, which we promptly secured.

At Milledgeville we found newspapers from all the South, and learned the consternation which had filled the Southern mind at our temerity; many charging that we were actually fleeing for our lives and seeking safety at the hands of our fleet on the sea-coast. All demanded that we should be assailed, "front, flank, and rear;" that provisions should be destroyed in advance, so that we would starve; that bridges should be burned, roads obstructed, and no mercy shown us. Judging from the tone of the Southern press of that day, the outside world must have supposed us ruined and lost. I give a few of these appeals as samples, which to-day must sound strange to the parties who made them:

CORINTH, MISSISSIPPI, *November* 18, 1864.
To the People of Georgia:
Arise for the defense of your native soil! Rally around your patriotic Governor and gallant soldiers! Obstruct and destroy all the roads in Sherman's front, flank, and rear, and his army will soon starve in your midst. Be confident. Be resolute. Trust in an overruling Providence, and success will soon crown your efforts. I hasten to join you in the defense of your homes and firesides.

G. T. BEAUREGARD.

RICHMOND, *November* 18, 1864.
To the People of Georgia:
You have now the best opportunity ever yet presented to destroy the enemy. Put every thing at the disposal of our generals; remove all provisions from the path of the invader, and put all obstructions in his path.

Every citizen with his gun, and every negro with his spade and axe, can do the work of a soldier. You can destroy the enemy by retarding his march.

Georgians, be firm! Act promptly, and fear not!

B. H. HILL, *Senator.*

I most cordially approve the above.

JAMES A. SEDDON, *Secretary of War.*

RICHMOND, *November* 19, 1864.

To the People of Georgia:

We have had a special conference with President Davis and the Secretary of War, and are able to assure you that they have done and are still doing all that can be done to meet the emergency that presses upon you. Let every man fly to arms! Remove your negroes, horses, cattle, and provisions from Sherman's army, and burn what you cannot carry. Burn all bridges, and block up the roads in his route. Assail the invader in front, flank, and rear, by night and by day. Let him have no rest.

JULIAN HARTRIDGE,	MARK BLANDFORD,
J. H. ECHOLS,	GEO. N. LESTER,
JOHN T. SHUEMAKE,	JAS. M. SMITH,
	Members of Congress.

Of course, we were rather amused than alarmed at these threats, and made light of the feeble opposition offered to our progress. Some of the officers (in the spirit of mischief) gathered together in the vacant hall of Representatives, elected a Speaker, and constituted themselves the Legislature of the State of Georgia! A proposition was made to repeal the ordinance of secession, which was well debated, and resulted in its repeal by a fair vote! I was not present at these frolics, but heard of them at the time, and enjoyed the joke.

Meantime orders were made for the total destruction of the arsenal and its contents, and of such public buildings as could be easily converted to hostile uses. But little or no damage was done to private property, and General Slocum, with my approval, spared several mills, and many thousands of bales of cotton, taking what he knew to be worthless bonds, that the cotton should not be used for the Confederacy. Meantime the right wing continued its movement along the railroad toward Savannah, tearing up the track and destroying its iron. At the Oconee was met a feeble resistance from Harry Wayne's troops, but soon the pontoon-bridge was laid, and that wing crossed over. Kilpatrick's cavalry was brought into Milledgeville, and crossed the Oconee by the bridge near the town; and on the 23d I made the general orders for the next stage of the march as far as Millen. These were, substantially, for the right wing to follow the Savannah Railroad, by roads on its south; the left wing was to move to Sandersville, by Davisboro' and Louisville, while the cavalry was ordered by a circuit to the north, and to march rapidly for Millen, to rescue our prisoners of war confined there. The distance was about a hundred miles.

General Wheeler, with his division of rebel cavalry, had succeeded in getting ahead of us between Milledgeville and Augusta; and General W. J. Hardee had been dispatched by General Beauregard from Hood's army to oppose our progress directly in front. He had, however, brought with him no troops, but relied on his influence with the Georgians (of whose State he was a native) to arouse the people, and with them to annihilate Sherman's army!

On the 24th we renewed the march, and I accompanied the Twentieth Corps, which took the direct road to Sandersville, which we reached simultaneously with the Fourteenth Corps, on the 26th. A brigade of rebel cavalry was deployed before the town, and was driven in and through it by our skirmish-line. I myself saw the rebel cavalry apply fire to stacks of fodder standing in the fields at Sandersville, and gave orders to burn some unoccupied dwellings close by. On entering the town, I told certain citizens (who would be sure to spread the report) that, if the enemy attempted to carry out their threat to burn their food, corn, and fodder, in our route, I would most undoubtedly execute to the letter the general orders of devastation made at the outset of the campaign. With this exception, and one or two minor cases near Savannah, the people did not destroy food, for they saw clearly that it would be ruin to themselves.

At Sandersville I halted the left wing until I heard that the right wing was abreast of us on the railroad. During the evening a negro was brought to me, who had that day been to the station (Tenille), about six miles south of the town. I inquired of him if there were any Yankees there, and he answered, "Yes." He described in his own way what he had seen. "First, there come along some cavalry-men, and they burned the depot; then come along some infantry-men, and they tore up the track, and burned it;" and just before he left they had "sot fire to the well!"

The next morning, viz., the 27th, I rode down to the station, and found General Corse's division (of the Fifteenth Corps) engaged in destroying the railroad, and saw the well which my negro informant had seen "burnt." It was a square pit about twenty-five feet deep, boarded up, with wooden steps leading to the bottom, wherein was a fine copper pump, to lift the water to a tank above. The soldiers had broken up the pump, heaved in the steps and lining, and set fire to the mass of lumber in the bottom of the well, which corroborated the negro's description.

From this point Blair's corps, the Seventeenth, took up the work of destroying the railroad, the Fifteenth Corps following another road leading eastward, farther to the south of the railroad. While the left wing was marching toward Louisville, north of the railroad, General Kilpatrick had, with his cavalry division, moved rapidly toward Waynesboro', on the branch railroad leading from Millen to Augusta. He found Wheeler's division of rebel cavalry there, and had considerable skirmishing with it; but, learning that our prisoners had been removed two days before from Millen, he returned to Louisville on the 29th, where he found the left wing. Here he remained a couple of days to rest his horses, and, receiving orders from me to engage Wheeler and give him all the fighting he wanted, he procured from General Slocum the assistance of the infantry division of General Baird, and moved back for Waynesboro' on the 2d of December, the remainder of the left wing continuing its march on toward Millen. Near Waynesboro' Wheeler was again encountered, and driven through the town and beyond Brier Creek, toward Augusta, thus keeping up the delusion that the main army was moving toward Augusta. General Kilpatrick's fighting and movements about Waynesboro' and Brier Creek were spirited, and produced a good effect by relieving the infantry column and the wagon-trains of all molestation during their march on Millen. Having thus covered that flank, he turned south and followed the movement of the Fourteenth Corps to Buckhead Church, north of Millen and near it.

On the 3d of December I entered Millen with the Seven-

teenth Corps (General Frank P. Blair), and there paused one
day, to communicate with all parts of the army. General
Howard was south of the Ogeechee River, with the Fifteenth
Corps, opposite Scarboro'. General Slocum was at Buckhead
Church, four miles north of Millen, with the Twentieth
Corps. The Fourteenth (General Davis) was at Lumpkin's
Station, on the Augusta road, about ten miles north of
Millen, and the cavalry division was within easy support of
this wing. Thus the whole army was in good position and in
good condition. We had largely subsisted on the country; our
wagons were full of forage and provisions; but, as we approached the sea-coast, the country became more sandy and
barren, and food became more scarce; still, with little or no
loss, we had traveled two-thirds of our distance, and I concluded to push on for Savannah. At Millen I learned that
General Bragg was in Augusta, and that General Wade
Hampton had been ordered there from Richmond, to organize a large cavalry force with which to resist our progress.

General Hardee was ahead, between us and Savannah, with
McLaw's division, and other irregular troops, that could not,
I felt assured, exceed ten thousand men. I caused the fine depot at Millen to be destroyed, and other damage done, and
then resumed the march directly on Savannah, by the four
main roads. The Seventeenth Corps (General Blair) followed
substantially the railroad, and, along with it, on the 5th of
December, I reached Ogeechee Church, about fifty miles
from Savannah, and found there fresh earthworks, which had
been thrown up by McLaw's division; but he must have seen
that both his flanks were being turned, and prudently retreated to Savannah without a fight. All the columns then
pursued leisurely their march toward Savannah, corn and forage becoming more and more scarce, but rice-fields beginning
to occur along the Savannah and Ogeechee Rivers, which
proved a good substitute, both as food and forage. The
weather was fine, the roads good, and every thing seemed to
favor us. Never do I recall a more agreeable sensation than
the sight of our camps by night, lit up by the fires of fragrant
pine-knots. The trains were all in good order, and the men
seemed to march their fifteen miles a day as though it were
nothing. No enemy opposed us, and we could only occasion-

ally hear the faint reverberation of a gun to our left rear, where we knew that General Kilpatrick was skirmishing with Wheeler's cavalry, which persistently followed him. But the infantry columns had met with no opposition whatsoever. McLaw's division was falling back before us, and we occasionally picked up a few of his men as prisoners, who insisted that we would meet with strong opposition at Savannah.

On the 8th, as I rode along, I found the column turned out of the main road, marching through the fields. Close by, in the corner of a fence, was a group of men standing around a handsome young officer, whose foot had been blown to pieces by a torpedo planted in the road. He was waiting for a surgeon to amputate his leg, and told me that he was riding along with the rest of his brigade-staff of the Seventeenth Corps, when a torpedo trodden on by his horse had exploded, killing the horse and literally blowing off all the flesh from one of his legs. I saw the terrible wound, and made full inquiry into the facts. There had been no resistance at that point, nothing to give warning of danger, and the rebels had planted eight-inch shells in the road, with friction-matches to explode them by being trodden on. This was not war, but murder, and it made me very angry. I immediately ordered a lot of rebel prisoners to be brought from the provost-guard, armed with picks and spades, and made them march in close order along the road, so as to explode their own torpedoes, or to discover and dig them up. They begged hard, but I reiterated the order, and could hardly help laughing at their stepping so gingerly along the road, where it was supposed sunken torpedoes might explode at each step, but they found no other torpedoes till near Fort McAllister. That night we reached Pooler's Station, eight miles from Savannah, and during the next two days, December 9th and 10th, the several corps reached the defenses of Savannah—the Fourteenth Corps on the left, touching the river; the Twentieth Corps next; then the Seventeenth; and the Fifteenth on the extreme right; thus completely investing the city. Wishing to reconnoitre the place in person, I rode forward by the Louisville road, into a dense wood of oak, pine, and cypress, left the horses, and walked down to the railroad-track, at a place where there was a side-track, and a cut about four feet deep.

From that point the railroad was straight, leading into Savannah, and about eight hundred yards off were a rebel parapet and battery. I could see the cannoneers preparing to fire, and cautioned the officers near me to scatter, as we would likely attract a shot. Very soon I saw the white puff of smoke, and, watching close, caught sight of the ball as it rose in its flight, and, finding it coming pretty straight, I stepped a short distance to one side, but noticed a negro very near me in the act of crossing the track at right angles. Some one called to him to look out; but, before the poor fellow understood his danger, the ball (a thirty-two-pound round shot) struck the ground, and rose in its first ricochet, caught the negro under the right jaw, and literally carried away his head, scattering blood and brains about. A soldier close by spread an overcoat over the body, and we all concluded to get out of that railroad-cut. Meantime, General Mower's division of the Seventeenth Corps had crossed the canal to the right of the Louisville road, and had found the line of parapet continuous; so at Savannah we had again run up against the old familiar parapet, with its deep ditches, canals, and bayous, full of water; and it looked as though another siege was inevitable. I accordingly made a camp or bivouac near the Louisville road, about five miles from Savannah, and proceeded to invest the place closely, pushing forward reconnoissances at every available point.

As soon as it was demonstrated that Savannah was well fortified, with a good garrison, commanded by General William J. Hardee, a competent soldier, I saw that the first step was to open communication with our fleet, supposed to be waiting for us with supplies and clothing in Ossabaw Sound.

General Howard had, some nights previously, sent one of his best scouts, Captain Duncan, with two men, in a canoe, to drift past Fort McAllister, and to convey to the fleet a knowledge of our approach. General Kilpatrick's cavalry had also been transferred to the south bank of the Ogeechee, with orders to open communication with the fleet. Leaving orders with General Slocum to press the siege, I instructed General Howard to send a division with all his engineers to King's Bridge, fourteen and a half miles southwest from Savannah, to rebuild it. On the evening of the 12th I rode over myself, and spent the night at Mr. King's house, where I found General Howard, with General Hazen's division of the Fifteenth Corps. His engineers were hard at work on the bridge, which they finished that night, and at sunrise Hazen's division passed over. I gave General Hazen, in person, his orders to march rapidly down the right bank of the Ogeechee, and without hesitation to assault and carry Fort McAllister by storm. I knew it to be strong in heavy artillery, as against an approach from the sea, but believed it open and weak to the rear. I explained to General Hazen, fully, that on his action depended the safety of the whole army, and the success of the campaign. Kilpatrick had already felt the fort, and had gone farther down the coast to Kilkenny Bluff, or St. Catharine's Sound, where, on the same day, he had communication with a vessel belonging to the blockading fleet; but, at the time, I was not aware of this fact, and trusted entirely to General Hazen and his division of infantry, the Second of the Fifteenth Corps, the same old division which I had commanded at Shiloh and Vicksburg, in which I felt a special pride and confidence.

Having seen General Hazen fairly off, accompanied by General Howard, I rode with my staff down the left bank of the Ogeechee, ten miles to the rice-plantation of a Mr. Cheeves, where General Howard had established a signal-station to overlook the lower river, and to watch for any vessel of the blockading squadron, which the negroes reported to be expecting us, because they nightly sent up rockets, and daily dispatched a steamboat up the Ogeechee as near to Fort McAllister as it was safe.

On reaching the rice-mill at Cheeves's, I found a guard and a couple of twenty-pound Parrott guns, of De Gres's battery, which fired an occasional shot toward Fort McAllister, plainly seen over the salt-marsh, about three miles distant. Fort McAllister had the rebel flag flying, and occasionally sent a heavy shot back across the marsh to where we were, but otherwise every thing about the place looked as peaceable and quiet as on the Sabbath.

The signal-officer had built a platform on the ridge-pole of the rice-mill. Leaving our horses behind the stacks of rice-straw, we all got on the roof of a shed attached to the mill, wherefrom I could communicate with the signal-officer above, and at the same time look out toward Ossabaw Sound, and across the Ogeechee River at Fort McAllister. About 2 P.M. we observed signs of commotion in the fort, and noticed one or two guns fired inland, and some musket-skirmishing in the woods close by.

This betokened the approach of Hazen's division, which had been anxiously expected, and soon thereafter the signal-officer discovered about three miles above the fort a signal-flag, with which he conversed, and found it to belong to General Hazen, who was preparing to assault the fort, and wanted to know if I were there. On being assured of this fact, and that I expected the fort to be carried before night, I received by signal the assurance of General Hazen that he was making his preparations, and would soon attempt the assault. The sun was rapidly declining, and I was dreadfully impatient. At that very moment some one discovered a faint cloud of smoke, and an object gliding, as it were, along the horizon above the tops of the sedge toward the sea, which little by little grew till it was pronounced to be the smoke-stack of a steamer coming up the river. "It must be one of our squadron!" Soon the flag of the United States was plainly visible, and our attention was divided between this approaching steamer and the expected assault. When the sun was about an hour high, another signal-message came from General Hazen that he was all ready, and I replied to go ahead, as a friendly steamer was approaching from below. Soon we made out a group of officers on the deck of this vessel, signaling with a flag, "Who are you?" The answer went back promptly, "General Sherman." Then followed the question, "Is Fort McAllister taken?" "Not yet, but it will be in a minute!" Almost at that instant of time, we saw Hazen's troops come out of the dark fringe of woods that encompassed the fort, the lines dressed as on parade, with colors flying, and moving forward with a quick, steady pace. Fort McAllister was then all alive, its big guns belching forth dense clouds of smoke, which soon enveloped our assaulting lines. One color went down, but was up in a moment. On the lines advanced, faintly seen in the white, sulphurous smoke; there was a pause, a cessation of fire; the smoke cleared away, and the parapets were blue with our men, who fired their muskets in the air, and shouted so that we actually heard them, or felt that we did. Fort McAllister was taken, and the good news was instantly sent by the signal-officer to our navy friends on the approaching gunboat, for a point of timber had shut out Fort McAllister from their view, and they had not seen the action at all, but must have heard the cannonading.

During the progress of the assault, our little group on Cheeves's mill hardly breathed; but no sooner did we see our flags on the parapet than I exclaimed, in the language of the poor negro at Cobb's plantation, "This nigger will have no sleep this night!"

I was resolved to communicate with our fleet that night, which happened to be a beautiful moonlight one. At the wharf belonging to Cheeves's mill was a small skiff, that had been used by our men in fishing or in gathering oysters. I was there in a minute, called for a volunteer crew, when several young officers, Nichols and Merritt among the number, said they were good oarsmen, and volunteered to pull the boat down to Fort McAllister. General Howard asked to accompany me; so we took seats in the stern of the boat, and our crew of officers pulled out with a will. The tide was setting in strong, and they had a hard pull, for, though the distance was but three miles in an air-line, the river was so crooked that the actual distance was fully six miles. On the way down we passed the wreck of a steamer which had been sunk some years before, during a naval attack on Fort McAllister.

Night had fairly set in when we discovered a soldier on the beach. I hailed him, and inquired if he knew where General Hazen was. He answered that the general was at the house of the overseer of the plantation (McAllister's), and that he could guide me to it. We accordingly landed, tied our boat to a drift-log, and followed our guide through bushes to a frame-house, standing in a grove of live-oaks, near a row of negro quarters. General Hazen was there with his staff, in the act of getting supper; he invited us to join them, which we accepted promptly, for we were really very hungry. Of course, I congratulated Hazen most heartily on his brilliant success, and praised its execution very highly, as it deserved, and he explained to me more in detail the exact results. The fort was an inclosed work, and its land-front was in the nature of a bastion and curtains, with good parapet, ditch, *fraise*, and *chevaux-de-frise*, made out of the large branches of live-oaks. Luckily, the rebels had left the larger and unwieldy trunks on the ground, which served as a good cover for the skirmish-line, which crept behind these logs, and from them kept the artillerists from loading and firing their guns accurately.

The assault had been made by three parties in line, one from below, one from above the fort, and the third directly in rear, along the capital. All were simultaneous, and had to pass a good abatis and line of torpedoes, which actually killed more of the assailants than the heavy guns of the fort, which generally overshot the mark. Hazen's entire loss was reported, killed and wounded, ninety-two. Each party reached the parapet about the same time, and the garrison inside, of about two hundred and fifty men (about fifty of them killed or wounded), were in his power. The commanding officer, Major Anderson, was at that moment a prisoner, and General Hazen invited him in to take supper with us, which he did.

Up to this time General Hazen did not know that a gun-boat was in the river below the fort; for it was shut off from sight by a point of timber, and I was determined to board her that night, at whatever risk or cost, as I wanted some news of what was going on in the outer world. Accordingly, after supper, we all walked down to the fort, nearly a mile from the house where we had been, entered Fort McAllister, held by a regiment of Hazen's troops, and the sentinel cautioned us to be very careful, as the ground outside the fort was full of torpedoes. Indeed, while we were there, a torpedo exploded, tearing to pieces a poor fellow who was hunting for a dead comrade. Inside the fort lay the dead as they had fallen, and they could hardly be distinguished from their living comrades, sleeping soundly side by side in the pale moonlight. In the river, close by the fort, was a good yawl tied to a stake, but the tide was high, and it required some time to get it in to the bank; the commanding officer, whose name I cannot recall, manned the boat with a good crew of his men, and, with

General Howard, I entered, and pulled down-stream, regardless of the warnings of all about the torpedoes.

The night was unusually bright, and we expected to find the gunboat within a mile or so; but, after pulling down the river fully three miles, and not seeing the gunboat, I began to think she had turned and gone back to the sound; but we kept on, following the bends of the river, and about six miles below McAllister we saw her light, and soon were hailed by the vessel at anchor. Pulling alongside, we announced ourselves, and were received with great warmth and enthusiasm on deck by half a dozen naval officers, among them Captain Williamson, United States Navy. She proved to be the Dandelion, a tender of the regular gunboat Flag, posted at the mouth of the Ogeechee. All sorts of questions were made and answered, and we learned that Captain Duncan had safely reached the squadron, had communicated the good news of our approach, and they had been expecting us for some days. They explained that Admiral Dahlgren commanded the South-Atlantic Squadron, which was then engaged in blockading the coast from Charleston south, and was on his flagship, the Harvest Moon, lying in Wassaw Sound; that General J. G. Foster was in command of the Department of the South, with his headquarters at Hilton Head; and that several ships loaded with stores for the army were lying in Tybee Roads and in Port Royal Sound. From these officers I also learned that General Grant was still besieging Petersburg and Richmond, and that matters and things generally remained pretty much the same as when we had left Atlanta. All thoughts seemed to have been turned to us in Georgia, cut off from all communication with our friends; and the rebel papers had reported us to be harassed, defeated, starving, and fleeing for safety to the coast. I then asked for pen and paper, and wrote several hasty notes to General Foster, Admiral Dahlgren, General Grant, and the Secretary of War, giving in general terms the actual state of affairs, the fact of the capture of Fort McAllister, and of my desire that means should be taken to establish a line of supply from the vessels in port up the Ogeechee to the rear of the army. As a sample, I give one of these notes, addressed to the Secretary of War, intended for publication to relieve the anxiety of our friends at the North generally:

ON BOARD DANDELION, OSSABAW SOUND, ⎫
December 13, 1864 — 11.50 P.M.⎭

To Hon. E. M. STANTON, *Secretary of War, Washington, D. C.:*

To-day, at 5 P.M., General Hazen's division of the Fifteenth Corps carried Fort McAllister by assault, capturing its entire garrison and stores. This opened to us Ossabaw Sound, and I pushed down to this gunboat to communicate with the fleet. Before opening communication we had completely destroyed all the railroads leading into Savannah, and invested the city. The left of the army is on the Savannah River three miles above the city, and the right on the Ogeechee, at King's Bridge. The army is in splendid order, and equal to any thing. The weather has been fine, and supplies were abundant. Our march was most agreeable, and we were not at all molested by guerrillas.

We reached Savannah three days ago, but, owing to Fort McAllister, could not communicate; but, now that we have McAllister, we can go ahead.

We have already captured two boats on the Savannah River, and prevented their gunboats from coming down.

I estimate the population of Savannah at twenty-five thousand, and the garrison at fifteen thousand. General Hardee commands.

We have not lost a wagon on the trip; but have gathered a large supply of negroes, mules, horses, etc., and our teams are in far better condition than when we started.

My first duty will be to clear the army of surplus negroes, mules, and horses. We have utterly destroyed over two hundred miles of rails, and consumed stores and provisions that were essential to Lee's and Hood's armies.

The quick work made with McAllister, the opening of communication with our fleet, and our consequent independence as to supplies, dissipate all their boasted threats to head us off and starve the army.

I regard Savannah as already *gained*. Yours truly,

W. T. SHERMAN, *Major-General.*

By this time the night was well advanced, and the tide was running ebb-strong; so I asked Captain Williamson to tow us up as near Fort McAllister as he would venture for the torpedoes, of which the navy-officers had a wholesome dread. The

Dandelion steamed up some three or four miles, till the lights of Fort McAllister could be seen, when she anchored, and we pulled to the fort in our own boat. General Howard and I then walked up to the McAllister House, where we found General Hazen and his officers asleep on the floor of one of the rooms. Lying down on the floor, I was soon fast asleep, but shortly became conscious that some one in the room was inquiring for me among the sleepers. Calling out, I was told that an officer of General Foster's staff had just arrived from a steamboat anchored below McAllister; that the general was extremely anxious to see me on important business, but that he was lame from an old Mexican-War wound, and could not possibly come to me. I was extremely weary from the incessant labor of the day and night before, but got up, and again walked down the sandy road to McAllister, where I found a boat awaiting us, which carried us some three miles down the river, to the steamer W. W. Coit (I think), on board of which we found General Foster. He had just come from Port Royal, expecting to find Admiral Dahlgren in Ossabaw Sound, and, hearing of the capture of Fort McAllister, he had come up to see me. He described fully the condition of affairs with his own command in South Carolina. He had made several serious efforts to effect a lodgment on the railroad which connects Savannah with Charleston near Pocotaligo, but had not succeeded in reaching the railroad itself, though he had a full division of troops, strongly intrenched, near Broad River, within cannon-range of the railroad. He explained, moreover, that there were at Port Royal abundant supplies of bread and provisions, as well as of clothing, designed for our use. We still had in our wagons and in camp abundance of meat, but we needed bread, sugar, and coffee, and it was all-important that a route of supply should at once be opened, for which purpose the aid and assistance of the navy were indispensable. We accordingly steamed down the Ogeechee River to Ossabaw Sound, in hopes to meet Admiral Dahlgren, but he was not there, and we continued on by the inland channel to Wassaw Sound, where we found the Harvest Moon, and Admiral Dahlgren. I was not personally acquainted with him at the time, but he was so extremely kind and courteous that I was at once attracted to him. There was nothing in his power, he said, which he would not do to assist us, to make our campaign absolutely successful. He undertook at once to find vessels of light draught to carry our supplies from Port Royal to Cheeves's Mill, or to King's Bridge above, whence they could be hauled by wagons to our several camps; he offered to return with me to Fort McAllister, to superintend the removal of the torpedoes, and to relieve me of all the details of this most difficult work. General Foster then concluded to go on to Port Royal, to send back to us six hundred thousand rations, and all the rifled guns of heavy calibre, and ammunition on hand, with which I thought we could reach the city of Savannah, from the positions already secured. Admiral Dahlgren then returned with me in the Harvest Moon to Fort McAllister. This consumed all of the 14th of December; and by the 15th I had again reached Cheeves's Mill, where my horse awaited me, and rode on to General Howard's headquarters at Anderson's plantation, on the plank-road, about eight miles back of Savannah. I reached this place about noon, and immediately sent orders to my own headquarters, on the Louisville road, to have them brought over to the plank-road, as a place more central and convenient; gave written notice to Generals Slocum and Howard of all the steps taken, and ordered them to get ready to receive the siege-guns, to put them in position to bombard Savannah, and to prepare for the general assault. The country back of Savannah is very low, and intersected with innumerable salt-water creeks, swamps, and rice-fields. Fortunately the weather was good and the roads were passable, but, should the winter rains set in, I knew that we would be much embarrassed. Therefore, heavy details of men were at once put to work to prepare a wharf and depot at King's Bridge, and the roads leading thereto were corduroyed in advance. The Ogeechee Canal was also cleared out for use; and boats, such as were common on the river plantations, were collected, in which to float stores from our proposed base on the Ogeechee to the points most convenient to the several camps.

Slocum's wing extended from the Savannah River to the canal, and Howard's wing from the canal to the extreme right, along down the Little Ogeechee. The enemy occupied not only the city itself, with its long line of outer works, but the many forts which had been built to guard the approaches from the sea—such as at Beaulieu, Rosedew, White Bluff, Bonaventura, Thunderbolt, Cansten's Bluff, Forts Tatnall, Boggs, etc., etc. I knew that General Hardee could not have a garrison strong enough for all these purposes, and I was therefore anxious to break his lines before he could receive reënforcements from Virginia or Augusta. General Slocum had already captured a couple of steamboats trying to pass down the Savannah River from Augusta, and had established some of his men on Argyle and Hutchinson Islands above the city, and wanted to transfer a whole corps to the South Carolina bank; but, as the enemy had iron-clad gunboats in the river, I did not deem it prudent, because the same result could be better accomplished from General Foster's position at Broad River.

Fort McAllister was captured as described, late in the evening of December 13th, and by the 16th many steamboats had passed up as high as King's Bridge; among them one which General Grant had dispatched with the mails for the army, which had accumulated since our departure from Atlanta, under charge of Colonel A. H. Markland. These mails were most welcome to all the officers and soldiers of the army, which had been cut off from friends and the world for two months, and this prompt receipt of letters from home had an excellent effect, making us feel that home was near. By this vessel also came Lieutenant Dunn, aide-de-camp, with the following letter of December 3d, from General Grant, and on the next day Colonel Babcock, United States Engineers, arrived with the letter of December 6th, both of which are in General Grant's own handwriting, and are given entire:

HEADQUARTERS ARMIES OF THE UNITED STATES, ⎱
CITY POINT, VIRGINIA, *December* 3, 1864. ⎰

Major-General W. T. SHERMAN, *commanding Armies near Savannah, Georgia.*

GENERAL: The little information gleaned from the Southern press indicating no great obstacle to your progress, I have directed your mails (which had been previously collected in Baltimore by Colonel

Markland, special agent of the Post-Office Department) to be sent as far as the blockading squadron off Savannah, to be forwarded to you as soon as heard from on the coast.

Not liking to rejoice before the victory is assured, I abstain from congratulating you and those under your command, until bottom has been struck. I have never had a fear, however, for the result.

Since you left Atlanta no very great progress has been made here. The enemy has been closely watched, though, and prevented from detaching against you. I think not one man has gone from here, except some twelve or fifteen hundred dismounted cavalry. Bragg has gone from Wilmington. I am trying to take advantage of his absence to get possession of that place. Owing to some preparations Admiral Porter and General Butler are making to blow up Fort Fisher (which, while hoping for the best, I do not believe a particle in), there is a delay in getting this expedition off. I hope they will be ready to start by the 7th, and that Bragg will not have started back by that time.

In this letter I do not intend to give you any thing like directions for future action, but will state a general idea I have, and will get your views after you have established yourself on the sea-coast. With your veteran army I hope to get control of the only two through routes from east to west possessed by the enemy before the fall of Atlanta. The condition will be filled by holding Savannah and Augusta, or by holding any other port to the east of Savannah and Branchville. If Wilmington falls, a force from there can coöperate with you.

Thomas has got back into the defenses of Nashville, with Hood close upon him. Decatur has been abandoned, and so have all the roads, except the main one leading to Chattanooga. Part of this falling back was undoubtedly necessary, and all of it may have been. It did not look so, however, to me. In my opinion, Thomas far outnumbers Hood in infantry. In cavalry Hood has the advantage in *morale* and numbers. I hope yet that Hood will be badly crippled, if not destroyed. The general news you will learn from the papers better than I can give it.

After all becomes quiet, and roads become so bad up here that there is likely to be a week or two when nothing can be done, I will run down the coast to see you. If you desire it, I will ask Mrs. Sherman to go with me.

Yours truly,

U. S. GRANT, *Lieutenant-General.*

HEADQUARTERS ARMIES OF THE UNITED STATES, ⎱
CITY POINT, VIRGINIA, *December* 6, 1864.   ⎰

Major-General W. T. SHERMAN, *commanding Military Division of the Mississippi.*

GENERAL: On reflection since sending my letter by the hands of Lieutenant Dunn, I have concluded that the most important operation toward closing out the rebellion will be to close out Lee and his army.

You have now destroyed the roads of the South so that it will probably take them three months without interruption to reëstablish a through line from east to west. In that time I think the job here will be effectually completed.

My idea now is that you establish a base on the sea-coast, fortify and leave in it all your artillery and cavalry, and enough infantry to protect them, and at the same time so threaten the interior that the militia of the South will have to be kept at home. With the balance of your command come here by water with all dispatch. Select yourself the officer to leave in command, but you I want in person. Unless you see objections to this plan which I cannot see, use every vessel going to you for purposes of transportation.

Hood has Thomas close in Nashville. I have said all I can to force him to attack, without giving the positive order until to-day. To-day, however, I could stand it no longer, and gave the order without any reserve. I think the battle will take place to-morrow. The result will probably be known in New York before Colonel Babcock (the bearer of this) will leave it. Colonel Babcock will give you full information of all operations now in progress. Very respectfully your obedient servant,

U. S. GRANT, *Lieutenant-General.*

The contents of these letters gave me great uneasiness, for I had set my heart on the capture of Savannah, which I believed to be practicable, and to be near; for me to embark for Virginia by sea was so complete a change from what I had supposed would be the course of events that I was very much concerned. I supposed, as a matter of course, that a fleet of vessels would soon pour in, ready to convey the army to Virginia, and as General Grant's orders contemplated my leaving the cavalry, trains, and artillery, behind, I judged Fort McAllister to be the best place for the purpose, and sent my chief-engineer, Colonel Poe, to that fort, to reconnoitre the ground, and to prepare it so as to make a fortified camp large enough to accommodate the vast herd of mules and horses that would thus be left behind. And as some time might be required to collect the necessary shipping, which I estimated at little less than a hundred steamers and sailing-vessels, I determined to push operations, in hopes to secure the city of Savannah before the necessary fleet could be available. All these ideas are given in my answer to General Grant's letters (dated December 16, 1864) herewith, which is a little more full than the one printed in the report of the Committee on the Conduct of the War, because in that copy I omitted the matter concerning General Thomas, which now need no longer be withheld:

HEADQUARTERS MILITARY DIVISION OF THE MISSISSIPPI, ⎱
    IN THE FIELD, NEAR SAVANNAH, *December* 16, 1864. ⎰

Lieutenant-General U. S. GRANT, *Commander-in-Chief, City Point, Virginia.*

GENERAL: I received, day before yesterday, at the hands of Lieutenant Dunn, your letter of December 3d, and last night, at the hands of Colonel Babcock, that of December 6th. I had previously made you a hasty scrawl from the tugboat Dandelion, in Ogeechee River, advising you that the army had reached the sea-coast, destroying all the railroads across the State of Georgia, investing closely the city of Savannah, and had made connection with the fleet.

Since writing that note, I have in person met and conferred with General Foster and Admiral Dahlgren, and made all the arrangements which were deemed essential for reducing the city of Savannah to our possession. But, since the receipt of yours of the 6th, I have initiated measures looking principally to coming to you with fifty or sixty thousand infantry, and incidentally to capture Savannah, if time will allow.

At the time we carried Fort McAllister by assault so handsomely, with its twenty-two guns and entire garrison, I was hardly aware of its importance; but, since passing down the river with General Foster and up with Admiral Dahlgren, I realize how admirably adapted are Ossabaw Sound and Ogeechee River to supply an army operating against Savannah. Sea-going vessels can easily come to King's Bridge, a point on Ogeechee River, fourteen and a half miles due west of Savannah, from which point we have roads leading to all our camps. The country is low and sandy, and cut up with marshes, which in wet weather will be very bad, but we have been so favored with weather that they are all now comparatively good, and heavy details are constantly employed in double-corduroying the marshes, so that I have no fears even of bad weather. Fortunately, also, by liberal and judicious foraging, we reached the sea-coast abundantly supplied with forage and provisions, needing nothing on arrival except bread. Of this we started from Atlanta, with from eight to twenty days' supply per corps, and some of the troops only had one day's issue of bread during the trip of thirty days; yet they did not want, for sweet-potatoes were very abundant, as well as corn-meal, and our soldiers took to them naturally. We started with about five thousand head of cattle, and arrived with over ten thousand, of course consuming mostly turkeys, chickens, sheep, hogs, and the cattle of the country. As to our mules and horses, we left Atlanta with about twenty-five hundred wagons, many of which were drawn by mules which had not recovered from the Chattanooga starvation, all of which were replaced, the poor mules shot, and our transportation is now in superb condition. I have no doubt the State of Georgia has lost, by our operations, fifteen thousand first-rate mules. As to horses, Kilpatrick collected all his remounts, and it looks to me, in riding along our columns, as though every officer had three or four led horses, and each regiment seems to be followed by at least fifty negroes and foot-sore soldiers, riding on horses and mules. The custom was for each brigade to send out daily a foraging-party of about fifty men, on foot, who invariably returned mounted, with several wagons loaded with poultry, potatoes, etc., and as the army is composed of about forty brigades, you can estimate approximately the number of horses collected. Great numbers of these were shot by my order, because of the disorganizing effect on our infantry of having too many idlers mounted. General Easton is now engaged in collecting statistics on this subject, but I know the Government will never receive full accounts of our captures, although the result aimed at was fully attained, viz., to deprive our enemy of them. All these animals I will have sent to Port Royal, or collected behind Fort McAllister, to be used by General Saxton in his farming operations, or by the Quartermaster's Department, after they are systematically accounted for. While General Easton is collecting transportation for my troops to James River, I will throw to Port Royal Island all our means of transportation I can, and collect the rest near Fort McAllister, covered by the Ogeechee River and intrenchments to be erected, and for which Captain Poe, my chief-engineer, is now reconnoitring the ground, but in the mean time will act as I have begun, as though the city of Savannah were my objective: namely, the troops will continue to invest Savannah closely, making attacks and feints wherever we have fair ground to stand upon, and I will place some thirty-pound Parrotts, which I have got from General Foster, in position, near enough to reach the centre of the city, and then will demand its surrender. If General Hardee is alarmed, or fears starvation, he may surrender; otherwise I will bombard the city, but not risk the lives of our men by assaults across the narrow causeways, by which alone I can now reach it.

If I had time, Savannah, with all its dependent fortifications, would surely fall into our possession, for we hold all its avenues of supply.

The enemy has made two desperate efforts to get boats from above to the city, in both of which he has been foiled — General Slocum (whose left flank rests on the river) capturing and burning the first boat, and in the second instance driving back two gunboats and capturing the steamer Resolute, with seven naval officers and a crew of twenty-five seamen. General Slocum occupies Argyle Island and the upper end of Hutchinson Island, and has a brigade on the South Carolina shore opposite, and is very urgent to pass one of his corps over to that shore. But, in view of the change of plan made necessary by your order of the 6th, I will maintain things *in statu quo* till I have got all my transportation to the rear and out of the way, and until I have sea-transportation for the troops you require at James River, which I will accompany and command in person. Of course, I will leave Kilpatrick, with his cavalry (say five thousand three hundred), and, it may be, a division of the Fifteenth Corps; but, before determining on this, I must see General Foster, and may arrange to shift his force (now over above the Charleston Railroad, at the head of Broad River) to the Ogeechee, where, in coöperation with Kilpatrick's cavalry, he can better threaten the State of Georgia than from the direction of Port Royal. Besides, I would much prefer not to detach from my regular corps any of its veteran divisions, and would even prefer that other less valuable troops should be sent to reënforce Foster from some other quarter. My four corps, full of experience and full of ardor, coming to you *en masse*, equal to sixty thousand fighting-men, will be a reënforcement that Lee cannot disregard. Indeed, with my present command, I had expected, after reducing Savannah, instantly to march to Columbia, South Carolina; thence to Raleigh, and thence to report to you. But this would consume, it may be, six weeks' time after the fall of Savannah; whereas, by sea, I can probably reach you with my men and arms before the middle of January.

I myself am somewhat astonished at the attitude of things in Tennessee. I purposely delayed at Kingston until General Thomas assured me that he was all ready, and my last dispatch from him of the

12th of November was full of confidence, in which he promised me that he would ruin Hood if he dared to advance from Florence, urging me to go ahead, and give myself no concern about Hood's army in Tennessee.

Why he did not turn on him at Franklin, after checking and discomfiting him, surpasses my understanding. Indeed, I do not approve of his evacuating Decatur, but think he should have assumed the offensive against Hood from Pulaski, in the direction of Waynesburg. I know full well that General Thomas is slow in mind and in action; but he is judicious and brave, and the troops feel great confidence in him. I still hope he will outmanœuvre and destroy Hood.

As to matters in the Southeast, I think Hardee, in Savannah, has good artillerists, some five or six thousand good infantry, and, it may be, a mongrel mass of eight to ten thousand militia. In all our marching through Georgia, he has not forced us to use any thing but a skirmish-line, though at several points he had erected fortifications and tried to alarm us by bombastic threats. In Savannah he has taken refuge in a line constructed behind swamps and overflowed rice-fields, extending from a point on the Savannah River about three miles above the city, around by a branch of the Little Ogeechee, which stream is impassable from its salt-marshes and boggy swamps, crossed only by narrow causeways or common corduroy-roads.

There must be twenty-five thousand citizens, men, women, and children, in Savannah, that must also be fed, and how he is to feed them beyond a few days I cannot imagine. I know that his requisitions for corn on the interior counties were not filled, and we are in possession of the rice-fields and mills, which could alone be of service to him in this neighborhood. He can draw nothing from South Carolina, save from a small corner down in the southeast, and that by a disused wagon-road. I could easily get possession of this, but hardly deem it worth the risk of making a detachment, which would be in danger by its isolation from the main army. Our whole army is in fine condition as to health, and the weather is splendid. For that reason alone I feel a personal dislike to turning northward. I will keep Lieutenant Dunn here until I know the result of my demand for the surrender of Savannah, but, whether successful or not, shall not delay my execution of your order of the 6th, which will depend alone upon the time it will require to obtain transportation by sea.

I am, with respect, etc., your obedient servant,

W. T. SHERMAN, *Major-General United States Army.*

Having concluded all needful preparations, I rode from my headquarters, on the plank-road, over to General Slocum's headquarters, on the Macon road, and thence dispatched (by flag of truce) into Savannah, by the hands of Colonel Ewing, inspector-general, a demand for the surrender of the place. The following letters give the result. General Hardee refused to surrender, and I then resolved to make the attempt to break his line of defense at several places, trusting that some one would succeed.

HEADQUARTERS MILITARY DIVISION OF THE MISSISSIPPI, IN THE FIELD, SAVANNAH, GEORGIA, *December* 17, 1864.

General WILLIAM J. HARDEE, *commanding Confederate Forces in Savannah.*

GENERAL: You have doubtless observed, from your station at Rosedew, that sea-going vessels now come through Ossabaw Sound and up the Ogeechee to the rear of my army, giving me abundant supplies of all kinds, and more especially heavy ordnance necessary for the reduction of Savannah. I have already received guns that can cast heavy and destructive shot as far as the heart of your city; also, I have for some days held and controlled every avenue by which the people and garrison of Savannah can be supplied, and I am therefore justified in demanding the surrender of the city of Savannah, and its dependent forts, and shall wait a reasonable time for your answer, before opening with heavy ordnance. Should you entertain the proposition, I am prepared to grant liberal terms to the inhabitants and garrison; but should I be forced to resort to assault, or the slower and surer process of starvation, I shall then feel justified in resorting to the harshest measures, and shall make little effort to restrain my army—burning to avenge the national wrong which they attach to Savannah and other large cities which have been so prominent in dragging our country into civil war. I inclose you a copy of General Hood's demand for the surrender of the town of Resaca, to be used by you for what it is worth.

I have the honor to be your obedient servant,

W. T. SHERMAN, *Major-General.*

HEADQUARTERS DEPARTMENT SOUTH CAROLINA, GEORGIA, AND FLORIDA, SAVANNAH, GEORGIA, *December* 17, 1864.

Major-General W. T. SHERMAN, *commanding Federal Forces near Savannah, Georgia.*

GENERAL: I have to acknowledge the receipt of a communication from you of this date, in which you demand "the surrender of

Savannah and its dependent forts," on the ground that you "have received guns that can cast heavy and destructive shot into the heart of the city," and for the further reason that you "have, for some days, held and controlled every avenue by which the people and garrison can be supplied." You add that, should you be "forced to resort to assault, or to the slower and surer process of starvation, you will then feel justified in resorting to the harshest measures, and will make little effort to restrain your army," etc., etc. The position of your forces (a half-mile beyond the outer line for the land-defense of Savannah) is, at the nearest point, at least four miles from the heart of the city. That and the interior line are both intact.

Your statement that you have, for some days, held and controlled every avenue by which the people and garrison can be supplied, is incorrect. I am in free and constant communication with my department.

Your demand for the surrender of Savannah and its dependent forts is refused.

With respect to the threats conveyed in the closing paragraphs of your letter (of what may be expected in case your demand is not complied with), I have to say that I have hitherto conducted the military operations intrusted to my direction in strict accordance with the rules of civilized warfare, and I should deeply regret the adoption of any course by you that may force me to deviate from them in future. I have the honor to be, very respectfully, your obedient servant,

W. J. HARDEE, *Lieutenant-General.*

HEADQUARTERS MILITARY DIVISION OF THE MISSISSIPPI,
IN THE FIELD, NEAR SAVANNAH, GEORGIA,
December 18, 1864—8 P.M.

Lieutenant-General U. S. GRANT, *City Point, Virginia.*

GENERAL: I wrote you at length (by Colonel Babcock) on the 16th instant. As I therein explained my purpose, yesterday I made a demand on General Hardee for the surrender of the city of Savannah, and to-day received his answer—refusing; copies of both letters are herewith inclosed. You will notice that I claim that my lines are within easy cannon-range of the heart of Savannah; but General Hardee asserts that we are four and a half miles distant. But I myself have been to the intersection of the Charleston and Georgia Central Railroads, and the three-mile post is but a few yards beyond, within the line of our pickets. The enemy has no pickets outside of his fortified line (which is a full quarter of a mile within the three-mile post), and I have the evidence of Mr. R. R. Cuyler, President of the Georgia Central Railroad (who was a prisoner in our hands), that the mile-posts are measured from the Exchange, which is but two squares back from the river. By to-morrow morning I will have six thirty-pound Parrotts in position, and General Hardee will learn whether I am right or not. From the left of our line, which is on the Savannah River, the spires can be plainly seen; but the country is so densely wooded with pine and live-oak, and lies so flat, that we can see nothing from any other portion of our lines. General Slocum feels confident that he can make a successful assault at one or two points in front of General Davis's (Fourteenth) corps. All of General Howard's troops (the right wing) lie behind the Little Ogeechee, and I doubt if it can be passed by troops in the face of an enemy. Still, we can make strong feints, and if I can get a sufficient number of boats, I shall make a coöperative demonstration up Vernon River or Wassaw Sound. I should like very much indeed to take Savannah before coming to you; but, as I wrote to you before, I will do nothing rash or hasty, and will embark for the James River as soon as General Easton (who is gone to Port Royal for that purpose) reports to me that he has an approximate number of vessels for the transportation of the contemplated force. I fear even this will cost more delay than you anticipate, for already the movement of our transports and the gunboats has required more time than I had expected. We have had dense fogs; there are more mud-banks in the Ogeechee than were reported, and there are no pilots whatever. Admiral Dahlgren promised to have the channel buoyed and staked, but it is not done yet. We find only six feet of water up to King's Bridge at low tide, about ten feet up to the rice-mill, and sixteen to Fort McAllister. All these points may be used by us, and we have a good, strong bridge across Ogeechee at King's, by which our wagons can go to Fort McAllister, to which point I am sending all wagons not absolutely necessary for daily use, the negroes, prisoners of war, sick, etc., *en route* for Port Royal. In relation to Savannah, you will remark that General Hardee refers to his still being in communication with his department. This language he thought would deceive me; but I am confirmed in the belief that the route to which he refers (the Union Plank-road on the South Carolina shore) is inadequate to feed his army and the people of Savannah, and General Foster assures me that he has his force on that very road, near the head of Broad River, so that cars no longer run between Charleston and Savannah. We hold this end of the Charleston Railroad, and have destroyed it from the three-mile post back to the bridge (about twelve miles). In anticipation of leaving this country, I am continuing the destruction of their railroads, and at this moment have two divisions and the cavalry at work breaking up the Gulf Railroad from the Ogeechee to the Altamaha; so that, even if I do not take Savannah, I will leave it in a bad way. But I still hope that events will give me time to take Savannah, even if I have to assault with some loss. I am satisfied that, unless we take it, the gunboats never will, for they can make no impression upon the batteries which guard every approach from the sea. I have a faint belief that, when Colonel Babcock reaches you, you will delay operations long enough to enable me to succeed here. With Savannah in our possession, at some future time if not now, we can punish South Carolina as she deserves, and as thousands of the people in Georgia hoped we would do. I do sincerely believe that the whole United States, North and South, would rejoice to have this army turned loose on South Carolina, to devastate that State in the manner we have done in Georgia, and it would have a direct and immediate bearing on your campaign in Virginia.

I have the honor to be your obedient servant,

W. T. SHERMAN, *Major-General United States Army.*

As soon as the army had reached Savannah, and had opened communication with the fleet, I endeavored to ascertain what had transpired in Tennessee since our departure. We received our letters and files of newspapers, which contained full accounts of all the events there up to about the 1st of December. As before described, General Hood had three full corps of infantry—S. D. Lee's, A. P. Stewart's, and Cheatham's, at Florence, Alabama—with Forrest's corps of cavalry, numbering in the aggregate about forty-five thousand men. General Thomas was in Nashville, Tennessee, quietly engaged in reorganizing his army out of the somewhat broken forces at his disposal. He had posted his only two regular corps, the Fourth and Twenty-third, under the general command of Major-General J. M. Schofield, at Pulaski, directly in front of Florence, with the three brigades of cavalry (Hatch, Croxton, and Capron), commanded by Major-General Wilson, watching closely for Hood's initiative.

This force aggregated about thirty thousand men, was therefore inferior to the enemy; and General Schofield was instructed, in case the enemy made a general advance, to fall back slowly toward Nashville, fighting, till he should be re-enforced by General Thomas in person. Hood's movement was probably hurried by reason of my advance into Georgia; for on the 17th his infantry columns marched from Florence in the direction of Waynesboro', turning Schofield's position at Pulaski. The latter at once sent his trains to the rear, and on the 21st fell back to Columbia, Tennessee. General Hood followed up this movement, skirmished lightly with Schofield at Columbia, began the passage of Duck River, below the town, and Cheatham's corps reached the vicinity of Spring Hill, whither General Schofield had sent General Stanley, with two of his divisions, to cover the movement of his trains. During the night of November 29th General Schofield passed Spring Hill with his trains and army, and took post at Franklin, on the south side of Harpeth River. General Hood now attaches serious blame to General Cheatham for not attacking General Schofield in flank while in motion at Spring Hill, for he was bivouacked within eight hundred yards of the road at the time of the passage of our army. General Schofield reached Franklin on the morning of November 30th, and posted his army in front of the town, where some rifle-intrenchments had been constructed in advance. He had the two corps of Stanley and Cox (Fourth and Twenty-third), with Wilson's cavalry on his flanks, and sent his trains behind the Harpeth.

General Hood closed upon him the same day, and assaulted his position with vehemence, at one time breaking the line and wounding General Stanley seriously; but our men were veterans, cool and determined, and fought magnificently. The rebel officers led their men in person to the several persistent assaults, continuing the battle far into the night, when they drew off, beaten and discomfited.

Their loss was very severe, especially in general officers; among them Generals Cleburn and Adams, division commanders. Hood's loss on that day was afterward ascertained to be (Thomas's report): Buried on the field, seventeen hundred and fifty; left in hospital at Franklin, thirty-eight hundred; and seven hundred and two prisoners captured and held: aggregate, six thousand two hundred and fifty-two. General Schofield's loss, reported officially, was one hundred and eighty-nine killed, one thousand and thirty-three wounded, and eleven hundred and four prisoners or missing: aggregate, twenty-three hundred and twenty-six. The next day General Schofield crossed the Harpeth without trouble, and fell back to the defenses of Nashville.

Meantime General Thomas had organized the employés of the Quartermaster's Department into a corps, commanded by the chief-quartermaster, General J. L. Donaldson, and placed them in the fortifications of Nashville, under the general direction of Major-General Z. B. Tower, now of the United States Engineers. He had also received the two veteran divisions of the Sixteenth Corps, under General A. J. Smith, long absent and long expected; and he had drawn from Chattanooga and Decatur (Alabama) the divisions of Steedman and of R. S. Granger. These, with General Schofield's army and about ten thousand good cavalry, under General J. H. Wilson, constituted a strong army, capable not only of defending Nashville, but of beating Hood in the open field. Yet Thomas remained inside of Nashville, seemingly passive, until General Hood had closed upon him and had intrenched his position.

General Thomas had furthermore held fast to the railroad leading from Nashville to Chattanooga, leaving strong guards at its principal points, as at Murfreesboro', Deckerd, Stevenson, Bridgeport, Whitesides, and Chattanooga. At Murfreesboro' the division of Rousseau was reënforced and strengthened up to about eight thousand men.

At that time the weather was cold and sleety, the ground was covered with ice and snow, and both parties for a time rested on the defensive. Thus matters stood at Nashville, while we were closing down on Savannah, in the early part of December, 1864; and the country, as well as General Grant, was alarmed at the seeming passive conduct of General Thomas; and General Grant at one time considered the situation so dangerous that he thought of going to Nashville in person, but General John A. Logan, happening to be at City Point, was sent out to supersede General Thomas; luckily for the latter, he acted in time, gained a magnificent victory, and thus escaped so terrible a fate.

On the 18th of December, at my camp by the side of the plank-road, eight miles back of Savannah, I received General Hardee's letter declining to surrender, when nothing remained but to assault. The ground was difficult, and, as all former assaults had proved so bloody, I concluded to make one more effort to completely surround Savannah on all sides, so as further to excite Hardee's fears, and, in case of success, to capture the whole of his army. We had already completely invested the place on the north, west, and south, but there remained to the enemy, on the east, the use of the old dike or plank-road leading into South Carolina, and I knew that Hardee would have a pontoon-bridge across the river. On examining my maps, I thought that the division of John P. Hatch, belonging to General Foster's command, might be moved from its then position at Broad River, by water, down to Bluffton, from which it could reach this plank-road, fortify and hold it—at some risk, of course, because Hardee could avail himself of his central position to fall on this detachment with his whole army. I did not want to make a mistake like "Ball's Bluff" at that period of the war; so, taking one or two of my personal staff, I rode back to King's Bridge, leaving with Generals Howard and Slocum orders to make all possible preparations, but not to attack, during my two or three days' absence; and there I took a boat for Wassaw Sound, whence Admiral Dahlgren conveyed me in his own boat (the Harvest Moon) to Hilton Head, where I represented the matter to General Foster, and he promptly agreed to give his personal attention to it. During the night of the 20th we started back, the wind blowing strong, Admiral Dahlgren ordered the pilot of the Harvest Moon to run into Tybee, and to work his way through to Wassaw Sound and the Ogeechee River by the Romney Marshes. We were caught by a low tide and stuck in the mud. After laboring some time, the admiral ordered out his barge; in it we pulled through this intricate and shallow channel, and toward evening of December 21st we discovered, coming toward us, a tug, called the Red Legs, belonging to the Quartermaster's Department, with a staff-officer on board, bearing letters from Colonel Dayton to myself and the admiral, reporting that the city of Savannah had been found evacuated on the morning of December 21st, and was then in our possession. General Hardee had crossed the Savannah River by a pontoon-bridge, carrying off his men and light artillery, blowing up his iron-clads and navy-yard, but leaving for us all the heavy guns, stores, cotton, railway-cars, steamboats, and an immense amount of public and private property. Admiral Dahlgren concluded to go toward a vessel (the Sonoma) of his blockading fleet, which lay at anchor near Beaulieu, and I transferred to the Red Legs, and hastened up the Ogeechee River to King's Bridge, whence I rode to my camp that same night. I there learned that, early on the morning of December 21st, the skirmishers had detected the absence of the enemy, and had occupied his lines simultaneously along their whole extent; but the left flank (Slocum), especially Geary's division of the Twentieth Corps, claimed to have been the first to reach the heart of the city.

Generals Slocum and Howard moved their headquarters at once into the city, leaving the bulk of their troops in camps outside. On the morning of December 22d I followed with my own headquarters, and rode down Bull Street to the custom-house, from the roof of which we had an extensive view over the city, the river, and the vast extent of marsh and rice-fields on the South Carolina side. The navy-yard, and the wreck of the iron-clad ram Savannah, were still smouldering, but all else looked quiet enough. Turning back, we rode to the Pulaski Hotel, which I had known in years long gone, and found it kept by a Vermont man with a lame leg, who used to be a clerk in the St. Louis Hotel, New Orleans, and I inquired about the capacity of his hotel for headquarters. He was very anxious to have us for boarders, but I soon explained to him that we had a full mess equipment along, and that we were not in the habit of paying board; that one wing of the building would suffice for our use, while I would allow him to keep an hotel for the accommodation of officers and gentlemen in the remainder. I then dispatched an officer to look around for a livery-stable that could accommodate our horses, and, while waiting there, an English gentleman, Mr. Charles Green, came and said that he had a fine house completely furnished, for which he had no use, and offered it as headquarters. He explained, moreover, that General Howard had informed him, the day before, that I would want his house for headquarters. At first I felt strongly disinclined to make use of any private dwelling, lest complaints should arise of damage and loss of furniture, and so expressed myself to

Mr. Green; but, after riding about the city, and finding his house so spacious, so convenient, with large yard and stabling, I accepted his offer, and occupied that house during our stay in Savannah. He only reserved for himself the use of a couple of rooms above the dining-room, and we had all else, and a most excellent house it was in all respects.

I was disappointed that Hardee had escaped with his army, but on the whole we had reason to be content with the substantial fruits of victory. The Savannah River was found to be badly obstructed by torpedoes, and by log piers stretched across the channel below the city, which piers were filled with the cobble stones that formerly paved the streets. Admiral Dahlgren was extremely active, visited me repeatedly in the city, while his fleet still watched Charleston, and all the avenues, for the blockade-runners that infested the coast, which were notoriously owned and managed by Englishmen, who used the island of New Providence (Nassau) as a sort of entrepot. One of these small blockade-runners came into Savannah after we were in full possession, and the master did not discover his mistake till he came ashore to visit the custom-house. Of course his vessel fell a prize to the navy. A heavy force was at once set to work to remove the torpedoes and obstructions in the main channel of the river, and, from that time forth, Savannah became the great depot of supply for the troops operating in that quarter.

Meantime, on the 15th and 16th of December, were fought, in front of Nashville, the great battles in which General Thomas so nobly fulfilled his promise to ruin Hood, the details of which are fully given in his own official reports, long since published. Rumors of these great victories reached us at Savannah by piecemeal, but his official report came on the 24th of December, with a letter from General Grant, giving in general terms the events up to the 18th, and I wrote at once through my chief of staff, General Webster, to General Thomas, complimenting him in the highest terms. His brilliant victory at Nashville was necessary to mine at Savannah to make a complete whole, and this fact was perfectly comprehended by Mr. Lincoln, who recognized it fully in his personal letter of December 26th, hereinbefore quoted at length,

and which is also claimed at the time, in my Special Field
Order No. 6, of January 8, 1865, here given:

[Special Field Order No. 6.]
HEADQUARTERS MILITARY DIVISION OF THE MISSISSIPPI, ⎱
IN THE FIELD, SAVANNAH, GEORGIA, *January* 8, 1865.⎰

The general commanding announces to the troops composing the
Military Division of the Mississippi that he has received from the
President of the United States, and from Lieutenant-General Grant,
letters conveying their high sense and appreciation of the campaign
just closed, resulting in the capture of Savannah and the defeat of
Hood's army in Tennessee.

In order that all may understand the importance of events, it is
proper to revert to the situation of affairs in September last. We held
Atlanta, a city of little value to us, but so important to the enemy
that Mr. Davis, the head of the rebellious faction in the South, visited his army near Palmetto, and commanded it to regain the place
and also to ruin and destroy us, by a series of measures which he
thought would be effectual. That army, by a rapid march, gained our
railroad near Big Shanty, and afterward about Dalton. We pursued
it, but it moved so rapidly that we could not overtake it, and General
Hood led his army successfully far over toward Mississippi, in hope
to decoy us out of Georgia. But we were not thus to be led away by
him, and preferred to lead and control events ourselves. Generals
Thomas and Schofield, commanding the departments to our rear,
returned to their posts and prepared to decoy General Hood into
their meshes, while we came on to complete the original journey. We
quietly and deliberately destroyed Atlanta, and all the railroads
which the enemy had used to carry on war against us, occupied his
State capital, and then captured his commercial capital, which had
been so strongly fortified from the sea as to defy approach from that
quarter. Almost at the moment of our victorious entry into Savannah came the welcome and expected news that our comrades in Tennessee had also fulfilled nobly and well their part, had decoyed
General Hood to Nashville and then turned on him, defeating his
army thoroughly, capturing all his artillery, great numbers of prisoners, and were still pursuing the fragments down in Alabama. So
complete a success in military operations, extending over half a continent, is an achievement that entitles it to a place in the military
history of the world. The armies serving in Georgia and Tennessee,
as well as the local garrisons of Decatur, Bridgeport, Chattanooga,
and Murfreesboro', are alike entitled to the common honors, and

each regiment may inscribe on its colors, at pleasure, the word "Savannah" or "Nashville." The general commanding embraces, in the same general success, the operations of the cavalry under Generals Stoneman, Burbridge, and Gillem, that penetrated into Southwest Virginia, and paralyzed the efforts of the enemy to disturb the peace and safety of East Tennessee. Instead of being put on the defensive, we have at all points assumed the bold offensive, and have completely thwarted the designs of the enemies of our country.

By order of Major-General W. T. Sherman,

L. M. DAYTON, *Aide-de-Camp.*

Here terminated the "March to the Sea," and I only add a few letters, selected out of many, to illustrate the general feeling of rejoicing throughout the country at the time. I only regarded the march from Atlanta to Savannah as a "shift of base," as the transfer of a strong army, which had no opponent, and had finished its then work, from the interior to a point on the sea-coast, from which it could achieve other important results. I considered this march as a means to an end, and not as an essential act of war. Still, then, as now, the march to the sea was generally regarded as something extraordinary, something anomalous, something out of the usual order of events; whereas, in fact, I simply moved from Atlanta to Savannah, as one step in the direction of Richmond, a movement that had to be met and defeated, or the war was necessarily at an end.

Were I to express my measure of the relative importance of the march to the sea, and of that from Savannah northward, I would place the former at one, and the latter at ten, or the maximum.

I now close this long chapter by giving a tabular statement of the losses during the march, and the number of prisoners captured. The property captured consisted of horses and mules by the thousand, and of quantities of subsistence stores that aggregate very large, but may be measured with sufficient accuracy by assuming that sixty-five thousand men obtained abundant food for about forty days, and thirty-five thousand animals were fed for a like period, so as to reach Savannah in splendid flesh and condition. I also add a few of the more important letters that passed between Generals Grant,

Halleck, and myself, which illustrate our opinions at that stage of the war:

STATEMENT OF CASUALTIES AND PRISONERS CAPTURED BY THE
ARMY IN THE FIELD, CAMPAIGN OF GEORGIA.

COMMANDS.	KILLED.		W'UND'D.		MISSING.			CAPTURED.		
	Commissioned Officers.	Enlisted Men.	Commissioned Officers.	Enlisted Men.	Commissioned Officers.	Enlisted Men.	Aggregate.	Commissioned Officers.	Enlisted Men.	Aggregate.
Right Wing, Army of the Tennessee, Major-General O. O. Howard commanding.	5	35	11	172	. . .	19	242	34	632	666
Left Wing, Fourteenth and Twentieth Corps, Major-General H. W. Slocum commanding. . .	2	23	6	112	1	258	402	30	409	439
Cavalry Division, Brigadier-General J. Kilpatrick commanding.	3	35	7	120	. . .	. . .	120	13	220	233
Total.	10	93	24	404	1	277	764	77	1,261	1,338

L. M. DAYTON, *Assistant Adjutant-General.*

HEADQUARTERS OF THE ARMY, ⎱
WASHINGTON, *December* 16, 1864.⎰

Major-General SHERMAN (*via Hilton Head*).

GENERAL: Lieutenant-General Grant informs me that, in his last dispatch sent to you, he suggested the transfer of your infantry to Richmond. He now wishes me to say that you will retain your entire force, at least for the present, and, with such assistance as may be given you by General Foster and Admiral Dahlgren, operate from such base as you may establish on the coast. General Foster will obey such instructions as may be given by you.

Should you have captured Savannah, it is thought that by transferring the water-batteries to the land side that place may be made a good depot and base of operations on Augusta, Branchville, or Charleston. If Savannah should not be captured, or if captured and not deemed suitable for this purpose, perhaps Beaufort would serve as a depot. As the rebels have probably removed their most valuable property from Augusta, perhaps Branchville would be the most important point at which to strike in order to sever all connection between Virginia and the Southwestern Railroad.

General Grant's wishes, however, are, that this whole matter of your future actions should be entirely left to your discretion.

We can send you from here a number of complete batteries of field-artillery, with or without horses, as you may desire; also, as soon as General Thomas can spare them, all the fragments, convalescents, and furloughed men of your army. It is reported that Thomas defeated Hood yesterday, near Nashville, but we have no particulars nor official reports, telegraphic communication being interrupted by a heavy storm.

Our last advices from you was General Howard's note, announcing his approach to Savannah. Yours truly,

H. W. HALLECK, *Major-General, Chief-of-Staff.*

HEADQUARTERS OF THE ARMY, }
WASHINGTON, *December* 18, 1864.}

Major-General W. T. SHERMAN, *Savannah* (*via Hilton Head*).

MY DEAR GENERAL: Yours of the 13th, by Major Anderson, is just received. I congratulate you on your splendid success, and shall very soon expect to hear of the crowning work of your campaign—the capture of Savannah. Your march will stand out prominently as the great one of this great war. When Savannah falls, then for another wide swath through the centre of the Confederacy. But I will not anticipate. General Grant is expected here this morning, and will probably write you his own views.

I do not learn from your letter, or from Major Anderson, that you are in want of any thing which we have not provided at Hilton Head. Thinking it probable that you might want more field-artillery, I had prepared several batteries, but the great difficulty of foraging horses on the sea-coast will prevent our sending any unless you actually need them. The hay-crop this year is short, and the Quartermaster's Department has great difficulty in procuring a supply for our animals.

General Thomas has defeated Hood, near Nashville, and it is hoped that he will completely crush his army. Breckenridge, at last accounts, was trying to form a junction near Murfreesboro', but, as

Thomas is between them, Breckenridge must either retreat or be defeated.

General Rosecrans made very bad work of it in Missouri, allowing Price with a small force to overrun the State and destroy millions of property. ˙

Orders have been issued for all officers and detachments having three months or more to serve, to rejoin your army *via* Savannah. Those having less than three months to serve, will be retained by General Thomas.

Should you capture Charleston, I hope that by *some accident* the place may be destroyed, and, if a little salt should be sown upon its site, it may prevent the growth of future crops of nullification and secession.

Yours truly,
H. W. HALLECK, *Major-General, Chief-of-Staff.*

[CONFIDENTIAL.]
HEADQUARTERS ARMIES OF THE UNITED STATES, ⎱
WASHINGTON, D. C., *December* 18, 1864.   ⎰

To Major-General W. T. SHERMAN, *commanding Military Division of the Mississippi.*

MY DEAR GENERAL: I have just received and read, I need not tell you with how much gratification, your letter to General Halleck. I congratulate you and the brave officers and men under your command on the successful termination of your most brilliant campaign. I never had a doubt of the result. When apprehensions for your safety were expressed by the President, I assured him with the army you had, and you in command of it, there was no danger but you would *strike* bottom on salt-water some place; that I would not feel the same security—in fact, would not have intrusted the expedition to any other living commander.

It has been very hard work to get Thomas to attack Hood. I gave him the most peremptory order, and had started to go there myself, before he got off. He has done magnificently, however, since he started. Up to last night, five thousand prisoners and forty-nine pieces of captured artillery, besides many wagons and innumerable small-arms, had been received in Nashville. This is exclusive of the enemy's loss at Franklin, which amounted to thirteen general officers killed, wounded, and captured. The enemy probably lost five thousand men at Franklin, and ten thousand in the last three days' operations. Breckenridge is said to be making for Murfreesboro'.

I think he is in a most excellent place. Stoneman has nearly wiped out John Morgan's old command, and five days ago entered Bristol.

I did think the best thing to do was to bring the greater part of your army here, and wipe out Lee. The turn affairs now seem to be taking has shaken me in that opinion. I doubt whether you may not accomplish more toward that result where you are than if brought here, especially as I am informed, since my arrival in the city, that it would take about two months to get you here with all the other calls there are for ocean transportation.

I want to get your views about what ought to be done, and what can be done. If you capture the garrison of Savannah, it certainly will compel Lee to detach from Richmond, or give us nearly the whole South. My own opinion is that Lee is averse to going out of Virginia, and if the cause of the South is lost he wants Richmond to be the last place surrendered. If he has such views, it may be well to indulge him until we get every thing else in our hands.

Congratulating you and the army again upon the splendid results of your campaign, the like of which is not read of in past history, I subscribe myself, more than ever, if possible, your friend,

U. S. GRANT, Lieutenant-General.

HEADQUARTERS ARMIES OF THE UNITED STATES,
CITY POINT, VIRGINIA, December 26, 1864. }

Major-General W. T. SHERMAN, *Savannah, Georgia.*

GENERAL: Your very interesting letter of the 22d inst., brought by Major Gray, of General Foster's staff, is just at hand. As the major starts back at once, I can do no more at present than simply acknowledge its receipt. The capture of Savannah, with all its immense stores, must tell upon the people of the South. All well here.

Yours truly,

U. S. GRANT, Lieutenant-General.

HEADQUARTERS MILITARY DIVISION OF THE MISSISSIPPI,
SAVANNAH, GEORGIA, December 24, 1864. }

Lieutenant-General U. S. GRANT, *City Point, Virginia.*

GENERAL: Your letter of December 18th is just received. I feel very much gratified at receiving the handsome commendation you pay my army. I will, in general orders, convey to the officers and men the substance of your note.

I am also pleased that you have modified your former orders, for I feared that the transportation by sea would very much disturb the unity and *morale* of my army, now so perfect.

The occupation of Savannah, which I have heretofore reported, completes the first part of our game, and fulfills a great part of your instructions; and we are now engaged in dismantling the rebel forts which bear upon the sea-channels, and transferring the heavy ordnance and ammunition to Fort Pulaski and Hilton Head, where they can be more easily guarded than if left in the city.

The rebel inner lines are well adapted to our purpose, and with slight modifications can be held by a comparatively small force; and in about ten days I expect to be ready to sally forth again. I feel no doubt whatever as to our future plans. I have thought them over so long and well that they appear as clear as daylight. I left Augusta untouched on purpose, because the enemy will be in doubt as to my objective point, after we cross the Savannah River, whether it be Augusta or Charleston, and will naturally divide his forces. I will then move either on Branchville or Columbia, by any curved line that gives us the best supplies, breaking up in our course as much railroad as possible; then, ignoring Charleston and Augusta both, I would occupy Columbia and Camden, pausing there long enough to observe the effect. I would then strike for the Charleston & Wilmington Railroad, somewhere between the Santee and Cape Fear Rivers, and, if possible, communicate with the fleet under Admiral Dahlgren (whom I find a most agreeable gentleman, accommodating himself to our wishes and plans). Then I would favor an attack on Wilmington, in the belief that Porter and Butler will fail in their present undertaking. Charleston is now a mere desolated wreck, and is hardly worth the time it would take to starve it out. Still, I am aware that, historically and politically, much importance is attached to the place, and it may be that, apart from its military importance, both you and the Administration may prefer I should give it more attention; and it would be well for you to give me some general idea on that subject, for otherwise I would treat it as I have expressed, as a point of little importance, after all its railroads leading into the interior have been destroyed or occupied by us. But, on the hypothesis of ignoring Charleston and taking Wilmington, I would then favor a movement direct on Raleigh. The game is then up with Lee, unless he comes out of Richmond, avoids you and fights me; in which case I should reckon on your being on his heels. Now that Hood is used up by Thomas, I feel disposed to bring the matter to an issue as quick as possible. I feel confident that I can break up the whole railroad system of South Carolina and North Carolina, and be on the Roanoke, either at Raleigh or Weldon, by the time spring fairly opens; and, if you feel confident that you can whip Lee outside of his intrenchments, I feel equally confident that I can handle him in the open country.

One reason why I would ignore Charleston is this: that I believe Hardee will reduce the garrison to a small force, with plenty of provisions; I know that the neck back of Charleston can be made impregnable to assault, and we will hardly have time for siege operations.

I will have to leave in Savannah a garrison, and, if Thomas can spare them, I would like to have all detachments, convalescents, etc., belonging to these four corps, sent forward at once. I do not want to cripple Thomas, because I regard his operations as all-important, and I have ordered him to pursue Hood down into Alabama, trusting to the country for supplies.

I reviewed one of my corps to-day, and shall continue to review the whole army. I do not like to boast, but believe this army has a confidence in itself that makes it almost invincible. I wish you could run down and see us; it would have a good effect, and show to both armies that they are acting on a common plan. The weather is now cool and pleasant, and the general health very good. Your true friend,

W. T. SHERMAN, *Major-General.*

HEADQUARTERS MILITARY DIVISION OF THE MISSISSIPPI, ⎱
IN THE FIELD, SAVANNAH, *December* 24, 1864. ⎰

Major-General H. W. HALLECK, *Chief-of-Staff, Washington, D. C.*

GENERAL: I had the pleasure of receiving your two letters of the 16th and 18th instant to-day, and feel more than usually flattered by the high encomiums you have passed on our recent campaign, which is now complete by the occupation of Savannah.

I am also very glad that General Grant has changed his mind about embarking my troops for James River, leaving me free to make the broad swath you describe through South and North Carolina, and still more gratified at the news from Thomas, in Tennessee, because it fulfills my plans, which contemplated his being able to dispose of Hood, in case he ventured north of the Tennessee River. So, I think, on the whole, I can chuckle over Jeff. Davis's disappointment in not turning my Atlanta campaign into a "Moscow disaster."

I have just finished a long letter to General Grant, and have explained to him that we are engaged in shifting our base from the Ogeechee to the Savannah River, dismantling all the forts made by the enemy to bear upon the salt-water channels, transferring the heavy ordnance, etc., to Fort Pulaski and Hilton Head, and in re-modeling the enemy's interior lines to suit our future plans and purposes. I have also laid down the programme for a campaign which I can make this winter, and which will put me in the spring on the Roanoke, in direct communication with General Grant on James River. In general terms, my plan is to turn over to General Foster the city of Savannah, to sally forth with my army resupplied, cross the Savannah, feign on Charleston and Augusta, but strike between, breaking *en route* the Charleston & Augusta Railroad, also a large part of that from Branchville and Camden toward North Carolina, and then rapidly to move for some point of the railroad from Charleston to Wilmington, between the Santee and Cape Fear Rivers; then, communicating with the fleet in the neighborhood of Georgetown, I would turn upon Wilmington or Charleston, according to the importance of either. I rather prefer Wilmington, as a live place, over Charleston, which is dead and unimportant when its railroad communications are broken. I take it for granted that the present movement on Wilmington will fail. If I should determine to take Charleston, I would turn across the country (which I have hunted over many a time) from Santee to Mount Pleasant, throwing one wing on the peninsula between the Ashley and Cooper. After accomplishing one or other of these ends, I would make a bee-line for Raleigh or Weldon, when Lee would be forced to come out of Richmond, or acknowledge himself beaten. He would, I think, by the use of the Danville Railroad, throw himself rapidly between me and Grant, leaving Richmond in the hands of the latter. This would not alarm me, for I have an army which I think can manœuvre, and I would force him to attack me at a disadvantage, always under the supposition that Grant would be on his heels; and, if the worst come to the worst, I can fight my way down to Albermarle Sound, or Newbern.

I think the time has come now when we should attempt the boldest moves, and my experience is, that they are easier of execution than more timid ones, because the enemy is disconcerted by them— as, for instance, my recent campaign.

I also doubt the wisdom of concentration beyond a certain extent, for the roads of this country limit the amount of men that can be brought to bear in any one battle, and I do not believe that any one general can handle more than sixty thousand men in battle.

I think our campaign of the last month, as well as every step I take from this point northward, is as much a direct attack upon Lee's army as though we were operating within the sound of his artillery.

I am very anxious that Thomas should follow up his success to the very utmost point. My orders to him before I left Kingston were, after beating Hood, to follow him as far as Columbus, Mississippi, or Selma, Alabama, both of which lie in districts of country which are rich in corn and meat.

I attach more importance to these deep incisions into the enemy's country, because this war differs from European wars in this particular: we are not only fighting hostile armies, but a hostile people, and must make old and young, rich and poor, feel the hard hand of war, as well as their organized armies. I know that this recent movement of mine through Georgia has had a wonderful effect in this respect. Thousands who had been deceived by their lying newspapers to believe that we were being whipped all the time now realize the truth, and have no appetite for a repetition of the same experience. To be sure, Jeff. Davis has his people under pretty good discipline, but I think faith in him is much shaken in Georgia, and before we have done with her South Carolina will not be quite so tempestuous.

I will bear in mind your hint as to Charleston, and do not think "salt" will be necessary. When I move, the Fifteenth Corps will be on the right of the right wing, and their position will naturally bring them into Charleston first; and, if you have watched the history of that corps, you will have remarked that they generally do their work pretty well. The truth is, the whole army is burning with an insatiable desire to wreak vengeance upon South Carolina. I almost tremble at her fate, but feel that she deserves all that seems in store for her.

Many and many a person in Georgia asked me why we did not go to South Carolina; and, when I answered that we were *en route* for that State, the invariable reply was, "Well, if you will make those people feel the utmost severities of war, we will pardon you for your desolation of Georgia."

I look upon Columbia as quite as bad as Charleston, and I doubt if we shall spare the public buildings there as we did at Milledgeville.

I have been so busy lately that I have not yet made my official report, and I think I had better wait until I get my subordinate reports before attempting it, as I am anxious to explain clearly not only the reasons for every step, but the amount of execution done, and this I cannot do until I get the subordinate reports; for we marched the whole distance in four or more columns, and, of course, I could only be present with one, and generally that one engaged in destroying railroads. This work of destruction was performed better than usual, because I had an engineer-regiment, provided with claws to twist the bars after being heated. Such bars can never be used again, and the only way in which a railroad line can be reconstructed across Georgia is, to make a new road from Fairburn Station (twenty-four miles southwest of Atlanta) to Madison, a distance of one hundred miles; and, before that can be done, I propose to be on the road from Augusta to Charleston, which is a continuation of the same. I felt somewhat disappointed at Hardee's escape, but really am not to blame. I moved as quickly as possible to close up the "Union Cause-way," but intervening obstacles were such that, before I could get troops on the road, Hardee had slipped out. Still, I know that the men that were in Savannah will be lost in a measure to Jeff. Davis, for the Georgia troops, under G. W. Smith, declared they would not fight in South Carolina, and they have gone north, *en route* for Augusta, and I have reason to believe the North Carolina troops have gone to Wilmington; in other words, they are scattered. I have reason to believe that Beauregard was present in Savannah at the time of its evacuation, and think that he and Hardee are now in Charleston, making preparations for what they suppose will be my next step.

Please say to the President that I have received his kind message (through Colonel Markland), and feel thankful for his high favor. If I disappoint him in the future, it shall not be from want of zeal or love to the cause.

From you I expect a full and frank criticism of my plans for the future, which may enable me to correct errors before it is too late. I do not wish to be rash, but want to give my rebel friends no chance to accuse us of want of enterprise or courage.

Assuring you of my high personal respect, I remain, as ever, your friend,

W. T. SHERMAN, *Major-General*.

[General Order No. 3.]
WAR DEPARTMENT, ADJUTANT-GENERAL'S OFFICE,
WASHINGTON, *January* 14, 1865.

The following resolution of the Senate and House of Representatives is published to the army:

[PUBLIC RESOLUTION—No. 4.]

Joint resolution tendering the thanks of the people and of Congress to Major-General William T. Sherman, and the officers and soldiers of his command, for their gallant conduct in their late brilliant movement through Georgia.

Be it resolved by the Senate and House of Representatives of the United States of America in Congress assembled, That the thanks of the people and of the Congress of the United States are due and are hereby tendered to Major-General William T. Sherman, and through him to the officers and men under his command, for their gallantry and good conduct in their late campaign from Chattanooga to Atlanta, and the triumphal march thence through Georgia to Savannah, terminating in the capture and occupation of that city; and that the President cause a copy of this joint resolution to be engrossed and forwarded to Major-General Sherman. Approved, January 10, 1865.

By order of the Secretary of War,

W. A. NICHOLS, *Assistant Adjutant-General.*

Chapter XXII.

SAVANNAH AND POCOTALIGO.

December, 1864, and January, 1865.

THE CITY of Savannah was an old place, and usually accounted a handsome one. Its houses were of brick or frame, with large yards, ornamented with shrubbery and flowers; its streets perfectly regular, crossing each other at right angles; and at many of the intersections were small inclosures in the nature of parks. These streets and parks were lined with the handsomest shade-trees of which I have knowledge, viz., the willow-leaf live-oak, evergreens of exquisite beauty; and these certainly entitled Savannah to its reputation as a handsome town more than the houses, which, though comfortable, would hardly make a display on Fifth Avenue or the Boulevard Haussmann of Paris. The city was built on a plateau of sand about forty feet above the level of the sea, abutting against the river, leaving room along its margin for a street of stores and warehouses. The custom-house, court-house, post-office, etc., were on the plateau above. In rear of Savannah was a large park, with a fountain, and between it and the court-house was a handsome monument, erected to the memory of Count Pulaski, who fell in 1779 in the assault made on the city at the time it was held by the English during the Revolutionary War. Outside of Savannah there was very little to interest a stranger, except the cemetery of Bonaventura, and the ride along the Wilmington Channel by way of Thunderbolt, where might be seen some groves of the majestic live-oak trees, covered with gray and funereal moss, which were truly sublime in grandeur, but gloomy after a few days' camping under them.

Within an hour of taking up my quarters in Mr. Green's house, Mr. A. G. Browne, of Salem, Massachusetts, United States Treasury agent for the Department of the South, made his appearance to claim possession, in the name of the Treasury Department, of all captured cotton, rice, buildings, etc. Having use for these articles ourselves, and having fairly earned them, I did not feel inclined to surrender possession,

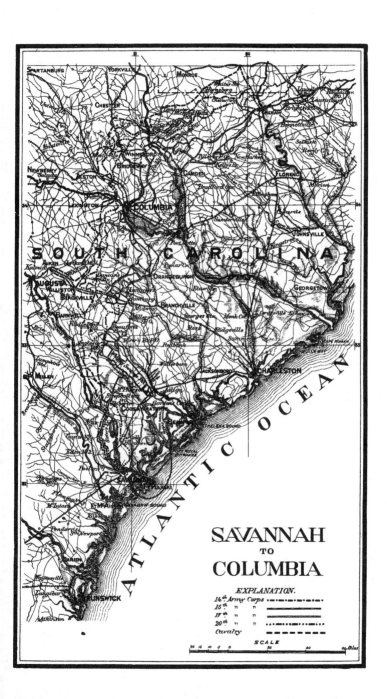

SAVANNAH
TO
COLUMBIA

EXPLANATION.

14th Army Corps ⋅—⋅—⋅—⋅—
15th   „   „   ——————
17th   „   „   ——————
20th   „   „   ⋅⋅⋅—⋅⋅⋅—⋅⋅⋅
Cavalry   ————————

SCALE
20 15 10 5 0   20   40   60 Miles

and explained to him that the quartermaster and commissary could manage them more to my liking than he; but I agreed, after the proper inventories had been prepared, if there remained any thing for which we had no special use, I would turn it over to him. It was then known that in the warehouses were stored at least twenty-five thousand bales of cotton, and in the forts one hundred and fifty large, heavy sea-coast guns: although afterward, on a more careful count, there proved to be more than two hundred and fifty sea-coast or siege guns, and thirty-one thousand bales of cotton. At that interview Mr. Browne, who was a shrewd, clever Yankee, told me that a vessel was on the point of starting for Old Point Comfort, and, if she had good weather off Cape Hatteras, would reach Fortress Monroe by Christmas-day, and he suggested that I might make it the occasion of sending a welcome Christmas gift to the President, Mr. Lincoln, who peculiarly enjoyed such pleasantry. I accordingly sat down and wrote on a slip of paper, to be left at the telegraph-office at Fortress Monroe for transmission, the following:

SAVANNAH, GEORGIA, *December* 22, 1864.
To His Excellency President LINCOLN, *Washington, D. C.:*
I beg to present you as a Christmas-gift the city of Savannah, with one hundred and fifty heavy guns and plenty of ammunition, also about twenty-five thousand bales of cotton.
W. T. SHERMAN, *Major-General.*

This message actually reached him on Christmas-eve, was extensively published in the newspapers, and made many a household unusually happy on that festive day; and it was in the answer to this dispatch that Mr. Lincoln wrote me the letter of December 28th, already given, beginning with the words, "Many, many thanks," etc., which he sent at the hands of General John A. Logan, who happened to be in Washington, and was coming to Savannah, to rejoin his command.

On the 23d of December were made the following general orders for the disposition of the troops in and about Savannah:

[Special Field Order No. 139.]
HEADQUARTERS MILITARY DIVISION OF THE MISSISSIPPI,⎱
IN THE FIELD, SAVANNAH, GEORGIA, *December* 23, 1864.⎰

Savannah, being now in our possession, the river partially cleared out, and measures having been taken to remove all obstructions, will at once be made a grand depot for future operations:

1. The chief-quartermaster, General Easton, will, after giving the necessary orders touching the transports in Ogeechee River and Ossabaw Sound, come in person to Savannah, and take possession of all public buildings, vacant storerooms, warehouses, etc., that may be now or hereafter needed for any department of the army. No rents will be paid by the Government of the United States during the war, and all buildings must be distributed according to the accustomed rules of the Quartermaster's Department, as though they were public property.

2. The chief commissary of subsistence, Colonel A. Beckwith, will transfer the grand depot of the army to the city of Savannah, secure possession of the needful buildings and offices, and give the necessary orders, to the end that the army may be supplied abundantly and well.

3. The chief-engineer, Captain Poe, will at once direct which of the enemy's forts are to be retained for our use, and which dismantled and destroyed. The chief ordnance-officer, Captain Baylor, will in like manner take possession of all property pertaining to his department captured from the enemy, and cause the same to be collected and conveyed to points of security; all the heavy coast-guns will be dismounted and carried to Fort Pulaski.

4. The troops, for the present, will be grouped about the city of Savannah, looking to convenience of camps; General Slocum taking from the Savannah River around to the seven-mile post on the canal, and General Howard thence to the sea; General Kilpatrick will hold King's Bridge until Fort McAllister is dismantled, and the troops withdrawn from the south side of the Ogeechee, when he will take post about Anderson's plantation, on the plank-road, and picket all the roads leading from the north and west.

5. General Howard will keep a small guard at Forts Rosedale, Beaulieu, Wimberley, Thunderbolt, and Bonaventura, and he will cause that shore and Skidaway Island to be examined very closely, with a view to finding many and convenient points for the embarkation of troops and wagons on sea-going vessels.

By order of Major-General W. T. Sherman,

L. M. DAYTON, *Aide-de-Camp*.

[Special Field Order No. 143.]
HEADQUARTERS MILITARY DIVISION OF THE MISSISSIPPI, }
IN THE FIELD, SAVANNAH, GEORGIA, *December* 26, 1864.}

The city of Savannah and surrounding country will be held as a military post, and adapted to future military uses, but, as it contains a population of some twenty thousand people, who must be provided for, and as other citizens may come, it is proper to lay down certain general principles, that all within its military jurisdiction may understand their relative duties and obligations.

1. During war, the military is superior to civil authority, and, where interests clash, the civil must give way; yet, where there is no conflict, every encouragement should be given to well-disposed and peaceful inhabitants to resume their usual pursuits. Families should be disturbed as little as possible in their residences, and tradesmen allowed the free use of their shops, tools, etc.; churches, schools, and all places of amusement and recreation, should be encouraged, and streets and roads made perfectly safe to persons in their pursuits. Passes should not be exacted within the line of outer pickets, but if any person shall abuse these privileges by communicating with the enemy, or doing any act of hostility to the Government of the United States, he or she will be punished with the utmost rigor of the law. Commerce with the outer world will be resumed to an extent commensurate with the wants of the citizens, governed by the restrictions and rules of the Treasury Department.

2. The chief quartermaster and commissary of the army may give suitable employment to the people, white and black, or transport them to such points as they may choose where employment can be had; and may extend temporary relief in the way of provisions and vacant houses to the worthy and needy, until such time as they can help themselves. They will select first the buildings for the necessary uses of the army; next, a sufficient number of stores, to be turned over to the Treasury agent for trade-stores. All vacant storehouses or dwellings, and all buildings belonging to absent rebels, will be construed and used as belonging to the United States, until such time as their titles can be settled by the courts of the United States.

3. The Mayor and City Council of Savannah will continue to exercise their functions, and will, in concert with the commanding officer of the post and the chief-quartermaster, see that the fire-companies are kept in organization, the streets cleaned and lighted, and keep up a good understanding between the citizens and soldiers. They will ascertain and report to the chief commissary of subsistence, as soon as possible, the names and number of worthy families that need

assistance and support. The mayor will forthwith give public notice that the time has come when all must choose their course, viz., remain within our lines, and conduct themselves as good citizens, or depart in peace. He will ascertain the names of all who choose to leave Savannah, and report their names and residence to the chief-quartermaster, that measures may be taken to transport them beyond our lines.

4. Not more than two newspapers will be published in Savannah; their editors and proprietors will be held to the strictest accountability, and will be punished severely, in person and property, for any libelous publication, mischievous matter, premature news, exaggerated statements, or any comments whatever upon the acts of the constituted authorities; they will be held accountable for such articles, even though copied from other papers.

By order of Major-General W. T. Sherman,

L. M. DAYTON, *Aide-de-Camp*.

It was estimated that there were about twenty thousand inhabitants in Savannah, all of whom had participated more or less in the war, and had no special claims to our favor, but I regarded the war as rapidly drawing to a close, and it was becoming a political question as to what was to be done with the people of the South, both white and black, when the war was actually over. I concluded to give them the option to remain or to join their friends in Charleston or Augusta, and so announced in general orders. The mayor, Dr. Arnold, was completely "subjugated," and, after consulting with him, I authorized him to assemble his City Council to take charge generally of the interests of the people; but warned all who remained that they must be strictly subordinate to the military law, and to the interests of the General Government. About two hundred persons, mostly the families of men in the Confederate army, prepared to follow the fortunes of their husbands and fathers, and these were sent in a steamboat under a flag of truce, in charge of my aide Captain Audenried, to Charleston harbor, and there delivered to an officer of the Confederate army. But the great bulk of the inhabitants chose to remain in Savannah, generally behaved with propriety, and good social relations at once arose between them and the army. Shortly after our occupation of Savannah, a lady was announced at my headquarters by the orderly or sentinel at the front-door, who was ushered into the parlor, and proved to be the wife of General G. W. Smith, whom I had known about 1850, when Smith was on duty at West Point. She was a native of New London, Connecticut, and very handsome. She began her interview by presenting me a letter from her husband, who then commanded a division of the Georgia militia in the rebel army, which had just quitted Savannah, which letter began, "DEAR SHERMAN: The fortunes of war, etc., compel me to leave my wife in Savannah, and I beg for her your courteous protection," etc., etc. I inquired where she lived, and if anybody was troubling her. She said she was boarding with a lady whose husband had, in like manner with her own, gone off with Hardee's army; that a part of the house had been taken for the use of Major-General Ward, of Kentucky; that her landlady was approaching her confinement, and was nervous at the noise which the younger staff-officers made at night, etc. I explained to her that I could give but little personal attention to such matters, and referred her to General Slocum, whose troops occupied the city. I afterward visited her house, and saw, personally, that she had no reason to complain. Shortly afterward Mr. Hardee, a merchant of Savannah, came to me and presented a letter from his brother, the general, to the same effect, alleging that his brother was a civilian, had never taken up arms, and asked of me protection for his family, his cotton, etc. To him I gave the general assurance that no harm was designed to any of the people of Savannah who would remain quiet and peaceable, but that I could give him no guarantee as to his cotton, for over it I had no absolute control; and yet still later I received a note from the wife of General A. P. Stewart (who commanded a corps in Hood's army), asking me to come to see her. This I did, and found her to be a native of Cincinnati, Ohio, wanting protection, and who was naturally anxious about the fate of her husband, known to be with General Hood, in Tennessee, retreating before General Thomas. I remember that I was able to assure her that he had not been killed or captured, up to that date, and think that I advised her, instead of attempting to go in pursuit of her husband, to go to Cincinnati, to her uncle, Judge Storer, there await the issue of events.

Before I had reached Savannah, and during our stay there, the rebel officers and newspapers represented the conduct of the men of our army as simply infamous; that we respected neither age nor sex; that we burned every thing we came across—barns, stables, cotton-gins, and even dwelling-houses; that we ravished the women and killed the men, and perpetrated all manner of outrages on the inhabitants. Therefore it struck me as strange that Generals Hardee and Smith should commit their families to our custody, and even be-speak our personal care and attention. These officers knew well that these reports were exaggerated in the extreme, and yet tacitly assented to these publications, to arouse the droop-ing energies of the people of the South.

As the division of Major-General John W. Geary, of the Twentieth Corps, was the first to enter Savannah, that officer was appointed to command the place, or to act as a sort of governor. He very soon established a good police, maintained admirable order, and I doubt if Savannah, either before or since, has had a better government than during our stay. The guard-mountings and parades, as well as the greater reviews, became the daily resorts of the ladies, to hear the music of our excellent bands; schools were opened, and the churches every Sunday were well filled with most devout and respectful con-gregations; stores were reopened, and markets for provisions, meat, wood, etc., were established, so that each family, re-gardless of race, color, or opinion, could procure all the nec-essaries and even luxuries of life, provided they had money. Of course, many families were actually destitute of this, and to these were issued stores from our own stock of supplies. I remember to have given to Dr. Arnold, the mayor, an order for the contents of a large warehouse of rice, which he con-fided to a committee of gentlemen, who went North (to Boston), and soon returned with one or more cargoes of flour, hams, sugar, coffee, etc., for gratuitous distribution, which relieved the most pressing wants until the revival of trade and business enabled the people to provide for them-selves.

A lady, whom I had known in former years as Miss Josephine Goodwin, told me that, with a barrel of flour and some sugar which she had received gratuitously from the commissary, she had baked cakes and pies, in the sale of which she realized a profit of fifty-six dollars.

Meantime Colonel Poe had reconnoitred and laid off new lines of parapet, which would enable a comparatively small garrison to hold the place, and a heavy detail of soldiers was put to work thereon; Generals Easton and Beckwith had organized a complete depot of supplies; and, though vessels arrived almost daily with mails and provisions, we were hardly ready to initiate a new and hazardous campaign. I had not yet received from General Grant or General Halleck any modification of the orders of December 6, 1864, to embark my command for Virginia by sea; but on the 2d of January, 1865, General J. G. Barnard, United States Engineers, arrived direct from General Grant's headquarters, bearing the following letter, in the general's own handwriting, which, with my answer, is here given:

HEADQUARTERS ARMIES OF THE UNITED STATES,
CITY POINT, VIRGINIA, *December* 27, 1864.

Major-General W. T. SHERMAN, *commanding Military Division of the Mississippi.*

GENERAL: Before writing you definite instructions for the next campaign, I wanted to receive your answer to my letter written from Washington. Your confidence in being able to march up and join this army pleases me, and I believe it can be done. The effect of such a campaign will be to disorganize the South, and prevent the organization of new armies from their broken fragments. Hood is now retreating, with his army broken and demoralized. His loss in men has probably not been far from twenty thousand, besides deserters. If time is given, the fragments may be collected together and many of the deserters reassembled. If we can, we should act to prevent this. Your spare army, as it were, moving as proposed, will do it.

In addition to holding Savannah, it looks to me that an intrenched camp ought to be held on the railroad between Savannah and Charleston. Your movement toward Branchville will probably enable Foster to reach this with his own force. This will give us a position in the South from which we can threaten the interior without marching over long, narrow causeways, easily defended, as we have heretofore been compelled to do. Could not such a camp be established about Pocotaligo or Coosawhatchie?

I have thought that, Hood being so completely wiped out for present harm, I might bring A. J. Smith here, with fourteen to fifteen thousand men. With this increase I could hold my lines, and move out with a greater force than Lee has. It would compel Lee to retain all his present force in the defenses of Richmond or abandon them entirely. This latter contingency is probably the only danger to the easy success of your expedition. In the event you should meet Lee's army, you would be compelled to beat it or find the sea-coast. Of course, I shall not let Lee's army escape if I can help it, and will not let it go without following to the best of my ability.

Without waiting further directions, then, you may make your preparations to start on your northern expedition without delay. Break up the railroads in South and North Carolina, and join the armies operating against Richmond as soon as you can. I will leave out all suggestions about the route you should take, knowing that your information, gained daily in the course of events, will be better than any that can be obtained now.

It may not be possible for you to march to the rear of Petersburg; but, failing in this, you could strike either of the sea-coast ports in North Carolina held by us. From there you could take shipping. It would be decidedly preferable, however, if you could march the whole distance.

From the best information I have, you will find no difficulty in supplying your army until you cross the Roanoke. From there here is but a few days' march, and supplies could be collected south of the river to bring you through. I shall establish communication with you there, by steamboat and gunboat. By this means your wants can be partially supplied. I shall hope to hear from you soon, and to hear your plan, and about the time of starting.

Please instruct Foster to hold on to all the property in Savannah, and especially the cotton. Do not turn it over to citizens or Treasury agents, without orders of the War Department.

Very respectfully, your obedient servant,

U. S. GRANT, *Lieutenant-General.*

HEADQUARTERS MILITARY DIVISION OF THE MISSISSIPPI, ⎱
IN THE FIELD, SAVANNAH, GEORGIA, *January* 2, 1865.⎰

Lieutenant-General U. S. GRANT, *City Point.*

GENERAL: I have received, by the hands of General Barnard, your note of 26th and letter of 27th December.

I herewith inclose to you a copy of a *projet* which I have this morning, in strict confidence, discussed with my immediate commanders.

I shall need, however, larger supplies of stores, especially grain. I will inclose to you, with this, letters from General Easton, quartermaster, and Colonel Beckwith, commissary of subsistence, setting forth what will be required, and trust you will forward them to Washington with your sanction, so that the necessary steps may be taken at once to enable me to carry out this plan on time.

I wrote you very fully on the 24th, and have nothing to add. Every thing here is quiet, and if I can get the necessary supplies in our wagons, shall be ready to start at the time indicated in my *projet* (January 15th). But, until those supplies are in hand, I can do nothing; after they are, I shall be ready to move with great rapidity.

I have heard of the affair at Cape Fear. It has turned out as you will remember I expected.

I have furnished General Easton a copy of the dispatch from the Secretary of War. He will retain possession of all cotton here, and ship it as fast as vessels can be had to New York.

I shall immediately send the Seventeenth Corps over to Port Royal, by boats, to be furnished by Admiral Dahlgren and General Foster (without interfering with General Easton's vessels), to make a lodgment on the railroad at Pocotaligo.

General Barnard will remain with me a few days, and I send this by a staff-officer, who can return on one of the vessels of the supply-fleet. I suppose that, now that General Butler has got through with them, you can spare them to us.

My report of recent operations is nearly ready, and will be sent you in a day or two, as soon as some further subordinate reports come in.

I am, with great respect, very truly, your friend,

W. T. SHERMAN, *Major-General.*

[ENTIRELY CONFIDENTIAL.]

PROJET FOR JANUARY.

1. Right wing to move men and artillery by transports to head of Broad River and Beaufort; reëstablish Port Royal Ferry, and mass the wing at or in the neighborhood of Pocotaligo.

Left wing and cavalry to work slowly across the causeway toward Hardeeville, to open a road by which wagons can reach their corps about Broad River; also, by a rapid movement of the left, to secure Sister's Ferry, and Augusta road out to Robertsville.

In the mean time, all guns, shot, shell, cotton, etc., to be moved to a safe place, easy to guard, and provisions and wagons got ready for another *swath*, aiming to have our army in hand about the head of Broad River, say Pocotaligo, Robertsville, and Coosawhatchie, by the 15th January.

2. The whole army to move with loaded wagons by the roads leading in the direction of Columbia, which afford the best chance of forage and provisions. Howard to be at Pocotaligo by the 15th January, and Slocum to be at Robertsville, and Kilpatrick at or near Coosawhatchie about the same date. General Foster's troops to occupy Savannah, and gunboats to protect the rivers as soon as Howard gets Pocotaligo.

W. T. SHERMAN, *Major-General.*

Therefore, on the 2d of January, I was authorized to march with my entire army north by land, and concluded at once to secure a foothold or starting-point on the South Carolina side, selecting Pocotaligo and Hardeeville as the points of rendezvous for the two wings; but I still remained in doubt as to the wishes of the Administration, whether I should take Charleston *en route*, or confine my whole attention to the incidental advantages of breaking up the railways of South and North Carolina, and the greater object of uniting my army with that of General Grant before Richmond.

General Barnard remained with me several days, and was regarded then, as now, one of the first engineers of the age, perfectly competent to advise me on the strategy and objects of the new campaign. He expressed himself delighted with the high spirit of the army, the steps already taken, by which we had captured Savannah, and he personally inspected some of the forts, such as Thunderbolt and Causten's Bluff, by which the enemy had so long held at bay the whole of our navy, and had defeated the previous attempts made in April, 1862, by the army of General Gillmore, which had bombarded and captured Fort Pulaski, but had failed to reach the city of Savannah. I think General Barnard expected me to invite him to accompany us northward in his official capacity; but Colonel Poe, of my staff, had done so well, and was so perfectly competent, that I thought it unjust to supersede him by a senior in his own corps. I therefore said nothing of this to General Barnard, and soon after he returned to his post with

General Grant, at City Point, bearing letters and full personal messages of our situation and wants.

We were very much in want of light-draught steamers for navigating the shallow waters of the coast, so that it took the Seventeenth Corps more than a week to transfer from Thunderbolt to Beaufort, South Carolina. Admiral Dahlgren had supplied the Harvest Moon and the Pontiac, and General Foster gave us a couple of hired steamers; I was really amused at the effect this short sea-voyage had on our men, most of whom had never before looked upon the ocean. Of course, they were fit subjects for sea-sickness, and afterward they begged me never again to send them to sea, saying they would rather march a thousand miles on the worst roads of the South than to spend a single night on the ocean. By the 10th General Howard had collected the bulk of the Seventeenth Corps (General Blair) on Beaufort Island, and began his march for Pocotaligo, twenty-five miles inland. They crossed the channel between the island and main-land during Saturday, the 14th of January, by a pontoon-bridge, and marched out to Garden's Corners, where there was some light skirmishing; the next day, Sunday, they continued on to Pocotaligo, finding the strong fort there abandoned, and accordingly made a lodgment on the railroad, having lost only two officers and eight men.

About the same time General Slocum crossed two divisions of the Twentieth Corps over the Savannah River, above the city, occupied Hardeeville by one division and Purysburg by another. Thus, by the middle of January, we had effected a lodgment in South Carolina, and were ready to resume the march northward; but we had not yet accumulated enough provisions and forage to fill the wagons, and other causes of delay occurred, of which I will make mention in due order.

On the last day of December, 1864, Captain Breese, United States Navy, flag-officer to Admiral Porter, reached Savannah, bringing the first news of General Butler's failure at Fort Fisher, and that the general had returned to James River with his land-forces, leaving Admiral Porter's fleet anchored off Cape Fear, in that tempestuous season. Captain Breese brought me a letter from the admiral, dated December 29th, asking me to send him from Savannah one of my old divisions, with which he said he would make short work of Fort Fisher; that he had already bombarded and silenced its guns, and that General Butler had failed because he was afraid to attack, or even give the order to attack, after (as Porter insisted) the guns of Fort Fisher had been actually silenced by the navy.

I answered him promptly on the 31st of December, that I proposed to march north *inland*, and that I would prefer to leave the rebel garrisons on the coast, instead of dislodging and piling them up in my front as we progressed. From the chances, as I then understood them, I supposed that Fort Fisher was garrisoned by a comparatively small force, while the whole division of General Hoke remained about the city of Wilmington; and that, if Fort Fisher were captured, it would leave General Hoke free to join the larger force that would naturally be collected to oppose my progress northward. I accordingly answered Admiral Porter to this effect, declining to loan him the use of one of my divisions. It subsequently transpired, however, that, as soon as General Butler reached City Point, General Grant was unwilling to rest under a sense of failure, and accordingly dispatched back the same troops, reënforced and commanded by General A. H. Terry, who, on the 15th day of January, successfully assaulted and captured Fort Fisher, with its entire garrison. After the war was over, about the 20th of May, when I was giving my testimony before the Congressional Committee on the Conduct of the War, the chairman of the committee, Senator B. F. Wade, of Ohio, told me that General Butler had been summoned before that committee during the previous January, and had just finished his demonstration to their entire satisfaction that Fort Fisher could not be carried by assault, when they heard the newsboy in the hall crying out an "extra." Calling him in, they inquired the news, and he answered, "Fort Fisher done took!" Of course, they all laughed, and none more heartily than General Butler himself.

On the 11th of January there arrived at Savannah a revenue-cutter, having on board Simeon Draper, Esq., of New York City, the Hon. E. M. Stanton, Secretary of War, Quartermaster-General Meigs, Adjutant-General Townsend, and a retinue of civilians, who had come down from the North to regulate the civil affairs of Savannah.

I was instructed by Mr. Stanton to transfer to Mr. Draper the custom-house, post-office, and such other public buildings as these civilians needed in the execution of their office, and to cause to be delivered into their custody the captured cotton. This was accomplished by—

[Special Field Orders, No. 10.]
HEADQUARTERS MILITARY DIVISION OF THE MISSISSIPPI, ⎫
    IN THE FIELD, SAVANNAH, GEORGIA, *January* 12, 1865.⎭

1. Brevet Brigadier-General Easton, chief-quartermaster, will turn over to Simeon Draper, Esq., agent of the United States Treasury Department, all cotton now in the city of Savannah, prize of war, taking his receipt for the same in gross, and returning for it to the quartermaster-general. He will also afford Mr. Draper all the facilities in his power in the way of transportation, labor, etc., to enable him to handle the cotton with expedition.

2. General Easton will also turn over to Mr. Draper the custom-house, and such other buildings in the city of Savannah as he may need in the execution of his office.

By order of General W. T. Sherman,

L. M. DAYTON, *Aide-de-Camp.*

Up to this time all the cotton had been carefully guarded, with orders to General Easton to ship it by the return-vessels to New York, for the adjudication of the nearest prize-court, accompanied with invoices and all evidence of title to ownership. Marks, numbers, and other figures, were carefully preserved on the bales, so that the court might know the history of each bale. But Mr. Stanton, who surely was an able lawyer, changed all this, and ordered the obliteration of all the marks; so that no man, friend or foe, could trace his identical cotton. I thought it strange at the time, and think it more so now; for I am assured that claims, real and fictitious, have been *proved up* against this identical cotton of three times the quantity actually captured, and that reclamations on the Treasury have been *allowed* for more than the actual quantity captured, viz., thirty-one thousand bales.

Mr. Stanton staid in Savannah several days, and seemed very curious about matters and things in general. I walked with him through the city, especially the bivouacs of the several regiments that occupied the vacant squares, and he seemed particularly pleased at the ingenuity of the men in constructing their temporary huts. Four of the "dog-tents," or *tentes d'abri*, buttoned together, served for a roof, and the sides were made of clapboards, or rough boards brought from demolished houses or fences. I remember his marked admiration for the hut of a soldier who had made his door out of a handsome parlor mirror, the glass gone and its gilt frame serving for his door.

He talked to me a great deal about the negroes, the former slaves, and I told him of many interesting incidents, illustrating their simple character and faith in our arms and progress. He inquired particularly about General Jeff. C. Davis, who, he said, was a Democrat, and hostile to the negro. I assured him that General Davis was an excellent soldier, and I did not believe he had any hostility to the negro; that in our army we had no negro soldiers, and, as a rule, we preferred white soldiers, but that we employed a large force of them as servants, teamsters, and pioneers, who had rendered admirable service. He then showed me a newspaper account of General Davis taking up his pontoon-bridge across Ebenezer Creek, leaving sleeping negro men, women, and children, on the other side, to be slaughtered by Wheeler's cavalry. I had heard such a rumor, and advised Mr. Stanton, before becoming prejudiced, to allow me to send for General Davis, which he did, and General Davis explained the matter to his entire satisfaction. The truth was, that, as we approached the seaboard, the freedmen in droves, old and young, followed the several columns to reach a place of safety. It so happened that General Davis's route into Savannah followed what was known as the "River-road," and he had to make constant use of his pontoon-train—the head of his column reaching some deep, impassable creek before the rear was fairly over another. He had occasionally to use the pontoons both day and night. On the occasion referred to, the bridge was taken up from Ebenezer Creek while some of the camp-followers remained asleep on the farther side, and these were picked up by Wheeler's cavalry. Some of them, in their fright, were drowned in trying to swim over, and others may have been cruelly killed by

Wheeler's men, but this was a mere supposition. At all events, the same thing might have resulted to General Howard, or to any other of the many most humane commanders who filled the army. General Jeff. C. Davis was strictly a soldier, and doubtless hated to have his wagons and columns encumbered by these poor negroes, for whom we all felt sympathy, but a sympathy of a different sort from that of Mr. Stanton, which was not of pure humanity, but of *politics*. The negro question was beginning to loom up among the political eventualities of the day, and many foresaw that not only would the slaves secure their freedom, but that they would also have votes. I did not dream of such a result then, but knew that slavery, as such, was dead forever, and did not suppose that the former slaves would be suddenly, without preparation, manufactured into voters, equal to all others, politically and socially. Mr. Stanton seemed desirous of coming into contact with the negroes to confer with them, and he asked me to arrange an interview for him. I accordingly sent out and invited the most intelligent of the negroes, mostly Baptist and Methodist preachers, to come to my rooms to meet the Secretary of War. Twenty responded, and were received in my room up-stairs in Mr. Green's house, where Mr. Stanton and Adjutant-General Townsend took down the conversation in the form of questions and answers. Each of the twenty gave his name and partial history, and then selected Garrison Frazier as their spokesman:

First Question. State what your understanding is in regard to the acts of Congress and President Lincoln's proclamation touching the colored people in the rebel States?
Answer. So far as I understand President Lincoln's proclamation to the rebel States, it is, that if they will lay down their arms and submit to the laws of the United States, before the 1st of January, 1863, all should be well; but if they did not, then all the slaves in the Southern States should be free, henceforth and forever. That is what I understood.
Second Question. State what you understand by slavery, and the freedom that was to be given by the President's proclamation?
Answer. Slavery is receiving by irresistible power the work of another man, and not by his consent. The freedom, as I understand it, promised by the proclamation, is taking us from under the yoke of

bondage and placing us where we can reap the fruit of our own labor, and take care of ourselves and assist the Government in maintaining our freedom.

.   .   .   .

Fourth Question. State in what manner you would rather live—whether scattered among the whites, or in colonies by yourselves?

Answer. I would prefer to live by ourselves, for there is a prejudice against us in the South that will take years to get over; but I do not know that I can answer for my brethren.

(All but Mr. Lynch, a missionary from the North, agreed with Frazier, but he thought they ought to live together, along with the whites.)

.   .   .   .

Eighth Question. If the rebel leaders were to arm the slaves, what would be its effect?

Answer. I think they would fight as long as they were before the "bayonet," and just as soon as they could get away they would desert, in my opinion.

.   .   .   .

Tenth Question. Do you understand the mode of enlistment of colored persons in the rebel States by State agents, under the act of Congress; if yes, what is your understanding?

Answer. My understanding is, that colored persons enlisted by State agents are enlisted as substitutes, and give credit to the State and do not swell the army, because every black man enlisted by a State agent leaves a white man at home; and also that larger bounties are given, or promised, by the State agents than are given by the United States. The great object should be to push through this rebellion the shortest way; and there seems to be something wanting in the enlistment by State agents, for it don't strengthen the army, but takes one away for every colored man enlisted.

Eleventh Question. State what, in your opinion, is the best way to enlist colored men as soldiers?

Answer. I think, sir, that all compulsory operations should be put a stop to. The ministers would talk to them, and the young men would enlist. It is my opinion that it would be far better for the State agents to stay at home and the enlistments be made for the United States under the direction of General Sherman.

Up to this time I was present, and, on Mr. Stanton's intimating that he wanted to ask some questions affecting me, I withdrew, and then he put the twelfth and last question:

Twelfth Question. State what is the feeling of the colored people

toward General Sherman, and how far do they regard his sentiments and actions as friendly to their rights and interests, or
otherwise?

Answer. We looked upon General Sherman, prior to his arrival, as
a man, in the providence of God, specially set apart to accomplish
this work, and we unanimously felt inexpressible gratitude to him,
looking upon him as a man who should be honored for the faithful
performance of his duty. Some of us called upon him immediately
upon his arrival, and it is probable he did not meet the secretary with
more courtesy than he did us. His conduct and deportment toward
us characterized him as a friend and gentleman. We have confidence
in General Sherman, and think what concerns us could not be in
better hands. This is our opinion now, from the short acquaintance
and intercourse we have had.

It certainly was a strange fact that the great War Secretary
should have catechized negroes concerning the character of a
general who had commanded a hundred thousand men in
battle, had captured cities, conducted sixty-five thousand men
successfully across four hundred miles of hostile territory, and
had just brought tens of thousands of freedmen to a place of
security; but because I had not loaded down my army by
other hundreds of thousands of poor negroes, I was construed by others as hostile to the black race. I had received
from General Halleck, at Washington, a letter warning me
that there were certain influential parties near the President
who were torturing him with suspicions of my fidelity to him
and his negro policy; but I shall always believe that Mr. Lincoln, though a civilian, knew better, and appreciated my motives and character. Though this letter of General Halleck has
always been treated by me as confidential, I now insert it here
at length:

HEADQUARTERS OF THE ARMY, ⎱
WASHINGTON, D. C., *December* 30, 1864.⎰

Major-General W. T. SHERMAN, *Savannah.*

MY DEAR GENERAL: I take the liberty of calling your attention, in
this private and friendly way, to a matter which may possibly hereafter be of more importance to you than either of us may now
anticipate.

While almost every one is praising your great march through
Georgia, and the capture of Savannah, there is a certain class having

now great influence with the President, and very probably anticipating still more on a change of cabinet, who are decidedly disposed to make a point against you. I mean in regard to "inevitable Sambo." They say that you have manifested an almost *criminal* dislike to the negro, and that you are not willing to carry out the wishes of the Government in regard to him, but repulse him with contempt! They say you might have brought with you to Savannah more than fifty thousand, thus stripping Georgia of that number of laborers, and opening a road by which as many more could have escaped from their masters; but that, instead of this, you drove them from your ranks, prevented their following you by cutting the bridges in your rear, and thus caused the massacre of large numbers by Wheeler's cavalry.

To those who know you as I do, such accusation will pass as the idle winds, for we presume that you discouraged the negroes from following you because you had not the means of supporting them, and feared they might seriously embarrass your march. But there are others, and among them some in high authority, who think or pretend to think otherwise, and they are decidedly disposed to make a point against you.

I do not write this to induce you to conciliate this class of men by doing any thing which you do not deem right and proper, and for the interest of the Government and the country; but simply to call your attention to certain things which are viewed here somewhat differently than from your stand-point. I will explain as briefly as possible:

Some here think that, in view of the scarcity of labor in the South, and the probability that a part, at least, of the able-bodied slaves will be called into the military service of the rebels, it is of the greatest importance to open outlets by which these slaves can escape into our lines, and they say that the route you have passed over should be made the route of escape, and Savannah the great place of refuge. These, I know, are the views of some of the leading men in the Administration, and they now express dissatisfaction that you did not carry them out in your great raid.

Now that you are in possession of Savannah, and there can be no further fears about supplies, would it not be possible for you to reopen these avenues of escape for the negroes, without interfering with your military operations? Could not such escaped slaves find at least a partial supply of food in the rice-fields about Savannah, and cotton plantations on the coast?

I merely throw out these suggestions. I know that such a course would be approved by the Government, and I believe that a manifestation on your part of a desire to bring the slaves within our lines will do much to silence your opponents. You will appreciate my motives in writing this private letter.

Yours truly,
H. W. HALLECK.

There is no doubt that Mr. Stanton, when he reached Savannah, shared these thoughts, but luckily the negroes themselves convinced him that he was in error, and that they understood their own interests far better than did the men in Washington, who tried to make political capital out of this negro question. The idea that such men should have been permitted to hang around Mr. Lincoln, to torture his life by suspicions of the officers who were toiling with the single purpose to bring the war to a successful end, and thereby to liberate *all* slaves, is a fair illustration of the influences that poison a political capital.

My aim then was, to whip the rebels, to humble their pride, to follow them to their inmost recesses, and make them fear and dread us. "Fear of the Lord is the beginning of wisdom." I did not want them to cast in our teeth what General Hood had once done in Atlanta, that we had to call on *their* slaves to help us to subdue them. But, as regards kindness to the race, encouraging them to patience and forbearance, procuring them food and clothing, and providing them with land whereon to labor, I assert that no army ever did more for that race than the one I commanded in Savannah. When we reached Savannah, we were beset by ravenous State agents from Hilton Head, who enticed and carried away our servants, and the corps of pioneers which we had organized, and which had done such excellent service. On one occasion, my own aide-de-camp, Colonel Audenried, found at least a hundred poor negroes shut up in a house and pen, waiting for the night, to be conveyed stealthily to Hilton Head. They appealed to him for protection, alleging that they had been told that they *must be* soldiers, that "Massa Lincoln" wanted them, etc. I never denied the slaves a full opportunity for voluntary enlistment, but I did prohibit force to be used, for I knew that the State agents were more influenced by the profit they derived from the large bounties then being paid than by any love of country or of the colored race. In the language of Mr. Frazier, the enlistment of every black man "did not strengthen the army, but took away one white man from the ranks."

During Mr. Stanton's stay in Savannah we discussed this negro question very fully; he asked me to draft an order on the subject, in accordance with my own views, that would meet the pressing necessities of the case, and I did so. We went over this order, No. 15, of January 16, 1865, very carefully. The secretary made some verbal modifications, when it was approved by him in all its details, I published it, and it went into operation at once. It provided fully for the enlistment of colored troops, and gave the freedmen certain possessory rights to land, which afterward became matters of judicial inquiry and decision. Of course, the military authorities at that day, when war prevailed, had a perfect right to grant the possession of any vacant land to which they could extend military protection, but we did not undertake to give a fee-simple title; and all that was designed by these special field orders was to make temporary provisions for the freedmen and their families during the rest of the war, or until Congress should take action in the premises. All that I now propose to assert is, that Mr. Stanton, Secretary of War, saw these orders in the rough, and approved every paragraph thereof, before they were made public:

[Special Field Orders, No. 15.]
HEADQUARTERS MILITARY DIVISION OF THE MISSISSIPPI, ⎫
IN THE FIELD, SAVANNAH, GEORGIA, *January* 16, 1865.⎭

1. The islands from Charleston south, the abandoned rice-fields along the rivers for thirty miles back from the sea, and the country bordering the St. John's River, Florida, are reserved and set apart for the settlement of the negroes now made free by the acts of war and the proclamation of the President of the United States.

2. At Beaufort, Hilton Head, Savannah, Fernandina, St. Augustine, and Jacksonville, the blacks may remain in their chosen or accustomed vocations; but on the islands, and in the settlements hereafter to be established, no white person whatever, unless military officers and soldiers detailed for duty, will be permitted to reside; and the sole and exclusive management of affairs will be left to the freed people themselves, subject only to the United States military authority, .

and the acts of Congress. By the laws of war, and orders of the President of the United States, the negro is free, and must be dealt with as such. He cannot be subjected to conscription, or forced military service, save by the written orders of the highest military authority of the department, under such regulations as the President or Congress may prescribe. Domestic servants, blacksmiths, carpenters, and other mechanics, will be free to select their own work and residence, but the young and able-bodied negroes must be encouraged to enlist as soldiers in the service of the United States, to contribute their share toward maintaining their own freedom, and securing their rights as citizens of the United States.

Negroes so enlisted will be organized into companies, battalions, and regiments, under the orders of the United States military authorities, and will be paid, fed, and clothed, according to law. The bounties paid on enlistment may, with the consent of the recruit, go to assist his family and settlement in procuring agricultural implements, seed, tools, boots, clothing, and other articles necessary for their livelihood.

3. Whenever three respectable negroes, heads of families, shall desire to settle on land, and shall have selected for that purpose an island or a locality clearly defined within the limits above designated, the Inspector of Settlements and Plantations will himself, or by such subordinate officer as he may appoint, give them a license to settle such island or district, and afford them such assistance as he can to enable them to establish a peaceable agricultural settlement. The three parties named will subdivide the land, under the supervision of the inspector, among themselves, and such others as may choose to settle near them, so that each family shall have a plot of not more than forty acres of tillable ground, and, when it borders on some water-channel, with not more than eight hundred feet water-front, in the possession of which land the military authorities will afford them protection until such time as they can protect themselves, or until Congress shall regulate their title. The quartermaster may, on the requisition of the Inspector of Settlements and Plantations, place at the disposal of the inspector one or more of the captured steamers to ply between the settlements and one or more of the commercial points heretofore named, in order to afford the settlers the opportunity to supply their necessary wants, and to sell the products of their land and labor.

4. Whenever a negro has enlisted in the military service of the United States, he may locate his family in any one of the settlements at pleasure, and acquire a homestead, and all other rights and privileges of a settler, as though present in person. In like manner,

negroes may settle their families and engage on board the gunboats, or in fishing, or in the navigation of the inland waters, without losing any claim to land or other advantages derived from this system. But no one, unless an actual settler as above defined, or unless absent on Government service, will be entitled to claim any right to land or property in any settlement by virtue of these orders.

5. In order to carry out this system of settlement, a general officer will be detailed as Inspector of Settlements and Plantations, whose duty it shall be to visit the settlements, to regulate their police and general arrangement, and who will furnish personally to each head of a family, subject to the approval of the President of the United States, a possessory title in writing, giving as near as possible the description of boundaries; and who shall adjust all claims or conflicts that may arise under the same, subject to the like approval, treating such titles altogether as possessory. The same general officer will also be charged with the enlistment and organization of the negro recruits, and protecting their interests while absent from their settlements; and will be governed by the rules and regulations prescribed by the War Department for such purposes.

6. Brigadier-General R. Saxton is hereby appointed Inspector of Settlements and Plantations, and will at once enter on the performance of his duties. No change is intended or desired in the settlement now on Beaufort Island, nor will any rights to property heretofore acquired be affected thereby.

By order of Major-General W. T. Sherman,

L. M. DAYTON, *Assistant Adjutant-General.*

I saw a good deal of the secretary socially, during the time of his visit to Savannah. He kept his quarters on the revenue-cutter with Simeon Draper, Esq., which cutter lay at a wharf in the river, but he came very often to my quarters at Mr. Green's house. Though appearing robust and strong, he complained a good deal of internal pains, which he said threatened his life, and would compel him soon to quit public office. He professed to have come from Washington purposely for rest and recreation, and he spoke unreservedly of the bickerings and jealousies at the national capital; of the interminable quarrels of the State Governors about their quotas, and more particularly of the financial troubles that threatened the very existence of the Government itself. He said that the price of every thing had so risen in comparison with the depreciated money, that there was danger of national bankruptcy, and he appealed to me, as a soldier and patriot, to hurry up matters so as to bring the war to a close.

He left for Port Royal about the 15th of January, and promised to go North without delay, so as to hurry back to me the supplies I had called for, as indispensable for the prosecution of the next stage of the campaign. I was quite impatient to get off myself, for a city-life had become dull and tame, and we were all anxious to get into the pine-woods again, free from the importunities of rebel women asking for protection, and of the civilians from the North who were coming to Savannah for cotton and all sorts of profit.

On the 18th of January General Slocum was ordered to turn over the city of Savannah to General J. G. Foster, commanding the Department of the South, who proposed to retain his own headquarters at Hilton Head, and to occupy Savannah by General Grover's division of the Nineteenth Corps, just arrived from James River; and on the next day, viz., January 19th, I made the first general orders for the move.

These were substantially to group the right wing of the army at Pocotaligo, already held by the Seventeenth Corps, and the left wing and cavalry at or near Robertsville, in South Carolina. The army remained substantially the same as during the march from Atlanta, with the exception of a few changes in the commanders of brigades and divisions, the addition of some men who had joined from furlough, and the loss of others from the expiration of their term of service. My own personal staff remained the same, with the exception that General W. F. Barry had rejoined us at Savannah, perfectly recovered from his attack of erysipelas, and continued with us to the end of the war. Generals Easton and Beckwith remained at Savannah, in charge of their respective depots, with orders to follow and meet us by sea with supplies when we should reach the coast at Wilmington or Newbern, North Carolina.

Of course, I gave out with some ostentation, especially among the rebels, that we were going to Charleston or Augusta; but I had long before made up my mind to waste no time on either, further than to play off on their fears, thus to retain for their protection a force of the enemy which would otherwise concentrate in our front, and make the passage of some of the great rivers that crossed our route more difficult and bloody.

Having accomplished all that seemed necessary, on the 21st of January, with my entire headquarters, officers, clerks, orderlies, etc., with wagons and horses, I embarked in a steamer for Beaufort, South Carolina, touching at Hilton Head, to see General Foster. The weather was rainy and bad, but we reached Beaufort safely on the 23d, and found some of General Blair's troops there. The bulk of his corps (Seventeenth) was, however, up on the railroad about Pocotaligo, near the head of Broad River, to which their supplies were carried from Hilton Head by steamboats. General Hatch's division (of General Foster's command) was still at Coosawhatchie or Tullafinny, where the Charleston & Savannah Railroad crosses the river of that name. All the country between Beaufort and Pocotaligo was low alluvial land, cut up by an infinite number of salt-water sloughs and fresh-water creeks, easily susceptible of defense by a small force; and why the enemy had allowed us to make a lodgment at Pocotaligo so easily I did not understand, unless it resulted from fear or ignorance. It seemed to me then that the terrible energy they had displayed in the earlier stages of the war was beginning to yield to the slower but more certain industry and discipline of our Northern men. It was to me manifest that the soldiers and people of the South entertained an undue fear of our Western men, and, like children, they had invented such ghostlike stories of our prowess in Georgia, that they were scared by their own inventions. Still, this was a power, and I intended to utilize it. Somehow, our men had got the idea that South Carolina was the cause of all our troubles; her people were the first to fire on Fort Sumter, had been in a great hurry to precipitate the country into civil war; and therefore on them should fall the scourge of war in its worst form. Taunting messages had also come to us, when in Georgia, to the effect that, when we should reach South Carolina, we would find a people less passive, who would fight us to the bitter end, daring us to come over, etc.; so that I saw and felt that we would not be able longer to restrain our men as we had done in Georgia.

Personally I had many friends in Charleston, to whom I would gladly have extended protection and mercy, but they were beyond my personal reach, and I would not restrain the army lest its vigor and energy should be impaired; and I had every reason to expect bold and strong resistance at the many broad and deep rivers that lay across our path.

General Foster's Department of the South had been enlarged to embrace the coast of North Carolina, so that the few troops serving there, under the command of General Innis N. Palmer, at Newbern, became subject to my command. General A. H. Terry held Fort Fisher, and a rumor came that he had taken the city of Wilmington; but this was premature. He had about eight thousand men. General Schofield was also known to be *en route* from Nashville for North Carolina, with the entire Twenty-third Corps, so that I had every reason to be satisfied that I would receive additional strength as we progressed northward, and before I should need it.

General W. J. Hardee commanded the Confederate forces in Charleston, with the Salkiehatchie River as his line of defense. It was also known that General Beauregard had come from the direction of Tennessee, and had assumed the general command of all the troops designed to resist our progress.

The heavy winter rains had begun early in January, rendered the roads execrable, and the Savannah River became so swollen that it filled its many channels, overflowing the vast extent of rice-fields that lay on the east bank. This flood delayed our departure two weeks; for it swept away our pontoon-bridge at Savannah, and came near drowning John E. Smith's division of the Fifteenth Corps, with several heavy trains of wagons that were *en route* from Savannah to Pocotaligo by the old causeway.

General Slocum had already ferried two of his divisions across the river, when Sister's Ferry, about forty miles above Savannah, was selected for the passage of the rest of his wing and of Kilpatrick's cavalry. The troops were in motion for that point before I quitted Savannah, and Captain S. B. Luce, United States Navy, had reported to me with a gunboat (the Pontiac) and a couple of transports, which I requested him to use in protecting Sister's Ferry during the passage of Slocum's wing, and to facilitate the passage of the troops all he could. The utmost activity prevailed at all points, but it was manifest we could not get off much before the 1st day of

February; so I determined to go in person to Pocotaligo, and there act as though we were bound for Charleston. On the 24th of January I started from Beaufort with a part of my staff, leaving the rest to follow at leisure, rode across the island to a pontoon-bridge that spanned the channel between it and the main-land, and thence rode by Garden's Corners to a plantation not far from Pocotaligo, occupied by General Blair. There we found a house, with a majestic avenue of live-oaks, whose limbs had been cut away by the troops for firewood, and desolation marked one of those splendid South Carolina estates where the proprietors formerly had dispensed a hospitality that distinguished the old *régime* of that proud State. I slept on the floor of the house, but the night was so bitter cold that I got up by the fire several times, and when it burned low I rekindled it with an old mantel-clock and the wreck of a bedstead which stood in a corner of the room—the only act of vandalism that I recall done by myself personally during the war.

The next morning I rode to Pocotaligo, and thence reconnoitred our entire line down to Coosawhatchie. Pocotaligo Fort was on low, alluvial ground, and near it began the sandy pine-land which connected with the firm ground extending inland, constituting the chief reason for its capture at the very first stage of the campaign. Hatch's division was ordered to that point from Coosawhatchie, and the whole of Howard's right wing was brought near by, ready to start by the 1st of February. I also reconnoitred the point of the Salkiehatchie River, where the Charleston Railroad crossed it, found the bridge protected by a rebel battery on the farther side, and could see a few men about it; but the stream itself was absolutely impassable, for the whole bottom was overflowed by its swollen waters to the breadth of a full mile. Nevertheless, Force's and Mower's divisions of the Seventeenth Corps were kept active, seemingly with the intention to cross over in the direction of Charleston, and thus to keep up the delusion that that city was our immediate "objective." Meantime, I had reports from General Slocum of the terrible difficulties he had encountered about Sister's Ferry, where the Savannah River was reported nearly three miles wide, and it seemed for a time almost impossible for him to span it at all with his frail pontoons. About this time (January 25th), the weather cleared away bright and cold, and I inferred that the river would soon run down, and enable Slocum to pass the river before February 1st. One of the divisions of the Fifteenth Corps (Corse's) had also been cut off by the loss of the pontoon-bridge at Savannah, so that General Slocum had with him, not only his own two corps, but Corse's division and Kilpatrick's cavalry, without which it was not prudent for me to inaugurate the campaign. We therefore rested quietly about Pocotaligo, collecting stores and making final preparations, until the 1st of February, when I learned that the cavalry and two divisions of the Twentieth Corps were fairly across the river, and then gave the necessary orders for the march northward.

Before closing this chapter, I will add a few original letters that bear directly on the subject, and tend to illustrate it:

HEADQUARTERS ARMIES OF THE UNITED STATES, ⎰
WASHINGTON, D. C., *January* 21, 1865. ⎱

Major-General W. T. SHERMAN, *commanding Military*
   Division of the Mississippi.

GENERAL: Your letters brought by General Barnard were received at City Point, and read with interest. Not having them with me, however, I cannot say that in this I will be able to satisfy you on all points of recommendation. As I arrived here at 1 P.M., and must leave at 6 P.M., having in the mean time spent over three hours with the secretary and General Halleck, I must be brief. Before your last request to have Thomas make a campaign into the heart of Alabama, I had ordered Schofield to Annapolis, Maryland, with his corps. The advance (six thousand) will reach the seaboard by the 23d, the remainder following as rapidly as railroad transportation can be procured from Cincinnati. The corps numbers over twenty-one thousand men.

·   ·   ·   ·   ·   ·   ·   ·

Thomas is still left with a sufficient force, surplus to go to Selma under an energetic leader. He has been telegraphed to, to know whether he could go, and, if so, by which of several routes he would select. No reply is yet received. Canby has been ordered to act offensively from the sea-coast to the interior, toward Montgomery and Selma. Thomas's forces will move from the north at an early day, or some of his troops will be sent to Canby. Without further reënforcement Canby will have a moving column of twenty thousand men.

Fort Fisher, you are aware, has been captured. We have a force there of eight thousand effective. At Newbern about half the number. It is rumored, through deserters, that Wilmington also has fallen. I am inclined to believe the rumor, because on the 17th we knew the enemy were blowing up their works about Fort Caswell, and that on the 18th Terry moved on Wilmington.

If Wilmington is captured, Schofield will go there. If not, he will be sent to Newbern. In either event, all the surplus forces at the two points will move to the interior, toward Goldsboro', in coöperation with your movements. From either point, railroad communications can be run out, there being here abundance of rolling-stock suited to the gauge of those roads.

There have been about sixteen thousand men sent from Lee's army south. Of these, you will have fourteen thousand against you, if Wilmington is not held by the enemy, casualties at Fort Fisher having overtaken about two thousand.

All other troops are subject to your orders as you come in communication with them. They will be so instructed. From about Richmond I will watch Lee closely, and if he detaches many men, or attempts to evacuate, will pitch in. In the mean time, should you be brought to a halt anywhere, I can send two corps of thirty thousand effective men to your support, from the troops about Richmond.

To resume: Canby is ordered to operate to the interior from the Gulf. A. J. Smith may go from the north, but I think it doubtful. A force of twenty-eight or thirty thousand will coöperate with you from Newbern or Wilmington, or both. You can call for reënforcements.

This will be handed you by Captain Hudson, of my staff, who will return with any message you may have for me. If there is any thing I can do for you in the way of having supplies on shipboard, at any point on the sea-coast, ready for you, let me know it.

Yours truly,

U. S. GRANT, *Lieutenant-General.*

HEADQUARTERS MILITARY DIVISION OF THE MISSISSIPPI, ⎫
IN THE FIELD, POCOTALIGO, SOUTH CAROLINA, *January* 29, 1865.⎭

Lieutenant-General U. S. GRANT, *City Point, Virginia.*

DEAR GENERAL: Captain Hudson has this moment arrived with your letter of January 21st, which I have read with interest.

The capture of Fort Fisher has a most important bearing on my campaign, and I rejoice in it for many reasons, because of its intrinsic importance, and because it gives me another point of security on the seaboard. I hope General Terry will follow it up by the capture of Wilmington, although I do not look for it, from Admiral Porter's dispatch to me. I rejoice that Terry was not a West-Pointer, that he belonged to your army, and that he had the same troops with which Butler feared to make the attempt.

Admiral Dahlgren, whose fleet is reënforced by some more iron-clads, wants to make an assault *à la* Fisher on Fort Moultrie, but I withhold my consent, for the reason that the capture of all Sullivan's Island is not conclusive as to Charleston; the capture of James Island would be, but all pronounce that impossible at this time. Therefore, I am moving (as hitherto designed) for the railroad west of Branch-ville, then will swing across to Orangeburg, which will interpose my army between Charleston and the interior. Contemporaneous with this, Foster will demonstrate up the Edisto, and afterward make a lodgment at Bull's Bay, and occupy the common road which leads from Mount Pleasant toward Georgetown. When I get to Co-lumbia, I think I shall move straight for Goldsboro', *via* Fayetteville. By this circuit I cut all roads, and devastate the land; and the forces along the coast, commanded by Foster, will follow my movement, taking any thing the enemy lets go, or so occupy his attention that he cannot detach all his forces against me. I feel sure of getting Wilmington, and may be Charleston, and being at Goldsboro', with its railroads finished back to Morehead City and Wilmington, I can easily take Raleigh, when it seems that Lee must come out. If Scho-field comes to Beaufort, he should be pushed out to Kinston, on the Neuse, and may be Goldsboro' (or, rather, a point on the Wilming-ton road, south of Goldsboro'). It is not necessary to storm Golds-boro', because it is in a distant region, of no importance in itself, and, if its garrison is forced to draw supplies from its north, it will be eating up the same stores on which Lee depends for his command.

I have no doubt Hood will bring his army to Augusta. Canby and Thomas should penetrate Alabama as far as possible, to keep em-ployed at least a part of Hood's army; or, what would accomplish the same thing, Thomas might reoccupy the railroad from Chatta-nooga forward to the Etowah, viz., Rome, Kingston, and Allatoona, thereby threatening Georgia. I know that the Georgia troops are disaffected. At Savannah I met delegates from several counties of the southwest, who manifested a decidedly hostile spirit to the Confed-erate cause. I nursed the feeling as far as possible, and instructed Grover to keep it up.

My left wing must now be at Sister's Ferry, crossing the Savannah River to the east bank. Slocum has orders to be at Robertsville to-morrow, prepared to move on Barnwell. Howard is here, all ready to start for the Augusta Railroad at Midway.

We find the enemy on the east side of the Salkiehatchie, and cavalry in our front; but all give ground on our approach, and seem to be merely watching us. If we start on Tuesday, in one week we shall be near Orangeburg, having broken up the Augusta road from the Edisto westward twenty or twenty-five miles. I will be sure that every rail is twisted. Should we encounter too much opposition near Orangeburg, then I will for a time neglect that branch, and rapidly move on Columbia, and fill up the triangle formed by the Congaree and Wateree (tributaries of the Santee), breaking up that great centre of the Carolina roads. Up to that point I feel full confidence, but from there may have to manœuvre some, and will be guided by the questions of weather and supplies.

You remember we had fine weather last February for our Meridian trip, and my memory of the weather at Charleston is, that February is usually a fine month. Before the March storms come we should be within striking distance of the coast. The months of April and May will be the best for operations from Goldsboro' to Raleigh and the Roanoke. You may rest assured that I will keep my troops well in hand, and, if I get worsted, will aim to make the enemy pay so dearly that you will have less to do. I know that this trip is necessary; it must be made sooner or later; I am on time, and in the right position for it. My army is large enough for the purpose, and I ask no reënforcement, but simply wish the utmost activity to be kept up at all other points, so that concentration against me may not be universal.

I expect that Jeff. Davis will move heaven and earth to catch me, for success to this column is fatal to his dream of empire. Richmond is not more vital to his cause than Columbia and the heart of South Carolina.

If Thomas will not move on Selma, order him to occupy Rome, Kingston, and Allatoona, and again threaten Georgia in the direction of Athens.

I think the "poor white trash" of the South are falling out of their ranks by sickness, desertion, and every available means; but there is a large class of vindictive Southerners who will fight to the last. The squabbles in Richmond, the howls in Charleston, and the disintegration elsewhere, are all good omens for us; we must not relax one iota, but, on the contrary, pile up our efforts. I would, ere this, have been off, but we had terrific rains, which caught us in motion, and nearly drowned some of the troops in the rice-fields of the Savannah, swept away our causeway (which had been carefully corduroyed), and made the swamps hereabout mere lakes of slimy mud. The weather is now good, and I have the army on *terra firma*. Supplies, too, came for a long time by daily driblets instead of in bulk; this is now all remedied, and I hope to start on Tuesday.

I will issue instructions to General Foster, based on the reënforcements of North Carolina; but if Schofield come, you had better relieve Foster, who cannot take the field, and needs an operation on his leg. Let Schofield take command, with his headquarters at Beaufort, North Carolina, and with orders to secure Goldsboro' (with its railroad communication back to Beaufort and Wilmington). If Lee lets us get that position, he is gone up.

I will start with my Atlanta army (sixty thousand), supplied as before, depending on the country for all food in excess of thirty days. I will have less cattle on the hoof, but I hear of hogs, cows, and calves, in Barnwell and the Columbia districts. Even here we have found some forage. Of course, the enemy will carry off and destroy some forage, but I will burn the houses where the people burn their forage, and they will get tired of it.

I must risk Hood, and trust to you to hold Lee or be on his heels if he comes south. I observe that the enemy has some respect for my name, for they gave up Pocotaligo without a fight when they heard that the attacking force belonged to my army. I will try and keep up that feeling, which is a real power. With respect, your friend,

W. T. SHERMAN, *Major-General commanding*.

P.S.—I leave my chief-quartermaster and commissary behind to follow coastwise.   W. T. S.

[Dispatch No. 6.]
FLAG-STEAMER PHILADELPHIA, ⎱
SAVANNAH RIVER, *January* 4, 1865.⎰

Hon. GIDEON WELLES, *Secretary of the Navy.*

SIR: I have already apprised the Department that the army of General Sherman occupied the city of Savannah on the 21st of December.

The rebel army, hardly respectable in numbers or condition, escaped by crossing the river and taking the Union Causeway toward the railroad.

I have walked about the city several times, and can affirm that its tranquillity is undisturbed. The Union soldiers who are stationed within its limits are as orderly as if they were in New York or Boston. . . . One effect of the march of General Sherman through Georgia has been to satisfy the people that their credulity has been

imposed upon by the lying assertions of the rebel Government, af-
firming the inability of the United States Government to withstand
the armies of rebeldom. They have seen the old flag of the United
States carried by its victorious legions through their State, almost
unopposed, and placed in their principal city without a blow.

Since the occupation of the city General Sherman has been occupied in making arrangements for its security after he leaves it for the
march that he meditates. My attention has been directed to such
measures of coöperation as the number and quality of my force
permit.

On the 2d I arrived here from Charleston, whither, as I stated in
my dispatch of the 29th of December, I had gone in consequence of
information from the senior officer there that the rebels contemplated issuing from the harbor, and his request for my presence.
Having placed a force there of seven monitors, sufficient to meet
such an emergency, and not perceiving any sign of the expected raid,
I returned to Savannah, to keep in communication with General
Sherman and be ready to render any assistance that might be desired.
General Sherman has fully informed me of his plans, and, so far as
my means permit, they shall not lack assistance by water.

On the 3d the transfer of the right wing to Beaufort was begun,
and the only suitable vessel I had at hand (the Harvest Moon) was
sent to Thunderbolt to receive the first embarkation. This took place
about 3 P.M., and was witnessed by General Sherman and General
Barnard (United States Engineers) and myself. The Pontiac is ordered around to assist, and the army transports also followed the first
move by the Harvest Moon.

I could not help remarking the unbroken silence that prevailed in
the large array of troops; not a voice was to be heard, as they gathered in masses on the bluff to look at the vessels. The notes of a
solitary bugle alone came from their midst.

General Barnard made a brief visit to one of the rebel works
(Causten's Bluff) that dominated this water-course—the best approach of the kind to Savannah.

I am collecting data that will fully exhibit to the Department the
powerful character of the defenses of the city and its approaches.
General Sherman will not retain the extended limits they embrace,
but will contract the line very much.

General Foster still holds the position near the Tullifinny. With his
concurrence I have detached the fleet brigade, and the men belonging to it have returned to their vessels. The excellent service performed by this detachment has fully realized my wishes, and
exemplified the efficiency of the organization—infantry and light

artillery handled as skirmishers. The howitzers were always landed as quickly as the men, and were brought into action before the light pieces of the land-service could be got ashore.

I regret very much that the reduced complements of the vessels prevent me from maintaining the force in constant organization. With three hundred more marines and five hundred seamen I could frequently operate to great advantage, at the present time, when the attention of the rebels is so engrossed by General Sherman.

It is said that they have a force at Hardeeville, the pickets of which were retained on the Union Causeway until a few days since, when some of our troops crossed the river and pushed them back. Concurrently with this, I caused the Sonoma to anchor so as to sweep the ground in the direction of the causeway.

The transfer of the right wing (thirty thousand men) to Beaufort will so imperil the rebel force at Hardeeville that it will be cut off or dispersed, if not moved in season.

Meanwhile I will send the Dai-Ching to St. Helena, to meet any want that may arise in that quarter, while the Mingo and Pontiac will be ready to act from Broad River.

The general route of the army will be northward; but the exact direction must be decided more or less by circumstances which it may not be possible to foresee.

My coöperation will be confined to assistance in attacking Charleston, or in establishing communication at Georgetown, in case the army pushes on without attacking Charleston, and time alone will show which of these will eventuate.

The weather of the winter first, and the condition of the ground in spring, would permit little advantage to be derived from the presence of the army at Richmond until the middle of May. So that General Sherman has no reason to move in haste, but can choose such objects as he prefers, and take as much time as their attainment may demand. The Department will learn the objects in view of General Sherman more precisely from a letter addressed by him to General Halleck, which he read to me a few days since.

I have the honor to be, very respectfully, your obedient servant,

J. A. DAHLGREN,
Rear-Admiral, commanding South-Atlantic Blockading Squadron.

HEADQUARTERS MILITARY DIVISION OF THE MISSISSIPPI, }
IN THE FIELD, POCOTALIGO, SOUTH CAROLINA, *January* 29, 1865.}

Major-General J. G. FOSTER, *commanding Department of the South.*
GENERAL: I have just received dispatches from General Grant,

stating that Schofield's corps (the Twenty-third), twenty-one thousand strong, is ordered east from Tennessee, and will be sent to Beaufort, North Carolina. That is well; I want that force to secure a point on the railroad about Goldsboro', and then to build the railroad out to that point. If Goldsboro' be too strong to carry by a rapid movement, then a point near the Neuse, south of Goldsboro', will answer, but the bridge and position about Kinston, should be held and fortified strong. The movement should be masked by the troops already at Newbern. Please notify General Palmer that these troops are coming, and to be prepared to receive them. Major-General Schofield will command in person, and is admirably adapted for the work. If it is possible, I want him to secure Goldsboro', with the railroad back to Morehead City and Wilmington. As soon as General Schofield reaches Fort Macon, have him to meet some one of your staff, to explain in full the details of the situation of affairs with me; and you can give him the chief command of all troops at Cape Fear and in North Carolina. If he finds the enemy has all turned south against me, he need not follow, but turn his attention against Raleigh; if he can secure Goldsboro' and Wilmington, it will be as much as I expect before I have passed the Santee. Send him all detachments of men that have come to join my army. They can be so organized and officered as to be efficient, for they are nearly all old soldiers who have been detached or on furlough. Until I pass the Santee, you can better use these detachments at Bull's Bay, Georgetown, etc.

I will instruct General McCallum, of the Railroad Department, to take his men up to Beaufort, North Carolina, and employ them on the road out. I do not know that he can use them on any road here. I did instruct him, while awaiting information from North Carolina, to have them build a good trestle-bridge across Port Royal ferry; but I now suppose the pontoon-bridge will do. If you move the pontoons, be sure to make a good road out to Garden's Corners, and mark it with sign-boards—obstructing the old road, so that, should I send back any detachments, they would not be misled.

I prefer that Hatch's force should not be materially weakened until I am near Columbia, when you may be governed by the situation of affairs about Charleston. If you can break the railroad between this and Charleston, then this force could be reduced.

I am, with respect, etc.,

W. T. SHERMAN, *Major-General commanding.*

Hon. EDWIN M. STANTON, *Secretary of War, Washington, D. C.*

SIR: When you left Savannah a few days ago, you forgot the map which General Geary had prepared for you, showing the route by which his division entered the city of Savannah, being the first troops to occupy that city. I now send it to you.

I avail myself of the opportunity also to inclose you copies of all my official orders touching trade and intercourse with the people of Georgia, as well as for the establishment of the negro settlements.

Delegations of the people of Georgia continue to come in, and I am satisfied that, by judicious handling and by a little respect shown to their prejudices, we can create a schism in Jeff. Davis's dominions. All that I have conversed with realize the truth that slavery as an institution is defunct, and the only questions that remain are what disposition shall be made of the negroes themselves. I confess myself unable to offer a complete solution for these questions, and prefer to leave it to the slower operations of time. We have given the initiative, and can afford to await the working of the experiment.

As to trade-matters, I also think it is to our interest to keep the Southern people somewhat dependent on the articles of commerce to which they have hitherto been accustomed. General Grover is now here, and will, I think, be able to handle this matter judiciously, and may gradually relax, and invite cotton to come in in large quantities. But at first we should manifest no undue anxiety on that score; for the rebels would at once make use of it as a power against us. We should assume a tone of perfect contempt for cotton and every thing else in comparison with the great object of the war—*the restoration of the Union, with all its rights and power.* If the rebels burn cotton as a war measure, they simply play into our hands by taking away the only product of value they have to exchange in foreign ports for war-ships and munitions. By such a course, also, they alienate the feelings of a large class of small farmers who look to their little parcels of cotton to exchange for food and clothing for their families. I hope the Government will not manifest too much anxiety to obtain cotton in large quantities, and especially that the President will not indorse the contracts for the purchase of large quantities of cotton. Several contracts, involving from six to ten thousand bales, indorsed by Mr. Lincoln, have been shown me, but were not in such a form as to amount to an order to compel me to facilitate their execution.

As to Treasury agents, and agents to take charge of confiscated and abandoned property, whose salaries depend on their fees, I can only say that, as a general rule, they are mischievous and disturbing elements to a military government, and it is almost impossible for us to study the law and regulations so as to understand fully their powers and duties. I rather think the Quartermaster's Department of the army could better fulfill all their duties and accomplish all that is aimed at by the law. Yet on this subject I will leave Generals Foster and Grover to do the best they can.

I am, with great respect, your obedient servant,

W. T. SHERMAN, *Major-General commanding.*

HEADQUARTERS MILITARY DIVISION OF THE MISSISSIPPI,⎱
IN THE FIELD, SAVANNAH, GEORGIA, *January* 2, 1865. ⎰

Hon. EDWIN M. STANTON, *Secretary of War, Washington, D. C.*

SIR: I have just received from Lieutenant-General Grant a copy of that part of your telegram to him of December 26th relating to cotton, a copy of which has been immediately furnished to General Easton, chief-quartermaster, who will be strictly governed by it.

I had already been approached by all the consuls and half the people of Savannah on this cotton question, and my invariable answer was that all the cotton in Savannah was prize of war, belonged to the United States, and nobody should recover a bale of it with my consent; that, as cotton had been one of the chief causes of this war, it should help to pay its expenses; that all cotton became tainted with treason from the hour the first act of hostility was committed against the United States some time in December, 1860; and that no bill of sale subsequent to that date could convey title.

My orders were that an officer of the Quartermaster's Department, United States Army, might furnish the holder, agent, or attorney, a mere certificate of the fact of seizure, with description of the bales' marks, etc., the cotton then to be turned over to the agent of the Treasury Department, to be shipped to New York for sale. But, since the receipt of your dispatch, I have ordered General Easton to make the shipment himself to the quartermaster at New York, where you can dispose of it at pleasure. I do not think the Treasury Department ought to bother itself with the prizes or captures of war.

Mr. Barclay, former consul at New York, representing Mr. Molyneux, former consul here, but absent a long time, called on me with reference to cotton claimed by English subjects. He seemed amazed when I told him I should pay no respect to consular certificates, that in no event would I treat an English subject with more favor than one of our own deluded citizens, and that for my part I was unwilling to fight for cotton for the benefit of Englishmen openly engaged in smuggling arms and instruments of war to kill us; that, on the contrary, it would afford me great satisfaction to conduct my army to Nassau, and wipe out that nest of pirates. I explained to him, however, that I was not a diplomatic agent of the General Government of the United States, but that my opinion, so frankly expressed, was that of a soldier, which it would be well for him to heed. It appeared, also, that he owned a plantation on the line of investment of Savannah, which, of course, was pillaged, and for which he expected me to give some certificate entitling him to indemnification, which I declined emphatically.

I have adopted in Savannah rules concerning property—severe but just—founded upon the laws of nations and the practice of civilized governments, and am clearly of opinion that we should claim all the belligerent rights over conquered countries, that the people may realize the truth that war is no child's play.

I embrace in this a copy of a letter, dated December 31, 1864, in answer to one from Solomon Cohen (a rich lawyer) to General Blair, his personal friend, as follows:

Major-General F. P. BLAIR, *commanding Seventeenth Army Corps.*

GENERAL: Your note, inclosing Mr. Cohen's of this date, is received, and I answer frankly through you his inquiries.

1. No one can practise law as an attorney in the United States without acknowledging the supremacy of our Government. If I am not in error, an attorney is as much an officer of the court as the clerk, and it would be a novel thing in a government to have a court to administer law which denied the supremacy of the government itself.

2. No one will be allowed the privileges of a merchant, or, rather, to trade is a privilege which no one should seek of the Government without in like manner acknowledging its supremacy.

3. If Mr. Cohen remains in Savannah as a denizen, his property, real and personal, will not be disturbed unless its temporary use be necessary for the military authorities of the city. The title to property will not be disturbed in any event, until adjudicated by the courts of the United States.

4. If Mr. Cohen leaves Savannah under my Special Order No. 143, it is a public acknowledgment that he "adheres to the enemies of the United States," and all his property becomes forfeited to the United States. But, as a matter of favor, he will be allowed to carry with him clothing and furniture for the use of himself, his family, and servants, and will be transported within the enemy's lines, but not by way of Port Royal.

These rules will apply to all parties, and from them no exception will be made.

I have the honor to be, general, your obedient servant,

W. T. SHERMAN, *Major-General.*

This letter was in answer to specific inquiries; it is clear, and covers all the points, and, should I leave before my orders are executed,

I will endeavor to impress upon my successor, General Foster, their wisdom and propriety.

I hope the course I have taken in these matters will meet your approbation, and that the President will not refund to parties claiming cotton or other property, without the strongest evidence of loyalty and friendship on the part of the claimant, or unless some other positive end is to be gained.

I am, with great respect, your obedient servant,

W. T. Sherman, *Major-General commanding.*

Chapter XXIII.

Campaign of the Carolinas.

February and March, 1865.

O N THE 1ST DAY of February, as before explained, the army designed for the active campaign from Savannah northward was composed of two wings, commanded respectively by Major-Generals Howard and Slocum, and was substantially the same that had marched from Atlanta to Savannah. The same general orders were in force, and this campaign may properly be classed as a continuance of the former.

The right wing, less Corse's division, Fifteenth Corps, was grouped at or near Pocotaligo, South Carolina, with its wagons filled with food, ammunition, and forage, all ready to start, and only waiting for the left wing, which was detained by the flood in the Savannah River. It was composed as follows:

Fifteenth Corps, Major-General JOHN A. LOGAN.

First Division, Brigadier-General Charles R. Woods; Second Division, Major-General W. B. Hazen; Third Division, Brigadier-General John E. Smith; Fourth Division, Brigadier-General John M. Corse. Artillery brigade, eighteen guns, Lieutenant-Colonel W. H. Ross, First Michigan Artillery.

Seventeenth Corps, Major-General FRANK P. BLAIR, JR.

First Division, Major-General Joseph A. Mower; Second Division, Brigadier-General M. F. Force; Fourth Division, Brigadier-General Giles A. Smith. Artillery brigade, fourteen guns, Major A. C. Waterhouse, First Illinois Artillery.

The left wing, with Corse's division and Kilpatrick's cavalry, was at and near Sister's Ferry, forty miles above the city of Savannah, engaged in crossing the river, then much swollen. It was composed as follows:

Fourteenth Corps, Major-General JEFF. C. DAVIS.

First Division, Brigadier-General W. P. Carlin; Second Division, Brigadier-General John D. Morgan; Third Division, Brigadier-

General A. Baird. Artillery brigade, sixteen guns, Major Charles Houghtaling, First Illinois Artillery.

Twentieth Corps, Brigadier-General A. S. WILLIAMS.

First Division, Brigadier-General N. I. Jackson; Second Division, Brigadier-General J. W. Geary; Third Division, Brigadier-General W. T. Ward. Artillery brigade, sixteen guns, Major J. A. Reynolds, First New York Artillery.

Cavalry Division, Brigadier-General JUDSON KILPATRICK.

First Brigade, Colonel T. J. Jordan, Ninth Pennsylvania Cavalry; Second Brigade, Colonel S. D. Atkins, Ninety-second Illinois Volunteers; Third Brigade, Colonel George E. Spencer, First Alabama Cavalry. One battery of four guns.

The actual strength of the army, as given in the following official tabular statements, was at the time sixty thousand and seventy-nine men, and sixty-eight guns. The trains were made up of about twenty-five hundred wagons, with six mules to each wagon, and about six hundred ambulances, with two horses each. The contents of the wagons embraced an ample supply of ammunition for a great battle; forage for about seven days, and provisions for twenty days, mostly of bread, sugar, coffee, and salt, depending largely for fresh meat on beeves driven on the hoof and such cattle, hogs, and poultry, as we expected to gather along our line of march.

RECAPITULATION—CAMPAIGN OF THE CAROLINAS.

ARM.	February 1.	March 1.	April 1.	April 10.
Infantry.	53,923	51,598	74,105	80,968
Cavalry	4,438	4,401	4,781	5,537
Artillery	1,718	1,677	2,264	2,443
Aggregate	60,079	57,676	81,150	88,948

The enemy occupied the cities of Charleston and Augusta, with garrisons capable of making a respectable if not successful defense, but utterly unable to meet our veteran columns in the open field. To resist or delay our progress north, General Wheeler had his division of cavalry (reduced to the size of a brigade by his hard and persistent fighting ever since the

Effective Strength of the Army under General W. T. SHERMAN, during the Campaign of the Carolinas, 1865.

COMMANDS.	FEBRUARY 1. Infantry Comm. Off.	Enl. Men	Cavalry Comm. Off.	Enl. Men	Artillery Comm. Off.	Enl. Men	MARCH 1. Infantry Comm. Off.	Enl. Men	Cavalry Comm. Off.	Enl. Men	Artillery Comm. Off.	Enl. Men	APRIL 1. Infantry Comm. Off.	Enl. Men	Cavalry Comm. Off.	Enl. Men	Artillery Comm. Off.	Enl. Men	APRIL 10. Infantry Comm. Off.	Enl. Men	Cavalry Comm. Off.	Enl. Men	Artillery Comm. Off.	Enl. Men
Fifteenth Ar'y C'rps.	720	14,638	2	14	10	371	733	14,076	2	12	14	348	747	14,668	2	11	15	366	708	14,536	2	21	13	390
Seventeenth A. C's.	466	11,220	4	43	6	238	441	10,675	4	42	5	266	475	11,614	4	42	7	252	478	12,395	2	28	8	253
Total, Right Wing.	1,186	25,858	6	57	16	629	1,174	24,751	6	54	19	614	1,222	26,282	6	53	22	618	1,186	26,931	4	49	21	643
Fourteenth A. C'rps.	596	13,372	. .	. .	8	444	571	12,192	. .	. .	7	438	516	12,193	. .	. .	6	408	561	14,092	. .	. .	8	437
Twentieth A. Corps.	579	12,332	. .	. .	22	501	610	12,300	. .	. .	23	481	614	11,375	. .	. .	23	486	639	11,832	. .	. .	18	476
Total, Left Wing.	1,175	25,704	. .	. .	30	945	1,181	24,492	. .	. .	30	919	1,130	23,568	. .	. .	29	894	1,200	25,924	. .	. .	26	913
Tenth Army Corps.	. .	. .	. .	. .	. .	. .	. .	. .	. .	. .	. .	. .	372	9,841	15	559	3	124	392	11,335	. .	. .	6	366
Twenty-third A. C.	. .	. .	. .	. .	. .	. .	. .	. .	. .	. .	. .	. .	547	11,143	. .	. .	13	480	641	13,359	. .	. .	11	282
Kilpatrick's Cav'ry.	. .	. .	180	4,195	4	94	. .	. .	173	4,168	4	91	. .	. .	155	3,993	4	77	. .	. .	178	5,306	5	170
Grand Aggregate.	2,361	51,562	186	4,252	50	1,668	2,355	49,243	179	4,222	53	1,624	3,271	70,834	176	4,605	71	2,193	3,419	77,549	182	5,355	69	2,374

beginning of the Atlanta campaign), and General Wade Hampton had been dispatched from the Army of Virginia to his native State of South Carolina, with a great flourish of trumpets, and extraordinary powers to raise men, money, and horses, with which "to stay the progress of the invader," and "to punish us for our insolent attempt to invade the glorious State of South Carolina!" He was supposed at the time to have, at and near Columbia, two small divisions of cavalry commanded by himself and General Butler.

Of course, I had a species of contempt for these scattered and inconsiderable forces, knew that they could hardly delay us an hour; and the only serious question that occurred to me was, would General Lee sit down in Richmond (besieged by General Grant), and permit us, almost unopposed, to pass through the States of South and North Carolina, cutting off and consuming the very supplies on which he depended to feed his army in Virginia, or would he make an effort to escape from General Grant, and endeavor to catch us inland somewhere between Columbia and Raleigh? I knew full well at the time that the broken fragments of Hood's army (which had escaped from Tennessee) were being hurried rapidly across Georgia, by Augusta, to make junction in my front; estimating them at the maximum twenty-five thousand men, and Hardee's, Wheeler's, and Hampton's forces at fifteen thousand, made forty thousand; which, if handled with spirit and energy, would constitute a formidable force, and might make the passage of such rivers as the Santee and Cape Fear a difficult undertaking. Therefore, I took all possible precautions, and arranged with Admiral Dahlgren and General Foster to watch our progress inland by all the means possible, and to provide for us points of security along the coast; as, at Bull's Bay, Georgetown, and the mouth of Cape Fear River. Still, it was extremely desirable in *one* march to reach Goldsboro' in the State of North Carolina (distant four hundred and twenty-five miles), a point of great convenience for ulterior operations, by reason of the two railroads which meet there, coming from the sea-coast at Wilmington and Newbern. Before leaving Savannah I had sent to Newbern Colonel W. W. Wright, of the Engineers, with orders to look to these railroads, to collect rolling-stock, and to have the roads repaired out as far as possible in six weeks—the time estimated as necessary for us to march that distance.

The question of supplies remained still the one of vital importance, and I reasoned that we might safely rely on the country for a considerable quantity of forage and provisions, and that, if the worst came to the worst, we could live several months on the mules and horses of our trains. Nevertheless, time was equally material, and the moment I heard that General Slocum had finished his pontoon-bridge at Sister's Ferry, and that Kilpatrick's cavalry was over the river, I gave the general orders to march, and instructed all the columns to aim for the South Carolina Railroad to the west of Branchville, about Blackville and Midway.

The right wing moved up the Salkiehatchie, the Seventeenth Corps on the right, with orders on reaching Rivers's Bridge to cross over, and the Fifteenth Corps by Hickory Hill to Beaufort's Bridge. Kilpatrick was instructed to march by way of Barnwell; Corse's division and the Twentieth Corps to take such roads as would bring them into communication with the Fifteenth Corps about Beaufort's Bridge. All these columns started promptly on the 1st of February. We encountered Wheeler's cavalry, which had obstructed the road by felling trees, but our men picked these up and threw them aside, so that this obstruction hardly delayed us an hour. In person I accompanied the Fifteenth Corps (General Logan) by McPhersonville and Hickory Hill, and kept couriers going to and fro to General Slocum with instructions to hurry as much as possible, so as to make a junction of the whole army on the South Carolina Railroad about Blackville.

I spent the night of February 1st at Hickory Hill Post-Office, and that of the 2d at Duck Branch Post-Office, thirty-one miles out from Pocotaligo. On the 3d the Seventeenth Corps was opposite Rivers's Bridge, and the Fifteenth approached Beaufort's Bridge. The Salkiehatchie was still over its banks, and presented a most formidable obstacle. The enemy appeared in some force on the opposite bank, had cut away all the bridges which spanned the many deep channels of the swollen river, and the only available passage seemed to be along the narrow causeways which constituted the common roads. At Rivers's Bridge Generals Mower and Giles A.

Smith led their heads of column through this swamp, the water up to their shoulders, crossed over to the pine-land, turned upon the rebel brigade which defended the passage, and routed it in utter disorder. It was in this attack that General Wager Swayne lost his leg, and he had to be conveyed back to Pocotaligo. Still, the loss of life was very small, in proportion to the advantages gained, for the enemy at once abandoned the whole line of the Salkiehatchie, and the Fifteenth Corps passed over at Beaufort's Bridge, without opposition.

On the 5th of February I was at Beaufort's Bridge, by which time General A. S. Williams had got up with five brigades of the Twentieth Corps; I also heard of General Kilpatrick's being abreast of us, at Barnwell, and then gave orders for the march straight for the railroad at Midway. I still remained with the Fifteenth Corps, which, on the 6th of February, was five miles from Bamberg. As a matter of course, I expected severe resistance at this railroad, for its loss would sever all the communications of the enemy in Charleston with those in Augusta.

Early on the 7th, in the midst of a rain-storm, we reached the railroad, almost unopposed, striking it at several points. General Howard told me a good story concerning this, which will bear repeating: He was with the Seventeenth Corps, marching straight for Midway, and when about five miles distant he began to deploy the leading division, so as to be ready for battle. Sitting on his horse by the road-side, while the deployment was making, he saw a man coming down the road, riding as hard as he could, and as he approached he recognized him as one of his own "foragers," mounted on a white horse, with a rope bridle and a blanket for saddle. As he came near he called out, "Hurry up, general; we have got the railroad!" So, while we, the generals, were proceeding deliberately to prepare for a serious battle, a parcel of our foragers, in search of plunder, had got ahead and actually captured the South Carolina Railroad, a line of vital importance to the rebel Government.

As soon as we struck the railroad, details of men were set to work to tear up the rails, to burn the ties and twist the bars. This was a most important railroad, and I proposed to de-

stroy it completely for fifty miles, partly to prevent a possibility of its restoration and partly to utilize the time necessary
for General Slocum to get up.

The country thereabouts was very poor, but the inhabitants
mostly remained at home. Indeed, they knew not where to
go. The enemy's cavalry had retreated before us, but his infantry was reported in some strength at Branchville, on the
farther side of the Edisto; yet on the appearance of a mere
squad of our men they burned their own bridges—the very
thing I wanted, for we had no use for them, and they had.

We all remained strung along this railroad till the 9th of
February—the Seventeenth Corps on the right, then the Fifteenth, Twentieth, and cavalry, at Blackville. General Slocum
reached Blackville that day, with Geary's division of the
Twentieth Corps, and reported the Fourteenth Corps (General Jeff. C. Davis's) to be following by way of Barnwell. On
the 10th I rode up to Blackville, where I conferred with Generals Slocum and Kilpatrick, became satisfied that the whole
army would be ready within a day, and accordingly made orders for the next movement north to Columbia, the right
wing to strike Orangeburg *en route*. Kilpatrick was ordered to
demonstrate strongly toward Aiken, to keep up the delusion
that we might turn to Augusta; but he was notified that Columbia was the next objective, and that he should cover the
left flank against Wheeler, who hung around it. I wanted to
reach Columbia before any part of Hood's army could possibly get there. Some of them were reported as having reached
Augusta, under the command of General Dick Taylor.

Having sufficiently damaged the railroad, and effected the
junction of the entire army, the general march was resumed
on the 11th, each corps crossing the South Edisto by separate
bridges, with orders to pause on the road leading from Orangeburg to Augusta, till it was certain that the Seventeenth
Corps had got possession of Orangeburg. This place was simply important as its occupation would sever the communications between Charleston and Columbia. All the heads of
column reached this road, known as the Edgefield road, during the 12th, and the Seventeenth Corps turned to the right,
against Orangeburg. When I reached the head of column opposite Orangeburg, I found Giles A. Smith's division halted,

with a battery unlimbered, exchanging shots with a party on the opposite side of the Edisto. He reported that the bridge was gone, and that the river was deep and impassable. I then directed General Blair to send a strong division below the town, some four or five miles, to effect a crossing there. He laid his pontoon-bridge, but the bottom on the other side was overflowed, and the men had to wade through it, in places as deep as their waists. I was with this division at the time, on foot, trying to pick my way across the overflowed bottom; but, as soon as the head of column reached the sand-hills, I knew that the enemy would not long remain in Orangeburg, and accordingly returned to my horse, on the west bank, and rode rapidly up to where I had left Giles A. Smith. I found him in possession of the broken bridge, abreast of the town, which he was repairing, and I was among the first to cross over and enter the town. By and before the time either Force's or Giles A. Smith's skirmishers entered the place, several stores were on fire, and I am sure that some of the towns-people told me that a Jew merchant had set fire to his own cotton and store, and from this the fire had spread. This, however, was soon put out, and the Seventeenth Corps (General Blair) occupied the place during that night. I remember to have visited a large hospital, on the hill near the railroad depot, which was occupied by the orphan children who had been removed from the asylum in Charleston. We gave them protection, and, I think, some provisions. The railroad and depot were destroyed by order, and no doubt a good deal of cotton was burned, for we all regarded cotton as hostile property, a thing to be destroyed. General Blair was ordered to break up this railroad, forward to the point where it crossed the Santee, and then to turn for Columbia. On the morning of the 13th I again joined the Fifteenth Corps, which crossed the North Edisto by Snilling's Bridge, and moved straight for Columbia, around the head of Caw-Caw Swamp. Orders were sent to all the columns to turn for Columbia, where it was supposed the enemy had concentrated all the men they could from Charleston, Augusta, and even from Virginia. That night I was with the Fifteenth Corps, twenty-one miles from Columbia, where my aide, Colonel Audenried, picked up a rebel officer on the road, who, supposing him to be of the same service with himself, answered all his questions frankly, and revealed the truth that there was nothing in Columbia except Hampton's cavalry. The fact was, that General Hardee, in Charleston, took it for granted that we were after Charleston; the rebel troops in Augusta supposed they were "our objective;" so they abandoned poor Columbia to the care of Hampton's cavalry, which was confused by the rumors that poured in on it, so that both Beauregard and Wade Hampton, who were in Columbia, seem to have lost their heads.

On the 14th the head of the Fifteenth Corps, Charles R. Woods's division, approached the Little Congaree, a broad, deep stream, tributary to the Main Congaree, six or eight miles below Columbia. On the opposite side of this stream was a newly-constructed fort, and on our side a wide extent of old cotton-fields, which had been overflowed, and was covered with a deep slime. General Woods had deployed his leading brigade, which was skirmishing forward, but he reported that the bridge was gone, and that a considerable force of the enemy was on the other side. I directed General Howard or Logan to send a brigade by a circuit to the left, to see if this stream could not be crossed higher up, but at the same time knew that General Slocum's route would bring him to Columbia behind this stream, and that his approach would uncover it. Therefore, there was no need of exposing much life. The brigade, however, found means to cross the Little Congaree, and thus uncovered the passage by the main road, so that General Woods's skirmishers at once passed over, and a party was set to work to repair the bridge, which occupied less than an hour, when I passed over with my whole staff. I found the new fort unfinished and unoccupied, but from its parapet could see over some old fields bounded to the north and west by hills skirted with timber. There was a plantation to our left, about half a mile, and on the edge of the timber was drawn up a force of rebel cavalry of about a regiment, which advanced, and charged upon some of our foragers, who were plundering the plantation; my aide, Colonel Audenried, who had ridden forward, came back somewhat hurt and bruised, for, observing this charge of cavalry, he had turned for us, and his horse fell with him in attempting to leap a ditch. General Woods's skirmish-line met this charge of cavalry, and drove it back into the woods and beyond. We remained on that ground during the night of the 15th, and I camped on the nearest dry ground behind the Little Congaree, where on the next morning were made the written orders for the government of the troops while occupying Columbia. These are dated February 16, 1865, in these words:

> General Howard will cross the Saluda and Broad Rivers as near their mouths as possible, occupy Columbia, destroy the public buildings, railroad property, manufacturing and machine shops; but will spare libraries, asylums, and private dwellings. He will then move to Winnsboro', destroying *en route* utterly that section of the railroad. He will also cause all bridges, trestles, water-tanks, and depots on the railroad back to the Wateree to be burned, switches broken, and such other destruction as he can find time to accomplish consistent with proper celerity.

These instructions were embraced in General Order No. 26, which prescribed the routes of march for the several columns as far as Fayetteville, North Carolina, and is conclusive that I then regarded Columbia as simply one point on our general route of march, and not as an important conquest.

During the 16th of February the Fifteenth Corps reached the point opposite Columbia, and pushed on for the Saluda Factory three miles above, crossed that stream, and the head of column reached Broad River just in time to find its bridge in flames, Butler's cavalry having just passed over into Columbia. The head of Slocum's column also reached the point opposite Columbia the same morning, but the bulk of his army was back at Lexington. I reached this place early in the morning of the 16th, met General Slocum there, and explained to him the purport of General Order No. 26, which contemplated the passage of his army across Broad River at Alston, fifteen miles above Columbia. Riding down to the river-bank, I saw the wreck of the large bridge which had been burned by the enemy, with its many stone piers still standing, but the superstructure gone. Across the Congaree River lay the city of Columbia, in plain, easy view. I could see the unfinished State-House, a handsome granite structure, and the ruins of the railroad depot, which were still smouldering.

Occasionally a few citizens or cavalry could be seen running across the streets, and quite a number of negroes were seemingly busy in carrying off bags of grain or meal, which were piled up near the burned depot.

Captain De Gres had a section of his twenty-pound Parrott guns unlimbered, firing into the town. I asked him what he was firing for; he said he could see some rebel cavalry occasionally at the intersections of the streets, and he had an idea that there was a large force of infantry concealed on the opposite bank, lying low, in case we should attempt to cross over directly into the town. I instructed him not to fire any more into the town, but consented to his bursting a few shells near the depot, to scare away the negroes who were appropriating the bags of corn and meal which we wanted, also to fire three shots at the unoccupied State-House. I stood by and saw these fired, and then all firing ceased. Although this matter of firing into Columbia has been the subject of much abuse and investigation, I have yet to hear of any single person having been killed in Columbia by our cannon. On the other hand, the night before, when Woods's division was in camp in the open fields at Little Congaree, it was shelled all night by a rebel battery from the other side of the river. This provoked me much at the time, for it was wanton mischief, as Generals Beauregard and Hampton must have been convinced that they could not prevent our entrance into Columbia. I have always contended that I would have been justified in retaliating for this unnecessary act of war, but did not, though I always characterized it as it deserved.

The night of the 16th I camped near an old prison bivouac opposite Columbia, known to our prisoners of war as "Camp Sorghum," where remained the mud-hovels and holes in the ground which our prisoners had made to shelter themselves from the winter's cold and the summer's heat. The Fifteenth Corps was then ahead, reaching to Broad River, about four miles above Columbia; the Seventeenth Corps was behind, on the river-bank opposite Columbia; and the left wing and cavalry had turned north toward Alston.

The next morning, viz., February 17th, I rode to the head of General Howard's column, and found that during the night he had ferried Stone's brigade of Woods's division of the Fifteenth Corps across by rafts made of the pontoons, and that brigade was then deployed on the opposite bank to cover the construction of a pontoon-bridge nearly finished.

I sat with General Howard on a log, watching the men lay this bridge; and about 9 or 10 A.M. a messenger came from Colonel Stone on the other side, saying that the Mayor of Columbia had come out of the city to surrender the place, and asking for orders. I simply remarked to General Howard that he had his orders, to let Colonel Stone go on into the city, and that we would follow as soon as the bridge was ready. By this same messenger I received a note in pencil from the Lady Superioress of a convent or school in Columbia, in which she claimed to have been a teacher in a convent in Brown County, Ohio, at the time my daughter Minnie was a pupil there, and therefore asking special protection. My recollection is, that I gave the note to my brother-in-law, Colonel Ewing, then inspector-general on my staff, with instructions to see this lady, and assure her that we contemplated no destruction of any private property in Columbia at all.

As soon as the bridge was done, I led my horse over it, followed by my whole staff. General Howard accompanied me with his, and General Logan was next in order, followed by General C. R. Woods, and the whole of the Fifteenth Corps. Ascending the hill, we soon emerged into a broad road leading into Columbia, between old fields of corn and cotton, and, entering the city, we found seemingly all its population, white and black, in the streets. A high and boisterous wind was prevailing from the north, and flakes of cotton were flying about in the air and lodging in the limbs of the trees, reminding us of a Northern snow-storm. Near the market-square we found Stone's brigade halted, with arms stacked, and a large detail of his men, along with some citizens, engaged with an old fire-engine, trying to put out the fire in a long pile of burning cotton-bales, which I was told had been fired by the rebel cavalry on withdrawing from the city that morning. I know that, to avoid this row of burning cotton-bales, I had to ride my horse on the sidewalk. In the market-square had collected a large crowd of whites and blacks, among whom was the mayor of the city, Dr. Goodwin, quite a respectable old gentleman, who was extremely anxious to protect the interests of the citizens. He was on foot, and I on horseback, and it is probable I told him then not to be uneasy, that we did not intend to stay long, and had no purpose to injure the private citizens or private property. About this time I noticed several men trying to get through the crowd to speak with me, and called to some black people to make room for them; when they reached me, they explained that they were officers of our army, who had been prisoners, had escaped from the rebel prison and guard, and were of course overjoyed to find themselves safe with us. I told them that, as soon as things settled down, they should report to General Howard, who would provide for their safety, and enable them to travel with us. One of them handed me a paper, asking me to read it at my leisure; I put it in my breast-pocket and rode on. General Howard was still with me, and, riding down the street which led by the right to the Charleston depot, we found it and a large storehouse burned to the ground, but there were, on the platform and ground near by, piles of cotton bags filled with corn and corn-meal, partially burned.

A detachment of Stone's brigade was guarding this, and separating the good from the bad. We rode along the railroad-track, some three or four hundred yards, to a large foundery, when some man rode up and said the rebel cavalry were close by, and he warned us that we might get shot. We accordingly turned back to the market-square, and *en route* noticed that several of the men were evidently in liquor, when I called General Howard's attention to it. He left me and rode toward General Woods's head of column, which was defiling through the town. On reaching the market-square, I again met Dr. Goodwin, and inquired where he proposed to quarter me, and he said that he had selected the house of Blanton Duncan, Esq., a citizen of Louisville, Kentucky, then a resident there, who had the contract for manufacturing the Confederate money, and had fled with Hampton's cavalry. We all rode some six or eight squares back from the new State-House, and found a very good modern house, completely furnished, with stabling and a large yard, took it as our headquarters, and occupied it during our stay. I considered General Howard as in command of the place, and referred the many applicants for guards and protection to him. Before our headquarter-wagons had got up, I strolled through the streets of Columbia, found sentinels posted at the principal intersections, and generally good order prevailing, but did not again return to the main street, because it was filled with a crowd of citizens watching the soldiers marching by.

During the afternoon of that day, February 17th, the whole of the Fifteenth Corps passed through the town and out on the Camden and Winnsboro' roads. The Seventeenth Corps did not enter the city at all, but crossed directly over to the Winnsboro' road from the pontoon-bridge at Broad River, which was about four miles above the city.

After we had got, as it were, settled in Blanton Duncan's house, say about 2 P.M., I overhauled my pocket according to custom, to read more carefully the various notes and memoranda received during the day, and found the paper which had been given me, as described, by one of our escaped prisoners. It proved to be the song of "Sherman's March to the Sea," which had been composed by Adjutant S. H. M. Byers, of the Fifth Iowa Infantry, when a prisoner in the asylum at Columbia, which had been beautifully written off by a fellow-prisoner, and handed to me in person. This appeared to me so good that I at once sent for Byers, attached him to my staff, provided him with horse and equipment, and took him as far as Fayetteville, North Carolina, whence he was sent to Washington as bearer of dispatches. He is now United States consul at Zurich, Switzerland, where I have since been his guest. I insert the song here for convenient reference and preservation. Byers said that there was an excellent glee-club among the prisoners in Columbia, who used to sing it well, with an audience often of rebel ladies:

SHERMAN'S MARCH TO THE SEA.

Composed by Adjutant BYERS, *Fifth Iowa Infantry. Arranged and sung by the Prisoners in Columbia Prison.*

I.

Our camp-fires shone bright on the mountain
   That frowned on the river below,
As we stood by our guns in the morning,
   And eagerly watched for the foe;

When a rider came out of the darkness
　That hung over mountain and tree,
And shouted, "Boys, up and be ready!
　For Sherman will march to the sea!"

Chorus.
　Then sang we a song of our chieftain,
　　That echoed over river and lea;
　And the stars of our banner shone brighter
　　When Sherman marched down to the sea!

II.
Then cheer upon cheer for bold Sherman
　Went up from each valley and glen,
And the bugles reëchoed the music
　That came from the lips of the men;
For we knew that the stars in our banner
　More bright in their splendor would be,
And that blessings from Northland would greet us,
　When Sherman marched down to the sea!
　　　　　Then sang we a song, etc.

III.
Then forward, boys! forward to battle!
　We marched on our wearisome way,
We stormed the wild hills of Resaca—
　God bless those who fell on that day!
Then Kenesaw frowned in its glory,
　Frowned down on the flag of the free;
But the East and the West bore our standard,
　And Sherman marched on to the sea!
　　　　　Then sang we a song, etc.

IV.
Still onward we pressed, till our banners
　Swept out from Atlanta's grim walls,
And the blood of the patriot dampened
　The soil where the traitor-flag falls;
But we paused not to weep for the fallen,

Who slept by each river and tree,
Yet we twined them a wreath of the laurel,
  As Sherman marched down to the sea!
              Then sang we a song, etc.

V.

Oh, proud was our army that morning,
  That stood where the pine darkly towers,
When Sherman said, "Boys, you are weary,
  But to-day fair Savannah is ours!"
Then sang we the song of our chieftain,
  That echoed over river and lea,
And the stars in our banner shone brighter
  When Sherman camped down by the sea!

Toward evening of February 17th, the mayor, Dr. Goodwin, came to my quarters at Duncan's house, and remarked that there was a lady in Columbia who professed to be a special friend of mine. On his giving her name, I could not recall it, but inquired as to her maiden or family name. He answered Poyas. It so happened that, when I was a lieutenant at Fort Moultrie, in 1842–'46, I used very often to visit a family of that name on the east branch of Cooper River, about forty miles from Fort Moultrie, and to hunt with the son, Mr. James Poyas, an elegant young fellow and a fine sportsman. His father, mother, and several sisters, composed the family, and were extremely hospitable. One of the ladies was very fond of painting in water-colors, which was one of my weaknesses, and on one occasion I had presented her with a volume treating of water-colors. Of course, I was glad to renew the acquaintance, and proposed to Dr. Goodwin that we should walk to her house and visit this lady, which we did. The house stood beyond the Charlotte depot, in a large lot, was of frame, with a high porch, which was reached by a set of steps outside. Entering this yard, I noticed ducks and chickens, and a general air of peace and comfort that was really pleasant to behold at that time of universal desolation; the lady in question met us at the head of the steps and invited us into a parlor which was perfectly neat and well furnished. After inquiring about her father, mother, sisters, and especially her brother James, my special friend, I could not help saying that I was pleased to notice that our men had not handled her house and premises as roughly as was their wont. "I owe it to you, general," she answered. "Not at all. I did not know you were here till a few minutes ago." She reiterated that she was indebted to me for the perfect safety of her house and property, and added, "You remember, when you were at our house on Cooper River in 1845, you gave me a book;" and she handed me the book in question, on the fly-leaf of which was written: "To Miss —— Poyas, with the compliments of W. T. Sherman, First-lieutenant Third Artillery." She then explained that, as our army approached Columbia, there was a doubt in her mind whether the terrible Sherman who was devastating the land were W. T. Sherman or T. W. Sherman, both known to be generals in the Northern army; but, on the supposition that he was her old acquaintance, when Wade Hampton's cavalry drew out of the city, calling out that the Yankees were coming, she armed herself with this book, and awaited the crisis. Soon the shouts about the market-house announced that the Yankees had come; very soon men were seen running up and down the streets; a parcel of them poured over the fence, began to chase the chickens and ducks, and to enter her house. She observed one large man, with full beard, who exercised some authority, and to him she appealed in the name of "his general." "What do you know of Uncle Billy?" "Why," she said, "when he was a young man he used to be our friend in Charleston, and here is a book he gave me." The officer or soldier took the book, looked at the inscription, and, turning to his fellows, said: "Boys, that's so; that's Uncle Billy's writing, for I have seen it often before." He at once commanded the party to stop pillaging, and left a man in charge of the house, to protect her until the regular provost-guard should be established. I then asked her if the regular guard or sentinel had been as good to her. She assured me that he was a very nice young man; that he had been telling her all about his family in Iowa; and that at that very instant of time he was in another room minding her baby. Now, this lady had good sense and tact, and had thus turned aside a party who, in five minutes more, would have rifled her premises of all that was good to eat or wear. I made her a long social visit, and, before leaving Columbia, gave her a half-tierce of rice and about one hundred pounds of ham from our own mess-stores.

In like manner, that same evening I found in Mrs. Simons another acquaintance—the wife of the brother of Hon. James Simons, of Charleston, who had been Miss Wragg. When Columbia was on fire that night, and her house in danger, I had her family and effects carried to my own headquarters, gave them my own room and bed, and, on leaving Columbia the next day, supplied her with a half-barrel of hams and a half-tierce of rice. I mention these specific facts to show that, personally, I had no malice or desire to destroy that city or its inhabitants, as is generally believed at the South.

Having walked over much of the suburbs of Columbia in the afternoon, and being tired, I lay down on a bed in Blanton Duncan's house to rest. Soon after dark I became conscious that a bright light was shining on the walls; and, calling some one of my staff (Major Nichols, I think) to inquire the cause, he said there seemed to be a house on fire down about the market-house. The same high wind still prevailed, and, fearing the consequences, I bade him go in person to see if the provost-guard were doing its duty. He soon returned, and reported that the block of buildings directly opposite the burning cotton of that morning was on fire, and that it was spreading; but he had found General Woods on the ground, with plenty of men trying to put the fire out, or, at least, to prevent its extension. The fire continued to increase, and the whole heavens became lurid. I dispatched messenger after messenger to Generals Howard, Logan, and Woods, and received from them repeated assurances that all was being done that could be done, but that the high wind was spreading the flames beyond all control. These general officers were on the ground all night, and Hazen's division had been brought into the city to assist Woods's division, already there. About eleven o'clock at night I went down-town myself, Colonel Dayton with me; we walked to Mr. Simons's house, from which I could see the flames rising high in the air, and could hear the roaring of the fire. I advised the ladies to move to my headquarters, had our own headquarter-wagons hitched up, and their effects carried there, as a place

of greater safety. The whole air was full of sparks and of flying masses of cotton, shingles, etc., some of which were carried four or five blocks, and started new fires. The men
seemed generally under good control, and certainly labored
hard to girdle the fire, to prevent its spreading; but, so long
as the high wind prevailed, it was simply beyond human possibility. Fortunately, about 3 or 4 A.M., the wind moderated,
and gradually the fire was got under control; but it had
burned out the very heart of the city, embracing several
churches, the old State-House, and the school or asylum of
that very Sister of Charity who had appealed for my personal
protection. Nickerson's Hotel, in which several of my staff
were quartered, was burned down, but the houses occupied
by myself, Generals Howard and Logan, were not burned at
all. Many of the people thought that this fire was deliberately
planned and executed. This is not true. It was accidental, and
in my judgment began with the cotton which General Hampton's men had set fire to on leaving the city (whether by his
orders or not is not material), which fire was partially subdued early in the day by our men; but, when night came, the
high wind fanned it again into full blaze, carried it against the
frame-houses, which caught like tinder, and soon spread beyond our control.

This whole subject has since been thoroughly and judicially
investigated, in some cotton cases, by the mixed commission
on American and British claims, under the Treaty of Washington, which commission failed to award a verdict in favor of
the English claimants, and thereby settled the fact that the
destruction of property in Columbia, during that night, did
not result from the acts of the General Government of the
United States—that is to say, from my army. In my official
report of this conflagration, I distinctly charged it to General
Wade Hampton, and confess I did so pointedly, to shake the
faith of his people in him, for he was in my opinion boastful,
and professed to be the special champion of South Carolina.

The morning sun of February 18th rose bright and clear
over a ruined city. About half of it was in ashes and in smouldering heaps. Many of the people were houseless, and
gathered in groups in the suburbs, or in the open parks
and spaces, around their scanty piles of furniture. General

Howard, in concert with the mayor, did all that was possible to provide other houses for them; and by my authority he turned over to the Sisters of Charity the Methodist College, and to the mayor five hundred beef-cattle, to help feed the people; I also gave the mayor (Dr. Goodwin) one hundred muskets, with which to arm a guard to maintain order after we should leave the neighborhood. During the 18th and 19th we remained in Columbia, General Howard's troops engaged in tearing up and destroying the railroad, back toward the Wateree, while a strong detail, under the immediate supervision of Colonel O. M. Poe, United States Engineers, destroyed the State Arsenal, which was found to be well supplied with shot, shell, and ammunition. These were hauled in wagons to the Saluda River, under the supervision of Colonel Baylor, chief of ordnance, and emptied into deep water, causing a very serious accident by the bursting of a percussion-shell, as it struck another on the margin of the water. The flame followed back a train of powder which had sifted out, reached the wagons, still partially loaded, and exploded them, killing sixteen men and destroying several wagons and teams of mules. We also destroyed several valuable founderies and the factory of Confederate money. The dies had been carried away, but about sixty hand-presses remained. There was also found an immense quantity of money, in various stages of manufacture, which our men spent and gambled with in the most lavish manner.

Having utterly ruined Columbia, the right wing began its march northward, toward Winnsboro', on the 20th, which we reached on the 21st, and found General Slocum, with the left wing, who had come by the way of Alston. Thence the right wing was turned eastward, toward Cheraw, and Fayetteville, North Carolina, to cross the Catawba River at Peay's Ferry. The cavalry was ordered to follow the railroad north as far as Chester, and then to turn east to Rocky Mount, the point indicated for the passage of the left wing. In person I reached Rocky Mount on the 22d, with the Twentieth Corps, which laid its pontoon-bridge and crossed over during the 23d. Kilpatrick arrived the next day, in the midst of heavy rain, and was instructed to cross the Catawba at once, by night, and to move up to Lancaster, to make believe we were bound for

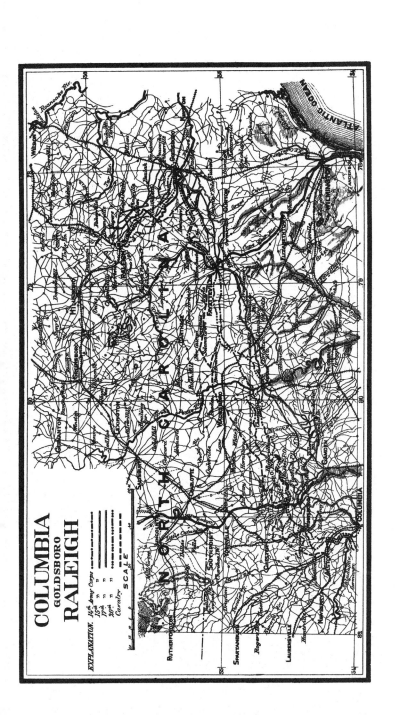

COLUMBIA
GOLDSBORO
RALEIGH

EXPLANATION.
14th Army Corps ▪▬▪▬▪▬
15th " "
17th " "
20th " "
Cavalry

SCALE

NORTH CAROLINA

ATLANTIC OCEAN

RUTHERFORDTON
SPARTANBURG
LAURENSVILLE
COLUMBIA
CAMDEN

Charlotte, to which point I heard that Beauregard had directed all his detachments, including a corps of Hood's old army, which had been marching parallel with us, but had failed to make junction with the forces immediately opposing us. Of course, I had no purpose of going to Charlotte, for the right wing was already moving rapidly toward Fayetteville, North Carolina. The rain was so heavy and persistent that the Catawba River rose fast, and soon after I had crossed the pontoon-bridge at Rocky Mount it was carried away, leaving General Davis, with the Fourteenth Corps, on the west bank. The roads were infamous, so I halted the Twentieth Corps at Hanging Rock for some days, to allow time for the Fourteenth to get over.

General Davis had infinite difficulty in reconstructing his bridge, and was compelled to use the fifth chains of his wagons for anchor-chains, so that we were delayed nearly a week in that neighborhood. While in camp at Hanging Rock two prisoners were brought to me—one a chaplain, the other a boy, son of Richard Bacot, of Charleston, whom I had known as a cadet at West Point. They were just from Charleston, and had been sent away by General Hardee in advance, because he was, they said, evacuating Charleston. Rumors to the same effect had reached me through the negroes, and it was, moreover, reported that Wilmington, North Carolina, was in possession of the Yankee troops; so that I had every reason to be satisfied that our march was fully reaping all the fruits we could possibly ask for. Charleston was, in fact, evacuated by General Hardee on the 18th of February, and was taken possession of by a brigade of General Foster's troops, commanded by General Schimmelpfennig, the same day. Hardee had availed himself of his only remaining railroad, by Florence to Cheraw; had sent there much of his ammunition and stores, and reached it with the effective part of the garrison in time to escape across the Pedee River before our arrival. Wilmington was captured by General Terry on the 22d of February; but of this important event we only knew by the vague rumors which reached us through rebel sources.

General Jeff. C. Davis got across the Catawba during the 27th, and the general march was resumed on Cheraw. Kilpatrick remained near Lancaster, skirmishing with Wheeler's and Hampton's cavalry, keeping up the delusion that we proposed to move on Charlotte and Salisbury, but with orders to watch the progress of the Fourteenth Corps, and to act in concert with it, on its left rear. On the 1st of March I was at Finlay's Bridge across Lynch's Creek, the roads so bad that we had to corduroy nearly every foot of the way; but I was in communication with all parts of the army, which had met no serious opposition from the enemy. On the 2d of March we entered the village of Chesterfield, skirmishing with Butler's cavalry, which gave ground rapidly. There I received a message from General Howard, who reported that he was already in Cheraw with the Seventeenth Corps, and that the Fifteenth was near at hand.

General Hardee had retreated eastward across the Pedee, burning the bridge. I therefore directed the left wing to march for Sneedsboro', about ten miles above Cheraw, to cross the Pedee there, while I in person proposed to cross over and join the right wing in Cheraw. Early in the morning of the 3d of March I rode out of Chesterfield along with the Twentieth Corps, which filled the road, forded Thompson's Creek, and, at the top of the hill beyond, found a road branching off to the right, which corresponded with the one on my map leading to Cheraw. Seeing a negro standing by the road-side, looking at the troops passing, I inquired of him what road that was. "Him lead to Cheraw, master!" "Is it a good road, and how far?" "A very good road, and eight or ten miles." "Any guerrillas?" "Oh! no, master, dey is gone two days ago; you could have played cards on der coat-tails, dey was in sich a hurry!" I was on my Lexington horse, who was very handsome and restive, so I made signal to my staff to follow, as I proposed to go without escort. I turned my horse down the road, and the rest of the staff followed. General Barry took up the questions about the road, and asked the same negro what he was doing there. He answered, "Dey say Massa Sherman will be along soon!" "Why," said General Barry, "that was General Sherman you were talking to." The poor negro, almost in the attitude of prayer, exclaimed: "De great God! just look at his horse!" He ran up and trotted by my side for a mile or so, and gave me all the information he possessed, but he seemed to admire the horse more than the rider.

We reached Cheraw in a couple of hours in a drizzling rain, and, while waiting for our wagons to come up, I staid with General Blair in a large house, the property of a blockade-runner, whose family remained. General Howard occupied another house farther down-town. He had already ordered his pontoon-bridge to be laid across the Pedee, there a large, deep, navigable stream, and Mower's division was already across, skirmishing with the enemy about two miles out. Cheraw was found to be full of stores which had been sent up from Charleston prior to its evacuation, and which could not be removed. I was satisfied, from inquiries, that General Hardee had with him only the Charleston garrison, that the enemy had not divined our movements, and that conse-quently they were still scattered from Charlotte around to Florence, then behind us. Having thus secured the passage of the Pedee, I felt no uneasiness about the future, because there remained no further great impediment between us and Cape Fear River, which I felt assured was by that time in possession of our friends. The day was so wet that we all kept in-doors; and about noon General Blair invited us to take lunch with him. We passed down into the basement dining-room, where the regular family table was spread with an excellent meal; and during its progress I was asked to take some wine, which stood upon the table in venerable bottles. It was so very good that I inquired where it came from. General Blair simply asked, "Do you like it?" but I insisted upon knowing where he had got it; he only replied by asking if I liked it, and wanted some. He afterward sent to my bivouac a case containing a dozen bottles of the finest madeira I ever tasted; and I learned that he had captured, in Cheraw, the wine of some of the old aristocratic families of Charleston, who had sent it up to Cheraw for safety, and heard afterward that Blair had found about eight wagon-loads of this wine, which he distributed to the army generally, in very fair pro-portions.

After finishing our lunch, as we passed out of the dining-room, General Blair asked me if I did not want some saddle-blankets, or a rug for my tent, and, leading me into the hall to a space under the stairway, he pointed out a pile of carpets which had also been sent up from Charleston for safety. After our headquarter-wagons got up, and our bivouac was established in a field near by, I sent my orderly (Walter) over to General Blair, and he came back staggering under a load of carpets, out of which the officers and escort made excellent tent-rugs, saddle-cloths, and blankets. There was an immense amount of stores in Cheraw, which were used or destroyed; among them twenty-four guns, two thousand muskets, and thirty-six hundred barrels of gunpowder. By the carelessness of a soldier, an immense pile of this powder was exploded, which shook the town badly, and killed and maimed several of our men.

We remained in or near Cheraw till the 6th of March, by which time the army was mostly across the Pedee River, and was prepared to resume the march on Fayetteville. In a house where General Hardee had been, I found a late *New York Tribune*, of fully a month later date than any I had seen. It contained a mass of news of great interest to us, and one short paragraph which I thought extremely mischievous. I think it was an editorial, to the effect that at last the editor had the satisfaction to inform his readers that General Sherman would next be heard from about Goldsboro', because his supply-vessels from Savannah were known to be rendezvousing at Morehead City. Now, I knew that General Hardee had read that same paper, and that he would be perfectly able to draw his own inferences. Up to that moment I had endeavored so to feign to our left that we had completely misled our antagonists; but this was no longer possible, and I concluded that we must be ready for the concentration in our front of all the force subject to General Jos. Johnston's orders, for I was there also informed that he had been restored to the full command of the Confederate forces in South and North Carolina.

On the 6th of March I crossed the Pedee, and all the army marched for Fayetteville: the Seventeenth Corps kept well to the right, to make room; the Fifteenth Corps marched by a direct road; the Fourteenth Corps also followed a direct road from Sneedsboro', where it had crossed the Pedee; and the Twentieth Corps, which had come into Cheraw for the convenience of the pontoon-bridge, diverged to the left, so as to enter Fayetteville next after the Fourteenth Corps, which was appointed to lead into Fayetteville. Kilpatrick held his cavalry still farther to the left rear on the roads from Lancaster, by way of Wadesboro' and New Gilead, so as to cover our trains from Hampton's and Wheeler's cavalry, who had first retreated toward the north. I traveled with the Fifteenth Corps, and on the 8th of March reached Laurel Hill, North Carolina. Satisfied that our troops must be at Wilmington, I determined to send a message there; I called for my man, Corporal Pike, whom I had rescued as before described, at Columbia, who was then traveling with our escort, and instructed him in disguise to work his way to the Cape Fear River, secure a boat, and float down to Wilmington to convey a letter, and to report our approach. I also called on General Howard for another volunteer, and he brought me a very clever young sergeant, who is now a commissioned officer in the regular army. Each of these got off during the night by separate routes, bearing the following message, reduced to the same cipher we used in telegraphic messages:

HEADQUARTERS MILITARY DIVISION OF THE MISSISSIPPI, ⎫
    IN THE FIELD, LAUREL HILL, *Wednesday, March* 8, 1865.⎰

Commanding Officer, Wilmington, North Carolina:
    We are marching for Fayetteville, will be there Saturday, Sunday, and Monday, and will then march for Goldsboro'.
    If possible, send a boat up Cape Fear River, and have word conveyed to General Schofield that I expect to meet him about Goldsboro'. We are all well and have done finely. The rains make our roads difficult, and may delay us about Fayetteville, in which case I would like to have some bread, sugar, and coffee. We have abundance of all else. I expect to reach Goldsboro' by the 20th instant.
                                        W. T. SHERMAN, *Major-General.*

    On the 9th I was with the Fifteenth Corps, and toward evening reached a little church called Bethel, in the woods, in which we took refuge in a terrible storm of rain, which poured all night, making the roads awful. All the men were at work corduroying the roads, using fence-rails and split saplings, and every foot of the way had thus to be corduroyed to enable the artillery and wagons to pass. On the 10th we made some little progress; on the 11th I reached Fayetteville, and found that General Hardee, followed by Wade Hampton's cavalry, had barely escaped across Cape Fear River, burning the bridge which I had hoped to save. On reaching Fayetteville I found General Slocum already in possession with the Fourteenth Corps, and all the rest of the army was near at hand. A day or two before, General Kilpatrick, to our left rear, had divided his force into two parts, occupying roads behind the Twentieth Corps, interposing between our infantry columns and Wade Hampton's cavalry. The latter, doubtless to make junction with General Hardee, in Fayetteville, broke across this line, captured the house in which General Kilpatrick and the brigade-commander, General Spencer, were, and for a time held possession of the camp and artillery of the brigade. However, General Kilpatrick and most of his men escaped into a swamp with their arms, reorganized and returned, catching Hampton's men in turn, scattered and drove them away, recovering most of his camp and artillery; but Hampton got off with Kilpatrick's private horses and a couple hundred prisoners, of which he boasted much in passing through Fayetteville.

It was also reported that, in the morning after Hardee's army was all across the bridge at Cape Fear River, Hampton, with a small body-guard, had remained in town, ready to retreat and burn the bridge as soon as our forces made their appearance. He was getting breakfast at the hotel when the alarm was given, when he and his escort took saddle, but soon realized that the alarm came from a set of our foragers, who, as usual, were extremely bold and rash. On these he turned, scattered them, killing some and making others prisoners; among them General Howard's favorite scout, Captain Duncan. Hampton then crossed the bridge and burned it.

I took up my quarters at the old United States Arsenal, which was in fine order, and had been much enlarged by the Confederate authorities, who never dreamed that an invading army would reach it from the west; and I also found in Fayetteville the widow and daughter of my first captain (General Childs), of the Third Artillery, learned that her son Fred had been the ordnance-officer in charge of the arsenal, and had of course fled with Hardee's army.

During the 11th the whole army closed down upon Fayetteville, and immediate preparations were made to lay two pontoon-bridges, one near the burned bridge, and another about four miles lower down.

Sunday, March 12th, was a day of Sabbath stillness in Fayetteville. The people generally attended their churches, for they were a very pious people, descended in a large measure from the old Scotch Covenanters, and our men too were resting from the toils and labors of six weeks of as hard marching as ever fell to the lot of soldiers. Shortly after noon was heard in the distance the shrill whistle of a steamboat, which came nearer and nearer, and soon a shout, long and continuous, was raised down by the river, which spread farther and farther, and we all felt that it meant a messenger from home. The effect was electric, and no one can realize the feeling unless, like us, he has been for months cut off from all communication with friends, and compelled to listen to the croakings and prognostications of open enemies. But in a very few minutes came up through the town to the arsenal on the plateau behind a group of officers, among whom was a large, florid seafaring man, named Ainsworth, bearing a small mail-bag from General Terry, at Wilmington, having left at 2 P.M. the day before. Our couriers had got through safe from Laurel Hill, and this was the prompt reply.

As in the case of our former march from Atlanta, intense anxiety had been felt for our safety, and General Terry had been prompt to open communication. After a few minutes' conference with Captain Ainsworth about the capacity of his boat, and the state of facts along the river, I instructed him to be ready to start back at 6 P.M., and ordered Captain Byers to get ready to carry dispatches to Washington. I also authorized General Howard to send back by this opportunity some of the fugitives who had traveled with his army all the way from Columbia, among whom were Mrs. Feaster and her two beautiful daughters.

I immediately prepared letters for Secretary Stanton, Generals Halleck and Grant, and Generals Schofield, Foster, Easton, and Beckwith, all of which have been published, but I include here only those to the Secretary of War, and Generals Grant and Terry, as samples of the whole.

HEADQUARTERS MILITARY DIVISION OF THE MISSISSIPPI,
IN THE FIELD, FAYETTEVILLE, NORTH CAROLINA,
Sunday, March 12, 1865.

Hon. E. M. STANTON, *Secretary of War.*

DEAR SIR: I know you will be pleased to hear that my army has reached this point, and has opened communication with Wilmington. A tug-boat came up this morning, and will start back at 6 P.M.

I have written a letter to General Grant, the substance of which he will doubtless communicate, and it must suffice for me to tell you what I know will give you pleasure—that I have done all that I proposed, and the fruits seem to me ample for the time employed. Charleston, Georgetown, and Wilmington, are incidents, while the utter demolition of the railroad system of South Carolina, and the utter destruction of the enemy's arsenals of Columbia, Cheraw, and Fayetteville, are the principals of the movement. These points were regarded as inaccessible to us, and now no place in the Confederacy is safe against the army of the West. Let Lee hold on to Richmond, and we will destroy his country; and then of what use is Richmond? He must come out and fight us on open ground, and for that we must ever be ready. Let him stick behind his parapets, and he will perish.

I remember well what you asked me, and think I am on the right road, though a long one. My army is as united and cheerful as ever, and as full of confidence in itself and its leaders. It is utterly impossible for me to enumerate what we have done, but I inclose a slip just handed me, which is but partial. At Columbia and Cheraw we destroyed nearly all the gunpowder and cartridges which the Confederacy had in this part of the country. This arsenal is in fine order, and has been much enlarged. I cannot leave a detachment to hold it, therefore shall burn it, blow it up with gunpowder, and then with rams knock down its walls. I take it for granted the United States will never again trust North Carolina with an arsenal to appropriate at her pleasure.

Hoping that good fortune may still attend my army, I remain your servant,

W. T. SHERMAN, *Major-General.*

HEADQUARTERS MILITARY DIVISION OF THE MISSISSIPPI,
IN THE FIELD, FAYETTEVILLE, NORTH CAROLINA, *March* 12, 1865.

Lieutenant-General U. S. GRANT, *commanding United States Army, City Point, Virginia.*

DEAR GENERAL: We reached this place yesterday at noon;

Hardee, as usual, retreating across the Cape Fear, burning his bridges; but our pontoons will be up to-day, and, with as little delay as possible, I will be after him toward Goldsboro'.

A tug has just come up from Wilmington, and before I get off from here, I hope to get from Wilmington some shoes and stockings, sugar, coffee, and flour. We are abundantly supplied with all else, having in a measure lived off the country.

The army is in splendid health, condition, and spirits, though we have had foul weather, and roads that would have stopped travel to almost any other body of men I ever heard of.

Our march was substantially what I designed—straight on Columbia, feigning on Branchville and Augusta. We destroyed, in passing, the railroad from the Edisto nearly up to Aiken; again, from Orangeburg to the Congaree; again, from Columbia down to Kingsville on the Wateree, and up toward Charlotte as far as the Chester line; thence we turned east on Cheraw and Fayetteville. At Columbia we destroyed immense arsenals and railroad establishments, among which were forty-three cannon. At Cheraw we found also machinery and material of war sent from Charleston, among which were twenty-five guns and thirty-six hundred barrels of powder; and here we find about twenty guns and a magnificent United States' arsenal.

We cannot afford to leave detachments, and I shall therefore destroy this valuable arsenal, so the enemy shall not have its use; and the United States should never again confide such valuable property to a people who have betrayed a trust.

I could leave here to-morrow, but want to clear my columns of the vast crowd of refugees and negroes that encumber us. Some I will send down the river in boats, and the rest to Wilmington by land, under small escort, as soon as we are across Cape Fear River.

I hope you have not been uneasy about us, and that the fruits of this march will be appreciated. It had to be made not only to destroy the valuable depots by the way, but for its incidents in the necessary fall of Charleston, Georgetown, and Wilmington. If I can now add Goldsboro' without too much cost, I will be in a position to aid you materially in the spring campaign.

Jos. Johnston may try to interpose between me here and Schofield about Newbern; but I think he will not try that, but concentrate his scattered armies at Raleigh, and I will go straight at him as soon as I get our men reclothed and our wagons reloaded.

Keep everybody busy, and let Stoneman push toward Greensboro' or Charlotte from Knoxville; even a feint in that quarter will be most important.

The railroad from Charlotte to Danville is all that is left to the enemy, and it will not do for me to go there, on account of the red-clay hills which are impassable to wheels in wet weather.

I expect to make a junction with General Schofield in ten days.

Yours truly,

W. T. SHERMAN, *Major-General.*

HEADQUARTERS MILITARY DIVISION OF THE MISSISSIPPI, }
IN THE FIELD, FAYETTEVILLE, NORTH CAROLINA, *March* 12, 1865.}

Major-General TERRY, *commanding United States Forces. Wilmington, North Carolina.*

GENERAL: I have just received your message by the tug which left Wilmington at 2 P.M. yesterday, which arrived here without trouble. The scout who brought me your cipher-message started back last night with my answers, which are superseded by the fact of your opening the river.

General Howard just reports that he has secured one of the enemy's steamboats below the city, General Slocum will try to secure two others known to be above, and we will load them with refugees (white and black) who have clung to our skirts, impeded our movements, and consumed our food.

We have swept the country well from Savannah to here, and the men and animals are in fine condition. Had it not been for the foul weather, I would have caught Hardee at Cheraw or here; but at Columbia, Cheraw, and here, we have captured immense stores, and destroyed machinery, guns, ammunition, and property, of inestimable value to our enemy. At all points he has fled from us, "standing not on the order of his going."

The people of South Carolina, instead of feeding Lee's army, will now call on Lee to feed them.

I want you to send me all the shoes, stockings, drawers, sugar, coffee, and flour, you can spare; finish the loads with oats or corn. Have the boats escorted, and let them run at night at any risk. We must not give time for Jos. Johnston to concentrate at Goldsboro'. We cannot prevent his concentrating at Raleigh, but he shall have no rest. I want General Schofield to go on with his railroad from Newbern as far as he can, and you should do the same from Wilmington. If we can get the roads to and secure Goldsboro' by April 10th, it will be soon enough; but every day now is worth a million of dollars. I can whip Jos. Johnston provided he does not catch one of my corps in flank, and I will see that the army marches hence to Goldsboro' in compact form.

I must rid our army of from twenty to thirty thousand useless mouths; as many to go down Cape Fear as possible, and the rest to go in vehicles or on captured horses *via* Clinton to Wilmington.

I thank you for the energetic action that has marked your course, and shall be most happy to meet you. I am, truly your friend,

W. T. SHERMAN, *Major-General.*

In quick succession I received other messages from General Terry, of older date, and therefore superseded by that brought by the tug Davidson, viz., by two naval officers, who had come up partly by canoes and partly by land; General Terry had also sent the Thirteenth Pennsylvania Cavalry to search for us, under Colonel Kerwin, who had dispatched Major Berks with fifty men, who reached us at Fayetteville; so that, by March 12th, I was in full communication with General Terry and the outside world. Still, I was anxious to reach Goldsboro', there to make junction with General Schofield, so as to be ready for the next and last stage of the war. I then knew that my special antagonist, General Jos. E. Johnston, was back, with part of his old army; that he would not be misled by feints and false reports, and would somehow compel me to exercise more caution than I had hitherto done. I then over-estimated his force at thirty-seven thousand infantry, supposed to be made up of S. D. Lee's corps, four thousand; Cheatham's, five thousand; Hoke's, eight thousand; Hardee's, ten thousand; and other detachments, ten thousand; with Hampton's, Wheeler's, and Butler's cavalry, about eight thousand. Of these, only Hardee and the cavalry were immediately in our front, while the bulk of Johnston's army was supposed to be collecting at or near Raleigh. I was determined, however, to give him as little time for organization as possible, and accordingly crossed Cape Fear River, with all the army, during the 13th and 14th, leaving one division as a rear-guard, until the arsenal could be completely destroyed. This was deliberately and completely leveled on the 14th, when fire was applied to the wreck. Little other damage was done at Fayetteville.

On the 14th the tug Davidson again arrived from Wilmington, with General Dodge, quartermaster, on board, reporting that there was no clothing to be had at Wilmington; but he brought up some sugar and coffee, which were most welcome, and some oats. He was followed by a couple of gun-boats, under command of Captain Young, United States Navy, who reached Fayetteville after I had left, and undertook to patrol the river as long as the stage of water would permit; and General Dodge also promised to use the captured steam-boats for a like purpose. Meantime, also, I had sent orders to General Schofield, at Newbern, and to General Terry, at Wil-mington, to move with their effective forces straight for Golds-boro', where I expected to meet them by the 20th of March.

On the 15th of March the whole army was across Cape Fear River, and at once began its march for Goldsboro'; the Sev-enteenth Corps still on the right, the Fifteenth next in order, then the Fourteenth and Twentieth on the extreme left; the cavalry acting in close concert with the left flank. With almost a certainty of being attacked on this flank, I had instructed General Slocum to send his corps-trains under strong escort by an interior road, holding four divisions ready for immedi-ate battle. General Howard was in like manner ordered to keep his trains well to his right, and to have four divisions unencumbered, about six miles ahead of General Slocum, within easy support.

In the mean time, I had dispatched by land to Wilmington a train of refugees who had followed the army all the way from Columbia, South Carolina, under an escort of two hundred men, commanded by Major John A. Winson (One Hundred and Sixteenth Illinois Infantry), so that we were disencumbered, and prepared for instant battle on our left and exposed flank.

In person I accompanied General Slocum, and during the night of March 15th was thirteen miles out on the Raleigh road. This flank followed substantially a road along Cape Fear River north, encountered pretty stubborn resistance by Har-dee's infantry, artillery, and cavalry, and the ground favored our enemy; for the deep river, Cape Fear, was on his right, and North River on his left, forcing us to attack him square in front. I proposed to drive Hardee well beyond Averysboro', and then to turn to the right by Bentonsville for Goldsboro'. During the day it rained very hard, and I had taken refuge in an old cooper-shop, where a prisoner of war was brought to me (sent back from the skirmish-line by General Kilpatrick), who proved to be Colonel Albert Rhett, former commander of Fort Sumter. He was a tall, slender, and handsome young man, dressed in the most approved rebel uniform, with high jack-boots beautifully stitched, and was dreadfully mortified to find himself a prisoner in our hands. General Frank Blair happened to be with me at the moment, and we were much amused at Rhett's outspoken disgust at having been captured without a fight. He said he was a brigade commander, and that his brigade that day was Hardee's rear-guard; that his command was composed mostly of the recent garrisons of the batteries of Charleston Harbor, and had little experience in woodcraft; that he was giving ground to us as fast as Hardee's army to his rear moved back, and during this operation he was with a single aide in the woods, and was captured by two men of Kilpatrick's skirmish-line that was following up his retrograde movement. These men called on him to surrender, and ordered him, in language more forcible than polite, to turn and ride back. He first supposed these men to be of Hampton's cavalry, and threatened to report them to General Hampton for disrespectful language; but he was soon undeceived, and was conducted to Kilpatrick, who sent him back to General Slocum's guard.

The rain was falling heavily, and, our wagons coming up, we went into camp there, and had Rhett and General Blair to take supper with us, and our conversation was full and quite interesting. In due time, however, Rhett was passed over by General Slocum to his provost-guard, with orders to be treated with due respect, and was furnished with a horse to ride.

The next day (the 16th) the opposition continued stubborn, and near Averysboro' Hardee had taken up a strong position, before which General Slocum deployed Jackson's division (of the Twentieth Corps), with part of Ward's. Kilpatrick was on his right front. Coming up, I advised that a brigade should make a wide circuit by the left, and, if possible, catch this line in flank. The movement was completely successful, the first line of the enemy was swept away, and we captured the larger part of Rhett's brigade, two hundred and seventeen men, including Captain Macbeth's battery of three guns, and buried one hundred and eight dead.

The deployed lines (Ward's and Jackson's) pressed on, and found Hardee again intrenched; but the next morning he was gone, in full retreat toward Smithfield. In this action, called the battle of Averysboro', we lost twelve officers and sixty-five men killed, and four hundred and seventy-seven men wounded; a serious loss, because every wounded man had to be carried in an ambulance. The rebel wounded (sixty-eight) were carried to a house near by, all surgical operations necessary were performed by our surgeons, and then these wounded men were left in care of an officer and four men of the rebel prisoners, with a scanty supply of food, which was the best we could do for them. In person I visited this house while the surgeons were at work, with arms and legs lying around loose, in the yard and on the porch; and in a room on a bed lay a pale, handsome young fellow, whose left arm had just been cut off near the shoulder. Some one used my name, when he asked, in a feeble voice, if I were General Sherman. He then announced himself as Captain Macbeth, whose battery had just been captured; and said that he remembered me when I used to visit his father's house, in Charleston. I inquired about his family, and enabled him to write a note to his mother, which was sent her afterward from Goldsboro'. I have seen that same young gentleman since in St. Louis, where he was a clerk in an insurance-office.

While the battle of Averysboro' was in progress, and I was sitting on my horse, I was approached by a man on foot, without shoes or coat, and his head bandaged by a handkerchief. He announced himself as the Captain Duncan who had been captured by Wade Hampton in Fayetteville, but had escaped; and, on my inquiring how he happened to be in that plight, he explained that when he was a prisoner Wade Hampton's men had made him "get out of his coat, hat, and shoes," which they appropriated to themselves. He said Wade Hampton had seen them do it, and he had appealed to him personally for protection, as an officer, but Hampton answered him with a curse. I sent Duncan to General Kilpatrick, and heard afterward that Kilpatrick had applied to General Slocum for his prisoner, Colonel Rhett, whom he made march on foot the rest of the way to Goldsboro', in retaliation. There was a story afloat that Kilpatrick made him "get out" of those fine boots, but restored them because none of his own officers had feet delicate enough to wear them. Of course, I know nothing of this personally, and have never seen Rhett since that night by the cooper-shop; and suppose that he is the editor who recently fought a duel in New Orleans.

From Averysboro' the left wing turned east, toward Goldsboro', the Fourteenth Corps leading. I remained with this wing until the night of the 18th, when we were within twenty-seven miles of Goldsboro' and five from Bentonsville; and, supposing that all danger was over, I crossed over to join Howard's column, to the right, so as to be nearer to Generals Schofield and Terry, known to be approaching Goldsboro'. I overtook General Howard at Falling-Creek Church, and found his column well drawn out, by reason of the bad roads. I had heard some cannonading over about Slocum's head of column, and supposed it to indicate about the same measure of opposition by Hardee's troops and Hampton's cavalry before experienced; but during the day a messenger overtook me, and notified me that near Bentonsville General Slocum had run up against *Johnston's whole army.* I sent back orders for him to fight defensively to save time, and that I would come up with reënforcements from the direction of Cox's Bridge, by the road which we had reached near Falling-Creek Church. The country was very obscure, and the maps extremely defective.

By this movement I hoped General Slocum would hold Johnston's army facing west, while I would come on his rear from the east. The Fifteenth Corps, less one division (Hazen's), still well to the rear, was turned at once toward Bentonsville; Hazen's division was ordered to Slocum's flank, and orders were also sent for General Blair, with the Seventeenth Corps, to come to the same destination. Meantime the sound of cannon came from the direction of Bentonsville.

The night of the 19th caught us near Falling-Creek Church; but early the next morning the Fifteenth Corps, General C. R. Woods's division leading, closed down on Bentonsville, near which it was brought up by encountering a line of fresh parapet, crossing the road and extending north, toward Mill Creek. After deploying, I ordered General Howard to proceed with due caution, using skirmishers alone, till he had made junction with General Slocum, on his left. These deployments occupied all day, during which two divisions of the Seventeenth Corps also got up. At that time General Johnston's army occupied the form of a V, the angle reaching the road leading from Averysboro' to Goldsboro', and the flanks resting on Mill Creek, his lines embracing the village of Bentonsville.

General Slocum's wing faced one of these lines and General Howard's the other; and, in the uncertainty of General Johnston's strength, I did not feel disposed to invite a general battle, for we had been out from Savannah since the latter part of January, and our wagon-trains contained but little food. I had also received messages during the day from General Schofield, at Kinston, and General Terry, at Faison's Depot, approaching Goldsboro', both expecting to reach it by March 21st. During the 20th we simply held our ground and started our trains back to Kinston for provisions, which would be needed in the event of being forced to fight a general battle at Bentonsville. The next day (21st) it began to rain again, and we remained quiet till about noon, when General Mower, ever rash, broke through the rebel line on his extreme left flank, and was pushing straight for Bentonsville and the bridge across Mill Creek. I ordered him back to connect with his own corps; and, lest the enemy should concentrate on him, ordered the whole rebel line to be engaged with a strong skirmish-fire.

I think I made a mistake there, and should rapidly have followed Mower's lead with the whole of the right wing, which would have brought on a general battle, and it could not have resulted otherwise than successfully to us, by reason of our vastly superior numbers; but at the moment, for the reasons given, I preferred to make junction with Generals Terry and Schofield, before engaging Johnston's army, the strength of which was utterly unknown. The next day he was gone, and had retreated on Smithfield; and, the roads all being clear, our army moved to Goldsboro'. The heaviest fighting at Bentonsville was on the first day, viz., the 19th, when Johnston's army struck the head of Slocum's columns, knocking back Carlin's division; but, as soon as General Slocum had brought up the rest of the Fourteenth Corps into line, and afterward the Twentieth on its left, he received and repulsed all attacks, and held his ground as ordered, to await the coming back of the right wing. His loss, as reported, was nine officers and one hundred and forty-five men killed, eight hundred and sixteen wounded, and two hundred and twenty-six missing. He reported having buried of the rebel dead one hundred and sixty-seven, and captured three hundred and thirty-eight prisoners.

The loss of the right wing was two officers and thirty-five men killed, twelve officers and two hundred and eighty-nine men wounded, and seventy missing. General Howard reported that he had buried one hundred of the rebel dead, and had captured twelve hundred and eighty-seven prisoners.

Our total loss, therefore, at Bentonsville was:

	Officers.	Men.
Killed.	11	180
Wounded.	12	1,105
Missing.	. . .	296
Total	23	1,581

Aggregate Loss 1,604

General Johnston, in his "Narrative" (p. 392), asserts that his entire force at Bentonsville, omitting Wheeler's and Butler's cavalry, only amounted to fourteen thousand one hundred infantry and artillery; and (p. 393) states his losses as follows:

DATE.	Killed.	Wounded.	Missing.
On the 19th	180	1,220	515
On the 20th	6	90	31
On the 21th	37	157	107
Total	223	1,467	653

Aggregate Loss 2,343

Wide discrepancies exist in these figures: for instance, General Slocum accounts for three hundred and thirty-eight prisoners captured, and General Howard for twelve hundred and eighty-seven, making sixteen hundred and twenty-five in all, to Johnston's six hundred and fifty-three—a difference of eight hundred and seventy-two. I have always accorded to General Johnston due credit for boldness in his attack on our exposed flank at Bentonsville, but I think he understates his strength, and doubt whether at the time he had accurate returns from his miscellaneous army, collected from Hoke, Bragg, Hardee, Lee, etc. After the first attack on Carlin's division, I doubt if the fighting was as desperate as described by him, p. 385, *et seq.* I was close up with the Fifteenth Corps, on the 20th and 21st, considered the fighting as mere skirmishing, and know that my orders were to avoid a general battle, till we could be sure of Goldsboro', and of opening up a new base of supply. With the knowledge now possessed of his small force, of course I committed an error in not overwhelming Johnston's army on the 21st of March, 1865. But I was content then to let him go, and on the 22d of March rode to Cox's Bridge, where I met General Terry, with his two divisions of the Tenth Corps; and the next day we rode into Goldsboro', where I found General Schofield with the Twenty-third Corps, thus effecting a perfect junction of all the army at that point, as originally contemplated. During the 23d and 24th the whole army was assembled at Goldsboro'; General Terry's two divisions encamped at Faison's Depot to the south, and General Kilpatrick's cavalry at Mount Olive Station, near him, and there we all rested, while I directed my special attention to replenishing the army for the next and last stage of the campaign. Colonel W. W. Wright had been so indefatigable, that the Newbern Railroad was done, and a locomotive arrived in Goldsboro' on the 25th of March.

Thus was concluded one of the longest and most important marches ever made by an organized army in a civilized country. The distance from Savannah to Goldsboro' is four hundred and twenty-five miles, and the route traversed embraced five large navigable rivers, viz., the Edisto, Broad, Catawba, Pedee, and Cape Fear, at either of which a comparatively small force, well handled, should have made the passage most difficult, if not impossible. The country generally was in a state of nature, with innumerable swamps, with simply mud roads, nearly every mile of which had to be corduroyed. In our route we had captured Columbia, Cheraw, and Fayetteville, important cities and depots of supplies, had compelled the evacuation of Charleston City and Harbor, had utterly broken up all the railroads of South Carolina, and had consumed a vast amount of food and forage, essential to the enemy for the support of his own armies. We had in mid-winter accomplished the whole journey of four hundred and twenty-five miles in fifty days, averaging ten miles per day, allowing ten lay-days, and had reached Goldsboro' with the army in superb order, and the trains almost as fresh as when we had started from Atlanta.

It was manifest to me that we could resume our march, and come within the theatre of General Grant's field of operations in all April, and that there was no force in existence that could delay our progress, unless General Lee should succeed in eluding General Grant at Petersburg, make junction with General Johnston, and thus united meet me alone; and now that we had effected a junction with Generals Terry and Schofield, I had no fear even of that event. On reaching Goldsboro', I learned from General Schofield all the details of his operations about Wilmington and Newbern; also of the fight of the Twenty-third Corps about Kinston, with General Bragg. I also found Lieutenant Dunn, of General Grant's staff, awaiting me, with the general's letter of February 7th, covering instructions to Generals Schofield and Thomas; and his letter of March 16th, in answer to mine of the 12th, from Fayetteville.

These are all given here to explain the full reasons for the events of the war then in progress, with two or three letters from myself, to fill out the picture.

HEADQUARTERS ARMIES OF THE UNITED STATES,⎱
CITY POINT, VIRGINIA, *February* 7, 1865.⎰

Major-General W. T. SHERMAN, *commanding Military Division of the Mississippi.*

GENERAL: Without much expectation of it reaching you in time to be of any service, I have mailed to you copies of instructions to

Schofield and Thomas. I had informed Schofield by telegraph of the departure of Mahone's division, south from the Petersburg front. These troops marched down the Weldon road, and, as they apparently went without baggage, it is doubtful whether they have not returned. I was absent from here when they left. Just returned yesterday morning from Cape Fear River. I went there to determine where Schofield's corps had better go to operate against Wilmington and Goldsboro'. The instructions with this will inform you of the conclusion arrived at.

Schofield was with me, and the plan of the movement against Wilmington fully determined before we started back; hence the absence of more detailed instructions to him. He will land one division at Smithville, and move rapidly up the south side of the river, and secure the Wilmington & Charlotte Railroad, and with his pontoon train cross over to the island south of the city, if he can. With the aid of the gunboats, there is no doubt but this move will drive the enemy from their position eight miles east of the city, either back to their line or away altogether. There will be a large force on the north bank of Cape Fear River, ready to follow up and invest the garrison, if they should go inside.

The railroads of North Carolina are four feet eight and one-half inches gauge. I have sent large parties of railroad-men there to build them up, and have ordered stock to run them. We have abundance of it idle from the non-use of the Virginia roads. I have taken every precaution to have supplies ready for you wherever you may turn up. I did this before when you left Atlanta, and regret that they did not reach you promptly when you reached salt-water. . . .

Alexander Stephens, R. M. T. Hunter, and Judge Campbell, are now at my headquarters, very desirous of going to Washington to see Mr. Lincoln, informally, on the subject of peace. The peace feeling within the rebel lines is gaining ground rapidly. This, however, should not relax our energies in the least, but should stimulate us to greater activity.

I have received your very kind letters, in which you say you would decline, or are opposed to, promotion. No one would be more pleased at your advancement than I, and if you should be placed in my position, and I put subordinate, it would not change our personal relations in the least. I would make the same exertions to support you that you have ever done to support me, and would do all in my power to make our cause win.

Yours truly,
U. S. GRANT, Lieutenant-General.

HEADQUARTERS ARMIES OF THE UNITED STATES,
CITY POINT, VIRGINIA, *January* 31, 1865.

Major-General G. H. THOMAS, *commanding Army of the*
Cumberland.

GENERAL: With this I send you a letter from General Sherman. At the time of writing it, General Sherman was not informed of the depletion of your command by my orders. It will be impossible at present for you to move south as he contemplated, with the force of infantry indicated.

General Slocum is advised before this of the changes made, and that for the winter you will be on the defensive. I think, however, an expedition from East Tennessee, under General Stoneman might penetrate South Carolina, well down toward Columbia, destroying the railroad and military resources of the country, thus visiting a portion of the State which will not be reached by Sherman's forces. He might also be able to return to East Tennessee by way of Salisbury, North Carolina, thus releasing some of our prisoners of war in rebel hands.

Of the practicability of doing this, General Stoneman will have to be the judge, making up his mind from information obtained while executing the first part of his instructions. Sherman's movements will attract the attention of all the force the enemy can collect, thus facilitating the execution of this.

Three thousand cavalry would be a sufficient force to take. This probably can be raised in the old Department of the Ohio, without taking any now under General Wilson. It would require, though, the reorganization of the two regiments of Kentucky Cavalry, which Stoneman had in his very successful raid into Southwestern Virginia.

It will be necessary, probably, for you to send, in addition to the force now in East Tennessee, a small division of infantry, to enable General Gillem to hold the upper end of Holston Valley, and the mountain-passes in rear of Stevenson.

You may order such an expedition. To save time, I will send a copy of this to General Stoneman, so that he can begin his preparations without loss of time, and can commence his correspondence with you as to these preparations.

As this expedition goes to destroy and not to fight battles, but to avoid them when practicable, particularly against any thing like equal forces, or where a great object is to be gained, it should go as light as possible. Stoneman's experience in raiding will teach him in this matter better than he can be directed.

Let there be no delay in the preparations for this expedition, and keep me advised of its progress. Very respectfully, your obedient servant,

U. S. GRANT, *Lieutenant-General.*

HEADQUARTERS ARMIES OF THE UNITED STATES, } CITY POINT, VIRGINIA, *January* 31, 1865. }

Major-General J. M. SCHOFIELD, *commanding Army of the Ohio.*

GENERAL: I have requested by telegraph that, for present purposes, North Carolina be erected into a department, and that you be placed in command of it, subject to Major-General Sherman's orders. Of course, you will receive orders from me direct until such time as General Sherman gets within communicating distance of you. This obviates the necessity of my publishing the order which I informed you would meet you at Fortress Monroe. If the order referred to should not be published from the Adjutant-General's office, you will read these instructions as your authority to assume command of all the troops in North Carolina, dating all official communications, "Headquarters Army of the Ohio." Your headquarters will be in the field, and with the portion of the army where you feel yourself most needed. In the first move you will go to Cape Fear River.

Your movements are intended as coöperative with Sherman's movement through the States of South and North Carolina. The first point to be obtained is to secure Wilmington. Goldsboro' will then be your objective point, moving either from Wilmington or Newbern, or both, as you may deem best. Should you not be able to reach Goldsboro', you will advance on the line or lines of railway connecting that place with the sea-coast, as near to it as you can, building the road behind you. The enterprise under you has two objects: the first is, to give General Sherman material aid, if needed, in his march north; the second, to open a base of supplies for him on the line of his march. As soon, therefore, as you can determine which of the two points, Wilmington or Newbern, you can best use for throwing supplies from to the interior, you will commence the accumulation of twenty days' rations and forage for sixty thousand men and twenty thousand animals. You will get of these as many as you can house and protect, to such point in the interior as you may be able to occupy.

I believe General Innis N. Palmer has received some instructions directly from General Sherman, on the subject of securing supplies for his army. You can learn what steps he has taken, and be governed in your requisitions accordingly. A supply of ordnance-stores will also be necessary.

Make all your requisitions upon the chiefs of their respective departments, in the field, with me at City Point. Communicate with me by every opportunity, and, should you deem it necessary at any time, send a special boat to Fortress Monroe, from which point you can communicate by telegraph.

The supplies referred to in these instructions are exclusive of those required by your own command.

The movements of the enemy may justify you, or even make it your imperative duty, to cut loose from your base and strike for the interior, to aid Sherman. In such case you will act on your own judgment, without waiting for instructions. You will report, however, what you propose doing. The details for carrying out these instructions are necessarily left to you. I would urge, however, if I did not know that you are already fully alive to the importance of it, prompt action. Sherman may be looked for in the neighborhood of Goldsboro' any time from the 22d to the 28th of February. This limits your time very materially.

If rolling-stock is not secured in the capture of Wilmington, it can be supplied from Washington. A large force of railroad-men has already been sent to Beaufort, and other mechanics will go to Fort Fisher in a day or two. On this point I have informed you by telegraph.

Very respectfully, your obedient servant,

U. S. GRANT, *Lieutenant-General.*

HEADQUARTERS ARMIES OF THE UNITED STATES, ⎱
CITY POINT, VIRGINIA, *March* 16, 1865. ⎰

Major-General W. T. SHERMAN, *commanding Military Division of the Mississippi.*

GENERAL: Your interesting letter of the 12th inst. is just received. I have never felt any uneasiness for your safety, but I have felt great anxiety to know just how you were progressing. I knew, or thought I did, that, with the magnificent army with you, you would come out safely somewhere.

To secure certain success, I deemed the capture of Wilmington of the greatest importance. Butler came near losing that prize to us. But Terry and Schofield have since retrieved his blunders, and I do not know but the first failure has been as valuable a success for the country as the capture of Fort Fisher. Butler may not see it in that light.

Ever since you started on the last campaign, and before, I have been attempting to get something done in the West, both to coöperate

with you and to take advantage of the enemy's weakness there—
to accomplish results favorable to us. Knowing Thomas to be slow
beyond excuse, I depleted his army to reënforce Canby, so that he
might act from Mobile Bay on the interior. With all I have said, he
had not moved at last advices. Canby was sending a cavalry force, of
about seven thousand, from Vicksburg toward Selma. I ordered
Thomas to send Wilson from Eastport toward the same point, and
to get him off as soon after the 20th of February as possible. He
telegraphed me that he would be off by that date. He has not yet
started, or had not at last advices. I ordered him to send Stoneman
from East Tennessee into Northwest South Carolina, to be there
about the time you would reach Columbia. He would either have
drawn off the enemy's cavalry from you, or would have succeeded in
destroying railroads, supplies, and other material, which you could
not reach. At that time the Richmond papers were full of the accounts of your movements, and gave daily accounts of movements in
West North Carolina. I supposed all the time it was Stoneman. You
may judge my surprise when I afterward learned that Stoneman was
still in Louisville, Kentucky, and that the troops in North Carolina
were Kirk's forces! In order that Stoneman might get off without
delay, I told Thomas that three thousand men would be sufficient for
him to take. In the mean time I had directed Sheridan to get his
cavalry ready, and, as soon as the snow in the mountains melted
sufficiently, to start for Staunton, and go on and destroy the Virginia
Central Railroad and canal. Time advanced, until he set the 28th of
February for starting. I informed Thomas, and directed him to
change the course of Stoneman toward Lynchburg, to destroy the
road in Virginia up as near to that place as possible. Not hearing
from Thomas, I telegraphed to him about the 12th, to know if Stoneman was yet off. He replied not, but that he (Thomas) would start
that day for Knoxville, to get him off as soon as possible.

Sheridan has made his raid, and with splendid success, so far as
heard. I am looking for him at "White House" to-day. Since about
the 20th of last month the Richmond papers have been prohibited
from publishing accounts of army movements. We are left to our
own resources, therefore, for information. You will see from the
papers what Sheridan has done; if you do not, the officer who bears
this will tell you all.

Lee has depleted his army but very little recently, and I learn of
none going south. Some regiments may have been detached, but I
think no division or brigade. The determination seems to be to hold
Richmond as long as possible. I have a force sufficient to leave
enough to hold our lines (all that is necessary of them), and move

out with plenty to whip his whole army. But the roads are entirely impassable. Until they improve, I shall content myself with watching Lee, and be prepared to pitch into him if he attempts to evacuate the place. I may bring Sheridan over—think I will—and break up the Danville and Southside Railroads. These are the last avenues left to the enemy.

Recruits have come in so rapidly at the West that Thomas has now about as much force as he had when he attacked Hood. I have stopped all who, under previous orders, would go to him, except those from Illinois.

Fearing the possibility of the enemy falling back to Lynchburg, and afterward attempting to go into East Tennessee or Kentucky, I have ordered Thomas to move the Fourth Corps to Bull's Gap, and to fortify there, and to hold out to the Virginia line, if he can. He has accumulated a large amount of supplies in Knoxville, and has been ordered not to destroy any of the railroad west of the Virginia line. I told him to get ready for a campaign toward Lynchburg, if it became necessary. He never can make one there or elsewhere; but the steps taken will prepare for any one else to take his troops and come east or go toward Rome, whichever may be necessary. I do not believe either will.

When I hear that you and Schofield are together, with your back upon the coast, I shall feel that you are entirely safe against any thing the enemy can do. Lee may evacuate Richmond, but he cannot get there with force enough to touch you. His army is now demoralized and deserting very fast, both to us and to their homes. A retrograde movement would cost him thousands of men, even if we did not follow.

Five thousand men, belonging to the corps with you, are now on their way to join you. If more reënforcements are necessary, I will send them. My notion is, that you should get Raleigh as soon as possible, and hold the railroad from there back. This may take more force than you now have.

From that point all North Carolina roads can be made useless to the enemy, without keeping up communications with the rear.

Hoping to hear soon of your junction with the forces from Wilmington and Newbern, I remain, very respectfully, your obedient servant,

U. S. GRANT, *Lieutenant-General.*

HEADQUARTERS MILITARY DIVISION OF THE MISSISSIPPI,
IN THE FIELD, COX'S BRIDGE, NEUSE RIVER,
NORTH CAROLINA, *March* 22, 1865.

Lieutenant-General U. S. GRANT, *Commander-in-Chief, City Point, Virginia.*

GENERAL: I wrote you from Fayetteville, North Carolina, on Tuesday, the 14th instant, that I was all ready to start for Goldsboro', to which point I had also ordered General Schofield, from Newbern, and General Terry, from Wilmington. I knew that General Jos. Johnston was supreme in command against me, and that he would have time to concentrate a respectable army to oppose the last stage of this march. Accordingly, General Slocum was ordered to send his main supply-train, under escort of two divisions, straight for Bentonsville, while he, with his other four divisions, disencumbered of all unnecessary wagons, should march toward Raleigh, by way of threat, as far as Averysboro'. General Howard, in like manner, sent his trains with the Seventeenth Corps, well to the right, and, with the four divisions of the Fifteenth Corps, took roads which would enable him to come promptly to the exposed left flank. We started on the 15th, but again the rains set in, and the roads, already bad enough, became horrible.

On Tuesday, the 15th, General Slocum found Hardee's army, from Charleston, which had retreated before us from Cheraw, in position across the narrow, swampy neck between Cape Fear and North Rivers, where the road branches off to Goldsboro'. There a pretty severe fight occurred, in which General Slocum's troops carried handsomely the advanced line, held by a South Carolina brigade, commanded by a Colonel Butler. Its commander, Colonel Rhett, of Fort Sumter notoriety, with one of his staff, had the night before been captured, by Kilpatrick's scouts, from his very skirmish-line. The next morning Hardee was found gone, and was pursued through and beyond Averysboro'. General Slocum buried one hundred and eight dead rebels, and captured and destroyed three guns. Some eighty wounded rebels were left in our hands, and, after dressing their wounds, we left them in a house, attended by a Confederate officer and four privates, detailed out of our prisoners and paroled for the purpose.

We resumed the march toward Goldsboro'. I was with the left wing until I supposed all danger had passed; but, when General Slocum's head of column was within four miles of Bentonsville, after skirmishing as usual with cavalry, he became aware that there was infantry in his front. He deployed a couple of brigades, which, on advancing, sustained a partial repulse, but soon rallied, when he formed a line of the two leading divisions (Morgan's and Carlin's) of Jeff. C. Davis's corps. The enemy attacked these with violence, but was repulsed. This was in the forenoon of Sunday, the 19th. General Slocum brought forward the two divisions of the Twentieth Corps, hastily disposed of them for defense, and General Kilpatrick massed his cavalry on the left.

General Jos. Johnston had, the night before, marched his whole army (Bragg, Cheatham, S. D. Lee, Hardee, and all the troops he had drawn from every quarter), determined, as he told his men, to crush one of our corps, and then defeat us in detail. He attacked General Slocum in position from 3 P.M. on the 19th till dark; but was everywhere repulsed, and lost heavily. At the time, I was with the Fifteenth Corps, marching on a road more to the right; but, on hearing of General Slocum's danger, directed that corps toward Cox's Bridge, in the night brought Blair's corps over, and on the 20th marched rapidly on Johnston's flank and rear. We struck him about noon, forced him to assume the defensive, and to fortify. Yesterday we pushed him hard, and came very near crushing him, the right division of the Seventeenth Corps (Mower's) having broken in to within a hundred yards of where Johnston himself was, at the bridge across Mill Creek. Last night he retreated, leaving us in possession of the field, dead, and wounded. We have over two thousand prisoners from this affair and the one at Averysboro', and I am satisfied that Johnston's army was so roughly handled yesterday that we could march right on to Raleigh; but we have now been out six weeks, living precariously upon the collections of our foragers, our men "dirty, ragged, and saucy," and we must rest and fix up a little. Our entire losses thus far (killed, wounded, and prisoners) will be covered by twenty-five hundred, a great part of which are, as usual, slight wounds. The enemy has lost more than double as many, and we have in prisoners alone full two thousand.

I limited the pursuit, this morning, to Mill Creek, and will forthwith march the army to Goldsboro', there to rest, reclothe, and get some rations.

Our combinations were such that General Schofield entered Goldsboro' from Newbern; General Terry got Cox's Bridge, with pontoons laid, and a brigade across Neuse River intrenched; and we whipped Jos. Johnston—all on the same day.

After riding over the field of battle to-day, near Bentonsville, and making the necessary orders, I have ridden down to this place (Cox's Bridge) to see General Terry, and to-morrow shall ride into Goldsboro'.

I propose to collect there my army proper; shall post General

Terry about Faison's Depot, and General Schofield about Kinston, partly to protect the road, but more to collect such food and forage as the country affords, until the railroads are repaired leading into Goldsboro'.

I fear these have not been pushed with the vigor I had expected; but I will soon have them both going. I shall proceed at once to organize three armies of twenty-five thousand men each, and will try and be all ready to march to Raleigh or Weldon, as we may determine, by or before April 10th.

I inclose you a copy of my orders of to-day. I would like to be more specific, but have not the data. We have lost no general officers nor any organization. General Slocum took three guns at Averysboro', and lost three others at the first dash on him at Bentonsville. We have all our wagons and trains in good order.

Yours truly,

W. T. SHERMAN, *Major-General.*

HEADQUARTERS MILITARY DIVISION OF THE MISSISSIPPI, ⎫
IN THE FIELD, GOLDSBORO', NORTH CAROLINA, *March* 23, 1865.⎭

Lieutenant-General U. S. GRANT, *commanding the Armies of the United States, City Point, Virginia.*

GENERAL: On reaching Goldsboro' this morning, I found Lieutenant Dunn awaiting me with your letter of March 16th and dispatch of the 17th. I wrote you fully from Cox's Bridge yesterday, and since reaching Goldsboro' have learned that my letter was sent punctually to Newbern, whence it will be dispatched to you.

I am very glad to hear that General Sheridan did such good service between Richmond and Lynchburg, and hope he will keep the ball moving. I know that these raids and dashes disconcert our enemy and discourage him much.

General Slocum's two corps (Fourteenth and Twentieth) are now coming in. I will dispose of them north of Goldsboro', between the Weldon road and Little River. General Howard to-day is marching south of the Neuse, and to-morrow will come in and occupy ground north of Goldsboro', extending from the Weldon Railroad to that leading to Kinston.

I have ordered all the provisional divisions, made up of troops belonging to the regular corps, to be broken up, and the men to join their proper regiments and organizations; and have ordered General Schofield to guard the railroads back to Newbern and Wilmington, and to make up a movable column equal to twenty-five thousand men, with which to take the field. His army will be the centre, as on the Atlanta campaign. I do not think I want any more troops (other than absentees and recruits) to fill up the present regiments, and I can make up an army of eighty thousand men by April 10th. I will post General Kilpatrick at Mount Olive Station on the Wilmington road, and then allow the army some rest.

We have sent all our empty wagons, under escort, with the proper staff-officers, to bring up from Kinston clothing and provisions. As long as we move we can gather food and forage; but, the moment we stop, trouble begins.

I feel sadly disappointed that our railroads are not done. I do not like to say there has been any neglect until I make inquiries; but it does seem to me the repairs should have been made ere this, and the road properly stocked. I can only hear of one locomotive (besides the four old ones) on the Newbern road, and two damaged locomotives (found by General Terry) on the Wilmington road. I left Generals Easton and Beckwith purposely to make arrangements in anticipation of my arrival, and have heard from neither, though I suppose them both to be at Morehead City.

At all events, we have now made a junction of all the armies, and if we can maintain them, will, in a short time, be in a position to march against Raleigh, Gaston, Weldon, or even Richmond, as you may determine.

If I get the troops all well placed, and the supplies working well, I may run up to see you for a day or two before diving again into the bowels of the country.

I will make, in a very short time, accurate reports of our operations for the past two months. Yours truly,

W. T. SHERMAN, *Major-General commanding.*

HEADQUARTERS MILITARY DIVISION OF THE MISSISSIPPI, ⎫
IN THE FIELD, GOLDSBORO', NORTH CAROLINA, *March* 24, 1865.⎰

Lieutenant-General U. S. GRANT, *City Point, Virginia.*

GENERAL: I have kept Lieutenant Dunn over to-day that I might report further. All the army is now in, save the cavalry (which I have posted at Mount Olive Station, south of the Neuse) and General Terry's command (which to-morrow will move from Cox's Ferry to Faison's Depot, also on the Wilmington road). I send you a copy of my orders of this morning, the operation of which will, I think, soon complete our roads. The telegraph is now done to Morehead City, and by it I learn that stores have been sent to Kinston in boats, and that our wagons are loading with rations and clothing. By using the

Neuse as high up as Kinston, hauling from there twenty-six miles, and by equipping the two roads to Morehead City and Wilmington, I feel certain we can not only feed and equip the army, but in a short time fill our wagons for another start. I feel certain, from the character of the fighting, that we have got Johnston's army afraid of us. He himself acts with timidity and caution. His cavalry alone manifests spirit, but limits its operations to our stragglers and foraging-parties. My marching columns of infantry do not pay the cavalry any attention, but walk right through it.

I think I see pretty clearly how, in one more move, we can checkmate Lee, forcing him to unite Johnston with him in the defense of Richmond, or to abandon the *cause*. I feel certain, if he leaves Richmond, Virginia leaves the Confederacy. I will study my maps a little more before giving my positive views. I want all possible information of the Roanoke as to navigability, how far up, and with what draught.

We find the country sandy, dry, with good roads, and more corn and forage than I had expected. The families remain, but I will gradually push them all out to Raleigh or Wilmington. We will need every house in the town. Lieutenant Dunn can tell you of many things of which I need not write. Yours truly,

W. T. SHERMAN, *Major-General.*

HEADQUARTERS MILITARY DIVISION OF THE MISSISSIPPI, ⎫
IN THE FIELD, GOLDSBORO', NORTH CAROLINA, *April* 5, 1865.⎭

Major-General GEORGE H. THOMAS, *commanding Department of the Cumberland.*

DEAR GENERAL: I can hardly help smiling when I contemplate my command—it is decidedly mixed. I believe, but am not certain, that you are in my jurisdiction, but I certainly cannot help you in the way of orders or men; nor do I think you need either. General Cruft has just arrived with his provisional division, which will at once be broken up and the men sent to their proper regiments, as that of Meagher was on my arrival here.

You may have some feeling about my asking that General Slocum should have command of the two corps that properly belong to you, viz., the Fourteenth and Twentieth, but you can recall that he was but a corps commander, and could not legally make orders of discharge, transfer, etc., which was imperatively necessary. I therefore asked that General Slocum should be assigned to command "an army in the field," called the Army of Georgia, composed of the Fourteenth and Twentieth Corps. The order is not yet made by the President, though I have recognized it because both General Grant and the President have sanctioned it, and promised to have the order made.

My army is now here, pretty well clad and provided, divided into three parts, of two corps each—much as our old Atlanta army was.

I expect to move on in a few days, and propose (if Lee remains in Richmond) to pass the Roanoke, and open communication with the Chowan and Norfolk. This will bring me in direct communication with General Grant.

This is an admirable point—country open, and the two railroads in good order back to Wilmington and Beaufort. We have already brought up stores enough to fill our wagons, and only await some few articles, and the arrival of some men who are marching up from the coast, to be off.

General Grant explained to me his orders to you, which, of course, are all right. You can make reports direct to Washington or to General Grant, but keep me advised occasionally of the general state of affairs, that I may know what is happening. I must give my undivided attention to matters here. You will hear from a thousand sources pretty fair accounts of our next march. Yours truly,

W. T. SHERMAN, *Major-General.*

[LETTER FROM ADMIRAL DAHLGREN.]
SOUTH-ATLANTIC SQUADRON,
FLAG-SHIP PHILADELPHIA, CHARLESTON, *April* 20, 1865.}

Major-General W. T. SHERMAN, *commanding Armies of the Tennessee, Georgia, and Mississippi.*

MY DEAR GENERAL: I was much gratified by a sight of your handwriting, which has just reached me from Goldsboro'; it was very suggestive of a past to me, when these regions were the scene of your operations.

As you progressed through South Carolina, there was no manifestation of weakness or of an intention to abandon Charleston, until within a few hours of the fact. On the 11th of February I was at Stono, and a spirited demonstration was made by General Schimmelpfennig and the vessels. He drove the rebels from their rifle-pits in front of the lines, extending from Fort Pringle, and pushed them vigorously. The next day I was at Bull's Bay, with a dozen steamers, among them the finest of the squadron. General Potter had twelve to fifteen hundred men, the object being to carry out your views. We made as much fuss as possible, and with better success than I anticipated, for it seems that the rebs conceived Stono to be a feint, and the real object at Bull's Bay, supposing, from the number of steamers and boats, that we had several thousand men. Now came an aide from General Gillmore, at Port Royal, with your cipher-dispatch from Midway, so I steamed down to Port Royal to see him. Next day was spent in vain efforts to decipher—finally it was accomplished. You thought that the state of the roads *might* force you to turn upon Charleston; so I went there on the 15th, but there was no sign yet of flinching. Then I went to Bull's Bay next day (16th), and found that the troops were not yet ashore, owing to the difficulties of shoal water. One of the gunboats had contrived to get up to within shelling range, and both soldiers and sailors were working hard. On the evening of the 16th I steamed down to Stono to see how matters were going there. Passing Charleston, I noticed two large fires, well inside—probably preparing to leave. On the 17th, in Stono, rumors were flying about loose of evacuation. In course of the morning, General Schimmelpfennig telegraphed me, from Morris Island, that there were symptoms of leaving; that he would again make a push at Stono, and asked for monitors. General Schimmelpfennig came down in the afternoon, and we met in the Folly Branch, near Secessionville. He was sure that the rebs would be off that night, so he was to assault them in front, while a monitor and gunboats stung their flanks both sides. I also sent an aide to order my battery of five eleven-inch guns, at Cumming's Point, to fire steadily all night on Sullivan's Island, and two monitors to close up to the island for the same object. Next morning (18th) the rascals were found to be off, and we broke in from all directions, by land and water. The main bodies had left at eight or nine in the evening, leaving detachments to keep up a fire from the batteries. I steamed round quickly, and soon got into the city, threading the streets with a large group of naval captains who had joined me. All was silent as the grave. No one to be seen but a few firemen.

No one can question the excellence of your judgment in taking the track you did, and I never had any misgivings, but it was natural to desire to go into the place with a strong hand, for, if any one spot in the land was foremost in the trouble, it was Charleston.

Your campaign was the final blow, grand in conception, complete in execution; and now it is yours to secure the last army which rebeldom possesses. I hear of your being in motion by the 9th, and hope that the result may be all that you wish.

Tidings of the murder of the President have just come, and shocked every mind. Can it be that such a resort finds root in any stratum of American opinion? Evidently it has not been the act of one man, nor of a madman. Who have prompted him?

I am grateful for your remembrance of my boy; the thought of him is ever nearest to my heart. Generous, brave, and noble, as I ever knew him to be, that he should close his young life so early, even under the accepted conditions of a soldier's life, as a son of the Union, would have been grief sufficient for me to bear; but that his precious remains should have been so treated by the brutes into whose hands they fell, adds even to the bitterness of death. I am now awaiting the hour when I can pay my last duties to his memory.

With my best and sincere wishes, my dear general, for your success and happiness, I am, most truly, your friend,

J. A. DAHLGREN.

[General Order No. 50.]
WAR DEPARTMENT, ADJUTANT-GENERAL'S OFFICE, }
WASHINGTON, *March* 27, 1865. }

Ordered—1. That at the hour of noon, on the 14th day of April, 1865, Brevet Major-General Anderson will raise and plant upon the ruins of Fort Sumter, in Charleston Harbor, the same United States flag which floated over the battlements of that fort during the rebel assault, and which was lowered and saluted by him and the small force of his command when the works were evacuated on the 14th day of April, 1861.

2. That the flag, when raised, be saluted by one hundred guns from Fort Sumter, and by a national salute from every fort and rebel battery that fired upon Fort Sumter.

3. That suitable ceremonies be had upon the occasion, under the direction of Major-General William T. Sherman, whose military operations compelled the rebels to evacuate Charleston, or, in his absence, under the charge of Major-General Q. A. Gillmore, commanding the department. Among the ceremonies will be the delivery of a public address by the Rev. Henry Ward Beecher.

4. That the naval forces at Charleston, and their commander on that station, be invited to participate in the ceremonies of the occasion.

By order of the President of the United States,

EDWIN M. STANTON, *Secretary of War.*

[General Order No. 41.]
HEADQUARTERS DEPARTMENT OF THE SOUTH, }
HILTON HEAD, SOUTH CAROLINA, *April* 10, 1865. }

Friday next, the 14th inst., will be the fourth anniversary of the capture of Fort Sumter by the rebels. A befitting celebration on that day, in honor of its reoccupation by the national forces, has been ordered by the President, in pursuance of which Brevet Major-General Robert Anderson, United States Army, will restore to its original place on the fort the identical flag which, after an honorable and gallant defense, he was compelled to lower to the insurgents in South Carolina, in April, 1861.

The ceremonies for the occasion will commence with prayer, at thirty minutes past eleven o'clock A.M.

At noon precisely, the flag will be raised and saluted with one hundred guns from Fort Sumter, and with a national salute from Fort Moultrie and Battery Bee on Sullivan's Island, Fort Putnam on Morris Island, and Fort Johnson on James's Island; it being eminently appropriate that the places which were so conspicuous in the inauguration of the rebellion should take a part not less prominent in this national rejoicing over the restoration of the national authority.

After the salutes, the Rev. Henry Ward Beecher will deliver an address.

The ceremonies will close with prayer and a benediction.

Colonel Stewart L. Woodford, chief of staff, under such verbal instructions as he may receive, is hereby charged with the details of the celebration, comprising all the arrangements that it may be necessary to make for the accommodation of the orator of the day, and the comfort and safety of the invited guests from the army and navy, and from civil life.

By command of Major-General Q. A. Gillmore,

> W. L. M. BURGER, *Assistant Adjutant-General.*

Copy of Major ANDERSON'S *Dispatch, announcing the Surrender of Fort Sumter, April 14, 1861.*

> STEAMSHIP BALTIC, OFF SANDY HOOK, }
> *April* 18, 1861, 10.30 A.M. — *Via* NEW YORK. }

Honorable S. CAMERON, *Secretary of War, Washington:*

Having defended Fort Sumter for thirty-four hours, until the quarters were entirely burned, the main gates destroyed by fire, the gorge-walls seriously injured, the magazine surrounded by flames, and its door closed from the effect of heat, four barrels and three cartridges of powder only being available, and no provisions remaining but pork, I accepted terms of evacuation offered by General Beauregard, being the same offered by him on the 11th inst., prior to the commencement of hostilities, and marched out of the fort,

Sunday afternoon, the 14th inst., with colors flying and drums beating, bringing away company and private property, and saluting my flag with fifty guns.

ROBERT ANDERSON, *Major First Artillery, commanding*.

Chapter XXIV.

END OF THE WAR. — FROM GOLDSBORO' TO RALEIGH
AND WASHINGTON.
April and May, 1865.

As before described, the armies commanded respectively by Generals J. M. Schofield, A. H. Terry, and
myself, effected a junction in and about Goldsboro', North
Carolina, during the 22d and 23d of March, 1865, but it required a few days for all the troops and trains of wagons to
reach their respective camps. In person I reached Goldsboro'
on the 23d, and met General Schofield, who described fully his
operations in North Carolina up to that date; and I also found
Lieutenant Dunn, aide-de-camp to General Grant, with a letter from him of March 16th, giving a general description of
the state of facts about City Point. The next day I received
another letter, more full, dated the 22d, which I give herewith.

Nevertheless, I deemed it of great importance that I should
have a personal interview with the general, and determined to
go in person to City Point as soon as the repairs of the railroad, then in progress under the personal direction of Colonel
W. W. Wright, would permit:

HEADQUARTERS ARMIES OF THE UNITED STATES, }
CITY POINT, VIRGINIA, *March* 22, 1865. }

Major-General W. T. SHERMAN, *commanding Military Division of the
Mississippi.*

GENERAL: Although the Richmond papers do not communicate
the fact, yet I saw enough in them to satisfy me that you occupied
Goldsboro' on the 19th inst. I congratulate you and the army on
what may be regarded as the successful termination of the third campaign since leaving the Tennessee River, less than one year ago.

Since Sheridan's very successful raid north of the James, the enemy
are left dependent on the Southside and Danville roads for all their
supplies. These I hope to cut next week. Sheridan is at "White
House," shoeing up and resting his cavalry. I expect him to finish by
Friday night and to start the following morning, *via* Long Bridge,
Newmarket, Bermuda Hundred, and the extreme left of the army
around Petersburg. He will make no halt with the armies operating
here, but will be joined by a division of cavalry, five thousand five

RALEIGH
TO
WASHINGTON

END OF THE WAR

EXPLANATION.

14th Army Corps
15th   ,,   ,,
17th   ,,   ,,
20th   ,,   ,,
Cavalry

SCALE

hundred strong, from the Army of the Potomac, and will proceed directly to the Southside and Danville roads. His instructions will be to strike the Southside road as near Petersburg as he can, and destroy it so that it cannot be repaired for three or four days, and push on to the Danville road, as near to the Appomattox as he can get. Then I want him to destroy the road toward Burkesville as far as he can; then push on to the Southside road, west of Burkesville, and destroy it effectually. From that point I shall probably leave it to his discretion either to return to this army, crossing the Danville road south of Burkesville, or go and join you, passing between Danville and Greensboro'. When this movement commences I shall move out by my left, with all the force I can, holding present intrenched lines. I shall start with no distinct view, further than holding Lee's forces from following Sheridan. But I shall be along myself, and will take advantage of any thing that turns up. If Lee detaches, I will attack; or if he comes out of his lines I will endeavor to repulse him, and follow it up to the best advantage.

It is most difficult to understand what the rebels intend to do; so far but few troops have been detached from Lee's army. Much machinery has been removed, and material has been sent to Lynchburg, showing a disposition to go there. Points, too, have been fortified on the Danville road.

Lee's army is much demoralized, and great numbers are deserting. Probably, from returned prisoners, and such conscripts as can be picked up, his numbers may be kept up. I estimate his force now at about sixty-five thousand men.

Wilson started on Monday, with twelve thousand cavalry, from Eastport. Stoneman started on the same day, from East Tennessee, toward Lynchburg. Thomas is moving the Fourth Corps to Bull's Gap. Canby is moving with a formidable force on Mobile and the interior of Alabama.

I ordered Gillmore, as soon as the fall of Charleston was known, to hold all important posts on the sea-coast, and to send to Wilmington all surplus forces. Thomas was also directed to forward to Newbern all troops belonging to the corps with you. I understand this will give you about five thousand men, besides those brought east by Meagher.

I have been telegraphing General Meigs to hasten up locomotives and cars for you. General McCallum, he informs me, is attending to it. I fear they are not going forward as fast as I would like.

Let me know if you want more troops, or any thing else.

Very respectfully, your obedient servant,

U. S. GRANT, *Lieutenant-General.*

The railroad was repaired to Goldsboro' by the evening of March 25th, when, leaving General Schofield in chief command, with a couple of staff-officers I started for City Point, Virginia, on a locomotive, in company with Colonel Wright, the constructing engineer. We reached Newbern that evening, which was passed in the company of General Palmer and his accomplished lady, and early the next morning we continued on to Morehead City, where General Easton had provided for us the small captured steamer Russia, Captain Smith. We put to sea at once and steamed up the coast, reaching Fortress Monroe on the morning of the 27th, where I landed and telegraphed to my brother, Senator Sherman, at Washington, inviting him to come down and return with me to Goldsboro'. We proceeded on up James River to City Point, which we reached the same afternoon. I found General Grant, with his family and staff, occupying a pretty group of huts on the bank of James River, overlooking the harbor, which was full of vessels of all classes, both war and merchant, with wharves and warehouses on an extensive scale. The general received me most heartily, and we talked over matters very fully. After I had been with him an hour or so, he remarked that the President, Mr. Lincoln, was then on board the steamer River Queen, lying at the wharf, and he proposed that we should call and see him. We walked down to the wharf, went on board, and found Mr. Lincoln alone, in the after-cabin. He remembered me perfectly, and at once engaged in a most interesting conversation. He was full of curiosity about the many incidents of our great march, which had reached him officially and through the newspapers, and seemed to enjoy very much the more ludicrous parts—about the "bummers," and their devices to collect food and forage when the outside world supposed us to be starving; but at the same time he expressed a good deal of anxiety lest some accident might happen to the army in North Carolina during my absence. I explained to him that that army was snug and comfortable, in good camps, at Goldsboro'; that it would require some days to collect forage and food for another march; and that General Schofield was fully competent to command it in my absence. Having made a good, long, social visit, we took our leave and returned to General Grant's quarters, where Mrs.

Grant had provided tea. While at the table, Mrs. Grant inquired if we had seen *Mrs*. Lincoln. "No," said the general, "I did not ask for her;" and I added that I did not even know that she was on board. Mrs. Grant then exclaimed, "Well, you are a pretty pair!" and added that our neglect was unpardonable; when the general said we would call again the next day, and make amends for the unintended slight.

Early the next day, March 28th, all the principal officers of the army and navy called to see me, Generals Meade, Ord, Ingalls, etc., and Admiral Porter. At this time the River Queen was at anchor out in the river, abreast of the wharf, and we again started to visit Mr. and *Mrs*. Lincoln. Admiral Porter accompanied us. We took a small tug at the wharf, which conveyed us on board, where we were again received most courteously by the President, who conducted us to the after-cabin. After the general compliments, General Grant inquired after *Mrs*. Lincoln, when the President went to her state-room, returned, and begged us to excuse her, as she was not well. We then again entered upon a general conversation, during which General Grant explained to the President that at that very instant of time General Sheridan was crossing James River from the north, by a pontoon-bridge below City Point; that he had a large, well-appointed force of cavalry, with which he proposed to strike the Southside and Danville Railroads, by which alone General Lee, in Richmond, supplied his army; and that, in his judgment, matters were drawing to a crisis, his only apprehension being that General Lee would not wait long enough. I also explained that my army at Goldsboro' was strong enough to fight Lee's army and Johnston's combined, provided that General Grant could come up within a day or so; that if Lee would only remain in Richmond another fortnight, I could march up to Burkesville, when Lee would have to starve inside of his lines, or come out from his intrenchments and fight us on equal terms.

Both General Grant and myself supposed that one or the other of us would have to fight one more bloody battle, and that it would be the *last*. Mr. Lincoln exclaimed, more than once, that there had been blood enough shed, and asked us if another battle could not be avoided. I remember well to have said that we could not control that event; that this necessarily rested with our enemy; and I inferred that both Jeff. Davis and General Lee would be forced to fight one more desperate and bloody battle. I rather supposed it would fall on me, somewhere near Raleigh; and General Grant added that, if Lee would only wait a few more days, he would have his army so disposed that if the enemy should abandon Richmond, and attempt to make junction with General Jos. Johnston in North Carolina, he (General Grant) would be on his heels. Mr. Lincoln more than once expressed uneasiness that I was not with my army at Goldsboro', when I again assured him that General Schofield was fully competent to command in my absence; that I was going to start back that very day, and that Admiral Porter had kindly provided for me the steamer Bat, which he said was much swifter than my own vessel, the Russia. During this interview I inquired of the President if he was all ready for the end of the war. What was to be done with the rebel armies when defeated? And what should be done with the political leaders, such as Jeff. Davis, etc.? Should we allow them to escape, etc.? He said he was all ready; all he wanted of us was to defeat the opposing armies, and to get the men composing the Confederate armies back to their homes, at work on their farms and in their shops. As to Jeff. Davis, he was hardly at liberty to speak his mind fully, but intimated that he ought to clear out, "escape the country," only it would not do for him to say so openly. As usual, he illustrated his meaning by a story: "A man once had taken the total-abstinence pledge. When visiting a friend, he was invited to take a drink, but declined, on the score of his pledge; when his friend suggested lemonade, which was accepted. In preparing the lemonade, the friend pointed to the brandy-bottle, and said the lemonade would be more palatable if he were to pour in a little brandy; when his guest said, if he could do so 'unbeknown' to him, he would not object." From which illustration I inferred that Mr. Lincoln wanted Davis to escape, "unbeknown" to him.

I made no notes of this conversation at the time, but Admiral Porter, who was present, did, and in 1866 he furnished me an account thereof, which I insert below, but the admiral describes the first visit, of the 27th, whereas my memory puts

Admiral Porter's presence on the following day. Still he may be right, and he may have been with us the day before, as I write this chiefly from memory. There were two distinct interviews; the first was late in the afternoon of March 27th, and the other about noon of the 28th, both in the after-cabin of the steamer River Queen; on both occasions Mr. Lincoln was full and frank in his conversation, assuring me that in his mind he was all ready for the civil reorganization of affairs at the South as soon as the war was over; and he distinctly authorized me to assure Governor Vance and the people of North Carolina that, as soon as the rebel armies laid down their arms, and resumed their civil pursuits, they would at once be guaranteed all their rights as citizens of a common country; and that to avoid anarchy the State governments then in existence, with their civil functionaries, would be recognized by him as the government *de facto* till Congress could provide others.

I know, when I left him, that I was more than ever impressed by his kindly nature, his deep and earnest sympathy with the afflictions of the whole people, resulting from the war, and by the march of hostile armies through the South; and that his earnest desire seemed to be to end the war speedily, without more bloodshed or devastation, and to restore all the men of both sections to their homes. In the language of his second inaugural address, he seemed to have "charity for all, malice toward none," and, above all, an absolute faith in the courage, manliness, and integrity of the armies in the field. When at rest or listening, his legs and arms seemed to hang almost lifeless, and his face was care-worn and haggard; but, the moment he began to talk, his face lightened up, his tall form, as it were, unfolded, and he was the very impersonation of good-humor and fellowship. The last words I recall as addressed to me were that he would feel better when I was back at Goldsboro'. We parted at the gangway of the River Queen, about noon of March 28th, and I never saw him again. Of all the men I ever met, he seemed to possess more of the elements of greatness, combined with goodness, than any other.

ADMIRAL PORTER'S ACCOUNT OF THE INTERVIEW WITH MR. LINCOLN.

THE day of General Sherman's arrival at City Point (I think the 27th of March, 1865), I accompanied him and General Grant on board the President's flag-ship, the Queen, where the President received us in the upper saloon, no one but ourselves being present.

The President was in an exceedingly pleasant mood, and delighted to meet General Sherman, whom he cordially greeted.

It seems that this was the first time he had met Sherman, to remember him, since the beginning of the war, and did not remember when he had seen him before, until the general reminded him of the circumstances of their first meeting.

This was rather singular on the part of Mr. Lincoln, who was, I think, remarkable for remembering people, having that kingly quality in an eminent degree. Indeed, such was the power of his memory, that he seemed never to forget the most minute circumstance.

The conversation soon turned on the events of Sherman's campaign through the South, with every movement of which the President seemed familiar.

He laughed over some of the stories Sherman told of his "bummers," and told others in return, which illustrated in a striking manner the ideas he wanted to convey. For example, he would often express his wishes by telling an apt story, which was quite a habit with him, and one that I think he adopted to prevent his committing himself seriously.

The interview between the two generals and the President lasted about an hour and a half, and, as it was a remarkable one, I jotted down what I remembered of the conversation, as I have made a practice of doing during the rebellion, when any thing interesting occurred.

I don't regret having done so, as circumstances afterward occurred (Stanton's ill-conduct toward Sherman) which tended to cast odium on General Sherman for allowing such liberal terms to Jos. Johnston.

Could the conversation that occurred on board the Queen, between the President and General Sherman, have been known, Sherman would not, and could not, have been censured. Mr. Lincoln, had he lived, would have acquitted the general of any blame, for he was only carrying out the President's wishes.

My opinion is, that Mr. Lincoln came down to City Point with the most liberal views toward the rebels. He felt confident that we would be successful, and was willing that the enemy should capitulate on the most favorable terms.

I don't know what the President would have done had he been left to himself, and had our army been unsuccessful, but he was then wrought up to a high state of excitement. He wanted peace on almost any terms, and there is no knowing what proposals he might have been willing to listen to. His heart was tenderness throughout, and, as long as the rebels laid down their arms, he did not care how it was done. I do not know how far he was influenced by General Grant, but I presume, from their long conferences, that they must have understood each other perfectly, and that the terms given to Lee after his surrender were authorized by Mr. Lincoln. I know that the latter was delighted when he heard that they had been given, and exclaimed, a dozen times, "Good!" "All right!" "Exactly the thing!" and other similar expressions. Indeed, the President more than once told me what he supposed the terms would be: if Lee and Johnston surrendered, he considered the war ended, and that all the other rebel forces would lay down their arms at once.

In this he proved to be right. Grant and Sherman were both of the same opinion, and so was every one else who knew any thing about the matter.

What signified *the terms* to them, so long as we obtained the actual surrender of people who only wanted a good opportunity to give up gracefully? The rebels had fought "to the last ditch," and all that they had left them was the hope of being handed down in history as having received honorable terms.

After hearing General Sherman's account of his own position, and that of Johnston, at that time, the President expressed fears that the rebel general would escape south again by the railroads, and that General Sherman would have to chase him anew, over the same ground; but the general pronounced this to be impracticable. He remarked: "I have him where he cannot move without breaking up his army, which, once disbanded, can never again be got together; and I have destroyed the Southern railroads, so that they cannot be used again for a long time." General Grant remarked, "What is to prevent their laying the rails again?" "Why," said General Sherman, "my 'bummers' don't do things by halves. Every rail, after having been placed over a hot fire, has been twisted as crooked as a ram's-horn, and they never can be used again."

This was the only remark made by General Grant during the interview, as he sat smoking a short distance from the President, intent, no doubt, on his own plans, which were being brought to a successful termination.

The conversation between the President and General Sherman,

about the terms of surrender to be allowed Jos. Johnston, continued. Sherman energetically insisted that he could command his own terms, and that Johnston would have to yield to his demands; but the President was very decided about the matter, and insisted that the surrender of Johnston's army must be obtained on any terms.

General Grant was evidently of the same way of thinking, for, although he did not join in the conversation to any extent, yet he made no objections, and I presume had made up his mind to allow the best terms himself.

He was also anxious that Johnston should not be driven into Richmond, to reënforce the rebels there, who, from behind their strong intrenchments, would have given us incalculable trouble.

Sherman, as a subordinate officer, yielded his views to those of the President, and the terms of capitulation between himself and Johnston were exactly in accordance with Mr. Lincoln's wishes. He could not have done any thing which would have pleased the President better.

Mr. Lincoln did, in fact, arrange the (so considered) liberal terms offered General Jos. Johnston, and, whatever may have been General Sherman's private views, I feel sure that he yielded to the wishes of the President in every respect. It was Mr. Lincoln's policy that was carried out, and, had he lived long enough, he would have been but too glad to have acknowledged it. Had Mr. Lincoln lived, Secretary Stanton would have issued no false telegraphic dispatches, in the hope of killing off another general in the regular army, one who by his success had placed himself in the way of his own succession.

The disbanding of Jos. Johnston's army was so complete, that the pens and ink used in the discussion of the matter were all wasted.

It was asserted, by the rabid ones, that General Sherman had given up all that we had been fighting for, had conceded every thing to Jos. Johnston, and had, as the boys say, "knocked the fat into the fire;" but sober reflection soon overruled these harsh expressions, and, with those who knew General Sherman, and appreciated him, he was still the great soldier, patriot, and gentleman. In future times this matter will be looked at more calmly and dispassionately. The bitter animosities that have been engendered during the rebellion will have died out for want of food on which to live, and the very course Grant, Sherman, and others pursued, in granting liberal terms to the defeated rebels, will be applauded. The fact is, they met an old beggar in the road, whose crutches had broken from under him: they let him have only the broken crutches to get home with!

I sent General Sherman back to Newbern, North Carolina, in the steamer Bat.

While he was absent from his command he was losing no time, for he was getting his army fully equipped with stores and clothing; and, when he returned, he had a rested and regenerated army, ready to swallow up Jos. Johnston and all his ragamuffins.

Johnston was cornered, could not move without leaving every thing behind him, and could not go to Richmond without bringing on a famine in that destitute city.

I was with Mr. Lincoln all the time he was at City Point, and until he left for Washington. He was more than delighted with the surrender of Lee, and with the terms Grant gave the rebel general; and would have given Jos. Johnston twice as much, had the latter asked for it, and could he have been certain that the rebel would have surrendered without a fight. I again repeat that, had Mr. Lincoln lived, he would have shouldered *all* the responsibility.

One thing is certain: had Jos. Johnston escaped and got into Richmond, and caused a larger list of killed and wounded than we had, General Sherman would have been blamed. Then why not give him the full credit of capturing on the best terms the enemy's last important army and its best general, and putting an end to the rebellion?

It was a *finale* worthy of Sherman's great march through the swamps and deserts of the South, a march not excelled by any thing we read of in modern military history.

D. D. PORTER, Vice-Admiral.

(Written by the admiral in 1866, at the United States Naval Academy at Annapolis, Md., and mailed to General Sherman at St. Louis, Mo.)

As soon as possible, I arranged with General Grant for certain changes in the organization of my army; and the general also undertook to send to North Carolina some tug-boats and barges to carry stores from Newbern up as far as Kinston, whence they could be hauled in wagons to our camps, thus relieving our railroads to that extent. I undertook to be ready to march north by April 10th, and then embarked on the steamer Bat, Captain Barnes, for North Carolina. We steamed down James River, and at Old Point Comfort took on board my brother, Senator Sherman, and Mr. Edwin Stanton, son of the Secretary of War, and proceeded at once to our destination. On our way down the river, Captain Barnes expressed himself extremely obliged to me for taking his vessel, as it had relieved him of a most painful dilemma. He explained that he had been detailed by Admiral Porter to escort the President's unarmed boat, the River Queen, in which capacity it became his special duty to look after Mrs. Lincoln. The day before my arrival at City Point, there had been a grand review of a part of the Army of the James, then commanded by General Ord. The President rode out from City Point with General Grant on horseback, accompanied by a numerous staff, including Captain Barnes and Mrs. Ord; but Mrs. Lincoln and Mrs. Grant had followed in a carriage.

The cavalcade reached the review-ground some five or six miles out from City Point, found the troops all ready, drawn up in line, and after the usual presentation of arms, the President and party, followed by Mrs. Ord and Captain Barnes on horseback, rode the lines, and returned to the reviewing stand, which meantime had been reached by Mrs. Lincoln and Mrs. Grant in their carriage, which had been delayed by the driver taking a wrong road. Mrs. Lincoln, seeing Mrs. Ord and Captain Barnes riding with the retinue, and supposing that Mrs. Ord had personated her, turned on Captain Barnes and gave him a fearful scolding; and even indulged in some pretty sharp upbraidings to Mrs. Ord.

This made Barnes's position very unpleasant, so that he felt much relieved when he was sent with me to North Carolina. The Bat was very fast, and on the morning of the 29th we were near Cape Hatteras; Captain Barnes, noticing a propeller coming out of Hatteras Inlet, made her turn back and pilot us in. We entered safely, steamed up Pamlico Sound into Neuse River, and the next morning, by reason of some derangement of machinery, we anchored about seven miles below Newbern, whence we went up in Captain Barnes's barge. As soon as we arrived at Newbern, I telegraphed up to General Schofield at Goldsboro' the fact of my return, and that I had arranged with General Grant for the changes made necessary in the reorganization of the army, and for the boats necessary to carry up the provisions and stores we needed, prior to the renewal of our march northward.

These changes amounted to constituting the left wing a distinct army, under the title of "the Army of Georgia," under command of General Slocum, with his two corps commanded by General Jeff. C. Davis and General Joseph A. Mower; the Tenth and Twenty-third Corps already constituted another army, "of the Ohio," under the command of Major-General Schofield, and his two corps were commanded by Generals J. D. Cox and A. H. Terry. These changes were necessary, because army commanders only could order courts-martial, grant discharges, and perform many other matters of discipline and administration which were indispensable; but my chief purpose was to prepare the whole army for what seemed among the probabilities of the time—to fight both Lee's and Johnston's armies combined, in case their junction could be formed before General Grant could possibly follow Lee to North Carolina.

General George H. Thomas, who still remained at Nashville, was not pleased with these changes, for the two corps with General Slocum, viz., the Fourteenth and Twentieth, up to that time, had remained technically a part of his "Army of the Cumberland;" but he was so far away, that I had to act to the best advantage with the troops and general officers actually present. I had specially asked for General Mower to command the Twentieth Corps, because I regarded him as one of the boldest and best fighting generals in the whole army. His predecessor, General A. S. Williams, the senior division commander present, had commanded the corps well from Atlanta to Goldsboro', and it may have seemed unjust to replace him at that precise moment; but I was resolved to be prepared for a most desperate and, as then expected, a final battle, should it fall on me.

I returned to Goldsboro' from Newbern by rail the evening of March 30th, and at once addressed myself to the task of reorganization and replenishment of stores, so as to be ready to march by April 10th, the day agreed on with General Grant.

The army was divided into the usual three parts, right and left wings, and centre. The tabular statements herewith will give the exact composition of these separate armies, which by the 10th of April gave the following effective strength:

RIGHT WING—ARMY OF THE TENNESSEE—GENERAL O. O. HOWARD.

COMMANDS.	Infantry.	Cavalry.	Artillery.	Total.
Fifteenth Corps	15,244	23	403	15,670
Seventeenth Corps . . .	12,873	30	261	13,164
Aggregate	28,117	53	664	28,834

LEFT WING—ARMY OF GEORGIA—GENERAL H. W. SLOCUM.

COMMANDS.	Infantry.	Cavalry.	Artillery.	Total.
Fourteenth Corps	14,653	. . .	445	15,098
Twentieth Corps	12,471	. . .	494	12,965
Aggregate	27,124	. . .	939	28,063

CENTRE—ARMY OF THE OHIO—GENERAL J. M. SCHOFIELD.

COMMANDS.	Infantry.	Cavalry.	Artillery.	Total.
Tenth Corps	11,727	. . .	372	12,099
Twenty-third Corps. . .	14,000	. . .	293	14,293
Aggregate	25,727	. . .	665	26,392

CAVALRY DIVISION—BRIGADIER-GENERAL J. KILPATRICK.

	Infantry.	Cavalry.	Artillery.	Total.
Aggregate	. . .	5,484	175	5,659

Totals.

Infantry.	80,968
Artillery	2,443
Cavalry	5,537
Aggregate	88,948

Total number of guns, 91.

ARMY OF THE TENNESSEE.

MAJOR-GENERAL O. O. HOWARD COMMANDING.

Fifteenth Army Corps—Major-General JOHN A. LOGAN *commanding.*

FIRST DIVISION.

Brevet Major-General C. R. WOODS.

First Brigade.	Second Brigade.	Third Brigade.
Brevet Brig.-Gen. W. B. Woods.	Colonel R. F. Catterson.	Colonel G. A. Stone.
27th Missouri Infantry.	40th Illinois Infantry.	4th Iowa Infantry.
12th Indiana Infantry.	46th Ohio Infantry.	9th Iowa Infantry.
76th Ohio Infantry.	103d Illinois Infantry.	25th Iowa Infantry.
26th Iowa Infantry.	6th Iowa Infantry.	30th Iowa Infantry.
31st Missouri Infantry.	97th Indiana Infantry.	31st Iowa Infantry.
32d Missouri Infantry.	26th Illinois Infantry.	
	100th Indiana Infantry.	

SECOND DIVISION.

Major-General WILLIAM B. HAZEN.

First Brigade.	Second Brigade.	Third Brigade.
Colonel T. Jones.	Colonel W. S. Jones.	Brigadier-General J. M. Oliver.
6th Missouri Infantry.	37th Ohio Infantry.	15th Michigan Infantry.
55th Illinois Infantry.	47th Ohio Infantry.	70th Ohio Infantry.
116th Illinois Infantry.	53d Ohio Infantry.	48th Illinois Infantry.
127th Illinois Infantry.	54th Ohio Infantry.	90th Illinois Infantry.
30th Ohio Infantry.	83d Indiana Infantry.	99th Indiana Infantry.
57th Ohio Infantry.	111th Illinois Infantry.	

THIRD DIVISION.

Brevet Major-General J. E. SMITH.

First Brigade.	Second Brigade.
Brigadier-General W. T. Clark	Colonel J. E. Tourtellotte
18th Wisconsin Infantry.	56th Illinois Infantry.
59th Indiana Infantry.	10th Iowa Infantry.
63d Illinois Infantry.	80th Ohio Infantry.
48th Indiana Infantry.	17th Iowa Infantry.
93d Illinois Infantry.	Battalion 26th Missouri Infantry.
	Battalion 10th Missouri Infantry.
	4th Minnesota Infantry.

FOURTH DIVISION.

Brevet Major-General JOHN M. CORSE.

First Brigade.	Second Brigade.	Third Brigade.
Brig.-Gen. E. W. Rice.	Colonel R. N. Adams.	Colonel F. J. Hurlbut.
2d Iowa Infantry.	12th Illinois Infantry.	7th Illinois Infantry.
7th Iowa Infantry.	66th Illinois Infantry.	39th Iowa Infantry.
66th Indiana Infantry.	81st Ohio Infantry.	50th Illinois Infantry.
52d Illinois Infantry.		57th Illinois Infantry.
		110th U. S. Col'd Inf.

DETACHMENTS.

Artillery Brigade.

Lieutenant-Colonel WILLIAM H. ROSS.

H, 1st Illinois Artillery.	H, 1st Missouri Artillery.
12th Wisconsin Battery.	B, 1st Michigan Artillery.

29th Missouri Infantry.
Signal Detachment.

Seventeenth Army Corps—Major-General F. P. BLAIR *commanding.*

FIRST DIVISION.

Brigadier-General M. F. FORCE.

First Brigade.	Second Brigade.	Third Brigade.
Brig.-General	Brig.-General	Lieut.-Colonel
J. W. Fuller.	J. W. Sprague.	J. S. Wright
18th Missouri Infantry.	25th Wisconsin Infantry.	10th Illinois Infantry.
27th Ohio Infantry.	35th New Jersey Infantry.	25th Indiana Infantry.
39th Ohio Infantry.	43d Ohio Infantry.	32d Wisconsin Infantry.
64th Illinois Infantry.	63d Ohio Infantry.	

THIRD DIVISION.

Brevet Major-General M. D. LEGGETT.

First Brigade.	Second Brigade.
Brigadier-General Charles Ewing.	Brigadier-General R. K. Scott.
16th Wisconsin Infantry.	20th Ohio Infantry.
45th Illinois Infantry.	68th Ohio Infantry.
31st Illinois Infantry.	78th Ohio Infantry.
20th Illinois Infantry.	19th Wisconsin Infantry.
30th Illinois Infantry.	
12th Wisconsin Infantry.	

FOURTH DIVISION.

Brevet Major-General G. A. SMITH.

<table>
<tr><td>First Brigade.</td><td>Third Brigade.</td></tr>
<tr><td>Brigadier-General B. F. Potts.</td><td>Brigadier-General W. W. Belknap.</td></tr>
<tr><td>23d Indiana Infantry.</td><td>11th Iowa Infantry.</td></tr>
<tr><td>32d Ohio Infantry.</td><td>13th Iowa Infantry.</td></tr>
<tr><td>53d Indiana Infantry.</td><td>15th Iowa Infantry.</td></tr>
<tr><td>14th Illinois Infantry.</td><td>16th Iowa Infantry.</td></tr>
<tr><td>53d Illinois Infantry.</td><td>32d Illinois Infantry.</td></tr>
<tr><td>15th Illinois Infantry.</td><td></td></tr>
</table>

DETACHMENTS.

Artillery Brigade.

Major FREDERICK WELKER.

<table>
<tr><td>C Battalion, 1st Michigan Artillery.</td><td>9th Illinois Mounted Infantry.</td></tr>
<tr><td>1st Minnesota Battery.</td><td>G Company, 11th Illinois Cavalry.</td></tr>
<tr><td>15th Ohio Battery.</td><td>Signal Detachment.</td></tr>
</table>

ARMY OF GEORGIA.

MAJOR-GENERAL H. W. SLOCUM COMMANDING.

Fourteenth Army Corps—Brevet Major-General J. C. DAVIS *commanding*

FIRST DIVISION.

Brigadier-General C. C. WALCOTT.

<table>
<tr><td>First Brigade.</td><td>Second Brigade.</td><td>Third Brigade.</td></tr>
<tr><td>Brevet Brig.-General Hobart.</td><td>Brevet Brig.-General Buell.</td><td>Colonel Hambright.</td></tr>
<tr><td>21st Wisconsin Volunteers.</td><td>21st Michigan Volunteers.</td><td>21st Ohio Volunteers.</td></tr>
<tr><td>33d Ohio Volunteers.</td><td>13th Michigan Volunteers.</td><td>74th Ohio Volunteers.</td></tr>
<tr><td>94th Ohio Volunteers.</td><td>69th Ohio Volunteers.</td><td>78th Pennsylvania Volun.</td></tr>
<tr><td>42d Indiana Volunteers.</td><td></td><td>79th Pennsylvania Volun.</td></tr>
<tr><td>88th Indiana Volunteers.</td><td></td><td></td></tr>
<tr><td>104th Illinois Volunteers.</td><td></td><td></td></tr>
</table>

SECOND DIVISION.

Brigadier-General J. D. MORGAN.

First Brigade. Brigadier-General Vandever.	Second Brigade. Brigadier-General Mitchell.	Third Brigade. Lieutenant-Colonel Langley.
10th Michigan Volunteers.	121st Ohio Volunteers.	85th Illinois Volunteers.
14th Michigan Volunteers.	113th Ohio Volunteers.	86th Illinois Volunteers.
16th Illinois Volunteers.	108th Ohio Volunteers.	110th Illinois Volunteers.
60th Illinois Volunteers.	98th Ohio Volunteers.	125th Illinois Volunteers.
17th New York Volunteers.	78th Illinois Volunteers.	52d Ohio Volunteers.
	34th Illinois Volunteers.	22d Indiana Volunteers.
		37th Indiana (Det.) Volun.

THIRD DIVISION.

Brevet Major-General A. BAIRD.

First Brigade. Colonel M. C. Hunter.	Second Brigade. Lieutenant-Colonel Doan.	Third Brigade. Brig.-General George S. Greene.
17th Ohio Volunteers.	2d Minnesota Volunteers.	14th Ohio Volunteers.
31st Ohio Volunteers.	105th Ohio Volunteers.	38th Ohio Volunteers.
89th Ohio Volunteers.	75th Indiana Volunteers.	10th Kentucky Volunteers.
92d Ohio Volunteers.	87th Indiana Volunteers.	18th Kentucky Volunteers.
82d Indiana Volunteers.	101st Indiana Volunteers.	74th Indiana Volunteers.
23d Missouri (Det.) Volun.		
11th Ohio Volunteers.		

DETACHMENTS.

Artillery Brigade.

Major CHARLES HOUGHTALING.

Battery I, 2d Illinois.	5th Wisconsin Battery.
Battery C, 1st Illinois.	19th Indiana Battery.

Twentieth Army Corps—Major-General J. A. MOWER commanding.

FIRST DIVISION.
Brevet Major-General A. S. WILLIAMS.

First Brigade.	Second Brigade.	Third Brigade.
Colonel J. L. Selfridge.	Colonel William Hawley.	Brig.-General J. S. Robinson.
4th Pennsylvania Volunt'rs.	2d Massachusetts Volun.	31st Wisconsin Volunteers.
5th Connecticut Volunteers.	3d Wisconsin Volunteers.	61st Ohio Volunteers.
123d New York Volunteers.	13th New Jersey Volunt'rs.	82nd Ohio Volunteers.
141st New York Volunteers.	107th New York Volunt'rs.	82nd Illinois Volunteers
	150th New York Volunt'rs.	101st Illinois Volunteers.
		143d New York Volun.

SECOND DIVISION.
Brevet Major-General JOHN W. GEARY.

First Brigade.	Second Brigade.	Third Brigade.
Brevet Brig.-Gen. N. Pardee, Jr.	Colonel P. H. Jones.	Brevet Brig.-General Barnum.
5th Ohio Volunteers.	33d New Jersey Volunteers.	29th Pennsylvania Volun.
29th Ohio Volunteers.	73d Pennsylvania Volun.	111th Pennsylvania Volun.
66th Ohio Volunteers.	109th Pennsylvania Volun.	60th New York Volunteers.
28th Pennsylvania Volun.	119th New York Volun.	102d New York Volunt'rs.
147th Pennsylvania Volun.	134th New York Volun.	137th New York Volunt'rs
Detachment K. P. B.	154th New York Volun.	149th New York Volunt'rs.

THIRD DIVISION.
Brevet Major-General W. T. WARD.

First Brigade.	Second Brigade.	Third Brigade.
Colonel H. Case.	Colonel Daniel Dustin.	Brevet Brig.-General Coggswell.
70th Indiana Volunteers.	19th Michigan Volunteers.	20th Connecticut Volun.
79th Ohio Volunteers.	22d Wisconsin Volunteers.	26th Wisconsin Volunt'rs.
102d Illinois Volunteers.	33d Indiana Volunteers.	33d Massachusetts Volun.
105th Illinois Volunteers.	85th Indiana Volunteers.	55th Ohio Volunteers.
129th Illinois Volunteers.		73d Ohio Volunteers.
		136th New York Volunt'rs.

DETACHMENTS.
Artillery Brigade.
Captain WINNEGAR.

Battery I, 1st New York.   Battery C, 1st Ohio.
Battery M, 1st New York.   Battery E, Independent Pennsylvania.
Pontoniers, 58th Indiana Veteran Volunteers.
Mechanics and Engineers, 1st Michigan.

ARMY OF THE OHIO.

MAJOR-GENERAL JOHN M. SCHOFIELD COMMANDING.

Tenth Army Corps — Major-General A. H. TERRY *commanding.*

FIRST DIVISION.

Brevet Major-General H. W. BIRGE.

First Brigade. Colonel H. D. Washburn.	Second Brigade. Colonel Harvey Graham.	Third Brigade. Colonel N. W. Day.
8th Indiana Volunteers.	159th New York Volunteers.	38th Massachusetts Vol.
18th Indiana Volunteers.	13th Connecticut Volunt'rs.	156th New York Volun.
9th Connecticut Volunteers.	22d Iowa Volunteers.	128th New York Volun.
14th New Hampshire Volun.	131st New York Volunteers.	175th New York Volun.
12th Maine Volunteers.	28th Iowa Volunteers.	176th New York Volun.
14th Maine Volunteers.		24th Iowa Volunteers.
75th New York Volunteers.		

SECOND DIVISION.

Brevet Major-General A. AMES.

First Brigade. Colonel R. Daggett.	Second Brigade. Colonel J. S. Littell.	Third Brigade. Colonel G. F. Granger.
3d New York Volunteers.	47th New York Volunteers.	4th New Hampshire Vol.
112th New York Volunteers.	48th New York Volunteers.	9th Maine Volunteers.
117th New York Volunteers.	203d Pennsylvania Volun.	13th Indiana Volunteers.
142d New York Volunteers.	97th Pennsylvania Volun.	115th New York Volun.
	76th Pennsylvania Volun.	169th New York Volun.

THIRD DIVISION.

Brigadier-General C. J. PAINE.

First Brigade.	Second Brigade.	Third Brigade.
Brevet Brig.-General D. Bates.	Brevet Brig.-Gen. S. Duncan.	Colonel J. H. Holman.
1st U. S. C. T.	4th U. S. C. T.	5th U. S. C. T.
30th U. S. C. T.	6th U. S. C. T.	27th U. S. C. T.
107th U. S. C. T.	39th U. S. C. T.	37th U. S. C. T.

DETACHMENTS.

Brigade (not numbered)

Brevet Brigadier-General J. C. ABBOTT.

3d New Hampshire Volunteers.   6th Connecticut Volunteers.
7th New Hampshire Volunteers.   7th Connecticut Volunteers.
16th New York Heavy Artillery (six companies).
16th New York Independent Battery.
22d Indiana Battery.
Light Company E, 3d United States Artillery.
Company A, 2d Pennsylvania Heavy Artillery.
Companies E and K, 12th New York Cavalry.
Detachment Signal Corps.

Twenty-third Army Corps—Major-General J. D. Cox *commanding.*

FIRST DIVISION.

Brigadier-General THOMAS H. RUGER.

First Brigade.	Second Brigade.	Third Brigade.
Brevet Brig.-General J. N. Stiles.	Colonel J. C. McQuiston.	Colonel M. T. Thomas.
120th Indiana Vol. Infantry.	123d Indiana Vol. Infantry.	8th Minnesota Vol. Infan.
124th Indiana Vol. Infantry.	129th Indiana Vol. Infan'y.	174th Ohio Vol. Infantry.
128th Indiana Vol. Infantry.	130th Indiana Vol. Infan'y.	178th Ohio Vol. Infantry.
180th Ohio Volun. Infantry.	28th Michigan Vol. Infan'y.	

Battery Elgin, Illinois Volunteers.

SECOND DIVISION.

Major-General D. N. COUCH.

First Brigade.	Second Brigade.	Third Brigade.
Colonel O. H. Moore.	Colonel J. Mehringer.	Colonel S. A. Strickland.

25th Michigan Vol. Infantry.	23d Michigan Vol. Infantry.	91st Indiana Vol. Infantry.
26th Kentucky Vol. Infantry.	80th Indiana Vol. Infantry.	183d Ohio Vol. Infantry.
	118th Ohio Vol. Infantry.	181st Ohio Vol. Infantry.
	107th Illinois Vol. Infantry.	50th Ohio Vol. Infantry.
	111th Ohio Vol. Infantry.	
	19th Ohio Battery.	

THIRD DIVISION.

Brigadier-General S. P. CARTER.

First Brigade.	Second Brigade.	Third Brigade.
Colonel O. W. Steel.	Colonel J. S. Casement.	Colonel T. J. Henderson.

8th Tennessee Vol. Infantry.	177th Ohio Vol. Infantry.	112th Illinois Vol. Infan'y.
12th Kentucky Vol. Infantry.	65th Indiana Vol. Infantry.	63d Indiana Vol. Infantry.
16th Kentucky Vol. Infantry.	65th Illinois Vol. Infantry.	140th Indiana Vol. Infan'y.
100th Ohio Volun. Infantry.	103d Ohio Volun. Infantry.	
104th Ohio Volun. Infantry.		

Battery D, 1st Ohio Light Artillery.

Cavalry Division — *Major-General* JUDSON KILPATRICK *commanding.*

First Brigade.	Second Brigade.	Third Brigade.
Brev. Brig.-Gen. Thos. J. Jordan.	Brevet Brig.-Gen. S. D. Atkins.	Colonel George E. Spencer.

9th Pennsylvania Cavalry.	92d Illinois Mounted Infan.	5th Kentucky Cavalry.
3d Kentucky Cavalry.	10th Ohio Cavalry.	5th Ohio Cavalry.
2d Kentucky Cavalry.	9th Ohio Cavalry.	1st Alabama Cavalry.
8th Indiana Cavalry.	1st Ohio Squadron.	13th Pennsylvania Cav.
3d Indiana Cavalry	9th Michigan Cavalry.	

ARTILLERY.

Captain Y. V. BEEBE.

10th Wisconsin Battery.

The railroads to our rear had also been repaired, so that stores were arriving very fast, both from Morehead City and Wilmington. The country was so level that a single locomotive could haul twenty-five and thirty cars to a train, instead of only ten, as was the case in Tennessee and Upper Georgia.

By the 5th of April such progress had been made, that I issued the following Special Field Orders, No. 48, prescribing the time and manner of the next march:

[Special Field Orders, No. 48.]
HEADQUARTERS MILITARY DIVISION OF THE MISSISSIPPI, }
IN THE FIELD, GOLDSBORO', NORTH CAROLINA, *April* 5, 1865.}

*Confidential to Army Commanders, Corps Commanders, and Chiefs of
Staff Departments:*
The next grand objective is to place this army (with its full equipment) north of Roanoke River, facing west, with a base for supplies at Norfolk, and at Winton or Murfreesboro' on the Chowan, and in full communication with the Army of the Potomac, about Petersburg; and also to do the enemy as much harm as possible *en route*:

1. To accomplish this result the following general plan will be followed, or modified only by written orders from these headquarters, should events require a change:

(1.) On Monday, the 10th of April, all preparations are presumed to be complete, and the outlying detachments will be called in, or given directions to meet on the next march. All preparations will also be complete to place the railroad-stock back of Kinston on the one road, and below the Northeast Branch on the other.

(2.) On Tuesday, the 11th, the columns will draw out on their lines of march, say, about seven miles, and close up.

(3.) On Wednesday the march will begin in earnest, and will be kept up at the rate, say, of about twelve miles a day, or according to the amount of resistance. All the columns will dress to the left (which is the exposed flank), and commanders will study always to find roads by which they can, if necessary, perform a general left wheel, the wagons to be escorted to some place of security on the direct route of march. Foraging and other details may continue as heretofore, only more caution and prudence should be observed; and foragers should not go in advance of the *advance-guard*, but look more to our right rear for corn, bacon, and meal.

2. The left wing (Major-General Slocum commanding) will aim

straight for the railroad-bridge near Smithfield; thence along up the Neuse River to the railroad-bridge over Neuse River, northeast of Raleigh (Powell's); thence to Warrenton, the general point of concentration.

The centre (Major-General Schofield commanding) will move to Whitley's Mill, ready to support the left until it is past Smithfield, when it will follow up (substantially) Little River to about Rolesville, ready at all times to move to the support of the left; after passing Tar River, to move to Warrenton.

The right wing (Major-General Howard commanding), preceded by the cavalry, will move rapidly on Pikeville and Nahunta, then swing across to Bulah to Folk's Bridge, ready to make junction with the other armies in case the enemy offers battle this side of Neuse River, about Smithfield; thence, in case of no serious opposition on the left, will work up toward Earpsboro', Andrews, B——, and Warrenton.

The cavalry (General Kilpatrick commanding), leaving its encumbrances with the right wing, will push as though straight for Weldon, until the enemy is across Tar River, and that bridge burned; then it will deflect toward Nashville and Warrenton, keeping up communication with general headquarters.

3. As soon as the army starts, the chief-quartermaster and commissary will prepare a resupply of stores at some point on Pamlico or Albemarle Sounds, ready to be conveyed to Kinston or Winton and Murfreesboro', according to developments. As soon as they have satisfactory information that the army is north of the Roanoke, they will forthwith establish a depot at Winton, with a sub-depot at Murfreesboro'. Major-General Schofield will hold, as heretofore, Wilmington (with the bridge across Northern Branch as an outpost), Newbern (and Kinston as its outpost), and will be prepared to hold Winton and Murfreesboro' as soon as the time arrives for that move. The navy has instructions from Admiral Porter to coöperate, and any commanding officer is authorized to call on the navy for assistance and coöperation, always in writing, setting forth the reasons, of which necessarily the naval commander must be the judge.

4. The general-in-chief will be with the centre habitually, but may in person shift to either flank where his presence may be needed, leaving a staff-officer to receive reports. He requires, absolutely, a report of each army or grand detachment each night, whether any thing material has occurred or not, for often the absence of an enemy is a very important fact in military prognostication.

By order of Major-General W. T. Sherman,

L. M. DAYTON, *Assistant Adjutant-General.*

But the whole problem became suddenly changed by the news of the fall of Richmond and Petersburg, which reached us at Goldsboro', on the 6th of April. The Confederate Government, with Lee's army, had hastily abandoned Richmond, fled in great disorder toward Danville, and General Grant's whole army was in close pursuit. Of course, I inferred that General Lee would succeed in making junction with General Johnston, with at least a fraction of his army, somewhere to my front. I at once altered the foregoing orders, and prepared on the day appointed, viz., April 10th, to move straight on Raleigh, against the army of General Johnston, known to be at Smithfield, and supposed to have about thirty-five thousand men. Wade Hampton's cavalry was on his left front and Wheeler's on his right front, simply watching us and awaiting our initiative. Meantime the details of the great victories in Virginia came thick and fast, and on the 8th I received from General Grant this communication, in the form of a cipher-dispatch:

HEADQUARTERS ARMIES OF THE UNITED STATES, ⎱
WILSON'S STATION, *April* 5, 1865.   ⎰

Major-General SHERMAN, *Goldsboro', North Carolina:*
All indications now are that Lee will attempt to reach Danville with the remnant of his force. Sheridan, who was up with him last night, reports all that is left with him—horse, foot, and dragoons—at twenty thousand, much demoralized. We hope to reduce this number one-half. I will push on to Burkesville, and, if a stand is made at Danville, will, in a very few days, go there. If you can possibly do so, push on from where you are, and let us see if we cannot finish the job with Lee's and Johnston's armies. Whether it will be better for you to strike for Greensboro' or nearer to Danville, you will be better able to judge when you receive this. Rebel armies now are the only strategic points to strike at.

U. S. GRANT, *Lieutenant-General.*

I answered immediately that we would move on the 10th, prepared to follow Johnston wherever he might go. Promptly on Monday morning, April 10th, the army moved straight on Smithfield; the right wing making a circuit by the right, and the left wing, supported by the centre, moving on the two direct roads toward Raleigh, distant fifty miles. General Terry's and General Kilpatrick's troops moved from their positions on the south or west bank of the Neuse River in the same general direction, by Cox's Bridge. On the 11th we reached Smithfield, and found it abandoned by Johnston's army, which had retreated hastily on Raleigh, burning the bridges. To restore these consumed the remainder of the day, and during that night I received a message from General Grant, at Appomattox, that General Lee had surrendered to him his whole army, which I at once announced to the troops in orders:

[Special Field Orders, No. 54.]
HEADQUARTERS MILITARY DIVISION OF THE MISSISSIPPI, ⎱
IN THE FIELD, SMITHFIELD, NORTH CAROLINA, *April* 12, 1865.⎰

The general commanding announces to the army that he has official notice from General Grant that General Lee surrendered to him his entire army, on the 9th inst., at Appomattox Court-House, Virginia.

Glory to God and our country, and all honor to our comrades in arms, toward whom we are marching!

A little more labor, a little more toil on our part, the great race is won, and our Government stands regenerated, after four long years of war.

W. T. SHERMAN, *Major-General commanding*.

Of course, this created a perfect *furore* of rejoicing, and we all regarded the war as over, for I knew well that General Johnston had no army with which to oppose mine. So that the only questions that remained were, would he surrender at Raleigh? or would he allow his army to disperse into guerrilla-bands, to "die in the last ditch," and entail on his country an indefinite and prolonged military occupation, and of consequent desolation? I knew well that Johnston's army could not be caught; the country was too open; and, without wagons, the men could escape us, disperse, and assemble again at some place agreed on, and thus the war might be prolonged indefinitely.

I then remembered Mr. Lincoln's repeated expression that he wanted the rebel soldiers not only defeated, but "back at their homes, engaged in their civil pursuits." On the evening of the 12th I was with the head of Slocum's column, at

Gulley's, and General Kilpatrick's cavalry was still ahead, fighting Wade Hampton's rear-guard, with orders to push it through Raleigh, while I would give a more southerly course to the infantry columns, so as, if possible, to prevent a retreat southward. On the 13th, early, I entered Raleigh, and ordered the several heads of column toward Ashville, in the direction of Salisbury or Charlotte. Before reaching Raleigh, a locomotive came down the road to meet me, passing through both Wade Hampton's and Kilpatrick's cavalry, bringing four gentlemen, with a letter from Governor Vance to me, asking protection for the citizens of Raleigh. These gentlemen were, of course, dreadfully excited at the dangers through which they had passed. Among them were ex-Senator Graham, Mr. Swain, president of Chapel Hill University, and a Surgeon Warren, of the Confederate army. They had come with a flag of truce, to which they were not entitled; still, in the interest of peace, I respected it, and permitted them to return to Raleigh with their locomotive, to assure the Governor and the people that the war was substantially over, and that I wanted the civil authorities to remain in the execution of their office till the pleasure of the President could be ascertained. On reaching Raleigh I found these same gentlemen, with Messrs. Badger, Bragg, Holden, and others, but Governor Vance had fled, and could not be prevailed on to return, because he feared an arrest and imprisonment. From the Raleigh newspapers of the 10th I learned that General Stoneman, with his division of cavalry, had come across the mountains from East Tennessee, had destroyed the railroad at Salisbury, and was then supposed to be approaching Greensboro'. I also learned that General Wilson's cavalry corps was "smashing things" down about Selma and Montgomery, Alabama, and was pushing for Columbus and Macon, Georgia; and I also had reason to expect that General Sheridan would come down from Appomattox to join us at Raleigh with his superb cavalry corps. I needed more cavalry to check Johnston's retreat, so that I could come up to him with my infantry, and therefore had good reason to delay. I ordered the railroad to be finished up to Raleigh, so that I could operate from it as a base, and then made—

[Special Field Orders, No. 55.]

HEADQUARTERS MILITARY DIVISION OF THE MISSISSIPPI, ⎫
IN THE FIELD, RALEIGH, NORTH CAROLINA, *April* 14, 1865. ⎭

The next movement will be on Ashboro', to turn the position of the enemy at the "Company's Shops" in rear of Haw River Bridge, and at Greensboro', and to cut off his only available line of retreat by Salisbury and Charlotte:

1. General Kilpatrick will keep up a show of pursuit in the direction of Hillsboro' and Graham, but be ready to cross Haw River on General Howard's bridge, near Pittsboro', and thence will operate toward Greensboro', on the right front of the right wing.

2. The right wing, Major-General Howard commanding, will move out on the Chapel Hill road, and send a light division up in the direction of Chapel Hill University to act in connection with the cavalry; but the main columns and trains will move *via* Hackney's Cross-Roads, and Trader's Hill, Pittsboro', St. Lawrence, etc., to be followed by the cavalry and light division, as soon as the bridge is laid over Haw River.

3. The centre, Major-General Schofield commanding, will move *via* Holly Springs, New Hill, Haywood, and Moffitt's Mills.

4. The left wing, Major-General Slocum commanding, will move rapidly by the Aven's Ferry road, Carthage, Caledonia, and Cox's Mills.

5. All the troops will draw well out on the roads designated during to-day and to-morrow, and on the following day will move with all possible rapidity for Ashboro'. No further destruction of railroads, mills, cotton, and produce, will be made without the specific orders of an army commander, and the inhabitants will be dealt with kindly, looking to an early reconciliation. The troops will be permitted, however, to gather forage and provisions as heretofore; only more care should be taken not to strip the poorer classes too closely.

By order of General W. T. Sherman,

L. M. DAYTON, *Assistant Adjutant-General*.

Thus matters stood, when on the morning of the 14th General Kilpatrick reported from Durham's Station, twenty-six miles up the railroad toward Hillsboro', that a flag of truce had come in from the enemy with a package from General Johnston addressed to me. Taking it for granted that this was preliminary to a surrender, I ordered the message to be sent me at Raleigh, and on the 14th received from General Johnston a letter dated April 13, 1865, in these words:

The results of the recent campaign in Virginia have changed the relative military condition of the belligerents. I am, therefore, induced to address you in this form the inquiry whether, to stop the further effusion of blood and devastation of property, you are willing to make a temporary suspension of active operations, and to communicate to Lieutenant-General Grant, commanding the armies of the United States, the request that he will take like action in regard to other armies, the object being to permit the civil authorities to enter into the needful arrangements to terminate the existing war.

To which I replied as follows:

HEADQUARTERS MILITARY DIVISION OF THE MISSISSIPPI, IN THE FIELD, RALEIGH, NORTH CAROLINA, *April* 14, 1865.

General J. E. JOHNSTON, *commanding Confederate Army*.

GENERAL: I have this moment received your communication of this date. I am fully empowered to arrange with you any terms for the suspension of further hostilities between the armies commanded by you and those commanded by myself, and will be willing to confer with you to that end. I will limit the advance of my main column, to-morrow, to Morrisville, and the cavalry to the university, and expect that you will also maintain the present position of your forces until each has notice of a failure to agree.

That a basis of action may be had, I undertake to abide by the same terms and conditions as were made by Generals Grant and Lee at Appomattox Court-House, on the 9th instant, relative to our two armies; and, furthermore, to obtain from General Grant an order to suspend the movements of any troops from the direction of Virginia. General Stoneman is under my command, and my order will suspend any devastation or destruction contemplated by him. I will add that I really desire to save the people of North Carolina the damage they would sustain by the march of this army through the central or western parts of the State.

I am, with respect, your obedient servant,

W. T. SHERMAN, *Major-General*.

I sent my aide-de-camp, Colonel McCoy, up to Durham's Station with this letter, with instructions to receive the answer, to telegraph its contents back to me at Raleigh, and to arrange for an interview. On the 16th I received a reply from General Johnston, agreeing to meet me the next day at a point midway between our advance at Durham and his rear at Hillsboro'. I ordered a car and locomotive to be prepared to convey me up to Durham's at eight o'clock of the morning of April 17th. Just as we were entering the car, the telegraph-operator, whose office was up-stairs in the depot-building, ran down to me and said that he was at that instant of time receiving a most important dispatch in cipher from Morehead City, which I ought to see. I held the train for nearly half an hour, when he returned with the message translated and written out. It was from Mr. Stanton, announcing the assassination of Mr. Lincoln, the attempt on the life of Mr. Seward and son, and a suspicion that a like fate was designed for General Grant and all the principal officers of the Government. Dreading the effect of such a message at that critical instant of time, I asked the operator if any one besides himself had seen it; he answered no. I then bade him not to reveal the contents by word or look till I came back, which I proposed to do the same afternoon. The train then started, and, as we passed Morris's Station, General Logan, commanding the Fifteenth Corps, came into my car, and I told him I wanted to see him on my return, as I had something very important to communicate. He knew I was going to meet General Johnston, and volunteered to say that he hoped I would succeed in obtaining his surrender, as the whole army dreaded the long march to Charlotte (one hundred and seventy-five miles), already begun, but which had been interrupted by the receipt of General Johnston's letter of the 13th. We reached Durham's, twenty-six miles, about 10 A.M., where General Kilpatrick had a squadron of cavalry drawn up to receive me. We passed into the house in which he had his headquarters, and soon after mounted some led horses, which he had prepared for myself and staff. General Kilpatrick sent a man ahead with a white flag, followed by a small platoon, behind which we rode, and were followed by the rest of the escort. We rode up the Hillsboro' road for about five miles, when our flag-bearer discovered another coming to meet him. They met, and word was passed back to us that General Johnston was near at hand, when we rode forward and met General Johnston on horseback, riding side by side with General Wade Hampton. We shook hands, and introduced our respective attendants. I asked if there was a place convenient where we could be private, and General Johnston said he had passed a small farm-house a short distance back, when we rode back to it together side by side, our staff-officers and escorts following. We had never met before, though we had been in the regular army together for thirteen years; but it so happened that we had never before come together. He was some twelve or more years my senior; but we knew enough of each other to be well acquainted at once. We soon reached the house of a Mr. Bennett, dismounted, and left our horses with orderlies in the road. Our officers, on foot, passed into the yard, and General Johnston and I entered the small frame-house. We asked the farmer if we could have the use of his house for a few minutes, and he and his wife withdrew into a smaller log-house, which stood close by.

As soon as we were alone together I showed him the dispatch announcing Mr. Lincoln's assassination, and watched him closely. The perspiration came out in large drops on his forehead, and he did not attempt to conceal his distress. He denounced the act as a disgrace to the age, and hoped I did not charge it to the Confederate Government. I told him I could not believe that he or General Lee, or the officers of the Confederate army, could possibly be privy to acts of assassination; but I would not say as much for Jeff. Davis, George Sanders, and men of that stripe. We talked about the effect of this act on the country at large and on the armies, and he realized that it made my situation extremely delicate. I explained to him that I had not yet revealed the news to my own personal staff or to the army, and that I dreaded the effect when made known in Raleigh. Mr. Lincoln was peculiarly endeared to the soldiers, and I feared that some foolish woman or man in Raleigh might say something or do something that would madden our men, and that a fate worse than that of Columbia would befall the place.

I then told Johnston that he must be convinced that he could not oppose my army, and that, since Lee had surrendered, he could do the same with honor and propriety. He plainly and repeatedly admitted this, and added that any further fighting would be "*murder;*" but he thought that, instead of surrendering piecemeal, we might arrange terms that would embrace *all* the Confederate armies. I asked him if he could control other armies than his own; he said, not then, but intimated that he could procure authority from Mr. Davis. I then told him that I had recently had an interview with General Grant and President Lincoln, and that I was possessed of their views; that with them and the people North there seemed to be no vindictive feeling against the Confederate armies, but there was against Davis and his political adherents; and that the terms that General Grant had given to General Lee's army were certainly most generous and liberal. All this he admitted, but always recurred to the idea of a universal surrender, embracing his own army, that of Dick Taylor in Louisiana and Texas, and of Maury, Forrest, and others, in Alabama and Georgia. General Johnston's account of our interview in his "Narrative" (page 402, *et seq.*) is quite accurate and correct, only I do not recall his naming the capitulation of Loeben, to which he refers. Our conversation was very general and extremely cordial, satisfying me that it could have but one result, and that which we all desired, viz., to end the war as quickly as possible; and, being anxious to return to Raleigh before the news of Mr. Lincoln's assassination could be divulged, on General Johnston's saying that he thought that, during the night, he could procure authority to act in the name of all the Confederate armies in existence, we agreed to meet again the next day at noon at the same place, and parted, he for Hillsboro' and I for Raleigh.

We rode back to Durham's Station in the order we had come, and then I showed the dispatch announcing Mr. Lincoln's death. I cautioned the officers to watch the soldiers closely, to prevent any violent retaliation by them, leaving that to the Government at Washington; and on our way back to Raleigh in the cars I showed the same dispatch to General Logan and to several of the officers of the Fifteenth Corps that were posted at Morrisville and Jones's Station, all of whom were deeply impressed by it; but all gave their opinion that this sad news should not change our general course of action.

As soon as I reached Raleigh I published the following orders to the army, announcing the assassination of the President, and I doubt if, in the whole land, there were more sincere mourners over his sad fate than were then in and about Raleigh. I watched the effect closely, and was gratified that there was no single act of retaliation; though I saw and felt that one single word by me would have laid the city in ashes, and turned its whole population houseless upon the country, if not worse:

[Special Field Orders, No. 56.]
HEADQUARTERS MILITARY DIVISION OF THE MISSISSIPPI, ⎫
IN THE FIELD, RALEIGH, NORTH CAROLINA, *April* 17, 1865.⎰

The general commanding announces, with pain and sorrow, that on the evening of the 14th instant, at the theatre in Washington city, his Excellency the President of the United States, Mr. Lincoln, was assassinated by one who uttered the State motto of Virginia. At the same time, the Secretary of State, Mr. Seward, while suffering from a broken arm, was also stabbed by another murderer in his own house, but still survives, and his son was wounded, supposed fatally. It is believed, by persons capable of judging, that other high officers were designed to share the same fate. Thus it seems that our enemy, despairing of meeting us in open, manly warfare, begins to resort to the assassin's tools.

Your general does not wish you to infer that this is universal, for he knows that the great mass of the Confederate army would scorn to sanction such acts, but he believes it the legitimate consequence of rebellion against rightful authority.

We have met every phase which this war has assumed, and must now be prepared for it in its last and worst shape, that of assassins and guerrillas; but woe unto the people who seek to expend their wild passions in such a manner, for there is but one dread result!

By order of Major-General W. T. Sherman,
L. M. DAYTON, *Assistant Adjutant-General.*

During the evening of the 17th and morning of the 18th I saw nearly all the general officers of the army (Schofield, Slocum, Howard, Logan, Blair), and we talked over the matter of the conference at Bennett's house of the day before, and, without exception, all advised me to agree to some terms, for they all dreaded the long and harassing march in pursuit of a dissolving and fleeing army—a march that might carry us back again over the thousand miles that we had just accomplished. We all knew that if we could bring Johnston's army to bay, we could destroy it in an hour, but that was simply impossible in the country in which we found ourselves. We discussed all the probabilities, among which was, whether, if Johnston made a point of it, I should assent to the escape from the country of Jeff. Davis and his fugitive cabinet; and some one of my general officers, either Logan or Blair, insisted that, if asked for, we should even provide a vessel to carry them to Nassau from Charleston.

The next morning I again started in the cars to Durham's Station, accompanied by most of my personal staff, and by Generals Blair, Barry, Howard, etc., and, reaching General Kilpatrick's headquarters at Durham's, we again mounted, and rode, with the same escort of the day before, to Bennett's house, reaching there punctually at noon. General Johnston had not yet arrived, but a courier shortly came, and reported him as on the way. It must have been nearly 2 P.M. when he arrived, as before, with General Wade Hampton. He had halted his escort out of sight, and we again entered Bennett's house, and I closed the door. General Johnston then assured me that he had authority over all the Confederate armies, so that they would obey his orders to surrender on the same terms with his own, but he argued that, to obtain so cheaply this desirable result, I ought to give his men and officers some assurance of their political rights after their surrender. I explained to him that Mr. Lincoln's proclamation of amnesty, of December 8, 1863, still in force, enabled every Confederate soldier and officer, below the rank of colonel, to obtain an absolute pardon, by simply laying down his arms, and taking the common oath of allegiance, and that General Grant, in accepting the surrender of General Lee's army, had extended the same principle to *all* the officers, General Lee included; such a pardon, I understood, would restore to them all their rights of citizenship. But he insisted that the officers and men of the Confederate army were unnecessarily alarmed about this matter, as a sort of bugbear. He then said that Mr. Breckenridge was near at hand, and he thought that it would be well for him to be present. I objected, on the score that he was then in Davis's cabinet, and our negotiations should be confined strictly to belligerents. He then said Breckenridge was a major-general in the Confederate army, and might sink his character of Secretary of War. I consented, and he sent one

of his staff-officers back, who soon returned with Breckenridge, and he entered the room. General Johnston and I then
again went over the whole ground, and Breckenridge confirmed what he had said as to the uneasiness of the Southern
officers and soldiers about their political rights in case of surrender. While we were in consultation, a messenger came
with a parcel of papers, which General Johnston said were
from Mr. Reagan, Postmaster-General. He and Breckenridge
looked over them, and, after some side conversation, he
handed one of the papers to me. It was in Reagan's handwriting, and began with a long preamble and terms, so general
and verbose, that I said they were inadmissible. Then recalling
the conversation of Mr. Lincoln, at City Point, I sat down at
the table, and wrote off the terms, which I thought concisely
expressed his views and wishes, and explained that I was willing to submit these terms to the new President, Mr. Johnson,
provided that both armies should remain *in statu quo* until the
truce therein declared should expire. I had full faith that General Johnston would religiously respect the truce, which he
did; and that I would be the gainer, for in the few days it
would take to send the papers to Washington, and receive an
answer, I could finish the railroad up to Raleigh, and be the
better prepared for a long chase.

Neither Mr. Breckenridge nor General Johnston wrote one
word of that paper. I wrote it myself, and announced it as the
best I could do, and they readily assented.

While copies of this paper were being made for signature,
the officers of our staffs commingled in the yard at Bennett's
house, and were all presented to Generals Johnston and
Breckenridge. All without exception were rejoiced that the
war was over, and that in a very few days we could turn our
faces toward home. I remember telling Breckenridge that he
had better get away, as the feeling of our people was utterly
hostile to the political element of the South, and to him especially, because he was the Vice-President of the United States,
who had as such announced Mr. Lincoln, of Illinois, duly and
properly elected the President of the United States, and yet
that he had afterward openly rebelled and taken up arms
against the Government. He answered me that he surely

would give us no more trouble, and intimated that he would speedily leave the country forever. I may have also advised him that Mr. Davis too should get abroad as soon as possible.

The papers were duly signed; we parted about dark, and my party returned to Raleigh. Early the next morning, April 19th, I dispatched by telegraph to Morehead City to prepare a fleet-steamer to carry a messenger to Washington, and sent Major Henry Hitchcock down by rail, bearing the following letters, and agreement with General Johnston, with instructions to be very careful to let nothing escape him to the greedy newspaper correspondents, but to submit his papers to General Halleck, General Grant, or the Secretary of War, and to bring me back with all expedition their orders and instructions.

On their face they recited that I had no authority to make final terms involving civil or political questions, but that I submitted them to the proper quarter in Washington for their action; and the letters fully explained that the military situation was such that the delay was an advantage to us. I cared little whether they were approved, modified, or disapproved *in toto*; only I wanted instructions. Many of my general officers, among whom, I am almost positive, were Generals Logan and Blair, urged me to accept the "terms," without reference at all to Washington, but I preferred the latter course:

HEADQUARTERS MILITARY DIVISION OF THE MISSISSIPPI, ⎱
IN THE FIELD, RALEIGH, NORTH CAROLINA, *April* 18, 1865. ⎰

General H. W. HALLECK, *Chief of Staff, Washington, D. C.*

GENERAL: I received your dispatch describing the man Clark, detailed to assassinate me. He had better be in a hurry, or he will be too late.

The news of Mr. Lincoln's death produced a most intense effect on our troops. At first I feared it would lead to excesses; but now it has softened down, and can easily be guided. None evinced more feeling than General Johnston, who admitted that the act was calculated to stain his cause with a dark hue; and he contended that the loss was most serious to the South, who had begun to realize that Mr. Lincoln was the best friend they had.

I cannot believe that even Mr. Davis was privy to the diabolical plot, but think it the emanation of a set of young men of the South, who are very devils. I want to throw upon the South the care of this class of men, who will soon be as obnoxious to their industrial classes as to us.

Had I pushed Johnston's army to an extremity, it would have dispersed, and done infinite mischief. Johnston informed me that General Stoneman had been at Salisbury, and was now at Statesville. I have sent him orders to come to me.

General Johnston also informed me that General Wilson was at Columbus, Georgia, and he wanted me to arrest his progress. I leave that to you.

Indeed, if the President sanctions my agreement with Johnston, our interest is to cease all destruction.

Please give all orders necessary according to the views the Executive may take, and influence him, if possible, not to vary the terms at all, for I have considered every thing, and believe that, the Confederate armies once dispersed, we can adjust all else fairly and well. I am, yours, etc.,

W. T. SHERMAN, *Major-General commanding.*

HEADQUARTERS MILITARY DIVISION OF THE MISSISSIPPI,
IN THE FIELD, RALEIGH, NORTH CAROLINA, *April* 18, 1865.

Lieutenant-General U. S. GRANT, *or Major-General* HALLECK,
    Washington, D. C.

GENERAL: I inclose herewith a copy of an agreement made this day between General Joseph E. Johnston and myself, which, if approved by the President of the United States, will produce peace from the Potomac to the Rio Grande. Mr. Breckenridge was present at our conference, in the capacity of major-general, and satisfied me of the ability of General Johnston to carry out to their full extent the terms of this agreement; and if you will get the President to simply indorse the copy, and commission me to carry out the terms, I will follow them to the conclusion.

You will observe that it is an absolute submission of the enemy to the lawful authority of the United States, and disperses his armies absolutely; and the point to which I attach most importance is, that the dispersion and disbandment of these armies is done in such a manner as to prevent their breaking up into guerrilla bands. On the other hand, we can retain just as much of an army as we please. I agreed to the mode and manner of the surrender of arms set forth, as it gives the States the means of repressing guerrillas, which we could not expect them to do if we stripped them of all arms.

Both Generals Johnston and Breckenridge admitted that slavery was dead, and I could not insist on embracing it in such a paper, because it can be made with the States in detail. I know that all the men of substance South sincerely want peace, and I do not believe they will resort to war again during this century. I have no doubt that they will in the future be perfectly subordinate to the laws of the United States. The moment my action in this matter is approved, I can spare five corps, and will ask for orders to leave General Schofield here with the Tenth Corps, and to march myself with the Fourteenth, Fifteenth, Seventeenth, Twentieth, and Twenty-third Corps *via* Burkesville and Gordonsville to Frederick or Hagerstown, Maryland, there to be paid and mustered out.

The question of finance is now the chief one, and every soldier and officer not needed should be got home at work. I would like to be able to begin the march north by May 1st.

I urge, on the part of the President, speedy action, as it is important to get the Confederate armies to their homes as well as our own.

I am, with great respect, your obedient servant,

W. T. SHERMAN, *Major-General commanding*.

Memorandum, or Basis of Agreement, made this 18th day of April, A.D. 1865, near Durham's Station, in the State of North Carolina, by and between General JOSEPH E. JOHNSTON, *commanding the Confederate Army, and Major-General* WILLIAM T. SHERMAN, *commanding the Army of the United States in North Carolina, both present:*

1. The contending armies now in the field to maintain the *statu quo* until notice is given by the commanding general of any one to its opponent, and reasonable time—say, forty-eight hours—allowed.

2. The Confederate armies now in existence to be disbanded and conducted to their several State capitals, there to deposit their arms and public property in the State Arsenal; and each officer and man to execute and file an agreement to cease from acts of war, and to abide the action of the State and Federal authority. The number of arms and munitions of war to be reported to the Chief of Ordnance at Washington City, subject to the future action of the Congress of the United States, and, in the mean time, to be used solely to maintain peace and order within the borders of the States respectively.

3. The recognition, by the Executive of the United States, of the several State governments, on their officers and Legislatures taking the oaths prescribed by the Constitution of the United States, and, where conflicting State governments have resulted from the war, the legitimacy of all shall be submitted to the Supreme Court of the United States.

4. The reëstablishment of all the Federal Courts in the several

States, with powers as defined by the Constitution of the United States and of the States respectively.

5. The people and inhabitants of all the States to be guaranteed, so far as the Executive can, their political rights and franchises, as well as their rights of person and property, as defined by the Constitution of the United States and of the States respectively.

6. The Executive authority of the Government of the United States not to disturb any of the people by reason of the late war, so long as they live in peace and quiet, abstain from acts of armed hostility, and obey the laws in existence at the place of their residence.

7. In general terms — the war to cease; a general amnesty, so far as the Executive of the United States can command, on condition of the disbandment of the Confederate armies, the distribution of the arms, and the resumption of peaceful pursuits by the officers and men hitherto composing said armies.

Not being fully empowered by our respective principals to fulfill these terms, we individually and officially pledge ourselves to promptly obtain the necessary authority, and to carry out the above programme.

W. T. SHERMAN, *Major-General,*
Commanding Army of the United States in North Carolina.
J. E. JOHNSTON, *General,*
Commanding Confederate States Army in North Carolina.

Major Hitchcock got off on the morning of the 20th, and I reckoned that it would take him four or five days to go to Washington and back. During that time the repairs on all the railroads and telegraph-lines were pushed with energy, and we also got possession of the railroad and telegraph from Raleigh to Weldon, in the direction of Norfolk. Meantime the troops remained *statu quo,* our cavalry occupying Durham's Station and Chapel Hill. General Slocum's head of column was at Aven's Ferry on Cape Fear River, and General Howard's was strung along the railroad toward Hillsboro'; the rest of the army was in and about Raleigh.

On the 20th I reviewed the Tenth Corps, and was much pleased at the appearance of General Paines's division of black troops, the first I had ever seen as a part of an organized army; and on the 21st I reviewed the Twenty-third Corps, which had been with me to Atlanta, but had returned to Nashville, had formed an essential part of the army which fought at Franklin, and with which General Thomas had defeated General Hood in Tennessee. It had then been transferred rapidly by rail to Baltimore and Washington by General Grant's orders, and thence by sea to North Carolina. Nothing of interest happened at Raleigh till the evening of April 23d, when Major Hitchcock reported by telegraph his return to Morehead City, and that he would come up by rail during the night. He arrived at 6 A.M., April 24th, accompanied by General Grant and one or two officers of his staff, who had not telegraphed the fact of their being on the train, for prudential reasons. Of course, I was both surprised and pleased to see the general, soon learned that my terms with Johnston had been disapproved, was instructed by him to give the forty-eight hours' notice required by the terms of the truce, and afterward to proceed to attack or follow him. I immediately telegraphed to General Kilpatrick, at Durham's, to have a mounted courier ready to carry the following message, then on its way up by rail, to the rebel lines:

HEADQUARTERS MILITARY DIVISION OF THE MISSISSIPPI, IN ⎫
THE FIELD, RALEIGH, NORTH CAROLINA, *April* 24, 1865 — 6 A.M. ⎭

General JOHNSTON, *commanding Confederate Army, Greensboro':*
You will take notice that the truce or suspension of hostilities agreed to between us will cease in forty-eight hours after this is received at your lines, under the first of the articles of agreement.
W. T. SHERMAN, *Major-General.*

At the same time I wrote another short note to General Johnston, of the same date:

I have replies from Washington to my communications of April 18th. I am instructed to limit my operations to your immediate command, and not to attempt civil negotiations. I therefore demand the surrender of your army on the same terms as were given to General Lee at Appomattox, April 9th instant, purely and simply.

Of course, both these papers were shown to General Grant at the time, before they were sent, and he approved of them.
At the same time orders were sent to all parts of the army to be ready to resume the pursuit of the enemy on the expiration of the forty-eight hours' truce, and messages were sent to General Gillmore (at Hilton Head) to the same effect, with

instructions to get a similar message through to General Wilson, at Macon, by some means.

General Grant had brought with him, from Washington, written answers from the Secretary of War, and of himself, to my communications of the 18th, which I still possess, and here give the originals. They embrace the copy of a dispatch made by Mr. Stanton to General Grant, when he was pressing Lee at Appomattox, which dispatch, if sent me at the same time (as should have been done), would have saved a world of trouble. I did not understand that General Grant had come down to supersede me in command, nor did he intimate it, nor did I receive these communications as a serious reproof, but promptly acted on them, as is already shown; and in this connection I give my answer made to General Grant, at Raleigh, before I had received any answer from General Johnston to the demand for the surrender of his own army, as well as my answer to Mr. Stanton's letter, of the same date, both written on the supposition that I might have to start suddenly in pursuit of Johnston, and have no other chance to explain.

WAR DEPARTMENT, WASHINGTON CITY, *April* 21, 1865.
Lieutenant-General GRANT.

GENERAL: The memorandum or basis agreed upon between General Sherman and General Johnston having been submitted to the President, they are disapproved. You will give notice of the disapproval to General Sherman, and direct him to resume hostilities at the earliest moment.

The instructions given to you by the late President, Abraham Lincoln, on the 3d of March, by my telegraph of that date, addressed to you, express substantially the views of President Andrew Johnson, and will be observed by General Sherman. A copy is herewith appended.

The President desires that you proceed immediately to the headquarters of Major-General Sherman, and direct operations against the enemy.

Yours truly,
EDWIN M. STANTON, *Secretary of War.*

The following telegram was received 2 P.M., City Point, March 4, 1865 (from Washington, 12 M., March 3, 1865):

[CIPHER.]
OFFICE UNITED STATES MILITARY TELEGRAPH, ⎫
HEADQUARTERS ARMIES OF THE UNITED STATES.⎰

Lieutenant-General GRANT:

The President directs me to say to you that he wishes you to have no conference with General Lee, unless it be for the capitulation of Lee's army or on solely minor and purely military matters.

He instructs me to say that you are not to decide, discuss, or confer upon any political question; such questions the President holds in his own hands, and will submit them to no military conferences or conventions.

Meantime you are to press to the utmost your military advantages.

EDWIN M. STANTON, *Secretary of War.*

HEADQUARTERS ARMIES OF THE UNITED STATES, ⎫
WASHINGTON, D. C., *April* 21, 1865. ⎰

Major-General W. T. SHERMAN, *commanding Military Division
    of the Mississippi.*

GENERAL: The basis of agreement entered into between yourself and General J. E. Johnston, for the disbandment of the Southern army, and the extension of the authority of the General Government over all the territory belonging to it, sent for the approval of the President, is received.

I read it carefully myself before submitting it to the President and Secretary of War, and felt satisfied that it could not possibly be approved. My reason for these views I will give you at another time, in a more extended letter.

Your agreement touches upon questions of such vital importance that, as soon as read, I addressed a note to the Secretary of War, notifying him of their receipt, and the importance of immediate action by the President; and suggested, in view of their importance, that the entire Cabinet be called together, that all might give an expression of their opinions upon the matter. The result was a disapproval by the President of the basis laid down; a disapproval of the negotiations altogether—except for the surrender of the army commanded by General Johnston, and directions to me to notify you of this decision. I cannot do so better than by sending you the inclosed copy of a dispatch (penned by the late President, though signed by the Secretary of War) in answer to me, on sending a letter received from General Lee, proposing to meet me for the purpose of submitting the question of peace to a convention of officers.

Please notify General Johnston, immediately on receipt of this, of the termination of the truce, and resume hostilities against his army at the earliest moment you can, acting in good faith.

Very respectfully your obedient servant,

U. S. GRANT, *Lieutenant-General.*

HEADQUARTERS MILITARY DIVISION OF THE MISSISSIPPI, }
IN THE FIELD, RALEIGH, NORTH CAROLINA, *April* 25, 1865.}

Lieutenant-General U. S. GRANT, *present.*

GENERAL: I had the honor to receive your letter of April 21st, with inclosures, yesterday, and was well pleased that you came along, as you must have observed that I held the military control so as to adapt it to any phase the case might assume.

It is but just I should record the fact that I made my terms with General Johnston under the influence of the liberal terms you extended to the army of General Lee at Appomattox Court-House on the 9th, and the seeming policy of our Government, as evinced by the call of the Virginia Legislature and Governor back to Richmond, under yours and President Lincoln's very eyes.

It now appears this last act was done without any consultation with you or any knowledge of Mr. Lincoln, but rather in opposition to a previous policy well considered.

I have not the least desire to interfere in the civil policy of our Government, but would shun it as something not to my liking; but occasions do arise when a prompt seizure of results is forced on military commanders not in immediate communication with the proper authority. It is probable that the terms signed by General Johnston and myself were not clear enough on the point, well understood between us, that our negotiations did not apply to any parties outside the officers and men of the Confederate armies, which could easily have been remedied.

No surrender of any army not actually at the mercy of an antagonist was ever made without "terms," and these always define the military status of the surrendered. Thus you stipulated that the officers and men of Lee's army should not be molested at their homes so long as they obeyed the laws at the place of their residence.

I do not wish to discuss these points involved in our recognition of the State governments in actual existence, but will merely state my conclusions, to await the solution of the future.

Such action on our part in no manner recognizes for a moment the so-called Confederate Government, or makes us liable for its debts or acts.

The laws and acts done by the several States during the period of rebellion are void, because done without the oath prescribed by our Constitution of the United States, which is a "condition precedent."

We have a right to use any sort of machinery to produce military results; and it is the commonest thing for military commanders to use the civil governments *in actual existence* as a means to an end. I do believe we could and can use the present State governments lawfully, constitutionally, and as the very best possible means to produce the object desired, viz., entire and complete submission to the lawful authority of the United States.

As to punishment for past crimes, that is for the judiciary, and can in no manner of way be disturbed by our acts; and, so far as I can, I will use my influence that rebels shall suffer all the personal punishment prescribed by law, as also the civil liabilities arising from their past acts.

What we now want is the new form of law by which common men may regain the positions of industry, so long disturbed by the war.

I now apprehend that the rebel armies will disperse; and, instead of dealing with six or seven States, we will have to deal with numberless bands of desperadoes, headed by such men as Mosby, Forrest, Red Jackson, and others, who know not and care not for danger and its consequences.

I am, with great respect, your obedient servant,

W. T. SHERMAN, *Major-General commanding.*

HEADQUARTERS MILITARY DIVISION OF THE MISSISSIPPI,
IN THE FIELD, RALEIGH, NORTH CAROLINA, *April 25, 1865.*

Hon. E. M. STANTON, *Secretary of War, Washington.*

DEAR SIR: I have been furnished a copy of your letter of April 21st to General Grant, signifying your disapproval of the terms on which General Johnston proposed to disarm and disperse the insurgents, on condition of amnesty, etc. I admit my folly in embracing in a military convention any civil matters; but, unfortunately, such is the nature of our situation that they seem inextricably united, and I understood from you at Savannah that the financial state of the country demanded military success, and would warrant a little bending to policy.

When I had my conference with General Johnston I had the public examples before me of General Grant's terms to Lee's army, and General Weitzel's invitation to the Virginia Legislature to assemble at Richmond.

I still believe the General Government of the United States has made a mistake; but that is none of my business—mine is a different task; and I had flattered myself that, by four years of patient, unremitting, and successful labor, I deserved no reminder such as is contained in the last paragraph of your letter to General Grant. You may assure the President that I heed his suggestion. I am truly, etc.,

W. T. SHERMAN, *Major-General commanding.*

On the same day, but later, I received an answer from General Johnston, agreeing to meet me again at Bennett's house the next day, April 26th, at noon. He did not even know that General Grant was in Raleigh.

General Grant advised me to meet him, and to accept his surrender on the same terms as his with General Lee; and on the 26th I again went up to Durham's Station by rail, and rode out to Bennett's house, where we again met, and General Johnston, without hesitation, agreed to, and we executed, the following final terms:

Terms of a Military Convention, entered into this 26th day of April, 1865, at Bennett's House, near Durham's Station, North Carolina, between General JOSEPH E. JOHNSTON, commanding the Confederate Army, and Major-General W. T. SHERMAN, commanding the United States Army in North Carolina:

1. All acts of war on the part of the troops under General Johnston's command to cease from this date.

2. All arms and public property to be deposited at Greensboro', and delivered to an ordnance-officer of the United States Army.

3. Rolls of all the officers and men to be made in duplicate; one copy to be retained by the commander of the troops, and the other to be given to an officer to be designated by General Sherman. Each officer and man to give his individual obligation in writing not to take up arms against the Government of the United States, until properly released from this obligation.

4. The side-arms of officers, and their private horses and baggage, to be retained by them.

5. This being done, all the officers and men will be permitted to return to their homes, not to be disturbed by the United States authorities, so long as they observe their obligation and the laws in force where they may reside.

W. T. SHERMAN, *Major-General,*
Commanding United States Forces in North Carolina.
J. E. JOHNSTON, *General,*
Commanding Confederate States Forces in North Carolina.
Approved: U. S. GRANT, *Lieutenant-General.*

I returned to Raleigh the same evening, and, at my request, General Grant wrote on these terms his approval, and then I thought the matter was surely at an end. He took the original copy, on the 27th returned to Newbern, and thence went back to Washington.

I immediately made all the orders necessary to carry into effect the terms of this convention, devolving on General Schofield the details of granting the parols and making the muster-rolls of prisoners, inventories of property, etc., of General Johnston's army at and about Greensboro', North Carolina, and on General Wilson the same duties in Georgia; but, thus far, I had been compelled to communicate with the latter through rebel sources, and General Wilson was necessarily confused by the conflict of orders and information. I deemed it of the utmost importance to establish for him a more reliable base of information and supply, and accordingly resolved to go in person to Savannah for that purpose. But, before starting, I received a *New York Times*, of April 24th, containing the following extraordinary communications:

[First Bulletin.]
WAR DEPARTMENT, WASHINGTON, *April* 22, 1865.

Yesterday evening a bearer of dispatches arrived from General Sherman. An agreement for a suspension of hostilities, and a memorandum of what is called a basis for peace, had been entered into on the 18th inst. by General Sherman, with the rebel General Johnston. Brigadier-General Breckenridge was present at the conference.

A cabinet meeting was held at eight o'clock in the evening, at which the action of General Sherman was disapproved by the President, by the Secretary of War, by General Grant, and by every member of the cabinet. General Sherman was ordered to resume hostilities immediately, and was directed that the instructions given by the late President, in the following telegram, which was penned by Mr. Lincoln himself, at the Capitol, on the night of the 3d of March, were approved by President Andrew Johnson, and were reiterated to govern the action of military commanders.

On the night of the 3d of March, while President Lincoln and his cabinet were at the Capitol, a telegram from General Grant was brought to the Secretary of War, informing him that General Lee had requested an interview or conference, to make an arrangement for terms of peace. The letter of General Lee was published in a letter to Davis and to the rebel Congress. General Grant's telegram was submitted to Mr. Lincoln, who, after pondering a few minutes, took up his pen and wrote with his own hand the following reply, which he submitted to the Secretary of State and Secretary of War. It was then dated, addressed, and signed, by the Secretary of War, and telegraphed to General Grant:

WASHINGTON, *March* 3, 1865—12 P.M.
Lieutenant-General GRANT:

The President directs me to say to you that he wishes you to have no conference with General Lee, unless it be for the capitulation of General Lee's army, or on some minor or purely military matter. He instructs me to say that you are not to decide, discuss, or confer upon any political questions. Such questions the President holds in his own hands, and will submit them to no military conferences or conventions.

Meantime you are to press to the utmost your military advantages.
EDWIN M. STANTON, *Secretary of War*.

The orders of General Sherman to General Stoneman to withdraw from Salisbury and join him will probably open the way for Davis to escape to Mexico or Europe with his plunder, which is reported to be very large, including not only the plunder of the Richmond banks, but previous accumulations.

A dispatch received by this department from Richmond says: "It is stated here, by respectable parties, that the amount of specie taken south by Jeff. Davis and his partisans is very large, including not only the plunder of the Richmond banks, but previous accumulations. They hope, it is said, to make terms with General Sherman, or some other commander, by which they will be permitted, with their effects, including this gold plunder, to go to Mexico or Europe. Johnston's negotiations look to this end."

After the cabinet meeting last night, General Grant started for North Carolina, to direct operations against Johnston's army.
EDWIN M. STANTON, *Secretary of War*.

Here followed the terms, and Mr. Stanton's ten reasons for rejecting them.

The publication of this bulletin by authority was an outrage on me, for Mr. Stanton had failed to communicate to me in advance, as was his duty, the purpose of the Administration to limit our negotiations to purely military matters; but, on the contrary, at Savannah he had authorized me to control all matters, *civil* and military.

By this bulletin, he implied that I had previously been furnished with a copy of his dispatch of March 3d to General Grant, which was not so; and he gave warrant to the impression, which was sown broadcast, that I might be bribed by banker's gold to permit Davis to escape. Under the influence of this, I wrote General Grant the following letter of April 28th, which has been published in the Proceedings of the Committee on the Conduct of the War.

I regarded this bulletin of Mr. Stanton as a personal and official insult, which I afterward publicly resented.

HEADQUARTERS MILITARY DIVISION OF THE MISSISSIPPI,
IN THE FIELD, RALEIGH, NORTH CAROLINA, *April* 28, 1865.

Lieutenant-General U. S. GRANT, *General-in-Chief,*
    Washington, D. C.

GENERAL: Since you left me yesterday, I have seen the *New York Times* of the 24th, containing a budget of military news, authenticated by the signature of the Secretary of War, Hon. E. M. Stanton, which is grouped in such a way as to give the public very erroneous impressions. It embraces a copy of the basis of agreement between myself and General Johnston, of April 18th, with comments, which it will be time enough to discuss two or three years hence, after the Government has experimented a little more in the machinery by which power reaches the scattered people of the vast country known as the "South."

In the mean time, however, I did think that my rank (if not past services) entitled me at least to trust that the Secretary of War would keep secret what was communicated for the use of none but the cabinet, until further inquiry could be made, instead of giving publicity to it along with documents which I never saw, and drawing therefrom inferences wide of the truth. I never saw or had furnished me a copy of President Lincoln's dispatch to you of the 3d of March, nor did Mr. Stanton or any human being ever convey to me its substance, or any thing like it. On the contrary, I had seen General Weitzel's invitation to the Virginia Legislature, made in Mr. Lincoln's very presence, and failed to discover any other official hint of a plan of reconstruction, or any ideas calculated to allay the fears of the people of the South, after the destruction of their armies and civil authorities would leave them without any government whatever.

We should not drive a people into anarchy, and it is simply impossible for our military power to reach all the masses of their un-happy country.

I confess I did not desire to drive General Johnston's army into bands of armed men, going about without purpose, and capable only of infinite mischief. But you saw, on your arrival here, that I had my army so disposed that his escape was only possible in a dis-organized shape; and as you did not choose to "direct military oper-ations in this quarter," I inferred that you were satisfied with the military situation; at all events, the instant I learned what was proper enough, the disapproval of the President, I acted in such a manner as to compel the surrender of General Johnston's whole army on the same terms which you had prescribed to General Lee's army, when you had it surrounded and in your absolute power.

Mr. Stanton, in stating that my orders to General Stoneman were likely to result in the escape of "Mr. Davis to Mexico or Europe," is in deep error. General Stoneman was not at "Salisbury," but had gone back to "Statesville." Davis was between us, and therefore Stoneman was beyond him. By turning toward me he was approach-ing Davis, and, had he joined me as ordered, I would have had a mounted force greatly needed for Davis's capture, and for other pur-poses. Even now I don't know that Mr. Stanton wants Davis caught, and as my official papers, deemed sacred, are hastily published to the world, it will be imprudent for me to state what has been done in that regard.

As the editor of the *Times* has (it may be) logically and fairly drawn from this singular document the conclusion that I am insub-ordinate, I can only deny the intention.

I have never in my life questioned or disobeyed an order, though many and many a time have I risked my life, health, and reputation, in obeying orders, or even hints to execute plans and purposes, not to my liking. It is not fair to withhold from me the plans and policy of Government (if any there be), and expect me to guess at them; for facts and events appear quite different from different stand-points. For four years I have been in camp dealing with soldiers, and I can assure you that the conclusion at which the cabinet arrived with such singular unanimity differs from mine. I conferred freely with the best officers in this army as to the points involved in this controversy, and, strange to say, they were singularly unanimous in the other conclusion. They will learn with pain and amazement that I am deemed insubordinate, and wanting in common-sense; that I, who for four years have labored day and night, winter and summer, who have brought an army of seventy thousand men in magnificent con-dition across a country hitherto deemed impassable, and placed it just where it was wanted, on the day appointed, have brought discredit on our Government! I do not wish to boast of this, but I do say that it entitled me to the courtesy of being consulted, before publishing to the world a proposition rightfully submitted to higher authority for adjudication, and then accompanied by statements which invited the dogs of the press to be let loose upon me. It is true that non-combatants, men who sleep in comfort and security while we watch on the distant lines, are better able to judge than we poor soldiers, who rarely see a newspaper, hardly hear from our families, or stop long enough to draw our pay. I envy not the task of "reconstruction," and am delighted that the Secretary of War has relieved me of it.

As you did not undertake to assume the management of the affairs of this army, I infer that, on personal inspection, your mind arrived at a different conclusion from that of the Secretary of War. I will therefore go on to execute your orders to the conclusion, and, when done, will with intense satisfaction leave to the civil authorities the execution of the task of which they seem so jealous. But, as an honest man and soldier, I invite them to go back to Nashville and follow my path, for they will see some things and hear some things that may disturb their philosophy.

With sincere respect,

W. T. SHERMAN, *Major-General commanding.*

P. S.—As Mr. Stanton's most singular paper has been published, I demand that this also be made public, though I am in no manner responsible to the press, but to the law, and my proper superiors.

W. T. S., *Major-General.*

On the 28th I summoned all the army and corps commanders together at my quarters in the Governor's mansion at Raleigh, where every thing was explained to them, and all orders for the future were completed. Generals Schofield, Terry, and Kilpatrick, were to remain on duty in the Department of North Carolina, already commanded by General Schofield, and the right and left wings were ordered to march under their respective commanding generals North by easy stages to Richmond, Virginia, there to await my return from the South.

On the 29th of April, with a part of my personal staff, I proceeded by rail to Wilmington, North Carolina, where I found Generals Hawley and Potter, and the little steamer Russia, Captain Smith, awaiting me. After a short pause in

Wilmington, we embarked, and proceeded down the coast to Port Royal and the Savannah River, which we reached on the 1st of May. There Captain Hosea, who had just come from General Wilson at Macon, met us, bearing letters for me and General Grant, in which General Wilson gave a brief summary of his operations up to date. He had marched from Eastport, Mississippi, "five hundred miles in thirty days, took six thousand three hundred prisoners, twenty-three colors, and one hundred and fifty-six guns, defeating Forrest, scattering the militia, and destroying every railroad, iron establishment, and factory, in North Alabama and Georgia."

He spoke in the highest terms of his cavalry, as "cavalry," claiming that it could not be *excelled*, and he regarded his corps as a model for modern cavalry in organization, armament, and discipline. Its strength was given at thirteen thousand five hundred men and horses on reaching Macon. Of course I was extremely gratified at his just confidence, and saw that all he wanted for efficient action was a sure base of supply, so that he need no longer depend for clothing, ammunition, food, and forage, on the country, which, now that war had ceased, it was our solemn duty to protect, instead of plunder. I accordingly ordered the captured steamer Jeff. Davis to be loaded with stores, to proceed at once up the Savannah River to Augusta, with a small detachment of troops to occupy the arsenal, and to open communication with General Wilson at Macon; and on the next day, May 2d, this steamer was followed by another with a full cargo of clothing, sugar, coffee, and bread, sent from Hilton Head by the department commander, General Gillmore, with a stronger guard commanded by General Molineux. Leaving to General Gillmore, who was present, and in whose department General Wilson was, to keep up the supplies at Augusta, and to facilitate as far as possible General Wilson's operations inland, I began my return on the 2d of May. We went into Charleston Harbor, passing the ruins of old Forts Moultrie and Sumter without landing. We reached the city of Charleston, which was held by part of the division of General John P. Hatch, the same that we had left at Pocotaligo. We walked the old familiar streets—Broad, King, Meeting, etc.—but desolation and ruin were everywhere. The heart of the city had been burned during the bombardment, and the rebel garrison at the time of its final evacuation had fired the railroad-depots, which fire had spread, and was only subdued by our troops after they had reached the city.

I inquired for many of my old friends, but they were dead or gone, and of them all I only saw a part of the family of Mrs. Pettigru. I doubt whether any city was ever more terribly punished than Charleston, but, as her people had for years been agitating for war and discord, and had finally inaugurated the civil war by an attack on the small and devoted garrison of Major Anderson, sent there by the General Government to defend them, the judgment of the world will be, that Charleston deserved the fate that befell her. Resuming our voyage, we passed into Cape Fear River by its mouth at Fort Caswell and Smithville, and out by the new channel at Fort Fisher, and reached Morehead City on the 4th of May. We found there the revenue-cutter Wayanda, on board of which were the Chief-Justice, Mr. Chase, and his daughter Nettie, now Mrs. Hoyt. The Chief-Justice at that moment was absent on a visit to Newbern, but came back the next day. Meantime, by means of the telegraph, I was again in correspondence with General Schofield at Raleigh. He had made great progress in parolling the officers and men of Johnston's army at Greensboro', but was embarrassed by the utter confusion and anarchy that had resulted from a want of understanding on many minor points, and on the political questions that had to be met at the instant. In order to facilitate the return to their homes of the Confederate officers and men, he had been forced to make with General Johnston the following supplemental terms, which were of course ratified and approved:

MILITARY CONVENTION OF APRIL 26, 1865.

SUPPLEMENTAL TERMS.

1. The field transportation to be loaned to the troops for their march to their homes, and for subsequent use in their industrial pursuits. Artillery-horses may be used in field-transportation, if necessary.

2. Each brigade or separate body to retain a number of arms equal to *one-seventh* of its effective strength, which, when the troops reach

the capitals of their States, will be disposed of as the general commanding the department may direct.

3. Private horses, and other private property of both officers and men, to be retained by them.

4. The commanding general of the Military Division of West Mississippi, Major-General Canby, will be requested to give transportation by water, from Mobile or New Orleans, to the troops from Arkansas and Texas.

5. The obligations of officers and soldiers to be signed by their immediate commanders.

6. Naval forces within the limits of General Johnston's command to be included in the terms of this convention.

J. M. SCHOFIELD, *Major-General,*
Commanding United States Forces in North Carolina.
J. E. JOHNSTON, *General,*
Commanding Confederate States Forces in North Carolina.

The total number of prisoners of war parolled by General
    Schofield, at Greensboro', North Carolina, as afterward
    officially reported, amounted to 36,817
And the total number who surrendered in Georgia
    and Florida, as reported by General J. H. Wilson, was . . 52,453

    Aggregate surrendered under the capitulation of
       General J. E. Johnston 89,270

On the morning of the 5th I also received from General Schofield this dispatch:

RALEIGH, NORTH CAROLINA, *May* 5, 1865.
To Major-General W. T. SHERMAN, *Morehead City:*
When General Grant was here, as you doubtless recollect, he said the lines (for trade and intercourse) had been extended to embrace this and other States south. The order, it seems, has been modified so as to include only Virginia and Tennessee. I think it would be an act of wisdom to open this State to trade at once.

I hope the Government will make known its policy as to the organs of State government without delay. Affairs must necessarily be in a very unsettled state until that is done. The people are now in a mood to accept almost any thing which promises a definite settlement. "What is to be done with the freedmen?" is the question of all, and it is the all-important question. It requires prompt and wise action to prevent the negroes from becoming a huge elephant on our hands. If I am to govern this State, it is important for me to know it at once. If another is to be sent here, it cannot be done too soon, for he probably will undo the most that I shall have done. I shall be glad to hear from you fully, when you have time to write. I will send your message to General Wilson at once.

J. M. SCHOFIELD, *Major-General.*

I was utterly without instructions from any source on the points of General Schofield's inquiry, and under the existing state of facts could not even advise him, for by this time I was in possession of the second bulletin of Mr. Stanton, published in all the Northern papers, with comments that assumed that I was a common traitor and a public enemy; and high officials had even instructed my own subordinates to disobey my lawful orders. General Halleck, who had so long been in Washington as the chief of staff, had been sent on the 21st of April to Richmond, to command the armies of the Potomac and James, in place of General Grant, who had transferred his headquarters to the national capital, and he (General Halleck) was therefore in supreme command in Virginia, while my command over North Carolina had never been revoked or modified.

[Second Bulletin.]
WAR DEPARTMENT, WASHINGTON, *April* 27—9.30 A.M.
To Major-General DIX:
The department has received the following dispatch from Major-General Halleck, commanding the Military Division of the James. Generals Canby and Thomas were instructed some days ago that Sherman's arrangements with Johnston were disapproved by the President, and they were ordered to disregard it and push the enemy in every direction.

E. M. STANTON, *Secretary of War.*

RICHMOND, VIRGINIA, *April* 26—9.30 P.M.
Hon. E. M. STANTON, *Secretary of War:*
Generals Meade, Sheridan, and Wright, are acting under orders to pay no regard to any truce or orders of General Sherman respecting hostilities, on the ground that Sherman's agreement could bind his command only, and no other.

They are directed to push forward, regardless of orders from any one except from General Grant, and cut off Johnston's retreat.

Beauregard has telegraphed to Danville that a new arrangement has been made with Sherman, and that the advance of the Sixth Corps was to be suspended until further orders.

I have telegraphed back to obey no orders of Sherman, but to push forward as rapidly as possible.

The bankers here have information to-day that Jeff. Davis's specie is moving south from Goldsboro', in wagons, as fast as possible.

I suggest that orders be telegraphed, through General Thomas, that Wilson obey no orders from Sherman, and notifying him and Canby, and all commanders on the Mississippi, to take measures to intercept the rebel chiefs and their plunder.

The specie taken with them is estimated here at from six to thirteen million dollars.

H. W. HALLECK, *Major-General commanding.*

Subsequently, before the Committee on the Conduct of the War, in Washington, on the 22d of May, I testified fully on this whole matter, and will abide the judgment of the country on the patriotism and wisdom of my public conduct in this connection. General Halleck's measures to capture General Johnston's army, actually surrendered to me at the time, at Greensboro', on the 26th of April, simply excited my contempt for a judgment such as he was supposed to possess. The assertion that Jeff. Davis's specie-train, of six to thirteen million dollars, was reported to be moving south from Goldsboro' in wagons as fast as possible, found plenty of willing ears, though my army of eighty thousand men had been at Goldsboro' from March 22d to the date of his dispatch, April 26th; and such a train would have been composed of from fifteen to thirty-two six-mule teams to have hauled this specie, even if it all were in gold. I suppose the exact amount of treasure which Davis had with him is now known to a cent; some of it was paid to his escort, when it disbanded at and near Washington, Georgia, and at the time of his capture he had a small parcel of gold and silver coin, not to exceed ten thousand dollars, which is now retained in the United States Treasury-vault at Washington, and shown to the curious.

The thirteen millions of treasure, with which Jeff. Davis was to corrupt our armies and buy his escape, dwindled down to the contents of a hand-valise!

To say that I was merely angry at the tone and substance of these published bulletins of the War Department, would hardly express the state of my feelings. I was outraged beyond measure, and was resolved to resent the insult, cost what it might. I went to the Wayanda and showed them to Mr. Chase, with whom I had a long and frank conversation, during which he explained to me the confusion caused in Washington by the assassination of Mr. Lincoln, the sudden accession to power of Mr. Johnson, who was then supposed to be bitter and vindictive in his feelings toward the South, and the wild pressure of every class of politicians to enforce on the new President their pet schemes. He showed me a letter of his own, which was in print, dated Baltimore, April 11th, and another of April 12th, addressed to the President, urging him to recognize the freedmen as equal in all respects to the whites. He was the first man, of any authority or station, who ever informed me that the Government of the United States would insist on extending to the former slaves of the South the elective franchise, and he gave as a reason the fact that the slaves, grateful for their freedom, for which they were indebted to the armies and Government of the North, would, by their votes, offset the disaffected and rebel element of the white population of the South. At that time quite a storm was prevailing at sea, outside, and our two vessels lay snug at the wharf at Morehead City. I saw a good deal of Mr. Chase, and several notes passed between us, of which I have the originals yet. Always claiming that the South had herself freed all her slaves by rebellion, and that Mr. Lincoln's proclamation of freedom (of September 22, 1862) was binding on all officers of the General Government, I doubted the wisdom of at once clothing them with the elective franchise, without some previous preparation and qualification; and then realized the national loss in the death at that critical moment of Mr. Lincoln, who had long pondered over the difficult questions involved, who, at all events, would have been honest and frank, and would not have withheld from his army commanders at least a hint that would have been to them a guide. It was plain to me, therefore, that the manner of his assassination had stampeded the civil authorities in Washington, had unnerved them, and that they were then undecided as to the measures indispensably necessary to prevent anarchy at the South.

On the 7th of May the storm subsided, and we put to sea, Mr. Chase to the south, on his proposed tour as far as New Orleans, and I for James River. I reached Fortress Monroe on the 8th, and thence telegraphed my arrival to General Grant, asking for orders. I found at Fortress Monroe a dispatch from General Halleck, professing great friendship, and inviting me to accept his hospitality at Richmond. I answered by a cipher-dispatch that I had seen his dispatch to Mr. Stanton, of April 26th, embraced in the second bulletin, which I regarded as insulting, declined his hospitality, and added that I preferred we should not meet as I passed through Richmond. I thence proceeded to City Point in the Russia, and on to Manchester, opposite Richmond, *via* Petersburg, by rail. I found that both wings of the army had arrived from Raleigh, and were in camp in and around Manchester, whence I again telegraphed General Grant, on the 9th of May, for orders, and also reported my arrival to General Halleck by letter. I found that General Halleck had ordered General Davis's corps (the Fourteenth) for review by himself. This I forbade. All the army knew of the insult that had been made me by the Secretary of War and General Halleck, and watched me closely to see if I would tamely submit. During the 9th I made a full and complete report of all these events, from the last report made at Goldsboro' up to date, and the next day received orders to continue the march to Alexandria, near Washington.

On the morning of the 11th we crossed the pontoon-bridge at Richmond, marched through that city, and out on the Hanover Court-House road, General Slocum's left wing leading. The right wing (General Logan) followed the next day, viz., the 12th. Meantime, General O. O. Howard had been summoned to Washington to take charge of the new Bureau of Refugees, Freedmen, and Abandoned Lands, and, from that time till the army was finally disbanded, General John A. Logan was in command of the right wing, and of the Army of the Tennessee. The left wing marched through Hanover Court-House, and thence took roads well to the left by Chilesburg; the Fourteenth Corps by New Market and Culpepper, Manassas, etc.; the Twentieth Corps by Spotsylvania Court-House and Chancellorsville. The right wing followed the more direct road by Fredericksburg. On my way north I endeavored to see as much of the battle-fields of the Army of the Potomac as I could, and therefore shifted from one column to the other, visiting *en route* Hanover Court-House, Spotsylvania, Fredericksburg, Dumfries, etc., reaching Alexandria during the afternoon of May 19th, and pitched my camp by the road-side, about half-way between Alexandria and the Long Bridge. During the same and next day the whole army reached Alexandria, and camped round about it; General Meade's Army of the Potomac had possession of the camps above, opposite Washington and Georgetown.

The next day (by invitation) I went over to Washington and met many friends—among them General Grant and President Johnson. The latter occupied rooms in the house on the corner of Fifteenth and H Streets, belonging to Mr. Hooper. He was extremely cordial to me, and knowing that I was chafing under the censures of the War Department, especially of the two war bulletins of Mr. Stanton, he volunteered to say that he knew of neither of them till seen in the newspapers, and that Mr. Stanton had shown neither to him nor to any of his associates in the cabinet till they were published. Nearly all the members of the cabinet made similar assurances to me afterward, and, as Mr. Stanton made no friendly advances, and offered no word of explanation or apology, I declined General Grant's friendly offices for a reconciliation, but, on the contrary, resolved to resent what I considered an insult, as publicly as it was made. My brother, Senator Sherman, who was Mr. Stanton's neighbor, always insisted that Mr. Stanton had been frightened by the intended assassination of himself, and had become embittered thereby. At all events, I found strong military guards around his house, as well as all the houses occupied by the cabinet and by the principal officers of Government; and a sense of insecurity pervaded Washington, for which no reason existed.

On the 19th I received a copy of War Department Special Order No. 239, Adjutant-General's office, of May 18th, ordering a grand review, by the President and cabinet, of all the armies then near Washington; General Meade's to occur on Tuesday, May 23d, mine on Wednesday, the 24th; and on the 20th I made the necessary orders for my part. Meantime I had also arranged (with General Grant's approval) to remove, after the review, my armies from the south side of the Potomac to the north; both for convenience and because our men had found that the grounds assigned them had been used so long for camps that they were foul and unfit.

By invitation I was on the reviewing-stand, and witnessed the review of the Army of the Potomac (on the 23d), commanded by General Meade in person. The day was beautiful, and the pageant was superb. Washington was full of strangers, who filled the streets in holiday-dress, and every house was decorated with flags. The army marched by divisions in close column around the Capitol, down Pennsylvania Avenue, past the President and cabinet, who occupied a large stand prepared for the occasion, directly in front of the White House.

I had telegraphed to Lancaster for Mrs. Sherman, who arrived that day, accompanied by her father, the Hon. Thomas Ewing, and my son Tom, then eight years old.

During the afternoon and night of the 23d, the Fifteenth, Seventeenth, and Twentieth Corps, crossed Long Bridge, bivouacked in the streets about the Capitol, and the Fourteenth Corps closed up to the bridge. The morning of the 24th was extremely beautiful, and the ground was in splendid order for our review. The streets were filled with people to see the pageant, armed with bouquets of flowers for their favorite regiments or heroes, and every thing was propitious. Punctually at 9 A.M. the signal-gun was fired, when in person, attended by General Howard and all my staff, I rode slowly down Pennsylvania Avenue, the crowds of men, women, and children, densely lining the sidewalks, and almost obstructing the way. We were followed close by General Logan and the head of the Fifteenth Corps. When I reached the Treasury-building, and looked back, the sight was simply magnificent. The column was compact, and the glittering muskets looked like a solid mass of steel, moving with the regularity of a pendulum. We passed the Treasury-building, in front of which and of the White House was an immense throng of people, for whom extensive stands had been prepared on both sides of the avenue. As I neared the brick-house opposite the lower corner of Lafayette Square, some one asked me to notice Mr. Seward, who, still feeble and bandaged for his wounds, had been removed there that he might behold the troops. I moved in that direction and took off my hat to Mr. Seward, who sat at an upper window. He recognized the salute, returned it, and then we rode on steadily past the President, saluting with our swords. All on his stand arose and acknowledged the salute. Then, turning into the gate of the presidential grounds, we left our horses with orderlies, and went upon the stand, where I found Mrs. Sherman, with her father and son. Passing them, I shook hands with the President, General Grant, and each member of the cabinet. As I approached Mr. Stanton, he offered me his hand, but I declined it publicly, and the fact was universally noticed. I then took my post on the left of the President, and for six hours and a half stood, while the army passed in the order of the Fifteenth, Seventeenth, Twentieth, and Fourteenth Corps. It was, in my judgment, the most magnificent army in existence—sixty-five thousand men, in splendid *physique*, who had just completed a march of nearly two thousand miles in a hostile country, in good drill, and who realized that they were being closely scrutinized by thousands of their fellow-countrymen and by foreigners. Division after division passed, each commander of an army corps or division coming on the stand during the passage of his command, to be presented to the President, cabinet, and spectators. The steadiness and firmness of the tread, the careful dress on the guides, the uniform intervals between the companies, all eyes directly to the front, and the tattered and bullet-riven flags, festooned with flowers, all attracted universal notice. Many good people, up to that time, had looked upon our Western army as a sort of mob; but the world then saw, and recognized the fact, that it was an army in the proper sense, well organized, well commanded and disciplined; and there was no wonder that it had swept through the South like a tornado. For six hours and a half that strong tread of the Army of the West resounded along Pennsylvania Avenue; not a soul of that vast crowd of spectators left his place; and, when the rear of the column had passed by, thousands of the spectators still lingered to express their sense of confidence in the strength of a Government which could claim such an army.

Some little scenes enlivened the day, and called for the laughter and cheers of the crowd. Each division was followed

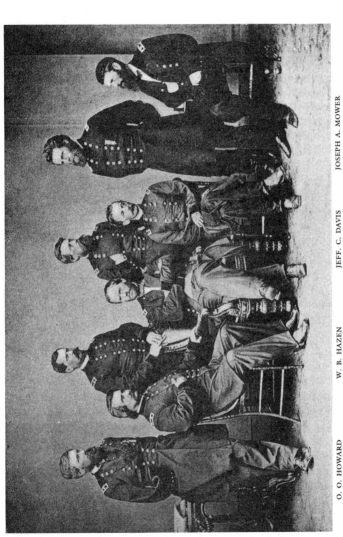

O. O. HOWARD   W. B. HAZEN   JEFF. C. DAVIS   JOSEPH A. MOWER

JOHN A. LOGAN   W. T. SHERMAN   H. W. SLOCUM   FRANK BLAIR

ARMY AND CORPS COMMANDERS—END OF THE WAR.

by six ambulances, as a representative of its baggage-train. Some of the division commanders had added, by way of variety, goats, milch-cows, and pack-mules, whose loads consisted of game-cocks, poultry, hams, etc., and some of them had the families of freed slaves along, with the women leading their children. Each division was preceded by its corps of black pioneers, armed with picks and spades. These marched abreast in double ranks, keeping perfect dress and step, and added much to the interest of the occasion. On the whole, the grand review was a splendid success, and was a fitting conclusion to the campaign and the war.

I will now conclude by a copy of my general orders taking leave of the army, which ended my connection with the war, though I afterward visited and took a more formal leave of the officers and men on July 4, 1865, at Louisville, Kentucky:

[Special Field Orders, No. 76.]
HEADQUARTERS MILITARY DIVISION OF THE MISSISSIPPI,
IN THE FIELD, WASHINGTON, D. C., *May* 30, 1865.

The general commanding announces to the Armies of the Tennessee and Georgia that the time has come for us to part. Our work is done, and armed enemies no longer defy us. Some of you will go to your homes, and others will be retained in military service till further orders.

And now that we are all about to separate, to mingle with the civil world, it becomes a pleasing duty to recall to mind the situation of national affairs when, but little more than a year ago, we were gathered about the cliffs of Lookout Mountain, and all the future was wrapped in doubt and uncertainty.

Three armies had come together from distant fields, with separate histories, yet bound by one common cause—the union of our country, and the perpetuation of the Government of our inheritance. There is no need to recall to your memories Tunnel Hill, with Rocky-Face Mountain and Buzzard-Roost Gap, and the ugly forts of Dalton behind.

We were in earnest, and paused not for danger and difficulty, but dashed through Snake-Creek Gap and fell on Resaca; then on to the Etowah, to Dallas, Kenesaw; and the heats of summer found us on the banks of the Chattahoochee, far from home, and dependent on a single road for supplies. Again we were not to be held back by any obstacle, and crossed over and fought four hard battles for the possession of the citadel of Atlanta. That was the crisis of our history. A doubt still clouded our future, but we solved the problem, destroyed Atlanta, struck boldly across the State of Georgia, severed all the main arteries of life to our enemy, and Christmas found us at Savannah.

Waiting there only long enough to fill our wagons, we again began a march which, for peril, labor, and results, will compare with any ever made by an organized army. The floods of the Savannah, the swamps of the Combahee and Edisto, the "high hills" and rocks of the Santee, the flat quagmires of the Pedee and Cape Fear Rivers, were all passed in mid-winter, with its floods and rains, in the face of an accumulating enemy; and, after the battles of Averysboro' and Bentonsville, we once more came out of the wilderness, to meet our friends at Goldsboro'. Even then we paused only long enough to get new clothing, to reload our wagons, again pushed on to Raleigh and beyond, until we met our enemy suing for peace, instead of war, and offering to submit to the injured laws of his and our country. As long as that enemy was defiant, nor mountains nor rivers, nor swamps, nor hunger, nor cold, had checked us; but when he, who had fought us hard and persistently, offered submission, your general thought it wrong to pursue him farther, and negotiations followed, which resulted, as you all know, in his surrender.

How far the operations of this army contributed to the final overthrow of the Confederacy and the peace which now dawns upon us, must be judged by others, not by us; but that you have done all that men could do has been admitted by those in authority, and we have a right to join in the universal joy that fills our land because the war is *over*, and our Government stands vindicated before the world by the joint action of the volunteer armies and navy of the United States.

To such as remain in the service, your general need only remind you that success in the past was due to hard work and discipline, and that the same work and discipline are equally important in the future. To such as go home, he will only say that our favored country is so grand, so extensive, so diversified in climate, soil, and productions, that every man may find a home and occupation suited to his taste; none should yield to the natural impatience sure to result from our past life of excitement and adventure. You will be invited to seek new adventures abroad; do not yield to the temptation, for it will lead only to death and disappointment.

Your general now bids you farewell, with the full belief that, as in war you have been good soldiers, so in peace you will make good citizens; and if, unfortunately, new war should arise in our country, "Sherman's army" will be the first to buckle on its old armor, and come forth to defend and maintain the Government of our inheritance.

By order of Major-General W. T. Sherman,

L. M. DAYTON, *Assistant Adjutant-General*.

List of the Average Number of Miles marched by the Different Army Corps of the United States Forces under Command of Major-General W. T. SHERMAN, United States Army, during his Campaigns in 1863-'64-'65.

ROUTE.	NUMBER OF MILES.						
	Fourth Corps.	Fourteenth Corps.	Fifteenth Corps.	Sixteenth Corps.	Sixteenth Corps (Left Wing).	Seventeenth Corps.	Twentieth Corps.
From Vicksburg to Meridian, and back.	…	…	…	…	…	335	…
From Memphis to Chattanooga.	…	…	330	330	…	…	…
From Chattanooga to Knoxville, and back.	110	…	230	…	…	…	…
From Chattanooga to Huntsville (Paint Rock), Langston, etc., and back.	…	…	240	…	…	…	…
From Clifton to Rome.	…	…	…	…	…	261	…
From Chattanooga to Atlanta (average distance traversed in manoeuvring).	…	178	178	…	178	89	178
Pursuit of Hood, and back to Atlanta.	…	270	270	…	…	270	270
From Atlanta to Savannah.	…	283	285	…	…	290	287
From Savannah to Goldsboro'.	…	425	423	…	…	478	420
From Goldsboro' to Washington, D. C.	…	430	333	…	…	353	370
Total distance in miles.	110	1,586	2,289	330	178	2,076	1,525

Compiled from campaign maps at headquarters Military Division of the Mississippi, St. Louis, Missouri.

WILLIAM KOSSACK, Captain, Additional Aide-de-Camp on Engineer Duty.

Chapter XXV.

CONCLUSION—MILITARY LESSONS OF THE WAR.

HAVING THUS recorded a summary of events, mostly under my own personal supervision, during the years from 1846 to 1865, it seems proper that I should add an opinion of some of the useful military lessons to be derived therefrom.

That civil war, by reason of the existence of slavery, was apprehended by most of the leading statesmen of the half-century preceding its outbreak, is a matter of notoriety. General Scott told me on my arrival at New York, as early as 1850, that the country was on the eve of civil war; and the Southern politicians openly asserted that it was their purpose to accept as a *casus belli* the election of General Fremont in 1856; but, fortunately or unfortunately, he was beaten by Mr. Buchanan, which simply postponed its occurrence for four years. Mr. Seward had also publicly declared that no government could possibly exist half slave and half free; yet the Government made no military preparation, and the Northern people generally paid no attention, took no warning of its coming, and would not realize its existence till Fort Sumter was fired on by batteries of artillery, handled by declared enemies, from the surrounding islands and from the city of Charleston.

General Bragg, who certainly was a man of intelligence, and who, in early life, ridiculed a thousand times, in my hearing, the threats of the people of South Carolina to secede from the Federal Union, said to me in New Orleans, in February, 1861, that he was convinced that the feeling between the slave and free States had become so embittered that it was better to part in peace; better to part anyhow; and, as a separation was inevitable, that the South should begin at once, because the possibility of a successful effort was yearly lessened by the rapid and increasing inequality between the two sections, from the fact that all the European immigrants were coming to the Northern States and Territories, and none to the Southern.

The slave population in 1860 was near four millions, and

the money value thereof not far from twenty-five hundred million dollars. Now, ignoring the moral side of the question, a cause that endangered so vast a moneyed interest was an adequate cause of anxiety and preparation, and the Northern leaders surely ought to have foreseen the danger and prepared for it. After the election of Mr. Lincoln in 1860, there was no concealment of the declaration and preparation for war in the South. In Louisiana, as I have related, men were openly enlisted, officers were appointed, and war was actually begun, in January, 1861. The forts at the mouth of the Mississippi were seized, and occupied by garrisons that hauled down the United States flag and hoisted that of the State. The United States Arsenal at Baton Rouge was captured by New Orleans militia, its garrison ignominiously sent off, and the contents of the arsenal distributed. These were as much acts of war as was the subsequent firing on Fort Sumter, yet no public notice was taken thereof; and when, months afterward, I came North, I found not one single sign of preparation. It was for this reason, somewhat, that the people of the South became convinced that those of the North were pusillanimous and cowardly, and the Southern leaders were thereby enabled to commit their people to the war, nominally in defense of their slave property. Up to the hour of the firing on Fort Sumter, in April, 1861, it does seem to me that our public men, our politicians, were blamable for not sounding the note of alarm.

Then, when war was actually begun, it was by a call for seventy-five thousand "ninety-day" men, I suppose to fulfill Mr. Seward's prophecy that the war would last but ninety days.

The earlier steps by our political Government were extremely wavering and weak, for which an excuse can be found in the fact that many of the Southern representatives remained in Congress, sharing in the public councils, and influencing legislation. But as soon as Mr. Lincoln was installed, there was no longer any reason why Congress and the cabinet should have hesitated. They should have measured the cause, provided the means, and left the Executive to apply the remedy.

At the time of Mr. Lincoln's inauguration, viz., March 4, 1861, the Regular Army, by law, consisted of two regiments of dragoons, two regiments of cavalry, one regiment of mounted rifles, four regiments of artillery, and ten regiments of infantry, admitting of an aggregate strength of thirteen thousand and twenty-four officers and men. On the subsequent 4th of May the President, by his own orders (afterward sanctioned by Congress), added a regiment of cavalry, a regiment of artillery, and eight regiments of infantry, which, with the former army, admitted of a strength of thirty-nine thousand nine hundred and seventy-three; but at no time during the war did the Regular Army attain a strength of twenty-five thousand men.

To the new regiments of infantry was given an organization differing from any that had heretofore prevailed in this country—of three battalions of eight companies each; but at no time did more than one of these regiments attain its full standard; nor in the vast army of volunteers that was raised during the war were any of the regiments of infantry formed on the three-battalion system, but these were universally single battalions of ten companies; so that, on the reorganization of the Regular Army at the close of the war, Congress adopted the form of twelve companies for the regiments of cavalry and artillery, and that of ten companies for the infantry, which is the present standard.

Inasmuch as the Regular Army will naturally form the standard of organization for any increase or for new regiments of volunteers, it becomes important to study this subject in the light of past experience, and to select that form which is best for peace as well as war.

A cavalry regiment is now composed of twelve companies, usually divided into six squadrons, of two companies each, or better subdivided into three battalions of four companies each. This is an excellent form, easily admitting of subdivision as well as union into larger masses.

A single battalion of four companies, with a field-officer, will compose a good body for a garrison, for a separate expedition, or for a detachment; and, in war, three regiments would compose a good brigade, three brigades a division, and three divisions a strong cavalry corps, such as was formed and fought by Generals Sheridan and Wilson during the war.

In the artillery arm, the officers differ widely in their

opinion of the true organization. A single company forms a battery, and habitually each battery acts separately, though sometimes several are united or "massed;" but these always act in concert with cavalry or infantry.

Nevertheless, the regimental organization for artillery has always been maintained in this country for classification and promotion. Twelve companies compose a regiment, and, though probably no colonel ever commanded his full regiment in the form of twelve batteries, yet in peace they occupy our heavy sea-coast forts or act as infantry; then the regimental organization is both necessary and convenient.

But the infantry composes the great mass of all armies, and the true form of the regiment or unit has been the subject of infinite discussion; and, as I have stated, during the civil war the regiment was a single battalion of ten companies. In olden times the regiment was composed of eight battalion companies and two flank companies. The first and tenth companies were armed with rifles, and were styled and used as "skirmishers;" but during the war they were never used exclusively for that special purpose, and in fact no distinction existed between them and the other eight companies.

The ten-company organization is awkward in practice, and I am satisfied that the infantry regiment should have the same identical organization as exists for the cavalry and artillery, viz., twelve companies, so as to be susceptible of division into three battalions of four companies each.

These companies should habitually be about one hundred men strong, giving twelve hundred to a regiment, which in practice would settle down to about one thousand men.

Three such regiments would compose a brigade, three brigades a division, and three divisions a corps. Then, by allowing to an infantry corps a brigade of cavalry and six batteries of field-artillery, we would have an efficient *corps d'armée* of thirty thousand men, whose organization would be simple and most efficient, and whose strength should never be allowed to fall below twenty-five thousand men.

The corps is the true unit for grand campaigns and battle, should have a full and perfect staff, and every thing requisite for separate action, ready at all times to be detached and sent off for any nature of service. The general in command should have the rank of lieutenant-general, and should be, by experience and education, equal to any thing in war. Habitually with us he was a major-general, specially selected and assigned to the command by an order of the President, constituting, in fact, a separate grade.

The division is the unit of administration, and is the legitimate command of a major-general.

The brigade is the next subdivision, and is commanded by a brigadier-general.

The regiment is the family. The colonel, as the father, should have a personal acquaintance with every officer and man, and should instill a feeling of pride and affection for himself, so that his officers and men would naturally look to him for personal advice and instruction. In war the regiment should never be subdivided, but should always be maintained entire. In peace this is impossible.

The company is the true unit of discipline, and the captain is the company. A good captain makes a good company, and he should have the power to reward as well as punish. The fact that soldiers would naturally like to have a good fellow for their captain is the best reason why he should be appointed by the colonel, or by some superior authority, instead of being elected by the men.

In the United States the people are the "sovereign," all power originally proceeds from them, and therefore the election of officers by the men is the common rule. This is wrong, because an army is not a popular organization, but an animated machine, an instrument in the hands of the Executive for enforcing the law, and maintaining the honor and dignity of the nation; and the President, as the constitutional commander-in-chief of the army and navy, should exercise the power of appointment (subject to the confirmation of the Senate) of the officers of "volunteers," as well as of "regulars."

No army can be efficient unless it be a unit for action; and the power must come from above, not from below: the President usually delegates his power to the commander-in-chief, and he to the next, and so on down to the lowest actual commander of troops, however small the detachment. No matter how troops come together, when once united, the highest officer in rank is held responsible, and should be consequently armed with the fullest power of the Executive, subject only to law and existing orders. The more simple the principle, the greater the likelihood of determined action; and the less a commanding officer is circumscribed by bounds or by precedent, the greater is the probability that he will make the best use of his command and achieve the best results.

The Regular Army and the Military Academy at West Point have in the past provided, and doubtless will in the future provide an ample supply of good officers for future wars; but, should their numbers be insufficient, we can always safely rely on the great number of young men of education and force of character throughout the country, to supplement them. At the close of our civil war, lasting four years, some of our best corps and division generals, as well as staff-officers, were from civil life; but I cannot recall any of the most successful who did not express a regret that he had not received in early life instruction in the elementary principles of the art of war, instead of being forced to acquire this knowledge in the dangerous and expensive school of actual war.

But the real difficulty was, and will be again, to obtain an adequate number of good soldiers. We tried almost every system known to modern nations, all with more or less success—voluntary enlistments, the draft, and bought substitutes—and I think that all officers of experience will confirm my assertion that the men who voluntarily enlisted at the outbreak of the war were the best, better than the conscript, and far better than the bought substitute. When a regiment is once organized in a State, and mustered into the service of the United States, the officers and men become subject to the same laws of discipline and government as the regular troops. They are in no sense "militia," but compose a part of the Army of the United States, only retain their State title for convenience, and yet may be principally recruited from the neighborhood of their original organization. Once organized, the regiment should be kept full by recruits, and when it becomes difficult to obtain more recruits the pay should be raised by Congress, instead of tempting new men by exaggerated bounties. I believe it would have been more economical to have raised the pay of the soldier to thirty or even fifty dollars a month than to have held out the promise of three hundred and even six hundred dollars in the form of bounty. Toward the close of the war, I have often heard the soldiers complain that the "stay-at-home" men got better pay, bounties, and food, than they who were exposed to all the dangers and vicissitudes of the battles and marches at the front. The feeling of the soldier should be that, in every event, the sympathy and preference of his government is for him who fights, rather than for him who is on provost or guard duty to the rear, and, like most men, he measures this by the amount of pay. Of course, the soldier must be trained to obedience, and should be "content with his wages;" but whoever has commanded an army in the field knows the difference between a willing, contented mass of men, and one that feels a cause of grievance. There is a soul to an army as well as to the individual man, and no general can accomplish the full work of his army unless he commands the soul of his men, as well as their bodies and legs.

The greatest mistake made in our civil war was in the mode of recruitment and promotion. When a regiment became reduced by the necessary wear and tear of service, instead of being filled up at the bottom, and the vacancies among the officers filled from the best non-commissioned officers and men, the habit was to raise new regiments, with new colonels, captains, and men, leaving the old and experienced battalions to dwindle away into mere skeleton organizations. I believe with the volunteers this matter was left to the States exclusively, and I remember that Wisconsin kept her regiments filled with recruits, whereas other States generally filled their quotas by new regiments, and the result was that we estimated a Wisconsin regiment equal to an ordinary brigade. I believe that five hundred new men added to an old and experienced regiment were more valuable than a thousand men in the form of a new regiment, for the former by association with good, experienced captains, lieutenants, and non-commissioned officers, soon became veterans, whereas the latter were generally unavailable for a year. The German method of recruitment is simply perfect, and there is no good reason why we should not follow it substantially.

On a road, marching by the flank, it would be considered "good order" to have five thousand men to a mile, so that a full corps of thirty thousand men would extend six miles, but with the average trains and batteries of artillery the probabilities are that it would draw out to ten miles. On a long and regular march the divisions and brigades should alternate in the lead, the leading division should be on the road by the earliest dawn, and march at the rate of about two miles, or, at most, two and a half miles an hour, so as to reach camp by noon. Even then the rear divisions and trains will hardly reach camp much before night. Theoretically, a marching column should preserve such order that by simply halting and facing to the right or left, it would be in line of battle; but this is rarely the case, and generally deployments are made "forward," by conducting each brigade by the flank obliquely to the right or left to its approximate position in line of battle, and there deployed. In such a line of battle, a brigade of three thousand infantry would occupy a mile of "front;" but for a strong line of battle five thousand men with two batteries should be allowed to each mile, or a division would habitually constitute a double line with skirmishers and a reserve on a mile of "front."

The "feeding" of an army is a matter of the most vital importance, and demands the earliest attention of the general intrusted with a campaign. To be strong, healthy, and capable of the largest measure of physical effort, the soldier needs about three pounds gross of food per day, and the horse or mule about twenty pounds. When a general first estimates the quantity of food and forage needed for an army of fifty or one hundred thousand men, he is apt to be dismayed, and here a good staff is indispensable, though the general cannot throw off on them the responsibility. He must give the subject his personal attention, for the army reposes in him alone, and should never doubt the fact that their existence overrides in importance all other considerations. Once satisfied of this, and that all has been done that can be, the soldiers are always willing to bear the largest measure of privation. Probably no army ever had a more varied experience in this regard than the one I commanded in 1864–'65.

Our base of supply was at Nashville, supplied by railways and the Cumberland River, thence by rail to Chattanooga, a "secondary base," and thence forward a single-track railroad.

The stores came forward daily, but I endeavored to have on hand a full supply for twenty days in advance. These stores were habitually in the wagon-trains, distributed to corps, divisions, and regiments, in charge of experienced quartermasters and commissaries, and became subject to the orders of the generals commanding these bodies. They were generally issued on provision returns, but these had to be closely scrutinized, for too often the colonels would make requisitions for provisions for more men than they reported for battle. Of course, there are always a good many non-combatants with an army, but, after careful study, I limited their amount to twenty-five per cent. of the "effective strength," and that was found to be liberal. An ordinary army-wagon drawn by six mules may be counted on to carry three thousand pounds net, equal to the food of a full regiment for one day, but, by driving along beef-cattle, a commissary may safely count the contents of one wagon as sufficient for two days' food for a regiment of a thousand men; and as a corps should have food on hand for twenty days ready for detachment, it should have three hundred such wagons, as a provision-train; and for forage, ammunition, clothing, and other necessary stores, it was found necessary to have three hundred more wagons, or six hundred wagons in all, for a *corps d'armée.*

These should be absolutely under the immediate control of the corps commander, who will, however, find it economical to distribute them in due proportion to his divisions, brigades, and even regiments. Each regiment ought usually to have at least one wagon for convenience to distribute stores, and each company two pack-mules, so that the regiment may always be certain of a meal on reaching camp without waiting for the larger trains.

On long marches the artillery and wagon-trains should always have the right of way, and the troops should improvise roads to one side, unless forced to use a bridge in common, and all trains should have escorts to protect them, and to assist them in bad places. To this end there is nothing like actual experience, only, unless the officers in command give the subject their personal attention, they will find their wagon-trains loaded down with tents, personal baggage, and even the arms and knapsacks of the escort. Each soldier should, if not actually "sick or wounded," carry his musket and equipments containing from forty to sixty rounds of ammunition, his shelter-tent, a blanket or overcoat, and an extra pair of pants, socks, and drawers, in the form of a scarf, worn from the left shoulder to the right side in lieu of knapsack, and in his haversack he should carry some bread, cooked meat, salt, and coffee. I do not believe a soldier should be loaded down too much, but, including his clothing, arms, and equipment, he can carry about fifty pounds without impairing his health or activity. A simple calculation will show that by such a distribution a corps will thus carry the equivalent of five hundred wagon-loads—an immense relief to the trains.

Where an army is near one of our many large navigable rivers, or has the safe use of a railway, it can usually be supplied with the full army ration, which is by far the best furnished to any army in America or Europe; but when it is compelled to operate away from such a base, and is dependent on its own train of wagons, the commanding officer must exercise a wise discretion in the selection of his stores. In my opinion there is no better food for man than beef-cattle driven on the hoof, issued liberally, with salt, bacon, and bread. Coffee has also become almost indispensable, though many substitutes were found for it, such as Indian-corn, roasted, ground, and boiled as coffee; the sweet-potato, and the seed of the okra-plant prepared in the same way. All these were used by the people of the South, who for years could procure no coffee, but I noticed that the women always begged of us some *real* coffee, which seems to satisfy a natural yearning or craving more powerful than can be accounted for on the theory of habit. Therefore I would always advise that the coffee and sugar ration be carried along, even at the expense of bread, for which there are many substitutes. Of these, Indian-corn is the best and most abundant. Parched in a frying-pan, it is excellent food, or if ground, or pounded and boiled with meat of any sort, it makes a most nutritious meal. The potato, both Irish and sweet, forms an excellent substitute for bread, and at Savannah we found the rice also suitable, both for men and animals. For the former it should be cleaned of its husk in a hominy block, easily prepared out of a log, and sifted with a coarse corn-bag; but for horses it should be fed in the straw. During the Atlanta campaign we were supplied by our regular commissaries with all sorts of patent compounds, such as desiccated vegetables, and concentrated milk, meat-biscuit, and sausages, but somehow the men preferred the simpler and more familiar forms of food, and usually styled these "desecrated vegetables and consecrated milk." We were also supplied liberally with lime-juice, sauerkraut, and pickles, as an antidote to scurvy, and I now recall the extreme anxiety of my medical director, Dr. Kittoe, about the scurvy, which he reported at one time as spreading and imperiling the army. This occurred at a crisis about Kenesaw, when the railroad was taxed to its utmost capacity to provide the necessary ammunition, food, and forage, and could not possibly bring us an adequate supply of potatoes and cabbage, the usual antiscorbutics, when providentially the blackberries ripened and proved an admirable antidote, and I have known the skirmish-line, without orders, to fight a respectable battle for the possession of some old fields that were full of blackberries. Soon, thereafter, the green corn or roasting-ear came into season, and I heard no more of the scurvy. Our country abounds with plants which can be utilized for a prevention to the scurvy; besides the above are the persimmon, the sassafras root and bud, the wild-mustard, the "agave," turnip-tops, the dandelion cooked as greens, and a decoction of the ordinary pine-leaf.

For the more delicate and costly articles of food for the sick we relied mostly on the agents of the Sanitary Commission. I do not wish to doubt the value of these organizations, which gained so much applause during our civil war, for no one can question the motives of these charitable and generous people; but to be honest I must record an opinion that the Sanitary Commission should limit its operations to the hospitals at the rear, and should never appear at the front. They were generally local in feeling, aimed to furnish their personal friends and neighbors with a better class of food than the Government supplied, and the consequence was, that one regiment of a brigade would receive potatoes and fruit which would be denied another regiment close by. Jealousy would be the inevitable result, and in an army all parts should be equal; there should be no "partiality, favor, or affection." The Government should supply all essential wants, and in the hospitals to the rear will be found abundant opportunities for the exercise of all possible charity and generosity. During the war I several times gained the ill-will of the agents of the Sanitary Commission because I forbade their coming to the front unless they would consent to distribute their stores equally among all, regardless of the parties who had contributed them.

The sick, wounded, and dead of an army are the subjects of the greatest possible anxiety, and add an immense amount of labor to the well men. Each regiment in an active campaign should have a surgeon and two assistants always close at hand, and each brigade and division should have an experienced surgeon as a medical director. The great majority of wounds and of sickness should be treated by the regimental surgeon, on the ground, under the eye of the colonel. As few should be sent to the brigade or division hospital as possible, for the men always receive better care with their own regiment than with strangers, and as a rule the cure is more certain; but when men receive disabling wounds, or have sickness likely to become permanent, the sooner they go far to the rear the better for all. The tent or the shelter of a tree is a better hospital than a house, whose walls absorb fetid and poisonous emanations, and then give them back to the atmosphere. To men accustomed to the open air, who live on the plainest food, wounds seem to give less pain, and are attended with less danger to life than to ordinary soldiers in barracks.

Wounds which, in 1861, would have sent a man to the hospital for months, in 1865 were regarded as mere scratches, rather the subject of a joke than of sorrow. To new soldiers the sight of blood and death always has a sickening effect, but soon men become accustomed to it, and I have heard them exclaim on seeing a dead comrade borne to the rear, "Well, Bill has turned up *his* toes to the daisies." Of course, during a skirmish or battle, armed men should *never* leave their ranks to attend a dead or wounded comrade—this should be seen to in advance by the colonel, who should designate his musicians or company cooks as hospital attendants, with a white rag on their arm to indicate their office. A wounded man should go himself (if able) to the surgeon near at hand, or, if he need help, he should receive it from one of the attendants and not a comrade. It is wonderful how soon the men accustom themselves to these simple rules. In great battles these matters call for a more enlarged attention, and then it becomes the duty of the division general to see that proper stretchers and field-hospitals are ready for the wounded, and trenches are dug for the dead. There should be no real neglect of the dead, because it has a bad effect on the living; for each soldier values himself and comrade as highly as though he were living in a good house at home.

The regimental chaplain, if any, usually attends the burials from the hospital, should make notes and communicate details to the captain of the company, and to the family at home. Of course it is usually impossible to mark the grave with names, dates, etc., and consequently the names of the "unknown" in our national cemeteries equal about one-half of all the dead.

Very few of the battles in which I have participated were fought as described in European text-books, viz., in great masses, in perfect order, manœuvring by corps, divisions, and brigades. We were generally in a wooded country, and, though our lines were deployed according to tactics, the men generally fought in strong skirmish-lines, taking advantage of the shape of ground, and of every cover. We were generally the assailants, and in wooded and broken countries the "defensive" had a positive advantage over us, for they were always ready, had cover, and always knew the ground to their immediate front; whereas we, their assailants, had to grope our way over unknown ground, and generally found a cleared field or prepared entanglements that held us for a time under a close and withering fire. Rarely did the opposing lines in compact order come into actual contact, but when, as at Peach-Tree Creek and Atlanta, the lines did become commingled, the men fought individually in every possible style, more frequently with the musket clubbed than with the bayonet, and in some instances the men clinched like wrestlers, and went to the ground together. Europeans frequently criticised our war, because we did not always take full advantage of a victory; the true reason was, that habitually the woods served as a screen, and we often did not realize the fact that our enemy had retreated till he was already miles away and was again intrenched, having left a mere skirmish-line to cover the movement, in turn to fall back to the new position.

Our war was fought with the muzzle-loading rifle. Toward the close I had one brigade (Walcutt's) armed with breech-loading "Spencer's;" the cavalry generally had breech-loading carbines, "Spencer's" and "Sharp's," both of which were good arms.

The only change that breech-loading arms will probably make in the art and practice of war will be to increase the amount of ammunition to be expended, and necessarily to be carried along; to still further "thin out" the lines of attack, and to reduce battles to short, quick, decisive conflicts. It does not in the least affect the grand strategy, or the necessity for perfect organization, drill, and discipline. The companies and battalions will be more dispersed, and the men will be less under the immediate eye of their officers, and therefore a higher order of intelligence and courage on the part of the individual soldier will be an element of strength.

When a regiment is deployed as skirmishers, and crosses an open field or woods, under heavy fire, if each man runs forward from tree to tree, or stump to stump, and yet preserves a good general alignment, it gives great confidence to the men themselves, for they always keep their eyes well to the right and left, and watch their comrades; but when some few hold back, stick too close or too long to a comfortable log, it often stops the line and defeats the whole object. Therefore, the more we improve the fire-arm the more will be the necessity for good organization, good discipline and intelligence on the part of the individual soldier and officer. There is, of course, such a thing as individual courage, which has a value in war, but familiarity with danger, experience in war and its common attendants, and personal habit, are equally valuable traits, and these are the qualities with which we usually have to deal in war. All men naturally shrink from pain and danger, and only incur their risk from some higher motive, or from habit; so that I would define true courage to be a perfect sensibility of the measure of danger, and a mental willingness to incur it, rather than that insensibility to danger of which I have heard far more than I have seen. The most courageous men are generally unconscious of possessing the quality;

therefore, when one professes it too openly, by words or bearing, there is reason to mistrust it. I would further illustrate my meaning by describing a man of true courage to be one who possesses all his faculties and senses perfectly when serious danger is actually present.

Modern wars have not materially changed the relative values or proportions of the several arms of service: infantry, artillery, cavalry, and engineers. If any thing, the infantry has been increased in value. The danger of cavalry attempting to charge infantry armed with breech-loading rifles was fully illustrated at Sedan, and with us very frequently. So improbable has such a thing become that we have omitted the infantry-square from our recent tactics. Still, cavalry against cavalry, and as auxiliary to infantry, will always be valuable, while all great wars will, as heretofore, depend chiefly on the infantry. Artillery is more valuable with new and inexperienced troops than with veterans. In the early stages of the war the field-guns often bore the proportion of six to a thousand men; but toward the close of the war one gun, or at most two, to a thousand men, was deemed enough. Sieges, such as characterized the wars of the last century, are too slow for this period of the world, and the Prussians recently almost ignored them altogether, penetrated France between the forts, and left a superior force "in observation," to watch the garrison and accept its surrender when the greater events of the war ahead made further resistance useless; but earth-forts, and especially field-works, will hereafter play an important part in wars, because they enable a minor force to hold a superior one in check for a *time*, and time is a most valuable element in all wars. It was one of Prof. Mahan's maxims that the spade was as useful in war as the musket, and to this I will add the axe. The habit of intrenching certainly does have the effect of making new troops timid. When a line of battle is once covered by a good parapet, made by the engineers or by the labor of the men themselves, it does require an effort to make them leave it in the face of danger; but when the enemy is intrenched, it becomes absolutely necessary to permit each brigade and division of the troops immediately opposed to throw up a corresponding trench for their own protection in case of a sudden sally. We invariably did this in all our recent campaigns, and it had no ill effect, though sometimes our troops were a little too slow in leaving their well-covered lines to assail the enemy in position or on retreat. Even our skirmishers were in the habit of rolling logs together, or of making a lunette of rails, with dirt in front, to cover their bodies; and, though it revealed their position, I cannot say that it worked a bad effect; so that, as a rule, it may safely be left to the men themselves. On the "defensive," there is no doubt of the propriety of fortifying; but in the assailing army the general must watch closely to see that his men do not neglect an opportunity to drop his precautionary defenses, and act promptly on the "offensive" at every chance.

I have many a time crept forward to the skirmish-line to avail myself of the cover of the pickets' "little fort," to observe more closely some expected result; and always talked familiarly with the men, and was astonished to see how well they comprehended the general object, and how accurately they were informed of the state of facts existing miles away from their particular corps. Soldiers are very quick to catch the general drift and purpose of a campaign, and are always sensible when they are well commanded or well cared for. Once impressed with this fact, and that they are making progress, they bear cheerfully any amount of labor and privation.

In camp, and especially in the presence of an active enemy, it is much easier to maintain discipline than in barracks in time of peace. Crime and breaches of discipline are much less frequent, and the necessity for courts-martial far less. The captain can usually inflict all the punishment necessary, and the colonel *should* always. The field-officers' court is the best form for war, viz., one of the field-officers—the lieutenant-colonel or major—can examine the case and report his verdict, and the colonel should execute it. Of course, there are statutory offenses which demand a general court-martial, and these must be ordered by the division or corps commander; but the presence of one of our regular civilian judge-advocates in an army in the field would be a first-class nuisance, for technical courts always work mischief. Too many courts-martial in any command are evidence of poor discipline and inefficient officers.

For the rapid transmission of orders in an army covering a

large space of ground, the magnetic telegraph is by far the best, though habitually the paper and pencil, with good mounted orderlies, answer every purpose. I have little faith in the signal-service by flags and torches, though we always used them; because, almost invariably when they were most needed, the view was cut off by intervening trees, or by mists and fogs. There was one notable instance in my experience, when the signal-flags carried a message of vital importance over the heads of Hood's army, which had interposed between me and Allatoona, and had broken the telegraph-wires—as recorded in Chapter XIX.; but the value of the magnetic telegraph in war cannot be exaggerated, as was illustrated by the perfect concert of action between the armies in Virginia and Georgia during 1864. Hardly a day intervened when General Grant did not know the exact state of facts with me, more than fifteen hundred miles away as the wires ran. So on the field a thin insulated wire may be run on improvised stakes or from tree to tree for six or more miles in a couple of hours, and I have seen operators so skillful, that by cutting the wire they would receive a message with their tongues from a distant station. As a matter of course, the ordinary commercial wires along the railways form the usual telegraph-lines for an army, and these are easily repaired and extended as the army advances, but each army and wing should have a small party of skilled men to put up the field-wire, and take it down when done. This is far better than the signal-flags and torches. Our commercial telegraph-lines will always supply for war enough skillful operators.

The value of railways is also fully recognized in war quite as much as, if not more so than, in peace. The Atlanta campaign would simply have been impossible without the use of the railroads from Louisville to Nashville—one hundred and eighty-five miles—from Nashville to Chattanooga—one hundred and fifty-one miles—and from Chattanooga to Atlanta—one hundred and thirty-seven miles. Every mile of this "single track" was so delicate, that one man could in a minute have broken or moved a rail, but our trains usually carried along the tools and means to repair such a break. We had, however, to maintain strong guards and garrisons at each important bridge or trestle—the destruction of which would have necessitated time for rebuilding. For the protection of a bridge, one or two log block-houses, two stories high, with a piece of ordnance and a small infantry guard, usually sufficed. The block-house had a small parapet and ditch about it, and the roof was made shot-proof by earth piled on. These points could usually be reached only by a dash of the enemy's cavalry, and many of these block-houses successfully resisted serious attacks by both cavalry and artillery. The only block-house that was actually captured on the main was the one described near Allatoona.

Our trains from Nashville forward were operated under military rules, and ran about ten miles an hour in gangs of four trains of ten cars each. Four such groups of trains daily made one hundred and sixty cars, of ten tons each, carrying sixteen hundred tons, which exceeded the absolute necessity of the army, and allowed for the accidents that were common and inevitable. But, as I have recorded, that single stem of railroad, four hundred and seventy-three miles long, supplied an army of one hundred thousand men and thirty-five thousand animals for the period of one hundred and ninety-six days, viz., from May 1 to November 12, 1864. To have delivered regularly that amount of food and forage by ordinary wagons would have required thirty-six thousand eight hundred wagons of six mules each, allowing each wagon to have hauled two tons twenty miles each day, a simple impossibility in roads such as then existed in that region of country. Therefore, I reiterate that the Atlanta campaign was an impossibility without these railroads; and only then, because we had the men and means to maintain and defend them, in addition to what were necessary to overcome the enemy. Habitually, a passenger-car will carry fifty men with their necessary baggage. Box-cars, and even platform-cars, answer the purpose well enough, but they should always have rough board-seats. For sick and wounded men, box-cars filled with straw or bushes were usually employed. Personally, I saw but little of the practical working of the railroads, for I only turned back once as far as Resaca; but I had daily reports from the engineer in charge, and officers who came from the rear often explained to me the whole thing, with a description of the wrecked trains all the way from Nashville to Atlanta. I am convinced that the risk to life to the engineers and men on that railroad fully equaled that on the skirmish-line, called for as high an order of courage, and fully equaled it in importance. Still, I doubt if there be any necessity in time of peace to organize a corps specially to work the military railroads in time of war, because in peace these same men gain all the necessary experience, possess all the daring and courage of soldiers, and only need the occasional protection and assistance of the necessary train-guard, which may be composed of the furloughed men coming and going, or of details made from the local garrisons to the rear.

For the transfer of large armies by rail, from one theatre of action to another by the rear—the cases of the transfer of the Eleventh and Twelfth Corps—General Hooker, twenty-three thousand men—from the East to Chattanooga, eleven hundred and ninety-two miles in seven days, in the fall of 1863; and that of the Army of the Ohio—General Schofield, fifteen thousand men—from the valley of the Tennessee to Washington, fourteen hundred miles in eleven days, *en route* to North Carolina in January, 1865, are the best examples of which I have any knowledge, and reference to these is made in the report of the Secretary of War, Mr. Stanton, dated November 22, 1865.

Engineer troops attached to an army are habitually employed in supervising the construction of forts or field works of a nature more permanent than the lines used by the troops in motion, and in repairing roads and making bridges. I had several regiments of this kind that were most useful, but as a rule we used the infantry, or employed parties of freedmen, who worked on the trenches at night while the soldiers slept, and these in turn rested by day. Habitually the repair of the railroad and its bridges was committed to hired laborers, like the English navvies, under the supervision of Colonel W. W. Wright, a railroad-engineer, who was in the military service at the time, and his successful labors were frequently referred to in the official reports of the campaign.

For the passage of rivers, each army corps had a pontoon-train with a detachment of engineers, and, on reaching a river, the leading infantry division was charged with the labor of putting it down. Generally the single pontoon-train could provide for nine hundred feet of bridge, which sufficed; but when the rivers were very wide two such trains would be brought together, or the single train was supplemented by a trestle-bridge, or bridges made on crib-work, out of timber found near the place. The pontoons in general use were skeleton frames, made with a hinge, so as to fold back and constitute a wagon-body. In this same wagon were carried the cotton canvas cover, the anchor and chains, and a due proportion of the balks, chesses, and lashings. All the troops became very familiar with their mechanism and use, and we were rarely delayed by reason of a river, however broad. I saw, recently, in Aldershot, England, a very complete pontoon-train; the boats were sheathed with wood and felt, made very light; but I think these were more liable to chafing and damage in rough handling than were our less expensive and rougher boats. On the whole, I would prefer the skeleton frame and canvas cover to any style of pontoon that I have ever seen.

In relation to guards, pickets, and vedettes, I doubt if any discoveries or improvements were made during our war, or in any of the modern wars in Europe. These precautions vary with the nature of the country and the situation of each army. When advancing or retreating in line of battle, the usual skirmish-line constitutes the picket-line, and may have "reserves," but usually the main line of battle constitutes the reserve; and in this connection I will state that the recent innovation introduced into the new infantry tactics by General Upton is admirable, for by it each regiment, brigade, and division deployed, sends forward as "skirmishers" the one man of each set of fours, to cover its own front, and these can be recalled or reënforced at pleasure by the bugle-signal.

For flank-guards and rear-guards, one or more companies should be detached under their own officers, instead of making up the guard by detailing men from the several companies.

For regimental or camp guards, the details should be made according to existing army regulations; and all the guards should be posted early in the evening, so as to afford each sentinel or vedette a chance to study his ground before it becomes too dark.

In like manner as to the staff. The more intimately it comes into contact with the troops, the more useful and valuable it becomes. The almost entire separation of the staff from the line, as now practised by us, and hitherto by the French, has proved mischievous, and the great retinues of staff-officers with which some of our earlier generals began the war were simply ridiculous. I don't believe in a chief of staff at all, and any general commanding an army, corps, or division, that has a staff-officer who professes to know more than his chief, is to be pitied. Each regiment should have a competent adjutant, quartermaster, and commissary, with two or three medical officers. Each brigade commander should have the same staff, with the addition of a couple of young aides-de-camp, habitually selected from the subalterns of the brigade, who should be good riders, and intelligent enough to give and explain the orders of their general.

The same staff will answer for a division. The general in command of a separate army, and of a *corps d'armée*, should have the same professional assistance, with two or more good engineers, and his adjutant-general should exercise all the functions usually ascribed to a chief of staff, viz., he should possess the ability to comprehend the scope of operations, and to make verbally and in writing all the orders and details necessary to carry into effect the views of his general, as well as to keep the returns and records of events for the information of the next higher authority, and for history. A bulky staff implies a division of responsibility, slowness of action, and indecision, whereas a small staff implies activity and concentration of purpose. The smallness of General Grant's staff throughout the civil war forms the best model for future imitation. So of tents, officers' furniture, etc., etc. In real war these should all be discarded, and an army is efficient for action and motion exactly in the inverse ratio of its *impedimenta*. Tents should be omitted altogether, save one to a regiment for an office, and a few for the division hospital. Officers should be content with a tent fly, improvising poles and shelter out of bushes. The *tente d'abri*, or shelter-tent, carried by the soldier himself, is all-sufficient. Officers should never seek for houses, but share the condition of their men.

A recent message (July 18, 1874) made to the French As-

894 MEMOIRS OF W. T. SHERMAN

sembly by Marshal MacMahon, President of the French Republic, submits a *projet de loi*, with a report prepared by a board
of French generals on "army administration," which is full
of information, and is as applicable to us as to the French.
I quote from its very beginning: "The misfortunes of the
campaign of 1870 have demonstrated the inferiority of our
system. . . . Two separate organizations existed with parallel
functions—the 'general' more occupied in giving direction to
his troops than in providing for their material wants, which
he regarded as the special province of the staff, and the 'inten-
dant' (staff) often working at random, taking on his shoulders
a crushing burden of functions and duties, exhausting himself
with useless efforts, and aiming to accomplish an insufficient
service, to the disappointment of everybody. This separation
of the administration and command, this coexistence of two
wills, each independent of the other, which paralyzed both
and annulled the dualism," was condemned. It was decided by
the board that this error should be "proscribed" in the new
military system. The report then goes on at great length discussing the provisions of the "new law," which is described to
be a radical change from the old one on the same subject.
While conceding to the Minister of War in Paris the general
control and supervision of the entire military establishment
primarily, especially of the annual estimates or budget, and
the great depots of supply, it distributes to the commanders
of the *corps d'armée* in time of peace, and to all army commanders generally in time of war, the absolute command of
the money, provisions, and stores, with the necessary staff-
officers to receive, issue, and account for them. I quote further: "The object of this law is to confer on the commander
of troops whatever liberty of action the case demands. He has
the power even to go beyond the regulations, in circumstances of urgency and pressing necessity. The extraordinary
measures he may take on these occasions may require their
execution without delay. The staff-officer has but one duty
before obeying, and that is to submit his observations to the
general, and to ask his orders in writing. With this formality
his responsibility ceases, and the responsibility for the extraordinary act falls solely on the general who gives the order. The
officers and agents charged with supplies are placed under the

orders of the general in command of the troops, that is, they are obliged both in war and peace to obey, with the single qualification above named, of first making their observations and securing the written order of the general."

With us, to-day, the law and regulations are that, no matter what may be the emergency, the commanding general in Texas, New Mexico, and the remote frontiers, cannot draw from the arsenals a pistol-cartridge, or any sort of ordnance-stores, without first procuring an order of the Secretary of War in Washington. The commanding general—though intrusted with the lives of his soldiers and with the safety of a frontier in a condition of chronic war—cannot touch or be trusted with ordnance-stores or property, and that is declared to be the law! Every officer of the old army remembers how, in 1861, we were hampered with the old blue army-regulations, which tied our hands, and that to do any thing positive and necessary we had to tear it all to pieces—cut the red-tape, as it was called—a dangerous thing for an army to do, for it was calculated to bring the law and authority into contempt; but war was upon us, and overwhelming necessity overrides all law.

This French report is well worth the study of our army-officers, of all grades and classes, and I will only refer again, casually, to another part, wherein it discusses the subject of military correspondence: whether the staff-officer should correspond directly with his chief in Paris, submitting to his general copies, or whether he should be required to carry on his correspondence through his general, so that the latter could promptly forward the communication, indorsed with his own remarks and opinions. The latter is declared by the board to be the only safe rule, because "the general should never be ignorant of any thing that is transpiring that concerns his command."

In this country, as in France, Congress controls the great questions of war and peace, makes all laws for the creation and government of armies, and votes the necessary supplies, leaving to the President to execute and apply these laws, especially the harder task of limiting the expenditure of public money to the amount of the annual appropriations. The executive power is further subdivided into the seven great depart-

ments, and to the Secretary of War is confided the general care
of the military establishment, and his powers are further subdivided into ten distinct and separate bureaus.

The chiefs of these bureaus are under the immediate orders
of the Secretary of War, who, through them, in fact commands the army from "his office," but cannot do so "in the
field"—an absurdity in military if not civil law.

The subordinates of these staff-corps and departments are
selected and chosen from the army itself, or fresh from West
Point, and too commonly construe themselves into the *élite*, as
made of better clay than the common soldier. Thus they separate themselves more and more from their comrades of the
line, and in process of time realize the condition of that old
officer of artillery who thought the army would be a delightful place for a gentleman if it were not for the d——d soldier; or, better still, the conclusion of the young lord in
"Henry IV.," who told Harry Percy (Hotspur) that "but for
these vile guns he would himself have been a soldier." This is
all wrong; utterly at variance with our democratic form of
government and of universal experience; and now that the
French, from whom we had copied the system, have utterly
"proscribed" it, I hope that our Congress will follow suit. I
admit, in its fullest force, the strength of the maxim that the
civil law should be superior to the military in time of peace;
that the army should be at all times subject to the direct control of Congress; and I assert that, from the formation of our
Government to the present day, the Regular Army has set the
highest example of obedience to law and authority; but, for
the very reason that our army is comparatively so very small, I
hold that it should be the best possible, organized and governed on true military principles, and that in time of peace we
should preserve the "habits and usages of war," so that, when
war does come, we may not again be compelled to suffer the
disgrace, confusion, and disorder of 1861.

The commanding officers of divisions, departments, and
posts, should have the amplest powers, not only to command
their troops, but all the stores designed for their use, and the
officers of the staff necessary to administer them, within the
area of their command; and then with fairness they could be
held to the most perfect responsibility. The President and

Secretary of War can command the army quite as well through these generals as through the subordinate staff-officers. Of course, the Secretary would, as now, distribute the funds according to the appropriation bills, and reserve to himself the absolute control and supervision of the larger arsenals and depots of supply. The error lies in the law, or in the judicial interpretation thereof, and no code of army regulations can be made that meets the case, until Congress, like the French *Corps Législatif*, utterly annihilates and "proscribes" the old law and the system which has grown up under it.

It is related of Napoleon that his last words were, "Tête-d'armée!" Doubtless, as the shadow of death obscured his memory, the last thought that remained for speech was of some event when he was directing an important "head of column." I believe that every general who has handled armies in battle must recall from his own experience the intensity of thought on some similar occasion, when by a single command he had given the finishing stroke to some complicated action; but to me recurs another thought that is worthy of record, and may encourage others who are to follow us in our profession. I never saw the rear of an army engaged in battle but I feared that some calamity had happened at the front—the apparent confusion, broken wagons, crippled horses, men lying about dead and maimed, parties hastening to and fro in seeming disorder, and a general apprehension of something dreadful about to ensue; all these signs, however, lessened as I neared the front, and there the contrast was complete—perfect order, men and horses full of confidence, and it was not unusual for general hilarity, laughing, and cheering. Although cannon might be firing, the musketry clattering, and the enemy's shot hitting close, there reigned a general feeling of strength and security that bore a marked contrast to the bloody signs that had drifted rapidly to the rear; therefore, for comfort and safety, I surely would rather be at the front than the rear line of battle. So also on the march, the head of a column moves on steadily, while the rear is alternately halting and then rushing forward to close up the gap; and all sorts of rumors, especially the worst, float back to the rear. Old troops invariably deem it a special privilege to be in the front—to be at the "head of column"—because experience has taught them that it is the easiest and most comfortable place, and danger only adds zest and stimulus to this fact.

The hardest task in war is to lie in support of some position or battery, under fire without the privilege of returning it; or to guard some train left in the rear, within hearing but out of danger; or to provide for the wounded and dead of some corps which is too busy ahead to care for its own.

To be at the head of a strong column of troops, in the execution of some task that requires brain, is the highest pleasure of war—a grim one and terrible, but which leaves on the mind and memory the strongest mark; to detect the weak point of an enemy's line; to break through with vehemence and thus lead to victory; or to discover some key-point and hold it with tenacity; or to do some other distinct act which is afterward recognized as the real cause of success. These all become matters that are never forgotten. Other great difficulties, experienced by every general, are to measure truly the thousand-and-one reports that come to him in the midst of conflict; to preserve a clear and well-defined purpose at every instant of time, and to cause all efforts to converge to that end.

To do these things he must know perfectly the strength and quality of each part of his own army, as well as that of his opponent, and must be where he can personally see and observe with his own eyes, and judge with his own mind. No man can properly command an army from the rear, he must be "at its front;" and when a detachment is made, the commander thereof should be informed of the object to be accomplished, and left as free as possible to execute it in his own way; and when an army is divided up into several parts, the superior should always attend that one which he regards as most important. Some men think that modern armies may be so regulated that a general can sit in an office and play on his several columns as on the keys of a piano; this is a fearful mistake. The directing mind must be at the very head of the army—must be seen there, and the effect of his mind and personal energy must be felt by every officer and man present with it, to secure the best results. Every attempt to make war easy and safe will result in humiliation and disaster.

Lastly, mail facilities should be kept up with an army if possible, that officers and men may receive and send letters to their friends, thus maintaining the home influence of infinite assistance to discipline. Newspaper correspondents with an army, as a rule, are mischievous. They are the world's gossips, pick up and retail the camp scandal, and gradually drift to the headquarters of some general, who finds it easier to make reputation at home than with his own corps or division. They are also tempted to prophesy events and state facts which, to an enemy, reveal a purpose in time to guard against it. Moreover, they are always bound to see facts colored by the partisan or political character of their own patrons, and thus bring army officers into the political controversies of the day, which are always mischievous and wrong. Yet, so greedy are the people at large for war news, that it is doubtful whether any army commander can exclude all reporters, without bringing down on himself a clamor that may imperil his own safety. Time and moderation must bring a just solution to this modern difficulty.

Chapter XXVI.

AFTER THE WAR.

IN THE FOREGOING PAGES I have endeavored to describe the public events in which I was an actor or spectator before and during the civil war of 1861–'65, and it now only remains for me to treat of similar matters of general interest subsequent to the civil war. Within a few days of the grand review of May 24, 1865, I took leave of the army at Washington, and with my family went to Chicago to attend a fair held in the interest of the families of soldiers impoverished by the war. I remained there about two weeks; on the 22d of June was at South Bend, Indiana, where two of my children were at school, and reached my native place, Lancaster, Ohio, on the 24th. On the 4th of July I visited at Louisville, Kentucky, the Fourteenth, Fifteenth, Sixteenth, and Seventeenth Army Corps, which had come from Washington, under the command of General John A. Logan, for "muster out," or "further orders." I then made a short visit to General George H. Thomas at Nashville, and returned to Lancaster, where I remained with the family till the receipt of General Orders No. 118 of June 27, 1865, which divided the whole territory of the United States into nineteen departments and five military divisions, the second of which was the military division of the "Mississippi," afterward changed to "Missouri," Major-General W. T. Sherman to command, with headquarters at St. Louis, to embrace the Departments of the Ohio, Missouri, and Arkansas.

This territorial command included the States north of the Ohio River, and the States and Territories north of Texas, as far west as the Rocky Mountains, including Montana, Utah, and New Mexico, but the part east of the Mississippi was soon transferred to another division. The department commanders were General E. O. C. Ord, at Detroit; General John Pope, at Fort Leavenworth; and General J. J. Reynolds, at Little Rock, but these also were soon changed. I at once assumed command, and ordered my staff and headquarters from Washington to St. Louis, Missouri, going there in person on the 16th of July.

My thoughts and feelings at once reverted to the construction of the great Pacific Railway, which had been chartered by Congress in the midst of war, and was then in progress. I put myself in communication with the parties engaged in the work, visiting them in person, and assured them that I would afford them all possible assistance and encouragement. Dr. Durant, the leading man of the Union Pacific, seemed to me a person of ardent nature, of great ability and energy, enthusiastic in his undertaking, and determined to build the road from Omaha to San Francisco. He had an able corps of assistants, collecting materials, letting out contracts for ties, grading, etc., and I attended the celebration of the first completed division of sixteen and a half miles, from Omaha to Papillon. When the orators spoke so confidently of the determination to build two thousand miles of railway across the plains, mountains, and desert, devoid of timber, with no population, but on the contrary raided by the bold and bloody Sioux and Cheyennes, who had almost successfully defied our power for half a century, I was disposed to treat it jocularly, because I could not help recall our California experience of 1855–'56, when we celebrated the completion of twenty-two and a half miles of the same road eastward of Sacramento; on which occasion Edward Baker had electrified us by his unequalled oratory, painting the glorious things which would result from uniting the Western coast with the East by bands of iron. Baker then, with a poet's imagination, saw the vision of the mighty future, but not the gulf which meantime was destined to swallow up half a million of the brightest and best youth of our land, and that he himself would be one of the first victims far away on the banks of the Potomac (he was killed in battle at Balls Bluff, October 21, 1861).

The Kansas Pacific was designed to unite with the main branch about the 100° meridian, near Fort Kearney. Mr. Shoemaker was its general superintendent and building contractor, and this branch in 1865 was finished about forty miles to a point near Lawrence, Kansas. I may not be able to refer to these roads again except incidentally, and will, therefore, record here that the location of this branch afterward was changed from the Republican to the Smoky Hill Fork of the Kansas River, and is now the main line to Denver. The Union and Central Railroads from the beginning were pushed with a skill, vigor, and courage which always commanded my admiration, the two meeting at Promontory Point, Utah, July 15, 1869, and in my judgment constitute one of the greatest and most beneficent achievements of man on earth.

The construction of the Union Pacific Railroad was deemed so important that the President, at my suggestion, constituted on the 5th of March, 1866, the new Department of the Platte, General P. St. George Cooke commanding, succeeded by General C. C. Augur, headquarters at Omaha, with orders to give ample protection to the working-parties, and to afford every possible assistance in the construction of the road; and subsequently in like manner the Department of Dakota was constituted. General A. H. Terry commanding, with headquarters at St. Paul, to give similar protection and encouragement to the Northern Pacific Railroad. These departments, with changed commanders, have continued up to the present day, and have fulfilled perfectly the uses for which they were designed.

During the years 1865 and 1866 the great plains remained almost in a state of nature, being the pasture-fields of about ten million buffalo, deer, elk, and antelope, and were in full possession of the Sioux, Cheyennes, Arapahoes, and Kiowas, a race of bold Indians, who saw plainly that the construction of two parallel railroads right through their country would prove destructive to the game on which they subsisted, and consequently fatal to themselves.

The troops were posted to the best advantage to protect the parties engaged in building these roads, and in person I reconnoitred well to the front, traversing the buffalo regions from south to north, and from east to west, often with a very small escort, mingling with the Indians whenever safe, and thereby gained personal knowledge of matters which enabled me to use the troops to the best advantage. I am sure that without the courage and activity of the department commanders with the small bodies of regular troops on the plains during the years 1866–'69, the Pacific Railroads could not have been built; but once built and in full operation the fate of the buffalo and Indian was settled for all time to come.

At the close of the civil war there were one million five hundred and sixteen names on the muster-rolls, of which seven hundred and ninety-seven thousand eight hundred and seven were present, and two hundred and two thousand seven hundred and nine absent, of which twenty-two thousand nine hundred and twenty-nine were regulars, the others were volunteers, colored troops, and veteran reserves. The regulars consisted of six regiments of cavalry, five of artillery, and nineteen of infantry. By the act of July 28, 1866, the peace establishment was fixed at one general (Grant), one lieutenant-general (Sherman), five major-generals (Halleck, Meade, Sheridan, Thomas, and Hancock), ten brigadiers (McDowell, Cooke, Pope, Hooker, Schofield, Howard, Terry, Ord, Canby, and Rousseau), ten regiments of cavalry, five of artillery, and forty-five of infantry, admitting of an aggregate force of fifty-four thousand six hundred and forty-one men.

All others were mustered out, and thus were remanded to their homes nearly a million of strong, vigorous men who had imbibed the somewhat erratic habits of the soldier; these were of every profession and trade in life, who, on regaining their homes, found their places occupied by others, that their friends and neighbors were different, and that they themselves had changed. They naturally looked for new homes to the great West, to the new Territories and States as far as the Pacific coast, and we realize to-day that the vigorous men who control Kansas, Nebraska, Dakota, Montana, Colorado, etc., etc., were soldiers of the civil war. These men flocked to the plains, and were rather stimulated than retarded by the danger of an Indian war. This was another potent agency in producing the result we enjoy to-day, in having in so short a time replaced the wild buffaloes by more numerous herds of tame cattle, and by substituting for the useless Indians the intelligent owners of productive farms and cattle-ranches.

While these great changes were being wrought at the West, in the East politics had resumed full sway, and all the methods of anti-war times had been renewed. President Johnson had differed with his party as to the best method of recon-

structing the State governments of the South, which had been
destroyed and impoverished by the war, and the press began
to agitate the question of the *next* President. Of course, all
Union men naturally turned to General Grant, and the result
was jealousy of him by the personal friends of President
Johnson and some of his cabinet. Mr. Johnson always seemed
very patriotic and friendly, and I believed him honest and sincere in his declared purpose to follow strictly the Constitution
of the United States in restoring the Southern States to their
normal place in the Union; but the same cordial friendship
subsisted between General Grant and myself, which was the
outgrowth of personal relations dating back to 1839. So I resolved to keep out of this conflict. In September, 1866, I was
in the mountains of New Mexico, when a message reached
me that I was wanted at Washington. I had with me a couple
of officers and half a dozen soldiers as escort, and traveled
down the Arkansas, through the Kiowas, Comanches, Cheyennes, and Arapahoes, all more or less disaffected, but
reached St. Louis in safety, and proceeded to Washington,
where I reported to General Grant.

He explained to me that President Johnson wanted to see
me. He did not know the why or wherefore, but supposed it
had some connection with an order he (General Grant) had
received to escort the newly appointed Minister, Hon. Lew
Campbell, of Ohio, to the court of Juarez, the President-elect
of Mexico, which country was still in possession of the
Emperor Maximilian, supported by a corps of French troops
commanded by General Bazaine. General Grant denied the
right of the President to order him on a diplomatic mission
unattended by troops; said that he had thought the matter
over, would disobey the order, and stand the consequences.
He manifested much feeling, and said it was a plot to get rid
of him. I then went to President Johnson, who treated me
with great cordiality, and said that he was very glad I had
come; that General Grant was about to go to Mexico on business of importance, and he wanted me at Washington to command the army in General Grant's absence. I then informed
him that General Grant *would not go*, and he seemed amazed;
said that it was generally understood that General Grant
construed the occupation of the territories of our neighbor,

Mexico, by French troops, and the establishment of an empire therein, with an Austrian prince at its head, as hostile to republican America, and that the Administration had arranged with the French Government for the withdrawal of Bazaine's troops, which would leave the country free for the President-elect Juarez to reoccupy the city of Mexico, etc., etc.; that Mr. Campbell had been accredited to Juarez, and the fact that he was accompanied by so distinguished a soldier as General Grant would emphasize the act of the United States. I simply reiterated that General Grant *would not go*, and that he, Mr. Johnson, could not afford to quarrel with him at that time. I further argued that General Grant was at the moment engaged on the most delicate and difficult task of reorganizing the army under the act of July 28, 1866; that if the real object was to put Mr. Campbell in official communication with President Juarez, supposed to be at El Paso or Monterey, either General Hancock, whose command embraced New Mexico, or General Sheridan, whose command included Texas, could fulfil the object perfectly; or, in the event of neither of these alternates proving satisfactory to the Secretary of State, that I could be easier spared than General Grant. "Certainly," answered the President, "if you will go, that will answer perfectly."

The instructions of the Secretary of State, W. H. Seward, to Hon. Lewis D. Campbell, Minister to Mexico, dated October 25, 1866; a letter from President Johnson to Secretary of War Stanton, dated October 26, 1866; and the letter of Edwin M. Stanton, Secretary of War, to General Grant, dated October 27th, had been already prepared and printed, and the originals or copies were furnished me; but on the 30th of October, 1866, the following letter passed:

EXECUTIVE MANSION, ⎫
WASHINGTON, D. C., *October* 30, 1866. ⎭

SIR: General Ulysses S. Grant having found it inconvenient to assume the duties specified in my letter to you of the 26th inst., you will please relieve him, and assign them in all respects to William T. Sherman, Lieutenant-General of the Army of the United States. By way of guiding General Sherman in the performance of his duties, you will furnish him with a copy of your special orders to General

Grant made in compliance with my letter of the 26th inst., together with a copy of the instructions of the Secretary of State to Lewis D. Campbell, Esq., therein mentioned.

The lieutenant-general will proceed to the execution of his duties without delay.   Very respectfully yours,

ANDREW JOHNSON.

To the HON. EDWIN M. STANTON, *Secretary of War.*

At the Navy Department I learned that the United States ship Susquehanna, Captain Alden, was fitting out in New York for the use of this mission, and that there would be time for me to return to St. Louis to make arrangements for a prolonged absence, as also to communicate with Mr. Campbell, who was still at his home in Hamilton, Ohio. By correspondence we agreed to meet in New York, November 8th, he accompanied by Mr. Plumb, secretary of legation, and I by my aide, Colonel Audenried.

We embarked November 10th, and went to sea next day, making for Havana and Vera Cruz, and, as soon as we were outside of Sandy Hook, I explained to Captain Alden that my mission was ended, because I believed by substituting myself for General Grant I had prevented a serious quarrel between him and the Administration, which was unnecessary. We reached Havana on the 18th, with nothing to vary the monotony of an ordinary sea-voyage, except off Hatteras we picked up one woman and twenty men from open boats, who had just abandoned a propeller bound from Baltimore to Charleston which foundered. The sea was very rough, but by the personal skill and supervision of Captain Alden every soul reached our deck safely, and was carried to our consul at Havana. At Havana we were very handsomely entertained, especially by Señor Aldama, who took us by rail to his sugar-estates at Santa Rosa, and back by Matanzas.

We took our departure thence on the 25th, and anchored under Isla Verde, off Vera Cruz, on the 29th.

Everything about Vera Cruz indicated the purpose of the French to withdraw, and also that the Emperor Maximilian would precede them, for the Austrian frigate Dandolo was in port, and an Austrian bark, on which were received, according to the report of our consul, Mr. Lane, as many as eleven hundred packages of private furniture to be transferred to

Miramar, Maximilian's home; and Lieutenant Clarin, of the French navy, who visited the Susquehanna from the French commodore, Clouet, told me, without reserve, that, if we had delayed eight days more, we would have found Maximilian gone. General Bazaine was reported to be in the city of Mexico with about twenty-eight thousand French troops; but instead of leaving Mexico in three detachments, viz., November, 1866, March, 1867, and November, 1867, as described in Mr. Seward's letter to Mr. Campbell, of October 25, 1866, it looked to me that, as a soldier, he would evacuate at some time before November, 1867, *all at once*, and not by detachments. Lieutenant Clarin telegraphed Bazaine at the city of Mexico the fact of our arrival, and he sent me a most courteous and pressing invitation to come up to the city; but, as we were accredited to the government of Juarez, it was considered *un*diplomatic to establish friendly relations with the existing authorities. Meantime we could not hear a word of Juarez, and concluded to search for him along the coast northward. (When I was in Versailles, France, July, 1872, learning that General Bazaine was in arrest for the surrender of his army and post at Metz, in 1870, I wanted to call on him to thank him for his courteous invitation to me at Vera Cruz in 1866. I inquired of President Thiers if I could with propriety call on the marshal. He answered that it would be very acceptable, no doubt, but suggested for form's sake that I should consult the Minister of War, General de Cissey, which I did, and he promptly assented. Accordingly, I called with my aide, Colonel Audenried, on Marshal Bazaine, who occupied a small, two-story stone house at Versailles, in an inclosure with a high garden wall, at the front gate or door of which was a lodge, in which was a military guard. We were shown to a good room on the second floor, where was seated the marshal in military half-dress, with large head, full face, short neck, and evidently a man of strong physique. He did not speak English, but spoke Spanish perfectly. We managed to carry on a conversation in which I endeavored to convey my sense of his politeness in inviting me so cordially up to the city of Mexico, and my regret that the peculiar duty on which I was engaged did not admit of a compliance, or even of an intelligent explanation, at the time. He spoke of the whole

Mexican business as a "sad affair," that the empire necessarily fell with the result of our civil war, and that poor Maximilian was sacrificed to his own high sense of honor.)

While on board the Susquehanna, on the 1st day of December, 1866, we received the proclamation made by the Emperor Maximilian at Orizaba, in which, notwithstanding the near withdrawal of the French troops, he declared his purpose to remain and "shed the last drop of his blood in defense of his dear country." Undoubtedly many of the most substantial people of Mexico, having lost all faith in the stability of the native government, had committed themselves to what they considered the more stable government of Maximilian, and Maximilian, a man of honor, concluded at the last moment he could not abandon them; the consequence was his death.

Failing to hear of Juarez, we steamed up the coast to the Island of Lobos, and on to Tampico, off which we found the United States steamer Paul Jones, which, drawing less water than the Susquehanna, carried us over the bar to the city, then in possession of the Liberal party, which recognized Juarez as their constitutional President, but of Juarez and his whereabout we could hear not a word; so we continued up the coast and anchored off Brazos Santiago, December 7th. Going ashore in small boats, we found a railroad, under the management of General J. R. West, now one of the commissioners of the city of Washington, who sent us up to Brownsville, Texas. We met on the way General Sheridan, returning from a tour of inspection of the Rio Grande frontier. On Sunday, December 9th, we were all at Matamoras, Mexico, where we met General Escobedo, one of Juarez's trusty lieutenants, who developed to us the general plan agreed on for the overthrow of the empire, and the reëstablishment of the republican government of Mexico. He asked of us no assistance, except the loan of some arms, ammunition, clothing, and camp-equipage. It was agreed that Mr. Campbell should, as soon as he could get his baggage off the Susquehanna, return to Matamoras, and thence proceed to Monterey, to be received by Juarez in person as the accredited Minister of the United States to the Republic of Mexico. Meantime the weather off the coast was stormy, and the Susquehanna parted a cable, so that we were delayed some days at Brazos;

but in due time Mr. Campbell got his baggage, and we regained the deck of the Susquehanna, which got up steam and started for New Orleans. We reached New Orleans December 20th, whence I reported fully everything to General Grant, and on the 21st received the following dispatch:

WASHINGTON, *December* 21, 1866.
Lieutenant-General SHERMAN, *New Orleans.*
Your telegram of yesterday has been submitted to the President. You are authorized to proceed to St. Louis at your convenience. Your proceedings in the special and delicate duties assigned you are cordially approved by the President and Cabinet and this department.

EDWIN M. STANTON.

And on the same day I received this dispatch:

GALVESTON, *December* 21, 1866.
To General SHERMAN, *or General* SHERIDAN.
Will be in New Orleans to-morrow. Wish to see you both on arrival, on matters of importance.

LEWIS D. CAMPBELL, *Minister to Mexico.*

Mr. Campbell arrived on the 22d, but had nothing to tell of the least importance, save that he was generally disgusted with the whole thing, and had not found Juarez at all.

I am sure this whole movement was got up for the purpose of getting General Grant away from Washington, on the pretext of his known antagonism to the French occupation of Mexico, because he was looming up as a candidate for President, and nobody understood the *animus* and purpose better than did Mr. Stanton. He himself was not then on good terms with President Johnson, and with several of his associates in the Cabinet. By Christmas I was back in St. Louis.

By this time the conflict between President Johnson and Congress had become open and unconcealed. Congress passed the bill known as the "Tenure of Civil Office" on the 2d of March, 1867 (over the President's veto), the first clause of which, now section 1767 of the Revised Statutes, reads thus: "Every person who holds any civil office to which he has been or hereafter may be appointed, by and with the advice and consent of the Senate, and who shall have become duly qualified to act therein, shall be entitled to hold such office during the term for which he was appointed, unless sooner removed by and with the advice and consent of the Senate, or by the appointment with the like advice and consent of a successor in his place, except as herein otherwise provided."

General E. D. Townsend, in his "Anecdotes of the Civil War," states tersely and correctly the preliminary circumstances of which I must treat. He says: "On Monday morning, August 5, 1867, President Johnson invited Mr. Stanton to resign as Secretary of War. Under the tenure-of-civil-office law, Mr. Stanton declined. The President a week after suspended him, and appointed General Grant, General-in-Chief of the Army, to exercise the functions. This continued until January 13, 1868, when according to the law the Senate passed a resolution *not* sustaining the President's action. The next morning General Grant came to my office and handed me the key of the Secretary's room, saying: 'I am to be found over at my office at army headquarters. I was served with a copy of the Senate resolution last evening.' I then went up-stairs and delivered the key of his room to Mr. Stanton."

The mode and manner of Mr. Stanton's regaining his office, and of General Grant's surrendering it, were at the time subjects of bitter controversy. Unhappily I was involved, and must bear testimony. In all January, 1868, I was a member of a board ordered to compile a code of articles of war and army regulations, of which Major-General Sheridan and Brigadier-General C. C. Augur were associate members. Our place of meeting was in the room of the old War Department, second floor, next to the corner room occupied by the Secretary of War, with a door of communication. While we were at work it was common for General Grant and, afterward, for Mr. Stanton to drop in and chat with us on the social gossip of the time.

On Saturday, January 11th, General Grant said that he had more carefully read the law (tenure of civil office), and it was different from what he had supposed; that in case the Senate did not consent to the removal of Secretary of War Stanton, and he (Grant) should hold on, he should incur a liability of ten thousand dollars and five years' imprisonment. We all expected the resolution of Senator Howard, of Michigan, virtually restoring Mr. Stanton to his office, would pass the Senate, and knowing that the President expected General Grant to *hold on*, I inquired if he had given notice of his change of purpose; he answered that there was no hurry, because he supposed Mr. Stanton would pursue toward him (Grant) the same course which he (Stanton) had required of him the preceding August, viz., would address him a letter claiming the office, and allow him a couple of days for the change. Still, he said he would go to the White House the same day and notify the President of his intended action.

That afternoon I went over to the White House to present General Pope, who was on a visit to Washington, and we found the President and General Grant together. We made our visit and withdrew, leaving them still together, and I always supposed the subject of this conference was the expected decision of the Senate, which would in effect restore Mr. Stanton to his civil office of Secretary of War. That evening I dined with the Hon. Reverdy Johnson, Senator from Maryland, and suggested to him that the best way to escape a conflict was for the President to nominate some good man as Secretary of War whose confirmation by the Senate would fall within the provisions of the law, and named General J. D. Cox, then Governor of Ohio, whose term of office was drawing to a close, who would, I knew, be acceptable to General Grant and the army generally. Mr. Johnson was most favorably impressed with this suggestion, and promised to call on the President the next day (Sunday), which he did, but President Johnson had made up his mind to meet the conflict boldly. I saw General Grant that afternoon at his house on I Street, and told him what I had done, and so anxious was he about it that he came to our room at the War Department the next morning (Monday), the 13th, and asked me to go in person to the White House to urge the President to send in the name of General Cox. I did so, saw the President, and inquired if he had seen Mr. Reverdy Johnson the day before about General Cox. He answered that he had, and thought well of General Cox, but would say no further.

Tuesday, January 14, 1868, came, and with it Mr. Stanton. He resumed possession of his former office; came into that where General Sheridan, General Augur, and I were at work, and greeted us very cordially. He said he wanted to see me when at leisure, and at half-past 10 A.M. I went into his office and found him and General Grant together. Supposing they had some special matters of business, I withdrew, with the remark that I was close at hand, and could come in at any moment. In the afternoon I went again into Mr. Stanton's office, and we had a long and most friendly conversation, but not one word was spoken about the "tenure-of-office" matter. I then crossed over Seventeenth Street to the headquarters of the army, where I found General Grant, who expressed himself as by no means pleased with the manner in which Mr. Stanton had regained his office, saying that he had sent a messenger for him that morning as of old, with word that "he wanted to see him." We then arranged to meet at his office the next morning at half-past nine, and go together to see the President.

That morning the *National Intelligencer* published an article accusing General Grant of acting in bad faith to the President, and of having prevaricated in making his personal explanation to the Cabinet, so that General Grant at first felt unwilling to go, but we went. The President received us promptly and kindly. Being seated, General Grant said, "Mr. President, whoever gave the facts for the article of the *Intelligencer* of this morning has made some serious mistakes." The President: "General Grant, let me interrupt you just there. I have not seen the *Intelligencer* of this morning, and have no knowledge of the contents of any article therein." General Grant then went on: "Well, the idea is given there that I have not kept faith with you. Now, Mr. President, I remember, when you spoke to me on this subject last summer, I did say that, like the case of the Baltimore police commissioners, I did suppose Mr. Stanton could not regain his office except by a process through the courts." To this the President assented, saying he "remembered the reference to the case of the Baltimore commissioners," when General Grant resumed: "I said if I changed my opinion I would give you notice, and put things as they were before my appointment as Secretary of War *ad interim*."

We then entered into a general friendly conversation, both parties professing to be satisfied, the President claiming that he had always been most friendly to General Grant, and the latter insisting that he had taken the office, not for honor or profit, but in the general interests of the army.

As we withdrew, at the very door, General Grant said, "Mr. President, you should make some order that we of the army are not bound to obey the orders of Mr. Stanton as Secretary of War," which the President intimated he would do.

No such "orders" were ever made; many conferences were held, and the following letters are selected out of a great mass to show the general feeling at the time:

1321 K STREET, WASHINGTON, *January* 28, 1868, *Saturday.*
To the President:

I neglected this morning to say that I had agreed to go down to Annapolis to spend Sunday with Admiral Porter. General Grant also has to leave for Richmond on Monday morning at 6 A.M.

At a conversation with the General after our interview, wherein I offered to go with him on Monday morning to Mr. Stanton, and to say that it was our joint opinion he should resign, it was found impossible by reason of his (General Grant) going to Richmond and my going to Annapolis. The General proposed this course: He will call on you to-morrow, and offer to go to Mr. Stanton to say, for the good of the Army and of the country, he ought to resign. This on Sunday. On Monday I will again call on you, and, if you think it necessary, I will do the same, viz., go to Mr. Stanton and tell him he should resign.

If he will not, then it will be time to contrive ulterior measures. In the mean time it so happens that no necessity exists for precipitating matters.

Yours truly,   W. T. SHERMAN, *Lieutenant-General.*

DEAR GENERAL: On the point of starting, I have written the above, and will send a fair copy of it to the President. Please retain this, that in case of necessity I may have a copy. The President clearly stated to me that he relied on us in this category.

Think of the propriety of your putting in writing what you have to say to-morrow, even if you have to put it in the form of a letter to hand him in person, retaining a copy. I'm afraid that acting as a go-between for three persons, I may share the usual fate of meddlers, at last get kicks from all. We ought not to be involved in politics, but for the sake of the Army we are justified in trying at least to cut this Gordian knot, which they do not appear to have any practicable plan to do. In haste as usual,

W. T. SHERMAN.

HEADQUARTERS ARMIES OF THE UNITED STATES, }
January 29, 1868.}

DEAR SHERMAN: I called on the President and Mr. Stanton to-day, but without any effect.

I soon found that to recommend resignation to Mr. Stanton would have no effect, unless it was to incur further his displeasure; and, therefore, did not directly suggest it to him. I explained to him, however, the course I supposed he would pursue, and what I expected to do in that case, namely, to notify the President of his intentions, and thus leave him to violate the "Tenure-of-Office Bill" if he chose, instead of having me do it.

I would advise that you say nothing to Mr. Stanton on the subject unless he asks your advice. It will do no good, and may embarrass you. I did not mention your name to him, at least not in connection with his position, or what you thought upon it.

All that Mr. Johnson said was pacific and compromising. While I think he wanted the constitutionality of the "Tenure Bill" tested, I think now he would be glad either to get the vacancy of Secretary of War, or have the office just where it was during suspension. Yours truly,   U. S. GRANT.

WASHINGTON, D. C., *January* 27, 1868.
To the President.

DEAR SIR: As I promised, I saw Mr. Ewing yesterday, and after a long conversation asked him to put down his opinion in writing, which he has done and which I now inclose.

I am now at work on these Army Regulations, and in the course of preparation have laid down the Constitution and laws now in force, clearer than I find them elsewhere; and beg leave herewith to inclose you three pages of printed matter for your perusal. My opinion is, if you will adopt these rules and make them an executive order to General Grant, they will so clearly define the duties of all concerned that no conflict can arise. I hope to get through this task in the course of this week, and want very much to go to St. Louis. For eleven years I have been tossed about so much that I really do want to rest, study, and make the acquaintance of my family. I do not think, since 1857, I have averaged thirty days out of three hundred and sixty-five at home.

Next summer also, in fulfillment of our promise to the Sioux, I must go to Fort Phil Kearney early in the spring, so that, unless I can spend the next two months at home, I might as well break up my house at St. Louis, and give up all prospect of taking care of my family.

For these reasons especially I shall soon ask leave to go to St. Louis, to resume my proper and legitimate command. With great respect,

W. T. SHERMAN, *Lieutenant-General.*

[INCLOSURE.]

WASHINGTON, D. C., *January* 25, 1868.

MY DEAR GENERAL: I am quite clear in the opinion that it is not expedient for the President to take any action now in the case of Stanton. So far as he and his interests are concerned, things are in the best possible condition. Stanton is in the Department, *not* his secretary, but the secretary of the Senate, who have taken upon themselves his sins, and who place him there under a large salary to annoy and obstruct the operations of the Executive. This the people well enough understand, and he is a stench in the nostrils of their own party.

I thought the nomination of Cox at the proper juncture would have been wise as a peace-offering, but perhaps it would have let off the Senate too easily from the effect of their arbitrary act. Now the dislodging of Stanton and filling the office even temporarily without the consent of the Senate would raise a question as to the legality of the President's acts, and he would belong to the attacked instead of the attacking party. If the war between Congress and the President is to go on, as I suppose it is, Stanton should be ignored by the President, left to perform his clerical duties which the law requires him to perform, and let the party bear the odium which is already upon them for placing him where he is. So much for the President.

As to yourself, I wish you as far as possible to keep clear of political complications. I do not think the President will require you to do an act of doubtful legality. Certainly he will not without sanction of the opinion of his Attorney-General; and you should have time, in a questionable case, to consult with me before called upon to act. The office of Secretary of War is a civil office, as completely so as that of Secretary of State; and you as a military officer cannot, I think, be required to assume or exercise it. This may, if necessary, be a subject for further consideration. Such, however, will not, I think, be the case. The appeal is to the people, and it is better for the President to persist in the course he has for some time pursued—let the aggressions all come from the other side; and I think there is no doubt he will do so. Affectionately,

T. EWING.

To Lieutenant-General SHERMAN.

LIBRARY-ROOM, WAR DEPARTMENT, }
WASHINGTON, D. C., *January* 31, 1868.}

To the President:

Since our interview of yesterday I have given the subject of our conversation all my thoughts, and I beg you will pardon my reducing the same to writing.

My personal preferences, as expressed, were to be allowed to return to St. Louis to resume my present command, because my command was important, large, suited to my rank and inclination, and because my family was well provided for there in house, facilities, schools, living, and agreeable society; while, on the other hand, Washington was for many (to me) good reasons highly objectionable, especially because it is the political capital of the country, and focus of intrigue, gossip, and slander. Your personal preferences were, as expressed, to make a new department East adequate to my rank, with headquarters at Washington, and assign me to its command, to remove my family here, and to avail myself of its schools, etc.; to remove Mr. Stanton from his office as Secretary of War, and have me to discharge the duties.

To effect his removal two modes were indicated: to simply cause him to quit the War-Office Building, and notify the Treasury Department and the Army Staff Departments no longer to respect him as Secretary of War; or to remove him and submit my name to the Senate for confirmation.

Permit me to discuss these points a little, and I will premise by saying that I have spoken to no one on the subject, and have not even seen Mr. Ewing, Mr. Stanbery, or General Grant, since I was with you.

It has been the rule and custom of our army, since the organization of the government, that the second officer of the army should be at the second (in importance) command, and remote from general headquarters. To bring me to Washington would put three heads to an army, yourself, General Grant, and myself, and we would be more than human if we were not to differ. In my judgment it would ruin the army, and would be fatal to one or two of us.

Generals Scott and Taylor proved themselves soldiers and patriots in the field, but Washington was fatal to both. This city, and the influences that centre here, defeated every army that had its headquarters here from 1861 to 1864, and would have overwhelmed General Grant at Spottsylvania and Petersburg, had he not been fortified by a strong reputation, already hard-earned, and because no one then living coveted the place; whereas, in the West, we made progress from the start, because there was no political capital near enough to poison our minds, and kindle into life that craving, itching for fame which has killed more good men than bullets. I have been with General Grant in the midst of death and slaughter—when the howls of people reached him after Shiloh; when messengers were speeding to and from his army to Washington, bearing slanders, to induce his removal before he took Vicksburg; in Chattanooga, when the soldiers were stealing the corn of the starving mules to satisfy their own hunger; at Nashville, when he was ordered to the "forlorn hope" to command the Army of the Potomac, so often defeated— and yet I never saw him more troubled than since he has been in Washington, and been compelled to read himself a "sneak and deceiver," based on reports of four of the Cabinet, and apparently with your knowledge. If this political atmosphere can disturb the equanimity of one so guarded and so prudent as he is, what will be the result with me, so careless, so outspoken as I am? Therefore, with my consent, Washington never.

As to the Secretary of War, his office is twofold. As a Cabinet officer he should not be there without your hearty, cheerful assent, and I believe that is the judgment and opinion of every fair-minded man. As the holder of a civil office, having the supervision of moneys appropriated by Congress and of contracts for army supplies, I do think Congress, or the Senate by delegation from Congress, has a lawful right to be consulted. At all events, I would not risk a suit or contest on that phase of the question. The law of Congress, of March 2, 1867, prescribing the manner in which orders and instructions relating to "military movements" shall reach the army, gives you as constitutional Commander-in-Chief the very power you want to exercise, and enables you to prevent the Secretary from making any such orders and instructions; and consequently he cannot control the army, but is limited and restricted to a duty that an Auditor of the Treasury could perform. You certainly can afford to await the result. The Executive power is not weakened, but rather strengthened. Surely he is not such an obstruction as would warrant violence, or even a show of force, which would produce the very reaction and clamor that he hopes for to save him from the absurdity of holding an empty office "for the safety of the country."

This is as much as I ought to say, and more too, but if it produces the result I will be more than satisfied, viz., that I be simply allowed to resume my proper post and duties in St. Louis. With great respect, yours truly,

W. T. SHERMAN, *Lieutenant-General.*

On the 1st of February, the board of which I was the president submitted to the adjutant-general our draft of the

"Articles of War and Army Regulations," condensed to a small compass, the result of our war experience. But they did not suit the powers that were, and have ever since slept the sleep that knows no waking, to make room for the ponderous document now in vogue, which will not stand the strain of a week's campaign in real war.

I hurried back to St. Louis to escape the political storm I saw brewing. The President repeatedly said to me that he wanted me in Washington, and I as often answered that nothing could tempt me to live in that center of intrigue and excitement; but soon came the following:

HEADQUARTERS ARMY OF THE UNITED STATES,
WASHINGTON, *February* 10, 1868.

DEAR GENERAL: I have received at last the President's reply to my last letter. He attempts to substantiate his statements by his Cabinet. In this view it is important that I should have a letter from you, if you are willing to give it, of what I said to you about the effect of the "Tenure-of-Office Bill," and my object in going to see the President on Saturday before the installment of Mr. Stanton. What occurred after the meeting of the Cabinet on the Tuesday following is not a subject under controversy now; therefore, if you choose to write down your recollection (and I would like to have it) on Wednesday, when you and I called on the President, and your conversation with him the last time you saw him, make that a separate communication.

Your order to come East was received several days ago, but the President withdrew it, I supposed to make some alteration, but it has not been returned.   Yours truly,

U. S. GRANT.

[TELEGRAM.]
WASHINGTON, D. C., *February* 13, 1868.

Lieutenant-General W. T. SHERMAN, *St. Louis.*
    The order is issued ordering you to Atlantic Division.

U. S. GRANT, *General.*

[TELEGRAM.]
HEADQUARTERS MILITARY DIVISION OF THE MISSOURI,
ST. LOUIS, *February* 14, 1868.

General U. S. GRANT, *Washington, D. C.*
    Your dispatch is received informing me that the order for the

Atlantic Division has been issued, and that I am assigned to its command. I was in hopes I had escaped the danger, and now were I prepared I should resign on the spot, as it requires no foresight to predict such must be the inevitable result in the end. I will make one more desperate effort by mail, which please await.

W. T. SHERMAN, *Lieutenant-General.*

[TELEGRAM.]
WASHINGTON, *February* 14, 1868.
Lieutenant-General W. T. SHERMAN, *St. Louis.*

I think it due to you that your letter of January 31st to the President of the United States should be published, to correct misapprehension in the public mind about your willingness to come to Washington. It will not be published against your will.

U. S. GRANT, *General.*

(Sent in cipher.)

[TELEGRAM.]
HEADQUARTERS MILITARY DIVISION OF THE MISSOURI,
ST. LOUIS, MISSOURI, *February* 14, 1868.

General U. S. GRANT, *Washington, D. C.*

Dispatch of to-day received. Please await a letter I address this day through you to the President, which will in due time reach the public, covering the very point you make.

I don't want to come to Washington at all.

W. T. SHERMAN, *Lieutenant-General.*

[TELEGRAM.]
HEADQUARTERS MILITARY DIVISION OF THE MISSOURI,
ST. LOUIS, MISSOURI, *February* 14, 1868.

Hon. JOHN SHERMAN, *United States Senate, Washington, D. C.*

Oppose confirmation of myself as brevet general, on ground that it is unprecedented, and that it is better not to extend the system of brevets above major-general. If I can't avoid coming to Washington, I may have to resign.

W. T. SHERMAN, *Lieutenant-General.*

HEADQUARTERS OF THE ARMY,
WASHINGTON, D. C., *February* 12, 1868.

The following orders are published for the information and guidance of all concerned:

EXECUTIVE MANSION,
WASHINGTON, D. C., *February* 12, 1868.

GENERAL: You will please issue an order creating a military division to be styled the Military Division of the Atlantic, to be composed of the Department of the Lakes, the Department of the East, and the Department of Washington, to be commanded by Lieutenant-General W. T. Sherman, with his headquarters at Washington. Until further orders from the President, you will assign no officer to the permanent command of the Military Division of the Missouri.   Respectfully yours,

ANDREW JOHNSON.

GENERAL U. S. GRANT,
  Commanding Armies of the United States, Washington, D. C.

Major-General P. H. Sheridan, the senior officer in the Military Division of the Missouri, will temporarily perform the duties of commander of the Military Division of the Missouri in addition to his duties of department commander.

By command of General Grant:

E. D. TOWNSEND, *Assistant Adjutant-General.*

This order, if carried into effect, would have grouped in Washington:

1. The President, constitutional Commander-in-Chief.

2. The Secretary of War, congressional Commander-in-Chief.

3. The General of the Armies of the United States.

4. The Lieutenant-General of the Army.

5. The Commanding General of the Department of Washington.

6. The commander of the post of Washington.

At that date the garrison of Washington was a brigade of infantry and a battery of artillery. I never doubted Mr. Johnson's sincerity in wishing to befriend me, but this was the broadest kind of a farce, or meant mischief. I therefore appealed to him by letter to allow me to remain where I was, and where I could do service, *real service*, and received his most satisfactory answer.

HEADQUARTERS MILITARY DIVISION OF THE MISSOURI,
ST. LOUIS, MISSOURI, *February* 14, 1868.

General U. S. GRANT, *Washington, D. C.*

DEAR GENERAL: Last evening, just before leaving my office, I received your note of the 10th, and had intended answering it according to your request; but, after I got home, I got your dispatch of yesterday, announcing that the order I dreaded so much was issued. I never felt so troubled in my life. Were it an order to go to Sitka, to the devil, to battle with rebels or Indians, I think you would not hear a whimper from me, but it comes in such a questionable form that, like Hamlet's ghost, it curdles my blood and mars my judgment. My first thoughts were of resignation, and I had almost made up my mind to ask Dodge for some place on the Pacific road, or on one of the Iowa roads, and then again various colleges ran through my memory, but hard times and an expensive family have brought me back to staring the proposition square in the face, and I have just written a letter to the President, which I herewith transmit through you, on which I will hang a hope of respite till you telegraph me its effect. The uncertainties ahead are too great to warrant my incurring the expense of breaking up my house and family here, and therefore in no event will I do this till I can be assured of some permanence elsewhere. If it were at all certain that you would accept the nomination of President in May, I would try and kill the intervening time, and then judge of the chances, but I do not want you to reveal your plans to me till you choose to do so.

I have telegraphed to John Sherman to oppose the nomination which the papers announce has been made of me for brevet general.

I have this minute received your cipher dispatch of to-day, which I have just answered and sent down to the telegraph-office, and the clerk is just engaged in copying my letter to the President to go with this. If the President or his friends pretend that I seek to go to Washington, it will be fully rebutted by letters I have written to the President, to you, to John Sherman, to Mr. Ewing, and to Mr. Stanbery. You remember that in our last talk you suggested I should write again to the President. I thought of it, and concluded my letter of January 31st, already delivered, was full and emphatic. Still, I did write again to Mr. Stanbery, asking him as a friend to interpose in my behalf. There are plenty of people who know my wishes, and I would avoid, if possible, the publication of a letter so confidential as that of January 31st, in which I notice I allude to the President's purpose of removing Mr. Stanton by force, a fact that ought not to be drawn out through me if it be possible to avoid it. In the letter herewith I confine myself to purely private matters, and will not object if it reaches the public in any proper way. My opinion is, the President thinks Mrs. Sherman would like to come to Washington by reason of her father and brothers being there. This is true, for Mrs. Sherman has an idea that St. Louis is unhealthy for our children, and because most of the Catholics here are tainted with the old secesh feeling. But I know better what is to our common interest, and prefer to judge of the proprieties myself. What I do object to is the false position I would occupy as between you and the President. Were there an actual army at or near Washington, I could be withdrawn from the most unpleasant attitude of a "go-between," but there is no army there, nor any military duties which you with a host of subordinates can not perform. Therefore I would be there with naked, informal, and sinecure duties, and utterly out of place. This you understand well enough, and the army too, but the President and the politicians, who flatter themselves they are saving the country, cannot and will not understand. My opinion is, the country is doctored to death, and if President and Congress would go to sleep like Rip Van Winkle, the country would go on under natural influences, and recover far faster than under their joint and several treatment. This doctrine would be accounted by Congress, and by the President too, as high treason, and therefore I don't care about saying so to either of them, but I know you can hear anything, and give it just what thought or action it merits.

Excuse this long letter, and telegraph me the result of my letter to the President as early as you can. If he holds my letter so long as to make it improper for me to await his answer, also telegraph me.

The order, when received, will, I suppose, direct me as to whom and how I am to turn over this command, which should, in my judgment, not be broken up, as the three departments composing the division should be under one head.

I expect my staff-officers to be making for me within the hour to learn their fate, so advise me all you can as quick as possible.

With great respect, yours truly,

W. T. SHERMAN, *Lieutenant-General*.

HEADQUARTERS MILITARY DIVISION OF THE MISSOURI, ⎱
ST. LOUIS, MISSOURI, *February* 14, 1868.   ⎰

To the President.

DEAR SIR: It is hard for me to conceive you would purposely do me an unkindness unless under the pressure of a sense of public duty, or because you do not believe me sincere. I was in hopes, since my letter to you of the 31st of January, that you had concluded to pass over that purpose of yours expressed more than once in conversation—to organize a new command for me in the East, with headquarters in Washington; but a telegram from General Grant of yesterday says that "the order was issued ordering you" (me) "to

Atlantic Division"; and the newspapers of this morning contain the same information, with the addition that I have been nominated as brevet general. I have telegraphed my own brother in the Senate to oppose my confirmation, on the ground that the two higher grades in the army ought not to be complicated with brevets, and I trust you will conceive my motives aright. If I could see my way clear to maintain my family, I should not hesitate a moment to resign my present commission, and seek some business wherein I would be free from these unhappy complications that seem to be closing about me, spite of my earnest efforts to avoid them; but necessity ties my hands, and I must submit with the best grace I can till I make other arrangements.

In Washington are already the headquarters of a department, and of the army itself, and it is hard for me to see wherein I can render military service there. Any staff-officer with the rank of major could surely fill any gap left between these two military officers; and, by being placed in Washington, I will be universally construed as a rival to the General-in-Chief, a position damaging to me in the highest degree. Our relations have always been most confidential and friendly, and if, unhappily, any cloud of difference should arise between us, my sense of personal dignity and duty would leave me no alternative but resignation. For this I am not yet prepared, but I shall proceed to arrange for it as rapidly as possible, so that when the time does come (as it surely will if this plan is carried into effect) I may act promptly.

Inasmuch as the order is now issued, I cannot expect a full revocation of it, but I beg the privilege of taking post at New York, or any point you may name within the new military division other than Washington. This privilege is generally granted to all military commanders, and I see no good reason why I too may not ask for it, and this simple concession, involving no public interest, will much soften the blow, which, right or wrong, I construe as one of the hardest I have sustained in a life somewhat checkered with adversity. With great respect, yours truly,

W. T. SHERMAN, *Lieutenant-General*.

WASHINGTON, D. C., 2 P.M., *February* 19, 1868.
Lieutenant-General W. T. SHERMAN, *St. Louis, Missouri:*

I have just received, with General Grant's indorsement of reference, your letter to me of the fourteenth (14th) inst.

The order to which you refer was made in good faith, and with a view to the best interests of the country and the service; as, however, your assignment to a new military division seems so objectionable, you will retain your present command.

ANDREW JOHNSON.

On that same 19th of February he appointed Adjutant-General Lorenzo Thomas to be Secretary of War *ad interim*, which finally resulted in the articles of impeachment and trial of President Johnson before the Senate. I was a witness on that trial, but of course the lawyers would not allow me to express any opinion of the President's motives or intentions, and restricted me to the facts set forth in the articles of impeachment, of which I was glad to know nothing. The final test vote revealed less than two thirds, and the President was consequently acquitted. Mr. Stanton resigned. General Schofield, previously nominated, was confirmed as Secretary of War, thus putting an end to what ought never to have happened at all.

Indian Peace Commission.

On the 20th of July, 1867, President Johnson approved an act to establish peace with certain hostile Indian tribes, the first section of which reads as follows: "Be it enacted, etc., that the President of the United States be and is hereby authorized to appoint a commission to consist of three (3) officers of the army not below the rank of brigadier-general, who, together with N. G. Taylor, Commissioner of Indian Affairs, John B. Henderson, chairman of the Committee of Indian Affairs of the Senate, S. F. Tappan, and John B. Sanborn, shall have power and authority to call together the chiefs and head men of such bands or tribes of Indians as are now waging war against the United States, or committing depredations on the people thereof, to ascertain the alleged reasons for their acts of hostility, and in their discretion, under the direction of the President, to make and conclude with said bands or tribes such treaty stipulations, subject to the action of the Senate, as may remove all just causes of complaint on their part, and at the same time establish security for person and property along the lines of railroad now being constructed to the Pacific and other thoroughfares of travel to the Western Territories, and such as will most likely insure civilization for the Indians, and peace and safety for the whites."

The President named as the military members Lieutenant-General Sherman, Brigadier-Generals A. H. Terry and W. S.

Harney. Subsequently, to insure a full attendance, Brigadier-General C. C. Augur was added to the commission, and his name will be found on most of the treaties. The commissioners met at St. Louis and elected N. G. Taylor, the Commissioner of Indian Affairs, president; J. B. Sanborn, treasurer; and A. S. H. White, Esq., of Washington, D. C., secretary. The year 1867 was too far advanced to complete the task assigned during that season, and it was agreed that a steamboat (St. John's) should be chartered to convey the commission up the Missouri River, and we adjourned to meet at Omaha. In the St. John's the commission proceeded up the Missouri River, holding informal "talks" with the Santees at their agency near the Niobrara, the Yanktonnais at Fort Thompson, and the Ogallallas, Minneconjous, Sans Arcs, etc., at Fort Sully. From this point runners were sent out to the Sioux occupying the country west of the Missouri River, to meet us in council at the Forks of the Platte that fall, and to Sitting Bull's band of outlaw Sioux, and the Crows on the upper Yellowstone, to meet us in May, 1868, at Fort Laramie. We proceeded up the river to the mouth of the Cheyenne and turned back to Omaha, having ample time on this steamboat to discuss and deliberate on the problems submitted to our charge.

We all agreed that the nomad Indians should be removed from the vicinity of the two great railroads then in rapid construction, and be localized on one or other of the two great reservations south of Kansas and north of Nebraska; that agreements, not treaties, should be made for their liberal maintenance as to food, clothing, schools, and farming implements for ten years, during which time we believed that these Indians should become self-supporting. To the north we proposed to remove the various bands of Sioux, with such others as could be induced to locate near them; and to the south, on the Indian Territory already established, we proposed to remove the Cheyennes, Arapahoes, Kiowas, Comanches, and such others as we could prevail on to move thither.

At that date the Union Pacific construction had reached the Rocky Mountains at Cheyenne, and the Kansas Pacific to about Fort Wallace. We held council with the Ogallallas at the Forks of the Platte, and arranged to meet them all the next spring, 1868. In the spring of 1868 we met the Crows in council at Fort Laramie, the Sioux at the North Platte, the Shoshones or Snakes at Fort Hall, the Navajos at Fort Sumner, on the Pecos, and the Cheyennes and Arapahoes at Medicine Lodge. To accomplish these results the commission divided up into committees, General Augur going to the Shoshones, Mr. Tappan and I to the Navajos, and the remainder to Medicine Lodge. In that year we made treaties or arrangements with all the tribes which before had followed the buffalo in their annual migrations, and which brought them into constant conflict with the whites.

Mr. Tappan and I found it impossible to prevail on the Navajos to remove to the Indian Territory, and had to consent to their return to their former home, restricted to a limited reservation west of Santa Fé, about old Fort Defiance, and there they continue unto this day, rich in the possession of herds of sheep and goats, with some cattle and horses; and they have remained at peace ever since.

A part of our general plan was to organize the two great reservations into regular Territorial governments, with Governor, Council, courts, and civil officers. General Harney was temporarily assigned to that of the Sioux at the north, and General Hazen to that of the Kiowas, Comanches, Cheyennes, Arapahoes, etc., etc., at the south, but the patronage of the Indian Bureau was too strong for us, and that part of our labor failed. Still, the Indian Peace Commission of 1867–'68 did prepare the way for the great Pacific Railroads, which, for better or worse, have settled the fate of the buffalo and Indian forever. There have been wars and conflicts since with these Indians up to a recent period too numerous and complicated in their detail for me to unravel and record, but they have been the dying struggles of a singular race of brave men fighting against destiny, each less and less violent, till now the wild game is gone, the whites too numerous and powerful; so that the Indian question has become one of sentiment and charity, but not of war.

The peace, or "Quaker" policy, of which so much has been said, originated about thus: By the act of Congress, approved March 3, 1869, the forty-five regiments of infantry were reduced to twenty-five, and provision was made for the "muster out" of many of the surplus officers, and for retaining others to be absorbed by the usual promotions and casualties. On the 7th of May of that year, by authority of an act of Congress approved *June 30, 1834,* nine field-officers and fifty-nine captains and subalterns were detached and ordered to report to the Commissioner of Indian Affairs, to serve as Indian superintendents and agents. Thus by an old law surplus army officers were made to displace the usual civil appointees, undoubtedly a change for the better, but most distasteful to members of Congress, who looked to these appointments as part of their proper patronage. The consequence was the law of July 15, 1870, which vacated the military commission of any officer who accepted or exercised the functions of a civil officer. I was then told that certain politicians called on President Grant, informing him that this law was chiefly designed to prevent his using army officers for Indian agents, "civil offices," which he believed to be both judicious and wise; army officers, as a rule, being better qualified to deal with Indians than the average political appointees. The President then quietly replied: "Gentlemen, you have defeated my plan of Indian management; but you shall not succeed in *your* purpose, for I will divide these appointments up among the religious churches, with which you dare not contend." The army officers were consequently relieved of their "civil offices," and the Indian agencies were apportioned to the several religious churches in about the proportion of their supposed strength—some to the Quakers, some to the Methodists, to the Catholics, Episcopalians, Presbyterians, etc., etc.—and thus it remains to the present time, these religious communities selecting the agents to be appointed by the Secretary of the Interior. The Quakers, being first named, gave name to the policy, and it is called the "Quaker" policy to-day. Meantime railroads and settlements by hardy, bold pioneers have made the character of Indian agents of small concern, and it matters little who are the beneficiaries.

As was clearly foreseen, General U. S. Grant was duly nominated, and on the 7th of November, 1868, was elected President of the United States for the four years beginning with March 4, 1869.

On the 15th and 16th of December, 1868, the four societies

of the Armies of the Cumberland, Tennessee, Ohio, and Georgia, held a joint reunion at Chicago, at which were present over two thousand of the surviving officers and soldiers of the war. The ceremonies consisted of the joint meeting in Crosby's magnificent opera-house, at which General George H. Thomas presided. General W. W. Belknap was the orator for the Army of the Tennessee, General Charles Cruft for the Army of the Cumberland, General J. D. Cox for the Army of the Ohio, and General William Cogswell for the Army of Georgia. The banquet was held in the vast Chamber of Commerce, at which I presided. General Grant, President-elect, General J. M. Schofield, Secretary of War, General H. W. Slocum, and nearly every general officer of note was present except General Sheridan, who at the moment was fighting the Cheyennes in Southern Kansas and the Indian country.

At that time we discussed the army changes which would necessarily occur in the following March, and it was generally understood that I was to succeed General Grant as general-in-chief, but as to my successor, Meade, Thomas, and Sheridan were candidates. And here I will remark that General Grant, afterward famous as the "silent man," used to be very gossipy, and no one was ever more fond than he of telling anecdotes of our West Point and early army life. At the Chicago reunion he told me that I would have to come to Washington, that he wanted me to effect a change as to the general staff, which he had long contemplated, and which was outlined in his letter to Mr. Stanton of January 29, 1866, given hereafter, which had been repeatedly published, and was well known to the military world; that on being inaugurated President on the 4th of March he would retain General Schofield as his Secretary of War until the change had become habitual; that the modern custom of the Secretary of War giving military orders to the adjutant-general and other staff officers was positively wrong and should be stopped. Speaking of General Grant's personal characteristics at that period of his life, I recall a conversation in his carriage, when, riding down Pennsylvania Avenue, he inquired of me in a humorous way, "Sherman, what special hobby do you intend to adopt?" I inquired what he meant, and he explained that all men had their special weakness or vanity, and that it was wiser to choose one's own than to leave the newspapers to affix one less acceptable, and that for his part he had chosen the "horse," so that when any one tried to pump him he would turn the conversation to his "horse." I answered that I would stick to the "theatre and balls," for I was always fond of seeing young people happy, and did actually acquire a reputation for "dancing," though I had not attempted the waltz, or anything more than the ordinary cotillon, since the war.

On the 24th of February, 1869, I was summoned to Washington, arriving on the 26th, taking along my aides, Lieutenant-Colonels Dayton and Audenried.

On the 4th of March General Grant was duly inaugurated President of the United States, and I was nominated and confirmed as General of the Army.

Major-General P. H. Sheridan was at the same time nominated and confirmed as lieutenant-general, with orders to command the Military Division of the Missouri, which he did, moving the headquarters from St. Louis to Chicago; and General Meade was assigned to command the Military Division of the Atlantic, with headquarters at Philadelphia.

At that moment General Meade was in Atlanta, Georgia, commanding the Third Military District under the "Reconstruction Act;" and General Thomas, whose post was in Nashville, was in Washington on a court of inquiry investigating certain allegations against General A. B. Dyer, Chief of Ordnance. He occupied the room of the second floor in the building on the corner of H and Fifteenth Streets, since become Wormley's Hotel. I at the time was staying with my brother, Senator Sherman, at his residence, 1321 K Street, and it was my habit each morning to stop at Thomas's room on my way to the office in the War Department to tell him the military news, and to talk over matters of common interest. We had been intimately associated as "man and boy" for thirty-odd years, and I profess to have had better opportunities to know him than any man then living. His fame as the "Rock of Chickamauga" was perfect, and by the world at large he was considered as the embodiment of strength, calmness, and imperturbability. Yet of all my acquaintances Thomas worried and fretted over what he construed neglects or acts of favoritism more than any other. At that time he was much worried by what he supposed was injustice in the promotion of General Sheridan, and still more that General Meade should have an Eastern station, which compelled him to remain at Nashville or go to the Pacific. General Thomas claimed that all his life he had been stationed in the South or remote West, and had not had a fair share of Eastern posts, whereas that General Meade had always been there. I tried to get him to go with me to see President Grant and talk the matter over frankly, but he would not, and I had to act as a friendly mediator. General Grant assured me at the time that he not only admired and respected General Thomas, but actually loved him as a man, and he authorized me in making up commands for the general officers to do anything and everything to favor him, only he could not recede from his former action in respect to Generals Sheridan and Meade.

Prior to General Grant's inauguration the army register showed as major-generals Halleck, Meade, Sheridan, Thomas, and Hancock. Therefore, the promotion of General Sheridan to be lieutenant-general did not "overslaugh" Thomas, but it did Meade and Halleck. The latter did not expect promotion; General Meade did, but was partially, not wholly, reconciled by being stationed at Philadelphia, the home of his family; and President Grant assured me that he knew of his own knowledge that General Sheridan had been nominated major-general before General Meade, but had waived dates out of respect for his age and longer service, and that he had nominated him as lieutenant-general by reason of his special fitness to command the Military Division of the Missouri, embracing all the wild Indians, at that very moment in a state of hostility. I gave General Thomas the choice of every other command in the army, and of his own choice he went to San Francisco, California, where he died, March 28, 1870. The truth is, Congress should have provided by law for three lieutenant-generals for these three pre-eminent soldiers, and should have dated their commissions with "Gettysburg," "Winchester," and "Nashville." It would have been a graceful act, and might have prolonged the lives of two most popular officers, who died soon after, feeling that they had experienced ingratitude and neglect.

Soon after General Grant's inauguration as President, and, as I supposed, in fulfilment of his plan divulged in Chicago the previous December, were made the following:

HEADQUARTERS OF THE ARMY, ⎱
WASHINGTON, *March* 8, 1869.⎰

General Orders No. 11:
The following orders of the President of the United States are published for the information and government of all concerned:

WAR DEPARTMENT, ⎱
WASHINGTON CITY, *March* 5, 1869.⎰

By direction of the President, General William T. Sherman will assume command of the Army of the United States.

The chiefs of staff corps, departments, and bureaus will report to and act under the immediate orders of the general commanding the army.

Any official business which by law or regulation requires the action of the President or Secretary of War will be submitted by the General of the Army to the Secretary of War, and in general all orders from the President or Secretary of War to any portion of the army, line or staff, will be transmitted through the General of the Army.

J. M. SCHOFIELD, *Secretary of War.*
By command of the General of the Army.
E. D. TOWNSEND, *Assistant Adjutant-General.*

On the same day I issued my General Orders No. 12, assuming command and naming all the heads of staff departments and bureaus as members of my staff, adding to my then three aides, Colonels McCoy, Dayton, and Audenried, the names of Colonels Comstock, Horace Porter, and Dent, agreeing with President Grant that the two latter could remain with him till I should need their personal services or ask their resignations.

I was soon made aware that the heads of several of the staff corps were restive under this new order of things, for by long usage they had grown to believe themselves not officers of the army in a technical sense, but a part of the War Department, the civil branch of the Government which connects the army with the President and Congress.

In a short time General John A. Rawlins, General Grant's

former chief of staff, was nominated and confirmed as Secretary of War; and soon appeared this order:

HEADQUARTERS OF THE ARMY,
ADJUTANT-GENERAL'S OFFICE,
WASHINGTON, *March* 27, 1869.

General Orders No. 28:

The following orders received for the War Department are published for the government of all concerned:

WAR DEPARTMENT,
WASHINGTON CITY, *March* 26, 1869.

By direction of the President, the order of the Secretary of War, dated War Department, March 5, 1869, and published in General Orders No. 11, headquarters of the army, Adjutant-General's Office, dated March 8, 1869, except so much as directs General W. T. Sherman to assume command of the Army of the United States, is hereby rescinded.

All official business which by law or regulations requires the action of the President or Secretary of War will be submitted by the chiefs of staff corps, departments, and bureaus to the Secretary of War.

All orders and instructions relating to military operations issued by the President or Secretary of War will be issued through the General of the Army.

JOHN A. RAWLINS, *Secretary of War.*

By command of General SHERMAN:

E. D. TOWNSEND, *Assistant Adjutant-General.*

Thus we were thrown back on the old method in having a double- if not a treble-headed machine. Each head of a bureau in daily consultation with the Secretary of War, and the general to command without an adjutant, quartermaster, commissary, or any staff except his own aides, often reading in the newspapers of military events and orders before he could be consulted or informed. This was the very reverse of what General Grant, after four years' experience in Washington as general-in-chief, seemed to want, different from what he had explained to me in Chicago, and totally different from the demand he had made on Secretary of War Stanton in his complete letter of January 29, 1866. I went to him to know the cause. He said he had been informed by members of Congress that his action, as defined by his order of March 5th, was regarded as a violation of laws making provision for the bureaus of the War Department; that he had repealed his own orders, but not mine, and that he had no doubt that General Rawlins and I could draw the line of separation satisfactorily to us both. General Rawlins was very conscientious, but a very sick man when appointed Secretary of War. Several times he made orders through the adjutant-general to individuals of the army without notifying me, but always when his attention was called to it he apologized, and repeatedly said to me that he understood from his experience on General Grant's staff how almost insulting it was for orders to go to individuals of a regiment, brigade, division, or an army of any kind without the commanding officer being consulted or even advised. This habit is more common at Washington than any place on earth, unless it be in London, where nearly the same condition of facts exists. Members of Congress daily appeal to the Secretary of War for the discharge of some soldier on the application of a mother, or some young officer has to be dry-nursed, withdrawn from his company on the plains to be stationed near home. The Secretary of War, sometimes moved by private reasons, or more likely to oblige the member of Congress, grants the order, of which the commanding general knows nothing till he reads it in the newspapers. Also, an Indian tribe, goaded by the pressure of white neighbors, breaks out in revolt. The general-in-chief must reënforce the local garrisons not only with men, but horses, wagons, ammunition, and food. All the necessary information is in the staff bureaus in Washington, but the general has no *right* to call for it, and generally finds it more practicable to ask by telegraph of the distant division or department commanders for the information before making the formal orders. The general in actual command of the army should have a full staff, subject to his own command. If not, he cannot be held responsible for results.

General Rawlins sank away visibly, rapidly, and died in Washington, September 6, 1869, and I was appointed to perform the duties of his office till a successor could be selected. I realized how much easier and better it was to have both offices conjoined. The army then had one constitutional commander-in-chief of both army and navy, and one actual commanding general, bringing all parts into real harmony. An army to be useful must be a unit, and out of this has grown the saying, attributed to Napoleon, but doubtless spoken before the days of Alexander, that an army with an inefficient commander was better than one with two able heads. Our political system and methods, however, demanded a separate Secretary of War, and in October President Grant asked me to scan the list of the volunteer generals of good record who had served in the civil war, preferably from the "West." I did so, and submitted to him in writing the names of W. W. Belknap, of Iowa; G. M. Dodge, the Chief Engineer of the Union Pacific Railroad; and Lucius Fairchild, of Madison, Wisconsin. I also named General John W. Sprague, then employed by the Northern Pacific Railroad in Washington Territory. General Grant knew them all personally, and said if General Dodge were not connected with the Union Pacific Railroad, with which the Secretary of War must necessarily have large transactions, he would choose him, but as the case stood, and remembering the very excellent speech made by General Belknap at the Chicago reunion of December, 1868, he authorized me to communicate with him to ascertain if he were willing to come to Washington as Secretary of War. General Belknap was then the collector of internal revenue at Keokuk, Iowa. I telegraphed him and received a prompt and favorable answer. His name was sent to the Senate, promptly confirmed, and he entered on his duties October 25, 1869. General Belknap surely had at that date as fair a fame as any officer of volunteers of my personal acquaintance. He took up the business where it was left off, and gradually fell into the current which led to the command of the army itself as of the legal and financial matters which properly pertain to the War Department. Orders granting leaves of absence to officers, transfers, discharges of soldiers for favor, and all the old abuses, which had embittered the life of General Scott in the days of Secretaries of War Marcy and Davis, were renewed. I called his attention to these facts, but without sensible effect. My office was under his in the old War Department, and one day I sent my aide-de-camp, Colonel Audenried, up to him with some message, and when he returned red as a beet, very much agitated, he asked me as a personal favor never again to send him to General Belknap. I inquired his reason, and he explained that he had been treated with a rudeness and discourtesy he had never seen displayed by any officer to a soldier. Colonel Audenried was one of the most polished gentlemen in the army, noted for his personal bearing and deportment, and I had some trouble to impress on him the patience necessary for the occasion, but I promised on future occasions to send some other or go myself. Things went on from bad to worse, till in 1870 I received from Mr. Hugh Campbell, of St. Louis, a personal friend and an honorable gentleman, a telegraphic message complaining that I had removed from his position Mr. Ward, post-trader at Fort Laramie, with only a month in which to dispose of his large stock of goods, to make room for his successor.

It so happened that we of the Indian Peace Commission had been much indebted to this same trader, Ward, for advances of flour, sugar, and coffee, to provide for the Crow Indians, who had come down from their reservation on the Yellowstone to meet us in 1868, before our own supplies had been received. For a time I could not comprehend the nature of Mr. Campbell's complaint, so I telegraphed to the department commander, General C. C. Augur, at Omaha, to know if any such occurrence had happened, and the reasons therefor. I received a prompt answer that it was substantially true, and had been ordered by the Secretary of War. It so happened that during General Grant's command of the army Congress had given to the general of the army the appointment of "post-traders." He had naturally devolved it on the subordinate division and department commanders, but the legal power remained with the general of the army. I went up to the Secretary of War, showed him the telegraphic correspondence, and pointed out the existing law in the Revised Statutes. General Belknap was visibly taken aback, and explained that he had supposed the right of appointment rested with him, that Ward was an old rebel Democrat, etc.; whereas Ward had been in fact the sutler of Fort Laramie, a United States military post, throughout the civil war. I told him that I should revoke his orders, and leave the matter where it belonged, to the local council of administration and commanding officers. Ward was unanimously reëlected and reinstated. He remained the trader of the post until Congress repealed the law, and gave back the power of appointment to the Secretary of War, when of course he had to go. But meantime he was able to make the necessary business arrangements which saved him and his partners the sacrifice which would have been necessary in the first instance. I never had any knowledge whatever of General Belknap's transactions with the traders at Fort Sill and Fort Lincoln which resulted in his downfall. I have never sought to ascertain his motives for breaking with me, because he knew I had always befriended him while under my military command, and in securing him his office of Secretary of War. I spoke frequently to President Grant of the growing tendency of his Secretary of War to usurp all the powers of the commanding general, which would surely result in driving me away. He as frequently promised to bring us together to agree upon a just line of separation of our respective offices, but never did.

Determined to bring the matter to an issue, I wrote the following letter:

HEADQUARTERS ARMY OF THE UNITED STATES,
WASHINGTON, D. C., *August* 17, 1870.

General W. W. BELKNAP, *Secretary of War.*

GENERAL: I must urgently and respectfully invite your attention when at leisure to a matter of deep interest to future commanding generals of the army more than to myself, of the imperative necessity of fixing and clearly defining the limits of the powers and duties of the general of the army or of whomsoever may succeed to the place of commander-in-chief.

The case is well stated by General Grant in his letter of January 29, 1866, to the Secretary of War, Mr. Stanton, hereto appended, and though I find no official answer recorded, I remember that General Grant told me that the Secretary of War had promptly assured him in conversation that he fully approved of his views as expressed in this letter.

At that time the subject was much discussed, and soon after Congress enacted the bill reviving the grade of general, which bill was approved July 25, 1866, and provided that the general, when commissioned, may be authorized under the direction and during the pleasure of the President to command the armies of the United States; and a few days after, viz., July 28, 1866, was enacted the law which defined the military peace establishment. The enacting clause reads: "That the military peace establishment of the United States shall hereafter consist of five regiments of artillery, ten regiments of cavalry, forty-five regiments of infantry, the professors and Corps of Cadets of the United States Military Academy, and such other forces as shall be provided for by this act, to be known as the army of the United States."

The act then recites in great detail all the parts of the army, making no distinction between the line and staff, but clearly makes each and every part an element of the whole.

Section 37 provides for a board to revise the army regulations and report; and declares that the regulations then in force, viz., those of 1863, should remain until Congress "shall act on said report;" and section 38 and last enacts that all laws and parts of laws inconsistent with the provisions of this act be and the same are hereby repealed.

Under the provisions of this law my predecessor, General Grant, did not hesitate to command and make orders to all parts of the army, the Military Academy, and staff, and it was under his advice that the new regulations were compiled in 1868 that drew the line more clearly between the high and responsible duties of the Secretary of War and the general of the army. He assured me many a time before I was called here to succeed him that he wanted me to perfect the distinction, and it was by his express orders that on assuming the command of the army I specifically placed the heads of the staff corps here in Washington in the exact relation to the army which they would bear to an army in the field.

I am aware that subsequently, in his orders of March 26th, he modified his former orders of March 5th, but only as to the heads of bureaus in Washington, who have, he told me, certain functions of office imposed on them by special laws of Congress, which laws, of course, override all orders and regulations, but I did not either understand from him in person, or from General Rawlins, at whose instance this order was made, that it was designed in any way to modify, alter, or change his purposes that division and department commanders, as well as the general of the army, should exercise the same command of the staff as they did of the line of the army.

I need not remind the Secretary that orders and reports are made to and from the Military Academy which the general does not even see, though the Military Academy is specifically named as a part of that army which he is required to command. Leaves of absence are granted, the stations of officers are changed, and other orders are now made directly to the army, not through the general, but direct through other officials and the adjutant-general.

So long as this is the case I surely do not command the army of the United States, and am not responsible for it.

I am aware that the confusion results from the fact that the thirty-seventh section of the act of July 28, 1866, clothes the army regulations of 1863 with the sanction of law, but the next section repeals all laws and parts of laws inconsistent with the provisions of this act. The regulations of 1863 are but a compilation of orders made prior to the war, when such men as Davis and Floyd took pleasure in stripping General Scott of even the semblance of power, and purposely reduced him to a cipher in the command of the army.

Not one word can be found in those regulations speaking of the duties of the lieutenant-general commanding the army, or defining a single act of authority rightfully devolving on him. Not a single mention is made of the rights and duties of a commander-in-chief of the army. He is ignored, and purposely, too, as a part of the programme resulting in the rebellion, that the army without a legitimate head should pass into the anarchy which these men were shaping for the whole country.

I invite your attention to the army regulations of 1847, when our best soldiers lived, among whom was your own father, and see paragraphs 48 and 49, page 8, and they are so important that I quote them entire:

"48. The military establishment is placed under the orders of the major-general commanding in chief in all that regards its discipline and military control. Its fiscal arrangements properly belong to the administrative departments of the staff and to the Treasury Department under the direction of the Secretary of War.

"49. The general of the army will watch over the economy of the service in all that relates to the expenditure of money, supply of arms, ordnance and ordnance stores, clothing, equipments, camp-equipage, medical and hospital stores, barracks, quarters, transportation, Military Academy, pay, and subsistence: in short, everything which enters into the expenses of the military establishment, whether personal or material. He will also see that the estimates for the military service are based on proper data, and made for the objects contemplated by law, and necessary to the due support and useful employment of the army. In carrying into effect these important duties, he will call to his counsel and assistance the staff, and those officers proper, in his opinion, to be employed in verifying and inspecting all the objects which may require attention. The rules and regulations established for the government of the army, and the laws relating to the military establishment, are the guides to the commanding general in the performance of his duties."

Why was this, or why was all mention of any field of duty for the head of the army left out of the army regulations? Simply because Jefferson Davis had a purpose, and absorbed to himself, as Secretary of War, as General Grant well says, all the powers of commander-in-chief. Floyd succeeded him, and the last regulations of 1863 were but a new compilation of *their* orders, hastily collected and published to supply a vast army with a new edition.

I contend that all parts of these regulations inconsistent with the law of July 28, 1866, are repealed.

I surely do not ask for any power myself, but I hope and trust, now when we have a military President and a military Secretary of War, that in the new regulations to be laid before Congress next session the functions and duties of the commander-in-chief will be so clearly marked out and defined that they may be understood by himself and the army at large.

I am, with great respect, your obedient servant,

W. T. SHERMAN, *General.*

[INCLOSURE.]

WASHINGTON, *January* 29, 1866.
Hon. E. M. STANTON, *Secretary of War:*

From the period of the difficulties between Major-General (now Lieutenant-General) Scott with Secretary Marcy, during the administration of President Polk, the command of the army virtually passed into the hands of the Secretary of War.

From that day to the breaking out of the rebellion the general-in-chief never kept his headquarters in Washington, and could not, consequently, with propriety resume his proper functions. To administer the affairs of the army properly, headquarters and the adjutant-general's office must be in the same place.

During the war, while in the field, my functions as commander of all the armies was never impaired, but were facilitated in all essential matters by the Administration and by the War Department. Now, however, that the war is over, and I have brought my headquarters to the city, I find my present position embarrassing and, I think, out of place. I have been intending, or did intend, to make the beginning of the New Year the time to bring this matter before you, with the view of asking to have the old condition of affairs restored, but from diffidence about mentioning the matter have delayed. In a few words

I will state what I conceive to be my duties and my place, and ask respectfully to be restored to them and it.

The entire adjutant-general's office should be under the entire control of the general-in-chief of the army. No orders should go to the army, or the adjutant-general, except through the general-in-chief. Such as require the action of the President would be laid before the Secretary of War, whose actions would be regarded as those of the President. In short, in my opinion, the general-in-chief stands between the President and the army in all official matters, and the Secretary of War is between the army (through the general-in-chief) and the President.

I can very well conceive that a rule so long disregarded could not, or would not, be restored without the subject being presented, and I now do so respectfully for your consideration.

U. S. GRANT, *Lieutenant-General.*

General Belknap never answered that letter.

In August, 1870, was held at Des Moines, Iowa, an encampment of old soldiers which I attended, *en route* to the Pacific, and at Omaha received this letter:

LONG BRANCH, NEW JERSEY, *August* 18, 1870.
General W. T. SHERMAN.

DEAR GENERAL: Your letter of the 7th inst. did not reach Long Branch until after I had left for St. Louis, and consequently is just before me for the first time. I do not know what changes recent laws, particularly the last army bill passed, make in the relations between the general of the army and the Secretary of War.

Not having this law or other statutes here, I cannot examine the subject now, nor would I want to without consultation with the Secretary of War. On our return to Washington I have no doubt but that the relations between the Secretary and yourself can be made pleasant, and the duties of each be so clearly defined as to leave no doubt where the authority of one leaves off and the other commences.

My own views, when commanding the army, were that orders to the army should go through the general. No changes should be made, however, either of the location of troops or officers, without the knowledge of the Secretary of War.

In peace, the general commanded them without reporting to the Secretary further than he chose the specific orders he gave from time to time, but subjected himself to orders from the Secretary, the latter deriving his authority to give orders from the President. As Congress has the right, however, to make rules and regulations for the government of the army, rules made by them whether they are as they should be or not, will have to govern. As before stated, I have not examined the recent law.

Yours truly,
U. S. GRANT.

To which I replied:

OMAHA, NEBRASKA, *September* 2, 1870.
General U. S. GRANT, *Washington, D. C.*
DEAR GENERAL: I have received your most acceptable letter of August 18th, and assure you that I am perfectly willing to abide by any decision you may make. We had a most enthusiastic meeting at Des Moines, and General Belknap gave us a fine, finished address. I have concluded to go over to San Francisco to attend the annual celebration of the Pioneers, to be held on the 9th instant; from there I will make a short tour, aiming to get back to St. Louis by the 1st of October, and so on to Washington without unnecessary delay.

Conscious of the heavy burdens already on you, I should refrain from adding one ounce to your load of care, but it seems to me now is the time to fix clearly and plainly the field of duty for the Secretary of War and the commanding general of the army, so that we may escape the unpleasant controversy that gave so much scandal in General Scott's time, and leave to our successors a clear field.

No matter what the result, I promise to submit to whatever decision you may make. I also feel certain that General Belknap thinks he is simply executing the law as it now stands, but I am equally certain that he does not interpret the law reviving the grade of general, and that fixing the "peace establishment" of 1868, as I construe them.

For instance, I am supposed to control the discipline of the Military Academy as a part of the army, whereas General Belknap ordered a court of inquiry in the case of the colored cadet, made the detail, reviewed the proceedings, and made his order, without my knowing a word of it, except through the newspapers; and more recently, when I went to Chicago to attend to some division business, I found the inspector-general (Hardie) under orders from the Secretary of War to go to Montana on some claim business.

All I ask is that such orders should go through me. If all the staff-officers are subject to receive orders direct from the Secretary of War it will surely clash with the orders they may be in the act of executing from me, or from their immediate commanders.

I ask that General Belknap draw up some clear, well-defined rules for my action, that he show them to me before publication, that I make on them my remarks, and then that you make a final decision. I promise faithfully to abide by it, or give up my commission.

Please show this to General Belknap, and I will be back early in October. With great respect, your friend,

W. T. SHERMAN.

I did return about October 15th, saw President Grant, who said nothing had been done in the premises, but that he would bring General Belknap and me together and settle this matter. Matters went along pretty much as usual till the month of August, 1871, when I dined at the Arlington with Admiral Alden and General Belknap. The former said he had been promoted to rear-admiral and appointed to command the European squadron, then at Villa Franca, near Nice, and that he was going out in the frigate Wabash, inviting me to go along. I had never been to Europe, and the opportunity was too tempting to refuse. After some preliminaries I agreed to go along, taking with me as aides-de-camp Colonel Audenried and Lieutenant Fred Grant. The Wabash was being overhauled at the Navy-Yard at Boston, and was not ready to sail till November, when she came to New York, where we all embarked Saturday, November 11th.

I have very full notes of the whole trip, and here need only state that we went out to the Island of Madeira, and thence to Cadiz and Gibraltar. Here my party landed, and the Wabash went on to Villa Franca. From Gibraltar we made the general tour of Spain to Bordeaux, through the south of France to Marseilles, Toulon, etc., to Nice, from which place we rejoined the Wabash and brought ashore our baggage.

From Nice we went to Genoa, Turin, the Mont Cenis Tunnel, Milan, Venice, etc., to Rome. Thence to Naples, Messina, and Syracuse, where we took a steamer to Malta. From Malta to Egypt and Constantinople, to Sebastopol, Poti, and Tiflis. At Constantinople and Sebastopol my party was increased by Governor Curtin, his son, and Mr. McGahan.

It was my purpose to have reached the Caspian, and taken boats to the Volga, and up that river as far as navigation would permit, but we were dissuaded by the Grand-Duke Michael, Governor-General of the Caucasas, and took carriages six hundred miles to Taganrog, on the Sea of Azof, to which point the railroad system of Russia was completed. From Taganrog we took cars to Moscow and St. Petersburg. Here Mr. Curtin and party remained, he being our Minister at that court; also Fred Grant left us to visit his aunt at Copenhagen. Colonel Audenried and I then completed the tour of interior Europe, taking in Warsaw, Berlin, Vienna, Switzerland, France, England, Scotland, and Ireland, embarking for home in the good steamer Baltic, Saturday, September 7, 1872, reaching Washington, D. C., September 22d. I refrain from dwelling on this trip, because it would swell this chapter beyond my purpose.

When I regained my office I found matters unchanged since my departure, the Secretary of War exercising all the functions of commander-in-chief, and I determined to allow things to run to their necessary conclusion. In 1873 my daughter Minnie also made a trip to Europe, and I resolved as soon as she returned that I would simply move back to St. Louis to execute my office there as best I could. But I was embarrassed by being the possessor of a large piece of property in Washington on I Street, near the corner of Third, which I could at the time neither sell nor give away. It came into my possession as a gift from friends in New York and Boston, who had purchased it of General Grant and transferred to me at the price of $65,000.

The house was very large, costly to light, heat, and maintain, and Congress had reduced my pay four or five thousand dollars a year, so that I was gradually being impoverished. Taxes, too, grew annually, from about four hundred dollars a year to fifteen hundred, besides all sorts of special taxes.

Finding myself caught in a dilemma, I added a new hall, and made out of it two houses, one of which I occupied, and the other I rented, and thus matters stood in 1873–'74. By the agency of Mr. Hall, a neighbor and broker, I effected a sale of the property to the present owner, Mr. Emory, at a fair price, accepting about half payment in notes, and the other half in a piece of property on E Street, which I afterward exchanged for a place in Côte Brilliante, a suburb of St. Louis, which I still own. Being thus foot-loose, and having repeatedly notified President Grant of my purpose, I wrote the Secretary of War on the 8th day of May, 1874, asking the authority of the

President and the War Department to remove my headquarters to St. Louis.

On the 11th day of May General Belknap replied that I had the assent of the President and himself, inclosing the rough draft of an order to accomplish this result, which I answered on the 15th, expressing my entire satisfaction, only requesting delay in the publication of the orders till August or September, as I preferred to make the changes in the month of October.

On the 3d of September these orders were made:

WAR DEPARTMENT, ADJUTANT-GENERAL'S OFFICE,
WASHINGTON, *September* 3, 1874.

General Orders No. 108.

With the assent of the President, and at the request of the General, the headquarters of the armies of the United States will be established at St. Louis, Missouri, in the month of October next.

The regulations and orders now governing the functions of the General of the Army, and those in relation to transactions of business with the War Department and its bureaus, will continue in force.

By order of the Secretary of War:

E. D. TOWNSEND, *Adjutant-General.*

Our daughter Minnie was married October 1, 1874, to Thomas W. Fitch, United States Navy, and we all forthwith packed up and regained our own house at St. Louis, taking an office on the corner of Tenth and Locust Streets. The only staff I brought with me were the aides allowed by law, and, though we went through the forms of "command," I realized that it was a farce, and it did not need a prophet to foretell it would end in a tragedy. We made ourselves very comfortable, made many pleasant excursions into the interior, had a large correspondence, and escaped the mortification of being slighted by men in Washington who were using their temporary power for selfish ends.

Early in March, 1876, appeared in all the newspapers of the day the sensational report from Washington that Secretary of War Belknap had been detected in selling sutlerships in the army; that he had confessed it to Representative Blackburn, of Kentucky; that he had tendered his resignation, which had been accepted by the President; and that he was still subject to impeachment, would be impeached and tried by the Senate. I was surprised to learn that General Belknap was dishonest in money matters, for I believed him a brave soldier, and I surely thought him honest; but the truth was soon revealed from Washington, and very soon after I received from Judge Alphonso Taft, of Cincinnati, a letter informing me that he had been appointed Secretary of War, and should insist on my immediate return to Washington. I answered that I was ready to go to Washington, or anywhere, if assured of decent treatment.

I proceeded to Washington, when, on the 6th of April, were published these orders:

WAR DEPARTMENT, ADJUTANT-GENERAL'S OFFICE, }
            WASHINGTON, *April* 6, 1876. }

General Orders No. 28.

The following orders of the President of the United States are hereby promulgated for the information and guidance of all concerned:

The headquarters of the army are hereby reëstablished at Washington City, and all orders and instructions relative to military operations or affecting the military control and discipline of the army issued by the President through the Secretary of War, shall be promulgated through the General of the Army, and the departments of the Adjutant-General and the Inspector-General shall report to him, and be under his control in all matters relating thereto.

By order of the Secretary of War:

E. D. TOWNSEND, *Adjutant-General.*

This was all I had ever asked; accordingly my personal staff were brought back to Washington, where we resumed our old places; only I did not, for some time, bring back the family, and then only to a rented house on Fifteenth Street, which we occupied till we left Washington for good. During the period from 1876 to 1884 we had as Secretaries of War in succession, the Hons. Alphonso Taft, J. D. Cameron, George W. McCrary, Alexander Ramsey, and R. T. Lincoln, with each and all of whom I was on terms of the most intimate and friendly relations.

And here I will record of Washington that I saw it, under

the magic hand of Alexander R. Shepherd, grow from a straggling, ill-paved city, to one of the cleanest, most beautiful, and attractive cities of the whole world. Its climate is salubrious, with as much sunshine as any city of America. The country immediately about it is naturally beautiful and romantic, especially up the Potomac, in the region of the Great Falls; and, though the soil be poor as compared with that of my present home, it is susceptible of easy improvement and embellishment. The social advantages cannot be surpassed even in London, Paris, or Vienna; and among the resident population, the members of the Supreme Court, Senate, House of Representatives, army, navy, and the several executive departments, may be found an intellectual class one cannot encounter in our commercial and manufacturing cities. The student may, without tax and without price, have access, in the libraries of Congress and of the several departments, to books of every nature and kind; and the museums of natural history are rapidly approaching a standard of comparison with the best of the world. Yet it is the usual and proper center of political intrigue, from which the army especially should keep aloof, because the army must be true and faithful to the powers that be, and not be subjected to a temptation to favor one or other of the great parties into which our people have divided, and will continue to divide, it may be, with advantage to the whole.

It would be a labor of love for me, in this connection, to pay a tribute of respect, by name, to the many able and most patriotic officers with whom I was so long associated as the commanding generals of military divisions and departments, as well as staff-officers; but I must forego the temptation, because of the magnitude of the subject, certain that each and all of them will find biographers better posted and more capable than myself; and I would also like to make recognition of the hundreds of acts of most graceful hospitality on the part of the officers and families at our remote military posts in the days of the "adobe," the "jacal," and "dug-out," when a board floor and a shingle roof were luxuries expected by none except the commanding officer. I can see, in memory, a beautiful young city-bred lady, who had married a poor second-lieutenant, and followed him to his post on the plains, whose quarters were in a "dug-out" ten feet by about fifteen, seven feet high, with a dirt roof; four feet of the walls were the natural earth, the other three of sod, with holes for windows and corn-sacks for curtains. This little lady had her Saratoga trunk, which was the chief article of furniture; yet, by means of a rug on the ground-floor, a few candle-boxes covered with red cotton calico for seats, a table improvised out of a barrel-head, and a fire-place and chimney excavated in the back wall or bank, she had transformed her "hole in the ground" into a most attractive home for her young warrior husband; and she entertained me with a supper consisting of the best of coffee, fried ham, cakes, and jellies from the commissary, which made on my mind an impression more lasting than have any one of the hundreds of magnificent banquets I have since attended in the palaces and mansions of our own and foreign lands.

Still more would I like to go over again the many magnificent trips made across the interior plains, mountains, and deserts before the days of the completed Pacific Railroad, with regular "Doughertys" drawn by four smart mules, one soldier with carbine or loaded musket in hand seated alongside the driver; two in the back seat with loaded rifles swung in the loops made for them; the lightest kind of baggage, and generally a bag of oats to supplement the grass, and to attach the mules to their camp. With an outfit of two, three, or four of such, I have made journeys of as much as eighteen hundred miles in a single season, usually from post to post, averaging in distance about two hundred miles a week, with as much regularity as is done to-day by the steam-car its five hundred miles a day; but those days are gone, and, though I recognize the great national advantages of the more rapid locomotion, I cannot help occasionally regretting the change. One instance in 1866 rises in my memory, which I must record: Returning eastward from Fort Garland, we ascended the Rocky Mountains to the Sangre-de-Cristo Pass. The road descending the mountain was very rough and sidling. I got out with my rifle, and walked ahead about four miles, where I awaited my "Dougherty." After an hour or so I saw, coming down the road, a wagon, and did not recognize it as my own till quite near. It had been upset, the top all mashed in, and no means at hand for repairs. I consequently turned aside from the main road to a camp of cavalry near the Spanish Peaks, where we were most hospitably received by Major A—— and his accomplished wife. They occupied a large hospital-tent, which about a dozen beautiful greyhounds were free to enter at will. The ambulance was repaired, and the next morning we renewed our journey, escorted by the major and his wife on their fine saddle-horses. They accompanied us about ten miles of the way; and, though age has since begun to tell on them, I shall ever remember them in their pride and strength as they galloped alongside our wagons down the long slopes of the Spanish Peaks in a driving snow-storm.

And yet again would it be a pleasant task to recall the many banquets and feasts of the various associations of officers and soldiers, who had fought the good battles of the civil war, in which I shared as a guest or host, when we could indulge in a reasonable amount of glorification at deeds done and recorded, with wit, humor, and song; these when memory was fresh, and when the old soldiers were made welcome to the best of cheer and applause in every city and town of the land. But no! I must hurry to my conclusion, for this journey has already been sufficiently prolonged.

I had always intended to divide time with my natural successor, General P. H. Sheridan, and early notified him that I should about the year 1884 retire from the command of the army, leaving him about an equal period of time for the highest office in the army. It so happened that Congress had meantime by successive "enactments" cut down the army to twenty-five thousand men, the usual strength of a *corps d'armée*, the legitimate command of a lieutenant-general. Up to 1882 officers not disabled by wounds or sickness could only avail themselves of the privileges of retirement on application, after thirty years of service, at sixty-two years of age; but on the 30th of June, 1882, a bill was passed which, by operation of the law itself, compulsorily retired all army-officers, regardless of rank, at the age of sixty-four years. At the time this law was debated in Congress, I was consulted by Senators and others in the most friendly manner, representing that, if I wanted it, an exception could justly and easily be made in favor of the general and lieutenant-general, whose commissions expired with their lives; but I invariably replied that I did not ask or expect an exception in my case, because no man could know or realize when his own mental and physical powers began to decline. I remembered well the experience of Gil Blas with the Bishop of Granada, and favored the passage of the law fixing a positive period for retirement, to obviate in the future special cases of injustice such as I had seen in the recent past. The law was passed, and every officer then knew the very day on which he *must* retire, and could make his preparations accordingly. In my own case the law was liberal in the extreme, being "without reduction in his current pay and allowances."

I would be sixty-four years old on the 8th of February, 1884, a date inconvenient to move, and not suited to other incidents; so I resolved to retire on the 1st day of November, 1883, to resume my former home at St. Louis, and give my successor ample time to meet the incoming Congress. But, preliminary thereto, I concluded to make one more tour of the continent, going out to the Pacific by the Northern route, and returning by that of the thirty-fifth parallel. This we accomplished, beginning at Buffalo, June 21st, and ending at St. Louis, Missouri, September 30, 1883, a full and most excellent account of which can be found in Colonel Tidball's "Diary," which forms part of the report of the General of the Army for the year 1883.

Before retiring also, as was my duty, I desired that my aides-de-camp who had been so faithful and true to me should not suffer by my act. All were to retain the rank of colonels of cavalry till the last day, February 8, 1884; but meantime each secured places, as follows:

Colonel O. M. Poe was lieutenant-colonel of the Engineer Corps United States Army, and was by his own choice assigned to Detroit in charge of the engineering works on the Upper Lakes, which duty was most congenial to him.

Colonel J. C. Tidball was assigned to command the Artillery School at Fort Monroe, by virtue of his commission as lieutenant-colonel, Third Artillery, a station for which he was specially qualified.

Colonel John E. Tourtelotte was then entitled to promotion to major of the Seventh Cavalry, a rank in which he could be certain of an honorable command.

The only remaining aide-de-camp was Colonel John M.

Bacon, who utterly ignored self in his personal attachment to me. He was then a captain of the Ninth Cavalry, but with almost a certainty of promotion to be major of the Seventh before the date of my official retirement, which actually resulted. The last two accompanied me to St. Louis, and remained with me to the end.* Having previously accomplished

---

*It is but just that I should account for the other most zealous and friendly officers who had served as aides-de-camp near me during my command of the army.

Colonel James C. McCoy was a first lieutenant in the Forty-sixth Ohio Volunteers, and adjutant of his regiment at the time I made up my brigade at Paducah, Kentucky, March, 1862. I selected him as one of my two aides. He was a brave, patient officer, always ready for work of any kind, was with me throughout the war and afterward, until failing health compelled him to seek relief in Florida. At the close of the war, on the disbandment of the volunteer army, he was appointed second lieutenant of the Fourth Artillery, to enable him legally to continue as a staff-officer, and in fact he remained with me, sharing my fortunes, rising from first lieutenant to colonel, until his death in New York City, May 29, 1875.

Colonel L. M. Dayton was also an officer of volunteers, joined me as aide-de-camp before the battle of Shiloh, and continued with me throughout the war, much of the time acting as adjutant-general. Nearly all my records of that period are in his handwriting. Soon after the close of the war he married a most accomplished and wealthy lady of Cincinnati, and resigned December 31, 1870. He is now a well-known citizen and manufacturer of Cincinnati, Ohio.

Colonel J. C. Audenried was a graduate of West Point, class of 1861, served with the Army of the Potomac, and on the staff of General Sumner until his death, March 31, 1863; soon after which he was sent with dispatches to General Grant at Vicksburg. In July, 1863, General Grant sent him with dispatches to me at Jackson, Mississippi. Impressed by his handsome appearance and soldierly demeanor, I soon after offered him a place on my staff, which he accepted, and he remained with me until his death, in Washington, June 3, 1880. A more honorable, chivalrous, and courteous gentleman never lived than Colonel J. C. Audenried.

The vacancy created by the death of Colonel McCoy was filled, at my invitation, by Lieutenant-Colonel Alexander McDowell McCook, of the Tenth Infantry, one of the most loyal and enthusiastic of the army officers who had promptly, in 1861, joined the volunteers. This officer had been in continuous service from 1852, had filled every commission from second lieutenant up to a corps commander, which by the military usage of the world is recognized by the rank of lieutenant-general; yet, on the "reduction" of 1866, he was thrown back to the grade of lieutenant-colonel, and continued with the same cheerfulness and hearty zeal which had characterized his whole life. He remained with me until his promotion to the colonelcy of the Sixth

the removal of my family to St. Louis, and having completed
my last journey to the Pacific, I wrote the following letter:

HEADQUARTERS ARMY UNITED STATES, ⎫
WASHINGTON, D. C., *October* 8, 1883.   ⎭

Hon. R. T. LINCOLN, *Secretary of War.*

SIR: By the act of Congress, approved June 30, 1882, all army-
officers are retired on reaching the age of sixty-four years. If living, I
will attain that age on the 8th day of February, 1884; but as that
period of the year is not suited for the changes necessary on my
retirement, I have contemplated anticipating the event by several
months, to enable the President to meet these changes at a more
convenient season of the year, and also to enable my successor to be
in office before the assembling of the next Congress.

I therefore request authority to turn over the command of the
army to Lieutenant-General Sheridan on the 1st day of November,
1883, and that I be ordered to my home at St. Louis, Missouri, there
to await the date of my legal retirement; and inasmuch as for a long

---

Infantry, December 15, 1880. He is now in command of that regiment at Fort
Douglas, Salt Lake City.

In like manner the vacancy made by Colonel McCook was filled by
Lieutenant-Colonel Richard Irving Dodge, Twenty-third Infantry, then serving at a cantonment on the Upper Canadian—an officer who had performed
cheerfully and well a full measure of frontier service, was a capital sportsman,
and of a perfect war record. He also remained with me until his promotion as
colonel of the Eleventh Infantry, January 26, 1882. He is now commanding his
regiment and post at Fort Sully, Dakota. Anticipating my retirement, I never
filled his vacancy.

As I have heretofore recorded, at the time I succeeded General Grant in the
command of the army, March 5, 1869, I offered to provide for three of his
then six aides-de-camp, viz., Colonels Horace Porter, Fred T. Dent, and Cyrus
B. Comstock. The two former never officiated a day near me as aides-de-
camp, but remained at the White House with President Grant until their resignation, January 1, 1873. Colonel Comstock did serve in my office until his resignation, May 3, 1870, to resume his appropriate functions in the Engineer Corps.
He is an officer of great ability, of perfect integrity, and is still in the service.

Colonel W. D. Whipple, of the Adjutant-General's Department, also
served on my staff as an aide-de-camp from January 1, 1873, until January 1,
1881, when his services were called for in his own corps, in which he is now
serving, with a fair prospect to become its chief.

I beg, at this late date, to express my great respect for all these officers,
who were faithful, intelligent, and patriotic—not only an official respect, but
a personal affection for their qualities as men, in the full belief that they were
model soldiers and gentlemen, such as should ever characterize the headquarters of the Army of the United States.

time I must have much correspondence about war and official matters, I also ask the favor to have with me for a time my two present aides-de-camp, Colonels J. E. Tourtelotte and J. M. Bacon.

The others of my personal staff, viz., Colonels O. M. Poe and J. C. Tidball, have already been assigned to appropriate duties in their own branches of the military service, the engineers and artillery. All should retain the rank and pay as aides-de-camp until February 8, 1884. By or before the 1st day of November I can complete all official reports, and believe I can surrender the army to my successor in good shape and condition, well provided in all respects, and distributed for the best interests of the country.

I am grateful that my physical and mental strength remain unimpaired by years, and am thankful for the liberal provision made by Congress for my remaining years, which will enable me to respond promptly to any call the President may make for my military service or judgment as long as I live.

I have the honor to be your obedient servant,

W. T. SHERMAN, *General*.

The answer was:

WAR DEPARTMENT, ⎫
WASHINGTON CITY, *October* 10, 1883.⎭

General W. T. SHERMAN, *Washington, D. C.*

GENERAL: I have submitted to the President your letter of the 8th instant, requesting that you be relieved of the command of the army on the 1st of November next, as a more convenient time for making the changes in military commands which must follow your retirement from active service, than would be the date of your retirement under the law.

In signifying his approval of your request, the President directs me to express to you his earnest hope that there may be given you many years of health and happiness in which to enjoy the gratitude of your fellow-citizens, well earned by your most distinguished public services.

It will give me pleasure to comply with your wishes respecting your aides-de-camp, and the necessary orders will be duly issued.

I have the honor to be, General, your obedient servant,

ROBERT T. LINCOLN, *Secretary of War*.

On the 27th day of October I submitted to the Secretary of War, the Hon. R. T. Lincoln, my last annual report, embracing among other valuable matters the most interesting and condensed report of Colonel O. M. Poe, A. D. C., of the "original conception, progress, and completion" of the four great trans-continental railways, which have in my judgment done more for the subjugation and civilization of the Indians than all other causes combined, and have made possible the utilization of the vast area of pasture-lands and mineral regions which before were almost inaccessible, for my agency in which I feel as much pride as for my share in any of the battles in which I took part.

Promptly on the 1st of November were made the following general orders, and the command of the Army of the United States passed from me to Lieutenant-General P. H. Sheridan, with as little ceremony as would attend the succession of the lieutenant-colonel of a regiment to his colonel about to take a leave of absence:

HEADQUARTERS OF THE ARMY,
WASHINGTON, *November* 1, 1883.

General Orders No. 77:

By and with the consent of the President, as contained in General Orders No. 71, of October 13, 1883, the undersigned relinquishes command of the Army of the United States.

In thus severing relations which have hitherto existed between us, he thanks all officers and men for their fidelity to the high trust imposed on them during his official life, and will, in his retirement, watch with parental solicitude their progress upward in the noble profession to which they have devoted their lives.

W. T. SHERMAN, *General.*

Official: R. C. DRUM, *Adjutant-General.*

HEADQUARTERS OF THE ARMY,
WASHINGTON, *November* 1, 1883.

General Orders No. 78:

In obedience to orders of the President, promulgated in General Orders No. 71, October 13, 1883, from these headquarters, the undersigned hereby assumes command of the Army of the United States.

The following-named officers compose the personal staff of the Lieutenant-General: Major Michael V. Sheridan, Assistant Adjutant-General and Military Secretary; Captain William J. Volkmar, of the Fifth Cavalry, Aide-de-Camp; Captain James F. Gregory, of the Corps of Engineers, Aide-de-Camp.

P. H. SHERIDAN, *Lieutenant-General.*

Official: R. C. DRUM, *Adjutant-General.*

After a few days in which to complete my social visits, and after a short visit to my daughter, Mrs. A. M. Thackara, at Philadelphia, I quietly departed for St. Louis; and, as I hope, for "good and all," the family was again reunited in the same place from which we were driven by a cruel, unnecessary civil war initiated in Charleston Harbor in April, 1861.

On the 8th day of February, 1884, I was sixty-four years of age, and therefore *retired* by the operation of the act of Congress, approved June 30, 1882; but the fact was gracefully noticed by President Arthur in the following general orders:

WAR DEPARTMENT, ADJUTANT-GENERAL'S OFFICE, }
WASHINGTON, *February* 8, 1884.   }

The following order of the President is published to the army:

EXECUTIVE MANSION, *February* 8, 1884.

General William T. Sherman, General of the Army, having this day reached the age of sixty-four years, is, in accordance with the law, placed upon the retired list of the army, without reduction in his current pay and allowances.

The announcement of the severance from the command of the army of one who has been for so many years its distinguished chief, can but awaken in the minds, not only of the army, but of the people of the United States, mingled emotions of regret and gratitude— regret at the withdrawal from active military service of an officer whose lofty sense of duty has been a model for all soldiers since he first entered the army in July, 1840; and gratitude, freshly awakened, for the services of incalculable value rendered by him in the war for the Union, which his great military genius and daring did so much to end.

The President deems this a fitting occasion to give expression, in this manner, to the gratitude felt toward General Sherman by his fellow-citizens, and to the hope that Providence may grant him many years of health and happiness in the relief from the active duties of his profession.

CHESTER A. ARTHUR.

By order of the Secretary of War:
R. C. DRUM, *Adjutant-General*.

To which I replied:

St. Louis, *February* 9, 1884.
His Excellency CHESTER A. ARTHUR, *President of the United States.*

DEAR SIR: Permit me with a soldier's frankness to thank you personally for the handsome compliment bestowed in general orders of yesterday, which are reported in the journals of the day. To me it was a surprise and a most agreeable one. I had supposed the actual date of my retirement would form a short paragraph in the common series of special orders of the War Department; but as the honored Executive of our country has made it the occasion for his own hand to pen a tribute of respect and affection to an officer passing from the active stage of life to one of ease and rest, I can only say I feel highly honored, and congratulate myself in thus rounding out my record of service in a manner most gratifying to my family and friends. Not only this, but I feel sure, when the orders of yesterday are read on parade to the regiments and garrisons of the United States, many a young hero will tighten his belt, and resolve anew to be brave and true to the starry flag, which we of our day have carried safely through one epoch of danger, but which may yet be subjected to other trials, which may demand similar sacrifices, equal fidelity and courage, and a larger measure of intelligence. Again thanking you for so marked a compliment, and reciprocating the kind wishes for the future,

I am, with profound respect, your friend and servant,

W. T. SHERMAN, *General.*

This I construe as the end of my military career. In looking back upon the past I can only say, with millions of others, that I have done many things I should not have done, and have left undone still more which ought to have been done; that I can see where hundreds of opportunities have been neglected, but on the whole am content; and feel sure that I can travel this broad country of ours, and be each night the welcome guest in palace or cabin; and, as

"all the world's a stage,
And all the men and women merely players,"

I claim the privilege to ring down the curtain.

W. T. SHERMAN, *General.*

Appendix to Volume II.

UNIVERSITY, WASHINGTON SQUARE,
NEW YORK, *May* 24, 1875.

MY DEAR GENERAL: Now, I suppose, there can be no doubt that your decision to publish your war memoirs was correct. One would have supposed that, whatever else might be denied, your origination of the "march to the sea" would never have been called in question. Yet you see it is! If there is to be a battle upon that or any other point, it is better that it should be fought now, while you who know all the facts of the case are here to take care of your own reputation. If claims that every one has for the last ten years admitted to be just can be called in question now, what would not be possible hereafter?

I do not see with what face the persons who are engaged in this disreputable attempt can proceed. How are they going to get over your letter of October 10th to Grant, or those of the same day to Howard and to Thomas? Surely you would not have presumed, in writing to Grant on October 10th, to say, "Had I better not execute *the plan of my* letter," if the operation contemplated had been advised by him. Nor would you the next day have sent him the cipher dispatch that you did. To the same effect is your letter to Halleck of October 19th, and that of November 2d to Grant. Grant in his letter to you of that same date does not say, "Go on as *I* proposed," but "Go on as *you* propose."

So I repeat, as there is to be a controversy, let it come now. Of course, it is a disagreeable thing to have such an affair on one's hands—an affair which one would very gladly avoid if possible, but I think you are fortunate in discovering what envious rivals are ready to do.

I received from Appletons this morning a copy of the "Memoirs" as presented by yourself, and heartily thank you for bearing me in mind. They have got the book up in very good style, and in that respect have left nothing to be desired. In the course of this and the next week I shall read it through, but I did not care to delay writing to congratulate you on the event.

General Grant could by half a dozen words stifle all these shameful claims, and do you justice. He ought to do so.

With kindest regards to your family, believe me, my dear general,

Very truly yours,

J. W. DRAPER.

General SHERMAN.

WEST POINT, *May* 29, 1875.

DEAR GENERAL: The presentation to me of a copy of your "Memoirs" was no less pleasing than unexpected.

I have refrained from writing until I could finish the book, which I have read with absorbing interest. I feel personally indebted to you for this contribution to history, which will not only enhance your reputation, but, what will be more gratifying to you, will attract the attention of Europe to the achievements of our army and open up a fertile field of illustration to the future students of strategy and grand tactics. I see there are some criticisms in the press, but all lovers of the truth will be glad that you have been faithful in your narration. I can safely say, from my knowledge of the character of some of the delinquent officers, that you have treated them with tender consideration. I am glad to have read your book before going abroad, as it has made clear and well defined my knowledge of operations in the West and South, which before was but vague and shadowy, and will thus enable me to talk intelligently with all officers who may seek information. I wrote a few days since to the Secretary of War about my tour, and mentioned Audenried as a desirable officer to accompany me. The Secretary replied that Audenried had been abroad once, and that he thought it ought to be given to some officer serving with troops. I owe this tour entirely to you, and would be glad to have you suggest some one to accompany me—Alexander might like to go, but I doubt if he would like to leave his family so long. With many thanks for the "Memoirs," ever

Very respectfully yours,

E. UPTON.

NOTE.—Lieutenant-Colonel George A. Forsyth, of Lieutenant-General Sheridan's staff, and Captain Joseph P. Sanger, of the First Artillery, accompanied General Upton on his tour around the world, and have since contributed largely of military knowledge to the profession.   W. T. S.

ST. LOUIS, 1885.

NEW YORK, *December* 12, 1875.

MY DEAR GENERAL: It has often been a subject of discussion between not only officers of the volunteer and regular army, but military critics, as to how far General Lee's plans and movements during the campaign immediately preceding his surrender were influenced by your "march to the sea." Thinking the following extract of a letter written by General Lee, three years after the close of the war, might not have come under your notice, and regarding it as having a most important bearing upon the discussion referred to, being the unprejudiced testimony of the only person who could give the facts and reasons which controlled the movements of the Confederate forces operating for the defense of the Confederate capital, I have made a transcript of the following:

"WARM SPRINGS, VIRGINIA, *July* 27, 1868.
"*General* W. S. SMITH.

. . . .

"As regards the movements of General Sherman, it was easy to see that, unless they were interrupted, I should be compelled to abandon the defense of Richmond, and with a view of arresting his progress I so weakened my force by sending reënforcements to South and North Carolina that I had not sufficient men to man my lines.

"Had they not been broken, I should have abandoned them as soon as General Sherman reached the Roanoke.

(Signed) "R. E. LEE."

Yours truly, G. A. CUSTER,
Brevet Major-General, United States Army.
General W. T. SHERMAN, *United States Army.*

11 GROSVENOR MANSION, ⎫
VICTORIA STREET, S. W., LONDON, *December* 25, 1875.⎭

General W. T. SHERMAN.

MY DEAR SIR: There could be no more desirable gift than that which has just reached me of your (red) second volume from the publishers. I thank you again heartily, and add special thanks for your valuable remarks touching European war. I have nothing at present to offer you in return if it was at all possible to balance such a work, which it assuredly is not. I have been writing a little again on the Prussians, but mainly in the "Edinburgh," which I know is regularly republished with you. The newest foreign thing, however, is Ducrot's little book on "Tirailleurs," interesting mainly as showing how close the best French officers are copying the Germans. I am taking the liberty of sending you a copy, one of the first got over here.

Mrs. Chesney desires me to thank you heartily for the promise of the photograph, for which she will look anxiously. She unites with me in best wishes, and I am always   Yours very sincerely,
C. C. CHESNEY.

P. S.—I ought not to close this without adding that, deep as is my interest in your book, I never thought of *your* campaign as "all confusion." Indeed, may I not hope you remember my lecturing on your Atlanta advance very soon after it had taken place? One part only I had been very doubtful about—your Meridian campaign. I, of course, am the more pleased to now have it fully cleared.

C. C. C.
(*Colonel of Engineers, English Army*).

STAFF COLLEGE, FARNBRO STATION, }
(NEAR ALDERSHOT, ENGLAND), *July* 28, 1875.}

DEAR GENERAL SHERMAN: I have just had the greatest satisfaction to receive a copy of your "Memoirs," most valuable in any case; but my pleasure is greatly increased by the book being your own gift. I shall look with pride at its place on my shelves after my careful and profitable study of it. I was on the point of ordering it from a publisher's when it arrived. The world is greatly indebted to you for furnishing such important and authentic material toward the record of the second great historical epoch of your country, and students of military art owe you much for the clear narrative of matters essential to be known, but generally omitted from the histories of wars. Coming from whatever hand, the details of transport movement and supply would be of great value; but from you, who devised the plans and gave the orders, they are inestimable.

Last September, I and the officers under my charge went through a little sham campaign as training for staff duties, and I afterward published the record of it. I can scarcely expect that a leader who has conducted such famous operations will care to look at it; but I venture to send it for your kind acceptance, as well as a pamphlet I lately published on what may be called the philosophy of outposts, and I should consider it a great honor if you think them worthy of a glance. With renewed thanks for the kind favor, believe me, dear general, Yours sincerely,

E. B. HAMLEY.

SONOMA, CALIFORNIA, *December* 15, 1880.

FRIEND SHERMAN: From time to time I have observed some unfavorable criticism of your "Memoirs," which is accounted for by your just estimate of newspaper correspondents in the closing of your "Military Lessons of the War." Those writers, having found employment on newspapers in every part of the country, never forget or forgive. However, as falsehood and ridicule are ephemeral, and truth eternal, you have the best of it.

I have just finished reading the volumes of your "Memoirs," and find them the most interesting pages I have ever perused. All the facts and circumstances, given as they occurred, are so faithfully and plainly related that they fairly photograph themselves upon the understanding.

It was a wise conclusion of yours to write that book, for I am now well convinced that justice never would have been meted out to you by future historians; the envy of others would have warped their judgment. The fact is, no one else could have given such details, for they could not be concentrated in the brains of any other individual.

If the history of the war was to be written for the schools, yours could not be condensed to advantage; and if for a standard library work, yours could not be improved as far as it goes.

Your triumphs never have been and never will be equaled, your glory will never be dim, and generations yet unborn will do honor to your name. Like every true American, I am proud of you, and take this occasion to say so.

Being now seventy, I am living on borrowed time. I see you will be sixty-two next April. I shall, on the 27th of that month, be seventy-one. Please reply. I want your signature. Remember me kindly to your wife and children.   Your friend,
                                                          A. M. WINN.
General W. T. SHERMAN, *Washington, D. C.*

COLUMBIA, SOUTH CAROLINA, *June* 22, 1872.
General W. T. SHERMAN, *Washington, D. C.*

GENERAL: I have just finished reading your "Memoirs," written by yourself, and have been so much pleased with them that I cannot resist the temptation to write you a line. I never before in my life became so much interested in a book. I could not put it down after commencing it, especially the second volume. It carries with it the stamp of truth in every line, and no one reading it can fail to see it. When your army moved in the spring of 1864, I was a captain in the Seventh Connecticut (General A. H. Terry's old regiment); was captured June 2d, and taken to Macon, Georgia; was there, and never shall I forget the day, when McPherson was killed. Not a prisoner but seemed to feel it as though he had been a brother. The feeling was, I assure you, not confined to Western soldiers. I remember well Stoneman's coming into stockade. When you took Atlanta I was in Charleston. The papers there tried to convince the people that Atlanta did not amount to much anyhow, and it was better on the whole that you should have it. On October 4th I was sent to this place, and with the rest of the officers, about eighteen hundred, sent into stockade on the Lexington side of the Congaree River. I made an unsuccessful attempt at escape on the 4th of November; was recaptured and brought back. Got out again on the night of 28th

November, reached gunboat off Georgetown on morning of December 8th, and was at Hilton Head when you took Fort McAllister. On our passage down the river we laid up our boat in the day and traveled nights, and were furnished with provisions by the negroes, and never knew one to fail to respond with the best he or she could obtain when asked. We had been unable for some time to hear from you, or to know what was going on. I felt sure, however, you would go to Savannah. One morning I came across an old negro with more than ordinary intelligence, and I said to him, "Do you hear anything from General Sherman?" "Oh, yes, we hear young massa talk about Mr. Sherman" (it was and is now to a great extent the custom to call you Mr. Sherman by both whites and blacks, instead of General). "What does he say?" "He says Mr. Sherman cross de river, and dey don't know whar he's gwine, but dat dey got a army behind that can't catch up with him, and de army in front of him can't get out de way." I am much pleased with your plain talk about some of the rebel generals. The feeling of the people in this State toward the United States Government has not changed one *iota*, or toward those who fought in the Union cause, no matter how much they try, and do gloss it over at the centennials, where they are fêted and treated. I have lived here nine years among them, and know. I think every lover of the Union should have in his house your book, and that his children should read it as soon as they can read anything, to see and to know what it cost in life, hardship, and treasure to preserve for them this Government.

Very respectfully, your obedient servant,

JOHN B. DENNIS,
Late Brevet Brigadier-General U. S. Volunteers.

TREASURY OF THE UNITED STATES, ⎫
WASHINGTON, *June* 22, 1875.⎭

MY DEAR GENERAL: I have just finished your "Memoirs." It is the only book, save one, that I have read in twenty years. You cannot imagine how I enjoyed it from beginning to end, for which please accept my thanks.

I was residing in the city of New York in 1846 when the "armed emigration" under Colonel Stevenson was organized, and saw the regiment leave for the Pacific coast. So I was able to follow you all the way through for twenty years to the close of the war of the rebellion, in which you acted so very conspicuous a part, and added so much to the glorious history of our country.

Entertained, instructed, and pleased as I was all the way through your narrative, I was particularly struck with the justice of your ideas and the force with which you expressed them, at the conclusion, in regard to your staff.

But comparatively, the evils flowing from this branch of the public service are to a degree limited, and show themselves in a mild form in the army, while in the civil departments they are intolerable.

The lowest clerk, and even a messenger, in the office proper of the head of a department is considered competent, and authorized to direct the official actions of the chiefs of the various bureaus.

This is utterly subversive of efficiency in the offices, and an absolute obstruction and hinderance to the correct and proper transaction of the public business.

Again thanking you for the enjoyment the reading of your book has afforded me, I am, most sincerely,

Your friend, F. E. SPINNER.

General WILLIAM T. SHERMAN, *St. Louis, Missouri.*

WASHINGTON, D. C., *July* 5, 1875.

MY DEAR GENERAL: Since I parted with you at Columbus, I have read your two volumes of "Memoirs" very carefully, and I cannot let the occasion pass without telling you how much pleasure they have given me. Though the general history of the war was very familiar to me, I read these volumes with a keenness of interest which I have rarely experienced. The fresh and vivid style, the graphic description of persons and events would make your book attractive even were the subject-matter less interesting than it is. While you have very frankly given your opinion of your associates in the war, I do not believe that a just criticism will charge you with doing any intentional injustice to any one. It was not possible that such great events could have transpired without bringing into sharp collision individual interests and opinions; and I believe it is far better that all controverted opinions should be debated while the actors are living. Judging from the effect of your book upon myself, I cannot doubt that it will greatly strengthen the affection with which you are cherished by the American people. With kindest regards, I am very truly yours,

J. A. GARFIELD.

General W. T. SHERMAN, *St. Louis, Missouri.*

ATHENS, OHIO, *July* 12, 1875.

General W. T. SHERMAN.

DEAR SIR: I have from time to time read the ingenious and rather bitter reviews of certain portions of your "Memoirs" by General Boynton, in the *Cincinnati Gazette.*

So much as relates to your published comments and historical statements of the campaigns of General George H. Thomas, and more especially his last great campaign of 1864, I have read with great interest. Neither to General Boynton nor any one else do I yield the palm for devotion to the memory and history of General Thomas. I served under him, often under his observation, from October, 1862, until the end of the war, and until November 22, 1865. I commanded a brigade at Nashville, and served all through his campaigns of that year.

It may be in some degree gratifying to you that, jealous as I am of the fame of Thomas, gratified as I am for his unsought indorsement of my own character as a soldier, and confident as I am that his record is without a blemish, or "spot, or wrinkle, or any such thing," yet nothing that you have written of him and his campaigns do I criticise as untrue, unjust, or even injudicious and ill-timed.

The misgivings you had in your tent away off from us pressed heavily upon us around our camp-fires at Nashville. We who were in inferior positions of command felt, or at least feared, that the long delays were likely to be fatal in the end; and often, between November 30th and December 15th, as I rode along the familiar lines of our army, and saw the solid works of Hood going up, I felt the moments of delay were golden, and perhaps fatal ones to us.

That my impatience and misgiving was without reasonable cause now appears affirmatively; and yet it existed, and was reasonable at the time. Our apprehensions did not take the shape of doubts of the zeal or competency of Thomas, so much as a dread of some obstacles to our progress, of the existence and magnitude of which we did not know and comprehend.

I am, general, your obedient servant,

C. H. GROSVENOR.

KALAMA, WASHINGTON TERRITORY, *July* 13, 1875.

DEAR GENERAL: I have just finished reading your "Memoirs," and want to thank you for that valuable addition to the literature of our country. Many of the critics seem surprised that you should publish *facts* instead of fiction, and I don't wonder, as the latter has become so fashionable. The *facts* of your book will be invaluable in the future to the conscientious historian. I could but wonder at the ill-natured criticisms of some, without regard to your comments on Generals Blair and Logan. Your views of these gentlemen as soldiers are precisely the same as those expressed by hundreds of volunteer officers during the war, and who felt for both those gentlemen only the highest respect and most kindly feelings.

I am sure every soldier who had the good fortune to serve with you in the late war will, if possible, feel an increased affection for you, and wonder that you were able to draw so true a picture of the scenes of which you were the central figure.

Please accept, general, my grateful thanks, and believe me,

Respectfully, your sincere friend, JOHN W. SPRAGUE.

General W. T. SHERMAN, *United States Army, St. Louis, Missouri.*

LOUISIANA STATE UNIVERSITY, ⎫
BATON ROUGE, LOUISIANA, *July* 17, 1875.⎭

General W. T. SHERMAN, *St. Louis, Missouri.*

DEAR GENERAL: I have read your book pretty carefully, especially the chapter on Louisiana.

The book will no doubt prove what you design it to be, a valuable contribution to the future historian who may wish to write of the origin and conduct of our great civil war.

The chapter on California I could almost anticipate page after page. I had heard you talk it all in 1860–'61, and the California story is, I think, the best part of the work. I am sorry you left out Florida and West Point; and it would have been all the better had you gone back to Ohio, and "Nosey Josey," and other old Western characters that you used to have us laugh at.

As to the Louisiana portion of the "Memoirs," it is true in its aim and purpose, and almost faultless even in its details, and you know I had a good opportunity of testing its accuracy. From January 1, 1860, until you left the seminary, in February, 1861, I knew you very intimately, officially and personally. Our isolation in the pine-woods, and messing together, enabled our little party of professors to see and know more of each other than would otherwise have been the case. And, with the exception of a few minor and unimportant details, your account of our school, yourself, and your relations to it and to the State, and of Louisiana affairs generally, as given in your book, is true—given with remarkable fidelity. You may recollect that I staid at the seminary for you during the vacation of 1860, while you visited your family in Ohio. You necessarily wrote me on business frequently, and as the country (North and South) was then in considerable agitation, pending the presidential election, you wrote a good deal also of politics. All those letters I have preserved, as well as those you did me the honor to write me after you had left us in 1861, from New Orleans and St. Louis, as late as May 13th, and they bear you out in what you say in your book on Louisiana. Regarding what I knew of your opinions and intentions, gathered from daily talk and discussions, you were a Clay Whig (if you were of any party at all), and I a Calhoun Democrat; you denying the right of secession, and I maintaining it. I need only say that, for six months *before* Louisiana seceded, you even then, and at all times, denounced secession as *treason*; said if Louisiana did secede, you would resign your superintendency of our school, and go away, and you did so. All the while, however, you expressed the hope that there would be no *secession* of any of the Southern States; and I shall never forget how you received the news of the secession of South Carolina. I happened to be in your room with you when the mail was brought in, and when you read of the actual passage of the formal and solemn withdrawal by that State from the Union, *you cried like a little child*, exclaiming: "My God, you Southern people don't know what you are doing! Peaceable secession! There can be no *peaceable secession*. Secession means war. The North will fight you, and fight you hard, and God only knows how or where it will end!" Yet, even after that, you seemed to have a vague hope that something would take place to bring back the seceding States, and to prevent actual war, and your letters to me show that to have been your hope, as late as April 4, 1861. But all the while, before you left Louisiana and afterward, you said that, if war did come, every *true* man must take sides one way or the other; and, as for you, you would go with the North, or the Union, as it was then understood. Nevertheless, your letters from St. Louis, of April and May, show clearly that you were then checked, or restrained, from actively taking sides with the North, by what you believed to be the *partisan* nature of Mr. Lincoln's Administration, and from feelings of friendship for us in the South. I remember well how it grieved you to leave us, and how sorry were we to see you go, and how great an influence was brought to bear on you to keep you at your post at the head of our school.

Moore and Bragg and Beauregard and Dick Taylor all wrote you most urgently to stay. Some of these letters, left by you among the *official* letters, I recollect seeing as late as 1863. One of a very friendly nature from Beauregard, particularly, I remember seeing there. And General Taylor told me, during the war, that he had thought you would *not* leave the seminary after you had received a certain letter from him. All these gentlemen, so distinguished afterward, seemed attached to you personally, and were very anxious that you should remain as president of our school; and my impression then was, and now is, that they thought you could do so without compromising yourself in politics, or taking actively any part for the South, should war take place. I recollect a little incident at Manassas that tends to confirm me in this view. A few days after the battle, some of us from Louisiana spoke of the false rumor that you had been captured, when Dr. S. A. Smith, our Vice-President of the Board of Supervisors, said: "By *Gemminy*, I wish it had been so; I would like to have a good long talk with him, and then make him go back home to the seminary!" The letters of Beauregard, Bragg, and others alluded to, you might possibly find. Major Gillespie, of Macon, Missouri, says that he removed all the books, papers, apparatus, etc., from the old seminary in 1864, by order of General T. Kilby Smith, of the Federal army, and that General Smith took charge of some of the articles himself. Who knows but he may have preserved those letters? [He did. — W. T. S.]

Any account of the war, however accurate and liberal, must be, to even Confederates, full of sadness. We made a struggle such as history may never tell of again. We lost so much of our best blood, only to *fail*!

There are some few things in your book that I regret. You have mistaken the character of some of the Confederate leaders. If you had known Mr. Davis and General Hampton personally and well, I know you well enough to say that you would not have done them the injustice you have in your book.

The burning of Columbia accounts for itself—one army retreating, stragglers falling behind; the other advancing, bummers in front, Confederate storehouses fired, and *cotton* (which the Confederates were afraid to burn, lest they would burn the town) *unbaled and scattered through the streets*, with *liquor* everywhere! Nothing but a miracle could have saved Columbia from burning. Such is the account given me in 1866, by one who was present, a Southern lad, a son of a prominent New Orleans gentleman; and I have always felt that neither you nor Hampton were to blame, and that there ought never to have been a word between you about it.

Mr. Jefferson Davis, whatever else may be said of him, is a humane, Christian gentleman. He was really opposed to the war, thought secession premature, but, as a States-rights man, went along with Mississippi into the Confederacy, and became, without his seeking, its president. He entered into the great struggle with his whole soul, and *failed* simply because God seems not to have meant us (of the South) to break up the Union! How else can you account for the death of Albert Sidney Johnston, from a mere *scratch*, just in the height of his victory at Shiloh; and the calling back of Jackson, by Lee, when in the act of making his final rush on McClellan at Harrison's Bar, when McClellan says (under oath) he expected to surrender his whole army? And the killing of Jackson, by *his own men*, when Hooker's condition was so desperate at Chancellorsville? And Ewell standing still in the streets of Gettysburg and quietly looking on at Meade slowly and timidly crowning the heights with men and guns? And a *commissioned officer five days slow* in carrying to Dick Taylor and Kirby Smith the terrible straits of General Banks's army and Admiral Porter's fleet at Grand Ecore, after the defeat at Mansfield? And, that army captured and that fleet destroyed, would not the blockade of the Mississippi River have been raised, and Nashville fallen to Hood, and Jubal Early have taken Washington? The issues of war turn often upon trifles too small for man to see or consider; but God observes them all, integrates all such differentials, and uses them for His own wise purposes. He never meant us of the Confederacy to succeed, and it is the duty of every true Confederate soldier to acquiesce in *His* decision; to thank Him for the abolition of slavery, and the preservation of the American Union.

But I have wandered off from Mr. Davis. He had no more to do with the assassination of Mr. Lincoln than you had; and the sensible, far-seeing man he is must, for the sake of his own dear South, have regretted his death even more than you could have done. For then Mr. Lincoln's good sense and firmness had saved the Union; and we needed his kindness of heart and liberal views to save the South. It was a sad day for the South (and for the Union) when Mr. Lincoln was killed (by a crazy actor), and the national government fell into the hands of partisans and demagogues, and cowards and thieves, and nobody knew that better than Jefferson Davis; no one so soon *felt it in his own person*, and ever since, the *outrageous and ignominious treatment* which he received at Fortress Monroe, from men who would have done you likewise, if they had dared—an indignity imposed upon him merely because he was the able and conscientious bearer of a gallant and earnest (though unfortunate) people. I loved Jefferson Davis dearly, and I shall teach my children to love him and to revere his memory.

Please pardon the liberty I have taken as a friend to speak to you frankly, not too fully, about your book. In the last letter I had from you at St. Louis (May 13, 1861), before you had entered actively into the war, you say, "No matter what happens, I will ever consider you my personal friend." I am proud to know that this promise shown to me has been verified, and in all this great country, outside of your own immediate family, there is not one who rejoices more in your personal success and great fame than

Your humble but devoted friend,   D. F. BOYD.

FORT WAYNE, MICHIGAN, *September* 24, 1875.
General W. T. SHERMAN.

DEAR GENERAL: I have carefully read your "Memoirs," and desire to express my admiration of the work as a vivid picture of the great part of the war your experience was made in. It is not to be supposed, indeed it is not possible, that all the actors in their varied scenes should be satisfied with the parts assigned them, neither is it possible that you could have a perfect and personal acquaintance of the circumstances of every portion of your widely extended theatres of movements and battles.

On page 581, second volume of the "Memoirs," it is stated: "General Stanley had come up on the left of General Davis, and was deploying, though there could not have been on his front more than a skirmish-line. Had he moved straight by the flank, or by a slight circuit to his left, he would have inclosed the whole ground occupied by Hardee's corps, and that corps could not have escaped us." I have no copy of my official report with me, but have a copy of the daily journal of my chief of staff, Colonel J. S. Fullerton, written the night of September 1, 1864. I also ask you to read the inclosed extracts from letters to me from General Nathan Kimball, John Newton, and William Grose, to each of whom I addressed a note in order to get their recollections of the day's movements, and the state of the case. I give only extracts, as each of these letters contains private matter only interesting to myself.

In regard to the day's result at Jonesboro', I assure you I felt at the time, and have since felt, as discontented as yourself. I urged the movement in person, and at the time thought Newton unnecessarily slow (I think since he did all he could under the circumstances). The only criticism I have to make is the one made by General Grose, that "too much time was spent tearing up railroads." About 2, or half-past 2, P.M., Colonel Willard Warner came to me and said that you directed that a thorough destruction of the railroad be made. If we had marched on the enemy during the hours we spent burning ties, and making bows and loops of iron rails, we would have ruined Hardee's corps, sure enough. General Thomas never came near me, nor did I meet any one that afternoon who could give me the least information with regard to the situation of affairs. I accompanied Newton's division in its deployment, and urged them on. Just at dark I received a contused wound from a musket-ball in the groin that disabled me for the remainder of that day. I submit these papers to you, with the utmost good nature, to show you that your supposition in regard to the force of the enemy upon my front is a mistaken one. The great difficulty was the dense tangle of underbrush we had to traverse under artillery-fire, and the impossibility in consequence of the ranking generals being able to push the advance rapidly by any personal influence.

I am aware that there was much severe criticism made upon the Fourth Corps at the time, but I have always felt we had a record that could stand a little hammering, and this communication is intended only for yourself.

I am, very respectfully, your obedient servant,

D. S. STANLEY, *Colonel Twenty-second Infantry,*
Brevet Major-General, U. S. Army.

[INCLOSURES.]

Extract from Diary of Brevet Brigadier-General J. S. Fullerton, Chief of Staff, Fourth Army Corps, U. S. Army, for the 1st day of September, 1864.

ATLANTA & MACON RAILROAD, BELOW }
ROUGH AND READY, GEORGIA.   }

4 A.M. — Our working parties commenced to destroy the railroads.

4.30 A.M. — Received a note from department headquarters, of which the following is a copy:

"RENFREWS, GEORGIA, *August* 31, 1864.
"Major-General D. S. STANLEY,
    "Commanding Fourth Army Corps.
"GENERAL: The major-general commanding directs that to-morrow morning early you commence the destruction of the Macon & Western Railroad in connection with General Schofield, who will receive orders from General Sherman.

"You will destroy, as far as you can, in the direction of Jonesboro', or until you meet with General Baird's division of the Fourteenth Corps, which you will probably find engaged in the same kind of work. Should you meet or overtake General Baird, you will report for further orders. Brigadier-General Garrard has been ordered to cover the flank of your column during your march down the road.
            "Very respectfully,
                "WILLIAM D. WHIPPLE, *A. A. G.*
    "P. S. — General Baird struck the railroad at 5 P.M. to-day, and went to work immediately breaking the road.   W. D. W."

5.30 A.M. — Directed division commanders to make immediate preparations to march. General Kimball's division to move down the railroad toward Jonesboro', followed by General Newton, these two divisions to destroy the railroad. General Wood's division to march carefully down the Griffin road (which runs parallel with the railroad) toward Jonesboro', and to take the artillery with him, all save two guns, which are to move with the column down the railroad.

8 A.M.—Kimball commenced to move down the railroad, followed by Newton, destroying the road as they marched.

10 A.M.—Arrived at the point on the railroad where Baird had destroyed it; he only destroyed about three hundred yards of it, and that partially. Went over to report our arrival at this point to General Thomas; this is at Morris Station.

11 A.M.—Found General Thomas; he said he had sent General Wood from the Macon (or Griffin) road to join the rest of the corps at Morris Station, and that, as soon as he arrived there, for General Stanley to put his troops in column, and to send a man on and report his readiness to move to him (General Thomas) as soon as he can. Gave the message to General Stanley at 12.15 P.M.

12.45 P.M.—General Wood has joined the command and started to General Thomas to inform him of the fact; found him near Jonesboro' with General Howard at 2.30 P.M. He sent word to General Stanley to push forward down the railroad for Jonesboro' at once. This message was delivered to General Stanley at 3.30 P.M., and the column commenced to move at 3.40 P.M., General Kimball leading, followed by Newton, then Wood.

4.45 P.M.—Head of the column arrived at a point near Jonesboro', where the enemy was fortified. General Davis's corps (Fourteenth) was then going into position (his formations are made) on the right of the railroad to assault the enemy's works. (Kimball and Newton only.)

4.50 P.M.—Orders were given division commanders to deploy on the left of the railroad, and to advance immediately after their formations were made upon the enemy's position, for the purpose of assaulting the same and assisting General Davis. These orders were obeyed, and the troops commenced to form for advance immediately—Kimball's division on the right and Newton's on the left, while Wood's division was massed close in the rear of our line for support to any part of the same. The troops of the First and Second Divisions made their formations and moved forward as rapidly as possible. In front of the First Division the underbrush was so thick that it was almost impossible to move through it, and Newton could not go before this division. It was necessary to keep up connection with it.

5.30 P.M.—We drove in the enemy's skirmishers after a brisk fight, and Kimball's division came up to the enemy's works at about

5.40 P.M. They were in a strong place, and just beyond a deep ravine, and he thought it not practicable to assault them; he made a feeble attempt to do so, and found he could not succeed. Newton moved up as fast as possible through such thick wood between, it was dark before he reached the enemy. He had completely turned his right flank, but it was too late in the day to accomplish anything.

7 P.M.—We commenced to barricade along our front.

7.30 P.M.—Received instructions to move upon the enemy's works tomorrow morning at daylight. At once directed division commanders to prepare for an assault at daylight, to get up plenty of ammunition, etc. We lost in killed and wounded about one hundred and fifteen to-day. Day clear and very hot. Thoroughly destroyed about five miles of the Macon railroad-track to-day. Took seventy enlisted men and five commissioned officers prisoners to-day.

A true copy:

D. S. STANLEY, *Colonel Twenty-second Infantry.*

Letter from Major-General Nathan Kimball.

SALT LAKE CITY, UTAH, *July* 3, 1875.
General D. S. STANLEY, *Fort Wayne, Michigan.*

DEAR GENERAL: Yours of June 14th ult. was duly received, but, being necessarily absent, I could not answer earlier. I note your reference to General Sherman's "Memoirs," which I have read, and regret that he has made such a great mistake.

Your recollection of the disposition of the enemy's force, and especially as to his position and strength at Jonesboro', to which you call my attention, is correct, as I remember it, and, though I have not my notes, journal, or any of my papers here to refresh my memory, I am certain that General Sherman is mistaken. My division, the First of the Fourth Corps, was deployed, my right resting on the railroad, and joined to Jeff. C. Davis's left. I found the enemy well posted on a ridge, or hill, being the bluff bank of a ravine, and in great force— whether Hardee's corps alone or more, I do not know. Their works or positions extended beyond my left, so that General Newton's division, which deployed and formed on my left, found them in his front, or at least in front of his right. Newton's left came round, when the enemy were yet resisting us, and captured their hospital just after dark. I know that my entire line was resisted by both infantry and artillery. You remember what difficulty I had in getting my battery in position under the fire from theirs. You were slightly wounded at that point just at dark. The line of works, barricade of logs and earth made and occupied by the enemy, continued from the railroad, at a point immediately opposite, to the line of works carried by Morgan's brigade of Jeff. C. Davis's command diagonally to the left along the ridge or bluff mentioned. The only way we could have passed around them by a flank movement would have been to march miles away to make the circuit, and left Jeff. C. Davis's left entirely exposed, and this would have enabled Hardee to turn Davis's flank and attack our line (Davis) in rear. After deploying we met a heavy skirmish-line, which retired to their main line, and fought us with as much determination as they ever did in any engagement. My own impression was, at the time, that the enemy was preparing to move around Davis's left, and believe that he would if we had not come up at the time we did. Their line of works encountered by us were freshly made, seemingly designed to retire to in case of failure to flank Davis, or on meeting a resisting column. Sherman is much mistaken in his ideas of that fight, so far as my division was concerned, and of your movement.

I am, as ever, truly your friend,

A true copy: NATHAN KIMBALL.

D. S. STANLEY, *Colonel Twenty-second Infantry.*

Extract from Letter of Brevet Major-General John Newton.

NEW YORK, June 22, 1875.

General D. S. STANLEY.

DEAR GENERAL: Yours of the 14th came to hand, and I have been trying to refresh my memory of the events spoken of.

Most of the details have escaped my mind. My impression is, that the order to you, having to come through several hands, was delayed in delivery. I remember this, because that, while the facts were fresh in my mind, I defended you against Sherman himself, who thought you were slow in coming up that day.

I remember the difficult ground through which my division forced its way, and how it was urged on both by you and myself, and that no time was lost, but we came in too late, i. e., at dark. I have only a slight remembrance about Kimball's action that day. For him to have advanced by a flank would have been absurd.   Yours truly,

JOHN NEWTON.

A true copy:

D. S. STANLEY, *Colonel Twenty-second Infantry.*

Extract from Letter of Brigadier-General William Grose.

NEWCASTLE, July 2, 1875.

General D. S. STANLEY.

MY DEAR GENERAL: Your kind note of 30th ult. came last evening.

Truly glad and surprised to hear from you. It would do me so much good to see you and talk over old times.

General Sherman's "Memoirs" are creating quite a buzz. I inclose you an extract from my official report of the campaign covering the Jonesboro' day. I always thought the fault of that day's work lay in spending too much time in destroying railroads. From the time I had orders to leave the railroad and prolong line of First Brigade, it would have been impossible, even with a *slight circuit to the left*, to have gained Hardee's rear in daylight of that day by one unacquainted with the situation of the grounds.

Believe me, your humble friend and obedient servant,

WILLIAM GROSE.

A true copy:

D. S. STANLEY, *Colonel Twenty-second Infantry.*

Extract from Report of General William Grose, commanding Third Brigade, First Division, Fourth Army Corps.

ATLANTA, GEORGIA, *September 5,* 1864.

.   .   .   .

September 1st. —Our division marched at 6 A.M., First Brigade in advance, moving on the railroad toward Jonesboro', and under orders spent most of the day in destruction of railroad as we advanced. At about four o'clock, P.M., the advance brigade of our division made junction with the left of the Fourteenth Corps on the railroad at a point about two miles north of Jonesboro', the First Brigade forward in line, its right near or upon the railroad. I was ordered by General Kimball to prolong the left of the First Brigade, which I did without halting until my advance was checked by getting into a thick bramble of underbrush and a swamp in a dense woodland, through which it was impossible to ride, and the enemy, with a heavy skirmish-line in our front, and his artillery in reach playing upon us, contributed to impede our progress. The course or direction when I entered the woods seemed to be about south, and upon emerging from it, at a distance from one-half to three-fourths of a mile, the brigade to my right had shifted to the right such an extent that I had to move right oblique to fill the space, and my left swinging around, so that when my lines came upon the lines of the enemy behind barricades, my front was about southwest, and by the time we got the lines straightened up, and the enemy's driven back, and the position of the enemy discovered, night came on. Yet my lines, Seventy-seventh Pennsylvania, Eighty-fourth and Eightieth Illinois, and Ninth Indiana in front line, pressed forward under a heavy canister-fire from the enemy's guns to within three hundred yards of their barricaded lines, when the fighting ceased at dark. One of General Newton's brigades had moved up toward my left, and his skirmish-line connected with the left of my front battle-line. The barricade of the enemy ceased opposite the left of my lines. During the night the enemy withdrew.

. . . .

A true copy:
   D. S. STANLEY, *Colonel Twenty-second Infantry.*

TOLEDO, *October* 19, 1875.

MY DEAR GENERAL: I have seen it stated in the newspapers that you are preparing a second edition of your "Memoirs," and that you have intimated you would add, as an appendix, the letters of any officers explaining acts or events in which they deemed you had not done them justice. I hope I am not too late to be heard when I advise you to do no such thing. There can be no good reason for making your book the vehicle of unlimited controversy. You are under no obligations to square your account of affairs by other men's memory, or to gauge your judgment of their conduct by their own estimate of it. Your book is your testimony, based on your memory, aided by orders and other memoranda, of what occurred under your own eye and command. As such it has very great historical value, though you would yourself be probably the last man to claim that it is infallible, or that other witnesses will not be examined by future historians. The time will come when not only public documents will be minutely scrutinized, but even for centuries new evidence will be discovered in private diaries, soldiers' correspondence, both Union and Confederate, and in the thousand-and-one unsuspected and unthought-of sources of circumstantial evidence, which will throw strong direct or side lights upon the events of the war. You cannot, if you would, embody all these in your book, and the controversy, if opened in the form hinted at in the beginning of this letter, would weigh your book down with bulky matter, which should be published, if at all, in some other form.

It is to be hoped that every officer who would be likely to contribute to the "Appendix" will give his own narrative of events in which he took part. He need not write a history. A pamphlet in the form of a *"mémoire pour servir"* would find a welcome place on the shelves of every public library, where it will be safe against the day when the case will be authoritatively and judicially made up by an historian worthy of the theme. Meanwhile, however, your book is your contribution to this material, and, in my opinion, it ought to be kept in its integrity as such.

I assume that in the cases in which you have expressed opinions of men's capacity, character, or efficiency, you would not be likely to change your mind by anything they could write. In nearly every instance in which your book expresses your judgment of men, I know from my personal intercourse with you that you held the same opinion in 1864–'65, and at all times since. Such rooted opinions must therefore be accepted as a fixed judgment from which the appeal should be taken, if any one feels wronged, by means of separate publications, and not through an appendix to your book. While on this subject permit me to say further that in my opinion it is too late to consider the question whether on the whole you would prefer not to have anything to say which could wound personal pride or feeling. If you were convinced that you had erred, I am confident you would take pleasure in admitting it frankly; but, if you are not, you owe it to yourself, in all good temper, to stand firmly by what you have said. No omissions from a new edition could take the facts away from the possession of the public. You used your best judgment in giving what you thought it would be useful and interesting to the world to know. We, who know you intimately, know that you have done it without rancor or desire to harm any one, and that you felt that the lesson of the war would not be properly taught if you did not have the courage of your opinions enough to say when a subordinate failed as well as when he succeeded. Instead of omitting anything which you still believe to be true, you should rather, as it seems to me, support your former statement by such circumstantial matters as will more perfectly put others in a position to understand the grounds of your conclusions. There are several instances in the book in which, judging from the impression left on my own mind, I think this should be done.

I have read the book with some care, and I can honestly say I have noticed but a single and that an unimportant instance, in which my memory of your opinion at the time differs from that you now express, and only one in which you seem to have made a slight mistake as to a fact within my personal knowledge. The latter I will mention, as it involves the credit due to another person. On page 629 of the second volume you speak of the reconnaissance made from Rome in October, 1864, to determine the course taken by Hood's army, and say that it was made by General Corse, and resulted in the capture of two guns and some prisoners, besides obtaining the information desired. The guns and prisoners were in fact taken by Kenner Garrard's cavalry, acting under my command, on the northwest side of the

Coosa, Corse being on the southeast side. On first reading the passage, I thought it was a mere typographical error; but, on looking back at your special field order No. 90, I find (what I had forgotten) that Corse was ordered to make the reconnaissance on the southeast side of the river, and *Elliot* (paragraph II) to send cavalry on the other side, which he did by detaching Garrard's division. But from news you had you changed the order after it was written, and directed me orally and in person to follow Garrard out with the Twenty-third Corps, and take command of the whole reconnaissance on that side. We found the enemy's cavalry in position behind a fence-barricade, and at Garrard's request I let his dismounted cavalry charge them, simply keeping my own infantry in supporting distance. Garrard's work was very handsomely done, and I think you will recollect on reflection how pleased Elliot was when I reported the gallantry of the cavalry and their capture of the guns, for you were at the time feeling a little dissatisfied with what the mounted troops had accomplished for a little while before that. We brought you the definite news that Hood was on our side of the Coosa, making toward Resaca. It would be a miracle if in some small matters of this kind there should be absolutely no error of remembrance, especially as the written order seemed to accord best with the statement you have given. It is one of the exceptions which prove the rule.

I need not say what by this time so many have told you, that the country is your debtor for the writing of the book, and that, despite some irritations and heart-burnings, you will in the end find abundant reason to be glad of having written it.

Sincerely yours,
J. D. Cox.

General W. T. SHERMAN.

314 EAST 120TH STREET, }
NEW YORK CITY, *October* 30, 1876. }

General W. T. SHERMAN, *Washington, D. C.*

GENERAL: Having read your "Memoirs," I confess to being disappointed at the entire absence of any notice of the operations of my command (Second Division, Sixteenth Army Corps, Army of the Tennessee) during the Atlanta campaign of 1864. Knowing your high sense of justice, and that it is your intention to correct any mistakes or errors you may have unintentionally made in your first edition, I have the honor to inclose herewith extracts from my military history submitted to the Retiring Board, by which I was retired in May, 1870.

Hoping you will give this matter a favorable consideration, I have the honor to subscribe myself, general,

Your most obedient servant,

T. W. SWEENY, *Brigadier-General, U. S. Army.*

NOTE.—The "Atlanta army" consisted of three separate armies, embracing six corps, made up of nineteen divisions of infantry and four of cavalry. To have embraced these latter in the "Memoirs" would have swelled them to an unwieldy size, and I aimed to limit my narrative to the main armies, with occasional reference to the corps and detachments, leaving to history to collect the details.   W. T. S.

St. Louis, 1885.

Extracts of my Military Record, submitted to the Retiring Board, by which I was retired in May, 1870.

Left Pulaski, Tennessee, with my division (Second Division, Sixteenth Army Corps) April 29, 1864; passed through Huntsville, Alabama, on the 2d of May, and encamped on Chickamauga Creek on the 7th; took possession of Snake-Creek Gap on the afternoon of the 8th, skirmishing heavily with the enemy. At daylight on the morning of the 9th the rebels attacked me with vigor and drove back my advance guard some distance, wounding the commanding officer, Lieutenant-Colonel Phillips, Ninth Illinois Mounted Infantry; but I finally succeeded in clearing the "Gap" and driving them before me into the works of Resaca. I held the heights commanding them the greater part of the day, and was prevented from making an assault by the orders of General G. M. Dodge. Prisoners captured that morning informed me that Resaca was garrisoned by one brigade of infantry and ten guns. Soon after my arrival, however, column after column of rebels came down on the run, and late in the afternoon we received orders to fall back to the mouth of the "Gap" and fortify. My division were the first troops of our army that entered the "Gap."

On the 14th of May my division was detached and ordered to force a passage across the Oostenaula River at "Lay's Ferry." I made feints at two points, one above and the other below the real point of attack, and, while the enemy's attention was distracted, succeeded in throwing a few companies across in pontoon-boats. At this stage of affairs I received information from our cavalry that the enemy were laying a pontoon-bridge at Calhoun Ferry, about three miles above, evidently with the intention of crossing a large force to attack me. At the same time I received a message from our signal corps that heavy columns of the enemy's infantry were moving down on the opposite side of the river in the direction of Lay's Ferry, and cautioned me to be on my guard. I hastily recalled the companies I had thrown across the river, and sent a brigade to watch the enemy at Calhoun Ferry and report positively whether they intended to cross there or not. After a careful reconnaissance I discovered that the enemy were fortifying the other side, but showing no disposition to cross. I saw at once they concluded that that was the real point of attack, and I made my preparations accordingly. The withdrawal of the troops I had thrown across the river helped to strengthen this idea in their minds. At daylight on the morning of the 15th I commenced crossing in a flat-boat I had brought from the other side the evening before, and, when I had two regiments over, commenced laying my pontoon-bridges and fortifying on both sides. The bridges were soon laid, and two brigades crossed, when my artillery was put in position on the north bank so as to sweep the ground in front of the troops on the opposite side, the trees that obstructed the river having been cut down for the purpose. The enemy did not allow me to carry out my plans, however, unmolested. General Walker's division of Hardee's corps made a fierce charge just as I had got my two brigades across, with the intention of driving me into the river, but was handsomely repulsed, not without considerable loss to us, however. I then crossed the Third Brigade of my division, strengthened my position, my artillery remaining on the right bank of the river, and received orders from General Sherman through General Corse, who was with me, to hold the position at all hazards. I knew General Johnson had to do one of two things, as my position threatened his main line of retreat—either to mass heavily in my front during the night and drive me across the river, or abandon his position at Resaca. I therefore threw out a thin line of skirmishers selected for the purpose, with instructions to advance cautiously and feel the enemy and find out what he was doing. The movement commenced about midnight, and at two o'clock on the morning of the 16th I received the report that General Johnson's army was in full retreat south. When General Sherman heard it, he sent me orders to move out at daylight as far as the Rome and Calhoun cross-roads (about two and a half miles) and strike the enemy's flank. I did, and had Hardee's corps hurled at me in order to protect the railroad by which they were retreating. A sharp fight took place here, in which I lost several valuable officers, among them General Burke (Sixty-sixth Illinois and captain in the Fourteenth Regulars) and one of my brigade commanders. I held my position, however, until the rest of the Army of the Tennessee came to my assistance.

.   .   .   .

Engaged in the battle of the 22d of July, 1864, in front of Atlanta, when General McPherson was killed. On the 21st Garrard's cavalry was sent about forty miles south to destroy part of the Augusta Railroad, leaving our left flank entirely exposed. The enemy was not slow in taking advantage of it. Blair's and Logan's corps were intrenched, and my division was moving from the right of the Fifteenth to the left of the Seventeenth Corps, when I learned from a scout of General Thomas that the enemy's columns were then forming in the woods with the intention of making a flank attack on the Army of the Tennessee while they attacked in front at the same time. I immediately moved forward, threw my division into position so as to receive the attack, and, after a severe fight which lasted between five and six hours, repulsed the enemy at every point, capturing nine hundred prisoners, four battle-flags, and killed the rebel General Walker. After the repulse, the Second Brigade of my division, Colonel Mersey, Ninth Illinois, commanding, was ordered by General Logan to recapture the works lost by the Second Division, Fifteenth Army Corps, and still held by the rebels, which they did in a very handsome manner, and recovered Captain De Gress's battery of twenty-pound Parrott guns.

T. W. SWEENY, *Brigadier-General, U. S. Army.*

BURNING OF COLUMBIA.

BEFORE THE MIXED COMMISSION ON AMERICAN AND BRITISH CLAIMS.

(Composed of Count Corti, of Italy; Hon. Russell Gurney, M. P., of London; and Hon. James S. Fraser, of Indiana.)

WOOD AND HEYWORTH
vs.   } No. 103.
UNITED STATES.

COWLAM GRAVELEY
vs.   } No. 292.
UNITED STATES.

Depositions for Defence.

WASHINGTON, *December* 10, 1872.
Commission met pursuant to notice.

.   .   .   .

Deposition of O. O. Howard.

The deposition of O. O. Howard, a witness produced, sworn, and examined on the part and behalf of the United States in the cause above entitled, now depending before the above-named Commission, taken before me, a United States Commissioner, in and for the District of Columbia, at Washington, in said District, on the 10th day of December, 1872, pursuant to a notice to that effect duly given by the agent and counsel for the United States.

Mr. A. S. Worthington appeared on behalf of the United States; Messrs. George R. Walker, Bartley, Denver, Mackay, and Wells, on behalf of claimants.

The said O. O. Howard, having been first by me duly sworn to tell the truth, the whole truth, and nothing but the truth, deposes and says:

My name is O. O. Howard; my age is forty-two years; my residence is District of Columbia; I am a native of Maine; my position is that of a brigadier-general in the United States Army.

Preliminary questions propounded by the officer taking this deposition:

Have you any interest, direct or indirect, in the claim which is the subject-matter of the above-entitled cause, or of this examination? If so, state the nature and extent of such interest.

Answer. I have no interest.

Being examined by Mr. Worthington, of counsel for the United States, the witness further deposes and says:

Question. State what your rank in the United States Army was in February, 1865.

A. I was major-general of volunteers at that time; I think I was not a brigadier-general in the regular army until March following.

Q. What was your command in February, 1865?

A. I commanded the Army of the Tennessee, constituting the right wing of General Sherman's army.

Q. Operating in the State of South Carolina?

A. Yes, sir.

Q. Please state the principal points through which your command passed in the march from Savannah to Goldsboro.

A. The principal portion of my command was transported to Beaufort, South Carolina; thence (marched) northward through

Pocotaligo, Orangeburg, Columbia, Cheraw, Fayetteville; subordinate columns swept into different towns; General Slocum had the left wing; he was at the north of me; mine was the right line of march.

Q. During that march, under what orders from General Sherman were you acting in respect to private property?

A. They were to take such provisions as were necessary for the subsistence of the army, but generally to spare private property, with some few exceptions; cotton was excepted; I was directly instructed again and again to destroy the cotton.

(Objected to by Mr. Walker, as the orders will show for themselves, they being the best testimony.)

A. (Continued.) I will put in evidence the orders I received from General Sherman, and the orders I issued on the subject, if it be desired.

Q. On what day did you enter the town of Columbia yourself?

A. The 17th of February, 1865.

Q. Please state, in your own way, your recollection of the circumstances attending the occupation of that city, and the destruction of a portion of it.

A. On the 15th of February, in the vicinity of Columbia, opposite thereto, across the Congaree, we met with much resistance at Little Congaree Creek, and had to push our way very slowly, the enemy retiring before us; when we arrived opposite Columbia, we found the bridge across the Congaree destroyed by fire; we moved up to where the two rivers, the Saluda and the Broad, conjoined to form the Congaree; the bridge across the Saluda was destroyed by fire by the enemy; we bridged that and crossed our troops; the other bridge, when we reached the land intervening between the two rivers, was still standing, but as we attempted to cross it, it was set on fire by the enemy, and having been covered with rosin, was in flames in a moment, so that even the Confederate cavalry rushed northward to save themselves, some of them without crossing; our troops spent the whole night getting across the Broad, which was a very difficult river; we ferried over a brigade at the beginning by means of ropes and boats; that brigade was the brigade of Colonel Stone, and pushed its way up the hill slowly against the enemy, retiring; the enemy passed through Columbia, and the mayor came to the outside of the city and surrendered the city, I think between ten and eleven o'clock, say ten o'clock; in the mean time a regular bridge was laid across the Broad River, and General Sherman and myself crossed over, riding side by side, before any other troops than this leading brigade had passed; it was about half-past ten that General Sherman and I rode over ahead of all the remaining portion of the troops that had not been ferried over, and rode directly on to the city, a distance of about three miles, entering it in what we called the main street; I believe the name, as it appears on the map, is Richardson Street; it was the one that leads directly to the Capitol; at every corner of the street we met crowds of people, principally negroes; not very far from the market-house we met the mayor of the city, who had a short conversation with General Sherman; as my troops alone were to have charge of the city, I observed very carefully the disposition of the guards of the leading brigade, Colonel Stone's; sentinels were located in front of buildings of any considerable importance, and on the main street the principal portion of the brigade was in rest, waiting for orders; there was only that one brigade; we were ahead of all the rest; near the brigade was an immense pile of cotton; bales were broken open in the middle of the streets, and were on fire; an engine was playing upon the fire, and soldiers and citizens were engaged apparently in extinguishing it; General Sherman was met with much enthusiasm by a company of soldiers; observing them closely, I saw that some of them were under the influence of drink.

Mr. Walker:

Q. How do you know that?

A. Only from the testimony of a great many who saw it. [The statement of the witness as to the rebel soldiers having set the depot on fire, was objected to by Mr. Walker, on the ground that the witness does not know it of his own personal knowledge.]

A. (Continued.) We rode to a foundry where guns had been cast, and observed that, and went afterward through several streets together, when I separated from General Sherman, selected my headquarters, and gave the necessary orders for the thorough care of the troops and of the city for the night. General Sherman took his headquarters at the house of Blanton Duncan, and I mine at a house near the university, belonging to one of the professors; after this disposition I lay down to take a little rest, and was awaked first about dark by one of my aides, who said the city was on fire. I sent the aide, Captain Gilbreth, immediately to ascertain where the fire was, and to call upon General Charles R. Wood, the division commander, who had the immediate command of the city, to prevent the extension of the fire; I then at once dressed myself and went to the scene; there I met General John A. Logan, who was my next in rank, and who commanded the corps; we consulted together, and took every precautionary measure we could think of to prevent the extension of the flames, sometimes ordering the tearing down of sheds and small buildings, protecting citizens, assisting them in the care of their property, and guarding it; much of the property was thrown into the streets; personally I set a great many soldiers during the night to extinguish the flames from the houses, and they went to the tops of the houses where water was passed up to them; nearly everything in my immediate vicinity was saved; a perfect gale from the northwest had commenced about the time we crossed the bridge, or before that, and continued all night or until, I should say, between two and three o'clock in the morning; it seemed at first utterly useless to attempt to stop the flames; they were so hot that many of our own soldiers were burnt up that night; when the wind changed, however, it was easy to prevent any further extension of the fire; it was done; some of our men behaved badly on account of being under the influence of drink, but they were replaced by fresh men as soon as their conduct came to the knowledge of the officer in charge; the first brigade—Stone's—was relieved by another brigade of General Wood's division, and finally the entire division of General Hazen was brought into the city to assist; all the men who misbehaved that we could seize upon were kept under guard until the next day and punished; there were quite a number of our men who had been taken prisoners and were held by the Confederates; they appeared in the streets of Columbia soon after our arrival; I do not know myself where they were confined; the penitentiary was also opened, and all its prisoners loosed; I found, during the night, a reckless mob very often, sometimes insulting ladies, and sometimes rushing into houses and pillaging; I did not see anybody setting fires; General Sherman himself staid up with us for the most of the night; General Logan and General Wood were on the ground all the time until the fire abated, and I believe did everything they could to prevent it. General Sherman's order to me to destroy certain classes of property is a part of our record, and I remember the tenor of it.

[Objected to, on the ground that the record testimony should be produced.]

A. (Continued.) I would like to make it a part of my testimony.

Mr. Worthington:

Q. State your recollection of it, General Howard.

A. It was that certain buildings of a certain nature should be destroyed, such as arsenals, armories, powder-mills, depots; but that private property and asylums so called should be protected. I saw that the wind was so high that it would be impossible to destroy that class of buildings by fire on the evening of the 17th of February, and therefore refrained at that time from putting the order into practical execution; on the 18th and 19th those buildings of that class that were left from the flames were destroyed. I have in my report an accurate list of them; the flames of this burning of the night of the

17th had destroyed a part of these other buildings included in the order. We destroyed also the railroad-track. Though the order was to destroy cotton in South Carolina, yet no cotton remained that I know of after this fire to be destroyed; none was destroyed, according to my recollection.

Q. State what actual hostilities occurred near Columbia immediately before its occupation, if any.

A. We had very heavy resistance on the other side in the vicinity of Congaree Creek, and all the way along; we had also very heavy resistance in crossing the Broad—the last river—the enemy's troops being posted in a very covered position; we hardly could reach them; they annoyed our troops and killed many; then we had our sleeping-camp shelled during the preceding night—the night of the 15th, if I remember correctly—from the Columbia side, from a battery in the vicinity of Columbia; it excited the hostile feeling of the officers and soldiers very much indeed; they thought it was contrary to the rules of war. After we crossed the river there was scarcely any resistance; I think there was none in the immediate vicinity of Columbia after the mayor met us.

Q. Do you know where those drunken soldiers obtained their liquor?

A. I know they obtained it in Columbia.

Mr. Walker: I would like the witness to state how he knew this; whether it is hearsay, or what.

The witness. It was not hearsay; I know the troops obtained it in Columbia; I know they had not any until they went into the city; I have testimony—for I investigated very thoroughly—that citizens carried pails of whiskey along the ranks, and that the men of the leading brigade of Colonel Stone drank with dippers out of pails.

Mr. Worthington:

Q. You have said that you made every disposition for the security of the private property immediately after your entry into the city. I wish you would state more particularly what measures you took for the security of private property.

A. The orders were general as to the manner of locating a brigade or division in a city, and this brigade or division conformed to the general order; I saw them, by my own observation, taking up a central place for the main portion of the brigade, and distributing different detachments to different parts of the city; locating sentinels very much as policemen are located in a city for its care: then I gave verbal instructions to General Charles R. Wood, General Logan not happening to be near me; they should have been given to General

Logan, but I gave them directly to General Wood, and he, doubtless, reported my orders to General Logan; he, at any rate, obeyed the order. Seeing some of these men in the First Brigade under the influence of drink, my first order to him was to send in another brigade that had not had any drink, which he did; my next order went through General Logan, to send a division into the city, which was General Hazen's division; General Logan himself took the immediate disposition of those two divisions; they were under his command and formed a part of it; he had four divisions, and these were two of them; the sentinels I tested myself as to the orders that had been given them, and those in front of houses told me that they had orders to watch against all fires, or against any pillaging parties, and to see that no wrong should be done to private property where they were located; one or two executed the orders so thoroughly that after fire had caught roofs they hindered people from going in, but those sentinels were at once replaced, as it was the effect of the whiskey which did that; I took pains myself, as did my staff, to go about and to see as far as possible that everything was done rightly as ordered, for it was a fearful condition of things with such a fire, and with so many women and children in the city.

I would further say, to show our disposition toward the inhabitants, that, though we were in war, we left five hundred cattle for the people who had been burned out, and who were without food, and also provisions, and had them carted to the State-House, and we also assisted the mayor in a method by which he could get provisions from those outside the city.

Q. Were any applications made to you by the citizens before or during the war for guards to protect their property?

A. Constantly.

Q. What was your reply to them?

A. I always sent them; where we had not soldiers immediately at hand, my aides themselves went; Lieutenant McQueen, one of my staff-officers, stood sentinel the whole night, and protected the property of the Rev. A. T. Porter, of the Episcopal Church, and received his gratitude for it.

Q. Do I understand you to say that no cotton was burned in Columbia by your order?

A. None whatever.

Q. If the fire had not occurred, what would you have done with the cotton in Columbia?

Mr. Walker: I object to all answers to that question, and to all testimony elicited by it.

A. I had no specific orders to burn the cotton in Columbia, and I should not have burned it without consulting with the general-in-chief; if he had ordered it to be burned, I should have burned it; and if he had ordered it to be spared, I should have spared it.

By Mr. Worthington:

Q. Do you know anything about some rockets having been sent up in the vicinity of the State-House on the night of the 17th of February?

A. I do.

Q. State what you know about that.

A. The rockets were sent up by the signal corps; the left wing was quite a distance from us. General Blair's corps was located outside of the city, and one-half of General Logan's, and it was customary for the signal officers attached to each division or corps to communicate with their neighbors as to where they were, or to give any events of the day; they did it in the daytime by flags, and at night by rockets, and this was done at night; the signals meant nothing else, that I know of.

Q. Do you know of any understanding before the occupation of Columbia, or after it was occupied, that it was to be destroyed?

A. On the part of whom?

Q. On the part of anybody?

A. By the officers there was a distinct understanding that it should not be destroyed, and those were the orders; that is, the private property, asylums, etc.; on the part of the men I don't know anything about it; I have no knowledge whatever; they always had to obey orders.

. . . .

I, James O. Clephane, United States Commissioner for the District of Columbia, do hereby certify that, at the request of counsel for the United States, I caused the above-mentioned O. O. Howard, deponent in the foregoing deposition, to come before me at the time and place in the caption mentioned; that said deponent was by me sworn to tell the truth, the whole truth, and nothing but the truth; that said deposition was reduced to writing by me, and was carefully read to or by deponent before being signed by him, and deponent then and there, in my presence, subscribed the same; and I further certify that I have no interest, direct or indirect, in the claim to which the above deposition relates, and am not the agent or attorney of any person having any interest therein.

Witness my hand, at the city of Washington, D. C., this 10th day of December, 1872. JAMES O. CLEPHANE.

. . . .

NOTE.—Judgment in these cases was for the United States. W. T. S.

ALBANY, NEW YORK, *May* 15, 1876.

MY DEAR GENERAL: If you revise your "Memoirs," and wish to strengthen your position regarding the burning of Columbia, you are welcome to my testimony, etc. I was a prisoner of war at Columbia, and escaped at the time, and in the same manner and with Adjutant Byers, author of "The March to the Sea." From time of escape till the occupation, I was concealed in a barn on the outskirts of Columbia, and was an eye-witness to the going out of town of Hampton's troops, and their firing the depot, or surrounding warehouses, previous to departure. I was in the streets of the city before your coming in personally, and saw the cotton burning then. I am, general, very truly yours,

IRA B. SAMPSON,

Formerly Captain Company G, Second Massachusetts Artillery, at time of capture, March, 1864, Chief of Artillery sub-district of the Albemarle, North Carolina, under General H. W. Wessels.
To General W. T. SHERMAN, *St. Louis.*

POMEROY, OHIO, *August* 31, 1875.
General W. T. SHERMAN, *General of the Army.*

GENERAL: In your "Memoirs," giving the grand movements of the war, it is, of course, not to be expected that you could take time to verify all small details. And yet most of the officers as well as men were engaged only in details. It is a matter of little moment to history whether the commander is called Smith or Brown; but to the commander the difference is, whether he really was present in the war or not.

I confess when I first read your book I was vexed, because it looked as if you intentionally blotted me out of the war; not by mere omission to mention, for that might easily happen, but by describing some things I did, and giving credit for them to others.

I certainly was present in your command. From Acworth to the 21st July my brigade was the very whip-lash of the army: it always constituted the very extreme of one of the flanks, sometimes the right, sometimes the left. Though I then commanded only a brigade, General McPherson used to send orders directing me by name to command little expeditions. I had only four staff-officers besides a quartermaster. Yet, from Kenesaw to Pocotaligo, three of my staff were killed outright; one was mortally wounded; one was taken prisoner; and two were sent to hospital, broken down with exhaustion. I was myself wounded on the 22d July; at the time it was supposed to be a mortal wound. The Seventeenth Corps forced a crossing at

Orangeburg; you say it was done by the divisions of Mower and Giles Smith. My division is not named or in any way referred to.

On the 10th February, the Seventeenth Corps lay in camp on the south fork of the Edisto, below Binnaker's Bridge. In the afternoon my division was moved across the river, and two miles beyond. At seven o'clock A.M. next day, I set out under orders to push to the crossing of the north fork at Orangeburg, and save the bridge, but not attempt to cross. I moved so rapidly that General Howard coming up found a gap of four miles between the rear of my train and the head of the next following division. On reaching the swamp bordering the river, I detached the Twentieth Ohio, which double-quicked over the causeway, charging and driving the hostile cavalry so that they could not pause to injure the causeway or the bridges over the small streams of the Edisto. Near the main stream the road bends, and a battery on the farther side of the river commanded the bridge and the road to the bend. I drew the men off the road at this point, and posted the Twentieth Ohio in the water under the trees that skirted the main stream, so as to cover the bridge with their rifles. Four of the enemy, dead, were picked up, and seven unhurt were captured in the swamp. I sent a party under Colonel Wiles, of the Second Brigade, up-stream, and a party from the First Brigade (Colonel Fairchild) down-stream, to find a place for crossing. Colonel Wiles found a place where, by clambering over fallen trees, men could scramble over singly. The other party found a place little more than a mile below the bridge, which, on their report, I went to examine, and found solid ground on our side extended to the river, while the farther side was a stretch of swamp. After supper I reported to General Blair. You and General Howard were both present. The instant I finished my verbal report to General Blair, you said to him: "Yes, the lower place is the place to cross; make your movement there—your feint at the bridge, your diversion above." My division was withdrawn from the bridge in the night, relieved by Giles Smith; and a road constructed for the pontoon train to the proposed crossing. In the morning I marched to the crossing-place. The pontoon-bridge was laid; I crossed over; General Mower's division was brought down to be in readiness in case of need, but did not cross. Emerging from the swamp on the farther side, I formed the division in lines in a long, open field, which extended all the way to the town. The enemy's battery was meanwhile playing across the river, over the bridge on to Giles Smith. I sent the Second Brigade, by a by-road across the woods, to the railroad below the town, and marched with the other brigade on to the enemy's battery at the bridge-head. It then turned its fire on to me, and withdrew as I approached. My skirmishers, dashing on through the town, fired on the train that left with the last of the enemy's infantry. I took possession of the town, and detailed the Twelfth Wisconsin, Colonel Proudfit, as provost guard. When my skirmish-line was passing through the town, and the first brigade was ascending the slope between the bridge and the town, an officer and three men from Giles Smith's division scrambled over the scantling of the bridge (for the enemy in the night had succeeded in burning some of the planking of the bridge without injuring the timbers) and joined me at the edge of the town. The bridge was repaired, and Giles Smith and Mower, later in the afternoon, marched their divisions over it. General Mower stood ready to support me, just as, on the night of the 9th, I stood ready to support him at Binnaker's Bridge, but my division alone made the crossing at Orangeburg; and, moreover, I there saved the bridge, the only instance in your campaign where a contested bridge was saved and used by the army in crossing. I happened to be in advance the day we reached Orangeburg, and so made the crossing there; just as Mower and Giles Smith made the crossing of the rivers when they happened to be in advance.

You say that General Blair, while lying at Pocotaligo, kept General Mower busy making demonstrations upon the river to amuse and deceive the enemy. The fact is, one day General Mower took his division out to make a demonstration, but the country was so overflowed by water that he could not approach the river. Another day I made a demonstration on the high ground near the railroad-bridge. On the 30th January, the day we moved, I was sent to the river to make another. Next day, the Army of the Tennessee lying in camp, I was sent back to where the enemy had a work on the farther side of the river and silenced its fire. The work was reënforced, and kept up such a racket with artillery, that General Howard sent a staff-officer to inquire if there was a gunboat in the river. This was the only one of the four "demonstrations" that amounted to anything. Of the four, I made three, General Mower one, and you name General Mower as the only officer employed.

You give quite a detailed account of the battle of Atlanta of the 22d of July and the preliminary movements. On the 20th the Seventeenth Corps moved out from Decatur, General Gresham in front, my brigade (of General Leggett's division) supporting *en échelon* on his left; the rest of General Leggett's division in reserve. In the skirmishing during this advance General Gresham was wounded in the ankle and sent to the rear. At sunset his division halted at the base of a ridge, and I went into line and bivouacked on its left. The enemy, slightly intrenched on the summit of the hill, kept up a dropping fire through the night, so that I had to change my sleeping-place on the ground, my blankets being cut by their balls. Early next morning, the 21st, General Leggett came to the front and said to me, "I think I shall have to ask you to carry this hill." I made my own dispositions, formed the brigade into two lines with fixed bayonets, sent a skirmish-line dashing up the smooth surface of the hill to distract the fire of General Cleburne's men, who held it. I went up myself with the first line; Captain Walker, my adjutant, with the second. The men fell in groups under the fire, but closed continually on their colors, and swept over the works with a line as precise as on parade. The Twelfth and Sixteenth Wisconsin formed the first; Twentieth, Thirtieth, and Thirty-first Illinois the second line. The enemy fell back along the line some distance, but, as my brigade had no support, and I occupied only the extreme right of their line, they soon returned to the rest of their line, and I was subjected to a severe enfilading fire. I asked General Leggett to send up some twenty-four-pound howitzers attached to the division, and with them cleared out the woods until my men could throw up a line of work facing Atlanta, with a refused line from my right running down-hill toward my rear, so as to protect my right flank. General Leggett then brought up the rest of his division on to my left, extending the line that way, as it was threatened by bodies of troops in front. The night of the 21st I threw up heavy traverses, five to each regiment, and strengthened the works. In the night the enemy abandoned their line; and next morning, the 22d, the Fifteenth Corps moved up to my right, and Giles Smith, having succeeded General Gresham, moved out to General Leggett's left. In the battle of the 22d the enemy rolled up our line till they came to my brigade, intrenched in the traverses, and advanced no farther. In the two days forty per cent. of my brigade was lost. The Twentieth Illinois marched up the hill on the 21st over one hundred and fifty strong. At sunset of the 22d it numbered one officer and seventeen men, but held its place. Captain Walker, my assistant adjutant-general, was wounded. After ten years of suffering, he died of his wounds last winter. While making a tourniquet for him on the field, I was shot through the face. I was brevetted major-general "for especial gallantry before Atlanta on the 22d July"—the only brevet entitled "for especial gallantry" in that campaign. You mention General Gresham as the general officer who was wounded; and go so far into detail as to mention that Colonel Reynolds (lieutenant-colonel of one of my regiments) was wounded, yet my name is nowhere referred to in any way.

I might mention other similar instances. Taken together they all have an air of an intentional exclusion of my name as a participant in the war. Of course, there is nothing of the sort. You simply have not bothered yourself with details. But, if another edition of your book should be published, I hope this memorandum may secure a revision of these matters, of little moment to the world, or, indeed, to history, but of some moment to

Very respectfully and truly yours,
M. F. FORCE.

NOTE.—This may be another instance in which, by attempting to avoid details, which would swell the bulk of my intended volume into too large proportions, I may seem to have done individual injustice. There was not in the whole army a more intelligent, conscientious, zealous, or brave officer than General Force, for whom I always entertained the most profound respect and personal affection. I indorse all he says, have made the corrections, and publish his letter entire in this the final edition of my "Memoirs."

ST. LOUIS, 1883.   W. T. S.

General G. M. Dodge's account of the part taken by the Sixteenth Army Corps in the movement on Resaca. Attack of the 4th of July, and battle of Atlanta, July 22, 1864.

General W. T. SHERMAN, *St. Louis, Missouri.*

DEAR GENERAL: Your suggestion to send you a brief *résumé* of the part taken by my corps (the Sixteenth) of the Army of the Tennessee, in the Atlanta campaign, was received some time ago. I reply as early as possible, in view of absence and other engagements.

I wish to refer to only such parts of the Atlanta campaign as have been to some extent the subject of public comment, through your "Memoirs," and to which my personal testimony may contribute light.

I shall therefore confine myself to the attempted surprise of Resaca, May 9, 1864, and some following events, and to the repulse of General Hood's rear movement at Atlanta, July 22d.

The Sixteenth Corps, as the vanguard of General McPherson's army, penetrated, first, through the Chattanooga Mountains, and made the attack of Resaca. The same corps, while moving to a new position around Atlanta, fell across the way of Hood's army, and met him on such opportunely good ground that the battle was accepted on the spot. I have never published my official report of the operations of the corps. I state these general facts to save you the trouble of explaining them again if you should ever make use of this letter. Your rapid and general summary of a maze of events, in which the part of a corps is more or less lost in the movement of several armies, has attracted my admiration for its clearness, and I can well see how the limitations of your book have compelled a severe distribution of prominence to the many detachments.

The left wing of the Sixteenth Corps (Dodge's), the other wing not being in this campaign, arrived at Chattanooga May 5th, in the evening, in the cars, the batteries and transportation following by road from Pulaski, Tennessee, and Athens, Alabama.

The same evening General McPherson's orders arrived to take the initiative for his army, and to move to Gordon's Mills. While marching there the next day, verbal orders came to push a portion of my command forward toward Villanow, and seize Ship's Gap. Sprague's brigade, of the Fourth Division, did this at midnight of the same day, and the next day we had passed through and occupied Villanow.

The third day (May 8th) my command, with the Second Division in advance, moved rapidly to Snake-Creek Gap, one day before my orders had contemplated, they advising me to march when the Fifteenth Army Corps had closed upon me. I had heard from General McPherson personally, however, that the object was to threaten Johnston's flank and communications, and the Ninth Illinois Mounted Infantry, supported by the Thirty-ninth Iowa Infantry, went forward through the gap to Sugar-Creek Valley, a portion of the corps without transportation following, and intrenching that night, thus holding its eastern outlet. On the evening of May 8th, instead of May 9th, I was astonished to find this strong position, the side-gate to Johnston's rear, not only undefended but unoccupied, though a few men might have held it long. Having reported the fact to General McPherson, and also that Colonel Phillips reported Resaca occupied by a brigade of the enemy, I received his orders to march at six o'clock next morning, the 9th of May, toward Resaca, and to advance as far as Rome cross-roads in Sugar-Creek Valley, and there await specific orders and instructions. The object of the movement was stated to be a demonstration upon Resaca, while other troops cut the railroad north of that place.

At daylight on the 9th my advance, as before—a regiment of mounted infantry, supported by a regiment of infantry—was attacked by Ferguson's brigade of the enemy's cavalry, and Colonel Phillips was severely wounded. We drove the enemy rapidly before us to Rome cross-roads, where I received orders to advance upon Resaca, to press forward until I should succeed in developing the enemy in line of battle, or in his fortifications, but not to attack him there without orders. I was also ordered to hold the Calhoun and

Dalton cross-roads, about two miles west of Resaca, if I became possessed of it, until the Fifteenth Army Corps arrived. These orders were obeyed, my force skirmishing heavily the entire distance to the Calhoun cross-roads.

The enemy was discovered in line of battle on a bald hill, three-quarters of a mile west of Resaca, and also in his works at Resaca.

I placed the Fourth Division at the cross-roads, formed the Second Division in two lines, and carried the hill, and holding there under instructions, awaited my orders from General McPherson, to whom I had promptly reported, sending, I think, my staff-officer, Captain Edward Jonas, telling General McPherson that, if we could make a prompt attack, we could carry Resaca, as the enemy in my front gave way readily, and that though prisoners had reported the arrival of Canty's brigade, the night before, I did not believe it, as no such force as a division showed in our front. General McPherson soon came upon the ground in person; he directed me to send some mounted men up the Dalton road to reconnoitre the country, and find an approach to the railroad, while he would go back and bring up the Fifteenth (Logan's) Corps. Until that corps arrived, I was to hold the bald hill indicated, and the Dalton and Calhoun cross-roads. I sent all the mounted men I had with me at the time, eighteen in number (of the Ninth Illinois), under Captain Hughes. They proceeded toward Dalton, struck the railroad two miles south of Tilton, and found it strongly patrolled by cavalry; they cut the telegraph-wires, burned a wood station, and reported to me again at dark. Meantime the enemy came marching out of Resaca up the Dalton Railroad, and I ordered the Fourth Division to march from Calhoun cross-roads and to intercept them, and to take position on the railroad north of Resaca. This order was reported to General McPherson promptly; he replied that I must hold the cross-roads until relieved. It was about four o'clock when I finally received from one of General McPherson's staff-officers the information that the Fifteenth Army Corps was closing up, and that I was now at liberty to carry out my movement against the railroad. It was intrusted by me to General Veatch, with Fuller's and Sprague's brigades of his division, the Fourth. The Second Division was stationed on the bald hill I had occupied about noon, and the left of this division was now assailed with musketry, while the marching division was fired upon as they advanced in column in full view of the enemy. Fuller, in the advance, moved with spirit across the west fork of Mill Creek, crossed an open field, and the skirmish-line was up to the timber skirting the railroad, when another order came from General McPherson to look well to my right, as the enemy was massing to strike me there. I was with Fuller's advance at this time, and the enemy that had come out of Resaca had opened on Fuller's troops in the open field. Near by was a good cover of woods on the east side of the creek, to attain which I changed the direction of Fuller's column more to the north; his skirmish-line took some prisoners; the morning rumor was confirmed by them that Canty's brigade had arrived. Fuller steadily advanced, however, and as soon as his skirmish-lines debouched from the woods, a regiment of the enemy's infantry and a battery in position opened directly upon his right and front. Another notice had been received from General McPherson, as we got to the roads, that Sprague's brigade was not following us, having been arrested by him to hold the space between the Second and the advance of the Fourth Division. While Fuller was executing the movement to gain the railroad, a final order came to me from General McPherson to halt the column, and to repair in person to him back of the bald hill occupied by the Second Division. There I found General McPherson and General Logan with the advance of Logan's Fifteenth Corps. They were discussing the propriety of an attack upon Resaca. General Logan asked me what I thought of the situation, and if we could carry the place. I replied, I thought we could. Logan responded that he was glad I had so much faith. McPherson appeared to feel the responsibility of his orders from the commander of the army, as well as the responsibility of holding the gap we had already seized. He listened attentively to the conversation, to my description of the position, and to the nature of the orders I had given. He reluctantly gave us orders to immediately return. The Sixteenth Corps withdrew over the eight miles they had already marched that day, reaching the eastern *débouche* of the gap at midnight. I had with the entire corps only seventeen wagons since leaving Chattanooga. My transportation had not yet come up, and the men and the animals had been without other food for a day and a half than what could be afforded by the poor and picked country we had marched over.

A day or two after our return to the gap, General McPherson stated to me the contents of a letter or letters from General Sherman commenting upon the march to Resaca. He seemed to feel that their criticism amounted to censure, but he had assumed the responsibility. He said a part of one of his corps was still west of the gap, guarding trains, that he could not have thrown his whole force across the railroad, as they were situated, and that he looked for his vindication to the successful termination of the campaign. He said: "We had ascertained, from prisoners taken the day of the advance to Resaca, that the enemy knew just what force had passed through the

gap, and where the balance of the army was. He made the final decision to return to the gap between five and six o'clock in the afternoon, being satisfied nothing could be accomplished by attacking an
intrenched post that late in the day."

At Snake-Creek Gap we waited three days, seeing the whole army
move through the pass we had captured "to Johnston's complete surprise," and fortifying Sugar-Creek Valley. May 13th, the Fourth Division of my corps formed on the right of the Fifteenth Corps, resting
on the Oostenaula River, and took part in the attack on Resaca. My
second division, Sweeney's, May 14th went on to Lay's Ferry, below
Resaca, to cross the Oostenaula River and threaten Johnston's communications. General Rice with the advanced brigade crossed in the
face of Walker's division. As soon as this movement in the rear was
accomplished, Johnston began to retreat from Resaca, which he had
defended a second time, and now with his whole army, and which
he "only evacuated because his safety demanded it."

Attack of July 4, 1864.

I desire only to refer to the action of July 4th, described in the
"Memoirs" as "noisy but not desperate."

The Fourth Division of my corps, under General Fuller, pressed
forward on that day, crossing the Nickajack Creek at Ruff's Mill,
driving the enemy before us, until, after two miles of skirmishing,
we developed him in strong intrenchments, and in very heavy
force. The "Memoirs" imply that this was the head of column of
the Army of the Cumberland, and unintentionally leave it to be
inferred that the storming of the works was General Thomas's performance. It was General McPherson who sent me a message to attack at discretion, or if I thought I could carry the works. Prisoners
informed me that Hood's corps was before me, and I proceeded to
reconnoitre their works, which I found very strong, but, as I observed a singular confusion there, indicative of retreating, and knew
that the 4th of July would be a good day to assault, I formed a
charging column of a part of the Fourth Division, the Thirty-ninth
and Twenty-seventh Ohio, and the Sixty-fourth Illinois Infantry of
my corps, under command of Colonel E. F. Noyes. A supporting
column was made up of the Sixty-sixth Illinois and the Second Iowa
infantry, of the Second Division. Noyes moved forward with gallantry, although he fell at the first fire, and lost his leg, but through
almost impenetrable abatis and fallen timber, the men went over the
intrenchments, and took one hundred prisoners, and they so settled
the enemy's confusion, if any there was, that the whole of that line
was soon abandoned.

I come, now, to the last subject of my letter, the battle of the 22d of July, where General McPherson lost his life.

Battle of Atlanta.

The movement ordered by General Sherman, of the transfer of the Army of the Tennessee from the right to the extreme left of the combined armies, began June 9th.

Marching from Sand Town, by the rear to the left, on the 9th of July, the Sixteenth Corps bivouacked, at ten o'clock at night, near Marietta, continued on, at three o'clock, in the dark of the morning, and that second day had crossed the Chattahoochee, spanned it with a foot-bridge, seven hundred feet long, covered it with a long *tête-du-pont*, and intrenched on the Atlanta side. The march was thirty-one miles, the heat was intense, yet the men were uncomplaining and ardent, and for nearly three days more they worked in reliefs of one thousand in the mud and water until we completed, July 13th, at Roswell, Georgia, a double-track trestle-bridge, fourteen feet high and seven hundred and ten feet long. The material used was standing timber and some cotton-mills; over this bridge the entire Army of the Tennessee, with trains and artillery, passed.

On the 17th the command moved toward Decatur, cutting a new road so as not to infringe upon the Seventeenth and Twenty-third corps, which took the old roads; keeping its communication with those corps, the Sixteenth advanced behind its pioneers, preceded by the Ninth Illinois mounted infantry, which skirmished with the enemy at Nancy's Creek, and drove them across; and here, one of my scouts, who had left Atlanta that morning, brought the first intelligence of Hood's having superseded Johnston, which was at once sent to Generals Sherman and McPherson. Decatur was occupied July 19th, after a heavy skirmish and artillery-fighting, and Colonel Sprague, with Second Brigade of Fourth Division, was placed there to relieve General Garrard's cavalry division and guard the trains. As we approached Atlanta the converging corps forced the Sixteenth Corps out of line, and a series of transfers began. On the 21st of July General Fuller, with First Brigade, Fourth Division, was put in reserve to the Seventeenth Army Corps, and United States Regular Battery F, of the Fourth Division, was put in front line of General Giles A. Smith's division of the Seventeenth Corps. My second division, under General Sweeny, moved forward three quarters of a mile beyond its old position, to a range of hills, the enemy contesting this advance very sharply, and intrenched there. At four o'clock the next morning General Sweeny reported to me that the enemy had disappeared from his front; whereupon I ordered him to push forward a heavy skirmish-line. He soon found the enemy in force, in works surrounding Atlanta. The Second Division being displaced by the contraction of the lines, and the Fifteenth and Twenty-third Corps closing upon each other, General McPherson ordered me to move to the left of the army, and place Fuller's first brigade on the left of the new position to be assumed by the Seventeenth Corps, and hold the rest of the command in reserve on the extreme left. Before this was done, I rode with General McPherson from his headquarters to the front on the direct Decatur and Atlanta road. It was quite early in the morning, the day of the battle of Atlanta. The sudden evacuation of the enemy was surprising to both of us, and gave General McPherson serious concern. He requested me to return immediately to my command, and get the troops upon the ground they were to occupy, and first to examine that ground myself, and choose a position on the left of the Seventeenth Corps, and also to feel toward the wagon-road running from Atlanta south. I started at once. There was a cross-road leading to the left from the Atlanta road, in the rear of the Fifteenth, and passing through the left of the Seventeenth Army Corps, by which I gave orders for the Sixteenth Corps to march, while I went forward rapidly with my engineers and a part of my staff to select the new position. I rode out beyond the Seventeenth Corps, far in the advance, and within easy musket-range of the works of Atlanta, passing the pioneers of the Seventeenth Corps intrenching the new line. The stillness was oppressive, and, I thought, almost ominous. I could plainly see the enemy's troops working on their fortifications, on the south side of Atlanta, and they allowed myself and staff to approach within easy musket-range, not firing upon us until we turned about to return, after having picked out the ground for the corps. As we retired, the enemy opened on us briskly with musket and artillery. I at once sent word to General Fuller to send out working-parties to intrench his line on the new position, and for the Second Division to move to the rear of the Seventeenth Army Corps and bivouac.

While passing through the Seventeenth Army Corps, I left an order for Murray's Second United States Battery to join its command, and also met General Giles A. Smith, commanding the left division of the Seventeenth Army Corps, who told me that the Seventeenth Corps would not move into their new position until night. Immediately on receiving this information I sent General Sweeny orders to halt and bivouac his division (the Second) where he then was, viz., about three-fourths of a mile in the rear of the Fifteenth Army Corps (General Logan's), and on the right and rear of the Seventeenth

(General Blair's). At noon I reached General Fuller's headquarters, in the rear of the Seventeenth Corps, and almost directly on an extension of the line of Sweeny's division, which had halted upon receiving my order, and was resting by the road-side. While at Fuller's headquarters I heard straggling shots fired to the east and to the left of General Sweeny's division, which warned me, and I ordered General Fuller to put his command immediately in position, and spoke to him of the gap that existed of about one-quarter of a mile between him and General Giles A. Smith, and of the exposed condition of the left flank of our army. I called his attention to the position of the ammunition-train of the army on the right of Fuller and in the rear of General Smith, where they were very much exposed; but I had scarcely given General Fuller his orders, when the report came in that the enemy was in force in our rear, and developing far behind General Sweeny. I sent a staff-officer to General Sweeny on the minute, with orders to immediately close on Fuller, and to form to repel an attack. General Sweeny anticipated the order, and had already sent forward skirmishers in the direction of the enemy's fire, and he developed the enemy in large force. The Second Division had just got into position when Hood's army appeared in force, advancing in three columns. I waited until the enemy was fully developed, then dispatched a staff-officer to General Giles A. Smith, telling him that the enemy was attacking in his rear, that he must refuse his left and join with Fuller. My staff-officer came back with the information that General Smith would comply with the request. Smith had not then been attacked, and the enemy was all developed beyond my right in the timber, covering Fuller's right flank, with their skirmish-line extending around to the left of Sweeny. I observed no movement of General Smith, and became very anxious for the safety of that flank. I sent another staff-officer to General Smith, giving him fully the position of the enemy, and telling him that a very large force was upon our rear. General Smith was by this time apprised of the fact of the enemy's intentions, from the general attack which had been made along my whole line. It afterward was made plain to me by General Smith why he hesitated to comply with my first request. He was in the act of refusing his left, when General McPherson sent him orders to hold his ground, and that reënforcements would be sent to him, or his left protected. General McPherson had evidently sent this order before arriving on the ground, without knowing the position of the enemy as fully as I did. I received no orders from General McPherson during the battle. In moving out of the timber into the open field in my front, now the rear of the army, one of the enemy's columns of attack (the centre column) struck a mill-pond, or some other obstruction, just on the edge of an open field, and became entangled, retarding its progress and exposing the flank of the other column. I saw that something had confused the enemy, and immediately ordered Colonel Mersey's brigade to charge the advance column on the exposed flank, and also sent orders to Fuller to instantly charge the enemy in his front, and to take advantage of their embarrassment. Both commands moved promptly, and fell upon the enemy and drove them back across the field, and I have no doubt saved my command. While this attack was progressing, not hearing from the staff-officer I sent to General Giles A. Smith, and seeing that the enemy was passing to my right in the rear, and far down the line of the Seventeenth Army Corps, I sent another staff-officer to that flank who must have passed up the road a short time before General McPherson, for he found General Giles A. Smith hotly engaged and unable to move. Fortunately, two batteries that were in line were in the centre of Sweeny's division, on a knoll naturally strong and commanding, and giving a sweeping fire across an open field, covering both the right and left of Sweeny's division; this knoll being the apex of the formation of Sweeny, the road bent to the west at that point, and Sweeny followed the direction of the road, forming his line right where his men were resting. These two batteries fired very effectively upon the enemy's advance forces, pouring into them canister at short range. The fire was so destructive and Mersey's charge so furious that the enemy very soon gave way on their front and fell back to the timber. General Fuller advanced rapidly across the field, driving the enemy before him, developed them in the gap between General Smith and his right, and drawing a rapid fire on his right flank, from the body of the enemy that had poured around the left of the Seventeenth Corps, he promptly changed front with a portion of his division, and, under a galling fire, moved on the enemy in the timber, clearing that point. The Sixty-fourth Illinois Infantry pushed in between the main column of the enemy and their advance in the timber, and captured their skirmish-line, the same that had killed General McPherson a few minutes before, and were then in possession of his papers and effects, including his orders, which we obtained. The fighting in General Fuller's front was very severe, and the ground contested inch by inch, his artillery doing very effective service. Finally, the enemy fell back along Fuller's whole line, and I swung my right in order to bring it into line with the brigade that McPherson had ordered up to General Giles A. Smith's aid, which had been forced to take position to the right, and somewhat in rear of Fuller's advance. The Seventeenth Army Corps reformed its left at right angles with the original line, and joined this brigade. This brought the enemy well to our front, and there we kept them the rest of the day. Major-General McPherson arrived on the ground during the attack on me, stood near the ammunition-train on right of my line, watching the result of my counter-charge upon the enemy. As soon as the tide turned in my favor, he followed a road through the timber leading from Fuller's right before his advance to the left of the Seventeenth Army Corps, still unaware of the advance of the enemy into the gap between Fuller's right and the Seventeenth Corps. About half an hour after my first repulse of the enemy I received a report that General McPherson was wounded, and it was about 3 P.M. before I was aware he was dead. About 4 P.M. General Logan called in person for aid to drive back the enemy on the Decatur and Atlanta road, where he had made a sortie and gained a temporary advantage, breaking through General Morgan L. Smith's division of the Fifteenth Army Corps. I sent the Second Brigade of the Second Division under Colonel Mersey, accompanied by Captain Jonas of my staff. Mersey's brigade immediately went into line and moved down the main road, participating in the charge with General Wood's division of the Fifteenth Army Corps, retook the works and batteries that had been lost, Colonel Mersey receiving a wound in his leg, having his horse killed under him. General Morgan L. Smith, who witnessed Colonel Mersey's attack, sent by Captain Jonas a very complimentary message as to Colonel Mersey's charge and its success. When General Logan called for Mersey's brigade, he told me that if the enemy again attacked me and I needed help to call upon General J. D. Cox, of the Twenty-third Corps. At 5 P.M. the enemy made a demonstration on my extreme left, and I requested General Cox to send me a brigade, which he promptly did. The enemy, however, only opened with artillery. Again Mersey's brigade was called into action about midnight, when General Logan ordered two regiments from it to occupy the hill that had been hotly contested in line of the Seventeenth Army Corps and relieve the troops of that command. Mersey's troops promptly executed the request, crawling in on their hands and knees, finding the enemy in the ditches on the outside, and driving them out. The time of Colonel Mersey's brigade had expired; they were exempt from participating in this battle had they chosen to avail themselves of this right, and were awaiting transportation North. They fought successfully on different parts of the field, suffering heavy loss in killed and wounded. General Sprague, who was at Decatur holding that town, covering the trains of the Army of the Tennessee with three regiments of his brigade and six guns of the Chicago Board of Trade Battery and one section of the Eighth Michigan Artillery, was attacked by the enemy in overwhelming numbers. Two divisions of Wheeler's cavalry, dismounted, charged upon Sprague from three different directions. General Sprague concentrated his command, and, after a doubtful and determined contest, held the enemy in check and gained a position north of the town, which he was able to keep. In their charge the enemy twice got possession of Sprague's artillery, but were immediately driven from it. General Sprague, by his good generalship and hard fighting, saved the trains of the Fifteenth, Sixteenth, and Seventeenth Army Corps at Decatur and *en route* from Roswell to the army. The trains on the march were guarded by the Ninth Illinois Infantry and the Forty-third Ohio Infantry, which regiments, upon their arrival at Decatur, went promptly into the action. The Sixteenth Army Corps, at the time of Hood's attack, was in the rear of the Fifteenth and Seventeenth Corps, stretched out upon a common wagon-road. Three brigades disposed in single line, numbering about forty-five hundred men, and not in line with the other corps, had met the attack of the rebel army, staggered it at the first onset, and driven it back with great slaughter, leaving the dead and wounded of the enemy in our hands. Any failure on the part of the Sixteenth Corps to check the enemy's advance when he was already in our rear and certain of success, would have been disastrous to the whole Army of the Tennessee. The fortunate topography of the ground, the intelligence of the commanders, and the alacrity and bravery of the troops, enabled us to take advantage of the confusion created in the enemy's ranks in finding this corps prepared for the attack, and to rout the enemy.

The disparity of forces can be seen from the fact that in the charge made by the two brigades under Fuller and Mersey they took three hundred and fifty-one prisoners, representing forty-nine different regiments, eight brigades, and three divisions. These two brigades brought back eight battle-flags from the enemy.

After the fight, four hundred and twenty-two of the enemy's dead were buried in my front, and large numbers of the wounded were cared for in my hospitals.

The Sixteenth Army Corps suffered terribly in the battle of Atlanta. Their loss in killed and wounded was eight hundred and fifty-four out of fifty-four hundred men engaged, and nearly every field-officer of my command was killed or wounded.

I am, general, very respectfully, your obedient servant,

G. M. DODGE.

COUNCIL BLUFFS, IOWA, *November* 30, 1875.

TECUMSEH, ALABAMA, *February* 22, 1876.
Mrs. General W. T. SHERMAN.

MY DEAR MADAM: I have read with great interest General Sherman's "Memoirs," and some of the criticisms made upon it, and venture to give my testimony in regard to some of the disputed points falling within my personal knowledge, as of interest possibly to some of my comrades in arms, if not to the general public and history.

The March to the Sea.

On the 5th of May, 1864, I reported to General Sherman at Ringgold, Georgia, for duty as inspector-general on his staff. The general, with his map before him, explained the general course of his proposed campaign against General Johnston, ending with the capture of Atlanta. I remember that he had his coat and hat off, and his slippers on. When he had done his explanations, he began walking the floor of the room, smoking a cigar. I said to him that when he got to Atlanta he would be four hundred and fifty miles from his real base of supplies, with one railroad as his only means of transportation, and every mile of that liable to be broken by the enemy, and that it would absorb the whole of his army to hold Atlanta and protect the road, and asked him what he proposed after the capture of Atlanta. Stopping short in his walk, and snapping the ashes off his cigar in a quick, nervous way, he replied in two words—"Salt water." I did not comprehend his meaning, but after a little further examination of the map I asked him if he meant Savannah or Charleston, and he said, "Yes."

Again, soon after the capture of Atlanta, he called Colonel Beckwith, his chief commissary, and myself into his room in Judge Lyon's house in Atlanta, and, locking the door, laid his map on the floor, and indicated his proposed march to Savannah. Colonel Beckwith's first question naturally was, "How about supplies?" The general replied that there were one million of people in Georgia, and that where they could live his army would not starve.

Snake-Creek Gap.

Before and during the movements against General Johnston, at Rocky Face, General Sherman explained to me and others of his staff that the demonstrations on Johnston's front and right were feints to cover and hide the real movement of attack by General McPherson through Snake-Creek Gap. In speaking of the danger that Johnston might fall on McPherson with his whole force, and crush him before help could be got to him, he said that the twenty-three thousand muskets of the Army of the Tennessee could not "be run over by anybody in a hurry," and that the moment Johnston let go of Rocky Face, Thomas and Schofield would be on his rear, and thus place him between two fires, when ruin would be sure.

On the night of May 9th, as we were at supper at the brick house, by the spring near Tunnel Hill Station, a letter was brought to the general. Reading it, he instantly left the table, and bade me follow him. When we had got a little way from the house, he stopped short, and, with a vehement gesture of his right hand clinched, said: "I have got Joe Johnston dead. This letter is from McPherson. At one o'clock to-day he was within one and a half mile of the railroad. He must be on it now. I want to go over and see 'Tom' "—meaning General Thomas. On his way he said that Johnston would be compelled to abandon the railroad and most of his artillery and trains, and retreat to the east through the mountains (Pigeon Mountains, I think they were called); that we would follow the railroad, and beat Johnston to Atlanta.

Arriving at General Thomas's headquarters, we found him at supper, and General Sherman repeated to him the same expressions he used to me. General Thomas was also greatly pleased, and my recollection is that he said he thought Johnston would fortify and defend the gap. Sherman and Thomas agreed that Johnston must now let go Rocky Face, and that Thomas and Schofield must push him hard in the morning to crush him and prevent his crushing McPherson. This understanding had, we returned to our headquarters, General Sherman being in high spirits.

Late that night word came from McPherson that he had failed to seize the railroad, and had fallen back to the mouth of the gap and fortified. I think that all the members of the staff will remember how disappointed and excited the general was on receipt of this news, and how cross he was the next day, and that we all thought he might relieve McPherson of his command, though the general gave no intimation of such intent—to me, at least. We simply inferred it from McPherson's failure to execute the work expected of him.

I was present when General Sherman and McPherson first met after this, and well remember that General Sherman's manner toward McPherson was one of sadness rather than anger, and that his first remark was, "Well, Mac, you have missed the great opportunity of your life." General Adkins and Colonel Hickenlooper, both of whom were in good position to know the truth, express, I think, the general judgment of the Army of the Tennessee—that if certain other division commanders had been in the lead, the railroad would have been seized and held, and Johnston ruined.

That the failure to do this was by far the most grievous disappointment which General Sherman met with during the Atlanta campaign, will, I think, be admitted by all who participated in it, and were familiar with its history.

The Battle of the 22d of July, or "Atlanta."

Perhaps I cannot better state my knowledge of this battle than by quoting some remarks made by me in the Ohio Senate in 1866, when the facts were all fresh in my memory, and repeated in the United States Senate May 4, 1870. Though not all exactly pertinent to the points in issue about the battle of Atlanta, I will copy the whole of these remarks, as affording the conclusive proof of my high regard and admiration for all three of these true men and great soldiers — Sherman, Thomas, and McPherson — and how incapable I am of seeking to lessen in the slightest degree their well-earned fame. Grant, Sherman, Thomas, McPherson, and Sheridan, are names that will be illustrious throughout the world while the history of our late great war is preserved.

The joint resolution appropriating condemned cannon for the use of the McPherson Monument Association having been taken up, Senator Warner said:

"I claim the indulgence of the Senate for a few minutes.

"Mr. President, I speak on this resolution with feelings of unusual interest, growing out of the remarkable character of the man whom it is intended to honor, and of my long association during the late war with him. I first met him just after we had fought so successfully the battle of Fort Donelson, when he was a lieutenant-colonel on the staff of General Grant; and from that time until the hour of his death I was in the same army, campaigns, and battles, with him. During the ever-memorable and brilliant Atlanta campaign, it was my honor to serve as an inspector-general on the staff of General Sherman, and, as such, was brought much in contact with General McPherson, and had large opportunities of learning his character and services, and the regard in which he was held by the army and by his military peers and superiors. That esteem was in some respects peculiar. General Sherman had, above all others, the supreme confidence of the entire army in his military skill and bold energy, and none stood higher for personal patriotism, purity, and integrity — an integrity of Roman firmness, rigidity, and self-denial. These qualities are well shown in his refusal to accept, in the beginning of the Atlanta campaign, a commission as major-general in the regular army, on the ground that the Government had already sufficiently rewarded and honored him for his services, and that it should be held up as a prize for the most meritorious service during the campaigns then about to be begun, of Atlanta and the Wilderness.

"General Thomas, in his Washingtonian greatness, solidity, and purity, had universal respect and confidence throughout the army. General Schofield, though less widely known than either Sherman or Thomas, yet had the entire confidence and perfect respect of his own army, and of all who were competent to judge him, as a soldier of skill and courage, and as a pure patriot and just man. But McPherson, added to the utmost confidence in his military skill and personal courage, had such noble beauty of form and countenance, such winning gentleness of expression and manner; his face, which in repose had an expression of almost womanly sweetness, would so light up and blaze with fiercest courage and daring in the moment of battle, that in danger he was worshiped as a hero; in quiet regarded in tenderest love as a man—it seemed as though the love of the beautiful one whom he worshiped, but whom the Fates in blind cruelty decreed he might never wed, so lighted the noble soul which God gave him, as to illuminate his face, and make gentle and true and winning his life, his own love attracting to him the love of all other men.

"And then the circumstances of his life and death were so touching and tragic! At two o'clock of the morning of the memorable 22d of July, 1864, when General Sherman's army was laying close siege to Atlanta, I was called by him and ordered to go to McPherson, some six miles distant on our left, and inform him that the enemy had evacuated his works in front of our centre, and with directions for him to pursue, by certain roads, in case the enemy had abandoned his whole line and Atlanta. I found him at daylight in bed. Waking him up, he gave instantly the necessary orders for a reconnaissance to ascertain the movements of the enemy. We ate breakfast together, mounted our horses, rode to the front, and found the enemy had only retired about a mile to an inner and shorter line. We rode to his skirmish-line and outside of it, and a mile in front of the line on which the great battle was fought later in the day, passing twice over the spot on which he fell a few hours later. Very near this spot we met General G. M. Dodge, and then General McPherson gave him the order to halt his two divisions of the Sixteenth Corps, which were then marching by the flank in a direction at right angles to our line, the head of the column being less than a mile from our extreme left. Neither McPherson nor Dodge nor General Frank P. Blair, who was with us, then comprehended the mighty and happy influence which this order, given only to await the intrenching by working parties of the extended and advanced line on our left, which Dodge

was to occupy, was to have on the day's battle, whose stillness was
even then upon us. One may well regard it as providential. No one
then knew or thought that Hood had, during the night before, contracted his line so as to be able to spare Hardee with a corps of ten
to fifteen thousand men, to make by a night march of fifteen miles a
circuit round our left to attack us in flank and rear, and who was
then, just out of our sight, forming his troops for the attack. We left
the field on our left and rode rapidly to the centre to General Sherman, at the Howard House, an abandoned private dwelling near the
centre of our line, and within easy reach of the enemy's rifles. On
our way we halted for a few moments at the tent of Major-General
Frank P. Blair. While there, Blair's surgeon reported that rebel cavalry had been seen near the hospital of the Seventeenth Corps, which
held our left. It was also reported to McPherson that rebel cavalry
had been seen near his headquarters, located in the rear of our left,
on Decatur road. The necessary orders were given by McPherson
and Blair to guard against dashes of bands of cavalry, but no importance was attached by any one to the fact of their appearance, as it
was so common, though, in fact, it was the first pattering of the
great storm of battle which was soon to burst upon the two armies,
and prostrate in wounds and death ten thousand brave men. A few
moments after dismounting at General Sherman's headquarters, the
sharp, rattling fire of musketry was heard in the direction of our left
rear. Sherman and McPherson listened to it attentively for a few
moments, both detecting in it the decisive sound of coming battle,
when McPherson quickly mounted his horse and rode rapidly toward it. In less than two hours his dead body was laid at Sherman's
feet on the porch of the Howard House. In riding from the right of
General Dodge's line through the interval that separated it from the
left of Leggett's division of the Seventeenth Corps by a blind road
through the woods, attended only by an orderly, his staff having all
been sent away with orders for the conduct of the battle, he was
halted by a squad of rebel infantry and ordered to surrender. Raising
his hat as if in token of surrender, he essayed to rein his horse
quickly away and plunge into the woods and escape. The rebels,
instantly detecting his purpose, fired a volley, and the brave and
chivalrous McPherson fell to rise no more.

"I can never forget the touching scene at the Howard House as his
body lay there, still and beautiful in death. McPherson was betrothed
to a girl of rare beauty and worth in Baltimore, and had the promise
of a leave of absence in the spring of 1864 to go to Baltimore and be
married. The exigencies of the military service, in connection with
the grand movements of the Atlanta and Wilderness campaigns,

which General Grant directed should be begun simultaneously, compelled General Sherman to the painful necessity of denying this leave. He wrote a kind and touching letter to the girl, taking the whole responsibility, and begging her to consider that General McPherson had no option but obedience or soldierly dishonor, and promising him leave the earliest time the service would allow. As we looked on his face, pale and cold in death, even the remembrance of his virtues, and his value to the army and to the country, was hushed in the thought of the deep love which, but a few hours before, had lent such light to his eyes and such geniality to his manners, and of the irreparable sorrow soon to come to one from whom death had so cruelly snatched her beautiful hero. Sherman slowly paced the floor, frequently stopping short to receive reports of the progress of the fight, or to give orders for its conduct, or to gaze into the lifeless face of his beloved captain, the tears meanwhile rapidly coursing down his war-worn face.

"Mr. President, the tears shed on the battle-field over his dead body by his great chief Tecumseh and his brave men would have made his most fitting monument, had the skill of other than a divine artist been equal to the task of gathering them in the form in which they fell, and of giving them the perpetuity as they had the radiance of diamonds, of fashioning them into 'a form of beauty,' sparkling in God's light, while time shall last, the story of his virtues. But earth caught them, mingled with the blood of those who shed them, and her flowers, nourished by them, will be Nature's sympathetic testimony to his kindred beauty of form and soul.

"The high military renown of General McPherson, together with the possession by him of those gentle qualities which won for him the *sobriquet* of 'the beloved McPherson,' so peculiarly distinguished him as to warrant us in making this contribution, to aid in raising a monument which shall tell to all future ages of his services and fame."

On my way to General McPherson's headquarters, on the morning of the 22d of July, I passed General Logan's quarters at daylight, and seeing him in front of his tent, told him my errand, and my recollection is that he at once proceeded to reconnoitre his front, without waiting for orders from General McPherson, which were sent by a staff-officer on my arrival at General McPherson's, perhaps a mile distant and to the left rear.

When news came of General McPherson's death, and of the partial turning of our left, General Sherman said to me, "Warner, you have been over all this ground to-day; go quickly and see how matters stand, and report to me." I went and saw Generals Dodge, Blair, and

Leggett. Blair's left had been turned, but he had reformed it refused from Leggett's Hill, and had made connection, or nearly so, with Dodge's divisions, and the three stood firm and were confident of holding their positions, which they did, and repulsed the enemy with great slaughter. General Blair said to me, on my asking him of the condition of matters, "We have had a d——d hard fight, but we whipped them, and can do it again if they come back at us."

As I returned I had to ride, in order to pass a fence, up the main wagon-road alongside the railroad from Atlanta to Decatur to within one or two hundred yards of our main line on our centre, when it crossed the wagon and rail roads near the brick house. The enemy were just attacking our centre with great energy, and their artillery enfiladed the road up which I was riding—three solid shots or shells striking in the road in front of me and ricochetting over me, in going a distance of half a mile. Just as I passed nearest our line, the enemy issued from the railroad-cut in the rear of our line and captured a part of it belonging to General Morgan L. Smith's division, and not to General Wood's, as General Kilpatrick erroneously states. General Wood's line was nowhere broken, nor seriously attacked, as I remember. The splendid fighting of his division was done later in aiding General Smith's division to recover the lost part of their line.

Reaching General Sherman a few minutes later at the Howard House, I informed him of the condition of affairs on the left, as stated by Generals Blair, Dodge, and Leggett, and as seen by myself, and said to him that Leggett's Hill was the key of our entire left from the railroad, and that it would be held—that, in fact, the enemy were already repulsed and beaten on that part of the field.

General C. R. Wood had just reported the breaking of our line to his left, but General Sherman was incredulous, and sent him back to be sure. I confirmed the report, and presently General Wood returned and again confirmed it. Then it was that General Wood's troops were formed *en échelon* and advanced in such splendid style to the left to the attack of the enemy's left flank, swinging to the right up to the breastworks as the enemy were driven from the opposite side by the enfilading fire of Wood, aided by Schofield's guns on the hill in front of the Howard House trained on the enemy's flank. I directed the fire of one of these guns, by watching with my glass where the shots struck and hinting accordingly to the officer sighting the gun. To understand all this it must be borne in mind that the guns were on a high hill, Wood's troops in a deep hollow, and the enemy on the face of the hill opposite—the line of breastworks crossing the hollow at right angles. All this was done by the orders and under the eye of General Sherman.

The result was that our entire line was speedily recovered, and the day closed with the enemy completely foiled of his object, and everywhere repulsed and beaten with great loss.

The next morning General Sherman, soon followed by General Logan, rode along our entire line to the left of the Howard House, and both were received with the wildest enthusiasm by the troops which had done such severe and splendid fighting the day before.

The sight of the great number of Confederate dead in front of our lines was appalling, and never to be forgotten by those who saw it.

As showing General Sherman's estimate of General McPherson, I will say that, as we rode to our quarters from the battle-field late that night, General Sherman said: "The army and the country have sustained a great loss by the death of McPherson. I had expected him to finish the war. Grant and I are likely to be killed, or set aside after some failure to meet popular expectation, and McPherson would have come into chief command at the right time to end the war. He had no enemies."

Successor to McPherson.

General Sherman talked to me freely about this matter at the time, and the considerations that seemed to influence him were that General Howard was a soldier of education and training, with a larger experience than General Logan, and therefore better fitted for such high command; but he seemed to regret that these reasons compelled him to prefer General Howard to so brave and daring a soldier as General Logan.

Removal of the People of Atlanta.

The following letter, the original of which is in my possession, throws some light on this matter, in regard to which General Sherman was so sharply censured at the South. The fact is, that not more than half the people of Atlanta obeyed the order, and no force was used to compel obedience. I was detailed by the general to attend to the delivery of the people to General Hood at Rough and Ready, where he sent Colonel Clare, of his staff, to receive them. The inhabitants had choice of transportation by rail or wagons—Colonel Le Duc, of General Geary's command, having control of all the transportation of the army for the purpose, and sending as many wagons to each house as were asked for. I had a train of cars standing on the track in Atlanta every day from 8 A.M. to 3 P.M., and the people were allowed to put on what they chose. The only limit to amount of goods to be taken was Hood's ability to transport from Rough and Ready. This letter Colonel Clare handed to me sealed and addressed to myself, when we parted, with request that I would not open it until I reached Atlanta. It illustrates his generous nature.

"ROUGH AND READY, GEORGIA, ⎫
                September 21, 1864.⎭

"COLONEL: Our official connection is about to cease. You will permit me to bear testimony to the uniform courtesy you have shown on all occasions to me and my people; and the promptness with which you have corrected all irregularities arising in our intercourse.

"Hoping, sir, to be able at some future time to reciprocate your courtesy and in many instances your positive kindness,

      "I am, with respect, your obedient servant,

            "W. CLARE, *Major and Assistant Inspector-General,*
                        General Hood's Staff.
   "Colonel WARNER, *Inspector-General, Major-General Sherman's Staff."*

General Thomas.

General Sherman has been censured for not doing General Thomas justice in his "Memoirs," and particularly for speaking of him as "slow." That General Sherman is rapid and bold, and that Thomas was slow and cautious, in thought and action, in word and deed, in constitutional habit of mind, certainly no sane and honest man acquainted with each will deny.

This is certainly as well known as that General Grant was quicker and bolder than McClellan, and Sheridan than Buell. Which was the better general, on the whole, is a question not here in dispute.

On the 5th of May, 1864, General Thomas came to General Sherman's headquarters at Ringgold, Georgia. I did not then know him, but asked General Sherman if that were not General Thomas. He said, "Yes," and I then asked him if there was any truth in the rumor that Thomas felt aggrieved at having him (Sherman) put in command over him. He replied: "No, not a bit! It don't make much difference which of us commands. I would obey 'Tom's' orders to-morrow as cheerfully as he obeys mine to-day, but I think I can give an army a little more impetus than 'Tom' can." Here was the whole truth and difference in a nut-shell.

Their consultations were frequent, frank, and free, and I never saw any sign of bad feeling between them. After the battle of Nashville, General Thomas complained to me, as I understood he did to others, that injustice was done him in sending General Logan to relieve him of command; that those who gave and allowed the order did not and could not know the facts of his position, and that results had justified and vindicated him.

After the war he complained to me of the treatment of President Grant. I well remember his grand old figure, as he leaned on the little marble pedestal that used to stand in the vestibule of Willard's Hotel, in Washington, at the Fourteenth Street entrance, and said sadly: "I think that I have done the country some service, and something toward the success of the Republican party, and the only thing I have asked of this Administration was the appointment of my old commissary, Paul, as postmaster at Nashville, and that was refused, as the place was needed for some politician. I shall never ask for anything more."

WILLARD WARNER,
Late Brigadier-General of Volunteers,
and late United States Senator of Alabama.

Official account of the people sent south, their numbers and luggage, under Special Field Order No. 67, issued by Major-General W. T. Sherman, Atlanta, Georgia, September 4, 1864.

DATE.	No.	NAME.	ADULTS, CHILDREN, AND SERVANTS.	BAGGAGE.
1864 Sept. 10.	1	J. M. Bryant	3 adults, 6 children, 1 servant	30 packages.
	·2	Mrs. B. Ogletree. . . .	2 adults	27 "
	3	Mrs. Bookout	1 adult and 1 child . . .	18 "
	4	Mrs. M. R. Thronton .	1 adult, 5 children, 1 servant	41 "
	5	Mrs. F. Winkfield . . .	1 adult and 1 child . . .	12 "
	6	Mrs. S. Hood	1 adult and 3 children .	11 "
	7	Mrs. J. P. Brooks . . .	1 adult and 1 child . . .	14 "
	8	Mrs. L. C. Kent	1 adult and 1 child . . .	10 "
	9	Mrs. J. W. Thurman .	1 adult and 1 child . . .	6 "
	10	Mrs. N. Eason	1 adult and 1 child . . .	5 "
	11	Mrs. M. F. McDuffie .	1 adult and 4 children .	14 "
	12	Mrs. S. E. Bell	1 adult and 2 children .	12 "
	13	Mrs. J. S. Johnson . . .	1 adult	5 "
	14	Mrs. Blanchard.	1 adult, 2 children, 1 servant	40 "
	15	Mrs. C. E. Harris . . .	1 adult	2 "
	16	Mrs. M. Struce.	2 adults and 1 child. . .	11 "
	17	Mrs. G. E. Forrest. . .	2 adults and 2 children.	12 "
	18	Mrs. C. Grubbs	1 adult and 2 children .	4 "

Official account of the people sent south, etc.—(CONTINUED.)

DATE.	No.	NAME.	ADULTS, CHILDREN, AND SERVANTS.	BAGGAGE.
1864. Sept. 10.	18½	Mrs. M. A. P. Jones . .	1 adult	4 packages
	19	Josiah Kent	2 adults	15 "
	20	Mrs. M. Huggen- bottom	1 adult and 2 children .	11 "
Sept. 11.	21	Mrs. Stafford	2 adults and 1 child . . .	14 "
	22	Mrs. M. Blackburn . .	2 adults and 3 children	12 "
	23	B. Evans	1 adult and 1 child . . .	18 "
	24	Mrs. B. Thompson . Mrs. E. Lee . . . . . Mrs. M. Lee . . . . . Mrs. Cook	5 adults and 7 children .	44 pack- ages and 1 old horse and wagon.
	25	Mrs. S. Lee	1 adult and 6 children	17 packages.
	26	Mrs S. Abrams	1 adult	7 "
	27	Mrs. M. Wright	1 adult and 1 servant . .	17 "
	28	Miss J. Combs	1 adult	14 "
	29	Mrs. Sims and Davis .	2 adults and 1 child . . .	24 "
	30	John Cassen	2 adults	22 "
	31	Mrs. M. Higgens . . .	1 adult and 2 children .	23 "
	32	Mrs S. A. Gossett . . .	1 adult	15 "
	33	Mrs. E. J. Lofton . . .	1 adult and 1 child . . .	14 "
	34	Mrs. M. Johnson	1 adult and 5 children .	21 "
	35 ·	Mrs. S. McDuffie . . Mrs. M. J. Self . . .	3 adults and 4 children	20 packages and 1 cow.
	36	Mrs. E. McGriff	1 adult and 1 child . . .	13 packages.
	37	G. M. Lester	1 adult and 2 servants .	26 "
	38	Mrs. A. Patterson . . .	1 adult and 2 children .	15 "
	39	Mrs. M. Ballard	1 adult and 4 children .	23 "
	40	Mrs. F. C. House . . .	1 adult and 2 children .	23 "
	41	Mrs. C. Johnson	1 adult and 6 children .	25 "
	42	Mrs. S. Ellis	1 adult and 1 child . . .	13 "
	43	Mrs. M. Wilson	1 adult and 5 children .	23 "
	44	Mrs. E. Phillips	4 adults	17 "
	45	Mrs. G. W. Adair . . .	2 adults, 4 children, 2 servants	53 packages, and 2 horses, carriage, cow, and calf.

Official account of the people sent south, etc. — (CONTINUED.)

DATE.	No.	NAME.	ADULTS, CHILDREN, AND SERVANTS.	BAGGAGE.
1864. Sept. 11.	46	Mrs. M. Ball . . . . .⎱ Mrs. Brooks . . . . .⎰	2 adults and 4 children.	35 packages.
	47	Mrs. C. Johnson	1 adult and 1 child . . .	9 "
	48	Mrs. J. Kramer.	1 adult and 3 children .	4 "
	49	Miss L. Miller	1 adult	14 "
	50	Mrs. J. Kilby	1 adult and 5 children .	35 "
	51	J. M. Blackburn	2 adults	15 "
	52	Mrs. F. Witcher	1 adult and 1 child . . .	18 "
	53	Mrs. S. Freeman. . . .	1 adult	7 "
	54	Mrs. E. L. Mill	1 adult, 3 children, 1 servant	27 packages and 1 cow.
	55	Mrs. N. Mayson	1 adult, 1 child, 1 servant	28 packages and cow and calf.
	56	Mrs. N. McTeer	1 adult	8 packages.
	57	Mrs. A. M. McTeer . .	1 adult and 6 children .	27 "
	58	Mrs. S. Mayson	1 adult and 5 children .	22 packages, and 1 old horse and dray, cow, and calf.
	59	Mrs. A. J. Mayson. . .	1 adult	10 packages.
	60	Mrs. S. A. Moss	2 adults and 1 child. . .	17 "
	61	Mrs. S. Armstrong . .	1 adult, 2 children, 1 servant	19 "
	62	J. L. Mayson	2 adults and 1 servant .	34 packages and horse & dray.
	63	Mrs. E. Gilham	1 adult	10 packages.
	64	A. H. Webb	2 adults, 2 children, 4 servants	21 "
	65	Mrs. M. Waier	1 adult	17 "
	66	Mrs. E. Harper	1 adult and 5 children .	27 "
	67	Mrs. M. Brady.	1 adult and 2 children .	17 "
	68	Benjamin Gaum	2 adults and 8 children.	31 "
	69	Mrs. N. Ireland	1 adult and 4 children .	19 "
	70	Mrs. N. Waddail. . . .	2 adults	15 "

Official account of the people sent south, etc.—(CONTINUED.)

DATE.	No.	NAME.	ADULTS, CHILDREN, AND SERVANTS.	BAGGAGE.
1864. Sept. 11.	71	Mrs. Preckett.	1 adult, 2 children, 1 servant	18 packages.
	72	J. Hawkins	1 adult	4 "
	73	R. W. T. Denham . . .	1 adult and 5 children .	12 "
	74	Mrs. M. A. Franklin. .	1 adult and 2 children .	8 "
	75	Mrs. N. M. Franklin .	1 adult and 2 children .	8 "
	76	Mrs. S. Saul	1 adult	7 "
	77	Mrs. S. Clownes	2 adults and 1 servant .	9 "
	78	B. Eustell	2 adults and 4 children	41 packages and cow and calf.
	79	Mrs. F. Crawford . . .	1 adult	7 packages.
	80	Mrs. Makridge	1 adult and 5 children .	23 "
	81	Mrs. R. Corsey	1 adult and 3 children .	7 "
	82	Mrs. A. M. Rollo . . .	1 adult	10 "
	83	Mrs. L. Smith	1 adult and 4 children .	12 "
	84	Mrs. J. Sheppard . . .	1 adult and 5 children .	20 "
	85	Mrs. L. Whitmire . . .	1 adult and 2 children .	13 "
	86	Mrs. E. Lee	1 adult	1 package.
	87	Miss C. Powers	1 adult	1 "
Sept. 12.	88	Mrs. S. Corsey	1 adult	11 packages.
	89	Mrs. M. Grubbs	1 adult and 4 children .	15 "
	90	S. Robinson	2 adults and 2 children .	14 "
	91	Mrs. E. Hill	1 adult and 1 child . . .	10 "
	92	Mrs. L. Patterson . . .	1 adult and 3 children .	24 "
	93	Mrs. P. Jones	1 adult	5 "
	94	Mrs. C. Grubbs	1 adult and 2 children .	11 "
	95	Mrs. E. Cook	1 adult and 1 child . . .	12 "
	96	Mrs. M. H. Atkinson .	1 adult and 4 children .	16 "
	97	Mrs. T. Harebork . . .	2 adults and 4 children	18 "
	98	Mrs. A. Hall	2 adults and 1 child . . .	1 package.
	99	Mrs. E. Sears	1 adult and 4 children .	7 packages.
	100	Mrs. A. Willard	1 adult and 3 children .	7 "
	101	J. Haslett	2 adults	22 "
	102	R. McCowan.	2 adults and 1 child . . .	17 "
	103	Mrs. J. Atkins	1 adult and 1 child . . .	16 "
	104	Mrs. M. Wing	1 adult and 1 child . . .	7 "
	105	B. Knott	2 adults	33 "
	106	Mrs. S. Johnson	1 adult and 1 child . . .	10 "
	107	J. M. Knott	2 adults and 1 child . . .	7 "

Official account of the people sent south, etc.—(CONTINUED.)

DATE.	NO.	NAME.	ADULTS, CHILDREN, AND SERVANTS.	BAGGAGE.
1864. Sept. 12.	108	Mrs. C. Knott	1 adult and 1 child . . .	22 packages.
	109	B. Thrower.	2 adults and 2 children.	32 "
	110	Mrs. M. E. Sharpe. . .	1 adult and 4 children .	26 "
	111	Mrs. E. Glenn	1 adult and 3 children .	31 packages and cow and calf.
	112	Mrs. L. Wing	1 adult and 1 child . . .	21 packages.
	113	W. H. H. Dorsey . . .	2 adults and 1 child. . .	16 "
	114	Mrs. M. A. Gober. . .	2 adults	14 packages and cow and calf.
Sept. 13.	115	Mrs. J. I. Shaw	2 adults and 3 children.	17 packages.
	116	Mrs. S. Banks	1 adult and 2 children .	16 "
	117	Mrs. M. Kelly	2 adults and 4 children.	19 "
	118	Mrs. L. Dean	1 adult and 3 children .	7 "
	119	Mrs. M. Kelly	2 adults and 2 children.	14 "
	120	Mrs. E. Bellew.	1 adult	none.
	121	Mrs. J. S. McWaters. .	1 adult and 4 children .	31 packages and 1 cow.
	122	Mrs. N. Reeves	1 adult and 2 children .	21 packages.
	123	Mrs. M. L. Holbrook.	1 adult and 3 children .	33 "
	124	Mrs. S. Hewitt.	1 adult	13 "
	125	Mrs. L. Bowls	1 adult	2 "
	126	Mrs. A. Blackman . . .	2 adults and 1 child. . .	19 "
	127	Mrs. E. Winfield. . . .	1 adult and 2 children .	15 "
	128	Mrs. D. Defoor	3 adults and 2 children.	22 "
	129	Mrs. E. N. Hilton. . .	1 adult and 1 child . . .	12 packages and 1 cow.
	130	J. B. McDaniel.	1 adult	2 packages.
	131	Mrs. C. J. Lamb. . . .	1 adult and 9 children .	21 "
	132	Mrs. P. Campbell . . .	1 adult, 3 children, 1 servant	3 "
	133	Miss G. Timmons . . .	1 adult	1 package.
	134	Mrs. M. Richards . . .	1 adult	1 "
	135	Mrs. J. Johns.	2 adults and 5 children .	15 packages.
	136	Mrs. S. Williams. . . .	1 adult and 2 children .	1 package.
	137	Mrs. C. Jenkins	1 adult and 2 children .	4 packages.
	138	Mrs. M. Kilpatrick . .	2 adults and 9 children.	12 "

Official account of the people sent south, etc.— (CONTINUED.)

DATE.	No.	NAME.	ADULTS, CHILDREN, AND SERVANTS.	BAGGAGE.
1864. Sept. 13.	139	Miss M. Teall.	3 adults	7 packages.
	140	Mrs. M. Edwards . . .	1 adult and 1 child . . .	10 "
	141	Mrs. S. Blalcek.	1 adult	11 "
	142	A. Grist.	4 adults and 3 children	34 "
	143	Mrs. N. C. White . . .	1 adult	22 "
	144	Mrs. M. E. Hutchens .	1 adult and 2 children .	9 "
	145	Mrs. N. Studevent. . .	1 adult and 1 child . . .	19 "
	146	Mrs. M. C. Seale . . .	2 adults and 2 children.	20 "
	147	Mrs. S. P. Baggerly	1 adult	4 "
	148	Mrs. P. Rothwell. . . .	1 adult	6 "
	149	Mrs. C. McHugh . . .	2 adults	8 "
	150	W. L. White	2 adults	1 package.
	151	Miss E. Taylor	1 adult	5 packages.
	152	Mrs. J. M. Taylor . . .	1 adult and 3 children .	15 "
	153	Mrs. M. Wooding . . .	1 adult and 2 children .	11 "
	154	Thomas Byne	1 adult	1 horse.
	155	W. G. Grist	2 adults and 1 child. . .	28 packages.
	156	J. Thompson.	3 adults	13 "
	157	Mrs. M. E. Brace . . .	1 adult and 2 children .	16 "
	158	Mrs. E. Brace	1 adult and 3 children .	17 "
	159	Mrs. S. P. Wilson	1 adult, 4 children, 2 servants	37 "
	160	Mrs. J. McLaughlin . .	5 adults and 4 children.	7 "
	161	Mrs. L. Loren	1 adult and 2 children .	18 "
	162	Mrs. A. Gerrett	1 adult	7 "
	163	Mrs. P. S. Jenkins . . .	1 adult and 7 children .	30 "
	164	Joseph Coker.	1 adult	10 "
	165	Mrs. Mary Harper. . .	2 adults and 3 children.	19 packages and 1 cow.
	166	Mrs. L. Knight	1 adult and 2 children .	11 packages.
	167	John Bash . . . .⎫ W. L. Bash . . . . . ⎭	4 adults and 4 children.	40 "
Sept. 14.	168	Mrs. E. Robinson . . .	2 adults	13 "
	169	Mrs. J. Williams	2 adults	19 "
	170	Mrs. M. Bell	3 adults and 7 children.	38 packages and 1 cow.
	171	Mrs. L. Plummer . . .	3 adults and 3 children.	13 packages.
	172	W. D. Crockett	2 adults	16 "

Official account of the people sent south, etc.—(Continued.)

Date.	No.	Name.	Adults, Children, and Servants.	Baggage.
1864. Sept. 14.	173	Mrs. W. D. Mitchell .	1 adult, 3 children, 1 servant	25 packages.
	174	Miss Drum	1 adult and 1 child . . .	8 "
	175	Mrs. S. Smith	1 adult and 4 children .	26 "
	176	Mrs. N. Johnson	1 adult and 1 child . . .	17 "
	177	Miss L. Buffington . .	2 adults	5 "
	178	Mrs. M. A. Miner . . .	1 adult and 3 children .	25 "
	179	J. G. Mitchell	2 adults, 1 child, 2 servants	40 "
	180	T. H. Wilson	2 adults	21 packages and 1 cow.
	181	Mrs. M. Johnson	3 adults and 3 children .	18 "
	182	Mrs. E. M. Tweely . .	1 adult and 1 child . . .	20 "
	183	Mrs. A. Robinson . . .	1 adult	4 "
	184	J. Wilson	2 adults	9 "
	185	Mrs. M. Faulkner . . .	1 adult	13 "
	186	Mrs. Oslin	3 adults	49 "
	187	W. C. Parker	2 adults	none.
	188	A. W. Weaver	2 adults, 4 children, 2 servants	30 packages.
	189	W. Kenodle	2 adults and 5 children .	18 packages and 1 cow.
	190	J. L. Mathews	1 adult	2 packages.
	191	Mrs. J. Whaley	1 adult and 3 children .	38 "
	192	E. Daniel	2 adults and 6 children .	19 "
	193	Mrs. H. B. Hutchens .	1 adult	26 "
	194	Mrs. S. Robinson . . .	1 adult	39 "
	195	Mrs. C. Bell	1 adult and 2 children .	28 "
	196	J. Carmichael	2 adults	31 "
	197	W. Whitaker	3 adults and 5 children .	35 "
	198	George Kidd	2 adults	19 "
	199	Debby Wall	1 adult, 2 children, 1 servant	19 "
	200	L. L. Bird	1 adult and 2 servants .	10 "
	201	P. W. Carter	1 adult	8 "
	202	C. Emmet	1 adult	25 "
	203	E. D. Graff	3 adults and 1 child . . .	26 "
	204	J. A. Timmons	2 adults and 3 children .	15 "
	205	Daniel Sanders	2 adults	5 "

Official account of the people sent south, etc.—(CONTINUED.)

DATE.	NO.	NAME.	ADULTS, CHILDREN, AND SERVANTS.	BAGGAGE.
1864.				
Sept. 14.	206	Mary Richards	1 adult and 2 children .	16 packages.
	207	Mrs. M. Shields	2 adults and 2 children.	10 "
	208	Mrs. J. Batterns	3 adults and 1 child. . .	13 "
	209	T. M. Jones.	2 adults, 4 children, 6 servants	70 "
	210	Mrs. M. Crawford. . .	1 adult and 1 child . . .	19 "
	211	Mrs. M. C. Morris . .	1 adult and 6 children .	43 "
	212	M. E. Grey	1 adult and 2 children .	20 "
	213	E. Carmichael	1 adult and 5 children .	12 "
	214	J. W. Rucker.	2 adults	20 "
	215	Mrs. L. V. Rucker . . .	2 adults	15 "
	216	S. A. Bridwell	1 adult	7 "
	217	Mrs. M. Coker.	1 adult and 2 children .	16 "
	218	Henry Buise	2 adults and 2 children.	27 "
	219	Mrs. W. Rushton . . .	1 adult and 7 children .	39 "
	220	Mrs. Rose	1 adult, 2 children, 1 servant	4 "
	221	Jos. Herndon.	2 adults and 3 children.	18 "
	222	Mrs. Zimmerman . . .	2 adults and 1 child. . .	10 "
	223	J. L. Wilson	1 adult	1 package.
	224	W. C. Nelson	2 adults and 1 child. . .	14 packages.
	225	C. Harden	2 adults	20 "
	226	J. C. Reves	3 adults	7 "
	227	Mrs. M. J. Corsey . . .	1 adult and 4 children .	6 "
	228	Alfred Lamb	5 adults and 1 child. . .	17 "
	229	Mrs. M. Paine	3 adults and 7 children.	19 "
	230	Mrs. T. H. Greyson. .	1 adult and 4 children .	21 "
	231	Mrs. R. Nichols	2 adults	10 "
	232	Mrs. M. G. Wickner .	1 adult and 1 child . . .	6 "
	233	S. Hopper	3 adults and 4 children.	43 packages and 1 cow.
	234	E. T. Hunnecut	2 adults, 4 children, 2 servants	43 packages.
	235	Mrs. N. Pulient	1 adult and 1 child . . .	17 "
	236	Sarah Fry.	1 adult, 2 children, 1 servant	17 "
	237	J. Veals	2 adults, 2 children, 2 servants	22 "
	238	C. A. Martin	1 adult	none.
	239	D. O. Driscoe	3 adults	37 packages.

Official account of the people sent south, etc. — (CONTINUED.)

DATE.	NO.	NAME.	ADULTS, CHILDREN, AND SERVANTS.	BAGGAGE.
1864.				
Sept. 14.	240	Jane Lofton	1 adult and 1 child . . .	
				18 packages.
	241	Mrs. N. A. Bray. . . .	1 adult	29 "
	242	Mrs. E. J. Frederick. .	2 adults and 4 children.	25 "
	243	Mrs. E. Leach	1 adult and 4 children .	23 "
	244	H. H. Richards	2 adults, 1 child, 1 servant	18 "
	245	J. A. Rush	2 adults and 4 children	23 "
	246	James Lester	2 adults	22 "
	247	Mrs. N. Christean. . .	1 adult	4 "
	247½	Mrs. W. A. Norris . .	1 adult	6 "
	248	Mrs. C. P. O'Keefe . .	1 adult, 2 children, 1 servant	45 "
	249	J. Caldwell	5 adults	50 "
	250	Mrs. B. F. Bennett . .	2 adults and 2 children.	40 "
	251	Mrs. E. C. Smith . . .	1 adult and 4 children .	40 "
	252	G. Stewart	3 adults and 6 children.	33 "
	253	Mrs. Cook	1 adult, 2 children, 2 servants	47 "
	254	Mrs. N. Simpson	5 adults	22 "
	255	Mrs. A. Smith	2 adults and 3 children.	1 package.
	256	Wm. Christean	1 adult	none.
	257	Mrs. E. Adams	2 adults and 1 child. . .	10 packages.
	258	J. C. Rogers	1 adult	2 "
	259	Mrs. S. E. Osborne . .	1 adult, 4 children, 1 servant	13 "
	260	Mrs. Collins	1 adult and 4 children .	13 "
	261	Miss Reeves	1 adult	12 "
	262	J. J. Whitly.	1 adult	1 package.
	263	Dr. Biggers	2 adults and 1 child. . .	60 packages.
	264	A. F. Cuming	2 adults and 1 child. . .	10 "
	265	G. A. Pilgrim	3 adults and 2 children.	35 "
	266	W. M. Bryant	2 adults and 5 children.	25 "
	267	Jos. Coker	1 adult	10 "
	268	E. B. Bachus	3 adults and 6 children.	40 "
	269	Mrs. N. Carroll	1 adult and 3 children .	20 "
	270	Mrs. E. Grubb.	2 adults and 1 child. . .	20 "
	271	Mrs. M. Heton	1 adult and 4 children .	23 "
	272	Mrs. E. Aiken	1 adult and 1 child . . .	13 "
	273	Mrs. N. A. Williams .	1 adult and 4 children .	18 "

Official account of the people sent south, etc.—(CONTINUED.)

DATE.	NO.	NAME.	ADULTS, CHILDREN, AND SERVANTS.	BAGGAGE.
1864.				
Sept. 14.	274	Mrs. M. Hartman . . .	1 adult	7 packages.
	275	John Ealeman	2 adults, 1 child, 1 servant	37 "
	276	Mrs. L. Taylor	1 adult	15 "
	277	Mrs. S. A. Trout. . . .	3 adults and 4 children.	8 "
	278	W. A. Packett	2 adults, 3 children, 3 servants	42 "
	279	Mrs. L. Ford.	1 adult and 6 children .	42 "
	280	N. McPherson	2 adults and 4 children.	17 "
	281	H. Wilson	2 adults and 7 children.	10 "
	282	W. King	1 adult	2 "
	283	Mrs. C. C. Rhodes . .	1 adult and 3 children .	23 "
	284	Mrs. M. Combs	1 adult	12 "
	285	James Kile	2 adults and 1 child. . .	19 "
	286	Mrs. A. F. Powers . . .	1 adult	16 "
	287	S. Hamilton	3 adults and 2 children.	16 "
	288	Henry Gaum.	2 adults and 5 children.	25 "
	289	W. F. Simpson.	2 adults and 5 children.	17 "
	290	Mrs. Robinson.	1 adult, 2 children, 1 servant	20 "
	291	Mrs. Scruchen	1 adult, 1 child, 1 servant	40 "
	292	Mrs. C. A. Jett	2 adults and 4 children.	30 "
	293	J. T. Coppage	2 adults and 5 children.	25 "
	294	J. H. Smith.	2 adults and 2 children.	56 "
	295	Mrs. L. Simpson. . . .	1 adult and 5 children .	24 "
	296	Mrs. L. Williams. . . .	1 adult and 5 children .	16 "
	297	Mrs. J. Berry	1 adult and 7 children .	20 "
	298	Miss Cole.	4 adults	18 "
	299	R. J. Maynard	2 adults and 4 children.	41 "
	300	R. Faulkner	2 adults, 1 child, 1 servant.	45 packages and 1 cow.
	301	D. Howard.	2 adults and 3 children.	30 packages.
	302	A. H. Bramlett.	1 adult	1 package.
	303	T. J. London.	2 adults and 4 children.	26 packages.
	304	Mrs. E. Green	2 adults and 2 children.	50 "

Official account of the people sent south, etc.—(CONTINUED.)

DATE.	NO.	NAME.	ADULTS, CHILDREN, AND SERVANTS.	BAGGAGE.
1864.				
Sept. 14.	305	W. B. Webb	4 adults, 3 children, 1 servant	35 packages.
	306	J. E. Webb	2 adults	17 "
	307	A. M. Johnson	3 adults	37 "
	308	J. A. Jett	1 adult	10 packages, wagon & horses.
	309	Mrs. R. Otto.	2 adults	10 packages.
	310	W. R. Venable	2 adults and 3 children .	25 "
Sept. 16.	311	Mrs. L. Pain	1 adult and 1 child . . .	10 "
	312	G. W. Croft	2 adults and 6 children.	52 "
	313	E. W. Marsh	3 adults, 4 children, 1 servant	67 "
	314	Mrs. H. Ward	1 adult	3 "
	315	Mrs. General Bowen.⎫ Mrs. Joyner . . . . . ⎭	2 adults, 3 children, 1 servant	26 "
	316	Mrs. Darst	1 adult and 2 children .	5 "
	317	J. R. Crew	2 adults and 3 servants	15 "
	318	W. J. Ballard	1 adult	1 package.
	319	P. Broadshaw.	2 adults	10 packages.
	320	T. E. Jones	1 adult and 1 child . . .	1 package.
	321	Mrs. E. Grey	1 adult	2 packages.
	322	Mrs. M. A. Hoosins. .	1 adult and 1 child . . .	none.
	323	Mrs. E. Skinner	1 adult and 4 children .	20 packages.
	324	G. O. Reed.	1 adult	none.
	325	J. C. Johnson.	2 adults and 2 children.	25 packages.
	326	P. J. McCullough . . .	1 adult	2 "
	327	G. Slaton	2 adults and 4 children.	25 "
	328	Mrs. E. Warrick	3 adults and 6 children.	32 "
	329	M. Solomen	2 adults	35 "
	330	Mrs. E. Buice	3 adults and 2 children.	50 "
	331	Mrs. M. A. Haygood .	2 adults	60 "
	332	Mrs. E. Roberts	1 adult	2 "
	333	Mrs. M. E. Martin . .	1 adult and 5 children .	42 "
	334	F. P. Rice.	2 adults	3 "
	335	Mrs. M. Denny	1 adult and 4 children .	28 "
	336	A. J. Pouder	2 adults and 3 children.	18 "
	337	Mrs. E. Leach	1 adult and 4 children .	26 "
	338	W. C. Hueghton . . .	3 adults and 5 children .	40 "

Official account of the people sent south, etc. — (CONTINUED.)

DATE.	No.	NAME.	ADULTS, CHILDREN, AND SERVANTS.	BAGGAGE.
1864.				
Sept. 16.	339	Sam Farrar	2 adults	17 packages.
	340	Mrs. E. Sewell	7 adults and 1 servant .	48 packages and 1 cow.
	341	J. J. Hunt.	2 adults	2 packages.
	342	Mrs. McCormack . . .	1 adult and 4 children	11 "
	343	Mrs. M. Davis	1 adult and 1 servant . .	41 "
	344	W. W. Roack	1 adult and 3 children .	60 "
	345	T. C. Bradbury	3 adults	25 "
	346	M. E. Smith	1 adult and 2 children .	35 "
	347	Mrs. R. P. Reid	1 adult and 3 children .	30 "
	348	Mrs. L. Underwood . .	1 adult	1 package.
	349	Mrs. E. Curtis	1 adult and 6 children .	60 packages.
	350	Mrs. J. Winship	1 adult	54 "
	351	J. L. Smith	5 adults and 1 servant. .	72 "
	352	Mrs. M. J. Johnson . .	4 adults	39 "
	353	P. Maddox	4 adults	50 "
	354	Miss Born	1 adult	25 "
	355	Mrs. E. C. Trail	4 adults	25 "
	356	Mrs. N. Loveless . . .	1 adult	30 "
	357	Mrs. T. C. Jackson. . .	1 adult and 1 child . . .	39 "
	358	J. C. Rasboy	2 adults and 6 children.	62 packages.
	359	J. M. Clark	2 adults and 3 servants	10 "
	360	J. M. Bramlett	2 adults, 4 children, 1 servant	20 "
	361	W. H. McMillen. . . .	1 adult	12 "
	362	C. Rinehart.	2 adults and 3 children.	27 "
	363	E. M. Monday	2 adults and 4 children.	48 packages and horse & buggy.
	364	Mrs. F. W. Johnson . .	1 adult, 5 children, 2 servants	35 packages.
	365	Mrs. E. Phillips	1 adult and 1 child . . .	23 "
	366	B. Mullegan	3 adults	12 "
	367	Mrs. M. Owens	2 adults and 6 children.	30 packages and 1 cow.
	368	Mrs. A. C. Trehelem .	3 adults and 1 child. . .	11 packages.

Official account of the people sent south, etc.—(CONTINUED.)

DATE.	NO.	NAME.	ADULTS, CHILDREN, AND SERVANTS.	BAGGAGE.
1864.				
Sept. 16.	369	Wm. Garvin	2 adults and 4 children.	15 packages.
	370	Mrs. C. C. Pain	1 adult and 2 children .	11 "
	371	Mrs. M. Tubb	1 adult and 1 servant . .	10 "
	372	R. Powens	1 adult and 3 children .	10 packages and "negro."
	373	Mrs. J. Wilson	1 adult	3 packages.
	374	Mrs. E. Farr	1 adult and 5 children .	20 "
	375	B. J. Austin.	2 adults, 1 child, 1 servant	40 "
	376	Mrs. J. Hall	1 adult	20 "
	377	Mrs. S. Sumerlin. . . .	1 adult and 2 children .	25 "
	378	J. E. Buchanan.	2 adults and 5 children .	none.
	379	Mrs. M. Merritt	1 adult	10 packages.
	380	Mrs. Wilson	1 adult	5 "
	381	S. N. Biggers.	1 adult	25 "
	382	Miss M. Burke.	1 adult	20 "
	383	J. Ormend	1 adult	1 package.
	384	Mrs. S. Ament	2 adults and 4 children.	20 packages.
	385	Mrs. Emma Rince . . .	2 adults and 2 children.	10 "
	386	T. P. Fleming	3 adults and 3 servants	30 "
	387	Mrs. N. Ray	1 adult and 5 children .	20 "
	388	Mrs. Coleman	1 adult and 4 children .	25 "
	389	Mrs. A. G. Ware	1 adult	2 "
	390	Mrs. F. Glave	1 adult	1 package.
	391	Mrs. J. R. Wilson . . .	1 adult	2 packages.
Sept. 17.	392	Mrs. N. Thompson . .	2 adults	20 "
	393	T. S. Denney.	2 adults and 1 child. . .	30 "
	394	Mrs. A. Manion	1 adult	36 "
	395	J. M. Calhoun	1 adult and 4 servants .	30 "
	396	E. J. Clark	1 adult	1 package.
	397	J. F. Trout	2 adults and 5 children.	60 packages.
	398	Mrs. Solomon	1 adult	2 "
	399	M. A. McCaian	1 adult and 2 children .	2 "
	400	Mrs. N. Wilder	2 adults	58 "
	401	Mrs. M. D. Wormack .	1 adult and 3 children .	22 "
	402	Mrs. C. Kill	1 adult	17 "

Official account of the people sent south, etc.— (CONTINUED.)

DATE.	NO.	NAME.	ADULTS, CHILDREN, AND SERVANTS.	BAGGAGE.
1864.				
Sept. 17.	403	Mrs. E. Sheirs	1 adult and 3 children .	18 packages.
	404	J. Langston.	3 adults and 4 children.	50 "
	405	J. J. Jenkins.	2 adults and 7 children.	55 "
	406	Mrs. F. W. Flynn . . .	2 adults, 3 children, 1 servant	20 "
	407	Mrs. C. Flynn	1 adult	10 "
	408	Mrs. C. M. Winn . . .	1 adult, 2 children, 1 servant	30 "
	409	Mrs. C. Caldwell . . .	4 adults and 9 children.	20 packages and 1 cow.
	410	W. N. Kirkpatrick . . .	2 adults and 3 children.	40 packages.
	411	Mrs. F. Glave	1 adult	1 package.
	412	Mrs. M. Maddox . . .	1 adult, 5 children, 1 servant	20 packages.
	413	A. F. Morrison.	2 adults and 4 children.	10 "
	414	E. Monday	2 adults and 6 children.	50 packages (did not go).
	415	A. J. Blackham.	1 adult	50 packages.
	416	Mrs. N. D. Wood . . .	2 adults	25 "
Sept. 18.	417	Mrs. C. Wood	2 adults	20 "
	418	Mrs. L. Cox	1 adult	none.
	419	Frank Berry	2 adults and 2 children.	50 packages.
	420	James Turner	1 adult	1 package.
	421	Miss E. Simpson. . . .	1 adult	3 packages.
	422	A. D. Westmoreland. .	1 adult and 1 servant . .	20 "
	423	Mrs. L. Ross	1 adult, 3 children, 1 servant	40 "
	424	Mrs. Morgan.	2 adults and 10 children.	12 "
	425	Mrs. M. Holnyd. . . .	2 adults	100 "
	426	Mrs. M. E. Clements .	1 adult, 3 children, 1 servant	50 "
	427	J. B. Colen	1 adult	1 package.
	428	Mrs. L. L. Grant . . .	1 adult, 2 children, 1 servant	50 packages.
	429	F. M. Jeffrys	1 adult	none.
	430	J. J. Ford	1 adult	none.

Official account of the people sent south, etc. — (CONCLUDED.)

DATE.	No.	NAME.	ADULTS, CHILDREN, AND SERVANTS.	BAGGAGE.
1864.				
Sept. 18.	431	Mrs. N. McDaniel. . .	1 adult and 5 children .	10 packages.
	432	E. Kennedy.	2 adults, 1 child, 2 servants	35 "
	433	Mrs. Kennedy	3 adults	22 "
	434	Mrs. V. Williams	1 adult and 4 children .	20 "
	435	W. Terry	1 adult	20 "
	436	Mrs. Dolman.	1 adult and 6 children .	10 "
	437	Mrs. Robbins	1 adult and 1 child . . .	3 "
	438	Miss E. Johns	2 adults	10 "
	439	Mrs. Gilmore.	1 adult and 2 children .	20 "
	440	G. M. Barry	1 adult	none.
Sept. 20.	441	Mrs. F. Carr	1 adult	10 packages.
	442	Mrs. J. Powell	1 adult and 3 children .	12 "
	(A)	Mrs. J. Dudley.	1 adult	3 "
	(B)	Mrs. A. Knight	1 adult and 3 children .	4 "
	(C)	Mrs. K. Bouls . . . . } Mrs. M. Bouls. . . . }	2 adults	14 "
	(D)	R. A. Davis	1 adult	none.

RECAPITULATION.

Adults	705		Packages of baggage.	8,842
Children	860		Horses	9
Servants	86		Cows	19
			Calves.	6
Total	1,651		Wagons.	2
			Drays	2
			Carriages	1
			Buggies.	1

Respectfully submitted:

(Signed)   WILLIAM G. LE DUC,

Lieutenant-Colonel and Chief Quartermaster Twentieth Army Corps.

Statement showing the organizations actually participating in the movement on Atlanta, Georgia, under General W. T. Sherman, in May, 1864.

ARMY OF THE CUMBERLAND.

MAJOR-GENERAL GEORGE H. THOMAS.

Fourth Army Corps.—Major-General O. O. HOWARD, *commanding.*

FIRST DIVISION.

Major-General D. S. STANLEY.

First Brigade. Brigadier-General Charles Cruft.	Second Brigade. Brig.-General W. C. Whitaker.	Third Brigade. Colonel William Grose.
1st Kentucky Infantry.	96th Illinois Infantry.	59th Illinois Infantry.
2d Kentucky Infantry.	115th Illinois Infantry.	75th Illinois Infantry.
90th Ohio Infantry.	35th Indiana Infantry.	80th Illinois Infantry.
101st Ohio Infantry.	84th Indiana Infantry.	84th Illinois Infantry.
31st Indiana Infantry.	40th Ohio Infantry.	9th Indiana Infantry.
81st Indiana Infantry.	51st Ohio Infantry.	30th Indiana Infantry.
21st Illinois Infantry.	99th Ohio Infantry.	36th Indiana Infantry.
38th Illinois Infantry.	21st Kentucky Infantry.	77th Pennsylvania Infantry.

Artillery.

5th Indiana Battery Light Artillery; Independent Battery B, Pennsylvania Light Artillery.

SECOND DIVISION.

Major-General JOHN NEWTON.

First Brigade. Brigadier-General N. Kimball.	Second Brigade. Brig.-General G. D. Wagner.	Third Brigade. Brig.-General C. G. Harker.
2d Missouri Infantry.	40th Indiana Infantry.	3d Kentucky Infantry.
15th Missouri Infantry.	57th Indiana Infantry.	64th Ohio Infantry.
24th Wisconsin Infantry.	26th Ohio Infantry.	65th Ohio Infantry.
36th Illinois Infantry.	97th Ohio Infantry.	125th Ohio Infantry.
44th Illinois Infantry.	100th Illinois Infantry.	22d Illinois Infantry.
73d Illinois Infantry.	28th Kentucky Infantry.	27th Illinois Infantry.
74th Illinois Infantry.		42d Illinois Infantry.
88th Illinois Infantry.		51st Illinois Infantry.
		79th Illinois Infantry.

Artillery.

M, 1st Illinois Light Artillery; A, Ohio Light Artillery.

THIRD DIVISION.

Brigadier-General T. J. WOOD.

First Brigade.	Second Brigade.	Third Brigade.
Colonel W. H. Gibson	Brig.-General W. B. Hazen.	Colonel Fred Knefler.

First Brigade.	Second Brigade.	Third Brigade.
8th Kansas Infantry.	1st Ohio Infantry.	9th Kentucky Infantry.
15th Wisconsin Infantry.	6th Ohio Infantry.	17th Kentucky Infantry.
15th Ohio Infantry.	41st Ohio Infantry.	13th Ohio Infantry.
49th Ohio Infantry.	93d Ohio Infantry.	19th Ohio Infantry.
32d Indiana Infantry.	124th Ohio Infantry.	59th Ohio Infantry.
25th Illinois Infantry.	5th Kentucky Infantry.	79th Indiana Infantry.
35th Illinois Infantry.	6th Kentucky Infantry.	86th Indiana Infantry.
89th Illinois Infantry.	23d Kentucky Infantry.	
	6th Indiana Infantry.	

Artillery.

6th Battery Ohio Light Artillery; Bridge's Battery, Illinois Light Artillery.

Fourteenth Army Corps.—*Major-General* JOHN M. PALMER, commanding.

FIRST DIVISION.

Brigadier-General R. W. JOHNSON.

First Brigade.	Second Brigade.	Third Brigade.
Brigadier-General W. P. Carlin.	Brigadier-General J. H. King.	Colonel B. F. Scribner.

First Brigade.	Second Brigade.	Third Brigade.
21st Wisconsin Infantry.	1st Bat. 15th U.S. Infantry.	78th Pennsylvania Infant'y.
10th Wisconsin Infantry.	2d Bat. 15th U.S. Infantry.	79th Pennsylvania Infant'y.
33d Ohio Infantry.	1st Bat. 16th U.S. Infantry.	21st Ohio Infantry.
94th Ohio Infantry.	2d Bat. 16th U.S. Infantry.	74th Ohio Infantry.
2d Ohio Infantry.	1st Bat. 18th U.S. Infantry.	37th Indiana Infantry.
42d Indiana Infantry.	2d Bat. 18th U.S. Infantry.	1st Wisconsin Infantry.
88th Indiana Infantry.	1st Bat. 19th U.S. Infantry.	38th Indiana Infantry.
104th Illinois Infantry.	69th Ohio Infantry.	
15th Kentucky Infantry.	11th Michigan Infantry.	

Artillery.

C, 1st Illinois Light Artillery; I, 1st Ohio Light Artillery.

SECOND DIVISION.

Brigadier-General J. C. DAVIS.

First Brigade. Brigadier-General J. D. Morgan.	Second Brigade. Colonel J. G. Mitchell.	Third Brigade. Colonel Daniel McCook.
10th Illinois Infantry.	121st Ohio Infantry.	52d Ohio Infantry.
16th Illinois Infantry.	113th Ohio Infantry.	85th Illinois Infantry.
60th Illinois Infantry.	98th Ohio Infantry.	86th Illinois Infantry.
10th Michigan Infantry.	108th Ohio Infantry.	110th Illinois Infantry.
14th Michigan Infantry.	3d Ohio Infantry.	125th Illinois Infantry.
	78th Illinois Infantry.	22d Indiana Infantry.
	34th Illinois Infantry.	

Artillery.

I, 2d Illinois Light Artillery; 5th Wisconsin Battery.

THIRD DIVISION.

Brigadier-General ABSALOM BAIRD.

First Brigade. Brigadier-General J. B. Turchin.	Second Brigade. Colonel R. Van Derveer.	Third Brigade. Colonel George P. Este.
11th Ohio Infantry.	35th Ohio Infantry.	4th Kentucky Infantry.
17th Ohio Infantry.	2d Minnesota Infantry.	10th Kentucky Infantry.
31st Ohio Infantry.	9th Ohio Infantry.	18th Kentucky Infantry.
89th Ohio Infantry.	87th Indiana Infantry.	10th Indiana Infantry.
92d Ohio Infantry.	105th Ohio Infantry.	74th Indiana Infantry.
82d Indiana Infantry.	101st Indiana Infantry.	14th Ohio Infantry.
19th Illinois Infantry.	75th Indiana Infantry.	38th Ohio Infantry.
24th Illinois Infantry.		

Artillery.

7th Indiana Battery; 19th Indiana Battery.

Twentieth Army Corps.—Major-General JOSEPH HOOKER, *commanding.*

Escort. K, 15th Illinois Cavalry.

FIRST DIVISION.

Brigadier-General A. S. WILLIAMS.

First Brigade. Brigadier-General J. F. Knipe.	Second Brigade. Brigadier-General T. H. Ruger.	Third Brigade. Colonel J. S. Robinson.
123d New York Infantry. 3d Maryland Infantry (det.). 141st New York Infantry. 5th Connecticut Infantry. 46th Pennsylvania Infantry.	2d Massachusetts Infantry. 3d Wisconsin Infantry. 107th New York Infantry. 150th New York Infantry. 27th Indiana Infantry. 13th New Jersey Infantry.	82d Ohio Infantry. 61st Ohio Infantry. 143d New York Infantry. 45th New York Infantry. 82d Illinois Infantry. 101st Illinois Infantry.

Artillery.

I and M, 1st New York Light Artillery.

SECOND DIVISION.

Brigadier-General JOHN W. GEARY.

First Brigade. Colonel Charles Candy.	Second Brigade. Colonel J. F. Lockman.	Third Brigade. Colonel David Ireland.
5th Ohio Infantry. 7th Ohio Infantry. 29th Ohio Infantry. 66th Ohio Infantry. 28th Pennsylvania Infantry. 147th Pennsylvania Infan'y.	73d Pennsylvania Infantry. 109th Pennsylva. Infantry. 33d New Jersey Infantry. 119th New York Infantry. 134th New York Infantry. 154th New York Infantry.	60th New York Infantry. 78th New York Infantry. 102d New York Infantry. 137th New York Infantry. 149th New York Infantry. 29th Pennsylvania Infant'y. 111th Pennsylvania Infan'y.

Artillery.

13th New York Battery—Independent; E, Pennsylvania Light Artillery.

THIRD DIVISION.

Major-General DANIEL BUTTERFIELD.

First Brigade.	Second Brigade.	Third Brigade.
Brigadier-General W. T. Ward.	Colonel John Coburn.	Colonel James Wood, Jr.

70th Indiana Infantry.	33d Indiana Infantry.	136th New York Infantry.
102d Illinois Infantry.	85th Indiana Infantry.	33d Massachusetts Infan'y.
105th Illinois Infantry.	19th Michigan Infantry.	55th Ohio Infantry.
129th Illinois Infantry.	22d Wisconsin Infantry.	73d Ohio Infantry.
79th Ohio Infantry.		26th Wisconsin Infantry.
		20th Connecticut Infantry.

Artillery.

C, 1st Ohio Light Artillery; I, 1st Michigan Light Artillery.

Cavalry Corps.—Brigadier-General W. L. ELLIOTT.

FIRST DIVISION.

Colonel E. M. McCook.

First Brigade.	Second Brigade.
Colonel Joseph B. Dorr.	Colonel O. H. La Grange.
2d Michigan Cavalry.	1st Wisconsin Cavalry.
8th Iowa Cavalry.	2d Indiana Cavalry.
1st East Tennessee Cavalry.	4th Indiana Cavalry.

18th Indiana Battery.

SECOND DIVISION.

Brigadier-General KENNER GARRARD.

First Brigade.	Second Brigade.	Third Brigade.
Colonel R. H. G. Minty.	Colonel Eli Long.	Colonel John T. Wilder.

4th U.S. Cavalry.	1st Ohio Cavalry.	17th Indiana Mounted Infantry.
4th Michigan Cavalry.	3d Ohio Cavalry.	72d Indiana Mounted Infantry.
7th Pennsylvania Cavalry.	4th Ohio Cavalry.	98th Illinois Mounted Infantry.
		123 Illinois Mounted Infantry.

Chicago Board of Trade Battery.

THIRD DIVISION.

Brigadier-General JUDSON KILPATRICK.

First Brigade.	Second Brigade. Colonel Charles C. Smith.	Third Brigade. Colonel E. H. Murray.
5th Iowa Cavalry.	10th Ohio Cavalry.	92d Illinois M'nted Infantry.
3d Indiana Cavalry.	2d Kentucky Cavalry.	3d Kentucky Cavalry.
9th Pennsylvania Cavalry.	8th Indiana Cavalry.	5th Kentucky Cavalry.

Artillery.
10th Wisconsin Battery.

Reserve Brigade. Colonel H. Le Favour.	Pioneer Brigade. Colonel George P. Buell.
9th Michigan Infantry.	58th Indiana Infantry.
22d Michigan Infantry.	Pontoon Battalion.

Unassigned Artillery.
11th Indiana Battery.

ARMY OF THE TENNESSEE.

MAJOR-GENERAL JAMES B. McPHERSON.

Fifteenth Army Corps.—*Major-General* JOHN A. LOGAN,
commanding.

FIRST DIVISION.

Brigadier-General P. J. OSTERHAUS.

First Brigade. Brigadier-General C. R. Woods.	Second Brigade. Colonel J. A. Williamson.	Third Brigade. Colonel H. Wangelin.
76th Ohio Infantry.	4th Iowa Infantry.	3d Missouri Infantry.
26th Iowa Infantry.	9th Iowa Infantry.	12th Missouri Infantry.
30th Iowa Infantry.	25th Iowa Infantry.	17th Missouri Infantry.
27th Missouri Infantry.	31st Iowa Infantry.	29th Missouri Infantry.
		31st Missouri Infantry.
		32d Missouri Infantry.

Artillery.
F, 2d Missouri Light Artillery; 4th Ohio Battery.

SECOND DIVISION.

Brigadier-General MORGAN L. SMITH.

First Brigade.	Second Brigade.
Brigadier-General	Brigadier-General
Giles A. Smith.	J. A. J. Lightburn.
6th Missouri Infantry.	30th Ohio Infantry.
8th Missouri Infantry.	37th Ohio Infantry.
55th Illinois Infantry.	47th Ohio Infantry.
111th Illinois Infantry.	53d Ohio Infantry.
127th Illinois Infantry.	54th Ohio Infantry.
57th Ohio Infantry.	83d Indiana Infantry.
	4th West Virginia Infantry.

Artillery.

A, B, and H, 1st Illinois Light Artillery.

FOURTH DIVISION.

Brigadier-General WILLIAM HARROW.

First Brigade.	Second Brigade.	Third Brigade.
Colonel R. Williams.	Brig.-General	Colonel John M. Oliver.
	John M. Corse.	
12th Indiana Infantry.	46th Ohio Infantry.	15th Michigan Infantry.
100th Indiana Infantry.	6th Iowa Infantry.	70th Ohio Infantry.
26th Illinois Infantry.	40th Illinois Infantry.	48th Illinois Infantry.
90th Illinois Infantry.	103d Illinois Infantry.	99th Indiana Infantry.
	97th Indiana Infantry.	

Artillery.

1st Iowa Battery; F, 1st Illinois Light Artillery.

Sixteenth Army Corps (Left Wing).—Brigadier-General G. M. DODGE, *commanding.*

SECOND DIVISION.

Brigadier-General T. W. SWEENY.

First Brigade.	Second Brigade.	Third Brigade.
Colonel E. W. Rice.	Colonel Augustus Mersy.	Colonel M. M. Bane.
2d Iowa Infantry.	9th Illinois Infantry.	7th Illinois Infantry.
7th Iowa Infantry.	12th Illinois Infantry.	50th Illinois Infantry.
52d Illinois Infantry.	66th Illinois Infantry.	57th Illinois Infantry.
66th Indiana Infantry.	81st Ohio Infantry.	39th Iowa Infantry.

Artillery.

H, 1st Missouri Light Artillery; B, 1st Michigan Light Artillery.

FOURTH DIVISION.

Brigadier-General JAMES C. VEATCH.

First Brigade.	Second Brigade.
Brigadier-General	Colonel John W. Sprague.
J. W. Fuller.	
18th Missouri Infantry.	25th Wisconsin Infantry.
27th Ohio Infantry.	35th New Jersey Infantry.
39th Ohio Infantry.	43d Ohio Infantry.
64th Illinois Infantry.	63d Ohio Infantry.

Cavalry.

1st Alabama Cavalry.

Artillery.

14th Ohio Battery; C, 1st Michigan, and F, 2d U.S. Artillery.

*Seventeenth Army Corps.—Major-General F. P. BLAIR, *Jr.,*
commanding.

THIRD DIVISION.

Brigadier-General M. D. LEGGETT.

First Brigade.	Second Brigade.	Third Brigade.
Brigadier-General	Colonel R. K. Scott.	Colonel A. G. Molloy.
M. F. Force.		
20th Illinois Infantry.	20th Ohio Infantry.	17th Wisconsin Infantry.
30th Illinois Infantry.	32d Ohio Infantry..	⌠14th Wisconsin Infantry.
31st Illinois Infantry.	68th Ohio Infantry.	Det's.⟨81st Illinois Infantry.
45th Illinois Infantry.	78th Ohio Infantry.	⌡95th Illinois Infantry.
16th Wisconsin		
Infantry.		

Artillery.

D, 1st Illinois; H, 1st Michigan and 3d Ohio Battery.

*Joined in June, 1864.

FOURTH DIVISION.
Brigadier-General W. Q. GRESHAM.

First Brigade.	Second Brigade.	Third Brigade.
Colonel W. S. Sanderson.	Colonel J. C. Rogers.	Colonel William Hall.
3d Iowa Infantry.	14th Illinois Infantry.	11th Iowa Infantry.
12th Wisconsin Infantry.	15th Illinois Infantry.	13th Iowa Infantry.
23d Indiana Infantry.	41st Illinois Infantry.	15th Iowa Infantry.
32d Illinois Infantry.	53d Illinois Infantry.	16th Iowa Infantry.
53d Indiana Infantry.	33d Wisconsin Infantry.	

Cavalry.

G, 11th Illinois Cavalry.

Artillery.

10th and 15th Ohio Batteries; 1st Minnesota Battery;
C, 1st Missouri, and F, 2d Illinois Batteries.

Army of the Ohio (Twenty-third Army Corps).—Major-General J. M. SCHOFIELD, *commanding.*

FIRST DIVISION.
Brigadier-General A. P. HOVEY.

First Brigade.	Second Brigade.
Colonel Richard Baxter.	Colonel J. C. McQuiston.
120th Indiana Infantry.	123d Indiana Infantry.
124th Indiana Infantry.	129th Indiana Infantry.
128th Indiana Infantry.	130th Indiana Infantry.

Artillery.

23d and 24th Indiana Batteries.

SECOND DIVISION.
Brigadier-General M. S. HASCALL.

First Brigade.	Second Brigade.
Brigadier-General N. C. McLean	Colonel John A. Bond.
25th Michigan Infantry.	23d Michigan Infantry.
80th Indiana Infantry.	111th Ohio Infantry.
13th Kentucky Infantry.	107th Illinois Infantry.
3d Tennessee Infantry.	118th Ohio Infantry.
6th Tennessee Infantry.	

Artillery.

19th Ohio Battery, and F, 1st Michigan Light Artillery.

THIRD DIVISION.

Brigadier-General J. D. Cox.

First Brigade.	Second Brigade.
Colonel J. W. Reilly.	Brigadier-General M. D. Manson.
100th Ohio Infantry.	65th Indiana Infantry.
104th Ohio Infantry.	63d Indiana Infantry.
112th Illinois Infantry.	24th Kentucky Infantry.
16th Kentucky Infantry.	5th Tennessee Infantry.
8th Tennessee Infantry.	103d Ohio Infantry.

Artillery.

D, 1st Ohio and 15th Indiana Battery.

CAVALRY DIVISION.

Major-General GEORGE STONEMAN.

First Brigade.	Second Brigade.
Colonel C. D. Pannabaker.	Colonel Israel Garrard.
1st Kentucky Cavalry.	7th Ohio Cavalry.
11th Kentucky Cavalry.	9th Michigan Cavalry.
8th Michigan Cavalry.	5th Indiana Cavalry.
6th Indiana Cavalry.	16th Kentucky Cavalry.
12th Kentucky Cavalry.	
16th Illinois Cavalry.	

List of regiments, etc., belonging to the Armies of the Cumberland, Tennessee, and Ohio, left in Tennessee, Kentucky, Alabama, and Mississippi, when General W. T. Sherman commenced his advance on Atlanta, Georgia, in May, 1864.

ARMY OF THE CUMBERLAND.
AT WAUHATCHIE.

Third Brigade, First Cavalry Division —Col. L. D. WATKINS,
commanding.

4th, 5th, and 6th Kentucky Cavalry.

AT NASHVILLE, TULLAHOMA, AND GALLATIN, TENNESSEE.

Fourth Cavalry Division —Brigadier-General A. C. GILLEM, commanding.

First Brigade.	Second Brigade.	Third Brigade.
(Nashville.)	(Tullahoma.)	(Gallatin.)
Lieut.-Col.	Lieut.-Colonel	Colonel J. K. Miller.
D. G. Thornburgh.	George Spalding.	
2d Tennessee Cavalry.	5th Tennessee Cavalry.	8th Tennessee Cavalry.
3d Tennessee Cavalry.	11th Tennessee Cavalry.	9th Tennessee Cavalry.
4th Tennessee Cavalry.	12th Tennessee Cavalry.	13th Tennessee Cavalry.

A, 1st Tennessee Light Artillery.

District of Nashville —General L. H. ROUSSEAU, commanding.

FIRST BRIGADE, FOURTH DIVISION, TWENTIETH CORPS.
Brigadier-General R. S. GRANGER.
AT NASHVILLE.

18th Michigan Infantry.	10th Tennessee Infantry.
102d Ohio Infantry.	73d Indiana Infantry.
13th Wisconsin Infantry.	

UNASSIGNED REGIMENTS, FOURTH DIVISION, TWENTIETH CORPS.
At Murfreesboro, Tennessee, 115th Ohio Infantry.
At Duck River Bridge, Tennessee, 31st Wisconsin Infantry.
At McMinnville, Tennessee, 23d Missouri Infantry.
At Clarksville, Tennessee, 83d Illinois Infantry (Right Wing).
At Fort Donelson, Tennessee, 83d Illinois Infantry (Left Wing).
At Elk River Bridge, Tennessee, 71st Ohio Infantry.
At Bridgeport, Alabama, 58th and 68th New York, 75th Pennsylvania and
106th Ohio Infantry, 9th Ohio and 20th Indiana Batteries.

POST FORCES, NASHVILLE, TENNESSEE.
Brigadier-General R. S. GRANGER.

15th United States Colored Infantry.
17th United States Colored Infantry.
15th Pennsylvania Cavalry.
8th Indiana Cavalry.

Garrison Artillery.

C, 1st Tennessee Light Artillery.
D, 1st Tennessee Light Artillery.
G, 1st Tennessee Light Artillery.
E, 1st Michigan Light Artillery.
I, 4th United States Light Artillery.
12th Indiana Light Artillery.

Artillery Reserve, D. C.

F, 4th United States Artillery.
G, 4th United States Artillery.
H, 4th United States Artillery.
M, 4th United States Artillery.
H, 5th United States Artillery.
K, 5th United States Artillery.
F, 1st Ohio Artillery.
G, 1st Ohio Artillery.
M, 1st Ohio Artillery.
1st Kentucky Battery.
18th Ohio Battery.

22d Indiana Battery.
M, 2d Illinois Light Artillery. } Temporarily at post.
I, 1st Missouri Light Artillery.

POST FORCES, FORT DONELSON, TENNESSEE.
Lieutenant-Colonel E. C. BROTT, *commanding.*
C, 2d Illinois Light Artillery.

POST FORCES, CLARKSVILLE, TENNESSEE.
Colonel A. A. SMITH, *commanding.*
H, 2d Illinois Light Artillery.

POST FORCES, GALLATIN, TENNESSEE.
Lieutenant-Colonel A. I. BROWN, *commanding.*
13th Indiana Battery.

POST FORCES, COLUMBIA, TENNESSEE.
Colonel —— FUNKHOUSER, *commanding.*
21st Indiana Battery.

POST FORCES, MURFREESBORO, TENNESSEE.
Brigadier-General H. P. VAN CLEVE, *commanding.*
D, 1st Michigan Artillery.
12th Ohio Battery.
8th Wisconsin Battery.

POST FORCES, BRIDGEPORT, ALABAMA.
Colonel W. KRZYZANOWSKI, *commanding.*
133d Indiana Infantry.

TROOPS ON THE NASHVILLE & NORTHWESTERN RAILROAD.
Brigadier-General A. C. GILLEM, *commanding.*
12th United States Colored Infantry. 1st Missouri Engineers and Mechanics.
13th United States Colored Infantry. 1st Kansas Battery.

GARRISON ARTILLERY, BRIDGEPORT, ALABAMA.
Major W. EDGARTON, *commanding.*
B and E, 1st Ohio Light Artillery.

ENGINEER BRIGADE, CHATTANOOGA, TENNESSEE.
Colonel W. B. McCREERY, *commanding.*

18th Ohio Infantry.   21st Michigan Infantry.
13th Michigan Infantry.   22d Michigan Infantry.

PIONEER BRIGADE.
Colonel GEORGE P. BUELL, *commanding.*
58th Indiana Infantry (with army in the field).
1st Battalion Pioneers (at Chattanooga).
2d Battalion Pioneers (at Chattanooga).
Pontoon Battalion (with army in the field).

POST FORCES, CHATTANOOGA, TENNESSEE.
Brigadier-General J. B. STEEDMAN, *commanding.*

15th Indiana Infantry.   68th Indiana Infantry.
29th Indiana Infantry.   3d Ohio Infantry.
44th Indiana Infantry.   24th Ohio Infantry.
51st Indiana Infantry.   8th Kentucky Infantry.

GARRISON ARTILLERY, CHATTANOOGA, TENNESSEE.
Major C. S. COTTER, *commanding.*

20th Ohio Battery.   3d Wisconsin Battery.
K, 1st Michigan Light Artillery.   G, 1st Missouri Light Artillery.
C, 1st Wisconsin Heavy Artillery.   8th Indiana Battery.
A, 1st Michigan Light Artillery.   4th Indiana Battery.

WESTERN RESERVE CORPS, NASHVILLE, TENNESSEE.
Major A. W. GAZZAM, *commanding.*
139th, 148th, 149th, 150th, 151st, 152d, 153d, 154th, 155th, 160th, and 165th Co's.

SIGNAL CORPS.
Captain CHARLES R. CASE, *Chief Signal-Officer.*

ARMY OF THE TENNESSEE.

Third Division, Fifteenth Army Corps — Brigadier-General JOHN E. SMITH, *commanding.*

First Brigade. (At Huntsville, Alabama.)	Second Brigade. (At Larkinsville, Alabama.)	Third Brigade. (At Decatur, Alabama.)
Colonel J. J. Alexander.	Colonel G. B. Raum.	Colonel B. D. Dean.
59th Indiana Infantry.	56th Illinois Infantry.	26th Missouri Infantry.
48th Indiana Infantry.	17th Iowa Infantry.	5th Iowa Infantry.
4th Minnesota Infantry.	10th Missouri Infantry.	10th Iowa Infantry.
18th Wisconsin Infantry.	80th Ohio Infantry.	93d Illinois Infantry.
63d Illinois Infantry.	E, 24th Missouri Infantry.	

Cavalry.	*Artillery.*
5th Ohio Cavalry.	D, 1st Missouri Light Artillery.
F, 4th Missouri Cavalry.	6th Wisconsin Battery.
	12th Wisconsin Battery.

Third Brigade, Fourth Division, Sixteenth Army Corps — Colonel JOHN H. HOWE, *commanding.*

AT DECATUR, ALABAMA.
32d Wisconsin Infantry.
17th New York Infantry.
25th Indiana Infantry.
D, 2d Illinois Light Artillery.

First Division, Sixteenth Army Corps — Brigadier-General J. A. MOWER, *commanding.*

First Brigade. (At Memphis.) Colonel W. L. McMillen.	Second Brigade. (At Vicksburg.) Colonel L. B. Hubbard.	Third Brigade. (At Vicksburg.) Colonel S. G. Hill.
72d Ohio Infantry.	11th Missouri Infantry.	8th Iowa Infantry.
95th Ohio Infantry.	47th Illinois Infantry.	12th Iowa Infantry.
114th Illinois Infantry.	8th Wisconsin Infantry.	33d Missouri Infantry.
93d Indiana Infantry.	5th Minnesota Infantry.	35th Iowa Infantry.
E, 1st Illinois Light Art'y.	2d Iowa Battery.	6th Indiana Battery.

Third Division, Sixteenth Army Corps—Colonel DAVID MOORE, com'ding.

AT VICKSBURG, MISSISSIPPI.

First Brigade.	Second Brigade.	Third Brigade.
Colonel C. D. Murray.	Colonel W. T. Shaw.	Colonel E. H. Wolfe.
89th Indiana Infantry.	14th Iowa Infantry.	117th Illinois Infantry.
119th Illinois Infantry.	27th Iowa Infantry.	178th New York Infantry.
58th Illinois Infantry.	32d Iowa Infantry.	52d Indiana Infantry.
21st Missouri Infantry.	24th Missouri Infantry.	49th Illinois Infantry.
9th Indiana Battery.	3d Indiana Battery.	

District of West Tennessee—Major-General C. C. WASHBURNE, command'g.

CAVALRY DIVISION, SIXTEENTH ARMY CORPS.

Brigadier-General B. H. GRIERSON, commanding.

First Brigade.	Second Brigade.	Third Brigade.
(At White's Station, Tennessee.)	(At Memphis, Tennessee.)	(At Memphis, Tennessee.)
Colonel George E. Waring.	Colonel E. F. Winslow.	Lieutenant-Colonel H. B. Burgh.
4th Missouri Cavalry.	4th Iowa Cavalry.	9th Illinois Cavalry.
2d New Jersey Cavalry.	3d Iowa Cavalry.	6th Illinois Cavalry.
19th Pennsylvania Cavalry.	10th Missouri Cavalry.	3d Illinois Cavalry.
7th Indiana Cavalry.	K, 1st Illinois Light Art'y.	
6th Tennessee Cavalry.		

District of Memphis—Brigadier-General R. P. BUCKLAND, commanding.

113th Illinois Infantry.	61st U.S. Colored Inf'try.	3d U.S. Col'd Heavy Art'y.
108th Illinois Infantry.	55th U.S. Colored Inf'try.	7th U.S. Col'd Heavy Art'y.
120th Illinois Infantry.	63d U.S. Col'd (det.) Inf'y.	G, 1st Illinois Light Artil'y.
11th Missouri Infantry.	14th Indiana Battery.	B, 2d Illinois Light Artil'y.
59th U.S. Colored Inf'try.	F, 2d U.S. Col'd L't Art'y.	7th Wisconsin Battery.

District of Columbus — Brigadier-General HENRY PRINCE, *commanding.*

122d Illinois Infantry.	4th U.S. Col'd Heavy Ar'y.	8th U.S. Col'd Heavy
34th New Jersey	C, 2d Illinois Light Artil'y.	Art'y.
Infantry.	7th Minnesota Infantry.	7th Tennessee Cav'y
10th Minnesota Infantry.		(det.).

District of Vicksburg — Major-General H. W. SLOCUM, *commanding.*

FIRST DIVISION, SEVENTEENTH ARMY CORPS.

Brigadier-General E. S. DENNIS, *commanding.*

AT VICKSBURG, MISSISSIPPI.

First Brigade.	Second Brigade.	Second Brigade
Colonel F. A. Starring.	Colonel J. H. Coates.	(4th Division).
		Colonel B. Dornblaser.
30th Missouri Infantry.	11th Illinois Infantry.	46th Illinois Infantry.
58th Ohio Infantry.		76th Illinois Infantry.
72d Illinois Infantry.		
1st Kansas Infantry.		

Artillery.

7th Ohio Battery.
L, 2d Illinois Light Artillery.
M, 1st Missouri Light Artillery.

First Division, U.S. Colored Troops — Brigadier-General J. P. HAWKINS, *commanding.*

First Brigade. (Vicksburg, Mississippi.)	Second Brigade. (Vicksburg, Mississippi.)	United States Forces. (Goodrich's Landing, Louisiana.)
Brigadier-General J. F. Shepard.	Colonel H. Schofield.	Colonel A. W. Webber.
48th U.S. Colored Inf'y.	47th U.S. Colored Inf'y.	51st U.S. Colored Infantry.
49th U.S. Colored Inf'y.	50th U.S. Colored Inf'y.	66th U.S. Colored Infantry.
53d U.S. Colored Inf'y.	52d U.S. Colored Inf'y.	D, 2d U.S. Col'd Light Ar'y.
46th U.S. Colored Inf'y.	C, 2d U.S. Col'd Light Ar'y.	

5th United States Colored Heavy Artillery. (Garrison of Vicksburg.)

United States Forces at Milliken's Bend, Louisiana — Colonel W. F. WOOD, *commanding*.

46th United States Colored Infantry.

Cavalry Brigade —Colonel T. STEPHENS, *commanding*.

2d Wisconsin Cavalry.
5th Illinois Cavalry.
11th Illinois Cavalry.

10th Missouri Cavalry.
3d U.S. Colored Cavalry.

Garrison of Vicksburg —Brigadier-General J. A. MALTBY, *commanding*.

8th Illinois Infantry.
124th Illinois Infantry.
17th Illinois Infantry (det.).
81st Illinois Infantry.

7th Missouri Infantry (det.).
8th Ohio Battery.
26th Ohio Battery.

District of Natchez —Colonel B. G. FARRAR, *commanding*.

29th Illinois Infantry.
28th Illinois Infantry.
4th Illinois Cavalry.
K, 2d Illinois Light Artillery.
58th U.S. Colored Infantry.

71st U.S. Colored Infantry.
70th U.S. Colored Infantry.
63d U.S. Colored Infantry.
64th U.S. Colored Infantry.
6th U.S. Colored Heavy Art'y.

Mississippi Marine Brigade —Brigadier General A. W. ELLET, *com'ding*.

ARMY OF THE OHIO.

Fourth Division, Twenty-third Army Corps—Brigadier-General
JACOB AMMEN, *commanding*.

First Brigade.	Second Brigade.	Third Brigade.
(Cumberland Gap, Tennessee.)	(Knoxville, Tennessee.)	(Loudon, Tennessee.)
Colonel W. Y. Dillard.	Brigadier-General D. Tillson.	Colonel B. P. Runkle.
34th Kentucky Infantry.	2d East Tennessee Inf'y.	50th Ohio Infantry.
2d N. C. Mounted Infantry.	1st Ohio Heavy Artillery.	1st Tennessee Infantry.
9th Indiana Infantry.	1st U.S. Col'd Heavy Ar'y.	11th Kentucky Infantry.
L, 1st Michigan Light Ar'y.	21st Ohio Battery.	27th Kentucky Infantry.
M, 1st Michigan Light Ar'y.	Colvin's Illinois Battery.	4th Tennessee Infantry.
B, 1st Tenn'see Light Ar'y.	Elgin's Illinois Battery.	Henshaw's Illinois Battery.
22d Ohio Battery.	Wilder's Indiana Battery.	14th Illinois Cavalry.
11th Tennessee Cavalry.	10th Michigan Cavalry.	

NOTE.—The 91st Indiana, 50th Ohio, 1st Tennessee, and the 11th and 27th Kentucky, of this command, were ordered to join the army in the field, May 17, 1864.

District of Kentucky, or Fifth Division, Twenty-third Army Corps—Brigadier-General S. G. BURBRIDGE, *commanding*.

FIRST DIVISION.

Brigadier-General E. H. HOBSON, *commanding*.

First Brigade.	Second Brigade.	Third Brigade.
Colonel S. Brown.	Colonel C. J. True.	Colonel C. S. Hanson.
39th Kent'y Mounted Inf'y.	40th Kent'y Mounted Inf'y.	37th Kent'y Mounted Inf'y.
11th Michigan Cavalry.	12th Ohio Cavalry.	52d Kent'y Mounted Inf'y.
14th Kentucky Infantry.	13th Kentucky Cavalry.	

FOURTH BRIGADE.

Colonel J. M. BROWN, *commanding*.

30th Kentucky Mounted Infantry.	49th Kentucky Infantry.
45th Kentucky Mounted Infantry.	1st Wisconsin Heavy Artillery.
47th Kentucky Infantry.	

SECOND DIVISION.

Brigadier-General HUGH EWING, *commanding*.

First Brigade.	Second Brigade.
Lieutenant-Colonel	Colonel C. Maxwell.
T. B. Fairleigh.	

77th Co., 2d Battalion, V. R. C.   26th Kentucky Infantry.
56th Co., 2d Battalion, V. R. C.   35th Kentucky Infantry.
40th Co., 2d Battalion, V. R. C.   (mounted).
D, 23d Regiment, V. R. C.   2d Ohio Heavy Artillery (det.).
48th Kentucky Infantry.
2d Ohio Heavy Artillery (det.).
20th Kentucky Infantry.
27th Kentucky Infantry.

Newport Barracks, Kentucky—Captain CHARLES SMITH,
commanding.
Permanent party.

SAVANNAH, GEORGIA, *October* 23, 1875.
General W. T. SHERMAN, *United States Army, St. Louis, Missouri.*

GENERAL: I read in a paper yesterday that you were bringing out a second edition of your "Memoirs." If this be so, permit me to correct a few errors in your first edition in regard to your march through Georgia, which, though of no moment to you in comparison with your grand operations, are pertinent to the truth of history, and to me in connection with it.

On page 665, second volume, you say, "But these hastily retreated east across the Oconee River, leaving a good bridge, which we promptly secured."

I did not cross the Oconee River, as you state, but moved by rail to the support of General Cobb at Macon, with a company of mounted scouts, one battery of field-artillery, and about five hundred men, composed as you have stated. Before leaving Milledgeville, I ordered the bridge you refer to to be burned; but, on the representation to me by leading citizens that the bridge was essential to the town for supplies, and for a way of escape at the last, and knowing that its destruction would offer but a slight impediment to your well-appointed army, in the absence of all opposition, I revoked the order for its destruction. On arrival at Gordon, I learned that the wires between it and Macon had been cut about twenty minutes before, which caused me to halt, as I apprehended you had anticipated me, and that a portion of your command was in my way. Scouts were sent forward, and about midnight I learned from them and from citizens who came in of the repulse at Macon, and of General G. W. Smith's affair at Griswold. I was completely cut off from all communication with Macon I knew, and awaited further information and instructions, intrenching meanwhile. None, however, came to me, and learning from my scouts that a force of the enemy, of between four and five thousand, were close upon me, which my few hundreds could not contend with in the flat, open country, I fell back about sunset to the railroad crossing of the Ogeechee River, where a battalion of Confederate troops and a field-battery of Confederate artillery were stationed under command of Major Alfred L. Hartridge, of the Confederate army. The advance of your troops entered Gordon as I left, but failed in its attempt to head and cut me off. On arriving at the Ogeechee I assumed the command of the mixed troops, and spent Monday and Tuesday in strengthening my position at the bridge and at Ball's Ferry, eight miles below. My force numbered twelve hundred men, all told.

On Wednesday morning, at half-past ten, your advance opened upon me at the bridge, and about 3 P.M. at the ferry below. I held my ground, repulsing every attempt to carry the bridge and the ferry throughout Wednesday, Thursday, and Friday, when at dusk I learned that your left wing was closing my rear. In consequence, I withdrew my troops at the ferry, and abandoning the bridge at 1 A.M. Saturday, I fell back toward Millen, passing at Tenille within three miles of Slocum's advance. While at the bridge I had acquired from my scouts, who examined your columns closely, accurate information of your strength and movements, all of which was telegraphed to General Hardee at Savannah. But so possessed was he with the idea that my reports were exaggerated, and that you were making the best escape you could to the protection of the gunboats at Port Royal or Ossabaw, that my advice with regard to his action was not heeded. He was induced, however, to run up to me at the bridge, arriving Friday evening, but even there and at Tenille, where I had a consultation with him again, he could not comprehend the situation, so prejudiced had his mind become by telegrams from General Bragg at Augusta. At Millen I again halted until a courier from General Wheeler advised me to fall back to the crossing of the Little Ogeechee, as General Kilpatrick was working to get behind me.

At the Little Ogeechee I again took up position until your right wing lapped me, when I fell back. On receiving my telegram to that effect, General Hardee peremptorily ordered me to return to my position at the Little Ogeechee, adding that he would send up four thousand Confederate troops to my assistance. I returned as ordered, although my officers, in a body, protested against it, resumed my abandoned lines, and was reënforced as promised. The troops were disposed to make the best fight against overwhelming odds that could be made, and I grimly awaited the result. Your advance began skirmishing in the morning. In the course of the day General McLaws arrived with orders from General Hardee to relieve me in the command. I rode with McLaws along the lines, explaining my positions and the reasons for them, and the condition of affairs, and, returning to the telegraph station on the line of the railroad, resigned the command and retired to sleep, of which I stood in need. Hardly had I closed my eyes, when a request from General McLaws took me again to the telegraph station. Taking me aside, he told me that he had come up under a total misconception of the state of affairs; that their true condition had not been represented to him, and that under the circumstances he would not take the command, and that I must get out of the scrape. I told him that General Hardee had my telegrams representing Sherman's force at over seventy thousand men, marching leisurely along; that I had got out of the scrape once, but was sent back with increased numbers to complicate the problem, and that I was truly glad to be relieved from such (in my opinion) unwise operations. He positively refused to continue in command, and immediately returned to Savannah. Skirmishing in front was continuing, and from my advanced line I observed your position and movements to flank my right, the river being fordable, about waist-deep, above. Keeping my own counsel, I waited until eleven o'clock at night, when I sent for the generals of divisions and brigades, explained to them the position, and gave orders for withdrawing immediately and silently. The orders were well executed, and by 2 A.M. I had extricated my men and was in retreat; the cavalry, with a battery of field-artillery, covering it. At daybreak I saw my anticipations realized. You had flanked me, ready to close upon my right wing and rear. Escaping from your troops, I found my retreat embarrassed by an unexpected and dangerous obstruction. Civilians had been sent out from Savannah to burn the bridges in your front, and had commenced by destroying them in my rear, instead of waiting for me to pass. This nearly cost me my artillery, which was only saved by the coolness and energy of the officer in command of it. At about fifteen miles from Savannah my retreat was arrested by orders to take position behind a line of rifle-pits that had been dug there, and to occupy the line between the railroad and the Savannah River. Reconnoitring the position, I returned to my command and began my dispositions, when orders came to me to fall back upon the city, and occupy a line between the Augusta road and the river.

On arriving in Savannah I reported in person at headquarters, and found there General Beauregard, who had come over from Charleston. Making my report to him, in which your strength was included, he threw his hands up and exclaimed: "My God, Harry! what has come over you? You did not use to be so nervous! General Bragg telegraphs me from Augusta that Sherman has not more than twenty-one thousand men with him, that he hardly has eighteen thousand muskets, and is making a hasty retreat for his gunboats, either across Sister's Ferry to Port Royal, or to Ossabaw." I replied: "General, I don't know what reliable sources of information General Bragg may have in Augusta, but General Wheeler and I, who are the only general officers who have been in front of the enemy for the past fifteen days, have both reported that General Sherman has with him a force of more than seventy thousand men, well organized and equipped, marching leisurely, and showing no signs of haste. He cannot cross the Savannah River at Sister's Ferry, as there is a freshet, and the South Carolina side is flooded for three miles and more beyond it. Believe me, that Savannah is his objective point, and that on Friday night he will invest the city." My words seemed, unfortunately, to have no weight, and General G. W. Smith recovering from a slight attack of illness, I turned over to him the next day my command, and awaited the inevitable result of your movements.

On Friday morning early, my cousin, Colonel George Gordon, of the Sixtieth Georgia, temporarily attached to headquarters, called upon me in much concern, for he was sincerely attached to me, and expressed great regret at the position I held in the public estimation, saying that scouts had gone seventy miles up the right bank of the Ogeechee without encountering a sign of an enemy, and that I must certainly be mistaken. To which I answered that I was fully aware of the public feeling toward me and was sorry for it, but that I was right and not mistaken, as events would show, and that, though unpleasant, I had to bear like a man present contumely, knowing that I was right; and added: "Mark my words! at 2 P.M. to-day some of Osterhaus's men will break up the little command of North Carolinians at No. 2, and at nine to-night Savannah will be surrounded. I hear that your uncle, Mr. Cuyler, the President of the Central Railroad, intends leaving by a special train this evening on the Gulf Railroad for Macon. Beg him, from me, not to attempt it, for if he does he will run into Sherman's lines." He went, however, and was captured. Learning toward evening that General Beauregard intended to return that night to Charleston by the railroad, I called upon him and urged him not to attempt it, but cross at Screven's Ferry, below Savannah, and take the road at Hardeeville. My advice, however, was rejected, and he left by rail. Fortunately, the conductor thought there might be some danger, and ran slowly, stopping his train within about a mile of Slocum's lines. General Beauregard returned to Savannah and crossed at Screven's Ferry. The next morning revealed to the incredulous that Savannah was invested. The capture of McAllister settled the doubts as to your object completely.

The defense of Savannah should have been made, as I advised at the time, along the line of the Great Ogeechee. There you might have been checked, as my own slight resistance subsequently convinced me. That river passed, however, there was no serious impediment in your way to the sea. And had a strong fight been made there, I question if you could have made your way through the Carolinas unless reënforced strongly at Savannah. At no time was General Hardee in the field with ten thousand men, as you state on page 669, second volume. He was not in the field at all with any troops. And what you state on the same page with regard to McLaws at Ogeechee Church (the Little Ogeechee I call it) I have already explained in this narrative.

In all the incidents of this, my little campaign, I owe whatever merit may attach to them largely to my chief-of-staff, General Capers; and in resistance at the bridge and Ball's Ferry, to him, and to Major Alfred L. Hartridge, an *élève* of the Georgia Military Institute, in immediate command of the Confederate troops under me.

If I have been prolix, attribute it to the necessity for explaining, in justice to myself and my family, that which has not yet been understood, until this the first opportunity for explanation has been properly presented to me. Very respectfully, your obedient servant,

HENRY C. WAYNE.

SAVANNAH, GEORGIA, *January,* 1865.
Hon. GERRIT SMITH, *Peterboro, New York.*

MY DEAR SIR: You have heard, I know, of our occupation of this place, and many of the incidents connected with it must be familiar to you, but there is one which I wish you could have witnessed. I chanced on two or three consecutive days after our arrival to be in General Sherman's rooms when he was receiving the negroes of the place. Poor creatures! they came to him as their deliverer, and one black preacher told him, like Simeon in the Bible, he had prayed for this day, and all he now wanted was to see Mr. Lincoln. Some of them wanted to kneel before him, but the general would not permit it, and told them they must not kneel to any one but their Maker. To the white rebels, particularly those in high official positions, swelling, as they are apt to do, with their own self-importance, Sherman is not conciliatory. He tells them plainly of their crime and of the penalties which they must expect, and his treatment is the same of those who attempt to shield themselves under the garb of foreign allegiance or foreign official position; but to these humble creatures, overflowing with gratitude to God and to him, he was a different person, all kindness and goodness. He detained them with him, and their simple talk seemed to give him a pleasure which I have not seen him display in his intercourse with those of more pretension. While I was with him a negro recruiting officer came in to exhibit his papers. The general did not encourage him, and the other blacks present at once appealed to the general to know whether they were all liable to be conscripted and carried off, as armed parties were then circulating through the city, seizing every one they could, doubtless to speculate upon the bounties offered by the Government. General Sherman at once dispatched his staff-officers to put a stop to this outrage, and told the negroes that they were now free, that they must look for their living, and that, if they chose to enter the army and fight, they could do so, but should not be compelled to enlist or be treated otherwise than white men were; and that, so far as his feelings were concerned, he would rather for some time yet use them as laborers and pioneers than as soldiers.

You and I, who have been abolitionists of the strictest school for so many years—I since 1834, and you longer—may be permitted to be critical respecting the faith of new converts, and I am willing to take this display of General Sherman's feelings before the louder professions of many others. Previous to this interview with the blacks, which I witnessed, I had regarded General Sherman as a pro-slavery man—for most of the men I meet are pro-slavery—but since then I have looked upon him as not simply a great man but a good man as well.

I wish you would let your friend Phillips, and others thinking as we do, know these facts, since a man having the ability to do so much good, and having his heart in the right direction, should have all possible encouragement and support. Most affectionately yours,

A. BAIRD.

NOTE.—To this letter Mr. Smith made a prompt reply, expressing great gratification on his part and on that of Mr. Wendell Phillips, to whom he sent the letter, at this exhibition of General Sherman's feelings. I forwarded Mr. Smith's reply to General Sherman, and he promptly sent me the following reply: A. B.

HEADQUARTERS MILITARY DIVISION OF THE MISSISSIPPI, }
IN THE FIELD, GOLDSBORO, NORTH CAROLINA, *April* 3, 1865. }

General A. BAIRD, *present*.

DEAR BAIRD: I thank you for the perusal of Gerrit Smith's letter. I doubt not he feels the joy he expresses at our progress, because we free the slaves in the same ratio that we manifest the power of our Government.

It seems impossible for citizens to understand us of the *old army*. In our private circles we may be gentle, kind, and forbearing, but when mutiny and war show their horrid heads we may seem very devils. As to the negro, I know I will do as much to ameliorate his political and social condition as Mr. Gerrit Smith, Wendell Phillips, Greeley, and others who seem to me mere theorists and not practical workers. If the people of the South had stood by the Constitution, I for one would have fought for the protection of the slave property, just as much as for any other kind of property, because the Constitution was a contract, signed, sealed, and delivered, and we had no right to go behind it. The right or wrong of slavery in the abstract had nothing to do with the contract made by our forefathers, for reasons good enough for them, and which we were bound in honor and law to abide by. But when the people and States of the South undertook to save their slave property by themselves breaking the Constitution, they themselves released us of our honorary and legal obligation, and we are free to deal with slavery as we please. They were slaves, but are now free, made so by their former owners breaking the bonds by which their slave property alone could be held.

Slavery as of old in this land is, in my judgment, long since determined, but we live in a busy world, and people won't be still. No sooner is one point gained than new ones arise, and we find plenty of people contending to make negroes voters, and even, with the legal right and encouragement, to commingle their blood with ours. On these points I think men may honestly differ very widely, and I for one would be slow in going to such extremes. The negro should, of course, be protected in his industry and encouraged to acquire property, knowledge, trade, and every means possible to better his condition, but I think we should all be rather too slow than too fast in extending political rights. These in time will adjust themselves according to the laws of Nature and experience. "Festina lente" is a good old maxim, and we, who have to catch the buffeting of political factions fighting their battles over our shoulders, ought to have a voice in questions which involve prejudices that influence the actions of men quite as much as pure reason.

I believe you and I have practically done more acts of kindness to the negroes of America than all the philanthropists put together; but our acts are quiet and unknown, whereas theirs have been noisy and demonstrative. I do not say this of Gerrit Smith, but of others who make the negro a hobby, and keep their precious persons well out of harm's way in the bloody struggle they have had their share in making, but not in subduing.

Your friend,   W. T. SHERMAN, Major-General.

Appendix B.

"HISTORY OF THE CIVIL WAR IN AMERICA." COMTE DE PARIS. Translated by Louis F. Tasistro, edited by Professor Coppée, and published by J. H. Coates & Co., Philadelphia, 1876. Vol. III., page 853:

"Let us quote, in short, among our authors, the most illustrious of all, General Sherman, to whom we owe, under the form of 'Memoirs,' the pages the most original, brilliant, and instructive, which have ever been written on the war. General Sherman, who has never been ambitious for any political post, nor solicited the votes of any political party, has had the rare courage to say frankly in these 'Memoirs' what he thought of the officers who served near or under him. Judgments without any reticence, thus expressed by the commander of an army, clash with many feelings of self-love, and sometimes wound legitimate susceptibilities, and excite some manifestations of anger; but they have, in the eyes of the historian, an incomparable value."

"AROUND THE WORLD WITH GENERAL GRANT." JOHN RUSSELL YOUNG. Vol. II., pages 290 and 291:

"So far as the war is concerned," said the general, "I think history will more than approve the places given to Sherman and Sheridan. Sherman I have known for thirty-five years. During that time there never was but one cloud over our friendship, and that," said the general, laughing, "lasted about three weeks. When Sherman's book came out, General Boynton, the correspondent, printed some letters about it. In these, Sherman was made to disparage his comrades, and to disparage me especially. I cannot tell you how much I was shocked. But there were the letters and the extracts. I could not believe it in Sherman, the man whom I had always found so true and knightly, more anxious to honor others than win honor for himself. So I sent for the book, and I resolved to read it over, with paper and pencil, and make careful notes, and in justice to my comrades and myself prepare a reply. I do not think I ever ventured upon a more painful duty. I was some time about it. I was moving to Long Branch. I had official duties, and I am a slow reader. Then I missed the books when I reached the Branch, and had to send for them. So it was three weeks before I was through. During these weeks," replied the general, laughing, "I did not see Sherman, and I am glad I did not. My mind was so set by Boynton's extracts that I should certainly have been cold to him. But, when I finished the book, I found that I approved every word; that, apart from a few mistakes that any writer would make in so voluminous a work, it was a true book, an honorable book, creditable to Sherman, just to his companions—to myself particularly so—just such a book as I expected Sherman would write. Then it was accurate, because Sherman keeps a diary, and he compiled the book from notes made at the time. Then he is a very accurate man. You cannot imagine how pleased I was, for my respect and affection for Sherman were so great, that I look on these three weeks as among the most painful in my remembrance. I wrote Sherman my opinion of the book. I told him the only points I objected to were his criticisms upon some of our civil soldiers, like Logan and Blair. As a matter of fact, there were in the army no two men more loyal than John A. Logan and Frank Blair. I knew that Sherman did not mean to disparage either of them, and that he wrote hastily. Logan did a great work for the Union in bringing Egypt out of the Confederacy, which he did; and he was an admirable soldier, and is, as he always has been, an honorable, true man—a perfectly just and fair man, whose record in the army was brilliant. Blair also did a work in the war entitling him to the gratitude of every Northern man, and the respect of every soldier. Sherman did not do justice to Burnside; Burnside's fine character has sustained him in the respect and esteem of all who knew him through the most surprising reverses of fortune. There was a mistake in Sherman's book as to the suggestion of the Fort Henry and Donelson campaign coming from Halleck. But these are mistakes natural to a large book, which Sherman would be the last to commit, and the first to correct. Taking Sherman's book as a whole, it is a sound, true, honest work, and a valuable contribution to the history of the war."

NOTE.—The only allusion to General Burnside in my "Memoirs," to which his friends have ever taken exception, is found on pages 393 and 394, Vol. I., where I describe our reception at Knoxville, December 4, 1863, ending with a handsome "turkey-dinner." This occurred after the Fifteenth Corps had marched about four hundred and fifty miles from Memphis, and fought two or three days from Mission Ridge back to Ringgold, when I was required to march it still another one hundred and twenty miles to Knoxville, Tennessee, by order of General Grant, furnished with copies of dispatches from General Burnside, to the effect that his provisions could only hold out until December 3d, by which time he must have relief, or could not be held responsible for the consequences.

General Burnside himself never took offense at this, but, on the contrary, many a time since the war we have, at his most hospitable table and mine, in

Washington enjoyed "turkey-dinners," at which we have laughed over the "Knoxville affair."

As to Generals Logan and Blair, the newspaper critics quoted, as from the "Memoirs," the offensive words "political generals." Such words never did exist in the "Memoirs," and the simple truth was this:

When General McPherson was killed in battle, July 22, 1864, it was the office of the President to appoint his successor—mine simply to recommend. On pages 558 and 559, Vol. II., I endeavor to describe simply and truthfully the circumstances which influenced *my own action*. I would most gladly change the language if thereby I could purge it of all offense, but find it impossible; and I deny that a fair interpretation of the words used contains any just cause of offense to these most distinguished officers. I indorse fully every word General Grant says in reference to the value of their services before, during the war, and after; and go further, because I had a better opportunity to witness their individual conduct in the field. I have on many a public occasion borne willing testimony to their transcendent courage and ability in actual battle, and insist that the "Memoirs" contain many evidences of the high estimation in which I personally held them.

And where, afterward, I record that these two most prominent commanders of corps went back to take part in the presidential campaign, then at its crisis—General Logan went by President Lincoln's express and positive orders, and General Blair to resume his seat in Congress—I meant no reflection on these officers, but referred to the circumstance to explain *my own* embarrassment in preparing for the final campaign, which was bound to be fatal to the Southern Confederacy, or to me.

Finally, as to the movement of General Grant's army up the Tennessee in January and February, 1862, one of the most skillful and the most fruitful in results of the whole war, I simply describe, on pages 238, Vol. I., a scene which I personally witnessed in General Halleck's room, at the Planters' House, in St. Louis, and drew from it the only logical inference, that he, General Halleck, then in supreme command, was the author of that movement. I did not and could not know who had suggested it to him; nor do I now attach as much importance to the conception of a plan of military operations as to the execution of the plan. This latter was unquestionably wholly General Grant's.

W. T. SHERMAN.

Index

belief that the Northwestern States would join in, 171; ordinances of, passed, 172; of Louisiana, 172, 173; correspondence in consequence of, 174–179; perplexity of Union officers in reference to, 173; opinion that it would be peaceably accomplished, 181; prospects of, in the spring of 1861, 184, 185; of the border States, 188.

Secretary of War, functions of, 895.

Sedalia, Missouri, 233–236.

Sedgwick, Captain John, 107.

Selfridge, Colonel J. L., 825.

Seminoles, war with the, 18 et seq.; removal of the, 25.

Semple, Dr., founder of the "Alta California," 78–79, 100.

Seton, Mr., 96, 98.

Settlements and plantations, inspector of, 732.

Seward, Wm. H., 207, 208, 590, 865.

Shepherd, Alexander R., 946.

Sheridan, Major M. V., 953.

Sheridan, General P. H., 794, 831, 833; made major-general, 903; 910, 928; made lieutenant-general, 929; Grant's grounds for the promotion, 930; assumes command, 953.

Sherman, Charles R., father of General W. T., 9, 10; appointed judge, 11; his death, 13.

Sherman, Charles T., 11, 12, 13.

Sherman, Daniel, 9, 10.

Sherman, Elizabeth, 13.

Sherman, Fanny (Moulton), 113.

Sherman family, the, 9–11.

Sherman, Colonel Frank, captured, 539.

Sherman, James, 11, 12.

Sherman, Hon. John, 166, 184, 185, 195.

Sherman, Lizzie, 122, 123, 136.

Sherman, Minnie, 136, 417, 943, 944.

Sherman, Roger, 9.

Sherman, Judge Taylor, 9, 10.

Sherman, Tom, 370, 374.

Sherman, General Thomas W., 35, 271, 425.

Sherman, General W. T.: scope and purpose of his "Memoirs," 3 et seq.; his ancestry, 9 et seq.; boyhood, 12 et

seq.; adopted by Hon. T. Ewing, 13; at West Point, 15 et seq.; in Florida, 17 et seq.; in South Carolina, Georgia, and Alabama, 27 et seq.; value of his knowledge of those States, 30; accident to, 31; recruits for the Mexican War, 35; sent to California, 37; mission to Sonoma, 56 et seq.; visits the gold-mines and reports to the Government, 71 et seq.; at Monterey, 84 et seq.; desires to leave the service, 86; adjutant, 86; removes to San Francisco, 88 et seq.; surveying by, 95 et seq.; purchases of, in Sacramento, 99; goes to New York, 103; in Washington, 104–105; his marriage, 106; sent to St. Louis, 109; to New Orleans, 113; trip to California, 114; shipwrecked, 116–120; resigns his commission to go into business, 122; removes to San Francisco, 122; major-general of militia, 139; resigns, 149; removes to New York, 153; retires from the business, 158; practices law in Leavenworth, 159; becomes superintendent of a military college, 160; correspondence on secession, 174 et seq.; his resignation, 174 et seq.; removes to St. Louis, 184; declines offices offered, 188, 189; his letter to the Secretary of War, 189; appointed colonel, 190; ordered to Washington, 192; removes from St. Louis, 193; begins service in the civil war, 194; reasons for not writing a history of the war, 194; assigned to Washington, 194; to the command of a brigade, 197; march of his command, 198; official report on Bull Run, 199; made brigadier, 209; assigned to the Department of the Ohio (afterward Cumberland), 210, 211; appointed to succeed General Anderson, 216; his "insane" request for troops, 220, 223; official report of forces in Kentucky, 223–226; dispatches, 226; General Wood's statement, 228; transferred to Missouri, 232; at Sedalia, 233; charge of insanity, 233, 234; recalled from Sedalia, 233–236; placed in charge of camp of

Chronology

1820 Born February 8 in New Lancaster (present-day Lancaster), Ohio, sixth child of attorney Charles Robert Sherman (b. 1788) and Mary Hoyt Sherman (b. 1787). Named Tecumseh (Shooting Star) after the Shawnee leader who had been killed in the battle of the Thames in 1813, and called "Cump" by his family. (Parents were both from Norwalk, Connecticut, where they were married in 1810 before moving west. Siblings are Charles Taylor, b. 1811; Mary Elizabeth, b. 1813; James, b. 1814; Amelia, b. 1816; and Julia Ann, b. 1818.)

1822 Brother Lampson born.

1823 Father is elected by the legislature to the Supreme Court of Ohio and begins riding its circuit. Brother John born.

1825 Sherman enters Lancaster Academy, a private school whose curriculum includes Latin, Greek, and French.

1826 Sister Susan born.

1827 Brother Hoyt born.

1829 Sister Fanny born in early May. Father dies, probably from typhoid fever, in Lebanon, Ohio, on June 24. Due to his mother's straitened finances, Sherman moves into the home of family friends and close neighbors Thomas Ewing (b. 1789), a successful attorney later active in Whig politics, and Maria Boyle Ewing (b. 1801), and their children Philemon (b. 1820), Eleanor (b. 1824, called Ellen), and Hugh Boyle (b. 1826). Thomas Ewing, Jr., born in August.

1830 At the instigation of Maria Boyle Ewing and with his mother's consent, Sherman is baptized by a Roman Catholic priest, and William is added to his name; he never becomes a practicing Roman Catholic, however. Visits relatives in Mansfield, Ohio, with his mother.

1831   Thomas Ewing is elected to the U.S. Senate (serves until 1837). Brother John moves to Mount Vernon, Ohio, to live with a cousin of their father's. Sherman hunts rabbits, squirrels, and pigeons.

1833   Notified by Thomas Ewing to prepare to enter the U.S. Military Academy in 1836.

1834   Works during the fall on surveying team for canal in the Hocking Valley of Ohio for fifty cents a day. Forms, with other Lancaster boys, the Lancaster Academical Institute, evidently a reading and discussion society.

1835   Charles Ewing born in March. Sherman works as canal surveyor in the spring. Concentrates studies on mathematics and French in preparation for the military academy. John returns to Lancaster for 18 months.

1836   Travels in May to Washington, D.C., where he visits Senator Ewing, tours the city, and sees President Andrew Jackson. Visits family of William J. Reese, husband of his sister Mary Elizabeth, in Philadelphia, and his uncles Charles and James Hoyt in New York City. Sees first professional theater productions (will attend plays and concerts whenever possible for remainder of his life). Enters the U.S. Military Academy at West Point, New York, in June. Studies mathematics and French. Becomes friends with classmates George H. Thomas and Stewart Van Vliet. Begins regular correspondence with Ellen Ewing.

1837   Maria Teresa Ewing born in May. Sherman ranks 5th of 76 cadets in his class academically but 9th overall because of conduct demerits; ranks 124th of 211 cadets in conduct. Spends summer in training encampment. Studies mathematics, French, and drawing.

1838   Ranks 6th of 58 in his class. Rises to 78th of all cadets in conduct. Ranks 7th in mathematics, 4th in French, 1st in drawing. Returns to Lancaster on summer furlough in July. Stays at his mother's house and begins using some of his cadet pay ($28 per month) to help her financially (support continues until her death). Returns to West Point by way of Niagara Falls. Studies natural philosophy (physics), chemistry, and drawing (including map-making).

1839   Ranks 6th in his class, 115th of all cadets in conduct. Meets Ulysses S. Grant, who enters the academy as a first-year cadet. Studies civil and military engineering, moral philosophy, rhetoric, international and common law, mineralogy and geology, artillery, and infantry tactics.

1840   Graduates 6th of 43 in his class, standing 4th academically. Visits Ellen Ewing at the Academy of the Visitation, a convent school in Georgetown, D.C., before going to Lancaster for a three-month furlough. Commissioned as second lieutenant in Company A, Third Artillery Regiment, with pay of $64 per month. Reports for duty at Governor's Island, New York, in September and is assigned to Fort Pierce, Florida. Deplores what he considers demagoguery in the presidential campaign between Whig William Henry Harrison and Democrat Martin Van Buren.

1841   Thomas Ewing is appointed secretary of the treasury by William Henry Harrison (serves until September, when he resigns from the Tyler administration). Sherman takes part in expeditions to capture and remove Seminole Indians to Indian Territory (present-day Oklahoma). Assists in the seizure of Coacoochee, a Seminole leader, and about 20 men, which leads to the removal of about 150 men, women, and children. Seeks transfer to western frontier. Promoted to first lieutenant on November 30. Transferred to Company G, Third Artillery Regiment, at Picolata, Florida, 18 miles from St. Augustine.

1842   Company G is transferred in February to Fort Morgan, Mobile, Alabama. Sherman enjoys visiting with wealthy Mobile families. Transferred in June with Companies D and G to Fort Moultrie, five miles from Charleston, South Carolina. Captain Robert Anderson takes command of Company G. Sherman becomes acquainted with many planters' families, explores much of eastern South Carolina on hunting and fishing trips, and visits North Carolina twice. Briefly takes up painting.

1843   Takes three-month furlough in the autumn. Visits family
            and friends in Ohio, and discusses marriage with Ellen
            Ewing. While returning to Charleston in November and
            December, goes down the Ohio River, stopping at Cin-
            cinnati and Louisville, then down the Mississippi River,
            stopping for a week at both St. Louis and New Orleans.
            Travels eastward by way of Mobile, Montgomery, Macon,
            and Savannah.

1844   Receives a letter from Ellen Ewing in February agreeing
            to marry him. Reports to Colonel Sylvester Churchill, in-
            spector general of the army, in Marietta, Georgia, and be-
            gins taking depositions from volunteer soldiers claiming
            compensation for the loss of horses and equipment during
            Seminole War. Writes to Thomas Ewing on March 4 ask-
            ing for his consent to the marriage, which Ewing gives.
            Rides on horseback by way of Rome, Georgia, to Belle-
            fonte, Alabama, where he takes depositions for two
            months, then rides across northern Georgia to Augusta,
            making topographical sketches and notes on terrain.
            Reads Blackstone's *Commentaries* and considers becoming
            a lawyer, but decides to remain in the army. Spends au-
            tumn at the Augusta arsenal. Writes to John, disapproving
            of his stump-speaking for Whig candidates but expressing
            wish that Henry Clay, the Whig nominee, be elected
            president.

1845   Dislocates shoulder while hunting in January and takes
            convalescent furlough. Visits Washington and Lancaster,
            returning to Fort Moultrie in March. Sherman and Ellen
            Ewing decide to defer their wedding for reasons of her
            health and his low pay.

1846   Ordered in April to recruiting service in Pittsburgh and
            arrives there in May. Congress declares war against Mex-
            ico, May 11–12. Eager to see active service, Sherman takes
            his recruits, without authorization, to Newport, Ken-
            tucky; the superintendent of the western recruiting service
            reprimands him and sends him back to Pittsburgh. Or-
            dered to join Company F of the Third Artillery Regiment,
            assigned to California. Leaves New York aboard the
            U.S.S. *Lexington* on July 14; fellow officers onboard
            include Lieutenants Edward O. C. Ord and Henry W.
            Halleck. En route to California, the ship stops at Rio de

Janeiro, Brazil, and Valparaiso, Chile; Sherman tours both. Reads Washington Irving, Charles Dickens' *Pickwick Papers* and *Barnaby Rudge* (will read and reread Dickens' novels throughout his life), Shakespeare, the Bible, and histories of the Protestant Reformation. (Reading at other times includes works by Walter Scott, Robert Burns, Captain Frederick Marryat, Charles Lever, William Makepeace Thackeray, and later, Bret Harte and Mark Twain, as well as British and American histories, scientific and geographic treatises, the Duke of Wellington's dispatches and other military writings, census and explorers' reports, and ethnographic studies.)

1847   Arrives at Monterey, California, January 26. Makes scouting trip inland with Ord in February. Meets explorer Captain John C. Frémont. Sails to Los Angeles in May with General Stephen Watts Kearny, military commander in California, and returns to Monterey overland. With Kearny's departure for the East, Colonel Richard B. Mason becomes civil and military governor of California and names Sherman his assistant adjutant. Goes to Sonoma by way of Yerba Buena (later San Francisco) in July, where he carries out Mason's order to arrest the mayor the American settlers had illegally elected and to install his replacement, appointed by Mason. Hunts deer, bear, ducks, and geese.

1848   Learns in spring of discovery of gold at sawmill owned by John A. Sutter at Coloma, 45 miles from Sutter's Fort (later Sacramento), and inspects samples sent to Mason by Sutter. Travels to quicksilver mines near San José with Mason, who adjudicates land title disputes. Meets scout Christopher "Kit" Carson, who has brought the first overland mail to California. Accompanies Mason on an inspection tour of gold fields in the Sacramento Valley during June and July. Drafts an official report, signed by Mason, August 17, on the discovery of gold. Learns in August of the peace treaty ending the Mexican War, which was ratified on May 30; considers the terms too generous to Mexico. Concludes that his military career has been damaged by his having no combat experience. Revisits the gold fields in September and October. Invests $500 in a store at Coloma and earns profit of $1,500.

1849   Becomes adjutant to General Persifor F. Smith, newly
            arrived commander of the Division of the Pacific, in Feb-
            ruary. Thomas Ewing becomes secretary of the interior.
            Sherman accompanies Smith to new headquarters at San
            Francisco, then returns to Monterey in May because of the
            high cost of living in the city. Helps transfer division
            headquarters to Sonoma, then becomes an aide-de-camp
            to Smith when new adjutant, Major Joseph Hooker,
            arrives. Takes a two-month furlough and works with Ord
            as a surveyor for land speculators and ranchers, making
            $6,000. Invited by Sutter to become his agent for selling
            city lots in Sacramento. Reads army promotion list, which
            does not include his name, and writes letter of resignation,
            but then withdraws it. Attends California constitutional
            convention in Monterey as Smith's observer in September
            and October. Spends the remainder of the autumn in Sac-
            ramento, observing the arrival of gold-rush immigrants.
            Receives orders in San Francisco in late December to take
            dispatches to New York.

1850   Travels by way of the Isthmus of Panama to New York
            during January. Reports to General Winfield Scott and
            then takes dispatches to Washington in February. Lives
            with Thomas Ewing in the Blair House at 1651 Pennsylva-
            nia Avenue, NW. Reports to President Zachary Taylor on
            California. Takes a six-month leave of absence. Goes to
            Philadelphia to visit his sister Mary Elizabeth Reese, who
            is in financial difficulty, and loans her $1,500. Sees his
            mother and relatives in Ohio. Returns to Washington and
            in March attends Senate debates on the Compromise of
            1850. Married to Ellen Ewing by Father James Ryder, pres-
            ident of Georgetown College, on the evening of May 1 at
            the Blair House; the wedding guests include President
            Taylor, his Cabinet, Senators Daniel Webster, Thomas
            Hart Benton, Henry Clay, and Stephen A. Douglas. Trav-
            els with his wife to Baltimore, New York, Niagara Falls,
            and Ohio, returning to Washington on July 1. Attends
            funeral of President Taylor, who died on July 9. Thomas
            Ewing resigns from the Cabinet and is chosen to fill the
            remainder of Thomas Corwin's term in the U.S. Senate
            (serves until 1851). Sherman and his wife return to Lan-
            caster, where he is ordered to report to Company C,
            Third Artillery, commanded by Captain Braxton Bragg, at
            Jefferson Barracks near St. Louis in September. Ellen, who

is pregnant, stays with her family in Lancaster. Receives commission, dated September 27, as captain in the Commissary Corps, with offices in St. Louis. Lives at the Planters' House hotel.

1851   Daughter Maria Ewing Sherman ("Minnie") born January 28. (She is baptized and raised a Catholic and educated in Catholic schools, as are all of Sherman's children.) Sherman returns to Lancaster in March and takes Ellen and Minnie to St. Louis. Leases a house on Chouteau Avenue, near 12th Street. Thomas Ewing visits St. Louis on legal business in June, September, and November; he and Ellen urge Sherman to resign from the army. Purchases small tracts of land in St. Louis and in western Illinois. Suffers acute attacks of asthma (episodes will recur intermittently for the rest of his life). Through his army friend Henry S. Turner, meets James H. Lucas, a wealthy St. Louis property owner and banker.

1852   Receives financial assistance from his brother John and Thomas Ewing. Makes inspection trip to Fort Leavenworth, spending one night in a Shawnee settlement. Ellen, who is again pregnant, returns to Lancaster. Moves to a rented room on Market Street, opposite the courthouse. Ordered in August to become the commissary officer at New Orleans and to eradicate corruption in its depot. Learns in St. Louis on September 30 of the death of his mother in Mansfield, Ohio, September 23. Moves to New Orleans, living in the St. Louis Hotel. Daughter Mary Elizabeth Sherman ("Lizzie") born November 17. Rents a house on Magazine Street in preparation for the arrival of his family.

1853   Wife and children arrive in New Orleans on January 1. Henry S. Turner visits New Orleans en route to California and offers Sherman the position of manager of Lucas, Turner, & Co., a new bank in San Francisco. Takes six-month leave of absence to provisionally accept Turner's offer. Ellen and the daughters return to Lancaster in February. Leaves in March for San Francisco by way of Nicaragua. His ship runs aground north of San Francisco on April 9; Sherman goes ashore, finds a schooner that takes him to San Francisco, where it capsizes in the bay; picked up by a small boat, he reaches the city and summons help. Finds San Francisco prosperous and decides to accept the Lucas, Turner offer. Returns by way of Nicaragua to New York, then to St. Louis and Lancaster. Resigns his commission, effective September 6. Travels with Ellen and Lizzie, by way of New York and Nicaragua, to San Francisco, arriving in mid-October; Minnie stays with the Ewings. Operates the bank in a rented office on Montgomery Street between Sacramento and California streets, and rents a house on Stockton Street near Green Street.

1854   Has building constructed for bank at intersection of Montgomery and Jackson streets at cost of $82,000. Estimates the bank's profits at $10,000 per month. Buys a house on Green Street for $3,500. Agrees to invest money for friends, mostly army officers (eventually invests approximately $130,000 of their funds). Son William Ewing Sherman born June 8. The flight of financier and timber merchant Henry (Honest Harry) Meiggs to South America in October, leaving over $800,000 in unpaid debts, precipitates bankruptcies and the start of financial instability in San Francisco. Family expenses for the year are approximately $13,000; Sherman's income is $5,000 per year plus 10 percent of the bank's profits; his personal account in the bank is overdrawn by $8,000 in October. Suffers from severe attacks of asthma, which often prevent sleep. John is elected as a Republican to the U.S. House of Representatives from the 13th congressional district of Ohio. Sherman writes to him that slavery should be accepted where it exists, but that it should not and will not be extended to the West.

1855   In February rumors of the failure of St. Louis bankers Page, Bacon & Company lead to a run on its San Francisco branch; when it closes on February 22, runs begin on other banks. Sherman meets all withdrawals from Lucas, Turner on February 23. Buys a lot on Harrison Street between Fremont and First streets, builds a house on it at a total cost of $10,000, and moves into it April 9. Ellen leaves to visit Lancaster on April 17; Lizzie and Willie stay in San Francisco. Gold production declines, and property values, rents, and commercial activity drop in San Francisco. Sherman refuses in May to be the Democratic candidate for city treasurer. Serves as chairman of the Committee to Memorialize Congress for the Building of an Overland Wagon Road to California. Buys stock in and serves as vice-president of the Sacramento Valley Railroad, which lays 22 miles of track eastward from Folsom, California (track later becomes part of the Central Pacific Railroad). Ellen returns to San Francisco on November 29.

1856   Advises John not to speak against slavery in Congress, and predicts that the growing prosperity of the free states will eventually settle the issue. Accepts appointment as major general in the California militia from Governor J. Neely Johnson in early May. After the fatal shooting of newspaper editor James King of William by James Casey on May 14, the San Francisco Vigilance Committee seizes control of the city. Casey, along with Charles Cora, the killer of a U.S. marshal, is hanged by the Committee on May 22, and on June 1 it defies a writ of habeas corpus issued by Judge David S. Terry for the release of a man it had seized. Sherman publishes orders on June 4 summoning the militia in preparation for opposing the Committee. Brigadier General John E. Wool, commander of the Department of the Pacific, refuses to provide arms for the militia. Sherman resigns militia commission on June 6. Receives public criticism for opposing the Committee and anticipates that the businessmen who are its main supporters will hurt the business of Lucas, Turner in retaliation. The Vigilance Committee hangs two more men, expels others from the city, and remains the effective government of San Francisco until the fall election. Sherman predicts that continued agitation of the slavery issue will lead to civil war. Moves the offices of Lucas, Turner to Battery Street at Washington Street in October. Son Thomas Ewing Sherman born October 12. Votes for Democrat James Buchanan for president over Republican John C. Frémont and Whig-American Millard Fillmore (the only time Sherman ever votes in a presidential election).

1857   Receives a letter from Turner in January saying that Lucas and Turner have decided to close their bank in San Francisco. Gives notice in the newspapers in April and closes the bank on May 1. Rents house and leaves San Francisco with his family on May 20, traveling to New York by way of Panama with money borrowed from Thomas Ewing. Opens Lucas, Turner, & Company, a bank at 12 Wall Street, on July 21. Rents rooms at 100 Prince Street (wife and children stay with the Ewings in Lancaster). Financial and commercial panic begins on Wall Street on August 24 and soon becomes nationwide. Lucas's bank in St. Louis closes, and Sherman receives instructions on October 7 to close the New York branch. Works in St. Louis during October and November on the closing of Lucas's banks. Encounters Ulysses S. Grant, who is living at Hardscrabble, his small farm outside the city. Sherman applies for a commission in the army. Spends part of December with his family in Lancaster, then leaves after Christmas for San Francisco by way of New York.

1858   Arrives in San Francisco January 28. Liquidates the bank's remaining assets in California and tries to recoup as much as possible of the $13,000 remaining of the investments he had made for friends. Repays entire amount, leaving himself with about $1,000 in savings. Provisionally accepts offer from Thomas Ewing to become manager of his salt works in the Hocking Valley of Ohio. Leaves San Francisco on July 3 and travels to Lancaster. Decides to join Hugh Boyle Ewing and Thomas Ewing, Jr., in a Leavenworth, Kansas, law firm. Goes to Leavenworth in September and is hired by Stewart Van Vliet, now the Fort Leavenworth quartermaster, to superintend repairs on a military road near Fort Riley, Kansas. Manages collections and real estate transactions for the firm, Sherman & Ewing, whose office is on Main Street, between Shawnee and Delaware streets. Becomes a member of the Kansas bar and a notary public. Ellen and the children, except Minnie, arrive in Leavenworth on November 12; family lives in the home of Thomas Ewing, Jr., on the corner of Third and Pottawatomie streets, while the Ewings are away. Hoping to return to St. Louis, considers entering real estate partnerships or opening a grocery there.

1859   Daniel McCook joins the law firm, which becomes Sherman, Ewing, and McCook. Sherman writes a report on the logistics and financing of a transcontinental railroad for John, who arranges for its publication in the Washington *National Intelligencer* on January 18. Ellen and the children return to Lancaster in March. Clears land owned by Thomas Ewing, Sr., on Indian Creek, 40 miles west of Leavenworth, and builds farm which he works with tenants. Invests $2,000 of his own and $3,340 of Thomas Ewing, Sr.'s, money in the purchase of 7,200 bushels of corn to sell to emigrants on their way to the recently discovered Colorado gold fields, but is left with 4,000 bushels unsold. Decides to leave Leavenworth and writes to Major Don Carlos Buell at the War Department, June 11, seeking position as an army paymaster. Travels to Lancaster. Learns from Buell of the position of superintendent at the newly created Louisiana Seminary of Learning and Military Academy and applies for it. Offered banking position in London by Cincinnati banker William R. Roelofson. Accepts offer of the superintendency in August at salary of $3,500 per year. Daughter Eleanor Mary Sherman ("Ellie") born September 5. Earns $5,600 from sale of house in San Francisco, easing financial pressure. Travels to Louisiana in October. Meets Governor-elect Thomas O. Moore and other members of the Seminary's board of supervisors, including its vice-chairman, George Mason Graham, half-brother of Richard B. Mason, Sherman's commander in California. Purchases books and supplies in New Orleans for the Seminary, which is at Pineville, Rapides Parish, near Alexandria. In December John becomes the Republican candidate for Speaker of the House of Representatives in a bitter contest dominated by his endorsement of an anti-slavery tract drawn from Hinton Rowan Helper's *The Impending Crisis of the South: How to Meet It* (1857). Sherman resolves not to tolerate criticism of his brother while also deploring abolitionist agitation, and tells the board of supervisors that he will accept slavery in the South but not disunion. Writes to Ellen predicting a terrible civil war if the South secedes.

1860   The Louisiana Seminary of Learning and Military Academy opens on January 2 with 56 cadets and faculty of five (later six), including Sherman as professor of engineering. Quells insubordination among the students; five cadets resign or are expelled. Becomes friends with David F. Boyd, professor of ancient languages. John loses contest for Speaker of the House. Roelofson travels to Alexandria in February to renew offer of banking position in London, which would pay $7,500 a year. Sherman works with legislators in Baton Rouge to improve the financing and operation of the Seminary. Reconsiders taking London position; travels to Cincinnati and Lancaster, and finally rejects Roelofson's offer. Returns to Louisiana, where he hopes to permanently settle his family, but Ellen is reluctant to move there because she fears yellow fever outbreaks and refuses to own slaves (Sherman had written her that it was impossible to hire white servants in the parish). After the Seminary's examinations, July 30–31, Sherman travels to Lancaster, then to Washington, where he secures from Secretary of War John B. Floyd a promise to ship 200 muskets to the Seminary for the cadets' use in drill. Goes to New York to purchase uniforms, textbooks, and books for a library, then to Lancaster, where he remains until his return to Louisiana in October for the start of the Seminary's fall session. After the victory of Abraham Lincoln in the presidential election, November 6, Sherman talks with many people who predict the secession of the Southern states. Receives on December 24 a newspaper reporting the secession of South Carolina on December 20. Weeps and predicts to Boyd a bitter civil war, ending in subjugation of the South.

1861   Deplores the inaction of President Buchanan in the face of secession. Louisiana militiamen seize the federal arsenal and barracks in Baton Rouge on January 10. Submits his resignation on January 18, to take effect when Louisiana secedes. Louisiana state convention votes for secession on January 26. Clears his accounts in New Orleans and goes to Lancaster at the end of February. The Ohio legislature elects John Sherman to the U.S. Senate. Travels to Washington in March and, accompanied by his brother, meets President Lincoln; Sherman is unimpressed. Moves with his family to St. Louis, renting a house at 226 Locust Street. Becomes president of the Fifth Street Railroad, a street railway in which Lucas holds stock, at salary of $2,000 a year. Declines on April 8 offer of the chief clerkship of the War Department. Regards Lincoln's call on April 15 for 75,000 three-month volunteers as inadequate and rejects proposal that he raise and lead an Ohio regiment. Watches with his son Willie on May 10 as Unionist volunteers escort captured secessionist militia through St. Louis, and takes cover when they open fire on the crowd.

Receives commission as colonel of the 13th U.S. Infantry, new regular army regiment, dated May 14. Travels to Washington while Ellen and children go to Lancaster. Assumes command of the Third Brigade, First Division, on June 30. Daughter Rachel born July 5. Commands his brigade in the first battle of Bull Run, July 21, and helps cover the retreat into the fortifications around Washington after the Union defeat. Trains and disciplines his troops. Promoted to brigadier general of volunteers on August 3. Ordered on August 24 to serve in Kentucky under Brigadier General Robert Anderson as second in command of the Department of the Cumberland. Visits Indianapolis, Indiana, Springfield, Illinois, and St. Louis before reporting to Louisville, Kentucky; finds a shortage of arms for recruits in all these places. Commands 5,000 men at Muldraugh's Hill, 40 miles south of Louisville. Expects a Confederate attack and a general uprising of pro-Confederate citizens. General Anderson resigns because of ill health, and Sherman assumes command on October 8, with headquarters at Louisville, where he lives in the Galt House hotel. Attempts to exclude newspaper reporters from his department in order to keep military secrets from appearing in the press. Anticipates Confederate attacks in Kentucky and sends dispatches to Lincoln and to the War Department reporting his force at less than 20,000 men and saying that he needs 60,000 men and arms. Cancels planned expedition into East Tennessee to assist Unionists resisting the Confederacy. Stays at the telegraph office until 3 A.M., gets little sleep, smokes cigars constantly, and drinks excessively. Tells Secretary of War Simon Cameron and Adjutant General Lorenzo Thomas in October that expulsion of the Confederates from Kentucky will require 60,000 men and that a successful offensive in his theater of operations will eventually require 200,000. The adjutant general's report of this conversation is published in the *New-York Tribune*, October 30, angering Sherman. Continues to send pessimistic dispatches to Washington. Warns Governor William Dennison of Ohio on November 6 that the Confederates cannot be stopped from over-running Kentucky if they attack in the numbers reported. Telegraphs Major General George B. McClellan, general-in-chief of the army, asking to be relieved of command. Learns that East Tennessee Unionists have been repressed by Confederate troops, with many arrested and five hanged. Brigadier General Don Carlos Buell succeeds Sherman on November 15, becoming commander of the Department of the Ohio. Reports for duty under Major General Henry W. Halleck, commander of the Department of the Missouri, in St. Louis. Inspects troops at Sedalia, Missouri, and orders them concentrated in anticipation of Confederate attack. Halleck countermands Sherman's orders, recalls him, and sends him to Lancaster for a 20-day furlough, telling McClellan on December 2 that Sherman is unfit for duty at present. The *Cincinnati Commercial* reports on December 11 that Sherman is "insane . . . stark mad," and the charge is repeated in other newspapers. Philemon B. Ewing writes a refutation of the report, which the *Commercial* prints on December 13. Sherman returns to St. Louis and assumes command of Benton Barracks, a training camp, on December 23.

1862   Tells John in letter on January 4 that his sense of disgrace over having exaggerated Confederate strength in Kentucky has caused him to think of suicide. Ordered on February 13 to take command of the District of Cairo at Paducah, Kentucky. Supervises the forwarding of men and supplies up the Cumberland and Tennessee rivers to Brigadier General Ulysses S. Grant during Grant's operations against Fort Donelson, which surrenders on February 16, and then in preparation for an advance against Corinth, Mississippi. Assumes command of the Fifth Division, Army of the Tennessee, on March 1. Arrives with his division at Pittsburg Landing, Tennessee, on March 15. Grant (now a major general) arrives in nearby Savannah, Tennessee, on March 17 and directs Sherman to organize the reinforcements arriving at Pittsburg Landing. Sherman commands his division and rallies troops from other units during repeated Confederate assaults on the first day of the battle of Shiloh, April 6, withdrawing his line toward the Tennessee River twice and sustaining a slight wound in the hand. Participates in the Union counterattack on April 7 by the combined armies of Grant and Buell, ending in Confederate withdrawal toward Corinth. Newspapers generally praise Sherman for his battlefield leadership but attack Grant for falling victim to a surprise attack and sustaining heavy casualties; Sherman defends Grant in public and private letters. Halleck assumes command at Pittsburg Landing and begins advancing on Corinth. Sherman is promoted to major general of volunteers on May 1. Recommends Captain Philip H. Sheridan, who had known Ewing family in Ohio, for appointment as colonel of an Ohio regiment (recommendation is rejected, and Sheridan becomes commander of the 2nd Michigan Cavalry). Confederates evacuate Corinth May 29–30. Advises Grant not to take leave of absence despite Halleck's having put him in the powerless position of second-in-command; Grant is restored to command of the Army of the Tennessee on June 10. Commands the Fourth and Fifth Divisions in repairing the railroad between Grand Junction and Memphis, Tennessee, in June and July. Assumes command of the District of Memphis on July 21 and reinstates the city's civilian government under his supervision. Oversees the feeding and employing of fugitive slaves, sends expeditions against guerrillas, and permits, under orders from Washington, the purchase of cotton by agents from the North. Has Randolph, Tennessee, burned on September 24 in reprisal for guerrillas' firing on a boat in the Mississippi River. Issues Special Order Number 254 on September 27, announcing that ten families of Confederate soldiers or sympathizers will be expelled from Memphis for each boat fired on. After guerrillas fire on four boats, Sherman orders on October 18 the expulsion of 40 families from the city and the destruction of all houses, farms, and cornfields on the Arkansas bank of the Mississippi River for 15 miles downriver from Memphis. Confers with Grant in Oxford, Mississippi, on December 8, and is ordered to move against Vicksburg with four divisions, while Grant advances along the Mississippi Central Railroad against the Confederate forces under Lieutenant General John C. Pemberton. Leaves Memphis with about 100 transport vessels on December 19 and proceeds downriver, unaware that the Confederate raid on the supply depot at Holly Springs, Mississippi, on December 20 has induced Grant to turn back and has freed Pemberton to reinforce Vicksburg. Reaches the Yazoo River, north of Vicksburg, on December 26, and goes up it to face Confederate defenses on the bluffs above Chickasaw Bayou. Attacks with approximately 30,000 men on December 29; the assault fails. Plans further offensive moves, but cancels them due to heavy rains and increasing Confederate strength.

1863   Reembarks his troops on transports and returns to the Mississippi River on January 2. Many newspapers denounce Sherman for the assault at Chickasaw Bayou and renew the accusation that he is insane. Major General John A. McClernand, a former Illinois congressman, arrives and assumes command on January 4, and Sherman becomes commander of the 15th Army Corps under him. Plans attack on Fort Hindman, 50 miles up the Arkansas River, and leads troops under McClernand in assault on the fort, which surrenders January 11. Grant orders McClernand's force downriver to Milliken's Bend, Louisiana, about 15 miles above Vicksburg, and assumes personal command of the Vicksburg expedition. Sherman writes John that suffrage among men of military age should be restricted to soldiers. Arrests Thomas W. Knox, a New York *Herald* reporter who had severely criticized the Chickasaw Bayou attack, on January 31 and has him court-martialed for publishing military news without permission, publishing false accusations against army officers, and violating Sherman's order that excluded reporters from the Vicksburg expedition in December 1862. Sherman testifies at his trial as the sole prosecution witness. On February 18 Knox is convicted of the third charge and expelled from the army's lines. Sherman has his troops work on canal across bend in the river bank opposite Vicksburg designed to let boats pass downriver out of range of Confederate artillery. Commands three regiments in support of Acting Rear Admiral David D. Porter's unsuccessful attempt to open a route through the Mississippi Delta, by way of Steele's Bayou, to the Yazoo River east of Vicksburg, March 16–27. Resumes digging canal until heavy rains and rising water force its abandonment. Advises Grant to take the army back to Memphis and to approach Vicksburg overland along the line of the Mississippi Central Railroad; instead, Grant has Porter run his fleet past the Confederate guns on April 16 and then marches with most of his army down the west bank of the Mississippi below Vicksburg. Sherman feints an attack on Vicksburg's northern defenses with ten regiments on April 29 as a diversion from Grant's crossing of the Mississippi, then

marches his men below Vicksburg and crosses near Grand
Gulf, Mississippi, on May 7. Joins Grant, McClernand's
13th Corps, and Major General James B. McPherson's 17th
Corps in march toward Jackson, Mississippi, during which
the troops supply themselves by foraging on the countryside. Jackson falls on May 14. Sherman's corps destroys
railroads, the arsenal, and factories in the town on May
15–16. Commands the 15th Corps in a skirmish pushing
Confederates west from the Big Black River on May 17.
Begins, with McClernand and McPherson, the investment
of Vicksburg on May 18. The three corps mount an assault
against the Vicksburg defenses on May 19, which fails;
Grant orders a second assault on May 22, which also fails.
On June 17 and 18 Sherman and McPherson strongly protest McClernand's publication of a self-congratulatory
order in the newspapers without authorization. Grant,
already unhappy with McClernand's performance, removes him from command on June 18 and appoints Major
General Edward O. C. Ord as his successor. Sherman
commands three divisions at the Big Black River, guarding the Union rear against Confederate forces under General Joseph E. Johnston, from June 20 until the fall of
Vicksburg on July 4. Commands the 15th, the 13th, and the
recently arrived 9th Army Corps in pursuit of Johnston to
Jackson; Johnston abandons the town on July 16. Sherman
destroys railroads and warehouses in Jackson and then
breaks off the pursuit due to the extreme heat and drought
of summer. Returns to his camps on the west bank of the
Big Black River and remains there during July, August,
and September. Promoted to brigadier general in the regular army, dating from July 4. Ellen and the four oldest
children arrive in camp on August 14, remaining until
September 28. Begins, on September 25, to send troops to
Chattanooga, Tennessee, to reinforce the Army of the
Cumberland after its defeat in the battle of Chickamauga,
September 19–20. Son Willie contracts typhoid fever and
dies in Memphis on October 3. While en route by train to
Corinth, Mississippi, on October 11, Sherman and 600
men hold off an attack by approximately 3,000 Confederates at Collierville, Tennessee, until the approach of Union
reinforcements causes the Confederates to leave. Continues to move eastward through northern Mississippi
and Alabama. Learns on October 24 that Grant, now

commander of the Military Division of the Mississippi,
has given him command of the Army of the Tennessee.
Reaches Chattanooga on November 15. Crosses the Tennessee River with four divisions on the night of November 23–24 to threaten the right flank of General Braxton
Bragg's Army of Tennessee, entrenched along Missionary
Ridge overlooking Chattanooga. Advances on the Confederate right on November 24 but finds that the position
he has occupied is separated from Missionary Ridge by a
ravine. Attacks Tunnel Hill, the north end of Missionary
Ridge, on November 25. Makes little headway, but troops
of the Army of the Cumberland under Major General
George H. Thomas break the Confederate center, and
Bragg's men retreat into northwest Georgia. Marches to
Knoxville, Tennessee, which is besieged by Confederates
under Lieutenant General James Longstreet. Sherman's
cavalry reaches Knoxville on December 3; the Confederates withdraw toward Virginia. Marches to Bridgeport,
Alabama, and disposes his troops in winter quarters in
northern Alabama and southern Tennessee. Arrives in
Lancaster December 25 and spends a week with his family.

1864   Takes Minnie to Mount Notre Dame, a convent school at
Reading, Ohio. Arrives in Memphis on January 10. Organizes a force of 25,000 men to march into central Mississippi. Orders Brigadier General William Sooy Smith to
leave Memphis with 7,000 cavalry and destroy the Mobile
& Ohio Railroad, defeat the smaller force of Major General Nathan Bedford Forrest, then meet Sherman at Meridian, Mississippi. Marches to Meridian from Vicksburg,
February 3–14, destroying the railroad, doing extensive
damage to property, and fighting five skirmishes en route.
Destroys Confederate supply depot, an arsenal, gristmills,
cotton, and railroads at Meridian, February 14–20; Smith
never arrives due to unsuccessful fighting with Forrest.
Returns to Vicksburg, followed by hundreds of former
slaves. Mother-in-law Maria Boyle Ewing dies February
20. On February 21 Congress passes a joint resolution of
thanks to Sherman and his men for the march to Chattanooga and the battle of Missionary Ridge. Confers with
Major General Nathaniel P. Banks in New Orleans, March
2–3, and agrees to lend Banks 10,000 soldiers for use in
the Red River campaign. Travels to Nashville to confer

with Grant, who has been made general-in-chief of the
Union army, on March 17. Assumes command of the Military Division of the Mississippi on March 18. Confers
with Grant in Cincinnati, where they plan the spring
campaign—Grant to move against the Army of Northern
Virginia while in Georgia Sherman simultaneously moves
against the Army of Tennessee. Organizes logistical system
to build reserves of supplies for the Union forces in northern Georgia. Arranges for the newspaper publication of a
letter in which he warns Southern civilians of the severe
consequences of continued rebellion. Begins the Atlanta
campaign May 7, advancing along the railroad line that
runs from Chattanooga to Atlanta. Commands approximately 100,000 men divided into the Army of the Tennessee (McPherson), the Army of the Cumberland (Thomas),
and the Army of the Ohio (Major General John Schofield), facing the Army of Tennessee (General Joseph E.
Johnston), which numbers approximately 40,000 (later reinforced to about 60,000). Sends McPherson around the
left of the Confederate defenses west of Dalton, Georgia,
on May 9. Johnston withdraws to Resaca on the night of
May 12. Assaults Johnston's line, May 14–15. Sends a cavalry division to threaten the railroad in the Confederates'
rear. Johnston withdraws to Cassville, May 16, and then to
Allatoona Pass, May 19. Sherman begins moving away
from the railroad on May 23 in attempt to outflank the
Confederate positions, resulting in heavy fighting at New
Hope Church, May 25, and at Pickett's Mill, May 27.
Moves back to the rail line by steady skirmishing and entrenching. Obstructs efforts of Northern recruiting agents
to fill their state quotas by enlisting Southern blacks. Son
Charles Celestine Sherman born June 11. Orders Union
commanders at Memphis to devastate the areas of western
Tennessee and northern Mississippi that support the cavalry raids of Forrest. Johnston falls back through a series
of new defensive positions until his army reaches Kenesaw
Mountain, near Marietta, on June 18. Sherman orders assault on the center of the Confederate line, June 27, which
is repulsed. Sends McPherson around the left flank of the
Confederate position, July 1–2. Johnston withdraws to fortifications on the north bank of the Chattahoochee River.
Sherman sends Schofield across the Chattahoochee upriver from Johnston's position. Johnston withdraws into

the fortifications of Atlanta, July 9, and is removed from command and replaced by General John B. Hood on July 17. Hood orders assaults on the Army of the Cumberland, July 20, and the Army of the Tennessee, July 22, both of which are repulsed; McPherson is killed on July 22. Major General John A. Logan, a volunteer officer and former Illinois congressman, assumes temporary command of the Army of the Tennessee until Sherman names Major General Oliver O. Howard, a West Point graduate, as McPherson's replacement on July 24. Orders cavalry raids to cut the rail line into Atlanta from Macon, which fail in the last week of July. Directs Howard to march south to cut the rail line; Howard encounters and repulses a Confederate attack at Ezra Church, July 28. Writes a widely published letter to a Massachusetts recruiting agent, July 30, opposing the recruitment of blacks into the Union army on the grounds that they are not the equal of white soldiers, that their use offends white soldiers, that their enlistment allows Northern states to reduce the number of whites they must conscript to fulfill their draft quotas, and that they are better used as paid construction laborers with the armies in the field. Maintains continuous artillery fire into Atlanta and extends entrenchments toward the Atlanta–Macon rail line. Refuses on August 12 to give Indiana troops, who are not allowed to vote in the field, a furlough to go home to vote in state elections. Promoted to major general in the regular army on August 12. Orders another cavalry raid on the rail line, August 18–22, which also fails. Moves his army south of Atlanta, August 25–30, to cut the rail line. Repulses Lieutenant General William J. Hardee's corps in fighting near Jonesboro, Georgia, August 31–September 1. Hood evacuates Atlanta on September 1 and Union forces enter September 2. Sherman's telegram announcing city's capture is widely quoted ("Atlanta is ours and fairly won"), and the victory revives hopes of Lincoln's supporters for his reelection. Orders expulsion of all civilians from Atlanta so it can be held solely as a military depot; his subsequent correspondence with Hood and the mayor of Atlanta debating the morality of the order is widely printed and praised in the North. Conveys to Governor Joseph E. Brown a proposal to restrain damage to civilian property in Georgia in return for Brown's withdrawing Georgia troops from the Confederate army; the proposal is not acted on. Hood breaks Sherman's supply line on the Chattanooga–Atlanta railroad, October 2–4, but is repulsed by the Union garrison at Allatoona Pass, October 5. Skirmishing continues as Hood moves westward toward Alabama. Proposes to Grant on October 9 a destructive march across Georgia to Savannah. Pursues Hood as far as Gaylesville, Alabama, where Sherman stays, October 21–28. After corresponding with Sherman, Grant approves the march across Georgia, November 2. Sherman orders reinforcements to Nashville, where Thomas will command two corps against Hood, leaving four corps (approximately 60,000 men) under his command in Georgia. Leaves Atlanta on November 16, destroying railroads, factories, and part of the city. Accompanies the left wing of his army as it feints toward Augusta, while the right wing threatens Macon, destroying or confiscating railroads, government buildings, cotton gins, crops, livestock, and much private property. Converging at the state capital, Milledgeville, on November 23, the two wings march toward Savannah at the rate of about ten miles a day, continuing devastations across a path 50–60 miles wide, and fighting skirmishes with Confederate cavalry and militia. Many former slaves follow the army eastward. Sherman's forces reach the outskirts of Savannah on December 10. Orders assault on Fort McAllister December 13; its fall opens a supply line to naval vessels offshore. Summons Hardee to surrender the garrison on December 17, threatening to destroy Savannah and show no quarter if he resists. Hardee refuses, then evacuates Savannah and moves into South Carolina on December 20–21. Sherman enters Savannah, where he learns on December 24 that Thomas has decisively defeated Hood outside Nashville on December 15–16. Learns from a New York newspaper that his son Charles had died on December 4 (had previously been told that the baby was ill).

1865   Receives on January 2 Grant's approval for his proposed march north through the Carolinas. Congress passes on January 10 a joint resolution of thanks for the Atlanta campaign and march to the sea. Secretary of War Edwin M. Stanton arrives in Savannah on January 11 to dispose of captured cotton, to confer with Sherman and with black leaders, and to investigate charges that Sherman and other

officers had been cruel to black refugees. Sherman defends
as militarily necessary Brigadier General Jefferson C.
Davis's decision to take up his pontoon bridge at Ebenezer
Creek during the march to Savannah, leaving many refugees behind (newspapers had reported that hundreds of
refugees had subsequently either drowned trying to cross
the creek or been reenslaved by the Confederates). Issues
Special Field Order Number 15, January 16, reserving a
coastal strip 30 miles wide from Charleston to St. John's
River, Florida, for the use of blacks and granting possessory title of 40-acre plots to families that settle there.
Issues orders on January 19 for the march to Goldsboro,
North Carolina. Begins main advance on February 1, sending the left wing toward Augusta and the right wing
toward Charleston to mask his intention to go to Columbia. Despite heavy rains, swollen rivers, and intermittent
skirmishing, the columns average ten miles per day. Destruction of homes and property is more severe than in
Georgia. Enters Columbia on February 17. On the night
of February 17–18 much of central Columbia is destroyed
by fire and looted by soldiers; Sherman and other soldiers
try to control fires. Orders destruction of arsenals, munitions, and other government facilities in Columbia. Leaves
Columbia on February 20, the army continuing northward in a path usually about 30 miles wide. Reaches
Fayetteville, North Carolina, on March 11 and orders
destruction of its arsenal. Confederate forces under Joseph
E. Johnston, numbering approximately 21,000, attack the
left wing of Sherman's army near Bentonville, North
Carolina, on March 19 and are repulsed. Prepares on
March 20 to move his whole force against Johnston, who
withdraws on the night of March 21. Reaches Goldsboro
on March 23, establishing a supply line to the coast and
joining up with forces under Schofield, giving him total
command of 89,000 men. Travels to City Point, Virginia,
on March 27 and meets with Lincoln, Grant, and Porter,
planning the spring offensive and discussing possible
terms of Southern surrender. Returns to Goldsboro on
March 31. Learns on April 6 of the fall of Richmond on
April 3 and the westward retreat of the Army of Northern
Virginia, pursued by Grant. Begins march west in pursuit
of Johnston on April 10. Learns on April 12 of the surrender of the Army of Northern Virginia to Grant on April 9.

Enters Raleigh on April 13. Receives Johnston's proposal
of a cease-fire on April 14. Learns en route to meet
Johnston on April 17 that Lincoln was assassinated on
April 14. Meets with Johnston outside Durham, North
Carolina, April 17–18. Sherman drafts on April 18 an agreement, which he and Johnston sign, entailing not only the
military surrender of all Confederate forces but also political terms of peace, including recognition of existing
Southern state governments, guarantees of political rights,
and a general amnesty. President Andrew Johnson and his
Cabinet reject the agreement on April 21, and send Grant
to North Carolina. Grant arrives in Raleigh on April 24
and orders Sherman to demand Johnston's surrender on
the same terms given to the Army of Northern Virginia;
Sherman receives Johnston's surrender on April 26. Sherman learns that Stanton has published a report implying
that he had been willfully insubordinate and possibly disloyal in his negotiations with Johnston. Many newspapers
denounce Sherman in the following days and some again
question his sanity. Travels to Savannah by boat and
makes arrangements for the supply of Union forces in
Georgia and the feeding of destitute civilians, then goes to
Richmond, where he meets his army on May 9. Marches
with them to Alexandria, Virginia, viewing en route the
major battlefields in Virginia. Watches the grand review of
the Army of the Potomac in Washington on May 23. Leads
the grand review of the western armies on May 24. Refuses to shake Stanton's hand on the reviewing stand.
Travels to New York on May 31, visits West Point on June
5, and attends the Sanitary Fair in Chicago on June 9; enthusiastic crowds greet him at many places. Declares his
opposition to granting the franchise to blacks and depre-
cates reconstruction measures designed to change the
South, stating that there are not enough troops to occupy
it for long, that Southern attitudes cannot be changed by
force, and that blacks and poor whites are incapable of
ruling Southern states. Bids farewell at Louisville on July 4
to four corps of his army, who are about to be mustered
out. Receives orders in Lancaster assigning him to the
command of the Military Division of the Mississippi (renamed the Military Division of the Missouri in 1866),
which includes the area from the Mississippi River to the
Rocky Mountains between the Canadian and Mexican

borders, excluding Texas. Moves with his family to St. Louis, living at 912 Garrison Avenue. Travels to Omaha, Nebraska, and Leavenworth, Kansas, in September and October to inspect the construction of the Union Pacific Railroad. Recommends that the control of Indian affairs be transferred from the Interior Department to the War Department (continues to recommend this change often in the following years, but it is never approved). Prepares extensive report on his wartime operations, and makes inspection tour of Arkansas.

1866   Visits Washington, D.C., in February. Supports President Johnson's veto of the Freedmen's Bureau Bill. Oversees the army's regulation of wagon traffic across the Great Plains, protecting a limited number of routes because of troop shortages, and gives priority to the construction of the transcontinental railroad, which he considers the key to controlling the West. Makes inspection tour through eastern Nebraska and Minnesota, May–June. Visits Yale College in New Haven, Connecticut, and receives honorary LL.D. degree from Dartmouth College in Hanover, New Hampshire, on July 25. Promoted to lieutenant general on July 25, ranking second after Grant, who is promoted to general. Strength of army is set by act of Congress at approximately 54,000 men. Makes inspection tour through Wyoming and Colorado, August–October. Confers on Indian situation with Kit Carson at Fort Garland in southern Colorado. Recommends restricting Plains Indians to reservations north of the Platte River and south of the Arkansas River in order to keep them away from the main transcontinental travel routes. In October President Johnson orders Sherman to Washington and Grant to accompany Lewis D. Campbell on a diplomatic mission to establish relations with President Benito Juárez of Mexico. Grant refuses to go and Sherman takes his place, leaving New York on November 10. Visits Vera Cruz, Tampico, and Matamoros without finding Juárez and then goes to New Orleans, arriving December 20. Advocates harsh measures against the Sioux after Captain William J. Fetterman and 80 of his men are killed in battle in northwestern Wyoming on December 21.

1867   Son Philemon Tecumseh Sherman ("Cump") born January 9. Plans offensives against northern and southern Plains tribes and cautions commanders against killing unresisting Indians (attacks are later curtailed to allow for new peace efforts). Resists calls for raising volunteer troops in the West, considering them undisciplined. Reads John William Draper's *Thoughts on the Future Civil Policy of America*, *A History of the Intellectual Development of Europe*, and the recently published first volume of his *History of the American Civil War*. Gives Draper source material, reminiscences, and critical readings for Volumes II (published 1868) and III (published 1870); Draper urges Sherman to write his memoirs. Appointed in July to the seven-man military and civilian Peace Commission to negotiate with western Indians. Meets Sioux and Northern Cheyenne leaders in Dakota Territory, Wyoming, and Nebraska. Warns them that they must make permanent settlements and become an agricultural people. Ordered to Washington in October by President Johnson. Declines to become secretary of war and advises Johnson to seek support of moderates in Congress. Rejects suggestions that he remain in Washington and returns to St. Louis. Travels to Washington in December to serve with Major General Philip H. Sheridan and Brigadier General Christopher C. Augur on a commission that is to review the articles of war and army regulations.

1868   Declines again to become secretary of war, as Johnson tries to remove Stanton from the office against the will of the Senate. Commission recommends in February that the army's independent administrative bureaus and staff corps be placed under the control of the commanding general. Sherman returns to St. Louis in February and resists Johnson's proposal to give him the rank of brevet general and create a command that would put him in Washington; threatens to resign his commission. Called as a defense witness at the impeachment trial of Johnson and testifies about Johnson's attempts to make him secretary of war, April 11–13. Travels with peace commissioners to meet Sioux leaders in Wyoming and Navajos and Utes in New Mexico. Attends meeting of the Peace Commission in Chicago in October and wins majority approval for policy of confining Indians on reservations and ending their treatment as separate, independent nations under the law. Approves Sheridan's plan for winter offensive against the Southern Cheyenne and Arapaho who had raided in

Kansas and Colorado during the summer. Grant wins the presidential election on November 3.

1869   Visits Seminary at Pineville, near Alexandria, Louisiana, and finds his portrait hanging in the main hall. Moves to Washington in February, accepting a group of business-men's gift of a house at 205 I Street, NW, which had pre-viously belonged to Grant (Ellen and the children join him in April). Promoted to general and becomes com-manding general of the army on March 5; Sheridan suc-ceeds him as commander of the Division of the Missouri. Grant's General Order Number II of March 8 places army administrative bureaus and staff corps, as well as line units, under the control of the commanding general, and specifies that all orders will go through Sherman. Grant's long-time friend and aide, John A. Rawlins, becomes sec-retary of war on March 11. With the encouragement of members of Congress, Rawlins induces Grant to rescind the order on March 26, restoring the independence of bureaus and staff corps from the commanding general. Sherman disapproves of Grant's policy of assigning supervision of Indian reservations to religious denomina-tions. Listens in the War Office on May 10 to the tele-graphic signal triggered by the driving of the spike that completes the transcontinental railroad. Declines financier Jay Cooke's offer of a one-percent share in the Northern Pacific Railroad for $2,500. Delivers the commencement address at the U.S. Military Academy. Rawlins dies on September 6 and Sherman serves as secretary of war until the confirmation in October of William Worth Belknap, who had commanded a brigade in Sherman's army during the war. On September 22, Thomas Ewing collapses while arguing a case before the U.S. Supreme Court, beginning long period of declining health. Sherman is elected presi-dent of the Society of the Army of the Tennessee at the annual reunion in Louisville, November 17–18 (is reelected annually for the rest of his life and will regularly attend its reunions, as well as those of other Union veterans' groups).

1870   Defends army attack on Piegan village in Montana in which 120 men and 53 women and children were killed. Denounces in March the army bill sponsored by Illinois congressman John A. Logan, which in its final form cuts the enlisted strength of the army from 54,000 to 30,000 men and reduces Sherman's pay and allowances from $18,700 to $16,500 per year. Protests Belknap's practice of making appointments and issuing orders through the adjutant general's office without consulting him. Privately deplores Grant's susceptibility to the influence of corrupt politicians. Complains that the office of commanding general has been made a sinecure and speaks of resigning.

1871   Becomes regent of the Smithsonian Institution in Washington, D.C. (serves until 1874, and again from 1879 to 1885). Visits New Orleans in April on the way to Texas. Gives a speech critical of Republican Reconstruction policies and suggests that reports of Ku Klux Klan activity have been exaggerated. Several Southern newspapers, as well as the New York *Herald*, endorse Sherman for the presidency, but he publicly disavows interest in the nomination of either party. Learns at Fort Richardson, Texas, during inspection trip in May, of a Kiowa attack on a wagon train in which seven teamsters were killed. Goes to Fort Sill, Indian Territory, arrests Kiowa leaders Satanta, Big Tree, and Satank during armed confrontation on May 27, and has them sent to Texas for civil trial. Returns to Washington and considers moving his headquarters to St. Louis. Orders army protection for surveying crews of the Northern Pacific Railroad. Thomas Ewing, Sr., dies on October 26. Leaves New York, November 11, for a tour of Europe and the Mediterranean.

1872   Travels through Spain, France, Italy, Malta, Egypt, Turkey, Russia, Germany, Austria, Switzerland, England, Scotland, and Ireland. Attends operas and concerts and tours battlefields, including those of the Crimean and the Franco-Prussian wars. Returns to the United States in September. Grant is reelected president on November 5.

1873   Begins writing his memoirs. Recommends in February the abrogation of the 1868 treaty with the Sioux, which had allowed them to hunt buffalo in northern Wyoming and Montana, and their confinement to the vicinity of the Missouri River in Dakota Territory. Endorses severe retaliation against resisting Modoc Indians in northeastern

California after their leader Kintpuash (Captain Jack) kills Brigadier General Edward R. S. Canby, who had served with Sherman in California, during a truce meeting on April 11. (Kintpuash and three other Modocs are later hanged, and 155 prisoners are sent to the Indian Territory.) Submits a brief annual report, November 7, saying that no part of the army is under his immediate control and that all command and responsibility belong to Secretary of War Belknap. Divides his house in two and rents out one half to reduce the expense of living and entertaining in Washington.

1874   Testifies before the House Committee on Military Affairs in January. Opposes further reduction in the enlisted strength of the army from 30,000 to 25,000 and tells the committee that Belknap is its real commander. Congress reduces the army by 5,000. Asks Grant to define the extent of the commanding general's authority, but Grant does not do so. On May 8 requests approval to move his headquarters to St. Louis, which Grant gives. Belknap retains control over assignment of commanders and movement of troops, as well as bureaus and staff corps. Daughter Maria marries Lieutenant Thomas W. Fitch, U.S. Navy, on October 1. Sells the house on I Street, NW, and moves to 912 Garrison Avenue in St. Louis in October, establishing an office at the intersection of Locust and 10th streets. Son Thomas graduates from Georgetown College and enters the Sheffield Scientific School of Yale College.

1875   Completes his memoirs, dating the dedication January 21; they are published as *Memoirs of General W. T. Sherman. By Himself.* in two volumes by D. Appleton & Company in May and sell 10,000 copies before the end of the month. Receives many letters of praise, as well as letters of criticism and correction. Orville Babcock, Grant's personal secretary, employs Washington journalist Henry Van Ness Boynton, a veteran of the Army of the Cumberland, to write an attack on the memoirs and on Sherman's war record with the aid of official documents copied by War Department clerks. Boynton's work appears first as series of newspaper articles, then as a book, *Sherman's Historical Raid; The Memoirs in the Light of the Record*, and accuses Sherman of being "intensely egotistical" and of unfairly slighting or blaming Grant, Thomas, Buell, Stanton, and many of his subordinates. Sherman provides criticisms of Boynton's work to Charles William Moulton, who writes a pamphlet rebuttal of it, *The Review of General Sherman's Memoirs Examined Chiefly in the Light of Its Own Evidence*. Sherman's first grandchild, William Sherman Fitch, born June 24. Sends Lieutenant Colonel Emory Upton, instructor in tactics at West Point, on a two-year inspection tour of foreign armies (tour results in Upton's book *The Armies of Asia and Europe*, published in 1878, which recommends a modified version of Prussian organization and training for the U.S. Army). Privately criticizes Grant's administration as a failure and censures Republican Reconstruction policies, including the enfranchisement of blacks. Repeatedly says that he will not accept nomination for the presidency. Considers revising *Memoirs* in response to his critics, but decides against it.

1876   Testimony to the House Special Committee on Expenditures in the War Department in February reveals that Belknap and his family had received money from army post traders in return for their appointments. Belknap resigns as secretary of war on March 2. Alphonso Taft, the new secretary of war, issues orders on April 6 recalling Sherman to Washington and specifying that all military orders will go through Sherman, who will also control the adjutant general's and inspector general's departments. Army begins campaign to force the Sioux and Northern Cheyenne onto their reservation; Sherman expresses concern that the Indians will not stand and fight, leading to a long and inconclusive pursuit. Family moves to Washington in May, living in several suites at the Ebbitt House hotel. Attends Thomas's commencement at Yale and receives an honorary LL.D. degree on June 29. Learns in early July of the 7th Cavalry's defeat in Montana on June 25 by the Sioux and Northern Cheyenne in the battle of the Little Big Horn, ending in the deaths of Lieutenant Colonel George A. Custer and 262 of his men. Sherman refuses to use civilian volunteers for war against the Sioux. Congress authorizes an increase of 2,500 in the army's strength. Orders offensive to resume (campaign continues until surrender of surviving Indians in 1877). Thomas enters the St. Louis Law School of Washington University and manages Sherman's Missouri investments for him.

Privately disapproves of continued use of federal troops to support Republican state administrations in the South. The presidential election between Republican Rutherford B. Hayes and Democrat Samuel J. Tilden on November 7 ends in a disputed electoral count. Sherman privately deplores the prospect of victory by Tilden. Orders troops to Washington to quell any disturbances during the resolution of the presidential election.

1877   Grant threatens to declare martial law in the event of violent action by political protestors. Joint session of Congress accepts on March 2 decision of electoral commission declaring that Hayes received a majority of the electoral votes. John Sherman becomes secretary of the treasury in Hayes's Cabinet. Hayes returns troops supporting Republican state governments in Louisiana and South Carolina to their barracks in April, ending the army's role in Southern politics. Sherman takes son Thomas on an inspection trip through the Northwest and California. Praises the military skill and humane conduct toward white settlers shown by the Nez Percé during their resistance to resettlement on an Idaho reservation and subsequent 1,000-mile flight across the Northwest, July–October. Orders the Nez Percé sent to Indian Territory. Privately criticizes Congress for failing to make an army appropriation until November and for opposing the use of troops in violent labor disputes.

1878   Continues to oppose reduction in the army's strength as Congress considers its reorganization. Thomas graduates from law school, May 13, and tells his father in a letter, May 20, that he intends to enter a Jesuit seminary in England and become a priest. Sherman reacts bitterly to his son's decision, accusing Thomas of deserting the family, and writes many private letters denouncing the Roman Catholic Church and its clergy. Delivers the commencement address at the College of New Jersey (later Princeton University) on June 19. Ellen, after a visit to Thomas in St. Louis and to Maria in Lancaster, moves to Baltimore with Rachel and Philemon, and writes to Sherman angrily about the social demands placed on her by his position. Sherman continues to live at the Ebbitt House hotel in Washington. Reports to Secretary of War George W.

McCrary after an inspection tour of the West that new settlement is proceeding rapidly, that the buffalo have been nearly exterminated, and that the government's provisions for Indians confined on reservations are dangerously inadequate.

1879   Travels across the South, January–March, from Savannah and St. Augustine in the east to New Orleans and Baton Rouge in the west. Writes a letter, February 4, at the request of Evan P. Howell of *The Atlanta Constitution*, describing his courteous reception in the South and encouraging investment and settlement in Atlanta, eastern Tennessee, and northern Georgia and Alabama; it is reprinted in other Southern newspapers. Receives title Duke of Louisiana during Mardi Gras festivities in New Orleans and has friendly meeting with John B. Hood. Visits Louisiana State University at Baton Rouge (the successor to the Seminary near Alexandria, which burned down in October 1869 and was then relocated). Continues north by way of Vicksburg and Jackson. Rents a house in Washington on 15th Street, NW, near H Street; Ellen and the younger children move in with him.

1880   Sherman renews controversy with journalist Henry Van Ness Boynton when he tells the *Cleveland Leader* in January that Boynton slanders for pay. Boynton asks Hayes to court-martial Sherman, but Hayes refuses, and Boynton does not file civil suit for libel or slander. Daughter Eleanor marries Lieutenant Alexander M. Thackara, U.S. Navy, on May 5. Attends veterans' reunion in Columbus, Ohio, on August 11 and says in his speech, "There is many a boy here today who looks on war as all glory, but, boys, it is all hell." Thomas Sherman arrives in Washington in the last week of August and is reconciled with his father, who continues to regret Thomas's decision to become a priest. Travels with Hayes, August–November, across the Northwest to Seattle, Washington, south through Oregon and California, and across the Southwest. Defends investigation conducted by Major General John Schofield of alleged assault upon Johnson C. Whittaker, the only black cadet at the U.S. Military Academy, which concludes that Whittaker's injuries had been self-inflicted. Sherman denies that there is more racial prejudice at West Point than

elsewhere and that the academy is an undemocratic institution. Recommends against keeping black soldiers only
in separate all-black regiments, which he considers contrary to the Fourteenth Amendment. Angered by Hayes's
decision to forcibly retire Edward O. C. Ord in order to
promote Nelson A. Miles to brigadier general.

1881   John Sherman is returned to the U.S. Senate from Ohio,
January 18. Sherman orders on May 7 the establishment of
the School of Application for Infantry and Cavalry at Fort
Leavenworth, Kansas (school later becomes the U.S.
Army Command and General Staff College). Publicly criticizes inaccuracies in Jefferson Davis's *The Rise and Fall of
the Confederate Government*. President James A. Garfield is
fatally wounded on July 2; Sherman orders troops to
guard the jail in which the assassin, Charles J. Guiteau, is
held and to patrol Washington. Visits Atlanta in November to see the International Cotton Exposition, to which
he had subscribed $2,000. Speaks to the Georgia Mexican
Veterans Association in Atlanta.

1882   Makes an inspection trip through the Southwest to Los
Angeles, March–April. Declines offer from some members of Congress that he be exempted from the provisions
of a new law requiring army officers to retire at age 64.
Visits Montreal in September. Praises the Southern Pacific
Railroad as an influence for settlement and for suppression
of Indian resistance in Texas, New Mexico, and Arizona.
President Chester A. Arthur decides on army promotions
to general officer rank without consulting Sherman.

1883   Orders Brigadier General George Crook to pursue and destroy, without regard to departmental or international
boundaries, the Apaches who raided from Mexico into
Arizona and New Mexico in March. With Mexican permission, Crook moves into Sierra Madre with force of
Apache scouts and regular cavalry and successfully negotiates with Geronimo and other leaders for their return to
the reservation in Arizona. (Apache warfare resumes in
1885–86, ending only when Geronimo and his followers
are imprisoned in Florida after their final surrender.) Sherman decides in June to turn over command of the army to
Sheridan in November. Receives many letters urging him

to seek the Republican nomination for the presidency. Travels through the Northwest, the Pacific coastal states, and the Southwest in the summer. Turns over command to Sheridan on November 1 and moves to St. Louis, returning to house at 912 Garrison Avenue. Writes to D. Appleton & Company on December 28, suggesting the publication of a second edition of his *Memoirs*.

1884   Retires from the army on February 8. Sends telegrams to the Republican national convention on June 3 and 5 ("I will not accept if nominated and will not serve if elected") to forestall the possibility of his nomination for president in case the convention deadlocks. Calls for reform of the state militia system at a meeting of the Military Service Institution, Governor's Island, New York, December 24 (paper is published as "The Militia" in the *Journal of the Military Service Institution*, March 1885). Visits Grant, who is writing his memoirs and is suffering from cancer, in New York City.

1885   Works on revision of his *Memoirs*, including new chapters on the first 26 years of his life and on his activities from 1865 until 1883. Declines to go on the professional lecture circuit. Grant dies July 23. Takes part in the funeral procession in New York City on August 8. Sends Samuel L. Clemens a 300-page manuscript on his tour of Europe. Clemens calls manuscript a "skeleton" and advises against publishing it while praising Sherman's *Memoirs* as *"fat"* in letter on October 5 (manuscript remains unpublished). Sherman privately criticizes President Grover Cleveland for appointing too many former Confederates to federal office.

1886   Censures the railroad strike by the Knights of Labor, March–May. D. Appleton & Company publishes a second edition of his *Memoirs*. Delivers an address to the reunion of the Grand Army of the Republic in San Francisco, August 4, and calls the American desire to acquire California the true cause of the Mexican War. Travels from San Francisco to Vancouver, British Columbia, and returns east on the Canadian Pacific Railroad. Moves to New York City in September so that Ellen can be closer to their son Philemon while he attends the Sheffield

Scientific School. Lives at the Fifth Avenue Hotel, joins the Union League Club, helps found the Players' Club, and enjoys taking his grandchildren to Central Park and museums. Speaks at a banquet on November 3 in honor of the dedication of the Statue of Liberty (becomes popular after-dinner speaker in New York).

1887   Ellen's health declines as she suffers from effects of worsening heart disease. Sherman goes to Woodbury, Connecticut, with his brother John in April to see the sites of 17th- and 18th-century Sherman family residences and graves. In response to article by British general Viscount Wolseley praising Robert E. Lee as George Washington's equal, publishes "Grant, Thomas, Lee" in the May *North American Review*, describing Grant as a strategist superior to Lee and praising George H. Thomas, a Virginian, for remaining loyal to the Union. Delivers the commencement address at the U.S. Military Academy, May 11. Sits for a bust by the sculptor Augustus Saint-Gaudens in December (bust is used by Saint-Gaudens as model for Sherman's head in 1903 equestrian statue at southeast corner of Central Park in New York City).

1888   Publishes "The Grand Strategy of the War of the Rebellion" in the February *Century Magazine* (appears in revised form as "The Grand Strategy of the Last Year of the War" in Volume IV of *Battles and Leaders of the Civil War*, published in 1889). Son Philemon Tecumseh graduates from the Sheffield Scientific School and begins studying law at Columbia University. Buys a house at 75 West 71st Street, New York City, in August and moves into it in September. Publishes "Old Shady, with a Moral" in the October *North American Review*, arguing that either blacks should be assured the right to vote or the federal government should reduce the representation in Congress of states that deny that right and warning of another civil war if suffrage is permanently denied to blacks. Publishes "Camp-Fires of the G.A.R." in the November *North American Review* and "Hon. James G. Blaine," a tribute, in the December number. Ellen suffers heart attacks on November 7 and 25 and dies on November 28. Travels to St. Louis for her burial in Calvary Cemetery. Suffers severe attacks of asthma.

1889   Asks President Benjamin Harrison to retain Joseph E.
          Johnston in the office of U.S. Railroad Commissioner, to
          which Cleveland had appointed him, but Johnston is
          asked to resign. Publishes "Old Times in California" in the
          March *North American Review*. Serves in June on the New
          York City committee to raise relief funds for survivors of
          the Johnstown flood in Pennsylvania. Attends Inde-
          pendence Day ceremonies in Denver; does not attend
          Thomas's ordination in Philadelphia on July 7.

1890   Gives Thomas instructions on the gravestone that he has
          designed for himself, bearing epitaph "Faithful and Hon-
          orable" and the insignia of five Union army corps. Re-
          ceives hundreds of messages congratulating him on his
          70th birthday, and spends a week in February answering
          them with the help of a clerk. Visits Washington in May
          and dines at the White House with President Harrison,
          who had been a brigade commander in Sherman's army
          during the Civil War. Publishes "Our Army and Militia"
          in the August *North American Review*, calling for nation-
          wide modernization of state militias.

1891   Develops erysipelas on February 4, followed by pneumo-
          nia and continued attacks of asthma. Spends 71st birthday
          rereading Dickens' *Great Expectations*. Dies at 1:50 P.M.,
          February 14. Thomas officiates at a private service on Feb-
          ruary 19. Funeral procession in New York City includes
          President Harrison and former presidents Hayes and
          Cleveland. Among the 12 pallbearers is 84-year-old Joseph
          E. Johnston, who refuses to cover his head against the
          cold (Johnston dies of pneumonia March 21). Crowds as-
          semble along the route as a special train carries the body
          to St. Louis where, after a funeral procession and ceremo-
          nies on February 21, Sherman is buried in Calvary Ceme-
          tery next to Willie, Charles, and Ellen.

Note on the Text

This volume presents the text of the corrected, expanded, and slightly revised version of the *Memoirs of General William T. Sherman*, published by D. Appleton and Company in 1886.

Sherman began to write his memoirs at least as early as 1873 but feared they would be too controversial for publication. He finally decided to go ahead with the project and on January 23, 1875, wrote his brother, Senator John Sherman, about his decision: "You will be surprised and maybe alarmed, that I have at last agreed to publish in book form my Memoirs of a period from 1846–65, in two volumes. . . . I have carefully eliminated everything calculated to raise controversy, except where sustained by documents embraced in the work itself, and then only with minor parties." He was encouraged to do so, he said, by the reaction of the few people to whom he had earlier shown the manuscript, one of whom was "emphatic that it ought to be published in the interest of history."

He had first discussed publication with Robert Clarke & Company but then made arrangements with William Appleton, who came to St. Louis to meet with him. The completed manuscript was in the publisher's office in New York by March 1875, and the *Memoirs of General William T. Sherman. By Himself* was published in two volumes in May 1875 by D. Appleton and Company. According to what Sherman later told U. S. Grant, who passed it on to Samuel L. Clemens (Mark Twain), 25,000 sets were sold at $7 a set, for which Sherman was paid $25,000.

The *Memoirs* proved to be very controversial, and Sherman received numerous letters, ranging from praise to demands for extensive revisions. After consulting with friends and family, he decided that, though he would correct factual errors in future printings, he would not actually revise the work. Instead, he announced his intention to bring out a "second edition" that would include an appendix of letters in which other people would have the opportunity to give their own versions of the events he described. A few corrections were made in the cheaper one-volume version brought out by Appleton the next year. Sherman collected material for the "second edition" but did not work on it until after his retirement from the army in 1884. To the 1875 printing he added a second preface, two new chapters, one at the beginning and the other at the end, an appendix to volume I, two appendixes to volume II, and an index. Sherman corrected further factual errors and made a few revisions. Portraits were also added, as well as maps that had been unavailable at the time of the 1875 printing. By the spring of 1885 his work was completed, but he asked D. Appleton and Company to delay publication until after the *Personal Memoirs of U. S. Grant* was published in 1885–86. The expanded, corrected, and slightly revised version of the 1875 printing was published by D. Appleton and Company in New York as the *Memoirs of General William T. Sherman*, "Second edition, revised and corrected, in two volumes," in 1886. Sherman made no further corrections or revisions, and though later versions were issued containing additional conclusions and tributes, and are described on the title pages as "third edition," or "fourth edition," all of them are printed from the same plates as the 1886 version, or from the original uncorrected 1875 printing, as in the case of the 1891 Appleton version, which appeared after Sherman had transferred the publication rights in 1890 to Clemens's publishing firm, Charles L. Webster & Company.

Aside from the supplemental material, almost all of the fifty or so differences between the 1875 and 1886 versions of the *Memoirs* are corrections of fact, such as the change from "Louis Philippe of France" to "the King of Sicily," at 39.36; or "1849" to "1850" at 88.2 (made in the 1876 printing); or "Taos, New Mexico" to "Santa Fé, New Mexico" at 111.38 (made in the 1876 printing). Some corrections were made in spelling, such as the change of "Quimby" to "Quinby" at 197.22 and elsewhere. Others supply omissions; for example, in 1875 Sherman spoke of "Marshall and his family" but was informed that the family really belonged to "Mr. Wimmer," and so he revised the passage at 73.34–35 to read "Marshall and the family of Mr. Wimmer." Other passages where "Mr. Wimmer" was added are at 74.35–36 and 77.31–32. Two omissions of General Force were corrected: at 547.30–31, "because General Leggett's division had carried" was changed to "which Leggett's and Force's divisions had carried"; and at 736.32–33, "Nevertheless, a division (Mower's) of the Seventeenth Corps was kept" became "Nevertheless, Force's and Mower's divisions of the Seventeenth Corps were kept" in the 1886 version. The omission of the command of Major-General Pope in 1875 at 239.38–240.8 and 241.9–10 was corrected in the first case by revision of the passage (see notes to this volume), and in the second case by adding a line to the page. Other changes involved correcting the names of persons involved in a particular event; for example, at 513.18, 529.14, and 529.37, "Ward" was changed to "Williams," and at 629.20, "Corse" was changed to "Cox." In a few instances, Sherman made his wording less abrasive: for example, at 73.23, "Sutter was very 'tight,'" was changed to "Sutter was enthusiastic"; at 500.20, in a description of McPherson, the word "timid" was changed to "cautious"; and at 716.14, "assented to these false publications" was changed to "assented to these publications." (For a few more extensive revisions of this kind see the notes to this volume at 232.38–41 and 560.9–17 and 23–24.) Because this version is the last one that Sherman himself prepared, the 1886 D. Appleton and Company text of the *Memoirs of General William T. Sherman* is printed here.

This volume presents the text of the 1886 printing but does not attempt to reproduce features of its typographic design. The text, including the index, is printed without alteration except for the correction of typographical errors and the change of page numbers to conform to this edition. Spelling, punctuation, and capitalization are often expressive features, and they are not altered, even when inconsistent or irregular. The following is a list of typographical errors corrected, cited by page and line number: 47.10, *chilc*; 123.28, Francisco;; 127.12, house which,; 172.2, al/although; 181.12, 1860; 198.22, forward; 200.3, Quinby's; 201.18–19, Quinby,s; 376.8, Resecrans's; 886.1, shirmish-line; 886.5, breach-loading; 1079.26B, Johnson. Errors corrected third printing: 718.42, *project* (*LOA*); 719.19, Seveneenth (*LOA*). Errors corrected fifth printing: 846.7–8, accompanied General (*LOA*); 1072.7b, Tennessee.

Notes

In the notes that follow, the reference numbers denote page and line of this volume (the line count includes chapter headings). No note is made for material included in a standard desk-reference book. Notes within the text are Sherman's own. For further identification of persons and events mentioned in the *Memoirs*, see Mark Mayo Boatner III, *The Civil War Dictionary*, revised edition (New York: David McKay Company, Inc., 1988), and Stewart Sifakis, *Who Was Who in the Civil War* (New York: Facts On File, Inc., 1988).

5.15   Napier, . . . Hume] Sir William Francis Napier (1785–1860), *History of the War in the Peninsula* (1828–40) and *History of the Conquest of Scinde* (1844–46); Sir Archibald Alison (1792–1867), *History of Europe during the French Revolution* (1833–42; 1852–59); and David Hume (1711–76), *History of Great Britain* (1754–62).

6.14–16   these publications . . . 1862.] *The War of the Rebellion: A Compilation of the Official Records of the Union and Confederate Armies*, 70 vols. (1880–1901).

16.18   Mahan] Dennis Hart Mahan (1802–71) was professor of engineering at the Military Academy from 1832 to 1871 and wrote extensively on military subjects. His course offered the only instruction in strategy given during Sherman's time at the Academy.

22.31–32   black . . . Joe] Many escaped slaves found refuge among the Seminoles in Florida and fought with them against the U.S. Army.

28.10   Henry Stanberry] Henry Stanbery (1803–81) practiced law with Thomas Ewing in Lancaster, Ohio. He was attorney general under President Andrew Johnson, 1866–68, before resigning to represent Johnson at his Senate impeachment trial.

33.27   counterscarp] A wall or slope in front of a defensive ditch.

42.15–16   Wilkes's . . . Missions."] Charles Wilkes (1798–1877), *Narrative of the United States Exploring Expedition. During the Years 1838, 1839, 1840, 1841, 1842*, 5 vols. (1844); Richard Henry Dana (1815–82), *Two Years Before the Mast. A Personal Narrative of Life at Sea* (1840); Alexander Forbes (1778–1862), *California: A History of Upper and Lower California from Their First Discovery to the Present Time* (1839).

43.33   alcalde] Mayor.

45.35–37   her brother . . . claim.]   Vicente Gómez, who asserted in 1853
that the rich New Indria quicksilver mine, established in San Benito County
in 1851, was on land granted to him by the Mexican governor of California in
1844. In 1857 Gómez sold his claim to William McGarrahan. The claim was
repeatedly brought before the courts and Congress by McGarrahan and his
heirs until 1900, but it was never confirmed. Accusations of corruption were
leveled against both McGarrahan and his opponents in connection with their
lobbying efforts.

46.3–4   *costumbres del pais*]   Customs of the country.

48.31   Colonel Benton]   Thomas Hart Benton (1782–1858) served as a
colonel in the War of 1812 and was a Democratic senator from Missouri,
1821–51. His daughter Jessie had married Frémont in 1841.

55.18   Sloat . . . occupation]   Commodore John D. Sloat (1781–1867)
landed a party at Monterey on July 7, 1846, that proclaimed California to be
an American possession under American law.

67.9   McAdam-stone]   The macadam roadway, made of layers of stone
broken into uniform size, was invented by John McAdam (1756–1836). The
roadway and materials used in making it were also called McAdam and
MacAdam.

70.6   *alforjas*]   Saddle bags.

107.37–38   Mr. Calhoun . . . end]   Senator John C. Calhoun of South
Carolina died on March 31, 1850.

107.39–40   Mr. Webster's . . . speech]   Webster delivered his last speech
on July 17, 1850.

118.32   Baulinas Bay]   Bolinas Bay.

132.29–30   like Hotspur's . . . come.]   Cf. *1 Henry IV*, III, i, 52–54.

139.5   "Eatanswill"]   In chapter 13 of Charles Dickens' *Pickwick Papers*
(1836–37), the fictional borough of Eatanswill is the scene of a parliamentary
election. Its partisan newspapers, the *Eatanswill Gazette* and the *Eatanswill
Independent*, engage in "spirited attacks" on each other, viz., " 'Our worthless
contemporary, the *Gazette*—' 'That disgraceful and dastardly journal, the *Independent*—' 'That false and scurrilous print, the *Independent*—' 'That vile
and slanderous calumniator, the *Gazette*.' "

154.16   Aspinwall]   Founded in 1850 and named for the railroad builder
William H. Aspinwall, the city, now called Colón, is located at what became
the northern entrance to the Panama Canal.

158.26   Hugh and T. E., Jr.,]   Hugh Boyle Ewing (1826–1905) and Thomas

Ewing, Jr., (1829–96) became Union brigadier generals during the Civil War, as did their brother Charles Ewing (1835–83).

166.25–27   Sherman . . . Bocock]   On February 1, 1860, William Penning-ton of New Jersey, a Whig recently turned Republican, was elected Speaker of the House on the forty-fourth ballot taken during the contest.

170.13–14   Bell . . . compromise]   John Bell of Tennessee and Edward Everett of Massachusetts, both former Whigs, were nominated for president and vice-president by the Constitutional Union convention in Baltimore on May 9, 1860. The convention adopted no platform, but pledged itself to uphold the Constitution, the Union, and the enforcement of the laws. Bell and Everett carried Virginia, Kentucky, and Tennessee in the presidential election.

171.6   "Knights . . . Circle,"]   A secret organization, formed around 1855, that advocated the annexation of Mexico and the creation of a slaveholding "empire" extending in a "golden circle" from the tip of Florida around the Gulf of Mexico to the Yucatán Peninsula. The name was later used in 1862–63 by a secret society of Confederate sympathizers in the Midwest.

172.16   Haskins]   Joseph A. Haskin (1817–74). He became a Union briga-dier general in the Civil War, serving in the Washington, D.C., fortifications.

172.23   clamor . . . Brownsville]   On September 28, 1859, a group of Mexican-Americans led by rancher Juan Cortina (1824–92) occupied Browns-ville, Texas, and proclaimed a "Republic of the Rio Grande." The rebellion dispersed after U.S. Army reinforcements reached the Rio Grande Valley, and Cortina went into exile in Mexico, where he later served as a military gover-nor under President Benito Juárez.

173.14   Jäger rifles]   Name commonly given to the first muzzle-loading, percussion-cap rifle widely issued to the U.S. Army, beginning in 1846. Jäger ("hunter") troops were the skirmishing and scouting riflemen in German armies.

174.9   *esto perpetua*]   May it be perpetual.

175.30–31   offer of employment]   Sherman had been offered a position in London with a new banking venture.

181.13   seven . . . states]   Texas, Louisiana, Mississippi, Alabama, Florida, Georgia, and South Carolina.

197.35   difficulty . . . Baltimore]   On April 19, 1861, secessionist sympa-thizers in Baltimore attacked Union volunteers en route to Washington. Six-teen people were killed in the ensuing riot.

206.17   sinks]   Latrines.

213.34   senator]   Frémont represented California in the U.S. Senate from September 1850 to March 1851.

219.29   Springfield muskets]   Muzzle-loading rifles made at the armory in Springfield, Massachusetts.

228.30   Wilkinson, or Wilkerson]   Samuel Wilkeson (1817–89).

231.6   *onus faciendi*]   Burden of acting.

232.38–41   It was . . . name.]   In the 1875 edition, this passage read: "Still, on a review of the only official documents before the War Department at the time, it was cruel for a Secretary of War to give a tacit credence to a rumor which probably started without his wish or intention, yet through his instrumentality."

234.19   Halsted]   Murat Halstead (1829–1908).

234.26–27   12th of November]   The date and text of Halleck's reply, as well as the chronology of the events discussed in this passage, indicate that Sherman's letter was written on December 12.

239.32   Island No. Ten]   A fortified island in the Mississippi River near New Madrid, Missouri.

239.38–240.8   About . . . 10.]   This passage replaced one in the 1875 edition that read: "From the time I had left Kentucky, General Buell had really made no substantial progress, though strongly reënforced beyond even what I had asked for. General Albert Sidney Johnston had remained at Bowling Green until his line was broken at Henry and Donelson, when he let go Bowling Green and fell back hastily to Nashville; and, on Buell's approach, he did not even tarry there, but continued his retreat southward."

298.11   Bolivar army]   Union forces based at Bolivar, Tennessee.

326.7–9   Dr. Draper . . . Grant."]   John William Draper (1811–82), *History of the American Civil War*, 3 vols. (1867–1870); Adam Badeau (1831–95), *Military History of Ulysses S. Grant, from April, 1861, to April, 1865*, 3 vols. (1868–1881). Sherman assisted Draper in the preparation of his second and third volumes. Badeau was Grant's military secretary, 1864–66, and drew on Grant's records when writing his history.

351.34   epaulements]   Embankments raised for protection from enemy fire.

352.10   Orion P. Howe]   Howe was a 12-year-old drummer boy serving with the 55th Illinois Volunteer Infantry.

353.23   Sevastopol]   During the Crimean War the Russian garrison was besieged by British and French armies from September 28, 1854, until September 9, 1855. The Russians abandoned the city after the fall of the Malakov, an important part of the defensive fortifications. Sherman toured the Crimean battlefields in 1872.

357.32–33   Lincoln . . . sea.''] In an August 26, 1863, letter to a meeting of Union supporters in Springfield, Illinois, Lincoln wrote: "The Father of Waters again goes unvexed to the sea."

362.22   *tiers état*] Third estate or class; in pre-revolutionary France, the commons (in practice, the burghers) as distinct from the nobility and the higher clergy.

363.11–12   Stewart . . . Jackson] Major General J.E.B. Stuart (1833–64); Brigadier General William H. (Red) Jackson (1835–1903).

366.43–367.1   Napoleon's . . . Mexico] French troops captured Mexico City in June 1863. Napoleon III then arranged for Mexican conservatives to offer the Austrian archduke Ferdinand Maximilian the imperial throne of Mexico in July 1863.

368.24–25   *Polonius* . . . thee."] *Hamlet*, I, iii, 65–67.

381.2   Perryville] The battle of Perryville was fought on October 8, 1862.

381.5   Stone River] The battle of Stones River (also known as Murfreesboro) was fought from December 31, 1862 to January 2, 1863.

398.41   balks and chesses] Balks are beams laid lengthwise along a pontoon bridge, and chesses are planks laid across them.

400.19   *tête du pont*] Bridgehead.

402.22   *place d'armes*] An assembly point for troops.

403.12   Napoleon battery] The Napoleon was a smoothbore, muzzle-loading cannon, developed in France under Napoleon III. It was the most commonly used artillery piece on both sides of the Civil War. Most Napoleons fired a 12-pound projectile.

419.4   (Bishop) Polk] Leonidas Polk (1806–64) graduated from the U.S. Military Academy in 1827 and then resigned from the army to become an Episcopal minister. He became Bishop of Louisiana in 1841 and joined the Confederate army in 1861.

425.28   "Anvil Chorus"] Opening chorus in Act II of the opera *Il Trovatore* (1853) by Giuseppe Verdi (1813–1901).

463.22–23   McCook . . . Crittenden] Major General Alexander M. McCook (1831–1903), brother of Sherman's former law partner Daniel McCook, Major General James S. Negley (1826–1901), and Major General Thomas L. Crittenden (1815–93) all lost control of their commands during the rout of the

Union right wing on the second day of the battle of Chickamauga, September 20, 1863.

490.40–41   Sigel . . . skins.]   In his *Personal Memoirs* (1885–86) Grant wrote that when he explained to Lincoln his reasons for ordering several simultaneous Union advances in the spring campaign, the President replied: "Oh, yes! I see that. As we say out West, if a man can't skin he must hold a leg while somebody else does." Lincoln's personal secretary, John Hay, recorded the remark (as retold to him by the President) in his diary on April 30, 1864, as: "Those not skinning, can hold a leg."

491.5   two letters]   The second letter approved command changes Sherman had recommended (see page 466.9–19 in this volume).

492.30   General Jackson's army]   Andrew Jackson campaigned in northern Alabama against the Creek Indians in 1813–14.

496.35   *débouché*]   Outlet of a pass or gorge.

500.20–21   McPherson . . . cautious.]   In the 1875 edition, this passage read: "McPherson seems to have been a little timid."

503.13   Oostenaula]   Oostanaula.

508.25   spring of 1870]   Sherman visited New Orleans en route to Texas in 1871.

520.21   somewhat refused]   Moved back, away from the enemy line.

524.23   Johnston . . . "Narrative,"]   Joseph E. Johnston (1807–91), *Narrative of Military Operations Directed During the Late War Between the States* (1874).

530.4   "battle above the clouds,"]   The name popularly given to the fighting on Lookout Mountain on November 24, 1863, during which the battlefield was covered by mist.

541.34–35   "Well, . . . side?"]   Major General Lovell H. Rousseau (1818–69) was from Kentucky, as were many men in the Confederate army.

547.15   *fraise* . . . abatis,]   A *fraise* is a slanted or horizontal palisade pointing out from a fortified position, *chevaux-de-frise* are logs or barrels with protruding spikes, used in front of fortified positions, and an abatis is an obstruction made of felled trees with sharpened branches.

559.33–35   Howard . . . Hooker]   Howard was junior to Hooker and had served as a corps commander under him in the Army of the Potomac.

560.1   Slocum . . . displaced]   Relations between Slocum and Hooker had been strained since Slocum's bitter criticism of Hooker's leadership during the Union defeat at Chancellorsville, May 1–4, 1863.

560.9–17   I had . . . us.]   This passage replaced one in the 1875 edition that read: "I am told that he says that Thomas and I were jealous of him; but this is hardly probable, for we on the spot did not rate his fighting qualities as high as he did, and I am, moreover, convinced that both he and General Butterfield went to the rear for personal reasons." Major General Daniel Butterfield (1831–1901) served as Hooker's chief of staff in the Army of the Potomac, January–June 1863, and in the Army of the Cumberland, October 1863–April 1864. He commanded a division in Hooker's corps from April 14 to June 29, 1864, when he left the field because of illness.

560.23–24   fairly earned.] At this point in the 1875 edition there was a sentence that read: "General Hooker, moreover, when he got back to Cincinnati, reported (I was told) that we had run up against a rock at Atlanta, and that the country ought to be prepared to hear of disaster from that quarter."

575.10   parallels] Trenches dug so as to gradually approach an enemy line.

583.1   "Atlanta . . . won."] Sherman's telegram to Halleck announcing the city's capture contained the phrase "Atlanta is ours and fairly won."

590.6   Your letter] Sherman wrote a widely published letter to John Spooner, a Massachusetts recruiting agent, on July 30, 1864, criticizing the recruitment of Southern blacks by Northern states as a means of fulfilling their enlistment quotas.

590.22   B—— . . . S——] The manuscript of the letter reads: "Belmont, Vallandigham, Wood, Seymour," referring to August Belmont (1816–90), New York financier and chairman of the Democratic national committee; Clement L. Vallandigham (1820–71), former Ohio congressman and leader of the Peace Democrats; Fernando Wood (1812–81), Democratic congressman from New York and an opponent of the war; and Horatio Seymour (1810–86), Democratic governor of New York and chairman of the Chicago convention.

590.23–27   platform . . . letter] The Democratic national convention adopted a platform on August 30, 1864, that denounced the war as "four years of failure" and called for the immediate cessation of hostilities and negotiations to restore the Union. McClellan accepted the Democratic presidential nomination on September 8 in a letter that repudiated the platform's description of the war as a failure and its call for an immediate end to the fighting, but which endorsed the restoration of the Union through a negotiated peace.

590.33   W.B. . . . worthies.] The manuscript of the letter reads: "Wilkes, Butterfield, & such worthies." George Wilkes (1817–85) was the publisher of *Wilkes' Spirit of the Times*, where he supported Hooker. For Butterfield, see note 560.9–17.

590.35   relieved . . . occasion] Hooker had been relieved as commander of the Army of the Potomac on June 28, 1863.

603.41   General Hunter's course] Major General David Hunter (1802–86) ordered the burning of Confederate public buildings and private property in the Shenandoah Valley while commanding Union forces in western Virginia, May 21–August 8, 1864.

614.3   JOSEPH C. BROWN.] Joseph E. Brown (1821–94) was governor of Georgia from 1857 to 1865.

654.36–37   Alabama cavalry] Recruited from among Alabama Unionists, most of whom lived in the northern hill counties.

655.37–38   "John . . . on;"] The common title of the song is "John Brown's Body"; its author is unknown. Julia Ward Howe wrote "The Battle Hymn of the Republic" (1862) for the same tune.

656.7   never . . . since.] Sherman visited Atlanta in November 1881, but did not revise this passage when preparing the 1886 edition of his *Memoirs*.

675.12   the capital] An imaginary line bisecting the salient angle of a fortification.

684.33   General Saxton . . . operations] Brigadier General Rufus Saxton (1824–1908) commanded Union forces on the South Carolina Sea Islands, where freed slaves were farming abandoned plantations under army supervision.

693.16   "Ball's Bluff"] On October 21, 1861, a Union brigade crossed the Potomac at Ball's Bluff, near Leesburg, Virginia, while another brigade crossed nearby at Edward's Ferry. The Confederates were able to reinforce their Ball's Bluff position from a central location between the two crossings without being detected, and launched a counterattack that drove the Union troops back across the Potomac with heavy losses.

700.11   salt . . . sown] At the close of the Third Punic War (149–146 B.C.), the Romans burned and razed Carthage, then plowed and salted the ground on which it had stood to prevent the site from ever being resettled.

716.14   these publications] In the 1875 edition: "these false publications."

729.19–20   "Fear . . . wisdom."] Psalm 111:10.

732.12–14   possessory . . . approval] In the fall of 1865 President Andrew Johnson ordered almost all of the land set aside under Special Field Order No. 15 restored to its former owners.

780.25–26   "standing . . . going."] Cf. *Macbeth*, III, iv, 118–119: "Stand not upon the order of your going, / But go at once."

789.35   *February* 7] The original of this letter, now in the Library of Congress, is dated "Feb.y 1865." Sherman assigned it the date of February 7, but its contents better support the date of February 1.

790.35   decline . . . promotion.]   Sherman had written Grant on January 21, 1865, expressing his disapproval of attempts in Congress to create a second lieutenant general in the U.S. Army.

794.20   Kirk's forces]   North Carolina Unionists commanded by Lieutenant Colonel George W. Kirk.

802.43–803.6   remembrance . . . death.]   Admiral Dahlgren's son, Colonel Ulric Dahlgren (1842–64), lost a leg while serving on General George G. Meade's staff during the Gettysburg campaign. In February 1864 he volunteered to accompany Brigadier General Judson Kilpatrick on a cavalry raid designed to free Union prisoners held in Richmond. The raid failed and Dahlgren was killed on March 1. The Confederates claimed to have found on his body documents proving that Dahlgren planned to burn Richmond and kill Jefferson Davis and his Cabinet. Dahlgren's body was stripped, his artificial leg was stolen, and one of his fingers was cut off.

827.6   U. S. C. T.]   United States Colored Troops.

838.12–15   General . . . refers.]   Johnston wrote in his *Narrative of Military Operations* that he suggested to Sherman "that, instead of a partial suspension of hostilities, we might, as other generals had done, arrange the terms of a permanent peace, and among other precedents reminded him of the preliminaries of Leoben, and the terms in which Napoleon, then victorious, proposed negotiation to the Archduke Charles; and the sentiment he expressed, that the civic crown earned by preserving the life of one citizen confers truer glory than the highest achievement merely military. General Sherman replied, with heightened color, that he appreciated such a sentiment and that to put an end to further devastation and bloodshed, and restore the Union, and with it the prosperity of the country, were to him objects of ambition." In 1797 Napoleon led his army over the Alps from Italy into Austria and on April 7 reached Leoben, about 80 miles southwest of Vienna, where he entered into negotiations. On April 18 he ratified an armistice and signed preliminary peace terms, acting without instructions or authority from the Directory in Paris. The territorial concessions made by the Austrians at Leoben were confirmed by the treaty of Campo Formio, signed on October 17, 1797.

849.16   call . . . Richmond]   On April 6, 1865, Lincoln gave permission for "the gentlemen who have acted as the Legislature of Virginia" to assemble in Richmond for the purpose of withdrawing Virginia troops from the Confederate armies. However, Lincoln withdrew his permission on April 12 after learning that the legislature planned to seek peace terms from the United States.

879.36–37   German . . . recruitment]   German regiments, excluding those in the guard-corps, recruited men from specific geographic districts. Each regiment maintained a depot battalion in its home district, which in wartime would train new recruits and send them to the regiment in the field as replacements for casualties.

887.11   Sedan] The site of a decisive German victory in the Franco-Prussian War on September 1, 1870.

892.27–28   new . . . Upton] Emory Upton (1839–81), *A New System of Infantry Tactics, Double and Single Rank, Adapted to American Topography and Improved Firearms* (1867, revised edition 1874).

894.2   *projet de loi*] A drafted bill or proposed law.

896.17–18   "Henry . . . soldier."]   *1 Henry IV*, I, iii, 63–64.

897.9   *Corps Législatif*]   The legislature of France under the Second Empire, 1852–70. In 1874 the legislature was the *Assemblée nationale*.

907.20–21   General Bazaine . . . 1870]   During the Franco-Prussian War the fortress of Metz was besieged by the Prussians from August 19 to October 29, 1870, when Marshal Achille François Bazaine (1811–88) surrendered it with 150,000 men. Denounced as a traitor, Bazaine later asked for a committee of inquiry into his actions, resulting in his censure in the spring of 1872. He then asked to be tried before a military court and was convicted of treason in 1873. His death sentence was commuted to confinement for 20 years. In 1874 he escaped to Italy and lived in exile for the remainder of his life.

908.14   his death]   Maximilian was captured by Juárez's forces at Querétaro on May 15, 1867, court-martialed, and shot on June 19, 1867.

910.6–7   General E. D. . . . War,"]   Edward Davis Townsend (1817–93), *Anecdotes of the Civil War in the United States* (1884).

912.31   Baltimore police commissioners]   Maryland governor Thomas Swann replaced two Republican police commissioners, who were responsible for enforcing voter registration laws, with two conservatives shortly before the November 1866 election. The ousted commissioners then obtained a writ from a federal circuit judge arresting their replacements. Election-day violence was averted when Grant went to Baltimore at Swann and Johnson's request and negotiated an agreement between the rival parties on poll-watching procedures.

914.40   Fort Phil Kearney]   A post in the Powder River country of northern Wyoming Territory, abandoned in the summer of 1868 as part of a treaty with the Sioux. Sherman went in May 1868 to Fort Laramie in southeastern Wyoming, where the treaty was being signed.

917.12   four . . . Cabinet]   Secretary of the Treasury Hugh McCulloch, Postmaster General Alexander W. Randall, Secretary of the Interior Orville H. Browning, and Secretary of the Navy Gideon Welles.

922.12–13   Rip Van Winkle]   Protagonist of Washington Irving's short story "Rip Van Winkle" (first published in *The Sketch Book of Geoffrey Crayon,*

Gent., 1819–20), who sleeps for 20 years, awakening to find the changes brought by the American Revolution.

929.23–24   "Reconstruction Act;"] Passed over President Johnson's veto on March 2, 1867, the act divided the former Confederate states (excluding Tennessee) into five military districts and placed them under the administration of the district commanders.

929.25–26   court . . . Dyer] Contractors and inventors made allegations of improper conduct against Brigadier General Alexander B. Dyer (1815–74), who then requested a court of inquiry. It exonerated him, and Dyer continued to serve as chief of ordnance until his death.

930.39   died soon after] Meade died on November 6, 1872, at the age of 56.

934.36   Marcy and Davis] William L. Marcy (1786–1857) served as secretary of war, 1845–49, under President James K. Polk. Jefferson Davis was secretary of war from 1853 to 1857 under President Franklin Pierce.

938.22   your own father] Lieutenant Colonel William G. Belknap (1794–1851), who fought in the War of 1812, the Seminole War, and the Mexican War.

941.31   case . . . cadet] James W. Smith was the first black cadet at the United States Military Academy. His continual harassment by fellow cadets led to a court of inquiry in the summer of 1870, which issued several reprimands. Smith withstood further harassment and survived several disciplinary proceedings brought against him, but left the Academy after failing an unfairly administered examination.

942.18   Fred Grant] Frederick Dent Grant (1850–1912), Ulysses S. Grant's oldest son, who had graduated from the Military Academy in 1871.

947.19   "Doughertys"] Canvas-sided wagons, with seats that could be converted into beds, pulled by four-mule teams.

949.3–4   Gil . . . Granada] Alain Réné Le Sage (1668–1747), *L'Histoire de Gil Blas de Santillane* (1715–35). In Book VII, chapters 3 and 4 of the novel, the archbishop of Granada employs Gil Blas and asks to be told whenever his homilies or writings show signs of deterioration due to old age. After suffering a stroke the archbishop declines mentally. Gil Blas says so, and the archbishop rejects his statement and dismisses him.

955.33–34   "all . . . players,"] *As You Like It*, II, vii, 139–40.

959.30   Ducrot's . . . "Tirailleurs,"] August Alexandre Ducrot (1817–82), *Guerre des Frontieres. Wissembourg. Réponse du Général Ducrot a l'État-Major Allemand* (1873). *Tirailleurs* are separate formations of skirmishers and sharpshooters.

961.21   1872] This date appeared in the 1886 edition by error. The correct year of the letter is probably 1875, when the first edition of the *Memoirs* appeared.

975.39   *"mémoire pour servir"*] Memoir regarding service.

1049.30   *élève*] Student.

1050.5   Simeon . . . Bible] Cf. Luke 2:25–35.

1052.5   "Festina lente"] Make haste slowly.

1054.16–17   Logan . . . Confederacy] The southern, or southernmost, region of Illinois, where many Southerners and descendants of Southerners lived, was colloquially known as "Egypt." Logan was a Democratic congressman from the area in 1859–62, and in 1861 helped rally support there for the Union war effort.

THE LIBRARY OF AMERICA SERIES

Library of America fosters appreciation of America's literary heritage by publishing, and keeping permanently in print, authoritative editions of America's best and most significant writing. An independent nonprofit organization, it was founded in 1979 with seed funding from the National Endowment for the Humanities and the Ford Foundation.

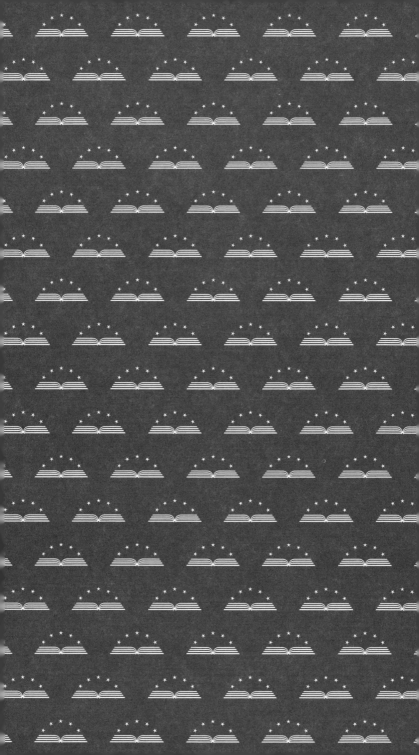

Library of America, a nonprofit organization,
champions our nation's cultural heritage
by publishing America's greatest writing in
authoritative new editions and providing resources
for readers to explore this rich, living legacy.

ULYSSES S. GRANT

ULYSSES S. GRANT

MEMOIRS AND SELECTED LETTERS

Personal Memoirs of U. S. Grant
Selected Letters 1839–1865

Edited by
Mary Drake McFeely
William S. McFeely

THE LIBRARY OF AMERICA

Published in the United States by Library of America.
Visit our website at www.loa.org.

Texts of the letters are reprinted from THE PAPERS OF
ULYSSES S. GRANT, edited by John Y. Simon, Volumes 1–14, copyright
1967–1985, by The Ulysses S. Grant Association, published by
Southern Illinois University Press. Reprinted by
permission of the publisher.

Facsimile on pages 742–43 courtesy of The New-York Historical Society.

This paper exceeds the requirements of
ANSI/NISO Z39.48–1992 (Permanence of Paper).

Distributed to the trade in the United States
by Penguin Random House Inc.
and in Canada by Penguin Random House Canada Ltd.

Library of Congress Catalog Card Number: 90–60013
For cataloging information, see end of Notes.
ISBN: 978–0–940450–58–5
ISBN: 0–940450–58–5

———

Sixteenth Printing
The Library of America—50

Manufactured in the United States of America

The publishers wish to thank John Y. Simon, editor of The Papers of Ulysses S. Grant, published by Southern Illinois University Press, for editorial assistance.

Contents

PERSONAL MEMOIRS

OF

U. S. GRANT.

IN TWO VOLUMES.

VOL. I.

U. S. Grant
Bvt. 2d Lt. 4th Infy.

These volumes are dedicated to the American Soldier and Sailor.

U. S. Grant.

New York City
May 23d 1885.

Preface.

M AN proposes and God disposes." There are but few important events in the affairs of men brought about by
their own choice.

Although frequently urged by friends to write my memoirs
I had determined never to do so, nor to write anything for
publication. At the age of nearly sixty-two I received an injury
from a fall, which confined me closely to the house while it
did not apparently affect my general health. This made study
a pleasant pastime. Shortly after, the rascality of a business
partner developed itself by the announcement of a failure.
This was followed soon after by universal depression of all
securities, which seemed to threaten the extinction of a good
part of the income still retained, and for which I am indebted
to the kindly act of friends. At this juncture the editor of the
Century Magazine asked me to write a few articles for him. I
consented for the money it gave me; for at that moment I was
living upon borrowed money. The work I found congenial,
and I determined to continue it. The event is an important
one for me, for good or evil; I hope for the former.

In preparing these volumes for the public, I have entered
upon the task with the sincere desire to avoid doing injustice
to any one, whether on the National or Confederate side,
other than the unavoidable injustice of not making mention
often where special mention is due. There must be many errors of omission in this work, because the subject is too large
to be treated of in two volumes in such way as to do justice to
all the officers and men engaged. There were thousands of
instances, during the rebellion, of individual, company, regimental and brigade deeds of heroism which deserve special
mention and are not here alluded to. The troops engaged in
them will have to look to the detailed reports of their individual commanders for the full history of those deeds.

The first volume, as well as a portion of the second, was
written before I had reason to suppose I was in a critical condition of health. Later I was reduced almost to the point of
death, and it became impossible for me to attend to anything

for weeks. I have, however, somewhat regained my strength, and am able, often, to devote as many hours a day as a person should devote to such work. I would have more hope of satisfying the expectation of the public if I could have allowed myself more time. I have used my best efforts, with the aid of my eldest son, F. D. Grant, assisted by his brothers, to verify from the records every statement of fact given. The comments are my own, and show how I saw the matters treated of whether others saw them in the same light or not.

With these remarks I present these volumes to the public, asking no favor but hoping they will meet the approval of the reader.

U. S. GRANT.

MOUNT MACGREGOR, NEW YORK, *July* 1, 1885.

Contents.

VOLUME I.

Chapter XXXVIII.

Chapter XXXIX.

Maps and Illustrations.

VOLUME I.

Chapter I.

M Y FAMILY is American, and has been for generations, in all its branches, direct and collateral.

Mathew Grant, the founder of the branch in America, of which I am a descendant, reached Dorchester, Massachusetts, in May, 1630. In 1635 he moved to what is now Windsor, Connecticut, and was the surveyor for that colony for more than forty years. He was also, for many years of the time, town clerk. He was a married man when he arrived at Dorchester, but his children were all born in this country. His eldest son, Samuel, took lands on the east side of the Connecticut River, opposite Windsor, which have been held and occupied by descendants of his to this day.

I am of the eighth generation from Mathew Grant, and seventh from Samuel. Mathew Grant's first wife died a few years after their settlement in Windsor, and he soon after married the widow Rockwell, who, with her first husband, had been fellow-passengers with him and his first wife, on the ship *Mary and John,* from Dorchester, England, in 1630. Mrs. Rockwell had several children by her first marriage, and others by her second. By intermarriage, two or three generations later, I am descended from both the wives of Mathew Grant.

In the fifth descending generation my great grandfather, Noah Grant, and his younger brother, Solomon, held commissions in the English army, in 1756, in the war against the French and Indians. Both were killed that year.

My grandfather, also named Noah, was then but nine years old. At the breaking out of the war of the Revolution, after the battles of Concord and Lexington, he went with a Connecticut company to join the Continental army, and was present at the battle of Bunker Hill. He served until the fall of Yorktown, or through the entire Revolutionary war. He must, however, have been on furlough part of the time — as I believe most of the soldiers of that period were — for he married in Connecticut during the war, had two children, and was a widower at the close. Soon after this he emigrated to

Westmoreland County, Pennsylvania, and settled near the town of Greensburg in that county. He took with him the younger of his two children, Peter Grant. The elder, Solomon, remained with his relatives in Connecticut until old enough to do for himself, when he emigrated to the British West Indies.

Not long after his settlement in Pennsylvania, my grandfather, Captain Noah Grant, married a Miss Kelly, and in 1799 he emigrated again, this time to Ohio, and settled where the town of Deerfield now stands. He had now five children, including Peter, a son by his first marriage. My father, Jesse R. Grant, was the second child—oldest son, by the second marriage.

Peter Grant went early to Maysville, Kentucky, where he was very prosperous, married, had a family of nine children, and was drowned at the mouth of the Kanawha River, Virginia, in 1825, being at the time one of the wealthy men of the West.

My grandmother Grant died in 1805, leaving seven children. This broke up the family. Captain Noah Grant was not thrifty in the way of "laying up stores on earth," and, after the death of his second wife, he went, with the two youngest children, to live with his son Peter, in Maysville. The rest of the family found homes in the neighborhood of Deerfield, my father in the family of Judge Tod, the father of the late Governor Tod, of Ohio. His industry and independence of character were such, that I imagine his labor compensated fully for the expense of his maintenance.

There must have been a cordiality in his welcome into the Tod family, for to the day of his death he looked upon Judge Tod and his wife, with all the reverence he could have felt if they had been parents instead of benefactors. I have often heard him speak of Mrs. Tod as the most admirable woman he had ever known. He remained with the Tod family only a few years, until old enough to learn a trade. He went first, I believe, with his half-brother, Peter Grant, who, though not a tanner himself, owned a tannery in Maysville, Kentucky. Here he learned his trade, and in a few years returned to Deerfield and worked for, and lived in the family of a Mr. Brown, the father of John Brown—"whose body lies mouldering in the grave, while his soul goes marching on." I have often heard my father speak of John Brown, particularly since the events at Harper's Ferry. Brown was a boy when they lived in the same house, but he knew him afterwards, and regarded him as a man of great purity of character, of high moral and physical courage, but a fanatic and extremist in whatever he advocated. It was certainly the act of an insane man to attempt the invasion of the South, and the overthrow of slavery, with less than twenty men.

My father set up for himself in business, establishing a tannery at Ravenna, the county seat of Portage County. In a few years he removed from Ravenna, and set up the same business at Point Pleasant, Clermont County, Ohio.

During the minority of my father, the West afforded but poor facilities for the most opulent of the youth to acquire an education, and the majority were dependent, almost exclusively, upon their own exertions for whatever learning they obtained. I have often heard him say that his time at school was limited to six months, when he was very young, too young, indeed, to learn much, or to appreciate the advantages of an education, and to a "quarter's schooling" afterwards, probably while living with Judge Tod. But his thirst for education was intense. He learned rapidly, and was a constant reader up to the day of his death—in his eightieth year. Books were scarce in the Western Reserve during his youth, but he read every book he could borrow in the neighborhood where he lived. This scarcity gave him the early habit of studying everything he read, so that when he got through with a book, he knew everything in it. The habit continued through life. Even after reading the daily papers—which he never neglected—he could give all the important information they contained. He made himself an excellent English scholar, and before he was twenty years of age was a constant contributor to Western newspapers, and was also, from that time until he was fifty years old, an able debater in the societies for this purpose, which were common in the West at that time. He always took an active part in politics, but was never a candidate for office, except, I believe, that he was the first Mayor of Georgetown. He supported Jackson for the Presidency; but he was a Whig, a great admirer of Henry Clay, and never voted for any other democrat for high office after Jackson.

My mother's family lived in Montgomery County, Pennsylvania, for several generations. I have little information about her ancestors. Her family took no interest in genealogy, so that my grandfather, who died when I was sixteen years old, knew only back to his grandfather. On the other side, my father took a great interest in the subject, and in his researches, he found that there was an entailed estate in Windsor, Connecticut, belonging to the family, to which his nephew, Lawson Grant—still living—was the heir. He was so much interested in the subject that he got his nephew to empower him to act in the matter, and in 1832 or 1833, when I was a boy ten or eleven years old, he went to Windsor, proved the title beyond dispute, and perfected the claim of the owners for a consideration—three thousand dollars, I think. I remember the circumstance well, and remember, too, hearing him say on his return that he found some widows living on the property, who had little or nothing beyond their homes. From these he refused to receive any recompense.

My mother's father, John Simpson, moved from Montgomery County, Pennsylvania, to Clermont County, Ohio, about the year 1819, taking with him his four children, three daughters and one son. My mother, Hannah Simpson, was the third of these children, and was then over twenty years of age. Her oldest sister was at that time married, and had several children. She still lives in Clermont County at this writing, October 5th, 1884, and is over ninety years of age. Until her memory failed her, a few years ago, she thought the country ruined beyond recovery when the Democratic party lost control in 1860. Her family, which was large, inherited her views, with the exception of one son who settled in Kentucky before the war. He was the only one of the children who entered the volunteer service to suppress the rebellion.

Her brother, next of age and now past eighty-eight, is also still living in Clermont County, within a few miles of the old homestead, and is as active in mind as ever. He was a supporter of the Government during the war, and remains a firm believer, that national success by the Democratic party means irretrievable ruin.

In June, 1821, my father, Jesse R. Grant, married Hannah Simpson. I was born on the 27th of April, 1822, at Point Pleasant, Clermont County, Ohio. In the fall of 1823 we moved to Georgetown, the county seat of Brown, the adjoining county east. This place remained my home, until at the age of seventeen, in 1839, I went to West Point.

The schools, at the time of which I write, were very indifferent. There were no free schools, and none in which the scholars were classified. They were all supported by subscription, and a single teacher—who was often a man or a woman incapable of teaching much, even if they imparted all they knew—would have thirty or forty scholars, male and female, from the infant learning the A B C's up to the young lady of eighteen and the boy of twenty, studying the highest branches taught—the three R's, "Reading, 'Riting, 'Rithmetic." I never saw an algebra, or other mathematical work higher than the arithmetic, in Georgetown, until after I was appointed to West Point. I then bought a work on algebra in Cincinnati; but having no teacher it was Greek to me.

My life in Georgetown was uneventful. From the age of five or six until seventeen, I attended the subscription schools of the village, except during the winters of 1836–7 and 1838–9. The former period was spent in Maysville, Kentucky, attending the school of Richardson and Rand; the latter in Ripley, Ohio, at a private school. I was not studious in habit, and probably did not make progress enough to compensate for the outlay for board and tuition. At all events both winters were spent in going over the same old arithmetic which I knew every word of before, and repeating: "A noun is the name of a thing," which I had also heard my Georgetown teachers repeat, until I had come to believe it—but I cast no reflections upon my old teacher, Richardson. He turned out bright scholars from his school, many of whom have filled conspicuous places in the service of their States. Two of my cotemporaries there—who, I believe, never attended any other institution of learning—have held seats in Congress, and one, if not both, other high offices; these are Wadsworth and Brewster.

My father was, from my earliest recollection, in comfortable circumstances, considering the times, his place of residence, and the community in which he lived. Mindful of his own lack of facilities for acquiring an education, his greatest desire in maturer years was for the education of his children. Consequently, as stated before, I never missed a quarter from school from the time I was old enough to attend till the time of leaving home. This did not exempt me from labor. In my early days, every one labored more or less, in the region where my youth was spent, and more in proportion to their private means. It was only the very poor who were exempt. While my father carried on the manufacture of leather and worked at the trade himself, he owned and tilled considerable land. I detested the trade, preferring almost any other labor; but I was fond of agriculture, and of all employment in which horses were used. We had, among other lands, fifty acres of forest within a mile of the village. In the fall of the year choppers were employed to cut enough wood to last a twelve-month. When I was seven or eight years of age, I began hauling all the wood used in the house and shops. I could not load it on the wagons, of course, at that time, but I could drive, and the choppers would load, and some one at the house unload. When about eleven years old, I was strong enough to hold a plough. From that age until seventeen I did all the work done with horses, such as breaking up the land, furrowing, ploughing corn and potatoes, bringing in the crops when harvested, hauling all the wood, besides tending two or three horses, a cow or two, and sawing wood for stoves, etc., while still attending school. For this I was compensated by the fact that there was never any scolding or punishing by my parents; no objection to rational enjoyments, such as fishing, going to the creek a mile away to swim in summer, taking a horse and visiting my grandparents in the adjoining county, fifteen miles off, skating on the ice in winter, or taking a horse and sleigh when there was snow on the ground.

While still quite young I had visited Cincinnati, forty-five miles away, several times, alone; also Maysville, Kentucky,

BIRTH-PLACE OF GENERAL U.S. GRANT.

POINT PLEASANT, OHIO.

often, and once Louisville. The journey to Louisville was a big one for a boy of that day. I had also gone once with a two-horse carriage to Chilicothe, about seventy miles, with a neighbor's family, who were removing to Toledo, Ohio, and returned alone; and had gone once, in like manner, to Flat Rock, Kentucky, about seventy miles away. On this latter occasion I was fifteen years of age. While at Flat Rock, at the house of a Mr. Payne, whom I was visiting with his brother, a neighbor of ours in Georgetown, I saw a very fine saddle horse, which I rather coveted, and proposed to Mr. Payne, the owner, to trade him for one of the two I was driving. Payne hesitated to trade with a boy, but asking his brother about it, the latter told him that it would be all right, that I was allowed to do as I pleased with the horses. I was seventy miles from home, with a carriage to take back, and Mr. Payne said he did not know that his horse had ever had a collar on. I asked to have him hitched to a farm wagon and we would soon see whether he would work. It was soon evident that the horse had never worn harness before; but he showed no viciousness, and I expressed a confidence that I could manage him. A trade was at once struck, I receiving ten dollars difference.

The next day Mr. Payne, of Georgetown, and I started on our return. We got along very well for a few miles, when we encountered a ferocious dog that frightened the horses and made them run. The new animal kicked at every jump he made. I got the horses stopped, however, before any damage was done, and without running into anything. After giving them a little rest, to quiet their fears, we started again. That instant the new horse kicked, and started to run once more. The road we were on, struck the turnpike within half a mile of the point where the second runaway commenced, and there there was an embankment twenty or more feet deep on the opposite side of the pike. I got the horses stopped on the very brink of the precipice. My new horse was terribly frightened and trembled like an aspen; but he was not half so badly frightened as my companion, Mr. Payne, who deserted me after this last experience, and took passage on a freight wagon for Maysville. Every time I attempted to start, my new horse would commence to kick. I was in quite a dilemma for a time.

Once in Maysville I could borrow a horse from an uncle who lived there; but I was more than a day's travel from that point. Finally I took out my bandanna—the style of handkerchief in universal use then—and with this blindfolded my horse. In this way I reached Maysville safely the next day, no doubt much to the surprise of my friend. Here I borrowed a horse from my uncle, and the following day we proceeded on our journey.

About half my school-days in Georgetown were spent at the school of John D. White, a North Carolinian, and the father of Chilton White who represented the district in Congress for one term during the rebellion. Mr. White was always a Democrat in politics, and Chilton followed his father. He had two older brothers—all three being school-mates of mine at their father's school—who did not go the same way. The second brother died before the rebellion began; he was a Whig, and afterwards a Republican. His oldest brother was a Republican and brave soldier during the rebellion. Chilton is reported as having told of an earlier horse-trade of mine. As he told the story, there was a Mr. Ralston living within a few miles of the village, who owned a colt which I very much wanted. My father had offered twenty dollars for it, but Ralston wanted twenty-five. I was so anxious to have the colt, that after the owner left, I begged to be allowed to take him at the price demanded. My father yielded, but said twenty dollars was all the horse was worth, and told me to offer that price; if it was not accepted I was to offer twenty-two and a half, and if that would not get him, to give the twenty-five. I at once mounted a horse and went for the colt. When I got to Mr. Ralston's house, I said to him: "Papa says I may offer you twenty dollars for the colt, but if you won't take that, I am to offer twenty-two and a half, and if you won't take that, to give you twenty-five." It would not require a Connecticut man to guess the price finally agreed upon. This story is nearly true. I certainly showed very plainly that I had come for the colt and meant to have him. I could not have been over eight years old at the time. This transaction caused me great heart-burning. The story got out among the boys of the village, and it was a long time before I heard the last of it. Boys enjoy the misery of their companions, at least village boys in that day did, and in later life I have found that all adults are not free from the peculiarity. I kept the horse until he was four years old, when he went blind, and I sold him for twenty dollars. When I went to Maysville to school, in 1836, at the age of fourteen, I recognized my colt as one of the blind horses working on the tread-wheel of the ferry-boat.

I have described enough of my early life to give an impression of the whole. I did not like to work; but I did as much of it, while young, as grown men can be hired to do in these days, and attended school at the same time. I had as many privileges as any boy in the village, and probably more than most of them. I have no recollection of ever having been punished at home, either by scolding or by the rod. But at school the case was different. The rod was freely used there, and I was not exempt from its influence. I can see John D. White— the school teacher—now, with his long beech switch always in his hand. It was not always the same one, either. Switches were brought in bundles, from a beech wood near the school house, by the boys for whose benefit they were intended. Often a whole bundle would be used up in a single day. I never had any hard feelings against my teacher, either while attending the school, or in later years when reflecting upon my experience. Mr. White was a kind-hearted man, and was much respected by the community in which he lived. He only followed the universal custom of the period, and that under which he had received his own education.

Chapter II.

WEST POINT—GRADUATION.

IN THE WINTER of 1838–9 I was attending school at Ripley, only ten miles distant from Georgetown, but spent the Christmas holidays at home. During this vacation my father received a letter from the Honorable Thomas Morris, then United States Senator from Ohio. When he read it he said to me, "Ulysses, I believe you are going to receive the appointment." "What appointment?" I inquired. "To West Point; I have applied for it." "But I won't go," I said. He said he thought I would, *and I thought so too, if he did.* I really had no objection to going to West Point, except that I had a very exalted idea of the acquirements necessary to get through. I did not believe I possessed them, and could not bear the idea of failing. There had been four boys from our village, or its immediate neighborhood, who had been graduated from West Point, and never a failure of any one appointed from Georgetown, except in the case of the one whose place I was to take. He was the son of Dr. Bailey, our nearest and most intimate neighbor. Young Bailey had been appointed in 1837. Finding before the January examination following, that he could not pass, he resigned and went to a private school, and remained there until the following year, when he was reappointed. Before the next examination he was dismissed. Dr. Bailey was a proud and sensitive man, and felt the failure of his son so keenly that he forbade his return home. There were no telegraphs in those days to disseminate news rapidly, no railroads west of the Alleghanies, and but few east; and above all, there were no reporters prying into other people's private affairs. Consequently it did not become generally known that there was a vacancy at West Point from our district until I was appointed. I presume Mrs. Bailey confided to my mother the fact that Bartlett had been dismissed, and that the doctor had forbidden his son's return home.

The Honorable Thomas L. Hamer, one of the ablest men Ohio ever produced, was our member of Congress at the time, and had the right of nomination. He and my father had been members of the same debating society (where they were generally pitted on opposite sides), and intimate personal friends from their early manhood up to a few years before. In politics they differed. Hamer was a life-long Democrat, while my father was a Whig. They had a warm discussion, which finally became angry—over some act of President Jackson, the removal of the deposit of public moneys, I think—after which they never spoke until after my appointment. I know both of them felt badly over this estrangement, and would have been glad at any time to come to a reconciliation; but neither would make the advance. Under these circumstances my father would not write to Hamer for the appointment, but he wrote to Thomas Morris, United States Senator from Ohio, informing him that there was a vacancy at West Point from our district, and that he would be glad if I could be appointed to fill it. This letter, I presume, was turned over to Mr. Hamer, and, as there was no other applicant, he cheerfully appointed me. This healed the breach between the two, never after reopened.

Besides the argument used by my father in favor of my going to West Point—that "he thought I would go"—there was another very strong inducement. I had always a great desire to travel. I was already the best travelled boy in Georgetown, except the sons of one man, John Walker, who had emigrated to Texas with his family, and immigrated back as soon as he could get the means to do so. In his short stay in Texas he acquired a very different opinion of the country from what one would form going there now.

I had been east to Wheeling, Virginia, and north to the Western Reserve, in Ohio, west to Louisville, and south to Bourbon County, Kentucky, besides having driven or ridden pretty much over the whole country within fifty miles of home. Going to West Point would give me the opportunity of visiting the two great cities of the continent, Philadelphia and New York. This was enough. When these places were visited I would have been glad to have had a steamboat or railroad collision, or any other accident happen, by which I might have received a temporary injury sufficient to make me ineligible, for a time, to enter the Academy. Nothing of the kind occurred, and I had to face the music.

Georgetown has a remarkable record for a western village. It is, and has been from its earliest existence, a democratic town. There was probably no time during the rebellion when, if the opportunity could have been afforded, it would not have voted for Jefferson Davis for President of the United States, over Mr. Lincoln, or any other representative of his party; unless it was immediately after some of John Morgan's men, in his celebrated raid through Ohio, spent a few hours in the village. The rebels helped themselves to whatever they could find, horses, boots and shoes, especially horses, and many ordered meals to be prepared for them by the families. This was no doubt a far pleasanter duty for some families than it would have been to render a like service for Union soldiers. The line between the Rebel and Union element in Georgetown was so marked that it led to divisions even in the churches. There were churches in that part of Ohio where treason was preached regularly, and where, to secure membership, hostility to the government, to the war and to the liberation of the slaves, was far more essential than a belief in the authenticity or credibility of the Bible. There were men in Georgetown who filled all the requirements for membership in these churches.

Yet this far-off western village, with a population, including old and young, male and female, of about one thousand— about enough for the organization of a single regiment if all had been men capable of bearing arms—furnished the Union army four general officers and one colonel, West Point graduates, and nine generals and field officers of Volunteers, that I can think of. Of the graduates from West Point, all had citizenship elsewhere at the breaking out of the rebellion, except possibly General A. V. Kautz, who had remained in the army from his graduation. Two of the colonels also entered the service from other localities. The other seven, General McGroierty, Colonels White, Fyffe, Loudon and Marshall, Majors King and Bailey, were all residents of Georgetown when the war broke out, and all of them, who were alive at the close, returned there. Major Bailey was the cadet who had preceded me at West Point. He was killed in West Virginia, in his first engagement. As far as I know, every boy who has entered West Point from that village since my time has been graduated.

I took passage on a steamer at Ripley, Ohio, for Pittsburg, about the middle of May, 1839. Western boats at that day did not make regular trips at stated times, but would stop anywhere, and for any length of time, for passengers or freight. I have myself been detained two or three days at a place after steam was up, the gang planks, all but one, drawn in, and after the time advertised for starting had expired. On this occasion we had no vexatious delays, and in about three days Pittsburg was reached. From Pittsburg I chose passage by the canal to Harrisburg, rather than by the more expeditious stage. This gave a better opportunity of enjoying the fine scenery of Western Pennsylvania, and I had rather a dread of reaching my destination at all. At that time the canal was much patronized by travellers, and, with the comfortable packets of the period, no mode of conveyance could be more pleasant, when time was not an object. From Harrisburg to Philadelphia there was a railroad, the first I had ever seen, except the one on which I had just crossed the summit of the Alleghany Mountains, and over which canal boats were transported. In travelling by the road from Harrisburg, I thought the perfection of rapid transit had been reached. We travelled at least eighteen miles an hour, when at full speed, and made the whole distance averaging probably as much as twelve miles an hour. This seemed like annihilating space. I stopped five days in Philadelphia, saw about every street in the city, attended the theatre, visited Girard College (which was then in course of construction), and got reprimanded from home afterwards, for dallying by the way so long. My sojourn in New York was shorter, but long enough to enable me to see the city very well. I reported at West Point on the 30th or 31st of May, and about two weeks later passed my examination for admission, without difficulty, very much to my surprise.

A military life had no charms for me, and I had not the faintest idea of staying in the army even if I should be graduated, which I did not expect. The encampment which preceded the commencement of academic studies was very wearisome and uninteresting. When the 28th of August came—the date for breaking up camp and going into barracks—I felt as though I had been at West Point always, and that if I staid to graduation, I would have to remain always. I did not take hold of my studies with avidity, in fact I rarely ever read over a lesson the second time during my entire cadetship. I could not sit in my room doing nothing. There is a fine library connected with the Academy from which cadets can get books to read in their quarters. I devoted more time to these, than to books relating to the course of studies. Much of the time, I am sorry to say, was devoted to novels, but not those of a trashy sort. I read all of Bulwer's then published, Cooper's, Marryat's, Scott's, Washington Irving's works, Lever's, and many others that I do not now remember. Mathematics was very easy to me, so that when January came, I passed the examination, taking a good standing in that branch. In French, the only other study at that time in the first year's course, my standing was very low. In fact, if the class had been turned the other end foremost I should have been near head. I never succeeded in getting squarely at either end of my class, in any one study, during the four years. I came near it in French, artillery, infantry and cavalry tactics, and conduct.

Early in the session of the Congress which met in December, 1839, a bill was discussed abolishing the Military Academy. I saw in this an honorable way to obtain a discharge, and read the debates with much interest, but with impatience at the delay in taking action, for I was selfish enough to favor the bill. It never passed, and a year later, although the time hung drearily with me, I would have been sorry to have seen it succeed. My idea then was to get through the course, secure a detail for a few years as assistant professor of mathematics at the Academy, and afterwards obtain a permanent position as professor in some respectable college; but circumstances always did shape my course different from my plans.

At the end of two years the class received the usual furlough, extending from the close of the June examination to the 28th of August. This I enjoyed beyond any other period of my life. My father had sold out his business in Georgetown—where my youth had been spent, and to which my day-dreams carried me back as my future home, if I should ever be able to retire on a competency. He had moved to Bethel, only twelve miles away, in the adjoining county of Clermont, and had bought a young horse that had never been in harness, for my special use under the saddle during my furlough. Most of my time was spent among my old school-mates—these ten weeks were shorter than one week at West Point.

Persons acquainted with the Academy know that the corps of cadets is divided into four companies for the purpose of military exercises. These companies are officered from the cadets, the superintendent and commandant selecting the officers for their military bearing and qualifications. The adjutant, quartermaster, four captains and twelve lieutenants are taken from the first, or Senior class; the sergeants from the second, or Junior class; and the corporals from the third, or Sophomore class. I had not been "called out" as a corporal, but when I returned from furlough I found myself the last but one—about my standing in all the tactics—of eighteen sergeants. The promotion was too much for me. That year my standing in the class—as shown by the number of demerits of the year—was about the same as it was among the sergeants, and I was dropped, and served the fourth year as a private.

During my first year's encampment General Scott visited West Point, and reviewed the cadets. With his commanding figure, his quite colossal size and showy uniform, I thought him the finest specimen of manhood my eyes had ever beheld, and the most to be envied. I could never resemble him in appearance, but I believe I did have a presentiment for a moment that some day I should occupy his place on review—although I had no intention then of remaining in the army. My experience in a horse-trade ten years before, and the ridicule it caused me, were too fresh in my mind for me to communicate this presentiment to even my most intimate chum. The next summer Martin Van Buren, then President of the United States, visited West Point and reviewed the cadets; he did not impress me with the awe which Scott had inspired. In fact I regarded General Scott and Captain C. F. Smith, the Commandant of Cadets, as the two men most to be envied in the nation. I retained a high regard for both up to the day of their death.

The last two years wore away more rapidly than the first two, but they still seemed about five times as long as Ohio years, to me. At last all the examinations were passed, and the members of the class were called upon to record their choice of arms of service and regiments. I was anxious to enter the cavalry, or dragoons as they were then called, but there was only one regiment of dragoons in the Army at that time, and attached to that, besides the full complement of officers, there were at least four brevet second lieutenants. I recorded therefore my first choice, dragoons; second, 4th infantry; and got the latter. Again there was a furlough—or, more properly speaking, leave of absence for the class were now commissioned officers—this time to the end of September. Again I went to Ohio to spend my vacation among my old schoolmates; and again I found a fine saddle horse purchased for my special use, besides a horse and buggy that I could drive—but I was not in a physical condition to enjoy myself quite as well as on the former occasion. For six months before graduation I had had a desperate cough ("Tyler's grip" it was called), and I was very much reduced, weighing but one hundred and seventeen pounds, just my weight at entrance, though I had grown six inches in stature in the mean time. There was consumption in my father's family, two of his brothers having died of that disease, which made my symptoms more alarming. The brother and sister next younger than myself died, during the rebellion, of the same disease, and I seemed the most promising subject for it of the three in 1843.

Having made alternate choice of two different arms of service with different uniforms, I could not get a uniform suit until notified of my assignment. I left my measurement with a tailor, with directions not to make the uniform until I notified him whether it was to be for infantry or dragoons. Notice did not reach me for several weeks, and then it took at least a week to get the letter of instructions to the tailor and two more to make the clothes and have them sent to me. This was a time of great suspense. I was impatient to get on my uniform and see how it looked, and probably wanted my old school-mates, particularly the girls, to see me in it.

The conceit was knocked out of me by two little circumstances that happened soon after the arrival of the clothes, which gave me a distaste for military uniform that I never recovered from. Soon after the arrival of the suit I donned it, and put off for Cincinnati on horseback. While I was riding along a street of that city, imagining that every one was looking at me, with a feeling akin to mine when I first saw General Scott, a little urchin, bareheaded, barefooted, with dirty and ragged pants held up by a single gallows—that's what suspenders were called then—and a shirt that had not seen a wash-tub for weeks, turned to me and cried: "Soldier! will you work? No, sir—ee; I'll sell my shirt first!!" The horse trade and its dire consequences were recalled to mind.

The other circumstance occurred at home. Opposite our house in Bethel stood the old stage tavern where "man and beast" found accommodation. The stable-man was rather dissipated, but possessed of some humor. On my return I found him parading the streets, and attending in the stable, barefooted, but in a pair of sky-blue nankeen pantaloons—just the color of my uniform trousers—with a strip of white cotton sheeting sewed down the outside seams in imitation of mine. The joke was a huge one in the mind of many of the people, and was much enjoyed by them; but I did not appreciate it so highly.

During the remainder of my leave of absence, my time was spent in visiting friends in Georgetown and Cincinnati, and occasionally other towns in that part of the State.

Chapter III.

O N THE 30th of September I reported for duty at Jefferson Barracks, St. Louis, with the 4th United States infantry. It was the largest military post in the country at that time, being garrisoned by sixteen companies of infantry, eight of the 3d regiment, the remainder of the 4th. Colonel Steven Kearney, one of the ablest officers of the day, commanded the post, and under him discipline was kept at a high standard, but without vexatious rules or regulations. Every drill and roll-call had to be attended, but in the intervals officers were permitted to enjoy themselves, leaving the garrison, and going where they pleased, without making written application to state where they were going for how long, etc., so that they were back for their next duty. It did seem to me, in my early army days, that too many of the older officers, when they came to command posts, made it a study to think what orders they could publish to annoy their subordinates and render them uncomfortable. I noticed, however, a few years later, when the Mexican war broke out, that most of this class of officers discovered they were possessed of disabilities which entirely incapacitated them for active field service. They had the moral courage to proclaim it, too. They were right; but they did not always give their disease the right name.

At West Point I had a class-mate — in the last year of our studies he was room-mate also — F. T. Dent, whose family resided some five miles west of Jefferson Barracks. Two of his unmarried brothers were living at home at that time, and as I had taken with me from Ohio, my horse, saddle and bridle, I soon found my way out to White Haven, the name of the Dent estate. As I found the family congenial my visits became frequent. There were at home, besides the young men, two daughters, one a school miss of fifteen, the other a girl of eight or nine. There was still an older daughter of seventeen, who had been spending several years at boarding-school in St. Louis, but who, though through school, had not yet returned home. She was spending the winter in the city with connections, the family of Colonel John O'Fallon, well known in St. Louis. In February she returned to her country home. After that I do not know but my visits became more frequent; they certainly did become more enjoyable. We would often take walks, or go on horseback to visit the neighbors, until I became quite well acquainted in that vicinity. Sometimes one of the brothers would accompany us, sometimes one of the younger sisters. If the 4th infantry had remained at Jefferson Barracks it is possible, even probable, that this life might have continued for some years without my finding out that there was anything serious the matter with me; but in the following May a circumstance occurred which developed my sentiment so palpably that there was no mistaking it.

The annexation of Texas was at this time the subject of violent discussion in Congress, in the press, and by individuals. The administration of President Tyler, then in power, was making the most strenuous efforts to effect the annexation, which was, indeed, the great and absorbing question of the day. During these discussions the greater part of the single rifle regiment in the army—the 2d dragoons, which had been dismounted a year or two before, and designated "Dismounted Rifles"—was stationed at Fort Jessup, Louisiana, some twenty-five miles east of the Texas line, to observe the frontier. About the 1st of May the 3d infantry was ordered from Jefferson Barracks to Louisiana, to go into camp in the neighborhood of Fort Jessup, and there await further orders. The troops were embarked on steamers and were on their way down the Mississippi within a few days after the receipt of this order. About the time they started I obtained a leave of absence for twenty days to go to Ohio to visit my parents. I was obliged to go to St. Louis to take a steamer for Louisville or Cincinnati, or the first steamer going up the Ohio River to any point. Before I left St. Louis orders were received at Jefferson Barracks for the 4th infantry to follow the 3d. A messenger was sent after me to stop my leaving; but before he could reach me I was off, totally ignorant of these events. A day or two after my arrival at Bethel I received a letter from a class-mate and fellow lieutenant in the 4th, informing me of the circumstances related above, and advising me not to open any letter post marked St. Louis or Jefferson Barracks, until the expiration of my leave, and saying that he would pack up my things and take them along for me. His advice was not necessary, for no other letter was sent to me. I now discovered that I was exceedingly anxious to get back to Jefferson Barracks, and I understood the reason without explanation from any one. My leave of absence required me to report for duty, at Jefferson Barracks, at the end of twenty days. I knew my regiment had gone up the Red River, but I was not disposed to break the letter of my leave; besides, if I had proceeded to Louisiana direct, I could not have reached there until after the expiration of my leave. Accordingly, at the end of the twenty days, I reported for duty to Lieutenant Ewell, commanding at Jefferson Barracks, handing him at the same time my leave of absence. After noticing the phraseology of the order—leaves of absence were generally worded, "at the end of which time he will report for duty with his proper command"—he said he would give me an order to join my regiment in Louisiana. I then asked for a few days' leave before starting, which he readily granted. This was the same Ewell who acquired considerable reputation as a Confederate general during the rebellion. He was a man much esteemed, and deservedly so, in the old army, and proved himself a gallant and efficient officer in two wars—both in my estimation unholy.

I immediately procured a horse and started for the country, taking no baggage with me, of course. There is an insignificant creek—the Gravois—between Jefferson Barracks and the place to which I was going, and at that day there was not a bridge over it from its source to its mouth. There is not water enough in the creek at ordinary stages to run a coffee mill, and at low water there is none running whatever. On this occasion it had been raining heavily, and, when the creek was reached, I found the banks full to overflowing, and the current rapid. I looked at it a moment to consider what to do. One of my superstitions had always been when I started to go any where, or to do anything, not to turn back, or stop until the thing intended was accomplished. I have frequently started to go to places where I had never been and to which I did not know the way, depending upon making inquiries on the road, and if I got past the place without knowing it, instead of turning back, I would go on until a road was found turning in the right direction, take that, and come in by the other side. So I struck into the stream, and in an instant the horse was swimming and I being carried down by the current. I headed the horse towards the other bank and soon reached it, wet through and without other clothes on that side of the stream. I went on, however, to my destination and borrowed a dry suit from my—future—brother-in-law. We were not of the same size, but the clothes answered every purpose until I got more of my own.

Before I returned I mustered up courage to make known, in the most awkward manner imaginable, the discovery I had made on learning that the 4th infantry had been ordered away from Jefferson Barracks. The young lady afterwards admitted that she too, although until then she had never looked upon me other than as a visitor whose company was agreeable to her, had experienced a depression of spirits she could not account for when the regiment left. Before separating it was definitely understood that at a convenient time we would join our fortunes, and not let the removal of a regiment trouble us. This was in May, 1844. It was the 22d of August, 1848, before the fulfilment of this agreement. My duties kept me on the frontier of Louisiana with the Army of Observation during the pendency of Annexation; and afterwards I was absent through the war with Mexico, provoked by the action of the army, if not by the annexation itself. During that time there was a constant correspondence between Miss Dent and myself, but we only met once in the period of four years and three months. In May, 1845, I procured a leave for twenty days, visited St. Louis, and obtained the consent of the parents for the union, which had not been asked for before.

As already stated, it was never my intention to remain in the army long, but to prepare myself for a professorship in some college. Accordingly, soon after I was settled at Jefferson Barracks, I wrote a letter to Professor Church—Professor of Mathematics at West Point—requesting him to ask my designation as his assistant, when next a detail had to be made. Assistant professors at West Point are all officers of the army, supposed to be selected for their special fitness for the particular branch of study they are assigned to teach. The answer from Professor Church was entirely satisfactory, and no doubt I should have been detailed a year or two later but for the Mexican War coming on. Accordingly I laid out for myself a course of studies to be pursued in garrison, with regularity, if not persistency. I reviewed my West Point course of mathematics during the seven months at Jefferson Barracks, and read many valuable historical works, besides an occasional novel. To help my memory I kept a book in which I would write up, from time to time, my recollections of all I had read since last posting it. When the regiment was ordered away, I being absent at the time, my effects were packed up by Lieutenant Haslett, of the 4th infantry, and taken along. I never saw my journal after, nor did I ever keep another, except for a portion of the time while travelling abroad. Often since a fear has crossed my mind lest that book might turn up yet, and fall into the hands of some malicious person who would publish it. I know its appearance would cause me as much heart-burning as my youthful horse-trade, or the later rebuke for wearing uniform clothes.

The 3d infantry had selected camping grounds on the reservation at Fort Jessup, about midway between the Red River and the Sabine. Our orders required us to go into camp in the same neighborhood, and await further instructions. Those authorized to do so selected a place in the pine woods, between the old town of Natchitoches and Grand Ecore, about three miles from each, and on high ground back from the river. The place was given the name of Camp Salubrity, and proved entitled to it. The camp was on a high, sandy, pine ridge, with spring branches in the valley, in front and rear. The springs furnished an abundance of cool, pure water, and the ridge was above the flight of mosquitoes, which abound in that region in great multitudes and of great voracity. In the valley they swarmed in myriads, but never came to the summit of the ridge. The regiment occupied this camp six months before the first death occurred, and that was caused by an accident.

There was no intimation given that the removal of the 3d and 4th regiments of infantry to the western border of Louisiana was occasioned in any way by the prospective annexation of Texas, but it was generally understood that such was the case. Ostensibly we were intended to prevent filibustering into Texas, but really as a menace to Mexico in case she appeared to contemplate war. Generally the officers of the army were indifferent whether the annexation was consummated or not; but not so all of them. For myself, I was bitterly opposed to the measure, and to this day regard the war, which resulted, as one of the most unjust ever waged by a stronger against a weaker nation. It was an instance of a republic following the bad example of European monarchies, in not considering justice in their desire to acquire additional territory.

Texas was originally a state belonging to the republic of Mexico. It extended from the Sabine River on the east to the Rio Grande on the west, and from the Gulf of Mexico on the south and east to the territory of the United States and New Mexico—another Mexican state at that time—on the north and west. An empire in territory, it had but a very sparse population, until settled by Americans who had received authority from Mexico to colonize. These colonists paid very little attention to the supreme government, and introduced slavery into the state almost from the start, though the constitution of Mexico did not, nor does it now, sanction that institution. Soon they set up an independent government of their own, and war existed, between Texas and Mexico, in name from that time until 1836, when active hostilities very nearly ceased upon the capture of Santa Anna, the Mexican President. Before long, however, the same people—who with permission of Mexico had colonized Texas, and afterwards set up slavery there, and then seceded as soon as they felt strong enough to do so—offered themselves and the State to the United States, and in 1845 their offer was accepted. The occupation, separation and annexation were, from the inception of the movement to its final consummation, a conspiracy to acquire territory out of which slave states might be formed for the American Union.

Even if the annexation itself could be justified, the manner in which the subsequent war was forced upon Mexico cannot. The fact is, annexationists wanted more territory than they could possibly lay any claim to, as part of the new acquisition.

Texas, as an independent State, never had exercised jurisdiction over the territory between the Nueces River and the Rio Grande. Mexico had never recognized the independence of Texas, and maintained that, even if independent, the State had no claim south of the Nueces. I am aware that a treaty, made by the Texans with Santa Anna while he was under duress, ceded all the territory between the Nueces and the Rio Grande; but he was a prisoner of war when the treaty was made, and his life was in jeopardy. He knew, too, that he deserved execution at the hands of the Texans, if they should ever capture him. The Texans, if they had taken his life, would have only followed the example set by Santa Anna himself a few years before, when he executed the entire garrison of the Alamo and the villagers of Goliad.

In taking military possession of Texas after annexation, the army of occupation, under General Taylor, was directed to occupy the disputed territory. The army did not stop at the Nueces and offer to negotiate for a settlement of the boundary question, but went beyond, apparently in order to force Mexico to initiate war. It is to the credit of the American nation, however, that after conquering Mexico, and while practically holding the country in our possession, so that we could have retained the whole of it, or made any terms we chose, we paid a round sum for the additional territory taken; more than it was worth, or was likely to be, to Mexico. To us it was an empire and of incalculable value; but it might have been obtained by other means. The Southern rebellion was largely the outgrowth of the Mexican war. Nations, like individuals, are punished for their transgressions. We got our punishment in the most sanguinary and expensive war of modern times.

The 4th infantry went into camp at Salubrity in the month of May, 1844, with instructions, as I have said, to await further orders. At first, officers and men occupied ordinary tents. As the summer heat increased these were covered by sheds to break the rays of the sun. The summer was whiled away in social enjoyments among the officers, in visiting those stationed at, and near, Fort Jessup, twenty-five miles away, visiting the planters on the Red River, and the citizens of Natchitoches and Grand Ecore. There was much pleasant intercourse between the inhabitants and the officers of the army. I retain very agreeable recollections of my stay at Camp Salubrity, and of the acquaintances made there, and no doubt my feeling is shared by the few officers living who were there at the time. I can call to mind only two officers of the 4th infantry, besides myself, who were at Camp Salubrity with the regiment, who are now alive.

With a war in prospect, and belonging to a regiment that had an unusual number of officers detailed on special duty away from the regiment, my hopes of being ordered to West Point as instructor vanished. At the time of which I now write, officers in the quartermaster's, commissary's and adjutant-general's departments were appointed from the line of the army, and did not vacate their regimental commissions until their regimental and staff commissions were for the same grades. Generally lieutenants were appointed to captaincies to fill vacancies in the staff corps. If they should reach a captaincy in the line before they arrived at a majority in the staff, they would elect which commission they would retain. In the 4th infantry, in 1844, at least six line officers were on duty in the staff, and therefore permanently detached from the regiment. Under these circumstances I gave up everything like a special course of reading, and only read thereafter for my own amusement, and not very much for that, until the war was over. I kept a horse and rode, and staid out of doors most of the time by day, and entirely recovered from the cough which I had carried from West Point, and from all indications of consumption. I have often thought that my life was saved, and my health restored, by exercise and exposure, enforced by an administrative act, and a war, both of which I disapproved.

As summer wore away, and cool days and colder nights came upon us, the tents we were occupying ceased to afford comfortable quarters; and "further orders" not reaching us, we began to look about to remedy the hardship. Men were put to work getting out timber to build huts, and in a very short time all were comfortably housed—privates as well as officers. The outlay by the government in accomplishing this was nothing, or nearly nothing. The winter was spent more agreeably than the summer had been. There were occasional parties given by the planters along the "coast"—as the bottom lands on the Red River were called. The climate was delightful.

Near the close of the short session of Congress of 1844–5, the bill for the annexation of Texas to the United States was passed. It reached President Tyler on the 1st of March, 1845, and promptly received his approval. When the news reached us we began to look again for "further orders." They did not arrive promptly, and on the 1st of May following I asked and obtained a leave of absence for twenty days, for the purpose of visiting St. Louis. The object of this visit has been before stated.

Early in July the long expected orders were received, but they only took the regiment to New Orleans Barracks. We reached there before the middle of the month, and again waited weeks for still further orders. The yellow fever was raging in New Orleans during the time we remained there, and the streets of the city had the appearance of a continuous well-observed Sunday. I recollect but one occasion when this observance seemed to be broken by the inhabitants. One morning about daylight I happened to be awake, and, hearing the discharge of a rifle not far off, I looked out to ascertain where the sound came from. I observed a couple of clusters of men near by, and learned afterwards that "it was nothing; only a couple of gentlemen deciding a difference of opinion with rifles, at twenty paces." I do not remember if either was killed, or even hurt, but no doubt the question of difference was settled satisfactorily, and "honorably," in the estimation of the parties engaged. I do not believe I ever would have the courage to fight a duel. If any man should wrong me to the extent of my being willing to kill him, I would not be willing to give him the choice of weapons with which it should be done, and of the time, place and distance separating us, when I executed him. If I should do another such a wrong as to justify him in killing me, I would make any reasonable atonement within my power, if convinced of the wrong done. I place my opposition to duelling on higher grounds than any here stated. No doubt a majority of the duels fought have been for want of moral courage on the part of those engaged to decline.

At Camp Salubrity, and when we went to New Orleans Barracks, the 4th infantry was commanded by Colonel Vose, then an old gentleman who had not commanded on drill for a number of years. He was not a man to discover infirmity in the presence of danger. It now appeared that war was imminent, and he felt that it was his duty to brush up his tactics. Accordingly, when we got settled down at our new post, he took command of the regiment at a battalion drill. Only two or three evolutions had been gone through when he dismissed the battalion, and, turning to go to his own quarters, dropped dead. He had not been complaining of ill health, but no doubt died of heart disease. He was a most estimable man, of exemplary habits, and by no means the author of his own disease.

Chapter IV.

EARLY IN SEPTEMBER the regiment left New Orleans for Corpus Christi, now in Texas. Ocean steamers were not then common, and the passage was made in sailing vessels. At that time there was not more than three feet of water in the channel at the outlet of Corpus Christi Bay; the debarkation, therefore, had to take place by small steamers, and at an island in the channel called Shell Island, the ships anchoring some miles out from shore. This made the work slow, and as the army was only supplied with one or two steamers, it took a number of days to effect the landing of a single regiment with its stores, camp and garrison equipage, etc. There happened to be pleasant weather while this was going on, but the land-swell was so great that when the ship and steamer were on opposite sides of the same wave they would be at considerable distance apart. The men and baggage were let down to a point higher than the lower deck of the steamer, and when ship and steamer got into the trough between the waves, and were close together, the load would be drawn over the steamer and rapidly run down until it rested on the deck.

After I had gone ashore, and had been on guard several days at Shell Island, quite six miles from the ship, I had occasion for some reason or other to return on board. While on the *Suviah*—I think that was the name of our vessel—I heard a tremendous racket at the other end of the ship, and much and excited sailor language, such as "damn your eyes," etc. In a moment or two the captain, who was an excitable little man, dying with consumption, and not weighing much over a hundred pounds, came running out, carrying a sabre nearly as large and as heavy as he was, and crying that his men had mutinied. It was necessary to sustain the captain without question, and in a few minutes all the sailors charged with mutiny were in irons. I rather felt for a time a wish that I had not gone aboard just then. As the men charged with mutiny submitted to being placed in irons without resistance,

I always doubted if they knew that they had mutinied until they were told.

By the time I was ready to leave the ship again I thought I had learned enough of the working of the double and single pulley, by which passengers were let down from the upper deck of the ship to the steamer below, and determined to let myself down without assistance. Without saying anything of my intentions to any one, I mounted the railing, and taking hold of the centre rope, just below the upper block, I put one foot on the hook below the lower block, and stepped off. Just as I did so some one called out "hold on." It was too late. I tried to "hold on" with all my might, but my heels went up, and my head went down so rapidly that my hold broke, and I plunged head foremost into the water, some twenty-five feet below, with such velocity that it seemed to me I never would stop. When I came to the surface again, being a fair swimmer, and not having lost my presence of mind, I swam around until a bucket was let down for me, and I was drawn up without a scratch or injury. I do not believe there was a man on board who sympathized with me in the least when they found me uninjured. I rather enjoyed the joke myself. The captain of the *Suviah* died of his disease a few months later, and I believe before the mutineers were tried. I hope they got clear, because, as before stated, I always thought the mutiny was all in the brain of a very weak and sick man.

After reaching shore, or Shell Island, the labor of getting to Corpus Christi was slow and tedious. There was, if my memory serves me, but one small steamer to transport troops and baggage when the 4th infantry arrived. Others were procured later. The distance from Shell Island to Corpus Christi was some sixteen or eighteen miles. The channel to the bay was so shallow that the steamer, small as it was, had to be dragged over the bottom when loaded. Not more than one trip a day could be effected. Later this was remedied, by deepening the channel and increasing the number of vessels suitable to its navigation.

Corpus Christi is near the head of the bay of the same name, formed by the entrance of the Nueces River into tidewater, and is on the west bank of that bay. At the time of its first occupancy by United States troops there was a small

Mexican hamlet there, containing probably less than one hundred souls. There was, in addition, a small American trading post, at which goods were sold to Mexican smugglers. All goods were put up in compact packages of about one hundred pounds each, suitable for loading on pack mules. Two of these packages made a load for an ordinary Mexican mule, and three for the larger ones. The bulk of the trade was in leaf tobacco, and domestic cotton-cloths and calicoes. The Mexicans had, before the arrival of the army, but little to offer in exchange except silver. The trade in tobacco was enormous, considering the population to be supplied. Almost every Mexican above the age of ten years, and many much younger, smoked the cigarette. Nearly every Mexican carried a pouch of leaf tobacco, powdered by rolling in the hands, and a roll of corn husks to make wrappers. The cigarettes were made by the smokers as they used them.

Up to the time of which I write, and for years afterwards— I think until the administration of President Juarez—the cultivation, manufacture and sale of tobacco constituted a government monopoly, and paid the bulk of the revenue collected from internal sources. The price was enormously high, and made successful smuggling very profitable. The difficulty of obtaining tobacco is probably the reason why everybody, male and female, used it at that time. I know from my own experience that when I was at West Point, the fact that tobacco, in every form, was prohibited, and the mere possession of the weed severely punished, made the majority of the cadets, myself included, try to acquire the habit of using it. I failed utterly at the time and for many years afterward; but the majority accomplished the object of their youthful ambition.

Under Spanish rule Mexico was prohibited from producing anything that the mother-country could supply. This rule excluded the cultivation of the grape, olive and many other articles to which the soil and climate were well adapted. The country was governed for "revenue only;" and tobacco, which cannot be raised in Spain, but is indigenous to Mexico, offered a fine instrumentality for securing this prime object of government. The native population had been in the habit of using "the weed" from a period, back of any recorded history of this continent. Bad habits—if not restrained by law or public opinion—spread more rapidly and universally than good ones, and the Spanish colonists adopted the use of tobacco almost as generally as the natives. Spain, therefore, in order to secure the largest revenue from this source, prohibited the cultivation, except in specified localities—and in these places farmed out the privilege at a very high price. The tobacco when raised could only be sold to the government, and the price to the consumer was limited only by the avarice of the authorities, and the capacity of the people to pay.

All laws for the government of the country were enacted in Spain, and the officers for their execution were appointed by the Crown, and sent out to the New El Dorado. The Mexicans had been brought up ignorant of how to legislate or how to rule. When they gained their independence, after many years of war, it was the most natural thing in the world that they should adopt as their own the laws then in existence. The only change was, that Mexico became her own executor of the laws and the recipient of the revenues. The tobacco tax, yielding so large a revenue under the law as it stood, was one of the last, if not the very last, of the obnoxious imposts to be repealed. Now, the citizens are allowed to cultivate any crops the soil will yield. Tobacco is cheap, and every quality can be produced. Its use is by no means so general as when I first visited the country.

Gradually the "Army of Occupation" assembled at Corpus Christi. When it was all together it consisted of seven companies of the 2d regiment of dragoons, four companies of light artillery, five regiments of infantry—the 3d, 4th, 5th, 7th and 8th—and one regiment of artillery acting as infantry—not more than three thousand men in all. General Zachary Taylor commanded the whole. There were troops enough in one body to establish a drill and discipline sufficient to fit men and officers for all they were capable of in case of battle. The rank and file were composed of men who had enlisted in time of peace, to serve for seven dollars a month, and were necessarily inferior as material to the average volunteers enlisted later in the war expressly to fight, and also to the volunteers in the war for the preservation of the Union. The men engaged in the Mexican war were brave, and the officers of the regular army, from highest to lowest, were educated in their profession. A more efficient army for its number and armament, I do not believe ever fought a battle than the one commanded by General Taylor in his first two engagements on Mexican— or Texan soil.

The presence of United States troops on the edge of the disputed territory furthest from the Mexican settlements, was not sufficient to provoke hostilities. We were sent to provoke a fight, but it was essential that Mexico should commence it. It was very doubtful whether Congress would declare war; but if Mexico should attack our troops, the Executive could announce, "Whereas, war exists by the acts of, etc.," and prosecute the contest with vigor. Once initiated there were but few public men who would have the courage to oppose it. Experience proves that the man who obstructs a war in which his nation is engaged, no matter whether right or wrong, occupies no enviable place in life or history. Better for him, individually, to advocate "war, pestilence, and famine," than to act as obstructionist to a war already begun. The history of the defeated rebel will be honorable hereafter, compared with that of the Northern man who aided him by conspiring against his government while protected by it. The most favorable posthumous history the stay-at-home traitor can hope for is—oblivion.

Mexico showing no willingness to come to the Nueces to drive the invaders from her soil, it became necessary for the "invaders" to approach to within a convenient distance to be struck. Accordingly, preparations were begun for moving the army to the Rio Grande, to a point near Matamoras. It was desirable to occupy a position near the largest centre of population possible to reach, without absolutely invading territory to which we set up no claim whatever.

The distance from Corpus Christi to Matamoras is about one hundred and fifty miles. The country does not abound in fresh water, and the length of the marches had to be regulated by the distance between water supplies. Besides the streams, there were occasional pools, filled during the rainy season, some probably made by the traders, who travelled constantly between Corpus Christi and the Rio Grande, and some by the buffalo. There was not at that time a single habitation, culti-

vated field, or herd of domestic animals, between Corpus
Christi and Matamoras. It was necessary, therefore, to have a
wagon train sufficiently large to transport the camp and garrison equipage, officers' baggage, rations for the army, and part
rations of grain for the artillery horses and all the animals
taken from the north, where they had been accustomed to
having their forage furnished them. The army was but indifferently supplied with transportation. Wagons and harness
could easily be supplied from the north; but mules and horses
could not so readily be brought. The American traders and
Mexican smugglers came to the relief. Contracts were made
for mules at from eight to eleven dollars each. The smugglers
furnished the animals, and took their pay in goods of the description before mentioned. I doubt whether the Mexicans
received in value from the traders five dollars per head for the
animals they furnished, and still more, whether they paid anything but their own time in procuring them. Such is trade;
such is war. The government paid in hard cash to the contractor the stipulated price.

Between the Rio Grande and the Nueces there was at that
time a large band of wild horses feeding; as numerous, probably, as the band of buffalo roaming further north was before
its rapid extermination commenced. The Mexicans used to
capture these in large numbers and bring them into the American settlements and sell them. A picked animal could be purchased at from eight to twelve dollars, but taken at wholesale,
they could be bought for thirty-six dollars a dozen. Some of
these were purchased for the army, and answered a most useful purpose. The horses were generally very strong, formed
much like the Norman horse, and with very heavy manes and
tails. A number of officers supplied themselves with these, and
they generally rendered as useful service as the northern animal; in fact they were much better when grazing was the only
means of supplying forage.

There was no need for haste, and some months were consumed in the necessary preparations for a move. In the meantime the army was engaged in all the duties pertaining to the
officer and the soldier. Twice, that I remember, small trains
were sent from Corpus Christi, with cavalry escorts, to San
Antonio and Austin, with paymasters and funds to pay off

small detachments of troops stationed at those places. General Taylor encouraged officers to accompany these expeditions. I accompanied one of them in December, 1845. The distance from Corpus Christi to San Antonio was then computed at one hundred and fifty miles. Now that roads exist it is probably less. From San Antonio to Austin we computed the distance at one hundred and ten miles, and from the latter place back to Corpus Christi at over two hundred miles. I know the distance now from San Antonio to Austin is but little over eighty miles, so that our computation was probably too high.

There was not at the time an individual living between Corpus Christi and San Antonio until within about thirty miles of the latter point, where there were a few scattering Mexican settlements along the San Antonio River. The people in at least one of these hamlets lived underground for protection against the Indians. The country abounded in game, such as deer and antelope, with abundance of wild turkeys along the streams and where there were nut-bearing woods. On the Nueces, about twenty-five miles up from Corpus Christi, were a few log cabins, the remains of a town called San Patricio, but the inhabitants had all been massacred by the Indians, or driven away.

San Antonio was about equally divided in population between Americans and Mexicans. From there to Austin there was not a single residence except at New Braunfels, on the Guadalupe River. At that point was a settlement of Germans who had only that year come into the State. At all events they were living in small huts, about such as soldiers would hastily construct for temporary occupation. From Austin to Corpus Christi there was only a small settlement at Bastrop, with a few farms along the Colorado River; but after leaving that, there were no settlements except the home of one man, with one female slave, at the old town of Goliad. Some of the houses were still standing. Goliad had been quite a village for the period and region, but some years before there had been a Mexican massacre, in which every inhabitant had been killed or driven away. This, with the massacre of the prisoners in the Alamo, San Antonio, about the same time, more than three hundred men in all, furnished the strongest justification the Texans had for carrying on the war with so much cruelty.

In fact, from that time until the Mexican war, the hostilities between Texans and Mexicans was so great that neither was safe in the neighborhood of the other who might be in superior numbers or possessed of superior arms. The man we found living there seemed like an old friend; he had come from near Fort Jessup, Louisiana, where the officers of the 3d and 4th infantry and the 2d dragoons had known him and his family. He had emigrated in advance of his family to build up a home for them.

Chapter V.

WHEN OUR PARTY left Corpus Christi it was quite large, including the cavalry escort, Paymaster, Major Dix, his clerk and the officers who, like myself, were simply on leave; but all the officers on leave, except Lieutenant Benjamin— afterwards killed in the valley of Mexico—Lieutenant, now General, Augur, and myself, concluded to spend their allotted time at San Antonio and return from there. We were all to be back at Corpus Christi by the end of the month. The paymaster was detained in Austin so long that, if we had waited for him, we would have exceeded our leave. We concluded, therefore, to start back at once with the animals we had, and having to rely principally on grass for their food, it was a good six days' journey. We had to sleep on the prairie every night, except at Goliad, and possibly one night on the Colorado, without shelter and with only such food as we carried with us, and prepared ourselves. The journey was hazardous on account of Indians, and there were white men in Texas whom I would not have cared to meet in a secluded place. Lieutenant Augur was taken seriously sick before we reached Goliad and at a distance from any habitation. To add to the complication, his horse—a mustang that had probably been captured from the band of wild horses before alluded to, and of undoubted longevity at his capture—gave out. It was absolutely necessary to get forward to Goliad to find a shelter for our sick companion. By dint of patience and exceedingly slow movements, Goliad was at last reached, and a shelter and bed secured for our patient. We remained over a day, hoping that Augur might recover sufficiently to resume his travels. He did not, however, and knowing that Major Dix would be along in a few days, with his wagon-train, now empty, and escort, we arranged with our Louisiana friend to take the best of care of the sick lieutenant until thus relieved, and went on.

I had never been a sportsman in my life; had scarcely ever gone in search of game, and rarely seen any when looking for

it. On this trip there was no minute of time while travelling
between San Patricio and the settlements on the San Antonio
River, from San Antonio to Austin, and again from the Colorado River back to San Patricio, when deer or antelope
could not be seen in great numbers. Each officer carried a
shot-gun, and every evening, after going into camp, some
would go out and soon return with venison and wild turkeys
enough for the entire camp. I, however, never went out, and
had no occasion to fire my gun; except, being detained over a
day at Goliad, Benjamin and I concluded to go down to the
creek—which was fringed with timber, much of it the pe-
can—and bring back a few turkeys. We had scarcely reached
the edge of the timber when I heard the flutter of wings overhead, and in an instant I saw two or three turkeys flying
away. These were soon followed by more, then more, and
more, until a flock of twenty or thirty had left from just over
my head. All this time I stood watching the turkeys to see
where they flew—with my gun on my shoulder, and never
once thought of levelling it at the birds. When I had time to
reflect upon the matter, I came to the conclusion that as a
sportsman I was a failure, and went back to the house. Benjamin remained out, and got as many turkeys as he wanted to
carry back.

After the second night at Goliad, Benjamin and I started to
make the remainder of the journey alone. We reached Corpus
Christi just in time to avoid "absence without leave." We met
no one—not even an Indian—during the remainder of our
journey, except at San Patricio. A new settlement had been
started there in our absence of three weeks, induced possibly
by the fact that there were houses already built, while the
proximity of troops gave protection against the Indians. On
the evening of the first day out from Goliad we heard the
most unearthly howling of wolves, directly in our front. The
prairie grass was tall and we could not see the beasts, but the
sound indicated that they were near. To my ear it appeared
that there must have been enough of them to devour our
party, horses and all, at a single meal. The part of Ohio that I
hailed from was not thickly settled, but wolves had been
driven out long before I left. Benjamin was from Indiana, still
less populated, where the wolf yet roamed over the prairies.

He understood the nature of the animal and the capacity of a few to make believe there was an unlimited number of them. He kept on towards the noise, unmoved. I followed in his trail, lacking moral courage to turn back and join our sick companion. I have no doubt that if Benjamin had proposed returning to Goliad, I would not only have "seconded the motion" but have suggested that it was very hard-hearted in us to leave Augur sick there in the first place; but Benjamin did not propose turning back. When he did speak it was to ask: "Grant, how many wolves do you think there are in that pack?" Knowing where he was from, and suspecting that he thought I would over-estimate the number, I determined to show my acquaintance with the animal by putting the estimate below what possibly could be correct, and answered: "Oh, about twenty," very indifferently. He smiled and rode on. In a minute we were close upon them, and before they saw us. There were just *two* of them. Seated upon their haunches, with their mouths close together, they had made all the noise we had been hearing for the past ten minutes. I have often thought of this incident since when I have heard the noise of a few disappointed politicians who had deserted their associates. There are always more of them before they are counted.

A week or two before leaving Corpus Christi on this trip, I had been promoted from brevet second-lieutenant, 4th infantry, to full second-lieutenant, 7th infantry. Frank Gardner,* of the 7th, was promoted to the 4th in the same orders. We immediately made application to be transferred, so as to get back to our old regiments. On my return, I found that our application had been approved at Washington. While in the 7th infantry I was in the company of Captain Holmes, afterwards a Lieutenant-general in the Confederate army. I never came in contact with him in the war of the Rebellion, nor did he render any very conspicuous service in his high rank. My transfer carried me to the company of Captain McCall, who resigned from the army after the Mexican war and settled in Philadelphia. He was prompt, however, to volunteer when the rebellion broke out, and soon rose to the rank of major-

*Afterwards General Gardner, C.S.A.

general in the Union army. I was not fortunate enough to meet him after he resigned. In the old army he was esteemed very highly as a soldier and gentleman. Our relations were always most pleasant.

The preparations at Corpus Christi for an advance progressed as rapidly in the absence of some twenty or more lieutenants as if we had been there. The principal business consisted in securing mules, and getting them broken to harness. The process was slow but amusing. The animals sold to the government were all young and unbroken, even to the saddle, and were quite as wild as the wild horses of the prairie. Usually a number would be brought in by a company of Mexicans, partners in the delivery. The mules were first driven into a stockade, called a *corral*, inclosing an acre or more of ground. The Mexicans,—who were all experienced in throwing the lasso,—would go into the *corral* on horseback, with their lassos attached to the pommels of their saddles. Soldiers detailed as teamsters and blacksmiths would also enter the *corral*, the former with ropes to serve as halters, the latter with branding irons and a fire to keep the irons heated. A lasso was then thrown over the neck of a mule, when he would immediately go to the length of his tether, first one end, then the other in the air. While he was thus plunging and gyrating, another lasso would be thrown by another Mexican, catching the animal by a fore-foot. This would bring the mule to the ground, when he was seized and held by the teamsters while the blacksmith put upon him, with hot irons, the initials "U. S." Ropes were then put about the neck, with a slip-noose which would tighten around the throat if pulled. With a man on each side holding these ropes, the mule was released from his other bindings and allowed to rise. With more or less difficulty he would be conducted to a picket rope outside and fastened there. The delivery of that mule was then complete. This process was gone through with every mule and wild horse with the army of occupation.

The method of breaking them was less cruel and much more amusing. It is a well-known fact that where domestic animals are used for specific purposes from generation to generation, the descendants are easily, as a rule, subdued to the same uses. At that time in Northern Mexico the mule, or his ancestors, the horse and the ass, was seldom used except for the saddle or pack. At all events the Corpus Christi mule resisted the new use to which he was being put. The treatment he was subjected to in order to overcome his prejudices was summary and effective.

The soldiers were principally foreigners who had enlisted in our large cities, and, with the exception of a chance drayman among them, it is not probable that any of the men who reported themselves as competent teamsters had ever driven a mule-team in their lives, or indeed that many had had any previous experience in driving any animal whatever to harness. Numbers together can accomplish what twice their number acting individually could not perform. Five mules were allotted to each wagon. A teamster would select at the picket rope five animals of nearly the same color and general appearance for his team. With a full corps of assistants, other teamsters, he would then proceed to get his mules together. In two's the men would approach each animal selected, avoiding as far as possible its heels. Two ropes would be put about the neck of each animal, with a slip noose, so that he could be choked if too unruly. They were then led out, harnessed by force and hitched to the wagon in the position they had to keep ever after. Two men remained on either side of the leader, with the lassos about its neck, and one man retained the same restraining influence over each of the others. All being ready, the hold would be slackened and the team started. The first motion was generally five mules in the air at one time, backs bowed, hind feet extended to the rear. After repeating this movement a few times the leaders would start to run. This would bring the breeching tight against the mules at the wheels, which these last seemed to regard as a most unwarrantable attempt at coercion and would resist by taking a seat, sometimes going so far as to lie down. In time all were broken in to do their duty submissively if not cheerfully, but there never was a time during the war when it was safe to let a Mexican mule get entirely loose. Their drivers were all teamsters by the time they got through.

I recollect one case of a mule that had worked in a team under the saddle, not only for some time at Corpus Christi, where he was broken, but all the way to the point opposite

Matamoras, then to Camargo, where he got loose from his fastenings during the night. He did not run away at first, but staid in the neighborhood for a day or two, coming up sometimes to the feed trough even; but on the approach of the teamster he always got out of the way. At last, growing tired of the constant effort to catch him, he disappeared altogether. Nothing short of a Mexican with his lasso could have caught him. Regulations would not have warranted the expenditure of a dollar in hiring a man with a lasso to catch that mule; but they did allow the expenditure "of the mule," on a certificate that he had run away without any fault of the quartermaster on whose returns he was borne, and also the purchase of another to take his place. I am a competent witness, for I was regimental quartermaster at the time.

While at Corpus Christi all the officers who had a fancy for riding kept horses. The animals cost but little in the first instance, and when picketed they would get their living without any cost. I had three not long before the army moved, but a sad accident bereft me of them all at one time. A colored boy who gave them all the attention they got—besides looking after my tent and that of a class-mate and fellow-lieutenant and cooking for us, all for about eight dollars per month, was riding one to water and leading the other two. The led horses pulled him from his seat and all three ran away. They never were heard of afterwards. Shortly after that some one told Captain Bliss, General Taylor's Adjutant-General, of my misfortune. "Yes; I heard Grant lost five or six dollars' worth of horses the other day," he replied. That was a slander; they were broken to the saddle when I got them and cost nearly twenty dollars. I never suspected the colored boy of malicious intent in letting them get away, because, if they had not escaped, he could have had one of them to ride on the long march then in prospect.

Chapter VI.

ADVANCE OF THE ARMY—CROSSING THE COLORADO—
THE RIO GRANDE.

A T LAST the preparations were complete and orders were
issued for the advance to begin on the 8th of March.
General Taylor had an army of not more than three thousand
men. One battery, the siege guns and all the convalescent
troops were sent on by water to Brazos Santiago, at the
mouth of the Rio Grande. A guard was left back at Corpus
Christi to look after public property and to take care of those
who were too sick to be removed. The remainder of the army,
probably not more than twenty-five hundred men, was divided into three brigades, with the cavalry independent. Colonel Twiggs, with seven companies of dragoons and a battery
of light artillery, moved on the 8th. He was followed by the
three infantry brigades, with a day's interval between the
commands. Thus the rear brigade did not move from Corpus
Christi until the 11th of March. In view of the immense bodies
of men moved on the same day over narrow roads, through
dense forests and across large streams, in our late war, it
seems strange now that a body of less than three thousand
men should have been broken into four columns, separated
by a day's march.

General Taylor was opposed to anything like plundering by
the troops, and in this instance, I doubt not, he looked upon
the enemy as the aggrieved party and was not willing to injure them further than his instructions from Washington demanded. His orders to the troops enjoined scrupulous regard
for the rights of all peaceable persons and the payment of the
highest price for all supplies taken for the use of the army.

All officers of foot regiments who had horses were permitted to ride them on the march when it did not interfere with
their military duties. As already related, having lost my "five
or six dollars' worth of horses" but a short time before I determined not to get another, but to make the journey on foot.
My company commander, Captain McCall, had two good
American horses, of considerably more value in that country,

where native horses were cheap, than they were in the States. He used one himself and wanted the other for his servant. He was quite anxious to know whether I did not intend to get me another horse before the march began. I told him No; I belonged to a foot regiment. I did not understand the object of his solicitude at the time, but, when we were about to start, he said: "There, Grant, is a horse for you." I found that he could not bear the idea of his servant riding on a long march while his lieutenant went a-foot. He had found a mustang, a three-year-old colt only recently captured, which had been purchased by one of the colored servants with the regiment for the sum of three dollars. It was probably the only horse at Corpus Christi that could have been purchased just then for any reasonable price. Five dollars, sixty-six and two-thirds per cent. advance, induced the owner to part with the mustang. I was sorry to take him, because I really felt that, belonging to a foot regiment, it was my duty to march with the men. But I saw the Captain's earnestness in the matter, and accepted the horse for the trip. The day we started was the first time the horse had ever been under saddle. I had, however, but little difficulty in breaking him, though for the first day there were frequent disagreements between us as to which way we should go, and sometimes whether we should go at all. At no time during the day could I choose exactly the part of the column I would march with; but after that, I had as tractable a horse as any with the army, and there was none that stood the trip better. He never ate a mouthful of food on the journey except the grass he could pick within the length of his picket rope.

A few days out from Corpus Christi, the immense herd of wild horses that ranged at that time between the Nueces and the Rio Grande was seen directly in advance of the head of the column and but a few miles off. It was the very band from which the horse I was riding had been captured but a few weeks before. The column was halted for a rest, and a number of officers, myself among them, rode out two or three miles to the right to see the extent of the herd. The country was a rolling prairie, and, from the higher ground, the vision was obstructed only by the earth's curvature. As far as the eye could reach to our right, the herd extended. To the left, it extended equally. There was no estimating the number of animals in it; I have no idea that they could all have been corralled in the State of Rhode Island, or Delaware, at one time. If they had been, they would have been so thick that the pasturage would have given out the first day. People who saw the Southern herd of buffalo, fifteen or twenty years ago, can appreciate the size of the Texas band of wild horses in 1846.

At the point where the army struck the Little Colorado River, the stream was quite wide and of sufficient depth for navigation. The water was brackish and the banks were fringed with timber. Here the whole army concentrated before attempting to cross. The army was not accompanied by a pontoon train, and at that time the troops were not instructed in bridge building. To add to the embarrassment of the situation, the army was here, for the first time, threatened with opposition. Buglers, concealed from our view by the brush on the opposite side, sounded the "assembly," and other military calls. Like the wolves before spoken of, they gave the impression that there was a large number of them and that, if the troops were in proportion to the noise, they were sufficient to devour General Taylor and his army. There were probably but few troops, and those engaged principally in watching the movements of the "invader." A few of our cavalry dashed in, and forded and swam the stream, and all opposition was soon dispersed. I do not remember that a single shot was fired.

The troops waded the stream, which was up to their necks in the deepest part. Teams were crossed by attaching a long rope to the end of the wagon tongue, passing it between the two swing mules and by the side of the leader, hitching his bridle as well as the bridle of the mules in rear to it, and carrying the end to men on the opposite shore. The bank down to the water was steep on both sides. A rope long enough to cross the river, therefore, was attached to the back axle of the wagon, and men behind would hold the rope to prevent the wagon "beating" the mules into the water. This latter rope also served the purpose of bringing the end of the forward one back, to be used over again. The water was deep enough for a short distance to swim the little Mexican mules which the army was then using, but they, and the wagons, were pulled through so fast by the men at the end of the rope ahead, that no time was left them to show their obstinacy. In this manner the artillery and transportation of the "army of occupation" crossed the Little Colorado River.

About the middle of the month of March the advance of the army reached the Rio Grande and went into camp near the banks of the river, opposite the city of Matamoras and almost under the guns of a small fort at the lower end of the town. There was not at that time a single habitation from Corpus Christi until the Rio Grande was reached.

The work of fortifying was commenced at once. The fort was laid out by the engineers, but the work was done by the soldiers under the supervision of their officers, the chief engineer retaining general directions. The Mexicans now became so incensed at our near approach that some of their troops crossed the river above us, and made it unsafe for small bodies of men to go far beyond the limits of camp. They captured two companies of dragoons, commanded by Captains Thornton and Hardee. The latter figured as a general in the late war, on the Confederate side, and was author of the tactics first used by both armies. Lieutenant Theodric Porter, of the 4th infantry, was killed while out with a small detachment; and Major Cross, the assistant quartermaster-general, had also been killed not far from camp.

There was no base of supplies nearer than Point Isabel, on the coast, north of the mouth of the Rio Grande and twenty-five miles away. The enemy, if the Mexicans could be called such at this time when no war had been declared, hovered about in such numbers that it was not safe to send a wagon train after supplies with any escort that could be spared. I have already said that General Taylor's whole command on the Rio Grande numbered less than three thousand men. He had, however, a few more troops at Point Isabel or Brazos Santiago. The supplies brought from Corpus Christi in wagons were running short. Work was therefore pushed with great vigor on the defences, to enable the minimum number of troops to hold the fort. All the men who could be employed, were kept at work from early dawn until darkness closed the labors of the day. With all this the fort was not completed until the supplies grew so short that further delay in obtaining more could not be thought of. By the latter part of April the work was in a partially defensible condition, and the 7th infantry, Major Jacob Brown commanding, was marched in to garrison it, with some few pieces of artillery. All the supplies on hand, with the exception of enough to carry the rest of the army to Point Isabel, were left with the garrison, and the march was commenced with the remainder of the command, every wagon being taken with the army. Early on the second day after starting the force reached its destination, without opposition from the Mexicans. There was some delay in getting supplies ashore from vessels at anchor in the open roadstead.

Chapter VII.

THE MEXICAN WAR—THE BATTLE OF PALO ALTO—THE
BATTLE OF RESACA DE LA PALMA—ARMY OF INVASION
—GENERAL TAYLOR—MOVEMENT ON CAMARGO.

WHILE GENERAL TAYLOR was away with the bulk of his
army, the little garrison up the river was besieged. As
we lay in our tents upon the sea-shore, the artillery at the fort
on the Rio Grande could be distinctly heard.

The war had begun.

There were no possible means of obtaining news from the
garrison, and information from outside could not be otherwise than unfavorable. What General Taylor's feelings were
during this suspense I do not know; but for myself, a young
second-lieutenant who had never heard a hostile gun before, I
felt sorry that I had enlisted. A great many men, when they
smell battle afar off, chafe to get into the fray. When they say
so themselves they generally fail to convince their hearers that
they are as anxious as they would like to make believe, and as
they approach danger they become more subdued. This rule
is not universal, for I have known a few men who were always
aching for a fight when there was no enemy near, who were
as good as their word when the battle did come. But the
number of such men is small.

On the 7th of May the wagons were all loaded and General
Taylor started on his return, with his army reinforced at Point
Isabel, but still less than three thousand strong, to relieve the
garrison on the Rio Grande. The road from Point Isabel to
Matamoras is over an open, rolling, treeless prairie, until the
timber that borders the bank of the Rio Grande is reached.
This river, like the Mississippi, flows through a rich alluvial
valley in the most meandering manner, running towards all
points of the compass at times within a few miles. Formerly
the river ran by Resaca de la Palma, some four or five miles
east of the present channel. The old bed of the river at Resaca
had become filled at places, leaving a succession of little lakes.
The timber that had formerly grown upon both banks, and
for a considerable distance out, was still standing. This timber

was struck six or eight miles out from the besieged garrison, at a point known as Palo Alto—"Tall trees" or "woods."

Early in the forenoon of the 8th of May as Palo Alto was approached, an army, certainly outnumbering our little force, was seen, drawn up in line of battle just in front of the timber. Their bayonets and spearheads glistened in the sunlight formidably. The force was composed largely of cavalry armed with lances. Where we were the grass was tall, reaching nearly to the shoulders of the men, very stiff, and each stock was pointed at the top, and hard and almost as sharp as a darning-needle. General Taylor halted his army before the head of column came in range of the artillery of the Mexicans. He then formed a line of battle, facing the enemy. His artillery, two batteries and two eighteen-pounder iron guns, drawn by oxen, were placed in position at intervals along the line. A battalion was thrown to the rear, commanded by Lieutenant-Colonel Childs, of the artillery, as reserves. These preparations completed, orders were given for a platoon of each company to stack arms and go to a stream off to the right of the command, to fill their canteens and also those of the rest of their respective companies. When the men were all back in their places in line, the command to advance was given. As I looked down that long line of about three thousand armed men, advancing towards a larger force also armed, I thought what a fearful responsibility General Taylor must feel, commanding such a host and so far away from friends. The Mexicans immediately opened fire upon us, first with artillery and then with infantry. At first their shots did not reach us, and the advance was continued. As we got nearer, the cannon balls commenced going through the ranks. They hurt no one, however, during this advance, because they would strike the ground long before they reached our line, and ricochetted through the tall grass so slowly that the men would see them and open ranks and let them pass. When we got to a point where the artillery could be used with effect, a halt was called, and the battle opened on both sides.

The infantry under General Taylor was armed with flint-lock muskets, and paper cartridges charged with powder, buck-shot and ball. At the distance of a few hundred yards a man might fire at you all day without your finding it out.

The artillery was generally six-pounder brass guns throwing only solid shot; but General Taylor had with him three or four twelve-pounder howitzers throwing shell, besides his eighteen-pounders before spoken of, that had a long range. This made a powerful armament. The Mexicans were armed about as we were so far as their infantry was concerned, but their artillery only fired solid shot. We had greatly the advantage in this arm.

The artillery was advanced a rod or two in front of the line, and opened fire. The infantry stood at order arms as spectators, watching the effect of our shots upon the enemy, and watching his shots so as to step out of their way. It could be seen that the eighteen-pounders and the howitzers did a great deal of execution. On our side there was little or no loss while we occupied this position. During the battle Major Ringgold, an accomplished and brave artillery officer, was mortally wounded, and Lieutenant Luther, also of the artillery, was struck. During the day several advances were made, and just at dusk it became evident that the Mexicans were falling back. We again advanced, and occupied at the close of the battle substantially the ground held by the enemy at the beginning. In this last move there was a brisk fire upon our troops, and some execution was done. One cannon-ball passed through our ranks, not far from me. It took off the head of an enlisted man, and the under jaw of Captain Page of my regiment, while the splinters from the musket of the killed soldier, and his brains and bones, knocked down two or three others, including one officer, Lieutenant Wallen,—hurting them more or less. Our casualties for the day were nine killed and forty-seven wounded.

At the break of day on the 9th, the army under Taylor was ready to renew the battle; but an advance showed that the enemy had entirely left our front during the night. The chaparral before us was impenetrable except where there were roads or trails, with occasionally clear or bare spots of small dimensions. A body of men penetrating it might easily be ambushed. It was better to have a few men caught in this way than the whole army, yet it was necessary that the garrison at the river should be relieved. To get to them the chaparral had to be passed. Thus I assume General Taylor reasoned. He halted the army not far in advance of the ground occupied by the Mexicans the day before, and selected Captain C. F. Smith, of the artillery, and Captain McCall, of my company, to take one hundred and fifty picked men each and find where the enemy had gone. This left me in command of the company, an honor and responsibility I thought very great.

Smith and McCall found no obstruction in the way of their advance until they came up to the succession of ponds, before described, at Resaca. The Mexicans had passed them and formed their lines on the opposite bank. This position they had strengthened a little by throwing up dead trees and brush in their front, and by placing artillery to cover the approaches and open places. Smith and McCall deployed on each side of the road as well as they could, and engaged the enemy at long range. Word was sent back, and the advance of the whole army was at once commenced. As we came up we were deployed in like manner. I was with the right wing, and led my company through the thicket wherever a penetrable place could be found, taking advantage of any clear spot that would carry me towards the enemy. At last I got pretty close up without knowing it. The balls commenced to whistle very thick overhead, cutting the limbs of the chaparral right and left. We could not see the enemy, so I ordered my men to lie down, an order that did not have to be enforced. We kept our position until it became evident that the enemy were not firing at us, and then withdrew to find better ground to advance upon.

By this time some progress had been made on our left. A section of artillery had been captured by the cavalry, and some prisoners had been taken. The Mexicans were giving way all along the line, and many of them had, no doubt, left early. I at last found a clear space separating two ponds. There seemed to be a few men in front and I charged upon them with my company. There was no resistance, and we captured a Mexican colonel, who had been wounded, and a few men. Just as I was sending them to the rear with a guard of two or three men, a private came from the front bringing back one of our officers, who had been badly wounded in advance of where I was. The ground had been charged over before. My exploit was equal to that of the soldier who boasted that he had cut off the leg of one of the enemy. When asked why he did not cut off his head, he replied: "Some one had done that before." This left no doubt in my mind but that the battle of Resaca de la Palma would have been won, just as it was, if I had not been there.

There was no further resistance. The evening of the 9th the army was encamped on its old ground near the Fort, and the garrison was relieved. The siege had lasted a number of days, but the casualties were few in number. Major Jacob Brown, of the 7th infantry, the commanding officer, had been killed, and in his honor the fort was named. Since then a town of considerable importance has sprung up on the ground occupied by the fort and troops, which has also taken his name.

The battles of Palo Alto and Resaca de la Palma seemed to us engaged, as pretty important affairs; but we had only a faint conception of their magnitude until they were fought over in the North by the Press and the reports came back to us. At the same time, or about the same time, we learned that war existed between the United States and Mexico, by the acts of the latter country. On learning this fact General Taylor transferred our camps to the south or west bank of the river, and Matamoras was occupied. We then became the "Army of Invasion."

Up to this time Taylor had none but regular troops in his command; but now that invasion had already taken place, volunteers for one year commenced arriving. The army remained at Matamoras until sufficiently reinforced to warrant a movement into the interior. General Taylor was not an officer to trouble the administration much with his demands, but was inclined to do the best he could with the means given him. He felt his responsibility as going no further. If he had thought that he was sent to perform an impossibility with the means given him, he would probably have informed the authorities of his opinion and left them to determine what should be done. If the judgment was against him he would have gone on and done the best he could with the means at hand without parading his grievance before the public. No soldier could face either danger or responsibility more calmly than he. These are qualities more rarely found than genius or physical courage.

General Taylor never made any great show or parade, either of uniform or retinue. In dress he was possibly too plain, rarely wearing anything in the field to indicate his rank, or even that he was an officer; but he was known to every soldier in his army, and was respected by all. I can call to mind only one instance when I saw him in uniform, and one other when I heard of his wearing it. On both occasions he was unfortunate. The first was at Corpus Christi. He had concluded to review his army before starting on the march and gave orders accordingly. Colonel Twiggs was then second in rank with the army, and to him was given the command of the review. Colonel and Brevet Brigadier-General Worth, a far different soldier from Taylor in the use of the uniform, was next to Twiggs in rank, and claimed superiority by virtue of his brevet rank when the accidents of service threw them where one or the other had to command. Worth declined to attend the review as subordinate to Twiggs until the question was settled by the highest authority. This broke up the review, and the question was referred to Washington for final decision.

General Taylor was himself only a colonel, in real rank, at that time, and a brigadier-general by brevet. He was assigned to duty, however, by the President, with the rank which his brevet gave him. Worth was not so assigned, but by virtue of commanding a division he must, under the army regulations of that day, have drawn the pay of his brevet rank. The question was submitted to Washington, and no response was received until after the army had reached the Rio Grande. It was decided against General Worth, who at once tendered his resignation and left the army, going north, no doubt, by the same vessel that carried it. This kept him out of the battles of Palo Alto and Resaca de la Palma. Either the resignation was not accepted, or General Worth withdrew it before action had been taken. At all events he returned to the army in time to command his division in the battle of Monterey, and served with it to the end of the war.

The second occasion on which General Taylor was said to have donned his uniform, was in order to receive a visit from the Flag Officer of the naval squadron off the mouth of the Rio Grande. While the army was on that river the Flag Officer sent word that he would call on the General to pay his respects on a certain day. General Taylor, knowing that naval officers habitually wore all the uniform the "law allowed" on all occasions of ceremony, thought it would be only civil to receive his guest in the same style. His uniform was therefore got out, brushed up, and put on, in advance of the visit. The Flag Officer, knowing General Taylor's aversion to the wearing of the uniform, and feeling that it would be regarded as a compliment should he meet him in civilian's dress, left off his uniform for this occasion. The meeting was said to have been embarrassing to both, and the conversation was principally apologetic.

The time was whiled away pleasantly enough at Matamoras, while we were waiting for volunteers. It is probable that all the most important people of the territory occupied by our army left their homes before we got there, but with those remaining the best of relations apparently existed. It was the policy of the Commanding General to allow no pillaging, no taking of private property for public or individual use without satisfactory compensation, so that a better market was afforded than the people had ever known before.

Among the troops that joined us at Matamoras was an Ohio regiment, of which Thomas L. Hamer, the Member of Congress who had given me my appointment to West Point, was major. He told me then that he could have had the colonelcy, but that as he knew he was to be appointed a brigadier-general, he preferred at first to take the lower grade. I have said before that Hamer was one of the ablest men Ohio ever produced. At that time he was in the prime of life, being less than fifty years of age, and possessed an admirable physique, promising long life. But he was taken sick before Monterey, and died within a few days. I have always believed that had his life been spared, he would have been President of the United States during the term filled by President Pierce. Had Hamer filled that office his partiality for me was such, there is but little doubt I should have been appointed to one of the staff corps of the army—the Pay Department probably—and would therefore now be preparing to retire. Neither of these speculations is unreasonable, and they are mentioned to show how little men control their own destiny.

Reinforcements having arrived, in the month of August the movement commenced from Matamoras to Camargo, the head of navigation on the Rio Grande. The line of the Rio Grande was all that was necessary to hold, unless it was intended to invade Mexico from the North. In that case the most natural route to take was the one which General Taylor selected. It entered a pass in the Sierra Madre Mountains, at Monterey, through which the main road runs to the City of Mexico. Monterey itself was a good point to hold, even if the line of the Rio Grande covered all the territory we desired to occupy at that time. It is built on a plain two thousand feet above tide water, where the air is bracing and the situation healthy.

On the 19th of August the army started for Monterey, leaving a small garrison at Matamoras. The troops, with the exception of the artillery, cavalry, and the brigade to which I belonged, were moved up the river to Camargo on steamers. As there were but two or three of these, the boats had to make a number of trips before the last of the troops were up. Those who marched did so by the south side of the river. Lieutenant-Colonel Garland, of the 4th infantry, was the brigade commander, and on this occasion commanded the entire marching force. One day out convinced him that marching by day in that latitude, in the month of August, was not a beneficial sanitary measure, particularly for Northern men. The order of marching was changed and night marches were substituted with the best results.

When Camargo was reached, we found a city of tents outside the Mexican hamlet. I was detailed to act as quartermaster and commissary to the regiment. The teams that had proven abundantly sufficient to transport all supplies from Corpus Christi to the Rio Grande over the level prairies of Texas, were entirely inadequate to the needs of the reinforced army in a mountainous country. To obviate the deficiency, pack mules were hired, with Mexicans to pack and drive them. I had charge of the few wagons allotted to the 4th infantry and of the pack train to supplement them. There were not men enough in the army to manage that train without the help of Mexicans who had learned how. As it was the difficulty was great enough. The troops would take up their march at an early hour each day. After they had started, the tents and cooking utensils had to be made into packages, so that they could be lashed to the backs of the mules. Sheet-iron kettles, tent-poles and mess chests were inconvenient articles to transport in that way. It took several hours to get ready to start each morning, and by the time we were ready some of the mules first loaded would be tired of standing so long with their loads on their backs. Sometimes one would start to run, bowing his back and kicking up until he scattered his load; others would lie down and try to disarrange their loads by attempting to get on the top of them by rolling on them; others with tent-poles for part of their loads would manage to run a tent-pole on one side of a sapling while they would take the other. I am not aware of ever having used a profane expletive in my life; but I would have the charity to excuse those who may have done so, if they were in charge of a train of Mexican pack mules at the time.

Chapter VIII.

ADVANCE ON MONTEREY — THE BLACK FORT — THE
BATTLE OF MONTEREY — SURRENDER OF THE CITY.

THE ADVANCE from Camargo was commenced on the 5th
of September. The army was divided into four columns,
separated from each other by one day's march. The advance
reached Cerralvo in four days and halted for the remainder of
the troops to come up. By the 13th the rear-guard had arrived,
and the same day the advance resumed its march, followed as
before, a day separating the divisions. The forward division
halted again at Marin, twenty-four miles from Monterey.
Both this place and Cerralvo were nearly deserted, and men,
women and children were seen running and scattered over the
hills as we approached; but when the people returned they
found all their abandoned property safe, which must have
given them a favorable opinion of *Los Grengos* — "the Yankees." From Marin the movement was in mass. On the 19th
General Taylor, with his army, was encamped at Walnut
Springs, within three miles of Monterey.

The town is on a small stream coming out of the mountain-
pass, and is backed by a range of hills of moderate elevation.
To the north, between the city and Walnut Springs, stretches
an extensive plain. On this plain, and entirely outside of the
last houses of the city, stood a strong fort, enclosed on all
sides, to which our army gave the name of "Black Fort." Its
guns commanded the approaches to the city to the full extent
of their range. There were two detached spurs of hills or
mountains to the north and north-west of the city, which
were also fortified. On one of these stood the Bishop's Palace.
The road to Saltillo leaves the upper or western end of the
city under the fire of the guns from these heights. The lower
or eastern end was defended by two or three small detached
works, armed with artillery and infantry. To the south was the
mountain stream before mentioned, and back of that the
range of foot-hills. The plaza in the centre of the city was the
citadel, properly speaking. All the streets leading from it were
swept by artillery, cannon being intrenched behind temporary

parapets. The house-tops near the plaza were converted into infantry fortifications by the use of sand-bags for parapets. Such were the defences of Monterey in September, 1846. General Ampudia, with a force of certainly ten thousand men, was in command.

General Taylor's force was about six thousand five hundred strong, in three divisions, under Generals Butler, Twiggs and Worth. The troops went into camp at Walnut Springs, while the engineer officers, under Major Mansfield—a General in the late war—commenced their reconnoissance. Major Mansfield found that it would be practicable to get troops around, out of range of the Black Fort and the works on the detached hills to the north-west of the city, to the Saltillo road. With this road in our possession, the enemy would be cut off from receiving further supplies, if not from all communication with the interior. General Worth, with his division somewhat reinforced, was given the task of gaining possession of the Saltillo road, and of carrying the detached works outside the city, in that quarter. He started on his march early in the afternoon of the 20th. The divisions under Generals Butler and Twiggs were drawn up to threaten the east and north sides of the city and the works on those fronts, in support of the movement under General Worth. Worth's was regarded as the main attack on Monterey, and all other operations were in support of it. His march this day was uninterrupted; but the enemy was seen to reinforce heavily about the Bishop's Palace and the other outside fortifications on their left. General Worth reached a defensible position just out of range of the enemy's guns on the heights north-west of the city, and bivouacked for the night. The engineer officers with him—Captain Sanders and Lieutenant George G. Meade, afterwards the commander of the victorious National army at the battle of Gettysburg—made a reconnoissance to the Saltillo road under cover of night.

During the night of the 20th General Taylor had established a battery, consisting of two twenty-four-pounder howitzers and a ten-inch mortar, at a point from which they could play upon Black Fort. A natural depression in the plain, sufficiently deep to protect men standing in it from the fire from the fort, was selected and the battery established on the crest nearest the enemy. The 4th infantry, then consisting of but six reduced companies, was ordered to support the artillerists while they were intrenching themselves and their guns. I was regimental quartermaster at the time and was ordered to remain in charge of camp and the public property at Walnut Springs. It was supposed that the regiment would return to its camp in the morning.

The point for establishing the siege battery was reached and the work performed without attracting the attention of the enemy. At daylight the next morning fire was opened on both sides and continued with, what seemed to me at that day, great fury. My curiosity got the better of my judgment, and I mounted a horse and rode to the front to see what was going on. I had been there but a short time when an order to charge was given, and lacking the moral courage to return to camp—where I had been ordered to stay—I charged with the regiment. As soon as the troops were out of the depression they came under the fire of Black Fort. As they advanced they got under fire from batteries guarding the east, or lower, end of the city, and of musketry. About one-third of the men engaged in the charge were killed or wounded in the space of a few minutes. We retreated to get out of fire, not backward, but eastward and perpendicular to the direct road running into the city from Walnut Springs. I was, I believe, the only person in the 4th infantry in the charge who was on horseback. When we got to a place of safety the regiment halted and drew itself together—what was left of it. The adjutant of the regiment, Lieutenant Hoskins, who was not in robust health, found himself very much fatigued from running on foot in the charge and retreat, and, seeing me on horseback, expressed a wish that he could be mounted also. I offered him my horse and he accepted the offer. A few minutes later I saw a soldier, a quartermaster's man, mounted, not far away. I ran to him, took his horse and was back with the regiment in a few minutes. In a short time we were off again; and the next place of safety from the shots of the enemy that I recollect of being in, was a field of cane or corn to the north-east of the lower batteries. The adjutant to whom I had loaned my horse was killed, and I was designated to act in his place.

This charge was ill-conceived, or badly executed. We belonged to the brigade commanded by Lieutenant-Colonel Garland, and he had received orders to charge the lower batteries of the city, and carry them if he could without too much loss, for the purpose of creating a diversion in favor of Worth, who was conducting the movement which it was intended should be decisive. By a movement by the left flank Garland could have led his men beyond the range of the fire from Black Fort and advanced towards the northeast angle of the city, as well covered from fire as could be expected. There was no undue loss of life in reaching the lower end of Monterey, except that sustained by Garland's command.

Meanwhile Quitman's brigade, conducted by an officer of engineers, had reached the eastern end of the city, and was placed under cover of the houses without much loss. Colonel Garland's brigade also arrived at the suburbs, and, by the assistance of some of our troops that had reached house-tops from which they could fire into a little battery covering the approaches to the lower end of the city, the battery was speedily captured and its guns were turned upon another work of the enemy. An entrance into the east end of the city was now secured, and the houses protected our troops so long as they were inactive.

On the west General Worth had reached the Saltillo road after some fighting but without heavy loss. He turned from his new position and captured the forts on both heights in that quarter. This gave him possession of the upper or west end of Monterey. Troops from both Twiggs's and Butler's divisions were in possession of the east end of the town, but the Black Fort to the north of the town and the plaza in the centre were still in the possession of the enemy. Our camps at Walnut Springs, three miles away, were guarded by a company from each regiment. A regiment of Kentucky volunteers guarded the mortars and howitzers engaged against Black Fort. Practically Monterey was invested.

There was nothing done on the 22d by the United States troops; but the enemy kept up a harmless fire upon us from Black Fort and the batteries still in their possession at the east end of the city. During the night they evacuated these; so that on the morning of the 23d we held undisputed possession of the east end of Monterey.

Twiggs's division was at the lower end of the city, and well covered from the fire of the enemy. But the streets leading to the plaza—all Spanish or Spanish-American towns have near their centres a square called a plaza—were commanded from all directions by artillery. The houses were flat-roofed and but one or two stories high, and about the plaza the roofs were manned with infantry, the troops being protected from our fire by parapets made of sand-bags. All advances into the city were thus attended with much danger. While moving along streets which did not lead to the plaza, our men were protected from the fire, and from the view, of the enemy except at the crossings; but at these a volley of musketry and a discharge of grape-shot were invariably encountered. The 3d and 4th regiments of infantry made an advance nearly to the plaza in this way and with heavy loss. The loss of the 3d infantry in commissioned officers was especially severe. There were only five companies of the regiment and not over twelve officers present, and five of these officers were killed. When within a square of the plaza this small command, ten companies in all, was brought to a halt. Placing themselves under cover from the shots of the enemy, the men would watch to detect a head above the sand-bags on the neighboring houses. The exposure of a single head would bring a volley from our soldiers.

We had not occupied this position long when it was discovered that our ammunition was growing low. I volunteered to go back* to the point we had started from, report our position to General Twiggs, and ask for ammunition to be forwarded. We were at this time occupying ground off from the street, in rear of the houses. My ride back was an exposed one. Before starting I adjusted myself on the side of my horse furthest from the enemy, and with only one foot holding to

---

*General Garland expressed a wish to get a message back to General Twiggs, his division commander, or General Taylor, to the effect that he was nearly out of ammunition and must have more sent to him, or otherwise be reinforced. Deeming the return dangerous he did not like to order any one to carry it, so he called for a volunteer. Lieutenant Grant offered his services, which were accepted.—PUBLISHERS.

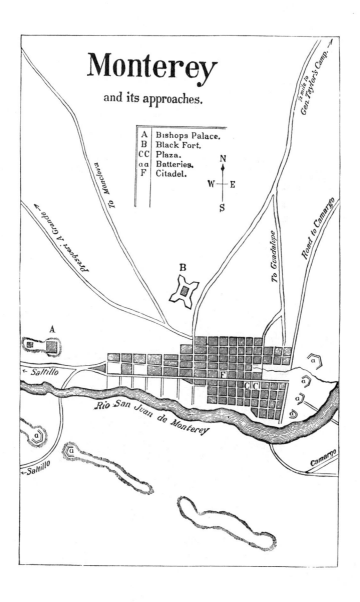

Monterey

and its approaches.

A	Bishops Palace.
B	Black Fort.
CC	Plaza.
a a	Batteries.
F	Citadel.

N
W — E
S

½ mile to Gen. Taylor's Camp.

To Monclova

Presquet A Grande

To Guadalupe

Road to Camargo

B

A

← Saltillo

F

C C

Rio San Juan de Monterey

a

a

a

a

a

← Saltillo

Camargo

the cantle of the saddle, and an arm over the neck of the horse exposed, I started at full run. It was only at street crossings that my horse was under fire, but these I crossed at such a flying rate that generally I was past and under cover of the next block of houses before the enemy fired. I got out safely without a scratch.

At one place on my ride, I saw a sentry walking in front of a house, and stopped to inquire what he was doing there. Finding that the house was full of wounded American officers and soldiers, I dismounted and went in. I found there Captain Williams, of the Engineer Corps, wounded in the head, prob-ably fatally, and Lieutenant Territt, also badly wounded, his bowels protruding from his wound. There were quite a num-ber of soldiers also. Promising them to report their situation, I left, readjusted myself to my horse, recommenced the run, and was soon with the troops at the east end. Before ammu-nition could be collected, the two regiments I had been with were seen returning, running the same gauntlet in getting out that they had passed in going in, but with comparatively little loss. The movement was countermanded and the troops were withdrawn. The poor wounded officers and men I had found, fell into the hands of the enemy during the night, and died.

While this was going on at the east, General Worth, with a small division of troops, was advancing towards the plaza from the opposite end of the city. He resorted to a better expedient for getting to the plaza—the citadel—than we did on the east. Instead of moving by the open streets, he ad-vanced through the houses, cutting passage-ways from one to another. Without much loss of life, he got so near the plaza during the night that before morning, Ampudia, the Mexican commander, made overtures for the surrender of the city and garrison. This stopped all further hostilities. The terms of sur-render were soon agreed upon. The prisoners were paroled and permitted to take their horses and personal property with them.

My pity was aroused by the sight of the Mexican garrison of Monterey marching out of town as prisoners, and no doubt the same feeling was experienced by most of our army who witnessed it. Many of the prisoners were cavalry, armed with lances, and mounted on miserable little half-starved horses that did not look as if they could carry their riders out of town. The men looked in but little better condition. I thought how little interest the men before me had in the results of the war, and how little knowledge they had of "what it was all about."

After the surrender of the garrison of Monterey a quiet camp life was led until midwinter. As had been the case on the Rio Grande, the people who remained at their homes fraternized with the "Yankees" in the pleasantest manner. In fact, under the humane policy of our commander, I question whether the great majority of the Mexican people did not regret our departure as much as they had regretted our coming. Property and person were thoroughly protected, and a market was afforded for all the products of the country such as the people had never enjoyed before. The educated and wealthy portion of the population here, as elsewhere, abandoned their homes and remained away from them as long as they were in the possession of the invaders; but this class formed a very small percentage of the whole population.

Chapter IX.

THE MEXICAN WAR was a political war, and the administration conducting it desired to make party capital out of it. General Scott was at the head of the army, and, being a soldier of acknowledged professional capacity, his claim to the command of the forces in the field was almost indisputable and does not seem to have been denied by President Polk, or Marcy, his Secretary of War. Scott was a Whig and the administration was democratic. General Scott was also known to have political aspirations, and nothing so popularizes a candidate for high civil positions as military victories. It would not do therefore to give him command of the "army of conquest." The plans submitted by Scott for a campaign in Mexico were disapproved by the administration, and he replied, in a tone possibly a little disrespectful, to the effect that, if a soldier's plans were not to be supported by the administration, success could not be expected. This was on the 27th of May, 1846. Four days later General Scott was notified that he need not go to Mexico. General Gaines was next in rank, but he was too old and feeble to take the field. Colonel Zachary Taylor — a brigadier-general by brevet — was therefore left in command. He, too, was a Whig, but was not supposed to entertain any political ambitions; nor did he; but after the fall of Monterey, his third battle and third complete victory, the Whig papers at home began to speak of him as the candidate of their party for the Presidency. Something had to be done to neutralize his growing popularity. He could not be relieved from duty in the field where all his battles had been victories: the design would have been too transparent. It was finally decided to send General Scott to Mexico in chief command, and to authorize him to carry out his own original plan: that is, capture Vera Cruz and march upon the capital of the country. It was no doubt supposed that Scott's ambition would lead him to slaughter Taylor or destroy his chances for the Presidency, and yet it was hoped that he would not make sufficient capital himself to secure the prize.

The administration had indeed a most embarrassing problem to solve. It was engaged in a war of conquest which must be carried to a successful issue, or the political object would be unattained. Yet all the capable officers of the requisite rank belonged to the opposition, and the man selected for his lack of political ambition had himself become a prominent candidate for the Presidency. It was necessary to destroy his chances promptly. The problem was to do this without the loss of conquest and without permitting another general of the same political party to acquire like popularity. The fact is, the administration of Mr. Polk made every preparation to disgrace Scott, or, to speak more correctly, to drive him to such desperation that he would disgrace himself.

General Scott had opposed conquest by the way of the Rio Grande, Matamoras and Saltillo from the first. Now that he was in command of all the forces in Mexico, he withdrew from Taylor most of his regular troops and left him only enough volunteers, as he thought, to hold the line then in possession of the invading army. Indeed Scott did not deem it important to hold anything beyond the Rio Grande, and authorized Taylor to fall back to that line if he chose. General Taylor protested against the depletion of his army, and his subsequent movement upon Buena Vista would indicate that he did not share the views of his chief in regard to the unimportance of conquest beyond the Rio Grande.

Scott had estimated the men and material that would be required to capture Vera Cruz and to march on the capital of the country, two hundred and sixty miles in the interior. He was promised all he asked and seemed to have not only the confidence of the President, but his sincere good wishes. The promises were all broken. Only about half the troops were furnished that had been pledged, other war material was withheld and Scott had scarcely started for Mexico before the President undertook to supersede him by the appointment of Senator Thomas H. Benton as lieutenant-general. This being refused by Congress, the President asked legislative authority to place a junior over a senior of the same grade, with the view of appointing Benton to the rank of major-general and then placing him in command of the army, but Congress failed to accede to this proposition as well, and Scott remained in command: but every general appointed to serve under him was politically opposed to the chief, and several were personally hostile.

General Scott reached Brazos Santiago or Point Isabel, at the mouth of the Rio Grande, late in December, 1846, and proceeded at once up the river to Camargo, where he had written General Taylor to meet him. Taylor, however, had gone to, or towards Tampico, for the purpose of establishing a post there. He had started on this march before he was aware of General Scott being in the country. Under these circumstances Scott had to issue his orders designating the troops to be withdrawn from Taylor, without the personal consultation he had expected to hold with his subordinate.

General Taylor's victory at Buena Vista, February 22d, 23d, and 24th, 1847, with an army composed almost entirely of volunteers who had not been in battle before, and over a vastly superior force numerically, made his nomination for the Presidency by the Whigs a foregone conclusion. He was nominated and elected in 1848. I believe that he sincerely regretted this turn in his fortunes, preferring the peace afforded by a quiet life free from abuse to the honor of filling the highest office in the gift of any people, the Presidency of the United States.

When General Scott assumed command of the army of invasion, I was in the division of General David Twiggs, in Taylor's command; but under the new orders my regiment was transferred to the division of General William Worth, in which I served to the close of the war. The troops withdrawn from Taylor to form part of the forces to operate against Vera Cruz, were assembled at the mouth of the Rio Grande preparatory to embarkation for their destination. I found General Worth a different man from any I had before served directly under. He was nervous, impatient and restless on the march, or when important or responsible duty confronted him. There was not the least reason for haste on the march, for it was known that it would take weeks to assemble shipping enough at the point of our embarkation to carry the army, but General Worth moved his division with a rapidity that would have

been commendable had he been going to the relief of a beleaguered garrison. The length of the marches was regulated by
the distances between places affording a supply of water for the
troops, and these distances were sometimes long and sometimes short. General Worth on one occasion at least, after having made the full distance intended for the day, and after the
troops were in camp and preparing their food, ordered tents
struck and made the march that night which had been intended for the next day. Some commanders can move troops
so as to get the maximum distance out of them without fatigue, while others can wear them out in a few days without
accomplishing so much. General Worth belonged to this latter
class. He enjoyed, however, a fine reputation for his fighting
qualities, and thus attached his officers and men to him.

The army lay in camp upon the sand-beach in the neighborhood of the mouth of the Rio Grande for several weeks,
awaiting the arrival of transports to carry it to its new field of
operations. The transports were all sailing vessels. The passage was a tedious one, and many of the troops were on ship-
board over thirty days from the embarkation at the mouth of
the Rio Grande to the time of debarkation south of Vera
Cruz. The trip was a comfortless one for officers and men.
The transports used were built for carrying freight and possessed but limited accommodations for passengers, and the
climate added to the discomfort of all.

The transports with troops were assembled in the harbor of
Anton Lizardo, some sixteen miles south of Vera Cruz, as
they arrived, and there awaited the remainder of the fleet,
bringing artillery, ammunition and supplies of all kinds from
the North. With the fleet there was a little steam propeller
dispatch-boat—the first vessel of the kind I had ever seen,
and probably the first of its kind ever seen by any one then
with the army. At that day ocean steamers were rare, and
what there were were side-wheelers. This little vessel, going
through the fleet so fast, so noiselessly and with its propeller
under water out of view, attracted a great deal of attention. I
recollect that Lieutenant Sidney Smith, of the 4th infantry, by
whom I happened to be standing on the deck of a vessel
when this propeller was passing, exclaimed, "Why, the thing
looks as if it was propelled by the force of circumstances."

Finally on the 7th of March, 1847, the little army of ten or twelve thousand men, given Scott to invade a country with a population of seven or eight millions, a mountainous country affording the greatest possible natural advantages for defence, was all assembled and ready to commence the perilous task of landing from vessels lying in the open sea.

The debarkation took place inside of the little island of Sacrificios, some three miles south of Vera Cruz. The vessels could not get anywhere near shore, so that everything had to be landed in lighters or surf-boats; General Scott had provided these before leaving the North. The breakers were sometimes high, so that the landing was tedious. The men were got ashore rapidly, because they could wade when they came to shallow water; but the camp and garrison equipage, provisions, ammunition and all stores had to be protected from the salt water, and therefore their landing took several days. The Mexicans were very kind to us, however, and threw no obstacles in the way of our landing except an occasional shot from their nearest fort. During the debarkation one shot took off the head of Major Albertis. No other, I believe, reached anywhere near the same distance. On the 9th of March the troops were landed and the investment of Vera Cruz, from the Gulf of Mexico south of the city to the Gulf again on the north, was soon and easily effected. The landing of stores was continued until everything was got ashore.

Vera Cruz, at the time of which I write and up to 1880, was a walled city. The wall extended from the water's edge south of the town to the water again on the north. There were fortifications at intervals along the line and at the angles. In front of the city, and on an island half a mile out in the Gulf, stands San Juan de Ulloa, an enclosed fortification of large dimensions and great strength for that period. Against artillery of the present day the land forts and walls would prove elements of weakness rather than strength. After the invading army had established their camps out of range of the fire from the city, batteries were established, under cover of night, far to the front of the line where the troops lay. These batteries were intrenched and the approaches sufficiently protected. If a sortie had been made at any time by the Mexicans, the men serving the batteries could have been quickly reinforced without great exposure to the fire from the enemy's main line. No serious attempt was made to capture the batteries or to drive our troops away.

The siege continued with brisk firing on our side till the 27th of March, by which time a considerable breach had been made in the wall surrounding the city. Upon this General Morales, who was Governor of both the city and of San Juan de Ulloa, commenced a correspondence with General Scott looking to the surrender of the town, forts and garrison. On the 29th Vera Cruz and San Juan de Ulloa were occupied by Scott's army. About five thousand prisoners and four hundred pieces of artillery, besides large amounts of small arms and ammunition, fell into the hands of the victorious force. The casualties on our side during the siege amounted to sixty-four officers and men, killed and wounded.

Chapter X.

MARCH TO JALAPA—BATTLE OF CERRO GORDO—
PEROTE—PUEBLA—SCOTT AND TAYLOR.

GENERAL SCOTT had less than twelve thousand men at
Vera Cruz. He had been promised by the administration a very much larger force, or claimed that he had, and he
was a man of veracity. Twelve thousand was a very small army
with which to penetrate two hundred and sixty miles into an
enemy's country, and to besiege the capital; a city, at that
time, of largely over one hundred thousand inhabitants.
Then, too, any line of march that could be selected led
through mountain passes easily defended. In fact, there were
at that time but two roads from Vera Cruz to the City of
Mexico that could be taken by an army; one by Jalapa and
Perote, the other by Cordova and Orizaba, the two coming
together on the great plain which extends to the City of Mexico after the range of mountains is passed.

It was very important to get the army away from Vera
Cruz as soon as possible, in order to avoid the yellow fever,
or vomito, which usually visits that city early in the year,
and is very fatal to persons not acclimated; but transportation, which was expected from the North, was arriving very
slowly. It was absolutely necessary to have enough to supply
the army to Jalapa, sixty-five miles in the interior and above
the fevers of the coast. At that point the country is fertile,
and an army of the size of General Scott's could subsist
there for an indefinite period. Not counting the sick, the
weak and the garrisons for the captured city and fort, the
moving column was now less than ten thousand strong. This
force was composed of three divisions, under Generals
Twiggs, Patterson, and Worth. The importance of escaping
the vomito was so great that as soon as transportation enough
could be got together to move a division the advance was
commenced. On the 8th of April, Twiggs's division started
for Jalapa. He was followed very soon by Patterson, with his
division. General Worth was to bring up the rear with his
command as soon as transportation enough was assembled to

carry six days' rations for his troops with the necessary ammunition and camp and garrison equipage. It was the 13th of April before this division left Vera Cruz.

The leading division ran against the enemy at Cerro Gordo, some fifty miles west, on the road to Jalapa, and went into camp at Plan del Rio, about three miles from the fortifications. General Patterson reached Plan del Rio with his division soon after Twiggs arrived. The two were then secure against an attack from Santa Anna, who commanded the Mexican forces. At all events they confronted the enemy without reinforcements and without molestation, until the 18th of April. General Scott had remained at Vera Cruz to hasten preparations for the field; but on the 12th, learning the situation at the front, he hastened on to take personal supervision. He at once commenced his preparations for the capture of the position held by Santa Anna and of the troops holding it.

Cerro Gordo is one of the higher spurs of the mountains some twelve to fifteen miles east of Jalapa, and Santa Anna had selected this point as the easiest to defend against an invading army. The road, said to have been built by Cortez, zigzags around the mountain-side and was defended at every turn by artillery. On either side were deep chasms or mountain walls. A direct attack along the road was an impossibility. A flank movement seemed equally impossible. After the arrival of the commanding-general upon the scene, reconnoissances were sent out to find, or to make, a road by which the rear of the enemy's works might be reached without a front attack. These reconnoissances were made under the supervision of Captain Robert E. Lee, assisted by Lieutenants P. G. T. Beauregard, Isaac I. Stevens, Z. B. Tower, G. W. Smith, George B. McClellan, and J. G. Foster, of the corps of engineers, all officers who attained rank and fame, on one side or the other, in the great conflict for the preservation of the unity of the nation. The reconnoissance was completed, and the labor of cutting out and making roads by the flank of the enemy was effected by the 17th of the month. This was accomplished without the knowledge of Santa Anna or his army, and over ground where he supposed it impossible. On the same day General Scott issued his order for the attack on the 18th.

The attack was made as ordered, and perhaps there was not a battle of the Mexican war, or of any other, where orders issued before an engagement were nearer being a correct report of what afterwards took place. Under the supervision of the engineers, roadways had been opened over chasms to the right where the walls were so steep that men could barely climb them. Animals could not. These had been opened under cover of night, without attracting the notice of the enemy. The engineers, who had directed the opening, led the way and the troops followed. Artillery was let down the steep slopes by hand, the men engaged attaching a strong rope to the rear axle and letting the guns down, a piece at a time, while the men at the ropes kept their ground on top, paying out gradually, while a few at the front directed the course of the piece. In like manner the guns were drawn by hand up the opposite slopes. In this way Scott's troops reached their assigned position in rear of most of the intrenchments of the enemy, unobserved. The attack was made, the Mexican reserves behind the works beat a hasty retreat, and those occupying them surrendered. On the left General Pillow's command made a formidable demonstration, which doubtless held a part of the enemy in his front and contributed to the victory. I am not pretending to give full details of all the battles fought, but of the portion that I saw. There were troops engaged on both sides at other points in which both sustained losses; but the battle was won as here narrated.

The surprise of the enemy was complete, the victory overwhelming; some three thousand prisoners fell into Scott's hands, also a large amount of ordnance and ordnance stores. The prisoners were paroled, the artillery parked and the small arms and ammunition destroyed. The battle of Buena Vista was probably very important to the success of General Scott at Cerro Gordo and in his entire campaign from Vera Cruz to the great plains reaching to the City of Mexico. The only army Santa Anna had to protect his capital and the mountain passes west of Vera Cruz, was the one he had with him confronting General Taylor. It is not likely that he would have gone as far north as Monterey to attack the United States troops when he knew his country was threatened with invasion further south. When Taylor moved to Saltillo and then advanced on to Buena Vista, Santa Anna crossed the desert confronting the invading army, hoping no doubt to crush it and get back in time to meet General Scott in the mountain passes west of Vera Cruz. His attack on Taylor was disastrous to the Mexican army, but, notwithstanding this, he marched his army to Cerro Gordo, a distance not much short of one thousand miles by the line he had to travel, in time to in-trench himself well before Scott got there. If he had been successful at Buena Vista his troops would no doubt have made a more stubborn resistance at Cerro Gordo. Had the battle of Buena Vista not been fought Santa Anna would have had time to move leisurely to meet the invader further south and with an army not demoralized nor depleted by defeat.

After the battle the victorious army moved on to Jalapa, where it was in a beautiful, productive and healthy country, far above the fevers of the coast. Jalapa, however, is still in the mountains, and between there and the great plain the whole line of the road is easy of defence. It was important, therefore, to get possession of the great highway between the sea-coast and the capital up to the point where it leaves the mountains, before the enemy could have time to re-organize and fortify in our front. Worth's division was selected to go forward to secure this result. The division marched to Perote on the great plain, not far from where the road debouches from the mountains. There is a low, strong fort on the plain in front of the town, known as the Castle of Perote. This, however, offered no resistance and fell into our hands, with its armament.

General Scott having now only nine or ten thousand men west of Vera Cruz, and the time of some four thousand of them being about to expire, a long delay was the conse-quence. The troops were in a healthy climate, and where they could subsist for an indefinite period even if their line back to Vera Cruz should be cut off. It being ascertained that the men whose time would expire before the City of Mexico could possibly fall into the hands of the American army, would not remain beyond the term for which they had volunteered, the commanding-general determined to discharge them at once, for a delay until the expiration of their time would have compelled them to pass through Vera Cruz during the season of the vomito. This reduced Scott's force in the field to about five thousand men.

Early in May, Worth, with his division, left Perote and marched on to Puebla. The roads were wide and the country open except through one pass in a spur of mountains coming up from the south, through which the road runs. Notwithstanding this the small column was divided into two bodies, moving a day apart. Nothing occurred on the march of special note, except that while lying at the town of Amozoque—an easy day's march east of Puebla—a body of the enemy's cavalry, two or three thousand strong, was seen to our right, not more than a mile away. A battery or two, with two or three infantry regiments, was sent against them and they soon disappeared. On the 15th of May we entered the city of Puebla.

General Worth was in command at Puebla until the latter end of May, when General Scott arrived. Here, as well as on the march up, his restlessness, particularly under responsibilities, showed itself. During his brief command he had the enemy hovering around near the city, in vastly superior numbers to his own. The brigade to which I was attached changed quarters three different times in about a week, occupying at first quarters near the plaza, in the heart of the city; then at the western entrance; then at the extreme east. On one occasion General Worth had the troops in line, under arms, all day, with three days' cooked rations in their haversacks. He galloped from one command to another proclaiming the near proximity of Santa Anna with an army vastly superior to his own. General Scott arrived upon the scene the latter part of the month, and nothing more was heard of Santa Anna and his myriads. There were, of course, bodies of mounted Mexicans hovering around to watch our movements and to pick up stragglers, or small bodies of troops, if they ventured too far out. These always withdrew on the approach of any considerable number of our soldiers. After the arrival of General Scott I was sent, as quartermaster, with a large train of wagons, back two days' march at least, to procure forage. We had less than a thousand men as escort, and never thought of danger. We procured full loads for our entire train at two plantations, which could easily have furnished as much more.

There had been great delay in obtaining the authority of Congress for the raising of the troops asked for by the administration. A bill was before the National Legislature from early in the session of 1846–7, authorizing the creation of ten additional regiments for the war to be attached to the regular army, but it was the middle of February before it became a law. Appointments of commissioned officers had then to be made; men had to be enlisted, the regiments equipped and the whole transported to Mexico. It was August before General Scott received reinforcement sufficient to warrant an advance. His moving column, not even now more than ten thousand strong, was in four divisions, commanded by Generals Twiggs, Worth, Pillow and Quitman. There was also a cavalry corps under General Harney, composed of detachments of the 1st, 2d, and 3d dragoons. The advance commenced on the 7th of August with Twiggs's division in front. The remaining three divisions followed, with an interval of a day between. The marches were short, to make concentration easier in case of attack.

I had now been in battle with the two leading commanders conducting armies in a foreign land. The contrast between the two was very marked. General Taylor never wore uniform, but dressed himself entirely for comfort. He moved about the field in which he was operating to see through his own eyes the situation. Often he would be without staff officers, and when he was accompanied by them there was no prescribed order in which they followed. He was very much given to sit his horse side-ways—with both feet on one side—particularly on the battle-field. General Scott was the reverse in all these particulars. He always wore all the uniform prescribed or allowed by law when he inspected his lines; word would be sent to all division and brigade commanders in advance, notifying them of the hour when the commanding general might be expected. This was done so that all the army might be under arms to salute their chief as he passed. On these occasions he wore his dress uniform, cocked hat, aiguillettes, sabre and spurs. His staff proper, besides all officers constructively on his staff—engineers, inspectors, quartermasters, etc., that could be spared—followed, also in uniform and in prescribed order. Orders were prepared with great care and evidently with the view that they should be a history of what followed.

In their modes of expressing thought, these two generals contrasted quite as strongly as in their other characteristics. General Scott was precise in language, cultivated a style peculiarly his own; was proud of his rhetoric; not averse to speaking of himself, often in the third person, and he could bestow praise upon the person he was talking about without the least embarrassment. Taylor was not a conversationalist, but on paper he could put his meaning so plainly that there could be no mistaking it. He knew how to express what he wanted to say in the fewest well-chosen words, but would not sacrifice meaning to the construction of high-sounding sentences. But with their opposite characteristics both were great and successful soldiers; both were true, patriotic and upright in all their dealings. Both were pleasant to serve under—Taylor was pleasant to serve with. Scott saw more through the eyes of his staff officers than through his own. His plans were deliberately prepared, and fully expressed in orders. Taylor saw for himself, and gave orders to meet the emergency without reference to how they would read in history.

Chapter XI.

ADVANCE ON THE CITY OF MEXICO — BATTLE OF
CONTRERAS — ASSAULT AT CHURUBUSCO — NEGOTIATIONS
FOR PEACE — BATTLE OF MOLINO DEL REY — STORMING
OF CHAPULTEPEC — SAN COSME — EVACUATION OF THE
CITY — HALLS OF THE MONTEZUMAS.

THE ROUTE followed by the army from Puebla to the
City of Mexico was over Rio Frio mountain, the road
leading over which, at the highest point, is about eleven
thousand feet above tide water. The pass through this mountain might have been easily defended, but it was not; and the
advanced division reached the summit in three days after
leaving Puebla. The City of Mexico lies west of Rio Frio
mountain, on a plain backed by another mountain six miles
farther west, with others still nearer on the north and south.
Between the western base of Rio Frio and the City of Mexico
there are three lakes, Chalco and Xochimilco on the left and
Texcoco on the right, extending to the east end of the City of
Mexico. Chalco and Texcoco are divided by a narrow strip of
land over which the direct road to the city runs. Xochimilco is
also to the left of the road, but at a considerable distance
south of it, and is connected with Lake Chalco by a narrow
channel. There is a high rocky mound, called El Peñon, on the
right of the road, springing up from the low flat ground dividing the lakes. This mound was strengthened by intrenchments at its base and summit, and rendered a direct attack
impracticable.

Scott's army was rapidly concentrated about Ayotla and
other points near the eastern end of Lake Chalco. Reconnoissances were made up to within gun-shot of El Peñon, while
engineers were seeking a route by the south side of Lake
Chalco to flank the city, and come upon it from the south and
south-west. A way was found around the lake, and by the 18th
of August troops were in St. Augustin Tlalpam, a town about
eleven miles due south from the plaza of the capital. Between
St. Augustin Tlalpam and the city lie the hacienda of San Antonio and the village of Churubusco, and south-west of them

is Contreras. All these points, except St. Augustin Tlalpam, were intrenched and strongly garrisoned. Contreras is situated on the side of a mountain, near its base, where volcanic rocks are piled in great confusion, reaching nearly to San Antonio. This made the approach to the city from the south very difficult.

The brigade to which I was attached—Garland's, of Worth's division—was sent to confront San Antonio, two or three miles from St. Augustin Tlalpam, on the road to Churubusco and the City of Mexico. The ground on which San Antonio stands is completely in the valley, and the surface of the land is only a little above the level of the lakes, and, except to the south-west, it was cut up by deep ditches filled with water. To the south-west is the Pedregal—the volcanic rock before spoken of—over which cavalry or artillery could not be passed, and infantry would make but poor progress if confronted by an enemy. From the position occupied by Garland's brigade, therefore, no movement could be made against the defences of San Antonio except to the front, and by a narrow causeway, over perfectly level ground, every inch of which was commanded by the enemy's artillery and infantry. If Contreras, some three miles west and south, should fall into our hands, troops from there could move to the right flank of all the positions held by the enemy between us and the city. Under these circumstances General Scott directed the holding of the front of the enemy without making an attack until further orders.

On the 18th of August, the day of reaching San Augustin Tlalpam, Garland's brigade secured a position within easy range of the advanced intrenchments of San Antonio, but where his troops were protected by an artificial embankment that had been thrown up for some other purpose than defence. General Scott at once set his engineers reconnoitring the works about Contreras, and on the 19th movements were commenced to get troops into positions from which an assault could be made upon the force occupying that place. The Pedregal on the north and north-east, and the mountain on the south, made the passage by either flank of the enemy's defences difficult, for their work stood exactly between those natural bulwarks; but a road was completed during the day and night of the 19th, and troops were got to the north and west of the enemy.

This affair, like that of Cerro Gordo, was an engagement in which the officers of the engineer corps won special distinction. In fact, in both cases, tasks which seemed difficult at first sight were made easier for the troops that had to execute them than they would have been on an ordinary field. The very strength of each of these positions was, by the skill of the engineers, converted into a defence for the assaulting parties while securing their positions for final attack. All the troops with General Scott in the valley of Mexico, except a part of the division of General Quitman at San Augustin Tlalpam and the brigade of Garland (Worth's division) at San Antonio, were engaged at the battle of Contreras, or were on their way, in obedience to the orders of their chief, to reinforce those who were engaged. The assault was made on the morning of the 20th, and in less than half an hour from the sound of the advance the position was in our hands, with many prisoners and large quantities of ordnance and other stores. The brigade commanded by General Riley was from its position the most conspicuous in the final assault, but all did well, volunteers and regulars.

From the point occupied by Garland's brigade we could see the progress made at Contreras and the movement of troops toward the flank and rear of the enemy opposing us. The Mexicans all the way back to the city could see the same thing, and their conduct showed plainly that they did not enjoy the sight. We moved out at once, and found them gone from our immediate front. Clarke's brigade of Worth's division now moved west over the point of the Pedregal, and after having passed to the north sufficiently to clear San Antonio, turned east and got on the causeway leading to Churubusco and the City of Mexico. When he approached Churubusco his left, under Colonel Hoffman, attacked a tête-de-pont at that place and brought on an engagement. About an hour after, Garland was ordered to advance directly along the causeway, and got up in time to take part in the engagement. San Antonio was found evacuated, the evacuation having probably taken place immediately upon the enemy seeing the stars and stripes waving over Contreras.

The troops that had been engaged at Contreras, and even then on their way to that battle-field, were moved by a causeway west of, and parallel to the one by way of San Antonio and Churubusco. It was expected by the commanding general that these troops would move north sufficiently far to flank the enemy out of his position at Churubusco, before turning east to reach the San Antonio road, but they did not succeed in this, and Churubusco proved to be about the severest battle fought in the valley of Mexico. General Scott coming upon the battle-field about this juncture, ordered two brigades, under Shields, to move north and turn the right of the enemy. This Shields did, but not without hard fighting and heavy loss. The enemy finally gave way, leaving in our hands prisoners, artillery and small arms. The balance of the causeway held by the enemy, up to the very gates of the city, fell in like manner. I recollect at this place that some of the gunners who had stood their ground, were deserters from General Taylor's army on the Rio Grande.

Both the strategy and tactics displayed by General Scott in these various engagements of the 20th of August, 1847, were faultless as I look upon them now, after the lapse of so many years. As before stated, the work of the engineer officers who made the reconnoissances and led the different commands to their destinations, was so perfect that the chief was able to give his orders to his various subordinates with all the precision he could use on an ordinary march. I mean, up to the points from which the attack was to commence. After that point is reached the enemy often induces a change of orders not before contemplated. The enemy outside the city outnumbered our soldiery quite three to one, but they had become so demoralized by the succession of defeats this day, that the City of Mexico could have been entered without much further bloodshed. In fact, Captain Philip Kearney — afterwards a general in the war of the rebellion — rode with a squadron of cavalry to the very gates of the city, and would no doubt have entered with his little force, only at that point he was badly wounded, as were several of his officers. He had not heard the call for a halt.

General Franklin Pierce had joined the army in Mexico, at Puebla, a short time before the advance upon the capital commenced. He had consequently not been in any of the engagements of the war up to the battle of Contreras. By an unfortunate fall of his horse on the afternoon of the 19th he was painfully injured. The next day, when his brigade, with the other troops engaged on the same field, was ordered against the flank and rear of the enemy guarding the different points of the road from San Augustin Tlalpam to the city, General Pierce attempted to accompany them. He was not sufficiently recovered to do so, and fainted. This circumstance gave rise to exceedingly unfair and unjust criticisms of him when he became a candidate for the Presidency. Whatever General Pierce's qualifications may have been for the Presidency, he was a gentleman and a man of courage. I was not a supporter of him politically, but I knew him more intimately than I did any other of the volunteer generals.

General Scott abstained from entering the city at this time, because Mr. Nicholas P. Trist, the commissioner on the part of the United States to negotiate a treaty of peace with Mexico, was with the army, and either he or General Scott thought—probably both of them—that a treaty would be more possible while the Mexican government was in possession of the capital than if it was scattered and the capital in the hands of an invader. Be this as it may, we did not enter at that time. The army took up positions along the slopes of the mountains south of the city, as far west as Tacubaya. Negotiations were at once entered into with Santa Anna, who was then practically *the Government* and the immediate commander of all the troops engaged in defence of the country. A truce was signed which denied to either party the right to strengthen its position, or to receive reinforcements during the continuance of the armistices, but authorized General Scott to draw supplies for his army from the city in the meantime.

Negotiations were commenced at once and were kept up vigorously, between Mr. Trist and the commissioners appointed on the part of Mexico, until the 2d of September. At that time Mr. Trist handed in his ultimatum. Texas was to be given up absolutely by Mexico, and New Mexico and California ceded to the United States for a stipulated sum to be afterwards determined. I do not suppose Mr. Trist had any discretion whatever in regard to boundaries. The war was one of conquest, in the interest of an institution, and the probabilities are that private instructions were for the acquisition of territory out of which new States might be carved. At all events the Mexicans felt so outraged at the terms proposed that they commenced preparations for defence, without giving notice of the termination of the armistice. The terms of the truce had been violated before, when teams had been sent into the city to bring out supplies for the army. The first train entering the city was very severely threatened by a mob. This, however, was apologized for by the authorities and all responsibility for it denied; and thereafter, to avoid exciting the Mexican people and soldiery, our teams with their escorts were sent in at night, when the troops were in barracks and the citizens in bed. The circumstance was overlooked and negotiations continued. As soon as the news reached General Scott of the second violation of the armistice, about the 4th of September, he wrote a vigorous note to President Santa Anna, calling his attention to it, and, receiving an unsatisfactory reply, declared the armistice at an end.

General Scott, with Worth's division, was now occupying Tacubaya, a village some four miles south-west of the City of Mexico, and extending from the base up the mountain-side for the distance of half a mile. More than a mile west, and also a little above the plain, stands Molino del Rey. The mill is a long stone structure, one story high and several hundred feet in length. At the period of which I speak General Scott supposed a portion of the mill to be used as a foundry for the casting of guns. This, however, proved to be a mistake. It was valuable to the Mexicans because of the quantity of grain it contained. The building is flat roofed, and a line of sand-bags over the outer walls rendered the top quite a formidable defence for infantry. Chapultepec is a mound springing up from the plain to the height of probably three hundred feet, and almost in a direct line between Molino del Rey and the western part of the city. It was fortified both on the top and on the rocky and precipitous sides.

The City of Mexico is supplied with water by two aqueducts, resting on strong stone arches. One of these aqueducts draws its supply of water from a mountain stream coming into it at or near Molino del Rey, and runs north close to the west base of Chapultepec; thence along the centre of a wide road, until it reaches the road running east into the city by the Garita San Cosme; from which point the aqueduct and road both run east to the city. The second aqueduct starts from the east base of Chapultepec, where it is fed by a spring, and runs north-east to the city. This aqueduct, like the other, runs in the middle of a broad road-way, thus leaving a space on each side. The arches supporting the aqueduct afforded protection for advancing troops as well as to those engaged defensively. At points on the San Cosme road parapets were thrown across, with an embrasure for a single piece of artillery in each. At the point where both road and aqueduct turn at right angles from north to east, there was not only one of these parapets supplied by one gun and infantry supports, but the houses to the north of the San Cosme road, facing south and commanding a view of the road back to Chapultepec, were covered with infantry, protected by parapets made of sand-bags. The roads leading to garitas (the gates) San Cosme and Belen, by which these aqueducts enter the city, were strongly intrenched. Deep, wide ditches, filled with water, lined the sides of both roads. Such were the defences of the City of Mexico in September, 1847, on the routes over which General Scott entered.

Prior to the Mexican war General Scott had been very partial to General Worth—indeed he continued so up to the close of hostilities—but, for some reason, Worth had become estranged from his chief. Scott evidently took this coldness somewhat to heart. He did not retaliate, however, but on the contrary showed every disposition to appease his subordinate. It was understood at the time that he gave Worth authority to plan and execute the battle of Molino del Rey without dictation or interference from any one, for the very purpose of restoring their former relations. The effort failed, and the two generals remained ever after cold and indifferent towards each other, if not actually hostile.

The battle of Molino del Rey was fought on the 8th of September. The night of the 7th, Worth sent for his brigade and regimental commanders, with their staffs, to come to his quarters to receive instructions for the morrow. These orders contemplated a movement up to within striking distance of the Mills before daylight. The engineers had reconnoitred the ground as well as possible, and had acquired all the information necessary to base proper orders both for approach and attack.

By daylight on the morning of the 8th, the troops to be engaged at Molino were all at the places designated. The ground in front of the Mills, to the south, was commanded by the artillery from the summit of Chapultepec as well as by the lighter batteries at hand; but a charge was made, and soon all was over. Worth's troops entered the Mills by every door, and the enemy beat a hasty retreat back to Chapultepec. Had this victory been followed up promptly, no doubt Americans and Mexicans would have gone over the defences of Chapultepec so near together that the place would have fallen into our hands without further loss. The defenders of the works could not have fired upon us without endangering their own men. This was not done, and five days later more valuable lives were sacrificed to carry works which had been so nearly in our possession on the 8th. I do not criticise the failure to capture Chapultepec at this time. The result that followed the first assault could not possibly have been foreseen, and to profit by the unexpected advantage, the commanding general must have been on the spot and given the necessary instructions at the moment, or the troops must have kept on without orders. It is always, however, in order to follow a retreating foe, unless stopped or otherwise directed. The loss on our side at Molino del Rey was severe for the numbers engaged. It was especially so among commissioned officers.

I was with the earliest of the troops to enter the Mills. In passing through to the north side, looking towards Chapultepec, I happened to notice that there were armed Mexicans still on top of the building, only a few feet from many of our men. Not seeing any stairway or ladder reaching to the top of the building, I took a few soldiers, and had a cart that happened to be standing near brought up, and, placing the shafts against the wall and chocking the wheels so that the cart could not back, used the shafts as a sort of ladder extending to within three or four feet of the top. By this I climbed to the roof of the building, followed by a few men, but found a private soldier had preceded me by some other way. There were still quite a number of Mexicans on the roof, among them a major and five or six officers of lower grades, who had not succeeded in getting away before our troops occupied the building. They still had their arms, while the soldier before mentioned was walking as sentry, guarding the prisoners he had *surrounded*, all by himself. I halted the sentinel, received the swords from the commissioned officers, and proceeded, with the assistance of the soldiers now with me, to disable the muskets by striking them against the edge of the wall, and throw them to the ground below.

Molino del Rey was now captured, and the troops engaged, with the exception of an appropriate guard over the captured position and property, were marched back to their quarters in Tacubaya. The engagement did not last many minutes, but the killed and wounded were numerous for the number of troops engaged.

During the night of the 11th batteries were established which could play upon the fortifications of Chapultepec. The bombardment commenced early on the morning of the 12th, but there was no further engagement during this day than that of the artillery. General Scott assigned the capture of Chapultepec to General Pillow, but did not leave the details to his judgment. Two assaulting columns, two hundred and fifty men each, composed of volunteers for the occasion, were formed. They were commanded by Captains McKinzie and Casey respectively. The assault was successful, but bloody.

In later years, if not at the time, the battles of Molino del Rey and Chapultepec have seemed to me to have been wholly unnecessary. When the assaults upon the garitas of San Cosme and Belen were determined upon, the road running east to the former gate could have been reached easily, without an engagement, by moving along south of the Mills until west of them sufficiently far to be out of range, thence north to the road above mentioned; or, if desirable to keep the two attacking columns nearer together, the troops could have been turned east so as to come on the aqueduct road out of range of the guns from Chapultepec. In like manner, the troops designated to act against Belen could have kept east of

Chapultepec, out of range, and come on to the aqueduct, also out of range of Chapultepec. Molino del Rey and Chapultepec would both have been necessarily evacuated if this course had been pursued, for they would have been turned.

General Quitman, a volunteer from the State of Mississippi, who stood well with the army both as a soldier and as a man, commanded the column acting against Belen. General Worth commanded the column against San Cosme. When Chapultepec fell the advance commenced along the two aqueduct roads. I was on the road to San Cosme, and witnessed most that took place on that route. When opposition was encountered our troops sheltered themselves by keeping under the arches supporting the aqueduct, advancing an arch at a time. We encountered no serious obstruction until within gun-shot of the point where the road we were on intersects that running east to the city, the point where the aqueduct turns at a right angle. I have described the defences of this position before. There were but three commissioned officers besides myself, that I can now call to mind, with the advance when the above position was reached. One of these officers was a Lieutenant Semmes, of the Marine Corps. I think Captain Gore, and Lieutenant Judah, of the 4th infantry, were the others. Our progress was stopped for the time by the single piece of artillery at the angle of the roads and the infantry occupying the house-tops back from it.

West of the road from where we were, stood a house occupying the south-west angle made by the San Cosme road and the road we were moving upon. A stone wall ran from the house along each of these roads for a considerable distance and thence back until it joined, enclosing quite a yard about the house. I watched my opportunity and skipped across the road and behind the south wall. Proceeding cautiously to the west corner of the enclosure, I peeped around and seeing nobody, continued, still cautiously, until the road running east and west was reached. I then returned to the troops, and called for volunteers. All that were close to me, or that heard me, about a dozen, offered their services. Commanding them to carry their arms at a trail, I watched our opportunity and got them across the road and under cover of the wall beyond, before the enemy had a shot at us. Our men under cover of the arches kept a close watch on the intrenchments that crossed our path and the house-tops beyond, and whenever a head showed itself above the parapets they would fire at it. Our crossing was thus made practicable without loss.

When we reached a safe position I instructed my little command again to carry their arms at a trail, not to fire at the enemy until they were ordered, and to move very cautiously following me until the San Cosme road was reached; we would then be on the flank of the men serving the gun on the road, and with no obstruction between us and them. When we reached the south-west corner of the enclosure before described, I saw some United States troops pushing north through a shallow ditch near by, who had come up since my reconnaissance. This was the company of Captain Horace Brooks, of the artillery, acting as infantry. I explained to Brooks briefly what I had discovered and what I was about to do. He said, as I knew the ground and he did not, I might go on and he would follow. As soon as we got on the road leading to the city the troops serving the gun on the parapet retreated, and those on the house-tops near by followed; our men went after them in such close pursuit—the troops we had left under the arches joining—that a second line across the road, about half-way between the first and the garita, was carried. No reinforcements had yet come up except Brooks's company, and the position we had taken was too advanced to be held by so small a force. It was given up, but retaken later in the day, with some loss.

Worth's command gradually advanced to the front now open to it. Later in the day in reconnoitring I found a church off to the south of the road, which looked to me as if the belfry would command the ground back of the garita San Cosme. I got an officer of the voltigeurs, with a mountain howitzer and men to work it, to go with me. The road being in possession of the enemy, we had to take the field to the south to reach the church. This took us over several ditches breast deep in water and grown up with water plants. These ditches, however, were not over eight or ten feet in width. The howitzer was taken to pieces and carried by the men to its destination. When I knocked for admission a priest came to the door, who, while extremely polite, declined to admit

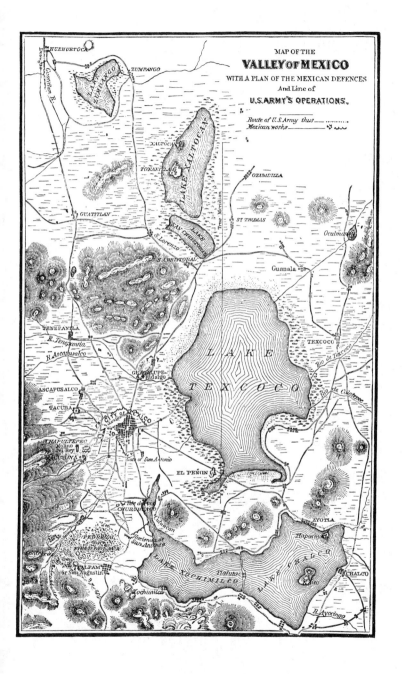

MAP OF THE
VALLEY of MEXICO
WITH A PLAN OF THE MEXICAN DEFENCES
And Line of
U.S.ARMY'S OPERATIONS.

Route of U.S.Army thus _____
Mexican works _____

us. With the little Spanish then at my command, I explained
to him that he might save property by opening the door, and
he certainly would save himself from becoming a prisoner, for
a time at least; and besides, I intended to go in whether he
consented or not. He began to see his duty in the same light
that I did, and opened the door, though he did not look as if
it gave him special pleasure to do so. The gun was carried to
the belfry and put together. We were not more than two or
three hundred yards from San Cosme. The shots from our
little gun dropped in upon the enemy and created great confusion. Why they did not send out a small party and capture
us, I do not know. We had no infantry or other defences besides our one gun.

The effect of this gun upon the troops about the gate of the
city was so marked that General Worth saw it from his
position.* He was so pleased that he sent a staff officer, Lieutenant Pemberton—later Lieutenant-General commanding
the defences of Vicksburg—to bring me to him. He expressed his gratification at the services the howitzer in the
church steeple was doing, saying that every shot was effective,
and ordered a captain of voltigeurs to report to me with another howitzer to be placed along with the one already rendering so much service. I could not tell the General that there
was not room enough in the steeple for another gun, because
he probably would have looked upon such a statement as a
contradiction from a second lieutenant. I took the captain
with me, but did not use his gun.

The night of the 13th of September was spent by the troops
under General Worth in the houses near San Cosme, and in
line confronting the general line of the enemy across to Belen.
The troops that I was with were in the houses north of the
road leading into the city, and were engaged during the night
in cutting passage-ways from one house to another towards
the town. During the night Santa Anna, with his army—except the deserters—left the city. He liberated all the convicts
confined in the town, hoping, no doubt, that they would inflict upon us some injury before daylight; but several hours

---

*Mentioned in the reports of Major Lee, Colonel Garland and General
Worth.—Publishers.

after Santa Anna was out of the way, the city authorities sent a delegation to General Scott to ask—if not demand—an armistice, respecting church property, the rights of citizens and the supremacy of the city government in the management of municipal affairs. General Scott declined to trammel himself with conditions, but gave assurances that those who chose to remain within our lines would be protected so long as they behaved themselves properly.

General Quitman had advanced along his line very successfully on the 13th, so that at night his command occupied nearly the same position at Belen that Worth's troops did about San Cosme. After the interview above related between General Scott and the city council, orders were issued for the cautious entry of both columns in the morning. The troops under Worth were to stop at the Alameda, a park near the west end of the city. Quitman was to go directly to the Plaza, and take possession of the Palace—a mass of buildings on the east side in which Congress has its sessions, the national courts are held, the public offices are all located, the President resides, and much room is left for museums, receptions, etc. This is the building generally designated as the "Halls of the Montezumas."

Chapter XII.

O N ENTERING the city the troops were fired upon by the
released convicts, and possibly by deserters and hostile
citizens. The streets were deserted, and the place presented
the appearance of a "city of the dead," except for this firing by
unseen persons from house-tops, windows, and around corners. In this firing the lieutenant-colonel of my regiment, Garland, was badly wounded, Lieutenant Sidney Smith, of the
4th infantry, was also wounded mortally. He died a few days
after, and by his death I was promoted to the grade of first
lieutenant. I had gone into the battle of Palo Alto in May,
1846, a second lieutenant, and I entered the city of Mexico
sixteen months later with the same rank, after having been in
all the engagements possible for any one man and in a regiment that lost more officers during the war than it ever had
present at any one engagement. My regiment lost four commissioned officers, all senior to me, by steamboat explosions
during the Mexican war. The Mexicans were not so discriminating. They sometimes picked off my juniors.

General Scott soon followed the troops into the city, in
state. I wonder that he was not fired upon, but I believe he
was not; at all events he was not hurt. He took quarters at
first in the "Halls of the Montezumas," and from there issued
his wise and discreet orders for the government of a conquered city, and for suppressing the hostile acts of liberated

---

NOTE.—It had been a favorite idea with General Scott for a great many
years before the Mexican war to have established in the United States a soldiers' home, patterned after something of the kind abroad, particularly, I
believe, in France. He recommended this uniformly, or at least frequently, in
his annual reports to the Secretary of War, but never got any hearing. Now,
as he had conquered the state, he made assessments upon the different large
towns and cities occupied by our troops, in proportion to their capacity to
pay, and appointed officers to receive the money. In addition to the sum thus
realized he had derived, through capture at Cerro Gordo, sales of captured

convicts already spoken of—orders which challenge the respect of all who study them. Lawlessness was soon suppressed, and the City of Mexico settled down into a quiet, law-abiding place. The people began to make their appearance upon the streets without fear of the invaders. Shortly afterwards the bulk of the troops were sent from the city to the villages at the foot of the mountains, four or five miles to the south and south-west.

Whether General Scott approved of the Mexican war and the manner in which it was brought about, I have no means of knowing. His orders to troops indicate only a soldierly spirit, with probably a little regard for the perpetuation of his own fame. On the other hand, General Taylor's, I think, indicate that he considered the administration accountable for the war, and felt no responsibility resting on himself further than for the faithful performance of his duties. Both generals deserve the commendations of their countrymen and to live in the grateful memory of this people to the latest generation.

Earlier in this narrative I have stated that the plain, reached after passing the mountains east of Perote, extends to the cities of Puebla and Mexico. The route travelled by the army before reaching Puebla, goes over a pass in a spur of mountain coming up from the south. This pass is very susceptible of defence by a smaller against a larger force. Again, the highest point of the road-bed between Vera Cruz and the City of Mexico is over Rio Frio mountain, which also might have been successfully defended by an inferior against a superior force. But by moving north of the mountains, and about thirty miles north of Puebla, both of these passes would have been avoided. The road from Perote to the City of Mexico, by

government tobacco, etc., sums which swelled the fund to a total of about $220,000. Portions of this fund were distributed among the rank and file, given to the wounded in hospital, or applied in other ways, leaving a balance of some $118,000 remaining unapplied at the close of the war. After the war was over and the troops all home, General Scott applied to have this money, which had never been turned into the Treasury of the United States, expended in establishing such homes as he had previously recommended. This fund was the foundation of the Soldiers' Home at Washington City, and also one at Harrodsburgh, Kentucky.

The latter went into disuse many years ago. In fact it never had many soldiers in it, and was, I believe, finally sold.

this latter route, is as level as the prairies in our West. Arriving due north from Puebla, troops could have been detached to take possession of that place, and then proceeding west with the rest of the army no mountain would have been encountered before reaching the City of Mexico. It is true this road would have brought troops in by Guadalupe—a town, church and detached spur of mountain about two miles north of the capital, all bearing the same general name—and at this point Lake Texcoco comes near to the mountain, which was fortified both at the base and on the sides: but troops could have passed north of the mountain and come in only a few miles to the north-west, and so flanked the position, as they actually did on the south.

It has always seemed to me that this northern route to the City of Mexico, would have been the better one to have taken. But my later experience has taught me two lessons: first, that things are seen plainer after the events have occurred; second, that the most confident critics are generally those who know the least about the matter criticised. I know just enough about the Mexican war to approve heartily of most of the generalship, but to differ with a little of it. It is natural that an important city like Puebla should not have been passed with contempt; it may be natural that the direct road to it should have been taken; but it could have been passed, its evacuation insured and possession acquired without danger of encountering the enemy in intricate mountain defiles. In this same way the City of Mexico could have been approached without any danger of opposition, except in the open field.

But General Scott's successes are an answer to all criticism. He invaded a populous country, penetrating two hundred and sixty miles into the interior, with a force at no time equal to one-half of that opposed to him; he was without a base; the enemy was always intrenched, always on the defensive; yet he won every battle, he captured the capital, and conquered the government. Credit is due to the troops engaged, it is true, but the plans and the strategy were the general's.

I had now made marches and been in battle under both General Scott and General Taylor. The former divided his force of 10,500 men into four columns, starting a day apart, in

moving from Puebla to the capital of the nation, when it was
known that an army more than twice as large as his own
stood ready to resist his coming. The road was broad and the
country open except in crossing the Rio Frio mountain. General Taylor pursued the same course in marching toward an
enemy. He moved even in smaller bodies. I never thought at
the time to doubt the infallibility of these two generals in all
matters pertaining to their profession. I supposed they moved
in small bodies because more men could not be passed over a
single road on the same day with their artillery and necessary
trains. Later I found the fallacy of this belief. The rebellion,
which followed as a sequence to the Mexican war, never could
have been suppressed if larger bodies of men could not have
been moved at the same time than was the custom under
Scott and Taylor.

The victories in Mexico were, in every instance, over vastly
superior numbers. There were two reasons for this. Both
General Scott and General Taylor had such armies as are not
often got together. At the battles of Palo Alto and Resaca-de-
la-Palma, General Taylor had a small army, but it was composed exclusively of regular troops, under the best of drill and
discipline. Every officer, from the highest to the lowest, was
educated in his profession, not at West Point necessarily, but
in the camp, in garrison, and many of them in Indian wars.
The rank and file were probably inferior, as material out of
which to make an army, to the volunteers that participated in
all the later battles of the war; but they were brave men, and
then drill and discipline brought out all there was in them. A
better army, man for man, probably never faced an enemy
than the one commanded by General Taylor in the earliest
two engagements of the Mexican war. The volunteers who
followed were of better material, but without drill or discipline at the start. They were associated with so many disciplined men and professionally educated officers, that when
they went into engagements it was with a confidence they
would not have felt otherwise. They became soldiers themselves almost at once. All these conditions we would enjoy
again in case of war.

The Mexican army of that day was hardly an organization.
The private soldier was picked up from the lower class of the

inhabitants when wanted; his consent was not asked; he was poorly clothed, worse fed, and seldom paid. He was turned adrift when no longer wanted. The officers of the lower grades were but little superior to the men. With all this I have seen as brave stands made by some of these men as I have ever seen made by soldiers. Now Mexico has a standing army larger than that of the United States. They have a military school modelled after West Point. Their officers are educated and, no doubt, generally brave. The Mexican war of 1846–8 would be an impossibility in this generation.

The Mexicans have shown a patriotism which it would be well if we would imitate in part, but with more regard to truth. They celebrate the anniversaries of Chapultepec and Molino del Rey as of very great victories. The anniversaries are recognized as national holidays. At these two battles, while the United States troops were victorious, it was at very great sacrifice of life compared with what the Mexicans suffered. The Mexicans, as on many other occasions, stood up as well as any troops ever did. The trouble seemed to be the lack of experience among the officers, which led them after a certain time to simply quit, without being particularly whipped, but because they had fought enough. Their authorities of the present day grow enthusiastic over their theme when telling of these victories, and speak with pride of the large sum of money they forced us to pay in the end. With us, now twenty years after the close of the most stupendous war ever known, we have writers—who profess devotion to the nation—engaged in trying to prove that the Union forces were not victorious; practically, they say, we were slashed around from Donelson to Vicksburg and to Chattanooga; and in the East from Gettysburg to Appomattox, when the physical rebellion gave out from sheer exhaustion. There is no difference in the amount of romance in the two stories.

I would not have the anniversaries of our victories celebrated, nor those of our defeats made fast days and spent in humiliation and prayer; but I would like to see truthful history written. Such history will do full credit to the courage, endurance and soldierly ability of the American citizen, no matter what section of the country he hailed from, or in what ranks he fought. The justice of the cause which in the end prevailed, will, I doubt not, come to be acknowledged by every citizen of the land, in time. For the present, and so long as there are living witnesses of the great war of sections, there will be people who will not be consoled for the loss of a cause which they believed to be holy. As time passes, people, even of the South, will begin to wonder how it was possible that their ancestors ever fought for or justified institutions which acknowledged the right of property in man.

After the fall of the capital and the dispersal of the government of Mexico, it looked very much as if military occupation of the country for a long time might be necessary. General Scott at once began the preparation of orders, regulations and laws in view of this contingency. He contemplated making the country pay all the expenses of the occupation, without the army becoming a perceptible burden upon the people. His plan was to levy a direct tax upon the separate states, and collect, at the ports left open to trade, a duty on all imports. From the beginning of the war private property had not been taken, either for the use of the army or of individuals, without full compensation. This policy was to be pursued. There were not troops enough in the valley of Mexico to occupy many points, but now that there was no organized army of the enemy of any size, reinforcements could be got from the Rio Grande, and there were also new volunteers arriving from time to time, all by way of Vera Cruz. Military possession was taken of Cuernavaca, fifty miles south of the City of Mexico; of Toluca, nearly as far west, and of Pachuca, a mining town of great importance, some sixty miles to the northeast. Vera Cruz, Jalapa, Orizaba, and Puebla were already in our possession.

Meanwhile the Mexican government had departed in the person of Santa Anna, and it looked doubtful for a time whether the United States commissioner, Mr. Trist, would find anybody to negotiate with. A temporary government, however, was soon established at Queretaro, and Trist began negotiations for a conclusion of the war. Before terms were finally agreed upon he was ordered back to Washington, but General Scott prevailed upon him to remain, as an arrangement had been so nearly reached, and the administration must approve his acts if he succeeded in making such a treaty as had been contemplated in his instructions. The treaty was finally signed the 2d of February, 1848, and accepted by the government at Washington. It is that known as the "Treaty of Guadalupe Hidalgo," and secured to the United States the Rio Grande as the boundary of Texas, and the whole territory then included in New Mexico and Upper California, for the sum of $15,000,000.

Soon after entering the city of Mexico, the opposition of Generals Pillow, Worth and Colonel Duncan to General Scott became very marked. Scott claimed that they had demanded of the President his removal. I do not know whether this is so or not, but I do know of their unconcealed hostility to their chief. At last he placed them in arrest, and preferred charges against them of insubordination and disrespect. This act brought on a crisis in the career of the general commanding. He had asserted from the beginning that the administration was hostile to him; that it had failed in its promises of men and war material; that the President himself had shown duplicity if not treachery in the endeavor to procure the appointment of Benton: and the administration now gave open evidence of its enmity. About the middle of February orders came convening a court of inquiry, composed of Brevet Brigadier-General Towson, the paymaster-general of the army, Brigadier-General Cushing and Colonel Belknap, to inquire into the conduct of the accused and the accuser, and shortly afterwards orders were received from Washington, relieving Scott of the command of the army in the field and assigning Major-General William O. Butler of Kentucky to the place. This order also released Pillow, Worth and Duncan from arrest.

If a change was to be made the selection of General Butler was agreeable to every one concerned, so far as I remember to have heard expressions on the subject. There were many who regarded the treatment of General Scott as harsh and unjust. It is quite possible that the vanity of the General had led him to say and do things that afforded a plausible pretext to the administration for doing just what it did and what it had wanted to do from the start. The court tried the accuser quite as much as the accused. It was adjourned before completing its labors, to meet in Frederick, Maryland. General Scott left the country, and never after had more than the nominal command of the army until early in 1861. He certainly was not sustained in his efforts to maintain discipline in high places.

The efforts to kill off politically the two successful generals, made them both candidates for the Presidency. General Taylor was nominated in 1848, and was elected. Four years later General Scott received the nomination but was badly beaten, and the party nominating him died with his defeat.*

---

*The Mexican war made three presidential candidates, Scott, Taylor and Pierce—and any number of aspirants for that high office. It made also governors of States, members of the cabinet, foreign ministers and other officers of high rank both in state and nation. The rebellion, which contained more war in a single day, at some critical periods, than the whole Mexican war in two years, has not been so fruitful of political results to those engaged on the Union side. On the other side, the side of the South, nearly every man who holds office of any sort whatever, either in the state or in the nation, was a Confederate soldier; but this is easily accounted for from the fact that the South was a military camp, and there were very few people of a suitable age to be in the army who were not in it.

Chapter XIII.

TREATY OF PEACE—MEXICAN BULL FIGHTS—
REGIMENTAL QUARTERMASTER—TRIP TO POPOCATAPETL
—TRIP TO THE CAVES OF MEXICO.

THE TREATY OF PEACE between the two countries was signed by the commissioners of each side early in February, 1848. It took a considerable time for it to reach Washington, receive the approval of the administration, and be finally ratified by the Senate. It was naturally supposed by the army that there would be no more fighting, and officers and men were of course anxious to get home, but knowing there must be delay they contented themselves as best they could. Every Sunday there was a bull fight for the amusement of those who would pay their fifty cents. I attended one of them—just one—not wishing to leave the country without having witnessed the national sport. The sight to me was sickening. I could not see how human beings could enjoy the sufferings of beasts, and often of men, as they seemed to do on these occasions.

At these sports there are usually from four to six bulls sacrificed. The audience occupies seats around the ring in which the exhibition is given, each seat but the foremost rising higher than the one in front, so that every one can get a full view of the sport. When all is ready a bull is turned into the ring. Three or four men come in, mounted on the merest skeletons of horses blind or blind-folded and so weak that they could not make a sudden turn with their riders without danger of falling down. The men are armed with spears having a point as sharp as a needle. Other men enter the arena on foot, armed with red flags and explosives about the size of a musket cartridge. To each of these explosives is fastened a barbed needle which serves the purpose of attaching them to the bull by running the needle into the skin. Before the animal is turned loose a lot of these explosives are attached to him. The pain from the pricking of the skin by the needles is exasperating; but when the explosions of the cartridges commence the animal becomes frantic. As he makes a lunge towards one horseman, another runs a spear into him. He turns towards his last tormentor when a man on foot holds out a red flag; the bull rushes for this and is allowed to take it on his horns. The flag drops and covers the eyes of the animal so that he is at a loss what to do; it is jerked from him and the torment is renewed. When the animal is worked into an uncontrollable frenzy, the horsemen withdraw, and the matadores—literally murderers—enter, armed with knives having blades twelve or eighteen inches long, and sharp. The trick is to dodge an attack from the animal and stab him to the heart as he passes. If these efforts fail the bull is finally lassoed, held fast and killed by driving a knife blade into the spinal column just back of the horns. He is then dragged out by horses or mules, another is let into the ring, and the same performance is renewed.

On the occasion when I was present one of the bulls was not turned aside by the attacks in the rear, the presentations of the red flag, etc., etc., but kept right on, and placing his horns under the flanks of a horse threw him and his rider to the ground with great force. The horse was killed and the rider lay prostrate as if dead. The bull was then lassoed and killed in the manner above described. Men came in and carried the dead man off in a litter. When the slaughtered bull and horse were dragged out, a fresh bull was turned into the ring. Conspicuous among the spectators was the man who had been carried out on a litter but a few minutes before. He was only dead so far as that performance went; but the corpse was so lively that it could not forego the chance of witnessing the discomfiture of some of his brethren who might not be so fortunate. There was a feeling of disgust manifested by the audience to find that he had come to life again. I confess that I felt sorry to see the cruelty to the bull and the horse. I did not stay for the conclusion of the performance; but while I did stay, there was not a bull killed in the prescribed way.

Bull fights are now prohibited in the Federal District—embracing a territory around the City of Mexico, somewhat larger than the District of Columbia—and they are not an institution in any part of the country. During one of my recent visits to Mexico, bull fights were got up in my honor at Puebla and at Pachuca. I was not notified in advance so as to be able to decline and thus prevent the performance; but in both cases I civilly declined to attend.

Another amusement of the people of Mexico of that day, and one which nearly all indulged in, male and female, old and young, priest and layman, was Monte playing. Regular feast weeks were held every year at what was then known as St. Augustin Tlalpam, eleven miles out of town. There were dealers to suit every class and condition of people. In many of the booths *tlacos*—the copper coin of the country, four of them making six and a quarter cents of our money—were piled up in great quantities, with some silver, to accommodate the people who could not bet more than a few pennies at a time. In other booths silver formed the bulk of the capital of the bank, with a few doubloons to be changed if there should be a run of luck against the bank. In some there was no coin except gold. Here the rich were said to bet away their entire estates in a single day. All this is stopped now.

For myself, I was kept somewhat busy during the winter of 1847–8. My regiment was stationed in Tacubaya. I was regimental quartermaster and commissary. General Scott had been unable to get clothing for the troops from the North. The men were becoming—well, they needed clothing. Material had to be purchased, such as could be obtained, and people employed to make it up into "Yankee uniforms." A quartermaster in the city was designated to attend to this special duty; but clothing was so much needed that it was seized as fast as made up. A regiment was glad to get a dozen suits at a time. I had to look after this matter for the 4th infantry. Then our regimental fund had run down and some of the musicians in the band had been without their extra pay for a number of months.

The regimental bands at that day were kept up partly by pay from the government, and partly by pay from the regimental fund. There was authority of law for enlisting a certain number of men as musicians. So many could receive the pay of non-commissioned officers of the various grades, and the remainder the pay of privates. This would not secure a band leader, nor good players on certain instruments. In garrison

there are various ways of keeping up a regimental fund sufficient to give extra pay to musicians, establish libraries and
ten-pin alleys, subscribe to magazines and furnish many extra
comforts to the men. The best device for supplying the fund
is to issue bread to the soldiers instead of flour. The ration
used to be eighteen ounces per day of either flour or bread;
and one hundred pounds of flour will make one hundred and
forty pounds of bread. This saving was purchased by the commissary for the benefit of the fund. In the emergency the 4th
infantry was laboring under, I rented a bakery in the city,
hired bakers—Mexicans—bought fuel and whatever was necessary, and I also got a contract from the chief commissary of
the army for baking a large amount of hard bread. In two
months I made more money for the fund than my pay
amounted to during the entire war. While stationed at Monterey I had relieved the post fund in the same way. There,
however, was no profit except in the saving of flour by converting it into bread.

In the spring of 1848 a party of officers obtained leave to
visit Popocatapetl, the highest volcano in America, and to take
an escort. I went with the party, many of whom afterwards
occupied conspicuous positions before the country. Of those
who "went south," and attained high rank, there was Lieutenant Richard Anderson, who commanded a corps at Spottsylvania; Captain Sibley, a major-general, and, after the war,
for a number of years in the employ of the Khédive of Egypt;
Captain George Crittenden, a rebel general; S. B. Buckner,
who surrendered Fort Donelson; and Mansfield Lovell, who
commanded at New Orleans before that city fell into the
hands of the National troops. Of those who remained on our
side there were Captain Andrew Porter, Lieutenant C. P.
Stone and Lieutenant Z. B. Tower. There were quite a number of other officers, whose names I cannot recollect.

At a little village (Ozumba) near the base of Popocatapetl,
where we purposed to commence the ascent, we procured
guides and two pack mules with forage for our horses. High
up on the mountain there was a deserted house of one room,
called the Vaqueria, which had been occupied years before by
men in charge of cattle ranging on the mountain. The pasturage up there was very fine when we saw it, and there were still

some cattle, descendants of the former domestic herd, which had now become wild. It was possible to go on horseback as far as the Vaqueria, though the road was somewhat hazardous in places. Sometimes it was very narrow with a yawning precipice on one side, hundreds of feet down to a roaring mountain torrent below, and almost perpendicular walls on the other side. At one of these places one of our mules loaded with two sacks of barley, one on each side, the two about as big as he was, struck his load against the mountain-side and was precipitated to the bottom. The descent was steep but not perpendicular. The mule rolled over and over until the bottom was reached, and we supposed of course the poor animal was dashed to pieces. What was our surprise, not long after we had gone into bivouac, to see the lost mule, cargo and owner coming up the ascent. The load had protected the animal from serious injury; and his owner had gone after him and found a way back to the path leading up to the hut where we were to stay.

The night at the Vaqueria was one of the most unpleasant I ever knew. It was very cold and the rain fell in torrents. A little higher up the rain ceased and snow began. The wind blew with great velocity. The log-cabin we were in had lost the roof entirely on one side, and on the other it was hardly better than a sieve. There was little or no sleep that night. As soon as it was light the next morning, we started to make the ascent to the summit. The wind continued to blow with violence and the weather was still cloudy, but there was neither rain nor snow. The clouds, however, concealed from our view the country below us, except at times a momentary glimpse could be got through a clear space between them. The wind carried the loose snow around the mountain-sides in such volumes as to make it almost impossible to stand up against it. We labored on and on, until it became evident that the top could not be reached before night, if at all in such a storm, and we concluded to return. The descent was easy and rapid, though dangerous, until we got below the snow line. At the cabin we mounted our horses, and by night were at Ozumba.

The fatigues of the day and the loss of sleep the night before drove us to bed early. Our beds consisted of a place on the dirt-floor with a blanket under us. Soon all were asleep; but long before morning first one and then another of our party began to cry out with excruciating pain in the eyes. Not one escaped it. By morning the eyes of half the party were so swollen that they were entirely closed. The others suffered pain equally. The feeling was about what might be expected from the prick of a sharp needle at a white heat. We remained in quarters until the afternoon bathing our eyes in cold water. This relieved us very much, and before night the pain had entirely left. The swelling, however, continued, and about half the party still had their eyes entirely closed; but we concluded to make a start back, those who could see a little leading the horses of those who could not see at all. We moved back to the village of Ameca Ameca, some six miles, and stopped again for the night. The next morning all were entirely well and free from pain. The weather was clear and Popocatapetl stood out in all its beauty, the top looking as if not a mile away, and inviting us to return. About half the party were anxious to try the ascent again, and concluded to do so. The remainder — I was with the remainder — concluded that we had got all the pleasure there was to be had out of mountain climbing, and that we would visit the great caves of Mexico, some ninety miles from where we then were, on the road to Acapulco.

The party that ascended the mountain the second time succeeded in reaching the crater at the top, with but little of the labor they encountered in their first attempt. Three of them — Anderson, Stone and Buckner — wrote accounts of their journey, which were published at the time. I made no notes of this excursion, and have read nothing about it since, but it seems to me that I can see the whole of it as vividly as if it were but yesterday. I have been back at Ameca Ameca, and the village beyond, twice in the last five years. The scene had not changed materially from my recollection of it.

The party which I was with moved south down the valley to the town of Cuantla, some forty miles from Ameca Ameca. The latter stands on the plain at the foot of Popocatapetl, at an elevation of about eight thousand feet above tide water. The slope down is gradual as the traveller moves south, but one would not judge that, in going to Cuantla, descent enough had been made to occasion a material change in the climate and productions of the soil; but such is the case. In the morning we left a temperate climate where the cereals and fruits are those common to the United States; we halted in the evening in a tropical climate where the orange and banana, the coffee and the sugar-cane were flourishing. We had been travelling, apparently, on a plain all day, but in the direction of the flow of water.

Soon after the capture of the City of Mexico an armistice had been agreed to, designating the limits beyond which troops of the respective armies were not to go during its continuance. Our party knew nothing about these limits. As we approached Cuantla bugles sounded the assembly, and soldiers rushed from the guard-house in the edge of the town towards us. Our party halted, and I tied a white pocket handkerchief to a stick and, using it as a flag of truce, proceeded on to the town. Captains Sibley and Porter followed a few hundred yards behind. I was detained at the guard-house until a messenger could be dispatched to the quarters of the commanding general, who authorized that I should be conducted to him. I had been with the general but a few minutes when the two officers following announced themselves. The Mexican general reminded us that it was a violation of the truce for us to be there. However, as we had no special authority from our own commanding general, and as we knew nothing about the terms of the truce, we were permitted to occupy a vacant house outside the guard for the night, with the promise of a guide to put us on the road to Cuernavaca the next morning.

Cuernavaca is a town west of Cuantla. The country through which we passed, between these two towns, is tropical in climate and productions and rich in scenery. At one point, about half-way between the two places, the road goes over a low pass in the mountains in which there is a very quaint old town, the inhabitants of which at that day were nearly all full-blooded Indians. Very few of them even spoke Spanish. The houses were built of stone and generally only one story high. The streets were narrow, and had probably been paved before Cortez visited the country. They had not been graded, but the paving had been done on the natural surface. We had with us one vehicle, a cart, which was probably the first wheeled vehicle that had ever passed through that town.

On a hill overlooking this town stands the tomb of an ancient king; and it was understood that the inhabitants venerated this tomb very highly, as well as the memory of the ruler who was supposed to be buried in it. We ascended the mountain and surveyed the tomb; but it showed no particular marks of architectural taste, mechanical skill or advanced civilization. The next day we went into Cuernavaca.

After a day's rest at Cuernavaca our party set out again on the journey to the great caves of Mexico. We had proceeded but a few miles when we were stopped, as before, by a guard and notified that the terms of the existing armistice did not permit us to go further in that direction. Upon convincing the guard that we were a mere party of pleasure seekers desirous of visiting the great natural curiosities of the country which we expected soon to leave, we were conducted to a large hacienda near by, and directed to remain there until the commanding general of that department could be communicated with and his decision obtained as to whether we should be permitted to pursue our journey. The guard promised to send a messenger at once, and expected a reply by night. At night there was no response from the commanding general, but the captain of the guard was sure he would have a reply by morning. Again in the morning there was no reply. The second evening the same thing happened, and finally we learned that the guard had sent no message or messenger to the department commander. We determined therefore to go on unless stopped by a force sufficient to compel obedience.

After a few hours' travel we came to a town where a scene similar to the one at Cuantla occurred. The commanding officer sent a guide to conduct our party around the village and to put us upon our road again. This was the last interruption: that night we rested at a large coffee plantation, some eight miles from the cave we were on the way to visit. It must have been a Saturday night; the peons had been paid off, and spent part of the night in gambling away their scanty week's earnings. Their coin was principally copper, and I do not believe there was a man among them who had received as much as twenty-five cents in money. They were as much excited, however, as if they had been staking thousands. I recollect one poor fellow, who had lost his last tlaco, pulled off his shirt and, in the most excited manner, put that up on the turn of a card. Monte was the game played, the place out of doors, near the window of the room occupied by the officers of our party.

The next morning we were at the mouth of the cave at an early hour, provided with guides, candles and rockets. We explored to a distance of about three miles from the entrance, and found a succession of chambers of great dimensions and of great beauty when lit up with our rockets. Stalactites and stalagmites of all sizes were discovered. Some of the former were many feet in diameter and extended from ceiling to floor; some of the latter were but a few feet high from the floor; but the formation is going on constantly, and many centuries hence these stalagmites will extend to the ceiling and become complete columns. The stalagmites were all a little concave, and the cavities were filled with water. The water percolates through the roof, a drop at a time—often the drops several minutes apart—and more or less charged with mineral matter. Evaporation goes on slowly, leaving the mineral behind. This in time makes the immense columns, many of them thousands of tons in weight, which serve to support the roofs over the vast chambers. I recollect that at one point in the cave one of these columns is of such huge proportions that there is only a narrow passage left on either side of it. Some of our party became satisfied with their explorations before we had reached the point to which the guides were accustomed to take explorers, and started back without guides. Coming to the large column spoken of, they followed it entirely around, and commenced retracing their steps into the bowels of the mountain, without being aware of the fact. When the rest of us had completed our explorations, we started out with our guides, but had not gone far before we saw the torches of an approaching party. We could not conceive who these could be, for all of us had come in together, and there were none but ourselves at the entrance when we started in. Very soon we found it was our friends. It took them some time to conceive how they had got where they were. They were sure they had kept straight on for the mouth of the cave, and had gone about far enough to have reached it.

Chapter XIV.

MY EXPERIENCE in the Mexican war was of great advantage to me afterwards. Besides the many practical lessons it taught, the war brought nearly all the officers of the regular army together so as to make them personally acquainted. It also brought them in contact with volunteers, many of whom served in the war of the rebellion afterwards. Then, in my particular case, I had been at West Point at about the right time to meet most of the graduates who were of a suitable age at the breaking out of the rebellion to be trusted with large commands. Graduating in 1843, I was at the military academy from one to four years with all cadets who graduated between 1840 and 1846—seven classes. These classes embraced more than fifty officers who afterwards became generals on one side or the other in the rebellion, many of them holding high commands. All the older officers, who became conspicuous in the rebellion, I had also served with and known in Mexico: Lee, J. E. Johnston, A. S. Johnston, Holmes, Hebért and a number of others on the Confederate side; McCall, Mansfield, Phil. Kearney and others on the National side. The acquaintance thus formed was of immense service to me in the war of the rebellion—I mean what I learned of the characters of those to whom I was afterwards opposed. I do not pretend to say that all movements, or even many of them, were made with special reference to the characteristics of the commander against whom they were directed. But my appreciation of my enemies was certainly affected by this knowledge. The natural disposition of most people is to clothe a commander of a large army whom they do not know, with almost superhuman abilities. A large part of the National army, for instance, and most of the press of the country, clothed General Lee with just such qualities, but I had known him personally, and knew that he was mortal; and it was just as well that I felt this.

The treaty of peace was at last ratified, and the evacuation of Mexico by United States troops was ordered. Early in June the troops in the City of Mexico began to move out. Many of them, including the brigade to which I belonged, were assembled at Jalapa, above the vomito, to await the arrival of transports at Vera Cruz: but with all this precaution my regiment and others were in camp on the sand beach in a July sun, for about a week before embarking, while the fever raged with great virulence in Vera Cruz, not two miles away. I can call to mind only one person, an officer, who died of the disease. My regiment was sent to Pascagoula, Mississippi, to spend the summer. As soon as it was settled in camp I obtained a leave of absence for four months and proceeded to St. Louis. On the 22d of August, 1848, I was married to Miss Julia Dent, the lady of whom I have before spoken. We visited my parents and relations in Ohio, and, at the end of my leave, proceeded to my post at Sackett's Harbor, New York. In April following I was ordered to Detroit, Michigan, where two years were spent with but few important incidents.

The present constitution of the State of Michigan was ratified during this time. By the terms of one of its provisions, all citizens of the United States residing within the State at the time of the ratification became citizens of Michigan also. During my stay in Detroit there was an election for city officers. Mr. Zachariah Chandler was the candidate of the Whigs for the office of Mayor, and was elected, although the city was then reckoned democratic. All the officers stationed there at the time who offered their votes were permitted to cast them. I did not offer mine, however, as I did not wish to consider myself a citizen of Michigan. This was Mr. Chandler's first entry into politics, a career he followed ever after with great success, and in which he died enjoying the friendship, esteem and love of his countrymen.

In the spring of 1851 the garrison at Detroit was transferred to Sackett's Harbor, and in the following spring the entire 4th infantry was ordered to the Pacific Coast. It was decided that Mrs. Grant should visit my parents at first for a few months, and then remain with her own family at their St. Louis home until an opportunity offered of sending for

her. In the month of April the regiment was assembled at
Governor's Island, New York Harbor, and on the 5th of July
eight companies sailed for Aspinwall. We numbered a little
over seven hundred persons, including the families of officers
and soldiers. Passage was secured for us on the old steamer
Ohio, commanded at the time by Captain Schenck, of the
navy. It had not been determined, until a day or two before
starting, that the 4th infantry should go by the *Ohio*; consequently, a complement of passengers had already been
secured. The addition of over seven hundred to this list
crowded the steamer most uncomfortably, especially for the
tropics in July.

In eight days Aspinwall was reached. At that time the
streets of the town were eight or ten inches under water, and
foot passengers passed from place to place on raised foot-
walks. July is at the height of the wet season, on the Isthmus.
At intervals the rain would pour down in streams, followed in
not many minutes by a blazing, tropical summer's sun. These
alternate changes, from rain to sunshine, were continuous in
the afternoons. I wondered how any person could live many
months in Aspinwall, and wondered still more why any one
tried.

In the summer of 1852 the Panama railroad was completed
only to the point where it now crosses the Chagres River.
From there passengers were carried by boats to Gorgona, at
which place they took mules for Panama, some twenty-five
miles further. Those who travelled over the Isthmus in those
days will remember that boats on the Chagres River were
propelled by natives not inconveniently burdened with clothing. These boats carried thirty to forty passengers each. The
crews consisted of six men to a boat, armed with long poles.
There were planks wide enough for a man to walk on conveniently, running along the sides of each boat from end to end.
The men would start from the bow, place one end of their
poles against the river bottom, brace their shoulders against
the other end, and then walk to the stern as rapidly as they
could. In this way from a mile to a mile and a half an hour
could be made, against the current of the river.

I, as regimental quartermaster, had charge of the public
property and had also to look after the transportation. A con-

tract had been entered into with the steamship company in New York for the transportation of the regiment to California, including the Isthmus transit. A certain amount of baggage was allowed per man, and saddle animals were to be furnished to commissioned officers and to all disabled persons. The regiment, with the exception of one company left as guards to the public property—camp and garrison equipage principally—and the soldiers with families, took boats, propelled as above described, for Gorgona. From this place they marched to Panama, and were soon comfortably on the steamer anchored in the bay, some three or four miles from the town. I, with one company of troops and all the soldiers with families, all the tents, mess chests and camp kettles, was sent to Cruces, a town a few miles higher up the Chagres River than Gorgona. There I found an impecunious American who had taken the contract to furnish transportation for the regiment at a stipulated price per hundred pounds for the freight and so much for each saddle animal. But when we reached Cruces there was not a mule, either for pack or saddle, in the place. The contractor promised that the animals should be on hand in the morning. In the morning he said that they were on the way from some imaginary place, and would arrive in the course of the day. This went on until I saw that he could not procure the animals at all at the price he had promised to furnish them for. The unusual number of passengers that had come over on the steamer, and the large amount of freight to pack, had created an unprecedented demand for mules. Some of the passengers paid as high as forty dollars for the use of a mule to ride twenty-five miles, when the mule would not have sold for ten dollars in that market at other times. Meanwhile the cholera had broken out, and men were dying every hour. To diminish the food for the disease, I permitted the company detailed with me to proceed to Panama. The captain and the doctors accompanied the men, and I was left alone with the sick and the soldiers who had families. The regiment at Panama was also affected with the disease; but there were better accommodations for the well on the steamer, and a hospital, for those taken with the disease, on an old hulk anchored a mile off. There were also hospital tents on shore on the island of Flamingo, which stands in the bay.

I was about a week at Cruces before transportation began to come in. About one-third of the people with me died, either at Cruces or on the way to Panama. There was no agent of the transportation company at Cruces to consult, or to take the responsibility of procuring transportation at a price which would secure it. I therefore myself dismissed the contractor and made a new contract with a native, at more than double the original price. Thus we finally reached Panama. The steamer, however, could not proceed until the cholera abated, and the regiment was detained still longer. Altogether, on the Isthmus and on the Pacific side, we were delayed six weeks. About one-seventh of those who left New York harbor with the 4th infantry on the 5th of July, now lie buried on the Isthmus of Panama or on Flamingo island in Panama Bay.

One amusing circumstance occurred while we were lying at anchor in Panama Bay. In the regiment there was a Lieutenant Slaughter who was very liable to sea-sickness. It almost made him sick to see the wave of a table-cloth when the servants were spreading it. Soon after his graduation, Slaughter was ordered to California and took passage by a sailing vessel going around Cape Horn. The vessel was seven months making the voyage, and Slaughter was sick every moment of the time, never more so than while lying at anchor after reaching his place of destination. On landing in California he found orders which had come by the Isthmus, notifying him of a mistake in his assignment; he should have been ordered to the northern lakes. He started back by the Isthmus route and was sick all the way. But when he arrived at the East he was again ordered to California, this time definitely, and at this date was making his third trip. He was as sick as ever, and had been so for more than a month while lying at anchor in the bay. I remember him well, seated with his elbows on the table in front of him, his chin between his hands, and looking the picture of despair. At last he broke out, "I wish I had taken my father's advice; he wanted me to go into the navy; if I had done so, I should not have had to go to sea so much." Poor Slaughter! it was his last sea voyage. He was killed by Indians in Oregon.

By the last of August the cholera had so abated that it was

deemed safe to start. The disease did not break out again on the way to California, and we reached San Francisco early in September.

Chapter XV.

SAN FRANCISCO at that day was a lively place. Gold, or placer digging as it was called, was at its height. Steamers plied daily between San Francisco and both Stockton and Sacramento. Passengers and gold from the southern mines came by the Stockton boat; from the northern mines by Sacramento. In the evening when these boats arrived, Long Wharf — there was but one wharf in San Francisco in 1852 — was alive with people crowding to meet the miners as they came down to sell their "dust" and to "have a time." Of these some were runners for hotels, boarding houses or restaurants; others belonged to a class of impecunious adventurers, of good manners and good presence, who were ever on the alert to make the acquaintance of people with some ready means, in the hope of being asked to take a meal at a restaurant. Many were young men of good family, good education and gentlemanly instincts. Their parents had been able to support them during their minority, and to give them good educations, but not to maintain them afterwards. From 1849 to 1853 there was a rush of people to the Pacific coast, of the class described. All thought that fortunes were to be picked up, without effort, in the gold fields on the Pacific. Some realized more than their most sanguine expectations; but for one such there were hundreds disappointed, many of whom now fill unknown graves; others died wrecks of their former selves, and many, without a vicious instinct, became criminals and outcasts. Many of the real scenes in early California life exceed in strangeness and interest any of the mere products of the brain of the novelist.

Those early days in California brought out character. It was a long way off then, and the journey was expensive. The fortunate could go by Cape Horn or by the Isthmus of Panama; but the mass of pioneers crossed the plains with their ox-teams. This took an entire summer. They were very lucky when they got through with a yoke of worn-out cattle. All other means were exhausted in procuring the outfit on the Missouri River. The immigrant, on arriving, found himself a stranger, in a strange land, far from friends. Time pressed, for the little means that could be realized from the sale of what was left of the outfit would not support a man long at California prices. Many became discouraged. Others would take off their coats and look for a job, no matter what it might be. These succeeded as a rule. There were many young men who had studied professions before they went to California, and who had never done a day's manual labor in their lives, who took in the situation at once and went to work to make a start at anything they could get to do. Some supplied carpenters and masons with material—carrying plank, brick, or mortar, as the case might be; others drove stages, drays, or baggage wagons, until they could do better. More became discouraged early and spent their time looking up people who would "treat," or lounging about restaurants and gambling houses where free lunches were furnished daily. They were welcomed at these places because they often brought in miners who proved good customers.

My regiment spent a few weeks at Benicia barracks, and then was ordered to Fort Vancouver, on the Columbia River, then in Oregon Territory. During the winter of 1852–3 the territory was divided, all north of the Columbia River being taken from Oregon to make Washington Territory.

Prices for all kinds of supplies were so high on the Pacific coast from 1849 until at least 1853—that it would have been impossible for officers of the army to exist upon their pay, if it had not been that authority was given them to purchase from the commissary such supplies as he kept, at New Orleans wholesale prices. A cook could not be hired for the pay of a captain. The cook could do better. At Benicia, in 1852, flour was 25 cents per pound; potatoes were 16 cents; beets, turnips and cabbage, 6 cents; onions, 37½ cents; meat and other articles in proportion. In 1853 at Vancouver vegetables were a little lower. I with three other officers concluded that we would raise a crop for ourselves, and by selling the surplus realize something handsome. I bought a pair of horses that had crossed the plains that summer and were very poor. They recuperated rapidly, however, and proved a good team to break up the ground with. I performed all the labor of breaking up the ground while the other officers planted the potatoes. Our crop was enormous. Luckily for us the Columbia River rose to a great height from the melting of the snow in the mountains in June, and overflowed and killed most of our crop. This saved digging it up, for everybody on the Pacific coast seemed to have come to the conclusion at the same time that agriculture would be profitable. In 1853 more than three-quarters of the potatoes raised were permitted to rot in the ground, or had to be thrown away. The only potatoes we sold were to our own mess.

While I was stationed on the Pacific coast we were free from Indian wars. There were quite a number of remnants of tribes in the vicinity of Portland in Oregon, and of Fort Vancouver in Washington Territory. They had generally acquired some of the vices of civilization, but none of the virtues, except in individual cases. The Hudson's Bay Company had held the North-west with their trading posts for many years before the United States was represented on the Pacific coast. They still retained posts along the Columbia River and one at Fort Vancouver, when I was there. Their treatment of the Indians had brought out the better qualities of the savages. Farming had been undertaken by the company to supply the Indians with bread and vegetables; they raised some cattle and horses; and they had now taught the Indians to do the labor of the farm and herd. They always compensated them for their labor, and always gave them goods of uniform quality and at uniform price.

Before the advent of the American, the medium of exchange between the Indian and the white man was pelts. Afterward it was silver coin. If an Indian received in the sale of a horse a fifty dollar gold piece, not an infrequent occurrence, the first thing he did was to exchange it for American half dollars. These he could count. He would then commence his purchases, paying for each article separately, as he got it. He would not trust any one to add up the bill and pay it all at once. At that day fifty dollar gold pieces, not the issue of the government, were common on the Pacific coast. They were called slugs.

The Indians, along the lower Columbia as far as the Cascades and on the lower Willamette, died off very fast during
the year I spent in that section; for besides acquiring the vices
of the white people they had acquired also their diseases. The
measles and the small-pox were both amazingly fatal. In their
wild state, before the appearance of the white man among
them, the principal complaints they were subject to were
those produced by long involuntary fasting, violent exercise in
pursuit of game, and over-eating. Instinct more than reason
had taught them a remedy for these ills. It was the steam
bath. Something like a bake-oven was built, large enough to
admit a man lying down. Bushes were stuck in the ground in
two rows, about six feet long and some two or three feet
apart; other bushes connected the rows at one end. The tops
of the bushes were drawn together to interlace, and confined
in that position; the whole was then plastered over with wet
clay until every opening was filled. Just inside the open end of
the oven the floor was scooped out so as to make a hole that
would hold a bucket or two of water. These ovens were always built on the banks of a stream, a big spring, or pool of
water. When a patient required a bath, a fire was built near
the oven and a pile of stones put upon it. The cavity at the
front was then filled with water. When the stones were sufficiently heated, the patient would draw himself into the oven;
a blanket would be thrown over the open end, and hot stones
put into the water until the patient could stand it no longer.
He was then withdrawn from his steam bath and doused into
the cold stream near by. This treatment may have answered
with the early ailments of the Indians. With the measles or
small-pox it would kill every time.

During my year on the Columbia River, the small-pox exterminated one small remnant of a band of Indians entirely,
and reduced others materially. I do not think there was a
case of recovery among them, until the doctor with the
Hudson Bay Company took the matter in hand and established a hospital. Nearly every case he treated recovered. I
never, myself, saw the treatment described in the preceding
paragraph, but have heard it described by persons who have
witnessed it. The decimation among the Indians I knew of
personally, and the hospital, established for their benefit,

was a Hudson's Bay building not a stone's throw from my own quarters.

The death of Colonel Bliss, of the Adjutant General's department, which occurred July 5th, 1853, promoted me to the captaincy of a company then stationed at Humboldt Bay, California. The notice reached me in September of the same year, and I very soon started to join my new command. There was no way of reaching Humboldt at that time except to take passage on a San Francisco sailing vessel going after lumber. Red wood, a species of cedar, which on the Pacific coast takes the place filled by white pine in the East, then abounded on the banks of Humboldt Bay. There were extensive saw-mills engaged in preparing this lumber for the San Francisco market, and sailing vessels, used in getting it to market, furnished the only means of communication between Humboldt and the balance of the world.

I was obliged to remain in San Francisco for several days before I found a vessel. This gave me a good opportunity of comparing the San Francisco of 1852 with that of 1853. As before stated, there had been but one wharf in front of the city in 1852—Long Wharf. In 1853 the town had grown out into the bay beyond what was the end of this wharf when I first saw it. Streets and houses had been built out on piles where the year before the largest vessels visiting the port lay at anchor or tied to the wharf. There was no filling under the streets or houses. San Francisco presented the same general appearance as the year before; that is, eating, drinking and gambling houses were conspicuous for their number and publicity. They were on the first floor, with doors wide open. At all hours of the day and night in walking the streets, the eye was regaled, on every block near the water front, by the sight of players at faro. Often broken places were found in the street, large enough to let a man down into the water below. I have but little doubt that many of the people who went to the Pacific coast in the early days of the gold excitement, and have never been heard from since, or who were heard from for a time and then ceased to write, found watery graves beneath the houses or streets built over San Francisco Bay.

Besides the gambling in cards there was gambling on a

larger scale in city lots. These were sold "On Change," much as stocks are now sold on Wall Street. Cash, at time of purchase, was always paid by the broker; but the purchaser had only to put up his margin. He was charged at the rate of two or three per cent. a month on the difference, besides commissions. The sand hills, some of them almost inaccessible to foot-passengers, were surveyed off and mapped into fifty vara lots—a vara being a Spanish yard. These were sold at first at very low prices, but were sold and resold for higher prices until they went up to many thousands of dollars. The brokers did a fine business, and so did many such purchasers as were sharp enough to quit purchasing before the final crash came. As the city grew, the sand hills back of the town furnished material for filling up the bay under the houses and streets, and still further out. The temporary houses, first built over the water in the harbor, soon gave way to more solid structures. The main business part of the city now is on solid ground, made where vessels of the largest class lay at anchor in the early days. I was in San Francisco again in 1854. Gambling houses had disappeared from public view. The city had become staid and orderly.

Chapter XVI.

M Y FAMILY, all this while, was at the East. It consisted now of a wife and two children. I saw no chance of supporting them on the Pacific coast out of my pay as an army officer. I concluded, therefore, to resign, and in March applied for a leave of absence until the end of the July following, tendering my resignation to take effect at the end of that time. I left the Pacific coast very much attached to it, and with the full expectation of making it my future home. That expectation and that hope remained uppermost in my mind until the Lieutenant-Generalcy bill was introduced into Congress in the winter of 1863–4. The passage of that bill, and my promotion, blasted my last hope of ever becoming a citizen of the further West.

In the late summer of 1854 I rejoined my family, to find in it a son whom I had never seen, born while I was on the Isthmus of Panama. I was now to commence, at the age of thirty-two, a new struggle for our support. My wife had a farm near St. Louis, to which we went, but I had no means to stock it. A house had to be built also. I worked very hard, never losing a day because of bad weather, and accomplished the object in a moderate way. If nothing else could be done I would load a cord of wood on a wagon and take it to the city for sale. I managed to keep along very well until 1858, when I was attacked by fever and ague. I had suffered very severely and for a long time from this disease, while a boy in Ohio. It lasted now over a year, and, while it did not keep me in the house, it did interfere greatly with the amount of work I was able to perform. In the fall of 1858 I sold out my stock, crops and farming utensils at auction, and gave up farming.

In the winter I established a partnership with Harry Boggs, a cousin of Mrs. Grant, in the real estate agency business. I spent that winter at St. Louis myself, but did not take my family into town until the spring. Our business might have become prosperous if I had been able to wait for it to grow.

As it was, there was no more than one person could attend to, and not enough to support two families. While a citizen of St. Louis and engaged in the real estate agency business, I was a candidate for the office of county engineer, an office of respectability and emolument which would have been very acceptable to me at that time. The incumbent was appointed by the county court, which consisted of five members. My opponent had the advantage of birth over me (he was a citizen by adoption) and carried off the prize. I now withdrew from the co-partnership with Boggs, and, in May, 1860, removed to Galena, Illinois, and took a clerkship in my father's store.

While a citizen of Missouri, my first opportunity for casting a vote at a Presidential election occurred. I had been in the army from before attaining my majority and had thought but little about politics, although I was a Whig by education and a great admirer of Mr. Clay. But the Whig party had ceased to exist before I had an opportunity of exercising the privilege of casting a ballot; the Know-Nothing party had taken its place, but was on the wane; and the Republican party was in a chaotic state and had not yet received a name. It had no existence in the Slave States except at points on the borders next to Free States. In St. Louis City and County, what afterwards became the Republican party was known as the Free-Soil Democracy, led by the Honorable Frank P. Blair. Most of my neighbors had known me as an officer of the army with Whig proclivities. They had been on the same side, and, on the death of their party, many had become Know-Nothings, or members of the American party. There was a lodge near my new home, and I was invited to join it. I accepted the invitation; was initiated; attended a meeting just one week later, and never went to another afterwards.

I have no apologies to make for having been one week a member of the American party; for I still think native-born citizens of the United States should have as much protection, as many privileges in their native country, as those who voluntarily select it for a home. But all secret, oath-bound political parties are dangerous to any nation, no matter how pure or how patriotic the motives and principles which first bring them together. No political party can or ought to exist when one of its corner-stones is opposition to freedom of thought and to the right to worship God "according to the dictate of one's own conscience," or according to the creed of any religious denomination whatever. Nevertheless, if a sect sets up its laws as binding above the State laws, wherever the two come in conflict this claim must be resisted and suppressed at whatever cost.

Up to the Mexican war there were a few out and out abolitionists, men who carried their hostility to slavery into all elections, from those for a justice of the peace up to the Presidency of the United States. They were noisy but not numerous. But the great majority of people at the North, where slavery did not exist, were opposed to the institution, and looked upon its existence in any part of the country as unfortunate. They did not hold the States where slavery existed responsible for it; and believed that protection should be given to the right of property in slaves until some satisfactory way could be reached to be rid of the institution. Opposition to slavery was not a creed of either political party. In some sections more anti-slavery men belonged to the Democratic party, and in others to the Whigs. But with the inauguration of the Mexican war, in fact with the annexation of Texas, "the inevitable conflict" commenced.

As the time for the Presidential election of 1856—the first at which I had the opportunity of voting—approached, party feeling began to run high. The Republican party was regarded in the South and the border States not only as opposed to the extension of slavery, but as favoring the compulsory abolition of the institution without compensation to the owners. The most horrible visions seemed to present themselves to the minds of people who, one would suppose, ought to have known better. Many educated and, otherwise, sensible persons appeared to believe that emancipation meant social equality. Treason to the Government was openly advocated and was not rebuked. It was evident to my mind that the election of a Republican President in 1856 meant the secession of all the Slave States, and rebellion. Under these circumstances I preferred the success of a candidate whose election would prevent or postpone secession, to seeing the country plunged into a war the end of which no man could foretell.

With a Democrat elected by the unanimous vote of the Slave States, there could be no pretext for secession for four years. I very much hoped that the passions of the people would subside in that time, and the catastrophe be averted altogether; if it was not, I believed the country would be better prepared to receive the shock and to resist it. I therefore voted for James Buchanan for President. Four years later the Republican party was successful in electing its candidate to the Presidency. The civilized world has learned the consequence. Four millions of human beings held as chattels have been liberated; the ballot has been given to them; the free schools of the country have been opened to their children. The nation still lives, and the people are just as free to avoid social intimacy with the blacks as ever they were, or as they are with white people.

While living in Galena I was nominally only a clerk supporting myself and family on a stipulated salary. In reality my position was different. My father had never lived in Galena himself, but had established my two brothers there, the one next younger than myself in charge of the business, assisted by the youngest. When I went there it was my father's intention to give up all connection with the business himself, and to establish his three sons in it: but the brother who had really built up the business was sinking with consumption, and it was not thought best to make any change while he was in this condition. He lived until September, 1861, when he succumbed to that insidious disease which always flatters its victims into the belief that they are growing better up to the close of life. A more honorable man never transacted business. In September, 1861, I was engaged in an employment which required all my attention elsewhere.

During the eleven months that I lived in Galena prior to the first call for volunteers, I had been strictly attentive to my business, and had made but few acquaintances other than customers and people engaged in the same line with myself. When the election took place in November, 1860, I had not been a resident of Illinois long enough to gain citizenship and could not, therefore, vote. I was really glad of this at the time, for my pledges would have compelled me to vote for Stephen A. Douglas, who had no possible chance of election. The contest was really between Mr. Breckinridge and Mr. Lincoln;

between minority rule and rule by the majority. I wanted, as between these candidates, to see Mr. Lincoln elected. Excitement ran high during the canvass, and torch-light processions enlivened the scene in the generally quiet streets of Galena many nights during the campaign. I did not parade with either party, but occasionally met with the "wide awakes"— Republicans—in their rooms, and superintended their drill. It was evident, from the time of the Chicago nomination to the close of the canvass, that the election of the Republican candidate would be the signal for some of the Southern States to secede. I still had hopes that the four years which had elapsed since the first nomination of a Presidential candidate by a party distinctly opposed to slavery extension, had given time for the extreme pro-slavery sentiment to cool down; for the Southerners to think well before they took the awful leap which they had so vehemently threatened. But I was mistaken.

The Republican candidate was elected, and solid substantial people of the North-west, and I presume the same order of people throughout the entire North, felt very serious, but determined, after this event. It was very much discussed whether the South would carry out its threat to secede and set up a separate government, the corner-stone of which should be, protection to the "Divine" institution of slavery. For there were people who believed in the "divinity" of human slavery, as there are now people who believe Mormonism and Polygamy to be ordained by the Most High. We forgive them for entertaining such notions, but forbid their practice. It was generally believed that there would be a flurry; that some of the extreme Southern States would go so far as to pass ordinances of secession. But the common impression was that this step was so plainly suicidal for the South, that the movement would not spread over much of the territory and would not last long.

Doubtless the founders of our government, the majority of them at least, regarded the confederation of the colonies as an experiment. Each colony considered itself a separate government; that the confederation was for mutual protection against a foreign foe, and the prevention of strife and war among themselves. If there had been a desire on the part of any single State to withdraw from the compact at any time while the number of States was limited to the original thirteen, I do not suppose there would have been any to contest the right, no matter how much the determination might have been regretted. The problem changed on the ratification of the Constitution by all the colonies; it changed still more when amendments were added; and if the right of any one State to withdraw continued to exist at all after the ratification of the Constitution, it certainly ceased on the formation of new States, at least so far as the new States themselves were concerned. It was never possessed at all by Florida or the States west of the Mississippi, all of which were purchased by the treasury of the entire nation. Texas and the territory brought into the Union in consequence of annexation, were purchased with both blood and treasure; and Texas, with a domain greater than that of any European state except Russia, was permitted to retain as state property all the public lands within its borders. It would have been ingratitude and injustice of the most flagrant sort for this State to withdraw from the Union after all that had been spent and done to introduce her; yet, if separation had actually occurred, Texas must necessarily have gone with the South, both on account of her institutions and her geographical position. Secession was illogical as well as impracticable; it was revolution.

Now, the right of revolution is an inherent one. When people are oppressed by their government, it is a natural right they enjoy to relieve themselves of the oppression, if they are strong enough, either by withdrawal from it, or by overthrowing it and substituting a government more acceptable. But any people or part of a people who resort to this remedy, stake their lives, their property, and every claim for protection given by citizenship—on the issue. Victory, or the conditions imposed by the conqueror—must be the result.

In the case of the war between the States it would have been the exact truth if the South had said,—"We do not want to live with you Northern people any longer; we know our institution of slavery is obnoxious to you, and, as you are growing numerically stronger than we, it may at some time in the future be endangered. So long as you permitted us to control the government, and with the aid of a few friends at the North to enact laws constituting your section a guard against the escape of our property, we were willing to live with you. You have been submissive to our rule heretofore; but it looks now as if you did not intend to continue so, and we will remain in the Union no longer." Instead of this the seceding States cried lustily,—"Let us alone; you have no constitutional power to interfere with us." Newspapers and people at the North reiterated the cry. Individuals might ignore the constitution; but the Nation itself must not only obey it, but must enforce the strictest construction of that instrument; the construction put upon it by the Southerners themselves. The fact is the constitution did not apply to any such contingency as the one existing from 1861 to 1865. Its framers never dreamed of such a contingency occurring. If they had foreseen it, the probabilities are they would have sanctioned the right of a State or States to withdraw rather than that there should be war between brothers.

The framers were wise in their generation and wanted to do the very best possible to secure their own liberty and independence, and that also of their descendants to the latest days. It is preposterous to suppose that the people of one generation can lay down the best and only rules of government for all who are to come after them, and under unforeseen contingencies. At the time of the framing of our constitution the only physical forces that had been subdued and made to serve man and do his labor, were the currents in the streams and in the air we breathe. Rude machinery, propelled by water power, had been invented; sails to propel ships upon the waters had been set to catch the passing breeze—but the application of steam to propel vessels against both wind and current, and machinery to do all manner of work had not been thought of. The instantaneous transmission of messages around the world by means of electricity would probably at that day have been attributed to witchcraft or a league with the Devil. Immaterial circumstances had changed as greatly as material ones. We could not and ought not to be rigidly bound by the rules laid down under circumstances so different for emergencies so utterly unanticipated. The fathers themselves would have been the first to declare that their prerogatives were not irrevocable. They would surely have resisted secession could they have lived to see the shape it assumed.

I travelled through the Northwest considerably during the winter of 1860–1. We had customers in all the little towns in south-west Wisconsin, south-east Minnesota and north-east Iowa. These generally knew I had been a captain in the regular army and had served through the Mexican war. Consequently wherever I stopped at night, some of the people would come to the public-house where I was, and sit till a late hour discussing the probabilities of the future. My own views at that time were like those officially expressed by Mr. Seward at a later day, that "the war would be over in ninety days." I continued to entertain these views until after the battle of Shiloh. I believe now that there would have been no more battles at the West after the capture of Fort Donelson if all the troops in that region had been under a single commander who would have followed up that victory.

There is little doubt in my mind now that the prevailing sentiment of the South would have been opposed to secession in 1860 and 1861, if there had been a fair and calm expression of opinion, unbiased by threats, and if the ballot of one legal voter had counted for as much as that of any other. But there was no calm discussion of the question. Demagogues who were too old to enter the army if there should be a war, others who entertained so high an opinion of their own ability that they did not believe they could be spared from the direction of the affairs of state in such an event, declaimed vehemently and unceasingly against the North; against its aggressions upon the South; its interference with Southern rights, etc., etc. They denounced the Northerners as cowards, poltroons, negro-worshippers; claimed that one Southern man was equal to five Northern men in battle; that if the South would stand up for its rights the North would back down. Mr. Jefferson Davis said in a speech, delivered at La Grange, Mississippi, before the secession of that State, that he would agree to drink all the blood spilled south of Mason and Dixon's line if there should be a war. The young men who would have the fighting to do in case of war, believed all these statements, both in regard to the aggressiveness of the North and its cowardice. They, too, cried out for a separation from such people. The great bulk of the legal voters of the South were men who owned no slaves; their homes were generally in the hills and poor country; their facilities for educating their children, even up to the point of reading and writing, were very limited; their interest in the contest was very meagre—what there was, if they had been capable of seeing it, was with the North; they too needed emancipation. Under the old régime they were looked down upon by those who controlled all the affairs in the interest of slave-owners, as poor white trash who were allowed the ballot so long as they cast it according to direction.

I am aware that this last statement may be disputed and individual testimony perhaps adduced to show that in ante-bellum days the ballot was as untrammelled in the South as in any section of the country; but in the face of any such contradiction I reassert the statement. The shot-gun was not resorted to. Masked men did not ride over the country at night intimidating voters; but there was a firm feeling that a class existed in every State with a sort of divine right to control public affairs. If they could not get this control by one means they must by another. The end justified the means. The co-ercion, if mild, was complete.

There were two political parties, it is true, in all the States, both strong in numbers and respectability, but both equally loyal to the institution which stood paramount in Southern eyes to all other institutions in state or nation. The slave-owners were the minority, but governed both parties. Had politics ever divided the slave-holders and the non-slave-holders, the majority would have been obliged to yield, or internecine war would have been the consequence. I do not know that the Southern people were to blame for this condition of affairs. There was a time when slavery was not profitable, and the discussion of the merits of the institution was confined almost exclusively to the territory where it existed. The States of Virginia and Kentucky came near abolishing slavery by their own acts, one State defeating the measure by a tie vote and the other only lacking one. But when the institution became profitable, all talk of its abolition ceased where it existed; and naturally, as human nature is constituted, arguments were adduced in its support. The cotton-gin probably had much to do with the justification of slavery.

The winter of 1860–1 will be remembered by middle-aged people of to-day as one of great excitement. South Carolina promptly seceded after the result of the Presidential election was known. Other Southern States proposed to follow. In some of them the Union sentiment was so strong that it had to be suppressed by force. Maryland, Delaware, Kentucky and Missouri, all Slave States, failed to pass ordinances of secession; but they were all represented in the so-called congress of the so-called Confederate States. The Governor and Lieutenant-Governor of Missouri, in 1861, Jackson and Reynolds, were both supporters of the rebellion and took refuge with the enemy. The governor soon died, and the lieutenant-governor assumed his office; issued proclamations as governor of the State; was recognized as such by the Confederate Government, and continued his pretensions until the collapse of the rebellion. The South claimed the sovereignty of States, but claimed the right to coerce into their confederation such States as they wanted, that is, all the States where slavery existed. They did not seem to think this course inconsistent. The fact is, the Southern slave-owners believed that, in some way, the ownership of slaves conferred a sort of patent of nobility—a right to govern independent of the interest or wishes of those who did not hold such property. They convinced themselves, first, of the divine origin of the institution and, next, that that particular institution was not safe in the hands of any body of legislators but themselves.

Meanwhile the Administration of President Buchanan looked helplessly on and proclaimed that the general government had no power to interfere; that the Nation had no power to save its own life. Mr. Buchanan had in his cabinet two members at least, who were as earnest—to use a mild term—in the cause of secession as Mr. Davis or any Southern statesman. One of them, Floyd, the Secretary of War, scattered the army so that much of it could be captured when hostilities should commence, and distributed the cannon and small arms from Northern arsenals throughout the South so as to be on hand when treason wanted them. The navy was scattered in like manner. The President did not prevent his cabinet preparing for war upon their government, either by destroying its resources or storing them in the South until a de facto government was established with Jefferson Davis as its President, and Montgomery, Alabama, as the Capital. The secessionists had then to leave the cabinet. In their own estimation they were aliens in the country which had given them birth. Loyal men were put into their places. Treason in the executive branch of the government was estopped. But the harm had already been done. The stable door was locked after the horse had been stolen.

During all of the trying winter of 1860–1, when the Southerners were so defiant that they would not allow within their borders the expression of a sentiment hostile to their views, it was a brave man indeed who could stand up and proclaim his loyalty to the Union. On the other hand men at the North— prominent men—proclaimed that the government had no power to coerce the South into submission to the laws of the land; that if the North undertook to raise armies to go south, these armies would have to march over the dead bodies of the speakers. A portion of the press of the North was constantly proclaiming similar views. When the time arrived for the President-elect to go to the capital of the Nation to be sworn into office, it was deemed unsafe for him to travel, not only as a President-elect, but as any private citizen should be allowed to do. Instead of going in a special car, receiving the good wishes of his constituents at all the stations along the road, he was obliged to stop on the way and to be smuggled into the capital. He disappeared from public view on his journey, and the next the country knew, his arrival was announced at the capital. There is little doubt that he would have been assassinated if he had attempted to travel openly throughout his journey.

Chapter XVII.

THE 4TH OF MARCH, 1861, came, and Abraham Lincoln
was sworn to maintain the Union against all its enemies.
The secession of one State after another followed, until eleven
had gone out. On the 11th of April Fort Sumter, a National
fort in the harbor of Charleston, South Carolina, was fired
upon by the Southerners and a few days after was captured.
The Confederates proclaimed themselves aliens, and thereby
debarred themselves of all right to claim protection under the
Constitution of the United States. We did not admit the fact
that they were aliens, but all the same, they debarred themselves of the right to expect better treatment than people of
any other foreign state who make war upon an independent
nation. Upon the firing on Sumter President Lincoln issued
his first call for troops and soon after a proclamation convening Congress in extra session. The call was for 75,000 volunteers for ninety days' service. If the shot fired at Fort Sumter
"was heard around the world," the call of the President for
75,000 men was heard throughout the Northern States. There
was not a state in the North of a million of inhabitants that
would not have furnished the entire number faster than arms
could have been supplied to them, if it had been necessary.

As soon as the news of the call for volunteers reached
Galena, posters were stuck up calling for a meeting of the
citizens at the court-house in the evening. Business ceased
entirely; all was excitement; for a time there were no party
distinctions; all were Union men, determined to avenge the
insult to the national flag. In the evening the court-house was
packed. Although a comparative stranger I was called upon to
preside; the sole reason, possibly, was that I had been in the
army and had seen service. With much embarrassment and
some prompting I made out to announce the object of the
meeting. Speeches were in order, but it is doubtful whether it

would have been safe just then to make other than patriotic ones. There was probably no one in the house, however, who felt like making any other. The two principal speeches were by B. B. Howard, the post-master and a Breckinridge Democrat at the November election the fall before, and John A. Rawlins, an elector on the Douglas ticket. E. B. Washburne, with whom I was not acquainted at that time, came in after the meeting had been organized, and expressed, I understood afterwards, a little surprise that Galena could not furnish a presiding officer for such an occasion without taking a stranger. He came forward and was introduced, and made a speech appealing to the patriotism of the meeting.

After the speaking was over volunteers were called for to form a company. The quota of Illinois had been fixed at six regiments; and it was supposed that one company would be as much as would be accepted from Galena. The company was raised and the officers and non-commissioned officers elected before the meeting adjourned. I declined the captaincy before the balloting, but announced that I would aid the company in every way I could and would be found in the service in some position if there should be a war. I never went into our leather store after that meeting, to put up a package or do other business.

The ladies of Galena were quite as patriotic as the men. They could not enlist, but they conceived the idea of sending their first company to the field uniformed. They came to me to get a description of the United States uniform for infantry; subscribed and bought the material; procured tailors to cut out the garments, and the ladies made them up. In a few days the company was in uniform and ready to report at the State capital for assignment. The men all turned out the morning after their enlistment, and I took charge, divided them into squads and superintended their drill. When they were ready to go to Springfield I went with them and remained there until they were assigned to a regiment.

There were so many more volunteers than had been called for that the question whom to accept was quite embarrassing to the governor, Richard Yates. The legislature was in session at the time, however, and came to his relief. A law was enacted authorizing the governor to accept the services of ten additional regiments, one from each congressional district, for one month, to be paid by the State, but pledged to go into the service of the United States if there should be a further call during their term. Even with this relief the governor was still very much embarrassed. Before the war was over he was like the President when he was taken with the varioloid: "at last he had something he could give to all who wanted it."

In time the Galena company was mustered into the United States service, forming a part of the 11th Illinois volunteer infantry. My duties, I thought, had ended at Springfield, and I was prepared to start home by the evening train, leaving at nine o'clock. Up to that time I do not think I had been introduced to Governor Yates, or had ever spoken to him. I knew him by sight, however, because he was living at the same hotel and I often saw him at table. The evening I was to quit the capital I left the supper room before the governor and was standing at the front door when he came out. He spoke to me, calling me by my old army title "Captain," and said he understood that I was about leaving the city. I answered that I was. He said he would be glad if I would remain over-night and call at the Executive office the next morning. I complied with his request, and was asked to go into the Adjutant-General's office and render such assistance as I could, the governor saying that my army experience would be of great service there. I accepted the proposition.

My old army experience I found indeed of very great service. I was no clerk, nor had I any capacity to become one. The only place I ever found in my life to put a paper so as to find it again was either a side coat-pocket or the hands of a clerk or secretary more careful than myself. But I had been quartermaster, commissary and adjutant in the field. The army forms were familiar to me and I could direct how they should be made out. There was a clerk in the office of the Adjutant-General who supplied my deficiencies. The ease with which the State of Illinois settled its accounts with the government at the close of the war is evidence of the efficiency of Mr. Loomis as an accountant on a large scale. He remained in the office until that time.

As I have stated, the legislature authorized the governor to accept the services of ten additional regiments. I had charge of mustering these regiments into the State service. They were assembled at the most convenient railroad centres in their respective congressional districts. I detailed officers to muster in a portion of them, but mustered three in the southern part of the State myself. One of these was to assemble at Belleville, some eighteen miles south-east of St. Louis. When I got there I found that only one or two companies had arrived. There was no probability of the regiment coming together under five days. This gave me a few idle days which I concluded to spend in St. Louis.

There was a considerable force of State militia at Camp Jackson, on the outskirts of St. Louis, at the time. There is but little doubt that it was the design of Governor Claiborn Jackson to have these troops ready to seize the United States arsenal and the city of St. Louis. Why they did not do so I do not know. There was but a small garrison, two companies I think, under Captain N. Lyon at the arsenal, and but for the timely services of the Hon. F. P. Blair, I have little doubt that St. Louis would have gone into rebel hands, and with it the arsenal with all its arms and ammunition.

Blair was a leader among the Union men of St. Louis in 1861. There was no State government in Missouri at the time that would sanction the raising of troops or commissioned officers to protect United States property, but Blair had probably procured some form of authority from the President to raise troops in Missouri and to muster them into the service of the United States. At all events, he did raise a regiment and took command himself as Colonel. With this force he reported to Captain Lyon and placed himself and regiment under his orders. It was whispered that Lyon thus reinforced intended to break up Camp Jackson and capture the militia. I went down to the arsenal in the morning to see the troops start out. I had known Lyon for two years at West Point and in the old army afterwards. Blair I knew very well by sight. I had heard him speak in the canvass of 1858, possibly several times, but I had never spoken to him. As the troops marched out of the enclosure around the arsenal, Blair was on his horse outside forming them into line preparatory to their march. I introduced myself to him and had a few moments' conversation and expressed my sympathy with his purpose.

This was my first personal acquaintance with the Honorable—afterwards Major-General F. P. Blair. Camp Jackson surrendered without a fight and the garrison was marched down to the arsenal as prisoners of war.

Up to this time the enemies of the government in St. Louis had been bold and defiant, while Union men were quiet but determined. The enemies had their head-quarters in a central and public position on Pine Street, near Fifth—from which the rebel flag was flaunted boldly. The Union men had a place of meeting somewhere in the city, I did not know where, and I doubt whether they dared to enrage the enemies of the government by placing the national flag outside their head-quarters. As soon as the news of the capture of Camp Jackson reached the city the condition of affairs was changed. Union men became rampant, aggressive, and, if you will, intolerant. They proclaimed their sentiments boldly, and were impatient at anything like disrespect for the Union. The secessionists became quiet but were filled with suppressed rage. They had been playing the bully. The Union men ordered the rebel flag taken down from the building on Pine Street. The command was given in tones of authority and it was taken down, never to be raised again in St. Louis.

I witnessed the scene. I had heard of the surrender of the camp and that the garrison was on its way to the arsenal. I had seen the troops start out in the morning and had wished them success. I now determined to go to the arsenal and await their arrival and congratulate them. I stepped on a car standing at the corner of 4th and Pine streets, and saw a crowd of people standing quietly in front of the head-quarters, who were there for the purpose of hauling down the flag. There were squads of other people at intervals down the street. They too were quiet but filled with suppressed rage, and muttered their resentment at the insult to, what they called, "their" flag. Before the car I was in had started, a dapper little fellow—he would be called a dude at this day—stepped in. He was in a great state of excitement and used adjectives freely to express his contempt for the Union and for those who had just perpetrated such an outrage upon the rights of a free people. There was only one other passenger in the car besides myself when this young man entered. He evidently expected to find nothing but sympathy when he got away from the "mud sills" engaged in compelling a "free people" to pull down a flag they adored. He turned to me saying: "Things have come to a ―― pretty pass when a free people can't choose their own flag. Where I came from if a man dares to say a word in favor of the Union we hang him to a limb of the first tree we come to." I replied that "after all we were not so intolerant in St. Louis as we might be; I had not seen a single rebel hung yet, nor heard of one; there were plenty of them who ought to be, however." The young man subsided. He was so crestfallen that I believe if I had ordered him to leave the car he would have gone quietly out, saying to himself: "More Yankee oppression."

By nightfall the late defenders of Camp Jackson were all within the walls of the St. Louis arsenal, prisoners of war. The next day I left St. Louis for Mattoon, Illinois, where I was to muster in the regiment from that congressional district. This was the 21st Illinois infantry, the regiment of which I subsequently became colonel. I mustered one regiment afterwards, when my services for the State were about closed.

Brigadier-General John Pope was stationed at Springfield, as United States mustering officer, all the time I was in the State service. He was a native of Illinois and well acquainted with most of the prominent men in the State. I was a carpet-bagger and knew but few of them. While I was on duty at Springfield the senators, representatives in Congress, ex-governors and the State legislators were nearly all at the State capital. The only acquaintance I made among them was with the governor, whom I was serving, and, by chance, with Senator S. A. Douglas. The only members of Congress I knew were Washburne and Philip Foulk. With the former, though he represented my district and we were citizens of the same town, I only became acquainted at the meeting when the first company of Galena volunteers was raised. Foulk I had known in St. Louis when I was a citizen of that city. I had been three years at West Point with Pope and had served with him a short time during the Mexican war, under General Taylor. I saw a good deal of him during my service with the State. On one occasion he said to me that I ought to go into the United States service. I told him I intended to do so if there was a war. He spoke of his acquaintance with the public men of the State, and said he could get them to recommend me for a position and that he would do all he could for me. I declined to receive endorsement for permission to fight for my country.

Going home for a day or two soon after this conversation with General Pope, I wrote from Galena the following letter to the Adjutant-General of the Army.

GALENA, ILLINOIS,
May 24, 1861.

COL. L. THOMAS,
     Adjt. Gen. U. S. A.,
        Washington, D. C.

SIR: — Having served for fifteen years in the regular army, including four years at West Point, and feeling it the duty of every one who has been educated at the Government expense to offer their services for the support of that Government, I have the honor, very respectfully, to tender my services, until the close of the war, in such capacity as may be offered. I would say, in view of my present age and length of service, I feel myself competent to command a regiment, if the President, in his judgment, should see fit to intrust one to me

Since the first call of the President I have been serving on the staff of the Governor of this State, rendering such aid as I could in the organization of our State militia, and am still engaged in that capacity. A letter addressed to me at Springfield, Illinois, will reach me.

I am very respectfully,
Your obt. svt.,
U. S. GRANT.

This letter failed to elicit an answer from the Adjutant-General of the Army. I presume it was hardly read by him, and certainly it could not have been submitted to higher authority. Subsequent to the war General Badeau having heard of this letter applied to the War Department for a copy of it. The letter could not be found and no one recollected ever having seen it. I took no copy when it was written. Long after the application of General Badeau, General Townsend, who had become Adjutant-General of the Army, while packing up papers preparatory to the removal of his office, found this letter in some out-of-the-way place. It had not been destroyed, but it had not been regularly filed away.

I felt some hesitation in suggesting rank as high as the colo-nelcy of a regiment, feeling somewhat doubtful whether I would be equal to the position. But I had seen nearly every colonel who had been mustered in from the State of Illinois, and some from Indiana, and felt that if they could command a regiment properly, and with credit, I could also.

Having but little to do after the muster of the last of the regiments authorized by the State legislature, I asked and ob-tained of the governor leave of absence for a week to visit my parents in Covington, Kentucky, immediately opposite Cin-cinnati. General McClellan had been made a major-general and had his headquarters at Cincinnati. In reality I wanted to see him. I had known him slightly at West Point, where we served one year together, and in the Mexican war. I was in hopes that when he saw me he would offer me a position on his staff. I called on two successive days at his office but failed to see him on either occasion, and returned to Springfield.

Chapter XVIII.

APPOINTED COLONEL OF THE 21ST ILLINOIS—PERSONNEL
OF THE REGIMENT—GENERAL LOGAN—MARCH TO
MISSOURI—MOVEMENT AGAINST HARRIS AT
FLORIDA, MO.—GENERAL POPE IN COMMAND—
STATIONED AT MEXICO, MO.

WHILE I WAS ABSENT from the State capital on this occasion the President's second call for troops was issued. This time it was for 300,000 men, for three years or the war. This brought into the United States service all the regiments then in the State service. These had elected their officers from highest to lowest and were accepted with their organizations as they were, except in two instances. A Chicago regiment, the 19th infantry, had elected a very young man to the colonelcy. When it came to taking the field the regiment asked to have another appointed colonel and the one they had previously chosen made lieutenant-colonel. The 21st regiment of infantry, mustered in by me at Mattoon, refused to go into the service with the colonel of their selection in any position. While I was still absent Governor Yates appointed me colonel of this latter regiment. A few days after I was in charge of it and in camp on the fair grounds near Springfield.

My regiment was composed in large part of young men of as good social position as any in their section of the State. It embraced the sons of farmers, lawyers, physicians, politicians, merchants, bankers and ministers, and some men of maturer years who had filled such positions themselves. There were also men in it who could be led astray; and the colonel, elected by the votes of the regiment, had proved to be fully capable of developing all there was in his men of recklessness. It was said that he even went so far at times as to take the guard from their posts and go with them to the village near by and make a night of it. When there came a prospect of battle the regiment wanted to have some one else to lead them. I found it very hard work for a few days to bring all the men into anything like subordination; but the great majority favored discipline, and by the application of a little regular army punishment all were reduced to as good discipline as one could ask.

The ten regiments which had volunteered in the State service for thirty days, it will be remembered, had done so with a pledge to go into the National service if called upon within that time. When they volunteered the government had only called for ninety days' enlistments. Men were called now for three years or the war. They felt that this change of period released them from the obligation of re-volunteering. When I was appointed colonel, the 21st regiment was still in the State service. About the time they were to be mustered into the United States service, such of them as would go, two members of Congress from the State, McClernand and Logan, appeared at the capital and I was introduced to them. I had never seen either of them before, but I had read a great deal about them, and particularly about Logan, in the newspapers. Both were democratic members of Congress, and Logan had been elected from the southern district of the State, where he had a majority of eighteen thousand over his Republican competitor. His district had been settled originally by people from the Southern States, and at the breaking out of secession they sympathized with the South. At the first outbreak of war some of them joined the Southern army; many others were preparing to do so; others rode over the country at night denouncing the Union, and made it as necessary to guard railroad bridges over which National troops had to pass in southern Illinois, as it was in Kentucky or any of the border slave states. Logan's popularity in this district was unbounded. He knew almost enough of the people in it by their Christian names, to form an ordinary congressional district. As he went in politics, so his district was sure to go. The Republican papers had been demanding that he should announce where he stood on the questions which at that time engrossed the whole of public thought. Some were very bitter in their denunciations of his silence. Logan was not a man to be coerced into an utterance by threats. He did, however, come out in a speech before the adjournment of the special session of Congress which was convened by the President soon after his inauguration, and announced his undying loyalty and devotion to the Union. But I had not happened to see that speech, so that when I first met Logan my impressions were those formed from reading denunciations of him. McClernand, on the other hand, had early taken strong grounds for the maintenance of the Union and had been praised accordingly by the Republican papers. The gentlemen who presented these two members of Congress asked me if I would have any objections to their addressing my regiment. I hesitated a little before answering. It was but a few days before the time set for mustering into the United States service such of the men as were willing to volunteer for three years or the war. I had some doubt as to the effect a speech from Logan might have; but as he was with McClernand, whose sentiments on the all-absorbing questions of the day were well known, I gave my consent. McClernand spoke first; and Logan followed in a speech which he has hardly equalled since for force and eloquence. It breathed a loyalty and devotion to the Union which inspired my men to such a point that they would have volunteered to remain in the army as long as an enemy of the country continued to bear arms against it. They entered the United States service almost to a man.

General Logan went to his part of the State and gave his attention to raising troops. The very men who at first made it necessary to guard the roads in southern Illinois became the defenders of the Union. Logan entered the service himself as colonel of a regiment and rapidly rose to the rank of major-general. His district, which had promised at first to give much trouble to the government, filled every call made upon it for troops, without resorting to the draft. There was no call made when there were not more volunteers than were asked for. That congressional district stands credited at the War Department to-day with furnishing more men for the army than it was called on to supply.

I remained in Springfield with my regiment until the 3d of July, when I was ordered to Quincy, Illinois. By that time the regiment was in a good state of discipline and the officers and men were well up in the company drill. There was direct railroad communication between Springfield and Quincy, but I thought it would be good preparation for the troops to march there. We had no transportation for our camp and garrison equipage, so wagons were hired for the occasion and on the 3d of July we started. There was no hurry, but fair marches were made every day until the Illinois River was crossed. There I was overtaken by a dispatch saying that the destination of the regiment had been changed to Ironton, Missouri, and ordering me to halt where I was and await the arrival of a steamer which had been dispatched up the Illinois River to take the regiment to St. Louis. The boat, when it did come, grounded on a sand-bar a few miles below where we were in camp. We remained there several days waiting to have the boat get off the bar, but before this occurred news came that an Illinois regiment was surrounded by rebels at a point on the Hannibal and St. Joe Railroad some miles west of Palmyra, in Missouri, and I was ordered to proceed with all dispatch to their relief. We took the cars and reached Quincy in a few hours.

When I left Galena for the last time to take command of the 21st regiment I took with me my oldest son, Frederick D. Grant, then a lad of eleven years of age. On receiving the order to take rail for Quincy I wrote to Mrs. Grant, to relieve what I supposed would be her great anxiety for one so young going into danger, that I would send Fred home from Quincy by river. I received a prompt letter in reply decidedly disapproving my proposition, and urging that the lad should be allowed to accompany me. It came too late. Fred was already on his way up the Mississippi bound for Dubuque, Iowa, from which place there was a railroad to Galena.

My sensations as we approached what I supposed might be "a field of battle" were anything but agreeable. I had been in all the engagements in Mexico that it was possible for one person to be in; but not in command. If some one else had been colonel and I had been lieutenant-colonel I do not think I would have felt any trepidation. Before we were prepared to cross the Mississippi River at Quincy my anxiety was relieved; for the men of the besieged regiment came straggling into town. I am inclined to think both sides got frightened and ran away.

I took my regiment to Palmyra and remained there for a few days, until relieved by the 19th Illinois infantry. From Palmyra I proceeded to Salt River, the railroad bridge over which had been destroyed by the enemy. Colonel John M.

Palmer at that time commanded the 13th Illinois, which was acting as a guard to workmen who were engaged in rebuilding this bridge. Palmer was my senior and commanded the two regiments as long as we remained together. The bridge was finished in about two weeks, and I received orders to move against Colonel Thomas Harris, who was said to be encamped at the little town of Florida, some twenty-five miles south of where we then were.

At the time of which I now write we had no transportation and the country about Salt River was sparsely settled, so that it took some days to collect teams and drivers enough to move the camp and garrison equipage of a regiment nearly a thousand strong, together with a week's supply of provision and some ammunition. While preparations for the move were going on I felt quite comfortable; but when we got on the road and found every house deserted I was anything but easy. In the twenty-five miles we had to march we did not see a person, old or young, male or female, except two horsemen who were on a road that crossed ours. As soon as they saw us they decamped as fast as their horses could carry them. I kept my men in the ranks and forbade their entering any of the deserted houses or taking anything from them. We halted at night on the road and proceeded the next morning at an early hour. Harris had been encamped in a creek bottom for the sake of being near water. The hills on either side of the creek extend to a considerable height, possibly more than a hundred feet. As we approached the brow of the hill from which it was expected we could see Harris' camp, and possibly find his men ready formed to meet us, my heart kept getting higher and higher until it felt to me as though it was in my throat. I would have given anything then to have been back in Illinois, but I had not the moral courage to halt and consider what to do; I kept right on. When we reached a point from which the valley below was in full view I halted. The place where Harris had been encamped a few days before was still there and the marks of a recent encampment were plainly visible, but the troops were gone. My heart resumed its place. It occurred to me at once that Harris had been as much afraid of me as I had been of him. This was a view of the question I had never taken before; but it was one I never forgot afterwards. From that event to the close of the war, I never experienced trepidation upon confronting an enemy, though I always felt more or less anxiety. I never forgot that he had as much reason to fear my forces as I had his. The lesson was valuable.

Inquiries at the village of Florida divulged the fact that Colonel Harris, learning of my intended movement, while my transportation was being collected took time by the forelock and left Florida before I had started from Salt River. He had increased the distance between us by forty miles. The next day I started back to my old camp at Salt River bridge. The citizens living on the line of our march had returned to their houses after we passed, and finding everything in good order, nothing carried away, they were at their front doors ready to greet us now. They had evidently been led to believe that the National troops carried death and devastation with them wherever they went.

In a short time after our return to Salt River bridge I was ordered with my regiment to the town of Mexico. General Pope was then commanding the district embracing all of the State of Missouri between the Mississippi and Missouri rivers, with his headquarters in the village of Mexico. I was assigned to the command of a sub-district embracing the troops in the immediate neighborhood, some three regiments of infantry and a section of artillery. There was one regiment encamped by the side of mine. I assumed command of the whole and the first night sent the commander of the other regiment the parole and countersign. Not wishing to be outdone in courtesy, he immediately sent me the countersign for his regiment for the night. When he was informed that the countersign sent to him was for use with his regiment as well as mine, it was difficult to make him understand that this was not an unwarranted interference of one colonel over another. No doubt he attributed it for the time to the presumption of a graduate of West Point over a volunteer pure and simple. But the question was soon settled and we had no further trouble.

My arrival in Mexico had been preceded by that of two or three regiments in which proper discipline had not been maintained, and the men had been in the habit of visiting houses without invitation and helping themselves to food and drink, or demanding them from the occupants. They carried their muskets while out of camp and made every man they found take the oath of allegiance to the government. I at once published orders prohibiting the soldiers from going into private houses unless invited by the inhabitants, and from appropriating private property to their own or to government uses. The people were no longer molested or made afraid. I received the most marked courtesy from the citizens of Mexico as long as I remained there.

Up to this time my regiment had not been carried in the school of the soldier beyond the company drill, except that it had received some training on the march from Springfield to the Illinois River. There was now a good opportunity of exercising it in the battalion drill. While I was at West Point the tactics used in the army had been Scott's and the musket the flint lock. I had never looked at a copy of tactics from the time of my graduation. My standing in that branch of studies had been near the foot of the class. In the Mexican war in the summer of 1846, I had been appointed regimental quartermaster and commissary and had not been at a battalion drill since. The arms had been changed since then and Hardee's tactics had been adopted. I got a copy of tactics and studied one lesson, intending to confine the exercise of the first day to the commands I had thus learned. By pursuing this course from day to day I thought I would soon get through the volume.

We were encamped just outside of town on the common, among scattering suburban houses with enclosed gardens, and when I got my regiment in line and rode to the front I soon saw that if I attempted to follow the lesson I had studied I would have to clear away some of the houses and garden fences to make room. I perceived at once, however, that Hardee's tactics—a mere translation from the French with Hardee's name attached—was nothing more than common sense and the progress of the age applied to Scott's system. The commands were abbreviated and the movement expedited. Under the old tactics almost every change in the order of march was preceded by a "halt," then came the change, and then the "forward march." With the new tactics all these changes could be made while in motion. I found no trouble in giving commands that would take my regiment where I wanted it to go and carry it around all obstacles. I do not believe that the officers of the regiment ever discovered that I had never studied the tactics that I used.

Chapter XIX.

I HAD NOT BEEN in Mexico many weeks when, reading a St. Louis paper, I found the President had asked the Illinois delegation in Congress to recommend some citizens of the State for the position of brigadier-general, and that they had unanimously recommended me as first on a list of seven. I was very much surprised because, as I have said, my acquaintance with the Congressmen was very limited and I did not know of anything I had done to inspire such confidence. The papers of the next day announced that my name, with three others, had been sent to the Senate, and a few days after our confirmation was announced.

When appointed brigadier-general I at once thought it proper that one of my aides should come from the regiment I had been commanding, and so selected Lieutenant C. B. Lagow. While living in St. Louis, I had had a desk in the law office of McClellan, Moody and Hillyer. Difference in views between the members of the firm on the questions of the day, and general hard times in the border cities, had broken up this firm. Hillyer was quite a young man, then in his twenties, and very brilliant. I asked him to accept a place on my staff. I also wanted to take one man from my new home, Galena. The canvass in the Presidential campaign the fall before had brought out a young lawyer by the name of John A. Rawlins, who proved himself one of the ablest speakers in the State. He was also a candidate for elector on the Douglas ticket. When Sumter was fired upon and the integrity of the Union threatened, there was no man more ready to serve his country than he. I wrote at once asking him to accept the position of assistant adjutant-general with the rank of captain, on my staff. He was about entering the service as major of a new regiment then organizing in the north-western part of the State; but he threw this up and accepted my offer.

Neither Hillyer nor Lagow proved to have any particular taste or special qualifications for the duties of the soldier, and the former resigned during the Vicksburg campaign; the latter I relieved after the battle of Chattanooga. Rawlins remained with me as long as he lived, and rose to the rank of brigadier-general and chief-of-staff to the General of the Army—an office created for him—before the war closed. He was an able man, possessed of great firmness, and could say "no" so emphatically to a request which he thought should not be granted that the person he was addressing would understand at once that there was no use of pressing the matter. General Rawlins was a very useful officer in other ways than this. I became very much attached to him.

Shortly after my promotion I was ordered to Ironton, Missouri, to command a district in that part of the State, and took the 21st Illinois, my old regiment, with me. Several other regiments were ordered to the same destination about the same time. Ironton is on the Iron Mountain railroad, about seventy miles south of St. Louis, and situated among hills rising almost to the dignity of mountains. When I reached there, about the 8th of August, Colonel B. Gratz Brown—afterwards Governor of Missouri and in 1872 Vice-Presidential candidate—was in command. Some of his troops were ninety days' men and their time had expired some time before. The men had no clothing but what they had volunteered in, and much of this was so worn that it would hardly stay on. General Hardee—the author of the tactics I did not study—was at Greenville, some twenty-five miles further south, it was said, with five thousand Confederate troops. Under these circumstances Colonel Brown's command was very much demoralized. A squadron of cavalry could have ridden into the valley and captured the entire force. Brown himself was gladder to see me on that occasion than he ever has been since. I relieved him and sent all his men home, within a day or two, to be mustered out of service.

Within ten days after reaching Ironton I was prepared to take the offensive against the enemy at Greenville. I sent a column east out of the valley we were in, with orders to swing around to the south and west and come into the Greenville road ten miles south of Ironton. Another column marched on the direct road and went into camp at the point designated for the two columns to meet. I was to ride out the next morning and take personal command of the movement. My experience against Harris, in northern Missouri, had inspired me with confidence. But when the evening train came in, it brought General B. M. Prentiss with orders to take command of the district. His orders did not relieve me, but I knew that by law I was senior, and at that time even the President did not have the authority to assign a junior to command a senior of the same grade. I therefore gave General Prentiss the situation of the troops and the general condition of affairs, and started for St. Louis the same day. The movement against the rebels at Greenville went no further.

From St. Louis I was ordered to Jefferson City, the capital of the State, to take command. General Sterling Price, of the Confederate army, was thought to be threatening the capital, Lexington, Chillicothe and other comparatively large towns in the central part of Missouri. I found a good many troops in Jefferson City, but in the greatest confusion, and no one person knew where they all were. Colonel Mulligan, a gallant man, was in command, but he had not been educated as yet to his new profession and did not know how to maintain discipline. I found that volunteers had obtained permission from the department commander, or claimed they had, to raise, some of them, regiments; some battalions; some companies—the officers to be commissioned according to the number of men they brought into the service. There were recruiting stations all over town, with notices, rudely lettered on boards over the doors, announcing the arm of service and length of time for which recruits at that station would be received. The law required all volunteers to serve for three years or the war. But in Jefferson City in August, 1861, they were recruited for different periods and on different conditions; some were enlisted for six months, some for a year, some without any condition as to where they were to serve, others were not to be sent out of the State. The recruits were principally men from regiments stationed there and already in the service, bound for three years if the war lasted that long.

The city was filled with Union fugitives who had been driven by guerilla bands to take refuge with the National troops. They were in a deplorable condition and must have starved but for the support the government gave them. They had generally made their escape with a team or two, sometimes a yoke of oxen with a mule or a horse in the lead. A little bedding besides their clothing and some food had been thrown into the wagon. All else of their worldly goods were abandoned and appropriated by their former neighbors; for the Union man in Missouri who staid at home during the rebellion, if he was not immediately under the protection of the National troops, was at perpetual war with his neighbors. I stopped the recruiting service, and disposed the troops about the outskirts of the city so as to guard all approaches. Order was soon restored.

I had been at Jefferson City but a few days when I was directed from department headquarters to fit out an expedition to Lexington, Booneville and Chillicothe, in order to take from the banks in those cities all the funds they had and send them to St. Louis. The western army had not yet been supplied with transportation. It became necessary therefore to press into the service teams belonging to sympathizers with the rebellion or to hire those of Union men. This afforded an opportunity of giving employment to such of the refugees within our lines as had teams suitable for our purposes. They accepted the service with alacrity. As fast as troops could be got off they were moved west some twenty miles or more. In seven or eight days from my assuming command at Jefferson City, I had all the troops, except a small garrison, at an advanced position and expected to join them myself the next day.

But my campaigns had not yet begun, for while seated at my office door, with nothing further to do until it was time to start for the front, I saw an officer of rank approaching, who proved to be Colonel Jefferson C. Davis. I had never met him before, but he introduced himself by handing me an order for him to proceed to Jefferson City and relieve me of the command. The orders directed that I should report at department headquarters at St. Louis without delay, to receive important special instructions. It was about an hour before the only regular train of the day would start. I therefore turned over to Colonel Davis my orders, and hurriedly stated to him the progress that had been made to carry out the department instructions already described. I had at that time but one staff officer,* doing myself all the detail work usually performed by an adjutant-general. In an hour after being relieved from the command I was on my way to St. Louis, leaving my single staff officer to follow the next day with our horses and baggage.

The "important special instructions" which I received the next day, assigned me to the command of the district of south-east Missouri, embracing all the territory south of St. Louis, in Missouri, as well as all southern Illinois. At first I was to take personal command of a combined expedition that had been ordered for the capture of Colonel Jeff. Thompson, a sort of independent or partisan commander who was disputing with us the possession of south-east Missouri. Troops had been ordered to move from Ironton to Cape Girardeau, sixty or seventy miles to the south-east, on the Mississippi River; while the forces at Cape Girardeau had been ordered to move to Jacksonville, ten miles out towards Ironton; and troops at Cairo and Bird's Point, at the junction of the Ohio and Mississippi rivers, were to hold themselves in readiness to go down the Mississippi to Belmont, eighteen miles below, to be moved west from there when an officer should come to command them. I was the officer who had been selected for this purpose. Cairo was to become my headquarters when the expedition terminated.

In pursuance of my orders I established my temporary headquarters at Cape Girardeau and sent instructions to the commanding officer at Jackson, to inform me of the approach of General Prentiss from Ironton. Hired wagons were kept moving night and day to take additional rations to Jackson, to supply the troops when they started from there. Neither General Prentiss nor Colonel Marsh, who commanded at Jackson, knew their destination. I drew up all the instructions for the contemplated move, and kept them in my pocket until I should hear of the junction of our troops at Jackson. Two or three days after my arrival at Cape Girardeau, word came that General Prentiss was approaching that place (Jackson). I

*C. B. Lagow, the others not yet having joined me.

started at once to meet him there and to give him his orders. As I turned the first corner of a street after starting, I saw a column of cavalry passing the next street in front of me. I turned and rode around the block the other way, so as to meet the head of the column. I found there General Prentiss himself, with a large escort. He had halted his troops at Jackson for the night, and had come on himself to Cape Girardeau, leaving orders for his command to follow him in the morning. I gave the General his orders—which stopped him at Jackson—but he was very much aggrieved at being placed under another brigadier-general, particularly as he believed himself to be the senior. He had been a brigadier, in command at Cairo, while I was mustering officer at Springfield without any rank. But we were nominated at the same time for the United States service, and both our commissions bore date May 17th, 1861. By virtue of my former army rank I was, by law, the senior. General Prentiss failed to get orders to his troops to remain at Jackson, and the next morning early they were reported as approaching Cape Girardeau. I then ordered the General very peremptorily to countermarch his command and take it back to Jackson. He obeyed the order, but bade his command adieu when he got them to Jackson, and went to St. Louis and reported himself. This broke up the expedition. But little harm was done, as Jeff. Thompson moved light and had no fixed place for even nominal headquarters. He was as much at home in Arkansas as he was in Missouri and would keep out of the way of a superior force. Prentiss was sent to another part of the State.

General Prentiss made a great mistake on the above occasion, one that he would not have committed later in the war. When I came to know him better, I regretted it much. In consequence of this occurrence he was off duty in the field when the principal campaign at the West was going on, and his juniors received promotion while he was where none could be obtained. He would have been next to myself in rank in the district of south-east Missouri, by virtue of his services in the Mexican war. He was a brave and very earnest soldier. No man in the service was more sincere in his devotion to the cause for which we were battling; none more ready to make sacrifices or risk life in it.

On the 4th of September I removed my headquarters to Cairo and found Colonel Richard Oglesby in command of the post. We had never met, at least not to my knowledge. After my promotion I had ordered my brigadier-general's uniform from New York, but it had not yet arrived, so that I was in citizen's dress. The Colonel had his office full of people, mostly from the neighboring States of Missouri and Kentucky, making complaints or asking favors. He evidently did not catch my name when I was presented, for on my taking a piece of paper from the table where he was seated and writing the order assuming command of the district of south-east Missouri, Colonel Richard J. Oglesby to command the post at Bird's Point, and handing it to him, he put on an expression of surprise that looked a little as if he would like to have some one identify me. But he surrendered the office without question.

The day after I assumed command at Cairo a man came to me who said he was a scout of General Fremont. He reported that he had just come from Columbus, a point on the Mississippi twenty miles below on the Kentucky side, and that troops had started from there, or were about to start, to seize Paducah, at the mouth of the Tennessee. There was no time for delay; I reported by telegraph to the department commander the information I had received, and added that I was taking steps to get off that night to be in advance of the enemy in securing that important point. There was a large number of steamers lying at Cairo and a good many boatmen were staying in the town. It was the work of only a few hours to get the boats manned, with coal aboard and steam up. Troops were also designated to go aboard. The distance from Cairo to Paducah is about forty-five miles. I did not wish to get there before daylight of the 6th, and directed therefore that the boats should lie at anchor out in the stream until the time to start. Not having received an answer to my first dispatch, I again telegraphed to department headquarters that I should start for Paducah that night unless I received further orders. Hearing nothing, we started before midnight and arrived early the following morning, anticipating the enemy by probably not over six or eight hours. It proved very fortunate that the expedition against Jeff. Thompson had been broken up. Had it not been, the enemy would have seized Paducah and fortified it, to our very great annoyance.

When the National troops entered the town the citizens were taken by surprise. I never after saw such consternation depicted on the faces of the people. Men, women and children came out of their doors looking pale and frightened at the presence of the invader. They were expecting rebel troops that day. In fact, nearly four thousand men from Columbus were at that time within ten or fifteen miles of Paducah on their way to occupy the place. I had but two regiments and one battery with me; but the enemy did not know this and returned to Columbus. I stationed my troops at the best points to guard the roads leading into the city, left gunboats to guard the river fronts and by noon was ready to start on my return to Cairo. Before leaving, however, I addressed a short printed proclamation to the citizens of Paducah assuring them of our peaceful intentions, that we had come among them to protect them against the enemies of our country, and that all who chose could continue their usual avocations with assurance of the protection of the government. This was evidently a relief to them; but the majority would have much preferred the presence of the other army. I reinforced Paducah rapidly from the troops at Cape Girardeau; and a day or two later General C. F. Smith, a most accomplished soldier, reported at Cairo and was assigned to the command of the post at the mouth of the Tennessee. In a short time it was well fortified and a detachment was sent to occupy Smithland, at the mouth of the Cumberland.

The State government of Kentucky at that time was rebel in sentiment, but wanted to preserve an armed neutrality between the North and the South, and the governor really seemed to think the State had a perfect right to maintain a neutral position. The rebels already occupied two towns in the State, Columbus and Hickman, on the Mississippi; and at the very moment the National troops were entering Paducah from the Ohio front, General Lloyd Tilghman—a Confederate—with his staff and a small detachment of men, were getting out in the other direction, while, as I have already said, nearly four thousand Confederate troops were on Kentucky soil on their way to take possession of the town. But, in the estimation of the governor and of those who thought with him, this did not justify the National authorities in invading the soil of Kentucky. I informed the legislature of the State of what I was doing, and my action was approved by the majority of that body. On my return to Cairo I found authority from department headquarters for me to take Paducah "if I felt strong enough," but very soon after I was reprimanded from the same quarters for my correspondence with the legislature and warned against a repetition of the offence.

Soon after I took command at Cairo, General Fremont entered into arrangements for the exchange of the prisoners captured at Camp Jackson in the month of May. I received orders to pass them through my lines to Columbus as they presented themselves with proper credentials. Quite a number of these prisoners I had been personally acquainted with before the war. Such of them as I had so known were received at my headquarters as old acquaintances, and ordinary routine business was not disturbed by their presence. On one occasion when several were present in my office my intention to visit Cape Girardeau the next day, to inspect the troops at that point, was mentioned. Something transpired which postponed my trip; but a steamer employed by the government was passing a point some twenty or more miles above Cairo, the next day, when a section of rebel artillery with proper escort brought her to. A major, one of those who had been at my headquarters the day before, came at once aboard and after some search made a direct demand for my delivery. It was hard to persuade him that I was not there. This officer was Major Barrett, of St. Louis. I had been acquainted with his family before the war.

Chapter XX.

GENERAL FREMONT IN COMMAND—MOVEMENT AGAINST
BELMONT—BATTLE OF BELMONT—A NARROW
ESCAPE—AFTER THE BATTLE.

FROM THE OCCUPATION of Paducah up to the early part of
November nothing important occurred with the troops
under my command. I was reinforced from time to time and
the men were drilled and disciplined preparatory for the service which was sure to come. By the 1st of November I had
not fewer than 20,000 men, most of them under good drill
and ready to meet any equal body of men who, like themselves, had not yet been in an engagement. They were growing impatient at lying idle so long, almost in hearing of the
guns of the enemy they had volunteered to fight against. I
asked on one or two occasions to be allowed to move against
Columbus. It could have been taken soon after the occupation of Paducah; but before November it was so strongly
fortified that it would have required a large force and a long
siege to capture it.

In the latter part of October General Fremont took the field
in person and moved from Jefferson City against General
Sterling Price, who was then in the State of Missouri with a
considerable command. About the first of November I was
directed from department headquarters to make a demonstration on both sides of the Mississippi River with the view of
detaining the rebels at Columbus within their lines. Before
my troops could be got off, I was notified from the same
quarter that there were some 3,000 of the enemy on the St.
Francis River about fifty miles west, or south-west, from
Cairo, and was ordered to send another force against them. I
dispatched Colonel Oglesby at once with troops sufficient to
compete with the reported number of the enemy. On the 5th
word came from the same source that the rebels were about
to detach a large force from Columbus to be moved by boats
down the Mississippi and up the White River, in Arkansas, in
order to reinforce Price, and I was directed to prevent this
movement if possible. I accordingly sent a regiment from

Bird's Point under Colonel W. H. L. Wallace to overtake and reinforce Oglesby, with orders to march to New Madrid, a point some distance below Columbus, on the Missouri side. At the same time I directed General C. F. Smith to move all the troops he could spare from Paducah directly against Columbus, halting them, however, a few miles from the town to await further orders from me. Then I gathered up all the troops at Cairo and Fort Holt, except suitable guards, and moved them down the river on steamers convoyed by two gunboats, accompanying them myself. My force consisted of a little over 3,000 men and embraced five regiments of infantry, two guns and two companies of cavalry. We dropped down the river on the 6th to within about six miles of Columbus, debarked a few men on the Kentucky side and established pickets to connect with the troops from Paducah.

I had no orders which contemplated an attack by the National troops, nor did I intend anything of the kind when I started out from Cairo; but after we started I saw that the officers and men were elated at the prospect of at last having the opportunity of doing what they had volunteered to do— fight the enemies of their country. I did not see how I could maintain discipline, or retain the confidence of my command, if we should return to Cairo without an effort to do something. Columbus, besides being strongly fortified, contained a garrison much more numerous than the force I had with me. It would not do, therefore, to attack that point. About two o'clock on the morning of the 7th, I learned that the enemy was crossing troops from Columbus to the west bank to be dispatched, presumably, after Oglesby. I knew there was a small camp of Confederates at Belmont, immediately opposite Columbus, and I speedily resolved to push down the river, land on the Missouri side, capture Belmont, break up the camp and return. Accordingly, the pickets above Columbus were drawn in at once, and about daylight the boats moved out from shore. In an hour we were debarking on the west bank of the Mississippi, just out of range of the batteries at Columbus.

The ground on the west shore of the river, opposite Columbus, is low and in places marshy and cut up with sloughs.

The soil is rich and the timber large and heavy. There were some small clearings between Belmont and the point where we landed, but most of the country was covered with the native forests. We landed in front of a cornfield. When the debarkation commenced, I took a regiment down the river to post it as a guard against surprise. At that time I had no staff officer who could be trusted with that duty. In the woods, at a short distance below the clearing, I found a depression, dry at the time, but which at high water became a slough or bayou. I placed the men in the hollow, gave them their instructions and ordered them to remain there until they were properly relieved. These troops, with the gunboats, were to protect our transports.

Up to this time the enemy had evidently failed to divine our intentions. From Columbus they could, of course, see our gunboats and transports loaded with troops. But the force from Paducah was threatening them from the land side, and it was hardly to be expected that if Columbus was our object we would separate our troops by a wide river. They doubtless thought we meant to draw a large force from the east bank, then embark ourselves, land on the east bank and make a sudden assault on Columbus before their divided command could be united.

About eight o'clock we started from the point of debarkation, marching by the flank. After moving in this way for a mile or a mile and a half, I halted where there was marshy ground covered with a heavy growth of timber in our front, and deployed a large part of my force as skirmishers. By this time the enemy discovered that we were moving upon Belmont and sent out troops to meet us. Soon after we had started in line, his skirmishers were encountered and fighting commenced. This continued, growing fiercer and fiercer, for about four hours, the enemy being forced back gradually until he was driven into his camp. Early in this engagement my horse was shot under me, but I got another from one of my staff and kept well up with the advance until the river was reached.

The officers and men engaged at Belmont were then under fire for the first time. Veterans could not have behaved better than they did up to the moment of reaching the rebel camp.

At this point they became demoralized from their victory and failed to reap its full reward. The enemy had been followed so closely that when he reached the clear ground on which his camp was pitched he beat a hasty retreat over the river bank, which protected him from our shots and from view. This precipitate retreat at the last moment enabled the National forces to pick their way without hinderance through the abatis—the only artificial defence the enemy had. The moment the camp was reached our men laid down their arms and commenced rummaging the tents to pick up trophies. Some of the higher officers were little better than the privates. They galloped about from one cluster of men to another and at every halt delivered a short eulogy upon the Union cause and the achievements of the command.

All this time the troops we had been engaged with for four hours, lay crouched under cover of the river bank, ready to come up and surrender if summoned to do so; but finding that they were not pursued, they worked their way up the river and came up on the bank between us and our transports. I saw at the same time two steamers coming from the Columbus side towards the west shore, above us, black—or gray—with soldiers from boiler-deck to roof. Some of my men were engaged in firing from captured guns at empty steamers down the river, out of range, cheering at every shot. I tried to get them to turn their guns upon the loaded steamers above and not so far away. My efforts were in vain. At last I directed my staff officers to set fire to the camps. This drew the fire of the enemy's guns located on the heights of Columbus. They had abstained from firing before, probably because they were afraid of hitting their own men; or they may have supposed, until the camp was on fire, that it was still in the possession of their friends. About this time, too, the men we had driven over the bank were seen in line up the river between us and our transports. The alarm "surrounded" was given. The guns of the enemy and the report of being surrounded, brought officers and men completely under control. At first some of the officers seemed to think that to be surrounded was to be placed in a hopeless position, where there was nothing to do but surrender. But when I announced that we had cut our way in and could cut our way out just as well, it seemed a

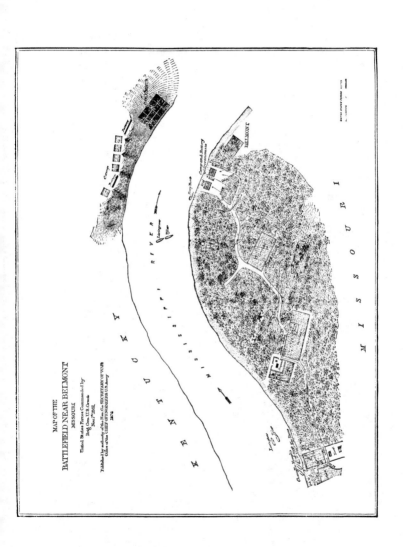

MAP OF THE
BATTLEFIELD NEAR BELMONT
MISSOURI

United States Forces Commanded by
Brig. Gen. U.S. Grant
Nov. 7th 1861.

Published by authority of the from the SECRETARY OF WAR
Office of the CHIEF OF ENGINEERS U.S. Army
1874

KENTUCKY

Mississippi River

MISSOURI

BELMONT

new revelation to officers and soldiers. They formed line rapidly and we started back to our boats, with the men deployed as skirmishers as they had been on entering camp. The enemy was soon encountered, but his resistance this time was feeble. Again the Confederates sought shelter under the river banks. We could not stop, however, to pick them up, because the troops we had seen crossing the river had debarked by this time and were nearer our transports than we were. It would be prudent to get them behind us; but we were not again molested on our way to the boats.

From the beginning of the fighting our wounded had been carried to the houses at the rear, near the place of debarkation. I now set the troops to bringing their wounded to the boats. After this had gone on for some little time I rode down the road, without even a staff officer, to visit the guard I had stationed over the approach to our transports. I knew the enemy had crossed over from Columbus in considerable numbers and might be expected to attack us as we were embarking. This guard would be encountered first and, as they were in a natural intrenchment, would be able to hold the enemy for a considerable time. My surprise was great to find there was not a single man in the trench. Riding back to the boat I found the officer who had commanded the guard and learned that he had withdrawn his force when the main body fell back. At first I ordered the guard to return, but finding that it would take some time to get the men together and march them back to their position, I countermanded the order. Then fearing that the enemy we had seen crossing the river below might be coming upon us unawares, I rode out in the field to our front, still entirely alone, to observe whether the enemy was passing. The field was grown up with corn so tall and thick as to cut off the view of even a person on horseback, except directly along the rows. Even in that direction, owing to the overhanging blades of corn, the view was not extensive. I had not gone more than a few hundred yards when I saw a body of troops marching past me not fifty yards away. I looked at them for a moment and then turned my horse towards the river and started back, first in a walk, and when I thought myself concealed from the view of the enemy, as fast as my horse could carry me.

When at the river bank I still had to ride a few hundred yards to the point where the nearest transport lay.

The cornfield in front of our transports terminated at the edge of a dense forest. Before I got back the enemy had entered this forest and had opened a brisk fire upon the boats. Our men, with the exception of details that had gone to the front after the wounded, were now either aboard the transports or very near them. Those who were not aboard soon got there, and the boats pushed off. I was the only man of the National army between the rebels and our transports. The captain of a boat that had just pushed out but had not started, recognized me and ordered the engineer not to start the engine; he then had a plank run out for me. My horse seemed to take in the situation. There was no path down the bank and every one acquainted with the Mississippi River knows that its banks, in a natural state, do not vary at any great angle from the perpendicular. My horse put his fore feet over the bank without hesitation or urging, and with his hind feet well under him, slid down the bank and trotted aboard the boat, twelve or fifteen feet away, over a single gang plank. I dismounted and went at once to the upper deck.

The Mississippi River was low on the 7th of November, 1861, so that the banks were higher than the heads of men standing on the upper decks of the steamers. The rebels were some distance back from the river, so that their fire was high and did us but little harm. Our smoke-stack was riddled with bullets, but there were only three men wounded on the boats, two of whom were soldiers. When I first went on deck I entered the captain's room adjoining the pilot-house, and threw myself on a sofa. I did not keep that position a moment, but rose to go out on the deck to observe what was going on. I had scarcely left when a musket ball entered the room, struck the head of the sofa, passed through it and lodged in the foot.

When the enemy opened fire on the transports our gunboats returned it with vigor. They were well out in the stream and some distance down, so that they had to give but very little elevation to their guns to clear the banks of the river. Their position very nearly enfiladed the line of the enemy while he was marching through the cornfield. The execution was very great, as we could see at the time and as I afterwards learned more positively. We were very soon out of range and went peacefully on our way to Cairo, every man feeling that Belmont was a great victory and that he had contributed his share to it.

Our loss at Belmont was 485 in killed, wounded and missing. About 125 of our wounded fell into the hands of the enemy. We returned with 175 prisoners and two guns, and spiked four other pieces. The loss of the enemy, as officially reported, was 642 men, killed, wounded and missing. We had engaged about 2,500 men, exclusive of the guard left with the transports. The enemy had about 7,000; but this includes the troops brought over from Columbus who were not engaged in the first defence of Belmont.

The two objects for which the battle of Belmont was fought were fully accomplished. The enemy gave up all idea of detaching troops from Columbus. His losses were very heavy for that period of the war. Columbus was beset by people looking for their wounded or dead kin, to take them home for medical treatment or burial. I learned later, when I had moved further south, that Belmont had caused more mourning than almost any other battle up to that time. The National troops acquired a confidence in themselves at Belmont that did not desert them through the war.

The day after the battle I met some officers from General Polk's command, arranged for permission to bury our dead at Belmont and also commenced negotiations for the exchange of prisoners. When our men went to bury their dead, before they were allowed to land they were conducted below the point where the enemy had engaged our transports. Some of the officers expressed a desire to see the field; but the request was refused with the statement that we had no dead there.

While on the truce-boat I mentioned to an officer, whom I had known both at West Point and in the Mexican war, that I was in the cornfield near their troops when they passed; that I had been on horseback and had worn a soldier's overcoat at the time. This officer was on General Polk's staff. He said both he and the general had seen me and that Polk had said to his men, "There is a Yankee; you may try your marksmanship on him if you wish," but nobody fired at me.

Belmont was severely criticised in the North as a wholly unnecessary battle, barren of results, or the possibility of them from the beginning. If it had not been fought, Colonel Oglesby would probably have been captured or destroyed with his three thousand men. Then I should have been culpable indeed.

Chapter XXI.

GENERAL HALLECK IN COMMAND—COMMANDING THE
DISTRICT OF CAIRO—MOVEMENT ON FORT
HENRY—CAPTURE OF FORT HENRY.

WHILE AT CAIRO I had frequent opportunities of meeting the rebel officers of the Columbus garrison. They seemed to be very fond of coming up on steamers under flags of truce. On two or three occasions I went down in like manner. When one of their boats was seen coming up carrying a white flag, a gun would be fired from the lower battery at Fort Holt, throwing a shot across the bow as a signal to come no farther. I would then take a steamer and, with my staff and occasionally a few other officers, go down to receive the party. There were several officers among them whom I had known before, both at West Point and in Mexico. Seeing these officers who had been educated for the profession of arms, both at school and in actual war, which is a far more efficient training, impressed me with the great advantage the South possessed over the North at the beginning of the rebellion. They had from thirty to forty per cent. of the educated soldiers of the Nation. They had no standing army and, consequently, these trained soldiers had to find employment with the troops from their own States. In this way what there was of military education and training was distributed throughout their whole army. The whole loaf was leavened.

The North had a greater number of educated and trained soldiers, but the bulk of them were still in the army and were retained, generally with their old commands and rank, until the war had lasted many months. In the Army of the Potomac there was what was known as the "regular brigade," in which, from the commanding officer down to the youngest second lieutenant, every one was educated to his profession. So, too, with many of the batteries; all the officers, generally four in number to each, were men educated for their profession. Some of these went into battle at the beginning under division commanders who were entirely without military training. This state of affairs gave me an idea which I expressed

while at Cairo; that the government ought to disband the regular army, with the exception of the staff corps, and notify the
disbanded officers that they would receive no compensation
while the war lasted except as volunteers. The register should
be kept up, but the names of all officers who were not in the
volunteer service at the close, should be stricken from it.

On the 9th of November, two days after the battle of Belmont, Major-General H. W. Halleck superseded General Fremont in command of the Department of the Missouri. The
limits of his command took in Arkansas and west Kentucky
east to the Cumberland River. From the battle of Belmont
until early in February, 1862, the troops under my command
did little except prepare for the long struggle which proved to
be before them.

The enemy at this time occupied a line running from the
Mississippi River at Columbus to Bowling Green and Mill
Springs, Kentucky. Each of these positions was strongly fortified, as were also points on the Tennessee and Cumberland
rivers near the Tennessee state line. The works on the Tennessee were called Fort Heiman and Fort Henry, and that on the
Cumberland was Fort Donelson. At these points the two
rivers approached within eleven miles of each other. The lines
of rifle pits at each place extended back from the water at
least two miles, so that the garrisons were in reality only
seven miles apart. These positions were of immense importance to the enemy; and of course correspondingly important
for us to possess ourselves of. With Fort Henry in our hands
we had a navigable stream open to us up to Muscle Shoals, in
Alabama. The Memphis and Charleston Railroad strikes the
Tennessee at Eastport, Mississippi, and follows close to the
banks of the river up to the shoals. This road, of vast importance to the enemy, would cease to be of use to them for
through traffic the moment Fort Henry became ours. Fort
Donelson was the gate to Nashville—a place of great military
and political importance—and to a rich country extending far
east in Kentucky. These two points in our possession the enemy would necessarily be thrown back to the Memphis and
Charleston road, or to the boundary of the cotton states, and,
as before stated, that road would be lost to them for through
communication.

The designation of my command had been changed after Halleck's arrival, from the District of South-east Missouri to the District of Cairo, and the small district commanded by General C. F. Smith, embracing the mouths of the Tennessee and Cumberland rivers, had been added to my jurisdiction. Early in January, 1862, I was directed by General McClellan, through my department commander, to make a reconnoissance in favor of Brigadier-General Don Carlos Buell, who commanded the Department of the Ohio, with headquarters at Louisville, and who was confronting General S. B. Buckner with a larger Confederate force at Bowling Green. It was supposed that Buell was about to make some move against the enemy, and my demonstration was intended to prevent the sending of troops from Columbus, Fort Henry or Donelson to Buckner. I at once ordered General Smith to send a force up the west bank of the Tennessee to threaten forts Heiman and Henry; McClernand at the same time with a force of 6,000 men was sent out into west Kentucky, threatening Columbus with one column and the Tennessee River with another. I went with McClernand's command. The weather was very bad; snow and rain fell; the roads, never good in that section, were intolerable. We were out more than a week splashing through the mud, snow and rain, the men suffering very much. The object of the expedition was accomplished. The enemy did not send reinforcements to Bowling Green, and General George H. Thomas fought and won the battle of Mill Springs before we returned.

As a result of this expedition General Smith reported that he thought it practicable to capture Fort Heiman. This fort stood on high ground, completely commanding Fort Henry on the opposite side of the river, and its possession by us, with the aid of our gunboats, would insure the capture of Fort Henry. This report of Smith's confirmed views I had previously held, that the true line of operations for us was up the Tennessee and Cumberland rivers. With us there, the enemy would be compelled to fall back on the east and west entirely out of the State of Kentucky. On the 6th of January, before receiving orders for this expedition, I had asked permission of the general commanding the department to go to see him at St. Louis. My object was to lay this plan of campaign before him. Now that my views had been confirmed by so able a general as Smith, I renewed my request to go to St. Louis on what I deemed important military business. The leave was granted, but not graciously. I had known General Halleck but very slightly in the old army, not having met him either at West Point or during the Mexican war. I was received with so little cordiality that I perhaps stated the object of my visit with less clearness than I might have done, and I had not uttered many sentences before I was cut short as if my plan was preposterous. I returned to Cairo very much crestfallen.

Flag-officer Foote commanded the little fleet of gunboats then in the neighborhood of Cairo and, though in another branch of the service, was subject to the command of General Halleck. He and I consulted freely upon military matters and he agreed with me perfectly as to the feasibility of the campaign up the Tennessee. Notwithstanding the rebuff I had received from my immediate chief, I therefore, on the 28th of January, renewed the suggestion by telegraph that "if permitted, I could take and hold Fort Henry on the Tennessee." This time I was backed by Flag-officer Foote, who sent a similar dispatch. On the 29th I wrote fully in support of the proposition. On the 1st of February I received full instructions from department headquarters to move upon Fort Henry. On the 2d the expedition started.

In February, 1862, there were quite a good many steamers laid up at Cairo for want of employment, the Mississippi River being closed against navigation below that point. There were also many men in the town whose occupation had been following the river in various capacities, from captain down to deck hand. But there were not enough of either boats or men to move at one time the 17,000 men I proposed to take with me up the Tennessee. I loaded the boats with more than half the force, however, and sent General McClernand in command. I followed with one of the later boats and found McClernand had stopped, very properly, nine miles below Fort Henry. Seven gunboats under Flag-officer Foote had accompanied the advance. The transports we had with us had to return to Paducah to bring up a division from there, with General C. F. Smith in command.

Before sending the boats back I wanted to get the troops as near to the enemy as I could without coming within range of their guns. There was a stream emptying into the Tennessee on the east side, apparently at about long range distance below the fort. On account of the narrow watershed separating the Tennessee and Cumberland rivers at that point, the stream must be insignificant at ordinary stages, but when we were there, in February, it was a torrent. It would facilitate the investment of Fort Henry materially if the troops could be landed south of that stream. To test whether this could be done I boarded the gunboat *Essex* and requested Captain Wm. Porter commanding it, to approach the fort to draw its fire. After we had gone some distance past the mouth of the stream we drew the fire of the fort, which fell much short of us. In consequence I had made up my mind to return and bring the troops to the upper side of the creek, when the enemy opened upon us with a rifled gun that sent shot far beyond us and beyond the stream. One shot passed very near where Captain Porter and I were standing, struck the deck near the stern, penetrated and passed through the cabin and so out into the river. We immediately turned back, and the troops were debarked below the mouth of the creek.

When the landing was completed I returned with the transports to Paducah to hasten up the balance of the troops. I got back on the 5th with the advance, the remainder following as rapidly as the steamers could carry them. At ten o'clock at night, on the 5th, the whole command was not yet up. Being anxious to commence operations as soon as possible before the enemy could reinforce heavily, I issued my orders for an advance at 11 A.M. on the 6th. I felt sure that all the troops would be up by that time.

Fort Henry occupies a bend in the river which gave the guns in the water battery a direct fire down the stream. The camp outside the fort was intrenched, with rifle pits and outworks two miles back on the road to Donelson and Dover. The garrison of the fort and camp was about 2,800, with strong reinforcements from Donelson halted some miles out. There were seventeen heavy guns in the fort. The river was very high, the banks being overflowed except where the bluffs come to the water's edge. A portion of the ground on which Fort Henry stood was two feet deep in water. Below, the water extended into the woods several hundred yards back from the bank on the east side. On the west bank Fort Heiman stood on high ground, completely commanding Fort Henry. The distance from Fort Henry to Donelson is but eleven miles. The two positions were so important to the enemy, *as he saw his interest*, that it was natural to suppose that reinforcements would come from every quarter from which they could be got. Prompt action on our part was imperative.

The plan was for the troops and gunboats to start at the same moment. The troops were to invest the garrison and the gunboats to attack the fort at close quarters. General Smith was to land a brigade of his division on the west bank during the night of the 5th and get it in rear of Heiman.

At the hour designated the troops and gunboats started. General Smith found Fort Heiman had been evacuated before his men arrived. The gunboats soon engaged the water batteries at very close quarters, but the troops which were to invest Fort Henry were delayed for want of roads, as well as by the dense forest and the high water in what would in dry weather have been unimportant beds of streams. This delay made no difference in the result. On our first appearance Tilghman had sent his entire command, with the exception of about one hundred men left to man the guns in the fort, to the outworks on the road to Dover and Donelson, so as to have them out of range of the guns of our navy; and before any attack on the 6th he had ordered them to retreat on Donelson. He stated in his subsequent report that the defence was intended solely to give his troops time to make their escape.

Tilghman was captured with his staff and ninety men, as well as the armament of the fort, the ammunition and whatever stores were there. Our cavalry pursued the retreating column towards Donelson and picked up two guns and a few stragglers; but the enemy had so much the start, that the pursuing force did not get in sight of any except the stragglers.

All the gunboats engaged were hit many times. The damage, however, beyond what could be repaired by a small expenditure of money, was slight, except to the *Essex*. A shell penetrated the boiler of that vessel and exploded it, killing

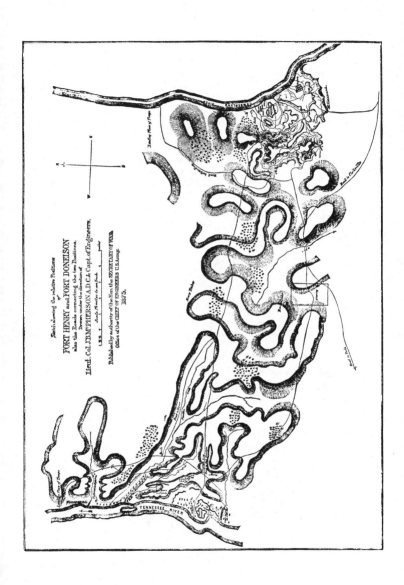

Sketch showing the relative Positions of
FORT HENRY and FORT DONELSON
also the Roads connecting the two Positions.
Drawn under the direction of
Lieut. Col. J.B. McPHERSON A.D.C. & Capt. of Engineers.
1875.
Published by authority of the Hon. the SECRETARY OF WAR
Office of the CHIEF OF ENGINEERS U.S. Army.
1875.

TENNESSEE RIVER

and wounding forty-eight men, nineteen of whom were soldiers who had been detailed to act with the navy. On several occasions during the war such details were made when the complement of men with the navy was insufficient for the duty before them. After the fall of Fort Henry Captain Walke, commanding the iron-clad *Carondelet*, at my request ascended the Tennessee River and thoroughly destroyed the bridge of the Memphis and Ohio Railroad.

Chapter XXII.

INVESTMENT OF FORT DONELSON—THE NAVAL
OPERATIONS—ATTACK OF THE ENEMY—ASSAULTING
THE WORKS—SURRENDER OF THE FORT.

I INFORMED the department commander of our success at Fort Henry and that on the 8th I would take Fort Donelson. But the rain continued to fall so heavily that the roads became impassable for artillery and wagon trains. Then, too, it would not have been prudent to proceed without the gunboats. At least it would have been leaving behind a valuable part of our available force.

On the 7th, the day after the fall of Fort Henry, I took my staff and the cavalry—a part of one regiment—and made a reconnoissance to within about a mile of the outer line of works at Donelson. I had known General Pillow in Mexico, and judged that with any force, no matter how small, I could march up to within gunshot of any intrenchments he was given to hold. I said this to the officers of my staff at the time. I knew that Floyd was in command, but he was no soldier, and I judged that he would yield to Pillow's pretensions. I met, as I expected, no opposition in making the reconnoissance and, besides learning the topography of the country on the way and around Fort Donelson, found that there were two roads available for marching; one leading to the village of Dover, the other to Donelson.

Fort Donelson is two miles north, or down the river, from Dover. The fort, as it stood in 1861, embraced about one hundred acres of land. On the east it fronted the Cumberland; to the north it faced Hickman's creek, a small stream which at that time was deep and wide because of the back-water from the river; on the south was another small stream, or rather a ravine, opening into the Cumberland. This also was filled with back-water from the river. The fort stood on high ground, some of it as much as a hundred feet above the Cumberland. Strong protection to the heavy guns in the water batteries had been obtained by cutting away places for them in the bluff. To the west there was a line of rifle-pits some two miles back from the river at the farthest point. This line ran generally along the crest of high ground, but in one place crossed a ravine which opens into the river between the village and the fort. The ground inside and out-side of this intrenched line was very broken and generally wooded. The trees outside of the rifle-pits had been cut down for a considerable way out, and had been felled so that their tops lay outwards from the intrenchments. The limbs had been trimmed and pointed, and thus formed an abatis in front of the greater part of the line. Outside of this intrenched line, and extending about half the entire length of it, is a ravine running north and south and opening into Hickman creek at a point north of the fort. The entire side of this ravine next to the works was one long abatis.

General Halleck commenced his efforts in all quarters to get reinforcements to forward to me immediately on my de-parture from Cairo. General Hunter sent men freely from Kansas, and a large division under General Nelson, from Buell's army, was also dispatched. Orders went out from the War Department to consolidate fragments of companies that were being recruited in the Western States so as to make full companies, and to consolidate companies into regiments. General Halleck did not approve or disapprove of my going to Fort Donelson. He said nothing whatever to me on the subject. He informed Buell on the 7th that I would march against Fort Donelson the next day; but on the 10th he di-rected me to fortify Fort Henry strongly, particularly to the land side, saying that he forwarded me intrenching tools for that purpose. I received this dispatch in front of Fort Donelson.

I was very impatient to get to Fort Donelson because I knew the importance of the place to the enemy and supposed he would reinforce it rapidly. I felt that 15,000 men on the 8th would be more effective than 50,000 a month later. I asked Flag-officer Foote, therefore, to order his gunboats still about Cairo to proceed up the Cumberland River and not to wait for those gone to Eastport and Florence; but the others got back in time and we started on the 12th. I had moved McCler-nand out a few miles the night before so as to leave the road as free as possible.

Just as we were about to start the first reinforcement reached me on transports. It was a brigade composed of six full regiments commanded by Colonel Thayer, of Nebraska. As the gunboats were going around to Donelson by the Tennessee, Ohio and Cumberland rivers, I directed Thayer to turn about and go under their convoy.

I started from Fort Henry with 15,000 men, including eight batteries and part of a regiment of cavalry, and, meeting with no obstruction to detain us, the advance arrived in front of the enemy by noon. That afternoon and the next day were spent in taking up ground to make the investment as complete as possible. General Smith had been directed to leave a portion of his division behind to guard forts Henry and Heiman. He left General Lew. Wallace with 2,500 men. With the remainder of his division he occupied our left, extending to Hickman creek. McClernand was on the right and covered the roads running south and south-west from Dover. His right extended to the back-water up the ravine opening into the Cumberland south of the village. The troops were not intrenched, but the nature of the ground was such that they were just as well protected from the fire of the enemy as if rifle-pits had been thrown up. Our line was generally along the crest of ridges. The artillery was protected by being sunk in the ground. The men who were not serving the guns were perfectly covered from fire on taking position a little back from the crest. The greatest suffering was from want of shelter. It was midwinter and during the siege we had rain and snow, thawing and freezing alternately. It would not do to allow camp-fires except far down the hill out of sight of the enemy, and it would not do to allow many of the troops to remain there at the same time. In the march over from Fort Henry numbers of the men had thrown away their blankets and overcoats. There was therefore much discomfort and absolute suffering.

During the 12th and 13th, and until the arrival of Wallace and Thayer on the 14th, the National forces, composed of but 15,000 men, without intrenchments, confronted an intrenched army of 21,000, without conflict further than what was brought on by ourselves. Only one gunboat had arrived. There was a little skirmishing each day, brought on by the

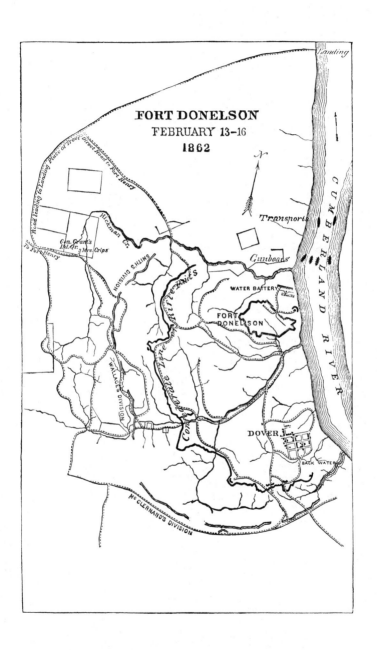

FORT DONELSON
FEBRUARY 13–16
1862

movement of our troops in securing commanding positions; but there was no actual fighting during this time except once, on the 13th, in front of McClernand's command. That general had undertaken to capture a battery of the enemy which was annoying his men. Without orders or authority he sent three regiments to make the assault. The battery was in the main line of the enemy, which was defended by his whole army present. Of course the assault was a failure, and of course the loss on our side was great for the number of men engaged. In this assault Colonel William Morrison fell badly wounded. Up to this time the surgeons with the army had no difficulty in finding room in the houses near our line for all the sick and wounded; but now hospitals were overcrowded. Owing, however, to the energy and skill of the surgeons the suffering was not so great as it might have been. The hospital arrangements at Fort Donelson were as complete as it was possible to make them, considering the inclemency of the weather and the lack of tents, in a sparsely settled country where the houses were generally of but one or two rooms.

On the return of Captain Walke to Fort Henry on the 10th, I had requested him to take the vessels that had accompanied him on his expedition up the Tennessee, and get possession of the Cumberland as far up towards Donelson as possible. He started without delay, taking, however, only his own gunboat, the *Carondelet*, towed by the steamer *Alps*. Captain Walke arrived a few miles below Donelson on the 12th, a little after noon. About the time the advance of troops reached a point within gunshot of the fort on the land side, he engaged the water batteries at long range. On the 13th I informed him of my arrival the day before and of the establishment of most of our batteries, requesting him at the same time to attack again that day so that I might take advantage of any diversion. The attack was made and many shots fell within the fort, creating some consternation, as we now know. The investment on the land side was made as complete as the number of troops engaged would admit of.

During the night of the 13th Flag-officer Foote arrived with the iron-clads *St. Louis*, *Louisville* and *Pittsburg* and the wooden gunboats *Tyler* and *Conestoga*, convoying Thayer's brigade. On the morning of the 14th Thayer was landed. Wallace, whom I had ordered over from Fort Henry, also arrived about the same time. Up to this time he had been commanding a brigade belonging to the division of General C. F. Smith. These troops were now restored to the division they belonged to, and General Lew. Wallace was assigned to the command of a division composed of the brigade of Colonel Thayer and other reinforcements that arrived the same day. This new division was assigned to the centre, giving the two flanking divisions an opportunity to close up and form a stronger line.

The plan was for the troops to hold the enemy within his lines, while the gunboats should attack the water batteries at close quarters and silence his guns if possible. Some of the gunboats were to run the batteries, get above the fort and above the village of Dover. I had ordered a reconnoissance made with the view of getting troops to the river above Dover in case they should be needed there. That position attained by the gunboats it would have been but a question of time—and a very short time, too—when the garrison would have been compelled to surrender.

By three in the afternoon of the 14th Flag-officer Foote was ready, and advanced upon the water batteries with his entire fleet. After coming in range of the batteries of the enemy the advance was slow, but a constant fire was delivered from every gun that could be brought to bear upon the fort. I occupied a position on shore from which I could see the advancing navy. The leading boat got within a very short distance of the water battery, not further off I think than two hundred yards, and I soon saw one and then another of them dropping down the river, visibly disabled. Then the whole fleet followed and the engagement closed for the day. The gunboat which Flag-officer Foote was on, besides having been hit about sixty times, several of the shots passing through near the water-line, had a shot enter the pilot-house which killed the pilot, carried away the wheel and wounded the flag-officer himself. The tiller-ropes of another vessel were carried away and she, too, dropped helplessly back. Two others had their pilot-houses so injured that they scarcely formed a protection to the men at the wheel.

The enemy had evidently been much demoralized by the assault, but they were jubilant when they saw the disabled vessels dropping down the river entirely out of the control of the men on board. Of course I only witnessed the falling back of our gunboats and felt sad enough at the time over the repulse. Subsequent reports, now published, show that the enemy telegraphed a great victory to Richmond. The sun went down on the night of the 14th of February, 1862, leaving the army confronting Fort Donelson anything but comforted over the prospects. The weather had turned intensely cold; the men were without tents and could not keep up fires where most of them had to stay, and, as previously stated, many had thrown away their overcoats and blankets. Two of the strongest of our gunboats had been disabled, presumably beyond the possibility of rendering any present assistance. I retired this night not knowing but that I would have to intrench my position, and bring up tents for the men or build huts under the cover of the hills.

On the morning of the 15th, before it was yet broad day, a messenger from Flag-officer Foote handed me a note, expressing a desire to see me on the flag-ship and saying that he had been injured the day before so much that he could not come himself to me. I at once made my preparations for starting. I directed my adjutant-general to notify each of the division commanders of my absence and instruct them to do nothing to bring on an engagement until they received further orders, but to hold their positions. From the heavy rains that had fallen for days and weeks preceding and from the constant use of the road between the troops and the landing four to seven miles below, these roads had become cut up so as to be hardly passable. The intense cold of the night of the 14th–15th had frozen the ground solid. This made travel on horseback even slower than through the mud; but I went as fast as the roads would allow.

When I reached the fleet I found the flag-ship was anchored out in the stream. A small boat, however, awaited my arrival and I was soon on board with the flag-officer. He explained to me in short the condition in which he was left by the engagement of the evening before, and suggested that I should intrench while he returned to Mound City with his disabled boats, expressing at the time the belief that he could have the necessary repairs made and be back in ten days. I saw the absolute necessity of his gunboats going into hospital and did not know but I should be forced to the alternative of going through a siege. But the enemy relieved me from this necessity.

When I left the National line to visit Flag-officer Foote I had no idea that there would be any engagement on land unless I brought it on myself. The conditions for battle were much more favorable to us than they had been for the first two days of the investment. From the 12th to the 14th we had but 15,000 men of all arms and no gunboats. Now we had been reinforced by a fleet of six naval vessels, a large division of troops under General L. Wallace and 2,500 men brought over from Fort Henry belonging to the division of C. F. Smith. The enemy, however, had taken the initiative. Just as I landed I met Captain Hillyer of my staff, white with fear, not for his personal safety, but for the safety of the National troops. He said the enemy had come out of his lines in full force and attacked and scattered McClernand's division, which was in full retreat. The roads, as I have said, were unfit for making fast time, but I got to my command as soon as possible. The attack had been made on the National right. I was some four or five miles north of our left. The line was about three miles long. In reaching the point where the disaster had occurred I had to pass the divisions of Smith and Wallace. I saw no sign of excitement on the portion of the line held by Smith; Wallace was nearer the scene of conflict and had taken part in it. He had, at an opportune time, sent Thayer's brigade to the support of McClernand and thereby contributed to hold the enemy within his lines.

I saw everything favorable for us along the line of our left and centre. When I came to the right appearances were different. The enemy had come out in full force to cut his way out and make his escape. McClernand's division had to bear the brunt of the attack from this combined force. His men had stood up gallantly until the ammunition in their cartridge-boxes gave out. There was abundance of ammunition near by lying on the ground in boxes, but at that stage of the war it was not all of our commanders of regiments, brigades, or even divisions, who had been educated up to the point of seeing that their men were constantly supplied with ammunition during an engagement. When the men found themselves without ammunition they could not stand up against troops who seemed to have plenty of it. The division broke and a portion fled, but most of the men, as they were not pursued, only fell back out of range of the fire of the enemy. It must have been about this time that Thayer pushed his brigade in between the enemy and those of our troops that were without ammunition. At all events the enemy fell back within his intrenchments and was there when I got on the field.

I saw the men standing in knots talking in the most excited manner. No officer seemed to be giving any directions. The soldiers had their muskets, but no ammunition, while there were tons of it close at hand. I heard some of the men say that the enemy had come out with knapsacks, and haversacks filled with rations. They seemed to think this indicated a determination on his part to stay out and fight just as long as the provisions held out. I turned to Colonel J. D. Webster, of my staff, who was with me, and said: "Some of our men are pretty badly demoralized, but the enemy must be more so, for he has attempted to force his way out, but has fallen back: the one who attacks first now will be victorious and the enemy will have to be in a hurry if he gets ahead of me." I determined to make the assault at once on our left. It was clear to my mind that the enemy had started to march out with his entire force, except a few pickets, and if our attack could be made on the left before the enemy could redistribute his forces along the line, we would find but little opposition except from the intervening abatis. I directed Colonel Webster to ride with me and call out to the men as we passed: "Fill your cartridge-boxes, quick, and get into line; the enemy is trying to escape and he must not be permitted to do so." This acted like a charm. The men only wanted some one to give them a command. We rode rapidly to Smith's quarters, when I explained the situation to him and directed him to charge the enemy's works in his front with his whole division, saying at the same time that he would find nothing but a very thin line to con-tend with. The general was off in an incredibly short time, going in advance himself to keep his men from firing while they were working their way through the abatis intervening between them and the enemy. The outer line of rifle-pits was passed, and the night of the 15th General Smith, with much of his division, bivouacked within the lines of the enemy. There was now no doubt but that the Confederates must surrender or be captured the next day.

There seems from subsequent accounts to have been much consternation, particularly among the officers of high rank, in Dover during the night of the 15th. General Floyd, the commanding officer, who was a man of talent enough for any civil position, was no soldier and, possibly, did not possess the elements of one. He was further unfitted for command, for the reason that his conscience must have troubled him and made him afraid. As Secretary of War he had taken a solemn oath to maintain the Constitution of the United States and to uphold the same against all its ene-mies. He had betrayed that trust. As Secretary of War he was reported through the northern press to have scattered the little army the country had so that the most of it could be picked up in detail when secession occurred. About a year before leaving the Cabinet he had removed arms from north-ern to southern arsenals. He continued in the Cabinet of President Buchanan until about the 1st of January, 1861, while he was working vigilantly for the establishment of a confederacy made out of United States territory. Well may he have been afraid to fall into the hands of National troops. He would no doubt have been tried for misappropriating public property, if not for treason, had he been captured. General Pillow, next in command, was conceited, and prided himself much on his services in the Mexican war. He tele-graphed to General Johnston, at Nashville, after our men were within the rebel rifle-pits, and almost on the eve of his making his escape, that the Southern troops had had great success all day. Johnston forwarded the dispatch to Rich-mond. While the authorities at the capital were reading it Floyd and Pillow were fugitives.

A council of war was held by the enemy at which all agreed

that it would be impossible to hold out longer. General Buckner, who was third in rank in the garrison but much the most capable soldier, seems to have regarded it a duty to hold the fort until the general commanding the department, A. S. Johnston, should get back to his headquarters at Nashville. Buckner's report shows, however, that he considered Donelson lost and that any attempt to hold the place longer would be at the sacrifice of the command. Being assured that Johnston was already in Nashville, Buckner too agreed that surrender was the proper thing. Floyd turned over the command to Pillow, who declined it. It then devolved upon Buckner, who accepted the responsibility of the position. Floyd and Pillow took possession of all the river transports at Dover and before morning both were on their way to Nashville, with the brigade formerly commanded by Floyd and some other troops, in all about 3,000. Some marched up the east bank of the Cumberland; others went on the steamers. During the night Forrest also, with his cavalry and some other troops, about a thousand in all, made their way out, passing between our right and the river. They had to ford or swim over the back-water in the little creek just south of Dover.

Before daylight General Smith brought to me the following letter from General Buckner:

HEADQUARTERS, FORT DONELSON,
February 16, 1862.

Sir:—In consideration of all the circumstances governing the present situation of affairs at this station, I propose to the Commanding Officer of the Federal forces the appointment of Commissioners to agree upon terms of capitulation of the forces and fort under my command, and in that view suggest an armistice until 12 o'clock to-day.

I am, sir, very respectfully,
Your ob't se'v't,
S. B. BUCKNER,
Brig. Gen. C. S. A.

To Brigadier-General U. S. GRANT,
    Com'ding U. S. Forces,
        Near Fort Donelson.

To this I responded as follows:

> HEADQUARTERS ARMY IN THE FIELD,
> Camp near Donelson,
> *February* 16, 1862.

General S. B. BUCKNER,
> Confederate Army.

SIR: — Yours of this date, proposing armistice and appointment of Commissioners to settle terms of capitulation, is just received. No terms except an unconditional and immediate surrender can be accepted. I propose to move immediately upon your works.

> I am, sir, very respectfully,
> Your ob't se'v't,
> U. S. GRANT,
> Brig. Gen.

To this I received the following reply:

> HEADQUARTERS, DOVER, TENNESSEE,
> *February* 16, 1862.

To Brig. Gen'l U. S. GRANT,
> U. S. Army.

SIR: —The distribution of the forces under my command, incident to an unexpected change of commanders, and the overwhelming force under your command, compel me, notwithstanding the brilliant success of the Confederate arms yesterday, to accept the ungenerous and unchivalrous terms which you propose.

> I am, sir,
> Your very ob't se'v't,
> S. B. BUCKNER,
> Brig. Gen. C. S. A.

General Buckner, as soon as he had dispatched the first of the above letters, sent word to his different commanders on the line of rifle-pits, notifying them that he had made a proposition looking to the surrender of the garrison, and directing them to notify National troops in their front so that all fighting might be prevented. White flags were stuck at intervals along the line of rifle-pits, but none over the fort. As soon as the last letter from Buckner was received I mounted my horse and rode to Dover. General Wallace, I found, had preceded me an hour or more. I presume that, seeing white flags exposed in his front, he rode up to see what they meant and,

Hd. Qrs. Fort Donelson,
Febry 16 1862.

Sir:

In consideration of all the
circumstances governing the present
situation of affairs at this Station
I propose to the Commanding officer
of the Federal forces the appointment
of Commissioners to agree upon terms
of Capitulation of the forces and fort
under my
command, and in that view suggest
an armistice until 12 O'clock to-day.

I am, Sir, very respectfully,
Your Obsvt.

S. B. Buckner.
Brig. Genl. C.S.A.

To
Brig Genl. U.S. Grant
Comdg. U.S. Forces,
Near Fort Donelson.

Hd Qrs, Army in the Field
Camp near Donelson, Feby 16th 1862

Gen. S. B. Buckner,
  Confed. Army,
        Sir,

        Yours of this date proposing
Armistice, and appointment of Commissioners
to settle terms of Capitulation is just received.
No terms except an unconditional and immediate
surrender can be accepted.

    I propose to move immediately upon
your works.

            I am sir; very respectfully
              Your obt. Sert.
                U. S. Grant
                Brig. Gen

Head Quarters, Dover, Tenn,
Febry. 16. 1862.

To Brig, Gen. U. S. Grant, U.S. Army.
        Sir,
                The ~~condition~~ distribution
of the forces under my command, incident
to an unexpected change of commanders, and
the overwhelming force under your command,
compel me, notwithstanding the brilliant
success of the Confederate arms yesterday, to
accept the ungenerous and unchivalrous
terms which you propose.
        I am, sir,
                Your very obt. set.
                        S. B. Buckner.
                        Brig. Gen. C.S.A.

not being fired upon or halted, he kept on until he found himself at the headquarters of General Buckner.

I had been at West Point three years with Buckner and afterwards served with him in the army, so that we were quite well acquainted. In the course of our conversation, which was very friendly, he said to me that if he had been in command I would not have got up to Donelson as easily as I did. I told him that if he had been in command I should not have tried in the way I did: I had invested their lines with a smaller force than they had to defend them, and at the same time had sent a brigade full 5,000 strong, around by water; I had relied very much upon their commander to allow me to come safely up to the outside of their works. I asked General Buckner about what force he had to surrender. He replied that he could not tell with any degree of accuracy; that all the sick and weak had been sent to Nashville while we were about Fort Henry; that Floyd and Pillow had left during the night, taking many men with them; and that Forrest, and probably others, had also escaped during the preceding night: the number of casualties he could not tell; but he said I would not find fewer than 12,000, nor more than 15,000.

He asked permission to send parties outside of the lines to bury his dead, who had fallen on the 15th when they tried to get out. I gave directions that his permit to pass our limits should be recognized. I have no reason to believe that this privilege was abused, but it familiarized our guards so much with the sight of Confederates passing to and fro that I have no doubt many got beyond our pickets unobserved and went on. The most of the men who went in that way no doubt thought they had had war enough, and left with the intention of remaining out of the army. Some came to me and asked permission to go, saying that they were tired of the war and would not be caught in the ranks again, and I bade them go.

The actual number of Confederates at Fort Donelson can never be given with entire accuracy. The largest number admitted by any writer on the Southern side, is by Colonel Preston Johnston. He gives the number at 17,000. But this must be an underestimate. The commissary general of prisoners reported having issued rations to 14,623 Fort Donelson prisoners at Cairo, as they passed that point. General Pillow reported the killed and wounded at 2,000; but he had less opportunity of knowing the actual numbers than the officers of McClernand's division, for most of the killed and wounded fell outside their works, in front of that division, and were buried or cared for by Buckner after the surrender and when Pillow was a fugitive. It is known that Floyd and Pillow escaped during the night of the 15th, taking with them not less than 3,000 men. Forrest escaped with about 1,000 and others were leaving singly and in squads all night. It is probable that the Confederate force at Donelson, on the 15th of February, 1862, was 21,000 in round numbers.

On the day Fort Donelson fell I had 27,000 men to confront the Confederate lines and guard the road four or five miles to the left, over which all our supplies had to be drawn on wagons. During the 16th, after the surrender, additional reinforcements arrived.

During the siege General Sherman had been sent to Smithland, at the mouth of the Cumberland River, to forward reinforcements and supplies to me. At that time he was my senior in rank and there was no authority of law to assign a junior to command a senior of the same grade. But every boat that came up with supplies or reinforcements brought a note of encouragement from Sherman, asking me to call upon him for any assistance he could render and saying that if he could be of service at the front I might send for him and he would waive rank.

Chapter XXIII.

PROMOTED MAJOR-GENERAL OF VOLUNTEERS—
UNOCCUPIED TERRITORY—ADVANCE UPON NASHVILLE
—SITUATION OF THE TROOPS—CONFEDERATE RETREAT
—RELIEVED OF THE COMMAND—RESTORED TO THE
COMMAND—GENERAL SMITH.

THE NEWS of the fall of Fort Donelson caused great delight all over the North. At the South, particularly in Richmond, the effect was correspondingly depressing. I was promptly promoted to the grade of Major-General of Volunteers, and confirmed by the Senate. All three of my division commanders were promoted to the same grade and the colonels who commanded brigades were made brigadier-generals in the volunteer service. My chief, who was in St. Louis, telegraphed his congratulations to General Hunter in Kansas for the services he had rendered in securing the fall of Fort Donelson by sending reinforcements so rapidly. To Washington he telegraphed that the victory was due to General C. F. Smith; "promote him," he said, "and the whole country will applaud." On the 19th there was published at St. Louis a formal order thanking Flag-officer Foote and myself, and the forces under our command, for the victories on the Tennessee and the Cumberland. I received no other recognition whatever from General Halleck. But General Cullum, his chief of staff, who was at Cairo, wrote me a warm congratulatory letter on his own behalf. I approved of General Smith's promotion highly, as I did all the promotions that were made.

My opinion was and still is that immediately after the fall of Fort Donelson the way was opened to the National forces all over the South-west without much resistance. If one general who would have taken the responsibility had been in command of all the troops west of the Alleghanies, he could have marched to Chattanooga, Corinth, Memphis and Vicksburg with the troops we then had, and as volunteering was going on rapidly over the North there would soon have been force enough at all these centres to operate offensively against any body of the enemy that might be found near them. Rapid movements and the acquisition of rebellious territory would have promoted volunteering, so that reinforcements could have been had as fast as transportation could have been obtained to carry them to their destination. On the other hand there were tens of thousands of strong able-bodied young men still at their homes in the South-western States, who had not gone into the Confederate army in February, 1862, and who had no particular desire to go. If our lines had been extended to protect their homes, many of them never would have gone. Providence ruled differently. Time was given the enemy to collect armies and fortify his new positions; and twice afterwards he came near forcing his north-western front up to the Ohio River.

I promptly informed the department commander of our success at Fort Donelson and that the way was open now to Clarksville and Nashville; and that unless I received orders to the contrary I should take Clarksville on the 21st and Nashville about the 1st of March. Both these places are on the Cumberland River above Fort Donelson. As I heard nothing from headquarters on the subject, General C. F. Smith was sent to Clarksville at the time designated and found the place evacuated. The capture of forts Henry and Donelson had broken the line the enemy had taken from Columbus to Bowling Green, and it was known that he was falling back from the eastern point of this line and that Buell was following, or at least advancing. I should have sent troops to Nashville at the time I sent to Clarksville, but my transportation was limited and there were many prisoners to be forwarded north.

None of the reinforcements from Buell's army arrived until the 24th of February. Then General Nelson came up, with orders to report to me with two brigades, he having sent one brigade to Cairo. I knew General Buell was advancing on Nashville from the north, and I was advised by scouts that the rebels were leaving that place, and trying to get out all the supplies they could. Nashville was, at that time, one of the best provisioned posts in the South. I had no use for reinforcements now, and thinking Buell would like to have his troops again, I ordered Nelson to proceed to Nashville without debarking at Fort Donelson. I sent a gunboat also as a convoy. The Cumberland River was very high at the time; the railroad bridge at Nashville had been burned, and all river craft had been destroyed, or would be before the enemy left. Nashville is on the west bank of the Cumberland, and Buell was approaching from the east. I thought the steamers carrying Nelson's division would be useful in ferrying the balance of Buell's forces across. I ordered Nelson to put himself in communication with Buell as soon as possible, and if he found him more than two days off from Nashville to return below the city and await orders. Buell, however, had already arrived in person at Edgefield, opposite Nashville, and Mitchell's division of his command reached there the same day. Nelson immediately took possession of the city.

After Nelson had gone and before I had learned of Buell's arrival, I sent word to department headquarters that I should go to Nashville myself on the 28th if I received no orders to the contrary. Hearing nothing, I went as I had informed my superior officer I would do. On arriving at Clarksville I saw a fleet of steamers at the shore—the same that had taken Nelson's division—and troops going aboard. I landed and called on the commanding officer, General C. F. Smith. As soon as he saw me he showed an order he had just received from Buell in these words:

NASHVILLE, *February* 25, 1862.

GENERAL C. F. SMITH,
     Commanding U. S. Forces, Clarksville.

GENERAL:—The landing of a portion of our troops, contrary to my intentions, on the south side of the river has compelled me to hold this side at every hazard. If the enemy should assume the offensive, and I am assured by reliable persons that in view of my position such is his intention, my force present is altogether inadequate, consisting of only 15,000 men. I have to request you, therefore, to come forward with all the available force under your command. So important do I consider the occasion that I think it necessary to give this communication all the force of orders, and I send four boats, the *Diana, Woodford, John Rain,* and *Autocrat,* to bring you up. In five or six days my force will probably be sufficient to relieve you.

Very respectfully, your ob't srv't,
D. C. BUELL,
Brigadier-General Comd'g.

P. S.—The steamers will leave here at 12 o'clock to-night.

General Smith said this order was nonsense. But I told him it was better to obey it. The General replied, "of course I must obey," and said his men were embarking as fast as they could. I went on up to Nashville and inspected the position taken by Nelson's troops. I did not see Buell during the day, and wrote him a note saying that I had been in Nashville since early morning and had hoped to meet him. On my return to the boat we met. His troops were still east of the river, and the steamers that had carried Nelson's division up were mostly at Clarksville to bring Smith's division. I said to General Buell my information was that the enemy was retreating as fast as possible. General Buell said there was fighting going on then only ten or twelve miles away. I said: "Quite probably; Nashville contained valuable stores of arms, ammunition and provisions, and the enemy is probably trying to carry away all he can. The fighting is doubtless with the rearguard who are trying to protect the trains they are getting away with." Buell spoke very positively of the danger Nashville was in of an attack from the enemy. I said, in the absence of positive information, I believed my information was correct. He responded that he "knew." "Well," I said, "I do not know; but as I came by Clarksville General Smith's troops were embarking to join you."

Smith's troops were returned the same day. The enemy were trying to get away from Nashville and not to return to it.

At this time General Albert Sidney Johnston commanded all the Confederate troops west of the Alleghany Mountains, with the exception of those in the extreme south. On the National side the forces confronting him were divided into, at first three, then four separate departments. Johnston had greatly the advantage in having supreme command over all troops that could possibly be brought to bear upon one point, while the forces similarly situated on the National side, divided into independent commands, could not be brought into harmonious action except by orders from Washington.

At the beginning of 1862 Johnston's troops east of the Mississippi occupied a line extending from Columbus, on his left, to Mill Springs, on his right. As we have seen, Columbus, both banks of the Tennessee River, the west bank of the Cumberland and Bowling Green, all were strongly fortified. Mill

Springs was intrenched. The National troops occupied no territory south of the Ohio, except three small garrisons along its bank and a force thrown out from Louisville to confront that at Bowling Green. Johnston's strength was no doubt numerically inferior to that of the National troops; but this was compensated for by the advantage of being sole commander of all the Confederate forces at the West, and of operating in a country where his friends would take care of his rear without any detail of soldiers. But when General George H. Thomas moved upon the enemy at Mill Springs and totally routed him, inflicting a loss of some 300 killed and wounded, and forts Henry and Heiman fell into the hands of the National forces, with their armaments and about 100 prisoners, those losses seemed to dishearten the Confederate commander so much that he immediately commenced a retreat from Bowling Green on Nashville. He reached this latter place on the 14th of February, while Donelson was still besieged. Buell followed with a portion of the Army of the Ohio, but he had to march and did not reach the east bank of the Cumberland opposite Nashville until the 24th of the month, and then with only one division of his army.

The bridge at Nashville had been destroyed and all boats removed or disabled, so that a small garrison could have held the place against any National troops that could have been brought against it within ten days after the arrival of the force from Bowling Green. Johnston seemed to lie quietly at Nashville to await the result at Fort Donelson, on which he had staked the possession of most of the territory embraced in the States of Kentucky and Tennessee. It is true, the two generals senior in rank at Fort Donelson were sending him encouraging dispatches, even claiming great Confederate victories up to the night of the 16th when they must have been preparing for their individual escape. Johnston made a fatal mistake in intrusting so important a command to Floyd, who he must have known was no soldier even if he possessed the elements of one. Pillow's presence as second was also a mistake. If these officers had been forced upon him and designated for that particular command, then he should have left Nashville with a small garrison under a trusty officer, and with the remainder of his force gone to Donelson himself. If he had been captured the result could not have been worse than it was.

Johnston's heart failed him upon the first advance of National troops. He wrote to Richmond on the 8th of February, "I think the gunboats of the enemy will probably take Fort Donelson without the necessity of employing their land force in co-operation." After the fall of that place he abandoned Nashville and Chattanooga without an effort to save either, and fell back into northern Mississippi, where, six weeks later, he was destined to end his career.

From the time of leaving Cairo I was singularly unfortunate in not receiving dispatches from General Halleck. The order of the 10th of February directing me to fortify Fort Henry strongly, particularly to the land side, and saying that intrenching tools had been sent for that purpose, reached me after Donelson was invested. I received nothing direct which indicated that the department commander knew we were in possession of Donelson. I was reporting regularly to the chief of staff, who had been sent to Cairo, soon after the troops left there, to receive all reports from the front and to telegraph the substance to the St. Louis headquarters. Cairo was at the southern end of the telegraph wire. Another line was started at once from Cairo to Paducah and Smithland, at the mouths of the Tennessee and Cumberland respectively. My dispatches were all sent to Cairo by boat, but many of those addressed to me were sent to the operator at the end of the advancing wire and he failed to forward them. This operator afterwards proved to be a rebel; he deserted his post after a short time and went south taking his dispatches with him. A telegram from General McClellan to me of February 16th, the day of the surrender, directing me to report in full the situation, was not received at my headquarters until the 3d of March.

On the 2d of March I received orders dated March 1st to move my command back to Fort Henry, leaving only a small garrison at Donelson. From Fort Henry expeditions were to be sent against Eastport, Mississippi, and Paris, Tennessee. We started from Donelson on the 4th, and the same day I was back on the Tennessee River. On March 4th I also received the following dispatch from General Halleck:

Maj.-Gen. U. S. Grant,
     Fort Henry:
  You will place Maj.-Gen. C. F. Smith in command of expedition,
and remain yourself at Fort Henry. Why do you not obey my orders
to report strength and positions of your command?
                                        H. W. HALLECK,
                                              Major-General.

  I was surprised. This was the first intimation I had received
that General Halleck had called for information as to the
strength of my command. On the 6th he wrote to me again.
"Your going to Nashville without authority, and when your
presence with your troops was of the utmost importance, was
a matter of very serious complaint at Washington, so much so
that I was advised to arrest you on your return." This was the
first I knew of his objecting to my going to Nashville. That
place was not beyond the limits of my command, which, it
had been expressly declared in orders, were "not defined."
Nashville is west of the Cumberland River, and I had sent
troops that had reported to me for duty to occupy the place. I
turned over the command as directed and then replied to
General Halleck courteously, but asked to be relieved from
further duty under him.
  Later I learned that General Halleck had been calling lustily
for more troops, promising that he would do something important if he could only be sufficiently reinforced. McClellan
asked him what force he then had. Halleck telegraphed me to
supply the information so far as my command was concerned,
but I received none of his dispatches. At last Halleck reported
to Washington that he had repeatedly ordered me to give the
strength of my force, but could get nothing out of me; that I
had gone to Nashville, beyond the limits of my command,
without his authority, and that my army was more demoralized by victory than the army at Bull Run had been by defeat.
General McClellan, on this information, ordered that I should
be relieved from duty and that an investigation should be
made into any charges against me. He even authorized my
arrest. Thus in less than two weeks after the victory at Donelson, the two leading generals in the army were in correspondence as to what disposition should be made of me, and in

less than three weeks I was virtually in arrest and without a command.

On the 13th of March I was restored to command, and on the 17th Halleck sent me a copy of an order from the War Department which stated that accounts of my misbehavior had reached Washington and directed him to investigate and report the facts. He forwarded also a copy of a detailed dispatch from himself to Washington entirely exonerating me; but he did not inform me that it was his own reports that had created all the trouble. On the contrary, he wrote to me, "Instead of relieving you, I wish you, as soon as your new army is in the field, to assume immediate command, and lead it to new victories." In consequence I felt very grateful to him, and supposed it was his interposition that had set me right with the government. I never knew the truth until General Badeau unearthed the facts in his researches for his history of my campaigns.

General Halleck unquestionably deemed General C. F. Smith a much fitter officer for the command of all the forces in the military district than I was, and, to render him available for such command, desired his promotion to antedate mine and those of the other division commanders. It is probable that the general opinion was that Smith's long services in the army and distinguished deeds rendered him the more proper person for such command. Indeed I was rather inclined to this opinion myself at that time, and would have served as faithfully under Smith as he had done under me. But this did not justify the dispatches which General Halleck sent to Washington, or his subsequent concealment of them from me when pretending to explain the action of my superiors.

On receipt of the order restoring me to command I proceeded to Savannah on the Tennessee, to which point my troops had advanced. General Smith was delighted to see me and was unhesitating in his denunciation of the treatment I had received. He was on a sick bed at the time, from which he never came away alive. His death was a severe loss to our western army. His personal courage was unquestioned, his judgment and professional acquirements were unsurpassed, and he had the confidence of those he commanded as well as of those over him.

Chapter XXIV.

THE ARMY AT PITTSBURG LANDING—INJURED BY A
FALL—THE CONFEDERATE ATTACK AT SHILOH—THE
FIRST DAY'S FIGHT AT SHILOH—GENERAL SHERMAN—
CONDITION OF THE ARMY—CLOSE OF THE FIRST DAY'S
FIGHT—THE SECOND DAY'S FIGHT—RETREAT AND
DEFEAT OF THE CONFEDERATES.

WHEN I REASSUMED command on the 17th of March I found the army divided, about half being on the east bank of the Tennessee at Savannah, while one division was at Crump's landing on the west bank about four miles higher up, and the remainder at Pittsburg landing, five miles above Crump's. The enemy was in force at Corinth, the junction of the two most important railroads in the Mississippi valley— one connecting Memphis and the Mississippi River with the East, and the other leading south to all the cotton states. Still another railroad connects Corinth with Jackson, in west Tennessee. If we obtained possession of Corinth the enemy would have no railroad for the transportation of armies or supplies until that running east from Vicksburg was reached. It was the great strategic position at the West between the Tennessee and the Mississippi rivers and between Nashville and Vicksburg.

I at once put all the troops at Savannah in motion for Pittsburg landing, knowing that the enemy was fortifying at Corinth and collecting an army there under Johnston. It was my expectation to march against that army as soon as Buell, who had been ordered to reinforce me with the Army of the Ohio, should arrive; and the west bank of the river was the place to start from. Pittsburg is only about twenty miles from Corinth, and Hamburg landing, four miles further up the river, is a mile or two nearer. I had not been in command long before I selected Hamburg as the place to put the Army of the Ohio when it arrived. The roads from Pittsburg and Hamburg to Corinth converge some eight miles out. This disposition of the troops would have given additional roads to march over when the advance commenced, within supporting distance of each other.

Before I arrived at Savannah, Sherman, who had joined the Army of the Tennessee and been placed in command of a division, had made an expedition on steamers convoyed by gunboats to the neighborhood of Eastport, thirty miles south, for the purpose of destroying the railroad east of Corinth. The rains had been so heavy for some time before that the low-lands had become impassable swamps. Sherman debarked his troops and started out to accomplish the object of the expedition; but the river was rising so rapidly that the back-water up the small tributaries threatened to cut off the possibility of getting back to the boats, and the expedition had to return without reaching the railroad. The guns had to be hauled by hand through the water to get back to the boats.

On the 17th of March the army on the Tennessee River consisted of five divisions, commanded respectively by Generals C. F. Smith, McClernand, L. Wallace, Hurlbut and Sherman. General W. H. L. Wallace was temporarily in command of Smith's division, General Smith, as I have said, being confined to his bed. Reinforcements were arriving daily and as they came up they were organized, first into brigades, then into a division, and the command given to General Prentiss, who had been ordered to report to me. General Buell was on his way from Nashville with 40,000 veterans. On the 19th of March he was at Columbia, Tennessee, eighty-five miles from Pittsburg. When all reinforcements should have arrived I expected to take the initiative by marching on Corinth, and had no expectation of needing fortifications, though this subject was taken into consideration. McPherson, my only military engineer, was directed to lay out a line to intrench. He did so, but reported that it would have to be made in rear of the line of encampment as it then ran. The new line, while it would be nearer the river, was yet too far away from the Tennessee, or even from the creeks, to be easily supplied with water, and in case of attack these creeks would be in the hands of the enemy. The fact is, I regarded the campaign we were engaged in as an offensive one and had no idea that the enemy would leave strong intrenchments to take the initiative when he knew he would be attacked where he was if he remained. This view, however, did not prevent every precaution being taken and every effort made to keep advised of all movements of the enemy.

Johnston's cavalry meanwhile had been well out towards our front, and occasional encounters occurred between it and our outposts. On the 1st of April this cavalry became bold and approached our lines, showing that an advance of some kind was contemplated. On the 2d Johnston left Corinth in force to attack my army. On the 4th his cavalry dashed down and captured a small picket guard of six or seven men, stationed some five miles out from Pittsburg on the Corinth road. Colonel Buckland sent relief to the guard at once and soon followed in person with an entire regiment, and General Sherman followed Buckland taking the remainder of a brigade. The pursuit was kept up for some three miles beyond the point where the picket guard had been captured, and after nightfall Sherman returned to camp and reported to me by letter what had occurred.

At this time a large body of the enemy was hovering to the west of us, along the line of the Mobile and Ohio railroad. My apprehension was much greater for the safety of Crump's landing than it was for Pittsburg. I had no apprehension that the enemy could really capture either place. But I feared it was possible that he might make a rapid dash upon Crump's and destroy our transports and stores, most of which were kept at that point, and then retreat before Wallace could be reinforced. Lew. Wallace's position I regarded as so well chosen that he was not removed.

At this time I generally spent the day at Pittsburg and returned to Savannah in the evening. I was intending to remove my headquarters to Pittsburg, but Buell was expected daily and would come in at Savannah. I remained at this point, therefore, a few days longer than I otherwise should have done, in order to meet him on his arrival. The skirmishing in our front, however, had been so continuous from about the 3d of April that I did not leave Pittsburg each night until an hour when I felt there would be no further danger before the morning.

On Friday the 4th, the day of Buckland's advance, I was very much injured by my horse falling with me, and on me, while I was trying to get to the front where firing had been heard. The night was one of impenetrable darkness, with rain pouring down in torrents; nothing was visible to the eye except as revealed by the frequent flashes of lightning. Under these circumstances I had to trust to the horse, without guidance, to keep the road. I had not gone far, however, when I met General W. H. L. Wallace and Colonel (afterwards General) McPherson coming from the direction of the front. They said all was quiet so far as the enemy was concerned. On the way back to the boat my horse's feet slipped from under him, and he fell with my leg under his body. The extreme softness of the ground, from the excessive rains of the few preceding days, no doubt saved me from a severe injury and protracted lameness. As it was, my ankle was very much injured, so much so that my boot had to be cut off. For two or three days after I was unable to walk except with crutches.

On the 5th General Nelson, with a division of Buell's army, arrived at Savannah and I ordered him to move up the east bank of the river, to be in a position where he could be ferried over to Crump's landing or Pittsburg as occasion required. I had learned that General Buell himself would be at Savannah the next day, and desired to meet me on his arrival. Affairs at Pittsburg landing had been such for several days that I did not want to be away during the day. I determined, therefore, to take a very early breakfast and ride out to meet Buell, and thus save time. He had arrived on the evening of the 5th, but had not advised me of the fact and I was not aware of it until some time after. While I was at breakfast, however, heavy firing was heard in the direction of Pittsburg landing, and I hastened there, sending a hurried note to Buell informing him of the reason why I could not meet him at Savannah. On the way up the river I directed the dispatch-boat to run in close to Crump's landing, so that I could communicate with General Lew. Wallace. I found him waiting on a boat apparently expecting to see me, and I directed him to get his troops in line ready to execute any orders he might receive. He replied that his troops were already under arms and prepared to move.

Up to that time I had felt by no means certain that Crump's landing might not be the point of attack. On reaching the front, however, about eight A.M., I found that the attack on Pittsburg was unmistakable, and that nothing more than a small guard, to protect our transports and stores, was needed at Crump's. Captain Baxter, a quartermaster on my staff, was accordingly directed to go back and order General Wallace to march immediately to Pittsburg by the road nearest the river. Captain Baxter made a memorandum of this order. About one P.M., not hearing from Wallace and being much in need of reinforcements, I sent two more of my staff, Colonel McPherson and Captain Rowley, to bring him up with his division. They reported finding him marching towards Purdy, Bethel, or some point west from the river, and farther from Pittsburg by several miles than when he started. The road from his first position to Pittsburg landing was direct and near the river. Between the two points a bridge had been built across Snake Creek by our troops, at which Wallace's command had assisted, expressly to enable the troops at the two places to support each other in case of need. Wallace did not arrive in time to take part in the first day's fight. General Wallace has since claimed that the order delivered to him by Captain Baxter was simply to join the right of the army, and that the road over which he marched would have taken him to the road from Pittsburg to Purdy where it crosses Owl Creek on the right of Sherman; but this is not where I had ordered him nor where I wanted him to go.

I never could see and do not now see why any order was necessary further than to direct him to come to Pittsburg landing, without specifying by what route. His was one of three veteran divisions that had been in battle, and its absence was severely felt. Later in the war General Wallace would not have made the mistake that he committed on the 6th of April, 1862. I presume his idea was that by taking the route he did he would be able to come around on the flank or rear of the enemy, and thus perform an act of heroism that would re-dound to the credit of his command, as well as to the benefit of his country.

Some two or three miles from Pittsburg landing was a log meeting-house called Shiloh. It stood on the ridge which di-vides the waters of Snake and Lick creeks, the former empty-ing into the Tennessee just north of Pittsburg landing, and the latter south. This point was the key to our position and was held by Sherman. His division was at that time wholly raw, no part of it ever having been in an engagement; but I thought this deficiency was more than made up by the superiority of the commander. McClernand was on Sherman's left, with troops that had been engaged at forts Henry and Donelson and were therefore veterans so far as western troops had become such at that stage of the war. Next to McClernand came Prentiss with a raw division, and on the extreme left, Stuart with one brigade of Sherman's division. Hurlbut was in rear of Prentiss, massed, and in reserve at the time of the onset. The division of General C. F. Smith was on the right, also in reserve. General Smith was still sick in bed at Savannah, but within hearing of our guns. His services would no doubt have been of inestimable value had his health permitted his presence. The command of his division devolved upon Brigadier-General W. H. L. Wallace, a most estimable and able officer; a veteran too, for he had served a year in the Mexican war and had been with his command at Henry and Donelson. Wallace was mortally wounded in the first day's engagement, and with the change of commanders thus necessarily effected in the heat of battle the efficiency of his division was much weakened.

The position of our troops made a continuous line from Lick Creek on the left to Owl Creek, a branch of Snake Creek, on the right, facing nearly south and possibly a little west. The water in all these streams was very high at the time and contributed to protect our flanks. The enemy was compelled, therefore, to attack directly in front. This he did with great vigor, inflicting heavy losses on the National side, but suffering much heavier on his own.

The Confederate assaults were made with such a disregard of losses on their own side that our line of tents soon fell into their hands. The ground on which the battle was fought was undulating, heavily timbered with scattered clearings, the woods giving some protection to the troops on both sides. There was also considerable underbrush. A number of attempts were made by the enemy to turn our right flank, where Sherman was posted, but every effort was repulsed with heavy loss. But the front attack was kept up so vigorously that, to prevent the success of these attempts to get on our flanks, the National troops were compelled, several times, to take positions to the rear nearer Pittsburg landing. When the firing ceased at night the National line was all of a mile in rear of the position it had occupied in the morning.

In one of the backward moves, on the 6th, the division commanded by General Prentiss did not fall back with the others. This left his flanks exposed and enabled the enemy to capture him with about 2,200 of his officers and men. General Badeau gives four o'clock of the 6th as about the time this capture took place. He may be right as to the time, but my recollection is that the hour was later. General Prentiss him-self gave the hour as half-past five. I was with him, as I was with each of the division commanders that day, several times, and my recollection is that the last time I was with him was about half-past four, when his division was standing up firmly and the General was as cool as if expecting victory. But no matter whether it was four or later, the story that he and his command were surprised and captured in their camps is with-out any foundation whatever. If it had been true, as currently reported at the time and yet believed by thousands of people, that Prentiss and his division had been captured in their beds, there would not have been an all-day struggle, with the loss of thousands killed and wounded on the Confederate side.

With the single exception of a few minutes after the capture of Prentiss, a continuous and unbroken line was maintained all day from Snake Creek or its tributaries on the right to Lick Creek or the Tennessee on the left above Pittsburg. There was no hour during the day when there was not heavy firing and generally hard fighting at some point on the line, but seldom at all points at the same time. It was a case of Southern dash against Northern pluck and endurance. Three of the five divi-sions engaged on Sunday were entirely raw, and many of the men had only received their arms on the way from their States to the field. Many of them had arrived but a day or two be-fore and were hardly able to load their muskets according to the manual. Their officers were equally ignorant of their duties. Under these circumstances it is not astonishing that many of the regiments broke at the first fire. In two cases, as I now

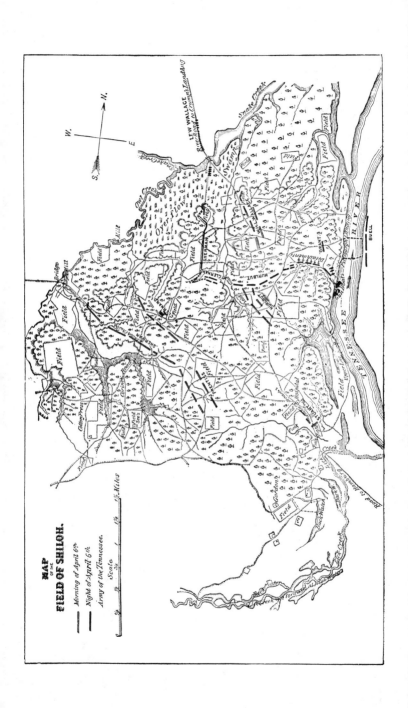

MAP
OF THE
FIELD OF SHILOH.

Morning of April 6th

Night of April 6th.

Army of the Tennessee.

Scale
⅛   ¼   ½   1   1¼   1½ Miles

remember, colonels led their regiments from the field on first hearing the whistle of the enemy's bullets. In these cases the colonels were constitutional cowards, unfit for any military position; but not so the officers and men led out of danger by them. Better troops never went upon a battle-field than many of these, officers and men, afterwards proved themselves to be, who fled panic-stricken at the first whistle of bullets and shell at Shiloh.

During the whole of Sunday I was continuously engaged in passing from one part of the field to another, giving directions to division commanders. In thus moving along the line, however, I never deemed it important to stay long with Sherman. Although his troops were then under fire for the first time, their commander, by his constant presence with them, inspired a confidence in officers and men that enabled them to render services on that bloody battle-field worthy of the best of veterans. McClernand was next to Sherman, and the hardest fighting was in front of these two divisions. McClernand told me on that day, the 6th, that he profited much by having so able a commander supporting him. A casualty to Sherman that would have taken him from the field that day would have been a sad one for the troops engaged at Shiloh. And how near we came to this! On the 6th Sherman was shot twice, once in the hand, once in the shoulder, the ball cutting his coat and making a slight wound, and a third ball passed through his hat. In addition to this he had several horses shot during the day.

The nature of this battle was such that cavalry could not be used in front; I therefore formed ours into line in rear, to stop stragglers—of whom there were many. When there would be enough of them to make a show, and after they had recovered from their fright, they would be sent to reinforce some part of the line which needed support, without regard to their companies, regiments or brigades.

On one occasion during the day I rode back as far as the river and met General Buell, who had just arrived; I do not remember the hour, but at that time there probably were as many as four or five thousand stragglers lying under cover of the river bluff, panic-stricken, most of whom would have been shot where they lay, without resistance, before they

would have taken muskets and marched to the front to protect themselves. This meeting between General Buell and myself was on the dispatch-boat used to run between the landing
and Savannah. It was brief, and related specially to his getting
his troops over the river. As we left the boat together, Buell's
attention was attracted by the men lying under cover of the
river bank. I saw him berating them and trying to shame
them into joining their regiments. He even threatened them
with shells from the gunboats near by. But it was all to no
effect. Most of these men afterward proved themselves as gallant as any of those who saved the battle from which they had
deserted. I have no doubt that this sight impressed General
Buell with the idea that a line of retreat would be a good
thing just then. If he had come in by the front instead of
through the stragglers in the rear, he would have thought and
felt differently. Could he have come through the Confederate
rear, he would have witnessed there a scene similar to that at
our own. The distant rear of an army engaged in battle is not
the best place from which to judge correctly what is going on
in front. Later in the war, while occupying the country between the Tennessee and the Mississippi, I learned that the
panic in the Confederate lines had not differed much from
that within our own. Some of the country people estimated
the stragglers from Johnston's army as high as 20,000. Of
course this was an exaggeration.

The situation at the close of Sunday was as follows: along
the top of the bluff just south of the log-house which stood at
Pittsburg landing, Colonel J. D. Webster, of my staff, had
arranged twenty or more pieces of artillery facing south or up
the river. This line of artillery was on the crest of a hill overlooking a deep ravine opening into the Tennessee. Hurlbut
with his division intact was on the right of this artillery, extending west and possibly a little north. McClernand came
next in the general line, looking more to the west. His division was complete in its organization and ready for any duty.
Sherman came next, his right extending to Snake Creek. His
command, like the other two, was complete in its organization and ready, like its chief, for any service it might be called
upon to render. All three divisions were, as a matter of
course, more or less shattered and depleted in numbers from

the terrible battle of the day. The division of W. H. L. Wallace, as much from the disorder arising from changes of division and brigade commanders, under heavy fire, as from any other cause, had lost its organization and did not occupy a place in the line as a division. Prentiss' command was gone as a division, many of its members having been killed, wounded or captured; but it had rendered valiant services before its final dispersal, and had contributed a good share to the defence of Shiloh.

The right of my line rested near the bank of Snake Creek, a short distance above the bridge which had been built by the troops for the purpose of connecting Crump's landing and Pittsburg landing. Sherman had posted some troops in a loghouse and out-buildings which overlooked both the bridge over which Wallace was expected and the creek above that point. In this last position Sherman was frequently attacked before night, but held the point until he voluntarily abandoned it to advance in order to make room for Lew. Wallace, who came up after dark.

There was, as I have said, a deep ravine in front of our left. The Tennessee River was very high and there was water to a considerable depth in the ravine. Here the enemy made a last desperate effort to turn our flank, but was repelled. The gunboats *Tyler* and *Lexington*, Gwin and Shirk commanding, with the artillery under Webster, aided the army and effectually checked their further progress. Before any of Buell's troops had reached the west bank of the Tennessee, firing had almost entirely ceased; anything like an attempt on the part of the enemy to advance had absolutely ceased. There was some artillery firing from an unseen enemy, some of his shells passing beyond us; but I do not remember that there was the whistle of a single musket-ball heard. As his troops arrived in the dusk General Buell marched several of his regiments part way down the face of the hill where they fired briskly for some minutes, but I do not think a single man engaged in this firing received an injury. The attack had spent its force.

General Lew. Wallace, with 5,000 effective men, arrived after firing had ceased for the day, and was placed on the right. Thus night came, Wallace came, and the advance of Nelson's division came; but none—unless night—in time to be of material service to the gallant men who saved Shiloh on that first day against large odds. Buell's loss on the 6th of April was two men killed and one wounded, all members of the 36th Indiana infantry. The Army of the Tennessee lost on that day at least 7,000 men. The presence of two or three regiments of Buell's army on the west bank before firing ceased had not the slightest effect in preventing the capture of Pittsburg landing.

So confident was I before firing had ceased on the 6th that the next day would bring victory to our arms if we could only take the initiative, that I visited each division commander in person before any reinforcements had reached the field. I directed them to throw out heavy lines of skirmishers in the morning as soon as they could see, and push them forward until they found the enemy, following with their entire divisions in supporting distance, and to engage the enemy as soon as found. To Sherman I told the story of the assault at Fort Donelson, and said that the same tactics would win at Shiloh. Victory was assured when Wallace arrived, even if there had been no other support. I was glad, however, to see the reinforcements of Buell and credit them with doing all there was for them to do. During the night of the 6th the remainder of Nelson's division, Buell's army, crossed the river and were ready to advance in the morning, forming the left wing. Two other divisions, Crittenden's and McCook's, came up the river from Savannah in the transports and were on the west bank early on the 7th. Buell commanded them in person. My command was thus nearly doubled in numbers and efficiency.

During the night rain fell in torrents and our troops were exposed to the storm without shelter. I made my headquarters under a tree a few hundred yards back from the river bank. My ankle was so much swollen from the fall of my horse the Friday night preceding, and the bruise was so painful, that I could get no rest. The drenching rain would have precluded the possibility of sleep without this additional cause. Some time after midnight, growing restive under the storm and the continuous pain, I moved back to the loghouse under the bank. This had been taken as a hospital, and all night wounded men were being brought in, their wounds dressed, a leg or an arm amputated as the case might require, and everything being done to save life or alleviate suffering. The sight was more unendurable than encountering the enemy's fire, and I returned to my tree in the rain.

The advance on the morning of the 7th developed the enemy in the camps occupied by our troops before the battle began, more than a mile back from the most advanced position of the Confederates on the day before. It is known now that they had not yet learned of the arrival of Buell's command. Possibly they fell back so far to get the shelter of our tents during the rain, and also to get away from the shells that were dropped upon them by the gunboats every fifteen minutes during the night.

The position of the Union troops on the morning of the 7th was as follows: General Lew. Wallace on the right; Sherman on his left; then McClernand and then Hurlbut. Nelson, of Buell's army, was on our extreme left, next to the river. Crittenden was next in line after Nelson and on his right; McCook followed and formed the extreme right of Buell's command. My old command thus formed the right wing, while the troops directly under Buell constituted the left wing of the army. These relative positions were retained during the entire day, or until the enemy was driven from the field.

In a very short time the battle became general all along the line. This day everything was favorable to the Union side. We had now become the attacking party. The enemy was driven back all day, as we had been the day before, until finally he beat a precipitate retreat. The last point held by him was near the road leading from the landing to Corinth, on the left of Sherman and right of McClernand. About three o'clock, being near that point and seeing that the enemy was giving way everywhere else, I gathered up a couple of regiments, or parts of regiments, from troops near by, formed them in line of battle and marched them forward, going in front myself to prevent premature or long-range firing. At this point there was a clearing between us and the enemy favorable for charging, although exposed. I knew the enemy were ready to break and only wanted a little encouragement from us to go quickly and join their friends who had started earlier. After marching to within musket-range I stopped and let the troops pass. The command, *Charge*, was given, and was executed with loud cheers and with a run; when the last of the enemy broke.

NOTE.—Since writing this chapter I have received from Mrs. W. H. L. Wallace, widow of the gallant general who was killed in the first day's fight on the field of Shiloh, a letter from General Lew. Wallace to him dated the morning of the 5th. At the date of this letter it was well known that the Confederates had troops out along the Mobile & Ohio railroad west of Crump's landing and Pittsburg landing, and were also collecting near Shiloh. This letter shows that at that time General Lew. Wallace was making preparations for the emergency that might happen for the passing of reinforcements between Shiloh and his position, extending from Crump's landing westward, and he sends it over the road running from Adamsville to the Pittsburg landing and Purdy road. These two roads intersect nearly a mile west of the crossing of the latter over Owl Creek, where our right rested. In this letter General Lew. Wallace advises General W. H. L. Wallace that he will send "to-morrow" (and his letter also says "April 5th," which is the same day the letter was dated and which, therefore, must have been written on the 4th) some cavalry to report to him at his headquarters, and suggesting the propriety of General W. H. L. Wallace's sending a company back with them for the purpose of having the cavalry at the two landings familiarize themselves with the road so that they could "act promptly in case of emergency as guides to and from the different camps."

This modifies very materially what I have said, and what has been said by others, of the conduct of General Lew. Wallace at the battle of Shiloh. It shows that he naturally, with no more experience than he had at the time in the profession of arms, would take the particular road that he did start upon in the absence of orders to move by a different road.

The mistake he made, and which probably caused his apparent dilatoriness, was that of advancing some distance after he found that the firing, which would be at first directly to his front and then off to the left, had fallen back until it had got very much in rear of the position of his advance. This falling back had taken place before I sent General Wallace orders to move up to Pittsburg landing and, naturally, my order was to follow the road nearest the river. But my order was verbal, and to a staff officer who was to deliver it to General Wallace, so that I am not competent to say just what order the General actually received.

General Wallace's division was stationed, the First brigade at Crump's landing, the Second out two miles, and the Third two and a half miles out. Hearing the sounds of battle General Wallace early ordered his First and Third brigades to concentrate on the Second. If the position of our front had not changed, the road which Wallace took would have been somewhat shorter to our right than the River road.

U. S. GRANT.

MOUNT MACGREGOR, NEW YORK, *June* 21, 1885.

Chapter XXV.

DURING THIS SECOND DAY of the battle I had been moving from right to left and back, to see for myself the
progress made. In the early part of the afternoon, while riding
with Colonel McPherson and Major Hawkins, then my chief
commissary, we got beyond the left of our troops. We were
moving along the northern edge of a clearing, very leisurely,
toward the river above the landing. There did not appear to
be an enemy to our right, until suddenly a battery with musketry opened upon us from the edge of the woods on the
other side of the clearing. The shells and balls whistled about
our ears very fast for about a minute. I do not think it took us
longer than that to get out of range and out of sight. In the
sudden start we made, Major Hawkins lost his hat. He did
not stop to pick it up. When we arrived at a perfectly safe
position we halted to take an account of damages. McPherson's horse was panting as if ready to drop. On examination it
was found that a ball had struck him forward of the flank
just back of the saddle, and had gone entirely through. In
a few minutes the poor beast dropped dead; he had given
no sign of injury until we came to a stop. A ball had struck
the metal scabbard of my sword, just below the hilt, and
broken it nearly off; before the battle was over it had broken
off entirely. There were three of us: one had lost a horse,
killed; one a hat and one a sword-scabbard. All were thankful
that it was no worse.

After the rain of the night before and the frequent and
heavy rains for some days previous, the roads were almost impassable. The enemy carrying his artillery and supply trains over
them in his retreat, made them still worse for troops following. I wanted to pursue, but had not the heart to order the
men who had fought desperately for two days, lying in the mud
and rain whenever not fighting, and I did not feel disposed
to positively order Buell, or any part of his command, to

pursue. Although the senior in rank at the time I had been so only a few weeks. Buell was, and had been for some time past, a department commander, while I commanded only a district. I did not meet Buell in person until too late to get troops ready and pursue with effect; but had I seen him at the moment of the last charge I should have at least requested him to follow.

I rode forward several miles the day after the battle, and found that the enemy had dropped much, if not all, of their provisions, some ammunition and the extra wheels of their caissons, lightening their loads to enable them to get off their guns. About five miles out we found their field hospital abandoned. An immediate pursuit must have resulted in the capture of a considerable number of prisoners and probably some guns.

Shiloh was the severest battle fought at the West during the war, and but few in the East equalled it for hard, determined fighting. I saw an open field, in our possession on the second day, over which the Confederates had made repeated charges the day before, so covered with dead that it would have been possible to walk across the clearing, in any direction, stepping

---

NOTE: In an article on the battle of Shiloh which I wrote for the *Century* Magazine, I stated that General A. McD. McCook, who commanded a division of Buell's army, expressed some unwillingness to pursue the enemy on Monday, April 7th, because of the condition of his troops. General Badeau, in his history, also makes the same statement, on my authority. Out of justice to General McCook and his command, I must say that they left a point twenty-two miles east of Savannah on the morning of the 6th. From the heavy rains of a few days previous and the passage of trains and artillery, the roads were necessarily deep in mud, which made marching slow. The division had not only marched through this mud the day before, but it had been in the rain all night without rest. It was engaged in the battle of the second day and did as good service as its position allowed. In fact an opportunity occurred for it to perform a conspicuous act of gallantry which elicited the highest commendation from division commanders in the Army of the Tennessee. General Sherman both in his memoirs and report makes mention of this fact. General McCook himself belongs to a family which furnished many volunteers to the army. I refer to these circumstances with minuteness because I did General McCook injustice in my article in the *Century*, though not to the extent one would suppose from the public press. I am not willing to do any one an injustice, and if convinced that I have done one, I am always willing to make the fullest admission.

on dead bodies, without a foot touching the ground. On our side National and Confederate troops were mingled together in about equal proportions; but on the remainder of the field nearly all were Confederates. On one part, which had evidently not been ploughed for several years, probably because the land was poor, bushes had grown up, some to the height of eight or ten feet. There was not one of these left standing unpierced by bullets. The smaller ones were all cut down.

Contrary to all my experience up to that time, and to the experience of the army I was then commanding, we were on the defensive. We were without intrenchments or defensive advantages of any sort, and more than half the army engaged the first day was without experience or even drill as soldiers. The officers with them, except the division commanders and possibly two or three of the brigade commanders, were equally inexperienced in war. The result was a Union victory that gave the men who achieved it great confidence in themselves ever after.

The enemy fought bravely, but they had started out to defeat and destroy an army and capture a position. They failed in both, with very heavy loss in killed and wounded, and must have gone back discouraged and convinced that the "Yankee" was not an enemy to be despised.

After the battle I gave verbal instructions to division commanders to let the regiments send out parties to bury their own dead, and to detail parties, under commissioned officers from each division, to bury the Confederate dead in their respective fronts and to report the numbers so buried. The latter part of these instructions was not carried out by all; but they were by those sent from Sherman's division, and by some of the parties sent out by McClernand. The heaviest loss sustained by the enemy was in front of these two divisions.

The criticism has often been made that the Union troops should have been intrenched at Shiloh. Up to that time the pick and spade had been but little resorted to at the West. I had, however, taken this subject under consideration soon after re-assuming command in the field, and, as already stated, my only military engineer reported unfavorably. Besides this, the troops with me, officers and men, needed discipline and drill more than they did experience with the pick, shovel and axe. Reinforcements were arriving almost daily, composed of troops that had been hastily thrown together into companies and regiments—fragments of incomplete organizations, the men and officers strangers to each other. Under all these circumstances I concluded that drill and discipline were worth more to our men than fortifications.

General Buell was a brave, intelligent officer, with as much professional pride and ambition of a commendable sort as I ever knew. I had been two years at West Point with him, and had served with him afterwards, in garrison and in the Mexican war, several years more. He was not given in early life or in mature years to forming intimate acquaintances. He was studious by habit, and commanded the confidence and respect of all who knew him. He was a strict disciplinarian, and perhaps did not distinguish sufficiently between the volunteer who "enlisted for the war" and the soldier who serves in time of peace. One system embraced men who risked life for a principle, and often men of social standing, competence, or wealth and independence of character. The other includes, as a rule, only men who could not do as well in any other occupation. General Buell became an object of harsh criticism later, some going so far as to challenge his loyalty. No one who knew him ever believed him capable of a dishonorable act, and nothing could be more dishonorable than to accept high rank and command in war and then betray the trust. When I came into command of the army in 1864, I requested the Secretary of War to restore General Buell to duty.

After the war, during the summer of 1865, I travelled considerably through the North, and was everywhere met by large numbers of people. Every one had his opinion about the manner in which the war had been conducted: who among the generals had failed, how, and why. Correspondents of the press were ever on hand to hear every word dropped, and were not always disposed to report correctly what did not confirm their preconceived notions, either about the conduct of the war or the individuals concerned in it. The opportunity frequently occurred for me to defend General Buell against what I believed to be most unjust charges. On one occasion a correspondent put in my mouth the very charge I had so often refuted—of disloyalty. This brought from General Buell a very severe retort, which I saw in the New York *World* some time before I received the letter itself. I could very well understand his grievance at seeing untrue and disgraceful charges apparently sustained by an officer who, at the time, was at the head of the army. I replied to him, but not through the press. I kept no copy of my letter, nor did I ever see it in print; neither did I receive an answer.

General Albert Sidney Johnston, who commanded the Confederate forces at the beginning of the battle, was disabled by a wound on the afternoon of the first day. This wound, as I understood afterwards, was not necessarily fatal, or even dangerous. But he was a man who would not abandon what he deemed an important trust in the face of danger and consequently continued in the saddle, commanding, until so exhausted by the loss of blood that he had to be taken from his horse, and soon after died. The news was not long in reaching our side and I suppose was quite an encouragement to the National soldiers.

I had known Johnston slightly in the Mexican war and later as an officer in the regular army. He was a man of high character and ability. His contemporaries at West Point, and officers generally who came to know him personally later and who remained on our side, expected him to prove the most formidable man to meet that the Confederacy would produce.

I once wrote that nothing occurred in his brief command of an army to prove or disprove the high estimate that had been placed upon his military ability; but after studying the orders and dispatches of Johnston I am compelled to materially modify my views of that officer's qualifications as a soldier. My judgment now is that he was vacillating and undecided in his actions.

All the disasters in Kentucky and Tennessee were so discouraging to the authorities in Richmond that Jefferson Davis wrote an unofficial letter to Johnston expressing his own anxiety and that of the public, and saying that he had made such defence as was dictated by long friendship, but that in the absence of a report he needed facts. The letter was not a reprimand in direct terms, but it was evidently as much felt as though it had been one. General Johnston raised another army as rapidly as he could, and fortified or strongly intrenched at Corinth. He knew the National troops were preparing to attack him in his chosen position. But he had evidently become so disturbed at the results of his operations that he resolved to strike out in an offensive campaign which would restore all that was lost, and if successful accomplish still more. We have the authority of his son and biographer for saying that his plan was to attack the forces at Shiloh and crush them; then to cross the Tennessee and destroy the army of Buell, and push the war across the Ohio River. The design was a bold one; but we have the same authority for saying that in the execution Johnston showed vacillation and indecision. He left Corinth on the 2d of April and was not ready to attack until the 6th. The distance his army had to march was less than twenty miles. Beauregard, his second in command, was opposed to the attack for two reasons: first, he thought, if let alone the National troops would attack the Confederates in their intrenchments; second, we were in ground of our own choosing and would necessarily be intrenched. Johnston not only listened to the objection of Beauregard to an attack, but held a council of war on the subject on the morning of the 5th. On the evening of the same day he was in consultation with some of his generals on the same subject, and still again on the morning of the 6th. During this last consultation, and before a decision had been reached, the battle began by the National troops opening fire on the enemy. This seemed to settle the question as to whether there was to be any battle of Shiloh. It also seems to me to settle the question as to whether there was a surprise.

I do not question the personal courage of General Johnston, or his ability. But he did not win the distinction predicted for him by many of his friends. He did prove that as a general he was over-estimated.

General Beauregard was next in rank to Johnston and succeeded to the command, which he retained to the close of the battle and during the subsequent retreat on Corinth, as well as in the siege of that place. His tactics have been severely criticised by Confederate writers, but I do not believe his fallen chief could have done any better under the circumstances.

Some of these critics claim that Shiloh was won when Johnston fell, and that if he had not fallen the army under me would have been annihilated or captured. *Ifs* defeated the Confederates at Shiloh. There is little doubt that we would have been disgracefully beaten *if* all the shells and bullets fired by us had passed harmlessly over the enemy and *if* all of theirs had taken effect. Commanding generals are liable to be killed during engagements; and the fact that when he was shot Johnston was leading a brigade to induce it to make a charge which had been repeatedly ordered, is evidence that there was neither the universal demoralization on our side nor the unbounded confidence on theirs which has been claimed. There was, in fact, no hour during the day when I doubted the eventual defeat of the enemy, although I was disappointed that reinforcements so near at hand did not arrive at an earlier hour.

The description of the battle of Shiloh given by Colonel Wm. Preston Johnston is very graphic and well told. The reader will imagine that he can see each blow struck, a demoralized and broken mob of Union soldiers, each blow sending the enemy more demoralized than ever towards the Tennessee River, which was a little more than two miles away at the beginning of the onset. If the reader does not stop to inquire why, with such Confederate success for more than twelve hours of hard fighting, the National troops were not all killed, captured or driven into the river, he will regard the pen picture as perfect. But I witnessed the fight from the National side from eight o'clock in the morning until night closed the contest. I see but little in the description that I can recognize. The Confederate troops fought well and deserve commendation enough for their bravery and endurance on the 6th of April, without detracting from their antagonists or claiming anything more than their just dues.

The reports of the enemy show that their condition at the end of the first day was deplorable; their losses in killed and wounded had been very heavy, and their stragglers had been quite as numerous as on the National side, with the difference that those of the enemy left the field entirely and were not brought back to their respective commands for many days. On the Union side but few of the stragglers fell back further than the landing on the river, and many of these were in line for duty on the second day. The admissions of the highest Confederate officers engaged at Shiloh make the claim of a victory for them absurd. The victory was not to either party until the battle was over. It was then a Union victory, in which the Armies of the Tennessee and the Ohio both participated. But the Army of the Tennessee fought the entire rebel army on the 6th and held it at bay until near night; and night alone closed the conflict and not the three regiments of Nelson's division.

The Confederates fought with courage at Shiloh, but the particular skill claimed I could not and still cannot see; though there is nothing to criticise except the claims put forward for it since. But the Confederate claimants for superiority in strategy, superiority in generalship and superiority in dash and prowess are not so unjust to the Union troops engaged at Shiloh as are many Northern writers. The troops on both sides were American, and united they need not fear any foreign foe. It is possible that the Southern man started in with a little more dash than his Northern brother; but he was correspondingly less enduring.

The endeavor of the enemy on the first day was simply to hurl their men against ours—first at one point, then at another, sometimes at several points at once. This they did with daring and energy, until at night the rebel troops were worn out. Our effort during the same time was to be prepared to resist assaults wherever made. The object of the Confederates on the second day was to get away with as much of their army and material as possible. Ours then was to drive them from our front, and to capture or destroy as great a part as possible of their men and material. We were successful in driving them back, but not so successful in captures as if farther pursuit could have been made. As it was, we captured or recaptured on the second day about as much artillery as we lost on the first; and, leaving out the one great capture of Prentiss, we took more prisoners on Monday than the enemy gained from us on Sunday. On the 6th Sherman lost seven pieces of artillery, McClernand six, Prentiss eight, and Hurlbut two batteries. On the 7th Sherman captured seven guns, McClernand three and the Army of the Ohio twenty.

At Shiloh the effective strength of the Union forces on the morning of the 6th was 33,000 men. Lew. Wallace brought 5,000 more after nightfall. Beauregard reported the enemy's strength at 40,955. According to the custom of enumeration in the South, this number probably excluded every man enlisted as musician or detailed as guard or nurse, and all commissioned officers—everybody who did not carry a musket or serve a cannon. With us everybody in the field receiving pay from the government is counted. Excluding the troops who fled, panic-stricken, before they had fired a shot, there was not a time during the 6th when we had more than 25,000 men in line. On the 7th Buell brought 20,000 more. Of his remaining two divisions, Thomas's did not reach the field during the engagement; Wood's arrived before firing had ceased, but not in time to be of much service.

Our loss in the two days' fight was 1,754 killed, 8,408 wounded and 2,885 missing. Of these, 2,103 were in the Army of the Ohio. Beauregard reported a total loss of 10,699, of whom 1,728 were killed, 8,012 wounded and 957 missing. This estimate must be incorrect. We buried, by actual count, more of the enemy's dead in front of the divisions of McClernand and Sherman alone than here reported, and 4,000 was the estimate of the burial parties for the whole field. Beauregard reports the Confederate force on the 6th at over 40,000, and their total loss during the two days at 10,699; and at the same time declares that he could put only 20,000 men in battle on the morning of the 7th.

The navy gave a hearty support to the army at Shiloh, as indeed it always did both before and subsequently when I was in command. The nature of the ground was such, however, that on this occasion it could do nothing in aid of the troops until sundown on the first day. The country was broken and heavily timbered, cutting off all view of the battle from the river, so that friends would be as much in danger from fire from the gunboats as the foe. But about sundown, when the National troops were back in their last position, the right of the enemy was near the river and exposed to the fire of the two gun-boats, which was delivered with vigor and effect. After nightfall, when firing had entirely ceased on land, the commander of the fleet informed himself, approximately, of the position of our troops and suggested the idea of dropping a shell within the lines of the enemy every fifteen minutes during the night. This was done with effect, as is proved by the Confederate reports.

Up to the battle of Shiloh I, as well as thousands of other citizens, believed that the rebellion against the Government would collapse suddenly and soon, if a decisive victory could be gained over any of its armies. Donelson and Henry were such victories. An army of more than 21,000 men was captured or destroyed. Bowling Green, Columbus and Hickman, Kentucky, fell in consequence, and Clarksville and Nashville, Tennessee, the last two with an immense amount of stores, also fell into our hands. The Tennessee and Cumberland rivers, from their mouths to the head of navigation, were secured. But when Confederate armies were collected which not only attempted to hold a line farther south, from Memphis to Chattanooga, Knoxville and on to the Atlantic, but assumed the offensive and made such a gallant effort to regain what had been lost, then, indeed, I gave up all idea of saving the Union except by complete conquest. Up to that time it had been the policy of our army, certainly of that portion commanded by me, to protect the property of the citizens whose territory was invaded, without regard to their sentiments, whether Union or Secession. After this, however, I regarded it as humane to both sides to protect the persons of those found at their homes, but to consume everything that could be used to support or supply armies. Protection was still continued over such supplies as were within lines held by us and which we expected to continue to hold; but such supplies within the reach of Confederate armies I regarded as much contraband as arms or ordnance stores. Their destruction was accomplished without bloodshed and tended to the same result as the destruction of armies. I continued this policy to the close of the war. Promiscuous pillaging, however, was discouraged and punished. Instructions were always given to take provisions and forage under the direction of commissioned officers who should give receipts to owners, if at home, and turn the property over to officers of the quartermaster or commissary departments to be issued as if furnished from our Northern dépôts. But much was destroyed without receipts to owners, when it could not be brought within our lines and would otherwise have gone to the support of secession and rebellion.

This policy I believe exercised a material influence in hastening the end.

The battle of Shiloh, or Pittsburg landing, has been perhaps less understood, or, to state the case more accurately, more persistently misunderstood, than any other engagement between National and Confederate troops during the entire rebellion. Correct reports of the battle have been published, notably by Sherman, Badeau and, in a speech before a meeting of veterans, by General Prentiss; but all of these appeared long subsequent to the close of the rebellion and after public opinion had been most erroneously formed.

I myself made no report to General Halleck, further than was contained in a letter, written immediately after the battle informing him that an engagement had been fought and announcing the result. A few days afterwards General Halleck moved his headquarters to Pittsburg landing and assumed command of the troops in the field. Although next to him in rank, and nominally in command of my old district and army, I was ignored as much as if I had been at the most distant point of territory within my jurisdiction; and although I was in command of all the troops engaged at Shiloh I was not permitted to see one of the reports of General Buell or his subordinates in that battle, until they were published by the War Department long after the event. For this reason I never made a full official report of this engagement.

Chapter XXVI.

HALLECK ASSUMES COMMAND IN THE FIELD—THE
ADVANCE UPON CORINTH—OCCUPATION OF
CORINTH—THE ARMY SEPARATED.

GENERAL HALLECK arrived at Pittsburg landing on the 11th of April and immediately assumed command in the field. On the 21st General Pope arrived with an army 30,000 strong, fresh from the capture of Island Number Ten in the Mississippi River. He went into camp at Hamburg landing five miles above Pittsburg. Halleck had now three armies: the Army of the Ohio, Buell commanding; the Army of the Mississippi, Pope commanding; and the Army of the Tennessee. His orders divided the combined force into the right wing, reserve, centre and left wing. Major-General George H. Thomas, who had been in Buell's army, was transferred with his division to the Army of the Tennessee and given command of the right wing, composed of all of that army except McClernand's and Lew. Wallace's divisions. McClernand was assigned to the command of the reserve, composed of his own and Lew. Wallace's divisions. Buell commanded the centre, the Army of the Ohio; and Pope the left wing, the Army of the Mississippi. I was named second in command of the whole, and was also supposed to be in command of the right wing and reserve.

Orders were given to all the commanders engaged at Shiloh to send in their reports without delay to department headquarters. Those from officers of the Army of the Tennessee were sent through me; but from the Army of the Ohio they were sent by General Buell without passing through my hands. General Halleck ordered me, verbally, to send in my report, but I positively declined on the ground that he had received the reports of a part of the army engaged at Shiloh without their coming through me. He admitted that my refusal was justifiable under the circumstances, but explained that he had wanted to get the reports off before moving the command, and as fast as a report had come to him he had forwarded it to Washington.

Preparations were at once made upon the arrival of the new commander for an advance on Corinth. Owl Creek, on our right, was bridged, and expeditions were sent to the northwest and west to ascertain if our position was being threatened from those quarters; the roads towards Corinth were corduroyed and new ones made; lateral roads were also constructed, so that in case of necessity troops marching by different routes could reinforce each other. All commanders were cautioned against bringing on an engagement and informed in so many words that it would be better to retreat than to fight. By the 30th of April all preparations were complete; the country west to the Mobile and Ohio railroad had been reconnoitred, as well as the road to Corinth as far as Monterey twelve miles from Pittsburg. Everywhere small bodies of the enemy had been encountered, but they were observers and not in force to fight battles.

Corinth, Mississippi, lies in a south-westerly direction from Pittsburg landing and about nineteen miles away as the bird would fly, but probably twenty-two by the nearest wagon-road. It is about four miles south of the line dividing the States of Tennessee and Mississippi, and at the junction of the Mississippi and Chattanooga railroad with the Mobile and Ohio road which runs from Columbus to Mobile. From Pittsburg to Corinth the land is rolling, but at no point reaching an elevation that makes high hills to pass over. In 1862 the greater part of the country was covered with forest with intervening clearings and houses. Underbrush was dense in the low grounds along the creeks and ravines, but generally not so thick on the high land as to prevent men passing through with ease. There are two small creeks running from north of the town and connecting some four miles south, where they form Bridge Creek which empties into the Tuscumbia River. Corinth is on the ridge between these streams and is a naturally strong defensive position. The creeks are insignificant in volume of water, but the stream to the east widens out in front of the town into a swamp, impassable in the presence of an enemy. On the crest of the west bank of this stream the enemy was strongly intrenched.

Corinth was a valuable strategic point for the enemy to

hold, and consequently a valuable one for us to possess ourselves of. We ought to have seized it immediately after the
fall of Donelson and Nashville, when it could have been
taken without a battle, but failing then it should have been
taken, without delay, on the concentration of troops at Pittsburg landing after the battle of Shiloh. In fact the arrival of
Pope should not have been awaited. There was no time from
the battle of Shiloh up to the evacuation of Corinth when
the enemy would not have left if pushed. The demoralization among the Confederates from their defeats at Henry and
Donelson; their long marches from Bowling Green, Columbus, and Nashville, and their failure at Shiloh; in fact from
having been driven out of Kentucky and Tennessee, was so
great that a stand for the time would have been impossible.
Beauregard made strenuous efforts to reinforce himself and
partially succeeded. He appealed to the people of the South-
west for new regiments, and received a few. A. S. Johnston
had made efforts to reinforce in the same quarter, before the
battle of Shiloh, but in a different way. He had negroes sent
out to him to take the place of teamsters, company cooks
and laborers in every capacity, so as to put all his white men
into the ranks. The people, while willing to send their sons
to the field, were not willing to part with their negroes. It is
only fair to state that they probably wanted their blacks to
raise supplies for the army and for the families left at home.

Beauregard, however, was reinforced by Van Dorn immediately after Shiloh with 17,000 men. Interior points, less exposed, were also depleted to add to the strength at Corinth.
With these reinforcements and the new regiments, Beauregard had, during the month of May, 1862, a large force on
paper, but probably not much over 50,000 effective men. We
estimated his strength at 70,000. Our own was, in round
numbers, 120,000. The defensible nature of the ground at
Corinth, and the fortifications, made 50,000 then enough to
maintain their position against double that number for an indefinite time but for the demoralization spoken of.

On the 30th of April the grand army commenced its advance from Shiloh upon Corinth. The movement was a siege
from the start to the close. The National troops were always

behind intrenchments, except of course the small reconnoitring parties sent to the front to clear the way for an advance.
Even the commanders of these parties were cautioned, "not to
bring on an engagement." "It is better to retreat than to
fight." The enemy were constantly watching our advance, but
as they were simply observers there were but few engagements that even threatened to become battles. All the engagements fought ought to have served to encourage the
enemy. Roads were again made in our front, and again corduroyed; a line was intrenched, and the troops were advanced
to the new position. Cross roads were constructed to these
new positions to enable the troops to concentrate in case of
attack. The National armies were thoroughly intrenched all
the way from the Tennessee River to Corinth.

For myself I was little more than an observer. Orders were
sent direct to the right wing or reserve, ignoring me, and
advances were made from one line of intrenchments to another without notifying me. My position was so embarrassing
in fact that I made several applications during the siege to be
relieved.

General Halleck kept his headquarters generally, if not all
the time, with the right wing. Pope being on the extreme
left did not see so much of his chief, and consequently got
loose as it were at times. On the 3d of May he was at Seven
Mile Creek with the main body of his command, but threw
forward a division to Farmington, within four miles of
Corinth. His troops had quite a little engagement at Farmington on that day, but carried the place with considerable
loss to the enemy. There would then have been no difficulty
in advancing the centre and right so as to form a new line
well up to the enemy, but Pope was ordered back to conform with the general line. On the 8th of May he moved
again, taking his whole force to Farmington, and pushed out
two divisions close to the rebel line. Again he was ordered
back. By the 4th of May the centre and right wing reached
Monterey, twelve miles out. Their advance was slow from
there, for they intrenched with every forward movement.
The left wing moved up again on the 25th of May and intrenched itself close to the enemy. The creek, with the

marsh before described, separated the two lines. Skirmishers thirty feet apart could have maintained either line at this point.

Our centre and right were, at this time, extended so that the right of the right wing was probably five miles from Corinth and four from the works in their front. The creek, which was a formidable obstacle for either side to pass on our left, became a very slight obstacle on our right. Here the enemy occupied two positions. One of them, as much as two miles out from his main line, was on a commanding elevation and defended by an intrenched battery with infantry supports. A heavy wood intervened between this work and the National forces. In rear to the south there was a clearing extending a mile or more, and south of this clearing a log-house which had been loop-holed and was occupied by infantry. Sherman's division carried these two positions with some loss to himself, but with probably greater to the enemy, on the 28th of May, and on that day the investment of Corinth was complete, or as complete as it was ever made. Thomas' right now rested west of the Mobile and Ohio railroad. Pope's left commanded the Memphis and Charleston railroad east of Corinth.

Some days before I had suggested to the commanding general that I thought if he would move the Army of the Mississippi at night, by the rear of the centre and right, ready to advance at daylight, Pope would find no natural obstacle in his front and, I believed, no serious artificial one. The ground, or works, occupied by our left could be held by a thin picket line, owing to the stream and swamp in front. To the right the troops would have a dry ridge to march over. I was silenced so quickly that I felt that possibly I had suggested an unmilitary movement.

Later, probably on the 28th of May, General Logan, whose command was then on the Mobile and Ohio railroad, said to me that the enemy had been evacuating for several days and that if allowed he could go into Corinth with his brigade. Trains of cars were heard coming in and going out of Corinth constantly. Some of the men who had been engaged in various capacities on railroads before the war claimed that they could tell, by putting their ears to the rail, not only which

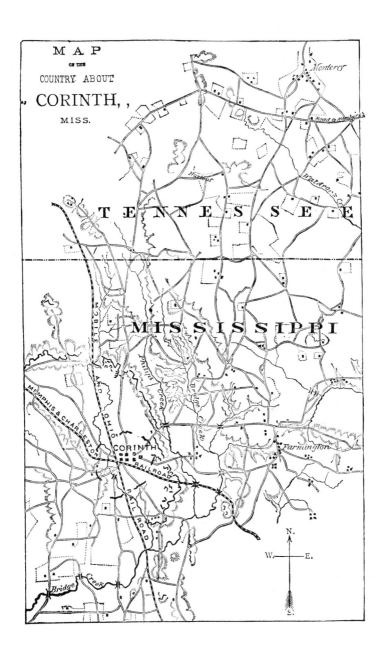

MAP
OF THE
COUNTRY ABOUT
CORINTH,,
MISS.

TENNESSEE

MISSISSIPPI

Monterey

Road to Hamburg

Waldron

Hickory

MOBILE AND OHIO RAILROAD

MEMPHIS & CHARLESTON

CORINTH

RAILROAD

Phillis Creek

Bridge Creek

Farmington

RAIL ROAD

Bridge Creek

N.

W.—E.

S.

way the trains were moving but which trains were loaded and which were empty. They said loaded trains had been going out for several days and empty ones coming in. Subsequent events proved the correctness of their judgment. Beauregard published his orders for the evacuation of Corinth on the 26th of May and fixed the 29th for the departure of his troops, and on the 30th of May General Halleck had his whole army drawn up prepared for battle and announced in orders that there was every indication that our left was to be attacked that morning. Corinth had already been evacuated and the National troops marched on and took possession without opposition. Everything had been destroyed or carried away. The Confederate commander had instructed his soldiers to cheer on the arrival of every train to create the impression among the Yankees that reinforcements were arriving. There was not a sick or wounded man left by the Confederates, nor stores of any kind. Some ammunition had been blown up—not removed—but the trophies of war were a few Quaker guns, logs of about the diameter of ordinary cannon, mounted on wheels of wagons and pointed in the most threatening manner towards us.

The possession of Corinth by the National troops was of strategic importance, but the victory was barren in every other particular. It was nearly bloodless. It is a question whether the *morale* of the Confederate troops engaged at Corinth was not improved by the immunity with which they were permitted to remove all public property and then withdraw themselves. On our side I know officers and men of the Army of the Tennessee—and I presume the same is true of those of the other commands—were disappointed at the result. They could not see how the mere occupation of places was to close the war while large and effective rebel armies existed. They believed that a well-directed attack would at least have partially destroyed the army defending Corinth. For myself I am satisfied that Corinth could have been captured in a two days' campaign commenced promptly on the arrival of reinforcements after the battle of Shiloh.

General Halleck at once commenced erecting fortifications around Corinth on a scale to indicate that this one point must be held if it took the whole National army to do it. All com-

manding points two or three miles to the south, south-east
and south-west were strongly fortified. It was expected in case
of necessity to connect these forts by rifle-pits. They were laid
out on a scale that would have required 100,000 men to fully
man them. It was probably thought that a final battle of the
war would be fought at that point. These fortifications were
never used. Immediately after the occupation of Corinth by
the National troops, General Pope was sent in pursuit of the
retreating garrison and General Buell soon followed. Buell
was the senior of the two generals and commanded the entire
column. The pursuit was kept up for some thirty miles, but
did not result in the capture of any material of war or prisoners, unless a few stragglers who had fallen behind and were
willing captives. On the 10th of June the pursuing column was
all back at Corinth. The Army of the Tennessee was not engaged in any of these movements.

The Confederates were now driven out of West Tennessee,
and on the 6th of June, after a well-contested naval battle, the
National forces took possession of Memphis and held the
Mississippi river from its source to that point. The railroad
from Columbus to Corinth was at once put in good condition and held by us. We had garrisons at Donelson, Clarksville
and Nashville, on the Cumberland River, and held the Tennessee River from its mouth to Eastport. New Orleans and
Baton Rouge had fallen into the possession of the National
forces, so that now the Confederates at the west were narrowed down for all communication with Richmond to the
single line of road running east from Vicksburg. To dispossess
them of this, therefore, became a matter of the first importance. The possession of the Mississippi by us from Memphis
to Baton Rouge was also a most important object. It would
be equal to the amputation of a limb in its weakening effects
upon the enemy.

After the capture of Corinth a movable force of 80,000
men, besides enough to hold all the territory acquired, could
have been set in motion for the accomplishment of any great
campaign for the suppression of the rebellion. In addition to
this fresh troops were being raised to swell the effective force.
But the work of depletion commenced. Buell with the Army
of the Ohio was sent east, following the line of the Memphis

and Charleston railroad. This he was ordered to repair as he advanced—only to have it destroyed by small guerilla bands or other troops as soon as he was out of the way. If he had been sent directly to Chattanooga as rapidly as he could march, leaving two or three divisions along the line of the railroad from Nashville forward, he could have arrived with but little fighting, and would have saved much of the loss of life which was afterwards incurred in gaining Chattanooga. Bragg would then not have had time to raise an army to contest the possession of middle and east Tennessee and Kentucky; the battles of Stone River and Chickamauga would not necessarily have been fought; Burnside would not have been besieged in Knoxville without the power of helping himself or escaping; the battle of Chattanooga would not have been fought. These are the negative advantages, if the term negative is applicable, which would probably have resulted from prompt movements after Corinth fell into the possession of the National forces. The positive results might have been: a bloodless advance to Atlanta, to Vicksburg, or to any other desired point south of Corinth in the interior of Mississippi.

Chapter XXVII.

M Y POSITION at Corinth, with a nominal command and
yet no command, became so unbearable that I asked
permission of Halleck to remove my headquarters to Memphis. I had repeatedly asked, between the fall of Donelson and
the evacuation of Corinth, to be relieved from duty under
Halleck; but all my applications were refused until the occupation of the town. I then obtained permission to leave the
department, but General Sherman happened to call on me as I
was about starting and urged me so strongly not to think of
going, that I concluded to remain. My application to be permitted to remove my headquarters to Memphis was, however,
approved, and on the 21st of June I started for that point with
my staff and a cavalry escort of only a part of one company.
There was a detachment of two or three companies going
some twenty-five miles west to be stationed as a guard to the
railroad. I went under cover of this escort to the end of their
march, and the next morning proceeded to La Grange with
no convoy but the few cavalry men I had with me.

From La Grange to Memphis the distance is forty-seven
miles. There were no troops stationed between these two
points, except a small force guarding a working party which
was engaged in repairing the railroad. Not knowing where
this party would be found I halted at La Grange. General
Hurlbut was in command there at the time and had his headquarters tents pitched on the lawn of a very commodious
country house. The proprietor was at home and, learning of
my arrival, he invited General Hurlbut and me to dine with
him. I accepted the invitation and spent a very pleasant afternoon with my host, who was a thorough Southern gentleman

fully convinced of the justice of secession. After dinner, seated in the capacious porch, he entertained me with a recital of the services he was rendering the cause. He was too old to be in the ranks himself—he must have been quite seventy then—but his means enabled him to be useful in other ways. In ordinary times the homestead where he was now living produced the bread and meat to supply the slaves on his main plantation, in the low-lands of Mississippi. Now he raised food and forage on both places, and thought he would have that year a surplus sufficient to feed three hundred families of poor men who had gone into the war and left their families dependent upon the "patriotism" of those better off. The crops around me looked fine, and I had at the moment an idea that about the time they were ready to be gathered the "Yankee" troops would be in the neighborhood and harvest them for the benefit of those engaged in the suppression of the rebellion instead of its support. I felt, however, the greatest respect for the candor of my host and for his zeal in a cause he thoroughly believed in, though our views were as wide apart as it is possible to conceive.

The 23d of June, 1862, on the road from La Grange to Memphis was very warm, even for that latitude and season. With my staff and small escort I started at an early hour, and before noon we arrived within twenty miles of Memphis. At this point I saw a very comfortable-looking white-haired gentleman seated at the front of his house, a little distance from the road. I let my staff and escort ride ahead while I halted and, for an excuse, asked for a glass of water. I was invited at once to dismount and come in. I found my host very genial and communicative, and staid longer than I had intended, until the lady of the house announced dinner and asked me to join them. The host, however, was not pressing, so that I declined the invitation and, mounting my horse, rode on.

About a mile west from where I had been stopping a road comes up from the south-east, joining that from La Grange to Memphis. A mile west of this junction I found my staff and escort halted and enjoying the shade of forest trees on the lawn of a house located several hundred feet back from the road, their horses hitched to the fence along the line of the road. I, too, stopped and we remained there until the cool of the afternoon, and then rode into Memphis.

The gentleman with whom I had stopped twenty miles from Memphis was a Mr. De Loche, a man loyal to the Union. He had not pressed me to tarry longer with him because in the early part of my visit a neighbor, a Dr. Smith, had called and, on being presented to me, backed off the porch as if something had hit him. Mr. De Loche knew that the rebel General Jackson was in that neighborhood with a detachment of cavalry. His neighbor was as earnest in the southern cause as was Mr. De Loche in that of the Union. The exact location of Jackson was entirely unknown to Mr. De Loche; but he was sure that his neighbor would know it and would give information of my presence, and this made my stay unpleasant to him after the call of Dr. Smith.

I have stated that a detachment of troops was engaged in guarding workmen who were repairing the railroad east of Memphis. On the day I entered Memphis, Jackson captured a small herd of beef cattle which had been sent east for the troops so engaged. The drovers were not enlisted men and he released them. A day or two after one of these drovers came to my headquarters and, relating the circumstances of his capture, said Jackson was very much disappointed that he had not captured me; that he was six or seven miles south of the Memphis and Charleston railroad when he learned that I was stopping at the house of Mr. De Loche, and had ridden with his command to the junction of the road he was on with that from La Grange and Memphis, where he learned that I had passed three-quarters of an hour before. He thought it would be useless to pursue with jaded horses a well-mounted party with so much of a start. Had he gone three-quarters of a mile farther he would have found me with my party quietly resting under the shade of trees and without even arms in our hands with which to defend ourselves.

General Jackson of course did not communicate his disappointment at not capturing me to a prisoner, a young drover; but from the talk among the soldiers the facts related were learned. A day or two later Mr. De Loche called on me in Memphis to apologize for his apparent incivility in not insisting on my staying for dinner. He said that his wife accused him of marked discourtesy, but that, after the call of his neighbor, he had felt restless until I got away. I never met General Jackson before the war, nor during it, but have met him since at his very comfortable summer home at Manitou Springs, Colorado. I reminded him of the above incident, and this drew from him the response that he was thankful now he had not captured me. I certainly was very thankful too.

My occupation of Memphis as district headquarters did not last long. The period, however, was marked by a few incidents which were novel to me. Up to that time I had not occupied any place in the South where the citizens were at home in any great numbers. Dover was within the fortifications at Fort Donelson, and, as far as I remember, every citizen was gone. There were no people living at Pittsburg landing, and but very few at Corinth. Memphis, however, was a populous city, and there were many of the citizens remaining there who were not only thoroughly impressed with the justice of their cause, but who thought that even the "Yankee soldiery" must entertain the same views if they could only be induced to make an honest confession. It took hours of my time every day to listen to complaints and requests. The latter were generally reasonable, and if so they were granted; but the complaints were not always, or even often, well founded. Two instances will mark the general character. First: the officer who commanded at Memphis immediately after the city fell into the hands of the National troops had ordered one of the churches of the city to be opened to the soldiers. Army chaplains were authorized to occupy the pulpit. Second: at the beginning of the war the Confederate Congress had passed a law confiscating all property of "alien enemies" at the South, including the debts of Southerners to Northern men. In consequence of this law, when Memphis was occupied the provost-marshal had forcibly collected all the evidences he could obtain of such debts.

Almost the first complaints made to me were these two outrages. The gentleman who made the complaints informed me first of his own high standing as a lawyer, a citizen and a Christian. He was a deacon in the church which had been defiled by the occupation of Union troops, and by a Union chaplain filling the pulpit. He did not use the word "defile," but he expressed the idea very clearly. He asked that the church be restored to the former congregation. I told him that no order had been issued prohibiting the congregation attending the church. He said of course the congregation could not hear a Northern clergyman who differed so radically with them on questions of government. I told him the troops would continue to occupy that church for the present, and that they would not be called upon to hear disloyal sentiments proclaimed from the pulpit. This closed the argument on the first point.

Then came the second. The complainant said that he wanted the papers restored to him which had been surrendered to the provost-marshal under protest; he was a lawyer, and before the establishment of the "Confederate States Government" had been the attorney for a number of large business houses at the North; that "his government" had confiscated all debts due "alien enemies," and appointed commissioners, or officers, to collect such debts and pay them over to the "government": but in his case, owing to his high standing, he had been permitted to hold these claims for collection, the responsible officials knowing that he would account to the "government" for every dollar received. He said that his "government," when it came in possession of all its territory, would hold him personally responsible for the claims he had surrendered to the provost-marshal. His impudence was so sublime that I was rather amused than indignant. I told him, however, that if he would remain in Memphis I did not believe the Confederate government would ever molest him. He left, no doubt, as much amazed at my assurance as I was at the brazenness of his request.

On the 11th of July General Halleck received telegraphic orders appointing him to the command of all the armies, with headquarters in Washington. His instructions pressed him to proceed to his new field of duty with as little delay as was consistent with the safety and interests of his previous command. I was next in rank, and he telegraphed me the same day to report at department headquarters at Corinth. I was not informed by the dispatch that my chief had been ordered to a different field and did not know whether to move my headquarters or not. I telegraphed asking if I was to take my staff with me, and received word in reply: "This place will be your headquarters. You can judge for yourself." I left Memphis for my new field without delay, and reached Corinth on the 15th of the month. General Halleck remained until the 17th of July; but he was very uncommunicative, and gave me no information as to what I had been called to Corinth for.

When General Halleck left to assume the duties of general-in-chief I remained in command of the district of West Tennessee. Practically I became a department commander, because no one was assigned to that position over me and I made my reports direct to the general-in-chief; but I was not assigned to the position of department commander until the 25th of October. General Halleck while commanding the Department of the Mississippi had had control as far east as a line drawn from Chattanooga north. My district only embraced West Tennessee and Kentucky west of the Cumberland River. Buell, with the Army of the Ohio, had, as previously stated, been ordered east towards Chattanooga, with instructions to repair the Memphis and Charleston railroad as he advanced. Troops had been sent north by Halleck along the line of the Mobile and Ohio railroad to put it in repair as far as Columbus. Other troops were stationed on the railroad from Jackson, Tennessee, to Grand Junction, and still others on the road west to Memphis.

The remainder of the magnificent army of 120,000 men which entered Corinth on the 30th of May had now become so scattered that I was put entirely on the defensive in a territory whose population was hostile to the Union. One of the first things I had to do was to construct fortifications at Corinth better suited to the garrison that could be spared to man them. The structures that had been built during the months of May and June were left as monuments to the skill of the engineer, and others were constructed in a few days, plainer in design but suited to the command available to defend them.

I disposed the troops belonging to the district in conformity with the situation as rapidly as possible. The forces at Donelson, Clarksville and Nashville, with those at Corinth and along the railroad eastward, I regarded as sufficient for protection against any attack from the west. The Mobile and

Ohio railroad was guarded from Rienzi, south of Corinth, to Columbus; and the Mississippi Central railroad from Jackson, Tennessee, to Bolivar. Grand Junction and La Grange on the Memphis railroad were abandoned.

South of the Army of the Tennessee, and confronting it, was Van Dorn, with a sufficient force to organize a movable army of thirty-five to forty thousand men, after being reinforced by Price from Missouri. This movable force could be thrown against either Corinth, Bolivar or Memphis; and the best that could be done in such event would be to weaken the points not threatened in order to reinforce the one that was. Nothing could be gained on the National side by attacking elsewhere, because the territory already occupied was as much as the force present could guard. The most anxious period of the war, to me, was during the time the Army of the Tennessee was guarding the territory acquired by the fall of Corinth and Memphis and before I was sufficiently reinforced to take the offensive. The enemy also had cavalry operating in our rear, making it necessary to guard every point of the railroad back to Columbus, on the security of which we were dependent for all our supplies. Headquarters were connected by telegraph with all points of the command except Memphis and the Mississippi below Columbus. With these points communication was had by the railroad to Columbus, then down the river by boat. To reinforce Memphis would take three or four days, and to get an order there for troops to move elsewhere would have taken at least two days. Memphis therefore was practically isolated from the balance of the command. But it was in Sherman's hands. Then too the troops were well intrenched and the gunboats made a valuable auxiliary.

During the two months after the departure of General Halleck there was much fighting between small bodies of the contending armies, but these encounters were dwarfed by the magnitude of the main battles so as to be now almost forgotten except by those engaged in them. Some of them, however, estimated by the losses on both sides in killed and wounded, were equal in hard fighting to most of the battles of the Mexican war which attracted so much of the attention of the public when they occurred. About the 23d of July Colonel Ross, commanding at Bolivar, was threatened by a large force of the enemy so that he had to be reinforced from Jackson and Corinth. On the 27th there was skirmishing on the Hatchie River, eight miles from Bolivar. On the 30th I learned from Colonel P. H. Sheridan, who had been far to the south, that Bragg in person was at Rome, Georgia, with his troops moving by rail (by way of Mobile) to Chattanooga and his wagon train marching overland to join him at Rome. Price was at this time at Holly Springs, Mississippi, with a large force, and occupied Grand Junction as an outpost. I proposed to the general-in-chief to be permitted to drive him away, but was informed that, while I had to judge for myself, the best use to make of my troops *was not to scatter them*, but hold them ready to reinforce Buell.

The movement of Bragg himself with his wagon trains to Chattanooga across country, while his troops were transported over a long round-about road to the same destination, without need of guards except when in my immediate front, demonstrates the advantage which troops enjoy while acting in a country where the people are friendly. Buell was marching through a hostile region and had to have his communications thoroughly guarded back to a base of supplies. More men were required the farther the National troops penetrated into the enemy's country. I, with an army sufficiently powerful to have destroyed Bragg, was purely on the defensive and accomplishing no more than to hold a force far inferior to my own.

On the 2d of August I was ordered from Washington to live upon the country, on the resources of citizens hostile to the government, so far as practicable. I was also directed to "handle rebels within our lines without gloves," to imprison them, or to expel them from their homes and from our lines. I do not recollect having arrested and confined a citizen (not a soldier) during the entire rebellion. I am aware that a great many were sent to northern prisons, particularly to Joliet, Illinois, by some of my subordinates with the statement that it was my order. I had all such released the moment I learned of their arrest; and finally sent a staff officer north to release every prisoner who was said to be confined by my order. There were many citizens at home who deserved punishment because they were soldiers when an opportunity was afforded to inflict an injury to the National cause. This class was not of the kind that were apt to get arrested, and I deemed it better that a few guilty men should escape than that a great many innocent ones should suffer.

On the 14th of August I was ordered to send two more divisions to Buell. They were sent the same day by way of Decatur. On the 22d Colonel Rodney Mason surrendered Clarksville with six companies of his regiment.

Colonel Mason was one of the officers who had led their regiments off the field at almost the first fire of the rebels at Shiloh. He was by nature and education a gentleman, and was terribly mortified at his action when the battle was over. He came to me with tears in his eyes and begged to be allowed to have another trial. I felt great sympathy for him and sent him, with his regiment, to garrison Clarksville and Donelson. He selected Clarksville for his headquarters, no doubt because he regarded it as the post of danger, it being nearer the enemy. But when he was summoned to surrender by a band of guerillas, his constitutional weakness overcame him. He inquired the number of men the enemy had, and receiving a response indicating a force greater than his own he said if he could be satisfied of that fact he would surrender. Arrangements were made for him to count the guerillas, and having satisfied himself that the enemy had the greater force he surrendered and informed his subordinate at Donelson of the fact, advising him to do the same. The guerillas paroled their prisoners and moved upon Donelson, but the officer in command at that point marched out to meet them and drove them away.

Among other embarrassments, at the time of which I now write, was the fact that the government wanted to get out all the cotton possible from the South and directed me to give every facility toward that end. Pay in gold was authorized, and stations on the Mississippi River and on the railroad in our possession had to be designated where cotton would be received. This opened to the enemy not only the means of converting cotton into money, which had a value all over the world and which they so much needed, but it afforded them means of obtaining accurate and intelligent information in regard to our position and strength. It was also demoralizing to the troops. Citizens obtaining permits from the treasury department had to be protected within our lines and given facilities to get out cotton by which they realized enormous profits. Men who had enlisted to fight the battles of their country did not like to be engaged in protecting a traffic which went to the support of an enemy they had to fight, and the profits of which went to men who shared none of their dangers.

On the 30th of August Colonel M. D. Leggett, near Bolivar, with the 20th and 29th Ohio volunteer infantry, was attacked by a force supposed to be about 4,000 strong. The enemy was driven away with a loss of more than one hundred men. On the 1st of September the bridge guard at Medon was attacked by guerillas. The guard held the position until reinforced, when the enemy were routed leaving about fifty of their number on the field dead or wounded, our loss being only two killed and fifteen wounded. On the same day Colonel Dennis, with a force of less than 500 infantry and two pieces of artillery, met the cavalry of the enemy in strong force, a few miles west of Medon, and drove them away with great loss. Our troops buried 179 of the enemy's dead, left upon the field. Afterwards it was found that all the houses in the vicinity of the battle-field were turned into hospitals for the wounded. Our loss, as reported at the time, was forty-five killed and wounded. On the 2d of September I was ordered to send more reinforcements to Buell. Jackson and Bolivar were yet threatened, but I sent the reinforcements. On the 4th I received direct orders to send Granger's division also to Louisville, Kentucky.

General Buell had left Corinth about the 10th of June to march upon Chattanooga; Bragg, who had superseded Beauregard in command, sent one division from Tupelo on the 27th of June for the same place. This gave Buell about seventeen days' start. If he had not been required to repair the railroad as he advanced, the march could have been made in eighteen days at the outside, and Chattanooga must have been reached by the National forces before the rebels could have possibly got there. The road between Nashville and Chattanooga could easily have been put in repair by other troops, so that communication with the North would have been opened in a short time after the occupation of the place by the National troops. If Buell had been permitted to move in the first instance, with the whole of the Army of the Ohio and that portion of the Army of the Mississippi afterwards sent to him, he could have thrown four divisions from his own command along the line of road to repair and guard it.

Granger's division was promptly sent on the 4th of September. I was at the station at Corinth when the troops reached that point, and found General P. H. Sheridan with them. I expressed surprise at seeing him and said that I had not expected him to go. He showed decided disappointment at the prospect of being detained. I felt a little nettled at his desire to get away and did not detain him.

Sheridan was a first lieutenant in the regiment in which I had served eleven years, the 4th infantry, and stationed on the Pacific coast when the war broke out. He was promoted to a captaincy in May, 1861, and before the close of the year managed in some way, I do not know how, to get East. He went to Missouri. Halleck had known him as a very successful young officer in managing campaigns against the Indians on the Pacific coast, and appointed him acting-quartermaster in south-west Missouri. There was no difficulty in getting supplies forward while Sheridan served in that capacity; but he got into difficulty with his immediate superiors because of his stringent rules for preventing the use of public transportation for private purposes. He asked to be relieved from further duty in the capacity in which he was engaged and his request was granted. When General Halleck took the field in April, 1862, Sheridan was assigned to duty on his staff. During the advance on Corinth a vacancy occurred in the colonelcy of the 2d Michigan cavalry. Governor Blair, of Michigan, telegraphed General Halleck asking him to suggest the name of a professional soldier for the vacancy, saying he would appoint a good man without reference to his State. Sheridan was named; and was so conspicuously efficient that when Corinth was reached he was assigned to command a cavalry brigade in the Army of the Mississippi. He was in command at Booneville on the 1st of July with two small regiments, when he was attacked by a force full three times as numerous as his own. By very skilful manœuvres and boldness of attack he completely routed the enemy. For this he was made a brigadier-general and became a conspicuous figure in the army about Corinth. On this account I was sorry to see him leaving me. His departure was probably fortunate, for he rendered distinguished services in his new field.

Granger and Sheridan reached Louisville before Buell got there, and on the night of their arrival Sheridan with his command threw up works around the railroad station for the defence of troops as they came from the front.

Chapter XXVIII.

ADVANCE OF VAN DORN AND PRICE — PRICE
ENTERS IUKA — BATTLE OF IUKA.

AT THIS TIME, September 4th, I had two divisions of the Army of the Mississippi stationed at Corinth, Rienzi, Jacinto and Danville. There were at Corinth also Davies' division and two brigades of McArthur's, besides cavalry and artillery. This force constituted my left wing, of which Rosecrans was in command. General Ord commanded the centre, from Bethel to Humboldt on the Mobile and Ohio railroad and from Jackson to Bolivar where the Mississippi Central is crossed by the Hatchie River. General Sherman commanded on the right at Memphis with two of his brigades back at Brownsville, at the crossing of the Hatchie River by the Memphis and Ohio railroad. This made the most convenient arrangement I could devise for concentrating all my spare forces upon any threatened point. All the troops of the command were within telegraphic communication of each other, except those under Sherman. By bringing a portion of his command to Brownsville, from which point there was a railroad and telegraph back to Memphis, communication could be had with that part of my command within a few hours by the use of couriers. In case it became necessary to reinforce Corinth, by this arrangement all the troops at Bolivar, except a small guard, could be sent by rail by the way of Jackson in less than twenty-four hours; while the troops from Brownsville could march up to Bolivar to take their place.

On the 7th of September I learned of the advance of Van Dorn and Price, apparently upon Corinth. One division was brought from Memphis to Bolivar to meet any emergency that might arise from this move of the enemy. I was much concerned because my first duty, after holding the territory acquired within my command, was to prevent further reinforcing of Bragg in Middle Tennessee. Already the Army of Northern Virginia had defeated the army under General Pope and was invading Maryland. In the Centre General Buell was on his way to Louisville and Bragg marching parallel to him with a large Confederate force for the Ohio River.

I had been constantly called upon to reinforce Buell until at this time my entire force numbered less than 50,000 men, of all arms. This included everything from Cairo south within my jurisdiction. If I too should be driven back, the Ohio River would become the line dividing the belligerents west of the Alleghanies, while at the East the line was already farther north than when hostilities commenced at the opening of the war. It is true Nashville was never given up after its first capture, but it would have been isolated and the garrison there would have been obliged to beat a hasty retreat if the troops in West Tennessee had been compelled to fall back. To say at the end of the second year of the war the line dividing the contestants at the East was pushed north of Maryland, a State that had not seceded, and at the West beyond Kentucky, another State which had been always loyal, would have been discouraging indeed. As it was, many loyal people despaired in the fall of 1862 of ever saving the Union. The administration at Washington was much concerned for the safety of the cause it held so dear. But I believe there was never a day when the President did not think that, in some way or other, a cause so just as ours would come out triumphant.

Up to the 11th of September Rosecrans still had troops on the railroad east of Corinth, but they had all been ordered in. By the 12th all were in except a small force under Colonel Murphy of the 8th Wisconsin. He had been detained to guard the remainder of the stores which had not yet been brought in to Corinth.

On the 13th of September General Sterling Price entered Iuka, a town about twenty miles east of Corinth on the Memphis and Charleston railroad. Colonel Murphy with a few men was guarding the place. He made no resistance, but evacuated the town on the approach of the enemy. I was apprehensive lest the object of the rebels might be to get troops into Tennessee to reinforce Bragg, as it was afterwards ascertained to be. The authorities at Washington, including the general-in-chief of the army, were very anxious, as I have said, about affairs both in East and Middle Tennessee; and my anxiety was quite as great on their account as for any danger threatening my command. I had not force enough at Corinth to attack Price even by stripping everything; and there was danger that before troops could be got from other points he might be far on his way across the Tennessee. To prevent this all spare forces at Bolivar and Jackson were ordered to Corinth, and cars were concentrated at Jackson for their transportation. Within twenty-four hours from the transmission of the order the troops were at their destination, although there had been a delay of four hours resulting from the forward train getting off the track and stopping all the others. This gave a reinforcement of near 8,000 men, General Ord in command. General Rosecrans commanded the district of Corinth with a movable force of about 9,000, independent of the garrison deemed necessary to be left behind. It was known that General Van Dorn was about a four days' march south of us, with a large force. It might have been part of his plan to attack at Corinth, Price coming from the east while he came up from the south. My desire was to attack Price before Van Dorn could reach Corinth or go to his relief.

General Rosecrans had previously had his headquarters at Iuka, where his command was spread out along the Memphis and Charleston railroad eastward. While there he had a most excellent map prepared showing all the roads and streams in the surrounding country. He was also personally familiar with the ground, so that I deferred very much to him in my plans for the approach. We had cars enough to transport all of General Ord's command, which was to go by rail to Burnsville, a point on the road about seven miles west of Iuka. From there his troops were to march by the north side of the railroad and attack Price from the north-west, while Rosecrans was to move eastward from his position south of Corinth by way of the Jacinto road. A small force was to hold the Jacinto road where it turns to the north-east, while the main force moved on the Fulton road which comes into Iuka further east. This plan was suggested by Rosecrans.

Bear Creek, a few miles to the east of the Fulton road, is a formidable obstacle to the movement of troops in the absence of bridges, all of which, in September, 1862, had been destroyed in that vicinity. The Tennessee, to the north-east, not many miles away, was also a formidable obstacle for an army

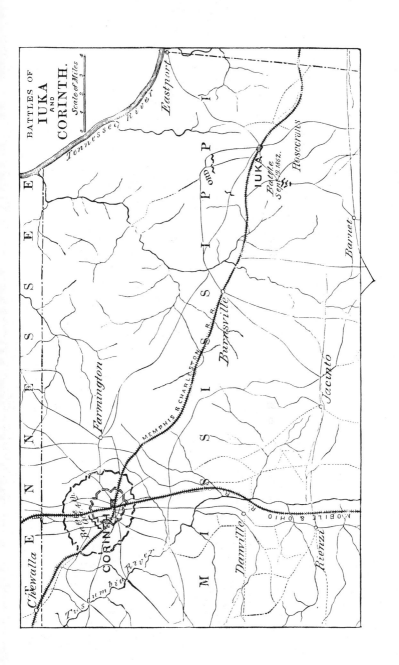

followed by a pursuing force. Ord was on the north-west, and even if a rebel movement had been possible in that direction it could have brought only temporary relief, for it would have carried Price's army to the rear of the National forces and isolated it from all support. It looked to me that, if Price would remain in Iuka until we could get there, his annihilation was inevitable.

On the morning of the 18th of September General Ord moved by rail to Burnsville, and there left the cars and moved out to perform his part of the programme. He was to get as near the enemy as possible during the day and intrench himself so as to hold his position until the next morning. Rosecrans was to be up by the morning of the 19th on the two roads before described, and the attack was to be from all three quarters simultaneously. Troops enough were left at Jacinto and Rienzi to detain any cavalry that Van Dorn might send out to make a sudden dash into Corinth until I could be notified. There was a telegraph wire along the railroad, so there would be no delay in communication. I detained cars and locomotives enough at Burnsville to transport the whole of Ord's command at once, and if Van Dorn had moved against Corinth instead of Iuka I could have thrown in reinforcements to the number of 7,000 or 8,000 before he could have arrived. I remained at Burnsville with a detachment of about 900 men from Ord's command and communicated with my two wings by courier. Ord met the advance of the enemy soon after leaving Burnsville. Quite a sharp engagement ensued, but he drove the rebels back with considerable loss, including one general officer killed. He maintained his position and was ready to attack by daylight the next morning. I was very much disappointed at receiving a dispatch from Rosecrans after midnight from Jacinto, twenty-two miles from Iuka, saying that some of his command had been delayed, and that the rear of his column was not yet up as far as Jacinto. He said, however, that he would still be at Iuka by two o'clock the next day. I did not believe this possible because of the distance and the condition of the roads, which was bad; besides, troops after a forced march of twenty miles are not in a good condition for fighting the moment they get through. It might do in marching to relieve a beleaguered garrison, but not to make an assault. I immediately sent Ord a copy of Rosecrans' dispatch and ordered him to be in readiness to attack the moment he heard the sound of guns to the south or south-east. He was instructed to notify his officers to be on the alert for any indications of battle. During the 19th the wind blew in the wrong direction to transmit sound either towards the point where Ord was, or to Burnsville where I had remained.

A couple of hours before dark on the 19th Rosecrans arrived with the head of his column at Barnets, the point where the Jacinto road to Iuka leaves the road going east. He here turned north without sending any troops to the Fulton road. While still moving in column up the Jacinto road he met a force of the enemy and had his advance badly beaten and driven back upon the main road. In this short engagement his loss was considerable for the number engaged, and one battery was taken from him. The wind was still blowing hard and in the wrong direction to transmit sound towards either Ord or me. Neither he nor I nor any one in either command heard a gun that was fired upon the battle-field. After the engagement Rosecrans sent me a dispatch announcing the result. This was brought by a courier. There was no road between Burnsville and the position then occupied by Rosecrans and the country was impassable for a man on horseback. The courier bearing the message was compelled to move west nearly to Jacinto before he found a road leading to Burnsville. This made it a late hour of the night before I learned of the battle that had taken place during the afternoon. I at once notified Ord of the fact and ordered him to attack early in the morning. The next morning Rosecrans himself renewed the attack and went into Iuka with but little resistance. Ord also went in according to orders, without hearing a gun from the south of town but supposing the troops coming from the south-west must be up by that time. Rosecrans, however, had put no troops upon the Fulton road, and the enemy had taken advantage of this neglect and retreated by that road during the night. Word was soon brought to me that our troops were in Iuka. I immediately rode into town and found that the enemy was not being pursued even by the cavalry. I ordered pursuit by the whole of Rosecrans' command and went on with him a few miles in person. He followed only a few miles after I left him and then went into camp, and the pursuit was continued no further. I was disappointed at the result of the battle of Iuka—but I had so high an opinion of General Rosecrans that I found no fault at the time.

Chapter XXIX.

ON THE 19TH of September General Geo. H. Thomas
was ordered east to reinforce Buell. This threw the army
at my command still more on the defensive. The Memphis
and Charleston railroad was abandoned, except at Corinth,
and small forces were left at Chewalla and Grand Junction.
Soon afterwards the latter of these two places was given up
and Bolivar became our most advanced position on the Mississippi Central railroad. Our cavalry was kept well to the
front and frequent expeditions were sent out to watch the
movements of the enemy. We were in a country where nearly
all the people, except the negroes, were hostile to us and
friendly to the cause we were trying to suppress. It was easy,
therefore, for the enemy to get early information of our every
move. We, on the contrary, had to go after our information in
force, and then often returned without it.

On the 22d Bolivar was threatened by a large force from
south of Grand Junction, supposed to be twenty regiments of
infantry with cavalry and artillery. I reinforced Bolivar, and
went to Jackson in person to superintend the movement of
troops to whatever point the attack might be made upon. The
troops from Corinth were brought up in time to repel the
threatened movement without a battle. Our cavalry followed
the enemy south of Davis' mills in Mississippi.

On the 30th I found that Van Dorn was apparently endeavoring to strike the Mississippi River above Memphis. At the
same time other points within my command were so threatened that it was impossible to concentrate a force to drive
him away. There was at this juncture a large Union force at
Helena, Arkansas, which, had it been within my command, I
could have ordered across the river to attack and break up the
Mississippi Central railroad far to the south. This would not
only have called Van Dorn back, but would have compelled
the retention of a large rebel force far to the south to prevent

a repetition of such raids on the enemy's line of supplies. Geographical lines between the commands during the rebellion were not always well chosen, or they were too rigidly adhered to.

Van Dorn did not attempt to get upon the line above Memphis, as had apparently been his intention. He was simply covering a deeper design; one much more important to his cause. By the 1st of October it was fully apparent that Corinth was to be attacked with great force and determination, and that Van Dorn, Lovell, Price, Villepigue and Rust had joined their strength for this purpose. There was some skirmishing outside of Corinth with the advance of the enemy on the 3d. The rebels massed in the north-west angle of the Memphis and Charleston and the Mobile and Ohio railroads, and were thus between the troops at Corinth and all possible reinforcements. Any fresh troops for us must come by a circuitous route.

On the night of the 3d, accordingly, I ordered General McPherson, who was at Jackson, to join Rosecrans at Corinth with reinforcements picked up along the line of the railroad equal to a brigade. Hurlbut had been ordered from Bolivar to march for the same destination; and as Van Dorn was coming upon Corinth from the north-west some of his men fell in with the advance of Hurlbut's and some skirmishing ensued on the evening of the 3d. On the 4th Van Dorn made a dashing attack, hoping, no doubt, to capture Rosecrans before his reinforcements could come up. In that case the enemy himself could have occupied the defences of Corinth and held at bay all the Union troops that arrived. In fact he could have taken the offensive against the reinforcements with three or four times their number and still left a sufficient garrison in the works about Corinth to hold them. He came near success, some of his troops penetrating the National lines at least once, but the works that were built after Halleck's departure enabled Rosecrans to hold his position until the troops of both McPherson and Hurlbut approached towards the rebel front and rear. The enemy was finally driven back with great slaughter: all their charges, made with great gallantry, were repulsed. The loss on our side was heavy, but nothing to compare with Van Dorn's. McPherson came up with the train of cars bearing his command as close to the enemy as was prudent, debarked on the rebel flank and got in to the support of Rosecrans just after the repulse. His approach, as well as that of Hurlbut, was known to the enemy and had a moral effect. General Rosecrans, however, failed to follow up the victory, although I had given specific orders in advance of the battle for him to pursue the moment the enemy was repelled. He did not do so, and I repeated the order after the battle. In the first order he was notified that the force of 4,000 men which was going to his assistance would be in great peril if the enemy was not pursued.

General Ord had joined Hurlbut on the 4th and being senior took command of his troops. This force encountered the head of Van Dorn's retreating column just as it was crossing the Hatchie by a bridge some ten miles out from Corinth. The bottom land here was swampy and bad for the operations of troops, making a good place to get an enemy into. Ord attacked the troops that had crossed the bridge and drove them back in a panic. Many were killed, and others were drowned by being pushed off the bridge in their hurried retreat. Ord followed and met the main force. He was too weak in numbers to assault, but he held the bridge and compelled the enemy to resume his retreat by another bridge higher up the stream. Ord was wounded in this engagement and the command devolved on Hurlbut.

Rosecrans did not start in pursuit till the morning of the 5th and then took the wrong road. Moving in the enemy's country he travelled with a wagon train to carry his provisions and munitions of war. His march was therefore slower than that of the enemy, who was moving towards his supplies. Two or three hours of pursuit on the day of battle, without anything except what the men carried on their persons, would have been worth more than any pursuit commenced the next day could have possibly been. Even when he did start, if Rosecrans had followed the route taken by the enemy, he would have come upon Van Dorn in a swamp with a stream in front and Ord holding the only bridge; but he took the road leading north and towards Chewalla instead of west, and, after having marched as far as the enemy had moved to get to the Hatchie, he was as far from battle as when he started. Hurlbut had not the numbers to meet any such force as Van Dorn's if they had been in any mood for fighting, and he might have been in great peril.

I now regarded the time to accomplish anything by pursuit as past and, after Rosecrans reached Jonesboro, I ordered him to return. He kept on to Ripley, however, and was persistent in wanting to go farther. I thereupon ordered him to halt and submitted the matter to the general-in-chief, who allowed me to exercise my judgment in the matter, but inquired "why not pursue?" Upon this I ordered Rosecrans back. Had he gone much farther he would have met a greater force than Van Dorn had at Corinth and behind intrenchments or on chosen ground, and the probabilities are he would have lost his army.

The battle of Corinth was bloody, our loss being 315 killed, 1,812 wounded and 232 missing. The enemy lost many more. Rosecrans reported 1,423 dead and 2,225 prisoners. We fought behind breastworks, which accounts in some degree for the disparity. Among the killed on our side was General Hackelman. General Oglesby was badly, it was for some time supposed mortally, wounded. I received a congratulatory letter from the President, which expressed also his sorrow for the losses.

This battle was recognized by me as being a decided victory, though not so complete as I had hoped for, nor nearly so complete as I now think was within the easy grasp of the commanding officer at Corinth. Since the war it is known that the result, as it was, was a crushing blow to the enemy, and felt by him much more than it was appreciated at the North. The battle relieved me from any further anxiety for the safety of the territory within my jurisdiction, and soon after receiving reinforcements I suggested to the general-in-chief a forward movement against Vicksburg.

On the 23d of October I learned of Pemberton's being in command at Holly Springs and much reinforced by conscripts and troops from Alabama and Texas. The same day General Rosecrans was relieved from duty with my command, and shortly after he succeeded Buell in the command of the army in Middle Tennessee. I was delighted at the promotion of General Rosecrans to a separate command, because I still believed that when independent of an immediate superior the qualities which I, at that time, credited him with possessing, would show themselves. As a subordinate I found that I could not make him do as I wished, and had determined to relieve him from duty that very day.

At the close of the operations just described my force, in round numbers, was 48,500. Of these 4,800 were in Kentucky and Illinois, 7,000 in Memphis, 19,200 from Mound City south, and 17,500 at Corinth. General McClernand had been authorized from Washington to go north and organize troops to be used in opening the Mississippi. These new levies with other reinforcements now began to come in.

On the 25th of October I was placed in command of the Department of the Tennessee. Reinforcements continued to come from the north and by the 2d of November I was prepared to take the initiative. This was a great relief after the two and a half months of continued defence over a large district of country, and where nearly every citizen was an enemy ready to give information of our every move. I have described very imperfectly a few of the battles and skirmishes that took place during this time. To describe all would take more space than I can allot to the purpose; to make special mention of all the officers and troops who distinguished themselves, would take a volume.

NOTE.—For gallantry in the various engagements, from the time I was left in command down to 26th of October and on my recommendation, Generals McPherson and C. S. Hamilton were promoted to be Major-Generals, and Colonels C. C. Marsh, 20th Illinois, M. M. Crocker, 13th Iowa, J. A. Mower, 11th Missouri, M. D. Leggett, 78th Ohio, J. D. Stevenson, 7th Missouri, and John E. Smith, 45th Illinois, to be Brigadiers.

Chapter XXX.

THE CAMPAIGN AGAINST VICKSBURG—EMPLOYING THE
FREEDMEN—OCCUPATION OF HOLLY SPRINGS—
SHERMAN ORDERED TO MEMPHIS—SHERMAN'S
MOVEMENTS DOWN THE MISSISSIPPI—VAN DORN
CAPTURES HOLLY SPRINGS—COLLECTING
FORAGE AND FOOD.

VICKSBURG WAS IMPORTANT to the enemy because it occupied the first high ground coming close to the river below Memphis. From there a railroad runs east, connecting with other roads leading to all points of the Southern States. A railroad also starts from the opposite side of the river, extending west as far as Shreveport, Louisiana. Vicksburg was the only channel, at the time of the events of which this chapter treats, connecting the parts of the Confederacy divided by the Mississippi. So long as it was held by the enemy, the free navigation of the river was prevented. Hence its importance. Points on the river between Vicksburg and Port Hudson were held as dependencies; but their fall was sure to follow the capture of the former place.

The campaign against Vicksburg commenced on the 2d of November as indicated in a dispatch to the general-in-chief in the following words: "I have commenced a movement on Grand Junction, with three divisions from Corinth and two from Bolivar. Will leave here [Jackson, Tennessee] to-morrow, and take command in person. If found practicable, I will go to Holly Springs, and, may be, Grenada, completing railroad and telegraph as I go."

At this time my command was holding the Mobile and Ohio railroad from about twenty-five miles south of Corinth, north to Columbus, Kentucky; the Mississippi Central from Bolivar north to its junction with the Mobile and Ohio; the Memphis and Charleston from Corinth east to Bear Creek, and the Mississippi River from Cairo to Memphis. My entire command was no more than was necessary to hold these lines, and hardly that if kept on the defensive. By moving against the enemy and into his unsubdued, or not yet captured, territory, driving their army before us, these lines would nearly hold themselves; thus affording a large force for field operations. My moving force at that time was about 30,000 men, and I estimated the enemy confronting me, under Pemberton, at about the same number. General McPherson commanded my left wing and General C. S. Hamilton the centre, while Sherman was at Memphis with the right wing. Pemberton was fortified at the Tallahatchie, but occupied Holly Springs and Grand Junction on the Mississippi Central railroad. On the 8th we occupied Grand Junction and La Grange, throwing a considerable force seven or eight miles south, along the line of the railroad. The road from Bolivar forward was repaired and put in running order as the troops advanced.

Up to this time it had been regarded as an axiom in war that large bodies of troops must operate from a base of supplies which they always covered and guarded in all forward movements. There was delay therefore in repairing the road back, and in gathering and forwarding supplies to the front.

By my orders, and in accordance with previous instructions from Washington, all the forage within reach was collected under the supervision of the chief quartermaster and the provisions under the chief commissary, receipts being given when there was any one to take them; the supplies in any event to be accounted for as government stores. The stock was bountiful, but still it gave me no idea of the possibility of supplying a moving column in an enemy's country from the country itself.

It was at this point, probably, where the first idea of a "Freedman's Bureau" took its origin. Orders of the government prohibited the expulsion of the negroes from the protection of the army, when they came in voluntarily. Humanity forbade allowing them to starve. With such an army of them, of all ages and both sexes, as had congregated about Grand Junction, amounting to many thousands, it was impossible to advance. There was no special authority for feeding them unless they were employed as teamsters, cooks and pioneers with the army; but only able-bodied young men were suitable for such work. This labor would support but a very limited percentage of them. The plantations were all deserted; the cotton and corn were ripe: men, women and children above ten years of age could be employed in saving these crops. To do this work with contrabands, or to have it done, organization under a competent chief was necessary. On inquiring for such a man Chaplain Eaton, now and for many years the very able United States Commissioner of Education, was suggested. He proved as efficient in that field as he has since done in his present one. I gave him all the assistants and guards he called for. We together fixed the prices to be paid for the negro labor, whether rendered to the government or to individuals. The cotton was to be picked from abandoned plantations, the laborers to receive the stipulated price (my recollection is twelve and a half cents per pound for picking and ginning) from the quartermaster, he shipping the cotton north to be sold for the benefit of the government. Citizens remaining on their plantations were allowed the privilege of having their crops saved by freedmen on the same terms.

At once the freedmen became self-sustaining. The money was not paid to them directly, but was expended judiciously and for their benefit. They gave me no trouble afterwards.

Later the freedmen were engaged in cutting wood along the Mississippi River to supply the large number of steamers on that stream. A good price was paid for chopping wood used for the supply of government steamers (steamers chartered and which the government had to supply with fuel). Those supplying their own fuel paid a much higher price. In this way a fund was created not only sufficient to feed and clothe all, old and young, male and female, but to build them comfortable cabins, hospitals for the sick, and to supply them with many comforts they had never known before.

At this stage of the campaign against Vicksburg I was very much disturbed by newspaper rumors that General McClernand was to have a separate and independent command within mine, to operate against Vicksburg by way of the Mississippi River. Two commanders on the same field are always one too many, and in this case I did not think the general selected had either the experience or the qualifications to fit him for so important a position. I feared for the safety of the troops intrusted to him, especially as he was to raise new levies, raw troops, to execute so important a trust. But on the 12th I received a dispatch from General Halleck saying that I had command of all the troops sent to my department and authorizing me to fight the enemy where I pleased. The next day my cavalry was in Holly Springs, and the enemy fell back south of the Tallahatchie.

Holly Springs I selected for my dépot of supplies and munitions of war, all of which at that time came by rail from Columbus, Kentucky, except the few stores collected about La Grange and Grand Junction. This was a long line (increasing in length as we moved south) to maintain in an enemy's country. On the 15th of November, while I was still at Holly Springs, I sent word to Sherman to meet me at Columbus. We were but forty-seven miles apart, yet the most expeditious way for us to meet was for me to take the rail to Columbus and Sherman a steamer for the same place. At that meeting, besides talking over my general plans I gave him his orders to join me with two divisions and to march them down the Mississippi Central railroad if he could. Sherman, who was always prompt, was up by the 29th to Cottage Hill, ten miles north of Oxford. He brought three divisions with him, leaving a garrison of only four regiments of infantry, a couple of pieces of artillery and a small detachment of cavalry. Further reinforcements he knew were on their way from the north to Memphis. About this time General Halleck ordered troops from Helena, Arkansas (territory west of the Mississippi was not under my command then) to cut the road in Pemberton's rear. The expedition was under Generals Hovey and C. C. Washburn and was successful so far as reaching the railroad was concerned, but the damage done was very slight and was soon repaired.

The Tallahatchie, which confronted me, was very high, the railroad bridge destroyed and Pemberton strongly fortified on the south side. A crossing would have been impossible in the presence of an enemy. I sent the cavalry higher up the stream and they secured a crossing. This caused the enemy to evacuate their position, which was possibly accelerated by the expedition of Hovey and Washburn. The enemy was followed as far south as Oxford by the main body of troops, and some seventeen miles farther by McPherson's command. Here the pursuit was halted to repair the railroad from the Tallahatchie northward, in order to bring up supplies. The piles on which the railroad bridge rested had been left standing. The work of constructing a roadway for the troops was but a short matter, and, later, rails were laid for cars.

During the delay at Oxford in repairing railroads I learned that an expedition down the Mississippi now was inevitable and, desiring to have a competent commander in charge, I ordered Sherman on the 8th of December back to Memphis to take charge. The following were his orders:

Headquarters 13th Army Corps, Department of the Tennessee.
OXFORD, MISSISSIPPI, *December* 8, 1862.
MAJOR-GENERAL W. T. SHERMAN,
    Commanding Right Wing:
You will proceed, with as little delay as possible, to Memphis, Tennessee, taking with you one division of your present command. On your arrival at Memphis you will assume command of all the troops there, and that portion of General Curtis's forces at present east of the Mississippi River, and organize them into brigades and divisions in your own army. As soon as possible move with them down the river to the vicinity of Vicksburg, and with the co-operation of the gunboat fleet under command of Flag-officer Porter proceed to the reduction of that place in such manner as circumstances, and your own judgment, may dictate.

The amount of rations, forage, land transportation, etc., necessary to take, will be left entirely with yourself. The Quartermaster at St. Louis will be instructed to send you transportation for 30,000 men; should you still find yourself deficient, your quartermaster will be authorized to make up the deficiency from such transports as may come into the port of Memphis.

On arriving in Memphis, put yourself in communication with Admiral Porter, and arrange with him for his co-operation.

Inform me at the earliest practicable day of the time when you will embark, and such plans as may then be matured. I will hold the forces here in readiness to co-operate with you in such manner as the movements of the enemy may make necessary.

Leave the District of Memphis in the command of an efficient officer, and with a garrison of four regiments of infantry, the siege guns, and whatever cavalry may be there.

U. S. GRANT,
Major-General.

This idea had presented itself to my mind earlier, for on the 3d of December I asked Halleck if it would not be well to hold the enemy south of the Yallabusha and move a force from Helena and Memphis on Vicksburg. On the 5th again I suggested, from Oxford, to Halleck that if the Helena troops were at my command I thought it would be possible to take them and the Memphis forces south of the mouth of the Yazoo River, and thus secure Vicksburg and the State of Mississippi. Halleck on the same day, the 5th of December, directed me not to attempt to hold the country south of the Tallahatchie, but to collect 25,000 troops at Memphis by the 20th for the Vicksburg expedition. I sent Sherman with two divisions at once, informed the general-in-chief of the fact, and asked whether I should command the expedition down the river myself or send Sherman. I was authorized to do as I thought best for the accomplishment of the great object in view. I sent Sherman and so informed General Halleck.

As stated, my action in sending Sherman back was expedited by a desire to get him in command of the forces separated from my direct supervision. I feared that delay might bring McClernand, who was his senior and who had authority from the President and Secretary of War to exercise that particular command,—and independently. I doubted McClernand's fitness; and I had good reason to believe that in forestalling him I was by no means giving offence to those whose authority to command was above both him and me.

Neither my orders to General Sherman, nor the correspondence between us or between General Halleck and myself, contemplated at the time my going further south than the Yallabusha. Pemberton's force in my front was the main part of the garrison of Vicksburg, as the force with me was the defence of the territory held by us in West Tennessee and Kentucky. I hoped to hold Pemberton in my front while Sherman should get in his rear and into Vicksburg. The further north the enemy could be held the better.

It was understood, however, between General Sherman and myself that our movements were to be co-operative; if Pemberton could not be held away from Vicksburg I was to follow him; but at that time it was not expected to abandon the railroad north of the Yallabusha. With that point as a secondary base of supplies, the possibility of moving down the Yazoo until communications could be opened with the Mississippi was contemplated.

It was my intention, and so understood by Sherman and his command, that if the enemy should fall back I would follow him even to the gates of Vicksburg. I intended in such an event to hold the road to Grenada on the Yallabusha and cut loose from there, expecting to establish a new base of supplies on the Yazoo, or at Vicksburg itself, with Grenada to fall back upon in case of failure. It should be remembered that at the time I speak of it had not been demonstrated that an army could operate in an enemy's territory depending upon the country for supplies. A halt was called at Oxford with the advance seventeen miles south of there, to bring up the road to the latter point and to bring supplies of food, forage and munitions to the front.

On the 18th of December I received orders from Washington to divide my command into four army corps, with General McClernand to command one of them and to be assigned to that part of the army which was to operate down the Mississippi. This interfered with my plans, but probably resulted in my ultimately taking the command in person. McClernand was at that time in Springfield, Illinois. The order was obeyed without any delay. Dispatches were sent to him the same day in conformity.

On the 20th General Van Dorn appeared at Holly Springs, my secondary base of supplies, captured the garrison of 1,500 men commanded by Colonel Murphy, of the 8th Wisconsin regiment, and destroyed all our munitions of war, food and forage. The capture was a disgraceful one to the officer commanding but not to the troops under him. At the same time Forrest got on our line of railroad between Jackson, Tennessee, and Columbus, Kentucky, doing much damage to it. This cut me off from all communication with the north for more than a week, and it was more than two weeks before rations or forage could be issued from stores obtained in the regular way. This demonstrated the impossibility of maintaining so long a line of road over which to draw supplies for an army moving in an enemy's country. I determined, therefore, to abandon my campaign into the interior with Columbus as a base, and returned to La Grange and Grand Junction destroying the road to my front and repairing the road to Memphis, making the Mississippi river the line over which to draw supplies. Pemberton was falling back at the same time.

The moment I received the news of Van Dorn's success I sent the cavalry at the front back to drive him from the country. He had start enough to move north destroying the railroad in many places, and to attack several small garrisons intrenched as guards to the railroad. All these he found warned of his coming and prepared to receive him. Van Dorn did not succeed in capturing a single garrison except the one at Holly Springs, which was larger than all the others attacked by him put together. Murphy was also warned of Van Dorn's approach, but made no preparations to meet him. He did not even notify his command.

Colonel Murphy was the officer who, two months before, had evacuated Iuka on the approach of the enemy. General Rosecrans denounced him for the act and desired to have him tried and punished. I sustained the colonel at the time because his command was a small one compared with that of the enemy—not one-tenth as large—and I thought he had done well to get away without falling into their hands. His leaving large stores to fall into Price's possession I looked upon as an oversight and excused it on the ground of inexperience in military matters. He should, however, have destroyed them. This last surrender demonstrated to my mind that Rosecrans' judgment of Murphy's conduct at Iuka was correct. The surrender of Holly Springs was most reprehensible and showed either the disloyalty of Colonel Murphy to the cause which he professed to serve, or gross cowardice.

After the war was over I read from the diary of a lady who accompanied General Pemberton in his retreat from the Tallahatchie, that the retreat was almost a panic. The roads were bad and it was difficult to move the artillery and trains. Why there should have been a panic I do not see. No expedition had yet started down the Mississippi River. Had I known the demoralized condition of the enemy, or the fact that central Mississippi abounded so in all army supplies, I would have been in pursuit of Pemberton while his cavalry was destroying the roads in my rear.

After sending cavalry to drive Van Dorn away, my next order was to dispatch all the wagons we had, under proper escort, to collect and bring in all supplies of forage and food from a region of fifteen miles east and west of the road from our front back to Grand Junction, leaving two months' supplies for the families of those whose stores were taken. I was amazed at the quantity of supplies the country afforded. It showed that we could have subsisted off the country for two months instead of two weeks without going beyond the limits designated. This taught me a lesson which was taken advantage of later in the campaign when our army lived twenty days with the issue of only five days' rations by the commissary. Our loss of supplies was great at Holly Springs, but it was more than compensated for by those taken from the country and by the lesson taught.

The news of the capture of Holly Springs and the destruction of our supplies caused much rejoicing among the people remaining in Oxford. They came with broad smiles on their faces, indicating intense joy, to ask what I was going to do now without anything for my soldiers to eat. I told them that I was not disturbed; that I had already sent troops and wagons to collect all the food and forage they could find for fifteen miles on each side of the road. Countenances soon changed, and so did the inquiry. The next was, "What are *we* to do?" My response was that we had endeavored to feed ourselves from our own northern resources while visiting them; but their friends in gray had been uncivil enough to destroy what we had brought along, and it could not be expected that men, with arms in their hands, would starve in the midst of plenty. I advised them to emigrate east, or west, fifteen miles and assist in eating up what we left.

Chapter XXXI.

HEADQUARTERS MOVED TO HOLLY SPRINGS—GENERAL
M'CLERNAND IN COMMAND—ASSUMING COMMAND
AT YOUNG'S POINT—OPERATIONS ABOVE
VICKSBURG—FORTIFICATIONS ABOUT VICKSBURG—
THE CANAL—LAKE PROVIDENCE—OPERATIONS
AT YAZOO PASS.

THIS INTERRUPTION in my communications north—I was really cut off from communication with a great part of my own command during this time—resulted in Sherman's moving from Memphis before McClernand could arrive, for my dispatch of the 18th did not reach McClernand. Pemberton got back to Vicksburg before Sherman got there. The rebel positions were on a bluff on the Yazoo River, some miles above its mouth. The waters were high so that the bottoms were generally overflowed, leaving only narrow causeways of dry land between points of debarkation and the high bluffs. These were fortified and defended at all points. The rebel position was impregnable against any force that could be brought against its front. Sherman could not use one-fourth of his force. His efforts to capture the city, or the high ground north of it, were necessarily unavailing.

Sherman's attack was very unfortunate, but I had no opportunity of communicating with him after the destruction of the road and telegraph to my rear on the 20th. He did not know but what I was in the rear of the enemy and depending on him to open a new base of supplies for the troops with me. I had, before he started from Memphis, directed him to take with him a few small steamers suitable for the navigation of the Yazoo, not knowing but that I might want them to supply me after cutting loose from my base at Grenada.

On the 23d I removed my headquarters back to Holly Springs. The troops were drawn back gradually, but without haste or confusion, finding supplies abundant and no enemy following. The road was not damaged south of Holly Springs by Van Dorn, at least not to an extent to cause any delay. As I had resolved to move headquarters to Memphis, and to repair the road to that point, I remained at Holly Springs until this work was completed.

On the 10th of January, the work on the road from Holly Springs to Grand Junction and thence to Memphis being completed, I moved my headquarters to the latter place. During the campaign here described, the losses (mostly captures) were about equal, crediting the rebels with their Holly Springs capture, which they could not hold.

When Sherman started on his expedition down the river he had 20,000 men, taken from Memphis, and was reinforced by 12,000 more at Helena, Arkansas. The troops on the west bank of the river had previously been assigned to my command. McClernand having received the orders for his assignment reached the mouth of the Yazoo on the 2d of January, and immediately assumed command of all the troops with Sherman, being a part of his own corps, the 13th, and all of Sherman's, the 15th. Sherman, and Admiral Porter with the fleet, had withdrawn from the Yazoo. After consultation they decided that neither the army nor navy could render service to the cause where they were, and learning that I had withdrawn from the interior of Mississippi, they determined to return to the Arkansas River and to attack Arkansas Post, about fifty miles up that stream and garrisoned by about five or six thousand men. Sherman had learned of the existence of this force through a man who had been captured by the enemy with a steamer loaded with ammunition and other supplies intended for his command. The man had made his escape. McClernand approved this move reluctantly, as Sherman says. No obstacle was encountered until the gunboats and transports were within range of the fort. After three days' bombardment by the navy an assault was made by the troops and marines, resulting in the capture of the place, and in taking 5,000 prisoners and 17 guns. I was at first disposed to disapprove of this move as an unnecessary side movement having no especial bearing upon the work before us; but when the result was understood I regarded it as very important. Five thousand Confederate troops left in the rear might have caused us much trouble and loss of property while navigating the Mississippi.

Immediately after the reduction of Arkansas Post and the capture of the garrison, McClernand returned with his entire force to Napoleon, at the mouth of the Arkansas River. From here I received messages from both Sherman and Admiral Porter, urging me to come and take command in person, and expressing their distrust of McClernand's ability and fitness for so important and intricate an expedition.

On the 17th I visited McClernand and his command at Napoleon. It was here made evident to me that both the army and navy were so distrustful of McClernand's fitness to command that, while they would do all they could to insure success, this distrust was an element of weakness. It would have been criminal to send troops under these circumstances into such danger. By this time I had received authority to relieve McClernand, or to assign any person else to the command of the river expedition, or to assume command in person. I felt great embarrassment about McClernand. He was the senior major-general after myself within the department. It would not do, with his rank and ambition, to assign a junior over him. Nothing was left, therefore, but to assume the command myself. I would have been glad to put Sherman in command, to give him an opportunity to accomplish what he had failed in the December before; but there seemed no other way out of the difficulty, for he was junior to McClernand. Sherman's failure needs no apology.

On the 20th I ordered General McClernand with the entire command, to Young's Point and Milliken's Bend, while I returned to Memphis to make all the necessary preparation for leaving the territory behind me secure. General Hurlbut with the 16th corps was left in command. The Memphis and Charleston railroad was held, while the Mississippi Central was given up. Columbus was the only point between Cairo and Memphis, on the river, left with a garrison. All the troops and guns from the posts on the abandoned railroad and river were sent to the front.

On the 29th of January I arrived at Young's Point and assumed command the following day. General McClernand took exception in a most characteristic way—for him. His correspondence with me on the subject was more in the nature of a reprimand than a protest. It was highly insubordinate, but I overlooked it, as I believed, for the good of the service. General McClernand was a politician of very

considerable prominence in his State; he was a member of
Congress when the secession war broke out; he belonged to
that political party which furnished all the opposition there
was to a vigorous prosecution of the war for saving the
Union; there was no delay in his declaring himself for the
Union at all hazards, and there was no uncertain sound in his
declaration of where he stood in the contest before the country. He also gave up his seat in Congress to take the field in
defence of the principles he had proclaimed.

The real work of the campaign and siege of Vicksburg now
began. The problem was to secure a footing upon dry ground
on the east side of the river from which the troops could operate against Vicksburg. The Mississippi River, from Cairo
south, runs through a rich alluvial valley of many miles in
width, bound on the east by land running from eighty up to
two or more hundred feet above the river. On the west side
the highest land, except in a few places, is but little above the
highest water. Through this valley the river meanders in the
most tortuous way, varying in direction to all points of the
compass. At places it runs to the very foot of the bluffs. After
leaving Memphis, there are no such highlands coming to the
water's edge on the east shore until Vicksburg is reached.

The intervening land is cut up by bayous filled from the
river in high water—many of them navigable for steamers.
All of them would be, except for overhanging trees, narrowness and tortuous course, making it impossible to turn the
bends with vessels of any considerable length. Marching
across this country in the face of an enemy was impossible;
navigating it proved equally impracticable. The strategical
way according to the rule, therefore, would have been to go
back to Memphis; establish that as a base of supplies; fortify it
so that the storehouses could be held by a small garrison, and
move from there along the line of railroad, repairing as we
advanced, to the Yallabusha, or to Jackson, Mississippi. At this
time the North had become very much discouraged. Many
strong Union men believed that the war must prove a failure.
The elections of 1862 had gone against the party which was
for the prosecution of the war to save the Union if it took the
last man and the last dollar. Voluntary enlistments had ceased
throughout the greater part of the North, and the draft had

been resorted to to fill up our ranks. It was my judgment at the time that to make a backward movement as long as that from Vicksburg to Memphis, would be interpreted, by many of those yet full of hope for the preservation of the Union, as a defeat, and that the draft would be resisted, desertions ensue and the power to capture and punish deserters lost. There was nothing left to be done but to *go forward to a decisive victory*. This was in my mind from the moment I took command in person at Young's Point.

The winter of 1862–3 was a noted one for continuous high water in the Mississippi and for heavy rains along the lower river. To get dry land, or rather land above the water, to encamp the troops upon, took many miles of river front. We had to occupy the levees and the ground immediately behind. This was so limited that one corps, the 17th, under General McPherson, was at Lake Providence, seventy miles above Vicksburg.

It was in January the troops took their position opposite Vicksburg. The water was very high and the rains were incessant. There seemed no possibility of a land movement before the end of March or later, and it would not do to lie idle all this time. The effect would be demoralizing to the troops and injurious to their health. Friends in the North would have grown more and more discouraged, and enemies in the same section more and more insolent in their gibes and denunciation of the cause and those engaged in it.

I always admired the South, as bad as I thought their cause, for the boldness with which they silenced all opposition and all croaking, by press or by individuals, within their control. War at all times, whether a civil war between sections of a common country or between nations, ought to be avoided, if possible with honor. But, once entered into, it is too much for human nature to tolerate an enemy within their ranks to give aid and comfort to the armies of the opposing section or nation.

Vicksburg, as stated before, is on the first high land coming to the river's edge, below that on which Memphis stands. The bluff, or high land, follows the left bank of the Yazoo for some distance and continues in a southerly direction to the Mississippi River, thence it runs along the Mississippi to

Warrenton, six miles below. The Yazoo River leaves the high land a short distance below Haines' Bluff and empties into the Mississippi nine miles above Vicksburg. Vicksburg is built on this high land where the Mississippi washes the base of the hill. Haines' Bluff, eleven miles from Vicksburg, on the Yazoo River, was strongly fortified. The whole distance from there to Vicksburg and thence to Warrenton was also intrenched, with batteries at suitable distances and rifle-pits connecting them.

From Young's Point the Mississippi turns in a north-easterly direction to a point just above the city, when it again turns and runs south-westerly, leaving vessels, which might attempt to run the blockade, exposed to the fire of batteries six miles below the city before they were in range of the up-per batteries. Since then the river has made a cut-off, leaving what was the peninsula in front of the city, an island. North of the Yazoo was all a marsh, heavily timbered, cut up with bayous, and much overflowed. A front attack was therefore impossible, and was never contemplated; certainly not by me. The problem then became, how to secure a landing on high ground east of the Mississippi without an apparent retreat. Then commenced a series of experiments to consume time, and to divert the attention of the enemy, of my troops and of the public generally. I, myself, never felt great confidence that any of the experiments resorted to would prove successful. Nevertheless I was always prepared to take advantage of them in case they did.

In 1862 General Thomas Williams had come up from New Orleans and cut a ditch ten or twelve feet wide and about as deep, straight across from Young's Point to the river below. The distance across was a little over a mile. It was Williams' expectation that when the river rose it would cut a navigable channel through; but the canal started in an eddy from both ends, and, of course, it only filled up with water on the rise without doing any execution in the way of cutting. Mr. Lin-coln had navigated the Mississippi in his younger days and understood well its tendency to change its channel, in places, from time to time. He set much store accordingly by this canal. General McClernand had been, therefore, directed before I went to Young's Point to push the work of widening and deepening this canal. After my arrival the work was diligently pushed with about 4,000 men—as many as could be used to advantage—until interrupted by a sudden rise in the river that broke a dam at the upper end, which had been put there to keep the water out until the excavation was completed. This was on the 8th of March.

Even if the canal had proven a success, so far as to be navigable for steamers, it could not have been of much advantage to us. It runs in a direction almost perpendicular to the line of bluffs on the opposite side, or east bank, of the river. As soon as the enemy discovered what we were doing he established a battery commanding the canal throughout its length. This battery soon drove out our dredges, two in number, which were doing the work of thousands of men. Had the canal been completed it might have proven of some use in running transports through, under the cover of night, to use below; but they would yet have to run batteries, though for a much shorter distance.

While this work was progressing we were busy in other directions, trying to find an available landing on high ground on the east bank of the river, or to make water-ways to get below the city, avoiding the batteries.

On the 30th of January, the day after my arrival at the front, I ordered General McPherson, stationed with his corps at Lake Providence, to cut the levee at that point. If successful in opening a channel for navigation by this route, it would carry us to the Mississippi River through the mouth of the Red River, just above Port Hudson and four hundred miles below Vicksburg by the river.

Lake Providence is a part of the old bed of the Mississippi, about a mile from the present channel. It is six miles long and has its outlet through Bayou Baxter, Bayou Macon, and the Tensas, Washita and Red Rivers. The last three are navigable streams at all seasons. Bayous Baxter and Macon are narrow and tortuous, and the banks are covered with dense forests overhanging the channel. They were also filled with fallen timber, the accumulation of years. The land along the Mississippi River, from Memphis down, is in all instances highest next to the river, except where the river washes the bluffs which form the boundary of the valley through which it winds. Bayou Baxter, as it reaches lower land, begins to spread out and disappears entirely in a cypress swamp before it reaches the Macon. There was about two feet of water in this swamp at the time. To get through it, even with vessels of the lightest draft, it was necessary to clear off a belt of heavy timber wide enough to make a passage way. As the trees would have to be cut close to the bottom—under water—it was an undertaking of great magnitude.

On the 4th of February I visited General McPherson, and remained with him several days. The work had not progressed so far as to admit the water from the river into the lake, but the troops had succeeded in drawing a small steamer, of probably not over thirty tons' capacity, from the river into the lake. With this we were able to explore the lake and bayou as far as cleared. I saw then that there was scarcely a chance of this ever becoming a practicable route for moving troops through an enemy's country. The distance from Lake Providence to the point where vessels going by that route would enter the Mississippi again, is about four hundred and seventy miles by the main river. The distance would probably be greater by the tortuous bayous through which this new route would carry us. The enemy held Port Hudson, below where the Red River debouches, and all the Mississippi above to Vicksburg. The Red River, Washita and Tensas were, as has been said, all navigable streams, on which the enemy could throw small bodies of men to obstruct our passage and pick off our troops with their sharpshooters. I let the work go on, believing employment was better than idleness for the men. Then, too, it served as a cover for other efforts which gave a better prospect of success. This work was abandoned after the canal proved a failure.

Lieutenant-Colonel Wilson of my staff was sent to Helena, Arkansas, to examine and open a way through Moon Lake and the Yazoo Pass if possible. Formerly there was a route by way of an inlet from the Mississippi River into Moon Lake, a mile east of the river, thence east through Yazoo Pass to Coldwater, along the latter to the Tallahatchie, which joins the Yallabusha about two hundred and fifty miles below Moon Lake and forms the Yazoo River. These were formerly navigated by steamers trading with the rich plantations along their banks; but the State of Mississippi had built a strong levee across the inlet some years before, leaving the only entrance for vessels into this rich region the one by way of the mouth of the Yazoo several hundreds of miles below.

On the 2d of February this dam, or levee, was cut. The river being high the rush of water through the cut was so great that in a very short time the entire obstruction was washed away. The bayous were soon filled and much of the country was overflowed. This pass leaves the Mississippi River but a few miles below Helena. On the 24th General Ross, with his brigade of about 4,500 men on transports, moved into this new water-way. The rebels had obstructed the navigation of Yazoo Pass and the Coldwater by felling trees into them. Much of the timber in this region being of greater specific gravity than water, and being of great size, their removal was a matter of great labor; but it was finally accomplished, and on the 11th of March Ross found himself, accompanied by two gunboats under the command of Lieutenant-Commander Watson Smith, confronting a fortification at Greenwood, where the Tallahatchie and Yallabusha unite and the Yazoo begins. The bends of the rivers are such at this point as to almost form an island, scarcely above water at that stage of the river. This island was fortified and manned. It was named Fort Pemberton after the commander at Vicksburg. No land approach was accessible. The troops, therefore, could render no assistance towards an assault further than to establish a battery on a little piece of ground which was discovered above water. The gunboats, however, attacked on the 11th and again on the 13th of March. Both efforts were failures and were not renewed. One gunboat was disabled and we lost six men killed and twenty-five wounded. The loss of the enemy was less.

Fort Pemberton was so little above the water that it was thought that a rise of two feet would drive the enemy out. In hope of enlisting the elements on our side, which had been so much against us up to this time, a second cut was made in the Mississippi levee, this time directly opposite Helena, or six miles above the former cut. It did not accomplish the desired result, and Ross, with his fleet, started back. On the 22d he met Quinby with a brigade at Yazoo Pass. Quinby was the senior of Ross, and assumed command. He was not satisfied with returning to his former position without seeing for himself whether anything could be accomplished. Accordingly Fort Pemberton was revisited by our troops; but an inspection was sufficient this time without an attack. Quinby, with his command, returned with but little delay. In the meantime I was much exercised for the safety of Ross, not knowing that Quinby had been able to join him. Reinforcements were of no use in a country covered with water, as they would have to remain on board of their transports. Relief had to come from another quarter. So I determined to get into the Yazoo below Fort Pemberton.

Steel's Bayou empties into the Yazoo River between Haines' Bluff and its mouth. It is narrow, very tortuous, and fringed with a very heavy growth of timber, but it is deep. It approaches to within one mile of the Mississippi at Eagle Bend, thirty miles above Young's Point. Steel's Bayou connects with Black Bayou, Black Bayou with Deer Creek, Deer Creek with Rolling Fork, Rolling Fork with the Big Sunflower River, and the Big Sunflower with the Yazoo River about ten miles above Haines' Bluff in a right line but probably twenty or twenty-five miles by the winding of the river. All these waterways are of about the same nature so far as navigation is concerned, until the Sunflower is reached; this affords free navigation.

Admiral Porter explored this waterway as far as Deer Creek on the 14th of March, and reported it navigable. On the next day he started with five gunboats and four mortar-boats. I went with him for some distance. The heavy, overhanging timber retarded progress very much, as did also the short turns in so narrow a stream. The gunboats, however, ploughed their way through without other damage than to their appearance. The transports did not fare so well although they followed behind. The road was somewhat cleared for them by the gunboats. In the evening I returned to headquarters to hurry up reinforcements. Sherman went in person on the 16th, taking with him Stuart's division of the 15th corps. They took large river transports to Eagle Bend on the Mississippi, where they debarked and marched across to Steel's Bayou, where they re-embarked on the transports. The river steamers, with their tall smoke-stacks and light guards extending out, were so much impeded that the gunboats got far ahead. Porter, with his fleet, got within a few hundred yards of where the sailing would have been clear and free from the obstructions caused by felling trees into the water, when he encountered rebel sharp-shooters, and his progress was delayed by obstructions in his front. He could do nothing with gunboats against sharp-shooters. The rebels, learning his route, had sent in about 4,000 men—many more than there were sailors in the fleet.

Sherman went back, at the request of the admiral, to clear out Black Bayou and to hurry up reinforcements, which were far behind. On the night of the 19th he received notice from the admiral that he had been attacked by sharp-shooters and was in imminent peril. Sherman at once returned through Black Bayou in a canoe, and passed on until he met a steamer, with the last of the reinforcements he had, coming up. They tried to force their way through Black Bayou with their steamer, but, finding it slow and tedious work, debarked and pushed forward on foot. It was night when they landed, and intensely dark. There was but a narrow strip of land above water, and that was grown up with underbrush or cane. The troops lighted their way through this with candles carried in their hands for a mile and a half, when they came to an open plantation. Here the troops rested until morning. They made twenty-one miles from this resting-place by noon the next day, and were in time to rescue the fleet. Porter had fully made up his mind to blow up the gunboats rather than have them fall into the hands of the enemy. More welcome visitors he probably never met than the "boys in blue" on this occasion. The vessels were backed out and returned to their rendezvous on the Mississippi; and thus ended in failure the fourth attempt to get in rear of Vicksburg.

Chapter XXXII.

THE BAYOUS WEST OF THE MISSISSIPPI—CRITICISMS OF
THE NORTHERN PRESS—RUNNING THE BATTERIES—LOSS
OF THE INDIANOLA—DISPOSITION OF THE TROOPS.

THE ORIGINAL canal scheme was also abandoned on the 27th of March. The effort to make a waterway through Lake Providence and the connecting bayous was abandoned as wholly impracticable about the same time.

At Milliken's Bend, and also at Young's Point, bayous or channels start, which, connecting with other bayous passing Richmond, Louisiana, enter the Mississippi at Carthage twenty-five or thirty miles above Grand Gulf. The Mississippi levee cuts the supply of water off from these bayous or channels, but all the rainfall behind the levee, at these points, is carried through these same channels to the river below. In case of a crevasse in this vicinity, the water escaping would find its outlet through the same channels. The dredges and laborers from the canal having been driven out by overflow and the enemy's batteries, I determined to open these other channels, if possible. If successful the effort would afford a route, away from the enemy's batteries, for our transports. There was a good road back of the levees, along these bayous, to carry the troops, artillery and wagon trains over whenever the water receded a little, and after a few days of dry weather. Accordingly, with the abandonment of all the other plans for reaching a base heretofore described, this new one was undertaken.

As early as the 4th of February I had written to Halleck about this route, stating that I thought it much more practicable than the other undertaking (the Lake Providence route), and that it would have been accomplished with much less labor if commenced before the water had got all over the country.

The upper end of these bayous being cut off from a water supply, further than the rainfall back of the levees, was grown up with dense timber for a distance of several miles from their source. It was necessary, therefore, to clear this out before letting in the water from the river. This work was continued until the waters of the river began to recede and the road to Richmond, Louisiana, emerged from the water. One small steamer and some barges were got through this channel, but no further use could be made of it because of the fall in the river. Beyond this it was no more successful than the other experiments with which the winter was whiled away. All these failures would have been very discouraging if I had expected much from the efforts; but I had not. From the first the most I hoped to accomplish was the passage of transports, to be used below Vicksburg, without exposure to the long line of batteries defending that city.

This long, dreary and, for heavy and continuous rains and high water, unprecedented winter was one of great hardship to all engaged about Vicksburg. The river was higher than its natural banks from December, 1862, to the following April. The war had suspended peaceful pursuits in the South, further than the production of army supplies, and in consequence the levees were neglected and broken in many places and the whole country was covered with water. Troops could scarcely find dry ground on which to pitch their tents. Malarial fevers broke out among the men. Measles and small-pox also attacked them. The hospital arrangements and medical attendance were so perfect, however, that the loss of life was much less than might have been expected. Visitors to the camps went home with dismal stories to relate; Northern papers came back to the soldiers with these stories exaggerated. Because I would not divulge my ultimate plans to visitors, they pronounced me idle, incompetent and unfit to command men in an emergency, and clamored for my removal. They were not to be satisfied, many of them, with my simple removal, but named who my successor should be. McClernand, Fremont, Hunter and McClellan were all mentioned in this connection. I took no steps to answer these complaints, but continued to do my duty, as I understood it, to the best of my ability. Every one has his superstitions. One of mine is that in positions of great responsibility every one should do his duty to the best of his ability where assigned by competent authority, without application or the use of influence to change his position. While at Cairo I had watched with very great interest the operations of the Army of the Potomac, looking upon that as the main field of the war. I had no idea, myself, of ever having any large command, nor did I suppose that I was equal to one; but I had the vanity to think that as a cavalry officer I might succeed very well in the command of a brigade. On one occasion, in talking about this to my staff officers, all of whom were civilians without any military education whatever, I said that I would give anything if I were commanding a brigade of cavalry in the Army of the Potomac and I believed I could do some good. Captain Hillyer spoke up and suggested that I make application to be transferred there to command the cavalry. I then told him that I would cut my right arm off first, and mentioned this superstition.

In time of war the President, being by the Constitution Commander-in-chief of the Army and Navy, is responsible for the selection of commanders. He should not be embarrassed in making his selections. I having been selected, my responsibility ended with my doing the best I knew how. If I had sought the place, or obtained it through personal or political influence, my belief is that I would have feared to undertake any plan of my own conception, and would probably have awaited direct orders from my distant superiors. Persons obtaining important commands by application or political influence are apt to keep a written record of complaints and predictions of defeat, which are shown in case of disaster. Somebody must be responsible for their failures.

With all the pressure brought to bear upon them, both President Lincoln and General Halleck stood by me to the end of the campaign. I had never met Mr. Lincoln, but his support was constant.

At last the waters began to recede; the roads crossing the peninsula behind the levees of the bayous, were emerging from the waters; the troops were all concentrated from distant points at Milliken's Bend preparatory to a final move which was to crown the long, tedious and discouraging labors with success.

I had had in contemplation the whole winter the movement by land to a point below Vicksburg from which to operate, subject only to the possible but not expected success of some one of the expedients resorted to for the purpose of giving us a different base. This could not be undertaken until the waters receded. I did not therefore communicate this plan, even to an officer of my staff, until it was necessary to make preparations for the start. My recollection is that Admiral Porter was the first one to whom I mentioned it. The co-operation of the navy was absolutely essential to the success (even to the contemplation) of such an enterprise. I had no more authority to command Porter than he had to command me. It was necessary to have part of his fleet below Vicksburg if the troops went there. Steamers to use as ferries were also essential. The navy was the only escort and protection for these steamers, all of which in getting below had to run about fourteen miles of batteries. Porter fell into the plan at once, and suggested that he had better superintend the preparation of the steamers selected to run the batteries, as sailors would probably understand the work better than soldiers. I was glad to accept his proposition, not only because I admitted his argument, but because it would enable me to keep from the enemy a little longer our designs. Porter's fleet was on the east side of the river above the mouth of the Yazoo, entirely concealed from the enemy by the dense forests that intervened. Even spies could not get near him, on account of the undergrowth and overflowed lands. Suspicions of some mysterious movements were aroused. Our river guards discovered one day a small skiff moving quietly and mysteriously up the river near the east shore, from the direction of Vicksburg, towards the fleet. On overhauling the boat they found a small white flag, not much larger than a handkerchief, set up in the stern, no doubt intended as a flag of truce in case of discovery. The boat, crew and passengers were brought ashore to me. The chief personage aboard proved to be Jacob Thompson, Secretary of the Interior under the administration of President Buchanan. After a pleasant conversation of half an hour or more I allowed the boat and crew, passengers and all, to return to Vicksburg, without creating a suspicion that there was a doubt in my mind as to the good faith of Mr. Thompson and his flag.

Admiral Porter proceeded with the preparation of the steamers for their hazardous passage of the enemy's batteries.

The great essential was to protect the boilers from the ene-my's shot, and to conceal the fires under the boilers from view. This he accomplished by loading the steamers, between the guards and boilers on the boiler deck up to the deck above, with bales of hay and cotton, and the deck in front of the boilers in the same way, adding sacks of grain. The hay and grain would be wanted below, and could not be trans-ported in sufficient quantity by the muddy roads over which we expected to march.

Before this I had been collecting, from St. Louis and Chi-cago, yawls and barges to be used as ferries when we got below. By the 16th of April Porter was ready to start on his perilous trip. The advance, flagship *Benton*, Porter command-ing, started at ten o'clock at night, followed at intervals of a few minutes by the *Lafayette* with a captured steamer, the *Price*, lashed to her side, the *Louisville*, *Mound City*, *Pittsburgh* and *Carondelet*—all of these being naval vessels. Next came the transports—*Forest Queen*, *Silver Wave* and *Henry Clay*, each towing barges loaded with coal to be used as fuel by the naval and transport steamers when below the batteries. The gunboat *Tuscumbia* brought up the rear. Soon after the start a battery between Vicksburg and Warrenton opened fire across the intervening peninsula, followed by the upper batteries, and then by batteries all along the line. The gunboats ran up close under the bluffs, delivering their fire in return at short distances, probably without much effect. They were under fire for more than two hours and every vessel was struck many times, but with little damage to the gunboats. The transports did not fare so well. The *Henry Clay* was disabled and de-serted by her crew. Soon after a shell burst in the cotton packed about the boilers, set the vessel on fire and burned her to the water's edge. The burning mass, however, floated down to Carthage before grounding, as did also one of the barges in tow.

The enemy were evidently expecting our fleet, for they were ready to light up the river by means of bonfires on the east side and by firing houses on the point of land opposite the city on the Louisiana side. The sight was magnificent, but terrible. I witnessed it from the deck of a river transport, run out into the middle of the river and as low down as it was prudent to go. My mind was much relieved when I learned that no one on the transports had been killed and but few, if any, wounded. During the running of the batteries men were stationed in the holds of the transports to partially stop with cotton shot-holes that might be made in the hulls. All damage was afterwards soon repaired under the direction of Admiral Porter.

The experiment of passing batteries had been tried before this, however, during the war. Admiral Farragut had run the batteries at Port Hudson with the flagship *Hartford* and one iron-clad and visited me from below Vicksburg. The 13th of February Admiral Porter had sent the gunboat *Indianola*, Lieutenant-Commander George Brown commanding, below. She met Colonel Ellet of the Marine brigade below Natchez on a captured steamer. Two of the Colonel's fleet had previously run the batteries, producing the greatest consternation among the people along the Mississippi from Vicksburg* to the Red River.

The *Indianola* remained about the mouth of the Red River some days, and then started up the Mississippi. The Confederates soon raised the *Queen of the West*,† and repaired her. With this vessel and the ram *Webb*, which they had had for some time in the Red River, and two other steamers, they followed the *Indianola*. The latter was encumbered with barges of coal in tow, and consequently could make but little speed against the rapid current of the Mississippi. The Confederate fleet overtook her just above Grand Gulf, and attacked her after dark on the 24th of February. The *Indianola* was superior to all the others in armament, and probably would have destroyed them or driven them away, but for her encumbrance. As it was she fought them for an hour

---

*Colonel Ellet reported having attacked a Confederate battery on the Red River two days before with one of his boats, the *De Soto*. Running aground, he was obliged to abandon his vessel. However, he reported that he set fire to her and blew her up. Twenty of his men fell into the hands of the enemy. With the balance he escaped on the small captured steamer, the *New Era*, and succeeded in passing the batteries at Grand Gulf and reaching the vicinity of Vicksburg.

†One of Colonel Ellet's vessels which had run the blockade on February the 2d and been sunk in the Red River.

and a half, but, in the dark, was struck seven or eight times by the ram and other vessels, and was finally disabled and reduced to a sinking condition. The armament was thrown overboard and the vessel run ashore. Officers and crew then surrendered.

I had started McClernand with his corps of four divisions on the 29th of March, by way of Richmond, Louisiana, to New Carthage, hoping that he might capture Grand Gulf before the balance of the troops could get there; but the roads were very bad, scarcely above water yet. Some miles from New Carthage the levee to Bayou Vidal was broken in several places, overflowing the roads for the distance of two miles. Boats were collected from the surrounding bayous, and some constructed on the spot from such material as could be collected, to transport the troops across the overflowed interval. By the 6th of April McClernand had reached New Carthage with one division and its artillery, the latter ferried through the woods by these boats. On the 17th I visited New Carthage in person, and saw that the process of getting troops through in the way we were doing was so tedious that a better method must be devised. The water was falling, and in a few days there would not be depth enough to use boats; nor would the land be dry enough to march over. McClernand had already found a new route from Smith's plantation where the crevasse occurred, to Perkins' plantation, eight to twelve miles below New Carthage. This increased the march from Milliken's Bend from twenty-seven to nearly forty miles. Four bridges had to be built across bayous, two of them each over six hundred feet long, making about two thousand feet of bridging in all. The river falling made the current in these bayous very rapid, increasing the difficulty of building and permanently fastening these bridges; but the ingenuity of the "Yankee soldier" was equal to any emergency. The bridges were soon built of such material as could be found near by, and so substantial were they that not a single mishap occurred in crossing all the army with artillery, cavalry and wagon trains, except the loss of one siege gun (a thirty-two pounder). This, if my memory serves me correctly, broke through the only pontoon bridge we had in all our march across the peninsula. These bridges were all built by McClernand's command, under the supervision of Lieutenant Hains of the Engineer Corps.

I returned to Milliken's Bend on the 18th or 19th, and on the 20th issued the following final order for the movement of troops:

HEADQUARTERS DEPARTMENT OF THE TENNESSEE,
MILLIKEN'S BEND, LOUISIANA,
April 20, 1863.

Special Orders, No. 110.

*   *   *   *   *   *   *

VIII. The following orders are published for the information and guidance of the "Army in the Field," in its present movement to obtain a foothold on the east bank of the Mississippi River, from which Vicksburg can be approached by practicable roads.

First. — The Thirteenth army corps, Major-General John A. McClernand commanding, will constitute the right wing.

Second. — The Fifteenth army corps, Major-General W. T. Sherman commanding, will constitute the left wing.

Third. — The Seventeenth army corps, Major-General James B. McPherson commanding, will constitute the centre.

Fourth. — The order of march to New Carthage will be from right to left.

Fifth. — Reserves will be formed by divisions from each army corps; or, an entire army corps will be held as a reserve, as necessity may require. When the reserve is formed by divisions, each division will remain under the immediate command of its respective corps commander, unless otherwise specially ordered for a particular emergency.

Sixth. — Troops will be required to bivouac, until proper facilities can be afforded for the transportation of camp equipage.

Seventh. — In the present movement, one tent will be allowed to each company for the protection of rations from rain; one wall tent for each regimental headquarters; one wall tent for each brigade headquarters; and one wall tent for each division headquarters; corps commanders having the books and blanks of their respective commands to provide for, are authorized to take such tents as are absolutely necessary, but not to exceed the number allowed by General Orders No. 160, A. G. O., series of 1862.

Eighth. — All the teams of the three army corps, under the immediate charge of the quartermasters bearing them on their returns, will constitute a train for carrying supplies and ordnance and the authorized camp equipage of the army.

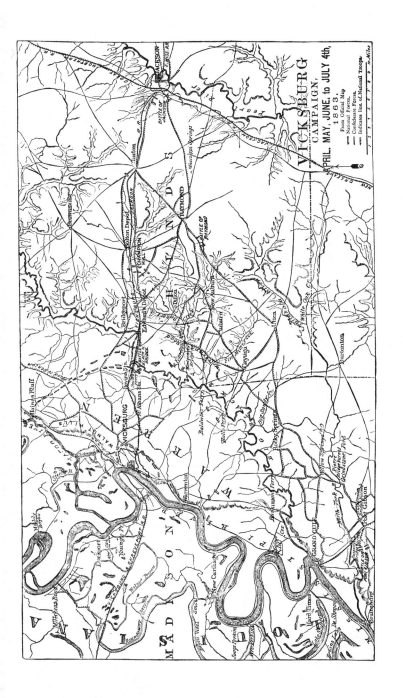

VICKSBURG
CAMPAIGN,
APRIL, MAY, JUNE, to JULY 4th,
1863.
From Official Map.
━━━ Confederate Forces.
═══ National Forces.
⌇⌇⌇ Indicates line of National Troops

Ninth.—As fast as the Thirteenth army corps advances, the Seventeenth army corps will take its place; and it, in turn, will be followed in like manner by the Fifteenth army corps.

Tenth.—Two regiments from each army corps will be detailed by corps commanders, to guard the lines from Richmond to New Carthage.

Eleventh.—General hospitals will be established by the medical director, between Duckport and Milliken's Bend. All sick and disabled soldiers will be left in these hospitals. Surgeons in charge of hospitals will report convalescents as fast as they become fit for duty. Each corps commander will detail an intelligent and good drill officer, to remain behind and take charge of the convalescents of their respective corps; officers so detailed will organize the men under their charge into squads and companies, without regard to the regiments they belong to; and in the absence of convalescent commissioned officers to command them, will appoint non-commissioned officers or privates. The force so organized will constitute the guard of the line from Duckport to Milliken's Bend. They will furnish all the guards and details required for general hospitals, and with the contrabands that may be about the camps, will furnish all the details for loading and unloading boats.

Twelfth.—The movement of troops from Milliken's Bend to New Carthage will be so conducted as to allow the transportation of ten days' supply of rations, and one-half the allowance of ordnance, required by previous orders.

Thirteenth.—Commanders are authorized and enjoined to collect all the beef cattle, corn and other necessary supplies on the line of march; but wanton destruction of property, taking of articles useless for military purposes, insulting citizens, going into and searching houses without proper orders from division commanders, are positively prohibited. All such irregularities must be summarily punished.

Fourteenth.—Brigadier-General J. C. Sullivan is appointed to the command of all the forces detailed for the protection of the line from here to New Carthage. His particular attention is called to General Orders, No. 69, from Adjutant-General's Office, Washington, of date March 20, 1863.

By order of
Major-General U. S. GRANT.

McClernand was already below on the Mississippi. Two of McPherson's divisions were put upon the march immediately. The third had not yet arrived from Lake Providence; it was on its way to Milliken's Bend and was to follow on arrival.

Sherman was to follow McPherson. Two of his divisions were at Duckport and Young's Point, and the third under Steele was under orders to return from Greenville, Mississippi, where it had been sent to expel a rebel battery that had been annoying our transports.

It had now become evident that the army could not be rationed by a wagon train over the single narrow and almost impassable road between Milliken's Bend and Perkins' plantation. Accordingly six more steamers were protected as before, to run the batteries, and were loaded with supplies. They took twelve barges in tow, loaded also with rations. On the night of the 22d of April they ran the batteries, five getting through more or less disabled while one was sunk. About half the barges got through with their needed freight.

When it was first proposed to run the blockade at Vicksburg with river steamers there were but two captains or masters who were willing to accompany their vessels, and but one crew. Volunteers were called for from the army, men who had had experience in any capacity in navigating the western rivers. Captains, pilots, mates, engineers and deck-hands enough presented themselves to take five times the number of vessels we were moving through this dangerous ordeal. Most of them were from Logan's division, composed generally of men from the southern part of Illinois and from Missouri. All but two of the steamers were commanded by volunteers from the army, and all but one so manned. In this instance, as in all others during the war, I found that volunteers could be found in the ranks and among the commissioned officers to meet every call for aid whether mechanical or professional. Colonel W. S. Oliver was master of transportation on this occasion by special detail.

Chapter XXXIII.

ATTACK ON GRAND GULF — OPERATIONS BELOW VICKSBURG.

On the 24TH my headquarters were with the advance at Perkins' plantation. Reconnoissances were made in boats to ascertain whether there was high land on the east shore of the river where we might land above Grand Gulf. There was none practicable. Accordingly the troops were set in motion for Hard Times, twenty-two miles farther down the river and nearly opposite Grand Gulf. The loss of two steamers and six barges reduced our transportation so that only 10,000 men could be moved by water. Some of the steamers that had got below were injured in their machinery, so that they were only useful as barges towed by those less severely injured. All the troops, therefore, except what could be transported in one trip, had to march. The road lay west of Lake St. Joseph. Three large bayous had to be crossed. They were rapidly bridged in the same manner as those previously encountered.

On the 27th McClernand's corps was all at Hard Times, and McPherson's was following closely. I had determined to make the attempt to effect a landing on the east side of the river as soon as possible. Accordingly, on the morning of the 29th, McClernand was directed to embark all the troops from his corps that our transports and barges could carry. About 10,000 men were so embarked. The plan was to have the navy silence the guns at Grand Gulf, and to have as many men as possible ready to debark in the shortest possible time under cover of the fire of the navy and carry the works by storm. The following order was issued:

NOTE. — On this occasion Governor Richard Yates, of Illinois, happened to be on a visit to the army, and accompanied me to Carthage. I furnished an ambulance for his use and that of some of the State officers who accompanied him.

PERKINS' PLANTATION, LA., $\left.\right\}$
April 27, 1863.

MAJOR-GENERAL J. A. McCLERNAND,
        Commanding 13th A. C.

Commence immediately the embarkation of your corps, or so much of it as there is transportation for. Have put aboard the artillery and every article authorized in orders limiting baggage, except the men, and hold them in readiness, with their places assigned, to be moved at a moment's warning.

All the troops you may have, except those ordered to remain behind, send to a point nearly opposite Grand Gulf, where you see, by special orders of this date, General McPherson is ordered to send one division.

The plan of the attack will be for the navy to attack and silence all the batteries commanding the river. Your corps will be on the river, ready to run to and debark on the nearest eligible land below the promontory first brought to view passing down the river. Once on shore, have each commander instructed beforehand to form his men the best the ground will admit of, and take possession of the most commanding points, but avoid separating your command so that it cannot support itself. The first object is to get a foothold where our troops can maintain themselves until such time as preparations can be made and troops collected for a forward movement.

Admiral Porter has proposed to place his boats in the position indicated to you a few days ago, and to bring over with them such troops as may be below the city after the guns of the enemy are silenced.

It may be that the enemy will occupy positions back from the city, out of range of the gunboats, so as to make it desirable to run past Grand Gulf and land at Rodney. In case this should prove the plan, a signal will be arranged and you duly informed, when the transports are to start with this view. Or, it may be expedient for the boats to run past, but not the men. In this case, then, the transports would have to be brought back to where the men could land and move by forced marches to below Grand Gulf, re-embark rapidly and proceed to the latter place. There will be required, then, three signals; one, to indicate that the transports can run down and debark the troops at Grand Gulf; one, that the transports can run by without the troops; and the last, that the transports can run by with the troops on board.

Should the men have to march, all baggage and artillery will be left to run the blockade.

If not already directed, require your men to keep three days' rations in their haversacks, not to be touched until a movement commences.

U. S. GRANT,
Major-General.

At 8 o'clock A.M., 29th, Porter made the attack with his entire strength present, eight gunboats. For nearly five and a half hours the attack was kept up without silencing a single gun of the enemy. All this time McClernand's 10,000 men were huddled together on the transports in the stream ready to attempt a landing if signalled. I occupied a tug from which I could see the effect of the battle on both sides, within range of the enemy's guns; but a small tug, without armament, was not calculated to attract the fire of batteries while they were being assailed themselves. About half-past one the fleet withdrew, seeing their efforts were entirely unavailing. The enemy ceased firing as soon as we withdrew. I immediately signalled the Admiral and went aboard his ship. The navy lost in this engagement eighteen killed and fifty-six wounded. A large proportion of these were of the crew of the flagship, and most of those from a single shell which penetrated the ship's side and exploded between decks where the men were working their guns. The sight of the mangled and dying men which met my eye as I boarded the ship was sickening.

Grand Gulf is on a high bluff where the river runs at the very foot of it. It is as defensible upon its front as Vicksburg and, at that time, would have been just as impossible to capture by a front attack. I therefore requested Porter to run the batteries with his fleet that night, and to take charge of the transports, all of which would be wanted below.

There is a long tongue of land from the Louisiana side extending towards Grand Gulf, made by the river running nearly east from about three miles above and nearly in the opposite direction from that point for about the same distance below. The land was so low and wet that it would not have been practicable to march an army across but for a levee. I had had this explored before, as well as the east bank below to ascertain if there was a possible point of debarkation north of Rodney. It was found that the top of the levee afforded a good road to march upon.

Porter, as was always the case with him, not only acquiesced in the plan, but volunteered to use his entire fleet as
transports. I had intended to make this request, but he anticipated me. At dusk, when concealed from the view of the
enemy at Grand Gulf, McClernand landed his command on
the west bank. The navy and transports ran the batteries successfully. The troops marched across the point of land under
cover of night, unobserved. By the time it was light the enemy saw our whole fleet, iron-clads, gunboats, river steamers
and barges, quietly moving down the river three miles below
them, black, or rather blue, with National troops.

When the troops debarked, the evening of the 29th, it
was expected that we would have to go to Rodney, about
nine miles below, to find a landing; but that night a colored
man came in who informed me that a good landing would
be found at Bruinsburg, a few miles above Rodney, from
which point there was a good road leading to Port Gibson
some twelve miles in the interior. The information was found
correct, and our landing was effected without opposition.

Sherman had not left his position above Vicksburg yet. On
the morning of the 27th I ordered him to create a diversion by
moving his corps up the Yazoo and threatening an attack on
Haines' Bluff.

My object was to compel Pemberton to keep as much force
about Vicksburg as I could, until I could secure a good footing on high land east of the river. The move was eminently
successful and, as we afterwards learned, created great confusion about Vicksburg and doubts about our real design. Sherman moved the day of our attack on Grand Gulf, the 29th,
with ten regiments of his command and eight gunboats which
Porter had left above Vicksburg.

He debarked his troops and apparently made every preparation to attack the enemy while the navy bombarded the
main forts at Haines' Bluff. This move was made without a
single casualty in either branch of the service. On the first of
May Sherman received orders from me (sent from Hard
Times the evening of the 29th of April) to withdraw from the
front of Haines' Bluff and follow McPherson with two divisions as fast as he could.

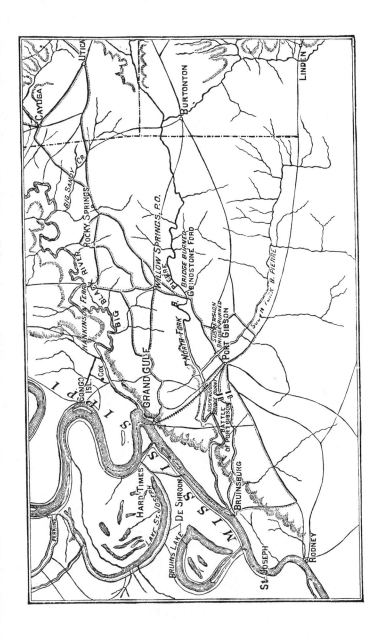

I had established a depot of supplies at Perkins' plantation. Now that all our gunboats were below Grand Gulf it was possible that the enemy might fit out boats in the Big Black with improvised armament and attempt to destroy these supplies. McPherson was at Hard Times with a portion of his corps, and the depot was protected by a part of his command. The night of the 29th I directed him to arm one of the transports with artillery and send it up to Perkins' plantation as a guard; and also to have the siege guns we had brought along moved there and put in position.

The embarkation below Grand Gulf took place at De Shroon's, Louisiana, six miles above Bruinsburg, Mississippi. Early on the morning of 30th of April McClernand's corps and one division of McPherson's corps were speedily landed.

When this was effected I felt a degree of relief scarcely ever equalled since. Vicksburg was not yet taken it is true, nor were its defenders demoralized by any of our previous moves. I was now in the enemy's country, with a vast river and the stronghold of Vicksburg between me and my base of supplies. But I was on dry ground on the same side of the river with the enemy. All the campaigns, labors, hardships and exposures from the month of December previous to this time that had been made and endured, were for the accomplishment of this one object.

I had with me the 13th corps, General McClernand commanding, and two brigades of Logan's division of the 17th corps, General McPherson commanding—in all not more than twenty thousand men to commence the campaign with. These were soon reinforced by the remaining brigade of Logan's division and Crocker's division of the 17th corps. On the 7th of May I was further reinforced by Sherman with two divisions of his, the 15th corps. My total force was then about thirty-three thousand men.

The enemy occupied Grand Gulf, Haines' Bluff and Jackson with a force of nearly sixty thousand men. Jackson is fifty miles east of Vicksburg and is connected with it by a railroad. My first problem was to capture Grand Gulf to use as a base.

Bruinsburg is two miles from high ground. The bottom at that point is higher than most of the low land in the valley of the Mississippi, and a good road leads to the bluff. It was natural to expect the garrison from Grand Gulf to come out to meet us and prevent, if they could, our reaching this solid base. Bayou Pierre enters the Mississippi just above Bruinsburg and, as it is a navigable stream and was high at the time, in order to intercept us they had to go by Port Gibson, the nearest point where there was a bridge to cross upon. This more than doubled the distance from Grand Gulf to the high land back of Bruinsburg. No time was to be lost in securing this foothold. Our transportation was not sufficient to move all the army across the river at one trip, or even two; but the landing of the 13th corps and one division of the 17th was effected during the day, April 30th, and early evening. Mc-Clernand was advanced as soon as ammunition and two days' rations (to last five) could be issued to his men. The bluffs were reached an hour before sunset and McClernand was pushed on, hoping to reach Port Gibson and save the bridge spanning the Bayou Pierre before the enemy could get there; for crossing a stream in the presence of an enemy is always difficult. Port Gibson, too, is the starting point of roads to Grand Gulf, Vicksburg and Jackson.

McClernand's advance met the enemy about five miles west of Port Gibson at Thompson's plantation. There was some firing during the night, but nothing rising to the dignity of a battle until daylight. The enemy had taken a strong natural position with most of the Grand Gulf garrison, numbering about seven or eight thousand men, under General Bowen. His hope was to hold me in check until reinforcements under Loring could reach him from Vicksburg; but Loring did not come in time to render much assistance south of Port Gibson. Two brigades of McPherson's corps followed McClernand as fast as rations and ammunition could be issued, and were ready to take position upon the battle-field whenever the 13th corps could be got out of the way.

The country in this part of Mississippi stands on edge, as it were, the roads running along the ridges except when they occasionally pass from one ridge to another. Where there are no clearings the sides of the hills are covered with a very heavy growth of timber and with undergrowth, and the ravines are filled with vines and canebrakes, almost impenetrable. This makes it easy for an inferior force to delay, if not defeat, a far superior one.

Near the point selected by Bowen to defend, the road to Port Gibson divides, taking two ridges which do not diverge more than a mile or two at the widest point. These roads unite just outside the town. This made it necessary for Mc-Clernand to divide his force. It was not only divided, but it was separated by a deep ravine of the character above described. One flank could not reinforce the other except by marching back to the junction of the roads. McClernand put the divisions of Hovey, Carr and A. J. Smith upon the right-hand branch and Osterhaus on the left. I was on the field by ten A.M., and inspected both flanks in person. On the right the enemy, if not being pressed back, was at least not repulsing our advance. On the left, however, Osterhaus was not faring so well. He had been repulsed with some loss. As soon as the road could be cleared of McClernand's troops I ordered up McPherson, who was close upon the rear of the 13th corps, with two brigades of Logan's division. This was about noon. I ordered him to send one brigade (General John E. Smith's was selected) to support Osterhaus, and to move to the left and flank the enemy out of his position. This movement carried the brigade over a deep ravine to a third ridge and, when Smith's troops were seen well through the ravine, Osterhaus was directed to renew his front attack. It was successful and unattended by heavy loss. The enemy was sent in full retreat on their right, and their left followed before sunset. While the movement to our left was going on, McClernand, who was with his right flank, sent me frequent requests for reinforcements, although the force with him was not being pressed. I had been upon the ground and knew it did not admit of his engaging all the men he had. We followed up our victory until night overtook us about two miles from Port Gibson; then the troops went into bivouac for the night.

Chapter XXXIV.

WE STARTED next morning for Port Gibson as soon as it was light enough to see the road. We were soon in the town, and I was delighted to find that the enemy had not stopped to contest our crossing further at the bridge, which he had burned. The troops were set to work at once to construct a bridge across the South Fork of the Bayou Pierre. At this time the water was high and the current rapid. What might be called a raft-bridge was soon constructed from material obtained from wooden buildings, stables, fences, etc., which sufficed for carrying the whole army over safely. Colonel J. H. Wilson, a member of my staff, planned and superintended the construction of this bridge, going into the water and working as hard as any one engaged. Officers and men generally joined in this work. When it was finished the army crossed and marched eight miles beyond to the North Fork that day. One brigade of Logan's division was sent down the stream to occupy the attention of a rebel battery, which had been left behind with infantry supports to prevent our repairing the burnt railroad bridge. Two of his brigades were sent up the bayou to find a crossing and reach the North Fork to repair the bridge there. The enemy soon left when he found we were building a bridge elsewhere. Before leaving Port Gibson we were reinforced by Crocker's division, McPherson's corps, which had crossed the Mississippi at Bruinsburg and come up without stopping except to get two days' rations. McPherson still had one division west of the Mississippi River, guarding the road from Milliken's Bend to the river below until Sherman's command should relieve it.

On leaving Bruinsburg for the front I left my son Frederick, who had joined me a few weeks before, on board one of the gunboats asleep, and hoped to get away without him until after Grand Gulf should fall into our hands; but on waking up he learned that I had gone, and being guided by the sound of the battle raging at Thompson's Hill—called the Battle of Port Gibson—found his way to where I was. He had no horse to ride at the time, and I had no facilities for even preparing a meal. He, therefore, foraged around the best he could until we reached Grand Gulf. Mr. C. A. Dana, then an officer of the War Department, accompanied me on the Vicksburg campaign and through a portion of the siege. He was in the same situation as Fred so far as transportation and mess arrangements were concerned. The first time I call to mind seeing either of them, after the battle, they were mounted on two enormous horses, grown white from age, each equipped with dilapidated saddles and bridles.

Our trains arrived a few days later, after which we were all perfectly equipped.

My son accompanied me throughout the campaign and siege, and caused no anxiety either to me or to his mother, who was at home. He looked out for himself and was in every battle of the campaign. His age, then not quite thirteen, enabled him to take in all he saw, and to retain a recollection of it that would not be possible in more mature years.

When the movement from Bruinsburg commenced we were without a wagon train. The train still west of the Mississippi was carried around with proper escort, by a circuitous route from Milliken's Bend to Hard Times seventy or more miles below, and did not get up for some days after the battle of Port Gibson. My own horses, headquarters' transportation, servants, mess chest, and everything except what I had on, was with this train. General A. J. Smith happened to have an extra horse at Bruinsburg which I borrowed, with a saddletree without upholstering further than stirrups. I had no other for nearly a week.

It was necessary to have transportation for ammunition. Provisions could be taken from the country; but all the ammunition that can be carried on the person is soon exhausted when there is much fighting. I directed, therefore, immediately on landing that all the vehicles and draft animals, whether horses, mules, or oxen, in the vicinity should be collected and loaded to their capacity with ammunition. Quite a train was collected during the 30th, and a motley train it was. In it could be found fine carriages, loaded nearly to the top

with boxes of cartridges that had been pitched in promiscu-
ously, drawn by mules with plough-harness, straw collars,
rope-lines, etc.; long-coupled wagons, with racks for carrying
cotton bales, drawn by oxen, and everything that could be
found in the way of transportation on a plantation, either for
use or pleasure. The making out of provision returns was
stopped for the time. No formalities were to retard our
progress until a position was secured when the time could be
spared to observe them.

It was at Port Gibson I first heard through a Southern
paper of the complete success of Colonel Grierson, who was
making a raid through central Mississippi. He had started
from La Grange April 17th with three regiments of about
1,700 men. On the 21st he had detached Colonel Hatch with
one regiment to destroy the railroad between Columbus and
Macon and then return to La Grange. Hatch had a sharp fight
with the enemy at Columbus and retreated along the railroad, destroying it at Okalona and Tupelo, and arriving in La
Grange April 26. Grierson continued his movement with
about 1,000 men, breaking the Vicksburg and Meridian railroad and the New Orleans and Jackson railroad, arriving at
Baton Rouge May 2d. This raid was of great importance, for
Grierson had attracted the attention of the enemy from the
main movement against Vicksburg.

During the night of the 2d of May the bridge over the
North Fork was repaired, and the troops commenced crossing
at five the next morning. Before the leading brigade was over
it was fired upon by the enemy from a commanding position;
but they were soon driven off. It was evident that the enemy
was covering a retreat from Grand Gulf to Vicksburg. Every
commanding position from this (Grindstone) crossing to
Hankinson's ferry over the Big Black was occupied by the
retreating foe to delay our progress. McPherson, however,
reached Hankinson's ferry before night, seized the ferry boat,
and sent a detachment of his command across and several
miles north on the road to Vicksburg. When the junction of
the road going to Vicksburg with the road from Grand Gulf
to Raymond and Jackson was reached, Logan with his division was turned to the left towards Grand Gulf. I went with
him a short distance from this junction. McPherson had en-

countered the largest force yet met since the battle of Port Gibson and had a skirmish nearly approaching a battle; but the road Logan had taken enabled him to come up on the enemy's right flank, and they soon gave way. McPherson was ordered to hold Hankinson's ferry and the road back to Willow Springs with one division; McClernand, who was now in the rear, was to join in this as well as to guard the line back down the bayou. I did not want to take the chances of having an enemy lurking in our rear.

On the way from the junction to Grand Gulf, where the road comes into the one from Vicksburg to the same place six or seven miles out, I learned that the last of the enemy had retreated past that place on their way to Vicksburg. I left Logan to make the proper disposition of his troops for the night, while I rode into the town with an escort of about twenty cavalry. Admiral Porter had already arrived with his fleet. The enemy had abandoned his heavy guns and evacuated the place.

When I reached Grand Gulf May 3d I had not been with my baggage since the 27th of April and consequently had had no change of underclothing, no meal except such as I could pick up sometimes at other headquarters, and no tent to cover me. The first thing I did was to get a bath, borrow some fresh underclothing from one of the naval officers and get a good meal on the flag-ship. Then I wrote letters to the general-in-chief informing him of our present position, dispatches to be telegraphed from Cairo, orders to General Sullivan commanding above Vicksburg, and gave orders to all my corps commanders. About twelve o'clock at night I was through my work and started for Hankinson's ferry, arriving there before daylight. While at Grand Gulf I heard from Banks, who was on the Red River, and who said that he could not be at Port Hudson before the 10th of May and then with only 15,000 men. Up to this time my intention had been to secure Grand Gulf, as a base of supplies, detach McClernand's corps to Banks and co-operate with him in the reduction of Port Hudson.

The news from Banks forced upon me a different plan of campaign from the one intended. To wait for his co-operation would have detained me at least a month. The reinforcements would not have reached ten thousand men after deducting casualties and necessary river guards at all high points close to the river for over three hundred miles. The enemy would have strengthened his position and been reinforced by more men than Banks could have brought. I therefore determined to move independently of Banks, cut loose from my base, destroy the rebel force in rear of Vicksburg and invest or capture the city.

Grand Gulf was accordingly given up as a base and the authorities at Washington were notified. I knew well that Halleck's caution would lead him to disapprove of this course; but it was the only one that gave any chance of success. The time it would take to communicate with Washington and get a reply would be so great that I could not be interfered with until it was demonstrated whether my plan was practicable. Even Sherman, who afterwards ignored bases of supplies other than what were afforded by the country while marching through four States of the Confederacy with an army more than twice as large as mine at this time, wrote me from Hankinson's ferry, advising me of the impossibility of supplying our army over a single road. He urged me to "stop all troops till your army is partially supplied with wagons, and then act as quick as possible; for this road will be jammed, as sure as life." To this I replied: "I do not calculate upon the possibility of supplying the army with full rations from Grand Gulf. I know it will be impossible without constructing additional roads. What I do expect is to get up what rations of hard bread, coffee and salt we can, and make the country furnish the balance." We started from Bruinsburg with an average of about two days' rations, and received no more from our own supplies for some days; abundance was found in the mean time. A delay would give the enemy time to reinforce and fortify.

McClernand's and McPherson's commands were kept substantially as they were on the night of the 2d, awaiting supplies sufficient to give them three days' rations in haversacks. Beef, mutton, poultry and forage were found in abundance. Quite a quantity of bacon and molasses was also secured from the country, but bread and coffee could not be obtained in quantity sufficient for all the men. Every plantation, however, had a run of stone, propelled by mule power, to grind corn for the owners and their slaves. All these were kept running while we were stopping, day and night, and when we were marching, during the night, at all plantations covered by the troops. But the product was taken by the troops nearest by, so that the majority of the command was destined to go without bread until a new base was established on the Yazoo above Vicksburg.

While the troops were awaiting the arrival of rations I ordered reconnoissances made by McClernand and McPherson, with the view of leading the enemy to believe that we intended to cross the Big Black and attack the city at once.

On the 6th Sherman arrived at Grand Gulf and crossed his command that night and the next day. Three days' rations had been brought up from Grand Gulf for the advanced troops and were issued. Orders were given for a forward movement the next day. Sherman was directed to order up Blair, who had been left behind to guard the road from Milliken's Bend to Hard Times with two brigades.

The quartermaster at Young's Point was ordered to send two hundred wagons with Blair, and the commissary was to load them with hard bread, coffee, sugar, salt and one hundred thousand pounds of salt meat.

On the 3d Hurlbut, who had been left at Memphis, was ordered to send four regiments from his command to Milliken's Bend to relieve Blair's division, and on the 5th he was ordered to send Lauman's division in addition, the latter to join the army in the field. The four regiments were to be taken from troops near the river so that there would be no delay.

During the night of the 6th McPherson drew in his troops north of the Big Black and was off at an early hour on the road to Jackson, viâ Rocky Springs, Utica and Raymond. That night he and McClernand were both at Rocky Springs ten miles from Hankinson's ferry. McPherson remained there during the 8th, while McClernand moved to Big Sandy and Sherman marched from Grand Gulf to Hankinson's ferry. The 9th, McPherson moved to a point within a few miles west of Utica; McClernand and Sherman remained where they were. On the 10th McPherson moved to Utica, Sherman to Big

Sandy; McClernand was still at Big Sandy. The 11th, McClernand was at Five Mile Creek; Sherman at Auburn; McPherson five miles advanced from Utica. May 12th, McClernand was at Fourteen Mile Creek; Sherman at Fourteen Mile Creek; McPherson at Raymond after a battle.

After McPherson crossed the Big Black at Hankinson's ferry Vicksburg could have been approached and besieged by the south side. It is not probable, however, that Pemberton would have permitted a close besiegement. The broken nature of the ground would have enabled him to hold a strong defensible line from the river south of the city to the Big Black, retaining possession of the railroad back to that point. It was my plan, therefore, to get to the railroad east of Vicksburg, and approach from that direction. Accordingly, McPherson's troops that had crossed the Big Black were withdrawn and the movement east to Jackson commenced.

As has been stated before, the country is very much broken and the roads generally confined to the tops of the hills. The troops were moved one (sometimes two) corps at a time to reach designated points out parallel to the railroad and only from six to ten miles from it. McClernand's corps was kept with its left flank on the Big Black guarding all the crossings. Fourteen Mile Creek, a stream substantially parallel with the railroad, was reached and crossings effected by McClernand and Sherman with slight loss. McPherson was to the right of Sherman, extending to Raymond. The cavalry was used in this advance in reconnoitring to find the roads: to cover our advances and to find the most practicable routes from one command to another so they could support each other in case of an attack. In making this move I estimated Pemberton's movable force at Vicksburg at about eighteen thousand men, with smaller forces at Haines' Bluff and Jackson. It would not be possible for Pemberton to attack me with all his troops at one place, and I determined to throw my army between his and fight him in detail. This was done with success, but I found afterwards that I had entirely under-estimated Pemberton's strength.

Up to this point our movements had been made without serious opposition. My line was now nearly parallel with the Jackson and Vicksburg railroad and about seven miles south of it. The right was at Raymond eighteen miles from Jackson, McPherson commanding; Sherman in the centre on Fourteen Mile Creek, his advance thrown across; McClernand to the left, also on Fourteen Mile Creek, advance across, and his pickets within two miles of Edward's station, where the enemy had concentrated a considerable force and where they undoubtedly expected us to attack. McClernand's left was on the Big Black. In all our moves, up to this time, the left had hugged the Big Black closely, and all the ferries had been guarded to prevent the enemy throwing a force on our rear.

McPherson encountered the enemy, five thousand strong with two batteries under General Gregg, about two miles out of Raymond. This was about two P.M. Logan was in advance with one of his brigades. He deployed and moved up to engage the enemy. McPherson ordered the road in rear to be cleared of wagons, and the balance of Logan's division, and Crocker's, which was still farther in rear, to come forward with all dispatch. The order was obeyed with alacrity. Logan got his division in position for assault before Crocker could get up, and attacked with vigor, carrying the enemy's position easily, sending Gregg flying from the field not to appear against our front again until we met at Jackson.

In this battle McPherson lost 66 killed, 339 wounded, and 37 missing—nearly or quite all from Logan's division. The enemy's loss was 100 killed, 305 wounded, besides 415 taken prisoners.

I regarded Logan and Crocker as being as competent division commanders as could be found in or out of the army and both equal to a much higher command. Crocker, however, was dying of consumption when he volunteered. His weak condition never put him on the sick report when there was a battle in prospect, as long as he could keep on his feet. He died not long after the close of the rebellion.

Chapter XXXV.

MOVEMENT AGAINST JACKSON — FALL OF
JACKSON — INTERCEPTING THE ENEMY — BATTLE
OF CHAMPION'S HILL.

WHEN THE NEWS reached me of McPherson's victory at Raymond about sundown my position was with Sherman. I decided at once to turn the whole column towards Jackson and capture that place without delay.

Pemberton was now on my left, with, as I supposed, about 18,000 men; in fact, as I learned afterwards, with nearly 50,000. A force was also collecting on my right, at Jackson, the point where all the railroads communicating with Vicksburg connect. All the enemy's supplies of men and stores would come by that point. As I hoped in the end to besiege Vicksburg I must first destroy all possibility of aid. I therefore determined to move swiftly towards Jackson, destroy or drive any force in that direction and then turn upon Pemberton. But by moving against Jackson, I uncovered my own communication. So I finally decided to have none — to cut loose altogether from my base and move my whole force eastward. I then had no fears for my communications, and if I moved quickly enough could turn upon Pemberton before he could attack me in the rear.

Accordingly, all previous orders given during the day for movements on the 13th were annulled by new ones. McPherson was ordered at daylight to move on Clinton, ten miles from Jackson; Sherman was notified of my determination to capture Jackson and work from there westward. He was ordered to start at four in the morning and march to Raymond. McClernand was ordered to march with three divisions by Dillon's to Raymond. One was left to guard the crossing of the Big Black.

On the 10th I had received a letter from Banks, on the Red River, asking reinforcements. Porter had gone to his assistance with a part of his fleet on the 3d, and I now wrote to him describing my position and declining to send any troops. I looked upon side movements as long as the enemy held Port Hudson and Vicksburg as a waste of time and material.

General Joseph E. Johnston arrived at Jackson in the night of the 13th from Tennessee, and immediately assumed command of all the Confederate troops in Mississippi. I knew he was expecting reinforcements from the south and east. On the 6th I had written to General Halleck: "Information from the other side leaves me to believe the enemy are bringing forces from Tullahoma."

Up to this time my troops had been kept in supporting distances of each other, as far as the nature of the country would admit. Reconnoissances were constantly made from each corps to enable them to acquaint themselves with the most practicable routes from one to another in case a union became necessary.

McPherson reached Clinton with the advance early on the 13th and immediately set to work destroying the railroad. Sherman's advance reached Raymond before the last of McPherson's command had got out of the town. McClernand withdrew from the front of the enemy, at Edward's station, with much skill and without loss, and reached his position for the night in good order. On the night of the 13th, McPherson was ordered to march at early dawn upon Jackson, only fifteen miles away. Sherman was given the same order; but he was to move by the direct road from Raymond to Jackson, which is south of the road McPherson was on and does not approach within two miles of it at the point where it crossed the line of intrenchments which, at that time, defended the city. McClernand was ordered to move one division of his command to Clinton, one division a few miles beyond Mississippi Springs following Sherman's line, and a third to Raymond. He was also directed to send his siege guns, four in number, with the troops going by Mississippi Springs. McClernand's position was an advantageous one in any event. With one division at Clinton he was in position to reinforce McPherson, at Jackson, rapidly if it became necessary; the division beyond Mississippi Springs was equally available to reinforce Sherman; the one at Raymond could take either road. He still had two other divisions farther back, now that Blair had come up, available within a day at Jackson. If this last command should not be wanted at Jackson, they were already one day's march from there on their way to Vicksburg and on three different roads leading to the latter city. But the most important consideration in my mind was to have a force confronting Pemberton if he should come out to attack my rear. This I expected him to do; as shown further on, he was directed by Johnston to make this very move.

I notified General Halleck that I should attack the State capital on the 14th. A courier carried the dispatch to Grand Gulf through an unprotected country.

Sherman and McPherson communicated with each other during the night and arranged to reach Jackson at about the same hour. It rained in torrents during the night of the 13th and the fore part of the day of the 14th. The roads were intolerable, and in some places on Sherman's line, where the land was low, they were covered more than a foot deep with water. But the troops never murmured. By nine o'clock Crocker, of McPherson's corps, who was now in advance, came upon the enemy's pickets and speedily drove them in upon the main body. They were outside of the intrenchments in a strong position, and proved to be the troops that had been driven out of Raymond. Johnston had been reinforced during the night by Georgia and South Carolina regiments, so that his force amounted to eleven thousand men, and he was expecting still more.

Sherman also came upon the rebel pickets some distance out from the town, but speedily drove them in. He was now on the south and south-west of Jackson confronting the Confederates behind their breastworks, while McPherson's right was nearly two miles north, occupying a line running north and south across the Vicksburg railroad. Artillery was brought up and reconnoissances made preparatory to an assault. McPherson brought up Logan's division while he deployed Crocker's for the assault. Sherman made similar dispositions on the right. By eleven A.M. both were ready to attack. Crocker moved his division forward, preceded by a strong skirmish line. These troops at once encountered the enemy's advance and drove it back on the main body, when they returned to their proper regiment and the whole division charged, routing the enemy completely and driving him into

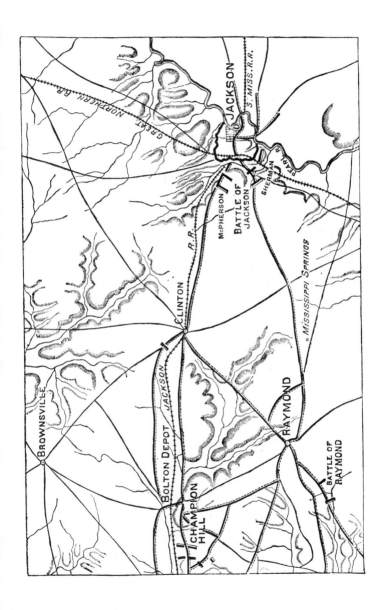

this main line. This stand by the enemy was made more than two miles outside of his main fortifications. McPherson followed up with his command until within range of the guns of the enemy from their intrenchments, when he halted to bring his troops into line and reconnoitre to determine the next move. It was now about noon.

While this was going on Sherman was confronting a rebel battery which enfiladed the road on which he was marching—the Mississippi Springs road—and commanded a bridge spanning a stream over which he had to pass. By detaching right and left the stream was forced and the enemy flanked and speedily driven within the main line. This brought our whole line in front of the enemy's line of works, which was continuous on the north, west and south sides from the Pearl River north of the city to the same river south. I was with Sherman. He was confronted by a force sufficient to hold us back. Appearances did not justify an assault where we were. I had directed Sherman to send a force to the right, and to reconnoitre as far as to the Pearl River. This force, Tuttle's division, not returning I rode to the right with my staff, and soon found that the enemy had left that part of the line. Tuttle's movement or McPherson's pressure had no doubt led Johnston to order a retreat, leaving only the men at the guns to retard us while he was getting away. Tuttle had seen this and, passing through the lines without resistance, came up in the rear of the artillerists confronting Sherman and captured them with ten pieces of artillery. I rode immediately to the State House, where I was soon followed by Sherman. About the same time McPherson discovered that the enemy was leaving his front, and advanced Crocker, who was so close upon the enemy that they could not move their guns or destroy them. He captured seven guns and, moving on, hoisted the National flag over the rebel capital of Mississippi. Stevenson's brigade was sent to cut off the rebel retreat, but was too late or not expeditious enough.

Our loss in this engagement was: McPherson, 37 killed, 228 wounded; Sherman, 4 killed and 21 wounded and missing. The enemy lost 845 killed, wounded and captured. Seventeen guns fell into our hands, and the enemy destroyed by fire their store-houses, containing a large amount of commissary stores.

On this day Blair reached New Auburn and joined McClernand's 4th division. He had with him two hundred wagons loaded with rations, the only commissary supplies received during the entire campaign.

I slept that night in the room that Johnston was said to have occupied the night before.

About four in the afternoon I sent for the corps commanders and directed the dispositions to be made of their troops. Sherman was to remain in Jackson until he destroyed that place as a railroad centre, and manufacturing city of military supplies. He did the work most effectually. Sherman and I went together into a manufactory which had not ceased work on account of the battle nor for the entrance of Yankee troops. Our presence did not seem to attract the attention of either the manager or the operatives, most of whom were girls. We looked on for a while to see the tent cloth which they were making roll out of the looms, with "C. S. A." woven in each bolt. There was an immense amount of cotton, in bales, stacked outside. Finally I told Sherman I thought they had done work enough. The operatives were told they could leave and take with them what cloth they could carry. In a few minutes cotton and factory were in a blaze. The proprietor visited Washington while I was President to get his pay for this property, claiming that it was private. He asked me to give him a statement of the fact that his property had been destroyed by National troops, so that he might use it with Congress where he was pressing, or proposed to press, his claim. I declined.

On the night of the 13th Johnston sent the following dispatch to Pemberton at Edward's station: "I have lately arrived, and learn that Major-General Sherman is between us with four divisions at Clinton. It is important to establish communication, that you may be reinforced. If practicable, come up in his rear at once. To beat such a detachment would be of immense value. All the troops you can quickly assemble should be brought. Time is all-important." This dispatch was sent in triplicate, by different messengers. One of the messengers happened to be a loyal man who had been expelled from

Memphis some months before by Hurlbut for uttering disloyal and threatening sentiments. There was a good deal of
parade about his expulsion, ostensibly as a warning to those
who entertained the sentiments he expressed; but Hurlbut
and the expelled man understood each other. He delivered his
copy of Johnston's dispatch to McPherson who forwarded it
to me.

Receiving this dispatch on the 14th I ordered McPherson
to move promptly in the morning back to Bolton, the nearest
point where Johnston could reach the road. Bolton is about
twenty miles west of Jackson. I also informed McClernand of
the capture of Jackson and sent him the following order: "It is
evidently the design of the enemy to get north of us and cross
the Big Black, and beat us into Vicksburg. We must not allow
them to do this. Turn all your forces towards Bolton station,
and make all dispatch in getting there. Move troops by the
most direct road from wherever they may be on the receipt of
this order."

And to Blair I wrote: "Their design is evidently to cross the
Big Black and pass down the peninsula between the Big Black
and Yazoo rivers. We must beat them. Turn your troops
immediately to Bolton; take all the trains with you. Smith's
division, and any other troops now with you, will go to the
same place. If practicable, take parallel roads, so as to divide
your troops and train."

Johnston stopped on the Canton road only six miles north
of Jackson, the night of the 14th. He sent from there to Pemberton dispatches announcing the loss of Jackson, and the following order:

"As soon as the reinforcements are all up, they must be
united to the rest of the army. I am anxious to see a force
assembled that may be able to inflict a heavy blow upon the
enemy. Can Grant supply himself from the Mississippi? Can
you not cut him off from it, and above all, should he be compelled to fall back for want of supplies, beat him."

The concentration of my troops was easy, considering the
character of the country. McPherson moved along the road
parallel with and near the railroad. McClernand's command
was, one division (Hovey's) on the road McPherson had to
take, but with a start of four miles. One (Osterhaus) was at

Raymond, on a converging road that intersected the other near Champion's Hill; one (Carr's) had to pass over the same road with Osterhaus, but being back at Mississippi Springs, would not be detained by it; the fourth (Smith's) with Blair's division, was near Auburn with a different road to pass over. McClernand faced about and moved promptly. His cavalry from Raymond seized Bolton by half-past nine in the morning, driving out the enemy's pickets and capturing several men.

The night of the 15th Hovey was at Bolton; Carr and Osterhaus were about three miles south, but abreast, facing west; Smith was north of Raymond with Blair in his rear.

McPherson's command, with Logan in front, had marched at seven o'clock, and by four reached Hovey and went into camp; Crocker bivouacked just in Hovey's rear on the Clinton road. Sherman with two divisions, was in Jackson, completing the destruction of roads, bridges and military factories. I rode in person out to Clinton. On my arrival I ordered McClernand to move early in the morning on Edward's station, cautioning him to watch for the enemy and not bring on an engagement unless he felt very certain of success.

I naturally expected that Pemberton would endeavor to obey the orders of his superior, which I have shown were to attack us at Clinton. This, indeed, I knew he could not do; but I felt sure he would make the attempt to reach that point. It turned out, however, that he had decided his superior's plans were impracticable, and consequently determined to move south from Edward's station and get between me and my base. I, however, had no base, having abandoned it more than a week before. On the 15th Pemberton had actually marched south from Edward's station, but the rains had swollen Baker's Creek, which he had to cross, so much that he could not ford it, and the bridges were washed away. This brought him back to the Jackson road, on which there was a good bridge over Baker's Creek. Some of his troops were marching until midnight to get there. Receiving here early on the 16th a repetition of his order to join Johnston at Clinton, he concluded to obey, and sent a dispatch to his chief, informing him of the route by which he might be expected.

About five o'clock in the morning (16th) two men, who had been employed on the Jackson and Vicksburg railroad, were brought to me. They reported that they had passed through Pemberton's army in the night, and that it was still marching east. They reported him to have eighty regiments of infantry and ten batteries; in all, about twenty-five thousand men.

I had expected to leave Sherman at Jackson another day in order to complete his work; but getting the above information I sent him orders to move with all dispatch to Bolton, and to put one division with an ammunition train on the road at once, with directions to its commander to march with all possible speed until he came up to our rear. Within an hour after receiving this order Steele's division was on the road. At the same time I dispatched to Blair, who was near Auburn, to move with all speed to Edward's station. McClernand was directed to embrace Blair in his command for the present. Blair's division was a part of the 15th army corps (Sherman's); but as it was on its way to join its corps, it naturally struck our left first, now that we had faced about and were moving west. The 15th corps, when it got up, would be on our extreme right. McPherson was directed to get his trains out of the way of the troops, and to follow Hovey's division as closely as possible. McClernand had two roads about three miles apart, converging at Edward's station, over which to march his troops. Hovey's division of his corps had the advance on a third road (the Clinton) still farther north. McClernand was directed to move Blair's and A. J. Smith's divisions by the southernmost of these roads, and Osterhaus and Carr by the middle road. Orders were to move cautiously with skirmishers to the front to feel for the enemy.

Smith's division on the most southern road was the first to encounter the enemy's pickets, who were speedily driven in. Osterhaus, on the middle road, hearing the firing, pushed his skirmishers forward, found the enemy's pickets and forced them back to the main line. About the same time Hovey encountered the enemy on the northern or direct wagon road from Jackson to Vicksburg. McPherson was hastening up to join Hovey, but was embarrassed by Hovey's trains occupying the roads. I was still back at Clinton. McPherson sent me word of the situation, and expressed the wish that I was up. By half-past seven I was on the road and proceeded rapidly to the front, ordering all trains that were in front of troops off the road. When I arrived Hovey's skirmishing amounted almost to a battle.

McClernand was in person on the middle road and had a shorter distance to march to reach the enemy's position than McPherson. I sent him word by a staff officer to push forward and attack. These orders were repeated several times without apparently expediting McClernand's advance.

Champion's Hill, where Pemberton had chosen his position to receive us, whether taken by accident or design, was well selected. It is one of the highest points in that section, and commanded all the ground in range. On the east side of the ridge, which is quite precipitous, is a ravine running first north, then westerly, terminating at Baker's Creek. It was grown up thickly with large trees and undergrowth, making it difficult to penetrate with troops, even when not defended. The ridge occupied by the enemy terminated abruptly where the ravine turns westerly. The left of the enemy occupied the north end of this ridge. The Bolton and Edward's station wagon-road turns almost due south at this point and ascends the ridge, which it follows for about a mile; then turning west, descends by a gentle declivity to Baker's Creek, nearly a mile away. On the west side the slope of the ridge is gradual and is cultivated from near the summit to the creek. There was, when we were there, a narrow belt of timber near the summit west of the road.

From Raymond there is a direct road to Edward's station, some three miles west of Champion's Hill. There is one also to Bolton. From this latter road there is still another, leaving it about three and a half miles before reaching Bolton and leads direct to the same station. It was along these two roads that three divisions of McClernand's corps, and Blair of Sherman's, temporarily under McClernand, were moving. Hovey of McClernand's command was with McPherson, farther north on the road from Bolton direct to Edward's station. The middle road comes into the northern road at the point where the latter turns to the west and descends to Baker's Creek; the southern road is still several miles south and does

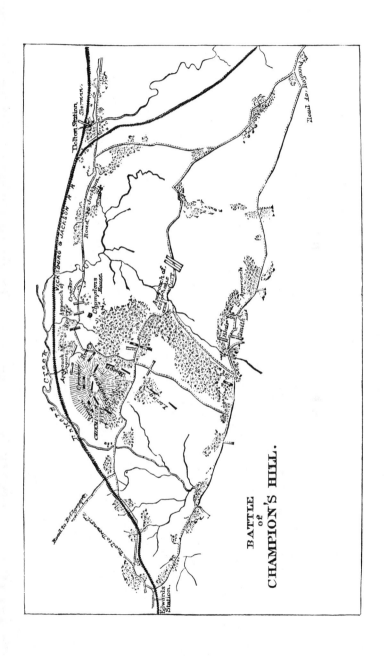

BATTLE
of
CHAMPION'S HILL.

not intersect the others until it reaches Edward's station. Pemberton's lines covered all these roads, and faced east. Hovey's line, when it first drove in the enemy's pickets, was formed parallel to that of the enemy and confronted his left.

By eleven o'clock the skirmishing had grown into a hard-contested battle. Hovey alone, before other troops could be got to assist him, had captured a battery of the enemy. But he was not able to hold his position and had to abandon the artillery. McPherson brought up his troops as fast as possible, Logan in front, and posted them on the right of Hovey and across the flank of the enemy. Logan reinforced Hovey with one brigade from his division; with his other two he moved farther west to make room for Crocker, who was coming up as rapidly as the roads would admit. Hovey was still being heavily pressed, and was calling on me for more reinforcements. I ordered Crocker, who was now coming up, to send one brigade from his division. McPherson ordered two batteries to be stationed where they nearly enfiladed the enemy's line, and they did good execution.

From Logan's position now a direct forward movement carried him over open fields, in rear of the enemy and in a line parallel with them. He did make exactly this move, attacking, however, the enemy through the belt of woods covering the west slope of the hill for a short distance. Up to this time I had kept my position near Hovey where we were the most heavily pressed; but about noon I moved with a part of my staff by our right around, until I came up with Logan himself. I found him near the road leading down to Baker's Creek. He was actually in command of the only road over which the enemy could retreat; Hovey, reinforced by two brigades from McPherson's command, confronted the enemy's left; Crocker, with two brigades, covered their left flank; McClernand two hours before, had been within two miles and a half of their centre with two divisions, and the two divisions, Blair's and A. J. Smith's, were confronting the rebel right; Ransom, with a brigade of McArthur's division of the 17th corps (McPherson's), had crossed the river at Grand Gulf a few days before, and was coming up on their right flank. Neither Logan nor I knew that we had cut off the retreat of the enemy. Just at this juncture a messenger came from Hovey, asking for more reinforcements. There were none to spare. I then gave an order to move McPherson's command by the left flank around to Hovey. This uncovered the rebel line of retreat, which was soon taken advantage of by the enemy.

During all this time, Hovey, reinforced as he was by a brigade from Logan and another from Crocker, and by Crocker gallantly coming up with two other brigades on his right, had made several assaults, the last one about the time the road was opened to the rear. The enemy fled precipitately. This was between three and four o'clock. I rode forward, or rather back, to where the middle road intersects the north road, and found the skirmishers of Carr's division just coming in. Osterhaus was farther south and soon after came up with skirmishers advanced in like manner. Hovey's division, and McPherson's two divisions with him, had marched and fought from early dawn, and were not in the best condition to follow the retreating foe. I sent orders to Osterhaus to pursue the enemy, and to Carr, whom I saw personally, I explained the situation and directed him to pursue vigorously as far as the Big Black, and to cross it if he could; Osterhaus to follow him. The pursuit was continued until after dark.

The battle of Champion's Hill lasted about four hours, hard fighting, preceded by two or three hours of skirmishing, some of which almost rose to the dignity of battle. Every man of Hovey's division and of McPherson's two divisions was engaged during the battle. No other part of my command was engaged at all, except that as described before. Osterhaus's and A. J. Smith's divisions had encountered the rebel advanced pickets as early as half-past seven. Their positions were admirable for advancing upon the enemy's line. McClernand, with two divisions, was within a few miles of the battle-field long before noon, and in easy hearing. I sent him repeated orders by staff officers fully competent to explain to him the situation. These traversed the wood separating us, without escort, and directed him to push forward; but he did not come. It is true, in front of McClernand there was a small force of the enemy and posted in a good position behind a ravine obstructing his advance; but if he had moved to the right by the road my staff officers had followed the enemy must either have fallen back or been cut off. Instead of this he sent orders to Hovey, who belonged to his corps, to join on to his right flank. Hovey was bearing the brunt of the battle at the time. To obey the order he would have had to pull out from the front of the enemy and march back as far as McClernand had to advance to get into battle, and substantially over the same ground. Of course I did not permit Hovey to obey the order of his intermediate superior.

We had in this battle about 15,000 men absolutely engaged. This excludes those that did not get up, all of McClernand's command except Hovey. Our loss was 410 killed, 1,844 wounded and 187 missing. Hovey alone lost 1,200 killed, wounded and missing—more than one-third of his division.

Had McClernand come up with reasonable promptness, or had I known the ground as I did afterwards, I cannot see how Pemberton could have escaped with any organized force. As it was he lost over three thousand killed and wounded and about three thousand captured in battle and in pursuit. Loring's division, which was the right of Pemberton's line, was cut off from the retreating army and never got back into Vicksburg. Pemberton himself fell back that night to the Big Black River. His troops did not stop before midnight and many of them left before the general retreat commenced, and no doubt a good part of them returned to their homes. Logan alone captured 1,300 prisoners and eleven guns. Hovey captured 300 under fire and about 700 in all, exclusive of 500 sick and wounded whom he paroled, thus making 1,200.

McPherson joined in the advance as soon as his men could fill their cartridge-boxes, leaving one brigade to guard our wounded. The pursuit was continued as long as it was light enough to see the road. The night of the 16th of May found McPherson's command bivouacked from two to six miles west of the battle-field, along the line of the road to Vicksburg. Carr and Osterhaus were at Edward's station, and Blair was about three miles south-east; Hovey remained on the field where his troops had fought so bravely and bled so freely. Much war material abandoned by the enemy was picked up on the battle-field, among it thirty pieces of artillery. I pushed through the advancing column with my staff and kept in advance until after night. Finding ourselves alone we stopped and took possession of a vacant house. As no troops came up we moved back a mile or more until we met the head of the column just going into bivouac on the road. We had no tents, so we occupied the porch of a house which had been taken for a rebel hospital and which was filled with wounded and dying who had been brought from the battle-field we had just left.

While a battle is raging one can see his enemy mowed down by the thousand, or the ten thousand, with great composure; but after the battle these scenes are distressing, and one is naturally disposed to do as much to alleviate the suffering of an enemy as a friend.

Chapter XXXVI.

BATTLE OF BLACK RIVER BRIDGE—CROSSING THE BIG
BLACK—INVESTMENT OF VICKSBURG—ASSAULTING
THE WORKS.

W E WERE now assured of our position between Johnston
and Pemberton, without a possibility of a junction of
their forces. Pemberton might have made a night march to the
Big Black, crossed the bridge there and, by moving north on
the west side, have eluded us and finally returned to Johnston.
But this would have given us Vicksburg. It would have been
his proper move, however, and the one Johnston would have
made had he been in Pemberton's place. In fact it would have
been in conformity with Johnston's orders to Pemberton.

Sherman left Jackson with the last of his troops about noon
on the 16th and reached Bolton, twenty miles west, before
halting. His rear guard did not get in until two A.M. the 17th,
but renewed their march by daylight. He paroled his prisoners at Jackson, and was forced to leave his own wounded in
care of surgeons and attendants. At Bolton he was informed
of our victory. He was directed to commence the march early
next day, and to diverge from the road he was on to Bridgeport on the Big Black River, some eleven miles above the
point where we expected to find the enemy. Blair was ordered
to join him there with the pontoon train as early as possible.

This movement brought Sherman's corps together, and at a
point where I hoped a crossing of the Big Black might be
effected and Sherman's corps used to flank the enemy out of
his position in our front, thus opening a crossing for the remainder of the army. I informed him that I would endeavor
to hold the enemy in my front while he crossed the river.

The advance division, Carr's (McClernand's corps), resumed the pursuit at half-past three A.M. on the 17th, followed closely by Osterhaus, McPherson bringing up the rear
with his corps. As I expected, the enemy was found in position on the Big Black. The point was only six miles from
that where my advance had rested for the night, and was
reached at an early hour. Here the river makes a turn to the

west, and has washed close up to the high land; the east side is a low bottom, sometimes overflowed at very high water, but was cleared and in cultivation. A bayou runs irregularly across this low land, the bottom of which, however, is above the surface of the Big Black at ordinary stages. When the river is full water runs through it, converting the point of land into an island. The bayou was grown up with timber, which the enemy had felled into the ditch. At this time there was a foot or two of water in it. The rebels had constructed a parapet along the inner bank of this bayou by using cotton bales from the plantation close by and throwing dirt over them. The whole was thoroughly commanded from the height west of the river. At the upper end of the bayou there was a strip of uncleared land which afforded a cover for a portion of our men. Carr's division was deployed on our right, Lawler's brigade forming his extreme right and reaching through these woods to the river above. Osterhaus' division was deployed to the left of Carr and covered the enemy's entire front. McPherson was in column on the road, the head close by, ready to come in wherever he could be of assistance.

While the troops were standing as here described an officer from Banks' staff came up and presented me with a letter from General Halleck, dated the 11th of May. It had been sent by the way of New Orleans to Banks to be forwarded to me. It ordered me to return to Grand Gulf and to co-operate from there with Banks against Port Hudson, and then to return with our combined forces to besiege Vicksburg. I told the officer that the order came too late, and that Halleck would not give it now if he knew our position. The bearer of the dispatch insisted that I ought to obey the order, and was giving arguments to support his position when I heard great cheering to the right of our line and, looking in that direction, saw Lawler in his shirt sleeves leading a charge upon the enemy. I immediately mounted my horse and rode in the direction of the charge, and saw no more of the officer who delivered the dispatch; I think not even to this day.

The assault was successful. But little resistance was made. The enemy fled from the west bank of the river, burning the

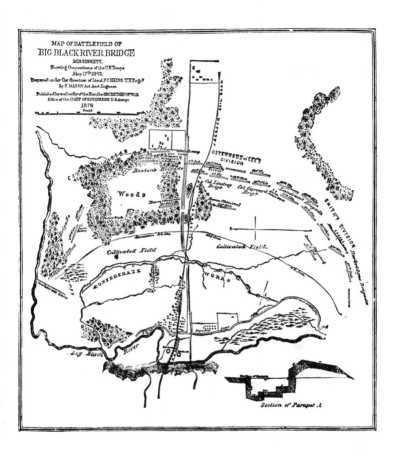

MAP OF BATTLEFIELD OF
BIG BLACK RIVER BRIDGE
MISSISSIPPI.
Showing the positions of the U.S. Troops
May 17th 1863.
Prepared under the direction of Lieut. P.C. HAINS U.S. Engr
by F. MASON Act Asst Engineer.
Published by authority of the Hon. the SECRETARY OF WAR
Office of the CHIEF OF ENGINEERS U.S. Army.
1876
Scale

Section of Parapet A

bridge behind him and leaving the men and guns on the east side to fall into our hands. Many tried to escape by swimming the river. Some succeeded and some were drowned in the attempt. Eighteen guns were captured and 1,751 prisoners. Our loss was 39 killed, 237 wounded and 3 missing. The enemy probably lost but few men except those captured and drowned. But for the successful and complete destruction of the bridge, I have but little doubt that we should have followed the enemy so closely as to prevent his occupying his defences around Vicksburg.

As the bridge was destroyed and the river was high, new bridges had to be built. It was but little after nine o'clock A.M. when the capture took place. As soon as work could be commenced, orders were given for the construction of three bridges. One was taken charge of by Lieutenant Hains, of the Engineer Corps, one by General McPherson himself and one by General Ransom, a most gallant and intelligent volunteer officer. My recollection is that Hains built a raft bridge; McPherson a pontoon, using cotton bales in large numbers, for pontoons; and that Ransom felled trees on opposite banks of the river, cutting only on one side of the tree, so that they would fall with their tops interlacing in the river, without the trees being entirely severed from their stumps. A bridge was then made with these trees to support the roadway. Lumber was taken from buildings, cotton gins and wherever found, for this purpose. By eight o'clock in the morning of the 18th all three bridges were complete and the troops were crossing.

Sherman reached Bridgeport about noon of the 17th and found Blair with the pontoon train already there. A few of the enemy were intrenched on the west bank, but they made little resistance and soon surrendered. Two divisions were crossed that night and the third the following morning.

On the 18th I moved along the Vicksburg road in advance of the troops and as soon as possible joined Sherman. My first anxiety was to secure a base of supplies on the Yazoo River above Vicksburg. Sherman's line of march led him to the very point on Walnut Hills occupied by the enemy the December before when he was repulsed. Sherman was equally anxious with myself. Our impatience led us to move in advance of the column and well up with the advanced skirmishers. There were some detached works along the crest of the hill. These were still occupied by the enemy, or else the garrison from Haines' Bluff had not all got past on their way to Vicksburg. At all events the bullets of the enemy whistled by thick and fast for a short time. In a few minutes Sherman had the plea-sure of looking down from the spot coveted so much by him the December before on the ground where his command had lain so helpless for offensive action. He turned to me, saying that up to this minute he had felt no positive assurance of success. This, however, he said was the end of one of the greatest campaigns in history and I ought to make a report of it at once. Vicksburg was not yet captured, and there was no telling what might happen before it was taken; but whether captured or not, this was a complete and successful campaign. I do not claim to quote Sherman's language; but the sub-stance only. My reason for mentioning this incident will appear further on.

McPherson, after crossing the Big Black, came into the Jackson and Vicksburg road which Sherman was on, but to his rear. He arrived at night near the lines of the enemy, and went into camp. McClernand moved by the direct road near the railroad to Mount Albans, and then turned to the left and put his troops on the road from Baldwin's ferry to Vicksburg. This brought him south of McPherson. I now had my three corps up to the works built for the defence of Vicksburg, on three roads—one to the north, one to the east and one to the south-east of the city. By the morning of the 19th the invest-ment was as complete as my limited number of troops would allow. Sherman was on the right, and covered the high ground from where it overlooked the Yazoo as far south-east as his troops would extend. McPherson joined on to his left, and occupied ground on both sides of the Jackson road. Mc-Clernand took up the ground to his left and extended as far towards Warrenton as he could, keeping a continuous line.

On the 19th there was constant skirmishing with the enemy while we were getting into better position. The enemy had been much demoralized by his defeats at Champion's Hill and the Big Black, and I believed he would not make much effort to hold Vicksburg. Accordingly, at two o'clock I ordered an assault. It resulted in securing more advanced positions for all our troops where they were fully covered from the fire of the enemy.

The 20th and 21st were spent in strengthening our position and in making roads in rear of the army, from Yazoo River or Chickasaw Bayou. Most of the army had now been for three weeks with only five days' rations issued by the commissary. They had an abundance of food, however, but began to feel the want of bread. I remember that in passing around to the left of the line on the 21st, a soldier, recognizing me, said in rather a low voice, but yet so that I heard him, "Hard tack." In a moment the cry was taken up all along the line, "Hard tack! Hard tack!" I told the men nearest to me that we had been engaged ever since the arrival of the troops in building a road over which to supply them with everything they needed. The cry was instantly changed to cheers. By the night of the 21st all the troops had full rations issued to them. The bread and coffee were highly appreciated.

I now determined on a second assault. Johnston was in my rear, only fifty miles away, with an army not much inferior in numbers to the one I had with me, and I knew he was being reinforced. There was danger of his coming to the assistance of Pemberton, and after all he might defeat my anticipations of capturing the garrison if, indeed, he did not prevent the capture of the city. The immediate capture of Vicksburg would save sending me the reinforcements which were so much wanted elsewhere, and would set free the army under me to drive Johnston from the State. But the first consideration of all was—the troops believed they could carry the works in their front, and would not have worked so patiently in the trenches if they had not been allowed to try.

The attack was ordered to commence on all parts of the line at ten o'clock A.M. on the 22d with a furious cannonade from every battery in position. All the corps commanders set their time by mine so that all might open the engagement at the same minute. The attack was gallant, and portions of each of the three corps succeeded in getting up to the very parapets of the enemy and in planting their battle flags upon them; but at no place were we able to enter. General McClernand reported that he had gained the enemy's intrenchments at several points, and wanted reinforcements. I occupied a position from which I believed I could see as well as he what took place in his front, and I did not see the success he reported. But his request for reinforcements being repeated I could not ignore it, and sent him Quinby's division of the 17th corps. Sherman and McPherson were both ordered to renew their assaults as a diversion in favor of McClernand. This last attack only served to increase our casualties without giving any benefit whatever. As soon as it was dark our troops that had reached the enemy's line and been obliged to remain there for security all day, were withdrawn; and thus ended the last assault upon Vicksburg.

Chapter XXXVII.

SIEGE OF VICKSBURG.

I NOW DETERMINED upon a regular siege—to "out-camp the enemy," as it were, and to incur no more losses. The experience of the 22d convinced officers and men that this was best, and they went to work on the defences and approaches with a will. With the navy holding the river, the investment of Vicksburg was complete. As long as we could hold our position the enemy was limited in supplies of food, men and munitions of war to what they had on hand. These could not last always.

The crossing of troops at Bruinsburg commenced April 30th. On the 18th of May the army was in rear of Vicksburg. On the 19th, just twenty days after the crossing, the city was completely invested and an assault had been made: five distinct battles (besides continuous skirmishing) had been fought and won by the Union forces; the capital of the State had fallen and its arsenals, military manufactories and everything useful for military purposes had been destroyed; an average of about one hundred and eighty miles had been marched by the troops engaged; but five days' rations had been issued, and no forage; over six thousand prisoners had been captured, and as many more of the enemy had been killed or wounded; twenty-seven heavy cannon and sixty-one field-pieces had fallen into our hands; and four hundred miles of the river, from Vicksburg to Port Hudson, had become ours. The Union force that had crossed the Mississippi River up to this time was less than forty-three thousand men. One division of these, Blair's, only arrived in time to take part in the battle of Champion's Hill, but was not engaged there; and one brigade, Ransom's of McPherson's corps, reached the field after the battle. The enemy had at Vicksburg, Grand Gulf, Jackson, and on the roads between these places, over sixty thousand men. They were in their own country, where no rear guards were necessary. The country is admirable for defence, but difficult for the conduct of an offensive campaign. All their troops had to be met. We were fortunate, to say the least, in meeting them in detail: at Port Gibson seven or eight thousand; at Raymond, five thousand; at Jackson, from eight to eleven thousand; at Champion's Hill, twenty-five thousand; at the Big Black, four thousand. A part of those met at Jackson were all that was left of those encountered at Raymond. They were beaten in detail by a force smaller than their own, upon their own ground. Our loss up to this time was:

AT	KILLED.	WOUNDED.	MISSING.
Port Gibson	131	719	25
South Fork Bayou Pierre .	. .	1	. .
Skirmishes, May 3	1	9	. .
Fourteen Mile Creek . . .	6	24	. .
Raymond	66	339	37
Jackson	42	251	7
Champion's Hill	410	1,844	187
Big Black	39	237	3
Bridgeport	. .	1	. .
Total	695	3,425	259

Of the wounded many were but slightly so, and continued on duty. Not half of them were disabled for any length of time.

After the unsuccessful assault of the 22d the work of the regular siege began. Sherman occupied the right starting from the river above Vicksburg, McPherson the centre (McArthur's division now with him) and McClernand the left, holding the road south to Warrenton. Lauman's division arrived at this time and was placed on the extreme left of the line.

In the interval between the assaults of the 19th and 22d, roads had been completed from the Yazoo River and Chickasaw Bayou, around the rear of the army, to enable us to bring up supplies of food and ammunition; ground had been selected and cleared on which the troops were to be encamped, and tents and cooking utensils were brought up. The troops had been without these from the time of crossing the Mississippi up to this time. All was now ready for the pick and spade. Prentiss and Hurlbut were ordered to send forward every man that could be spared. Cavalry especially was wanted to watch the fords along the Big Black, and to observe Johnston. I knew that Johnston was receiving reinforcements from Bragg, who was confronting Rosecrans in Tennessee. Vicksburg was so important to the enemy that I believed he would make the most strenuous efforts to raise the siege, even at the risk of losing ground elsewhere.

My line was more than fifteen miles long, extending from Haines' Bluff to Vicksburg, thence to Warrenton. The line of the enemy was about seven. In addition to this, having an enemy at Canton and Jackson, in our rear, who was being constantly reinforced, we required a second line of defence facing the other way. I had not troops enough under my command to man these. General Halleck appreciated the situation and, without being asked, forwarded reinforcements with all possible dispatch.

The ground about Vicksburg is admirable for defence. On the north it is about two hundred feet above the Mississippi River at the highest point and very much cut up by the washing rains; the ravines were grown up with cane and underbrush, while the sides and tops were covered with a dense forest. Farther south the ground flattens out somewhat, and was in cultivation. But here, too, it was cut up by ravines and small streams. The enemy's line of defence followed the crest of a ridge from the river north of the city eastward, then southerly around to the Jackson road, full three miles back of the city; thence in a southwesterly direction to the river. Deep ravines of the description given lay in front of these defences. As there is a succession of gullies, cut out by rains along the side of the ridge, the line was necessarily very irregular. To follow each of these spurs with intrenchments, so as to command the slopes on either side, would have lengthened their line very much. Generally therefore, or in many places, their line would run from near the head of one gully nearly straight to the head of another, and an outer work triangular in shape, generally open in the rear, was thrown up on the point; with a few men in this outer work they commanded the approaches to the main line completely.

The work to be done, to make our position as strong against the enemy as his was against us, was very great. The problem was also complicated by our wanting our line as near that of the enemy as possible. We had but four engineer officers with us. Captain Prime, of the Engineer Corps, was the chief, and the work at the beginning was mainly directed by him. His health soon gave out, when he was succeeded by Captain Comstock, also of the Engineer Corps. To provide assistants on such a long line I directed that all officers who had graduated at West Point, where they had necessarily to study military engineering, should in addition to their other duties assist in the work.

The chief quartermaster and the chief commissary were graduates. The chief commissary, now the Commissary-General of the Army, begged off, however, saying that there was nothing in engineering that he was good for unless he would do for a sap-roller. As soldiers require rations while working in the ditches as well as when marching and fighting, and as we would be sure to lose him if he was used as a sap-roller, I let him off. The general is a large man; weighs two hundred and twenty pounds, and is not tall.

We had no siege guns except six thirty-two pounders, and there were none at the West to draw from. Admiral Porter, however, supplied us with a battery of navy-guns of large calibre, and with these, and the field artillery used in the campaign, the siege began. The first thing to do was to get the artillery in batteries where they would occupy commanding positions; then establish the camps, under cover from the fire of the enemy but as near up as possible; and then construct rifle-pits and covered ways, to connect the entire command by the shortest route. The enemy did not harass us much while we were constructing our batteries. Probably their artillery ammunition was short; and their infantry was kept down by our sharpshooters, who were always on the alert and ready to fire at a head whenever it showed itself above the rebel works.

In no place were our lines more than six hundred yards from the enemy. It was necessary, therefore, to cover our men

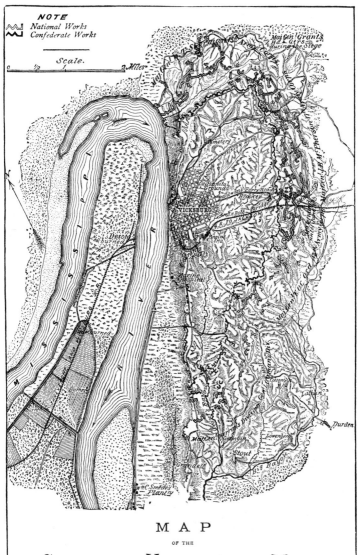

NOTE

National Works
Confederate Works

Scale.

0   ½   1   2 Miles

MAP

OF THE

SIEGE OF VICKSBURG, MISS.

From the 18th of May to the 4th of July, 1863.

by something more than the ordinary parapet. To give additional protection sand bags, bullet-proof, were placed along the tops of the parapets far enough apart to make loop-holes for musketry. On top of these, logs were put. By these means the men were enabled to walk about erect when off duty, without fear of annoyance from sharpshooters. The enemy used in their defence explosive musket-balls, no doubt thinking that, bursting over our men in the trenches, they would do some execution; but I do not remember a single case where a man was injured by a piece of one of these shells. When they were hit and the ball exploded, the wound was terrible. In these cases a solid ball would have hit as well. Their use is barbarous, because they produce increased suffering without any corresponding advantage to those using them.

The enemy could not resort to our method to protect their men, because we had an inexhaustible supply of ammunition to draw upon and used it freely. Splinters from the timber would have made havoc among the men behind.

There were no mortars with the besiegers, except what the navy had in front of the city; but wooden ones were made by taking logs of the toughest wood that could be found, boring them out for six or twelve pound shells and binding them with strong iron bands. These answered as coehorns, and shells were successfully thrown from them into the trenches of the enemy.

The labor of building the batteries and intrenching was largely done by the pioneers, assisted by negroes who came within our lines and who were paid for their work; but details from the troops had often to be made. The work was pushed forward as rapidly as possible, and when an advanced position was secured and covered from the fire of the enemy the batteries were advanced. By the 30th of June there were two hundred and twenty guns in position, mostly light field-pieces, besides a battery of heavy guns belonging to, manned and commanded by the navy. We were now as strong for defence against the garrison of Vicksburg as they were against us; but I knew that Johnston was in our rear, and was receiving constant reinforcements from the east. He had at this time a larger force than I had had at any time prior to the battle of Champion's Hill.

As soon as the news of the arrival of the Union army behind Vicksburg reached the North, floods of visitors began to pour in. Some came to gratify curiosity; some to see sons or brothers who had passed through the terrible ordeal; members of the Christian and Sanitary Associations came to minister to the wants of the sick and the wounded. Often those coming to see a son or brother would bring a dozen or two of poultry. They did not know how little the gift would be appreciated. Many of the soldiers had lived so much on chickens, ducks and turkeys without bread during the march, that the sight of poultry, if they could get bacon, almost took away their appetite. But the intention was good.

Among the earliest arrivals was the Governor of Illinois, with most of the State officers. I naturally wanted to show them what there was of most interest. In Sherman's front the ground was the most broken and most wooded, and more was to be seen without exposure. I therefore took them to Sherman's headquarters and presented them. Before starting out to look at the lines—possibly while Sherman's horse was being saddled—there were many questions asked about the late campaign, about which the North had been so imperfectly informed. There was a little knot around Sherman and another around me, and I heard Sherman repeating, in the most animated manner, what he had said to me when we first looked down from Walnut Hills upon the land below on the 18th of May, adding: "Grant is entitled to every bit of the credit for the campaign; I opposed it. I wrote him a letter about it." But for this speech it is not likely that Sherman's opposition would have ever been heard of. His untiring energy and great efficiency during the campaign entitle him to a full share of all the credit due for its success. He could not have done more if the plan had been his own.

NOTE.—When General Sherman first learned of the move I proposed to make, he called to see me about it. I recollect that I had transferred my headquarters from a boat in the river to a house a short distance back from the levee. I was seated on the piazza engaged in conversation with my staff when Sherman came up. After a few moments' conversation he said that he would like to see me alone. We passed into the house together and shut the door after us. Sherman then expressed his alarm at the move I had ordered, saying that I was putting myself in a position voluntarily which an enemy

On the 26th of May I sent Blair's division up the Yazoo to drive out a force of the enemy supposed to be between the Big Black and the Yazoo. The country was rich and full of supplies of both food and forage. Blair was instructed to take all of it. The cattle were to be driven in for the use of our army, and the food and forage to be consumed by our troops or destroyed by fire; all bridges were to be destroyed, and the roads rendered as nearly impassable as possible. Blair went

---

would be glad to manœuvre a year—or a long time—to get me in. I was going into the enemy's country, with a large river behind me and the enemy holding points strongly fortified above and below. He said that it was an axiom in war that when any great body of troops moved against an enemy they should do so from a base of supplies, which they would guard as they would the apple of the eye, etc. He pointed out all the difficulties that might be encountered in the campaign proposed, and stated in turn what would be the true campaign to make. This was, in substance, to go back until high ground could be reached on the east bank of the river; fortify there and establish a depot of supplies, and move from there, being always prepared to fall back upon it in case of disaster. I said this would take us back to Memphis. Sherman then said that was the very place he would go to, and would move by railroad from Memphis to Grenada, repairing the road as we advanced. To this I replied, the country is already disheartened over the lack of success on the part of our armies; the last election went against the vigorous prosecution of the war, voluntary enlistments had ceased throughout most of the North and conscription was already resorted to, and if we went back so far as Memphis it would discourage the people so much that bases of supplies would be of no use: neither men to hold them nor supplies to put in them would be furnished. The problem for us was to move forward to a decisive victory, or our cause was lost. No progress was being made in any other field, and we had to go on.

Sherman wrote to my adjutant general, Colonel J. A. Rawlins, embodying his views of the campaign that should be made, and asking him to advise me to at least get the views of my generals upon the subject. Colonel Rawlins showed me the letter, but I did not see any reason for changing my plans. The letter was not answered and the subect was not subsequently mentioned between Sherman and myself to the end of the war, that I remember of. I did not regard the letter as official, and consequently did not preserve it. General Sherman furnished a copy himself to General Badeau, who printed it in his history of my campaigns. I did not regard either the conversation between us or the letter to my adjutant-general as protests, but simply friendly advice which the relations between us fully justified. Sherman gave the same energy to make the campaign a success that he would or could have done if it had been ordered by himself. I make this statement here to correct an impression which was circulated at the close of the war to Sherman's prejudice, and for which there was no fair foundation.

forty-five miles and was gone almost a week. His work was effectually done. I requested Porter at this time to send the marine brigade, a floating nondescript force which had been assigned to his command and which proved very useful, up to Haines' Bluff to hold it until reinforcements could be sent.

On the 26th I also received a letter from Banks, asking me to reinforce him with ten thousand men at Port Hudson. Of course I could not comply with his request, nor did I think he needed them. He was in no danger of an attack by the garrison in his front, and there was no army organizing in his rear to raise the siege.

On the 3d of June a brigade from Hurlbut's command arrived, General Kimball commanding. It was sent to Mechanicsburg, some miles north-east of Haines' Bluff and about midway between the Big Black and the Yazoo. A brigade of Blair's division and twelve hundred cavalry had already, on Blair's return from the Yazoo, been sent to the same place with instructions to watch the crossings of the Big Black River, to destroy the roads in his (Blair's) front, and to gather or destroy all supplies.

On the 7th of June our little force of colored and white troops across the Mississippi, at Milliken's Bend, were attacked by about 3,000 men from Richard Taylor's trans-Mississippi command. With the aid of the gunboats they were speedily repelled. I sent Mower's brigade over with instructions to drive the enemy beyond the Tensas Bayou; and we had no further trouble in that quarter during the siege. This was the first important engagement of the war in which colored troops were under fire. These men were very raw, having all been enlisted since the beginning of the siege, but they behaved well.

On the 8th of June a full division arrived from Hurlbut's command, under General Sooy Smith. It was sent immediately to Haines' Bluff, and General C. C. Washburn was assigned to the general command at that point.

On the 11th a strong division arrived from the Department of the Missouri under General Herron, which was placed on our left. This cut off the last possible chance of communication between Pemberton and Johnston, as it enabled

Lauman to close up on McClernand's left while Herron in-trenched from Lauman to the water's edge. At this point the water recedes a few hundred yards from the high land. Through this opening no doubt the Confederate commanders had been able to get messengers under cover of night.

On the 14th General Parke arrived with two divisions of Burnside's corps, and was immediately dispatched to Haines' Bluff. These latter troops—Herron's and Parke's—were the reinforcements already spoken of sent by Halleck in anticipa-tion of their being needed. They arrived none too soon.

I now had about seventy-one thousand men. More than half were disposed across the peninsula, between the Yazoo at Haines' Bluff and the Big Black, with the division of Oster-haus watching the crossings of the latter river farther south and west from the crossing of the Jackson road to Baldwin's ferry and below.

There were eight roads leading into Vicksburg, along which and their immediate sides, our work was specially pushed and batteries advanced; but no commanding point within range of the enemy was neglected.

On the 17th I received a letter from General Sherman and one on the 18th from General McPherson, saying that their respective commands had complained to them of a fulsome, congratulatory order published by General McClernand to the 13th corps, which did great injustice to the other troops engaged in the campaign. This order had been sent North and published, and now papers containing it had reached our camps. The order had not been heard of by me, and certainly not by troops outside of McClernand's command until brought in this way. I at once wrote to McClernand, direct-ing him to send me a copy of this order. He did so, and I at once relieved him from the command of the 13th army corps and ordered him back to Springfield, Illinois. The publication of his order in the press was in violation of War Department orders and also of mine.

Chapter XXXVIII.

O N THE 22D of June positive information was received
that Johnston had crossed the Big Black River for
the purpose of attacking our rear, to raise the siege and release Pemberton. The correspondence between Johnston and
Pemberton shows that all expectation of holding Vicksburg had by this time passed from Johnston's mind. I
immediately ordered Sherman to the command of all the
forces from Haines' Bluff to the Big Black River. This
amounted now to quite half the troops about Vicksburg. Besides these, Herron and A. J. Smith's divisions were ordered
to hold themselves in readiness to reinforce Sherman.
Haines' Bluff had been strongly fortified on the land side,
and on all commanding points from there to the Big Black
at the railroad crossing batteries had been constructed. The
work of connecting by rifle-pits where this was not already
done, was an easy task for the troops that were to defend
them.

We were now looking west, besieging Pemberton, while
we were also looking east to defend ourselves against an expected siege by Johnston. But as against the garrison of
Vicksburg we were as substantially protected as they were
against us. Where we were looking east and north we were
strongly fortified, and on the defensive. Johnston evidently
took in the situation and wisely, I think, abstained from
making an assault on us because it would simply have inflicted loss on both sides without accomplishing any result.
We were strong enough to have taken the offensive against
him; but I did not feel disposed to take any risk of losing
our hold upon Pemberton's army, while I would have re-

joiced at the opportunity of defending ourselves against an attack by Johnston.

From the 23d of May the work of fortifying and pushing forward our position nearer to the enemy had been steadily progressing. At three points on the Jackson road, in front of Leggett's brigade, a sap was run up to the enemy's parapet, and by the 25th of June we had it undermined and the mine charged. The enemy had countermined, but did not succeed in reaching our mine. At this particular point the hill on which the rebel work stands rises abruptly. Our sap ran close up to the outside of the enemy's parapet. In fact this parapet was also our protection. The soldiers of the two sides occasionally conversed pleasantly across this barrier; sometimes they exchanged the hard bread of the Union soldiers for the tobacco of the Confederates; at other times the enemy threw over hand-grenades, and often our men, catching them in their hands, returned them.

Our mine had been started some distance back down the hill; consequently when it had extended as far as the parapet it was many feet below it. This caused the failure of the enemy in his search to find and destroy it. On the 25th of June at three o'clock, all being ready, the mine was exploded. A heavy artillery fire all along the line had been ordered to open with the explosion. The effect was to blow the top of the hill off and make a crater where it stood. The breach was not sufficient to enable us to pass a column of attack through. In fact, the enemy having failed to reach our mine had thrown up a line farther back, where most of the men guarding that point were placed. There were a few men, however, left at the advance line, and others working in the countermine, which was still being pushed to find ours. All that were there were thrown into the air, some of them coming down on our side, still alive. I remember one colored man, who had been under ground at work when the explosion took place, who was thrown to our side. He was not much hurt, but terribly frightened. Some one asked him how high he had gone up. "Dun no, massa, but t'ink 'bout t'ree mile," was his reply. General Logan commanded at this point and took this colored man to his quarters, where he did service to the end of the siege.

As soon as the explosion took place the crater was seized by two regiments of our troops who were near by, under cover, where they had been placed for the express purpose. The enemy made a desperate effort to expel them, but failed, and soon retired behind the new line. From here, however, they threw hand-grenades, which did some execution. The compliment was returned by our men, but not with so much effect. The enemy could lay their grenades on the parapet, which alone divided the contestants, and roll them down upon us; while from our side they had to be thrown over the parapet, which was at considerable elevation. During the night we made efforts to secure our position in the crater against the missiles of the enemy, so as to run trenches along the outer base of their parapet, right and left; but the enemy continued throwing their grenades, and brought boxes of field ammunition (shells), the fuses of which they would light with port-fires, and throw them by hand into our ranks. We found it impossible to continue this work. Another mine was consequently started which was exploded on the 1st of July, destroying an entire rebel redan, killing and wounding a considerable number of its occupants and leaving an immense chasm where it stood. No attempt to charge was made this time, the experience of the 25th admonishing us. Our loss in the first affair was about thirty killed and wounded. The enemy must have lost more in the two explosions than we did in the first. We lost none in the second.

From this time forward the work of mining and pushing our position nearer to the enemy was prosecuted with vigor, and I determined to explode no more mines until we were ready to explode a number at different points and assault immediately after. We were up now at three different points, one in front of each corps, to where only the parapet of the enemy divided us.

At this time an intercepted dispatch from Johnston to Pemberton informed me that Johnston intended to make a determined attack upon us in order to relieve the garrison at Vicksburg. I knew the garrison would make no formidable effort to relieve itself. The picket lines were so close to each other—where there was space enough between the lines to post pickets—that the men could converse. On the 21st of

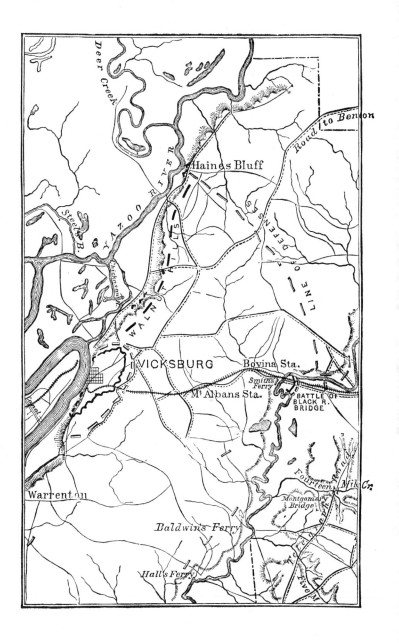

June I was informed, through this means, that Pemberton was preparing to escape, by crossing to the Louisiana side under cover of night; that he had employed workmen in making boats for that purpose; that the men had been canvassed to ascertain if they would make an assault on the "Yankees" to cut their way out; that they had refused, and almost mutinied, because their commander would not surrender and relieve their sufferings, and had only been pacified by the assurance that boats enough would be finished in a week to carry them all over. The rebel pickets also said that houses in the city had been pulled down to get material to build these boats with. Afterwards this story was verified: on entering the city we found a large number of very rudely constructed boats.

All necessary steps were at once taken to render such an attempt abortive. Our pickets were doubled; Admiral Porter was notified, so that the river might be more closely watched; material was collected on the west bank of the river to be set on fire and light up the river if the attempt was made; and batteries were established along the levee crossing the peninsula on the Louisiana side. Had the attempt been made the garrison of Vicksburg would have been drowned, or made prisoners on the Louisiana side. General Richard Taylor was expected on the west bank to co-operate in this movement, I believe, but he did not come, nor could he have done so with a force sufficient to be of service. The Mississippi was now in our possession from its source to its mouth, except in the immediate front of Vicksburg and of Port Hudson. We had nearly exhausted the country, along a line drawn from Lake Providence to opposite Bruinsburg. The roads west were not of a character to draw supplies over for any considerable force.

By the 1st of July our approaches had reached the enemy's ditch at a number of places. At ten points we could move under cover to within from five to one hundred yards of the enemy. Orders were given to make all preparations for assault on the 6th of July. The debouches were ordered widened to afford easy egress, while the approaches were also to be widened to admit the troops to pass through four abreast. Plank, and bags filled with cotton packed in tightly, were ordered prepared, to enable the troops to cross the ditches.

On the night of the 1st of July Johnston was between Brownsville and the Big Black, and wrote Pemberton from there that about the 7th of the month an attempt would be made to create a diversion to enable him to cut his way out. Pemberton was a prisoner before this message reached him.

On July 1st Pemberton, seeing no hope of outside relief, addressed the following letter to each of his four division commanders:

"Unless the siege of Vicksburg is raised, or supplies are thrown in, it will become necessary very shortly to evacuate the place. I see no prospect of the former, and there are many great, if not insuperable obstacles in the way of the latter. You are, therefore, requested to inform me with as little delay as possible, as to the condition of your troops and their ability to make the marches and undergo the fatigues necessary to accomplish a successful evacuation."

Two of his generals suggested surrender, and the other two practically did the same. They expressed the opinion that an attempt to evacuate would fail. Pemberton had previously got a message to Johnston suggesting that he should try to negotiate with me for a release of the garrison with their arms. Johnston replied that it would be a confession of weakness for him to do so; but he authorized Pemberton to use his name in making such an arrangement.

On the 3d about ten o'clock A.M. white flags appeared on a portion of the rebel works. Hostilities along that part of the line ceased at once. Soon two persons were seen coming towards our lines bearing a white flag. They proved to be General Bowen, a division commander, and Colonel Montgomery, aide-de-camp to Pemberton, bearing the following letter to me:

"I have the honor to propose an armistice for —— hours, with the view to arranging terms for the capitulation of Vicksburg. To this end, if agreeable to you, I will appoint three commissioners, to meet a like number to be named by yourself, at such place and hour to-day as you may find convenient. I make this proposition to save the further effusion of blood, which must otherwise be shed to a frightful extent, feeling myself fully able to maintain my position for a yet indefinite period. This communication will be handed you under a flag of truce, by Major-General John S. Bowen."

It was a glorious sight to officers and soldiers on the line where these white flags were visible, and the news soon spread to all parts of the command. The troops felt that their long and weary marches, hard fighting, ceaseless watching by night and day, in a hot climate, exposure to all sorts of weather, to diseases and, worst of all, to the gibes of many Northern papers that came to them saying all their suffering was in vain, that Vicksburg would never be taken, were at last at an end and the Union sure to be saved.

Bowen was received by General A. J. Smith, and asked to see me. I had been a neighbor of Bowen's in Missouri, and knew him well and favorably before the war; but his request was refused. He then suggested that I should meet Pemberton. To this I sent a verbal message saying that, if Pemberton desired it, I would meet him in front of McPherson's corps at three o'clock that afternoon. I also sent the following written reply to Pemberton's letter:

"Your note of this date is just received, proposing an armistice for several hours, for the purpose of arranging terms of capitulation through commissioners, to be appointed, etc. The useless effusion of blood you propose stopping by this course can be ended at any time you may choose, by the unconditional surrender of the city and garrison. Men who have shown so much endurance and courage as those now in Vicksburg, will always challenge the respect of an adversary, and I can assure you will be treated with all the respect due to prisoners of war. I do not favor the proposition of appointing commissioners to arrange the terms of capitulation, because I have no terms other than those indicated above."

At three o'clock Pemberton appeared at the point suggested in my verbal message, accompanied by the same officers who had borne his letter of the morning. Generals Ord, McPherson, Logan and A. J. Smith, and several officers of my staff, accompanied me. Our place of meeting was on a hillside within a few hundred feet of the rebel lines. Near by stood a stunted oak-tree, which was made historical by the event. It was but a short time before the last vestige of its body, root and limb had disappeared, the fragments taken as trophies. Since then the same tree has furnished as many cords of wood, in the shape of trophies, as "The True Cross."

Pemberton and I had served in the same division during part of the Mexican War. I knew him very well therefore, and greeted him as an old acquaintance. He soon asked what terms I proposed to give his army if it surrendered. My answer was the same as proposed in my reply to his letter. Pemberton then said, rather snappishly, "The conference might as well end," and turned abruptly as if to leave. I said, "Very well." General Bowen, I saw, was very anxious that the surrender should be consummated. His manner and remarks while Pemberton and I were talking, showed this. He now proposed that he and one of our generals should have a conference. I had no objection to this, as nothing could be made binding upon me that they might propose. Smith and Bowen accordingly had a conference, during which Pemberton and I, moving a short distance away towards the enemy's lines were in conversation. After a while Bowen suggested that the Confederate army should be allowed to march out with the honors of war, carrying their small arms and field artillery. This was promptly and unceremoniously rejected. The interview here ended, I agreeing, however, to send a letter giving final terms by ten o'clock that night.

Word was sent to Admiral Porter soon after the correspondence with Pemberton commenced, so that hostilities might be stopped on the part of both army and navy. It was agreed on my parting with Pemberton that they should not be renewed until our correspondence ceased.

When I returned to my headquarters I sent for all the corps and division commanders with the army immediately confronting Vicksburg. Half the army was from eight to twelve miles off, waiting for Johnston. I informed them of the contents of Pemberton's letters, of my reply and the substance of the interview, and that I was ready to hear any suggestion; but would hold the power of deciding entirely in my own hands. This was the nearest approach to a "council of war" I ever held. Against the general, and almost unanimous judgment of the council I sent the following letter:

"In conformity with agreement of this afternoon, I will submit the following proposition for the surrender of the City of Vicksburg, public stores, etc. On your accepting the terms proposed, I will march in one division as a guard, and take possession at eight A.M. to-morrow. As soon as rolls can be made out, and paroles be signed by officers and men, you will be allowed to march out of our lines, the officers taking with them their side-arms and clothing, and the field, staff and cavalry officers one horse each. The rank and file will be allowed all their clothing, but no other property. If these conditions are accepted, any amount of rations you may deem necessary can be taken from the stores you now have, and also the necessary cooking utensils for preparing them. Thirty wagons also, counting two two-horse or mule teams as one, will be allowed to transport such articles as cannot be carried along. The same conditions will be allowed to all sick and wounded officers and soldiers as fast as they become able to travel. The paroles for these latter must be signed, however, whilst officers present are authorized to sign the roll of prisoners."

By the terms of the cartel then in force, prisoners captured by either army were required to be forwarded as soon as possible to either Aiken's landing below Dutch Gap on the James River, or to Vicksburg, there to be exchanged, or paroled until they could be exchanged. There was a Confederate commissioner at Vicksburg, authorized to make the exchange. I did not propose to take him a prisoner, but to leave him free to perform the functions of his office. Had I insisted upon an unconditional surrender there would have been over thirty thousand men to transport to Cairo, very much to the inconvenience of the army on the Mississippi. Thence the prisoners would have had to be transported by rail to Washington or Baltimore; thence again by steamer to Aiken's—all at very great expense. At Aiken's they would have had to be paroled, because the Confederates did not have Union prisoners to give in exchange. Then again Pemberton's army was largely composed of men whose homes were in the South-west; I knew many of them were tired of the war and would get home just as soon as they could. A large number of them had voluntarily come into our lines during the siege, and requested to be sent north where they could get employment until the war was over and they could go to their homes.

Late at night I received the following reply to my last letter:

"I have the honor to acknowledge the receipt of your communication of this date, proposing terms of capitulation for this garrison and post. In the main your terms are accepted; but, in justice both to the honor and spirit of my troops, manifested in the defence of Vicksburg, I have to submit the following amendments, which, if acceded to by you, will perfect the agreement between us. At ten o'clock A.M. to-morrow, I propose to evacuate the works in and around Vicksburg, and to surrender the city and garrison under my command, by marching out with my colors and arms, stacking them in front of my present lines. After which you will take possession. Officers to retain their side-arms and personal property, and the rights and property of citizens to be respected."

This was received after midnight. My reply was as follows:

"I have the honor to acknowledge the receipt of your communication of 3d July. The amendment proposed by you cannot be acceded to in full. It will be necessary to furnish every officer and man with a parole signed by himself, which, with the completion of the roll of prisoners, will necessarily take some time. Again, I can make no stipulations with regard to the treatment of citizens and their private property. While I do not propose to cause them any undue annoyance or loss, I cannot consent to leave myself under any restraint by stipulations. The property which officers will be allowed to take with them will be as stated in my proposition of last evening; that is, officers will be allowed their private baggage and side-arms, and mounted officers one horse each. If you mean by your proposition for each brigade to march to the front of the lines now occupied by it, and stack arms at ten o'clock A.M., and then return to the inside and there remain as prisoners until properly paroled, I will make no objection to it. Should no notification be received of your acceptance of my terms by nine o'clock A.M. I shall regard them as having been rejected, and shall act accordingly. Should these terms be accepted, white flags should be displayed along your lines to prevent such of my troops as may not have been notified, from firing upon your men."

Pemberton promptly accepted these terms.

During the siege there had been a good deal of friendly sparring between the soldiers of the two armies, on picket and where the lines were close together. All rebels were known as "Johnnies," all Union troops as "Yanks." Often "Johnny" would call: "Well, Yank, when are you coming into town?"

The reply was sometimes: "We propose to celebrate the 4th of July there." Sometimes it would be: "We always treat our prisoners with kindness and do not want to hurt them;" or, "We are holding you as prisoners of war while you are feeding yourselves." The garrison, from the commanding general down, undoubtedly expected an assault on the fourth. They knew from the temper of their men it would be successful when made; and that would be a greater humiliation than to surrender. Besides it would be attended with severe loss to them.

The Vicksburg paper, which we received regularly through the courtesy of the rebel pickets, said prior to the fourth, in speaking of the "Yankee" boast that they would take dinner in Vicksburg that day, that the best receipt for cooking a rabbit was "First ketch your rabbit." The paper at this time and for some time previous was printed on the plain side of wall paper. The last number was issued on the fourth and announced that we had "caught our rabbit."

I have no doubt that Pemberton commenced his correspondence on the third with a two-fold purpose: first, to avoid an assault, which he knew would be successful, and second, to prevent the capture taking place on the great national holiday, the anniversary of the Declaration of American Independence. Holding out for better terms as he did he defeated his aim in the latter particular.

At the appointed hour the garrison of Vicksburg marched out of their works and formed line in front, stacked arms and marched back in good order. Our whole army present witnessed this scene without cheering. Logan's division, which had approached nearest the rebel works, was the first to march in; and the flag of one of the regiments of his division was soon floating over the court-house. Our soldiers were no sooner inside the lines than the two armies began to fraternize. Our men had had full rations from the time the siege commenced, to the close. The enemy had been suffering, particularly towards the last. I myself saw our men taking bread from their haversacks and giving it to the enemy they had so recently been engaged in starving out. It was accepted with avidity and with thanks.

Pemberton says in his report:

"If it should be asked why the 4th of July was selected as the day for surrender, the answer is obvious. I believed that upon that day I should obtain better terms. Well aware of the vanity of our foe, I knew they would attach vast importance to the entrance on the 4th of July into the stronghold of the great river, and that, to gratify their national vanity, they would yield then what could not be extorted from them at any other time."

This does not support my view of his reasons for selecting the day he did for surrendering. But it must be recollected that his first letter asking terms was received about 10 o'clock A.M., July 3d. It then could hardly be expected that it would take twenty-four hours to effect a surrender. He knew that Johnston was in our rear for the purpose of raising the siege, and he naturally would want to hold out as long as he could. He knew his men would not resist an assault, and one was expected on the fourth. In our interview he told me he had rations enough to hold out for some time—my recollection is two weeks. It was this statement that induced me to insert in the terms that he was to draw rations for his men from his own supplies.

On the 4th of July General Holmes, with an army of eight or nine thousand men belonging to the trans-Mississippi department, made an attack upon Helena, Arkansas. He was totally defeated by General Prentiss, who was holding Helena with less than forty-two hundred soldiers. Holmes reported his loss at 1,636, of which 173 were killed; but as Prentiss buried 400, Holmes evidently understated his losses. The Union loss was 57 killed, 127 wounded, and between 30 and 40 missing. This was the last effort on the part of the Confederacy to raise the siege of Vicksburg.

On the third, as soon as negotiations were commenced, I notified Sherman and directed him to be ready to take the offensive against Johnston, drive him out of the State and destroy his army if he could. Steele and Ord were directed at the same time to be in readiness to join Sherman as soon as the surrender took place. Of this Sherman was notified.

I rode into Vicksburg with the troops, and went to the river to exchange congratulations with the navy upon our joint victory. At that time I found that many of the citizens had been living under ground. The ridges upon which Vicksburg is built, and those back to the Big Black, are composed of a deep yellow clay of great tenacity. Where roads and streets are cut through, perpendicular banks are left and stand as well as if composed of stone. The magazines of the enemy were made by running passage-ways into this clay at places where there were deep cuts. Many citizens secured places of safety for their families by carving out rooms in these embankments. A door-way in these cases would be cut in a high bank, starting from the level of the road or street, and after running in a few feet a room of the size required was carved out of the clay, the dirt being removed by the door-way. In some instances I saw where two rooms were cut out, for a single family, with a door-way in the clay wall separating them. Some of these were carpeted and furnished with considerable elaboration. In these the occupants were fully secure from the shells of the navy, which were dropped into the city night and day without intermission.

I returned to my old headquarters outside in the afternoon, and did not move into the town until the sixth. On the afternoon of the fourth I sent Captain Wm. M. Dunn of my staff to Cairo, the nearest point where the telegraph could be reached, with a dispatch to the general-in-chief. It was as follows:

"The enemy surrendered this morning. The only terms allowed is their parole as prisoners of war. This I regard as a great advantage to us at this moment. It saves, probably, several days in the capture, and leaves troops and transports ready for immediate service. Sherman, with a large force, moves immediately on Johnston, to drive him from the State. I will send troops to the relief of Banks, and return the 9th army corps to Burnside."

This news, with the victory at Gettysburg won the same day, lifted a great load of anxiety from the minds of the President, his Cabinet and the loyal people all over the North. The fate of the Confederacy was sealed when Vicksburg fell. Much hard fighting was to be done afterwards and many precious lives were to be sacrificed; but the *morale* was with the supporters of the Union ever after.

I at the same time wrote to General Banks informing him of the fall and sending him a copy of the terms; also saying I would send him all the troops he wanted to insure the capture of the only foothold the enemy now had on the Mississippi River. General Banks had a number of copies of this letter printed, or at least a synopsis of it, and very soon a copy fell into the hands of General Gardner, who was then in command of Port Hudson. Gardner at once sent a letter to the commander of the National forces saying that he had been informed of the surrender of Vicksburg and telling how the information reached him. He added that if this was true, it was useless for him to hold out longer. General Banks gave him assurances that Vicksburg had been surrendered, and General Gardner surrendered unconditionally on the 9th of July. Port Hudson with nearly 6,000 prisoners, 51 guns, 5,000 small-arms and other stores fell into the hands of the Union forces: from that day to the close of the rebellion the Mississippi River, from its source to its mouth, remained in the control of the National troops.

Pemberton and his army were kept in Vicksburg until the whole could be paroled. The paroles were in duplicate, by organization (one copy for each, Federals and Confederates), and signed by the commanding officers of the companies or regiments. Duplicates were also made for each soldier and signed by each individually, one to be retained by the soldier signing and one to be retained by us. Several hundred refused to sign their paroles, preferring to be sent to the North as prisoners to being sent back to fight again. Others again kept out of the way, hoping to escape either alternative.

Pemberton appealed to me in person to compel these men to sign their paroles, but I declined. It also leaked out that many of the men who had signed their paroles, intended to desert and go to their homes as soon as they got out of our lines. Pemberton hearing this, again appealed to me to assist him. He wanted arms for a battalion, to act as guards in keeping his men together while being marched to a camp of instruction, where he expected to keep them until exchanged. This request was also declined. It was precisely what I expected and hoped that they would do. I told him, however, that I would see that they marched beyond our lines in good order. By the eleventh, just one week after the surrender, the paroles were completed and the Confederate garrison marched out. Many deserted, and fewer of them were ever returned to the ranks to fight again than would have been the case had the surrender been unconditional and the prisoners sent to the James River to be paroled.

As soon as our troops took possession of the city guards were established along the whole line of parapet, from the river above to the river below. The prisoners were allowed to occupy their old camps behind the intrenchments. No restraint was put upon them, except by their own commanders. They were rationed about as our own men, and from our supplies. The men of the two armies fraternized as if they had been fighting for the same cause. When they passed out of the works they had so long and so gallantly defended, between lines of their late antagonists, not a cheer went up, not a remark was made that would give pain. Really, I believe there was a feeling of sadness just then in the breasts of most of the Union soldiers at seeing the dejection of their late antagonists.

The day before the departure the following order was issued:

"Paroled prisoners will be sent out of here to-morrow. They will be authorized to cross at the railroad bridge, and move from there to Edward's Ferry,* and on by way of Raymond. Instruct the commands to be orderly and quiet as these prisoners pass, to make no offensive remarks, and not to harbor any who fall out of ranks after they have passed."

---

*Meant Edward's Station.

Chapter XXXIX.

RETROSPECT OF THE CAMPAIGN—SHERMAN'S
MOVEMENTS—PROPOSED MOVEMENT UPON MOBILE—A
PAINFUL ACCIDENT—ORDERED TO REPORT AT CAIRO.

THE CAPTURE of Vicksburg, with its garrison, ordnance and ordnance stores, and the successful battles fought in reaching them, gave new spirit to the loyal people of the North. New hopes for the final success of the cause of the Union were inspired. The victory gained at Gettysburg, upon the same day, added to their hopes. Now the Mississippi River was entirely in the possession of the National troops; for the fall of Vicksburg gave us Port Hudson at once. The army of northern Virginia was driven out of Pennsylvania and forced back to about the same ground it occupied in 1861. The Army of the Tennessee united with the Army of the Gulf, dividing the Confederate States completely.

The first dispatch I received from the government after the fall of Vicksburg was in these words:

"I fear your paroling the prisoners at Vicksburg, without actual delivery to a proper agent as required by the seventh article of the cartel, may be construed into an absolute release, and that the men will immediately be placed in the ranks of the enemy. Such has been the case elsewhere. If these prisoners have not been allowed to depart, you will detain them until further orders."

Halleck did not know that they had already been delivered into the hands of Major Watts, Confederate commissioner for the exchange of prisoners.

At Vicksburg 31,600 prisoners were surrendered, together with 172 cannon, about 60,000 muskets and a large amount of ammunition. The small-arms of the enemy were far superior to the bulk of ours. Up to this time our troops at the West had been limited to the old United States flint-lock muskets changed into percussion, or the Belgian musket imported early in the war—almost as dangerous to the person firing it as to the one aimed at—and a few new and improved arms. These were of many different calibers, a fact that caused much trouble in distributing ammunition during an engagement. The enemy had generally new arms which had run the blockade and were of uniform caliber. After the surrender I authorized all colonels whose regiments were armed with inferior muskets, to place them in the stack of captured arms and replace them with the latter. A large number of arms turned in to the Ordnance Department as captured, were thus arms that had really been used by the Union army in the capture of Vicksburg.

In this narrative I have not made the mention I should like of officers, dead and alive, whose services entitle them to special mention. Neither have I made that mention of the navy which its services deserve. Suffice it to say, the close of the siege of Vicksburg found us with an army unsurpassed, in proportion to its numbers, taken as a whole of officers and men. A military education was acquired which no other school could have given. Men who thought a company was quite enough for them to command properly at the beginning, would have made good regimental or brigade commanders; most of the brigade commanders were equal to the command of a division, and one, Ransom, would have been equal to the command of a corps at least. Logan and Crocker ended the campaign fitted to command independent armies.

General F. P. Blair joined me at Milliken's Bend a full-fledged general, without having served in a lower grade. He commanded a division in the campaign. I had known Blair in Missouri, where I had voted against him in 1858 when he ran for Congress. I knew him as a frank, positive and generous man, true to his friends even to a fault, but always a leader. I dreaded his coming; I knew from experience that it was more difficult to command two generals desiring to be leaders than it was to command one army officered intelligently and with subordination. It affords me the greatest pleasure to record now my agreeable disappointment in respect to his character. There was no man braver than he, nor was there any who obeyed all orders of his superior in rank with more unquestioning alacrity. He was one man as a soldier, another as a politician.

The navy under Porter was all it could be, during the entire campaign. Without its assistance the campaign could not have

been successfully made with twice the number of men engaged. It could not have been made at all, in the way it was,
with any number of men without such assistance. The most
perfect harmony reigned between the two arms of the service.
There never was a request made, that I am aware of, either of
the flag-officer or any of his subordinates, that was not
promptly complied with.

The campaign of Vicksburg was suggested and developed
by circumstances. The elections of 1862 had gone against the
prosecution of the war. Voluntary enlistments had nearly
ceased and the draft had been resorted to; this was resisted,
and a defeat or backward movement would have made its execution impossible. A forward movement to a decisive victory
was necessary. Accordingly I resolved to get below Vicksburg, unite with Banks against Port Hudson, make New Orleans a base and, with that base and Grand Gulf as a starting
point, move our combined forces against Vicksburg. Upon
reaching Grand Gulf, after running its batteries and fighting a
battle, I received a letter from Banks informing me that he
could not be at Port Hudson under ten days, and then with
only fifteen thousand men. The time was worth more than
the reinforcements; I therefore determined to push into the
interior of the enemy's country.

With a large river behind us, held above and below by the
enemy, rapid movements were essential to success. Jackson
was captured the day after a new commander had arrived, and
only a few days before large reinforcements were expected. A
rapid movement west was made; the garrison of Vicksburg
was met in two engagements and badly defeated, and driven
back into its stronghold and there successfully besieged. It
looks now as though Providence had directed the course of
the campaign while the Army of the Tennessee executed the
decree.

Upon the surrender of the garrison of Vicksburg there
were three things that required immediate attention. The first
was to send a force to drive the enemy from our rear, and out
of the State. The second was to send reinforcements to Banks
near Port Hudson, if necessary, to complete the triumph of
opening the Mississippi from its source to its mouth to the
free navigation of vessels bearing the Stars and Stripes. The

third was to inform the authorities at Washington and the North of the good news, to relieve their long suspense and strengthen their confidence in the ultimate success of the cause they had so much at heart.

Soon after negotiations were opened with General Pemberton for the surrender of the city, I notified Sherman, whose troops extended from Haines' Bluff on the left to the crossing of the Vicksburg and Jackson road over the Big Black on the right, and directed him to hold his command in readiness to advance and drive the enemy from the State as soon as Vicksburg surrendered. Steele and Ord were directed to be in readiness to join Sherman in his move against General Johnston, and Sherman was advised of this also. Sherman moved promptly, crossing the Big Black at three different points with as many columns, all concentrating at Bolton, twenty miles west of Jackson.

Johnston heard of the surrender of Vicksburg almost as soon as it occurred, and immediately fell back on Jackson. On the 8th of July Sherman was within ten miles of Jackson and on the 11th was close up to the defences of the city and shelling the town. The siege was kept up until the morning of the 17th, when it was found that the enemy had evacuated during the night. The weather was very hot, the roads dusty and the water bad. Johnston destroyed the roads as he passed and had so much the start that pursuit was useless; but Sherman sent one division, Steele's, to Brandon, fourteen miles east of Jackson.

The National loss in the second capture of Jackson was less than one thousand men, killed, wounded and missing. The Confederate loss was probably less, except in captured. More than this number fell into our hands as prisoners.

Medicines and food were left for the Confederate wounded and sick who had to be left behind. A large amount of rations was issued to the families that remained in Jackson. Medicine and food were also sent to Raymond for the destitute families as well as the sick and wounded, as I thought it only fair that we should return to these people some of the articles we had taken while marching through the country. I wrote to Sherman: "Impress upon the men the importance of going through the State in an orderly manner, abstaining from taking anything not absolutely necessary for their subsistence while travelling. They should try to create as favorable an impression as possible upon the people." Provisions and forage, when called for by them, were issued to all the people, from Bruinsburg to Jackson and back to Vicksburg, whose resources had been taken for the supply of our army. Very large quantities of groceries and provisions were so issued.

Sherman was ordered back to Vicksburg, and his troops took much the same position they had occupied before— from the Big Black to Haines' Bluff.

Having cleaned up about Vicksburg and captured or routed all regular Confederate forces for more than a hundred miles in all directions, I felt that the troops that had done so much should be allowed to do more before the enemy could recover from the blow he had received, and while important points might be captured without bloodshed. I suggested to the General-in-chief the idea of a campaign against Mobile, starting from Lake Pontchartrain. Halleck preferred another course. The possession of the trans-Mississippi by the Union forces seemed to possess more importance in his mind than almost any campaign east of the Mississippi. I am well aware that the President was very anxious to have a foothold in Texas, to stop the clamor of some of the foreign governments which seemed to be seeking a pretext to interfere in the war, at least so far as to recognize belligerent rights to the Confederate States. This, however, could have been easily done without wasting troops in western Louisiana and eastern Texas, by sending a garrison at once to Brownsville on the Rio Grande.

Halleck disapproved of my proposition to go against Mobile, so that I was obliged to settle down and see myself put again on the defensive as I had been a year before in west Tennessee. It would have been an easy thing to capture Mobile at the time I proposed to go there. Having that as a base of operations, troops could have been thrown into the interior to operate against General Bragg's army. This would necessarily have compelled Bragg to detach in order to meet this fire in his rear. If he had not done this the troops from Mobile could have inflicted inestimable damage upon much of the country from which his army and Lee's were yet receiving their supplies. I was so much impressed with this idea that I renewed my request later in July and again about the 1st of August, and proposed sending all the troops necessary, asking only the assistance of the navy to protect the debarkation of troops at or near Mobile. I also asked for a leave of absence to visit New Orleans, particularly if my suggestion to move against Mobile should be approved. Both requests were refused. So far as my experience with General Halleck went it was very much easier for him to refuse a favor than to grant one. But I did not regard this as a favor. It was simply in line of duty, though out of my department.

The General-in-chief having decided against me, the depletion of an army, which had won a succession of great victories, commenced, as had been the case the year before after the fall of Corinth when the army was sent where it would do the least good. By orders, I sent to Banks a force of 4,000 men; returned the 9th corps to Kentucky and, when transportation had been collected, started a division of 5,000 men to Schofield in Missouri where Price was raiding the State. I also detached a brigade under Ransom to Natchez, to garrison that place permanently. This latter move was quite fortunate as to the time when Ransom arrived there. The enemy happened to have a large number, about 5,000 head, of beef cattle there on the way from Texas to feed the Eastern armies, and also a large amount of munitions of war which had probably come through Texas from the Rio Grande and which were on the way to Lee's and other armies in the East.

The troops that were left with me around Vicksburg were very busily and unpleasantly employed in making expeditions against guerilla bands and small detachments of cavalry which infested the interior, and in destroying mills, bridges and rolling stock on the railroads. The guerillas and cavalry were not there to fight but to annoy, and therefore disappeared on the first approach of our troops.

The country back of Vicksburg was filled with deserters from Pemberton's army and, it was reported, many from Johnston's also. The men determined not to fight again while the war lasted. Those who lived beyond the reach of the Confederate army wanted to get to their homes. Those who did not, wanted to get North where they could work for their support till the war was over. Besides all this there was quite a peace feeling, for the time being, among the citizens of that part of Mississippi, but this feeling soon subsided. It is not probable that Pemberton got off with over 4,000 of his army to the camp where he proposed taking them, and these were in a demoralized condition.

On the 7th of August I further depleted my army by sending the 13th corps, General Ord commanding, to Banks. Besides this I received orders to co-operate with the latter general in movements west of the Mississippi. Having received this order I went to New Orleans to confer with Banks about the proposed movement. All these movements came to naught.

During this visit I reviewed Banks' army a short distance above Carrollton. The horse I rode was vicious and but little used, and on my return to New Orleans ran away and, shying at a locomotive in the street, fell, probably on me. I was rendered insensible, and when I regained consciousness I found myself in a hotel near by with several doctors attending me. My leg was swollen from the knee to the thigh, and the swelling, almost to the point of bursting, extended along the body up to the arm-pit. The pain was almost beyond endurance. I lay at the hotel something over a week without being able to turn myself in bed. I had a steamer stop at the nearest point possible, and was carried to it on a litter. I was then taken to Vicksburg, where I remained unable to move for some time afterwards.

While I was absent General Sherman declined to assume command because, he said, it would confuse the records; but he let all the orders be made in my name, and was glad to render any assistance he could. No orders were issued by my staff, certainly no important orders, except upon consultation with and approval of Sherman.

On the 13th of September, while I was still in New Orleans, Halleck telegraphed to me to send all available forces to Memphis and thence to Tuscumbia, to co-operate with Rosecrans for the relief of Chattanooga. On the 15th he telegraphed again for all available forces to go to Rosecrans. This was received on the 27th. I was still confined to my bed, unable to rise from it without assistance; but I at once ordered Sherman to send one division to Memphis as fast as transports could be provided. The division of McPherson's corps, which had got off and was on the way to join Steele in Arkansas, was recalled and sent, likewise, to report to Hurlbut at Memphis. Hurlbut was directed to forward these two divisions with two others from his own corps at once, and also to send any other troops that might be returning there. Halleck suggested that some good man, like Sherman or McPherson, should be sent to Memphis to take charge of the troops going east. On this I sent Sherman, as being, I thought, the most suitable person for an independent command, and besides he was entitled to it if it had to be given to any one. He was directed to take with him another division of his corps. This left one back, but having one of McPherson's divisions he had still the equivalent.

Before the receipt by me of these orders the battle of Chickamauga had been fought and Rosecrans forced back into Chattanooga. The administration as well as the General-in-chief was nearly frantic at the situation of affairs there. Mr. Charles A. Dana, an officer of the War Department, was sent to Rosecrans' headquarters. I do not know what his instructions were, but he was still in Chattanooga when I arrived there at a later period.

It seems that Halleck suggested that I should go to Nashville as soon as able to move and take general direction of the troops moving from the west. I received the following dispatch dated October 3d: "It is the wish of the Secretary of War that as soon as General Grant is able he will come to Cairo and report by telegraph." I was still very lame, but started without delay. Arriving at Columbus on the 16th I reported by telegraph: "Your dispatch from Cairo of the 3d directing me to report from Cairo was received at 11.30 on the 10th. Left the same day with staff and headquarters and am here en route for Cairo."

END OF VOL. I.

PERSONAL MEMOIRS

OF

U. S. GRANT.

IN TWO VOLUMES.

VOL. II.

Contents.

VOLUME II.

Maps and Illustrations.

VOLUME II.

Chapter XL.

THE REPLY (to my telegram of October 16, 1863, from Cairo, announcing my arrival at that point) came on the morning of the 17th, directing me to proceed immediately to the Galt House, Louisville, where I would meet an officer of the War Department with my instructions. I left Cairo within an hour or two after the receipt of this dispatch, going by rail via Indianapolis. Just as the train I was on was starting out of the depot at Indianapolis a messenger came running up to stop it, saying the Secretary of War was coming into the station and wanted to see me.

I had never met Mr. Stanton up to that time, though we had held frequent conversations over the wires the year before, when I was in Tennessee. Occasionally at night he would order the wires between the War Department and my headquarters to be connected, and we would hold a conversation for an hour or two. On this occasion the Secretary was accompanied by Governor Brough of Ohio, whom I had never met, though he and my father had been old acquaintances. Mr. Stanton dismissed the special train that had brought him to Indianapolis, and accompanied me to Louisville.

Up to this time no hint had been given me of what was wanted after I left Vicksburg, except the suggestion in one of Halleck's dispatches that I had better go to Nashville and superintend the operation of troops sent to relieve Rosecrans. Soon after we started the Secretary handed me two orders, saying that I might take my choice of them. The two were identical in all but one particular. Both created the "Military Division of the Mississippi," (giving me the command) composed of the Departments of the Ohio, the Cumberland, and the Tennessee, and all the territory from the Alleghanies to the Mississippi River north of Banks's command in the southwest. One order left the department commanders as they were, while the other relieved Rosecrans and assigned Thomas to his place. I accepted the latter. We reached Louisville after night and, if I remember rightly, in a cold, drizzling rain. The Secretary of War told me afterwards that he caught a cold on that occasion from which he never expected to recover. He never did.

A day was spent in Louisville, the Secretary giving me the military news at the capital and talking about the disappointment at the results of some of the campaigns. By the evening of the day after our arrival all matters of discussion seemed exhausted, and I left the hotel to spend· the evening away, both Mrs. Grant (who was with me) and myself having relatives living in Louisville. In the course of the evening Mr. Stanton received a dispatch from Mr. C. A. Dana, then in Chattanooga, informing him that unless prevented Rosecrans would retreat, and advising peremptory orders against his doing so.

As stated before, after the fall of Vicksburg I urged strongly upon the government the propriety of a movement against Mobile. General Rosecrans had been at Murfreesboro', Tennessee, with a large and well-equipped army from early in the year 1863, with Bragg confronting him with a force quite equal to his own at first, considering it was on the defensive. But after the investment of Vicksburg Bragg's army was largely depleted to strengthen Johnston, in Mississippi, who was being reinforced to raise the siege. I frequently wrote General Halleck suggesting that Rosecrans should move against Bragg. By so doing he would either detain the latter's troops where they were or lay Chattanooga open to capture. General Halleck strongly approved the suggestion, and finally wrote me that he had repeatedly ordered Rosecrans to advance, but that the latter had constantly failed to comply with the order, and at last, after having held a council of war, had replied in effect that it was a military maxim "not to fight two decisive battles at the same time." If true, the maxim was not applicable in this case. It would be bad to be defeated in two decisive battles fought the same day, but it would not be bad to win them. I, however, was fighting no battle, and the siege of Vicksburg had drawn from Rosecrans' front so many of the enemy that his chances of victory were much greater than they would be if he waited until the siege was over, when these troops could be returned. Rosecrans was ordered to move against the army that was detaching troops to raise the siege. Finally he did move, on the 24th of June, but ten days afterwards Vicksburg surrendered, and the troops sent from Bragg were free to return.

It was at this time that I recommended to the general-in-chief the movement against Mobile. I knew the peril the Army of the Cumberland was in, being depleted continually, not only by ordinary casualties, but also by having to detach troops to hold its constantly extending line over which to draw supplies, while the enemy in front was as constantly being strengthened. Mobile was important to the enemy, and in the absence of a threatening force was guarded by little else than artillery. If threatened by land and from the water at the same time the prize would fall easily, or troops would have to be sent to its defence. Those troops would necessarily come from Bragg. My judgment was overruled, and the troops under my command were dissipated over other parts of the country where it was thought they could render the most service.

Soon it was discovered in Washington that Rosecrans was in trouble and required assistance. The emergency was now too immediate to allow us to give this assistance by making an attack in rear of Bragg upon Mobile. It was therefore necessary to reinforce directly, and troops were sent from every available point.

Rosecrans had very skilfully manœuvred Bragg south of the Tennessee River, and through and beyond Chattanooga. If he had stopped and intrenched, and made himself strong there, all would have been right and the mistake of not moving earlier partially compensated. But he pushed on, with his forces very much scattered, until Bragg's troops from Mississippi began to join him. Then Bragg took the initiative. Rosecrans had to fall back in turn, and was able to get his army together at Chickamauga, some miles south-east of Chattanooga, before the main battle was brought on. The battle was fought on the 19th and 20th of September, and Rosecrans was badly defeated, with a heavy loss in artillery and some sixteen thousand men killed, wounded and captured. The corps under

Major-General George H. Thomas stood its ground, while Rosecrans, with Crittenden and McCook, returned to Chattanooga. Thomas returned also, but later, and with his troops in good order. Bragg followed and took possession of Missionary Ridge, overlooking Chattanooga. He also occupied Lookout Mountain, west of the town, which Rosecrans had abandoned, and with it his control of the river and the river road as far back as Bridgeport. The National troops were now strongly intrenched in Chattanooga Valley, with the Tennessee River behind them and the enemy occupying commanding heights to the east and west, with a strong line across the valley from mountain to mountain, and with Chattanooga Creek, for a large part of the way, in front of their line.

On the 29th Halleck telegraphed me the above results, and directed all the forces that could be spared from my department to be sent to Rosecrans. Long before this dispatch was received Sherman was on his way, and McPherson was moving east with most of the garrison of Vicksburg.

A retreat at that time would have been a terrible disaster. It would not only have been the loss of a most important strategic position to us, but it would have been attended with the loss of all the artillery still left with the Army of the Cumberland and the annihilation of that army itself, either by capture or demoralization.

All supplies for Rosecrans had to be brought from Nashville. The railroad between this base and the army was in possession of the government up to Bridgeport, the point at which the road crosses to the south side of the Tennessee River; but Bragg, holding Lookout and Raccoon mountains west of Chattanooga, commanded the railroad, the river and the shortest and best wagon-roads, both south and north of the Tennessee, between Chattanooga and Bridgeport. The distance between these two places is but twenty-six miles by rail; but owing to the position of Bragg, all supplies for Rosecrans had to be hauled by a circuitous route north of the river and over a mountainous country, increasing the distance to over sixty miles.

This country afforded but little food for his animals, nearly ten thousand of which had already starved, and not enough

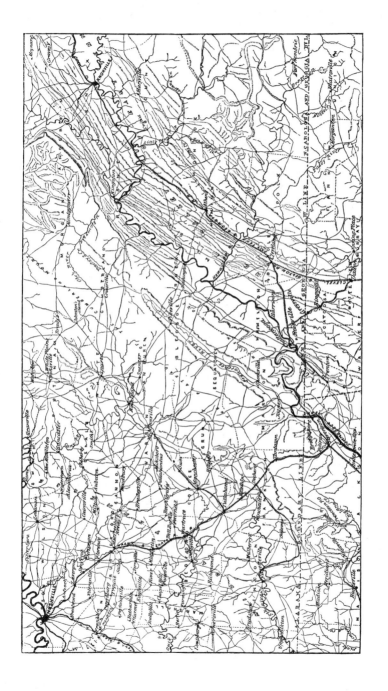

were left to draw a single piece of artillery or even the ambulances to convey the sick. The men had been on half rations of hard bread for a considerable time, with but few other supplies except beef driven from Nashville across the country. The region along the road became so exhausted of food for the cattle that by the time they reached Chattanooga they were much in the condition of the few animals left alive there—"on the lift." Indeed, the beef was so poor that the soldiers were in the habit of saying, with a faint facetiousness, that they were living on "half rations of hard bread and *beef dried on the hoof.*"

Nothing could be transported but food, and the troops were without sufficient shoes or other clothing suitable for the advancing season. What they had was well worn. The fuel within the Federal lines was exhausted, even to the stumps of trees. There were no teams to draw it from the opposite bank, where it was abundant. The only way of supplying fuel, for some time before my arrival, had been to cut trees on the north bank of the river at a considerable distance up the stream, form rafts of it and float it down with the current, effecting a landing on the south side within our lines by the use of paddles or poles. It would then be carried on the shoulders of the men to their camps.

If a retreat had occurred at this time it is not probable that any of the army would have reached the railroad as an organized body, if followed by the enemy.

On the receipt of Mr. Dana's dispatch Mr. Stanton sent for me. Finding that I was out he became nervous and excited, inquiring of every person he met, including guests of the house, whether they knew where I was, and bidding them find me and send me to him at once. About eleven o'clock I returned to the hotel, and on my way, when near the house, every person met was a messenger from the Secretary, apparently partaking of his impatience to see me. I hastened to the room of the Secretary and found him pacing the floor rapidly in his dressing-gown. Saying that the retreat must be prevented, he showed me the dispatch. I immediately wrote an order assuming command of the Military Division of the Mississippi, and telegraphed it to General Rosecrans. I then telegraphed to him the order from Washington assigning Thomas to the command of the Army of the Cumberland; and to Thomas that he must hold Chattanooga at all hazards, informing him at the same time that I would be at the front as soon as possible. A prompt reply was received from Thomas, saying, "We will hold the town till we starve." I appreciated the force of this dispatch later when I witnessed the condition of affairs which prompted it. It looked, indeed, as if but two courses were open: one to starve, the other to surrender or be captured.

On the morning of the 20th of October I started, with my staff, and proceeded as far as Nashville. At that time it was not prudent to travel beyond that point by night, so I remained in Nashville until the next morning. Here I met for the first time Andrew Johnson, Military Governor of Tennessee. He delivered a speech of welcome. His composure showed that it was by no means his maiden effort. It was long, and I was in torture while he was delivering it, fearing something would be expected from me in response. I was relieved, however, the people assembled having apparently heard enough. At all events they commenced a general hand-shaking, which, although trying where there is so much of it, was a great relief to me in this emergency.

From Nashville I telegraphed to Burnside, who was then at Knoxville, that important points in his department ought to be fortified, so that they could be held with the least number of men; to Admiral Porter at Cairo, that Sherman's advance had passed Eastport, Mississippi, that rations were probably on their way from St. Louis by boat for supplying his army, and requesting him to send a gunboat to convoy them; and to Thomas, suggesting that large parties should be put at work on the wagon-road then in use back to Bridgeport.

On the morning of the 21st we took the train for the front, reaching Stevenson, Alabama, after dark. Rosecrans was there on his way north. He came into my car and we held a brief interview, in which he described very clearly the situation at Chattanooga, and made some excellent suggestions as to what should be done. My only wonder was that he had not carried them out. We then proceeded to Bridgeport, where we stopped for the night. From here we took horses and made our way by Jasper and over Waldron's Ridge to Chattanooga.

There had been much rain, and the roads were almost impassable from mud, knee-deep in places, and from wash-outs on
the mountain sides. I had been on crutches since the time of
my fall in New Orleans, and had to be carried over places
where it was not safe to cross on horseback. The roads were
strewn with the *débris* of broken wagons and the carcasses of
thousands of starved mules and horses. At Jasper, some ten or
twelve miles from Bridgeport, there was a halt. General O. O.
Howard had his headquarters there. From this point I telegraphed Burnside to make every effort to secure five hundred
rounds of ammunition for his artillery and small-arms. We
stopped for the night at a little hamlet some ten or twelve
miles farther on. The next day we reached Chattanooga a little
before dark. I went directly to General Thomas's headquarters, and remaining there a few days, until I could establish
my own.

During the evening most of the general officers called in to
pay their respects and to talk about the condition of affairs.
They pointed out on the map the line, marked with a red or
blue pencil, which Rosecrans had contemplated falling back
upon. If any of them had approved the move they did not say
so to me. I found General W. F. Smith occupying the position of chief engineer of the Army of the Cumberland. I had
known Smith as a cadet at West Point, but had no recollection
of having met him after my graduation, in 1843, up to this
time. He explained the situation of the two armies and the
topography of the country so plainly that I could see it without an inspection. I found that he had established a saw-mill
on the banks of the river, by utilizing an old engine found in
the neighborhood; and, by rafting logs from the north side
of the river above, had got out the lumber and completed
pontoons and roadway plank for a second bridge, one flying
bridge being there already. He was also rapidly getting out
the materials and constructing the boats for a third bridge. In
addition to this he had far under way a steamer for plying
between Chattanooga and Bridgeport whenever we might get
possession of the river. This boat consisted of a scow, made of
the plank sawed out at the mill, housed in, and a stern wheel
attached which was propelled by a second engine taken from
some shop or factory.

I telegraphed to Washington this night, notifying General Halleck of my arrival, and asking to have General Sherman assigned to the command of the Army of the Tennessee, headquarters in the field. The request was at once complied with.

Chapter XLI.

ASSUMING THE COMMAND AT CHATTANOOGA — OPENING
A LINE OF SUPPLIES — BATTLE OF WAUHATCHIE —
ON THE PICKET LINE.

THE NEXT DAY, the 24th, I started out to make a personal inspection, taking Thomas and Smith with me, besides most of the members of my personal staff. We crossed to the north side of the river, and, moving to the north of detached spurs of hills, reached the Tennessee at Brown's Ferry, some three miles below Lookout Mountain, unobserved by the enemy. Here we left our horses back from the river and approached the water on foot. There was a picket station of the enemy on the opposite side, of about twenty men, in full view, and we were within easy range. They did not fire upon us nor seem to be disturbed by our presence. They must have seen that we were all commissioned officers. But, I suppose, they looked upon the garrison of Chattanooga as prisoners of war, feeding or starving themselves, and thought it would be inhuman to kill any of them except in self-defence.

That night I issued orders for opening the route to Bridge-port — *a cracker line*, as the soldiers appropriately termed it. They had been so long on short rations that my first thought was the establishment of a line over which food might reach them.

Chattanooga is on the south bank of the Tennessee, where that river runs nearly due west. It is at the northern end of a valley five or six miles in width, through which Chattanooga Creek runs. To the east of the valley is Missionary Ridge, rising from five to eight hundred feet above the creek and terminating somewhat abruptly a half mile or more before reaching the Tennessee. On the west of the valley is Lookout Mountain, twenty-two hundred feet above-tide water. Just be-low the town the Tennessee makes a turn to the south and runs to the base of Lookout Mountain, leaving no level ground between the mountain and river. The Memphis and Charleston Railroad passes this point, where the mountain stands nearly perpendicular. East of Missionary Ridge flows the South Chickamauga River; west of Lookout Mountain is Lookout Creek; and west of that, Raccoon Mountains. Lookout Mountain, at its northern end, rises almost perpendicularly for some distance, then breaks off in a gentle slope of cultivated fields to near the summit, where it ends in a palisade thirty or more feet in height. On the gently sloping ground, between the upper and lower palisades, there is a single farmhouse, which is reached by a wagon-road from the valley east.

The intrenched line of the enemy commenced on the north end of Missionary Ridge and extended along the crest for some distance south, thence across Chattanooga valley to Lookout Mountain. Lookout Mountain was also fortified and held by the enemy, who also kept troops in Lookout valley west, and on Raccoon Mountain, with pickets extending down the river so as to command the road on the north bank and render it useless to us. In addition to this there was an intrenched line in Chattanooga valley extending from the river east of the town to Lookout Mountain, to make the investment complete. Besides the fortifications on Mission Ridge, there was a line at the base of the hill, with occasional spurs of rifle-pits half-way up the front. The enemy's pickets extended out into the valley towards the town, so far that the pickets of the two armies could converse. At one point they were separated only by the narrow creek which gives its name to the valley and town, and from which both sides drew water. The Union lines were shorter than those of the enemy.

Thus the enemy, with a vastly superior force, was strongly fortified to the east, south, and west, and commanded the river below. Practically, the Army of the Cumberland was besieged. The enemy had stopped with his cavalry north of the river the passing of a train loaded with ammunition and medical supplies. The Union army was short of both, not having ammunition enough for a day's fighting.

General Halleck had, long before my coming into this new field, ordered parts of the 11th and 12th corps, commanded respectively by Generals Howard and Slocum, Hooker in command of the whole, from the Army of the Potomac to reinforce Rosecrans. It would have been folly to send them to

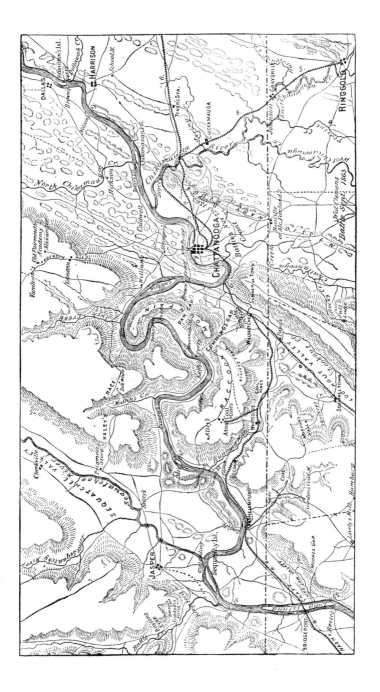

Chattanooga to help eat up the few rations left there. They were consequently left on the railroad, where supplies could be brought to them. Before my arrival, Thomas ordered their concentration at Bridgeport.

General W. F. Smith had been so instrumental in preparing for the move which I was now about to make, and so clear in his judgment about the manner of making it, that I deemed it but just to him that he should have command of the troops detailed to execute the design, although he was then acting as a staff officer and was not in command of troops.

On the 24th of October, after my return to Chattanooga, the following details were made: General Hooker, who was now at Bridgeport, was ordered to cross to the south side of the Tennessee and march up by Whitesides and Wauhatchie to Brown's Ferry. General Palmer, with a division of the 14th corps, Army of the Cumberland, was ordered to move down the river on the north side, by a back road, until opposite Whitesides, then cross and hold the road in Hooker's rear after he had passed. Four thousand men were at the same time detailed to act under General Smith directly from Chattanooga. Eighteen hundred of them, under General Hazen, were to take sixty pontoon boats, and under cover of night float by the pickets of the enemy at the north base of Lookout, down to Brown's Ferry, then land on the south side and capture or drive away the pickets at that point. Smith was to march with the remainder of the detail, also under cover of night, by the north bank of the river to Brown's Ferry, taking with him all the material for laying the bridge as soon as the crossing was secured.

On the 26th, Hooker crossed the river at Bridgeport and commenced his eastward march. At three o'clock on the morning of the 27th, Hazen moved into the stream with his sixty pontoons and eighteen hundred brave and well-equipped men. Smith started enough in advance to be near the river when Hazen should arrive. There are a number of detached spurs of hills north of the river at Chattanooga, back of which is a good road parallel to the stream, sheltered from the view from the top of Lookout. It was over this road Smith marched. At five o'clock Hazen landed at Brown's Ferry, surprised the picket guard, and captured most of it. By seven o'clock the whole of Smith's force was ferried over and in possession of a height commanding the ferry. This was speedily fortified, while a detail was laying the pontoon bridge. By ten o'clock the bridge was laid, and our extreme right, now in Lookout valley, was fortified and connected with the rest of the army. The two bridges over the Tennessee River—a flying one at Chattanooga and the new one at Brown's Ferry—with the road north of the river, covered from both the fire and the view of the enemy, made the connection complete. Hooker found but slight obstacles in his way, and on the afternoon of the 28th emerged into Lookout valley at Wauhatchie. Howard marched on to Brown's Ferry, while Geary, who commanded a division in the 12th corps, stopped three miles south. The pickets of the enemy on the river below were now cut off, and soon came in and surrendered.

The river was now opened to us from Lookout valley to Bridgeport. Between Brown's Ferry and Kelly's Ferry the Tennessee runs through a narrow gorge in the mountains, which contracts the stream so much as to increase the current beyond the capacity of an ordinary steamer to stem it. To get up these rapids, steamers must be cordelled; that is, pulled up by ropes from the shore. But there is no difficulty in navigating the stream from Bridgeport to Kelly's Ferry. The latter point is only eight miles from Chattanooga and connected with it by a good wagon-road, which runs through a low pass in the Raccoon Mountains on the south side of the river to Brown's Ferry, thence on the north side to the river opposite Chattanooga. There were several steamers at Bridgeport, and abundance of forage, clothing and provisions.

On the way to Chattanooga I had telegraphed back to Nashville for a good supply of vegetables and small rations, which the troops had been so long deprived of. Hooker had brought with him from the east a full supply of land transportation. His animals had not been subjected to hard work on bad roads without forage, but were in good condition. In five days from my arrival in Chattanooga the way was open to Bridgeport and, with the aid of steamers and Hooker's teams, in a week the troops were receiving full rations. It is hard for any one not an eye-witness to realize the relief this brought.

The men were soon reclothed and also well fed; an abundance of ammunition was brought up, and a cheerfulness prevailed not before enjoyed in many weeks. Neither officers nor men looked upon themselves any longer as doomed. The weak and languid appearance of the troops, so visible before, disappeared at once. I do not know what the effect was on the other side, but assume it must have been correspondingly depressing. Mr. Davis had visited Bragg but a short time before, and must have perceived our condition to be about as Bragg described it in his subsequent report. "These dispositions," he said, "faithfully sustained, insured the enemy's speedy evacuation of Chattanooga for want of food and forage. Possessed of the shortest route to his depot, and the one by which reinforcements must reach him, we held him at our mercy, and his destruction was only a question of time." But the dispositions were not "faithfully sustained," and I doubt not but thousands of men engaged in trying to "sustain" them now rejoice that they were not. There was no time during the rebellion when I did not think, and often say, that the South was more to be benefited by its defeat than the North. The latter had the people, the institutions, and the territory to make a great and prosperous nation. The former was burdened with an institution abhorrent to all civilized people not brought up under it, and one which degraded labor, kept it in ignorance, and enervated the governing class. With the outside world at war with this institution, they could not have extended their territory. The labor of the country was not skilled, nor allowed to become so. The whites could not toil without becoming degraded, and those who did were denominated "poor white trash." The system of labor would have soon exhausted the soil and left the people poor. The non-slaveholders would have left the country, and the small slaveholder must have sold out to his more fortunate neighbor. Soon the slaves would have outnumbered the masters, and, not being in sympathy with them, would have risen in their might and exterminated them. The war was expensive to the South as well as to the North, both in blood and treasure, but it was worth all it cost.

The enemy was surprised by the movements which secured to us a line of supplies. He appreciated its importance, and hastened to try to recover the line from us. His strength on Lookout Mountain was not equal to Hooker's command in the valley below. From Missionary Ridge he had to march twice the distance we had from Chattanooga, in order to reach Lookout Valley; but on the night of the 28th and 29th an attack was made on Geary at Wauhatchie by Longstreet's corps. When the battle commenced, Hooker ordered Howard up from Brown's Ferry. He had three miles to march to reach Geary. On his way he was fired upon by rebel troops from a foot-hill to the left of the road and from which the road was commanded. Howard turned to the left, charged up the hill and captured it before the enemy had time to intrench, taking many prisoners. Leaving sufficient men to hold this height, he pushed on to reinforce Geary. Before he got up, Geary had been engaged for about three hours against a vastly superior force. The night was so dark that the men could not distinguish one from another except by the light of the flashes of their muskets. In the darkness and uproar, Hooker's teamsters became frightened and deserted their teams. The mules also became frightened, and breaking loose from their fastenings stampeded directly towards the enemy. The latter, no doubt, took this for a charge, and stampeded in turn. By four o'clock in the morning the battle had entirely ceased, and our "cracker line" was never afterward disturbed.

In securing possession of Lookout Valley, Smith lost one man killed and four or five wounded. The enemy lost most of his pickets at the ferry, captured. In the night engagement of the 28th—9th Hooker lost 416 killed and wounded. I never knew the loss of the enemy, but our troops buried over one hundred and fifty of his dead and captured more than a hundred.

After we had secured the opening of a line over which to bring our supplies to the army, I made a personal inspection to see the situation of the pickets of the two armies. As I have stated, Chattanooga Creek comes down the centre of the valley to within a mile or such a matter of the town of Chattanooga, then bears off westerly, then north-westerly, and enters the Tennessee River at the foot of Lookout Mountain. This creek, from its mouth up to where it bears off west, lay between the two lines of pickets, and the guards of both armies drew their water from the same stream. As I would be under short-range fire and in an open country, I took nobody with me, except, I believe, a bugler, who stayed some distance to the rear. I rode from our right around to our left. When I came to the camp of the picket guard of our side, I heard the call, "Turn out the guard for the commanding general." I replied, "Never mind the guard," and they were dismissed and went back to their tents. Just back of these, and about equally distant from the creek, were the guards of the Confederate pickets. The sentinel on their post called out in like manner, "Turn out the guard for the commanding general," and, I believe, added, "General Grant." Their line in a moment front-faced to the north, facing me, and gave a salute, which I returned.

The most friendly relations seemed to exist between the pickets of the two armies. At one place there was a tree which had fallen across the stream, and which was used by the soldiers of both armies in drawing water for their camps. General Longstreet's corps was stationed there at the time, and wore blue of a little different shade from our uniform. Seeing a soldier in blue on this log, I rode up to him, commenced conversing with him, and asked whose corps he belonged to. He was very polite, and, touching his hat to me, said he belonged to General Longstreet's corps. I asked him a few questions—but not with a view of gaining any particular information—all of which he answered, and I rode off.

Chapter XLII.

HAVING GOT the Army of the Cumberland in a comfortable position, I now began to look after the remainder of my new command. Burnside was in about as desperate a condition as the Army of the Cumberland had been, only he was not yet besieged. He was a hundred miles from the nearest possible base, Big South Fork of the Cumberland River, and much farther from any railroad we had possession of. The roads back were over mountains, and all supplies along the line had long since been exhausted. His animals, too, had been starved, and their carcasses lined the road from Cumberland Gap, and far back towards Lexington, Ky. East Tennessee still furnished supplies of beef, bread and forage, but it did not supply ammunition, clothing, medical supplies, or small rations, such as coffee, sugar, salt and rice.

Sherman had started from Memphis for Corinth on the 11th of October. His instructions required him to repair the road in his rear in order to bring up supplies. The distance was about three hundred and thirty miles through a hostile country. His entire command could not have maintained the road if it had been completed. The bridges had all been destroyed by the enemy, and much other damage done. A hostile community lived along the road; guerilla bands infested the country, and more or less of the cavalry of the enemy was still in the West. Often Sherman's work was destroyed as soon as completed, and he only a short distance away.

The Memphis and Charleston Railroad strikes the Tennessee River at Eastport, Mississippi. Knowing the difficulty Sherman would have to supply himself from Memphis, I had previously ordered supplies sent from St. Louis on small steamers, to be convoyed by the navy, to meet him at Eastport. These he got. I now ordered him to discontinue his work of repairing roads and to move on with his whole force to Stevenson, Alabama, without delay. This order was borne to Sherman by a messenger, who paddled down the Tennessee in a canoe and floated over Muscle Shoals; it was delivered at Iuka on the 27th. In this Sherman was notified that the rebels were moving a force towards Cleveland, East Tennessee, and might be going to Nashville, in which event his troops were in the best position to beat them there. Sherman, with his characteristic promptness, abandoned the work he was engaged upon and pushed on at once. On the 1st of November he crossed the Tennessee at Eastport, and that day was in Florence, Alabama, with the head of column, while his troops were still crossing at Eastport, with Blair bringing up the rear.

Sherman's force made an additional army, with cavalry, artillery, and trains, all to be supplied by the single track road from Nashville. All indications pointed also to the probable necessity of supplying Burnside's command in East Tennessee, twenty-five thousand more, by the same route. A single track could not do this. I gave, therefore, an order to Sherman to halt General G. M. Dodge's command, of about eight thousand men, at Athens, and subsequently directed the latter to arrange his troops along the railroad from Decatur north towards Nashville, and to rebuild that road. The road from Nashville to Decatur passes over a broken country, cut up with innumerable streams, many of them of considerable width, and with valleys far below the road-bed. All the bridges over these had been destroyed, and the rails taken up and twisted by the enemy. All the cars and locomotives not carried off had been destroyed as effectually as they knew how to destroy them. All bridges and culverts had been destroyed between Nashville and Decatur, and thence to Stevenson, where the Memphis and Charleston and the Nashville and Chattanooga roads unite. The rebuilding of this road would give us two roads as far as Stevenson over which to supply the army. From Bridgeport, a short distance farther east, the river supplements the road.

General Dodge, besides being a most capable soldier, was an experienced railroad builder. He had no tools to work with except those of the pioneers—axes, picks, and spades. With these he was able to intrench his men and protect them against surprises by small parties of the enemy. As he had no base of supplies until the road could be completed back to Nashville, the first matter to consider after protecting his men was the getting in of food and forage from the surrounding country. He had his men and teams bring in all the grain they could find, or all they needed, and all the cattle for beef, and such other food as could be found. Millers were detailed from the ranks to run the mills along the line of the army. When these were not near enough to the troops for protection they were taken down and moved up to the line of the road. Blacksmith shops, with all the iron and steel found in them, were moved up in like manner. Blacksmiths were detailed and set to work making the tools necessary in railroad and bridge building. Axemen were put to work getting out timber for bridges and cutting fuel for locomotives when the road should be completed. Car-builders were set to work repairing the locomotives and cars. Thus every branch of railroad building, making tools to work with, and supplying the workmen with food, was all going on at once, and without the aid of a mechanic or laborer except what the command itself furnished. But rails and cars the men could not make without material, and there was not enough rolling stock to keep the road we already had worked to its full capacity. There were no rails except those in use. To supply these deficiencies I ordered eight of the ten engines General McPherson had at Vicksburg to be sent to Nashville, and all the cars he had except ten. I also ordered the troops in West Tennessee to points on the river and on the Memphis and Charleston road, and ordered the cars, locomotives and rails from all the railroads except the Memphis and Charleston to Nashville. The military manager of railroads also was directed to furnish more rolling stock and, as far as he could, bridge material. General Dodge had the work assigned him finished within forty days after receiving his orders. The number of bridges to rebuild was one hundred and eighty-two, many of them over deep and wide chasms; the length of road repaired was one hundred and two miles.

The enemy's troops, which it was thought were either moving against Burnside or were going to Nashville, went no farther than Cleveland. Their presence there, however, alarmed the authorities at Washington, and, on account of our helpless condition at Chattanooga, caused me much uneasiness. Dispatches were constantly coming, urging me to do something for Burnside's relief; calling attention to the importance of holding East Tennessee; saying the President was much concerned for the protection of the loyal people in that section, etc. We had not at Chattanooga animals to pull a single piece of artillery, much less a supply train. Reinforcements could not help Burnside, because he had neither supplies nor ammunition sufficient for them; hardly, indeed, bread and meat for the men he had. There was no relief possible for him except by expelling the enemy from Missionary Ridge and about Chattanooga.

On the 4th of November Longstreet left our front with about fifteen thousand troops, besides Wheeler's cavalry, five thousand more, to go against Burnside. The situation seemed desperate, and was more aggravating because nothing could be done until Sherman should get up. The authorities at Washington were now more than ever anxious for the safety of Burnside's army, and plied me with dispatches faster than ever, urging that something should be done for his relief. On the 7th, before Longstreet could possibly have reached Knoxville, I ordered Thomas peremptorily to attack the enemy's right, so as to force the return of the troops that had gone up the valley. I directed him to take mules, officers' horses, or animals wherever he could get them, to move the necessary artillery. But he persisted in the declaration that he could not move a single piece of artillery, and could not see how he could possibly comply with the order. Nothing was left to be done but to answer Washington dispatches as best I could; urge Sherman forward, although he was making every effort to get forward, and encourage Burnside to hold on, assuring him that in a short time he should be relieved. All of Burnside's dispatches showed the greatest confidence in his ability to hold his position as long as his ammunition held out. He even suggested the propriety of abandoning the territory he held south and west of Knoxville, so as to draw the enemy farther from his base and make it more difficult for him to get back to Chattanooga when the battle should begin.

Longstreet had a railroad as far as Loudon; but from there to Knoxville he had to rely on wagon trains. Burnside's suggestion, therefore, was a good one, and it was adopted. On the 14th I telegraphed him:

"Sherman's advance has reached Bridgeport. His whole force will be ready to move from there by Tuesday at farthest. If you can hold Longstreet in check until he gets up, or by skirmishing and falling back can avoid serious loss to yourself and gain time, I will be able to force the enemy back from here and place a force between Longstreet and Bragg that must inevitably make the former take to the mountain-passes by every available road, to get to his supplies. Sherman would have been here before this but for high water in Elk River driving him some thirty miles up that river to cross."

And again later in the day, indicating my plans for his relief, as follows:

"Your dispatch and Dana's just received. Being there, you can tell better how to resist Longstreet's attack than I can direct. With your showing you had better give up Kingston at the last moment and save the most productive part of your possessions. Every arrangement is now made to throw Sherman's force across the river, just at and below the mouth of Chickamauga Creek, as soon as it arrives. Thomas will attack on his left at the same time, and together it is expected to carry Missionary Ridge, and from there push a force on to the railroad between Cleveland and Dalton. Hooker will at the same time attack, and, if he can, carry Lookout Mountain. The enemy now seems to be looking for an attack on his left flank. This favors us. To further confirm this, Sherman's advance division will march direct from Whiteside to Trenton. The remainder of his force will pass over a new road just made from Whiteside to Kelly's Ferry, thus being concealed from the enemy, and leave him to suppose the whole force is going up Lookout Valley. Sherman's advance has only just reached Bridgeport. The rear will only reach there on the 16th. This will bring it to the 19th as the earliest day for making the combined movement as desired. Inform me if you think you can sustain yourself until this time. I can hardly conceive of the enemy breaking through at Kingston and pushing for Kentucky. If they should, however, a new problem would be left for solution. Thomas has ordered a division of cavalry to the vicinity of Sparta. I will ascertain if they have started, and inform you. It will be entirely out of the question to send you ten thousand men, not because they cannot be spared, but how would they be fed after they got even one day east from here?"

Longstreet, for some reason or other, stopped at Loudon until the 13th. That being the terminus of his railroad communications, it is probable he was directed to remain there awaiting orders. He was in a position threatening Knoxville, and at the same time where he could be brought back speedily to Chattanooga. The day after Longstreet left Loudon, Sherman reached Bridgeport in person and proceeded on to see me that evening, the 14th, and reached Chattanooga the next day.

My orders for battle were all prepared in advance of Sherman's arrival,* except the dates, which could not be fixed while troops to be engaged were so far away. The possession of Lookout Mountain was of no special advantage to us now. Hooker was instructed to send Howard's corps to the north side of the Tennessee, thence up behind the hills on the north side, and to go into camp opposite Chattanooga; with the remainder of the command, Hooker was, at a time to be afterwards appointed, to ascend the western slope between the upper and lower palisades, and so get into Chattanooga valley.

The plan of battle was for Sherman to attack the enemy's right flank, form a line across it, extend our left over South Chickamauga River so as to threaten or hold the railroad in Bragg's rear, and thus force him either to weaken his lines elsewhere or lose his connection with his base at Chickamauga Station. Hooker was to perform like service on our right. His problem was to get from Lookout Valley to Chattanooga Valley in the most expeditious way possible; cross the

---

*CHATTANOOGA, *November* 18, 1863.
MAJOR-GENERAL W. T. SHERMAN:

Enclosed herewith I send you copy of instructions to Major-General Thomas. You having been over the ground in person, and having heard the whole matter discussed, further instructions will not be necessary for you. It is particularly desirable that a force should be got through to the railroad between Cleveland and Dalton, and Longstreet thus cut off from communication with the South; but being confronted by a large force here, strongly located, it is not easy to tell how this is to be effected until the result of our first effort is known.

I will add, however, what is not shown in my instructions to Thomas, that

latter valley rapidly to Rossville, south of Bragg's line on Missionary Ridge, form line there across the ridge facing north, with his right flank extended to Chickamauga Valley east of the ridge, thus threatening the enemy's rear on that flank and compelling him to reinforce this also. Thomas, with the Army of the Cumberland, occupied the centre, and was to assault while the enemy was engaged with most of his forces on his two flanks.

To carry out this plan, Sherman was to cross the Tennessee at Brown's Ferry and move east of Chattanooga to a point opposite the north end of Mission Ridge, and to place his command back of the foot-hills out of sight of the enemy on the ridge. There are two streams called Chickamauga emptying into the Tennessee River east of Chattanooga—North Chickamauga, taking its rise in Tennessee, flowing south, and emptying into the river some seven or eight miles east; while the South Chickamauga, which takes its rise in Georgia, flows

---

a brigade of cavalry has been ordered here which, if it arrives in time, will be thrown across the Tennessee above Chickamauga, and may be able to make the trip to Cleveland or thereabouts.

U. S. GRANT,
Maj.-Gen'l.

CHATTANOOGA, *November* 18, 1863.
MAJOR-GENERAL GEO. H. THOMAS,
        Chattanooga:

All preparations should be made for attacking the enemy's position on Missionary Ridge by Saturday at daylight. Not being provided with a map giving names of roads, spurs of the mountains, and other places, such definite instructions cannot be given as might be desirable. However, the general plan, you understand, is for Sherman, with the force brought with him strengthened by a division from your command, to effect a crossing of the Tennessee River just below the mouth of Chickamauga; his crossing to be protected by artillery from the heights on the north bank of the river (to be located by your chief of artillery), and to secure the heights on the northern extremity to about the railroad tunnel before the enemy can concentrate against him. You will co-operate with Sherman. The troops in Chattanooga Valley should be well concentrated on your left flank, leaving only the necessary force to defend fortifications on the right and centre, and a movable column of one division in readiness to move wherever ordered. This division should show itself as threateningly as possible on the most practicable

northward, and empties into the Tennessee some three or four miles above the town. There were now one hundred and sixteen pontoons in the North Chickamauga River, their presence there being unknown to the enemy.

At night a division was to be marched up to that point, and at two o'clock in the morning moved down with the current, thirty men in each boat. A few were to land east of the mouth of the South Chickamauga, capture the pickets there, and then lay a bridge connecting the two banks of the river. The rest were to land on the south side of the Tennessee, where Missionary Ridge would strike it if prolonged, and a sufficient number of men to man the boats were to push to the north side to ferry over the main body of Sherman's command while those left on the south side intrenched themselves. Thomas was to move out from his lines facing the ridge, leaving enough of Palmer's corps to guard against an attack down the valley. Lookout Valley being of no present value to us, and being untenable by the enemy if we should secure Missionary Ridge, Hooker's orders were changed. His revised orders brought him to Chattanooga by the established

---

line for making an attack up the valley. Your effort then will be to form a junction with Sherman, making your advance well towards the northern end of Missionary Ridge, and moving as near simultaneously with him as possible. The junction once formed and the ridge carried, communications will be at once established between the two armies by roads on the south bank of the river. Further movements will then depend on those of the enemy. Lookout Valley, I think, will be easily held by Geary's division and what troops you may still have there belonging to the old Army of the Cumberland. Howard's corps can then be held in readiness to act either with you at Chattanooga or with Sherman. It should be marched on Friday night to a position on the north side of the river, not lower down than the first pontoon-bridge, and there held in readiness for such orders as may become necessary. All these troops will be provided with two days' cooked rations in haversacks, and one hundred rounds of ammunition on the person of each infantry soldier. Special care should be taken by all officers to see that ammunition is not wasted or unnecessarily fired away. You will call on the engineer department for such preparations as you may deem necessary for carrying your infantry and artillery over the creek.

U. S. GRANT,
Major-General.

route north of the Tennessee. He was then to move out to the right to Rossville.

Hooker's position in Lookout Valley was absolutely essential to us so long as Chattanooga was besieged. It was the key to our line for supplying the army. But it was not essential after the enemy was dispersed from our front, or even after the battle for this purpose was begun. Hooker's orders, therefore, were designed to get his force past Lookout Mountain and Chattanooga Valley, and up to Missionary Ridge. By crossing the north face of Lookout the troops would come into Chattanooga Valley in rear of the line held by the enemy across the valley, and would necessarily force its evacuation. Orders were accordingly given to march by this route. But days before the battle began the advantages as well as the disadvantages of this plan of action were all considered. The passage over the mountain was a difficult one to make in the face of an enemy. It might consume so much time as to lose us the use of the troops engaged in it at other points where they were more wanted. After reaching Chattanooga Valley, the creek of the same name, quite a formidable stream to get an army over, had to be crossed. I was perfectly willing that the enemy should keep Lookout Mountain until we got through with the troops on Missionary Ridge. By marching Hooker to the north side of the river, thence up the stream, and recrossing at the town, he could be got in position at any named time; when in this new position, he would have Chattanooga Creek behind him, and the attack on Missionary Ridge would unquestionably cause the evacuation by the enemy of his line across the valley and on Lookout Mountain. Hooker's order was changed accordingly. As explained elsewhere, the original order had to be reverted to, because of a flood in the river rendering the bridge at Brown's Ferry unsafe for the passage of troops at the exact juncture when it was wanted to bring all the troops together against Missionary Ridge.

The next day after Sherman's arrival I took him, with Generals Thomas and Smith and other officers, to the north side of the river, and showed them the ground over which Sherman had to march, and pointed out generally what he was expected to do. I, as well as the authorities in Washington, was still in a great state of anxiety for Burnside's safety. Burnside himself, I believe, was the only one who did not share in this anxiety. Nothing could be done for him, however, until Sherman's troops were up. As soon, therefore, as the inspection was over, Sherman started for Bridgeport to hasten matters, rowing a boat himself, I believe, from Kelly's Ferry. Sherman had left Bridgeport the night of the 14th, reached Chattanooga the evening of the 15th, made the above-described inspection on the morning of the 16th, and started back the same evening to hurry up his command, fully appreciating the importance of time.

His march was conducted with as much expedition as the roads and season would admit of. By the 20th he was himself at Brown's Ferry with the head of column, but many of his troops were far behind, and one division (Ewing's) was at Trenton, sent that way to create the impression that Lookout was to be taken from the south. Sherman received his orders at the ferry, and was asked if he could not be ready for the assault the following morning. News had been received that the battle had been commenced at Knoxville. Burnside had been cut off from telegraphic communications. The President, the Secretary of War, and General Halleck, were in an agony of suspense. My suspense was also great, but more endurable, because I was where I could soon do something to relieve the situation. It was impossible to get Sherman's troops up for the next day. I then asked him if they could not be got up to make the assault on the morning of the 22d, and ordered Thomas to move on that date. But the elements were against us. It rained all the 20th and 21st. The river rose so rapidly that it was difficult to keep the pontoons in place.

General Orlando B. Willcox, a division commander under Burnside, was at this time occupying a position farther up the valley than Knoxville—about Maynardville—and was still in telegraphic communication with the North. A dispatch was received from him saying that he was threatened from the east. The following was sent in reply:

"If you can communicate with General Burnside, say to him that our attack on Bragg will commence in the morning. If successful, such a move will be made as I think will relieve East Tennessee, if he can hold out. Longstreet passing through our lines to Kentucky need not cause alarm. He would find the country so bare that he would lose his transportation and artillery before reaching Kentucky, and would meet such a force before he got through, that he could not return."

Meantime, Sherman continued his crossing without intermission as fast as his troops could be got up. The crossing had to be effected in full view of the enemy on the top of Lookout Mountain. Once over, however, the troops soon disappeared behind the detached hills on the north side, and would not come to view again, either to watchmen on Lookout Mountain or Missionary Ridge, until they emerged between the hills to strike the bank of the river. But when Sherman's advance reached a point opposite the town of Chattanooga, Howard, who, it will be remembered, had been concealed behind the hills on the north side, took up his line of march to join the troops on the south side. His crossing was in full view both from Missionary Ridge and the top of Lookout, and the enemy of course supposed these troops to be Sherman's. This enabled Sherman to get to his assigned position without discovery.

Chapter XLIII.

PREPARATIONS FOR BATTLE — THOMAS CARRIES THE
FIRST LINE OF THE ENEMY — SHERMAN CARRIES
MISSIONARY RIDGE — BATTLE OF LOOKOUT
MOUNTAIN — GENERAL HOOKER'S FIGHT.

O N THE 20TH, when so much was occurring to discourage — rains falling so heavily as to delay the passage of troops over the river at Brown's Ferry and threatening the entire breaking of the bridge; news coming of a battle raging at Knoxville; of Willcox being threatened by a force from the east — a letter was received from Bragg which contained these words: "As there may still be some non-combatants in Chattanooga, I deem it proper to notify you that prudence would dictate their early withdrawal." Of course, I understood that this was a device intended to deceive; but I did not know what the intended deception was. On the 22d, however, a deserter came in who informed me that Bragg was leaving our front, and on that day Buckner's division was sent to reinforce Longstreet at Knoxville, and another division started to follow but was recalled. The object of Bragg's letter, no doubt, was in some way to detain me until Knoxville could be captured, and his troops there be returned to Chattanooga.

During the night of the 21st the rest of the pontoon boats, completed, one hundred and sixteen in all, were carried up to and placed in North Chickamauga. The material for the roadway over these was deposited out of view of the enemy within a few hundred yards of the bank of the Tennessee, where the north end of the bridge was to rest.

Hearing nothing from Burnside, and hearing much of the distress in Washington on his account, I could no longer defer operations for his relief. I determined, therefore, to do on the 23d, with the Army of the Cumberland, what had been intended to be done on the 24th.

The position occupied by the Army of the Cumberland had been made very strong for defence during the months it had been besieged. The line was about a mile from the town, and

extended from Citico Creek, a small stream running near the
base of Missionary Ridge and emptying into the Tennessee
about two miles below the mouth of the South Chickamauga,
on the left, to Chattanooga Creek on the right. All commanding points on the line were well fortified and well equipped
with artillery. The important elevations within the line had all
been carefully fortified and supplied with a proper armament.
Among the elevations so fortified was one to the east of the
town, named Fort Wood. It owed its importance chiefly to
the fact that it lay between the town and Missionary Ridge,
where most of the strength of the enemy was. Fort Wood had
in it twenty-two pieces of artillery, most of which would
reach the nearer points of the enemy's line. On the morning
of the 23d Thomas, according to instructions, moved Granger's corps of two divisions, Sheridan and T. J. Wood commanding, to the foot of Fort Wood, and formed them into
line as if going on parade, Sheridan on the right, Wood to the
left, extending to or near Citico Creek. Palmer, commanding
the 14th corps, held that part of our line facing south and
south-west. He supported Sheridan with one division
(Baird's), while his other division under Johnson remained in
the trenches, under arms, ready to be moved to any point.
Howard's corps was moved in rear of the centre. The picket
lines were within a few hundred yards of each other. At two
o'clock in the afternoon all were ready to advance. By this
time the clouds had lifted so that the enemy could see from
his elevated position all that was going on. The signal for
advance was given by a booming of cannon from Fort Wood
and other points on the line. The rebel pickets were soon
driven back upon the main guards, which occupied minor and
detached heights between the main ridge and our lines. These
too were carried before halting, and before the enemy had
time to reinforce their advance guards. But it was not without
loss on both sides. This movement secured to us a line fully a
mile in advance of the one we occupied in the morning, and
the one which the enemy had occupied up to this time. The
fortifications were rapidly turned to face the other way. During the following night they were made strong. We lost in this
preliminary action about eleven hundred killed and wounded,
while the enemy probably lost quite as heavily, including the

prisoners that were captured. With the exception of the firing of artillery, kept up from Missionary Ridge and Fort Wood until night closed in, this ended the fighting for the first day

The advantage was greatly on our side now, and if I could only have been assured that Burnside could hold out ten days longer I should have rested more easily. But we were doing the best we could for him and the cause.

By the night of the 23d Sherman's command was in a position to move, though one division (Osterhaus's) had not yet crossed the river at Brown's Ferry. The continuous rise in the Tennessee had rendered it impossible to keep the bridge at that point in condition for troops to cross; but I was determined to move that night even without this division. Orders were sent to Osterhaus accordingly to report to Hooker, if he could not cross by eight o'clock on the morning of the 24th. Because of the break in the bridge, Hooker's orders were again changed, but this time only back to those first given to him.

General W. F. Smith had been assigned to duty as Chief Engineer of the Military Division. To him were given the general direction of moving troops by the boats from North Chickamauga, laying the bridge after they reached their position, and generally all the duties pertaining to his office of chief engineer. During the night General Morgan L. Smith's division was marched to the point where the pontoons were, and the brigade of Giles A. Smith was selected for the delicate duty of manning the boats and surprising the enemy's pickets on the south bank of the river. During this night also General J. M. Brannan, chief of artillery, moved forty pieces of artillery, belonging to the Army of the Cumberland, and placed them on the north side of the river so as to command the ground opposite, to aid in protecting the approach to the point where the south end of the bridge was to rest. He had to use Sherman's artillery horses for this purpose, Thomas having none.

At two o'clock in the morning, November 24th, Giles A. Smith pushed out from the North Chickamauga with his one hundred and sixteen boats, each loaded with thirty brave and well-armed men. The boats with their precious freight dropped down quietly with the current to avoid attracting the attention of any one who could convey information to the enemy, until arriving near the mouth of South Chickamauga. Here a few boats were landed, the troops debarked, and a rush was made upon the picket guard known to be at that point. The guard were surprised, and twenty of their number captured. The remainder of the troops effected a landing at the point where the bridge was to start, with equally good results. The work of ferrying over Sherman's command from the north side of the Tennessee was at once commenced, using the pontoons for the purpose. A steamer was also brought up from the town to assist. The rest of M. L. Smith's division came first, then the division of John E. Smith. The troops as they landed were put to work intrenching their position. By daylight the two entire divisions were over, and well covered by the works they had built.

The work of laying the bridge, on which to cross the artillery and cavalry, was now begun. The ferrying over the infantry was continued with the steamer and the pontoons, taking the pontoons, however, as fast as they were wanted to put in their place in the bridge. By a little past noon the bridge was completed, as well as one over the South Chickamauga connecting the troops left on that side with their comrades below, and all the infantry and artillery were on the south bank of the Tennessee.

Sherman at once formed his troops for assault on Missionary Ridge. By one o'clock he started with M. L. Smith on his left, keeping nearly the course of Chickamauga River; J. E. Smith next to the right and a little to the rear; and Ewing still farther to the right and also a little to the rear of J. E. Smith's command, in column, ready to deploy to the right if an enemy should come from that direction. A good skirmish line preceded each of these columns. Soon the foot of the hill was reached; the skirmishers pushed directly up, followed closely by their supports. By half-past three Sherman was in possession of the height without having sustained much loss. A brigade from each division was now brought up, and artillery was dragged to the top of the hill by hand. The enemy did not seem to be aware of this movement until the top of the hill was gained. There had been a drizzling rain during the

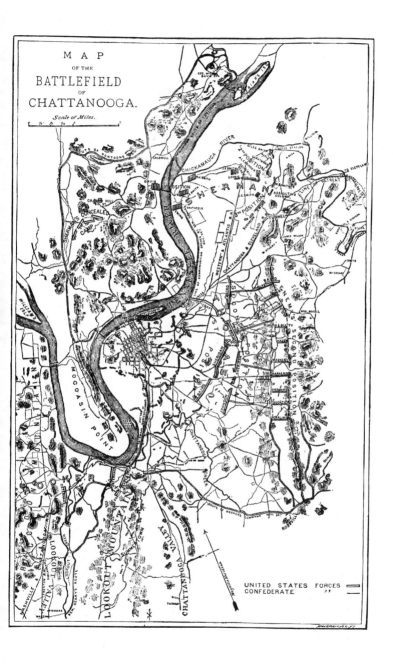

MAP
OF THE
BATTLEFIELD
OF
CHATTANOOGA.

Scale of Miles.

UNITED STATES FORCES
CONFEDERATE.

day, and the clouds were so low that Lookout Mountain and the top of Missionary Ridge were obscured from the view of persons in the valley. But now the enemy opened fire upon their assailants, and made several attempts with their skirmishers to drive them away, but without avail. Later in the day a more determined attack was made, but this, too, failed, and Sherman was left to fortify what he had gained.

Sherman's cavalry took up its line of march soon after the bridge was completed, and by half-past three the whole of it was over both bridges and on its way to strike the enemy's communications at Chickamauga Station. All of Sherman's command was now south of the Tennessee. During the afternoon General Giles A. Smith was severely wounded and carried from the field.

Thomas having done on the 23d what was expected of him on the 24th, there was nothing for him to do this day except to strengthen his position. Howard, however, effected a crossing of Citico Creek and a junction with Sherman, and was directed to report to him. With two or three regiments of his command he moved in the morning along the banks of the Tennessee, and reached the point where the bridge was being laid. He went out on the bridge as far as it was completed from the south end, and saw Sherman superintending the work from the north side and moving himself south as fast as an additional boat was put in and the roadway put upon it. Howard reported to his new chief across the chasm between them, which was now narrow and in a few minutes closed.

While these operations were going on to the east of Chattanooga, Hooker was engaged on the west. He had three divisions: Osterhaus's, of the 15th corps, Army of the Tennessee; Geary's, 12th corps, Army of the Potomac; and Cruft's, 14th corps, Army of the Cumberland. Geary was on the right at Wauhatchie, Cruft at the centre, and Osterhaus near Brown's Ferry. These troops were all west of Lookout Creek. The enemy had the east bank of the creek strongly picketed and intrenched, and three brigades of troops in the rear to reinforce them if attacked. These brigades occupied the summit of the mountain. General Carter L. Stevenson was in command of the whole. Why any troops, except artillery with a small infantry guard, were kept on the mountain-top, I do not see. A hundred men could have held the summit—which is a palisade for more than thirty feet down—against the assault of any number of men from the position Hooker occupied.

The side of Lookout Mountain confronting Hooker's command was rugged, heavily timbered, and full of chasms, making it difficult to advance with troops, even in the absence of an opposing force. Farther up, the ground becomes more even and level, and was in cultivation. On the east side the slope is much more gradual, and a good wagon road, zig-zagging up it, connects the town of Chattanooga with the summit.

Early on the morning of the 24th Hooker moved Geary's division, supported by a brigade of Cruft's, up Lookout Creek, to effect a crossing. The remainder of Cruft's division was to seize the bridge over the creek, near the crossing of the railroad. Osterhaus was to move up to the bridge and cross it. The bridge was seized by Gross's brigade after a slight skirmish with the pickets guarding it. This attracted the enemy so that Geary's movement farther up was not observed. A heavy mist obscured him from the view of the troops on the top of the mountain. He crossed the creek almost unobserved, and captured the picket of over forty men on guard near by. He then commenced ascending the mountain directly in his front. By this time the enemy was seen coming down from their camps on the mountain slope, and filing into their rifle-pits to contest the crossing of the bridge. By eleven o'clock the bridge was complete. Osterhaus was up, and after some sharp skirmishing the enemy was driven away with considerable loss in killed and captured.

While the operations at the bridge were progressing, Geary was pushing up the hill over great obstacles, resisted by the enemy directly in his front, and in face of the guns on top of the mountain. The enemy, seeing their left flank and rear menaced, gave way, and were followed by Cruft and Osterhaus. Soon these were up abreast of Geary, and the whole command pushed up the hill, driving the enemy in advance. By noon Geary had gained the open ground on the north slope of the mountain, with his right close up to the base of the upper palisade, but there were strong fortifications in his front. The rest of the command coming up, a line was formed from the base of the upper palisade to the mouth of Chattanooga Creek.

Thomas and I were on the top of Orchard Knob. Hooker's advance now made our line a continuous one. It was in full view, extending from the Tennessee River, where Sherman had crossed, up Chickamauga River to the base of Mission Ridge, over the top of the north end of the ridge to Chattanooga Valley, then along parallel to the ridge a mile or more, across the valley to the mouth of Chattanooga Creek, thence up the slope of Lookout Mountain to the foot of the upper palisade. The day was hazy, so that Hooker's operations were not visible to us except at moments when the clouds would rise. But the sound of his artillery and musketry was heard incessantly. The enemy on his front was partially fortified, but was soon driven out of his works. During the afternoon the clouds, which had so obscured the top of Lookout all day as to hide whatever was going on from the view of those below, settled down and made it so dark where Hooker was as to stop operations for the time. At four o'clock Hooker reported his position as impregnable. By a little after five direct communication was established, and a brigade of troops was sent from Chattanooga to reinforce him. These troops had to cross Chattanooga Creek and met with some opposition, but soon overcame it, and by night the commander, General Carlin, reported to Hooker and was assigned to his left. I now telegraphed to Washington: "The fight to-day progressed favorably. Sherman carried the end of Missionary Ridge, and his right is now at the tunnel, and his left at Chickamauga Creek. Troops from Lookout Valley carried the point of the mountain, and now hold the eastern slope and a point high up. Hooker reports two thousand prisoners taken, besides which a small number have fallen into our hands from Missionary Ridge." The next day the President replied: "Your dispatches as to fighting on Monday and Tuesday are here. Well done. Many thanks to all. Remember Burnside." And Halleck also telegraphed: "I congratulate you on the success thus far of your plans. I fear that Burnside is hard pushed, and that any further delay may prove fatal. I know you will do all in your power to relieve him."

The division of Jefferson C. Davis, Army of the Cumberland, had been sent to the North Chickamauga to guard the pontoons as they were deposited in the river, and to prevent all ingress or egress of citizens. On the night of the 24th his division, having crossed with Sherman, occupied our extreme left from the upper bridge over the plain to the north base of Missionary Ridge. Firing continued to a late hour in the night, but it was not connected with an assault at any point.

Chapter XLIV.

BATTLE OF CHATTANOOGA—A GALLANT
CHARGE—COMPLETE ROUT OF THE ENEMY—PURSUIT
OF THE CONFEDERATES—GENERAL BRAGG—REMARKS
ON CHATTANOOGA.

AT TWELVE O'CLOCK at night, when all was quiet, I began to give orders for the next day, and sent a dispatch to Willcox to encourage Burnside. Sherman was directed to attack at daylight. Hooker was ordered to move at the same hour, and endeavor to intercept the enemy's retreat if he still remained; if he had gone, then to move directly to Rossville and operate against the left and rear of the force on Missionary Ridge. Thomas was not to move until Hooker had reached Missionary Ridge. As I was with him on Orchard Knob, he would not move without further orders from me.

The morning of the 25th opened clear and bright, and the whole field was in full view from the top of Orchard Knob. It remained so all day. Bragg's headquarters were in full view, and officers—presumably staff officers—could be seen coming and going constantly.

The point of ground which Sherman had carried on the 24th was almost disconnected from the main ridge occupied by the enemy. A low pass, over which there is a wagon road crossing the hill, and near which there is a railroad tunnel, intervenes between the two hills. The problem now was to get to the main ridge. The enemy was fortified on the point; and back farther, where the ground was still higher, was a second fortification commanding the first. Sherman was out as soon as it was light enough to see, and by sunrise his command was in motion. Three brigades held the hill already gained. Morgan L. Smith moved along the east base of Missionary Ridge; Loomis along the west base, supported by two brigades of John E. Smith's division; and Corse with his brigade was between the two, moving directly towards the hill to be captured. The ridge is steep and heavily wooded on the east side, where M. L. Smith's troops were advancing, but cleared and with a more gentle slope on the west side. The troops advanced rapidly and carried the extreme end of the rebel works. Morgan L. Smith advanced to a point which cut the enemy off from the railroad bridge and the means of bringing up supplies by rail from Chickamauga Station, where the main depot was located. The enemy made brave and strenuous efforts to drive our troops from the position we had gained, but without success. The contest lasted for two hours. Corse, a brave and efficient commander, was badly wounded in this assault. Sherman now threatened both Bragg's flank and his stores, and made it necessary for him to weaken other points of his line to strengthen his right. From the position I occupied I could see column after column of Bragg's forces moving against Sherman. Every Confederate gun that could be brought to bear upon the Union forces was concentrated upon him. J. E. Smith, with two brigades, charged up the west side of the ridge to the support of Corse's command, over open ground and in the face of a heavy fire of both artillery and musketry, and reached the very parapet of the enemy. He lay here for a time, but the enemy coming with a heavy force upon his right flank, he was compelled to fall back, followed by the foe. A few hundred yards brought Smith's troops into a wood, where they were speedily reformed, when they charged and drove the attacking party back to his intrenchments.

Seeing the advance, repulse, and second advance of J. E. Smith from the position I occupied, I directed Thomas to send a division to reinforce him. Baird's division was accordingly sent from the right of Orchard Knob. It had to march a considerable distance directly under the eyes of the enemy to reach its position. Bragg at once commenced massing in the same direction. This was what I wanted. But it had now got to be late in the afternoon, and I had expected before this to see Hooker crossing the ridge in the neighborhood of Rossville and compelling Bragg to mass in that direction also.

The enemy had evacuated Lookout Mountain during the night, as I expected he would. In crossing the valley he burned the bridge over Chattanooga Creek, and did all he could to obstruct the roads behind him. Hooker was off bright and early, with no obstructions in his front but distance and the destruction above named. He was detained four

hours crossing Chattanooga Creek, and thus was lost the immediate advantage I expected from his forces. His reaching
Bragg's flank and extending across it was to be the signal for
Thomas's assault of the ridge. But Sherman's condition was
getting so critical that the assault for his relief could not be
delayed any longer.

Sheridan's and Wood's divisions had been lying under arms
from early morning, ready to move the instant the signal was
given. I now directed Thomas to order the charge at once.* I
watched eagerly to see the effect, and became impatient at last
that there was no indication of any charge being made. The
centre of the line which was to make the charge was near
where Thomas and I stood, but concealed from view by an
intervening forest. Turning to Thomas to inquire what caused
the delay, I was surprised to see Thomas J. Wood, one of the
division commanders who was to make the charge, standing
talking to him. I spoke to General Wood, asking him why he
did not charge as ordered an hour before. He replied very
promptly that this was the first he had heard of it, but that he
had been ready all day to move at a moment's notice. I told
him to make the charge at once. He was off in a moment, and
in an incredibly short time loud cheering was heard, and he
and Sheridan were driving the enemy's advance before them
towards Missionary Ridge. The Confederates were strongly
intrenched on the crest of the ridge in front of us, and had a
second line half-way down and another at the base. Our men
drove the troops in front of the lower line of rifle-pits so
rapidly, and followed them so closely, that rebel and Union
troops went over the first line of works almost at the same
time. Many rebels were captured and sent to the rear under
the fire of their own friends higher up the hill. Those that
were not captured retreated, and were pursued. The retreating hordes being between friends and pursuers caused the enemy to fire high to avoid killing their own men. In fact, on
that occasion the Union soldier nearest the enemy was in the
safest position. Without awaiting further orders or stopping
to reform, on our troops went to the second line of works;

*In this order authority was given for the troops to reform after taking the
first line of rifle-pits preparatory to carrying the ridge.

over that and on for the crest—thus effectually carrying out my orders of the 18th for the battle and of the 24th* for this charge.

I watched their progress with intense interest. The fire along the rebel line was terrific. Cannon and musket balls filled the air: but the damage done was in small proportion to the ammunition expended. The pursuit continued until the crest was reached, and soon our men were seen climbing over the Confederate barriers at different points in front of both Sheridan's and Wood's divisions. The retreat of the enemy along most of his line was precipitate and the panic so great that Bragg and his officers lost all control over their men. Many were captured, and thousands threw away their arms in their flight.

Sheridan pushed forward until he reached the Chickamauga River at a point above where the enemy crossed. He met some resistance from troops occupying a second hill in rear of Missionary Ridge, probably to cover the retreat of the main body and of the artillery and trains. It was now getting dark, but Sheridan, without halting on that account pushed his men forward up this second hill slowly and without attracting the attention of the men placed to defend it, while he detached to the right and left to surround the position. The enemy discovered the movement before these dispositions were complete, and beat a hasty retreat, leaving artillery, wagon trains, and many prisoners in our hands. To Sheridan's

---

*CHATTANOOGA, *November* 24, 1863.

MAJOR-GENERAL GEO. H. THOMAS,
        Chattanooga:

General Sherman carried Missionary Ridge as far as the tunnel with only slight skirmishing. His right now rests at the tunnel and on top of the hill, his left at Chickamauga Creek. I have instructed General Sherman to advance as soon as it is light in the morning, and your attack, which will be simultaneous, will be in co-operation. Your command will either carry the rifle-pits and ridge directly in front of them, or move to the left, as the presence of the enemy may require. If Hooker's position on the mountain [cannot be maintained] with a small force, and it is found impracticable to carry the top from where he is, it would be advisable for him to move up the valley with all the force he can spare, and ascend by the first practicable road.

                                        U. S. GRANT,
                                                Major-General.

prompt movement the Army of the Cumberland, and the nation, are indebted for the bulk of the capture of prisoners, artillery, and small-arms that day. Except for his prompt pursuit, so much in this way would not have been accomplished.

While the advance up Mission Ridge was going forward, General Thomas with staff, General Gordon Granger, commander of the corps making the assault, and myself and staff occupied Orchard Knob, from which the entire field could be observed. The moment the troops were seen going over the last line of rebel defences, I ordered Granger to join his command, and mounting my horse I rode to the front. General Thomas left about the same time. Sheridan on the extreme right was already in pursuit of the enemy east of the ridge. Wood, who commanded the division to the left of Sheridan, accompanied his men on horseback in the charge, but did not join Sheridan in the pursuit. To the left, in Baird's front where Bragg's troops had massed against Sherman, the resistance was more stubborn and the contest lasted longer. I ordered Granger to follow the enemy with Wood's division, but he was so much excited, and kept up such a roar of musketry in the direction the enemy had taken, that by the time I could stop the firing the enemy had got well out of the way. The enemy confronting Sherman, now seeing everything to their left giving way, fled also. Sherman, however, was not aware of the extent of our success until after nightfall, when he received orders to pursue at daylight in the morning.

As soon as Sherman discovered that the enemy had left his front he directed his reserves, Davis's division of the Army of the Cumberland, to push over the pontoon-bridge at the mouth of the Chickamauga, and to move forward to Chickamauga Station. He ordered Howard to move up the stream some two miles to where there was an old bridge, repair it during the night, and follow Davis at four o'clock in the morning. Morgan L. Smith was ordered to reconnoitre the tunnel to see if that was still held. Nothing was found there but dead bodies of men of both armies. The rest of Sherman's command was directed to follow Howard at daylight in the morning to get on to the railroad towards Graysville.

Hooker, as stated, was detained at Chattanooga Creek by the destruction of the bridge at that point. He got his troops over, with the exception of the artillery, by fording the stream at a little after three o'clock. Leaving his artillery to follow when the bridge should be reconstructed, he pushed on with the remainder of his command. At Rossville he came upon the flank of a division of the enemy, which soon commenced a retreat along the ridge. This threw them on Palmer. They could make but little resistance in the position they were caught in, and as many of them as could do so escaped. Many, however, were captured. Hooker's position during the night of the 25th was near Rossville, extending east of the ridge. Palmer was on his left, on the road to Graysville.

During the night I telegraphed to Willcox that Bragg had been defeated, and that immediate relief would be sent to Burnside if he could hold out; to Halleck I sent an announcement of our victory, and informed him that forces would be sent up the valley to relieve Burnside.

Before the battle of Chattanooga opened I had taken measures for the relief of Burnside the moment the way should be clear. Thomas was directed to have the little steamer that had been built at Chattanooga loaded to its capacity with rations and ammunition. Granger's corps was to move by the south bank of the Tennessee River to the mouth of the Holston, and up that to Knoxville, accompanied by the boat. In addition to the supplies transported by boat, the men were to carry forty rounds of ammunition in their cartridge-boxes, and four days' rations in haversacks.

In the battle of Chattanooga, troops from the Army of the Potomac, from the Army of the Tennessee, and from the Army of the Cumberland participated. In fact, the accidents growing out of the heavy rains and the sudden rise in the Tennessee River so mingled the troops that the organizations were not kept together, under their respective commanders, during the battle. Hooker, on the right, had Geary's division of the 12th corps, Army of the Potomac; Osterhaus's division of the 15th corps, Army of the Tennessee; and Cruft's division of the Army of the Cumberland. Sherman had three divisions of his own army, Howard's corps from the Army of the Potomac, and Jefferson C. Davis's division of the Army of the Cumberland. There was no jealousy—hardly rivalry. Indeed, I doubt whether officers or men took any note at the time of the fact of this intermingling of commands. All saw a defiant foe surrounding them, and took it for granted that every move was intended to dislodge him, and it made no difference where the troops came from so that the end was accomplished.

The victory at Chattanooga was won against great odds, considering the advantage the enemy had of position, and was accomplished more easily than was expected by reason of Bragg's making several grave mistakes: first, in sending away his ablest corps commander with over twenty thousand troops; second, in sending away a division of troops on the eve of battle; third, in placing so much of a force on the plain in front of his impregnable position.

It was known that Mr. Jefferson Davis had visited Bragg on Missionary Ridge a short time before my reaching Chattanooga. It was reported and believed that he had come out to reconcile a serious difference between Bragg and Longstreet, and finding this difficult to do, planned the campaign against Knoxville, to be conducted by the latter general. I had known both Bragg and Longstreet before the war, the latter very well. We had been three years at West Point together, and, after my graduation, for a time in the same regiment. Then we served together in the Mexican War. I had known Bragg in Mexico, and met him occasionally subsequently. I could well understand how there might be an irreconcilable difference between them.

Bragg was a remarkably intelligent and well-informed man, professionally and otherwise. He was also thoroughly upright. But he was possessed of an irascible temper, and was naturally disputatious. A man of the highest moral character and the most correct habits, yet in the old army he was in frequent trouble. As a subordinate he was always on the lookout to catch his commanding officer infringing his prerogatives; as a post commander he was equally vigilant to detect the slightest neglect, even of the most trivial order.

I have heard in the old army an anecdote very characteristic of Bragg. On one occasion, when stationed at a post of several companies commanded by a field officer, he was himself commanding one of the companies and at the same time acting as post quartermaster and commissary. He was first lieutenant at the time, but his captain was detached on other duty. As commander of the company he made a requisition upon the quartermaster—himself—for something he wanted. As quartermaster he declined to fill the requisition, and endorsed on the back of it his reasons for so doing. As company commander he responded to this, urging that his requisition called for nothing but what he was entitled to, and that it was the duty of the quartermaster to fill it. As quartermaster he still persisted that he was right. In this condition of affairs Bragg referred the whole matter to the commanding officer of the post. The latter, when he saw the nature of the matter referred, exclaimed: "My God, Mr. Bragg, you have quarrelled with every officer in the army, and now you are quarrelling with yourself!"

Longstreet was an entirely different man. He was brave, honest, intelligent, a very capable soldier, subordinate to his superiors, just and kind to his subordinates, but jealous of his own rights, which he had the courage to maintain. He was never on the lookout to detect a slight, but saw one as soon as anybody when intentionally given.

It may be that Longstreet was not sent to Knoxville for the reason stated, but because Mr. Davis had an exalted opinion of his own military genius, and thought he saw a chance of "killing two birds with one stone." On several occasions during the war he came to the relief of the Union army by means of his *superior military genius*.

I speak advisedly when I say Mr. Davis prided himself on his military capacity. He says so himself, virtually, in his answer to the notice of his nomination to the Confederate presidency. Some of his generals have said so in their writings since the downfall of the Confederacy.

My recollection is that my first orders for the battle of Chattanooga were as fought. Sherman was to get on Missionary Ridge, as he did; Hooker to cross the north end of Lookout Mountain, as he did, sweep across Chattanooga Valley and get across the south end of the ridge near Rossville. When Hooker had secured that position the Army of the Cumberland was to assault in the centre. Before Sherman arrived, however, the order was so changed as that Hooker was directed to come to Chattanooga by the north bank of the Tennessee River. The waters in the river, owing to heavy rains, rose so fast that the bridge at Brown's Ferry could not be maintained in a condition to be used in crossing troops upon it. For this reason Hooker's orders were changed by telegraph back to what they were originally.

NOTE.—From this point on this volume was written (with the exception of the campaign in the Wilderness, which had been previously written) by General Grant after his great illness in April, and the present arrangement of the subject-matter was made by him between the 10th and 18th of July, 1885.

Chapter XLV.

C HATTANOOGA now being secure to the National troops
beyond any doubt, I immediately turned my attention
to relieving Knoxville, about the situation of which the President, in particular, was very anxious. Prior to the battles, I
had made preparations for sending troops to the relief of
Burnside at the very earliest moment after securing Chattanooga. We had there two little steamers which had been built
and fitted up from the remains of old boats and put in condition to run. General Thomas was directed to have one of
these boats loaded with rations and ammunition and move up
the Tennessee River to the mouth of the Holston, keeping the
boat all the time abreast of the troops. General Granger, with
the 4th corps reinforced to make twenty thousand men, was
to start the moment Missionary Ridge was carried, and under
no circumstances were the troops to return to their old
camps. With the provisions carried, and the little that could
be got in the country, it was supposed he could hold out until
Longstreet was driven away, after which event East Tennessee
would furnish abundance of food for Burnside's army and his
own also.

While following the enemy on the 26th, and again on the
morning of the 27th, part of the time by the road to Ringgold, I directed Thomas, verbally, not to start Granger until
he received further orders from me; advising him that I was
going to the front to more fully see the situation. I was not
right sure but that Bragg's troops might be over their stampede by the time they reached Dalton. In that case Bragg
might think it well to take the road back to Cleveland, move
thence towards Knoxville, and, uniting with Longstreet, make
a sudden dash upon Burnside.

When I arrived at Ringgold, however, on the 27th, I
saw that the retreat was most earnest. The enemy had been
throwing away guns, caissons and small-arms, abandoning

452

provisions, and, altogether, seemed to be moving like a disorganized mob, with the exception of Cleburne's division, which was acting as rear-guard to cover the retreat.

When Hooker moved from Rossville toward Ringgold Palmer's division took the road to Graysville, and Sherman moved by the way of Chickamauga Station toward the same point. As soon as I saw the situation at Ringgold I sent a staff officer back to Chattanooga to advise Thomas of the condition of affairs, and direct him by my orders to start Granger at once. Feeling now that the troops were already on the march for the relief of Burnside I was in no hurry to get back, but stayed at Ringgold through the day to prepare for the return of our troops.

Ringgold is in a valley in the mountains, situated between East Chickamauga Creek and Taylor's Ridge, and about twenty miles south-east from Chattanooga. I arrived just as the artillery that Hooker had left behind at Chattanooga Creek got up. His men were attacking Cleburne's division, which had taken a strong position in the adjacent hills so as to cover the retreat of the Confederate army through a narrow gorge which presents itself at that point. Just beyond the gorge the valley is narrow, and the creek so tortuous that it has to be crossed a great many times in the course of the first mile. This attack was unfortunate, and cost us some men unnecessarily. Hooker captured, however, 3 pieces of artillery and 230 prisoners, and 130 rebel dead were left upon the field.

I directed General Hooker to collect the flour and wheat in the neighboring mills for the use of the troops, and then to destroy the mills and all other property that could be of use to the enemy, but not to make any wanton destruction.

At this point Sherman came up, having reached Graysville with his troops, where he found Palmer had preceded him. Palmer had picked up many prisoners and much abandoned property on the route. I went back in the evening to Graysville with Sherman, remained there over night and did not return to Chattanooga until the following night, the 29th. I then found that Thomas had not yet started Granger, thus having lost a full day which I deemed of so much importance in determining the fate of Knoxville. Thomas and Granger were aware that on the 23d of the month Burnside had telegraphed that his supplies would last for ten or twelve days and during that time he could hold out against Longstreet, but if not relieved within the time indicated he would be obliged to surrender or attempt to retreat. To effect a retreat would have been an impossibility. He was already very low in ammunition, and with an army pursuing he would not have been able to gather supplies.

Finding that Granger had not only not started but was very reluctant to go, he having decided for himself that it was a very bad move to make, I sent word to General Sherman of the situation and directed him to march to the relief of Knoxville. I also gave him the problem that we had to solve—that Burnside had now but four to six days supplies left, and that he must be relieved within that time.

Sherman, fortunately, had not started on his return from Graysville, having sent out detachments on the railroad which runs from Dalton to Cleveland and Knoxville to thoroughly destroy that road, and these troops had not yet returned to camp. I was very loath to send Sherman, because his men needed rest after their long march from Memphis and hard fighting at Chattanooga. But I had become satisfied that Burnside would not be rescued if his relief depended upon General Granger's movements.

Sherman had left his camp on the north side of the Tennessee River, near Chattanooga, on the night of the 23d, the men having two days' cooked rations in their haversacks. Expecting to be back in their tents by that time and to be engaged in battle while out, they took with them neither overcoats nor blankets. The weather was already cold, and at night they must have suffered more or less. The two days' rations had already lasted them five days; and they were now to go through a country which had been run over so much by Confederate troops that there was but little probability of finding much food. They did, however, succeed in capturing some flour. They also found a good deal of bran in some of the mills, which the men made up into bread; and in this and other ways they eked out an existence until they could reach Knoxville.

I was so very anxious that Burnside should get news of the

steps being taken for his relief, and thus induce him to hold out a little longer if it became necessary, that I determined to send a message to him. I therefore sent a member of my staff, Colonel J. H. Wilson, to get into Knoxville if he could, report to Burnside the situation fully, and give him all the encouragement possible. Mr. Charles A. Dana was at Chattanooga during the battle, and had been there even before I assumed command. Mr. Dana volunteered to accompany Colonel Wilson, and did accompany him. I put the information of what was being done for the relief of Knoxville into writing, and directed that in some way or other it must be secretly managed so as to have a copy of this fall into the hands of General Longstreet. They made the trip safely; General Longstreet did learn of Sherman's coming in advance of his reaching there, and Burnside was prepared to hold out even for a longer time if it had been necessary.

Burnside had stretched a boom across the Holston River to catch scows and flats as they floated down. On these, by previous arrangements with the loyal people of East Tennessee, were placed flour and corn, with forage and provisions generally, and were thus secured for the use of the Union troops. They also drove cattle into Knoxville by the east side, which was not covered by the enemy; so that when relief arrived Burnside had more provisions on hand than when he had last reported.

Our total loss (not including Burnside's) in all these engagements amounted to 757 killed, 4,529 wounded and 330 missing. We captured 6,142 prisoners—about 50 per cent. more than the enemy reported for their total loss—40 pieces of artillery, 69 artillery carriages and caissons and over 7,000 stands of small-arms. The enemy's loss in arms was probably much greater than here reported, because we picked up a great many that were found abandoned.

I had at Chattanooga, in round numbers, about 60,000 men. Bragg had about half this number, but his position was supposed to be impregnable. It was his own fault that he did not have more men present. He had sent Longstreet away with his corps swelled by reinforcements up to over twenty thousand men, thus reducing his own force more than one-third and depriving himself of the presence of the ablest general of his command. He did this, too, after our troops had opened a line of communication by way of Brown's and Kelly's ferries with Bridgeport, thus securing full rations and supplies of every kind; and also when he knew reinforcements were coming to me. Knoxville was of no earthly use to him while Chattanooga was in our hands. If he should capture Chattanooga, Knoxville with its garrison would have fallen into his hands without a struggle. I have never been able to see the wisdom of this move.

Then, too, after Sherman had arrived, and when Bragg knew that he was on the north side of the Tennessee River, he sent Buckner's division to reinforce Longstreet. He also started another division a day later, but our attack having commenced before it reached Knoxville Bragg ordered it back. It had got so far, however, that it could not return to Chattanooga in time to be of service there. It is possible this latter blunder may have been made by Bragg having become confused as to what was going on on our side. Sherman had, as already stated, crossed to the north side of the Tennessee River at Brown's Ferry, in full view of Bragg's troops from Lookout Mountain, a few days before the attack. They then disappeared behind foot hills, and did not come to the view of the troops on Missionary Ridge until they met their assault. Bragg knew it was Sherman's troops that had crossed, and, they being so long out of view, may have supposed that they had gone up the north bank of the Tennessee River to the relief of Knoxville and that Longstreet was therefore in danger. But the first great blunder, detaching Longstreet, cannot be accounted for in any way I know of. If he had captured Chattanooga, East Tennessee would have fallen without a struggle. It would have been a victory for us to have got our army away from Chattanooga safely. It was a manifold greater victory to drive away the besieging army; a still greater one to defeat that army in his chosen ground and nearly annihilate it.

The probabilities are that our loss in killed was the heavier, as we were the attacking party. The enemy reported his loss in killed at 361: but as he reported his missing at 4,146 while we held over 6,000 of them as prisoners, and there must have been hundreds if not thousands who deserted, but little reliance can be placed on this report. There was certainly great dissatisfaction with Bragg on the part of the soldiers for his harsh treatment of them, and a disposition to get away if they could. Then, too, Chattanooga, following in the same half year with Gettysburg in the East and Vicksburg in the West, there was much the same feeling in the South at this time that there had been in the North the fall and winter before. If the same license had been allowed the people and press in the South that was allowed in the North, Chattanooga would probably have been the last battle fought for the preservation of the Union.

General William F. Smith's services in these battles had been such that I thought him eminently entitled to promotion. I was aware that he had previously been named by the President for promotion to the grade of major-general, but that the Senate had rejected the nomination. I was not aware of the reasons for this course, and therefore strongly recommended him for a major-generalcy. My recommendation was heeded and the appointment made.

Upon the raising of the siege of Knoxville I, of course, informed the authorities at Washington—the President and Secretary of War—of the fact, which caused great rejoicing there. The President especially was rejoiced that Knoxville had been relieved* without further bloodshed. The safety of Burnside's army and the loyal people of East Tennessee had been the subject of much anxiety to the President for several months, during which time he was doing all he could to relieve the situation; sending a new commander† with a few thousand troops by the way of Cumberland Gap, and tele-

---

*WASHINGTON, D. C.,
December 8, 1863, 10.2 A.M.

MAJ.-GENERAL U. S. GRANT:

Understanding that your lodgment at Knoxville and at Chattanooga is now secure, I wish to tender you, and all under your command, my more than thanks, my profoundest gratitude for the skill, courage, and perseverance with which you and they, over so great difficulties, have effected that important object. God bless you all.

A. LINCOLN,
President U. S.

†General John G. Foster.

graphing me daily, almost hourly, to "remember Burnside," "do something for Burnside," and other appeals of like tenor. He saw no escape for East Tennessee until after our victory at Chattanooga. Even then he was afraid that Burnside might be out of ammunition, in a starving condition, or overpowered: and his anxiety was still intense until he heard that Longstreet had been driven from the field.

Burnside followed Longstreet only to Strawberry Plains, some twenty miles or more east, and then stopped, believing that Longstreet would leave the State. The latter did not do so, however, but stopped only a short distance farther on and subsisted his army for the entire winter off East Tennessee. Foster now relieved Burnside. Sherman made disposition of his troops along the Tennessee River in accordance with instructions. I left Thomas in command at Chattanooga, and, about the 20th of December, moved my headquarters to Nashville, Tennessee.

Nashville was the most central point from which to communicate with my entire military division, and also with the authorities at Washington. While remaining at Chattanooga I was liable to have my telegraphic communications cut so as to throw me out of communication with both my command and Washington.

Nothing occurred at Nashville worthy of mention during the winter,* so I set myself to the task of having troops in positions from which they could move to advantage, and in collecting all necessary supplies so as to be ready to claim a due share of the enemy's attention upon the appearance of the first good weather in the spring. I expected to retain the command I then had, and prepared myself for the campaign against Atlanta. I also had great hopes of having a campaign made against Mobile from the Gulf. I expected after Atlanta

---

*During this winter the citizens of Jo Davies County, Ill., subscribed for and had a diamond-hilted sword made for General Grant, which was always known as the Chattanooga sword. The scabbard was of gold, and was ornamented with a scroll running nearly its entire length, displaying in engraved letters the names of the battles in which General Grant had participated.

Congress also gave him a vote of thanks for the victories at Chattanooga, and voted him a gold medal for Vicksburg and Chattanooga. All such things are now in the possession of the government at Washington.

fell to occupy that place permanently, and to cut off Lee's army from the West by way of the road running through Augusta to Atlanta and thence south-west. I was preparing to hold Atlanta with a small garrison, and it was my expectation to push through to Mobile if that city was in our possession: if not, to Savannah; and in this manner to get possession of the only east and west railroad that would then be left to the enemy. But the spring campaign against Mobile was not made.

The Army of the Ohio had been getting supplies over Cumberland Gap until their animals had nearly all starved. I now determined to go myself to see if there was any possible chance of using that route in the spring, and if not to abandon it. Accordingly I left Nashville in the latter part of December by rail for Chattanooga. From Chattanooga I took one of the little steamers previously spoken of as having been built there, and, putting my horses aboard, went up to the junction of the Clinch with the Tennessee. From that point the railroad had been repaired up to Knoxville and out east to Strawberry Plains. I went by rail therefore to Knoxville, where I remained for several days. General John G. Foster was then commanding the Department of the Ohio. It was an intensely cold winter, the thermometer being down as low as zero every morning for more than a week while I was at Knoxville and on my way from there on horseback to Lexington, Kentucky, the first point where I could reach rail to carry me back to my headquarters at Nashville.

The road over Cumberland Gap, and back of it, was strewn with *débris* of broken wagons and dead animals, much as I had found it on my first trip to Chattanooga over Waldron's Ridge. The road had been cut up to as great a depth as clay could be by mules and wagons, and in that condition frozen; so that the ride of six days from Strawberry Plains to Lexington over these holes and knobs in the road was a very cheerless one, and very disagreeable.

I found a great many people at home along that route, both in Tennessee and Kentucky, and, almost universally, intensely loyal. They would collect in little places where we would stop of evenings, to see me, generally hearing of my approach before we arrived. The people naturally expected to see the commanding general the oldest person in the party. I was then forty-one years of age, while my medical director was gray-haired and probably twelve or more years my senior. The crowds would generally swarm around him, and thus give me an opportunity of quietly dismounting and getting into the house. It also gave me an opportunity of hearing passing remarks from one spectator to another about their general. Those remarks were apt to be more complimentary to the cause than to the appearance of the supposed general, owing to his being muffled up, and also owing to the travel-worn condition we were all in after a hard day's ride. I was back in Nashville by the 13th of January, 1864.

When I started on this trip it was necessary for me to have some person along who could turn dispatches into cipher, and who could also read the cipher dispatches which I was liable to receive daily and almost hourly. Under the rules of the War Department at that time, Mr. Stanton had taken entire control of the matter of regulating the telegraph and determining how it should be used, and of saying who, and who alone, should have the ciphers. The operators possessed of the ciphers, as well as the ciphers used, were practically independent of the commanders whom they were serving immediately under, and had to report to the War Department through General Stager all the dispatches which they received or forwarded.

I was obliged to leave the telegraphic operator back at Nashville, because that was the point at which all dispatches to me would come, to be forwarded from there. As I have said, it was necessary for me also to have an operator during this inspection who had possession of this cipher to enable me to telegraph to my division and to the War Department without my dispatches being read by all the operators along the line of wires over which they were transmitted. Accordingly I ordered the cipher operator to turn over the key to Captain Cyrus B. Comstock, of the Corps of Engineers, whom I had selected as a wise and discreet man who certainly could be trusted with the cipher if the operator at my headquarters could.

The operator refused point blank to turn over the key to Captain Comstock as directed by me, stating that his orders from the War Department were not to give it to anybody—

the commanding general or any one else. I told him I would see whether he would or not. He said that if he did he would be punished. I told him if he did not he most certainly would be punished. Finally, seeing that punishment was certain if he refused longer to obey my order, and being somewhat remote (even if he was not protected altogether from the consequences of his disobedience to his orders) from the War Department, he yielded. When I returned from Knoxville I found quite a commotion. The operator had been reprimanded very severely and ordered to be relieved. I informed the Secretary of War, or his assistant secretary in charge of the telegraph, Stager, that the man could not be relieved, for he had only obeyed my orders. It was absolutely necessary for me to have the cipher, and the man would most certainly have been punished if he had not delivered it; that they would have to punish me if they punished anybody, or words to that effect.

This was about the only thing approaching a disagreeable difference between the Secretary of War and myself that occurred until the war was over, when we had another little spat. Owing to his natural disposition to assume all power and control in all matters that he had anything whatever to do with, he boldly took command of the armies, and, while issuing no orders on the subject, prohibited any order from me going out of the adjutant-general's office until he had approved it. This was done by directing the adjutant-general to hold any orders that came from me to be issued from the adjutant-general's office until he had examined them and given his approval. He never disturbed himself, either, in examining my orders until it was entirely convenient for him; so that orders which I had prepared would often lie there three or four days before he would sanction them. I remonstrated against this in writing, and the Secretary apologetically restored me to my rightful position of General-in-Chief of the Army. But he soon lapsed again and took control much as before.

After the relief of Knoxville Sherman had proposed to Burnside that he should go with him to drive Longstreet out of Tennessee; but Burnside assured him that with the troops which had been brought by Granger, and which were to be left, he would be amply prepared to dispose of Longstreet without availing himself of this offer. As before stated Sherman's command had left their camps north of the Tennessee, near Chattanooga, with two days' rations in their haversacks, without coats or blankets, and without many wagons, expecting to return to their camps by the end of that time. The weather was now cold and they were suffering, but still they were ready to make the further sacrifice, had it been required, for the good of the cause which had brought them into service. Sherman, having accomplished the object for which he was sent, marched back leisurely to his old camp on the Tennessee River.

Chapter XLVI.

OPERATIONS IN MISSISSIPPI—LONGSTREET IN EAST
TENNESSEE—COMMISSIONED LIEUTENANT-GENERAL—
COMMANDING THE ARMIES OF THE UNITED STATES—
FIRST INTERVIEW WITH PRESIDENT LINCOLN.

SOON AFTER his return from Knoxville I ordered Sherman to distribute his forces from Stevenson to Decatur and thence north to Nashville; Sherman suggested that he be permitted to go back to Mississippi, to the limits of his own department and where most of his army still remained, for the purpose of clearing out what Confederates might still be left on the east bank of the Mississippi River to impede its navigation by our boats. He expected also to have the co-operation of Banks to do the same thing on the west shore. Of course I approved heartily.

About the 10th of January Sherman was back in Memphis, where Hurlbut commanded, and got together his Memphis men, or ordered them collected and sent to Vicksburg. He then went to Vicksburg and out to where McPherson was in command, and had him organize his surplus troops so as to give him about 20,000 men in all.

Sherman knew that General (Bishop) Polk was occupying Meridian with his headquarters, and had two divisions of infantry with a considerable force of cavalry scattered west of him. He determined, therefore, to move directly upon Meridian.

I had sent some 2,500 cavalry under General Sooy Smith to Sherman's department, and they had mostly arrived before Sherman got to Memphis. Hurlbut had 7,000 cavalry, and Sherman ordered him to reinforce Smith so as to give the latter a force of about 7,000 with which to go against Forrest, who was then known to be south-east from Memphis. Smith was ordered to move about the 1st of February.

While Sherman was waiting at Vicksburg for the arrival of Hurlbut with his surplus men, he sent out scouts to ascertain the position and strength of the enemy and to bring back all the information they could gather. When these scouts returned it was through them that he got the information of General Polk's being at Meridian, and of the strength and disposition of his command.

Forrest had about 4,000 cavalry with him, composed of thoroughly well-disciplined men, who under so able a leader were very effective. Smith's command was nearly double that of Forrest, but not equal, man to man, for the lack of a successful experience such as Forrest's men had had. The fact is, troops who have fought a few battles and won, and followed up their victories, improve upon what they were before to an extent that can hardly be counted by percentage. The difference in result is often decisive victory instead of inglorious defeat. This same difference, too, is often due to the way troops are officered, and for the particular kind of warfare which Forrest had carried on neither army could present a more effective officer than he was.

Sherman got off on the 3d of February and moved out on his expedition, meeting with no opposition whatever until he crossed the Big Black, and with no great deal of opposition after that until he reached Jackson, Mississippi. This latter place he reached on the 6th or 7th, Brandon on the 8th, and Morton on the 9th. Up to this time he moved in two columns to enable him to get a good supply of forage, etc., and expedite the march. Here, however, there were indications of the concentration of Confederate infantry, and he was obliged to keep his army close together. He had no serious engagement; but he met some of the enemy who destroyed a few of his wagons about Decatur, Mississippi, where, by the way, Sherman himself came near being picked up.

He entered Meridian on the 14th of the month, the enemy having retreated toward Demopolis, Alabama. He spent several days in Meridian in thoroughly destroying the railroad to the north and south, and also for the purpose of hearing from Sooy Smith, who he supposed had met Forrest before this time and he hoped had gained a decisive victory because of a superiority of numbers. Hearing nothing of him, however, he started on his return trip to Vicksburg. There he learned that Smith, while waiting for a few of his men who had been ice-bound in the Ohio River, instead of getting off on the 1st as expected, had not left until the 11th. Smith did meet Forrest, but the result was decidedly in Forrest's favor.

Sherman had written a letter to Banks, proposing a co-operative movement with him against Shreveport, subject to my approval. I disapproved of Sherman's going himself, because I had other important work for him to do, but consented that he might send a few troops to the aid of Banks, though their time to remain absent must be limited. We must have them for the spring campaign. The trans-Mississippi movement proved abortive.

My eldest son, who had accompanied me on the Vicksburg campaign and siege, had while there contracted disease, which grew worse, until he had grown so dangerously ill that on the 24th of January I obtained permission to go to St. Louis, where he was staying at the time, to see him, hardly expecting to find him alive on my arrival. While I was permitted to go, I was not permitted to turn over my command to any one else, but was directed to keep the headquarters with me and to communicate regularly with all parts of my division and with Washington, just as though I had remained at Nashville.

When I obtained this leave I was at Chattanooga, having gone there again to make preparations to have the troops of Thomas in the southern part of Tennessee co-operate with Sherman's movement in Mississippi. I directed Thomas, and Logan who was at Scottsboro, Alabama, to keep up a threatening movement to the south against J. E. Johnston, who had again relieved Bragg, for the purpose of making him keep as many troops as possible there.

I learned through Confederate sources that Johnston had already sent two divisions in the direction of Mobile, presumably to operate against Sherman, and two more divisions to Longstreet in East Tennessee. Seeing that Johnston had depleted in this way, I directed Thomas to send at least ten thousand men, besides Stanley's division which was already to the east, into East Tennessee, and notified Schofield, who was now in command in East Tennessee, of this movement of troops into his department and also of the reinforcements Longstreet had received. My object was to drive Longstreet out of East Tennessee as a part of the preparations for my spring campaign.

About this time General Foster, who had been in command of the Department of the Ohio after Burnside until Schofield relieved him,* advised me that he thought it would be a good thing to keep Longstreet just where he was; that he was perfectly quiet in East Tennessee, and if he was forced to leave there, his whole well-equipped army would be free to go to any place where it could effect the most for their cause. I thought the advice was good, and, adopting that view, countermanded the orders for pursuit of Longstreet.

On the 12th of February I ordered Thomas to take Dalton and hold it, if possible; and I directed him to move without delay. Finding that he had not moved, on the 17th I urged him again to start, telling him how important it was, that the object of the movement was to co-operate with Sherman, who was moving eastward and might be in danger. Then again on the 21st, he not yet having started, I asked him if he could not start the next day. He finally got off on the 22d or 23d. The enemy fell back from his front without a battle, but took a new position quite as strong and farther to the rear. Thomas reported that he could not go any farther, because it was impossible with his poor teams, nearly starved, to keep up supplies until the railroads were repaired. He soon fell back.

Schofield also had to return for the same reason. He could not carry supplies with him, and Longstreet was between him and the supplies still left in the country. Longstreet, in his retreat, would be moving towards his supplies, while our forces, following, would be receding from theirs. On the 2d of March, however, I learned of Sherman's success, which eased my mind very much. The next day, the 3d, I was ordered to Washington.

----

*Washington, D. C.,
December 29, 1863.

Maj.-General U. S. Grant:

General Foster has asked to be relieved from his command on account of disability from old wounds. Should his request be granted, who would you like as his successor? It is possible that Schofield will be sent to your command.

H. W. HALLECK,
General-in-Chief.

(*Official.*)

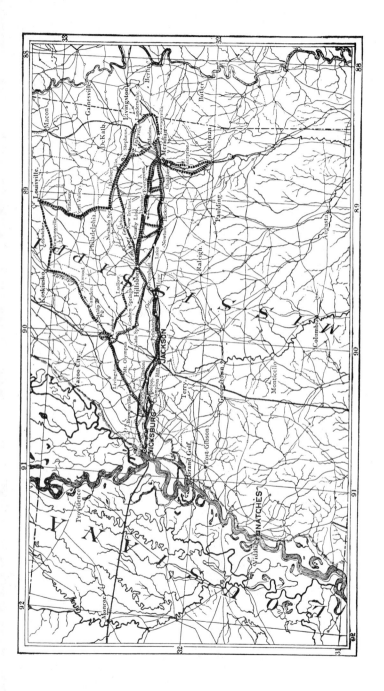

The bill restoring the grade of lieutenant-general of the army had passed through Congress and became a law on the 26th of February. My nomination had been sent to the Senate on the 1st of March and confirmed the next day (the 2d). I was ordered to Washington on the 3d to receive my commission, and started the day following that. The commission was handed to me on the 9th. It was delivered to me at the Executive Mansion by President Lincoln in the presence of his Cabinet, my eldest son, those of my staff who were with me and a few other visitors.

The President in presenting my commission read from a paper—stating, however, as a preliminary, and prior to the delivery of it, that he had drawn that up on paper, knowing my disinclination to speak in public, and handed me a copy in advance so that I might prepare a few lines of reply. The President said:

"General Grant, the nation's appreciation of what you have done, and its reliance upon you for what remains to be done in the existing great struggle, are now presented, with this commission constituting you lieutenant-general in the Army of the United States. With this high honor, devolves upon you, also, a corresponding responsibility. As the country herein trusts you, so, under God, it will sustain you. I scarcely need to add, that, with what I here speak for the nation, goes my own hearty personal concurrence."

To this I replied: "Mr. President, I accept the commission, with gratitude for the high honor conferred. With the aid of the noble armies that have fought in so many fields for our common country, it will be my earnest endeavor not to disappoint your expectations. I feel the full weight of the responsibilities now devolving on me; and I know that if they are met, it will be due to those armies, and above all, to the favor of that Providence which leads both nations and men."

On the 10th I visited the headquarters of the Army of the Potomac at Brandy Station; then returned to Washington, and pushed west at once to make my arrangements for turning over the commands there and giving general directions for the preparations to be made for the spring campaign.

It had been my intention before this to remain in the West, even if I was made lieutenant-general; but when I got to

Washington and saw the situation it was plain that here was
the point for the commanding general to be. No one else
could, probably, resist the pressure that would be brought to
bear upon him to desist from his own plans and pursue
others. I determined, therefore, before I started back to have
Sherman advanced to my late position, McPherson to Sherman's in command of the department, and Logan to the command of McPherson's corps. These changes were all made on
my recommendation and without hesitation. My commission
as lieutenant-general was given to me on the 9th of March,
1864. On the following day, as already stated, I visited General Meade, commanding the Army of the Potomac, at his
headquarters at Brandy Station, north of the Rapidan. I had
known General Meade slightly in the Mexican war, but had
not met him since until this visit. I was a stranger to most of
the Army of the Potomac, I might say to all except the officers
of the regular army who had served in the Mexican war.
There had been some changes ordered in the organization of
that army before my promotion. One was the consolidation
of five corps into three, thus throwing some officers of rank
out of important commands. Meade evidently thought that I
might want to make still one more change not yet ordered.
He said to me that I might want an officer who had served
with me in the West, mentioning Sherman specially, to take
his place. If so, he begged me not to hesitate about making
the change. He urged that the work before us was of such
vast importance to the whole nation that the feeling or wishes
of no one person should stand in the way of selecting the
right men for all positions. For himself, he would serve to the
best of his ability wherever placed. I assured him that I had
no thought of substituting any one for him. As to Sherman,
he could not be spared from the West.

This incident gave me even a more favorable opinion of
Meade than did his great victory at Gettysburg the July before. It is men who wait to be selected, and not those who
seek, from whom we may always expect the most efficient
service.

Meade's position afterwards proved embarrassing to me if
not to him. He was commanding an army and, for nearly a
year previous to my taking command of all the armies, was in

supreme command of the Army of the Potomac—except from the authorities at Washington. All other general officers occupying similar positions were independent in their commands so far as any one present with them was concerned. I tried to make General Meade's position as nearly as possible what it would have been if I had been in Washington or any other place away from his command. I therefore gave all orders for the movements of the Army of the Potomac to Meade to have them executed. To avoid the necessity of having to give orders direct, I established my headquarters near his, unless there were reasons for locating them elsewhere. This sometimes happened, and I had on occasions to give orders direct to the troops affected. On the 11th I returned to Washington and, on the day after, orders were published by the War Department placing me in command of all the armies. I had left Washington the night before to return to my old command in the West and to meet Sherman whom I had telegraphed to join me in Nashville.

Sherman assumed command of the military division of the Mississippi on the 18th of March, and we left Nashville together for Cincinnati. I had Sherman accompany me that far on my way back to Washington so that we could talk over the matters about which I wanted to see him, without losing any more time from my new command than was necessary. The first point which I wished to discuss was particularly about the co-operation of his command with mine when the spring campaign should commence. There were also other and minor points, minor as compared with the great importance of the question to be decided by sanguinary war—the restoration to duty of officers who had been relieved from important commands, namely McClellan, Burnside and Fremont in the East, and Buell, McCook, Negley and Crittenden in the West.

Some time in the winter of 1863–64 I had been invited by the general-in-chief to give my views of the campaign I thought advisable for the command under me—now Sherman's. General J. E. Johnston was defending Atlanta and the interior of Georgia with an army, the largest part of which was stationed at Dalton, about 38 miles south of Chattanooga. Dalton is at the junction of the railroad from Cleveland with the one from Chattanooga to Atlanta.

There could have been no difference of opinion as to the first duty of the armies of the military division of the Mississippi. Johnston's army was the first objective, and that important railroad centre, Atlanta, the second. At the time I wrote General Halleck giving my views of the approaching campaign, and at the time I met General Sherman, it was expected that General Banks would be through with the campaign which he had been ordered upon before my appointment to the command of all the armies, and would be ready to co-operate with the armies east of the Mississippi, his part in the programme being to move upon Mobile by land while the navy would close the harbor and assist to the best of its ability.* The plan therefore was for Sherman to attack Johnston and destroy his army if possible, to capture Atlanta and hold it, and with his troops and those of Banks to hold a line through to Mobile, or at least to hold Atlanta and command the railroad running east and west, and the troops from one or other of the armies to hold important points on the southern road, the only east and west road that would be left in the possession of the enemy. This would cut the Confederacy in two again, as our gaining possession of the Mississippi River had done before. Banks was not ready in time for the part assigned to him, and circumstances that could not be foreseen determined the campaign which was afterwards made, the success and grandeur of which has resounded throughout all lands.

In regard to restoring officers who had been relieved from important commands to duty again, I left Sherman to look after those who had been removed in the West while I looked out for the rest. I directed, however, that he should make no assignment until I could speak to the Secretary of War about the matter. I shortly after recommended to the Secretary the assignment of General Buell to duty. I received the assurance that duty would be offered to him; and afterwards the Secretary told me that he had offered Buell an assignment and that the latter had declined it, saying that it would be degradation to accept the assignment offered. I understood afterwards that he refused to serve under either Sherman or Canby because

---

*See letter to Banks, in General Grant's report, Appendix.

he had ranked them both. Both graduated before him and ranked him in the old army. Sherman ranked him as a brigadier-general. All of them ranked me in the old army, and Sherman and Buell did as brigadiers. The worst excuse a soldier can make for declining service is that he once ranked the commander he is ordered to report to.

On the 23d of March I was back in Washington, and on the 26th took up my headquarters at Culpeper Court-House, a few miles south of the headquarters of the Army of the Potomac.

Although hailing from Illinois myself, the State of the President, I never met Mr. Lincoln until called to the capital to receive my commission as lieutenant-general. I knew him, however, very well and favorably from the accounts given by officers under me at the West who had known him all their lives. I had also read the remarkable series of debates between Lincoln and Douglas a few years before, when they were rival candidates for the United States Senate. I was then a resident of Missouri, and by no means a "Lincoln man" in that contest; but I recognized then his great ability.

In my first interview with Mr. Lincoln alone he stated to me that he had never professed to be a military man or to know how campaigns should be conducted, and never wanted to interfere in them: but that procrastination on the part of commanders, and the pressure from the people at the North and Congress, *which was always with him*, forced him into issuing his series of "Military Orders"—one, two, three, etc. He did not know but they were all wrong, and did know that some of them were. All he wanted or had ever wanted was some one who would take the responsibility and act, and call on him for all the assistance needed, pledging himself to use all the power of the government in rendering such assistance. Assuring him that I would do the best I could with the means at hand, and avoid as far as possible annoying him or the War Department, our first interview ended.

The Secretary of War I had met once before only, but felt that I knew him better.

While commanding in West Tennessee we had occasionally held conversations over the wires, at night, when they were not being otherwise used. He and General Halleck both cautioned me against giving the President my plans of campaign, saying that he was so kind-hearted, so averse to refusing anything asked of him, that some friend would be sure to get from him all he knew. I should have said that in our interview the President told me he did not want to know what I proposed to do. But he submitted a plan of campaign of his own which he wanted me to hear and then do as I pleased about. He brought out a map of Virginia on which he had evidently marked every position occupied by the Federal and Confederate armies up to that time. He pointed out on the map two streams which empty into the Potomac, and suggested that the army might be moved on boats and landed between the mouths of these streams. We would then have the Potomac to bring our supplies, and the tributaries would protect our flanks while we moved out. I listened respectfully, but did not suggest that the same streams would protect Lee's flanks while he was shutting us up.

I did not communicate my plans to the President, nor did I to the Secretary of War or to General Halleck.

March the 26th my headquarters were, as stated, at Culpeper, and the work of preparing for an early campaign commenced.

Chapter XLVII.

THE MILITARY SITUATION—PLANS FOR THE CAMPAIGN—
SHERIDAN ASSIGNED TO COMMAND OF THE CAVALRY—
FLANK MOVEMENTS—FORREST AT FORT PILLOW—
GENERAL BANKS'S EXPEDITION—COLONEL MOSBY
—AN INCIDENT OF THE WILDERNESS CAMPAIGN.

WHEN I ASSUMED command of all the armies the situation was about this: the Mississippi River was guarded
from St. Louis to its mouth; the line of the Arkansas was
held, thus giving us all the North-west north of that river. A
few points in Louisiana not remote from the river were held
by the Federal troops, as was also the mouth of the Rio
Grande. East of the Mississippi we held substantially all north
of the Memphis and Charleston Railroad as far east as Chattanooga, thence along the line of the Tennessee and Holston
rivers, taking in nearly all of the State of Tennessee. West Virginia was in our hands; and that part of old Virginia north of
the Rapidan and east of the Blue Ridge we also held. On the
sea-coast we had Fortress Monroe and Norfolk in Virginia;
Plymouth, Washington and New Berne in North Carolina;
Beaufort, Folly and Morris islands, Hilton Head, Port Royal
and Fort Pulaski in South Carolina and Georgia; Fernandina,
St. Augustine, Key West and Pensacola in Florida. The balance of the Southern territory, an empire in extent, was still in
the hands of the enemy.

Sherman, who had succeeded me in the command of the
military division of the Mississippi, commanded all the troops
in the territory west of the Alleghanies and north of Natchez,
with a large movable force about Chattanooga. His command
was subdivided into four departments, but the commanders
all reported to Sherman and were subject to his orders. This
arrangement, however, insured the better protection of all
lines of communication through the acquired territory, for
the reason that these different department commanders could
act promptly in case of a sudden or unexpected raid within
their respective jurisdictions without awaiting the orders of
the division commander.

In the East the opposing forces stood in substantially the same relations towards each other as three years before, or when the war began; they were both between the Federal and Confederate capitals. It is true, footholds had been secured by us on the sea-coast, in Virginia and North Carolina, but, beyond that, no substantial advantage had been gained by either side. Battles had been fought of as great severity as had ever been known in war, over ground from the James River and Chickahominy, near Richmond, to Gettysburg and Chambersburg, in Pennsylvania, with indecisive results, sometimes favorable to the National army, sometimes to the Confederate army; but in every instance, I believe, claimed as victories for the South by the Southern press if not by the Southern generals. The Northern press, as a whole, did not discourage these claims; a portion of it always magnified rebel success and belittled ours, while another portion, most sincerely earnest in their desire for the preservation of the Union and the overwhelming success of the Federal armies, would nevertheless generally express dissatisfaction with whatever victories were gained because they were not more complete.

That portion of the Army of the Potomac not engaged in guarding lines of communication was on the northern bank of the Rapidan. The Army of Northern Virginia confronting it on the opposite bank of the same river, was strongly intrenched and commanded by the acknowledged ablest general in the Confederate army. The country back to the James River is cut up with many streams, generally narrow, deep, and difficult to cross except where bridged. The region is heavily timbered, and the roads narrow, and very bad after the least rain. Such an enemy was not, of course, unprepared with adequate fortifications at convenient intervals all the way back to Richmond, so that when driven from one fortified position they would always have another farther to the rear to fall back into.

To provision an army, campaigning against so formidable a foe through such a country, from wagons alone seemed almost impossible. System and discipline were both essential to its accomplishment.

The Union armies were now divided into nineteen departments, though four of them in the West had been concentrated into a single military division. The Army of the Potomac was a separate command and had no territorial limits. There were thus seventeen distinct commanders. Before this time these various armies had acted separately and independently of each other, giving the enemy an opportunity often of depleting one command, not pressed, to reinforce another more actively engaged. I determined to stop this. To this end I regarded the Army of the Potomac as the centre, and all west to Memphis along the line described as our position at the time, and north of it, the right wing; the Army of the James, under General Butler, as the left wing, and all the troops south, as a force in rear of the enemy. Some of these latter were occupying positions from which they could not render service proportionate to their numerical strength. All such were depleted to the minimum necessary to hold their positions as a guard against blockade runners; where they could not do this their positions were abandoned altogether. In this way ten thousand men were added to the Army of the James from South Carolina alone, with General Gillmore in command. It was not contemplated that General Gillmore should leave his department; but as most of his troops were taken, presumably for active service, he asked to accompany them and was permitted to do so. Officers and soldiers on furlough, of whom there were many thousands, were ordered to their proper commands; concentration was the order of the day, and to have it accomplished in time to advance at the earliest moment the roads would permit was the problem.

As a reinforcement to the Army of the Potomac, or to act in support of it, the 9th army corps, over twenty thousand strong, under General Burnside, had been rendezvoused at Annapolis, Maryland. This was an admirable position for such a reinforcement. The corps could be brought at the last moment as a reinforcement to the Army of the Potomac, or it could be thrown on the sea-coast, south of Norfolk, in Virginia or North Carolina, to operate against Richmond from that direction. In fact Burnside and the War Department both thought the 9th corps was intended for such an expedition up to the last moment.

My general plan now was to concentrate all the force

possible against the Confederate armies in the field. There were but two such, as we have seen, east of the Mississippi River and facing north. The Army of Northern Virginia, General Robert E. Lee commanding, was on the south bank of the Rapidan, confronting the Army of the Potomac; the second, under General Joseph E. Johnston, was at Dalton, Georgia, opposed to Sherman who was still at Chattanooga. Beside these main armies the Confederates had to guard the Shenandoah Valley, a great storehouse to feed their armies from, and their line of communications from Richmond to Tennessee. Forrest, a brave and intrepid cavalry general, was in the West with a large force; making a larger command necessary to hold what we had gained in Middle and West Tennessee. We could not abandon any territory north of the line held by the enemy because it would lay the Northern States open to invasion. But as the Army of the Potomac was the principal garrison for the protection of Washington even while it was moving on Lee, so all the forces to the west, and the Army of the James, guarded their special trusts when advancing from them as well as when remaining at them. Better indeed, for they forced the enemy to guard his own lines and resources at a greater distance from ours, and with a greater force. Little expeditions could not so well be sent out to destroy a bridge or tear up a few miles of railroad track, burn a storehouse, or inflict other little annoyances. Accordingly I arranged for a simultaneous movement all along the line. Sherman was to move from Chattanooga, Johnston's army and Atlanta being his objective points.* Crook, commanding in West Virginia, was to move from the mouth of the Gauley River with a cavalry force and some artillery, the Virginia and Tennessee

---

*[*Private and Confidential.*]

HEADQUARTERS ARMIES OF THE UNITED STATES,
WASHINGTON, D. C., *April* 4, 1864.

MAJOR-GENERAL W. T. SHERMAN,
    Commanding Military Division of the Mississippi.

General: — It is my design, if the enemy keep quiet and allow me to take the initiative in the spring campaign, to work all parts of the army together, and somewhat towards a common centre. For your information I now write you my programme, as at present determined upon.

Railroad to be his objective. Either the enemy would have to keep a large force to protect their communications, or see them destroyed and a large amount of forage and provision, which they so much needed, fall into our hands. Sigel was in command in the Valley of Virginia. He was to advance up the valley, covering the North from an invasion through that channel as well while advancing as by remaining near Harper's Ferry. Every mile he advanced also gave us possession of stores on which Lee relied. Butler was to advance by the James River, having Richmond and Petersburg as his objective.

Before the advance commenced I visited Butler at Fort

I have sent orders to Banks, by private messenger, to finish up his present expedition against Shreveport with all dispatch; to turn over the defence of Red River to General Steele and the navy, and to return your troops to you and his own to New Orleans; to abandon all of Texas, except the Rio Grande, and to hold that with not to exceed four thousand men; to reduce the number of troops on the Mississippi to the lowest number necessary to hold it, and to collect from his command not less than twenty-five thousand men. To this I will add five thousand men from Missouri. With this force he is to commence operations against Mobile as soon as he can. It will be impossible for him to commence too early.

Gillmore joins Butler with ten thousand men, and the two operate against Richmond from the south side of the James River. This will give Butler thirty-three thousand men to operate with, W. F. Smith commanding the right wing of his forces and Gillmore the left wing. I will stay with the Army of the Potomac, increased by Burnside's corps of not less than twenty-five thousand effective men, and operate directly against Lee's army, wherever it may be found.

Sigel collects all his available force in two columns, one, under Ord and Averell, to start from Beverly, Virginia, and the other, under Crook, to start from Charleston on the Kanawha, to move against the Virginia and Tennessee Railroad.

Crook will have all cavalry, and will endeavor to get in about Saltville, and move east from there to join Ord. His force will be all cavalry, while Ord will have from ten to twelve thousand men of all arms.

You I propose to move against Johnston's army, to break it up and to get into the interior of the enemy's country as far as you can, inflicting all the damage you can against their war resources.

I do not propose to lay down for you a plan of campaign, but simply lay down the work it is desirable to have done and leave you free to execute it in your own way. Submit to me, however, as early as you can, your plan of operations.

Monroe. This was the first time I had ever met him. Before giving him any order as to the part he was to play in the approaching campaign I invited his views. They were very much such as I intended to direct, and as I did direct,* in writing, before leaving.

General W. F. Smith, who had been promoted to the rank of major-general shortly after the battle of Chattanooga on my recommendation, had not yet been confirmed. I found a decided prejudice against his confirmation by a majority of the Senate, but I insisted that his services had been such that he should be rewarded. My wishes were now reluctantly complied with, and I assigned him to the command of one of the corps under General Butler. I was not long in finding out that the objections to Smith's promotion were well founded.

In one of my early interviews with the President I expressed my dissatisfaction with the little that had been accomplished by the cavalry so far in the war, and the belief that it was capable of accomplishing much more than it had done if under a thorough leader. I said I wanted the very best man in the army for that command. Halleck was present and spoke up, saying: "How would Sheridan do?" I replied: "The very man I want." The President said I could have anybody I

As stated, Banks is ordered to commence operations as soon as he can. Gillmore is ordered to report at Fortress Monroe by the 18th inst., or as soon thereafter as practicable. Sigel is concentrating now. None will move from their places of rendezvous until I direct, except Banks. I want to be ready to move by the 25th inst., if possible. But all I can now direct is that you get ready as soon as possible. I know you will have difficulties to encounter in getting through the mountains to where supplies are abundant, but I believe you will accomplish it.

From the expedition from the Department of West Virginia I do not calculate on very great results; but it is the only way I can take troops from there. With the long line of railroad Sigel has to protect, he can spare no troops except to move directly to his front. In this way he must get through to inflict great damage on the enemy, or the enemy must detach from one of his armies a large force to prevent it. In other words, if Sigel can't skin himself he can hold a leg while some one else skins.

I am, general, very respectfully, your obedient servant,

U. S. GRANT,
Lieutenant-General.

*See instructions to Butler, in General Grant's report, Appendix.

wanted. Sheridan was telegraphed for that day, and on his
arrival was assigned to the command of the cavalry corps with
the Army of the Potomac. This relieved General Alfred Pleas-
onton. It was not a reflection on that officer, however, for I
did not know but that he had been as efficient as any other
cavalry commander.

Banks in the Department of the Gulf was ordered to assemble all the troops he had at New Orleans in time to join in the
general move, Mobile to be his objective.

At this time I was not entirely decided as to whether I
should move the Army of the Potomac by the right flank of
the enemy, or by his left. Each plan presented advantages.*

----

*IN FIELD, CULPEPER C. H., VA.,
April 9, 1864.

MAJ.-GENERAL GEO. G. MEADE,
     Com'd'g Army of the Potomac.

For information and as instruction to govern your preparations for the
coming campaign, the following is communicated confidentially for your
own perusal alone.

So far as practicable all the armies are to move together, and towards one
common centre. Banks has been instructed to turn over the guarding of the
Red River to General Steele and the navy, to abandon Texas with the exception of the Rio Grande, and to concentrate all the force he can, not less than
25,000 men, to move on Mobile. This he is to do without reference to other
movements. From the scattered condition of his command, however, he cannot possibly get it together to leave New Orleans before the 1st of May, if so
soon. Sherman will move at the same time you do, or two or three days in
advance, Jo. Johnston's army being his objective point, and the heart of Georgia his ultimate aim. If successful he will secure the line from Chattanooga to
Mobile with the aid of Banks.

Sigel cannot spare troops from his army to reinforce either of the great
armies, but he can aid them by moving directly to his front. This he has been
directed to do, and is now making preparations for it. Two columns of his
command will make south at the same time with the general move; one from
Beverly, from ten to twelve thousand strong, under Major-General Ord; the
other from Charleston, Va., principally cavalry, under Brig.-General Crook.
The former of these will endeavor to reach the Tennessee and Virginia Railroad, about south of Covington, and if found practicable will work eastward
to Lynchburg and return to its base by way of the Shenandoah Valley, or join
you. The other will strike at Saltville, Va., and come eastward to join Ord.
The cavalry from Ord's command will try to force a passage southward, if
they are successful in reaching the Virginia and Tennessee Railroad, to cut
the main lines of the road connecting Richmond with all the South and
South-west.

If by his right—my left—the Potomac, Chesapeake Bay and tributaries would furnish us an easy line over which to bring all supplies to within easy hauling distance of every position the army could occupy from the Rapidan to the James River. But Lee could, if he chose, detach or move his whole army

---

Gillmore will join Butler with about 10,000 men from South Carolina. Butler can reduce his garrison so as to take 23,000 men into the field directly to his front. The force will be commanded by Maj.-General W. F. Smith. With Smith and Gillmore, Butler will seize City Point, and operate against Richmond from the south side of the river. His movement will be simultaneous with yours.

Lee's army will be your objective point. Wherever Lee goes, there you will go also. The only point upon which I am now in doubt is, whether it will be better to cross the Rapidan above or below him. Each plan presents great advantages over the other with corresponding objections. By crossing above, Lee is cut off from all chance of ignoring Richmond and going north on a raid. But if we take this route, all we do must be done whilst the rations we start with hold out. We separate from Butler so that he cannot be directed how to co-operate. By the other route Brandy Station can be used as a base of supplies until another is secured on the York or James rivers.

These advantages and objections I will talk over with you more fully than I can write them.

Burnside with a force of probably 25,000 men will reinforce you. Immediately upon his arrival, which will be shortly after the 20th inst., I will give him the defence of the road from Bull Run as far south as we wish to hold it. This will enable you to collect all your strength about Brandy Station and to the front.

There will be naval co-operation on the James River, and transports and ferries will be provided so that should Lee fall back into his intrenchments at Richmond, Butler's force and yours will be a unit, or at least can be made to act as such. What I would direct then, is that you commence at once reducing baggage to the very lowest possible standard. Two wagons to a regiment of five hundred men is the greatest number that should be allowed, for all baggage, exclusive of subsistence stores and ordnance stores. One wagon to brigade and one to division headquarters is sufficient and about two to corps headquarters.

Should by Lee's right flank be our route, you will want to make arrangements for having supplies of all sorts promptly forwarded to White House on the Pamunkey. Your estimates for this contingency should be made at once. If not wanted there, there is every probability they will be wanted on the James River or elsewhere.

If Lee's left is turned, large provision will have to be made for ordnance stores. I would say not much short of five hundred rounds of infantry ammunition would do. By the other, half the amount would be sufficient.

U. S. GRANT,
Lieutenant-General.

north on a line rather interior to the one I would have to take in following. A movement by his left—our right—would obviate this; but all that was done would have to be done with the supplies and ammunition we started with. All idea of adopting this latter plan was abandoned when the limited quantity of supplies possible to take with us was considered. The country over which we would have to pass was so exhausted of all food or forage that we would be obliged to carry everything with us.

While these preparations were going on the enemy was not entirely idle. In the West Forrest made a raid in West Tennessee up to the northern border, capturing the garrison of four or five hundred men at Union City, and followed it up by an attack on Paducah, Kentucky, on the banks of the Ohio. While he was able to enter the city he failed to capture the forts or any part of the garrison. On the first intelligence of Forrest's raid I telegraphed Sherman to send all his cavalry against him, and not to let him get out of the trap he had put himself into. Sherman had anticipated me by sending troops against him before he got my order.

Forrest, however, fell back rapidly, and attacked the troops at Fort Pillow, a station for the protection of the navigation of the Mississippi River. The garrison consisted of a regiment of colored troops, infantry, and a detachment of Tennessee cavalry. These troops fought bravely, but were overpowered. I will leave Forrest in his dispatches to tell what he did with them.

"The river was dyed," he says, "with the blood of the slaughtered for two hundred yards. The approximate loss was upward of five hundred killed, but few of the officers escaping. My loss was about twenty killed. It is hoped that these facts will demonstrate to the Northern people that negro soldiers cannot cope with Southerners." Subsequently Forrest made a report in which he left out the part which shocks humanity to read.

At the East, also, the rebels were busy. I had said to Halleck that Plymouth and Washington, North Carolina, were unnecessary to hold. It would be better to have the garrisons engaged there added to Butler's command. If success attended our arms both places, and others too, would fall into our hands naturally. These places had been occupied by Federal troops before I took command of the armies, and I knew that the Executive would be reluctant to abandon them, and therefore explained my views; but before my views were carried out the rebels captured the garrison at Plymouth. I then ordered the abandonment of Washington, but directed the holding of New Berne at all hazards. This was essential because New Berne was a port into which blockade runners could enter.

General Banks had gone on an expedition up the Red River long before my promotion to general command. I had opposed the movement strenuously, but acquiesced because it was the order of my superior at the time. By direction of Halleck I had reinforced Banks with a corps of about ten thousand men from Sherman's command. This reinforcement was wanted back badly before the forward movement commenced. But Banks had got so far that it seemed best that he should take Shreveport on the Red River, and turn over the line of that river to Steele, who commanded in Arkansas, to hold instead of the line of the Arkansas. Orders were given accordingly, and with the expectation that the campaign would be ended in time for Banks to return A. J. Smith's command to where it belonged and get back to New Orleans himself in time to execute his part in the general plan. But the expedition was a failure. Banks did not get back in time to take part in the programme as laid down. Nor was Smith returned until long after the movements of May, 1864, had been begun. The services of forty thousand veteran troops, over and above the number required to hold all that was necessary in the Department of the Gulf, were thus paralyzed. It is but just to Banks, however, to say that his expedition was ordered from Washington and he was in no way responsible except for the conduct of it. I make no criticism on this point. He opposed the expedition.

By the 27th of April spring had so far advanced as to justify me in fixing a day for the great move. On that day Burnside left Annapolis to occupy Meade's position between Bull Run and the Rappahannock. Meade was notified and directed to bring his troops forward to his advance. On the following day Butler was notified of my intended advance on the 4th of

May, and he was directed to move the night of the same day and get as far up the James River as possible by daylight, and push on from there to accomplish the task given him. He was also notified that reinforcements were being collected in Washington City, which would be forwarded to him should the enemy fall back into the trenches at Richmond. The same day Sherman was directed to get his forces up ready to advance on the 5th. Sigel was in Winchester and was notified to move in conjunction with the others.

The criticism has been made by writers on the campaign from the Rapidan to the James River that all the loss of life could have been obviated by moving the army there on transports. Richmond was fortified and intrenched so perfectly that one man inside to defend was more than equal to five outside besieging or assaulting. To get possession of Lee's army was the first great object. With the capture of his army Richmond would necessarily follow. It was better to fight him outside of his stronghold than in it. If the Army of the Potomac had been moved bodily to the James River by water Lee could have moved a part of his forces back to Richmond, called Beauregard from the south to reinforce it, and with the balance moved on to Washington. Then, too, I ordered a move, simultaneous with that of the Army of the Potomac, up the James River by a formidable army already collected at the mouth of the river.

While my headquarters were at Culpeper, from the 26th of March to the 4th of May, I generally visited Washington once a week to confer with the Secretary of War and President. On the last occasion, a few days before moving, a circumstance occurred which came near postponing my part in the campaign altogether. Colonel John S. Mosby had for a long time been commanding a partisan corps, or regiment, which operated in the rear of the Army of the Potomac. On my return to the field on this occasion, as the train approached Warrenton Junction, a heavy cloud of dust was seen to the east of the road as if made by a body of cavalry on a charge. Arriving at the junction the train was stopped and inquiries made as to the cause of the dust. There was but one man at the station, and he informed us that Mosby had crossed a few minutes before at full speed in pursuit of Federal cavalry. Had he seen our train coming, no doubt he would have let his prisoners escape to capture the train. I was on a special train, if I remember correctly, without any guard.

Since the close of the war I have come to know Colonel Mosby personally, and somewhat intimately. He is a different man entirely from what I had supposed. He is slender, not tall, wiry, and looks as if he could endure any amount of physical exercise. He is able, and thoroughly honest and truthful. There were probably but few men in the South who could have commanded successfully a separate detachment in the rear of an opposing army, and so near the border of hostilities, as long as he did without losing his entire command.

On this same visit to Washington I had my last interview with the President before reaching the James River. He had of course become acquainted with the fact that a general movement had been ordered all along the line, and seemed to think it a new feature in war. I explained to him that it was necessary to have a great number of troops to guard and hold the territory we had captured, and to prevent incursions into the Northern States. These troops could perform this service just as well by advancing as by remaining still; and by advancing they would compel the enemy to keep detachments to hold them back, or else lay his own territory open to invasion. His answer was: "Oh, yes! I see that. As we say out West, if a man can't skin he must hold a leg while somebody else does."

There was a certain incident connected with the Wilderness campaign of which it may not be out of place to speak; and to avoid a digression further on I will mention it here.

A few days before my departure from Culpeper the Honorable E. B. Washburne visited me there, and remained with my headquarters for some distance south, through the battle in the Wilderness and, I think, to Spottsylvania. He was accompanied by a Mr. Swinton, whom he presented as a literary gentleman who wished to accompany the army with a view of writing a history of the war when it was over. He assured me—and I have no doubt Swinton gave him the assurance— that he was not present as a correspondent of the press. I expressed an entire willingness to have him (Swinton) accompany the army, and would have allowed him to do so as a correspondent, restricted, however, in the character of the information he could give. We received Richmond papers with about as much regularity as if there had been no war, and knew that our papers were received with equal regularity by the Confederates. It was desirable, therefore, that correspondents should not be privileged spies of the enemy within our lines.

Probably Mr. Swinton expected to be an invited guest at my headquarters, and was disappointed that he was not asked to become so. At all events he was not invited, and soon I found that he was corresponding with some paper (I have now forgotten which one), thus violating his word either expressed or implied. He knew of the assurance Washburne had given as to the character of his mission. I never saw the man from the day of our introduction to the present that I recollect. He accompanied us, however, for a time at least.

The second night after crossing the Rapidan (the night of the 5th of May) Colonel W. R. Rowley, of my staff, was acting as night officer at my headquarters. A short time before midnight I gave him verbal instructions for the night. Three days later I read in a Richmond paper a verbatim report of these instructions.

A few nights still later (after the first, and possibly after the second, day's fighting in the Wilderness) General Meade came to my tent for consultation, bringing with him some of his staff officers. Both his staff and mine retired to the camp-fire some yards in front of the tent, thinking our conversation should be private. There was a stump a little to one side, and between the front of the tent and camp-fire. One of my staff, Colonel T. S. Bowers, saw what he took to be a man seated on the ground and leaning against the stump, listening to the conversation between Meade and myself. He called the attention of Colonel Rowley to it. The latter immediately took the man by the shoulder and asked him, in language more forcible than polite, what he was doing there. The man proved to be Swinton, the "historian," and his replies to the question were evasive and unsatisfactory, and he was warned against further eaves-dropping.

The next I heard of Mr. Swinton was at Cold Harbor. General Meade came to my headquarters saying that General Burnside had arrested Swinton, who at some previous time had given great offence, and had ordered him to be shot that afternoon. I promptly ordered the prisoner to be released, but that he must be expelled from the lines of the army not to return again on pain of punishment.

Chapter XLVIII.

COMMENCEMENT OF THE GRAND CAMPAIGN—GENERAL
BUTLER'S POSITION—SHERIDAN'S FIRST RAID.

THE ARMIES were now all ready to move for the accomplishment of a single object. They were acting as a unit so far as such a thing was possible over such a vast field. Lee, with the capital of the Confederacy, was the main end to which all were working. Johnston, with Atlanta, was an important obstacle in the way of our accomplishing the result aimed at, and was therefore almost an independent objective. It was of less importance only because the capture of Johnston and his army would not produce so immediate and decisive a result in closing the rebellion as would the possession of Richmond, Lee and his army. All other troops were employed exclusively in support of these two movements. This was the plan; and I will now endeavor to give, as concisely as I can, the method of its execution, outlining first the operations of minor detached but co-operative columns.

As stated before, Banks failed to accomplish what he had been sent to do on the Red River, and eliminated the use of forty thousand veterans whose co-operation in the grand campaign had been expected—ten thousand with Sherman and thirty thousand against Mobile.

Sigel's record is almost equally brief. He moved out, it is true, according to programme; but just when I was hoping to hear of good work being done in the valley I received instead the following announcement from Halleck: "Sigel is in full retreat on Strasburg. He will do nothing but run; never did anything else." The enemy had intercepted him about New Market and handled him roughly, leaving him short six guns, and some nine hundred men out of his six thousand.

The plan had been for an advance of Sigel's forces in two columns. Though the one under his immediate command failed ingloriously the other proved more fortunate. Under Crook and Averell his western column advanced from the Gauley in West Virginia at the appointed time, and with more happy results. They reached the Virginia and Tennessee Railroad at Dublin and destroyed a depot of supplies, besides tearing up several miles of road and burning the bridge over New River. Having accomplished this they recrossed the Alleghanies to Meadow Bluffs and there awaited further orders.

Butler embarked at Fort Monroe with all his command, except the cavalry and some artillery which moved up the south bank of the James River. His steamers moved first up Chesapeake Bay and York River as if threatening the rear of Lee's army. At midnight they turned back, and Butler by daylight was far up the James River. He seized City Point and Bermuda Hundred early in the day, without loss and, no doubt, very much to the surprise of the enemy.

This was the accomplishment of the first step contemplated in my instructions to Butler. He was to act from here, looking to Richmond as his objective point. I had given him to understand that I should aim to fight Lee between the Rapidan and Richmond if he would stand; but should Lee fall back into Richmond I would follow up and make a junction of the armies of the Potomac and the James on the James River. He was directed to secure a footing as far up the south side of the river as he could at as early a date as possible.

Butler was in position by the 6th of May and had begun intrenching, and on the 7th he sent out his cavalry from Suffolk to cut the Weldon Railroad. He also sent out detachments to destroy the railroad between Petersburg and Richmond, but no great success attended these latter efforts. He made no great effort to establish himself on that road and neglected to attack Petersburg, which was almost defenceless. About the 11th he advanced slowly until he reached the works at Drury's Bluff, about half way between Bermuda Hundred and Richmond. In the mean time Beauregard had been gathering reinforcements. On the 16th he attacked Butler with great vigor, and with such success as to limit very materially the further usefulness of the Army of the James as a distinct factor in the campaign. I afterward ordered a portion of it to join the Army of the Potomac, leaving a sufficient force with Butler to man his works, hold securely the footing he had already gained and maintain a threatening front toward the rear of the Confederate capital.

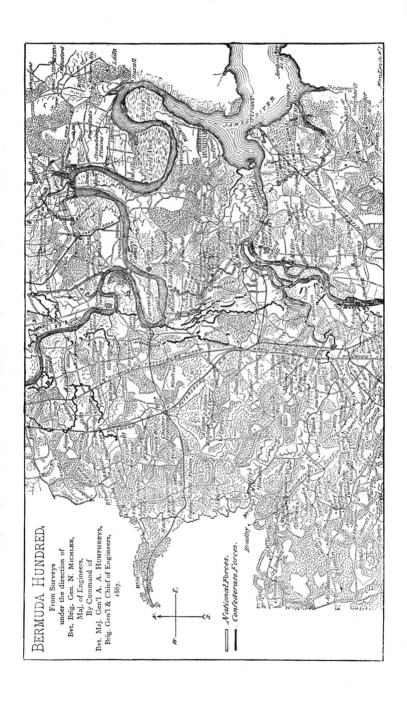

BERMUDA HUNDRED.
From Surveys
under the direction of
Bvt. Brig. Gen. N. MICHLER,
Maj. of Engineers,
By Command of
Bvt. Maj. Gen'l A. A. HUMPHREYS,
Brig. Gen'l & Chief of Engineers,
1867.

_____ National Forces.
_____ Confederate Forces.

The position which General Butler had chosen between the two rivers, the James and Appomattox, was one of great natural strength, one where a large area of ground might be thoroughly inclosed by means of a single intrenched line, and that a very short one in comparison with the extent of territory which it thoroughly protected. His right was protected by the James River, his left by the Appomattox, and his rear by their junction—the two streams uniting near by. The bends of the two streams shortened the line that had been chosen for intrenchments, while it increased the area which the line inclosed.

Previous to ordering any troops from Butler I sent my chief engineer, General Barnard, from the Army of the Potomac to that of the James to inspect Butler's position and ascertain whether I could again safely make an order for General Butler's movement in co-operation with mine, now that I was getting so near Richmond; or, if I could not, whether his position was strong enough to justify me in withdrawing some of his troops and having them brought round by water to White House to join me and reinforce the Army of the Potomac. General Barnard reported the position very strong for defensive purposes, and that I could do the latter with great security; but that General Butler could not move from where he was, in co-operation, to produce any effect. He said that the general occupied a place between the James and Appomattox rivers which was of great strength, and where with an inferior force he could hold it for an indefinite length of time against a superior; but that he could do nothing offensively. I then asked him why Butler could not move out from his lines and push across the Richmond and Petersburg Railroad to the rear and on the south side of Richmond. He replied that it was impracticable, because the enemy had substantially the same line across the neck of land that General Butler had. He then took out his pencil and drew a sketch of the locality, remarking that the position was like a bottle and that Butler's line of intrenchments across the neck represented the cork; that the enemy had built an equally strong line immediately in front of him across the neck; and it was therefore as if Butler was in a bottle. He was perfectly safe against an attack; but, as Barnard expressed it, the enemy had corked the bottle and with a small force could hold the cork in its place. This struck me as being very expressive of his position, particularly when I saw the hasty sketch which General Barnard had drawn; and in making my subsequent report I used that expression without adding quotation marks, never thinking that anything had been said that would attract attention—as this did, very much to the annoyance, no doubt, of General Butler and, I know, very much to my own. I found afterwards that this was mentioned in the notes of General Badeau's book, which, when they were shown to me, I asked to have stricken out; yet it was retained there, though against my wishes.

I make this statement here because, although I have often made it before, it has never been in my power until now to place it where it will correct history; and I desire to rectify all injustice that I may have done to individuals, particularly to officers who were gallantly serving their country during the trying period of the war for the preservation of the Union. General Butler certainly gave his very earnest support to the war; and he gave his own best efforts personally to the suppression of the rebellion.

The further operations of the Army of the James can best be treated of in connection with those of the Army of the Potomac, the two being so intimately associated and connected as to be substantially one body in which the individuality of the supporting wing is merged.

Before giving the reader a summary of Sherman's great Atlanta campaign, which must conclude my description of the various co-operative movements preparatory to proceeding with that of the operations of the centre, I will briefly mention Sheridan's first raid upon Lee's communications which, though an incident of the operations on the main line and not specifically marked out in the original plan, attained in its brilliant execution and results all the proportions of an independent campaign. By thus anticipating, in point of time, I will be able to more perfectly observe the continuity of events occurring in my immediate front when I shall have undertaken to describe our advance from the Rapidan.

On the 8th of May, just after the battle of the Wilderness and when we were moving on Spottsylvania I directed Sheridan verbally to cut loose from the Army of the Potomac, pass around the left of Lee's army and attack his cavalry: to cut the two roads—one running west through Gordonsville, Charlottesville and Lynchburg, the other to Richmond, and, when compelled to do so for want of forage and rations, to move on to the James River and draw these from Butler's supplies. This move took him past the entire rear of Lee's army. These orders were also given in writing through Meade.

The object of this move was three-fold. First, if successfully executed, and it was, he would annoy the enemy by cutting his line of supplies and telegraphic communications, and destroy or get for his own use supplies in store in the rear and coming up. Second, he would draw the enemy's cavalry after him, and thus better protect our flanks, rear and trains than by remaining with the army. Third, his absence would save the trains drawing his forage and other supplies from Fredericksburg, which had now become our base. He started at daylight the next morning, and accomplished more than was expected. It was sixteen days before he got back to the Army of the Potomac.

The course Sheridan took was directly to Richmond. Before night Stuart, commanding the Confederate cavalry, came on to the rear of his command. But the advance kept on, crossed the North Anna, and at Beaver Dam, a station on the Virginia Central Railroad, recaptured four hundred Union prisoners on their way to Richmond, destroyed the road and used and destroyed a large amount of subsistence and medical stores.

Stuart, seeing that our cavalry was pushing towards Richmond, abandoned the pursuit on the morning of the 10th and, by a detour and an exhausting march, interposed between Sheridan and Richmond at Yellow Tavern, only about six miles north of the city. Sheridan destroyed the railroad and more supplies at Ashland, and on the 11th arrived in Stuart's front. A severe engagement ensued in which the losses were heavy on both sides, but the rebels were beaten, their leader mortally wounded, and some guns and many prisoners were captured.

Sheridan passed through the outer defences of Richmond, and could, no doubt, have passed through the inner ones. But having no supports near he could not have remained. After caring for his wounded he struck for the James River below the city, to communicate with Butler and to rest his men and horses as well as to get food and forage for them.

He moved first between the Chickahominy and the James, but in the morning (the 12th) he was stopped by batteries at Mechanicsville. He then turned to cross to the north side of the Chickahominy by Meadow Bridge. He found this barred, and the defeated Confederate cavalry, reorganized, occupying the opposite side. The panic created by his first entrance within the outer works of Richmond having subsided troops were sent out to attack his rear.

He was now in a perilous position, one from which but few generals could have extricated themselves. The defences of Richmond, manned, were to the right, the Chickahominy was to the left with no bridge remaining and the opposite bank guarded, to the rear was a force from Richmond. This force was attacked and beaten by Wilson's and Gregg's divisions, while Sheridan turned to the left with the remaining division and hastily built a bridge over the Chickahominy under the fire of the enemy, forced a crossing and soon dispersed the Confederates he found there. The enemy was held back from the stream by the fire of the troops not engaged in bridge building.

On the 13th Sheridan was at Bottom's Bridge, over the Chickahominy. On the 14th he crossed this stream and on that day went into camp on the James River at Haxall's Landing. He at once put himself into communication with General Butler, who directed all the supplies he wanted to be furnished.

Sheridan had left the Army of the Potomac at Spottsylvania, but did not know where either this or Lee's army was now. Great caution therefore had to be exercised in getting back. On the 17th, after resting his command for three days, he started on his return. He moved by the way of White House. The bridge over the Pamunkey had been burned by the enemy, but a new one was speedily improvised and the cavalry crossed over it. On the 22d he was at Aylett's on the Matapony, where he learned the position of the two armies. On the 24th he joined us on the march

from North Anna to Cold Harbor, in the vicinity of Chesterfield.

Sheridan in this memorable raid passed entirely around
Lee's army: encountered his cavalry in four engagements, and
defeated them in all; recaptured four hundred Union prisoners and killed and captured many of the enemy; destroyed and
used many supplies and munitions of war; destroyed miles of
railroad and telegraph, and freed us from annoyance by the
cavalry of the enemy for more than two weeks.

Chapter XLIX.

SHERMAN'S CAMPAIGN IN GEORGIA—SIEGE OF
ATLANTA—DEATH OF GENERAL McPHERSON—ATTEMPT
TO CAPTURE ANDERSONVILLE—CAPTURE OF ATLANTA.

AFTER SEPARATING from Sherman in Cincinnati I went on
to Washington, as already stated, while he returned to
Nashville to assume the duties of his new command. His military division was now composed of four departments and
embraced all the territory west of the Alleghany Mountains
and east of the Mississippi River, together with the State of
Arkansas in the trans-Mississippi. The most easterly of these
was the Department of the Ohio, General Schofield commanding; the next was the Department of the Cumberland,
General Thomas commanding; the third the Department of
the Tennessee, General McPherson commanding; and General
Steele still commanded the trans-Mississippi, or Department
of Arkansas. The last-named department was so far away that
Sherman could not communicate with it very readily after
starting on his spring campaign, and it was therefore soon
transferred from his military division to that of the Gulf,
where General Canby, who had relieved General Banks, was
in command.

The movements of the armies, as I have stated in a former
chapter, were to be simultaneous, I fixing the day to start
when the season should be far enough advanced, it was
hoped, for the roads to be in a condition for the troops to
march.

General Sherman at once set himself to work preparing for
the task which was assigned him to accomplish in the spring
campaign. McPherson lay at Huntsville with about twenty-
four thousand men, guarding those points of Tennessee which
were regarded as most worth holding; Thomas, with over
sixty thousand men of the Army of the Cumberland, was at
Chattanooga; and Schofield, with about fourteen thousand
men, was at Knoxville. With these three armies, numbering
about one hundred thousand men in all, Sherman was to
move on the day fixed for the general advance, with a view of

destroying Johnston's army and capturing Atlanta. He visited each of these commands to inform himself as to their condition, and it was found to be, speaking generally, good.

One of the first matters to turn his attention to was that of getting, before the time arrived for starting, an accumulation of supplies forward to Chattanooga sufficiently large to warrant a movement. He found, when he got to that place, that the trains over the single-track railroad, which was frequently interrupted for a day or two at a time, were only sufficient to meet the daily wants of the troops without bringing forward any surplus of any kind. He found, however, that trains were being used to transport all the beef cattle, horses for the cavalry, and even teams that were being brought to the front. He at once changed all this, and required beef cattle, teams, cavalry horses, and everything that could travel, even the troops, to be marched, and used the road exclusively for transporting supplies. In this way he was able to accumulate an abundance before the time finally fixed upon for the move, the 4th of May.

As I have said already, Johnston was at Dalton, which was nearly one-fourth of the way between Chattanooga and Atlanta. The country is mountainous all the way to Atlanta, abounding in mountain streams, some of them of considerable volume. Dalton is on ground where water drains towards Atlanta and into one of the main streams rising north-east from there and flowing south-west—this being the general direction which all the main streams of that section take, with smaller tributaries entering into them. Johnston had been preparing himself for this campaign during the entire winter. The best positions for defence had been selected all the way from Dalton back to Atlanta, and very strongly intrenched; so that, as he might be forced to fall back from one position, he would have another to fall into in his rear. His position at Dalton was so very strongly intrenched that no doubt he expected, or at least hoped, to hold Sherman there and prevent him from getting any further. With a less skilful general, and one disposed to take no risks, I have no doubt that he would have succeeded.

Sherman's plan was to start Schofield, who was farthest back, a few days in advance from Knoxville, having him move on the direct road to Dalton. Thomas was to move out to Ringgold. It had been Sherman's intention to cross McPherson over the Tennessee River at Huntsville or Decatur, and move him south from there so as to have him come into the road running from Chattanooga to Atlanta a good distance to the rear of the point Johnston was occupying; but when that was contemplated it was hoped that McPherson alone would have troops enough to cope with Johnston, if the latter should move against him while unsupported by the balance of the army. In this he was disappointed. Two of McPherson's veteran divisions had re-enlisted on the express provision that they were to have a furlough. This furlough had not yet expired, and they were not back.

Then, again, Sherman had lent Banks two divisions under A. J. Smith, the winter before, to co-operate with the trans-Mississippi forces, and this with the express pledge that they should be back by a time specified, so as to be prepared for this very campaign. It is hardly necessary to say they were not returned. That department continued to absorb troops to no purpose to the end of the war. This left McPherson so weak that the part of the plan above indicated had to be changed. He was therefore brought up to Chattanooga and moved from there on a road to the right of Thomas—the two coming together about Dalton. The three armies were abreast, all ready to start promptly on time.

Sherman soon found that Dalton was so strongly fortified that it was useless to make any attempt to carry it by assault; and even to carry it by regular approaches was impracticable. There was a narrowing up in the mountain, between the National and Confederate armies, through which a stream, a wagon road and a railroad ran. Besides, the stream had been dammed so that the valley was a lake. Through this gorge the troops would have to pass. McPherson was therefore sent around by the right, to come out by the way of Snake Creek Gap into the rear of the enemy. This was a surprise to Johnston, and about the 13th he decided to abandon his position at Dalton.

On the 15th there was very hard fighting about Resaca; but our cavalry having been sent around to the right got near the road in the enemy's rear. Again Johnston fell back, our army

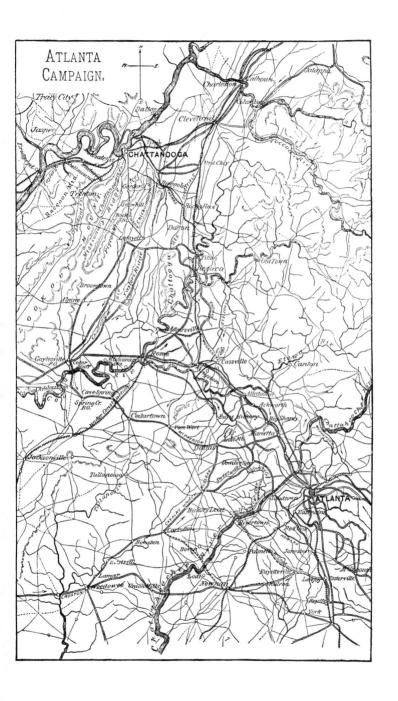

ATLANTA
CAMPAIGN.

pursuing. The pursuit was continued to Kingston, which was reached on the 19th with very little fighting, except that Newton's division overtook the rear of Johnston's army and engaged it. Sherman was now obliged to halt for the purpose of bringing up his railroad trains. He was depending upon the railroad for all of his supplies, and as of course the railroad was wholly destroyed as Johnston fell back, it had to be rebuilt. This work was pushed forward night and day, and caused much less delay than most persons would naturally expect in a mountainous country where there were so many bridges to be rebuilt.

The campaign to Atlanta was managed with the most consummate skill, the enemy being flanked out of one position after another all the way there. It is true this was not accomplished without a good deal of fighting—some of it very hard fighting, rising to the dignity of very important battles—neither were single positions gained in a day. On the contrary, weeks were spent at some; and about Atlanta more than a month was consumed.

It was the 23d of May before the road was finished up to the rear of Sherman's army and the pursuit renewed. This pursuit brought him up to the vicinity of Allatoona. This place was very strongly intrenched, and naturally a very defensible position. An assault upon it was not thought of, but preparations were made to flank the enemy out of it. This was done by sending a large force around our right, by the way of Dallas, to reach the rear of the enemy. Before reaching there, however, they found the enemy fortified in their way, and there resulted hard fighting for about a week at a place called New Hope Church. On the left our troops also were fortified, and as close up to the enemy as they could get. They kept working still farther around to the left toward the railroad. This was the case more particularly with the cavalry. By the 4th of June Johnston found that he was being hemmed in so rapidly that he drew off and Allatoona was left in our possession.

Allatoona, being an important place, was strongly intrenched for occupation by our troops before advancing farther, and made a secondary base of supplies. The railroad was finished up to that point, the intrenchments completed, storehouses provided for food, and the army got in readiness for a further advance. The rains, however, were falling in such torrents that it was impossible to move the army by the side roads which they would have to move upon in order to turn Johnston out of his new position.

While Sherman's army lay here, General F. P. Blair returned to it, bringing with him the two divisions of veterans who had been on furlough.

Johnston had fallen back to Marietta and Kenesaw Mountain, where strong intrenchments awaited him. At this latter place our troops made an assault upon the enemy's lines after having got their own lines up close to him, and failed, sustaining considerable loss. But during the progress of the battle Schofield was gaining ground to the left; and the cavalry on his left were gaining still more toward the enemy's rear. These operations were completed by the 3d of July, when it was found that Johnston had evacuated the place. He was pursued at once. Sherman had made every preparation to abandon the railroad, leaving a strong guard in his intrenchments. He had intended, moving out with twenty days' rations and plenty of ammunition, to come in on the railroad again at the Chattahoochee River. Johnston frustrated this plan by himself starting back as above stated. This time he fell back to the Chattahoochee.

About the 5th of July he was besieged again, Sherman getting easy possession of the Chattahoochee River both above and below him. The enemy was again flanked out of his position, or so frightened by flanking movements that on the night of the 9th he fell back across the river.

Here Johnston made a stand until the 17th, when Sherman's old tactics prevailed again and the final movement toward Atlanta began. Johnston was now relieved of the command, and Hood superseded him.

Johnston's tactics in this campaign do not seem to have met with much favor, either in the eyes of the administration at Richmond, or of the people of that section of the South in which he was commanding. The very fact of a change of commanders being ordered under such circumstances was an indication of a change of policy, and that now they would become the aggressors—the very thing our troops wanted.

For my own part, I think that Johnston's tactics were right. Anything that could have prolonged the war a year beyond the time that it did finally close, would probably have exhausted the North to such an extent that they might then have abandoned the contest and agreed to a separation.

Atlanta was very strongly intrenched all the way around in a circle about a mile and a half outside of the city. In addition to this, there were advanced intrenchments which had to be taken before a close siege could be commenced.

Sure enough, as indicated by the change of commanders, the enemy was about to assume the offensive. On the 20th he came out and attacked the Army of the Cumberland most furiously. Hooker's corps, and Newton's and Johnson's divisions were the principal ones engaged in this contest, which lasted more than an hour; but the Confederates were then forced to fall back inside their main lines. The losses were quite heavy on both sides. On this day General Gresham, since our Postmaster-General, was very badly wounded. During the night Hood abandoned his outer lines, and our troops were advanced. The investment had not been relinquished for a moment during the day.

During the night of the 21st Hood moved out again, passing by our left flank, which was then in motion to get a position farther in rear of him, and a desperate battle ensued, which lasted most of the day of the 22d. At first the battle went very much in favor of the Confederates, our troops being somewhat surprised. While our troops were advancing they were struck in flank, and their flank was enveloped. But they had become too thorough veterans to be thrown into irreparable confusion by an unexpected attack when off their guard, and soon they were in order and engaging the enemy, with the advantage now of knowing where their antagonist was. The field of battle continued to expand until it embraced about seven miles of ground. Finally, however, and before night, the enemy was driven back into the city.*

---

*General John A. Logan, upon whom devolved the command of the Army of the Tennessee during this battle, in his report gave our total loss in killed, wounded and missing at 3,521; and estimated that of the enemy to be not less than 10,000: and General G. M. Dodge, graphically describing to General

It was during this battle that McPherson, while passing from one column to another, was instantly killed. In his death the army lost one of its ablest, purest and best generals.

Garrard had been sent out with his cavalry to get upon the railroad east of Atlanta and to cut it in the direction of Augusta. He was successful in this, and returned about the time of the battle. Rousseau had also come up from Tennessee with a small division of cavalry, having crossed the Tennessee River about Decatur and made a raid into Alabama. Finally, when hard pressed, he had come in, striking the railroad in rear of Sherman, and reported to him about this time.

The battle of the 22d is usually known as the Battle of Atlanta, although the city did not fall into our hands until the 2d of September. Preparations went on, as before, to flank the enemy out of his position. The work was tedious, and the lines that had to be maintained were very long. Our troops were gradually worked around to the east until they struck the road between Decatur and Atlanta. These lines were strongly fortified, as were those to the north and west of the city—all as close up to the enemy's lines as practicable—in order to hold them with the smallest possible number of men, the design being to detach an army to move by our right and try to get upon the railroad down south of Atlanta.

On the 27th the movement by the right flank commenced. On the 28th the enemy struck our right flank, General Logan commanding, with great vigor. Logan intrenched himself hastily, and by that means was enabled to resist all assaults and inflict a great deal of damage upon the enemy. These assaults were continued to the middle of the afternoon, and resumed once or twice still later in the day. The enemy's losses in these unsuccessful assaults were fearful.

During that evening the enemy in Logan's front withdrew into the town. This now left Sherman's army close up to the

---

Sherman the enemy's attack, the full weight of which fell first upon and was broken by his depleted command, remarks: "The disparity of forces can be seen from the fact that in the charge made by my two brigades under Fuller and Mersy they took 351 prisoners, representing forty-nine different regiments, eight brigades and three divisions; and brought back eight battle flags from the enemy."

Confederate lines, extending from a point directly east of the city around by the north and west of it for a distance of fully ten miles; the whole of this line being intrenched, and made stronger every day they remained there.

In the latter part of July Sherman sent Stoneman to destroy the railroads to the south, about Macon. He was then to go east and, if possible, release our prisoners about Andersonville. There were painful stories current at the time about the great hardships these prisoners had to endure in the way of general bad treatment, in the way in which they were housed, and in the way in which they were fed. Great sympathy was felt for them; and it was thought that even if they could be turned loose upon the country it would be a great relief to them. But the attempt proved a failure. McCook, who commanded a small brigade, was first reported to have been captured; but he got back, having inflicted a good deal of damage upon the enemy. He had also taken some prisoners; but encountering afterwards a largely superior force of the enemy he was obliged to drop his prisoners and get back as best he could with what men he had left. He had lost several hundred men out of his small command. On the 4th of August Colonel Adams, commanding a little brigade of about a thousand men, returned reporting Stoneman and all but himself as lost. I myself had heard around Richmond of the capture of Stoneman, and had sent Sherman word, which he received. The rumor was confirmed there, also, from other sources. A few days after Colonel Adams's return Colonel Capron also got in with a small detachment and confirmed the report of the capture of Stoneman with something less than a thousand men.

It seems that Stoneman, finding the escape of all his force was impossible, had made arrangements for the escape of two divisions. He covered the movement of these divisions to the rear with a force of about seven hundred men, and at length surrendered himself and this detachment to the commanding Confederate. In this raid, however, much damage was inflicted upon the enemy by the destruction of cars, locomotives, army wagons, manufactories of military supplies, etc.

On the 4th and 5th Sherman endeavored to get upon the railroad to our right, where Schofield was in command, but

these attempts failed utterly. General Palmer was charged with
being the cause of this failure, to a great extent, by both General Sherman and General Schofield; but I am not prepared to
say this, although a question seems to have arisen with Palmer
as to whether Schofield had any right to command him. If he
did raise this question while an action was going on, that act
alone was exceedingly reprehensible.

About the same time Wheeler got upon our railroad north
of Resaca and destroyed it nearly up to Dalton. This cut Sherman off from communication with the North for several days.
Sherman responded to this attack on his lines of communication by directing one upon theirs.

Kilpatrick started on the night of the 18th of August to
reach the Macon road about Jonesboro. He succeeded in
doing so, passed entirely around the Confederate lines of
Atlanta, and was back again in his former position on our left
by the 22d. These little affairs, however, contributed but very
little to the grand result. They annoyed, it is true, but any
damage thus done to a railroad by any cavalry expedition is
soon repaired.

Sherman made preparations for a repetition of his tactics;
that is, for a flank movement with as large a force as could be
got together to some point in the enemy's rear. Sherman
commenced this last movement on the 25th of August, and on
the 1st of September was well up towards the railroad twenty
miles south of Atlanta. Here he found Hardee intrenched,
ready to meet him. A battle ensued, but he was unable to
drive Hardee away before night set in. Under cover of the
night, however, Hardee left of his own accord. That night
Hood blew up his military works, such as he thought would
be valuable in our hands, and decamped.

The next morning at daylight General H. W. Slocum, who
was commanding north of the city, moved in and took
possession of Atlanta, and notified Sherman. Sherman then
moved deliberately back, taking three days to reach the city,
and occupied a line extending from Decatur on the left to
Atlanta in the centre, with his troops extending out of the city
for some distance to the right.

The campaign had lasted about four months, and was one
of the most memorable in history. There was but little if any-

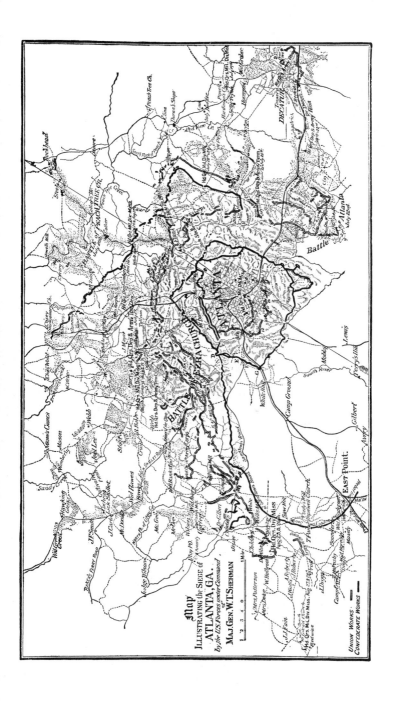

Map
ILLUSTRATING the SIEGE of
ATLANTA, GA.
by the U.S. Forces under Command
of
MAJ. GEN. W. T. SHERMAN

UNION WORKS ━━━
CONFEDERATE WORKS ━━━

thing in the whole campaign, now that it is over, to criticise at all, and nothing to criticise severely. It was creditable alike to the general who commanded and the army which had executed it. Sherman had on this campaign some bright, wide-awake division and brigade commanders whose alertness added a host to the efficiency of his command.

The troops now went to work to make themselves comfortable, and to enjoy a little rest after their arduous campaign. The city of Atlanta was turned into a military base. The citizens were all compelled to leave. Sherman also very wisely prohibited the assembling of the army of sutlers and traders who always follow in the wake of an army in the field, if permitted to do so, from trading with the citizens and getting the money of the soldiers for articles of but little use to them, and for which they are made to pay most exorbitant prices. He limited the number of these traders to one for each of his three armies.

The news of Sherman's success reached the North instantaneously, and set the country all aglow. This was the first great political campaign for the Republicans in their canvass of 1864. It was followed later by Sheridan's campaign in the Shenandoah Valley; and these two campaigns probably had more effect in settling the election of the following November than all the speeches, all the bonfires, and all the parading with banners and bands of music in the North.

Chapter L.

GRAND MOVEMENT OF THE ARMY OF THE POTOMAC—
CROSSING THE RAPIDAN—ENTERING THE WILDERNESS—
BATTLE OF THE WILDERNESS.

SOON AFTER MIDNIGHT, May 3d–4th, the Army of the
Potomac moved out from its position north of the Rapidan, to start upon that memorable campaign, destined to result in the capture of the Confederate capital and the army
defending it. This was not to be accomplished, however,
without as desperate fighting as the world has ever witnessed;
not to be consummated in a day, a week, a month, or a single
season. The losses inflicted, and endured, were destined to be
severe; but the armies now confronting each other had already been in deadly conflict for a period of three years, with
immense losses in killed, by death from sickness, captured and
wounded; and neither had made any real progress toward accomplishing the final end. It is true the Confederates had, so
far, held their capital, and they claimed this to be their sole
object. But previously they had boldly proclaimed their intention to capture Philadelphia, New York, and the National
Capital, and had made several attempts to do so, and once or
twice had come fearfully near making their boast good—too
near for complacent contemplation by the loyal North. They
had also come near losing their own capital on at least one
occasion. So here was a stand-off. The campaign now begun
was destined to result in heavier losses, to both armies, in a
given time, than any previously suffered; but the carnage was
to be limited to a single year, and to accomplish all that had
been anticipated or desired at the beginning in that time. We
had to have hard fighting to achieve this. The two armies had
been confronting each other so long, without any decisive result, that they hardly knew which could whip.

Ten days' rations, with a supply of forage and ammunition
were taken in wagons. Beef cattle were driven with the trains,
and butchered as wanted. Three days' rations in addition, in
haversacks, and fifty rounds of cartridges, were carried on the
person of each soldier.

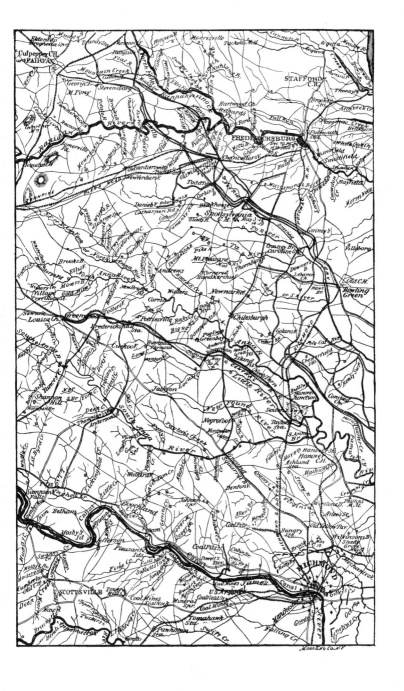

The country over which the army had to operate, from the Rapidan to the crossing of the James River, is rather flat, and is cut by numerous streams which make their way to the Chesapeake Bay. The crossings of these streams by the army were generally made not far above tide-water, and where they formed a considerable obstacle to the rapid advance of troops even when the enemy did not appear in opposition. The country roads were narrow and poor. Most of the country is covered with a dense forest, in places, like the Wilderness and along the Chickahominy, almost impenetrable even for infantry except along the roads. All bridges were naturally destroyed before the National troops came to them.

UNION ARMY ON THE RAPIDAN, MAY 5, 1864.

[COMPILED.]

LIEUTENANT-GENERAL U. S. GRANT, Commander-in-Chief.
MAJOR-GENERAL GEORGE G. MEADE, Commanding Army of the Potomac.

MAJ.-GEN. W. S. HANCOCK, commanding Second Army Corps.

First Division, Brig.-Gen. Francis C. Barlow.
- First Brigade, Col. Nelson A. Miles.
- Second Brigade, Col. Thomas A. Smyth.
- Third Brigade, Col. Paul Frank.
- Fourth Brigade, Col. John R. Brooke.

Second Division, Brig.-Gen. John Gibbon.
- First Brigade, Brig.-Gen. Alex. S. Webb.
- Second Brigade, Brig.-Gen. Joshua T. Owen.
- Third Brigade, Col. Samuel S. Carroll.

Third Division, Maj.-Gen. David B. Birney.
- First Brigade, Brig.-Gen. J. H. H. Ward.
- Second Brigade, Brig.-Gen. Alexander Hays.

Fourth Division, Brig.-Gen. Gershom Mott.
- First Brigade, Col. Robert McAllister.
- Second Brigade, Col. Wm. R. Brewster.

Artillery Brigade, Col. John C. Tidball.

The Army of the Potomac was composed of three infantry and one cavalry corps, commanded respectively by Generals W. S. Hancock, G. K. Warren, John Sedgwick and P. H. Sheridan. The artillery was commanded by General Henry J. Hunt. This arm was in such abundance that the fourth of it could not be used to advantage in such a country as we were destined to pass through. The surplus was much in the way, taking up as it did so much of the narrow and bad roads, and consuming so much of the forage and other stores brought up by the trains.

The 5th corps, General Warren commanding, was in advance on the right, and marched directly for Germania Ford, preceded by one division of cavalry, under General J. H. Wilson. General Sedgwick followed Warren with the 6th corps. Germania Ford was nine or ten miles below the right of Lee's line. Hancock, with the 2d corps, moved by another road,

MAJ.-GEN. G. K. WARREN, commanding Fifth Army Corps.

First Division, Brig.-Gen. Charles Griffin.
- First Brigade, Brig.-Gen. Romeyn B. Ayres.
- Second Brigade, Col. Jacob B. Sweitzer.
- Third Brigade, Brig.-Gen. J. J. Bartlett.

Second Division, Brig.-Gen. John C. Robinson.
- First Brigade, Col. Samuel H. Leonard.
- Second Brigade, Brig.-Gen. Henry Baxter.
- Third Brigade, Col. Andrew W. Denison.

Third Division, Brig.-Gen. Samuel W. Crawford.
- First Brigade, Col. Wm. McCandless.
- Third Brigade, Col. Joseph W. Fisher.

Fourth Division, Brig.-Gen. James S. Wadsworth.
- First Brigade, Brig.-Gen. Lysander Cutler.
- Second Brigade, Brig.-Gen. James C. Rice.
- Third Brigade, Col. Roy Stone.

Artillery Brigade, Col. C. S. Wainwright.

farther east, directly upon Ely's Ford, six miles below Germania, preceded by Gregg's division of cavalry, and followed by
the artillery. Torbert's division of cavalry was left north of the
Rapidan, for the time, to picket the river and prevent the

MAJ.-GEN. JOHN SEDGWICK, commanding Sixth Army Corps.	First Division, Brig.-Gen. H. G. Wright.	First Brigade, Col. Henry W. Brown. Second Brigade, Col. Emory Upton. Third Brigade, Brig.-Gen. D. A. Russell. Fourth Brigade, Brig.-Gen. Alexander Shaler.
	Second Division, Brig.-Gen. George W. Getty.	First Brigade, Brig.-Gen. Frank Wheaton. Second Brigade, Col. Lewis A. Grant. Third Brigade, Brig.-Gen. Thos. H. Neill. Fourth Brigade, Brig.-Gen. Henry L. Eustis.
	Third Division, Brig.-Gen. James B. Ricketts.	First Brigade, Brig.-Gen. Wm. H. Morris. Second Brigade, Brig.-Gen. T. Seymour.
		Artillery Brigade, Col. C. H. Tompkins.
MAJ.-GEN. P. H. SHERIDAN, commanding Cavalry Corps.	First Division, Brig.-Gen. A. T. A. Torbert.	First Brigade, Brig.-Gen. G. A. Custer. Second Brigade, Col. Thos. C. Devin. Reserve Brigade, Brig.-Gen. Wesley Merritt.
	Second Division, Brig.-Gen. D. McM. Gregg.	First Brigade, Brig.-Gen. Henry E. Davies, Jr. Second Brigade, Col. J. Irvin Gregg.
	Third Division, Brig.-Gen. J. H. Wilson.	First Brigade, Col. T. M. Bryan, Jr. Second Brigade, Col. Geo. H. Chapman.

enemy from crossing and getting into our rear. The cavalry seized the two crossings before daylight, drove the enemy's pickets guarding them away, and by six o'clock A.M. had the pontoons laid ready for the crossing of the infantry and artillery. This was undoubtedly a surprise to Lee. The fact that the movement was unopposed proves this.

Burnside, with the 9th corps, was left back at Warrenton, guarding the railroad from Bull Run forward to preserve

	First Division, Brig.-Gen. T. G. Stevenson.	First Brigade, Col. Sumner Carruth.
		Second Brigade, Col. Daniel Leasure.
	Second Division, Brig.-Gen. Robert B. Potter.	First Brigade, Col. Zenas R. Bliss.
		Second Brigade, Col. Simon G. Griffin.
MAJ.-GEN. A. E. BURNSIDE, commanding Ninth Army Corps.	Third Division, Brig.-Gen. Orlando B. Willcox.	First Brigade, Col. John F. Hartranft.
		Second Brigade, Col. Benj. C. Christ.
	Fourth Division, Brig.-Gen. Edward Ferrero.	First Brigade, Col. Joshua K. Sigfried.
		Second Brigade, Col. Henry G. Thomas.
		Provisional Brigade, Col. Elisha G. Marshall.
BRIG.-GEN. HENRY J. HUNT, commanding Artillery.	Reserve, Col. H. S. Burton.	First Brigade, Col. J. H. Kitching.
		Second Brigade, Maj. J. A. Tompkins
		First Brig. Horse Art., Capt J. M. Robertson.
		Second Brigade Horse Art., Capt. D. R. Ransom.
		Third Brigade, Maj. R. H. Fitzhugh.
GENERAL HEADQUARTERS		Provost Guard, Brig.-Gen. M. R. Patrick.
		Volunteer Engineers, Brig.-Gen. H. W. Benham.

control of it in case our crossing the Rapidan should be long delayed. He was instructed, however, to advance at once on

---

CONFEDERATE ARMY.

Organization of the Army of Northern Virginia, Commanded by GENERAL ROBERT E. LEE, August 31st, 1864.

First Army Corps: LIEUT.-GEN. R. H. ANDERSON, Commanding.

MAJ.-GEN. GEO. E. PICKETT'S Division.	Brig.-Gen. Seth M. Barton's Brigade. (a) " M. D. Corse's " " Eppa Hunton's " " Wm. R. Terry's "
MAJ.-GEN. C. W. FIELD'S Division. (b)	Brig.-Gen. G. T. Anderson's Brigade. " E. M. Law's (c) " " John Bratton's "
MAJ.-GEN. J. B. KERSHAW'S Division. (d)	Brig.-Gen. W. T. Wofford's Brigade. " B. G. Humphrey's " " Goode Bryan's " " Kershaw's (Old) "

Second Army Corps: MAJOR-GENERAL JUBAL A. EARLY, Commanding.

MAJ.-GEN. JOHN B. GORDON'S Division.	Brig.-Gen. H. T. Hays' Brigade. (e) " John Pegram's " (f) " Gordon's " (g) Brig.-Gen. R. F. Hoke's "
MAJ.-GEN. EDWARD JOHNSON'S Division.	Stonewall Brig. (Brig.-Gen. J. A. Walker). (h) Brig.-Gen. J. M. Jones' Brigade. (h) " Geo. H. Stewart's " (h) " L. A. Stafford's " (e)
MAJ.-GEN. R. E. RODES' Division.	Brig.-Gen. J. Daniel's Brigade. (i) " Geo. Dole's " (k) " S. D. Ramseur's Brigade. " C. A. Battle's " " R. D. Johnston's " (f)

NOTE.

(a) Col. W. R. Aylett was in command Aug. 29th, and probably at above date.
(b) Inspection report of this division shows that it also contained Benning's and Gregg's Brigades.
(c) Commanded by Colonel P. D. Bowles.
(d) Only two brigadier-generals reported for duty; names not indicated.
(e) Constituting York's Brigade. ⎫
(f) In Ramseur's Division. ⎪
(g) Evan's Brigade, Colonel E. N. Atkinson commanding, and containing 12th Georgia Battalion. ⎬ Organization of the Army
(h) The Virginia regiments constituted Terry's Brigade, ⎪ of the Valley District
    Gordon's Division. ⎪
(i) Grimes' Brigade. ⎪
(k) Cook's " ⎭

receiving notice that the army had crossed; and a dispatch was sent to him a little after one P.M. giving the information that our crossing had been successful.

The country was heavily wooded at all the points of crossing, particularly on the south side of the river. The battle-field from the crossing of the Rapidan until the final movement from the Wilderness toward Spottsylvania was of the same character. There were some clearings and small farms within what might be termed the battle-field; but generally the country

---

Third Army Corps: LIEUT.-GEN. A. P. HILL, Commanding.

MAJ.-GEN. WM. MAHONE'S Division. (*l*)	Brig.-Gen. J. C. C. Sanders' Brigade.
	    " Mahone's "
	Brig.-Gen. N. H. Harris's " (*m*)
	    " A. R. Wright's "
	    " Joseph Finegan's "

MAJ.-GEN. C. M. WILCOX'S Division.	Brig.-Gen. E. L. Thomas's Brigade (*n*)
	    " James H. Lane's "
	    " Sam'l McGowan's "
	    " Alfred M. Scale's "

MAJ.-GEN. H. HETH'S Division. (*o*)	Brig.-Gen. J. R. Davis's Brigade.
	    " John R. Cooke's "
	    " D. McRae's "
	    " J. J. Archer's "
	    " H. H. Walker's "

Unattached: 5th Alabama Battalion.

Cavalry Corps: LIEUTENANT-GENERAL WADE HAMPTON, Commanding. (*p*)

MAJ.-GEN. FITZHUGH LEE'S Division.	Brig.-Gen. W. C. Wickham's Brigade. " L. L. Lomax's "

MAJ.-GEN. M. C. BUTLER'S Division.	Brig.-Gen. John Dunovant's Brigade.
	    " P. M. B. Young's "
	    " Thomas L. Rosser's "

MAJ.-GEN. W. H. F. LEE'S Division.	Brig.-Gen. Rufus Barringer's Brigade. " J. R. Chambliss's "

NOTE.
(*l*) Returns report but one general officer present for duty; name not indicated.
(*m*) Colonel Joseph M. Jayne, commanding.
(*n*) Colonel Thomas J. Simmons, commanding.
(*o*) Four brigadier-generals reported present for duty; names not indicated.
(*p*) On face of returns appears to have consisted of Hampton's, Fitz-Lee's, and W. H. F. Lee's Division, and Dearing's Brigade.

was covered with a dense forest. The roads were narrow and bad. All the conditions were favorable for defensive operations.

Artillery Reserve: Brig.-Gen. W. N. Pendleton, Commanding.

Brig.-Gen. E. P. Alexander's Division.*	Cabell's Battalion.	Manly's Battery. 1st Co. Richmond Howitzers. Carleton's Battery. Calloway's Battery.
	Haskell's Battalion.	Branch's Battery. Nelson's " Garden's " Rowan "
	Huger's Battalion.	Smith's Battery. Moody " Woolfolk " Parker's " Taylor's " Fickling's " Martin's "
	Gibb's Battalion.	Davidson's Battery. Dickenson's " Otey's "
Brig.-Gen. A. L. Long's Division.	Braxton's Battalion.	Lee Battery. 1st Md. Artillery. Stafford " Alleghany "
	Cutshaw's Battalion.	Charlotteville Artillery.- Staunton " Courtney "
	Carter's Battalion.	Morris Artillery. Orange " King William Artillery. Jeff Davis "
	Nelson's Battalion.	Amherst Artillery. Milledge " Fluvauna "
	Brown's Battalion.	Powhatan Artillery. 2d Richmond Howitzers. 3d " " Rockbridge Artillery. Salem Flying Artillery.

*But one general officer reported present for duty in the artillery, and Alexander's name not on the original.

There are two roads, good for that part of Virginia, running from Orange Court House to the battle-field. The most southerly of these roads is known as the Orange Court House Plank Road, the northern one as the Orange Turnpike. There are also roads from east of the battle-field running to Spottsylvania Court House, one from Chancellorsville, branching at Aldrich's; the western branch going by Piney Branch Church, Alsop's, thence by the Brock Road to Spottsylvania; the east branch goes by Gates's, thence to Spottsylvania. The Brock Road runs from Germania Ford through the battle-field and on to the Court House. As Spottsylvania is approached the country is cut up with numerous roads, some going to the town direct, and others crossing so as to connect the farms with roads going there.

Lee's headquarters were at Orange Court House. From there to Fredericksburg he had the use of the two roads above described running nearly parallel to the Wilderness. This gave him unusual facilities, for that country, for concentrating his forces to his right. These roads strike the road from Germania Ford in the Wilderness.

COL. R. L. WALKER'S DIVISION.	Cutt's Battalion.	Ross's Battery. Patterson's Battery. Irwin Artillery.
	Richardson's Battalion.	Lewis Artillery. Donaldsonville Artillery. Norfolk Light " Huger "
	McIntosh's Battalion.	Johnson's Battery. Hardaway Artillery. Danville " 2d Rockbridge Artillery.
	Pegram's Battalion.	Peedee Artillery. Fredericksburg Artillery. Letcher Purcell Battery. Crenshaw's Battery.
	Poague's Battalion.	Madison Artillery. Albemarle " Brooke " Charlotte "

As soon as the crossing of the infantry was assured, the cavalry pushed forward, Wilson's division by Wilderness Tavern to Parker's store, on the Orange Plank Road; Gregg to the left towards Chancellorsville. Warren followed Wilson and reached the Wilderness Tavern by noon, took position there and intrenched. Sedgwick followed Warren. He was across the river and in camp on the south bank, on the right of Warren, by sundown. Hancock, with the 2d corps, moved parallel with Warren and camped about six miles east of him. Before night all the troops, and by the evening of the 5th the trains of more than four thousand wagons, were safely on the south side of the river.

There never was a corps better organized than was the quartermaster's corps with the Army of the Potomac in 1864. With a wagon-train that would have extended from the Rapidan to Richmond, stretched along in single file and separated as the teams necessarily would be when moving, we could still carry only three days' forage and about ten to twelve days' rations, besides a supply of ammunition. To overcome all difficulties, the chief quartermaster, General Rufus Ingalls, had marked on each wagon the corps badge with the division color and the number of the brigade. At a glance, the particular brigade to which any wagon belonged could be told. The wagons were also marked to note the contents: if ammunition, whether for artillery or infantry; if forage, whether grain or hay; if rations, whether bread, pork, beans, rice, sugar, coffee or whatever it might be. Empty wagons were never allowed to follow the army or stay in camp. As soon as a wagon was empty it would return to the base of supply for a load of precisely the same article that had been taken from it. Empty trains were obliged to leave the road free for loaded ones. Arriving near the army they would be parked in fields nearest to the brigades they belonged to. Issues, except of ammunition, were made at night in all cases. By this system the hauling of forage for the supply train was almost wholly dispensed with. They consumed theirs at the depots.

I left Culpeper Court House after all the troops had been put in motion, and passing rapidly to the front, crossed the Rapidan in advance of Sedgwick's corps; and established headquarters for the afternoon and night in a deserted house near the river.

Orders had been given, long before this movement began, to cut down the baggage of officers and men to the lowest point possible. Notwithstanding this I saw scattered along the road from Culpeper to Germania Ford wagon-loads of new blankets and overcoats, thrown away by the troops to lighten their knapsacks; an improvidence I had never witnessed before.

Lee, while his pickets and signal corps must have discovered at a very early hour on the morning of the 4th of May, that the Army of the Potomac was moving, evidently did not learn until about one o'clock in the afternoon by what route we would confront his army. This I judge from the fact that at 1.15 P.M., an hour and a quarter after Warren had reached Old Wilderness Tavern, our officers took off rebel signals which, when translated, were seen to be an order to his troops to occupy their intrenchments at Mine Run.

Here at night dispatches were received announcing that Sherman, Butler and Crook had moved according to programme.

On discovering the advance of the Army of the Potomac, Lee ordered Hill, Ewell and Longstreet, each commanding corps, to move to the right to attack us, Hill on the Orange Plank Road, Longstreet to follow on the same road. Longstreet was at this time—middle of the afternoon—at Gordonsville, twenty or more miles away. Ewell was ordered by the Orange Pike. He was near by and arrived some four miles east of Mine Run before bivouacking for the night.

My orders were given through General Meade for an early advance on the morning of the 5th. Warren was to move to Parker's store, and Wilson's cavalry—then at Parker's store—to move on to Craig's meeting-house. Sedgwick followed Warren, closing in on his right. The Army of the Potomac was facing to the west, though our advance was made to the south, except when facing the enemy. Hancock was to move south-westward to join on the left of Warren, his left to reach to Shady Grove Church.

At six o'clock, before reaching Parker's store, Warren discovered the enemy. He sent word back to this effect, and

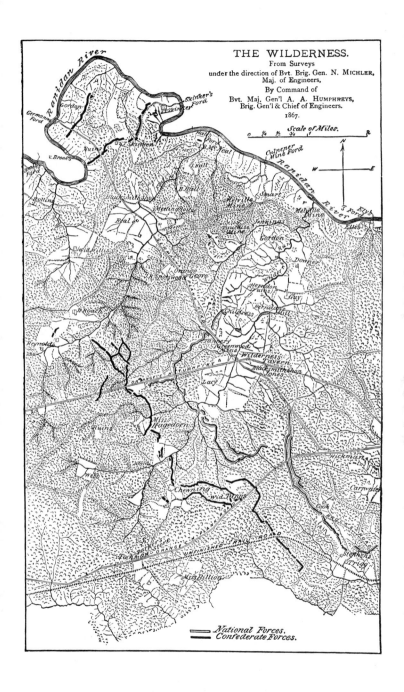

THE WILDERNESS.
From Surveys
under the direction of Bvt. Brig. Gen. N. MICHLER,
Maj. of Engineers,
By Command of
Bvt. Maj. Gen'l A. A. HUMPHREYS,
Brig. Gen'l & Chief of Engineers.
1867.

Scale of Miles.

National Forces.
Confederate Forces.

was ordered to halt and prepare to meet and attack him. Wright, with his division of Sedgwick's corps, was ordered, by any road he could find, to join on to Warren's right, and Getty with his division, also of Sedgwick's corps, was ordered to move rapidly by Warren's rear and get on his left. This was the speediest way to reinforce Warren who was confronting the enemy on both the Orange plank and turnpike roads.

Burnside had moved promptly on the 4th, on receiving word that the Army of the Potomac had safely crossed the Rapidan. By making a night march, although some of his troops had to march forty miles to reach the river, he was crossing with the head of his column early on the morning of the 5th.

Meade moved his headquarters on to Old Wilderness Tavern, four miles south of the river, as soon as it was light enough to see the road. I remained to hasten Burnside's crossing and to put him in position. Burnside at this time was not under Meade's command, and was his senior in rank. Getting information of the proximity of the enemy, I informed Meade, and without waiting to see Burnside, at once moved forward my headquarters to where Meade was.

It was my plan then, as it was on all other occasions, to take the initiative whenever the enemy could be drawn from his intrenchments if we were not intrenched ourselves. Warren had not yet reached the point where he was to halt, when he discovered the enemy near by. Neither party had any advantage of position. Warren was, therefore, ordered to attack as soon as he could prepare for it. At nine o'clock Hancock was ordered to come up to the support of Getty. He himself arrived at Getty's front about noon, but his troops were yet far in the rear. Getty was directed to hold his position at all hazards until relieved. About this hour Warren was ready, and attacked with favorable though not decisive results. Getty was somewhat isolated from Warren and was in a precarious condition for a time. Wilson, with his division of cavalry, was farther south, and was cut off from the rest of the army. At two o'clock Hancock's troops began to arrive, and immediately he was ordered to join Getty and attack the enemy. But the heavy timber and narrow roads prevented him from getting into position for attack as promptly as he generally did when receiving such orders. At four o'clock he again received his orders to attack, and General Getty received orders from Meade a few minutes later to attack whether Hancock was ready or not. He met the enemy under Heth within a few hundred yards.

Hancock immediately sent two divisions, commanded by Birney and Mott, and later two brigades, Carroll's and Owen's, to the support of Getty. This was timely and saved Getty. During the battle Getty and Carroll were wounded, but remained on the field. One of Birney's most gallant brigade commanders—Alexander Hays—was killed.

I had been at West Point with Hays for three years, and had served with him through the Mexican war, a portion of the time in the same regiment. He was a most gallant officer, ready to lead his command wherever ordered. With him it was "Come, boys," not "Go."

Wadsworth's division and Baxter's brigade of the 2d division were sent to reinforce Hancock and Getty; but the density of the intervening forest was such that, there being no road to march upon, they did not get up with the head of column until night, and bivouacked where they were without getting into position.

During the afternoon Sheridan sent Gregg's division of cavalry to Todd's Tavern in search of Wilson. This was fortunate. He found Wilson engaged with a superior force under General Rosser, supported by infantry, and falling back before it. Together they were strong enough to turn the tables upon the enemy and themselves become aggressive. They soon drove the rebel cavalry back beyond Corbin's Bridge.

Fighting between Hancock and Hill continued until night put a close to it. Neither side made any special progress.

After the close of the battle of the 5th of May my orders were given for the following morning. We knew Longstreet with 12,000 men was on his way to join Hill's right, near the Brock Road, and might arrive during the night. I was anxious that the rebels should not take the initiative in the morning, and therefore ordered Hancock to make an assault at 4.30 o'clock. Meade asked to have the hour changed to six. Deferring to his wishes as far as I was willing, the order was modified and five was fixed as the hour to move.

Hancock had now fully one-half of the Army of the Potomac. Wadsworth with his division, which had arrived the night before, lay in a line perpendicular to that held by Hill, and to the right of Hancock. He was directed to move at the same time, and to attack Hill's left.

Burnside, who was coming up with two divisions, was directed to get in between Warren and Wadsworth, and attack as soon as he could get in position to do so. Sedgwick and Warren were to make attacks in their front, to detain as many of the enemy as they could and to take advantage of any attempt to reinforce Hill from that quarter. Burnside was ordered if he should succeed in breaking the enemy's centre, to swing around to the left and envelop the right of Lee's army. Hancock was informed of all the movements ordered.

Burnside had three divisions, but one of them—a colored division—was sent to guard the wagon train, and he did not see it again until July.

Lee was evidently very anxious that there should be no battle on his right until Longstreet got up. This is evident from the fact that notwithstanding the early hour at which I had ordered the assault, both for the purpose of being the attacking party and to strike before Longstreet got up, Lee was ahead in his assault on our right. His purpose was evident, but he failed.

Hancock was ready to advance by the hour named, but learning in time that Longstreet was moving a part of his corps by the Catharpin Road, thus threatening his left flank, sent a division of infantry, commanded by General Barlow, with all his artillery, to cover the approaches by which Longstreet was expected. This disposition was made in time to attack as ordered. Hancock moved by the left of the Orange Plank Road, and Wadsworth by the right of it. The fighting was desperate for about an hour, when the enemy began to break up in great confusion.

I believed then, and see no reason to change that opinion now, that if the country had been such that Hancock and his command could have seen the confusion and panic in the lines of the enemy, it would have been taken advantage of so

effectually that Lee would not have made another stand outside of his Richmond defences.

Gibbon commanded Hancock's left, and was ordered to
attack, but was not able to accomplish much.

On the morning of the 6th Sheridan was sent to connect
with Hancock's left and attack the enemy's cavalry who were
trying to get on our left and rear. He met them at the intersection of the Furnace and Brock roads and at Todd's Tavern,
and defeated them at both places. Later he was attacked, and
again the enemy was repulsed.

Hancock heard the firing between Sheridan and Stuart, and
thinking the enemy coming by that road, still further reinforced his position guarding the entrance to the Brock Road.
Another incident happened during the day to further induce
Hancock to weaken his attacking column. Word reached him
that troops were seen moving towards him from the direction
of Todd's Tavern, and Brooke's brigade was detached to meet
this new enemy; but the troops approaching proved to be
several hundred convalescents coming from Chancellorsville,
by the road Hancock had advanced upon, to join their respective commands. At 6.50 o'clock A.M., Burnside, who had
passed Wilderness Tavern at six o'clock, was ordered to send a
division to the support of Hancock, but to continue with the
remainder of his command in the execution of his previous
order. The difficulty of making a way through the dense forests prevented Burnside from getting up in time to be of any
service on the forenoon of the sixth.

Hancock followed Hill's retreating forces, in the morning,
a mile or more. He maintained this position until, along in
the afternoon, Longstreet came upon him. The retreating column of Hill meeting reinforcements that had not yet been
engaged, became encouraged and returned with them. They
were enabled, from the density of the forest, to approach
within a few hundred yards of our advance before being discovered. Falling upon a brigade of Hancock's corps thrown
to the advance, they swept it away almost instantly. The enemy followed up his advantage and soon came upon Mott's
division, which fell back in great confusion. Hancock made
dispositions to hold his advanced position, but after holding
it for a time, fell back into the position that he had held in the

morning, which was strongly intrenched. In this engagement the intrepid Wadsworth while trying to rally his men was mortally wounded and fell into the hands of the enemy. The enemy followed up, but made no immediate attack.

The Confederate General Jenkins was killed and Longstreet seriously wounded in this engagement. Longstreet had to leave the field, not to resume command for many weeks. His loss was a severe one to Lee, and compensated in a great measure for the mishap, or misapprehensions, which had fallen to our lot during the day.

After Longstreet's removal from the field Lee took command of his right in person. He was not able, however, to rally his men to attack Hancock's position, and withdrew from our front for the purpose of reforming. Hancock sent a brigade to clear his front of all remnants that might be left of Longstreet's or Hill's commands. This brigade having been formed at right angles to the intrenchments held by Hancock's command, swept down the whole length of them from left to right. A brigade of the enemy was encountered in this move; but it broke and disappeared without a contest.

Firing was continued after this, but with less fury. Burnside had not yet been able to get up to render any assistance. But it was now only about nine in the morning, and he was getting into position on Hancock's right.

At 4.15 in the afternoon Lee attacked our left. His line moved up to within a hundred yards of ours and opened a heavy fire. This status was maintained for about half an hour. Then a part of Mott's division and Ward's brigade of Birney's division gave way and retired in disorder. The enemy under R. H. Anderson took advantage of this and pushed through our line, planting their flags on a part of the intrenchments not on fire. But owing to the efforts of Hancock, their success was but temporary. Carroll, of Gibbon's division, moved at a double quick with his brigade and drove back the enemy, inflicting great loss. Fighting had continued from five in the morning sometimes along the whole line, at other times only in places. The ground fought over had varied in width, but averaged three-quarters of a mile. The killed, and many of the severely wounded, of both armies, lay within this belt where it was impossible to reach them. The woods were set on fire by the bursting shells, and the conflagration raged. The wounded who had not strength to move themselves were either suffocated or burned to death. Finally the fire communicated with our breastworks, in places. Being constructed of wood, they burned with great fury. But the battle still raged, our men firing through the flames until it became too hot to remain longer.

Lee was now in distress. His men were in confusion, and his personal efforts failed to restore order. These facts, however, were learned subsequently, or we would have taken advantage of his condition and no doubt gained a decisive success. His troops were withdrawn now, but I revoked the order, which I had given previously to this assault, for Hancock to attack, because his troops had exhausted their ammunition and did not have time to replenish from the train, which was at some distance.

Burnside, Sedgwick, and Warren had all kept up an assault during all this time; but their efforts had no other effect than to prevent the enemy from reinforcing his right from the troops in their front.

I had, on the 5th, ordered all the bridges over the Rapidan to be taken up except one at Germania Ford.

The troops on Sedgwick's right had been sent to reinforce our left. This left our right in danger of being turned, and us of being cut off from all present base of supplies. Sedgwick had refused his right and intrenched it for protection against attack. But late in the afternoon of the 6th Early came out from his lines in considerable force and got in upon Sedgwick's right, notwithstanding the precautions taken, and created considerable confusion. Early captured several hundred prisoners, among them two general officers. The defence, however, was vigorous; and night coming on, the enemy was thrown into as much confusion as our troops, engaged, were. Early says in his Memoirs that if we had discovered the confusion in his lines we might have brought fresh troops to his great discomfort. Many officers, who had not been attacked by Early, continued coming to my headquarters even after Sedgwick had rectified his lines a little farther to the rear, with news of the disaster, fully impressed with the idea that the enemy was pushing on and would soon be upon me.

During the night all of Lee's army withdrew within their intrenchments. On the morning of the 7th General Custer drove the enemy's cavalry from Catharpin Furnace to Todd's Tavern. Pickets and skirmishers were sent along our entire front to find the position of the enemy. Some went as far as a mile and a half before finding him. But Lee showed no disposition to come out of his works. There was no battle during the day, and but little firing except in Warren's front; he being directed about noon to make a reconnoissance in force. This drew some sharp firing, but there was no attempt on the part of Lee to drive him back. This ended the Battle of the Wilderness.

Chapter LI.

AFTER THE BATTLE—TELEGRAPH AND SIGNAL SERVICE—
MOVEMENT BY THE LEFT FLANK.

MORE DESPERATE FIGHTING has not been witnessed on this continent than that of the 5th and 6th of May. Our victory consisted in having successfully crossed a formidable stream, almost in the face of an enemy, and in getting the army together as a unit. We gained an advantage on the morning of the 6th, which, if it had been followed up, must have proven very decisive. In the evening the enemy gained an advantage; but was speedily repulsed. As we stood at the close, the two armies were relatively in about the same condition to meet each other as when the river divided them. But the fact of having safely crossed was a victory.

Our losses in the Wilderness were very severe. Those of the Confederates must have been even more so; but I have no means of speaking with accuracy upon this point. The Germania Ford bridge was transferred to Ely's Ford to facilitate the transportation of the wounded to Washington.

It may be as well here as elsewhere to state two things connected with all movements of the Army of the Potomac: first, in every change of position or halt for the night, whether confronting the enemy or not, the moment arms were stacked the men intrenched themselves. For this purpose they would build up piles of logs or rails if they could be found in their front, and dig a ditch, throwing the dirt forward on the timber. Thus the digging they did counted in making a depression to stand in, and increased the elevation in front of them. It was wonderful how quickly they could in this way construct defences of considerable strength. When a halt was made with the view of assaulting the enemy, or in his presence, these would be strengthened or their positions changed under the direction of engineer officers. The second was, the use made of the telegraph and signal corps. Nothing could be more complete than the organization and discipline of this body of brave and intelligent men. Insulated wires—insulated so that they would transmit messages in a storm, on the ground or under water—were wound upon reels, making about two hundred pounds weight of wire to each reel. Two men and one mule were detailed to each reel. The pack-saddle on which this was carried was provided with a rack like a sawbuck placed crosswise of the saddle, and raised above it so that the reel, with its wire, would revolve freely. There was a wagon, supplied with a telegraph operator, battery and tele- graph instruments for each division, each corps, each army, and one for my headquarters. There were wagons also loaded with light poles, about the size and length of a wall tent pole, supplied with an iron spike in one end, used to hold the wires up when laid, so that wagons and artillery would not run over them. The mules thus loaded were assigned to brigades, and always kept with the command they were assigned to. The operators were also assigned to particular headquarters, and never changed except by special orders.

The moment the troops were put in position to go into camp all the men connected with this branch of service would proceed to put up their wires. A mule loaded with a coil of wire would be led to the rear of the nearest flank of the brigade he belonged to, and would be led in a line parallel thereto, while one man would hold an end of the wire and uncoil it as the mule was led off. When he had walked the length of the wire the whole of it would be on the ground. This would be done in rear of every brigade at the same time. The ends of all the wires would then be joined, making a continuous wire in the rear of the whole army. The men, at- tached to brigades or divisions, would all commence at once raising the wires with their telegraph poles. This was done by making a loop in the wire and putting it over the spike and raising the pole to a perpendicular position. At intervals the wire would be attached to trees, or some other permanent object, so that one pole was sufficient at a place. In the ab- sence of such a support two poles would have to be used, at intervals, placed at an angle so as to hold the wire firm in its place. While this was being done the telegraph wagons would take their positions near where the headquarters they be- longed to were to be established, and would connect with the wire. Thus, in a few minutes longer time than it took a mule to walk the length of its coil, telegraphic communication would be effected between all the headquarters of the army. No orders ever had to be given to establish the telegraph.

The signal service was used on the march. The men composing this corps were assigned to specified commands. When movements were made, they would go in advance, or on the flanks, and seize upon high points of ground giving a commanding view of the country, if cleared, or would climb tall trees on the highest points if not cleared, and would denote, by signals, the positions of different parts of our own army, and often the movements of the enemy. They would also take off the signals of the enemy and transmit them. It would sometimes take too long a time to make translations of intercepted dispatches for us to receive any benefit from them. But sometimes they gave useful information.

On the afternoon of the 7th I received news from Washington announcing that Sherman had probably attacked Johnston that day, and that Butler had reached City Point safely and taken it by surprise on the 5th. I had given orders for a movement by the left flank, fearing that Lee might move rapidly to Richmond to crush Butler before I could get there.

My order for this movement was as follows:

HEADQUARTERS ARMIES OF THE U. S.,

May 7, 1864, 6.30 A.M.

MAJOR-GENERAL MEADE,
    Commanding A. P.

Make all preparations during the day for a night march to take position at Spottsylvania C. H. with one army corps, at Todd's Tavern with one, and another near the intersection of the Piney Branch and Spottsylvania road with the road from Alsop's to Old Court House. If this move is made the trains should be thrown forward early in the morning to the Ny River.

I think it would be advisable in making the change to leave Hancock where he is until Warren passes him. He could then follow and become the right of the new line. Burnside will move to Piney Branch Church. Sedgwick can move along the pike to Chancellorsville and on to his destination. Burnside will move on the plank road to the intersection of it with the Orange and Fredericksburg plank road, then follow Sedgwick to his place of destination.

All vehicles should be got out of hearing of the enemy before the troops move, and then move off quietly.

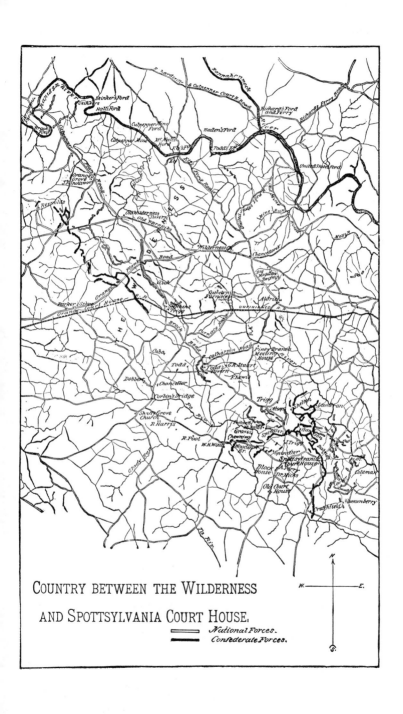

COUNTRY BETWEEN THE WILDERNESS
AND SPOTTSYLVANIA COURT HOUSE.

National Forces.
Confederate Forces.

It is more than probable that the enemy concentrate for a heavy attack on Hancock this afternoon. In case they do we must be prepared to resist them, and follow up any success we may gain, with our whole force. Such a result would necessarily modify these instructions.

All the hospitals should be moved to-day to Chancellorsville.

U. S. GRANT,
Lieut.-General.

During the 7th Sheridan had a fight with the rebel cavalry at Todd's Tavern, but routed them, thus opening the way for the troops that were to go by that route at night. Soon after dark Warren withdrew from the front of the enemy, and was soon followed by Sedgwick. Warren's march carried him immediately behind the works where Hancock's command lay on the Brock Road. With my staff and a small escort of cavalry I preceded the troops. Meade with his staff accompanied me. The greatest enthusiasm was manifested by Hancock's men as we passed by. No doubt it was inspired by the fact that the movement was south. It indicated to them that they had passed through the "beginning of the end" in the battle just fought. The cheering was so lusty that the enemy must have taken it for a night attack. At all events it drew from him a furious fusillade of artillery and musketry, plainly heard but not felt by us.

Meade and I rode in advance. We had passed but a little way beyond our left when the road forked. We looked to see, if we could, which road Sheridan had taken with his cavalry during the day. It seemed to be the right-hand one, and accordingly we took it. We had not gone far, however, when Colonel C. B. Comstock, of my staff, with the instinct of the engineer, suspecting that we were on a road that would lead us into the lines of the enemy, if he, too, should be moving, dashed by at a rapid gallop and all alone. In a few minutes he returned and reported that Lee was moving, and that the road we were on would bring us into his lines in a short distance. We returned to the forks of the road, left a man to indicate the right road to the head of Warren's column when it should come up, and continued our journey to Todd's Tavern, where we arrived after midnight.

My object in moving to Spottsylvania was twofold: first, I did not want Lee to get back to Richmond in time to attempt to crush Butler before I could get there; second, I wanted to get between his army and Richmond if possible; and, if not, to draw him into the open field. But Lee, by accident, beat us to Spottsylvania. Our wagon trains had been ordered easterly of the roads the troops were to march upon before the movement commenced. Lee interpreted this as a semi-retreat of the Army of the Potomac to Fredericksburg, and so informed his government. Accordingly he ordered Longstreet's corps— now commanded by Anderson—to move in the morning (the 8th) to Spottsylvania. But the woods being still on fire, Anderson could not go into bivouac, and marched directly on to his destination that night. By this accident Lee got possession of Spottsylvania. It is impossible to say now what would have been the result if Lee's orders had been obeyed as given; but it is certain that we would have been in Spottsylvania, and between him and his capital. My belief is that there would have been a race between the two armies to see which could reach Richmond first, and the Army of the Potomac would have had the shorter line. Thus, twice since crossing the Rapidan we came near closing the campaign, so far as battles were concerned, from the Rapidan to the James River or Richmond. The first failure was caused by our not following up the success gained over Hill's corps on the morning of the 6th, as before described: the second, when fires caused by that battle drove Anderson to make a march during the night of the 7th–8th which he was ordered to commence on the morning of the 8th. But accident often decides the fate of battle.

Sheridan's cavalry had had considerable fighting during the afternoon of the 7th, lasting at Todd's Tavern until after night, with the field his at the close. He issued the necessary orders for seizing Spottsylvania and holding the bridge over the Po River, which Lee's troops would have to cross to get to Spottsylvania. But Meade changed Sheridan's orders to Merritt—who was holding the bridge—on his arrival at Todd's Tavern, and thereby left the road free for Anderson when he came up. Wilson, who was ordered to seize the town, did so, with his division of cavalry; but he could not hold it against the Confederate corps which had not been detained at the crossing of the Po, as it would have been but for the unfortunate change in Merritt's orders. Had he been permitted to execute the orders Sheridan gave him, he would have been guarding with two brigades of cavalry the bridge over the Po River which Anderson had to cross, and must have detained him long enough to enable Warren to reinforce Wilson and hold the town.

Anderson soon intrenched himself—if indeed the intrenchments were not already made—immediately across Warren's front. Warren was not aware of his presence, but probably supposed it was the cavalry which Merritt had engaged earlier in the day. He assaulted at once, but was repulsed. He soon organized his men, as they were not pursued by the enemy, and made a second attack, this time with his whole corps. This time he succeeded in gaining a position immediately in the enemy's front, where he intrenched. His right and left divisions—the former Crawford's, the latter Wadsworth's, now commanded by Cutler—drove the enemy back some distance.

At this time my headquarters had been advanced to Piney Branch Church. I was anxious to crush Anderson before Lee could get a force to his support. To this end Sedgwick, who was at Piney Branch Church, was ordered to Warren's support. Hancock, who was at Todd's Tavern, was notified of Warren's engagement, and was directed to be in readiness to come up. Burnside, who was with the wagon trains at Aldrich's on our extreme left, received the same instructions. Sedgwick was slow in getting up for some reason—probably unavoidable, because he was never at fault when serious work was to be done—so that it was near night before the combined forces were ready to attack. Even then all of Sedgwick's command did not get into the engagement. Warren led the last assault, one division at a time, and of course it failed.

Warren's difficulty was twofold: when he received an order to do anything, it would at once occur to his mind how all the balance of the army should be engaged so as properly to co-operate with him. His ideas were generally good, but he would forget that the person giving him orders had thought of others at the time he had of him. In like manner, when he did get ready to execute an order, after giving most intelligent instructions to division commanders, he would go in with one division, holding the others in reserve until he could superintend their movements in person also, forgetting that division commanders could execute an order without his presence. His difficulty was constitutional and beyond his control. He was an officer of superior ability, quick perceptions, and personal courage to accomplish anything that could be done with a small command.

Lee had ordered Hill's corps—now commanded by Early—to move by the very road we had marched upon. This shows that even early in the morning of the 8th Lee had not yet become acquainted with my move, but still thought that the Army of the Potomac had gone to Fredericksburg. Indeed, he informed the authorities at Richmond that he had possession of Spottsylvania and was thus on my flank. Anderson was in possession of Spottsylvania, through no foresight of Lee, however. Early only found that he had been following us when he ran against Hancock at Todd's Tavern. His coming detained Hancock from the battle-field of Spottsylvania for that day; but he, in like manner, kept Early back and forced him to move by another route.

Had I ordered the movement for the night of the 7th by my left flank, it would have put Hancock in the lead. It would also have given us an hour or more earlier start. It took all that time for Warren to get the head of his column to the left of Hancock after he had got his troops out of their line confronting the enemy. This hour, and Hancock's capacity to use his whole force when necessary, would, no doubt, have enabled him to crush Anderson before he could be reinforced. But the movement made was tactical. It kept the troops in mass against a possible assault by the enemy. Our left occupied its intrenchments while the two corps to the right passed. If an attack had been made by the enemy he would have found the 2d corps in position, fortified, and, practically, the 5th and 6th corps in position as reserves, until his entire front was passed. By a left flank movement the army would have been scattered while still passing the front of the enemy, and before the extreme right had got by it would have been very much exposed. Then, too, I had not yet learned the special qualifications of the different corps commanders. At that time my judgment was that Warren was the man I would suggest to succeed Meade should anything happen to that gallant soldier to take him from the field. As I have before said, Warren was a gallant soldier, an able man; and he was beside thoroughly imbued with the solemnity and importance of the duty he had to perform.

Chapter LII.

THE MATTAPONY RIVER is formed by the junction of the Mat, the Ta, the Po and the Ny rivers, the last being the northernmost of the four. It takes its rise about a mile south and a little east of the Wilderness Tavern. The Po rises southwest of the same place, but farther away. Spottsylvania is on the ridge dividing these two streams, and where they are but a few miles apart. The Brock Road reaches Spottsylvania without crossing either of these streams. Lee's army coming up by the Catharpin Road, had to cross the Po at Wooden Bridge. Warren and Hancock came by the Brock Road. Sedgwick crossed the Ny at Catharpin Furnace. Burnside coming by Aldrich's to Gates's house, had to cross the Ny near the enemy. He found pickets at the bridge, but they were soon driven off by a brigade of Willcox's division, and the stream was crossed. This brigade was furiously attacked; but the remainder of the division coming up, they were enabled to hold their position, and soon fortified it.

About the time I received the news of this attack, word came from Hancock that Early had left his front. He had been forced over to the Catharpin Road, crossing the Po at Corbin's and again at Wooden Bridge. These are the ridges Sheridan had given orders to his cavalry to occupy on the 8th, while one division should occupy Spottsylvania. These movements of the enemy gave me the idea that Lee was about to make the attempt to get to, or towards, Fredericksburg to cut off my supplies. I made arrangements to attack his right and get between him and Richmond if he should try to execute this design. If he had any such intention it was abandoned as soon as Burnside was established south of the Ny.

The Po and the Ny are narrow little streams, but deep, with abrupt banks, and bordered by heavily wooded and marshy

bottoms—at the time we were there—and difficult to cross
except where bridged. The country about was generally
heavily timbered, but with occasional clearings. It was a much
better country to conduct a defensive campaign in than an
offensive one.

By noon of the 9th the position of the two armies was as
follows: Lee occupied a semicircle facing north, north-west
and north-east, inclosing the town. Anderson was on his left
extending to the Po, Ewell came next, then Early. Warren
occupied our right, covering the Brock and other roads
converging at Spottsylvania; Sedgwick was to his left and
Burnside on our extreme left. Hancock was yet back at Todd's
Tavern, but as soon as it was known that Early had left Hancock's front the latter was ordered up to Warren's right. He
formed a line with three divisions on the hill overlooking the
Po early in the afternoon, and was ordered to cross the Po and
get on the enemy's flank. The fourth division of Hancock's
corps, Mott commanding, was left at Todd's when the corps
first came up; but in the afternoon it was brought up and
placed to the left of Sedgwick's—now Wright's—6th corps.
In the morning General Sedgwick had been killed near the
right of his intrenchments by rebel sharp-shooters. His loss
was a severe one to the Army of the Potomac and to the Nation. General H. G. Wright succeeded him in the command
of his corps.

Hancock was now, nine P.M. of the 9th of May, across the
left flank of Lee's army, but separated from it, and also from
the remainder of Meade's army, by the Po River. But for the
lateness of the hour and the darkness of the night he would
have attempted to cross the river again at Wooden Bridge,
thus bringing himself on the same side with both friend and
foe.

The Po at the points where Hancock's corps crossed runs
nearly due east. Just below his lower crossing—the troops
crossed at three points—it turns due south, and after passing
under Wooden Bridge soon resumes a more easterly direction.
During the night this corps built three bridges over the Po;
but these were in rear.

The position assumed by Hancock's corps forced Lee to reinforce his left during the night. Accordingly on the morning

of the 10th, when Hancock renewed his effort to get over the
Po to his front, he found himself confronted by some of
Early's command, which had been brought from the extreme
right of the enemy during the night. He succeeded in effecting a crossing with one brigade, however, but finding the enemy intrenched in his front, no more were crossed.

Hancock reconnoitred his front on the morning of the
10th, with the view of forcing a crossing, if it was found that
an advantage could be gained. The enemy was found strongly
intrenched on the high ground overlooking the river, and
commanding the Wooden Bridge with artillery. Anderson's
left rested on the Po, where it turns south; therefore, for Hancock to cross over—although it would bring him to the same
side of the stream with the rest of the army—would still farther isolate him from it. The stream would have to be crossed
twice in the face of the enemy to unite with the main body.
The idea of crossing was therefore abandoned.

Lee had weakened the other parts of his line to meet this
movement of Hancock's, and I determined to take advantage
of it. Accordingly in the morning, orders were issued for
an attack in the afternoon on the centre by Warren's and
Wright's corps, Hancock to command all the attacking force.
Two of his divisions were brought to the north side of the Po.
Gibbon was placed to the right of Warren, and Birney in his
rear as a reserve. Barlow's division was left south of the
stream, and Mott of the same corps was still to the left of
Wright's corps. Burnside was ordered to reconnoitre his front
in force, and, if an opportunity presented, to attack with
vigor. The enemy seeing Barlow's division isolated from the
rest of the army, came out and attacked with fury. Barlow
repulsed the assault with great slaughter, and with considerable loss to himself. But the enemy reorganized and renewed
the assault. Birney was now moved to the high ground overlooking the river crossings built by our troops, and covered
the crossings. The second assault was repulsed, again with severe loss to the enemy, and Barlow was withdrawn without
further molestation. General T. G. Stevenson was killed in
this move.

Between the lines, where Warren's assault was to take place,
there was a ravine grown up with large trees and underbrush,

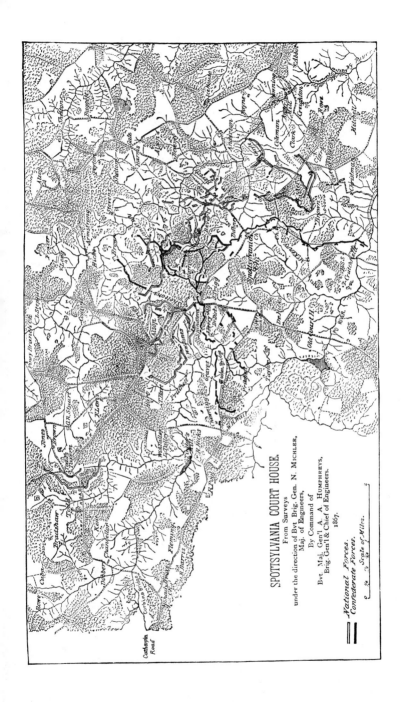

SPOTTSYLVANIA COURT HOUSE.
From Surveys
under the direction of Bvt. Brig. Gen. N. MICHLER,
Maj. of Engineers,
By Command of
Bvt. Maj. Gen'l A. A. HUMPHREYS,
Brig. Gen'l & Chief of Engineers.
1867.

National Forces.
Confederate Forces.

Scale of Miles.

making it almost impenetrable by man. The slopes on both sides were also covered with a heavy growth of timber. Warren, before noon, reconnoitred his front twice, the first time with one and the second with two divisions. He was repulsed on both occasions, but gained such information of the ground as to induce him to report recommending the assault.

Wright also reconnoitred his front and gained a considerably advanced position from the one he started from. He then organized a storming party, consisting of twelve regiments, and assigned Colonel Emory Upton, of the 121st New York Volunteers, to the command of it. About four o'clock in the afternoon the assault was ordered, Warren's and Wright's corps, with Mott's division of Hancock's corps, to move simultaneously. The movement was prompt, and in a few minutes the fiercest of struggles began. The battle-field was so densely covered with forest that but little could be seen, by any one person, as to the progress made. Meade and I occupied the best position we could get, in rear of Warren.

Warren was repulsed with heavy loss, General J. C. Rice being among the killed. He was not followed, however, by the enemy, and was thereby enabled to reorganize his command as soon as covered from the guns of the enemy. To the left our success was decided, but the advantage was lost by the feeble action of Mott. Upton with his assaulting party pushed forward and crossed the enemy's intrenchments. Turning to the right and left he captured several guns and some hundreds of prisoners. Mott was ordered to his assistance but failed utterly. So much time was lost in trying to get up the troops which were in the right position to reinforce, that I ordered Upton to withdraw; but the officers and men of his command were so averse to giving up the advantage they had gained that I withdrew the order. To relieve them, I ordered a renewal of the assault. By this time Hancock, who had gone with Birney's division to relieve Barlow, had returned, bringing the division with him. His corps was now joined with Warren's and Wright's in this last assault. It was gallantly made, many men getting up to, and over, the works of the enemy; but they were not able to hold them. At night they were withdrawn. Upton brought his prisoners with him, but the guns he had captured he was obliged to abandon.

Upton had gained an important advantage, but a lack in others of the spirit and dash possessed by him lost it to us. Before leaving Washington I had been authorized to promote officers on the field for special acts of gallantry. By this authority I conferred the rank of brigadier-general upon Upton on the spot, and this act was confirmed by the President. Upton had been badly wounded in this fight.

Burnside on the left had got up to within a few hundred yards of Spottsylvania Court House, completely turning Lee's right. He was not aware of the importance of the advantage he had gained, and I, being with the troops where the heavy fighting was, did not know of it at the time. He had gained his position with but little fighting, and almost without loss. Burnside's position now separated him widely from Wright's corps, the corps nearest to him. At night he was ordered to join on to this. This brought him back about a mile, and lost to us an important advantage. I attach no blame to Burnside for this, but I do to myself for not having had a staff officer with him to report to me his position.

The enemy had not dared to come out of his line at any point to follow up his advantage, except in the single instance of his attack on Barlow. Then he was twice repulsed with heavy loss, though he had an entire corps against two brigades. Barlow took up his bridges in the presence of this force.

On the 11th there was no battle and but little firing; none except by Mott who made a reconnoissance to ascertain if there was a weak point in the enemy's line.

I wrote the following letter to General Halleck:

NEAR SPOTTSYLVANIA C. H.,
May 11, 1864 — 8.30 A.M.
MAJOR-GENERAL HALLECK, Chief of Staff of the Army,
Washington, D. C.

We have now ended the 6th day of very hard fighting. The result up to this time is much in our favor. But our losses have been heavy as well as those of the enemy. We have lost to this time eleven general officers killed, wounded and missing, and probably twenty thousand men. I think the loss of the enemy must be greater — we having taken over four thousand prisoners in battle, whilst he has taken from us but few except a few stragglers. I am now sending back to

Belle Plain all my wagons for a fresh supply of provisions and ammunition, and purpose to fight it out on this line if it takes all summer.

The arrival of reinforcements here will be very encouraging to the men, and I hope they will be sent as fast as possible, and in as great numbers. My object in having them sent to Belle Plain was to use them as an escort to our supply trains. If it is more convenient to send them out by train to march from the railroad to Belle Plain or Fredericksburg, send them so.

I am satisfied the enemy are very shaky, and are only kept up to the mark by the greatest exertions on the part of their officers, and by keeping them intrenched in every position they take.

Up to this time there is no indication of any portion of Lee's army being detached for the defence of Richmond.

U. S. GRANT,
Lieut.-General.

And also, I received information, through the War Department, from General Butler that his cavalry under Kautz had cut the railroad south of Petersburg, separating Beauregard from Richmond, and had whipped Hill, killing, wounding and capturing many. Also that he was intrenched, and could maintain himself. On this same day came news from Sheridan to the effect that he had destroyed ten miles of the railroad and telegraph between Lee and Richmond, one and a half million rations, and most of the medical stores for his army.

On the 8th I had directed Sheridan verbally to cut loose from the Army of the Potomac and pass around the left of Lee's army and attack his cavalry and communications, which was successfully executed in the manner I have already described.

Chapter LIII.

HANCOCK'S ASSAULT — LOSSES OF THE CONFEDERATES —
PROMOTIONS RECOMMENDED — DISCOMFITURE OF THE
ENEMY — EWELL'S ATTACK — REDUCING THE ARTILLERY.

I N THE RECONNOISSANCE made by Mott on the 11th, a salient was discovered at the right centre. I determined that
an assault should be made at that point.* Accordingly in the
afternoon Hancock was ordered to move his command by the
rear of Warren and Wright, under cover of night, to Wright's
left, and there form it for an assault at four o'clock the next
morning. The night was dark, it rained heavily, and the road
was difficult, so that it was midnight when he reached the
point where he was to halt. It took most of the night to get
the men in position for their advance in the morning. The
men got but little rest. Burnside was ordered to attack† on

---

*HEADQUARTERS ARMIES U. S.,
May 11, 1864. — 3 P.M.

MAJOR-GENERAL MEADE,
    Commanding Army of the Potomac.
    Move three divisions of the 2d corps by the rear of the 5th and 6th corps,
under cover of night, so as to join the 9th corps in a vigorous assault on the
enemy at four o'clock A.M. to-morrow. I will send one or two staff officers
over to-night to stay with Burnside, and impress him with the importance of
a prompt and vigorous attack. Warren and Wright should hold their corps as
close to the enemy as possible, to take advantage of any diversion caused by
this attack, and to push in if any opportunity presents itself. There is but little
doubt in my mind that the assault last evening would have proved entirely
successful if it had commenced one hour earlier and had been heartily entered
into by Mott's division and the 9th corps.

U. S. GRANT,
Lieut.-General.

†HEADQUARTERS, ARMIES U. S.,
May 11, 1864. — 4 P.M.

MAJOR-GENERAL A. E. BURNSIDE,
    Commanding 9th Army Corps.
    Major-General Hancock has been ordered to move his corps under cover
of night to join you in a vigorous attack against the enemy at 4 o'clock A.M.
to-morrow. You will move against the enemy with your entire force promptly
and with all possible vigor at precisely 4 o'clock A.M. to-morrow the 12th

the left of the salient at the same hour. I sent two of my staff officers to impress upon him the importance of pushing forward vigorously. Hancock was notified of this. Warren and Wright were ordered to hold themselves in readiness to join in the assault if circumstances made it advisable. I occupied a central position most convenient for receiving information from all points. Hancock put Barlow on his left, in double column, and Birney to his right. Mott followed Birney, and Gibbon was held in reserve.

The morning of the 12th opened foggy, delaying the start more than half an hour.

The ground over which Hancock had to pass to reach the enemy, was ascending and heavily wooded to within two or three hundred yards of the enemy's intrenchments. In front of Birney there was also a marsh to cross. But, notwithstanding all these difficulties, the troops pushed on in quick time without firing a gun, and when within four or five hundred yards of the enemy's line broke out in loud cheers, and with a rush went up to and over the breastworks. Barlow and Birney entered almost simultaneously. Here a desperate hand-to-hand conflict took place. The men of the two sides were too close together to fire, but used their guns as clubs. The hand conflict was soon over. Hancock's corps captured some four thousand prisoners—among them a division and a brigade commander—twenty or more guns with their horses, caissons, and ammunition, several thousand stand of arms, and many colors. Hancock, as soon as the hand-to-hand conflict was over, turned the guns of the enemy against him and advanced inside the rebel lines. About six o'clock I ordered

inst. Let your preparations for this attack be conducted with the utmost secrecy and veiled entirely from the enemy.

I send two of my staff officers; Colonels Comstock and Babcock, in whom I have great confidence and who are acquainted with the direction the attack is to be made from here, to remain with you and General Hancock with instructions to render you every assistance in their power. Generals Warren and Wright will hold their corps as close to the enemy as possible, to take advantage of any diversion caused by yours and Hancock's attack, and will push in their whole force if any opportunity presents itself.

U. S. GRANT,
Lieut.-General.

Warren's corps to the support of Hancock's. Burnside, on the left, had advanced up east of the salient to the very parapet of the enemy. Potter, commanding one of his divisions, got over but was not able to remain there. However, he inflicted a heavy loss upon the enemy; but not without loss in return.

This victory was important, and one that Lee could not afford to leave us in full possession of. He made the most strenuous efforts to regain the position he had lost. Troops were brought up from his left and attacked Hancock furiously. Hancock was forced to fall back: but he did so slowly, with his face to the enemy, inflicting on him heavy loss, until behind the breastworks he had captured. These he turned, facing them the other way, and continued to hold. Wright was ordered up to reinforce Hancock, and arrived by six o'clock. He was wounded soon after coming up but did not relinquish the command of his corps, although the fighting lasted until one o'clock the next morning. At eight o'clock Warren was ordered up again, but was so slow in making his dispositions that his orders were frequently repeated, and with emphasis. At eleven o'clock I gave Meade written orders to relieve Warren from his command if he failed to move promptly. Hancock placed batteries on high ground in his rear, which he used against the enemy, firing over the heads of his own troops.

Burnside accomplished but little on our left of a positive nature, but negatively a great deal. He kept Lee from reinforcing his centre from that quarter. If the 5th corps, or rather if Warren, had been as prompt as Wright was with the 6th corps, better results might have been obtained.

Lee massed heavily from his left flank on the broken point of his line. Five times during the day he assaulted furiously, but without dislodging our troops from their new position. His losses must have been fearful. Sometimes the belligerents would be separated by but a few feet. In one place a tree, eighteen inches in diameter, was cut entirely down by musket balls. All the trees between the lines were very much cut to pieces by artillery and musketry. It was three o'clock next morning before the fighting ceased. Some of our troops had then been twenty hours under fire. In this engagement we did not lose a single organization, not even a company. The enemy lost one division with its commander, one brigade and one regiment, with heavy losses elsewhere.* Our losses were heavy, but, as stated, no whole company was captured. At night Lee took a position in rear of his former one, and by the following morning he was strongly intrenched in it.

Warren's corps was now temporarily broken up, Cutler's division sent to Wright, and Griffin's to Hancock. Meade ordered his chief of staff, General Humphreys, to remain with Warren and the remaining division, and authorized him to give it orders in his name.

During the day I was passing along the line from wing to wing continuously. About the centre stood a house which proved to be occupied by an old lady and her daughter. She showed such unmistakable signs of being strongly Union that I stopped. She said she had not seen a Union flag for so long a time that it did her heart good to look upon it again. She said her husband and son, being Union men, had had to leave early in the war, and were now somewhere in the Union army, if alive. She was without food or nearly so, so I ordered rations issued to her, and promised to find out if I could where the husband and son were.

There was no fighting on the 13th, further than a little skirmishing between Mott's division and the enemy. I was afraid that Lee might be moving out, and I did not want him to go without my knowing it. The indications were that he was moving, but it was found that he was only taking his new position back from the salient that had been captured. Our dead were buried this day. Mott's division was reduced to a brigade, and assigned to Birney's division.

---

*Headquarters Armies U. S.,
May 12, 1864, 6.30 P.M.

Major-General Halleck,
     Washington, D.C.

The eighth day of the battle closes, leaving between three and four thousand prisoners in our hands for the day's work, including two general officers, and over thirty pieces of artillery. The enemy are obstinate, and seem to have found the last ditch. We have lost no organizations, not even that of a company, whilst we have destroyed and captured one division (Johnson's), one brigade (Doles'), and one regiment entire from the enemy.

U. S. GRANT,
Lieut.-General.

During this day I wrote to Washington recommending Sherman and Meade* for promotion to the grade of Major-General in the regular army; Hancock for Brigadier-General; Wright, Gibbon and Humphreys to be Major-Generals of Volunteers; and Upton and Carroll to be Brigadiers. Upton had already been named as such, but the appointment had to be confirmed by the Senate on the nomination of the President.

The night of the 13th Warren and Wright were moved by the rear to the left of Burnside. The night was very dark and it rained heavily, the roads were so bad that the troops had to cut trees and corduroy the road a part of the way, to get through. It was midnight before they got to the point where they were to halt, and daylight before the troops could be organized to advance to their position in line. They gained their position in line, however, without any fighting, except a little in Wright's front. Here Upton had to contend for an elevation which we wanted and which the enemy was not

---

*SPOTTSYLVANIA C. H., *May* 13, 1864.
HON. E. M. STANTON, SECRETARY OF WAR,
        Washington, D. C.

I beg leave to recommend the following promotions be made for gallant and distinguished services in the last eight days' battles, to wit: Brigadier-General H. G. Wright and Brigadier-General John Gibbon to be Major-Generals; Colonel S. S. Carroll, 8th Ohio Volunteers; Colonel E. Upton, 121st New York Volunteers; Colonel William McCandless, 2d Pennsylvania Reserves, to be Brigadier-Generals. I would also recommend Major-General W. S. Hancock for Brigadier-General in the regular army. His services and qualifications are eminently deserving of this recognition. In making these recommendations I do not wish the claims of General G. M. Dodge for promotion forgotten, but recommend his name to be sent in at the same time. I would also ask to have General Wright assigned to the command of the Sixth Army Corps. I would further ask the confirmation of General Humphreys to the rank of Major-General.

General Meade has more than met my most sanguine expectations. He and Sherman are the fittest officers for large commands I have come in contact with. If their services can be rewarded by promotion to the rank of Major-Generals in the regular army the honor would be worthily bestowed, and I would feel personally gratified. I would not like to see one of these promotions at this time without seeing both.

                                            U. S. GRANT,
                                                Lieut.-General.

disposed to yield. Upton first drove the enemy, and was then repulsed in turn. Ayres coming to his support with his brigade (of Griffin's division, Warren's corps), the position was secured and fortified. There was no more battle during the 14th. This brought our line east of the Court House and running north and south and facing west.

During the night of the 14th–15th Lee moved to cover this new front. This left Hancock without an enemy confronting him. He was brought to the rear of our new centre, ready to be moved in any direction he might be wanted.

On the 15th news came from Butler and Averill. The former reported the capture of the outer works at Drury's Bluff, on the James River, and that his cavalry had cut the railroad and telegraph south of Richmond on the Danville road: and the latter, the destruction of a depot of supplies at Dublin, West Virginia, and the breaking of New River Bridge on the Virginia and Tennessee Railroad. The next day news came from Sherman and Sheridan. Sherman had forced Johnston out of Dalton, Georgia, and was following him south. The report from Sheridan embraced his operations up to his passing the outer defences of Richmond. The prospect must now have been dismal in Richmond. The road and telegraph were cut between the capital and Lee. The roads and wires were cut in every direction from the rebel capital. Temporarily that city was cut off from all communication with the outside except by courier. This condition of affairs, however, was of but short duration.

I wrote Halleck:

NEAR SPOTTSYLVANIA C. H.,
May 16, 1864, 8 A.M.

MAJOR-GENERAL HALLECK,
            Washington, D. C.:

We have had five days almost constant rain without any prospect yet of it clearing up. The roads have now become so impassable that ambulances with wounded men can no longer run between here and Fredericksburg. All offensive operations necessarily cease until we can have twenty-four hours of dry weather. The army is in the best of spirits, and feel the greatest confidence of ultimate success.

*   *   *   *   *   *

You can assure the President and Secretary of War that the ele-

ments alone have suspended hostilities, and that it is in no manner
due to weakness or exhaustion on our part.

                                    U. S. GRANT,
                                              Lieut.-General.

The condition of the roads was such that nothing was done
on the 17th. But that night Hancock and Wright were to
make a night march back to their old positions, and to make
an assault at four o'clock in the morning. Lee got troops back
in time to protect his old line, so the assault was unsuccessful.
On this day (18th) the news was almost as discouraging to us
as it had been two days before in the rebel capital. As stated
above, Hancock's and Wright's corps had made an unsuccessful assault. News came that Sigel had been defeated at New
Market, badly, and was retreating down the valley. Not two
hours before, I had sent the inquiry to Halleck whether Sigel
could not get to Staunton to stop supplies coming from there
to Lee. I asked at once that Sigel might be relieved, and some
one else put in his place. Hunter's name was suggested, and I
heartily approved. Further news from Butler reported him
driven from Drury's Bluff, but still in possession of the Petersburg road. Banks had been defeated in Louisiana, relieved,
and Canby put in his place. This change of commander was
not on my suggestion. All this news was very discouraging.
All of it must have been known by the enemy before it was by
me. In fact, the good news (for the enemy) must have been
known to him at the moment I thought he was in despair,
and his anguish had been already relieved when we were enjoying his supposed discomfiture. But this was no time for
repining. I immediately gave orders for a movement by the
left flank, on towards Richmond, to commence on the night
of the 19th. I also asked Halleck to secure the co-operation of
the navy in changing our base of supplies from Fredericksburg to Port Royal, on the Rappahannock.

Up to this time I had received no reinforcements, except six
thousand raw troops under Brigadier-General Robert O.
Tyler, just arrived. They had not yet joined their command,
Hancock's corps, but were on our right. This corps had been
brought to the rear of the centre, ready to move in any direction. Lee, probably suspecting some move on my part, and

seeing our right entirely abandoned, moved Ewell's corps about five o'clock in the afternoon, with Early's as a reserve, to attack us in that quarter. Tyler had come up from Fredericksburg, and had been halted on the road to the right of our line, near Kitching's brigade of Warren's corps. Tyler received the attack with his raw troops, and they maintained their position, until reinforced, in a manner worthy of veterans.

Hancock was in a position to reinforce speedily, and was the soldier to do it without waiting to make dispositions. Birney was thrown to Tyler's right and Crawford to his left, with Gibbon as a reserve; and Ewell was whirled back speedily and with heavy loss.

Warren had been ordered to get on Ewell's flank and in his rear, to cut him off from his intrenchments. But his efforts were so feeble that under the cover of night Ewell got back with only the loss of a few hundred prisoners, besides his killed and wounded. The army being engaged until after dark, I rescinded the order for the march by our left flank that night.

As soon as it was discovered that the enemy were coming out to attack, I naturally supposed they would detach a force to destroy our trains. The withdrawal of Hancock from the right uncovered one road from Spottsylvania to Fredericksburg over which trains drew our supplies. This was guarded by a division of colored troops, commanded by General Ferrero, belonging to Burnside's corps. Ferrero was therefore promptly notified, and ordered to throw his cavalry pickets out to the south and be prepared to meet the enemy if he should come; if he had to retreat to do so towards Fredericksburg. The enemy did detach as expected, and captured twenty-five or thirty wagons which, however, were soon retaken.

In consequence of the disasters that had befallen us in the past few days, Lee could be reinforced largely, and I had no doubt he would be. Beauregard had come up from the south with troops to guard the Confederate capital when it was in danger. Butler being driven back, most of the troops could be sent to Lee. Hoke was no longer needed in North Carolina; and Sigel's troops having gone back to Cedar Creek, whipped, many troops could be spared from the valley.

The Wilderness and Spottsylvania battles convinced me that we had more artillery than could ever be brought into action at any one time. It occupied much of the road in marching, and taxed the trains in bringing up forage. Artillery is very useful when it can be brought into action, but it is a very burdensome luxury where it cannot be used. Before leaving Spottsylvania, therefore, I sent back to the defences of Washington over one hundred pieces of artillery, with the horses and caissons. This relieved the roads over which we were to march of more than two hundred six-horse teams, and still left us more artillery than could be advantageously used. In fact, before reaching the James River I again reduced the artillery with the army largely.

I believed that, if one corps of the army was exposed on the road to Richmond, and at a distance from the main army, Lee would endeavor to attack the exposed corps before reinforcements could come up; in which case the main army could follow Lee up and attack him before he had time to intrench. So I issued the following orders:

NEAR SPOTTSYLVANIA C. H., VA.,
May 18, 1864.

MAJOR-GENERAL MEADE,
        Commanding Army of the Potomac.

Before daylight to-morrow morning I propose to draw Hancock and Burnside from the position they now hold, and put Burnside to the left of Wright. Wright and Burnside should then force their way up as close to the enemy as they can get without a general engagement, or with a general engagement if the enemy will come out of their works to fight, and intrench. Hancock should march and take up a position as if in support of the two left corps. To-morrow night, at twelve or one o'clock, he will be moved south-east with all his force and as much cavalry as can be given to him, to get as far towards Richmond on the line of the Fredericksburg Railroad as he can make, fighting the enemy in whatever force he can find him. If the enemy make a general move to meet this, they will be followed by the other three corps of the army, and attacked, if possible, before time is given to intrench.

Suitable directions will at once be given for all trains and surplus artillery to conform to this movement.

U. S. GRANT.

On the 20th, Lee showing no signs of coming out of his lines, orders were renewed for a left-flank movement, to commence after night.

Chapter LIV.

MOVEMENT BY THE LEFT FLANK — BATTLE OF NORTH
ANNA — AN INCIDENT OF THE MARCH — MOVING ON
RICHMOND — SOUTH OF THE PAMUNKEY — POSITION
OF THE NATIONAL ARMY.

WE WERE NOW to operate in a different country from
any we had before seen in Virginia. The roads were
wide and good, and the country well cultivated. No men were
seen except those bearing arms, even the black man having
been sent away. The country, however, was new to us, and
we had neither guides nor maps to tell us where the roads
were, or where they led to. Engineer and staff officers were
put to the dangerous duty of supplying the place of both
maps and guides. By reconnoitring they were enabled to locate the roads in the vicinity of each army corps. Our course
was south, and we took all roads leading in that direction
which would not separate the army too widely.

Hancock who had the lead had marched easterly to
Guiney's Station, on the Fredericksburg Railroad, thence
southerly to Bowling Green and Milford. He was at Milford
by the night of the 21st. Here he met a detachment of Pickett's division coming from Richmond to reinforce Lee. They
were speedily driven away, and several hundred captured.
Warren followed on the morning of the 21st, and reached
Guiney's Station that night without molestation. Burnside
and Wright were retained at Spottsylvania to keep up the appearance of an intended assault, and to hold Lee, if possible,
while Hancock and Warren should get start enough to interpose between him and Richmond.

Lee had now a superb opportunity to take the initiative
either by attacking Wright and Burnside alone, or by following by the Telegraph Road and striking Hancock's and
Warren's corps, or even Hancock's alone, before reinforcements could come up. But he did not avail himself of either
opportunity. He seemed really to be misled as to my designs;
but moved by his interior line — the Telegraph Road — to
make sure of keeping between his capital and the Army of the

Potomac. He never again had such an opportunity of dealing a heavy blow.

The evening of the 21st Burnside, 9th corps, moved out followed by Wright, 6th corps. Burnside was to take the Telegraph Road; but finding Stanard's Ford, over the Po, fortified and guarded, he turned east to the road taken by Hancock and Warren without an attempt to dislodge the enemy. The night of the 21st I had my headquarters near the 6th corps, at Guiney's Station, and the enemy's cavalry was between us and Hancock. There was a slight attack on Burnside's and Wright's corps as they moved out of their lines; but it was easily repulsed. The object probably was only to make sure that we were not leaving a force to follow upon the rear of the Confederates.

By the morning of the 22d Burnside and Wright were at Guiney's Station. Hancock's corps had now been marching and fighting continuously for several days, not having had rest even at night much of the time. They were, therefore, permitted to rest during the 22d. But Warren was pushed to Harris's Store, directly west of Milford, and connected with it by a good road, and Burnside was sent to New Bethel Church. Wright's corps was still back at Guiney's Station.

I issued the following order for the movement of the troops the next day:

NEW BETHEL, VA., *May* 22, 1864.
MAJOR-GENERAL MEADE,
    Commanding Army of the Potomac.

Direct corps commanders to hold their troops in readiness to march at five A.M. to-morrow. At that hour each command will send out cavalry and infantry on all roads to their front leading south, and ascertain, if possible, where the enemy is. If beyond the South Anna, the 5th and 6th corps will march to the forks of the road, where one branch leads to Beaver Dam Station, the other to Jericho Bridge, then south by roads reaching the Anna, as near to and east of Hawkins Creek as they can be found.

The 2d corps will move to Chesterfield Ford. The 9th corps will be directed to move at the same time to Jericho Bridge. The map only shows two roads for the four corps to march upon, but, no doubt, by the use of plantation roads, and pressing in guides, others can be found, to give one for each corps.

The troops will follow their respective reconnoitring parties. The trains will be moved at the same time to Milford Station.

Headquarters will follow the 9th corps.

U. S. GRANT,
Lieut.-General.

Warren's corps was moved from Harris's Store to Jericho Ford, Wright's following. Warren arrived at the ford early in the afternoon, and by five o'clock effected a crossing under the protection of sharp-shooters. The men had to wade in water up to their waists. As soon as enough troops were over to guard the ford, pontoons were laid and the artillery and the rest of the troops crossed. The line formed was almost perpendicular to the course of the river—Crawford on the left, next to the river, Griffin in the centre, and Cutler on the right. Lee was found intrenched along the front of their line. The whole of Hill's corps was sent against Warren's right before it had got in position. A brigade of Cutler's division was driven back, the enemy following, but assistance coming up the enemy was in turn driven back into his trenches with heavy loss in killed and wounded, with about five hundred prisoners left in our hands. By night Wright's corps was up ready to reinforce Warren.

On the 23d Hancock's corps was moved to the wooden bridge which spans the North Anna River just west of where the Fredericksburg Railroad crosses. It was near night when the troops arrived. They found the bridge guarded, with troops intrenched, on the north side. Hancock sent two brigades, Egan's and Pierce's, to the right and left, and when properly disposed they charged simultaneously. The bridge was carried quickly, the enemy retreating over it so hastily that many were shoved into the river, and some of them were drowned. Several hundred prisoners were captured. The hour was so late that Hancock did not cross until next morning.

Burnside's corps was moved by a middle road running between those described above, and which strikes the North Anna at Ox Ford, midway between Telegraph Road and Jericho Ford. The hour of its arrival was too late to cross that night.

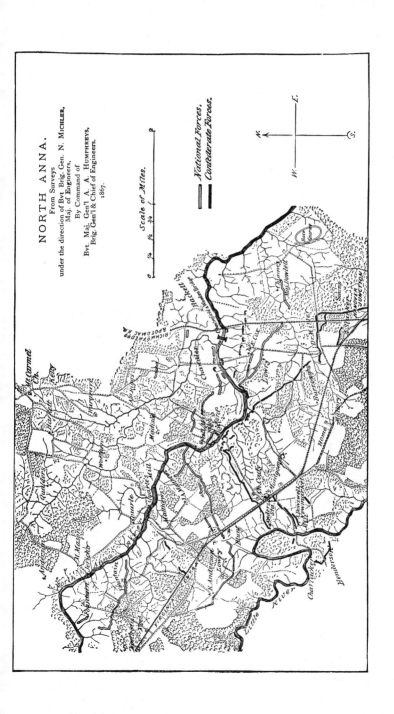

NORTH ANNA.

From Surveys

under the direction of Bvt. Brig. Gen. N. MICHLER,
Maj. of Engineers,

By Command of

Bvt. Maj. Gen'l A. A. HUMPHREYS,
Brig. Gen'l & Chief of Engineers.

1867.

Scale of Miles.

0   ¼   ½   ¾   2

━━━ National Forces.
━━━ Confederate Forces.

N
W ——— E
S

On the 24th Hancock's corps crossed to the south side of the river without opposition, and formed line facing nearly west. The railroad in rear was taken possession of and destroyed as far as possible. Wright's corps crossed at Jericho early the same day, and took position to the right of Warren's corps, extending south of the Virginia Central Railroad. This road was torn up for a considerable distance to the rear (west), the ties burned, and the rails bent and twisted by heating them over the burning ties. It was found, however, that Burnside's corps could not cross at Ox Ford. Lee had taken a position with his centre on the river at this point, with the two wings thrown back, his line making an acute angle where it overlooked the river.

Before the exact position of the whole of Lee's line was accurately known, I directed Hancock and Warren each to send a brigade to Ox Ford by the south side of the river. They found the enemy too strong to justify a serious attack. A third ford was found between Ox Ford and Jericho. Burnside was directed to cross a division over this ford, and to send one division to Hancock. Crittenden was crossed by this newly-discovered ford, and formed up the river to connect with Crawford's left. Potter joined Hancock by way of the wooden bridge. Crittenden had a severe engagement with some of Hill's corps on his crossing the river, and lost heavily. When joined to Warren's corps he was no further molested. Burnside still guarded Ox Ford from the north side.

Lee now had his entire army south of the North Anna. Our lines covered his front, with the six miles separating the two wings guarded by but a single division. To get from one wing to the other the river would have to be crossed twice. Lee could reinforce any part of his line from all points of it in a very short march; or could concentrate the whole of it wherever he might choose to assault. We were, for the time, practically two armies besieging.

Lee had been reinforced, and was being reinforced, largely. About this time the very troops whose coming I had predicted, had arrived or were coming in. Pickett with a full division from Richmond was up; Hoke from North Carolina had come with a brigade; and Breckinridge was there: in all probably not less than fifteen thousand men. But he did not attempt to drive us from the field.

On the 22d or 23d I received dispatches from Washington saying that Sherman had taken Kingston, crossed the Etowah River and was advancing into Georgia.

I was seated at the time on the porch of a fine plantation house waiting for Burnside's corps to pass. Meade and his staff, besides my own staff, were with me. The lady of the house, a Mrs. Tyler, and an elderly lady, were present. Burnside seeing us, came up on the porch, his big spurs and saber rattling as he walked. He touched his hat politely to the ladies, and remarked that he supposed they had never seen so many "live Yankees" before in their lives. The elderly lady spoke up promptly saying, "Oh yes, I have; many more." "Where?" said Burnside. "In Richmond." Prisoners, of course, was understood.

I read my dispatch aloud, when it was received. This threw the younger lady into tears. I found the information she had received (and I suppose it was the information generally in circulation through the South) was that Lee was driving us from the State in the most demoralized condition, and that in the South-west our troops were but little better than prisoners of war. Seeing our troops moving south was ocular proof that a part of her information was incorrect, and she asked me if my news from Sherman was true. I assured her that there was no doubt about it. I left a guard to protect the house from intrusion until the troops should have all passed, and assured her that if her husband was in hiding she could bring him in and he should be protected also. But I presume he was in the Confederate army.

On the 25th I gave orders, through Halleck, to Hunter, who had relieved Sigel, to move up the Valley of Virginia, cross over the Blue Ridge to Charlottesville and go as far as Lynchburg if possible, living upon the country and cutting the railroads and canal as he went. After doing this he could find his way back to his base, or join me.

On the same day news was received that Lee was falling back on Richmond. This proved not to be true. But we could do nothing where we were unless Lee would assume the offensive. I determined, therefore, to draw out of our present position and make one more effort to get between him and Richmond. I had no expectation now, however, of succeeding in this; but I did expect to hold him far enough west to enable me to reach the James River high up. Sheridan was now again with the Army of the Potomac.

On the 26th I informed the government at Washington of the position of the two armies; of the reinforcements the enemy had received; of the move I proposed to make;* and directed that our base of supplies should be shifted to White House, on the Pamunkey. The wagon train and guards moved

---

*QUARLES' MILLS, VA., *May* 26, 1864.

MAJOR-GENERAL HALLECK,
        Washington, D. C.

The relative position of the two armies is now as follows: Lee's right rests on a swamp east of the Richmond and Fredericksburg road and south of the North Anna, his centre on the river at Ox Ford, and his left at Little River with the crossings of Little River guarded as far up as we have gone. Hancock with his corps and one division of the 9th corps crossed at Chesterfield Ford and covers the right wing of Lee's army. One division of the 9th corps is on the north bank of the Anna at Ox Ford, with bridges above and below at points nearest to it where both banks are held by us, so that it could reinforce either wing of our army with equal facility. The 5th and 6th corps with one division of the 9th corps run from the south bank of the Anna from a short distance above Ox Ford to Little River, and parallel with and near to the enemy.

To make a direct attack from either wing would cause a slaughter of our men that even success would not justify. To turn the enemy by his right, between the two Annas, is impossible on account of the swamp upon which his right rests. To turn him by the left leaves Little River, New Found River and South Anna River, all of them streams presenting considerable obstacles to the movement of our army, to be crossed. I have determined therefore to turn the enemy's right by crossing at or near Hanover Town. This crosses all three streams at once, and leaves us still where we can draw supplies.

During the last night the teams and artillery not in position, belonging to the right wing of our army, and one division of that wing were quietly withdrawn to the north bank of the river and moved down to the rear of the left. As soon as it is dark this division with most of the cavalry will commence a forced march for Hanover Town to seize and hold the crossings. The balance of the right wing will withdraw at the same hour, and follow as rapidly as possible. The left wing will also withdraw from the south bank of the river to-night and follow in rear of the right wing.

Lee's army is really whipped. The prisoners we now take show it, and the action of his army shows it unmistakably. A battle with them outside of intrenchments cannot be had. Our men feel that they have gained the *morale*

directly from Port Royal to White House. Supplies moved around by water, guarded by the navy. Orders had previously been sent, through Halleck, for Butler to send Smith's corps to White House. This order was repeated on the 25th, with directions that they should be landed on the north side of the Pamunkey, and marched until they joined the Army of the Potomac.

It was a delicate move to get the right wing of the Army of the Potomac from its position south of the North Anna in the presence of the enemy. To accomplish it, I issued the following order:

QUARLES' MILLS, VA., *May 25, 1864.*

MAJOR GENERAL MEADE,
        Commanding A. P.

Direct Generals Warren and Wright to withdraw all their teams and artillery, not in position, to the north side of the river to-morrow. Send that belonging to General Wright's corps as far on the road to Hanover Town as it can go, without attracting attention to the fact. Send with it Wright's best division or division under his ablest commander. Have their places filled up in the line so if possible the enemy will not notice their withdrawal. Send the cavalry to-morrow afternoon, or as much of it as you may deem necessary, to watch and seize, if they can, Littlepage's Bridge and Taylor's Ford, and to remain on one or other side of the river at these points until the infantry and artillery all pass. As soon as it is dark to-morrow night start the division which you withdraw first from Wright's

---

over the enemy, and attack him with confidence. I may be mistaken, but I feel that our success over Lee's army is already assured. The promptness and rapidity with which you have forwarded reinforcements has contributed largely to the feeling of confidence inspired in our men, and to break down that of the enemy.

We are destroying all the rails we can on the Central and Fredericksburg roads. I want to leave a gap on the roads north of Richmond so big that to get a single track they will have to import rail from elsewhere.

Even if a crossing is not effected at Hanover Town it will probably be necessary for us to move on down the Pamunkey until a crossing is effected. I think it advisable therefore to change our base of supplies from Port Royal to the White House. I wish you would direct this change at once, and also direct Smith to put the railroad bridge there in condition for crossing troops and artillery and leave men to hold it.

U. S. GRANT,
Lieut.-General.

corps to make a forced march to Hanover Town, taking with them
no teams to impede their march. At the same time this division starts
commence withdrawing all of the 5th and 6th corps from the south
side of the river, and march them for the same place. The two divisions of the 9th corps not now with Hancock, may be moved down
the north bank of the river where they will be handy to support
Hancock if necessary, or will be that much on their road to follow
the 5th and 6th corps. Hancock should hold his command in readiness to follow as soon as the way is clear for him. To-morrow it will
leave nothing for him to do, but as soon as he can he should get all
his teams and spare artillery on the road or roads which he will have
to take. As soon as the troops reach Hanover Town they should get
possession of all the crossings they can in that neighborhood. I think
it would be well to make a heavy cavalry demonstration on the
enemy's left, to-morrow afternoon, also.

U. S. GRANT,
Lieut.-General.

Wilson's division of cavalry was brought up from the left
and moved by our right south to Little River. Here he manœuvred to give the impression that we were going to attack
the left flank of Lee's army.

Under cover of night our right wing was withdrawn to the
north side of the river, Lee being completely deceived by
Wilson's feint. On the afternoon of the 26th Sheridan moved,
sending Gregg's and Torbert's cavalry to Taylor's and Littlepage's fords towards Hanover. As soon as it was dark both
divisions moved quietly to Hanover Ferry, leaving small
guards behind to keep up the impression that crossings were
to be attempted in the morning. Sheridan was followed by a
division of infantry under General Russell. On the morning
of the 27th the crossing was effected with but little loss, the
enemy losing thirty or forty, taken prisoners. Thus a position
was secured south of the Pamunkey.

Russell stopped at the crossing while the cavalry pushed on
to Hanover Town. Here Barringer's, formerly Gordon's, brigade of rebel cavalry was encountered, but it was speedily
driven away.

Warren's and Wright's corps were moved by the rear of
Burnside's and Hancock's corps. When out of the way these
latter corps followed, leaving pickets confronting the enemy.
Wilson's cavalry followed last, watching all the fords until

everything had recrossed; then taking up the pontoons and destroying other bridges, became the rear-guard.

Two roads were traversed by the troops in this move. The one nearest to and north of the North Anna and Pamunkey was taken by Wright, followed by Hancock. Warren, followed by Burnside, moved by a road farther north, and longer. The trains moved by a road still farther north, and had to travel a still greater distance. All the troops that had crossed the Pamunkey on the morning of the 27th remained quiet during the rest of the day, while the troops north of that stream marched to reach the crossing that had been secured for them.

Lee had evidently been deceived by our movement from North Anna; for on the morning of the 27th he telegraphed to Richmond: "Enemy crossed to north side, and cavalry and infantry crossed at Hanover Town." The troops that had then crossed left his front the night of the 25th.

The country we were now in was a difficult one to move troops over. The streams were numerous, deep and sluggish, sometimes spreading out into swamps grown up with impenetrable growths of trees and underbrush. The banks were generally low and marshy, making the streams difficult to approach except where there were roads and bridges.

Hanover Town is about twenty miles from Richmond. There are two roads leading there; the most direct and shortest one crossing the Chickahominy at Meadow Bridge, near the Virginia Central Railroad, the second going by New and Old Cold Harbor. A few miles out from Hanover Town there is a third road by way of Mechanicsville to Richmond. New Cold Harbor was important to us because while there we both covered the roads back to White House (where our supplies came from), and the roads south-east over which we would have to pass to get to the James River below the Richmond defences.

On the morning of the 28th the army made an early start, and by noon all had crossed except Burnside's corps. This was left on the north side temporarily to guard the large wagon train. A line was at once formed extending south from the river, Wright's corps on the right, Hancock's in the centre,

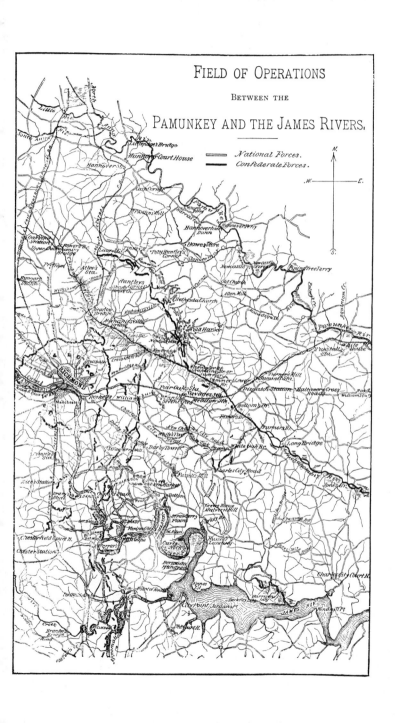

FIELD OF OPERATIONS

BETWEEN THE

PAMUNKEY AND THE JAMES RIVERS.

=== *National Forces.*
——— *Confederate Forces.*

N
W——E
S

and Warren's on the left, ready to meet the enemy if he should come.

At the same time Sheridan was directed to reconnoitre towards Mechanicsville to find Lee's position. At Hawes' Shop, just where the middle road leaves the direct road to Richmond, he encountered the Confederate cavalry dismounted and partially intrenched. Gregg attacked with his division, but was unable to move the enemy. In the evening Custer came up with a brigade. The attack was now renewed, the cavalry dismounting and charging as infantry. This time the assault was successful, both sides losing a considerable number of men. But our troops had to bury the dead, and found that more Confederate than Union soldiers had been killed. The position was easily held, because our infantry was near.

On the 29th a reconnoissance was made in force, to find the position of Lee. Wright's corps pushed to Hanover Court House. Hancock's corps pushed toward Totopotomoy Creek; Warren's corps to the left on the Shady Grove Church Road, while Burnside was held in reserve. Our advance was pushed forward three miles on the left with but little fighting. There was now an appearance of a movement past our left flank, and Sheridan was sent to meet it.

On the 30th Hancock moved to the Totopotomoy, where he found the enemy strongly fortified. Wright was moved to the right of Hancock's corps, and Burnside was brought forward and crossed, taking position to the left of Hancock. Warren moved up near Huntley Corners on the Shady Grove Church Road. There was some skirmishing along the centre, and in the evening Early attacked Warren with some vigor, driving him back at first, and threatening to turn our left flank. As the best means of reinforcing the left, Hancock was ordered to attack in his front. He carried and held the rifle-pits. While this was going on Warren got his men up, repulsed Early, and drove him more than a mile.

On this day I wrote to Halleck ordering all the pontoons in Washington to be sent to City Point. In the evening news was received of the arrival of Smith with his corps at White House. I notified Meade, in writing, as follows:

Near Hawes' Shop, Va.,
6.40 p.m., *May* 30, 1864.

Major-General Meade,
    Commanding A. P.

General Smith will debark his force at the White House to-night and start up the south bank of the Pamunkey at an early hour, probably at 3 a.m. in the morning. It is not improbable that the enemy, being aware of Smith's movement, will be feeling to get on our left flank for the purpose of cutting him off, or by a dash to crush him and get back before we are aware of it. Sheridan ought to be notified to watch the enemy's movements well out towards Cold Harbor, and also on the Mechanicsville road. Wright should be got well massed on Hancock's right, so that, if it becomes necessary, he can take the place of the latter readily whilst troops are being thrown east of the Totopotomoy if necessary.

I want Sheridan to send a cavalry force of at least half a brigade, if not a whole brigade, at 5 a.m. in the morning, to communicate with Smith and to return with him. I will send orders for Smith by the messenger you send to Sheridan with his orders.

U. S. GRANT.

I also notified Smith of his danger, and the precautions that would be taken to protect him.

The night of the 30th Lee's position was substantially from Atlee's Station on the Virginia Central Railroad south and east to the vicinity of Cold Harbor. Ours was: The left of Warren's corps was on the Shady Grove Road, extending to the Mechanicsville Road and about three miles south of the Totopotomoy. Burnside to his right, then Hancock, and Wright on the extreme right, extending towards Hanover Court House, six miles south-east of it. Sheridan with two divisions of cavalry was watching our left front towards Cold Harbor. Wilson with his division on our right was sent to get on the Virginia Central Railroad and destroy it as far back as possible. He got possession of Hanover Court House the next day after a skirmish with Young's cavalry brigade. The enemy attacked Sheridan's pickets, but reinforcements were sent up and the attack was speedily repulsed and the enemy followed some distance towards Cold Harbor.

CENTRAL VIRGINIA
SHOWING
Lieut. Gen'l U. S. Grant's
Campaign against
Richmond & Petersburg,
1864-'5.

Scale of Miles

Chapter LV.

ADVANCE ON COLD HARBOR—AN ANECDOTE OF THE
WAR—BATTLE OF COLD HARBOR—CORRESPONDENCE
WITH LEE—RETROSPECTIVE.

O N THE 31ST Sheridan advanced to near Old Cold Harbor. He found it intrenched and occupied by cavalry and infantry. A hard fight ensued but the place was carried. The enemy well knew the importance of Cold Harbor to us, and seemed determined that we should not hold it. He returned with such a large force that Sheridan was about withdrawing without making any effort to hold it against such odds; but about the time he commenced the evacuation he received orders to hold the place at all hazards, until reinforcements could be sent to him. He speedily turned the rebel works to face against them and placed his men in position for defence. Night came on before the enemy was ready for assault.

Wright's corps was ordered early in the evening to march directly to Cold Harbor passing by the rear of the army. It was expected to arrive by daylight or before; but the night was dark and the distance great, so that it was nine o'clock the 1st of June before it reached its destination. Before the arrival of Wright the enemy had made two assaults on Sheridan, both of which were repulsed with heavy loss to the enemy. Wright's corps coming up, there was no further assault on Cold Harbor.

Smith, who was coming up from White House, was also directed to march directly to Cold Harbor, and was expected early on the morning of the 1st of June; but by some blunder the order which reached Smith directed him to Newcastle instead of Cold Harbor. Through this blunder Smith did not reach his destination until three o'clock in the afternoon, and then with tired and worn-out men from their long and dusty march. He landed twelve thousand five hundred men from Butler's command, but a division was left at White House temporarily and many men had fallen out of ranks in their long march.

Before the removal of Wright's corps from our right, after dark on the 31st, the two lines, Federal and Confederate, were so close together at that point that either side could detect directly any movement made by the other. Finding at daylight that Wright had left his front, Lee evidently divined that he had gone to our left. At all events, soon after light on the 1st of June Anderson, who commanded the corps on Lee's left, was seen moving along Warren's front. Warren was ordered to attack him vigorously in flank, while Wright was directed to move out and get on his front. Warren fired his artillery at the enemy; but lost so much time in making ready that the enemy got by, and at three o'clock he reported the enemy was strongly intrenched in his front, and besides his lines were so long that he had no mass of troops to move with. He seemed to have forgotten that lines in rear of an army hold themselves while their defenders are fighting in their front. Wright reconnoitred some distance to his front: but the enemy finding Old Cold Harbor already taken had halted and fortified some distance west.

By six o'clock in the afternoon Wright and Smith were ready to make an assault. In front of both the ground was clear for several hundred yards, and then became wooded. Both charged across this open space and into the wood, capturing and holding the first line of rifle-pits of the enemy, and also capturing seven or eight hundred prisoners.

While this was going on, the enemy charged Warren three separate times with vigor, but were repulsed each time with loss. There was no officer more capable, nor one more prompt in acting, than Warren when the enemy forced him to it. There was also an attack upon Hancock's and Burnside's corps at the same time; but it was feeble and probably only intended to relieve Anderson who was being pressed by Wright and Smith.

During the night the enemy made frequent attacks with the view of dispossessing us of the important position we had gained, but without effecting their object.

Hancock was moved from his place in line during the night and ordered to the left of Wright. I expected to take the offensive on the morning of the 2d, but the night was so dark, the heat and dust so excessive and the roads so intricate and

COLD HARBOR.

From Surveys

under the direction of Bvt. Brig. Gen. N. Michler,
Maj. of Engineers.

By Command of

Bvt. Maj. Gen'l A. A. Humphreys,
Brig. Gen'l & Chief of Engineers.
1867.

National Forces.
Confederate Forces.

Scale of Miles.

0   ¼   ½   ¾   1   2   3

hard to keep, that the head of column only reached Old Cold Harbor at six o'clock, but was in position at 7.30 A.M. Preparations were made for an attack in the afternoon, but did not take place until the next morning. Warren's corps was moved to the left to connect with Smith: Hancock's corps was got into position to the left of Wright's, and Burnside was moved to Bethesda Church in reserve. While Warren and Burnside were making these changes the enemy came out several times and attacked them, capturing several hundred prisoners. The attacks were repulsed, but not followed up as they should have been. I was so annoyed at this that I directed Meade to instruct his corps commanders that they should seize all such opportunities when they occurred, and not wait for orders, all of our manœuvres being made for the very purpose of getting the enemy out of his cover.

On this day Wilson returned from his raid upon the Virginia Central Railroad, having damaged it considerably. But, like ourselves, the rebels had become experts in repairing such damage. Sherman, in his memoirs, relates an anecdote of his campaign to Atlanta that well illustrates this point. The rebel cavalry lurking in his rear to burn bridges and obstruct his communications had become so disgusted at hearing trains go whistling by within a few hours after a bridge had been burned, that they proposed to try blowing up some of the tunnels. One of them said, "No use, boys, Old Sherman carries duplicate tunnels with him, and will replace them as fast as you can blow them up; better save your powder."

Sheridan was engaged reconnoitring the banks of the Chickahominy, to find crossings and the condition of the roads. He reported favorably.

During the night Lee moved his left up to make his line correspond to ours. His lines extended now from the Totopotomoy to New Cold Harbor. Mine from Bethesda Church by Old Cold Harbor to the Chickahominy, with a division of cavalry guarding our right. An assault was ordered for the 3d, to be made mainly by the corps of Hancock, Wright and Smith; but Warren and Burnside were to support it by threatening Lee's left, and to attack with great earnestness if he should either reinforce more threatened points by drawing from that quarter or if a favorable opportunity should present itself.

The corps commanders were to select the points in their respective fronts where they would make their assaults. The move was to commence at half-past four in the morning. Hancock sent Barlow and Gibbon forward at the appointed hour, with Birney as a reserve. Barlow pushed forward with great vigor, under a heavy fire of both artillery and musketry, through thickets and swamps. Notwithstanding all the resistance of the enemy and the natural obstructions to overcome, he carried a position occupied by the enemy outside their main line where the road makes a deep cut through a bank affording as good a shelter for troops as if it had been made for that purpose. Three pieces of artillery had been captured here, and several hundred prisoners. The guns were immediately turned against the men who had just been using them. No assistance coming to him, he (Barlow) intrenched under fire and continued to hold his place. Gibbon was not so fortunate in his front. He found the ground over which he had to pass cut up with deep ravines, and a morass difficult to cross. But his men struggled on until some of them got up to the very parapet covering the enemy. Gibbon gained ground much nearer the enemy than that which he left, and here he intrenched and held fast.

Wright's corps moving in two lines captured the outer rifle-pits in their front, but accomplished nothing more. Smith's corps also gained the outer rifle-pits in its front. The ground over which this corps (18th) had to move was the most exposed of any over which charges were made. An open plain intervened between the contending forces at this point, which was exposed both to a direct and a cross fire. Smith,

---

NEAR COLD HARBOR, *June* 3, 1864, 7 A.M.

MAJOR-GENERAL MEADE,
Commanding A. P.

The moment it becomes certain that an assault cannot succeed, suspend the offensive; but when one does succeed, push it vigorously and if necessary pile in troops at the successful point from wherever they can be taken. I shall go to where you are in the course of an hour.

U. S. GRANT,
Lieut.-General.

however, finding a ravine running towards his front, sufficiently deep to protect men in it from cross fire, and somewhat from a direct fire, put Martindale's division in it, and
with Brooks supporting him on the left and Devens on the
right succeeded in gaining the outer—probably picket—rifle-
pits. Warren and Burnside also advanced and gained ground
—which brought the whole army on one line.

This assault cost us heavily and probably without benefit to
compensate: but the enemy was not cheered by the occurrence sufficiently to induce him to take the offensive. In fact,
nowhere after the battle of the Wilderness did Lee show any
disposition to leave his defences far behind him.

Fighting was substantially over by half-past seven in the
morning. At eleven o'clock I started to visit all the corps commanders to see for myself the different positions gained and
to get their opinion of the practicability of doing anything
more in their respective fronts.

Hancock gave the opinion that in his front the enemy was
too strong to make any further assault promise success.
Wright thought he could gain the lines of the enemy, but it
would require the co-operation of Hancock's and Smith's
corps. Smith thought a lodgment possible, but was not sanguine: Burnside thought something could be done in his
front, but Warren differed. I concluded, therefore, to make no
more assaults, and a little after twelve directed in the following letter that all offensive action should cease.

> COLD HARBOR, *June* 3, 1864. —12.30 P.M.
> MAJOR-GENERAL MEADE,
>   Commanding A. P.
>   The opinion of corps commanders not being sanguine of success
> in case an assault is ordered, you may direct a suspension of farther
> advance for the present. Hold our most advanced positions and
> strengthen them. Whilst on the defensive our line may be contracted
> from the right if practicable. Reconnoissances should be made in
> front of every corps and advances made to advantageous positions by
> regular approaches. To aid the expedition under General Hunter it is
> necessary that we should detain all the army now with Lee until the
> former gets well on his way to Lynchburg. To do this effectually it
> will be better to keep the enemy out of the intrenchments of Rich-
> mond than to have them go back there.

Wright and Hancock should be ready to assault in case the enemy should break through General Smith's lines, and all should be ready to resist an assault.

U. S. GRANT,

Lieutenant-General.

The remainder of the day was spent in strengthening the line we now held. By night we were as strong against Lee as he was against us.

During the night the enemy quitted our right front, abandoning some of their wounded, and without burying their dead. These we were able to care for. But there were many dead and wounded men between the lines of the contending forces, which were now close together, who could not be cared for without a cessation of hostilities.

So I wrote the following:

COLD HARBOR, VA., *June* 5, 1864.

GENERAL R. E. LEE,

      Commanding Confederate Army.

It is reported to me that there are wounded men, probably of both armies, now lying exposed and suffering between the lines occupied respectively by the two armies. Humanity would dictate that some provision should be made to provide against such hardships. I would propose, therefore, that hereafter, when no battle is raging, either party be authorized to send to any point between the pickets or skirmish lines, unarmed men bearing litters to pick up their dead or wounded, without being fired upon by the other party. Any other method, equally fair to both parties, you may propose for meeting the end desired will be accepted by me.

U. S. GRANT,

Lieut.-General.

Lee replied that he feared such an arrangement would lead to misunderstanding, and proposed that in future, when either party wished to remove their dead and wounded, a flag of truce be sent. I answered this immediately by saying:

COLD HARBOR, VA., *June* 6, 1864.

GENERAL R. E. LEE,

      Commanding Army of N. Va.

Your communication of yesterday's date is received. I will send immediately, as you propose, to collect the dead and wounded between the lines of the two armies, and will also instruct that you be

allowed to do the same. I propose that the time for doing this be
between the hours of 12 M. and 3 P.M. to-day. I will direct all parties
going out to bear a white flag, and not to attempt to go beyond
where we have dead or wounded, and not beyond or on ground
occupied by your troops.

U. S. GRANT,
Lieut.-General.

Lee's response was that he could not consent to the burial
of the dead and removal of the wounded in the way I proposed, but when either party desired such permission it
should be asked for by flag of truce; and he had directed that
any parties I may have sent out, as mentioned in my letter, to
be turned back. I answered:

COLD HARBOR, VA, *June* 6, 1864.
GENERAL R. E. LEE,
    Commanding Army, N. Va.
The knowledge that wounded men are now suffering from want
of attention, between the two armies, compels me to ask a suspension of hostilities for sufficient time to collect them in, say two
hours. Permit me to say that the hours you may fix upon for this will
be agreeable to me, and the same privilege will be extended to such
parties as you may wish to send out on the same duty without further application.

U. S. GRANT,
Lieut.-General.

Lee acceded to this; but delays in transmitting the correspondence brought it to the 7th of June—forty-eight hours
after it commenced—before parties were got out to collect
the men left upon the field. In the meantime all but two of
the wounded had died. And I wrote to Lee:

COLD HARBOR, VA., *June* 7, 1864.
10.30 A.M.
GEN. R. E. LEE,
    Commanding Army of N. Va.
I regret that your note of seven P.M. yesterday should have been
received at the nearest corps headquarters, to where it was delivered,
after the hour which had been given for the removal of the dead and
wounded had expired; 10.45 P.M. was the hour at which it was received at corps headquarters, and between eleven and twelve it
reached my headquarters. As a consequence, it was not understood

by the troops of this army that there was a cessation of hostilities for the purpose of collecting the dead and wounded, and none were collected. Two officers and six men of the 8th and 25th North Carolina Regts., who were out in search of the bodies of officers of their respective regiments, were captured and brought into our lines, owing to this want of understanding. I regret this, but will state that as soon as I learned the fact, I directed that they should not be held as prisoners, but must be returned to their commands. These officers and men having been carelessly brought through our lines to the rear, I have not determined whether they will be sent back the way they came, or whether they will be sent by some other route.

Regretting that all my efforts for alleviating the sufferings of wounded men left upon the battle-field have been rendered nugatory, I remain, &c.,

U. S. GRANT,
Lieutenant-General.

I have always regretted that the last assault at Cold Harbor was ever made. I might say the same thing of the assault of the 22d of May, 1863, at Vicksburg. At Cold Harbor no advantage whatever was gained to compensate for the heavy loss we sustained. Indeed, the advantages other than those of relative losses, were on the Confederate side. Before that, the Army of Northern Virginia seemed to have acquired a wholesome regard for the courage, endurance, and soldierly qualities generally of the Army of the Potomac. They no longer wanted to fight them "one Confederate to five Yanks." Indeed, they seemed to have given up any idea of gaining any advantage of their antagonist in the open field. They had come to much prefer breastworks in their front to the Army of the Potomac. This charge seemed to revive their hopes temporarily; but it was of short duration. The effect upon the Army of the Potomac was the reverse. When we reached the James River, however, all effects of the battle of Cold Harbor seemed to have disappeared.

There was more justification for the assault at Vicksburg. We were in a Southern climate, at the beginning of the hot season. The Army of the Tennessee had won five successive victories over the garrison of Vicksburg in the three preceding weeks. They had driven a portion of that army from Port Gibson with considerable loss, after having flanked them out of their stronghold at Grand Gulf. They had attacked another portion of the same army at Raymond, more than fifty miles farther in the interior of the State, and driven them back into Jackson with great loss in killed, wounded, captured and missing, besides loss of large and small arms: they had captured the capital of the State of Mississippi, with a large amount of materials of war and manufactures. Only a few days before, they had beaten the enemy then penned up in the town first at Champion's Hill, next at Big Black River Bridge, inflicting upon him a loss of fifteen thousand or more men (including those cut off from returning) besides large losses in arms and ammunition. The Army of the Tennessee had come to believe that they could beat their antagonist under any circumstances. There was no telling how long a regular siege might last. As I have stated, it was the beginning of the hot season in a Southern climate. There was no telling what the casualties might be among Northern troops working and living in trenches, drinking surface water filtered through rich vegetation, under a tropical sun. If Vicksburg could have been carried in May, it would not only have saved the army the risk it ran of a greater danger than from the bullets of the enemy, but it would have given us a splendid army, well equipped and officered, to operate elsewhere with. These are reasons justifying the assault. The only benefit we gained—and it was a slight one for so great a sacrifice—was that the men worked cheerfully in the trenches after that, being satisfied with digging the enemy out. Had the assault not been made, I have no doubt that the majority of those engaged in the siege of Vicksburg would have believed that had we assaulted it would have proven successful, and would have saved life, health and comfort.

Chapter LVI.

LEFT FLANK MOVEMENT ACROSS THE CHICKAHOMINY
AND JAMES—GENERAL LEE—VISIT TO BUTLER—
THE MOVEMENT ON PETERSBURG—THE INVESTMENT
OF PETERSBURG.

LEE'S POSITION was now so near Richmond, and the intervening swamps of the Chickahominy so great an obstacle to the movement of troops in the face of an enemy, that I
determined to make my next left flank move carry the Army
of the Potomac south of the James River.* Preparations for
this were promptly commenced. The move was a hazardous
one to make: the Chickahominy River, with its marshy and
heavily timbered approaches, had to be crossed; all the
bridges over it east of Lee were destroyed; the enemy had a
shorter line and better roads to travel on to confront me in
crossing; more than fifty miles intervened between me and
Butler, by the roads I should have to travel, with both the
James and the Chickahominy unbridged to cross; and last, the
Army of the Potomac had to be got out of a position but a
few hundred yards from the enemy at the widest place. Lee, if
he did not choose to follow me, might, with his shorter distance to travel and his bridges over the Chickahominy and the
James, move rapidly on Butler and crush him before the army
with me could come to his relief. Then too he might spare
troops enough to send against Hunter who was approaching
Lynchburg, living upon the country he passed through, and
without ammunition further than what he carried with him.

---

*COLD HARBOR, *June* 5, 1864.
MAJOR-GENERAL HALLECK, Chief of Staff of the Army,
        Washington, D. C.
    A full survey of all the ground satisfies me that it would be impracticable to
hold a line north-east of Richmond that would protect the Fredericksburg
Railroad to enable us to use that road for supplying the army. To do so
would give us a long vulnerable line of road to protect, exhausting much of
our strength to guard it, and would leave open to the enemy all of his lines of
communication on the south side of the James. My idea from the start has
been to beat Lee's army if possible north of Richmond; then after destroying

But the move had to be made, and I relied upon Lee's not seeing my danger as I saw it. Besides we had armies on both sides of the James River and not far from the Confederate capital. I knew that its safety would be a matter of the first consideration with the executive, legislative and judicial branches of the so-called Confederate government, if it was not with the military commanders. But I took all the precaution I knew of to guard against all dangers.

Sheridan was sent with two divisions, to communicate with Hunter and to break up the Virginia Central Railroad and the James River Canal, on the 7th of June, taking instructions to

his lines of communication on the north side of the James River to transfer the army to the south side and besiege Lee in Richmond, or follow him south if he should retreat.

I now find, after over thirty days of trial, the enemy deems it of the first importance to run no risks with the armies they now have. They act purely on the defensive behind breastworks, or feebly on the offensive immediately in front of them, and where in case of repulse they can instantly retire behind them. Without a greater sacrifice of human life than I am willing to make all cannot be accomplished that I had designed outside of the city. I have therefore resolved upon the following plan:

I will continue to hold substantially the ground now occupied by the Army of the Potomac, taking advantage of any favorable circumstance that may present itself until the cavalry can be sent west to destroy the Virginia Central Railroad from about Beaver Dam for some twenty-five or thirty miles west. When this is effected I will move the army to the south side of the James River, either by crossing the Chickahominy and marching near to City Point, or by going to the mouth of the Chickahominy on north side and crossing there. To provide for this last and most possible contingency, several ferry-boats of the largest class ought to be immediately provided.

Once on the south side of the James River, I can cut off all sources of supply to the enemy except what is furnished by the canal. If Hunter succeeds in reaching Lynchburg, that will be lost to him also. Should Hunter not succeed, I will still make the effort to destroy the canal by sending cavalry up the south side of the river with a pontoon train to cross wherever they can.

The feeling of the two armies now seems to be that the rebels can protect themselves only by strong intrenchments, whilst our army is not only confident of protecting itself without intrenchments, but that it can beat and drive the enemy wherever and whenever he can be found without this protection.

U. S. GRANT,
Lieutenant-General.

Hunter to come back with him.* Hunter was also informed by way of Washington and the Valley that Sheridan was on the way to meet him. The canal and Central Road, and the regions penetrated by them, were of vast importance to the enemy, furnishing and carrying a large per cent. of all the supplies for the Army of Northern Virginia and the people of Richmond. Before Sheridan got off on the 7th news was received from Hunter reporting his advance to Staunton and successful engagement with the enemy near that place on the 5th, in which the Confederate commander, W. S. Jones, was killed. On the 4th of June the enemy having withdrawn his left corps, Burnside on our right was moved up between Warren and Smith. On the 5th Birney returned to Hancock, which extended his left now to the Chickahominy, and Warren was withdrawn to Cold Harbor. Wright was directed to send two divisions to the left to extend down the banks of that stream to Bottom's Bridge. The cavalry extended still farther east to Jones's Bridge.

---

*COLD HARBOR, VA., *June* 6, 1864.

MAJOR-GENERAL D. HUNTER,
      Commanding Dept. W. Va.

General Sheridan leaves here to-morrow morning, with instructions to proceed to Charlottesville, Va., and to commence there the destruction of the Va. Cen. R. R., destroying this way as much as possible. The complete destruction of this road and of the canal on James River is of great importance to us. According to the instructions I sent to General Halleck for your guidance, you were to proceed to Lynchburg and commence there. It would be of great value to us to get possession of Lynchburg for a single day. But that point is of so much importance to the enemy, that in attempting to get it such resistance may be met as to defeat your getting onto the road or canal at all. I see, in looking over the letter to General Halleck on the subject of your instructions, that it rather indicates that your route should be from Staunton via Charlottesville. If you have so understood it, you will be doing just what I want. The direction I would now give is, that if this letter reaches you in the valley between Staunton and Lynchburg, you immediately turn east by the most practicable road until you strike the Lynchburg branch of the Va. Central road. From thence move eastward along the line of the road, destroying it completely and thoroughly, until you join General Sheridan. After the work laid out for General Sheridan and yourself is thoroughly done, proceed to join the Army of the Potomac by the route laid out in General Sheridan's instructions.

If any portion of your force, especially your cavalry, is needed back in your Department, you are authorized to send it back.

On the 7th Abercrombie—who was in command at White House, and who had been in command at our base of supplies in all the changes made from the start—was ordered to take up the iron from the York River Railroad and put it on boats, and to be in readiness to move by water to City Point.

On the 8th Meade was directed to fortify a line down the bank overlooking the Chickahominy, under cover of which the army could move.

On the 9th Abercrombie was directed to send all organized troops arriving at White House, without debarking from their transports, to report to Butler. Halleck was at this time instructed to send all reinforcements to City Point.

On the 11th I wrote:

> COLD HARBOR, VA., *June* 11, 1864.
> MAJOR-GEN. B. F. BUTLER,
>   Commanding Department of Va. and N. C.
>   The movement to transfer this army to the south side of the James River will commence after dark to-morrow night. Col. Comstock, of my staff, was sent specially to ascertain what was necessary to make your position secure in the interval during which the enemy might use most of his force against you, and also, to ascertain what point on the river we should reach to effect a crossing if it should not be practicable to reach this side of the river at Bermuda Hundred. Colonel Comstock has not yet returned, so that I cannot make instructions as definite as I would wish, but the time between this and Sunday night being so short in which to get word to you, I must do the best I can. Colonel Dent goes to make arrangements for gunboats and transportation to send up the Chickahominy to take to you the 18th corps. The corps will leave its position in the trenches as early in the evening, to-morrow, as possible, and make a forced march to Cole's Landing or Ferry, where it should reach by ten A.M. the following morning. This corps numbers now 15,300 men. They take with them neither wagons nor artillery; these latter marching with the balance of the army to the James River. The remainder of

---

If on receipt of this you should be near to Lynchburg and deem it practicable to reach that point, you will exercise your judgment about going there.

If you should be on the railroad between Charlottesville and Lynchburg, it may be practicable to detach a cavalry force to destroy the canal. Lose no opportunity to destroy the canal.

U. S. GRANT,
Lieut.-General.

the army will cross the Chickahominy at Long Bridge and at Jones's, and strike the river at the most practicable crossing below City Point.

I directed several days ago that all reinforcements for the army should be sent to you. I am not advised of the number that may have gone, but suppose you have received from six to ten thousand. General Smith will also reach you as soon as the enemy could, going by the way of Richmond.

The balance of the force will not be more than one day behind, unless detained by the whole of Lee's army, in which case you will be strong enough.

I wish you would direct the proper staff officers, your chief-engineer and your chief-quartermaster, to commence at once the collection of all the means in their reach for crossing the army on its arrival. If there is a point below City Point where a pontoon bridge can be thrown, have it laid.

Expecting the arrival of the 18th corps by Monday night, if you deem it practicable from the force you have to seize and hold Petersburg, you may prepare to start, on the arrival of troops to hold your present lines. I do not want Petersburg visited, however, unless it is held, nor an attempt to take it, unless you feel a reasonable degree of confidence of success. If you should go there, I think troops should take nothing with them except what they can carry, depending upon supplies being sent after the place is secured. If Colonel Dent should not succeed in securing the requisite amount of transportation for the 18th corps before reaching you, please have the balance supplied.

U. S. GRANT,
Lieut.-General.

P. S.—On reflection I will send the 18th corps by way of White House. The distance which they will have to march will be enough shorter to enable them to reach you about the same time, and the uncertainty of navigation on the Chickahominy will be avoided.

U. S. GRANT.

COLD HARBOR, VA., *June* 11, 1864.
MAJOR-GENERAL G. G. MEADE,
     Commanding Army of the Potomac.

Colonel Comstock, who visited the James River for the purpose of ascertaining the best point below Bermuda Hundred to which to march the army has not yet returned. It is now getting so late, however, that all preparations may be made for the move to-morrow night without waiting longer.

The movement will be made as heretofore agreed upon, that is, the 18th corps make a rapid march with the infantry alone, their wagons and artillery accompanying the balance of the army to Cole's Landing or Ferry, and there embark for City Point, losing no time for rest until they reach the latter point.

The 5th corps will seize Long Bridge and move out on the Long Bridge Road to its junction with Quaker Road, or until stopped by the enemy.

The other three corps will follow in such order as you may direct, one of them crossing at Long Bridge, and two at Jones's Bridge. After the crossing is effected, the most practicable roads will be taken to reach about Fort Powhattan. Of course, this is supposing the enemy makes no opposition to our advance. The 5th corps, after securing the passage of the balance of the army, will join or follow in rear of the corps which crosses the same bridge with themselves. The wagon trains should be kept well east of the troops, and if a crossing can be found, or made lower down than Jones's they should take it.

U. S. GRANT,
Lieut.-General.

P. S.—In view of the long march to reach Cole's Landing, and the uncertainty of being able to embark a large number of men there, the direction of the 18th corps may be changed to White House. They should be directed to load up transports, and start them as fast as loaded without waiting for the whole corps or even whole divisions to go together.

U. S. GRANT.

About this time word was received (through the Richmond papers of the 11th) that Crook and Averell had united and were moving east. This, with the news of Hunter's successful engagement near Staunton, was no doubt known to Lee before it was to me. Then Sheridan leaving with two divisions of cavalry, looked indeed threatening, both to Lee's communications and supplies. Much of his cavalry was sent after Sheridan, and Early with Ewell's entire corps was sent to the Valley. Supplies were growing scarce in Richmond, and the sources from which to draw them were in our hands. People from outside began to pour into Richmond to help eat up the little on hand. Consternation reigned there.

On the 12th Smith was ordered to move at night to White House, not to stop until he reached there, and to take boats at once for City Point, leaving his trains and artillery to move by land.

Soon after dark some of the cavalry at Long Bridge effected a crossing by wading and floundering through the water and mud, leaving their horses behind, and drove away the cavalry pickets. A pontoon bridge was speedily thrown across, over which the remainder of the army soon passed and pushed out for a mile or two to watch and detain any advance that might be made from the other side. Warren followed the cavalry, and by the morning of the 13th had his whole corps over. Hancock followed Warren. Burnside took the road to Jones's Bridge, followed by Wright. Ferrero's division, with the wagon train, moved farther east, by Window Shades and Cole's Ferry, our rear being covered by cavalry.

It was known that the enemy had some gunboats at Richmond. These might run down at night and inflict great damage upon us before they could be sunk or captured by our navy. General Butler had, in advance, loaded some vessels with stone ready to be sunk so as to obstruct the channel in an emergency. On the 13th I sent orders to have these sunk as high up the river as we could guard them, and prevent their removal by the enemy.

As soon as Warren's corps was over the Chickahominy it marched out and joined the cavalry in holding the roads from Richmond while the army passed. No attempt was made by the enemy to impede our march, however, but Warren and Wilson reported the enemy strongly fortified in their front. By the evening of the 13th Hancock's corps was at Charles City Court House on the James River. Burnside's and Wright's corps were on the Chickahominy, and crossed during the night, Warren's corps and the cavalry still covering the army. The material for a pontoon bridge was already at hand and the work of laying it was commenced immediately, under the superintendence of Brigadier-General Benham, commanding the engineer brigade. On the evening of the 14th the crossing commenced, Hancock in advance, using both the bridge and boats.

When the Wilderness campaign commenced the Army of the Potomac, including Burnside's corps—which was a separate command until the 24th of May when it was incorporated with the main army—numbered about 116,000 men. During the progress of the campaign about 40,000 reinforcements were received. At the crossing of the James River June 14th—15th the army numbered about 115,000. Besides the ordinary losses incident to a campaign of six weeks' nearly constant fighting or skirmishing, about one-half of the artillery was sent back to Washington, and many men were discharged by reason of the expiration of their term of service.* In estimating our strength every enlisted man and every commissioned officer present is included, no matter how employed; in bands, sick in field hospitals, hospital attendants, company cooks and all. Operating in an enemy's country, and being supplied always from a distant base, large detachments had at all times to be sent from the front, not only to guard the base of supplies and the roads to it, but all the roads leading to our flanks and rear. We were also operating in a country unknown to us, and without competent guides or maps showing the roads accurately.

The manner of estimating numbers in the two armies differs materially. In the Confederate army often only bayonets are taken into account, never, I believe, do they estimate more than are handling the guns of the artillery and armed with muskets or carbines. Generally the latter are far enough away to be excluded from the count in any one field. Officers and details of enlisted men are not included. In the Northern armies the estimate is most liberal, taking in all connected with the army and drawing pay.

Estimated in the same manner as ours, Lee had not less than 80,000 men at the start. His reinforcements were about equal to ours during the campaign, deducting the discharged men and those sent back. He was on the defensive, and in a country in which every stream, every road, every obstacle to

---

*FROM A STATEMENT OF LOSSES COMPILED IN THE ADJUTANT-GENERAL'S OFFICE.

FIELD OF ACTION AND DATE.	KILLED.	WOUNDED.	MISSING.	AGGREGATE.
Wilderness, May 5th to 7th . . .	2,261	8,785	2,902	13,948
Spottsylvania, May 8th to 21st. . .	2,271	9,360	1,970	13,601
North Anna, May 23d to 27th. . .	186	792	165	1,143
Totopotomoy, May 27th to 31st . .	99	358	52	509
Cold Harbor, May 31st to June 12th .	1,769	6,752	1,537	10,058
Total.	6,586	26,047	6,626	39,259

the movement of troops and every natural defence was familiar to him and his army. The citizens were all friendly to him
and his cause, and could and did furnish him with accurate
reports of our every move. Rear guards were not necessary
for him, and having always a railroad at his back, large wagon
trains were not required. All circumstances considered we did
not have any advantage in numbers.

General Lee, who had led the Army of Northern Virginia
in all these contests, was a very highly estimated man in the
Confederate army and States, and filled also a very high place
in the estimation of the people and press of the Northern
States. His praise was sounded throughout the entire North
after every action he was engaged in: the number of his forces
was always lowered and that of the National forces exaggerated. He was a large, austere man, and I judge difficult of
approach to his subordinates. To be extolled by the entire
press of the South after every engagement, and by a portion
of the press North with equal vehemence, was calculated to
give him the entire confidence of his troops and to make him
feared by his antagonists. It was not an uncommon thing for
my staff-officers to hear from Eastern officers, "Well, Grant
has never met Bobby Lee yet." There were good and true
officers who believe now that the Army of Northern Virginia
was superior to the Army of the Potomac man to man. I do
not believe so, except as the advantages spoken of above made
them so. Before the end I believe the difference was the other
way. The Army of Northern Virginia became despondent and
saw the end. It did not please them. The National army saw
the same thing, and were encouraged by it.

The advance of the Army of the Potomac reached the James
on the 14th of June. Preparations were at once commenced for
laying the pontoon bridges and crossing the river. As already
stated, I had previously ordered General Butler to have two
vessels loaded with stone and carried up the river to a point
above that occupied by our gunboats, where the channel was
narrow, and sunk there so as to obstruct the passage and prevent Confederate gunboats from coming down the river. Butler had had these boats filled and put in position, but had not
had them sunk before my arrival. I ordered this done, and
also directed that he should turn over all material and boats

not then in use in the river to be used in ferrying the troops across.

I then, on the 14th, took a steamer and ran up to Bermuda Hundred to see General Butler for the purpose of directing a movement against Petersburg, while our troops of the Army of the Potomac were crossing.

I had sent General W. F. Smith back from Cold Harbor by the way of White House, thence on steamers to City Point for the purpose of giving General Butler more troops with which to accomplish this result. General Butler was ordered to send Smith with his troops reinforced, as far as that could be conveniently done, from other parts of the Army of the James. He gave Smith about six thousand reinforcements, including some twenty-five hundred cavalry under Kautz, and about thirty-five hundred colored infantry under Hinks.

The distance which Smith had to move to reach the enemy's lines was about six miles, and the Confederate advance line of works was but two miles outside of Petersburg. Smith was to move under cover of night, up close to the enemy's works, and assault as soon as he could after daylight. I believed then, and still believe, that Petersburg could have been easily captured at that time. It only had about 2,500 men in the defences besides some irregular troops, consisting of citizens and employees in the city who took up arms in case of emergency. Smith started as proposed, but his advance encountered a rebel force intrenched between City Point and their lines outside of Petersburg. This position he carried, with some loss to the enemy; but there was so much delay that it was daylight before his troops really got off from there. While there I informed General Butler that Hancock's corps would cross the river and move to Petersburg to support Smith in case the latter was successful, and that I could reinforce there more rapidly than Lee could reinforce from his position.

I returned down the river to where the troops of the Army of the Potomac now were, communicated to General Meade, in writing, the directions I had given to General Butler and directed him (Meade) to cross Hancock's corps over under cover of night, and push them forward in the morning to Petersburg; halting them, however, at a designated point until they could hear from Smith. I also informed General Meade that I had ordered rations from Bermuda Hundred for Hancock's corps, and desired him to issue them speedily, and to lose no more time than was absolutely necessary. The rations did not reach him, however, and Hancock, while he got all his corps over during the night, remained until half-past ten in the hope of receiving them. He then moved without them, and on the road received a note from General W. F. Smith, asking him to come on. This seems to be the first information that General Hancock had received of the fact that he was to go to Petersburg, or that anything particular was expected of him. Otherwise he would have been there by four o'clock in the afternoon.

Smith arrived in front of the enemy's lines early in the forenoon of the 15th, and spent the day until after seven o'clock in the evening in reconnoitering what appeared to be empty works. The enemy's line consisted of redans occupying commanding positions, with rifle-pits connecting them. To the east side of Petersburg, from the Appomattox back, there were thirteen of these redans extending a distance of several miles, probably three. If they had been properly manned they could have held out against any force that could have attacked them, at least until reinforcements could have got up from the north of Richmond.

Smith assaulted with the colored troops, and with success. By nine o'clock at night he was in possession of five of these redans and, of course, of the connecting lines of rifle-pits. All of them contained artillery, which fell into our hands. Hancock came up and proposed to take any part assigned to him; and Smith asked him to relieve his men who were in the trenches.

Next morning, the 16th, Hancock himself was in command, and captured another redan. Meade came up in the afternoon and succeeded Hancock, who had to be relieved, temporarily, from the command of his corps on account of the breaking out afresh of the wound he had received at Gettysburg. During the day Meade assaulted and carried one more redan to his right and two to his left. In all this we lost very heavily. The works were not strongly manned, but they all had guns in them which fell into our hands, together with the men who were handling them in the effort to repel these assaults.

Up to this time Beauregard, who had commanded south of Richmond, had received no reinforcements, except Hoke's division from Drury's Bluff,* which had arrived on the morning of the 16th; though he had urged the authorities very strongly to send them, believing, as he did, that Petersburg would be a valuable prize which we might seek.

During the 17th the fighting was very severe and the losses heavy; and at night our troops occupied about the same position they had occupied in the morning, except that they held a redan which had been captured by Potter during the day. During the night, however, Beauregard fell back to the line which had been already selected, and commenced fortifying it. Our troops advanced on the 18th to the line which he had abandoned, and found that the Confederate loss had been very severe, many of the enemy's dead still remaining in the ditches and in front of them.

Colonel J. L. Chamberlain, of the 20th Maine, was wounded on the 18th. He was gallantly leading his brigade at the time, as he had been in the habit of doing in all the engagements in which he had previously been engaged. He had several times been recommended for a brigadier-generalcy for gallant and meritorious conduct. On this occasion, however, I promoted him on the spot, and forwarded a copy of my order to the War Department, asking that my act might be confirmed and Chamberlain's name sent to the Senate for confir-

---

*CITY POINT, VA., *June* 17, 1864 — 11 A.M.

MAJOR-GEN. HALLECK,
          Washington, D. C.

*   *   *   *   *   *

The enemy in their endeavor to reinforce Petersburg abandoned their intrenchments in front of Bermuda Hundred. They no doubt expected troops from north of the James River to take their place before we discovered it. General Butler took advantage of this and moved a force at once upon the railroad and plank road between Richmond and Petersburg, which I hope to retain possession of. Too much credit cannot be given to the troops and their commanders for the energy and fortitude displayed during the last five days. Day and night has been all the same, no delays being allowed on any account.

U. S. GRANT,
Lieut.-General.

mation without any delay. This was done, and at last a gallant and meritorious officer received partial justice at the hands of his government, which he had served so faithfully and so well.

If General Hancock's orders of the 15th had been communicated to him, that officer, with his usual promptness, would undoubtedly have been upon the ground around Petersburg as early as four o'clock in the afternoon of the 15th. The days were long and it would have given him considerable time before night. I do not think there is any doubt that Petersburg itself could have been carried without much loss; or, at least, if protected by inner detached works, that a line could have been established very much in rear of the one then occupied by the enemy. This would have given us control of both the Weldon and South Side railroads. This would also have saved an immense amount of hard fighting which had to be done from the 15th to the 18th, and would have given us greatly the advantage in the long siege which ensued.

I now ordered the troops to be put under cover and allowed some of the rest which they had so long needed. They remained quiet, except that there was more or less firing every day, until the 22d, when General Meade ordered an advance towards the Weldon Railroad. We were very anxious to get to that road, and even round to the South Side Railroad if possible.

Meade moved Hancock's corps, now commanded by Birney, to the left, with a view to at least force the enemy to stay within the limits of his own line. General Wright, with the 6th corps, was ordered by a road farther south, to march directly for the Weldon road. The enemy passed in between these two corps and attacked vigorously, and with very serious results to the National troops, who were then withdrawn from their advanced position.

The Army of the Potomac was given the investment of Petersburg, while the Army of the James held Bermuda Hundred and all the ground we possessed north of the James River. The 9th corps, Burnside's, was placed upon the right at Petersburg; the 5th, Warren's, next; the 2d, Birney's, next; then the 6th, Wright's, broken off to the left and south. Thus began the siege of Petersburg.

Chapter LVII.

O N THE 7TH of June, while at Cold Harbor, I had as already indicated sent Sheridan with two divisions of cavalry to destroy as much as he could of the Virginia Central Railroad. General Hunter had been operating up the Shenandoah Valley with some success, having fought a battle near Staunton where he captured a great many prisoners, besides killing and wounding a good many men. After the battle he formed a junction at Staunton with Averell and Crook, who had come up from the Kanawha, or Gauley River. It was supposed, therefore, that General Hunter would be about Charlottesville, Virginia, by the time Sheridan could get there, doing on the way the damage that he was sent to do.

I gave Sheridan instructions to have Hunter, in case he should meet him about Charlottesville, join and return with him to the Army of the Potomac. Lee, hearing of Hunter's success in the valley, started Breckinridge out for its defence at once. Learning later of Sheridan's going with two divisions, he also sent Hampton with two divisions of cavalry, his own and Fitz-Hugh Lee's.

Sheridan moved to the north side of the North Anna to get out west, and learned of the movement of these troops to the south side of the same stream almost as soon as they had started. He pushed on to get to Trevilian Station to commence his destruction at that point. On the night of the 10th he bivouacked some six or seven miles east of Trevilian, while Fitz-Hugh Lee was the same night at Trevilian Station and Hampton but a few miles away.

During the night Hampton ordered an advance on Sheridan, hoping, no doubt, to surprise and very badly cripple him. Sheridan, however, by a counter move sent Custer on a rapid march to get between the two divisions of the enemy and into their rear. This he did successfully, so that at daylight, when the assault was made, the enemy found himself at the same time resisted in front and attacked in rear, and broke in some confusion. The losses were probably very light on both sides in killed and wounded, but Sheridan got away with some five hundred prisoners and sent them to City Point.

During that day, the 11th, Sheridan moved into Trevilian Station, and the following day proceeded to tear up the road east and west. There was considerable fighting during the whole of the day, but the work of destruction went on. In the meantime, at night, the enemy had taken possession of the crossing which Sheridan had proposed to take to go north when he left Trevilian. Sheridan learned, however, from some of the prisoners he had captured here, that General Hunter was about Lynchburg, and therefore that there was no use of his going on to Charlottesville with a view to meet him.

Sheridan started back during the night of the 12th, and made his way north and farther east, coming around by the north side of White House, and arriving there on the 21st. Here he found an abundance of forage for his animals, food for his men, and security while resting. He had been obliged to leave about ninety of his own men in the field-hospital which he had established near Trevilian, and these necessarily fell into the hands of the enemy.

White House up to this time had been a depot; but now that our troops were all on the James River, it was no longer wanted as a store of supplies. Sheridan was, therefore, directed to break it up; which he did on the 22d of June, bringing the garrison and an immense wagon train with him. All these were over the James River by the 26th of the month, and Sheridan ready to follow.

In the meantime Meade had sent Wilson's division on a raid to destroy the Weldon and South Side roads. Now that Sheridan was safe and Hampton free to return to Richmond with his cavalry, Wilson's position became precarious. Meade therefore, on the 27th, ordered Sheridan over the river to make a demonstration in favor of Wilson. Wilson got back, though not without severe loss, having struck both roads, but the damage done was soon repaired.

After these events comparative quiet reigned about Petersburg until late in July. The time, however, was spent in strengthening the intrenchments and making our position generally more secure against a sudden attack. In the meantime I had to look after other portions of my command, where things had not been going on so favorably, always, as I could have wished.

General Hunter who had been appointed to succeed Sigel in the Shenandoah Valley immediately took up the offensive. He met the enemy on the 5th of June at Piedmont, and defeated him. On the 8th he formed a junction with Crook and Averell at Staunton, from which place he moved direct on Lynchburg, via Lexington, which he reached and invested on the 16th. Up to this time he was very successful; and but for the difficulty of taking with him sufficient ordnance stores over so long a march, through a hostile country, he would, no doubt, have captured Lynchburg. The destruction of the enemy's supplies and manufactories had been very great. To meet this movement under General Hunter, General Lee sent Early with his corps, a part of which reached Lynchburg before Hunter. After some skirmishing on the 17th and 18th, General Hunter, owing to a want of ammunition to give battle, retired from before the place. Unfortunately, this want of ammunition left him no choice of route for his return but by the way of the Gauley and Kanawha rivers, thence up the Ohio River, returning to Harper's Ferry by way of the Baltimore and Ohio Railroad. A long time was consumed in making this movement. Meantime the valley was left open to Early's troops, and others in that quarter; and Washington also was uncovered. Early took advantage of this condition of affairs and moved on Washington.

In the absence of Hunter, General Lew Wallace, with headquarters at Baltimore, commanded the department in which the Shenandoah lay. His surplus of troops with which to move against the enemy was small in number. Most of these were raw and, consequently, very much inferior to our veterans and to the veterans which Early had with him; but the situation of Washington was precarious, and Wallace moved with commendable promptitude to meet the enemy at the Monocacy. He could hardly have expected to defeat him badly, but he hoped to cripple and delay him until Washington could be put into a state of preparation for his reception. I had previously ordered General Meade to send a division to Baltimore for the purpose of adding to the defences of Washington, and he had sent Ricketts's division of the 6th corps (Wright's), which arrived in Baltimore on the 8th of July. Finding that Wallace had gone to the front with his command, Ricketts immediately took the cars and followed him to the Monocacy with his entire division. They met the enemy and, as might have been expected, were defeated; but they succeeded in stopping him for the day on which the battle took place. The next morning Early started on his march to the capital of the Nation, arriving before it on the 11th.

Learning of the gravity of the situation I had directed General Meade to also order Wright with the rest of his corps directly to Washington for the relief of that place, and the latter reached there the very day that Early arrived before it. The 19th corps, which had been stationed in Louisiana, having been ordered up to reinforce the armies about Richmond, had about this time arrived at Fortress Monroe, on their way to join us. I diverted them from that point to Washington, which place they reached, almost simultaneously with Wright, on the 11th. The 19th corps was commanded by Major-General Emory.

Early made his reconnoissance with a view of attacking on the following morning, the 12th; but the next morning he found our intrenchments, which were very strong, fully manned. He at once commenced to retreat, Wright following. There is no telling how much this result was contributed to by General Lew Wallace's leading what might well be considered almost a forlorn hope. If Early had been but one day earlier he might have entered the capital before the arrival of the reinforcements I had sent. Whether the delay caused by the battle amounted to a day or not, General Wallace contributed on this occasion, by the defeat of the troops under him a greater benefit to the cause than often falls to the lot of a commander of an equal force to render by means of a victory.

Farther west also the troubles were threatening. Some time before, Forrest had met Sturgis in command of some of our cavalry in Mississippi and handled him very roughly, gaining a very great victory over him. This left Forrest free to go almost where he pleased, and to cut the roads in rear of Sherman who was then advancing. Sherman was abundantly able to look after the army that he was immediately with, and all of his military division so long as he could communicate with it; but it was my place to see that he had the means with which to hold his rear. Two divisions under A. J. Smith had been sent to Banks in Louisiana some months before. Sherman ordered these back, with directions to attack Forrest. Smith met and defeated him very badly. I then directed that Smith should hang to Forrest and not let him go; and to prevent by all means his getting upon the Memphis and Nashville Railroad. Sherman had anticipated me in this matter, and given the same orders in substance; but receiving my directions for this order to Smith, he repeated it.

On the 25th of June General Burnside had commenced running a mine from about the centre of his front under the Confederate works confronting him. He was induced to do this by Colonel Pleasants, of the Pennsylvania Volunteers, whose regiment was mostly composed of miners, and who was himself a practical miner. Burnside had submitted the scheme to Meade and myself, and we both approved of it, as a means of keeping the men occupied. His position was very favorable for carrying on this work, but not so favorable for the operations to follow its completion. The position of the two lines at that point were only about a hundred yards apart with a comparatively deep ravine intervening. In the bottom of this ravine the work commenced. The position was unfavorable in this particular: that the enemy's line at that point was re-entering, so that its front was commanded by their own lines both to the right and left. Then, too, the ground was sloping upward back of the Confederate line for a considerable distance, and it was presumable that the enemy had, at least, a detached work on this highest point.

The work progressed, and on the 23d of July the mine was finished ready for charging; but I had this work of charging deferred until we were ready for it.

On the 17th of July several deserters came in and said that there was great consternation in Richmond, and that Lee was coming out to make an attack upon us—the object being to put us on the defensive so that he might detach troops to go to Georgia where the army Sherman was operating against was said to be in great trouble. I put the army commanders, Meade and Butler, on the lookout, but the attack was not made.

I concluded, then, a few days later, to do something in the way of offensive movement myself, having in view something of the same object that Lee had had. Wright's and Emory's corps were in Washington, and with this reduction of my force Lee might very readily have spared some troops from the defences to send West. I had other objects in view, however, besides keeping Lee where he was. The mine was constructed and ready to be exploded, and I wanted to take that occasion to carry Petersburg if I could. It was the object, therefore, to get as many of Lee's troops away from the south side of the James River as possible. Accordingly, on the 26th, we commenced a movement with Hancock's corps and Sheridan's cavalry to the north side by the way of Deep Bottom, where Butler had a pontoon bridge laid. The plan, in the main, was to let the cavalry cut loose and, joining with Kautz's cavalry of the Army of the James, get by Lee's lines and destroy as much as they could of the Virginia Central Railroad, while, in the mean time, the infantry was to move out so as to protect their rear and cover their retreat back when they should have got through with their work. We were successful in drawing the enemy's troops to the north side of the James as I expected. The mine was ordered to be charged, and the morning of the 30th of July was the time fixed for its explosion. I gave Meade minute orders* on the 24th directing

---

*City Point, Va., *July* 24, 1864.
Major-General Meade,
         Commanding, etc.

The engineer officers who made a survey of the front from Bermuda Hundred report against the probability of success from an attack there. The

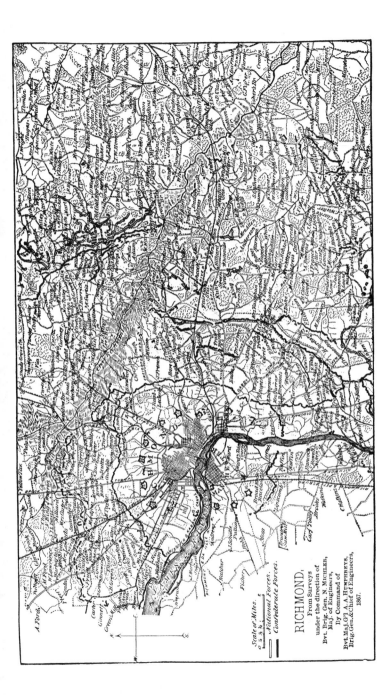

RICHMOND,

From Surveys
under the direction of
Bvt. Brig. Gen. N. MICHLER,
Maj. of Engineers,
By Command of
Bvt. Maj. Gen. A. A. HUMPHREYS,
Brig. Gen. & Chief of Engineers,
1867.

Scale of Miles.
0 ¼ ½ ¾ 1

National Forces.
Confederate Forces.

how I wanted the assault conducted, which orders he amplified into general instructions for the guidance of the troops that were to be engaged.

Meade's instructions, which I, of course, approved most heartily, were all that I can see now was necessary. The only further precaution which he could have taken, and which he could not foresee, would have been to have different men to execute them.

The gallery to the mine was over five hundred feet long from where it entered the ground to the point where it was under the enemy's works, and with a cross gallery of something over eighty feet running under their lines. Eight chambers had been left, requiring a ton of powder each to charge them. All was ready by the time I had prescribed; and on the 29th Hancock and Sheridan were brought back near the James River with their troops. Under cover of night they started to recross the bridge at Deep Bottom, and to march directly for that part of our lines in front of the mine.

Warren was to hold his line of intrenchments with a sufficient number of men and concentrate the balance on the right

chances they think will be better on Burnside's front. If this is attempted it will be necessary to concentrate all the force possible at the point in the enemy's line we expect to penetrate. All officers should be fully impressed with the absolute necessity of pushing entirely beyond the enemy's present line, if they should succeed in penetrating it, and of getting back to their present line promptly if they should not succeed in breaking through.

To the right and left of the point of assault all the artillery possible should be brought to play upon the enemy in front during the assault. Their lines would be sufficient for the support of the artillery, and all the reserves could be brought on the flanks of their commands nearest to the point of assault, ready to follow in if successful. The field artillery and infantry held in the lines during the first assault should be in readiness to move at a moment's notice either to their front or to follow the main assault, as they should receive orders. One thing, however, should be impressed on corps commanders. If they see the enemy giving away on their front or moving from it to reinforce a heavily assaulted portion of their line, they should take advantage of such knowledge and act promptly without waiting for orders from army commanders. General Ord can co-operate with his corps in this movement, and about five thousand troops from Bermuda Hundred can be sent to reinforce you or can be used to threaten an assault between the Appomattox and James rivers, as may be deemed best.

This should be done by Tuesday morning, if done at all. If not at-next to Burnside's corps, while Ord, now commanding the 18th corps, temporarily under Meade, was to form in the rear of Burnside to support him when he went in. All were to clear off the parapets and the *abatis* in their front so as to leave the space as open as possible, and be able to charge the moment the mine had been sprung and Burnside had taken possession. Burnside's corps was not to stop in the crater at all but push on to the top of the hill, supported on the right and left by Ord's and Warren's corps.

Warren and Ord fulfilled their instructions perfectly so far as making ready was concerned. Burnside seemed to have paid no attention whatever to the instructions, and left all the obstruction in his own front for his troops to get over in the best way they could. The four divisions of his corps were commanded by Generals Potter, Willcox, Ledlie and Ferrero. The last was a colored division; and Burnside selected it to make the assault. Meade interfered with this. Burnside then took Ledlie's division—a worse selection than the first could have been. In fact, Potter and Willcox were the only division commanders Burnside had who were equal to the occasion. Ledlie besides being otherwise inefficient, proved also to possess disqualification less common among soldiers.

There was some delay about the explosion of the mine so that it did not go off until about five o'clock in the morning. When it did explode it was very successful, making a crater twenty feet deep and something like a hundred feet in length. Instantly one hundred and ten cannon and fifty mortars, which had been placed in the most commanding positions covering the ground to the right and left of where the troops were to enter the enemy's lines, commenced playing. Ledlie's division marched into the crater immediately on the explosion, but most of the men stopped there in the absence of any

---

tempted, we will then start at the date indicated to destroy the railroad as far as Hicksford at least, and to Weldon if possible.

*   *   *   *   *   *   *

Whether we send an expedition on the road or assault at Petersburg, Burnside's mine will be blown up. . . .

U. S. GRANT,
Lieutenant-General.

one to give directions; their commander having found some safe retreat to get into before they started. There was some delay on the left and right in advancing, but some of the troops did get in and turn to the right and left, carrying the rifle-pits as I expected they would do.

There had been great consternation in Petersburg, as we were well aware, about a rumored mine that we were going to explode. They knew we were mining, and they had failed to cut our mine off by countermining, though Beauregard had taken the precaution to run up a line of intrenchments to the rear of that part of their line fronting where they could see that our men were at work. We had learned through deserters who had come in that the people had very wild rumors about what was going on on our side. They said that we had undermined the whole of Petersburg; that they were resting upon a slumbering volcano and did not know at what moment they might expect an eruption. I somewhat based my calculations upon this state of feeling, and expected that when the mine was exploded the troops to the right and left would flee in all directions, and that our troops, if they moved promptly, could get in and strengthen themselves before the enemy had come to a realization of the true situation. It was just as I expected it would be. We could see the men running without any apparent object except to get away. It was half an hour before musketry firing, to amount to anything, was opened upon our men in the crater. It was an hour before the enemy got artillery up to play upon them; and it was nine o'clock before Lee got up reinforcements from his right to join in expelling our troops.

The effort was a stupendous failure. It cost us about four thousand men, mostly, however, captured; and all due to inefficiency on the part of the corps commander and the incompetency of the division commander who was sent to lead the assault.

After being fully assured of the failure of the mine, and finding that most of that part of Lee's army which had been drawn north of the James River were still there, I gave Meade directions to send a corps of infantry and the cavalry next morning, before Lee could get his forces back, to destroy fifteen or twenty miles of the Weldon Railroad. But misfortunes never come singly. I learned during that same afternoon that Wright's pursuit of Early was feeble because of the constant and contrary orders he had been receiving from Washington, while I was cut off from immediate communication by reason of our cable across Chesapeake Bay being broken. Early, however, was not aware of the fact that Wright was not pursuing until he had reached Strasburg. Finding that he was not pursued he turned back to Winchester, where Crook was stationed with a small force, and drove him out. He then pushed north until he had reached the Potomac, then he sent McCausland across to Chambersburg, Pa., to destroy that town. Chambersburg was a purely defenceless town with no garrison whatever, and no fortifications; yet McCausland, under Early's orders, burned the place and left about three hundred families houseless. This occurred on the 30th of July. I rescinded my orders for the troops to go out to destroy the Weldon Railroad, and directed them to embark for Washington City. After burning Chambersburg McCausland retreated, pursued by our cavalry, towards Cumberland. They were met and defeated by General Kelley and driven into Virginia.

The Shenandoah Valley was very important to the Confederates, because it was the principal store-house they now had for feeding their armies about Richmond. It was well known that they would make a desperate struggle to maintain it. It had been the source of a great deal of trouble to us heretofore to guard that outlet to the north, partly because of the incompetency of some of the commanders, but chiefly because of interference from Washington. It seemed to be the policy of General Halleck and Secretary Stanton to keep any force sent there, in pursuit of the invading army, moving right and left so as to keep between the enemy and our capital; and, generally speaking, they pursued this policy until all knowledge of the whereabouts of the enemy was lost. They were left, therefore, free to supply themselves with horses, beef cattle, and such provisions as they could carry away from Western Maryland and Pennsylvania. I determined to put a stop to this. I started Sheridan at once for that field of operation, and on the following day sent another division of his cavalry.

I had previously asked to have Sheridan assigned to that command, but Mr. Stanton objected, on the ground that he was too young for so important a command. On the 1st of August when I sent reinforcements for the protection of Washington, I sent the following orders:

> CITY POINT, VA.,
> *August* 1, 1864, 11.30 A.M.

MAJOR-GENERAL HALLECK,
      Washington, D. C.

I am sending General Sheridan for temporary duty whilst the enemy is being expelled from the border. Unless General Hunter is in the field in person, I want Sheridan put in command of all the troops in the field, with instructions to put himself south of the enemy and follow him to the death. Wherever the enemy goes let our troops go also. Once started up the valley they ought to be followed until we get possession of the Virginia Central Railroad. If General Hunter is in the field, give Sheridan direct command of the 6th corps and cavalry division. All the cavalry, I presume, will reach Washington in the course of to-morrow.

> U. S. GRANT,
> Lieutenant-General.

The President in some way or other got to see this dispatch of mine directing certain instructions to be given to the commanders in the field, operating against Early, and sent me the following very characteristic dispatch:

> OFFICE U. S. MILITARY TELEGRAPH,
> WAR DEPARTMENT,
> WASHINGTON, D. C., *August* 3, 1864.

Cypher. 6 P.M.,
      LT.-GENERAL GRANT,
            City Point, Va.

I have seen your despatch in which you say, "I want Sheridan put in command of all the troops in the field, with instructions to put himself south of the enemy, and follow him to the death. Wherever the enemy goes, let our troops go also." This, I think, is exactly right, as to how our forces should move. But please look over the despatches you may have received from here, even since you made that order, and discover, if you can, that there is any idea in the head of any one here, of "putting our army *south* of the enemy," or of "following him to the *death*" in any direction. I repeat to you it will neither be done nor attempted unless you watch it every day, and hour, and force it.

A. LINCOLN.

I replied to this that "I would start in two hours for Washington," and soon got off, going directly to the Monocacy without stopping at Washington on my way. I found General Hunter's army encamped there, scattered over the fields along the banks of the Monocacy, with many hundreds of cars and locomotives, belonging to the Baltimore and Ohio Railroad, which he had taken the precaution to bring back and collect at that point. I asked the general where the enemy was. He replied that he did not know. He said the fact was, that he was so embarrassed with orders from Washington moving him first to the right and then to the left that he had lost all trace of the enemy.

I then told the general that I would find out where the enemy was, and at once ordered steam got up and trains made up, giving directions to push for Halltown, some four miles above Harper's Ferry, in the Shenandoah Valley. The cavalry and the wagon trains were to march, but all the troops that could be transported by the cars were to go in that way. I knew that the valley was of such importance to the enemy that, no matter how much he was scattered at that time, he would in a very short time be found in front of our troops moving south.

I then wrote out General Hunter's instructions.* I told him that Sheridan was in Washington, and still another division was on its way; and suggested that he establish the headquarters of the department at any point that would suit him best, Cumberland, Baltimore, or elsewhere, and give Sheridan command of the troops in the field. The general replied to this, that he thought he had better be relieved entirely. He said that General Halleck seemed so much to distrust his fitness for the position he was in that he thought somebody else ought to be there. He did not want, in any way, to embarrass the cause; thus showing a patriotism that was none too common in the army. There were not many major-generals who

---

*See letter, August 5th, Appendix.

would voluntarily have asked to have the command of a department taken from them on the supposition that for some particular reason, or for any reason, the service would be better performed. I told him, "very well then," and telegraphed at once for Sheridan to come to the Monocacy, and suggested that I would wait and meet him there.

Sheridan came at once by special train, but reached there after the troops were all off. I went to the station and remained there until he arrived. Myself and one or two of my staff were about all the Union people, except General Hunter and his staff, who were left at the Monocacy when Sheridan arrived. I hastily told Sheridan what had been done and what I wanted him to do, giving him, at the same time, the written instructions which had been prepared for General Hunter and directed to that officer.

Sheridan now had about 30,000 men to move with, 8,000 of them being cavalry. Early had about the same number, but the superior ability of the National commander over the Confederate commander was so great that all the latter's advantage of being on the defensive was more than counterbalanced by this circumstance. As I had predicted, Early was soon found in front of Sheridan in the valley, and Pennsylvania and Maryland were speedily freed from the invaders. The importance of the valley was so great to the Confederates that Lee reinforced Early, but not to the extent that we thought and feared he would.

To prevent as much as possible these reinforcements from being sent out from Richmond, I had to do something to compel Lee to retain his forces about his capital. I therefore gave orders for another move to the north side of the James River, to threaten Richmond. Hancock's corps, part of the 10th corps under Birney, and Gregg's division of cavalry were crossed to the north side of the James during the night of the 13th–14th of August. A threatening position was maintained for a number of days, with more or less skirmishing, and some tolerably hard fighting; although it was my object and my instructions that anything like a battle should be avoided, unless opportunities should present themselves which would insure great success. General Meade was left in command of the few troops around Petersburg, strongly intrenched; and was instructed to keep a close watch upon the enemy in that quarter, and himself to take advantage of any weakening that might occur through an effort on the part of the enemy to reinforce the north side. There was no particular victory gained on either side; but during that time no more reinforcements were sent to the valley.

I informed Sheridan of what had been done to prevent reinforcements being sent from Richmond against him, and also that the efforts we had made had proven that one of the divisions which we supposed had gone to the valley was still at Richmond, because we had captured six or seven hundred prisoners from that division, each of its four brigades having contributed to our list of captures. I also informed him that but one division had gone, and it was possible that I should be able to prevent the going of any more.

To add to my embarrassment at this time Sherman, who was now near Atlanta, wanted reinforcements. He was perfectly willing to take the raw troops then being raised in the North-west, saying that he could teach them more soldiering in one day among his troops than they would learn in a week in a camp of instruction. I therefore asked that all troops in camps of instruction in the North-west be sent to him. Sherman also wanted to be assured that no Eastern troops were moving out against him. I informed him of what I had done and assured him that I would hold all the troops there that it was possible for me to hold, and that up to that time none had gone. I also informed him that his real danger was from Kirby Smith, who commanded the trans-Mississippi Department. If Smith should escape Steele, and get across the Mississippi River, he might move against him. I had, therefore, asked to have an expedition ready to move from New Orleans against Mobile in case Kirby Smith should get across. This would have a tendency to draw him to the defence of that place, instead of going against Sherman.

Right in the midst of all these embarrassments Halleck informed me that there was an organized scheme on foot in the North to resist the draft, and suggested that it might become necessary to draw troops from the field to put it down. He also advised taking in sail, and not going too fast.

The troops were withdrawn from the north side of the

James River on the night of the 20th. Before they were withdrawn, however, and while most of Lee's force was on that side of the river, Warren had been sent with most of the 5th corps to capture the Weldon Railroad. He took up his line of march well back to the rear, south of the enemy, while the troops remaining in the trenches extended so as to cover that part of the line which he had vacated by moving out. From our left, near the old line, it was about three miles to the Weldon Railroad. A division was ordered from the right of the Petersburg line to reinforce Warren, while a division was brought back from the north side of the James River to take its place.

This road was very important to the enemy. The limits from which his supplies had been drawn were already very much contracted, and I knew that he must fight desperately to protect it. Warren carried the road, though with heavy loss on both sides. He fortified his new position, and our trenches were then extended from the left of our main line to connect with his new one. Lee made repeated attempts to dislodge Warren's corps, but without success, and with heavy loss.

As soon as Warren was fortified and reinforcements reached him, troops were sent south to destroy the bridges on the Weldon Railroad; and with such success that the enemy had to draw in wagons, for a distance of about thirty miles, all the supplies they got thereafter from that source. It was on the 21st that Lee seemed to have given up the Weldon Railroad as having been lost to him; but along about the 24th or 25th he made renewed attempts to recapture it; again he failed and with very heavy losses to him as compared with ours.

On the night of the 20th our troops on the north side of the James were withdrawn, and Hancock and Gregg were sent south to destroy the Weldon Railroad. They were attacked on the 25th at Reams's Station, and after desperate fighting a part of our line gave way, losing five pieces of artillery. But the Weldon Railroad never went out of our possession from the 18th of August to the close of the war.

Chapter LVIII.

W E HAD our troops on the Weldon Railroad contending
against a large force that regarded this road of so much
importance that they could afford to expend many lives in
retaking it; Sherman just getting through to Atlanta with
great losses of men from casualties, discharges and detachments left along as guards to occupy and hold the road in rear
of him; Washington threatened but a short time before, and
now Early being strengthened in the valley so as, probably, to
renew that attempt. It kept me pretty active in looking after
all these points.

On the 10th of August Sheridan had advanced on Early up
the Shenandoah Valley, Early falling back to Strasburg. On
the 12th I learned that Lee had sent twenty pieces of artillery,
two divisions of infantry and a considerable cavalry force to
strengthen Early. It was important that Sheridan should be
informed of this, so I sent the information to Washington by
telegraph, and directed a courier to be sent from there to
get the message to Sheridan at all hazards, giving him the
information. The messenger, an officer of the army, pushed
through with great energy and reached Sheridan just in time.
The officer went through by way of Snicker's Gap, escorted
by some cavalry. He found Sheridan just making his preparations to attack Early in his chosen position. Now, however,
he was thrown back on the defensive.

On the 15th of September I started to visit General Sheridan
in the Shenandoah Valley. My purpose was to have him attack
Early, or drive him out of the valley and destroy that source
of supplies for Lee's army. I knew it was impossible for me to
get orders through Washington to Sheridan to make a move,
because they would be stopped there and such orders as
Halleck's caution (and that of the Secretary of War) would
suggest would be given instead, and would, no doubt, be

contradictory to mine. I therefore, without stopping at Washington, went directly through to Charlestown, some ten miles above Harper's Ferry, and waited there to see General Sheridan, having sent a courier in advance to inform him where to meet me.

When Sheridan arrived I asked him if he had a map showing the positions of his army and that of the enemy. He at once drew one out of his side pocket, showing all roads and streams, and the camps of the two armies. He said that if he had permission he would move so and so (pointing out how) against the Confederates, and that he could "whip them." Before starting I had drawn up a plan of campaign for Sheridan, which I had brought with me; but, seeing that he was so clear and so positive in his views and so confident of success, I said nothing about this and did not take it out of my pocket.

Sheridan's wagon trains were kept at Harper's Ferry, where all of his stores were. By keeping the teams at that place, their forage did not have to be hauled to them. As supplies of ammunition, provisions and rations for the men were wanted, trains would be made up to deliver the stores to the commissaries and quartermasters encamped at Winchester. Knowing that he, in making preparations to move at a given day, would have to bring up wagon trains from Harper's Ferry, I asked him if he could be ready to get off by the following Tuesday. This was on Friday. "O yes," he said, he "could be off before daylight on Monday." I told him then to make the attack at that time and according to his own plan; and I immediately started to return to the army about Richmond. After visiting Baltimore and Burlington, New Jersey, I arrived at City Point on the 19th.

On the way out to Harper's Ferry I had met Mr. Robert Garrett, President of the Baltimore and Ohio Railroad. He seemed very anxious to know when workmen might be put upon the road again so as to make repairs and put it in shape for running. It was a large piece of property to have standing idle. I told him I could not answer then positively but would try and inform him before a great while. On my return Mr. Garrett met me again with the same question and I told him I thought that by the following Wednesday he might send his workmen out on his road. I gave him no further information however, and he had no suspicion of how I expected to have the road cleared for his workmen.

Sheridan moved at the time he had fixed upon. He met Early at the crossing of Opequon Creek, and won a most decisive victory—one which electrified the country. Early had invited this attack himself by his bad generalship and made the victory easy. He had sent G. T. Anderson's division east of the Blue Ridge before I went to Harper's Ferry; and about the time I arrived there he started with two other divisions (leaving but two in their camps) to march to Martinsburg for the purpose of destroying the Baltimore and Ohio Railroad at that point. Early here learned that I had been with Sheridan and, supposing there was some movement on foot, started back as soon as he got the information. But his forces were separated and, as I have said, he was very badly defeated. He fell back to Fisher's Hill, Sheridan following.

The valley is narrow at that point, and Early made another stand there, behind works which extended across. But Sheridan turned both his flanks and again sent him speeding up the valley, following in hot pursuit. The pursuit was continued up the valley to Mount Jackson and New Market. Sheridan captured about eleven hundred prisoners and sixteen guns. The houses which he passed all along the route were found to be filled with Early's wounded, and the country swarmed with his deserters. Finally, on the 25th, Early turned from the valley eastward, leaving Sheridan at Harrisonburg in undisputed possession.

Now one of the main objects of the expedition began to be accomplished. Sheridan went to work with his command, gathering in the crops, cattle, and everything in the upper part of the valley required by our troops; and especially taking what might be of use to the enemy. What he could not take away he destroyed, so that the enemy would not be invited to come back there. I congratulated Sheridan upon his recent great victory and had a salute of a hundred guns fired in honor of it, the guns being aimed at the enemy around Petersburg. I also notified the other commanders throughout the country, who also fired salutes in honor of his victory.

I had reason to believe that the administration was a little afraid to have a decisive battle fought at that time, for fear it

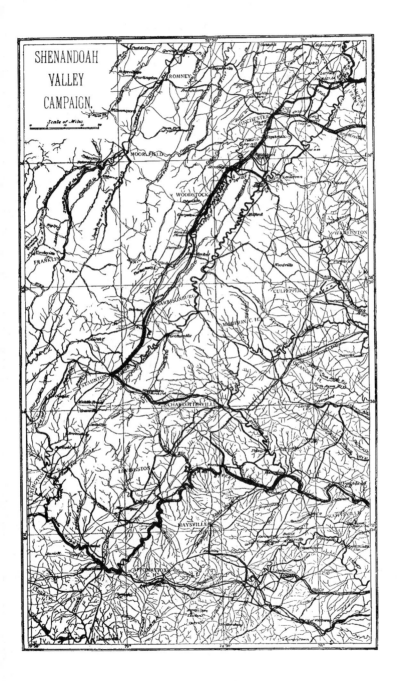

SHENANDOAH
VALLEY
CAMPAIGN.

Scale of Miles

might go against us and have a bad effect on the November elections. The convention which had met and made its nomination of the Democratic candidate for the presidency had declared the war a failure. Treason was talked as boldly in Chicago at that convention as ever it had been in Charleston. It was a question whether the government would then have had the power to make arrests and punish those who thus talked treason. But this decisive victory was the most effective campaign argument made in the canvass.

Sheridan, in his pursuit, got beyond where they could hear from him in Washington, and the President became very much frightened about him. He was afraid that the hot pursuit had been a little like that of General Cass was said to have been, in one of our Indian wars, when he was an officer of the army. Cass was pursuing the Indians so closely that the first thing he knew he found himself in their front, and the Indians pursuing him. The President was afraid that Sheridan had got on the other side of Early and that Early was in behind him. He was afraid that Sheridan was getting so far away that reinforcements would be sent out from Richmond to enable Early to beat him. I replied to the President that I had taken steps to prevent Lee from sending reinforcements to Early, by attacking the former where he was.

On the 28th of September, to retain Lee in his position, I sent Ord with the 18th corps and Birney with the 10th corps to make an advance on Richmond, to threaten it. Ord moved with the left wing up to Chaffin's Bluff; Birney with the 10th corps took a road farther north; while Kautz with the cavalry took the Darby road, still farther to the north. They got across the river by the next morning, and made an effort to surprise the enemy. In that, however, they were unsuccessful.

The enemy's lines were very strong and very intricate. Stannard's division of the 18th corps with General Burnham's brigade leading, tried an assault against Fort Harrison and captured it with sixteen guns and a good many prisoners. Burnham was killed in the assault. Colonel Stevens who succeeded him was badly wounded; and his successor also fell in the same way. Some works to the right and left were also carried with the guns in them—six in number—and a few more prisoners. Birney's troops to the right captured the enemy's intrenched picket-lines, but were unsuccessful in their efforts upon the main line.

Our troops fortified their new position, bringing Fort Harrison into the new line and extending it to the river. This brought us pretty close to the enemy on the north side of the James, and the two opposing lines maintained their relative positions to the close of the siege.

In the afternoon a further attempt was made to advance, but it failed. Ord fell badly wounded, and had to be relieved; the command devolved upon General Heckman, and later General Weitzel was assigned to the command of the 18th corps. During the night Lee reinforced his troops about Fort Gilmer, which was at the right of Fort Harrison, by transferring eight additional brigades from Petersburg, and attempted to retake the works which we had captured by concentrating ten brigades against them. All their efforts failed, their attacks being all repulsed with very heavy loss. In one of these assaults upon us General Stannard, a gallant officer, who was defending Fort Harrison, lost an arm. Our casualties during these operations amounted to 394 killed, 1,554 wounded and 324 missing.

Whilst this was going on General Meade was instructed to keep up an appearance of moving troops to our extreme left. Parke and Warren were kept with two divisions, each under arms, ready to move, leaving their enclosed batteries manned, with a scattering line on the other intrenchments. The object of this was to prevent reinforcements from going to the north side of the river. Meade was instructed to watch the enemy closely and, if Lee weakened his lines, to make an attack.

On the 30th these troops moved out, under Warren, and captured an advanced intrenched camp at Peeble's farm, driving the enemy back to the main line. Our troops followed and made an attack in the hope of carrying the enemy's main line; but in this they were unsuccessful and lost a large number of men, mostly captured. The number of killed and wounded was not large. The next day our troops advanced again and established themselves, intrenching a new line about a mile in front of the enemy. This advanced Warren's position on the Weldon Railroad very considerably.

Sheridan having driven the enemy out of the valley, and taken the productions of the valley so that instead of going there for supplies the enemy would have to bring his provisions with him if he again entered it, recommended a reduction of his own force, the surplus to be sent where it could be of more use. I approved of his suggestion, and ordered him to send Wright's corps back to the James River. I further directed him to repair the railroad up the Shenandoah Valley towards the advanced position which we would hold with a small force. The troops were to be sent to Washington by the way of Culpeper, in order to watch the east side of the Blue Ridge, and prevent the enemy from getting into the rear of Sheridan while he was still doing his work of destruction.

The valley was so very important, however, to the Confederate army that, contrary to our expectations, they determined to make one more strike, and save it if possible before the supplies should be all destroyed. Reinforcements were sent therefore to Early, and this before any of our troops had been withdrawn. Early prepared to strike Sheridan at Harrisonburg; but the latter had not remained there.

On the 6th of October Sheridan commenced retiring down the valley, taking or destroying all the food and forage and driving the cattle before him, Early following. At Fisher's Hill Sheridan turned his cavalry back on that of Early, which, under the lead of Rosser, was pursuing closely, and routed it most completely, capturing eleven guns and a large number of prisoners. Sheridan lost only about sixty men. His cavalry pursued the enemy back some twenty-five miles. On the 10th of October the march down the valley was again resumed, Early again following.

I now ordered Sheridan to halt, and to improve the opportunity if afforded by the enemy's having been sufficiently weakened, to move back again and cut the James River Canal and Virginia Central Railroad. But this order had to go through Washington where it was intercepted; and when Sheridan received what purported to be a statement of what I wanted him to do it was something entirely different. Halleck informed Sheridan that it was my wish for him to hold a forward position as a base from which to act against Charlottesville and Gordonsville; that he should fortify this position and provision it.

Sheridan objected to this most decidedly; and I was impelled to telegraph him, on the 14th, as follows:

CITY POINT, VA.,
October 14, 1864. —12.30 P.M.

MAJOR-GENERAL SHERIDAN,
Cedar Creek, Va.

What I want is for you to threaten the Virginia Central Railroad and canal in the manner your judgment tells you is best, holding yourself ready to advance, if the enemy draw off their forces. If you make the enemy hold a force equal to your own for the protection of those thoroughfares, it will accomplish nearly as much as their destruction. If you cannot do this, then the next best thing to do is to send here all the force you can. I deem a good cavalry force necessary for your offensive, as well as defensive operations. You need not therefore send here more than one division of cavalry.

U. S. GRANT,
Lieutenant-General.

Sheridan having been summoned to Washington City, started on the 15th leaving Wright in command. His army was then at Cedar Creek, some twenty miles south of Winchester. The next morning while at Front Royal, Sheridan received a dispatch from Wright, saying that a dispatch from Longstreet to Early had been intercepted. It directed the latter to be ready to move and to crush Sheridan as soon as he, Longstreet, arrived. On the receipt of this news Sheridan ordered the cavalry up the valley to join Wright.

On the 18th of October Early was ready to move, and during the night succeeded in getting his troops in the rear of our left flank, which fled precipitately and in great confusion down the valley, losing eighteen pieces of artillery and a thousand or more prisoners. The right under General Getty maintained a firm and steady front, falling back to Middletown where it took a position and made a stand. The cavalry went to the rear, seized the roads leading to Winchester and held them for the use of our troops in falling back, General Wright having ordered a retreat back to that place.

Sheridan having left Washington on the 18th, reached Winchester that night. The following morning he started to join his command. He had scarcely got out of town, when he met his men returning in panic from the front and also heard heavy firing to the south. He immediately ordered the cavalry at Winchester to be deployed across the valley to stop the stragglers. Leaving members of his staff to take care of Winchester and the public property there, he set out with a small escort directly for the scene of battle. As he met the fugitives he ordered them to turn back, reminding them that they were going the wrong way. His presence soon restored confidence. Finding themselves worse frightened than hurt the men did halt and turn back. Many of those who had run ten miles got back in time to redeem their reputation as gallant soldiers before night.

When Sheridan got to the front he found Getty and Custer still holding their ground firmly between the Confederates and our retreating troops. Everything in the rear was now ordered up. Sheridan at once proceeded to intrench his position; and he awaited an assault from the enemy. This was made with vigor, and was directed principally against Emory's corps, which had sustained the principal loss in the first attack. By one o'clock the attack was repulsed. Early was so badly damaged that he seemed disinclined to make another attack, but went to work to intrench himself with a view to holding the position he had already gained. He thought, no doubt, that Sheridan would be glad enough to leave him unmolested; but in this he was mistaken.

About the middle of the afternoon Sheridan advanced. He sent his cavalry by both flanks, and they penetrated to the enemy's rear. The contest was close for a time, but at length the left of the enemy broke, and disintegration along the whole line soon followed. Early tried to rally his men, but they were followed so closely that they had to give way very quickly every time they attempted to make a stand. Our cavalry, having pushed on and got in the rear of the Confederates, captured twenty-four pieces of artillery, besides retaking what had been lost in the morning. This victory pretty much closed the campaigning in the Valley of Virginia. All the Confederate troops were sent back to Richmond with the exception of one division of infantry and a little cavalry. Wright's corps was ordered back to the Army of the Potomac, and two other divisions were withdrawn from the valley. Early had lost more men in killed, wounded and captured in the valley than Sheridan had commanded from first to last.

On more than one occasion in these engagements General R. B. Hayes, who succeeded me as President of the United States, bore a very honorable part. His conduct on the field was marked by conspicuous gallantry as well as the display of qualities of a higher order than that of mere personal daring. This might well have been expected of one who could write at the time he is said to have done so: "Any officer fit for duty who at this crisis would abandon his post to electioneer for a seat in Congress, ought to be scalped." Having entered the army as a Major of Volunteers at the beginning of the war, General Hayes attained by meritorious service the rank of Brevet Major-General before its close.

On the north side of the James River the enemy attacked Kautz's cavalry on the 7th of October, and drove it back with heavy loss in killed, wounded and prisoners, and the loss of all the artillery. This was followed up by an attack on our intrenched infantry line, but was repulsed with severe slaughter. On the 13th a reconnoissance was sent out by General Butler, with a view to drive the enemy from some new works he was constructing, which resulted in heavy loss to us.

On the 24th I ordered General Meade to attempt to get possession of the South Side Railroad, and for that purpose to advance on the 27th. The attempt proved a failure, however, the most advanced of our troops not getting nearer than within six miles of the point aimed for. Seeing the impossibility of its accomplishment I ordered the troops to withdraw, and they were all back in their former positions the next day.

Butler, by my directions, also made a demonstration on the north side of the James River in order to support this move, by detaining there the Confederate troops who were on that side. He succeeded in this, but failed of further results by not marching past the enemy's left before turning in on the Darby road and by reason of simply coming up against their lines in place.

This closed active operations around Richmond for the winter. Of course there was frequent skirmishing between pickets, but no serious battle was fought near either Petersburg or Richmond. It would prolong this work to give a detailed account of all that took place from day to day around Petersburg and at other parts of my command, and it would not interest the general reader if given. All these details can be found by the military student in a series of books published by the Scribners, Badeau's history of my campaigns, and also in the publications of the War Department, including both the National and Confederate reports.

In the latter part of November General Hancock was relieved from the command of the 2d corps by the Secretary of War and ordered to Washington, to organize and command a corps of veteran troops to be designated the 1st corps. It was expected that this would give him a large command to cooperate with in the spring. It was my expectation, at the time, that in the final operations Hancock should move either up the valley, or else east of the Blue Ridge to Lynchburg; the idea being to make the spring campaign the close of the war. I expected, with Sherman coming up from the South, Meade south of Petersburg and around Richmond, and Thomas's command in Tennessee with depots of supplies established in the eastern part of that State, to move from the direction of Washington or the valley towards Lynchburg. We would then have Lee so surrounded that his supplies would be cut off entirely, making it impossible for him to support his army.

General Humphreys, chief-of-staff of the Army of the Potomac, was assigned to the command of the 2d corps, to succeed Hancock.

Chapter LIX.

LET US now return to the operations in the military division of the Mississippi, and accompany Sherman in his march to the sea.

The possession of Atlanta by us narrowed the territory of the enemy very materially and cut off one of his two remaining lines of roads from east to west.

A short time after the fall of Atlanta Mr. Davis visited Palmetto and Macon and made speeches at each place. He spoke at Palmetto on the 20th of September, and at Macon on the 22d. Inasmuch as he had relieved Johnston and appointed Hood, and Hood had immediately taken the initiative, it is natural to suppose that Mr. Davis was disappointed with General Johnston's policy. My own judgment is that Johnston acted very wisely: he husbanded his men and saved as much of his territory as he could, without fighting decisive battles in which all might be lost. As Sherman advanced, as I have shown, his army became spread out, until, if this had been continued, it would have been easy to destroy it in detail. I know that both Sherman and I were rejoiced when we heard of the change. Hood was unquestionably a brave, gallant soldier and not destitute of ability; but unfortunately his policy was to fight the enemy wherever he saw him, without thinking much of the consequences of defeat.

In his speeches Mr. Davis denounced Governor Brown, of Georgia, and General Johnston in unmeasured terms, even insinuating that their loyalty to the Southern cause was doubtful. So far as General Johnston is concerned, I think Davis did him a great injustice in this particular. I had known the general before the war and strongly believed it would be impossible for him to accept a high commission for the purpose of betraying the cause he had espoused. Then, as I have said, I think that his policy was the best one that could have been pursued by the whole South—protract the war, which was all that was necessary to enable them to gain recognition in the end. The North was already growing weary, as the South evidently was also, but with this difference. In the North the people governed, and could stop hostilities whenever they chose to stop supplies. The South was a military camp, controlled absolutely by the government with soldiers to back it, and the war could have been protracted, no matter to what extent the discontent reached, up to the point of open mutiny of the soldiers themselves. Mr. Davis's speeches were frank appeals to the people of Georgia and that portion of the South to come to their relief. He tried to assure his frightened hearers that the Yankees were rapidly digging their own graves; that measures were already being taken to cut them off from supplies from the North; and that with a force in front, and cut off from the rear, they must soon starve in the midst of a hostile people. Papers containing reports of these speeches immediately reached the Northern States, and they were republished. Of course, that caused no alarm so long as telegraphic communication was kept up with Sherman.

When Hood was forced to retreat from Atlanta he moved to the south-west and was followed by a portion of Sherman's army. He soon appeared upon the railroad in Sherman's rear, and with his whole army began destroying the road. At the same time also the work was begun in Tennessee and Kentucky which Mr. Davis had assured his hearers at Palmetto and Macon would take place. He ordered Forrest (about the ablest cavalry general in the South) north for this purpose; and Forrest and Wheeler carried out their orders with more or less destruction, occasionally picking up a garrison. Forrest indeed performed the very remarkable feat of capturing, with cavalry, two gunboats and a number of transports, something the accomplishment of which is very hard to account for. Hood's army had been weakened by Governor Brown's withdrawing the Georgia State troops for the purpose of gathering in the season's crops for the use of the people and for the use of the army. This not only depleted Hood's forces but it served a most excellent purpose in gathering in supplies of food and forage for the use of our army in its subsequent march. Sherman was obliged to push on with his force and go himself with portions of it hither and thither, until it was clearly demonstrated to him that with the army he then had it would be impossible to hold the line from Atlanta back and leave him any force whatever with which to take the offensive. Had that plan been adhered to, very large reinforcements would have been necessary; and Mr. Davis's prediction of the destruction of the army would have been realized, or else Sherman would have been obliged to make a successful retreat, which Mr. Davis said in his speeches would prove more disastrous than Napoleon's retreat from Moscow.

These speeches of Mr. Davis were not long in reaching Sherman. He took advantage of the information they gave, and made all the preparation possible for him to make to meet what now became expected, attempts to break his communications. Something else had to be done: and to Sherman's sensible and soldierly mind the idea was not long in dawning upon him, not only that something else had to be done, but what that something else should be.

On September 10th I telegraphed Sherman as follows:

CITY POINT, VA., *Sept.* 10, 1864.

MAJOR-GENERAL SHERMAN,
        Atlanta, Georgia.

So soon as your men are sufficiently rested, and preparations can be made, it is desirable that another campaign should be commenced. We want to keep the enemy constantly pressed to the end of the war. If we give him no peace whilst the war lasts, the end cannot be distant. Now that we have all of Mobile Bay that is valuable, I do not know but it will be the best move to transfer Canby's troops to act upon Savannah, whilst you move on Augusta. I should like to hear from you, however, in this matter.

U. S. GRANT,
        Lieutenant-General.

Sherman replied promptly:

"If I could be sure of finding provisions and ammunition at Augusta, or Columbus, Georgia, I can march to Milledgeville, and compel Hood to give up Augusta or Macon, and then turn on the other. * * * If you can manage to take the Savannah River as high up as Augusta, or the Chattahoochee as far up as Columbus, I can sweep the whole State of Georgia."

On the 12th I sent a special messenger, one of my own staff, with a letter inviting Sherman's views about the next campaign.

CITY POINT, VA., *Sept.* 12, 1864.

MAJOR-GENERAL W. T. SHERMAN,

Commanding Mil. Division of the Mississippi.

I send Lieutenant-Colonel Porter, of my staff, with this. Colonel Porter will explain to you the exact condition of affairs here better than I can do in the limits of a letter. Although I feel myself strong enough for offensive operations, I am holding on quietly to get advantage of recruits and convalescents, who are coming forward very rapidly. My lines are necessarily very long, extending from Deep Bottom north of the James across the peninsula formed by the Appomattox and the James, and south of the Appomattox to the Weldon Road. This line is very strongly fortified, and can be held with comparatively few men, but from its great length takes many in the aggregate. I propose, when I do move, to extend my left so as to control what is known as the South Side, or Lynchburg and Petersburg Road, then if possible to keep the Danville Road cut. At the same time this move is made, I want to send a force of from six to ten thousand men against Wilmington.

The way I propose to do this is to land the men north of Fort Fisher, and hold that point. At the same time a large naval fleet will be assembled there, and the iron-clads will run the batteries as they did at Mobile. This will give us the same control of the harbor of Wilmington that we now have of the harbor of Mobile. What you are to do with the forces at your command, I do not see. The difficulties of supplying your army, except when you are constantly moving, beyond where you are, I plainly see. If it had not been for Price's movements Canby would have sent twelve thousand more men to Mobile. From your command on the Mississippi an equal number could have been taken. With these forces my idea would have been to divide them, sending one half to Mobile and the other half to Savannah. You could then move as proposed in your telegram, so as to threaten Macon and Augusta equally. Whichever was abandoned by the enemy you could take and open up a new base of supplies. My object now in sending a staff officer is not so much to suggest operations for you, as to get your views and have plans matured by the time everything can be got ready. It will probably be the 5th of October before any of the plans herein indicated will be executed.

If you have any promotions to recommend, send the names forward and I will approve them. * * *

U. S. GRANT,
Lieutenant-General.

This reached Sherman on September 20th.

On the 25th of September Sherman reported to Washington that Hood's troops were in his rear. He had provided against this by sending a division to Chattanooga and a division to Rome, Georgia, which was in the rear of Hood, supposing that Hood would fall back in the direction from which he had come to reach the railroad. At the same time Sherman and Hood kept up a correspondence relative to the exchange of prisoners, the treatment of citizens, and other matters suitable to be arranged between hostile commanders in the field. On the 27th of September I telegraphed Sherman as follows:

CITY POINT, VA.,
September 27, 1864. — 10.30 A.M.

MAJOR-GENERAL SHERMAN:

I have directed all recruits and new troops from the Western States to be sent to Nashville, to receive their further orders from you. * * *

U. S. GRANT,
Lieutenant-General.

On the 29th Sherman sent Thomas back to Chattanooga, and afterwards to Nashville, with another division (Morgan's) of the advanced army. Sherman then suggested that, when he was prepared, his movements should take place against Milledgeville and then to Savannah. His expectation at that time was, to make this movement as soon as he could get up his supplies. Hood was moving in his own country, and was moving light so that he could make two miles to Sherman's one. He depended upon the country to gather his supplies, and so was not affected by delays.

As I have said, until this unexpected state of affairs happened, Mobile had been looked upon as the objective point of Sherman's army. It had been a favorite move of mine from 1862, when I first suggested to the then commander-in-chief that the troops in Louisiana, instead of frittering away their time in the trans-Mississippi, should move against Mobile. I recommended this from time to time until I came into command of the army, the last of March 1864. Having the power in my own hands, I now ordered the concentration of supplies, stores and troops, in the department of the Gulf about New Orleans, with a view to a move against Mobile, in support of, and in conjunction with, the other armies operating in the field. Before I came into command, these troops had been scattered over the trans-Mississippi department in such a way that they could not be, or were not, gotten back in time to take any part in the original movement; hence the consideration, which had caused Mobile to be selected as the objective point for Sherman's army to find his next base of supplies after having cut loose from Atlanta, no longer existed.

General G. M. Dodge, an exceedingly efficient officer, having been badly wounded, had to leave the army about the first of October. He was in command of two divisions of the 16th corps, consolidated into one. Sherman then divided his army into the right and left wings—the right commanded by General O. O. Howard and the left by General Slocum. General Dodge's two divisions were assigned, one to each of these wings. Howard's command embraced the 15th and 17th corps, and Slocum's the 14th and 20th corps, commanded by Generals Jeff. C. Davis and A. S. Williams. Generals Logan and Blair commanded the two corps composing the right wing. About this time they left to take part in the presidential election, which took place that year, leaving their corps to Osterhaus and Ransom. I have no doubt that their leaving was at the earnest solicitation of the War Department. General Blair got back in time to resume his command and to proceed with it throughout the march to the sea and back to the grand review at Washington. General Logan did not return to his command until after it reached Savannah.

Logan felt very much aggrieved at the transfer of General Howard from that portion of the Army of the Potomac which was then with the Western Army, to the command of the Army of the Tennessee, with which army General Logan had served from the battle of Belmont to the fall of Atlanta—having passed successively through all grades from colonel commanding a regiment to general commanding a brigade, division and army corps, until upon the death of McPherson the command of the entire Army of the Tennessee devolved upon him in the midst of a hotly contested battle. He conceived that he had done his full duty as commander in that engagement; and I can bear testimony, from personal observation, that he had proved himself fully equal to all the lower positions which he had occupied as a soldier. I will not pretend to question the motive which actuated Sherman in taking an officer from another army to supersede General Logan. I have no doubt, whatever, that he did this for what he considered would be to the good of the service, which was more important than that the personal feelings of any individual should not be aggrieved; though I doubt whether he had an officer with him who could have filled the place as Logan would have done. Differences of opinion must exist between the best of friends as to policies in war, and of judgment as to men's fitness. The officer who has the command, however, should be allowed to judge of the fitness of the officers under him, unless he is very manifestly wrong.

Sherman's army, after all the depletions, numbered about sixty thousand effective men. All weak men had been left to hold the rear, and those remaining were not only well men, but strong and hardy, so that he had sixty thousand as good soldiers as ever trod the earth; better than any European soldiers, because they not only worked like a machine but the machine thought. European armies know very little what they are fighting for, and care less. Included in these sixty thousand troops, there were two small divisions of cavalry, numbering altogether about four thousand men. Hood had about thirty-five to forty thousand men, independent of Forrest, whose forces were operating in Tennessee and Kentucky, as Mr. Davis had promised they should. This part of Mr. Davis's military plan was admirable, and promised the best results of anything he could have done, according to my judgment. I say this because I have criticised his military judgment in the removal of Johnston, and also in the appointment of Hood. I am aware, however, that there was high feeling existing at that time between Davis and his subordinate, whom I regarded as one of his ablest lieutenants.

On the 5th of October the railroad back from Atlanta was again very badly broken, Hood having got on the track with his army. Sherman saw after night, from a high point, the road burning for miles. The defence of the railroad by our troops was very gallant, but they could not hold points between their intrenched positions against Hood's whole army; in fact they made no attempt to do so; but generally the intrenched positions were held, as well as important bridges, and stores located at them. Allatoona, for instance, was defended by a small force of men under the command of General Corse, one of the very able and efficient volunteer officers produced by the war. He, with a small force, was cut off from the remainder of the National army and was attacked with great vigor by many times his own number. Sherman from his high position could see the battle raging, with the Confederate troops between him and his subordinate. He sent men, of course, to raise the temporary siege, but the time that would be necessarily consumed in reaching Corse, would be so great that all occupying the intrenchments might be dead. Corse was a man who would never surrender. From a high position some of Sherman's signal corps discovered a signal flag waving from a hole in the block house at Allatoona. It was from Corse. He had been shot through the face, but he signalled to his chief a message which left no doubt of his determination to hold his post at all hazards. It was at this point probably, that Sherman first realized that with the forces at his disposal, the keeping open of his line of communications with the North would be impossible if he expected to retain any force with which to operate offensively beyond Atlanta. He proposed, therefore, to destroy the roads back to Chattanooga, when all ready to move, and leave the latter place garrisoned. Yet, before abandoning the railroad, it was necessary that he should repair damages already done, and hold the road until he could get forward such supplies, ordnance stores and small rations, as he wanted to carry with him on his proposed march, and to return to the north his surplus artillery; his object being to move light and to have no more artillery than could be used to advantage on the field.

Sherman thought Hood would follow him, though he proposed to prepare for the contingency of the latter moving the other way while he was moving south, by making Thomas strong enough to hold Tennessee and Kentucky. I, myself, was thoroughly satisfied that Hood would go north, as he did. On the 2d of November I telegraphed Sherman authorizing him definitely to move according to the plan he had proposed: that is, cutting loose from his base, giving up Atlanta and the railroad back to Chattanooga. To strengthen Thomas he sent Stanley (4th corps) back, and also ordered Schofield, commanding the Army of the Ohio, twelve thousand strong, to report to him. In addition to this, A. J. Smith, who, with two divisions of Sherman's army, was in Missouri aiding Rosecrans in driving the enemy from that State, was under orders to return to Thomas and, under the most unfavorable circumstances, might be expected to arrive there long before Hood could reach Nashville.

In addition to this, the new levies of troops that were being raised in the North-west went to Thomas as rapidly as enrolled and equipped. Thomas, without any of these additions spoken of, had a garrison at Chattanooga—which had been strengthened by one division—and garrisons at Bridgeport, Stevenson, Decatur, Murfreesboro, and Florence. There were already with him in Nashville ten thousand soldiers in round numbers, and many thousands of employees in the quartermaster's and other departments who could be put in the intrenchments in front of Nashville, for its defence. Also, Wilson was there with ten thousand dismounted cavalrymen, who were being equipped for the field. Thomas had at this time about forty-five thousand men without any of the reinforcements here above enumerated. These reinforcements gave him altogether about seventy thousand men, without counting what might be added by the new levies already spoken of.

About this time Beauregard arrived upon the field, not to supersede Hood in command, but to take general charge over the entire district in which Hood and Sherman were, or might be, operating. He made the most frantic appeals to the citizens for assistance to be rendered in every way: by sending reinforcements, by destroying supplies on the line of march of the invaders, by destroying the bridges over which they would have to cross, and by, in every way, obstructing the roads to their front. But it was hard to convince the people of the propriety of destroying supplies which were so much

needed by themselves, and each one hoped that his own possessions might escape.

Hood soon started north, and went into camp near Decatur, Alabama, where he remained until the 29th of October,
but without making an attack on the garrison of that place.

The Tennessee River was patrolled by gunboats, from Muscle Shoals east; and, also, below the second shoals out to the
Ohio River. These, with the troops that might be concentrated from the garrisons along the river at any point where
Hood might choose to attempt to cross, made it impossible
for him to cross the Tennessee at any place where it was navigable. But Muscle Shoals is not navigable, and below them
again is another shoal which also obstructs navigation. Hood
therefore moved down to a point nearly opposite Florence,
Alabama, crossed over and remained there for some time, collecting supplies of food, forage and ammunition. All of these
had to come from a considerable distance south, because the
region in which he was then situated was mountainous, with
small valleys which produced but little, and what they had
produced had long since been exhausted. On the 1st of November I suggested to Sherman, and also asked his views
thereon, the propriety of destroying Hood before he started
on his campaign.

On the 2d of November, as stated, I approved definitely his
making his proposed campaign through Georgia, leaving
Hood behind to the tender mercy of Thomas and the troops
in his command. Sherman fixed the 10th of November as the
day of starting.

Sherman started on that day to get back to Atlanta, and on
the 15th the real march to the sea commenced. The right wing,
under Howard, and the cavalry went to Jonesboro, Milledgeville, then the capital of Georgia, being Sherman's objective or stopping place on the way to Savannah. The left wing
moved to Stone Mountain, along roads much farther east
than those taken by the right wing. Slocum was in command,
and threatened Augusta as the point to which he was moving,
but he was to turn off and meet the right wing at Milledgeville.

Atlanta was destroyed so far as to render it worthless for
military purposes before starting, Sherman himself remaining

over a day to superintend the work, and see that it was well done. Sherman's orders for this campaign were perfect. Before starting, he had sent back all sick, disabled and weak men, retaining nothing but the hardy, well-inured soldiers to accompany him on his long march in prospect. His artillery was reduced to sixty-five guns. The ammunition carried with them was two hundred rounds for musket and gun. Small rations were taken in a small wagon train, which was loaded to its capacity for rapid movement. The army was expected to live on the country, and to always keep the wagons full of forage and provisions against a possible delay of a few days.

The troops, both of the right and left wings, made most of their advance along the line of railroads, which they destroyed. The method adopted to perform this work, was to burn and destroy all the bridges and culverts, and for a long distance, at places, to tear up the track and bend the rails. Soldiers to do this rapidly would form a line along one side of the road with crowbars and poles, place these under the rails and, hoisting all at once, turn over many rods of road at one time. The ties would then be placed in piles, and the rails, as they were loosened, would be carried and put across these log heaps. When a sufficient number of rails were placed upon a pile of ties it would be set on fire. This would heat the rails very much more in the middle, that being over the main part of the fire, than at the ends, so that they would naturally bend of their own weight; but the soldiers, to increase the damage, would take tongs and, one or two men at each end of the rail, carry it with force against the nearest tree and twist it around, thus leaving rails forming bands to ornament the forest trees of Georgia. All this work was going on at the same time, there being a sufficient number of men detailed for that purpose. Some piled the logs and built the fire; some put the rails upon the fire; while others would bend those that were sufficiently heated: so that, by the time the last bit of road was torn up, that it was designed to destroy at a certain place, the rails previously taken up were already destroyed.

The organization for supplying the army was very complete. Each brigade furnished a company to gather supplies of

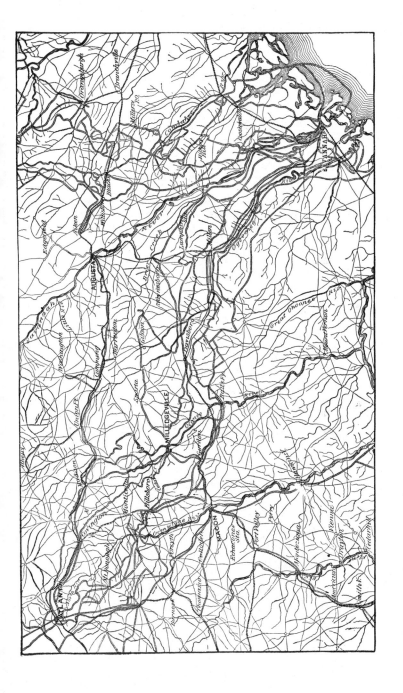

forage and provisions for the command to which they belonged. Strict injunctions were issued against pillaging, or otherwise unnecessarily annoying the people; but everything in shape of food for man and forage for beast was taken. The supplies were turned over to the brigade commissary and quartermaster, and were issued by them to their respective commands precisely the same as if they had been purchased. The captures consisted largely of cattle, sheep, poultry, some bacon, cornmeal, often molasses, and occasionally coffee or other small rations.

The skill of these men, called by themselves and the army "bummers," in collecting their loads and getting back to their respective commands, was marvellous. When they started out in the morning, they were always on foot; but scarcely one of them returned in the evening without being mounted on a horse or mule. These would be turned in for the general use of the army, and the next day these men would start out afoot and return again in the evening mounted.

Many of the exploits of these men would fall under the head of romance; indeed, I am afraid that in telling some of their experiences, the romance got the better of the truth upon which the story was founded, and that, in the way many of these anecdotes are told, very little of the foundation is left. I suspect that most of them consist chiefly of the fiction added to make the stories better. In one instance it was reported that a few men of Sherman's army passed a house where they discovered some chickens under the dwelling. They immediately proceeded to capture them, to add to the army's supplies. The lady of the house, who happened to be at home, made piteous appeals to have these spared, saying they were a few she had put away to save by permission of other parties who had preceded and who had taken all the others that she had. The soldiers seemed moved at her appeal; but looking at the chickens again they were tempted and one of them replied: "The rebellion must be suppressed if it takes the last chicken in the Confederacy," and proceeded to appropriate the last one.

Another anecdote characteristic of these times has been told. The South, prior to the rebellion, kept bloodhounds to pursue runaway slaves who took refuge in the neighboring swamps, and also to hunt convicts. Orders were issued to kill all these animals as they were met with. On one occasion a soldier picked up a poodle, the favorite pet of its mistress, and was carrying it off to execution when the lady made a strong appeal to him to spare it. The soldier replied, "Madam, our orders are to kill every bloodhound." "But this is not a bloodhound," said the lady. "Well, madam, we cannot tell what it will grow into if we leave it behind," said the soldier as he went off with it.

Notwithstanding these anecdotes, and the necessary hardship they would seem to imply, I do not believe there was much unwarrantable pillaging considering that we were in the enemy's territory and without any supplies except such as the country afforded.

On the 23d Sherman, with the left wing, reached Milledgeville. The right wing was not far off: but proceeded on its way towards Savannah destroying the road as it went. The troops at Milledgeville remained over a day to destroy factories, buildings used for military purposes, etc., before resuming its march.

The governor, who had been almost defying Mr. Davis before this, now fled precipitately, as did the legislature of the State and all the State officers. The governor, Sherman says, was careful to carry away even his garden vegetables, while he left the archives of the State to fall into our hands. The only military force that was opposed to Sherman's forward march was the Georgia militia, a division under the command of General G. W. Smith, and a battalion under Harry Wayne. Neither the quality of the forces nor their numbers was sufficient to even retard the progress of Sherman's army.

The people at the South became so frantic at this time at the successful invasion of Georgia that they took the cadets from the military college and added them to the ranks of the militia. They even liberated the State convicts under promise from them that they would serve in the army. I have but little doubt that the worst acts that were attributed to Sherman's army were committed by these convicts, and by other Southern people who ought to have been under sentence—such people as could be found in every community, North and South—who took advantage of their country being invaded to commit crime. They were in but little danger of detection, or of arrest even if detected.

The Southern papers in commenting upon Sherman's movements pictured him as in the most deplorable condition: stating that his men were starving, that they were demoralized and wandering about almost without object, aiming only to reach the sea coast and get under the protection of our navy. These papers got to the North and had more or less effect upon the minds of the people, causing much distress to all loyal persons—particularly to those who had husbands, sons or brothers with Sherman. Mr. Lincoln seeing these accounts, had a letter written asking me if I could give him anything that he could say to the loyal people that would comfort them. I told him there was not the slightest occasion for alarm; that with 60,000 such men as Sherman had with him, such a commanding officer as he was could not be cut off in the open country. He might possibly be prevented from reaching the point he had started out to reach, but he would get through somewhere and would finally get to his chosen destination: and even if worst came to worst he could return North. I heard afterwards of Mr. Lincoln's saying, to those who would inquire of him as to what he thought about the safety of Sherman's army, that Sherman was all right: "Grant says they are safe with such a general, and that if they cannot get out where they want to, they can crawl back by the hole they went in at."

While at Milledgeville the soldiers met at the State House, organized a legislature, and proceeded to business precisely as if they were the legislative body belonging to the State of Georgia. The debates were exciting, and were upon the subject of the situation the South was in at that time, particularly the State of Georgia. They went so far as to repeal, after a spirited and acrimonious debate, the ordinance of secession.

The next day (24th) Sherman continued his march, going by the way of Waynesboro and Louisville, Millen being the next objective and where the two columns (the right and left wings) were to meet. The left wing moved to the left of the direct road, and the cavalry still farther off so as to make it look as though Augusta was the point they were aiming for.

They moved on all the roads they could find leading in that direction. The cavalry was sent to make a rapid march in hope of surprising Millen before the Union prisoners could be carried away; but they failed in this.

The distance from Milledgeville to Millen was about one hundred miles. At this point Wheeler, who had been ordered from Tennessee, arrived and swelled the numbers and efficiency of the troops confronting Sherman. Hardee, a native of Georgia, also came, but brought no troops with him. It was intended that he should raise as large an army as possible with which to intercept Sherman's march. He did succeed in raising some troops, and with these and those under the command of Wheeler and Wayne, had an army sufficient to cause some annoyance but no great detention. Our cavalry and Wheeler's had a pretty severe engagement, in which Wheeler was driven towards Augusta, thus giving the idea that Sherman was probably making for that point.

Millen was reached on the 3d of December, and the march was resumed the following day for Savannah, the final objective. Bragg had now been sent to Augusta with some troops. Wade Hampton was there also trying to raise cavalry sufficient to destroy Sherman's army. If he ever raised a force it was too late to do the work expected of it. Hardee's whole force probably numbered less than ten thousand men.

From Millen to Savannah the country is sandy and poor, and affords but very little forage other than rice straw, which was then growing. This answered a very good purpose as forage, and the rice grain was an addition to the soldier's rations. No further resistance worthy of note was met with, until within a few miles of Savannah. This place was found to be intrenched and garrisoned. Sherman proceeded at once on his arrival to invest the place, and found that the enemy had placed torpedoes in the ground, which were to explode when stepped on by man or beast. One of these exploded under an officer's horse, blowing the animal to pieces and tearing one of the legs of the officer so badly that it had to be amputated. Sherman at once ordered his prisoners to the front, moving them in a compact body in advance, to either explode the torpedoes or dig them up. No further explosion took place.

On the 10th of December the siege of Savannah commenced. Sherman then, before proceeding any further with operations for the capture of the place, started with some troops to open communication with our fleet, which he expected to find in the lower harbor or as near by as the forts of the enemy would permit. In marching to the coast he encountered Fort McAllister, which it was necessary to reduce before the supplies he might find on shipboard could be made available. Fort McAllister was soon captured by an assault made by General Hazen's division. Communication was then established with the fleet. The capture of Savannah then only occupied a few days, and involved no great loss of life. The garrison, however, as we shall see, was enabled to escape by crossing the river and moving eastward.

When Sherman had opened communication with the fleet he found there a steamer, which I had forwarded to him, carrying the accumulated mails for his army, also supplies which I supposed he would be in need of. General J. G. Foster, who commanded all the troops south of North Carolina on the Atlantic sea-board, visited General Sherman before he had opened communication with the fleet, with the view of ascertaining what assistance he could be to him. Foster returned immediately to his own headquarters at Hilton Head, for the purpose of sending Sherman siege guns, and also if he should find he had them to spare, supplies of clothing, hard bread, etc., thinking that these articles might not be found outside. The mail on the steamer which I sent down, had been collected by Colonel A. H. Markland of the Post Office Department, who went in charge of it. On this same vessel I sent an officer of my staff (Lieutenant Dunn) with the following letter to General Sherman:

CITY POINT, VA., *Dec.* 3, 1864.
MAJOR-GENERAL W. T. SHERMAN,
Commanding Armies near Savannah, Ga.
The little information gleaned from the Southern press, indicating no great obstacle to your progress, I have directed your mails (which had been previously collected at Baltimore by Colonel Markland, Special Agent of the Post Office Department) to be sent as far as the blockading squadron off Savannah, to be forwarded to you as soon as heard from on the coast.

Not liking to rejoice before the victory is assured, I abstain from congratulating you and those under your command, until bottom has been struck. I have never had a fear, however, for the result.

Since you left Atlanta, no very great progress has been made here. The enemy has been closely watched though, and prevented from detaching against you. I think not one man has gone from here, except some twelve or fifteen hundred dismounted cavalry. Bragg has gone from Wilmington. I am trying to take advantage of his absence to get possession of that place. Owing to some preparations Admiral Porter and General Butler are making to blow up Fort Fisher (which, while hoping for the best, I do not believe a particle in), there is a delay in getting this expedition off. I hope they will be ready to start by the 7th, and that Bragg will not have started back by that time.

In this letter I do not intend to give you anything like directions for future action, but will state a general idea I have, and will get your views after you have established yourself on the sea-coast. With your veteran army I hope to get control of the only two through routes from east to west possessed by the enemy before the fall of Atlanta. The condition will be filled by holding Savannah and Augusta, or by holding any other port to the east of Savannah and Branchville. If Wilmington falls, a force from there can co-operate with you.

Thomas has got back into the defences of Nashville, with Hood close upon him. Decatur has been abandoned, and so have all the roads except the main one leading to Chattanooga. Part of this falling back was undoubtedly necessary, and all of it may have been. It did not look so, however, to me. In my opinion, Thomas far outnumbers Hood in infantry. In cavalry, Hood has the advantage in *morale* and numbers. I hope yet that Hood will be badly crippled if not destroyed. The general news you will learn from the papers better than I could give it.

After all becomes quiet, and roads become so bad up here that there is likely to be a week or two when nothing can be done, I will run down the coast to see you. If you desire it, I will ask Mrs. Sherman to go with me.

Yours truly,
U. S. GRANT,
Lieutenant-General.

I quote this letter because it gives the reader a full knowledge of the events of that period.

Sherman now (the 15th) returned to Savannah to complete

its investment and insure the surrender of the garrison. The country about Savannah is low and marshy, and the city was well intrenched from the river above to the river below, and assaults could not be made except along a comparatively narrow causeway. For this reason assaults must have resulted in serious destruction of life to the Union troops, with the chance of failing altogether. Sherman therefore decided upon a complete investment of the place. When he believed this investment completed, he summoned the garrison to surrender. General Hardee, who was in command, replied in substance that the condition of affairs was not such as Sherman had described. He said he was in full communication with his department and was receiving supplies constantly.

Hardee, however, was cut off entirely from all communication with the west side of the river, and by the river itself to the north and south. On the South Carolina side the country was all rice fields, through which it would have been impossible to bring supplies—so that Hardee had no possible communication with the outside world except by a dilapidated plank road starting from the west bank of the river. Sherman, receiving this reply, proceeded in person to a point on the coast, where General Foster had troops stationed under General Hatch, for the purpose of making arrangements with the latter officer to go through by one of the numerous channels running inland along that part of the coast of South Carolina, to the plank road which General Hardee still possessed, and thus to cut him off from the last means he had of getting supplies, if not of communication.

While arranging for this movement, and before the attempt to execute the plan had been commenced, Sherman received information through one of his staff officers that the enemy had evacuated Savannah the night before. This was the night of the 21st of December. Before evacuating the place Hardee had blown up the navy yard. Some iron-clads had been destroyed, as well as other property that might have been valuable to us; but he left an immense amount of stores untouched, consisting of cotton, railroad cars, workshops, numerous pieces of artillery, and several thousand stands of small arms.

A little incident occurred, soon after the fall of Savannah,

which Sherman relates in his Memoirs, and which is worthy
of repetition. Savannah was one of the points where blockade
runners entered. Shortly after the city fell into our possession,
a blockade runner came sailing up serenely, not doubting but
the Confederates were still in possession. It was not molested,
and the captain did not find out his mistake until he had tied
up and gone to the Custom House, where he found a new
occupant of the building, and made a less profitable disposition of his vessel and cargo than he had expected.

As there was some discussion as to the authorship of Sherman's march to the sea, by critics of his book when it appeared before the public, I want to state here that no question
upon that subject was ever raised between General Sherman
and myself. Circumstances made the plan on which Sherman
expected to act impracticable, and as commander of the forces
he necessarily had to devise a new one which would give
more promise of success: consequently he recommended the
destruction of the railroad back to Chattanooga, and that he
should be authorized then to move, as he did, from Atlanta
forward. His suggestions were finally approved, although
they did not immediately find favor in Washington. Even
when it came to the time of starting, the greatest apprehension, as to the propriety of the campaign he was about to
commence, filled the mind of the President, induced no doubt
by his advisers. This went so far as to move the President to
ask me to suspend Sherman's march for a day or two until I
could think the matter over. My recollection is, though I find
no record to show it, that out of deference to the President's
wish I did send a dispatch to Sherman asking him to wait a
day or two, or else the connections between us were already
cut so that I could not do so. However this may be, the question of who devised the plan of march from Atlanta to Savannah is easily answered: it was clearly Sherman, and to him
also belongs the credit of its brilliant execution. It was hardly
possible that any one else than those on the spot could have
devised a new plan of campaign to supersede one that did not
promise success.*

***

*See Appendix, letters of Oct. 11th.

I was in favor of Sherman's plan from the time it was first submitted to me. My chief of staff, however, was very bitterly opposed to it and, as I learned subsequently, finding that he could not move me, he appealed to the authorities at Washington to stop it.

Chapter LX.

A S WE have seen, Hood succeeded in crossing the Tennessee River between Muscle Shoals and the lower shoals
at the end of October, 1864. Thomas sent Schofield with the
4th and 23d corps, together with three brigades of Wilson's
cavalry to Pulaski to watch him. On the 17th of November
Hood started and moved in such a manner as to avoid Schofield, thereby turning his position. Hood had with him three
infantry corps, commanded respectively by Stephen D. Lee,
Stewart and Cheatham. These, with his cavalry, numbered
about forty-five thousand men. Schofield had, of all arms,
about thirty thousand. Thomas's orders were, therefore, for
Schofield to watch the movements of the enemy, but not to
fight a battle if he could avoid it; but to fall back in case of an
advance on Nashville, and to fight the enemy, as he fell back,
so as to retard the enemy's movements until he could be reinforced by Thomas himself. As soon as Schofield saw this
movement of Hood's, he sent his trains to the rear, but did
not fall back himself until the 21st, and then only to Columbia. At Columbia there was a slight skirmish but no battle.
From this place Schofield then retreated to Franklin. He had
sent his wagons in advance, and Stanley had gone with them
with two divisions to protect them. Cheatham's corps of
Hood's army pursued the wagon train and went into camp at
Spring Hill, for the night of the 29th.

Schofield retreating from Columbia on the 29th, passed
Spring Hill, where Cheatham was bivouacked, during the
night without molestation, though within half a mile of
where the Confederates were encamped. On the morning of
the 30th he had arrived at Franklin.

Hood followed closely and reached Franklin in time to
make an attack the same day. The fight was very desperate
and sanguinary. The Confederate generals led their men in
the repeated charges, and the loss among them was of unusual
proportions. This fighting continued with great severity until
long after the night closed in, when the Confederates drew

off. General Stanley, who commanded two divisions of the Union troops, and whose troops bore the brunt of the battle, was wounded in the fight, but maintained his position.

The enemy's loss at Franklin, according to Thomas's report, was 1,750 buried upon the field by our troops, 3,800 in the hospital, and 702 prisoners besides. Schofield's loss, as officially reported, was 189 killed, 1,033 wounded, and 1,104 captured and missing.

Thomas made no effort to reinforce Schofield at Franklin, as it seemed to me at the time he should have done, and fight out the battle there. He simply ordered Schofield to continue his retreat to Nashville, which the latter did during that night and the next day.

Thomas, in the meantime, was making his preparations to receive Hood. The road to Chattanooga was still well guarded with strong garrisons at Murfreesboro, Stevenson, Bridgeport and Chattanooga. Thomas had previously given up Decatur and had been reinforced by A. J. Smith's two divisions just returned from Missouri. He also had Steedman's division and R. S. Granger's, which he had drawn from the front. His quartermaster's men, about ten thousand in number, had been organized and armed under the command of the chief quartermaster, General J. L. Donaldson, and placed in the fortifications under the general supervision of General Z. B. Tower, of the United States Engineers.

Hood was allowed to move upon Nashville, and to invest that place almost without interference. Thomas was strongly fortified in his position, so that he would have been safe against the attack of Hood. He had troops enough even to annihilate him in the open field. To me his delay was unaccountable—sitting there and permitting himself to be invested, so that, in the end, to raise the siege he would have to fight the enemy strongly posted behind fortifications. It is true the weather was very bad. The rain was falling and freezing as it fell, so that the ground was covered with a sheet of ice, that made it very difficult to move. But I was afraid that the enemy would find means of moving, elude Thomas and manage to get north of the Cumberland River. If he did this, I apprehended most serious results from the campaign in the North, and was afraid we might even have to send troops from the East to head him off if he got there, General Thomas's movements being always so deliberate and so slow, though effective in defence.

I consequently urged Thomas in frequent dispatches sent from City Point* to make the attack at once. The country was alarmed, the administration was alarmed, and I was alarmed lest the very thing would take place which I have just described—that is, Hood would get north. It was all without avail further than to elicit dispatches from Thomas saying that he was getting ready to move as soon as he could,

---

*City Point, Va., *December* 2, 1864.

Major-General Thomas,
    Nashville, Tenn.

If Hood is permitted to remain quietly about Nashville, you will lose all the road back to Chattanooga and possibly have to abandon the line of the Tennessee. Should he attack you it is all well, but if he does not you should attack him before he fortifies. Arm and put in the trenches your quartermaster employees, citizens, etc.

U. S. GRANT,
Lieutenant-General.

City Point, Va., *December* 2, 1864.—1.30 p.m.

Major-General Thomas,
    Nashville, Tenn.

With your citizen employees armed, you can move out of Nashville with all your army and force the enemy to retire or fight upon ground of your own choosing. After the repulse of Hood at Franklin, it looks to me that instead of falling back to Nashville we should have taken the offensive against the enemy where he was. At this distance, however, I may err as to the best method of dealing with the enemy. You will now suffer incalculable injury upon your railroads if Hood is not speedily disposed of. Put forth therefore every possible exertion to attain this end. Should you get him to retreating give him no peace.

U. S. GRANT,
Lieutenant-General.

City Point, Va., *December* 5, 1864.

Major-General Thomas,
    Nashville, Tenn.

Is there not danger of Forrest moving down the Cumberland to where he can cross it? It seems to me whilst you should be getting up your cavalry as rapidly as possible to look after Forrest, Hood should be attacked where he is. Time strengthens him in all possibility as much as it does you.

U. S. GRANT,
Lieutenant-General.

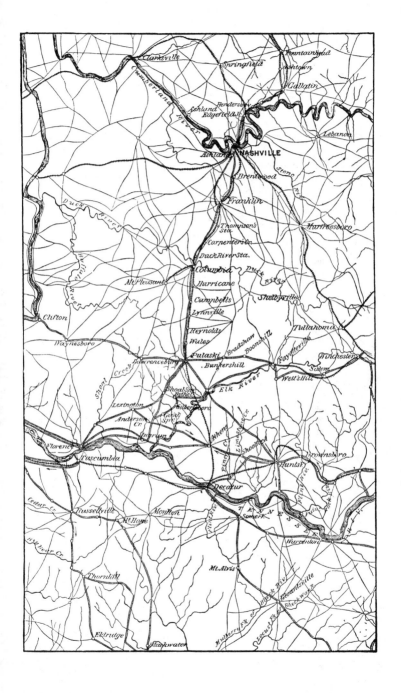

that he was making preparations, etc. At last I had to say to General Thomas that I should be obliged to remove him unless he acted promptly. He replied that he was very sorry, but he would move as soon as he could.

General Logan happening to visit City Point about that time, and knowing him as a prompt, gallant and efficient officer, I gave him an order to proceed to Nashville to relieve Thomas. I directed him, however, not to deliver the order or

---

CITY POINT, VA., *December* 6, 1864. — 4 P.M.

MAJOR-GENERAL THOMAS,
    Nashville, Tenn.

Attack Hood at once and wait no longer for a remnant of your cavalry. There is great danger of delay resulting in a campaign back to the Ohio River.

U. S. GRANT,
Lieutenant-General.

CITY POINT, VA., *December* 8, 1864. — 8.30 P.M.

MAJOR-GENERAL THOMAS,
    Nashville, Tenn.

Your dispatch of yesterday received. It looks to me evident the enemy are trying to cross the Cumberland River, and are scattered. Why not attack at once? By all means avoid the contingency of a foot race to see which, you or Hood, can beat to the Ohio. If you think necessary call on the governors of States to send a force into Louisville to meet the enemy if he should cross the river. You clearly never should cross except in rear of the enemy. Now is one of the finest opportunities ever presented of destroying one of the three armies of the enemy. If destroyed he never can replace it. Use the means at your command, and you can do this and cause a rejoicing that will resound from one end of the land to the other.

U. S. GRANT,
Lieutenant-General.

CITY POINT, VA., *December* 11, 1864. — 4 P.M.

MAJOR-GENERAL THOMAS,
    Nashville, Tenn.

If you delay attack longer the mortifying spectacle will be witnessed of a rebel army moving for the Ohio River, and you will be forced to act, accepting such weather as you find. Let there be no further delay. Hood cannot even stand a drawn battle so far from his supplies of ordnance stores. If he retreats and you follow, he must lose his material and much of his army. I am in hopes of receiving a dispatch from you to-day announcing that you have moved. Delay no longer for weather or reinforcements.

U. S. GRANT,
Lieutenant-General.

publish it until he reached there, and if Thomas had moved, then not to deliver it at all, but communicate with me by telegraph. After Logan started, in thinking over the situation, I became restless, and concluded to go myself. I went as far as Washington City, when a dispatch was received from General Thomas announcing his readiness at last to move, and designating the time of his movement. I concluded to wait until that time. He did move, and was successful from the start. This was on the 15th of December. General Logan was at Louisville at the time this movement was made, and telegraphed the fact to Washington, and proceeded no farther himself.

The battle during the 15th was severe, but favorable to the Union troops, and continued until night closed in upon the combat. The next day the battle was renewed. After a successful assault upon Hood's men in their intrenchments the enemy fled in disorder, routed and broken, leaving their dead, their artillery and small arms in great numbers on the field, besides the wounded that were captured. Our cavalry had fought on foot as infantry, and had not their horses with them; so that they were not ready to join in the pursuit the moment the enemy retreated. They sent back, however, for their horses, and endeavored to get to Franklin ahead of Hood's broken army by the Granny White Road, but too much time was consumed in getting started. They had got but a few miles beyond the scene of the battle when they found the enemy's cavalry dismounted and behind intrenchments covering the road on which they were advancing. Here another battle ensued, our men dismounting and fighting on

---

WASHINGTON, D. C., *December* 15, 1864.

MAJOR-GENERAL THOMAS,
        Nashville, Tenn.

I was just on my way to Nashville, but receiving a dispatch from Van Dutzer detailing your splendid success of to-day, I shall go no further. Push the enemy now and give him no rest until he is entirely destroyed. Your army will cheerfully suffer many privations to break up Hood's army and render it useless for future operations. Do not stop for trains or supplies, but take them from the country as the enemy have done. Much is now expected.

U. S. GRANT,
Lieutenant-General.

foot, in which the Confederates were again routed and driven in great disorder. Our cavalry then went into bivouac, and renewed the pursuit on the following morning. They were too late. The enemy already had possession of Franklin, and was beyond them. It now became a chase in which the Confederates had the lead.

Our troops continued the pursuit to within a few miles of Columbia, where they found the rebels had destroyed the railroad bridge as well as all other bridges over Duck River. The heavy rains of a few days before had swelled the stream into a mad torrent, impassable except on bridges. Unfortunately, either through a mistake in the wording of the order or otherwise, the pontoon bridge which was to have been sent by rail out to Franklin, to be taken thence with the pursuing column, had gone toward Chattanooga. There was, consequently, a delay of some four days in building bridges out of the remains of the old railroad bridge. Of course Hood got such a start in this time that farther pursuit was useless, although it was continued for some distance, but without coming upon him again.

Chapter LXI.

EXPEDITION AGAINST FORT FISHER—ATTACK ON THE
FORT—FAILURE OF THE EXPEDITION—SECOND
EXPEDITION AGAINST THE FORT—CAPTURE OF
FORT FISHER.

U P TO JANUARY, 1865, the enemy occupied Fort Fisher, at the mouth of Cape Fear River and below the City of Wilmington. This port was of immense importance to the Confederates, because it formed their principal inlet for blockade runners by means of which they brought in from abroad such supplies and munitions of war as they could not produce at home. It was equally important to us to get possession of it, not only because it was desirable to cut off their supplies so as to insure a speedy termination of the war, but also because foreign governments, particularly the British Government, were constantly threatening that unless ours could maintain the blockade of that coast they should cease to recognize any blockade. For these reasons I determined, with the concurrence of the Navy Department, in December, to send an expedition against Fort Fisher for the purpose of capturing it.

To show the difficulty experienced in maintaining the blockade, I will mention a circumstance that took place at Fort Fisher after its fall. Two English blockade runners came in at night. Their commanders, not supposing the fort had fallen, worked their way through all our fleet and got into the river unobserved. They then signalled the fort, announcing their arrival. There was a colored man in the fort who had been there before and who understood these signals. He informed General Terry what reply he should make to have them come in, and Terry did as he advised. The vessels came in, their officers entirely unconscious that they were falling into the hands of the Union forces. Even after they were brought in to the fort they were entertained in conversation for some little time before suspecting that the Union troops were occupying the fort. They were finally informed that their vessels and cargoes were prizes.

I selected General Weitzel, of the Army of the James, to go with the expedition, but gave instructions through General Butler. He commanded the department within whose geographical limits Fort Fisher was situated, as well as Beaufort and other points on that coast held by our troops; he was, therefore, entitled to the right of fitting out the expedition against Fort Fisher.

General Butler conceived the idea that if a steamer loaded heavily with powder could be run up to near the shore under the fort and exploded, it would create great havoc and make the capture an easy matter. Admiral Porter, who was to command the naval squadron, seemed to fall in with the idea, and it was not disapproved of in Washington; the navy was therefore given the task of preparing the steamer for this purpose. I had no confidence in the success of the scheme, and so expressed myself; but as no serious harm could come of the experiment, and the authorities at Washington seemed desirous to have it tried, I permitted it. The steamer was sent to Beaufort, North Carolina, and was there loaded with powder and prepared for the part she was to play in the reduction of Fort Fisher.

General Butler chose to go in command of the expedition himself, and was all ready to sail by the 9th of December (1864). Very heavy storms prevailed, however, at that time along that part of the sea-coast, and prevented him from getting off until the 13th or 14th. His advance arrived off Fort Fisher on the 15th. The naval force had been already assembled, or was assembling, but they were obliged to run into Beaufort for munitions, coal, etc.; then, too, the powder-boat was not yet fully prepared. The fleet was ready to proceed on the 18th; but Butler, who had remained outside from the 15th up to that time, now found himself out of coal, fresh water, etc., and had to put into Beaufort to replenish. Another storm overtook him, and several days more were lost before the army and navy were both ready at the same time to co-operate.

On the night of the 23d the powder-boat was towed in by a gunboat as near to the fort as it was safe to run. She was then propelled by her own machinery to within about five hundred yards of the shore. There the clockwork, which was to explode her within a certain length of time, was set and she was abandoned. Everybody left, and even the vessels put out to sea to prevent the effect of the explosion upon them. At two o'clock in the morning the explosion took place—and produced no more effect on the fort, or anything else on land, than the bursting of a boiler anywhere on the Atlantic Ocean would have done. Indeed when the troops in Fort Fisher heard the explosion they supposed it was the bursting of a boiler in one of the Yankee gunboats.

Fort Fisher was situated upon a low, flat peninsula north of Cape Fear River. The soil is sandy. Back a little the peninsula is very heavily wooded, and covered with fresh-water swamps. The fort ran across this peninsula, about five hundred yards in width, and extended along the sea coast about thirteen hundred yards. The fort had an armament of 21 guns and 3 mortars on the land side, and 24 guns on the sea front. At that time it was only garrisoned by four companies of infantry, one light battery and the gunners at the heavy guns—less than seven hundred men—with a reserve of less than a thousand men five miles up the peninsula. General Whiting of the Confederate army was in command, and General Bragg was in command of the force at Wilmington. Both commenced calling for reinforcements the moment they saw our troops landing. The Governor of North Carolina called for everybody who could stand behind a parapet and shoot a gun, to join them. In this way they got two or three hundred additional men into Fort Fisher; and Hoke's division, five or six thousand strong, was sent down from Richmond. A few of these troops arrived the very day that Butler was ready to advance.

On the 24th the fleet formed for an attack in arcs of concentric circles, their heavy iron-clads going in very close range, being nearest the shore, and leaving intervals or spaces so that the outer vessels could fire between them. Porter was thus enabled to throw one hundred and fifteen shells per minute. The damage done to the fort by these shells was very slight, only two or three cannon being disabled in the fort. But the firing silenced all the guns by making it too hot for the men to maintain their positions about them and compelling them to seek shelter in the bomb-proofs.

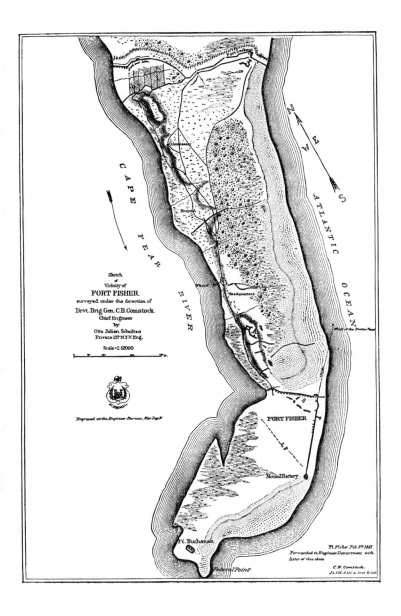

Sketch
of
Vicinity of
FORT FISHER
surveyed under the direction of
Brvt. Brig. Gen. C.B. Comstock
Chief Engineer
by
Otto Julian Schultze
Private 15ᵗʰ N.Y.V. Eng.

Scale = 1:12000

Engraved at the Engineer Bureau, War Dep't

FORT FISHER

Ft. Fisher Feb. 3ᵈ 1865
Forwarded to Engineer Department with
letter of this date
C.B. Comstock,
Lt. Col. A.D.C & Bvvt B. Gen.

CAPE FEAR RIVER

ATLANTIC OCEAN

Commissary

Hospital

Wharf Sᵗᵉ

Headquarters

Wreck of the Powder Vessel

Mound Battery

F.Y. Buchanan

Federal Point

Fort Lamb

On the next day part of Butler's troops under General Adelbert Ames effected a landing out of range of the fort without difficulty. This was accomplished under the protection of gunboats sent for the purpose, and under cover of a renewed attack upon the fort by the fleet. They formed a line across the peninsula and advanced, part going north and part toward the fort, covering themselves as they did so. Curtis pushed forward and came near to Fort Fisher, capturing the small garrison at what was called the Flag Pond Battery. Weitzel accompanied him to within a half a mile of the works. Here he saw that the fort had not been injured, and so reported to Butler, advising against an assault. Ames, who had gone north in his advance, captured 228 of the reserves. These prisoners reported to Butler that sixteen hundred of Hoke's division of six thousand from Richmond had already arrived and the rest would soon be in his rear.

Upon these reports Butler determined to withdraw his troops from the peninsula and return to the fleet. At that time there had not been a man on our side injured except by one of the shells from the fleet. Curtis had got within a few yards of the works. Some of his men had snatched a flag from the parapet of the fort, and others had taken a horse from the inside of the stockade. At night Butler informed Porter of his withdrawal, giving the reasons above stated, and announced his purpose as soon as his men could embark to start for Hampton Roads. Porter represented to him that he had sent to Beaufort for more ammunition. He could fire much faster than he had been doing, and would keep the enemy from showing himself until our men were within twenty yards of the fort, and he begged that Butler would leave some brave fellows like those who had snatched the flag from the parapet and taken the horse from the fort.

Butler was unchangeable. He got all his troops aboard, except Curtis's brigade, and started back. In doing this, Butler made a fearful mistake. My instructions to him, or to the officer who went in command of the expedition, were explicit in the statement that to effect a landing would be of itself a great victory, and if one should be effected, the foothold must not be relinquished; on the contrary, a regular siege of the fort must be commenced and, to guard against interference by reason of storms, supplies of provisions must be laid in as soon as they could be got on shore. But General Butler seems to have lost sight of this part of his instructions, and was back at Fort Monroe on the 28th.

I telegraphed to the President as follows:

CITY POINT, VA.,
Dec. 28, 1864. —8.30 P.M.

The Wilmington expedition has proven a gross and culpable failure. Many of the troops are back here. Delays and free talk of the object of the expedition enabled the enemy to move troops to Wilmington to defeat it. After the expedition sailed from Fort Monroe, three days of fine weather were squandered, during which the enemy was without a force to protect himself. Who is to blame will, I hope, be known.

U. S. GRANT,
Lieutenant-General.

Porter sent dispatches to the Navy Department in which he complained bitterly of having been abandoned by the army just when the fort was nearly in our possession, and begged that our troops might be sent back again to co-operate, but with a different commander. As soon as I heard this I sent a messenger to Porter with a letter asking him to hold on. I assured him that I fully sympathized with him in his disappointment, and that I would send the same troops back with a different commander, with some reinforcements to offset those which the enemy had received. I told him it would take some little time to get transportation for the additional troops; but as soon as it could be had the men should be on their way to him, and there would be no delay on my part. I selected A. H. Terry to command.

It was the 6th of January before the transports could be got ready and the troops aboard. They sailed from Fortress Monroe on that day. The object and destination of the second expedition were at the time kept a secret to all except a few in the Navy Department and in the army to whom it was necessary to impart the information. General Terry had not the slightest idea of where he was going or what he was to do. He simply knew that he was going to sea and that he had his orders with him, which were to be opened when out at sea.

He was instructed to communicate freely with Porter and have entire harmony between army and navy, because the work before them would require the best efforts of both arms of the service. They arrived off Beaufort on the 8th. A heavy storm, however, prevented a landing at Fort Fisher until the 13th. The navy prepared itself for attack about as before, and at the same time assisted the army in landing, this time five miles away. Only iron-clads fired at first; the object being to draw the fire of the enemy's guns so as to ascertain their positions. This object being accomplished, they then let in their shots thick and fast. Very soon the guns were all silenced, and the fort showed evident signs of being much injured.

Terry deployed his men across the peninsula as had been done before, and at two o'clock on the following morning was up within two miles of the fort with a respectable *abatis* in front of his line. His artillery was all landed on that day, the 14th. Again Curtis's brigade of Ames's division had the lead. By noon they had carried an unfinished work less than a half mile from the fort, and turned it so as to face the other way.

Terry now saw Porter and arranged for an assault on the following day. The two commanders arranged their signals so that they could communicate with each other from time to time as they might have occasion. At daylight the fleet commenced its firing. The time agreed upon for the assault was the middle of the afternoon, and Ames who commanded the assaulting column moved at 3.30. Porter landed a force of sailors and marines to move against the sea-front in co-operation with Ames's assault. They were under Commander Breese of the navy. These sailors and marines had worked their way up to within a couple of hundred yards of the fort before the assault. The signal was given and the assault was made; but the poor sailors and marines were repulsed and very badly handled by the enemy, losing 280 killed and wounded out of their number.

Curtis's brigade charged successfully though met by a heavy fire, some of the men having to wade through the swamp up to their waists to reach the fort. Many were wounded, of course, and some killed; but they soon reached the palisades. These they cut away, and pushed on through. The other troops then came up, Pennypacker's following Curtis, and Bell, who commanded the 3d brigade of Ames's division, following Pennypacker. But the fort was not yet captured though the parapet was gained.

The works were very extensive. The large parapet around the work would have been but very little protection to those inside except when they were close up under it. Traverses had, therefore, been run until really the work was a succession of small forts enclosed by a large one. The rebels made a desperate effort to hold the fort, and had to be driven from these traverses one by one. The fight continued till long after night. Our troops gained first one traverse and then another, and by 10 o'clock at night the place was carried. During this engagement the sailors, who had been repulsed in their assault on the bastion, rendered the best service they could by reinforcing Terry's northern line—thus enabling him to send a detachment to the assistance of Ames. The fleet kept up a continuous fire upon that part of the fort which was still occupied by the enemy. By means of signals they could be informed where to direct their shots.

During the succeeding nights the enemy blew up Fort Caswell on the opposite side of Cape Fear River, and abandoned two extensive works on Smith's Island in the river.

Our captures in all amounted to 169 guns, besides small-arms, with full supplies of ammunition, and 2,083 prisoners. In addition to these, there were about 700 dead and wounded left there. We had lost 110 killed and 536 wounded.

In this assault on Fort Fisher, Bell, one of the brigade commanders, was killed, and two, Curtis and Pennypacker, were badly wounded.

Secretary Stanton, who was on his way back from Savannah, arrived off Fort Fisher soon after it fell. When he heard the good news he promoted all the officers of any considerable rank for their conspicuous gallantry. Terry had been nominated for major-general, but had not been confirmed. This confirmed him; and soon after I recommended him for a brigadier-generalcy in the regular army, and it was given to him for this victory.

Chapter LXII.

WHEN NEWS of Sherman being in possession of Savannah reached the North, distinguished statesmen and visitors began to pour in to see him. Among others who went was the Secretary of War, who seemed much pleased at the result of his campaign. Mr. Draper, the collector of customs of New York, who was with Mr. Stanton's party, was put in charge of the public property that had been abandoned and captured. Savannah was then turned over to General Foster's command to hold, so that Sherman might have his own entire army free to operate as might be decided upon in the future. I sent the chief engineer of the Army of the Potomac (General Barnard) with letters to General Sherman. He remained some time with the general, and when he returned brought back letters, one of which contained suggestions from Sherman as to what ought to be done in co-operation with him, when he should have started upon his march northward.

I must not neglect to state here the fact that I had no idea originally of having Sherman march from Savannah to Richmond, or even to North Carolina. The season was bad, the roads impassable for anything except such an army as he had, and I should not have thought of ordering such a move. I had, therefore, made preparations to collect transports to carry Sherman and his army around to the James River by water, and so informed him. On receiving this letter he went to work immediately to prepare for the move, but seeing that it would require a long time to collect the transports, he suggested the idea then of marching up north through the Carolinas. I was only too happy to approve this; for if successful, it promised every advantage. His march through Georgia had thoroughly destroyed all lines

of transportation in that State, and had completely cut the
enemy off from all sources of supply to the west of it. If
North and South Carolina were rendered helpless so far as
capacity for feeding Lee's army was concerned, the Confederate garrison at Richmond would be reduced in territory, from which to draw supplies, to very narrow limits in
the State of Virginia; and, although that section of the country was fertile, it was already well exhausted of both forage and food. I approved Sherman's suggestion therefore at
once.

The work of preparation was tedious, because supplies, to
load the wagons for the march, had to be brought from a
long distance. Sherman would now have to march through a
country furnishing fewer provisions than that he had previously been operating in during his march to the sea. Besides,
he was confronting, or marching toward, a force of the
enemy vastly superior to any his troops had encountered on
their previous march; and the territory through which he
had to pass had now become of such vast importance to the
very existence of the Confederate army, that the most desperate efforts were to be expected in order to save it.

Sherman, therefore, while collecting the necessary supplies
to start with, made arrangements with Admiral Dahlgren,
who commanded that part of the navy on the South Carolina
and Georgia coast, and General Foster, commanding the
troops, to take positions, and hold a few points on the sea
coast, which he (Sherman) designated, in the neighborhood
of Charleston.

This provision was made to enable him to fall back upon
the sea coast, in case he should encounter a force sufficient
to stop his onward progress. He also wrote me a letter, making suggestions as to what he would like to have done in
support of his movement farther north. This letter was
brought to City Point by General Barnard at a time when I
happened to be going to Washington City, where I arrived
on the 21st of January. I cannot tell the provision I had already made to co-operate with Sherman, in anticipation of
his expected movement, better than by giving my reply to
this letter.

HEADQUARTERS ARMIES OF THE UNITED STATES,
Washington, D. C., *Jan.* 21, 1865.

MAJOR-GENERAL W. T. SHERMAN,
Commanding Mil. Div. of the Mississippi.

GENERAL: — Your letters brought by General Barnard were received at City Point, and read with interest. Not having them with me, however, I cannot say that in this I will be able to satisfy you on all points of recommendation. As I arrived here at one P.M., and must leave at six P.M., having in the meantime spent over three hours with the Secretary and General Halleck, I must be brief. Before your last request to have Thomas make a campaign into the heart of Alabama, I had ordered Schofield to Annapolis, Md., with his corps. The advance (six thousand) will reach the seaboard by the 23d, the remainder following as rapidly as railroad transportation can be procured from Cincinnati. The corps numbers over twenty-one thousand men. I was induced to do this because I did not believe Thomas could possibly be got off before spring. His pursuit of Hood indicated a sluggishness that satisfied me that he would never do to conduct one of your campaigns. The command of the advance of the pursuit was left to subordinates, whilst Thomas followed far behind. When Hood had crossed the Tennessee, and those in pursuit had reached it, Thomas had not much more than half crossed the State, from whence he returned to Nashville to take steamer for Eastport. He is possessed of excellent judgment, great coolness and honesty, but he is not good on a pursuit. He also reported his troops fagged, and that it was necessary to equip up. This report and a determination to give the enemy no rest determined me to use his surplus troops elsewhere.

Thomas is still left with a sufficient force surplus to go to Selma under an energetic leader. He has been telegraphed to, to know whether he could go, and, if so, which of the several routes he would select. No reply is yet received. Canby has been ordered to act offensively from the sea-coast to the interior, towards Montgomery and Selma. Thomas's forces will move from the north at an early day, or some of his troops will be sent to Canby. Without further reinforcements Canby will have a moving column of twenty thousand men.

Fort Fisher, you are aware, has been captured. We have a force there of eight thousand effective. At New Bern about half the number. It is rumored, through deserters, that Wilmington also has fallen. I am inclined to believe the rumor, because on the 17th we knew the enemy were blowing up their works about Fort Caswell, and that on the 18th Terry moved on Wilmington.

If Wilmington is captured, Schofield will go there. If not, he will be sent to New Bern. In either event, all the surplus forces at the two points will move to the interior toward Goldsboro' in co-operation with your movements. From either point, railroad communications can be run out, there being here abundance of rolling-stock suited to the gauge of those roads.

There have been about sixteen thousand men sent from Lee's army south. Of these, you will have fourteen thousand against you, if Wilmington is not held by the enemy, casualties at Fort Fisher having overtaken about two thousand.

All these troops are subject to your orders as you come in communication with them. They will be so instructed. From about Richmond I will watch Lee closely, and if he detaches much more, or attempts to evacuate, will pitch in. In the meantime, should you be brought to a halt anywhere, I can send two corps of thirty thousand effective men to your support, from the troops about Richmond.

To resume: Canby is ordered to operate to the interior from the Gulf. A. J. Smith may go from the north, but I think it doubtful. A force of twenty-eight or thirty thousand will co-operate with you from New Bern or Wilmington, or both. You can call for reinforcements.

This will be handed you by Captain Hudson, of my staff, who will return with any message you may have for me. If there is anything I can do for you in the way of having supplies on ship-board, at any point on the sea-coast, ready for you, let me know it.

Yours truly,
U. S. GRANT,
Lieut.-General.

I had written on the 18th of January to General Sherman, giving him the news of the battle of Nashville. He was much pleased at the result, although, like myself, he had been very much disappointed at Thomas for permitting Hood to cross the Tennessee River and nearly the whole State of Tennessee, and come to Nashville to be attacked there. He, however, as I had done, sent Thomas a warm congratulatory letter.

On the 10th of January, 1865, the resolutions of thanks to Sherman and his army passed by Congress were approved.

Sherman, after the capture, at once had the *débris* in Savannah cleared up, commencing the work by removing the piling and torpedoes from the river, and taking up all other obstructions. He had then intrenched the city, so that it could be held by a small garrison. By the middle of January all his work was done, except the accumulation of supplies to commence his movements with.

He proposed to move in two columns, one from Savannah, going along by the river of the same name, and the other by roads farther east, threatening Charleston. He commenced the advance by moving his right wing to Beaufort, South Carolina, then to Pocotaligo by water. This column, in moving north, threatened Charleston, and, indeed, it was not determined at first that they would not have a force visit Charleston. South Carolina had done so much to prepare the public mind of the South for secession, and had been so active in precipitating the decision of the question before the South was fully prepared to meet it, that there was, at that time, a feeling throughout the North and also largely entertained by people of the South, that the State of South Carolina, and Charleston, the hot-bed of secession in particular, ought to have a heavy hand laid upon them. In fact, nothing but the decisive results that followed, deterred the radical portion of the people from condemning the movement, because Charleston had been left out. To pass into the interior would, however, be to insure the evacuation of the city, and its possession by the navy and Foster's troops. It is so situated between two formidable rivers that a small garrison could have held it against all odds as long as their supplies would hold out. Sherman therefore passed it by.

By the first of February all preparations were completed for the final march, Columbia, South Carolina, being the first objective; Fayetteville, North Carolina, the second; and Goldsboro, or neighborhood, the final one, unless something further should be determined upon. The right wing went from Pocotaligo, and the left from about Hardeeville on the Savannah River, both columns taking a pretty direct route for Columbia. The cavalry, however, were to threaten Charleston on the right, and Augusta on the left.

On the 15th of January Fort Fisher had fallen, news of which Sherman had received before starting out on his march. We already had New Bern and had soon Wilmington, whose fall followed that of Fort Fisher; as did other points on the sea coast, where the National troops were now in readiness to co-operate with Sherman's advance when he had passed Fayetteville.

On the 18th of January I ordered Canby, in command at New Orleans, to move against Mobile, Montgomery and Selma, Alabama, for the purpose of destroying roads, machine shops, etc. On the 8th of February I ordered Sheridan, who was in the Valley of Virginia, to push forward as soon as the weather would permit and strike the canal west of Richmond at or about Lynchburg; and on the 20th I made the order to go to Lynchburg as soon as the roads would permit, saying: "As soon as it is possible to travel, I think you will have no difficulty about reaching Lynchburg with a cavalry force alone. From there you could destroy the railroad and canal in every direction, so as to be of no further use to the rebellion. * * * This additional raid, with one starting from East Tennessee under Stoneman, numbering about four or five thousand cavalry; one from Eastport, Mississippi, ten thousand cavalry; Canby, from Mobile Bay, with about eighteen thousand mixed troops—these three latter pushing for Tuscaloosa, Selma and Montgomery; and Sherman with a large army eating out the vitals of South Carolina—is all that will be wanted to leave nothing for the rebellion to stand upon. I would advise you to overcome great obstacles to accomplish this. Charleston was evacuated on Tuesday last."

On the 27th of February, more than a month after Canby had received his orders, I again wrote to him, saying that I was extremely anxious to hear of his being in Alabama. I notified him, also, that I had sent Grierson to take command of his cavalry, he being a very efficient officer. I further suggested that Forrest was probably in Mississippi, and if he was there, he would find him an officer of great courage and capacity whom it would be difficult to get by. I still further informed him that Thomas had been ordered to start a cavalry force into Mississippi on the 20th of February, or as soon as possible thereafter. This force did not get off however.

All these movements were designed to be in support of Sherman's march, the object being to keep the Confederate troops in the West from leaving there. But neither Canby nor Thomas could be got off in time. I had some time before

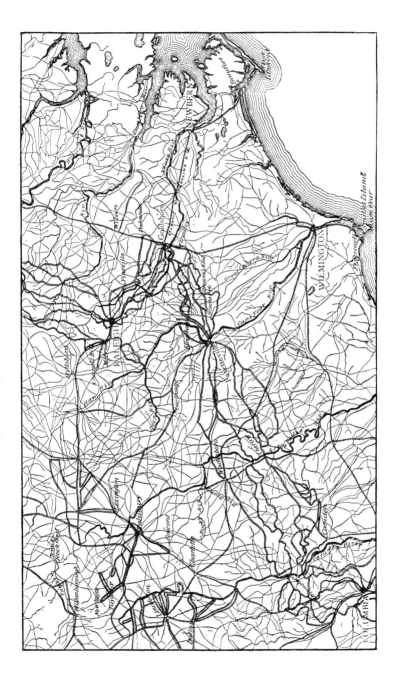

depleted Thomas's army to reinforce Canby, for the reason that Thomas had failed to start an expedition which he had been ordered to send out, and to have the troops where they might do something. Canby seemed to be equally deliberate in all of his movements. I ordered him to go in person; but he prepared to send a detachment under another officer. General Granger had got down to New Orleans, in some way or other, and I wrote Canby that he must not put him in command of troops. In spite of this he asked the War Department to assign Granger to the command of a corps.

Almost in despair of having adequate service rendered to the cause in that quarter, I said to Canby: "I am in receipt of a dispatch * * * informing me that you have made requisitions for a construction corps and material to build seventy miles of railroad. I have directed that none be sent. Thomas's army has been depleted to send a force to you that they might be where they could act in winter, and at least detain the force the enemy had in the West. If there had been any idea of repairing railroads, it could have been done much better from the North, where we already had the troops. I expected your movements to be co-operative with Sherman's last. This has now entirely failed. I wrote to you long ago, urging you to push promptly and to live upon the country, and destroy railroads, machine shops, etc., not to build them. Take Mobile and hold it, and push your forces to the interior—to Montgomery and to Selma. Destroy railroads, rolling stock, and everything useful for carrying on war, and, when you have done this, take such positions as can be supplied by water. By this means alone you can occupy positions from which the enemy's roads in the interior can be kept broken."

Most of these expeditions got off finally, but too late to render any service in the direction for which they were designated.

The enemy, ready to intercept his advance, consisted of Hardee's troops and Wheeler's cavalry, perhaps less than fifteen thousand men in all; but frantic efforts were being made in Richmond, as I was sure would be the case, to retard Sherman's movements. Everything possible was being done to raise troops in the South. Lee dispatched against Sherman the troops which had been sent to relieve Fort Fisher, which, including those of the other defences of the harbor and its neighborhood, amounted, after deducting the two thousand killed, wounded and captured, to fourteen thousand men. After Thomas's victory at Nashville what remained, of Hood's army were gathered together and forwarded as rapidly as possible to the east to co-operate with these forces; and, finally, General Joseph E. Johnston, one of the ablest commanders of the South though not in favor with the administration (or at least with Mr. Davis), was put in command of all the troops in North and South Carolina.

Schofield arrived at Annapolis in the latter part of January, but before sending his troops to North Carolina I went with him down the coast to see the situation of affairs, as I could give fuller directions after being on the ground than I could very well have given without. We soon returned, and the troops were sent by sea to Cape Fear River. Both New Bern and Wilmington are connected with Raleigh by railroads which unite at Goldsboro. Schofield was to land troops at Smithville, near the mouth of the Cape Fear River on the west side, and move up to secure the Wilmington and Charlotteville Railroad. This column took their pontoon bridges with them, to enable them to cross over to the island south of the city of Wilmington. A large body was sent by the north side to co-operate with them. They succeeded in taking the city on the 22d of February. I took the precaution to provide for Sherman's army, in case he should be forced to turn in toward the sea coast before reaching North Carolina, by forwarding supplies to every place where he was liable to have to make such a deflection from his projected march. I also sent railroad rolling stock, of which we had a great abundance, now that we were not operating the roads in Virginia. The gauge of the North Carolina railroads being the same as the Virginia railroads had been altered too; these cars and locomotives were ready for use there without any change.

On the 31st of January I countermanded the orders given to Thomas to move south to Alabama and Georgia. (I had previously reduced his force by sending a portion of it to Terry.) I directed in lieu of this movement, that he should send Stoneman through East Tennessee, and push him well down toward Columbia, South Carolina, in support of Sherman.

Thomas did not get Stoneman off in time, but, on the contrary, when I had supposed he was on his march in support of Sherman I heard of his being in Louisville, Kentucky. I immediately changed the order, and directed Thomas to send him toward Lynchburg. Finally, however, on the 12th of March, he did push down through the north-western end of South Carolina, creating some consternation. I also ordered Thomas to send the 4th corps (Stanley's) to Bull Gap and to destroy no more roads east of that. I also directed him to concentrate supplies at Knoxville, with a view to a probable movement of his army through that way toward Lynchburg.

Goldsboro is four hundred and twenty-five miles from Savannah. Sherman's march was without much incident until he entered Columbia, on the 17th of February. He was detained in his progress by having to repair and corduroy the roads, and rebuild the bridges. There was constant skirmishing and fighting between the cavalry of the two armies, but this did not retard the advance of the infantry. Four days, also, were lost in making complete the destruction of the most important railroads south of Columbia; there was also some delay caused by the high water, and the destruction of the bridges on the line of the road. A formidable river had to be crossed near Columbia, and that in the face of a small garrison under General Wade Hampton. There was but little delay, however, further than that caused by high water in the stream. Hampton left as Sherman approached, and the city was found to be on fire.

There has since been a great deal of acrimony displayed in discussions of the question as to who set Columbia on fire. Sherman denies it on the part of his troops, and Hampton denies it on the part of the Confederates. One thing is certain: as soon as our troops took possession, they at once proceeded to extinguish the flames to the best of their ability with the limited means at hand. In any case, the example set by the Confederates in burning the village of Chambersburg, Pa., a town which was not garrisoned, would seem to make a defence of the act of firing the seat of government of the State most responsible for the conflict then raging, not imperative.

The Confederate troops having vacated the city, the mayor took possession, and sallied forth to meet the commander of the National forces for the purpose of surrendering the town, making terms for the protection of property, etc. Sherman paid no attention at all to the overture, but pushed forward and took the town without making any conditions whatever with its citizens. He then, however, co-operated with the mayor in extinguishing the flames and providing for the people who were rendered destitute by this destruction of their homes. When he left there he even gave the mayor five hundred head of cattle to be distributed among the citizens, to tide them over until some arrangement could be made for their future supplies. He remained in Columbia until the roads, public buildings, work-shops and everything that could be useful to the enemy were destroyed. While at Columbia, Sherman learned for the first time that what remained of Hood's army was confronting him, under the command of General Beauregard.

Charleston was evacuated on the 18th of February, and Foster garrisoned the place. Wilmington was captured on the 22d. Columbia and Cheraw farther north, were regarded as so secure from invasion that the wealthy people of Charleston and Augusta had sent much of their valuable property to these two points to be stored. Among the goods sent there were valuable carpets, tons of old Madeira, silverware, and furniture. I am afraid much of these goods fell into the hands of our troops. There was found at Columbia a large amount of powder, some artillery, small-arms and fixed ammunition. These, of course, were among the articles destroyed. While here, Sherman also learned of Johnston's restoration to command. The latter was given, as already stated, all troops in North and South Carolina. After the completion of the destruction of public property about Columbia, Sherman proceeded on his march and reached Cheraw without any special opposition and without incident to relate. The railroads, of course, were thoroughly destroyed on the way. Sherman remained a day or two at Cheraw; and, finally, on the 6th of March crossed his troops over the Pedee and advanced straight for Fayetteville. Hardee and Hampton were there, and barely escaped. Sherman reached Fayetteville on the 11th of March. He had dispatched scouts from Cheraw with letters to General Terry, at Wilmington, asking him to send a

steamer with some supplies of bread, clothing and other articles which he enumerated. The scouts got through successfully, and a boat was sent with the mail and such articles for
which Sherman had asked as were in store at Wilmington;
unfortunately, however, those stores did not contain clothing.

Four days later, on the 15th, Sherman left Fayetteville for
Goldsboro. The march, now, had to be made with great caution, for he was approaching Lee's army and nearing the
country that still remained open to the enemy. Besides, he
was confronting all that he had had to confront in his previous march up to that point, reinforced by the garrisons along
the road and by what remained of Hood's army. Frantic appeals were made to the people to come in voluntarily and
swell the ranks of our foe. I presume, however, that Johnston
did not have in all over 35,000 or 40,000 men. The people
had grown tired of the war, and desertions from the Confederate army were much more numerous than the voluntary
accessions.

There was some fighting at Averysboro on the 16th between
Johnston's troops and Sherman's, with some loss; and at Bentonville on the 19th and 21st of March, but Johnston withdrew
from the contest before the morning of the 22d. Sherman's
loss in these last engagements in killed, wounded, and missing, was about sixteen hundred. Sherman's troops at last
reached Goldsboro on the 23d of the month and went into
bivouac; and there his men were destined to have a long rest.
Schofield was there to meet him with the troops which had
been sent to Wilmington.

Sherman was no longer in danger. He had Johnston confronting him; but with an army much inferior to his own,
both in numbers and morale. He had Lee to the north of him
with a force largely superior; but I was holding Lee with a
still greater force, and had he made his escape and gotten
down to reinforce Johnston, Sherman, with the reinforcements he now had from Schofield and Terry, would have been
able to hold the Confederates at bay for an indefinite period.
He was near the sea-shore with his back to it, and our navy
occupied the harbors. He had a railroad to both Wilmington
and New Bern, and his flanks were thoroughly protected by
streams, which intersect that part of the country and deepen

as they approach the sea. Then, too, Sherman knew that if Lee should escape me I would be on his heels, and he and Johnston together would be crushed in one blow if they attempted to make a stand. With the loss of their capital, it is doubtful whether Lee's army would have amounted to much as an army when it reached North Carolina. Johnston's army was demoralized by constant defeat and would hardly have made an offensive movement, even if they could have been induced to remain on duty. The men of both Lee's and Johnston's armies were, like their brethren of the North, as brave as men can be; but no man is so brave that he may not meet such defeats and disasters as to discourage him and dampen his ardor for any cause, no matter how just he deems it.

Chapter LXIII.

ARRIVAL OF THE PEACE COMMISSIONERS—LINCOLN
AND THE PEACE COMMISSIONERS—AN ANECDOTE
OF LINCOLN—THE WINTER BEFORE
PETERSBURG—SHERIDAN DESTROYS THE RAILROAD—
GORDON CARRIES THE PICKET LINE—PARKE
RECAPTURES THE LINE—THE BATTLE OF
WHITE OAK ROAD.

O N THE LAST of January, 1865, peace commissioners from the so-called Confederate States presented themselves on our lines around Petersburg, and were immediately conducted to my headquarters at City Point. They proved to be Alexander H. Stephens, Vice-President of the Confederacy, Judge Campbell, Assistant-Secretary of War, and R. M. T. Hunter, formerly United States Senator and then a member of the Confederate Senate.

It was about dark when they reached my headquarters, and I at once conducted them to the steamer *Mary Martin*, a Hudson River boat which was very comfortably fitted up for the use of passengers. I at once communicated by telegraph with Washington and informed the Secretary of War and the President of the arrival of these commissioners and that their object was to negotiate terms of peace between the United States and, as they termed it, the Confederate Government. I was instructed to retain them at City Point, until the President, or some one whom he would designate, should come to meet them. They remained several days as guests on board the boat. I saw them quite frequently, though I have no recollection of having had any conversation whatever with them on the subject of their mission. It was something I had nothing to do with, and I therefore did not wish to express any views on the subject. For my own part I never had admitted, and never was ready to admit, that they were the representatives of a *government*. There had been too great a waste of blood and treasure to concede anything of the kind. As long as they remained there, however, our relations were pleasant and I found them all very agreeable gentlemen. I directed the captain to furnish them with the best the boat afforded, and to administer to their comfort in every way possible. No guard was placed over them and no restriction was put upon their movements; nor was there any pledge asked that they would not abuse the privileges extended to them. They were permitted to leave the boat when they felt like it, and did so, coming up on the bank and visiting me at my headquarters.

I had never met either of these gentlemen before the war, but knew them well by reputation and through their public services, and I had been a particular admirer of Mr. Stephens. I had always supposed that he was a very small man, but when I saw him in the dusk of the evening I was very much surprised to find so large a man as he seemed to be. When he got down on to the boat I found that he was wearing a coarse gray woollen overcoat, a manufacture that had been introduced into the South during the rebellion. The cloth was thicker than anything of the kind I had ever seen, even in Canada. The overcoat extended nearly to his feet, and was so large that it gave him the appearance of being an average-sized man. He took this off when he reached the cabin of the boat, and I was struck with the apparent change in size, in the coat and out of it.

After a few days, about the 2d of February, I received a dispatch from Washington, directing me to send the commissioners to Hampton Roads to meet the President and a member of the cabinet. Mr. Lincoln met them there and had an interview of short duration. It was not a great while after they met that the President visited me at City Point. He spoke of his having met the commissioners, and said he had told them that there would be no use in entering into any negotiations unless they would recognize, first: that the Union as a whole must be forever preserved, and second: that slavery must be abolished. If they were willing to concede these two points, then he was ready to enter into negotiations and was almost willing to hand them a blank sheet of paper with his signature attached for them to fill in the terms upon which they were willing to live with us in the Union and be one people. He always showed a generous and kindly spirit toward the Southern people, and I never heard him abuse an enemy. Some of the cruel things said about President Lincoln, particularly in the North, used to pierce him to the heart; but never in my presence did he evince a revengeful disposition—and I saw a great deal of him at City Point, for he seemed glad to get away from the cares and anxieties of the capital.

Right here I might relate an anecdote of Mr. Lincoln. It was on the occasion of his visit to me just after he had talked with the peace commissioners at Hampton Roads. After a little conversation, he asked me if I had seen that overcoat of Stephens's. I replied that I had. "Well," said he, "did you see him take it off?" I said yes. "Well," said he, "didn't you think it was the biggest shuck and the littlest ear that ever you did see?" Long afterwards I told this story to the Confederate General J. B. Gordon, at the time a member of the Senate. He repeated it to Stephens, and, as I heard afterwards, Stephens laughed immoderately at the simile of Mr. Lincoln.

The rest of the winter, after the departure of the peace commissioners, passed off quietly and uneventfully, except for two or three little incidents. On one occasion during this period, while I was visiting Washington City for the purpose of conferring with the administration, the enemy's cavalry under General Wade Hampton, passing our extreme left and then going to the south, got in east of us. Before their presence was known, they had driven off a large number of beef cattle that were grazing in that section. It was a fair capture, and they were sufficiently needed by the Confederates. It was only retaliating for what we had done, sometimes for many weeks at a time, when out of supplies—taking what the Confederate army otherwise would have gotten. As appears in this book, on one single occasion we captured five thousand head of cattle which were crossing the Mississippi River near Port Hudson on their way from Texas to supply the Confederate army in the East.

One of the most anxious periods of my experience during the rebellion was the last few weeks before Petersburg. I felt that the situation of the Confederate army was such that they would try to make an escape at the earliest practicable moment, and I was afraid, every morning, that I would awake from my sleep to hear that Lee had gone, and that nothing was left but a picket line. He had his railroad by the way of

Danville south, and I was afraid that he was running off his men and all stores and ordnance except such as it would be necessary to carry with him for his immediate defence. I knew he could move much more lightly and more rapidly than I, and that, if he got the start, he would leave me behind so that we would have the same army to fight again farther south—and the war might be prolonged another year.

I was led to this fear by the fact that I could not see how it was possible for the Confederates to hold out much longer where they were. There is no doubt that Richmond would have been evacuated much sooner than it was, if it had not been that it was the capital of the so-called Confederacy, and the fact of evacuating the capital would, of course, have had a very demoralizing effect upon the Confederate army. When it was evacuated (as we shall see further on), the Confederacy at once began to crumble and fade away. Then, too, desertions were taking place, not only among those who were with General Lee in the neighborhood of their capital, but throughout the whole Confederacy. I remember that in a conversation with me on one occasion long prior to this, General Butler remarked that the Confederates would find great difficulty in getting more men for their army; possibly adding, though I am not certain as to this, "unless they should arm the slave."

The South, as we all knew, were conscripting every able-bodied man between the ages of eighteen and forty-five; and now they had passed a law for the further conscription of boys from fourteen to eighteen, calling them the junior reserves, and men from forty-five to sixty to be called the senior reserves. The latter were to hold the necessary points not in immediate danger, and especially those in the rear. General Butler, in alluding to this conscription, remarked that they were thus "robbing both the cradle and the grave," an expression which I afterwards used in writing a letter to Mr. Washburn.

It was my belief that while the enemy could get no more recruits they were losing at least a regiment a day, taking it throughout the entire army, by desertions alone. Then by casualties of war, sickness, and other natural causes, their losses were much heavier. It was a mere question of arithmetic to calculate how long they could hold out while that rate of depletion was going on. Of course long before their army would be thus reduced to nothing the army which we had in the field would have been able to capture theirs. Then too I knew from the great number of desertions, that the men who had fought so bravely, so gallantly and so long for the cause which they believed in—and as earnestly, I take it, as our men believed in the cause for which they were fighting—had lost hope and become despondent. Many of them were making application to be sent North where they might get employment until the war was over, when they could return to their Southern homes.

For these and other reasons I was naturally very impatient for the time to come when I could commence the spring campaign, which I thoroughly believed would close the war.

There were two considerations I had to observe, however, and which detained me. One was the fact that the winter had been one of heavy rains, and the roads were impassable for artillery and teams. It was necessary to wait until they had dried sufficiently to enable us to move the wagon trains and artillery necessary to the efficiency of an army operating in the enemy's country. The other consideration was that General Sheridan with the cavalry of the Army of the Potomac was operating on the north side of the James River, having come down from the Shenandoah. It was necessary that I should have his cavalry with me, and I was therefore obliged to wait until he could join me south of the James River.

Let us now take account of what he was doing.

On the 5th of March I had heard from Sheridan. He had met Early between Staunton and Charlottesville and defeated him, capturing nearly his entire command. Early and some of his officers escaped by finding refuge in the neighboring houses or in the woods.

On the 12th I heard from him again. He had turned east, to come to White House. He could not go to Lynchburg as ordered, because the rains had been so very heavy and the streams were so very much swollen. He had a pontoon train with him, but it would not reach half way across some of the streams, at their then stage of water, which he would have to get over in going south as first ordered.

I had supplies sent around to White House for him, and kept the depot there open until he arrived. We had intended to abandon it because the James River had now become our base of supplies.

Sheridan had about ten thousand cavalry with him, divided into two divisions commanded respectively by Custer and Devin. General Merritt was acting as chief of cavalry. Sheridan moved very light, carrying only four days' provisions with him, with a larger supply of coffee, salt and other small rations, and a very little else besides ammunition. They stopped at Charlottesville and commenced tearing up the railroad back toward Lynchburg. He also sent a division along the James River Canal to destroy locks, culverts, etc. All mills and factories along the lines of march of his troops were destroyed also.

Sheridan had in this way consumed so much time that his making a march to White House was now somewhat hazardous. He determined therefore to fight his way along the railroad and canal till he was as near to Richmond as it was possible to get, or until attacked. He did this, destroying the canal as far as Goochland, and the railroad to a point as near Richmond as he could get. On the 10th he was at Columbia. Negroes had joined his column to the number of two thousand or more, and they assisted considerably in the work of destroying the railroads and the canal. His cavalry was in as fine a condition as when he started, because he had been able to find plenty of forage. He had captured most of Early's horses and picked up a good many others on the road. When he reached Ashland he was assailed by the enemy in force. He resisted their assault with part of his command, moved quickly across the South and North Anna, going north, and reached White House safely on the 19th.

The time for Sherman to move had to be fixed with reference to the time he could get away from Goldsboro where he then was. Supplies had to be got up to him which would last him through a long march, as there would probably not be much to be obtained in the country through which he would pass. I had to arrange, therefore, that he should start from where he was, in the neighborhood of Goldsboro, on the 18th of April, the earliest day at which he supposed he could be ready.

Sherman was anxious that I should wait where I was until he could come up, and make a sure thing of it; but I had determined to move as soon as the roads and weather would admit of my doing so. I had been tied down somewhat in the matter of fixing any time at my pleasure for starting, until Sheridan, who was on his way from the Shenandoah Valley to join me, should arrive, as both his presence and that of his cavalry were necessary to the execution of the plans which I had in mind. However, having arrived at White House on the 19th of March, I was enabled to make my plans.

Prompted by my anxiety lest Lee should get away some night before I was aware of it, and having the lead of me, push into North Carolina to join with Johnston in attempting to crush out Sherman, I had, as early as the 1st of the month of March, given instructions to the troops around Petersburg to keep a sharp lookout to see that such a movement should not escape their notice, and to be ready to strike at once if it was undertaken.

It is now known that early in the month of March Mr. Davis and General Lee had a consultation about the situation of affairs in and about Richmond and Petersburg, and they both agreed that these places were no longer tenable for them, and that they must get away as soon as possible. They, too, were waiting for dry roads, or a condition of the roads which would make it possible to move.

General Lee, in aid of his plan of escape, and to secure a wider opening to enable them to reach the Danville Road with greater security than he would have in the way the two armies were situated, determined upon an assault upon the right of our lines around Petersburg. The night of the 24th of March was fixed upon for this assault, and General Gordon was assigned to the execution of the plan. The point between Fort Stedman and Battery No. 10, where our lines were closest together, was selected as the point of his attack. The attack was to be made at night, and the troops were to get possession of the higher ground in the rear where they supposed we had intrenchments, then sweep to the right and left, create a panic in the lines of our army, and force me to contract my lines. Lee hoped this would detain me a few days longer and give him an opportunity of escape. The plan was well conceived and the execution of it very well done indeed, up to the point of carrying a portion of our line.

Gordon assembled his troops under the cover of night, at the point at which they were to make their charge, and got possession of our picket-line, entirely without the knowledge of the troops inside of our main line of intrenchments; this reduced the distance he would have to charge over to not much more than fifty yards. For some time before the deserters had been coming in with great frequency, often bringing their arms with them, and this the Confederate general knew. Taking advantage of this knowledge he sent his pickets, with their arms, creeping through to ours as if to desert. When they got to our lines they at once took possession and sent our pickets to the rear as prisoners. In the main line our men were sleeping serenely, as if in great security. This plan was to have been executed and much damage done before daylight; but the troops that were to reinforce Gordon had to be brought from the north side of the James River and, by some accident on the railroad on their way over, they were detained for a considerable time; so that it got to be nearly daylight before they were ready to make the charge.

The charge, however, was successful and almost without loss, the enemy passing through our lines between Fort Stedman and Battery No. 10. Then turning to the right and left they captured the fort and the battery, with all the arms and troops in them. Continuing the charge, they also carried batteries Eleven and Twelve to our left, which they turned toward City Point.

Meade happened to be at City Point that night, and this break in his line cut him off from all communication with his headquarters. Parke, however, commanding the 9th corps when this breach took place, telegraphed the facts to Meade's headquarters, and learning that the general was away, assumed command himself and with commendable promptitude made all preparations to drive the enemy back. General Tidball gathered a large number of pieces of artillery and planted them in rear of the captured works so as to sweep the narrow space of ground between the lines very thoroughly. Hartranft was soon out with his division, as also was Willcox. Hartranft to the right of the breach headed the rebels off in that direction and rapidly drove them back into Fort Sted- man. On the other side they were driven back into the in- trenchments which they had captured, and batteries eleven and twelve were retaken by Willcox early in the morning.

Parke then threw a line around outside of the captured fort and batteries, and communication was once more established. The artillery fire was kept up so continuously that it was im- possible for the Confederates to retreat, and equally impossi- ble for reinforcements to join them. They all, therefore, fell captives into our hands. This effort of Lee's cost him about four thousand men, and resulted in their killing, wounding and capturing about two thousand of ours.

After the recapture of the batteries taken by the Confeder- ates, our troops made a charge and carried the enemy's in- trenched picket line, which they strengthened and held. This, in turn, gave us but a short distance to charge over when our attack came to be made a few days later.

The day that Gordon was making dispositions for this at- tack (24th of March) I issued my orders for the movement to commence on the 29th. Ord, with three divisions of infantry and Mackenzie's cavalry, was to move in advance on the night of the 27th, from the north side of the James River and take his place on our extreme left, thirty miles away. He left Weit- zel with the rest of the Army of the James to hold Bermuda Hundred and the north of the James River. The engineer bri- gade was to be left at City Point, and Parke's corps in the lines about Petersburg.*

Ord was at his place promptly. Humphreys and Warren were then on our extreme left with the 2d and 5th corps. They were directed on the arrival of Ord, and on his getting into position in their places, to cross Hatcher's Run and extend out west toward Five Forks, the object being to get into a position from which we could strike the South Side Railroad and ultimately the Danville Railroad. There was considerable

*See orders to Major-Generals Meade, Ord, and Sheridan, March 24th, Appendix.

fighting in taking up these new positions for the 2d and 5th corps, in which the Army of the James had also to participate somewhat, and the losses were quite severe.

This was what was known as the battle of White Oak Road.

Chapter LXIV.

SHERIDAN reached City Point on the 26th day of March. His horses, of course, were jaded and many of them had lost their shoes. A few days of rest were necessary to recuperate the animals and also to have them shod and put in condition for moving. Immediately on General Sheridan's arrival at City Point I prepared his instructions for the move which I had decided upon. The movement was to commence on the 29th of the month.

After reading the instructions I had given him, Sheridan walked out of my tent, and I followed to have some conversation with him by himself—not in the presence of anybody else, even of a member of my staff. In preparing his instructions I contemplated just what took place; that is to say, capturing Five Forks, driving the enemy from Petersburg and Richmond and terminating the contest before separating from the enemy. But the Nation had already become restless and discouraged at the prolongation of the war, and many believed that it would never terminate except by compromise. Knowing that unless my plan proved an entire success it would be interpreted as a disastrous defeat, I provided in these instructions that in a certain event he was to cut loose from the Army of the Potomac and his base of supplies, and living upon the country proceed south by the way of the Danville Railroad, or near it, across the Roanoke, get in the rear of Johnston, who was guarding that road, and co-operate with Sherman in destroying Johnston; then with these combined forces to help carry out the instructions which Sherman already had received, to act in co-operation with the armies around Petersburg and Richmond.

I saw that after Sheridan had read his instructions he seemed somewhat disappointed at the idea, possibly, of having to cut loose again from the Army of the Potomac, and place himself between the two main armies of the enemy. I said to him: "General, this portion of your instructions I have put in merely as a blind;" and gave him the reason for doing so, heretofore described. I told him that, as a matter of fact, I intended to close the war right here, with this movement, and that he should go no farther. His face at once brightened up, and slapping his hand on his leg he said: "I am glad to hear it, and we can do it."

Sheridan was not however to make his movement against Five Forks until he got further instructions from me.

One day, after the movement I am about to describe had commenced, and when his cavalry was on our extreme left and far to the rear, south, Sheridan rode up to where my headquarters were then established, at Dabney's Mills. He met some of my staff officers outside, and was highly jubilant over the prospects of success, giving reasons why he believed this would prove the final and successful effort. Although my chief-of-staff had urged very strongly that we return to our position about City Point and in the lines around Petersburg, he asked Sheridan to come in to see me and say to me what he had been saying to them. Sheridan felt a little modest about giving his advice where it had not been asked; so one of my staff came in and told me that Sheridan had what they considered important news, and suggested that I send for him. I did so, and was glad to see the spirit of confidence with which he was imbued. Knowing as I did from experience, of what great value that feeling of confidence by a commander was, I determined to make a movement at once, although on account of the rains which had fallen after I had started out the roads were still very heavy. Orders were given accordingly.

Finally the 29th of March came, and fortunately there having been a few days free from rain, the surface of the ground was dry, giving indications that the time had come when we could move. On that date I moved out with all the army available after leaving sufficient force to hold the line about Petersburg. It soon set in raining again however, and in a very short time the roads became practically impassable for teams, and almost so for cavalry. Sometimes a horse or mule would be standing apparently on firm ground, when all at once one foot would sink, and as he commenced scrambling to catch himself all his feet would sink and he would have to be drawn by hand out of the quicksands so common in that part of Virginia and other southern States. It became necessary therefore to build corduroy roads every foot of the way as we advanced, to move our artillery upon. The army had become so accustomed to this kind of work, and were so well prepared for it, that it was done very rapidly. The next day, March 30th, we had made sufficient progress to the south-west to warrant me in starting Sheridan with his cavalry over by Dinwiddie with instructions to then come up by the road leading north-west to Five Forks, thus menacing the right of Lee's line.

This movement was made for the purpose of extending our lines to the west as far as practicable towards the enemy's extreme right, or Five Forks. The column moving detached from the army still in the trenches was, excluding the cavalry, very small. The forces in the trenches were themselves extending to the left flank. Warren was on the extreme left when the extension began, but Humphreys was marched around later and thrown into line between him and Five Forks.

My hope was that Sheridan would be able to carry Five Forks, get on the enemy's right flank and rear, and force them to weaken their centre to protect their right so that an assault in the centre might be successfully made. General Wright's corps had been designated to make this assault, which I intended to order as soon as information reached me of Sheridan's success. He was to move under cover as close to the enemy as he could get.

It is natural to suppose that Lee would understand my design to be to get up to the South Side and ultimately to the Danville Railroad, as soon as he had heard of the movement commenced on the 29th. These roads were so important to his very existence while he remained in Richmond and Petersburg, and of such vital importance to him even in case of retreat, that naturally he would make most strenuous efforts to defend them. He did on the 30th send Pickett with five brigades to reinforce Five Forks. He also sent around to the right of his army some two or three other divisions, besides directing that other troops be held in readiness on the north side of the James River to come over on call. He came over himself to superintend in person the defence of his right flank.

Sheridan moved back to Dinwiddie Court-House on the night of the 30th, and then took a road leading north-west to Five Forks. He had only his cavalry with him. Soon encountering the rebel cavalry he met with a very stout resistance. He gradually drove them back however until in the neighborhood of Five Forks. Here he had to encounter other troops besides those he had been contending with, and was forced to give way.

In this condition of affairs he notified me of what had taken place and stated that he was falling back toward Dinwiddie gradually and slowly, and asked me to send Wright's corps to his assistance. I replied to him that it was impossible to send Wright's corps because that corps was already in line close up to the enemy, where we should want to assault when the proper time came, and was besides a long distance from him; but the 2d (Humphreys's) and 5th (Warren's) corps were on our extreme left and a little to the rear of it in a position to threaten the left flank of the enemy at Five Forks, and that I would send Warren.

Accordingly orders were sent to Warren to move at once that night (the 31st) to Dinwiddie Court House and put himself in communication with Sheridan as soon as possible, and report to him. He was very slow in moving, some of his troops not starting until after 5 o'clock next morning. When he did move it was done very deliberately, and on arriving at Gravelly Run he found the stream swollen from the recent rains so that he regarded it as not fordable. Sheridan of course knew of his coming, and being impatient to get the troops up as soon as possible, sent orders to him to hasten. He was also hastened or at least ordered to move up rapidly by General Meade. He now felt that he could not cross that creek without bridges, and his orders were changed to move so as to strike the pursuing enemy in flank or get in their rear; but he was so late in getting up that Sheridan determined to move forward without him. However, Ayres's division of Warren's corps reached him in time to be in the fight all day, most of

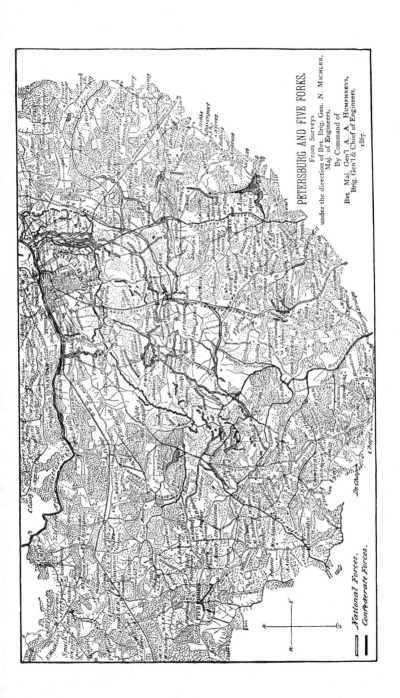

PETERSBURG AND FIVE FORKS.

From Surveys
under the direction of Bvt. Brig. Gen. N. MICHLER,
Maj. of Engineers,
By Command of
Bvt. Maj. Gen'l A. A. HUMPHREYS,
Brig. Gen'l & Chief of Engineers.
1867.

National Forces.
Confederate Forces.

the time separated from the remainder of the 5th corps and fighting directly under Sheridan.

Warren reported to Sheridan about 11 o'clock on the 1st, but the whole of his troops were not up so as to be much engaged until late in the afternoon. Griffin's division in backing to get out of the way of a severe cross fire of the enemy was found marching away from the fighting. This did not continue long, however; the division was brought back and with Ayres's division did most excellent service during the day. Crawford's division of the same corps had backed still farther off, and although orders were sent repeatedly to bring it up, it was late before it finally got to where it could be of material assistance. Once there it did very excellent service.

Sheridan succeeded by the middle of the afternoon or a little later, in advancing up to the point from which to make his designated assault upon Five Forks itself. He was very impatient to make the assault and have it all over before night, because the ground he occupied would be untenable for him in bivouac during the night. Unless the assault was made and was successful, he would be obliged to return to Dinwiddie Court-House, or even further than that for the night.

It was at this junction of affairs that Sheridan wanted to get Crawford's division in hand, and he also wanted Warren. He sent staff officer after staff officer in search of Warren, directing that general to report to him, but they were unable to find him. At all events Sheridan was unable to get that officer to him. Finally he went himself. He issued an order relieving Warren and assigning Griffin to the command of the 5th Corps. The troops were then brought up and the assault successfully made.

I was so much dissatisfied with Warren's dilatory movements in the battle of White Oak Road and in his failure to reach Sheridan in time, that I was very much afraid that at the last moment he would fail Sheridan. He was a man of fine intelligence, great earnestness, quick perception, and could make his dispositions as quickly as any officer, under difficulties where he was forced to act. But I had before discovered a defect which was beyond his control, that was very prejudicial to his usefulness in emergencies like the one just before us. He could see every danger at a glance before he had encountered it. He would not only make preparations to meet the danger which might occur, but he would inform his commanding officer what others should do while he was executing his move.

I had sent a staff officer to General Sheridan to call his attention to these defects, and to say that as much as I liked General Warren, now was not a time when we could let our personal feelings for any one stand in the way of success; and if his removal was necessary to success, not to hesitate. It was upon that authorization that Sheridan removed Warren. I was very sorry that it had been done, and regretted still more that I had not long before taken occasion to assign him to another field of duty.

It was dusk when our troops under Sheridan went over the parapets of the enemy. The two armies were mingled together there for a time in such manner that it was almost a question which one was going to demand the surrender of the other. Soon, however, the enemy broke and ran in every direction; some six thousand prisoners, besides artillery and small-arms in large quantities, falling into our hands. The flying troops were pursued in different directions, the cavalry and 5th corps under Sheridan pursuing the larger body which moved northwest.

This pursuit continued until about nine o'clock at night, when Sheridan halted his troops, and knowing the importance to him of the part of the enemy's line which had been captured, returned, sending the 5th corps across Hatcher's Run to just south-west of Petersburg, and facing them toward it. Merritt, with the cavalry, stopped and bivouacked west of Five Forks.

This was the condition which affairs were in on the night of the 1st of April. I then issued orders for an assault by Wright and Parke at four o'clock on the morning of the 2d. I also ordered the 2d corps, General Humphreys, and General Ord with the Army of the James, on the left, to hold themselves in readiness to take any advantage that could be taken from weakening in their front.

I notified Mr. Lincoln at City Point of the success of the day; in fact I had reported to him during the day and evening as I got news, because he was so much interested in the movements taking place that I wanted to relieve his mind as much as I could. I notified Weitzel on the north side of the James River, directing him, also, to keep close up to the enemy, and take advantage of the withdrawal of troops from there to promptly enter the city of Richmond.

I was afraid that Lee would regard the possession of Five Forks as of so much importance that he would make a last desperate effort to retake it, risking everything upon the cast of a single die. It was for this reason that I had ordered the assault to take place at once, as soon as I had received the news of the capture of Five Forks. The corps commanders, however, reported that it was so dark that the men could not see to move, and it would be impossible to make the assault then. But we kept up a continuous artillery fire upon the enemy around the whole line including that north of the James River, until it was light enough to move, which was about a quarter to five in the morning.

At that hour Parke's and Wright's corps moved out as directed, brushed the *abatis* from their front as they advanced under a heavy fire of musketry and artillery, and went without flinching directly on till they mounted the parapets and threw themselves inside of the enemy's line. Parke, who was on the right, swept down to the right and captured a very considerable length of line in that direction, but at that point the outer was so near the inner line which closely enveloped the city of Petersburg that he could make no advance forward and, in fact, had a very serious task to turn the lines which he had captured to the defence of his own troops and to hold them; but he succeeded in this.

Wright swung around to his left and moved to Hatcher's Run, sweeping everything before him. The enemy had traverses in rear of his captured line, under cover of which he made something of a stand, from one to another, as Wright moved on; but the latter met no serious obstacle. As you proceed to the left the outer line becomes gradually much farther from the inner one, and along about Hatcher's Run they must be nearly two miles apart. Both Parke and Wright captured a considerable amount of artillery and some prisoners — Wright about three thousand of them.

In the meantime Ord and Humphreys, in obedience to the instructions they had received, had succeeded by daylight, or very early in the morning, in capturing the intrenched picket-lines in their front; and before Wright got up to that point, Ord had also succeeded in getting inside of the enemy's intrenchments. The second corps soon followed; and the outer works of Petersburg were in the hands of the National troops, never to be wrenched from them again. When Wright reached Hatcher's Run, he sent a regiment to destroy the South Side Railroad just outside of the city.

My headquarters were still at Dabney's saw-mills. As soon as I received the news of Wright's success, I sent dispatches announcing the fact to all points around the line, including the troops at Bermuda Hundred and those on the north side of the James, and to the President at City Point. Further dispatches kept coming in, and as they did I sent the additional news to these points. Finding at length that they were all in, I mounted my horse to join the troops who were inside the works. When I arrived there I rode my horse over the parapet just as Wright's three thousand prisoners were coming out. I was soon joined inside by General Meade and his staff.

Lee made frantic efforts to recover at least part of the lost ground. Parke on our right was repeatedly assaulted, but repulsed every effort. Before noon Longstreet was ordered up from the north side of the James River, thus bringing the bulk of Lee's army around to the support of his extreme right. As soon as I learned this I notified Weitzel and directed him to keep up close to the enemy and to have Hartsuff, commanding the Bermuda Hundred front, to do the same thing, and if they found any break to go in; Hartsuff especially should do so, for this would separate Richmond and Petersburg.

Sheridan, after he had returned to Five Forks, swept down to Petersburg, coming in on our left. This gave us a continuous line from the Appomattox River below the city to the same river above. At eleven o'clock, not having heard from Sheridan, I reinforced Parke with two brigades from City Point. With this additional force he completed his captured works for better defence, and built back from his right, so as to protect his flank. He also carried in and made an *abatis* between himself and the enemy. Lee brought additional troops and artillery against Parke even after this was done, and made several assaults with very heavy losses.

The enemy had in addition to their intrenched line close up to Petersburg, two enclosed works outside of it, Fort Gregg and Fort Whitworth. We thought it had now become necessary to carry them by assault. About one o'clock in the day, Fort Gregg was assaulted by Foster's division of the 24th corps (Gibbon's), supported by two brigades from Ord's command. The battle was desperate and the National troops were repulsed several times; but it was finally carried, and immediately the troops in Fort Whitworth evacuated the place. The guns of Fort Gregg were turned upon the retreating enemy, and the commanding officer with some sixty of the men of Fort Whitworth surrendered.

I had ordered Miles in the morning to report to Sheridan. In moving to execute this order he came upon the enemy at the intersection of the White Oak Road and the Claiborne Road. The enemy fell back to Sutherland Station on the South Side Road and were followed by Miles. This position, naturally a strong and defensible one, was also strongly entrenched. Sheridan now came up and Miles asked permission from him to make the assault, which Sheridan gave. By this time Humphreys had got through the outer works in his front, and came up also and assumed command over Miles, who commanded a division in his corps. I had sent an order to Humphreys to turn to his right and move towards Petersburg. This order he now got, and started off, thus leaving Miles alone. The latter made two assaults, both of which failed, and he had to fall back a few hundred yards.

Hearing that Miles had been left in this position, I directed Humphreys to send a division back to his relief. He went himself.

Sheridan before starting to sweep down to Petersburg had sent Merritt with his cavalry to the west to attack some Confederate cavalry that had assembled there. Merritt drove them north to the Appomattox River. Sheridan then took the enemy at Sutherland Station on the reverse side from where Miles was, and the two together captured the place, with a large number of prisoners and some pieces of artillery, and put the remainder, portions of three Confederate corps, to flight. Sheridan followed, and drove them until night, when further pursuit was stopped. Miles bivouacked for the night on the ground which he with Sheridan had carried so handsomely by assault. I cannot explain the situation here better than by giving my dispatch to City Point that evening:

BOYDTON ROAD, NEAR PETERSBURG,
April 2, 1865. —4.40 P.M.
COLONEL T. S. BOWERS,
City Point.

We are now up and have a continuous line of troops, and in a few hours will be intrenched from the Appomattox below Petersburg to the river above. Heth's and Wilcox's divisions, such part of them as were not captured, were cut off from town, either designedly on their part or because they could not help it. Sheridan with the cavalry and 5th corps is above them. Miles's division, 2d corps, was sent from the White Oak Road to Sutherland Station on the South Side Railroad, where he met them, and at last accounts was engaged with them. Not knowing whether Sheridan would get up in time, General Humphreys was sent with another division from here. The whole captures since the army started out gunning will amount to not less than twelve thousand men, and probably fifty pieces of artillery. I do not know the number of men and guns accurately however. * * * I think the President might come out and pay us a visit to-morrow.

U. S. GRANT,
Lieutenant-General.

During the night of April 2d our line was intrenched from the river above to the river below. I ordered a bombardment to be commenced the next morning at five A.M., to be followed by an assault at six o'clock; but the enemy evacuated Petersburg early in the morning.

Chapter LXV.

GENERAL MEADE and I entered Petersburg on the morning of the 3d and took a position under cover of a house which protected us from the enemy's musketry which was flying thick and fast there. As we would occasionally look around the corner we could see the streets and the Appomattox bottom, presumably near the bridge, packed with the Confederate army. I did not have artillery brought up, because I was sure Lee was trying to make his escape, and I wanted to push immediately in pursuit. At all events I had not the heart to turn the artillery upon such a mass of defeated and fleeing men, and I hoped to capture them soon.

Soon after the enemy had entirely evacuated Petersburg, a man came in who represented himself to be an engineer of the Army of Northern Virginia. He said that Lee had for some time been at work preparing a strong enclosed intrenchment, into which he would throw himself when forced out of Petersburg, and fight his final battle there; that he was actually at that time drawing his troops from Richmond, and falling back into this prepared work. This statement was made to General Meade and myself when we were together. I had already given orders for the movement up the south side of the Appomattox for the purpose of heading off Lee; but Meade was so much impressed by this man's story that he thought we ought to cross the Appomattox there at once and move against Lee in his new position. I knew that Lee was no fool, as he would have been to have put himself and his army between two formidable streams like the James and Appomattox rivers, and between two such armies as those of the Potomac and the James. Then these streams coming together as they did to the east of him, it would be only necessary to close up in the west to have him thoroughly cut off from all supplies or possibility of reinforcement. It would only have been a question of days, and not many of them, if he had taken the position assigned to him by the so-called engineer, when he would have been obliged to surrender his army. Such is one of the ruses resorted to in war to deceive your antagonist. My judgment was that Lee would necessarily have to evacuate Richmond, and that the only course for him to pursue would be to follow the Danville Road. Accordingly my object was to secure a point on that road south of Lee, and I told Meade this. He suggested that if Lee was going that way we would follow him. My reply was that we did not want to follow him; we wanted to get ahead of him and cut him off, and if he would only stay in the position he (Meade) believed him to be in at that time, I wanted nothing better; that when we got in possession of the Danville Railroad, at its crossing of the Appomattox River, if we still found him between the two rivers, all we had to do was to move eastward and close him up. That we would then have all the advantage we could possibly have by moving directly against him from Petersburg, even if he remained in the position assigned him by the engineer officer.

I had held most of the command aloof from the intrenchments, so as to start them out on the Danville Road early in the morning, supposing that Lee would be gone during the night. During the night I strengthened Sheridan by sending him Humphreys's corps.

Lee, as we now know, had advised the authorities at Richmond, during the day, of the condition of affairs, and told them it would be impossible for him to hold out longer than night, if he could hold out that long. Davis was at church when he received Lee's dispatch. The congregation was dismissed with the notice that there would be no evening service. The rebel government left Richmond about two o'clock in the afternoon of the 2d.

At night Lee ordered his troops to assemble at Amelia Court House, his object being to get away, join Johnston if possible, and to try to crush Sherman before I could get there. As soon as I was sure of this I notified Sheridan and directed him to move out on the Danville Railroad to the south side of the Appomattox River as speedily as possible. He replied that he already had some of his command nine

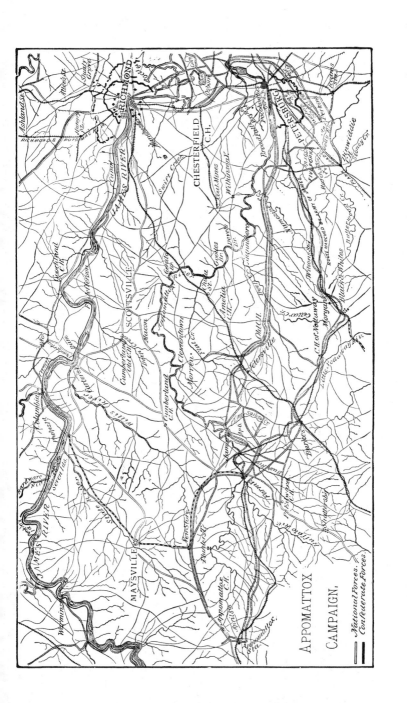

APPOMATTOX CAMPAIGN,

National Forces.
Confederate Forces.

miles out. I then ordered the rest of the Army of the Potomac under Meade to follow the same road in the morning. Parke's corps followed by the same road, and the Army of the James was directed to follow the road which ran alongside of the South Side Railroad to Burke's Station, and to repair the railroad and telegraph as they proceeded. That road was a 5 feet gauge, while our rolling stock was all of the 4 feet 8½ inches gauge; consequently the rail on one side of the track had to be taken up throughout the whole length and relaid so as to conform to the gauge of our cars and locomotives.

Mr. Lincoln was at City Point at the time, and had been for some days. I would have let him know what I contemplated doing, only while I felt a strong conviction that the move was going to be successful, yet it might not prove so; and then I would have only added another to the many disappointments he had been suffering for the past three years. But when we started out he saw that we were moving for a purpose, and bidding us Godspeed, remained there to hear the result.

The next morning after the capture of Petersburg, I telegraphed Mr. Lincoln asking him to ride out there and see me, while I would await his arrival. I had started all the troops out early in the morning, so that after the National army left Petersburg there was not a soul to be seen, not even an animal in the streets. There was absolutely no one there, except my staff officers and, possibly, a small escort of cavalry. We had selected the piazza of a deserted house, and occupied it until the President arrived.

About the first thing that Mr. Lincoln said to me, after warm congratulations for the victory, and thanks both to myself and to the army which had accomplished it, was: "Do you know, general, that I have had a sort of a sneaking idea for some days that you intended to do something like this." Our movements having been successful up to this point, I no longer had any object in concealing from the President all my movements, and the objects I had in view. He remained for some days near City Point, and I communicated with him frequently and fully by telegraph.

Mr. Lincoln knew that it had been arranged for Sherman to join me at a fixed time, to co-operate in the destruction of

Lee's army. I told him that I had been very anxious to have the Eastern armies vanquish their old enemy who had so long resisted all their repeated and gallant attempts to subdue them or drive them from their capital. The Western armies had been in the main successful until they had conquered all the territory from the Mississippi River to the State of North Carolina, and were now almost ready to knock at the back door of Richmond, asking admittance. I said to him that if the Western armies should be even upon the field, operating against Richmond and Lee, the credit would be given to them for the capture, by politicians and non-combatants from the section of country which those troops hailed from. It might lead to disagreeable bickerings between members of Congress of the East and those of the West in some of their debates. Western members might be throwing it up to the members of the East that in the suppression of the rebellion they were not able to capture an army, or to accomplish much in the way of contributing toward that end, but had to wait until the Western armies had conquered all the territory south and west of them, and then come on to help them capture the only army they had been engaged with.

Mr. Lincoln said he saw that now, but had never thought of it before, because his anxiety was so great that he did not care where the aid came from so the work was done.

The Army of the Potomac has every reason to be proud of its four years' record in the suppression of the rebellion. The army it had to fight was the protection to the capital of a people which was attempting to found a nation upon the territory of the United States. Its loss would be the loss of the cause. Every energy, therefore, was put forth by the Confederacy to protect and maintain their capital. Everything else would go if it went. Lee's army had to be strengthened to enable it to maintain its position, no matter what territory was wrested from the South in another quarter.

I never expected any such bickering as I have indicated, between the soldiers of the two sections; and, fortunately, there has been none between the politicians. Possibly I am the only one who thought of the liability of such a state of things in advance.

When our conversation was at an end Mr. Lincoln mounted his horse and started on his return to City Point, while I and my staff started to join the army, now a good many miles in advance. Up to this time I had not received the report of the capture of Richmond.

Soon after I left President Lincoln I received a dispatch from General Weitzel which notified me that he had taken possession of Richmond at about 8.15 o'clock in the morning of that day, the 3d, and that he had found the city on fire in two places. The city was in the most utter confusion. The authorities had taken the precaution to empty all the liquor into the gutter, and to throw out the provisions which the Confederate government had left, for the people to gather up. The city had been deserted by the authorities, civil and military, without any notice whatever that they were about to leave. In fact, up to the very hour of the evacuation the people had been led to believe that Lee had gained an important victory somewhere around Petersburg.

Weitzel's command found evidence of great demoralization in Lee's army, there being still a great many men and even officers in the town. The city was on fire. Our troops were directed to extinguish the flames, which they finally succeeded in doing. The fire had been started by some one connected with the retreating army. All authorities deny that it was authorized, and I presume it was the work of excited men who were leaving what they regarded as their capital and may have felt that it was better to destroy it than have it fall into the hands of their enemy. Be that as it may, the National troops found the city in flames, and used every effort to extinguish them.

The troops that had formed Lee's right, a great many of them, were cut off from getting back into Petersburg, and were pursued by our cavalry so hotly and closely that they threw away caissons, ammunition, clothing, and almost everything to lighten their loads, and pushed along up the Appomattox River until finally they took water and crossed over.

I left Mr. Lincoln and started, as I have already said, to join the command, which halted at Sutherland Station, about nine miles out. We had still time to march as much farther, and time was an object; but the roads were bad and the trains belonging to the advance corps had blocked up the road so that it was impossible to get on. Then, again, our cavalry had struck some of the enemy and were pursuing them; and the orders were that the roads should be given up to the cavalry whenever they appeared. This caused further delay.

General Wright, who was in command of one of the corps which were left back, thought to gain time by letting his men go into bivouac and trying to get up some rations for them, and clearing out the road, so that when they did start they would be uninterrupted. Humphreys, who was far ahead, was also out of rations. They did not succeed in getting them up through the night; but the Army of the Potomac, officers and men, were so elated by the reflection that at last they were following up a victory to its end, that they preferred marching without rations to running a possible risk of letting the enemy elude them. So the march was resumed at three o'clock in the morning.

Merritt's cavalry had struck the enemy at Deep Creek, and driven them north to the Appomattox, where, I presume, most of them were forced to cross.

On the morning of the 4th I learned that Lee had ordered rations up from Danville for his famishing army, and that they were to meet him at Farmville. This showed that Lee had already abandoned the idea of following the railroad down to Danville, but had determined to go farther west, by the way of Farmville. I notified Sheridan of this and directed him to get possession of the road before the supplies could reach Lee. He responded that he had already sent Crook's division to get upon the road between Burkesville and Jetersville, then to face north and march along the road upon the latter place; and he thought Crook must be there now. The bulk of the army moved directly for Jetersville by two roads.

After I had received the dispatch from Sheridan saying that Crook was on the Danville Road, I immediately ordered Meade to make a forced march with the Army of the Potomac, and to send Parke's corps across from the road they were on to the South Side Railroad, to fall in the rear of the Army of the James and to protect the railroad which that army was repairing as it went along.

Our troops took possession of Jetersville and in the telegraph office, they found a dispatch from Lee, ordering two hundred thousand rations from Danville. The dispatch had not been sent, but Sheridan sent a special messenger with it to Burkesville and had it forwarded from there. In the meantime, however, dispatches from other sources had reached Danville, and they knew there that our army was on the line of the road; so that they sent no further supplies from that quarter.

At this time Merritt and Mackenzie, with the cavalry, were off between the road which the Army of the Potomac was marching on and the Appomattox River, and were attacking the enemy in flank. They picked up a great many prisoners and forced the abandonment of some property.

Lee intrenched himself at Amelia Court House, and also his advance north of Jetersville, and sent his troops out to collect forage. The country was very poor and afforded but very little. His foragers scattered a great deal; many of them were picked up by our men, and many others never returned to the Army of Northern Virginia.

Griffin's corps was intrenched across the railroad south of Jetersville, and Sheridan notified me of the situation. I again ordered Meade up with all dispatch, Sheridan having but the one corps of infantry with a little cavalry confronting Lee's entire army. Meade, always prompt in obeying orders, now pushed forward with great energy, although he was himself sick and hardly able to be out of bed. Humphreys moved at two, and Wright at three o'clock in the morning, without rations, as I have said, the wagons being far in the rear.

I stayed that night at Wilson's Station on the South Side Railroad. On the morning of the 5th I sent word to Sheridan of the progress Meade was making, and suggested that he might now attack Lee. We had now no other objective than the Confederate armies, and I was anxious to close the thing up at once.

On the 5th I marched again with Ord's command until within about ten miles of Burkesville, where I stopped to let his army pass. I then received from Sheridan the following dispatch:

"The whole of Lee's army is at or near Amelia Court House, and on this side of it. General Davies, whom I sent out to Painesville on their right flank, has just captured six pieces of artillery and some wagons. We can capture the Army of Northern Virginia if force enough can be thrown to this point, and then advance upon it. My cavalry was at Burkesville yesterday, and six miles beyond, on the Danville Road, last night. General Lee is at Amelia Court House in person. They are out of rations, or nearly so. They were advancing up the railroad towards Burkesville yesterday, when we intercepted them at this point."

It now became a life and death struggle with Lee to get south to his provisions.

Sheridan, thinking the enemy might turn off immediately towards Farmville, moved Davies's brigade of cavalry out to watch him. Davies found the movement had already commenced. He attacked and drove away their cavalry which was escorting wagons to the west, capturing and burning 180 wagons. He also captured five pieces of artillery. The Confederate infantry then moved against him and probably would have handled him very roughly, but Sheridan had sent two more brigades of cavalry to follow Davies, and they came to his relief in time. A sharp engagement took place between these three brigades of cavalry and the enemy's infantry, but the latter was repulsed.

Meade himself reached Jetersville about two o'clock in the afternoon, but in advance of all his troops. The head of Humphreys's corps followed in about an hour afterwards. Sheridan stationed the troops as they came up, at Meade's request, the latter still being very sick. He extended two divisions of this corps off to the west of the road to the left of Griffin's corps, and one division to the right. The cavalry by this time had also come up, and they were put still farther off to the left, Sheridan feeling certain that there lay the route by which the enemy intended to escape. He wanted to attack, feeling that if time was given, the enemy would get away; but Meade prevented this, preferring to wait till his troops were all up.

At this juncture Sheridan sent me a letter which had been handed to him by a colored man, with a note from himself saying that he wished I was there myself. The letter was dated Amelia Court House, April 5th, and signed by Colonel Taylor. It was to his mother, and showed the demoralization of the Confederate army. Sheridan's note also gave me the information as here related of the movements of that day. I received a second message from Sheridan on the 5th, in which he urged more emphatically the importance of my presence. This was brought to me by a scout in gray uniform. It was written on tissue paper, and wrapped up in tin-foil such as chewing tobacco is folded in. This was a precaution taken so that if the scout should be captured he could take this tin-foil out of his pocket and putting it into his mouth, chew it. It would cause no surprise at all to see a Confederate soldier chewing tobacco. It was nearly night when this letter was received. I gave Ord directions to continue his march to Burkesville and there intrench himself for the night, and in the morning to move west to cut off all the roads between there and Farmville.

I then started with a few of my staff and a very small escort of cavalry, going directly through the woods, to join Meade's army. The distance was about sixteen miles; but the night being dark our progress was slow through the woods in the absence of direct roads. However, we got to the outposts about ten o'clock in the evening, and after some little parley convinced the sentinels of our identity and were conducted in to where Sheridan was bivouacked. We talked over the situation for some little time, Sheridan explaining to me what he thought Lee was trying to do, and that Meade's orders, if carried out, moving to the right flank, would give him the coveted opportunity of escaping us and putting us in rear of him.

We then together visited Meade, reaching his headquarters about midnight. I explained to Meade that we did not want to follow the enemy; we wanted to get ahead of him, and that his orders would allow the enemy to escape, and besides that, I had no doubt that Lee was moving right then. Meade changed his orders at once. They were now given for an advance on Amelia Court House, at an early hour in the morning, as the army then lay; that is, the infantry being across the railroad, most of it to the west of the road, with the cavalry swung out still farther to the left.

Chapter LXVI.

BATTLE OF SAILOR'S CREEK — ENGAGEMENT AT
FARMVILLE — CORRESPONDENCE WITH GENERAL LEE —
SHERIDAN INTERCEPTS THE ENEMY.

THE APPOMATTOX, going westward, takes a long sweep to the south-west from the neighborhood of the Richmond and Danville Railroad bridge, and then trends north-westerly. Sailor's Creek, an insignificant stream, running northward, empties into the Appomattox between the High Bridge and Jetersville. Near the High Bridge the stage road from Petersburg to Lynchburg crosses the Appomattox River, also on a bridge. The railroad runs on the north side of the river to Farmville, a few miles west, and from there, recrossing, continues on the south side of it. The roads coming up from the south-east to Farmville cross the Appomattox River there on a bridge and run on the north side, leaving the Lynchburg and Petersburg Railroad well to the left.

Lee, in pushing out from Amelia Court House, availed himself of all the roads between the Danville Road and Appomattox River to move upon, and never permitted the head of his columns to stop because of any fighting that might be going on in his rear. In this way he came very near succeeding in getting to his provision trains and eluding us with at least part of his army.

As expected, Lee's troops had moved during the night before, and our army in moving upon Amelia Court House soon encountered them. There was a good deal of fighting before Sailor's Creek was reached. Our cavalry charged in upon a body of theirs which was escorting a wagon train in order to get it past our left. A severe engagement ensued, in which we captured many prisoners, and many men also were killed and wounded. There was as much gallantry displayed by some of the Confederates in these little engagements as was displayed at any time during the war, notwithstanding the sad defeats of the past week.

The armies finally met on Sailor's Creek, when a heavy engagement took place, in which infantry, artillery and cavalry were all brought into action. Our men on the right, as they were brought in against the enemy, came in on higher ground, and upon his flank, giving us every advantage to be derived from the lay of the country. Our firing was also very much more rapid, because the enemy commenced his retreat westward and in firing as he retreated had to turn around every time he fired. The enemy's loss was very heavy, as well in killed and wounded as in captures. Some six general officers fell into our hands in this engagement, and seven thousand men were made prisoners. This engagement was commenced in the middle of the afternoon of the 6th, and the retreat and pursuit were continued until nightfall, when the armies bivouacked upon the ground where the night had overtaken them.

When the move towards Amelia Court House had commenced that morning, I ordered Wright's corps, which was on the extreme right, to be moved to the left past the whole army, to take the place of Griffin's, and ordered the latter at the same time to move by and place itself on the right. The object of this movement was to get the 6th corps, Wright's, next to the cavalry, with which they had formerly served so harmoniously and so efficiently in the valley of Virginia.

The 6th corps now remained with the cavalry and under Sheridan's direct command until after the surrender.

Ord had been directed to take possession of all the roads southward between Burkesville and the High Bridge. On the morning of the 6th he sent Colonel Washburn with two infantry regiments with instructions to destroy High Bridge and to return rapidly to Burkesville Station; and he prepared himself to resist the enemy there. Soon after Washburn had started Ord became a little alarmed as to his safety and sent Colonel Read, of his staff, with about eighty cavalrymen, to overtake him and bring him back. Very shortly after this he heard that the head of Lee's column had got up to the road between him and where Washburn now was, and attempted to send reinforcements, but the reinforcements could not get through. Read, however, had got through ahead of the enemy. He rode on to Farmville and was on his way back again when he found his return cut off, and Washburn confronting apparently the advance of Lee's army. Read drew his

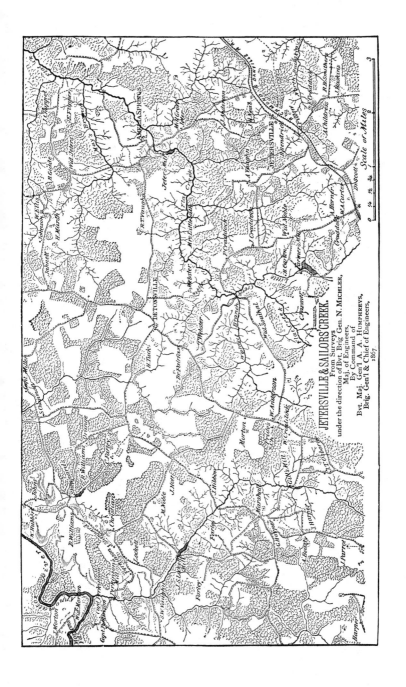

JETERSVILLE & SAILORS' CREEK.
From Surveys
under the direction of Bvt. Brig. Gen. N. MICHLER,
Maj. of Engineers,
By Command of
Bvt. Maj. Gen'l A. A. HUMPHREYS,
Brig. Gen'l & Chief of Engineers,
1867

Scale of Miles

men up into line of battle, his force now consisting of less than six hundred men, infantry and cavalry, and rode along their front, making a speech to his men to inspire them with the same enthusiasm that he himself felt. He then gave the order to charge. This little band made several charges, of course unsuccessful ones, but inflicted a loss upon the enemy more than equal to their own entire number. Colonel Read fell mortally wounded, and then Washburn; and at the close of the conflict nearly every officer of the command and most of the rank and file had been either killed or wounded. The remainder then surrendered. The Confederates took this to be only the advance of a larger column which had headed them off, and so stopped to intrench; so that this gallant band of six hundred had checked the progress of a strong detachment of the Confederate army.

This stoppage of Lee's column no doubt saved to us the trains following. Lee himself pushed on and crossed the wagon road bridge near the High Bridge, and attempted to destroy it. He did set fire to it, but the flames had made but little headway when Humphreys came up with his corps and drove away the rear-guard which had been left to protect it while it was being burned up. Humphreys forced his way across with some loss, and followed Lee to the intersection of the road crossing at Farmville with the one from Petersburg. Here Lee held a position which was very strong, naturally, besides being intrenched. Humphreys was alone, confronting him all through the day, and in a very hazardous position. He put on a bold face, however, and assaulted with some loss, but was not assaulted in return.

Our cavalry had gone farther south by the way of Prince Edward's Court House, along with the 5th corps (Griffin's), Ord falling in between Griffin and the Appomattox. Crook's division of cavalry and Wright's corps pushed on west of Farmville. When the cavalry reached Farmville they found that some of the Confederates were in ahead of them, and had already got their trains of provisions back to that point; but our troops were in time to prevent them from securing any-thing to eat, although they succeeded in again running the trains off, so that we did not get them for some time. These troops retreated to the north side of the Appomattox to join

Lee, and succeeded in destroying the bridge after them. Considerable fighting ensued there between Wright's corps and a portion of our cavalry and the Confederates, but finally the cavalry forded the stream and drove them away. Wright built a foot-bridge for his men to march over on and then marched out to the junction of the roads to relieve Humphreys, arriving there that night. I had stopped the night before at Burkesville Junction. Our troops were then pretty much all out of the place, but we had a field hospital there, and Ord's command was extended from that point towards Farmville.

Here I met Dr. Smith, a Virginian and an officer of the regular army, who told me that in a conversation with General Ewell, one of the prisoners and a relative of his, Ewell had said that when we had got across the James River he knew their cause was lost, and it was the duty of their authorities to make the best terms they could while they still had a right to claim concessions. The authorities thought differently, however. Now the cause was lost and they had no right to claim anything. He said further, that for every man that was killed after this in the war somebody is responsible, and it would be but very little better than murder. He was not sure that Lee would consent to surrender his army without being able to consult with the President, but he hoped he would.

I rode in to Farmville on the 7th, arriving there early in the day. Sheridan and Ord were pushing through, away to the south. Meade was back towards the High Bridge, and Humphreys confronting Lee as before stated. After having gone into bivouac at Prince Edward's Court House, Sheridan learned that seven trains of provisions and forage were at Appomattox, and determined to start at once and capture them; and a forced march was necessary in order to get there before Lee's army could secure them. He wrote me a note telling me this. This fact, together with the incident related the night before by Dr. Smith, gave me the idea of opening correspondence with General Lee on the subject of the surrender of his army. I therefore wrote to him on this day, as follows:

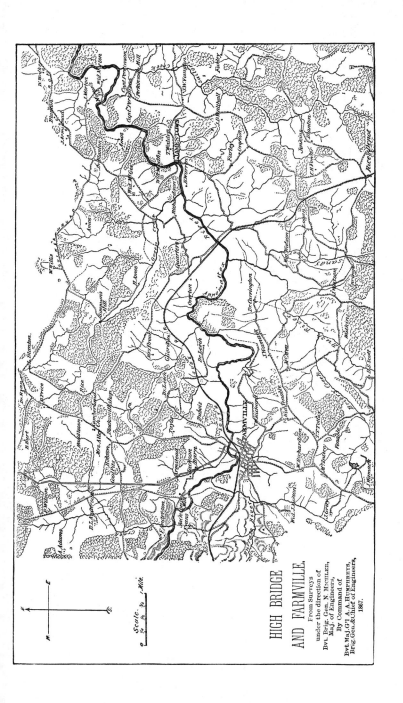

HIGH BRIDGE
AND FARMVILLE,
From Surveys
under the direction of
Bvt. Brig. Gen. N. Michler,
Maj. of Engineers,
By Command of
Bvt. Maj.G⁴ A. A. Humphreys,
Brig. Gen. & Chief of Engineers,
1867.

Scale ¾ 1 Mile.

HEADQUARTERS ARMIES OF THE U. S.,
5 P.M., *April* 7, 1865.

GENERAL R. E. LEE,
Commanding C. S. A.

The results of the last week must convince you of the hopelessness of further resistance on the part of the Army of Northern Virginia in this struggle. I feel that it is so, and regard it as my duty to shift from myself the responsibility of any further effusion of blood, by asking of you the surrender of that portion of the Confederate States army known as the Army of Northern Virginia.

U. S. GRANT,
Lieut.-General.

Lee replied on the evening of the same day as follows:

April 7, 1865.

GENERAL: — I have received your note of this day. Though not entertaining the opinion you express on the hopelessness of further resistance on the part of the Army of Northern Virginia, I reciprocate your desire to avoid useless effusion of blood, and therefore before considering your proposition, ask the terms you will offer on condition of its surrender.

R. E. LEE,
General.

LIEUT.-GENERAL U. S. GRANT,
Commanding Armies of the U.S.

This was not satisfactory, but I regarded it as deserving another letter and wrote him as follows:

April 8, 1865.

GENERAL R. E. LEE,
Commanding C. S. A.

Your note of last evening in reply to mine of same date, asking the condition on which I will accept the surrender of the Army of Northern Virginia is just received. In reply I would say that, peace being my great desire, there is but one condition I would insist upon, namely: that the men and officers surrendered shall be disqualified for taking up arms again against the Government of the United States until properly exchanged. I will meet you, or will designate officers to meet any officers you may name for the same purpose, at any point agreeable to you, for the purpose of arranging definitely the terms upon which the surrender of the Army of Northern Virginia will be received.

U.S. GRANT,
Lieut.-General.

Lee's army was rapidly crumbling. Many of his soldiers had enlisted from that part of the State where they now were, and were continually dropping out of the ranks and going to their homes. I know that I occupied a hotel almost destitute of furniture at Farmville, which had probably been used as a Confederate hospital. The next morning when I came out I found a Confederate colonel there, who reported to me and said that he was the proprietor of that house, and that he was a colonel of a regiment that had been raised in that neighborhood. He said that when he came along past home, he found that he was the only man of the regiment remaining with Lee's army, so he just dropped out, and now wanted to surrender himself. I told him to stay there and he would not be molested. That was one regiment which had been eliminated from Lee's force by this crumbling process.

Although Sheridan had been marching all day, his troops moved with alacrity and without any straggling. They began to see the end of what they had been fighting four years for. Nothing seemed to fatigue them. They were ready to move without rations and travel without rest until the end. Straggling had entirely ceased, and every man was now a rival for the front. The infantry marched about as rapidly as the cavalry could.

Sheridan sent Custer with his division to move south of Appomattox Station, which is about five miles south-west of the Court House, to get west of the trains and destroy the roads to the rear. They got there the night of the 8th, and succeeded partially; but some of the train men had just discovered the movement of our troops and succeeded in running off three of the trains. The other four were held by Custer.

The head of Lee's column came marching up there on the morning of the 9th, not dreaming, I suppose, that there were any Union soldiers near. The Confederates were surprised to find our cavalry had possession of the trains. However, they were desperate and at once assaulted, hoping to recover them. In the melée that ensued they succeeded in burning one of the trains, but not in getting anything from it. Custer then ordered the other trains run back on the road towards Farmville, and the fight continued.

So far, only our cavalry and the advance of Lee's army were engaged. Soon, however, Lee's men were brought up from the rear, no doubt expecting they had nothing to meet but our cavalry. But our infantry had pushed forward so rapidly that by the time the enemy got up they found Griffin's corps and the Army of the James confronting them. A sharp engagement ensued, but Lee quickly set up a white flag.

Chapter LXVII.

NEGOTIATIONS AT APPOMATTOX—INTERVIEW WITH
LEE AT McLEAN'S HOUSE—THE TERMS OF
SURRENDER—LEE'S SURRENDER—INTERVIEW
WITH LEE AFTER THE SURRENDER.

O<small>N THE</small> 8<small>TH</small> I had followed the Army of the Potomac in
rear of Lee. I was suffering very severely with a sick
headache, and stopped at a farmhouse on the road some distance in rear of the main body of the army. I spent the night
in bathing my feet in hot water and mustard, and putting
mustard plasters on my wrists and the back part of my neck,
hoping to be cured by morning. During the night I received
Lee's answer to my letter of the 8th, inviting an interview
between the lines on the following morning.* But it was for a
different purpose from that of surrendering his army, and I
answered him as follows:

H<small>EADQUARTERS</small> A<small>RMIES OF THE</small> U. S.,
April 9, 1865.

G<small>ENERAL</small> R. E. L<small>EE</small>,
   Commanding C. S. A.

Your note of yesterday is received. As I have no authority to treat
on the subject of peace, the meeting proposed for ten A.M. to-day
could lead to no good. I will state, however, General, that I am
equally anxious for peace with yourself, and the whole North entertains the same feeling. The terms upon which peace can be had are
well understood. By the South laying down their arms they will hasten that most desirable event, save thousands of human lives, and
hundreds of millions of property not yet destroyed. Sincerely hoping
that all our difficulties may be settled without the loss of another life,
I subscribe myself, etc.,

U. S. GRANT,
Lieutenant-General.

I proceeded at an early hour in the morning, still suffering
with the headache, to get to the head of the column. I was
not more than two or three miles from Appomattox Court

---

*See Appendix.

House at the time, but to go direct I would have to pass through Lee's army, or a portion of it. I had therefore to move south in order to get upon a road coming up from another direction.

When the white flag was put out by Lee, as already described, I was in this way moving towards Appomattox Court House, and consequently could not be communicated with immediately, and be informed of what Lee had done. Lee, therefore, sent a flag to the rear to advise Meade and one to the front to Sheridan, saying that he had sent a message to me for the purpose of having a meeting to consult about the surrender of his army, and asked for a suspension of hostilities until I could be communicated with. As they had heard nothing of this until the fighting had got to be severe and all going against Lee, both of these commanders hesitated very considerably about suspending hostilities at all. They were afraid it was not in good faith, and we had the Army of Northern Virginia where it could not escape except by some deception. They, however, finally consented to a suspension of hostilities for two hours to give an opportunity of communicating with me in that time, if possible. It was found that, from the route I had taken, they would probably not be able to communicate with me and get an answer back within the time fixed unless the messenger should pass through the rebel lines.

Lee, therefore, sent an escort with the officer bearing this message through his lines to me.

April 9, 1865.

GENERAL:—I received your note of this morning on the picket-line whither I had come to meet you and ascertain definitely what terms were embraced in your proposal of yesterday with reference to the surrender of this army. I now request an interview in accordance with the offer contained in your letter of yesterday for that purpose.

R. E. LEE, General.

LIEUTENANT-GENERAL U. S. GRANT,
        Commanding U. S. Armies.

When the officer reached me I was still suffering with the sick headache; but the instant I saw the contents of the note I was cured. I wrote the following note in reply and hastened on:

April 9, 1865.

GENERAL R. E. LEE,
    Commanding C. S. Armies.

Your note of this date is but this moment (11.50 A.M.) received, in consequence of my having passed from the Richmond and Lynchburg road to the Farmville and Lynchburg road. I am at this writing about four miles west of Walker's Church and will push forward to the front for the purpose of meeting you. Notice sent to me on this road where you wish the interview to take place will meet me.

U. S. GRANT,
Lieutenant-General.

I was conducted at once to where Sheridan was located with his troops drawn up in line of battle facing the Confederate army near by. They were very much excited, and expressed their view that this was all a ruse employed to enable the Confederates to get away. They said they believed that Johnston was marching up from North Carolina now, and Lee was moving to join him; and they would whip the rebels where they now were in five minutes if I would only let them go in. But I had no doubt about the good faith of Lee, and pretty soon was conducted to where he was. I found him at the house of a Mr. McLean, at Appomattox Court House, with Colonel Marshall, one of his staff officers, awaiting my arrival. The head of his column was occupying a hill, on a portion of which was an apple orchard, beyond a little valley which separated it from that on the crest of which Sheridan's forces were drawn up in line of battle to the south.

Before stating what took place between General Lee and myself, I will give all there is of the story of the famous apple tree.

Wars produce many stories of fiction, some of which are told until they are believed to be true. The war of the rebellion was no exception to this rule, and the story of the apple tree is one of those fictions based on a slight foundation of fact. As I have said, there was an apple orchard on the side of the hill occupied by the Confederate forces. Running diagonally up the hill was a wagon road, which, at one point, ran very near one of the trees, so that the wheels of vehicles had, on that side, cut off the roots of this tree, leaving a little embankment. General Babcock, of my staff, reported to me that

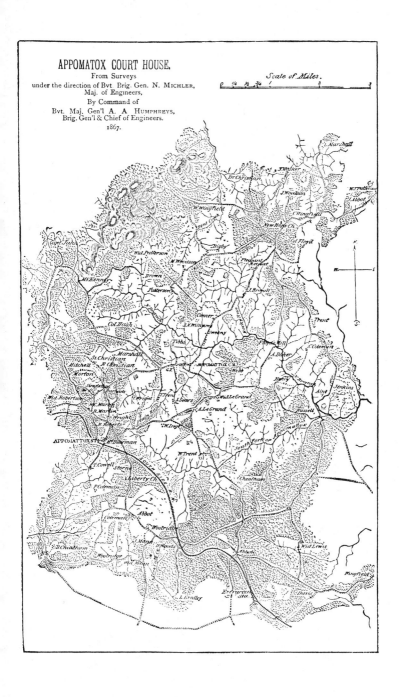

APPOMATOX COURT HOUSE.

From Surveys
under the direction of Bvt. Brig. Gen. N. Michler,
Maj. of Engineers,
By Command of
Bvt. Maj. Gen'l A. A. Humphreys,
Brig. Gen'l & Chief of Engineers.
1867.

Scale of Miles.

when he first met General Lee he was sitting upon this embankment with his feet in the road below and his back resting against the tree. The story had no other foundation than that. Like many other stories, it would be very good if it was only true.

I had known General Lee in the old army, and had served with him in the Mexican War; but did not suppose, owing to the difference in our age and rank, that he would remember me; while I would more naturally remember him distinctly, because he was the chief of staff of General Scott in the Mexican War.

When I had left camp that morning I had not expected so soon the result that was then taking place, and consequently was in rough garb. I was without a sword, as I usually was when on horseback on the field, and wore a soldier's blouse for a coat, with the shoulder straps of my rank to indicate to the army who I was. When I went into the house I found General Lee. We greeted each other, and after shaking hands took our seats. I had my staff with me, a good portion of whom were in the room during the whole of the interview.

What General Lee's feelings were I do not know. As he was a man of much dignity, with an impassible face, it was impossible to say whether he felt inwardly glad that the end had finally come, or felt sad over the result, and was too manly to show it. Whatever his feelings, they were entirely concealed from my observation; but my own feelings, which had been quite jubilant on the receipt of his letter, were sad and depressed. I felt like anything rather than rejoicing at the downfall of a foe who had fought so long and valiantly, and had suffered so much for a cause, though that cause was, I believe, one of the worst for which a people ever fought, and one for which there was the least excuse. I do not question, however, the sincerity of the great mass of those who were opposed to us.

General Lee was dressed in a full uniform which was entirely new, and was wearing a sword of considerable value, very likely the sword which had been presented by the State of Virginia; at all events, it was an entirely different sword from the one that would ordinarily be worn in the field. In my rough traveling suit, the uniform of a private with the straps of a lieutenant-general, I must have contrasted very strangely with a man so handsomely dressed, six feet high and of faultless form. But this was not a matter that I thought of until afterwards.

We soon fell into a conversation about old army times. He remarked that he remembered me very well in the old army; and I told him that as a matter of course I remembered him perfectly, but from the difference in our rank and years (there being about sixteen years' difference in our ages), I had thought it very likely that I had not attracted his attention sufficiently to be remembered by him after such a long interval. Our conversation grew so pleasant that I almost forgot the object of our meeting. After the conversation had run on in this style for some time, General Lee called my attention to the object of our meeting, and said that he had asked for this interview for the purpose of getting from me the terms I proposed to give his army. I said that I meant merely that his army should lay down their arms, not to take them up again during the continuance of the war unless duly and properly exchanged. He said that he had so understood my letter.

Then we gradually fell off again into conversation about matters foreign to the subject which had brought us together. This continued for some little time, when General Lee again interrupted the course of the conversation by suggesting that the terms I proposed to give his army ought to be written out. I called to General Parker, secretary on my staff, for writing materials, and commenced writing out the following terms:

APPOMATTOX C. H., VA.,
Ap l 9th, 1865.

GEN. R. E. LEE,
        Comd'g C. S. A.

GEN: In accordance with the substance of my letter to you of the 8th inst., I propose to receive the surrender of the Army of N. Va. on the following terms, to wit: Rolls of all the officers and men to be made in duplicate. One copy to be given to an officer designated by me, the other to be retained by such officer or officers as you may designate. The officers to give their individual paroles not to take up arms against the Government of the United States until properly

Eng. by A. Dresher

McLean's house at Appomattox in which General Lee signed the terms of surrender

exchanged, and each company or regimental commander sign a like parole for the men of their commands. The arms, artillery and public property to be parked and stacked, and turned over to the officer appointed by me to receive them. This will not embrace the side-arms of the officers, nor their private horses or baggage. This done, each officer and man will be allowed to return to their homes, not to be disturbed by United States authority so long as they observe their paroles and the laws in force where they may reside.

Very respectfully,
U. S. GRANT,
Lt. Gen.

When I put my pen to the paper I did not know the first word that I should make use of in writing the terms. I only knew what was in my mind, and I wished to express it clearly, so that there could be no mistaking it. As I wrote on, the thought occurred to me that the officers had their own private horses and effects, which were important to them, but of no value to us; also that it would be an unnecessary humiliation to call upon them to deliver their side arms.

No conversation, not one word, passed between General Lee and myself, either about private property, side arms, or kindred subjects. He appeared to have no objections to the terms first proposed; or if he had a point to make against them he wished to wait until they were in writing to make it. When he read over that part of the terms about side arms, horses and private property of the officers, he remarked, with some feeling, I thought, that this would have a happy effect upon his army.

Then, after a little further conversation, General Lee remarked to me again that their army was organized a little differently from the army of the United States (still maintaining by implication that we were two countries); that in their army the cavalrymen and artillerists owned their own horses; and he asked if he was to understand that the men who so owned their horses were to be permitted to retain them. I told him that as the terms were written they would not; that only the officers were permitted to take their private property. He then, after reading over the terms a second time, remarked that that was clear.

I then said to him that I thought this would be about the last battle of the war—I sincerely hoped so; and I said further I took it that most of the men in the ranks were small farmers. The whole country had been so raided by the two armies that it was doubtful whether they would be able to put in a crop to carry themselves and their families through the next winter without the aid of the horses they were then riding. The United States did not want them and I would, therefore, instruct the officers I left behind to receive the paroles of his troops to let every man of the Confederate army who claimed to own a horse or mule take the animal to his home. Lee remarked again that this would have a happy effect.

He then sat down and wrote out the following letter:

> HEADQUARTERS ARMY OF NORTHERN VIRGINIA,
> *April 9, 1865.*
> GENERAL:—I received your letter of this date containing the terms of the surrender of the Army of Northern Virginia as proposed by you. As they are substantially the same as those expressed in your letter of the 8th inst., they are accepted. I will proceed to designate the proper officers to carry the stipulations into effect.
> R. E. LEE, General.
> LIEUT.-GENERAL U. S. GRANT.

While duplicates of the two letters were being made, the Union generals present were severally presented to General Lee.

The much talked of surrendering of Lee's sword and my handing it back, this and much more that has been said about it is the purest romance. The word sword or side arms was not mentioned by either of us until I wrote it in the terms. There was no premeditation, and it did not occur to me until the moment I wrote it down. If I had happened to omit it, and General Lee had called my attention to it, I should have put it in the terms precisely as I acceded to the provision about the soldiers retaining their horses.

General Lee, after all was completed and before taking his leave, remarked that his army was in a very bad condition for want of food, and that they were without forage; that his men had been living for some days on parched corn exclusively, and that he would have to ask me for rations and forage. I told him "certainly," and asked for how many men he wanted rations. His answer was "about twenty-five thousand:" and I authorized him to send his own commissary and quartermaster to Appomattox Station, two or three miles away, where he could have, out of the trains we had stopped, all the provisions wanted. As for forage, we had ourselves depended almost entirely upon the country for that.

Generals Gibbon, Griffin and Merritt were designated by me to carry into effect the paroling of Lee's troops before they should start for their homes—General Lee leaving Generals Longstreet, Gordon and Pendleton for them to confer with in order to facilitate this work. Lee and I then separated as cordially as we had met, he returning to his own lines, and all went into bivouac for the night at Appomattox.

Soon after Lee's departure I telegraphed to Washington as follows:

HEADQUARTERS APPOMATTOX C. H., VA.,
April 9th, 1865, 4.30 P.M.

HON. E. M. STANTON, Secretary of War,
Washington.

General Lee surrendered the Army of Northern Virginia this afternoon on terms proposed by myself. The accompanying additional correspondence will show the conditions fully.

U. S. GRANT,
Lieut.-General.

When news of the surrender first reached our lines our men commenced firing a salute of a hundred guns in honor of the victory. I at once sent word, however, to have it stopped. The Confederates were now our prisoners, and we did not want to exult over their downfall.

I determined to return to Washington at once, with a view to putting a stop to the purchase of supplies, and what I now deemed other useless outlay of money. Before leaving, however, I thought I would like to see General Lee again; so next morning I rode out beyond our lines towards his headquarters, preceded by a bugler and a staff-officer carrying a white flag.

Lee soon mounted his horse, seeing who it was, and met me. We had there between the lines, sitting on horseback, a

(2)

Appomattox C.H. Va.
Apl. 9th 1865

Gen. R. E. Lee
Comdg C.S.A.

Gen.

In accordance
with the substance of my letter
to you of the 8th inst I propose to
receive the surrender of the Army of
N. Va. on the following terms; towit

Rolls of all the officers and
men to be made in duplicate
one copy to be given to an officer
designated by me the other to be
retained by such officer or officers
as you may designate. The officers
to give their individual paroles
not to take up arms against the

Government of the United States, nor each company officer commanded, may give a like parole for the men of their own commands.

The arms, artillery, and public property, to be parked and stacked and turned over to the officer appointed by me to receive them. This will not embrace the side arms of the officers, nor their private horses *or baggage*. This done, each officer and man will be allowed to return to their homes not to be disturbed by United States authority so long as they observe their parole and the laws in force where they may reside.

Very respectfully,

U. S. Grant, Lt.

very pleasant conversation of over half an hour, in the course of which Lee said to me that the South was a big country and that we might have to march over it three or four times before the war entirely ended, but that we would now be able to do it as they could no longer resist us. He expressed it as his earnest hope, however, that we would not be called upon to cause more loss and sacrifice of life; but he could not foretell the result. I then suggested to General Lee that there was not a man in the Confederacy whose influence with the soldiery and the whole people was as great as his, and that if he would now advise the surrender of all the armies I had no doubt his advice would be followed with alacrity. But Lee said, that he could not do that without consulting the President first. I knew there was no use to urge him to do anything against his ideas of what was right.

I was accompanied by my staff and other officers, some of whom seemed to have a great desire to go inside the Confederate lines. They finally asked permission of Lee to do so for the purpose of seeing some of their old army friends, and the permission was granted. They went over, had a very pleasant time with their old friends, and brought some of them back with them when they returned.

When Lee and I separated he went back to his lines and I returned to the house of Mr. McLean. Here the officers of both armies came in great numbers, and seemed to enjoy the meeting as much as though they had been friends separated for a long time while fighting battles under the same flag. For the time being it looked very much as if all thought of the war had escaped their minds. After an hour pleasantly passed in this way I set out on horseback, accompanied by my staff and a small escort, for Burkesville Junction, up to which point the railroad had by this time been repaired.

Chapter LXVIII.

MORALE OF THE TWO ARMIES — RELATIVE CONDITIONS
OF THE NORTH AND SOUTH — PRESIDENT LINCOLN
VISITS RICHMOND — ARRIVAL AT WASHINGTON —
PRESIDENT LINCOLN'S ASSASSINATION — PRESIDENT
JOHNSON'S POLICY.

AFTER THE FALL of Petersburg, and when the armies of the
Potomac and the James were in motion to head off Lee's
army, the *morale* of the National troops had greatly improved.
There was no more straggling, no more rear guards. The men
who in former times had been falling back, were now, as I
have already stated, striving to get to the front. For the first
time in four weary years they felt that they were now nearing
the time when they could return to their homes with their
country saved. On the other hand, the Confederates were
more than correspondingly depressed. Their despondency increased with each returning day, and especially after the battle
of Sailor's Creek. They threw away their arms in constantly
increasing numbers, dropping out of the ranks and betaking
themselves to the woods in the hope of reaching their homes.
I have already instanced the case of the entire disintegration
of a regiment whose colonel I met at Farmville. As a result of
these and other influences, when Lee finally surrendered at
Appomattox, there were only 28,356 officers and men left to
be paroled, and many of these were without arms. It was
probably this latter fact which gave rise to the statement
sometimes made, North and South, that Lee surrendered a
smaller number of men than what the official figures show. As
a matter of official record, and in addition to the number paroled as given above, we captured between March 29th and
the date of surrender 19,132 Confederates, to say nothing of
Lee's other losses, killed, wounded and missing, during the
series of desperate conflicts which marked his headlong and
determined flight. The same record shows the number of
cannon, including those at Appomattox, to have been 689
between the dates named.

There has always been a great conflict of opinion as to the number of troops engaged in every battle, or all important battles, fought between the sections, the South magnifying the number of Union troops engaged and belittling their own. Northern writers have fallen, in many instances, into the same error. I have often heard gentlemen, who were thoroughly loyal to the Union, speak of what a splendid fight the South had made and successfully continued for four years before yielding, with their twelve million of people against our twenty, and of the twelve four being colored slaves, non-combatants. I will add to their argument. We had many regiments of brave and loyal men who volunteered under great difficulty from the twelve million belonging to the South.

But the South had rebelled against the National government. It was not bound by any constitutional restrictions. The whole South was a military camp. The occupation of the colored people was to furnish supplies for the army. Conscription was resorted to early, and embraced every male from the age of eighteen to forty-five, excluding only those physically unfit to serve in the field, and the necessary number of civil officers of State and intended National government. The old and physically disabled furnished a good portion of these. The slaves, the non-combatants, one-third of the whole, were required to work in the field without regard to sex, and almost without regard to age. Children from the age of eight years could and did handle the hoe; they were not much older when they began to hold the plough. The four million of colored non-combatants were equal to more than three times their number in the North, age for age and sex for sex, in supplying food from the soil to support armies. Women did not work in the fields in the North, and children attended school.

The arts of peace were carried on in the North. Towns and cities grew during the war. Inventions were made in all kinds of machinery to increase the products of a day's labor in the shop, and in the field. In the South no opposition was allowed to the government which had been set up and which would have become real and respected if the rebellion had been successful. No rear had to be protected. All the troops in service could be brought to the front to contest every inch of ground threatened with invasion. The press of the South, like the people who remained at home, were loyal to the Southern cause.

In the North, the country, the towns and the cities presented about the same appearance they do in time of peace. The furnace was in blast, the shops were filled with workmen, the fields were cultivated, not only to supply the population of the North and the troops invading the South, but to ship abroad to pay a part of the expense of the war. In the North the press was free up to the point of open treason. The citizen could entertain his views and express them. Troops were necessary in the Northern States to prevent prisoners from the Southern army being released by outside force, armed and set at large to destroy by fire our Northern cities. Plans were formed by Northern and Southern citizens to burn our cities, to poison the water supplying them, to spread infection by importing clothing from infected regions, to blow up our river and lake steamers—regardless of the destruction of innocent lives. The copperhead disreputable portion of the press magnified rebel successes, and belittled those of the Union army. It was, with a large following, an auxiliary to the Confederate army. The North would have been much stronger with a hundred thousand of these men in the Confederate ranks and the rest of their kind thoroughly subdued, as the Union sentiment was in the South, than we were as the battle was fought.

As I have said, the whole South was a military camp. The colored people, four million in number, were submissive, and worked in the field and took care of the families while the able-bodied white men were at the front fighting for a cause destined to defeat. The cause was popular, and was enthusiastically supported by the young men. The conscription took all of them. Before the war was over, further conscriptions took those between fourteen and eighteen years of age as junior reserves, and those between forty-five and sixty as senior reserves. It would have been an offence, directly after the war, and perhaps it would be now, to ask any able-bodied man in the South, who was between the ages of fourteen and sixty at any time during the war, whether he had been in the Confederate army. He would assert that he had, or account for his absence from the ranks. Under such circumstances it is hard to conceive how the North showed such a superiority of force in every battle fought. I know they did not.

During 1862 and '3, John H. Morgan, a partisan officer, of no military education, but possessed of courage and endurance, operated in the rear of the Army of the Ohio in Kentucky and Tennessee. He had no base of supplies to protect, but was at home wherever he went. The army operating against the South, on the contrary, had to protect its lines of communication with the North, from which all supplies had to come to the front. Every foot of road had to be guarded by troops stationed at convenient distances apart. These guards could not render assistance beyond the points where stationed. Morgan was foot-loose and could operate where his information—always correct—led him to believe he could do the greatest damage. During the time he was operating in this way he killed, wounded and captured several times the number he ever had under his command at any one time. He destroyed many millions of property in addition. Places he did not attack had to be guarded as if threatened by him. Forrest, an abler soldier, operated farther west, and held from the National front quite as many men as could be spared for offensive operations. It is safe to say that more than half the National army was engaged in guarding lines of supplies, or were on leave, sick in hospital or on detail which prevented their bearing arms. Then, again, large forces were employed where no Confederate army confronted them. I deem it safe to say that there were no large engagements where the National numbers compensated for the advantage of position and intrenchment occupied by the enemy.

While I was in pursuit of General Lee, the President went to Richmond in company with Admiral Porter, and on board his flagship. He found the people of that city in great consternation. The leading citizens among the people who had remained at home surrounded him, anxious that something should be done to relieve them from suspense. General Weitzel was not then in the city, having taken offices in one of the neighboring villages after his troops had succeeded in subduing the conflagration which they had found in progress on entering the Confederate capital. The President sent for him, and, on his arrival, a short interview was had on board the vessel, Admiral Porter and a leading citizen of Virginia being also present. After this interview the President wrote an order in about these words, which I quote from memory: "General Weitzel is authorized to permit the body calling itself the Legislature of Virginia to meet for the purpose of recalling the Virginia troops from the Confederate armies."

Immediately some of the gentlemen composing that body wrote out a call for a meeting and had it published in their papers. This call, however, went very much further than Mr. Lincoln had contemplated, as he did not say the "Legislature of Virginia" but "the body which called itself the Legislature of Virginia." Mr. Stanton saw the call as published in the Northern papers the very next issue and took the liberty of countermanding the order authorizing any meeting of the Legislature, or any other body, and this notwithstanding the fact that the President was nearer the spot than he was.

This was characteristic of Mr. Stanton. He was a man who never questioned his own authority, and who always did in war time what he wanted to do. He was an able constitutional lawyer and jurist; but the Constitution was not an impediment to him while the war lasted. In this latter particular I entirely agree with the view he evidently held. The Constitution was not framed with a view to any such rebellion as that of 1861–5. While it did not authorize rebellion it made no provision against it. Yet the right to resist or suppress rebellion is as inherent as the right of self-defence, and as natural as the right of an individual to preserve his life when in jeopardy. The Constitution was therefore in abeyance for the time being, so far as it in any way affected the progress and termination of the war.

Those in rebellion against the government of the United States were not restricted by constitutional provisions, or any other, except the acts of their Congress, which was loyal and devoted to the cause for which the South was then fighting. It would be a hard case when one-third of a nation, united in rebellion against the national authority, is entirely untrammeled, that the other two-thirds, in their efforts to maintain the Union intact, should be restrained by a Constitution prepared by our ancestors for the express purpose of insuring the permanency of the confederation of the States.

After I left General Lee at Appomattox Station, I went with my staff and a few others directly to Burkesville Station on my way to Washington. The road from Burkesville back having been newly repaired and the ground being soft, the train got off the track frequently, and, as a result, it was after midnight of the second day when I reached City Point. As soon as possible I took a dispatch-boat thence to Washington City.

While in Washington I was very busy for a time in preparing the necessary orders for the new state of affairs; communicating with my different commanders of separate departments, bodies of troops, etc. But by the 14th I was pretty well through with this work, so as to be able to visit my children, who were then in Burlington, New Jersey, attending school. Mrs. Grant was with me in Washington at the time, and we were invited by President and Mrs. Lincoln to accompany them to the theatre on the evening of that day. I replied to the President's verbal invitation to the effect, that if we were in the city we would take great pleasure in accompanying them; but that I was very anxious to get away and visit my children, and if I could get through my work during the day I should do so. I did get through and started by the evening train on the 14th, sending Mr. Lincoln word, of course, that I would not be at the theatre.

At that time the railroad to New York entered Philadelphia on Broad Street; passengers were conveyed in ambulances to the Delaware River, and then ferried to Camden, at which point they took the cars again. When I reached the ferry, on the east side of the City of Philadelphia, I found people awaiting my arrival there; and also dispatches informing me of the assassination of the President and Mr. Seward, and of the probable assassination of the Vice-President, Mr. Johnson, and requesting my immediate return.

It would be impossible for me to describe the feeling that overcame me at the news of these assassinations, more especially the assassination of the President. I knew his goodness of heart, his generosity, his yielding disposition, his desire to have everybody happy, and above all his desire to see all the people of the United States enter again upon the full privileges of citizenship with equality among all. I knew also the feeling that Mr. Johnson had expressed in speeches and conversation against the Southern people, and I feared that his course towards them would be such as to repel, and make them unwilling citizens; and if they became such they would remain so for a long while. I felt that reconstruction had been set back, no telling how far.

I immediately arranged for getting a train to take me back to Washington City; but Mrs. Grant was with me; it was after midnight and Burlington was but an hour away. Finding that I could accompany her to our house and return about as soon as they would be ready to take me from the Philadelphia station, I went up with her and returned immediately by the same special train. The joy that I had witnessed among the people in the street and in public places in Washington when I left there, had been turned to grief; the city was in reality a city of mourning. I have stated what I believed then the effect of this would be, and my judgment now is that I was right. I believe the South would have been saved from very much of the hardness of feeling that was engendered by Mr. Johnson's course towards them during the first few months of his administration. Be this as it may, Mr. Lincoln's assassination was particularly unfortunate for the entire nation.

Mr. Johnson's course towards the South did engender bitterness of feeling. His denunciations of treason and his ever-ready remark, "Treason is a crime and must be made odious," was repeated to all those men of the South who came to him to get some assurances of safety so that they might go to work at something with the feeling that what they obtained would be secure to them. He uttered his denunciations with great vehemence, and as they were accompanied with no assurances of safety, many Southerners were driven to a point almost beyond endurance.

The President of the United States is, in a large degree, or ought to be, a representative of the feeling, wishes and judgment of those over whom he presides; and the Southerners who read the denunciations of themselves and their people must have come to the conclusion that he uttered the sentiments of the Northern people; whereas, as a matter of fact, but for the assassination of Mr. Lincoln, I believe the great majority of the Northern people, and the soldiers unanimously, would have been in favor of a speedy reconstruction on terms that would be the least humiliating to the people who had rebelled against their government. They believed, I have no doubt, as I did, that besides being the mildest, it was also the wisest, policy.

The people who had been in rebellion must necessarily come back into the Union, and be incorporated as an integral part of the nation. Naturally the nearer they were placed to an equality with the people who had not rebelled, the more reconciled they would feel with their old antagonists, and the better citizens they would be from the beginning. They surely would not make good citizens if they felt that they had a yoke around their necks.

I do not believe that the majority of the Northern people at that time were in favor of negro suffrage. They supposed that it would naturally follow the freedom of the negro, but that there would be a time of probation, in which the ex-slaves could prepare themselves for the privileges of citizenship before the full right would be conferred; but Mr. Johnson, after a complete revolution of sentiment, seemed to regard the South not only as an oppressed people, but as the people best entitled to consideration of any of our citizens. This was more than the people who had secured to us the perpetuation of the Union were prepared for, and they became more radical in their views. The Southerners had the most power in the executive branch, Mr. Johnson having gone to their side; and with a compact South, and such sympathy and support as they could get from the North, they felt that they would be able to control the nation at once, and already many of them acted as if they thought they were entitled to do so.

Thus Mr. Johnson, fighting Congress on the one hand, and receiving the support of the South on the other, drove Congress, which was overwhelmingly republican, to the passing of first one measure and then another to restrict his power. There being a solid South on one side that was in accord with the political party in the North which had sympathized with the rebellion, it finally, in the judgment of Congress and of the majority of the legislatures of the States, became necessary to enfranchise the negro, in all his ignorance. In this work, I shall not discuss the question of how far the policy of Congress in this particular proved a wise one. It became an absolute necessity, however, because of the foolhardiness of the President and the blindness of the Southern people to their own interest. As to myself, while strongly favoring the course that would be the least humiliating to the people who had been in rebellion, I had gradually worked up to the point where, with the majority of the people, I favored immediate enfranchisement.

Chapter LXIX.

SHERMAN AND JOHNSTON — JOHNSTON'S SURRENDER
TO SHERMAN — CAPTURE OF MOBILE — WILSON'S
EXPEDITION — CAPTURE OF JEFFERSON DAVIS — GENERAL
THOMAS'S QUALITIES — ESTIMATE OF GENERAL CANBY.

WHEN I LEFT Appomattox I ordered General Meade to proceed leisurely back to Burkesville Station with the Army of the Potomac and the Army of the James, and to go into camp there until further orders from me. General Johnston, as has been stated before, was in North Carolina confronting General Sherman. It could not be known positively, of course, whether Johnston would surrender on the news of Lee's surrender, though I supposed he would; and if he did not, Burkesville Station was the natural point from which to move to attack him. The army which I could have sent against him was superior to his, and that with which Sherman confronted him was also superior; and between the two he would necessarily have been crushed, or driven away. With the loss of their capital and the Army of Northern Virginia it was doubtful whether Johnston's men would have had the spirit to stand. My belief was that he would make no such attempt; but I adopted this course as a precaution against what might happen, however improbable.

Simultaneously with my starting from City Point, I sent a messenger to North Carolina by boat with dispatches to General Sherman, informing him of the surrender of Lee and his army; also of the terms which I had given him; and I authorized Sherman to give the same terms to Johnston if the latter chose to accept them. The country is familiar with the terms that Sherman agreed to *conditionally*, because they embraced a political question as well as a military one and he would therefore have to confer with the government before agreeing to them definitely.

General Sherman had met Mr. Lincoln at City Point while visiting there to confer with me about our final movement, and knew what Mr. Lincoln had said to the peace commissioners when he met them at Hampton Roads, viz.: that before he could enter into negotiations with them they would have to agree to two points: one being that the Union should be preserved, and the other that slavery should be abolished; and if they were ready to concede these two points he was almost ready to sign his name to a blank piece of paper and permit them to fill out the balance of the terms upon which we would live together. He had also seen notices in the newspapers of Mr. Lincoln's visit to Richmond, and had read in the same papers that while there he had authorized the convening of the Legislature of Virginia.

Sherman thought, no doubt, in adding to the terms that I had made with General Lee, that he was but carrying out the wishes of the President of the United States. But seeing that he was going beyond his authority, he made it a point that the terms were only conditional. They signed them with this understanding, and agreed to a truce until the terms could be sent to Washington for approval; if approved by the proper authorities there, they would then be final; if not approved, then he would give due notice, before resuming hostilities. As the world knows, Sherman, from being one of the most popular generals of the land (Congress having even gone so far as to propose a bill providing for a second lieutenant-general for the purpose of advancing him to that grade), was denounced by the President and Secretary of War in very bitter terms. Some people went so far as to denounce him as a traitor—a most preposterous term to apply to a man who had rendered so much service as he had, even supposing he had made a mistake in granting such terms as he did to Johnston and his army. If Sherman had taken authority to send Johnston with his army home, with their arms to be put in the arsenals of their own States, without submitting the question to the authorities at Washington, the suspicions against him might have some foundation. But the feeling against Sherman died out very rapidly, and it was not many weeks before he was restored to the fullest confidence of the American people.

When, some days after my return to Washington, President Johnson and the Secretary of War received the terms which General Sherman had forwarded for approval, a cabinet meeting was immediately called and I was sent for. There seemed to be the greatest consternation, lest Sherman would commit the government to terms which they were not willing to accede to and which he had no right to grant. A message went out directing the troops in the South not to obey General Sherman. I was ordered to proceed at once to North Carolina and take charge of matters there myself. Of course I started without delay, and reached there as soon as possible. I repaired to Raleigh, where Sherman was, as quietly as possible, hoping to see him without even his army learning of my presence.

When I arrived I went to Sherman's headquarters, and we were at once closeted together. I showed him the instructions and orders under which I visited him. I told him that I wanted him to notify General Johnston that the terms which they had conditionally agreed upon had not been approved in Washington, and that he was authorized to offer the same terms I had given General Lee. I sent Sherman to do this himself. I did not wish the knowledge of my presence to be known to the army generally; so I left it to Sherman to negotiate the terms of the surrender solely by himself, and without the enemy knowing that I was anywhere near the field. As soon as possible I started to get away, to leave Sherman quite free and untrammelled.

At Goldsboro', on my way back, I met a mail, containing the last newspapers, and I found in them indications of great excitement in the North over the terms Sherman had given Johnston; and harsh orders that had been promulgated by the President and Secretary of War. I knew that Sherman must see these papers, and I fully realized what great indignation they would cause him, though I do not think his feelings could have been more excited than were my own. But like the true and loyal soldier that he was, he carried out the instructions I had given him, obtained the surrender of Johnston's army, and settled down in his camp about Raleigh, to await final orders.

There were still a few expeditions out in the South that could not be communicated with, and had to be left to act according to the judgment of their respective commanders. With these it was impossible to tell how the news of the surrender of Lee and Johnston, of which they must have heard, might affect their judgment as to what was best to do.

The three expeditions which I had tried so hard to get off from the commands of Thomas and Canby did finally get off: one under Canby himself, against Mobile, late in March; that under Stoneman from East Tennessee on the 20th; and the one under Wilson, starting from Eastport, Mississippi, on the 22d of March. They were all eminently successful, but without any good result. Indeed much valuable property was destroyed and many lives lost at a time when we would have liked to spare them. The war was practically over before their victories were gained. They were so late in commencing operations, that they did not hold any troops away that otherwise would have been operating against the armies which were gradually forcing the Confederate armies to a surrender. The only possible good that we may have experienced from these raids was by Stoneman's getting near Lynchburg about the time the armies of the Potomac and the James were closing in on Lee at Appomattox.

Stoneman entered North Carolina and then pushed north to strike the Virginia and Tennessee Railroad. He got upon that road, destroyed its bridges at different places and rendered the road useless to the enemy up to within a few miles of Lynchburg. His approach caused the evacuation of that city about the time we were at Appomattox, and was the cause of a commotion we heard of there. He then pushed south, and was operating in the rear of Johnston's army about the time the negotiations were going on between Sherman and Johnston for the latter's surrender. In this raid Stoneman captured and destroyed a large amount of stores, while fourteen guns and nearly two thousand prisoners were the trophies of his success.

Canby appeared before Mobile on the 27th of March. The city of Mobile was protected by two forts, besides other intrenchments — Spanish Fort, on the east side of the bay, and Fort Blakely, north of the city. These forts were invested. On the night of the 8th of April, the National troops having carried the enemy's works at one point, Spanish Fort was evacuated; and on the 9th, the very day of Lee's surrender, Blakely was carried by assault, with a considerable loss to us. On the 11th the city was evacuated.

I had tried for more than two years to have an expedition sent against Mobile when its possession by us would have been of great advantage. It finally cost lives to take it when its possession was of no importance, and when, if left alone, it would within a few days have fallen into our hands without any bloodshed whatever

Wilson moved out with full 12,000 men, well equipped and well armed. He was an energetic officer and accomplished his work rapidly. Forrest was in his front, but with neither his old-time army nor his old-time prestige. He now had principally conscripts. His conscripts were generally old men and boys. He had a few thousand regular cavalry left, but not enough to even retard materially the progress of Wilson's cavalry. Selma fell on the 2d of April, with a large number of prisoners and a large quantity of war material, machine shops, etc., to be disposed of by the victors. Tuscaloosa, Montgomery and West Point fell in quick succession. These were all important points to the enemy by reason of their railroad connections, as depots of supplies, and because of their manufactories of war material. They were fortified or intrenched, and there was considerable fighting before they were captured. Macon surrendered on the 21st of April. Here news was received of the negotiations for the surrender of Johnston's army. Wilson belonged to the military division commanded by Sherman, and of course was bound by his terms. This stopped all fighting.

General Richard Taylor had now become the senior Confederate officer still at liberty east of the Mississippi River, and on the 4th of May he surrendered everything within the limits of this extensive command. General E. Kirby Smith surrendered the trans-Mississippi department on the 26th of May, leaving no other Confederate army at liberty to continue the war.

Wilson's raid resulted in the capture of the fugitive president of the defunct confederacy before he got out of the country. This occurred at Irwinsville, Georgia, on the 11th of May. For myself, and I believe Mr. Lincoln shared the feeling, I would have been very glad to have seen Mr. Davis succeed

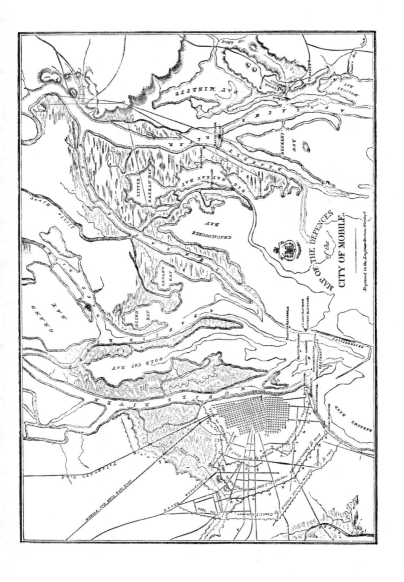

MAP OF THE DEFENCES
of the
CITY OF MOBILE.

Engraved in the Engineer Bureau Printing Office.

in escaping, but for one reason: I feared that if not captured, he might get into the trans-Mississippi region and there set up a more contracted confederacy. The young men now out of homes and out of employment might have rallied under his standard and protracted the war yet another year. The Northern people were tired of the war, they were tired of piling up a debt which would be a further mortgage upon their homes.

Mr. Lincoln, I believe, wanted Mr. Davis to escape, because he did not wish to deal with the matter of his punishment. He knew there would be people clamoring for the punishment of the ex-Confederate president, for high treason. He thought blood enough had already been spilled to atone for our wickedness as a nation. At all events he did not wish to be the judge to decide whether more should be shed or not. But his own life was sacrificed at the hands of an assassin before the ex-president of the Confederacy was a prisoner in the hands of the government which he had lent all his talent and all his energies to destroy.

All things are said to be wisely directed, and for the best interest of all concerned. This reflection does not, however, abate in the slightest our sense of bereavement in the untimely loss of so good and great a man as Abraham Lincoln.

He would have proven the best friend the South could have had, and saved much of the wrangling and bitterness of feeling brought out by reconstruction under a President who at first wished to revenge himself upon Southern men of better social standing than himself, but who still sought their recognition, and in a short time conceived the idea and advanced the proposition to become their Moses to lead them triumphantly out of all their difficulties.

The story of the legislation enacted during the reconstruction period to stay the hands of the President is too fresh in the minds of the people to be told now. Much of it, no doubt, was unconstitutional; but it was hoped that the laws enacted would serve their purpose before the question of constitutionality could be submitted to the judiciary and a decision obtained. These laws did serve their purpose, and now remain "a dead letter" upon the statute books of the United States, no one taking interest enough in them to give them a passing thought.

Much was said at the time about the garb Mr. Davis was wearing when he was captured. I cannot settle this question from personal knowledge of the facts; but I have been under the belief, from information given to me by General Wilson shortly after the event, that when Mr. Davis learned that he was surrounded by our cavalry he was in his tent dressed in a gentleman's dressing gown. Naturally enough, Mr. Davis wanted to escape, and would not reflect much how this should be accomplished provided it might be done successfully. If captured, he would be no ordinary prisoner. He represented all there was of that hostility to the government which had caused four years of the bloodiest war—and the most costly in other respects of which history makes any record. Every one supposed he would be tried for treason if captured, and that he would be executed. Had he succeeded in making his escape in any disguise it would have been adjudged a good thing afterwards by his admirers.

As my official letters on file in the War Department, as well as my remarks in this book, reflect upon General Thomas by dwelling somewhat upon his tardiness, it is due to myself, as well as to him, that I give my estimate of him as a soldier. The same remark will apply also in the case of General Canby. I had been at West Point with Thomas one year, and had known him later in the old army. He was a man of commanding appearance, slow and deliberate in speech and action; sensible, honest and brave. He possessed valuable soldierly qualities in an eminent degree. He gained the confidence of all who served under him, and almost their love. This implies a very valuable quality. It is a quality which calls out the most efficient services of the troops serving under the commander possessing it.

Thomas's dispositions were deliberately made, and always good. He could not be driven from a point he was given to hold. He was not as good, however, in pursuit as he was in action. I do not believe that he could ever have conducted Sherman's army from Chattanooga to Atlanta against the defences and the commander guarding that line in 1864. On the other hand, if it had been given him to hold the line which Johnston tried to hold, neither that general nor Sherman, nor any other officer could have done it better.

Thomas was a valuable officer, who richly deserved, as he has received, the plaudits of his countrymen for the part he played in the great tragedy of 1861−5.

General Canby was an officer of great merit. He was naturally studious, and inclined to the law. There have been in the army but very few, if any, officers who took as much interest in reading and digesting every act of Congress and every regulation for the government of the army as he. His knowledge gained in this way made him a most valuable staff officer, a capacity in which almost all his army services were rendered up to the time of his being assigned to the Military Division of the Gulf. He was an exceedingly modest officer, though of great talent and learning. I presume his feelings when first called upon to command a large army against a fortified city, were somewhat like my own when marching a regiment against General Thomas Harris in Missouri in 1861. Neither of us would have felt the slightest trepidation in going into battle with some one else commanding. Had Canby been in other engagements afterwards, he would, I have no doubt, have advanced without any fear arising from a sense of the responsibility. He was afterwards killed in the lava beds of Southern Oregon, while in pursuit of the hostile Modoc Indians. His character was as pure as his talent and learning were great. His services were valuable during the war, but principally as a bureau officer. I have no idea that it was from choice that his services were rendered in an office, but because of his superior efficiency there.

Chapter LXX.

THINGS BEGAN to quiet down, and as the certainty that there would be no more armed resistance became clearer, the troops in North Carolina and Virginia were ordered to march immediately to the capital, and go into camp there until mustered out. Suitable garrisons were left at the prominent places throughout the South to insure obedience to the laws that might be enacted for the government of the several States, and to insure security to the lives and property of all classes. I do not know how far this was necessary, but I deemed it necessary, at that time, that such a course should be pursued. I think now that these garrisons were continued after they ceased to be absolutely required; but it is not to be expected that such a rebellion as was fought between the sections from 1861 to 1865 could terminate without leaving many serious apprehensions in the mind of the people as to what should be done.

Sherman marched his troops from Goldsboro, up to Manchester, on the south side of the James River, opposite Richmond, and there put them in camp, while he went back to Savannah to see what the situation was there.

It was during this trip that the last outrage was committed upon him. Halleck had been sent to Richmond to command Virginia, and had issued orders prohibiting even Sherman's own troops from obeying his, Sherman's, orders. Sherman met the papers on his return, containing this order of Halleck, and very justly felt indignant at the outrage. On his arrival at Fortress Monroe returning from Savannah, Sherman received an invitation from Halleck to come to Richmond and be his guest. This he indignantly refused, and informed Halleck, furthermore, that he had seen his order. He also stated that he was coming up to take command of his troops, and as he marched through it would probably be as well for Halleck not to show himself, because he (Sherman) would not be responsible for what some rash person might do through indignation for the treatment he had received. Very soon after that, Sherman received orders from me to proceed to Washington City, and to go into camp on the south side of the city pending the mustering-out of the troops.

There was no incident worth noting in the march northward from Goldsboro, to Richmond, or in that from Richmond to Washington City. The army, however, commanded by Sherman, which had been engaged in all the battles of the West and had marched from the Mississippi through the Southern States to the sea, from there to Goldsboro, and thence to Washington City, had passed over many of the battle-fields of the Army of the Potomac, thus having seen, to a greater extent than any other body of troops, the entire theatre of the four years' war for the preservation of the Union.

The march of Sherman's army from Atlanta to the sea and north to Goldsboro, while it was not accompanied with the danger that was anticipated, yet was magnificent in its results, and equally magnificent in the way it was conducted. It had an important bearing, in various ways, upon the great object we had in view, that of closing the war. All the States east of the Mississippi River up to the State of Georgia, had felt the hardships of the war. Georgia, and South Carolina, and almost all of North Carolina, up to this time, had been exempt from invasion by the Northern armies, except upon their immediate sea coasts. Their newspapers had given such an account of Confederate success, that the people who remained at home had been convinced that the Yankees had been whipped from first to last, and driven from pillar to post, and that now they could hardly be holding out for any other purpose than to find a way out of the war with honor to themselves.

Even during this march of Sherman's the newspapers in his front were proclaiming daily that his army was nothing better than a mob of men who were frightened out of their wits and hastening, panic-stricken, to try to get under the cover of our navy for protection against the Southern people. As the army was seen marching on triumphantly, however, the minds of the people became disabused and they saw the true state of affairs. In turn they became disheartened, and would have been glad to submit without compromise.

Another great advantage resulting from this march, and which was calculated to hasten the end, was the fact that the great storehouse of Georgia was entirely cut off from the Confederate armies. As the troops advanced north from Savannah, the destruction of the railroads in South Carolina and the southern part of North Carolina, further cut off their resources and left the armies still in Virginia and North Carolina dependent for supplies upon a very small area of country, already very much exhausted of food and forage.

In due time the two armies, one from Burkesville Junction and the other from the neighborhood of Raleigh, North Carolina, arrived and went into camp near the Capital, as directed. The troops were hardy, being inured to fatigue, and they appeared in their respective camps as ready and fit for duty as they had ever been in their lives. I doubt whether an equal body of men of any nation, take them man for man, officer for officer, was ever gotten together that would have proved their equal in a great battle.

The armies of Europe are machines: the men are brave and the officers capable; but the majority of the soldiers in most of the nations of Europe are taken from a class of people who are not very intelligent and who have very little interest in the contest in which they are called upon to take part. Our armies were composed of men who were able to read, men who knew what they were fighting for, and could not be induced to serve as soldiers, except in an emergency when the safety of the nation was involved, and so necessarily must have been more than equal to men who fought merely because they were brave and because they were thoroughly drilled and inured to hardships.

There was nothing of particular importance occurred during the time these troops were in camp before starting North.

I remember one little incident which I will relate as an anecdote characteristic of Mr. Lincoln. It occurred a day after I reached Washington, and about the time General Meade reached Burkesville with the army. Governor Smith of Virginia had left Richmond with the Confederate States government, and had gone to Danville. Supposing I was necessarily with the army at Burkesville, he addressed a letter to me there informing me that, as governor of the Commonwealth of the State of Virginia, he had temporarily removed the State capital from Richmond to Danville, and asking if he would be permitted to perform the functions of his office there without molestation by the Federal authorities. I give this letter only in substance. He also inquired of me whether in case he was not allowed to perform the duties of his office, he with a few others might not be permitted to leave the country and go abroad without interference. General Meade being informed that a flag of truce was outside his pickets with a letter to me, at once sent out and had the letter brought in without informing the officer who brought it that I was not present. He read the letter and telegraphed me its contents. Meeting Mr. Lincoln shortly after receiving this dispatch, I repeated its contents to him. Mr. Lincoln, supposing I was asking for instructions, said, in reply to that part of Governor Smith's letter which inquired whether he with a few friends would be permitted to leave the country unmolested, that his position was like that of a certain Irishman (giving the name) he knew in Springfield who was very popular with the people, a man of considerable promise, and very much liked. Unfortunately he had acquired the habit of drinking, and his friends could see that the habit was growing on him. These friends determined to make an effort to save him, and to do this they drew up a pledge to abstain from all alcoholic drinks. They asked Pat to join them in signing the pledge, and he consented. He had been so long out of the habit of using plain water as a beverage that he resorted to soda-water as a substitute. After a few days this began to grow distasteful to him. So holding the glass behind him, he said: "Doctor, couldn't you drop a bit of brandy in that unbeknownst to myself."

I do not remember what the instructions were the President gave me, but I know that Governor Smith was not permitted to perform the duties of his office. I also know that if Mr. Lincoln had been spared, there would have been no efforts made to prevent any one from leaving the country who desired to do so. He would have been equally willing to permit the return of the same expatriated citizens after they had time to repent of their choice.

On the 18th of May orders were issued by the adjutant-general for a grand review by the President and his cabinet of Sherman's and Meade's armies. The review commenced on the 23d and lasted two days. Meade's army occupied over six hours of the first day in passing the grand stand which had been erected in front of the President's house. Sherman witnessed this review from the grand stand which was occupied by the President and his cabinet. Here he showed his resentment for the cruel and harsh treatment that had unnecessarily been inflicted upon him by the Secretary of War, by refusing to take his extended hand.

Sherman's troops had been in camp on the south side of the Potomac. During the night of the 23d he crossed over and bivouacked not far from the Capitol. Promptly at ten o'clock on the morning of the 24th, his troops commenced to pass in review. Sherman's army made a different appearance from that of the Army of the Potomac. The latter had been operating where they received directly from the North full supplies of food and clothing regularly: the review of this army therefore was the review of a body of 65,000 well-drilled, well-disciplined and orderly soldiers inured to hardship and fit for any duty, but without the experience of gathering their own food and supplies in an enemy's country, and of being ever on the watch. Sherman's army was not so well-dressed as the Army of the Potomac, but their marching could not be excelled; they gave the appearance of men who had been thoroughly drilled to endure hardships, either by long and continuous marches or through exposure to any climate, without the ordinary shelter of a camp. They exhibited also some of the order of march through Georgia where the "sweet potatoes sprung up from the ground" as Sherman's army went marching through. In the rear of a company there would be a captured horse or mule loaded with small cooking utensils, captured chickens and other food picked up for the use of the men. Negro families who had followed the army would sometimes come along in the rear of a company, with three or four children packed upon a single mule, and the mother leading it.

The sight was varied and grand: nearly all day for two successive days, from the Capitol to the Treasury Building, could be seen a mass of orderly soldiers marching in columns of companies. The National flag was flying from almost every house and store; the windows were filled with spectators; the door-steps and side-walks were crowded with colored people and poor whites who did not succeed in securing better quarters from which to get a view of the grand armies. The city was about as full of strangers who had come to see the sights as it usually is on inauguration day when a new President takes his seat.

It may not be out of place to again allude to President Lincoln and the Secretary of War, Mr. Stanton, who were the great conspicuous figures in the executive branch of the government. There is no great difference of opinion now, in the public mind, as to the characteristics of the President. With Mr. Stanton the case is different. They were the very opposite of each other in almost every particular, except that each possessed great ability. Mr. Lincoln gained influence over men by making them feel that it was a pleasure to serve him. He preferred yielding his own wish to gratify others, rather than to insist upon having his own way. It distressed him to disappoint others. In matters of public duty, however, he had what he wished, but in the least offensive way. Mr. Stanton never questioned his own authority to command, unless resisted. He cared nothing for the feeling of others. In fact it seemed to be pleasanter to him to disappoint than to gratify. He felt no hesitation in assuming the functions of the executive, or in acting without advising with him. If his act was not sustained, he would change it—if he saw the matter would be followed up until he did so.

It was generally supposed that these two officials formed the complement of each other. The Secretary was required to prevent the President's being imposed upon. The President was required in the more responsible place of seeing that injustice was not done to others. I do not know that this view of these two men is still entertained by the majority of the people. It is not a correct view, however, in my estimation. Mr. Lincoln did not require a guardian to aid him in the fulfilment of a public trust.

Mr. Lincoln was not timid, and he was willing to trust his generals in making and executing their plans. The Secretary was very timid, and it was impossible for him to avoid interfering with the armies covering the capital when it was sought to defend it by an offensive movement against the army guarding the Confederate capital. He could see our weakness, but he could not see that the enemy was in danger. The enemy would not have been in danger if Mr. Stanton had been in the field. These characteristics of the two officials were clearly shown shortly after Early came so near getting into the capital.

Among the army and corps commanders who served with me during the war between the States, and who attracted much public attention, but of whose ability as soldiers I have not yet given any estimate, are Meade, Hancock, Sedgwick, Burnside, Terry and Hooker. There were others of great merit, such as Griffin, Humphreys, Wright and Mackenzie. Of those first named, Burnside at one time had command of the Army of the Potomac, and later of the Army of the Ohio. Hooker also commanded the Army of the Potomac for a short time.

General Meade was an officer of great merit, with drawbacks to his usefulness that were beyond his control. He had been an officer of the engineer corps before the war, and consequently had never served with troops until he was over forty-six years of age. He never had, I believe, a command of less than a brigade. He saw clearly and distinctly the position of the enemy, and the topography of the country in front of his own position. His first idea was to take advantage of the lay of the ground, sometimes without reference to the direction we wanted to move afterwards. He was subordinate to his superiors in rank to the extent that he could execute an order which changed his own plans with the same zeal he would have displayed if the plan had been his own. He was brave and conscientious, and commanded the respect of all who knew him. He was unfortunately of a temper that would get beyond his control, at times, and make him speak to officers of high rank in the most offensive manner. No one saw this fault more plainly than he himself, and no one regretted it more. This made it unpleasant at times, even in battle, for those around him to approach him even with information. In spite of this defect he was a most valuable officer and deserves a high place in the annals of his country.

General Burnside was an officer who was generally liked and respected. He was not, however, fitted to command an army. No one knew this better than himself. He always admitted his blunders, and extenuated those of officers under him beyond what they were entitled to. It was hardly his fault that he was ever assigned to a separate command.

Of Hooker I saw but little during the war. I had known him very well before, however. Where I did see him, at Chattanooga, his achievement in bringing his command around the point of Lookout Mountain and into Chattanooga Valley was brilliant. I nevertheless regarded him as a dangerous man. He was not subordinate to his superiors. He was ambitious to the extent of caring nothing for the rights of others. His disposition was, when engaged in battle, to get detached from the main body of the army and exercise a separate command, gathering to his standard all he could of his juniors.

Hancock stands the most conspicuous figure of all the general officers who did not exercise a separate command. He commanded a corps longer than any other one, and his name was never mentioned as having committed in battle a blunder for which he was responsible. He was a man of very conspicuous personal appearance. Tall, well-formed and, at the time of which I now write, young and fresh-looking, he presented an appearance that would attract the attention of an army as he passed. His genial disposition made him friends, and his personal courage and his presence with his command in the thickest of the fight won for him the confidence of troops serving under him. No matter how hard the fight, the 2d corps always felt that their commander was looking after them.

Sedgwick was killed at Spottsylvania before I had an opportunity of forming an estimate of his qualifications as a soldier from personal observation. I had known him in Mexico when both of us were lieutenants, and when our service gave no indication that either of us would ever be equal to the command of a brigade. He stood very high in the army, however, as an officer and a man. He was brave and conscientious. His ambition was not great, and he seemed to dread responsibility. He was willing to do any amount of battling, but always wanted some one else to direct. He declined the command of the Army of the Potomac once, if not oftener.

General Alfred H. Terry came into the army as a volunteer without a military education. His way was won without political influence up to an important separate command—the expedition against Fort Fisher, in January, 1865. His success there was most brilliant, and won for him the rank of brigadier-general in the regular army and of major-general of volunteers. He is a man who makes friends of those under him by his consideration of their wants and their dues. As a commander, he won their confidence by his coolness in action and by his clearness of perception in taking in the situation under which he was placed at any given time.

Griffin, Humphreys, and Mackenzie were good corps commanders, but came into that position so near to the close of the war as not to attract public attention. All three served as such, in the last campaign of the armies of the Potomac and the James, which culminated at Appomattox Court House, on the 9th of April, 1865. The sudden collapse of the rebellion monopolized attention to the exclusion of almost everything else. I regarded Mackenzie as the most promising young officer in the army. Graduating at West Point, as he did, during the second year of the war, he had won his way up to the command of a corps before its close. This he did upon his own merit and without influence.

Conclusion.

THE CAUSE of the great War of the Rebellion against the United States will have to be attributed to slavery. For some years before the war began it was a trite saying among some politicians that "A state half slave and half free cannot exist." All must become slave or all free, or the state will go down. I took no part myself in any such view of the case at the time, but since the war is over, reviewing the whole question, I have come to the conclusion that the saying is quite true.

Slavery was an institution that required unusual guarantees for its security wherever it existed; and in a country like ours where the larger portion of it was free territory inhabited by an intelligent and well-to-do population, the people would naturally have but little sympathy with demands upon them for its protection. Hence the people of the South were dependent upon keeping control of the general government to secure the perpetuation of their favorite institution. They were enabled to maintain this control long after the States where slavery existed had ceased to have the controlling power, through the assistance they received from odd men here and there throughout the Northern States. They saw their power waning, and this led them to encroach upon the prerogatives and independence of the Northern States by enacting such laws as the Fugitive Slave Law. By this law every Northern man was obliged, when properly summoned, to turn out and help apprehend the runaway slave of a Southern man. Northern marshals became slave-catchers, and Northern courts had to contribute to the support and protection of the institution.

This was a degradation which the North would not permit any longer than until they could get the power to expunge such laws from the statute books. Prior to the time of these encroachments the great majority of the people of the North had no particular quarrel with slavery, so long as they were not forced to have it themselves. But they were not willing to play the rôle of police for the South in the protection of this particular institution.

In the early days of the country, before we had railroads, telegraphs and steamboats—in a word, rapid transit of any sort—the States were each almost a separate nationality. At that time the subject of slavery caused but little or no disturbance to the public mind. But the country grew, rapid transit was established, and trade and commerce between the States got to be so much greater than before, that the power of the National government became more felt and recognized and, therefore, had to be enlisted in the cause of this institution.

It is probably well that we had the war when we did. We are better off now than we would have been without it, and have made more rapid progress than we otherwise should have made. The civilized nations of Europe have been stimulated into unusual activity, so that commerce, trade, travel, and thorough acquaintance among people of different nationalities, has become common; whereas, before, it was but the few who had ever had the privilege of going beyond the limits of their own country or who knew anything about other people. Then, too, our republican institutions were regarded as experiments up to the breaking out of the rebellion, and monarchical Europe generally believed that our republic was a rope of sand that would part the moment the slightest strain was brought upon it. Now it has shown itself capable of dealing with one of the greatest wars that was ever made, and our people have proven themselves to be the most formidable in war of any nationality.

But this war was a fearful lesson, and should teach us the necessity of avoiding wars in the future.

The conduct of some of the European states during our troubles shows the lack of conscience of communities where the responsibility does not come upon a single individual. Seeing a nation that extended from ocean to ocean, embracing the better part of a continent, growing as we were growing in population, wealth and intelligence, the European nations thought it would be well to give us a check. We might, possibly, after a while threaten their peace, or, at least, the perpetuity of their institutions. Hence, England was constantly finding fault with the administration at Washington because we were not able to keep up an effective blockade.

She also joined, at first, with France and Spain in setting up an Austrian prince upon the throne in Mexico, totally disregarding any rights or claims that Mexico had of being treated as an independent power. It is true they trumped up grievances as a pretext, but they were only pretexts which can always be found when wanted.

Mexico, in her various revolutions, had been unable to give that protection to the subjects of foreign nations which she would have liked to give, and some of her revolutionary leaders had forced loans from them. Under pretence of protecting their citizens, these nations seized upon Mexico as a foothold for establishing a European monarchy upon our continent, thus threatening our peace at home. I, myself, regarded this as a direct act of war against the United States by the powers engaged, and supposed as a matter of course that the United States would treat it as such when their hands were free to strike. I often spoke of the matter to Mr. Lincoln and the Secretary of War, but never heard any special views from them to enable me to judge what they thought or felt about it. I inferred that they felt a good deal as I did, but were unwilling to commit themselves while we had our own troubles upon our hands.

All of the powers except France very soon withdrew from the armed intervention for the establishment of an Austrian prince upon the throne of Mexico; but the governing people of these countries continued to the close of the war to throw obstacles in our way. After the surrender of Lee, therefore, entertaining the opinion here expressed, I sent Sheridan with a corps to the Rio Grande to have him where he might aid Juarez in expelling the French from Mexico. These troops got off before they could be stopped; and went to the Rio Grande, where Sheridan distributed them up and down the river, much to the consternation of the troops in the quarter of Mexico bordering on that stream. This soon led to a request from France that we should withdraw our troops from the Rio Grande and to negotiations for the withdrawal of theirs. Finally Bazaine was withdrawn from Mexico by order of the French Government. From that day the empire began to totter. Mexico was then able to maintain her independence without aid from us.

France is the traditional ally and friend of the United States. I did not blame France for her part in the scheme to erect a monarchy upon the ruins of the Mexican Republic. That was the scheme of one man, an imitator without genius or merit. He had succeeded in stealing the government of his country, and made a change in its form against the wishes and instincts of his people. He tried to play the part of the first Napoleon, without the ability to sustain that rôle. He sought by new conquests to add to his empire and his glory; but the signal failure of his scheme of conquest was the precursor of his own overthrow.

Like our own war between the States, the Franco-Prussian war was an expensive one; but it was worth to France all it cost her people. It was the completion of the downfall of Napoleon III. The beginning was when he landed troops on this continent. Failing here, the prestige of his name—all the prestige he ever had—was gone. He must achieve a success or fall. He tried to strike down his neighbor, Prussia—and fell.

I never admired the character of the first Napoleon; but I recognize his great genius. His work, too, has left its impress for good on the face of Europe. The third Napoleon could have no claim to having done a good or just act.

To maintain peace in the future it is necessary to be prepared for war. There can scarcely be a possible chance of a conflict, such as the last one, occurring among our own people again; but, growing as we are, in population, wealth and military power, we may become the envy of nations which led us in all these particulars only a few years ago; and unless we are prepared for it we may be in danger of a combined movement being some day made to crush us out. Now, scarcely twenty years after the war, we seem to have forgotten the lessons it taught, and are going on as if in the greatest security, without the power to resist an invasion by the fleets of fourth-rate European powers for a time until we could prepare for them.

We should have a good navy, and our sea-coast defences should be put in the finest possible condition. Neither of these cost much when it is considered where the money goes, and what we get in return. Money expended in a fine navy, not only adds to our security and tends to prevent war in the future, but is very material aid to our commerce with foreign nations in the meantime. Money spent upon sea-coast defences is spent among our own people, and all goes back again among the people. The work accomplished, too, like that of the navy, gives us a feeling of security.

England's course towards the United States during the rebellion exasperated the people of this country very much against the mother country. I regretted it. England and the United States are natural allies, and should be the best of friends. They speak one language, and are related by blood and other ties. We together, or even either separately, are better qualified than any other people to establish commerce between all the nationalities of the world.

England governs her own colonies, and particularly those embracing the people of different races from her own, better than any other nation. She is just to the conquered, but rigid. She makes them self-supporting, but gives the benefit of labor to the laborer. She does not seem to look upon the colonies as outside possessions which she is at liberty to work for the support and aggrandizement of the home government.

The hostility of England to the United States during our rebellion was not so much real as it was apparent. It was the hostility of the leaders of one political party. I am told that there was no time during the civil war when they were able to get up in England a demonstration in favor of secession, while these were constantly being gotten up in favor of the Union, or, as they called it, in favor of the North. Even in Manchester, which suffered so fearfully by having the cotton cut off from her mills, they had a monster demonstration in favor of the North at the very time when their workmen were almost famishing.

It is possible that the question of a conflict between races may come up in the future, as did that between freedom and slavery before. The condition of the colored man within our borders may become a source of anxiety, to say the least. But he was brought to our shores by compulsion, and he now should be considered as having as good a right to remain here as any other class of our citizens. It was looking to a settlement of this question that led me to urge the annexation of Santo Domingo during the time I was President of the United States.

Santo Domingo was freely offered to us, not only by the administration, but by all the people, almost without price. The island is upon our shores, is very fertile, and is capable of supporting fifteen millions of people. The products of the soil are so valuable that labor in her fields would be so compensated as to enable those who wished to go there to quickly repay the cost of their passage. I took it that the colored people would go there in great numbers, so as to have independent states governed by their own race. They would still be States of the Union, and under the protection of the General Government; but the citizens would be almost wholly colored.

By the war with Mexico, we had acquired, as we have seen, territory almost equal in extent to that we already possessed. It was seen that the volunteers of the Mexican war largely composed the pioneers to settle up the Pacific coast country. Their numbers, however, were scarcely sufficient to be a nucleus for the population of the important points of the territory acquired by that war. After our rebellion, when so many young men were at liberty to return to their homes, they found they were not satisfied with the farm, the store, or the work-shop of the villages, but wanted larger fields. The mines of the mountains first attracted them; but afterwards they found that rich valleys and productive grazing and farming lands were there. This territory, the geography of which was not known to us at the close of the rebellion, is now as well mapped as any portion of our country. Railroads traverse it in every direction, north, south, east, and west. The mines are worked. The high lands are used for grazing purposes, and rich agricultural lands are found in many of the valleys. This is the work of the volunteer. It is probable that the Indians would have had control of these lands for a century yet but for the war. We must conclude, therefore, that wars are not always evils unmixed with some good.

Prior to the rebellion the great mass of the people were satisfied to remain near the scenes of their birth. In fact an immense majority of the whole people did not feel secure against coming to want should they move among entire strangers. So much was the country divided into small communities that localized idioms had grown up, so that you could almost tell what section a person was from by hearing him speak. Before, new territories were settled by a "class"; people who shunned contact with others; people who, when the country began to settle up around them, would push out farther from civilization. Their guns furnished meat, and the cultivation of a very limited amount of the soil, their bread and vegetables. All the streams abounded with fish. Trapping would furnish pelts to be brought into the States once a year, to pay for necessary articles which they could not raise— powder, lead, whiskey, tobacco and some store goods. Occasionally some little articles of luxury would enter into these purchases—a quarter of a pound of tea, two or three pounds of coffee, more of sugar, some playing cards, and if anything was left over of the proceeds of the sale, more whiskey.

Little was known of the topography of the country beyond the settlements of these frontiersmen. This is all changed now. The war begot a spirit of independence and enterprise. The feeling now is, that a youth must cut loose from his old surroundings to enable him to get up in the world. There is now such a commingling of the people that particular idioms and pronunciation are no longer localized to any great extent; the country has filled up "from the centre all around to the sea"; railroads connect the two oceans and all parts of the interior; maps, nearly perfect, of every part of the country are now furnished the student of geography.

The war has made us a nation of great power and intelligence. We have but little to do to preserve peace, happiness and prosperity at home, and the respect of other nations. Our experience ought to teach us the necessity of the first; our power secures the latter.

I feel that we are on the eve of a new era, when there is to be great harmony between the Federal and Confederate. I cannot stay to be a living witness to the correctness of this prophecy; but I feel it within me that it is to be so. The universally kind feeling expressed for me at a time when it was supposed that each day would prove my last, seemed to me the beginning of the answer to "Let us have peace."

The expressions of these kindly feelings were not restricted to a section of the country, nor to a division of the people. They came from individual citizens of all nationalities; from all denominations—the Protestant, the Catholic, and the Jew; and from the various societies of the land—scientific, educational, religious, or otherwise. Politics did not enter into the matter at all.

I am not egotist enough to suppose all this significance should be given because I was the object of it. But the war between the States was a very bloody and a very costly war. One side or the other had to yield principles they deemed dearer than life before it could be brought to an end. I commanded the whole of the mighty host engaged on the victorious side. I was, no matter whether deservedly so or not, a representative of that side of the controversy. It is a significant and gratifying fact that Confederates should have joined heartily in this spontaneous move. I hope the good feeling inaugurated may continue to the end.

APPENDIX.

REPORT OF LIEUTENANT-GENERAL U. S. GRANT,
OF THE
UNITED STATES ARMIES — 1864 – '65.

HEADQUARTERS ARMIES OF THE UNITED STATES,
WASHINGTON, D. C., *July* 22, 1865.

HON. E. M. STANTON, Secretary of War.

SIR: — I have the honor to submit the following report of the operations of the Armies of the United States from the date of my appointment to command the same.

From an early period in the rebellion I had been impressed with the idea that active and continuous operations of all the troops that could be brought into the field, regardless of season and weather, were necessary to a speedy termination of the war. The resources of the enemy and his numerical strength were far inferior to ours; but as an offset to this, we had a vast territory, with a population hostile to the government, to garrison, and long lines of river and railroad communications to protect, to enable us to supply the operating armies.

The armies in the East and West acted independently and without concert, like a balky team, no two ever pulling together, enabling the enemy to use to great advantage his interior lines of communication for transporting troops from East to West, reinforcing the army most vigorously pressed, and to furlough large numbers, during seasons of inactivity on our part, to go to their homes and do the work of producing, for the support of their armies. It was a question whether our numerical strength and resources were not more than balanced by these disadvantages and the enemy's superior position.

From the first, I was firm in the conviction that no peace could be had that would be stable and conducive to the happiness of the people, both North and South, until the military power of the rebellion was entirely broken.

I therefore determined, first, to use the greatest number of troops practicable against the armed force of the enemy; preventing him from using the same force at different seasons against first one and then another of our armies, and the possibility of repose for refitting and producing necessary supplies for carrying on resistance. Second, to hammer continuously against the armed force of the enemy and his resources, until by mere attrition, if in no other way, there should be nothing left to him but an equal submission with the loyal section of our common country to the constitution and laws of the land.

These views have been kept constantly in mind, and orders given and campaigns made to carry them out. Whether they might have been better in conception and execution is for the people, who mourn the loss of friends fallen, and who have to pay the pecuniary cost, to say. All I can say is, that what I have done has been done conscientiously, to the best of my ability, and in what I conceived to be for the best interests of the whole country.

At the date when this report begins, the situation of the contending forces was about as follows: The Mississippi River was strongly garrisoned by Federal troops, from St. Louis, Missouri, to its mouth. The line of the Arkansas was also held, thus giving us armed possession of all west of the Mississippi, north of that stream. A few points in Southern Louisiana, not remote from the river, were held by us, together with a small garrison at and near the mouth of the Rio Grande. All the balance of the vast territory of Arkansas, Louisiana, and Texas was in the almost undisputed possession of the enemy, with an army of probably not less than eighty thousand effective men, that could have been brought into the field had there been sufficient opposition to have brought them out. The let-alone policy had demoralized this force so that probably but little more than one-half of it was ever present in garrison at any one time. But the one-half, or forty thousand men, with the bands of guerillas scattered through Missouri, Arkansas, and along the Mississippi River, and the disloyal character of much of the population, compelled the use of a large number of troops to keep navigation open on the river, and to protect the loyal people to the west of it. To the east of the Mississippi we held substantially with the line of the Tennessee and Holston rivers, running eastward to include nearly all of the State of Tennessee. South of Chattanooga, a small foothold had been obtained in Georgia, sufficient to protect East Tennessee from incursions from the enemy's force at Dalton, Georgia. West Virginia was substantially within our lines. Virginia, with the exception of the northern border, the Potomac River, a small area about the mouth of James River, covered by the troops at Norfolk and Fort Monroe, and the territory covered by the Army of the Potomac lying along the Rapidan, was in the possession of the enemy. Along the sea-coast footholds had been obtained at Plymouth, Washington, and New Bern, in North Carolina; Beaufort, Folly and Morris Islands, Hilton Head, Fort Pulaski, and Port Royal, in South Carolina; Fernandina and St. Augustine, in Florida. Key West and Pensacola were also in our possession, while all the important ports were blockaded by the navy. The accompanying map, a copy of which was sent to General Sherman and other commanders in March, 1864, shows by red lines the territory occupied by us at the beginning of the rebellion, and at the opening of the campaign of 1864, while those in blue are the lines which it was proposed to occupy.

Behind the Union lines there were many bands of guerillas and a large population disloyal to the government, making it necessary to guard every foot of road or river used in supplying our armies. In the South, a reign of military despotism prevailed, which made every man and boy capable of bearing arms a soldier; and those who could not bear arms in the field acted as provosts for collecting deserters and returning them. This enabled the enemy to bring almost his entire strength into the field.

The enemy had concentrated the bulk of his forces east of the Mississippi into two armies, commanded by Generals R. E. Lee and J. E. Johnston, his ablest and best generals. The army commanded by Lee occupied the south bank of the Rapidan, extending from Mine Run westward, strongly intrenched, covering and defending Richmond, the rebel capital, against the Army of the Potomac. The army under Johnston occupied a strongly intrenched position at Dalton, Georgia, covering and defending Atlanta, Georgia, a place of great importance as a railroad centre, against the armies under Major-General W. T. Sherman. In addition to these armies he had a large cavalry force under Forrest, in North-east Mississippi; a considerable force, of all arms, in the Shenandoah Valley, and in the western part of Virginia and extreme eastern part of Tennessee; and also confronting our sea-coast garrisons, and holding blockaded ports where we had no foothold upon land.

These two armies, and the cities covered and defended by them, were the main objective points of the campaign.

Major-General W. T. Sherman, who was appointed to the command of the Military Division of the Mississippi, embracing all the armies and territory east of the Mississippi River to the Alleghanies and the Department of Arkansas, west of the Mississippi, had the immediate command of the armies operating against Johnston.

Major-General George G. Meade had the immediate command of the Army of the Potomac, from where I exercised general supervision of the movements of all our armies.

General Sherman was instructed to move against Johnston's army, to break it up, and to go into the interior of the enemy's country as far as he could, inflicting all the damage he could upon their war resources. If the enemy in his front showed signs of joining Lee, to follow him up to the full extent of his ability, while I would prevent the concentration of Lee upon him, if it was in the power of the Army of the Potomac to do so. More specific written instructions were not given, for the reason that I had talked over with him the plans of the campaign, and was satisfied that he understood them and would execute them to the fullest extent possible.

Major-General N. P. Banks, then on an expedition up Red River against Shreveport, Louisiana (which had been organized previous to my appointment to command), was notified by me on the 15th of March, of the importance it was that Shreveport should be taken at the earliest possible day, and that if he found that the taking of it would occupy from ten to fifteen days' more time than General Sherman had given his troops to be absent from their command, he would send them back at the time specified by General Sherman, even if it led to the abandonment of the main object of the Red River expedition, for this force was necessary to movements east of the Mississippi; that should his expedition prove successful, he would hold Shreveport and the Red River with such force as he might deem necessary, and return the balance of his troops to the neighborhood of New Orleans, commencing no move for the further acquisition of territory, unless it was to make that then held by him more easily held; that it might be a part of the spring campaign to move against Mobile; that it certainly would be, if troops enough could be obtained to make it without embarrassing other movements; that New Orleans would be the point of departure for such an expedition; also, that I had directed General Steele to make a real move from Arkansas, as suggested by him (General Banks), instead of a demonstration, as Steele thought advisable.

On the 31st of March, in addition to the foregoing notification and directions, he was instructed as follows:

"1st. If successful in your expedition against Shreveport, that you turn over the defence of the Red River to General Steele and the navy.

"2d. That you abandon Texas entirely, with the exception of your hold upon the Rio Grande. This can be held with four thousand men, if they will turn their attention immediately to fortifying their positions. At least one-half of the force required for this service might be taken from the colored troops.

"3d. By properly fortifying on the Mississippi River, the force to guard it from Port Hudson to New Orleans can be reduced to ten thousand men, if not to a less number. Six thousand more would then hold all the rest of the territory necessary to hold until active operations can again be resumed west of the river. According to your last return, this would give you a force of over thirty thousand effective men with which to move against Mobile. To this I expect to add five thousand men from Missouri. If, however, you think the force here stated too small to hold the territory regarded as necessary to hold possession of, I would say concentrate at least twenty-five thousand men of your present command for operations against Mobile. With these and such additions as I can give you from elsewhere, lose no time in making a demonstration, to be followed by an attack upon Mobile. Two or more iron-clads will be ordered to report to Admiral Farragut. This gives him a strong naval fleet with which to co-operate. You can make your own arrangements with the admiral for his co-operation, and select your own line of approach. My own idea of the matter is that Pascagoula should be your base; but, from your long service in the Gulf Department, you will know best about the matter. It is intended that your movements shall be co-operative with movements elsewhere, and you cannot now start too soon. All I would now add is, that you commence the concentration of your forces at once. Preserve a profound secrecy of what you intend doing, and start at the earliest possible moment.

"U. S. GRANT, Lieutenant-General.

"MAJOR-GENERAL N. P. BANKS."

Major-General Meade was instructed that Lee's army would be his objective point; that wherever Lee went he would go also. For his movement two plans presented themselves: One to cross the Rapidan below Lee, moving by his right flank; the other above, moving by his left. Each presented advantages over the other, with corresponding objections. By crossing above, Lee would be cut off from all chance of ignoring Richmond or going north on a raid. But if we took this route, all we did would have to be done whilst the rations we started with held out; besides, it separated us from Butler, so that he could not be directed how to co-operate. If we took the other route, Brandy Station could be used as a base of supplies until another was secured on the York or James rivers. Of these, however, it was decided to take the lower route.

The following letter of instruction was addressed to Major-General B. F. Butler:

"FORT MONROE, VIRGINIA, *April* 2, 1864.

"GENERAL: — In the spring campaign, which it is desirable shall commence at as early a day as practicable, it is proposed to have co-operative action of all the armies in the field, as far as this object can be accomplished.

"It will not be possible to unite our armies into two or three large ones to act as so many units, owing to the absolute necessity of holding on to the territory already taken from the enemy. But, generally speaking, concentration can be practically effected by armies moving to the interior of the enemy's country from the territory they have to guard. By such movement, they interpose themselves between the enemy and the country to be guarded, thereby reducing the number necessary to guard important points, or at least occupy the attention of a part of the enemy's force, if no greater object is gained. Lee's army and Richmond being the greater objects towards which our attention must be directed in the next campaign, it is desirable to unite all the force we can against them. The necessity of covering Washington with the

Army of the Potomac, and of covering your department with your army, makes it impossible to unite these forces at the beginning of any move. I propose, therefore, what comes nearest this of anything that seems practicable: The Army of the Potomac will act from its present base, Lee's army being the objective point. You will collect all the forces from your command that can be spared from garrison duty—I should say not less than twenty thousand effective men—to operate on the south side of James River, Richmond being your objective point. To the force you already have will be added about ten thousand men from South Carolina, under Major-General Gillmore, who will command them in person. Major-General W. F. Smith is ordered to report to you, to command the troops sent into the field from your own department.

"General Gillmore will be ordered to report to you at Fortress Monroe, with all the troops on transports, by the 18th instant, or as soon thereafter as practicable. Should you not receive notice by that time to move, you will make such disposition of them and your other forces as you may deem best calculated to deceive the enemy as to the real move to be made.

"When you are notified to move, take City Point with as much force as possible. Fortify, or rather intrench, at once, and concentrate all your troops for the field there as rapidly as you can. From City Point directions cannot be given at this time for your further movements.

"The fact that has already been stated—that is, that Richmond is to be your objective point, and that there is to be co-operation between your force and the Army of the Potomac—must be your guide. This indicates the necessity of your holding close to the south bank of the James River as you advance. Then, should the enemy be forced into his intrenchments in Richmond, the Army of the Potomac would follow, and by means of transports the two armies would become a unit.

"All the minor details of your advance are left entirely to your direction. If, however, you think it practicable to use your cavalry south of you, so as to cut the railroad about Hicksford, about the time of the general advance, it would be of immense advantage.

"You will please forward for my information, at the earliest practicable day, all orders, details, and instructions you may give for the execution of this order.

"U. S. GRANT, Lieutenant-General.
"MAJOR-GENERAL B. F. BUTLER."

On the 16th these instructions were substantially reiterated. On the 19th, in order to secure full co-operation between his army and that of General Meade, he was informed that I expected him to move from Fort Monroe the same day that General Meade moved from Culpeper. The exact time I was to telegraph him as soon as it was fixed, and that it would not be earlier than the 27th of April; that it was my intention to fight Lee between Culpeper and Richmond, if he would stand. Should he, however, fall back into Richmond, I would follow up and make a junction with his (General Butler's) army on the James River; that, could I be certain he would be able to invest Richmond on the south side, so as to have his left resting on the James, above the city, I would form the junction there; that circumstances might make this course advisable anyhow; that he should use every exertion to secure footing as far up the south side of the river as he could, and as soon as possible after the receipt of orders to move; that if he could not carry the city, he should at least detain as large a force there as possible.

In co-operation with the main movements against Lee and Johnston, I was desirous of using all other troops necessarily kept in departments remote from the fields of immediate operations, and also those kept in the background for the protection of our extended lines between the loyal States and the armies operating against them.

A very considerable force, under command of Major-General Sigel, was so held for the protection of West Virginia, and the frontiers of Maryland and Pennsylvania. Whilst these troops could not be withdrawn to distant fields without exposing the North to invasion by comparatively small bodies of the enemy, they could act directly to their front, and give better protection than if lying idle in garrison. By such a movement they would either compel the enemy to detach largely for the protection of his supplies and lines of communication, or he would lose them. General Sigel was therefore directed to organize all his available force into two expeditions, to move from Beverly and Charleston, under command of Generals Ord and Crook, against the East Tennessee and Virginia Railroad. Subsequently, General Ord having been relieved at his own request, General Sigel was instructed, at his own suggestion, to give up the expedition by Beverly, and to form two columns, one under General Crook, on the Kanawha, numbering about ten thousand men, and one on the Shenandoah, numbering about seven thousand men. The one on the Shenandoah to assemble between Cumberland and the Shenandoah, and the infantry and artillery advanced to Cedar Creek with such cavalry as could be made available at the moment, to threaten the enemy in the Shenandoah Valley, and advance as far as possible; while General Crook would take possession of Lewisburg with part of his force and move down the Tennessee Railroad, doing as much damage as he could, destroying the New River Bridge and the salt-works, at Saltville, Va.

Owing to the weather and bad condition of the roads, operations were delayed until the 1st of May, when, everything being in readiness and the roads favorable, orders were given for a general movement of all the armies not later than the 4th of May.

My first object being to break the military power of the rebellion, and capture the enemy's important strongholds, made me desirous that General Butler should succeed in his movement against Richmond, as that would tend more than anything else, unless it were the capture of Lee's army, to accomplish this desired result in the East. If he failed, it was my determination, by hard fighting, either to compel Lee to retreat, or to so cripple him that he could not detach a large force to go north, and still retain enough for the defence of Richmond. It was well understood, by both Generals Butler and Meade, before starting on the campaign, that it was my intention to put both their armies south of the James River, in case of failure to destroy Lee without it.

Before giving General Butler his instructions, I visited him at Fort Monroe, and in conversation pointed out the apparent importance of getting possession of Petersburg, and destroying railroad communication as far south as possible. Believing, however, in the practicability of capturing Richmond unless it was reinforced, I made that the objective point of his operations. As the Army of the Potomac was to move simultaneously with him, Lee could not detach from his army with safety, and the enemy did not have troops elsewhere to bring to the defence of the city in time to meet a rapid movement from the north of James River.

I may here state that, commanding all the armies as I did, I tried, as far as possible, to leave General Meade in independent command of the Army of the Potomac. My instructions for that army were all through him, and were general in their nature, leaving all the details and the execution to him. The campaigns that followed proved him to be the right man in the right place. His commanding always in the presence of an officer superior to him in rank, has drawn from him much of that public attention that his zeal and ability entitle him to, and which he would otherwise have received.

The movement of the Army of the Potomac commenced early on the morning of the 4th of May, under the immediate direction and orders of Major-General Meade, pursuant to instructions. Before night, the whole army was across the Rapidan (the fifth and sixth corps crossing at Germania Ford, and the second corps at Ely's Ford, the cavalry, under Major-General Sheridan, moving in advance,) with the greater part of its trains, numbering about four thousand wagons, meeting with but slight opposition. The average distance travelled by the troops that day was about twelve miles. This I regarded as a great success, and it removed from my mind the most serious apprehensions I had entertained, that of crossing the river in the face of an active, large, well-appointed, and ably commanded army, and how so large a train was to be carried through a hostile country, and protected. Early on the 5th, the advance corps (the fifth, Major-General G. K. Warren commanding,) met and engaged the enemy outside his intrenchments near Mine Run. The battle raged furiously all day, the whole army being brought into the fight as fast as the corps could be got upon the field, which, considering the density of the forest and narrowness of the roads, was done with commendable promptness.

General Burnside, with the ninth corps, was, at the time the Army of the Potomac moved, left with the bulk of his corps at the crossing of the Rappahannock River and Alexandria Railroad, holding the road back to Bull Run, with instructions not to move until he received notice that a crossing of the Rapidan was secured, but to move promptly as soon as such notice was received. This crossing he was apprised of on the afternoon of the 4th. By six o'clock of the morning of the 6th he was leading his corps into action near the Wilderness Tavern, some of his troops having marched a distance of over thirty miles, crossing both the Rappahannock and Rapidan rivers. Considering that a large proportion, probably two-thirds of his command, was composed of new troops, unaccustomed to marches, and carrying the accoutrements of a soldier, this was a remarkable march.

The battle of the Wilderness was renewed by us at five o'clock on the morning of the 6th, and continued with unabated fury until darkness set in, each army holding substantially the same position that they had on the evening of the 5th. After dark, the enemy made a feeble attempt to turn our right flank, capturing several hundred prisoners and creating considerable confusion. But the promptness of General Sedgwick, who was personally present and commanded that part of our line, soon reformed it and restored order. On the morning of the 7th, reconnoissances showed that the enemy had fallen behind his intrenched lines, with pickets to the front, covering a part of the battle-field. From this it was evident to my mind that the two days' fighting had satisfied him of his inability to further maintain the contest in the open field, notwithstanding his advantage of position, and that he would wait an attack behind his works. I therefore determined to push on and put my whole force between him and Richmond; and orders were at once issued for a movement by his right flank. On the night of the 7th, the march was commenced towards Spottsylvania Court House, the fifth corps moving on the most direct road. But the enemy having become apprised of our movement, and having the shorter line, was enabled to reach there first. On the 8th, General Warren met a force of the enemy, which had been sent out to oppose and delay his advance, to gain time to fortify the line taken up at Spottsylvania. This force was steadily driven back on the main force, within the recently constructed works, after considerable fighting, resulting in severe loss to both sides. On the morning of the 9th, General Sheridan started on a raid against the enemy's lines of communication with Richmond. The 9th, 10th, and 11th were spent in manœuvring and fighting, without decisive results. Among the killed on the 9th was that able and distinguished soldier Major-General John Sedgwick, commanding the sixth army corps. Major-General H. G. Wright succeeded him in command. Early on the morning of the 12th a general attack was made on the enemy in position. The second corps, Major-General Hancock commanding, carried a salient of his line, capturing most of Johnson's division of Ewell's corps and twenty pieces of artillery. But the resistance was so obstinate that the advantage gained did not prove decisive. The 13th, 14th, 15th, 16th, 17th, and 18th, were consumed in manœuvring and awaiting the arrival of re-inforcements from Washington. Deeming it impracticable to make any further attack upon the enemy at Spottsylvania Court House, orders were issued on the 18th with a view to a movement to the North Anna, to commence at twelve o'clock on the night of the 19th. Late in the afternoon of the 19th, Ewell's corps came out of its works on our extreme right flank; but the attack was promptly repulsed, with heavy loss. This delayed the movement to the North Anna until the night of the 21st, when it was commenced. But the enemy again, having the shorter line, and being in possession of the main roads, was enabled to reach the North Anna in advance of us, and took position behind it. The fifth corps reached the North Anna on the afternoon of the 23d, closely followed by the sixth corps. The second and ninth corps got up about the same time, the second holding the railroad bridge, and the ninth lying between that and Jericho Ford. General Warren effected a crossing the same afternoon, and got a position without much opposition. Soon after getting into position he was violently attacked, but repulsed the enemy with great slaughter. On the 25th, General Sheridan rejoined the Army of the Potomac from the raid on which he started from Spottsylvania, having destroyed the depots at Beaver Dam and Ashland stations, four trains of cars, large supplies of rations, and many miles of railroad-track; recaptured about four hundred of our men on their way to Richmond as prisoners of war; met and defeated the enemy's cavalry at Yellow Tavern; carried the first line of works around Richmond (but finding the second line too strong to be carried by assault), recrossed to the north bank of the Chickahominy at Meadow Bridge under heavy fire, and moved by a detour to Haxall's Landing, on the James

River, where he communicated with General Butler. This raid had the effect of drawing off the whole of the enemy's cavalry force, making it comparatively easy to guard our trains.

General Butler moved his main force up the James River, in pursuance of instructions, on the 4th of May, General Gillmore having joined him with the tenth corps. At the same time he sent a force of one thousand eight hundred cavalry, by way of West Point, to form a junction with him wherever he might get a foothold, and a force of three thousand cavalry, under General Kautz, from Suffolk, to operate against the road south of Petersburg and Richmond. On the 5th, he occupied, without opposition, both City Point and Bermuda Hundred, his movement being a complete surprise. On the 6th, he was in position with his main army, and commenced intrenching. On the 7th he made a reconnoissance against the Petersburg and Richmond Railroad, destroying a portion of it after some fighting. On the 9th he telegraphed as follows:

"HEADQUARTERS, NEAR BERMUDA LANDING,
May 9, 1864.

"HON. E. M. STANTON, Secretary of War.

"Our operations may be summed up in a few words. With one thousand seven hundred cavalry we have advanced up the Peninsula, forced the Chickahominy, and have safely brought them to their present position. These were colored cavalry, and are now holding our advance pickets towards Richmond.

"General Kautz, with three thousand cavalry from Suffolk, on the same day with our movement up James River, forced the Black Water, burned the railroad bridge at Stony Creek, below Petersburg, cutting into Beauregard's force at that point.

"We have landed here, intrenched ourselves, destroyed many miles of railroad, and got a position which, with proper supplies, we can hold out against the whole of Lee's army. I have ordered up the supplies.

"Beauregard, with a large portion of his force, was left south by the cutting of the railroads by Kautz. That portion which reached Petersburg under Hill I have whipped to-day, killing and wounding many, and taking many prisoners, after a severe and well-contested fight.

"General Grant will not be troubled with any further reinforcements to Lee from Beauregard's force.

"BENJ. F. BUTLER, Major-General."

On the evening of the 13th and morning of the 14th he carried a portion of the enemy's first line of defences at Drury's Bluff, or Fort Darling, with small loss. The time thus consumed from the 6th lost to us the benefit of the surprise and capture of Richmond and Petersburg, enabling, as it did, Beauregard to collect his loose forces in North and South Carolina, and bring them to the defence of those places. On the 16th, the enemy attacked General Butler in his position in front of Drury's Bluff. He was forced back, or drew back, into his intrenchments between the forks of the James and Appomattox rivers, the enemy intrenching strongly in his front, thus covering his railroads, the city, and all that was valuable to him. His army, therefore, though in a position of great security, was as completely shut off from further operations directly against Richmond as if it had been in a bottle strongly corked. It required but a comparatively small force of the enemy to hold it there.

On the 12th, General Kautz, with his cavalry, was started on a raid against the Danville Railroad, which he struck at Coalfield, Powhatan, and Chula Stations, destroying them, the railroad-track, two freight trains, and one locomotive, together with large quantities of commissary and other stores; thence, crossing to the South Side Road, struck it at Wilson's, Wellsville, and Black's and White's Stations, destroying the road and station-houses; thence he proceeded to City Point, which he reached on the 18th.

On the 19th of April, and prior to the movement of General Butler, the enemy, with a land force under General Hoke and an iron-clad ram, attacked Plymouth, N. C., commanded by General H. W. Wessells, and our gunboats there; and, after severe fighting, the place was carried by assault, and the entire garrison and armament captured. The gunboat *Smithfield* was sunk, and the *Miami* disabled.

The army sent to operate against Richmond having hermetically sealed itself up at Bermuda Hundred, the enemy was enabled to bring the most, if not all, the reinforcements brought from the south by Beauregard against the Army of the Potomac. In addition to this reinforcement, a very considerable one, probably not less than fifteen thousand men, was obtained by calling in the scattered troops under Breckinridge from the western part of Virginia.

The position of Bermuda Hundred was as easy to defend as it was difficult to operate from against the enemy. I determined, therefore, to bring from it all available forces, leaving enough only to secure what had been gained; and accordingly, on the 22d, I directed that they be sent forward, under command of Major-General W. F. Smith, to join the Army of the Potomac.

On the 24th of May, the 9th army corps, commanded by Major-General A. E. Burnside, was assigned to the Army of the Potomac, and from this time forward constituted a portion of Major-General Meade's command.

Finding the enemy's position on the North Anna stronger than either of his previous ones, I withdrew on the night of the 26th to the north bank of the North Anna, and moved *via* Hanover Town to turn the enemy's position by his right.

Generals Torbert's and Merritt's divisions of cavalry, under Sheridan, and the 6th corps, led the advance; crossed the Pamunkey River at Hanover Town, after considerable fighting, and on the 28th the two divisions of cavalry had a severe, but successful engagement with the enemy at Hawes's Shop. On the 29th and 30th we advanced, with heavy skirmishing, to the Hanover Court House and Cold Harbor Road, and developed the enemy's position north of the Chickahominy. Late on the evening of the last day the enemy came out and attacked our left, but was repulsed with very considerable loss. An attack was immediately ordered by General Meade, along his whole line, which resulted in driving the enemy from a part of his intrenched skirmish line.

On the 31st, General Wilson's division of cavalry destroyed the railroad bridges over the South Anna River, after defeating the enemy's cavalry. General Sheridan, on the same day, reached Cold Harbor, and held it until relieved by the 6th corps and General Smith's command, which had just arrived, *via* White House, from General Butler's army.

On the 1st day of June an attack was made at five P.M. by the 6th corps and the troops under General Smith, the other corps being held in readiness to advance on the receipt of orders. This resulted in our carrying and holding the enemy's first line of works in front of the right of the 6th corps, and in front of General Smith. During the attack the enemy made repeated assaults on each of the corps not engaged in the main attack, but was repulsed with heavy loss in every instance. That night he made several assaults to regain what he had lost in the day, but failed. The 2d was spent in getting troops into position for an attack on the 3d. On the 3d of June we again assaulted the enemy's works, in the hope of driving him from his position. In this attempt our loss was heavy, while that of the enemy, I have reason to believe, was comparatively light. It was the only general attack made from the Rapidan to the James which did not inflict upon the enemy losses to compensate for our own losses. I would not be understood as saying that all previous attacks resulted in victories to our arms, or accomplished as much as I had hoped from them; but they inflicted upon the enemy severe losses, which tended, in the end, to the complete overthrow of the rebellion.

From the proximity of the enemy to his defences around Richmond, it was impossible, by any flank movement, to interpose between him and the city. I was still in a condition to either move by his left flank, and invest Richmond from the north side, or continue my move by his right flank to the south side of the James. While the former might have been better as a covering for Washington, yet a full survey of all the ground satisfied me that it would be impracticable to hold a line north and east of Richmond that would protect the Fredericksburg Railroad, a long, vulnerable line, which would exhaust much of our strength to guard, and that would have to be protected to supply the army, and would leave open to the enemy all his lines of communication on the south side of the James. My idea, from the start, had been to beat Lee's army north of Richmond, if possible. Then, after destroying his lines of communication north of the James River, to transfer the army to the south side, and besiege Lee in Richmond, or follow him south if he should retreat. After the battle of the Wilderness, it was evident that the enemy deemed it of the first importance to run no risks with the army he then had. He acted purely on the defensive, behind breastworks, or feebly on the offensive immediately in front of them, and where, in case of repulse, he could easily retire behind them. Without a greater sacrifice of life than I was willing to make, all could not be accomplished that I had designed north of Richmond. I therefore determined to continue to hold substantially the ground we then occupied, taking advantage of any favorable circumstances that might present themselves, until the cavalry could be sent to Charlottesville and Gordonsville to effectually break up the railroad connection between Richmond and the Shenandoah Valley and Lynchburg; and when the cavalry got well off, to move the army to the south side of the James River, by the enemy's right flank, where I felt I could cut off all his sources of supply, except by the canal.

On the 7th, two divisions of cavalry, under General Sheridan, got off on the expedition against the Virginia Central Railroad, with instructions to Hunter, whom I hoped he would meet near Charlottesville, to join his forces to Sheridan's, and after the work laid out for them was thoroughly done, to join the Army of the Potomac by the route laid down in Sheridan's instructions.

On the 10th of June, General Butler sent a force of infantry, under General Gillmore, and of cavalry under General Kautz, to capture Petersburg, if possible, and destroy the railroad and common bridges across the Appomattox. The cavalry carried the works on the south side, and penetrated well in towards the town, but were forced to retire. General Gillmore, finding the works which he approached very strong, and deeming an assault impracticable, returned to Bermuda Hundred without attempting one.

Attaching great importance to the possession of Petersburg, I sent back to Bermuda Hundred and City Point, General Smith's command by water, *via* the White House, to reach there in advance of the Army of the Potomac. This was for the express purpose of securing Petersburg before the enemy, becoming aware of our intention, could reinforce the place.

The movement from Cold Harbor commenced after dark on the evening of the 12th. One division of cavalry, under General Wilson, and the 5th corps, crossed the Chickahominy at Long Bridge, and moved out to White Oak Swamp, to cover the crossings of the other corps. The advance corps reached James River, at Wilcox's Landing and Charles City Court House, on the night of the 13th.

During three long years the Armies of the Potomac and Northern Virginia had been confronting each other. In that time they had fought more desperate battles than it probably ever before fell to the lot of two armies to fight, without materially changing the vantage ground of either. The Southern press and people, with more shrewdness than was displayed in the North, finding that they had failed to capture Washington and march on to New York, as they had boasted they would do, assumed that they only defended their Capital and Southern territory. Hence, Antietam, Gettysburg, and all the other battles that had been fought, were by them set down as failures on our part, and victories for them. Their army believed this. It produced a morale which could only be overcome by desperate and continuous hard fighting. The battles of the Wilderness, Spottsylvania, North Anna and Cold Harbor, bloody and terrible as they were on our side, were even more damaging to the enemy, and so crippled him as to make him wary ever after of taking the offensive. His losses in men were probably not so great, owing to the fact that we were, save in the Wilderness, almost invariably the attacking party; and when he did attack, it was in the open field. The details of these battles, which for endurance and bravery on the part of the soldiery, have rarely been surpassed, are given in the report of Major-General Meade, and the subordinate reports accompanying it.

During the campaign of forty-three days, from the Rapidan to the James River, the army had to be supplied from an ever-shifting base, by wagons, over narrow roads, through a densely wooded country, with a lack of wharves at each new base from which to conveniently discharge vessels. Too much credit cannot, therefore, be awarded to the quartermaster and commissary departments for the zeal and efficiency displayed by them. Under the general supervision of the chief quartermaster, Brigadier-General R. Ingalls, the trains were made to occupy all the available roads between the army and our water-base, and but little difficulty was experienced in protecting them.

The movement in the Kanawha and Shenandoah valleys, under

General Sigel, commenced on the 1st of May. General Crook, who had the immediate command of the Kanawha expedition, divided his forces into two columns, giving one, composed of cavalry, to General Averell. They crossed the mountains by separate routes. Averell struck the Tennessee and Virginia Railroad, near Wytheville, on the 10th, and proceeding to New River and Christiansburg, destroyed the road, several important bridges and depots, including New River Bridge, forming a junction with Crook at Union on the 15th. General Sigel moved up the Shenandoah Valley, met the enemy at New Market on the 15th, and, after a severe engagement, was defeated with heavy loss, and retired behind Cedar Creek. Not regarding the operations of General Sigel as satisfactory, I asked his removal from command, and Major-General Hunter was appointed to supersede him. His instructions were embraced in the following dispatches to Major-General H. W. Halleck, chief of staff of the army:

"NEAR SPOTTSYLVANIA COURT HOUSE, VA.,
May 20, 1864.

*   *   *   *   *   *   *

"The enemy are evidently relying for supplies greatly on such as are brought over the branch road running through Staunton. On the whole, therefore, I think it would be better for General Hunter to move in that direction; reach Staunton and Gordonsville or Charlottesville, if he does not meet too much opposition. If he can hold at bay a force equal to his own, he will be doing good service. * * *

"U. S. GRANT, Lieutenant-General.
"MAJOR-GENERAL H. W. HALLECK."

JERICHO FORD, VA., *May* 25, 1864.
"If Hunter can possibly get to Charlottesville and Lynchburg, he should do so, living on the country. The railroads and canal should be destroyed beyond possibility of repairs for weeks. Completing this, he could find his way back to his original base, or from about Gordonsville join this army.

"U. S. GRANT, Lieutenant-General.
"MAJOR-GENERAL H. W. HALLECK."

General Hunter immediately took up the offensive, and, moving up the Shenandoah Valley, met the enemy on the 5th of June at Piedmont, and, after a battle of ten hours, routed and defeated him, capturing on the field of battle one thousand five hundred men, three pieces of artillery, and three hundred stand of small arms. On the 8th of the same month he formed a junction with Crook and Averell at Staunton, from which place he moved direct on Lynchburg, *via* Lexington, which place he reached and invested on the 16th day of June. Up to this time he was very successful; and but for the difficulty of taking with him sufficient ordnance stores over so long a march, through a hostile country, he would, no doubt, have captured that, to the enemy important, point. The destruction of the enemy's supplies and manufactories was very great. To meet this movement under General Hunter, General Lee sent a force, perhaps equal to a corps, a part of which reached Lynchburg a short time before Hunter. After some skirmishing on the 17th and 18th, General Hunter, owing to a want of ammunition to give battle, retired from before the place. Unfortunately, this want of ammunition left him no choice of route for his return but by way of Kanawha. This lost to us the use of his troops for several weeks from the defence of the North.

Had General Hunter moved by way of Charlottesville, instead of Lexington, as his instructions contemplated, he would have been in a position to have covered the Shenandoah Valley against the enemy, should the force he met have seemed to endanger it. If it did not, he would have been within easy distance of the James River Canal, on the main line of communication between Lynchburg and the force sent for its defence. I have never taken exception to the operations of General Hunter, and am not now disposed to find fault with him, for I have no doubt he acted within what he conceived to be the spirit of his instructions and the interests of the service. The promptitude of his movements and his gallantry should entitle him to the commendation of his country.

To return to the Army of the Potomac: The 2d corps commenced crossing the James River on the morning of the 14th by ferry-boats at Wilcox's Landing. The laying of the pontoon-bridge was completed about midnight of the 14th, and the crossing of the balance of the army was rapidly pushed forward by both bridge and ferry.

After the crossing had commenced, I proceeded by steamer to Bermuda Hundred to give the necessary orders for the immediate capture of Petersburg.

The instructions to General Butler were verbal, and were for him to send General Smith immediately, that night, with all the troops he could give him without sacrificing the position he then held. I told him that I would return at once to the Army of the Potomac, hasten its crossing, and throw it forward to Petersburg by divisions as rapidly as it could be done; that we could reinforce our armies more rapidly there than the enemy could bring troops against us. General Smith got off as directed, and confronted the enemy's pickets near Petersburg before daylight next morning, but for some reason that I have never been able to satisfactorily understand, did not get ready to assault his main lines until near sundown. Then, with a part of his command only, he made the assault, and carried the lines north-east of Petersburg from the Appomattox River, for a distance of over two and a half miles, capturing fifteen pieces of artillery and three hundred prisoners. This was about seven P.M. Between the line thus captured and Petersburg there were no other works, and there was no evidence that the enemy had reinforced Petersburg with a single brigade from any source. The night was clear—the moon shining brightly—and favorable to further operations. General Hancock, with two divisions of the 2d corps, reached General Smith just after dark, and offered the service of these troops as he (Smith) might wish, waiving rank to the named commander, who he naturally supposed knew best the position of affairs, and what to do with the troops. But instead of taking these troops and pushing at once into Petersburg, he requested General Hancock to relieve a part of his line in the captured works, which was done before midnight.

By the time I arrived the next morning the enemy was in force. An attack was ordered to be made at six o'clock that evening by the troops under Smith and the 2d and 9th corps. It required until that time for the 9th corps to get up and into position. The attack was made as ordered, and the fighting continued with but little intermission until six o'clock the next morning, and resulted in our carrying the advance and some of the main works of the enemy to the right (our left) of those previously captured by General Smith, several pieces of artillery, and over four hundred prisoners.

The 5th corps having got up, the attacks were renewed and persisted in with great vigor on the 17th and 18th, but only resulted in forcing the enemy into an interior line, from which he could not be dislodged. The advantages of position gained by us were very great. The army then proceeded to envelop Petersburg towards the South Side Railroad, as far as possible without attacking fortifications.

On the 16th the enemy, to reinforce Petersburg, withdrew from a part of his intrenchment in front of Bermuda Hundred, expecting, no doubt, to get troops from north of the James to take the place of those withdrawn before we could discover it. General Butler, taking advantage of this, at once moved a force on the railroad between Petersburg and Richmond. As soon as I was apprised of the advantage thus gained, to retain it I ordered two divisions of the 6th corps, General Wright commanding, that were embarking at Wilcox's Landing, under orders for City Point, to report to General Butler at Bermuda Hundred, of which General Butler was notified, and the importance of holding a position in advance of his present line urged upon him.

About two o'clock in the afternoon General Butler was forced back to the line the enemy had withdrawn from in the morning.

General Wright, with his two divisions, joined General Butler on the forenoon of the 17th, the latter still holding with a strong picket-line the enemy's works. But instead of putting these divisions into the enemy's works to hold them, he permitted them to halt and rest some distance in the rear of his own line. Between four and five o'clock in the afternoon the enemy attacked and drove in his pickets and re-occupied his old line.

On the night of the 20th and morning of the 21st a lodgment was effected by General Butler, with one brigade of infantry, on the north bank of the James, at Deep Bottom, and connected by pontoon-bridge with Bermuda Hundred.

On the 19th, General Sheridan, on his return from his expedition against the Virginia Central Railroad, arrived at the White House just as the enemy's cavalry was about to attack it, and compelled it to retire. The result of this expedition was, that General Sheridan met the enemy's cavalry near Trevilian Station, on the morning of the 11th of June, whom he attacked, and after an obstinate contest drove from the field in complete rout. He left his dead and nearly all his wounded in our hands, and about four hundred prisoners and several hundred horses. On the 12th he destroyed the railroad from Trevilian Station to Louisa Court House. This occupied until three o'clock P.M., when he advanced in the direction of Gordonsville. He found the enemy reinforced by infantry, behind well-constructed rifle-pits, about five miles from the latter place, and too strong to successfully assault. On the extreme right, however, his reserve brigade carried the enemy's works twice, and was twice driven therefrom by infantry. Night closed the contest. Not having sufficient ammunition to continue the engagement, and his animals being without forage (the country furnishing but inferior grazing), and hearing nothing from General Hunter, he withdrew his command to the north side of the North Anna, and commenced his return march, reaching White House at the time before stated. After breaking up the depot at that place, he moved to the James River, which he reached safely after heavy fighting. He commenced crossing on the 25th, near Fort Powhatan, without further molestation, and rejoined the Army of the Potomac.

On the 22d, General Wilson, with his own division of cavalry of the Army of the Potomac, and General Kautz's division of cavalry of the Army of the James, moved against the enemy's railroads south of Richmond. Striking the Weldon Railroad at Reams's Station, destroying the depot and several miles of the road, and the South Side road about fifteen miles from Petersburg, to near Nottoway Station, where he met and defeated a force of the enemy's cavalry. He reached Burkesville Station on the afternoon of the 23d, and from there destroyed the Danville Railroad to Roanoke Bridge, a distance of twenty-five miles, where he found the enemy in force, and in a position from which he could not dislodge him. He then commenced his return march, and on the 28th met the enemy's cavalry in force at the Weldon Railroad crossing of Stony Creek, where he had a severe but not decisive engagement. Thence he made a detour from his left with a view of reaching Reams's Station (supposing it to be in our possession). At this place he was met by the enemy's cavalry, supported by infantry, and forced to retire, with the loss of his artillery and trains. In this last encounter, General Kautz, with a part of his command, became separated, and made his way into our lines. General Wilson, with the remainder of his force, succeeded in crossing the Nottoway River and coming in safely on our left and rear. The damage to the enemy in this expedition more than compensated for the losses we sustained. It severed all connection by railroad with Richmond for several weeks.

With a view of cutting the enemy's railroad from near Richmond to the Anna rivers, and making him wary of the situation of his army in the Shenandoah, and, in the event of failure in this, to take advantage of his necessary withdrawal of troops from Petersburg, to explode a mine that had been prepared in front of the 9th corps and assault the enemy's lines at that place, on the night of the 26th of July the 2d corps and two divisions of the cavalry corps and Kautz's cavalry were crossed to the north bank of the James River and joined the force General Butler had there. On the 27th the enemy was driven from his intrenched position, with the loss of four pieces of artillery. On the 28th our lines were extended from Deep Bottom to New Market Road, but in getting this position were attacked by the enemy in heavy force. The fighting lasted for several hours, resulting in considerable loss to both sides. The first object of this move having failed, by reason of the very large force thrown there by the enemy, I determined to take advantage of the diversion made, by assaulting Petersburg before he could get his force back there. One division of the 2d corps was withdrawn on the night of the 28th, and moved during the night to the rear of the 18th corps, to relieve that corps in the line, that it might be foot-loose in the assault to be made. The other two divisions of the 2d corps and Sheridan's cavalry were crossed over on the night of the 29th and moved in front of Petersburg. On the morning of the 30th, between four and five o'clock, the mine was sprung, blowing up a battery and most of a regiment, and the advance of the assaulting column, formed of the 9th corps, immediately took possession of the crater made by the explosion, and the line for some distance to the right and left of it, and a detached line in front of it, but for some cause failed to advance promptly to the ridge beyond. Had they done this, I have every reason to believe that Petersburg would have fallen. Other troops were immediately pushed forward, but the time consumed in getting them up enabled the enemy to rally from his surprise (which had been complete), and get forces to this point for its defence. The captured line thus held being untenable, and of no advantage to us, the troops were withdrawn, but not without heavy loss. Thus terminated in disaster what promised to be the most successful assault of the campaign.

Immediately upon the enemy's ascertaining that General Hunter was retreating from Lynchburg by way of the Kanawha River, thus laying the Shenandoah Valley open for raids into Maryland and Pennsylvania, he returned northward and moved down that valley. As soon as this movement of the enemy was ascertained, General Hunter, who had reached the Kanawha River, was directed to move his troops without delay, by river and railroad, to Harper's Ferry; but owing to the difficulty of navigation by reason of low water and breaks in the railroad, great delay was experienced in getting there. It became necessary, therefore, to find other troops to check this movement of the enemy. For this purpose the 6th corps was taken from the armies operating against Richmond, to which was added the 19th corps, then fortunately beginning to arrive in Hampton Roads from the Gulf Department, under orders issued immediately after the ascertainment of the result of the Red River expedition. The garrisons of Baltimore and Washington were at this time made up of heavy-artillery regiments, hundred days' men, and detachments from the invalid corps. One division under command of General Ricketts, of the 6th corps, was sent to Baltimore, and the remaining two divisions of the 6th corps, under General Wright, were subsequently sent to Washington. On the 3d of July the enemy approached Martinsburg. General Sigel, who was in command of our forces there, retreated across the Potomac at Shepherdstown; and General Weber, commanding at Harper's Ferry, crossed the river and occupied Maryland Heights. On the 6th the enemy occupied Hagerstown, moving a strong column towards Frederick City. General Wallace, with Ricketts's division and his own command, the latter mostly new and undisciplined troops, pushed out from Baltimore with great promptness, and met the enemy in force on the Monocacy, near the crossing of the railroad bridge. His force was not sufficient to insure success, but he fought the enemy nevertheless, and although it resulted in a defeat to our arms, yet it detained the enemy, and thereby served to enable General Wright to reach Washington with two divisions of the 6th corps, and the advance of the 19th corps, before him. From Monocacy the enemy moved on Washington, his cavalry advance reaching Rockville on the evening of the 10th. On the 12th a reconnoissance was thrown out in front of Fort Stevens, to ascertain the enemy's position and force. A severe skirmish ensued, in which we lost about two hundred and eighty in killed and wounded. The enemy's loss was probably greater. He commenced retreating during the night. Learning the exact condition of affairs at Washington, I requested by telegraph, at forty-five minutes past eleven P.M., on the 12th, the assignment of Major-General H. G. Wright to the command of all the troops that could be made available to operate in the field against the enemy, and directed that he should get outside of the trenches with all the force he could, and push Early to the last moment. General Wright commenced the pursuit on the 13th; on the 18th the enemy was overtaken at Snicker's Ferry, on the Shenandoah, when a sharp skirmish occurred; and on the 20th, General Averell encountered and defeated a portion of the rebel army at Winchester, capturing four pieces of artillery and several hundred prisoners.

Learning that Early was retreating south towards Lynchburg or Richmond, I directed that the 6th and 19th corps be got back to the armies operating against Richmond, so that they might be used in a movement against Lee before the return of the troops sent by him into the valley; and that Hunter should remain in the Shenandoah Valley, keeping between any force of the enemy and Washington, acting on the defensive as much as possible. I felt that if the enemy had any notion of returning, the fact would be developed before the 6th and 19th corps could leave Washington. Subsequently, the 19th corps was excepted from the order to return to the James.

About the 25th it became evident that the enemy was again advancing upon Maryland and Pennsylvania, and the 6th corps, then at Washington, was ordered back to the vicinity of Harper's Ferry. The rebel force moved down the valley, and sent a raiding party into Pennsylvania which on the 30th burned Chambersburg, and then retreated, pursued by our cavalry, towards Cumberland. They were met and defeated by General Kelley, and with diminished numbers escaped into the mountains of West Virginia. From the time of the first raid the telegraph wires were frequently down between Washington and City Point, making it necessary to transmit messages a part of the way by boat. It took from twenty-four to thirty-six hours to get dispatches through and return answers back; so that often orders would be given, and then information would be received showing a different state of facts from those on which they were based, causing a confusion and apparent contradiction of orders that must have considerably embarrassed those who had to execute them, and rendered operations against the enemy less effective than they otherwise would have been. To remedy this evil, it was evident to my mind that some person should have the supreme command of all the forces in the Departments of West Virginia, Washington, Susquehanna, and the Middle Department, and I so recommended.

On the 2d of August, I ordered General Sheridan to report in person to Major-General Halleck, chief of staff, at Washington, with a view to his assignment to the command of all the forces against Early. At this time the enemy was concentrated in the neighborhood of Winchester, while our forces, under General Hunter, were concentrated on the Monocacy, at the crossing of the Baltimore and Ohio Railroad, leaving open to the enemy Western Maryland and Southern Pennsylvania. From where I was, I hesitated to give positive orders for the movement of our forces at Monocacy, lest by so doing I should expose Washington. Therefore, on the 4th, I left City Point to visit Hunter's command, and determine for myself what was best to be done. On arrival there, and after consultation with General Hunter, I issued to him the following instructions:

"MONOCACY BRIDGE, MARYLAND,
August 5, 1864—8 P.M.

"GENERAL:—Concentrate all your available force without delay in the vicinity of Harper's Ferry, leaving only such railroad guards and garrisons for public property as may be necessary. Use, in this concentrating, the railroad, if by so doing time can be saved. From Harper's Ferry, if it is found that the enemy has moved north of the Potomac in large force, push north, following him and attacking him wherever found; follow him, if driven south of the Potomac, as long as it is safe to do so. If it is ascertained that the enemy has but a small force north of the Potomac, then push south with the main force, detaching under a competent commander a sufficient force to look after the raiders, and drive them to their homes. In detaching such a force, the brigade of cavalry now *en route* from Washington *via* Rockville may be taken into account.

"There are now on their way to join you three other brigades of the best cavalry, numbering at least five thousand men and horses. These will be instructed, in the absence of further orders, to join you by the south side of the Potomac. One brigade will probably start to-morrow. In pushing up the Shenandoah Valley, where it is expected you will have to go first or last, it is desirable that nothing should be left to invite the enemy to return. Take all provisions, forage, and stock wanted for the use of your command; such as cannot be consumed, destroy. It is not desirable that the buildings should be destroyed—they should rather be protected; but the people should be informed that, so long as an army can subsist among them, recurrences of these raids must be expected, and we are determined to stop them at all hazards.

"Bear in mind, the object is to drive the enemy south; and to do this, you want to keep him always in sight. Be guided in your course by the course he takes.

"Make your own arrangements for supplies of all kinds, giving regular vouchers for such as may be taken from loyal citizens in the country through which you march.

"U. S. GRANT, Lieutenant-General.

"MAJOR-GENERAL D. HUNTER."

The troops were immediately put in motion, and the advance reached Halltown that night.

General Hunter having, in our conversation, expressed a willingness to be relieved from command, I telegraphed to have General Sheridan, then at Washington, sent to Harper's Ferry by the morning train, with orders to take general command of all the troops in the field, and to call on General Hunter at Monocacy, who would turn over to him my letter of instructions. I remained at Monocacy until General Sheridan arrived, on the morning of the 6th, and, after a conference with him in relation to military affairs in that vicinity, I returned to City Point by way of Washington.

On the 7th of August, the Middle Department, and the Departments of West Virginia, Washington, and Susquehanna, were constituted into the "Middle Military Division," and Major-General Sheridan was assigned to temporary command of the same.

Two divisions of cavalry, commanded by Generals Torbert and Wilson, were sent to Sheridan from the Army of the Potomac. The first reached him at Harper's Ferry about the 11th of August.

His operations during the month of August and the fore part of September were both of an offensive and defensive character, resulting in many severe skirmishes, principally by the cavalry, in which we were generally successful, but no general engagement took place. The two armies lay in such a position—the enemy on the west bank of the Opequon Creek covering Winchester, and our forces in front of Berryville—that either could bring on a battle at any time. Defeat to us would lay open to the enemy the States of Maryland and Pennsylvania for long distances before another army could be interposed to check him. Under these circumstances I hesitated about allowing the initiative to be taken. Finally, the use of the Baltimore and Ohio Railroad, and the Chesapeake and Ohio Canal, which were both obstructed by the enemy, became so indispensably necessary to us, and the importance of relieving Pennsylvania and Maryland from continuously threatened invasion so great, that I determined the risk should be taken. But fearing to telegraph the order for an attack without knowing more than I did of General Sheridan's feelings as to what would be the probable result, I left City Point on the 15th of September to visit him at his headquarters, to decide, after conference with him, what should be done. I met him at Charlestown, and he pointed out so distinctly how each army lay; what he could do the moment he was authorized, and expressed such confidence of success, that I saw there were but two words of instructions necessary—Go in! For the conveniences of forage, the teams for supplying the army were kept at Harper's Ferry. I asked him if he could get out his teams and supplies in time to make an attack on the ensuing Tuesday morning. His reply was, that he could before daylight on Monday. He was off promptly to time, and I may here add, that the result was such that I have never since deemed it necessary to visit General Sheridan before giving him orders.

Early on the morning of the 19th, General Sheridan attacked General Early at the crossing on the Opequon Creek, and after a most sanguinary and bloody battle, lasting until five o'clock in the evening, defeated him with heavy loss, carrying his entire position from Opequon Creek to Winchester, capturing several thousand prisoners and five pieces of artillery. The enemy rallied, and made a stand in a strong position at Fisher's Hill, where he was attacked, and again defeated with heavy loss on the 20th [22d]. Sheridan pursued him with great energy through Harrisonburg, Staunton, and the gaps of the Blue Ridge. After stripping the upper valley of most of the supplies and provisions for the rebel army, he returned to Strasburg, and took position on the north side of Cedar Creek.

Having received considerable reinforcements, General Early again returned to the valley, and, on the 9th of October, his cavalry encountered ours near Strasburg, where the rebels were defeated, with the loss of eleven pieces of artillery and three hundred and fifty prisoners. On the night of the 18th, the enemy crossed the mountains which separate the branches of the Shenandoah, forded the North Fork, and early on the morning of the 19th, under cover of the darkness and the fog, surprised and turned our left flank, and captured the batteries which enfiladed our whole line. Our troops fell back with heavy loss and in much confusion, but were finally rallied between Middletown and Newtown. At this juncture, General Sheridan, who was at Winchester when the battle commenced, arrived on the field, arranged his lines just in time to repulse a heavy attack of the enemy, and immediately assuming the offensive, he attacked in turn with great vigor. The enemy was defeated with great slaughter, and the loss of most of his artillery and trains, and the trophies he had captured in the morning. The wreck of his army escaped during the night, and fled in the direction of Staunton and Lynchburg. Pursuit was made to Mount Jackson. Thus ended this, the enemy's last attempt to invade the North *via* the Shenandoah Valley. I was now enabled to return the 6th corps to the Army of the Potomac, and to send one division from Sheridan's army to the Army of the James, and another to Savannah, Georgia, to hold Sherman's new acquisitions on the sea-coast, and thus enable him to move without detaching from his force for that purpose.

Reports from various sources led me to believe that the enemy had detached three divisions from Petersburg to reinforce Early in the Shenandoah Valley. I therefore sent the 2d corps and Gregg's division of cavalry, of the Army of the Potomac, and a force of General Butler's army, on the night of the 13th of August, to threaten Richmond from the north side of the James, to prevent him from sending troops away, and, if possible, to draw back those sent. In this move we captured six pieces of artillery and several hundred prisoners, detained troops that were under marching orders, and ascertained that but one division (Kershaw's), of the three reputed detached, had gone.

The enemy having withdrawn heavily from Petersburg to resist this movement, the 5th corps, General Warren commanding, was moved out on the 18th, and took possession of the Weldon Railroad. During the day he had considerable fighting. To regain possession of the road, the enemy made repeated and desperate assaults, but was each time repulsed with great loss. On the night of the 20th, the troops on the north side of the James were withdrawn, and Hancock and Gregg returned to the front at Petersburg. On the 25th, the 2d corps and Gregg's division of cavalry, while at Reams's Station destroying the railroad, were attacked, and after desperate fighting, a part of our line gave way, and five pieces of artillery fell into the hands of the enemy.

By the 12th of September, a branch railroad was completed from the City Point and Petersburg Railroad to the Weldon Railroad, enabling us to supply, without difficulty, in all weather, the army in front of Petersburg.

The extension of our lines across the Weldon Railroad compelled the enemy to so extend his, that it seemed he could have but few troops north of the James for the defence of Richmond. On the night of the 28th, the 10th corps, Major-General Birney, and the 18th corps, Major-General Ord commanding, of General Butler's army, were crossed to the north side of the James, and advanced on the morning of the 29th, carrying the very strong fortifications and intrenchments below Chaffin's Farm, known as Fort Harrison, capturing fifteen pieces of artillery, and the New Market Road and intrenchments. This success was followed up by a gallant assault upon Fort Gilmer, immediately in front of the Chaffin Farm fortifications, in which we were repulsed with heavy loss. Kautz's cavalry was pushed forward on the road to the right of this, supported by infantry, and reached the enemy's inner line, but was unable to get further. The position captured from the enemy was so threatening to Richmond, that I determined to hold it. The enemy made several desperate attempts to dislodge us, all of which were unsuccessful, and for which he paid dearly. On the morning of the 30th, General Meade sent out a reconnoissance, with a view to attacking the enemy's line, if it was found sufficiently weakened by withdrawal of troops to the north side. In this reconnoissance we captured and held the enemy's works near Poplar Spring Church. In the afternoon, troops moving to get to the left of the point gained were attacked by the enemy in heavy force, and compelled to fall back until supported by the forces holding the captured works. Our cavalry under Gregg was also attacked, but repulsed the enemy with great loss.

On the 7th of October, the enemy attacked Kautz's cavalry north of the James, and drove it back with heavy loss in killed, wounded, and prisoners, and the loss of all the artillery—eight or nine pieces. This he followed up by an attack on our intrenched infantry line, but was repulsed with severe slaughter. On the 13th, a reconnoissance was sent out by General Butler, with a view to drive the enemy from some new works he was constructing, which resulted in very heavy loss to us.

On the 27th, the Army of the Potomac, leaving only sufficient men to hold its fortified line, moved by the enemy's right flank. The 2d corps, followed by two divisions of the 5th corps, with the cavalry in advance and covering our left flank, forced a passage of Hatcher's Run, and moved up the south side of it towards the South Side Railroad, until the 2d corps and part of the cavalry reached the Boydton Plank Road where it crosses Hatcher's Run. At this point we were six miles distant from the South Side Railroad, which I had hoped by this movement to reach and hold. But finding that we had not reached the end of the enemy's fortifications, and no place presenting itself for a successful assault by which he might be doubled up and shortened, I determined to withdraw to within our fortified line. Orders were given accordingly. Immediately upon receiving a report that General Warren had connected with General Hancock, I returned to my headquarters. Soon after I left the enemy moved out across Hatcher's Run, in the gap between Generals Hancock and Warren, which was not closed as reported, and made a desperate attack on General Hancock's right and rear. General Hancock immediately faced his corps to meet it, and after a bloody combat drove the enemy within his works, and withdrew that night to his old position.

In support of this movement, General Butler made a demonstration on the north side of the James, and attacked the enemy on the Williamsburg Road, and also on the York River Railroad. In the former he was unsuccessful; in the latter he succeeded in carrying a work which was afterwards abandoned, and his forces withdrawn to their former positions.

From this time forward the operations in front of Petersburg and Richmond, until the spring campaign of 1865, were confined to the defence and extension of our lines, and to offensive movements for crippling the enemy's lines of communication, and to prevent his detaching any considerable force to send south. By the 7th of February, our lines were extended to Hatcher's Run, and the Weldon Railroad had been destroyed to Hicksford.

General Sherman moved from Chattanooga on the 6th of May, with the Armies of the Cumberland, Tennessee, and Ohio, commanded, respectively, by Generals Thomas, McPherson, and Schofield, upon Johnston's army at Dalton; but finding the enemy's position at Buzzard's Roost, covering Dalton, too strong to be assaulted, General McPherson was sent through Snake Gap to turn it, while Generals Thomas and Schofield threatened it in front and on the north. This movement was successful. Johnston, finding his retreat likely to be cut off, fell back to his fortified position at Resaca, where he was attacked on the afternoon of May 15th. A heavy battle ensued. During the night the enemy retreated south. Late on the 17th, his rear-guard was overtaken near Adairsville, and heavy skirmishing followed. The next morning, however, he had again disappeared. He was vigorously pursued, and was overtaken at Cassville on the 19th, but during the ensuing night retreated across the Etowah. While these operations were going on, General Jefferson C. Davis's division of Thomas's army was sent to Rome, capturing it with its forts and artillery, and its valuable mills and foundries. General Sherman, having given his army a few days' rest at this point, again put it in motion on the 23d, for Dallas, with a view of turning the difficult pass at Allatoona. On the afternoon of the 25th, the advance, under General Hooker, had a severe battle with the enemy, driving him back to New Hope Church, near Dallas. Several sharp encounters occurred at this point. The most important was on the 28th, when the enemy assaulted General McPherson at Dallas, but received a terrible and bloody repulse.

On the 4th of June, Johnston abandoned his intrenched position at New Hope Church, and retreated to the strong positions of Kenesaw, Pine, and Lost mountains. He was forced to yield the two last-named places, and concentrate his army on Kenesaw, where, on the 27th, Generals Thomas and McPherson made a determined but unsuccessful assault. On the night of the 2d of July, Sherman commenced moving his army by the right flank, and on the morning of the 3d, found that the enemy, in consequence of this movement, had abandoned Kenesaw and retreated across the Chattahoochee.

General Sherman remained on the Chattahoochee to give his men rest and get up stores until the 17th of July, when he resumed his operations, crossed the Chattahoochee, destroyed a large portion of the railroad to Augusta, and drove the enemy back to Atlanta. At this place General Hood succeeded General Johnston in command of the rebel army, and assuming the offensive-defensive policy, made several severe attacks upon Sherman in the vicinity of Atlanta, the most desperate and determined of which was on the 22d of July. About one P.M. of this day the brave, accomplished, and noble-hearted McPherson was killed. General Logan succeeded him, and commanded the Army of the Tennessee through this desperate battle, and until he was superseded by Major-General Howard, on the 26th, with the same success and ability that had characterized him in the command of a corps or division.

In all these attacks the enemy was repulsed with great loss. Finding it impossible to entirely invest the place, General Sherman, after securing his line of communications across the Chattahoochee, moved his main force round by the enemy's left flank upon the Montgomery and Macon roads, to draw the enemy from his fortifications. In this he succeeded, and after defeating the enemy near Rough-and-Ready, Jonesboro, and Lovejoy's, forcing him to retreat to the south, on the 2d of September occupied Atlanta, the objective point of his campaign.

About the time of this move, the rebel cavalry, under Wheeler, attempted to cut his communications in the rear, but was repulsed at Dalton, and driven into East Tennessee, whence it proceeded west to McMinnville, Murfreesboro', and Franklin, and was finally driven south of the Tennessee. The damage done by this raid was repaired in a few days.

During the partial investment of Atlanta, General Rousseau joined General Sherman with a force of cavalry from Decatur, having made a successful raid upon the Atlanta and Montgomery Railroad, and its branches near Opelika. Cavalry raids were also made by Generals McCook, Garrard, and Stoneman, to cut the remaining railroad communication with Atlanta. The first two were successful—the latter, disastrous.

General Sherman's movement from Chattanooga to Atlanta was prompt, skilful, and brilliant. The history of his flank movements and battles during that memorable campaign will ever be read with an interest unsurpassed by anything in history.

His own report, and those of his subordinate commanders, accompanying it, give the details of that most successful campaign.

He was dependent for the supply of his armies upon a single-track railroad from Nashville to the point where he was operating. This passed the entire distance through a hostile country, and every foot of it had to be protected by troops. The cavalry force of the enemy under Forrest, in Northern Mississippi, was evidently waiting for Sherman to advance far enough into the mountains of Georgia, to make a retreat disastrous, to get upon this line and destroy it beyond the possibility of further use. To guard against this danger, Sherman left what he supposed to be a sufficient force to operate against Forrest in West Tennessee. He directed General Washburn, who commanded there, to send Brigadier-General S. D. Sturgis in command of this force to attack him. On the morning of the 10th of June, General Sturgis met the enemy near Guntown, Mississippi, was badly beaten, and driven back in utter rout and confusion to Memphis, a distance of about one hundred miles, hotly pursued by the enemy. By this, however, the enemy was defeated in his designs upon Sherman's line of communications. The persistency with which he followed up this success exhausted him, and made a season for rest and repairs necessary. In the meantime, Major-General A. J. Smith, with the troops of the Army of the Tennessee that had been sent by General Sherman to General Banks, arrived at Memphis on their return from Red River, where they had done most excellent service. He was directed by General Sherman to immediately take the offensive against Forrest. This he did with the promptness and effect which has characterized his whole military career. On the 14th of July, he met the enemy at Tupelo, Mississippi, and whipped him badly. The fighting continued through three days. Our loss was small compared with that of the enemy. Having accomplished the object of his expedition, General Smith returned to Memphis.

During the months of March and April this same force under Forrest annoyed us considerably. On the 24th of March it captured Union City, Kentucky, and its garrison, and on the 24th attacked

Paducah, commanded by Colonel S. G. Hicks, 40th Illinois Volunteers. Colonel H., having but a small force, withdrew to the forts near the river, from where he repulsed the enemy and drove him from the place.

On the 13th of April, part of this force, under the rebel General Buford, summoned the garrison of Columbus, Kentucky, to surrender, but received for reply from Colonel Lawrence, 34th New Jersey Volunteers, that being placed there by his Government with adequate force to hold his post and repel all enemies from it, surrender was out of the question.

On the morning of the same day Forrest attacked Fort Pillow, Tennessee, garrisoned by a detachment of Tennessee cavalry and the 1st Regiment Alabama colored troops, commanded by Major Booth. The garrison fought bravely until about three o'clock in the afternoon, when the enemy carried the works by assault; and, after our men threw down their arms, proceeded to an inhuman and merciless massacre of the garrison.

On the 14th, General Buford, having failed at Columbus, appeared before Paducah, but was again driven off.

Guerillas and raiders, seemingly emboldened by Forrest's operations, were also very active in Kentucky. The most noted of these was Morgan. With a force of from two to three thousand cavalry, he entered the State through Pound Gap in the latter part of May. On the 11th of June they attacked and captured Cynthiana, with its entire garrison. On the 12th he was overtaken by General Burbridge, and completely routed with heavy loss, and was finally driven out of the State. This notorious guerilla was afterwards surprised and killed near Greenville, Tennessee, and his command captured and dispersed by General Gillem.

In the absence of official reports of the commencement of the Red River expedition, except so far as relates to the movements of the troops sent by General Sherman under General A. J. Smith, I am unable to give the date of its starting. The troops under General Smith, comprising two divisions of the 16th and a detachment of the 17th army corps, left Vicksburg on the 10th of March, and reached the designated point on Red River one day earlier than that appointed by General Banks. The rebel forces at Fort de Russy, thinking to defeat him, left the fort on the 14th to give him battle in the open field; but, while occupying the enemy with skirmishing and demonstrations, Smith pushed forward to Fort de Russy, which had been left with a weak garrison, and captured it with its garrison—about three hundred and fifty men, eleven pieces of artillery, and many small-arms. Our loss was but slight. On the 15th he pushed forward to Alexandria, which place he reached on the 18th. On the 21st he had an engagement with the enemy at Henderson's Hill, in which he defeated him, capturing two hundred and ten prisoners and four pieces of artillery.

On the 28th, he again attacked and defeated the enemy under the rebel General Taylor, at Cane River. By the 26th, General Banks had assembled his whole army at Alexandria, and pushed forward to Grand Ecore. On the morning of April 6th he moved from Grand Ecore. On the afternoon of the 7th, he advanced and met the enemy near Pleasant Hill, and drove him from the field. On the same afternoon the enemy made a stand eight miles beyond Pleasant Hill, but was again compelled to retreat. On the 8th, at Sabine Cross Roads and Peach Hill, the enemy attacked and defeated his advance, capturing nineteen pieces of artillery and an immense amount of transportation and stores. During the night, General Banks fell back to Pleasant Hill, where another battle was fought on the 9th, and the enemy repulsed with great loss. During the night, General Banks continued his retrograde movement to Grand Ecore, and thence to Alexandria, which he reached on the 27th of April. Here a serious difficulty arose in getting Admiral Porter's fleet which accompanied the expedition, over the rapids, the water having fallen so much since they passed up as to prevent their return. At the suggestion of Colonel (now Brigadier-General) Bailey, and under his superintendence, wing-dams were constructed, by which the channel was contracted so that the fleet passed down the rapids in safety.

The army evacuated Alexandria on the 14th of May, after considerable skirmishing with the enemy's advance, and reached Morganzia and Point Coupée near the end of the month. The disastrous termination of this expedition, and the lateness of the season, rendered impracticable the carrying out of my plans of a movement in force sufficient to insure the capture of Mobile.

On the 23d of March, Major-General Steele left Little Rock with the 7th army corps, to co-operate with General Banks's expedition on the Red River, and reached Arkadelphia on the 28th. On the 16th of April, after driving the enemy before him, he was joined, near Elkin's Ferry, in Washita County, by General Thayer, who had marched from Fort Smith. After several severe skirmishes, in which the enemy was defeated, General Steele reached Camden, which he occupied about the middle of April.

On learning the defeat and consequent retreat of General Banks on Red River, and the loss of one of his own trains at Mark's Mill, in Dallas County, General Steele determined to fall back to the Arkansas River. He left Camden on the 26th of April, and reached

Little Rock on the 2d of May. On the 30th of April, the enemy attacked him while crossing Saline River at Jenkins's Ferry, but was repulsed with considerable loss. Our loss was about six hundred in killed, wounded and prisoners.

Major-General Canby, who had been assigned to the command of the "Military Division of the West Mississippi," was therefore directed to send the 19th army corps to join the armies operating against Richmond, and to limit the remainder of his command to such operations as might be necessary to hold the positions and lines of communications he then occupied.

Before starting General A. J. Smith's troops back to Sherman, General Canby sent a part of it to disperse a force of the enemy that was collecting near the Mississippi River. General Smith met and defeated this force near Lake Chicot on the 5th of June. Our loss was about forty killed and seventy wounded.

In the latter part of July, General Canby sent Major-General Gordon Granger, with such forces as he could collect, to co-operate with Admiral Farragut against the defences of Mobile Bay. On the 8th of August, Fort Gaines surrendered to the combined naval and land forces. Fort Powell was blown up and abandoned.

On the 9th, Fort Morgan was invested, and, after a severe bombardment, surrendered on the 23d. The total captures amounted to one thousand four hundred and sixty-four prisoners, and one hundred and four pieces of artillery.

About the last of August, it being reported that the rebel General Price, with a force of about ten thousand men, had reached Jacksonport, on his way to invade Missouri, General A. J. Smith's command, then *en route* from Memphis to join Sherman, was ordered to Missouri. A cavalry force was also, at the same time, sent from Memphis, under command of Colonel Winslow. This made General Rosecrans's forces superior to those of Price, and no doubt was entertained he would be able to check Price and drive him back; while the forces under General Steele, in Arkansas, would cut off his retreat. On the 26th day of September, Price attacked Pilot Knob and forced the garrison to retreat, and thence moved north to the Missouri River, and continued up that river towards Kansas. General Curtis, commanding Department of Kansas, immediately collected such forces as he could to repel the invasion of Kansas, while General Rosecrans's cavalry was operating in his rear.

The enemy was brought to battle on the Big Blue and defeated, with the loss of nearly all his artillery and trains and a large number of prisoners. He made a precipitate retreat to Northern Arkansas. The impunity with which Price was enabled to roam over the State of Missouri for a long time, and the incalculable mischief done by him, shows to how little purpose a superior force may be used. There is no reason why General Rosecrans should not have concentrated his forces, and beaten and driven Price before the latter reached Pilot Knob.

September 20th, the enemy's cavalry, under Forrest, crossed the Tennessee near Waterloo, Alabama, and on the 23d attacked the garrison at Athens, consisting of six hundred men, which capitulated on the 24th. Soon after the surrender two regiments of reinforcements arrived, and after a severe fight were compelled to surrender. Forrest destroyed the railroad westward, captured the garrison at Sulphur Branch trestle, skirmished with the garrison at Pulaski on the 27th, and on the same day cut the Nashville and Chattanooga Railroad near Tullahoma and Dechard. On the morning of the 30th, one column of Forrest's command, under Buford, appeared before Huntsville, and summoned the surrender of the garrison. Receiving an answer in the negative, he remained in the vicinity of the place until next morning, when he again summoned its surrender, and received the same reply as on the night before. He withdrew in the direction of Athens, which place had been regarrisoned, and attacked it on the afternoon of the 1st of October, but without success. On the morning of the 2d he renewed his attack, but was handsomely repulsed.

Another column under Forrest appeared before Columbia on the morning of the 1st, but did not make an attack. On the morning of the 3d he moved towards Mount Pleasant. While these operations were going on, every exertion was made by General Thomas to destroy the forces under Forrest before he could recross the Tennessee, but was unable to prevent his escape to Corinth, Mississippi.

In September, an expedition under General Burbridge was sent to destroy the salt-works at Saltville, Virginia. He met the enemy on the 2d of October, about three miles and a half from Saltville, and drove him into his strongly intrenched position around the salt-works, from which he was unable to dislodge him. During the night he withdrew his command and returned to Kentucky.

General Sherman, immediately after the fall of Atlanta, put his armies in camp in and about the place, and made all preparations for refitting and supplying them for future service. The great length of road from Atlanta to the Cumberland River, however, which had to be guarded, allowed the troops but little rest.

During this time Jefferson Davis made a speech in Macon, Georgia, which was reported in the papers of the South, and soon became known to the whole country, disclosing the plans of the enemy, thus enabling General Sherman to fully meet them. He exhibited the weakness of supposing that an army that had been beaten and fearfully decimated in a vain attempt at the defensive, could successfully undertake the offensive against the army that had so often defeated it.

In execution of this plan, Hood, with this army, was soon reported to the south-west of Atlanta. Moving far to Sherman's right, he succeeded in reaching the railroad about Big Shanty, and moved north on it.

General Sherman, leaving a force to hold Atlanta, with the remainder of his army fell upon him and drove him to Gadsden, Alabama. Seeing the constant annoyance he would have with the roads to his rear if he attempted to hold Atlanta, General Sherman proposed the abandonment and destruction of that place, with all the railroads leading to it, and telegraphed me as follows:

> "CENTREVILLE, GEORGIA,
> *October* 10—noon.
>
> "Dispatch about Wilson just received. Hood is now crossing Coosa River, twelve miles below Rome, bound west. If he passes over the Mobile and Ohio road, had I not better execute the plan of my letter sent by Colonel Porter, and leave General Thomas with the troops now in Tennessee, to defend the State? He will have an ample force when the reinforcements ordered reach Nashville.
>
> "W. T. SHERMAN, Major-General.
>
> "LIEUTENANT-GENERAL GRANT."

For a full understanding of the plan referred to in this dispatch, I quote from the letter sent by Colonel Porter: "I will therefore give my opinion, that your army and Canby's should be reinforced to the maximum; that after you get Wilmington, you strike for Savannah and the river; that Canby be instructed to hold the Mississippi River, and send a force to get Columbus, Georgia, either by the way of the Alabama or the Appalachicola, and that I keep Hood employed and put my army in final order for a march on Augusta, Columbia, and Charleston, to be ready as soon as Wilmington is sealed as to commerce, and the city of Savannah is in our possession." This was in reply to a letter of mine of date September 12th, in answer to a dispatch of his containing substantially the same proposition, and in which I informed him of a proposed movement against Wilmington, and of the situation in Virginia, etc.

> "CITY POINT, VIRGINIA,
> *October* 11, 1864—11 A.M.
>
> "Your dispatch of October 10th received. Does it not look as if Hood was going to attempt the invasion of Middle Tennessee, using the Mobile and Ohio and Memphis and Charleston roads to supply his base on the Tennessee

River, about Florence or Decatur? If he does this, he ought to be met and prevented from getting north of the Tennessee River. If you were to cut loose, I do not believe you would meet Hood's army, but would be bush-whacked by all the old men and little boys, and such railroad guards as are still left at home. Hood would probably strike for Nashville, thinking that by going north he could inflict greater damage upon us than we could upon the rebels by going south. If there is any way of getting at Hood's army, I would prefer that, but I must trust to your own judgment. I find I shall not be able to send a force from here to act with you on Savannah. Your movements, therefore, will be independent of mine; at least until the fall of Richmond takes place. I am afraid Thomas, with such lines of road as he has to protect, could not prevent Hood from going north. With Wilson turned loose, with all your cavalry, you will find the rebels put much more on the defensive than heretofore.

"U. S. GRANT, Lieutenant-General.
"MAJOR-GENERAL W. T. SHERMAN."

"KINGSTON, GEORGIA,
October 11—11 A.M.

"Hood moved his army from Palmetto Station across by Dallas and Cedar-town, and is now on the Coosa River, south of Rome. He threw one corps on my road at Acworth, and I was forced to follow. I hold Atlanta with the 20th corps, and have strong detachments along my line. This reduces my active force to a comparatively small army. We cannot remain here on the defensive. With the twenty-five thousand men, and the bold cavalry he has, he can constantly break my roads. I would infinitely prefer to make a wreck of the road, and of the country from Chattanooga to Atlanta, including the latter city—send back all my wounded and worthless, and with my effective army, move through Georgia, smashing things, to the sea. Hood may turn into Tennessee and Kentucky, but I believe he will be forced to follow me. Instead of my being on the defensive, I would be on the offensive; instead of guessing at what he means to do, he would have to guess at my plans. The difference in war is full twenty-five per cent. I can make Savannah, Charles-ton, or the mouth of the Chattahoochee.

"Answer quick, as I know we will not have the telegraph long.

"W. T. SHERMAN, Major-General.
"LIEUTENANT-GENERAL GRANT."

"CITY POINT, VIRGINIA,
October 11, 1864—11.30 P.M.

"Your dispatch of to-day received. If you are satisfied the trip to the sea-coast can be made, holding the line of the Tennessee River firmly, you may make it, destroying all the railroad south of Dalton or Chattanooga, as you think best.

"U. S. GRANT, Lieutenant-General.
"MAJOR-GENERAL W. T. SHERMAN."

It was the original design to hold Atlanta, and by getting through to the coast, with a garrison left on the southern railroads, leading east and west, through Georgia, to effectually sever the east from the west. In other words, cut the would-be Confederacy in two again, as it had been cut once by our gaining possession of the Mississippi River. General Sherman's plan virtually effected this object.

General Sherman commenced at once his preparations for his proposed movement, keeping his army in position in the meantime to watch Hood. Becoming satisfied that Hood had moved westward from Gadsden across Sand Mountain, General Sherman sent the 4th corps, Major-General Stanley commanding, and the 23d corps, Major-General Schofield commanding, back to Chattanooga to report to Major-General Thomas, at Nashville, whom he had placed in command of all the troops of his military division, save the four army corps and cavalry division he designed to move with through Georgia. With the troops thus left at his disposal, there was little doubt that General Thomas could hold the line of the Tennessee, or, in the event Hood should force it, would be able to concentrate and beat him in battle. It was therefore readily consented to that Sherman should start for the sea-coast.

Having concentrated his troops at Atlanta by the 14th of November, he commenced his march, threatening both Augusta and Macon. His coming-out point could not be definitely fixed. Having to gather his subsistence as he marched through the country, it was not impossible that a force inferior to his own might compel him to head for such point as he could reach, instead of such as he might prefer. The blindness of the enemy, however, in ignoring his movement, and sending Hood's army, the only considerable force he had west of Richmond and east of the Mississippi River, northward on an offensive campaign, left the whole country open, and Sherman's route to his own choice.

How that campaign was conducted, how little opposition was met with, the condition of the country through which the armies passed, the capture of Fort McAllister, on the Savannah River, and the occupation of Savannah on the 21st of December, are all clearly set forth in General Sherman's admirable report.

Soon after General Sherman commenced his march from Atlanta, two expeditions, one from Baton Rouge, Louisiana, and one from Vicksburg, Mississippi, were started by General Canby to cut the enemy's lines of communication with Mobile and detain troops in that field. General Foster, commanding Department of the South, also sent an expedition, *via* Broad River, to destroy the railroad between Charleston and Savannah. The expedition from Vicksburg, under command of Brevet Brigadier-General E. D. Osband (colonel 3d United States colored cavalry), captured, on the 27th of November, and destroyed the Mississippi Central Railroad bridge and trestle-work over Big Black River, near Canton, thirty miles of the road, and two locomotives, besides large amounts of stores. The expedition from Baton Rouge was without favorable results. The expedition from the Department of the South, under the immediate command of Brigadier-General John P. Hatch, consisting of about five thousand men of all arms, including a brigade from the navy, proceeded up Broad River and debarked at Boyd's Neck on the 29th of November, from where it moved to strike the railroad at Grahamsville. At Honey Hill, about three miles from Grahamsville, the enemy was found and attacked in a strongly fortified position, which resulted, after severe fighting, in our repulse with a loss of seven hundred and forty-six in killed, wounded, and missing. During the night General Hatch withdrew. On the 6th of December General Foster obtained a position covering the Charleston and Savannah Railroad, between the Coosawhatchie and Tulifinny rivers.

Hood, instead of following Sherman, continued his move northward, which seemed to me to be leading to his certain doom. At all events, had I had the power to command both armies, I should not have changed the orders under which he seemed to be acting. On the 26th of October, the advance of Hood's army attacked the garrison at Decatur, Alabama, but failing to carry the place, withdrew towards Courtland, and succeeded, in the face of our cavalry, in effecting a lodgment on the north side of the Tennessee River, near Florence. On the 28th, Forrest reached the Tennessee, at Fort Heiman, and captured a gunboat and three transports. On the 2d of November he planted batteries above and below Johnsonville, on the opposite side of the river, isolating three gunboats and eight transports. On the 4th the enemy opened his batteries upon the place, and was replied to from the gunboats and the garrison. The gunboats becoming disabled were set on fire, as also were the transports, to prevent their falling into the hands of the enemy. About a million and a half dollars' worth of stores and property on the levee and in storehouses was consumed by fire. On the 5th the enemy disappeared and crossed to the north side of the Tennessee River, above Johnsonville, moving towards Clifton, and subsequently joined Hood. On the night of the 5th, General Schofield, with the advance of the 23d corps, reached Johnsonville, but finding the enemy gone, was ordered to Pulaski, and put in command of all the troops there, with instructions to watch the movements of Hood and retard his advance, but not to risk a general engagement until the arrival of

General A. J. Smith's command from Missouri, and until General Wilson could get his cavalry remounted.

On the 19th, General Hood continued his advance. General Thomas, retarding him as much as possible, fell back towards Nashville for the purpose of concentrating his command and gaining time for the arrival of reinforcements. The enemy coming up with our main force, commanded by General Schofield, at Franklin, on the 30th, assaulted our works repeatedly during the afternoon until late at night, but were in every instance repulsed. His loss in this battle was one thousand seven hundred and fifty killed, seven hundred and two prisoners, and three thousand eight hundred wounded. Among his losses were six general officers killed, six wounded, and one captured. Our entire loss was two thousand three hundred. This was the first serious opposition the enemy met with, and I am satisfied was the fatal blow to all his expectations. During the night, General Schofield fell back towards Nashville. This left the field to the enemy—not lost by battle, but voluntarily abandoned—so that General Thomas's whole force might be brought together. The enemy followed up and commenced the establishment of his line in front of Nashville on the 2d of December.

As soon as it was ascertained that Hood was crossing the Tennessee River, and that Price was going out of Missouri, General Rosecrans was ordered to send to General Thomas the troops of General A. J. Smith's command, and such other troops as he could spare. The advance of this reinforcement reached Nashville on the 30th of November.

On the morning of the 15th December, General Thomas attacked Hood in position, and, in a battle lasting two days, defeated and drove him from the field in the utmost confusion, leaving in our hands most of his artillery and many thousand prisoners, including four general officers.

Before the battle of Nashville I grew very impatient over, as it appeared to me, the unnecessary delay. This impatience was increased upon learning that the enemy had sent a force of cavalry across the Cumberland into Kentucky. I feared Hood would cross his whole army and give us great trouble there. After urging upon General Thomas the necessity of immediately assuming the offensive, I started West to superintend matters there in person. Reaching Washington City, I received General Thomas's dispatch announcing his attack upon the enemy, and the result as far as the battle had progressed. I was delighted. All fears and apprehensions were dispelled. I am not yet satisfied but that General Thomas, immediately upon the appearance of Hood before Nashville, and before he had time to fortify, should have moved out with his whole force and given him battle, instead of waiting to remount his cavalry, which delayed him until the inclemency of the weather made it impracticable to attack earlier than he did. But his final defeat of Hood was so complete, that it will be accepted as a vindication of that distinguished officer's judgment.

After Hood's defeat at Nashville he retreated, closely pursued by cavalry and infantry, to the Tennessee River, being forced to abandon many pieces of artillery and most of his transportation. On the 28th of December our advanced forces ascertained that he had made good his escape to the south side of the river.

About this time, the rains having set in heavily in Tennessee and North Alabama, making it difficult to move army transportation and artillery, General Thomas stopped the pursuit by his main force at the Tennessee River. A small force of cavalry, under Colonel W. J. Palmer, 15th Pennsylvania Volunteers, continued to follow Hood for some distance, capturing considerable transportation and the enemy's pontoon-bridge. The details of these operations will be found clearly set forth in General Thomas's report.

A cavalry expedition, under Brevet Major-General Grierson, started from Memphis on the 21st of December. On the 25th he surprised and captured Forrest's dismounted camp at Verona, Mississippi, on the Mobile and Ohio Railroad, destroyed the railroad, sixteen cars loaded with wagons and pontoons for Hood's army, four thousand new English carbines, and large amounts of public stores. On the morning of the 28th he attacked and captured a force of the enemy at Egypt, and destroyed a train of fourteen cars; thence turning to the south-west, he struck the Mississippi Central Railroad at Winona, destroyed the factories and large amounts of stores at Bankston, and the machine-shops and public property at Grenada, arriving at Vicksburg January 5th.

During these operations in Middle Tennessee, the enemy, with a force under General Breckinridge, entered East Tennessee. On the 13th of November he attacked General Gillem, near Morristown, capturing his artillery and several hundred prisoners. Gillem, with what was left of his command, retreated to Knoxville. Following up his success, Breckinridge moved to near Knoxville, but withdrew on the 18th, followed by General Ammen. Under the directions of General Thomas, General Stoneman concentrated the commands of Generals Burbridge and Gillem near Bean's Station, to operate against Breckinridge, and destroy or drive him into Virginia—destroy the salt-works at Saltville, and the railroad into Virginia as far as he could go without endangering his command. On the 12th of December he commenced his movement, capturing and dispersing the enemy's forces wherever he met them. On the 16th he struck the enemy, under Vaughn, at Marion, completely routing and pursuing him to Wytheville, capturing all his artillery, trains, and one hundred and ninety-eight prisoners; and destroyed Wytheville, with its stores and supplies, and the extensive lead-works near there. Returning to Marion, he met a force under Breckinridge, consisting, among other troops, of the garrison of Saltville, that had started in pursuit. He at once made arrangements to attack it the next morning; but morning found Breckinridge gone. He then moved directly to Saltville, and destroyed the extensive salt-works at that place, a large amount of stores, and captured eight pieces of artillery. Having thus successfully executed his instructions, he returned General Burbridge to Lexington and General Gillem to Knoxville.

Wilmington, North Carolina, was the most important sea-coast port left to the enemy through which to get supplies from abroad, and send cotton and other products out by blockade-runners, besides being a place of great strategic value. The navy had been making strenuous exertions to seal the harbor of Wilmington, but with only partial effect. The nature of the outlet of Cape Fear River was such, that it required watching for so great a distance that, without possession of the land north of New Inlet, or Fort Fisher, it was impossible for the navy to entirely close the harbor against the entrance of blockade-runners.

To secure the possession of this land required the co-operation of a land force, which I agreed to furnish. Immediately commenced the assemblage in Hampton Roads, under Admiral D. D. Porter, of the most formidable armada ever collected for concentration upon one given point. This necessarily attracted the attention of the enemy, as well as that of the loyal North; and through the imprudence of the public press, and very likely of officers of both branches of service, the exact object of the expedition became a subject of common discussion in the newspapers both North and South. The enemy, thus warned, prepared to meet it. This caused a postponement of the expedition until the later part of November, when, being again called upon by Hon. G. V. Fox, Assistant Secretary of the Navy, I agreed to furnish the men required at once, and went myself, in company with Major-General Butler, to Hampton Roads, where we had a conference with Admiral Porter as to the force required and the time of starting. A force of six thousand five hundred men was regarded as sufficient. The time of starting was not definitely arranged, but it was thought all would be ready by the 6th of December, if not before. Learning, on the 30th of

November, that Bragg had gone to Georgia, taking with him most of the forces about Wilmington, I deemed it of the utmost importance that the expedition should reach its destination before the return of Bragg, and directed General Butler to make all arrangements for the departure of Major-General Weitzel, who had been designated to command the land forces, so that the navy might not be detained one moment.

On the 6th of December, the following instructions were given:

"CITY POINT, VIRGINIA, *December* 6, 1864.

"GENERAL:—The first object of the expedition under General Weitzel is to close to the enemy the port of Wilmington. If successful in this, the second will be to capture Wilmington itself. There are reasonable grounds to hope for success, if advantage can be taken of the absence of the greater part of the enemy's forces now looking after Sherman in Georgia. The directions you have given for the numbers and equipment of the expedition are all right, except in the unimportant matter of where they embark and the amount of intrenching tools to be taken. The object of the expedition will be gained by effecting a landing on the main land between Cape Fear River and the Atlantic, north of the north entrance to the river. Should such landing be effected while the enemy still holds Fort Fisher and the batteries guarding the entrance to the river, then the troops should intrench themselves, and, by co-operating with the navy, effect the reduction and capture of those places. These in our hands, the navy could enter the harbor, and the port of Wilmington would be sealed. Should Fort Fisher and the point of land on which it is built fall into the hands of our troops immediately on landing, then it will be worth the attempt to capture Wilmington by a forced march and surprise. If time is consumed in gaining the first object of the expedition, the second will become a matter of after consideration.

"The details for execution are intrusted to you and the officer immediately in command of the troops.

"Should the troops under General Weitzel fail to effect a landing at or near Fort Fisher, they will be returned to the armies operating against Richmond without delay.

"U. S. GRANT, Lieutenant-General.

"MAJOR-GENERAL B. F. BUTLER."

General Butler commanding the army from which the troops were taken for this enterprise, and the territory within which they were to operate, military courtesy required that all orders and instructions should go through him. They were so sent; but General Weitzel has since officially informed me that he never received the foregoing instructions, nor was he aware of their existence, until he read General Butler's published official report of the Fort Fisher failure, with my indorsement and papers accompanying it. I had no idea of General Butler's accompanying the expedition until the evening before it got off from Bermuda Hundred, and then did not dream but that General Weitzel had received all the instructions, and would be in command. I rather formed the idea that General Butler was actuated by a desire to witness the effect of the explosion of the powder-boat. The expedition was detained several days at Hampton Roads, awaiting the loading of the powder-boat.

The importance of getting the Wilmington expedition off without any delay, with or without the powder-boat, had been urged upon General Butler, and he advised to so notify Admiral Porter.

The expedition finally got off on the 13th of December, and arrived at the place of rendezvous, off New Inlet, near Fort Fisher, on the evening of the 15th. Admiral Porter arrived on the evening of the 18th, having put in at Beaufort to get ammunition for the monitors. The sea becoming rough, making it difficult to land troops, and the supply of water and coal being about exhausted, the transport fleet put back to Beaufort to replenish; this, with the state of the weather, delayed the return to the place of rendezvous until the 24th. The powder-boat was exploded on the morning of the 24th, before the return of General Butler from Beaufort; but it would seem, from the notice taken of it in the Southern newspapers, that the enemy were never enlightened as to the object of the explosion until they were informed by the Northern press.

On the 25th a landing was effected without opposition, and a reconnoissance, under Brevet Brigadier-General Curtis, pushed up towards the fort. But before receiving a full report of the result of this reconnoissance, General Butler, in direct violation of the instructions given, ordered the re-embarkation of the troops and the return of the expedition. The re-embarkation was accomplished by the morning of the 27th.

On the return of the expedition, officers and men—among them Brevet Major-General (then Brevet Brigadier-General) N. M. Curtis, First-Lieutenant G. W. Ross, 117th Regiment New York Volunteers, First-Lieutenant William H. Walling, and Second-Lieutenant George Simpson, 142d New York Volunteers—voluntarily reported to me that when recalled they were nearly into the fort, and, in their opinion, it could have been taken without much loss.

Soon after the return of the expedition, I received a dispatch from the Secretary of the Navy, and a letter from Admiral Porter, informing me that the fleet was still off Fort Fisher, and expressing the conviction that, under a proper leader, the place could be taken. The natural supposition with me was, that when the troops abandoned the expedition, the navy would do so also. Finding it had not, however, I answered on the 30th of December, advising Admiral Porter to hold on, and that I would send a force and make another attempt to take the place. This time I selected Brevet Major-General (now Major-General) A. H. Terry to command the expedition. The troops composing it consisted of the same that composed the former, with the addition of a small brigade, numbering about one thousand five hundred, and a small siege train. The latter it was never found necessary to land. I communicated direct to the commander of the expedition the following instructions:

"CITY POINT, VIRGINIA, *January* 3, 1865.

"GENERAL:—The expedition intrusted to your command has been fitted out to renew the attempt to capture Fort Fisher, N. C., and Wilmington ultimately, if the fort falls. You will then proceed with as little delay as possible to the naval fleet lying off Cape Fear River, and report the arrival of yourself and command to Admiral D. D. Porter, commanding North Atlantic Blockading Squadron.

"It is exceedingly desirable that the most complete understanding should exist between yourself and the naval commander. I suggest, therefore, that you consult with Admiral Porter freely, and get from him the part to be performed by each branch of the public service, so that there may be unity of action. It would be well to have the whole programme laid down in writing. I have served with Admiral Porter, and know that you can rely on his judgment and his nerve to undertake what he proposes. I would, therefore, defer to him as much as is consistent with your own responsibilities. The first object to be attained is to get a firm position on the spit of land on which Fort Fisher is built, from which you can operate against that fort. You want to look to the practicability of receiving your supplies, and to defending yourself against superior forces sent against you by any of the avenues left open to the enemy. If such a position can be obtained, the siege of Fort Fisher will not be abandoned until its reduction is accomplished, or another plan of campaign is ordered from these headquarters.

"My own views are, that if you effect a landing, the navy ought to run a portion of their fleet into Cape Fear River, while the balance of it operates on the outside. Land forces cannot invest Fort Fisher, or cut it off from supplies or reinforcements, while the river is in possession of the enemy.

"A siege-train will be loaded on vessels and sent to Fort Monroe, in readiness to be sent to you if required. All other supplies can be drawn from Beaufort as you need them.

"Keep the fleet of vessels with you until your position is assured. When you find they can be spared, order them back, or such of them as you can spare, to Fort Monroe, to report for orders.

"In case of failure to effect a landing, bring your command back to Beaufort, and report to these headquarters for further instructions. You will not debark at Beaufort until so directed.

"General Sheridan has been ordered to send a division of troops to Baltimore and place them on sea-going vessels. These troops will be brought to

Fort Monroe and kept there on the vessels until you are heard from. Should you require them, they will be sent to you.

"U.S. GRANT, Lieutenant-General.

"BREVET MAJOR-GENERAL A. H. TERRY."

Lieutenant-Colonel C. B. Comstock, aide-de-camp (now brevet brigadier-general), who accompanied the former expedition, was assigned, in orders, as chief-engineer to this.

It will be seen that these instructions did not differ materially from those given for the first expedition; and that in neither instance was there an order to assault Fort Fisher. This was a matter left entirely to the discretion of the commanding officer.

The expedition sailed from Fort Monroe on the morning of the 6th, arriving at the rendezvous, off Beaufort, on the 8th, where, owing to the difficulties of the weather, it lay until the morning of the 12th, when it got under way and reached its destination that evening. Under cover of the fleet, the disembarkation of the troops commenced on the morning of the 13th, and by three o'clock P.M. was completed without loss. On the 14th a reconnoissance was pushed to within five hundred yards of Fort Fisher, and a small advance work taken possession of and turned into a defensive line against any attempt that might be made from the fort. This reconnoissance disclosed the fact that the front of the work had been seriously injured by the navy fire. In the afternoon of the 15th the fort was assaulted, and after most desperate fighting was captured, with its entire garrison and armament. Thus was secured, by the combined efforts of the navy and army, one of the most important successes of the war. Our loss was: killed, one hundred and ten; wounded, five hundred and thirty-six. On the 16th and 17th the enemy abandoned and blew up Fort Caswell and the works on Smith's Island, which were immediately occupied by us. This gave us entire control of the mouth of the Cape Fear River.

At my request, Major-General B. F. Butler was relieved, and Major-General E. O. C. Ord assigned to the Department of Virginia and North Carolina.

The defence of the line of the Tennessee no longer requiring the force which had beaten and nearly destroyed the only army now threatening it, I determined to find other fields of operation for General Thomas's surplus troops—fields from which they would co-operate with other movements. General Thomas was therefore directed to collect all troops, not essential to hold his communications at Eastport, in readiness for orders. On the 7th of January, General Thomas was directed, if he was assured of the departure of Hood south from Corinth, to send General Schofield with his corps east with as little delay as possible. This direction was promptly complied with, and the advance of the corps reached Washington on the 23d of the same month, whence it was sent to Fort Fisher and New Bern. On the 26th he was directed to send General A. J. Smith's command and a division of cavalry to report to General Canby. By the 7th of February the whole force was *en route* for its destination.

The State of North Carolina was constituted into a military department, and General Schofield assigned to command, and placed under the orders of Major-General Sherman. The following instructions were given him:

"CITY POINT, VA., January 31, 1865.

"GENERAL: — * * * Your movements are intended as co-operative with Sherman's through the States of South and North Carolina. The first point to be attained is to secure Wilmington. Goldsboro' will then be your objective point, moving either from Wilmington or New Bern, or both, as you deem best. Should you not be able to reach Goldsboro', you will advance on the line or lines of railway connecting that place with the sea-coast—as near to it as you can, building the road behind you. The enterprise under you has two objects: the first is to give General Sherman material aid, if needed, in his march north; the second, to open a base of supplies for him on his line of march. As soon, therefore, as you can determine which of the two points, Wilmington or New Bern, you can best use for throwing supplies from, to the interior, you will commence the accumulation of twenty days' rations and forage for sixty thousand men and twenty thousand animals. You will get of these as many as you can house and protect to such point in the interior as you may be able to occupy. I believe General Palmer has received some instructions direct from General Sherman on the subject of securing supplies for his army. You will learn what steps he has taken, and be governed in your requisitions accordingly. A supply of ordnance stores will also be necessary.

"Make all requisitions upon the chiefs of their respective departments in the field with me at City Point. Communicate with me by every opportunity, and should you deem it necessary at any time, send a special boat to Fortress Monroe, from which point you can communicate by telegraph.

"The supplies referred to in these instructions are exclusive of those required for your own command.

"The movements of the enemy may justify, or even make it your imperative duty, to cut loose from your base, and strike for the interior to aid Sherman. In such case you will act on your own judgment without waiting for instructions. You will report, however, what you purpose doing. The details for carrying out these instructions are necessarily left to you. I would urge, however, if I did not know that you are already fully alive to the importance of it, prompt action. Sherman may be looked for in the neighborhood of Goldsboro' any time from the 22d to the 28th of February; this limits your time very materially.

"If rolling-stock is not secured in the capture of Wilmington, it can be supplied from Washington. A large force of railroad men have already been sent to Beaufort, and other mechanics will go to Fort Fisher in a day or two. On this point I have informed you by telegraph.

"U. S. GRANT, Lieutenant-General.

"MAJOR GENERAL J. M. SCHOFIELD."

Previous to giving these instructions I had visited Fort Fisher, accompanied by General Schofield, for the purpose of seeing for myself the condition of things, and personally conferring with General Terry and Admiral Porter as to what was best to be done.

Anticipating the arrival of General Sherman at Savannah—his army entirely foot-loose, Hood being then before Nashville, Tennessee, the Southern railroads destroyed, so that it would take several months to re-establish a through line from west to east, and regarding the capture of Lee's army as the most important operation towards closing the rebellion—I sent orders to General Sherman on the 6th of December, that after establishing a base on the sea-coast, with necessary garrison, to include all his artillery and cavalry, to come by water to City Point with the balance of his command.

On the 18th of December, having received information of the defeat and utter rout of Hood's army by General Thomas, and that, owing to the great difficulty of procuring ocean transportation, it would take over two months to transport Sherman's army, and doubting whether he might not contribute as much towards the desired result by operating from where he was, I wrote to him to that effect, and asked him for his views as to what would be best to do. A few days after this I received a communication from General Sherman, of date 16th December, acknowledging the receipt of my order of the 6th, and informing me of his preparations to carry it into effect as soon as he could get transportation. Also that he had expected, upon reducing Savannah, instantly to march to Columbia, South Carolina, thence to Raleigh, and thence to report to me; but that this would consume about six weeks' time after the fall of Savannah, whereas by sea he could probably reach me by the middle of January. The confidence he manifested in this letter of being able to march up and join me pleased me, and, without waiting for a reply to my letter of the 18th, I directed him, on the 28th of December, to make preparations to start, as he proposed, without delay, to break up the railroads in North and South Carolina, and join the armies operating against Richmond as soon as he could.

On the 21st of January I informed General Sherman that I had ordered the 23d corps, Major-General Schofield commanding, east; that it numbered about twenty-one thousand men; that we had at Fort Fisher, about eight thousand men; at New Bern, about four thousand; that if Wilmington was captured, General Schofield would go there; if not, he would be sent to New Bern; that, in either event, all the surplus force at both points would move to the interior towards Goldsboro', in co-operation with his movement; that from either point railroad communication could be run out; and that all these troops would be subject to his orders as he came into communication with them.

In obedience to his instructions, General Schofield proceeded to reduce Wilmington, North Carolina, in co-operation with the navy under Admiral Porter, moving his forces up both sides of the Cape Fear River. Fort Anderson, the enemy's main defence on the west bank of the river, was occupied on the morning of the 19th, the enemy having evacuated it after our appearance before it.

After fighting on 20th and 21st, our troops entered Wilmington on the morning of the 22d, the enemy having retreated towards Goldsboro' during the night. Preparations were at once made for a movement on Goldsboro' in two columns—one from Wilmington, and the other from New Bern—and to repair the railroad leading there from each place, as well as to supply General Sherman by Cape Fear River, towards Fayetteville, if it became necessary. The column from New Bern was attacked on the 8th of March, at Wise's Forks, and driven back with the loss of several hundred prisoners. On the 11th the enemy renewed his attack upon our intrenched position, but was repulsed with severe loss, and fell back during the night. On the 14th the Neuse River was crossed and Kinston occupied, and on the 21st Goldsboro' was entered. The column from Wilmington reached Cox's Bridge, on the Neuse River, ten miles above Goldsboro', on the 22d.

By the 1st of February, General Sherman's whole army was in motion from Savannah. He captured Columbia, South Carolina, on the 17th; thence moved on Goldsboro', North Carolina, *via* Fayetteville, reaching the latter place on the 12th of March, opening up communication with General Schofield by way of Cape Fear River. On the 15th he resumed his march on Goldsboro'. He met a force of the enemy at Averysboro', and after a severe fight defeated and compelled it to retreat. Our loss in this engagement was about six hundred. The enemy's loss was much greater. On the 18th the combined forces of the enemy, under Joe Johnston, attacked his advance at Bentonville, capturing three guns and driving it back upon the main body. General Slocum, who was in the advance, ascertaining that the whole of Johnston's army was in the front, arranged his troops on the defensive, intrenched himself and awaited reinforcements, which were pushed forward. On the night of the 21st the enemy retreated to Smithfield, leaving his dead and wounded in our hands. From there Sherman continued to Goldsboro', which place had been occupied by General Schofield on the 21st (crossing the Neuse River ten miles above there, at Cox's Bridge, where General Terry had got possession and thrown a pontoon-bridge on the 22d), thus forming a junction with the columns from New Bern and Wilmington.

Among the important fruits of this campaign was the fall of Charleston, South Carolina. It was evacuated by the enemy on the night of the 17th of February, and occupied by our forces on the 18th.

On the morning of the 31st of January, General Thomas was directed to send a cavalry expedition, under General Stoneman, from East Tennessee, to penetrate South Carolina well down towards Columbia, to destroy the railroads and military resources of the country, and return, if he was able, to East Tennessee by way of Salisbury, North Carolina, releasing our prisoners there, if possible. Of the feasibility of this latter, however, General Stoneman was to judge. Sherman's movements, I had no doubt, would attract the attention of all the force the enemy could collect, and facilitate the execution of this. General Stoneman was so late in making his start on this expedition (and Sherman having passed out of the State of South Carolina), on the 27th of February I directed General Thomas to change his course, and order him to repeat his raid of last fall, destroying the railroad towards Lynchburg as far as he could. This would keep him between our garrisons in East Tennessee and the enemy. I regarded it not impossible that in the event of the enemy being driven from Richmond, he might fall back to Lynchburg and attempt a raid north through East Tennessee. On the 14th of February the following communication was sent to General Thomas:

"CITY POINT, VA., *February* 14, 1865.

"General Canby is preparing a movement from Mobile Bay against Mobile and the interior of Alabama. His force will consist of about twenty thousand men, besides A. J. Smith's command. The cavalry you have sent to Canby will be debarked at Vicksburg. It, with the available cavalry already in that section, will move from there eastward, in co-operation. Hood's army has been terribly reduced by the severe punishment you gave it in Tennessee, by desertion consequent upon their defeat, and now by the withdrawal of many of them to oppose Sherman. (I take it a large portion of the infantry has been so withdrawn. It is so asserted in the Richmond papers, and a member of the rebel Congress said a few days since in a speech, that one-half of it had been brought to South Carolina to oppose Sherman.) This being true, or even if it is not true, Canby's movement will attract all the attention of the enemy, and leave the advance from your standpoint easy. I think it advisable, therefore, that you prepare as much of a cavalry force as you can spare, and hold it in readiness to go south. The object would be threefold: first, to attract as much of the enemy's force as possible, to insure success to Canby; second, to destroy the enemy's line of communications and military resources; third, to destroy or capture their forces brought into the field. Tuscaloosa and Selma would probably be the points to direct the expedition against. This, however, would not be so important as the mere fact of penetrating deep into Alabama. Discretion should be left to the officer commanding the expedition to go where, according to the information he may receive, he will best secure the objects named above.

"Now that your force has been so much depleted, I do not know what number of men you can put into the field. If not more than five thousand men, however, all cavalry, I think it will be sufficient. It is not desirable that you should start this expedition until the one leaving Vicksburg has been three or four days out, or even a week. I do not know when it will start, but will inform you by telegraph as soon as I learn. If you should hear through other sources before hearing from me, you can act on the information received.

"To insure success your cavalry should go with as little wagon-train as possible, relying upon the country for supplies. I would also reduce the number of guns to a battery, or the number of batteries, and put the extra teams to the guns taken. No guns or caissons should be taken with less than eight horses.

"Please inform me by telegraph, on receipt of this, what force you think you will be able to send under these directions.

"U. S. GRANT, Lieutenant-General.

"MAJOR-GENERAL G. H. THOMAS."

On the 15th, he was directed to start the expedition as soon after the 20th as he could get it off.

I deemed it of the utmost importance, before a general movement of the armies operating against Richmond, that all communications with the city, north of James River, should be cut off. The enemy having withdrawn the bulk of his force from the Shenandoah Valley and sent it south, or replaced troops sent from Richmond, and desiring to reinforce Sherman, if practicable, whose cavalry was greatly inferior in numbers to that of the enemy, I determined to make a move from the Shenandoah, which, if successful, would accomplish the first at least, and possibly the latter of these objects. I therefore telegraphed General Sheridan as follows:

"CITY POINT, VA., *February* 20, 1865—1 P.M.

"GENERAL:—As soon as it is possible to travel, I think you will have no difficulty about reaching Lynchburg with a cavalry force alone. From there you could destroy the railroad and canal in every direction, so as to be of no further use to the rebellion. Sufficient cavalry should be left behind to look after Mosby's gang. From Lynchburg, if information you might get there would justify it, you will strike south, heading the streams in Virginia to the westward of Danville, and push on and join General Sherman. This additional raid, with one now about starting from East Tennessee under Stoneman, numbering four or five thousand cavalry, one from Vicksburg, numbering seven or eight thousand cavalry, one from Eastport, Mississippi, ten thousand cavalry, Canby from Mobile Bay, with about thirty-eight thousand mixed troops, these three latter pushing for Tuscaloosa, Selma, and Montgomery, and Sherman with a large army eating out the vitals of South Carolina, is all that will be wanted to leave nothing for the rebellion to stand upon. I would advise you to overcome great obstacles to accomplish this. Charleston was evacuated on Tuesday last.

"U. S. GRANT, Lieutenant-General.

"MAJOR-GENERAL P. H. SHERIDAN."

On the 25th I received a dispatch from General Sheridan, inquiring where Sherman was aiming for, and if I could give him definite information as to the points he might be expected to move on, this side of Charlotte, North Carolina. In answer, the following telegram was sent him:

"CITY POINT, VA., *February* 25, 1865.

"GENERAL: — Sherman's movements will depend on the amount of opposition he meets with from the enemy. If strongly opposed, he may possibly have to fall back to Georgetown, S. C., and fit out for a new start. I think, however, all danger for the necessity of going to that point has passed. I believe he has passed Charlotte. He may take Fayetteville on his way to Goldsboro'. If you reach Lynchburg, you will have to be guided in your after movements by the information you obtain. Before you could possibly reach Sherman, I think you would find him moving from Goldsboro' towards Raleigh, or engaging the enemy strongly posted at one or the other of these places, with railroad communications opened from his army to Wilmington or New Bern.

"U. S. GRANT, Lieutenant-General.

"MAJOR-GENERAL P. H. SHERIDAN."

General Sheridan moved from Winchester on the 27th of February, with two divisions of cavalry, numbering about five thousand each. On the 1st of March he secured the bridge, which the enemy attempted to destroy, across the middle fork of the Shenandoah, at Mount Crawford, and entered Staunton on the 2d, the enemy having retreated on Waynesboro'. Thence he pushed on to Waynesboro', where he found the enemy in force in an intrenched position, under General Early. Without stopping to make a reconnoissance, an immediate attack was made, the position was carried, and sixteen hundred prisoners, eleven pieces of artillery, with horses and caissons complete, two hundred wagons and teams loaded with subsistence, and seventeen battle-flags, were captured. The prisoners, under an escort of fifteen hundred men, were sent back to Winchester. Thence he marched on Charlottesville, destroying effectually the railroad and bridges as he went, which place he reached on the 3d. Here he remained two days, destroying the railroad towards Richmond and Lynchburg, including the large iron bridges over the north and south forks of the Rivanna River and awaited the arrival of his trains. This necessary delay caused him to abandon the idea of capturing Lynchburg. On the morning of the 6th, dividing his force into two columns, he sent one to Scottsville, whence it marched up the James River Canal to New Market, destroying every lock, and in many places the bank of the canal. From here a force was pushed out from this column to Duiguidsville, to obtain possession of the bridge across the James River at that place, but failed. The enemy burned it on our approach. The enemy also burned the bridge across the river at Hardwicksville. The other column moved down the railroad towards Lynchburg, destroying it as far as Amherst Court House, sixteen miles from Lynchburg; thence across the country, uniting with the column at New Market. The river being very high, his pontoons would not reach across it; and the enemy having destroyed the bridges by which he had hoped to cross the river and get on the South Side Railroad about Farmville, and destroy it to Appomattox Court House, the only thing left for him was to return to Winchester or strike a base at the White House. Fortunately, he chose the latter. From New Market he took up his line of march, following the canal towards Richmond, destroying every lock upon it and cutting the banks wherever practicable, to a point eight miles east of Goochland, concentrating the whole force at Columbia on the 10th. Here he rested one day, and sent through by scouts information of his whereabouts and purposes, and a request for supplies to meet him at White House, which reached me on the night of the 12th. An infantry force was immediately sent to get possession of White House, and supplies were forwarded. Moving from Columbia in a direction to threaten Richmond, to near Ashland Station, he crossed the Annas, and after having destroyed all the bridges and many miles of the railroad, proceeded down the north bank of the Pamunkey to White House, which place he reached on the 19th.

Previous to this the following communication was sent to General Thomas:

"CITY POINT, VIRGINIA,
March 7, 1865—9.30 A.M.

"GENERAL.:—I think it will be advisable now for you to repair the railroad in East Tennessee, and throw a good force up to Bull's Gap and fortify there. Supplies at Knoxville could always be got forward as required. With Bull's Gap fortified, you can occupy as outposts about all of East Tennessee, and be prepared, if it should be required of you in the spring, to make a campaign towards Lynchburg, or into North Carolina. I do not think Stoneman should break the road until he gets into Virginia, unless it should be to cut off rolling-stock that may be caught west of that.

"U. S. GRANT, Lieutenant-General.

"Major General G. H. Thomas."

Thus it will be seen that in March, 1865, General Canby was moving an adequate force against Mobile and the army defending it under General Dick Taylor; Thomas was pushing out two large and well-appointed cavalry expeditions—one from Middle Tennessee under Brevet Major-General Wilson against the enemy's vital points in Alabama, the other from East Tennessee, under Major-General Stoneman, towards Lynchburg—and assembling the remainder of his available forces, preparatory to commence offensive operations from East Tennessee; General Sheridan's cavalry was at White House; the armies of the Potomac and James were confronting the enemy, under Lee, in his defences of Richmond and Petersburg; General Sherman with his armies, reinforced by that of General Schofield, was at Goldsboro'; General Pope was making preparations for a spring campaign against the enemy under Kirby Smith and Price, west of the Mississippi; and General Hancock was concentrating a force in the vicinity of Winchester, Virginia, to guard against invasion or to operate offensively, as might prove necessary.

After the long march by General Sheridan's cavalry over winter roads, it was necessary to rest and refit at White House. At this time the greatest source of uneasiness to me was the fear that the enemy would leave his strong lines about Petersburg and Richmond for the purpose of uniting with Johnston, before he was driven from them by battle, or I was prepared to make an effectual pursuit. On the 24th of March, General Sheridan moved from White House, crossed the James River at Jones's Landing, and formed a junction with the Army of the Potomac in front of Petersburg on the 27th. During this move, General Ord sent forces to cover the crossings of the Chickahominy.

On the 24th of March the following instructions for a general movement of the armies operating against Richmond were issued:

"City Point, Virginia,

March 24, 1865.

"General:—On the 29th instant the armies operating against Richmond will be moved by our left, for the double purpose of turning the enemy out of his present position around Petersburg, and to insure the success of the cavalry under General Sheridan, which will start at the same time, in its efforts to reach and destroy the South Side and Danville railroads. Two corps of the Army of the Potomac will be moved at first in two columns, taking the two roads crossing Hatcher's Run, nearest where the present line held by us strikes that stream, both moving towards Dinwiddie Court House.

"The cavalry under General Sheridan, joined by the division now under General Davies, will move at the same time by the Weldon Road and the Jerusalem Plank Road, turning west from the latter before crossing the Nottoway, and west with the whole column before reaching Stony Creek. General Sheridan will then move independently, under other instructions which will be given him. All dismounted cavalry belonging to the Army of the Potomac, and the dismounted cavalry from the Middle Military Division not required for guarding property belonging to their arm of service, will report to Brigadier-General Benham, to be added to the defences of City Point. Major-General Parke will be left in command of all the army left for holding the lines about Petersburg and City Point, subject of course to orders from the commander of the Army of the Potomac. The 9th army corps will be left intact, to hold the present line of works so long as the whole line now occupied by us is held. If, however, the troops to the left of the 9th corps are withdrawn, then the left of the corps may be thrown back so as to occupy the position held by the army prior to the capture of the Weldon Road. All troops to the left of the 9th corps will be held in readiness to move at the shortest notice by such route as may be designated when the order is given.

"General Ord will detach three divisions, two white and one colored, or so much of them as he can, and hold his present lines, and march for the present left of the Army of the Potomac. In the absence of further orders, or until further orders are given, the white divisions will follow the left column of the Army of the Potomac, and the colored division the right column. During the movement Major-General Weitzel will be left in command of all the forces remaining behind from the Army of the James.

"The movement of troops from the Army of the James will commence on the night of the 27th instant. General Ord will leave behind the minimum number of cavalry necessary for picket duty, in the absence of the main army. A cavalry expedition, from General Ord's command, will also be started from Suffolk, to leave there on Saturday, the 1st of April, under Colonel Sumner, for the purpose of cutting the railroad about Hicksford. This, if accomplished, will have to be a surprise, and therefore from three to five hundred men will be sufficient. They should, however, be supported by all the infantry that can be spared from Norfolk and Portsmouth, as far out as to where the cavalry crosses the Blackwater. The crossing should probably be at Uniten. Should Colonel Sumner succeed in reaching the Weldon Road, he will be instructed to do all the damage possible to the triangle of roads between Hicksford, Weldon, and Gaston. The railroad bridge at Weldon being fitted up for the passage of carriages, it might be practicable to destroy any accumulation of supplies the enemy may have collected south of the Roanoke. All the troops will move with four days' rations in haversacks and eight days' in wagons. To avoid as much hauling as possible, and to give the Army of the James the same number of days' supplies with the Army of the Potomac, General Ord will direct his commissary and quartermaster to have sufficient supplies delivered at the terminus of the road to fill up in passing. Sixty rounds of ammunition per man will be taken in wagons, and as much grain as the transportation on hand will carry, after taking the specified amount of other supplies. The densely wooded country in which the army has to operate making the use of much artillery impracticable, the amount taken with the army will be reduced to six or eight guns to each division, at the option of the army commanders.

"All necessary preparations for carrying these directions into operation may be commenced at once. The reserves of the 9th corps should be massed as much as possible. While I would not now order an unconditional attack on the enemy's line by them, they should be ready and should make the attack if the enemy weakens his line in their front, without waiting for orders. In case they carry the line, then the whole of the 9th corps could follow up so as to join or co-operate with the balance of the army. To prepare for this, the 9th corps will have rations issued to them, same as the balance of the army. General Weitzel will keep vigilant watch upon his front, and if found at all practicable to break through at any point, he will do so. A success north of the James should be followed up with great promptness. An attack will not be feasible unless it is found that the enemy has detached largely. In that case it may be regarded as evident that the enemy are relying upon their local reserves principally for the defence of Richmond. Preparations may be made for abandoning all the line north of the James, except inclosed works—only to be abandoned, however, after a break is made in the lines of the enemy.

"By these instructions a large part of the armies operating against Richmond is left behind. The enemy, knowing this, may, as an only chance, strip their lines to the merest skeleton, in the hope of advantage not being taken of it, while they hurl everything against the moving column, and return. It cannot be impressed too strongly upon commanders of troops left in the trenches not to allow this to occur without taking advantage of it. The very fact of the enemy coming out to attack, if he does so, might be regarded as almost conclusive evidence of such a weakening of his lines. I would have it particularly enjoined upon corps commanders that, in case of an attack from the enemy, those not attacked are not to wait for orders from the commanding officer of the army to which they belong, but that they will move promptly, and notify the commander of their action. I would also enjoin the same action on the part of division commanders when other parts of their corps are engaged. In like manner, I would urge the importance of following up a repulse of the enemy.

"U. S. GRANT, Lieutenant-General.
"Major-Generals Meade, Ord, and Sheridan."

Early on the morning of the 25th the enemy assaulted our lines in front of the 9th corps (which held from the Appomattox River towards our left), and carried Fort Stedman, and a part of the line to the right and left of it, established themselves and turned the guns of the fort against us; but our troops on either flank held their ground until the reserves were brought up, when the enemy was driven back with a heavy loss in killed and wounded, and one thousand nine hundred prisoners. Our loss was sixty-eight killed, three hundred and thirty-seven wounded, and five hundred and six missing. General Meade at once ordered the other corps to advance and feel the enemy in their respective fronts. Pushing forward, they captured and held the enemy's strongly intrenched picket-line in front of the 2d and 6th corps, and eight hundred and thirty-four prisoners. The enemy made desperate attempts to retake this line, but without success. Our loss in front of these was fifty-two killed, eight hundred and sixty-four wounded, and two hundred and seven missing. The enemy's loss in killed and wounded was far greater.

General Sherman having got his troops all quietly in camp about Goldsboro', and his preparations for furnishing supplies to them perfected, visited me at City Point on the 27th of March, and stated that he would be ready to move, as he had previously written me, by the 10th of April, fully equipped and rationed for twenty days, if it should become necessary to bring his command to bear against Lee's army, in co-operation with our forces in front of Richmond and Petersburg. General Sherman proposed in this movement to threaten Raleigh, and then, by turning suddenly to the right, reach the Roanoke at Gaston or thereabouts, whence he could move on to the Richmond and Danville Railroad, striking it in the vicinity of Burkesville, or join the armies operating against Richmond, as might be deemed best. This plan he was directed to carry into execution, if he received no further directions in the meantime. I explained to him the movement I had ordered to commence on the 29th of March. That if it should not prove as entirely successful as I hoped, I would cut the cavalry loose to destroy the Danville and South Side railroads, and thus deprive the enemy of further supplies, and also to prevent the rapid concentration of Lee's and Johnston's armies.

I had spent days of anxiety lest each morning should bring the report that the enemy had retreated the night before. I was firmly convinced that Sherman's crossing the Roanoke would be the signal for Lee to leave. With Johnston and him combined, a long, tedious, and expensive campaign, consuming most of the summer, might become necessary. By moving out I would put the army in better condition for pursuit, and would at least, by the destruction of the Danville Road, retard the concentration of the two armies of Lee and Johnston, and cause the enemy to abandon much material that he might otherwise save. I therefore determined not to delay the movement ordered.

On the night of the 27th, Major-General Ord, with two divisions of the 24th corps, Major-General Gibbon commanding, and one division of the 25th corps, Brigadier-General Birney commanding, and Mackenzie's cavalry, took up his line of march in pursuance of the foregoing instructions, and reached the position assigned him near Hatcher's Run on the morning of the 29th. On the 28th the following instructions were given to General Sheridan:

"CITY POINT, VA., *March* 28, 1865.

"GENERAL: — The 5th army corps will move by the Vaughn Road at three A.M. to-morrow morning. The 2d moves at about nine A.M., having but about three miles to march to reach the point designated for it to take on the right of the 5th corps, after the latter reaching Dinwiddie Court House. Move your cavalry at as early an hour as you can, and without being confined to any particular road or roads. You may go out by the nearest roads in rear of the 5th corps, pass by its left, and passing near to or through Dinwiddie, reach the right and rear of the enemy as soon as you can. It is not the intention to attack the enemy in his intrenched position, but to force him out, if possible. Should he come out and attack us, or get himself where he can be attacked, move in with your entire force in your own way, and with the full reliance that the army will engage or follow, as circumstances will dictate. I shall be on the field, and will probably be able to communicate with you. Should I not do so, and you find that the enemy keeps within his main intrenched line, you may cut loose and push for the Danville Road. If you find it practicable, I would like you to cross the South Side Road, between Petersburg and Burkesville, and destroy it to some extent. I would not advise much detention, however, until you reach the Danville Road, which I would like you to strike as near to the Appomattox as possible. Make your destruction on that road as complete as possible. You can then pass on to the South Side Road, west of Burkesville, and destroy that in like manner.

"After having accomplished the destruction of the two railroads, which are now the only avenues of supply to Lee's army, you may return to this army, selecting your road further south, or you may go on into North Carolina and join General Sherman. Should you select the latter course, get the information to me as early as possible, so that I may send orders to meet you at Goldsboro'.

"U. S. GRANT, Lieutenant-General.

"MAJOR-GENERAL P. H. SHERIDAN."

On the morning of the 29th the movement commenced. At night the cavalry was at Dinwiddie Court House, and the left of our infantry line extended to the Quaker Road, near its intersection with the Boydton Plank Road. The position of the troops from left to right was as follows: Sheridan, Warren, Humphreys, Ord, Wright, Parke.

Everything looked favorable to the defeat of the enemy and the capture of Petersburg and Richmond, if the proper effort was made. I therefore addressed the following communication to General Sheridan, having previously informed him verbally not to cut loose for the raid contemplated in his orders until he received notice from me to do so:

"GRAVELLY CREEK, *March* 29, 1865.

"GENERAL: — Our line is now unbroken from the Appomattox to Dinwiddie. We are all ready, however, to give up all, from the Jerusalem Plank Road to Hatcher's Run, whenever the forces can be used advantageously. After getting into line south of Hatcher's, we pushed forward to find the enemy's position. General Griffin was attacked near where the Quaker Road intersects the Boydton Road, but repulsed it easily, capturing about one hundred men. Humphreys reached Dabney's Mill, and was pushing on when last heard from.

"I now feel like ending the matter, if it is possible to do so, before going back. I do not want you, therefore, to cut loose and go after the enemy's roads at present. In the morning push around the enemy, if you can, and get on to his right rear. The movements of the enemy's cavalry may, of course, modify your action. We will act all together as one army here, until it is seen what can be done with the enemy. The signal-officer at Cobb's Hill reported, at half-past eleven A.M., that a cavalry column had passed that point from Richmond towards Petersburg, taking forty minutes to pass.

"U. S. GRANT, Lieutenant-General.

"MAJOR-GENERAL P. H. SHERIDAN."

From the night of the 29th to the morning of the 31st the rain fell in such torrents as to make it impossible to move a wheeled vehicle, except as corduroy roads were laid in front of them. During the 30th, Sheridan advanced from Dinwiddie Court House towards Five Forks, where he found the enemy in full force. General Warren advanced and extended his line across the Boydton Plank Road to near the White Oak Road, with a view of getting across the latter; but, finding the enemy strong in his front and extending beyond his left, was directed to hold on where he was, and fortify. General Humphreys drove the enemy from his front into his main line on the Hatcher, near Burgess's Mills. Generals Ord, Wright, and Parke made examinations in their fronts to determine the feasibility of an assault on the enemy's lines. The two latter reported favorably. The enemy confronting us as he did, at every point from Richmond to our extreme left, I conceived his lines must be weakly held, and could be penetrated if my estimate of his forces was correct. I determined, therefore, to extend our line no farther, but to reinforce General Sheridan with a corps of infantry, and thus enable him to cut loose and turn the enemy's right flank, and with the other corps assault the enemy's lines. The result of the offensive effort of the enemy the week before, when he assaulted Fort Stedman, particularly favored this. The enemy's intrenched picket-line captured by us at that time threw the lines occupied by the belligerents so close together at some points that it was but a moment's run from one to the other. Preparations were at once made to relieve General Humphreys's corps, to report to General Sheridan; but the condition of the roads prevented immediate movement. On the morning of the 31st, General Warren reported favorably to getting possession of the White Oak Road, and was directed to do so. To accomplish this, he moved with one division, instead of his whole corps, which was attacked by the enemy in superior force and driven back on the 2d division before it had time to form, and it, in turn, forced back upon the 3d division, when the enemy was checked. A division of the 2d corps was immediately sent to his support, the enemy driven back with heavy loss, and possession of the White Oak Road gained. Sheridan advanced, and with a portion of his cavalry got possession of the Five Forks; but the enemy, after the affair with the 5th corps, reinforced the rebel cavalry, defending that point with infantry, and forced him back towards Dinwiddie Court House. Here General Sheridan displayed great generalship. Instead of retreating with his whole command on the main army, to tell the story of superior forces encountered, he deployed his cavalry on foot, leaving only mounted men enough to take charge of the horses. This compelled the enemy to deploy over a vast extent of wooded and broken country, and made his progress slow. At this juncture he dispatched to me what had taken place, and that he was dropping back slowly on Dinwiddie Court House. General Mackenzie's cavalry and one division of the 5th corps were immediately ordered to his assistance. Soon after receiving a report from General Meade that Humphreys could hold our position on the Boydton Road, and that the other two divisions of the 5th corps could go to Sheridan, they were so ordered at once. Thus the operations of the day necessitated the sending of Warren, because of his accessibility, instead of Humphreys, as was intended, and precipitated intended movements. On the morning of the 1st of April, General Sheridan, reinforced by General Warren, drove the enemy back on Five Forks, where, late in the evening, he assaulted and carried his strongly fortified position, capturing all his artillery and between five and six thousand prisoners.

About the close of this battle, Brevet Major-General Charles Griffin relieved Major-General Warren in command of the 5th corps. The report of this reached me after nightfall. Some apprehensions filled my mind lest the enemy might desert his lines during the night, and by falling upon General Sheridan before assistance could reach him, drive him from his position and open the way for retreat. To guard against this, General Miles's division of Humphreys's corps was sent to reinforce him, and a bombardment was commenced and kept up until four o'clock in the morning (April 2), when an assault was ordered on the enemy's lines. General Wright penetrated the lines with his whole corps, sweeping everything before him, and to his left towards Hatcher's Run, capturing many guns and several thousand prisoners. He was closely followed by two divisions of General Ord's command, until he met the other division of General Ord's that had succeeded in forcing the enemy's lines near Hatcher's Run. Generals Wright and Ord immediately swung to the right, and closed all of the enemy on that side of them in Petersburg, while General Humphreys pushed forward with two divisions and joined General Wright on the left. General Parke succeeded in carrying the enemy's main line, capturing guns and prisoners, but was unable to carry his inner line. General Sheridan being advised of the condition of affairs, returned General Miles to his proper command. On reaching the enemy's lines immediately surrounding Petersburg, a portion of General Gibbon's corps, by a most gallant charge, captured two strong inclosed works—the most salient and commanding south of Petersburg—thus materially shortening the line of investment necessary for taking in the city. The enemy south of Hatcher's Run retreated westward to Sutherland's Station, where they were overtaken by Miles's division. A severe engagement ensued, and lasted until both his right and left flanks were threatened by the approach of General Sheridan, who was moving from Ford's Station towards Petersburg, and a division sent by General Meade from the front of Petersburg, when he broke in the utmost confusion, leaving in our hands his guns and many prisoners. This force retreated by the main road along the Appomattox River. During the night of the 2d the enemy evacuated Petersburg and Richmond, and retreated towards Danville. On the morning of the 3d pursuit was commenced. General Sheridan pushed for the Danville Road, keeping near the Appomattox, followed by General Meade with the 2d and 6th corps, while General Ord moved for Burkesville, along the South Side Road; the 9th corps stretched along that road behind him. On the 4th, General Sheridan struck the Danville Road near Jetersville, where he learned that Lee was at Amelia Court House. He immediately intrenched himself and awaited the arrival of General Meade, who reached there the next day. General Ord reached Burkesville on the evening of the 5th.

On the morning of the 5th, I addressed Major-General Sherman the following communication:

"WILSON'S STATION, *April* 5, 1865.

"GENERAL: — All indications now are that Lee will attempt to reach Danville with the remnant of his force. Sheridan, who was up with him last night, reports all that is left, horse, foot, and dragoons, at twenty thousand, much demoralized. We hope to reduce this number one-half. I shall push on to Burkesville, and if a stand is made at Danville, will in a very few days go there. If you can possibly do so, push on from where you are, and let us see if we cannot finish the job with Lee's and Johnston's armies. Whether it will be better for you to strike for Greensboro', or nearer to Danville, you will be better able to judge when you receive this. Rebel armies now are the only strategic points to strike at.

"U. S. GRANT, Lieutenant-General.
"MAJOR-GENERAL W. T. SHERMAN."

On the morning of the 6th, it was found that General Lee was moving west of Jetersville, towards Danville. General Sheridan moved with his cavalry (the 5th corps having been returned to General Meade on his reaching Jetersville) to strike his flank, followed by the 6th corps, while the 2d and 5th corps pressed hard after, forcing him to abandon several hundred wagons and several pieces of artillery. General Ord advanced from Burkesville towards Farmville, sending two regiments of infantry and a squadron of cavalry, under Brevet Brigadier-General Theodore Read, to reach and destroy the bridges. This advance met the head of Lee's column near Farmville, which it heroically attacked and detained until General Read was killed and his small force overpowered. This caused a delay in the enemy's movements, and enabled General Ord to get well up with the remainder of his force, on meeting which, the enemy immediately intrenched himself. In the afternoon, General Sheridan struck the enemy south of Sailors' Creek, captured sixteen pieces of artillery and about four hundred wagons, and detained him until the 6th corps got up, when a general attack of infantry and cavalry was made, which resulted in the capture of six or seven thousand prisoners, among whom were many general officers. The movements of the 2d corps and General Ord's command contributed greatly to the day's success.

On the morning of the 7th the pursuit was renewed, the cavalry, except one division, and the 5th corps moving by Prince Edward's Court House; the 6th corps, General Ord's command, and one division of cavalry, on Farmville; and the 2d corps by the High Bridge Road. It was soon found that the enemy had crossed to the north side of the Appomattox; but so close was the pursuit, that the 2d corps got possession of the common bridge at High Bridge before the enemy could destroy it, and immediately crossed over.

The 6th corps and a division of cavalry crossed at Farmville to its support.

Feeling now that General Lee's chance of escape was utterly hopeless, I addressed him the following communication from Farmville:

"April 7, 1865.

"GENERAL:—The result of the last week must convince you of the hopelessness of further resistance on the part of the Army of Northern Virginia in this struggle. I feel that it is so, and regard it as my duty to shift from myself the responsibility of any further effusion of blood, by asking of you the surrender of that portion of the Confederate States army known as the Army of Northern Virginia.

"U. S. GRANT, Lieutenant-General.

"GENERAL R. E. LEE."

Early on the morning of the 8th, before leaving, I received at Farmville the following:

"April 7, 1865.

"GENERAL:—I have received your note of this date. Though not entertaining the opinion you express on the hopelessness of further resistance on the part of the Army of Northern Virginia, I reciprocate your desire to avoid useless effusion of blood, and therefore, before considering your proposition, ask the terms you will offer on condition of its surrender.

"R. E. LEE, General.

"LIEUTENANT-GENERAL U. S. GRANT."

To this I immediately replied:

"April 8, 1865.

"GENERAL:—Your note of last evening, in reply to mine of same date, asking the condition on which I will accept the surrender of the Army of Northern Virginia, is just received. In reply, I would say, that *peace* being my great desire, there is but one condition I would insist upon—namely, That the men and officers surrendered shall be disqualified for taking up arms again against the Government of the United States until properly exchanged. I will meet you, or will designate officers to meet any officers you may name for the same purpose, at any point agreeable to you, for the purpose of arranging definitely the terms upon which the surrender of the Army of Northern Virginia will be received.

"U. S. GRANT, Lieutenant-General.

"GENERAL R. E. LEE."

Early on the morning of the 8th the pursuit was resumed. General Meade followed north of the Appomattox, and General Sheridan, with all the cavalry, pushed straight for Appomattox Station, followed by General Ord's command and the 5th corps. During the day General Meade's advance had considerable fighting with the enemy's rear-guard, but was unable to bring on a general engagement. Late in the evening General Sheridan struck the railroad at Appomattox Station, drove the enemy from there, and captured twenty-five pieces of artillery, a hospital-train, and four trains of cars loaded with supplies for Lee's army. During this day I accompanied General Meade's column, and about midnight received the following communication from General Lee:

"*April* 8, 1865.

"GENERAL:—I received, at a late hour, your note of to-day. In mine of yesterday I did not intend to propose the surrender of the Army of Northern Virginia, but to ask the terms of your proposition. To be frank, I do not think the emergency has arisen to call for the surrender of this army; but as the restoration of peace should be the sole object of all, I desired to know whether your proposals would lead to that end. I cannot, therefore, meet you with a view to surrender the Army of Northern Virginia; but as far as your proposal may affect the Confederates States forces under my command, and tend to the restoration of peace, I should be pleased to meet you at ten A.M. tomorrow on the old stage-road to Richmond, between the picket-lines of the two armies.

"R. E. LEE, General.

"LIEUTENANT-GENERAL U. S. GRANT."

Early on the morning of the 9th I returned him an answer as follows, and immediately started to join the column south of the Appomattox:

"*April* 9, 1865.

"GENERAL:—Your note of yesterday is received. I have no authority to treat on the subject of peace; the meeting proposed for ten A.M. to-day could lead to no good. I will state, however, general, that I am equally anxious for peace with yourself, and the whole North entertains the same feeling. The terms upon which peace can be had are well understood. By the South laying down their arms they will hasten that most desirable event, save thousands of human lives, and hundreds of millions of property not yet destroyed. Seriously hoping that all our difficulties may be settled without the loss of another life. I subscribe myself, etc.

"U. S. GRANT, Lieutenant-General.

"GENERAL R. E. LEE."

On the morning of the 9th, General Ord's command and the 5th corps reached Appomattox Station just as the enemy was making a desperate effort to break through our cavalry. The infantry was at once thrown in. Soon after a white flag was received, requesting a suspension of hostilities pending negotiations for a surrender.

Before reaching General Sheridan's headquarters, I received the following from General Lee:

"*April* 9, 1865.

"GENERAL:—I received your note of this morning on the picket-line, whither I had come to meet you, and ascertain definitely what terms were embraced in your proposal of yesterday with reference to the surrender of this army. I now ask an interview, in accordance with the offer contained in your letter of yesterday, for that purpose.

"R. E. LEE, General.

"LIEUTENANT-GENERAL U. S. GRANT."

The interview was held at Appomattox Court-House, the result of which is set forth in the following correspondence:

APPOMATTOX COURT-HOUSE, Virginia, *April* 9, 1865.

"GENERAL:—In accordance with the substance of my letter to you of the 8th instant, I propose to receive the surrender of the Army of Northern Virginia on the following terms, to wit: Rolls of all the officers and men to be made in duplicate, one copy to be given to an officer to be designated by me, the other to be retained by such officer or officers as you may designate. The officers to give their individual paroles not to take up arms against the Government of the United States until properly exchanged; and each company or regimental commander sign a like parole for the men of their commands. The arms, artillery, and public property to be parked and stacked, and turned over to the officers appointed by me to receive them. This will not embrace the side-arms of the officers, nor their private horses or baggage. This done, each officer and man will be allowed to return to his home, not to be disturbed by United States authority so long as they observe their paroles and the laws in force where they may reside.

"U. S. GRANT, Lieutenant-General.

"GENERAL R. E. LEE."

"HEADQUARTERS ARMY OF NORTHERN VIRGINIA, *April* 9, 1865.

"GENERAL:—I have received your letter of this date containing the terms of surrender of the Army of Northern Virginia as proposed by you. As they are substantially the same as those expressed in your letter of the 8th instant, they are accepted. I will proceed to designate the proper officers to carry the stipulations into effect.

"R. E. LEE, General.

"LIEUTENANT-GENERAL U. S. GRANT."

The command of Major-General Gibbon, the 5th army corps under Griffin, and Mackenzie's cavalry, were designated to remain at Appomattox Court-House until the paroling of the surrendered army was completed, and to take charge of the public property. The remainder of the army immediately returned to the vicinity of Burkesville.

General Lee's great influence throughout the whole South caused his example to be followed, and to-day the result is that the armies lately under his leadership are at their homes, desiring peace and quiet, and their arms are in the hands of our ordnance officers.

On the receipt of my letter of the 5th, General Sherman moved directly against Joe Johnston, who retreated rapidly on and through Raleigh, which place General Sherman occupied on the morning of the 13th. The day preceding, news of the surrender of General Lee reached him at Smithfield.

On the 14th a correspondence was opened between General Sherman and General Johnston, which resulted on the 18th in an agreement for a suspension of hostilities, and a memorandum or basis for peace, subject to the approval of the President. This agreement was disapproved by the President on the 21st, which disapproval, together with your instructions, was communicated to General Sherman by me in person on the morning of the 24th, at Raleigh, North Carolina, in obedience to your orders. Notice was at once given by him to General Johnston for the termination of the truce that had been entered into. On the 25th another meeting between them was agreed upon, to take place on the 26th, which terminated in the surrender and disbandment of Johnston's army upon substantially the same terms as were given to General Lee.

The expedition under General Stoneman from East Tennessee got off on the 20th of March, moving by way of Boone, North Carolina, and struck the railroad at Wytheville, Chambersburg, and Big Lick. The force striking it at Big Lick pushed on to within a few miles of Lynchburg, destroying the important bridges, while with the main force he effectually destroyed it between New River and Big Lick, and then turned for Greensboro', on the North Carolina Railroad; struck that road and destroyed the bridges between Danville and Greensboro', and between Greensboro' and the Yadkin, together with the depots of supplies along it, and captured four hundred prisoners. At Salisbury he attacked and defeated a force of the enemy under General Gardiner, capturing fourteen pieces of artillery and one thousand three hundred and sixty-four prisoners, and destroyed large amounts of army stores. At this place he destroyed fifteen miles of railroad and the bridges towards Charlotte. Thence he moved to Slatersville.

General Canby, who had been directed in January to make preparations for a movement from Mobile Bay against Mobile and the interior of Alabama, commenced his movement on the 20th of March. The 16th corps, Major-General A. J. Smith commanding, moved from Fort Gaines by water to Fish River; the 13th corps, under Major-General Gordon Granger, moved from Fort Morgan and joined the 16th corps on Fish River, both moving thence on

Spanish Fort and investing it on the 27th; while Major-General Steele's command moved from Pensacola, cut the railroad leading from Tensas to Montgomery, effected a junction with them, and partially invested Fort Blakely. After a severe bombardment of Spanish Fort, a part of its line was carried on the 8th of April. During the night the enemy evacuated the fort. Fort Blakely was carried by assault on the 9th, and many prisoners captured; our loss was considerable. These successes practically opened to us the Alabama River, and enabled us to approach Mobile from the north. On the night of the 11th the city was evacuated, and was taken possession of by our forces on the morning of the 12th.

The expedition under command of Brevet Major-General Wilson, consisting of twelve thousand five hundred mounted men, was delayed by rains until March 22d, when it moved from Chickasaw, Alabama. On the 1st of April, General Wilson encountered the enemy in force under Forrest near Ebenezer Church, drove him in confusion, captured three hundred prisoners and three guns, and destroyed the central bridge over the Cahawba River. On the 2d he attacked and captured the fortified city of Selma, defended by Forrest, with seven thousand men and thirty-two guns, destroyed the arsenal, armory, naval foundry, machine-shops, vast quantities of stores, and captured three thousand prisoners. On the 4th he captured and destroyed Tuscaloosa. On the 10th he crossed the Alabama River, and after sending information of his operations to General Canby, marched on Montgomery, which place he occupied on the 14th, the enemy having abandoned it. At this place many stores and five steamboats fell into our hands. Thence a force marched direct on Columbus, and another on West Point, both of which places were assaulted and captured on the 16th. At the former place we got one thousand five hundred prisoners and fifty-two field-guns, destroyed two gunboats, the navy yard, foundries, arsenal, many factories, and much other public property. At the latter place we got three hundred prisoners, four guns, and destroyed nineteen locomotives and three hundred cars. On the 20th he took possession of Macon, Georgia, with sixty field-guns, one thousand two hundred militia, and five generals, surrendered by General Howell Cobb. General Wilson, hearing that Jeff. Davis was trying to make his escape, sent forces in pursuit and succeeded in capturing him on the morning of May 11th.

On the 4th day of May, General Dick Taylor surrendered to General Canby all the remaining rebel forces east of the Mississippi.

A force sufficient to insure an easy triumph over the enemy under Kirby Smith, west of the Mississippi, was immediately put in motion for Texas, and Major-General Sheridan designated for its immediate command; but on the 26th day of May, and before they reached their destination, General Kirby Smith surrendered his entire command to Major-General Canby. This surrender did not take place, however, until after the capture of the rebel President and Vice-President; and the bad faith was exhibited of first disbanding most of his army and permitting an indiscriminate plunder of public property.

Owing to the report that many of those lately in arms against the government had taken refuge upon the soil of Mexico, carrying with them arms rightfully belonging to the United States, which had been surrendered to us by agreement—among them some of the leaders who had surrendered in person—and the disturbed condition of affairs on the Rio Grande, the orders for troops to proceed to Texas were not changed.

There have been severe combats, raids, expeditions, and movements to defeat the designs and purposes of the enemy, most of them reflecting great credit on our arms, and which contributed greatly to our final triumph, that I have not mentioned. Many of these will be found clearly set forth in the reports herewith submitted; some in the telegrams and brief dispatches announcing them, and others, I regret to say, have not as yet been officially reported.

For information touching our Indian difficulties, I would respectfully refer to the reports of the commanders of departments in which they have occurred.

It has been my fortune to see the armies of both the West and the East fight battles, and from what I have seen I know there is no difference in their fighting qualities. All that it was possible for men to do in battle they have done. The Western armies commenced their battles in the Mississippi Valley, and received the final surrender of the remnant of the principal army opposed to them in North Carolina. The armies of the East commenced their battles on the river from which the Army of the Potomac derived its name, and received the final surrender of their old antagonists at Appomattox Court House, Virginia. The splendid achievements of each have nationalized our victories, removed all sectional jealousies (of which we have unfortunately experienced too much), and the cause of crimination and recrimination that might have followed had either section failed in its duty. All have a proud record, and all sections can well congratulate themselves and each other for having done their full share in restoring the supremacy of law over every foot of territory belonging to the United States. Let them hope for perpetual peace and harmony with that enemy, whose manhood, however mistaken the cause, drew forth such herculean deeds of valor.

I have the honor to be,

Very respectfully, your obedient servant,

U. S. GRANT,

Lieutenant-General.

THE END

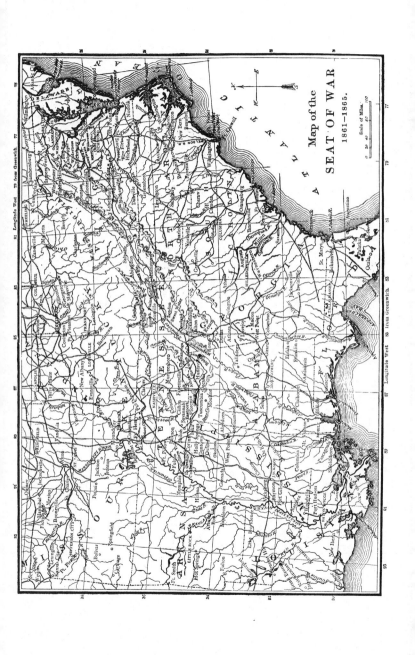

Map of the
SEAT OF WAR
1861—1865.

Scale of Miles.

Index

593; 601; 615; 616; 618; 620; 627; 673; 764.

Hamer, Thomas L., secures Grant's appointment to West Point, 28, 29; his ability, 71.

Hamilton, C. S., Major-General, 282; 284.

Hampton, Wade, General, 603; 604; 648; 681; 682; 687.

Hancock, W. S., General, 516; 523; 524; 527; at battle of Wilderness, 528, 529, 530, 531, 532; 539; 541; 542; at battle of Spottsylvania, 545, 546, 549; 552; 553; 554; 555; 556; 557; 558; 559; 560; 562; at battle of North Anna, 564, 565; 567; 571; 572; 575; 580; at battle of Cold Harbor, 583, 584; 592; 596; 599; 600; 602; 608; 611; 617; 619; 631; 770; his ability and courage, 771.

Hardee, Captain, 63; General, 169; 508; 648; 651; 679; 682.

Harney, General, 94.

Harris, Thomas, Colonel, 164; 165; General, 763.

Hartranft, General, 693.

Hartsuff, General, 704.

Haslett, Lieutenant, 40.

Hatch, Colonel, 326.

Hatch, General, 651.

Hawkins, Major, 237.

Hayes, R. B., General, his gallantry and efficiency, 630.

Hays, Alexander, General, at battle of Wilderness, his gallantry, 528.

Hazen, General, 417; captures Fort McAllister, 649.

Hebert, Colonel, 129.

Heckman, General, 626.

Herron, General, at siege of Vicksburg, 366, 367, 368.

Heth, General, at battle of Wilderness, 528; 706.

Hill, General, 524; at battle of Wilderness, 528, 529, 530; 540; 542; 551; 564; at battle of North Anna, 567.

Hillyer, Captain, 168; 204.

Hinks, General, 599.

Hoffman, Colonel, at capture of San Antonio, 98.

Hoke, General, 559; 567; 601; 664; 667.

Holly Springs, Miss., occupation of, 286; loss of, 289.

Holmes, Captain, 56; 129; General, 380.

Hood, General, supersedes Johnston, 504; 505; 508; his methods, 632; 633; 634; 636; 640; 641; 650; at battle of Franklin, 654, 655, 656; at battle of Nashville, 660, 661; 673; 674; 680; 682; 683.

Hooker, General, 414; 417; 418; 420; at battle of Wauhatchie, 420; 426; 427; 428; 429; 430; 435; 439; at battle of Lookout Mountain, 440; 441; at battle of Chattanooga, 444; 447; 448; 450; 451; 453; 505; 770; his character, 771.

Horses, Grant's experience with, 26–27; 38–39; 60–61; 390.

Hoskins, Lieutenant, at battle of Monterey, 76.

Hovey, General, 286; 323; 339; 340; 341; 342; at battle of Champion's Hill, 345, 346, 347.

Howard, B. B., 155.

Howard, O. O., General, 411; 414; 420; at battle of Wauhatchie, 427; 432; 434; 439; 447; 448; 637; 641.

Hudson, Captain, 674.

Humphreys, General, 555; 556; 631; at battle of White Oak Road, 693; 697; 698; 702; 704; 705; 706; 708; 714; 715; 723; 724; 770; 772.

Hunt, Henry J., General, 516.

Hunter, General, 197; 214; 304; 558; 568; 585; 590; 591; 592; 595; 603; 604; 605; 615; 616; 617.

Hunter, R. M. T., 685.

Hurlbut, General, 223; at battle of Shiloh, 227, 235, 244, 258; at battle of Corinth, 279, 280; 294; 329; 339; 359; 366; 391; 463.

INDIANS, their treatment by Hudson's Bay Company, their

SELECTED LETTERS
1839 – 1865

Contents

To R. McKinstry Griffith

Military Academy
West Point N.Y.
Sept. 22d 1839

Dear Coz.

I was just thinking that you would be right glad to hear from one of your relations who is so far away as I am so, I have put asaid my Algebra and French and am going to tell you a long story about this prettiest of places West Point. So far as it regards natural attractions it is decidedly the most beautiful place that I have ever seen; here are hills and dales, rocks and river; all pleasant to look upon. From the window near I can see the Hudson; that far famed, that beautiful river with its bosom studded with hundreds of snow sails. Again if I look another way I can see Fort Putnam frowning far above; a stern monument of a sterner age which seems placed there on purpose to tell us of the glorious deeds of our fathers and to bid us remember *their* sufferings—to follow their examples. In short this is the best of all places—the *place* of all *places* for an institution like this. I have not told you *half* its attractions. here is the house Washington used to live in—there Kosisuseko used to walk and think of *his* country and of *ours*. Over the river we are shown the duelling house of Arnold, that *base* and *heartless* traiter *to* his country and his God. I do love the *place*. it seems as though I could live here ferever if my friends would only come too. You might search the wide world over and then not find a better. Now all this sounds nice, very nice, "what a happy fellow you are" you will say, but I am not one to show fals colers the brightest side of the picture. So I will tell you about a few of the *drawbacks*. First, I slept for two months upon one single pair of blankets, now this sounds romantic and you may think it very easy. but I tell you what coz, it is *tremendeus hard*. suppose you try it by way of experiment for a night or two. I am pretty shure that you would be perfectly satisfied that is no easy matter. but glad am I these things are over. we are now in our quarters. I have a spleanded bed and get along very well. Our pay is nomonally about twenty eight dollars a month. but we never see one cent of it. if we want any thing from a shoestring to a coat we must go to the commandant of the post and get an order fer it or we cannot have it. We have tremendous long and hard lessons to get in both French and Algebra. I study hard and hope to get along so as to pass the examination in January. this examination is a hard one they say, but I am not frightened *yet*. If I am successful here you will not see me fer two long years. it seems a long while to me. but time passes off very fast. it seems but a few days since I came here. it is because every hour has it duty which must be performed. On the whole I like the place very much. so much that I would not go away on any account. The fact is if a man graduates here he safe fer life. let him go where he will. There is much to dislike but more to like. I mean to study hard and stay if it be possible. if I cannot—very well—the world is wide. I have now been here about four months and have not seen a single familier face or *spoken* to a single lady. I wish some of the pretty girles of Bethel were here just so I might look at them. but fudge! confound the girles. I have seen great men plenty of them. let us see. Gen Scott. M. Van Buren. Sec. of War and Navy. Washington Irving and lots of other big bugs. If I were to come home now with my uniform on. they way you would laugh at my appearance would be curious. My pants sit as tight to my skin as the bark to a tree and if I do not walk *military*. that is if I bend over quickly or run. they are very apt to crack with a report as loud as a pistol. my coat must always be buttoned up tight to the chin. it is made of sheeps grey cloth all covered with big round buttens. it makes me look very singulir. If you were to see me at a distance. the first question you would ask would be. "is that a Fish or an animal"? You must give my very best love and respects to all my friends particulaly you brothers. Uncle Ross & Sam'l Simpson. You must also write me a long. long letter in reply to this and till me about evry thing and every body including yourself. If you happen to see my folks just till them that I am happy, *alive* and *kicking*.

> I am truly your cousin
> and obedand servant
> U. H. GRANT

McKinstrey Griffith

N.B. In coming on I stopped five days in Philidelpha with my friends they are all well. Tell Grandmother Simpson that they always have expected to see here before. but have almost given up the idea now. they hope to hear from her often. U. H. GRANT

My very best respects to Grandmother Simpson. I think often her, I put this on the margen so that you may remember it better. I want you to show this letter and all others that I may write to you, to her

I am going to write to some of my friends in Philadelphia soon when they answer I shall write you again to tell you about them &c. &c. remember and write me very soon fer I want to here much

I came near forgetting to tell you about our demerit or "black marks" They give a man one of these "black marks" for almost nothing and if he gets 200 a year they dismiss him. To show how easy one can get these a man by the name of *Grant* of this state got *eight* of these "marks" fer not going to Church today. he was also put under arrest so he cannot leave his room perhaps fer a month, all this fer not going to Church. We are not only obliged to go to church but must *march* there by companys. This is not exactly republican. It is an Episcopal Church

Contrary to the prediction of you and rest of my Bethel friends I have not yet been the least *homesick* no! I would not go home on any account whatever. When I come home in two years (if I live) they way I shall astonish you *natives* will be *curious*. I hope you wont take me for a Babboon

To Julia Dent

Camp Salubrity
Near Nachitoches Louisiana
June 4th 1844

My Dear Julia

I have at length arrived here with the most pleasing recollections of the short leave of absence which prevented my accompanying my Regiment; and as well, with the consequences of the leave. I arrived here on Monday the 3d Ins; I believe just the day that I told you I thought I should arrive. My journey to N. Orleans was a pleasant one, on a pleasant boat, with pleasant passengers and officers, but was marked with no incident worth relating, except that as we approached the South the Musquetoes become troublesome, and by the time I left N. Orleans my hands and face bore the strongest testamony of their numbers and magnitude.—I spent something over a day in N. Orleans, and its being a tolerably large place, and my Bump of Acquisitiveness prompting me on to see as much of the place as possible, the result was that I went over the town just fast enough to see nothing as I went, stoped long enough at a time to find out nothing atall and at the end found found myself perfectly tired out. But I saw enough to convince me that a very pleasant season might be passed there; and if I *cant* get back to *Jeff. Bks* again will make no objections to the contemplated change which sends me there. But I am not disposed to give up a known good for an untried one, and as I *know* the climate &c. (&c. meaning much more than what precedes it) about St. Louis suits me well, I will by no means fail to take up with any offer which will take me back.—My journey up the Red River was not so pleasant as the other. The boat was quite small and considerably crouded with passengers, and they not of the most pleasant sort; a number of them being what are usually called *Black Legs* or Gamblers; and some of them with very cut throat appearances. There was some of them that I should very much dislike to meet unarmed, and in a retired place, their knowing I had a hundred dollars about me. Likely I judge harshly. The monotony of the Journey though was somewhat broken by the great difference in the appearance of the Red River country and anything else I had ever seen. The first hundred miles looks like a little deep and winding canal finding its way through a forest so thickly set, and of such heavy foliage that the eye cannot penetrate. The country is low and flat and overflown to the first limbs of the trees. Aligators and other revolting looking things occupy the swamps in thousands; and no doubt the very few people who live there shake with the ague all Summer. As far up the river as where we are the land is high and healthy, but too poor to bear any thing but one vast pine forest. Since Mr. Hazlitt wrote to you our Encampment has been moved to a much more pleasant and higher situation. We are on the top of a high ridge, with about the best spring of water in Louisiana runing near. There is nothing but pine woods surrounding us and they infested to an inormaus degree with Ticks, Red bugs, and a little creeping thing looking like a Lizard, that I dont know the name of. This last vermin is singularly partial to society, and become so very intimate and sociable on a short acquaintance as to visit our tents, crawl into our beds &c. &c. Tis said they are very innocent but I dont like the looks of them.—Nearly the first person I met here was Hazlitt, or Sly Bob, with one of those Stage driver's round top wool hats and a round jacket, trying to take the heat as comfortably as possible. He drew me into his tent; which by the way is a little linen affair just like your Fishing tent, with the ground covered with Pine leaves for a floore. It took me one day to answer his questions, and you may rest assured that a number of them were about Ellen and yourself together with the rest of the family. When you write to him tell him how Clarra is comeing on.—Since I first set down to write we have had a hard shower and I can tell you my tent is a poor protection. The rain run through in streams. But I will have a shed built in a few days then I will do better. You have been to Camp Meeting, and know just how the people cook, and sleep, and live there? Our life here is just about the same. Hazlitt probably told you all about how we live here. While I think of it he sends his love to you and Ellen and the rest of the family, and to Wrenshall Dent's family. Mine must go to the same.—

I was detained a day longer in St. Louis than I expected and to make time pleasantly pass away I called on Joe Shurlds and had a long talk of three or four hours, about—about!—let me see: What was the subject? I believe it was the usual topic. Nothing in particular, but matters generally. She pretends to have made a great discovery. Can you concieve what it was?

Julia! I cannot express the regrets that I feel at having to leave Jeff. Bks. at the time that I did. I was just learning how to enjoy the place and the *Society*, at least a part of it. Blank

———— ———— ———— ———— ———— ———— ————

———— ———— ———— ———— ———— ———— ————

———— ———— ———— ———— ———— ———— ———— Read these blank lines just as I intend them and they will express more than words.—You must not forget to write soon and what to seal with. Until I hear from you I shall be,—I dont know what I was going to say—but I recon it was your most humble [. . . . .] and Obt. Friend.

ULYSSES S GRANT

Miss Julia Dent
Gravois Mo.

P.S. Did you get the Magazines I sent you, one from Memphis the other from N. Orleans?   usg

To Mrs. George B. Bailey

Camp Salubrity
Near Nachitoches Louisiana
June 6th 1844

Mrs. Bailey

My journey fortunately is at an end, and agreeably to your request, and my own pleasure, I hasten to notify you of my safe arrival here   It always affords me pleasure to write to old acquaintances, and much more to hear from them, so I would be pleased if the correspondence would not stop here. As long as my letters are answered, if agreeable to you I will continue to write.—

My trip to this place "forty days journey in the wilderness" was marked with no incident, Save one, worth relating and that one is *laughable curious, important, surprising* &c. &c. but I cant tell it now. It is for the present a secret, but I will tell it to you some time. You must not guess what it is for you will go wrong. On my route I called arroune by the way of St Louis and Jefferson Barrack where I spent four or five days very pleasantly among my newly made acquaintances   From St Louis to N Orleans I had a very pleasant trip on a large and splendid boat, with pleasant passengers and not much crouded. As we approached the South the sun become sensibly warmer, and the Musquetoes desidedly more numerous   By the time we got to N Orleans my hands and face bore the strongest evidence of the number and size of this insect in a Southern climate   I was but one day in Orleans which was spent in runing over the city just fast enough to tire myself out and get but little good of my visit   But from what I saw I think it would be a pleasant place to live, and it is now contemplated that my Regiment will go in that neighborhood in case Texas should not be anexed to the U States, but in case of the anexation we will probably have to go much farther West than we are now. Probably to the Rio Colorado. From N. Orleans to Nachitoches I had the bad fortune to travel on a small boat considerably crouded, through a hot country, with gambling going on day and night. Some of the passengers had very cut throat appearances. From Nachitoches I had to walk (or pay an extravigant price for a conveyance) three miles through the hotest sun I think I ever felt   I found my Regiment Camping out in small linen tents on the top of a high Sandy ridge and in the midst of a pine forest   The great elevation of our situation and the fact that one of the best springs of water in the state puts out here are the only recommendations the place has. We are about three miles from any place, there is no conveyance to take us from on place to another and evry thing is so high that we cant afford to keep a horse or other conveyance of our own. I could walk myself but for the intensity of the heat. As for lodgings I have a small tent that the rain runs through as it would through a seive. For a bedstead I have four short pine sticks set upright and plank runing from the two at one end to the other. For chairs I use my trunk and bed, and as to a floor we have no such a luxury yet. Our meals are cooked in the woods by servants that know no more about culinary matters than I do myself. But with all these disadvantages my appetite is becoming extravigant. I would like to have our old West Point board again that you may have heard so much about. As for the troublesome insects of creation they abound here. The swamps are full of Aligators, and the wood full of Red bugs and ticks; insects the you are not trouble with in Ohio, but are the plague of this country. They crawl entirely unde the skin when they git on a person and it is impossible to keep them off.—So much for Camp Salubrity.—I should be happy to get an answer to this as early as possible; and if nothing more, a Post Script from the Young ladies. Ladies are always so much better at giving the news than others, and then there is nothing doing or said about Georgetown that I would not like to hear. They could tell me of all the weddings &c. &c. that are talked of. Give my love to evry body in Georgetown.

Lt. U S Grant
4th Infantry

To Mrs. G. B. Bailey
Georgetown Ohio

P. S. I give my title in signing this not because I wish people to know what it is, but because I want to get an answer to this and put it there that a letter may be directed so as to get to me

To Julia Dent

Camp Salubrity La.
Near Nachitoches
July 28th 1844

My Dear Julia.

Mr. Higgins has just arrived from Jefferson Barracks and brings word that he saw you well on the 4th Inst. He delivered your message and says that he promised to bring some letters from you but supposes that you expected him out at your house to recieve them. You can hardly immagine how acceptable your message was but when I found that I might have expected a letter from you by his calling for it, I took the Blues (You told me that you had experienced the same complaint) so badly that I could resort to no other means of expelling the dire feeling than by writing to My *Dear Julia.* It has been but few days since I wrote to you but I must write again. Be as punctual in writing to me Julia and then I will be compensated in a slight degree,—nothing could fully

compensate—for your absence.—In my mind I am constantly turning over plans to get back to Missouri, and until
today there has been strong grounds for hoping that the
whole of the 4th Regiment would be ordered back there; but
that hope is blasted now. Orders have arrive from Washington
City that no troops on the frontier will be removed. Fred's
Regiment as well as mine will have to remain. Mexico has
appropriated four millions of dollars for the purpose of raising an Army of thirty thousand men for the re-conquering of
Texas, and we are to remain here to preserve neutrality between the United States and the belligerent parties. Who
knows but Fred. and me may have something to do yet?
though it may be something short of the conquest of Mexico,
or the overpowering of some other big country. Would you
not be glad to hear of something of the kind after the difficulty was all over and we were safely out? I think there is no
danger however, from any present causes, of anything of the
kind taking place. Fred. and me are doomed to stay safe and
quietly in the woods for some time yet. I may be able to get
to the same post with Fred. by transfering with Lt. Elting   I
have written to Towson on the subject. If I should get there
Fred. and me will be great friends as we always have been,
and no doubt will spend many pleasant hours together talking
over the pleasant times both of us have spent on the Gravois.
No doubt your brother will have many pleasant things to relate of the place, and to me they will be doubly interesting
because Julia Dent is there. Many a pleasant hour have I spent
at Camp Salubrity thinking over my last visit to Mo. and its
results. Never before was I satisfied that my love for you was
returned, but you then assured me that it was. Does Mrs.
Dent know of the engagement between us? I believe from
Freds letter that he half suspects it, though he mentions nothing of the kind. I would be perfectly willing that he should be
acquainted with the fact though of course, would not tell him
myself.—Mr. Higgins gives us an account of the Barbecue on
the Gravois the 4th of July. No doubt Miss Fanny Morrison
was in all her glory with her returned intended! Does Fanny
call out to see you often? What does she say about me? What
is the reason I cant be there myself to hear? evry body els is
going. Col. Garland, Captain Morris & Capt. Barber are just

starting, and in a few days Capt. Morrison will be off.—Julia write to me soon and give a long account of how you pass your time. No doubt it is much more pleasantly spent than mine in the hot pine woods of Louisiana. Hazlitt and me visit each other, at our linen Mansions about three times per day, and our calls are so unfashionable that the three calls lasts from morning until bed time. The subjects of our conversations are usually Missouri   Turn over and commence reading the cross lines on the first page.

To Miss Julia Dent.   Yours most Constantly U S GRANT and the people of Missouri—Miss J. & E Dent in particular and our future prospects and plans. We have big plans laid for visiting Mixico and Texas this winter and Missouri too soon. Sometimes we get to talking about your house I almost immagine myself there. While speaking of Mr. Hazlitt let me tell you that he has just left my tent and the last words he said was for me to be sure and give you and Ellen, and the rest of the family his very best love. He says that he expects a partnership letter from you two.—I wish Julia that you and Ellen could be here for one hour to see our mode of living. When any body calls to see me we have very cozily to take our seats side by side on the bed for I have no chair. If I could only be in your parlor an hour per day what a recreation it would be. Since I arrived here it has been so very hot that I but seldom go out of Camp. Once I was over at Fort Jesup and saw Mr. Jarvis. Tell Ellen that he fell a good deal more than half in love with her. He seemed very anxious to know what word she had sent him by me. Has Miss Fanny ever tried to convince you *since*, that she is in possession of all my secrets and knows just who I love best? Dont you think it strange that a young lady will talk so. I am affraid that you will find difficulty in reading the crossed lines. I will therefore conclude on the page left for directing the letter. u.s.g.

Julia I would not presume so much as to send this letter without having recieved an answer to either of my others if Mr. Higgins had not mentioned that you told him you had rec'd letters from Mr Hazlitt and me, which led me to suppose that Mr. & Mrs. Dent knew of your recieving them and made no objection. I have too an opportunity of sending it to Jeff. Bks. to be mailed.—Be sure and answer it and all my others soon—and I am sorry Julia that I wrote the letter sent in one of Mrs. Porters. Burn it up wont you? I would feel much freer if the consent desired in that letter was obtained, but as it is not, I will have to wait until I get back there to get it; unless you can satisfy me that there is no parental objection.—What is the reason that John Dent has not written to me? He must have been much engaged electioneering this Summer! Give my love to Ellen and the rest of the family. Again, be sure and write soon and relieve from suspense your most *Devoted* and *Constant l*——

U S G

P. S. I have carefully preserved the lock of hair you gave me. Recollect when you write to seal with the ring I used to wear: I am anxious to see an impression of it once more.

u s g

To Julia Dent

Camp Necessity La.
Grand Ecore & Texas Road
Aug. 31st 1844

My Dear Julia

Your two letters of July and August have just been recieved and read you can scarsely immagine with how much pleasure. I have waited so long for an answer to my three letters (I have written you three times Julia one of them you probably had not time to get when you wrote yours) that I began to dispare of ever recieving a line from you; but it come at last and how agreeable the surprise! Take example in punctuality by me Julia, I have rec'd your letters only to day and now I am answering them. But I can forgive you since the tone of your last letter, the one in pencil, is so conclusive of constancy. I am sorry to hear that Mrs. Dent thinks there is nothing serious in our engagement with me nothing is more serious or half as pleasant to think of—Since the arrival of your letters I have read them over and over again and will continue to do so until another comes. I have not been into Camp Salubrity

yet to deliver to Mr. Hazlitt verbally the messages you sent
him, but I wrote him a note this morning containing them.
Mr. Hazlitt has been quite unwell for a few days past—You
probably have heard from Mr Porters letters that for the last
three weeks my company have been road making—The day
we came out it rained very hard all day—the men had heavy
Knap sacks to carry through the mud and rain for a distance
of about five miles and no shelter to go under at the end of
their journey—My fare was just the same only I had nothing
but myself to carry—The first night we had to lay our wet
beds on the still damper ground and make out the best we
could—Musketoes and Wood ticks by the hundreds pestered
us—On the whole I spent a few miserable nights and not
much better days at the begining of my first experience at
campaigning, but now I find it much better—We will probably be through and return to Camp Salubrity in ten days
more—I have just rec'd a letter from Fred, he is about my
most punctual correspondent, he speaks of Louise Stribling. I
think she certainly is not married nor wont be unless she gets
Fred—Fred is very well but hartily tired of Fort Towson—
He proposes that him and me should each get a leave of absence next Spring and go to Missouri I would accept his
proposal but I intend going sooner—I shall try very hard to
go in the Fall—The happiness of seeing you again can hardly
be realized, and then like you I have so much that I would
like to say and dont want to write.—Julia do tell me the secrets that Georgia M disclosed to you—I think I can guess
them from what follows in your letter—Georgia M is a very
nice modest and inexperienced girl and can very easily be
made to believe anything her oldest sister tells her—I know
very well that Fanny has told her that I was in love with her
and she foundes her reasons for thinking so upon what took
place at you house—You remember the occurrence of the apple seeds? Fany has tried to find out from Mr. Hazlitt which I
loved best Georgia or Julia—Mr. Hazlitt would not tell her
which he thought because to please her he would have to tell
what he believed to be a story, and to have said you (as he
believed though of course he new nothing about certain) he
thought would give an unnecessary offense. Hazlitt told me
of the conversation he had and it displeased me so much with

Miss F. that I said things of her which I would not commit to paper—Believe me my dear Julia what ever Miss Georgia may have told you she no doubt believed herself, but in believing she has allowed herself to be the dupe of one older than she is, but whose experience *in love affairs*, ought to be worth a great deel more than it is.—Tell me what she said in your next letter—Dont let Mrs. Dent see this part of my letter for of all things I dont like to have to speak ill of a third person, and if I do have to speak so I would like as few as possible to know it.—I am very far from having forgotten our promise to think of each other at sun seting—At that time I am most always on parade and no doubt I sometimes appear very absent minded—You say you were at a loss to ascribe a meaning to the blank lines in my first letter! Nothing is easyer, they were only intended to express an attachment which words would fail to express Julia do not keep anything a secret from me with persons standing in the relation that we do to each other there should be no backwardness about making any request—You commenced to make a request of me and checked yourself—Do not be affraid that any thing you may request will not be granted, and just think too the good you might do by giving good advice—No one is so capable of giving good advice as a lady, for they always practice just what they would preach—No doubt you have laid down to Fred. just the course he ought to take, and if he follows the advice he must do well—How fortunate he must feel himself to have a sister to correspond with I know I should have been proud to have had such a one to write to me all the years of my absence. My oldest sister is old enough to write now and I intend to direct all my home letters to her—She loves you and Ellen already without ever having seen you just from what she has heard me say—You say Julia that you often dream of me! do tell me some of your good ones; dont tell me any more of the bad ones; but it is an old saying that dreams go by contraries so I shall hope you will never find me in the condition you drempt I was in—And to think too that while I am writing this the ring I used to wear is on your hand—Parting with that ring Julia was the strongest evidence I could have given you (that is—in the way of a present) of the depth and sincerity of my love for you—Write to me

soon, much than the last time and if Mrs. Porter is not there,
or not writing at the time take a little ride and put your letter
in the Post Office—On the road think of some of the conversations we used to have when we rode out together

> Most Truly and Devotedly Your Lover
> ULYSSES

To Julia

P S I think in the course of a few days Julia I will write to
Col. Dent to obtain his consent to our correspondence; I will
ask nothing more at present but when I get back to St. Louis
I will lay the whole subject before him Julia do not let any
disclosed secrets such as Miss Georgia told you, make you
doubt for a moment the sincerity depth & constancy of my
feeling, for you and you alone out of the whole acquaintance.
Find some name beginning with "S" for me Julia You know I
have an 'S in my name and dont know what it stand for.

> U.S.G.

P.P.S. Tell Ellen that I have not been into Camp yet to see
the playthings she sent Mr. Hazlitt but I will go tomorrow
morning if I have to walk. I think there is no danger of us
quarreling since we have agreed so long together; but if we
do get into a scrape I will let her know it. Remember me to
Miss Ellen, Mrs. Porter Mrs. Mary Dent and your Fathers
family all.

> USG

To Julia Dent

> Camp Salubrity
> Near Nachitoches La.
> January 12th 1845

My Dear Julia
   It has now been nearly two months since I heard from you
and about four since I wrote the letter to your parents to
which I hoped so speedy an answer. Of course I cannot argue
any thing very strong in favor of my request being granted

from their not answering it, but at the same time they do not
say that I shall not write to you, at least as a friend, and ther-
fore I write you this Julia, and direct it to Sappington P. O.
expecting your Pa & Ma to know that you get it. The fact is I
thought I must hear from you again—The more than ordinary attachment that I formed for *yourself* and family during
my stay at Jeff. Bks. cannot be changed to forgetfulness by a
few months absence. But why should I use to you here the
language of flattery Julia, when we have spoken so much more
plainly of our feeling for each other? Indeed I have not
changed since and shall hope that you have not, nor will not,
at least untill I have seen all of you once more. I intend to
apply for a leave in the spring again and will go to St. Louis.
For three months now I have been the only officer with my
company and of course cannot leave even for one week. Julia
can we hope that you pa will be induced to change his opinion of an army life? I think he is mistaken about the army life
being such an unpleasant one. It is true the movements of the
troops from Jeff. Bks. so suddenly and to so outlandish a
place would rather create that opinion, but then such a thing
hardly occurs once a lifetime.

   Mr. Hazlitt returned about one month ago looking as lazy
and healthy as ever. I was away from camp when he returned
and did not get home until about midnight. I woke him up
and him and me had a long talk from that until morning. He
told me all about what a pleasant visit he had at Jeff. Bks. or
rather on the Gravois. Was he plagued much about Miss Clara
while there? You dont know how much I wished to be along
with him! He regrets very much that he didnot return by St
Louis.—I must tell you something about Mr. Hazlitt since he
returned. He has got him a little pony about the size of the
one I had at Jeff. Bks. it is a little "Jim a long Josy" of a thing
and if you were to see it you would think it was going to
drawl out "*y-e-s im* hisn" just as you know Mr. Hazlitt does
himself; he rode his pony to a Ball four or five mile from
camp a few days ago and as he was joging along the road,
neither pony nor man thinking of anything I suppose, the
little thing stumbled and away went Hazlitt over its head rolling in the dust and dirt. When he got up he found the pony
laying with its head in the other direction so it must have

turned a complete summer-set. I was not at the Ball myself,
and therefore didnot see Hazlitts exhibition and it was several
days before he told me of it. He could'nt keep it a secret. You
ought to be here a short time to see how we all live in our
winter houses. They are built by puting posts in the ground
as if for a fence and nailing up the outside with shingles. I
have plank for my house but there is but one or two other
officers that have. The chimneys are of mud and sticks and
generally are completed by puting a barrel or two on top to
make them high enough. Mr. Porter, Wallen, & Ridgley have
built themselves fine houses expecting their families here. Mr.
Porter went three or four weeks ago to visit his wife [. . . . .]
the mouth of Red river. If they were here they might live very
pleasantly for the weather is so warm that we need but little
or no fires. Mr. Hazlitt and me keep bachilors hall on a small
scale and get along very pleasantly. We have an old woman
about fifty years old to cook for us and a boy to take care of
our horses so that we live as well as though we were out of
the woods—Mr. Hazlitt wishes to be remembered to all of
you. He says that you must write to him right off.—I hear
from Fred. very often. He was well the last time he wrote.
Julia you must answer this quick wont you? I know you can.
Give my love to all the family

Fare well

ULYSSES

To Julia Dent

Camp Salubrity
Near Nachitoches La.
Tuesday, May 6th 1845

My Dear Julia

I have just arrived at Camp Salubrity after a tolerably pleasant trip of only one week from St. Louis, with one days detention at the mouth of Red River. I am here just in time; one
day later I would have probably an excuse to write. Whilst at
the mouth of Red river I met with Lt. Baker who is strait from
Fort Towson. He left there only about one week ago. Fred. is

very well, and would have been in Missouri with me but his commanding officer refused him a leave. It was right mean in him was'nt it?—Evry thing at Camp Salubrity Looks as usual only much greener from the contrast between the advancement of the season here and in the North. Though we are so far South and vegetation so far advanced a fire this evening is very comfortable. The officers are all collected in little parties discussing affairs of the nation. Annexation of Texas, war with Mexico, occupation of Orregon and difficulties with England are the general topics. Some of them expect and seem to contemplate with a great deal of pleasure some difficulty where they may be able to gain laurels and *advance a little in rank*. Any moove would be pleasant to me since I am so near promotion that a change of post would not affect me long. I have advanced three in rank very lately, leaving only five between me and promotion.—Mr. Hazlitt has gone to Fort Jesup and wont be back for a week; he left this morning before I got here.—It seems very strange for me to be siting here at Camp Salubrity writing to you when only a little more than one short week ago I was spending my time so pleasantly on the Gravois.—Mrs. Porter started a few days ago for Washita and of course took little Dave. along so that I could not give him the kiss you sent him. Mr. Porter was very particular in his enquiries about all of you, and if he knew that I was writing would send his love. When I got to Nachitoches I found Mr. Higgins and Beaman there just ready to start on a leave of absence. I am sorry that Miss Fanny dont know that he is on the way. I wanted him to tell me if he intended to bring her to Salubrity with him but he would not say yes nor no. Tell me what the probabilities are.—Have you heard yet from Col. Dent? I supose Brand must have written you a very amusing account of his adventuries in the East.—I supose Capt. Cotton has taken Lizzy to Green Bay before this. Does John pretend to be as much as ever in love?—The first thing I did after geting here was to get my letters from the Post Office. I found one from Miss J. B. D. that afforded me a great deel of pleasure, and one from home that had come by the way of St. Louis.—Is Miss Jemima Sappington married yet?—Tell John not to take it so hard as he appeared inclined to when he first heard of it. —I wrote to Fred. on my way down the Mississippi and told him of the pleasant visit I had, and how disappointed you all were that he was not along. I shall always look back to my short visit to Mo. as the most pleasant part of my life. In fact it seems more like a pleasant dream than reality. I can scarsely convince myself of the fact that I was there so short a time ago. My mind must be on this subject something like what Hercules Hardy's was whilst he was a prisoner among the Piannakataws in Guiana. I send you the story that you may read it. — Remember me very kindly to Mrs. Dent and Ellen and Emmy and your brothers and to your Aunt Fielding and your Cousins. Dont neglect to write as soon as you get this.

I am most devotedly your
ULYSSES S. GRANT

Julia

P. S. I promised to write to Lewis Dent as soon as I got here but I am so busily engaged building myself a new house that I will not have much time for a while. Mrs. Wallen is here safe and looks very delicate. — I am going to follow your advice Julia and have me a good and comfortable house.

U.

The letter you wrote me before I went to Mo. was very different from what I expected to find it. It was not near so cold and formal as you led me to believe. I should not have written this last Post script should I?

u

To Julia Dent

N. Orleans Barracks La.
July 6th 1845

My Dear Julia

I recieved your letter a day or two before leaving Camp Salubrity but after we knew that we were to go. You dont know how glad I was to get it at that time. A weeks longer delay in writing to me and I probably would not have heard from you for months, for there is no telling where we are going or how

letters will have to be directed so as to reach us. Our orders
are for the Western borders of Texas but how far up the Rio
Grand is hard to tell. My prediction that I would recieve but
few letters more at Camp Salubrity has proven very true. I
hope you have sent me a letter by Mr. Higgins. How unfor-
tune Miss Fanny has been. The Brevets that are going to
Texas are probably better off than those of higher rank. I am
perfectly rejoiced at the idea of going there myself for the
reason that in the course of five or six months I expect to be
promoted and there are seven chances out of eight that I will
not be promoted in the 4th so that at the end of that time I
shall hope to be back to the U. States, unless of course there
should be active service there to detain me and to take many
others there.—I was very much in hopes Julia that I would
recieve a letter from your pa before leaving Camp Salubrity
giving his full consent to our engagement. Now—that I am
going so far away and dont know how long it may be before I
can hear from you I shall be in a greatdeal of suspense on the
subject. Soldiering is a very pleasant occupation generally and
is so even on this occation except so far as it may be an obsti-
cle in the way of our gaining the unconditional consent of
your parents to what *we*, or at least I, believe is for our happiness.—Mrs. Wallen will soon go to Jefferson Barracks to
remain until her husband has quarters comfortably arranged
for her where the troops may be posted. She will be writing
to Mr. Wallen, wont you ask her how she directs her letters
and write to me? If you knew how happy I am to get a letter
from you you would write often. Mrs. Wallen asked me if I
would not have a letter for her to carry when she went to St.
Louis and I told her that I would so if you will call on her
when she arrives which will probably be about the 1st of
August you may find another letter from me.—From what I
have seen N. Orleans Barracks is the most pleasant place I
have ever been stationed at. It is about four miles below the
city, but it is so thickly settled all the way along that we appear to be in town from the start. The place is much more
handsomely fixed than Jeff. Bks.—In a few days the 3d Infantry will join us here, and not long after two companies are
expected from Fort Scott. I dont know what the probabilities
are for Fred. going to Texas, I know he is anxious to go and I

should be happy to meet him there.— You ask if Fred. has done any thing out of the way that his commanding officer would not give him a leave! Certainly he has not; the comd.g off. probably thinks that he has not been long enough in service to have a leave, or els there is too many officers absent already, or something of the kind. There are but few Commanding officers as indulgent about giving young officers leaves of absence as the one I am serving under. (Col. Vose). I recieved a letter from Fred. but a few weeks ago and he said nothing to me about being ordered farther into the wilderness. probably some of the Indians in those parts have been pestering the frontier setlers. Dont be frightened about his geting home again and I shall hope too to be with him. Next time I ask for a leave of absence it will be for six months, *to take a trip North*.

Give my love to all your family, and your Aunt Fieldings also. Mr. Hazlitt wishes to be remembered. He says that he was not two months in answering your letter.

Write without failing and I will trust to providence for geting the letter. for ever yours most devotedly

U S GRANT

Julia

P. S. Remind your pa about writing to me and you plead for us wont you Julia? I will keep an account of all the Mexicans and Comanches that we take in battle and give you a full account. I have a black boy to take along as my servant that has been in Mexico. He speaks English Spanish and French I think he may be very useful where we are going. fare well my Dear Julia for a scout among the Mexicans

U

To Julia Dent

N. Orleans Barracks La.
July 11th 1845

My Dear Julia

I wrote you a letter a few days ago in which I promised to write again by Mrs. Wallen. It was my intention then to write

you a very long one but she starts much sooner than I expected so that I will only trouble you with a short note, and it
too will probably reach you before the letter sent by Mail.
There is now no doubt Julia but we will all be in Texas in a
very short time. The 3d Infantry have arrived on their way
and in a week or so we will all be afloat on the Gulf of Mexico. When I get so far away you will still think of and write to
me I know and for my part I will avail my self of evry opportunity to send you a letter. It cannot well be many months
that I will be detained in that country unless I be promoted to
one of the Regiments stationed there and the chances are
much against that. I have never mentioned any thing about
love in any of the letters I have ever written you Julia, and
indeed it is not necessary that I should, for you know as well
as I can tell you that you alone have a place in my *my*—What
an out I make at expressing any thing like love or sentiment:
You know what I mean at all events, and you know too how
acquerdly I made known to you for the first time my love. It
is a scene that I often think of, and with how much pleasure
did I hear that my offer was not entirely unacceptable? In
going away now I feel as if I had some one els than myself to
live and strive to do well for. You can have but little idea of
the influance you have over me Julia, even while so far away.
If I feel tempted to do any thing that I think is not right I am
shure to think, "Well now if Julia saw me would I do so" and
thus it is absent or present I am more or less governed by
what I think is your will.

   Julia you know I have never written anything like this befor
and wont you keep any one from seeing it. It may not be
exactly right to keep it from your parents, but then you will
get a letter from me by Mail about the same time which they
will probably see. Am I giving you bad advice? if you think so
act just as you think you ought.—Mrs. Wallen will give you
all the news afloat here. Dont forget to ask her how she intends to direct her letters to Mr. Wallen and send mine to the
same address, and now I must close with sending the most
devotional love of
                              U S G
To Julia

To Julia Dent

Corpus Christi Texas
Sept. 14th 1845

My Dear Julia

I have just recieved your letter of the 21st ultimo in which you reproach me so heavily for not writing to you oftener. You know my Dear Julia that I never let two days pass over after recieving a letter from you without answering it; But we are so far separated now that we should not be contented with writing a letter and waiting an answer before we write again. Hereafter I will write evry two or three weeks at farthest, and wont you do the same Julia? I recieved your letter before the last only about three weeks ago and answered it immediately. Your letters always afford me a greatdeal of happiness because they assure me again that you love me still; I never doubted your love Julia for one instant but it is so pleasant to hear it repeated, for my own part I would sacrifice evrything Earthly [. . .] to make my Dear Julia my own forever. All that I would ask would be that my Regiment should be at a healthy post and you be with me, then I would be content though I might be out of the world. There are two things that you are mistaken in Julia, you say you know that I am in an unhealthy climate and in hourly expectation of War: The climate is delightful and very healthy, as much so as any climate in the world and as for war we dont believe a word of it. We are so numerous here now that we are in no fear of an attack upon our present ground. There are some such heavy storms here on the coast the later part of Sept. and October however that we will probably be moved up the Nuices river to San Patricio, an old deserted town, that the Indians have compelled the inhabitants to leave.—Since the troops have been at Corpus Christi there has not been a single death from sickness, but there has been two or three terrible visitations of providence. There has been one man drownd in the breakers; a few weeks ago a storm passed over camp and a flash of lightning struck a tent occupied by two black boys killing one and stuning the other, and day before yesterday the most terrible accidents of all occured. For the last few weeks there has been an old worn out Steam Boat, chartered by

government, runing across the bay here, and day before yesterday there happened to be several officers and a number of
soldiers aboard crossing the bay; the boat had scarsely got out
of sight when the boilers bursted tearing the boat into atoms
and througing almost evry one aboard from twenty to fifty
yards from the wreck into the Briny Deep. Some were struck
with iron bars and splinters and killed immediately others
swam and got hold of pieces of the wreck and were saved.
Among the killed was Lt. Higgins and Lt. Berry both of the
4th Infantry. It will drive Fanny almost mad I fear. Capt.
Morrison takes Mr. Higgins' death very hard. When he was
killed he was standing talking with several officers; the others
were uninjured. The number killed and wounded I have not
heard accurately stated, but I believe there was 9 killed and
about 17 wounded one or two probably mortally.

Do you hear much about War with Mexico? From the accounts we get here one would supposed that you all thought
the Mexicans were devouring us. The vacancies that have
lately occured brings me about first for promotion and if by
chance I should go back to the States I may have the pleasure
of seeing my Dear Julia again before the end of the year; what
happiness it would be to see you again so soon! I feel as
though my good fortune would take me back. If I should be
promoted to a Regt. in Texas I will have to remain untill
na[. . . .] affairs look a little more settled and we become
permanent in this country, which is a delightful one so far as
climate and soil is concerned, but where no one lives scarsely
except the troops, and then I will go back and either remain
there, or—May I flatter myself that one who I love so much
would return with me to this country, when all the families
that are now absent join there husbands?—If so Julia you
know what I would say.

The mail is just going to close so I must stop writing. I intended to have written another sheet but I will have to put off
my long letter until next time. Give my very best love to all
your family and also Mrs. Fieldings. Dont neglect writing to
me very soon Julia for you dont know anxious I always am to
get a letter from my *Dear Dear* Julia and how disappointed I
always feel when I am a long time without one from her. I
very often look at the name in the ring I wear and think how

much I would like to see again the one who gave it to me. I must close, so good by my Dear Julia

U S GRANT

To Julia Dent

Corpus Christi Texas
My Dear Julia

In my last letter I promised to write to you evry two or three weeks and it is now about that time since I wrote and you see how punctual I am. I fear Julia that there was a long time between the receipt of my letters from N. Orleans and my first from Texas but you must reflect that I had writen you three without having recieved an answer and before writing again I wanted to hear from my *Dear Dear* Julia. I always do and always will answer your letters immediately and if you knew how delighted I always am to hear from yourself you would write often too.

The late casualty in the 4th Infantry promotes me so that I am now permanently at home in this Regiment. I should have prefered being promoted to a Regiment that is now in the States, because then I would get to see again, *soon*, one who is much dearer to me than my commission, and because too, there is hardly a probability of active service in this remote quarter of our country, and there is nothing els, excepting a fine climate and soil, to make one wish to stay here. —There is now over half of the Army of the U. States at Corpus Christi, and there must of course be a breaking up and scatterment of this large force as soon as it is found that their services will not be required in this part of the country. It is the general opinion that on account of the length of time the 4th has already been encamped, here and at Camp Salubrity, and the general unsettled position that it has been in since the begining of the Florida war, that we will be the first out of Texas. Once in quarters again no doubt we will remain for a good long time.

The most of the talk of war now comes from the papers of the old portion of the U. States. There are constantly bands of Mexican Smugglers coming to this place to trade, and they seem to feel themselvs as secure from harm here as though they were citizens of Texas, and we on the other hand, although we are occupying disputed Territory, even acknowedging our right to Texas, feel as secure from attack as you do off in Missouri. There was a time since we have been here when we were in about half expectation of a fight and with a fare prospect of being whipped too; that was when there was but few of us here and we learned that General Arista and other officers of rank were on the Rio Grande ready to march down upon us. We began to make preparations to make as stout a defence as possible. Evry working man was turned out and an intrenchment began and continued for about a week and then abandoned.

Now my Dear Julia that a prospect is ahead for some perminancy in my situation dont you think it time for us to begin to settle upon some plan for consumating what we believe is for our mutual happiness? After an engagement of sixteen or seventeen months ought we not to think of bringing that engagement to an end, in the way that all true and constant lovers should? I have always expressed myself willing you know my Dear Julia to resign my appointment in the army for the sake of overcomeing the objections of your parents, and I would still do so; at the same time I think they mistake an army life very much. No set of ladies that I ever saw are better contented or more unwilling to change their condition than those of the Army; and you Julia would be contented knowing how much and how dearly devoted I am to you—I cannot help writing thus affectionately since you told me that no one but yourself reads my letters.

Your Pa asks what I could do out of the Army? I can tell you: I have at this time the offer of a professorship of mathematics in a tolerably well endowed College in Hillsboro, Ohio, a large and flourishing town, where my salery would probably equal or exceed my present pay. The Principle of the Institution got my father to write to me on the subject; he says I can have until next spring to think of this matter. The last letter I wrote was to make all the enquiries I could about the situation and if the answer proves favorable I shall give this matter serious concideration.

I am now reading the Wandering Jew, the copy that belonged to Mr. Higgins and the very same numbers read by
yourself. How often I think of you whilst reading it. I think
well Julia has read the very same words that I am now reading
and not long before me. Yesterday in reading the 9th No I saw
a sentence marked around with a pencil and the word *good*
written after it. I thought it had been marked by you and before I knew it I had read it over three or four times. The sentence was a sentiment expressed by the Indian Prince Djalmo
on the subject of the marriage of two loving hearts, making a
compareison you may recollect. Was it you that marked the
place. I have written so long a letter that I must close. Remember me to evry body on the Gravois. Mr. Hazlitt also
wishes to be remembered.

Give my love to Ellen. How is Ellen's soft eyed lover comeing on that she wanted me to quiz somebody down here
about? She did not say so but I know she wanted some of her
friends here to hear of him just to see how jealous she could
make them.

Good bye my Dear Julia and dont forget to write soon.

Yours most affectionately
ULYSSES

Julia

October 1845

To Julia Dent

Corpus Christi Texas
Feb 5th 1846

My Dear Julia

Two or three Mails have arrived at Corpus Christi in the
last few days and by each I confidently expected a letter from
you, but each time I was disappointed. As a consolation then
I come to my tent and got out all the letters you have ever
written me—How many do you think they amounted to?
only 11 Julia, and it is now twenty months that we have been
engaged. I read all of them over but two and now write to
you again Julia in hopes that hereafter I will get a letter from

you evry two or three weeks. You dont know with what pleasure I read your letters or you would write much oftener.

At present the prospect of the 4th Infantry, or any other
Regiment, geting back to civilization is by no means flattering. Our march is still onwards to the West. Orders have been
recieved here for the removal of the troops to the Rio Grand
(to Francis Isabel) and before you get this no doubt we will
be on our way.—Continue to direct your letters as before,
the care of Col. Hunt N. Orleans and they will reach me. In
all probability this movement to the Rio Grande will hasten
the settlement of the boundary question, either by treaty or
the sword, and in eather case we may hope for early peace and
a more settled life in the army, and then may *we—you and
I Julia*—hope for as speedy a consent on the part of your
parents to our union? You say they certainly will not refuse it.
I shall continue to hope and believe that it will be as you say.

I wrote to you a short time ago that I thought our engagement should be carried into effect as early as possible. I still
think so and would be very happy to have you set the time at
no very distant day, with the condition if the troops are not
actively emploid. Of course Julia I never even dremed of such
a thing as asking you to come to a Camp or a temporary and
distant post with me. I would not wish to take you from a
home where you are surrounded by evry comfort and where
you are among friends that you know and love. That is not
what I proposed. If you should consent that I might "clasp
that little hand and call it mine" while the troops are still in
their present unsettled state I would either resign as my father
is anxious to have me do, or return by myself leaving my Dear
Julia at a comfortable home while I was fighting the battles of
our Country.—Has John made application for an appointment in one of the new Regiments that are to be raised   I
hope he has not let the oportunity slip. With Mr. Bentons
influance he could probably get a Captaincy.—I got a letter
from Fred. a few days ago. He is well and is now looking out
for promotion. He is anxious to get to the 4th Inf.y and says
that if he is not promoted to it he intends to make a transfer
to get to it if he can.—Dont neglect to write to me often
Julia. If you have but a little to write say that, it gives me so
much pleasure even to see your name in your own hand

writing. About the time you get this I will be on the march (on foot of course) between this and San Isabel or Francis Isabel. In the evenings just think that one who loves you above all on this Earth is then resting on the ground (thinking of Julia) after a hard days march.—Give my love to Ellen Emmy and the rest at White Haven.

Your most affectionately
U S GRANT

Julia

To Julia Dent

Corpus Christi Texas
Feb. 7th 1846

Dearest Julia

I have just been delighted by a long and interesting letter from my Dear Julia and although I wrote to you but two or three days ago I answer this with my usual punctuality. You say you write me letter for letter well I am satisfied that my love is returned and you know how anxious one is to hear often from the one they love and it may appear to me that you do not write as often as you really do. Your letter was one of the sweetest you have ever written me and your answer to the question I have so often asked was so much like yourself, it was just what I wanted to hear you say; boldness indeed: no my Dear Julia that is a charge that can never be laid to you.—There is a part of your letter that is entirely incomprehensible to me. I dont know whether you are jesting or if you are serious. *** I first loved Julia I have loved no one els.—The chance of any of the troops geting out of Texas this spring is worse than ever, before long we will be on our way farther West but no doubt it will be but a few months until the boundary question will be settled and then we may look for a general dispersion of troops and I for one at least will see Missouri again.—Does your pa ever speak of me or of our engagement? I am so glad to hear you·say that you think his consent will be given when asked for. I shall never let an oportuntiy to do so pass.—As to resigning it would not be right in the present state of affairs and I shall not think of it again for the present. — So John is again a Bachilor without a string to his bow. no doubt he will remain single all his life The extract from some newspaper you send me is a gross exageration of the morals and health of Corpus Christi. I do not believe that there is a more healthy spot in the world. So much exposure in the winter season is of course attended with a goodeal of sickness but not of a serious nature. The letter was written I believe by a soldier of the 3d Inf.y. As to the poisning and robberies I believe they are entirely false. There has been several soldiers murdered since we have been here, but two of the number were shot by soldiers and there is no knowing that the others were not. Soldiers are a class of people who will drink and gamble let them be where they may, and they can always find houses to visit for these purposes. Upon the whole Corpus Christi is just the same as any other plase would be where there were so many troops. I think the man who wrote the letter you have been reading deservs to be put in the Guard house and kept there until we leave the country. There he would not see so much to write about. — Do you get the paper I send you evry week? — I know Julia if you could see me now you would not know me, I have allowed my beard to grow two or three inches long. Ellen would not have to be told now that I am trying to raise whiskers. Give my love to all at White Haven.

> Your Devoted lover
> ULYSSES

Julia

To Julia Dent

Corpus Christi Texas
March 3d 1846

My Dear Julia

I have not recieved a letter from you since my last, but as I may not have an opportunity of writing to you again for several weeks I must avail my self of this chance of writing to my dear Julia. This morning before I got awake I dreamed that I

was some place away from Corpus Christi walking with you
leaning upon my arm, your hand was in mine and I felt very
happy. How disappointed when I awoke and found that it
was but a dream. However I shall continue to hope that it
will not be a great while befor such enjoyment will be real
and no dream. — The troops have not yet left this place but
the movement is to commence now in a few days. The 4th
Inf.y is the last to leave. We are to go into camp on this side
of the Rio Grande just opposite to Matamoras, a town of
considerable importance in Mexico, and as we are informed,
occupied by several thousand troops who it is believed by
many will make us fight for our ground before we will be
allowed to occupy it. But fight or no fight evry one rejoises at
the idea of leaving Corpus Christi. It is to be hoped that our
troops being so close on the borders of Mexico will bring
about a speedy settlement of the boundary question; at all
events it is some consolation to know that we have now got
as far as we can go in this direction by any order from Government and therefore the next move will be for the better.
We may be taken prisoners it is true and taken to the City of
Mexico and then when we will be able to get away is entirely
uncertain. From the accounts recieved here I think the
chances of a fight on our first arrival on the Rio Grand are
about equal to the chances for peace, and if we are attacked in
the present reduced state of the troops here the consequences
may be much against us. — Fred is now about 2d or 3d for
promotion and I have no doubt but this moove will make
him a 2d Lieut. — But I have said enough on this subject for
the present. A few weeks more and we will know exactly what
is to take place and then the first thing, I will write to one
who in all difficulties is not out of my mind. My Dear Julia as
long as I must be separated from your dear self evry moove
that takes place I hail with joy. I am always rejoised when an
order comes for any change of position hoping that soon a
change will take place that will bring the 4th Inf.y to a post
where there are comfortable quarters, and where my Dear
Julia will be willing to accompany me. In my previous letters I
have spoken a great deal of resigning but of course I could
not think of such a thing now just at a time when it is probable that the services of evry officer will be called into requi-

sition; but I do not think that I will stand another year of idleness in camp.—You must write to me often Julia and direct your letters as heretofore. I will write to you very often and look forward with a great deal of anxiety—to the time when I may see you again and claim a kiss for my long absence.—Do you wear the ring with the letters U. S. G. in it Julia. I often take yours off to look at the name engraved in it.—While writing this I am on guard of course for the last time at this place.—Give my love to all at White Haven.

Mr. Hazlitt is well and also Capt Morrison. Tell John not to let his chance of geting into one of the new Reg.t that will probably be raised, slip by unimproved.

Your Most Devoted
ULYSSES

Julia

To Julia Dent

Camp Near Matamoras
March 29th 1846

My Dear Julia

A long and laborious march, and one that was threatened with opposition from the enemy too, has just been completed, and the Army now in this country are laying in camp just opposite to the town of Matamoras. The city from this side of the river bears a very imposing appearance and no doubt contains from four to five thousand inhabitants. Apparently there are a large force of Mexican troops preparing to attack us. Last night during the night they threw up a small Breast work of Sand Bags and this morning they have a piece of Artillery mounted on it and directed toward our camp. Whether they really intend anything or not is doubtful. Already they have boasted and threatened so much and executed so little that it is generally believed that all they are doing is mere bombast and show, intended to intimidate our troops. When our troops arrived at the Little Colorado, (a river of about 100 yards in width and near five feet deep where we forded it) they were met by a Mexican force, which was represented by there commander to be large and ready for an attack. A parly took place between Gen. Taylor and their commanding officer, whose name I have forgotten, the result of which was, that if we attempted to cross they would fire upon us. The Mexican officer said that however much he might be prepossessed in our favor himself he would have to obey the orders of his own Government, which were peremptory and left him but one course, and that was to defend the Colorado against our passing, and he pledged his honor that the moment we put foot into the water to cross he would fire upon us and war would commence. Gen. Taylor replied that he was going over and that he would allow them fifteen minuets to withdraw their troop and if one of them should show his head after he had started over, that he would fire upon them; whereupon they left and were seen no more until we were safely landed on this side. I think after making such threats and speaking so positivly of what they would do and then let so fine an opportunity to execute what they had threatened pass unimproved, shows anything but a decided disposition to drive us from the soil. When the troops were in the water up to their necks a small force on shore might have given them a greatdeel of trouble.—During our whole march we have been favored with fine weather, and alltogether the march has been a pleasant one. There are about forty miles between the Nuices and the Colorado rivers that is one continuous sandy desert waste, almost without wood, or water with the exception of Salt Lakes. Passing this the troops of course suffered considerably.—Here the soil is rich and the country beautiful for cultivation. When peace is established the most pleasant Military posts in our country I believe will be on the Banks of the Rio Grande. No doubt you suppose the Rio Grande, from its name and appearance on the map to be a large and magnificent stream, but instead of that it is a small muddy stream of probably from 150 to 200 yards in width and navigable for only small sized steamers. I forgot to mention that we recieved before we arrived here, the proclamation of Col. Majia the Commander-in-Chief I believe, of the Mexican forces. It was a long wordy and threatning document. He said that the citizens of Mexico were ready to expose their bare breasts to the Rifles of the Hunters of the

Mississippi, that the Invaders of the North would have to reap their Laurels at the points of their sharpened swords; if we continued our march the deep waters of the Rio Grande would be our Sepulcher the people of our Government should be driven East of the Sabine and Texas re-conquered &c. &c. all of which is thought to mean but very little.

The most beliggerent move that has taken place yet occured yesterday. When we had arrived near this place a party of Mexican soldiers siezed upon two of our Dragoons and the horse of a Bugler boy who had been sent in advance to keep an eye in the direction of the enemy and to communicate if they saw any movement towards our column. The prisoners are now confined in the city. It is quite possible that Gen. Taylor will demand the prisoners and if they are not given up march over and take the city or attempt it.

I am still in hopes notwithstand all warlike appearances that in a few months all difficulties will be settled and I will be permitted to see again My Dear Dear Julia. The time will appear long to me until this event but hope that has so long borne me out, the hope that one day we will meet to part no more for so long a time, will sustain me again. Give my love to all at White Haven and be sure to write soon and often. I have not heard from Fred. very lately. Vacancies have occured here which make him I think 2d from promotion and another will probably take place soon in the case of an officer who is to be tried for being drunk on duty.—I will write again in a few days, but dont put of answering this until you get my next.

ULYSSES

Julia

To Julia Dent

Head Quarters Mexican Army
May 11th 1846

My Dear Julia

After two hard fought battles against a force far superior to our own in numbers, Gen. Taylor has got possesion of the

Enemy's camp and now I am writing on the head of one of the captured drums. I wrote to you from Point Isabel and told you of the march we had and of the suspected attack upon the little force left near Matamoras. About two days after I wrote we left Point Isabel with about 300 waggons loaded with Army supplies. For the first 18 miles our course was uninterupted but at the end of that distance we found the Mexican Army, under the command of General Arista drawn up in line of battle waiting our approach. Our waggons were immediately parked and Gen. Taylor marched us up towards them. When we got in range of their Artillery they let us have it right and left. They had I believe 12 pieces. Our guns were then rounded at them and so the battle commenced. Our Artillery amounted to 8 guns of six pound calibre and 2 Eighteen pounders. Evry moment we could see the charges from our pieces cut a way through their ranks making a perfect road, but they would close up the interval without showing signs of retreat. Their officers made an attempt to charge upon us but the havoc had been so great that their soldiers could not be made to advance. Some of the prisoners that we have taken say that their officers cut and slashed among them with their Sabres at a dreadful rate to make them advance but it was no use, they would not come. This firing commenced at ½ past 2 o'clock and was nearly constant from that until Sun down.

Although the balls were whizing thick and fast about me I did not feel a sensation of fear until nearly the close of the firing a ball struck close by me killing one man instantly, it nocked Capt. Page's under Jaw entirely off and broke in the roof of his mouth, and nocked Lt. Wallen and one Sergeant down besides, but they were not much hurt. Capt. Page is still alive. When it become to dark to see the enemy we encamped upon the field of battle and expected to conclude the fight the next morning. Morning come and we found that the enemy had retreated under cover of the night. So ended the battle of the 8th of May. The enemy numbered three to our one besides we had a large waggon train to guard. It was a terrible sight to go over the ground the next day and see the amont of life that had been destroyed. The ground was litterally strewed with the bodies of dead men and horses. The loss of the enemy is variously estimated from about 300 to 500. Our loss was comparitively small. But two officers were badly wounded, two or three slightly. About 12 or 15 of our men were killed and probably 50 wounded. When I can learn the exact amount of loss I will write and correct the statements I have made if they are not right. On the 9th of May about noon we left the field of battle and started on our way to Matamoras. When we advanced about six miles we found that the enemy had taken up a new position in the midst of a dense wood, and as we have since learned they had recieved a reinforcement equal to our whole numbers. Grape shot and musket balls were let fly from both sides making dreadful havoc. Our men continued to advance and did advance in spite of their shots, to the very mouths of the cannon and killed and took prisoner the Mexicans with them, and drove off with their own teams, taking cannon ammunition and all, to our side. In this way nine of their big guns were taken and their own ammunition turned against them. The Mexicans fought very hard for an hour and a half but see-ing their means of war fall from their hands in spite of all their efforts they finally commenced to retreat helter skelter. A great many retreated to the banks of the Rio Grande and without looking for means of crossing plunged into this water and no doubt many of them were dround. Among the prisoners we have taken there are 14 officers and I have no idea how many privates. I understand that General Lavega, who is a prisoner in our camp has said that he has fought against several different nations but ours are the first that he ever saw who would charge up to the very mouths of cannon.

In this last affray we had we had three officers killed and some 8 or ten wounded. how many of our men suffered has not yet been learned. The Mexicans were so certain of sucsess that when we took their camp we found thir dinners on the fire cooking. After the battle the woods was strued with the dead. Waggons have been engaged drawing the bodies to bury. How many waggon loads have already come in and how many are still left would be hard to guess. I saw 3 large waggon loads at one time myself. We captured, besides the prisoners, 9 cannon, with a small amount of ammunition for them, probably 1000 or 1500 stand of fire arms sabres swords &c. Two hundred and fifty thousand rounds of ammunition for them over four hundred mules and pack saddles or harness. Drums, musical instruments camp equipage &c, &c. innumerable. The victory for us has been a very great one. No doubt you will see accounts enough of it in the papers. There is no great sport in having bullets flying about one in evry direction but I find they have less horror when among them than when in anticipation. Now that the war has commenced with such vengence I am in hopes my Dear Julia that we will soon be able to end it. In the thickest of it I thought of Julia. How much I should love to see you now to tell you all that happened. Mr. Hazlitt come out alive and whole. When we have another engagement, if we do have another atall, I will write again; that is if I am not one of the victims. Give my love to all at White Haven and do write soon my Dear Julia. I think you will find that history will count the victory just achieved one of the greatest on record. But I do not want to say to much about it until I see the accounts given by others. Dont forget to write soon to your most Devoted

ULYSSES

P. S. I forgot to tell you that the Fortifications left in charge of Maj. Brown in command of the 7th Inf.y was attacked while we were at Point Isabel and for five days the Mexicans continued to throw in shells. There was but 2 killed, Maj. Brown & one soldier, and 2 wounded.

To John W. Lowe

Matamoras Mexico
June 26th 1846

Dear Lowe

I have just recieved your letter of the 6th of June,: the first I have had from you since my Reg.t took the field in anticipation of the Annexation of Texas. Since that time the 4th Infantry has experienced but little of that ease and luxury of which the Hon. Mr. Black speaks so much. Besides hard marching, a great part of the time we have not even been blessed with a good tent as a protection against wind and weather. At Corpus Christi our troops were much exposed last winter which the citizens say was the severest season they have had for many years. From Corpus Christi to this place (a distance of about 180 miles) they had to march through a low sandy desert covered with salt ponds and in one or two instances ponds of drinkable water were separated by a whole days March. The troops suffered much but stood it like men who were able to fight many such battles as those of the 8th & 9th of May, that is without a murmur. On our arrival at the Rio Grande we found Matamoras occupied by a force superior to ours (in numbers) who might have made our march very uncomfortable if they had have had the spirit and courage to attempt it. But they confined their hostilities (except their paper ones) to small detached parties and single individuals as in the cases you mention in your letter, until they had their force augmented to thrible or quadrouple ours and then they made the bold efforts of which the papers are so full. About the last of April we got word of the enemy crossing the river no doubt with the intention of cuting us off from our supplies at Point Isabel. On the 1st of April at 3 o'clock General Taylor started with about 2000 men to go after and escort the Waggon train from Point Isabel and with the determination to cut his way, no matter how superior their numbers. Our march on this occation was as severe as could be made. Until 3 o'clock at night we scarsely halted, then we laid down in the grass and took a little sleep and marched the ballance of the way the next morning. Our March was mostly through grass up to the waist with a wet and uneven bottom yet we made 30 miles in much less than a day. I consider my march on that occation equal to a walk of sixty miles in one day on good roads and unencumbered with troops. The next morning after our arrival at Point Isabel we heard the enemies Artillery playing upon the little Field work which we had left Garrisoned by the 7th Inf.y and two Companies of Artillery. This bombardment was kept up for seven days with a loss of but two killed and four or five wounded on our side. The loss of the enemy was much greater though not serious. On the

7th of May General Taylor started from P. I. with his little force encumbered with a train of about 250 waggons loaded with provisions and ammunition. Although we knew the enemy was between us and Matamoras and in large numbers too, yet I did not believe, I was not able to appreciate the possibility of an attack from them. We had heard so much bombast and so many threats from the Mexicans that I began to believe that they were good for paper wars alone, but they stood up to their work manfully. On the 8th when within about 14 miles of Matamoras we found the enemy drawn up in line of battle on the edge of the prairie next a piece of woods Called Palo Alto. (Which is the Spanish for Tall Trees.) Even then I did not believe they were going to give battle. Our troops were halted out of range of Artillery and the waggons parked and the men allowed to fill their canteens with water. All preparations being made we marched forward in line of battle until we recieved a few shots from the enemy and then we were halted and our Artillery commenced. The first shot was fired about 3 o'clock P. M. and was kept up pretty equally on both sides until sun down or after, we then encamped on our own ground and the enemy on theirs. We supposed that the loss of the enemy had not been much greater than our own and expected of course that the fight would be renewed in the morning. During that night I believe all slept as soundly on the ground at Palo Alto as if they had been in a palace. For my own part I dont think I even dreamed of battles. During the days fight I scarsely thought of the probability or possibility of being touched myself (although 9 lb. shots were whistling all round,) until near the close of the evening a shot struck the ranks a little ways in front of me and nocked one man's head off, nocked the under Jaw of Capt. Page entirely away, and brought several others to the ground. Although Capt. Page rec'd so terrible a wound he is recovering from it. The under jaw is gone to the wind pipe and the tongue hangs down upon the throat. He will never be able to speak or to eat. The next morning we found to our surprise that the last rear guard of the enemy was just leaving their ground, the main body having left during the night. From Palo Alto to Matamoras there is for a great part of the way a dense forest of under growth, here called chapparel. The

Mexicans after having marched a few miles through this were reinforced by a conciderable body of troops. They chose a place on the opposite side from us of a long but narrow pond (called Resaca de la Palma) which gave them greatly the advantage of position   Here they made a stand. The fight was a pel mel affair evry body for himself. The chapparel is so dense that you may be within five feet of a person and not know it. Our troops rushed forward with shouts of victory and would kill and drive away the Mexicans from evry piece of Artillery they could get their eyes upon. The Mexicans stood this hot work for over two hours but with a great loss. When they did retreat there was such a panic among them that they only thought of safty in flight. They made the best of their way for the river and where ever they [. . . . .] it they would rush in. Many of them no doubt were drowned. Our loss in the two days was 182 killed & wounded. What the loss of the enemy was cannot be certainly ascertained but I know that acres of ground was strewed with the bodies of the dead and wounded. I think it would not be an over estimate to say that their loss from killed wounded, take prisoners, and missing was over 2,000; and of the remainder nothing now scarsely remains. So precipitate was their flight when they found that we were going to cross the river and take the town, that sickness broke out among them and as we have understood, they have but little effective force left. News has been recieved that Parades is about taking the field with a very large force. Daily, volunteers are arriving to reinforce us and soon we will be able to meet them in what ever force they choose to come. What will be our course has not been announced in orders, but no doubt we will carry the war into the interior. Monteray, distant about 300 miles from here, will no doubt be the first place where difficulties with an enemy await us. You want to know what my feelings were on the field of battle! I do not know that I felt any peculiar sensation. War seems much less horrible to persons engaged in it than to those who read of the battles. I forgot to tell you in the proper place of the amount of property taken. We took on the 9th Eight pieces of Artillery with all their ammunition something like 2,000 stand of arms, muskets, pistols, swords sabres Lances & 500 mules with their packs, camp equipage & provisions and in fact about evry thing they had. When we got into the camp of the enemy evrything showed the great confidence they had of sucsess. They were actually cooking their meal during the fight, and as we have since learned, the women of Matamoras were making preparations for a great festival upon the return of their victorious Army.—The people of Mexico are a very different race of people from ours. The better class are very proud and tyrinize over the lower and much more numerous class as much as a hard master does over his negroes, and they submit to it quite as humbly. The great majority inhabitants are either pure or more than half blooded Indians, and show but little more signs of neatness or comfort in their miserable dwellings than the uncivilized Indian.—Matamoras contains probably about 7,000 inhabitants, a great majority of them of the lower order. It is not a place of as much business impor-tance as our little towns of 1,000. But no doubt I will have an opportunity of knowing more of Mexico and the Mexicans before I leave the country and I will take another occation of telling you more of them.

Dont you think Mr. Polk has done the Officers of the Army injustice by filling up the new Regt. of Riflemen from citi-zens? It is plain to be seen that we have but little to expect from him.—I have now written you a long letter; as soon as any thing more is done I will write again. If you have an opportunity I wish you would let them know at home that I am well. I dont think I have written in the last few weeks.—I should like very much to see you here in command of a vol-unteer company. I think you would not be affected by the climate. So far our troops have had their health remarkably well—

Remember me to your own and Judge Fishback's family. I suppose Tom has grown so much that he almost thinks of volunteering for the Mexican Wars himself.—I shall be pleased to hear from you as often as you will make it conve-nient to write and will answer all your letters—

　　　　　　　　　　Yours Truly
　　　　　　　　　　U S GRANT
　　　　　　　　　　4th Inf.y

J. W. Lowe Esq.
Batavia O——

To Julia Dent

Matamoras Mexico
July 25th 1846

My Dearest Julia

It must be about two weeks since I have written to you, and as I am determined that a longer time shall never pass with my Dearest hearing from me, whilst I am in an enemie's country, I write to you again, notwithstanding I have not heard from you for some time. Do not understand me though to cast any censure upon you, for you may have written me a dozen letters and me not recieved one of them yet, for I believe it is about two weeks since we have had a Mail, and there is no telling when we will have another. You must not neglect to write often Dearest so that whenever a mail does reach this far-out-of-the-way country I can hear from the one single person who of all others occupies my thoughts. This is my last letter from Matamoras Julia. Already the most of the troops have left for Camargo and a very few days more will see the remainder of us off. Whether we will have much more fighting is a matter of much speculation. At present we are bound for Camargo and from thence to Monteray, where it is reported that there is several thousand Mexican troops engaged in throwing up Fortifications, and there is no doubt either but that Parades has left Mexico at the head of nine thousand more to reinforce them, but the latest news says that he has been obliged to return to the City of Mexico on account of some rupture there. But a few months more will determine what we have to do, and I will be careful to keep my Dear Julia advised of what the army in this quarter is about. Fred. has not arrived here yet but I am looking for him daily. His commission arrived some time ago, and also a letter from St. Louis for him. I have them both in my possession, and wrote to him to hasten on. His Reg.t. (the 5th Infantry) is already in Camargo. A few months more of fatigue and privation, I am much in hopes, will bring our difficulties to such a crisis that I will be able to see you again Julia, and then if my wishes prevailed, we would never part again as merely engaged, but as,—you know what I would say.—No doubt a hard march awaits us between Camargo and Monteray. The distance is over two hundred miles, and as I have understood, a great part of it without water. But a person cannot expect to make a Campaign without meeting with some privations.

Fred. and me will probably be near each other during the time and between us I am in hopes that I will hear from my Dear Julia evry week, but write oftener to me than to Fred.— Since we have been in Matamoras a great many murders have been committed, and what is strange there seemes to be but very week means made use of to prevent frequent repetitions. Some of the volunteers and about all the Texans seem to think it perfectly right to impose upon the people of a conquered City to any extent, and even to murder them where the act can be covered by the dark. And how much they seem to enjoy acts of violence too! I would not pretend to guess the number of murders that have been committed upon the persons of poor Mexicans and our soldiers, since we have been here, but the number would startle you.—Is Ellen married yet? I never hear you mention her name any more. John I suppose is on his way for the seat of war by this time. If we have to fight we may all meet next winter in the City of Mexico.

There is no telling whether it will be as prisoners of war or as a conquering force. From my experience I judge the latter much the most probable.—How pleasant it would be now for me to spend a day with you at White Haven. I envy you all very much, but still hope on that better times are coming. Remember me to all at White Haven and write very soon and very often to

ULYSSES

Julia

To Julia Dent

Camp Near Monteray Mex.
Oct. 3d 1846

My Dearest Julia

I wrote to you while we were still storming the city of Monteray and told you then that the town was not yet taken but that I thought the worst part was then over. I was right for the next day the Mexicans capitulated and we have been ever since the uninterupted holders of the beautiful city of Monteray. Monteray is a beautiful city enclosed on three sides by the mountains with a pass through them to the right and to the left. There are points around the city which command it and these the Mexicans fortified and armed. The city is built almost entirely of stone and with very thick walls. We found all their streets baricaded and the whole place well defended with artillery, and taking together the strength of the place and the means the Mexicans had of defending it it is almost incredible that the American army now are in possession here. But our victory was not gained without loss. 500, or near abouts, brave officers and men fell in the attack. Many of them were only wounded and will recover, but many is the leg or arm that will be buryed in this country while the owners will live to relate over and over again the scenes they witnessed during the siege of Monteray. I told you in my last letter the officers that you were acquainted with that suffered, but for fear the letter may not reach you I will inumerate them again. Capt. Morris of the 3d Inf.y Maj. Barbour Capt. Field Lt. Irwin Lt. Hazlitt Lt. Hoskins and Lt. Terrett & Dilworth since dead. Lt. Graham & Maj. Lier dangerously wounded. It is to be hoped that we are done fighting with Mexico for we have shown them now that we can whip them under evry disadvantage. I dont believe that we will ever advance beyond this place, for it is generally believed that Mexico has rec'd our Minister and a few months more will restore us to amity. I hope it may be so for fighting is no longer a pleasure. Fred. has not joined us yet and I think it a great pity too, for his Regiment was engaged at a point where they done the enemy as much harm probably as any other Reg.t but lost but very few men and no officer. Monteray is so full of Orange Lime and Pomgranite trees that the houses can scarsly be seen until you get into the town. If it was an American city I have no doubt it would be concidered the handsomest one in the Union. The climate is excellent and evry thing might be produced that any one could want *** I have written two pages and have not told you that I got a letter a few days ago from my Dear Dear Julia. It has been a long long time since I got one before but I do not say that you have not written often for I can very well conceive of letters loosing their way following us up. What made you ask me the question Dearest Julia "if I thought absence could conquer love"? You ought to be just as good a judge as me! I can only answer for myself alone, that Julia is as *dear* to me to-day as she was the day we visited St. Louis together, more than two years ago, when I first told her of my love. From that day to this I have loved you constantly and the same and with the hope too that long before this time I would have been able to call you *Wife*. Dearest Julia if you have been just as constant in your love it *shall not* [. . . .] long until I will be entitled to call you by the [. . . .] affectionate title. You have not told me for a long time Julia that you still loved me, but I never thought to doubt it. Write soon to me and continue to write often. Now that we are going to stay here some time I am in hopes that I will get a number of letters from you. I forgot to tell you that by the terms of the capitulation the Mexicans were to retire beyond Linariz within seven days and were not to fight again for eight weeks and we were not to advance for the same time. Fred. certainly will join soon and then I will make him write often. Give my love to all at White Haven

ULYSSES

Julia

P. S. I am going to write to you evry two weeks if I have an opportunity to write so you may know if you dont get letters that often that some of them are lost

U.

To Julia Dent

Castle of Perote Mexico
April 24th 1847

My Dear Julia

You see from the above that the great and long talked of Castle of Perote is at last in the hands of the Americans. On the 13th of this month the rear Division of Gen. Scott's army left Vera Cruz to drive Santa Anna and his army from the strong mountain passes which they had fortified, with the determination of driving back the Barbarians of the North, at all hazards. On the morning of the 17th our army met them at a pass called Cierra Gorda a mountain pass which to look at one would suppose impregnable. The road passes between mountains of rock the tops of which were all fortified and well armed with artillery. The road was Barricaded by a strong work with five pieces of artillery. Behind this was a peak of the mountains much higher than all the others and commanded them so that the Enemy calculated that even if the Americans should succeed in taking all the other hights, from this one they could fire upon us and be out of reach themselvs. But they were disappointed. Gen. Twiggs' Division worked its way around with a great deel of laibor and made the attack in the rear. With some loss on our side and great loss on the part of the Enemy this highest point was taken and soon the White flag of the enemy was seen to float. Of Generals and other officers and soldiers some Six thousand surrendered as prisoners of war   Their Artillery ammunition supplies and most of their small arms were captured. As soon as Santa Anna saw that the day was lost he made his escape with a portion of his army but he was pursued so closely that his carriage, a splendid affair, was taken and in it was his cork leg and some Thirty thousand dollars in gold. The pursuit was so close that the Mexicans could not establish themselvs in another strong pass which they had already fortified, and when they got to the strong Castle of Perote they passed on leaving it too with all of its artillery to fall into our hands. After so many victories on our part and so much defeat on the part of the Mexicans they certainly will agree to treat. For my part I do not believe there will be another fight unless we should pursue with a very small force.— From Vera Cruz to this place it is an almost constant rize Perote being about Eight thousand feet above the ocean. Around us are mountains covered with eternal snow and greatly the influance is felt too. Although we are in the Torrid zone it is never so warm as to be uncomfortable nor so cold as to make a fire necessary. From Vera Cruz to this place the road is one of the best and one that cost more

laibor probably than any other in the world. It was made a
great many years ago when Mexico was a province of Spain.
On the road there a great many specimens of beautiful table
land and a decided improvement in the appearance of the
people and the stile of building over any thing I had seen
before in Mexico. Jalapa is decidedly the most beautiful
place I ever saw in my life. From its low Latitude and great
elevation it is never hot nor never cold. The climate is said to
be the best in the world and from what I saw I would be
willing to make Jalapa my home for life with only one condition and that would be that I should be permitted to go and
bring my Dearest Julia.—The 5th Inf.y, Fred's Reg.t was
was not present at the fight of Cierra Gorda. A few days
before we left Vera Cruz the 5th Inf.y was ordered down
the coast to Alvarado to procure horses and mules for the
use of the army, and when we left they had not returned.
My Dearest Julia how very long it seems since we were
together and still our march is onward. In a few days no
doubt we will start for Puebla and then we will be within
from Eighty to a Hundred miles of the City of Mexico; there
the march must end. Three years now the 4th Inf.y has been
on the tented field and I think it is high time that I should
have a leave of absence. Just think Julia it is now three long
years that we have been engaged. Do you think I could endure another years separation loving you as I do now and
believing my love returned? At least commission and all will
go in less time or I will be permitted to see the one I have
loved so much for three long years. My Dearest dont you
think a soldiers life a hard one! But after a storm there must
be a calm. This war must end some time and the army scattered to occupy different places and I will be satisfied with
any place wher I can have you with me. Would you be willing
to go with me to some out-of-the-way post Dearest? But I
know you would for you have said so so often.—Your next
letter will probably reach me in Puebla the 3d city in size
in the Republic of Mexico. Write to me often Julia I always
get your letters. I will write again as soon as the army makes
another halt   Has your pa ever said anything more about
our engagement? You know in one of your sweet letters you
told me something he had said which argued that his consent

would be given. Remember me affectionately to you father and mother Miss Ellen & Emmy.

ULYSSES

Julia

P. S. Among the wounded on our side was Lt. Dana very dangerously. In the Rifle Reg.t one officer, Lt. Ewell, was killed Mr. Maury lost his hand Mason and Davis a leg each. A great many Volunteer officers were killed and wounded. I have not had a letter from you since the one I answered from Vera Cruz but there have been but few mails arrived since. I hope to get one soon.

U

To John W. Lowe

Tepey Ahualco Mexico
May 3d 1847

Dear Lowe

Just as the troops were leaving Vera Cruz I recieved a letter from my young friend Tom and yourself. Now that we will probably be stationary for four or five days I avail my self of the opportunity of answering. I see that you have written me several letters which you have not recieved answers to. I always make it a point to answer all your letters and am only sorry that I dont get more of them. You say you would like to hear more about the war. If you had seen as much of it as I have you would be tired of the subject. Of our success at Vera Cruz you have read evry thing. The strength of the town its Forts and Castle the papers are full and they do not exagerate. On the 13th of April the rear Division of Gen. Scotts army left Vera Cruze to ascend the mountains and drive Santa Anna from his strong position in one of the Passes. On the night of the 15th Gen. Worth arrived at Plana del Rio three miles from the Battle ground. Gen. Twiggs with his Division had been there several days prepairing for an attack. By the morning of the 17th the way was completed to go arround the Pass, Cierra Gordo, and make the attack in the rear as well as in front. The

difficulties to surmount made the undertaking almost equal to
Bonapartes Crossing the Alps. Cierra Gorda is a long narrow
Pass the mountains towring far above the road on either side.
Some five of the peaks were fortified and armed with Artillery
and Infantry. At the outlett of the Mountain Gorge a strong
Breast work was thrown up and 5 pieces placed into embrasure sweeping the road so that it would have been impossible
for any force in the world to have advanced. Immediately behind this is a peak of the Mountains several hundred feet
higher than any of the others and commanding them. It was
on this hight that Gen. Twiggs made his attack. As soon as
the Mexicans saw this hight taken they knew the day was up
with them. Santa Anna Vamoused with a small part of his
force leaving about 6000 to be taken prisoner with all their
arms supplies &c. Santa Anna's loss could not have been less
than 8000 killed, wounded taken prisoners and misen. The
pursuit was so close upon the retreating few that Santa Anna's
carriage and mules were taken and with them his wooden leg
and some 20 or 30 thousand dollars in money. Between the
thrashing the Mexicans have got at Buon Vista, Vera Cruz
and Cierra Gorde they are so completely broken up that if we
only had transportation we could go to the City of Mexico
and where ever els we liked without resistance. Garrisons
could be established in all the important towns and the Mexicans prevented from ever raising another army. Santa Anna is
said to be at Orazaba, at the foot of a mountain always covered with snow and of the same name. He has but a small
force. Orazaba looks from here as if you could almost throw a
stone to it, but it looked the same from Jalapa some fifty miles
back and was even visable from Vera Cruze. Since we left the
Sea Coast the improvement in the appearance of the people
and the stile of building has been very visable over any thing I
had seen in Mexico before. The road is one of the best in the
world. The scenery is beautiful and a great deal of magnificent
table land spreads out above you and below you. Jalapa is the
most beautiful place that I ever saw. It is about 4000 feet
above the sea and being in the Torrid zone, they have there
everlasting spring. Fruit and vegitables the year around. I saw
there a great many handsome ladies and more well dressed
men than I had ever seen before in the Republic. From Jalapa

we marched to Perote and walked quietly into the strong Castle that you no doubt have read about. It is a great work. One
Brigade, the one I belong to is now 20 miles in advance of
Perote. Soon no doubt we will advance upon Puebla. I am
Regtl Quarter Master appointed under the new law allowing
one to each Reg.t and giving extra allowances.—Remember
me to all your family and Judge Fishbacks. Tel Tom he must
write to me again

I will be much pleased to recieve all the letters you will write
to me and all that Tom will write too. I will write to Tom
from Puebla. I suppose we will be there in a few days. If you
see any of the Bethel people please remember me to them.
Tell them I am hartily tired of the wars. If you were to see me
now you would never recognize me in the world. I have a
beard more than four inches long and it is red.

                        Your Friend   U. S. GRANT
                        4th Inf.y

To Julia Dent

                                        City of Mexico
                                        September 1847

My Dearest Julia

   Because you have not heard from me for so long a time you
must not think that I have neglected to write or in the least
forgotten one who is so ever dear to me. For several months
no mail has gone to Vera Cruz except such as Editors of papers send by some Mexican they hire and these generally fall
into the hands of the enemy who infest the wole line from
here to the sea coast. Since my last letter to you four of the
hardest fougt battles that the world ever witnessed have taken
place, and the most astonishing victories have crowned the
American arms. But dearly have they paid for it! The loss of
officers and men killed and wounded is frightful. Among the
wounded you will find Fred's name but he is now walking
about and in the course of two weeks more will be entirely
well. I saw Fred. a moment after he received his wound but
escaped myself untouched. It is to be hoped that such fights it

will not be our misfortune to witness again during the war, and how can be? The whole Mexican army is destroyed or disbursed, they have lost nearly all their artillery and other munitions of war; we are occupying the rich and populace valley from which the great part of their revenues are collected and all their sea ports are cut off from them. Evry thing looks as if peace should be established soon; but perhaps my anxiety to get back to see again my Dearest Julia makes me argue thus. The idea of staying longer in this country is to me insupportable. Just think of the three long years that have passed since we met. My health has always been good, but exposure to weather and a Tropicle Sun had added ten years to my apparent age. At this rate I will soon be old.—Out of all the officers that left Jefferson Barracks with the 4th Infantry but three besides myself now remains with us, besides this four or five who joined since, are gone. Poor Sidney Smith was the last one killed. He was shot from one of the houses after we entered the city.

Mexico is one of the most beautiful cities in the world and being the capital no wonder that the Mexicans should have fought desperately to save it. But they deserve no credit. They fought us with evry advantage on their side. They doubled us in numbers, doubled us and more in artillery, they behind strong Breast-works had evry advantage and then they were fighting for their homes.*** It *** truly a great country. No country was ever so blessed by nature. There is no fruit nor no grain that cant be raised here nor no temperature that cant be found at any season. You have only to choose the degree of elevation to find perpetual snow or the hotest summer. But with all these advantages how anxious I am to get out of Mexico. You can redily solve the problem of my discontent Julia. If you were but here and me in the United States my anxiety would be just as great to come to Mexico as it now is to get out.

Oct. 25th   At last a mail is to leave here for the U States   I am glad at finally having an opportunity of leting you hear from me. A train is going to Vera Cruz and with it many of the wounded officers and men. Fred. is geting too well to be one of them. I am almost sorry that I was not one of the unfortunates so that now I could be going back. It is to be hoped that in future mails will be much more frequent though in fact it is generally believed that as soon as congress meets the whole army will be ordered from this valey of Mexico. There is no use of my teling you any more that I will take the first opportunity of geting back to Mo. for I have told you that so often, and yet no chance has occured. At present Gen. Scott will let no officer leave who is able for duty not even if he tenders his resignation. So you see it is not so easy to get out of the wars as it is to get into them. — Write to me often dearest Julia so if I cant have the pleasure of sending letters often to you let me at least enjoy the receipt of one from you by evry Mail coming this way. — No doubt before this the papers are teaming with accounts of the different battles and the courage and science shown by individuals. Even here one hears of individual exploits (which were never performed) sufficient to account for the taking of Mexico throwing out about four fifths of the army to do nothing. One bit of credit need not be given to accounts that are given except those taken from the reports of the different commanders.

Remember me my Dearest Julia to you father & mother and the rest of the family and pray that the time may not be far distant when we may take our walks again up and down the banks of the Gravois. Truly it will be a happy time for me when I see that stram again.

Farewell My Dearest Julia
U S Grant

To Julia Dent

Tacabaya Mexico
January 9th 1848

My Dear Julia

Since I wrote to you last one Brigade has moved to this place which is about four miles from the City of Mexico and from being so much higher than the City is much more healthy. One Brigade has gone to Toluca and it is rumored that before a great while we will move to some distant part, either Queretero, Zacetecus, San Louis Potosi or Guernivaca unless there is a strong probability of peace. It is now however strongly believed that peace will be established before many months. I hope it may be so for it is scarsely suportible for me to be separated from you so long my dearest Julia. A few weeks ago I went to the commanding officer of my Regiment and represented to him that when the 4th Inf.y left Jefferson Barracks, three years ago last May, I was engaged, and that I thought it high time that I should have a leave of absence to go back. He told me that he would approve it but I found that it would be impossible to get the Comd.g Gen. to give the leave so I never made the application. I have strong hopes though of going back in a few months. If peace is not made it is at all events about my turn to go on recruiting service. As to geting a sick leave that is out of the question for I am never sick a day. Mexico is a very pleasant place to live because it is never hot nor never cold, but I believe evry one is hartily tired of the war. There is no amusements except the Theatre and as the actors & actresses are Spanish but few of the officers can understand them. The better class of Mexicans dare not visit the Theatre or associate with the Americans lest they should be assassinated by their own people or banished by their Government as soon as we leave. A few weeks ago a Benefit was given to a favorite actress and the Govorner of Queretero hearing of it sent secret spies to take the names of such Mexicans as might be caught in indulging in amusements with the Americans for the purpose of banishing them as soon as the *Magnanimous Mexican Republic* should drive away the Barbarians of the North. I pity poor Mexico. With a soil and climate scarsely equaled in the world she has more poor and starving subjects who are willing and able to work than any country in the world. The rich keep down the poor with a hardness of heart that is incredible. Walk through the streets of Mexico for one day and you will see hundreds of begars, but you never see them ask alms of their own people, it is always of the Americans that they expect to recieve. I wish you could be here for one short day then I should be doubly gratified. Gratified at seeing you my dearest Julia, and gratified that you might see too the manners and customs of these people. You would see what you never dreamed of nor can you form a correct idea from reading.*** All gamble Priests & civilians, male & female and particularly so on Sundays.—But I will tell you all that I know about Mexico and the Mexicans when I see you which I do hope will not be a great while now. Fred. is in the same Brigade with me. I see him evry day. He like myself is in excellent health and has no prospect of geting out of the country on the plea of sickness.—I have one chance of geting out of Mexico soon besides going on recruiting service. Gen. Scott will grant leaves of absence to officers where there is over two to a Company. In my Reg.t there are three or four vacancies which will be filled soon [. . . .] h and will give an oportunity for one or two now here to go out. Give my love to all at White Haven and do not fail to write often dearest Julia. I write but seldom myself but it is because a mail but seldom goes from here to the sea coast. Coming this way it is different for the Volunteers are constantly arriving.

When you write next tell me if Mrs. Porter and Mrs. Higgins are married or likely to be.

Adieu My Dearest Julia
ULYSSES

To Julia Dent Grant

Detroit Michigan
April 27th 1849

My Dearest Julia

I recieved your Telagraphic dispach yesterday morning from which I see that you are on your way to St. Louis. I hope you may find all at home well, and get this soon after your arrival. This you know is my Birth day and I doubt if you will think of it once.—I have a room and am staying at present with Mr. Wallen. Wallen and family are as well as can be expected under present circumstances.

I have rented a neat little house in the same neighborhood with Wallen and Gore   In the lower part of the house there is a neat double parlour, a dining room, one small bedroom and kitchen. There is a nice upstares and a garden filled with the best kind of fruit. There is a long arbour grown over with vines that will bear fine grapes in abundance for us and to give away. There are currents and plum & peach trees and infact evrything that the place could want to make it comfortable.

I will have a soldier at work in the garden next week so that by the time you get here evrything will be in the nicest order. I find Detroit very dull as yet but I hope that it will appear better when I get better acquainted and you know dearest without *you* no place, or home, can be very pleasant to me. Now that we are fixed to go to hous keeping I will be after you sooner than we expected when you left. I think about the 1st of June you may look for me. Very likely Ellen will come along and spend the Summer with us. — I hope dearest that you had a very pleasant trip. I know that you have thought of me very often. *** I have dreamed of you several times since we parted.

I have nothing atal to do here. I have no company and consequently do not go on Guard or to Drills. Mr. Gore and myself are to commence fishing in a day or two and if sucsessful we will spend a great many pleasant hours in that way.

When I commence housekeeping I will probably get a soldier to cook for me, but in the mean time if any good girl offers I will engage her to come when you return.

Dearest I nothing more to write except to tell you how very very dear you are to me and how much I think of you. Give my love to all at home and write to me very soon and often. Yours devotedly

ULYS

P. S. I recieved two letters here for you which I opened and read; the one from Annie Walker I forwarded to you at Bethel. One from Elen I did not send inasmuch as you would be at home so soon. Give my love to Sallie & Annie.

U

To Julia Dent Grant

Detroit Michigan
Wednesday 28th May 1851

Dearest Julia

You will no doubt be astonished to learn that we have all been ordered away from Detroit. Maj. Gore goes with his company to Fort Gratioit. Col. Whistler is ordered to move his Head quarters to Fort Niagara; but as there are not sufficient quarters there he has represented the matter to Washington and no doubt our destination will be changed to Sacket's Harbor. Wont this be pleasant. I will write to you again before we leave here and tell you all about it. Dr. Tripler goes with us and Capt. McDowell goes to Jefferson Barracks. I will send your scarf by him.

Mrs. Gore is thoroughly disgusted at the idea of going to Gratiot. She seems really distressed at the idea of being separated from you. She starts to-day so as to be there before her troubles come on.

I think now I will send for you sooner than you expected to return when you left. When you come I will meet you at Detroit and we will spend a week here and at Fort Gratioit. If Ellen is not to be married this Fall get her to come with you and spend this Winter.

There is no possible news in Detroit. Evry thing is about as when you left. People all pretend to regret our depature very much and I presume some of them are sincere. For my part I am glad to go to Sackets Harbor. I anticipate pleasant housekeeping for the next year or two. I shall provide nothing in the way of furnature until you arrive except a carpet for one room.

I hope dearest Julia you have not been as unfortunate about geting letters this time as you was the last time you left me. I have had but one from you yet but I am expecting another now evry day.

You have none idea dearest how much I miss little Fred. I think I can see the little dog todeling along by himself and looking up and laughing as though it was something smart. Aint he walking? I know they will all dislike to see him leave Bethel.

Write to me very soon dearest and tell me all about what kind of a trip you had from Cincinnati, how you found all in St. Louis &c. &c.

Give my love to all of them and kiss them for me. Kiss Freddy and learn him to say papa before he comes back. Dont let him learn to say any bad words.—Mrs. Gore says Jim is learning to talk but I guess he talks about as he did when you left.

Good buy dearest Julia and dont forget to write very often. I will write punctually evry week as I promised.

ULYSSES

P. S. I am about selling my horse and if I do I will send you $50.00 by my next letter.

U

To Julia Dent Grant

Sacket's Harbor N. Y.
August 10th 1851

My Dearest Julia

My regular day for writing has come again but this time I have no letter of yours to answer. I am looking for a long letter now evry day. I am so sorry that you are not here now. Sacket's Harbor is one of the most pleasant places in the country to spend a summer. It is always cool and healthy. There are several pleasant families in garrison and the parade ground would be such a nice place for Fred. to run. I want to see the little dog very much. You will start now very soon will you not? Evry letter I get now I shall expect to hear that you are geting ready to start. I have not got a particle of news to write you only that I am well and want to see Fred. and you very much.

I have had some very nice furnature made in garrison and otherwise our quarters look very nice. All that we want now to go to housekeeping is the table furnature. That I will not buy until you come on lest I should not please you. The furnature made in garrison is nicer than I could buy in Watertown and more substantial. It consists of lounges, chairs and a center table.

I know dearest Julia you will dislike very much to leave home, and I know that they will miss you and Fred. very much; but you know that you must come after while and you might just as well leave soon as late. Write to Virginia and see if she will not come with you if you come that way. I have told you to ask Nelly two or three times but you never say anything about whether she can come or whether she is to be married this fall or anything about it. I suppose however from your always sending your letters by McKeever to the post office that she is to be married to him soon.—What news do the boys send from California? Are they doing as well as formerly? I suppose they say nothing more about comeing home now.

Col. Whistler confidantly expects to be ordered away from here in the spring. What leads him to think we will go I dont know. I hope his prediction may not prove true.

Tell Fred. to be a good boy and not annoy his grandpa & ma. Is he geting big enough to whip when he is a bad boy? I expect his aunt Ell. annoys him so as to make him act bad evry day. When he comes here I will get him his dog and little wagon so that he can ride about the garrison all day. You dont tell me, though I have asked so often, how many teeth he has.

I have not heard from home now for a long time, and to tell the truth I have not written since I was at Quebec.

I hope all are well at your house. Give my love to them all and write soon.

Dont forget to avail yourself of the first good opportunity to come on here.

Adieu dearest Julia. A thousand kisses to you and Fred.

ULYS.

To Julia Dent Grant

Steamer Ohio
July 15th 1852

My Dearest Julia;

What would I not give to know that you are well at this time? This is about the date when you expected to be sick and my being so far away I am afraid may affect you. I am very well, only sea-sick, and so are all the passengers, notwithstanding we are in latitude 10° North. We have been blessed

with remarkably fine weather from the begining; a very fortunate thing for a vessel coming to this latitude in July, with
1100 persons on board.

You see dearest Julia how bad it would have been had you
accompanied me to New York. The Regiment had but two
days notice before sailing and I had but a few hours. You
know I wrote to you Sunday afternoon from Philadelphia
when I knew nothing, nor suspected nothing, of the move.
The orders to sail were sent by Telegraph and obeyed before
there was time to correspond.

There is no insident of the voyage to relate that would interest you much, and then dearest I do not know how this
letter will find you. I hope for the best of course, but cannot
help fearing the worst. When I get on land and hear that you
are all over your troubles I will write you some long letters. I
cannot say when you may look for another letter from me.
This goes to New York by the vessel we come out upon. To-
morrow we commence crossing the Isthmus and I write you
this to-day because then I may not have an opportunity. I
write this on deck, standing up, because in the cabin it is so
insufferably hot that no one can stay there.

The vessel on the Pacific puts in at Acapulco, Mexico, and I
may find an opportunity of mailing a letter from there. If I do
you will hear from me again in about three weeks or less.

Before recieving this dearest I the little one will be born.
If it is a girl name it what you like, but if a boy name it after
me. I know you will do this Julia of your own choise but then
I want you to know it will please me too.

Dear little Fred. how is he now? I want to see him very
much. I imagine that he is begining to talk quite well. Is he
not? I know he is a great favorite with his Grandpa & ma and
his Aunts. Does he like them all? Kiss the little rascal for me.

My dearest Julia if I could only hear from you daily for the
next [. . .] days I would have nothing to regret in this move.
I expect by it to do something for myself.

The only ladies with us are Mrs. Gore, Mrs. Wallen, Mrs.
Slaughter, Mrs. Collins & Mrs. Underwood. They poor
things I fear will regret it before twenty four hours. It is now
in the midst of the rainy season and we have to cross the
mountains on mules, through passes which are too narrow

for two abreast, and the ascent and descent to precipitate for any other animal. Give my love to all at home dearest Julia. I hope you recieved the check for one hundred that I sent you. I have one hundred & fifty dollars in the hands of Col. Swords, Qr. Master in New York which I will direct him to send you.

Adieu Dearest, A thousand kisses for yourself, Fred. and our other little one. I will let no opportunity of mailing a letter pass unimproved. Write often dearest to your affectionate husband

ULYSS

To Julia Dent Grant

Steamer Golden Gate
Near Acapulco, Mexico, Aug. 9th 1852

My Dearest Julia;

I wish I could only know that you, and our dear little ones were as well as I am. Although we have had terrible sickness among the troops, and have lost one hundred persons, counting men, women & children, yet I have enjoyed good health. It has been the province of my place as Quarter Master to be exposed to the weather and climate on the Isthmus, while most of the others were quietly aboard ship, but to that very activity probably may be ascribed my good health. It no doubt will be a relief to you to know that we have been out from Panama over four days and no sickness has broken out aboard. All are healthy and evry minuet brings us towards a better climate.

Among the deaths was that of poor Maj. Gore. The Maj. was taken before daylight in the morning and in the afternoon was dead. Mrs. Gore took his death very hard and then to think too of the trip she had to undergo crossing the Isthmus again! My dearest you never could have crossed the Isthmus at this season, for the first time, let alone the second. The horrors of the road, in the rainy season, are beyond description.—Mrs. Gore will be at home, if she is so fortunate as to stand the trip, before you get this. I hope father and Gennie

will go and see her soon. Lieut. Macfeely, 2d Lt. of Maj.
Gore's Comp.y, accompanied Mrs. Gore and may go to our
house to see you. He promised me that he would. I gave him
an order on the Qr. Mr. in New York for $150 00 Mr. Hooker
owes me which he gets he will send you.

Mrs. Wallen and the other ladies along are tollerably well,
but a goodeal reduced. Mrs. Wallens weight when she got
across the Isthmus was 84 lbs. Her children, Harry Nanny &
Eddy look quite differently from what they did when they
left New York. But thank fortune we are fas approaching a
better climate. The Golden Gate takes us nearly 300 miles
per day.

We have seen from a Calafornia paper our destination. All
but one company goes to Oregon. Head Quarters (and of
course me with it) goes to Columbia Barracks, Fort Van Couver, Oregon. In consequence of one company of the Reg.t,
and all the sick being left at the Island Flamingo, near Panama, to follow on an other steamer, we will remain at Benecia
Cal. for probably a month. Benecia is within a days travels of
where John is and of course I shall see him.

You must not give yourself any uneasiness about me now
dearest for the time has passed for danger. I know you have
borrowed a goodeal of trouble and from the exagerated accounts which the papers will give you could not help it. From
Mrs. Gore however you can get the facts which are terrible
enough.

I have not given you any discription of any part of our
journey, and as I told you in all my letters dearest, I will not
until I hear of your being well. I will say however that there is
a great accountability some where for the loss which we have
sustained.—Out of the troops at Sackets Harbor some twelve
or fifteen are dead, none that you would recollect however
except O'Maley, and Sgt. Knox, the one you thought looked
so much like Maloney.

Elijah Camp is with us. He goes as sutler, probably with
Head Quarters.

Give my love to all at home dearest and kiss our dear little
ones for me. Fred, the little dog I know talks quite well by
this time. Is he not a great pet? You must not let them spoil
him dearest. A thousand kisses for yourself dear Julia. Dont

forget to write often and Direct, Hd Qrs. 4th Inf.y Columbia
Barracks Fort Van Couver, Oregon.

> Adieu dear wife,
> Your affectionate husband
> ULYS.

P. S. You may be anxious to hear from Maggy. She looks wors
than ever. She has been sea-sick ever since she started. She
regrets very much that she had not staid with you.

Mrs. Wallen was going to write to you from Panama but
Maj. Gore's taking sick prevented.

> Again adieu dear dear wife.
> U.

To Julia Dent Grant

> Benecia Calafornia
> August 20th 1852

My Dear Wife.

We have arrived, all safely, at this place where we will remain, probably, for some three weeks. When we leave here it
will be for Fort Van Couver as I have told you in all my
previous letters from Panama up to this place. — Benecia is a
nice healthy place where our troops will pick up what they
lost on the Isthmus in a very short time. I can assure you it
was no little that all lost in the way of flesh. Capt. McConnell
and myself when we got across were in prime order for riding
a race or doing anything where a light weight was required. I
have not been sick but the degree of prostration that I felt
could not be produced in any other latitude except that of the
tropics, and near the equator at that.

I should not write you now because there is no Mail going
for several days but I am going up to the Stanislands, to-
morrow, to see John and before I get back the Mail may leave,
and I can assure you dearest Julia that I shall never allow a
Mail to leave here without carrying a letter to you.

I am staying with Fred. Steel, a class-mate of mine, who
was at our wedding, and when I told him we had a little boy

named Fred. he was very much elated. McConnell, Russell
and Underwood all joined in telling what a nice boy Fred. is.
I really believe Fred. was much more of a favorite with the
officers than we thought.

I spent an hour or two with Mrs. Stevens in San Francisco,
and she would have come up with us only Stevens was sick.
They will be here in a day or two and make this their home.
Mrs. Stevens seemed very much disappointed at not seeing
you and Mrs. Gore. She sayd that she had heard you say so
much about Mrs. Gore that she felt almost like she was an old
acquaintance.

I have seen enough of Calafornia to know that it is a
different country from any thing that a person in the states
could imagine in their wildes dreams. There is no reason why
an active energetic person should not make a fortune evry
year. For my part I feel that I could quit the Army to-day
and in one year go home with enough to make us comfortable, on Gravois, all our life. Of course I do not contemplate doing any thing of the sort, because what I have is a
certainty, and what I might expect to do, might prove a
dream.

Jim. de Camp come aboard at San Francisco to see Mrs.
Wallen and he told her that John was making one hundred
dollars per day. This is Friday night and on Sunday night I
expect to be with John and then I will write to you, and make
him write also, and it is more than probable that you will get
the letters at the same time as you get this.

I wish dearest Julia that I could hear from you. — I cannot
hope to hear from, after your confinement, for at least a
month yet. It distresses me very much. If I could only know
that you and our little ones were well I would be perfectly
satisfied. Kiss them both for me dearest and dont let Fred.
forget his pa. No person can know the attachment that exists
between parent and child until they have been seperated for
some time. I am almost crazy sometimes to see Fred. I cannot
be seperated from him and his Ma for a long time.

Dearest I hope you have been well taken care of and contented at our house. I know they would do evrything to make
you comfortable. I have often feared that you would fret and
give yourself trouble because I was not there.

Give my love to all at home dear and kiss our little ones for their pa. Write me all about both of them.

Adieu dear dear Julia,

> Your affectionate husband
> ULYSS.

To Julia Dent Grant

Columbia Bks. Fort Vancouver O. T.
December 19th 1852

My Dear Wife;

The Mail Steamer very unexpectedly arrived this morning before I had half my correspondence completed. It brings no Mail however to this point but leaves it at Astoria to be brought up by the river steamer. As the Mail Steamer starts back before we will get the last Mail I cannot tell you whether I will recieve any letters or not; but I am very sure that there are letters for me.

I am, and have been, perfectly well in body since our arrival at Vancouver, but for the last few weeks I have suffered terribly from cramp in my feet and legs, and in one hand. You know I have always been subject to this affliction. I would recover from it entirely in a very short time if I could keep in the house and remain dry. My duties however have kept me out of doors a great deel, and as this is the rainy season I must necessarily suffer from wet and cold. I am now intending to spend one or two weeks indoors, on toast and tea, only going out once per day to see if the supply of wood is kept complete.

This is said by the old inhabitants of Origon to be a most terrible winter; the snow is now some ten inches in depth, and still snowing more, with a strong probability of much more falling. The Thermometer has been from Eigteen to twenty two degrees for several days. Ice has formed in the river to such an extent that it is extremly doubtful whether the Mail Steamer can get back here to take off the Mail by which I have been hoping to send this. You must know the Steamer comes here first, and then goes down the Columbia

about four miles, to the mouth of the Willamett river, and up
that some fifteen miles to Portland, the largest town in the
Territory, though an insignificant little place of but a few hundred inhabitants. I do not know enough of this country to
give you the account of it I would like to, having a desire to
say nothing that is calculated to mislead others in their opinions of it, but this I can say; so far as I have seen it it opens
the richest chances for poor persons who are willing, and
able, to work, either in cuting wood, saw logs, raising vegitables, poultry or stock of any kind, of any place I have ever
seen. Timber stands close to the banks of the river free for all.
Wood is worth five dollars per cord for steamers. The soil
produces almost double it does any place I have been before
with the finest market in the world for it after it is raised. For
instance beef gets fat without feeding and is worth at the
door from seventy to one hundred dollars per head, chickens
one dollar each, butter one dollar per pound, milk twenty five
cents per quart, wheat five dollars a bushel, oats two dollars,
onions four dollars, potatoes two dollars and evry thing in
the same proportion. You can see from this that mess bills
amount to something to speak of. I could not mess alone for
less than one hundred dollars per month, but by living as we
do, five or six together it does not cost probably much over
fifty. *** I have nearly filled this sheet dear Julia without saying one word about our dear little ones about whom I think
so much. If I could see Fred. and hear him talk, and see little
Ulys. I could then be contented for a month provided their
mother was with them. Learn them to be good boys and to
think of their Pa. If your brother does not come out there is
no telling when I am to see them and you. It cannot be a
great while however because I would prefer sacrifising my
commission and try something to continuing this seperation.
My hope is to get promotion and then orders to go to washington to settle my accounts. If you, Fred. and Ulys. were
only here I would not care to ever go back only to visit our
friends. Remember me most affectionately to all of them. Kiss
Fred. and Ulys. for their Pa and tell them to kiss their ma for
me. Maggy and Getz enquire a greatdeel after you and Fred.
They evidently think the world and all of him. I hope he is a
favorite with his grandpa and all his Uncles and Aunts. I have

no dought though the little rascal bothers them enough. When you write to me again dear Julia say a goodeal about Fred. and Ulys. You dont know what pleasure it gave me to read yours and Clara's account of them.

Has Jennie left yet? I suppose so however. How did they like her at your house? Adieu dear dear wife; think of me and dream of me often. I but seldom dream myself but I think of you none the less often.

> Your affectionate husband
> ULYS. to his dear wife Julia.

To Julia Dent Grant

Columbia Barracks O. T.
January 3d 1853

I wrote you a letter two weeks ago upon the arrival of the Mail Steamer at this place and told you that I had no doubt but that I would find letters. I was disappointed.

The weather has been very cold here and what is most unusual, the Colum river has been frozen over. Captain Ingalls and myself were the first to cross on it. It is now open however so you need not feel any alarm about my falling through. It either rains or snows here all the time at this place so I scarsely ever get a mile from home, and half the time do not go out of the house during the day. I am situated quite as comfortable as any body here, or in the Territory. The house I am living in is probably the best one in Oregon. Capt. Brent & Ingalls and their two clerks Mr. Bomford & myself live to gether and Maggy cooks for us and Getz assists about the house. Evry one says they are the best servants in the whole Territory. With Getz's pay, the sale of his rations, the wages we give and Maggy's washing, they get about 75 dollars per month. Living together as we do I suppose board, washing, and servant hire does not cost us over 61 dollars per month each, but alone it would require economy to get along inside of near twice that amount. For instance flour is 42 dollars per barrel and evry thing is proportionally dear. I expect to go to San Francisco in two or four weeks now, under orders to bring up public funds, and if I do I shall stay over one trip of the Steamer and go up and spend ten days with John and Wrenshall. You need not be atall surprised if my next letter should be from San Francisco.

I promised you to tell you all about Oregon, but I have seen so little of it that I know nothing that I have not told you. The country is very new but almost doubling its population yearly. The soil is generally very fertile but then there is but a very small proportion of it that can be cultivated.

My dearest I wish, if I am to be separated from you, and our little ones, that I could at least be where it did not take two months to get a letter. Just think, you write to me and tell me all Fred s pranks and how finely Ulys. is coming on all of which interests me exceedingly, but then I think what improvements must have taken place since the letter was written. I suppose that Ulys will be seting alone by the time you get this. Is Fred. very patronising towards him? I expect he wants to nurse him? The dear little dogs how much I wish I could see them. Is Fred. as fond of riding as he was in Bethel? How was Jennie pleased with her visit? and how were they all pleased with her? As a matter of course she had left before you will get this. Fred. and his bride no doubt have gone too. Does your Brother Lewis intend remaining in Missouri? or will he return to Calafornia? I have never recieved a line from your brother John since my arrival at Van-Couver although I wrote to him soon after we got here.

All the ladies here are quite well and the gentlemen also. Mrs. Wallen stays at home all the time and in fact she could not well do otherwise. She always enquires very particularly after you evry mail.

Give my love dearest Julia to your Pa & Ma and all the rest of the family. Tell Fred. to be a good boy and recollect his pa and mind evry thing his grand pa & ma tells him. Kiss him and Ulys for me and write a great deel about them. I will close here for the present hoping that before the Mail closes we will get the mail which has just come up and then I can let you know if I get anything.

Adieu dear wife
ULYS.

P. S. There is not a particle of hope of geting the Mail that come up in time to add anything to this   If the Mail should come in time to give me five minuets I will write you another letter if it is only to tell you whether or not I have heard from you. Do not fret dear Julia about me. I am perfectly well and have entirely recovered from those attacks of cramp which I had a few weeks since. They amounted to nothing except they were painful. Adieu again dear dear Julia.

Your affectionate husband
ULYS

To Julia Dent Grant

Columbia Barracks
Washington Territory
March 31st 1853

My Dearest Wife;

The Mail has just arrived bringing me a very short and very unsatisfactory letter. You speak of not joining me on this coast in a manner that would indicate that you have been reflecting upon a dream which you say you have had until you really imagine that it is true. Do not write so any more dearest. It is hard enough for us to be seperated so far without borrowing immaginary troubles. You know that it was entirely out of the question for you to have come with me at the time I had to come. I am doing all I can to put up a penny not only to enable you and our dear little boys to get here comfortably, but to enable you to be comfortable after you do get here.

You ask why I do not live with the bachilors? I do: that is there are two "messes" and I am in one. Capt.s Brent & Ingalls, Mr. Bomford, Brooke and Eastman are in the same mess that I am. If it is economy you think I should consult all I have to say is that my expenses are about twenty dollars per month less than if I was in the other. We all live and eat in the same house so that Maggy & Getz wash for us and wait upon us; and besides Maggy wastes nothing. The other "mess" is seperated from evry officer so that all expenses of servant hire &c. is surplus.

I am farming now in good earnest. All the ploughing and furrowing I do myself. There are two things that I have found out by working myself. One is that I can do as much, and do it better, than I can hire it done. The other is that by working myself those that are hired do a third more than if left alone.

I was surprised to find that I could run as strait a furrow now as I could fifteen years ago and work all day quite as well. I never worked before with so much pleasure either, because now I feel sure that evry day will bring a large reward.

I believe I told you that I have to do that detestable Quarter Master business this Summer? I dislike it very much. Mr. Camp become very much dissatisfied here and sold out. He was making money *** much faster than he will ever do again. Notwithstanding his bad luck having his store blown up he has cleared in the few months he has been here more than six thousand dollars, this without two thousand capital to start with.

Mrs. Wallen is quite well and so are all the officers. Capt. McConnell is here. Mr. Hunt is at Humbolt Bay, Russell at Fort Reading Calafornia. All were well when last heard from. Capt. Wallen met with a serious accident a few days since. He was riding in a wagon and the horse commenced kicking so to save himself he jumped out and fell throughing his right rist entirely out of joint. He will probably be lame in it all Summer.

You can tell your brother that we have had the news all the time that long beards were allowed, at least, on this coast. I have not shaved since I left Calafornia consequently my beard is several inches long. Why did you not tell me more about our dear little boys? I would like to hear some of Fred's sayings. I wish I could have him and his brother here. What does Fred. call Ulys.? What does the S stand for in Ulys.'s name? in mine you know it does not stand for anything! Give my love to all at your house. When you write again dearest write in better spirits.

Does Fred. and his Aunt Ellen get on harmoniously together? I expect she teases him. Cant you have your Dagueriotype taken with Fred. & Ulys. along? if you can send it by

Adam's and Co's Express, to Portland, O. T. I presume you have recieved your watch ere this? I have no opportunity of buying any pretty presents here to send you.

Adieu dear dear wife. I shall hope to get a long sweet letter from you next Mail. Kiss our little boys for their pa. A thousand kisses for yourself dear wife.

Your affectionate husband.
ULYS.

To Julia Dent Grant

Columbia Bks. W. T.
July 13th 1853

My Dearest Julia;

It is about 12 o'clock at night, but as the Mail is to leave here early in the morning I must write to-night.—I got your long sweet letter giving an account of our dear little boys at the pic nic where Fred. started behind his Grand ma, but wanted her to ride behinde him before he got through. You know before he could talk he would always persist in having his hands in front of mine when driving. The loose end of the lines never satisfied him.

My dear Julia if you could see the letters they write from my home about our dear little boys it would make you as proud as it does me. I am sure there never was one of my own brothers or sisters who have been more thought of than Fred. & Ulys. In the long letter I got from father he speaks of him as something more than boys of his age. You understand though that I can make allowances for his prejudices either in favor or against; where prejudices are strong predilections are generally right, so I must conclude that Fred. & Ulys. are more than I ever dreamed they were. I dreamed of you last night but not of either of our dear little boys. I mearly saw you for a minuet without having an opportunity of speaking to you and you were gone.

My dear julia I have spoken of speculations so much that the subject is becoming painful, but yet I know you feel interested in what I am doing.—In a former letter I told you, for the first time, of the *downs* of all I had done. (Before I had never met with a *down*.) Since that I have made several hundreds in speculations of various sorts. In groceries which I do not sell, and which are not retailed. I have now a large quantity of pork on hand which is worth to-day ten dollars pr. barrel more than I gave for it at the very place where it was bought. All this will help to buy dresses for Fred. & Ulys. but what interests me most is to know how it is to let their pa see them wear them, and their ma put them on to advantage.

I wrote you that Scott was appointed Inspector General and that it would take me to Fort Reading. — It turns out that he has not been appointed so I must await my place either for Alden's resignation, or for Col. Buchanan's promotion. The first would take me to Fort Jones, of which I have spoken, in former letters: the latter to a detestible place where the mails reach occationally. I should however have command of of the post, with double rations and two companies. Wallen is going to San Francisco before you recieve this letter with the intention of seting up a Dairy, Pigery, and market Garden, if practicable,. He will go on leave for a few months and then, if sucsessfull, strike out for himself.

You ask how many children Laura has? Before this you know. She has but two; Harry who is a healthy & smart boy, and Nancy who has always, until lately, been heathy.

My dear Julia I have said nothing about the pink leaves upon each of which you say you presed a sweet kiss. I cannot, in this, return the favor on flowers but you may rest assured that I will imprint them when we first meet upon your lips and those of our dear babes.

How can your pa & ma think that they are going to keep Fred. & Ulys always with them? I am growing impatient to see them myself. — Tell Fred. to say *Ugly Aunt Ell* I wont let you learn me anything. *** so Fred. might say the same to his Uncle. If you cant go your self send him to his other Grandpa's for tuition for a few months. — Indeed dear Julia you must either go with the children or make a very good excuse. Thy want to see you so much. If you have not got means enough I have still some in N. Y. I shall never draw it so long as I remain in this country except in your favor. I hope you got the hundred which I sent you, and also the begining of what Calender was to send you! Give my love to all at your house. I got the pink leaves that you kissed. A thousand kisses for our little boys and yourself.

Adieu dear julia. the Steamer is in sight that is to take this.

Your affectionate husband
ULYS.

To Osborn Cross

R. Q. Mrs. Office
Columbia Bks. W. T.
July 25th 1853

Maj;

The constant, and unremiting, calls upon the time, both of myself and clerk, consequent upon the fiting out of the expiditions connected with the Northern Pacific R. R. survey, in addition to the current duties of the office, have prevented the making out, and forwarding, of the annual report called for, by you, at an earlier date; and obliges me to enter far less than I should have done into detail had I not feared that the delay of another mail would be too late to serve your purposes.

As I have only been on duty at this Post, as Post Qr. Mr., since the first of May last (my previous duties here, in the Q. M. D, being merely nominal having neither funds nor stores in my charge) my Report can only embrace the operations of the Department here for the last two months of the past fical year.

I enclose a plan of the post marked "A" and a statement of the public buildings marked "B". With the exception of the shops, office & Qrs. in the immediate occupation of the Qr. Mr's Dept. & one cook house, the public buildings at this post are log buildings and most of them requiring repairs to make them comfortable.

By direction of the Com.g Genl. the Qrs. of the officers, and men, were chinked and daubed with mud, with a little lime to improve its consistency. The first heavy rains of winter swept this away and made new repairs necessary.

These Qrs. can only be made comfortable, permanently, by
being ceiled inside in a manner similar to those of the
Comd.g Officer & either weatherboarded, or at least chinked
& daubed with mortar made with plenty of lime & hair.

The Mechanics & Laborers employed have been one clerk,
two herdsmen, one blacksmith and one carpenter & boat-
builder—and the amount in round number paid—$670 00

The transportation furnished has been for Capt. Brent's
party, and "H" Co. hence to the Dalles at say a cost of $10 per
man and twenty five tons of public property, between the
same ponts, at an average cost of $60 00 per ton—with about
twelve tons from Portland at $8 00 per ton.

The manner of transportation has been by steamer between
Portland and this point, and between this point and the Cascades. Across the Cascade portage by R. R. & wagons; from
the Cascades to the Dalles by boats & steamer, all private
transportation.

The amt. of Lumber, Materials, Barley &c. is $2.342 00.
The lumber was required for repairs &c. at this post; the
materials & forage for the post & Depot.

The principle disbursments have been on account of other
posts and expiditions fitted out at this point. The amount expended for the Dept. purposes of the post has been very
small.

The soil on the borders of the river, where the banks are
not precipitous, and the lands are level for some distance
back, is exceedingly rich and productive, giving extraordinary
yieald of oats, wheat and potatoes, but unfortunately subject
to overflow during the June freshets. Farther back from the
river the soil is of a more gravely or sandy nature, easily cultivated when once cleared, but far less productive than the
bottom lands.

The country is heavily timbered, being, with the exception
of the river bottom, occational plains, and now and then an
occational clearing, almost entirely covered with a heavy
growth of fir with here and there a cedar, and on the banks of
the streams, groves of Oak, Cottonwood & Maple. The prevailing growth however is fir.

There are but few Indians in the vicinity of the post. These
few are of the Clickitat tribe with occational passing visits

from the Cowlitz and the Dalles, easily controlled and altogether to insignificant in prowess & numbers to need much
care or attention, and even this poor remnant of a once
powerful tribe is fast wasting away before those blessings of
civilization "whisky and Small pox.

There are no outstanding debts of the Department, at this
post, at the end of the fiscal year.

Very Respectfully
I am Maj.

To Maj. O. Cross   Your Obt. Svt.
Chf. Q. M. Pacific Div.   U. S. GRANT
San Francisco Cal.   Bvt. Capt. & R. Q. M. 4th Infy

To Julia Dent Grant

Fort Humboldt,
Humboldt Bay, Cal.
February 2d 1854

My Dear Wife.

You do not know how forsaken I feel here! The place is
good enough but I have interests at others which I cannot
help thinking about day and night; then to it is a long time
since I made application for orders to go on to Washington to
settle my accounts but not a word in reply do I get. Then I
feel again as if I had been separated from you. and Fred. long
enough and as to Ulys. I have never seen him. He must by
this time be talking about as Fred. did when I saw him last.
How very much I want to see all of you. I have made up
my mind what Ulys. looks like and I am anxious to see if
my presentiment is correct. Does he advance rapidly? Tell
me a great deel about him and Fred. and Freds pranks
with his Grandpa. How does he get along with his Uncle
Lewis?

I do nothing here but set in my room and read and occationally take a short ride on one of the public horses. There is
game here such as ducks, geese &c. which some of the officers
amuse themselves by shooting but I have not entered into the
sport. Within eight or ten miles Deer and occationally Elk

and black Bear are found. Further back the Grisley Bear are
quite numerous. I do not know if I have told you what officers are at this post? Col. Buchanan, Hunt, Collins, Dr.
Potts and Lt. Latimer to join. Expected soon. Col. B expects
promotion by evry Mail which, if he gets, will bring Montgomery, and leave me in command of the post. Mrs. Collins
is the only lady at the post. Dr. Potts however will have his
wife here in a short time. The quarters are comfortable frame
buildings, backed by a dense forest of immense trees. In front
is the Bay. We are on a bluff which gives us one of the most
commanding views that can be had from almost any point on
the whole Bay. Besides having a view of the Bay itself we can
look out to sea as far as the eye can extend. There are four
villeges on the Bay. One at the outlet, Humbolt Point is the
name, where there are probably not more than 50 inhabitants.
What they depend upon for support I do'nt know. They are
probably persons who supposed that it would be the point
for a City and they would realize a California fortune by the
rise of lots. Three miles up the Bay is Bucksport and this garrison Here geting out lumber is the occupation, and as it
finds a ready market in San Francisco this is a flourishing little
place of about 200. Three miles further up is Euricka with a
population of about 500 with the same resourses. The mills in
these two villeges have, for the last year, loaded an average of
19 vessels per month with lumber, and as they are building
several additional mills they will load a greater number this
year. Twelve miles further up, and at the head of the Bay, is
Union, the larges and best built town of the whole. From
there they pack provisions to the gold mines, and return with
the dust. Taking all of these villeges together there are about
enough ladies to get up a small sized Ball. There has been
several of them this winter.

I got one letter from you since I have been here but it was
some three months old. I fear very much that I shall loose
some before they get in the regular way of coming. There is
no regular mail between here and San Francisco so the only
way we have of geting letters off is to give them to some
Captain of a vessel to mail them after he gets down. In the
same way mails are recieved. This makes it very uncertain as
to the time a letter may be on the way. Sometimes, owing to

advers winds, vessels are 40 and even 60 days making the passage, while at others they make it in less than two days. So you need not be surprised if sometimes you would be a great while without a letter and then likely enough get three or four at once. I hope the next mail we get to have several from you. Be particular to pay postage on yours for otherwise they may refuse to deliver them at the San Francisco Post Office. I cant pay the postage here having no stamps and not being able to get them. I have sent below however for some.

I must finish by sending a great deel of love to all of you, your Pa. Ma. brother and sisters, niece and nepews. I have not yet fulfilled my promise to Emmy to write her a long letter from Humboldt.

Kiss our little ones for me. A thousand kisses for yourself dear Julia.

> Your affectionate husband
> ULYS

To Julia Dent Grant

> Fort Humboldt
> Humboldt Bay, Cal.
> Feb. 6th 1854.

My Dear Wife;

A mail come in this evening but brought me no news from you nor nothing in reply to my application for orders to go home. I cannot concieve what is the cause of the delay. The state of suspense that I am in is scarsely bearable. I think I have been from my family quite long enough and sometimes I feel as though I could almost *** go home "nolens volens." I presume, under ordinary circumstances, Humboldt would be a good enough place but the suspense I am in would make paradice form a bad picture. There is but one thing to console; misery loves company and there are a number in just the same fix with myself, and, with other Regiments, some who have been seperated much longer from their families than I have been.

It has only been a few days since I wrote to you but it will not do to let an opportunity pass of geting a letter into the San Francisco Post Office, and there is a vessel to leave here to-morrow. It is not all the vessels that it will do to entrust letters with. A few that come take the trouble, and expense, of going to the Post Office in San Francisco and geting all the mail directed to this bay and bring it without any remuneration either from the Post Office Department, or from individuals.

I have been suffering for the last few days most terribly. I am certain that if you were to see me now you would not know me. That tooth I had set in in Wattertown (You remember how much I suffered at the time) has been giving me the same trouble over again. Last evening I had it drawn and it was much harder to get out than any other tooth would have been. My face is swolen until it is as round as an apple and so tender that I do not feel as if I could shave, so, looking at the glass, I think I could pass readily for a person of forty five. Otherwise I am very well. You know what it is to suffer with teeth.

I am very much pleased with my company. All the men I have are old soldiers and very neat in their appearance. The contrast between them and the other company here is acknowledged as very great by the officers of the other company. The reason is that all my men are old soldiers while the other were recruits when they come here. I have however less than one third of the complement allowed by law and all of them will be discharged about the same time. I wish their times were out now so that I could go on recruiting service if no other way.

My dear wife you do not tell me whether you are contented or not! I hope you enjoy yourself very much. — Has Capt. Calender continued to send you money? Some three or four months since I bought two land warrants, one of which I want to send you but when I got to San Francisco I found that they were not negociable on account of not having on the transfer the Seal of the County Clerk. I sent them back to Vancouver to have this fixed and when I get them I will send you one. They are worth about forty dollars more there than I gave for them.

Do you think of going to Ohio this Spring? I hope you will

go. They want to see you very much. Evry letter I get from
home they speak of it.

In my letter written a few days ago I told you what officers
we had here, the amusements &c. so I have nothing more on
that head. Living here is extravigantly high besides being very
poor. Col. Buchanan, the Dr. and myself live together at an
expense of about $50 per month each including servant hire
and washing. Mr. Hunt lives by himself. Give my love to all
at home. Write me a great deel about our little boys. Tell me
all their pranks. I suppose Ulys. speaks a great many words
distinctly? Kiss both of them for me. — I believe I told you
that Mrs. Wallen had lost another child. I do not think Wallen
will ever raise either of his children. Harry & Nanny are large
fat children but they do not look right and they are forever
sick. If Wallen was out of the Army and had to pay his Doctor's bill it would amount to about as much as our entire
living. — Kiss Fred. and Ulys. for their pa. A great many
kisses for you dear wife.

Your affectionate husband
ULYS.

To Julia Dent Grant

Fort Humboldt
Humboldt Bay, Cal.
March 6th 1854.

My Dear Wife;

I have only had one letter from you in three months and
that had been a long time on the way so you may know how
anxious I am to hear from you. I know there are letters for me
in the Post Office department, someplace, but when shall I get
them. I sometimes get so anxious to see you, and our little
boys, that I am almost tempted to resign and trust to Providence, and my own exertions, for a living where I can have
you and them with me. It would only require the certainty of
a moderate competency to make me take the step. Whenever
I get to thinking upon the subject however *poverty, poverty,*
begins to stare me in the face and then I think what would

I do if you and our little ones should want for the necessaries of life.

I could be contented at Humboldt if it was possible to have you here but it is not. You could not do without a servant and a servant you could not have   This is to bad is it not? But you never complain of being lonesome so I infer that you are quite contented. I dreamed of you and our little boys the other night the first time for a long time I thought you were at a party when I arrived and before paying any attention to my arrival you said you must go you were engaged for that dance. Fred. and Ulys. did not seem half so large as I expected to see them. If I should see you it would not be as I dreamed, would it dearest? I know it would not.

I am geting to be as great a hand for staying in the house now as I used to be to run about. I have not been a hundred yards from my door but once in the last two weeks. I get so tired and out of patience with the lonliness of this place that I feel like volunteering for the first service that offers. It is likely a party will have to go from here for Cape Mendeceno in the course of a week and if so I think I shall go. I would be absent about two weeks. In the Summer I will try and make an exkursion out into the mines and in the fall another out on the immigrant trail. This will help pass off so much of the time.

This seems to be a very healthy place; all here are enjoying excellent health. The post has been occupied now for about fourteen months, by two Companies, and I believe there has been but two deaths. One by accidentally shooting himself and the other by a limb from a tree falling on a man.

Wallen has made up his mind to resign. Mrs. W. declared she would not go back to Vancouver that if he went he would go without her. W. has gone into the Coal business.— Stevens is going ahead at a rapid stride. A recent decission of the Courts in a land case made him one hundred thousand dollars better off than before. Mrs. Stevens & husband intended to have gone home last January but S. could not find time to go. Mrs. S. will soon be confined again. You recollect what she said at Sackets Harbor?

Mr. Hunt has just recently returned from San Francisco. While there he met John looking well.—There is no news here only occationally a disater at sea. A few days since a steamer went down just inside the Columbia river bar; vessel with all on board except one lost. I am in a great hurry to get this ready for the Mail so I must bid you all good buy for the present. Give my love to your pa, ma, sisters and brother. Kiss our little boys for me. Talk to them a great deel about their pa. A thousand kisses for yourself dearest.

I have some land warrants one of which I want to send you to sell but I am afraid to trust it to the mail. I will send it by the first favorable opportunity. They are worth about $180.00 in N. York; I do not know what you will be able to get in St. Louis.

Adieu dear wife.
ULYS.

To Frederick Dent

Galena, April 19th 1861

Mr. F. Dent;
Dear Sir:

I have but very little time to write but as in these exciting times we are very anxious to hear from you, and know of no other way but but by writing first to you, I must make time.—We get but little news, by telegraph, from St. Louis but from most all other points of the Country we are hearing all the time. The times are indeed startling but now is the time, particularly in the border Slave states, for men to prove their love of country. I know it is hard for men to apparently work with the Republican party but now all party distinctions should be lost sight of and evry true patriot be for maintaining the integrity of the glorious old *Stars & Stripes*, the Constitution and the Union. The North is responding to the Presidents call in such a manner that the rebels may truly quaik. I tell you there is no mistaking the feelings of the people. The Government can call into the field not only 75000 troops but ten or twenty times 75000 if it should be necessary and find the means of maintaining them too. It is all a mistake about the Northern pocket being so sensative. In times like the present no people are more ready to give their own time or of their abundant means. No impartial man can conceal from himself the fact that in all these troubles the South have been the aggressors and the Administration has stood purely on the defensive, more on the defensive than she would dared to have done but for her consiousness of strength and the certainty of right prevailing in the end. The news to-day is that Virginia has gone out of the Union. But for the influance she will have on the other border slave states this is not much to be regreted. Her position, or rather that of Eastern Virginia, has been more reprehensible from the begining than that of South Carolina. She should be made to bear a heavy portion of the burthen of the War for her guilt. — In all this I can but see the doom of Slavery. The North do not want, nor will they want, to interfere with the institution. But they will refuse for all time to give it protection unless the South shall return soon to their allegiance, and then too this disturbance will give such an impetus to the production of their staple, cotton, in other parts of the world that they can never recover the controll of the market again for that comodity. This will reduce the value of negroes so much that they will never be worth fighting over again. — I have just rec'd a letter from Fred. He breathes forth the most patriotic sentiments. He is for the old Flag as long as there is a Union of two states fighting under its banner and when they desolve he will go it alone. This is not his language but it is the idea not so well expressed as he expresses it.

Julia and the children are all well and join me in love to you all. I forgot to mention that Fred. has another heir, with some novel name that I have forgotten.

Yours Truly
U. S. GRANT

Get John or Lewis Sheets to write to me.

To Jesse Root Grant

Galena, April 21st 1861

Dear Father;

We are now in the midst of trying times when evry one must be for or against his country, and show his colors too,

by his every act. Having been educated for such an emergency, at the expense of the Government, I feel that it has
upon me superior claims, such claims as no ordinary motives
of self-interest can surmount. I do not wish to act hastily or
unadvisadly in the matter, and as there are more than enough
to respond to the first call of the President, I have not yet
offered myself. I have promised and am giving all the assistance I can in organizing the Company whose services have
been accepted from this place. I have promised further to go
with them to the state Capital and if I can be of service to the
Governer in organizing his state troops to do so. What I ask
now is your approval of the course I am taking, or advice in
the matter. A letter written this week will reach me in Springfield. I have not time to write you but a hasty line for though
Sunday as it is we are all busy here. In a few minuets I shall be
engaged in directing tailors in the style and trim of uniforms
for our men.

Whatever may have been my political opinions before I
have but one sentiment now. That is we have a Government,
and laws and a flag and they must all be sustained. There are
but two parties now, Traitors & Patriots and I want hereafter
to be ranked with the latter, and I trust, the stronger party.—
I do not know but you may be placed in an awkward position, and a dangerous one pecuniarily, but costs can not now
be counted. My advice would be to leave where you are if you
are not safe with the veiws you entertain. I would never stul-
tify my opinions for the sake of a little security.

I will say nothing about our business. Orvil & Lank will
keep you posted as to that.

Write soon and direct as above.

Yours Truly
U. S. GRANT.

To Julia Dent Grant

Springfield, Apl. 27th/61

Dear Julia;

On account of the cars not connecting promptly we did
not arrive here until evening yesterday, and as no mail gets

through as fast as passengers you will not probably get this until Tuesday morning. I fully made up my mind last night, and had not changed it this morning, to start home to-day and consequently did not intend to write to you atall. Mr. Washburn however come to me this morning and prevailed upon me to remain over for a day or two to see the result of a bill now before the legislature and which will no doubt pass to-day, authorizing the Governer to ration and pay the surplus troops now here, and to arrive, and to appoint suitable persons to take charge of them until such times as they may be organized into Companies and Regiments. All the Companies that have arrived so far, and that is near the whole number called for, have brought with them from twenty to sixty men more each than the law allows. The overplus have as a matter of course, to be cut off. These are the men the Legislature are providing for. The Governer told Mr Washburn last night that should the legislature pass the provision for them, he wanted me to take the command and drill them until they are organized into Companies and placed in Regiments. In case I should accept such a position I may remain here several weeks. In any event however I shall go home, if but for a day or two, so as to be there on next Sunday morning.—Our trip here was a perfect ovation, at evry station the whole population seemed to be out to greet the troops. There is such a feeling arroused through the country now as has not been known since the Revolution. Evry company called for in the Presidents proclimation has been organized, and filled to near double the amount that can be recieved. In addition to that evry town of 1000 inhabitants and over has from one to four additional companies organized ready to answer the next call that will be made.—I find but few old acquaintances here except from Galena. Capt. Pope of the army is here mustering in the volunteers.—I see by Telegraphic dispatch that K McKenzie died yesterday. So they go one at a time. I shall write to your father about Monday. Kiss all the children for me. Write as soon as you get this.

ULYS.

To Mary Grant

Springfield, April 29th, 1861

Dear Sister;

I come to this place several days ago fully expecting to find a letter here for me from father. As yet I have rec'd none. It was my intention to have returned to Galena last evening but the Governer detained, and I presume will want me to remain with him, until all the troops now called into service, or to be so called, are fully mustered in and completely organized. The enthusiasm through this state surpasses anything that could have been imagined three weeks ago. Only six Regiments are called for here while at least thirty could be promptly raised. The Governer, and all others in authority, are harrassed from morning until night with Patriotic men, and such political influance as they can bring, to obtain first promises of acceptance of their companies if there should be another call for troops. The eagerness to enter companies that were accepted by the Governer was so great that it has been impossible for commanders of companies to keep their numbers within the limits of the law consequently companies that have arrived here have all had from ten to sixty men more than can be accepted. The Legislature on Saturday last passed a bill providing for the maintenance and discipline of these surplus troops for one month, unless sooner mustered into service of the United States under a second call.—I am convinced that if the South knew the entire unanimity of the North for the Union and maintenance of Law, and how freely men and money are offered to the cause, they would lay down their arms at once in humble submission. There is no disposition to compromise now. Nearly every one is anxious to see the Government fully tested as to its strength, and see if it is not worth preserving. The conduct of eastern Virginia has been so abominable through the whole contest that there would be a great deal of disappointment here if matters should be settled before she is thoroughly punished. This is my feeling, and I believe it universal. Great allowance should be made for South Carolinians, for the last generation have been educated, from their infancy, to look upon their Government as oppressive and tyrannical and only to be endured till such time as they might have sufficient strength to strike it down. Virginia, and other border states, have no such excuse and are therefore traitors at heart as well as in act. I should like very much to see the letter Aunt Rachel wrote Clara! or a copy of it. Can't you send it?

When I left Galena, Julia and the children were very well. Jesse had been very sick for a few days but was getting much better. I have been very anxious that you should spend the summer with us. You have never visited us and I don't see why you can't. Two of you often travel together, and you might do so again, and come out with Clara. I do not like to urge anything of the kind, lest you should think that I ignored entirely the question of economy, but I do not do so. The fact is I have had my doubts whether or not it would not be more prudent for all of you to lock up and leave, until the present excitement subsides. If father were younger and Simpson strong and healthy, I would not advise such a course. On the contrary, I would like to see every Union man in the border slave states remain firm at his post. Every such man is equal to an armed volunteer at this time in defence of his country. There is very little that I can tell you that you do not get from the papers.

Remember me to all at home and write to me at once, to this place.

BROTHER ULYSSES.

To Julia Dent Grant

GENERAL HEAD QUARTERS—STATE OF ILLINOIS.
ADJUTANT GENERAL'S OFFICE,
SPRINGFIELD, MAY 1st *1861*.

Dear Julia;

I have an opportunity of sending a letter direct to Galena by Mr. Corwith and as it will probably reach you a day or two earlyer than if sent by Mail I avail myself of the chance. I enclose also a letter from father for you to read. As I shall probably be home on Saturday evening I shall say nothing about what my intentions are for the future, in fact my plans will have to mature from circumstances as they develop themselvs. At present I am on duty with the Governer, at his request, occupation principally smoking and occationally giving advice as to how an order should be communicated &c. I am going this morning however into the Adjutant General's Office to remain until some regularity is established there, if I can bring about that regularity. The fact is however, as I told the Governer, my bump of order is not largely developed and papers are not my forte and therefore my services may not be as valuable as he anticipates. However I am in to do all I can and will do my best.

We recieve the St. Louis morning papers here at 10 O'Clock a.m. evry day of the day issued and evry day some one is here from the city. The state of affairs there is terrible and no doubt a terrible calamity awaits them. Stationing Ill. Troops within striking distance of St Louis may possibly save the city. Business is entirely prostrated and the best houses are forced to close. I see by the Mo. Republican that Charless Blow & Co are among the number. But for the little piece of stratagem used to get the arms out of the arsenal, to this place, they would have fallen into the hands of the Secessionests and with their hands strengthened with these an attempt would have been made to take the city entirely under controll and terrible slaughter would have taken place. Great numbers of people are leaving Missouri now in evry direction, except South. In some of the Northern towns of the state merchants and business men are leaving with all their personal property. Missouri will be a great state ultimately but she is set back now for years. It will end in more rapid advancement however for she will be left a free state. Negroes are stampeding already and those who do not will be carried further South so that the destiny of the state, in that respect, may now be considered settled by fate and not political parties. Kiss the children for me. You need not write as I will be home so soon

ULYS.

To Jesse Root Grant

GENERAL HEAD QUARTERS—STATE OF ILLINOIS.
ADJUTANT GENERAL'S OFFICE,
SPRINGFIELD, May 2nd, *1861*.

Dear Father:

Your letter of the 24th inst was received the same evening one I had written to Mary was mailed. I would have answered earlier but for the fact I had just written.

I am not a volunteer, and indeed could not be, now that I did not go into the first Company raised in Galena. The call of the President was so promptly responded to that only those companies that organized at once, and telegraphed their application to come in, were received. All other applications were filed, and there are enough of them to furnish Illinois quota if the Army should be raised to 300,000 men. I am serving on the Governor's staff at present at his request, but suppose I shall not be here long.

I should have offered myself for the Colonelcy of one of the Regiments, but I find all those places are wanted by politicians who are up to log-rolling, and I do not care to be under such persons.

The war feeling is not abating here much, although hostilities appear more remote than they did a few days ago. Three of the six Regiments mustered in from this state are now at Cairo, and probably will be reinforced with two others within a few days.

Galena has several more companies organized but only one of them will be able to come in under a new call for ten regiments. Chicago has raised companies enough nearly to fill all the first call. The Northern feeling is so fully aroused that they will stop at no expense of money and men to insure the success of their cause.

I presume the feeling is just as strong on the other side, but they are infinitely in the minority in resources.

I have not heard from Galena since coming down here, but presume all is moving along smoothly. My advice was not to urge collections from such men as we knew to be good, and to make no efforts to sell in the present distracted state of our currency. The money will not buy Eastern exchange and is liable to become worse; I think that thirty days from this we shall have specie, and the bills of good foreign banks to do business on, and then will be the time to collect.

If Mary writes to me any time next week she may direct here to

ULYSSES.

To Julia Dent Grant

Springfield, May 3d/61

Dear Julia;

I thought I was going home this evening but when I told the Governer of it he objected because he had important duties for me in connexion with the organization of new Regiments provided for by the Legislature a day or two ago. I presume I shall be put on duty in Freeport mustering in a Regiment from that Congressional district. If so I will be within a few hours travel of Galena and can go down most any afternoon and return in the morning. It may be that I will remain there two or three weeks and then retire from the service. This place is within four hours travel of St. Louis and the Cars run here so that I could start at 5 o'clock a.m. be in St. Louis at 9, get a horse and buggy and go out and spend the day at your fathers and return here for breakfast the next morning. If I can get sent down to Alton on business I will try and go out and spend one day. All is buzz and excitement here, as well as confusion, and I dont see really that I am doing any good. But when I speak of going it is objected to by not only Governer Yates, but others. — I imagine it will do me no harm the time I spend here, for it has enabled me to become acquainted with the principle men in the state. I do not know that I shall receive any benefit from this but it does no harm.

Orvil enquires what compensation I receive: I presume it will be the pay of Capt. or $140 00 per month. At present I am at the Principle Hotel where I presume my board will be 10 or 12 dollars per week but if I remain I shall leave it. I have not had a line from you since I come here, how does this happen?

Kiss all the children for me. Tell Mary Duncan her beaux takes to soldiering very naturally. I have no doubt but he will send her a kiss by me when I go back.

Write to me Sunday the day you will get this.

ULYS.

To Julia Dent Grant

Anna, Ill.
May 21st 1861

Dear Julia;

I am through at this place and will leave in about one hour for Cairo, where I shall only remain until evening. I will then return to Springfield when I may be released from further duty. I am not however by any means certain of that for I know that I have been applied for for other service. I will write you again on Thursday if I am not at home. I might about as well volunteered in the first instance as to be detained the way I have and then I should have got the Colonelcy of a Regt. However my services have been quite as valuable, I presume the state thinks, as if I had been at the head of a Regt. and the duties are much more pleasant to me. —I have been agreeably disappointed in the people of Egypt. It is the prevailing opinion abroad that the people of this section of the State are ignorant, disloyal, intemperate and generally heathenish. The fact is the Regt. formed here is the equal, if not the superior, of any of the Regiments raised in the State, for all the virtues of which they are charged with being deficient. I have had no letter from you here but expect to find one at Springfield when I get there. I am anxious to hear from you and the children as well as see you. Somehow though I feel as if I was in for the War and cannot divest myself of the feeling. I will not go though for a position which I look upon as inferior to that of Col. of a Regt. and will not seek that. How much soever I might deem it my duty to give my services at this time I do not feel that the obligation, at present, calls for me to accept a lower position. —I see Jo Reynolds is in with the Indiana Volunteers. I do not expect to see Emma at Cairo but presume Jim. is there. My stay will be but about five hours there and my duties will occupy about half that time.

I hope you are geting along happily without me. I presume the last crash among the banks has startled Orvil. I expected it to come and when they wrote me that business was dull and collections ditto I was glad of it. No debts can be paid with the money they are geting and there is no use holding the depreciated stuff. Kiss the children for me and give my love to all our relations.

ULYS.

Orders No. 7

Head Quarters, Camp Yates June 18 1861.
Orders No. 7.

The undersigned having been duly appointed Colonel of the 7th Congl Dist Regt. of Ills Volts. Militia by order of Govr Richard Yates, duly promulgated hereby assumes command.

In accepting this command, your Commander will require the co-operation of all the commissioned and non-commissioned Officers in instructing the command, and in maintaining discipline, and hopes to receive also the hearty support of every enlisted man.

All orders now in force at this camp will be continued until countermanded.

By Order
U. S. GRANT Col. Comdg.

To Julia Dent Grant

Camp Yates, June 26th 1861
Dear Julia;

We arrived here on Monday evening all well. Fred. was delighted with his trip but I think is not so pleased here as while traveling. When I get a horse however so that he can ride out with me he will make up.

The probabilities are that we will not remain here longer than next week. I will write again before leaving here. — I am very much pleased with my officers generally. They are sober and attentive and anxious to learn their duties. The men I believe are pleased with the change that has taken place in their commander, or at least the greatest change has taken place in the order in camp. For Lieut. Colonel and Major I have two men that I think a greatdeal of but I can never have a game of Eucre with them. One is a preacher and the other a member of Church. For the Field officers of my regt. the 21st Ill. Volunteers one pint of liquor will do to the end of the war.

I am kept very busy from morning until night and no time for making acquaintances. No ladies have yet been to see me in camp and although I have been here most of the time for over two months I have not made the acquaintance of a single family.

Has Buck got used to being without Fred? When we get over to Quincy all of you will have an opportunity of trying camp life for a while.

Tell Orvil that I shall not buy another horse until I get to Quincy, in the mean time if he should see a very fine one in Galena I would rather buy there. Rondy will do me for the march, if we should make it which is by no means certain. Fred. will ride in a waggon if we should march. That part he will enjoy very much. It is a very uphill business for me to write this evening. — Is Simp. & Mother with you yet? When they come be sure and write me at once and tell me how Simp. stood the trip. I am very anxious that he should get out for I believe the trip will do him good if he can stand it. — Have you heard from any of your people since I left? I should like to hear from Dr. Sharp. I feel a little anxious to his sentiments on the present issues.

If you have an opportunity I wish you would send me McClellands report of battles in the Crimea. You will find it about the house. — Kiss all the children for me. Tell Mary Duncan to give you back that kiss you caught me giving her. The next time I write you may take back the one from Hellen.

This is a very poor letter but I have not written scarsely a single sentence without interruption.

Your Dodo

To Julia Dent Grant

Naples, Ill.
July 7th 1861

Dear Julia;

We are now laying in camp on the Illinois river spending sunday and will leave to-morrow on our way to Quincy. Up to this time my regiment have made their marches as well as troops ever do and the men have been very orderly. There have been a few men who show a disposition not to respect private property such as hen roosts and gardens, but I have kept such a watch on them, and punished offenders so, that I will venture that the same number of troops never marched through a thickly settled country like this committing fewer depridations. Fred. enjoys it hugely. Our Lieut. Col. was left behind and I am riding his horse so that Fred. has Rondy to ride. The Soldiers and officers call him Colonel and he seems to be quite a favorite.

From Springfield here is one of the most beautiful countries in the world. It is all settled and highly improved. It is all of it the district of the State that sends so much fine stock to St. Louis fair.

Passing through the towns the whole population would turn out to receive us. At Jacksonville, one of the prettyest towns with the most tasty houses that I ever saw, the ladies were all out waving their handkerchiefs, and one of them (I know she must be pretty) made up a boquet and sent me with her name, which by the way the messenger forgot before it come to me. So you see I shall probably never find who the fair donor was.

From present indications we will not remain long at

Quincy. There was four regiments ordered there with the expectation of remaining until frost. Two have arrived and been ordered into Missouri. I think my regiment cannot be ordered so soon because we have yet to get all our uniforms & equipments and a part of our arms. It will be at least two weeks before my regt. can be of much service and a month before it can do good service. It was in a terribly disorganized state when I took it but a very great change has taken place. Evry one says so and to me it is very observable. I dont believe there is a more orderly set of troops now in the volunteer service. I have been very strict with them and the men seem to like it. They appreciate that it is all for their own benefit. — Kiss the children for me. Fred. would send his love to all of you but he is out. He says he will answer Susy Felts letter but I am affraid that he will be slow about it. He writes sometimes but never copys letter.

Kisses to you.
ULYS.

To Jesse Root Grant

East Quincy, Mo.,
July 13th, 1861.

Dear Father:

I have just received yours and Mary's letters and really did not know that I had been so negligent as not to have written to you before. I did write from Camp Yates, but since receiving yours remember that I did not get to finish it at the time, and have neglected it since. The fact is that since I took command of this regiment I have had no spare time, and flatter myself, and believe I am sustained in my judgment by my officers and men, that I have done as much for the improvement and efficiency of this regiment as was ever done for a command in the same length of time. — You will see that I am in Missouri. Yesterday I went out as far as Palmyra and stationed my regiment along the railroad for the protection of the bridges, trestle work, etc. The day before I sent a small command, all I could spare, to relieve Colonel Smith who was surrounded by secessionists. He effected his relief, however, before they got there. Tomorrow I start for Monroe, where I shall fall in with Colonel Palmer and one company of horse and two pieces of artillery. One regiment and a battalion of infantry will move on to Mexico, North Missouri road, and all of us together will try to nab the notorious Tom Harris with his 1200 secessionists. His men are mounted, and I have but little faith in getting many of them. The notorious Jim Green who was let off on his parole of honor but a few days ago, has gone towards them with a strong company well armed. If he is caught it will prove bad work for him.

You no doubt saw from the papers that I started to march across the country for Quincy. My men behaved admirably, and the lesson has been a good one for them. They can now go into camp after a day's march with as much promptness as veteran troops; they can strike their tents and be on the march with equal celerity. At the Illinois River, I received a dispatch at eleven o'clock at night that a train of cars would arrive at half past eleven to move my regiment. All the men were of course asleep, but I had the drum beaten, and in forty minutes every tent and all the baggage was at the water's edge ready to put aboard the ferry to cross the river.

I will try to keep you posted from time to time, by writing either to you or to Mary, of my whereabouts and what I am doing. I hope you will have only a good account of me and the command under my charge. I assure you my heart is in the cause I have espoused, and however I may have disliked party Republicanism there has never been a day that I would not have taken up arms for a Constitutional Administration.

You ask if I should not like to go in the regular army. I should not. I want to bring my children up to useful employment, and in the army the chance is poor. There is at least the same objection that you find where slavery exists. Fred. has been with me until yesterday; I sent him home on a boat.

Yours &c.
U. S. GRANT.

To Julia Dent Grant

West Quincy, Mo.
July 13th 1861

Dear Julia;

A letter from you has just reached me. I join you in disappointment that you will not likely be able to make a trip to visit me this Summer. But our country calls me elswhere and I must obey. Secessionests are thick through this part of Missouri but so far they show themselves very scary about attacking. Their depridations are confined more to burning R. R. bridges, tearing up the track and where they can, surround small parties of Union troops. I come here to release Col. Smith who was surrounded but he effected his release too soon for me to assist him. Yesterday I went out as far as Palmyra and stationed my Regt. along at different points for the protection of the road. To-morrow I will be relieved by Col. Terchin and will start for Monroe where I will meet Col. Palmer with his Regt. and one company of horse & two pieces of Artillery. There will also be a Regt. & a half over at Mexico on the North Missouri road and all of us together will try and surround the notorious Tom Harris and his band. After that my Regt. goes down to St. Charles where we take a steamer for Alton there to go into Camp. I have no idea however that we will be allowed to remain long. I am kept very busy but with such a set of officers as I have they will learn their duties rapidly and relieve me of many of the cares I now have. My Regt. is a good one and deserves great credit for the progress it has made in the last three weeks. Our March from Springfield was conducted with as much dicipline, and our geting into camp at night and starting in the morning, was as prompt as I ever saw with regular troops. I have been strict with my men but it seems to have met with the approbation of them all. — Fred. started home yesterday and I did not telegraph you because I thought you would be in a perfect stew until he arrived. He did not want to go atall and I felt lothe at sending him but now that we are in the enemies country I thought you would be alarmed if he was with me. Fred. is a good boy and behaved very manly. Last night we had an alarm which kept me out all night with one of those terrible headaches which you know I am subject to. To-day I have laid up all day and taken medicine so that I feel pretty well.

Write your next letter to me at Alton. Fred. will have a budget of news to tell you. You must not fret about me. Of course there is more or less exposure in a call of the kind I am now obeying but the justness of it is a consolation.—It is geting late and I must go to bed. give my love to all at home. I hope Simp. will not abandon the idea of going to Lake Superior. I think it will do him a greatdeel of good. Kisses for yourself & children.

ULYS.

To Jesse Root Grant

Mexico Mo.
Aug 3, 1861

Dear Father;

I have written to you once from this place and received no answer, but as Orvil writes to me that you express great anxiety to hear from me often I will try and find time to drop you a line twice a month, and oftener when anything of special interest occurs.

The papers keep you posted as to Army Movements and as you are already in possession of my notions on Secession nothing more is wanted on that point. I find here however a different state of feeling from what I expected existed in any part of the South. The majority in this part of the State are Secessionists, as we would term them, but deplore the present state of affairs. They would make almost any sacrifice to have the Union restored, but regard it as disolved and nothing is left for them but to choose between two evils. Many too seem to be entirely ignorant of the object of present hostilities. You can't convince them but what the ultimate object is to extinguish, by force, slavery. Then too they feel that the Southern Confederacy will never consent to give up their State and as they, the South, are the strong party it is prudent to favor them from the start. There is never a movement of troops made that the Secession journals through the Country do not

give a startling account of their almost annihilation at the
hands of the States troops, whilst the facts are there are no
engagements. My Regt. has been reported cut to pieces once
that I know of, and I dont know but oftener, whilst a gun
has not been fired at us. These reports go uncontradicted here
and give confirmation to the conviction already entertained
that one Southron is equal to five Northerners. We believe
they are deluded and know that if they are not we are.

Since I have been in Command of this Military District
(two weeks) I have received the greatest hospitality and
attention from the Citizens about here. I have had every opportunity of conversing with them freely and learning their
sentiments and although I have confined myself strictly to the
truth as to what has been the result of the different engagements, the relative strength etc. and the objects of the Administration, and the North Generally, yet they dont believe a
word I dont think.

I see from the papers that my name has been sent in for
Brigadier Gen.! This is certainly very complimentary to me
particularly as I have never asked a friend to intercede in my
behalf. My only acquaintance with men of influence in the
State was whilst on duty at Springfield and I then saw much
pulling and hauling for favors that I determined never to ask
for anything, and never have, not even a Colonelcy. I wrote a
letter to Washington tendering my services but then declined
Gov. Yates' & Mr. Trumbull's endorsement.

My services with the Regt. I am now with have been highly
satisfactory to me. I took it in a very disorganized, demoralized and insubordinate condition and have worked it up to a
reputation equal to the best, and I believe with the good will
of all the officers and all the men. Hearing that I was likely to
be promoted the officers, with great unanimity, have requested to be attached to my Command. This I dont want
you to read to others for I very much dislike speaking of
myself.

We are now breaking up Camp here gradually. In a few
days the last of us will be on our way for the Mo. River, at
what point cannot be definitely determined, wood & water
being a concideration, as well as a healthy fine sight for a
large encampment. A letter addressed to me at Galena will

probably find me there. If I get my promotion I shall expect to go there for a few days.

Remember me to all at home and write to me.

Yours Truly
U. S. GRANT

To Julia Dent Grant

Mexico, Mo.
August 3d 1861

Dear Julia;

This is the last letter you will get from me from this point. We are now breaking up camp preparitory to moving on to the Missouri river. At what point I cannot yet say. From the accounts in the papers I may not go along however. I see some kind friends have been working to get me the Appointment of Brigadier General which, if confirmed may send me any place where there are Ill. troops.

I am glad to get away from here. The people have been remarkably polite if they are seceshers, but the weather is intolerably warm and dry and as there is neither wells nor springs in this country we have drank the whole place dry. People here will be glad to get clear of us notwithstanding their apparent hospitality. They are great fools in this section of country and will never rest until they bring upon themselvs all the horrors of war in its worst form. The people are inclined to carry on a guerilla Warfare that must eventuate in retaliation and when it does commence it will be hard to control. I hope from the bottom of my heart I may be mistaken but since the defeat of our troops at Manassas things look more gloomy here.

How long has it been since I wrote to you before? I am kept very busy and time passes off rapidly so that it seems but a day or two. I have received two letters from you since our arrival, one in which you gave me fits for sending Fred. home by himself and one of later date. Fred. will make a good General some day and I think you had better pack his valise and start him on now. I should like very much to see you and the children again.—The weather has been intolerably warm here for the last week.***

You need not write to me until you hear from me again. I will write soon and often if I do write short letters. Give my love to all at home. Kiss the children for me. Does Jess. talk about his pa or has he forgotten me. Little rascal I want to see him. Love and kisses for yourself.

U. S. GRANT

To Julia Dent Grant

Ironton Mo.
August 10th 1861

Dear Julia;

Night before last I come down to Jefferson Bks. with my old Regt. leaving my trunk at the Planter's House flattering myself that at 9 O'Clock the next day I would return to St. Louis, get a leave of absence for a few days and pop down upon you taking you by surprize. But my destination was suddenly changed, 9 O'Clock brought me orders, (and cars to carry a regiment) to proceed at once to this place and assume command. My present command here numbers about 3000 and will be increased to 4000 to-morrow and probably much larger the next day. When I come there was great talk of an attack upon this place and it was represented that there was 8000 rebels within a few miles but I am not ready to credit the report.

I have envited Mr. Rollins of Galena to accept a place on my Staff. I wish you would tell Orvil to say to him that I would like to have him come as soon as possible if he accepts the position.

I sent you some money the other day and requested Ford to write to you. Did he do it? The four gold dollars were thrown in extra for the four children. Bless their hearts I wish I could see them.

I certainly feel very greatful to the people of Ill. for the interest they seem to have taken in me and unasked too. Whilst I was about Springfield I certainly never blew my own trumpet and was not aware that I attracted any attention but it seems from what I have heard from there the people, who were perfect strangers to me up to the commencement of our present unhappy national difficulties, were very unanimous in recommending me for my present position. I shall do my very best not to disappoint them and shall hope by dilligence to render good account of some of the Ill. Vols. All my old Regt. expressed great regret at my leaving them and applied to be attached to my Brigade.

I called to see Harry Boggs the other day as I passed through St. Louis. He cursed and went on like a Madman. Told me that I would never be welcom in his hous; that the people of Illinois were a poor misserable set of Black Republicans, Abolition paupers that had to invade their state to get something to eat. Good joke that on something to eat. Harry is such a pittiful insignificant fellow that I could not get mad at him and told him so where upon he set the Army of Flanders far in the shade with his profanity.

Give my love to all the good people of Galena. I hope to be at home a day or two soon but dont you be disappointed if I am. Kiss the children for me. — Dont act upon the permission I gave you to go to Covington to board until you hear from me again on the subject.

ULYS.

To Mary Grant

Ironton Mo.
August 12th 1861

Dear Sister;

Your letter directed to me at Mexico, Mo. come to hand yesterday at this place. A glance at the map will show you where I am. When I come here it was reported that this place was to be attacked by 8,000 secessionests, under Gen. Hardee, within a day or two. Now Hardee's force seems to have reduced and his distance from here to have increased. Scouting parties however are constantly seen within a few miles of our Pickets. I have here about 3000 Vols. nearly all

Infantry, but our position being strong and our cause a good one, it would trouble a much larger force of the enemy to dislodge us.—You ask my views about the continuance of the war &c. Well I have changed my mind so much that I dont know what to think. That the Rebels will be so badly whipped by April next that they cannot make a stand anywhere I dont doubt. But they are so dogged that there is no telling when they may be subdued. Send Union troops among them and respect all their rights, pay for evrything you get and they become desperate and reckless because their state sovereignty is invaded. Troops of the opposite side march through and take evrything they want, leaving no pay but script, and they become desperate secession partisans because they have nothing more to loose. Evry change makes them more desperate. I should like to be sent to Western Virginia but my lot seems to be cast in this part of the world. I wanted to remain in St. Louis a day or two to get some books to read that might help me in my profession, and get my uniform &c. made. Mine has been a busy life from the begining and my new made friends in Ill. seem to give me great credit. I hope to deserve it and shall spare no pains on my part to do so.

It is precious little time I shall have for writing letters but I have subscribed for the Daily St. Louis Democrat to be sent to you, through which you may occationally hear from me.

Write to me often even though your letters are not answered. As I told father in my last, I will try and have you hear from me twice a month if I have to write after midnight.

I told Julia she might go to Covington and board whilst I am away but I dont know but she had better stay where she is. The people of Galena have always shown the greatest friendship for me and I would prefer keeping my home there. I would like very much though if you would go and stay with Julia.

If I get a uniform, and get where I can have my Dagueareotype taken your wish in that respect shall be gratified.

Your Brother
ULYS.

To Julia Dent Grant

Head Quarters, Jefferson City, Mo
August 26th 1861

Dear Julia;

The day Orvil arrived here I got a big batch of letters from you the first for a long time. I was surprised to learn that you had not heard from me for so long a time. I have been very particular to write often, and I think a single week has not passed without my writing at least once and generally twice. — Orvil can tell you how busy I have been. Evry night I am kept from 12 O'Clock to 2 in the morning. I stand it first rate however and never enjoyed better health in my life.

I receive a great many letters that I cannot answer and many that I do. Josh Sharp has applied to go on my Staff. He says that he will go on without pay and without position if I will let him go along.

My Staff are, J. A. Rawlins Clark B Lagow & W. S. Hillyer, three of the cleverest men that can be found anywhere. Father's recommendation come too late. I know the father of the young man he recommends and if the son is like him I could not get one that would suit better.

I am sorry that I did not keep Fred with me. He would have enjoyed it very much.

How long we will be here and whether I will get to go home is hard to tell. Gen. Fremont promised that I should but if a forward movement is to take place I fear I shall not. — When I was ordered away from Ironton nearly all the commanders of regiments expressed regret I am told. The fact is my whole career since the begining of present unhappy difficulties has been complimented in a very flattering manner. All my old friends in the Army and out seem to heartily congratulate me. I scarsely ever get to go out of the house and consequently see but little of the people here. There seems to be no stir however except among the troops and they are quiet. There is considerable apprehension of an attack soon but my means of information are certainly better than can be had by most others and my impression is that there is no force sufficiently strong to attempt anything of the kind under a weeks march.

I sent you ten dollars by Orvil to carry you through a few days until I can draw a months pay when I will send $75 or $100 more. I want you to have evrything comfortable and when I get some debts paid will supply you more liberally. My outfit costs $900 00 without being anything extra. This includes three horses saddles & bridles at $600 00.

Give my love to all at home. Remember me to the neighbors around you. I am very much in hopes I shall be able to pay you a short visit but fear I shall not. Kiss the children for me and accept the same for yourself.

Good night.
ULYS.

To Eleazer A. Paine

Head Quarters, Dist of Cairo
Cairo, Jany 11th 1862.

Brig Gen. E. A. Paine
Commdg Bird's Point, Mo.
General:

I undestand that four of our pickets were shot this morning. If this is so, and appearances indicate that the assassins were citizens, not regularly organized in the rebel Army, the whole country should be cleaned out, for six miles around, and word given that all citizens making their appearance within those limits are liable to be shot. To execute this, patrols should be sent out, in all directions, and bring into camp at Bird's Point all citizens, together with their Subsistence, and require them to remain, under pain of death and destruction of their property until properly relieved.

Let no harm befall these people, if they quietly submit but bring them in, and place them in camp below the breastworks and have them properly guarded.

The intention is not to make political prisoners of these people, but to cut off a dangerous class of spies.

This applies to all classes and conditions, Age and Sex. If however, Woman and Children, prefer other protection than we can afford them, they may be allowed to retire, beyond the limits indicated, not to return until authorized.

Report to me as soon as possibe every important occurrence within your command.

> Very Respectfully,
> Your Obt. Servant,
> U. S. GRANT.
> Brig. Gen'l. Commdg.

General Orders No. 3

Head Quarters Dist of Cairo
Cairo Ill. January 13. 1862

General Order No. 3

During the absence of the Expedition now starting upon soil hitherto occupied almost solely by the Rebel Army, and where it is a fair inference that every stranger met is our enemy, the following orders will be observed.

Troops, in marching, will be kept in the ranks, Company officers being held strictly accountable for all stragglers from their Companies.

No firing will be allowed in camp or on the march, not strictly required in the performance of duty.

Whilst in Camp, no permits will be granted to officers or soldiers to leave their regimental grounds, and all violations of this order must be promptly and summarily punished.

Disrepute having been brought upon our brave soldiers by the bad conduct of some of their numbers, showing on all occations, when marching through territory occupied by sympathisers of the enemy, a total disregard of rights of citizens, and being guilty of wanton destruction of private propety the Genl. commanding, desires and intends to enforce a change in this respect.

Interpreting Confiscation Acts by troops themselves, has a demoralizing effect, weakens them in exact proportion to the demoralization and makes open and armed enemies of many who, from opposite treatment would become friends or at worst non-combatants.

It is orded, therefore that the severest punishment, be inflicted upon every soldier, who is guilty of taking or dstroying private property, and any commissioned officer guilty of like conduct, or of countenancing it shall be deprived of his sword and expelled from the camp, not to be permitted to return.

On the march, Cavalry Advance guards will be well thrown out, also flank guards of Cavalry or Infantry when practicable.

A rear guard of Infantry will be required to see that no teams, baggage or disabled soldiers are left behind

It will be the duty of Company Commanders to see that rolls of their Companies are called immediatly upon going into camp each day and every member accounted for

By order
U. S. GRANT Brig. Gen'l Comdg.

To Julia Dent Grant

Camp Near Fort Henry, Ten.
Feb.y 5th 1862

Dear Julia,

We returned to-day with most of the remainder of our troops. The sight of our camp fires on either side of the river is beautiful and no doubt inspires the enemy, who is in full view of them, with the idea that we have full 4,000 men. To-morrow will come the tug of war. One side or the other must to-morrow night rest in quiet possession of Fort Henry. What the strength of Fort Henry is I do not know accurately, probably 10,000 men.

To-day our reconnoitering parties had a little skirmishing resulting in one killed & two slightly wounded on our side and one killed and a number wounded on the side of the rebels, and the balance badly frightened and driven into their fortifications.

I am well and in good spirits yet feeling confidance in the success of our enterprise. Probably by the time you receive this you will receive another announcing the result.

I received your letter last night just after I had written to you.

I have just written my order of battle. I hope it will be a report of the battle after it is fought.

Kiss the children for me. Kisses for yourself.

ULYS.

P. S. I was up til 5 o'clock this morning and awoke at 8 so I must try and get rest to-night. It is now 10½ however, and I cannot go to bed for some time yet.

U.

To Mary Grant

Fort Henry, Ten.
Feb.y 9th 1862.

Dear Sister,

I take my pen in hand "away down in Dixie" to let you know that I am still alive and well. What the next few days may bring forth however I cant tell you. I intend to keep the ball moving as lively as possible and have only been detained here from the fact that the Tennessee is very high and has been raising ever since we have been here overflowing the back land making it necessary to bridge it before we could move. — Before receiving this you will hear, by telegraph, of Fort Donaldson being attacked. — Yesterday I went up the Ten. river twenty odd miles and to-day crossed over to near the Cumberland river at Fort Donaldson. — Our men had a little engagement with the enemie's pickets killing five of them, wounding a number and, expressively speaking, "gobbeling up" some twenty-four more.

If I had your last letter at hand I would answer it. But I have not and therefore write you a very hasty and random letter simply to let you know that I believe you still remember me and am carrying on a conversation whilst writing with my Staff and others.

Julia will be with you in a few days and possibly I may accompany her. This is bearly possible, depending upon having full possession of the line from Fort Henry to Fort Donaldson and being able to quit for a few days without retarding any contemplated movement. This would not leave me free more than one day however.

You have no conception of the amount of labor I have to perform. An army of men all helpless looking to the commanding officer for every supply. Your plain brother however has, as yet, had no reason to feel himself unequal to the task and fully believes that he will carry on a successful campaign against our rebel enemy. I do not speak boastfully but utter a presentiment. The scare and fright of the rebels up here is beyond conception. Twenty three miles above here some were drowned in their haste to retreat thinking us such Vandals that neither life nor property would be respected. G. J. Pillow commands at Fort Donaldson. I hope to give him a tug before you receive this.

U. S. G.

To George W. Cullum

Head Quarters, Army in the Field
Fort Donelson, Feb. 16th 1862

Gen. G. W. Cullum
Chief of Staff, Dept. of the Mo.
Gen.

I am pleased to announce to you the unconditional surrender this morning of Fort Donelson, with twelve to fifteen thousand prisoners, at least forty pieces of Artillery and a large amount of stores, horses, mules and other public property. I left Fort Henry on the 12th inst. with a force of about 15000 men, divided into two Divisions under the commands of Gens. McClernand and Smith. Six regiments were sent around by water the day before, convoyed by a gun boat, or rather started one day later than one of the gunboats, and with instructions not to pass it.

The troops made the march in good order, the head of the colum arriving within two miles of the Fort, at 12 o'clock M. At this point the enemies pickets were met and driven in.

The fortifications of the enemy were from this point gradually approached and surrounded with occational skirmishing on the line. The following day owing to the nonarrival of the Gunboats and reinforcements sent by water no attack was made but the investment was extended on the flanks of the enemy and drawn closer to his works, with skirmishing all day. The evening of the 13th the Gunboats and reinforcements arrived. On the 14th a gallant attack was made by Flag Officer Foote, upon the enemies works, with his fleet. The engagement lasted probably one hour and a half and bid fair to result favorably to the cause of the Union when two unlucky shots disabled two of the Armoured boats so that they were carrid back by the tide. The remaining two were very much disabled also having received a number of heavy shots about the pilot houses and other parts of the vessels.

After these mishaps I concluded to make the investment of Fort Donelson as perfect as possible and partially fortify and await repairs to the gunboats. This plan was frustrated however by the enemy making a most vigorous attack upon our right wing, commanded by Gen. J. A. McClernands with a portion of the force under Gen. L. Wallace. The enemy were repelled after a closely contested battle of several hours in which our loss was heavy. The officers, and particularly field officers, suffered out of proportion. I have not the means yet of determining our loss even approximately but it cannot fall far short of 1200 killed wounded and missing. Of the latter I understand through Gen. Buckner about 250 were taken prisoners.—I shall retain enough of the enemy to exchange for them as they were immediately shipped off and not left for recapture.—About the close of this action the ammunition in cartridge boxes gave out, which with the loss of many of the Field officers produced great confusion in the ranks. Seeing that the enemy did not take advantage of it convinced me that equal confusion, and possibly great demoralization, existed with him. Taking advantage of this fact I ordered a charge upon the left,—Enemies right,—with the Division under Gen. C. F. Smith which was most brilliantly executed and gave to our arms full assurance of victory. The battle lasted until dark giving us possession of part of the entrenchments.—An attack was ordered from the other flank, after the charge by Gen. Smith was commenced, by the Divisions under Gens. McClernand & Wallace, which, notwithstanding the hours of exposure to a heavy fire in the fore part of the day, was gallantly made and the enemy further repulsed.

At the points thus gained, night having come on, all the troops encamped for the night feeling that a complete victory would crown their labors at an early hour in the morning.

This morning at a very early hour a note was received from Gen. S. B. Buckner, under a flag of truce, proposing an armistice &c. A copy of the correspondence which ensued is herewith accompanying.

I cannot mention individuals who specially distinguished themselvs but leave that to Division and Brigade Commanders, whos reports will be forwarded as soon as received.

To Division Commanders however, Gens McClernand, Smith and Wallace I must do the justice to say that each of them were with their commands in the midst of danger and were always ready to execute all orders no matter what the exposure to themselvs.

At the hour the attack was made on Gen. McClernand's command I was absent, having received a note from Flag Officer Foote requesting me to go and see him he being unable to call in consequence of a wound received the day before

My personal staff, Col. J. T. Webster, Chief of Staff Col. J. Riggin Jr Vol. Aid. Capt. J. A. Rawlins, A. A. Gen. Capts C. B Lagow & W. S. Hillyer Aids, and Lt. Col. J. B. McPherson Chief Engineer all are deserving of personal mention for their gallantry and services.

For full details see reports of Engineers, Medical Director and Commanders of Brigades & Divisions to follow.

> I am Gen. very respectfully
> your obt. svt.
> U. S. GRANT
> Brig. Gen

To Julia Dent Grant

Head Quarters, Fort Donelson Ten.
Feb.y 16th 1862

Dear Wife

I am most happy to write you from this very strongly fortified place, now in my possession, after the greatest victory of
the season. Some 12 or 15 thousand prisoners have fallen into
our possession to say nothing of 5 to 7 thousand that escaped
in the darkness of the night last night.

This is the largest capture I believe ever made on the continent.

You warn me against Capt. Kountz. He can do me no
harm. He is known as a venimous man whose hand is raised
against every man and is without friends or influance.***
—My impression is that I shall have one hard battle more to
fight and will find easy sailing after that. No telling though.
This was one of the most desperate affairs fought during this
war. Our men were out three terrible cold nights and fighting
through the day, without tents. Capt. Hillyer will explain all
to you. Kiss the children for me. I will direct my next letter to
Covington.

ULYS.

To Julia Dent Grant

Fort Donelson, Feb. 24th 1862.

Dear Julia,

I have just returned from Clarkesville. Yesterday some citizens of Nasville come down there ostensibly to bring surgeons to attend their wounded at that place but in reality no
doubt to get assurances that they would not be molested.
Johnson with his army of rebels have fallen back about forty
miles south from Nashville leaving the river clear to our
troops To-day a Division of Gen. Buells Army reported to
me for orders. As they were on Steamers I ordered them immediately up to Nashville. "Secesh" is now about on its last

legs in Tennessee. I want to push on as rapidly as possible to save hard fighting. These terrible battles are very good things to read about for persons who loose no friends but I am decidedly in favor of having as little of it as possible. The way to avoid it is to push forward as vigorously as possible.

Gen. Halleck is clearly the same way of thinking and with his clear head I think the Congressional Committee for investigating the Conduct of the War will have nothing to enquire about in the West.

I am writing you in great haste a boat being about leaving here. I will write you often to make up for the very short letters I send.

Give my love to all at home and write frequently. Tell me all about the children. I want to see rascal Jess already. Tell Mary she must write to me often. Kiss the children for me and the same for yourself

ULYS.

To Julia Dent Grant

Fort Donelson, Feby. 26th, 1862.

Dear Julia:

I am just starting to Nashville and will drop you a line before starting. Gen. Buell is there, or at least a portion of his command is, and I want to have an interview with the comdg. officer and learn what I can of the movements of the enemy. I shall be back here to-morrow evening and remain until some movement takes place. Since my promotion some change may take place in my command, but I do not know. I want however to remain in the field and be actively employed. But I shall never ask a favor or change. Whatever is ordered I will do independantly and as well as I know how. If a command inferior to my rank is given me it shall make no difference in my zeal. In spite of enemies, I have so far progressed satisfactorily to myself and the country and in reviewing the past can see but few changes that could have bettered the result. Perhaps I have done a little too much of the office duties and thereby lost time that might have been better employed in inspecting and reviewing troops.

I want to hear from you. I have not had a word since you left Cairo. My clothing &c. came up all right except the saddle cover. Do you know anything about it? Those covers cost $30 00 and I shall be compelled to buy another if that one is lost. I have written to Gen. Cullum to look it up. I am anxious to get a letter from Father to see his criticisms. I see his paper the Gazette gets off whole numbers without mentioning my name   That paper and the Cincinnati Commercial for some reason inexplicable to me have always apparently been my enemies   It never disturbed me however

Give my love to all at home. I write to you so often that you must be satisfied with short letters.

ULYS.

To Julia Dent Grant

Fort Henry Mach 11th/62

My Dear Julia,

I am just going down to Paducah looking after the interest of the expedition now gone up the Tennessee. Soon more troops will join us then I will go in command of the whole. What you are to look out for I cannot tell you but you may rely upon it that your husband will never disgrace you nor leave a defeated field. We all volunteered to be killed, if needs be, and whilst any of us are living there should be no feeling other than we are so far successful. This is my feeling and believe it is well inculcated among the troops.

My dear Julia I have but little idea from what point I shall next write you. If I knew I would hardly tell but I hope another mark will be made against rebelion.

There is a greatdeel that might be said, in a Military way, but that cannot be properly discussed. If I was ahead of the telegraph however I might say that I believe that I have the whole Tennessee river, to Florance Alabama, safe from any immediate attack. The enemy have preserved one Gunboat, the Dunbar, and may have run her up some creek, during the present high water, to bring out and destroy our transports. That would be my policy yet I do not think it has been adopted. Of course the steamer would be lost but she is lost anyhow and individuals should never take that into account.—We have such an inside track of the enemy that by following up our success we can go anywhere. To counteract us Tennessee at least is trying to bring out all her men. She is doing so so much against the feeling of the men themselvs that within my limited sphere I am giving all the protection possible to prevent forced enlistments. I have written you a military letter when only my love and kisses to the children, and to yourself, was intended. Tell Mary that her last letter was received and she must continue to write. Some day I will find a chance of answering

ULYS.

To Julia Dent Grant

Savanna Tennessee
March 18th 1862

My Dear Julia,

You will see by the above that I am far up South in the State of Ten. When you will hear of another great and important strike I cant tell you but it will be a big lick so far as numbers engaged is concerned. I have no misgivings myself as to the result and you must not feel the slightest alarm.—It is now 3 O'Clock in the morning but as a boat will be going down to-morrow and having just arrived I will have to much to do to write private letters in the morning. We got here about 4 O'Clock in the afternoon and I had necessarily many orders to write.

There is a strong manifestation of Union feeling in this section. Already some 500 have come in voluntarily and enlisted to prevent being drafted on the other side. Many more have come in to get the protection of our army for the same purpose.—With one more great success I do not see how the rebellion is to be sustained. War matters however must be an uninteresting subject to you so I will close on that.—I have been poorly for several weeks but began to feel better the very moment of arriving where there is so much to do and where it is so important that I should be able to do it.

I will try and have you hear from me often but it will not be possible to communicate as often as heretofore. I'm getting further from home. You are spending a pleasant time in Covington are you not? I should love very much to be there a day or two with you and the children. Does Jess talk of his pa? Kiss all the children for me and give my love to all at home.

Good night dear Julia.

ULYS.

To Elihu B. Washburne

Savanna, Tennessee
March 22d 1862.

Hon. E. B. Washburn
Washington D. C.
Dear Sir:

I have received two or three letters from you which I have not answered, because, at the time they were received I was unwell, and busy, and because at the time they were received either your brother or Rowley were about writing. I am now getting nearly well and ready for any immergency that may arise. A severe contest may be looked for in this quarter before many weeks, but of the result feel no alarm.

There are some things which I wish to say to you in my own vindication, not that I care one straw for what is said, individually, but because you have taken so much interest in my wellfare that I think you entitled to all facts connected with my acts.

I see by the papers that I am charged with giving up a certain number of slaves captured at Fort Donelson!

My published order on the occation shows that citizens were not permitted to pass through our camps to look for their slaves. There were some six or seven negroes at Donelson who represented that they had been brought from Ky. to work for officers, and had been kept a number of months without receiving pay. They expressed great anxiety to get back to their families and protested that they were free men. These I let go and none others.—I have studiously tried to prevent the running off of negroes from all outside places as I have tried to prevent all other marauding and plundering.

So long as I hold a commission in the Army I have no views of my own to carry out. Whatever may be the orders of my superiors, and law, I will execute. No man can be efficient as a commander who sets his own notions above law and those whom he is sworn to obey. When Congress enacts anything too odious for me to execute I will resign.

I see the credit of attacking the enemy by the way of the Tennessee and Cumberland is variously attributed! It is little to talk about it being the great wisdom of any Gen. that first brought forth this plan of attack.

Our gunboats were running up the Ten. and Cumberland rivers all fall and winter watching the progress of the rebels on these works. Gen. Halleck no doubt thought of this route long ago and I am shure I did. As to how the battles should be fought both McClellan and Halleck are too much of soldiers to suppose that they can plan how that should be done at a distance. This would presuppose that the enemy would make just the moves laid down for them. It would be a game of Chess the right hand against the left determining before hand that the right should win.

The job being an important one neither of the above Generals would have entrusted it to an officer who they had not confidance in. So far I was highly complimented by both.

After geting into Donelson Gen. Halleck did not hear from me for near two weeks. It was about the same time before I heard from him. I was writing every day and sometimes as often as three times a day. Reported every move and change, the condition of my troops &c. Not getting these Gen. Halleck very justly become dissatisfied and was, as I have since learned, sending me daily reprimands. Not receiving them they lost their sting. When one did reach me not seeing the justice of it I retorted and asked to be relieved. Three telegrams passed in this way each time ending by my requesting to be relieved. All is now understood however and I feel assured that Gen. Halleck is fully satisfied. In fact he wrote me a letter saying that I could not be relieved and otherwise quite complimentary. I will not tire you with a longer letter but assure you again that you shall not be disappointed in me if it is in my power to prevent it.

> I am sir, very respectfully
> your obt. svt.
> U. S. GRANT

To Julia Dent Grant

Savanna, March 23d/62

Dear Julia,

Two letters from you are just received. One of them a business letter and the other not. You do not say a word about the $700 00 I sent you since you left Cairo. I see plainly from your letter that it will be impossible for you to stay in Covington. Such unmittigated meanness as is shown by the girls makes me ashamed of them. You may go to Columbus and board or to Galena and keep house. It will be impossible for you to join me. It will be but a short time before I shall be in the tented field, *without a tent*, and after the enemy.

What the papers say about relieving me is all a falshood. For some reason to me entirely inexplicable Gen. Halleck did not hear from me for about two weeks after the fall of Donelson, nor did I hear from him for about the same time. I was writing daily and sometimes two or three times a day and the Gen. doing the same. At last a repremand come for not reporting as I had been frequently ordered.

I replied sharply that that was the first order I had but to relieve me. Gen. Halleck declined though he said my course had caused him to be repremanded from Washington. As I had been reporting daily I stated so and again asked to be relieved, and so again for the third time. All was understood however afterwards and though I say it myself I believe that I am the very last man in the Dept. Gen. Halleck would want to see taken out of it. Through some misrepresentations of jealous and disappointed persons, not belonging with my Army, false rumors were set afloat about what was done with captured property. I done all in my power to prevent any of it being carried off. I had sentinels placed to prevent it being carried aboard of boats, and send persons aboard of boats leaving to search and bring off all captured property they could find. This maddened the rascals engaged in the business and as much escaped my vigilence they have no doubt given currency to reports prejudicial to me. I am so consious of having done all things right myself that I borrow no trouble from the lies published. I say I dont care for what the papers say but I do. It annoys me very much when I see such barefaced falshoods published and then it distresses you.

I want to whip these rebels once more in a big fight and see what will then be said. I suppose such a result would make me a host of enemies.

I wrote to you last night and Capt. Lagow wrote the night before. Some day a big lot of letters will be turning up as I write from two to four letters a week.

If you go to Columbus to spend the summer put the children to school at once. I am sorry you cannot stay in Covington pleasantly for it is such a good place for the children. But it is too mortifying to me to hear of my sisters complaining about the amount paid for the board of their brothers children. If I should name the subject of board for one of them I could not raise my head again. How much better it would appear if they should never say a word on the subject. It would cost nothing either for them to hold their tongues.

You had better leave at once for some place. Tell them I direct it and the reason why.

Kiss the children for me and accept the same for yourself. It looks now as if the first place you could join me would be far down in Dixie.

ULYS.

To Henry W. Halleck

Savanna, March 24th 1862

Maj. Gen. H. W. Halleck
Comd.g Dept. of the Miss.
St. Louis Mo.
Gen.

Your letter enclosing correspondence between yourself and Adj. Gen. Thomas is just received. In regard to the plundering at Fort Donelson it is very much overestimated by disappointed persons who failed in getting off the trophies they had gathered. My orders of the time show that I did all in my power to prevent marauding. To execute these orders I kept a company on duty searching boats about leaving and to bring off all captured property found.

My great difficulty was with the rush of citizens, particularly the sanitary committee, who infested Donelson after its fall. They thought it an exceedingly hard case that patriotic gentleman like themselvs, who had gone to tender their services to the sick and wounded could not carry off what they pleased. Most of the wounded had reached hospitals before these gentlemen left Cairo. One of these men, a Dr. Fowler of Springfield, swore vengeance against me for this very act, of preventing trophies being carried off. How many more did the same thing I cant tell.

My going to Nashville I did not regard particularly as going beyond my District. After the fall of Donelson from information I had I knew that the way was clear to Clarkesville & Nashville. Accordingly I wrote to you, directed to your Chief of Staff, as was all my correspondence from the time of leaving Fort Henry until I learned you were not hearing from me, that by Friday following the fall of Donelson I should occupy Clarkesville, and by Saturday week following should be in Nashville if not prevented by orders from Hd Qrs. of the Dept. During all this time not one word was received from you and I accordingly occupied Clarkesville on the day indicated and two days after the time I was to occupy Nashville Gen. Nelson reported to me with a Division of Buell's Army. They being already on transports and knowing that Buells Column should have arrived opposite Nashville the day before, and having no use for these troops myself I ordered them immediately to Nashville.

It is perfectly plain to me that designing enemies are the cause of all the publications that appear and are the means of getting extracts sent to you. It is also a little remarkable that the Adj. Gen. should learn of my presence in Nashville before it was known in St. Louis where I reported that I was going before starting.

I do not feel that I have neglected a single duty. My reports to you have averaged at least one a day since leaving Cairo and there has been scarsely a single day that I have not either written or telegraphed to Hd Qrs.

I most fully appreciate your justness Gen. in the part you have taken and you may rely upon me to the utmost of my capacity for carrying out all your orders.

> I Am Gen. very respectfully
> your obt. svt.
> U. S. GRANT
> Maj. Gen. Com

To Julia Dent Grant

Savanna, March 29th 1862

Dear Julia,

I am again fully well. I have had the Diaoreah for several weeks and an inclination to Chills & Fever. We are all in *statu qua*. Dont know when we will move. Troops are constantly arriving so that I will soon have a very large army. A big fight may be looked for someplace before a great while which it appears to me will be the last in the West. This is all the time supposing that we will be successful which I never doubt for a single moment.

I heard of your arrival at Louisville several days ago through some Steamboat Capt. and before your letter was received stating that you would start the next day.

All my Staff are now well though most of them have suf-

fered same as myself. Rawlins & myself both being very unwell at the same time made our labors hard upon us. All that
were with me at Cairo are with me here, substuting Dr.
Brinton for Dr. Simons, and in addition Capt. Hawkins &
Capt. Rowley. Rowley has also been very unwell. Capt. Hillyer will probably return home and go to Washington. His
position on my Staff is not recognized and he will have to
quit or get it recognized.

Capt. Brinck is in the same category. All the slanders you
have seen against me originated away from where I was. The
only foundation was from the fact that I was ordered to remain at Fort Henry and send the expedition under command
of Maj. Gen. Smith. This was ordered because Gen. Halleck
received no report from me for near two weeks after the fall
of Fort Donelson. The same occured with me I received
nothing from him. The consequence was I apparently totally
disregarded his orders. The fact was he was ordering me every
day to report the condition of my command, I was not receiving the orders but knowing my duties was reporting daily,
and when anything occured to make it necessary, two or
three times a day. When I was ordered to remain behind it
was the cause of much astonishment among the troops of
my command and also disappointment. When I was again
ordered to join them they showed, I believe, heartfelt
joy. Knowing that for some reason I was relieved of the most
important part of my command the papers began to surmize
the cause, and the Abolition press, the New York Tribune
particularly, was willing to hear to no solution not unfavorable to me. Such men as Kountz busyed themselvs very
much. I never allowed a word of contridiction to go out
from my Head Quarters, thinking this the best course. I know,
though I do not like to speak of myself, that Gen. Halleck
would regard this army badly off if I was relieved. Not
but what there are Generals with it abundantly able to
command but because it would leave inexperienced officers
senior in rank. You need not fear but what I will come out
triumphantly. I am pulling no wires, as political Generals
do, to advance myself. I have no future ambition. My object is to carry on my part of this war successfully and I

am perfectly willing that others may make all the glory they can out of it.

Give my love to all at home. Kiss the children for me.

ULYS.

To Julia Dent Grant

Savanna, April 3d 1862

Dear Julia,

Letters from you drop along occationally, generally two or three at a time; sometimes one will be three weeks old whilst another will come in as many days.

I have received three written from Louisville one of them by Charles Page. I am very glad you are having a pleasant visit. I wish I could make a visit anywhere for a week or two. It would be a great relief not to have to think for a short time. Soon I hope to be permitted to move from here and when I do there will probably be the greatest battle fought of the War. I do not feel that there is the slightest doubt about the result and therefore, individually, feel as unconcerned about it as if nothing more than a review was to take place. Knowing however that a terrible sacrifice of life must take place I feel conserned for my army and their friends at home.

It will be impossible for you to join me at present. There are constantly ladies coming up here to see their husbands and consequencely destroying the efficiency of the army until I have determined to publish an order entirely excluding females from our lines. This is ungallant but necessary.

Mr. & Miss Safford were up here and returned a few days ago. I sent my watch by him to be expressed to you. I want you to keep it and not leave it with anyone els. I sent for a plain silver watch for myself. There would be no great danger in keeping the other but if it should be lost I never could forgive myself. I want to preserve it to the last day of my life, and want my children to do the same thing, in remembrance of poor Simp. who carried it in his lifetime.

Kiss Jess & Buck for me, and your cousin also, I mean the

young lady, if you want. *** Remember me kindly to Uncle & Aunt Page

ULYS.

To William T. Sherman

Head Quarters, Dist of West. Tenn.
Pittsburg, April 4th 1862.

Gen. W. T. Sherman
Commdg 5th Division
Gen:

Information just received would indicate that the enemy are sending a force to Purdy, and it may be with a view to attack Gen. Wallace at Crumps Landing. I have directed Gen. W. H. L. Wallace, Commdg 2nd Division, temporarily, to re-inforce Gen. L. Wallace in case of an attack with his entire Division, although, I look for nothing of the kind, but it is best to be prepared.

I would direct, therefore, that you advise your advance guards to keep a sharp look out for any movement in that direction, and should such a thing be attempted, give all the support of your Division, and Gen. Hurlbut's if necessary. I will return to Pittsburg at an early hour tomorrow, and will ride out to your camp.

I am, Gen, Very Respectfully
Your Obt Servant.
U. S. GRANT.
Major. Gen. Commdg

To Henry W. Halleck

Head Quarters, Dist. of West Ten.
Savanna, April 5th 1862.

Maj. Gen. H. W. Halleck,
Comd.g Dept. of the Miss.
St. Louis, Mo.
Gen.

Just as my letter of yesterday to Capt. McLean, A. A. Gen. was finished notes from Gens. McClernand's & Sherman's

A. A. Gens. were received stating that our outposts had been attacked by the enemy apparently in conciderable force. I immediately went up but found all quiet. The enemy took two officers and four or five of our men prisoners and wounded four. We took eight prisoners and killed several. Number of the enemy wounded not know.

They had with them three pieces of Artillery and Cavalry and Infantry. How much cannot of course be estimated.

I have scarsely the faintest idea of an attack, (general one,) being made upon us but will be prepared should such a thing take place.

Gen. Nelsons Division has arrived. The other two of Gen. Buells Column will arrive to-morrow and next day. It is my present intention to send them to Hamburg, some four miles above Pittsburg, when they all get here. From that point to Corinth the road is good and a junction can be formed with the troops from Pittsburg at almost any point.

Col. McPherson has gone with an escort to-day to examine the defensibility of the ground about Hamburg and to lay out the position of the Camps if advisable to occupy that place.

> I am Gen. very respectfully
> your obt. svt.
> U. S. GRANT
> Maj. Gen.

To Don Carlos Buell

Savanna, April 6th 1862

Gen. D. C. Buell,

Heavy firing is heard up the indicating plainly that an attack has been made upon our most advance positions. I have been looking for this but did not believe the attack could be made before Monday or Teusday.

This necessitates my joining the forces up the river instead of meeting you to-day as I had contemplated.

I have directed Gen. Nelson to move to the river with his Division. He can march to opposite Pittsburg.

> Respectfully your obt. svt.
> U. S. GRANT
> Maj. Gen Com

To Commanding Officer, Advance Forces

Pittsburg, April 6th 1862

Comd.g Officer
Advance Forces Near Pittsburg, Ten.
Gen.

The attack on my forces has been very spirited from early this morning. The appearance of fresh troops on the field now would have a powerful effect both by inspiring our men and disheartining the enemy. If you will get upon the field leaving all your baggage on the East bank of the river it will be a move to our advantage and possibly save the day to us.

The rebel forces is estimated at over 100.000 men.

My Hd Qrs. will be in the log building on top of the hill where you will be furnished a staff officer to guide you to your place on the field.

> Respectfully &c
> U. S. GRANT
> Maj. Gen.

To Henry W. Halleck

BY TELEGRAPH FROM Pittsburgh Tennessee 7th April *1862*
To Maj Gen Halleck

Yesterday the rebels attacked us here with an overwhelming force driving our troops in from their advanced position nearer to the landing—General Wallace was immy. ordered up from Crumps landing and in the evening one division of Buells Army and D C. Buell in person arrived, during the night one other division arrived, and still another today. This

morning at the break of day I ordered an attack which resulted in a fight that continued until late this afternoon with a
very heavy loss on both sides but a complete repulse of the
enemy. I shall follow tomorrow far enough to see that no
immediate renewal of attack is contemplated

U S GRANT

To Henry W. Halleck

BY TELEGRAPH FROM Pittsburg Tenn   *186*
To Maj. Genl. Halleck
Comdg. Dept.

Enemy badly routed & fleeing towards Corinth   Our
Cavalry supported by Infy. are now pursuing him with in-
structions to pursue to the swampy grounds near Pea Ridge.
I want transports sent here for our wounded.

U. S. GRANT

April 8, 1862

To Julia Dent Grant

Pittsburg, Ten. April 8th 1862
Dear Julia,

Again another terrible battle has occured in which our arms
have been victorious. For the number engaged and the tenacity with which both parties held on for two days, during an
incessant fire of musketry and artillery, it has no equal on this
continent. The best troops of the rebels were engaged to the
number of 162 regiments as stated by a deserter from their
camp, and their ablest generals. Beaurigard commanded in
person aided by A. S. Johnson, Bragg, Breckenridge and hosts
of other generals of less note but possibly of quite as much
merit. Gen. Johnson was killed and Bragg wounded. The loss
on both sides was heavy probably not less than 20,000 killed
and wounded altogether. The greatest loss was sustained by
the enemy. They suffered immensly by demoralization also

many of their men leaving the field who will not again be of value on the field.

I got through all safe having but one shot which struck my sword but did not touch me.

I am detaining a steamer to carry this and must cut it short.

Give my love to all at home. Kiss the children for me. The same for yourself.

Good night dear Julia.

ULYS.

To Nathaniel H. McLean

Head Quarters Disct of West Tenn
Pittsburgh April 9th 1862

Capt N H McLean
A A Genl Dept of the Mississippi
Saint Louis. Mo.
Capt

It becomes my duty again to report another battle fought between two great armies, one contending for the maintainance of the best Government ever devised the other for its destruction. It is pleasant to record the success of the army contending for the former principle.

On Sunday morning our pickets were attacked and driven in by the enemy. Immediately the five Divisions stationed at this place were drawn up in line of battle ready to meet them. The battle soon waxed warm on the left and center, varying at times to all parts of the line.

The most continuous firing of musketry and artillery ever heard on this Continent was kept up until night fall, the enemy having forced the entire line to fall back nearly half way from their Camps to the Landing. At a late hour in the afternoon a desperate effort was made by the enemy to turn our left and get possession of the Landing, transports &c. This point was guarded by the Gun boats Tyler and Lexington, Capt's Gwinn & Shirk U S N commanding Four 20 pounder Parrott guns and a battery of rifled guns. As there is a deep and impassable ravine for artillery or Cavalry and very difficult for Infantry at this point. No troops were stationed here except the neccessary Artillerists and a small Infantry force for their support Just at this moment the advance of Maj Genl Buells Column (a part of the Division under Genl Nelson) arrived, the two Generals named both being present. An advance was immediately made upon the point of attack and the enemy soon driven back.

In this repulse much is due to the presence of the Gun boats Tyler and Lexington and their able Commanders Capt Gwinn and Shirk.

During the night the Divisions under Genl Crittenden and McCook arrived. Genl Lew Wallace, at Crumps Landing six miles below, was ordered at an early hour in the morning to hold his Division in readiness to be moved in any direction to which it might be ordered. At about 11 oClock the order was delivered to move it up to Pittsburgh, but owing to its being led by a circuitous route did not arrive in time to take part in Sundays action.

During the night all was quiet, and feeling that a great moral advantage would be gained by becoming the attacking party, an advance was ordered as soon as day dawned. The result was a gradual repulse of the enemy at all parts of the line from morning until probably 5 oClock in the afternoon when it became evident the enemy was retreating. Before the close of the action the advance of Genl T J Woods Division arrived in time to take part in the action.

My force was too much fatigued from two days hard fighting and exposure in the open air to a drenching rain during the intervening night to pursue immediately.

Night closed in cloudy and with heavy rain making the roads impracticable for artillery by the next morning. Genl Sherman however followed the enemy finding that the main part of the army had retreated in good order.

Hospitals of the enemies wounded were found all along the road as far as pursuit was made. Dead bodies of the enemy and many graves were also found.

I enclose herewith report of Genl Sherman which will explain more fully the result of this pursuit.

Of the part taken by each seperate Command I cannot take

special notice in this report, but will do so more fully when reports of Division Commanders are handed in.

Genl Buell, coming on the Field with a distinct army, long under his command, and which did such efficient service, commanded by himself in person on the field, will be much better able to notice those of his command who particularly distinguished themselves than I possibly can.

I feel it a duty however to a gallant and able officer Brig Genl W T Sherman to make special mention. He not only was with his Command during the entire of the two days action, but displayed great judgment and skill in the management of his men. Altho severely wounded in the hand the first day, his place was never vacant. He was again wounded and had three horses killed under him. In making this mention of a gallant officer no disparagement is intended to the other Division Commanders Major Generals John A McClernand and Lew Wallace, and Brig Generals S A Hurlbut, B M. Prentiss and W H L Wallace, all of whom maintained their places with credit to themselves and the cause Genl Prentiss was taken prisoner in the first days action, and Genl W H L Wallace severely, probably mortally wounded. His Ass Adj Genl Capt William McMichael is missing, probably taken prisoner.

My personal Staff are all deserving of particular mention, they having been engaged during the entire two days in conveying orders to every part of the field. It consists of Col J D Webster, Chief of Staff, Lt Col J B McPherson Chief Engineer assisted by Lieuts W L B Jenney and William Kossack, Capt J A Rawlins A A Genl Capts W S Hillyer, W R Rowley and C B Lagow aides-de-Camp Col G. G. Pride Volunteer aide and Capt J P Hawkins Chief Commissary who accompanied me upon the field.

The Medical Department under the direction of Surgeon Hewitt Medical Director, showed great energy in providing for the wounded and in getting them from the field regardless of danger

Col Webster was placed in special charge of all the artillery and was constantly upon the field. He displayed, as always heretofore, both skill and bravery. At least in one instance he was the means of placing an entire Regiment in a position of doing most valuable service, and where it would not have been but for his exertions.

Lt Col McPherson attached to my staff as Chief Engineer deserves more than a passing notice for his activity and courage. All the grounds beyond our Camps for miles have been reconnoitred by him, and plats carefully prepared under his supervision, give accurate information of the nature of approaches to our lines. During the two days battle he was constantly in the saddle leading troops as they arrived to points where their services were required. During the engagement he had one horse shot under him.

The Country will have to mourn the loss of many brave men who fell at the battle of Pittsburgh, or Chilo more properly. The exact loss in killed and wounded will be known in a day or two. At present I can only give it approximately at 1500 killed and 3500 wounded.

The loss of Artillery was great, many pieces being disabled by the enemies shots and some loosing all their horses and many men. There was probably not less than two hundred horses killed.

The loss of the enemy in killed and left upon the field was greater than ours. In wounded the estimate cannot be made as many of them must have been sent back to Corinth and other points.

The enemy suffered terribly from demorilization and desertion. A flag of Truce was sent in to day from Genl Beaurigard. I enclose herewith a copy of the Correspondence.

I am. Very Respectfully
Your Obt Servt
U. S. GRANT
Major General Comdg

To Jesse Root Grant

Pittsburg Landing, Tenn., April 26, 1862.

I will go on, and do my duty to the very best of my ability, without praise, and do all I can to bring this war to a speedy close. I am not an aspirant for any thing at the close of the war.

There is one thing I feel well assured of; that is, that I have the confidence of every brave man in my command. Those who showed the white feather will do all in their power to attract attention from themselves. I had perhaps a dozen officers arrested for cowardice in the first day's fight at this place. These men are necessarily my enemies.

As to the talk about a surprise here, nothing could be more false. If the enemy had sent us word when and where they would attack us, we could not have been better prepared. Skirmishing had been going on for two days between our reconnoitering parties and the enemy's advance. I did not believe, however, that they intended to make a determined attack, but simply that they were making a reconnoisance in force.

My headquarters were in Savannah, though I usually spent the day here. Troops were constantly arriving to be assigned to brigades and divisions, all ordered to report at Savannah, making it necessary to keep an office and some one there. I was also looking for Buell to arrive, and it was important that I should have every arrangement complete for his speedy transit to this side of the river.

U. S. GRANT.

To Mrs. Charles F. Smith

Pittsburg Landing Tenn
April 26th 1862

Mrs C F Smith
No 191 East 4th St New York

It becomes my painful duty to announce to you the death of your lamented husband Major General Charles F Smith. He died at 4 Oclock P M yesterday at Savanna Tennessee

In his death the nation has lost one of its most gallant and most able defenders

It was my fortune to have gone through West Point with the Gen. (then Captain & Commandant of Cadets) and to have served with him in all his battles in Mexico, And in this rebellion, And I can bear honest testimony to his great worth as a soldier and friend. Where an entire nation condoles with you in your bereavement. no one can do so with more heart-felt grief than myself

> Very Truly Yours
> U S GRANT
> Maj Genl.

To Julia Dent Grant

Camp in the Field
Near Pittsburg Ten.
April 30th 1862

Dear Julia,

I move from here to-morrow. Before this reaches you prob-ably another battle, and I think the last big one, will have taken place or be near at hand. I mean the last in the Missis-sippi Valley and this of course implies if we are successful which no doubt we will be. You need give yourself no trouble about newspaper reports. They will all be understood and me come out all right without a single contradiction. Most or all that you have seen has been written by persons who were not here and thos few items collected from persons nominally present, eye witnesses, was from those who disgraced them-selvs and now want to draw off public attention. I am very sorry to say a greatdeel originates in jealousy. This is very far from applying however, I think, to our Chief, Halleck, who I look upon as one of the greatest men of the age. You enquire how I was hurt? For several days before the battle of Pitts-burg our out Pickets were skirmishing with the enemies ad-vance. I would remain up here all day and go back to Savanna in the evening where I was anxiously looking for the advance of Gen. Buell's column. My object was, if possible, to keep off an attack until Buell arrived otherwise I would have gone out and met the enemy on Friday before they could have got in position to use all their forces advantageously. Friday evening I went back to Savanna as usual and soon after dark a messenger arrived informing that we were attacked. I immediately returned here and started out onto the field on horseback, my staff with me. The night was intensely dark. I soon found that the firing had seased and started to go back to the river. Being very dark and in the woods we had to ride in a slow walk and at that got off the road. In geting back to it my horse's foot either cought or struck something and he fell flat on his side with my leg under him. Being wet and muddy I was not hurt much at the time but being in the saddle all of Sunday and Monday, and in the rain the intervening night without taking off boots or spurs my ancle swelled terribly and kept me on crutches for several days, unable to get on a boot. Col. Riggin is not with me. The rest of the gentlemen are. In addition I have Col. McPherson of the regular Army and one of the nicest gentleman you ever saw, Capt. Reynolds, regular, Lieuts Bowers & Rowley. We are all well and me as sober as a deacon no matter what is said to the contrary. Mrs. Turner & Miss Hadley run on the steamer Memphis carrying sick soldiers to hospital. As I am out from the river and they are only here about one day in eight or ten I rarely see them. There are no inhabitants here atall

Kiss all the children for me. Tell Jess I have a five shooter pistol for him. When you hear of me being on the Mississippi river join me leaving all the children except Jess. Draw the hundred dollars you have as a matter of course. If I had an opportunity I would send you $200 oo now. Give my love to all at home. Kisses for yourself.

Good buy
ULYS.

To Elihu B. Washburne

Camp Near Corinth, Miss.
May 14th 1862

Hon. E. B. Washburn,
Dear Sir:

The great number of attacks made upon me by the press of the country is my apology for not writing to you oftener, not desiring to give any contradiction to them myself.—You have interested yourself so much as my friend that should I say anything it would probably be made use of in my behalf. I would scorn being my own defender against such attacks except through the record which has been kept of all my official acts and which can be examined at Washington at any time.

To say that I have not been distressed at these attacks upon me would be false, for I have a father, mother, wife & children who read them and are distressed by them and I necessarily share with them in it. Then too all subject to my orders read these charges and it is calculated to weaken their confidance in me and weaken my ability to render efficient service in our present cause. One thing I will assure you of however; I can not be driven from rendering the best service within my ability to suppress the present rebellion, and when it is over retiring to the same quiet it, the rebellion, found me enjoying.

Notoriety has no charms for me and could I render the same services that I hope it has been my fortune to render our just cause, without being known in the matter, it would be infinately prefferable to me.

Those people who expect a field of battle to be maintained, for a whole day, with about 30,000 troops, most of them entirely raw, against 70,000, as was the case at Pittsburg Landing, whilst waiting for reinforcements to come up, without loss of life, know little of War. To have left the field of Pittsburg for the enemy to occupy until our force was sufficient to have gained a bloodless victory would have been to left the Tennessee to become a second Potomac.—There was nothing left for me but to occupy the West bank of the Tennessee and to hold it at all hazards. It would have set this war back six months to have failed and would have caused the necessity of raising, as it were, a new Army.

Looking back at the past I cannot see for the life of me any important point that could be corrected.—Many persons who have visited the different fields of battle may have gone away displeased because they were not permitted to carry off horses, fire arms, or other valuables as trophies. But they are no patriots who would base their enmity on such grounds. Such I assure you are the grounds of many bitter words that have been said against me by persons who at this day would not know me by sight yet profess to speak from a personal acquaintance.

I am sorry to write such a letter, infinately sorry that there should be grounds for it. My own justification does not demand it, but you, a friend, are entitled to know my feelings.

As a friend I would be pleased to give you a record, weekly at furthest, of all that transpires in that portion of the army that I am, or may be, connected with, but not to make public use of.

I am very truly Yours
U. S. GRANT.

To Julia Dent Grant

Corinth Miss.
June 12th 1862

Dear Julia

It is bright and early (before the morning mail leaves) and I thought to write you that in a few days, Monday the 16th probably, I would leave here. I hope to be off on Monday for Memphis and if so want you to join me there. I will write again however just before starting and it may be will have arranged to go after you instead of you coming by yourself.— I would love most dearly to get away from care for a week or two.

I am very well. This is apparently an exceedingly fine climate and one to enjoy health in.—Citizens are begining to return to Corinth and seem to think the Yankees a much less bloody, revengeful and to be dreaded people, than they had been led to think.

In my mind there is no question but that this war could be ended at once if the whole Southern people could express their unbiased feeling untramelled by by leaders. The feeling is kept up however by crying out Abolitionest against us and this is unfortunately sustained by the acts of a very few among us.—There has been instances of negro stealing, persons going to the houses of farmers who have remained at home, being inclined to Union sentiments, and before their eyes perswaid their blacks to mount up behind them and go off. Of course I can trace such conduct to no individual but believe the guilty parties have never heard the whistle of a single bullet nor intentionally never will.

Give my love to all at home. Kisses for yourself and children.

Your husband
ULYS.

To Henry W. Halleck

Memphis Tenn July 8 /62

Maj Gen Halleck

I commenced gathering contrabands last Saturday to work on fortifications They are now at work. On account of the limited force here we are only fortifying south end of city to protect stores & our own troops. Col Webster has been too unwell to push this matter & I have no other engineer.

Secessionists here have news from Richmond by the South which makes them jubilant. I would like to hear the truth

U S. GRANT
Maj Gen

July 7, 1862

To Salmon P. Chase

Head Qrs Disct of West Tenn
Corinth, Miss. July 31, 1862

To Hon S P Chase
Secretary of the Treasury
Washington, D. C.
Sir

Large quantities of salt flour, liquors and other articles of use and luxury are being shipped by the way of the Tennessee river and other lines of communication, to different points within our lines. It is presumed that these come under authority of regular permits from agents of the Treasury Department, and that the trade is so far legitimate. The collateral smuggling that goes on undoubtedly to a large extent is another matter not now under notice. It is however a very grave question in my mind whether this policy of "letting trade follow the flag" is not working injuriously to the Union Cause. Practically and really I think it is benefitting almost exclusively, first, a class of greedy traders whose first and only desire is gain, and to whom it would be idle to attribute the least patriotism, and secondly our enemies south of our lines. The quantities in which these goods are shipped clearly intimate that they are intended to be worked off into the enemys country thus administering to him the most essential "aid and comfort." Our lines are so extended that it is impossible for any military surveillance to contend successfully with the cunning of the traders, aided by the local knowledge and eager interest of the residents along the border. The enemy are thus receiving supplies of most necessary and useful articles which relieve their sufferings and strengthens them for resistance to our authority; while we are sure that the benefits thus conferred, tend in no degree to abate their rancorous hostility to our flag and Government. If any hopes have been entertained that a liberal commercial policy might have a conciliatory effect, I fear they will not be realized. The method of correcting the evil which first suggests itself is restriction of the quantity of these articles which may be allowed to be shipped under one invoice, together with more careful investigation of the loyalty of persons permitted to trade. Very limited amounts will be sufficient to supply the wants of the truly loyal men of the Districts within our lines, for unfortunately they are not numerous, and outside (south) of our lines, I fear it is little better than a unanimous rebellion. The evil is a great and growing one, and needs immediate attention.

I am sir, your obt. svt
U. S. GRANT
Maj. Gen. Com

Fragment on Shiloh

I cannot close this report without paying particular attention to the report of Brig. Gen (now Maj. Gen.) Nelson,

commanding the 4th Division of the Army of the Ohio. Not
having seen the report until within a few days attention could
not be paid it before.—The report is a tissue of unsupported
romance from begining to end some of which I will point
out.—Gen. Nelson says that "I left Savanna at 1.30 p.m. on
Sunday the 6th by my order, reiterated by Gen. Buell." My
order was given Gen. Nelson not later than 7 O'clock, must
have reached him not later than that hour, and was accompanied by a guide to show him the road. If not much mistaken
the most of his Division must have been on the march before
the arrival of Gen. Buell at Savanna. To say the least he
showed great want of promptness in not leaving Savanna
until 1.30 p.m. after receiving my orders and they given at so
early an hour.

In the second paragraph four days are mentioned as the
time consumed in making the march over most dreadful roads
resulting from previously overflowed bottoms. Four hours
were probably intended. Taking this charitable view of the
matter the head of his column had made the distance from
Savanna to Pittsburg Landing, had made the difficult fer-
rage at that point and were marching up the bank in just 30
minuets less time than the Gen.'s own statements show, that
through great exertion, and anxiety to participate in a battle
which they heard raging, took to march up the East bank of
the river.

The fire of the rebel artillery began to reach the landing
after the head of Gen. Nelsons column had assended the hill
at Pittsburg Landing.

The semicircle of artillery spoken of had been established at
an early hour in the day and were not unsupported at any
time. The left of the artillery spoken of was not turned at any
time and the abrupt nature of the ground and depth of back-
water in the slew immediately in front of the artillery would
have completely checked any attempt at such a movement.
The gunners never fled from their pieces.

The Gen. shows great fluancy in guessing at the large numbers he found cowering under the river bank when he crossed
placing the number at from 7000 to 10,000. I cannot see that
he was called on to make any report in this matter but if
he did he should have informed himself somewhat of the

necessity of men taking that position. He should recollect that large armies had been engaged in a terrible conflict all day compared with which the second days fight was mere childs play, and that the wounded were habitually carried back to the bank of the river. With them necessarily had to come men as nurses and supports who were not injured. This made a very large number; nearly equal to the Generals speculation who were back there lagitimately. In this I do not wish to shield the conduct of many who behaved badly and left the field on the first fire. Some excuse is to be found for them however, in the fact that they were perfectly raw having reached the ground but a few days before and having received their arms for the first time on their way to that scene of conflict.

Gen. Nelson claims to have directed Capt. Guinn of the gunboat service to throw an 8-inch shell in to the enemies camp every ten minuets during the night. This was great presumption in him if true his command being limited to a single division. The fact is I directed the gunboats to fire a shot into where we supposed the enemies camps to be every fifteen minuets and this is the order which was obeyed.

These are some of the glaring misstatements I would call attention. There are others with regard to who gave orders simply personal to myself which I abstain from noticing.

The statement of the killing of Gen. Johnson in front of the 4th Division of the Army of the Ohio on the 7th and of his body being in possession of the Federal troops might be mentioned. Southern official reports show that he was killed at about ½ past 2 O'clock on the day previous and was buried by his own friends.

August–September 1862?

To Jesse Root Grant

Corinth Mississippi
September 17th 1862

Dear Father,

A letter from you and one from Mary was received some time ago which I commenced answer in a letter addressed to

Mary, but being frequently interrupted by matters of business it was laid aside for some days, and finally torn up.—I now have all my time taxed. Although occupying a position attracting but little attention at this time there is probably no garrison more threatened to-day than this.

I expect to hold it and have never had any other feeling either here or elswhere but that of success. I would write you many particulars but you are so imprudent that I dare not trust you with them; and while on this subject let me say a word. I have not an enemy in the world who has done me so much injury as you in your efforts in my defence. I require no defenders and for my sake let me alone. I have heard this from various sources and persons who have returned to this Army and did not know that I had parents living near Cincinnati have said that they found the best feeling existing towards every place except there. You are constantly denouncing other General officers and the inference with people naturally is that you get your impressions for me.

Do nothing to correct what you have already done but for the future keep quiet on this subject.

Mary wrote to me about an appointment for Mr. Nixon! I have nothing in the world to do with any appointments, no power to make and nothing to do with recommending except for my own Staff. That is now already full.

If I can do anthing in the shape of lending any influence I may possess in Mr. Nixons behalf I will be most happy to do so on the strength of what Mary says in commendation, and should be most happy if it could so be that our lot would cast us near each other.

I do not know what Julia is going to do. I want her to go to Detroit and board. She has many pleasant acquaintances there and she would find good schools for the children.

I have no time for writing and scarsely to look over the telegraphic columns of the newspapers.

My love to all at home.

ULYS.

To Stephen A. Hurlbut

By Telegraph from Lagrange   *9 1862*

To Maj Gen Hurlbut

Refuse all permits to come south of Jackson for the present The Isrealites especially should be kept out   what troops have you now exclusive of stevensons brigade

U S Grant

Maj Genl

November 9, 1862

To Jesse Root Grant

Lagrange Ten.
Nov. 23d 1862

Dear Father,

A batch of letters from Covington, and among them one from you is just received.

I am only sorry your letter, and all that comes from you speaks so condescendingly of every thing Julia says, writes or thinks. You without probably being aware of it are so prejudiced against her that she could not please you. This is not pleasing to me.

Your letter speaks of Fred.s illness. Fred is a big stout looking boy but he is not healthy. The difference that has always been made between him and the other children has had a very bad influence on him. He is sensitive and notices these things. I hope no distinction will be made and he will in time recover from his diffidence caused by being scolded so much.

I wish you would have a bottle of Cod liver oil bought and have Fred. take a table spoonful three times a day in part of a glass of ale each dose. Dr. Pope of St. Louis says that he requires that treatment every little while and will continue to do so whilst he is growing. One of Mary's letters asks me for some explaination, about the Iuka battle. You can say that my report of that battle, and also of Corinth & the Hatchee went to Washington several weeks ago and I suppose will be printed. These will answer her question fully.

Before you receive this I will again be in motion. I feel every confidance of success but I know that a heavy force is now to my front. If it is my good fortune to come out successfully I will try and find time to write Mary a long letter.

Julia joins me in sending love to all of you.

ULYSSES.

To John C. Pemberton

Head Quarters, 13th Army Corps.
Dept of the Tennessee.
Oxford, Miss. Dec 14, 1862

Lieut. Gen. Pemberton,
Commdg Confederate Forces
Jackson, Tenn.
Genl:

Your communication in relation to the case of Col. Hedgepath is just received.

I did not even know that Col. Hedgepath was in the Hospital at Memphis and cannot answer as to the misfortunes that may possibly have befallen him in the way of losses sustained. Where there are large Armies, and particularly in large cities, there are always persons ready to *steal* where there is an opportunity occurs and especially have many of our Federal troops who have been so unfortunate as to fall into the hands of the Southern Army found this true.

As to the other, or any other bad treatment towards Col. Hedgepath you will find, when the facts are before you he has received none.

All prisoners of War are humanely treated by the Federal authorities and many a wounded or sick soldier has remonstrated against being sent back for exchange on the ground that the treatment received at the hands of the Union authorities was so much better than they could get among what they denominated their friends.

All prisoners who desire it are sent by the first opportunity that occurs to Vicksburg for exchange. Sick and wounded are paroled in Hospital and as soon as able to travel are furnished passes out of our lines, or are sent with other prisoners to the Depot agreed upon for exchange.

Unless there is some good reason for it Col. Hedgepath has not nor will not be made an exception to the rule

> I am, Sir, Very Respectfully
> Your Obt. Servant.
> U. S. GRANT
> Maj Genl.

To Henry W. Halleck

Head Quarters, Dept. of the Ten.
Before Vicksburg, Feb.y 18th 1863.

Maj. Gen. H. W. Halleck,
Gen. in Chief, Washington D. C.
Gen.

The work upon the canal here is progressing as well as possible with the excessively bad weather and high water we have had to contend against. Most of the time that troops could be out atall has been expended in keeping the water out of our camps. Five good working days would enable the force here to complete the canal sixty feet wide and of sufficient depth to admit any vessel here. Judging from the past it is fare to calculate that it will take ten or twelve days in which to get these five working days. Three more perhaps should be allowed from the fact that the work is being done by soldiers the most of whom under the most favorable circumstances could not come up to the calculations of the Engineer officers. McPherson's Army Corps is at Lake Providence prossecuting the work there. They could not be of any service in helping on the work here because there are already as many men as can be employed on it, and then he would have to go five or six miles above to find land above water to encamp on. I am using a few hundred contrabands on the work here, but have been compelled to prohibit any more coming in. Humanity dictates this policy. Planters have mostly deserted their plantations taking with them all their able bodied negroes and leaving the old and very young. Here they could not have shelter nor assurances of transportation when we leave.

I have sent one Division of troops from Helena to join the Yazoo expedition under Lt. Col. Wilson. Col. Wilson's last report was sent you a few days ago. If successful they will destroy the rail-road bridges at Grenada and capture or destroy all the transports in the Yazoo and tributaries.

The health of this command is not what is represented in the public press. It is as good as any previous calculation could have prognosticated. I believe too there is the best of feeling and greatest confidance of success among them. The greatest draw back to the spirits of the troops has been the great delay in paying them. Many of them have families at home who are no doubt in a suffering condition for want of the amounts due those bound for their support.

I am Gen. very respectfully
your obt. svt.
U. S. GRANT
Maj. Gen. Com

To David D. Porter

Feb.y 26th 1863.

Admiral,

I have changed the signal to the following. One rocket will denote the presence, in sight, of a rebel boat; two guns the presence of more than one. The same signals with the addition of a single gun that they are passing up stream above Warrenton and rapid firing that they are passing the batteries. Three rockets will indicate that rebel boats have turned back and followed by a single gun afterwards that. they have come to anchor below. Entire silence after three rockets will indicate that they have passed out of sight.

Very respectfully
U. S. GRANT
Maj. Gen.

To Isaac F. Quinby

Before Vicksburgh March 23d 1863

Brig Gen J. F. Quinby
Comm'dg. Yazoo Expedition

Learning of the slow progress in getting small steamers suitable for your expedition, I wrote to Gen McPherson to collect all of his forces not already in the Yazoo Pass and bring them to where he is.

Since sending this order I have learned of the arrival of a number of small boats at Helena and the probability that Smith's Division had started. As he may have made a start but not got so far but what orders could readily be sent for his return I hasten to change this and will instruct Gen Prentiss if Smith has gone to let him go. You will understand from Prentiss at the same time you receive this what force you are to expect. It is highly desirable that your expedition should clear out the Yazoo river and if possible effect a a lodgment from which we could act against Haines Bluff. You will be the best judge whether this can be done. You will also have to be governed by the disposition of the Navy to co-operate. We cannot order them but only ask their co-operation. I leave to you judgment to say whether the expedition with you should return from Greenwood or prosecute the attack further   It may be necessary for you to take more or less supplies from the citizens along the route but in doing so prevent all the plundering and destruction of property you can and only permit such things to be taken as are actually required for the use of the Army. Admiral Porter started about one week ago to try and reach the Yazoo river below Yazoo City with five Gunboats. His route was by way of Yazoo river to Steele's Bayou up the latter to Black Bayou through that to Deer Creek and up it to Rolling Fork thence across to Big Sunflower and down the Sunflower to the Yazoo. I sent Sherman with an army force of about equal to yours to co-operate. If successful they will come in below the enemy you contending against and between the two forces you would find no further difficulty before reaching the ground I so much desire. I have not heard from this expedition for several days. At last accounts they had got up Deer Creek but had not got through Rolling

Fork I cannot promise success to this expedition but it is possible that if it does get through such consternation will be created among the inhabitants and the troops on the Yazoo that you will hear of it. Feeling great anxiety for your success or speedy return if the object of the expedition shall prove impraticable

U S GRANT
Maj Genl

P. S. If not sanguine of success return immediately with your entire force and fleet. Banks is at Port Hudson but he writes with a force inadequate to the task. If I now had the forces in the Yazoo river upper and lower and I could send an army corps to co-operate with Banks and the two to-gether would easily take the place and every thing on the river from there to Warrenton just below Vicksburgh. The Lake Providence route through to Red river has proven a success and it is by this route I would send them I have neither transports or Gunboats suitable for this expedition all of them being in the Yazoo

U. S. G

To Thomas W. Knox

Head Quarters, Department of the Tennessee,
Before Vicksburg, April 6th 1863.

Thomas W. Knox,
Correspondent New York Herald. —
Sir. —

The letter of the President of the United States, authorizing you to return to these Head Quarters, and remain, with my consent, or leave if such consent is withheld, has been shown me.

You came here first in positive violation of an order from General Sherman. Because you were not pleased with his treatment of Army followers, who had violated his order, you attempted to break down his influence with his command, and to blast his reputation with the public. You made insinuations against his sanity, and said many things which were untrue, and so far as your letter had influence, calculated to effect the public service unfavorably.

General Sherman is one of the ablest Soldiers and purest men in the country. You have attacked him, and been sentenced to expulsion from this Department for the offence. Whilst I would conform to the slightest wish of the President, where it was founded upon a fair representation of both sides of any question, my respect for General Sherman is such, that in this case I must decline unless General Sherman first gives his consent to your remaining.

> I am, Sir,
> Yours &c.
> U. S. GRANT
> Maj. Gen.

To Stephen A. Hurlbut

> Head Quarters, Dept. of the Ten.
> Millikin's Bend, La, Apl. 9th/63

Maj. Gen. S. A. Hurlbut,
Comd.g 16th Army Corps,
Gen.

Suppress the entire press of Memphis for giving aid and comfort to the enemy by publishing in their columns every move made here by troops and every work commenced. Arrest the Editors of the Bulliten and send him here a prisoner, under guard, for his publication of present plans via New Carthage & Grand Gulf.

I am satisfied that much has found its way into the public press through that incoragibly gassy man Col. Bissell of the Eng. Regt. I sent him to you thinking he could not do so much harm there as here. His tongue will have to be tied if there is anything going on where he is which you dont want made public. I feel a strong inclination to arrest him and trust to find evidence against him afterwards.

> Very respectfully
> U. S. GRANT
> Maj. Gen Com

To Julia Dent Grant

Millikin's Bend La.
April 20th 1863.

Dear Julia,

I want you to go to St. Louis and stay there until you get the deed from your brother John for the 60 acres of land *where our house* is, and have it recorded. Also get the deed for 40 acres where your brother Lew's. house is and have it recorded. Be shure and have this done right. Then lease out the farm to some good and prompt tenant, for five years, giving them the privilege of taking off every stick of timber and puting the whole place in cultivation. Bind them to take care of the house, fences and fruit trees. Place Bass Sappington or Pardee in charge to collect the rent and when all is done say to your father that the house is for his use as long as he wants it and the rents are to go to him for the other place.

If John Dent wants to go to Calafornia you may offer him $1600 for 40 acres adjoining the 60 acres. If he desires this have this deed recorded also before you leave. I want it distinctly understood however that I do not desire this trade and only make the offer to enable him to go and look after other property he has. If it was not that I am poor and have not a dollar except my savings in the last two years I would not hesitate to furnish him all the necessary money without any other guarantee than the conciousnous that I had done him a favor.

In case you make this trade it will be necessary for you to go to Galena to get the money. You can explain to Orvil that I have purchased property and paid $3000 on it and have to pay $1600 more. You can settle the difference they make out against me at the store but try and have Lank. who kept the books, to make up the account. Ask Orvil how brother Simps estate was settled. Inform him that I should never have mentioned it in the world but some of them are seting so much higher merit upon money than any other earthly consideration that I feel it a duty to protect myself. If you go to Galena be patient and even tempered. Do not expose yourself to any misconstruction from a hasty remark. Be firm however. Give up no notes except what you get cashed unless they pay the whole with the interest accrued. In that case you can allow them for what they say I owe with the same interest upon the debt they pay you. Should you however get but a part of the money give only the notes they pay. Tell Orvil that on final settlement I will allow the same interest that I receive. So long as they hold money of mine they need not be afraid to trust me.

This business all settled you can visit any of your friends until you hear that I am in Vicksburg when you can join me as soon as possible. Try and engage a Governess to teach the children, one who speaks German if possible. Do not make a possitive bargain however until you write to me.

U. S. GRANT

To Jesse Root Grant

Millikins Bend La
April 21st 1863.

Dear Father,

Your letter of the 7th of April has just this day reached me. I hasten to answer your interogitories.

When I left Memphis with my past experiance I prohibited trade below Helena. Trade to that point had previously been opened by the Treasury Department. I give no permits to buy Cotton and if I find any one engaged in the business I send them out of the Department and seize their Cotton for the Government. I have given a few families permission to leave the country and to take with them as far as Memphis their Cotton. In doing this I have been decieved by unprincipled speculators who have smuggled themselves along with the Army in spite of orders prohibiting them and have been compelled to suspend this favor to persons anxious to get out of Dixie.

I understand that Govt has adopted some plan to regulate geting the Cotton out of the country. I do not know what plan they have adopted but am satisfied than any that can be adopted, except for Government to take the Cotton themselves, and rule out speculators altogether will be a bad one. I feel all Army followers who are engaged in speculating off the misfortunes of their country, and really aiding the enemy more than they possibly could do by open treason, should be drafted at once and put in the first forlorn hope.

I move my Head Quarters to New Carthage to-morrow. This whole country is under water except strips of land behind the levees along the river and bayous and makes opperations almost impossible. I struck upon a plan which I thought would give me a foot hold on the East bank of the Miss. before the enemy could offer any great resistance. But the difficulty of the last one & a half miles next to Carthage makes it so tedious that the enemy cannot fail to discover my plans. I am doing my best and am full of hope for complete success. Time has been consumed but it was absolutely impossible to avoid it. An attack upon the rebel works at any time since I arrived here must inevitably resulted in the loss of a large portion of my Army if not in an entire defeat. There was but two points of land, Hains Bluff & Vicksburg itself, out of water any place from which troops could march. These are thoroughly fortified and it would be folly to attack them as long as there is a prospect of turning their position. I never expect to have an army under my command whipped unless it is very badly whipped and cant help it but I have no idea of being driven to do a desperate or foolish act by the howlings of the press. It is painful to me as a matter of course to see the course pursued by some of the papers. But there is no one less disturbed by them than myself. I have never saught a large command and have no ambitious ends to accomplish. Was it not for the very natural desire of proving myself equal to anything expected of me, and the evidence my removal would afford that I was not thought equal to it, I would gladly accept a less responsible position. I have no desire to be an object of envy or jealousy, nor to have this war continue. I want, and will do my part towards it, to put down the rebellion in the shortest possible time without expecting or desiring any other recognition than a quiet approval of my course. I beg that you will destroy this letter. At least do not show it.

Julia and the children are here but will go up by the first good boat. I sent for her to come down and get instructions about some business I want attended to and see no immediate prospect of being able to attend to myself.

ULYSSES

To Peter J. Osterhaus

Head Quarters, Dept. of the Ten.
Near Vicksburg, May 29th 1863,

Brig. Gen. Osterhaus,
Comd.g at Black River Bridge,
Gen.

Burn up the remainder of Black River Bridge. Make details from the Negroes collected about your camp, and also from the troops and have as much of the road taken up, East of the river, as you can. Pile the ties up and lay the rails across them and burn them up. Wherever there is a bridge, or trestle work, as far East as you send troops have them destroyed. Effectually destroy the road, and particularly the rails, as far East as you can.

Very respectfully
U. S. GRANT
Maj. Gen. Com

To Jesse Root Grant

Vicksburg, July 6th 1863

Dear Father,

Vicksburg has at last surrendered after a siege of over forty days. The surrender took place on the morning of the 4th of July. I found I had continuously underestimated the force of the enemy both in men and Artillery. The number of prisoners surrendered was Thirty thousand & two hundred. The process of parolling is so tedious however that many who are desirous of getting to their homes will escape before the paroling officers get around to them. The Arms taken is about 180 pieces of Artillery and over 30 000 stand of small arms.

The enemy still had about four days rations of flour & meat
and a large quantity of sugar.

The weather now is excessively warm and the roads intolerably dusty. It can not be expected under these circumstances
that the health of this command can keep up as it has done.
My troops were not allowed one hours idle time after the
surrender but were at once started after other game.

My health has continued very good during the campaign
which has just closed.—Remember me to all at home.

ULYSSES

To Lorenzo Thomas

Vicksburg, Mississippi
July 11th, 1863.

Brig.-Genl. L. Thomas,
Adj. Gen. of the Army.
General:

Your letter of the 26th of last month, enclosing a letter from
Mrs Duncan, was received on the 9th. I have ordered an investigation of the matters complained of but think there must
be some mistake about the acts complained of having been
committed. About the date of your letter Mr Duncan the husband of Mrs Mary Duncan, called on me for a permit to ship
from the north, supplies of various kinds for the use of his
negroes. He then thanked me for the protection and courtesy
that had been extended to him by the Federal Authorities in
this Department. He made no complaint of even having been
annoyed.

All new organizations of negro regiments have been broken
up and their men transferred to those regiments for which
you had appointed officers. I found that the old regiments
never could be filled so long as authority was granted to form
new ones. I am anxious to get as many of these negro regiments as possible and to have them full and completely
equipped. The large amount of arms and equipments captured here will enable me to equip these regiments as rapidly
as they can be formed.

I am particularly desirous of organizing a regiment of Heavy Artillerists from the negroes to garrison this place, and shall do so as soon as possible, asking the authority and commissions for the officers named after it is organized. I will ask now if this course will be approved.

I caused an informal investigation to be had in the case of Col. Shepard. The result of it was, his release and restoration to duty. I will send the proceedings to your office for your information. I am satisfied that the whole difficulty arose from the outrageous treatment of the Black troops by some of the white ones, and the failure of their officers to punish the perpetrators when they were reported. Becoming exasperated Col. Shepard took the punishment in his own hands.

The long line of Plantations from Lake Providence to Millikens Bend, it has been perfectly impossible to give perfect protection to, during the siege of Vicksburg. Besides the gunboats, negro troops and six regiments of white troops left west of the Mississippi River in consequence of these Plantations being there, I sent an additional Brigade from the investing Army, and that at a time when the government was straining every nerve to send me troops to insure the success of the enterprise against Vicksburg. All has not been availing. I can now clean out the Tensas, and Bayou Macon country so that there will be but little difficulty in protecting what is left of the Plantations.

There are two of the Commissioners appointed by you, Field and Livermore who are doing a great deal of harm. The limits of a private letter would not suffice to describe their character, selfishness misrepresentations and impracticable characteristics for doing good to any cause. I have thought seriously of removing them from my Department and appointing officers to act in their stead until successors could be appointed by proper authority. Capt. Strickle I believe to be honest and enthusiastic in the cause which he is serving. He is probaby influenced by old theories of abolishing slavery and elevating the negro but withal very well qualified to carry out orders as he receives them without reference to his private views. The capture of Vicksburg has proved a bigger thing than I supposed it would. There was over thirty one thousand rebel troops still left when we entered the city. The number of small arms will reach 50,000 stands I think, and the amount of Ordnance and Ordnance stores is enormous. Since crossing the Miss. River an army of (60,000) sixty thousand men has, in the various battles been killed wounded, captured, and scattered so as to be lost to the Confederacy, and an armament for an army of (100,000) one hunderd thousand men has departed from there forever.

My surplus troops were held in a position menacing Johnston ready to move at a moments notice when Vicksburg should fall. The moment a surrendered was agreed upon the order was given. I hope to hear to day that Johnston's forces have been broken to pieces and much of his munition of War abandoned   I have not heard from Sherman since the morning of 9th. He was then near Jackson skirmishing with the cavalry of the enemy. What was intended as a private letter General has spun out into a long semi official one which I hope you will excuse

Thanking you kindly for the assurance given in your letter of the satisfaction my course has given the Administration I remain

> Your very oddt Servt
> U. S. GRANT
> Major General

To Salmon P. Chase

Head Qrs. Dept. of the Ten.
Vicksburg Miss. July 21st 1863.

Hon. S. P. Chase
Sec. of the Treasury,
Sir:

Your letter of the 4th inst. to me, enclosing copy of letter of same date to Mr. Mellen; Spl. Agt. of the Treasury is just received. — My Asst. Adj. Gen. by whom I shall send this letter is about starting for Washington hence I shall be very short in my reply.

My experiance in West Tennessee has convinced me that any trade whatever with the rebellious states is weakening to us of at least Thirty three per cent of our force. No matter what the restrictions thrown around trade if any whatever is allowed it will be made the means of supplying to the enemy all they want. Restrictions if lived up to make trade unproffitable and hence none but dishonest men go into it. I will venture that no honest man has made money in West Tennessee in the last year whilst many fortunes have been made there during the time.

The people in the Mississippi Valley are now nearly subjugated. Keep trade out for but a few months and I doubt not but that the work of subjugation will be so complete that trade can be opened freely with the states of Arkansas, La. & Mississippi. That the people of these states will be more anxious for the enforcement, and protection, of our laws than the people of the loyal states. They have experienced the misfortune of being without them and are now in a most happy condition to appreciate their blessing.

No theory of my own will ever stand in the way of my executing, in good faith, any order I may receive from those in authority over me. But my position has given me an opportunity of seeing what could not be know by persons away from the scene of War and I venture therefore to suggest great caution in opening trade with rebels.

> I am sir, very respectfully
> your obt. svt.
> U. S. GRANT
> Maj. Gen. Com

To Charles W. Ford

> Vicksburg Mississippi,
> July 28th 1863.

Dear Ford,

It will soon be time now for schools to open and as I am entirely broken up of a home from which to send my children I must look around for a place for them in time. If possible I would rather place my two oldest boys with Mr. Wyman of St. Louis. Not knowing his initials or address I want to ask the favor of you to see Mr. Wyman for me and know if he can take them and his conditions.

The oldest boy is thirteen years old and the other eleven. I want them to board with Mr. Wyman and have their washing done there also. My little girl I will send to Mrs. Boggs.

If you will attend to this for me you will place me under renewed obligations.

This breaking up of families is hard. But such is War. I have much less to complain of however than the majority. In this worlds goods I had nothing to loose, and in escaping wounds, or loss of health, I have been so far fortunate.

Everything is now quiet along the Mississippi. But there is still work for the Army. Little side expeditions will be required to clean out the country West of the Miss.—The state of Miss. is now completely subjugated. It would be easyer to preserve law and order in this state now than in Mo. or Ky. so far as the inhabitants are concerned. Ark. & Louisiana will soon be in the same happy frame of mind.

I shall hope to hear from you soon.

Yours Truly
U. S. GRANT

To Abraham Lincoln

Cairo Illinois
August 23d 1863,

His Excellency A. Lincoln
President of the United States,
Sir:

Your letter of the 9th inst. reached me at Vicksburg just as I was about starting for this place. Your letter of the 13th of July was also duly received.

After the fall of Vicksburg I did incline very much to an immediate move on Mobile. I believed then the place could be taken with but little effort, and with the rivers debouching there, in our possession, we would have such a base to opperate from on the very center of the Confederacy as would make them abandon entirely the states bound West by the Miss. I see however the importance of a movement into Texas just at this time.

I have reinforced Gen. Banks with the 13th Army Corps comprising ten Brigades of Infantry with a full proportion of Artillery.

I have given the subject of arming the negro my hearty support. This, with the emancipation of the negro, is the heavyest blow yet given the Confederacy. The South rave a greatdeel about it and profess to be very angry. But they were united in their action before and with the negro under subjection could spare their entire white population for the field. Now they complain that nothing can be got out of their negroes.

There has been great difficulty in getting able bodied negroes to fill up the colored regiments in consequence of the rebel cavalry runing off all that class to Georgia and Texas. This is especially the case for a distance of fifteen or twenty miles on each side of the river. I am now however sending two expeditions into Louisiana, one from Natchez to Harrisonburg and one from Goodriche's Landing to Monroe, that I expect will bring back a large number. I have ordered recruiting officers to accompany these expeditions. I am also moving a Brigade of Cavalry from Tennessee to Vicksburg which will enable me to move troops to a greater distance into the interior and will facilitate materially the *recruiting service*.

Gen. Thomas is now with me and you may rely on it I will give him all the aid in my power. I would do this whether the arming the negro seemed to me a wise policy or not, because it is an order that I am bound to obey and do not feel that in my position I have a right to question any policy of the Government. In this particular instance there is no objection however to my expressing an honest conviction. That is, by arming the negro we have added a powerful ally. They will make good soldiers and taking them from the enemy weaken him in the same proportion they strengthen us. I am therefore most decidedly in favor of pushing this policy to the enlistment of a force sufficient to hold all the South falling into our hands and to aid in capturing more.

Thanking you very kindly for the great favors you have ever shown me I remain, very truly and respectfully

> your obt. svt.
> U. S. GRANT
> Maj. Gn.

To John G. Thompson

> Head Quarters, Dept. of the Ten.
> Vicksburg Miss. Aug. 29th 1863,

Jno. G. Thompson, Esq.
Sir:

Your letter of the 10th inst. asking if "Democratic" newspapers, pamphlets &c. will be allowed to circulate within this Army, and stating that it is reported that such documents are destroyed by Postmasters, Provost Marshals &c. is received.

There can scarsely be a foundation for the report you speak of. If such a thing has ever been done in any one instance it has been without authority and has never been reported to me. This Army is composed of intelligent, reading, thinking men, capable of forming their own judgement, and acting accordingly. Papers of all pursuasions, political and religious, are received and freely read. Even those from Mobile & Selma are some times received and no effort is made to keep them out of the hands of soldiers. I will state however that whilst the troops in this command are left free to vote the ticket of their choice no electioneering or circulation of speaches of a disloyal character, or those calculated to create dissentions, will be tolerated if it can be avoided.

Disloyalty in the North should not be tolerated whilst such an expenditure of blood and treasure is going on to punish it in the South.

> I have the honor to be
> very respectfully
> your obt. svt.
> U. S. GRANT
> Maj. Gen Commanding

To Elihu B. Washburne

Vicksburg Mississippi
August 30th 1863.

Hon. E. B. Washburn,
Dear Sir;

Your letter of the 8th of August, enclosing one from Senator Wilson to you, reached here during my temporary absence to the Northern part of my command; hence my apparent delay in answering. I fully appreciate all Senator Wilson says. Had it not been for Gen. Halleck & Dana I think it altogether likely I would have been ordered to the Potomac. My going could do no possible good. They have there able officers who have been brought up with that army and to import a commander to place over them certainly could produce no good. Whilst I would not possitively disobey an order I would have objected most vehemently to taking that command, or any other except the one I have. I can do more with this army than it would be possible for me to do with any other without time to make the same acquaintance with others I have with this. I know that the soldiers of the Army of the Ten. can be relied on to the fullest extent. I believe I know the exact capacity of every General in my command to command troops, and just where to place them to get from them their best services. This is a matter of no small importance.

Your letter to Gen. Thomas has been delivered to him. I will make an effort to secure a Brigadiership for Col. Chetlain with the colored troops Before such a position will be open however more of these troops will have to be raised. This work will progress rapidly.

The people of the North need not quarrel over the institution of Slavery. What Vice President Stevens acknowledges the corner stone of the Confederacy is already knocked out. Slavery is already dead and cannot be resurrected. It would take a standing Army to maintain slavery in the South if we were to make peace to-day guaranteeing to the South all their former constitutional privileges.

I never was an Abolitionest, not even what could be called anti slavery, but I try to judge farely & honestly and it become patent to my mind early in the rebellion that the North & South could never live at peace with each other except as one nation, and that without Slavery. As anxious as I am to see peace reestablished I would not therefore be willing to see any settlement until this question is forever settled.

Rawlins & Maltby have been appointed Brigadier Generals. These are richly deserved promotions. Rawlins especially is no ordinary man. The fact is had he started in this war in the Line instead of in the Staff there is every probability he would be to-day one of our shining lights. As it is he is better and more favorably know than probably any other officer in the Army who has filled only staff appointments. Some men, to many of them, are only made by their Staff appointments whilst others give respectability to the position. Rawlins is of the latter class.

My kind regards to the citizens of Galena.

Your sincere friend
U. S. GRANT

To Henry W. Halleck

Head Quarters Military Div. of the Miss.
Chattanooga Ten. Oct. 26th 1863.

Maj. Gen. H. W. Halleck,
Gen. in Chief, Washington,
General,

I arrived here in the night of the 23d inst. after a ride on horseback of fifty miles, from Bridgeport, over the worst roads it is possible to concieve of, and through a continuous drenching rain. It is now clear and so long as it continues so it is bearly possible to supply this Army from its present base. But when Winter rains set in it will be impossible. — To guard against the possible contingency of having to abandon Chattanooga for want of supplies every precaution is being taken. The fortifications are being pushed to completion and when done a large part of the troops could be removed back near to their supplies. The troops at Bridgeport are engaged on the rail-road to Jaspar and can finish it in about two weeks. Rails are taken from one of the branch roads which we do not use. This shortens the distance to supplies twelve miles and avoids the worst part of the road in wet weather. Gen. Thomas had also set on foot, before my arrival, a plan for geting possession of the river from a point below Lookout Mountain to Bridgeport. If successful, and I think it will be the question of supplies will be fully settled.

The greatest apprehension I now have is that the enemy will move a large force up the river and force a passage through our line between Blyhe's Ferry and Cotton Port. Should he do this our Artillery horses are not in a condition to enable us to follow and neither is our larder. This part of the line is well watched but I cannot say guarded. To guard against this, in addition to the troops now on that part of the river, I have directed Gen. Thomas to increase the force at McMinnville immediately by one regiment of Cavalry with instructions to collect all the provisions and forage which the enemy would have to depend on for his subsistence, giving vouches payable at once when taken from loyal citizens, and payable at the end of the war, on proof of good conduct, when disloyal. As soon as the fortifications here are sufficiently defensable a Division will be sent there. I have also ordered Sherman to move Easward towards Stevenson until he recieved further orders, guarding nothing this side of Bear Creek, with the view of having his forces in a position to use if the enemy should attempt this move. Should this not be attempted when Sherman gets well up there will be force enough to insure a line for our supplies and enable me to move Thomas to the left thus securing Burnside's position and give a strong hold upon that part of the line from which I suppose a move will finally have to be made to turn Bragg. I think this will have to be done from the Northeast.

This leaves a gap to the West for the enemy to get into Middle Tennessee by, but he has no force to avail himself of this opportunity with except Cavalry, and our Cavalry can be held ready to oppose this.

I will endeavor to study up my position well and post the troops to the best of my judgement to meet all contingencies. I will also endeavor to get the troops in a state of readiness for a forward movement at the earlyest possible day.

What force the enemy have to my front I have no means of judging accurately. Deserters come in every day but their information is limited to their own Brigades or Divisions at furthest. The camps of the enemy are in sight and for the last few days there seems to have been some moving of troops. But where to I cannot tell. Some seem to have gone towards Cleveland whilst others moved in exactly an opposite direction.

> I am Gen. very respectfully
> your obt. svt.
> U. S. GRANT
> Maj. Gen.

To Julia Dent Grant

Chattanooga Tennessee
October 27th 1863.

Dear Julia,

The very hard ride over here and necessary exercise since to gain a full knowledge of location instead of making my injury worse has almost entirely cured me. I now walk without the use of a crutch or cane and mount my horse from the ground without difficulty. This is one of the wildest places you ever saw and without the use of rail-roads one of the most out-of-the way places. To give you an idea of its inaccessibility I have only to state that the waggons with our baggage left Bridgeport, the present rail-road turminus, fifty miles distant by the road they have to travel, on the 23d inst. It is now 10 O'Clock at night of the 27th and they have not yet arrived and I hardly expect them to-morrow. Then too six-mule teams are not loaded with what two would easily pull on ordinary dirt roads. We have not consequently been able to start Messes.— Ross remained back at Nashville to lay in supplies but as he has not yet come up to Bridgeport I suspect he has had to go, or send, to Louisville for them. When they will get up is hard to surmise. I am making a desperate effort however to get possession of the river from here to Bridgeport and if I do it will facilitate bringing supplies very much.

There are but very few people here and those few will have to leave soon. People about Vicksburg have not seen War yet, or at least not the suffering brought on by war.

I have received no line from you yet. I feel very anxious to hear from the children. Tell Fred and Buck they must write at least one letter each week to you or me.

Kisses for yourself and Jess.

ULYS.

When do you think of starting on your trip to Ohio? You ought to start soon or you will not be able to go this Fall.

U.

To Julia Dent Grant

Chattanooga Tennessee,
November 2d 1863,

Dear Julia,

I have received your second letter stating that you had not yet heard from me. Dr. Kittoe wrote to you the next day after our arrival and I wrote the same or next day. Since that I have written several times. You still ask to come to Nashville! I do not know what in the world you will do there. There is not a respectable hotel and I leave no one of my Staff there. You would be entirely among strangers and at an expensive and disagreeable place to live. Bowers is there now, but is there only to close up unfinished business and to pack up and dispose of papers useless to carry into the field. This is just as unsuitable a place for you to be as as Millikins Bend. More so for there you could get by Steamer and here you cannot.

I see the papers again team with all sorts of rumors of the reason for recent changes. This time however I do not see myself abused. I do not know whether this is a good omen or not. I have been so accustomed to seeing at least a portion of the press against me that I rather feel lost when not attacked from some quarter. The best of feeling seems to prevail with the Army here since the change. Thomas has the confidance of all the troops of Rosecrans late command. The consolidation of the three Departments into one command also seems to give general satisfaction.

I hope you have had a pleasant visit to Ohio. If I had thought of it I would have advised you to have asked Alice Tweed to have accompanied you. I hope you saw father & mother as you passed through Cincinnati? I would not have asked you to cross the river to see them. I know mother will feel very badly if she does not get to see you & Jess. Kiss the little rascal for me. Tell him to be a good boy and learn his lessons so that he can write letters to me. Kisses for yourself dear Julia.

ULYS.

To J. Russell Jones

Chattanooga Dec. 5th 1863,

Dear Jones,

Your letter of the 25th reached here about the time closing scenes of the late battles were taking place. I regret that you could not be here to witness the grand panorama. I presume a battle never took place on so large a scale where so much of it could be seen, or where every move proved so successful; and out of doors where there was an outlet to retreat by. An Army never was whipped so badly as Bragg was. So far as any opposition the enemy could make I could have marched to Atlanta or any other place in the Confederacy. But I was obliged to rescue Burnside. Again I had not rations to take nor the means of taking them and this mountain country will not support an Army. Altogether I feel well satisfied and the Army feel that they have accomplished great things. Well they may. By the end of this month I will have enough due me to pay you what you have laid out for me. In the mean time can you borrow, at my expense, the amount? It is rather hard to ask a friend to make an investment for you and then get him to borrow the money to make it. But I am so situated that I cannot attend to my own private affairs and hope I am not giving you too much trouble.

J. E. Smith, Rawlins, Dr. Kittoe, and the Galenaites are well and desire to be remembered.

> Yours Truly
> U. S. GRANT
> Maj. Gen.

To Barnabas Burns

Chattanooga Tennessee,
December 17th 1863.

B. Burns, Esq.
Chairman Dem. Cen. Com.
Dear Sir:

Your letter of the 7th inst. asking if you will be at liberty to use my name before the convention of the "War Democracy", as candidate for the office of the Presidency is just received. —The question astonishes me. I do not know of anything I have ever done or said which would indicate that I could be a candidate for any office whatever within the gift of the people.

I shall continue to do my duty, to the best of my ability, so long as permitted to remain in the Army, supporting whatever Administration may be in power, in their endeavor to suppress the rebellion and maintain National unity, and never desert it because my vote, if I had one, might have been cast for different candidates.

Nothing likely to happen would pain me so much as to see my name used in connection with a political office. I am not a candidate for any office nor for favors from any party. Let us succeed in crushing the rebellion, in the shortest possible time, and I will be content with whatever credit may then be given me, feeling assured that a just public will award all that is due.

Your letter I take to be private. Mine is also private. I wish to avoid notoriety as far as possible, and above all things desire to be spaired the pain of seeing my name mixed with politics. Do not therefore publish this letter but wherever, and by whatever party, you hear my name mentioned in connection with the candidacy for any office, say that you know from me direct that I am not "in the field," and cannot allow my name to be used before any convention.

> I am, with great respect,
> your obt. svt.
> U. S. GRANT

To Henry W. Halleck

> Head Quarters Mil. Div. of the Miss.
> Nashville Ten. Jan.y 15th 1864

Maj. Gen. H. W. Halleck,
Gen. in Chief, Washington D.C.
General,

I reached here the evening of the 12th on my return from East Tennessee. I felt a particular anxiety to have Longstreet driven from East Tennessee, and went there with the intention of taking such steps as would secure this end. I found however a large part of Foster's command suffering for want of clothing, especially shoes, so that in any advance not to exceed two thirds of his men could be taken. The difficulties of supplying them are such that to send reinforcements, at present, would be to put the whole on insufficient rations for their support. Under these circumstances I only made such changes of position of troops as would place Foster nearer the enemy when he did get in a condition to move, and would open to us new foraging grounds and diminish those held by the enemy. Having done this and seen the move across the Holston, at Strawberry Plains, commenced, I started on my return via Cumberland Gap, Barboursville, London & Richmond to Lexington Ky. The weather was intensly cold the thermometer standing a portion of the time below zero. But being desirous of seeing what portion of our supplies might be depended upon over that route, and it causing no loss of time, I determined to make the trip. From the personal inspection made I am satisfied that no portion of our supplies can be hawled by teams from Camp Nelson. Whilst forage could be got from the country to supply teams at the different stations on the road some supplies could be got through in this way. But the time is nearly at an end when this can be done.

On the first rise of the Cumberland 1.200,000 rations will be sent to the mouth of the Big South Fork. These I hope teams will be able to take. The distance to hawl is materially shortened, the road is said to be better than that by Cumberland Gap, and it is a new route and will furnish forage for a time. In the mean time troops in East Tennessee must depend for subsistence on what they can get from the country, and the little we can send them from Chattanooga. The rail road is now complete into Chattanooga and in a short time, say three weeks, the road by Decatur & Huntsville will be complete. Steamers then can be spared to supply the present force in E. Ten. well and to accumulate a store to support a large army for a short time if it should become necessary to send one there in the Spring. This contingency however I will do every thing in my power to avert.

Two steamers ply now tolerably regularly between Chattanooga and Loudon. From the latter place to Mossy Creek we have rail road. Some clothing has already reached Knoxville since my departure. A good supply will be got there with all dispatch. These, if necessary, and subsistence can by possibility be obtained, I will send force enough to secure Longstreets expulsion.

Sherman has gone down the Miss. to collect at Vicksburg all the force that can be spared for a separate movement from the Miss. He will probably have ready by the 24th of this month a force of 20.000 men that could be used East of the river. But to go West so large a force could not be spared.

The Red River, and all the streams West of the Miss. are now too low for navigation. I shall direct Sherman therefore to move out to Meredian with his spare force, the Cavalry going from Corinth and destroy the roads East & South of there so effectually that the enemy will not attempt to rebuild them during the rebellion. He will then return unless the opportunity of going into Mobile with the force he has appears perfectly plain. Owing to the large number of veterans furloughed I will not be able to do more at Chattanooga than to threaten an advance and try to detain the force now in Thomas' front.

Sherman will be instructed, whilst left with large discretionary powers, to take no extra hazard of loosing his army, or of getting it crippled too much for efficient service in the Spring.

I look upon the next line for me to secure to be that from Chattanooga to Mobile, Montgomery & Atlanta being the important intermediate points. To do this large supplies must be secured on the Tennessee River so as to be independent of the rail-roads from here to the Tennessee for a conciderable length of time. Mobile would be a second base. The destruction which Sherman will do the roads around Meredian will be of material importance to us in preventing the enemy from drawing supplies from Mississippi and in clearing that section of all large bodies of rebel troops.

I do not look upon any points except Mobile in the South and the Tennessee in the North as presenting practicable starting points from which to opperate against Atlanta and Montgomery. They are objectionable as starting points, to be all under one command from the fact that the time it will take to communicate from one to the other will be so great. But Sherman or McPherson, one of whom would be entrusted with the distant command, are officers of such experience and reliability that all objection on this score, except that of enabling the two armies to act as one unit, would be removed. The same objection will exist, probably not to so great an extent however, if a movement is made in more than one column. This will have to be with an army of the size we will be compelled to use.

Heretofore I have abstained from suggesting what might be done in other commands than my own, in co-operation with it, or even to think much over the matter. But as you have kindly asked me in your letter of the 8th of Jan.y, only just received, for an interchange of views on our present situation, I will write you again, in a day or two, going out side of my own operations.

> I am General, very respectfully,
> your obt. svt.
> U. S. GRANT
> Maj. Gen.

To George H. Thomas

Nashville Jany 16th 12 30 a m

Maj Genl Thomas

Longstreet is said to be marching towards Knoxville.

Enemy reinforced by one Div from Ewells Corps with another expected.

I have advised Foster to keep his force between Longstreet and you.

Should he be forced back south of the Tenn it may become necessary to reinforce him from your command.

In that case I would fill the place of troops taken away from Maj Genl W T Shermans Command

Send Foster all the provisions you can.

The question of provisions alone may decide the fate of East Tenn

Maj Genl GRANT

To Henry W. Halleck

Confidential   Head Quarters, Mil. Div. of the Miss.

Nashville Ten. Jan.y 19th 1864,

Maj. Gen. H. W. Halleck,
Gen. in Chief of the Army,
Washington, D. C.
General,

I would respectfully suggest whether an abandonment of all previously attempted lines to Richmond is not advisable, and in line of these one be taken further South. I would suggest Raleigh North Carolina as the objective point and Suffolk as the starting point. Raleigh once secured I would make New Bern the base of supplies until Wilmington is secured. A moving force of sixty thousand men would probably be required to start on such an expedition. This force would not have to be increased unless Lee should withdraw from his present position. In that case the necessity for so large a force on the Potomac would not exist.

A force moving from Suffolk would destroy first all the roads about Weldon, or even as far north as Hicksford. From Weldon to Raleigh they would scarsely meet with serious opposition. Once there the most interior line of rail way still left to the enemy, in fact the only one they would then have, would be so threatened as to force him to use a large portion of his army in guarding it. This would virtually force an evacuation of Virginia and indirectly of East Tennessee. It would throw our Armies into new fields where they could partially live upon the country and would reduce the stores of the enemy. It would cause thousands of the North Carolina troops to desert and return to their homes. It would give us possession of many Negroes who are now indirectly aiding the rebellion. It would draw the enemy from Campaigns of their own choosing, and for which they are prepared, to new lines of operations never expected to become necessary. It would effectually blockade Wilmington, the port now of more value to the enemy than all the balance of their sea coast. It would enable operations to commence at once by removing the war to a more southern climate instead of months of inactivity in winter quarters. Other advantages might be cited which would be likely to grow out of this plan, but these are enough. From your better opportunities of studying the country, and the Armies, that would be involved in this plan, you will be better able to judge of the practicability of it than I possibly can.

I have written this in accordance with what I understood to be an invitation from you to express my views about Military operations and not to insist that any plan of mine should be carried out. Whatever course is agreed upon I shall always believe is at least intended for the best and until fully tested will hope to have it prove so.

I am General, very respectfully your obt. svt.
U. S. GRANT
Maj. Gen.

To Rufus Ingalls

Nashville, Ten.
Feb.y 16th 1864.

Dear Ruf,

Your very welcom letter was received by due course of Mail and read with great interest and full intention to answer it right off. But since that time I have been moving about so much that I have neglected it. I have often wished that I could have you here to run the machinery of your department. This was on account of old acquaintance however. The Quartermaster's Dept. here has been well and satisfactorily managed so far as the heads are concerned. I did once apply to have you sent here as chief but it was thought you could not be spared from where you are. I have never had any cause of complaint either on account of deficiency in the Staff Deptmts or embarassments trown in the way by the Authorities at Washington. The fact is I believe complaints are generally made to shift responsibility of inaction from commanders to Staff Departments or Washington Authorities. Of course I only speak for the West. I am thankful my lot has not been cast where I could judge for any other section.

I am begining now to make preparations for attack or defence when Spring opens. Two important expeditions are now out, one under Sherman and the other under Thomas, which, if as successful as I expect them to be will have an important bearing on the Spring Campaign.

This war has developed some of our old acquaintances much differently from what we would have expected. Fred. Steele, a good fellow always but you would have supposed not much more, is really a splendid officer and would be fully capable of the management of the Army of the Potomac or any of the Departments. Some who much would have been expected from have proven rather failures. This class I do not like to mention by name.

I believe Ruf. you are still leading a bachilor's life? Don't you regret it? Now I have four children, three boys and one girl, in whos society I feel more enjoyment than I possibly can with any other company. They are a responsibility giving much more pleasure than anxiety. It may not be too late for you yet.

My respects to such old acquaintances as are with you.

Yours Truly
U. S. GRANT

To William T. Sherman

Nashville Tennessee,
March 4th 1864.

Dear Sherman,

The bill reviving the grade of Lieut. Gen. in the Army has become a law and my name has been sent to the Senate for the place. I now receive orders to report to Washington, *in person*, immediately, which indicates either a confirmation or a likelyhood of confirmation. I start in the morning to comply with the order but I shall say very distinctly on my arrival there that I accept no appointment which will require me to make that city my Hd Qrs. This however is not what I started out to write about.

Whilst I have been eminently successful in this War, in at least gaining the confidence of the public, no one feels more than me how much of this success is due to the energy, skill, and harmonious puting forth of that energy and skill, of those who it has been my good fortune to have occupying a subordinate position under me. There are many officers to whom these remarks are applicable to a greater or less degree, proportionate to their ability as soldiers, but what I want is to express my thanks to you and McPherson as *the men* to whom, above all others, I feel indebted for whatever I have had of success. How far your advice and suggestions have been of assistance you know. How far your execution of whatever has been given you to do entitles you to the reward I am receiving you cannot know as well as me. I feel all the gratitude this letter would express, giving it the most flattering construction.

The word *you* I use in the plural intending it for Mc. also. I should write to him, and will some day, but starting in the morning I do not know that I will find time just now.

Your friend

U. S. GRANT

Maj. Gen.

To Julia Dent Grant

Culpepper C. H. Va

March 25th 1864

Dear Julia,

I arrived here yesterday well but as on my former trip brought wet and bad weather. I have not been out of the house today and from appearances shall not be able to go out for several days. At present however I shall find enough to do in doors. From indications I would judge the best of feelings animate all the troops here towards the changes that have been made.—I find mails follow me up with remarkable promptitude. More letters reach me than I can answer.—I hope you have entirely recovered? It is poor enjoyment confined to bed in Washington.—There is one thing I learned in Washington just on leaving that wants attending to. You know breakfast lasts from early in the morning until about noon, and dinner from that time until night. Jess runs about the house loose and seeing the guests at meals thinks each time it is a new meal and that he must necessarily eat. In this way he eats five or six times each day and dips largely into deserts. If not looked after he will make himself sick.—Have you heard from Fred.? No doubt he got home safely. I shall go down to Washington on Sunday. You need not mention it however.—I have sent in my recommendations for staff appointments placing Fred's name among them. I will know by to-morrow if they are approved. No doubt they will be however. I have put in the name of Capt. H. Porter, a very valuable regular officer, about such as Comstock, and still left one vacancy so that if Wilson should fail in his confirmation

I can appoint him. I do not apprehend however any danger of his confirmation.

Kisses for yourself & Jess.

ULYS.

To Benjamin F. Butler

In field Culpeper C. H. Va. Apr. 17th 1864

Maj. Gen. B. F. Butler,
Com'd'g Dept. Va. & N. C.
Fortress Monroe, Va.
General:

Your report of negotiations with Mr. Ould, Confederate States Agent, touching the exchange of prisoners, has been referred to me by the Secretary of War, with directions to furnish you such instructions on the subject, as I may deem proper.

After a careful examination of your report, the only points on which I deem instructions necessary, are—

1st.: Touching the validity of the paroles of the prisoners captured at Vicksburg and Port Hudson.

2nd.: The status of colored prisoners.

As to the *first*. No Arrangement for the exchange of prisoners will be acceeded to that does not fully recognize the validity of these paroles, and provide for the release to us, of a sufficient number of prisoners now held by the Confederate Authorities to cancel any balance that may be in our favor by virtue of these paroles. Until there is released to us an equal number of officers and men as were captured and paroled at Vicksburg and Port Hudson, not another Confederate prisoner of war will be paroled or exchanged.

As to the *second*. No distinction whatever will be made in the exchange between white and colored prisoners; the only question being, were they, at the time of their capture, in the military service of the United States. If they were, the same terms as to treatment while prisoners and conditions of release and exchange must be exacted and had, in the case of colored soldiers as in the case of white soldiers.

Non-acquiescence by the Confederate Authorities in both

or either of these propositions, will be regarded as a refusal on their part to agree to the further exchange of prisoners, and will be so treated by us.

> I am General
> Very Respectfully
> Your Obt. Servant
> U. S. GRANT
> Lieut. General

To Julia Dent Grant

Culpepper Apl. 17th 1864

Dear Julia,

Bowers will leave here on Teusday, (Washington on Wednesday) for the West. If your mind is made up to accompany him telegraph me and I will go in to see you off. I dislike however very much going in again. In the first place I do not like being seen so much about Washington. In the second it is not altogether safe. I cannot move without it being known all over the country, and to the enemy who are hovering within a few miles of the rail-road all the time. I do not know that the enemy's attack on the road last Friday was with the view of ketching me, but it was well timed. If you intend going either get Mr. Stanton or Mr. Chadwick to telegraph me.

I understand Jess has been having a fight in the hall! How is that?—Fred has said nothing about Helen coming East. He told me that when you went out she would have to leave your fathers. Kisses for yourself and Jess. Gen. Hunter will deliver this and tell you how we are living. Plain and well, surrounded with mud. I do not say you must go but I see no particular reason for your remaining longer. I shall certainly go to Washington but once more and that will be to see you off. As soon as it is possible for me to settle I will send for you and the children. Should we be so fortunate as to whip the enemy well, I feel that after that there will be no campaigning that I cannot direct from some one place.

Kisses again.

> ULYS.

To William T. Sherman

Head Quarters, Armies in the Field,
Culpepper C. H. Va. Apl. 19th 1864

Maj. Gen. W. T. Sherman,
Comd.g Mil. Div. of the Miss.
General,

Since my letter to you I have seen no reason to change any portion of the general plan of Campaign if the enemy remain still and allow us to take the initiative. Rain has continued so uninteruptedly until the last day or two that it will be impossible to move however before the 27th even if no more should fall in the mean time. I think Saturday the 30th will probably be the day for our general move.

Col. Comstock, who will take this, can spend a day with you and fill up many little gaps of information not given in any of my letters.

What I now want more particularly to say is, that if the two main attacks, yours and the one from here, should promise great success the enemy may in a fit of desperation, abandon one part of their line of defence and throw their whole strength upon a single army, believing that a defeat with one victory to sustain them better than a defeat all along their line, and hoping too at the same time that the army meeting with no resistince will rest perfectly satisfied with their laurels having penetrated to a given point south thereby enabling them to throw their force first upon one and then on the other.

With the majority of Military commanders they might do this. But you have had too much experience in traveling light and subsisting upon the country to be caught by any such ruse. I hope my experience has not been thrown away. My directions then would be if the enemy in your front show signs of joining Lee follow him up to the full extent of your ability. I will prevent the concentration of Lee upon your front if it is in the power of this Army to do it.

The Army of the Potomac looks well and so far as I can judge officers and men feel well.

Yours Truly
U. S. GRANT
Lt. Gen.

To Julia Dent Grant

Culpepper April 24th/64

Dear Julia,

I see by the papers you are having a good time in New York. Hope you will enjoy it. But don't forget Jess and loose him in the streets in all the excitement, New York is a big place and you might not find him.—A telegraph dispatch announces that the sword has been voted to me! I am rather sorry for it, or rather regret that my name has been mixed up in such a contest. I could not help it however and therefore have nothing to blame myself for in the matter.

The weather has been very fine here for a few days and dried the roads up so as to make them quite passable. It has commenced raining again however, and is now raining so hard, that it will take a week to bring them back to what they were this afternoon.

Remember me kindly to Col. and Mrs. Hillyer and the children. Kisses for yourself and Jess. I rather expected a letter from you this evening, but none came. I will write to the children to-morrow evening. Don't forget to send me any letters you receive from them. I know they must be anxious to see you back.

ULYS.

To Henry W. Halleck

Head Qrs. Armies in the Field,
Culpepper C. H. Va. Apl. 29th 1864

Maj. Gen. Halleck,
Chief of Staff of the Army,
General,

If General Gilmore reaches Fortress Monroe in time, and if four of the Iron Clads promised by the Navy are also there, our advance will commence on the 4th of May. Gen. Butler will operate on the South side of James River, Richmond being his objective point. I will move against Lee's Army attempting to turn him by one flank or the other. Should Lee fall back within his fortifications at Richmond, either before or after giving battle, I will form a junction with Butler, and the two forces will draw supplies from the James River. My own notions about our line of march are entirely made up. But, as circumstances beyond my controll may change them I will only state that my effort will be to bring Butler's and Meade's forces together.

The Army will start with fifteen days supplies. All the country affords will be gathered as we go along. This will no doubt enable us to go twenty or twenty-five days, without further supplies, unless we should be forced to keep in the country between the Rapidan and Chickahominy, in which case supplies might be required by way of the York or the Rappahannock River. To provide for this contingency I would like to have about one million rations, and two hundred thousand forage rations, afloat to be sent wherever it may prove they will be required.

The late call for one hundred day men ought to give us all the old troops in the Northern States for the field. I think full two thousand of those in the West ought to be got to Nashville as soon as possible. Probably it would be as well to assemble all the balance of the reinforcements for the West at Cairo. Those that come to the East I think should come to Washington unless movements of the enemy, yet to develope, should require them elswhere. With all our reserves at two or three points you will know what to do with them when they come to be needed in the field.

If the enemy fall back it is probable General Butler will want all the force that can be sent to him. I have instructed him however to keep you constantly advised of his own movements, and those of the enemy, so far as he can.

General Burnside will not leave his present position, between Bull Run and the Rappahannock, until the 5th of May. By that time the troops to occupy the Blockhouses, with their rations, should be out. If they cannot be sent from Washington I will have to require Gen. Burnside to furnish the detail from his Corps. When we get once established on the James River there will be no further necessity of occupying the road South of Bull Run. I do not know even that it will be necessary to go so far South as that. In this matter your opportunity for knowing what is required being so far superior to mine I will leave it entirely to you.

> I am General, Very respectfully your obt. svt.
> U. S. GRANT
> Lt. Gen.

To Henry W. Halleck

Hd Qrs "Wilderness"
11 a. m. May 7. 1864.
By mail from Alexandria Va.

Maj Gen. H. W. Halleck,
Chief of Staff

We were engaged with the enemy nearly all day both on the 5th & 6th. Yesterday the enemy attacked our lines vigorously first at one point and then another from right to left. They were repulsed at all points before reaching our lines, except once during the afternoon on Hancock's front, and just after night on Sedgwick's front   In the former instance they were promptly and handsomely repulsed. The latter, Milroy's old brigade, was attacked & gave way in the greatest confusion almost without resistance, carrying good troops with them. Had there been daylight the enemy could have injured us very much in the confusion that prevailed, they however instead of getting through the break, attacked Gen Wright's Div of Sedgwick's Corps & were beaten back.

Our losses to this time in killed, wounded & prisoners will not probably exceed 12.000. of whom an unusually large proportion are but slightly wounded. Among the killed we have to deplore the loss of Genls Wadsworth & Hays, Genls Getty & Bartlett wounded & Genls Seymour & Shaler taken prisoners. We have about 2.000 prisoners. They report Gen Jenkins killed & Longstreet wounded. I think the loss of the enemy must exceed ours, but this is only a guess based upon the fact that they attacked & were repulsed so often.

I wish you would send me all the information you have of

Gen Sherman by Bull Run & also care of Genl Butler. Send by way of Bull Run all the information from the James River expedition.

At present we can claim no victory over the enemy, neither have they gained a single advantage

Enemy pushed out of their fortifications to prevent their position being turned & have been sooner or later driven back in every instance.

Up to this hour enemy have not shown themselves in force within a mile of our lines.

U. S. GRANT
Lt Genl

To Julia Dent Grant

Near Spotsylvania C. H. Va.
May 13th 1864

Dear Julia,

The ninth day of battle is just closing with victory so far on our side. But the enemy are fighting with great desperation entrenching themselves in every position they take up. We have lost many thousand men killed and wounded and the enemy have no doubt lost more. We have taken about eight thousand prisoners and lost likely three thousand. Among our wounded the great majority are but slightly hurt but most of them will be unfit for service in this battle. I have reinforcements now coming up which will greatly encourage our men and discourage the enemy correspondingly.

I am very well and full of hope. I see from the papers the country is also hopeful.

Remember me to your father and Aunt Fanny. Kisses for yourself and the children. The world has never seen so bloody or so protracted a battle as the one being fought and I hope never will again. The enemy were really whipped yesterday but their situation is desperate beyond anything heretofore known. To loose this battle they loose their cause. As bad as it is they have fought for it with a gallantry worthy of a better.

ULYS.

To Julia Dent Grant

June 1st 1864

Dear Julia,

There has been a very severe battle this afternoon and as I write, now 9 O'clock at night firing is still continued on some parts of the battle line. What the result of the days fighting has been I will know but little about before midnight and possibly not then. The rebels are making a desperate fight and I presume will continue to do so as long as they can get a respectable number of men to stand.

I send pay accounts for May to Washington by Col. Bowers, who starts in the morning, with directions to send you $800 00 of it. April pay I sent all to Jones in liquidation of my indebtedness. In June I hope to pay all up.—I see by the papers dear little Nellie acquitted herself very handsomely at the Sanitary Fair. I would like very much to see you and the children but cannot hope to do so until this Campaign is over. How long it will last is a problem. I can hardly hope to get through this month.—With the night booming of Artillery and musketry I do not feel much like writing so you must excuse a short letter this time. Dr. Sharp is with me apparently enjoying himself very much. Fred. has been suffering intensely for several days with rheumatism. He has to lay upon his back in the ambulance unable to turn himself. I think he will be well in a day or two. Orvil Grant is at the White House and will probably be here to morrow.

My love to all. Kisses for yourself and the children.

ULYS.

To Ellen Wrenshall Grant

Cold Harbor Va. June 4th 1864

My Dear little Nelly,

I received your pretty well written letter more than a week ago. You do not know how happy it made me feel to see how well my little girl not yet nine years old could write. I expect by the end of the year you and Buck will be able to speak

German and then I will have to buy you those nice gold watches I promised. I see in the papers, and also from Mamas letter, that you have been representing "the Old Woman that lived in a Shoe" at the Fair! I know you must have enjoyed it very much. You must send me one of your photographs taken at the Fair.

We have been fighting now for thirty days and have every prospect of still more fighting to do before we get into Richmond. When we do get there I shall go home to see you and Ma Fred, Buck and Jess. I expect Jess rides Little Rebel every day! I think when I go home I will get a little buggy to work Rebel in so that you and Jess can ride about the country during vacation. Tell Ma to let Fred learn French as soon as she thinks he is able to study it. It will be a great help to him when he goes to West Point. You must send this letter to Ma to read because I will not write to her to-day. Kiss Ma, Cousin Louisa and all the young ladies for pa. Be a good little girl as you have always been, study your lessons and you will be contented and happy.

From
PAPA

To Julia Dent Grant

June 7th/64

Dear Julia,

I wrote to you last night but having had my hair cut to-day and remembering that you asked me to send you a lock I now write again to send it. I have nothing to add. To-day has been the quietest since leaving Culpepper. There has been no fighting except a little Artillery firing and some skirmishing driving the enemy's pickets south of the Chickahominy at two of the bridges below our main line. War will get to be so common with me if this thing continues much longer that I will not be able to sleep after a while unless there is an occational gun shot near me during the night.

Love and kisses for you and the children.

ULYS.

To Julia Dent Grant

City Point Va. June 15th/64

Dear Julia,

Since Sunday we have been engaged in one of the most perilous movements ever executed by a large army, that of withdrawing from the front of an enemy and moving past his flank crossing two rivers over which the enemy has bridges and rail-roads whilst we have bridges to improvise. So far it has been eminently successful and I hope will prove so to the end. About one half my troops are now on the South side of James River. A few days now will enable me to form a judgement of the work before me. It will be hard and may be tedious however.

I am in excellent health and feel no doubt about holding the enemy in much greater alarm than I ever felt in my life. They are now on a strain that no people ever endured for any great length of time. As soon as I get a little settled I will write Buck and Missy. each a letter in answer to theirs and will write to Cousin Louisa who I have received another short letter from enclosing Buck's. I want the children to write to me often. It improves them very much. I forgot that I had received a letter from Fred. since I wrote to him. I will answer his first.

Give my love to all at home. Did you receive the draft for $800 00? It is all I can send you until the end of July.—Kisses for you and the children.

ULYS.

To Elihu B. Washburne

City Point Va. June 23d *1864.*

Hon. E. B. Washburn,

Dear Sir.

In answer to your letter of a few days ago asking what "S" stands for in my name I can only state *nothing*. It was a mistake made by Senator Morris of Ohio when application was first made for my appointment as Cadet to West Point. My mother's family name is Simpson and having a brother of that name Mr. Morris, who knew both of us as children, got the matter confounded and sent in the application for Cadet-ship for Ulysses S. Grant. I tried on entering West Point to correct this mistake but failing, after I received my Diploma and Commission, with the "S" inserted, adopted it and have so signed my name ever since.

Every thing progresses here slowly. The dispatches given by the Sec. of War contains all the news.

Yours Truly
U. S. GRANT

To Henry W. Halleck

City Point, Va. July 1st 1864.

Maj. Gen H. W. Halleck,
Chief of Staff of the Army
General,

Mr. Dana Asst. Sec. of War, has just returned. He informs me that he called attention to the necessity of sending Gen. Butler to another field of duty. Whilst I have no difficulty with Gen. Butler, finding him always clear in his conception of orders, and prompt to obey, yet there is a want of knowl-edge how to execute, and particularly a prejudice against him, as a commander, that operates against his usefulness. I have feared that it might become necessary to separate him and Gen. Smith. The latter is really one of the most efficient of-ficers in service, readiest in expedients and most skilful in the management of troops in action. I would dislike removing him from his present command unless it was to increase it, but as I say, may have it to do yet if Gen. Butler remains.

As an administrative officer Gen. Butler has no superior. In taking charge of a Dept.mt where there are no great battles to be fought, but a dissatisfied element to controll no one could manage it better than he. If a command could be cut out such as Mr Dana proposed, namely Ky. Ill. & Ia. or if the Depts. of the Mo. Kansas and the states of Ill. & Ia. could be merged together and Gen. Butler put over it I believe the good of the service would be subserved.

I regret the necessity of asking for a change in commander here, but Gen. Butler not being a soldier by education or experience, is in the hands of his subordinates in the execution of all operations Military. I would feel strengthened with Smith, Franklin or J. J. Reynolds commanding the right wing of this Army. At the same time, as I have here stated, Gen. Butler has always been prompt in his obedience to orders, with me, and clear in his understanding of them. I would not therefore be willing to recommend his retirement.

I send this by Mail for consideration but will telegraph if I think it absolutely necessary to make a change.

> I am General, very respectf.
> your obt. svt.
> U. S. GRANT
> Lt. Gen

To Julia Dent Grant

City Point, Va. July 7th *1864.*

Dear Julia,

I received two letters from you this evening, written after you had received mine stating that you could come to Fortress Monroe to spend the Summer. I am satisfied it is best you should not come. It would be expensive to furnish a house there and difficult supplying it afterwards. The camp life we are leading you would not be able to be where I am often and then only to come up and go immediately back, with an express boat that might be running at the time.

I wrote to you in my last why not make the same arrangement for the children as last year? Permanency is a great thing for children at school and you could not have a better home for them than with Louisa Boggs. If they were with her I should always feel easy for you to leave them for two or three months to stay with me if I was where you could possibly be with me. I want the children to prossecute their studies, and especially in languages. Speaking languages is a much greater accomplishment than the little parapharnalias of society such as music, dancing &c. I would have no objection to music being added to Nellies studies but with the boys I would never have it occupy one day of their time, or thought.

If you think it advisable to go some place where you can keep the children with you, and where they will be at a good school, I will not object. But I cannot settle for you where such a place would be, probably the City of St. Louis would be as good as any other, for the present. Love and Kisses for yourself and the children. How much I wish I could see you all.

ULYS.

To Charles E. Fuller

City Point July 16th 1864

Col. C. E. Fuller A. Q. M.
Bermuda Hundred

My Brother-in-law, who is now a prisoner in the south, is named John C. Dent. He was captured some place on the Miss. River not far from Vicksburg, and is now, or was when I last heard from him, at Columbia S. C. He is a citizen, never connected with the army since the breaking out of the War and I regret to say not a loyal man, otherwise I should have interested myself long ago for his exchange

U. S. GRANT Lt. Gen.

To Abraham Lincoln

(Cipher)   City Point Va. July 19th 1864

A. Lincoln, President,

In my opinion there ought to be an immediate call for say 300.000 men to be put in the field in the shortest possible time. The presence of this number of reinforcements would save the annoyance of raids and would enable us to drive the enemy back from his present front, particularly from Richmond, without attacking fortifications. The enemy now have their last man in the field. Every depletion of their Army is an irreparable loss. Desertions from it are now rapid. With the prospect of large additions to our force these desertions would increase. The greater number of men we have the shorter and less sanguinary will be the war.

I give this entirely as my view and not in any spirit of dictation, always holding myself in readiness to use the material given me to the best advantage I know how.

U. S. GRANT
Lt. Gen.

To Edwin M. Stanton

(Cipher) City Point July 20th/64
E. M. Stanton Sec. of War

I must enter my protest against States sending recruiting Agents into the Southern States for the purpose of filling their quotas. The negroes brought within our lines are rightfully recruits to the United States Service and should not go to benefit any particular state. It is simply allowing Massachusetts (I mention Mass. because I see the order of the Governor of that state for establishing recruiting agencies in the South and see no such order from any other state authority.) to fill her quota by paying an amount of money to recruits the United States have already got. I must also enter my protest against recruiting from prisoners of War. Each one enlisted robs us of a soldier and adds one to the enemy with a bounty paid in loyal money.

U. S. GRANT
Lt. Gen.

To Henry W. Halleck

City Point July 21st *1864.*
Maj. Gen. Halleck, Washington

There is no indication of any troops having been sent from here North. Deserters coming in daily indicate nearly the position of every Division of Hill's Longstreet's and Beaurigard's forces. Hill's Corps has withdrawn from its position on the extreme right and was yesterday in rear of the other part of the line held by the enemy. There is a rumor of some force having been sent to Georgia but if this is so it is most likely only regiments detached from their command.

U. S. GRANT
Lt. Gen.

To Winfield Scott

HEADQUARTERS, ARMIES OF THE UNITED STATES,
CITY POINT, Va, July 23, 1864.

Lieutenant General Winfield Scott, U. S. A.: —

My Dear General—Your letter of the 2d inst., addressed to the Hon. E. B Washburne, in which you informed him that you had heard that some one had told me that you had spoken slightingly of my appointment to my present rank, is just received. Allow me to assure you, General, that no one has ever given me such information. I have never heard of any speech of yours in connection with the present rebellion which did not show the great interest felt by you, both in our eminent success and in the success of all our commanders. In fact, all that I have heard of your saying in relation to myself has been more flattering to me than I probably deserve.

With assurance of great esteem for you personally, General, as well as for the services you have rendered our country throughout a long and eventful public career, I subscribe myself, very respectfully and truly, your obedient servant,

U. S. GRANT,
Lieutenant General U. S. A.

To Henry W. Halleck

(Cipher)   City Point Va. Aug. 1st *1864*

Maj. Gen Halleck, Washington,

The loss in the disaster of saturday last foots up about 3500 of whom 450 were killed and 2000 wounded. It was the saddest affair I have witnessed in this war. Such opportunity for carrying fortifications I have never seen and do not expect again to have. The enemy with a line of works five miles long had been reduced by our previous movements to the North side of James River to a force of only three Divisions. This line was undermined and blown up carrying a battery and most of a regiment with it. The enemy were taken completely by surprise and did not recover from it for more than an hour. The crater and several hundred yards of the enemys line to the right & left of it, and a short detached line in front of the crater, were occupied by our troops without opposition. Immediately in front of this and not 150 yards off, with clear ground intervening, was the crest of the ridge leading into town and which if carried the enemy would have made no resistance but would have continued a flight already commenced. It was three hours from the time our troops first occupied their works before the enemy took possession of this crest. I am constrained to believe that had instructions been promptly obeyed that Petersburg would have been carried with all the Artillery and a large number of prisoners without a loss of 300 men. It was in getting back to our lines that the loss was sustained. The enemy attempted to charge and retake the line captured from them and were repulsed, with heavy loss, by our Artillery. Their loss in killed must be greater than ours whilst our loss in wounded and captured is four times that of the enemy.

U. S. GRANT
Lt. Gn.

To Lydia Slocum

HEADQ'RS ARMIES OF THE UNITED STATES,
CITY POINT, VA., August 10.

Mrs. Lydia Slocum:

My Dear Madam: Your very welcome letter of the 3d instant has reached me. I am glad to know the relatives of the lamented Major General McPherson are aware of the more than friendship existing between him and myself. A nation grieves at the loss of one so dear to our nation's cause. It is a selfish grief, because the nation had more to expect from him than from almost any one living. I join in this selfish grief, and add the grief of personal love for the departed. He formed for some time one of my military family. I knew him well. To know him was but to love him. It may be some consolation to you, his aged grandmother, to know that every officer and every soldier who served under your grandson felt the highest reverence for his patriotism, his zeal, his great, almost unequalled ability, his amiability, and all the manly virtues that can adorn a commander. Your bereavement is great, but cannot exceed mine.

> Yours truly,
> U. S. GRANT,
> Lieutenant General.

To Elihu B. Washburne

City Point Va. Aug. 16th *1864.*

Hon. E. B. Washburn,
Dear Sir:

Your letter asking for Autographs to send to Mrs. Adams, the wife of our Minister to England, was duly received. She had also sent to Mr. Dana for the same thing and his requisition, he being with me at the time, was at once filled. I have directed Col. Bowers to send with this a few of the original dispatches telegraphed from here. They have all been hastily written and not with the expectation of ever being seen afterwards but will, I suppose, answer as well as any thing els, or as if they had been written specially for the purpose of sending.

We are progressing here slowly. The weather has been intolerably warm, so much so that marching troops is nearly death.

I state to all Citizens who visit me that all we want now to insure an early restoration of the Union is a determined unity of sentiment North. The rebels have now in their ranks their last man. The little boys and old men are guarding prisoners, guarding rail-road bridges and forming a good part of their garrisons for intrenched positions. A man lost by them can not be replaced. They have robbed the cradle and the grave equally to get their present force. Besides what they lose in frequent skirmishes and battles they are now loosing from desertions and other causes at least one regiment per day. With this drain upon them the end is visible if we will but be true to ourselves. Their only hope now is in a divided North. This might give them reinforcements from Tenn. Ky. Maryland and Mo. whilst it would weaken us. With the draft quietly enforced the enemy would become dispondent and would make but little resistence.

I have no doubt but the enemy are exceedingly anxious to hold out until after the Presidential election. They have many hopes from its effects. They hope a counter revolution. They hope the election of the peace candidate. In fact, like McCawber, they hope *something* to turn up.

Our peace friends, if they expect peace from separation, are much mistaken. It would be but the begining of war with thousands of Northern men joining the South because of our disgrace allowing separation. To have peace "on any terms" the South would demand the restoration of their slaves already freed. They would demand indemnity for losses sustained, and they would demand a treaty which would make the North slave hunters for the South. They would demand pay or the restoration of every slave escaping to the North.

Your Truly
U. S. GRANT

To William H. Seward

City Point, Va, Aug. 19th 1864.

Hon. W. H. Seward,
Sec. of State,
Washington D. C.
Dear Sir:

I am in receipt of copy of F. W. Morse letter of the 22d of July to you inclosing copy of statement of C. W. G. in relation to desertions from this Army. There are constant desertions, though but few of them go over to the enemy. Unlike the enemy however we do not loose our veterans and men who entered the service through patriotic motives. The men who desert are those who have just arrived and who have never done any fighting and never intended to when they enlisted. They are a class known as "Bounty Jumpers" or "Substitute" men, men who enlist for the money, desert and enlist again. After they have done this until they become fearful of punishment they join their regiments, in the field, and desert to the enemy.

Of this class of recruits we do not get one for every eight bounties paid to do good service. My Provost Marshal Gn. is preparing a statement on this subject which will show the reinforcements received from this class of recruits. Take the other side: the desertions from the enemy to us. Not a day passes but men come into our lines and men too who have been fighting for the South for more than three years. Not unfrequently a commissioned officer comes with them. Only a few days ago I sent a regiment, numbering one thousand men for duty, to Gen. Popes Department composed wholly of deserters from the rebel Army and prisoners who took the oath of allegiance and joined them.

There is no doubt but many prisoners of War have taken the oath of allegiance and enlisted as substitutes to get the bounty and effect their return to the South. These men are paraded abroad as deserters who want to join the south and fight her battles, and it is through our leniency that the South expects to reap great advantages.

We ought not to make a single exchange nor release a prisoner on any pretext whatever until the war closes. We have got to fight until the Military power of the South is exhausted and if we release or exchange prisoners captured it simply becomes a War of extermination.

> I have the honor to be
> Very respectfully
> your obt. svt.
> U. S. GRANT
> Lt. Gn

To Philip H. Sheridan

(Cipher)   City Point Va. Aug. 26th *1864. 2:30* P.M.
Maj. Gen. Sheridan, Halltown Va.

I telegraphed you that I had good reason for believing that Fitz Lee had been ordered back here? I now think it likely that all troops will be ordered back from the Valley except what they beleive to be the minimum number to detain you. My reason for supposing this is based upon the fact that yealding up the Welden road seems to be a blow to the enemy he can not stand. I think I do not overstate the loss of the enemy in the last two weeks at 10,000 killed & wounded. We have lost heavily but ours has been mostly in captures when the enemy gained temporay advantages.

Watch closely and if you find this theory correct push will all vigor   Give the enemy no rest and if it is possible to follow to the Va Central road follow that far. Do all the damage to rail-roads & crops you can. Carry off stock of all discreptions and negroes so as to prevent further planting. If the War is to last another year we want the Shenandoah valley to remain a barren waste.

U. S. GRANT
Lt. Gn.

To William T. Sherman

(Cipher)   City Point Va. Sept. 4th *1864*. 9 p. m.
Maj. Gen. Sherman, Atlanta Ga.

I have just received your dispatch announcing the capture of Atlanta. In honor of your great victory I have ordered a salute to be fired with shotted guns from every battery bearing upon the enemy. The salute will be fired within an hour amidst great rejoicing.

U. S. GRANT
Lt. Gen.

To Frederick Dent Grant
and Ulysses S. Grant, Jr.

City Point Va. Sept. 13th *1864.*

Dear Fred. & Buck,

I was very glad to get your letters the other day and still better pleased to see so few mistakes. There was some mistakes though. Write often to me and when you do write always keep a dictionary by you. When you feel any doubt about how a word should be spelled look at your dictionary and be sure to get it right. Missy did not write? Why did she not? She writes very pretty letters and by writing often now she will write a better letter at twelve years of age than most grown up yong ladies.

I have sent to get Jess' pony brought into town from your grand pa's. If he is left there long I am afraid he will be stolen.

I hope to be up to see you all before many weeks and before many months to be with you most of the time. Is Jess sorry he run off and left his pa the way he did? I thought he was going to be a brave boy and stay with me and ride Jeff Davis. Ask Jess if Jeff aint a bully horse.

Kiss your Ma, little Nelly & Jess for your

PA

To Julia Dent Grant

City Point Va. Sept. 14th *1864.*

Dear Julia,

Your letter speaking of the new embarassment which has arisen in not being able to send the boys to College without having them board away from home has just reached me. As school does not commence until the begining of next month it will not be necessary for me to write to the principle about it as I shall try to slip up there for a day and see him in person. As to Jess refusing to go to school I think you will have to show him that you are *boss.* How does he expect ever to write letters to his Pa, or get to be Aide de Camp if he does not go to school and learn to write. He will go I know. He was only joking when he said he would not. I hope you will be pleasantly situated. Burlington is said to be a very nice place and nice people. You will soon be more at home there than in Gravois where there is no body except your own family for whom you have much reason to care.—I hope Jennie will come on and at least spend the Winter with you. I have written to your father asking him to make his home with us. Love and kisses for you and the children. Good night.

ULYS.

To Edwin M. Stanton

(Cipher)   City Point Va. Sept. 20th *1864. 11:00* A.M.
Hon. E. M. Stanton, Sec. of War, Washington.

Please advise the President not to attempt to doctor up a state government for Georgia by the appointment of citizens in any capacity whatever. Leave Sherman to treat on all questions in his own way the President reserving his power to approve or disapprove of his action. Through Treasury Agents on the Mississippi and a very bad civil policy in Louisianna I have no doubt the war has been very conciderably protracted and the states bordering on that river thrown further from sympathy with the Government than they were before the river was opened to commerse. This is given as my private views.

U. S. GRANT
Lt. Gn.

To Elihu B. Washburne

City Point Va
Sept 21st 1864

Hon. E. B. Washburne—

I have no objection to the President using any thing I have ever written to him as he sees fit—I think however for him to attempt to answer all the charges the opposition will bring against him will be like setting a maiden to work to prove her chastity—

U. S. GRANT
Lieut. Genl

To Julia Dent Grant

City Point Va. Oct. 26th 1864

Dear Julia,

To-morrow a great battle will probably be fought. At all events I have made all the arrangements for one and unless I conclude through the day to change my programme it will take place. I do not like to predict results therefore will say nothing about what I expect to accomplish. The cake you sent by Mr. Smith come to hand but the other you speak of having sent by Express has not. In one of your letters you ask if I accepted the house in Chicago? I did not accept or decline. I stated that I had no disposition to give up Ill. as my place of residence but the probability being that my duties hereafter would keep me most of the time in the East I had selected Phila as a place where my children could have the benefit of good schools and I could expect often to visit my family. If they were in Chicago I could not expect to see them often. I have heard nothing further since.

All are well here. Rawlins appears to have entirely recovered. Shall I have Little Rebel sent to you? If you had him you could get a little buggy and sleigh expressly for him and the children could then ride as much as they pleased. I expect when this campaign ends to send all my horses home and stay there most of the time myself when I am not visiting the different Armies. I do wish I could tell when that would be.— Love and kisses for you and the children.

ULYS.

To Isaac S. Stewart

City Point, Va, Dec. 1st *1864*

Dear Major,

Your favor of the 29th ultimo enclosing draft for $47.50 and accounts for signature is just received. As I draw forage in kind I am not entitled to the $50 00 per month for horses. The accounts upon which you paid are therefore correct. Enclosed you will please find the draft returned.

The following is a discriptive list of my servants which you can have inserted in the accounts paid upon to perfect them

		ft	in	Eyes	Hair
James Guard, White		5.	11	Dark	
William	Black	5.	7	"	
Douglass	"	5.	9	"	
Georgianna	"	5.	4	"	

I am under obligations to you Major for your concideration and favor.

Yours Truly
U. S. GRANT
Lt. Gen

To Maj. I. S. Stewart
Paymaster U. S. A.

To William T. Sherman

Confidential — City Point, Va, Dec. 6th *1864*.
Maj. Gen. W. T. Sherman,
Comd.g Mil. Div. of the Miss.
General,

On reflection since sending my letter by the hands of Lieut. Dunn I have concluded that the most important operation towards closing out the rebellion will be to close out Lee and his Army. You have now destroyed the roads of the South so that it will probably take three months, without interruption, to reestablish a through line from East to West. In that time I think the job here will be effectually completed. My idea now then is that you establish a base on the Sea Coast. Fortify and leave in it all your Artillery and Cavalry and enough Infantry to protect them, and at the same time so threaten the interior that the Militia of the South will have to be kept at home. With the balance of your command come here by water with all dispatch. Select yourself the officer to leave in command, but you I want in person.

Unless you see objections to this plan which I can not see use every vessel going to you for purposes of transportation.

Hood has Thomas close in Nashville. I have said all I could to force him to attack without giving the possitive order until to-day. To-day however I could stand it no longer and gave the order without any reserve. I think the battle will take place to-morrow. The result will probably be known in New York before Col. Babcock, the bearer of this, will leaves New York. Col. B. will give you full information of all operations now in progress.

> Very respectfully
> your obt. svt.
> U. S. GRANT
> Lt. Gn.

To Abraham Lincoln

(Cipher)   City Point, Va, Dec. 7th 1864 *3:30* P.M.
A. Lincoln, President, Washington,

The best interests of the service require that the troops of the Northwest, Departments of the N. W. Mo. & Kansas, should all be under one head. Properly they should all be in one Department. Knowing however the difficulty of displacing Department commanders I have recommended these Departments be thrown together into a Military Division and Gen. Pope put in command. This is advisable for the fact that as a rule only one point is threatened at a time and if all that territory is commanded by one man he can take troops from one point to satisfy the wants of another. With separate Department commanders they want to keep what they have and get all they can. This will not be the case with Dodge who has been apponted to command Mo. nor will it be with Pope.

> U. S. GRANT
> Lt. Gn

To Henry W. Halleck

(Cipher) City Point, Va, Dec. 8th *1864. 10:00* P.M.
Maj. Gen. Halleck, Washington,

Your dispatch of 9 p. m. just received. I want Gen. Thomas reminded of the importance of immediate action. I sent him a dispatch this evening which will probably urge him on. I would not say relieve him until I hear further from him.

U. S. GRANT
Lt. Gn.

To Henry W. Halleck

(Cipher) City Point Va. Dec. 9th *1864. 11:00* A.M.
Maj. Gen. Halleck, Washington.

Dispatch of 8 p. m, last evening from Nashville shews the enemy scattered for more than seventy miles down the river and no attack yet made by Thomas. Please telegraph orders relieving him at once and placing Schofield in command. Thomas should be directed to turn over all orders and dispatches received since the battle of Franklin to Schofield.

U. S. GRANT
Lt. Gn.

To Henry W. Halleck

(Cipher) City Point, Va. Dec. 9th *1864. 5:30* P.M.
Maj. Gen. Halleck, Washington.

Gen. Thomas has been urged in every way possible to attack the enemy even to the giving the possitive order. He did say he thought he would be able to attack on the 7th but did not do so nor has he given a reason for not doing it. I am very unwilling to do injustice to an officer who has done as much good service as Gen. Thomas has, however and will therefore suspend the order relieving him until it is seen whether he will do anything.

U. S. GRANT
Lt. Gen.

To George H. Thomas

(Cipher)   City Point, Va, Dec. 9th 1864 *7:30* P.M.
Maj. Gn. Thomas, Nashville Tenn.

Your dispatch of 1 P. M. to-day received. I have as much confidence in your conducting a battle rightly as I have in any other officer. But it has seemed to me that you have been slow and I have had no explaination of affairs to convince me otherwise. Receiving your dispatch to Gen. Halleck of 2 p. m. before I did the one to me, I telegraphed to suspend the order relieving you until we should hear further. I hope most sincerely that there will be no necessity of repeating the order and that the facts will show that you have been right all the time.

U. S. GRANT
Lt. Gn.

To Edwin M. Stanton

Washington City,
Dec. 18th *1864*

Hon E M Stanton

In my opinion no General Order should be issued which would authorize subordinate Military Commanders to invade a foreign country, with which we are at peace, at their discretion. If such officers should pursue Marauders fitted out in Canada, to depridate upon our frontier, it should be the act of the officer himself to be justified or condemned afterwards upon the merits of the case. In all instances where to much delay will not ensue they should wait for the authority of the Comd.g Gn. of the Dept. at least, and then his action should be reported, through the proper channel, to the President at once.

U. S. GRANT
Lt. Gn.

To George H. Thomas

Washington City,
December 18th *1864*

Major General Thomas
Nashville, Tenn.

The armies operating against Richmond have fired two hundred guns in honor of your great victory. Sherman has fully established his base on Ossabaw Sound with Savannah fully invested. I hope to be able to fire a salute to-morrow in honor of the fall of Savannah. In all your operations we hear nothing of Forrest; Great precaution should be taken to prevent him crossing the Cumberland or Tennessee below Eastport. After Hood is driven as far as it is possible to follow him, you want to re-occupy Decatur and all other abandoned points.

U. S. GRANT
Lt. Gen.

To George H. Thomas

(Cipher)   City Point, Va, Dec. 22d *1864*. *11:00* P.M.

Maj. Gen. Thomas, Nashville Tenn.

You have the congratulations of the public for the energy with which you are pushing Hood. I hope you will succeed in reaching his pontoon bridge at Tuscumbia before he gets there. Should you do so it looks to me that Hood is cut off. If you succeed in destroying Hood's Army there will be but one Army left to the so called Confederacy capable of doing us harm. I will take care of that and try to draw the sting from it so that in the Spring we shall have easy sailing. You now have a big oportunity which I know you are availing yourself of. Let us push and do all we can before the enemy can derive benefit either from the rasing of Negro troops or the concentration of white troops now in the field.

U. S. GRANT
Lt. Gen.

To Julia Dent Grant

City Point, Va Jan 1st *1865*.

Dear Julia,

Happy New Year to you. Fred. starts home this morning and will tell you I am quite well. I must commence taking quinine however. Every one on the Staff have been sick, Col. Badeau and Col. Porter so much so that they had to be sent home.

I inclose you two strips of paper which I want you to read and preserve. Sherman's letter shows how noble a man he is. How few there are who when rising to popular favor as he now is would stop to say a word in defence of the only one between himself and the highest in command. I am glad to say that I appreciated Sherman from the first feeling him to be what he has proven to the world he is. Good buy.

                              ULYS.

Kisses for you and the children.

                              U.

To Julia Dent Grant

City Point, Va, Jan. 11th *1865*.

Dear Julia,

I have just rec'd a letter from Jones saying he had sent you $475 00 This however includes the gold which I do not want you to spend. If it is necessary for you to have more money I will try to send it. I have received a letter from Jim. Casey saying that $1400 00 back taxes are due on your fathers place and unless paid this month the place will be sold. Now I cannot afford to send $1400 there and get no return for it. I know if I pay up the taxes it will be the last I shall ever see of the money. Looking to my own interest in the matter I wrote to Ford to attend to the matter for me and to let the farm be sold for taxes and him to buy it in in my name. I at the same time arranged for borrowing the money to send to him. A tax title amounts to no title atall but it is good until the money paid is refunded. If I can I will force John to make Nelly and Emma deeds to their land and probably to Fred. also.

I receive all your letters. Some of them are rather cross.— Love and kisses for you and the children.

ULYS.

To Abraham Lincoln

(Cipher)   City Point, Va. Jan. 31st *1865*. *10:00* A.M.
A. Lincoln President
Washington

The following communication was received here last evening. Petersburg, Va, Jan. 30th 1865 LIEUT. GN. U. S. GRANT, SIR: We desire to pass your lines under safe conduct, and to proceed to Washington, to hold a conference with President Lincoln, upon the subject of the existing War, and with a view of ascertaining upon what terms it may be terminated, in pursuance of the course indicated by him in his letter to Mr. F. P. Blair of 18th of Jan.y 1865 of which we presume you have a copy; and if not we wish to see you in person, if convenient, and to confer with you upon the subject. (Signed) Yours very respectfully, ALEXANDER STEPHENS, J. A. CAMPBELL, R. M. T. HUNTER. I have sent directions to receive these gentlemen and expect to have them at my quarters this evening awaiting your instructions.

U. S. GRANT
Lt. Gn.

To Abraham Lincoln

From City Point Va Feb'y 1st 12 30 P. M *1865*.
His Excellency A. Lincoln
Prest U. S.

Your despatch received; there will be no armistice in consequence of the presence of Mr Stephens and others within our lines. The troops are kept in readiness to move at the shortest notice if occasion should justify it

U. S. GRANT
Lieut Genl

To William T. Sherman

City Point, Va, Feb.y *1865*.

Maj. Gen. W. T. Sherman,
Comd.g Mil. Div. of the Miss.
General.

Without much expectation of it reaching you in time to be of any service I have mailed to you copies of instructions to Schofield and Thomas. I had informed Schofield by telegraph of the departure of Mahones Division, South, from the Petersburg front. These troops marched down the Weldon road and as they apparently went without baggage it is doubtful whether they have not returned. I was absent from here when they left. Just returned yesterday morning from Cape Fear River. I went there to determine where Schofields Corps had better go to operate against Wilmington & Goldsboro   The instructions with this will inform you of the conclution arrived at. Schofield was with me and the plan of the movement against Wilmington fully determined before we started back, hence the absence of more detailed instructions to him. He will land one Division at Smithville and move rapidly up the south side of the river and secure the W & C rail-road and with his Pontoon train cross onto the Island south of the City if he can. With the aid of the gunboats there is no doubt but this move will drive the enemy from their position eight miles East of the City either back to their inner line or away altogether. There will be a large force on the North bank of Cape Fear river ready to follow up and invest the garrison if they should go inside.

The rail-roads of N. C. are 4 ft. 8½ in. gauge. I have sent large parties of rail-road men there to build them up and have ordered stock to run them. We have abundance of it idle from the non use of the Va. roads.

I have taken every precaution to have supplies ready for you wherever you may turn up. I did this before when you left Atlanta and regret that they did not reach you promptly when you reached Saltwater. The fact is Foster, from physical disability is entirely unfit for his command. I would like to change him for a man that can get about and see for himself.

Alexander Stevens, R. M. T. Hunter & Judge Campbelle are now at my Hd Qrs. very desirous of going to Washington to see Mr. Lincoln, informally, on the subject of peace. The Peace feeling within the rebel lines is gaining ground rapidly. This however should not relax our energies in the least, but should stimulate us to greater activity.

I have received your very kind letter in which you say you would decline, or are opposed, to promotion. No one would be more pleased at your advancement than I, and if you should be placed in my position and I put subordinate it would not change our personal relations in the least. I would make the same exertions to support you that you have ever done to support me, and would do all in my power to make our cause win

Yours Truly. U. S. Grant, Lt. Gn

February 1, 1865

To Edwin M. Stanton

City Point, Va., *February 6, 1865.*

Hon. E. M. Stanton:

The Richmond Dispatch to-day says that a rumor was current yesterday that Sherman had reached and was destroying the rail-road at Midway, ten miles west of Branchville. The Whig, however, says that the rumor was without foundation, as the tenor of official dispatches received at the War Department last evening renders it certain that such was not the case. On Saturday telegraphic communication was temporarily suspended with Augusta, but was resumed on yesterday. The Whig remarks that a repulse of Sherman, who is now apparently presumptuous on account of his unimpeded march through Georgia, would work wonders in bringing the North to its senses. The Confederate generals and the men under their commands on his front are commissioners to whose pacific exertions the country may well look with anxious and prayerful solicitude. The Enquirer reports that the salt-works are again in successful operation. C. C. Clay, jr., is reported having arrived in the Confederacy. The Peace Commissioners arrived in Richmond Saturday evening. The same evening a large war meeting was held, which was addressed by Henry A. Wise. Governor Smith issues a notice to-day to the citizens of Richmond, Va., and citizens of other States sojourning in Richmond, to meet this evening to respond to the answer made by President Lincoln to the Confederate deputies sent to confer with him on the subject of peace. It is expected that Stephens will be invited by the Confederate Congress to address them before leaving for Georgia, whither it is rumored he intends going to arouse the people of that State to renewed vigor in prosecuting the war. The general tone of all the Richmond papers to-day says that there is nothing left for the South to do but to fight it out.

U. S. GRANT,
Lieutenant-General.

To Abraham Lincoln

City Point, Va, March 2d 1865 *1:00* P.M.
A. Lincoln President, Washington,

Richmond papers are received daily. No bullitins were sent Teusday or Wednsday because there was not an item of either good or bad news in them. There is every indication that Sherman is perfectly safe. I am looking every day for direct news from him.

U. S. GRANT
Lt. Gen.

To Edwin M. Stanton

City Point Va, March 3d 1865 *12:30* P.M.
Hon, E, M, Stanton
Sec, of War, Washington

A great many deserters are coming in from the enemy bringing their Arms with them expecting the pay for them as the means of a little ready cash, Would there be any objection to amending my order so as to allow this? Now that the sources of supply are cutt off from the enemy it is a great object to deprive the enemy of present supply of Arms

U. S. GRANT
Lieut, General

To Jesse Root Grant

City Point, Va, March 19th *1865*

Dear Father,

I received your two letters announcing the death of Clara. Although I had known for some time that she was in a decline yet I was not expecting to hear of her death at this time. — I have had no heart to write earlyer. Your last letter made me feel very badly. I will not state the reason and hope I may be wrong in my judgement of its meaning.

We are now having fine weather and I think will be able to wind up matters about Richmond soon. I am anxious to have Lee hold on where he is a short time longer so that I can get him in a position where he must loose a great portion of his Army. The rebellion has lost its vitality and if I am not much mistaken there will be no rebel Army of any great dimentions a few weeks hence. Any great catastrophy to any one of our Armies would of course revive the enemy for a short time. But I expect no such thing to happen.

I do not know what I can do either for Will. Griffith's son or for Belville Simpson. I sent orders last Fall for John Simpson to come to these Hd Qrs. to run between here and Washington as a Mail Messenger. But he has not come. I hope this service to end now soon.

I am in excellent health but would enjoy a little respite from duty wonderfully. I hope it will come soon.

My kindest regards to all at home. I shall expect to make you a visit the coming Summer.

Yours Truly
ULYSSES.

To Edwin M. Stanton

(Cipher)   City Point, Va, March 21st *1865 2:30* P.M.
Hon. E. M. Stanton, Sec. of War, Washington.

I would recommend releiving Gen. Crook from command of his Dept. and ordering him to command the Cavalry of the A. P. I would call attention to the fact that our White troops are being paid whilst the Colored troops are not. If paymasters could be ordered here immediately to commence paying them it would have a fine affect.

U. S. GRANT
Lt. Gn.

To Philip H. Sheridan

City Point, Va. March 21, 1865

Maj. Gen. P. H. Sheridan
Com'dg Middle Military Division
General:

I do not wish to hurry you, and besides fully appreciate the necessity of both having your horses well shod and well rested before starting again on another long march. But there is now such a possibility, if not probability of Lee and Johnston attempting to unite, that I feel extremely desirous not only of cutting the lines of communication between them but of having a large and properly commanded cavalry force ready to act with in case such an attempt is made. I think that by Saturday next you had better start, even if you have to stop here to finish shoeing up

I will have a force moved out from north of the James, to take possession of Long Bridge crossing, and to lay a pontoon for you. Some of the troops will push up as far as Bottom Bridge if they do not meet with too much opposition. This move will not be made at the date indicated unless it is known that you are ready to start. It will be made earlier if you indicate a readiness to start earlier.

Stoneman started yesterday from Knoxville with a Cavalry force of probably 5000 men to penetrate S. W. Virginia as far towards Lynchburg as possible. Under his instructions he may strike from New river towards Danville. This however I do not expect him to do. Wilson started at the same time from Eastport towards Selma with a splendidly equipped Cavalry force of 12000 men. Canby is in motion and I have reason to believe that Sherman and Schofield have formed a junction at Goldsboro.

U. S. GRANT

To William T. Sherman

City Point, Va. March 22d 1865

Maj. Gen. W. T. Sherman,
Comd.g Mil. Div. of the Miss.
General,

Although the Richmond papers do not communicate the fact yet I saw enough in them to satisfy me that you occupied Goldsboro on the 19th inst. I congratulate you and the Army on what may be regarded as the sucsessful termination of the third Campaign since leaving the Tenn. river less than one year ago.

Since Sheridan's very sucsessful raid North of the James the enemy are left dependent on the South Side and Danville roads for all of their supplies. These I hope to cut next week. Sheridan is at "White House" shoeing up and resting his Cavalry. I expect him to finish by Friday night and to start the following morning via Long Bridge, New Market, Bermuda Hundred and the extreme left of the Army around Petersburg. He will make no halt with the Armies operating here, but will be joined by a Division of Cav.y, 5500 strong, from the Army of the Potomac, and will proceed directly to the S. S. & Danville roads. His instructions will be to strike the S. S. road as near Petersburg as he can and destroy it so that it cannot be repaired for three or four days, and push on to the Danville road as near to the Appomattox as he can get. Then I want him to destroy the road towards Burkesville as far as he can; then push on to the S. S. road, West of Burkesville, and destroy it effectually. From that point I shall probably leave it to his discretion either to return to this Army crossing the Danville road South of Burkeville, or go and join you passing between Danville and Greensboro?

When this movement commences I shall move out by my left with all the force I can, holding present intrenched lines. I shall start with no distinct view further than holding Lee's forces from following Sheridan. But I shall be along myself and will take advantage of any thing that turns up. If Lee detaches I will attack or if he comes out of his lines I will endeavor to repulse him and follow it up to the best advantage. It is most difficult to understand what the rebels intend to do. So far but few troops have been detached from Lee's Army. Much Machinery has been removed and materiel has been sent to Lynchburg showing a disposition to go there. Points too have been fortified on the Danville road.

Lee's Army is much demoralized and are deserting in great numbers. Probably from returned prisoners and such conscripts as can be picked up his numbers may be kept up. I estimate his force now at about 65.000 men.

Wilson started on Monday with 12.000 Cavalry from Eastport. Stoneman started on the same day from East Tenn. toward Lynchburg. Thomas is moving the 4th Corps to Bulls Gap. Canby is moving with a formidable force on Mobile and the interior of Alabama.

I ordered Gilmore, as soon as the fall of Charleston was known, to hold all important posts on the Seacoast and to send to Wilmington all surplus forces. Thomas was also directed to forward to New Berne all troops belonging to the corps with you. I understand this will give you about 5000 men besides those brought East by Meagher.

I have been telegraphing Gen. Meigs to hasten up locomotives and cars for you. Gen. McCallum he informs me is attending to it. I fear they are not going forward as fast as I would like.

Let me know if you want more troops or anything else.

>   Very respectfully
>   your obt. svt.
>   U. S. GRANT
>   Lt. Gn.

To Abraham Lincoln

Gravely Run, March 29th *1865*

A. Lincoln, President, City Point

Griffin was attacked near where the Quaker road intersects the Boydton plank road. At 5.50 p m. Warren reports the fighting pretty severe but the enemy repulsed leaving 100 prisoners in our hands. Warren advanced to attack at the hour named but found the enemy gone, he thinks inside of his main works. Warrens pickets on his left along Boydton plank road reported the enemy's Cavalry moving rapidly Northward and they though Sheridan after them. Sheridan was in Dinwiddie this afternoon—

U. S. GRANT
Lt. Gn—

To George G. Meade

Appomattox C. H.
April 9th 1865.

Agreement having been made for the Surrender of the Army of North Va. hostilities will not be resumed. General Lee desires that during the time the two Armies are laying near each other, the men of the two Armies be Kept separate, the sole object being to prevent unpleasant individual rencontres that may take place with a too free intercourse.

U. S. GRANT.

To Julia Dent Grant

Washington Apl. 16th *1865*

Dear Julia,

I got back here about 1 p. m. yesterday and was called immediately into the presence of our new President, who had already been qualified, and the Cabinet. I telegraphed you from Baltimore and told Beckwith to do the same thing from here. You no doubt received the dispatches. All seems very quiet here. There is but little doubt but that the plot contemplated the distruction of more than the President and Sec. of State. I think now however it has expended itself and there is but little to fear. For the present I shall occupy a room in the office which is well guarded and will be occupied by Bowers and probably two or three others. I shall only go to the Hotel twice a day for my meals and will stay indoors of evenings. The change which has come upon the country so suddenly will make it necessary for me to remain in the City for several days yet. Gen. Halleck will go to Richmond to command there and Ord to Charleston. Other changes which will have to be made, and the apparent feeling that I should remain here until everything gets into working order under the new régime will probably detain me here until next Saturday. If I can get home sooner I will do so. I hope you will be in your house in Phila when I do go home. The inconvenience of getting from the Phila depot to Burlington is about equal to the balance of the trip.

Love and kisses for you and the children.

ULYS.

To Edward O. C. Ord

Apl. 17th 1865 5:00 P.M.

Maj. Gen. Ord, Richmond, Va

Ford, Manager of the theatre where the President was assassinated is now in Richmond. Have him arrested and sent under guard to Washington. Do not let it be noised about that he is to be arrested until the work is done lest he escapes.

U. S. GRANT
Lt. Gn

To William T. Sherman

Washington, D. C., Apl. 21st *1865.*

Maj. Gen. W. T. Sherman,
Comd.g Mil. Div. of the Miss.
General,

The basis of agreement entered into between yourself and Gen. J. E. Johnston for the disbandment of the Southern Army and the extension of the authority of the general government over all the territory belonging to it, sent for the approval of the President, is received.

I read it carefully myself before submitting it to the President and secretary of War and felt satisfied that it could not possibly be approved. My reasons for these views I will give you at another time in a more extended letter.

Your agreement touches upon questions of such vital importance that as soon as read I addressed a note to the Sec. of War notifying him of their receipt and the importance of immediate action by the President, and suggested in view of their importance that the entire Cabinet be called together that all might give an expression of their opinions upon the matter. The result was a disapproval by the President of the basis laid down, a disapproval of the negociations altogether, except for the surrender of the Army commanded by Johnston, and directions to me to notify you of this decission. I cannot do so better than by sending you the enclosed copy of a dispatch penned by the late President, though signed by the Sec. of War, in answer to me on sending a letter received from Gen. Lee proposing to meet me for the purpose of submitting the question of peace to a convention of Officers.

Please notify General Johnston immediately on receipt of this of the termination of the truce and resume hostilities against his Army at the earlyest moment you can, acting in in good faith.

The rebels know well the terms upon which they can have peace and just where negociations can commence, namely: when they lay down their Arms and submit to the laws of the United States. Mr. Lincoln gave them full assurances of what he would do I believe in his conference with commissioners met in Hampton Roads.

> Very respectfully
> your obt. svt.
> U. S. GRANT
> Lt. Gn.

To Julia Dent Grant

Apl. 21st *1865*

Dear Julia,

It is now nearly 11 O'Clock at night and I have received directions from the Sec. of War, and President, to start at once for Raleigh North Carolina. I start in an hour. Gen. Meigs, Maj. Leet, Capt. Dunn, (Dunn is Capt. and Asst. Adj. Gn.) and Major Hudson go with me. I will write to you from Morehead City or New Berne.—I do hope you will have moved to Phila by the time I return. I can run up to Philadelphia easily; but to get to Burlington I have to give notice of my going to secure a train to take me the last end of the way.

I find my duties, anxieties, and the necessity for having all my wits about me, increasing instead of diminishing. I have a Herculean task to perform and shall endeavor to do it, not to please any one, but for the interests of our great country that is now begining to loom far above all other countries, modern or ancient. What a spectacle it will be to see a country able to put down a rebellion able to put half a Million of soldiers in the field, at one time, and maintain them! That will be done and is almost done already. That Nation, united, will have a strength which will enable it to dictate to all others, *conform to justice and right*. Power I think can go no further. The moment conscience leaves, physical strength will avail nothing, in the long run.

I only sat down to write you that I was suddenly required to leave on important duty, and not feeling willing to say what that duty is, you must await my return to know more.

Love and kisses for you and the children.

> U. S. GRANT

To Julia Dent Grant

In the Field Raleigh Apl. 25th *1865*

Dear Julia,

We arrived here yesterday and as I expected to return to-day did not intend to write until I returned. Now however matters have taken such a turn that I suppose Sherman will finish up matters by to-morrow night and I shall wait to see the result.

Raleigh is a very beautiful place. The grounds are large and filled with the most beautiful spreading oaks I ever saw. Nothing has been destroyed and the people are anxious to see peace restored so that further devastation need not take place in the country. The suffering that must exist in the South the next year, even with the war ending now, will be beyond conception. People who talk now of further retalliation and punishment, except of the political leaders, either do not conceive of the suffering endured already or they are heartless and unfeeling and wish to stay at home, out of danger, whilst the punishment is being inflicted.

Love and Kisses for you and the children,

ULYS,

Index to the Letters

Notes to the Doctor

*written while completing the Memoirs
at Mount McGregor, June – July 1885*

Notes to the Doctor

Dr. Since coming to this beautiful climate and getting a complete rest for about ten hours, I have watched my pains and compared them with those of the past few weeks. I can feel plainly that my system is preparing for dissolution in three ways; one by hemhorages, one by strangulation and the third by exaustion. The first and second are liable to come at any moment to relieve me of my earthly sufferings; the time for the arrival of the third can be computed with almost mathematical certainty. With an increase of daily food I have fallen off in weight and strength very rapidly for the last two weeks. There can not be a hope of going far beyond this time. All any physician, or any number of them do for me now is to make my burden of pain as light as possible. I do not want any physician but yourself but I tell you so that if you are unwilling to have me go without consultation with other professional men, you can send for them. I dread them however knowing that it means another desperate effort to save me, and more suffering.

June 17, 1885

I said I had been adding to my book and to my coffin. I presume every strain of the mind or body is one more nail in the coffin.

. . . . . .

Several more pages since, a portion of which I wrote out.

. . . . . .

I have now worked off all that I had notes of, and which often kept me thinking at night.

I will not push to make more notes for the present.

June 23, 1885, 5:30 P.M.

If this goes on I do not know but it will be best for me to take my first injection early. Three days ago I would scarsily have been able to endure the pain of to-day.

June 27, 1885

I am about as I every day at this hour. Papers are all read. I am drowsy without being able to sleep, and time passes heavily. No worse however only that my mouth has not been washed out to-day and the cocaine does not seem to relieve the pain.

June 29, 1885

This is always the trouble. No matter how well I get along the balance of the 24 hours, when the middle of the after-noon comes I begin to feel stuffy, stopped up and generally uncomfortable.

. . . . .

I do not feel the slightest desire to take morphine now. In fact when I do take it it is not from craving, but merely from a knowledge of the relief it gives. If I should go without it all night I would become restless I know, partly from the loss of it, and partly from the continuous pain I would have to endure.

June 29, 1885, 4:00 P.M.

I was frightened this morning because I felt so sleepy. I for-got that I had had nothing like the rest a well man requires. My feeling this am was what we want to produce: one that enables me to rest. But I was not quite conscious enough to reason correctly about what produced it.

June 30, 1885, 8:00 A.M.

12^{05} I will try to observe the effect of the last injection. Pain has ceased and slight drowsyness set in. Nothing however to indicate heavyness or the use of too much morphine.—At this hour, or a few minutes later, was given the minim of morphine. Went to sleep almost immediately. Awoke at 3^{30} feeling no effect of the injection.

. . . . .

It is a little hard giving up the use of cocoane when it gives so much relief. But I suppose that it may be used two or three times a day, without injury, and possibly with benefit, when the overuse of it has been counteracted.

. . . . . .

It will probably take several days to see the effect of discontinuing the use of cocoan? It might then be used once a day, might it not? say when I am retiring for the night. It is no trouble however to quit outright for the present.

June 30, 1885

I see the Times man keeps up the character of his dispatches to the paper. They are quite as untrue as they would be if he described me as getting better from day to day. I think he might spare my family at least from reading such stuff.

June 30, 1885, P.M.

I will have to be careful about my writing. I see ever person I give a piece of paper to puts it in his pocket. Some day they will be coming up against my English

June – July 1885

But you intend to go back to the hotel to-night whether I want an injection or not?
   I think then you had better run now. But we will see better in a few minuets. The probabilities are that I shall feel no more inclination to sleep for the next hour in any event, injection or no injection. I think my tongue has commenced to diminish.

June – July 1885

I see no effect whatever from the gas as yet. Mine is a different case from ordinary suffering.

June – July 1885

There was a week or such matter when I had but little acute pain. The newspapers gave that as a sure indication that I was declining rapidly.

June – July 1885

I feel weak from my exertions last night in throwing up. Then since that I can not help repeating two advertisements of the B & O railroad when I am half awake. The houses on their place at Deer Park are advertised as a sure cure for Malaria, or the place is signed Robt Garrett, Pres. The other is that the water—I think—is a sure cure for Catarrh. Signed same. There may be no such advertisement, but I keep dreaming them all the same. It strikes me as a very sharp dodge for a gentleman to advertise his own wares in such a way. When you consider Garrett owns the water and buildings at the park; is Pres. of the road over which invalids must pass to get to the place, and is a very large owner in the stock of the road it strikes me as another instance of what a man will do for money.

July 1, 1885, 8:00 A.M.

I have not taken any wine in six days. So far as I have tried I do not think alcoholic drinks agree with me. They seem to heat me up and have no other effect.

July 1, 1885, 10:00 A.M.

I talked a goodeal with my pencil. The wine I did take was not Madiera but Tokay, but since leaving N.Y. three small wine glasses of Old Port. I do not need or want either. Mrs. Grant and Fred thought they would help me.

July 1, 1885

I do not care about the doors being closed. I thought after coming down you might want to sit with me awhile. I have worked and feel a little weak from it, but I cannot sleep— since seven this am I have dosed off a few times, but not half hour in the aggregate.

July 2, 1885, A.M.

This is the first of the "jim-cracks" that has seemed to have real merit. I found it easy to-day to write upon for an hour without stopping. It also makes a good invalid table to get ones meals off of.

July 2, 1885

Cocain is a failure in my case now. It hurts very much to apply it and I do not feel that it does me much good. I do not see why it should have afforded so much relief heretofore and now stopped.

. . . . .

I have been writing up my views of some of our generals, and of the character of Lincoln & Stanton. I do not place Stanton as high as some people do. Mr. Lincoln cannot be extolled too highly.

July 2, 1885, P.M.

Dr. I ask you not to show this to any one, unless physicians you consult with, until the end. Particularly I want it kept from my family. If known to one man the papers will get it and they will get it. It would only distress them almost beyond endurance to know it, and, by reflex, would distress me.

I have not changed my mind materially since I wrote you before in the same strain. (Now however I know that I gain in strength some days, but when I do go back it is beyond when I started to improve.) I think the chances are very decidedly in favor of your being able to keep me alive until the change of weather towards the winter. Of course there are contingencies that might arise at any time that would carry me off very suddenly. The most probable of these are choking. Under these circumstances life is not worth living. I am very thankful to have been spared this long because it has enabled me to practically complete the work in which I take so much interest. I can not stir up strength enough to review it and make additions and subtractions that would suggest themselves to me and are not likely to to any one els.

Under the above circumstances I will be the happiest the most pain I can avoid. If there is to be an extraordinary cure, such as some people believe there is to be, it will develope itself. I would say therefore to you and your collegues to make me as comfortable as you can. If it is within Gods providence that I should go now I am ready to obey His call without a murmur. I should prefer going now to enduring my present suffering for a single day without hope of recovery. As I have stated I am thankful for the providential extension of my time to enable me to continue my work. I am further thankful, and in a much greater degree thankful, because it has enabled me to see for myself the happy harmony which has so suddenly sprung up between those engaged but a few short years ago in deadly conflict. It has been an inestimable blessing to me to hear the kind expressions towards me in person from all parts of our country; from people of all nationalities of all religions and of no religion, of Confederate and National troops alike; of soldiers organizations; of mechanical, scientific religious and all other societies, embracing almost every Citizen in the land. They have brought joy to my heart, if they have not effected a cure. To you and your collegues I acknowledge my indebtedness for having brought me through the "valley of the shadow of death" to enable me to witness these things.

U. S. GRANT

Mt. McGregor, N. Y.
July 2d 1885.

I have found so much difficulty in getting my breath this morning that I tried laudanum a few minuets ago, but with the same result as for some time past. The injection has not yet had any effect. The douche has not acted well for some time. Do you think it worth the experiment of trying. I imagine I feel the morphine commencing to act.

July 3, 1885

In coughing a while ago much blood came up— Has Dr. Sands gone. He takes a much more hopeful view of my case than I do— How old is he— I had to use the cocoan several times in quick succession this morning. I have not had to use it since. You used it once in the mean time, but that was more to let Dr. Sands see than for anything els. I did not need it.

July 4, 1885

I feel much relieved this morning. I had begun to feel that the work of getting my book to-gether was making but slow progress. I find it about completed, and the work now to be done is mostly after it gets back in gallies. It can be sent to the printer faster than he is ready for it. There from one hundred and fifty to two hundred pages more of it than I intended. Will not cut out anything of interest. It is possible we may find a little repetition. The whole of that however is not likely to amount to many pages. Then too there is more likelyhood of omissions.

July 5, 1885

I know that what you are doing will be as likely to cure me as any think els. Nature is given a good opportunity to act and if a cure is possible it will develope itself. All the medical scill in America, including Dr. Bron, could not find a cure.

July 6, 1885

I feel very badly probably because of a cross fire between opium and laudanum. If relieved of that I half hope to feel better.

I feel as if I cannot endure it any longer. The alcoholic stimulants must absolutely be given up.

July 7, 1885

If I live long enough I will become a sort of specialist in the use of certain medicines if not in the treatment of disease. It seems that one mans destiny in this world is quite as much a mystery as it is likely to be in the next. I never thought of acquiring rank in the profession I was educated for; yet it came with two grades higher prefixed to the rank of General officer for me. I certainly never had either ambition or taste for a political life; yet I was twice president of the United States. If any one had suggested the idea of my becoming an author, as they frequently did I was not sure whether they were making sport of me or not. I have now written a book which is in the hands of the manufacturers. I ask that you keep these notes very private lest I become authority with treatment of diseases. I have already to many trades to be proficent in any. Of course I feel very much better from your application of cocain, the first in three days, or I should never have thought of saying what I have said above.

July 8, 1885, 4:00 A.M.

I feel pretty well but get sleepy sitting in the air. Took a half hours nap. Do you want me to go in the house. I am as bright and well now, for a time at least, as I ever will be.

Will you tell Harrison to bring me the larger pad I have been using in my room.

July 8, 1885, 11:00 A.M.

Buck has brought up the last of first vol. in print. In two weeks if they work hard they can have the second vol. copied ready to go to the printer. I will then feel that my work is done.

. . . . . .

Gen. Buckner — Fort Donelson — will be here on the next train. He is coming up specially to pay his respects.

July 10, 1885, 11:30 A.M.

I do not feel a great deal of pain, but more than through the day. Not much pain but enough to be unpleasant. It is confined principally to the side of the tongue which cocain does not help, and to the place about where the right nostril enters the mouth.

I must try to get some soft pencils. I could then write plainer and more rapidly.

July 1885

Not sleeping does not disturb me because I have had so much sleep. And then too I have been comparitively free from pain. I know a sick person cannot feel just as he would like all the time; but I think it a duty to let the physician know from time to time just my feelings. It may benefit some other fellow sufferer hereafter. Wake the Dr. up and advise with him whether anything should be done. I cleared my mouth and throat very well just before twelve. I feel very well but have nearly a constant hicup. Whether this indicates anything or not I do not know, but it is inconvenient. I have not felt a desire or need of cocain since taking it to-day.

July 11, 1885, 1:00 A.M.

7^{45} am, July 11th woke up by biting my tongue, feeling perfectly fresh however as if I had had a good nights natural sleep. My breathing is less obstructed than usual at the same time of day and the head less filled up. In fact my breathing is not obstructed in the least. Have used no cocain during the night nor do I require any yet.

July 11, 1885, 7:45 A.M.

After all that however the disease is still there and must be fatal in the end. My life is precious of course to my family and would be to me if I could recover entirely. There never was one more willing to go than I am. I know most people have first one and then another little thing to fix up, and never get quite through. This was partially my case. I first wanted so many days to work on my book so the authorship would be clearly mine. It was graciously granted to me, after being apparently much lower than since, and with a capacity to do more work than I ever did in the same time. My work had been done so hastily that much was left out and I did all of it over from the crossing of the James river in June/64, to Appomattox in /65. Since that I have added as much as fifty pages to the book I should think. There is nothing more I should do to it now, and therefore I am not likely to be more ready to go than at this moment.

July 16, 1885

I have tried to study the question of the use of cocain as impartially as possible considering that I am the person effected by its use. The conclusion I have come to in my case is; taken properly it gives a wonderfull amount of relief from pain. Gradually the parts near those where the medicine is applied become numb and partially paralized. The feeling is unpleasant but not painful. Without the use of it the parts not effected with disease are pliable but of no use because their exercise moves the diseased parts and produces pain. When the medicine is being applied the tendency is to take more than there is any necessity for, and oftener. On the whole my conclusion is to take it when it seems to be so much needed as it was at times yesterday. I will try to limit its use. The latter you know how hard it is to do.

July 19, 1885

I can however write better seated with the board before me. I do not think I should take my medicine now. I might try to go to sleep and when I want the medicine call you.

July 19, 1885

What do you think of my taking the bath wagon and going down to overlook the south view?

July 20, 1885, 4:00 P.M.

I do not sleep though I sometimes dose off a little. If up I am talked to and in my efforts to answer cause pain. The fact is I think I am a verb instead of a personal pronoun. A verb is anything that signifies to be; to do; or to suffer. I signify all three.

July 1885

Chronology

1822   Born April 27 at Point Pleasant, Ohio, a small village along the Ohio River, first child of Jesse Root Grant and Hannah Simpson Grant. (Grandfather Noah Grant, a farmer and cobbler, moved from Connecticut to Westmoreland County in western Pennsylvania, where father, Jesse Root Grant, was born in 1794, and then to northeastern Ohio in 1799. After death of grandmother Rachel Kelly Grant in 1805 the family broke up, and father eventually was apprenticed to his half-brother Peter Grant's tannery in Maysville, Kentucky. In 1820 father began working in tannery at Point Pleasant and on June 24, 1821, married Hannah Simpson, b. 1798, the daughter of farmers who had moved to Ohio from eastern Pennsylvania in 1817.) Named Hiram Ulysses Grant and called Ulysses by his family (his father and mother's stepmother had read Fénelon's *Telemachus*).

1823   Father establishes tannery at Georgetown, Ohio, village 25 miles east of Point Pleasant and five miles from the Ohio River, and has two-story brick house built for his family, who move there in autumn.

1825   Brother Samuel Simpson Grant (called Simpson by family) born September 23.

1828   Begins attending subscription schools in Georgetown (may have started in 1827). Sister Clara Rachel Grant born December 11.

1830   Hauls cut wood from land owned by father. Enjoys working with horses; detests tannery.

1832   Sister Virginia Paine (Jennie) Grant born February 20.

1833   Begins working on family farm.

1835   Brother Orvil Lynch Grant born May 15.

1836–37   Attends Maysville Seminary, Maysville, Kentucky, living with father's relatives there.

1837–38   Attends subscription school in Georgetown.

1838–39   Attends Presbyterian Academy in Ripley, Ohio.

1839   Father arranges with Congressman Thomas L. Hamer
           for Grant to enter the U.S. Military Academy, and he is
           appointed on March 22. Arrives at West Point, New York,
           on May 29; however, due to Hamer's error, his appoint-
           ment is in the name of U. S. Grant, and he is officially
           registered under that name, though he will sign himself
           Ulysses H. (or U. H.) Grant while at the Academy. Passes
           entrance examination and spends summer in training
           encampment. Sister Mary Frances Grant born July 28.
           Studies mathematics and French when classes begin in
           fall. Reads novels and stories by Edward Bulwer (later Ed-
           ward Bulwer-Lytton), James Fenimore Cooper, Frederick
           Marryat, Walter Scott, and Washington Irving (later will
           read works of Charles Lever and Eugène Sue). Becomes a
           friend of roommate Rufus Ingalls (later quartermaster of
           the Army of the Potomac) and others, including Frederick
           Steele (later a Union major general) and James Longstreet
           (later a Confederate lieutenant general).

1840   Ranks 16th in mathematics and 49th in French in class of
           60 members and 147th in conduct in corps of 233 cadets;
           achieves overall standing of 27th in his class. Spends sum-
           mer in training encampment (will do so again in 1842).
           Studies mathematics, French, topographical and anatomi-
           cal drawing, and ethics. Does watercolor paintings for
           drawing class taught by well-known painter Robert Walter
           Weir. Distinguishes himself as a horseman, often riding
           difficult mounts.

1841   Ranks 10th in mathematics, 44th in French, 23rd in draw-
           ing, and 46th in ethics out of class of 53, and 144th in
           conduct out of corps of 219; stands 24th in his class over-
           all. Visits family, now living in Bethel, Ohio, ten miles
           northwest of Georgetown, and friends during ten-week
           summer furlough. Studies philosophy (physics), chemis-
           try, and landscape drawing.

1842   Ranks 15th in philosophy, 22nd in chemistry, and 19th in
           drawing in class of 41 and 157th in conduct in corps of 217;

achieves overall standing of 20th in his class. Studies military and civil engineering, ethics, artillery, infantry tactics, and mineralogy and geology. Rooms with friend Frederick T. Dent.

1843   Serves as president of Dialectic Society, cadet literary society. Ranks 16th in engineering, 28th in ethics, 25th in artillery, 28th in infantry tactics, and 17th in mineralogy and geology in class of 39, and 156th in conduct in corps of 223. Graduates 21st in his class in June and is commissioned brevet (provisional) second lieutenant in the 4th Infantry Regiment. Begins signing name as Ulysses S. Grant. Reports to Jefferson Barracks, outside of St. Louis, Missouri, on September 30. Visits White Haven, Dent family home near Jefferson Barracks (White Haven is adjacent to present-day Grantwood, Missouri). Meets Dent's parents, Frederick F. Dent, a slaveholding planter who had moved to Missouri from Maryland, and Ellen Wrenshall Dent. Grant studies mathematics in hopes of becoming assistant professor at the Military Academy.

1844   Begins courting Julia Boggs Dent (b. 1826), eldest daughter in the family, when she returns in late winter from stay in St. Louis. They often go riding together. While on leave in Bethel in early May, Grant learns that the 4th Infantry has been ordered to Louisiana. Returns to Missouri and proposes marriage to Julia Dent; she accepts. Joins regiment in June at Camp Salubrity, outside Natchitoches, Louisiana, near the Texas border. Plays cards with fellow officers and enjoys watching and betting on horse races.

1845   Congress votes to annex Texas, March 1. Grant takes leave in April to visit Julia Dent and receives her father's conditional consent to their marriage. Regiment is sent to Corpus Christi, Texas, in September. Grant is promoted to second lieutenant on September 30. Offered position as professor of mathematics at college in Hillsboro, Ohio, and considers resigning from the army to accept it. Visits San Antonio and Austin in December. Texas is admitted to the Union as a state, December 29.

1846   As part of force under Brevet Brigadier General Zachary Taylor (whom Grant will come to admire), Grant's regiment moves south on March 11 into territory between Nueces and Rio Grande rivers claimed by both Texas and Mexico. Troops reach Rio Grande opposite Matamoras on March 28. Mexico declares war, April 24. While on supply assignment at Point Isabel on the Gulf Coast, Grant hears sounds of fighting at Matamoros on May 3. Fights in battle of Palo Alto, May 8, and temporarily commands his company at battle of Resaca de la Palma, May 9. Mexicans retreat and Americans occupy Matamoros, May 18. Taylor's army begins advance on Monterrey on August 5. Grant becomes regimental quartermaster and commissary. Takes part in first American assault on Monterrey, September 21. Volunteers to ride through streets during heavy fighting on September 23, carrying message requesting ammunition resupply. Mexican defenders surrender, September 24. Grant remains in camp near Monterrey for remainder of the year.

1847   Regiment is assigned to Major General Winfield Scott's expedition against Veracruz and embarks at Point Isabel on February 13. Lands outside of Veracruz on March 9 and joins siege of the city, which surrenders March 27. Scott begins advance on Mexico City April 8. Grant takes part in the battle of Cerro Gordo, April 18, an American victory. Learns that Frederick F. Dent has given his final consent to his marriage to Julia. Fights at battles of Churubusco, August 20, and Molino del Rey, September 8, outside of Mexico City, and takes part in assault on the city, September 13; city surrenders on September 14. Promoted to first lieutenant September 16. Spends remainder of year outside of Mexico City as part of occupying force. (During the Mexican War, Grant serves with and gets to know many officers he will later command or fight against during the Civil War.)

1848   Peace negotiators sign Treaty of Guadalupe Hidalgo, February 2, and it is ratified by the U.S. Senate, March 10. Tours Valley of Mexico during armistice. Climbs Mount Popocatépetl, 17,887-foot volcano, in April with fellow officers, including his friend Simon Bolivar Buckner, but does not reach its summit because of bad weather; suffers temporary snow blindness. Visits Cacahuamilpa caverns near Cuernavaca. Mexican National Congress ratifies peace treaty May 30, officially ending war. On June 16, during the 4th Infantry's return to the United States, $1,000 in quartermaster's funds are stolen from the trunk of Grant's friend, Captain John H. Gore. Board of inquiry called at Grant's request exonerates him of blame for the theft, but he is not relieved of his obligation to reimburse the government. Returns to United States on July 23 and takes leave. Sees Julia Dent at White Haven, visits his family at Bethel, and then returns to Missouri. Marries Julia at Dent home at Fourth and Cerre streets in St. Louis on August 22; among the guests are Longstreet, Steele, and Cadmus M. Wilcox (later a Confederate major general). Returns to Bethel with Julia for extended stay, visiting Georgetown, Maysville, and Cincinnati. Reports for duty at Detroit, Michigan, on November 17, and is assigned to Madison Barracks at Sackets Harbor, New York, on the eastern shore of Lake Ontario near the Canadian border. Serves as company commander and post quartermaster. Plays chess and checkers with citizens of nearby Watertown.

1849   Successfully requests transfer back to regimental headquarters in Detroit and returns in April when lakes become navigable. Rents house at 253 E. Fort Street and is joined by Julia when she returns from visit to her family. Enjoys racing and betting on horses, plays cards, and entertains fellow officers and their wives at his home.

1850   On advice of regimental surgeon, Julia returns to her parents' home for the birth of her first child. Son Frederick Dent Grant (called "Fred" by the family) born May 30 in St. Louis. Grant takes extended leave to visit Missouri and Ohio and then returns to Detroit with wife and child.

1851   Reassigned to Sackets Harbor in June. Julia and son Frederick spend summer at White Haven. Grant takes leave in July and visits Quebec City, Montreal, Lake Champlain, New York City, and West Point. Rejoined by Julia and Frederick in late summer.

1852   4th Infantry is ordered to Pacific Northwest in May. Grant leaves Sackets Harbor in June and goes to Governor's Island in New York harbor; Julia, who is awaiting the birth of their second child, and Frederick go to stay with Grant's family in Bethel after Grant insists that they not accompany him. Grant goes to Washington, D.C., on July 1, seeking relief from his obligation to repay the quartermaster funds stolen in 1848. Finds government offices closed for Henry Clay's funeral; is later able to see several congressmen, but issue of lost funds remains unresolved. Sails from New York July 5 and reaches Aspinwall (now Colón, Panama) on July 16, where he makes arrangements for regiment and its dependents to cross the Isthmus. Helps tend the sick when cholera breaks out (about 100 people in regimental party die, including Captain John H. Gore and 17 children). Sails from Panama City on August 5 and arrives in San Francisco on August 18. Writes favorably to Julia about California. Reports on September 20 to Columbia Barracks (renamed Fort Vancouver in July 1853) on the Columbia River, near Portland, Oregon Territory (post becomes part of Washington Territory when it is created in March 1853). Serves as commissary officer. Likes Oregon but finds cost of living high. Realizes $1,500 profit from investment in store and speculates in cattle and hogs. Starts 100-acre farm with three fellow officers and plants potatoes and oats. Learns in early December of birth of Ulysses S. Grant, Jr., (later called "Buck" by the family) in Bethel on July 22.

1853   Sells cut wood to steamboats and rents out horses. Columbia floods in June, destroying much of his crop. Equips railroad surveying parties, including one led by Brevet Captain George B. McClellan. Promoted to captain on August 5. Resigns as regimental quartermaster and asks permission to go to Washington, D.C., to settle his accounts (including matter of stolen funds), hoping to return with his wife and children. Request is denied, and he is ordered to Fort Humboldt, California.

1854   Arrives at Fort Humboldt on January 5, and becomes commander of Company F of the 4th Infantry under Brevet Lieutenant Colonel Robert C. Buchanan, an officer he dislikes. Fort receives little mail; Grant is uncertain of status of his request for orders to return East and he becomes bored, lonely, and depressed (is alleged to have drunk heavily while at Fort Humboldt). Receives official commission as captain on April 11 and resigns from the army the same day, effective July 31. Settles army accounts, but is unable to collect $1,750 owed to him in San Francisco. Sails from San Francisco, June 1, and arrives in New York City by way of Nicaragua on June 25. Goes to Sackets Harbor in unsuccessful attempt to collect $800 owed to him by Elijah Camp, an army sutler Grant had invested with in Oregon. Army friend Captain Simon Bolivar Buckner lends him money. Joins wife and children at White Haven in late summer. Begins clearing 60 acres of land given to Julia by her father, cuts wood, and sells it on the streets of St. Louis (continues for several years to sell firewood as principal means of earning money).

1855   Plants wheat and corn and continues to clear land. Moves in spring to Wish-ton-wish, house on Dent property owned by brother-in-law Lewis Dent, who is in California. Hires and works with free blacks to cut and haul wood; in addition, Julia owns three slaves. Daughter Ellen Wrenshall (Nellie) Grant born July 4. Occasionally sees army friends in St. Louis who are stationed at Jefferson Barracks or traveling to and from western posts.

1856   Plants oats, corn, and potatoes, but is hampered by lack of money for seed. Builds two-story, six-room house (which Julia dislikes), names it Hardscrabble, and moves family into it in summer. Casts his first ballot in a presidential election, voting for Democrat James Buchanan over Whig-American party candidate Millard Fillmore (Republican John C. Frémont is not on the ballot in Missouri).

1857   Mother-in-law Ellen Wrenshall Dent dies January 14. Grant writes to father on February 7, asking for $500 loan with which to buy farm implements and seed for market crops. Financial panic in late August leads to nationwide economic depression. Meets William Tecumseh Sherman in St. Louis, where Sherman is helping close down the bank he had worked for since resigning from the army in 1853. Grant pawns gold watch for $22 on December 23.

1858   Son Jesse Root Grant born February 6. Father-in-law rents White Haven and 200 acres of ploughed land to Grant and moves into St. Louis; Grant rents out his 60 acres and Hardscrabble. Plants potatoes, corn, oats, and wheat, but farm suffers from unseasonably cold weather. Frederick is dangerously ill with typhoid fever in summer, and Grant develops recurrent fever and chills. Decides, with father-in-law, to auction off farm equipment and animals in fall, rent out cleared land, and sell woods on Dent property. Goes to work in St. Louis for Julia's cousin Harry Boggs in real estate firm, acting primarily as a rent collector.

1859   Lives in room in Boggs house until early March, then moves with family to rented cottage at Seventh and Lynch streets. Frees slave William Jones, whom he had bought from father-in-law (probably in 1858), on March 29. Seeks position as St. Louis County engineer, but is rejected by free-soil majority on county commission, which identifies him politically with the Democrats. Leaves real estate business, which has become increasingly unprofitable. Exchanges Hardscrabble for house on Ninth and Barton streets and note for $3,000, and moves there in October. Works briefly as clerk in the customhouse.

1860   Visits father (now living in Covington, Kentucky, across the Ohio from Cincinnati) and arranges to work as a clerk in his prosperous Galena, Illinois, leather-goods store, managed by younger brothers Simpson (who is suffering from tuberculosis) and Orvil. Moves to Galena with his family in May, renting house at 121 High Street. Becomes acquainted with attorney John A. Rawlins, an elector pledged to Democrat Stephen A. Douglas in the presidential race. Travels on business through northern Illinois, southern Wisconsin and Minnesota, and eastern Iowa. Does not meet Illinois residency requirement for voting in November 6 presidential election. In response to Abraham Lincoln's election, South Carolina secedes from the Union, December 20 (Mississippi, Florida, Alabama, Georgia, Louisiana, and Texas follow within two months).

1861   Confederates open fire on Fort Sumter on April 12. President Lincoln calls forth 75,000 militia on April 15. Grant attends public meeting in Galena on April 16 and presides at recruiting rally held on April 18. Declines to become captain of local company of volunteers, but agrees to drill them in Galena and at Camp Yates, Springfield, Illinois. Becomes military aide to Republican governor Richard Yates, April 29, partially through influence of Republican congressman Elihu B. Washburne, who represents Galena. Makes brief visit to Dent family in Missouri and watches as Union forces move against Confederate militia in St. Louis on May 10. Musters in three regiments of volunteers in central and southern Illinois. Applies on May 24 for commission as colonel and appointment as commander of regiment in regular army; request is not acted upon. Appointed commander of militia infantry regiment by Yates on June 15; troops are mustered into United States service as 21st Illinois Volunteers on June 28. Trains and disciplines troops at Springfield before crossing into northeastern Missouri on July 11. Guards railroad bridges and trestles against secessionist raids. Assigned command of several regiments in vicinity of Mexico, Missouri, on July 24. Appointed brigadier general of volunteers on August 5 at same time as several other colonels, after being recommended for promotion by Washburne. Names John A. Rawlins of Galena as his adjutant (Rawlins, whose wife is dying, does not join Grant's headquarters until early September, after her death). Commands troops at Ironton, Jefferson City, and Cape Girardeau, Missouri, before being appointed commander of the District of Southeast Missouri on September 1. Establishes his headquarters at Cairo, Illinois, at junction of Mississippi and Ohio rivers. Learns on September 5 that Confederates have entered previously neutral Kentucky and begun fortifying positions along the Mississippi at Columbus. Organizes expedition to occupy Paducah, Kentucky, near junction of Ohio and Tennessee rivers, and reaches town on September 6. Brother Samuel Simpson Grant dies of tuberculosis on September 13. Continues to train, discipline, and equip his forces and has fortifications built along the Ohio and the Mississippi. Attacks Confederate camp at Belmont, Missouri, on November 7. Joined in Cairo by Julia and their children. (Julia and some or all of the children will continue to stay with him during the war whenever it is practicable.) Major General Henry W. Halleck assumes command of the Department of the Missouri on November 19, becoming Grant's immediate superior. Grant attempts to stop contraband trade between Union and

Confederate-held territory and investigates corruption among army contractors. Tells subordinates to obey Department orders forbidding the sheltering of fugitive slaves in army camps, but also instructs them not to act as slave-catchers. Allegations begin circulating that Grant is often drunk. (Charge will recur throughout the war, although evidence indicates that, with a few exceptions, Grant abstained from drinking during the war.)

1862   Goes to St. Louis on January 23 and proposes immediate offensive up the Tennessee River against Fort Henry, Tennessee, to Halleck. Returns to Cairo on January 28 and sends telegram requesting permission to make attack, with the endorsement of Flag Officer Andrew H. Foote, commander of the Union riverboat flotilla. Halleck telegraphs his approval on January 30. Grant's expedition leaves Cairo on February 2. Confederates begin evacuating partially flooded Fort Henry on February 5, and the fort is surrendered to Foote after brief gunboat bombardment on February 6. Grant plans immediate attack on Fort Donelson, Tennessee, on the Cumberland River ten miles to the east, but it is delayed by bad roads and heavy rains. Writes to Washburne defending Brigadier General Charles F. Smith against accusations of disloyalty. (Smith, now a divisional commander under Grant, had been commandant of cadets when Grant was at West Point.) Union forces advance on Fort Donelson, February 12; their position outside the fort becomes difficult when temperature falls below freezing on February 13. Grant receives reinforcements and supplies sent from Paducah by Brigadier General William Tecumseh Sherman. On February 14 Grant is appointed commander of the District of West Tennessee; his troops become the Army of the Tennessee. Naval assault on Fort Donelson is repulsed on February 14. Confederates attack Grant's right on February 15; he orders counterattack along entire Union line, which captures portion of Confederate outer works. Confederate Brigadier General Simon Bolivar Buckner seeks terms of capitulation for the garrison before daybreak on February 16; Grant sends message demanding "unconditional and immediate surrender," which Buckner gives. Victory is hailed throughout North. Lincoln promotes Grant to major general of volunteers on February 19, making him second to Halleck in seniority in the western theater. Union forces move up the Cumberland and occupy Clarksville, Tennessee, on February 19. Grant orders occupation of Nashville on February 24; Union troops enter on February 25. Move angers Brigadier General Don Carlos Buell, commander of the Army of the Ohio, who had made Nashville the objective of his own advance. Halleck orders Grant on March 1 to send force up the Tennessee to disrupt Confederate railroads, then relieves him of command of expedition on March 4, accusing him of failing to report his strength and positions and naming Smith to command the river advance. Grant denies charge and stays at Fort Henry, making arrangements for expedition. Halleck repeats reprimand in telegram on March 6. Grant replies on March 7, defending his conduct and requesting to be relieved from further duty in Halleck's department; renews application on March 8. Halleck responds that he has been under pressure from Major General George B. McClellan, the Union general-in-chief, to forward reports and tells Grant that he will soon be restored to field command. Grant agrees on March 14 to serve in field under Halleck. Goes upriver (southward) to Savannah, Tennessee, on March 17. Sends reinforcements farther south to Pittsburg Landing, Tennessee, where Sherman, now a division commander, is organizing them for an advance against Corinth, Mississippi, while Grant awaits the arrival of Buell and the Army of the Ohio. On morning of April 6, Confederate army under General Albert Sidney Johnston attacks Union forces at Pittsburg Landing, beginning battle of Shiloh. Grant goes to Pittsburg Landing and takes command as Union troops fall back toward river. Johnston is killed in afternoon and General Pierre G. T. Beauregard assumes command of Confederates. By nightfall Union troops have been driven back to high ground along the river, but Confederates break off attack and reinforcements from Buell's army begin arriving. Grant orders counterattack on morning of April 7, and Confederates retreat toward Corinth in afternoon. Casualties during the two days at Shiloh are greater than the total losses in the four costliest battles of the Civil War until that time. Halleck arrives at Pittsburg Landing on April 11 and personally assumes command of Grant's and Buell's armies. Several newspapers severely criticize Grant for having been taken by surprise and suffering heavy losses at Shiloh. Washburne, Sherman, and his brother, Ohio senator John Sherman, publicly defend Grant's conduct. Grant mourns death on April 25 of Smith, who had fallen ill after injuring his leg in a minor boating accident. Halleck reorganizes his forces on April 30, making Grant his second in command while relieving him of authority over the Army of the Tennessee, and begins slow advance toward Corinth. Grant writes Halleck on May 11, asking to be either restored to field command or relieved from further duty; Halleck declines to do either. Confederates evacuate Corinth, May 29–30. Grant obtains leave of absence to visit his family and considers requesting transfer to another theater of operations, but is persuaded by Sherman to remain with army in hopes of being restored to independent command. Restored by Halleck to command of the Army of the Tennessee on June 10. Congress enacts legislation on June 17 relieving Grant of his obligations for missing Mexican War funds. Grant establishes headquarters in Memphis, June 23, and issues order on July 3 warning that Confederate guerillas captured out of uniform will not be treated as prisoners of war, and that Confederate sympathizers will have their property seized to compensate for losses caused by guerilla action. Halleck is appointed general-in-chief on July 11, and on July 16 appoints Grant to command all troops between the Mississippi and the Tennessee. Grant moves his headquarters to Corinth. Issues order, July 25, prohibiting government-licensed cotton dealers from making purchases with gold or silver (ban is soon countermanded by the administration). Repairs and guards railroads and begins to employ large numbers of escaped slaves as laborers. Sends reinforcements to Buell, who is deploying against Confederate advance through eastern Tennessee. Redeploys his troops to guard against Confederate forces in northern Mississippi under Major Generals Sterling Price and Earl Van Dorn, then attacks Price at Iuka, Mississippi, on September 19. Union forces capture town on September 20, but Price escapes and joins Van Dorn in attack on Corinth, which is repulsed, October 3–4. Grant is unhappy with his subordinate Major General William S. Rosecran's pursuit of the retreating Confederates and is pleased when Rosecrans replaces Buell on October 24 as commander of the

Army of the Ohio (command is renamed the Army of the Cumberland). Grant begins concentrating forces at Grand Junction, Tennessee, in early November, in preparation for advance south along the Mississippi Central Railroad. Directs John Eaton, chaplain of the 27th Ohio Volunteers, to set up camps for black refugees and to pay them to pick, bale, and ship cotton for the government. Angered by speculators in his military department, issues order on November 19 requiring all cotton traders to obtain permits from the army as well the Treasury Department; repeatedly criticizes the activities of Jewish cotton traders in his correspondence. Confers with Sherman in Oxford, Mississippi, on December 8, and orders him to move down the Mississippi against Vicksburg, while Grant advances south along the Mississippi Central Railroad against the Confederate forces under Lieutenant General John C. Pemberton. Issues General Order 11, December 17, expelling all Jews from the Department of the Tennessee. Recommends to the War Department that all cotton be purchased by the government at a fixed rate. Sherman leaves Memphis on December 19. Confederate cavalry under Van Dorn destroys Grant's main supply depot at Holly Springs, Mississippi, December 20. Grant orders a retreat but is unable to tell Sherman that he is turning back due to the cutting of telegraph lines by Confederate raiders. Sherman attacks Confederate positions along the Yazoo River, north of Vicksburg, on December 29 and is repulsed.

1863   Lincoln signs final Emancipation Proclamation on January 1. In response to protests, Lincoln revokes, through Halleck, General Order 11, expelling Jews, on January 4. Major General John A. McClernand, a politically influential War Democrat and former Illinois congressman who had been authorized by Lincoln to raise and lead troops against Vicksburg, assumes command of Sherman's expedition on January 4. Grant arrives in Memphis, January 10, and receives Halleck's approval on January 12 to relieve McClernand as commander of the Vicksburg expedition. Goes downriver and assumes personal command of the expedition on January 30, making his headquarters at Young's Point, Louisiana, several miles above Vicksburg. Assigns McClernand to lead one of the three corps in the river force (Sherman and Major General James B. McPherson command the other two). Grant attempts to bypass the Confederate batteries at Vicksburg by having a canal dug across a peninsula opposite the city and by opening a water route through Louisiana lakes, rivers, and bayous to the Mississippi below the city, and attempts to reach the Yazoo River above Vicksburg by opening two water routes through the rivers and bayous of the Mississippi Delta. Abandons all of these approaches by the end of March and begins preparing to cross the Mississippi below Vicksburg. Charles A. Dana, special emissary sent by Secretary of War Edwin M. Stanton, arrives on April 6 and begins to report favorably on Grant's performance to Stanton and Lincoln. Sherman advises Grant on April 8 to take the army back to Memphis and again approach Vicksburg overland along the line of the Mississippi Central Railroad. Instead, Grant has Acting Rear Admiral David D. Porter run his fleet past the Vicksburg shore batteries on April 16. Orders all commanders on April 22 to cooperate with efforts to raise black troops, and endorses the dismissal of three officers who sought to resign in protest against such a policy. Moves most of the army down the west bank of the Mississippi below Vicksburg, and then has Sherman feint attack north of the city on April 29. Grant crosses the river on April 30 and his troops win battle of Port Gibson, May 1. Sherman's corps crosses on May 7, and Grant's troops advance on Jackson, Mississippi, supplying themselves by foraging on the countryside. Jackson falls on May 14. Union forces win the battle of Champion's Hill, May 16, and capture crossings on the Big Black River, May 17, forcing Confederates back toward Vicksburg fortifications. Orders assault on Vicksburg defenses, May 19, which fails, and a second assault on May 22, which also fails. Begins siege operations against Vicksburg. Criticizes McClernand in letter to Halleck, May 24, as unfit to command his corps. After Sherman and McPherson strongly protest McClernand's publication of a self-congratulatory order in the newspapers without authorization, Grant removes him from command on June 18 and appoints Major General Edward O. C. Ord as his successor. Pemberton opens negotiations, July 3, and surrenders Vicksburg and its garrison on July 4. Grant is made a major general in the regular army on July 7. Sherman forces Confederates under General Joseph E.

Johnston to retreat east of Jackson, then breaks off pursuit. Grant rests his troops and works to secure Mississippi Valley. Sends Rawlins to Washington in late July to explain to Lincoln his reasons for removing McClernand. Goes to New Orleans to discuss strategy with Major General Nathaniel P. Banks, arriving on September 2. Injured when his horse falls on him, September 4. Returns to Vicksburg on September 16. Army of the Cumberland, commanded by Major General William S. Rosecrans, is defeated in battle of Chickamauga, September 19–20, and retreats to Chattanooga, Tennessee, which Confederates under General Braxton Bragg then besiege. On Halleck's orders, Grant begins sending troops to reinforce Rosecrans on September 22. Meets Secretary of War Stanton at the train station in Indianapolis, Indiana, on October 17, and goes with him to Louisville, Kentucky, where they confer on October 18. Grant is appointed commander of the Military Division of the Mississippi, covering territory between the Alleghenies and the Mississippi, except for Louisiana; replaces Rosecrans with Major General George H. Thomas and makes Sherman the new commander of the Army of the Tennessee. Still suffering effects of New Orleans injury, arrives in Chattanooga on October 23 after difficult ride over mountain trail, the only route still open into the town. Approves and implements plan drawn up by Thomas and his chief engineer, Brigadier General William F. Smith, to open new supply line into Chattanooga. Siege is broken on October 30, and Chattanooga garrison is reinforced by troops from the armies of the Potomac and the Tennessee. Grant plans offensive against Bragg, whose troops are entrenched on Missionary Ridge overlooking Chattanooga. Thomas's forces begin attack on November 23, capturing Confederate outposts below the ridge. On November 24 troops under Major General Joseph Hooker seize Lookout Mountain, overlooking southern end of Confederate position, while Sherman's troops occupy hill near northern end of ridge. Sherman's attack on November 25 makes little headway and Hooker's advance is delayed, but Thomas's troops break the Confederate center in the afternoon and Bragg's men retreat into northern Georgia. Grant sends force under Sherman to Knoxville, Tennessee, which is besieged by Confederates under Lieutenant General

James Longstreet; the Confederates begin retreating toward Virginia on December 3. Proposes winter campaign against Mobile and the interior of Alabama to Halleck on December 7, but administration does not act on plan because of concern over situation in East Tennessee and desire to mount campaign west of the Mississippi. Washburne introduces bill in Congress, December 14, to revive rank of lieutenant general, previously held only by George Washington and, by brevet, Winfield Scott. Responding on December 17 to letter from Barnabas Burns, an Ohio War Democrat, Grant privately disclaims any interest in the presidency.

1864   Returns to Nashville headquarters, January 12. Suggests abandoning attempts to take Richmond from the north or east in letter to Halleck on January 19, and proposes instead an advance from Suffolk, Virginia, toward Raleigh, North Carolina, with the aim of cutting rail lines into Virginia and forcing its evacuation. Learns that his son Frederick is dangerously ill in St. Louis and visits him there, January 27–February 1; Frederick begins to recover and Grant returns to Nashville. Continues to disavow any interest in the presidency in private letters, but considers a public statement to be incompatible with his military position. Halleck writes Grant on February 17 that proposed attack into North Carolina would open Maryland to Confederate invasion. Lincoln signs bill reviving rank of lieutenant general and nominates Grant for the position, February 29; he is confirmed by the U.S. Senate on March 2, with pay of $8,640 a year. Arrives in Washington on March 8 to receive commission and at the White House meets Lincoln for the first time. Assigned command of all Union armies, March 10. Confers in Virginia with Major General George G. Meade and decides to retain him as commander of the Army of the Potomac. Halleck becomes chief of staff and Sherman succeeds Grant as commander of the Military Division of the Mississippi. Grant plans spring campaign involving simultaneous advances by all Union forces in the field, with the Confederate armies in northern Georgia defending Atlanta and in northern Virginia defending Richmond as the main objectives. Returns to Nashville to consult with Sherman and other western commanders, goes back to Washington on March 23, and then joins the Army of the Potomac at Culpeper, Virginia. Orders halt in prisoner exchanges until the Confederates agree to recognize validity of the paroles given the Vicksburg garrison and to exchange black prisoners as well as white prisoners. On May 4 Grant and the Army of the Potomac cross the Rapidan River and begin advance on Richmond. Confederate General Robert E. Lee orders counteroffensive by the Army of Northern Virginia, leading to heavy losses on both sides in the battle of the Wilderness, May 5–6. Grant orders move southeast toward Spotsylvania Court House on May 7. Sherman begins advance toward Atlanta, May 7. Lee's troops reach Spotsylvania ahead of Union forces, May 8, and the two armies begin fighting there. Union assaults on May 10, 12, and 18 fail to achieve decisive break in Confederate line. Union forces are defeated in the Shenandoah Valley, May 15, and Union advance on Richmond along the James River is repulsed, May 16–17. Grant moves Army of the Potomac toward Richmond, May 20. Reaches the new Confederate lines near the North Anna River, May 23, but does not order a major attack. Begins disengaging on the night of May 26–27, and again moves toward Richmond, reaching new positions around Cold Harbor on May 31. Union attack on June 1 makes limited gains, and Grant orders second assault for June 2, which he then postpones until June 3. Attack is repulsed with severe loss. Army withdraws from Cold Harbor lines on June 12 and begins crossing the James River on June 14. Union troops attack Petersburg, rail center south of Richmond, June 15–18, capturing several Confederate defensive positions but failing to take the city itself. Grant decides against further frontal assaults and begins siege operations. Establishes headquarters at City Point, Virginia, sending and receiving most of his messages to and from other Union commanders through Washington. Makes unsuccessful attempt on June 22 to cut railroad running south from Petersburg (will make further attacks on Lee's flanks and supply routes into late October, resulting in the extension of siege lines to the north and west of Petersburg). Begins sending reinforcements to Washington on July 5 as Confederate force under Lieutenant General Jubal A. Early advances north through the Shenandoah Valley. Unsuccessfully tries to have politically influential Major General Benjamin F. Butler removed

from active command of Union forces along the James
River. After series of flanking maneuvers along the Chattanooga–Atlanta railroad, Sherman forces the Confederates to retreat inside Atlanta's fortifications on July 9.
Early's troops skirmish with Union forces on outskirts of
Washington, July 11–12, and then withdraw. Grant mourns
death of Major General James B. McPherson, Sherman's
successor as commander of the Army of the Tennessee,
who is killed outside of Atlanta on July 22. Union engineers explode mine at Petersburg on July 30, creating gap
in Confederate line, but Union troops fail to exploit it and
are severely repulsed; Grant describes it to Halleck as "the
saddest affair I have witnessed in this war." On August 1,
orders Major General Philip H. Sheridan to take command of Union field forces in the Shenandoah Valley and,
on Lincoln's suggestion, goes to Washington, August 5–7,
to simplify command arrangements in the upper Potomac
region. Recommends to Stanton on August 15 that Halleck be made commander of the Pacific Division, but Halleck is retained in Washington as chief of staff. Writes
Halleck on August 15 that he is unwilling to send troops
away from Petersburg to guard against possible uprisings
in the North against the draft, and receives telegram from
Lincoln on August 17 endorsing his decision. Sherman's
troops capture Atlanta, September 2. Confers with Sheridan in West Virginia, September 16–17, and approves his
plans for taking the offensive in the Shenandoah Valley.
Visits his family at Burlington, New Jersey, where they
have rented a house, before returning to City Point on September 19. Sheridan wins battles at Winchester, September
19, Fisher's Hill, September 22, and Cedar Creek, October
19, and devastates large parts of the Shenandoah Valley, a
major source of supplies for Lee's army; his success, along
with the fall of Atlanta, raises hopes of the administration's supporters for victory in the fall elections. Approves
on October 12 Sherman's proposed march from Atlanta to
the sea and endorses it in letter to Lincoln and Stanton on
October 13. Reconsiders when Confederate army under
General John B. Hood reaches the Tennessee River, but is
assured by Sherman that Hood can be defeated by forces
in Tennessee under Thomas and gives his final approval to
Sherman's plan on November 2. Lincoln is reelected, November 8. Sherman leaves Atlanta, November 16. Hood

reaches outskirts of Nashville, Tennessee, on December 2. Grant repeatedly urges Thomas to attack Hood, issues and cancels order relieving him on December 9, orders Major General John A. Logan to Nashville on December 13 to replace Thomas, then decides on December 14 to go to Nashville himself and reaches Washington on December 15. Thomas attacks and decisively defeats Hood, December 15–16; Grant congratulates Thomas and retains him in command. Visits his family in Burlington on December 17. Sherman captures Savannah, Georgia, December 21. Union expedition under Butler attacks Fort Fisher, guarding entrance to Wilmington, North Carolina, on December 25 and is repulsed. Grant approves on December 27 Sherman's proposal to march his army north through the Carolinas.

1865   Has Butler relieved from command and orders new expedition against Fort Fisher under Brigadier General Alfred H. Terry. Receives furnished house in Philadelphia as gift from group of citizens. Fort Fisher is captured January 15; Grant goes there, January 27–31, to plan attack on Wilmington. Sherman begins march through South Carolina, February 1. Grant recommends on February 1 that Lincoln meet with Confederate peace commissioners who had come to City Point on January 31. Lincoln has unsuccessful conference with them at Hampton Roads, February 3. Receives letter from Lee, March 3, proposing that they meet to negotiate peace terms. Asks Stanton for instructions, and is told by Lincoln that he has authority only to accept Lee's capitulation. Sister Clara Grant dies March 6. Sherman reaches Goldsboro, North Carolina, March 23. Grant meets with Lincoln, Sherman, and Porter at City Point, March 27, to discuss spring campaign and possible terms of Confederate surrender. Begins offensive southwest of Petersburg, March 29, leading to Union victory at Five Forks, April 1, and capture of much of the Petersburg entrenchments, April 2. Confederates evacuate Petersburg and Richmond, April 2, and Grant begins pursuit of retreating Army of Northern Virginia. Lee surrenders the Army of Northern Virginia to Grant at Appomattox Court House, Virginia, April 9. Grant meets with Lee, Longstreet, and other Confederate generals on April 10. Goes to Washington and confers with Stanton on April 13 and with Lincoln and the Cabinet on April 14. Declines invitation to join Lincolns at Ford's Theatre that evening and goes with Julia to visit their children in Burlington. Learns in Philadelphia that Lincoln has been fatally shot, and returns to Washington at Stanton's request on April 15. Stands at the catafalque during White House funeral service on April 19. Receives on April 21 an agreement signed by Sherman and General Joseph E. Johnston on April 18 that proposes political and military terms for the surrender of the remaining Confederate armies. Submits agreement to President Andrew Johnson and the Cabinet that evening; it is disapproved and Grant is ordered by Stanton and Johnson to go to Raleigh, North Carolina, and resume hostilities against Johnston's army. Arrives on April 24 and confers with Sherman, who on April 26 accepts Johnston's surrender under terms similar to those given to Lee at Appomattox. Grant returns to Washington, April 29. Family moves into Philadelphia home in early May. Confederates in Alabama, Mississippi, and eastern Louisiana surrender on May 4. Orders Sheridan to Texas on May 17 to force surrender of remaining Confederates and to exert pressure on the French to withdraw their army from Mexico. Watches grand review of the Union armies in Washington, May 23–24. Confederates in western Louisiana and Texas surrender on May 26. Endorses Lee's application for presidential pardon and amnesty, June 16, and protests his recent indictment for treason, arguing that it violates the Appomattox surrender terms (indictment is dropped). Directs mustering out of volunteer troops and the reorganization of the army; Sherman is assigned to command new Military Division of the Mississippi, covering the western plains. Urges President Johnson to sell arms and send officers to the liberal forces in Mexico fighting against Emperor Maximilian (will continue to advocate interventionist Mexican policy and oppose Secretary of State William H. Seward's attempts to achieve a French withdrawal through diplomacy). Makes extensive tour through the East and Midwest, July 24–October 6; is presented with a house by the citizens of Galena and cheered by crowds throughout his travels. Submits report on October 20 recommending establishment of peacetime army of 80,000 men. Stanton asks for reduction, and Grant submits new figure of 53,000 on November 3. Buys house in Washington at 205 I Street, N.W., for $30,000. Instructs military commanders to prevent Fenians (Irish nationalists) from attacking Canada (Fenian border incidents continue until 1871). Makes tour of South at Johnson's request, November 27–December 11, visiting Raleigh, North Carolina, Charleston, South Carolina, and Savannah and Augusta, Georgia. Submits report describing the majority of Southerners as submissive to the government's authority, recommending the withdrawal of black troops from the interior of the South, and criticizing some agents of the Freedmen's Bureau for encouraging blacks to believe that they will be given land by the government. Johnson sends report to the Senate on December 18 and cites it in his accompanying message describing the South as reconciled to its defeat.

1866   Issues order on January 12 protecting army officers, soldiers, and federal officials (including agents of the Freedmen's Bureau) acting in their official capacity, as well as Unionists charged for their wartime actions against the Confederates, from prosecution or suit in Southern local and state courts. Order also forbids the prosecution of blacks for offenses for which whites are not punished in the same manner or degree. Receives $50,000 in government bonds and $20,000 in cash as gift from committee of New York businessmen, who also pay mortgage on his Washington house. Son Frederick is appointed to the U.S. Military Academy in March. Concerned by increasing violence against freed blacks, issues orders on July 6 directing commanders in the South to arrest and hold for trial persons engaged in violence in cases where the civil authorities fail to act. Promoted on July 25 to rank of general, previously held only by George Washington. Strength of army is set by act of Congress, July 28, at approximately 54,000 men. Accompanies Johnson on tour of the North, August 28–September 17, ostensibly connected with the dedication in Chicago of a monument to Stephen A. Douglas. Johnson uses tour to rally support for National Union congressional candidates who support him in his struggle with the Republicans over Reconstruction and gives speeches violently attacking Republican leaders. Grant writes Julia that Johnson's speeches are disgraceful, but that his opinion of the President must be kept private. Orders surplus arms removed from Southern arsenals, and writes to Sheridan on October 12 expressing fear that Johnson's opposition to congressional Reconstruction policy may result in renewed rebellion against the Union. Repeatedly refuses Johnson's requests in late October that he accompany diplomatic mission to Mexico; Sherman goes in his place. Grant negotiates agreement between rival parties in Baltimore that prevents election-day violence. Urges Brigadier General Edward O. C. Ord to use his influence with the Arkansas legislature to gain ratification of the Fourteenth Amendment.

1867   Congress passes Reconstruction Act over Johnson's veto on March 2; it declares that no legal state governments exist in the former Confederate states (excluding Tennessee), divides these states into five military districts, and sets conditions necessary for their regaining congressional representation, including ratification of the Fourteenth Amendment and adoption of state constitutions providing for black suffrage. Congress also passes Command of the Army Act, requiring that all orders to the army go through Grant and protecting him from being removed against his will, and the Tenure of Office Act, restricting the power of the president to remove certain government officials without Senate approval. Johnson appoints district commanders recommended by Grant. Further legislation passed in March and July increases the role of Grant and the district commanders in implementing the Reconstruction Act. Grant rents seaside cottage at Long Branch, New Jersey (later buys summer home there, and family will return whenever possible for much of remainder of Grant's life). Congress adjourns July 20. Grant advises Johnson on August 1 not to remove Stanton as secretary of war for his support of congressional Reconstruction policy, but accepts appointment as secretary of war *ad interim* when Johnson suspends Stanton on August 12. When Johnson removes Sheridan as district commander for Louisiana and Texas for his forceful implementation of the Reconstruction acts, Grant protests in a letter that is soon made public, and continues to advise district commanders to execute congressional Reconstruction policy. Endorsements of Grant for the presidency increase in the Republican press after the Democrats make gains in the fall elections. Congress reconvenes on November 21 and begins considering Stanton's suspension.

1868   Grant tells Johnson on January 11 that he has recently learned that violation of the Tenure of Office Act is punishable by fine and imprisonment and therefore will not continue as secretary of war against the wishes of the Senate. Senate votes on January 13 not to sustain Stanton's suspension. Grant vacates office at the War Department on January 14 and Stanton reoccupies it. In exchange of letters, Johnson accuses Grant of breaking an earlier promise to retain the office so that Stanton would be forced to test constitutionality of Tenure of Office Act in court, and of not making his intentions known during their January 11 meeting; Grant denies accusations of bad faith. Correspondence is published, making their breach public. On February 21 Johnson appoints Adjutant General Lorenzo Thomas secretary of war *ad interim*, but Stanton refuses to leave his office in the War Department. House of Representatives votes eleven articles of impeachment of Johnson, March 2–3, nine of which concern his attempt to replace Stanton with Lorenzo Thomas. Senate acquits Johnson of the most comprehensive article of impeachment by one vote on May 16. Republican national convention meeting in Chicago unanimously nominates Grant for president on the first ballot, May 21, and nominates Speaker of the House Schuyler Colfax of Indiana for vice-president. Grant learns of his nomination at army headquarters in Washington. Johnson is acquitted of two further articles by one vote, May 26, and his trial is adjourned indefinitely. Stanton resigns and is succeeded as secretary of war by Brigadier General John M. Schofield. Grant accepts nomination on May 29 in letter that concludes, "Let us have peace"; phrase becomes main slogan of Republican campaign. On July 9 the Democrats nominate Horatio Seymour, former governor of New York, for president and Francis P. Blair, Jr., a former Missouri congressman who had commanded a division under Grant during the Vicksburg campaign, for vice-president. Fourteenth Amendment is declared ratified on July 28. Grant makes inspection tour of the West with Sherman and Sheridan in July, traveling mostly by train through Kansas, Nebraska, Wyoming, and Colorado. Visits Denver before returning to Galena, where he receives reports from Republican leaders. Makes no public political statements during campaign. Follows election returns at Washburne's home in Galena, November 3. Defeats Seymour, receiving 214 of 294 electoral votes and 52.7 percent of the popular vote. Returns to Washington in early November.

1869   On February 26 Congress proposes ratification of the Fifteenth Amendment, forbidding the denial of suffrage on account of race, color, or previous condition of servitude. Grant is inaugurated March 4. Delivers short address advocating full repayment of the national debt, redemption of government bonds and payment of their interest in gold, eventual restoration of the currency to a specie basis, and ratification of the Fifteenth Amendment. Names Sherman as commanding general of the army and issues order giving him authority over its administrative bureaus and staff corps. Makes Cabinet appointments without consulting Republican leaders or, in some cases, the nominees themselves. Washburne receives one-week courtesy appointment as secretary of state before becoming minister to France, and is succeeded by former New York governor, congressman, and senator Hamilton Fish. Grant withdraws nomination of wealthy New York department store owner Alexander T. Stewart to be secretary of the treasury because of 1789 law barring persons engaged in trade from holding the office, and names Massachusetts congressman George S. Boutwell in his place. Remainder of Cabinet includes Rawlins (secretary of war), Massachusetts state supreme court judge Ebenezer R. Hoar (attorney general), Maryland senator John A. J. Creswell (postmaster general), Philadelphia businessman Adolph E. Borie (secretary of the navy), who resigns in June and is succeeded by New Jersey state attorney general George E. Robeson, and former Ohio governor Jacob D. Cox (secretary of the interior). At Rawlins' request, Grant rescinds his earlier order and instructs the army administrative bureaus and staff corps to report to the secretary of war instead of the commanding general. On April 7 Grant proposes that referendums on new Virginia and Mississippi state constitutions be held with separate votes taken on disqualification clauses barring many former Confederates from voting or holding office. Signs appropriate legislation, April 10; act gives him power to schedule and

supervise elections previously held by district commanders. (Virginia and Mississippi approve constitutions and
reject disqualification clauses, July 6 and November 30;
Texas also adopts new constitution on November 30, and
all three states are readmitted, January–March 1870.)
Grant appoints Colonel Ely S. Parker (Donehogawa), a
Seneca Indian sachem and a member of his staff since
1864, as commissioner of Indian affairs, and begins reforming federal Indian policy. (New approach, known as
Grant's "peace policy," intended to resolve status of western Indian tribes, eventually includes their concentration
on reservations under the supervision of religious denominations, the conversion of nomadic hunting tribes to an
agricultural way of life, and the abolition of the treaty system that recognized tribes as separate nations; it is partially opposed by Sherman, who favors giving the army
sole control over Indian affairs and using force to drive
Indians onto the reservations. Despite new policy, however, fighting and raiding between Indians and settlers and
the army occur throughout Grant's administration.) Fi-
nanciers Jay Gould and James Fisk, Jr., plot with Abel R.
Corbin, who had recently married Grant's sister Virginia,
to corner the gold market and in June begin attempts to
persuade Grant to stop further government sale of gold.
Responding to overtures from President Buenaventura
Báez, Grant sends his personal secretary, Colonel Orville
E. Babcock, to the Dominican Republic (widely known in
the United States as Santo Domingo) on July 17 to investigate possible annexation of the country. Despite Rawlins'
advocacy of the cause of Cubans rebelling against Spain,
Grant agrees with Fish that the United States should not
support the rebels by granting them recognition as belligerents. (Diplomatic tensions caused by Americans involved in the Cuban rebellion persist for remainder of
Grant's presidency.) Rawlins dies of tuberculosis, September 6, and Grant loses closest adviser. Sherman serves as
secretary of war until confirmation in November of
William W. Belknap of Iowa, who had commanded a brigade under Sherman during the war. Babcock returns
from the Dominican Republic on September 14, having
signed treaty of annexation without diplomatic authority.
Gould, Fisk, and Corbin's speculations create gold market
panic in New York, September 24. Grant and Boutwell

decide to sell $4 million in government gold, restoring
financial stability. (Fish subsequently tells congressional
investigators that Julia Grant had been speculating in gold
with Gould and Corbin, but investigation exonerates both
her and Grant of wrongdoing in their contacts with the
conspirators.) Supports Radical Republicans for governor
in Mississippi, where brother-in-law Lewis Dent is conservative National Union candidate, and in Texas (Radicals
win in both states). Babcock returns to the Dominican
Republic carrying proper diplomatic credentials and signs
second treaty of annexation with Báez on November 29.
Grant nominates Stanton and Hoar to the Supreme
Court. Stanton is confirmed but dies on December 24;
Hoar fails to receive Senate confirmation. After months of
political unrest caused by the expulsion of black members
from the state legislature, Grant restores military rule in
Georgia on December 24 (black legislators regain their
seats and the state ratifies the Fifteenth Amendment before being readmitted in July 1870).

1870   Grant submits treaty for annexation of the Dominican Re-
            public to the Senate for ratification, January 10. Massachu-
            setts Republican Charles Sumner, chairman of the Senate
            Foreign Relations Committee, leads opposition to annex-
            ation, warning that it will involve the United States in Do-
            minican civil strife and threaten the independence of
            Haiti. Grant nominates William Strong of Pennsylvania
            and Joseph P. Bradley of New Jersey to the Supreme Court
            on February 7; both are soon confirmed. Foreign Rela-
            tions Committee unfavorably reports treaty to the Senate
            on March 15. Fifteenth Amendment is declared ratified,
            March 30. Grant signs first Enforcement Act, passed under
            the enforcement provision of the Fifteenth Amendment,
            on May 31. Act makes the denial of suffrage on racial
            grounds through force, fraud, bribery, and intimidation a
            federal offense. (Further acts, signed on July 14, 1870, and
            February 28, 1871, extend federal powers over elections, es-
            pecially in large cities; however, execution of the enforce-
            ment acts, particularly in the South, is sporadic and often
            ineffectual.) Grant sends message to the Senate, May 31,
            arguing that the annexation of the Dominican Republic
            will prevent further European intervention in the Carib-
            bean, guard American commerce through the Gulf of
            Mexico and the Isthmus of Panama, hasten the end of

slavery in Cuba, Puerto Rico, and Brazil, provide a market for American goods, and reduce the trade deficit. In bid for Southern Republican support for Dominican treaty, Grant asks for Hoar's resignation and names Amos T. Akerman of Georgia as new attorney general. Signs bill on June 22 establishing Department of Justice, increasing power of the federal government to enforce Reconstruction legislation. Senate fails to ratify Dominican treaty by vote of 28–28, June 30. Defeat embitters Grant's relations with Sumner and Missouri senator Carl Schurz and draws him into closer political alliance with congressional supporters, including Indiana senator Oliver P. Morton, New York senator Roscoe Conkling, and Benjamin F. Butler, now a Massachusetts congressman and Sumner's rival in that state's Republican party. Son Ulysses, Jr., enters Harvard College (graduates in 1874). Cox resigns as secretary of the interior in October to protest lack of civil service reform in Grant's administration and is replaced by Columbus Delano of Ohio, the commissioner of internal revenue. In his annual message to Congress, December 5, Grant again advocates acquiring the Dominican Republic and asks Congress to authorize a commission to negotiate a new treaty. (Congress funds commission for investigatory purposes only; it reports favorably on annexation in spring 1871, but Grant does not propose further action.)

1871   Grant submits report to Congress, January 13, on Ku Klux Klan outrages in the South; Congress begins investigation of Klan activities and debate over new enforcement law. Grant appoints Fish and four other commissioners on February 9 to negotiate American claims against Great Britain for damages caused by Confederate raiders built in British shipyards during the Civil War (popularly known as the *Alabama* claims, after a famous Confederate warship). Commissioners are also empowered to negotiate the water boundary between Washington Territory and British Columbia, disputes between the United States and Canada over trade, navigation on the St. Lawrence River, fishing rights, and claims against the United States resulting from the Fenian raids on Canada. Grant has administration's Senate supporters remove Sumner, who had advocated settling Civil War claims against Britain by annexing Canada, as chairman of the Foreign Relations Committee on March 10. Urges the passage of new enforcement bill in message to Congress, March 23, and signs it into law, April 20; act establishes criminal penalties for individuals who conspire to deprive citizens of their rights under the Fourteenth and Fifteenth Amendments, provides for prosecution in federal court in cases where state authorities fail to act, and gives the president power to suspend the writ of habeas corpus and declare martial law. Attorney General Akerman begins prosecution of Klansmen, concentrating on cases in North and South Carolina and Mississippi. Treaty of Washington, signed on May 8, submits commerce raider claims and western boundary dispute to arbitration, rejects claims arising from Fenian raids, and resolves other U.S.-Canadian issues. (Arbitration tribunal composed of American, British, Brazilian, Italian, and Swiss members awards the United States $15.5 million and Great Britain $1.9 million in Civil War claims on August 25, 1872; Emperor William I of Germany, the sole arbitrator of boundary dispute, settles it in favor of the United States on October 21, 1872.) Commissioner of Indian Affairs Parker submits his resignation on June 29 despite having been cleared in February of corruption charges brought before a congressional committee. Grant suspends the writ of habeas corpus in nine counties in South Carolina, October 17, and dispatches federal troops; Akerman supervises arrests of hundreds of suspected Klansmen (several dozen are eventually convicted). Grant replaces Akerman, who had ruled against western railroad companies in land-grant cases, as attorney general in December with former Oregon senator George H. Williams, who continues Klan prosecutions until 1873. (Klan declines as result of prosecutions, but other white supremacist groups continue acts of violence against blacks and white Republicans.)

1872   Signs act on March 1 establishing Yellowstone National Park (the first national park in the world). Convention of Liberal Republicans opposed to Grant's administration meets in Cincinnati on May 1. It nominates Horace Greeley, editor of the *New-York Tribune*, for president and Benjamin Gratz Brown, governor of Missouri, for vice-president, and adopts platform denouncing corruption in government and calling for civil service reform, universal political amnesty for former Confederates, and an end to federal intervention in the South. Grant is nominated for president on the first ballot by the Republican convention meeting in Philadelphia, June 5–6, which nominates Senator Henry Wilson of Massachusetts for vice-president. Democratic convention endorses Greeley and Brown on July 9. Grant is reelected on November 5, winning 286 of 352 electoral votes and over 55 percent of the popular vote. Voting in Louisiana results in two sets of election returns. On December 3 Grant authorizes use of the army to enforce U.S. circuit court orders regarding the Louisiana election. Attends funeral of Greeley, who died on November 29. Circuit court judge Edward H. Durell declares the Republican election returns valid, December 5, and orders statehouse seized; troops occupy it and admit Republican legislators, who declare William P. Kellogg to be the governor-elect. Grant appoints Ward Hunt of New York to the Supreme Court, December 11 (confirmed by the Senate, he is seated in 1873).

1873   Orders army to protect Kellogg's inauguration, but forbids it to disperse conservative group who declare themselves to be the legitimate state legislature and claim John McEnery to be governor. Signs Coinage Act, February 12, demonetizing the silver dollar, and salary act, March 3, which raises the president's salary from $25,000 to $50,000 and increases the pay of the vice-president, Cabinet members, Supreme Court justices, and members of Congress (measure is widely criticized and becomes known as the "Salary Grab" act). Inaugurated for second term on March 4. Concludes his address by describing his reelection as vindication against the abuse and slander to which he had been subjected during the war and his first term. Boutwell is elected to the Senate from Massachusetts and is replaced as secretary of the treasury by his assistant secretary, William A. Richardson, also from Massachusetts. Chief Justice Salmon P. Chase dies May 7. After months of worsening violence in Louisiana, Grant sends troop reinforcements to state and issues proclamation on May 22 ordering pro-McEnery forces to disperse. Father dies in Covington, Kentucky, on June 29. Series of financial failures in New York, September 8–18, leads to widespread panic and severe national economic depression (which continues to worsen for remainder of Grant's term). Grant and Richardson confer with bankers in New York in late September and moderately increase the supply of paper money irredeemable in gold ("greenbacks"). In December Grant nominates Attorney General Williams to be Chief Justice of the Supreme Court. Father-in-law dies in Washington on December 15.

1874   Withdraws nomination of Williams because of Senate opposition focusing on his wife's purchase of a carriage with government funds. Nominates Caleb Cushing of Massachusetts in his place, then withdraws nomination when letter Cushing wrote to Jefferson Davis in March 1861, recommending a former clerk for a Confederate position, is made public. Appoints Morrison R. Waite of Ohio, who is confirmed on January 21. On April 22 Grant vetoes bill to further increase the supply of irredeemable paper money. Sherman, frustrated by Belknap's increasing control of the army and Grant's reluctance to clearly define the commanding general's authority, receives permission from Belknap and Grant to move his headquarters from Washington, D.C., to St. Louis. Daughter Nellie marries Englishman Algernon Sartoris at the White House, May 21. Secretary of the Treasury Richardson resigns after being linked to a Massachusetts tax collection scandal; Grant nominates Benjamin H. Bristow of Kentucky, a former solicitor general, to replace him. Postmaster General Creswell resigns in June and is replaced in August by former Connecticut governor Marshall Jewell. White League militia overthrows Kellogg government in Louisiana and seizes control of New Orleans, September 14. Grant orders 5,000 troops sent to New Orleans, September 16. White League forces disperse and Kellogg is restored as governor. Fall elections give the Democrats a majority in the House of Representatives and reduce the Republican majority in the Senate. Louisiana legislative election again results in disputed count. Grant withdraws troops from the statehouse in New Orleans, November 17, but orders Sheridan to Louisiana on December 24 to observe situation there.

1875   Democrats attempt to gain control of Louisiana legislature on January 4 by forcibly installing five members in its lower chamber. At Kellogg's request, federal troops eject the five Democrats from the statehouse. Sheridan defends their removal and requests authority to try White League leaders by military tribunal. Action is widely denounced as an illegitimate military intervention in civil affairs. In message to the Senate, January 13, Grant reviews history of electoral fraud and violence in Louisiana, defends his previous interventions as constitutionally justified, states his belief that the military did not commit an "intentional wrong" by ousting the disputed legislators, and asks Congress to resolve the matter. (Congressional compromise, implemented in April 1875, gives control of the lower chamber of the legislature to the Democrats, the state senate to the Republicans, and retains Kellogg as governor.) Signs Specie Resumption Act, January 14, setting January 1, 1879, as date for restoration of currency to a specie basis. In message to Congress, February 8, Grant describes the revocation in 1874 of Arkansas's Reconstruction constitution as the illegal result of fraud and intimidation and asks Congress not to recognize it; instead, the House passes resolution accepting the new Arkansas state constitution and the Senate refuses to endorse federal intervention. Signs Civil Rights Act, March 1, which forbids racial discrimination in public accommodations, travel, and jury duty (law is overturned by Supreme Court in 1883). Attorney General Williams resigns and is replaced by New York lawyer Edwards Pierrepont. Bristow's investigation of the "whiskey rings" defrauding the treasury of excise taxes results in massive raids, May 10, and the subsequent indictment of over 200 distillers and revenue agents. Grant writes letter, published May 31, disavowing interest in a third term. First grandchild, Grant Sartoris, born at Long Branch on July 11 (child dies in England, May 21, 1876). Pierrepont warns Grant that Babcock is implicated in the St. Louis "whiskey ring"; Grant writes note directing the investigation to continue: "Let no guilty man escape if it can be avoided." Babcock and others tell Grant that the prosecutions are politically motivated. Mississippi governor Adelbert Ames calls on September 8 for federal troops to suppress violence by "White Liners" attempting to intimidate Republican voters in the state election. Pierrepont forwards message to Grant at Long Branch. Grant writes to Pierrepont on September 13 describing federal intervention in the South as unpopular but necessary and reluctantly agreeing to send troops. Pierrepont selectively quotes from Grant's letter in his reply to Ames on Sep-

tember 14, encouraging Ames to suppress disorders with
the state militia and promising federal intervention only
in case of direct rebellion against the state government.
(Democrats win control of Mississippi legislature in November, and Ames resigns in 1876 to avoid impeachment.)
Secretary of the Interior Delano resigns amid accusations
of nepotism and corruption in his department and is replaced in October by former Michigan senator Zachariah
Chandler. Grant abandons efforts to keep gold prospec-
tors out of the Black Hills despite treaty ceding it to the
Sioux. Democratic majority in House begins investigating
corruption in Grant's administration when new Congress
meets, December 6. Babcock is indicted in St. Louis
"whiskey ring" case, December 9.

1876   Grant has Pierrepont order U.S. attorneys prosecuting
           "whiskey ring" cases not to grant immunity to suspects in
           return for testimony. After being persuaded by his Cabi-
           net not to testify at Babcock's trial, Grant gives sworn
           deposition praising Babcock's character and Babcock is
           acquitted, February 24, but is forced to leave the White
           House staff. Secretary of War Belknap, under congres-
           sional investigation for taking bribes from an army post
           trader, resigns on the morning of March 2 and is im-
           peached by the House that afternoon; Grant is criticized
           for accepting his resignation. (Belknap is later acquitted
           by the Senate on the grounds that his resignation removed
           him from their jurisdiction.) Grant appoints Ohio attor-
           ney Alphonso Taft as new secretary of war; Taft restores
           Sherman's operational control of the army, and Sherman
           returns to Washington. Grant opens International Centen-
           nial Exposition in Philadelphia, May 10. Attorney General
           Pierrepont is made minister to Great Britain, and is suc-
           ceeded in May by Taft, who is replaced as secretary of war
           by James D. Cameron of Pennsylvania. First surviving
           grandchild, Julia Grant, daughter of Frederick Dent
           Grant, born June 7 (eight more grandchildren are born
           during Grant's lifetime). Secretary of the Treasury Bristow
           resigns on June 17 and is succeeded by Maine senator Lot
           M. Morrill. Lieutenant Colonel George A. Custer and 262
           of his men are killed in Montana, June 25, by the Sioux
           and Northern Cheyenne in the battle of the Little Big
           Horn (army soon resumes offensive, which continues
           until surviving Indians surrender in 1877). Postmaster

General Jewell resigns in July and is replaced by James N. Tyner of Connecticut. In October Grant sends troops to South Carolina and issues proclamation in attempt to control violence by white supremacist rifle clubs before the election. Presidential election between Democrat Samuel J. Tilden and Republican Rutherford B. Hayes on November 7 results in conflicting election returns in South Carolina, Florida, and Louisiana, and disqualification controversy over an Oregon elector, causing a disputed electoral count. Grant orders troops to guard the capitals of the three Southern states, allowing their Republican-controlled election boards to prepare and certify official returns, and promises to maintain order and work for a fair resolution of the electoral dispute. Reviews his administration's record in his final annual message to Congress, December 5, and describes his failures as "errors of judgment, not of intent." Defends his attempt to annex the Dominican Republic by arguing that it would have served as a refuge for persecuted Southern blacks and allowed them to secure their rights in the South by threatening to emigrate there.

1877   Supports creation of electoral commission to resolve presidential election and signs bill establishing 15-member panel on January 29. In series of 8–7 votes, commission awards all disputed electoral votes to Hayes, giving him electoral majority of one. Joint session of Congress declares Hayes the victor, March 2. Hayes privately takes oath of office on Saturday, March 3, and Grants leave the White House after public inaugural on March 5. Plans European tour. Visits Galena before sailing from Philadelphia on May 17 with Julia, son Jesse, and John Russell Young of the New York *Herald*. (Young's reports of Grant's travels and of their conversations about the Civil War and politics are widely reprinted in newspapers and are published in 1879 as part of travel account *Around the World with General Grant*.) Arrives in Liverpool, May 28, and visits Manchester and Leicester before going to London. Attends numerous banquets, receptions, and welcoming ceremonies, and meets prominent aristocrats and political leaders (will do so in many of the countries he visits). Sees Nellie and new grandson Algernon Edward Sartoris at her home in Southampton, and has dinner with Queen Victoria at Windsor Castle on June 27. Sails to

Ostend, July 5, and tours Belgium, western Germany, Switzerland, northern Italy, and Alsace and Lorraine before returning to Britain for tour of Scotland. Arrives in Edinburgh, August 31, and visits Glasgow and the Highlands. Goes to Newcastle-on-Tyne in northern England, September 20, where he watches procession of approximately 80,000 Northumberland and Durham miners, workers, and artisans in his honor on September 22 and is hailed for his role in ending slavery and upholding "the rights of man and the dignity of labor." Tours steel mills in Sheffield and factories in Birmingham and then stays with Nellie in Southampton for ten days. Arrives in Paris, October 24. Meets French republican leader Léon Gambetta, but is unable to see Victor Hugo, who considers Grant to have favored Prussia in the 1870–71 war. Remains in Paris until December, then sails for Italy from Marseilles. Arrives in Naples, December 17, goes up Mt. Vesuvius, and tours Pompeii. Spends Christmas in Palermo harbor, then sails for Egypt by way of Malta. Reads Mark Twain's *The Innocents Abroad* and Petroleum V. Nasby's *The Nasby Papers* on board ship.

1878   Arrives in Alexandria January 5. Meets explorer Henry Morton Stanley, who is returning from his recent expedition down the Congo River. Goes up the Nile to Cairo, Karnak, and Luxor, then sails for Palestine from Port Said in February 9, landing at Jaffa. Visits Jerusalem, Bethlehem, Nablus, Nazareth, and Damascus before sailing from Beirut. Arrives in Constantinople, March 5, and after short stay goes to Athens and Rome. Has audience with Pope Leo XIII, then goes to Florence, Venice, Milan, and Paris with Nellie. Jesse returns to the United States. Grant tours the Netherlands before arriving in Berlin on June 26 where congress of European powers is meeting to revise the peace terms of the Russo-Turkish War of 1877–78. Discusses the American Civil War with German chancellor Prince Otto von Bismarck, who equates the preservation of the Union with the wars of German unification (Grant later says that Gambetta and Bismarck were the two men in Europe he found most impressive). Meets sister Mary and brother-in-law Michael John Cramer, American minister to Denmark, in Copenhagen on July 6. Tours Norway and Sweden before sailing for Russia from Stockholm. Arrives in St. Petersburg July 30. Discusses American Indian

warfare with Tsar Alexander II, answers Grand Duke
Alexis' questions about Custer, and meets with Chancellor
Aleksandr M. Gorchakov. Visits Moscow and Warsaw be-
fore arriving in Vienna August 18. Tours Bavaria, southern
France, and northern Spain, reaching Madrid on October
28. Fall elections give Democrats control of both houses of
Congress and increase public speculation about Grant
seeking a third presidential term. Grant visits Lisbon, Cor-
dova, Seville, Cadiz, and Gibraltar before returning to
London by way of Paris.

1879   Grant arrives in Dublin, January 3, for tour of Ireland
while Julia stays with Nellie in England. Son Frederick
joins Grant and Julia, and they sail for India from
Marseilles on January 24. Arrives in Bombay, February 13,
and visits Allahabad, Agra, Jaipur, Delhi, Lucknow, and
Benares before reaching Calcutta on March 10, where he is
received by the viceroy, Lord Lytton (son of novelist Edward Bulwer-Lytton). Sails from Calcutta to Rangoon,
and then travels to Penang, Malacca, Singapore, Bangkok,
and Saigon before arriving in Hong Kong on April 30.
Goes to Canton and Macao, then north to Shanghai and
Tientsin. Discusses railroad and telegraph construction in
China with the viceroy of Tientsin, General Li Hung-
chang, who had helped suppress the Taiping rebellion in
1864. Meets Prince Kung, co-regent of the child emperor
Tsai-t'ien, in Peking. Kung and Li ask Grant for help in
Sino-Japanese dispute caused by the recent Japanese annexation of the Ryukyu Islands; Grant promises to raise
issue during his visit to Japan. Arrives on June 21 in Na-
gasaki, where Grant and Julia plant trees in fairgrounds
before sailing through Inland Sea to Yokohama. Meets
Emperor Mutsuhito (the Meiji emperor) and Empress
Haruko in Tokyo, July 4; the emperor and Grant shake
hands (reported to be the first time an emperor of Japan
had ever done so). In later private interview with the emperor, Grant recommends the gradual introduction of suffrage and a legislature to Japan, warns against incurring
foreign debt, condemns European control of Asian commerce, and urges a peaceful resolution of the Ryukyu
dispute without European intervention (conveys similar
advice to Kung and Li, and China eventually accepts Japanese annexation of islands; Grant will later write to Li
about Chinese-American issues). Visits shrines of early

Tokugawa shoguns at Nikko, but is unable to tour widely because of cholera outbreak. Praises Japanese schools and advises country to seek foreign investment while resisting unfair trade treaties. Unable to book passage for Australia, sails for California. Reads Victor Hugo's *Les Misérables* during voyage. Greeted by thousands of people in San Francisco, September 20. Visits Portland, Oregon, Fort Vancouver, and Yosemite, and descends with Julia into silver mine in Virginia City, Nevada. Returns to Galena, then attends reunion of Army of the Tennessee in Chicago on November 13, where he begins friendship with Samuel L. Clemens, who is the final speaker at the banquet. Travels to Philadelphia on December 16, completing his around-the-world trip.

1880   Continues traveling as supporters, including Conkling, Washburne, and Illinois senator John A. Logan, work for his nomination for a third term. Grant visits Florida and Cuba before going to Mexico in February. Lands at Vera-cruz and travels to Mexico City, where he shows Julia sites of 1847 battles. Returns to Galena in April by way of Texas, New Orleans, and the Mississippi Valley. Grant leads major rivals, Maine senator James G. Blaine and Ohio senator John Sherman, for 35 ballots in voting for presidential nomination at Republican national con-vention in Chicago, June 7–8, but loses on 36th ballot to dark-horse candidate, Ohio congressman James A. Gar-field. Washburne receives small number of votes, angering Grant and causing permanent breach between them. Visits Colorado in August to investigate possible mining invest-ments. Grant and Conkling meet with Garfield in Septem-ber at Mentor, Ohio, in attempt to reconcile Republican factions, and Grant campaigns for Garfield in New Jersey, New York, and Connecticut in October. Garfield defeats Democratic nominee Winfield S. Hancock, November 2. Grants go to New York City for the winter, staying at the Fifth Avenue Hotel.

1881   Grant makes recommendations on appointments to Garfield. Becomes president of the Mexican Southern Railroad on March 23, new company formed to build rail-road from Mexico City to Pacific Coast in Oaxaca, and goes to Mexico City to obtain government concessions. Partners in company include Grenville M. Dodge, for-

merly a Union major general and chief engineer of the
Union Pacific, and financier Russell Sage, both of whom
are business associates of Jay Gould, and Matías Romero,
former Mexican minister to the United States and a friend
of Grant's. Writes public letter protesting appointment by
Garfield of one of Conkling's opponents as collector of
customs in New York City. Returns from Mexico in late
spring and goes to Long Branch for the summer. Brother
Orvil dies August 4. Moves in fall to house at 3 East 66th
Street, New York City, bought with funds raised by group
of businessmen, and works at office at 2 Wall Street. Railroad does not attract sufficient capital to begin significant
track laying. Grant invests $100,000, his entire liquid cap-
ital, in Grant & Ward, private banking firm founded by
Ulysses, Jr., and Ferdinand Ward; Julia, Jesse, sister Virginia, and other family members also invest in the bank.
Firm appears to flourish, and Grant considers himself to
be financially secure.

1882   President Chester A. Arthur appoints Grant as one of
        two American commissioners to negotiate commercial
        treaty with Mexico; Romero is one of two Mexican com-
        missioners. Publishes article "An Undeserved Stigma," de-
        fending Major General Fitz-John Porter, who had been
        cashiered in 1863 for his role in the Union defeat at the
        second battle of Bull Run, in the December *North Amer-
        ican Review*.

1883   Commercial treaty eliminating tariffs on variety of goods
        is signed on January 20. Critics charge that treaty favors
        interests of Mexican Southern Railroad, and agreement is
        never put into effect by the U.S. Senate. Mother dies May
        11. Grant takes part in excursion made by group of politi-
        cal and business figures in late summer along newly com-
        pleted Northern Pacific Railroad. Leaves from Chicago
        and travels through Minnesota, North Dakota, Montana,
        Idaho, and Oregon to Tacoma, Washington. Shares plat-
        form with Sitting Bull in Bismarck, North Dakota. Visits
        British Columbia and Yellowstone National Park before
        returning to the East. Slips on sidewalk in New York City,
        December 24, and injures left leg and hip, which had
        been badly hurt in his 1863 riding accident in New Orleans
        (will regularly use crutches or cane for the remainder
        of his life).

1884   Develops pleurisy in January and is confined to bed for several weeks. Ward tells Grant on May 4 that he needs one-day loan of $150,000 to meet temporary demands on Marine National Bank, with which Grant & Ward is associated. Grant obtains personal check for the full amount from William H. Vanderbilt. Marine National Bank fails on May 6 and Grant & Ward suspends operations a few hours later (failures cause Mexican Southern Railroad to go bankrupt). Ward is revealed to have been defrauding his investors. Grant is financially ruined and is accused by some newspapers of being implicated in Ward's dishonesty. Gives Vanderbilt the deeds to all of his properties, his Civil War swords and trophies, and the gifts he had received on his world tour (move protects property from other creditors; Vanderbilt later gives Civil War collection and gifts to the Smithsonian). Agrees in June to write articles for *The Century Magazine* series on the Civil War, receiving $500 per article, and begins work at his Long Branch cottage. Submits draft of article on Shiloh, July 1, then rewrites it when *Century* editors ask him to provide a more personal perspective on the battle (article appears as "The Battle of Shiloh" in February 1885). Begins article on Vicksburg campaign, writing four hours a day. Discusses further articles on the Wilderness campaign and Lee's surrender with *Century* editor Robert U. Johnson on July 22, and tells Johnson that he intends to write a book about his campaigns. Begins suffering from dryness and pain in his throat during the summer, but postpones seeking medical attention until his family doctor returns from Europe. Works on draft of Vicksburg article with the assistance of Frederick, Johnson, and Adam Badeau, one of his former staff aides and author of the three-volume *Military History of Ulysses S. Grant*. Submits Vicksburg manuscript to *Century* in August and begins writing account of Chattanooga campaign. Meets with Roswell Smith, president of the Century Company, in early September and discusses his memoirs with him. Returns to New York in October and hires Badeau to assist him by locating documents, checking facts, and reviewing the manuscript. Family physician Dr. Fordyce Barker refers Grant to Dr. John H. Douglas, a leading throat specialist. Douglas finds inflammation on Grant's palate during examination on October 22. Grant asks if it is cancerous; Douglas tells him that he has a serious "epithelial" disease "sometimes capable of being cured." Continues work on his book and sees Douglas regularly for topical treatments. Receives draft contract from Century, offering him 10 percent royalty with expected sale of 25,000 copies. Grant gives up smoking in late November. Clemens learns of the Century offer and tells Grant that it is inadequate. Encourages Grant to sign with the company Clemens had recently founded with Charles L. Webster to publish *Adventures of Huckleberry Finn*. Grant makes no commitment to Clemens, and does not accept Webster's offer in early December of a $50,000 advance. Enjoys visits by Sherman.

1885   Receives extra $1,000 from *Century* for article on Shiloh. On February 3 Webster offers Grant choice of 20 percent royalty or 70 percent of net profits from his book. Grant develops throat ulcers, which doctors determine on February 19 to be cancerous and inoperable. Clemens learns during February 21 visit that Grant is dying, but renews offer to publish book. Grant signs contract with Charles L. Webster & Co., February 27, and chooses to receive 70 percent of the net profits; Clemens and Webster begin selling book by subscription canvassing (60,000 sets are ordered by May 1). After weeks of conflicting press reports concerning Grant's health, *The New York Times* confirms on March 1 that he has fatal cancer. Congress passes bill on March 4 placing Grant on army retired list as full general, with pay. Nellie arrives from Europe, March 20. Grant gives deposition on March 26 for trial of James D. Fish, an associate of Ferdinand Ward (Fish is convicted and sent to prison). Receives local injections of cocaine for pain and morphine to help him sleep. Has first of several violent choking and coughing fits on night of March 28, and is close to death for several days. Douglas and Dr. George F. Shrady keep his throat clear and Shrady administers brandy injections as stimulants. To please his family, receives baptism from Methodist minister John P. Newman. Press maintains vigil outside of house. Grant's condition unexpectedly improves after coughing fit brings on hemorrhage, and he is able to take carriage rides by late April. Webster & Co. begins printing proofs of first half of first volume. New York *World* reports on April 29 that Badeau is writing the memoirs from rough notes provided by Grant. Clemens wants to sue paper for libel, but instead Grant writes public letter declaring that the composition of the book is entirely his own. Begins giving dictation to a stenographer. Badeau writes Grant, May 2, offering to complete memoirs for $1,000 a month and 10 percent of the profits, and tells Grant that he is incapable of finishing the book on his own. Grant replies on May 5, dismissing Badeau as his assistant and insisting that he will finish the book himself. Continues dictation, giving 10,000 words in one session, then develops difficulty speaking and reverts to writing. Finishes draft of chapters covering the campaign from the Wilderness to Appomattox by early June. On advice of his doctors, goes to Mount McGregor, summer resort in Adirondacks near Saratoga Springs, New York, on June 16. Travels by special train in Vanderbilt's private car; crowds gather at stations along the route, and he is cheered by veterans while changing trains at Saratoga Springs. Stays in cottage with Julia, their children, and three grandchildren and is attended by Dr. Douglas. Newspapers print daily reports on his condition. Tells Douglas in note on June 17 that he does not expect to live much longer, but continues to work on memoirs, having proofs read aloud and writing revisions on slips of paper. Mostly communicates by writing notes, but manages to dictate extensive changes in proofs in a whisper on June 23. Clemens arrives on June 29. Grant tells him that second volume is nearly done, then writes preface and new section evaluating wartime generals and political leaders. Clemens leaves on July 2. Robert U. Johnson visits on July 8 and confirms arrangements, negotiated earlier by Clemens, for publishing three remaining articles in *Century Magazine* (they appear posthumously in September and November 1885 and February 1886). Simon Bolivar Buckner visits July 10; tells reporters his meeting with Grant is "too sacred" to recount. Last proofs of first volume are returned to the printer on July 11. Frederick prepares manuscript of second volume for the printer and discourages Grant from making further changes. Grant sits on porch of cottage, reading newspapers as visitors intent on seeing him pass by. Writes notes to doctors describing effects of medication. Manuscript of second volume is delivered to Webster on July 18. (First volume of *Personal Memoirs of U. S. Grant* is published by Charles L. Webster & Co. on

December 1, 1885, and the second volume on March 1, 1886. Over 300,000 sets are sold, and Julia eventually receives between $420,000 and $450,000 in profits.) On July 20 Grant has himself pushed in invalid's chair to outlook facing Hudson River and Green Mountains of Vermont; returns to cottage exhausted. Condition worsens on July 21. Dies surrounded by family at around 8:00 A.M., July 23. After funeral services at Mount McGregor on August 4 body is taken by train to New York City, where it lies in state at City Hall for two days. Funeral procession on August 8 carries body through Manhattan to Riverside Park, where it is interred in a temporary brick tomb (reinterred in permanent granite and marble tomb overlooking the Hudson River in 1897).

Note on the Texts

This volume presents the text of the *Personal Memoirs of U. S. Grant*, published in two volumes by Charles L. Webster & Company, 1885–86, and a selection of 175 letters, orders, and reports, written by Grant from 1839 to 1865, taken from the first 14 volumes of *The Papers of Ulysses S. Grant*, edited by John Y. Simon and published by Southern Illinois University Press, 1967–85.

Grant's *Personal Memoirs* grew out of the articles he had agreed to contribute to *The Century* as part of a series on the Civil War. He had earlier declined the offer, but after Grant & Ward, the private banking firm with which he was associated, failed on May 6, 1884, he was deeply in debt and in need of money. The agreement was for him to write four articles covering the battle of Shiloh, the Vicksburg and Wilderness campaigns, and Appomattox, for each of which he would be paid $500. He began writing in the middle of June 1884, and by July 1, 1884, he had sent a completed draft of "Shiloh" to *The Century*. This first version was very much like the official reports he had written during the Civil War. Robert U. Johnson, editor of *The Century*, visited him and explained that the readers of the series wanted a more personal story, told from his own point of view. Grant rewrote the article, and then began work on "Vicksburg." When Johnson visited him on July 22 and asked him if he had thought of turning the articles into a book, Grant replied that he had already "formed the intention" of writing a book during the coming winter. By mid-August, the Vicksburg article was given to *The Century*, and Grant had decided to contribute an article on his Chattanooga campaign rather than one on Appomattox. Aware that other publishers were beginning to hear about Grant's prospective book, Roswell Smith, president of the Century Company, accompanied by Johnson, visited Grant early in September to tentatively propose book publication. Though no definite arrangement was concluded, Grant said he would give them a chance to see the work when it was done. On October 22, 1884, the same day on which he learned that the sore throat he had been suffering from for several months was caused by a serious ailment (later diagnosed as cancer), Grant visited the Century office and said he would like the firm to publish his book. A contract was drawn up in November, offering him ten percent royalty on an expected sale of some 25,000 sets.

Grant was still considering this offer when his friend Samuel L. Clemens (Mark Twain) heard about the book. Clemens had recently formed his own subscription publishing company with his nephew and business associate, Charles L. Webster, whose name he used for the firm, in order to publish his own works, beginning with *Adventures of Huckleberry Finn*. Clemens told Grant that the terms offered in the Century's contract were not good enough and that he should not sign anything until he had had the chance to consider the offer Charles L. Webster & Co. would make. In early December 1884, Webster offered Grant a $50,000 advance: $25,000 for each volume. But Grant was still undecided; he had verbally agreed to let the Century Company publish his memoirs, and Johnson had helped him in the writing of the Shiloh article and had also encouraged him to write the book. Finally, Webster offered Grant on February 3, 1885, a choice of a twenty percent royalty or seventy percent of the profits. Grant chose seventy percent of the profits because that way, he said, no one would lose money on the deal. The contract was signed on February 27, 1885.

Grant's method of writing the book was similar to the way he had prepared his official reports during the Civil War. He would write the narrative, then his aides would read it over, suggest revisions, check the facts, and locate and insert the relevant documents. For this purpose, he had engaged in October the services of Adam Badeau, his former military secretary and the author of a three-volume history of Grant's war service; in addition, his son Frederick Dent Grant was already at work on the copying and researching. Meanwhile, Grant's health continued to deteriorate, and it was uncertain whether he would live to complete the work. When Clemens reviewed the progress of the manuscript in mid-March, he found that the first volume still lacked the last chapters and decided that, if necessary, the volume would end there, so

ensuring that at least one volume would have been written by
Grant. The second volume would be finished by someone else
(presumably Badeau). By the end of March, the first volume
was complete, and parts of the second volume were also
done: Grant had finished writing the Chattanooga section
and drafted an account of the Wilderness campaign. But then
his condition seriously worsened, and he was unable to work
for almost a month.

The Century series on the Civil War had begun in the November 1884 number. Grant's article, "The Battle of Shiloh,"
appearing in the February 1885 number, immediately increased
the magazine's circulation, and the Century Company voluntarily paid him an additional sum of $1,000. (In July, they
paid him an additional $1,500.) Clemens had looked over the
completed section on Vicksburg that Grant had submitted to
The Century and saw that it was at least twice as long as the
other articles. With the help of Frederick Grant he convinced
Grant that half the article, the section dealing with the siege
of Vicksburg, would be enough. Clemens was worried that
Grant's contributions to *The Century* series would not be recognized as excerpts from his forthcoming book. On April 15,
1885, Webster made an agreement with *The Century* that all
future articles by Grant appearing in the magazine would acknowledge that they were copyrighted by Grant and taken
from the *Personal Memoirs of U. S. Grant*. In return, Webster
was to allow all articles to appear before book publication:
the first volume was to be published December 1, 1885, and the
second to follow in March 1886. ("Vicksburg" appeared in the
September 1885 number, "Chattanooga" in the November 1885
number, and "Preparing for the Wilderness Campaign" in the
February 1886 number.)

By the middle of April 1885 the first part of Volume I was in
galleys. Proofs were sent to Clemens at the same time they
were sent to the Grant family, Clemens correcting only punctuation and grammar. To encourage Grant, he wrote him that
some of his chapters were like *Caesar's Commentaries* in their
"simplicity, naturalness & purity" of style. Grant's health
improved enough to continue work, and on April 30, using
a stenographer supplied by Webster & Co., he dictated
for three hours on the Appomattox campaign. On May 5

Clemens wrote to his friend William Dean Howells that Grant had dictated 50 pages, and thus "the Wilderness & Appomatox stand for all time in his own words."

Meanwhile, a disturbing story had appeared in late April in the New York *World* claiming that Grant was not writing his *Memoirs* himself, but only supplying information to Adam Badeau, who was actually doing the composition. With the knowledge that returns from the subscription canvass now showed that 60,000 sets of the *Personal Memoirs* were already sold, and Webster & Co. expected the total sales would be more than 300,000 sets, Adam Badeau wrote Grant a letter on May 2, 1885, asking that the terms of agreement between them be changed. Instead of the promise that he would receive $10,000 if the profits exceeded $30,000, he wanted to be paid $1,000 in advance each month until the work was finished, and then receive ten percent of the profits. He also preferred to have direct communication with Grant rather than through the stenographer. Grant, he said, did not have the strength to do his own research, and Badeau was the only one who could finish the book if Grant were not able to do so. Grant wrote to his publishers denying that anyone but himself was writing the book (this letter was printed in the newspapers), and privately wrote Badeau that he no longer needed his services and telling him that he was too petulant and demanded too much. He also said there had been a time when he was not sure that he would live to finish the book himself and had "supposed some one, whose name would necessarily be given to the public, and that name yours, would finish the book."

Though illness continued to interrupt his work, Grant could tell Clemens on May 26 that he had made the book too long by 200 pages. As proofs were received they were read to him; he made revisions, either dictating or writing them. By early June a great part of the Wilderness and Appomattox sections were set in galleys. A prospectus for the book, containing material from the early years to Appomattox, was given to the canvassers on June 8. Grant's son Frederick now acted as chief researcher, checking facts and finding particular letters and dispatches written during the war. Grant's other sons, Ulysses, Jr., and Jesse, also helped. This pattern of work continued even after Grant left New York on June 16 to spend the summer at Mount McGregor, New York. The Webster stenographer, Noble E. Dawson, accompanied the family and not only took dictation but helped Frederick Grant in copying and inserting new additions and revisions into the proofs. There were very few days now when Grant could dictate to the stenographer because the cancer in his throat made speaking too painful; instead, using a pencil and a special lap table, he wrote out his new sections and made notes for revisions. Clemens came to Mount McGregor the evening of June 29 and stayed until July 2, during which time Grant wrote the Preface. The first volume was completely set in type, but Grant continued to make last-minute revisions and notes for it until the first week of July. He was also organizing and rewriting the second volume. He was pleased with his revisions of the Appomattox section but felt that he did not have the time to revise other sections. At one point, in a note to his son Frederick, he wrote: "I should change Spotts. if I was able and could improve N. Ana and Cold Harbor." He also went over the contents of the Appendix with Frederick. The last two chapters were written at Mount McGregor. By July 10, all of Volume I was in page proofs and ready for the press, and by July 18, the text of Volume II was copied and ready for the printers, except for the documents that still had to be inserted, both in the work itself and in the Appendix. Grant died at Mount McGregor on July 23, 1885.

The first volume went to press in mid-July, but because more than 300,000 copies were needed, the total printing was not completed until December. Seven binderies were employed to bind the books. The first volume was published December 1, 1885, in five bindings: cloth at $7.00 a set; sheep, $9.00; half-morocco, $11.00; full-morocco, $18.00; and tree calf, $25.00. The second volume was still being set and revised in November. Clemens gave orders that "All on the Wilderness from the Rapidan to the James to come back in galleys. Insertions to be made in *corrected* galleys, & then printed *again* in galleys." This was the section that Grant had earlier wished he had more time to work on and improve. The insertions seem to be letters and dispatches; there are more of them in the second volume than in the first, and more of them are included as footnotes rather than inserted into the text. An index to both volumes was prepared. In addition, Frederick Grant was trying to make more revisions than Webster and Clemens wanted him to do. Webster reported to Clemens on December 25 that he had reversed some of Frederick's alterations, and Clemens agreed, saying, "It won't *do* to leave things out & make unnecessary alterations in the General's text." Though the full order of 300,000 copies of Volume II was not ready because of last-minute alterations, the publication date of March 1, 1886, was not officially changed. In all, over 300,000 sets were sold. Charles L. Webster & Co. paid Mrs. Grant $200,000, the largest single royalty payment ever made until then, on February 27, 1886, the anniversary of the signing of the contract. She later received another check for $150,000, and eventually received from $420,000 to $450,000.

The second volume of the *Personal Memoirs* contains an errata page correcting errors in the first volume, and these corrections, with one exception, are incorporated in the text printed here: at 62.8 and 63.3, "Little Colorado" replaces "Colorado"; at 65.24, "May" replaces "March"; at 75.3, "1846" replaces "1847"; at 117.23, "paymaster-general" replaces "surgeon-general"; at 121.11, "*tlacos*" replaces "*clackos*"; at 127.4, "tlacos" replaces "clackos"; at 170.15, "Sterling" replaces "Stirling"; at 198.19, "Cumberland" replaces "Tennessee"; and at 329.38, "9th" replaces "8th". Only at 195.6, where the errata page lists "Phelps" to replace "Walke", is the correction not made, since "Walke" is correct.

The letters, orders, and reports selected for this volume are from the years covered in Grant's *Personal Memoirs*, beginning with the earliest available letter written from West Point on September 22, 1839, and ending with a letter written to Julia Dent Grant from Raleigh, North Carolina, on April 25, 1865, where Grant had gone to confer with W. T. Sherman. *The Papers of Ulysses S. Grant*, edited by John Y. Simon, from which the texts of the 175 items included in this volume are taken, is the first inclusive collection of Grant's writings ever to be published. Eighty percent of the material contained in these volumes had never been published before. Except for his *Personal Memoirs* and two heavily edited volumes of his private letters—*General Grant's Letters to a Friend, 1861–1880*, edited by James Grant Wilson (New York, 1897), containing letters to Elihu Washburne, and *Letters of Ulysses S. Grant to his Father and his Youngest Sister, 1857–78*, edited by Jesse Grant Cramer (New York and London, 1912)—almost nothing outside of compilations of official documents was available to the interested reader. The largest repository of his official writings has been *The War of the Rebellion: A Compilation of the Official Records of the Union and Confederate Armies* (Washington, D.C., 1880–1901), and some of his presidential messages and addresses were available in various compilations made over the years. Most of the original material remained hidden, and the full extent of Grant's writings was unknown. This situation changed during the years 1953 to 1960 when Grant's grandson, Major General Ulysses S. Grant 3rd, gave to the Library of Congress his grandfather's headquarters records in 111 volumes and the letters Grant wrote his wife, Julia Dent Grant. In addition, new material in private hands, or owned by dealers, has been acquired by libraries across the country. In 1962, the Ulysses S. Grant Association was founded to collect, edit, and publish an edition of the Grant papers. John Y. Simon was made editor of the edition, and the first volume of *The Papers of Ulysses S. Grant* was published in 1967.

Simon's editorial policy in *The Papers* is to remain faithful to the original document. The items included in the edition are transcribed, whenever possible, from Grant's original manuscripts, and preserve Grant's own spelling, grammar, and punctuation. Some letters exist only in copies, and in these cases Simon has selected the one that he believes is the earliest. During the Civil War, aides copied out orders and dispatches by hand, and these were then copied in other quarters as well; the further removed a copy is from the original source, the more likely that it contains elements not originating with Grant. Beginning in the fall of 1864, Grant used a "Philp & Solomons' Highly Improved Manifold Writer," which allowed him to write multiple copies of his dispatches and reports, so a higher proportion of documents from this period are still extant in Grant's own handwriting.

Some of the original manuscript letters are in imperfect condition. Simon uses certain conventions to indicate particular problems, such as missing material and reconstructed texts. These conventions are adapted to suit the needs of the present volume in several ways. In *The Papers of Ulysses S. Grant*, when a word or letter is damaged, torn, or otherwise illegible, but there is no question about what the missing word or letter is, the missing material is set in roman type and enclosed in brackets; in these cases, the present volume accepts this editorial reconstruction and prints the word without brackets. When letters are missing, and reconstruction is not possible, Simon uses [. . .], the number of dots representing the missing letters; this practice is retained in the present volume. Grant also crossed out words. The *Papers* shows cancellations by printing the canceled words with lines through them; this volume does not print the crossed-out words. In addition, Julia Dent Grant deleted some sentences from Grant's letters to her, and her descendants requested that her wishes be followed. The *Papers* indicates these places in footnotes; the present volume uses three asterisks. *The Papers of Ulysses S. Grant* also indicates and offers corrections of errors, such as missing or incorrect dates and words, by printing corrections and conjectures in italic within brackets. The present volume omits the bracketed italic correction and usually prints the text as Grant wrote it; in some cases, however, the corrections are accepted and the word or date is printed without brackets. The following is a list of the corrections accepted in this volume, cited by page and line number: 888.19, [*s*]he; 913.1, ha[*r*]d; 920.9, ~~be~~fofore; 949.16, 1853 [*1854*]; 963.21, her[*e*]; 966.4, next [*week*]; 966.7, taken [*place*] in; 972.39, sigh[*t*]; 990.14, to[*o*]; 990.39, d[*a*]ily; 994.23, sever[*al*]. In addition, at 1065.17, "the" has been changed to "they."

This volume presents the texts of the editions chosen for inclusion here but does not attempt to reproduce features of their typographic design. The texts are printed without alteration except for the changes previously discussed and for the correction of typographical errors. Spelling, punctuation, and capitalization are often expressive features, and they are not altered, even when inconsistent or irregular. The following is a list of typographical errors corrected, cited by page and line number: 76.24, run,/ning; 121.2–3, as be; 191.3, empting; 376.32, suggest/tion; 480.41, Generals; 493.33, sameline; 498.2, SEIGE; 558.28, discomfiture,; 586.38, "Your; 707.8, enemies; 765.40, however; 773.36, rolé; 776.8, rolé; 797.32, vere; 816.10, ndependent; 839.6, possesions; 852.3b, surenders. Error corrected second printing: 1065.17, the. Errors corrected fifth printing: 279.5, Van Doren (LOA); 570.10, it. I.

Notes

In the notes below, the numbers refer to page and line of this volume (the line count includes chapter headings). No note is made for information available in a standard desk-reference book. All notes in the text appeared in the Charles L. Webster edition and are either Grant's own or were supplied by the publisher. For more detailed notes and references to other studies, see John Y. Simon, ed., *The Papers of Ulysses S. Grant* (16 vols. to date, Carbondale: University of Southern Illinois Press, 1967–88). For further identification of persons mentioned in the text, see E. B. Long and Barbara Long, *Civil War Day by Day: An Almanac, 1861–1865* (New York: Doubleday, 1971), and Mark Mayo Boatner III, *The Civil War Dictionary*, revised edition (New York: David McKay, 1988). For further biographical background than is provided in the Chronology, see Bruce Catton, *Grant Moves South* (Boston: Little, Brown, 1960) and *Grant Takes Command* (Boston: Little, Brown, 1969); William S. McFeely, *Grant: A Biography* (New York: Norton, 1981); and Thomas L. Pitkin, *The Captain Departs: Ulysses S. Grant's Last Campaign* (Carbondale: University of Southern Illinois Press, 1973).

PERSONAL MEMOIRS OF U. S. GRANT

5.2 MAN . . . disposes."] Early appearances of this proverb are in *Piers Plowman* by William Langland (c. 1332–c. 1400) and in *Imitation of Christ* by Thomas à Kempis (1379–1471).

5.10–11 rascality . . . failure.] Ferdinand Ward had formed the private banking firm of Grant & Ward with Ulysses S. Grant, Jr., in 1881. Grant then invested his entire liquid capital in his son's firm, which suspended its operations on May 6, 1884. Ward was subsequently imprisoned for fraud in connection with the bank's operations.

15.32 *Bridge* . . . 371] In the Charles L. Webster edition the following note appeared at this point:
"The Daguerreotype from which the frontispiece was engraved was furnished the publishers through the courtesy of Mr. George W. Childs.
"The fac-similes of General Buckner's dispatches at Fort Donelson are copied from the originals furnished the publishers through the courtesy of Mr. Ferdinand J. Dreer. General Grant's dispatch, 'I propose to move immediately upon your works,' was copied from the original document in the possession of the publishers."

18.25–26 Judge . . . Ohio] George Tod (1773–1841) of Youngstown served as a judge of the state supreme court, 1806–10, and state court of appeals, 1816–29, as well as a state senator, 1804–6, 1810–12. His son David (1805–68), a Democrat, was elected governor of Ohio on the Union party ticket in 1861 but was not renominated in 1863. When asked by Lincoln to succeed Salmon P. Chase as secretary of the treasury in 1864, he declined because of poor health.

18.40–19.1   John . . . on."]   The Civil War song most often known as "John Brown's Body," authorship unknown, was set to the music of a hymn (c. 1856) ascribed to the North Carolina musician William Steffe. "The Battle Hymn of the Republic" (1862), by Julia Ward Howe, is sung to the same tune.

19.25   Western Reserve]   A section of land in the northeast corner of Ohio reserved by the state of Connecticut when it dropped its claims to other western lands in 1786. In 1800 Connecticut transferred jurisdiction over the reserve to the federal government, and it became part of the newly created Ohio Territory.

21.37–22.2   Two . . . Brewster.]   William Henry Wadsworth (1821–93) of Kentucky served as a Unionist member of the House of Representatives, 1861–65, and as a Republican, 1885–87. No Brewster from the Richardson and Rand school is known to have served in the United States Congress.

28.6–7   Thomas . . . Senator]   Morris (1776–1844), elected as a Democrat, served from 1833 to 1839. He ran for vice-president with James G. Birney on the antislavery Liberty party ticket in 1844.

28.35–36   Thomas . . . Congress]   Thomas Hamer (1800–46) of Georgetown served in the House of Representatives from 1833 to 1839.

29.7   removal . . . moneys]   President Andrew Jackson withdrew all federal deposits from the Bank of the United States on October 1, 1833.

30.7–8   John . . . Ohio]   Confederate Brigadier General John Hunt Morgan (1825–64) led a large cavalry raid across the Ohio River into Indiana on July 8, 1863, then turned east and rode into southern Ohio. His troops passed through the area of Cincinnati and Georgetown on July 13–14, but were unable to elude their Union pursuers and find an unguarded ford across the Ohio. Morgan surrendered the remnants of his force at Salineville in northeastern Ohio on July 26 and was imprisoned in the Ohio state penitentiary at Columbus. He escaped on November 26, 1863, and rejoined the Confederate army, but was killed at Greeneville, Tennessee, on September 4, 1864.

31.26   Girard College]   The college—a home and primary and secondary schools—was built and endowed with the six million dollars in cash and real estate left in trust to the city of Philadelphia by Stephen Girard (1750–1831) for the education of orphaned white boys. It opened in 1848.

34.23–24   brother . . . rebellion]   Samuel Simpson Grant (called Simpson by his family), born September 23, 1825, died on September 13, 1861, in St. Paul, Minnesota, and Clara Rachel Grant, born December 11, 1828, died on March 6, 1865, in Covington, Kentucky.

36.27   F. T. Dent]   Frederick Tracy Dent (1820–92) fought in the Mexican War and served on the western frontier until 1863. He was on Grant's staff from March 1864 until April 1865, and retired from the army as a colonel in 1883.

37.2   Colonel John O'Fallon]   John O'Fallon (1791–1865), a nephew of Revolutionary War commander George Rogers Clark and explorer William Clark, was wounded at the battle of Tippecanoe in 1811 and served in the War of 1812. He resigned from the army in 1818 and became a wealthy St. Louis merchant and philanthropist.

39.36   Professor Church]   Albert E. Church had been professor of mathematics at the Academy while Grant was a cadet there.

42.5–6   treaty . . . Santa Anna]   President Antonio López de Santa Anna (1794–1876) was captured by the Texans after the battle of San Jacinto on April 21, 1836, and signed an armistice withdrawing the Mexican army beyond the Rio Grande.

42.14   Alamo . . . Goliad]   On March 6, 1836, Santa Anna's army stormed the Alamo mission in San Antonio, Texas, and killed all 187 of its defenders. Another Mexican force captured about 400 men near the village of Goliad on March 20, most of whom were volunteers from the southern United States. Having previously decreed that all foreigners caught under arms on Mexican soil would be treated as pirates, Santa Anna ordered their execution, and about 330 of the prisoners were shot on March 27, 1836.

63.18–19   Hardee . . . tactics]   *Rifle and Light Infantry Tactics* (1855) by William J. Hardee (1815–73).

63.20   Theodric Porter]   A younger brother of naval officer David D. Porter (1813–91), who commanded the Union riverboat squadron during the Vicksburg campaign in 1863.

71.31   died . . . days]   Hamer died of dysentery on December 2, 1846.

98.34–35   tête-de-pont]   Bridgehead.

105.20–21   Lieutenant Semmes]   Raphael Semmes (1809–77), an officer of the U.S. Navy, accompanied Winfield Scott's expedition to Mexico City on a mission to secure the parole of an American midshipman, captured during a shore raid, whom the Mexican authorities had threatened to treat as a spy. Although the midshipman successfully escaped in July 1847, Semmes remained with the army, serving as a volunteer aide to Brevet Major General William J. Worth. Semmes joined the Confederate navy in 1861 and commanded the commerce raider *Alabama* from its commissioning in August

1862 until its sinking off Cherbourg, France, by the U.S.S. *Kearsarge* on June 19, 1864.

105.38   carry . . . trail]   A weapon carried in trail position is held by the right hand along the side of the body, with its muzzle inclined obliquely upwards.

106.32   voltigeurs]   Skirmishers, sharpshooters.

109.38   Mentioned . . . Garland]   Grant received a brevet promotion to captain for his actions on September 13, 1847. Major Francis Lee commanded the 4th Infantry during the battle while Lieutenant Colonel John Garland of the 4th led a brigade.

117.5–6   the whole . . . California]   The treaty of Guadalupe Hidalgo, ratified in 1848, ended the Mexican War by ceding to the United States Nuevo Mexico, a territory including all of what is now Nevada and Utah, almost all of Arizona and New Mexico, and part of present-day Colorado and Wyoming, and Upper California, corresponding to the present-day American state.

118.8   party . . . defeat.]   Winfield Scott, the Whig party candidate, was defeated in 1852 by Democrat Franklin Pierce. In 1856 the Whig party endorsed Millard Fillmore, the nominee of the nativist American (Know-Nothing) party, although by then many Whigs had joined the new anti-slavery Republican party.

120.40–121.1   During . . . Mexico]   Grant visited Mexico in 1880 and in 1881.

124.3   excruciating . . . eyes]   The group was probably experiencing snow blindness.

130.31–33   Chandler's . . . success]   Zachariah Chandler (1813–79) was a Republican senator from Michigan from 1857 to 1875. He served as secretary of the interior, 1875–77, during Grant's second term, and was again elected to the U.S. Senate in 1879.

130.36   Sackett's Harbor]   A village on the eastern shore of Lake Ontario in upstate New York, near Watertown and about 20 miles from the Canadian border.

131.3–26   Aspinwall . . . Panama]   Aspinwall, now called Colón, was founded in 1850 and named for the railroad builder William H. Aspinwall. Grant's crossing of the Isthmus roughly followed the future route of the Panama Canal.

136.22   Benicia barracks]   Situated on a strait linking two northern extensions of San Francisco Bay, Benicia was the site of the army's main arsenal on the Pacific Coast.

139.3–4   Bliss . . . promoted] Captain William Wallace Smith Bliss (1815–53), a brevet lieutenant colonel, had been commissioned in the 4th Infantry after graduating from the Military Academy in 1833 and at the time of his death on August 5, 1853, was still officially an officer of that regiment, even though he had taught mathematics at the Academy from 1834 to 1840 and then served in the adjutant general's department for the remainder of his life.

141.5   two children] Frederick Dent Grant, born May 30, 1850, and Ulysses S. ("Buck") Grant, Jr., born July 22, 1852.

142.19   Know-Nothing party] Know-Nothing was the popular name of the nativist American party, organized in the 1850s to oppose Catholic and immigrant influence in American public life.

142.24–25   Free-Soil . . . Blair] Free-Soil Democrats opposed the extension of slavery into the western territories. Francis P. Blair, Jr. (1821–75), elected to Congress as a Free-Soiler in 1856, supported Abraham Lincoln in 1860 and was a Republican during the Civil War, but returned to the Democratic party during Reconstruction and was its nominee for vice-president in 1868.

144.18   my two brothers] Samuel Simpson Grant (1825–61) and Orvil Lynch Grant (1835–81).

144.39–40   Douglas . . . Lincoln] The Democratic national convention split along sectional lines in June 1860. Northern Democrats nominated Douglas for president while Southern Democrats chose John C. Breckinridge as their candidate. In the election Abraham Lincoln, the Republican candidate, won a majority of 180 of 303 electoral votes (all from free states) and a plurality of approximately 40 percent of the popular vote. Douglas received 12 electoral votes (from both slave and free states) and 21 percent of the popular vote, Breckinridge 72 electoral votes (all from slave states) and 14 percent of the popular vote, and John Bell of the Constitutional Union party 39 electoral votes (also all from slave states) and 12 percent of the popular vote. About 13 percent of the popular vote went to anti-Lincoln fusion tickets in the free states.

145.8   time . . . nomination] Lincoln won the nomination for president on May 18, 1860, on the third ballot taken at the Republican national convention.

149.35–36   States . . . acts] Emancipation measures were seriously debated in the Kentucky state constitutional conventions of 1792 and 1799 and in the Virginia House of Delegates in 1832. No record exists of their defeat by a tie or by one vote.

150.33   two . . . least] John B. Floyd (1806–63) of Virginia, who resigned on December 29, 1860, and Secretary of the Interior Jacob Thompson (1820–85) of Mississippi, who resigned January 8, 1861, were accused of using their Cabinet posts to aid secession. Secretary of the Treasury Howell Cobb

(1815–68) of Georgia resigned on December 10, 1860, so that he could return to his state in expectation of its secession; he was not accused of having acted in bad faith.

151.3–4   de facto . . . Capital.]   Delegates chosen by elected state conventions in South Carolina, Georgia, Florida, Alabama, Mississippi, and Louisiana met in Montgomery, Alabama, on February 4–9, 1861 (the Texas delegates arrived on February 8). Acting as the provisional Congress of the Confederate States of America, they adopted a provisional constitution and elected Jefferson Davis as president for a provisional one-year term. Davis was inaugurated on February 18; the Confederate capital was shifted to Richmond, Virginia, on May 21, 1861.

151.22–30   President-elect . . . capital.]   After leaving Springfield, Illinois, by train on February 11, 1861, Abraham Lincoln made brief speeches in Indiana, Ohio, Pennsylvania, New York, and New Jersey before being warned in Philadelphia of a possible attempt to assassinate him in Baltimore. Lincoln then traveled secretly to Washington, D.C., on the night of February 22–23.

152.22   "was . . . world,"]   Cf. Ralph Waldo Emerson, "Concord Hymn: Sung at the Completion of the Battle Monument, April 19, 1836," Stanza 1: "Here once the embattled farmers stood, / And fired the shot heard round the world."

153.6   Rawlins . . . Washburne]   Rawlins (1831–69) was appointed assistant adjutant general on Grant's staff with the rank of captain on August 30, 1861; see pp. 168.25–169.13 in this volume. Elihu B. Washburne (1816–87), a Galena resident, served in the U.S. House of Representatives as a Whig, 1853–56, and then as a Republican, 1856–69. By arrangement with Grant he served as secretary of state for a few days in March 1869 before becoming minister to France from 1869 to 1877.

154.6–7   President . . . wanted it."]   This remark is attributed to President Lincoln, who fell ill with varioloid, a mild form of smallpox, on his return to Washington after delivering his dedicatory address at Gettysburg on November 19, 1863.

157.31   Philip Foulk]   Philip B. Fouke (1818–76), Democratic congressman from Illinois, 1859–63, became a colonel in the Illinois volunteer infantry and served under Grant at the battle of Belmont, where he was wounded.

158.32   General Badeau]   Brevet Brigadier General Adam Badeau (1831–95), Grant's military secretary, was writing *Military History of Ulysses S. Grant* (3 vols., 1868–1881).

166.15   tactics . . . Scott's]   *Infantry Tactics,* revised and expanded by Winfield Scott (3 vols., 1835).

169.22–23   1872 . . . candidate]   Benjamin Gratz Brown (1826–75) was nominated by the Liberal Republicans to run with Horace Greeley against

Grant. The Liberal ticket was endorsed by the Democrats, but was decisively defeated in the election.

189.26–27   General . . . Mill Springs]   The battle was fought on January 19, 1862.

236.4   Since . . . chapter]   Chapters XXIV and XXV of the *Personal Memoirs of U. S. Grant* are a revised version of the article "The Battle of Shiloh," written by Grant in the summer of 1884, which appeared in the February 1885 *Century Magazine*.

238.23–24   I stated . . . unwillingness]   In his *Century* article Grant wrote: "The enemy had hardly started in retreat from his last position, when, looking back toward the river, I saw a division of troops coming up in beautiful order, as if going on parade or review. The commander was at the head of the column, and the staff seemed to be disposed about as they would have been had they been going on parade. When the head of the column came near where I was standing, it was halted, and the commanding officer, General A. McD. McCook, rode up to where I was and appealed to me not to send his division any farther, saying that they were worn out with marching and fighting. This division had marched on the 6th from a point ten or twelve miles east of Savanna, over bad roads. The men had also lost rest during the night while crossing the Tennessee, and had been engaged in the battle of the 7th. It was not, however, the rank and file or the junior officers who asked to be excused, but the division commander." This passage preceded the sentence beginning on p. 238.8 in this volume ("I rode forward several miles . . .").

238.34–36   conspicuous . . . report]   In his report of April 10, 1862, later printed in the *Memoirs of General William T. Sherman* (1875), Sherman praised McCook's division for driving the Confederates back along the Corinth road and singled out one of its brigades for capturing a heavily defended wood.

238.37–38   family . . . volunteers]   McCook's father, uncle, eight of his brothers, and four of his cousins served in the Union army, while another brother recruited and trained Ohio volunteers as a civilian and another cousin served as a Union naval officer. His father and three of his brothers were killed during the war.

240.40–241.2   correspondent . . . World]   Grant was reported in the New York *Herald* of August 3, 1865, as saying that Buell "was thoroughly versed in the theory of war, but knew nothing about handling men in an emergency," that his "heart was never in the war from the first," and that Buell's troops might have reached Pittsburg Landing several days earlier than they did. Buell wrote Grant on August 5 and December 27, asking for an explanation. Grant replied on December 29, 1865, that while he had no recollection of the conversation reported in the *Herald*, he was certain that he had been misquoted. Buell subsequently wrote a letter to Grant defending his movements before the battle of Shiloh, which appeared in the New York *World* on April 6, 1866.

241.27   I . . . wrote]   In his *Century* article Grant wrote: "Nothing occurred in his brief command of an army to prove or disprove the high estimate that had been placed upon his military ability." This sentence was followed by the paragraph beginning at p. 242.35 in this volume.

242.8   son and biographer]   William Preston Johnston (1831–99) wrote *The Life of Albert Sidney Johnston* (1880) and drew upon it in preparing "Albert Sidney Johnston and the Shiloh Campaign," which appeared in the February 1885 *Century* immediately following Grant's article on Shiloh.

247.28   full . . . report]   A fragment of the draft of a report appears on pp. 1011–13 in this volume.

284.29   "Freedman's Bureau"]   The Bureau of Refugees, Freedmen, and Abandoned Lands was established in the War Department by act of Congress on March 3, 1865. It provided provisions, clothing, and fuel to destitute former slaves and white refugees, leased abandoned and confiscated land (almost all of which was eventually restored to its former owners), founded schools and hospitals, regulated labor contracts, and attempted to mediate cases of racial conflict. President Andrew Johnson vetoed a bill extending its lifetime and expanding its powers on February 19, 1866, but another bill renewing the Bureau was passed over his veto on July 16, 1866. The Bureau ceased operations on July 1, 1869, except for its educational activities, which continued until June 30, 1872.

285.4   Chaplain Eaton]   John Eaton, Jr. (1829–1906) became an army chaplain in 1861. In May 1865 he was endorsed by Grant for commissioner of the Freedman's Bureau, but the post was given to Major General Oliver O. Howard, and Eaton was made assistant commissioner in charge of Washington, D.C., Maryland, and parts of Virginia. Grant appointed him commissioner of education in 1870, and he served until 1886.

286.26–27   C. C. Washburn]   Cadwallader C. Washburn (1818–82), a brother of Congressman Elihu B. Washburne.

306.32–33   Jacob Thompson]   See note 150.33.

313.34–35   General . . . No. 69]   An order providing for the organization of detachments of hospital invalids for limited duties.

360.16–17   chief . . . Army]   Robert Macfeely became commissary general in 1875.

360.19   sap-roller]   A large wickerwork cylinder filled with sticks that was rolled in front of trenches (saps) being dug toward enemy fortifications to protect the soldiers digging them from hostile fire.

363.23 coehorns] Small portable mortars, named after their Dutch inventor Baron Menno van Coehoorn (1641–1704).

370.20 redan] A V-shaped earthwork fortification, with its point projecting toward the enemy.

384.25–27 Halleck . . . prisoners.] A dispute over the validity of the paroles given to the Vicksburg garrison contributed to the eventual suspension of prisoner exchanges under the cartel. See Grant's letter to Benjamin F. Butler of April 17, 1864, pp. 1048–49 in this volume.

403.22 Governor Brough] John Brough (1811–65), a War Democrat nominated by the Republicans, was elected governor of Ohio on October 13, 1863, and was inaugurated on January 11, 1864.

409.35–36 pacing . . . dressing-gown] Grant wrote in his manuscript that Stanton had been "pacing the room rapidly in about the garb Mr. Davis was supposed to be wearing subsequently, when he was captured in a dressing gown," but then changed the passage in proof. Several Union officers who had helped capture Jefferson Davis near Irwinville, Georgia, on May 10, 1865, had described him as attempting to escape with a shawl over his head and a woman's waterproof cloak or robe, gathered at the waist, over his clothes.

458.33 Jo Davies County] Galena is the seat of Jo Daviess County.

461.32–33 remonstrated . . . writing] Grant wrote Stanton on January 29, 1866, that in his opinion "the Gen. in Chief stands between the President and the Army in all official matters and the Secretary of War is between the Army, (through the General in Chief,) and the President." He requested that Stanton adhere to this chain of command and not issue orders directly to the army through the adjutant general.

463.22 General (Bishop) Polk] Leonidas Polk (1806–64) graduated from the Military Academy in 1827 before resigning from the army to become an Episcopal minister. He became Bishop of Louisiana in 1841 and joined the Confederate army in 1861. Polk was killed by a Union shell at Pine Mountain, Georgia, on June 14, 1864.

469.1 restoring . . . lieutenant-general] George Washington was the only American previously to have held the permanent rank of lieutenant-general in the army; Winfield Scott had held it by brevet after 1855.

471.31–32 McClellan . . . Crittenden] Major General George B. McClellan (1826–85) had been relieved by Lincoln as commander of the Army of the Potomac on November 5, 1862. He received no further command during the war and was the Democratic candidate for president in 1864. Major General Ambrose E. Burnside (1824–81), McClellan's immediate successor as commander of the Army of the Potomac, was relieved by Lincoln on January 25, 1863. After commanding the Department of the Ohio for most of 1863,

Burnside returned to the East in April 1864 as commander of the 9th Corps. Major General John C. Frémont (1813–80) was relieved of his command in northwestern Virginia on June 28, 1862, when he refused to serve under Major General John Pope, and held no further command during the war; in 1864 he was briefly the presidential nominee of a splinter group of Republican radicals. Major General Don C. Buell (1818–98), relieved as commander of the Army of the Ohio on October 24, 1862, held no further command and resigned his commission on June 1, 1864 (see pp. 472.32–473.6 in this volume). Major General Alexander M. McCook (1831–1903), Major General James S. Negley (1826–1901), and Major General Thomas L. Crittenden (1815–93) all lost control of their commands in the rout of the Union right wing during the second day of the battle of Chickamauga, September 20, 1863. They were exonerated by a court of inquiry, but only Crittenden, who commanded a division in the Army of the Potomac in 1864, subsequently held a field command during the war.

480.36–37   In . . . skins.] See p. 486.13–25 and note 486.24–25 in this volume.

486.24–25   "Oh . . . does."] Cf. the version of this remark retold by Lincoln to his personal secretary John Hay and recorded by Hay in his diary on April 30, 1864: "Those not skinning, can hold a leg."

494.4–5   making . . . expression] See p. 792.7–9 in this volume.

507.14   McCook] Brigadier General Edward M. McCook (1833–1909), a cousin of Major General Alexander M. McCook.

519.23   Stonewall Brig.] The brigade, recruited from the Shenandoah Valley of Virginia in April 1861, was trained by Thomas J. Jackson and commanded by him at the first battle of Bull Run, July 21, 1861, where both the unit and its commander gained the nickname "Stonewall"; it became the brigade's official designation after Jackson's death in May 1863. After being reduced to regimental strength by the May 12, 1864, fighting at Spotsylvania, 210 survivors of the unit surrendered at Appomattox. Of the seven men who commanded it at brigade strength (including Jackson), five were killed during the war.

531.5–6   Jenkins . . . engagement.] In the confusion and poor visibility of the Wilderness battle, Jenkins and Longstreet were accidentally shot by Confederate troops, only a few miles from where Lieutenant General Thomas J. Jackson was mortally wounded by his own men on the night of May 2, 1863, during the battle of Chancellorsville.

532.26   refused his right] Moved it back, away from the enemy line.

612.17   Meade interfered] In his testimony about the Petersburg mine before the Congressional Joint Committee on the Conduct of the War on December 20, 1864, Grant said: "General Burnside wanted to put his colored division in front, and I believe if he had done so it would have been a success.

Still I agreed with General Meade in his objection to that plan. General Meade said that if we put the colored troops in front (we had only that one division) and it should prove a failure, it would then be said, and very properly, that we were shoving those people ahead to get killed because we did not care anything about them. But that could not be said if we put white troops in front. That is the only point he changed, to my knowledge, after he had given his orders to General Burnside. It was then that General Burnside left his three division commanders to toss coppers or draw straws which should and which should not go in front."

615.3   too young]   Sheridan was 33 years old.

621.29   Burlington, New Jersey]   The Grants had rented a house in Burlington.

631.6–9   series . . . reports]   "Campaigns of the Civil War," published by Charles Scribner's Sons, volume 12 of which is Andrew A. Humphreys' *The Virginia Campaign of '64 and '65; The Army of the Potomac and the Army of the James* (1883); Badeau's *Military History of Ulysses S. Grant* (1868–81); the Union and Confederate reports were later printed in *The War of the Rebellion: A Compilation of the Official Records of the Union and Confederate Armies* (70 vols., 1880–1901).

635.31   Price's movements]   See pp. 813.25–814.5 in this volume.

636.13   treatment of citizens]   Sherman had ordered the expulsion of all civilians from Atlanta so that it could be held solely as a military depot.

653.2   chief of staff]   John A. Rawlins.

685.13–15   Stephens . . . Hunter]   Alexander H. Stephens (1812–83) of Georgia served in the House of Representatives as a Whig, 1843–52, and then as a Democrat, 1852–59. He was vice-president of the Confederate States of America from 1861 to 1865. John A. Campbell (1811–89) of Alabama was an associate justice of the U.S. Supreme Court, 1853–61, and a Confederate assistant secretary of war, 1862–65. Robert M. T. Hunter (1809–87) of Virginia served in the House of Representatives from 1837 to 1843, first as a Whig and then as Democrat, and was its Speaker from 1839 to 1841. He returned to the House as a Democrat, 1845–47, before serving in the Senate from 1847 to 1861. Hunter was Confederate secretary of state, 1861–62, and a Confederate senator, 1862–65.

702.11   authorization . . . Warren.]   Gouverneur K. Warren (1830–82) held other commands before resigning his commission in the volunteers on May 27, 1865. He then served in the regular army as a major, and later lieutenant colonel, of engineers, and repeatedly asked for a court of inquiry into his relief at the battle of Five Forks. His request was finally granted on December 9, 1879, by President Rutherford B. Hayes. The court criticized Warren's performance in getting his troops into position on March 31, 1865, but exonerated him of misconduct in the battle on April 1. On November 21, 1881,

President Chester A. Arthur ordered the findings of the court published, but they were not made public until after Warren's death.

732.29–30   story . . . tree.]   According to a widespread report, Lee surrendered to Grant under an apple tree.

742.1   /2/ . . . Va.]   In the Charles L. Webster edition, the following publisher's note appeared at the bottom of the page facing the facsimile, which was printed on a fold-out page:

"The fac-simile of the terms of Lee's surrender inserted at this place, was copied from the original document furnished the publishers through the courtesy of General Ely S. Parker, Military Secretary on General Grant's staff at the time of the surrender.

"Three pages of paper were prepared in General Grant's manifold order book on which he wrote the terms, and the interlineations and erasures were added by General Parker at the suggestion of General Grant. After such alteration it was handed to General Lee, who put on his glasses, read it, and handed it back to General Grant. The original was then transcribed by General Parker upon official headed paper and a copy furnished to General Lee.

"The fac-simile herewith shows the color of the paper of the original document and all interlineations and erasures.

"There is a popular error to the effect that Generals Grant and Lee each signed the articles of surrender. The document in the form of a letter was signed only by General Grant, in the parlor of McLean's house while General Lee was sitting in the room, and General Lee immediately wrote a letter accepting the terms and handed it to General Grant. This letter is copied on page 494."

Lee's letter accepting the terms appears on p. 740.14–22 in this volume. The facsimile of the surrender terms in this volume does not reproduce the color of the original.

749.2   leading . . . Virginia]   Gustavus Myers, a member of the Confederate legislature of Virginia, accompanied by John A. Campbell, conferred with Lincoln.

754.29–30   terms . . . *conditionally*]   On April 18, 1865, Sherman and Johnston signed a "Memorandum, or Basis of Agreement" near Durham's Station, North Carolina, which set the following terms:

"1. The contending armies now in the field to maintain the *statu quo* until notice is given by the commanding general of any one to its opponent, and reasonable time—say, forty-eight hours—allowed.

"2. The Confederate armies now in existence to be disbanded and conducted to their several State capitals, there to deposit their arms and public property in the State Arsenal; and each officer and man to execute and file an agreement to cease from acts of war, and to abide the action of the State and Federal authority. The number of arms and munitions of war to be reported to the Chief of Ordnance at Washington City, subject to the future action of the Congress of the United States, and, in the mean time, to be used solely to maintain peace and order within the borders of the States respectively.

"3. The recognition, by the Executive of the United States, of the several State governments, on their officers and Legislatures taking the oaths prescribed by the Constitution of the United States, and, where conflicting State governments have resulted from the war, the legitimacy of all shall be submitted to the Supreme Court of the United States.

"4. The reëstablishment of all the Federal Courts in the several States, with powers as defined by the Constitution of the United States and of the States respectively.

"5. The people and inhabitants of all the States to be guaranteed, so far as the Executive can, their political rights and franchises, as well as their rights of person and property, as defined by the Constitution of the United States and of the States respectively.

"6. The Executive authority of the Government of the United States not to disturb any of the people by reason of the late war, so long as they live in peace and quiet, abstain from acts of armed hostility, and obey the laws in existence at the place of their residence.

"7. In general terms—the war to cease; a general amnesty, so far as the Executive of the United States can command, on condition of the disbandment of the Confederate armies, the distribution of arms, and the resumption of peaceful pursuits by the officers and men hitherto composing said armies.

"Not being fully empowered by our respective principals to fulfill these terms, we individually and officially pledge ourselves to promptly obtain the necessary authority, and to carry out the above programme."

762.1–2   garb . . . wearing]   See note 409.35–36.

768.33   "sweet . . . ground"]   Cf. the song "Marching through Georgia" (1865), words by Henry C. Work: "How the sweet potatoes even started from the ground."

772.23–26   Mackenzie . . . corps]   Ranald Slidell Mackenzie (1840–89), who graduated first in his class at the Military Academy in 1862, commanded the cavalry division of the Army of the James during the Appomattox campaign. After the Civil War he led the 4th Cavalry in campaigns against the Comanche, Kickapoo, and Cheyenne Indians. Wounded several times in action, Mackenzie was made a brigadier general in the regular army in 1882, but retired on disability in 1884 after having been judged insane. He was the son of Commander Alexander Slidell Mackenzie (1803–48), who had provoked a fierce controversy by hanging three suspected mutineers on board the brig *Somers* in 1842, and the nephew of John Slidell (1793–1871), the Confederate commissioner in France, 1862–65.

773.25   Fugitive . . . Law.]   Congress passed a new fugitive slave law in 1850.

774.40   effective blockade]   Under the Declaration of Paris, signed by France and Great Britain in 1856, a blockade had to be "maintained by a force sufficient really to prevent access to the coast of the enemy" in order to be considered legitimate by neutral powers; otherwise, the blockading power had no right to stop and search neutral shipping on the high seas, and attempts to do so became potential grounds for war.

775.2   Austrian prince]   After French troops captured Mexico City in June 1863, Napoleon III arranged for the Hapsburg archduke Maximilian (1832–67) to be offered the imperial throne of Mexico in July 1863. Maximilian was crowned in 1864 and ruled until 1867, when he was overthrown and executed by Mexicans led by Benito Juárez.

777.25   leaders . . . party]   Prime Minister Viscount Palmerston, Foreign Secretary Lord John Russell, and Chancellor of the Exchequer William E. Gladstone, leaders of the Liberal government in office from 1859 to 1865, were criticized in the North for taking actions and making statements favorable to the Confederate cause. Other prominent Liberals, including John Bright and Richard Cobden, were supporters of the Union.

778.1–2   annexation . . . President]   On January 10, 1870, Grant submitted a treaty calling for the annexation of the Dominican Republic for ratification by the Senate. It was defeated by a 28–28 vote on June 30, 1870. The opposition was led by Republicans Charles Sumner of Massachusetts, chairman of the Senate Foreign Relations Committee, and Carl Schurz of Missouri.

779.25–26   "from . . . sea"]   William Cowper (1731–1800), "Verses Supposed to be Written by Alexander Selkirk" (1782).

779.40   "Let . . . peace."]   The conclusion of Grant's letter of May 29, 1868, accepting the Republican nomination for the presidency, which became the party's main slogan during the ensuing campaign.

783.1   accompanying map]   This map was not printed in the Charles L. Webster edition of the *Personal Memoirs of U. S. Grant*.

801.28   hundred . . . men]   Men serving for 100 days were generally used to guard supply depots, rail lines, and prisoner-of-war camps.

SELECTED LETTERS 1839–1865

877.1   *R. McKinstry Griffith*]   Son of James Griffith and Mary Simpson Griffith, Grant's maternal aunt.

877.22   Kosisuseko]   Tadeusz Andrzej Bonawentura Kościuszko (1746–1817), a Polish officer, served as colonel of engineers with the Continental Army, 1776–83, and directed the fortification of West Point from 1778 to 1780. In 1794 he led an unsuccessful revolt against Russian rule in Poland.

880.10   Bump of Acquisitiveness] A reference to phrenology, in which the conformation of the skull reveals character traits and mental faculties, different "bumps" signifying specific attributes.

881.2   Mr. Hazlitt] Robert Hazlitt was an Academy classmate of Grant's. He was killed in the battle of Monterrey on September 21, 1846. See p. 919.20–23 in this volume.

881.20   Ellen] Julia Dent's sister, Ellen (Nellie) Wrenshall Dent (1824–1904).

881.30   Wrenshall Dent's family] George Wrenshall Dent (1819–99), Julia's brother, had married Mary Isabella Shurlds in 1841.

882.10   [. . . . .]] Bracketed ellipses indicate lost material in the original manuscripts that could not be reconstructed by the editors of *The Papers of Ulysses S. Grant*. The number of dots indicates the approximate number of missing letters.

882.16   *Mrs. George B. Bailey*] A Georgetown neighbor and the mother of Bartlett Bailey, whose departure from the Military Academy created the vacancy Grant filled.

884.24   Mr. Higgins] Second Lieutenant Thaddeus Higgins, an 1840 Military Academy graduate from Pennsylvania.

885.6–7   Fred's Regiment] Brevet Second Lieutenant Frederick T. Dent (1820–92), Julia's brother and Grant's roommate during his last year at the Military Academy, was stationed with the 6th Infantry at Fort Towson in Indian Territory (later Oklahoma).

885.36   Miss Fanny Morrison] Fanny Morrison, daughter of Captain Pitcairn Morrison of the 4th Infantry, married Lieutenant Higgins in 1845.

887.6   John Dent] Julia Dent's brother.

888.4   Mr. Porters] Second Lieutenant Theodoric H. Porter of the 4th Infantry. See p. 63.20–21 and note 63.20 in this volume.

889.29   My oldest sister] Clara Rachel Grant (1828–65).

890.9   Col. Dent] The title was honorific.

890.23   Mrs. Mary Dent] See note 881.30.

891.3   Sappington P. O.]   Sappington Post Office, the mailing address of White Haven, the Dent family home outside of St. Louis.

891.32   "Jim a long Josy"]   "Jim Along Josey" was the title of a minstrel song by Edward Harper, published in 1840.

893.9   occupation . . . England]   Treaties signed in 1818 and 1827 established joint Anglo-American occupation of the region west of the Rockies between 42° and 54°40′ latitude. In 1844–45 expansionist Democrats advocated annexation of the Pacific northwest up to the 54°40′ line and expressed the willingness to go to war with Great Britain over the issue. The question was resolved when the administration of President James K. Polk signed a treaty with Great Britain on June 18, 1846, that extended the boundary along the 49th parallel westward from the Rockies to the Strait of Georgia.

893.26   Beaman]   Second Lieutenant Jenks Beaman, an 1842 graduate of the Military Academy, was an officer in the 4th Infantry. He died of disease in Mexico in May 1848.

894.10   Emmy]   Julia's sister, Emily Marbury Dent (b. 1836).

900.17   promotes me]   Grant was promoted from brevet second lieutenant to second lieutenant on September 30, 1845.

900.32   Florida war]   Attempts by the United States to remove the Seminole Indians, and the Negroes who found refuge from slavery among them, from Florida Territory led to the outbreak of war in 1835. Fighting continued until 1842, by which time almost all of the surviving Seminoles had been sent to Indian Territory. The conflict, also known as the second Seminole War, cost the lives of approximately 1,500 American soldiers.

902.1   Wandering Jew]   *The Wandering Jew* (1844–45) by French novelist Eugène Sue (1804–75).

902.8–10 sentence . . . hearts,]   ". . . for two drops of dew blending in the cup of a flower are as hearts that mingle in a pure and virgin love; and two rays of light united in one inextinguishable flame, are as the burning and eternal joys of lovers joined in wedlock."

902.24   *October 1845*]   This letter, not dated by Grant, was postmarked in New Orleans on October 13, 1845.

903.33–34 Mr. Benton's influance]   Thomas Hart Benton (1782–1858) was a Democratic senator from Missouri, 1821–51.

904.27   ***]   In this volume, three asterisks indicate places where Julia Dent Grant later crossed out words or passages in the letters. The editors of *The Papers of Ulysses S. Grant* did not print this material at the request of Grant's descendants.

908.37   Col. Majia]   General Francisco Mejía.

910.31–32   Capt. Page . . . alive.]   Captain John Page died of his wounds on July 12, 1846.

911.26   General Lavega]   General R. Díaz de la Vega.

912.28   *John W. Lowe*]   Lowe, an Ohio lawyer and associate of Congressman Thomas L. Hamer, was a longtime friend of Grant and his father.

915.26   Parades]   General Mariano Paredes y Arrillaga (1797–1849), who opposed any compromise with the United States over territorial issues, overthrew President José Joaquín Herrera in December 1845 and became acting president on January 4, 1846. He stepped down on July 28, 1846, to lead troops in the field, but quickly lost all power. Santa Anna then returned from exile and assumed command of the Mexican army in September 1846.

916.21   new . . . Riflemen]   Congress added a regiment of Mounted Riflemen to the regular army on May 19, 1846.

919.22–23   Graham . . . wounded.]   First Lieutenant Richard H. Graham and Major William W. Lear died of their wounds in October 1846.

924.2   Bonapartes . . . Alps]   Napoleon Bonaparte led his reserve army from Switzerland through the Great St. Bernard Pass into Italy between May 14 and 25, 1800, and then moved on the rear of the Austrian army in Piedmont, defeating it at Marengo on June 14, 1800.

925.33   wounded . . . Fred's]   Frederick T. Dent was wounded in the thigh during the battle of Molino del Rey on September 8, 1847.

931.29   little Fred]   Grant's first child, Frederick Dent Grant, born May 30, 1850.

932.35   Virginia]   Grant's sister Virginia (Gennie, Jennie) Paine Grant (b. 1832).

933.33   date . . . sick]   Julia was expecting their second child. A son, Ulysses S. Grant, Jr., was born on July 22, 1852.

936.20   where John is]   Grant's brother-in-law John Dent (1816–89) operated a ferry, tavern, and stables at Knight's Ferry, California.

936.35   Elijah Camp]   Camp had been a special contractor at Sackets Harbor. He left Oregon Territory in 1853 owing Grant $800 from a joint business venture.

937.6   Maggy]   Margaret Getz and her husband, an enlisted soldier, had worked for the Grants at Sackets Harbor and now were with him in Oregon.

937.34   Fred. Steel] Frederick Steele (1819–68) became a Union major general of volunteers during the Civil War.

938.5   Mrs. Stevens] The wife of Lieutenant Thomas H. Stevens, a naval officer Grant had known at Sackets Harbor.

943.13   Washington Territory] On March 2, 1853, Congress created a new territory out of the northern portion of Oregon Territory.

944.21   Mr. Hunt . . . Russell] Unknown to Grant, first lieutenants Lewis C. Hunt and Edmund Russell had been killed on March 24, 1853, in a fight with Indians at Red Bluff, California.

946.22   Laura] Laura Wallen, the wife of First Lieutenant Henry Davies Wallen.

947.27–28   enclose . . . "B".] These attachments to Grant's report are not known to be extant.

948.40–949.1   Clickitat . . . Dalles] The Klikitat, a tribe in the Sahaptin linguistic group, lived north of the Columbia. In an adjacent region were the Cowlitz, a Salish tribe. The Dalles, a branch of the Wascos, a tribe in the Chinook linguistic group, lived upriver on the Columbia in The Dalles region.

949.20–21   long . . . application] Grant had made his request on September 8, 1853, in letters to the quartermaster general and the commissary general.

950.4–5   Col. B . . . promotion] Brevet Lieutenant Colonel Robert C. Buchanan (1811–78) held the permanent rank of captain until his promotion to major on February 3, 1855. He commanded a brigade in the Army of the Potomac, 1862–63.

952.31–32   Capt. Calender . . . money?] Grant had sold his stock in the Detroit & Saline and the Plymouth railroads to Franklin D. Callender, who was paying for it with interest.

955.14   *Frederick Dent*] Frederick F. Dent (1786–1873), Grant's father-in-law.

956.28   novel name] Sidney Johnston Dent was born in Walla Walla, Washington Territory, on February 18, 1861.

957.25–26   leave . . . safe] Jesse Root Grant (1794–1873) continued to live in Covington, Kentucky, across the Ohio River from Cincinnati, until his death.

957.28   Orvil] Grant's brother, Orvil Lynch Grant (1835–81).

958.16   The Governer]   Richard Yates (1818–73) was Republican governor
of Illinois from 1861 to 1865.

958.32   Capt. Pope]   John Pope (1822–92) was appointed brigadier general of volunteers on May 17, 1861, and made a major general in 1862.

958.34   K McKenzie]   Kenneth MacKenzie was a St. Louis merchant
who had endorsed Grant in 1859 for the position of county engineer.

960.5   Aunt . . . Clara!]   Rachel B. Grant Tompkins, a sister of Grant's
father, lived in Charleston, Virginia (now West Virginia). She had written to
Grant's sister Clara, "If you are with the accursed Lincolnites, the ties of
consanguinity shall be forever severed." In a subsequent letter of June 5, 1861,
she criticized Grant for "drawing his sword against those connected by the
ties of blood."

960.17–18   Simpson]   See p. 144.18–28 in this volume.

961.10   bump of order]   See note 880.10.

961.20–21   Charless Blow & Co]   A wholesale drug firm in St. Louis.

964.3   Mary Duncan]   The stepdaughter of a Galena grain merchant and
a neighbor of the Grant family.

964.24   Egypt]   A colloquial name for the southern, or southernmost,
counties of Illinois.

965.2   Jo Reynolds]   Joseph Jones Reynolds (1822–99), a friend and class-
mate of Grant's at the Military Academy, resigned from the army in 1857 to
become professor of mechanics and engineering at Washington University in
St. Louis and in 1859 endorsed Grant's unsuccessful candidacy for the post of
St. Louis County engineer. After serving as a major general of volunteers in
the Civil War, Reynolds rejoined the regular army as a colonel. He was court-
martialed and convicted in January 1877 on charges stemming from the failure
of his March 17, 1876, attack on an Indian village along the Powder River in
Montana, and sentenced to one year's suspension of rank and pay. President
Grant remitted the sentence, however, and Reynolds retired on disability in
July 1877.

965.3   Emma . . . Jim]   Julia's sister Emily had married James F. Casey
February 14, 1861. In 1869 Grant appointed Casey collector of customs at New
Orleans, where he took part in the bitter feuding within the Louisiana Republican party and was accused of running a corrupt ring in the custom-
house.

965.15   Camp Yates]   The camp was located in a fairgrounds outside of
Springfield, Illinois.

966.34   Dr. Sharp]   Dr. Alexander Sharp, husband of Julia's sister Ellen
and a resident of Lincoln County, Missouri. He remained loyal to the Union.

966.37   McClellands . . . Crimea.]   "Report of the Secretary of War, communicating the Report of Captain George B. McClellan (First Regiment United States Cavalry.) one of the Officers sent to the Seat of War in Europe in 1855 and 1856," published in *Senate Executive Documents* (1857).

968.14   Susy Felts]   Susan M. Felt was the eight-year-old daughter of a Galena grocer.

968.20   East Quincy, Mo.]   West Quincy, Missouri. This letter is taken from *Letters of Ulysses S. Grant to his Father and his Youngest Sister, 1857–78* (1912), edited by J. G. Cramer; the error may have occurred in transcription.

969.9   notorious Jim Green]   James S. Green (1817–70) was a Democratic congressman from Missouri, 1847–51, and then served in the U.S. Senate, 1857–61, where he defended the Buchanan administration's policy in Kansas.

972.26   Mr. Trumbull's]   Lyman Trumbull (1817–96) was a Republican senator from Illinois, 1855–73.

973.28   Manassas]   The first battle of Manassas (or Bull Run) was fought in northern Virginia on July 21, 1861.

974.26   Mr. Rollins]   John A. Rawlins. See note 153.6.

974.30   Ford]   Charles W. Ford, a lawyer, first met Grant at Sackets Harbor. Their friendship continued after Ford moved to St. Louis, and Ford often assisted Grant in business and financial transactions.

975.10   Harry Boggs]   Harry Boggs was Julia's cousin. Grant had worked for several months in 1858–59 as a bill collector in Boggs's real estate firm.

975.17–18   set . . . profanity.]   Cf. Laurence Sterne (1713–68), *Tristram Shandy*, Book III (1761–62), Chapter 11: " 'Our armies swore terribly in Flanders,' cried my uncle Toby—'But nothing to this.' "

975.22   Covington]   See note 957.25–26.

979.3   Report to me]   Paine reported on January 12, 1862, that his patrols would probably bring in 100 citizens by nightfall. On January 19, 1862, Grant ordered the release of all civilian prisoners at Bird's Point who had not been charged with a specific offense.

985.12   Capt. Kountz]   Captain William J. Kountz, the owner of a Pennsylvania steamboat fleet, had been reprimanded by Grant on December 21, 1861, for inspecting the river transportation at Cairo, Illinois, without first reporting to Grant and presenting his authorizing papers. Kountz was subsequently assigned by Major Robert Allen, quartermaster of the Department of the Missouri, to serve as master of river transportation at Cairo, where he quarreled with the civilian boatmen serving with the Union flotilla and caused several army officers to petition for his replacement. On January 14, 1862, Grant ordered his arrest for disobeying orders and applied to have him removed from his military district. Kountz then prepared charges against Grant, which Grant saw on January 30 before forwarding them to higher headquarters, accusing him of having been "beastly drunk" while meeting with Confederate officers under flag of truce and of having set an "evil example" to his command by repeated public drunkenness. These charges reached the War Department in Washington, D.C., but were never acted upon, and Kountz resigned his commission on March 13, 1862.

989.23   your brother] Colonel Cadwallader C. Washburn (1818–82), commander of the 2nd Wisconsin Cavalry. Washburn later became a major general of volunteers.

993.8   Thomas] Brigadier General Lorenzo Thomas (1804–75).

996.12   Charles Page] Charles Page was the son of Samuel K. Page, a prosperous Louisville builder, and Ellen Wrenshall Page, Julia's maternal aunt.

997.12   Gen. Wallace] Major General Lewis Wallace (1827–1905).

1004.27   the Correspondence] On April 8, 1862, Confederate General Pierre G. T. Beauregard wrote Grant, requesting permission to send a burial party to the Shiloh battlefield. Grant replied on April 9 that the warm weather had already caused him to order the immediate burial of the dead of both armies.

1004.32   *To Jesse Root Grant*] This letter appeared in the *Cincinnati Commercial* on May 2, 1862. Grant wrote to Julia on May 11, 1862, that he had seen "with pain" a letter to his father in the press and that its publication "should never have occured."

1010.16   news . . . Richmond] Confederate General Robert E. Lee had attacked the Army of the Potomac outside of Richmond in the Seven Days' Battles, June 25–July 1, 1862, causing Major General George B. McClellan to retreat to Harrison's Landing on the north bank of the James River.

1011.35   *Fragment on Shiloh*] This is printed from an undated manuscript draft, probably written between July 17, 1862, when William Nelson was confirmed as a major general of volunteers, and September 29, 1862, when Nelson was shot to death in Louisville, Kentucky, by Brigadier General Jefferson C. Davis during a quarrel.

1014.22   Mr. Nixon] John S. Nixon was a Covington, Kentucky, lawyer. With the help of Grant's father, he had written two letters praising Grant that were published in the *Cincinnati Gazette* in May 1862.

1015.1   *Stephen A. Hurlbut*] Hurlbut commanded the military district around Jackson, Tennessee. On November 10, 1862, Grant ordered that no Jews be allowed to travel south by railroad from any point within his department, and on December 17, 1862, authorized the issue of General Order No. 11, which expelled "Jews, as a class" from the Department of the Tennessee for "violating every regulation of trade established by the Treasury Department." President Lincoln, through Halleck, revoked General Order No. 11 on

January 4, 1863. For Grant's objections to the cotton trade, see pp. 266.30–267.8 in this volume.

1016.15–16   Col. Hedgepath]   Confederate Lieutenant Colonel Isaac N. Hedgpeth of the 6th Missouri Infantry was wounded and captured at Corinth, Mississippi, on October 3, 1862. Pemberton wrote Grant on December 10 that he had been "credibly informed" that Hedgpeth had been subjected to "unusually harsh treatment" and had had his parole, watch, and money taken from him.

1020.21   *Thomas W. Knox*]   Knox had accompanied Sherman's December 1862 movement against Vicksburg in violation of orders intended to exclude newspaper correspondents from the expedition. His dispatch in the New York *Herald* of January 18, 1863, criticized Sherman both for his failed attack against the bluffs above Chickasaw Bayou and for attempting to ban reporters from his operations. Sherman had Knox court-martialed for publishing military news without permission, making false accusations against army officers, and violating the exclusion order. On February 18, 1863, Knox was convicted of the third charge and expelled from the army's lines.

1020.27   letter . . . President]   In his letter of March 20, 1863, Lincoln wrote that he was conditionally revoking Knox's expulsion because Brigadier General John M. Thayer, president of the court-martial, Major General John McClernand, and "many other respectable persons" were of the opinion that Knox's offense was "technical, rather than wilfully wrong."

1021.9–10   Sherman . . . consent]   Sherman wrote Knox on April 7, 1863, that he would be allowed to rejoin Sherman's command as a soldier, but never as a correspondent.

1026.17–18   letter . . . Mrs Duncan]   Mary Duncan was the wife of Henry P. Duncan and the daughter-in-law of Dr. Stephen Duncan of Natchez, Mississippi, a wealthy planter and investor and staunch Unionist. She wrote Thomas on June 2, 1863, that despite protection papers issued by Grant and other Union commanders, freedmen now working for wages on her family's plantations had been forcibly removed by Union troops. On July 11 Grant ordered an investigation, which subsequently found that a number of soldiers in the 8th Louisiana Volunteers of African Descent claimed to have been forced into service from the Duncan plantations, but that the officer responsible had been killed in action on May 27. However, the commander of the 8th Louisiana Volunteers denied the charge of impressment and suggested that the claims had been made by soldiers who wanted to return to their families. Grant is not known to have taken any further action in this matter.

1027.13   Col. Shepard . . . punishment]   Colonel Isaac F. Shepard had ordered a white soldier tied to a tree and whipped by black soldiers under his command. In a letter of October 5, 1863, Thomas told Secretary of War Edwin M. Stanton that white troops had committed "acts of wantoness" against Shepard's soldiers and their families and that the "flagrant case under consideration" had been "one calling for the severest punishment, even to the loss of life . . ."

1027.26   Commissioners]   Commissioners in charge of plantations abandoned by their owners.

1028.30−31   Your letter . . . Mellen]   Chase asked Grant to confer with treasury agent William P. Mellen about the possibility of allowing civilians to trade in areas under military occupation after posting bonds to ensure their compliance with regulations.

1030.29   letter . . . 13th]   Lincoln had written to Grant from the White House on July 13, 1863:

"I do not remember that you and I ever met personally. I write this now as a grateful acknowledgment for the almost inestimable service you have done the country. I wish to say a word further. When you first reached the vicinity of Vicksburg, I thought you should do, what you finally did—march the troops across the neck, run the batteries with the transports, and thus go below; and I never had any faith, except a general hope that you knew better than I, that the Yazoo Pass expedition, and the like, could succeed. When you got below, and took Port-Gibson, Grand Gulf, and vicinity, I thought you should go down the river and join Gen. Banks; and when you turned Northward East of the Big Black, I feared it was a mistake. I now wish to make the personal acknowledgment that you were right, and I was wrong."

1031.1−2   importance . . . time]   See p. 388.11−28 in this volume and note 775.2.

1031.6−8   arming . . . Confederacy]   Cf. Lincoln's letter to a public meeting held in Springfield, Illinois, on September 3, 1863: "I know as fully as one can know the opinions of others, that some of the commanders of our armies in the field who have given us our most important successes, believe the emancipation policy, and the use of colored troops, constitute the heaviest blow yet dealt to the rebellion; . . ." This passage was part of a paragraph Lincoln added by telegram on August 31 to the main text of the letter, which he had sent to his friend James C. Conkling on August 26.

1032.6   *John G. Thompson*]   Thompson, a Columbus, Ohio, merchant, was chairman of the Ohio Democratic State Central Committee.

1032.24−26   vote . . . dissentions]   The Democratic nominee for governor of Ohio was Clement L. Vallandigham (1820−71), who had been exiled from the North by the administration in May 1863 for denouncing the prosecution of the war.

1033.7−9   Wilson . . . says]   Henry Wilson (1812−75), a Republican senator from Massachusetts from 1855 to 1873, was chairman of the Senate Military Affairs Committee. Wilson had written Washburne on July 25, 1863, praising Grant for favoring the overthrow of slavery and hoping that he would remain with the Army of the Tennessee and not accept a reported offer of the command of the Army of the Potomac, where, Wilson warned, Grant would be "ruined" by envious men "in and out of that army."

1036.18   my injury]   See p. 390.13–26 in this volume.

1038.13   *J. Russell Jones*]   Jones was a friend of Grant's from Galena, now living in Chicago, who advised Grant on investments.

1039.6   *Barnabas Burns*]   Burns was chairman of the State Central Committee of the Ohio "War Democracy," organized in opposition to the supporters of Clement L. Vallandigham (see note 1032.24–26). He had written Grant on December 7, 1863, asking permission to place Grant's name in nomination for the presidency at a state convention to be held in Columbus on January 8, 1864.

1044.25   you . . . judge]   On February 17, 1864, Halleck wrote Grant that an attack into North Carolina with 60,000 men would seriously weaken the Army of the Potomac and leave Maryland and Pennsylvania open to Confederate invasion. Halleck expressed his conviction that Lee's army, not Richmond, should be the objective of the next campaign and suggested that supply considerations favored making the advance over land through northern Virginia.

1045.1   *Rufus Ingalls*]   Ingalls (1820–93) was a friend and classmate of Grant's at the Military Academy and served with him at Fort Vancouver. He was chief quartermaster of the Army of the Potomac, 1862–64, and of the armies of the Potomac and the James, 1864–65.

1046.7   *To . . . Sherman*]   Sherman replied to Grant on March 10, 1864:
"Dear General: I have your more than kind and characteristic letter of the 4th—I will send a copy to General McPherson at once. You do yourself injustice and us too much honor in assigning to us so large a share of the merits which have led to your high advancement. I know you approve the friendship I have ever professed to you, and permit me to continue as heretofore to manifest it on all proper occasions. You are now Washington's legitimate successor and occupy a position of almost dangerous elevation, but if you can continue as heretofore to be yourself, simple, honest, and unpretending, you will enjoy through life the respect and love of friends, and the homage of millions of human beings that will award to you a large share in securing to them and their descendants a Government of Law and Stability. I repeat you do General McPherson and myself too much honor. At Belmont you manifested your traits, neither of us being near—at Donelson also you illustrated your whole character. I was not near, and Gen'l McPherson in too subordinate a capacity to influence you. Until you had won Donelson, I confess I was almost cowed by the terrible array of anarchial elements that presented themselves at every point, but that victory admitted the ray of light which I have followed ever since   I believe you are as brave, patriotic, and just, as the great prototype Washington—as unselfish, kindhearted and honest, as a man should be, but the chief characteristic in your nature is the

simple faith in success you have always manifested, which I can liken to nothing else than the faith a Christian has in a Savior. This faith gave you victory
at Shiloh and Vicksburg. Also when you have completed your best preparations you go into Battle without hesitation, as at Chattanooga—no doubts—
no reserve, and I tell you that it was this that made us act with confidence. I
knew wherever I was that you thought of me, and if I got in a tight place you
would come if alive   My only points of doubt were in your knowledge of
Grand Strategy and of Books of Science and History. But I confess your
common sense seems to have supplied all these. Now as to the future. Dont
stay in Washington. Halleck is better qualified than you are to stand the buffets of Intrigue and Policy. Come out West, take to yourself the whole Mississippi Valley. Let us make it dead sure, and I tell you the Atlantic slope and
Pacific shores will follow its destiny as sure as the limbs of a tree live or die
with the main trunk. We have done much, but still much remains to be done.
Time and times influences are all with us. We could almost afford to sit still
and let these influences work. Even in the Seceded States your word now
would go further than a Presidents Proclamation or an Act of Congress. For
Gods sake and for your Countrys sake come out of Washington. I foretold to
Gen'l Halleck before he left Corinth the inevitable result to him, and I now
exhort you to come out West. Here lies the seat of the coming Empire, and
from the West when our task is done, we will make short work of Charleston,
and Richmond, and the impoverished coast of the Atlantic. Your sincere
friend,

"W. T. Sherman"

1049.22   Mr. Chadwick]   A proprietor of Willard's Hotel in Washington, D.C.

1049.24   Helen]   Helen Louise Lynde Dent was the wife of Frederick T.
Dent.

1051.8   sword . . . voted]   Julia had been attending the New York Sanitary Fair, where donors of a dollar could vote to award an ornate sword to
either Grant or Major General George B. McClellan.

1052.18–19   one hundred . . . field]   See note 801.28.

1055.25–26   the White House]   White House, Virginia, a Union supply
base on the Pamunkey River.

1057.4   Sunday]   Sunday was June 12, 1864.

1058.24   Gen. Smith]   Major General William F. Smith (1824–1903),
commander of the 18th Corps, part of Butler's Army of the James.

1059.11   make a change]   Halleck suggested on July 3 retaining Butler as
commander of the Department of Virginia and North Carolina while assigning his troops along the James to Smith. Grant agreed on July 6, but found
the wording of the subsequent order issued from Washington unsatisfactory
and eventually abandoned his attempt to displace the politically influential

Butler. Instead, Grant relieved Smith, who had become increasingly critical of Major General George G. Meade, from command of the 18th Corps on July 19, 1864, replacing him with Major General Edward O. C. Ord.

1060.26−27   immediate call . . . 300.000]   On July 20, 1864, Lincoln telegraphed in reply: "Yours of yesterday about a call for 300,000 is received. I suppose you had not seen the call for 500,000 made the day before, and which I suppose covers the case. Always glad to have your suggestions."

1061.12   E. M. . . . War]   When drafting this telegram, Grant first addressed it to "A. Lincoln, President," but then changed its recipient to Stanton.

1061.13−15   protest . . . quotas.]   Stanton telegraphed Grant on July 20 that this practice was "neither reccommended nor sanctioned" by the War Department but was favored by the President. Later that day Stanton forwarded to Grant a copy of a telegram sent by Lincoln to Sherman on July 18, 1864:

"I have seen your despatches objecting to agents of Northern States opening recruiting stations near your camps. An act of congress authorizes this, giving the appointment of agents to the States, and not to this Executive government. It is not for the War Department, or myself, to restrain, or modify the law, in it's execution, further than actual necessity may require. To be candid, I was for the passage of the law, not apprehending at the time that it would produce such inconvenience to the armies in the field, as you now cause me to fear. Many of the States were very anxious for it, and I hoped that, with their State bounties, and active exertions, they would get out substantial additions to our colored forces, which, unlike white recruits, help us where they come from, as well as where they go to. I still hope advantage from the law; and being a law, it must be treated as such by all of us. We here, will do what we consistently can to save you from difficulties arising out of it. May I ask therefore that you will give your hearty co-operation?"

1061.22−23   protest . . . War.]   Stanton replied that the President had authorized Major General Benjamin F. Butler to recruit from prisoners of war. On August 9, 1864, Grant wrote Halleck that he was sending the first regiment recruited from Confederate prisoners to the northwest Indian frontier, where they would not risk punishment for desertion if taken prisoner. See Grant's letter to William H. Seward of August 19, 1864, pp. 1065−66 in this volume.

1063.29   To Lydia Slocum]   This letter was printed in the Washington Chronicle on August 29, 1864. Mrs. Slocum was the 87-year-old grandmother of Major General James B. McPherson, who was killed in the battle of Atlanta on July 22, 1864.

1064.20   Mrs. Adams]   Abigail Brooks Adams (1808−89), wife of Charles

Francis Adams, Sr., and mother of Charles Francis Adams, Jr., a captain serving in the Army of the Potomac, and Henry and Brooks Adams.

1064.33   I state]   The last three paragraphs of this letter were widely circulated in Republican campaign broadsides during the 1864 election.

1065.16–17   McCawber]   Wilkins Micawber, a character in Charles Dickens' *David Copperfield* (1849–50).

1065.35–36   F. W. Morse . . . C. W. G.]   Freeman H. Morse, a Whig
(1843–45) and later a Republican (1857–61) congressman from Maine, was
United States consul in London. C. W. Geddes, a Union agent, quoted the
secretary at the Confederate legation in London as saying that Union deserters wanted to fight against Grant because he had treated them so badly.

1066.21   Gen. Popes Department]   Major General John Pope commanded
the Department of the Northwest, which covered Iowa, Wisconsin, Minnesota, and the Nebraska and Dakota territories.

1069.2   Burlington]   See note 621.29.

1069.31   written to him]   Washburne telegraphed Grant on September 20,
1864, that publication of an exchange of letters between Grant and Lincoln in
the spring of 1864 would refute charges that the President had interfered with
Grant's arrangements. Lincoln had written Grant on April 30, 1864, expressing his "entire satisfaction with what you have done up to this time . . ."
The President continued: "The particulars of your plans I neither know, or
seek to know. You are vigilant and self-reliant; and, pleased with this, I wish
not to obtrude any constraints or restraints upon you." Grant replied on May
1, 1864, from his headquarters at Culpeper, Virginia, as follows:
    "Your very kind letter of yesterday is just received. The confidence you
express for the future, and satisfaction with the past, in my Military administration is acknowledged with pride. It will be my earnest endeavor that you,
and the country, shall not be disappointed.
    "From my first entrance into the volunteer service of the country, to the
present day, I have never had cause of complaint, have never expressed or
implied a complaint, against the Administration, or the Sec. of War, for
throwing any embarassment in the way of my vigerously prossecuting what
appeared to me my duty. Indeed since the promotion which placed me in
command of all the Armies, and in view of the great responsibility, and importance of success, I have been astonished at the readiness with which every
thing asked for has been yielded without even an explaination being asked.
Should my success be less than I desire, and expect, the least I can say is, the
fault is not with you."

1072.13   Col. Babcock]   Orville E. Babcock (1835–84) was an aide-de-
camp on Grant's staff. He served as President Grant's private secretary until

1876, when he was forced to resign because of his involvement in the "whiskey ring" tax fraud scandal.

1072.26–29   Knowing . . . command.]   On February 3, 1865, Pope assumed command of the new Division of the Missouri, covering the Department of the Missouri (into which the Department of Kansas had been merged) and the Department of the Northwest. Pope was succeeded in the Department of the Northwest by Major General Samuel R. Curtis (1805–66), previously the commander of the Department of Kansas.

1072.34–35   Dodge . . . Mo.]   Major General Grenville M. Dodge (1831–1916) was replacing Major General William S. Rosecrans (1819–98). Grant had long been critical of Curtis's and Rosecrans's performance as department commanders.

1073.4   dispatch of 9 p. m.]   Halleck had expressed his belief that while no one in Washington wished Thomas to be removed, no one there would interfere if Grant relieved Thomas on his own responsibility.

1074.4   dispatch of 1 P. M.]   Thomas telegraphed that a "terrible storm of freezing rain" had forced him to postpone an attack scheduled for the morning of December 10.

1074.8   dispatch . . . 2 p. m.]   Thomas justified his delay in his telegram to Halleck, but said he would "submit without a murmur" if Grant ordered his removal.

1079.8   decline . . . promotion.]   In a letter to Grant on January 21, 1865, Sherman expressed his disapproval of moves in Congress to create a second lieutenant general in the U.S. Army.

1079.35   C. C. Clay, jr.,]   Clement C. Clay, Jr. (1816–82) was a Democratic senator from Alabama, 1853–61, and served in the Confederate Senate, 1862–64. He was sent to Canada as a confidential agent of the Confederate government in April 1864, where he conferred with Northern opponents of the war. In July 1864 he met with newspaper editor Horace Greeley in an unsuccessful bid to open peace negotiations with the Lincoln administration.

1081.2   amending my order]   Grant had printed for circulation among Confederate troops his Special Order No. 82 of August 28, 1864, which offered subsistence and free transportation home, or to any point in the North, to Confederate deserters who took an oath not to take up arms again, and paid employment in the quartermaster department to deserters who took an oath of allegiance. The order promised that deserters would not be forced into military service, or into any service endangering them to capture by the Confederate army.

1081.10   death of Clara.]   See note 34.23–24.

1082.25   Saturday next]   March 25, 1865.

1086.28–29   arrested . . . escapes.]   Ord replied that Ford had left for Baltimore on the morning of April 17. Ford was eventually arrested and jailed for 39 days before being released.

1087.6   basis of agreement]   See note 754.29–30.

1087.26   copy . . . dispatch]   This message, sent on March 3, 1865, read: "The President directs me to say to you that he wishes you to have no conference with General Lee unless it be for the capitulation of Gen. Lee's army, or on some minor, and purely, military matter. He instructs me to say that you are not to decide, discuss, or confer upon any political question. Such questions the President holds in his own hands; and will submit them to no military conferences or conventions. Meantime you are to press to the utmost, your military advantages."

APPENDIX

1111.1   Notes . . . Doctor]   Dr. John Hancock Douglas (1824–92) was the throat specialist who diagnosed Grant's cancer on October 22, 1884, and attended him personally until his death. Dr. Douglas preserved these notes, written at Mount McGregor, New York, by Grant when he was unable to speak, describing the final stages of his illness. They are now in the Douglas Collection in the Library of Congress. The following are a selection from the Douglas Collection, transcribed from the originals, which were written in pencil. Grant's own spelling and punctuation have been preserved.

1116.31–32   Dr. Sands]   Henry B. Sands, called in for consultation in February 1885, was nearby in case of emergency during part of the time Grant was at Mount McGregor.

1118.10   Harrison]   Harrison Tyrrell, Grant's valet.

1119.2   the Dr.]   Dr. George F. Shrady, also attending Grant.

1120.18   bath wagon]   Bath chair; a large chair on wheels for invalids. The name derives from Bath, England, a fashionable health resort.

CATALOGING INFORMATION

Grant, Ulysses S., 1822–1885.
    Memoirs and selected letters: personal memoirs
    of U. S. Grant, selected letters 1839–1865 / Ulysses
    S. Grant.
    Edited by Mary Drake McFeely and William S. McFeely.

    (The Library of America ; 50)
    1. Grant, Ulysses S., 1822–1885. 2. Grant, Ulysses S.,
1822–1865—Correspondence. 3. Generals—United States—
Biography. 4. Presidents—United States—Biography.
5. United States. Army—Biography. I. Title. II. Series.

E660.G7562   1990   973.8'2'092—dc20   90-60013
ISBN 0-940450-58-5 (alk. paper)

THE LIBRARY OF AMERICA SERIES

Library of America fosters appreciation of America's literary heritage by publishing, and keeping permanently in print, authoritative editions of America's best and most significant writing. An independent nonprofit organization, it was founded in 1979 with seed funding from the National Endowment for the Humanities and the Ford Foundation.

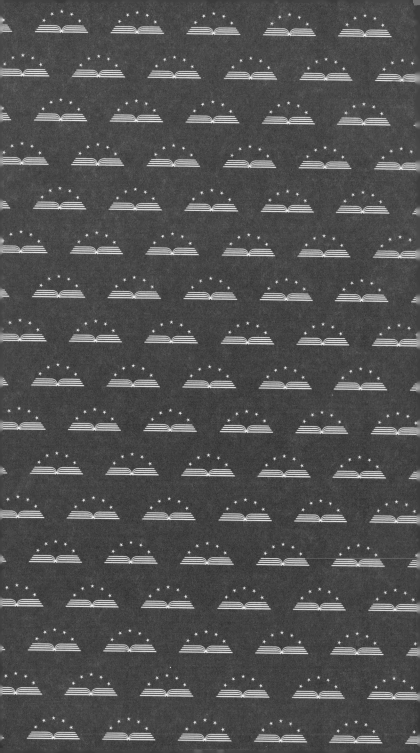